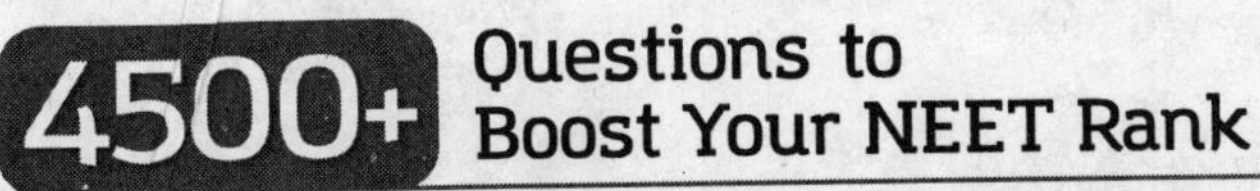

NEET power house Chemistry

Chapterwise Topicwise

Questions of Last 19 Years'

Authors
Saleha Pervez, Shahana Ansari
Vandana Kardam

ARIHANT PRAKASHAN (SERIES), MEERUT

卐 **Administrative & Production Offices**

Regd. Office

'Ramchhaya' 4577/15, Agarwal Road, Darya Ganj, New Delhi -110002
Tele: 011- 47630600, 43518550

Head Office

Kalindi, TP Nagar, Meerut (UP) - 250002 Tel: 0121-7156203, 7156204

卐 **Sales & Support Offices**

Agra, Ahmedabad, Bengaluru, Bareilly, Chennai, Delhi, Guwahati, Hyderabad, Jaipur, Jhansi, Kolkata, Lucknow, Nagpur & Pune.

卐 **PRICE** ₹795.00

Published by Arihant Publications (India) Ltd.

For further information about the books published by Arihant, log on to www.arihantbooks.com or e-mail at info@arihantbooks.com

Follow us on    

PREFACE

Once you have an idea of what you are going to be asked in a test, you are more comfortable to tackle it, and your performance in the test improves dramatically. Once you know the importance of different chapters and topics from the syllabi for a exam by going through chapterwise and topical segregation of previous years' questions, you can strategically plan out your preparation for the exam by allotting your time accordingly for the chapters or the topics of the chapters.

This book Chapterwise & Topicwise Medical Entrances Solved Papers Chemistry has Previous Years' Medical Entrance Questions with their Solutions to fulfill the above mentioned needs of understanding the nature & pattern of questions being asked in NEET and other Medical Entrances.

The Salient Features of the Book are

- It covers all the questions with explanations from year 2005 to 2023 for all Medical entrance exams in India (both National as well as Regional).
- Chapterwise division and topical categorisation has been done keeping in mind the syllabi of NEET & NCERT Textbooks and the learning facilitation to the students in the subject of Chemistry.
- Questions of all Medical entrances are grouped according to the year.
- Extreme care is taken, while solving the questions and compiling their answers for their accuracy.

We hope that the book will be of utmost help to you in your NEET Preparation and propel you to success. Suggestions for further improvement will be welcomed.

Publisher

CONTENTS

PART I *Based on Class XIth NCERT*

PART II *Based on Class XIIth NCERT*

01

Some Basic Concepts of Chemistry

Quick Review

All those things that have mass and a physical appearance can be considered as matter.

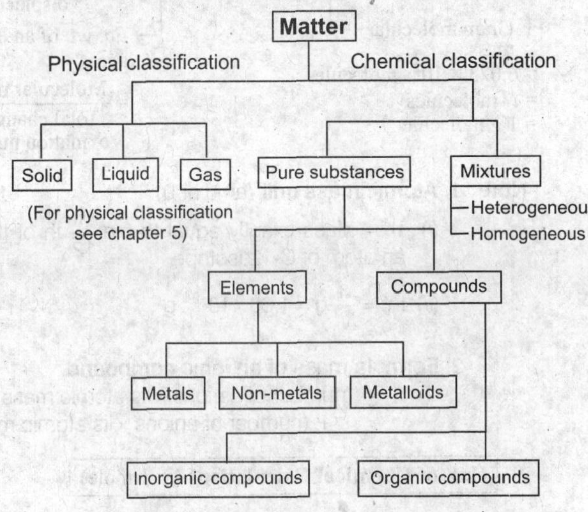

(*i*) **Mixture** is formed by mixing two or more substances together in any proportion. It can be **homogeneous** (uniform composition throughout) or **heterogeneous** (different composition throughout).

(*ii*) **Pure substances** have fixed composition and non-variable properties. An element is a substance that contains only one type of atoms, whereas a compound is formed when atoms of different elements combine in a fixed ratio.

Basic Physical Quantities and their Units

Physical quantity	SI unit
Length (l)	Metre (m)
Mass (m)	Kilogram (kg)
Time (t)	Second (s)
Electric current (I)	Ampere (A)
Thermodynamic temperature (T)	Kelvin (K)
Amount of substance (n)	Mole (mol)
Luminous intensity (I_v)	Candela (Cd)

Significant Figures

These are the total number of digits in a number including the last digit whose value is uncertain.

Rules for counting the number of significant figures are as follows :

(*i*) All digits are significant except zero at the beginning of the number.

(*ii*) The zeroes to the left of the first non-zero digit in a number are not significant.

(*iii*) The zeroes to the right of the decimal point are significant.

(*iv*) The above rules propose that, the numbers are expressed in scientific notation. In this term, every number is written as $N \times 10^n$.

where, N = a number with a single non-zero digit to the left of the decimal point

n = an integer

Significant figures in operational calculation are as follows:

(*i*) The result of an addition or subtraction should be reported to the same number of decimal places as that of the term with least number of decimal places.

(*ii*) The result of a multiplication or division should be reported to the same number of significant figures as is possessed by the least precise term used in the calculation.

(*iii*) If a calculation involves a number of steps, the result should contain the same number of significant figures as that of the least precise number involved other than the exact number.

Precision and Accuracy

Precision refers to how closely individual measurements agree with each other.

Accuracy refers to how closely a measured value agrees with the correct value.

Laws of Chemical Combinations

Elements combine to form molecules in accordance to the following six basic laws of chemical combinations.

Law of conservation of mass | **Antoine Lavoisier**

Matter can neither be created nor destroyed during the course of a chemical reaction, however its physical and chemical nature may change.

Law of definite proportions | **Joseph Proust**

A given compound always contains exactly the same proportion of elements by weight.

Law of multiple proportions | **John Dalton**

If two elements can combine to form more than one compound, the masses of one element that combine with a fixed mass of the other element, are in the ratio of small whole numbers.

Law of reciprocal proportions | **Richter**

If two different elements combine separately with the same weight of a third element, the ratio of the masses in which they do so, are either the same or simple multiple of the mass ratio in which they combine.

Law of gaseous volumes | **Gay Lussac**

When gases combine or are produced in a chemical reaction, they do so in a simple ratio by volume provided all gasses are at same temperature and pressure.

Avogadro's law | **Avogadro**

Equal volumes of all gases under the same condition of temperature and pressure should contain equal number of molecules.

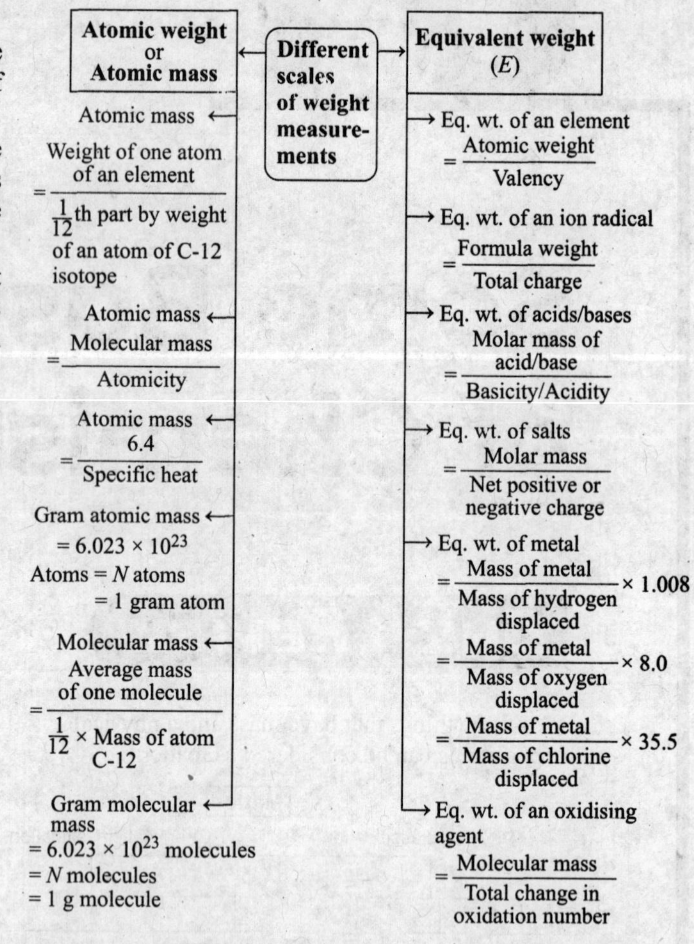

Note **1. Atomic mass unit** (amu or u)

(*i*) u = Mass exactly equal to the $\frac{1}{12}$ th of the weight of an atom of C-12 isotope.

(*ii*) $1\text{ u} = \frac{1}{N_A}\text{g} = 1.66 \times 10^{-24}\text{ g}$

2. Formula mass of an ionic compound

= (number of cations × its atomic mass) + (number of anions × its atomic mass)

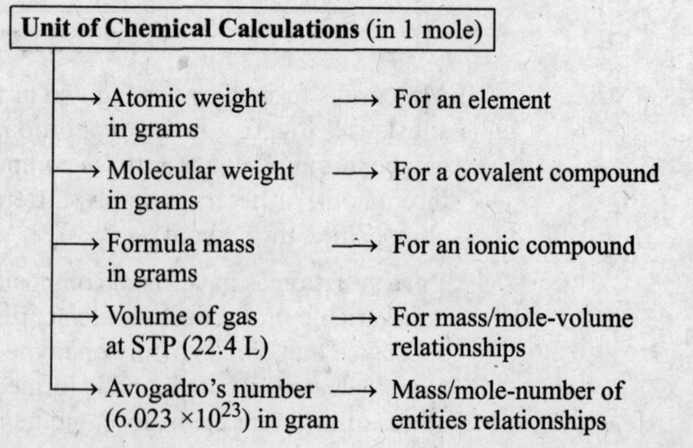

- **Percentage composition** or mass % of an element $= \dfrac{\text{Mass of that element in the compound}}{\text{Molar mass of the compound}} \times 100$
- **Empirical formula** of a chemical compound is the simplest positive integer ratio of atoms present in a compound.
- **Molecular formula** represents the exact number of atoms belonging to different elements in a molecule.

Molecular formula $= n \times$ Empirical formula

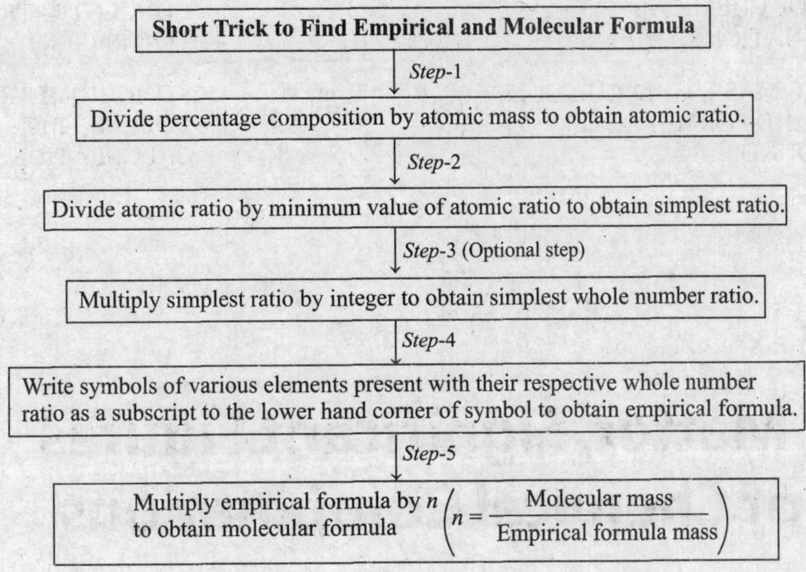

- **Stoichiometry** is the relationship between the relative quantities of substances taking part in a chemical reaction.
- The ratio in which the element or compound is represented in a balanced chemical reaction is known as the **stoichiometric ratio** or **coefficient**.
- *Type of stoichiometric relationship are given below :*
  (*i*) Mole – Mole relationship (*ii*) Mass – Mass relationship (*iii*) Mass – Mole relationship
  (*iv*) Mass – Volume relationship (*v*) Volume – Volume relationship

Limiting Reagent The reactant which is present in lesser amount and gets consumed after sometime and it limits the amount of product formed is called limiting reagent. While the reactant other than the limiting reagent, which is present in excess is called **excess reagent**.

Comparison between Concentration Terms

	Mass per cent	**Mole fraction** (χ)	**Molality** (m)	**Normality** (N)	**Molarity** (M), **Formality** (F)
Definition	The mass of a component per 100g of the solution.	The ratio of number of moles of a particular component to the total number of moles of the solution.	The number of moles of solute present in 1 kg of solvent.	The number of equivalents of solute present in one litre of the solution.	The number of moles of the solute in 1 litre of the solution.
Formula	$\dfrac{w_{\text{solute}}}{w_{\text{solution}}} \times 100$	$\chi_{\text{solute}} = \dfrac{n_{\text{solute}}}{n_{\text{solute}} + n_{\text{solvent}}} \times 100$ $\chi_{\text{solvent}} = \dfrac{n_{\text{solvent}}}{n_{\text{solute}} + n_{\text{solvent}}} \times 100$ $\chi_{\text{solute}} + \chi_{\text{solvent}} = 1$	$m = \dfrac{n_{\text{solute}}}{w_{\text{solvent}}\text{(in g)}} \times 1000$ $= \dfrac{w_{\text{solute}}\text{(in g)} \times 1000}{Mw_{\text{solute}} \times w_{\text{solvent}}\text{(in g)}}$	$N = \dfrac{\text{No. of g-equivalents of solute}}{V_{\text{solution}}\text{(in L)}}$ $= \dfrac{w_{\text{solute}}\text{(in g)}}{E \times V\text{(in L)}}$	$M \text{ or } F = \dfrac{n_{\text{solute}}}{V_{\text{solution}}\text{(in L)}}$ $M \text{ or } F = \dfrac{w_{\text{solute}}\text{(in g)}}{Mw_{\text{solute}} / Fw_{\text{solvent}} \times V_{\text{solution}}\text{(in L)}}$ $M = \dfrac{w_{\text{solute}} \% \times d_{\text{solution}} \times 10}{M_{\text{solute}}}$
Units	Unitless	Unitless	mol/kg	gram equiv./L	mol/L

Note (i) Normality of solution after dilution, $N_1V_1 = N_2V_2$
(ii) Molarity of solution after dilution, $M_1V_1 = M_2V_2$
(iii) Relation between molarity and normality is
normality of acid/base = molarity × basicity/acidity

Topical Practice Questions

All the exam questions of this chapter have been divided into four topics as listed below :

Topic 1

Nature of Matter, Significant Figures and Laws of Chemical Combinations

2014

1 Which one of the following data has only four significant figures? **[Kerala CEE]**

(a) 6.023×10^{23} (b) 285 cm
(c) 0.0025 L (d) 0.200 g
(e) 1.0×10^5 m

2012

2 An element **[OJEE]**

(a) is one type of atom
(b) is two or more types of atom
(c) has constant boiling point
(d) has constant melting point

2011

3 Which of the following sets of compounds correctly illustrate the law of reciprocal proportions? **[Kerala CEE]**

(a) P_2O_3, PH_3, H_2O (b) P_2O_5, PH_3, H_2O
(c) N_2O_5, NH_3, H_2O (d) N_2O, NH_3, H_2O
(e) NO_2, NH_3, H_2O

2009

4. The number of significant figures in 10.3406 g is **[Kerala CEE]**

(a) 2 (b) 3 (c) 1 (d) 4
(e) 6

5 The correctly reported answer of the addition of 4.523, 2.3 and 6.24 will have significant figures **[AFMC]**

(a) two (b) three (c) four (d) five

2006

6 The least count of an instrument is 0.01 cm. Taking all precautions, the most possible error in the measurement can be **[AMU]**

(a) 0.005 cm (b) 0.01 cm
(c) 0.0001 cm (d) 0.1 cm

7 Law of multiple proportions is illustrated by which of the following pairs. **[JCECE]**

(a) H_2S and SO_2 (b) NH_3 and NO_2
(c) Na_2S and Na_2O (d) N_2O and NO

Answers

1. (a) | 2. (a) | 3. (a) | 4. (e) | 5. (b) | 6. (b) | 7. (d)

Explanations

1. (*a*) 6.023×10^{23} has four significant figures. The total number of digits in a number including the last digit whose value is uncertain is called the number of significant figures.

2. (*a*) An element is a pure chemical substance which contains only one type of atom.

3. (*a*) P_2O_3, PH_3 and H_2O illustrates the law of reciprocal proportions.

(i) Ratio of masses of P to O in

$$P_2O_3 = \frac{62}{48} \text{ or } 31:24$$

(ii) Ratio of masses of P to H in

$$PH_3 = 31:3$$

(iii) Ratio of masses of H and O in

$$H_2O = 8:1$$

Ratio of H and O combining with fixed mass of P = 24 : 3 or 8 : 1

Thus, this illustrates the law of reciprocal proportion.

4 (*e*) All non-zero digits are significant. Hence, there are 6 significant figures in 10.3406 g.

5 (*b*) 4.523 + 2.3 + 6.24 = 13.063.

As 2.3 has least number of decimal places, i.e. one, therefore sum should be reported to one decimal place only. After rounding off, reported sum is 13.1 which has three significant figures.

6 (*b*) As we know that least count of an instrument is equal to the most possible error of the instrument, hence most possible error of the instrument will be 0.01 cm.

7 (*d*) According to law of multiple proportions, when two elements combine to form more than one compound, the fixed amount of one element combining with other element have simple whole number ratio.

In N_2O and NO, here 16 parts of oxygen react with 14 and 28 parts of nitrogen respectively, i.e. 14 : 28 or 1 : 2 which is simple whole number ratio.

∴ It follows law of multiple proportion.

Topic 2

Atomic Mass, Molecular Mass and Formulae of Compounds

2019

1 Find empirical formula of the compound, if $M = 68\%$ (atomic mass = 34) and remaining 32% oxygen. **[AIIMS]**

(a) MO (b) M_2O (c) MO_2 (d) M_2O_3

2013

2 The vapour density of a gas is 11.2. The volume occupied by one gram of the gas at STP is **[Manipal]**

(a) 1.0 L (b) 11.2 L
(c) 22.4 L (d) None of these

2012

3 The equivalent weight of potassium permanganate in alkaline solution is equal to **[AMU]**

(a) $1/5^{th}$ of the molar mass of $KMnO_4$

(b) $1/6^{th}$ of the molar mass of $KMnO_4$

(c) $1/3^{rd}$ of the molar mass of $KMnO_4$

(d) $1/10^{th}$ of the molar mass of $KMnO_4$

2010

4 When a metal is burnt, its weight is increased by 24 per cent. The equivalent weight of the metal will be **[BVP]**

(a) 2 (b) 24
(c) 33.3 (d) 76

5 In an experiment, 4 g of M_2O_x oxide was reduced to 2.8 g of the metal. If the atomic mass of the metal is 56 g mol^{-1}, the number of O-atoms in the oxide is **[AFMC]**

(a) 1 (b) 2 (c) 3 (d) 4

6 60 g of a compound on analysis produced 24 g carbon, 4 g hydrogen and 32 g oxygen. The empirical formula of the compound is **[BVP]**

(a) CH_2O_2 (b) CH_2O (c) CH_4O (d) $C_2H_4O_2$

7 1 u (amu) is equal to **[MHT CET]**

(a) 1.494×10^{-10} J (b) 1.492×10^{-7} J
(c) 1.492×10^{-13} J (d) 6.023×10^{23} J

8 74.5 g of a metallic chloride contain 35.5 g of chlorine. The equivalent weight of the metal is **[Manipal]**

(a) 19.5 (b) 35.5
(c) 39.0 (d) 78.0

9 In the reaction of sodium thiosulphate with I_2 in aqueous medium, the equivalent weight of sodium thiosulphate is equal to **[WB JEE]**

(a) molar mass of sodium thiosulphate
(b) the average of molar masses of $Na_2S_2O_3$ and I_2
(c) half the molar mass of sodium thiosulphate
(d) molar mass of sodium thiosulphate × 2

10 To dissolve 0.9 g metal, 100 mL of 1 N HCl is used. What is the equivalent weight of metal? **[MP PMT]**
(a) 7 (b) 9 (c) 10 (d) 6

11 During the conversion of $NH_2OH \longrightarrow N_2O$, the equivalent weight of NH_2OH is (molecular weight of NH_2OH is M.) **[AMU]**
(a) M (b) $M/2$ (c) $M/4$ (d) $M/5$

2009

12 One atom of an element weighs 1.8×10^{-22} g. Its atomic mass is **[Manipal]**
(a) 29.9 (b) 154 (c) 108.36 (d) 18

13 An organic compound made up of C, H and N contains 20% nitrogen. Its molecular weight is **[WB JEE]**
(a) 70 (b) 140 (c) 100 (d) 65

14 1.5 g of $CdCl_2$ was found to contain 0.9 g of Cd. Calculate the atomic weight of Cd. **[EAMCET]**
(a) 118 (b) 112 (c) 106.5 (d) 53.25

15 A bivalent metal has an equivalent mass of 32. The molecular mass of the metal nitrate is **[KCET]**
(a) 168 (b) 192 (c) 188 (d) 182

16 In the standardisation of $Na_2S_2O_3$ using $K_2Cr_2O_7$ by iodometry, the equivalent weight of $K_2Cr_2O_7$ is **[CG PMT, Haryana PMT]**
(a) $\frac{\text{molecular weight}}{2}$ (b) $\frac{\text{molecular weight}}{6}$
(c) $\frac{\text{molecular weight}}{3}$ (d) same as molecular weight

2008

17 **Assertion** (A) Equivalent weight of a base $= \frac{\text{molecular weight}}{\text{acidity}}$

Reason (R) Acidity is the number of replaceable hydrogen atom in one molecule of the base. **[AIIMS]**
(a) Both A and R are correct and R is the correct explanation of A
(b) Both A and R are correct but R is not the correct explanation of A
(c) A is correct but R is incorrect
(d) Both A and R are incorrect

18 The formula mass of Mohr's salt is 392. The iron present in it is oxidised by $KMnO_4$ in acidic medium. The equivalent mass of Mohr's salt is **[AFMC]**
(a) 392 (b) 31.6 (c) 278 (d) 156

19 A metal M of equivalent mass E forms an oxide of molecular formula M_xO_y. The atomic mass of the metal is given by which of the following equation. **[Kerala CEE]**
(a) $2E(y/x)$ (b) xyE (c) E/y (d) y/E
(e) $E_2(x/y)$

20 The equivalent weight of a metal is 9 and vapour density of its chloride is 59.25. The atomic weight of metal is **[DUMET]**
(a) 23.9 (b) 27.3
(c) 36.3 (d) 23.6

21 Out of two oxides of iron, the first contained 22% and the second contained 30% of oxygen by weight. The ratio of weights of iron in the two oxides that combine with the same weight of oxygen is **[J&K CET]**
(a) 3:2 (b) 2:1
(c) 1:2 (d) 1:1

22 1.520 g of hydroxide of a metal on ignition gave 0.995 g of oxide. The equivalent weight of metal is **[JCECE]**
(a) 1.52 (b) 0.995
(c) 190 (d) 9

23 The crystalline salt $Na_2SO_4 \cdot xH_2O$ on heating loses 55.9% of its weight. The formula of crystalline salt is **[Kerala CEE]**
(a) $Na_2SO_4 \cdot 5H_2O$ (b) $Na_2SO_4 \cdot 7H_2O$
(c) $Na_2SO_4 \cdot 2H_2O$ (d) $Na_2SO_4 \cdot 10H_2O$
(e) $Na_2SO_4 \cdot 6H_2O$

24 25 g of MCl_4 contains 0.5 mole chlorine then its molecular weight is **[Punjab PMET]**
(a) 100 g mol^{-1} (b) 200 g mol^{-1}
(c) 150 g mol^{-1} (d) 400 g mol^{-1}

25 What is the equivalent weight of $SnCl_2$ in the following reaction?
$SnCl_2 + Cl_2 \longrightarrow SnCl_4$ (mol. wt. of $SnCl_2 = 190$) **[KCET]**
(a) 95 (b) 45
(c) 60 (d) 30

26 What is the percentage of cation in ammonium dichromate? **[Kerala CEE]**
(a) 14.29% (b) 80% (c) 50.05% (d) 20.52%
(e) 25.62%

27 A gas is found to have a formula $(CO)_x$. If its vapour density is 70, the value of x is **[AMU]**
(a) 2.5 (b) 3.0 (c) 5.0 (d) 6.0

28 In the equation, $H_2S + 2HNO_3 \longrightarrow 2H_2O + 2NO_2 + S$, the equivalent weight of hydrogen sulphide is **[BCECE]**
(a) 18 (b) 68 (c) 34 (d) 17

29 The equivalent weight of phosphoric acid (H_3PO_4) in the reaction, **[BHU]**
$NaOH + H_3PO_4 \longrightarrow NaH_2PO_4 + H_2O$ is
(a) 59 (b) 49 (c) 25 (d) 98

30 The equivalent weight of $KMnO_4$ (in g eq.) in acidic medium is **[RPMT]**
(a) 158 (b) 52.67
(c) 31.6 (d) 49

Answers

1. (a)	2. (a)	3. (c)	4. (c)	5. (c)	6. (b)	7. (a)	8. (c)	9. (c)	10. (b)
11. (b)	12. (c)	13. (a)	14. (c)	15. (c)	16. (b)	17. (c)	18. (a)	19. (a)	20. (a)
21. (a)	22. (d)	23. (d)	24. (b)	25. (a)	26. (a)	27. (c)	28. (d)	29. (d)	30. (c)

Explanations

1. (*a*) Given,
% of element (M) = 68%
and of oxygen (O) = 32%
Atomic mass of M = 34 g/mol
Thus, empirical formula of M_xO_y is
element $\longrightarrow$ % of mass $\longrightarrow$ moles (n)
$M \longrightarrow 68 \longrightarrow 68/34 = 2$
$O \longrightarrow 32 \longrightarrow 32/16 = 2$
Hence, empirical formula of given compound is M_2O_2 or MO.
Thus, option (a) is correct.

2. (*a*) Here, vapour density of gas = 11.2
$\therefore$ Molecular weight
$= 2 \times$ vapour density
$= 2 \times 11.2 = 22.4$ g
22.4 g of gas occupied volume at STP
= 22.4 L
$\therefore$ 1 g gas occupied volume at STP
= 1 L

3. (*c*) $2K\overset{+7}{Mn}O_4 + H_2O \xrightarrow{\text{Alkaline}} 2\overset{+4}{Mn}O_2 + 2KOH + 3[O]$
(As change in oxidation number of Mn = 3)
So, equivalent mass $= \dfrac{\text{molar mass}}{3}$
Hence, the equivalent weight of $KMnO_4$ in alkaline solution is equal to $\frac{1}{3}$rd of the molar mass of $KMnO_4$.

4. (*c*) If 100 g of metal is burnt, then it combines with oxygen to form metal oxide. As its weight increases by 24%, then the mass of combined oxygen would be 24 g.
Thus, the equivalent weight of metal
$$= \frac{\text{weight of metal}}{\text{weight of oxygen combined}} \times 8$$
$$= \frac{100}{24} \times 8$$
$= 33.33$ g eq mol^{-1}
Hence, the equivalent weight of metal will be 33.3.

5. (*c*) Mass of oxygen in oxide
$= 4 - 2.8 = 1.2$ g
Eq. wt. of metal
$$= \frac{\text{mass of metal}}{\text{mass of oxygen combined}} \times 8$$
$$= \frac{2.8}{1.2} \times 8 = 18.67 \text{ g eq mol}^{-1}$$
Valency of metal
$$= \frac{\text{atomic weight of metal}}{\text{eq. wt. of metal}}$$
$$= \frac{56 \text{ (given)}}{18.67} = 2.99 \approx 3$$
Hence, the number of O-atoms in the oxide is 3.

6. (*b*) $C:H:O = \dfrac{24}{12} : \dfrac{4}{1} : \dfrac{32}{16} = 2:4:2$
or $1:2:1$
$\therefore$ Empirical formula = CH_2O

7. (*a*) 1 u (unified mass) is equal to exactly 1/12th of the mass of C^{12} atom.
Thus, $1\text{ u} = \dfrac{1}{12} \times \dfrac{12 \text{ g}}{6.023 \times 10^{23}}$
$\therefore$ $1 \text{ u} = 1.66 \times 10^{-24}$ g
$= 1.66 \times 10^{-27}$ kg
Since, $E = mc^2$, thus
$= 1.66 \times 10^{-27} \times (3 \times 10^8)^2$ kg m^{2}s^{-2}
$= 1.494 \times 10^{-10}$ J

8. (*c*) Eq. wt. of metal
$$= \frac{\text{weight of metal}}{\text{weight of chlorine combined}} \times 35.5$$
$\therefore$ Eq. wt. of metal
$$= \frac{(74.5 - 35.5)}{35.5} \times 35.5$$
$= 39.0$ g eq mol^{-1}

9. (*c*) $I_2 + 2S_2O_3^{2-} \longrightarrow 2I^- + S_4O_6^{2-}$
The change in valence factor of thiosulphate is 2.
Thus, equivalent weight of $Na_2S_2O_3$
$$= \frac{\text{molecular weight of } Na_2S_2O_3}{2}$$
Hence, equivalent weight of $Na_2S_2O_3$ is half the molecular weight (molar mass) of sodium thiosulphate.

10. (*b*) 1 N HCl solution means 36.5 g of HCl are dissolved in 1000 mL.
($\because$ equivalent weight of HCl = 36.5 g eq mol^{-1})
$\therefore$ 100 mL of HCl solution contains HCl = 3.65 g
Similarly, 100 mL of HCl solution contains metal = 0.9 g
Now, $\dfrac{\text{equivalent weight of metal}}{\text{weight of metal in solution}}$
$$= \frac{\text{equivalent weight of acid}}{\text{weight of acid in solution}}$$
or $\dfrac{\text{equivalent weight of metal}}{0.9} = \dfrac{36.5}{3.65}$
or equivalent weight of metal
$$= \frac{36.5}{3.65} \times 0.9 = 9 \text{ g eq mol}^{-1}$$

11. (*b*) $\overset{-1}{N}H_2OH \longrightarrow \overset{+1}{N}_2O$
Valence factor, $n = +1 - (-1) = +2$
Equivalent weight of
$NH_2OH = \dfrac{\text{molecular weight}}{\text{valence factor}} = \dfrac{M}{2}$

12. (*c*) Mass of 1 atom of an element
$= 1.8 \times 10^{-22}$ g
Mass of 6.023×10^{23} atoms of an element
$= 6.023 \times 10^{23} \times 1.8 \times 10^{-22}$ g
$= 6.023 \times 1.8 \times 10$ g $= 108.36$ g
Hence, atomic mass of element
= 108.36 g

13. (*a*) Mass % of N in organic compound
$$= \frac{\text{atomic mass of N}}{\text{molecular mass of compound}} \times 100$$
$$20 = \frac{14}{\text{molecular mass of compound}} \times 100$$
Molecular mass of compound
$$= \frac{14}{20} \times 100 = 70 \text{ g}$$

14. (*c*) Weight of Cd = 0.9 g

Weight of $CdCl_2$ = 1.5 g

Weight of chlorine combined = 1.5 − 0.9

⇒ 0.6 g

Now $\frac{0.9}{0.6} = \frac{\text{eq. wt. of metal}}{\text{eq. wt. of chlorine}}$

or $\frac{0.9}{0.6} = \frac{E}{35.5}$ or $E = 53.25\text{eq}$

Atomic weight = $E \times$ valency = 53.25 × 2 = 106.5 g

15. (*c*) Given, equivalent mass of bivalent metal, M^{2+} = 32 g-eq

∴ Atomic mass of M = 32 × 2 = 64 g

The metal nitrate formed has the formula $M(NO_3)_2$.

∴ Molecular mass of the metal nitrate

= 64 + 28 + 96 = 188 g/mol

16. (*b*) $Cr_2O_7^{2-} + 14H^+ + 6e^- \longrightarrow 2Cr^{3+} + 7H_2O$

$6I^- \longrightarrow 3I_2 + 6e^-$

$2Na_2S_2O_3 + I_2 \longrightarrow Na_2S_4O_6 + 2NaI$

In this reaction, equivalent weight of $K_2Cr_2O_7$

$= \frac{\text{molecular weight}}{3 \times 2}$

$= \frac{\text{molecular weight}}{6}$

17. (*c*) Equivalent weight of a base is calculated by dividing its molecular mass with its acidity. Acidity is defined as the number of replaceable hydroxyl group in one molecule of the base.

Hence, A is correct but R is incorrect.

18. (*a*) Mohr's salt is $(NH_4)_2SO_4 \cdot FeSO_4 \cdot 6H_2O$.

The equation is

$5Fe^{2+} + MnO_4^- + 8H^+ \longrightarrow 5Fe^{3+} + Mn^{2+} + 4H_2O$

Total change in oxidation number of iron = (+3) − (+2) = +1

So, equivalent weight of Mohr's salt

$= \frac{\text{molecular weight of Mohr's salt}}{\text{total change in oxidation number}} = \frac{392}{1} = 392 \text{ g-eq}$

19. (*a*) Let, the atomic mass of metal, 'M' = a

Given, equivalent mass of metal, $M = E$

$xM + yO \longrightarrow M_xO_y$

∴ 'xa' g metal 'M' reacts with oxygen = $16y$ g,

According to law of chemical equivalents,

$w \propto E \quad \Rightarrow \quad \frac{w_1}{w_2} = \frac{E_1}{E_2}$

$\frac{xa}{16y} = \frac{E}{8} \quad \Rightarrow \quad a = 2E\left(\frac{y}{x}\right)$

20. (*a*) Given, equivalent weight of metal = 9

Vapour density of metal chloride = 59.25

∴ Molecular weight of metal chloride = 2 × vapour density

= 2 × 59.25 = 118.50

Valency of metal = $\frac{\text{mol. wt. of metal chloride}}{\text{eq. wt. of metal} + 35.5}$

Valency of metal = $\frac{118.5}{9 + 35.5} = \frac{118.5}{44.5} = 2.66$

Therefore, atomic weight of the metal

= equivalent weight × valency

= 9 × 2.66 = 23.9 g

21. (*a*) For first oxide,

Element	% amount	Atomic weight	Number of moles	Simple molar ratio
O	22	16	$\frac{22}{16} = 1.375$	$\frac{1.375}{1.375} = 1$
Fe	78	56	$\frac{78}{56} = 1.392$	$\frac{1.392}{1.375} \approx 1$

∴ The formula of first oxide is FeO.

Similarly, for second oxide

Element	% amount	Atomic weight	Number of moles	Simple molar ratio
O	30	16	$\frac{30}{16} = 1.875$	$\frac{1.875}{1.25} \approx 1.5$
Fe	70	56	$\frac{70}{56} = 1.25$	$\frac{1.25}{1.25} = 1$

∴ The formula of second oxide is Fe_2O_3.

Suppose in both the oxides, iron reacts with x g oxygen.

∴ Equivalent weight of Fe in FeO = $\frac{\text{weight of Fe (II)}}{\text{weight of oxygen}} \times 8$

$\frac{56}{2} = \frac{\text{weight of Fe (II)}}{x} \times 8$ ...(i)

Similarly, equivalent weight of Fe in Fe_2O_3

$= \frac{\text{weight of Fe (III)}}{\text{weight of oxygen}} \times 8$

$\frac{56}{3} = \frac{\text{weight of Fe (III)}}{x} \times 8$ ...(ii)

From Eqs. (i) and (ii), $\frac{\text{weight of Fe (II)}}{\text{weight of Fe (III)}} = \frac{3}{2}$

22. (*d*) $\frac{E_{\text{hydroxide}}}{E_{\text{metal}} + E_{\text{OH}}} = \frac{E_{\text{oxide}}}{E_{\text{metal}} + E_{\text{O}}}$

$\frac{1.520}{E + 17} = \frac{0.995}{E + 8}$

or $1.52(E + 8) = 0.995(E + 17)$

$1.52E + 12.16 = 0.995E + 16.915$

$1.52E - 0.995E = 16.915 - 12.16$

$0.525E = 4.755$

$E = \frac{4.755}{0.525} \approx 9$

∴ The equivalent weight of metal is 9.

23. (*d*) As $Na_2SO_4 \cdot xH_2O$ on heating loses water, 55.9% ≈ 56% of its weight.

$\therefore$ % of weight of $Na_2SO_4 = 44\%$

Molecular weight of $Na_2SO_4 = 142$ g

$$\therefore \frac{w_{H_2O}}{w_{Na_2SO_4}} = \frac{56}{44}$$

or $w_{H_2O} = \frac{56}{44} \times 142 = 180$ g

As 18 g contains = 1 molecule of water

$\therefore$ 180 g contains = 10 molecules of water

Thus, the formula of crystalline salt is $Na_2SO_4 \cdot 10H_2O$.

24. (*b*) 0.5 mole chlorine is present in 25 g of MCl_4. Thus, 1 mole chlorine will be present in 50 g of MCl_4.

But MCl_4 contains 4 moles of chlorine, then molecular weight of MCl_4

$= 4 \times 50 = 200 \text{ g mol}^{-1}$.

25. (*a*) $\underset{190}{SnCl_2} + \underset{71}{Cl_2} \longrightarrow SnCl_4$

Eq. wt. of $SnCl_2$ ≡ Eq. wt. of Cl_2

$$\therefore \frac{190}{E_1} = \frac{71}{35.5} \text{ or } E_1 = 95 \text{ g eq}$$

26. (*a*) Molecular formula of ammonium dichromate is $(NH_4)_2Cr_2O_7$.

Molecular weight

$= 2 \times (14 + 4) + 2 \times 52 + 7 \times 16$

$= 252$ g/mol

Number of parts by weight of cation, $NH_4^+ = 2 \times (14 + 4) = 36$

$$\% \text{ of } NH_4^+ = \frac{36}{252} \times 100$$

$= 14.285\% \approx 14.29\%$

27. (*c*) Molecular weight = 2 × vapour density = 2 × 70 = 140 g mol^{-1}

$\because$ $(CO)_x = 140$

$\therefore$ $(12 + 16)_x = 140$

$\therefore$ $(28)_x = (28)_5$

$\therefore$ $x = 5$

28. (*d*) $H_2\overset{-2}{S} + 2HNO_3 \longrightarrow 2H_2O + 2NO_2 + \overset{0}{S}$

Hence, the equivalent weight of H_2S

$$= \frac{\text{molecular weight}}{\text{change in oxidation number}}$$

$$= \frac{34}{2} = 17 \text{ g-eq}$$

29. (*d*) $\underset{\substack{23+16+1 \\ = 40 \\ 1 \text{ g eq.}}}{NaOH} + \underset{\substack{1\times3+31+16\times4 \\ = 98 \\ 1 \text{ g eq.}}}{H_3\overset{+5}{P}O_4} \longrightarrow NaH_2\overset{+5}{P}O_4 + H_2O$

$\therefore$ Equivalent weight of H_3PO_4 is 98 g.

In the above reaction, no change occurs in the oxidation state of phosphorus. So, equivalent weight will be equal to its molecular weight.

30. (*c*) In acidic medium, $KMnO_4$ reacts as

$2KMnO_4 + 3H_2SO_4 \longrightarrow K_2SO_4 + 2MnSO_4 + 3H_2O + 5O$

or $\overset{+7}{Mn}O_4^- \longrightarrow Mn^{2+}$

$\because$ Change in oxidation number $= 7 - 2 = 5$

$\therefore$ Equivalent weight of $KMnO_4$

$$= \frac{\text{formula weight of } KMnO_4}{5}$$

$$= \frac{158}{5}$$

$= 31.6$ g-eq

Topic 3

Mole Concept and Some Important Concentration Terms

2019

1 Calculate the molarity of one litre solution of 22.2 g of $CaCl_2$ **[JIPMER]**

(a) 0.4 M (b) 0.2M (c) 0.8M (d) 0.6M

2 The density of 2 M aqueous solution of NaOH is 1.28 g/cm^3. The molality of the solution is [Given that molecular mass of NaOH = 40 g mol^{-1}] **[NEET (Odisha)]**

(a) 1.20 m (b) 1.56 m (c) 1.67 m (d) 1.32 m

2018

3 In which case is the number of molecules of water maximum? **[NEET]**

(a) 0.00224 L of water vapours at 1 atm and 273 K

(b) 0.18 g of water

(c) 18 mL of water (d) 10^{-3} mole of water

2017

4 The normality of 10% (*w*/*V*) of acetic acid is **[JIPMER]**

(a) 1 N (b) 1.3 N (c) 1.7 N (d) 1.9 N

5 Which of the following is dependent of temperature? **[NEET]**

(a) Molality (b) Molarity

(c) Mole fraction (d) Weight percentage

2014

6 What is the mass of one molecule of yellow phosphorus? (Atomic mass, P = 30) **[MHT CET]**

(a) 1.993×10^{-22} mg (b) 1.993×10^{-19} mg

(c) 4.983×10^{-20} mg (d) 4.983×10^{-23} mg

7 The system that contains the maximum number of atoms is **[WB JEE]**

(a) 4.25 g of NH_3 (b) 8 g of O_2

(c) 2 g of H_2 (d) 4 g of He

2013

8 The weight of 112 mL of oxygen at NTP is [Manipal]
(a) 0.64 g (b) 0.96 g (c) 0.32 g (d) 0.16 g

9 For 14 g of CO, the wrong statement is [Manipal]
(a) it occupies 2.24 L at NTP
(b) it corresponds to 1/2 mole of CO
(c) it corresponds to same mole of CO and nitrogen gas
(d) it corresponds to 3.01×10^{23} molecules of CO

10 What is the atomic weight of an element X for which a sample containing 1.58×10^{22} atoms weigh 1.05 g? [WB JEE]
(a) 28 g (b) 20 g
(c) 40 g (d) 23 g

11 The percentage of N_2 in urea is about [KCET]
(a) 28 (b) 18 (c) 85 (d) 46

12 Number of molecules in 1 L of water is close to [KCET]
(a) $18/22.4\times 10^{23}$ (b) $55.5\times 6.023\times 10^{23}$
(c) $6.023/23/4\times 10^{23}$ (d) $18\times 6.023\times 10^{23}$

13 The mass of 112 cm^3 of CH_4 gas at STP is [KCET]
(a) 0.16 g (b) 0.8 g (c) 0.08 g (d) 1.6 g

2012

14 How many moles of magnesium phosphate, $Mg_3(PO_4)_2$ will contain 0.25 mole of oxygen atom? [AFMC]
(a) 0.02 (b) 3.125×10^{-2}
(c) 1.25×10^{-2} (d) 2.5×10^{-2}

15 The number of sodium atoms in 2 moles of sodium ferrocyanide is [Manipal]
(a) 12×10^{23} (b) 26×10^{23}
(c) 34×10^{23} (d) 48×10^{23}

16. 10^{21} molecules are removed from 200 mg of CO_2. The moles of CO_2 left are [AIIMS]
(a) 2.88×10^{-3} (b) 28.8×10^{-3}
(c) 288×10^{-3} (d) 28.8×10^{3}

2011

17 The total number of electrons in 18 mL of water (density = $1 g mL^{-1}$) [KCET]
(a) 6.023×10^{25} (b) 6.023×10^{24}
(c) $6.023\times 18\times 10^{23}$ (d) 6.023×10^{23}

2010

18 1 L oxygen gas at STP will weigh [JCECE]
(a) 1.43 g (b) 2.24 g (c) 11.2 g (d) 22.4 g

19 If the density of water is $1 g cm^{-3}$ then the volume occupied by one molecule of water is approximately [CMC Ludhiyana]
(a) 18 cm^3 (b) 22400 cm^3
(c) 6.02×10^{-23} cm^3 (d) 3.0×10^{-23} cm^3

20 The number of atoms in 0.1 mole of a triatomic gas is ($N_A = 6.02\times 10^{23}$ mol^{-1}) [CBSE AIPMT]
(a) 6.026×10^{22} (b) 1.806×10^{23}
(c) 1.800×10^{22} (d) 3.600×10^{23}

21 Number of atoms present in 4.25 g of NH_3 is [AFMC]
(a) 6.023×10^{23} (b) $4\times 6.023\times 10^{23}$
(c) 1.7×10^{24} (d) $4.25\times 6.023\times 10^{23}$

22 The number of molecules in 100 mL of 0.02 N H_2SO_4 is [AMU]
(a) 6.023×10^{22} (b) 6.023×10^{21}
(c) 6.023×10^{20} (d) 6.023×10^{18}

23 If 1 mL of water contains 20 drops then number of molecules in one drop of water is [AFMC]
(a) 6.023×10^{23} molecules (b) 1.376×10^{26} molecules
(c) 1.344×10^{18} molecules (d) 4.346×10^{20} molecules

24 Volume of a gas at NTP is 1.12×10^{-7} cm^3. The number of molecules in it is [Manipal]
(a) 3.01×10^{12} (b) 3.01×10^{24}
(c) 3.01×10^{23} (d) 3.01×10^{20}

25 The volume of 2N H_2SO_4 solution is 0.1 dm^3. The volume of its decinormal solution (in dm^3) will be [MHT CET]
(a) 0.1 (b) 0.2 (c) 2 (d) 1.7

26 The number of molecules in 18 mg of water in terms of Avogadro number, N_A is [J&K CET]
(a) $10^{-3} N_A$ (b) $10^{-2} N_A$
(c) $10^{-1} N_A$ (d) $10 N_A$

27. The largest number of molecules is in [AMU]
(a) 34 g of H_2O (b) 28 g of CO_2
(c) 46 g of CH_3OH (d) 54 g of N_2O_5

28 Mass of 0.1 mole of methane is [KCET]
(a) 1 g (b) 16 g
(c) 1.6 g (d) 0.1 g

29 The maximum number of molecules are present in [BCECE]
(a) 15 L of H_2 gas at STP
(b) 5 L of N_2 gas at STP
(c) 0.5 g of H_2 gas
(d) 10 g of O_2 gas

30 Number of atoms of He in 100 u of He (atomic weight of He is 4) are [BCECE]
(a) 25 (b) 100
(c) 50 (d) $100\times 6\times 10^{-23}$

31 The weight of one molecule of a compound $C_{60}H_{122}$ is [KCET]
(a) 1.3×10^{-20} g (b) 5.01×10^{-21} g
(c) 3.72×10^{12} g (d) 1.4×10^{-21} g

32 The number of gram molecules of chlorine in 6.02×10^{25} hydrogen chloride molecules is **[KCET]**

(a) 10 (b) 100 (c) 50 (d) 5

33 Gram molecular volume of oxygen at STP is **[KCET]**

(a) 3200 cm^3 (b) 5600 cm^3
(c) 22400 cm^3 (d) 11200 cm^3

34 A gas mixture contains O_2 and N_2 in the ratio of 1:4 by weight. The ratio of their number of molecules is **[AFMC]**

(a) 1:8 (b) 1:4 (c) 3:16 (d) 7:32

35 Which among the following is the heaviest? **[Kerala CEE]**

(a) 1 mole of oxygen
(b) 1 molecule of sulphur trioxide
(c) 100 u of uranium
(d) 10 moles of hydrogen
(e) 44 g of carbon dioxide

36 Total number of atoms represented by the compound $CuSO_4 \cdot 5H_2O$ are **[BHU]**

(a) 27 (b) 21 (c) 5 (d) 8

37 Total number of protons in 10 g of calcium carbonate is ($N_A = 6.023 \times 10^{23}$) **[RPMT]**

(a) 12.04×10^{24} (b) 4.06×10^{24}
(c) 2.01×10^{24} (d) 3.24×10^{24}

38 The number of electrons required to reduce 4.5×10^{-5} g of Al is **[AFMC]**

(a) 1.03×10^{18} (b) 3.01×10^{18}
(c) 4.95×10^{26} (d) 7.31×10^{20}

39 How many grams of NaOH will be required to neutralise 12.2 g benzoic acid? **[KCET]**

(a) 12.2 g (b) 16 g (c) 40 g (d) 4 g

Answers

1. (b)	2. (c)	3. (c)	4. (c)	5. (b)	6. (b)	7. (c)	8. (d)	9. (a)	10. (c)
11. (d)	12. (b)	13. (c)	14. (b)	15. (d)	16. (a)	17. (b)	18. (a)	19. (d)	20. (b)
21. (a)	22. (c)	23. (c)	24. (a)	25. (c)	26. (a)	27. (a)	28. (c)	29. (a)	30. (a)
31. (d)	32. (b)	33. (c)	34. (d)	35. (e)	36. (b)	37. (d)	38. (b)	39. (d)	

Explanations

1. (*b*) Molarity (*M*)

$$= \frac{\text{Mass of solute (in g)}}{\text{Molecular weight of solute} \times \text{volume of solution (in L)}}$$

$$= \frac{22.2 \text{ g}}{111 \text{ g mol}^{-1} \times 1 \text{ L}}$$

[$\because$ Molecular weight of $CaCl_2 = 111 \text{ g mol}^{-1}$]

$= 0.2 \text{ mol L}^{-1} = 0.2$ M.

2. (*c*) Given, molarity = 2M
[i.e 2 moles NaOH is dissolved in 1 L solution]

Density (d) = 1.28 g/cm^3

Molecular weight of NaOH = 40 g mol^{-1}

We know that,

$$\text{density} = \frac{\text{mass of solution}}{\text{volume of solution}}$$

$\therefore$ Mass of solution = $1.28 \text{ g cm}^{-3} \times 1000 \text{ mL} = 1280$ g

Moreover,

Molarity

$$= \frac{\text{number of moles of solute}}{\text{volume of solution (in L)}}$$

$$\therefore 2 = \frac{\text{mass of solute}}{40 \times 1}$$

Mass of solute = 80 g

Now, mass of solution = mass of solvent + mass of solute

1280 g = mass of solvent + 80

$\therefore$ Mass of solvent = 1280 − 80 = 1200 g = 1.2 kg

Now, molality

$$= \frac{\text{number of moles of solute}}{\text{mass of solvent (in kg)}}$$

$$= \frac{2}{1.2} = \frac{20}{12} = \frac{5}{3} = 1.67 \text{ m}$$

Alternative method

$$\text{Molality } (m) = \frac{M}{1000d - M\text{wt.}} \times 1000$$

where, M = molarity, d = density of solution

Mwt. = molar mass of solute.

On substituting the given values

$$\text{Molality} = \frac{2}{1000 \times 1.28 - 40} \times 1000$$

$$= \frac{2}{1280 - 40} \times 1000 = \frac{2000}{1240} = 1.612 \text{ m}$$

3. (*c*) Number of molecules = mole × Avogadro's number (N_A)

The number of molecules of water in each of the given options is calculated as,

(a) $(V_{(H_2O)\,g})_{STP} = 0.00224$ L

$$n_{H_2O} = \frac{V}{22.4 \text{ L}} = \frac{0.00224}{22.4} = 0.0001$$

$\therefore$ Number of molecules of water $= 0.0001 \times N_A$

(b) 0.18 g of water

$$n_{H_2O} = \frac{w_{H_2O}}{M_{H_2O}} = \frac{0.18}{18} = 0.01$$

Number of molecules $= 0.01 \times N_A$

(c) 18 mL of water, number of moles (n_{H_2O})

$$= \frac{\text{mass of substance in g } (w_{H_2O})}{\text{molar mass in g mol}^{-1} (w_{H_2O})}$$

$w_{H_2O} = 18$ g/mol

[$\because$ Density of water (d_{H_2O}) = 1 g L^{-1}]

$$\therefore n_{H_2O} = \frac{18}{18} = 1$$

Number of molecules of water $= 1 \times N_A$

(d) $n_{H_2O} = 10^{-3}$

$\therefore$ Number of molecules of water $= 10^{-3} \times N_A$

Hence, maximum number of molecules are present in 18 mL of water.

4. (*c*) Normality $(N) = \dfrac{w \times 1000}{M \times V\,(\text{mL})}$

$= \dfrac{10 \times 1000}{60 \times 100} = 1.66$

$\therefore \quad N = 1.66\,\text{N} \Rightarrow N \approx 1.7\,\text{N}$

5. (*b*) Molarity and normality are temperature dependent entities because they involve volume of solution. Volume is dependent on temperature.

Molarity $(M) = \dfrac{\text{moles of solute}}{\text{volume of solution (in L)}}$

Molality, mole fraction and weight percentage do not depend on temperature because they involve masses of solute and solvent.

6. (*b*) Yellow phosphorus is an impure form of white phosphorus (P_4).

Molecular mass of yellow phosphorus (P_4) $= 4 \times 30 = 120\,\text{g mol}^{-1}$

$\therefore$ According to Avogadro's hypothesis,

Mass of 6.022×10^{23} molecules of P_4 $= 120\,\text{g}$

$\therefore$ Mass of 1 molecule of P_4

$= \dfrac{120 \times 1}{6.022 \times 10^{23}}\text{g} = 19.926 \times 10^{-23}\text{g}$

$\approx 1.993 \times 10^{-22}\text{g} = 1.993 \times 10^{-19}\text{mg}$

7. (*c*) Number of atoms $= \dfrac{\text{mass}}{\text{molar mass}} \times N_A$ $\times$ number of atoms present in 1 molecule (or atomicity)

(a) Number of atoms in 4.25 g of NH_3

$= \dfrac{4.25}{17} \times N_A \times 4 = N_A$

(b) Number of atoms in 8 g of O_2

$= \dfrac{8}{32} \times N_A \times 2 = \dfrac{N_A}{2}$

(c) Number of atoms in 2 g of H_2

$H_2 = \dfrac{2}{2} \times N_A \times 2 = 2N_A$

(d) Number of atoms in 4 g of He

$\text{He} = \dfrac{4}{4} \times N_A \times 1 = N_A$

Thus, 2 g of H_2 contains the maximum number of atoms among the given options.

8. (*d*) At NTP/STP

$\because \quad n = \dfrac{V}{22400\,(\text{mL})} = \dfrac{w}{M}$

$\therefore \quad w = \dfrac{V \times M}{22{,}400}$

Given, $V = 112$ mL and molar mass of oxygen = 32 g/mol

$\therefore \quad w = \dfrac{112 \times 32}{22400\,\text{mL}} \Rightarrow w = 0.16\,\text{g}$

Hence, weight of 112 mL of oxygen at NTP/STP = 0.16 g.

9. (*a*) (a) 28 g of CO occupies

= 22.4 L of CO at NTP

$\therefore$ 14 g of CO occupies

$= \dfrac{22.4}{28} \times 14$ L of CO at NTP

= 11.2 L of CO at NTP

Thus, 14 g of CO occupies 11.2 L volume at NTP.

(b) Number of moles of CO

$= \dfrac{\text{mass of CO}}{\text{molar mass of CO}}$

$= \dfrac{14\,\text{g}}{28\,\text{g mol}^{-1}} = \dfrac{1}{2}$ mole of CO

Thus, 14 g CO equal to $\dfrac{1}{2}$ mole of CO.

(c) As the molar mass of CO and N_2 gas are the same, thus 14 g of CO corresponds to same moles of N_2 gas.

(d) 28 g of CO contains $= 6.022 \times 10^{23}$ molecules

$\therefore$ 14 g of CO contains

$= \dfrac{6.022 \times 10^{23}}{28} \times 14$

$= 3.011 \times 10^{23}$ molecules

Thus, 14 g of CO corresponds to 3.011×10^{23} molecules.

Hence, option (a) is wrong, while rest of the options are correct.

10. (*c*) We know that, one mole of an element

$= 6.023 \times 10^{23}$ atoms

= atomic weight of the element

Now, 1.58×10^{22} atoms weigh 1.05 g

$\therefore$ 6.02×10^{23} atoms weigh

$= \dfrac{(1.05 \times 6.023 \times 10^{23})}{1.58 \times 10^{22}}$

$= 40.02\,\text{g} \sim 40\,\text{g}$

Atomic weight of $X = 40$ g

11. (*d*) The formula of urea = NH_2CONH_2

Molar mass of urea

$= 14 + (2 \times 1) + 12 + 16 + 14 + (2 \times 1)$

$= 60\,\text{g mol}^{-1}$

Molar mass of $N_2 = 28\,\text{g mol}^{-1}$

$\therefore$ % of N_2 in urea $= \dfrac{28}{60} \times 100 = 46.6\%$

Hence, the percentage of N_2 in urea $= 46.6\% \sim 46\%$

12. (*b*) 1 mole of water means 18 g of water which means 6.023×10^{23} molecules.

1 L of water means = 1000 g (as $d_{H_2O} = 1\,\text{g/mL}$)

1000 g of water $= \dfrac{1000}{18}$ mol

As, 1 mole of water $= 6.023 \times 10^{23}$ molecules

$\therefore \quad \dfrac{1000}{18}$ moles of water

$= \dfrac{1000}{18} \times 6.023 \times 10^{23}$

$= 55.5 \times 6.023 \times 10^{23}$ molecules

13. (*c*) At STP, 22400 cm^3 of

$CH_4 = 12 + 4 = 16\,\text{g}$ (1 mole)

At STP, 112 cm^3 of CH_4

$= \dfrac{16 \times 112}{22400} = 0.08\,\text{g}$

14. (*b*) As 8 moles of O-atoms are contained by 1 mole of $Mg_3(PO_4)_2$.

$\therefore$ The number of moles of $Mg_3(PO_4)_2$ that contains 0.25 mole of O-atoms.

$= \dfrac{1}{8} \times 0.25 = 3.125 \times 10^{-2}$ mol

15. (*d*) The formula of sodium ferrocyanide is $Na_4[Fe(CN)_6]$ suggests that it has four sodium atoms.

Number of Na-atoms

= number of moles $\times$ number of atoms per molecule $\times$ Avogadro's number

$= 2 \times 4 \times 6.023 \times 10^{23}$ Na-atoms

$= 48.2 \times 10^{23}$ Na-atoms

$\sim 48 \times 10^{23}$ Na-atoms

16. (*a*) 1 mole of CO_2 molecule

$= 6.023 \times 10^{23}$ molecules of CO_2

= 44 g of CO_2

$\therefore$ 10^{21} molecules of CO_2

$= \dfrac{44}{6.023 \times 10^{23}} \times 10^{21}\,\text{g}\,CO_2$

$= 7.31 \times 10^{-2}\,\text{g} = 73.1\,\text{mg}$

$\therefore$ CO_2 left $= 200 - 73.1 = 126.9$ mg

Hence, moles of CO_2 left $= \dfrac{\text{given mass}}{\text{molar mass}}$

$= \dfrac{126.9 \times 10^{-3}\,\text{g}}{44\,\text{g/mol}}$

$= 2.88 \times 10^{-3}$ mol

17. (*b*) In 18 mL, number of moles of water

$= \frac{\text{mass of } H_2O}{\text{molar mass of } H_2O}$

$= \frac{\text{density} \times \text{volume}}{\text{molar mass of } H_2O} = \frac{1 \times 18}{18} = 1 \text{ mol}$

Number of molecules present in 1 mole of $H_2O = 6.022 \times 10^{23}$ molecules

Number of electrons in 1 molecule of $H_2O = (1 \times 2) + 8 = 10$

$\therefore$ Number of electrons in 6.022×10^{23} molecules of H_2O

$= 6.023 \times 10^{23} \times 10$

$= 6.023 \times 10^{24}$ electrons

18. (*a*) Given, volume of $O_2 = 1$ L

$\because$ 22.4 L of O_2 at STP weigh = 32 g

$\therefore$ 1 L of O_2 at STP weigh

$= \frac{32}{22.4}$ g $= 1.428$ g ≈ 1.43 g

19. (*d*) Mass of one molecule of water

$= \frac{\text{molar mass}}{N_A} = \frac{18}{6.023 \times 10^{23}}$ g

$\therefore$ Volume of 1 molecule of water

$= \frac{\text{mass}}{\text{density}} = \frac{18 \times 10^{-23}}{6.023}$

$= 2.98 \times 10^{-23} \text{ cm}^3$ or $\approx 3 \times 10^{-23} \text{ cm}^3$

20. (*b*) The number of atoms in 0.1 mole of a triatomic gas = $NA \times$ number of moles $\times$ number of atoms in 1 molecule of gas

$= 6.023 \times 10^{23} \times 0.1 \times 3$

$= 1.806 \times 10^{23}$ atoms

21. (*a*) Number of atoms in 4.25 g of NH_3 = number of moles of NH_3 $\times$ Avogadro's number $\times$ number of atoms per molecule of NH_3.

$= \frac{4.25}{17} \times 6.023 \times 10^{23} \times 4$

$= 6.023 \times 10^{23}$ atoms

22. (*c*) As, normality = molarity $\times$ valence factor for H_2SO_4,

valence factor for $H_2SO_4 = 2$

$\therefore$ Normality, $N = M \times 2$

or $M = \frac{N}{2} = \frac{0.02}{2} = 0.01$ M

Moles of H_2SO_4

$= \frac{0.01 \times 100}{1000} = 1 \times 10^{-3}$ mol

[$\because$ Molarity $= \frac{\text{Number of moles of solute}}{\text{Volume in solution (in mL)}} \times 1000$]

$\therefore$ Number of molecules in 100 mL of 0.02 N H_2SO_4

$= 1 \times 10^{-3} \times N_A$

$= 1 \times 10^{-3} \times 6.023 \times 10^{23}$

$= 6.023 \times 10^{20}$ molecules

23. (*c*) $\because$ 22400 mL water contains water molecules $= 6.023 \times 10^{23}$ molecules

$\therefore$ In 1 mL, the number of water

molecules $= \frac{6.023 \times 10^{23}}{22400}$ molecules

Since, 1 mL contains 20 drops.

Therefore, number of water molecules in 1 drop

$= \frac{6.023 \times 10^{23}}{22400 \times 20}$

$= 1.344 \times 10^{18}$ molecules

24. (*a*) Given, $V = 1.12 \times 10^{-7} \text{ cm}^3$

$\because$ 22400 cm^3 of the gas at NTP has molecules $= 6.023 \times 10^{23}$

$\therefore$ $1.12 \times 10^{-7} \text{ cm}^3$ of the gas at NTP will have molecules.

$= \frac{6.023 \times 10^{23}}{22400} \times 1.12 \times 10^{-7}$

$= 3.01 \times 10^{12}$ molecules

25. (*c*) For solution of same substance,

$N_1V_1 = N_2V_2$

$\Rightarrow 2N \times 0.1 = \frac{N}{10} \times V_2$

$V_2 = 2 \text{ dm}^3$

26. (*a*) In 18 g of water, number of H_2O molecules is N_A.

So, in 18 mg of water, number of H_2O molecules would be

$= N_A \times \frac{18 \text{ mg}}{18 \times 10^3 \text{ mg}}$

$= 10^{-3} \times N_A$

27. (*a*)(a) 34 g of H_2O

$\because$ 18 g of $H_2O = 6.023 \times 10^{23}$ molecules

$\therefore$ 34 g of $H_2O = \frac{6.023 \times 10^{23} \times 34}{18}$

$= 11.37 \times 10^{23}$ molecules

(b) 28 g of CO_2

$\because$ 44 g of $CO_2 = 6.023 \times 10^{23}$ molecules

$\therefore$ 28 g of $CO_2 = \frac{6.023 \times 10^{23} \times 28}{44}$

$= 3.8 \times 10^{23}$ molecules

(c) 46 g of CH_3OH

$\because$ 32g of $CH_3OH = 6.023 \times 10^{23}$ molecules

$\therefore$ 46 g of $CH_3OH = \frac{6.023 \times 10^{23} \times 46}{32}$

$= 8.65 \times 10^{23}$ molecules

(d) 54 g of N_2O_5

$\because$ 108g of $N_2O_5 = 6.023 \times 10^{23}$ molecules

$\therefore$ 54 g of $N_2O_5 = \frac{6.023 \times 10^{23} \times 54}{108}$

$= 3.01 \times 10^{23}$ molecules

Thus, 34 g of H_2O contains the largest number of molecules.

28. (*c*) Mass of 1 mole of methane (CH_4)

$= 16$ g

Mass of 0.1 mole of methane

$= 16 \times 0.1$ g

$= 1.6$ g

29. (*a*) 22.4 L of gas at STP is occupied by 6.023×10^{23} molecules.

1 mole of substance = molar mass of that substance $= 6.023 \times 10^{23}$ molecules.

(a) In 15 L of H_2 gas at STP, the number of molecules

$= \frac{6.023 \times 10^{23}}{22.4} \times 15$

$= 4.033 \times 10^{23}$ molecules

(b) In 5 L of N_2 gas at STP, the number of molecules

$= \frac{6.023 \times 10^{23} \times 5}{22.4}$

$= 1.344 \times 10^{23}$ molecules

(c) In 0.5 g of H_2 gas, the number of molecules

$= \frac{6.023 \times 10^{23} \times 0.5}{2}$

$= 1.505 \times 10^{23}$ molecules

(d) In 10 g of O_2 gas, the number of molecules

$= \frac{6.023 \times 10^{23} \times 10}{32}$

$= 1.882 \times 10^{23}$ molecules

Thus, 15L of H_2 gas at STP has the maximum number of molecules.

30. (*a*) Mass of one He-atom = 4 u

or 4 u = 1 He-atom or $1\text{u} = \frac{1}{4}$ He-atom

$\therefore$ 100 u $= \frac{100}{4} = 25$ He-atoms

31. (*d*) The molecular weight of

$C_{60}H_{122} = (60 \times 12) + (122 \times 1)$
$= 720 + 122 = 842$ g/mol

Weight of 6.023×10^{23} molecules of $C_{60}H_{122} = 842$ g

$\therefore$ Weight of 1 molecule of $C_{60}H_{122}$

$$= \frac{842}{6.023 \times 10^{23}} \text{ g} = 1.39 \times 10^{-21} \text{ g}$$

$\approx 1.4 \times 10^{-21}$ g

Thus, the weight of one molecule of $C_{60}H_{122}$ is 1.4×10^{-21} g.

32. (*b*) Number of gram molecules of chlorine $= \frac{6.02 \times 10^{25}}{6.023 \times 10^{23}}$

$= 99.9 \sim 100$ gram molecules

33. (*c*) Gram molecular volume (standard molar volume) of a gas is the volume occupied by 1 mole of any gas at 273 K and 1 atm pressure (STP). It is equal to 22.4 L or 22400 cm^3. It is same for all gases.

34. (*d*) $\because$ The ratio of O_2 and N_2 by weight is 1 : 4.

$\therefore$ The ratio of O_2 and N_2 by moles

$$= \frac{1}{32} : \frac{4}{28}$$

Since,

number of molecules

= number of moles $\times 6.023 \times 10^{23}$

$\therefore$ Ratio of O_2 and N_2 by molecules

$$= \frac{\frac{1}{32} \times 6.023 \times 10^{23}}{\frac{4}{28} \times 6.023 \times 10^{23}}$$

$= 7:32$

35. (*e*) (a) The weight of 1 mole of oxygen

$= 16$ g

(b) Weight of 1 molecule of sulphur trioxide

$= 80 / (6.023 \times 10^{23})$ g

$= 1.328 \times 10^{-22}$ g

(c) Weight of 100 u of uranium

$= 100 \times 1.66 \times 10^{-24}$ g

$= 1.66 \times 10^{-22}$ g

(d) Weight of 10 moles of hydrogen

$= 10$ g

(e) Weight of $CO_2 = 44$ g

Hence, 44 g of carbon dioxide is the heaviest among these.

36. (*b*) Total number of atoms in $CuSO_4 \cdot 5H_2O$ are

$1 + 1 + 4 + 5(2 + 1) = 6 + 5 \times 3 = 21$

$\therefore$ $CuSO_4 \cdot 5H_2O$ has 21 atoms.

37. (*d*) Number of moles of $CaCO_3$

$$= \frac{10}{100} \text{ g} = 0.1 \text{ mol}$$

As 1 mole contains of $CaCO_3$
$= 6.023 \times 10^{23}$ molecules

$\therefore$ 0.1 mole contains $= 6.023 \times 10^{23} \times 0.1$
$= 6.023 \times 10^{22}$ molecules of $CaCO_3$

Also, it is known that protons in 1 mole or 6.023×10^{23} molecules of $CaCO_3$.
= atomic number of calcium + atomic number of carbon + 3 (atomic number of oxygen)

$= 20 + 6 + 3(8) = 50$

$\therefore$ Protons in 6.023×10^{22} molecules of $CaCO_3$
$= 6.023 \times 10^{22} \times 50 = 3.01 \times 10^{24}$

which is close to option (d).

Hence, option (d) is correct choice.

38. (*b*) $\underset{27\text{g}}{Al^{3+}} + 3e^- \longrightarrow \underset{27\text{g}}{Al}$

27 g of Al is reduced by $3 \times 6.023 \times 10^{23}$ electrons

$\therefore$ 4.5×10^{-5} g of Al will be reduced by

$$= \frac{3 \times 6.023 \times 10^{23} \times 4.5 \times 10^{-5}}{27}$$

$= 3.01 \times 10^{18}$ electrons

39. (*d*) $C_6H_5COOH + NaOH \longrightarrow C_6H_5COONa + H_2O$

For complete neutralisation,

Number of moles NaOH $\equiv$ Number of moles of benzoic acid

$$\frac{w}{40} = \frac{12.2}{122}$$

or $w = 4$ g

Topic 4

Stoichiometric and Volumetric Calculations

2019

1 The number of moles of hydrogen molecules required to produce 20 moles of ammonia through Haber's process is

(a) 20 (b) 30 (c) 40 (d) 10 [NEET]

2017

2 3.5 g of mixture of NaOH and KOH were dissolved and made up to 250 mL. 25 mL of this solution were completely neutralised by 17 mL of (N/2) HCl solution. Then, the percentage of KOH in mixture is [AIIMS]

(a) 80 (b) 10 (c) 34 (d) 56

2014

3 1.0 g of magnesium is burnt with 0.56 g O_2 in a closed vessel. Which reactant is left in excess and how much? (Atomic weight, Mg = 24, O = 16) [CBSE AIPMT]

(a) Mg, 0.16 g (b) O_2, 0.16 g
(c) Mg, 0.44 g (d) O_2, 0.28 g

4 When 22.4 L of $H_2(g)$ is mixed with 11.2 L of $Cl_2(g)$, each at STP, the moles of HCl (g) formed is equal to [CBSE AIPMT]

(a) 1 mole of HCl (g) (b) 2 moles of HCl (g)
(c) 0.5 mole of HCl (g) (d) 1.5 mole of HCl (g)

5 10 g of a mixture of BaO and CaO requires 100 cm^3 of 2.5 M HCl to react completely. The percentage of calcium oxide in the mixture is approximately (given, molar mass of BaO = 153) [KCET]
(a) 52.6 (b) 55.1 (c) 44.9 (d) 47.4

6 In a closed vessel, 5 moles of $A_2(g)$ and 7 moles of $B_2(g)$ are reacted in the following manner, [EAMCET]

$$A_2(g)+3B_2(g)\longrightarrow 2AB_3(g)$$

What is the total number of moles of gases present in the container at the end of the reaction?
(a) 22/3 (b) 7/3 (c) 14/3 (d) 8/3

2013

7 Cyclohexanol is dehydrated to cyclohexene on heating with conc. H_2SO_4. If the yield of this reaction is 75%, how much cyclohexene will be obtained from 100 g of cyclohexanol? [WB JEE]
(a) 61.5 g (b) 75.0 g (c) 20.0 g (d) 41.0g

8 In the synthesis of ammonia [KCET]

$$N_2(g)+3H_2 \rightleftharpoons 2NH_3(g)$$

If the quantity of N_2 reacted is 100 mL, the quantity of H_2 and NH_3 would be
(a) 300 mL H_2 and 200 mL NH_3
(b) 300 mL H_2 and 300 mL NH_3
(c) 300 mL H_2 and 100 mL NH_3
(d) 100 mL H_2 and 200 mL NH_3

2012

9 A metal oxide has the formula A_2O_3. It can be reduced by hydrogen to give free metal and water. 0.1596 g of this metal oxide requires 6 mg of hydrogen for complete reduction. What is the atomic weight of metal? [AIIMS]
(a) 52.3 (b) 57.3 (c) 55.8 (d) 59.3

10 20.0 kg of $N_2(g)$ and 3.0 kg of $H_2(g)$ are mixed to produce $NH_3(g)$. The amount of $NH_3(g)$ formed is [Kerala CEE]
(a) 17 kg (b) 34 kg (c) 20 kg
(d) 3 kg (e) 23 kg

11 Stoichiometric ratio of sodium dihydrogen orthophosphate and sodium hydrogen orthophosphate required for synthesis of $Na_5P_3O_{10}$ is [Guj CET]
(a) 1.5 : 3 (b) 3 : 1.5 (c) 1 : 1 (d) 2 : 3

2010

12 A mixture of $CaCl_2$ and NaCl weighing 4.44 g is treated with sodium carbonate solution to precipitate all the Ca^{2+} ions as calcium carbonate. The calcium carbonate, so obtained is heated strongly to get 0.56 g of CaO. The percentage of NaCl in the mixture (atomic mass of Ca = 40) is [KCET]
(a) 75 (b) 30.6 (c) 25 (d) 69.4

13 10 g of hydrogen and 64 g of oxygen were filled in a steel vessel and exploded. Amount of water produced in this reaction will be [CBSE AIPMT]
(a) 3 mol (b) 4 mol (c) 1 mol (d) 2 mol

14 x moles of potassium dichromate oxidises 1 mole of ferrous oxalate in acidic medium. Here x is [AIIMS]
(a) 3 (b) 1.5 (c) 0.5 (d) 1.0

15 What volume of CO_2 will be liberated at NTP, if 12 g of carbon is burnt in excess of oxygen? [AFMC]
(a) 11.2 L (b) 22.4 L
(c) 2.24 L (d) 1.12 L

16 The mass of oxygen that would be required to produce enough CO which completely reduces 1.6 kg Fe_2O_3 (atomic mass of Fe = 56), is [Manipal]
(a) 240 g (b) 480 g (c) 720 g (d) 960 g

17 How much volume of oxygen at STP (in litres) is required to burn 4 g of methane gas completely? [J&K CET]
(a) 11.2 (b) 5.6 (c) 2.8 (d) 82008

18 Excess of carbon dioxide is passed through 50 mL of 0.5 M calcium hydroxide solution. After the completion of the reaction, the solution was evaporated to dryness. The solid calcium carbonate was completely neutralised with 0.1N hydrochloric acid. The volume of hydrochloric acid required is (Atomic mass of calcium = 40) [KCET]
(a) 200 cm^3 (b) 500 cm^3
(c) 400 cm^3 (d) 300 cm^3

19 100 mL of PH_3 on heating forms P and H_2, the volume change in the reaction is [DUMET]
(a) an increase of 50 mL (b) an increase of 100 mL
(c) an increase of 150 mL (d) a decrease of 50 mL

2008

20 Number of moles of MnO_4^- required to oxidise one mole of ferrous oxalate completely in acidic medium will be [CBSE AIPMT]
(a) 0.6 mol (b) 0.4 mol
(c) 7.5 mol (d) 0.2 mol

21 What volume of oxygen gas (O_2) measured at 0°C and 1 atm, is needed to burn completely 1 L of propane gas (C_3H_8) measured under the same conditions? [CBSE AIPMT]
(a) 7 L (b) 6 L
(c) 5 L (d) 10 L

22 How many moles of lead (II) chloride will be formed from a reaction between 6.5 g of PbO and 3.2 g of HCl? [CBSE AIPMT]
(a) 0.044 (b) 0.333
(c) 0.011 (d) 0.029

23 The stoichiometry of the following reaction is

$$K_2S_2O_8(aq)+2KI(aq)\longrightarrow 2K_2SO_4(aq)+I_2(aq)$$

[J&K CET]
(a) 2 : 2 (b) 1 : 1
(c) 1 : 2 (d) 2 : 1

24 40 g of a sample of carbon on combustion left 10% of it unreacted. The volume of oxygen required at STP for this combustion reaction is [EAMCET]

(a) 22.4 L (b) 67.2 L (c) 11.2 L (d) 44.8 L

25 $Fe^{2+} \longrightarrow Fe^{3+} + e^-$,

$MnO_4^- + 5e^- \longrightarrow Mn^{2+}$

The ratio of stoichiometric coefficient of Fe^{2+} and MnO_4^- is [DUMET]

(a) 1 : 5 (b) 5 : 1 (c) 2 : 3 (d) 6 : 1

26 For the reaction, $Fe_2O_3 + 3CO \longrightarrow 2Fe + 3CO_2$, the volume of carbon monoxide required to reduce one mole of ferric oxide is [KCET]

(a) 22.4 dm^3 (b) 44.8 dm^3 (c) 67.2 dm^3 (d) 11.2 dm^3

2007

27 What is the stoichiometric coefficient of Ca in the reaction?

$Ca + Al^{3+} \longrightarrow Ca^{2+} + Al$ [UP CPMT]

(a) 2 (b) 1 (c) 3 (d) 4

28 10 L of O_2 gas is reacted with 30 L of CO gas at STP. The volumes of each gas present at the end of the reaction are [Kerala CEE]

(a) $CO = 10\,L, CO_2 = 20\,L$ (b) $O_2 = 10\,L, CO = 30\,L$
(c) $CO = 20\,L, CO_2 = 10\,L$ (d) $O_2 = 10\,L, CO_2 = 20\,L$
(e) $O_2 = 10\,L, CO = 10\,L$

29 If equal volumes of 1M $KMnO_4$ and 1M $K_2Cr_2O_7$ solutions are allowed to oxidise Fe (II) to Fe (III) in acidic medium then Fe (II) oxidised will be [EAMCET]

(a) more by $KMnO_4$ (b) more by $K_2Cr_2O_7$
(c) equal in both the cases (d) cannot be determined

30 2.76 g of silver carbonate on being strongly heated yield a residue weighing [BHU]

(a) 2.16 g (b) 2.48 g (c) 2.64 g (d) 2.32 g

31 Sodium bicarbonate on heating decomposes to form sodium carbonate, CO_2 and water. If 0.2 moles of sodium bicarbonate is completely decomposed, how many mole of sodium carbonate is formed? [J&K CET]

(a) 0.1 (b) 0.2 (c) 0.05 (d) 0.025

32 The decomposition of a certain mass of $CaCO_3$ gave 11.2 dm^3 of CO_2 gas at STP. The mass of KOH required to completely neutralise the gas is [KCET]

(a) 56 g (b) 28 g (c) 42 g (d) 20 g

33 What is the weight of oxygen that is required for the complete combustion of 2.8 kg of ethylene? [BCECE]

(a) 9.6 kg (b) 96.0 kg (c) 6.4 kg (d) 2.8 kg

34 2 g of O_2 at 27°C and 760 mm of Hg pressure has volume [BCECE]

(a) 1.4 L (b) 2.8 L
(c) 11.2 L (d) 22.4 L

Answers

1. (b)	2. (b)	3. (a)	4. (a)	5. (a)	6. (a)	7. (a)	8. (a)	9. (c)	10. (a)
11. (a)	12. (a)	13. (b)	14. (c)	15. (b)	16. (b)	17. (a)	18. (b)	19. (a)	20. (a)
21. (c)	22. (d)	23. (c)	24. (b)	25. (b)	26. (c)	27. (c)	28. (a)	29. (b)	30. (a)
31. (a)	32. (b)	33. (a)	34. (a)						

Explanations

1. (*b*) According to Haber's process,

$$N_2(g) + 3H_2(g) \rightleftharpoons 2NH_3(g)$$

Now, according to above equations 2 moles of ammonia (NH_3) require $= 3$ moles of H_2

$\therefore$ 1 mole of NH_3 require $= 3/2$ moles of H_2

or, 20 moles of NH_3 require $= \frac{3}{2} \times 20$ moles of H_2

$= 30$ moles of H_2.

Note Involvement of any limiting reagent is not mentioned in the question.

2. (*b*) Suppose the amount of NaOH in the mixture $= xg$

$\therefore$ Amount of KOH $= (3 \cdot 5 - x)$g

25 mL of alkali solution $= 17$ mL of ($N/2$) HCl

or, 250 mL of alkali solution $= 170$ mL of ($N/2$) HCl

1000 mL of (N) HCl contain 36.5 g of HCl

170 mL of $N/2$ HCl will contain

$$\frac{36 \cdot 5 \times 170}{1000 \times 2} = 3 \cdot 1025 \text{ g of HCl}$$

Eq. mass of NaOH $= 40$ g eq mol^{-1}

and that of KOH $= 56$ g eq mol^{-1}

40 g of NaOH require 36 · 5 g of HCl

x g of NaOH will require $\frac{36 \cdot 5 \times x}{40}$ g of HCl

Similarly, 56 g of KOH require 36 · 5 g of HCl

$(3.5 - x)$ of KOH will require

$$= \frac{36 \cdot 5(3 \cdot 5 - x)}{56} \text{ g of HCl}$$

Thus, $\frac{36 \cdot 5x}{40} + \frac{36 \cdot 5(3 \cdot 5 - x)}{56} = 3 \cdot 1025$ g of HCl

or $x = 3 \cdot 15$ g $=$ Amount of NaOH in the mixture

$\therefore$ Amount of KOH $= (3 \cdot 5 - 3 \cdot 15)$g $= 0.35$ g

3.5 g of the mixture contain 0 · 35 g of KOH

100 g of the mixture contain

$$= \frac{0 \cdot 35\text{g} \times 100}{3.5} = 10 \text{ g of KOH}$$

Hence, % of KOH $= 10\%$

3. (*a*) The balanced chemical equation is

$$\underset{24\text{g}}{Mg} + \underset{16\text{g}}{\frac{1}{2}O_2} \longrightarrow \underset{40\text{g}}{MgO}$$

From the above equation, it is clear that 24 g Mg reacts with 16 g O_2.

Thus, 1.0 g Mg reacts with

$\frac{16}{24}O_2 = 0.67\,g\,O_2$

But only 0.56 g O_2 is available which is less than 0.67 g. Thus, O_2 is the limiting reagent.

Further, 16 g O_2 reacts with 24 g Mg.

$\therefore$ 0.56 g O_2 will react with Mg

$= \frac{24}{16} \times 0.56 = 0.84$ g

$\therefore$ Amount of Mg left unreacted

$= 1.0 - 0.84$

$= 0.16$ g Mg

Hence, Mg is present in excess and 0.16 g Mg is left behind unreacted.

4. (*a*) The given problem is related to the concept of stoichiometry of chemical equations. Thus, we have to convert the given volumes into their moles and then, identify the limiting reagent (possessing minimum number of moles and gets completely used up in the reaction). The limiting reagent gives the moles of product formed in the reaction.

$\underset{22.4\,L}{H_2(g)} + \underset{11.2\,L}{Cl_2(g)} \longrightarrow \underset{2\,mol}{2HCl(g)}$

$\because$ 22.4 volume at STP is occupied by

$Cl_2 = 1$ mole,

$\therefore$ 11.2 L volume will be occupied by

$Cl_2 = \frac{1 \times 11.2}{22.4}$ mole

$= 0.5$ mol

Thus, $\underset{1\,mol}{H_2(g)} + \underset{0.5\,mol}{Cl_2(g)} \longrightarrow 2HCl(g)$

Since, Cl_2 possesses minimum number of moles, thus it is the limiting reagent.

As per equation,

1 mole Cl_2 = 2 mol HCl

$\therefore$ 0.5 mole $Cl_2 = 2 \times 0.5$ mol HCl

$= 1.0$ mole of HCl

Hence, 1.0 mole of HCl (*g*) is produced by 0.5 mole of Cl_2 (or 11.2 L).

5. (*a*) Let mass of CaO = *x* g

$\therefore$ Mass of BaO = $(10 - x)$g

Again, equivalent mass of BaO

$= \frac{\text{molar mass}}{2} = \frac{153}{2} = 76.5$

$\therefore$ Number of moles of BaO $= \frac{10-x}{76.5}$

and equivalent mass of CaO $= \frac{56}{2} = 28$

$\therefore$ Number of moles of CaO $= \frac{x}{28}$

Also, molarity

$= \frac{\text{moles of solute}}{\text{volume of solution (in L)}}$

$2.5 = \frac{\text{moles of solute}}{\frac{100}{1000}}$

$\therefore$ Moles of solute $= \frac{2.5 \times 100}{1000}$
$= 0.25$ mol

$\therefore$ For complete neutralisation (reaction), moles of BaO and CaO = moles of HCl (solute)

$\therefore \quad \frac{x}{28} + \frac{10-x}{76.5} = 0.25$

or $76.5x + 28(10 - x)$
$= 0.25 \times 28 \times 76.5$

or $\quad 48.5x = 255.5$

or $\quad x = \frac{255.5}{48.5} = 5.26$ g

$\therefore \quad$ % of CaO $= \frac{5.26}{10} \times 100 = 52.6\%$

6. (*a*) $\quad A_2 + 3B_2 \longrightarrow 2AB_3$
Initial 5 moles 7 mole 0

According to reaction, 1 mole A_2 requires 3 moles B_2.

Hence, 7 moles B_2 will react with 7/3 moles A_2

A_2 left $= 5 - \frac{7}{3} = 8/3$ moles A_2 (*g*)

1 mole A_2 produces 2 moles AB_3.

Hence, $\frac{7}{3}$ moles A_2 will produce $\frac{7}{3} \times 2$ moles AB_3

Total moles of gases in vessel

$= \frac{8}{3}$ moles $A_2(g) + \frac{14}{3}$ moles AB_3 (*g*)

$= \frac{22}{3}$ moles

7. (*a*) Cyclohexanol (OH) $\xrightarrow[\text{conc. } H_2SO_4]{\Delta}$ Cyclohexene
100 g $\qquad$ 82 g

100 g cyclohexanol produces = 82 g of cyclohexene

1 g cyclohexanol produces $= \frac{82}{100}$ g of cyclohexene

If reaction occurs 75% then weight of cyclohexene produced by 100 g of cyclohexanol is

$= \frac{82}{100} \times 100 \times \frac{75}{100} = 61.5$ g

8. (*a*) $N_2(g) + 3H_2(g) \rightleftharpoons 2NH_3(g)$

If the quantity of $N_2(g)$ reacted is 100 mL

$\therefore$ The quantity of $H_2(g)$ is three times i.e. 300 mL

and NH_3 produced = 200 mL

9. (*c*) The given oxide (A_2O_3) is a metal oxide, which gives free metal and water (H_2O) on reduction. The related reaction is as follows :

$A_2O_3 + \underset{\substack{6g \\ (3\times2=6)}}{3H_2} \longrightarrow \underset{(x)}{2A} + 3H_2O$

Given : ~ A_2O_3 (used) = 0.1596 g

H_2 (used) = 6 mg = 0.006 g

Also, $3H_2 = 6\,g\,(6 \times 1 = 6)$

and change in oxidation no. of $(A) = (3 \to 0) = 3$

$\because$ 0.006 g of H_2 is used to reduce 0.1596 g of A_2O_3

6 g of H_2 is used to reduce

$= \frac{0.1596 \times 6}{0.006}$ of A_2O_3

$= 159.6$ g of A_2O_3

$\because$ Mass of 1 mole = molar mass

$\therefore$ Mass of 1 mole of $A_2O_3 = 159.6$ g

Also, molar mass of A_2O_3 = sum of atomic masses of the present elements.

$\therefore$ $159.6 = 2x + 3 \times 16$

or $\quad x = 55.8$ g/mol

Hence, atomic mass of metal (*A*)
$= 55.8$ g/mol

10. (*a*) $\underset{28\,g}{N_2} + \underset{6\,g}{3H_2} \longrightarrow \underset{34\,g}{2NH_3}$

Mass of $N_2 = 20\,kg = 20000\,g$

Mass of $H_2 = 3\,kg = 3000\,g$

$n_{N_2} = \frac{w_{N_2}}{M_{N_2}} = \frac{20000}{28} = 714.28$ mol

$n_{H_2} = \frac{w_{H_2}}{M_{N_2}} = \frac{3000}{2} = 1500$ mol

According to the equation

$N_2 + 3H_2 \longrightarrow 2NH_3,$

1 mole of N_2 requires 3 moles of H_2

$\therefore$ 714.28 mole of N_2 requires 3×714.28 moles of H_2 = 2142.48 moles H_2

But there are only 1500 moles H_2.

So, limiting reactant is H_2.

Weight of NH_3 obtained from 6×10^{-3} kg of $H_2 = 34 \times 10^{-3}$ kg

$\therefore$ Weight of NH_3 obtained from 3 kg of H_2

$$= \frac{34 \times 10^{-3}}{6 \times 10^{-3}} \times 3 = 17 \text{ kg } NH_3$$

11. (*a*) $\underset{\text{Sodium dihydrogen orthophosphate}}{3NaH_2PO_4} + \underset{\text{Sodium hydrogen orthophosphate}}{6Na_2HPO_4}$

$$\longrightarrow 3Na_5P_3O_{10} + 6H_2O$$

Stoichiometric ratio = 3 : 6

$$= \frac{3}{2} : \frac{6}{2} = 1.5 : 3$$

Hence, stoichiometric ratio = 1.5 : 3

12. (*a*) Given, $CaCl_2 + NaCl = 4.44g$

The mixture when treated with Na_2CO_3, it gives $CaCO_3$, means $CaCl_2$ only react with Na_2CO_3 as follows :

$$CaCl_2(s) + Na_2CO_3 \longrightarrow CaCO_3 + 2NaCl \quad ...(i)$$

Again, when $CaCO_3$ thus formed is heated, it gives CaO(0.56 g) as follows

$$CaCO_3 \xrightarrow{\Delta} CaO + CO_2 \quad ...(ii)$$

On adding eq. no. (i) and (ii), we have,

$$CaCl_2 + Na_2CO_3 \longrightarrow \underset{1\text{ mole}}{CaO} + CO_2 + 2NaCl$$

$\because$ Moles of CaO = moles of $CaCl_2$

Also, molar mass of CaO = 56 g/mol

and molar mass of $CaCl_2$ = 111 g/mol

$\because$ 56 g of CaO = 111 g of $CaCl_2$

$\therefore$ 0.56 g of CaO = 1.11 g of $CaCl_2$

Hence, mass of NaCl

$$= 4.44 - 1.11 = 3.33 \text{ g}$$

and percentage of NaCl

$$= \frac{3.33 \times 100}{4.44} = 75\%$$

13. (*b*) $\underset{10g\text{ (5 moles)}}{2H_2} + \underset{64g\text{ (2 moles)}}{O_2} \longrightarrow 2H_2O$

2 moles H_2 reacts with 1 moles O_2

5 moles H_2 reacts with $\frac{1}{2} \times 5$ moles O_2

$$= 2.5 \text{ moles } O_2$$

But there are only 2 moles O_2.

Thus, O_2 act as a limiting reagent.

Thus, 1 mole of O_2 produces = 2 moles of H_2O

$\therefore$ 2 moles of O_2 produces = 4 moles of H_2O

14. (*c*) The reaction of oxidation of ferrous oxalate by potassium dichromate in acidic medium is written as

$$2FeC_2O_4 + Cr_2O_7^{2-} + 14H^+ \longrightarrow 2Fe^{3+} + 2Cr^{3+} + 4CO_2 + 7H_2O$$

$\because$ 2 moles of FeC_2O_4 are oxidised by = 1 mole of $Cr_2O_7^{2-}$.

$\therefore$ 1 mole of FeC_2O_4 will be oxidised by

$$= \frac{1}{2} = 0.5 \text{ mole of } Cr_2O_7^{2-}$$

15. (*b*) $\underset{\substack{1\text{ mol}\\12\text{ g}}}{C(g)} + O_2(g) \longrightarrow \underset{\substack{1\text{ mol}\\22.4\text{ L}}}{CO_2(g)}$

$\therefore$ If 12 g of carbon is burnt in excess of oxygen, 22.4 L of CO_2 will be liberated.

16. (*b*) $3C + \frac{3}{2}O_2 \longrightarrow 3CO$

$$Fe_2O_3 + 3CO \longrightarrow 2Fe + 3CO_2$$

$\because$ 1 mole of

$Fe_2O_3 \equiv 3$ moles of $CO \equiv \frac{3}{2}$ moles of O_2

$\therefore$ 160 g of Fe_2O_3 require

$$O_2 = \frac{3}{2} \times 32 = 48 \text{ g}$$

Thus, 1.6 kg (or 1600 g) of Fe_2O_3 will require O_2 = 480 g

17. (*a*) $CH_4 + 2O_2 \longrightarrow CO_2 + 2H_2O$

For 16 g of methane (2 × 22.4) L of O_2 is required.

For 4 g methane oxygen required

$$= \frac{2 \times 22.4 \times 4}{16} = 11.2 \text{ L of } O_2$$

18. (*b*) According to the question, the reaction occurs as

$$\underset{\substack{74\\(=1\text{ mole})}}{Ca(OH)_2} + \underset{\substack{44\\(=1\text{ mole})}}{CO_2} \longrightarrow \underset{\substack{100\\(=1\text{ mole})}}{CaCO_3} + \underset{\substack{18\\(=1\text{ mole})}}{H_2O}$$

Given, 50 mL of 0.5 M $Ca(OH)_2$ reacts with excess of CO_2.

$\therefore$ Number of millimoles of $Ca(OH)_2$ reacted = 25 m mol

$\because$ 1 mole of $Ca(OH)_2$ gives 1 mole of $CaCO_3$,

$\therefore$ Number of millimoles of $CaCO_3$ formed = 25 m mol

$\therefore$ Number of milliequivalent

$$= \frac{\text{weight (in mg)}}{\text{equivalent weight}} = \frac{25 \times 100}{50} = 50$$

Number of milliequivalents of $CaCO_3$ = 50

As, volume of $CaCO_3$ solution = 50 mL

So, normality of $CaCO_3$ solution = 1 N

[milliequivalent = $N \times V$ (in mL)]

Normality of HCl = 0.1 N (given)

Volume of HCl = ?

$$N_{HCl} \times V_{HCl} = N_{CaCO_3} \times V_{CaCO_3}$$

$$0.1 \times V_{HCl} = 1 \times 50$$

$$V_{HCl} = \frac{50}{0.1} = 500 \text{ mL or } 500 \text{ cm}^3$$

19. (*a*) $\underset{\substack{2\text{ mol}\\100\text{ mL}}}{2PH_3(g)} \longrightarrow 2P(s) + \underset{\substack{3\text{ mol}\\150\text{ mL}}}{3H_2(g)}$

$\therefore$ There is an increase of

$$150 - 100 = 50 \text{ mL}$$

20. (*a*) $3MnO_4^- + 5C_2O_4^{2-} + 5Fe^{2+} + 24H^+ \longrightarrow 3Mn^{2+} + 10CO_2 + 5Fe^{3+} + 12H_2O$

$\because$ Number of moles of MnO_4^- required to oxidise 5 moles of $C_2O_4^{2-} = 3$

$\therefore$ Number of moles of MnO_4^- required to oxidise 1 mole of $C_2O_4^{2-} = \frac{3}{5} = 0.6$ mol

21. (*c*) Volume of a gas at STP = 22.4 L

$$\underset{22.4\text{ L}}{C_3H_8} + \underset{5 \times 22.4\text{ L}}{5O_2} \longrightarrow 3CO_2 + 4H_2O$$

$\because$ To burn 22.4 L C_3H_8, the oxygen required

$$= 5 \times 22.4 \text{ L}$$

$\therefore$ To burn 1 L C_3H_8,

the oxygen required will be

$$= \frac{5 \times 22.4}{22.4} = 5 \text{ L}$$

22. (*d*) $\underset{\substack{207.2+16\\=223.2\\1\text{ mole}}}{PbO} + \underset{\substack{2(35.5+1)\\=73\\2\text{ mole}}}{2HCl} \longrightarrow \underset{\substack{207.2+71\\=278.2\\1\text{ mole}}}{PbCl_2} + H_2O$

Given,

mass of PbO = 6.5 g

mass of HCl = 3.2 g

$$n_{PbO} = \frac{W_{PbO}}{M_{PbO}} = \frac{6.5\text{g}}{223.2 \text{ g/mol}} = 0.029 \text{mol}$$

$$n_{HCl} = \frac{W_{HCl}}{M_{HCl}} = \frac{3.2\text{g}}{36.5 \text{ g/mol}} = 0.087 \text{mol}$$

2 moles of HCl reacts with 1 mole of PbO

∴ 0.087 mole of HCl reacts with

$\frac{1}{2} \times 0.087$ mole of PbO

= 0.0435 mol of PbO.

But the given number of mole of PbO is 0.029 mole

∴ PbO is the limiting reagent.

1 mole of PbO gives 1 mole of $PbCl_2$

∴ 0.029 mole of PbO gives 0.029 mole of $PbCl_2$.

23. (*c*) $K_2S_2O_8(aq) + 2KI(aq) \longrightarrow 2K_2SO_4(aq) + I_2(aq)$

In this reaction, one mole of $K_2S_2O_8$ reacts with 2 moles of KI, hence, the stoichiometry of this reaction is 1 : 2.

24. (*b*) $\underset{12\text{ g}}{C} + \underset{22.4\text{ L}}{O_2} \longrightarrow CO_2$

The amount of carbon unreacted

$= 40 \times \frac{10}{100} = 4$ g

So, the amount of carbon reacted

= (40 – 4) = 36 g

∵ At STP, for the combustion of 12 g of C, oxygen required

= 22.4 L

∴ For the combustion of 36 g of C, oxygen required will be

$= \frac{22.4}{12} \times 36\text{ L} = 67.2\text{ L}$

25. (*b*) $Fe^{2+} \longrightarrow Fe^{3+} + e^-$ (Oxidation) ...(i)

$8H^+ + MnO_4^- + 5e^- \longrightarrow Mn^{2+} + 4H_2O$ (Reduction) ...(ii)

Eq. (i) is multiplied by 5

$5Fe^{2+} \longrightarrow 5Fe^{3+} + 5e^-$

Then, balanced equation is

$8H^+ + 5Fe^{2+} + MnO_4^- \longrightarrow 5Fe^{3+} + Mn^{2+} + 4H_2O$

Thus, the ratio of stoichiometric coefficient of Fe^{2+} and MnO_4^- is 5 : 1.

26. (*c*) $\underset{1\text{ mole}}{Fe_2O_3} + \underset{3\text{ mole}}{3CO} \longrightarrow 2Fe + 3CO_2$

Volume of 1 mol carbon monoxide = 22.4 L (at STP)

1 mole of ferric oxide is reduced by 3 moles of CO

= 3 × 22.4 L of CO

= 67.2 L of CO

= 67.2 dm^3 of CO

27. (*c*) $Ca \longrightarrow Ca^{2+} + 2e^-$ (Oxidation) ...(i)

$Al^{3+} + 3e^- \longrightarrow Al$ (Reduction) ...(ii)

Eq. (i) is multiplied by 3 and Eq. (ii) is multiplied by 2. The two equations

$3Ca \longrightarrow 3Ca^{2+} + 6e^-$

$2Al^{3+} + 6e^- \longrightarrow 2Al$

Net reaction

$3Ca + 2Al^{3+} \longrightarrow 3Ca^{2+} + 2Al$

Therefore, the stoichiometric coefficient of Ca in the given reaction is 3.

28. (*a*) CO and O_2 reacts as follows

$\underset{20\text{ L}}{CO} + \underset{10\text{ L}}{\frac{1}{2}O_2} \longrightarrow \underset{20\text{L}}{CO_2}$

10L O_2 reacts with 20L CO to form 20L fo CO_2. The given volumes of O_2 and CO are 10L and 30L respectively.

Thus, left amount of CO will be (30 – 20) = 10 L at the end of the reaction.

29. (*b*) $\overset{+7}{Mn}O_4^- + 5e^- \longrightarrow Mn^{2+}$

$\overset{+6}{Cr_2}O_7^{2-} + 6e^- \longrightarrow 2Cr^{3+}$

Equal volumes of 1 M $KMnO_4$ and 1 M $K_2Cr_2O_7$ have equal number of moles of $KMnO_4$ and $K_2Cr_2O_7$.

As 1 mole of $KMnO_4$ accept 5 moles of electrons and 1 mole of $K_2Cr_2O_7$ accepts 6 moles of electrons, thus $K_2Cr_2O_7$ will oxidise more Fe^{2+} to Fe^{3+}.

30. (*a*) $\underset{2\times 276\text{ g}}{2Ag_2CO_3} \xrightarrow{\Delta} \underset{4\times 108\text{ g}}{4Ag\downarrow} + 2CO_2\uparrow + O_2\uparrow$

∵ 2 × 276 g of Ag_2CO_3 gives Ag = 4 × 108 g

∴ 1 g of Ag_2CO_3 will give Ag

$= \frac{4 \times 108}{2 \times 276}$ g

∴ 2.76 g of Ag_2CO_3 will give

$= \frac{4 \times 108 \times 2.76}{2 \times 276} = 2.16$ g Ag

31. (*a*) $\underset{2\text{ mole}}{2NaHCO_3} \xrightarrow{\Delta} \underset{1\text{ mole}}{Na_2CO_3} + H_2O + CO_2$

∵ 2 mole $NaHCO_3$ on decomposition gives 1 mole Na_2CO_3

∴ 0.2 mol $NaHCO_3$ on decomposition will give

$= \frac{1}{2} \times 0.2 = 0.1$ mole of Na_2CO_3

32. (*b*) $CaCO_3 \longrightarrow CaO + \underset{11.2\,dm^3}{CO_2}$

22.4 dm^3 of CO_2 occupied by

= 1 mol CO_2

∴ 11.2 dm^3 of CO_2 occupied by

$= \frac{1 \times 11.2}{22.4}$ mol CO_2

$= \frac{1 \times 11.2}{22.4} \times 44$ g

∴ Mass of CO_2 = 22 g CO_2

The reaction of neutralisation would be

$\underset{56\text{ g}}{KOH} + \underset{44\text{ g}}{CO_2} \longrightarrow KHCO_3$

56 g KOH required 44 g CO_2 for neutralisation.

KOH required for complete neutralisation of 22 g of CO_2

$= \frac{56}{44} \times 22 = 28$ g

33. (*a*) $\underset{12\times 2+4=28\text{ g}}{C_2H_4} + \underset{96\text{ g}}{3O_2} \longrightarrow 2CO_2 + 2H_2O$

∵ The weight of oxygen required for complete combustion of 28 g ethylene = 96 g

∴ Weight of oxygen required for combustion of 2800 g ethylene

$= \frac{96 \times 2800}{28}$

= 9600 g = 9.6 kg

34. (*a*) 1 mole of gas occupied 22.4 L at STP

Given, mass of O_2 = 2 g at 27°C and 760 mm Hg (or at STP)

As, 32 g of O_2 = 22.4 L at STP

∴ 2 g of $O_2 = \frac{22.4}{32} \times 2 = 1.4$ L

02

Structure of Atom

Quick Review

- An **atom** is defined as "the smallest particle of matter which may or may not exist independently but can take part in a chemical reaction."
- A **molecule** is defined as "the smallest particle of matter which can exist independently but cannot take part in a chemical reaction".
- A large number of subatomic particles have been discovered among which electron, proton and neutron are considered as **fundamental particles.**

Atomic and Mass Number

1. Atomic Number

The number of protons present in the nucleus of an atom is equal to its atomic number (Z). In order to maintain the electrical neutrality, the number of electrons in an atom is equal to the number of protons (atomic number $= Z$).

Thus, $(Z) =$ number of protons in the nucleus of an atom
$=$ number of electrons in a neutral atom

2. Mass Number

The sum of the number of neutrons and number of protons present in the nucleus of an atom is known as mass number.

Mass number (A) = Number of protons (Z) + Number of neutrons (n)

Different Atomic Species

The atomic species are of the following types :

(*i*) **Isoelectronic species** have same number of electrons. e.g., O^{2-}, F^-, Na^+ as they all have 10 electrons.

(*ii*) **Isotones** have same number of neutrons. e.g., ${}_6C^{14}$, ${}_7N^{15}$, ${}_8O^{16}$ all have 8 neutrons.

(*iii*) **Isotopes** have same atomic number (Z) but different mass number (A).
e.g., ${}_6C^{12}$, ${}_6C^{13}$, ${}_6C^{14}$ are isotopes of carbon.

(*iv*) **Isobars** have same mass number (A) but different atomic number (Z). e.g., ${}_6C^{14}$ and ${}_7N^{14}$.

Properties of the Fundamental Particles

Properties	Proton (p)	Neutron (n)	Electron (e^-)
Mass	1.67262×10^{-27} kg	1.67493×10^{-27} kg	9.1094×10^{-31} kg
Charge	1.6022×10^{-19} C	0	1.6022×10^{-19} C
Mass relative to the electron	1836	1839	1
Charge relative to the proton	+1	0	–1
Discoverer	Goldstein	Chadwick	Thomson

Planck's Quantum Theory

Early works of Thomson and Rutherford gave a direction to understand the atomic structure. However, its real basis was quantum theory.

The main postulates of this theory are as follows

(*i*) The radiant energy is emitted or absorbed not continuously, but discontinuously in the form of small discrete packets of energy, called a **quantum**. In case of light, the quantum of energy is known as **photon**.

(*ii*) The energy of each quantum is directly proportional to the frequency of the radiation,

i.e. $E \propto \nu$ or $E = h\nu$ ...(i)

where, h is the proportionality constant, called **Planck's constant.** Its value is approximately equal to 6.626×10^{-27} erg s or 6.626×10^{-34} J-s.

(*iii*) The total amount of energy emitted or absorbed by a body will be some whole number quanta, i.e. energy is quantised.

Hence, $E = nh\nu$, where n is any integer. ...(ii)

Photoelectric Effect

The phenomenon for ejection of electrons from the surface of a metal when light of suitable frequency falls on it, is called the photoelectric effect and the emitted electrons are called photoelectrons.

Einstein's photoelectric equation is

$$(\text{KE})_{\max} = h\nu - W$$

Here, $(\text{KE})_{\max}$ = maximum kinetic energy of free electrons,

ν = frequency of incident radiation

and W = work function for metal surface

(The minimum energy required to eject the electrons from the metal surface).

or
$$\frac{1}{2} m v_{\max}^2 = h\nu - h\nu_0$$

Here, $v_{\max}$ = maximum velocity of photoelectrons

and ν_0 = minimum frequency (threshold frequency) of incident radiation required to eject electrons.

Bohr's Model

Bohr gave the first and foremost model for the structure of atom. His model had the inputs of Planck's theory.

He gave the model of stationary energy orbits within an atom. It is applicable only for one electron system like H, He^+, Li^{2+} etc.

The important formulae's related to Bohr's model are

- Angular momentum, $(mvr) = \frac{nh}{2\pi}, n = 1, 2, 3, \ldots$
- Bohr's radius, $(r_n) = r_0 \frac{n^2}{Z}, r_0 = 0.529$ Å

$$r_n = 0.529 \times \frac{n^2}{Z} \text{ Å}$$

Energy of electron in n th Bohr's orbit,

$$(E_n) = -\frac{13.6 Z^2}{n^2} \text{ eV/atom}$$

- Potential energy, $(E_p) = \frac{-Ze^2}{4\pi\varepsilon_0 r}$
- Speed of electron in nth Bohr's orbit

$$v_n = \frac{2.18 \times 10^6 Z}{n} \text{ ms}^{-1}$$

- Number of revolutions made by an electron in nth Bohr's orbit $= \frac{v_n}{2\pi r}$ round/s
- Centrifugal force of orbiting electrons = Coulombic attraction by nucleus i.e. $\frac{mv^2}{r} = \frac{Ze^2}{4\pi\varepsilon_0 r^2}$
- Through this model, Bohr explained the emission spectrum of hydrogen atom.

Spectrum

A spectrum can be defined as the pictorial representation of arrangement of radiations in increasing order of wavelength or decreasing order of frequency.

Atomic Spectrum

The spectrum of atom is discontinuous and consists of sharp well defined lines or bonds corresponding to definite frequencies, called as **line spectrum.**

Depending upon the radiation absorbed or emitted, spectrum is classified as

(*i*) **Emission Spectrum** The spectrum of radiation emitted by a substance that has absorbed energy is called an emission spectrum. Atoms, molecules or ions that have absorbed radiation are said to be in excited state.

According to Bohr's theory, when an electron jumps from excited state to ground state, it emits radiation of definite frequency.

(*ii*) **Absorption Spectrum** To obtain an absorption spectra a continum of radiations is passed through a sample which absorbs radiation of certain wavelengths.

The missing wavelength which corresponds to the radiation absorbed by the matter, leave dark spaces in the bright continuous spectrum.

Depending upon the pictorial characteristics, spectrum can be mainly classified as :

(*i*) **Continuous Spectrum** In this spectrum, visible radiations do not have a definite boundary, i.e. one radiation merge into other without any gap. Thus, this spectrum appears like a continuous band of radiations.

(*ii*) **Discontinuous Spectrum** In this spectrum, shape and well defined lines of a particular wavelength are visible. These are separated completely from one other. Such lines readily give a discontinuous appearance.

Electromagnetic Spectrum

There are many types of electromagnetic radiations which differ from one another in wavelength (λ) or frequency (ν). When the electromagnetic radiations are arranged in order of their increasing wavelength or decreasing frequencies, the complete spectrum obtained is called **electromagnetic spectrum.**

Emission Spectrum of Hydrogen Atom

- The spectrum of hydrogen atom consists of several series of lines. Rydberg concluded that all series of lines could be described by the following expression :

$$\overline{\nu} = \frac{1}{\lambda} = R_H Z^2 \left[\frac{1}{n_1^2} - \frac{1}{n_2^2}\right];\ R_H = 1.09678 \times 10^7\ \text{m}^{-1}$$

- The **Rydberg constant** (R_H) represents the limiting value of highest wave number of any photon that can be emitted from hydrogen atom or hydrogen like species.

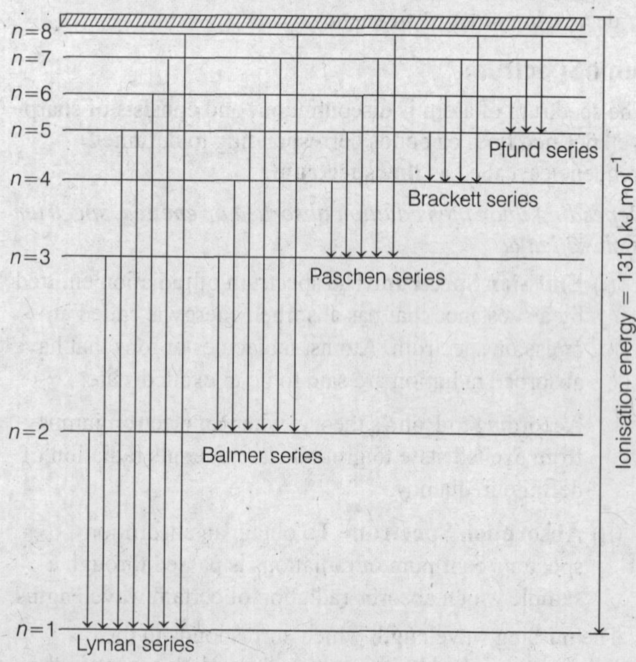

Spectrum lines in the hydrogen atom

(*i*) For Lyman series : $n_1 = 1, n_2 > 1$

(*ii*) For Balmer series : $n_1 = 2, n_2 > 2$

(*iii*) For Paschen series : $n_1 = 3, n_2 > 3$

(*iv*) For Brackett series : $n_1 = 4, n_2 > 4$

(*v*) For Pfund series : $n_1 = 5, n_2 > 5$

(*vi*) For Humphery series : $n_1 = 6, n_2 > 6$

- Number of spectral lines $= \frac{(n_2 - n_1)(n_2 - n_1 - 1)}{2}$

where $n_2 > n_1$ and n_2 and n_1 represents the number of energy levels from where the electron is undergoing transition.

Limitations of Bohr's Model

- Bohr's model could not explain **Zeeman effect** (splitting of spectral lines by magnetic field) and **Stark effect** (splitting of spectral lines by electric field).
- It could not explain spectrum of multi-electron atoms.
- It could not explain dual nature of electron.

de-Broglie Relationship

de-Broglie explain that the matter exhibit particle as well as wave like properties.

de-Broglie relationship, $\lambda = \frac{h}{p} = \frac{h}{mv}$

$$= \frac{h}{\sqrt{2m(\text{KE})}}$$

where, $p =$ momentum

Significance of de-Broglie Relationship

de-Broglie suggested that every object in motion has a wave character. But it is significant for microscopic bodies only. This is because the wavelengths associated with ordinary objects are so short due to their large masses ($\lambda \propto \frac{1}{m}$, for moving object) that their wave properties cannot be detected. Therefore, practically these bodies are said to have no wavelengths.

Heisenberg's Uncertainty Principle

According to this principle, it is impossible to determine simultaneously, the exact position and exact momentum (or velocity) of an electron.

$$\Delta x \cdot \Delta p \geq \frac{h}{4\pi}$$

where, $\Delta x =$ uncertainty in position and $\Delta p =$ uncertainty in momentum.

Significance of Uncertainty Principle

(i) Uncertainty principle is also called **principle of indeterminacy.** One of the important implications of this principle is that it rules out existence of definite paths or trajectories of electrons.

(ii) The effect of this principle is significant only for the motion of microscopic objects and is negligible for that of macroscopic objects.

Quantum Mechanical Model of Atom

It is given by Heisenberg and Schrodinger :

The important features of quantum mechanical model of atom are

(i) The energy of electrons in atoms is quantised.

(ii) An atomic orbital is the wave function ψ for an electron in an atom.

(iii) The probability of finding an electron at a point within an atom is proportional to the square of orbital wave function (ψ^2).

(iv) $|\psi^2|$ is known as probability density and is always positive.

- A node is a region of space, where probability of finding an electron is zero.

(i) $(n-l-1)$ = radial nodes (ii) l = angular nodes

(iii) $(n-1)$ = total nodes

- For H-atom, the Schrodinger equation is written as,

$$\hat{H}\psi = E\psi$$

where, $\hat{H}$ is a mathematical operator called Hamiltonian.

According to quantum mechanical model of atom, the structural features of an atom are as follows

- The orbitals or paths of different and definite energies in which the electrons revolve are called **shells**. Symbols K, L, M, N are used to represent various shells from lower to upper energy.
- Each orbit is made of **sub-orbits** or sub-shell. Each sub-shell is associated with one or more orbitals represented by s, p, d and f respectively.
- An **orbital** is the three dimensional space around the nucleus within which the probability of finding an electron is maximum.

Quantum Numbers

Schrodinger wave equation gave a set of quantum numbers to explain the properties of electron in an atom.

These are as follows

1. Principal Quantum Number (n)

- It describes principal shell to which the electron belongs.
- The values of n are integral (i.e., 1, 2, 3, 4, ...).
- It identifies,

(i) shell in which electron is revolving around the nucleus.

(ii) average distance of electron from the nucleus.

(iii) energy of shell that increases with increase in value of n.

(iv) maximum number of electrons present in a shell that is equal to $2n^2$.

2. Azimuthal (or Angular) Quantum Number (l)

- It is used to describe number of sub-shells in principal shell.
- For a given value of n, the value of l can vary from 0 to $(n-1)$.
- l also describes the shape of orbital occupied by the electron.

(i) When $l = 0$, the sub-shell is s and orbital is spherical in shape.

(ii) When $l = 1$, the sub-shell is p and orbital is dumb-bell shaped.

(iii) When $l = 2$, the sub-shell is d and orbital is double dumb-bell shaped.

(iv) When $l = 3$, the sub-shell is f and orbital is complicated in shape.

Any sub-shell is represented by 'nl' such that we write number for 'n' and name for l, e.g. $n = 1$, $l = 0$ indicates 1s sub-shell.

3. Magnetic Quantum Number (m)

- It shows the preferred orientation of orbital in three dimensional space.

Total value of $m = (2l + 1)$

- Magnetic quantum number describes behaviour of electron in magnetic field.
- With the help of magnetic quantum number, we can determine the number of preferred orientations of electrons in a sub-shell and also the shapes of orbitals.

(i) s-subshell ($m = 0$) will have only one **spherical orbital.**

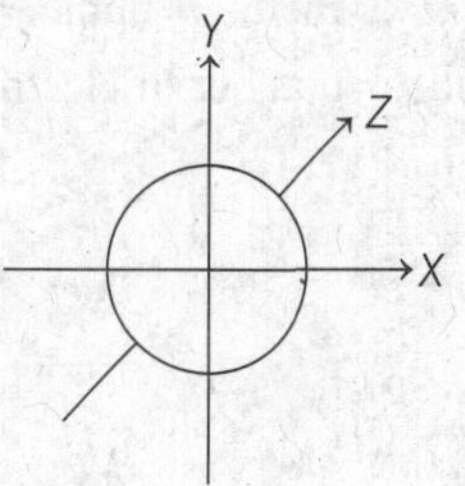

(*ii*) *p*-subshell ($m = -1, 0, +1$) has three orbitals (p_x, p_y, p_z).

They are identical in energy, shape and size which differ only in their directions in space.

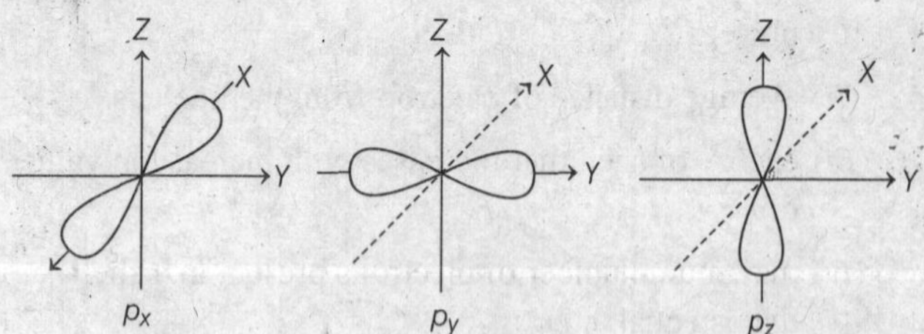

(*iii*) *d*-subshell ($m = -2, -1, 0, +1, +2$) has five orbitals ($d_{xy}, d_{yz}, d_{zx}, d_{x^2-y^2}$ and d_{z^2}). These are degenerate orbitals, i.e. equal in energy.

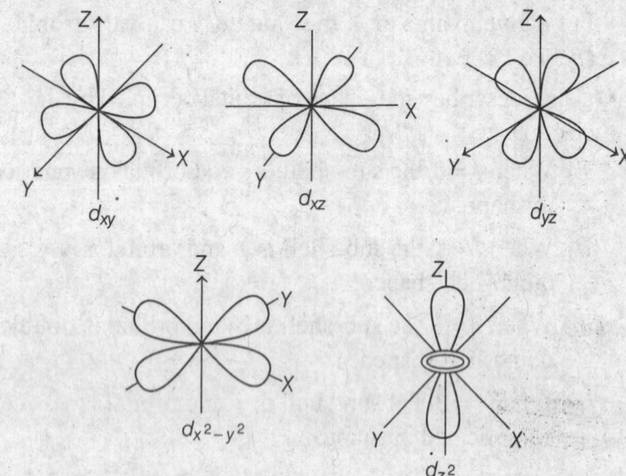

4. Spin Quantum Number (s)

- It shows the direction of spins of electrons, $s = \pm 1/2$.
- It helps to explain the magnetic properties of the nucleus like orbital motion and spinning.

Pauli's Exclusion Principle

This rule states that, in an atom, no two electrons can have the same set of four quantum numbers.

Electronic Configuration of Elements

- The arrangement of electrons in various shells, sub-shells and orbitals in an atom is termed as electronic configuration.
- It is written as nl^x, where n = number of shells l = sub-shell and x = number of electrons present.

Aufbau Principle

- According to this principle, electrons enter in the sub-shells of an atom in the increasing order of energy.
- Energy order of $1s, 2s, 2p, 3s$... sub-orbit is given in figure.

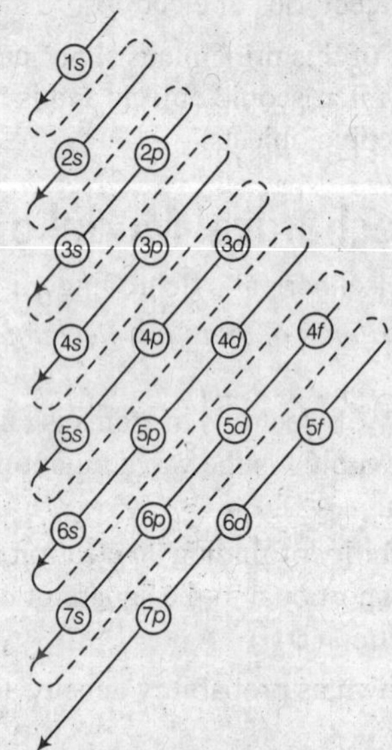

Order of filling of orbitals

- Thus, the order in which the energies of the sub-orbits increase and, hence the order in which the electrons are filled in the orbitals is as follows:

$$1s < 2s < 2p < 3s < 3p < 4s < 3d < 4p < 5s < 4d < 5p < 6s < 4f \ldots$$

Hund's Rule

This rule states that, "the pairing of electrons in the orbitals of a particular sub-shell does not take place until all the orbitals of a sub-shell are singly occupied".

Exchange Energy

When two or more electrons with the same spin are present in the degenerate orbitals of a subshell, they tend to exchange their position. The energy released in this exchange is called **exchange energy**. When the subshell is half-filled or completely filled, the number of exchanges can be maximum.

Thus, completely filled and half filled subshells are extra stable due to symmetrical distribution of electrons and high exchange energy.

Topical Practice Questions

All the exam questions of this chapter have been divided into four topics as listed below

Topic 1

Preliminary Models

2019

1 **Assertion** The chemical properties of different isotopes are same. **[AIIMS]**

Reason Isotopes having same number of neutron.

(a) Both Assertion and Reason are true and Reason is the correct explanation of Assertion
(b) Both Assertion and Reason are true, but Reason is not the correct explanation of Assertion
(c) Assertion is true, but Reason is false
(d) Both Assertion and Reason are false

2 A bulb emits electromagnetic radiation of 660 nm wavelength. The total energy of radiation is 3×10^{-18} J. The number of emitted photons will be ($h = 6.6\times 10^{-34}$ J×s, $c = 3\times 10^{8}$ m/s) **[AIIMS]**

(a) 1 (b) 10 (c) 100 (d) 1000

3 If two atoms have equal number of electrons, it is called **[JIPMER]**

(a) isoelectronic (b) isotone
(c) isobar (d) None of these

2018

4 The work function of a metal is 4.2 eV. If radiation of 2000Å falls on the metal, then the kinetic energy of the fastest photoelectron is **[AIIMS]**

(a) 1.6×10^{-19} J (b) 16×10^{-10} J
(c) 3.2×10^{-19} J (d) 6.4×10^{-10} J

2017

5 **Assertion** (A) Black body is an ideal body that emits and absorbs radiations of all frequencies.

Reason (R) The frequency of radiations emitted by a body goes from lower frequency to higher frequency with an increase in temperature. **[AIIMS]**

(a) Both A and R are correct and R is the correct explanation of the A.
(b) Both A and R are correct but R is not the correct explanation of the A.
(c) A is correct but R is incorrect
(d) Both A and R are incorrect

6 Number of photons emitted by a 100 W (Js^{-1}) yellow lamp in 1.0 s is (λ of yellow light is 560 nm) **[JIPMER]**

(a) 1.6×10^{18} (b) 1.4×10^{18}
(c) 2.8×10^{20} (d) 2.1×10^{20}

2014

7 Be^{2+} is isoelectronic with which of the following ions? **[CBSE AIPMT]**

(a) H^+ (b) Li^+ (c) Na^+ (d) Mg^{2+}

8 ($_{32}Ge^{76}$, $_{34}Se^{76}$) and ($_{14}Si^{30}$, $_{16}S^{32}$) are the examples of **[WB JEE]**

(a) isotopes and isobars (b) isobars and isotones
(c) isotones and isotopes (d) isobars and isotopes

9 Calculate the energy (in J) corresponding to light of wavelength 45 nm (Planck's constant, $h = 6.63\times 10^{-34}$ Js, speed of light, $c = 3\times 10^{8}\ ms^{-1}$). **[CBSE AIPMT]**

(a) 6.63×10^{8} (b) 6.67×10^{11}
(c) 4.42×10^{-15} (d) 4.42×10^{-18}

10 The value of Planck's constant is 6.63×10^{-34} Js. The speed of light is 3×10^{17} nm s^{-1}. Which value is closest to the wavelength (in nm) of a quantum of light with frequency of $6\times 10^{15}\ s^{-1}$? **[NEET]**

(a) 10 (b) 25 (c) 50 (d) 75

2013

11 Which of the following statements about electromagnetic spectrum is not correct? **[WB JEE]**

(a) Infrared radiations have larger wavelength than cosmic rays
(b) The frequency of microwaves is less than that of ultraviolet rays
(c) X-rays have larger wave number than microwaves
(d) The velocity of X-rays is more than that of microwaves

2012

12 The nitride ion in lithium nitride is composed of **[KCET]**
(a) 7 protons + 10 electrons (b) 10 protons + 10 electrons
(c) 7 protons + 7 electrons (d) 10 protons + 7 electrons

2011

13 The energies E_1 and E_2 of two radiations are 25 eV and 50 eV respectively. The relation between their wavelengths i.e., λ_1 and λ_2 will be **[CBSE AIPMT]**
(a) $\lambda_1 = \frac{1}{2}\lambda_2$ (b) $\lambda_1 = \lambda_2$ (c) $\lambda_1 = 2\lambda_2$ (d) $\lambda_1 = 4\lambda_2$

14 In which one of the following pairs, the two species are both isoelectronic and isotopic?
(Atomic numbers: Ca = 20, Ar = 18, K = 19, Mg = 12, Fe = 26, Na = 11) **[Kerala CEE]**
(a) $^{40}Ca^{2+}$ and ^{40}Ar (b) $^{39}K^+$ and $^{40}K^+$
(c) $^{24}Mg^{2+}$ and ^{25}Mg (d) ^{23}Na and $^{24}Na^+$
(e) $^{56}Fe^{3+}$ and $^{57}Fe^{2+}$

2010

15 The ratio between the neutrons in C and Si with respect to atomic masses 12 and 28 is **[BVP]**
(a) 2 : 3 (b) 3 : 2 (c) 3 : 7 (d) 7 : 3

16 If a species has 16 protons, 18 electrons and 16 neutrons, find the species and its charge. **[WB JEE]**
(a) S^- (b) Si^{2-} (c) S^{3-} (d) S^{2-}

17 Which of the following pairs is isoelectronic? **[VMMC]**
(a) Ne, Cl (b) Ca^{2+}, F^- (c) Mg^{2+}, K^+ (d) N^{3-}, Na^+

18 The relation between wave motion of photons and stream of particle is **[MP PMT]**
(a) $\Delta x . \Delta p \geq \frac{h}{4\pi}$ (b) $E = mc^2$ (c) $\lambda = \frac{h}{\bar{\nu}}$ (d) $E = h\nu$

2009

19 Electrons with a kinetic energy of 6.023×10^4 J/mol are evolved from a surface of a metal, when it is exposed to radiation of wavelength 600 nm. The minimum amount of energy required to remove an electron from the metal atom is **[EAMCET]**
(a) 2.3125×10^{-19} J (b) 3×10^{-19} J
(c) 6.02×10^{-19} J (d) 6.62×10^{-34} J

2008

20 The electronic configuration of a dipositive ion M^{2+} is 2, 8, 14 and its mass number is 56. The number of neutrons in M present is **[Manipal]**
(a) 32 (b) 42 (c) 30 (d) 34

21 Deflection back of a few particles on hitting thin foil of gold shows that **[Manipal]**
(a) nucleus is heavy
(b) nucleus is small
(c) Both (a) and (b)
(d) electrons create hindrance in movement of α-particles

22 The nucleus of an atom can be assumed to be spherical. The radius of the nucleus of mass number A is given by $1.25 \times 10^{-13} \times A^{1/3}$ cm. Radius of atom is 1.0 Å. If the mass number is 64 then the fraction of the atomic volume that is occupied by the nucleus is **[Manipal]**
(a) 1.0×10^{-3} (b) 5.0×10^{-5}
(c) 2.5×10^{-2} (d) 1.25×10^{-13}

23 In which one of the following, the number of protons is greater than the number of neutrons but number of protons is less than the number of electrons? **[Kerala CEE]**
(a) D_3O^+ (b) SO_2 (c) H_2O (d) S^{2-}
(e) OH^-

2007

24 An element X has the following isotopic composition,
^{200}X : 90% , ^{199}X : 8.0% , ^{202}X : 2.0%.
The weighted average atomic mass of the naturally occurring element X is closest to **[CBSE AIPMT]**
(a) 200 u (b) 201 u
(c) 202 u (d) 199 u

25 The energy ratio of a photon of wavelength 3000 Å and 6000 Å is **[BCECE]**
(a) 1 : 1 (b) 2 : 1 (c) 1 : 2 (d) 1 : 4

2006

26 Which pair is of isoelectronic species? **[BHU]**
(a) K^+, Cl^-, Na^+ (b) K^+, Cl^-, Ca^{2+}
(c) F^-, Al^{3+}, K^+ (d) Fe^{2+}, Cu^{2+}, V^{3+}

27 The lightest subatomic particle is **[Manipal]**
(a) α-particle (b) positron (c) proton (d) neutron

2005

28 The ratio of charge and mass would be greater for **[BHU]**
(a) proton (b) electron
(c) neutron (d) α-particle

29 Which among the following species have the same number of electrons in its outermost as well as penultimate shell? **[Manipal]**
(a) Mg^{2+} (b) O^{2-} (c) F^- (d) Ca^{2+}

30 The charge on an electron was discovered by **[Punjab PMET]**
(a) J.J. Thomson (b) Neil Bohr
(c) James Chadwick (d) Millikan

31 Particle nature of electron was experimentally demonstrated by **[AMU]**
(a) Max Bon (b) J.J. Thomson
(c) de-Broglie (d) Schrodinger

32 Which one of the following transitions have minimum wavelength? **[DUMET]**
(a) $n_4 \rightarrow n_1$ (b) $n_2 \rightarrow n_1$
(c) $n_4 \rightarrow n_2$ (d) $n_3 \rightarrow n_1$

Answers

1 (c)	2 (b)	3 (a)	4 (c)	5 (b)	6 (c)	7 (b)	8 (b)	9 (d)	10 (c)
11 (d)	12 (a)	13 (c)	14 (b)	15 (c)	16 (d)	17 (d)	18 (d)	19 (a)	20 (c)
21 (c)	22 (d)	23 (e)	24 (a)	25 (b)	26 (b)	27 (b)	28 (b)	29 (d)	30 (d)
31 (b)	32 (a)								

Explanations

1 (*c*) Isotopes are the elements having same number of protons but different number of neutrons. Their chemical properties are same.

Thus, Assertion is correct but Reason is incorrect.

Hence, option (c) is correct.

2 (*b*) Let, number of photons = n

$\therefore \quad E = nh\nu = n.\dfrac{hc}{\lambda}$

where, ν = frequency, c = velocity of light, λ = wavelength

$\therefore\ n = \dfrac{E \times \lambda}{hc}$

$= \dfrac{3\times10^{-18}\,\text{J}\times 660\times10^{-9}\,\text{m}}{626\times10^{-34}\,\text{Js}\times3\times10^{8}\,\text{ms}^{-1}} = 10$

$n = 10$

So, the number of emitted photon = 10

Hence, option (b) is the correct.

3 (*a*) The species having same number of electrons are called isoelectronic. For example, Na^+ and Mg^{2+} have 10 electrons thus are isoelectronic.

4 (*c*) Given, $E_0 = 4.2$ eV

$= 4.2\times1.60\times10^{-19}$ J

$= 6.72\times10^{-19}$ J

$\because \quad E = h\nu = \dfrac{hc}{\lambda}$

$\therefore \quad E = \dfrac{(6.63\times10^{-34})\times(3\times10^{8})}{2000\times10^{-10}}$

$= 9.94\times10^{-19}$ J

$\therefore$ Kinetic energy of electron emitted

$= (9.94 - 6.72)\times10^{-19}$ J

$= 3.22\times10^{-19}$ J

5 (*b*) The ideal body which emits and absorbs radiations of all frequencies is called a black body and the radiation emitted by such a body is called black body radiation. On increasing temperature, the frequency of emitted radiations also increases from lower frequency to higher frequency.

Thus, both A and R are individually correct but R is not the correct explanation of A.

6 (*c*) As we know that,

$$E = Nh\nu = N\frac{hc}{\lambda}$$

$$N = \frac{E\lambda}{hc} \quad \ldots\text{(i)}$$

$$E = 100\,\text{W}\,(\text{Js}^{-1})\times 1\,\text{s} = 100\,\text{J}$$

Putting the value in eq. (i) we get

$$N = \frac{100\,\text{J}\times560\times10^{-9}\,\text{m}}{6.626\times10^{-34}\,\text{Js}\times3\times10^{8}\,\text{ms}^{-1}}$$

$$= 2.82\times10^{20}\ \text{photons}$$

7 (*b*) Be^{2+} and Li^+ both have 2 electrons. Thus, both are isoelectronic species, whereas H^+ contains 0 electron, Na^+ contains 10 electrons and Mg^{+2} contains 10 electrons.

8 (*b*) $_{32}Ge^{76}$ and $_{34}Se^{76}$ have the same mass number but different atomic number, so they are isobars.

Number of neutrons in

$_{14}Si^{30} = 30 - 14 = 16$

Number of neutrons in

$_{16}S^{32} = 32 - 16 = 16$

Because of the presence of same number of neutrons, $_{14}Si^{30}$ and $_{16}S^{32}$ are called isotones.

Hence, ($_{32}Ge^{76}$, $_{34}Se^{76}$) and ($_{14}Si^{30}$, $_{16}S^{32}$) are the examples of isobars and isotones respectively.

9 (*d*) The wavelength of light is related to its energy by the equation,

$$E = \frac{hc}{\lambda}$$

Given, $\quad \lambda = 45\ \text{nm} = 45\times10^{-9}$ m

$[\because\ 1\ \text{nm} = 10^{-9}\ \text{m}]$

Hence,

$$E = \frac{6.63\times10^{-34}\,\text{Js}\times3\times10^{8}\,\text{ms}^{-1}}{45\times10^{-9}\,\text{m}}$$

$$= 4.42\times10^{-18}\ \text{J}$$

Hence, the energy corresponding to the light of wavelength 45 nm is 4.42×10^{-18} J.

10 (*c*) Given, Planck's constant (h) = 6.63×10^{-34} J s

Speed of light (c) = 3×10^{17} nm s^{-1}

Frequency of quanta, $\nu = 6\times10^{15}\,\text{s}^{-1}$

Wavelength (λ) = ?

We know that,

$$\nu = \frac{c}{\lambda},\ \lambda = \frac{c}{\nu}$$

$$= \frac{3\times10^{17}}{6\times10^{15}} = 0.5\times10^{2}\ \text{nm} = 50\ \text{nm}$$

11 (*d*) The velocity of electromagnetic waves depends upon the nature of medium through which it passes, while electromagnetic wave may have different wavelength, wave number and frequencies. So, the X-rays and microwaves (infact all electromagnetic waves) travel with the velocity of light and, thus have same velocity.

Therefore, the statement (d) is not correct, while the remaining statements are correct.

12 (*a*) Nitride ion can be represented as N^{3-}.

Number of protons = 7

Number of electrons = 7 + 3 = 10

Therefore, nitride ion contains 7 protons + 10 electrons.

13 (*c*) The energy of each quantum is directly proportional to frequency of the radiation.

i.e. $\quad E \propto \nu \Rightarrow E = h\nu$

or $\quad E = \dfrac{hc}{\lambda} \quad \left(\because \nu = \dfrac{c}{\lambda}\right)$

As, $\quad \lambda = \dfrac{hc}{E}$

$\therefore \quad \dfrac{E_1}{E_2} = \dfrac{\lambda_2}{\lambda_1} \Rightarrow \dfrac{25}{50} = \dfrac{\lambda_2}{\lambda_1}$

$\lambda_1 = 2\lambda_2$

14 (*b*) Isoelectronic species are those which have same number of electrons, while isotopic species are those which contains same number of protons.

(a) $^{40}Ca^{+2}$ contains 18 electrons and 20 protons

^{40}Ar contains 18 electrons and 18 protons.

(b) $^{39}K^{+}$ contains 18 electrons and 19 protons.

$^{40}K^{+}$ contains 18 electrons and 19 protons.

(c) $^{24}Mg^{+2}$ contains 10 electrons and 12 protons.

^{25}Mg contains 12 electrons and 12 protons.

(d) ^{23}Na contains 11 electrons and 11 protons.

$^{24}Na^{+}$ contains 10 electrons and 11 protons.

(e) $^{56}Fe^{+3}$ contains 23 electrons and 26 protons.

$^{57}Fe^{+2}$ contains 24 electrons and 26 protons.

Thus, option (b) i.e., $^{39}K^{+}$ and $^{40}K^{+}$ are both isoelectronic and isotopic species.

15 (*c*) Neutrons in $^{12}_{6}C = 6$,

Neutrons in $^{28}_{14}Si = 14$

$\therefore$ Ratio $= 6 : 14 = 3 : 7$

16 (*d*) $16p$ means $Z = 16$, $18e^{-}$ means 2 unit negative charge is present. Hence, species is S^{2-}.

17 (*d*) Isoelectronic species are those which have same number of electrons.

$\begin{bmatrix} Ne = \text{number of electrons} = 10 \\ Cl = \text{number of electrons} = 17 \end{bmatrix}$

$\begin{bmatrix} Ca^{+2} = \text{number of electrons} = 20 - 2 = 18 \\ F^{-} = \text{number of electrons} = 9 + 1 = 10 \end{bmatrix}$

$\begin{bmatrix} Mg^{+2} = \text{number of electrons} = 12 - 2 = 10 \\ K^{+} = \text{number of electrons} = 19 - 1 = 18 \end{bmatrix}$

$\begin{bmatrix} N^{-3} = \text{number of electrons} = 7 + 3 = 10 \\ Na^{+} = \text{number of electrons} = 11 - 1 = 10 \end{bmatrix}$

Thus, N^{3-} and Na^{+} are isoelectronic species.

18 (*d*) Planck's quantum theory, $E = h\nu$, describes the relationship between wave nature and particle nature of light.

19 (*a*) $\because$ 1 mole $= 6.023 \times 10^{23}$ electrons

KE of 1 mole of electrons

$= 6.023 \times 10^{4}$ J

$\therefore$ KE of 1 electron

$= \dfrac{6.023 \times 10^{4}}{6.023 \times 10^{23}}$

$= 1 \times 10^{-19}$ J

Energy, (E)

$= h\nu = \dfrac{hc}{\lambda} = \dfrac{6.626 \times 10^{-34} \times 3 \times 10^{8}}{600 \times 10^{-9}}$

$= 3.313 \times 10^{-19}$ J

Minimum energy required to remove an electron from the metal atom (i.e. threshold energy).

$h\nu - \text{KE} = 3.313 \times 10^{-19} - 1.0 \times 10^{-19}$

$= 2.313 \times 10^{-19}$ J

$\simeq 2.3125 \times 10^{-19}$ J

20 (*c*) Number of electrons in

$M^{2+} = 2 + 8 + 14 = 24$

$\therefore$ Number of electrons in $M = 26$

i.e., atomic number $(Z) = 26$

Mass number $(A) = 56$

$\therefore$ Number of neutrons

$= A - Z = 56 - 26 = 30$

21 (*c*) Deflection back of a few particles on hitting thin foil of gold is due to more repulsive forces of positive charge which is concentrated in a very small and heavy volume called nucleus and α-particles are also positively charged.

22 (*d*) Radius of nucleus

$= 1.25 \times 10^{-13} \times A^{1/3}$ cm

$= 1.25 \times 10^{-13} \times 64^{1/3}$ cm

$= 1.25 \times 10^{-13} \times 4$ cm $= 5 \times 10^{-13}$ cm

Radius of atom $= 1$ Å $= 10^{-8}$ cm

Volume of nucleus/volume of atom

$= \dfrac{4/3\pi r^{3}}{4/3\pi (r_A)^{3}}$

where, r = radius of nucleus

r_A = radius of atom.

$= \dfrac{(4/3)\pi\,(5 \times 10^{-13})^{3}}{(4/3)\pi\,(10^{-8})^{3}} = \dfrac{125 \times 10^{-39}}{10^{-24}}$

$= 125 \times 10^{-15}$

$= 1.25 \times 10^{-13}$

23 (*e*) (a) In D_3O^{+} = Number of protons

$= 3 + 8 = 11$

Number of neutrons $= 22 - 11 = 11$

Number of electrons $= 3 + 8 - 1 = 10$

(b) In SO_2 = Number of protons

$= 16 + (2 \times 8) = 32$

Number of neutrons $= 64 - 32 = 32$

Number of electrons $= 16 + (2 \times 8) = 32$

(c) In H_2O = Number of protons

$= 2 \times 1 + 8 = 10$

Number of neutrons $= 18 - 10 = 8$

Number of electrons $= 2 \times 1 + 8 = 10$

(d) In S^{2-} = Number of protons $= 16$

Number of neutrons $= 32 - 16 = 16$

Number of electrons $= 16 + 2 = 18$

(e) In OH^{-} = Number of protons

$= 8 + 1 = 9$

Number of neutrons $= 17 - 9 = 8$

Number of electrons $= 8 + 1 + 1 = 10$

Hence, in OH^{-}, the number of protons is greater than the number of neutrons but number of protons is less than the number of electrons.

24 (*a*) Weight of

$^{200}X = 0.90 \times 200 = 180.00$ u

Weight of $^{199}X = 0.08 \times 199 = 15.92$ u

Weight of $^{202}X = 0.02 \times 202 = 4.04$ u

Total weight $= 199.96\text{u} \approx 200$ u

25 (*b*) $\lambda_1 = 3000$ Å, $\lambda_2 = 6000$ Å

$E_1 = \dfrac{hc}{\lambda_1} = \dfrac{hc}{3000}$ ...(i)

$\Rightarrow E_2 = \dfrac{hc}{\lambda_2} = \dfrac{hc}{6000}$ ...(ii)

Divide Eq. (i) by Eq. (ii)

$\dfrac{E_1}{E_2} = \dfrac{\dfrac{hc}{3000}}{\dfrac{hc}{6000}}$

$= \dfrac{hc}{3000} \times \dfrac{6000}{hc} = \dfrac{2}{1}$

$\Rightarrow E_1 : E_2 = 2 : 1$

26 (*b*) Isoelectronic species have same number of electrons.

(a) K^{+} = number of electrons $= 19 - 1 = 18$
Cl^{-} = number of electrons $= 17 + 1 = 18$
Na^{+} = number of electrons $= 11 - 1 = 10$
— not isoelectronic

(b) K^+ = number of electrons = 19 − 1 = 18; Cl^- = number of electrons = 17 + 1 = 18; Ca^{2+} = number of electrons = 20 − 2 = 18 — isoelectronic

(c) F^- = number of electrons = 9 + 1 = 10; Al^{+3} = number of electrons = 13 − 3 = 10; K^+ = number of electrons = 19 − 1 = 18 — not isoelectronic

(d) Fe^{+2} = number of electrons = 26 − 2 = 24; Cu^{+2} = number of electrons = 29 − 2 = 27; V^{+3} = number of electrons = 23 − 3 = 20 — not isoelectronic

Hence, K^+, Cl^- and Ca^{2+} are isoelectronic species.

27 (*b*) α-particle have two neutrons and two protons. So, it is heaviest subatomic particle among all whereas, proton and neutron are of same weight as 1.6727×10^{-24} g.

While electron is of 9.1×10^{-28} g only and positron has same weight of electron with positive charge, thus both are lightest subatomic particles.

28 (*b*) The ratio of charge and mass would be greater for electron, as mass of the electron is least among the given species.

29 (*d*) (a) $Mg^{+2} = 1s^2\ 2s^2\ 2p^6$

Penultimate shell electron = 2

Outermost shell electron = 8,

(b) $O^{-2} = 1s^2\ 2s^2\ 2p^6$

Penultimate shell electron = 2

Outermost shell electron = 8,

(c) $F^- = 1s^2\ 2s^2\ 2p^6$

Penultimate shell electron = 8

Outermost shell electron = 8,

(d) $Ca^{+2} = 1s^2\ 2s^2\ 2p^6\ 3s^2\ 3p^6$

Penultimate shell electron =

Outermost shell electron = 8

Hence, Ca^{2+} has 8 electrons in outermost as well as in penultimate shell.

30 (*d*) J.J. Thomson gave the model of atom. Neil Bohr was first to explain structure of atom.

James Chadwick discovered neutron, while charge on an electron was given by R.A. Millikan by oil drop experiment.

31 (*b*) J.J. Thomson (1987) first experimentally demonstrated particle nature of electron. However, it was first time proposed by Millikan's oil drop experiment.

32 (*a*) $\because \quad E = \frac{hc}{\lambda}$

$\therefore \quad E \propto \frac{1}{\lambda}$

∴ Decrease in wavelength, increases the energy.

∵ Energy difference in $n_4 \rightarrow n_1$ transition is maximum.

∴ $n_4 \rightarrow n_1$ transition has minimum wavelength.

Topic 2

Bohr's Model and Hydrogen Spectrum

2019

1 Which of the following series of transitions in the spectrum of hydrogen atom fall in visible region? **[NEET]**

(a) Balmer series (b) Paschen series
(c) Brackett series (d) Lyman series

2017

2 Which transition in the hydrogen atomic spectrum will have the same wavelength as the Balmer transition (i.e. $n = 4$ to $n = 2$) of He^+ spectrum? **[AIIMS]**

(a) $n = 4$ to $n = 3$
(b) $n = 3$ to $n = 2$
(c) $n = 4$ to $n = 2$
(d) $n = 2$ to $n = 1$

3 Match the type of series given in Column I with the wavelength range given in Column II and choose the correct option. **[JIPMER]**

Column I	Column II
A. Lyman	1. Ultraviolet
B. Paschen	2. Near infrared
C. Balmer	3 Far infrared
D. Pfund	4. Visible

Codes

	A	B	C	D
(a)	1	2	4	3
(b)	4	3	1	2
(c)	3	1	2	4
(d)	4	3	2	1

2014

4 The emission spectrum of hydrogen discovered first and the region of the electromagnetic spectrum in which it belongs, respectively are **[WB JEE]**

(a) Lyman, ultraviolet (b) Lyman, visible
(c) Balmer, ultraviolet (d) Balmer, visible

2013

5 Based on equation, $E = -2.178 \times 10^{-18}\ (Z^2/n^2)$ J, certain conclusions are written. Which of them is not correct? **[NEET]**

(a) The negative sign in equation simply means that the energy of electron bound to the nucleus is lower than it would be if the electrons were at the infinite distance from the nucleus.
(b) Larger the value of n, larger is the radius of orbit.
(c) Equation can be used to calculate the change in energy when the electron changes orbit.
(d) For $n = 1$, the electron has a more negative energy than it does for $n = 6$ which means that the electron is more loosely bound in the smallest allowed orbit.

6 The velocity of electron in second shell of hydrogen atom is [AIIMS]

(a) $10.94\times10^6\ ms^{-1}$ (b) $18.88\times10^6\ ms^{-1}$
(c) $1.888\times10^6\ ms^{-1}$ (d) $1.094\times10^6\ ms^{-1}$

7 For which of the following species, Bohr's theory is not applicable? [WB JEE]

(a) Be^{3+} (b) Li^{2+}
(c) He^{2+} (d) H

8 If the first ionisation energy of H-atom is 13.6 eV, then the second ionisation energy of He-atom is [WB JEE]

(a) 27.2 eV (b) 40.8 eV
(c) 54.4 eV (d) 108.8 eV

2012

9 When the electrons of hydrogen atom return to L shell from shells of higher energy, we get a series of lines in the spectrum. This series is called [KCET]

(a) Balmer series
(b) Lyman series
(c) Brackett series
(d) Paschen series

2011

10 For Balmer series in the spectrum of atomic hydrogen, the wave number of each line is given by

$\overline{\nu} = R_H\left(\frac{1}{n_1^2} - \frac{1}{n_2^2}\right)$, where R_H is a constant and n_1 and n_2 are integers. Which of the following statement(s) is(are) correct?

I. As wavelength decreases, the lines in the series converge.
II. The integer n_1 is equal to 2.
III. The ionisation energy of hydrogen can be calculated from the wave number of these lines.
IV. The line of longest wavelength corresponds to $n_2 = 3$. [Kerala CEE]

(a) I, II and III (b) II, III and IV
(c) I, II and IV (d) II and IV
(e) Only II

2010

11 The wavelength of which series lie towards the ultraviolet region? [RPMT]

(a) Lyman (b) Balmer
(c) Paschen (d) None of these

12 When the electron of a hydrogen atom jumps from $n = 4$ to $n = 1$ state, the number of spectral lines emitted is [AMU]

(a) 15 (b) 9
(c) 6 (d) 3

13 The wave number of the spectral line in the emission spectrum of hydrogen will be equal to $\frac{8}{9}$ times the Rydberg constant if the electron jumps from [KCET]

(a) $n = 3$ to $n = 1$ (b) $n = 10$ to $n = 1$
(c) $n = 9$ to $n = 1$ (d) $n = 2$ to $n = 1$

14 Which one of the following statements does not belong to Bohr's model of atom? [CMC]

(a) The energy of the electrons in the orbit is quantised.
(b) The electron in the orbit nearest to the nucleus is in lowest energy state.
(c) The electrons revolve in different orbits around the nucleus.
(d) The electrons emit energy during revolution due to the presence of Coulombic forces of attraction

15 In Sommerfield's modification of Bohr's theory, the trajectory of an electron in a hydrogen atom is [WB JEE]

(a) a perfect ellipse
(b) a closed ellipse like curve, narrower at the perihelion position and flatter at the aphelion position
(c) a closed loop on spherical surface
(d) a rosette

2009

16 **Assertion** (A) In Lyman series of H-spectrum, the maximum wavelength of lines is 121.56 nm.
Reason (R) Wavelength is maximum if there is transition from the very next level. [AIIMS]

(a) Both A and R are correct and R is the correct explanation of A
(b) Both A and R are correct but R is not the correct explanation of A
(c) A is correct but R is incorrect
(d) Both A and R are incorrect

17 In hydrogen atomic spectrum, a series limit is found at $12186.3\ cm^{-1}$. Then, it belong to [Kerala CEE]

(a) Lyman series (b) Balmer series
(c) Paschen series (d) Brackett series
(e) Pfund series

18 For the Paschen series, the values of n_1 and n_2 in the expression, $\Delta E = R_H hc\left(\frac{1}{n_1^2} - \frac{1}{n_2^2}\right)$ [WB JEE]

(a) $n_1 = 1, n_2 = 2, 3, 4, \ldots$ (b) $n_1 = 2, n_2 = 3, 4, 5, \ldots$
(c) $n_1 = 3, n_2 = 4, 5, 6, \ldots$ (d) $n_1 = 4, n_2 = 5, 6, 7, \ldots$

19 The radius of the first Bohr orbit of the H-atom is r. Then, the radius of the first orbit of Li^{2+} will be [AMU]

(a) $r/9$ (b) $r/3$
(c) $3r$ (d) $9r$

2008

20 The scientist who proposed the atomic model based on the quantisation of energy for the first time is **[J&K CET]**

(a) Max Planck (b) Neil Bohr
(c) de-Broglie (d) Heisenberg

21 **Assertion** (A) A spectral line will be observed for a $2p_x$ - $2p_y$ transition.

Reason (R) The energy is released in the form of wave of light when electron drops from $2p_x$ to $2p_y$ orbital. **[AIIMS]**

(a) Both A and R are correct and R is the correct explanation of A.
(b) Both A and R are correct but R is not the correct explanation of A.
(c) A is correct but R is incorrect.
(d) Both A and R are incorrect.

22 What is the wave number of 4th line in Balmer series of hydrogen spectrum? ($R = 1{,}09{,}677\,\text{cm}^{-1}$) **[UP CPMT]**

(a) $24{,}630\,\text{cm}^{-1}$ (b) $24{,}360\,\text{cm}^{-1}$
(c) $24{,}730\,\text{cm}^{-1}$ (d) $24{,}372\,\text{cm}^{-1}$

23 What are the values of n_1 and n_2 respectively for H_β line in the Lyman series of hydrogen atomic spectrum?

(a) 3 and 5 (b) 2 and 3 **[UP CPMT]**
(c) 1 and 3 (d) 2 and 4

24 The wavelength (in Å) of an emission line obtained for Li^{2+} during an electronic transition from $n_2 = 2$ to $n_1 = 1$ is (R = Rydberg constant) **[EAMCET]**

(a) $\frac{3R}{4}$ (b) $\frac{27R}{4}$ (c) $\frac{4}{3R}$ (d) $\frac{4}{27R}$

25 In hydrogen atom, energy of first excited state is –3.4 eV. Then kinetic energy of same orbit of hydrogen atom is

(a) + 3.4 eV (b) + 6.8 eV **[Punjab PMET]**
(c) – 13.6 eV (d) + 13.6 eV

26 The maximum energy is possessed by an electron, when it is present **[AMU]**

(a) in nucleus
(b) in ground energy state
(c) in first excited state
(d) at infinite distance from the nucleus

27 Splitting of spectral lines under the influence of magnetic field is called **[DUMET]**

(a) Zeeman effect (b) Stark effect
(c) Photoelectric effect (d) None of these

28 The energy of second Bohr orbit of the hydrogen atom is $-328\,\text{kJ mol}^{-1}$, hence the energy of fourth Bohr orbit would be **[JCECE]**

(a) $-41\,\text{kJ mol}^{-1}$ (b) $-1312\,\text{kJ mol}^{-1}$
(c) $-164\,\text{kJ mol}^{-1}$ (d) $-82\,\text{kJ mol}^{-1}$

29 The wavelength of the radiation emitted, when in a hydrogen atom, the electron falls from infinity to the stationary state, would be
(Rydberg constant $= 1.097 \times 10^7\,\text{m}^{-1}$) **[JCECE]**

(a) 91 nm (b) 192 nm
(c) 406 nm (d) 9.1×10^{-8} nm

2007

30 The frequency of radiation emitted when the electron falls from $n = 4$ to $n = 1$ in a hydrogen atom, will be (given, ionisation energy of $H = 2.18 \times 10^{-18}$ J atom^{-1} and $h = 6.625 \times 10^{-34}$ J-s) **[Manipal]**

(a) $1.54 \times 10^{15}\,\text{s}^{-1}$ (b) $1.03 \times 10^{15}\,\text{s}^{-1}$
(c) $3.08 \times 10^{15}\,\text{s}^{-1}$ (d) $2.00 \times 10^{15}\,\text{s}^{-1}$

2006

31 Bohr's model can explain **[Manipal]**

(a) the solar spectrum
(b) the spectrum of hydrogen molecule
(c) spectrum of any atom or ion containing one electron only
(d) the spectrum of hydrogen atom only

32 The radius of hydrogen atom is 0.53 Å. The radius of $_3Li^{2+}$ is **[RPMT]**

(a) 1.27 Å (b) 0.17 Å
(c) 0.57 Å (d) 0.99 Å

33 The first emission line of hydrogen atomic spectrum in the Balmer series appears at (R = Rydberg constant) **[EAMCET]**

(a) $\frac{5R}{36}\,\text{cm}^{-1}$ (b) $\frac{3R}{4}\,\text{cm}^{-1}$
(c) $\frac{7R}{144}\,\text{cm}^{-1}$ (d) $\frac{9R}{400}\,\text{cm}^{-1}$

2005

34 What is the lowest energy of the spectral line emitted by the hydrogen atom in the Lyman series?
(h = Planck's constant, c = velocity of light, R_H = Rydberg constant) **[EAMCET]**

(a) $\frac{5hcR_H}{36}$ (b) $\frac{4hcR_H}{3}$ (c) $\frac{3hcR_H}{4}$ (d) $\frac{7hcR_H}{144}$

35 The radius of second Bohr orbit of hydrogen atom is

(a) 0.053 nm (b) 0.106 nm **[AMU]**
(c) 0.2116 nm (d) 0.4256 nm

36 Magnitude of kinetic energy in an orbit is equal to

(a) half of the potential energy **[BCECE]**
(b) twice of the potential energy
(c) one fourth of the potential energy
(d) None of the above

Answers

1 (a)	2 (d)	3 (a)	4 (d)	5 (d)	6 (d)	7 (c)	8 (c)	9 (a)	10 (c)
11 (a)	12 (c)	13 (a)	14 (d)	15 (b)	16 (a)	17 (c)	18 (c)	19 (b)	20 (b)
21 (d)	22 (d)	23 (c)	24 (d)	25 (a)	26 (d)	27 (a)	28 (d)	29 (a)	30 (c)
31 (c)	32 (b)	33 (a)	34 (c)	35 (c)	36 (a)				

Explanations

1 (*a*) Balmer series of transitions in the spectrum of hydrogen atom fall in visible region. Lyman series fall in ultraviolet while Paschen, Brackett and Pfund fall in infrared region.

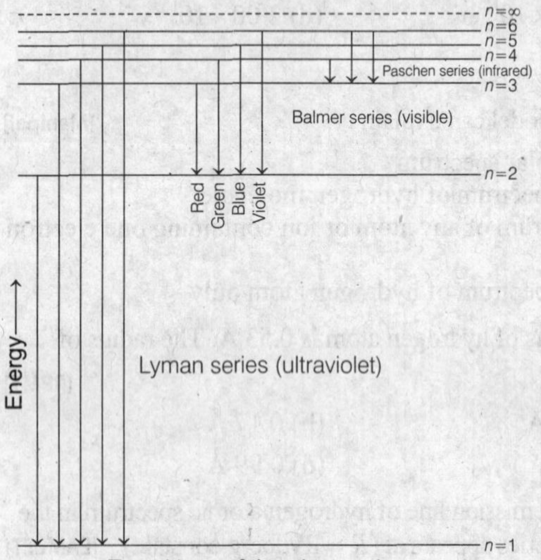

Transitions of the electron in the hydrogen atom

2 (*d*) $\because \frac{1}{\lambda} = Z^2 \cdot R\left[\frac{1}{n_1^2} - \frac{1}{n_2^2}\right]$

$\therefore$ For He^+ ion, $Z = 2$

$$\frac{1}{\lambda} = 2^2 \cdot R\left[\frac{1}{2^2} - \frac{1}{4^2}\right]$$

$$\frac{1}{\lambda} = 4 \times R \times \frac{3}{16} = \frac{3}{4}R$$

The same value for H-atom is possible when electron jumps from $n = 2$ to $n = 1$,

i.e. $\frac{1}{\lambda} = 1 \times R\left[\frac{1}{1} - \frac{1}{4}\right] \Rightarrow \frac{3}{4}R$

3 (*a*) The correct match is

(A) $\rightarrow$ Lyman $\rightarrow$ (1) $\rightarrow$ Ultraviolet

(B) $\rightarrow$ Paschen $\rightarrow$ (2) $\rightarrow$ Near infrared

(C) $\rightarrow$ Balmer $\rightarrow$ (4) $\rightarrow$ Visible

(D) $\rightarrow$ Pfund $\rightarrow$ (3) $\rightarrow$ Far infrared

4 (*d*) In 1885, Balmer for the first time showed that the wave numbers of spectral lines present in the visible region in hydrogen spectrum are given by

$$\bar{\nu}\ (\text{cm}^{-1}) = 109677\left(\frac{1}{(2)^2} - \frac{1}{n_2^2}\right)$$

Here, $n_2 = 3, 4, 5, \ldots$

Thus, Balmer spectrum of hydrogen was discovered first. It is the hydrogen spectrum which appear in the visible region of the electromagnetic spectrum.

5 (*d*) If $n = 1$,

$$E_1 = -2.178 \times 10^{-18}\left(\frac{Z^2}{1}\right) \text{ J}$$

If $n = 6$,

$$E_6 = \frac{-2.178 \times 10^{-18} Z^2}{36} = -6.05 \times 10^{-20} Z^2 \text{ J}$$

From the above calculation, it is obvious that, electron has a more negative energy in $n = 1$ than it does for $n = 6$. It means that electron is more strongly bound in the smallest allowed orbit.

All other given statements are correct.

6 (*d*) According to Bohr, velocity of an electron (v) $= 2.188 \times 10^6 \frac{Z}{n}$ m/s

For H, $Z = 1$

Given, $n = 2$

$$\therefore \quad v = \frac{2.188 \times 10^6 \times 1}{2} = 1.094 \times 10^6 \text{m/s}$$

7 (*c*) Bohr's atomic model is applicable only for hydrogen atom and H-like species, i.e. to the one electron system. Since, He^{2+} does not contain one electron while all other species have one electron each, thus Bohr's model is not applicable to He^{2+}.

8 (*c*) Ionisation energy for an atom of atomic number Z is given by

$$\text{IE} = \frac{(\text{IE})_\text{H} Z^2}{n^2} = 13.6 \times \frac{Z^2}{n^2} \text{ eV}$$

Thus, second ionisation energy for He-atom is given by

$$\text{IE} = \frac{13.6 \times (2)^2}{(1)^2} \text{ eV} = 13.6 \times 4 \text{ eV} = 54.4 \text{ eV}$$

9 (*a*) The spectral lines for atomic hydrogen is given as.

Series	n_1	n_2
Lyman	1	2, 3 ....
Balmer	2	3, 4 ....
Paschen	3	4, 5 ....
Brackett	4	5, 6 ....
Pfund	5	6, 7 ....

$\because$ L shell means $n = 2$,

thus, the series will be Balmer.

10 (*c*) Beyond a certain wavelength, line spectrum becomes band spectrum and, thus lines in the series converge as wavelength decreases.

For Balmer series, $n_1 = 2$

For the line of longest wavelength (lowest energy) in this series, $n_2 = 3$

11 (*a*) The spectral lines for atomic hydrogen is found in spectral region as:

Series	Region
Lyman	Ultraviolet
Balmer	Visible
Paschen	Infrared
Brackett	Infrared
Pfund	Infrared

Hence, the wavelength of Lyman series lie towards the ultraviolet region.

12 (*c*) When an electron jumps from higher energy level $n = 4$ to ground state (i.e. $n = 1$), the number of spectral lines $= \frac{n(n-1)}{2}$

$\therefore$ When an electron jumps from $n = 4$ level,

$$\text{number of spectral lines} = \frac{4(4-1)}{2} = \frac{4 \times 3}{2} = 6$$

13 (*a*) Wave number of spectral line in the emission spectrum of hydrogen,

$$\bar{\nu} = R_H\left(\frac{1}{n_1^2} - \frac{1}{n_2^2}\right) \quad \ldots\text{(i)}$$

Given, $\bar{\nu} = \frac{8}{9} R_H$

On putting the value of $\bar{\nu}$ in Eq. (i), we get

$$\frac{8}{9} R_H = R_H\left(\frac{1}{n_1^2} - \frac{1}{n_2^2}\right)$$

$$\frac{8}{9} = \frac{1}{(1)^2} - \frac{1}{n_2^2}$$

$$\frac{8}{9} - 1 = -\frac{1}{n_2^2} \Rightarrow \frac{1}{3} = \frac{1}{n_2}$$

$\therefore \quad n_2 = 3$

Hence, electron jumps from $n_2 = 3$ to $n_1 = 1$.

14 (*d*) According to Bohr's model of atom :

(i) Electron can move around the nucleus in fixed radius and energy. Orbits are quantised as electron can move only in those orbits for which angular momentum is integral multiple of $h/2\pi$.

(ii) Energy of electron in orbit is given as

$$E_n = -R_H\left(\frac{1}{n^2}\right)$$

R_H = Rydberg constant (2.18×10^{-18} J)

$$\boxed{E_n \propto \frac{1}{n^2}}$$

So, electron in the orbit nearest to the nucleus is in lowest energy state.

Only option (d) does not belong to Bohr's model.

15 (*b*) According to Sommerfield's modification, the trajectory of an electron in a hydrogen atom is a closed ellipse like curve in addition to circular orbits. The curve is narrower at the perihelion position and flatter at the aphelion position.

16 (*a*) $\frac{1}{\lambda} = R_H Z^2\left[\frac{1}{n_1^2} - \frac{1}{n_2^2}\right]$

For Lyman series, $n_1 = 1$ and $n_2 = 2$

($\because$ for maximum λ, transition is from very next level)

$$\therefore \quad \frac{1}{\lambda} = 109678 \times (1)^2\left[\frac{1}{(1)^2} - \frac{1}{(2)^2}\right]$$

$$= \frac{109678 \times 3}{4} \text{ cm}^{-1}$$

$$\lambda = \frac{4}{3 \times 109678} = 121.56 \times 10^{-7}$$

$$= 121.56 \text{ nm}$$

Hence, both A and R are correct and Reason is the correct explanation of Assertion.

17 (*c*) $\bar{\nu} = R_{\text{H}}\left[\frac{1}{n_1^2} - \frac{1}{n_2^2}\right]$

$$12186.3 = 109678\left[\frac{1}{n_1^2} - \frac{1}{\infty^2}\right]$$

$\therefore \quad n_1 = 3$

Since, $n_1 = 3$, it belong to Paschen series.

18 (*c*) For Paschen series,

$n_1 = 3, n_2 = 4, 5, 6, \ldots$

19 (*b*) Radius of H-like species,

$$r_n = 0.529 \times \frac{n^2}{Z} \text{ Å}$$

As $0.529 \times n^2$ is radius for first Bohr orbit of H-atom which is equal to r (given), so radius of first orbit of

Li^{2+}, $r_n = \frac{r}{3}$ ($n = 1, Z = 3$, for Li^{2+}).

20 (*b*) (a) **Max Planck** gave the concept of 'quantum', smallest quantity of energy. ($E = h\nu$)

h = Planck's constant = 6.626×10^{-34} J

(b) **Neil Bohr** gave the atomic model based on quantisation of energy.

(c) **de-Broglie** proposed that matter exhibits dual character i.e. both particle and wave like properties.

(d) **Heisenberg** gave uncertainty principle.

21 (*d*) Since, the $2p_x$ and $2p_y$ orbitals are degenerate orbitals, i.e. are of equal energy, so there is no possibility of electron transition.

Thus, both (A) and (R) are incorrect.

22 (*d*) $\bar{\nu} = R_H\left[\frac{1}{n_1^2} - \frac{1}{n_2^2}\right]$

For Balmer series, $n_1 = 2$ and for 4th line in Balmer series, $n_2 = 6$

$\because \quad R_H = 1{,}09{,}677 \text{ cm}^{-1}$

$$\bar{\nu} = 109677\left[\frac{1}{2^2} - \frac{1}{6^2}\right]$$

$$= 109677\left[\frac{1}{4} - \frac{1}{36}\right]$$

$$\bar{\nu} = 24{,}372 \text{ cm}^{-1}$$

23 (*c*) H_β line is formed when electron jumps from 3rd orbit to first orbit in Lyman series.

$\therefore \quad n_1 = 1, n_2 = 3$

24 (*d*) $\frac{1}{\lambda} = R_H Z^2\left(\frac{1}{n_1^2} - \frac{1}{n_2^2}\right)$

Where, $R_H = R$, $Z = 3$

($\because$ for Li^{2+}, atomic number = 3)

$n_2 = 2, n_1 = 1$

$$\frac{1}{\lambda} = R(3)^2\left(\frac{1}{(1)^2} - \frac{1}{(2)^2}\right)$$

$$= \frac{R \times 9 \times 3}{4}$$

$$\lambda = \frac{4}{27R}$$

25 (*a*) The total energy of the nth orbit is the sum of kinetic energy and potential energy

$\therefore \quad E_n = \text{KE} + \text{PE}$

The KE of the electron

$$= \frac{1}{2}mv^2 = \frac{1}{2}\frac{Zke^2}{r_n}$$

(where, k = constant)

For the first excited state of H-atom,

$$\text{KE} = \frac{1}{2}\frac{ke^2}{r}$$

Potential energy of the electron is equal to the work done when an electron is brought from an infinite distance to the orbit of the atom at a distance, r_n from the nucleus.

$$= \int_{\infty}^{r_n} \frac{kZe^2}{r_n}$$

$$= \frac{-kZe^2}{r_n}$$

(Here, negative sign indicates work done against force of attraction)

For the first excited state of H-atom,

$$\text{PE} = \frac{-ke^2}{r}$$

Thus, total energy $= \frac{1}{2}\frac{ke^2}{r} + \left(\frac{-ke^2}{r}\right)$

$$= \frac{-1}{2}\frac{ke^2}{r} = \text{KE}$$

But total energy is given as –3.4 eV.

Thus, $\text{KE} = \frac{-1}{2}\frac{ke^2}{r} = +3.4$ eV

$\Rightarrow \quad$ KE = 3.4 eV

Hence, kinetic energy of same orbit of H-atom is 3.4 eV.

Alternative solution

In first excited state, E_n

$$= \frac{1}{2}mv^2 + \left[-\frac{Ze^2}{r}\right]$$

$$= +\frac{1}{2}\frac{Ze^2}{r} - \frac{Ze^2}{r} = -\frac{1}{2}\frac{Ze^2}{r}$$

$$\therefore \quad KE = \frac{1}{2}\frac{Ze^2}{r} = +3.4 \text{ eV}$$

26 (*d*) As $E_n = -21.8 \times 10^{-19} \times Z^2/n^2$ J/atom

Thus, $E_n \propto \left[-\frac{1}{n^2}\right]$

where n is the number of orbits. Therefore, as the value of n increases, energy of the electron also increases. Therefore, when n becomes infinite, energy also becomes infinite. Due to this reason, maximum energy is possessed by an electron, when it is present at infinite distance from the nucleus.

27 (*a*) (a) The splitting of spectral line emitted by an excited electron under the influence of magnetic field is called **Zeeman effect.**

(b) Splitting of spectral lines under electric field is called **Stark effect**.

(c) The phenomenon of ejection of the electrons from the metal surface under the influence of incident radiation is called **photoelectric effect**.

28 (*d*) The energy of second Bohr orbit of hydrogen atom (E_2) is -328 kJ mol^{-1} because

$$E_2 = -\frac{1312}{2^2} \text{ kJ mol}^{-1}$$

$$\therefore \quad E_n = -\frac{1312}{n^2} \text{ kJ mol}^{-1}$$

If $\quad n = 4$

$$\therefore \quad E_4 = -\frac{1312}{4^2} = -82 \text{ kJ mol}^{-1}$$

29 (*a*) $\frac{1}{\lambda} = \bar{v}_H = R_H\left[\frac{1}{n_1^2} - \frac{1}{n_2^2}\right]$

$$= 1.097 \times 10^7 \left[\frac{1}{1^2} - \frac{1}{\infty^2}\right]$$

$$\therefore \quad \lambda = \frac{1}{1.097 \times 10^7}$$

$$= 9.11 \times 10^{-8} \text{ m}$$

$$= 91.1 \times 10^{-9} \text{ m} = 91.1 \text{ nm}$$

$$(\because 1 \text{ nm} = 10^{-9} \text{ m})$$

30 (*c*) Ionisation energy of H

$$= 2.18 \times 10^{-18} \text{ J atom}^{-1}$$

$\therefore$ E_1 (energy of Ist orbit of H-atom)

$$= -2.18 \times 10^{-18} \text{ J atom}^{-1}$$

$$\therefore E_n = \frac{-2.18 \times 10^{-18}}{n^2} \text{ J atom}^{-1} \text{ as}$$

$Z = 1$ for H-atom

$$\Delta E = E_4 - E_1$$

$$= \frac{-2.18 \times 10^{-18}}{4^2} - \frac{-2.18 \times 10^{-18}}{1^2}$$

$$= -2.18 \times 10^{-18} \times \left[\frac{1}{4^2} - \frac{1}{1^2}\right]$$

$$\Delta E = h\nu = -2.18 \times 10^{-18} \times -\frac{15}{16}$$

$$= +2.0437 \times 10^{-18} \text{ J atom}^{-1}$$

$$\therefore \nu = \frac{\Delta E}{h}$$

$$= \frac{2.0437 \times 10^{-18} \text{ J atom}^{-1}}{6.625 \times 10^{-34} \text{ Js}}$$

$$= 3.084 \times 10^{15} \text{ s}^{-1}$$

31 (*c*) As the Bohr's model is applicable only to hydrogen atom and hydrogen like species, i.e. to one electron system, thus Bohr's model can easily explain the spectrum of any atom or ion containing one electron only.

32 (*b*) Radius of nth Bohr orbit $(r) = \frac{n^2 a_0}{Z}$

where,

$$a_0 = 0.53 \text{ Å}$$

For hydrogen atom,

$$r = \frac{1^2 \times 0.53}{1} = 0.53 \text{ Å}$$

For $_3Li^{2+}$,

$$r = \frac{1^2 \times 0.529}{3} = 0.17 \text{ Å}$$

33 (*a*) Rydberg's equation,

$$\bar{\nu} = R_H\left[\frac{1}{n_1^2} - \frac{1}{n_2^2}\right]$$

For Balmer series,

$$n_1 = 2, n_2 = 3$$

$$\therefore \quad \bar{\nu} = R_H\left[\frac{9-4}{36}\right] = \frac{5R}{36} \text{ cm}^{-1}$$

34 (*c*) We know that,

$$\Delta E = hc \cdot R_H\left[\frac{1}{n_1^2} - \frac{1}{n_2^2}\right]$$

For lowest energy of spectral line in the Lyman series, $n_1 = 1, n_2 = 2$

$$\text{Hence, } \Delta E = hc \cdot R_H\left[\frac{1}{1^2} - \frac{1}{2^2}\right]$$

$$= \frac{3hcR_H}{4}$$

35 (*c*) Second Bohr orbit of hydrogen atom, i.e. $n = 2$

Atomic number of hydrogen $(Z) = 1$

By using, $r = \frac{0.529n^2}{Z}$

$$= \frac{0.529 \times (2)^2}{1}$$

$$= \frac{0.529 \times 4}{1}$$

$$= 2.116 \text{ Å}$$

$$= 0.2116 \text{ nm}$$

36 (*a*) Kinetic energy in an orbit

$$= \frac{Ze^2}{8\pi\varepsilon_0 r} \quad \ldots\text{(i)}$$

Potential energy in an orbit

$$= -\frac{Ze^2}{4\pi\varepsilon_0 r} \quad \ldots\text{(ii)}$$

On comparing Eqs. (i) and (ii), we get

$$KE = -\frac{1}{2} PE$$

Hence, the magnitude of kinetic energy in an orbit is equal to half of the potential energy.

Topic 3

Wave Particle Duality of Matter

(de-Broglie Relationship and Heisenberg's Uncertainity Principle)

2019

1 In hydrogen atom, the de-Broglie wavelength of an electron in the second Bohr orbit is
[Given that, Bohr radius, $a_0 = 52.9$ pm] **[NEET (Odisha)]**
(a) 211.6 pm (b) $211.6\,\pi$ pm
(c) $52.9\,\pi$ pm (d) 105.8 pm

2017

2 **Assertion** (A) It is impossible to determine the exact position and exact momentum of an electron, simultaneously.
Reason (R) The path of an electron is clearly defined. **[AIIMS]**
(a) Both A and R are correct and R is the correct explanation of the A.
(b) Both A and R are correct but R is not the correct explanation of the A.
(c) A is correct but R is incorrect.
(d) Both A and R are incorrect.

2014

3 The uncertainty in the velocity of a particle of mass 6.626×10^{-28} kg is $1 \times 10^{-6}\,\text{ms}^{-1}$. What is the uncertainty in its position (in nm)? ($h = 6.626 \times 10^{-34}$ Js) **[Kerala CEE]**
(a) $(1/2\pi)$ (b) $(2.5/\pi)$ (c) $(4/\pi)$ (d) $(1/4\pi)$
(e) $(5/\pi)$

4 The ratio of de-Broglie wavelengths of a deuterium atom to that of an α-particle, when the velocity of the former is five times greater than that of the latter is **[Kerala CEE]**
(a) 4 (b) 0.2 (c) 2 (d) 0.4
(e) 5

5 As per de-Broglie formula, a macroscopic particle of mass 100 g and moving at a velocity of $100\,\text{cm s}^{-1}$ will have a wavelength of **[WB JEE]**
(a) 6.6×10^{-29} cm (b) 6.6×10^{-30} cm
(c) 6.6×10^{-31} cm (d) 6.6×10^{-32} cm

2013

6 The de-Broglie wavelength associated with particle of mass 10^{-6} kg moving with a velocity of $10\,\text{m s}^{-1}$ is **[AIIMS]**
(a) 6.63×10^{-7} (b) 6.63×10^{-16}
(c) 6.63×10^{-21} (d) 6.63×10^{-29}

2012

7 If E_e, E_α and E_p represent the kinetic energies of an electron, α-particle and a proton respectively, each moving with same de-Broglie wavelength then **[OJEE]**
(a) $E_e = E_\alpha = E_p$ (b) $E_e > E_\alpha > E_p$
(c) $E_\alpha > E_p > E_e$ (d) $E_e > E_p > E_\alpha$

8 Which of the following does not represent the mathematical expression for the Heisenberg's uncertainty principle? **[WB JEE]**
(a) $\Delta x \cdot \Delta p \geq h/(4\pi)$ (b) $\Delta x \cdot \Delta v \geq h/(4\pi m)$
(c) $\Delta E \cdot \Delta t \geq h/(4\pi)$ (d) $\Delta E \cdot \Delta x \geq h/(4\pi)$

2011

9 Calculate the velocity of an electron having wavelength of 0.15 nm. Mass of an electron is 9.109×10^{-28} g. ($h = 6.626 \times 10^{-27}$ erg-s). **[Guj CET]**
(a) $4.85 \times 10^{8}\,\text{cm s}^{-1}$ (b) $2.062 \times 10^{-15}\,\text{cm s}^{-1}$
(c) $2.068 \times 10^{-10}\,\text{cm s}^{-1}$ (d) $4.85 \times 10^{-8}\,\text{cm s}^{-1}$

2010

10 The mass (in kg) of a photon with wavelength 3.6 Å is **[RPMT]**
(a) 6.135×10^{-19} (b) 5.6135×10^{-33}
(c) 6.100×10^{-19} (d) 6.135×10^{-33}

11 Calculate the wavelength of light required to break the bond between two chlorine atoms in a chlorine molecule. The Cl—Cl bond energy is 243 kJ mol^{-1}.
($h = 6.6 \times 10^{-34}$ Js, $c = 3 \times 10^{8}$ m/s, Avogadro's number $= 6.02 \times 10^{23}\,\text{mol}^{-1}$) **[DUMET]**
(a) 4.91×10^{-7} m (b) 4.11×10^{-6} m
(c) 8.81×10^{-31} m (d) 6.26×10^{-21} m

12 A particle having a mass of 1.0 mg has a velocity of the 3600 km/h. Calculate the wavelength of the particle. ($h = 6.626 \times 10^{-27}$ erg-s) **[Guj CET]**
(a) 6.626×10^{-28} cm (b) 6.626×10^{-29} cm
(c) 6.626×10^{-30} cm (d) 6.626×10^{-31} cm

2009

13 The de-Broglie wavelength of helium atom at room temperature is **[AIIMS]**
(a) 6.6×10^{-34} m (b) 4.39×10^{-10} m
(c) 7.34×10^{-11} m (d) 2.335×10^{-20} m

14 The uncertainty in the position of an electron (mass $= 9.1\times 10^{-28}$ g) moving with a velocity of 3.0×10^{4} cm s^{-1} accurate upto 0.011% will be **[Manipal]**

(a) 1.92 cm (b) 7.66 cm
(c) 0.175 cm (d) 3.84 cm

15 If uncertainty in position and velocity are equal then uncertainty in momentum will be **[Manipal]**

(a) $\frac{1}{2}\sqrt{\frac{mh}{\pi}}$ (b) $\frac{1}{2}\sqrt{\frac{h}{\pi m}}$
(c) $\frac{h}{4\pi m}$ (d) $\frac{mh}{4\pi}$

16 The velocity of particle A is 0.1 m s^{-1} and that of particle B is 0.05 m s^{-1}. If the mass of the particle B is five times that of particle A, the ratio of de-Broglie wavelengths associated with the particles A and B is **[Kerala CEE]**

(a) 2 : 5 (b) 3 : 4 (c) 6 : 4 (d) 4 : 3
(e) 5 : 2

17 If the de-Broglie wavelength of a particle of mass m is 100 times of its velocity then its value in terms of its mass (m) and Planck's constant (h) is **[J&K CET]**

(a) $\frac{1}{10}\sqrt{\frac{m}{h}}$ (b) $10\sqrt{\frac{h}{m}}$ (c) $\frac{1}{10}\sqrt{\frac{h}{m}}$ (d) $10\sqrt{\frac{m}{h}}$

18 A body of mass x kg is moving with a velocity of 100 m s^{-1}. Its de-Broglie wavelength is 6.62×10^{-35} m. Hence, x is ($h = 6.62\times 10^{-34}$ Js) **[KCET]**

(a) 0.25 kg (b) 0.15 kg
(c) 0.2 kg (d) 0.1 kg

19 The wavelengths of electron waves in two orbits is 3 : 5. The ratio of kinetic energy of electrons will be **[EAMCET]**

(a) 25 : 9 (b) 5 : 3 (c) 9 : 25 (d) 3 : 5

2008

20 If uncertainty in position and momentum are equal then uncertainty in velocity is **[CBSE AIPMT]**

(a) $\frac{1}{2m}\sqrt{\frac{h}{\pi}}$ (b) $\sqrt{\frac{h}{2\pi}}$ (c) $\frac{1}{m}\sqrt{\frac{h}{\pi}}$ (d) $\sqrt{\frac{h}{\pi}}$

21 The measurement of the electron position is associated with an uncertainty in momentum, which is equal to 1×10^{-18} g cm s^{-1}. The uncertainty in electron velocity is, (mass of an electron is 9×10^{-28} g) **[CBSE AIPMT]**

(a) 1×10^{9} cm s^{-1} (b) 1×10^{6} cm s^{-1}
(c) 1×10^{5} cm s^{-1} (d) 1×10^{11} cm s^{-1}

22 The energy of a photon is 3×10^{-12} erg. What is its wavelength in nm?
($h = 6.62\times 10^{-27}$ erg-s, $c = 3\times 10^{10}$ cm/s) **[AFMC]**

(a) 662 (b) 1324
(c) 66.2 (d) 5.62

23 Which of the following is incorrect statement? **[BHU]**

(a) Circumference of electron orbit $(2\pi r) = n\lambda$ (n = an integer)
(b) de-Broglie equation : $\lambda = h/mv$
(c) Angular momentum (mvr) of an electron is an integral multiple of $\frac{h}{2\pi}$
(d) Angular momentum of the electron is not quantised

24 Match the following columns. **[EAMCET]**

	Column I	Column II
A.	$mvr = \frac{nh}{2\pi}$	1. Paschen series
B.	Infrared	2. Electron's total energy
C.	$\lambda = \frac{h}{p}$	3. de-Broglie equation
D.	$\frac{-e^2}{2r}$	4. Schrodinger equation
E.	$H\psi = E\psi$	5. Bohr's equation

Codes

	A	B	C	D	E		A	B	C	D	E
(a)	5	2	3	1	4	(b)	3	2	5	4	1
(c)	5	1	3	2	4	(d)	4	1	2	3	5

2007

25 If the wavelength of photon is 2.2×10^{-11} m, $h = 6.6\times 10^{-34}$ Js, then momentum of photon is **[AFMC]**

(a) 3×10^{-23} kg ms^{-1} (b) 3.33×10^{22} kg ms^{-1}
(c) 1.452×10^{-44} kg ms^{-1} (d) 6.89×10^{43} kg ms^{-1}

26 The de-Broglie wavelength of a particle with mass 1 kg and velocity 100 m/s, is **[JCECE]**

(a) 6.6×10^{-33} m (b) 6.6×10^{-36} m
(c) 3.3×10^{33} m (d) 3.3×10^{-36} m

27 Which scientists diffracted the moving electron by using Ni metal crystal like X-rays? **[Guj CET]**

(a) de-Broglie and Schrodinger
(b) Max Planck and Hamilton
(c) Davisson and Germer
(d) Goldsmith and Unlenbeck

2006

28 Given, the mass of electron is 9.11×10^{-31} kg, Planck's constant is 6.626×10^{-34} Js, the uncertainty involved in the measurement of velocity within a distance of 0.1 Å is **[CBSE AIPMT]**

(a) 5.79×10^{6} ms^{-1}
(b) 5.79×10^{7} ms^{-1}
(c) 0.79×10^{8} ms^{-1}
(d) 5.79×10^{5} ms^{-1}

29 The de-Broglie wavelength associated with a ball of mass 1 kg having kinetic energy 0.5 J, is **[AIIMS]**

(a) 6.626×10^{-34} m (b) 13.20×10^{-34} m
(c) 10.38×10^{-21} m (d) 6.626×10^{-34} Å

30 Which of the following statement is true? **[Kerala CEE]**

(a) The kinetic energy of an electron is inversely proportional to square of its momentum
(b) de-Broglie wavelength associated with a particle is directly proportional to its mass
(c) de-Broglie wavelength associated with a particle is directly proportional to square of its velocity
(d) The wavelength associated with an electron is directly proportional to square root of accelerating potential
(e) The kinetic energy of an electron is directly proportional to accelerating potential

31 Wave nature of electrons was demonstrated by **[RPMT]**

(a) Schrodinger (b) de-Broglie
(c) Davisson and Germer (d) Heisenberg

32 The uncertainty in momentum of an electron is 1×10^{-5} kg ms^{-1}. The uncertainty in its position will be ($h = 6.63 \times 10^{-34}$ Js) **[DUMET]**

(a) 5.28×10^{-30} m (b) 5.25×10^{-28} m
(c) 1.05×10^{-26} m (d) 2.715×10^{-3} m

2005

33 What is the wavelength (in m) of a particle of mass 6.62×10^{-29} g moving with a velocity of 10^3 ms^{-1}? **[EAMCET]**

(a) 6.62×10^{-4} (b) 6.62×10^{-3}
(c) 10^{-5} (d) 10^5

34 For an electron, if the uncertainty in velocity is Δv, the uncertainty in its position (Δx) is given by **[DUMET]**

(a) $\dfrac{hm}{4\pi\Delta v}$ (b) $\dfrac{4\pi}{hm\Delta v}$
(c) $\dfrac{h}{4\pi m\Delta v}$ (d) $\dfrac{4\pi m}{h\Delta v}$

Answers

1 (b)	2 (c)	3 (d)	4 (d)	5 (c)	6 (d)	7 (d)	8 (d)	9 (a)	10 (d)
11 (a)	12 (b)	13 (c)	14 (c)	15 (a)	16 (a)	17 (b)	18 (d)	19 (a)	20 (a)
21 (a)	22 (a)	23 (d)	24 (c)	25 (a)	26 (b)	27 (c)	28 (a)	29 (a)	30 (e)
31 (b)	32 (a)	33 (c)	34 (c)						

Explanations

1 (*b*) According to Bohr,

$$mvr = \frac{nh}{2\pi}$$

$$2\pi r = \frac{nh}{mv} = n\lambda \quad \ldots\text{(i)}$$

$$\left[\because \lambda = \frac{h}{mv}\right]$$

where, r = radius,
λ = wavelength
n = number of orbit

Also, $$r = \frac{a_0 n^2}{Z} \quad \ldots\text{(ii)}$$

where, a_0 = Bohr radius = 52.9 pm
Z = atomic number

On substituting the value of 'r' from Eq. (ii) to Eq. (i), we get

$$n\lambda = \frac{2\pi n^2 a_0}{Z} \Rightarrow \lambda = \frac{2\pi n a_0}{Z}$$

$$\lambda = 2\pi \times 2 \times 52.9 \quad [\because n = 2, Z = 1]$$
$$= 211.6\pi \text{ pm}$$

2 (*c*) According to Heisenberg's uncertainty principle, the exact position and exact momentum of an electron cannot be determined simultaneously, thus path of an electron in an atom cannot be defined clearly.

Hence, (A) is correct but (R) is incorrect.

3 (*d*) According to Heisenberg's uncertainty principle,

$$m \cdot \Delta v \times \Delta x \geq \frac{h}{4\pi}$$

Given, $m = 6.626 \times 10^{-28}$ kg
$\Delta v = 10^{-6}$ m/s
$h = 6.626 \times 10^{-34}$ Js

$$6.626 \times 10^{-28} \times 10^{-6} \times \Delta x = \frac{6.626 \times 10^{-34}}{4\pi}$$

$$\Delta x = \frac{6.626 \times 10^{-34}}{4\pi \times 6.626 \times 10^{-34}} = \frac{1}{4\pi}$$

4 (*d*) $\lambda = \dfrac{h}{mv}$

Mass of α-particle = 4 u,
mass of deuterium = 2 u

$$v_D = 5v_\alpha$$

$$\lambda_D = \frac{1}{2 \times v_D}, \lambda_\alpha = \frac{1}{4v_\alpha}$$

$$\frac{\lambda_D}{\lambda\alpha} = \frac{4v_\alpha}{2v_D} = \frac{4}{2 \times 5} = 0.4$$

5 (*c*) According to de-Broglie equation,

wavelength, $(\lambda) = \dfrac{h}{mv}$

Given, $m = 100$ g, $v = 100$ cm s^{-1}
and $h = 6.6 \times 10^{-34}$ Js $= 6.6 \times 10^{-27}$ erg-s

On substituting values, we get

$$\lambda = \frac{6.6 \times 10^{-27}}{100 \times 100} = 6.6 \times 10^{-31} \text{ cm}$$

6 (*d*) According to de-Broglie relation

$$\lambda = \frac{h}{mv} = \frac{6.63 \times 10^{-34}}{10^{-6} \times 10} = 6.63 \times 10^{-29} \text{m}$$

7 (*d*) de-Broglie wavelength

$$\lambda = \frac{h}{mv} \Rightarrow v = \frac{h}{m\lambda} \quad ...(i)$$

$$KE = \frac{1}{2}mv^2 \quad ...(ii)$$

On putting the value of v in Eq. (ii), we get

$$KE = \frac{1}{2}m\left(\frac{h}{m \cdot \lambda}\right)^2$$

$$\Rightarrow \quad KE = \frac{1}{2}\left(\frac{h^2}{m \cdot \lambda^2}\right)$$

Hence, KE $\propto 1/m$ (if λ is same) and order of mass is as

$$m_e < m_p < m_\alpha$$

Thus, the order of KE is

$$E_e > E_p > E_\alpha$$

8 (*d*) From Heisenberg's uncertainty principle,

$$\Delta x \cdot \Delta p \ge \frac{h}{4\pi} \quad ...(i)$$

or $$\Delta x \cdot m\Delta v \ge \frac{h}{4\pi}$$

or $$\Delta x \cdot \Delta v \ge \frac{h}{4\pi m} \quad ...(ii)$$

This principle is also applicable for pairs like energy-time ($\Delta E \cdot \Delta t$) and angular momentum-angle ($\Delta\omega \cdot \Delta\theta$) alongwith position-momentum ($\Delta x \cdot \Delta p$).

Thus, $$\Delta E \cdot \Delta t \ge \frac{h}{4\pi} \quad ... (iii)$$

9 (*a*) According to de-Broglie, the wavelength λ of n electrons is inversely proportional to its momentum p.

$$\lambda \propto \frac{1}{p}$$

or $\lambda = \frac{h}{p}$ (where, h = Planck's constant and p = momentum of electron)

$\because$ Momentum (p) = Mass (m) $\times$ Velocity (v)

$$\Rightarrow \quad \lambda = \frac{h}{mv} \Rightarrow v = \frac{h}{m\lambda}$$

$$v = \frac{6.626 \times 10^{-27}}{0.15 \times 10^{-7} \times 9.109 \times 10^{-28}}$$

$$= 4.85 \times 10^8 \text{ cm s}^{-1}$$

10 (*d*) Here, $\lambda = 3.6$ Å $= 3.6 \times 10^{-10}$ m

As photon travels with the velocity of light, $v = 3.0 \times 10^8$ m s^{-1}

From de-Broglie equation,

$$\lambda = \frac{h}{mv}$$

or $$m = \frac{h}{\lambda v}$$

$$= \frac{6.626 \times 10^{-34} \text{ Js}}{(3.6 \times 10^{-10} \text{ m})(3.0 \times 10^8 \text{ m s}^{-1})}$$

$$= 6.135 \times 10^{-33} \text{ kg}$$

11 (*a*) Energy required to break one Cl—Cl bond

$$= \frac{\text{Bond energy per mole}}{\text{Avogadro's number}}$$

$$E = \frac{243 \times 10^3}{6.023 \times 10^{23}} \text{ J}$$

Let the wavelength of the photon to cause rupture of one Cl — Cl bond be λ.

$$\lambda = \frac{hc}{E} = \frac{6.6 \times 10^{-34} \times 3 \times 10^8 \times 6.023 \times 10^{23}}{243 \times 10^3}$$

$$= \frac{119.255}{243} \times 10^{-34} \times 10^{31} \times 10^{-3}$$

$$= 4.91 \times 10^{-7} \text{ m}$$

12 (*b*) $\lambda = \frac{h}{mv}$,

(according to de-Broglie relation.)

Here, $v = 3600$ km/h or 10^5 cm/s,

$m = 1.0$ mg $= 10^{-3}$ g

$$\lambda = \frac{6.626 \times 10^{-27}}{10^{-3} \times 10^5} = 6.626 \times 10^{-29} \text{ cm}$$

13 (*c*) $v_{rms} = \sqrt{\frac{3RT}{M}}$

Where, R (gas constant)

$= 8.314$ JK^{-1} mol^{-1}

M = molecular mass of helium atom

$= 4 \times 10^{-3}$ kg

$$\because v_{rms} = \sqrt{\frac{3 \times 8.314 \times 298}{4 \times 10^{-3}}} = 1363 \text{ ms}^{-1}$$

For one atom of He, de-Broglie wavelength is given as

$$\lambda = \frac{h}{mv}$$

$$= \frac{6.626 \times 10^{-34} \times 6.023 \times 10^{23}}{4 \times 10^{-3} \times 1363}$$

[$\because$ m is per particle mass of He, i.e. $m = M/N_A$]

$$= 7.32 \times 10^{-11} \text{ m} \approx 7.34 \times 10^{-11} \text{ m}$$

14 (*c*) $$\Delta x = \frac{h}{4\pi \times m \times \Delta v}$$

$$= \frac{6.6 \times 10^{-27} \times 100}{4 \times 3.14 \times 9.1 \times 10^{-28} \times 3 \times 10^4 \times 0.011}$$

$$= 0.175 \text{ cm}$$

15 (*a*) Here, $\Delta x = \Delta v$

$$\Delta x \times \Delta p \ge \frac{h}{4\pi}$$

$$\Delta x \times m \cdot \Delta v = \frac{h}{4\pi}$$

$$(\Delta v)^2 = \frac{h}{4\pi m} \quad (\because \Delta x = \Delta v)$$

$$\Delta v = \sqrt{\frac{h}{4\pi m}}$$

As, $$\Delta p = m \cdot \Delta v$$

$$\Delta p = m\sqrt{\frac{h}{4\pi m}} = \sqrt{\frac{mh}{4\pi}}$$

$$\therefore \quad \Delta p = \frac{1}{2}\sqrt{\frac{mh}{\pi}}$$

16 (*e*) Given, $v_A = 0.1$ ms^{-1},

$v_B = 0.05$ ms^{-1}, $m_B = 5 \times m_A$

de-Broglie wavelength, $(\lambda) = \frac{h}{mv}$

$$\lambda_A = \frac{h}{m_A \times 0.1},$$

$$\lambda_B = \frac{h}{5 \times m_A \times 0.05}$$

$$\frac{\lambda_A}{\lambda_B} = \frac{m_A \times 0.05 \times 5}{m_A \times 0.1} = \frac{5}{2}$$

17 (*b*) Let, the wavelength of particle be x,

Thus, $x = 100 \times$ velocity

Velocity $= \frac{x}{100}$, $\lambda = \frac{h}{mv}$, $x = \frac{h \times 100}{m \times x}$

$$x^2 = 100\frac{h}{m}$$

or $$x = 10\sqrt{\frac{h}{m}}$$

18 (*d*) According to de-Broglie equation,

$$\lambda = \frac{h}{mv}$$

Given, $\lambda = 6.62 \times 10^{-35}$ m

$v = 100$ m s^{-1}

$h = 6.62 \times 10^{-34}$ Js

and $m = x$ kg

$$\therefore \quad 6.62 \times 10^{-35} = \frac{6.62 \times 10^{-34}}{x \times 100}$$

$$x = 0.1 \text{ kg}$$

19 (*a*) de-Broglie equation is,

$$\lambda = \frac{h}{mv}$$

$$KE = \frac{1}{2}mv^2$$

or $$v = \sqrt{\frac{2KE}{m}}$$

$$\lambda = \frac{h}{\sqrt{2m\text{ KE}}}$$

$$\frac{(\text{KE})_1}{(\text{KE})_2} = \frac{\lambda_2^2}{\lambda_1^2} = \left(\frac{5}{3}\right)^2 = \frac{25}{9} \text{ or } 25:9$$

Hence, the ratio of kinetic energy of electrons will be 25 : 9.

20 (*a*) According to Heisenberg's uncertainty principle,

$$\Delta x \times \Delta p \geq \frac{h}{4\pi}$$

Here, $\Delta x = \Delta p$ and $\Delta p = m \cdot \Delta v$

$$\therefore \quad \Delta v^2 = \frac{h}{m^2 4\pi}$$

or $$\Delta v = \frac{1}{2m}\sqrt{\frac{h}{\pi}}$$

21 (*a*) $\Delta x \times \Delta p \geq \frac{h}{4\pi}$

But $\Delta p = m\Delta v$, $\Delta v = \frac{\Delta p}{m}$

Where, Δp = uncertainty in momentum

Δv = uncertainty in velocity

Here, $\Delta p = 1 \times 10^{-18}$ g cm s^{-1}

and $m = 9 \times 10^{-28}$ g

$$\Delta v = \frac{1 \times 10^{-18}}{9 \times 10^{-28}} = 1.1 \times 10^9$$

$$\approx 1.0 \times 10^9 \text{ cms}^{-1}$$

22 (*a*) We know that,

$E = hc/\lambda$

or $\lambda = hc/E$

Therefore,

wavelength

$$\lambda = \frac{hc}{E} = \frac{6.62 \times 10^{-27} \text{ erg-s} \times 3.0 \times 10^{10} \text{cm s}^{-1}}{3 \times 10^{-12} \text{erg}}$$

$= 6.62 \times 10^{-5}$ cm

Now, 1 cm = 10^7 nm

Therefore, the wavelength in nm

$= 6.62 \times 10^{-5} \times 10^7$ nm

$= 6.62 \times 10^2$ nm = 662 nm

23 (*d*) Angular momentum of an electron orienting around the nucleus is,

$mvr = n \cdot h/2\pi$

By substituting the values 1, 2, 3,… etc. for *n*, we can have respectively the angular momentum $h/2\pi, 2h/2\pi, 3h/2\pi$ etc. There can be no fractional value of $h/2\pi$.

Thus, the angular momentum is said to be quantised.

Rest of the statements are correct.

24 (*c*) A. According to Bohr, among the infinite number of possible circular orbits, an electron can revolve only in those orbits whose angular momentum (*mvr*) is an integral multiple of the factor $h/2\pi$, i.e. $mvr = nh/2\pi$

Hence, this equation is called Bohr's equation.

B. In infrared region, Paschen series of lines is obtained.

C. $\lambda = \frac{h}{p}$ is known as de-Broglie equation. (where, $p = mv$)

D. Total energy of an electron = KE + PE

$$= \frac{e^2}{2r} + \left(-\frac{e^2}{r}\right) = -\frac{e^2}{2r}$$

E. Schrodinger equation = $\hat{H}\psi = E\psi$.

25 (*a*) According to de-Broglie,

$$\lambda = \frac{h}{p}$$

or $$p = \frac{h}{\lambda} = \frac{6.6 \times 10^{-34}}{2.2 \times 10^{-11}}$$

$= 3 \times 10^{-23}$ kg m s^{-1}

26 (*b*) $\because \lambda = \frac{h}{mv}$

$$\therefore \quad \lambda = \frac{6.6 \times 10^{-34}}{1 \times 100}$$

$= 6.6 \times 10^{-36}$ m

27 (*c*) Davisson and Germer diffracted the moving electron by using Ni metal crystal like X-rays.

28 (*a*) By Heisenberg's uncertainty principle

$$\Delta v \times \Delta x \geq \frac{h}{4\pi m}$$

$\therefore$

$$\Delta v = \frac{6.626 \times 10^{-34}}{4 \times 3.14 \times 9.11 \times 10^{-31} \times 0.1 \times 10^{-10}} \text{ ms}^{-1}$$

$= 5.79 \times 10^6$ ms^{-1}

29 (*a*) $\lambda = \frac{h}{\sqrt{2m(\text{KE})}}$

$$= \frac{6.626 \times 10^{-34}}{\sqrt{2 \times 1 \times 0.5}}$$

$$= \frac{6.626 \times 10^{-34}}{\sqrt{1 \times 1}}$$

$= 6.626 \times 10^{-34}$ m

30 (*e*) The kinetic energy of an electron is directly proportional to accelerating potential.

$$\because \quad \frac{1}{2}mv^2 = eV$$

$$\therefore \quad \text{KE} \propto V$$

(where, V = potential difference)

The other corrected statements are

(a) The kinetic energy of an electron is directly proportional to the square of its velocity.

(b) de-Broglie wavelength associated with a particle is inversely proportional to its mass.

(c) de-Broglie wavelength associated with a particle is inversely proportional to its velocity.

(d) The wavelength associated with an electron is inversely proportional to accelerating potential.

31 (*b*) Wave nature of electrons was first demonstrated by de-Broglie who gave the following equation for the wavelength of electrons.

$$\lambda = h/mv$$

32 (*a*) According to Heisenberg's uncertainty principle,

$$\Delta x \cdot \Delta p = \frac{h}{4\pi}$$

$$\Delta x \text{ (uncertainty in position)} = \frac{h}{4\pi \times \Delta p}$$

$$= \frac{6.63 \times 10^{-34}}{4 \times 3.14 \times (1 \times 10^{-5})}$$

$= 5.28 \times 10^{-30}$ m

33 (*c*) According to de-Broglie equation,

$$\lambda = \frac{h}{mv}$$

$$= \frac{6.62 \times 10^{-34}}{6.62 \times 10^{-29} \times 10^{-3} \times 10^3}$$

$= 10^{-5}$ m

34 (*c*) According to Heisenberg's uncertainty principle,

$$\Delta x \cdot \Delta p \geq \frac{h}{4\pi}$$

But Δp (momentum) = $m\Delta v$

or $$\Delta x \cdot m\Delta v \geq \frac{h}{4\pi}$$

or $$\Delta x = \frac{h}{4\pi m \Delta v}$$

Topic 4

Quantum Mechanical Model

(Atom, Atomic Orbitals, Quantum Numbers and Electronic Configuration)

2019

1 Orbital having 3 angular nodes and 3 total nodes is [NEET (Odisha)]

(a) $5p$ (b) $3d$ (c) $4f$ (d) $6d$

2018

2 Which one is a wrong statement? [NEET]

(a) The electronic configuration of N-atom is

$1s^2$ $2s^2$ $2p_x^1$ $2p_y^1$ $2p^1$

[⇅] [⇅] [↑|↑|↓]

(b) An orbital is designated by three quantum numbers while an electron in an atom is designated by four quantum numbers

(c) Total orbital angular momentum of electron in '*s*' orbital is equal to zero

(d) The value of m for d_{z^2} is zero

2017

3 Among the following set of quantum numbers, the impossible set is [JIPMER]

	n	l	m	s
(a)	3	2	-3	$-\frac{1}{2}$
(b)	4	0	0	$\frac{1}{2}$
(c)	5	3	0	$-\frac{1}{2}$
(d)	3	2	-2	$\frac{1}{2}$

4 The electrons identified by quantum numbers n and l, are as follows

I. $n = 4$, $l = 1$ II. $n = 4$, $l = 0$

III. $n = 3$, $l = 2$ IV. $n = 3$, $l = 1$

If we arrange them in order of increasing energy, i.e. from lowest to highest, the correct order is [JIPMER]

(a) IV < II < III < I

(b) II < IV < I < III

(c) I < III < II < IV

(d) III < I < IV < II

5 Which one is the wrong statement? [NEET]

(a) de-Broglie's wavelength is given by $\lambda = \frac{h}{mv}$, where, m = mass of the particle v = group velocity of the particle

(b) The uncertainty principle is $\Delta E \times \Delta t \geq h/4\pi$

(c) Half-filled and fully filled orbitals have greater stability due to greater exchange energy, greater symmetry and more balanced arrangement

(d) The energy of 2*s*-orbital is less than the energy of 2*p*-orbital in case of hydrogen like atoms

2016

6 How many electrons can fit in the orbital for which $n = 3$ and $l = 1$? [NEET Phase II]

(a) 2 (b) 6 (c) 10 (d) 14

7 Two electrons occupying the same orbital are distinguished by [NEET]

(a) magnetic quantum number

(b) azimuthal quantum number

(c) spin quantum number

(d) principal quantum number

2015

8 The number of *d*-electrons in Fe^{2+} ($Z = 26$) is not equal to the number of electrons in which one of the following?

(a) *s*-electrons in Mg ($Z = 12$) [CBSE AIPMT 2015]

(b) *p*-electrons in Cl ($Z = 17$)

(c) *d*-electrons in Fe ($Z = 26$)

(d) *p*-electrons in Ne ($Z = 10$)

9 The angular momentum of electrons in *d* orbital is equal to [CBSE AIPMT, 2015]

(a) $\sqrt{6}\,\hbar$ (b) $\sqrt{2}\,\hbar$

(c) $2\sqrt{3}\,\hbar$ (d) $0\hbar$

2014

10 What is the maximum number of orbitals that can be identified with the following quantum numbers?

$n = 3, l = 1$ and $m_l = 0$ [CBSE AIPMT]

(a) 1 (b) 2 (c) 3 (d) 4

11 Magnetic moment 2.83 BM is given by which one of the following ions? **[CBSE AIPMT]**
(Atomic number of Ti = 22, Cr = 24, Mn = 25, Ni = 28)
(a) Ti^{3+} (b) Ni^{2+}
(c) Cr^{3+} (d) Mn^{2+}

12 What is the orbital angular momentum of an electron in *f*-orbital? **[MHT CET]**
(a) $\frac{1.5h}{\pi}$ (b) $\frac{\sqrt{6h}}{\pi}$ (c) $\frac{\sqrt{3h}}{\pi}$ (d) $\frac{\sqrt{3h}}{\pi}$

13 The magnetic moment of Ni^{2+} ion (atomic number of Ni is 28) in BM unit is **[Kerala CEE]**
(a) 1.73 (b) 4.81 (c) 5.96 (d) 2.84
(e) 3.86

14 The maximum number of electrons which can be held by subshell with azimuthal quantum number l in an atom is given by **[Kerala CEE]**
(a) $(2l+1)$ (b) $(2l+2)$ (c) $2(2l+1)$ (d) $2(2l+2)$
(e) $2l$

15 The electronic configuration of Cu is **[WB JEE]**
(a) [Ne] $3s^2, 3p^6, 3d^9, 4s^2$
(b) [Ne] $3s^2\ 3p^6, 3d^{10}\ 4s^1$
(c) [Ne] $3s^2, 3p^6, 3d^3, 4s^2, 4p^6$
(d) [Ne] $3s^2, 3p^6, 3d^5, 4s^2, 4p^4$

16 Which of the following statements is incorrect? **[KCET]**
(a) Angular quantum number signifies the shape of the orbital
(b) Energies of stationary states in hydrogen like atoms is inversely proportional to the square of the principal quantum number
(c) Total number of nodes for 3*s*-orbital is three
(d) The radius of the first orbit of He^+ is half that of the first orbit of hydrogen atom

2013

17 What is the maximum number of electrons that can be associated with the following set of quantum numbers? $n=3, l=1$ and $m=-1$ **[NEET]**
(a) 10 (b) 6
(c) 4 (d) 2

18 The quantum number *m* of a free gaseous atom is associated with **[AIIMS]**
(a) the effective volume of the orbital
(b) the shape of the orbital
(c) the spatial orientation of the orbital
(d) the energy of the orbital in the absence of a magnetic field

19 Which one of the following element is represented by electronic configuration $1s^2, 2s^2\ 2p_x^1\ 2p_y^1\ 2p_z^1$?
(a) Nitrogen (b) Oxygen **[AIIMS]**
(c) Fluorine (d) Sulphur

20 The atomic number of an element is 17. The number of orbitals containing paired electron pairs in its valence shell is **[UP CPMT]**
(a) 3 (b) 4 (c) 6 (d) 8

21 The total number of electrons present in all the *p*-orbitals of bromine is **[UP CPMT]**
(a) 5 (b) 15 (c) 17 (d) 35

22 The value of azimuthal quantum number (l) is 2 then the value of principal quantum number (n) is **[Manipal]**
(a) 2 (b) 3 (c) 4 (d) 5

23 The number of unpaired electrons in Fe^{3+} ($Z=26$) are
(a) 5 (b) 6 (c) 3 (d) 4 **[KCET]**

2012

24 The orbital angular momentum of a *p*-electron is given as **[CBSE AIPMT]**
(a) $\frac{h}{\sqrt{2}\pi}$ (b) $\frac{\sqrt{3}h}{2\pi}$
(c) $\sqrt{\frac{2}{2}\frac{h}{\pi}}$ (d) $\frac{\sqrt{6}\,h}{2\pi}$

25 Maximum number of electrons in a subshell with $l=3$ and $n=4$ is **[CBSE AIPMT]**
(a) 14 (b) 16 (c) 10 (d) 12

26 The correct set of four quantum numbers for the valence electron of rubidium atom ($Z=37$) is **[CBSE AIPMT]**
(a) $5, 1, 1, +\frac{1}{2}$ (b) $6, 0, 0, +\frac{1}{2}$
(c) $5, 0, 0, +\frac{1}{2}$ (d) $5, 1, 0, +\frac{1}{2}$

27 Number of exchanges occuring in a *f*-subshell containing 6 unpaired electrons are **[AIIMS]**
(a) 6 (b) 9
(c) 12 (d) 15

28 Which one of the following statements in relation to the hydrogen atom is correct? **[Manipal]**
(a) 3*s*, 3*p* and 3*d*-orbitals all have the same energy
(b) 3*s* and 3*p*-orbitals are of lower energy than 3*d*-orbital
(c) 3*p*-orbital is lower in energy than 3*d*-orbital
(d) 3*s*-orbital is lower in energy than 3*p*-orbital

29 Which of the following laws will represent the pairing of electrons in a subshell after each orbital is filled with one electron? **[OJEE]**
(a) Pauli's exclusion principle
(b) Hund's rule
(c) Heisenberg's uncertainty principle
(d) Hess's law

30 Out of the following electronic arrangements for outer electronic configuration. [AMU]

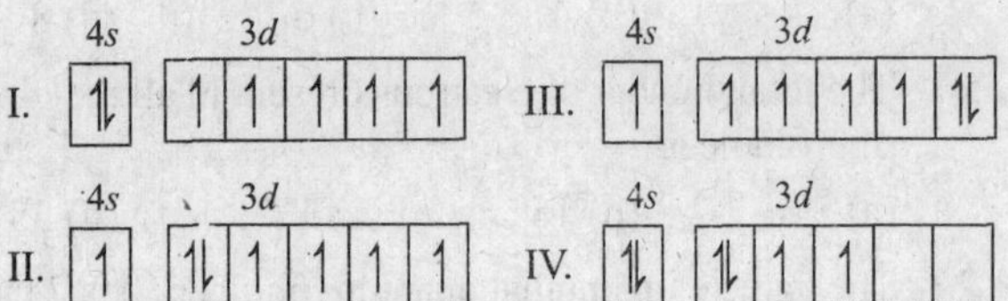

The most stable arrangement is

(a) I (b) II (c) III (d) IV

2011

31 The total number of atomic orbitals in fourth energy level of an atom is [CBSE AIPMT]

(a) 4 (b) 8 (c) 16 (d) 32

32 If $n = 6$, the correct sequence of filling of electrons will be [CBSE AIPMT]

(a) $ns \to np \to (n-1)d \to (n-2)f$

(b) $ns \to (n-2)f \to (n-1)d \to np$

(c) $ns \to (n-1)d \to (n-2)f \to np$

(d) $ns \to (n-2)f \to np \to (n-1)d$

33 Which one of the following sets of quantum numbers, represents the highest energy level in an atom? [KCET]

(a) $n = 4, l = 0, m = 0, s = +1/2$

(b) $n = 3, l = 1, m = 1, s = +1/2$

(c) $n = 3, l = 2, m = -2, s = +1/2$

(d) $n = 3, l = 0, m = 0, s = +1/2$

34 Which of the following is correct for number of electrons, number of orbitals and type of orbitals respectively in N-orbit? [Guj CET]

(a) 4, 4 and 8 (b) 4, 8 and 16

(c) 32, 16 and 4 (d) 4, 16 and 32

2010

35 For $n = 2$, the correct set of azimuthal and magnetic quantum numbers are [OJEE]

(a) $l = 2$; $m = -2, -1, 0, +1, +2$

(b) $l = 1$; $m = -2, -1, 0, +1, +2$

(c) $l = 0$; $m = -1, 0, +1$

(d) $l = 1$; $m = -1, 0, +1$

36 Which of the following orbitals will have zero probability of finding the electron in the *yz*-plane? [WB JEE]

(a) p_x (b) p_y

(c) p_z (b) d_{yz}

37 Magnetic quantum number specifies [WB JEE]

(a) size of orbitals

(b) shape of orbitals

(c) orientation of orbitals

(d) nuclear stability

38 The number of nodal planes that has 5*d*-orbital is [RPMT]

(a) zero (b) one (c) two (d) three

39 Pauli's exclusion principle states that [RPMT]

(a) the nucleus of an atom is negatively charged

(b) electrons revolve around the nucleus in circular orbits

(c) electrons enter into lowest energy orbitals

(d) no two electrons in an atom can have all the four quantum numbers identical

40 Principal, azimuthal and magnetic quantum numbers are respectively related to [RPMT]

(a) size, orientation and shape

(b) size, shape and orientation

(c) shape, size and orientation

(d) None of the above

41 Nitrogen has the electronic configuration $1s^2, 2s^2\ 2p_x^1\ 2p_y^1\ 2p_z^1$ and not $1s^2 2s^2\ 2p_x^2\ 2p_y^1\ 2p_z^0$ which is determined by [Haryana PMT]

(a) Pauli's exclusion principle

(b) Aufbau principle

(c) Hund's rule

(d) uncertainty principle

42 Which of the following sets of quantum numbers represents the 19th electron in chromium? ($Z = 24$ for Cr) [AMU]

(a) 4, 0, 0, 1/2 (b) 4, 1, –1, 1/2

(c) 3, 2, 2, 1/2 (d) 3, 2, –2, 1/2

2009

43 Which of the following is not permissible arrangement of electrons in an atom? [CBSE AIPMT]

(a) $n = 3, l = 2, m = -3, s = -1/2$

(b) $n = 5, l = 3, m = 0, s = +1/2$

(c) $n = 4, l = 0, m = 0, s = -1/2$

(d) $n = 3, l = 2, m = -2, s = -1/2$

44 Which of the following orbital diagram violates Pauli's exclusion principle? [AFMC]

(a) 2s ⇅ 2p ⇅ ↑ (b) 2s ⇈ 2p ↑ ↑ ↑

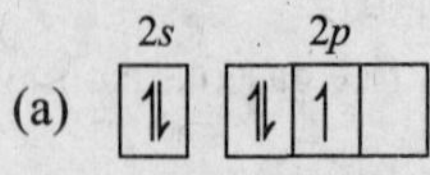

(c) 2s ⇅ 2p ↑ ↓ ↑ (d) 2s ↑ 2p ↑ ↑ ↑

45 The number of unpaired electrons in ferrous ion is [AFMC]

(a) 3 (b) 2 (c) 4 (d) 5

46 For *f*-orbital, the values of *m* are [Manipal]

(a) –2, –1, 0, +1, +2 (b) –3, –2, –1, 0, +1, +2, +3

(c) –1, 0, +1 (d) 0, +1, +2, +3

47 The number of nodal planes in p_x orbital is **[CG PMT, Haryana PMT]**

(a) 1 (b) 2 (c) 3 (d) 0

48 The number of radial nodes of $3s$ and $2p$-orbitals are **[CG PMT, Haryana PMT]**

(a) 2, 0 (b) 0, 2 (c) 1, 2 (d) 2, 1

49 The set of quantum numbers $n = 4, l = 0, m = 0$ and $s = +\frac{1}{2}$ corresponds to the most loosely bound, ground state electron of which one of the following atoms?

(a) Na (b) Cl (c) Cr (d) Rb **[J&K CET]**

50 Arrange in decreasing order, the energy of $2s$-orbitals in the following atoms H, Li, Na, K **[AMU]**

(a) $E_{2s(H)} > E_{2s(Li)} > E_{2s(Na)} > E_{2s(K)}$
(b) $E_{2s(H)} > E_{2s(Na)} > E_{2s(Li)} > E_{2s(K)}$
(c) $E_{2s(H)} > E_{2s(Na)} = E_{2s(K)} > E_{2s(Li)}$
(d) $E_{2s(K)} < E_{2s(Na)} < E_{2s(Li)} < E_{2s(H)}$

51 Probability of finding an electron at the nodal surface is **[AMU]**

(a) unity (b) low
(c) high (d) zero

52 The correct set of quantum numbers for the unpaired electron of a chlorine atom is **[DUMET]**

(a) 2, 0, 0, +1/2 (b) 2, 1, –1, +1/2
(c) 3, 1, –1, ±1/2 (d) 3, 0, 0, ±1/2

2008

53 The shape of the orbital with the value of $l = 2$ and $m = 0$ is **[AFMC]**

(a) spherical
(b) double dumbbell
(c) trigonal planar
(d) square planar

54 Which of the following is not possible for $4p$ or $3d$ electrons? **[BHU]**

(a) $n = 3, l = 2, m = +1, s = +1/2$
(b) $n = 4, l = 1, m = 0, s = +1/2$
(c) $n = 3, l = 3, m = +3, s = +1/2$
(d) $n = 4, l = 1, m = -1, s = +1/2$

55 The ground state electronic configuration of nitrogen is represented by **[BHU]**

(a) [⇅] [⇅] [↑|↑|↑] (b) [⇅] [⇅] [↑|↓|↑]

(c) [⇅] [⇅] [⇅|↓|] (d) [⇅] [⇅] [⇅|↑|]

56 The correct order of increasing energy of atomic orbitals is **[BHU]**

(a) $5p < 4f < 6s < 5d$ (b) $5p < 6s < 4f < 5d$
(c) $4f < 5p < 5d < 6s$ (d) $5p < 5d < 4f < 6s$

57 Electron density in yz-plane of $3d_{x^2-y^2}$ orbital is **[J&K CET]**

(a) zero (b) 0.50
(c) 0.75 (d) 0.90

58 When the azimuthal quantum number has the value of 2, the number of orbitals possible are **[KCET]**

(a) 7 (b) 5
(c) 3 (d) 0

59 The presence of unpaired electron in phosphorus atom is explained by which principle? **[Guj CET]**

(a) Aufbau principle
(b) Pauli's exclusion principle
(c) Hund's rule
(d) Heisenberg's principle

60 Which is not in accordance to Aufbau principle? **[BCECE]**

(a) 2s [⇅] 2p [⇅|↑|↑] (b) 2s [⇅] 2p [⇅|⇅|↑]

(c) 2s [↑] 2p [⇅|↑|↑] (d) 2s [⇅] 2p [↑|↑|↑]

2007

61 Consider the following sets of quantum numbers

	n	l	m	s		n	l	m	s
I.	3	0	0	+1/2	II.	2	2	1	+1/2
III.	4	3	–2	–1/2	IV.	1	0	–1	–1/2
V.	3	2	3	+1/2					

Which of the following sets of quantum number is not possible? **[CBSE AIPMT]**

(a) II, III and IV
(b) I, II, III and IV
(c) II, IV and V
(d) I and III

62 Which of the following electronic configuration is not possible? **[BHU]**

(a) $1s^2, 2s^2$
(b) $3d^{10}, 4s^2, 4p^2$
(c) $1s^2, 2s^2, 2p^6$
(d) $1s^2, 2s^2, 2p^2, 3s^1$

63 What is the electronic configuration of Mn^{2+}? **[UP CPMT]**

(a) [Ne] $3d^5 4s^0$ (b) [Ar] $3d^5 4s^2$
(c) [Ar] $3d^5 4s^0$ (d) [Ne] $3d^5 4s^2$

64 What is the maximum number of electrons in an atom that can have the following quantum numbers $n = 4, m_l = +1$? **[Kerala CEE]**

(a) 4 (b) 15
(c) 3 (d) 1 (e) 6

65 The number of electrons accommodated in an orbital with principal quantum number 2 is [J&K CET]

(a) 2 (b) 6 (c) 10 (d) 8

66 The total number of orbitals upto $n = 4$, are [DUMET]

(a) 2 (b) 16
(c) 32 (d) 30

67 $\psi^2 = 0$ represents [DUMET]

(a) node
(b) orbital
(c) angular wave function
(d) wave function

2006

68 Which of the following statement is correct? [DUMET]

(a) Greater the number of unpaired electrons, more is the paramagnetic character
(b) Greater the number of unpaired electrons, less is paramagnetic character
(c) Elements are mostly diamagnetic and compounds are paramagnetic
(d) Elements are mostly paramagnetic and compounds are diamagnetic

69. The atomic number of Ni and Cu are 28 and 29 respectively. The electronic configuration $1s^2, 2s^2, 2p^6, 3s^2, 3p^6 3d^{10}$ represents [KCET]

(a) Cu^+ (b) Cu^{2+}
(c) Ni^{2+} (d) Ni

70 Non-directional orbital is [BCECE]

(a) $4p$ (b) $4d$ (c) $4f$ (d) $3s$

2005

71 If highest magnetic quantum number of a given atom is represented by –3, what will be its principal quantum number? [BHU]

(a) 2 (b) 3 (c) 4 (d) 5

72 If $n = 3, l = 0$ and $m = 0$, then atomic number is [Punjab PMET]

(a) 12 or 13 (b) 13 or 14
(c) 10 or 11 (d) 11 or 12

73 Which of the following sequence is correct as per Aufbau principle? [DUMET]

(a) $3s < 3d < 4s < 4p$ (b) $1s < 2p < 4s < 3d$
(c) $2s < 5s < 4p < 5d$ (d) $2s < 2p < 3d < 3p$

Answers

1 (c)	2 (a)	3 (a)	4 (a)	5 (d)	6 (a)	7 (c)	8 (b)	9 (a)	10 (a)
11 (b)	12 (d)	13 (d)	14 (c)	15 (b)	16 (c)	17 (d)	18 (c)	19 (a)	20 (a)
21 (c)	22 (b)	23 (a)	24 (a)	25 (a)	26 (c)	27 (d)	28 (a)	29 (b)	30 (a)
31 (c)	32 (b)	33 (c)	34 (c)	35 (d)	36 (a)	37 (c)	38 (c)	39 (d)	40 (b)
41 (c)	42 (a)	43 (a)	44 (b)	45 (c)	46 (b)	47 (a)	48 (a)	49 (c)	50 (a)
51 (d)	52 (c)	53 (b)	54 (c)	55 (a)	56 (b)	57 (a)	58 (b)	59 (c)	60 (c)
61 (c)	62 (d)	63 (c)	64 (e)	65 (a)	66 (d)	67 (a)	68 (a)	69 (a)	70 (d)
71 (c)	72 (d)	73 (b)							

Explanations

1. (c) Angular node $(l) = 3$

Total node = radial node + angular node

$$3 = (n - l - 1) + l = n - 1 \Rightarrow n = 4$$

$\therefore$ Orbital having 3 angular nodes and 3 total nodes is $= nl = 4f$
[$\because l = 3$ for f- orbital]

2 (a) According to Hund's rule "the pairing of electrons in the orbitals of a particular subshell does not take place until, all the orbitals of a sub-shell are singly occupied. Moreover, the single orbitals must have the electrons with parallel spin. i.e.

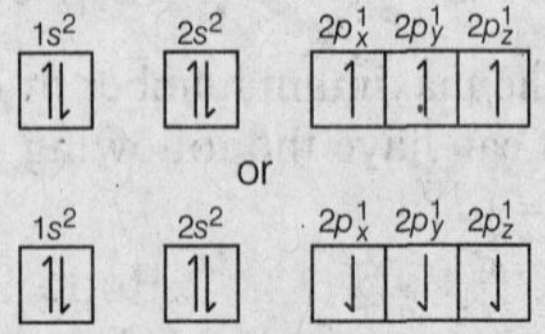

$\therefore$ Option (a) is the incorrect option.

3 (a) For each value of n, $l = 0$ to $n - 1$ (max) and for each value of l, $m = -l$ to $+l$.

Thus, for

(a) $n = 3; l = 0,1,2; m = -2, -1, 0, 1, 2$ and $m \neq -3; s = -\frac{1}{2}$ or $+\frac{1}{2}$

(b) $n = 4; l = 0,1,2,3; m = -3, -2, -1, 0, 1, 2, 3; s = \pm\frac{1}{2}$

(c) $n = 5; l = 0,1,2,3,4; m = -4, -3, -2, -1, 0, 1, 2, 3, 4; s = \pm\frac{1}{2}$

(d) $n = 3; l = 0,1,2; m = -2, -1, 0, 1, 2; s = \pm\frac{1}{2}$

Thus, option (a) contains impossible set.

4 (a) Greater the value of $n + l$, more will be the energy of electron. If the two electrons have same value for $(n + l)$, then one with lower value of n should be filled first because it possesses lower energy.

I. $n = 4, l = 1 \quad \therefore \quad n + l = 4 + 1 = 5$
II. $n = 4, l = 0 \quad \therefore \quad n + l = 4 + 0 = 4$
III. $n = 3, l = 2 \quad \therefore \quad n + l = 3 + 2 = 5$
IV. $n = 3, l = 1 \quad \therefore \quad n + l = 3 + 1 = 4$

$\therefore$ The correct order of energy is IV < II < III < I.

5 (*d*) (a) According to de-Broglie's equation,

$$\text{wavelength } (\lambda) = \frac{h}{mv}$$

where, h = Planck's constant.

Thus, statement (a) is correct.

(b) According to Heisenberg's uncertainty principle, the uncertainties of position (Δx) and momentum ($\Delta p = m\Delta v$) are related as,

$$\Delta x \cdot \Delta p \geq \frac{h}{4\pi} \text{ or, } \Delta x \cdot m\Delta v \geq \frac{h}{4\pi}$$

$$\Delta x \cdot m \cdot \Delta a \cdot \Delta t \geq \frac{h}{4\pi}$$

$$\left[\frac{\Delta v}{\Delta t} = \Delta a, a = \text{acceleration}\right]$$

$$\text{or } \Delta x \cdot F \cdot \Delta t \geq \frac{h}{4\pi} \quad [\because F = m \cdot \Delta a]$$

$$\text{or} \quad \Delta E \cdot \Delta t \geq \frac{h}{4\pi}$$

$$[\because \Delta E = F \cdot \Delta x, E = \text{energy}]$$

Thus, statement (b) is correct.

(c) The half and fully-filled orbitals have greater stability due to greater exchange energy, greater symmetry and more balanced arrangement. Thus, statement (c) is correct.

(d) For a single electronic species like H, energy depends on value of n and does not depend on l. Hence, energy of 2s-orbital and 2p-orbital is equal in case of hydrogen like species. Therefore, statement (d) is incorrect.

6 (*a*) According to Hund's rule of maximum multiplicity, an orbital can accommodate a maximum number of 2 electrons of exactly opposite spin. Hence, option (a) is correct.

Caution Remember maximum number of electrons in an orbital do not depend upon the quantum numbers as given in the question.

7 (*c*) Two electrons occupying the same orbital have equal spin but the directions of their spin are opposite. Hence, spin quantum number, s (represented +1/2 and – 1/2) distinguishes them.

8 (*b*) Electronic configuration of Fe^{2+} is $[Ar]3d^6 4s^0$.

$\therefore$ Number of d-electrons = 6

Mg – $1s^2 2s^2 2p^6 3s^2$

(*s*-electrons are 6)

It matches with the d-electrons in Fe^{2+}

Cl – $1s^2 2s^2 2p^6 3s^2 3p^5$

(*p*-electrons are 11)

It does not match with the d-electrons in Fe^{2+}

Fe – $[Ar]\,3d^6 4s^2$ (d-electrons are 6)

It matches with the d-electrons in Fe^{2+}

Ne – $1s^2 2s^2 2p^6$ (p-electrons are 6)

It matches with the d-electrons in Fe^{2+}.

Hence, Cl has 11 electrons in p-subshell which does not match with number of d-electrons in Fe^{2+}.

9 (*a*) Angular momentum of electrons in d-orbital is

$$= \sqrt{l(l+1)}\frac{h}{2\pi};$$

for d-orbital, $l = 2$

$$= \sqrt{2(2+1)}\,\hbar \qquad \left(\because \hbar = \frac{h}{2\pi}\right)$$

Angular momentum = $\sqrt{6}\,\hbar$

10 (*a*) The given value of $n = 3$ suggests that the shell is 3.

For $l = 1$, n has 3 values i.e. +1,0 and –1, hence, there occur 3 orbitals in p-subshell namely p_x, p_y and p_z along the x-axis, y-axis and z-axis respectively. Thus, the given values for $n = 3$, $l = 1$ and $m_l = 0$, suggests that the orbital is $3p_y$.

Hence, the maximum number of orbitals that can be represented by the given quantum numbers is only 1.

11 (*b*) Magnetic moment is given by,

$$\mu = \sqrt{n(n+2)}$$

Here, n = number of unpaired electrons

$$2.83 = \sqrt{n(n+2)}$$

or $(2.83)^2 = n(n+2)$

$\Rightarrow \quad 8.00 = n^2 + 2n$

$n^2 + 2n - 8 = 0$

$n^2 + 4n - 2n - 8 = 0$

$\Rightarrow \quad (n+4)(n-2) = 0$

$\therefore \quad n = 2 \quad (\because n \neq -4)$

Among the given ions

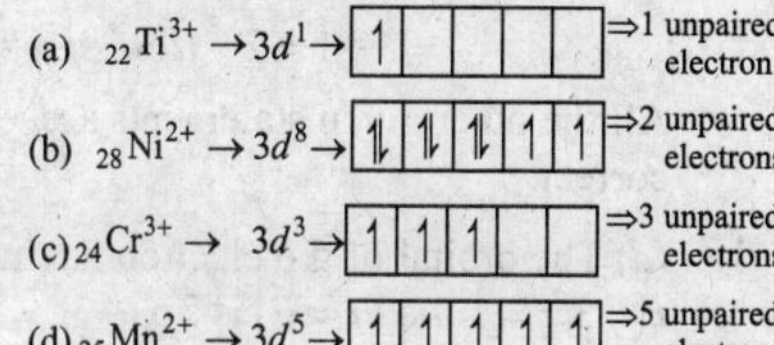

From the above configuration only Ni^{2+} ion contains 2 unpaired electrons. Hence, Ni^{2+} possesses a magnetic moment of 2.83 BM.

12 (*d*) Orbital angular momentum

$$= \frac{h}{2\pi}\sqrt{l(l+1)}$$

For f-orbital, $l = 3$ and for
s-orbital $l = 0$
p-orbital $l = 1$
d-orbital $l = 2$

$\therefore$ Orbital angular momentum

$$= \frac{h}{2\pi}\sqrt{3(3+1)} = \frac{\sqrt{3}h}{\pi}$$

13 (*d*) Electronic configuration of Ni_{28} is $[Ar]3d^8\,4s^2$.

Thus, outer orbital diagram for Ni^{2+} is

$3d^8$

⇅	⇅	⇅	↑	↑

Thus, Ni^{2+} has 2 unpaired electrons.

Magnetic moment, $\mu = \sqrt{n(n+2)}$

where, n = number of unpaired electrons.

$$\mu = \sqrt{2 \times 4} = 2.84 \text{ BM}$$

14 (*c*) The maximum number of electrons which can be held by sub-shell with azimuthal quantum number l in an atom is given by

$$= 2(2l+1)$$

15 (*b*) Atomic number of Cu is 29.

Thus , its electronic configuration can be written as,

$Cu_{29} = 1s^2, 2s^2\,2p^6, 3s^2\,3p^6, 3d^{10}\,4s^1$

(Since, fully-filled orbitals are more stable, so one electron from 4s orbital transfers into 3d-orbital.)

The electronic configuration of neon is

$Ne_{10} = 1s^2, 2s^2, 2p^6$

Thus, using inert gas, the configuration of Cu can also be represented as,

$Cu_{29} = [Ne]\,3s^2, 3p^6, 3d^{10}, 4s^1$

16 (*c*) $\because$ Total number of nodes $= n-1$

$\therefore$ For 3*s*-orbital, total nodes

$= 3-1 = 2$ (for 3*s*, $n = 3$)

All the other given statements are correct.

17 (*d*) The orbital of the electron having $n = 3$, $l = 1$ and $m = -1$ is $3p_x$ and an orbital can have a maximum of **two** electrons with opposite spins.

$m = -1\ (3p_x), 0\ (3p_y)$ and $+1\ (3p_z)$

Therefore, $3p_x$ orbital contains only two electrons or only 2 electrons are associated with $n = 3$, $l = 1$, $m = -1$.

18 (c) Magnetic quantum number, *m* is associated with spatial orientation of the orbital. Principal quantum number (n) determines energy of the electron and size (volume) of the atom. Azimuthal quantum number (l) determines shape of the orbital.

19 (*a*) Atomic number of element having electronic configuration

$1s^2, 2s^2 2p_x^1\ 2p_y^1\ 2p_z^1$ is 7 and nitrogen has atomic number 7.

It corresponds to N.

Oxygen (8) $= 1s^2, 2s^2\ 2p_x^2\ p_y^1\ p_z^1$

Fluorine (9) $= 1s^2, 2s^2\ 2p_x^2\ p_y^2\ p_z^1$

Sulphur (16) $= 1s^2, 2s^2\ 2p^6, 3s^2\ 3p_x^2 p_y^1 p_z^1$

20 (*a*) The electronic configuration of element with atomic number,

$17 = 1s^2, 2s^2\ 2p^6, 3s^2\ 3p^5$

Valence shell has $3s^2$ and $3p^5$-orbitals

3s	3p		
⥮	⥮	⥮	1

$\therefore$ Valence shell has 3 paired electrons.

21 (*c*) Write the electronic configuration of bromine, according to atomic orbital theory to find the total number of *p*-electrons in bromine.

$\therefore\ 1s^2, 2s^2\ 2p^6, 3s^2\ 3p^6\ 3d^{10}, 4s^2\ 4p^5$

$\therefore$ Total number of *p*-electrons in bromine is 17.

22 (*b*) The value of azimuthal quantum number is given by

$l = n-1, n = l+1$

Here, $l = 2$, thus, $n = 2+1 = 3$

Hence, the value of principal quantum number (n) is 3.

23 (*a*) The electronic configuration of

${}_{26}Fe = 1s^2, 2s^2\ 2p^6, 3s^2\ 3p^6\ 3d^6, 4s^2$

$Fe^{3+} = 1s^2, 2s^2\ 2p^6, 3s^2\ 3p^6\ 3d^5$

i.e. $3d^5$

1	1	1	1	1

Therefore, number of unpaired electrons = 5

24 (*a*) Orbital angular momentum

$= \sqrt{l(l+1)} \times \frac{h}{2\pi}$

Since, for *p*-electron, $l = 1$

$\therefore$ Orbital angular momentum

$= \sqrt{1(1+1)} \times \frac{h}{2\pi} = \frac{\sqrt{2}h}{2\pi} = \frac{h}{\sqrt{2}\pi}$

25 (*a*) *n* represents the main energy level and *l* represents the sub-shell.

If $n = 4$ and $l = 3$, the sub-shell is 4*f*.

In *f*-subshell, there are 7 orbitals and each orbital can accommodate a maximum of two electrons. So, maximum number of electrons in 4*f*-subshell $= 7 \times 2 = 14$.

26 (*c*) ${}_{37}Rb = {}_{36}[Kr]5s^1$. Its valence electronic configuration is $5s^1$.

So, quantum numbers for $5s^1$ electron are $n = 5$

$l = 0$ (for, *s*-orbital)

$m = 0$ (As, $m = -l$ to $+l$)

$s = +1/2$

27 (*d*) In order to attain stability, the electrons with same spin present in the degenerate orbitals tend to exchange their positions. The number of exchanges that can take place is maximum when the sub-shell is either half-filled or completely filled. The possible exchange for a f^6 configuration are

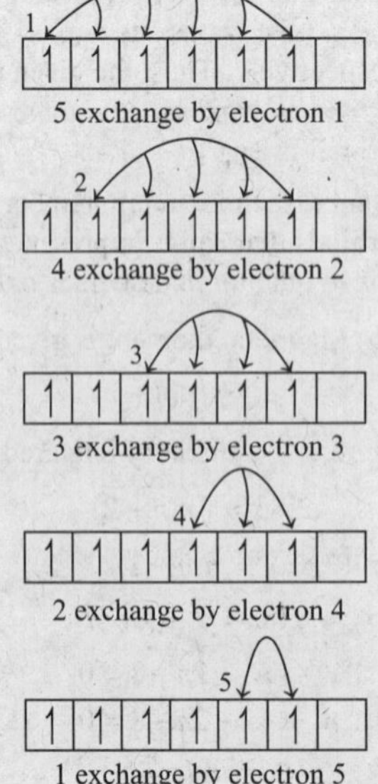

Thus, total number of exchanges for a f^6 configuration

$= 5+4+3+2+1 = 15$

28 (*a*) The hydrogen atom has the configuration $1s^1$ and 3*s*, 3*p* and 3*d*-orbitals will have same energy with respect to 1*s*-orbital.

29 (*b*) Hund's rule represents the pairing of electrons in a subshell after each orbital is filled with one electron. Thus, this rule states that 'during filling of electrons in a sub-shell, pairing of electrons cannot take place until there is no empty orbital available.' This rule is also called Hund's rule of maximum multiplicity.

30 (*a*) Most stable arrangement is

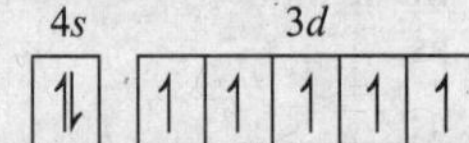

Because,

(i) According to Aufbau principle, electrons enter in the subshell of an atom in the increasing order of energy.

(ii) According to Hund's rule of maximum multiplicity, pairing of electrons in the orbitals of a sub-shell does not take place until all orbitals of a sub-shell are singly occupied.

31 (*c*) Total number of atomic orbitals in a shell $= n^2$

Given, $n = 4$, so atomic orbitals in 4th shell = 16

32 (*b*) The filling of electrons in different orbitals takes place in accordance with Aufbau principle. According to this principle, the electrons first occupy the lowest energy orbital and then enter into higher energy orbitals provided that lower energy orbitals are completely filled. For $n = 6$, the order in which the orbitals are filled is $6s, 4f, 5d, 6p$. The above order can be represented as

$ns \rightarrow (n-2)f \rightarrow (n-1)d \rightarrow np$

33 (*c*) The order of energy of orbitals can be calculated from $(n + l)$ rule.

The lower the value of $(n + l)$ for an orbital, lower in its energy.

If two orbitals have same $(n + l)$ value, the orbital with lower value of *n*, has the lower energy.

(a) $(n + l) = 4$ (b) $(n + l) = 4$

(c) $(n + l) = 5$ (d) $(n + l) = 3$

Thus, set given in option (c) represents the highest energy level.

34 (*c*) For *N* shell, types of orbitals

$$-4s, 4p, 4d, 4f$$

Number of orbitals $= 1 + 3 + 5 + 7 = 16$

Number of electrons $= 32$

35 (*d*) For $n = 2, l$ can be 0 and 1.

For $l = 0, m = 0$

and $l = 1, m = -1, 0, +1.$

36 (*a*) The electron density of p_x orbital lies along *x*-axis only.

Thus, the probability of finding an electron is maximum only in *x*-axis.

37 (*c*) Principal and azimuthal quantum numbers specify the size and shape of orbitals respectively. Magnetic quantum number specifies the orientation of orbitals while nuclear stability is explained by n/p ratio.

38 (*c*) Number of nodal planes in orbital $= l$

$\because$ 5*d* orbital has $l = 2$

So, number of nodal planes in 5*d* orbital $= 2$

39 (*d*) Pauli's exclusion principle states that "no two electrons in an atom can have the same set of four quantum numbers."

40 (*b*) Principal, azimuthal and magnetic quantum numbers are respectively related to size, shape and orientation of the shell, subshell and orbitals.

41 (*c*) According to Hund's rule, electron pairing in *p, d* and *f*-orbitals cannot occur until each orbital of a given subshell is singly occupied.'

Hence, $1s^2, 2s^2\ 2p_x^3\ 2p_y^1\ 2p_z^0$ electronic configuration is not possible for nitrogen.

42 (*a*) The atomic number of Cr is 24. Its electronic configuration can be written as : $1s^2 2s^2 2p^6 3s^2 3p^6 4s^1 3d^5$

(According to Aufbau's principle, 4*s* will be filled first and then 3*d* will be filled).

$\because$ The 19th electron enters in 4*s* subshell.

For $4s^1$, $n = 4, l = 0$

(for *s*-orbital, $l = 0$)

$m = 0$ $(\because m = -l \text{ to } +l)$

$$s = +\frac{1}{2}$$

43 (*a*) The value of *m* lies from $-l$ to $+l$ while value of *l* lies from 0 to $(n-1)$.

Thus, for $n = 3$, *l* and *m* values are,

Value of *l*	0	1	2
m	0	$-1, 0$	$-2, -1, 0, 1, 2$

Thus, $n = 3, l = 2, m = -2, s = -1/2$ is permissible but $n = 3, l = 2, m = -3, s = -1/2$ is not permissible

44 (*b*) According to Pauli's exclusion principle, within an orbital, the electrons must have opposite spin.

Therefore,

2*s* 2*p*

[↑↑] [↿ | ↿ | ↿] violates this principle.

45 (*c*) Suffix 'ous' with the name of iron shows that it is in +2 oxidation state.

$Fe^{2+} = [Ar]\,3d^6, 4s^0$. Its orbital diagram can be represented as,

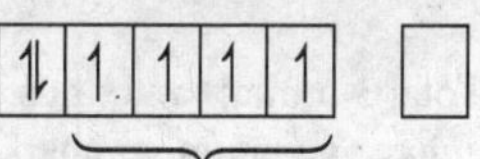

Four unpaired electrons

46 (*b*) For *f*-orbital, $l = 3$, thus *m* lies from -3 to $+3$.

Hence, $m = -3, -2, -1, 0, +1, +2, +3$

47 (*a*) Number of nodal planes $= l$

For p_x orbital, $l = 1$

$\therefore$ Number of nodal planes $= 1$

48 (*a*) Number of radial nodes,

$$x = n - l - 1$$

In 3*s*-orbital, $x = 3 - 0 - 1 = 2$

In 2*p*-orbital, $x = 2 - 1 - 1 = 0$

49 (*c*) (a) $_{11}Na \longrightarrow 1s^2, 2s^2\ 2p^6, 3s^1$

(b) $_{17}Cl \longrightarrow 1s^2, 2s^2\ 2p^6, 3s^2\ 3p^5$

(c) $_{24}Cr \longrightarrow 1s^2, 2s^2 2p^6, 3s^2 3p^6 3d^5, 4s^1$

(d) $_{37}Rb \longrightarrow 1s^2, 2s^2 2p^6, 3s^2 3p^6 3d^{10}, 4s^2\ 4p^6, 5s^1$

For $_{11}Na$ and $_{17}Cl$, there is no shell filled corresponding to $n = 4$, so not possible for $_{11}Na$ and $_{17}Cl$. In Cr, electrons are present corresponding to $n = 4$ shell and are loosely bound but in Rb, the electrons are present corresponding to $n = 5$ shell.

So, the all conditions are full-filled by Cr only.

50 (*a*) Energy of the similar orbitals of different atoms decreases with increase in nuclear charge. Nuclear charge increases with number of nucleons present in nucleus. So, order of nuclear charge decreases as K > Na > Li > H. Thus energy in decreasing order given as $E_{2s\,(H)} > E_{2s\,(Li)} > E_{2s\,(Na)} > E_{2s\,(K)}$.

51 (*d*) The region at which the probability of finding an electron is zero is called **node** or **nodal plane** or **nodal surface**. Thus, within the orbital (where probability of finding an electron is maximum) there is a space called node surrounding the nucleus where probability of finding electron is zero.

52 (*c*) Electronic configuration of Cl-atom $= 1s^2, 2s^2\ 2p^6, 3s^2\ 3p^5$

Unpaired electron is present in 3*p*-orbital that can be shown as,

$3p^5$

Cl = [⇅ | ⇅ | ↿]

Thus, for 3*p*, $n = 3$,

$l = 1, m = -1,$

$$s = \pm\frac{1}{2}$$

53 (*b*) For *s, p, d* and *f*-orbitals, the values of *l* are respectively, 0, 1, 2 and 3. Thus, if $l = 2$, then the orbital is *d*, which is double dumb-bell shaped.

54 (*c*) For 4*p*-orbital, $n = 4$ and $l = 1$ and for 3*d*-orbital, $n = 3$ and $l = 2$

So, option (c) does not show 4*p* and 3*d*-orbital, it indicates '3 *f* orbital which is not possible.

55 (*a*) $N_7 \longrightarrow 1s^2, 2s^2\ 2p^3$. Its orbital diagram can be shown as according to Hund's rule.

1*s* 2*s* 2*p*

[⇅] [⇅] [↿ | ↿ | ↿]

Electron pairing in *p, d* and *f*-orbitals cannot occur until each orbital is singly occupied.

56 (*b*) According to Aufbau principle, the order in which the energies of the orbitals increases is as follows:

1*s*, 2*s*, 2*p*, 3*s*, 3*p*, 4*s*, 3*d*, 4*p*, 5*s*, 4*d*, 5*p*, 6*s*, 4*f*, 5*d*, 6*p*, 7*s*, 5*f*, 6*d*, 7*p*, 8*s*

Hence, the correct order of increasing energy of orbital is

$5p > 6s > 4f > 5d$.

57 (*a*) Electron density in *yz*-plane of $3d_{x^2-y^2}$ orbital is zero, as this orbital lies in the *xy*-plane.

58 (*b*) Given, azimuthal quantum number $(l) = 2$
Number of orbitals
$= (2l + 1) = (2 \times 2 + 1)$
$= 4 + 1 = 5$

59 (*c*) The presence of unpaired electrons in phosphorus atom is explained by Hund's rule, which states that electron pairing in *p, d* and *f*-orbitals cannot occur until each orbital of a given sub-shell contains one electron or is singly occupied.

$_{15}P : 1s^2, 2s^2, 2p^6, 3s^2, 3p_x^1, 3p_y^1, 3p_z^1$

60 (*c*) Aufbau principle states that in the ground state of an atom, the orbital with lower energy is filled up first before the filling of orbitals with the higher energy.

Increasing order of energy of various orbitals is $1s, 2s, 2p, 3s, 3p, 4s, 3d, 4p, 5s, \ldots$ etc.

Therefore,

2s	2p		
1	1l	1	1

is not in accordance to Aufbau principle as without fully-filling of *s*-subshell, electrons cannot enter in *p*-subshell in ground state of an atom.

61 (*c*) The value of *l* varies from 0 to $(n-1)$ and the value of *m* varies from $-l$ to $+l$ through zero.

The value of *s* is $\pm \frac{1}{2}$ which signifies the spin of electron.

Hence, the sets of quantum number II, IV and V are not possible.

Thus, correct sets of these quantum numbers are as follows :

	n	l	m	s
II.	2	1	1	+ 1/2
IV.	1	0	0	− 1/2
V.	3	2	2	+ 1/2

62 (*d*) $1s^2, 2s^2, 2p^2, 3s^1$ configuration is not possible because electron cannot go in 3*s*-orbital without filling 2*p*-subshell.

63 (*c*) Electronic configuration of Mn (25) is

$1s^2, 2s^2, 2p^6, 3s^2, 3p^6, 3d^5, 4s^2$.

$\therefore$ Electronic configuration of Mn^{2+} is

$1s^2, 2s^2, 2p^6, 3s^2, 3p^6, 3d^5$

or $Mn^{2+} = [Ar]\, 3d^5\, 4s^0$

64 (*e*) For $n = 4$, 4 subshells (*s, p, d* and *f*) are possible.

m_l for *s*-subshell $= 0$
(i.e. number of orbitals = 1)

m_l for *p*-subshell $= -1, 0, +1$
(orbitals = 3)

m_l for *d*-subshell $= -2, -1, 0, +1, +2$
(orbitals = 5)

m_l for *f*-subshell
$= -3, -2, -1, 0, +1, +2, +3$
(orbitals = 7)

$\therefore$ Total 3 orbitals and, thus 6 electrons can have quantum numbers $n = 4$, $m_l = +1$.

65 (*a*) Whatever, the principal quantum number is the number of electrons accommodated in an orbital is always 2.

66 (*d*) Number of orbitals for principal quantum number $n = n^2$

$\therefore$ For $n = 1$, number of orbitals $= 1^2 = 1$
$n = 2$, number of orbitals $= 2^2 = 4$
$n = 3$, number of orbitals $= 3^2 = 9$
$n = 4$, number of orbitals $= 4^2 = 16$

Therefore, total number of orbitals up to $(n = 4)$ are $1 + 4 + 9 + 16 = 30$.

67 (*a*) $\psi^2 = 0$, means probability of finding an electron in the orbital is zero i.e. it represents a node.

68 (*a*) Substance which has unpaired electrons are paramagnetic. So, greater the number of unpaired electrons, more is the paramagnetic character.

Magnetic properties as paramagnetic and diamagnetic are not concerned with elements and compounds, both can have magnetic properties as well.

69 (*a*) Electronic configuration of given species are as shown below.

(i) $_{28}Ni = 1s^2, 2s^2, 2p^6, 3s^2, 3p^6, 3d^8, 4s^2$
$Ni^{2+} = 1s^2, 2s^2, 2p^6, 3s^2, 3p^6, 3d^8, 4s^0$

(ii) $_{29}Cu = 1s^2, 2s^2, 2p^6, 3s^2, 3p^6, 3d^{10}, 4s^1$
$Cu^+ = 1s^2, 2s^2 2p^6, 3s^2 3p^6 3d^{10}, 4s^0$

So, the given configuration is of Cu^+.

Note Half-filled and fully-filled orbitals are more stable.

70 (*d*) *s*-subshell has only one orbital and that is spherical in shape, hence *s*-orbitals are non-directional.

71 (*c*) If the highest value of magnetic quantum number $= -3$
Then $l = 3$ ($\because$ *m* has value from $-l$ to $+l$ including zero)

$\therefore \quad n = 4$
($\because$ *l* has values from 0 to $n - 1$)

Thus, the principal quantum number $(n) = 4$

72 (*d*) $n = 3 \rightarrow$ represents that the electron is in the third shell (*M*-shell)
$l = 0 \rightarrow$ represents that the electron is in the 3*s*-subshell (since, for $s, l = 0$)
$m = 0 \rightarrow$ represents that the electron is in the 3*s*-subshell (may be $3s^1$ or $3s^2$)

Hence, its complete electronic configuration is

$1s^2, 2s^2, 2p^6, 3s^{1 \text{ or } 2}$.

$\therefore$ The atomic number = 11 or 12

73 (*b*) According to Aufbau principle, orbitals of any atom are filled in increasing order of energy. The correct order is,

$1s < 2s < 2p < 3s < 3p < 4s < 3d < 4p < 5s < 4d < 5p < 6s\ 4f < 5d$

Hence, option (b) is correct.

Classification of Elements and Periodicity in Properties

Quick Review

To group different elements together on the basis of their properties is called classification of elements.

Earlier Attempt to Classify the Elements

Many attempts were made to classify the known elements from time to time.

The earlier attempts are as follows :

- **Dobereiner Triads** It is a group of three elements with similar physical and chemical properties. In these triads, the atomic mass of the middle element was arithmetic mean of the other two elements.

e.g.

Element	Li	Na	K
Atomic weight	7	23	39

$$\text{Mean of atomic masses} = \frac{7+39}{2} = 23$$

Cl, Br, I and Ca, Sr, Ba are other examples of such triads.

- **Newland's Law of Octaves** It was an arrangement of elements in the order of their increasing atomic weights in such a manner that every eighth element had properties similar to those of the first just like the eighth note in an octave of music.

- **Lothar Meyer's Atomic Volume Curve** It presented the classification of elements in the form of a curve between atomic volume and atomic masses. It is observed that, elements with similar properties occupied similar positions on the curve.

Mendeleev's Periodic Table

It is based upon Mendeleev's periodic law, which states that the physical and chemical properties of the elements are periodic function of their atomic weights. Thus, table consists of six periods and eight groups (group '0' for noble gases).

Note Mg, Al and Si (elements of third period) are called **bridge elements** since, division of each main group into subgroups (A and B) starts from these elements.

Modern Periodic Law and the Present Form of Periodic Table

- Henry Moseley showed that the atomic number is a more fundamental property of an element than its atomic mass and formulated modern periodic law.
- Modern periodic law can be stated as "the physical and chemical properties of the elements are periodic functions of their atomic numbers".

- Moseley arranged elements in the order of increasing atomic numbers. It consists of seven periods and nine groups. These groups are further sub-divided into A and B (groups I to VII), VIII and 0 groups.

Long Form of Periodic Table

It is based on electronic configuration of elements. It contains seven periods and eighteen groups.

Features of Long Form of Periodic Table

- The number of periods denote the number of outermost shell of that element. 1st period is **very short period,** contains two elements. 2nd and 3rd periods are **short periods**, contain eight elements each. 4th and 5th periods are **long periods**, contain eighteen elements each. 6th period contains 32 elements (very large period) and 7th period is still incomplete.
- Elements of group 1 are called **alkali metals**. Elements of group 2 are called **alkaline earth metals**. Elements of group 1 and 2 constitute ***s*-block**. The general electronic configuration of *s*-block elements is ns^{1-2}. These are highly reactive and soft metals.
- Elements of group 3 to 12 constitute ***d*-block**. These elements are **transition metals**. The general electronic configuration of *d*-block elements is $(n-1)\,d^{1-10}ns^{1-2}$. These elements show variable oxidation states, paramagnetism, form coloured complex ions and possess catalytic activity.
- Elements of group 13 to 18 constitute *p*-block. The general electronic configuration of *p*-block elements is ns^2np^{1-6}. This block includes metals, non-metals and few metalloids.
- The elements of two horizontal rows placed at the bottom of the periodic table are called ***f*-block elements**. These are also called **inner transition elements** (lanthanoids and actinoids). The general electronic configuration of *f*-block elements is $(n-2)\,f^{1-14}(n-1)\,d^{0-1}ns^2$. They are called **rare earth elements**.
- Two adjacent elements placed in a group differ by atomic numbers 2, 8, 18 or 32. These particular numbers are therefore, known as **magic numbers**.

Note The elements (e.g. silicon, germanium, arsenic, antimony and tellurium) show properties of both metals and non-metals. These elements are called **semi-metals** and **metalloids**.

Demerits of Long Form of Periodic Table

- Position of hydrogen is in appropriate as it resembles both alkali metals and halogens.
- Lanthanoids and actiniods are not merged in the main body of the table.

Classification of Elements

Depending upon the orbital in which last electron enters, the elements are classified as follows:

1. *s*-Block Elements

- Group I (alkali metals) and group II (alkaline earth metals) elements belong to this block, their last electron enters in *s*-orbital.
- General electronic configuration of *s*-block elements is ns^{1-2}.

2. *p*-Block Elements

- Groups 13th to 18th excluding He, belong to this block. Their last electron enters in *p*-block.
- General electronic configuration of *p*-block elements is ns^2, np^{1-6}.
- *s* and *p*-block elements are known as representative elements or main group elements.

Diagonal Relationship

The first member of each group of *s* and *p*-block elements shows different characteristics from the rest of the members of the same group.

However, the first three elements of second period (Li, Be, B) shows diagonal similarity with elements (Mg, Al, Si) of third period placed on the right hand side. This is called diagonal relationship.

2nd period		Li ↘	Be ↘	B ↘	C
3rd period	Na	Mg	Al	Si	

3. *d*-Block or Transition Elements

- Elements of group 3rd to 12th in periodic table belong to *d*-block. Their last electron enters in *d*-block.
- Two outermost shells of *d*-block elements are incomplete.
- General electronic configuration of *d*-block elements is $(n-1)d^{1-10}\ ns^{0-2}$

4. *f*-Block or Inner-Transition Elements

- General configuration $(n-2)f^{1-14}\ (n-1)d^{0-1}ns^2$.
- Last electron enters in *f*-orbital.
- Two series 4*f* (lanthanoids) and 5*f* (actinoids). Also known as rare earth elements.

Periodic Trends in Properties of Elements

The elements in the periodic table are arranged in order of increasing atomic number. All of these elements display several other trends and we can use the periodic law and table formation to predict their chemical, physical and atomic properties.

Some of the physical and chemical properties of the elements are discussed below :

1. Atomic Size/Radius

- The atomic radius is defined as 'the distance from the centre of the nucleus to the outermost shell containing electrons.'
  The order of different atomic radii is
  van der Waals' radius > metallic radius >> covalent radius.
- Ionic radius $\propto$ charge on anion $\propto \dfrac{1}{\text{charge on cation}}$
  [same for isoelectronic species]
- On moving across the period from left to right, the effective nuclear charge increases and thus, atomic radii decreases.
- On moving down the group, atomic radii increases.

Exception

- Transition elements show a little variation in their atomic radii due to poor shielding effect of *d*-electrons.
- For isoelectronic species (with same number of electrons), atomic radius is inversely proportional to atomic number. Due to lanthanoid contraction, there is greater than expected decrease in ionic radius of elements in lanthanoid series.

2. Ionisation Energy (IE) or Ionisation Potential (IP)

- The minimum amount of energy required to remove an electron from outermost orbit of an isolated gaseous atom resulting in the formation of positive ion is called the ionisation energy.
- Order of ionisation energy of various orbitals is
  $$s > p > d > f$$
- On moving across the period from left to right, ionisation energy increases with decrease in atomic radius.
- On moving down the group, ionisation energy decreases due to increase in atomic size.

Exception

- There are some exceptions to the general trend. e.g. IE of elements of group 2 is greater than that of group 3 due to stable configuration, i.e. ns^2. Similarly, IE of elements of group 15 is greater than that of group 16 because exactly half-filled orbitals possess extra stability.
- Cd and Hg have exceptionally high IE due to the greater stability of *s*-subshell.

Note IE is maximum (highest) for noble gases and lowest for alkali metals in a period.

3. Electron Gain Enthalpy [Electron Affinity (EA)]

- The process of change in enthalpy when an electron is added to an isolated neutral gaseous atom is called electron gain enthalpy.
- Electron gain enthalpy becomes more negative with increase in the atomic number across a period and less negative as we go down the group.
- On moving down the group, the magnitude of electron affinity decreases due to increase in atomic size.

Exception

- Electron affinities of group 2, 15 and 18 are less due to exactly half-filled or completely filled orbitals that are against the expected trend.
- $\Delta_{eg}H$ of elements having half-filled and completely filled orbitals is positive.
- $\Delta_{eg}H$ of O is less negative than S and that of F is less negative than Cl due to electron-electron repulsion.

4. Electronegativity

- It is a measure of the tendency of an element to attract the shared pair of electrons towards itself.
- As the absolute magnitude of electronegativity value of an element is not fixed, thus, different scales have been suggested, which are given below :

(a) Mulliken's Scale,

$$\chi_M = \frac{\text{IE} + A_e}{2}\ \text{kcal mol}^{-1}$$

or $$\frac{\text{IE} + A_e}{5.6}\ \text{eV}$$

where, IE = ionisation energy

(b) Pauling Scale

According to Pauling, the electronegativity difference between two atoms *A* and *B*,

$$(\chi_A - \chi_B) = 0.208\sqrt{\Delta E}$$

where, $$\Delta E = E_{A-B} - \sqrt{E_{A-A} \times E_{B-B}}$$

$\chi_A - \chi_B$ = electronegativity difference between two atoms *A* and *B*.

E_{A-A} and E_{B-B} are the bond energies of the molecules of A_2 and B_2 respectively.

(c) Allred and Rochow Scale

$$\chi_A = 0.744 + \frac{0.359\,Z_{\text{eff}}}{r^2}$$

- **Mulliken scale values** are ≈ 2.8 times greater than Pauling scale values.
  $$\chi_P = 0.336\,[\chi_M - 0.615]$$

Slater's Rule

The extent of screening of an electron by other electrons in the atom is calculated with the help of Slater's rule.

$$Z_{\text{eff}} = Z - \sigma^*$$

σ^* = screening or shielding constant.

σ^* = [0.35 × number of electrons in nth shell + 0.85 × number of electrons in $(n-1)$th shell + 1.00 × total number of electrons in inner shells].

Electronegativity increases along a period and decreases down a group.

5. Electropositive or Metallic Character

- The tendency of an element to form a cation by the loss of electron is called **electropositive** or **metallic character**.
- Metallic character increases down the group and decreases along a period whereas, non-metallic character increases along a period and decreases down the group in the periodic table.

6. Valency

- The combining capacity of an element is defined as the valency. In general, elements of same group show same type of valency. E.g. all alkali metals have valency equal to 1.
- In *p*-block elements, tendency to show higher valency decreases on going down the group due to inert pair effect.
- Transition and inner transition elements exhibit variable valency due to the involvement of electrons of *d* and *f* orbitals present in their outer as well as penultimate shell.

7. Chemical Reactivity

- Chemical reactivity of metal increases with decrease in IE, electronegativity and increase in atomic size as well as electropositive character.
- Reactivity of non-metals increases with increase in electronegativity as well as electron gain enthalpy and decrease in atomic radii.
- Across a period, the chemical reactivity of metals decreases while those of non-metals increases.
- On moving down the group, chemical reactivity increases for metals but for non-metals, it decreases.
- Reducing agents release electrons, thus, metals act as good reducing agents whereas oxidising agents accept electrons, thus, non-metals are good oxidising agents.
- Among *s*-block elements, the reducing property increases while oxidising property decreases down the group.
- However, in case of *p*-block elements, the oxidising character decreases while reducing character increases down the group.
- Metal oxides are basic while non-metal oxides are acidic in nature when dissolved in water.
- Basic character of oxides decreases along the period and increases down the group whereas acidic character of oxides increases along the period and decreases down the group in periodic table.

Diagonal Relationship

Certain elements of 2nd period show similarity in properties with their diagonal elements in the 3rd period. Thus, Li resembles Mg, Be resembles Al and B resembles Si. This is called **diagonal relationship**. These pairs of elements have almost identical ionic radii and polarising power.

Topical Practice Questions

All the exam questions of this chapter have been divided into two topics as listed below

Topic 1

Periodic Table and Classification of Elements

2019

1 An element with mass number 81 contains 31.7% more neutrons as compared to protons. Its symbol is **[JIPMER]**

(a) ${}_{40}X^{81}$ (b) ${}_{35}X^{81}$ (c) ${}_{81}X^{31.7}$ (d) ${}_{40}X^{81}$

2017

2 The element $(Z = 114)$ has been discovered recently. It will belong to which of the following family/group and electronic configuration? **[NEET]**

(a) Halogen family, [Rn] $5f^{14}\ 6d^{10}\ 7s^2\ 7p^5$

(b) Carbon family, [Rn] $5f^{14}\ 6d^{10}\ 7s^2\ 7p^2$

(c) Oxygen family, [Rn] $5f^{14}\ 6d^{10}\ 7s^2\ 7p^4$

(d) Nitrogen family, [Rn] $5f^{14}\ 6d^{10}\ 7s^2\ 7p^6$

3 The plot of square root of frequency of X-ray emitted against atomic number led to the suggestion of which law/rule? **[MHT CET]**

(a) Periodic law (b) Modern periodic law

(c) Hund's rule (d) Newland's law

4 Which of the following pairs contain metalloid elements in the periodic table? **[Kerala CEE]**

(a) Na and K (b) F and Cl

(c) Ca and Mg (d) As and Si

(e) Cu and Ag

5 Whose name is not associated with the development of periodic table? **[WB JEE]**

(a) Prout's (b) Newland's

(c) Rutherford (d) Lothar Meyer

6 Magic numbers are **[WB JEE]**

(a) principal quantum number

(b) azimuthal quantum number

(c) magnetic quantum number

(d) 2, 8, 18, 32

2012

7 Which of the following is not a periodic property? **[OJEE]**

(a) Atomic mass (b) Atomic volume

(c) Covalent radius (d) Electronegativity

2011

8 The number of naturally occurring *p*-block elements that are diamagnetic is **[KCET]**

(a) 18 (b) 6

(c) 5 (d) 7

2010

9 Which one of the following ions has electronic configuration [Ar] $3d^6$?

(Atomic numbers : Mn = 25, Fe = 26, Co = 27, Ni = 28) **[CBSE AIPMT]**

(a) Co^{3+} (b) Ni^{3+} (c) Mn^{3+} (d) Fe^{3+}

10 Electronic configuration of an element *X* having atomic number 24 is **[UP CPMT, OJEE]**

(a) [Ar] $3d^5\,4s^1$ (b) [Ar] $3d^4\,4s^2$

(c) [Ne] $2p^5\,3s^1$ (d) [Ar] $3d^6\,4s^2$

11 The element that shows diagonal relationship with B is

(a) Li (b) Al (c) Si (d) Mg **[OJEE]**

12 The electronic configuration of an element is $1s^2, 2s^2, 2p^6, 3s^2, 3p^6, 3d^{10}, 4s^2, 4p^6, 4d^{10}, 5s^2, 5p^3$.

From which group of the periodic table, it belongs?

(a) 2nd (b) 15th (c) 3rd (d) 7th **[KCET]**

13 What does the electronic configuration $1s^2, 2s^2, 2p^5, 3s^1$ indicate? **[Guj CET]**

(a) Ground state of fluorine

(b) Excited state of fluorine

(c) Excited state of neon

(d) Excited state of the O_2^- ion

14 The element with the electronic configuration as [Ar] $3d^{10}\ 4s^2, 4p^3$ represents a **[JCECE]**

(a) metal (b) non-metal

(c) metalloid (d) transition element

15 Mg and Li are similar in their properties due to **[VMMC]**

(a) same *e*/*m* ratio

(b) same electron affinity

(c) same group

(d) same ionisation potential

2009

16 Electronic configuration of Cu^{2+} ion is **[OJEE]**

(a) [Ar] $4s^1\,3d^8$ (b) [Ar] $4s^0\,3d^9$

(c) [Ar] $4s^2\,3d^7$ (d) [Ar] $4s^0\,3d^8$

17 The element with atomic number 117 has not been discovered yet. In which family, would you place this element, if discovered? **[Kerala CEE]**

(a) Alkali metals (b) Alkaline earth metals

(c) Halogens (d) Noble gases

(e) Coinage metals

2008

18 The discovery of which of the following group of elements gave death blow to the Newland's law of octaves? **[Manipal]**
(a) Inert gases (b) Alkaline earth metals
(c) Rare earths (d) Actinides

19 An element X belongs to fourth period and fifteenth group of the periodic table. Which one of the following is true regarding the outer electronic configuration of X? **[Kerala CEE]**
(a) It has partially filled d-orbitals and completely filled s-orbitals
(b) It has completely filled s-orbitals and completely filled p-orbitals
(c) It has completely filled s-orbitals and half-filled p-orbitals
(d) It has half-filled d-orbitals and completely filled s-orbitals
(e) It has completely filled d, s and p-orbitals

20 Element with atomic number 38, belongs to **[MP PMT]**
(a) II A group and 5th period
(b) II A group and 2nd period
(c) VA group and 2nd period
(d) III A group and 5th period

21 An element with atomic number 112 has been made recently. It should be **[Haryana PMT]**
(a) an actinide (b) a transition metal
(c) a noble gas (d) a lanthanide

2007

22 The long form of periodic table based on **[BHU]**
(a) atomic number (b) atomic mass
(c) electronic configuration (d) effective nuclear charge

23 The group of elements in which the differentiating electron enters in the anti-penultimate shell of atoms are called **[J&K CET]**
(a) f-block elements (b) p-block elements
(c) s-block elements (d) d-block elements

24 An atom has electronic configuration $1s^2, 2s^2, 2p^6, 3s^2, 3p^6, 3d^3, 4s^2$, you will place it in **[Punjab PMET]**
(a) fifth group (b) fifteenth group
(c) second group (d) third group

25 In the periodic table, metals usually used as catalysts belong to **[KCET]**
(a) f-block (b) d-block (c) p-block (d) s-block

2006

26 The electronic configuration of four elements are
I. $[Xe]\,6s^1$ II. $[Xe]\,4f^{14}, 5d^1, 6s^2$
III. $[Ar]\,4s^2, 4p^5$ IV. $[Ar]\,3d^7, 4s^2$.
Which one of the following statements about these elements is not correct? **[Kerala CEE]**
(a) I is a strong reducing agent
(b) II is a d-block element
(c) III has high electron affinity
(d) IV shows variable oxidation state
(e) The compound formed between I and III is ionic

2005

27 What is the name of the element with atomic number 105? **[MP PMT]**
(a) Kurchatovium (b) Dubnium
(c) Nobelium (d) Holmium

Answers

1 (b)	2 (b)	3 (b)	4 (d)	5 (c)	6 (d)	7 (a)	8 (a)	9 (a)	10 (a)
11 (c)	12 (b)	13 (c)	14 (c)	15 (a)	16 (b)	17 (c)	18 (a)	19 (c)	20 (a)
21 (b)	22 (c)	23 (a)	24 (a)	25 (b)	26 (b)	27 (b)			

Explanations

1 (*b*) Let, the number of protons = x

$\therefore$ Number of neutrons

$$= x + \frac{31.7x}{100} = \frac{131.7x}{100}$$

Mass number = number of protons + number of neutrons

$$81 = x + \frac{131.7x}{100}$$

$\Rightarrow \quad x = 35$

Thus, the symbol of the element is ${}_{35}X^{81}$.

2 (*b*) The element with atomic number, ($Z = 114$) is flerovium (Fl). It is a super heavy artificial chemical element. In the periodic table of the elements, it is a transactinide element in the *p*-block. It is a member of the 7th period and it is the heaviest known member of the carbon family.

Electronic configuration for $Z = 114$ is

$$[\text{Rn}]_{86}\, 5f^{14}, 6d^{10}, 7s^2, 7p^2$$

3 (*b*) Moseley gave a modern periodic law. He showed that atomic number is more fundamental property of an element than its atomic mass. He found that, "the square root of the frequency of a line (of X-ray spectrum) is related to the atomic number Z of the target material as",

$$\sqrt{v} = a(Z - b)$$

where, a = proportionality constant
Z = atomic number
b = another constant

(It has the same value for all the lines of X-ray spectrum)

4 (*d*) Arsenic (As) and Silicon (Si) is a metalloid pair of elements in the periodic table.

A metalloid is a chemical element that has properties of both metals and non-metals. The term semi-metal is sometimes used.

The six commonly recognised metalloids are silicon, germanium, arsenic, antimony and tellurium.

5 (*c*) (a) Prout's gave unitary theory for the classification of elements. He suggested that the atoms of all the elements are made up of hydrogen atom.

(b) Newland's gave law of octaves. According to him, "if elements are arranged in the increasing order of their atomic weights, the properties of eighth element starting from the given one is the repetition of the first, like the eighth note in an octave of music".

(c) Rutherford is associated with structure of atom, so he is not associated with the development of periodic table.

(d) Lothar Meyer plotted the curve between atomic volumes (i.e. atomic weight/density) of various elements against their atomic weights and pointed out that the similar elements occupy similar position on the curve.

6 (*d*) In the periodic table, two adjacent elements placed in a group differ by atomic numbers 2, 8, 18 or 32. These particular numbers (2, 8, 18 and 32) are therefore, called the magic numbers.

7 (*a*) In periodic table, after certain regular intervals, some properties are repeated. These properties are known as periodic properties, e.g. atomic volume, ionic and covalent radius, ionisation enthalpy, electron affinity, etc. Atomic mass is not a periodic property.

8 (*a*) Noble gases are naturally occurring diamagnetic *p*-block elements (*viz*. He, Ne, Ar, Kr, Xe and Rn). Thus, element with atomic number 18 is diamagnetic.

9 (*a*) Among the given options Co^{3+} possess [Ar] $3d^6$ electronic configuration.

$$\text{Co} = [\text{Ar}]\,3d^7, 4s^2$$

$$\therefore \text{Co}^{3+} = [\text{Ar}]\,3d^6$$

10 (*a*) The electronic configuration of element X (atomic number = 24) is $1s^2, 2s^2, 2p^6, 3s^2, 3p^6, 4s^1, 3d^5$.

(one electron jumps from 4*s*-orbital to 3*d*-orbital to gain more stability)

Hence, the electronic configuration of element X is $[\text{Ar}]\,3d^5, 4s^1$.

11 (*c*) Elements of second period show similarity in properties with the elements of third period, that are placed diagonally opposite.

This type of similarity is called diagonal relationship, e.g.

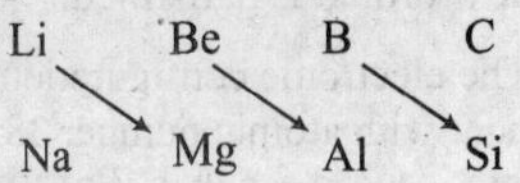

12 (*b*) The given configuration shows valence shell configuration as $5s^2, 5p^3$.

$\because$ It has five electrons in the valence shell.

$\therefore$ It belongs to group VA (or 15) of periodic table.

13 (*c*) The atomic number of neon is 10.

Ground state, Ne (10) – $1s^2, 2s^2, 2p^6$

Excited state,

Ne (10) – $1s^2, 2s^2, 2p^5, 3s^1$

Hence, $1s^2, 2s^2, 2p^5, 3s^1$ electronic configuration indicates the excited state of neon.

14 (*c*) Electronic configuration reveals that the *p*-orbital of the element is not complete. Therefore, it is a *p*-block element. Moreover, the atomic number of the element is 33(As). Therefore, it is a metalloid.

15 (*a*) Mg and Li are similar in their properties due to the similar electronegativity and polarising power, i.e. they have same charge/radius (*e*/*m*) ratio.

16 (*b*) Electronic configuration of copper is $\text{Cu}[29] = [\text{Ar}]\,4s^1, 3d^{10}$

$$\text{Cu}^{2+} = [\text{Ar}]\,4s^0, 3d^9$$

17 (*c*) The electronic configuration of the element with atomic number 117 is $[\text{Rn}]_{86}\, 5f^{14}, 6d^{10}, 7s^2, 7p^5$.

Name of this element is tennessine. This element contains 7 electrons in its outermost shell, so it belongs to VII A or (17) group of periodic table, i.e. it is a halogen. Its IUPAC symbol is Ts.

18 (*a*) With the discovery of inert gases (group zero in Mendeleev 's periodic table), the law of octaves lost its original significance. Since, it was now the ninth element which had properties similar to the first one, which is not in accordance to the law.

19 (*c*) Since, the element X belongs to fourth period and fifteenth group of periodic table, its outer **electronic configuration** is $4s^2, 4p^3$.

Its complete electronic configuration is $1s^2, 2s^2, 2p^6, 3s^2, 3p^6, 3d^{10}, 4s^2, 4p^3$.

Hence, its s-orbital is completely filled while p-orbital is half-filled.

20 (*a*) The electronic configuration of an element with atomic number 38 is

$X(38) = 1s^2, 2s^2, 2p^6, 3s^2, 3p^6, 4s^2, 3d^{10}, 4p^6, 5s^2$

As the outermost electron enters in s-orbital, hence, it belongs to II A group and 5th period. It is strontium (Sr).

21 (*b*) The electronic configuration of given element with atomic number 112 is $[Rn]_{86}\, 5f^{14}, 7s^2, 6d^{10}$. As its outermost electron enters in d-subshell, thus it belongs to d-block or a transition metal.

22 (*c*) The long form of periodic table is based on electronic configuration of elements, i.e. Bohr-Burry concept.

23 (*a*) The group of elements in which the differentiating electron enters in the anti-penultimate shell, inner to the penultimate shell, i.e. $(n-2)$ shell is called f-block elements or inner-transition elements.

24 (*a*) An atom has electronic configuration,

$1s^2, 2s^2, 2p^6, 3s^2, 3p^6, 3d^3, 4s^2$.

It is a member of d-block elements because the last electron is filled in d-subshell as $3d^3$. Group number of a d-block element = ns-electron + $(n-1)$ d-electrons = 2 + 3 = 5.

Hence, it is a member of fifth group.

25 (*b*) Metals which are usually used as catalysts belong to d-block of the periodic table. e.g. Ni, Pt, etc., as they have large surface area.

26 (*b*) $[Xe]\,4f^{14}, 5d^1, 6s^2$ is not a d-block element. It is lutetium and is present in lanthanide series. So, lutetium is a f-block element.

$[Xe]\,6s^1$ is a strong reducing agent as by losing one electron it acquires stable electronic configuration.

$[Ar]4s^2 4p^5$ has high electron affinity as by gaining one e^-, it acquires stable electronic configuration.

$[Ar]3d^7 4s^2$ is a d-block elements and it shows variable oxidation states.

Compound formed between $[Xe]6s^1$ (metal) and $[Ar]4s^2 4p^5$ (non-metal) is ionic.

Note The generalised electronic configuration of f-block elements is $(n-2)f^{1-14}(n-1)d^{0-1}ns^2$.

27 (*b*) The element with atomic number 105 is dubnium (Db). In IUPAC nomenclature, it is known as unnilpentium.

$Db(105) = [Rn]^{86} 5f^{14}\, 6d^3\, 7s^2$

Topic 2

Periodic Properties

2019

1 For the second period elements, the correct increasing order of first ionisation enthalpy is **[NEET]**

(a) Li < B < Be < C < O < N < F < Ne

(b) Li < B < Be < C < N < O < F < Ne

(c) Li < Be < B < C < O < N < F < Ne

(d) Li < Be < B < C < N < O < F < Ne

2 Which pair of elements has maximum electronegativity difference? **[AIIMS]**

(a) Li and F (b) Na and F (c) Na and Br (d) Na and Cl

3 Match the oxide given in Column A with its property given in Column B. **[NEET (Odisha)]**

	Column A		Column B
1.	Na_2O	(i)	Neutral
2.	Al_2O_3	(ii)	Basic
3.	N_2O	(iii)	Acidic
4.	Cl_2O_7	(iv)	Amphoteric

Which of the following options has all correct pairs?

	1	2	3	4
(a)	(ii)	(i)	(iv)	(iii)
(b)	(iii)	(ii)	(i)	(iv)
(c)	(i)	(ii)	(iv)	(iii)
(d)	(ii)	(iv)	(i)	(iii)

2018

4 Affinity for hydrogen decreases in the group from fluorine to iodine. Which of the halogen acids should have highest bond dissociation enthalpy? **[AIIMS]**

(a) HF (b) HCl

(c) HBr (d) HI

5 The ionic radii (Å) of C^{4-} and O^{2-} respectively are 2.60 and 1.40. The ionic radius of the isoelectronic ion N^{3-} would be **[AIIMS]**

(a) 1.31 Å (b) 2.83 Å

(c) 1.71 Å (d) 2.63 Å

6 Which of the following oxides is most acidic in nature? **[NEET]**

(a) BaO (b) BeO

(c) MgO (d) CaO

2017

7 Which of the following is the correct order of stability for the given superoxides? **[JIPMER]**

(a) $KO_2 < RbO_2 < CsO_2$

(b) $CsO_2 < RbO_2 < KO_2$

(c) $RbO_2 < CsO_2 < KO_2$

(d) $KO_2 < CsO_2 < RbO_2$

2016

8 Which one of the following orders is correct for the bond dissociation enthalpy of halogen molecules? **[NEET]**
(a) $Cl_2 > Br_2 > F_2 > I_2$
(b) $Br_2 > I_2 > F_2 > Cl_2$
(c) $F_2 > Cl_2 > Br_2 > I_2$
(d) $I_2 > Br_2 > Cl_2 > F_2$

2015

9 The species Ar, K^+ and Ca^{2+} contain the same number of electrons. In which order do their radii increase? **[CBSE AIPMT]**
(a) $Ar < K^+ < Ca^{2+}$ (b) $Ca^{2+} < Ar < K^+$
(c) $Ca^{2+} < K^+ < Ar$ (d) $K^+ < Ar < Ca^{2+}$

10 Which is the correct order of atomic radius? **[AIIMS]**
(a) Metallic radius > van der Waals' radius > covalent radius
(b) van der Waals' radius > covalent radius > metallic radius
(c) van der Waals' radius > metallic radius > covalent radius
(d) covalent radius > metallic radius > van der Waals' radius

2014

11 Which of the following orders of ionic radius is correctly represented? **[CBSE AIPMT]**
(a) $H^- > H > H^+$ (b) $Na^+ > F^- > O^{2-}$
(c) $F^- > O^{2-} > Na^+$ (d) $Al^{3+} > Mg^{2+} > N^{3-}$

12 Amongst the following, select the element having highest ionisation enthalpy. **[MHT CET]**
(a) Sodium (b) Potassium
(c) Beryllium (d) Magnesium

13 The compound not acting as a reducing agent is **[Manipal]**
(a) SO_2 (b) SeO_2
(c) TeO_2 (d) All of these

14 The correct order of acidic strength **[Manipal]**
(a) $Cl_2O_7 > SO_2 > P_4O_{10}$
(b) $CO_2 > N_2O_5 > SO_3$
(c) $Na_2O > MgO > Al_2O_3$
(d) $K_2O > CaO > MgO$

15 The correct arrangement for the ions in the increasing order of their radius is **[KCET]**
(a) Na^+, Cl^-, Ca^{2+} (b) Ca^{2+}, K^+, S^{2-}
(c) Na^+, Al^{3+}, Be^{2+} (d) Cl^-, F^-, S^{2-}

16 For the properties mentioned, the correct trend for the different species is in **[KCET]**
(a) strength as Lewis acid — $BCl_3 > AlCl_3 > GaCl_3$
(b) inert pair effect — $Al > Ga > In$
(c) oxidising property — $Al^{3+} > In^{3+} > Tl^{3+}$
(d) first ionisation enthalpy — $B > Al > Tl$

17 Elements *A*, *B* and *C* belong to the same period in the long form of the periodic table. The nature of the oxides of *A*, *B* and *C* is amphoteric, basic and acidic respectively. The correct order of the atomic numbers of these elements is **[EAMCET]**
(a) $C > B > A$ (b) $C > A > B$ (c) $A > B > C$ (d) $B > A > C$

18 Which one of the following is the correct order of the size of the ions? **[EAMCET]**
(a) $Na^+ > Mg^{2+} > F^- > O^{2-}$ (b) $O^{2-} > F^- > Na^+ > Mg^{2+}$
(c) $Mg^{2+} > Na^+ > F^- > O^{2-}$ (d) $O^{2-} > F^- > Mg^{2+} > Na^+$

2013

19 Sodium forms Na^+ ion but it does not form Na^{2+} because **[AIIMS]**
(a) very low value of 1st and IInd IE
(b) very high value of 1st and IInd IE
(c) high value of 1st IE and low value of IInd IE
(d) low value of 1st IE and high value of IInd IE

20 The electron affinity of Be is similar to **[UP CPMT]**
(a) He (b) B (c) Li (d) Na

21 The correct order of decreasing first ionisation potential is **[UP CPMT]**
(a) $Ca > K > Rb > Cs$ (b) $Cs > Rb > K > Ca$
(c) $Ca > Cs > Rb > K$ (d) $K > Rb > Cs > Ca$

2012

22 Identify the wrong statement in the following. **[CBSE AIPMT]**
(a) Amongst isoelectronic species, smaller the positive charge on the cation, smaller is the ionic radius.
(b) Amongst isoelectronic species, greater the negative charge on the anion, larger is the ionic radius.
(c) Atomic radius of the elements increases as one moves down the first group of the periodic table.
(d) Atomic radius of the elements decreases as one moves across from left to right in the 2nd period of the periodic table.

23 In which of the following arrangements, the given sequence is not strictly according to the property indicated against it? **[CBSE AIPMT]**
(a) $HF < HCl < HBr < HI$ (Increasing acidic strength)
(b) $H_2O < H_2S < H_2Se < H_2Te$ (Increasing pK_a values)
(c) $NH_3 < PH_3 < AsH_3 < SbH_3$ (Increasing acidic character)
(d) $CO_2 < SiO_2 < SnO_2 < PbO_2$ (Increasing oxidising power)

24 The electron affinity of halogens are F = 322, Cl = 349, Br = 324, I = 295 kJ mol^{-1}. The higher value for Cl as compared to that of F is due to **[AIIMS]**
(a) weaker electron-electron repulsion in Cl
(b) higher atomic radius of F
(c) smaller electronegativity of F
(d) more vacant *p*-subshell in Cl

25 **Assertion** (A) Removal of *s*-electron is relatively difficult than removal of *p*-electron of the same main shell.
Reason (R) *s*-electrons are closer to the nucleus than *p*-electrons of the same shell and hence, are more strongly attracted by nucleus. [AIIMS]
(a) Both A and R are correct and R is the correct explanation of A
(b) Both A and R are correct but R is not the correct explanation of A
(c) A is correct but R is incorrect
(d) Both A and R are incorrect

26 Which of the following is correct? [WB JEE]
(a) Radius of $Ca^{2+} < Cl^- < S^{2-}$
(b) Radius of $Cl^- < S^{2-} < Ca^{2+}$
(c) Radius of $S^{2-} < Cl^- = Ca^{2+}$
(d) Radius of $S^{2-} < Cl^- < Ca^{2+}$

2011

27 The bond enthalpy is the highest for [Kerala CEE]
(a) F_2 (b) Cl_2 (c) Br_2 (d) I_2
(e) H_2

28 The increasing order of the density of alkali metals is [Kerala CEE]
(a) Li < K < Na < Rb < Cs
(b) Li < Na < K < Rb < Cs
(c) Cs < Rb < Na < K < Li
(d) Cs < Rb < K < Na < Li
(e) Li < Na < Rb < K < Cs

29 The correct order of decreasing electronegativity values among the elements
I-beryllium, II-oxygen, III-nitrogen and IV-magnesium, is [Kerala CEE]
(a) II > III > I > IV (b) III > IV > II > I
(c) I > II > III > IV (d) I > II > IV > III
(e) II > III > IV > I

30 Which ion has the largest radius? [DUMET]
(a) Se^{2-} (b) F^- (c) O^{2-} (d) Rb^+

2010

31 The correct order of the decreasing ionic radius among the following isoelectronic species is [CBSE AIPMT, BVP]
(a) $K^+ > Ca^{2+} > Cl^- > S^{2-}$
(b) $Ca^{2+} > K^+ > S^{2-} > Cl^-$
(c) $Cl^- > S^{2-} > Ca^{2+} > K^+$
(d) $S^{2-} > Cl^- > K^+ > Ca^{2+}$

32 Which of the following represents the correct order of increasing electron gain enthalpy with negative sign for the elements O, S, F and Cl? [CBSE AIPMT]
(a) S < O < Cl < F (b) Cl < F < O < S
(c) O < S < F < Cl (d) F < S < O < Cl

33 Which of the following has the highest electron affinity?
(a) F^- (b) O^{2-} (c) O (d) Na [AFMC]

34 The electronegativity of the following elements increases in the order [AFMC]
(a) C, N, Si, P (b) N, Si, C, P
(c) Si, P, C, N (d) P, Si, N, C

35 Which of the following orders regarding ionisation energy is correct? [WB JEE]
(a) N > O > F (b) N < O < F
(c) N > O < F (d) N < O > F

36 In periodic table, the basic character of oxides [WB JEE]
(a) increases from left to right and decreases from top to bottom
(b) decreases from right to left and increases from top to bottom
(c) decreases from left to right and increases from top to bottom
(d) decreases from left to right and increases from bottom to top

37 Ease of formation of the cation is favoured by [RPMT]
(a) lower value of ionisation potential
(b) lower value of electron affinity
(c) higher value of electron affinity
(d) lower value of electronegativity

38 Which one of the following is correct order of the size? [Haryana PMT]
(a) $I > I^- > I^+$ (b) $I > I^+ > I^-$
(c) $I^+ > I^- > I$ (d) $I^- > I > I^+$

39 Among the following, the third ionisation energy is highest for [AMU]
(a) magnesium (b) boron
(c) beryllium (d) aluminium

40 Generally, the first ionisation energy increases along a period, but there are some exceptions. One which is not an exception is [KCET]
(a) N and O (b) Na and Mg
(c) Mg and Al (d) Be and B

41 The property of attracting electrons by the halogen atoms in a molecule is called [JCECE]
(a) ionisation potential (b) electron affinity
(c) electronegativity (d) electronic attraction

2009

42 The correct order of electron affinities of N, O, S and Cl is [AIIMS]
(a) N < O < S < Cl (b) O < N < Cl < S
(c) O ≈ Cl < N ≈ S (d) O < S < Cl < N

43 Which of the following pairs has almost same atomic radius? [AIIMS]
(a) Al, Ga (b) Be, Mg
(c) Mg, Al (d) B, Be

44 Which represents the correct order of first ionisation potential of third period elements? **[AFMC]**
(a) Na > Mg > Al > Si (b) Na < Mg < Al < Si
(c) Na < Si < Al < Mg (d) Na < Al < Mg < Si

45 Increasing order of ionic size for the ions, $F^-, O^{2-}, Na^+, Al^{3+}$ is **[AMU]**
(a) $O^{2-} < F^- < Na^+ < Al^{3+}$ (b) $Al^{3+} < Na^+ < F^- < O^{2-}$
(c) $O^{2-} < Na^+ < F^- < Al^{3+}$ (d) $Al^{3+} < F^- < Na^+ < O^{2-}$

46 In which of the following arrangements, the order is not according to the property indicated after it in bracket? **[Manipal]**
(a) $Al^{3+} < Mg^{2+} < Na^+ < F^-$ (Increasing ionic size)
(b) B < C < N < O (Increasing first ionisation energy)
(c) I < Br < F < Cl (Increasing electron gain enthalpy)
(d) Li < Na < K < Rb (Increasing metallic radius)

47 The oxide of an element whose electronic configuration is $1s^2, 2s^2, 2p^6, 3s^1$ is **[KCET]**
(a) amphoteric (b) basic
(c) acidic (d) neutral

48 The first ionisation energies of the elements of the first transition series (Ti ⟶ Cu) **[Manipal]**
(a) increase as the atomic number increases
(b) decrease as the atomic number increases
(c) do not show any change as the addition of electrons takes place in the inner $(n-1)d$-orbitals
(d) increase from Ti to Mn and then decrease from Mn to Cu

49 Amongst the elements with following electronic configurations, which one of them may have the highest ionisation energy? **[CBSE AIPMT]**
(a) $[Ne]\,3s^2, 3p^3$ (b) $[Ne]\,3s^2, 3p^2$
(c) $[Ar]\,3d^{10}, 4s^2, 4p^3$ (d) $[Ne]\,3s^2, 3p^1$

50 It is believed that atoms combine with each other such that the outermost shell acquires a stable configuration of 8 electrons. If stability were attained with 6 electrons rather than 8, what would be the formula of the stable fluoride ion? **[DUMET]**
(a) F^- (b) F^+ (c) F^{2+} (d) F^{3+}

2008

51 The correct order of decreasing second ionisation enthalpy of Ti(22), V(23), Cr(24) and Mn(25) is **[CBSE AIPMT]**
(a) Cr > Mn > V > Ti (b) V > Mn > Cr > Ti
(c) Mn > Cr > Ti > V (d) Ti > V > Cr > Mn

52 **Assertion** (A) The ionic size of $Mg^{2+} > Al^{3+}$.
Reason (R) In isoelectronic species, greater the nuclear charge, less is the size. **[AIIMS]**
(a) Both A and R are correct and R is the correct explanation of A
(b) Both A and R are correct but R is not the correct explanation of A
(c) A is correct but R is incorrect
(d) Both A and R are incorrect

53 Diagonal relationship is not shown by **[BHU]**
(a) Li and Mg (b) Be and Al
(c) B and Si (d) C and P

54 Which two elements in the periodic table, would you expect to combine in the most violent fashion? **[Kerala CEE]**
(a) H and O (b) Cl and F
(c) Mg and N (d) P and O
(e) Cs and F

55 In the graph given below, the one which represents an alkali metal with the higher atomic number is **[Kerala CEE]**

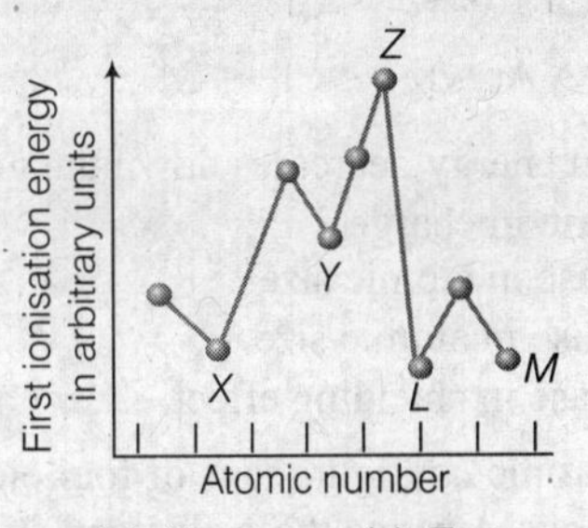

(a) X (b) Y (c) Z (d) L
(e) M

56 The atomic numbers of vanadium (V), chromium (Cr), manganese (Mn) and iron (Fe) are respectively 23, 24, 25 and 26. Which one of these may be expected to have the highest second ionisation enthalpy? **[RPMT]**
(a) V (b) Cr (c) Mn (d) Fe

57 Match Column I with Column II and select the correct answer using the codes given below. **[Punjab PMET]**

	Column I (Successive IE)			**Column II** (Elements)	
	IE_1	IE_2	IE_3 (kJ mol^{-1})		
A.	1312	—	—	1.	H
B.	520	7297	11810	2.	Li
C.	900	1758	14810	3.	Be
D.	800	2428	3660	4.	B

Codes

	A	B	C	D		A	B	C	D
(a)	2	1	4	3	(b)	3	4	2	1
(c)	4	3	1	2	(d)	1	2	3	4

58 Which one of the following ions has the highest value of ionic radius? **[DUMET]**
(a) O^{2-} (b) B^{3+} (c) Li^+ (d) F^-

59 Which metal has a greater tendency to form metal oxide? **[KCET]**
(a) Cr (b) Fe
(c) Al (d) Ca

60 The elements X, Y and Z form oxides which are acidic, basic and amphoteric respectively. The correct order of their electronegativity is **[EAMCET]**
(a) $X > Y > Z$ (b) $Z > Y > X$
(c) $X > Z > Y$ (d) $Y > X > Z$

61 Increase in atomic size down the group is due to **[JCECE]**
(a) increase in number of electrons
(b) increase in number of protons and neutrons
(c) increase in number of protons
(d) increase in number of protons, neutrons and electrons

2007

62 Identify the correct order of the size of the following **[CBSE AIPMT]**
(a) $Ca^{2+} < K^+ < Ar < S^{2-} < Cl^-$
(b) $Ca^{2+} < K^+ < Ar < Cl^- < S^{2-}$
(c) $Ar < Ca^{2+} < K^+ < Cl^- < S^{2-}$
(d) $Ca^{2+} < Ar < K^+ < Cl^- < S^{2-}$

63 Ionisation energy decreases down the group due to **[UP CPMT]**
(a) increase in charge
(b) increase in atomic size
(c) decrease in atomic size
(d) decrease in shielding effect

64 The electronic configurations of four elements are given below. Arrange these elements in the correct order of the magnitude (without sign) of their electron affinity.
I. $2s^2, 2p^5$ II. $3s^2, 3p^5$
III. $2s^2, 2p^4$ IV. $3s^2, 3p^4$
Select the correct answer using the codes given below : **[Kerala CEE]**
(a) I < II < III < IV
(b) II < I < IV < III
(c) I < III < IV < II
(d) III < IV < II < I
(e) III < IV < I < II

65 Which of the following order is wrong? **[Punjab PMET]**
(a) $NH_3 < PH_3 < AsH_3$ — Acidic
(b) Li < Be < B < C — First IP
(c) $Al_2O_3 < MgO < Na_2O < K_2O$ — Basic
(d) $Li^+ < Na^+ < K^+ < Cs^+$ — Ionic radius

66 Which of the following species has the highest electron affinity? **[AMU]**
(a) F (b) O (c) O^- (d) Na^+

2006

67 Which is chemically most active non-metal? **[Manipal]**
(a) S (b) O_2
(c) F_2 (d) N_2

68 Among the following transition elements, pick out the element/elements with highest second ionisation energy.
I. V (atomic number = 23)
II. Cr (atomic number = 24)
III. Mn (atomic number = 25)
IV. Cu (atomic number = 29)
V. Zn (atomic number = 30) **[Kerala CEE]**
(a) I and III (b) II and IV
(c) II and V (d) Only IV
(e) Only III

69 The value of electron gain enthalpy of Kr is **[J&KCET]**
(a) -83 kJ mol^{-1} (b) 96 kJ mol^{-1}
(c) -349 kJ mol^{-1} (d) -60 kJ mol^{-1}

70 Pauling's equation for determining the electronegativity of an element is
[X_A, X_B = electronegativity values of elements A and B
Δ represents polarity of A—B bond] **[J&K CET]**
(a) $X_A - X_B = 0.208\sqrt{\Delta}$ (b) $X_A + X_B = 0.208\sqrt{\Delta}$
(c) $X_A - X_B = 0.208\Delta^2$ (d) $X_A - X_B = \sqrt{\Delta}$

71 Atomic radii of F and Ne (in Å) are given by **[BCECE]**
(a) 0.72, 0.71 (b) 0.72, 1.6
(c) 1.6, 1.58 (d) 0.71, 0.72

72 Electron affinity is positive, when **[BCECE]**
(a) O changes into O^-
(b) O^- changes into O^{2-}
(c) O changes into O^+
(d) electron affinity is always negative

2005

73 **Assertion** (A) First ionisation energy for nitrogen is lower than that of oxygen.
Reason (R) Across a period, effective nuclear charge decreases. **[AIIMS]**
(a) Both A and R are correct and R is the correct explanation of A
(b) Both A and R are correct but R is not the correct explanation of A
(c) A is correct but R is incorrect
(d) Both A and R are incorrect

74 Among 3rd row elements, atomic size is maximum for **[MHT CET]**
(a) sodium (b) argon
(c) magnesium (d) chlorine

75 Which of the following element is a metalloid? **[MP PMT]**
(a) Bi (b) Sn (c) Sb (d) C

76 Identify the correct order in which the ionic radius of the following ions increases **[EAMCET]**
I. F^- II. Na^+ III. N^{3-}
(a) III, I and II (b) I, II and III
(c) II, III and I (d) II, I and III

Answers

1 (a)	2 (b)	3 (d)	4 (a)	5 (c)	6 (b)	7 (a)	8 (a)	9 (c)	10 (c)
11 (a)	12 (c)	13 (c)	14 (a)	15 (b)	16 (d)	17 (b)	18 (b)	19 (d)	20 (a)
21 (a)	22 (a)	23 (b)	24 (a)	25 (a)	26 (a)	27 (e)	28 (a)	29 (a)	30 (a)
31 (d)	32 (c)	33 (c)	34 (c)	35 (c)	36 (c)	37 (a)	38 (d)	39 (c)	40 (b)
41 (c)	42 (a)	43 (a)	44 (d)	45 (b)	46 (b)	47 (b)	48 (a)	49 (a)	50 (b)
51 (a)	52 (a)	53 (d)	54 (e)	55 (e)	56 (b)	57 (d)	58 (a)	59 (d)	60 (c)
61 (a)	62 (b)	63 (b)	64 (e)	65 (b)	66 (a)	67 (c)	68 (b)	69 (b)	70 (a)
71 (b)	72 (b)	73 (d)	74 (b)	75 (c)	76 (d)				

Explanations

1 (*a*) The increasing nuclear charge outweighs the shielding effect across a period. As a result, the outermost electrons are held more firmly. Hence, ionisation enthalpy (IE) increases across a period as:

Li < B < Be < C< O < N < F < Ne

Exceptions

(i) IE of boron (B) is less than IE of beryllium (Be). It is because of the presence of fully-filled 2*s*-orbitals in Be.

(ii) IE of oxygen (O) is less than that of nitrogen (N). It is because of the presence of half-filled *p*-orbitals in N which provides extra stability.

2 (*b*) Electronegativity decreases down the group and increases on moving from left to right in a period. Thus, Li is more electronegative than Na, and F is more electronegative than Cl and Br. Br is less electronegative than Cl because of its larger size. Also, lesser be the electronegativity of metal element and more is the electronegativity of halogen atom, then more will be the electronegativity difference of a given species.

Thus, Na and F shows the maximum electonegativity difference option (b) correct.

3 (*d*) Metal oxides are basic, non-metal oxides are acidic while semi-metal oxides are amphoteric in nature. Thus, the basic character of oxides decreases across the periods and increases down the groups.

The correct match of oxide with its property are as follows:

Na_2O-Basic

Al_2O_3-Amphoteric

N_2O-Neutral

Cl_2O_7-Acidic

Thus, option (d) is correct.

4 (*a*) As the size of the halogen atom increases from F to I, H—X bond length in halogen acids also increases from H—F to H—I as shown below. HF < HCl < HBr < HI. The increase in HX bond length decreases the strength of HX bond from HF to HI (HF > HCl > HBr > HI).

Due to successive decrease in the strength of HX bonds, bond dissociation enthalpy decreases from HF to HI.

HX :	HF	>	HCl	>	HBr	>	HI
Bond dissociation enthalpy (kJ/mol)	574.0		432		362.5		294.6

5 (*c*) C^{4-}, N^{3-} and O^{2-} are isoelectronic species. The ionic radius of isoelectronic species decreases with increase in nuclear charge. Hence, the order of ionic radius is

species : $C^{4-} > N^{3-} > O^{2-}$

ionic radii (Å) : 2.60 > 1.71 > 1.40

6 (*b*) Basic strength of the oxides of alkaline earth metals increases from BeO to BaO. Infact, BeO is amphoteric while all other oxides are basic. It is because all the alkaline earth metals are ionic in nature but BeO in addition to ionic character shows some covalent character also. Thus, BeO being amphoteric in nature behaves both as an acid and base.

$\underbrace{\text{MgO}}_{\text{Weak base}} \quad \underbrace{\text{CaO, SrO, BaO}}_{\text{Strong base}}$

7 (*a*) With progressive increase in the size of alkali metal ions, the stability of superoxides increases because the size of superoxide ion is large and large cation can be stabilised more by large anion. Therefore, the order of stability is $KO_2 < RbO_2 < CsO_2$.

8 (*a*) As the size increases, bond dissociation enthalpy becomes lower. Also, as the size of atoms get smaller, ion pairs on the two atoms get close enough together to experience repulsion. In case of F_2, this repulsion is bigger and bond becomes weaker.

Hence, correct order of bond dissociation enthalpy of halogen molecule is $Cl_2 > Br_2 > F_2 > I_2$.

9 (*c*) $Ca^{2+} < K^+ < Ar$.

Ar, K^+ and Ca^{2+} are isoelectronic i.e. with same number of electrons, 18. For isoelectronic species, ionic radii decreases with increase in effective (relative) positive charge. Also Ar, K and Ca belong to the same period (3rd period).

10 (*c*) Since, the internuclear distance between the atoms held by van der Waals' forces are larger than that between covalently bonded or metallic bonded atoms, van der Waals' radius is larger than metallic and covalent radius. In a covalent bond, the electron pairs are strongly attracted by the nuclei of two atoms due to which covalent radii is smaller than metallic radii. The correct order is van der Waals' radius > metallic radius > covalent radius.

11 (*a*) Option (a) is correct.

(a) $H^- > H > H^+$

It is known that radius of a cation is always smaller than that of a neutral atom because it has fewer electrons while its nuclear charge remains the same. Whereas, the radius of anion is always greater than neutral atom due to decrease in effective nuclear charge.

Hence, the given order is correct.

(b) $Na^+ > F^- > O^{2-}$

The given species are isoelectronic as they contain same number of electrons. For isoelectronic species,

$$\text{ionic radius} \propto \frac{1}{\text{atomic number}}$$

Ion	—	Na^+	F^-	O^{2-}
Atomic number	—	11	9	8

Hence, the correct order of ionic radius is

$$O^{2-} > F^- > Na^+$$

(c) Similarly, the correct option is

$$O^{2-} > F^- > Na^+.$$

(d)

Ion —	Al^{3+}	Mg^{2+}	N^{3-}
Atomic number —	13	12	7

Hence, the correct order is

$N^{3-} > Mg^{2+} > Al^{3+}$.

12 (*c*) Ionisation enthalpy increases on moving from left to right in a period and decreases on moving down in a group. Thus, order of ionisation enthalpy is Be > Mg > Na > K.

13 (*c*) Group 16 elements are O, S, Se, Te. Due to inert pair effect, stability of + 4, + 6 oxidation state decreases on moving down the group. Hence, Te^{4+} is more stable than Te^{6+}. Hence, TeO_2 will act as an oxidising agent and not as reducing agent.

14 (*a*) In a period, on moving from left to right along the same period, acidic nature of oxides increases.

Hence, the correct order of acidic strength is $Cl_2O_7 > SO_2 > P_4O_{10}$.

15 (*b*) Since, Ca^{2+}, K^+, S^{2-} have same number of electrons. so they are isoelectronic ions. It is know that the ion having greater number of protons will be smallest in size. Thus, the increasing order of ionic radii is

$$Ca^{2+} < K^+ < S^{2-}$$

16 (*d*) On moving down in a group, first ionisation enthalpy decreases. Therefore, order of first ionisation enthalpy for group 13 elements is B > Al > Ga > Tl > In.

17 (*b*)

A	*B*	*C*
Amphoteric	Basic	Acidic

On moving from left to right along the same period, acidic nature of oxide increases. Basically, basic nature of oxides changes from amphoteric to acidic on moving along a period. Hence, the correct order of the atomic numbers of these elements is

C > *A* > *B*

18 (*b*) For isoelectronic species,

$$\text{size} \propto \frac{1}{\text{atomic number}}$$

Thus, the correct order will be

$${}_8O^{2-} >{}_9F^- >{}_{11}Na^+ >{}_{12}Mg^{2+}$$

19 (*d*) Na (11) = $1s^2, 2s^2, 2p^6, 3s^1$

It readily gives one electron to attain stability, thus, value of 1st IE is less.

$$Na^+ = 1s^2, 2s^2, 2p^6$$

To form Na^{2+} ion, electron is to be isolated from a stable arrangement for which IE is very high.

Hence, to form Na^{2+} ion, second IE is extremely high.

20 (*a*) Electron affinity is the amount of energy given out when an electron is added to an isolated gaseous atom. Its value depends on the electronic configuration of valence shell.

On writing and comparing the electronic configuration of given elements, the element for which the electron affinity value is closer to Be can be obtained.

Be (4) = $1s^2, 2s^2$ He (2) = $1s^2$

B (5) = $1s^2, 2s^2, 2p^1$ Li (3) = $1s^2, 2s^1$

Na (11) = $1s^2, 2s^2, 2p^6, 3s^1$

∵ Electronic configuration of valence shell of Be and He is same.

∴ Electron affinity of Be is similar to that of He.

21 (*a*) $\text{Ionisation potential} \propto \frac{1}{\text{atomic size}}$

The atomic size increases down the group but decreases across a period.

∴ The correct order of decreasing first ionisation potential is

$$Ca > K > Rb > Cs.$$

22 (*a*) Atomic radius of the elements decreases across a period from left to right due to increase in effective nuclear charge. On moving down a group, since number of shells increases, so atomic radius also increases.

Amongst isoelectronic species, ionic radius increases with increase in negative charge and decrease in positive charge.

Hence, statement (a) is incorrect and all other statements are correct.

23 (*b*) As one moves from top to bottom in a group, acidic strength of hydrides increases.

Therefore, order of acidic strength of hydrides of VA and VII A group elements is

$$NH_3 < PH_3 < AsH_3 < SbH_3$$

$$HF < HCl < HBr < HI$$

According to option (b), as we move from top to bottom in a group, acidic nature (K_a) increases.

Therefore, pK_a decreases. Thus, order of pK_a values of hydrides of VI A group elements is

$$H_2O > H_2S > H_2Se > H_2Te$$

Hence, the arrangement given in option (b) is incorrect.

According to option (d), on moving from top to bottom, oxidising power of oxides increases.

Thus, order of oxidising power of oxides of IVA group elements is

$$CO_2 < SiO_2 < SnO_2 < PbO_2$$

24 (*a*) Electron affinity value of Cl is higher than that of F as Cl belongs to third period (have larger size) while F belongs to second period (have small size).

In Cl, electron-electron repulsion forces are weaker than that of F and hence, the extra electron which is to be added experiences less electronic repulsions.

25 (*a*) As *s*-electrons are more strongly attracted by nucleus, hence they are difficult to remove. Therefore, both (A) and (R) are correct and Reason is the correct explanation of Assertion.

26 (*a*)

Species	Atomic number	Number of electrons
Ca^{2+}	20	20 − 2 = 18
Cl^-	17	17 + 1 = 18
S^{2-}	16	16 + 2 = 18

In case of isoelectronic species, the cation with greater positive charge will have smaller radius and anion with greater negative charge will have larger radius.

Thus, order of radius will be

$$Ca^{2+} < Cl^- < S^{2-}$$

27 (*e*) H—H bond enthalpy is the highest. The enthalpy change accompanying the breaking of one mole of covalent bonds of gaseous covalent compound to give products in the gaseous phase is called the bond dissociation enthalpy.

e.g.
$H_2(g) \longrightarrow 2H(g);$

$\Delta_{H-H} H^\circ = 435.0 \text{ kJ mol}^{-1}$

$F_2(g) \longrightarrow 2F(g);$

$\Delta_{F-F} H^\circ = 158.8 \text{ kJ mol}^{-1}$

$Cl_2(g) \longrightarrow 2Cl(g);$

$\Delta_{Cl-Cl} H^\circ = 242.6 \text{ kJ mol}^{-1}$

$Br_2(g) \longrightarrow 2Br(g);$

$\Delta_{Br-Br} H^\circ = 193.0 \text{ kJ mol}^{-1}$

$I_2(g) \longrightarrow 2I(g);$

$\Delta_{I-I} H^\circ = 151.0 \text{ kJ mol}^{-1}$

28 (*a*) On moving downward in a group, density increases but the density of K is somewhat lesser than that of Na. Due to abnormal increase in size of K atom.

Thus, the order of density is Li < K < Na < Rb < Cs.

Densities are
Li – 0.53 g/cc, Na – 0.97 g/cc,
K – 0.86 g/cc, Rb – 1.53 g/cc and
Cs – 1.90 g/cc.

29 (*a*) Electronegativity increases along a period and decreases in a group. Thus, the order is II > III > I > IV.
Electronegativity of O = 3.5,
N = 3.0, Be = 1.5, Mg = 1.2

30 (*a*) On moving down the group, atomic radius increases, while it decreases on moving from left to right. However, for isoelectronic species, the atomic radius decreases with increase in atomic number. Further, larger the charge on the anion, greater is the radius.

Hence, on considering all the factors, Se^{2-} would possesses largest ionic radius among the given options.

31 (*d*) For isoelectronic species, the ionic radius decreases with increase in atomic number.

Thus, the order would be

$$\underset{(16)}{S^{2-}} > \underset{(17)}{Cl^-} > \underset{(19)}{K^+} > \underset{(20)}{Ca^{2+}}$$

32 (*c*) In general, electron affinity of group 17 elements is higher (or more negative) than that of group 16 elements. However, electron affinity of the elements of third period is higher than that of the elements of second period. Thus, on this basis, the correct order would be

$$\text{2nd period} \longleftarrow \underbrace{\underset{}{O} < \overset{\text{3rd period}}{\uparrow S}}_{\text{Group 16}} < \underbrace{\overset{\text{2nd period}}{\uparrow F} < \overset{\text{3rd period}}{\uparrow Cl}}_{\text{Group 17}}$$

33 (*c*) F^- and O^{2-} ions have stable electronic configuration, thus they will not accept further electrons, while O needs electrons to achieve stable arrangement, thus it has highest electron affinity. Further, Na is a metal, thus it does not have any electron affinity.

34 (*c*) On moving along a period from left to right in the periodic table, electronegativity increases (due to decrease in size). While on moving downward in a group, electronegativity decreases.
Thus, the correct order of electronegativity is

$$\underset{(1.8)}{Si} < \underset{(2.1)}{P} < \underset{(2.5)}{C} < \underset{(3.0)}{N}$$

35 (*c*) Ionisation energy is the energy required to remove an electron from outer shell of an atom. Since, on moving from left to right in a period, size decreases, thus larger amount of energy is required to remove an electron, i.e. ionisation energy increases.

Although, the size of O-atom is smaller as compared to that of N but the ionisation energy of N is higher.

This is because in case of N, the electron is to be removed from stable half-filled $2p^3$-orbital. Thus, the order of ionisation energy is O < N < F or N > O < F.

36 (*c*) On moving along a period, the tendency to lose electrons decreases and thus, the metallic character decreases. Since, the oxides of non-metals are acidic, it can be said that along a period from left to right, basic character decreases while on moving downward, basic character increases due to increase in metallic character.

37 (*a*) Lower the value of ionisation potential, higher will be the ease of formation of the cation.

Ionisation enthalpy (IE) The minimum amount of energy required to remove an electron from an isolated gaseous atom (X) in its ground state is called the ionisation enthalpy.

$$X(g) \longrightarrow X^+(g) + e^-, \Delta_i H = +\text{ve}$$

Hence, lower value of ionisation enthalpy favours the formation of cation.

38 (*d*) The size of the cation is always smaller than that of its parent atom and size of the anion is always larger than that of its parent atom.

∴ Size of the cation

$$\propto \frac{1}{\text{magnitude of positive charge}}$$

Size of the anion ∝ magnitude of negative charge

Hence, the correct order of the size is $I^- > I > I^+$.

39 (*c*) The electronic configuration of the given elements is as follows:

${}_{12}Mg = [Ne]\, 3s^2$ ${}_{5}B = [He]\, 2s^2, 2p^1$

${}_{4}Be = [He]\, 2s^2$ ${}_{13}Al = [Ne]\, 3s^2, 3p^1$

From the electronic configuration, it is clear that third ionisation energy of Mg and Be is higher than that of Al and B. In them, the third electron has to be removed from the stable inert gas configuration.

Between Mg and Be, third IE of Be is high because of its smaller size than Mg as both lie in the same group.

40 (*b*) Na belongs to I A group and Mg belongs to II A group. On moving from left to right in a period, first ionisation energy increases. Thus, IE of Mg is greater than the IE of Na.

IE order–Mg > Na

41 (*c*) The property of attracting electrons by an atom of a molecule is called electronegativity. However, electron affinity is the amount of energy liberated when an electron is added to an isolated gaseous atom.

42 (*a*) Generally, electron affinity increases on moving from left to right in a period and decreases on moving down in a group. Electron affinities of second period elements (such as N, O) are less negative as compared to corresponding third period element. This is because of the small atomic size of second period elements. Hence, the correct order of electron affinities is N < O < S < Cl.

43 (*a*) Electronic configuration of Al and Ga are written as

$$_{13}Al = [Ne]\, 3s^2, 3p^1$$
$$_{31}Ga = [Ar]\, 3d^{10}, 4s^2, 4p^1$$

Electronic configuration of Ga exhibits 10 electrons in *d*-orbitals which do not screen the nucleus effectively because of the diffused shape of *d*-orbitals. Consequently, the electrons are attracted by a greater force towards nucleus. Hence, the atomic radius of Ga decreases or Ga has almost same radius as that of Al.

44 (*d*) Generally, ionisation potential increases, as we move from left to right in a period. However, the ionisation potential of II A group elements is higher than that of the III A group elements. This is because of the fully-filled *s*-orbitals in II A group elements.

Hence, the correct order of ionisation potential is

$$Na < Al < Mg < Si$$

45 (*b*) For isoelectronic species,

$$\text{atomic size} \propto \frac{1}{\text{atomic number}}$$

Thus, the correct order would be

$$\underset{(13)}{Al^{3+}} < \underset{(11)}{Na^{+}} < \underset{(9)}{F^{-}} < \underset{(8)}{O^{2-}}$$

46 (*b*) IE increases on moving from left to right but, the order of IE_1 of B, C, O and N is as

$$B < C < O < N$$

IE_1 of N ($1s^2, 2s^2, 2p^3$) is more than that of O ($1s^2, 2s^2, 2p^4$) due to the presence of extra stable half-filled 2*p*-subshell of N.

Rest all arrangements are correct.

47 (*b*) The given element is sodium, which is an alkali metal and alkali metal oxides are strongly basic.

48 (*a*) The first ionisation energies of the elements of 3*d*-transition series increases as the atomic number increases. The increasing ionisation enthalpies are due to increased nuclear charge with increase in atomic number that reduces the size of the atom making the removal of outer electron difficult.

49 (*a*) Elements having electronic configurations [Ne] $3s^2, 3p^3$ and [Ar] $3d^{10} 4s^2, 4p^3$ have the higher ionisation energy than other given configurations because they contain exactly half-filled *p*-orbitals and these elements lie in the same group.

Ionisation energy decreases on moving down a group that's why, [Ne] $3s^2, 3p^3$ has higher ionisation energy than [Ar] $3d^{10} 4s^2, 4p^3$.

50 (*b*) Number of valence electrons in F are 7. Thus, in order to have 6 valence electrons, it must lose one electron and thus it would have the formula F^+.

51 (*a*) The second ionisation energies of the first transition series increase almost regularly with increase in atomic number. However, the value for Cr is sufficiently higher than those of its neighbour, i.e. Mn. This is due to stable configuration of Cr^+ ($3d^5$ exactly half-filled). Hence, the correct order of decreasing second ionisation enthalpy is

$$Cr > Mn > V > Ti$$

52 (*a*) The ionic size of Mg^{2+} is larger than Al^{3+}. Both the species are isoelectronic and in case of isoelectronic species as nuclear charge increases, attractive force between electron of valence shell and nucleus increases which results in decrease in ionic size.

Hence, both (A) and (R) are correct and (R) is the correct explanation of (A).

53 (*d*) Only metals of 2nd period and group 1, 2, 13 and 14 show diagonal relationship. So, C and P don't show diagonal relationship.

Group 1	Group 2	Group 13	Group 14
Li	Be	B	C
Na	Mg	Al	Si

(Diagonal relationships: Li → Mg, Be → Al, B → Si)

54 (*e*) There is a large difference between the electronegativities of Cs and F, thus forces of attraction will be strongest between them. Hence, they react violently.

55 (*e*) From the graph, it is clear that the atomic number is highest for metal *M* and lowest for metal *X*.

56 (*b*)
$$V(Z = 23) = [Ar]\, 3d^3, 4s^2$$
$$Cr(Z = 24) = [Ar]\, 3d^5, 4s^1$$
$$Mn(Z = 25) = [Ar]\, 3d^5, 4s^2$$
$$Fe(Z = 26) = [Ar]\, 3d^6, 4s^2$$

Since, Cr^+ has stable configuration ($3d^5$, exactly half- filled), thus it has the highest second ionisation enthalpy.

57 (*d*) Successive ionisation energies of the given elements are as follows:

	Electronic configuration	IE_1	IE_2	IE_3
H	$1s^1$	1312.0	—	—
Li	$1s^2, 2s^1$	520	7297	11810
Be	$1s^2, 2s^2$	900	1758	14810
B	$1s^2, 2s^2, 2p^1$	800	2428	3660

Thus, the correct option is $A \rightarrow 1, B \rightarrow 2, C \rightarrow 3, D \rightarrow 4$

58 (*a*) O^{2-} has the highest value of ionic radius and this can be explained on the basis of Z/e (nuclear charge/ number of electrons) ratio. When Z/e ratio increases, the size decreases and when *vice-versa* $\frac{Z}{e} \propto \frac{1}{r}$.

59 (*d*) Greater the stability of oxide, greater is the ease of its formation. Generally, ionic oxides are more stable than covalent oxides and among the given metals, only Ca forms ionic oxide. Hence, Ca has greater tendency to form metal oxide.

60 (*c*) Electronegativity $\propto$ Non-metallic character $\propto \frac{1}{\text{metallic character}}$

∵ The element *X* forms acidic oxide. So, it is a non-metal, while the element *Y* forms basic oxide, so *Y* is a metal. Thus, the order of their electronegativity is

$$X > Z > Y$$

61 (*a*) In a given group, atomic size increases due to addition of extra shell which outweighs the effect of increased nuclear charge. Number of shells increases with addition of extra electrons.

Hence, increase in atomic size down the group is due to increase in number of electrons.

62 (*b*) For isoelectronic species,

$$\text{atomic size} \propto \frac{1}{\text{atomic number}}$$

Since, all the given species have 18 electrons, thus these are isoelectronic. Hence, the correct order is,

$$\underset{(20)}{Ca^{2+}} < \underset{(19)}{K^+} < \underset{(18)}{Ar} < \underset{(17)}{Cl^-} < \underset{(16)}{S^{2-}}$$

63 (*b*) Ionisation energy decreases in a group as the atomic number increases. It is based on the fact that on moving down a group, the size of atom increases and the outer electrons become farther away from the nucleus. Thus, the force of attraction between electrons and nucleus decreases and hence ionisation energy decreases with increase in atomic size.

64 (*e*) In general, electron affinity of elements of third period is more negative than that of second period because elements of second period possesses smaller size due to which the incoming electron experiences electronic repulsions, thus releases less energy during addition of electron.

Further, electron affinity increases along a period and decreases down the group. Thus, the increasing order of electron affinity would be

$$\underset{\text{O (III)}}{2s^2, 2p^4} < \underset{\text{S (IV)}}{3s^2, 3p^4} < \underset{\text{F (I)}}{2s^2, 2p^5} < \underset{\text{Cl (II)}}{3s^2, 3p^5}$$

65 (*b*) Li, Be, B and C are present in IInd period. In a period from left to right, ionisation potential increases. But in case of Be and B, Be has higher IP than B due to stable configuration of Be. $_4Be = 1s^2, 2s^2$

[↿⇂] $1s^2$ [↿⇂] $2s^2$ Stable configuration

$_5B = 1s^2, 2s^2, 2p^1$

[↿⇂] $1s^2$ [↿⇂] $2s^2$ [↿| |] $2p^1$

So, the correct order of IP of given elements is

$$Li < B < Be < C.$$

Rest of the options are correct.

66 (*a*) Higher the energy released in the process of accepting an extra electron, the higher will be the electron affinity. Higher the value of electron affinity of an atom, the more is its tendency to change into anion. Halogens have more tendency to change into anion. Therefore, halogens have the highest electron affinity.
Thus, F has the highest electron affinity.

67 (*c*) F_2 is most reactive due to highest electronegativity, low bond dissociation energy and high heat of hydration of F^- ion.

68 (*b*) The second ionisation energy is higher in case of Cr and Cu due to extra stability of half-filled and completely filled set of *d*-orbitals in Cr and Cu respectively.

$$V^+ (Z = 23) = [Ar]\, 3d^3, 4s^1$$

$$Cr^+ (Z = 24) = [Ar]\, 3d^5, 4s^0$$

$$Mn^+ (Z = 25) = [Ar]\, 3d^5, 4s^1$$

$$Cu^+ (Z = 29) = [Ar]\, 3d^{10}, 4s^0$$

$$Zn^+ (Z = 30) = [Ar]\, 3d^{10}, 4s^1$$

69 (*b*) The value of electron gain enthalpy of Kr is +96 KJ mol^{-1}. This is because electron gain enthalpies of noble gases are positive as they have completely filled shells and an additional electron has to be added to the next higher shell.

70 (*a*) Pauling's equation for determining the electronegativity of an element is

$$X_A - X_B = 0.208\sqrt{\Delta}$$

where, X_A, X_B = Electronegativity values of element *A* and *B*

Δ = polarity of *A*—*B* bond

71 (*b*) Atomic radius decreases in a period from left to right, hence fluorine has very less atomic radius (covalent atomic radius = 0.72 Å).

But inert gases (like Ne) are monoatomic gases, hence their covalent atomic radius cannot be found. In fact, their calculated atomic radius is the van der Waals' radius, which is found almost double to covalent radius, hence the van der Waals' radius of neon (Ne) is about 1.60 Å.

72 (*b*) When O^- changes into O^{2-}, change is endothermic. The reason is that O^- repels the incoming electron due to similar charge and small size. Hence, it needs energy to accept the electron.

Thus, electron affinity is positive.

73 (*d*) In a period from left to right, effective nuclear charge increases and size decreases, as a result ionisation energy increases. But elements of II A and VA group on the account of their half-filled and completely filled orbitals have high IE than the elements of III A and VI A group, respectively.

74 (*b*) In a period, atomic size decreases from left to right. As sodium lies at extremely left of 3rd period hence, sodium has the largest atomic size among 3rd row elements. But it is also known that noble gases have van der Waals' radius which is larger than covalent and metallic radius.

Thus, Ar (argon) being a noble gas has maximum atomic size.

75 (*c*) Ge, As, Sb and Te are metalloids. Bismuth (Bi) and tin (Sn) are metals, while carbon (C) is a non-metal.

76 (*d*) These are all isoelectronic species. Among isoelectronic species, size increases with decrease in nuclear charge.

Hence, the correct order of size is

$$\underset{\text{II}}{Na^+} < \underset{\text{I}}{F^-} < \underset{\text{III}}{N^{3-}}$$

04

Chemical Bonding and Molecular Structures

Quick Review

Chemical bond can be defined as the force of attraction which holds various constituents together in different chemical species.

According to **Kossel-Lewis approach**, atoms, molecules or ions combine together, i.e. make chemical bond to complete their octet in their outermost shell or to gain stability. The chemical bond can be classified into ionic bond, covalent bond, coordinate bond, metallic bond and hydrogen bond.

Ionic Bond

It is formed as a result of electrostatic force of attraction between an electropositive atom and an electronegative atom due to complete transfer of electrons. To form an ionic bond, the electronegativity difference between two atoms should be ≥ 1.9.

Some important characteristics of ionic compounds are as follows :

(*i*) They are generally crystalline in nature. The constituent ions are arranged in a regular way in their crystal lattices.

(*ii*) They possess high melting and boiling points as they are held by strong electrostatic forces of attraction.

(*iii*) They are hard and brittle in nature.

(*iv*) In solid state, they do not conduct electricity. In molten state or in solution, they are good conductors of electricity due to the presence of free ions in aqueous state.

(*v*) They are soluble in polar solvent and insoluble in non-polar solvent.

(*vi*) The electrovalent bonds are non-rigid and non-directional. Thus, these compounds do not show configurational isomerism, i.e. geometrical and optical isomerism.

(*vii*) Electrovalent compounds show isomorphism (compounds with similar number of valence electrons, i.e. similar configuration of their cation and anion, e.g. NaF and MgO, both have same number of valence electrons in Na^+, F^-, Mg^{2+} and O^{2-}).

(*viii*) They show variable electrovalency. They differ in number of electrons used by an atom during the formation of bond. This occurs due to unstability of core.

Lattice Enthalpy

- It is defined as the energy required to completely separate one mole of a solid ionic compound into gaseous constituents.

(*i*) Charge on ions $\propto$ force of attraction between ions $\propto$ lattice energy

(*ii*) Size of ions (for a single cation *vs* many anions and *vice versa*) $\propto \dfrac{1}{\text{force of attraction between ions}} \propto \dfrac{1}{\text{lattice energy}}$

- The higher the magnitude of lattice energy, the greater is the tendency of the formation of an ionic bond.

Covalent Bond

It is formed by mutual sharing of electrons between the combining atoms of the same or different elements.

Characteristics of covalent compounds are as follows:

(*i*) These compounds are soft and less brittle than ionic compounds.

(*ii*) Covalent compounds have lower melting and boiling points than electrovalent compounds because of weak attractive forces.

(*iii*) Generally, covalent compounds are insoluble or sparingly soluble in polar solvents with few exceptions like H_2O, liquid NH_3 (due to H-bonding).
They are soluble in non-polar solvents like CCl_4, CS_2, benzene, toluene etc.

(*iv*) In solid state or molten state, covalent compounds do not conduct electricity because they do not contain mobile ions/free electrons.

(*v*) Some polar covalent compounds like HCl ionise in water and conduct electricity, e.g. H—Cl bond is polar and it ionises in water to give H^+ and Cl^- ions. Some non-polar covalent compounds (like $AlCl_3$) also ionise in water and conduct electricity.

(*vi*) These compounds undergo molecular reactions in which molecules take part as such. These reactions are slow as compared to ionic reactions.

(*vii*) Covalent molecules are directional in nature. Therefore, many covalent compounds show isomerism.

Coordinate Bond

It is formed by the shared pair of electrons. These are supplied by one atom (donor) and shared by both the atoms.

Characteristics of coordinate compounds are as follows

(*i*) These are usually insoluble in water but soluble in organic solvents.

(*ii*) The melting and boiling points of these compounds are higher than that of pure covalent compounds. They are poor conductors of electricity.

(*iii*) The coordinate bond is rigid and directional, thus coordinate compounds show isomerism.

(*iv*) The compounds containing coordinate bond possess high values of dielectric constant.

Formal Charge

It is based on pure covalent view of bonding in which electrons are shared equally by the atoms. In case of polyatomic molecules, formal charge is defined as the difference between the number of valence electrons in an isolated (free state) atom and the number of electrons assigned to that atom in the Lewis structure. It is an imaginary charge over an atom in a Lewis structure. It is represented as,

$$\text{Formal charge, } F = v - \frac{s}{2} - u$$

where,

v = total number of valence electrons in free atom

s = total number of shared pair of electrons

u = total number of non-bonding [i.e. lone pair of electrons]

Bond Parameters

The various characteristics shown by a bond are called parameters. *These are as follows*

(*i*) **Bond length** is defined as the equilibrium distance between the nuclei of two bonded atoms in a molecule.

$$\text{Bond length} \propto \text{size of atom} \propto \frac{1}{\text{bond multiplicity}}$$

(*ii*) **Bond angle** is defined as the angle between the orbitals containing bonding electron pairs around the central atom in a molecule or ion.

(*iii*) **Bond enthalpy** is defined as the amount of energy required to break one mole of bonds of a particular type between two atoms in a gaseous state.

$$\text{Bond enthalpy} \propto \frac{1}{\text{size of an atom}} \propto \text{bond multiplicity}$$

(*iv*) **Bond order** is given by the number of bonds between the two atoms in a molecule.

$$\text{Bond order} \propto \frac{1}{\text{bond length}} \propto \text{bond enthalpy}$$

Fajan's Rule

It is used to predict whether a chemical bond will be covalent or ionic.

Ionic character	Covalent character
Low charge on cation	High charge on cation
Large size of cation	Small size of cation
Small size of anion	Large size of anion

Dipole Moment

It is defined as the product of magnitude of the charge and the distance between the centres of positive and negative charges.

- Dipole moment (μ) = Charge (q) $\times$ distance between the charges (d).
- It's CGS unit is Debye (D).
- Symmetrical molecules have zero dipole moment.
- A molecule is said to be **polar**, if the net dipole moment is non zero and the other molecules having zero net dipole moment are non-polar.

Percentage ionic character

$$= \frac{\text{actual dipole moment}}{\text{dipole moment of pure ionic bond}} \times 100$$

Resonance

- According to the concept of resonance, whenever a single Lewis structure cannot describe a molecule accurately a number of canonical structures of hybrid are taken which describes the molecule accurately. Greater the resonance, more is the stability.
- Experimentally determined oxygen-oxygen bond lengths in the O_3 molecule are same (128 pm) which is not represented by either structure 'a' or 'b'. Thus, the oxygen-oxygen bond in O_3 molecule are intermediate between a double and a single bond and is represented by resonance hybrid (structure 'c').

121pm 148pm (a) ⟷ 148pm 121pm (b) ≡ 128pm 128pm (c)

VSEPR'S Theory

According to this theory, the shape of a molecule depends upon the number of bond pair and lone pair present around the central atom.

The main postulates of VSEPR theory are as follows :

(*i*) The shape of a molecule depends upon the number of valence shell electron pairs (bonded as well as non-bonded) around the central atom.

(*ii*) The electron pairs surrounding the central atom repel each other because of similar charge.

(*iii*) Pairs of electrons tend to occupy such positions in space where there is minimised repulsion. This results in maximum possible distance between them.

(*iv*) The repulsive interaction between electron pairs decreases in order :

lp-lp repulsion > *lp-bp* repulsion > *bp-bp* repulsion.

Shape of Some Molecules on the Basis of VSEPR Theory

Molecule type	No. of bonding pair	No. of lone pair	Arrangement of electron pairs and geometry of molecule	Shape	Examples
AB_2E	2	1	Trigonal planar	Bent	SO_2, O_3, $SnCl_2$, $PbCl_2$, NO_2^+
AB_3E	3	1	Tetrahedral	Trigonal pyramidal	PH_3, $BiCl_3$ NH_3, PCl_3, $AsCl_3$, XeO_3, ClO_3^-, SO_3^{2-}, $P(CH_3)_3$
AB_2E_2	2	2	Tetrahedral	Bent	H_2S $\bar{N}H_2$ H_2O, OF_2, Cl_2O $Cl_2\dot{O}$, ClO_2^-, $Cl\dot{O}F$, SCl_2
AB_4E	4	1	Trigonal bipyramidal	*see-saw*	SF_4, SCl_4, $TeCl_4$, XeO_2F_2

Molecule type	No. of bonding pair	No. of lone pair	Arrangement of electron pairs and geometry of molecule	Shape	Examples
AB_3E_2	3	2	Trigonal bipyramidal	T-shape	$ClF_3, IF_3, BrF_3, XeOF_2$
AB_5E	5	1	Octahedral	Square pyramidal	IF_5, BrF_5, SbF_5^{2-}
AB_4E_2	4	2	Octahedral	Square planar	XeF_4, ICl_4^-

Valence Bond Theory

This theory explains the bond formation in terms of overlapping of orbitals. *On the basis of overlapping, covalent bonds are of two types:*

(*i*) σ-**bond** formed by head to head overlapping of $s-s$, $s-p$ and $p_z - p_z$ orbitals.

(*ii*) π-**bond** formed by sideways overlapping of $p_y - p_y$ and $p_x - p_x$ orbitals.

Positive or in phase overlap Negative or out of phase overlap

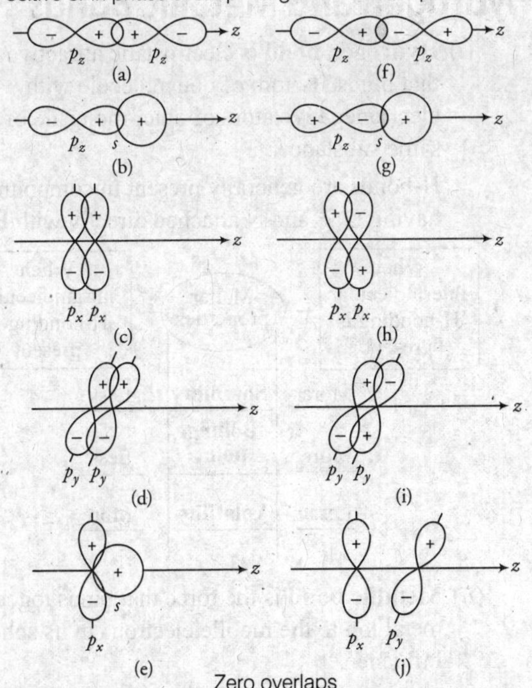

Zero overlaps

- Lateral or sideways overlapping is weaker than head on overlapping.
- Formation of π-bond never occurs alone. It is formed along with a σ bond.

Hybridisation

It is defined as the intermixing of atomic orbitals of same atomic energy and resulting in the formation of new atomic orbitals having identical shape, energy and size.

Hybridisation $= \frac{1}{2}$ [Number of valence electrons + number of monovalent atoms − charge on cation + charge on anion]

Salient Features of Hybridisation

The main features of hybridisation are as follows

(*i*) The number of hybrid orbitals generated is equal to the number of the atomic orbitals that get hybridised.

(*ii*) The hybridised orbitals are of equivalent energy and similar shape.

(*iii*) The hybrid orbitals are more effective in forming stable bonds than the pure atomic orbitals.

(*iv*) These hybrid orbitals are arranged in space in such a direction, so that there is minimum repulsion between electron pairs. This gives a stable arrangement of electrons. Thus, different types of hybridisation show different types the geometry of the molecules.

Important Conditions for Hybridisation

(*i*) The orbitals present in the valence shell of the atom are hybridised.

(*ii*) The orbitals taking part in hybridisation must have equal or only a small difference of energies.

(*iii*) Promotion of electron is not an essential condition prior to hybridisation.

(iv) It is not necessary that only half-filled orbitals participate in hybridisation. In some cases, even filled orbitals of valence or vacant orbitals can take part in hybridisation.

The geometry of a molecule can be determined by its hybridisation which is given in the table.

Number of lone pair	Hybridisation	Geometry	Examples
0	sp	Linear	$BeCl_2$, C_2H_2, BeF_2, CO_2, CS_2
0	sp^2	Trigonal planar	BF_3, $AlCl_3$, BCl_3, C_2H_4, NO_3^-, CO_3^{2-}
1	sp^2	Angular or V-shape	SO_2, O_3
0	sp^3	Tetrahedral	CH_4, ClO_4^-, SiF_4, NH_4^+, SO_4^{2-}
1	sp^3	Pyramidal	NH_3, XeO_3
2	sp^3	V-shape	H_2O, Cl_2O
3	sp^3d	Linear	XeF_2, I_3^-
0	sp^3d	Trigonal bipyramidal	PCl_5, PF_5, $[Fe(CO)_5]$
1	sp^3d	Distorted structure	XeO_2F_2
2	sp^3d	T-shape	ClF_3
0	sp^3d^2	Octahedral	SF_6, UF_6, TeF_6
1	sp^3d^2	Square pyramidal	IF_5
2	sp^3d^2	Square planar	XeF_4
0	sp^3d^3	Pentagonal bipyramidal	IF_7

Note $d_{x^2-y^2}$, orbital is involved in d_{sp^2}, d_{z^2} in sp^3d, $d_{x^2-y^2}$ and d_{z^2} in sp^3d^2 or d^2sp^3 and d_{xy}, d_{yz}, d_{xz} in sp^3d^3 hybridisation.

Molecular Orbital Theory

According to this theory, a molecule is supposed to have orbitals of varying energy levels in the same way as an isolated atom has. These orbitals are known as **molecular orbitals.**

- The molecular orbitals are formed due to the constructive and destructive interactions of atomic orbitals.
- Constructive interactions of orbitals give rise to orbitals of lower energy called **bonding orbitals** or HOMO (highly occupied molecular orbitals) $\sigma = \psi_A + \psi_B$.
- Destructive interactions give rise to orbitals of higher energy called **anti-orbital** or LUMO (lowest unoccupied molecular orbitals) $\sigma^* = \psi_A - \psi_B$.
- The condition of lower energy (bonding molecular orbital) is also called attractive state for electrons while condition of higher energy (anti-bonding molecular orbital) is also called **repulsive state** for electrons.

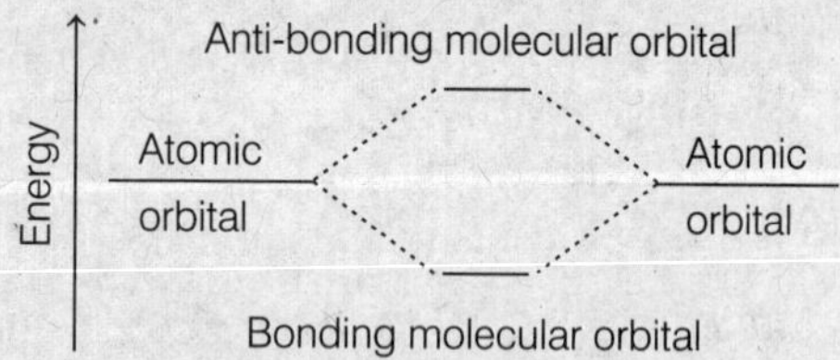

- The energy order of molecular orbitals, for number of electrons ≤ 14

$\sigma 1s, \sigma^* 1s, \sigma 2s, \sigma^* 2s, \pi 2p_x \approx \pi 2p_y, \sigma 2p_z, \pi^* 2p_x \approx \pi^* 2p_y, \sigma^* 2p_z$

for number of electrons > 14

$\sigma 1s, \sigma^* 1s, \sigma 2s, \sigma^* 2s, \sigma 2p_z, \pi 2p_x \approx \pi 2p_y, \pi^* 2p_x \approx \pi^* 2p_y, \sigma^* 2p_z$

- **Bond Order** (BO) $= \dfrac{N_b - N_a}{2}$

where, N_b = number of electrons in bonding molecular orbital.

N_a = number of electrons in anti-bonding molecular orbital.

Hydrogen and Metallic Bonds

(*i*) **Hydrogen bond** is electrostatic attractive force that binds H-atom of one molecule with electronegative atom of other molecule of the same substance.

H-bonds are generally present in compounds having O, F and N attached directly with H.

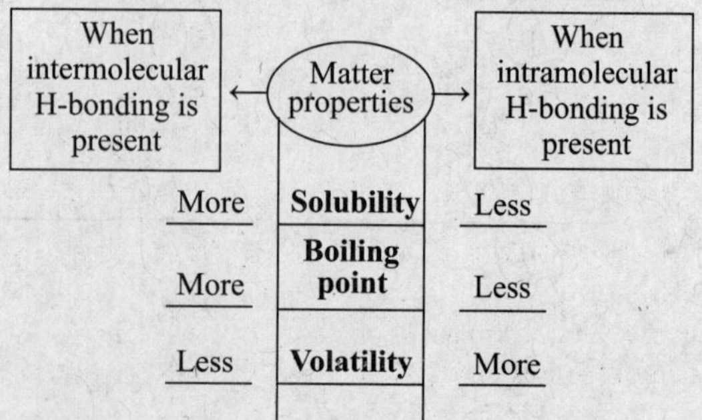

(*ii*) **Metallic bond** is the force that binds together the metal ion to the mobile electrons in its sphere of influence.

Note The metallic bonds are weaker and non-directional in character.

Topical Practice Questions

All the exam questions of this chapter have been divided into five topics as listed below.

Topic 1

Types of Bonds : Electrovalent, Covalent and Coordinate

2019

1 Which of the following has octet around central atom?
(a) PF_5 (b) SF_6 (c) CCl_4 (d) BF_3 [JIPMER]

2015

2 Which of the following species contains equal number of σ and π-bonds? [CBSE AIPMT]
(a) HCO_3^- (b) XeO_4 (c) $(CN)_2$ (d) $CH_2(CN)_2$

2014

3 The type of attractive forces that operate between gaseous HCl and chlorine molecule is [Kerala CEE]
(a) dipole-dipole forces (b) London forces
(c) induced dipole-induced dipole
(d) dipole-induced dipole forces
(e) electrostatic forces

4 Which one of the following exhibits the maximum covalent character? [EAMCET]
(a) $FeCl_2$ (b) $AlCl_3$ (c) $MgCl_2$ (d) $SnCl_2$

5 Covalent compounds have low melting point because
(a) covalent molecules are held by weak van der Waals' force of attraction [KCET]
(b) covalent bond is less exothermic
(c) covalent bond is weaker than ionic bond
(d) covalent molecules have definite shape

2012

6 During the formation of a chemical bond [UP CPMT]
(a) electron-electron repulsion becomes more than the nucleus-electron attraction
(b) energy of the system does not change
(c) energy increases (d) energy decreases

7 Which of the following forms stable coordinate bonds? [KCET]
(a) NH_3, H_2O (b) NH_3, BF_3
(c) NaOH, HCl (d) BF_3, BCl_3

2011

8 Which of the following is not the characteristic of a covalent compound? [KCET]
(a) No definite geometry
(b) Insoluble in polar solvent
(c) Small difference in electronegativity between the combining atoms
(d) Low melting point

2010

9 The compound containing coordinate bond is [AFMC]
(a) SO_3 (b) O_3 (c) H_2SO_4 (d) All of these

10 Which statement is not correct? [BVP]
(a) A sigma bond is weaker than a π-bond
(b) A sigma bond is stronger than a π-bond
(c) A double bond is stronger than a sigma bond
(d) A double bond is shorter than a single bond

11 Benzoic acid contains [UP CPMT]
(a) 15 σ and 2 π-bonds (b) 15 σ and 4 π-bonds
(c) 14 σ and 4 π-bonds (d) 13 σ and 4 π-bonds

12 Which of the following has electrovalent linkage? [MP PMT]
(a) $CaCl_2$ (b) $AlCl_3$ (c) $SiCl_2$ (d) PCl_3

13 The higher lattice energy corresponds to [AMU]
(a) MgO (b) CaO (c) SrO (d) BaO

14 Which of the following substance has the highest melting point? [VMMC]
(a) BaO (b) MgO (c) KCl (d) NaCl

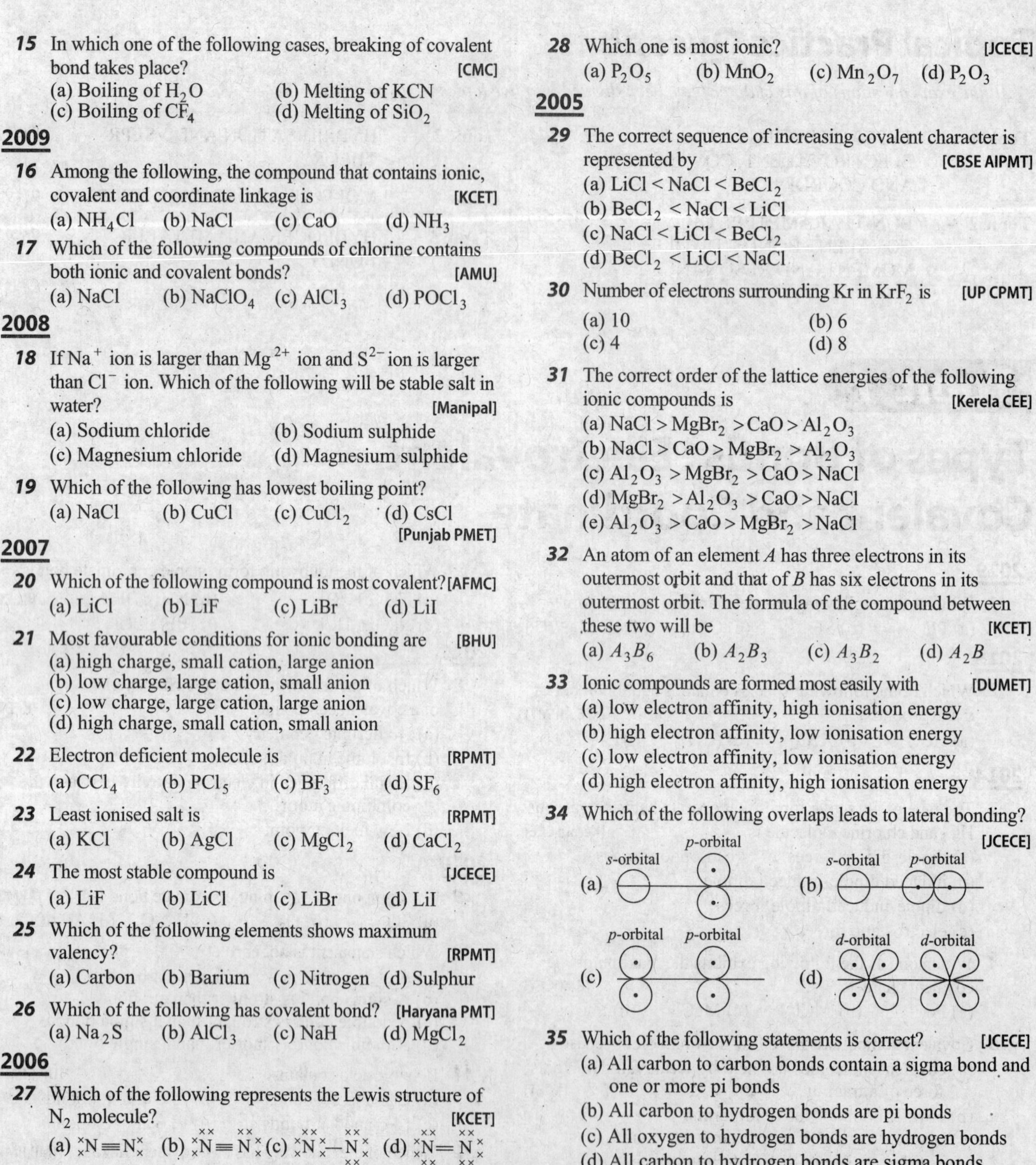

15 In which one of the following cases, breaking of covalent bond takes place? **[CMC]**
(a) Boiling of H_2O (b) Melting of KCN
(c) Boiling of CF_4 (d) Melting of SiO_2

2009

16 Among the following, the compound that contains ionic, covalent and coordinate linkage is **[KCET]**
(a) NH_4Cl (b) NaCl (c) CaO (d) NH_3

17 Which of the following compounds of chlorine contains both ionic and covalent bonds? **[AMU]**
(a) NaCl (b) $NaClO_4$ (c) $AlCl_3$ (d) $POCl_3$

2008

18 If Na^+ ion is larger than Mg^{2+} ion and S^{2-} ion is larger than Cl^- ion. Which of the following will be stable salt in water? **[Manipal]**
(a) Sodium chloride (b) Sodium sulphide
(c) Magnesium chloride (d) Magnesium sulphide

19 Which of the following has lowest boiling point?
(a) NaCl (b) CuCl (c) $CuCl_2$ (d) CsCl **[Punjab PMET]**

2007

20 Which of the following compound is most covalent? **[AFMC]**
(a) LiCl (b) LiF (c) LiBr (d) LiI

21 Most favourable conditions for ionic bonding are **[BHU]**
(a) high charge, small cation, large anion
(b) low charge, large cation, small anion
(c) low charge, large cation, large anion
(d) high charge, small cation, small anion

22 Electron deficient molecule is **[RPMT]**
(a) CCl_4 (b) PCl_5 (c) BF_3 (d) SF_6

23 Least ionised salt is **[RPMT]**
(a) KCl (b) AgCl (c) $MgCl_2$ (d) $CaCl_2$

24 The most stable compound is **[JCECE]**
(a) LiF (b) LiCl (c) LiBr (d) LiI

25 Which of the following elements shows maximum valency? **[RPMT]**
(a) Carbon (b) Barium (c) Nitrogen (d) Sulphur

26 Which of the following has covalent bond? **[Haryana PMT]**
(a) Na_2S (b) $AlCl_3$ (c) NaH (d) $MgCl_2$

2006

27 Which of the following represents the Lewis structure of N_2 molecule? **[KCET]**
(a) $\overset{\times}{\underset{\times}{}}N\equiv N\overset{\times}{\underset{\times}{}}$ (b) $\overset{\times}{\underset{\times}{}}\overset{\times\times}{N}\equiv \overset{\times\times}{N}\overset{\times}{\underset{\times}{}}$ (c) $\overset{\times}{\underset{\times}{}}\overset{\times\times}{N}-\underset{\times\times}{\overset{\times\times}{N}}\overset{\times}{\underset{\times}{}}$ (d) $\overset{\times}{\underset{\times}{}}\underset{\times\times}{\overset{\times\times}{N}}=\underset{\times\times}{\overset{\times\times}{N}}\overset{\times}{\underset{\times}{}}$

28 Which one is most ionic? **[JCECE]**
(a) P_2O_5 (b) MnO_2 (c) Mn_2O_7 (d) P_2O_3

2005

29 The correct sequence of increasing covalent character is represented by **[CBSE AIPMT]**
(a) $LiCl < NaCl < BeCl_2$
(b) $BeCl_2 < NaCl < LiCl$
(c) $NaCl < LiCl < BeCl_2$
(d) $BeCl_2 < LiCl < NaCl$

30 Number of electrons surrounding Kr in KrF_2 is **[UP CPMT]**
(a) 10 (b) 6
(c) 4 (d) 8

31 The correct order of the lattice energies of the following ionic compounds is **[Kerela CEE]**
(a) $NaCl > MgBr_2 > CaO > Al_2O_3$
(b) $NaCl > CaO > MgBr_2 > Al_2O_3$
(c) $Al_2O_3 > MgBr_2 > CaO > NaCl$
(d) $MgBr_2 > Al_2O_3 > CaO > NaCl$
(e) $Al_2O_3 > CaO > MgBr_2 > NaCl$

32 An atom of an element *A* has three electrons in its outermost orbit and that of *B* has six electrons in its outermost orbit. The formula of the compound between these two will be **[KCET]**
(a) A_3B_6 (b) A_2B_3 (c) A_3B_2 (d) A_2B

33 Ionic compounds are formed most easily with **[DUMET]**
(a) low electron affinity, high ionisation energy
(b) high electron affinity, low ionisation energy
(c) low electron affinity, low ionisation energy
(d) high electron affinity, high ionisation energy

34 Which of the following overlaps leads to lateral bonding? **[JCECE]**

35 Which of the following statements is correct? **[JCECE]**
(a) All carbon to carbon bonds contain a sigma bond and one or more pi bonds
(b) All carbon to hydrogen bonds are pi bonds
(c) All oxygen to hydrogen bonds are hydrogen bonds
(d) All carbon to hydrogen bonds are sigma bonds

Answers

1 (c)	2 (b)	3 (d)	4 (b)	5 (c)	6 (d)	7 (b)	8 (a)	9 (d)	10 (a)
11 (b)	12 (a)	13 (a)	14 (b)	15 (d)	16 (a)	17 (b)	18 (d)	19 (c)	20 (d)
21 (b)	22 (c)	23 (b)	24 (a)	25 (d)	26 (b)	27 (a)	28 (d)	29 (c)	30 (a)
31 (c)	32 (b)	33 (b)	34 (c)	35 (d)					

Explanations

1 (*c*) In a chemical bond, electrons are transferred or shared such that each atom attains an electronic configuration of a noble gas (ns^2np^6) i.e. having 8 outer shell (valency) electron. This arrangement is in accordance with octet rule. An outermost shell which had eight electrons is called octet. Carbon tetrachloride has octet around central atom. The number of valence electrons in given compounds are as follows: $PF_5(10e^-)$, $SF_6(12e^-)$, $CCl_4(8e^-)$, $BF_3(6e^-)$

2 (*b*)

	Structure	**σ and π bonds**
(a)	$O=C(-O)-O-H$	σ bond-4 π bond-1
(b)	XeO_4 (O=Xe with four O)	σ bond-4 π bond-4
(c)	$N\equiv C-C\equiv N$	σ bond-3 π bond-4
(d)	$N\equiv C-CH_2-C\equiv N$	σ bond-6 π bond-4

3 (*d*) HCl has electronegativity difference. Hence, it is polar, whereas Cl_2 is non-polar.Hence, HCl (permanent dipole) will induce a dipole in Cl_2 molecules.

4 (*b*) Smaller cation and larger anion shows more covalent character (Fajan's rule.)

Here, smallest ion is Al^{3+}. Hence, $AlCl_3$ has maximum covalent character.

5 (*c*) Covalent compounds have low melting point because covalent bond is weaker than ionic bond. While the ionic bonds tend to form a lattice structure that makes them much stronger.

6 (*d*) During the formation of a chemical bond, energy decreases because when bond forms, electrons are attracted in between the nuclei where, the electrostatic force of attraction is greater. As the electrons fall to a position of lower potential energy, the total mechanical energy of the molecular system decreases.

7 (*b*) NH_3 and BF_3 forms stable coordinate bond due to the presence of lone pair of electrons on N and electron deficiency on B.

$$H_3N: + BF_3 \longrightarrow H_3N \longrightarrow BF_3$$

8 (*a*) Covalent bonds are directional. Therefore, covalent compounds have definite shape (geometry), e.g. acetylene is linear, methane is tetrahedral in shape.

9 (*d*) The structure of the given compounds are as (arrow represents coordinate bond),

(a) SO_3: O=S(→O)=O (Coordinate bond)

(b) O_3: O=Ö→O (Coordinate bond)

(c) H_2SO_4: (HO)(HO)S(→O)(→O) (Coordinate bond)

Thus, all the given compounds contain coordinate bond.

10 (*a*) σ-bond is stronger than a π-bond because the former is formed by axial overlapping of orbitals (in it more surface is available for overlapping which results in strong bond).

11 (*b*) Single bond contains only one σ-bond, double bond contains one σ and one π-bond and triple bond contains one σ and two π-bonds. Thus,

$$H\overset{\sigma}{-}O\overset{\sigma}{-}C\overset{\sigma}{\underset{\pi}{=}}O \text{ attached to } C_6H_5 \text{ ring}$$

Thus, benzoic acid contains 15σ and 4π-bonds.

12 (*a*) In $CaCl_2$, Ca—Cl bonds are electrovalent or ionic bonds because of the higher electronegativity difference between Ca and Cl atom.

13 (*a*) Lattice energy ∝ charge of ion $\propto \frac{1}{\text{size of ion}}$

On moving downward, the size of alkaline earth metals increases due to increase in number of shells. Thus, Mg has the smallest size.

Hence, lattice energy is higher for MgO.

14 (*b*) Melting point depends upon lattice energy. NaCl and KCl have unit charge on their ions while MgO and BaO have two units of charge, therefore lattice energies of MgO and BaO are expected to be larger than those of NaCl and KCl. Since, Mg^{2+} is smaller than Ba^{2+}, therefore, MgO has the higher lattice energy and hence MgO has the highest melting point.

15 (*d*) SiO_2 is a covalent three dimensional network solid in which SiO_2 show tetrahedral geometry. In SiO_2, Si-atom is surrounded by 4 oxygen atoms. When SiO_2 is melted, the three dimensional network structure breaks due to breaking of covalent bond.

16 (*a*) In NH_4Cl, there are 3N—H covalent bonds, 1N ⟶ H coordinate bond and NH_4^+ — Cl^- ionic bond.

$$\left[H \leftarrow NH_3\right]^+ Cl^-$$

17 (*b*) In $NaClO_4$, bond between Cl and O is covalent bond and between Na^+ and ClO_4^-, ionic bond is present.

18 (*d*) Higher the lattice energy, lower the solubility. Out of the four combinations possible, the lattice energy of MgS is higher than those of Na_2S, $MgCl_2$ and NaCl. Hence, MgS is the least soluble.

19 (*c*) According to Fajan's rule, as the size of cation decreases, its polarising power increases and more will be the covalent character.

Hence, Cu^{2+} polarises Cl^- ions more than Cu^+. Therefore, $CuCl_2$ has more covalent character and hence, its boiling point is less.

20 (*d*) The magnitude of covalent character depends upon a number of factors. These factors are:
(i) Small size of cation.
(ii) Large size of anion.
(iii) Large charge on either of the two ions.

Hence, due to larger size of I^-, LiI is most covalent.

21 (*b*) According to Fajan's rule, most favourable conditions for ionic bonding are :
(i) Low charges on both cation and anion
(ii) Large size of cation
(iii) Small size of anion

22 (*c*) The compounds in which central atom has less than 8 electrons in its valence shell are electron deficient.

(a) CCl_4,

```
      Cl
      |
Cl—C—Cl
      |
      Cl
```

Carbon (central atom) has 8 electrons in the valence shell, 4 from carbon and 1 electron each from four chlorine atoms.

(b) PCl_5,

```
      Cl
      |  Cl
Cl—P
      |  Cl
      Cl
```

Phosphorus (central atom) has 10 electrons in valence shell, 5 from P and one each from five chlorine atoms.

(c) BF_3,

```
      F
      |
      B
     / \
    F   F
```

Boron (central atom) has 6 electrons in valence shell, 3 from boron and one each from three flourine atoms.

Boron in BF_3 has less than 8 electrons. So, it is electron deficient molecule.

(d) SF_6

```
      F
  F   |   F
    \ S /
  F / | \ F
      F
```

Sulphur (central atom) has 12 electrons in valence shell, 6 from sulphur and one each from six fluorine atoms.

23 (*b*) Least ionised salt will be the one which has highest covalent character.

$\because$ KCl, $MgCl_2$ and $CaCl_2$ are chlorides of members of group 1 and group 2 of periodic table.

$\therefore$ They are ionic.

AgCl is chloride of *d*-block element. So, it is least ionic and least ionised.

24 (*a*) The electronegativity of halogens is as:

$$F > Cl > Br > I$$

Among alkali metals, the electropositive character increases as:

$$Li < Na < K < Rb < Cs$$

Therefore, Li and F form strongest covalent bond with each other. As a result, LiF is least soluble in water.

Hence, LiF is the most stable compound.

25 (*d*) Sulphur belongs to group 16 of periodic table. Hence, it has maximum valency of 6.

26 (*b*) Al^{3+} cation is smaller than Na^+ (because of greater nuclear charge). According to Fajans' rule, small cation polarises anion upto greater extent.

Hence, Al^{3+} polarises Cl^- ions up to greater extent, therefore $AlCl_3$ has covalent bond between Al and Cl-atoms.

27 (*a*) Lewis structure of N_2 molecule is

(N)(N) or $\overset{\times}{\times}N \equiv N\overset{\times}{\times}$

28 (*d*) According to Fajan's rule, compounds having large charge on cation are more covalent or least electrovalent.

So, compounds having low charge on cation will be more electrovalent or ionic.

$\overset{+4}{Mn}O_2$ $\overset{+7}{Mn_2}O_7$ $\overset{+5}{P_2}O_5$ $\overset{+3}{P_2}O_3$

So, P_2O_3 will be most ionic.

29 (*c*) On the basis of Fajan's rule, lower the size of cation, higher will be its polarising power and higher will be covalent character.

$\therefore$ Polarising power $\propto \dfrac{1}{\text{size of cation}}$

Covalent character $\propto$ polarising power

(The order of size of cation is $Na^+ > Li^+ > Be^{2+}$)

So, the correct order is

$$NaCl < LiCl < BeCl_2$$

30 (*a*) Krypton (Kr) forms two covalent bonds with two fluorine atoms (one with each fluorine).

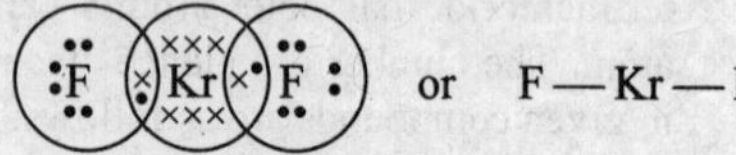

Number of electrons in valence shell of Kr = 8

Number of electrons its shares with two F-atoms = 2

$\therefore$ Total number of electrons found around Kr in KrF = 8 + 2 = 10

31 (*c*) Lattice energy depends upon
(i) the product of ionic charges.
(ii) the interionic distance.
(iii) nature of the crystal structure.

Hence, more is the ionic charge, more will be the lattice energy.

So, the correct order of lattice energy is $Al_2O_3 > MgBr_2 > CaO > NaCl$

32 (*b*) *A* has three electrons in its outermost orbit, its valency is 3.

B has six electrons in its outermost orbit, its valency is 2.

Element	*A*	*B*
Valency	3	2

$\therefore$ Formula of the compound = A_2B_3

33 (*b*) Formation of ionic bond is favoured by
(i) low ionisation potential of metal.
(ii) greater value of electronaffinity of non-metal.
(iii) higher value of lattice energy of resulting ionic compound.

34 (*c*) *p*-orbitals form bond by lateral overlapping.

35 (*d*) The first bond between any two atoms is sigma and rest are π-bonds.

Since, carbon and hydrogen form only 1 bond between them, hence all carbon-hydrogen bonds are sigma bonds.

Topic 2

Bond Parameters of Covalent Bonds, Dipole Moment and Resonance

2019

1 Which of the following is the correct order of dipole moment? **[NEET (Odisha)]**

(a) $NH_3 < BF_3 < NF_3 < H_2O$
(b) $BF_3 < NF_3 < NH_3 < H_2O$
(c) $BF_3 < NH_3 < NF_3 < H_2O$
(d) $H_2O < NF_3 < NH_3 < BF_3$

2017

2 The species, having bond angles of 120° is **[NEET]**

(a) PH_3 (b) ClF_3
(c) NCl_3 (d) BCl_3

2014

3 Which of the following molecules has the maximum dipole moment? **[CBSE AIPMT]**

(a) CO_2 (b) CH_4
(c) NH_3 (d) NF_3

4 Which one of the following has the lowest dipole moment? **[Kerala CEE]**

(a) CH_3F (b) CH_3Cl
(c) CH_3I (d) $CHCl_3$
(e) CH_3Br

5 The compound that will have a permanent dipole moment among the following is **[WB JEE]**

I: H, H and Cl, Cl on a central carbon (tetrahedral)
II: Cl(H)C=C(H)Cl
III: CCl_4
IV: Br—≡—Br

(a) I (b) II
(c) III (d) IV

6 The bond angle in NF_3 (102.3°) is smaller than NH_3 (107.2°). This is because of **[WB JEE]**

(a) large size of F compared to H
(b) large size of N compared to F
(c) opposite polarity of N in the two molecules
(d) small size of H compared to N

2013

7 Which of the following will have the maximum dipole moment? **[WB JEE]**

(a) CH_3F (b) CH_3Cl
(c) CH_3Br (d) CH_3I

8 Dipole-induced dipole interactions are present in which of the following pairs? **[NEET]**

(a) H_2O and alcohol
(b) Cl_2 and CCl_4
(c) HCl and He atoms
(d) SiF_4 and He atoms

9 Bond polarity of diatomic molecule is because of **[AIIMS]**

(a) difference in electron affinities of two atoms
(b) difference in electronegativities of two atoms
(c) difference in ionisation potentials
(d) All of the above

2012

10 The correct decreasing order of dipole moment in CH_3Cl, CH_3Br and CH_3F is **[DUMET]**

(a) $CH_3F > CH_3Cl > CH_3Br$
(b) $CH_3F > CH_3Br > CH_3Cl$
(c) $CH_3Cl > CH_3F > CH_3Br$
(d) $CH_3Cl > CH_3Br > CH_3F$

11 In the given structure of a compound, the correct directions of various bond moments are shown as **[DUMET]**

(a) $Br \leftleftarrows N \leftleftarrows CH_2 \rightrightarrows SiH_2 \leftleftarrows CH_2 \rightrightarrows O \leftleftarrows CH_3$
(b) $Br \leftleftarrows N \leftleftarrows CH_2 \leftleftarrows SiH_2 \leftleftarrows CH_2 \rightrightarrows O \leftleftarrows CH_3$
(c) $Br \leftleftarrows N \leftleftarrows CH_2 \leftleftarrows SiH_2 \rightrightarrows CH_2 \rightrightarrows O \leftleftarrows CH_3$
(d) $Br \leftleftarrows N \rightrightarrows CH_2 \leftleftarrows SiH_2 \leftleftarrows CH_2 \rightrightarrows O \rightrightarrows CH_3$

12 CO is practically non-polar. Since, **[WB JEE]**

(a) the σ-electron drift from C to O almost nullified by the π-electron drift from O to C
(b) the σ-electron drift from O to C is almost nullified by the π-electron drift from C to O
(c) the bond moment is low
(d) there is triple bond between C and O

2011

13 The units of dipole moment is [UP CPMT]
(a) esu (b) C-m
(c) Pascal (d) S-m

14 The correct order of increasing bond length of C—H, C—O, C—C and C=C is [CBSE AIPMT]
(a) $C—H < C—O < C—C < C=C$
(b) $C—H < C=C < C—O < C—C$
(c) $C—C < C=C < C—O < C—H$
(d) $C—O < C—H < C—C < C=C$

15 The covalent bond length is the shortest in which one of the following bonds? [Kerala CEE]
(a) C—O (b) C—C
(c) C≡N (d) O—H
(e) C≡C

16 Dipole moment of

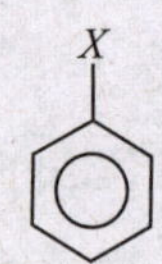

is 1.5 D. The dipole moment of

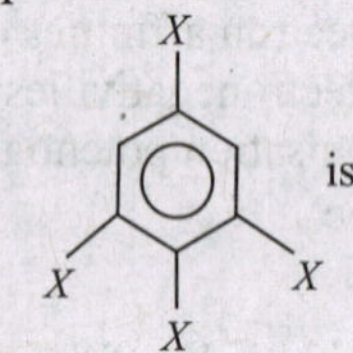

is
(a) 1.5 D (b) 2.35 D (c) 1 D (d) 3 D

17 The bond order of the N—O bonds in NO_3^- ion is [AMU]
(a) 0.33 (b) 1.00
(c) 1.33 (d) 1.50

18 Which of the following fluoride of xenon has zero dipole moment? [AMU]
(a) XeF_2 (b) XeF_3 (c) XeF_4 (d) XeF_6

19 The molecule which has zero dipole moment is [JCECE]
(a) CH_3Cl (b) NF_3
(c) BF_3 (d) ClO_2

20 The correct order of increasing bond angle in the following species is [CBSE AIPMT]
(a) $ClO_2^- < Cl_2O < ClO_2$
(b) $Cl_2O < ClO_2 < ClO_2^-$
(c) $ClO_2 < Cl_2O < ClO_2^-$
(d) $Cl_2O < ClO_2^- < ClO_2$

2009

21 Among the following, the molecule possessing highest dipole moment is [J&K CET]
(a) CO_2 (b) BF_3
(c) SO_2 (d) *trans*-2-butene

22 Dipole moments of HCl = 1.03 D, HI = 0.38 D. Bond length of HCl = 1.3 Å and HI = 1.6 Å. The ratio of fraction of an electric charge, *e* existing on each atom in HCl and HI is [EAMCET]
(a) 1.2 : 1 (b) 2.7 : 1
(c) 3.3 : 1 (d) 1 : 3.3

2008

23 The correct order of increasing dipole moment of
I. toluene,
II. *m*-dichlorobenzene,
III. *o*-dichlorobenzene and
IV. *p*-dichlorobenzene is [BHU]
(a) IV < II < I < III
(b) IV < I < II < III
(c) I < IV < II < III
(d) IV < I < III < II

24 In which of the following pairs, both molecules possess dipole moment? [UP CPMT]
(a) CO_2, SO_2 (b) BCl_3, PCl_3
(c) H_2O, SO_2 (d) CO_2, CS_2

25 The dipole moment of HBr is 1.6×10^{-30} C - m and interatomic spacing is 1 Å. The per cent ionic character of HBr is [Haryana PMT]
(a) 7 (b) 10 (c) 15 (d) 27

2008

26 H—O—H bond angle in H_2O is 104.5° and not 109° 28′ because of [UP CPMT]
(a) lone pair-lone pair repulsion
(b) lone pair-bond pair repulsion
(c) bond pair-bond pair repulsion
(d) high electronegativity of oxygen

27 Arrange the following ions in the order of decreasing *X*—O bond length, where *X* is the central atom in SiO_4^{4-}, ClO_4^-, PO_4^{3-}, SO_4^{2-} [Kerala CEE]
(a) $ClO_4^- > SO_4^{2-} > PO_4^{3-} > SiO_4^{4-}$
(b) $SiO_4^{4-} > PO_4^{3-} > SO_4^{2-} > ClO_4^-$
(c) $SiO_4^{4-} > PO_4^{3-} > ClO_4^- > SO_4^{2-}$
(d) $SiO_4^{4-} > SO_4^{2-} > PO_4^{3-} > ClO_4^-$
(e) $SO_4^{2-} > PO_4^{3-} > ClO_4^- > SiO_4^{4-}$

28 The bond angle in AsH_3 is greater than that in [Punjab PMET]
(a) NH_3 (b) H_2O
(c) BCl_3 (d) None of these

2007

29 Which of the following is polar? [DUMET]
(a) I_3^- (b) CO_3^{2-} (c) XeF_4 (d) PF_3

30 **Assertion** (A) H—S—H bond angle in H_2S is closer to 90° but H—O—H bond angle in H_2O is 104.5°.

Reason (R) Lone pair-lone pair repulsion is stronger in H_2S than in H_2O. **[AIIMS]**

(a) Both A and R are correct and R is the correct explanation of A
(b) Both A and R are correct but R is not the correct explanation of A
(c) A is correct but R is incorrect
(d) Both A and R are incorrect

31 The bond lengths and bond angles in the molecules of methane, ammonia and water are given below

This variation in bond angle is a result of **[Kerala CEE]**

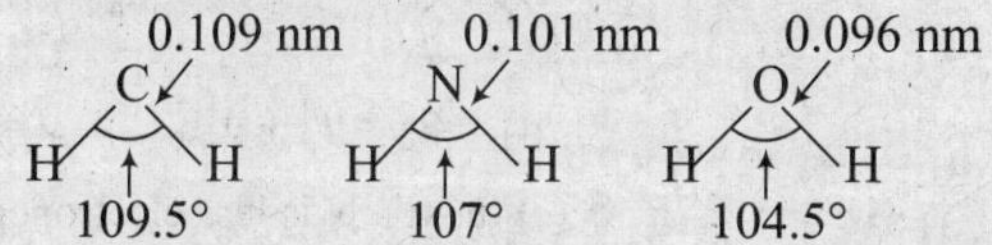

I. the increasing repulsion between hydrogen atoms as the bond length decreases.
II. the number of non-bonding electron pairs in the molecule.
III. a non-bonding electron pair having a greater repulsive force than a bonding electron pair.

(a) I, II and III are correct
(b) I and II are correct
(c) II and III are correct
(d) Only I is correct
(e) Only III is correct

2006

32 The electronegativity difference between N and F is greater than that between N and H yet the dipole moment of NH_3 (1.5 D) is larger than that of NF_3 (0.2 D). This is because **[CBSE AIPMT]**

(a) in NH_3 as well as in NF_3, the atomic dipole and bond dipole are in the same direction.
(b) in NH_3, the atomic dipole and bond dipole are in the same direction whereas in NF_3, these are in opposite directions.
(c) in NH_3 as well as in NF_3, the atomic dipole and bond dipole are in opposite directions.
(d) in NH_3, the atomic dipole and bond dipole are in the opposite directions whereas in NF_3, these are in the same directions.

2005

33 Which of the following would have a permanent dipole moment? **[CBSE AIPMT]**

(a) BF_3 (b) SiF_4 (c) SF_4 (d) XeF_4

34 The correct order in which the O—O bond length increases is **[CBSE AIPMT]**

(a) $H_2O_2 < O_2 < O_3$ (b) $O_3 < H_2O_2 < O_2$
(c) $O_2 < O_3 < H_2O_2$ (d) $O_2 < H_2O_2 < O_3$

35 The dipole moment of H_2S is 0.95 D. If the bond angle is 97°, the S—H bond moment would be (cos 48.5° = 0.66) **[Kerala CEE]**

(a) 0.95 D (b) 0.662 D
(c) 48.5 D (d) 0.72 D
(e) 7.2 D

36 What is the correct order of decreasing bond angle? **[VMMC]**

(a) $NH_4^+ > NH_3 > NH_2^-$ (b) $NH_3 > NH_2^- > NH_4^+$
(c) $NH_2^- < NH_3 > NH_4^+$ (d) $NH_3 > NH_4^+ > NH_2^-$

37 Correct order of bond angles for the following is **[OJEE]**

(a) $NH_3 > PCl_3 > BCl_3$ (b) $BCl_3 > NH_3 > PCl_3$
(c) $BCl_3 > PCl_3 > NH_3$ (d) $PCl_3 > BCl_3 > NH_3$

38 Which one of the following compounds has the smallest bond angle in its molecule? **[BCECE]**

(a) SO_2 (b) H_2O (c) H_2S (d) NH_3

Answers

1. (b)	2 (d)	3 (c)	4 (d)	5 (a)	6 (c)	7 (b)	8 (c)	9 (b)	10 (c)
11 (c)	12 (a)	13 (b)	14 (b)	15 (d)	16 (a)	17 (c)	18 (c)	19 (c)	20 (d)
21 (c)	22 (c)	23 (b)	24 (c)	25 (b)	26 (a)	27 (b)	28 (d)	29 (d)	30 (c)
31 (c)	32 (b)	33 (c)	34 (c)	35 (d)	36 (a)	37 (c)	38 (c)		

Explanations

1 (*b*) BF_3 has zero dipole moment as it is symmetrical in nature. H_2O has maximum dipole moment as it possess two lone pair of electrons. Between NH_3 and NF_3, NH_3 has greater dipole moment though in NH_3 and NF_3, possesses one lone pair of electrons. This is because in case of NH_3, the net N—H bond dipole is in the same direction as the direction of dipole of lone pair. But in case of NF_3, the direction of net dipole moment of three N—F bonds is opposite to that of the dipole moment of the lone pair. Thus, the correct order of dipole moment is

$(H_2O) > (NH_3) > (NF_3) > (BF_3)$

2 (*d*) The species having bond angles of 120° is BCl_3. It is sp^2-hybridised and central atom does not have any lone pair of electrons.

Chemical formula	Species	Bond angle
(a) PH_3	(Pyramidal)	93.5°
(b) ClF_3	(T-shaped)	90°
(c) NCl_3	(Pyramidal)	107.8°
(d) BCl_3	(Trigonal planar)	120°

3 (*c*) CO_2 and CH_4 have zero dipole moment as these are symmetrical in nature. Between NH_3 and NF_3, NH_3 has greater dipole moment though in NH_3 and NF_3 both, N possesses one lone pair of electrons. This is because in case of NH_3, the net N—H bond dipole is in the same direction as the direction of dipole of lone pair but in case of NF_3, the direction of net bond dipole moment of three N—F bonds is opposite to that of the dipole moment of the lone pair.

O=C=O $\mu_{net} = 0$; CH_4: $\mu = 0$

$\because \quad \mu_{res} = \mu_1 + \mu_2 + \mu_3 = -\mu_4$

$\therefore \quad \mu_{net} = \mu_1 + \mu_2 + \mu_3 + \mu_4 = -\mu_4 + \mu_4 = 0$

Resultant of 3 N—H bond lie in the same direction as μ_4

Resultant of 3 N—F bond lie opposite to μ_4, $\mu_{net} = 0.2$ D

4 (*d*) Among the given halides, $CHCl_3$ has the lowest dipole moment because here dipole moment of one C—Cl bond is cancelled by that of the other opposite to it, while such a condition is not found in others.

$\mu_{H-C} + \mu_{C-Cl} = (\mu_{net}) \quad \mu_{net} > (\mu_{net})_1$

5 (*a*) Symmetrical molecules and symmetrical *trans*-alkene have a net dipole moment zero.

CH_2Cl_2 *cis* is not a symmetrical molecule, thus it will have a permanent dipole.

$\mu_1 + \mu_2 - \mu_3 - \mu_4 = 0$

μ_3 and $\mu_4 > \mu_1$ and μ_2

$\mu_{net} = 0$ Symmetrical *trans*-alkene

Thus, $\mu_{net} \neq 0$

Br—C≡C—Br $\mu_{net} = 0$

$\mu_1 + \mu_2 = \mu_3 + \mu_4 \therefore \mu_{net} = 0$

6 (*c*) In NF_3, N is less electronegative as compared to F but in NH_3, it (N) is more electronegative than H.

In case of same central atom, as the electronegativity of other atoms increases, bond angle decreases.

Thus, bond angle in NF_3 is smaller than that in NH_3 because of the opposite polarity of N in these molecules.

7 (*b*) Although, F is the most electronegative, it is expected to have maximum dipole moment. However, it is too smaller in size to overpower its electronegative effect ($\mu = e \times d$), hence its dipole moment is lower than that of CH_3Cl. Thus, CH_3Cl has maximum dipole moment among all.

8 (*c*) Dipole-induced dipole interactions are present in the pair in which the first species is polar and the other is non-polar. H_2O and alcohol both are polar molecules, so there exists dipole-dipole interactions in between them.

Cl_2 and CCl_4 both are non-polar. So there exists induced dipole-induced dipole interactions in between them. Similar is true for $SiCl_4$ and He atoms pair. HCl is a polar molecule whereas

He atoms are non-polar, so in between them dipole-induced dipole interactions exist.

9 (*b*) Polarity is due to the difference in electronegativities of two atoms or molecules.

10 (*c*) CH_3F is expected to have highest dipole moment. But C—F bond length is smaller than C—Cl bond length, hence CH_3F dipole moment is less than CH_3Cl.

Hence, the correct decreasing order of dipole moment in CH_3Cl, CH_3Br_3, CH_3F is $CH_3Cl > CH_3F > CH_3Br$.

11 (*c*) Bond moment is shown from less electronegative to more electronegative atom.

12 (*a*) $\overset{\pi}{\overleftarrow{}}$ $C \underset{\sigma}{\overset{\pi}{\equiv}} O$

In CO molecule, C—O σ-moment and O—C π-moment cancels each other.

So that, practically it is non-polar.

13 (*b*) The dipole moment, μ is given as,

μ = charge × distance

= Coulomb × metre = C - m

14 (*b*) $C—H < C{=}C < C—O < C—C$

Bond length (pm) = 107 < 120 < 143 < 154

15 (*d*) O—H bond length is the shortest among the given set because of highest electronegativity difference between O and H.

16 (*a*) *X*

(benzene ring) μ_1= 1.5D (as it is unsymmetrical)

For (1,3,5-trisubstituted benzene) μ=0 (as it is symmetrical)

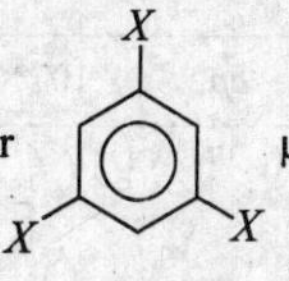

Hence, for (1,2,3,5-tetrasubstituted benzene) μ will be 1.5 D.

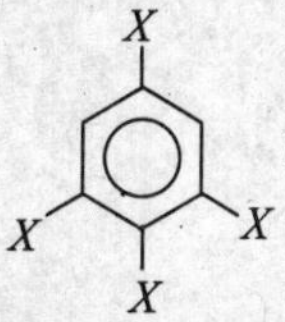

17 (*c*) The resonance structures of NO_3^- ions are as :

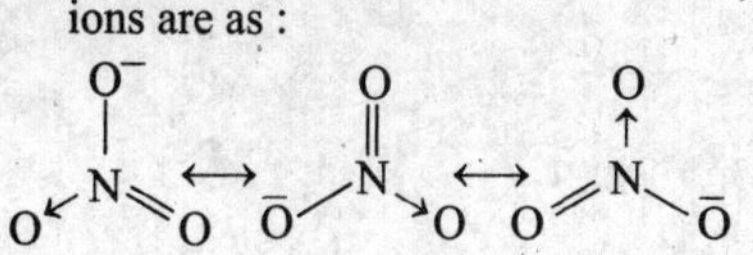

(three resonance structures of NO_3^-)

The N—O bond order

$$= \frac{\text{number of bonds between two atoms}}{\text{total number of resonating structure}}$$

$$= \frac{4}{3} = 1.33$$

18 (*c*) Symmetrical structures have zero dipole moment. Among the given compounds, XeF_4 has square planar structure as :

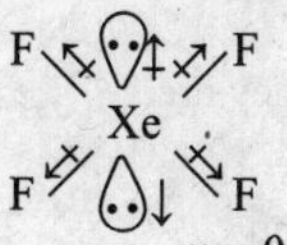

(structure of XeF_4) $\mu = 0$

Thus, its dipole moment is zero.

19 (*c*) The molecules having distorted geometry have dipole moment and those having regular geometry have zero dipole moment.

∵ NF_3, CH_3Cl and ClO_2 have distorted geometry.

∴ They have dipole moment.

∵ BF_3 has regular triangular planar geometry and thus the dipole moment of BF_3 is zero.

20 (*d*) OCl_2 (110°) < $[ClO_2]^-$ (110.9°) < ClO_2 (117.8°)

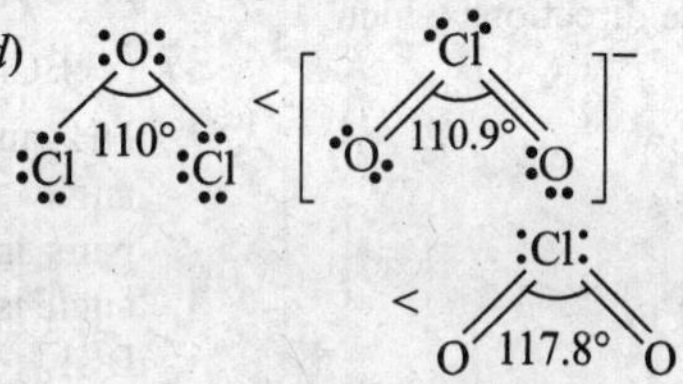

21 (*c*) $CO_2 \rightarrow$ zero dipole moment.

$BF_3 \rightarrow$ zero dipole moment.

$SO_2 \rightarrow$ non-zero dipole moment (1.85 D).

trans-2-butene → zero dipole moment

22 (*c*) Dipole moment, $\mu = e \times d$

where, e = magnitude of electric charge

d = distance between particles (here bond length)

$$\therefore \quad e = \frac{\mu}{d}$$

$$\text{or,} \quad \frac{e_{HCl}}{e_{HI}} = \frac{\mu_{HCl}}{d_{HCl}} \times \frac{d_{HI}}{\mu_{HI}} = \frac{1.03 \times 1.6}{1.3 \times 0.38}$$

$$= 3.3 : 1$$

23 (*b*) Dipole moment of *p*-dichlorobenzene is zero while that of *o*-dichlorobenzene is 2.54 D and for *m*-dichlorobenzene is 1.48 D. This shows that benzene ring is planar. In *p*-$C_6H_4Cl_2$, two C—Cl bonds are directed in the plane of the ring, thus on adding becomes zero.

In o-dichloro benzene, two C—Cl bonds contain an angle of 60° and in *m*-$C_6H_4Cl_2$, the two bonds C—Cl contains an angle of 120° and their dipole moments on vector addition give a higher value of dipole moment.

∴ Sequence of dipole moment is *p*-dichlorobenzene < toluene < *m*-dichlorobenzene < *o*-dichlorobenzene.

24 (*c*) H_2O and SO_2 both possess dipole moment due to bent structure (unsymmetrical).

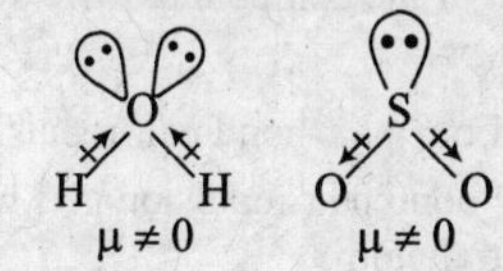

(H_2O) $\mu \neq 0$ (SO_2) $\mu \neq 0$

25 (*b*) Charge of electron = 1.6×10^{-19} C

Dipole moment of HBr = 1.6×10^{-30} C-m

Interatomic spacing = 1Å = 1×10^{-10} m

% ionic character in HBr

$$= \frac{\text{dipole moment of HBr} \times 100}{\text{Inter spacing distance} \times q}$$

$$= \frac{1.6 \times 10^{-30}}{1.6 \times 10^{-19} \times 10^{-10}} \times 100$$

$$= 10^{-30} \times 10^{29} \times 100$$

$$= 10^{-1} \times 100 = 0.1 \times 100 = 10\%$$

26 (*a*) The hybridisation of oxygen in water molecule is sp^3. So, water molecule must be tetrahedral and have bond angle 109°28′. But due to the presence of two lone pairs of electrons on oxygen atom (repulsion between lone pair-lone pair), the bond angle decreases to about 104.5° and the geometry becomes distorted tetrahedral or bent shaped.

27 (*b*) As the number of double bonds increases, *X*—O bond length decreases

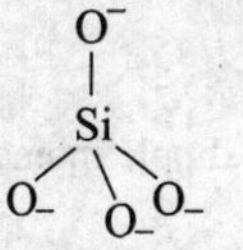

(no double bond) SiO_4^{4-}

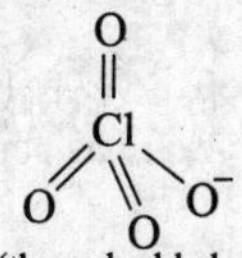

(three double bonds) ClO_4^-

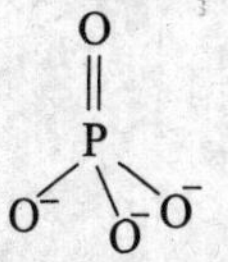

(one double bond) PO_4^{3-}

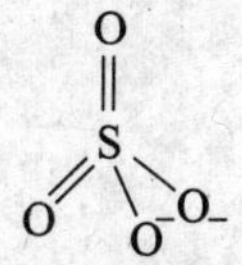

(two double bonds) SO_4^{2-}

Hence, the order of *X*—O bond length is $SiO_4^{4-} > PO_4^{3-} > SO_4^{2-} > ClO_4^-$

28 (*d*) BCl_3 has bond angle equal to 120° (trigonal planar), NH_3 and H_2O have sp^3 hybridisation but due to the presence of lone pair of electrons, they have bond angle less than 109°28′ (NH_3 : 107°, H_2O : 104.5°), AsH_3 (sp^3 hybridised) has smaller bond angle (91.8°) than NH_3 due to less electronegativity of As than N. Thus, none of these have smaller bond angle than AsH_3.

29 (*d*) PF_3 is triangular pyramidal, so its net dipole moment is not zero.

$\therefore$ PF_3 is polar.

Rest of the compounds have symmetrical shape. Thus, they are non-polar.

30 (*c*) Lone pair-bond pair repulsion is strong in H_2S as bond pair-bond pair repulsion gets weaker with increase in size of central atom.

Hence, (A) is correct but (R) is incorrect.

31 (*c*) The variation in bond angle in methane, ammonia and water is a result of the number of non-bonding pairs in the molecules. A lone pair (non-bonding electron pair) have greater repulsion force than bond pair. Thus, statement II and III are correct.

32 (*b*) Electronegativity of N is greater than that of H, but in NF_3 electronegativity of F is greater than that of that of N.

Yet dipole moment of NH_3 is larger than that of NF_3 because in NH_3, the atomic dipole and bond dipole are in the same direction whereas in NF_3, these are in opposite directions which cancel out each other.

33 (*c*)

$\mu = 0, (BF_3)$ $\quad$ $\mu = 0, (BF_3)$

$\mu > 0$ (more polar) (SF_4) $\quad$ $\mu = 0$ (non- polar) (XeF_4)

$\because$ SF_4 has $\mu > 0$.

$\therefore$ It has permanent dipole moment.

34 (*c*) Bond length of O—O in O_2 = 1.21 Å

Bond length of O—O in O_3 = 1.278 Å

Bond length of O—O in H_2O_2 = 1.49 Å

The bond length of a double bond in lesser than that of a single bond. A double bond is present between the two oxygen atoms in O_2 molecule. A single bond is present between the oxygen atoms in H_2O_2 molecule. Due to resonance, the bond length of O—O bond in O_3 is lesser than that of a single bond and greater than that of a doulbe bond.

Therefore, correct order of O—O bonds length is : (bond order decrease in the same order)

$$O_2 < O_3 < H_2O_2$$

35 (*d*) $\mu_{obs} = \mu_{S-H} \cos 97°$

$$2\mu_{S-H} \cos 48.5°$$

$$0.95 = 2\,\mu_{S-H} \times 0.662$$

$$\mu_{S-H} = \frac{0.95}{2 \times 0.662} = 0.72 \text{ D}$$

36 (*a*) The correct order of decreasing bond angle is

$$NH_4^+ > NH_3 > NH_2^-$$

this is because all of them involves sp^3 hybridisation. The number of lone pair of electrons present on N-atoms are 0, 1, 2 respectively. Greater the number of lone pairs, greater the repulsion between bond pairs and lone pairs , smaller is the bond angle.

37 (*c*) BCl_3 is trigonal in shape where bond angle is 120°. In NH_3 and PCl_3 (both are having pyramidal geometry bond angle < 120°), though the central atom has equal number of lone pairs and bond pairs, the size of P is relatively bigger and bond angle is lower. Hence, the correct order of bond angles is $BCl_3 > PCl_3 > NH_3$.

38 (*c*)

Molecule	Hybridisation	Repulsion	Bond angle
SO_2	sp^2	$lp - bp, bp - bp$	119°
H_2O	sp^3	$lp - lp, bp - lp, bp - bp$	104.5°
H_2S	sp^3	$lp - lp, bp - lp, bp - bp$	90°
NH_3	sp^3	$lp - bp, bp - bp$	107°

Topic 3

Hybridisation and VSEPR Theory

2019

1 What is hybridisation of 'O' in H_2O? **[JIPMER]**

(a) *sp* (b) sp^3
(c) sp^2 (d) No hybridisation

2 Which of the following is correct? **[JIPMER]**

(a) $SO_3^{2-} \Rightarrow$ Tetrahedral (b) $NO_2^- \Rightarrow$ Trigonal planar
(c) $ClO_4^- \Rightarrow$ Tetrahedral (d) $BrO_4^- \Rightarrow$ Tetrahedral

2018

3 Which of the following molecules represents the order of hybridisation sp^2, sp^2, sp, sp from left to right atoms? **[NEET]**

(a) $CH_2{=}CH{-}CH{=}CH_2$
(b) $CH_2{=}CH{-}C{\equiv}CH$
(c) $CH{\equiv}C{-}C{\equiv}CH$
(d) $CH_3{-}CH{=}CH{-}CH_3$

4 The structure of IF_7 is **[AIIMS]**

(a) square pyramidal (b) trigonal bipyramidal
(c) octahedral (d) pentagonal bipyramidal

2017

5 Pick out the correct statement with respect to $[Mn(CN)_6]^{3-}$. **[NEET]**

(a) It is sp^3d^2 hybridised and octahedral
(b) It is sp^3d^2 hybridised and tetrahedral
(c) It is d^2sp^3 hybridised and octahedral
(d) It is dsp^2 hybridised and square planar

6 Which of the following conversions involve change in both hybridisation and shape? **[AIIMS]**

(a) $CH_4 \longrightarrow C_2H_6$ (b) $NH_3 \longrightarrow NH_4^+$
(c) $BF_3 \longrightarrow BF_4^-$ (d) $H_2O \longrightarrow H_3O^+$

7 **Assertion** (A) The central atom of NH_3 and H_2O, are both sp^3-hybridised yet H—N—H bond angle is greater than that of H—O—H. **[AIIMS]**

Reason (R) In NH_3, N-atom has one lone pair of electron whereas in H_2O, oxygen atom has two lone pairs of electrons.

(a) Both A and R are correct and R is the correct explanation of A
(b) Both A and R are correct but R is not the correct explanation of A
(c) A is correct but R is incorrect
(d) Both A and R are incorrect

8 **Assertion** (A) In SF_6, molecule, F—S—F bond angle is 90°.

Reason (R) SF_6 molecule has octahedral geometry with sp^3d^2 hybridisation. **[AIIMS]**

(a) Both A and R are correct and R is the correct explanation of A
(b) Both A and R are correct but R is not the correct explanation of A
(c) A is correct but R is incorrect
(d) Both A and R are incorrect

2016

9 The hybridisation of atomic orbitals of nitrogen in NO_2^+, NO_3^- and NH_4^+ respectively are **[NEET Phase II]**

(a) sp, sp^2 and sp^2 (b) sp^2, sp^3 and sp
(c) sp, sp^2 and sp^3 (d) sp^2, sp and sp^3

10 The correct geometry and hybridisation of XeF_4 are

(a) octahedral sp^3d^2
(b) trigonal bipyramidal sp^3d
(c) planar triangle sp^3d^3
(d) square planar, sp^3d^2

11 The pair of electron in the given carbanion, $CH_3C \equiv C^-$, is present in which orbitals? **[NEET]**

(a) sp^3 (b) sp^2 (c) *sp* (d) 2*p*

12 Match the compounds given in Column I with the shape given in Column II and mark the correct option. **[NEET]**

	Column I		Column II
A.	XeF_6	1.	Distorted octahedral
B.	XeO_3	2.	Square planar
C.	$XeOF_4$	3.	Pyramidal
D.	XeF_4	4.	Square pyramidal

Codes

	A	B	C	D		A	B	C	D
(a)	1	2	4	3	(b)	4	3	1	2
(c)	4	1	2	3	(d)	1	3	4	2

2015

13 Which of the following pair of ions are isoelectronic and isostructural? **[NEET]**

(a) CO_3^{2-}, SO_3^{2-} (b) ClO_3^-, CO_3^{2-}
(c) SO_3^{2-}, NO_3^- (d) ClO_3^-, SO_3^{2-}

2014

14 Which one of the following species has triangular planar shape? [CBSE AIPMT]
(a) N_3 (b) NO_3^- (c) NO_2^- (d) CO_2

15 The percentage of s-character in the hybridised orbitals of B in BF_3 is [WB JEE]
(a) 25 (b) 50 (c) 75 (d) 33.3

16 The structure of XeF_6 is experimentally determined to be distorted octahedron. Its structure according to VSEPR theory is [WB JEE]
(a) octahedron
(b) trigonal bipyramidal
(c) pentagonal bipyramidal
(d) tetragonal bipyramidal

17 The pair of compounds having identical shapes for their molecules is [KCET]
(a) CH_4, SF_4 (b) BCl_3, ClF_3
(c) XeF_2, $ZnCl_2$ (d) SO_2, CO_2

18 If E = the number of lone pairs of electrons on Xe,
B = the number of bonding pairs of electrons,
S = shape of the molecule, [EAMCET]
then, what is the correct set of E, B and S of XeF_4?

	E	B	S
(a)	3	3	Octahedral
(b)	3	3	Square planar
(c)	2	4	Square planar
(d)	4	2	Square planar

19 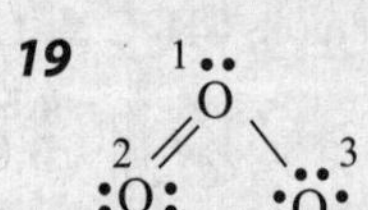

In the ozone molecule shown above, the formal charges of oxygen atoms 1, 2, 3 are respectively, [JCECE]
(a) 0, – 1, + 1 (b) 0, + 1, – 1
(c) + 1, 0, – 1 (d) – 1, 0, + 1

20 The number of bond pair and lone pair of electrons respectively in NH_3 molecule are [Manipal]
(a) 4 and 0 (b) 3 and 0
(c) 3 and 1 (d) 2 and 2

2013

21 The ion which is not tetrahedral in shape is [AIIMS]
(a) BF_4^- (b) NH_4^+
(c) $[Cu(NH_3)_4]^{2+}$ (d) $NiCl_4^{2-}$

22 The number of double bonds in gammexane is [UP CPMT]
(a) 0 (b) 1 (c) 2 (d) 3

23 Diagonal hybridisation is another name of
(a) sp^3-hybridisation (b) sp-hybridisation
(c) sp^2-hybridisation (d) All of these

24 Which of the following represents the given mode of hybridisation sp^2-sp^2-sp-sp from left to right? [WB JEE]
(a) $H_2C{=}CH{-}C{\equiv}N$ (b) $CH{\equiv}C{-}C{\equiv}CH$
(c) $H_2C{=}C{=}C{=}CH_2$ (d) 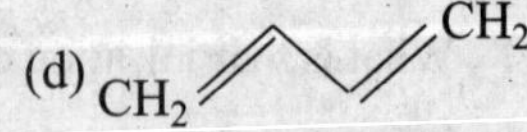

25 Geometry of SF_2Cl_2 molecule is [WB JEE]
(a) tetrahedral (b) octahedral
(c) square pyramidal (d) trigonal bipyramidal

26 Which of the following species contains three bond pairs and one lone pair around the central atom? [CBSE AIPMT]
(a) H_2O (b) BF_3
(c) NH_2^- (d) PCl_3

2012

27 Which one of the following pairs is isostructural (i.e. having the same shape and hybridisation)? [CBSE AIPMT]
(a) [BCl_3 and $BrCl_3$] (b) [NH_3 and NO_3^-]
(c) [NF_3 and BF_3] (d) [BF_4^- and NH_4^+]

28 All the four sigma bonds in perchlorate ion are [AMU]
(a) sp^3-sp^3 bond (b) sp^3-p bond
(c) sp^2-sp^2 bond (d) sp^2-p bond

29 In $XeOF_2$ molecule, the hybridisation of Xe-orbital is
(a) sp^3d^3 (b) sp^3d^2
(c) sp^3d (d) sp^3

30 The C—H bond and C—C bond in ethane are formed by which of the following types of overlap? [KCET]
(a) sp^2-s and sp^2-sp^2 (b) sp-s and sp-sp
(c) p-s and p-p (d) sp^3-s and sp^3-sp^3

31 Considering the state of hybridisation of carbon atoms, find out the molecule among the following which is linear? [CBSE AIPMT]
(a) $CH_3{-}CH_2{-}CH_2{-}CH_3$
(b) $CH_3{-}CH{=}CH{-}CH_3$
(c) $CH_3{-}C{\equiv}C{-}CH_3$
(d) $CH_2{=}CH{-}CH_2{-}C{\equiv}CH$

32 Which of the two ions from the list given below that have the geometry that is explained by the same hybridisation of orbitals, NO_2^-, NO_3^-, NH_2^-, NH_4^+, SCN^-? [CBSE AIPMT]
(a) NO_2^- and NH_2^- (b) NO_2^- and NO_3^-
(c) NH_4^+ and NO_3^- (d) SCN^- and NH_2^-

33 Among the following molecules : SO_2, SF_4, ClF_3, BrF_5 and XeF_4, which of the following shapes does not describe any of the molecules mentioned? **[Kerala CEE]**
(a) Bent (b) Trigonal bipyramidal
(c) *see-saw* (d) T-shape
(e) Square pyramidal

34 The geometry of electron pairs around I in IF_5 is **[DUMET]**
(a) octahedral (b) trigonal bipyramidal
(c) square pyramidal (d) pentagonal planar

35 Hybridisation shown by carbon and oxygen of —OH group in phenol are respectively, **[Guj CET]**
(a) sp^2, sp^2 (b) sp^3, sp^3 (c) sp, sp^2 (d) sp^2, sp^3

2010

36 In which one of the following species, the central atom has the type of hybridisation which is not the same as that present in the other three? **[CBSE AIPMT]**
(a) PCl_5 (b) SF_4 (c) I_3^- (d) $SbCl_5^{2-}$

37 In which of the following pairs of molecules/ions, the central atoms have sp^2 hybridisation? **[CBSE AIPMT]**
(a) BF_3 and NH_2^- (b) NO_2^- and NH_3
(c) BF_3 and NO_2^- (d) NH_2^- and H_2O

38 Match the following Columns. **[RPMT]**

	Column I (Compound)		Column II (Structure)
A.	ClF_3	1.	Square planar
B.	PCl_5	2.	Tetrahedral
C.	IF_5	3.	Trigonal bipyramidal
D.	CCl_4	4.	Square pyramidal
E.	XeF_4	5.	T-shaped

Codes

	A	B	C	D	E		A	B	C	D	E
(a)	5	4	3	2	1	(b)	5	3	4	2	1
(c)	5	3	4	1	2	(d)	4	3	5	2	1

39 Which one of the following conversions involve change in both hybridisation and shape? **[KCET]**
(a) $CH_4 \longrightarrow C_2H_6$ (b) $NH_3 \longrightarrow NH_4^+$
(c) $BF_3 \longrightarrow BF_4^-$ (d) $H_2O \longrightarrow H_3O^+$

40 The AsF_5 molecule is trigonal bipyramidal. The hybrid orbitals used by the As-atoms for bonding are **[JCECE]**
(a) $d_{x^2-y^2}, d_{z^2}, s, p_x, p_y$ (b) d_{xy}, s, p_x, p_y, p_z
(c) $s, p_x, p_y, p_z, d_{z^2}$ (d) $d_{x^2-y^2}, s, p_x, p_y$

41 The geometry of H_2S and its dipole moment are **[Haryana PMT]**
(a) angular and non-zero
(b) angular and zero
(c) linear and non-zero
(d) linear and zero

2009

42 The hybridisation scheme for the central atom includes a *d*-orbital contribution in **[AIIMS]**
(a) I_3^- (b) PCl_3
(c) NO_3^- (d) H_2Se

43 Out of $N_2O, SO_2, I_3^+, I_3^-, H_2O, NO_2^-$ and N_3^-, the linear species are **[OJEE]**
(a) NO_2^-, I_3^+, H_2O (b) N_2O, I_3^+, N_3^-
(c) N_2O, I_3^-, N_3^- (d) N^{3-}, I_3^+, SO_2

44 The molecular geometry and hybridisation of centralaton of IF_4 is **[OJEE]**
(a) Square planar, sp^3d^2
(b) T-shape, sp^3d
(c) Tetrahedral, sp^3
(d) Trigonal bipyramidal, sp^3d

45 Which are isoelectronic and isostructural? **[CG PMT, Haryana PMT]**
(a) NO_3^-, CO_3^{2-} (b) SO_3, NO_3^-
(c) ClO_3^-, CO_3^{2-} (d) CO_3^{2-}, SO_3

46 Total number of lone pairs of electrons on Xe in $XeOF_4$ is **[CG PMT, Haryana PMT]**
(a) 0 (b) 1
(c) 2 (d) 3

47 The shape of $XeOF_2$ on the basis of VSEPR theory is **[J&K CET]**
(a) *see-saw* (b) V-shaped
(c) trigonal planar (d) T-shaped

48 The '*d*' orbital involved in the hybridisation in the PCl_5 molecule is **[J&K CET]**
(a) $3d_{x^2-y^2}$ (b) $3d_{z^2}$
(c) $3d_{xy}$ (d) $4d_{x^2-y^2}$

49 If I_2 is dissolved in aqueous KI, the intense yellow species I_3^- is formed. The structure of I_3^- ions is **[DUMET]**
(a) square pyramidal
(b) trigonal bipyramidal
(c) octahedral
(d) pentagonal bipyramidal

50 Which of the following is incorrect match for hybridisation and geometry? **[BHU]**

	Hybridisation		Geometry
(a)	dsp^2	—	Planar
(b)	d^3s and sp^3	—	Tetrahedral
(c)	d^2sp^3 and sp^3d^2	—	Octahedral
(d)	d^3s	—	Planar

2008

51 The molecular shapes of SF_4, SiF_4 and ICl_4^- are **[Haryana PMT]**

(a) different with 1, 0 and 2 lone pairs of electrons on the central atoms, respectively
(b) different with 0, 1 and 2 lone pairs of electrons on the central atoms, respectively
(c) the same with 1, 1 and 1 lone pair of electrons on the central atoms, respectively
(d) the same with 2, 0 and 1 lone pairs of electrons on the central atoms, respectively

52 As the *s*-character of hybridised orbital increases, the bond angle **[AMU]**

(a) increases
(b) decreases
(c) becomes zero
(d) does not change

53 *X* and *Y* are anhydrides of sulphurous acid and sulphuric acid respectively. The hybridisation state and the shape of *X* and *Y* are **[EAMCET]**

	Hybridisation		Geometry
(a)	sp^2, sp^3	—	Angular, tetrahedral
(b)	sp^2, sp^2,	—	Angular, angular
(c)	sp^2, sp^2,	—	Angular, planar triangular
(d)	sp^3, sp^3,	—	Planar, planar

54 Match the following columns. **[EAMCET]**

	Column I		Column II
A.	BCl_3	1.	Linear
B.	$PdBr_4^{2-}$	2.	Triangular planar
C.	SF_6	3.	Tetrahedral
D.	I_3^-	4.	Octahedral
		5.	Square planar

Codes

	A	B	C	D
(a)	2	3	4	1
(b)	5	3	2	1
(c)	2	5	4	1
(d)	5	4	3	2

55 In NO_3^- ion, the number of bond pairs and lone pairs of electrons on nitrogen atom ae

(a) 2, 2 (b) 3, 1
(c) 1, 3 (d) 4, 0

2007

56 **Assertion** (A) C—H bond in ethyne is shorter than C—H bonds in ethene.
Reason (R) Carbon atom in ethene is *sp* hybridised while it is sp^2 in ethyne. **[AIIMS]**

(a) Both A and R are correct and R is the correct explanation of A
(b) Both A and R are correct but R is not the correct explanation of A
(c) A is correct but R is incorrect
(d) Both A and R are incorrect

57 Among the following, the pair in which the two species are not isostructural, is **[Manipal]**

(a) SiF_4 and SF_4 (b) IO_3^- and XeO_3
(c) BH_4^- and NH_4^+ (d) PF_6^- and SF_6

58 In a regular octahedral molecule MX_6, the number of *X*—*M*—*X* bonds at 180° is **[Manipal]**

(a) three (b) two
(c) six (d) four

59 In BrF_3 molecule, the lone pairs occupy equatorial positions to minimise **[Manipal]**

(a) lone pair-bond pair repulsion only
(b) bond pair-bond pair repulsion only
(c) lone pair-lone pair repulsion and lone pair-bond pair repulsion
(d) lone pair-lone pair repulsion only

60 Which of the following represents *pπ-dπ* back donation? **[MP PMT]**

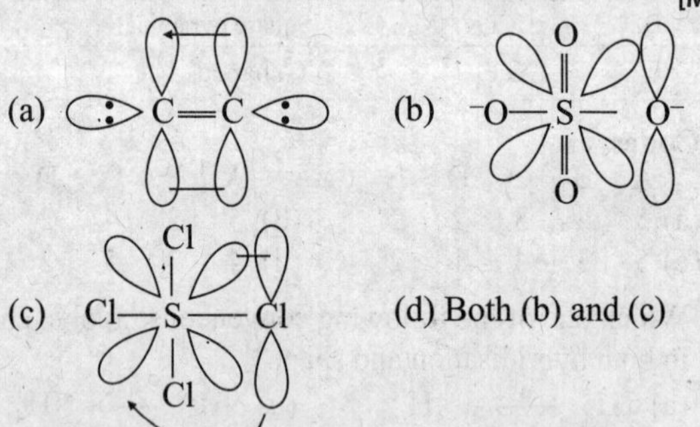

(d) Both (b) and (c)

61 H_2O is dipolar, whereas BeF_2 is not. It is because **[Manipal]**

(a) the electronegativity of F is greater than that of O
(b) H_2O involves hydrogen bonding whereas BeF_2 is a discrete molecule
(c) H_2O is linear and BeF_2 is angular
(d) H_2O is angular and BeF_2 is linear

62 Which of the following has $p\pi$-$d\pi$ bonding? **[Punjab PMET]**

(a) NO_3^- (b) SO_3^{2-}
(c) BO_3^{3-} (d) CO_3^{2-}

63 What will be the bond angle C—O—H in alcohol if hybridisation of C and O-atom possess sp^3 hybridisation? **[Guj CET]**

(a) 111°42′
(b) 109°28′
(c) 108°30′
(d) 109°

2006

64 Match the following columns.

	Column I (Species)		Column II (Geometry)
A.	H_3O^+	1.	Planar
B.	$H_2C=NH$	2.	Angular
C.	ClO_2^-	3.	Tetrahedral
D	NH_4^+	4.	Trigonal bipyramidal
E.	PCl_5	5.	Pyramidal

Codes **[Kerala CEE]**

	A	B	C	D	E
(a)	2	1	3	5	4
(b)	1	5	2	3	4
(c)	5	1	2	3	4
(d)	3	1	4	5	2
(e)	5	2	4	1	3

65 Which of the following set of properties belong to PCl_5? **[J&K CET]**

(a) sp^3, tetrahedral, 4 valence shell pairs of electrons
(b) sp^3d, trigonal bipyramidal, 5 valence shell pairs of electrons
(c) sp^3d^2, octahedral, 6 valence shell pairs of electrons
(d) sp^3d, square planar, 4 valence shell pairs of electrons

2005

66 **Assertion** (A) $SeCl_4$ does not have a tetrahedral structure.
Reason (R) Se in $SeCl_4$ has two lone pairs. **[AIIMS]**

(a) Both A and R are correct and R is the correct explanation of A
(b) Both A and R are correct but R is not the correct explanation of A
(c) A is correct but R is incorrect
(d) Both A and R are incorrect

67 Among the following molecules
I. XeO_3 II. $XeOF_4$ III. XeF_6
Those having same number of lone pairs on Xe are

(a) I and II (b) I and III
(c) II and III (d) I, II and III

68 With which of the given pairs CO_2 resembles in structure?

(a) $HgCl_2, C_2H_2$
(b) $HgCl_2, SnCl_4$
(c) C_2H_2, NO_2
(d) N_2O and NO_2

Answers

1 (b)	2 (c, d)	3 (b)	4 (d)	5 (c)	6 (c)	7 (a)	8 (a)	9 (c)	10 (a)
11 (c)	12 (d)	13 (d)	14 (b)	15 (d)	16 (c)	17 (c)	18 (c)	19 (c)	20 (c)
21 (c)	22 (a)	23 (b)	24 (a)	25 (d)	26 (d)	27 (d)	28 (b)	29 (c)	30 (d)
31 (c)	32 (b)	33 (b)	34 (c)	35 (d)	36 (d)	37 (c)	38 (b)	39 (c)	40 (c)
41 (a)	42 (a)	43 (c)	44 (a)	45 (a)	46 (b)	47 (d)	48 (b)	49 (b)	50 (d)
51 (a)	52 (a)	53 (c)	54 (c)	55 (d)	56 (c)	57 (a)	58 (a)	59 (d)	60 (d)
61 (d)	62 (b)	63 (c)	64 (c)	65 (b)	66 (d)	67 (d)	68 (a)		

Explanations

1 (*b*) In gaseous state, water exists as discrete H_2O molecule, in which the central O-atom contains four sp^3-hybridised orbitals, two of which are half - filled and used in overlapping with 1*s* orbital of H-atom to give two $sp^3 - s$, O–H, σ-bond while the remaining two exist as lone pair. The geometry of the molecule is angular or V-shape.

$2\delta^-$ 95.7 pm

δ^+H 104.5° $H\delta^+$

2 (*c*, *d*) The structure with hybridisation of given compounds are as follows :

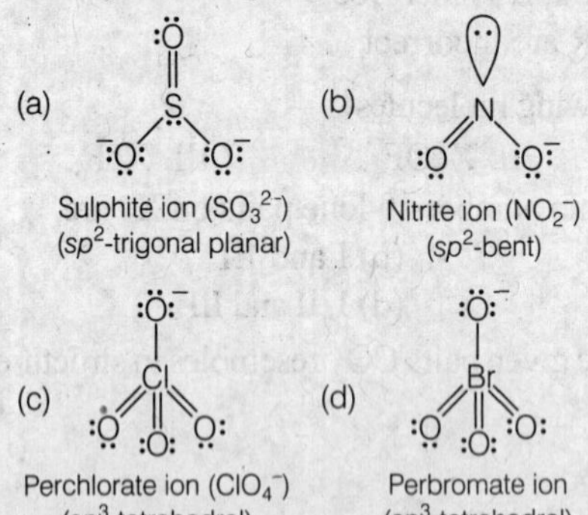

Sulphite ion (SO_3^{2-}) (sp^2-trigonal planar)

Nitrite ion (NO_2^-) (sp^2-bent)

Perchlorate ion (ClO_4^-) (sp^3-tetrahedral)

Perbromate ion (sp^3-tetrahedral)

3 (*b*) The hybridisation of the given molecules are :

(a) $\overset{sp^2}{CH_2}=\overset{sp^2}{CH}-\overset{sp^2}{CH}=\overset{sp^2}{CH_2}$

(b) $\overset{sp^2}{CH_2}=\overset{sp^2}{CH}-\overset{sp}{C}\equiv\overset{sp}{CH}$

(c) $\overset{sp}{CH}\equiv\overset{sp}{C}-\overset{sp}{C}\equiv\overset{sp}{CH}$

(d) $\overset{sp^3}{CH_3}-\overset{sp^2}{CH}=\overset{sp^2}{CH}-\overset{sp^3}{CH_3}$

Therefore, the correct option is (b).

4 (*d*) The structure of (IF_7) is pentagonal bipyramidal. It can be depicted as follows:

I (Z= 53) (Ground state) =

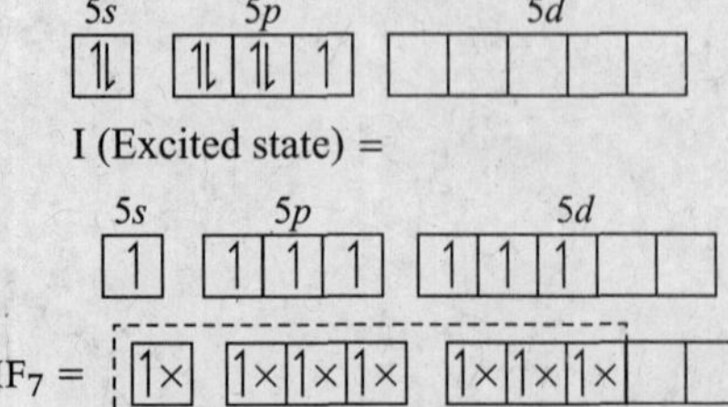

Here, X denotes electrons of F-atoms. The structure of IF_7 is shown below:

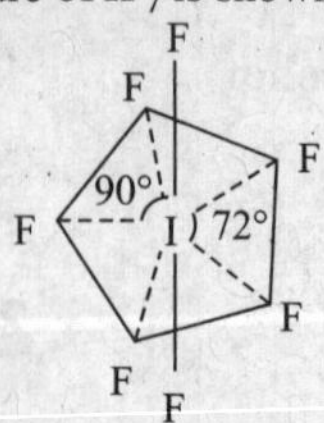

Pentagonal bipyramidal structure

5 (*c*) $[Mn(CN)_6]^{3-}$ is d^2sp^3-hybridised and octahedral. In $[Mn(CN)_6]^{3-}$, Mn is in +3 oxidation state.

$Mn^{3+} = 3d^4\ 4s^0$

Orbitals of Mn^{3+} ion

3*d* 4*s* 4*p*

= ⥮ 1 1 1 ☐ | ☐ | ☐☐☐

d^2sp^3-hybridised (Octahedral)

3*d* 4*s* 4*p*

$[Mn\ (CN)_6]^{3-}$ = ⥮ 1 1 ☒ ☒ | ☒ | ☒☒☒

d^2sp^3-hybridised (Octahedral)

6 (*c*) (a) $CH_4 \longrightarrow 4\,lp + 0\,lp$ (sp^3 and tetrahedral)

$C_2H_6 \longrightarrow$ each C-atom has $4\,lp + 0\,lp$ (sp^3 and tetrahedral)

(b) $NH_3 \longrightarrow 3bp + 1lp$ (sp^3 and pyramidal)

$NH_4^+ \longrightarrow 3\,bp + 1\,lp$ (sp^3 and tetrahedral)

(c) $BF_3 \longrightarrow 3bp + 0\,lp$ 5(sp^2 and trigonal planar)`

$BF_4^- \longrightarrow 4\,bp + 0\,lp$ (sp^3 and tetrahedral)`

(d) $H_2O \longrightarrow 2\,bp + 2\,lp$ (sp^3 and angular)

$H_3O^+ \longrightarrow 3\,bp + 1\,lp$ (sp^3 and pyramidal)

Hence, $BF_3 \longrightarrow BF_4^-$ conversion involve change in both hybridisation and shape.

7 (*a*) Due to presence of two lone pair of electrons over O-atom in H_2O, $lp - lp$ repulsion decreases the H— O—H bond angle.

Whereas in NH_3, there is only one lone pair of electrons present over N-atom, hence no $lp - lp$ repulsions. Thus, greater H—N—H bond angle.

$\because$ Magnitude for repulsion is in order $\rightarrow lp - lp > lp - bp > bp - bp$.

Hence, both (A) and (R) are true and (R) is the correct explanation of (A).

8 (*a*) Formation of SF_6 : In SF_6, the central sulphur atom has the ground state outer electronic configuration $3s^2 3p^4$. In the excited state, the available six orbitals i.e. one *s*, three *p* and two *d* are singly occupied by electrons. These orbitals hybridise to form six new sp^3d^2 hybrid orbitals which are projected towards the six corners of a regular octahedron in SF_6. In this, F—S—F bond angle are 90° and 180°.

9 (*c*)

Ion	Structure	Hybridisation
NO_2^+	$O=\overset{\oplus}{N}=O$	*sp*
NO_3^-	$O=N(\rightarrow O)-\overset{-}{O}$	sp^2
NH_4^+	$[NH_4]^+$ (N bonded to four H)	sp^3

Thus, option (c) is correct.

10 (*a*) Geometry is determined by electron pair arrangement whereas, shape is determined by arrangement of atoms around the central atom.

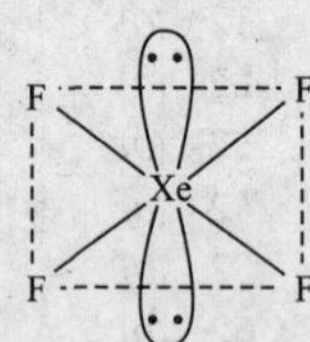

Geometry – octahedral

Hybridisation – sp^3d^2

Thus, option (a) is correct.

11 (*c*) Hybridisation

$$= \frac{\text{Number of } \sigma\text{- electrons}}{2}$$

$$= \frac{2 + 2\ (\text{negative ion})}{2}$$

$= 2 = sp$

Hence, in the carbanion, $CH_3C \equiv C^{\ominus}$, pair of electron as negative charge is present in *sp*-hybridised orbital.

12 (*d*) A – 1, B – 3, C – 4, D – 2

The structure of the xenon compounds are represented below:

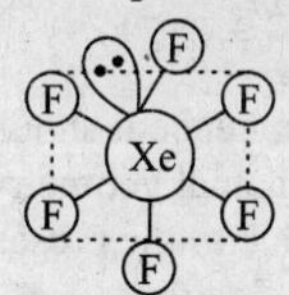

Distorted octahedral XeF_6

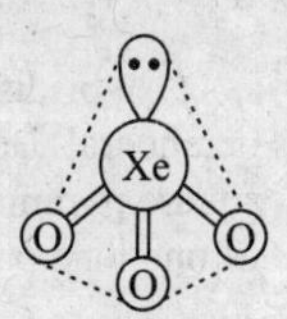

Pyramidal XeO_3

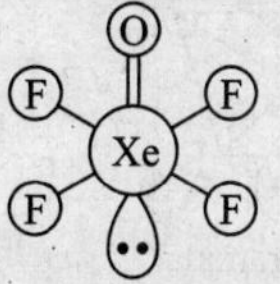

Square pyramidal $XeOF_4$

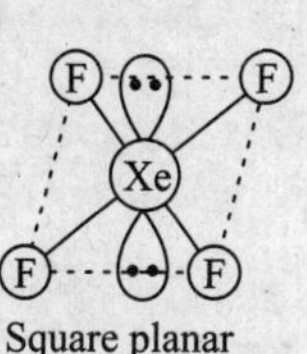

Square planar XeF_4

13 (*d*) ClO_3^-, $= SO_3^{2-}$

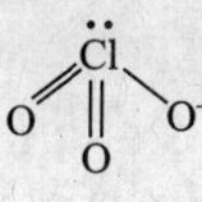

Number of electrons

$CO_3^{2-} = 6 + 2 + 24 = 32$

$SO_3^{2-} = 16 + 2 + 24 = 42$

$ClO_3^- = 17 + 24 + 1 = 42$

$NO_3^- = 7 + 1 + 24 = 32$

Hence, ClO_3^- and SO_3^{2-} are isoelectronic and are pyramidal in shape.

14 (*b*) Species with sp^2 hybridisation are planar triangular in shape. Among the given species NO_3^- is sp^2 hybridised with no lone pair of electrons on central atom, N. Whereas, N_3, NO_2^- and CO_2 are *sp* hybridised with a linear shape.

$[O—\ddot{N}=O]^-$, $O=C=O$

$:N=\overset{+}{N}=N\colon$

15 (*d*) BF_3 is sp^2 hybridised, where percentage of *s*-character is 33.3.

16 (*c*) In XeF_6, Xe, the central atom contains 8 valence electrons. Out of which 6 are utilised with fluorine in bonding (i.e. it contains six bond pairs of electrons) while one pair remains as lone pair.

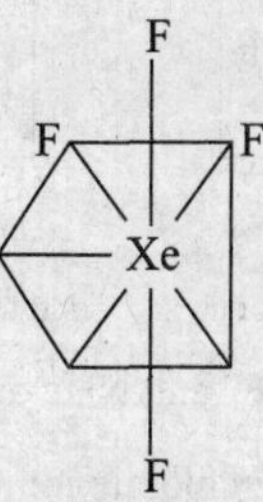

Thus, the total pairs = 6 + 1 = 7

Hence, its shape is pentagonal bipyramidal according to VSEPR theory.

17 (*c*)

Compound	Shape
CH_4	Tetrahedral
SF_4	*see-saw*
BCl_3	Triangular planar
ClF_3	T-shaped
XeF_2	Linear
$ZnCl_2$	Linear
SO_2	Bent
CO_2	Linear

18 (*c*) For XeF_4

E = 2 lone pairs on Xe

B = 4 bond pairs of electrons. Hybridisation sp^3d^2 because of 2 lone pairs of electrons, the regular octahedral shape is distorted to square planar.

19 (*c*) $O_1 = 6 - 2 - \frac{1}{2}(6) = 6 - 2 - 3 = 1$

$O_2 = 6 - 4 - \frac{1}{2}(4) = 6 - 4 - 2 = 0$

$O_3 = 6 - 6 - \frac{1}{2}(2) = 6 - 6 - 1 = -1$

20 (*c*) Electronic configuration of $_7N = 1s^2, 2s^2\,2p^3$ and $_1H = 1s^1$

$H \cdot \times \overset{\times\times}{N} \times \cdot H \Rightarrow H—\overset{\times\times}{N}—H$ (with H below N)

Hence, NH_3 has 3 bond pairs and 1 lone pair.

21 (*c*) BF_4^-, NH_4^+, $NiCl_4^{2-}$ all are tetrahedral in shape but $[Cu(NH_3)_4]^{2+}$ is not tetrahedral but square planar.

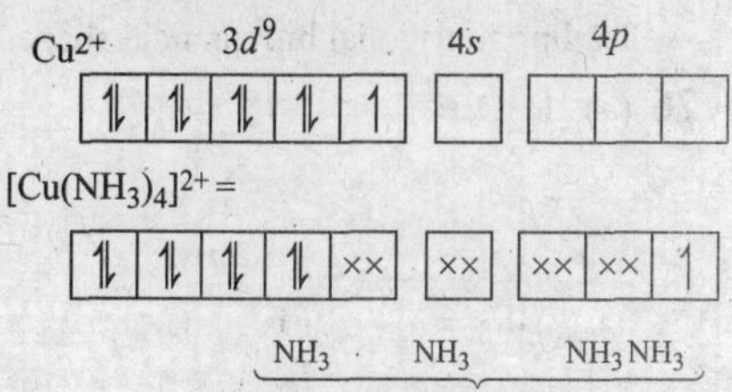

22 (*a*) Gammexane is chemically benzene hexachloride. Its formula is $C_6H_6Cl_6$. Its structure is as follows

∴ It has no double bond.

23 (*b*) In $_3Li$ additional electron is added in $1s^2 2s^1$.

In $_4Be$ additional electron is added in $1s^2, 2s^2$ (a stable state).

$_5B$ additional electron is added in $1s^2, 2s^2 2p^1$.

$_6C$ additional electron is added in $1s^2, 2s^2 2p^2$.

Thus, Be^- will be least stable.

24 (*a*) (a) $H_2C=CH—C\equiv N$ (sp^2, sp^2, sp, sp)

(b) $CH\equiv C—C\equiv CH$ (sp, sp, sp, sp)

(c) $H_2C=C=C=CH_2$ (sp^2, sp, sp, sp^2)

(d) $H_2C=CH—CH=CH_2$ (sp^2, sp^2, sp^2, sp^2)

The option (a) is represent the mode of hybridisation sp^2, sp^2, sp, sp from left to right. Hence, (a) is the correct option.

25 (*d*) Hybridisation

$= \frac{1}{2}(6 + 4 - 0 + 0) = 5$

Thus, the type of hybridisation is sp^3d leading to trigonal bipyramidal shape.

26 (*d*) $H_2O \Rightarrow$:O: with H, H

$(2bp + 2lp)$

$BF_3 \Rightarrow$ B with F, F, F

$(3bp + 0lp)$

$NH_2^- \Rightarrow$ [:N: with H, H]$^-$

$(2bp + 2lp)$

$PCl_3 \Rightarrow$ P (one lone pair) with Cl, Cl, Cl

$(3bp + 1lp)$

Thus, in PCl_3, the central atom P has three bond pairs and one lone pair.

27 (*d*) If number of bond pairs and lone pairs are same for the given pairs, they are isostructural.

(a) BCl_3 (B with three σ-bonded Cl) and ClF_3-type Cl—Br—Cl with Cl

3 σ-bonds
sp^2 hybridisation and trigonal planar geometry

3 σ-bonds + 2*lp*
sp^3d hybridisation and T-shape geometry

(b) NH_3 and NO_3^-

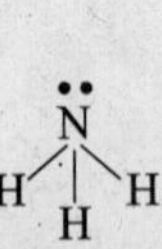

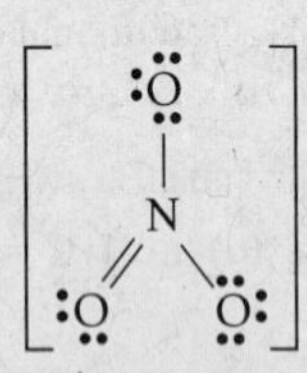

3σ-bonds + 1 *lp*, sp^3 hybridisation and pyramidal geometry

3σ-bonds, sp^2 hybridisation and trigonal planar geometry

(c) NF_3 and BF_3

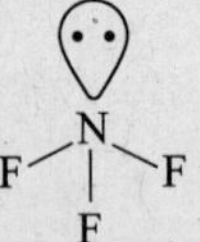

B with F, F, F

3σ-bonds + 1 *lp*, sp^3 hybridisation and pyramidal geometry

3σ-bonds, sp^2 hybridisation and triangular planar geometry

(d) BF_4^- and NH_4^+

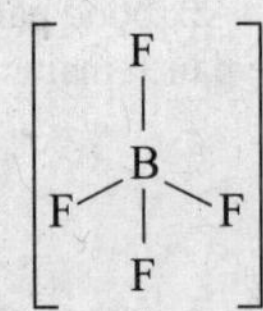

$[NH_4]^+$: N with H, H, H, H

4σ-bonds, sp^3 hybridisation tetrahedral geometry

4σ-bonds, sp^3 hybridisation and tetrahedral geometry

Thus, BF_4^- and NH_4^+ are isostructural.

28 (*b*) In perchlorate ion,

[Cl with O^-, O, O, O]

Central Cl-atom is sp^3 hybridised. So, all the four sigma bonds are $sp^3 - p$ bonds.

29 (*c*) In $XeOF_2$ molecule, Xe is sp^3d hybridised.

F—Xe(=O)—F with two lone pairs

$XeOF_2$
Trigonal pyramidal

30 (*d*)

$H_{(s)}—C_{sp^3}—C_{sp^3}—H_{(s)}$, with $H_{(s)}$ on each carbon above and below

C—H bond, C—C bond
$(sp^3 - s)$ $(sp^3 - sp^3)$

31 (*c*) $H_3C — \underset{sp}{C} \equiv \underset{sp}{C} — CH_3$ is linear due to *sp*-hybridisation of the two symmetric carbon.

32 (*b*)

Ions	Hybridisaton
NO_2^-	sp^2
NO_3^-	sp^2
NH_2^-	sp^3
NH_4^+	sp^3
SCN^-	*sp*

$\therefore NO_2^-$ and NO_3^- both have same hybridisation, i.e. sp^2 and trigonal planar geometry.

33 (*b*) SO_2 — Bent SF_4— *see-saw*

ClF_3 — T-shape

BrF_5 — Square pyramidal

XeF_4 — Square planar

34 (*c*) $H = \frac{1}{2}[V + Y - C + A]$

$= \frac{1}{2}[5 + 7] = 6$ or alternate way

$IF_5 = 7 + 5 \times 7 = \frac{42}{8} = 5 + 1$

sp^3d^2 hybridisation, hence it should be octahedral. But its actual geometry is square pyramidal due to the presence of one lone pair of electrons.

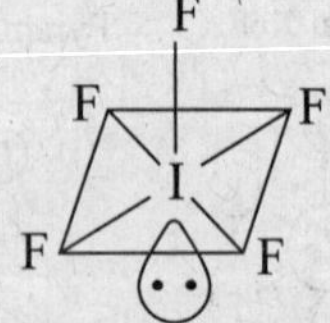

Square pyramidal

35 (*d*) Phenol: O—H on C of benzene ring (HC, CH, HC, CH, C—H)

sp^3 hybridised
sp^2 hybridised

36 (*d*) $SbCl_5^{2-} = sp^3d^2$; $PCl_5 = sp^3d$; $SF_4 = sp^3d$; $I_3^- = sp^3d$.

37 (*c*) BF_3 and NO_2^- are sp^2 hybridised while NH_2^-, NH_3 and H_2O are sp^3 hybridised.

38 (*b*)

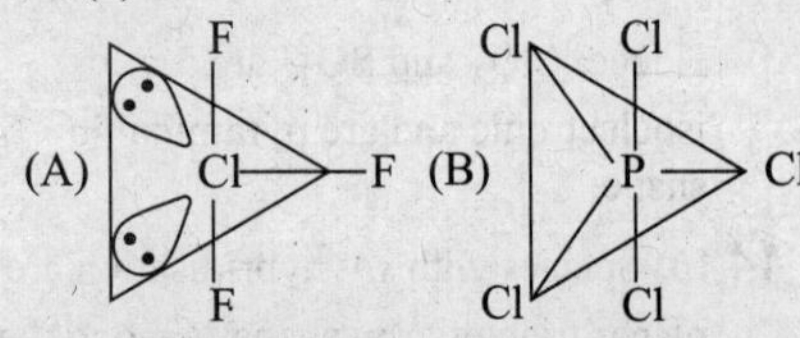

So, ClF_3–T-shaped, PCl_5–Trigonal bipyramidal.

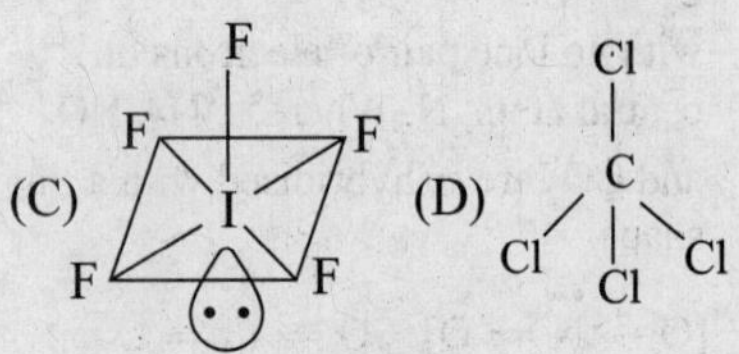

IF_5 : Square pyramidal CCl_4 : Tetrahedral

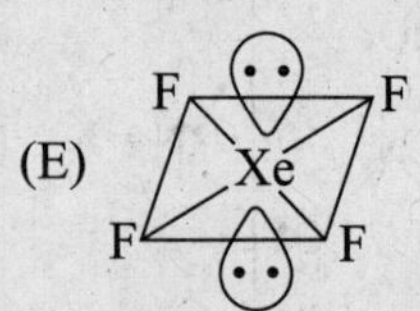

XeF_4 : Square planar

39 (*c*) (a) $CH_4 \longrightarrow CH_3—CH_3$

CH_4: $4bp + 0lp$, sp^3, Tetrahedral

$CH_3—CH_3$: $4bp$ $4bp$, sp^3 sp^3, Tetrahedral

(b)	NH_3 $3bp + 1lp$ sp^3 Pyramidal	$\longrightarrow$	NH_4^+ $4bp$ sp^3 Tetrahedral
(c)	BF_3 $3bp$ sp^2 Trigonal planar	$\longrightarrow$	BF_4^- $4bp$ sp^3 Tetrahedral
(d)	H_2O $2bp + 2lp$ sp^3 Angular	$\longrightarrow$	H_3O^+ $3bp + 1lp$ sp^3 Pyramidal

Thus, conversion of BF_3 into BF_4^- involves changes in both hybridisation and shape.

40 (*c*) Since, the geometry of AsF_5 molecule is trigonal bipyramidal, it is sp^3d hybridised. Thus, s, p_x, p_y, p_z and d_{z^2} orbitals are utilised by As-atom for bonding.

41 (*a*) Sulphur undergoes sp^3-hybridisation in H_2S but due to the presence of two lone pairs, it has angular geometry.

S, H, H

$\mu \neq 0$

42 (*a*)

(a) $I_3^- = [I—I—I]^-$ $= 2\sigma$-bonds + 3 lone pairs $= sp^3d$ hybridisation

(b) $PCl_3 =$ P, Cl, Cl, Cl $= 3\sigma$ bonds + 1 lone pair $= sp^3$ hybridisation

(c) $NO_3^- =$ [O=N(O)(O)]$^-$ $= 3\sigma$-bonds + 0 lone pair $= sp^2$ hybridisation

(d) H_2Se Se, H, H $= 2\sigma$-bonds + 2 lone pairs $= sp^3$ hydridisation

Hence, in I_3^-, *d*-orbitals are used in hybridisation.

43 (*c*) N_2O : $\overset{-}{N}{=}\overset{+}{N}{=}O$, hence it is linear.

I_3^- : With $2bp$ and $3lp$ around central atom it is linear.

N_3^- : With $2bp$ (stereo active pairs) around the central atom, it is linear.

44 (*a*) The molecular geometry and hybridisation of central atom in ICl_4^- is square planar and sp^3d^2 respectively.

45 (*a*) Isoelectronic means same number of electrons and isostructural means same structure.

[:Ö: — N — :O: , :Ö:]$^-$ [O=C(O)(O)]$^{2-}$

NO_3^- (No. of electrons = 32) CO_3^{2-} (No. of electrons = 32)

46 (*b*) Structure of $XeOF_4$ is,

O, F, F, Xe, F, F

one lone pair of electrons

47 (*d*) In $XeOF_2$, Number of σ-bonds = 3

Number of lone pairs = 2

F—Xe—F, O

$\therefore$ Total number of pairs of electrons = 3 + 2 = 5

Hybridisation $\rightarrow$ sp^3d

Shape $\rightarrow$ T-shaped

48 (*b*) PCl_5 molecule has trigonal bipyramidal shape and the P-atom is sp^3d hybridised. The *d*-orbital involved is $3d_{z^2}$.

49 (*b*) Total number of valence electrons in $I_3^- = 7 \times 3 + 1 = 22$

$$= \frac{22}{8} = \frac{2+6}{2}$$

$$= 2bp + 3lp$$

In triiodide ion, the central iodine atom is sp^3d hybridised and has trigonal bipyramidal structure in which the equatorial positions are occupied by lone pairs and the axial positions by iodine.

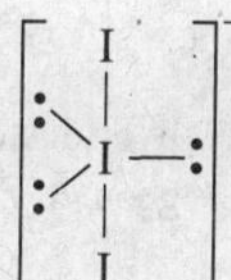

(Structure of I_3^- triangular bipyramidal)

50 (*d*) Hybridisation d^3s may have tetrahedral geometry, but not planar geometry.

51 (*a*)

Molecule	Structure	Hybridisation of central atom	Lone pair
SF_4	S with F, F, F, F and one lone pair	sp^3d	one
SiF_4	Si with F, F, F, F	sp^3	zero
ICl_4^-	[I with Cl, Cl, Cl, Cl and two lone pairs]$^-$	sp^3d^2	two

52 (*a*) Bond angle increases with increase in % *s*-character.

Hybridisation	% of *s*-character	Bond angle
sp	50	180°
sp^2	33.3	120°
sp^3	25	109°28′

53 (*c*)

$$\underset{\text{Sulphurous acid}}{H_2SO_3} \xrightarrow[-2H_2O]{P_2O_5} \underset{\substack{(X)\\ \text{(Anhydride of}\\ \text{sulphurous acid)}}}{SO_2}$$

Thus, hybridisation is sp^2 and shape is angular due to the presence of one lone pair of electrons.

$$\underset{\text{Sulphuric acid}}{H_2SO_4} \xrightarrow[-2H_2O]{P_2O_5} \underset{\substack{(Y)\\ \text{(Anhydride of}\\ \text{sulphuric acid)}}}{SO_3}$$

Thus, in SO_3, hybridisation of S is sp^2 and its shape is triangular planar.

54 (*c*) (A) $BCl_3 = 3bp + 0lp$
i.e. hybridisation is sp^2 and geometry is triangular planar.

(B) $[PdBr_4]^{2-}$

The outer electronic configuration of Pd is [Kr] $4d^{10}$, $5s^0$.

Geometry is square planar and it has $4bb + 0lp$

Pd^{2+} = [Kr] $4d^8$, $5s^0$

(C) $SF_6 = 6bp + 0lp$, i.e. hybridisation is sp^3d^2 and the geometry is octahedral.

(D) $I_3^- = 2bp + 3lp$, i.e. hybridisation is sp^3d but geometry is linear due to the presence of 3 lone pairs of electrons, that lie in equatorial plane.

55 (*d*) In N-atom, the number of valence electrons = 5. Due to presence of one negative charge, number of valence electrons = 5 + 1 = 6, one O-atom forms two bond (double bond) and two O-atom shared with two electrons of N-atom. Thus 3O atom shared with 8 electrons on N-atom.

∴ It has $4bp$ and $0lp$.

56 (*c*) The carbon atom is sp^2 hybridised in ethene and *sp* hybridised in ethyne.

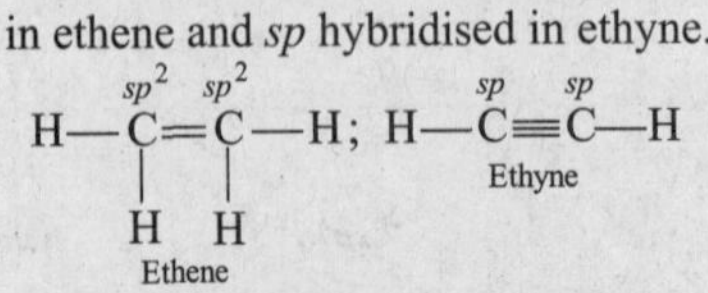

Hence, A is correct but R is incorrect.

57 (*a*) SiF_4 and SF_4 are not isostructural because SiF_4 is tetrahedral due to sp^3-hybridisation of Si.

$_{14}Si = 1s^2, 2s^2, 2p^6, 3s^2 3p^2$ (in ground state)

$_{14}Si = 1s^2, 2s^2\ 2p^6, 3s^1 3p^3$ (in excited state)

Hence, four equivalent sp^3-hybrid orbitals are obtained and they are overlapped by four *p*-orbitals of four fluorine atoms on their axis. Thus, it shows following structures.

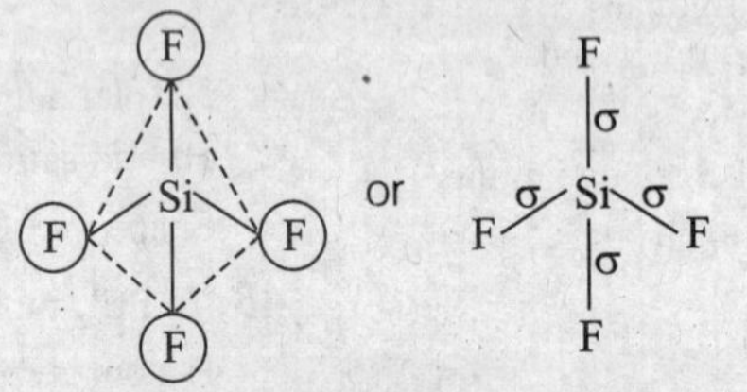

While SF_4 is not tetrahedral but it is distorted tetrahedral because in it, S is sp^3d hybridised.

$_{16}S = 1s^2, 2s^2 2p^6, 3s^2 3p_x^2 3p_y^1 3p_z^1$
(in ground state)
$= 1s^2, 2s^2 2p^6, 3s^2 3p_x^1 3p_y^1 3p_z^1 3d_{xy}^1$

sp^3d-hybridisation
(in first excitation state)

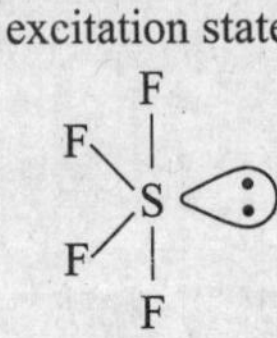

Hence, five sp^3d hybrid orbitals are obtained. One orbital is already paired and rest four are overlapped with four *p*-orbitals of four fluorine atoms on their axis in trigonal bipyramidal form.

This structure is distorted from trigonal bipyramidal to *see-saw* due to involvement of repulsion between lone pair and bond pair.

58 (*a*) In octahedral molecule MX_6, the six hybrid orbitals (sp^3d^2) are directed towards the corners of a regular octahedral with an angle of 90°. According to given structure of MX_6, the number of *X*—*M*—*X* bonds at 180° must be three.

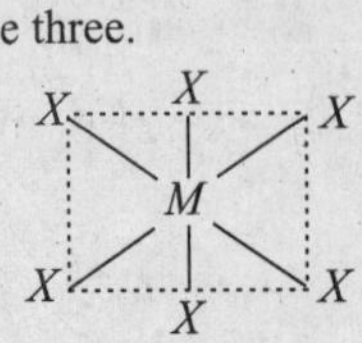

59 (*d*) In BrF_3 molecule, Br is sp^3d hybridised, but geometry is T-shaped due to distortion of geometry from trigonal bipyramidal to T-shaped by the involvement of lone pair-lone pair repulsion.

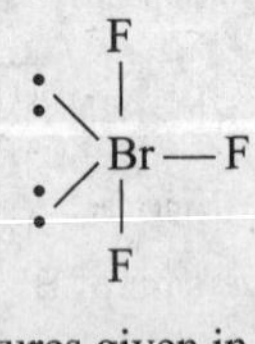

60 (*d*) Structures given in options (b) and (c) show the *pπ-dπ* back bonding as the *p*-orbitals of Cl and O donate electrons to the *d*-orbital of S.

61 (*d*) The structure of H_2O is angular (V-shape) with sp^3-hybridisation and bond angle is 104.5°. Its dipole moment value is positive or more than zero.

Hence,

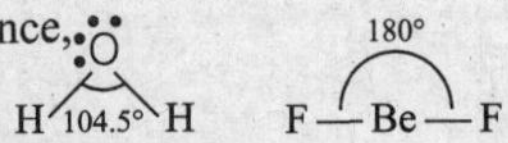

But in BeF_2, structure is linear due to *sp*-hybridisation (μ = 0)

Thus, due to μ > 0, H_2O is dipolar and due to μ = 0, BeF_2 is non-polar.

62 (*b*) In SO_3^{2-}, the S is sp^3 hybridised. So,

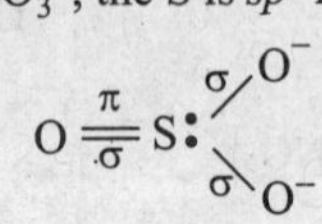

$_{16}S = 1s^2, 2s^2\ 2p^6\ , \underbrace{3s^2 3p_x^1 3p_y^1 3p_z^1}_{sp^3 \text{ hybridisation}}$, $\underset{\text{unhybridised}}{3d_{xy}^1}$
(Sulphur atom in excited state)

In 'S', the three *p*-orbitals form σ-bonds with three oxygen atoms and unhybridised *d*-orbital is involved in π-bond formation.

$_{16}O = 1s^2, 2s^2 2p_x^2 2p_y^1 2p_z^1$

In oxygen, two unpaired *p*-orbitals are present, one is involved in σ-bond formation while other is used in π-bond formation. Thus, in SO_3^{2-}, *pπ* and *dπ* orbitals are involved for *pπ* - *dπ* bonding.

63 (*c*) The bond angle C—O—H in alcohol is slightly less than tetrahedral angle (109°28′). This is due to larger repulsion between the lone pairs of oxygen. The bond angle C—O—H in alcohol is 108°30′.

64 (*c*)

List I (Species)	List II (Geometry)
H_3O^+	Pyramidal
$H_2C{=}NH$	Planar
ClO_2^-	Angular
NH_4^+	Tetrahedral
PCl_5	Trigonal bipyramidal

65 (*b*) PCl_5 molecule has sp^3d hybridisation. Its geometry is trigonal bipyramidal and it has 5 valence shell pairs of electrons.

66 (*d*) $SeCl_4$ has *see-saw* geometry, i.e. distorted trigonal pyramidal geometry (VSEPR theory). In this, molecule has only one lone pair and hence, it undergoes sp^3d hybridisation.

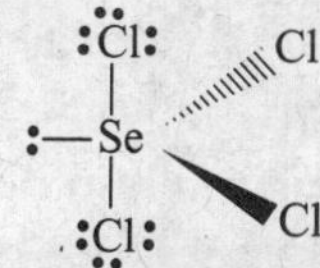

Hence, both A and R are incorrect.

67 (*d*)

(III)

$XeOF_4$, square planar (sp^3d^2 hybridisation)

(I)

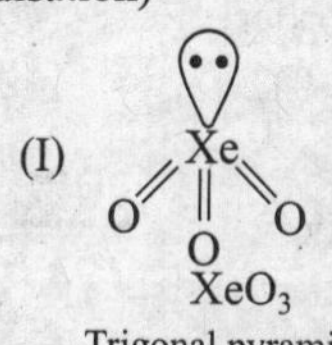

XeO_3
Trigonal pyramidal
(sp^3 hybridisation)

(II)

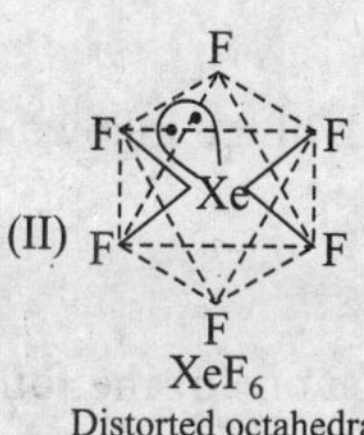

XeF_6
Distorted octahedral
(sp^3d^3 hybridisation)

As shown above, all the compounds have one lone pair.

68 (*a*) CO_2 is linear in structure.

(a) $HgCl_2$ and $HC{\equiv}CH(C_2H_2)$ both are linear in structure.

(b) $HgCl_2$ is linear but $SnCl_4$ is tetrahedral in structure.

(c) C_2H_2 is linear but NO_2 is bent.

(d) N_2O is linear but NO_2 is bent in structure.

Topic 4

Molecular Orbital Theory

2019

1 Which of the following diatomic molecular species has only π-bonds according to molecular orbital theory? [NEET]

(a) N_2 (b) C_2
(c) Be_2 (d) O_2

2 Which of the following is paramagnetic? [NEET (Odisha)]

(a) N_2 (b) H_2 (c) Li_2 (d) O_2

2017

3 Which one of the following pairs of species have the same bond order? [NEET]

(a) CO, NO (b) O_2, NO^+
(c) CN^-, CO (d) N_2, O_2^-

2014

4 Bond order of which among the following molecules is zero? [MHT CET]

(a) F_2 (b) O_2 (c) Be_2 (d) Li_2

5 The bond orders of O_2^+ and C_2 respectively are [Manipal]

(a) 2.5, 2 (b) 3, 2 (c) 2, 2.5 (d) 2, 3
(e) 3, 3

2012

6 The pair of species with the same bond order is [CBSE AIPMT]

(a) O_2^{2-}, B_2 (b) O_2^+, NO^+ (c) NO, CO (d) N_2, O_2

7 During change of O_2 to O_2^- ion, the electron adds on which one of the following orbitals? [CBSE AIPMT]

(a) $\overset{*}{\pi}$-orbital (b) π-orbital (c) $\overset{*}{\sigma}$-orbital (d) σ-orbital

8 Four diatomic species are listed below. Identify the correct order in which the bond order is increasing in them [CBSE AIPMT]

(a) $NO < O_2^- < C_2^{2-} < He_2^+$ (b) $O_2^- < NO < C_2^{2-} < He_2^+$
(c) $C_2^{2-} < He_2^+ < O_2^- < NO$ (d) $He_2^+ < O_2^- < NO < C_2^{2-}$

9 Which of the following molecules/ions does not contain unpaired electrons? [AFMC]

(a) O_2^{2-} (b) B_2 (c) N_2^- (d) O_2

10 The paramagnetic behaviour of B_2 is due to the presence of [WB JEE]

(a) 2 unpaired electrons in π_b MO
(b) 2 unpaired electrons in $\overset{*}{\pi}$ MO
(c) 2 unpaired electrons in $\overset{*}{\sigma}$ MO
(d) 2 unpaired electrons in σ_b MO

2011

11 Which of the following has minimum bond length? [CBSE AIPMT]

(a) O_2 (b) O_2^+ (c) O_2^- (d) O_2^{2-}

12 Which one of the following has the strong O—O bond? [DUMET]

(a) O_2^+ (b) O_2^0 (c) O_2^- (d) O_2^{2-}

13 When O_2 is converted into O_2^+, [KCET]

(a) both paramagnetic character and bond order increase.
(b) bond order decreases
(c) paramagnetic character increases
(d) paramagnetic character decreases and the bond order increases

2010

14 Which one of the following species does not exist under normal conditions? [CBSE AIPMT]

(a) Li_2 (b) Be_2^+ (c) Be_2 (d) B_2

15 Which of the following is paramagnetic with bond order 0.5? [Manipal, VMMC]

(a) F_2 (b) H_2^+ (c) N_2 (d) O_2^-

16 The number of anti-bonding electron pairs in O_2^{2-} molecular ion on the basis of molecular orbital theory is (atomic number of $O = 8$) [Haryana PMT]

(a) 2 (b) 3 (c) 4 (d) 5

17 In which of the following pairs, the two species have identical bond order? [RPMT]

(a) N_2^-, O_2^{2-} (b) N_2^-, O_2^- (c) N_2^-, O_2^+ (d) O_2^+, N_2^{2-}

18 Peroxide ion

I. has completely filled anti-bonding molecular orbitals
II. is diamagnetic.
III. has bond order one.
IV. is isoelectronic with neon.

Which of these are correct? [KCET]

(a) II and III (b) I, II and IV (c) I, II and III (d) I and IV

2009

19 According to molecular orbital theory, which is correct statement regarding O_2? [CG PMT, Haryana PMT]

(a) Paramagnetic and bond order $< O_2^-$
(b) Paramagnetic and bond order $> O_2^-$
(c) Diamagnetic and bond order $< O_2^-$
(d) Diamagnetic and bond order $> O_2^-$

20 The common features among the species CN^-, CO and NO^+ are [DUMET]

(a) bond order three and isoelectronic
(b) bond order three and weak field ligands
(c) bond order two and π-acceptor
(d) isoelectronic and weak field ligands

21 In the change of NO^+ to NO, the electron is added to [DUMET]

(a) σ-orbital (b) π-orbital (c) $\overset{*}{\pi}$-orbital (d) π-orbital

22 The correct statement with regards to H_2^+ and H_2^- is [KCET]

(a) both H_2^+ and H_2^- do not exist
(b) H_2^- is more stable than H_2^+
(c) H_2^+ is more stable than H_2^-
(d) both H_2^+ and H_2^- are equally stable

2008

23 **Assertion** (A) He_2 does not exist.
Reason (R) Bond order of He_2 is zero. [BHU]

(a) Both A and R are correct and R is the correct explanation of A
(b) Both A and R are correct but R is not the correct explanation of A
(c) A is correct but R is incorrect
(d) Both A and R are incorrect

24 The number of nodal planes present in σ^* *s* anti-bonding orbitals is [KCET]

(a) 1 (b) 2 (c) 0 (d) 3

2007

25 Which one of the following pairs consists of only paramagnetic species? [Kerala CEE]

(a) [O_2, NO] (b) [O_2^+, O_2^{2-}] (c) [CO, NO] (d) [NO, NO^+] (e) [O_2^{2-}, N_2^-]

26 According to MOT, C_2 molecule has [MP PMT]

(a) one σ and one π-bond (b) only two π-bonds (c) only two σ-bonds (d) one σ and two π-bonds

27 Which one of the following example exhibit transient existence? [J&K CET]

(a) H (b) H_2^+ (c) H^+ (d) He

28 Which of the following is correct based on molecular orbital theory for peroxide ion? [Guj CET]

(a) Its bond order is one and it is paramagnetic
(b) Its bond order is two and it is diamagnetic
(c) Its bond order is one and it is diamagnetic
(d) Its bond order is two and it is paramagnetic

29 The paramagnetic nature of oxygen molecule is best explained on the basis of [MHT CET]

(a) valence bond theory (b) resonance (c) molecular orbital theory (d) hybridisation

30 The paramagnetism of O_2^+ is due to the presence of an odd electron in the MO [Kerala CEE]

(a) $\overset{*}{\sigma} 2s$ (b) $\pi 2p_y$
(c) $\overset{*}{\pi} 2p_x$ (d) $\overset{*}{\sigma} 2p_x$
(e) $\pi 2p_x$

2006

31 Which of the following is diamagnetic? [KCET]

(a) H_2^+ (b) O_2
(c) Li_2 (d) He_2

2005

32 **Assertion** (A) B_2 molecule is diamagnetic.

Reason (R) The highest occupied molecule orbital is of σ type. [AIIMS]

(a) Both A and R are correct and R is the correct explanation of A
(b) Both A and R are correct but R is not the correct explanation of A
(c) A is correct but R is incorrect
(d) Both A and R are incorrect

Answers

1 (b)	2 (d)	3 (c)	4 (c)	5 (a)	6 (a)	7 (a)	8 (d)	9 (a)	10 (a)
11 (b)	12 (a)	13 (d)	14 (c)	15 (b)	16 (c)	17 (c)	18 (a)	19 (b)	20 (a)
21 (c)	22 (c)	23 (a)	24 (a)	25 (a)	26 (b)	27 (c)	28 (c)	29 (c)	30 (c)
31 (c)	32 (d)								

Explanations

1 (*b*) The molecular orbital configuration of C_2 is

$C_2(Z = 12) = \sigma 1s^2, \sigma^* 1s^2, \sigma 2s^2, \sigma^* 2s^2, \pi 2p_x^2 = \pi 2p_y^2$.

Double bond in C_2 consists of both π-bonds because of the presence of last (valence) four electrons in two π-molecular orbitals.

The configuration of N_2, Be_2 and O_2 are as follows:

$N_2(Z = 14) - \sigma 1s^2, \sigma^* 1s^2, \sigma 2s^2, \sigma^* 2s^2, \pi 2p_x^2 = \pi 2p_y^2, \sigma 2p_z^2$ (1 σ and 2π-bonds)

$Be_2(Z = 8) - \sigma 1s^2, \sigma^* 1s^2, \sigma 2s^2, \sigma^* 2s^2$ (σ bonds only)

$O_2(Z = 16) - \sigma 1s^2, \sigma^* 1s^2, \sigma 2s^2, \sigma^* 2s^2, \sigma^* 2p_z^2, \pi 2p_x^2 = \pi 2p_y^2, \pi^* 2p_x^1 = \pi^* 2p_z^1$

(σ, π and 1π* bond)

Hence, option (b) is correct.

2 (*d*) If all the electrons in a molecule are paired, the molecule is diamagnetic and if there are unpaired electrons in a molecule, it is paramagnetic.

Molecular orbital configuration of given molecules are as follows:

(a) $N_2(Z = 14) - \sigma 1s^2, \sigma^* 1s^2, \sigma 2s^2, \sigma^* 2s^2, \pi 2p_x^2 = \pi 2p_y^2, \sigma 2p_z^2$

It is a diamagnetic molecule due to absence of unpaired electron.

(b) $H_2 (Z = 2) - \sigma 1s^2$

It is a diamagnetic molecule.

(c) $Li_2 (Z = 6) - \sigma 1s^2, \sigma^* 1s^2, \sigma 2s^2$

It is a diamagnetic molecule.

(d) $O_2(Z = 16) - \sigma 1s^2, \sigma^* 1s^2, \sigma 2s^2, \sigma^* 2s^2, \sigma 2p_z^2, \pi 2p_x^2$

$= \pi 2p_y^2, \pi^* 2p_x^1$

$= \pi^* 2p_y^1$

It is a paramagnetic molecule due to presence of unpaired electrons in each orbital of degenerate levels.

Thus, option (d) is correct.

3 (*c*) The species that have same number of electrons have same bond order.

Species	Number of electrons
CO	6 + 8 = 14
NO	7 + 8 = 15
O_2	8 + 8 = 16
NO^+	7 + 8 − 1 = 14
CN^-	6 + 7 + 1 = 14
O_2^-	8 + 8 + 1 = 17

Thus, both CN^- and CO have equal number of electrons. So, their bond order will be same.

4 (*c*) (a) F_2 molecule

$= \sigma 1s^2, \overset{*}{\sigma} 1s^2, \sigma 2s^2 \overset{*}{\sigma} 2s^2, \sigma 2p_z^2, \pi 2p_x^2 \approx \pi 2p_y^2, \overset{*}{\pi} 2p_x^2 \approx \overset{*}{\pi} 2p_y^2$

$$\text{Bond order} = \frac{1}{2}(N_b - N_a)$$

$$= \frac{1}{2}(10 - 8) = 1$$

(b) O_2 molecule

$= \sigma 1s^2, \overset{*}{\sigma} 1s^2, \sigma 2s^2 \overset{*}{\sigma} 2s^2, \sigma 2p_z^2, \pi 2p_x^2 \approx \pi 2p_y^2, \overset{*}{\pi} 2p_x^1 \approx \overset{*}{\pi} 2p_y^1$

$$\text{Bond order} = \frac{1}{2}(10 - 6) = 2$$

(c) Be_2 molecule

$= \sigma 1s^2, \overset{*}{\sigma} 1s^2, \sigma 2s^2, \overset{*}{\sigma} 2s^2$

$$\text{Bond order} = \frac{1}{2}(4 - 4) = 0$$

(d) Li_2 molecule $= \sigma 1s^2, \overset{*}{\sigma} 1s^2, \sigma 2s^2$

$$\text{Bond order} = \frac{1}{2}(4 - 2) = 1$$

Therefore, Be_2 molecule has zero bond order.

5 (*a*) Bond order O_2^+

(total electrons 8 + 8 − 1 = 15)

$= \sigma 1s^2, \overset{*}{\sigma} 1s^2, \sigma 2s^2, \overset{*}{\sigma} 2s^2, \sigma 2p_z^2, \pi 2p_x{}^2 \approx 2p_y{}^2, \overset{*}{\pi} 2p_x{}^1 \approx \overset{*}{\pi} 2p_y{}^0$

$$\text{Bond order} = \frac{N_b - N_a}{2}$$

$$= \frac{10 - 5}{2} = 2.5$$

Bond order of C_2

(total electrons 6 + 6 = 12)

$= \sigma 1s^2, \overset{*}{\sigma} 1s^2, \sigma 2s^2, \overset{*}{\sigma} 2s^2, \pi 2p_x^2 \approx \pi 2p_y^2$

$$\text{Bond order} = \frac{N_b - N_a}{2} = \frac{8 - 4}{2} = 2$$

6 (*a*) O_2^{2-} (total electrons 8 + 8 + 2 = 18)

$= \sigma 1s^2, \overset{*}{\sigma} 1s^2, \sigma 2s^2, \overset{*}{\sigma} 2s^2, \sigma 2p_z^2, \pi 2p_x^2 \approx \pi 2p_y^2, \overset{*}{\pi} 2p_x^2 \approx \overset{*}{\pi} 2p_y^2$

Bond order (BO) $= \dfrac{N_b - N_a}{2} = \dfrac{10-8}{2} = 1$

$B_2 (5 + 5 = 10) = \sigma 1s^2, \overset{*}{\sigma} 1s^2, \sigma 2s^2 \overset{*}{\sigma} 2s^2, \pi 2p_x^1 \approx \pi 2p_y^1$

$BO = \dfrac{6-4}{2} = 1$

Thus, O_2^{2-} and B_2 have the same bond order.

Note BO of $O_2^+ = 2.5$, $NO^+ = 3$, $NO = 2.5$, $CO = 3$, $N_2 = 3$ and $O_2 = 2$

7 (*a*) During change of O_2 to O_2^-, the electronic configuration of O_2 (total electrons = 16) is

$\sigma(1s^2), \overset{*}{\sigma}(1s^2), \sigma(2s^2), \overset{*}{\sigma}(2s^2), \sigma(2p_z^2)$

$\pi(2p_x^2) \approx \pi(2p_y^2), \overset{*}{\pi}(2p_x^1) \approx \overset{*}{\pi}(2p_y^1)$

and configuration of O_2^-, (total electrons = 17)

$\sigma(1s^2), \overset{*}{\sigma}(1s^2), \sigma(2s^2), \overset{*}{\sigma}(2p_z^2), \pi(2p_x^2)$

$\approx \pi(2p_y^2), \overset{*}{\pi}(2p_x^2) \approx \overset{*}{\pi}(2p_y^1)$

Thus, electron goes in the $\overset{*}{\pi}$-orbital.

8 (*d*) Bond order $= (N_b - N_a)/2$

In NO, total electrons = 7 + 8 = 15

$\therefore$ Configuration of NO

$= KK^*, \sigma(2s^2), \overset{*}{\sigma}(2s^2), \sigma(2p_z^2), \pi(2p_x^2) \approx \pi(2p_y^2), \overset{*}{\pi}(2p_x^1)$

$\therefore$ Bond order $= \dfrac{8-3}{2} = \dfrac{5}{2} = 2.5$

In O_2^-, total electrons = 16 + 1 = 17

$\therefore$ Configuration of O_2^-

$= KK^*, \sigma(2s^2), \overset{*}{\sigma}(2s^2), \sigma(2p_z^2), \pi(2p_x^2) \approx \pi(2p_y^2), \overset{*}{\pi}(2p_x^2) \approx \overset{*}{\pi}(2p_y^1)$

$\therefore$ Bond order $= \dfrac{8-5}{2} = \dfrac{3}{2} = 1.5$

In C_2^{2-}, total electrons = 12 + 2 = 14

$\therefore$ Configuration of

$C_2^{2-} = K\overset{*}{K}; \sigma(2s^2), \overset{*}{\sigma}(2s^2)$

$\pi(2p_z^2) \approx \pi(2p_y^2), \sigma(2p_z^2)$

$\therefore$ Bond order $= \dfrac{8-2}{2} = \dfrac{6}{3} = 3$

In He_2^+, total electrons = 4 − 1 = 3

$\therefore$ Configuration of

$He_2^+ = \sigma(1s^2), \overset{*}{\sigma}(1s^1)$

$\therefore$ Bond order $= \dfrac{2-1}{2} = 1/2 = 0.5$

Hence, correct order of bond order is

$He_2^+ < O_2^- < NO < C_2^{2-}$

9 (*a*) O_2^{2-} (Number of electrons = 18 does not contain unpaired electrons)

O_2^{2-}

$= \sigma 1s^2, \overset{*}{\sigma} 1s^2, \sigma 2s^2, \overset{*}{\sigma} 2s^2, \sigma 2pz^2, \pi 2p_z^2 \approx \pi 2p_y^2, \overset{*}{\pi} 2p_x^2 \approx \overset{*}{\pi} 2p_y^2$

10 (*a*) $B_2 = 5 + 5 = 10e^-$

$= \sigma 1s^2 \overset{*}{\sigma} 1s^2, \sigma 2s^2 \overset{*}{\sigma} 2s^2, \pi 2p_x^1 \approx \pi 2p_y^1$

Due to the presence of 2 unpaired bonding electrons in π_b MO, B_2 shows paramagnetic behaviour.

11 (*b*) $O_2 (8 + 8 = 16) = \sigma 1s^2, \overset{*}{\sigma} 1s^2, \sigma 2s^2, \overset{*}{\sigma} 2s^2, \sigma 2p_z^2, \pi 2p_x^2 \approx \pi 2p_y^2, \overset{*}{\pi} 2p_x^1 \approx \overset{*}{\pi} 2p_y^1$

Bond order $= \dfrac{10-6}{2} = 2$

Similarly, O_2^+ (8 + 8 − 1 = 15),

$BO = \dfrac{10-5}{2} = 2.5$

$\Rightarrow$ $O_2^- (8 + 8 + 1 = 17)$,

$BO = \dfrac{10-7}{2} = 1.5$

$\Rightarrow$ $O_2^{2-} (8 + 8 + 2 = 18)$

$BO = \dfrac{10-8}{2} = 1$

$\therefore$ Bond order $\propto \dfrac{1}{\text{Bond length}}$

Thus, O_2^+ has the minimum bond length as its bond order is maximum.

12 (*a*) Bond order $\propto$ bond strength

From Q. 5, BO of $O_2^+ = 2.5$, and rest have BO less than 2.5.

Thus, it has the strongest O — O bond among the given.

13 (*d*) O_2^+ has one unpaired electron whereas O_2 has two unpaired electrons.

BO of $O_2^+ = \dfrac{10-5}{2} = 2.5$

$\Rightarrow$ BO of $O_2 = \dfrac{10-6}{2} = 2$

Therefore, during conversion of O_2 into O_2^+, number of unpaired electrons decreases from 2 to 1 i.e. paramagnetic character decreases and bond order increases.

14 (*c*) Bond order of Be_2 is zero, so it does not exist under normal condition.

15 (*b*) $H_2^+ = \sigma 1s^1$ (According to molecular orbital theory)

Bond order $= \dfrac{N_b - N_a}{2} = \dfrac{1-0}{2} = 0.5$

H_2^+ is paramagnetic due to the presence of one unpaired electron.

16 (*c*) The number of electrons in O_2^{2-} molecular ion is 18. Hence, the electronic configuration of O_2^{2-} ion will be

$KK^*, \sigma 2s^2, \overset{*}{\sigma} 2s^2, \sigma 2p_z^2, \pi 2p_x^2 \approx \pi 2p_y^2, \overset{*}{\pi} 2p_x^2 \approx \overset{*}{\pi} 2p_y^2$

Hence, the number of anti-bonding electron pairs in O_2^{2-} ion is 4.

17 (*c*) Total number of electrons in N_2^-

$= 7 + 7 + 1 = 15$

Total number of electrons in N_2^{2-}

$= 7 + 7 + 2 = 16$

Total number of electrons in O_2^-

$= 8 + 8 + 1 = 17$

Total number of electrons in O_2^{2-}

$= 8 + 8 + 2 = 18$

Total number of electrons in O_2^+

$= 8 + 8 - 1 = 15$

As N_2^- and O_2^+ contain the same total number of electrons, their MO electronic configuration will be same. Thus, N_2^- and O_2^+ have the same bond order.

18 (*a*) Peroxide ion is O_2^{2-}

$O_2^{2-}(18) = \sigma 1s^2, \overset{*}{\sigma} 1s^2, \sigma 2s^2, \overset{*}{\sigma} 2s^2, \sigma 2p_z^2, \pi 2p_x^2 \approx \pi 2p_y^2, \overset{*}{\pi} 2p_x^2 \approx \overset{*}{\pi} 2p_y^2$

Bond order $= \frac{N_b - N_a}{2} = \frac{10-8}{2} = 1$

O_2^{2-} is diamagnetic due to the absence of unpaired electrons and the number of anti-bonding electron pairs in O_2^{2-} ion is four. It is not isoelectronic with Ne(z = 10). Thus, option (a) is correct.

19 (b) $O_2(16) = \sigma 1s^2, \overset{*}{\sigma}1s^2, \sigma 2s^2, \overset{*}{\sigma}2s^2,$

$\sigma 2p_z^2, \pi 2p_x^2 \approx \pi 2p_y^2, \overset{*}{\pi}2p_x^1 \approx \overset{*}{\pi}2p_y^1$

Bond order $= \frac{10-6}{2} = 2$

Due to the presence of unpaired electrons, O_2 is paramagnetic.

$O_2^-(17) = \sigma 1s^2, \overset{*}{\sigma}1s^2, \sigma 2s^2, \overset{*}{\sigma}2s^2, \sigma 2p_z^2,$

$\pi 2p_x^2 \approx \pi 2p_y^2, \overset{*}{\pi}2p_x^2 \approx \pi^* 2p_y^1$

Bond order $= \frac{10-7}{2} = 1.5$

$\therefore$ BO of $O_2 > O_2^-$

20 (a) **CN^- ion** Total number of electrons $6+7+1=14$
MO configuration is

$\sigma 1s^2, \overset{*}{\sigma}1s^2, \sigma 2s^2, \overset{*}{\sigma}2s^2, \pi 2p_x^2 \approx \pi 2p_y^2, \sigma 2p_z^2$

Bond order $= \frac{10-4}{2} = 3$

CO molecule Total number of valence electrons $= 6+8=14$
MO configuration is

$\sigma 1s^2, \overset{*}{\sigma}1s^2, \sigma 2s^2, \overset{*}{\sigma}2s^2, \pi 2p_x^2 \approx \pi 2p_y^2, \sigma 2p_z^2$

Bond order $= \frac{10-4}{2} = 3$

NO^+ ion Total number of valence electrons $= 7+8-1=14$
MO configuration is

$\sigma 1s^2, \overset{*}{\sigma}1s^2, \sigma 2s^2, \overset{*}{\sigma}2s^2, \pi 2p_x^2, \approx \pi 2p_y^2, \sigma 2p_z^2$

Bond order $= \frac{10-4}{2} = 3$

All CN^-, CO and NO^+ ion have bond order 3 and they are isoelectronic.

21 (c) MO configuration of NO^+ is

$\sigma 1s^2, \overset{*}{\sigma}1s^2, \sigma 2s^2, \overset{*}{\sigma}2s^2, \sigma 2p_z^2, \pi 2p_x^2 \approx \pi 2p_y^2$

and MO configuration of NO is

$\sigma 1s^2, \overset{*}{\sigma}1s^2, \sigma 2s^2, \overset{*}{\sigma}2s^2, \sigma 2p_z^2, \pi 2p_x^2 \approx \pi 2p_y^2, \overset{*}{\pi}2p_x^1$

Hence, electron is added to $\overset{*}{\pi}$-orbital.

22 (c) $H_2^+ : (\sigma 1s^1)$

$\therefore \quad BO = \frac{1}{2}(1-0) = \frac{1}{2}$

$H_2^- : (\sigma 1s)^2(\overset{*}{\sigma}1s^1)$

$\therefore \quad BO = \frac{1}{2}(2-1) = \frac{1}{2}$

Even though, the bond order of H_2^+ and H_2^- are equal but H_2^+ is more stable than H_2^- as in the latter, an electron is present in the higher energy antibonding ($\overset{*}{\sigma}1s$) orbital.

23 (a) He_2 does not exist because bond order of He_2 is zero.
Molecular orbital configuration of

$He_2 = \sigma 1s^2, \overset{*}{\sigma}1s^2$

Bond order $= \frac{N_b - N_a}{2} = \frac{2-2}{2} = 0$

Hence, both A and R are correct and R is the correct explanation of A

24 (a) In an anti-bonding molecular orbital, most of the electron density is located away from the space between the nuclei, as a result of which there is a nodal plane (i.e. a plane at which the electron density is zero) between the nuclei.

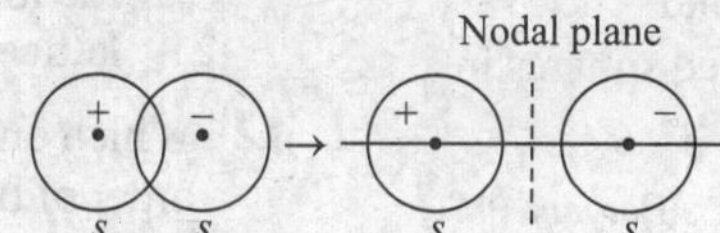

25 (a) According to MOT, $O_2(16)$

$\sigma 1s^2, \overset{*}{\sigma}1s^2, \sigma 2s^2, \overset{*}{\sigma}2s^2, \sigma 2p_z^2, \begin{cases}\pi 2p_x^2 \\ \pi 2p_y^2\end{cases}, \begin{cases}\overset{*}{\pi}2p_x^1 \\ \overset{*}{\pi}2p_y^1\end{cases},$

Electronic configuration of O_2 shows the presence of two unpaired electrons. So, it is paramagnetic in nature.

NO(15)
$\sigma 1s^2, \overset{*}{\sigma}1s^2, \sigma 2s^2, \overset{*}{\sigma}2s^2, \sigma 2p_z^2,$

$\begin{cases}\pi 2p_x^2 \\ \pi 2p_y^2\end{cases}, \begin{cases}\overset{*}{\pi}2p_x^1 \\ \overset{*}{\pi}2p_y^0\end{cases}$

Electronic configuration of NO shows the presence of one unpaired electrons/ So, it is also paramagnetic in nature.

26 (b) $C_2(12) = \sigma 1s^2, \overset{*}{\sigma}1s^2, \sigma 2s^2, \overset{*}{\sigma}2s^2, \pi 2p_x^2 \approx \pi 2p_y^2$

C_2 has two pairs of electrons in $\pi 2p_x$ and $\pi 2p_y$ therefore, it has only two π-bonds.

27 (c) The bond order of H, H_2^+ and He is positive. While the bond order of H^+ is zero. So, H^+ has transient existence.

28 (c) The electronic configuration of peroxide ion (O_2^{2-}) is as :

$O_2^{2-} : KK\ \sigma 2s^2, \overset{*}{\sigma}2s^2, \sigma 2p_z^2, \pi 2p_x^2 \approx \pi 2p_y^2, \overset{*}{\pi}2p_x^2 \approx \overset{*}{\pi}2p_y^2$

Bond order $= \frac{8-6}{2} = 1$

Since, all the electrons in molecular orbitals are paired, hence it is diamagnetic.

29 (c) The paramagnetic nature of oxygen molecule is best explained on the basis of molecular orbital theory. As there is one unpaired electron each in $\pi^* 2px$ and $\pi^* 2py$ orbitals.

30 (c) The electronic configuration of oxygen molecule ion is as

$O_2^+ : K\overset{*}{K}, \sigma 2s^2, \overset{*}{\sigma}2s^2, \sigma 2p_z^2, \pi 2p_x^2 \approx \pi 2p_y^2, \overset{*}{\pi}2p_x^1$

Due to the presence of an odd electron in the $\overset{*}{\pi}2p_x$ molecular orbital, O_2^+ is paramagnetic.

31 (c) Molecules or ions having no unpaired electrons are diamagnetic. e.g.

$Li_2 = 6e^- = \sigma 1s^2, \overset{*}{\sigma}1s^2, \sigma 2s^2.$

32 (d) The total number of electrons in $B_2 = 10$

$B_2 = \sigma 1s^2, \overset{*}{\sigma}1s^2, \sigma 2s^2, \overset{*}{\sigma}2s^2, \pi 2p_x^1 \approx \pi 2p_y^1$

It has two unpaired electrons.

$\therefore$ It is paramagnetic and the highest occupied molecular orbital is of π type.
Hence, both (A) and (R) are incorrect.

Topic 5

Hydrogen and Metallic Bonds

2019

1 Which of the following can form H-bond? **[JIPMER]**

(a) NH_3 (b) R-CN
(c) R-Br (d) R-B_4

2013

2 The hydrogen bond is shortest in **[Kerala CEE]**

(a) S—H---S (b) N—H---O
(c) S—H---O (d) F—H---O
(e) F—H---F

2011

3 The typical range of molar enthalpies for the strongest intermolecular (hydrogen) bond is **[DUMET]**

(a) 200-300 kJ (b) 300-500 kJ
(c) 4-25 kJ (d) 4-25 J

2010

4 Maximum number of H-bonds in one molecule of water is

(a) 1 (b) 2 (c) 3 (d) 4

5 Metallic bond is **[Manipal]**

(a) similar to ionic bond
(b) similar to covalent bond
(c) neither similar to ionic nor covalent bond
(d) formed by movement of positive charged spheres in a sea of electrons

6 Which of the following is least volatile? **[Haryana PMT]**

(a) H_2O (b) H_2S (c) H_2Se (d) H_2Te

2009

7 What is the dominant intermolecular force or bond that must be overcome in converting liquid CH_3OH to a gas? **[AIPMT]**

(a) Hydrogen bonding
(b) Dipole-dipole interaction
(c) Covalent bonds
(d) London dispersion force

8 NH_3 has higher boiling point than expected because **[Manipal]**

(a) it forms NH_4OH with water
(b) it has strong intermolecular hydrogen bonds
(c) it has intramolecular hydrogen bonds
(d) its density decreases on freezing

9 When two ice cubes are pressed over each other, they unite to form one cube. Which of the following forces is responsible to hold them together? **[DUMET]**

(a) Dipole forces (b) van der Waals' forces
(c) Covalent forces (d) Hydrogen bond forces

10 Out of the two compounds shown below, the volatile nature of B at a particular temperature is expected to be **[Manipal]**

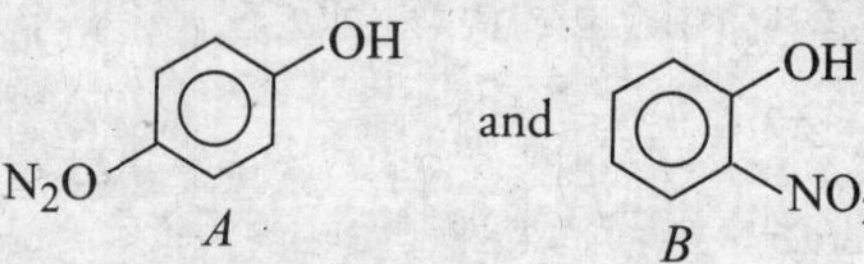

(a) higher than that of A
(b) lower than that of A
(c) same as that of A
(d) can be higher or lower depending upon the size of the vessel

2008

11 Malleability and ductility of metals can be accounted due to **[KCET]**

(a) the presence of electrostatic force
(b) the crystalline structure in metal
(c) the capacity of layers of metal ions to slide over the other
(d) the interaction of electrons with metal ions in the lattice

12 Which one of the following graphs represent the correct order of boiling points (b.p.) of ethane (1), ethyl alcohol (2) and acetic acid (3)? **[EAMCET]**

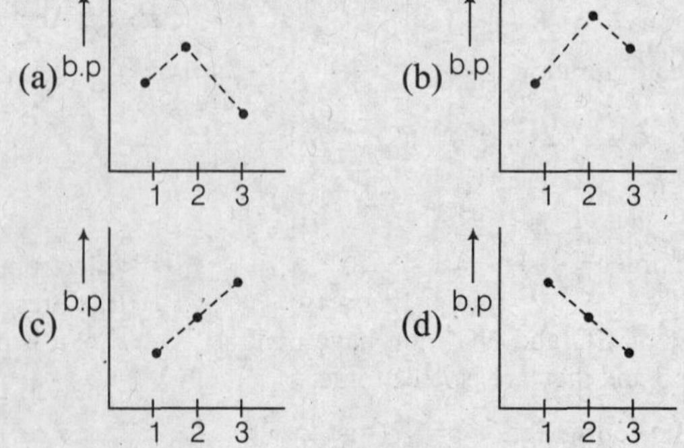

2007

13 The comparatively high boiling point of HF is due to **[MHT CET]**
(a) high reactivity of fluorine
(b) small size of hydrogen atom
(c) formation of hydrogen bonds and consequent association
(d) high IE of fluorine

2006

14 The higher boiling point of water is due to which reason? **[RPMT]**
(a) Coordinate bonding
(b) Covalent bonding
(c) Electrostatic force of attraction
(d) Hydrogen bonding

Answers

1 (a)	2 (e)	3 (c)	4 (d)	5 (c)	6 (a)	7 (a)	8 (b)	9 (d)	10 (a)
11 (c)	12 (c)	13 (c)	14 (d)						

Explanations

1 (*a*) The attractive electrostatic force between a hydrogen atom and an electronegative atom (F, O, N) is known as hydrogen bond. Thus, ammonia (NH_3) form hydrogen bond as

H—N(H)(H)······H—N(H)(H)······H—N(H)(H)······H

Intermolecular H–bonding in NH_3

2 (*e*) Strength of hydrogen bond between F—H---F is the strongest and hence, it has the shortest bond.

3 (*c*) The typical range of molar enthalpies for the strongest intermolecular (hydrogen) bond is 4-25 kJ.

4 (*d*) One water molecule is joined to 4 water molecules — two with H-atoms and other two with O-atom. Thus, the maximum number of hydrogen bonds that a molecule of water can have four as shown below:

$H_2^{\delta+}O^{\delta-}\cdots H^{\delta+}$—$O^{\delta-}$(H)(—H—O)$\cdots H^{\delta+}$—$O^{\delta-}H^{\delta+}$—H; O—$H^{\delta+}$

5 (*c*) A metallic bond consists of positive kernels arranged in a definite pattern in a sea of mobile electrons. It is quite different from ionic as well as covalent bond.

6 (*a*) Water (H_2O) is least volatile due to the association of H_2O molecules through hydrogen bonding.

H_2O---H—O(H)---H—O(H)---

However, hydrogen bonding is not present in other hydrides.

7 (*a*) The molecules of CH_3OH are associated by hydrogen bonding.

H—O(CH_3)---H—O(CH_3)---H—O(CH_3)---

8 (*b*) Ammonia has higher boiling point than excepted due to strong intermolecular hydrogen bonding between electronegative N atom of one NH_3 molecule and electro-positive H atom of another NH_3 molecule.

9 (*d*) Ice has H-bonding therefore, when two ice cubes are pressed over each other, they unite to form one cube.

10 (*a*) Due to intramolecular H-bonding in *o*-nitrophenol, it exists as a monomer while due to intermolecular H-bonding in p-nitrophenol, it exists as an associated molecule. As a result, volatile nature of *o*-nitrophenol is higher than that of *p*-nitrophenol.

11 (*c*) In metals, the valence shell electrons are delocalised and shared between many atoms. These delocalised electrons allow the metal atoms to slide over one another without being subjected to strong repulsive forces. The malleability and ductility of metals is due to this sliding capacity of the delocalised electrons.

12 (*c*) In both ethyl alcohol (2) and acetic acid (3), hydrogen bonding is present and the extent of H-bonding is more in acetic acid than ethyl alcohol due to formation of ring. Thus, acetic acid has higher boiling point than ethyl alcohol. Ethane (1) has lowest boiling point due to absence of H-bonding. Hence, the graph showing correct order of boiling points is

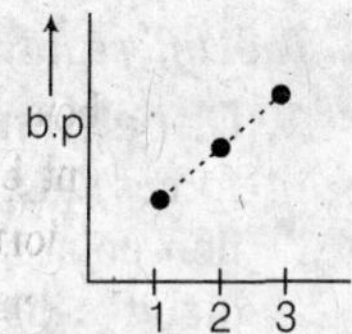

13 (*c*) Intermolecular hydrogen bonding is found in $(HF)_n$ due to higher electronegativity of fluorine atoms.

---H—F---H—H---H—F---

Hydrogen bonding

Hydrogen bonding is helpful in the association of HF molecule. So, HF is found in liquid form.

14 (*a*) The higher boiling point of water is due to hydrogen bonding. O-atom of each H_2O molecule is covalently linked with two H-atoms of its own molecule and with another H-atom of adjacent H_2O molecule by H-bonding.

05

States of Matter

Quick Review

Solid, liquid and gases are three general states of matter. In this chapter, we will discuss different characteristics of gaseous and liquid states of matter.

Intermolecular Forces

The attractive or repulsive forces that exist between interacting particles (i.e. atoms or molecules) are called **intermolecular forces**. These are the weak forces and generally affect the physical properties and some chemical properties of matter.

The different types of intermolecular forces are

1. **Dispersion Forces or London Forces** These forces exist in between neutral atoms and/or non-polar molecules as in them electronic charge cloud is distributed symmetrically and hence, have no dipole moment. But a dipole may develop momentarily even in such atoms and molecules. These forces are always attractive and work only over very short distances (~ 500 pm).
2. **Dipole-Dipole Forces** These forces exist between the molecules having permanent dipoles like HCl, NH_3 etc. Ends of such dipoles have "partial charges" (represented by Greek letter delta, δ), which are always less than the unit electronic charge (1.6×10^{-19} C).
3. **Dipole Induced Dipole Forces** These forces exist between the polar molecules having permanent dipole and the molecules lacking permanent dipole.
   The charged end of the polar molecule induces dipole in the non-polar molecule by deforming its electron cloud and hence, both the molecules get attracted by dipole-induced dipole forces.
4. **Ion-Dipole Forces** The force of attraction existing between an ion (cation or anion) and a dipole is called **ion-dipole forces**. The strength of force depends on the charge and size of the ion, on the magnitude of the dipole moment and size of the polar molecule.
5. **Repulsive Forces** These forces exist between the electron clouds or the nuclei of two molecules when they are in contact with each other. Magnitude of such forces increase as the distance between the molecules decreases.

Hydrogen Bond

It is a special case of dipole-dipole interaction. A hydrogen bond is formed (or such force exist) when a hydrogen is bonded to a more electronegative atom (like, N, O and F).

$$\overset{\delta^+}{H}-\overset{\delta^-}{F}\cdots\cdots\overset{\delta^+}{H}-\overset{\delta^-}{F}$$

H-bond

Although, size fo Cl is large but it may also participate in H-bonding to some extent.

Energy of hydrogen bond varies between 10 to 100 kJ mol^{-1} i.e. these are strong forces and play a key role in determining the structure and properties of many compounds like proteins, nucleic acid etc.

Thermal Energy

The energy of a body which arises because of the motion of its atoms or molecules, is called the **thermal energy**. It is infact the measure of average kinetic energy of the particles of the matter and hence, is responsible for their motion.

Intermolecular Forces *versus* Thermal Interactions

The intermolecular forces tend to keep the molecules together but thermal energy tend to keep them apart. Thus, these two compete and the competition between these two (i.e. intermolecular forces and thermal energy) result in three states of matter.

(*i*) In a solid, the intermolecular forces predominate over the thermal energy and hence, the particles are held together in rigid, highly-oriented and close-packed structure.

(*ii*) In liquids, the intermolecular forces are no longer strong enough, however, these are still sufficient so that particles remain in each other's environment, hence, liquids have sufficient mobility.

(*iii*) In gases, the thermal energy dominates over the effect of intermolecular forces, thus, the gas molecules acquire the unrestricted and independent mobility in the vapour state.

Predominance of thermal energy and the intermolecular interactions in the three states of matter is as follows.

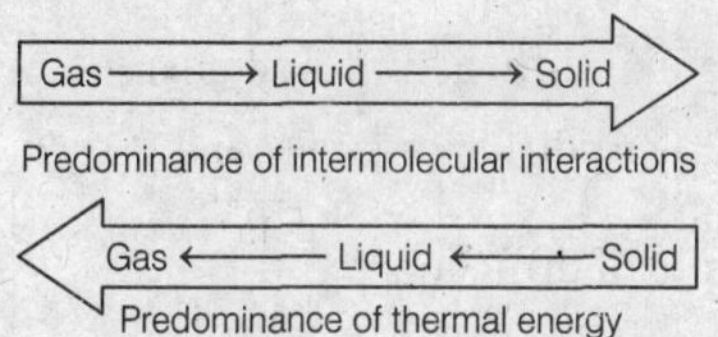

The melting and boiling points of solids are higher than room temperature but of gases are lower than room temperature. However, for liquids, the melting point is lower but boiling point is higher than room temperature.

Gaseous State

It is the most disordered state of matter. In this state, matter neither has fixed volume nor fixed shape. Gases exhibit dependency on temperature, pressure, volume and mass. The inter-relationship of these factors can be analysed through gas laws, *which are as follows*

1. Boyle's Law

- It states that "at a given temperature, the volume of a given mass of a gas is inversely proportional to its pressure."

i.e. $V \propto \frac{1}{p}$ or $pV = \text{constant}$

or $p_1V_1 = p_2V_2 = \text{constant}$

- Graph between p *versus* V or pV *versus* p at constant temperature is called **isotherm**.
- The different types of isotherms are given below:

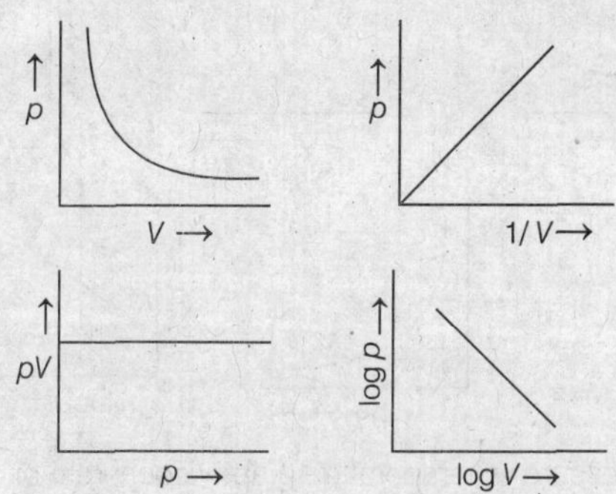

Graphical representation of Boyle's law

2. Charles' Law

- According to this law, the volume of a given mass of a gas is directly proportional to the absolute temperature at constant pressure.

i.e. $V \propto T$

(at constant pressure or $\frac{V}{T} = \text{constant}$ or $\frac{V_1}{T_1} = \frac{V_2}{T_2}$)

- A graph of V *versus* T at constant pressure is called **isobar.**
- Some important isobars are:

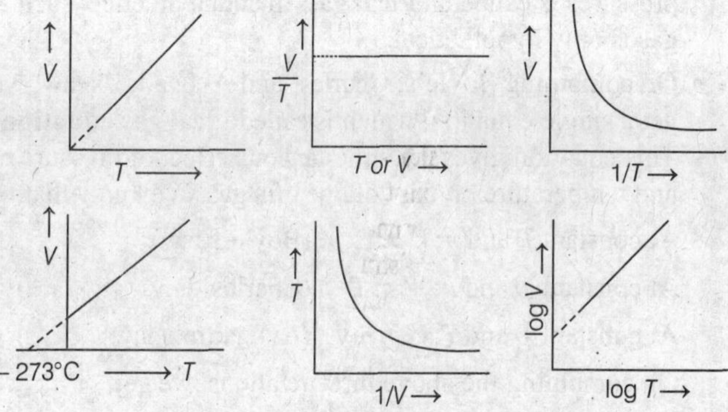

Graphical representation of Charles' law

3. Gay-Lussac's Law

- According to this law, at constant volume, the pressure of a given mass of a gas is directly proportional to its absolute temperature.

i.e. $p \propto T$

or $\frac{p}{T} = \text{constant (at constant } V)$

or $\frac{p_1}{T_1} = \frac{p_2}{T_2}$

- A graph of p *versus* T at constant volume is known as **isochore**.

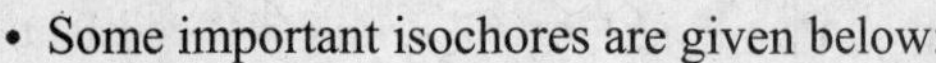

- Some important isochores are given below:

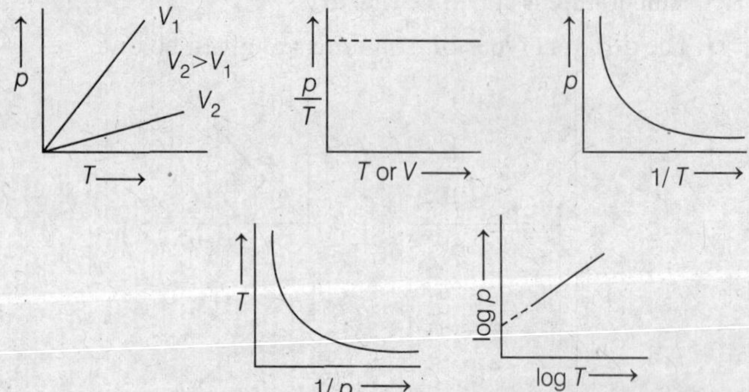

Pressure *vs* temperature graph (isochores) of a gas

4. Avogadro's Law

It states that, equal volumes of all gases, under same conditions of temperature and pressure contain equal number of molecules.

i.e. $V \propto n$

The volume of one mole of a gas at STP is known as molar gas volume.

Ideal Gas and Ideal Gas Equation

- A gas which follows Boyle's law, Charles' law and Avogadro's law at all conditions of temperatures and pressures is called an **ideal gas**. In actual practice, such a gas is only hypothetical.
- On combining Boyle's, Charles' and Avogadro's law, we get a single equation, which is called **ideal gas equation.** This equation gives the simultaneous effect of pressure and temperature on the volume of a gas. We know that,

  At constant T and n; $V \propto 1/p$ (Boyle's law)

  At constant p and n; $V \propto T$ (Charles' law)

  At constant p and T; $V \propto n$ (Avogadro's law)

  On combining the above three relations, we get

$$V \propto \frac{nT}{p} \quad \text{or} \quad V = R\frac{nT}{p} \qquad \ldots\text{(i)}$$

(Here, R = proportionality constant or gas constant)

On rearranging the equation (i), we get

$$\boxed{pV = nRT}$$

This equation is called **ideal gas equation** and is applicable for all gases that behave ideally. It describes the state of any gas, so it is also called **equation of state.**

Ideal gas equation in term of density is given as:

$$d = \frac{pM}{RT}$$

Relative molecular weight = 2× vapour density

Different Values of Universal Gas Constant, (*R*)

- $R = 0.0821$ L atm mol^{-1} K^{-1}
- $R = 8.314 \times 10^7$ erg K^{-1} mol^{-1}
- $R = 0.083$ L bar mol^{-1} K^{-1}
- $R = 1.987$ or 2 cal K^{-1} mol^{-1}
- $R = 8.314$ JK^{-1} mol^{-1}

Dalton's Law of Partial Pressure

At constant temperature, the total pressure exerted by a mixture of non-reacting gases is the sum of partial pressure of different gases present in the mixture.

$$p_{\text{total}} = p_1 + p_2 + p_3 + \ldots$$

where, partial pressures (p) = mole fraction × p_{total}

Mole fraction of gas (χ)

$$= \frac{\text{Partial pressure of gas } (p)}{\text{Total pressure } (p_t)}$$

Pressure of a dry gas can be determined by Dalton's law as:

$$p_{\substack{\text{gas}\\ \text{(dry)}}} = p_{\substack{\text{total}\\ \text{moist gas}}} - p_{\substack{\text{water}\\ \text{vapour}}}$$

Graham's Law of Diffusion

Under similar conditions of temperature and pressure, the rates of diffusion of gases are inversely proportional to the square root of their densities.

$$\frac{r_1}{r_2} = \sqrt{\frac{d_2}{d_1}} = \sqrt{\frac{M_2}{M_1}}$$

where, r_1 = rate of diffusion of first gas

and r_2 = rate of diffusion of second gas.

Therefore, rate of diffusion $\propto \sqrt{\frac{1}{M}}$

If two gases diffuse under different pressures,

$$\frac{r_1}{r_2} = \frac{p_1}{p_2}\sqrt{\frac{d_2}{d_1}} = \frac{p_1}{p_2}\sqrt{\frac{M_2}{M_1}}$$

Kinetic Theory of Gases

The molecular details regarding gases can be visualised with the help of kinetic molecular theory of gases which is based on following assumptions:

(*i*) A gas consists of extremely small discrete particles called the molecules.

(*ii*) The actual volume of the molecules is negligible as compared to the total volume of gas.

(*iii*) Gas molecules are in constant random motion with high velocities.

(*iv*) The intermolecular forces of attraction between gaseous molecules are negligible.

(*v*) All collisions are perfectly elastic, hence there is no loss of kinetic energy during the collision.

(*vi*) The effect of gravity on the motion of the molecules is negligible in comparison to the effect of collision.

(*vii*) The pressure of a gas is caused by the hits recorded by molecules on the walls of container.

(*viii*) Average kinetic energy of gas molecules is assumed to be directly proportional to the absolute temperature.

Kinetic Gas Equation

- On the basis of postulates of kinetic theory of gases, the following gas equation is derived.

$$pV = \frac{1}{3} mnv_{rms}^2$$

where, p = pressure exerted by the gas

and V = volume of the gas.

- Kinetic energy/mole $= \frac{3}{2} RT.$
- Average translational kinetic energy per molecule $= \frac{3}{2} k_B T$
- The different velocities possessed by gas molecules are:

(*i*) Most probable velocity $(\alpha) = \sqrt{\frac{2RT}{M}}$

(*ii*) Average velocity $(\bar{v}) = \sqrt{\frac{8RT}{\pi M}}$

(*iii*) Root mean square velocity $(u_{rms}) = \sqrt{\frac{3RT}{M}}$

- $\alpha : \bar{v} : u_{rms} = 1 : 1.128 : 1.224$

Behaviour of Real Gases : Deviation from Ideal Gas Behaviour

- Ideal gases are hypothetical gases whose pressure, volume and temperature behaviour can be completely accounted by ideal gas equation.
- This happens due to the two assumptions (*ii* and *iv*) of kinetic theory of gases which did not hold good in all conditions.
- Therefore, gases show deviation from the ideal behaviour and thus do not obey the gas laws. Such gases are called **real gases**.
- Real gases behave ideally under high temperature and low pressure.
- The temperature at which a real gas behaves like an ideal gas over an appreciable pressure range is called **Boyle's temperature** or **Boyle's point**.
- Extent of deviation of gases from ideal behaviour is decided by compressibility factor (Z).

$$Z = \frac{pV}{RT}$$

- In case of ideal gas, $pV = nRT, Z = 1$
- In case of real gas, $pV \neq nRT, Z \neq 1$

Negative Deviation In such case, $Z < 1$, gas is more compressible.

Positive Deviation In such case, $Z > 1$, gas is less compressible.

van der Waals' Equation

- Based on deviation in behaviour of real gas from ideal gas, a new equation is introduced known as van der Waal's equation.
- This equation explains the behaviour of a real gas correctly and is given as,

$$\left(p + \frac{n^2 a}{V^2}\right) \times (V - nb) = nRT$$

$\left(p + \frac{n^2 a}{V^2}\right)$ ↑ Pressure correction for molecular attraction, where n = number of moles.

$(V - nb)$ ↑ Volume correction for finite size of molecules

- a and b are called van der Waals' constants.
- a is the measure of force of attraction between gas molecules. Greater the value of 'a' easily would be the liquefication of the gas. Its unit is atm $L^2 mol^{-2}$.
- b is also called co-volume or excluded volume and is the measure of effective size of molecules. Its unit is L mol^{-1}

Liquefaction of Gases

- The conversion of a gas into liquid is called liquefaction.
- For a certain gas to liquefy, there is maximum limit of temperature and minimum limit of pressure. These limits are called critical constants.

Some of them are listed below.

(*i*) Critical temperature (*ii*) Critical pressure

(*iii*) Critical volume

Relation between these constants and van der Waals' constant is given as follows:

(*i*) Critical temperature $(T_c) = \frac{8a}{27Rb}$

(*ii*) Critical pressure$(p_c) = \frac{a}{27b^2}$

(*iii*) Critical volume $(V_c) = 3b$

Liquid State

- It is the state of matter in which molecules are held close to each other.
- Vapour pressure, surface tension and viscosity are some of the typical physical properties of liquids that arise due to two competing forces, the molecular interaction and thermal energy.

Vapour Pressure

It is the pressure exerted by the vapours above the liquid surface when these are in equilibrium with the liquid at a given temperature.

Variation of vapour pressure with temperature is given by Clausius-Clapeyron equation

$$\log p = \frac{-\Delta_{vap}H}{2.303RT} + \log A$$

Surface Tension

It is the force acting per unit length perpendicular to any line drawn on the surface of liquid. It decreases when substances such as soaps, detergents are dissolved in a liquid. Rise in temperature also decreases surface tension.

Viscosity

It is defined as the resistance of a liquid to flow. Usually, viscosity of a liquid decreases with the rise in temperature.

Topical Practice Questions

All the exam questions of this chapter have been divided into 5 topics as listed below

Topic 1

Gas Laws and Ideal Gas Equation

2019

1 **Assertion** The graph between p v/s $\frac{1}{V}$ is a straight line.

Reason For adiabatic process, $p \propto 1/V$ [AIIMS]

(a) Both A and R are correct and the R is the correct explanation of the A
(b) Both A and R are correct but the R is not the correct explanation of the A
(c) A is correct but R is incorrect
(d) Both A and R are incorrect

2 The volume occupied by 1.8 g of water vapour at 374°C and 1 bar pressure will be
[Use $R = 0.083$ bar L K^{-1} mol^{-1}] [NEET (Odisha)]

(a) 96.66 L (b) 55.87 L (c) 3.10 L (d) 5.37 L

3 In an ideal gas equation which is constant? [JIPMER]

(a) Temperature (b) Pressure
(c) Volume (d) Universal gas constant

2018

4 A 100 mL flask contained H_2 at 200 torr and a 200 mL flask contained He at 100 torr. The two flasks were then connected so that each gas filled their combined volume. Assume, no change in temperature, total pressure is [JIPMER]

(a) 104 torr
(b) 163.33 torr
(c) 279 torr
(d) 133.33 torr

2014

5 Equal masses of H_2, O_2 and methane have been taken in a container of volume V at temperature 27° C in identical conditions. The ratio of the volumes of gases $H_2:O_2:CH_4$ would be **[CBSE AIPMT]**

(a) 8 : 16 : 1 (b) 16 : 8 : 1
(c) 16 : 1 : 2 (d) 8 : 1 : 2

6 Density of carbon monoxide is maximum at **[KCET]**

(a) 2 atm and 600 K (b) 0.5 atm and 273 K
(c) 6 atm and 1092 K (d) 4 atm and 500 K

2011

7 Three different gases *X*, *Y* and *Z* of molecular masses 2, 16 and 64 were enclosed in a vessel at constant temperature till equilibrium is reached. Which of the following statement is correct? **[Kerala CEE]**

(a) Gas *Z* will be at the top of the vessel
(b) Gas *Y* will be at the top of the vessel
(c) Gas *Z* will be at the bottom and *X* will be at the top
(d) Gas *X* will be at the bottom and *Z* will be at the top
(e) Gases will form homogeneous mixture

2010

8 Which of the following expression is true regarding gas laws? (w = weight; M = molecular mass) **[UP CPMT]**

(a) $\frac{T_1}{T_2}=\frac{M_1w_2}{M_2w_1}$ (b) $\frac{T_1}{T_2}=\frac{M_2w_1}{M_1w_2}$

(c) $\frac{T_1}{T_2}=\frac{M_1w_1}{M_2w_2}$ (d) $\frac{T_2}{T_1}=\frac{M_1w_1}{M_2w_2}$

9 The temperature at which 28 g of N_2 will occupy a volume of 10.0 L at 2.46 atm is **[RPMT]**

(a) 299.6 K (b) 0°C
(c) 273 K (d) 10°C

10 If p, V, M, T and R are the symbols of pressure, volume, molecular weight, temperature and gas constant respectively. What is the equation of density of ideal gas? **[MP PMT]**

(a) $\frac{RT}{pM}$ (b) $\frac{p}{RT}$ (c) $\frac{M}{V}$ (d) $\frac{pM}{RT}$

11 In which one of the following, does the given amount of chlorine exert the least pressure in a vessel of capacity 1 dm^3 at 273 K? **[KCET]**

(a) 0.0355 g (b) 0.071 g
(c) 6.023×10^{21} molecules (d) 0.02 mol

2009

12 By the ideal gas law, the pressure of 0.60 mole NH_3 gas in a 3.00 L vessel at 25°C is **[AFMC]**

(a) 48.9 atm (b) 4.89 atm
(c) 0.489 atm (d) 489 atm

13 A certain mass of the oxygen gas occupies 7 L volume under a pressure of 380 mm Hg. The volume of the same mass of the gas at standard pressure, with temperature remaining constant, shall be **[UP CPMT]**

(a) 26.60 L (b) 54.28 L
(c) 3.5 L (d) 7 L

14 8.2 L of an ideal gas weighs 9.0 g at 300 K and 1 atm pressure. The molecular mass of the gas is **[Manipal]**

(a) 9 (b) 27
(c) 54 (d) 81

2008

15 The density of a gas is 1.964 g dm^{-3} at 273 K and 76 cm Hg. The gas is **[AFMC]**

(a) CH_4 (b) C_2H_6 (c) CO_2 (d) Xe

16 A 4.0 dm^3 flask containing N_2 at 4.0 bar was connected to a 6.0 dm^3 flask containing helium at 6.0 bar, and the gases were allowed to mix isothermally. Then, the total pressure of the resulting mixture will be **[Kerala CEE]**

(a) 10.0 bar (b) 5.2 bar
(c) 3.6 bar (d) 1.6 bar
(e) 5.0 bar

17 A cylinder of 5 L capacity, filled with air at NTP is connected with another evacuated cylinder of 30 L capacity. The resultant air pressure in both the cylinders will be **[AMU]**

(a) 10.8 cm of Hg (b) 14.9 cm of Hg
(c) 21.8 cm of Hg (d) 38.8 cm of Hg

18 The volume-temperature graphs of a given mass of an ideal gas at constant pressure are shown below:

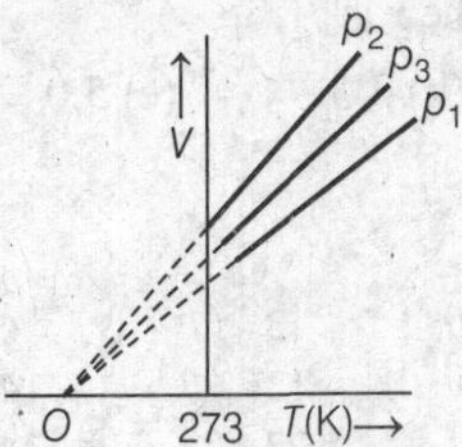

What is the correct order of pressure? **[DUMET]**

(a) $p_1 > p_3 > p_2$ (b) $p_1 > p_2 > p_3$
(c) $p_2 > p_3 > p_1$ (d) $p_2 > p_1 > p_3$

19 In order to increase the volume of a gas by 10%, the pressure of the gas should be **[KCET]**

(a) increased by 10% (b) increased by 1%
(c) decreased by 10% (d) decreased by 1%

2007

20 The pressure and temperature of 4 dm^3 of carbon dioxide gas are doubled. Then, volume of carbon dioxide gas would be **[AFMC]**

(a) 2 dm^3 (b) 3 dm^3
(c) 4 dm^3 (d) 8 dm^3

21 Which of the following diagram correctly describes the behaviour of a fixed mass of an ideal gas? (T is measured in K). **[Kerala CEE]**

(a) 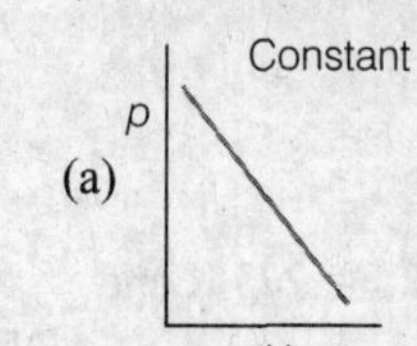

(b) 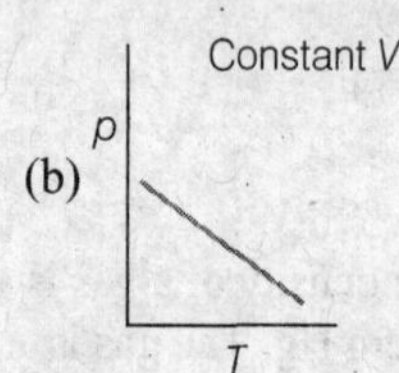

(c) 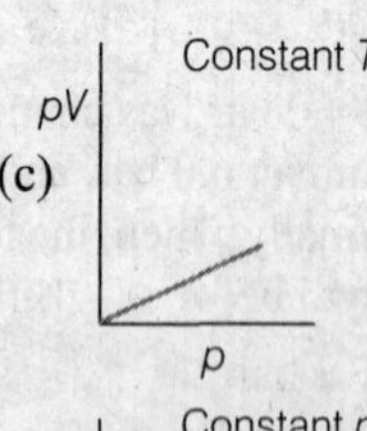

(d) 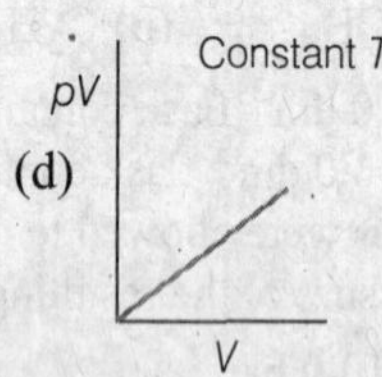

(e) 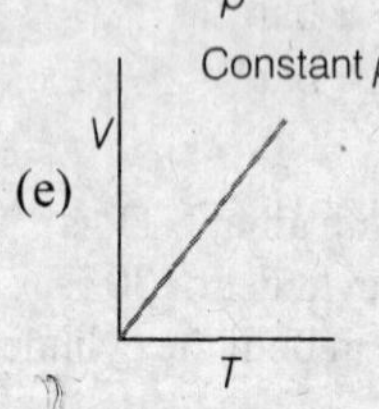

22 Gas equation $pV = nRT$ is obeyed by an ideal gas in **[BCECE]**

(a) adiabatic process (b) isothermal process
(c) Both (a) and (b) (d) None of these

23 A gas is found to have a formula $[CO]_x$. Its vapour density is 70, the x is **[BCECE]**

(a) 3.0 (b) 3.5 (c) 5.0 (d) 6.5

2005

24 An LPG cylinder, containing 15 kg butane at 27°C and 10 atm pressure, is leaking. After one day, its pressure decreased to 8 atm. The quantity of gas leaked is **[Haryana PMT]**

(a) 1 kg (b) 2 kg
(c) 3 kg (d) 4 kg

25 A gas has a vapour density 11.2. The volume occupied by 1 g of the gas at NTP is **[Punjab PMET]**

(a) 1 L (b) 11.2 L (c) 22.4 L (d) 4 L

26 Slope between pV and p at constant temperature is **[Punjab PMET]**

(a) slope between pV and p is zero
(b) slope between pV and p is 1
(c) slope between pV and p is 1/2
(d) slope between pV and p is $1/\sqrt{2}$

27 In the equation of state of an ideal gas $pV = nRT$, the value of the universal gas constant would depend only on **[KCET]**

(a) the nature of the gas
(b) the pressure of the gas
(c) the units of the measurememt
(d) None of the above

28 Avogadro's hypothesis states that **[JCECE]**

(a) the ideal gas consists of a large number of small particles called molecules
(b) under the same conditions of temperature and pressure equal volumes of all gases contain the same number of molecules
(c) volume of a definite quantity of gas at constant pressure, is directly proportional to absolute temperature
(d) a given mass of gas at constant pressure is directly proportional to absolute temperature

29 What will be the partial pressure of He and O_2 respectively, if 200 mL of He at 0.66 atm and 400 mL of O_2 at 0.52 atm pressure are mixed in 400 mL vessel at 20°C? **[AFMC]**

(a) 0.33 and 0.56 (b) 0.33 and 0.52
(c) 0.38 and 0.52 (d) 0.25 and 0.45

Answers

1 (c)	2 (d)	3 (d)	4 (d)	5 (c)	6 (d)	7 (e)	8 (a)	9 (a)	10 (d)
11 (a)	12 (b)	13 (c)	14 (b)	15 (c)	16 (b)	17 (a)	18 (a)	19 (c)	20 (c)
21 (e)	22 (c)	23 (c)	24 (c)	25 (a)	26 (a)	27 (c)	28 (b)	29 (b)	

Explanations

1 (*c*) The graph between p *v/s* $\frac{1}{V}$ is a straight line. The above statement is correct as it follows Boyle's law, i.e.

$$p \propto \frac{1}{V} \ (n, T)$$

where , n = moles, T = temperatrue,

or $$pV = \text{constant}$$

For adiabatic process, $p \propto \frac{1}{V}$ is not the correct statement, because for adiabatic process $\Delta q = 0$, i.e. q is constant (not temperature). Hence, Assertion is true but Reason is incorrect.

Thus, option (c) is the correct answer.

2 (*d*) According to ideal gas equation,

$$pV = nRT$$

or $$V = \frac{nRT}{p} = \frac{w}{M.wt} \frac{RT}{p} \quad \ldots\text{(i)}$$

$$\left[\because n = \frac{w}{M.wt}\right]$$

Given, $w = 1.8 \text{ g}, T = 374° \text{C}$

$= (374 + 273)\text{K} = 647 \text{ K}$

$p = 1 \text{ bar}, R = 0.083 \text{ bar LK}^{-1} \text{ mol}^{-1}$

On substituting the given values in Eq. (i) we get

$$V = \frac{1.8 \text{g}}{18 \text{ g mol}^{-1}} \times \frac{0.083 \text{ bar LK}^{-1} \text{ mol}^{-1} \times 647 \text{ K}}{1 \text{ bar}}$$

$= 5.37 \text{ L}$

3 (*d*) According to ideal gas equation,

$$pV = nRT$$

where, p = pressure, V = volume

n = no. of moles, T = temperature

R = universal gas constant

$R = 8.314 \text{ J mol}^{-1}\text{K}^{-1}$

$= 0.08205 \text{ L atm mol}^{-1}\text{K}^{-1}$

$= 1.99 \text{ cal mol}^{-1}\text{K}^{-1}$

$= 5.189 \times 10^{19} \text{ eV mol}^{-1}\text{K}^{-1}$

4 (*d*) Given, $p_{H_2} = 200$ torr, $V_{H_2} = 100$ mL

$p_{He} = 100$ torr, $V_{He} = 200$ mL

$\therefore \quad n_{H_2} = \frac{pV}{RT} = \frac{20000}{RT}$

$\therefore \quad n_{He} = \frac{pV}{RT} = \frac{20000}{RT}$

Total number of moles $= n_{H_2} + n_{He}$

$= \frac{20000}{RT} + \frac{20000}{RT} = \frac{40000}{RT}$

Total volume = 300 mL

Total pressure $(p) = \frac{n}{V} RT$

$= \frac{40000 \times RT}{RT \times 300} = \frac{400}{3} = 133.33$ torr

5 (*c*) At given temperature and pressure, volume of any gas is directly proportional to its number of moles.

i.e. $\quad V \propto n \, (T, P)$

The ratio of the volume of gases can be determined in terms of their moles.

The ratio of volumes of $H_2 : O_2 : CH_4$ is given by

Volume of H_2 : Volume of O_2 :

Volume of $CH_4 = \frac{w}{2} : \frac{w}{32} : \frac{w}{16}$

$(M_{H_2} = 2, M_{O_2} = 32, M_{CH_4} = 16)$

$= 16 : 1 : 2$

6 (*d*) From ideal gas equation, $d = \frac{pM}{RT}$

$\because$ M and R are constant for a particular gas

$\therefore \quad d \propto \frac{p}{T}$, i.e.

(a) $\frac{p}{T} = \frac{2}{600} = 0.0033$

(b) $\frac{p}{T} = \frac{0.5}{273} = 0.00183$

(c) $\frac{p}{T} = \frac{6}{1092} = 0.00549$

(d) $\frac{p}{T} = \frac{4}{500} = 0.0080$

$\because$ p/T ratio is highest at 4 atm and 500 K.

$\therefore$ Density of CO is maximum at this condition.

7 (*e*) The gases X, Y and Z are chemically unreactive, hence will form homogeneous mixture. All the gases occupy the available volume.

8 (*a*) Ideal gas equation,

$$pV = nRT, T \propto \frac{1}{n}$$

where, n = number of moles

$= \frac{\text{weight } (w)}{\text{molecular weight } (M)}$

$$\frac{T_1}{T_2} = \frac{n_2}{n_1} = \frac{w_2 \times M_1}{M_2 \times w_1}$$

9 (*a*) 28g of N_2 is equal to 1 mole of N_2

Applying, ideal gas equation

$$pV = nRT,$$

$$2.46 \times 10 = 1 \times 0.0821 \times T$$

$\therefore \quad T = 299.6 \text{ K}$

10 (*d*) Ideal gas equation, $pV = \frac{w}{M} RT$

$\Rightarrow \quad pM = \frac{w}{V} RT$

$\therefore \quad d = \frac{pM}{RT} \quad \left(\because \frac{w}{V} = \text{density } (d)\right)$

11 (*a*) Ideal gas equation, $pV = nRT$

When V and T are same, $p \propto n$

Thus, lower the number of moles of gas, lesser the pressure it will exert.

Hence,

(a) $n = \frac{\text{weight}}{\text{molecular weight}} = \frac{0.0355}{71}$

$= 5 \times 10^{-4}$ mol

(b) $n = \frac{0.071}{71} = 1 \times 10^{-3}$ mol

(c) $n = \frac{\text{number of molecules}}{N_A}$

$= \frac{6.023 \times 10^{21}}{6.023 \times 10^{23}} = 0.01$ mol

(d) $n = 0.02$ mol

Thus, 0.0355 g chlorine will exert the least pressure in a vessel.

12 (*b*) Given: $n = 0.60$ mol, $V = 3.00$ L

$T = 25°\text{C} \ (25° + 273 = 298 \text{ K})$

From ideal gas equation, we have

$pV = nRT$ or $p = \frac{nRT}{V}$

$= \frac{0.60 \times 0.0821 \times 298}{3} = 4.89$ atm

13 (*c*) Boyle's law relates the volume and the pressure of a given mass of a gas at constant temperature.

According to Boyle's law,

At constant temperature,

$$p_1V_1 = p_2V_2$$

$$380 \times 7 = 760 \times V_2$$

$\therefore \quad V_2 = \frac{380 \times 7}{760} = 3.5 \text{ L}$

14 (*b*) Given: $V = 8.2\text{L}, w = 9.0\text{g}, T = 300\text{K}$

Ideal gas equation is

$$pV = nRT \text{ or } pV = \frac{w}{M}RT$$

$$\therefore \quad M = \frac{wRT}{pV} = \frac{9.0 \times 0.082 \times 300}{1 \times 8.2}$$

$$= 27 \text{ g mol}^{-1}$$

15 (*c*) Ideal gas equation,

$$pV = nRT \Rightarrow pV = \frac{w}{M}RT$$

$$\left[\therefore n = \frac{w}{M}\right]$$

$$\Rightarrow \quad M = \frac{w}{V}\frac{RT}{p} \Rightarrow M = d\frac{RT}{p}$$

Here, $d = 1.964 \text{ g/dm}^3$

$= 1.964 \times 10^{-3} \text{ g/cc}$

$p = 76 \text{ cm} = 1 \text{ atm}$

$R = 0.0821 \text{ L atm K}^{-1} \text{ mol}^{-1}$

or $= 82.1 \text{ cc atm K}^{-1} \text{ mol}^{-1}$

$T = 273 \text{ K}$

$$\therefore M = \frac{1.964 \times 10^{-3} \times 82.1 \times 273}{1}$$

$= 44 \text{ g/mol}$

$\because$ The molecular weight of CO_2 is 44 g mol^{-1}.

$\therefore$ The gas is CO_2.

16 (*b*) Applying Boyle's law, (since, the temperature remains constant i.e., isothermal)

$p'_{N_2} V'_{N_2}$ (after mixing) $= p_{N_2} V_{N_2}$ (before mixing)

$$p'_{N_2} = \frac{p_{N_2} V_{N_2}}{V'_{N_2}} = \frac{4 \times 4.0}{10} = \frac{16}{10} = 1.6 \text{ bar}$$

Similarly, for He,

$p'_{He} V'_{He}$ (after mixing) $= p_{He} V_{He}$ (before mixing)

$$p'_{He} = \frac{pV_{He}}{V'_{He_2}}$$

$$= \frac{6 \times 6.0}{10} = \frac{36}{10} = 3.6 \text{ bar}$$

$\therefore$ Total pressure of mixture

$= 1.6 + 3.6 = 5.2 \text{ bar}$

17 (*a*) From Boyle's law,

$$p_1V_1 = p_2V_2 \Rightarrow 76 \times 5 = p_2 \times 35$$

[$\because$ at NTP $p = 76$ cm of Hg]

$$p_2 = \frac{76 \times 5}{35} = 10.8 \text{ cm of Hg}$$

18 (*a*) We know, $V_1 < V_3 < V_2$ at 273K (from figure)

$$p \propto \frac{1}{V}$$

Hence, $p_1 > p_3 > p_2$.

19 (*c*) According to Boyle's law, $p \propto \frac{1}{V}$

Hence, in order to increase the volume of a gas by 10%, the pressure of the gas should be decreased by 10%.

20 (*c*) $\frac{p_1V_1}{T_1} = \frac{p_2V_2}{T_2}$

$$\Rightarrow \frac{p_1 \times 4}{T_1} = \frac{2p_1 \times V_2}{2T_1}$$

$$V_2 = 4 \text{ dm}^3$$

21 (*e*) According to Charles' law, graph between V and T at constant pressure is called isobar and is always a straight line.

22 (*c*) Ideal gas equation, $pV = nRT$ is obeyed by ideal gas in both adiabatic process and isothermal process.

23 (*c*) Given, vapour density $= 70$

$\because$ Molecular weight

$= 2 \times$ vapour density

$\therefore$ Molecular weight $= 2 \times 70 = 140$

$[\text{CO}]_x = (12 + 16)_x = (28)_x$

$\because \quad (28)_x = 140$

$\therefore \quad (28)_x = (28)_5$

$x = 5$

Hence, formula is $(\text{CO})_5$.

$\therefore \quad x = 5$

24 (*c*) According to the question, temperature and volume are constant, hence, from ideal gas equation, we have

$$\frac{p_1}{p_2} = \frac{n_1}{n_2}$$

or $\frac{p_1}{p_2} = \frac{w_1}{w_2}$

[$\because M_2 = M_1$ as same gas is leaked]

$$\therefore \quad \frac{10}{8} = \frac{15}{w_2}$$

$\Rightarrow \quad w_2 = 12 \text{ kg}$

Hence, gas leaked $= 15 - 12 = 3$ kg

25 (*a*) Vapour density of gas $= 11.2$

$\because$ Molecular weight

$= 2 \times$ vapour density

$\therefore$ Molecular weight of the gas

$= 2 \times 11.2 = 22.4$ g

$\because$ 22.4 g of gas occupies

$= 22.4$ L volume

$\therefore$ 1 g of gas occupies $= \frac{22.4}{22.4} \times 1 = 1$ L

26 (*a*) Plot of pV against p is a straight line parallel to the X-axis, i.e. the slope will be zero.

27 (*c*) $\because \quad pV = nRT$

$$\therefore \quad R = \frac{pV}{nT}$$

Hence, the value of R depends only on the units of the measurement, e.g.

$R = 8.314 \text{ JK}^{-1}\text{mol}^{-1}$

$= 0.0821 \text{ L atm K}^{-1}\text{mol}^{-1}$

$= 1.987 \text{ cal K}^{-1}\text{mol}^{-1}$

28 (*b*) According to Avogadro's hypothesis, equal volumes of all gases under the same conditions of temperature and pressure contain equal number of molecules.

29 (*b*) Applying Boyle's law (since, the temperature remains constant)

$p'_{He} V'_{He}$ (after mixing) $= p_{He} V_{He}$ (before mixing)

$$p'_{He} = \frac{p_{He} V_{He}}{V'_{He}} = \frac{200 \times 0.66}{400} = 0.33 \text{ atm}$$

Similarly, for O_2,

$p'_{O_2} V'_{O_2}$ (after mixing)

$= p_{O_2} V_{O_2}$ (before mixing)

$$p'_{O_2} = \frac{400 \times 0.52}{400} = 0.52 \text{ atm}$$

Topic 2

Dalton's Law of Partial Pressure and Graham's Law of Diffusion

2014

1 At a certain temperature, the time required for the complete diffusion of 200 mL of H_2 gas is 30 min. The time required for the complete diffusion of 50 mL of O_2 gas at the same temperature will be **[WB JEE]**

(a) 60 min (b) 30 min (c) 45 min (d) 15 min

2 If 240 mL, of a gas x diffuse through a porous membrane in 20 min, whereas the same volume of methane diffuses in 10 min at the same temperature and pressure, the molar mass in g mol^{-1} of gas x is **[EAMCET]**

(a) 8 (b) 64 (c) 32 (d) 123

3 5.5 mg of nitrogen gas dissolves in 180 g of water at 273 K and 1 atm pressure due to nitrogen gas. The mole fraction of nitrogen in 180 g of water at 5 atm nitrogen pressure is approximately **[KCET]**

(a) 1×10^{-6} (b) 1×10^{-5} (c) 1×10^{-3} (d) 1×10^{-4}

2012

4 50 mL of each gas A and of gas B takes 150 and 200 s respectively for effusing through a pin hole under the similar conditions. If molecular mass of gas B is 36, the molecular mass of gas A will be **[CBSE AIPMT]**

(a) 96 (b) 128 (c) 32 (d) 64

5 A certain gas takes three times as long to effuse out as helium. Its molecular mass will be **[CBSE AIPMT]**

(a) 27 u (b) 36 u (c) 64 u (d) 9 u

6 Dalton's law of partial pressure is applicable to which one of the following systems? **[UP CPMT]**

(a) $NH_3 + HCl$ (b) $NO + O_2$
(c) $H_2 + Cl_2$ (d) $CO + H_2$

2011

7 Two gases A and B having the same volume diffuse through a porous partition in 20 and 10 s respectively. The molecular mass of A is 49 u. Molecular mass of B will be **[CBSE AIPMT]**

(a) 25.00 u (b) 50.00 u (c) 12.25 u (d) 6.50 u

8 A gaseous mixture was prepared by taking equal moles of CO and N_2. If the total pressure of the mixture was found 1 atm, the partial pressure of the nitrogen (N_2) in the mixture is **[CBSE AIPMT]**

(a) 1 atm (b) 0.5 atm (c) 0.8 atm (d) 0.9 atm

9 Equal weights of CH_4 and H_2 are mixed in a container at 25°C. Fraction of total pressure exerted by methane is

(a) $\frac{1}{2}$ (b) $\frac{1}{3}$ (c) $\frac{1}{9}$ (d) $\frac{8}{9}$ **[DUMET]**

2010

10 A gaseous mixture contains 2 moles of A and 3 moles of B. Total pressure of the mixture is 5 atm. The partial pressures of A and B are respectively. **[AFMC]**

(a) 2 atm and 4 atm (b) 2 atm and 3 atm
(c) 3 atm and 2 atm (d) 6 atm and 2 atm

11 2 g of hydrogen diffuse from a container in 10 min. How many gram of oxygen would diffuse through the same container in the same time under similar conditions?

(a) 0.5 g (b) 4 g (c) 6 g (d) 8 g **[Manipal]**

12 At identical temperature and pressure, the rate of diffusion of hydrogen gas is $3\sqrt{3}$ times that of a hydrocarbon having molecular formula C_nH_{2n-2}. What is the value of n? **[WB JEE]**

(a) 1 (b) 4 (c) 3 (d) 8

2009

13 The ratio of rates of diffusion of helium and methane under same conditions of temperature and pressure will be **[CG PMT, Haryana PMT]**

(a) 4 : 1 (b) 2 : 1 (c) 1 : 1 (d) 1 : 2

14 If the ratio of the rates of diffusion of two gases A and B is 4 : 1, then the ratio of their densities in the same order is

(a) 16 : 1 (b) 4 : 1 (c) 1 : 4 (d) 1 : 16 **[J&K CET]**

15 0.5 mole of each of H_2, SO_2 and CH_4 are kept in a container. A hole was made in the container. After 3 h, the order of partial pressures in the container will be **[KCET]**

(a) $p_{SO_2} > p_{CH_4} > p_{H_2}$ (b) $p_{H_2} > p_{SO_2} > p_{CH_4}$
(c) $p_{H_2} > p_{CH_4} > p_{SO_2}$ (d) $p_{SO_2} > p_{H_2} > p_{CH_4}$

2008

16 When a bottle of dry ammonia and a bottle of dry HCl connected through a long tube are opened simultaneously at both ends, at first **[Kerala CEE]**

(a) a white ring is formed at the centre of the tube
(b) a white ring is formed near the ammonia bottle
(c) entire length of tube turns white
(d) a white ring is formed near HCl bottle
(e) no white ring is formed

17 In a flask of 'V' litres, 0.2 mole of O_2, 0.4 mole of N_2, 0.1 mole of NH_3 and 0.3 mole of He gases are present at 27°C. If total pressure exerted by these non-reacting gases is 1 atm, the partial pressure exerted by N_2 gas is **[EAMCET]**

(a) 0.4 atm (b) 0.3 atm
(c) 0.2 atm (d) 0.1 atm

18 If two molecules of A and B have mass 100 kg and 64 kg and rate of diffusion of A is 12×10^{-3}, then what will be the rate of diffusion of B? **[BCECE]**

(a) 15×10^{-3} (b) 64×10^{-3}
(c) 5×10^{-3} (d) 46×10^{-3}

2007

19 At STP, a container has 1 mole of Ar, 2 moles of CO_2, 3 moles of O_2 and 4 moles of N_2. Without changing the total pressure if one mole of O_2 is removed, the partial pressure of O_2 is **[MHT CET]**

(a) changed by about 16% (b) halved
(c) changed by 26% (d) unchanged

20 If the ratio of masses of SO_3 and O_2 gases confined in a vessel is 1 : 1, then the ratio of their partial pressures would be **[Kerala CEE]**

(a) 5 : 2 (b) 2 : 5 (c) 2 : 1 (d) 1 : 2
(e) 1 : 1

21 Identify the pair of gases that have equal rates of diffusion. **[J&K CET]**

(a) NO, CO (b) N_2O, CO
(c) N_2O, CO_2 (d) CO_2, NO_2

22 A, B and C are ideal gases. Their molecular weights are 2, 4 and 28 respectively. The rate of diffusion of these gases follow the order **[J&K CET]**

(a) $C > A > B$ (b) $C > B > A$
(c) $A = B = C$ (d) $A > B > C$

23 If both oxygen and helium gases are at the same temperature, the rate of diffusion of O_2 is very close to **[BCECE]**

(a) 4 times that of He (b) 2 times that of He
(c) 0.35 times that of He (d) 8 times that of He

Answers

1 (b)	2 (b)	3 (d)	4 (*)	5 (b)	6 (d)	7 (c)	8 (b)	9 (c)	10 (b)
11 (d)	12 (b)	13 (b)	14 (d)	15 (a)	16 (d)	17 (a)	18 (a)	19 (c)	20 (b)
21 (c)	22 (d)	23 (c)							

Explanations

1 (*b*) According to Graham's law of diffusion,

Rate of diffusion, $r \propto 1/\sqrt{M} = V/t$

[Here, M = molecular mass
V = volume and t = time]

Thus, for H_2 gas,

$$200/30 = 1/\sqrt{2} \quad \text{...(i)}$$

For O_2 gas, $50/t = 1/\sqrt{32}$ ...(ii)

From Eq (i) and (ii), we get

$$\frac{200\times t}{30\times 50} = \frac{\sqrt{32}}{\sqrt{2}}$$

$$\Rightarrow t = \frac{\sqrt{16}\times 30\times 50}{200} = \frac{4\times 30}{4} = 30 \text{ min}$$

2 (*b*) According to Graham's law of diffusion

$$= \frac{V_1}{t_1}\frac{t_2}{V_2} = \sqrt{\frac{M_2}{M_1}} \Rightarrow \frac{240\times10}{20\times240} = \sqrt{\frac{16}{x}}$$

$\Rightarrow \quad 1/2 = \sqrt{16/x}$

$\Rightarrow \quad x = 16\times4$

$= 64 \text{ g mol}^{-1}$

3 (*d*) Amount of nitrogen gas at 5 atm

$= 5\times5.5 = 27.5 \text{ mg} = 27.5\times10^{-3}$ g

Mole fraction of N_2

$$= \frac{\text{Moles of } N_2}{\text{Moles of } H_2O + \text{Moles of } N_2}$$

$[\because n_{N_2} <<< n_{H_2O}]$

$$= \frac{27.5\times10^{-3}/28}{180/18} \approx 1\times10^{-4}$$

4 (*) Given, $V_A = V_B = 50$ mL

$t_A = 150\text{ s}$; $t_B = 200\text{ s}$;

$M_B = 36$; $M_A = ?$

From Graham's law of diffusion,

$$\frac{r_B}{r_A} = \sqrt{\frac{M_A}{M_B}} = \frac{V_B t_A}{t_B\cdot V_A}$$

$$\Rightarrow \sqrt{\frac{M_A}{36}} = \frac{V_A\times150}{200\times V_A}$$

$(\because V_B = V_A = 50\text{mL})$

$$\Rightarrow \sqrt{\frac{M_A}{36}} = \frac{15}{20} = \frac{3}{4} \Rightarrow \frac{M_A}{36} = \frac{9}{16}$$

$$M_A = \frac{9\times36}{16}$$

$$= \frac{9\times9}{4} = \frac{81}{4} = 20.25 \text{ g/mol}$$

(No option is correct).

Note If $T_A = 200$s and $T_B = 150$s, then $M_A = 64$, then option (d) comes out to be correct.

5 (*b*) From Graham's diffusion law,

$$\frac{r_1}{r_2} = \sqrt{\frac{M_2}{M_1}} \text{ or } \frac{V_{He}}{t_{He}}\times\frac{t_2}{V_2} = \sqrt{\frac{M_2}{M_{He}}}$$

$\because$ Volume is same, and $t_2 = 3t_{He}$,

$3/1 = \sqrt{M_2/4} \Rightarrow 9 = M_2/4$

$\therefore \quad M_2 = 9\times4 = 36$ u

6 (*d*) Dalton's law of partial pressure is applicable to two or more non-reacting gases.

(a) $NH_3 + HCl \longrightarrow NH_4Cl$

(b) $2NO + O_2 \longrightarrow 2NO_2$

(c) $H_2 + Cl_2 \longrightarrow 2HCl$

(d) $CO + H_2 \longrightarrow$ No reaction

$\because$ CO + H_2 are non-reacting gases. Hence, Dalton's law of partial pressure is applicable to this system.

7 (c) $\frac{r_A}{r_B} = \sqrt{\frac{M_B}{M_A}} \Rightarrow \frac{V_A}{t_A} \times \frac{t_B}{V_B} = \sqrt{\frac{M_B}{M_A}}$

If volumes are same, then,

$\frac{t_B}{t_A} = \sqrt{\frac{M_B}{M_A}} \Rightarrow \frac{10}{20} = \sqrt{\frac{M_B}{49}} \Rightarrow \frac{1}{4} = \frac{M_B}{49}$

$\therefore M_B = 49/4 = 12.25$ u

8 (b) Equal number of moles exert same partial pressure at same temperature and pressure. Therefore, partial pressure of N_2 in the mixture is 0.5 atm.

($\because p_{total} = p_1 + p_2$, 1 atm $= 2p_1$, $p_1 = 0.5$ atm)

9 (c) Suppose w kg of each is taken

$n_{CH_4} = w/16$ and $n_{H_2} = w/2$

$p_{CH_4} = p_{total} \times$ mole fraction

$= p_{total} \times \frac{w/16}{w/2 + w/16}$

$p_{CH_4} = p_{total} \times 1/9$

$\therefore$ Fraction of total pressure exerted by methane is 1/9.

10 (b) Mole fraction of $A = \frac{2}{2+3} = \frac{2}{5} = 0.4$

Mole fraction of $B = \frac{3}{2+3} = \frac{3}{5} = 0.6$

Partial pressure of gas A

$= P_{total} \times$ mole fraction of A

$= 5 \times 0.4 = 2$ atm

Partial pressure of gas B

$= P_{total} \times$ mole fraction of B

$= 5 \times 0.6 = 3$ atm

11 (d) Rate of diffusion, $r = \frac{V}{t} \propto \frac{1}{\sqrt{M}}$

$\Rightarrow = \frac{V_{H_2}}{V_{O_2}} = \frac{n_{H_2}}{n_{O_2}} = \sqrt{\frac{M_{O_2}}{M_{H_2}}}$ $[\because V \propto n]$

Thus, $\frac{w_{H_2}}{M_{H_2}} \times \frac{M_{O_2}}{w_{O_2}} = \sqrt{\frac{M_{O_2}}{M_{H_2}}}$

$[\because n = w/M]$

$\frac{2/2}{w/32} = \sqrt{\frac{32}{2}}, \frac{32}{w} = 4, w = 8$ g

12 (b) $\frac{r_{H_2}}{C_nH_{2n-2}} = \sqrt{\frac{M_{C_nH_{2n-2}}}{M_{H_2}}}$

$\because \sqrt{\frac{M_{C_nH_{2n-2}}}{2}} = 3\sqrt{3}; \frac{M_{C_nH_{2n-2}}}{2} = 27$

$\Rightarrow M_{C_nH_{2n-2}} = 27 \times 2 = 54$ g/mol

Hence, $12n + (2n-2) \times 1 = 54$

$\Rightarrow$ $14n = 56$ or $n = 4$

Thus, hydrocarbon is C_4H_6.

13 (b) According to Graham's law of diffusion,

rate of diffusion $\propto \sqrt{1/\text{Molecular mass}}$

$\therefore \frac{r_{He}}{r_{CH_4}} = \sqrt{\frac{M_{CH_4}}{M_{He}}} = \sqrt{\frac{16}{4}} = \sqrt{\frac{4}{1}} = 2:1$

14 (d) Rate of diffusion $\propto (1/\sqrt{d})$

$\frac{r_A}{r_B} = \sqrt{\frac{d_B}{d_A}} \Rightarrow \frac{4}{1} = \sqrt{\frac{d_B}{d_A}} \Rightarrow \frac{16}{1} = \frac{d_B}{d_A}$

$\therefore$ $d_A/d_B = 1/16$

15 (a) According to Graham's law of diffusion, rate of diffusion

$\propto \sqrt{\frac{1}{\text{molecular mass}}} \propto$ partial pressure

Since, equal moles of all gases were taken in the container, the rate of diffusion will be in the order

$H_2 > CH_4 > SO_2$

$\therefore$ The order of partial pressure of the gases remaining in the container will be $p_{SO_2} > p_{CH_4} > p_{H_2}$

16 (d) According to Graham's law of diffusion, $r \propto 1/\sqrt{M}$

Molecular weight of HCl

$= 1 + 35.5 = 36.5$ g/mol

Molecular weight of NH_3

$= 14 + 3 = 17$ g/mol

As, the molecular weight of dry ammonia is less, so it diffuses rapidly and forms a ring near HCl bottle at first.

17 (a) Total number of moles

$= 0.2 + 0.4 + 0.1 + 0.3 = 1.0$

Partial pressure of nitrogen = total pressure $\times$ mole fraction of nitrogen

$= 1 \text{ atm} \times \frac{\text{moles of nitrogen}}{\text{total number of moles}}$

$= 1 \times \frac{0.4}{1} = 0.4$ atm

18 (a) According to Graham's law,

$r_A/r_B = \sqrt{M_B/M_A}$

Here, $M_A = \left(\frac{100}{2}\right)$ kg/molecule,

$M_B = \left(\frac{64}{2}\right)$ kg/molecule

$r_A = 12 \times 10^{-3}$ and $r_B = ?$

$\frac{12 \times 10^{-3}}{r_B} = \sqrt{\frac{64/2}{100/2}} = \sqrt{\frac{64}{100}} = \frac{8}{10}$

$\therefore r_B = \frac{12 \times 10^{-3} \times 10}{8} = 15 \times 10^{-3}$

19 (c) Partial pressure of a gas $\propto$ mole fraction

Total moles $= 1 + 2 + 3 + 4 = 10$ moles

Initial mole fraction of $O_2 = 3/10$

Partial pressure $= \frac{3}{10} \times 100 = 30$ atm

Mole fraction of O_2 at final stage $\approx 2/9$

Change in partial pressure

$= \left(\frac{3}{10} - \frac{2}{9}\right) \times 100 = \frac{70}{9} \approx 8$

% change $= \frac{8}{30} \times 100 = 26\%$

20 (b) Ratio of masses of SO_3 and O_2 gases confined in a vessel is 1 : 1.

$\because$ Partial pressure

= total pressure $\times$ mole fraction

Partial pressure of SO_3

$= p° \times \frac{1/80}{1/32 + 1/80}$

$\therefore$ Partial pressure of O_2

$= p° \times \frac{1/32}{1/32 + 1/80}$

Ratio of partial pressure of SO_3 and $O_2(SO_3 : O_2) = \frac{1/80}{1/32} = 32 : 80 = 2 : 5$

21 (c) Rate of diffusion depends upon the molecular masses of gases. Therefore, the gases which have equal molecular mass have equal rates of diffusion.

$r_1/r_2 = \sqrt{M_2/M_1}$

Molecular mass of $N_2O = 28 + 16$

$= 44$ g/mol

Molecular mass of $CO_2 = 12 + 32$

$= 44$ g/mol

$\therefore$ $r_{N_2O}/r_{CO_2} = 1$ or $r_{N_2O} = r_{CO_2}$

22 (d) According to Graham's law of diffusion, $r \propto \frac{1}{\sqrt{M}}$

Hence, the order of rate of diffusion is

Gases : $A > B > C$

Molecular weight : 2 : 4 : 28

23 (c) According to Graham's law of diffusion,

$\frac{r_{O_2}}{r_{He}} = \sqrt{\frac{M_{He}}{M_{O_2}}} = \sqrt{\frac{4}{32}} = \frac{2}{5.65}$

$\therefore$ $r_{O_2} = 0.35\, r_{He}$

Topic 3

Kinetic Theory of Gases

2014

1 If average velocity of a sample of gas molecules at 300 K is 5 cm s^{-1}, what is RMS velocity of same sample of gas molecules at the same temperature?
(Given, $\alpha : u : v = 1 : 1.224 : 1.127$) **[MHT CET]**

(a) 6.112 cm/s (b) 4.605 cm/s
(c) 4.085 cm/s (d) 5.430 cm/s

2 Two gases X (molecular weight M_X) and Y (molecular weight $M_Y; M_Y > M_X$) are at the same temperature, T in two different containers. Their root mean square velocities are C_X and C_Y respectively. If the average kinetic energies per molecule of two gases X and Y are E_X and E_Y respectively then which of the following relation (s) is (are) true? **[WB JEE]**

(a) $E_X > E_Y$ (b) $C_X > C_Y$
(c) $E_X = E_Y = (3/2)RT$ (d) $E_X = E_Y = (3/2)k_B T$

3 The RMS speed of helium in ms^{-1} (atomic mass = 4.0 g mol^{-1}) at 400 K is **[EAMCET]**

(a) 15.8 (b) 50 (c) 158 (d) 1580

2013

4 At what temperature will the RMS velocity of SO_2 be the same as that of O_2 at 303K? **[KCET]**

(a) 403 K (b) 303 K (c) 606 K (d) 273 K

2012

5 One mole of oxygen at 273 K and one mole of sulphur dioxide at 546 K are taken in two separate containers, then **[UP CPMT]**

(a) kinetic energy of O_2 > kinetic energy of SO_2
(b) kinetic energy of SO_2 > kinetic energy of O_2
(c) kinetic energy of both are equal
(d) the temperature remains unaffected

2011

6 By what factor does the average velocity of a gaseous molecule increases, when the temperature (in kelvin) is doubled? **[CBSE AIPMT]**

(a) 1.4 (b) 2.0 (c) 2.8 (d) 4.0

2010

7 Average KE of CO_2 at 27°C is E. The average kinetic energy of N_2 at the same temperature will be **[BVP]**

(a) E (b) 22 E (c) $E/22$ (d) $3/\sqrt{2}$

8 At what temperature, the RMS velocity of gas shown at 50°C will be doubled? **[OJEE]**

(a) 626 K (b) 1019 K (c) 200°C (d) 1019°C

9 Given, RMS velocity of hydrogen at 300 K is 1.9×10^3 m/s. The RMS velocity of oxygen at 1200 K will be **[OJEE]**

(a) 7.6×10^3 m/s (b) 3.8×10^3 m/s
(c) 0.95×10^3 m/s (d) 0.475×10^3 m/s

10 If the temperature changes from 27°C to 127°C, the relative percentage change in RMS velocity is **[OJEE]**

(a) 1.56 (b) 2.56 (c) 15.6 (d) 82.4

11 For one mole of an ideal gas, increasing the temperature from 10°C to 20°C **[KCET]**

(a) increases the average kinetic energy by two times
(b) increases the RMS velocity by $\sqrt{2}$ times
(c) increases the RMS velocity by two times
(d) increases both the average kinetic energy and RMS velocity, but not significantly

12 The average kinetic energy of an ideal gas per molecule in SI units at 25°C will be **[CMC]**

(a) 6.17×10^{-21} JK^{-1} (b) 6.17×10^{-23} JK^{-1}
(c) 6.17×10^{-20} JK^{-1} (d) 7.16×10^{-20} JK^{-1}

2009

13 Which of the following comparisons of the average kinetic energy and the average molecular speeds of H_2 and N_2 gases at 300 K is correct? **[Kerala CEE]**

	Average kinetic energy	Average molecular speed
(a)	$H_2 = N_2$	$H_2 = N_2$
(b)	$H_2 < N_2$	$H_2 > N_2$
(c)	$H_2 = N_2$	$H_2 < N_2$
(d)	$H_2 > N_2$	$H_2 = N_2$
(e)	$H_2 = N_2$	$H_2 > N_2$

14 Different gases at the same temperature must have **[OJEE]**

(a) same volume
(b) same pressure
(c) same average KE
(d) same van der Waals' constant

15 The root mean square velocity of ideal gas at constant pressure varies with density (d) as **[CG PMT, Haryana PMT]**

(a) d^2 (b) d (c) $\sqrt{d}$ (d) $1/\sqrt{d}$

16 The average kinetic energy of one molecule of an ideal gas at 27°C and 1 atm pressure is [EAMCET]

(a) $900 \text{ cal K}^{-1} \text{ mol}^{-1}$
(b) $6.21 \times 10^{-21} \text{ JK}^{-1} \text{ molecule}^{-1}$
(c) $336.7 \text{ JK}^{-1} \text{ molecule}^{-1}$
(d) $3741.3 \text{ JK}^{-1} \text{ mol}^{-1}$

17 The RMS velocity of molecules of a gas of density 4 kg m^{-3} and pressure $1.2 \times 10^5 \text{ Nm}^{-2}$ is [KCET]

(a) 900 ms^{-1} (b) 120 ms^{-1} (c) 600 ms^{-1} (d) 300 ms^{-1}

2008

18 If a gas expands at constant temperature, it indicates that [CBSE AIPMT]

(a) kinetic energy of molecules decreases
(b) pressure of the gas increases
(c) kinetic energy of molecules remains the same
(d) number of the molecules of gas increases

19 If X is the total number of collisions which a gas molecule register with others per unit time under particular conditions, then the collision frequency of the gas containing N molecules per unit volume is [Manipal]

(a) $\frac{X}{N}$ (b) NX (c) $2NX$ (d) $\frac{NX}{2}$

20 The most probable velocity of a gas molecule at 298 K is 300 m/s. Its RMS velocity, (in m/s) is [Punjab PMET]

(a) 420
(b) 245
(c) 402
(d) 367

21 The average velocity (in cm/s) of hydrogen molecule at 27°C will be [DUMET]

(a) 19.3×10^4 (b) 17.8×10^4
(c) 24.93×10^9 (d) 17.8×10^8

2005

22 Kinetic energy of one mole of an ideal gas at 300 K is [AMU]

(a) 3.48 kJ
(b) 3.74 kJ
(c) 37.4 kJ
(d) 34.8 kJ

23 What is the ratio of kinetic energies of 3 g of hydrogen and 4 g of oxygen at T (K)? [EAMCET]

(a) 12 : 1 (b) 6 : 1
(c) 1 : 6 (d) 24 : 1

Answers

1 (d)	2 (b, d)	3 (d)	4 (c)	5 (b)	6 (a)	7 (a)	8 (d)	9 (c)	10 (c)
11 (d)	12 (a)	13 (e)	14 (c)	15 (d)	16 (b)	17 (d)	18 (c)	19 (d)	20 (d)
21 (b)	22 (b)	23 (a)							

Explanations

1 (*d*) Given that α (most probable velocity) : u(RMS velocity) : v (average velocity) = 1 : 1.224 : 1.127

$$\therefore \quad = \frac{1.224}{1.127} \Rightarrow \frac{u}{5} = \frac{1.224}{1.127}$$

$$\Rightarrow \quad u = \frac{1.224 \times 5}{1.127} = 5.430 \text{ cm/s}$$

2 (*b,d*) Given, molecular weight of $X = M_X$

Molecular weight of $Y = M_Y$ and $M_Y > M_X$

Root mean square velocities $= C_X$ and C_Y respectively.

Average KE/molecule $= E_X$ and E_Y respectively. We know that,

Root mean square velocity,

$$C = \sqrt{\frac{3RT}{M}} \quad \text{or} \quad C \propto \sqrt{\frac{1}{M}}$$

$$\Rightarrow \quad C_X/C_Y = \sqrt{M_Y/M_X}$$

Since, $M_Y > M_X \Rightarrow C_X > C_Y$

$$\text{KE/mole} = \frac{3}{2}RT$$

$$\Rightarrow \text{KE/mole} = \frac{3}{2}\left(\frac{R}{N_a}\right)T = \frac{3}{2}k_BT$$

$$\text{So,} \quad E_X = E_Y = \frac{3}{2}k_BT$$

3 (*d*) Given, $T = 400 \text{ K}$

Molar mass of helium = 0.004 kg

$R = 8.314 \text{ JK}^{-1} \text{ mol}^{-1}$(Gas constant)

$$v_{\text{rms}} = \sqrt{\frac{3RT}{M}} = \sqrt{\frac{3 \times 8.314 \times 400}{(4 \times 10^{-3}) \text{ kg}}}$$

$$= 1579.3 \text{ m/s} \approx 1580 \text{ m/s}$$

4 (*c*) The RMS velocity of SO_2

$$= \sqrt{\frac{3RT_{SO_2}}{M_{SO_2}}} = \sqrt{\frac{3RT_{SO_2}}{64}}$$

Here, molar mass of $SO_2 = 64$ g

The RMS velocity of O_2

$$= \sqrt{\frac{3RT_{O_2}}{M_{O_2}}} = \sqrt{\frac{3R \times 303}{32}}$$

Molar mass of $O_2 = 32$ g

$$\Rightarrow \quad \frac{3RT_{SO_2}}{64} = \frac{3R \times 303}{32}$$

$$\Rightarrow \quad T_{SO_2} = \frac{303 \times 64}{32}$$

$$\therefore \quad T_{SO_2} = 606 \text{ K}$$

5 (*b*) Kinetic energy, $\text{KE} = \frac{3}{2}RT$,

i.e. $\text{KE} \propto T$

$$\frac{\text{KE}_{O_2}}{\text{KE}_{SO_2}} = \frac{T_{O_2}}{T_{SO_2}} = \frac{273}{546} = \frac{1}{2}$$

$$\text{KE}_{SO_2} = 2\text{KE}_{O_2} \Rightarrow \text{KE}_{SO_2} > \text{KE}_{O_2}$$

6 (*a*) Average velocity, $v_{\text{av}} = \sqrt{8RT/\pi M}$

$$\therefore v_{\text{av}} \propto \sqrt{T} \Rightarrow \frac{v_1}{v_2} = \sqrt{\frac{T_1}{T_2}}$$

when temperature is doubled,

$$T_2 = 2T_1 \Rightarrow \frac{v_1}{v_2} = \sqrt{\frac{T_1}{2T_1}}$$

$$\Rightarrow v_2 = \sqrt{2}\, v_1 = 1.4\, v_1$$

7 (*a*) Average KE of a gas depends only on temperature.

$$KE = \frac{3}{2} kT$$

∴ At the same temperature,

KE of CO_2 = KE of $N_2 = E$

8 (*d*) $v_{rms} = \sqrt{\frac{3RT}{M}}$ or $v_{rms} \propto \sqrt{T}$

where, T is in Kelvin scale.

For RMS velocity to be doubled, T in Kelvin scale must be raised 4 times.

So, it should be

$$4 \times (50 + 273) = 1292 \text{ K}$$
$$= (1292 - 273)°\text{C}$$
$$= 1019°\text{C}$$

9 (*c*) $v_{rms}(H_2) = \sqrt{\frac{3R \times 300}{2}}$

$$= 1.9 \times 10^3 \text{ m/s}$$

$$v_{rms}(O_2) = \sqrt{\frac{3R \times 1200}{32}}$$

$$= \frac{1}{2}\left(\sqrt{\frac{3R \times 300}{2}}\right) = \frac{1}{2} \times v_{rms}(H_2)$$

$$= \frac{1}{2}(1.9 \times 10^3) \text{ m/s} = 0.95 \times 10^3 \text{ m/s}$$

10 (*c*) $v_{rms} = \sqrt{\frac{3RT}{M}}$ for a particular gas,

M is constant, $v_{rms} \propto \sqrt{T}$

$$v_{rms} \propto \sqrt{T} \Rightarrow v_{rms} = x \times \sqrt{T}$$

(where, $x = \sqrt{3R/M}$)

So, at 27°C (300 K),

$$v_{rms} = x\sqrt{300} = 17.3x$$

At 127°C (400 K),

$$v_{rms} = x\sqrt{400} = 20x$$

∴ Percentage increase

$$= \frac{(20x - 17.3x)}{17.3x} \times 100 = 15.6\%$$

11 (*d*) Given, $T_1 = 273 + 10 = 283$ K

$$T_2 = 273 + 20 = 293 \text{ K}$$

Average $KE = \frac{3}{2} kT \Rightarrow \frac{(KE_1)}{(KE_2)}$

$$= \frac{283}{293} = 0.96$$

Root mean square (RMS) velocity,

$$v_{rms} = \sqrt{\frac{3RT}{M}}$$

$$\Rightarrow \frac{v_{rms}(1)}{v_{rms}(2)} = \sqrt{\frac{T_1}{T_2}} = \sqrt{\frac{283}{293}} = 0.98$$

Thus, both average kinetic energy and root mean square velocity increases but not significantly when temperature is increased from 10°C to 20°C.

12 (*a*) Average kinetic energy per molecule

$$= \frac{3}{2} kT = \frac{3}{2} \times 1.38 \times 10^{-23} \times 298$$
$$= 6.17 \times 10^{-21} \text{ JK}^{-1} \text{ molecule}^{-1}$$

13 (*e*) Average kinetic energy,

$$KE = \frac{3}{2} kT$$

Since, temperature is same (300 K) for both H_2 and N_2.

$$KE_{(H_2)} = KE_{(N_2)}$$

Average velocity or molecular speed,

$$v_{av} = \sqrt{\frac{8RT}{\pi M}} \text{ or } v_{av} \propto \frac{1}{\sqrt{M}}$$

$$\frac{v_{av}(H_2)}{v_{av}(N_2)} = \sqrt{\frac{M_{(N_2)}}{M_{(H_2)}}} = \sqrt{\frac{28}{2}} = \sqrt{14}$$

$$v_{av}(H_2) = \sqrt{14} \times v_{av}(N_2)$$

$$\therefore v_{av}(H_2) > v_{av}(N_2)$$

14 (*c*) Since, $KE = \frac{3}{2} RT$ or $KE \propto T$

The value of kinetic energy depends only on temperature. Thus, different gases have similar KE at the same temperature.

15 (*d*) Root mean square velocity,

$$u = \sqrt{\frac{3RT}{M}}$$

$$\sqrt{\frac{3pV}{Mn}} = \sqrt{\frac{3pV}{M \times \frac{m}{M}}} \quad \left[\because \frac{pV}{n} = RT\right]$$

$$= \sqrt{\frac{3pV}{m}} = \sqrt{\frac{3p}{d}} \quad \left[\because \frac{m}{V} = d\right]$$

Thus, at constant pressure, $u \propto \sqrt{1/d}$.

16 (*b*) Average kinetic energy per molecule

$$= \frac{3}{2} kT \text{ or } = \frac{3}{2}\frac{R}{N_0} T \quad \left[k = \frac{R}{N_0}\right]$$

$$= \frac{3}{2} \times \frac{8.314}{6.023 \times 10^{23}} \times 300$$

$$= 6.21 \times 10^{-21} \text{ JK}^{-1} \text{ molecule}^{-1}$$

17 (*d*) The RMS velocity of a gas $= \sqrt{\frac{3p}{d}}$

Given, $p = 1.2 \times 10^5 \text{ Nm}^{-2}$,

$$d = 4 \text{ kg m}^{-3}$$

$$\therefore v_{rms} = \sqrt{\frac{3 \times 1.2 \times 10^5}{4}} = \sqrt{0.9 \times 10^5}$$

$$= \sqrt{9 \times 10^4} = 3 \times 10^2 = 300 \text{ m s}^{-1}$$

18 (*c*) Kinetic energy, $KE = \frac{3}{2} RT$

$$KE \propto T$$

Kinetic energy of gas depends upon temperature and is independent of pressure.

Here, the temperature of gas remains constant, hence, kinetic energy of molecules remains the same.

19 (*d*) Number of collisions of one molecule/unit time = X

Number of collisions of N molecules/unit time = NX

∴ Collision frequency = $NX/2$

20 (*d*) Most probable velocity

$$= \sqrt{2/3} \times \text{RMS velocity}$$

$$300 = \sqrt{2/3} \times \text{RMS velocity}$$

$$\text{RMS velocity} = \frac{\sqrt{3} \times 300}{\sqrt{2}}$$

$$= 367 \cdot 4 \text{m/s} = 367 \text{m/s}$$

21 (*b*) Average velocity $= \sqrt{8RT/\pi M}$

$$T = (27 + 273) = 300 \text{ K}$$

Molecular mass of $H_2 = 2 \text{ g mol}^{-1}$

∴ Average velocity

$$= \sqrt{\frac{8 \times 8.314 \times 10^7 \times 300}{3.14 \times 2}}$$

$$= 17.8 \times 10^4 \text{cm/s}$$

22 (*b*) Given that, $n = 1$, $T = 300$ K,

$$R = 8.314 \text{ JK}^{-1} \text{ mol}^{-1}$$

$$\therefore \text{KE (kinetic energy)} = \frac{3}{2} nRT$$

$$= \frac{3}{2} \times 1 \times 8.314 \times 300$$

$$= 3741 \cdot 3 \text{ J or } 3.74 \text{ kJ}$$

23 (*a*) $KE = \frac{3}{2} nRT$

Here (n = number of moles of the gas,
R = Universal gas constant,
T = temperature)

$$\therefore \frac{(KE)_{H_2}}{(KE)_{O_2}} = \frac{n_{H_2}}{n_{O_2}} = \frac{3/2}{4/32} = 12:1$$

Topic 4

Behaviour of Real Gases : Deviation from Ideal Behaviour

2019

1 A gas at 350 K and 15 bar has molar volume 20 percent smaller than that for an ideal gas under the same conditions. The correct option about the gas and its compressibility factor (Z) is

(a) $Z > 1$ and repulsive forces are dominant
(b) $Z < 1$ and attractive forces are dominant
(c) $Z < 1$ and repulsive forces are dominant
(d) $Z > 1$ and attractive forces are dominant

2018

2 The correction factor 'a' to the ideal gas equation corresponds to **[NEET 2018]**

(a) electric field present between the gas molecules
(b) volume of the gas molecules
(c) density of the gas molecules
(d) forces of attraction between the gas molecules

3 Given van der Waals' constant of NH_3, H_2, O_2 and CO_2 are respectively 4.17, 0.244, 1.36 and 3.59. Which one of the following gases is most easily liquefied? **[NEET 2018]**

(a) O_2 (b) H_2 (c) NH_3 (d) CO_2

2017

4 In van der Waals' equation of state for non-ideal gas, the term that accounts for intermolecular force is **[AIIMS]**

(a) $(V=b)$ (b) $(RT)^{-1}$ (c) $\left(p+\frac{a}{V^2}\right)$ (d) RT

2014

5 Which among the following gases can be liquefied easily? **[MHT CET]**

(a) Chlorine (b) Nitrogen
(c) Oxygen (d) Hydrogen

6 Four gases P, Q, R and S have almost same values of 'b' but their 'a' values (a and b are van der Waals' constants) are in the order $Q<R<S<P$. At a particular temperature, among the four gases, the most easily liquefiable one is **[WB JEE]**

(a) P (b) Q (c) R (d) S

7 The compressibility factor (Z) of one mole of a van der Waals' gas of negligible 'a' value is **[WB JEE]**

(a) 1 (b) $\frac{bp}{RT}$
(c) $1+\frac{bp}{RT}$ (d) $1-\frac{bp}{RT}$

2013

8 Maximum deviation from ideal gas is expected from **[NEET]**

(a) $H_2(g)$ (b) $N_2(g)$ (c) $CH_4(g)$ (d) $NH_3(g)$

9 van der Waals' equation for n mole of a gas is **[KCET]**

(a) $\left(p+\frac{n^2a}{V^2}\right)(V-nb)=nRT$ (b) $\left(p+\frac{na}{V^2}\right)(V-nb)=RT$
(c) $\left(p+\frac{a}{V^2}\right)(V-b)=nRT$ (d) $\left(p+\frac{an^2}{V^2}\right)(V-b)=RT$

2012

10 For real gases, van der Waals' equation is written as $\left(p+\frac{an^2}{V^2}\right)(V-nb)=nRT$, where '$a$' and '$b$' are van der Waals' constants. Two sets of gases are I. O_2, CO_2, H_2 and He II. CH_4, O_2 and H_2.
The gases given in set I are in increasing order of b and gases given in set II are in decreasing order of a are arranged below. Select the correct order from the following: **[CBSE AIPMT]**

(a) (I) $He<H_2<CO_2<O_2$, (II) $CH_4>H_2>O_2$
(b) (I) $O_2<He<H_2<CO_2$, (II) $H_2>O_2>CH_4$
(c) (I) $H_2<He<O_2<CO_2$, (II) $CH_4>O_2>H_2$
(d) (I) $H_2<O_2<He<CO_2$, (II) $O_2>CH_4>H_2$

11 Mark out the wrong expression. **[AFMC]**

(a) Boyle's temperature $T_b=a/R$
(b) Critical pressure $p_c=a/27b^2$
(c) Critical temperature $T_c=8a/27Rb$
(d) Critical volume $V_c=3b$

2010

12 The van der Waals' constant 'a' for different gases have been given as

Gas	a (atm L^2 mol^{-2})
O_2	1.36
N_2	1.39
CH_4	2.25
NH_3	4.17

The gas that can be most easily liquefied is **[OJEE]**

(a) O_2 (b) N_2
(c) CH_4 (d) NH_3

13 The compressibility factor for an ideal gas is **[OJEE]**

(a) 1 (b) <1 (c) >1 (d) ∞

14 In van der Waals' equation of state of the gas, the constant 'b' is a measure of **[JCECE]**

(a) intermolecular repulsions
(b) intermolecular attraction
(c) volume occupied by the molecules
(d) intermolecular collisions per unit volume

2009

15 At relatively high pressure, van der Waals' equation reduces to **[Manipal]**

(a) $pV = RT$ (b) $pV = RT - a/V$
(c) $pV = RT - a/V^2$ (d) $pV = RT + pb$

16 The van der Waals' constants for four gases P, Q, R and S are 4.17, 3.59, 6.17 and 3.8 atm L^2 mol^{-2}. Therefore, the ascending order of their liquefaction is **[J&K CET]**

(a) $R < P < S < Q$ (b) $Q < S < R < P$
(c) $Q < S < P < R$ (d) $R < P < Q < S$

17 The units of constants a in van der Waals' equation is **[AMU]**

(a) dm^6 atm mol^{-2} (b) dm^3 atm mol^{-1}
(c) dm atm mol^{-1} (d) atm mol^{-1}

18 Critical temperature of H_2O, NH_3, CO_2 and O_2 are 647 K, 405.6 K, 304.10 K and 154.2 K respectively. If the cooling starts from 500 K to their critical temperature, the gas that liquefies first is **[AMU]**

(a) H_2O (b) NH_3 (c) CO_2 (d) O_2

19 The critical temperatures of O_2, N_2, H_2 and CO_2 are 154.3 K, 126 K, 33.2 K and 304 K. The extent of adsorption on tungsten may be highest in case of **[AMU]**

(a) H_2 (b) N_2
(c) O_2 (d) CO_2

20 If helium is allowed to expand in vacuum, it liberates heat because **[DUMET]**

(a) helium is an inert gas
(b) helium is an ideal gas
(c) the inversion temperature of helium is very low
(d) helium is one of the lightest gases

21 The temperature at which real gases obey the ideal gas laws over a wide range of pressure is called **[DUMET]**

(a) critical temperature (b) inversion temperature
(c) Boyle temperature (d) reduced temperature

2008

22 Which of the following is incorrect? **[BHU]**

(a) A real gas behaves like an ideal gas over a wide range of pressure (~100 atm) at Boyle point
(b) A real gas behaves like an ideal gas over a wide range of pressure (~100 atm) at critical temperature of the gas
(c) $\left(\frac{\delta u}{\delta V}\right)_T = 0$ for an ideal gas
(d) $\left(\frac{\delta u}{\delta V}\right)_T = \frac{a}{V^2}$ for a real gas obeying van der Waals' equation

23 The units of van der Waals' constants a and b are respectively **[J&K CET]**

(a) L atm^2 mol^{-1} and mol L^{-1}
(b) L atm mol^2 and mol L
(c) L^2 atm mol^{-2} and mol^{-1} L
(d) L^{-2} atm^{-1} mol^{-1} and L mol^{-2}

2007

24 **Assertion** (A) At high pressure, the compressibility factor Z is $\left(1 + \frac{pb}{RT}\right)$.

Reason (R) At high pressure, van der Waals' equation is modified as $p(V - b) = RT$. **[AIIMS]**

(a) Both A and R are correct and R is the correct explanation of the A
(b) Both A and R are correct but R is not the correct explanation of A
(c) A is correct but R is incorrect
(d) Both A and R are incorrect

25 The compressibility of a gas is less than unity at STP. Therefore, **[RPMT]**

(a) $V_m > 22.4$ L
(b) $V_m < 22.4$ L
(c) $V_m = 22.4$ L
(d) $V_m = 44.8$ L

2006

26 Dominance of strong repulsive forces among the molecules of the gas (Z = compressibility factor) **[AIIMS]**

(a) depends on Z and indicated by $Z = 1$
(b) depends on Z and indicated by $Z > 1$
(c) depends on Z and indicated by $Z < 1$
(d) is independent of Z

27 The CO_2 gas does not follow gaseous laws at all ranges of pressure and temperature because **[MHT CET]**

(a) it is triatomic gas
(b) its internal energy is quite high
(c) there is attraction between its molecules
(d) it solidify at low temperature

2005

28 **Assertion** (A) Compressibility factor for hydrogen varies with pressure with positive slope at all pressures.

Reason (R) Even at low pressure, repulsive forces dominate in hydrogen gas. **[AIIMS]**

(a) Both A and R are correct and R is the correct explanation of the A
(b) Both A and R are correct but R is not the correct explanation of A
(c) A is correct but R incorrect
(d) Both A and R are incorrect

29 The van der Waals' equation for a real gas is given by the formula $(p + n^2 a / V^2)(V - nb) = nRT$;
where p, V, T and n are the pressure, volume, temperature and the number of moles of the gas. Which one is the correct interpretation for the parameter a? [JCECE]

(a) The parameter a accounts for the finite size of the molecule
(b) The parameter a accounts for the shape of gas phase molecules
(c) The parameter a accounts for intermolecular interactions present in the molecule
(d) The parameter a has no physical significance and van der Waals' introduced it as a numerical correction factor only

Answers

1 (b)	2 (d)	3 (c)	4 (c)	5 (a)	6 (a)	7 (c)	8 (d)	9 (a)	10 (c)
11 (a)	12 (d)	13 (a)	14 (c)	15 (d)	16 (c)	17 (a)	18 (b)	19 (d)	20 (c)
21 (c)	22 (b)	23 (c)	24 (a)	25 (b)	26 (b)	27 (c)	28 (a)	29 (c)	

Explanations

1 (b) Compressibility factor (Z) is the factor which decides the extent of deviation of real gases from ideal gases.

$$Z = \frac{V_{\text{real}}}{V_{\text{ideal}}}$$

Real gases deviate from ideal gas behaviour because for ideal gas, it is considered that there is no force of attraction between gas molecules.

Also, for ideal gas, volume of gas molecules is negligible as compared to volume of gas container.

Given, $V_{\text{real}} < V_{\text{ideal}}$

$\therefore \quad Z < 1$

If $Z < 1$, the gas is more compressible than expected from ideal behaviour. As a result, attractive forces are present between molecules and are dominant.

2 (d) According to van der Waals' equation,

$$\left[p + \frac{an^2}{V^2}\right](V - nb) = nRT$$

where, a and b are called van der Waals' constants. The term $\frac{an^2}{V^2}$ is called internal pressure of the gas.

where, 'a' is a measure of force of attraction between gas molecules.

'b' is also called co-volume or excluded volume.

The constants 'a' and 'b' are expressed in atm L^2 mol^{-2} and L mol^{-1}, respectively.

3 (c) In van der Waals' equation,

$$\left[p + \frac{an^2}{V^2}\right](V - nb) = nRT$$

'a' and 'b' are known as van der Waals' constant.

'a' is the measure of force of attraction between gas molecules. Greater the value of a, easier the liquefaction of the gas. Thus, among NH_3(4.17), H_2(0.244), O_2(1.36) and CO_2(3.59), the value of a is greatest in NH_3, hence it is most easily liquefied.

4 (c) Intermolecular forces are given by the term $(p + a/V^2)$. Value of 'a' is a measure of magnitude of intermolecular attractive foces within the gas.

5 (a) A gas can be liquefied by cooling or compressing it, when its temperature is below critical temperature. Gases which have high critical temperatures (such as Cl_2, NH_3, CO_2, SO_2, etc.,) can be liquefied by applying a suitable pressure alone. Permanent gases (such as H_2, N_2, O_2, etc.) cannot be liquefied by the action of pressure and cooling.

6 (a) The value of 'a' is a measure of force of attraction between the gas molecules.

Higher the value of a, more will be the tendency to get liquefied. Since, value of a is highest for P. Thus, P is the most liquefiable gas among the given gases.

7 (c) van der Waals' equation for 1 mole of a gas is

$$\left(p + \frac{a}{V^2}\right)(V - b) = RT \quad \text{(for 1 mole)}$$

If a is negligible, $p + \frac{a}{V^2} \approx p$

$$p(V - b) = RT$$
$$pV - pb = RT$$

or
$$\frac{pV}{RT} - \frac{pb}{RT} = 1$$

$$\therefore \quad Z = \frac{pV}{RT} = 1 + \frac{pb}{RT}$$

8 (d) Easily liquefiable gases like NH_3, SO_2, etc., exhibit maximum deviation from ideal gas as for them $Z <<< 1 \cdot CH_4$ also exhibits deviation but it is less as compared to NH_3. Moreover, permanent gases like H_2, N_2 cannot be liquefied, thus, shows no deviation.

9 (a) The van der Waals' equation for n moles of a gas is,

$$\left[p + \frac{an^2}{V^2}\right](V - nb) = nRT.$$

Here, a and b are van der Waals' constants.

10 (*c*) '*b*' is the measure of effective size of molecules.

Hence, correct order is

$H_2 < He < O_2 < CO_2$

'*a*' is the measure of force of attraction between gas molecules.

Easily liquefiable gases have greater value of van der Waals' constant (*a*).

Hence, correct order is $CH_4 > O_2 > H_2$.

11 (*a*) **Boyle's temperature** (T_b) The temperature at which a real gas tends to behave ideally over a wide range of pressure is known as Boyle's temperature.

$$T_b = \frac{a}{R \cdot b} = \left[\frac{\partial(pV)}{\partial p}\right]_{\lim p \to 0}$$

At this temperature the effect of size of molecular and intermolecular forces roughly compensate each other.

Thus option (a) is incorrect.

12 (*d*) The value of '*a*' is a measure of force of attraction between the molecules. Greater the value of '*a*', easier is the process of liquefaction.

Since, NH_3 has the largest value of *a* among the given molecules, thus, it can be most easily liquefied.

13 (*a*) Compressibility factor, $Z = \frac{V_{obs}}{V_{cal}}$

For ideal gas, $V_{obs} = V_{cal}$, so $Z = 1$

14 (*c*) van der Waals' equation for one mole of a gas is

$$\left(p + \frac{a}{V^2}\right)(V - b) = RT$$

where, *b* is volume correction term.. It arises due to effective size of molecules. Therefore, '*b*' is measure of volume occupied by the molecules.

15 (*d*) At high pressure, the pressure correction for 1 mole of gas is negligible.

$$\therefore \quad \frac{a}{V^2} = 0$$

However, the volume correction cannot be neglected. Hence, van der Waals' equation reduces to

$$(p + 0)(V - b) = RT$$

(For 1 mole)

$$pV - pb = RT$$

$$\therefore \quad pV = RT + pb$$

16 (*c*) Easily liquefiable gases have greater intermolecular forces which is represented by high value of *a*. The greater the value of *a*, more will be the liquefiability.

So, the order is $Q < S < P < R$.

17 (*a*) $p = \frac{n^2 a}{V^2}$

$$\Rightarrow a = \frac{pV^2}{n^2} = \text{dm}^6 \text{ atm mol}^{-2}$$

18 (*b*) Since, the cooling starts from 500 K, so water is not under consideration. As it is much easier to achieve 405·6 K from 500 K, the NH_3 will get liquefied first.

19 (*d*) More easily liquefiable gases, (i.e. gases having higher critical temperature) are readily adsorbed, as van der Waals' forces are stronger near the critical temperatures.

As, the value of critical temperature of CO_2 is the highest among the given values, the adsorption of CO_2 will be highest.

20 (*c*) Helium shows heating effect at room temperature as it possesses very low values of inversion temperature.

21 (*c*) The temperature at which real gas behaves like ideal gas and obeys the gas laws over a wide range of pressure is called Boyle temperature 'T_b'.

$T_b = \frac{a}{Rb}$ and where, *a* and *b* are van der Waals' constant.

22 (*b*) A real gas behaves like an ideal gas over a wide range of pressure above critical temperature of gas.

Rest of the given statements are correct.

23 (*c*) van der Waals' equation is

$$\left(p + \frac{n^2 a}{V^2}\right)(V - nb) = nRT$$

$$\therefore \text{ Units of } a = \frac{pV^2}{n^2}$$

$$= \frac{\text{atm} \times \text{L}^2}{\text{mol}^2}$$

$$= \text{L}^2 \text{ atm mol}^{-2}$$

$$\therefore \text{ Units of } b = \frac{V}{n}$$

$$= \frac{\text{L}}{\text{mol}} = \text{mol}^{-1} \text{ L}$$

24 (*a*) van der Waals' equation for 1 mole of gas is $\left(p + \frac{a}{V^2}\right)(V - b) = RT$

At high pressure, $p(V - b) = RT$

$$pV - pb = RT$$

$$\Rightarrow \quad \frac{pV}{RT} = \left(1 + \frac{pb}{RT}\right)$$

$$\text{if} \quad \frac{pV}{RT} = Z$$

$$\text{then} \quad Z = \left(1 + \frac{pb}{RT}\right)$$

25 (*b*) Given, $Z < 1$

$$\frac{pV_{\text{observed}}}{pV_{\text{ideal}}} < 1$$

$$\Rightarrow \quad pV_{\text{observed}} < pV_{\text{ideal}}$$

$$V_{\text{observed}} < V_{\text{ideal}}$$

$$\Rightarrow \quad V_{\text{observed}} < 22.4 \text{ L}$$

26 (*b*) $Z > 1$ shows that the gas is less compressible than expected. This is due to dominance of strong repulsive forces among the molecules.

27 (*c*) Real gases (like CO_2) do not follow gas laws at all temperature and pressure conditions due to two wrong assumptions in kinetic molecular theory of gases.

(*i*) The volume occupied by gas molecules is negligible. It is not true because gas molecules do occupy small volume.

(*ii*) The forces of attraction between gas molecules are zero. It is not true because attractive forces are present between molecules of real gases.

28 (*a*) In case of hydrogen, compressibility factor (*Z*) increases with pressure.

At 273 K, $Z > 1$, which shows that it is difficult to compress the gas as compared to ideal gas. In this case, repulsive forces dominate.

Note For ideal gases, $Z = 1$

For real gases $Z \neq 1$

If $Z < 1$, negative deviation and the gas is more compressible than expected.

If $Z > 1$, positive deviation and the gas is less compressible than expected.

29 (*c*) In van der Waals' equation for real gases, *a* accounts for intermolecular interactions present in the gases.

Topic 5

Liquid State

2019

1 **Assertion** A spherical water drops become flattened on flatter surface. [AIIMS]

Reason It become flat due to gravity.

(a) Both A and R are correct and the R is the correct explanation of the A
(b) Both A and R are correct but the R is not the correct explanation of the A
(c) A is correct but R is incorrect
(d) Both A and R are incorrect

2012

2 During the evaporation of liquid, [AIIMS]

(a) the temperature of the liquid will rise.
(b) the temperature of the liquid will fall.
(c) may rise or fall depending on the nature.
(d) the temperature remains unaffected.

2011

3 A bubble of gas released at the bottom of a lake increases to eight times its original volume when it reaches the surface. Assuming that atmospheric pressure is equivalent to the pressure exerted by a column of water, 10 m height, the depth of the lake is [Kerala CEE]

(a) 80 m (b) 90 m (c) 40 m (d) 10 m
(e) 70 m

4 Which of the following is a correct statement? [Kerala CEE]

(a) Surface tension of a liquid decreases with increase in temperature
(b) Vapour pressure of a liquid decreases with increase in temperature
(c) Viscosity of a liquid decreases with decrease in temperature
(d) In gravity free environments, droplets of a liquid on flat surface are slightly flattened

2008

5 **Assertion** (A) Meniscus of a liquid disappears at the critical temperature.

Reason (R) Density of liquid and its gaseous phase become equal at the critical temperature. [BHU]

(a) Both A and R are correct and R is the correct explanation of the A
(b) Both A and R are incorrect but R is not the correct explanation of A
(c) A is correct but R is incorrect
(d) Both A and R are incorrect

2007

6 **Assertion** (A) Viscosity of a liquid decreases on increasing the temperature.

Reason (R) Evaporation of liquid increases with rise in temperature. [AIIMS]

(a) Both A and R are correct and R is the correct explanation of the A
(b) Both A and R are correct but R is not the correct explanation of A
(c) A is correct but R is incorrect
(d) Both A and R are incorrect

7 The following is a method to determine the surface tension of liquids. [J&K CET]

(a) Single capillary method (b) Refractometric method
(c) Polarimetric method (d) Boiling point method

2006

8 Pick out the wrong statement(s).

I. Vapour pressure of a liquid is the measure of the strength of intermolecular attractive forces.
II. Surface tension of a liquid acts perpendicular to the surface of the liquid.
III. Vapour pressure of all liquids is same at their freezing points.
IV. Liquids with stronger intermolecular attractive forces are more viscous than those with weaker intermolecular forces. [Kerala CEE]

(a) II, III and IV (b) II and III
(c) I, II and III (d) Only III
(e) Only II

2005

9 Which of the following is not a property of liquid state? [BHU]

(a) Intermolecular force of attraction in a liquid is quite large
(b) All liquids are accompanied by cooling on evaporation
(c) Lower the boiling point of a liquid, greater is its vapour pressure at room temperature
(d) A liquid boils at high temperature at the top of a mountain than at the sea level

10 When a capillary tube of diameter 0.8 mm is dipped in a liquid having density 800 kg m^{-3}, then the height of liquid in the capillary tube rises to 4 cm. The surface tension of liquid is ($g = 9.8 \, m/s^2$) [AMU]

(a) 4.3×10^{-2} Nm^{-1} (b) 5.6×10^{-2} Nm^{-1}
(c) 6.3×10^{-2} Nm^{-1} (d) 7.3×10^{-2} Nm^{-1}

Answers

1 (a)	2 (b)	3 (e)	4 (a)	5 (a)	6 (b)	7 (a)	8 (d)	9 (d)	10 (c)

Explanations

1 (*a*) Due to surface tension, liquid tends to have a minimum surface area. For a given volume of a liquid, sphere has the minimum surface area. Therefore, the small drops of liquids are spherical on flat surfaces, the droplets get slightly flattened by the effect of gravity.

Thus, both Assertion and Reason are correct and Reason is the correct explanation for the Assertion.

2 (*b*) During evaporation, molecules having high energy leave the surface of the liquid. As a result, average kinetic energy of liquid decreases.

$$\text{KE} \propto T$$

$\therefore$ Temperature of liquid falls.

3 (*e*) $\underset{\text{(at bottom)}}{p_1V_1} = \underset{\text{(at surface)}}{p_2V_2}$

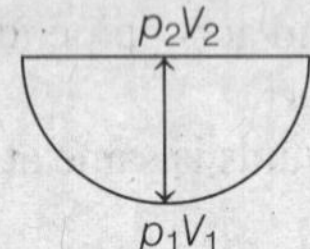

Here, let p_1 = pressure at the bottom,

V_1 = volume at the bottom,

p_2 = pressure at the surface

and V_2 = volume at the surface.

Temperature remains constant. So,

$$p = hdg$$

$$p_1V_1 = (p + p_1)V$$
$$= (hdg + 10\,g)V$$
$$= (hg + 10\,g)V$$

$[\because d \text{ of water} = 1\text{ g mL}^{-1}]$

$$p_1V_2 = 10\,g \times 8\,V$$

$$\Rightarrow (hg + 10\,g)V = 10\,g \times 8\,V$$

$$h + 10 = 80 \text{ or } h = 70\text{ m}$$

4 (*a*)

(a) Surface tension of a liquid decreases with increase in temperature. As the temperature increases, the kinetic energy of the molecules increases and hence, intermolecular attraction decreases which in turn decreases the surface tension.

(b) The vapour pressure of a liquid increases with increase in temperature. This is because at higher temperatures, more molecules in liquid will have the larger kinetic energy than the average values.

(c) Viscosity decreases with rise in temperature because increase in temperature increases the kinetic energy of molecules, this results in decrease in inter-layer friction.

(d) On flat surfaces, the droplets get slightly flattened by the effect of gravity.

Thus, the only correct option is (a).

5 (*a*) At critical temperature, it is not possible to state whether the substance is in the gaseous form or in the liquid form. In fact, both the states become indistinguishable at the critical point.

The surface of separation between liquid and gas disappears. At this point, the various physical properties such as density, refractive index etc., have identical values for both the states. Therefore, the meniscus of a liquid disappears at the critical temperature.

Hence, A and R are correct and R is the correct explanation of A.

6 (*b*) The correct reason is that molecules of liquid absorb heat energy, thus their kinetic energy or motion increases. This results in decrease in inter-layer friction which further decreases the viscosity of liquid. Also, as the temperature increases, evaporation of liquid also increases. Therefore, both A and R are correct but R is not the correct explanation of A.

7 (*a*) Single capillary method is used to determine the surface tension of liquids.

8 (*d*) The statement that vapour pressure of all liquids is same at their freezing points is not correct, because vapour pressure of different liquids is different at their freezing points.

Rest of the statements are correct.

9 (*d*) A liquid at mountain top boils at low temperature than at sea level. This is because the atmospheric pressure is low at the mountains and the vapour pressure of liquid (that boils) becomes equal to the atmospheric pressure faster.

10 (*c*) Given diameter of capillary tube is 0.8 mm. Hence, $r = 0.4\text{ mm} = 4\times10^{-4}\text{m}$

Density $= 800\text{ kgm}^{-3}$

The height of liquid in the capillary tube rises 4 cm or 0.04 m

$$T = \frac{rhdg}{2}$$

Gravity $(g) = 9.8\text{ m/s}^2$

Here, r = radius of capillary

h = height of liquid in the capillary.

d = density, g = gravity

$$\therefore\ T = \frac{(4\times10^{-4})\times(0.04)\times800\times9.8}{2}$$
$$= 4\times10^{-4}\times0.04\times400\times9.8$$
$$= 4\times4\times4\times98\times10^{-5}$$
$$= 6.3\times10^{-2}\text{ Nm}^{-1}$$

06

Thermodynamics

Quick Review

The branch of science which deals with the quantitative relationship between heat and other forms of energies is called **thermodynamics**.

Several terms used in thermodynamics are described below

- **System and surroundings** System is that part of the universe to which we focus our attention for studying the effect of applied change. Rest part of universe other than system is known as **surroundings**.
- The real or imaginary surface or lines separating two or more systems or a system from its surroundings is called **boundary**.

Depending upon the movement of matter or energy in or out of the system, *the system can be of the following types*

(*i*) **Open system** An open system can exchange matter as well as energy with its surroundings. The boundary here is not sealed and non-insulated thermally, i.e. it is generally imaginary.

For such a system, $\Delta m \neq \Delta E \neq 0$, i.e. change in mass and energy is not zero.

(*ii*) **Closed system** A closed system does not exchange matter with its surroundings but can exchange energy in the form of heat, work or radiations, i.e. here the boundary is sealed but not insulated.

For such a system, $\Delta m = 0, \Delta E \neq 0$

(*iii*) **Isolated system** An isolated system neither exchange matter nor energy with its surroundings, i.e. here the boundary is sealed as well as insulated, e.g. thermos flask.

For such a system, $\Delta m = 0, \Delta E = 0$.

The given processes can be easily understood by the following representation.

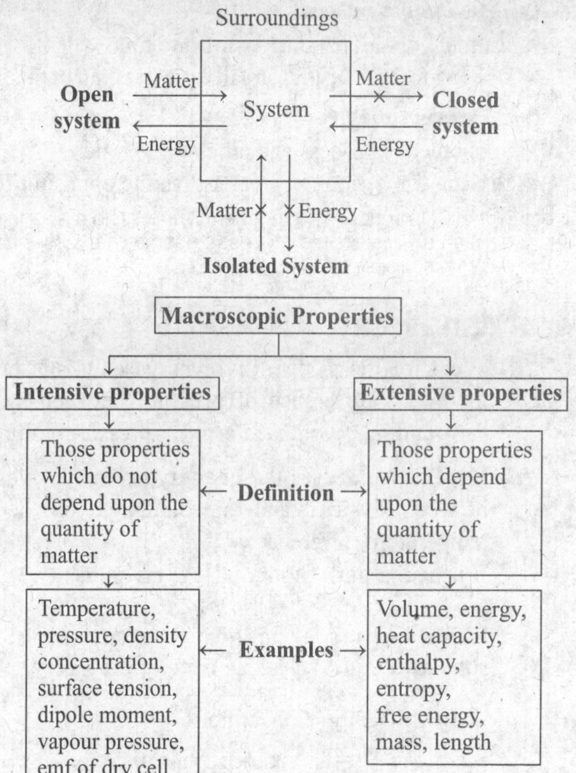

State and Path Functions

The property of a system whose value depends only upon the state of the system and is independent of the path by which the state is reached is called **state function**, while the properties that depend upon the path followed are called **path functions**.

Thermodynamic Process

A thermodynamic process is said to take place when some changes occur in the state of a thermodynamic system. Different thermodynamic processes are given below :

(*i*) **Adiabatic process**

- System does not exchange heat with surroundings
- $dq = 0$

(*ii*) **Isothermal process**

- Temperature remains fixed • $dT = 0$ and $dE = 0$

(*iii*) **Isobaric process**

- Pressure remains constant • $dp = 0$

(*iv*) **Isochoric process**

- Volume remains constant • $dV = 0$

(*v*) **Cyclic process**

- System has undergone a number of different states and finally returns to its initial state
- dE or $dU = 0$, $dH = 0$

(*vi*) **Reversible process**

- An ideal process and takes infinite time
- Driving force is infinitesimally greater than opposing forces

(*vii*) **Irreversible process**

- Spontaneous process and takes finite time
- Driving force is much greater than the opposing force

Note All natural processes are generally irreversible and the net work done in an irreversible process is somewhat less than that in a reversible process, i.e. $W_{irrev} < W_{rev}$

Work and Heat

(*i*) **Work** of the system involves gaseous substances and there is a difference of pressure between system and surroundings, work is referred as pressure-volume work.

(*ii*) **Heat** is defined as the quantity of energy which flows between system and surroundings on account of temperature difference.
It is also a path function. It is given as,

$$q = mc\,\Delta t$$

where, c is specific heat capacity, m is mass of substance and ΔE is rise in temperature.

Sign Convention

- q is +ve = heat is supplied to the system
- q is –ve = heat is lost by the system
- W is +ve = work done on the system
- W is –ve = work done by the system

Heat Capacity of a System (C)

It is defined as the amount of heat required to raise the temperature of a system by 1°C. *It is of following two types*

(*i*) **Molar heat capacity** (C_m) It is the heat capacity of 1 mole of substance of the system.

(*ii*) **Specific heat capacity** (c) It is the heat capacity of 1g of substance of the system.

$$q = mc\Delta T$$

- Molar heat capacity, at constant pressure,
$$C = C_p \times M$$
- Molar heat capacity at constant volume,
$$C_m = C_V \times M$$
- Relation between C_p and C_V, $C_p - C_V = nR$

Different Expressions for Pressure-Volume Work

Process	Isothermal	Adiabatic
Reversible	In isothermal reversible expansion, • $q = -W$ • $q = -2.303nRT \log\frac{V_2}{V_1}$ • $q = -2.303nRT \log\frac{p_1}{p_2}$	In adiabatic reversible expansion • $TV^{\gamma-1}$ = constant • pV^{γ} = constant • $p^{1-\gamma}T^{\gamma}$ = constant • $W = [nR/(\gamma-1)][T_2 - T_1]$
Irreversible	In isothermal irreversible expansion, • $q = -W$ • $q = p_{ext}\Delta V$	In adiabatic irreversible expansion • $W = -nRp_{ext}\left[\frac{T_2p_1 - T_1p_2}{p_1p_2}\right]$

Note γ is called atomicity $= \frac{C_p}{C_V}$

- For monoatomic gas : $\gamma = 1.66$
- For diatomic gas : $\gamma = 1.4$
- For triatomic gas : $\gamma = 1.3$

Internal Energy (ΔU or ΔE)

- It is the total energy within the substance. It is the sum of many types of energies like vibrational energy, translational energy etc.
- It is an extensive property and a state function.

$$\Delta U = \Sigma U_P - \Sigma U_R$$

Zeroth Law of Thermodynamics

This law states that, "when two objects are brought in thermal contact, they exchange heat with each other until they reach a state of thermal equilibrium."

First Law of Thermodynamics

This law states that energy can neither be created nor be destroyed but can be converted from one form to another.

$$\Delta U = q + W$$

where, ΔU = internal energy $= U_2 - U_1$

q = heat, W = work done

Enthalpy

- It is the total heat content of a system at constant pressure. Also, it is the sum of internal energy and pV-energy of the system. i.e. $H = U + pV$

- For exothermic reactions,
$\Delta H = -\text{ve}$ whereas for endothermic reactions, $\Delta H = +\text{ ve}$.
- The variation of heat evolved during exothermic reaction and heat absorbed during endothermic reaction with time is shown in the graph given below.

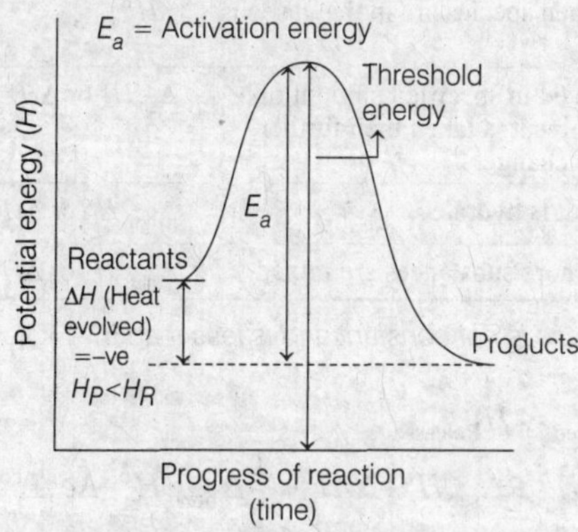

Energy evolved during an exothermic reaction

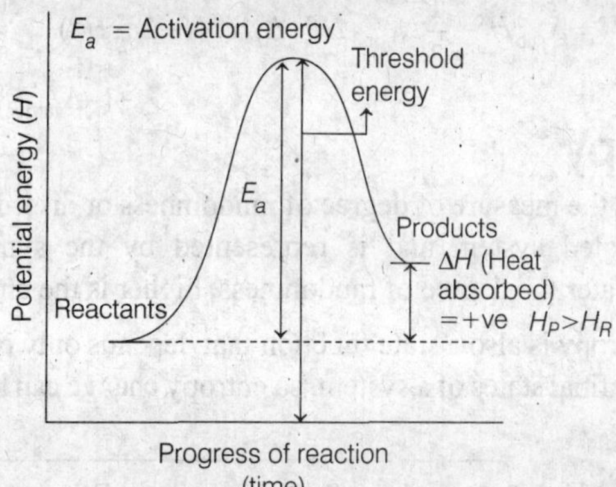

Energy absorbed during an endothermic reaction

Relationship between ΔH and ΔU or ΔE

$$\Delta H = \Delta U + \Delta n_g RT$$

where, Δn_g = change in the number of moles in gaseous state.

If, (i) $\Delta n_g = 0$, then $\Delta H = \Delta U$

(ii) $\Delta n_g < 0$ then $\Delta H < \Delta U$

(iii) $\Delta n_g > 0$ then $\Delta H > \Delta U$

Calorimeter

Enthalpy of the reaction is calculated experimentally by an apparatus called calorimeter.

- Two common types of calorimeter are water calorimeter and bomb calorimeter.
- Water calorimeter gives the heat at constant pressure while bomb calorimeter gives the heat at constant volume.

$$\Delta U = \frac{C \times \Delta T \times M}{w_1}$$

where, C = heat capacity of calorimeter

w_1 = mass of substance taken

M = molecular mass of the substance

Enthalpy Change of a Reaction ($\Delta_r H$)

It is the heat change that accompanies a chemical reaction represented by a balanced chemical equation.

$$\Delta_r H = \Sigma H_{(P)} - \Sigma H_{(R)}.$$

The variation of enthalpy of reaction with temperature is given by Kirchhoff's equation.

$$\Delta H_2 - \Delta H_1 = \Delta C_p (T_2 - T_1)$$

or $$\Delta U_2 - \Delta U_1 = \Delta C_V (T_2 - T_1)$$

Standard Enthalpy Changes for Different Types of Processes (based on IUPAC recommendations)

Transition enthalpy	Examples	Definition	Symbol
Enthalpy of formation	$Na(s) + (1/2)\, Cl_2(g) \longrightarrow NaCl(s)$	One mole of the compound formed from its elements.	$\Delta_f H°$ or $\Delta H°_f$
Enthalpy of combustion	$CH_4(g) + 2O_2(g) \longrightarrow CO_2(g) + 2H_2O(l)$	One mole of the compound (fuel) is burnt completely in oxygen (oxidation).	$\Delta_c H°$ or $\Delta H°_c$
Enthalpy of fusion	$H_2O(s) \longrightarrow H_2O(l)$	One mole of the liquid is formed from the solid without a change in temperature.	$\Delta_{fus} H°$ or $\Delta H°_{fus}$
Enthalpy of vaporisation	$H_2O(l) \longrightarrow H_2O(g)$	One mole of the vapour formed from the liquid without a change in temperature.	$\Delta_{vap} H°$ or $\Delta H°_{vap}$
Enthalpy of sublimation	$H_2O(s) \longrightarrow H_2O(g)$	One mole of the vapour formed from the solid.	$\Delta_{sub} H°$ or $\Delta H°_{sub}$
Enthalpy of transition	C (graphite) $\longrightarrow$ C (diamond)	One mole of one allotropic form changes to another.	$\Delta_{trans} H°$ or $\Delta H°_{trans}$
Enthalpy of atomisation	$H_2O(l) \longrightarrow 2H(g) + O(g)$	One mole of the substance broken into isolated atoms in the gas phase.	$\Delta_{at} H°$ or $\Delta H°_{at}$
Enthalpy of neutralisation	$HCl(aq) + NaOH(aq) \longrightarrow H_2O + NaCl(aq)$	One mole of an acid is neutralised by a base to form corresponding salt and water.	$\Delta_{next} H°$ or $\Delta H°_{next}$
Enthalpy of ionisation	$Na(g) \longrightarrow Na^+(g) + e^-$	One mole of an electrolyte completely dissociates into ions	$\Delta_{ion} H°$ or $\Delta H°_{ion}$

Transition enthalpy	Examples	Definition	Symbol
Electron-gain enthalpy	$X(g) + e^- \longrightarrow X^-(g)$	One mole of anions being formed from gaseous atom in its ground state.	$\Delta_{eg}H°$ or $\Delta H°_{e_g}$
Lattice enthalpy	$KCl(s) \longrightarrow K^+(g) + Cl^-(g)$	One mole of a crystal completely separated into isolated particles in the gaseous phase.	$\Delta_{lattice}H°$ or $\Delta H°_{lattice}$
Bond dissociation enthalpy (bond A — B)	$HX(g) \longrightarrow H(g) + X(g)$	One mole of bonds broken when species are in the gaseous phase.	$\Delta H°_{A-B}$
Enthalpy of solution	$A(s) + H_2O(\text{excess}) \longrightarrow A(aq)$	One mole of the solute dissolved in specified amount of solvent. If a large excess of solvent is taken then further dilution produces no enthalpy change.	$\Delta_{sol}H°$ or $\Delta H°_{sol}$
Enthalpy of hydration	X (anhydrous salt) $\longrightarrow X^{\pm}(aq)$	One mole of the anhydrous salt is hydrated.	$\Delta_{hyd}H°$ or $\Delta H°_{hyd}$
Enthalpy of mixing	Pure substances $\longrightarrow$ mixture	One mole each of the two or more substances are mixed.	$\Delta_{mix}H°$ or $\Delta H°_{mix}$

Note *Enthalpy of neutralisation of strong acid and weak base or weak acid and strong base is not constant and is less than* 57.1 kJ.

Hess's Law of Constant Heat Summation

According to this law, "the total heat change (ΔH) accompanying a chemical reaction is the same whether the reaction takes place in one or more steps".

Suppose, enthalpy change for direct conversion $A \longrightarrow B$ is ΔH, B can also be prepared from A through intermediates C and D, for which enthalpy changes are ΔH_1, ΔH_2 and ΔH_3 respectively as shown in the following figure:

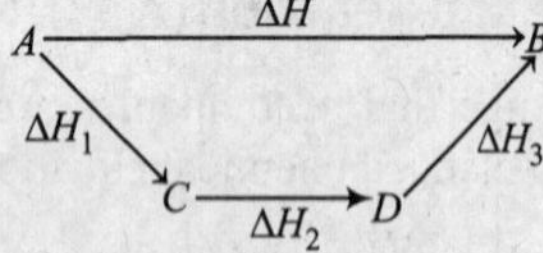

Then, according to Hess's law, $\Delta H = \Delta H_1 + \Delta H_2 + \Delta H_3$

Applications of Hess's Law

(*i*) For the determination of enthalpies of formation of compounds.

(*ii*) For the determination of enthalpies of extremely slow reactions.

(*iii*) For the determination of enthalpies of transformation of one allotropic form into another.

(*iv*) For the determination of bond energies.

$$\Delta H_{reaction} = \Sigma \text{ bond energies of reactants} - \Sigma \text{ bond energies of products}$$

Born-Haber Cycle

It is an approach to calculate energy involved during a process and is based on the Hess's law of constant heat summation.

It can be utilised to calculate lattice energy of crystals like NaCl.

Na (*s*) + 1/2 Cl_2 (*g*) $\xrightarrow{\Delta_f H°}$ Na^+Cl^- (*s*)
$\Delta_{sub} H°$
1/2 $\Delta_{bond} H°$
$\Delta_{lattice} H°$
Cl (*g*) $\xrightarrow{\Delta_{eg} H}$ Cl^- (*g*) + Na^+ (*g*)
Na (*g*) $\xrightarrow{\Delta_i H°}$

For spontaneous process,

$$H_{Required} \le H_{Released}$$

$$\therefore \ \Delta_{lattice}H° \le \Delta_{sub}H° + \Delta_i H° + \frac{1}{2}\Delta_{bond}H° - \Delta e_g H°$$

or

$$-\Delta_f H° = \Delta_{sub}H° + \frac{1}{2}\Delta_{bond}H° + \Delta_i H° + (-\Delta e_g H°) + (-\Delta_{lattice}H°)$$

Entropy

- It is the measure of degree of randomness or disorder in an isolated system and is represented by the symbol, S. Greater the degree of randomness, higher is the entropy.
- Entropy is also a state function that depends only on initial and final states of a system, so entropy change can be given as,

$$\Delta S = S_2 - S_1 = \Sigma S_{products} - \Sigma S_{reactants}$$

$$= \frac{q_{rev}}{T} = \frac{\Delta H}{T}$$

- Entropy change of an ideal gas is given by,

$$\Delta S = nC_V \ln\left(\frac{T_2}{T_1}\right) + nR \ln\left(\frac{V_2}{V_1}\right)$$

Spontaneity

- The **spontaneous process** may be defined as an irreversible process that can take place by itself under the given set of conditions, once it has been initiated.
- **Non-spontaneous process** include all the other processes which require a continuous supply of energy from external source.

Criteria For Spontaneity

The important condition for a reaction being a spontaneous or a non-spontaneous in terms of entropy are listed.

(*i*) If $\Delta S > 0$, the reaction is spontaneous.

(*ii*) If $\Delta S < 0$, the reaction is non-spontaneous.

(*iii*) If $\Delta S = 0$, the reaction is at equilibrium.

Sign of enthalpy, entropy and free energy changes and reaction spontaneity at constant temperature and pressure

ΔH	ΔS	$\Delta G = \Delta H - T\Delta S$	Reaction spontaneity
− − − **Exothermic**	+	−	Spontaneous at all temperatures.
	−	−	Spontaneous at low temperatures.
	−	+	Non-spontaneous at high temperatures.
+ + + **Endothermic**	+	+	Non-spontaneous at low temperatures.
	+	−	Spontaneous at high temperatures.
	−	+	Non-spontaneous at all temperatures.
$T\Delta S = \Delta H$		0	Equilibrium

Second Law of Thermodynamics

The second law of thermodynamics can be stated as :

- Whenever, a spontaneous process takes place, it is always accompanied by an increase in total entropy of the universe.
- It is impossible to take heat from a hotter reservoir and completely convert into work by a cyclic process without transferring a part of heat to a cooler reservoir. This statement of second law is called **Kelvin's statement.**

In statement (i) written above, the term universe means the system and the surroundings. Thus,

$$\boxed{\Delta S_{\text{univ}} = \Delta S_{\text{sys}} + \Delta S_{\text{surr}}}$$

Gibb's Free Energy

- The maximum amount of energy available to a system, during a process, that can be converted into useful work is called free energy or Gibb's free energy or Gibb's energy.
- Free energy is denoted by G and given as,

$$\boxed{G = H - TS}$$

where, H = enthalpy of the system

S = entropy of the system

T = absolute temperature

- Gibbs function, G is an extensive property and a state function. Hence, change in free energy (ΔG) for a process is independent of path

$$\Delta G = \Delta H - T\Delta S$$

This equation is called Gibb's equation.

- At equilibrium, $\Delta G = 0$

$$\Delta G = -RT \ln K = -2.303\, RT \log K$$

where, K is equilibrium constant.

Standard Free Energy Change

- The free energy change for a process at 298 K and 1 atm pressure in which the reactants in their standard state are converted into products in their standard state is called standard free energy change. It is denoted by $\Delta G°$.

$$\Delta_r G° = \begin{bmatrix}\text{Sum of the standard free energy}\\ \text{of formation of products}\end{bmatrix} - \begin{bmatrix}\text{Sum of the standard free energy of}\\ \text{formation of reactants}\end{bmatrix}$$

$$= \Sigma\Delta_f G° \text{ (products)} - \Sigma\Delta_f G° \text{ (reactants)}$$

Third Law of Thermodynamics

- According to this law, "the entropy of a perfectly crystalline substance approaches to zero as the absolute zero of temperature is approached".
- It forms the basis from which entropies at other temperatures can be measured.

Values to be Remembered

- 1 Joule = 1 Nm = 1 kg m^2s^{-2} = 0.239 Calorie = 10^7 Ergs
- 1 Calorie = 4.184 Joule
- 1 Litre atm = 101.3 Joule
- 1 Litre bar = 100 Joule
- 1 cal > 1 J > 1 erg > 1 eV

Topical Practice Questions

All the exam questions of this chapter have been divided into four topics as listed below

Topic 1

Generalised Terms Related to Thermodynamics

2019

1 An ideal gas expands isothermally from 10^{-3} m^3 to 10^{-2} m^3 at 300 K against a constant pressure of 10^5 Nm^{-2}. The work done on the gas is **[NEET (Odisha)]**

(a) + 270 kJ (b) – 900 J (c) + 900 kJ (d) – 900 kJ

2 What is the value of γ for monoatomic gas (ideal gas)? **[JIPMER]**

(a) $\frac{7}{5}$ (b) $\frac{4}{3}$ (c) $\frac{5}{2}$ (d) None

3 Under isothermal condition, a gas at 300 K expands from 0.1 L to 0.25 L against a constant external pressure of 2 bar. The work done by the gas is (Given that : 1 L bar = 100 J) **[NEET (National)]**

(a) 5 kJ (b) 25 J (c) 30 J (d) –30 J

2014

4 The work done when two moles of an ideal gas is compressed from a volume of 5 m^3 to 1 dm^3 at 300 K, under a pressure of 100 kPa is **[MHT CET]**

(a) 499.9 kJ (b) – 499.9 kJ
(c) – 99.5 kJ (d) 42495 kJ

5 **Assertion** (A) The increase in internal energy (ΔE) for the evaporation of one mole of water at 1 atm and 373 K is zero.
Reason (R) For all isothermal process, $\Delta E = 0$. **[Kerala CEE]**

(a) Both A and R are correct and R is the correct explanation of A
(b) Both A and R are correct but R is not the correct explanation of A
(c) A is correct but R is incorrect
(d) Both A and R are incorrect
(e) None of the above

2013

6 The four curves A_1, A_2, A_3 and A_4 are shown on p-V diagram. Which of the curves represents adiabatic process? **[Manipal]**

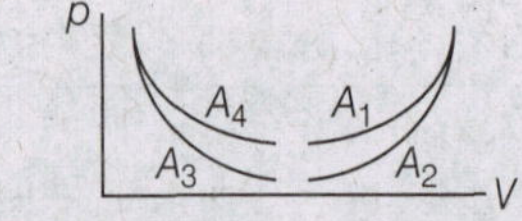

(a) A_3 (b) A_4 (c) A_1 (d) A_2

7 A chemical process is carried out in a thermostat maintained at 25°C, it is known as **[Manipal]**

(a) isothermal (b) isobaric (c) adiabatic (d) isotropic

8 Which of the following is not the extensive property? **[WB JEE]**

(a) Gibbs free energy (b) Enthalpy
(c) Entropy (d) Viscosity

2012

9 This graph expresses the various steps of the system containing 1 mole of gas. Which type of process does the system have when it moves from C to A? **[AIIMS]**

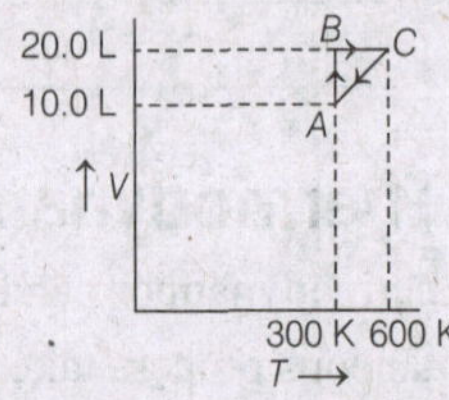

(a) Isochoric (b) Isobaric (c) Isothermal (d) Cyclic

10 Equal volumes of two monoatomic gases A and B at same temperature and pressure are mixed. The ratio of specific heats (C_p / C_V) of the mixture will be **[CBSE AIPMT]**

(a) 0.83 (b) 1.50 (c) 3.3 (d) 1.67

2010

11 4 L-atm is equal to **[MHT CET]**

(a) 40.50 cal (b) 78.75 cal (c) 95.23 cal (d) 96 cal

12 If W is the amount of work done by the system and q is the amount of heat supplied to the system, identify the type of the system. **[AMU]**

(a) Isolated system (b) Closed system
(c) Open system
(d) System with thermally conducting walls

13 If 1 mole of an ideal gas expands isothermally at 37°C from 15 L to 25 L, the maximum work obtained is **[AFMC]**

(a) 12.87 J (b) 6.43 J (c) 8.57 J (d) 2.92 J

14 The pressure of a gas is 100 kPa. If it is compressed from 1 m^3 to 10 dm^3, find the work done. **[MHT CET]**

(a) 990 J (b) 9990 J (c) 9900 J (d) 99000 J

15 An ideal gas expands in volume from 1×10^{-3} to 1×10^{-2} at 300 K against a constant pressure of 1×10^5 Nm^{-2}. The work done is **[JCECE]**

(a) – 900 J (b) – 900 kJ (c) 270 kJ (d) 900 kJ

2009

16 16 g of oxygen gas expands isothermally and reversibly at 300 K from 10 dm^3 to 100 dm^3. The work done is (in J) **[MHT CET]**

(a) zero (b) – 2875 J
(c) + 2875 J (d) infinite

17 At the same conditions of pressure, volume and temperature, work done is maximum for which gas if all gases have equal masses? **[MHT CET]**

(a) NH_3 (b) N_2
(c) Cl_2 (d) H_2S

18 ΔE is always positive, when **[OJEE]**

(a) system absorbs heat and work is done on it
(b) system emits heat and work is done by it
(c) system emits heat and no work is done on it
(d) system absorbs heat and work is done by it

19 Calculate the work done when 1 mole of an ideal gas is compressed reversibly from 1 bar to 4 bar at a constant temperature of 300 K. **[DUMET]**

(a) 4.01 kJ (b) –8.02 kJ
(c) 18.02 kJ (d) None of these

20 Under which of the following conditions is the relation $\Delta H = \Delta E + p\Delta V$ valid for a closed system? **[WB JEE]**

(a) Constant pressure
(b) Constant temperature
(c) Constant temperature and pressure
(d) Constant temperature, pressure and composition

21 In …… process, work is done at the expense of internal energy. **[MHT CET]**

(a) isothermal (b) isochoric
(c) adiabatic (d) isobaric

22 Which of the given properties depends on the manner in which a change is brought about? **[AMU]**

I. ΔE II. q III. W

(a) Only I (b) II and I
(c) II and III (d) Only III

23 In thermodynamics, a process is called reversible when **[CPMT, Haryana PMT]**

(a) surroundings and system change into each other
(b) there is no boundary between system and surroundings
(c) the surroundings are always in equilibrium with the system
(d) the system changes into surroundings spontaneously

2008

24 Which is included in thermodynamic equilibrium from the following? **[Guj CET]**

(a) Pressure equilibrium (b) Chemical equilibrium
(c) Thermo equilibrium (d) All of these

25 Which of the following is an intensive property? **[KCET]**

(a) Temperature
(b) Viscosity
(c) Surface tension
(d) All of the above

2007

26 Internal energy is the sum of **[UP CPMT]**

(a) kinetic energy and potential energy
(b) all types of energy of the system
(c) energy of internal system
(d) None of the above

27 The work done during the expansion of a gas from a volume of 4 dm^3 to 6 dm^3 against a constant external pressure of 3 atm is **[Manipal]**

(a) – 6 J (b) – 608 J
(c) + 304 J (d) – 304 J

28 Which of the following is a path function? **[MHT CET]**

(a) Internal energy (b) Enthalpy
(c) Work (d) Entropy

29 **Assertion** U is state function.
Reason T is an intensive property. **[AIIMS]**

(a) If both Assertion and Reason are true and Reason is the correct explanation of Assertion
(b) If both Assertion and Reason are true, but Reason is not the correct explanation of Assertion
(c) If Assertion is true, but Reason is false
(d) If both Assertion and Reason are false

2005

30 Five moles of a gas is put through a series of changes as shown graphically in a cyclic process. The process during $A \rightarrow B$, $B \rightarrow C$ and $C \rightarrow A$ respectively are **[Kerala CEE]**

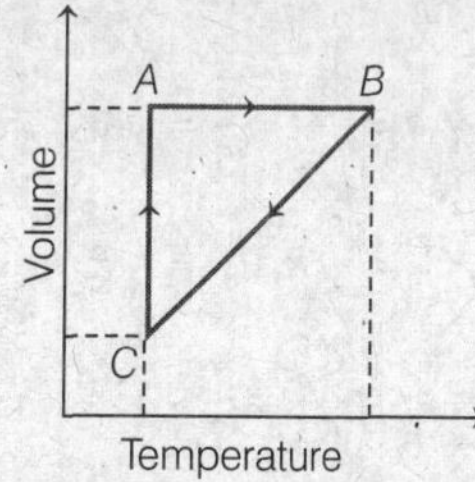

(a) isochoric, isobaric, isothermal
(b) isobaric, isochoric, isothermal
(c) isothermal, isobaric, isochoric
(d) isochoric, isothermal, isobaric
(e) isobaric, isothermal, isochoric

31 Which of the following are state variables? **[J&K CET]**

(a) Only pressure and volume
(b) Only volume and temperature
(c) Only pressure and temperature
(d) Pressure, volume and temperature

32 Minimum work is obtained when 1 kg of … gas expanded under 500 kPa to 200 kPa pressure at 0°C. **[MHT CET]**

(a) chlorine
(b) oxygen
(c) nitrogen
(d) methane

33 To calculate the amount of work done in joules during reversible expansion of an ideal gas, the volume must be expressed in **[AMU]**

(a) Only m^3 (b) Only dm^3
(c) Only cm^3 (d) All of these

Answers

1 (b)	2 (d)	3 (d)	4 (a)	5 (a)	6 (a)	7 (a)	8 (d)	9 (b)	10 (d)
11 (d)	12 (b)	13 (a)	14 (d)	15 (a)	16 (b)	17 (a)	.8 (a)	19 (d)	20 (a)
21 (c)	22 (c)	23 (c)	24 (d)	25 (d)	26 (b)	27 (b)	28 (c)	29 (b)	30 (a)
31 (d)	32 (a)	33 (d)							

Explanations

1 (*b*) For an isothermal irreversible expansion,

Work done $(W) = -p_{ext}(V_2 - V_1)$

where, V_1 = initial volume

V_2 = final volume

Given, $p_{ext} = 10^5\ Nm^{-2}, V_1 = 10^{-3} m^3$, $V_2 = 10^{-2}\ m^3$

On substituting the given values in Eq, (i),

$$W = -10^5 Nm^{-2}(10^{-2}m^3 - 10^{-3}m^3)$$
$$= -10^5 Nm^{-2} \times 10^{-3}\ (10-1)m^3$$
$$= -900\ Nm = -900\ J$$

2 (*d*) For monoatomic gas,

$$C_p = \frac{5}{2}R, C_V = \frac{3}{2}R$$
$$\gamma = \frac{C_p}{C_V} = \frac{5}{3} = 1.67$$

For diatomic gas, $C_p = \frac{7}{2}R, C_V = \frac{5}{2}R$

$$\gamma = \frac{C_p}{C_V} = \frac{7}{5} = 1.40$$

For triatomic gas, $C_p = \frac{9}{2}R, C_V = \frac{7}{2}R$

$$\gamma = \frac{C_p}{C_V} = \frac{9}{7} \sim 1.3$$

3 (*d*) For an isothermal irreversible expansion, $W_{irrev} = -p_{ext}(V_2 - V_1)$

Given, $V_1 = 0.1$ L, $V_2 = 0.25$ L,

$p_{ext} = 2$ bar

We know that, $W_{irrev} = -p_{ext}(V_2 - V_1)$

On substituting the given values in the above equation,

$$W_{irrev} = -2\text{ bar } (0.25 - 0.1)\text{ L}$$
$$= -2 \times 0.15 \text{ L bar} = -0.3 \text{ L bar}$$
$$= -0.3 \times 100\ J$$

[$\because$ 1 L bar = 100 J]

$$= -30\ J$$

4 (*a*) Work done, $W = -p_{ext}(V_2 - V_1)$

Here, $p_{ext} = 100$ kPa

$V_1 = 5\ m^3 = 5 \times 10^3$ L

$\Rightarrow V_2 = 1\ dm^3 = 1$ L

$W = -p_{ext}(V_2 - V_1)$

$\therefore W = -100 \times (1 - 5000)$

$= +499900$ kPa L

$= +499900$ J

$= +499.9$ kJ

5 (*a*) The Assertion that the increase in internal energy for vaporisation of one mole of water at 1 atm and 373 K is zero is true because for all isothermal process, change in internal energy is zero.

6 (*a*) An adiabatic process $(dq = 0)$ curve in a *p-V* diagram approaches both *V*-axis and *p*-axis. It represents a steep hyperbola, i.e. A_3 in the given diagram.

7 (*a*) A chemical process is carried out in a thermostat maintained at 25°C, i.e. at constant temperature so the process is isothermal.

8 (*d*) Gibbs free energy, enthalpy and entropy are extensive properties, but viscosity is an intensive property.

9 (*b*) At *A*, temperature = 300 K,

volume = 10 L, pressure = p_1

At *C*, temperature = 600 K,

volume = 20 L, pressure = p_2

$$\frac{p_1V_1}{T_1} = \frac{p_2V_2}{T_2}$$
$$\Rightarrow \frac{p_1 \times 10}{300} = \frac{p_2 \times 20}{600}$$
$$p_1 = p_2$$

Thus, the process is isobaric.

10 (*d*) For monoatomic gases,

$$\frac{C_p}{C_V} = \gamma = \frac{\frac{5}{2}R}{\frac{3}{2}R} = 1.67$$

$\because$ Equal volumes of two monoatomic gases are mixed.

So, γ will remain same.

11 (*d*) $\because$ 1 L-atm = 101.266 J

$\therefore$ 4 L-atm = 101.266 × 4

$$= 405.06\ J = \frac{405.06}{4.2}$$
$$= 96.4 \text{ cal} \approx 96 \text{ cal}$$

[$\because$ 1 cal = 4.2 J]

$\therefore$ 4 L-atm ≈ 96 cal.

12 (*b*) When amount of heat (*q*) is given to the system, the system does work (*W*), i.e. utilises heat but does not exchange matter, thus system is identified as closed system.

13 (*a*) $W_{rev} = -2.303 nRT \log\frac{V_2}{V_1}$

$$= -2.303 \times 1 \times 0.0821 \times (273 + 37) \log(25/15)$$
$$= -2.303 \times 0.0821 \times 310 \log\frac{5}{3}$$
$$= -13.003\ J$$

(–ve sign shows work of expansion)

This value is closer to the value given in option (a).

$\therefore$ Option (a) is correct.

14 (*d*) Given, pressure $p = 100$ kPa

$= 10^5$ Pa

Initial volume, $V_1 = 1\ m^3$

Final volume, $V_2 = 10 \times 10^{-3}\ m^3$

$= 10^{-2}\ m^3$

$$W = p\Delta V$$
$$= 10^5(1 - 10^{-2})$$
$$= 99000\ J$$

15 (*a*) Work done due to change in volume against constant pressure is,

$$W = -p_{ext}(V_2 - V_1)$$
$$= -1 \times 10^5 \text{ Nm}^{-2}$$
$$(1 \times 10^{-2} - 1 \times 10^{-3}) \text{ m}^3$$
$$= -900 \text{ Nm}$$
$$= -900 \text{ J} \qquad (1 \text{ Nm} = 1 \text{ J})$$

16 (*b*) $W = -2.303\, nRT \log (V_2 / V_1)$.

$$= -2.303 \times \frac{16}{32} \times 8.314 \times 300 \log \frac{100}{10}$$
$$= -2872 \text{ J} \approx -2875 \text{ J}$$

17 (*a*) When p, V and T are same and mass is also same, work done depends only upon molecular mass.

$$W \propto \frac{1}{M} \text{ (where, } M = \text{molecular mass)}$$

Among the given gases, NH_3 has lowest molecular mass, so work done is maximum for it.

18 (*a*) ΔE is positive, if heat passes in the system or the heat is absorbed by the system and work is done on it.

19 (*d*) Work done $= -2.303\, nRT \log \frac{p_1}{p_2}$

$$= -2.303 \times 8.314 \times 300 \log \frac{1}{4}$$
$$= -3458.3 \text{ J or } 3.458 \text{ kJ}$$

20 (a) $H = E + pV$

$\therefore \quad \Delta H = \Delta E + p\Delta V + V\Delta p$

At constant p, $V\Delta p = 0$

then $\quad \Delta H = \Delta E + p\Delta V$

21 (*c*) We know that, $\Delta U = q + W$

If heat is not supplied from the surroundings,

$$q = 0 \quad \text{(adiabatic process)}$$

$\therefore \quad \Delta E = W$

i.e. work is done at the expense of only internal energy in adiabatic process.

22 (*c*) ΔE is a state variable, i.e. it is independent of the manner in which change is brought about while q (heat) and W (work done) are path dependent, i.e. path functions.

23 (*c*) In case of a reversible process, an equilibrium exists between the system and surroundings. Such process takes infinite time to occur.

24 (*d*) Thermodynamic equilibrium includes pressure equilibrium, chemical equilibrium and thermo equilibrium.

25 (*d*) The properties of the system whose value is independent of the amount of substance present in the system are called intensive properties, e.g. viscosity, surface tension, temperature, pressure, etc.

26 (*b*) Every system having some quantity of matter is associated with a definite amount of energy. This energy is known as internal energy. It is the sum of many types of energies, such as translational energy, rotational energy, vibrational energy, electronic energy and bonding energy of the molecule.

$$E = E_{trans} + E_{rot} + E_{vib} + E_{bonding} + E_{electronic}$$

27 (*b*) Work done $(W) = -p_{ext}(V_2 - V_1)$

$$= -3 \times (6 - 4) = -6 \text{ L-atm}$$
$$= -6 \times 101.32 \text{ J } (\because \text{ 1 L-atm} = 101.32 \text{ J})$$
$$= -607.92 \approx -608 \text{ J}$$

28 (*b*) Internal energy, enthalpy and entropy are state functions but work and heat are path functions as they depend on the path by which the state is attained.

29 (*c*) Internal energy (U) is a state function as it depends only upon the states of the system (i.e. initial and final states) and does not depend on path. Temperature (T) is an intensive property as it does not depend on the quantity of matter.

Thus, both assertion and reason are correct but given reason is not the correct explanation for the given assertion.

Hence, option (b) is the correct answer.

30 (*a*) The process which does not show any change in volume is isochoric. So, graph $A \to B$ is isochoric.

The process which does not show any change in temperature is isothermal. So, graph $C \to A$ is isothermal.

When there is a change in temperature as well as in volume, then pressure remains constant, the process is isobaric. So, graph $B \to C$ is isobaric.

31 (*d*) The state of a system is described by its measurable properties such as T, V, p, etc. of the system. These properties of the system are called state variables.

32 (*a*) Work obtained in isothermal process is given below :

$$W = -2.303 nRT \log(p_1 / p_2)$$
$$\Rightarrow \quad -2.303 nRT \log \frac{500}{200} = W$$

$\therefore$ Minimum work will be obtained when number of moles (n) is minimum. Moles of substances, mass = 1kg = 1000 g

(a) Moles of $Cl_2 = 1000/71$

(b) Moles of $O_2 = 1000/32$

(c) Moles of $N_2 = 1000/28$

(d) Moles of $CH_4 = 1000/16$

$\because$ Moles of Cl_2 are least.

$\therefore$ Minimum work is obtained, when 1 kg of chlorine gas expands.

33 (*d*) Work done (W)

$$= -2.303\, nRT \log \frac{V_2}{V_1}$$

V_1 and V_2 are in ratio in the relation. So, unit may be expressed in any one of m^3, dm^3 or cm^3.

Topic 2
Laws of Thermodynamics

2019

1 Reversible expansion of an ideal gas under isothermal and adiabatic conditions are as shown in the figure. **[NEET (Odisha)]**

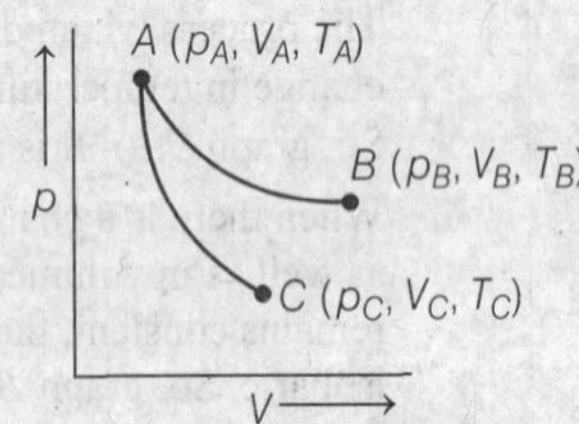

$AB \rightarrow$ Isothermal expansion
$AC \rightarrow$ Adiabatic expansion
Which of the following option is not correct?

(a) $\Delta S_{\text{isothermal}} > \Delta S_{\text{adiabatic}}$
(b) $T_A = T_B$
(c) $W_{\text{isothermal}} > W_{\text{adiabatic}}$
(d) $T_c > T_A$

2 What is the change in the energy of system if 500 cal of heat energy are added to a system and system does 350 cal of work on the surroundings. **[AIIMS]**

(a) -150 cal (b) $+150$ cal
(c) $+850$ cal (d) -850 cal

2018

3 In an adiabatic process, no transfer of heat takes place between system and surroundings. Choose the correct option for free expansion of an ideal gas under adiabatic condition from the following **[AIIMS]**

(a) $q=0, \Delta T \neq 0$ (b) $q \neq 0, \Delta T = 0$
(c) $q=0, \Delta T=0$ (d) $q=0, \Delta T<0$

4 In adiabatic conditions, 2 moles of CO_2 gas at 300 K is expanded such that its volume becomes 27 times. Then, the work done is ($C_V = 6$ cal mol^{-1} and $\gamma = 1.33$) **[JIPMER]**

(a) 1400 cal (b) 1000 cal
(c) 900 cal (d) 1200 cal

2017

5 A gas is allowed to expand in a well insulated container against a constant external pressure of 2.5 atm from an initial volume of 2.50 L to a final volume of 4.50 L. The change in internal energy ΔU of the gas in joules will be **[NEET]**

(a) 1136.25 J (b) -500 J
(c) -505 J (d) $+505$ J

2014

6 One mole of an ideal gas at 300 K is expanded isothermally from initial volume of 1 L to 10 L. The ΔE for this process is ($R = 2$ cal mol^{-1}K^{-1}) **[Manipal]**

(a) 163.7 cal (b) Zero
(c) 138.1 cal (d) 9 L atm

2013

7 Which law states that entropy of all pure crystalline solids is zero at absolute zero? **[UP CPMT]**

(a) First law of thermodynamics
(b) Second law of thermodynamics
(c) Third law of thermodynamics
(d) Hess's law

2012

8 Based on the first law of thermodynamics, which one of the following is correct? **[KCET]**

(a) For an isothermal process, $q = +W$
(b) For an isochoric process, $\Delta U = -q$
(c) For an adiabatic process, $\Delta U = -W$
(d) For a cyclic process, $q = -W$

2011

9 Which of the following is the correct option for free expansion of an ideal gas under adiabatic condition? **[CBSE AIPMT]**

(a) $q = 0, \Delta T < 0, W \neq 0$
(b) $q = 0, \Delta T \neq 0, W = 0$
(c) $q \neq 0, \Delta T = 0, W = 0$
(d) $q = 0, \Delta T = 0, W = 0$

2010

10 According to second law of thermodynamics, a process (reaction) is spontaneous, if during the process **[Manipal]**

(a) $\Delta S_{\text{universe}} > 0$ (b) $\Delta S_{\text{universe}} = 0$
(c) $\Delta H_{\text{system}} > 0$ (d) $\Delta S_{\text{universe}} = \Delta S_{\text{system}}$

11 The second law of thermodynamics says that in a cyclic process, **[WB JEE]**

(a) work cannot be converted into heat
(b) heat cannot be converted into work
(c) work cannot be completely converted into heat
(d) heat cannot be completely converted into work

2008

12 Change in internal energy, when 4 kJ of work is done on the system and 1 kJ of heat is given out by the system, is **[Kerala CEE]**

(a) + 1 kJ (b) – 5 kJ
(c) + 5 kJ (d) + 3 kJ
(e) – 3 kJ

2007

13 In a closed insulated container, a liquid is stirred with a paddle to increase the temperature, which of the following is true? **[Punjab PMET]**

(a) $\Delta E = \Delta W \neq 0, q = 0$ (b) $\Delta E = W = 0, q \neq 0$
(c) $\Delta E = 0, W = q \neq 0$ (d) $W = 0, \Delta E = q \neq 0$

14 A gas expands isothermally against a constant external pressure of 1 atm from a volume of $10\ dm^3$ to a volume of $20\ dm^3$. It absorbs 800 J of thermal energy from its surroundings. The ΔU is **[BCECE]**

(a) – 312 J (b) + 123 J (c) – 213 J (d) + 231 J

2006

15 The volume of a gas decreases from 500 cc to 300 cc when a sample of gas is compressed by an average pressure of 0.6 atm. During this process, 10 J of heat is liberated. The change in internal energy is **[BHU]**

(a) –2.16 J (b) 12.156 J (c) 2.16 J (d) 101.3 J

2005

16 One mole of an ideal gas is initially at 0°C and 1 atm pressure. If it absorbs 1000 cal heat during a reversible isothermal expansion, what will be its final volume? **[Haryana PMT]**

(a) 102.5 L (b) 242.5 L
(c) 22.4 L (d) 141.47 L

Answers

1 (d)	2 (b)	3 (c)	4 (d)	5 (c)	6 (b)	7 (c)	8 (d)	9 (d)	10 (a)
11 (d)	12 (d)	13 (a)	14 (c)	15 (c)	16 (d)				

Explanations

1 (*d*) From first law of thermodynamics,

$$\Delta U = q + W$$

In adiabatic expansion, $q = 0$

$\therefore \quad \Delta U = W$

During expansion of a gas, W is negative, i.e. $W < 0$ or $\Delta U < 0$.

We know that, $\Delta U = nC_V\Delta T$

$\therefore \quad nC_V\Delta T < 0$

or $\quad \Delta T < 0$

$\therefore \quad T_C - T_A < 0$

or $\quad T_C < T_A$

Thus, option (d) is incorrect while the remaining options are correct.

2 (*b*) Heat absorbed, $q = 500$ cal

Work done by the system,

$w = -350$ cal

According to the first law of thermodynamics,

$$\Delta E = q + w$$
$$= 500 + (-350)$$
$$= +150 \text{ cal}$$

3 (*c*) For free expansion, $W = 0$ and for adiabatic process, $q = 0$.

$\because \Delta U = q + W = 0$, this means that internal energy remains constant.

Therefore, $\Delta T = 0$ in ideal gas as there is no intermolecular attraction. Hence, when such a gas expands under adiabatic conditions into a vacuum, no heat is absorbed or evolved, since, no external work is done to separate the molecules.

4 (*d*) Given, $T_1 = 300$ K, $V_2 = 27\ V_1$, $n = 1$ mol, $C_V = 6$ cal mol^{-1}, $\gamma = 1.33$.

In adiabatic conditions, $\dfrac{T_2}{T_1} = \left(\dfrac{V_1}{V_2}\right)^{\gamma - 1}$

or, $\quad \dfrac{T_2}{T_1} = \left(\dfrac{1}{27}\right)^{1.33 - 1}$

$$= \left(\frac{1}{27}\right)^{0.33} = \left(\frac{1}{27}\right)^{1/3} = \frac{1}{3}$$

or, $\quad T_2 = 300 \times \dfrac{1}{3} = 100$ K

Thus, $T_2 < T_1$ hence, cooling takes place due to expansion under adiabatic condition.

$$\Delta U = q + W$$

$q = 0$ for adiabatic change

$\Delta U = -ve$ because gas expands.

Then, $W = -\Delta U$

$$= -C_V(T_2 - T_1)$$
$$= -6\ (100 - 300) = 1200 \text{ cal}$$

5 (*c*) According to first law of thermodynamics, $\Delta U = q + W$

where, ΔU = internal energy

q = heat absorbed or evolved,

W = work done.

Work done against constant external pressure (irreversible process).

$$W = -p_{ext}\ \Delta V$$
$$= -p_{ext}\ (V_2 - V_1)$$
$$= -2.5 \text{ atm } (4.5 \text{ L} - 2.5 \text{ L})$$
$$= -5 \text{ L atm}$$
$$= -5 \times 101.3 \text{ J}$$
$$= -506.5 \text{ J} \approx -505 \text{ J}$$

Since, the system is well insulated, $q = 0$

$\therefore \quad \Delta U = W = -505$ J

Hence, change in internal energy, ΔU of the gas is – 505 J, i.e. option (c) as it is the closest value.

6 (*b*) From first law of thermodynamics,

$$\Delta E = q + W$$

For isothermal process, $\Delta T = 0$

Hence, $\Delta E = 0$.

This means that for all isothermal process of an ideal gas, the value of $\Delta E = 0$.

7 (*c*) (a) The first law states that energy can neither be created nor destroyed.

(b) The second law of thermodynamics states that entropy of universe is continuously increasing.

(c) The third law of thermodynamics states that entropy of all crystalline solids is zero at absolute zero temperature.

(d) Hess's law states that total amount of heat evolved or absorbed in a reaction is independent of path.

8 (*d*) $\Delta U = q + W$

For an isothermal process,

$$\Delta U = 0, q = -W$$

For an isochoric process,

$$W\ (p\Delta V) = 0, \Delta U = q$$

For an adiabatic process, $q = 0, \Delta U = W$

For a cyclic process, $\Delta U = 0,\ q = -W$

9 (*d*) For free expansion of an ideal gas under adiabatic conditions, $q = 0$, $\Delta T = 0$ and $W = 0$. This is because no work is done in the case of free expansion of an ideal gas irrespective of the process being reversible or irreversible.

10 (*a*) When a spontaneous (naturally occurring) process takes place, it is accompanied by increase in entropy, i.e.

$$\Delta S_{\text{universe}} = \Delta S_{\text{system}} + \Delta S_{\text{surroundings}} > 0$$

11 (*d*) According to second law, work can always be completely converted into heat but heat cannot be completely converted into work.

12 (*d*) From first law of thermodynamics,

$$\Delta U = q + W$$

Here, $W = +4$ kJ

($\because$ Work is done on the system)

$$q = -1\text{ kJ}$$

($\because$ Heat is given out by the system)

$$\Delta U = q + W = -1 + 4 = +3\text{ kJ}$$

13 (*a*) In a closed insulated container, a liquid is stirred with a paddle to increase the temperature, therefore it behaves as adiabatic process, so $q = 0$. Hence, from first law of thermodynamics,

$$\Delta E = q + W$$

If $q = 0$

then, $\Delta E = W \neq 0$

14 (*c*) $W = -\int_{V_1}^{V_2} p dV = -p(V_2 - V_1)$

$$W = -1\ (20 - 10) = -10\text{ dm}^3\text{ atm}$$

$$= -1013\text{ J} \quad (\because 1\text{ L - atm} = 101.3\text{ J})$$

From first law of thermodynamics,

$$\Delta U = q + W$$

$$\Delta U = 800\text{ J} + (-1013\text{ J})$$

$$= -213\text{ J}$$

15 (*c*) $p\Delta V = 0.6 \times \frac{(500 - 300)}{1000} = 0.6 \times 0.2$

$$= 0.12\text{ L-atm} = 0.12 \times 101.3 = 12.16\text{ J}$$

$\because \Delta U = q + p\Delta V$

(First law of thermodynamics)

$\therefore \Delta U = -10 + 12.16 = 2.16$ J

16 (*d*) Since, the gas is under STP conditions hence, $V_1 = 22.4$ L, $V_2 = ?$

For isothermal and reversible expansion, $\Delta U = 0 \Rightarrow \Delta U = q + W$

$\because \Delta U = 0$, then $q = -W$

$\therefore q = -W$

$$= -[-nRT \times 2.303 \log V_2/V_1]$$

or 1000×4.184 J

$$= 1 \times 8.314 \times 273 \times 2.303 \times \log \frac{V_2}{22.4}$$

or $4184 = 5227.17 \log \frac{V_2}{22.4}$

$\therefore V_2 = 141.47$ L

Topic 3

Reactions Related to Enthalpies and Hess's Law

2018

1 Given that, for the reaction, $\frac{1}{2}H_2 + \frac{1}{2}Cl_2 \longrightarrow HCl$

$\Delta H_f(HCl) = -93$ kJ/mol BE $(H_2) = 434$ kJ/mol

BE $(Cl_2) = 242$ kJ/mol

The bond dissociation energy of HCl is **[JIPMER]**

(a) 232 kJ/mol (b) 331 kJ/mol

(c) 431 kJ/mol (d) 530 kJ/mol

2 ΔH and ΔE for the reaction,

$Fe_2O_3(s) + 3H_2(g) \longrightarrow 2Fe(s) + H_2O(l)$

at constant temperature are related as **[AIIMS]**

(a) $\Delta H = \Delta E$

(b) $\Delta H = \Delta E + RT$

(c) $\Delta H = \Delta E + 3RT$

(d) $\Delta H = \Delta E - 3RT$

3 The bond dissociation energies of X_2, Y_2 and XY are in the ratio of 1 : 0.5 : 1. ΔH for the formation of XY is -200 kJ mol^{-1}. The bond dissociation energy of X_2 will be **[NEET]**

(a) 800 kJ mol^{-1} (b) 100 kJ mol^{-1}

(c) 200 kJ mol^{-1} (d) 400 kJ mol^{-1}

4 The energy released when 6 moles of octane is burnt in air will be [Given, ΔH_f for $CO_2(g)$, $H_2O(g)$ and $C_8H_{18}(l)$, respectively are -490, -240 and -160 J/mol] **[JIPMER]**

(a) -37.4 kJ (b) -20 kJ (c) -6.2 kJ (d) -35.5 kJ

5 If at 298 K, the bond energies of C—H, C—C, C=C and H—H bonds are respectively 414, 347, 615 and 435 kJ mol^{-1}, the value of enthalpy change for the reaction;

$H_2C{=}CH_2 + H_2(g) \longrightarrow H_3C{-}CH_3(g)$

at 298 K, will be **[AIIMS]**

(a) $+250$ kJ (b) -250 kJ (c) $+125$ kJ (d) -125 kJ

2014

6 Assuming enthalpy of combustion of hydrogen at 273 K is −286 kJ and enthalpy of fusion of ice at the same temperature to be 6.0 kJ. Calculate enthalpy change during formation of 100 g of ice. **[MHT CET]**

(a) +1622 kJ (b) −1622 kJ (c) +292 kJ (d) −292 kJ

7 Enthalpy of combustion of carbon to CO_2 is −393.5 kJ mol^{-1}. What amount of heat will be released upon formation of 35.2 g of CO_2 from carbon and oxygen gas? **[Manipal]**

(a) 214.8 kJ (b) −314.8 kJ (c) 414.8 kJ (d) 514.8 kJ

8 A person inhales 640 g of O_2 per day. If all O_2 is used for converting sugar into CO_2 and H_2O, how much sucrose ($C_{12}H_{22}O_{11}$) is consumed in the body in one day and what is the heat evolved? [ΔH for combustion of sucrose = − 5645 kJ mol^{-1}] **[Manipal]**

(a) 530 g, 9403.34 kJ (b) 570 g, 9408.33 kJ
(c) 500 g, 9402.27 kJ (d) 1140 g, −18816 kJ

9 The enthalpy of formation of $CH_4(g)$, $H_2O(l)$ and $CO_2(g)$ are respectively −74.8 kJ mol^{-1}, − 285.5 kJ mol^{-1} and − 393.5 kJ mol^{-1}. Then, the standard enthalpy of combustion of $CH_4(g)$ is **[Kerala CEE]**

(a) + 890.3 kJ mol^{-1} (b) − 604.5 kJ mol^{-1}
(c) − 754.1 kJ mol^{-1} (d) + 604.5 kJ mol^{-1}
(e) − 890.3 kJ mol^{-1}

10 In the following reaction,
$4NO_2(g) + O_2(g) \longrightarrow 2N_2O_5(g)$, $\Delta H = -110$ kJ. If $N_2O_5(s)$ is formed instead of $N_2O_5(g)$ in the reaction, the enthalpy change (in kJ) would be (enthalpy of sublimation of $N_2O_5(s)$ is +53 kJ mol^{-1}) **[Kerala CEE]**

(a) −216 (b) −162 (c) +108 (d) +216
(e) +162

11 The value of ΔH for cooling 2 moles of an ideal monoatomic gas from 225° C to 125° C at constant pressure will be [given, $C_p = \frac{5}{2}R$] **[WB JEE]**

(a) 250 R (b) − 500 R (c) 500 R (d) − 250 R

12 Given that, $C + O_2 \longrightarrow CO_2; \Delta H° = -x$ kJ
$2CO + O_2 \longrightarrow 2CO_2; \Delta H° = -y$ kJ
The heat of formation of carbon monoxide will be **[WB JEE]**

(a) $\frac{y-2x}{2}$ (b) $y + 2x$
(c) $2x - y$ (d) $\frac{2x-y}{2}$

13 The ratio of heats liberated at 298 K from the combustion of 1 kg of coke and by burning water gas obtained from 1 kg of coke is (Assume coke to be 100% carbon). (Given, enthalpies of combustion of CO_2, CO and H_2 as 393.5 kJ, 285 kJ, 285 kJ, respectively all at 298 K) **[KCET]**

(a) 0.79:1 (b) 0.69:1 (c) 0.86:1 (d) 0.96:1

2013

14 **Assertion** (A) ΔH and ΔE are almost the same for the reaction, $N_2(g) + O_2(g) \rightleftharpoons 2NO(g)$

Reason (R) All reactants and products are gases. **[AIIMS]**

(a) Both A and R are correct and R is the correct explanation of A
(b) Both A and R are correct but R is not the correct explanation of A
(c) A is correct but R is incorrect
(d) Both A and R are incorrect

15 The heat of reaction for,
$C_{10}H_8(s) + 12O_2(g) \longrightarrow 10CO_2(g) + 4H_2O(l)$
at constant volume is −1228.2 kcal at 25° C. The heat of reaction at constant pressure and same temperature is **[AIIMS]**

(a) −1228.2 kcal (b) −1229.3 kcal
(c) −1232.9 kcal (d) −1242.6 kcal

16 The enthalpies of formation of $C_2H_2(g)$ and $C_6H_6(g)$ at 298 K are 230 and 85 kJ/mol respectively. The enthalpy change for the reaction is **[UP CPMT]**

(a) 605 kJ/mol (b) 865 kJ/mol
(c) − 605 kJ/mol (d) − 865 kJ/mol

17 $N_2(g) + 3H_2(g) \longrightarrow 2NH_3(g)$. For the above reaction, the correct statement is **[Manipal]**

(a) $\Delta H < \Delta E$ (b) $\Delta H = \Delta E$
(c) $\Delta H > \Delta E$ (d) None of these

18 $C(s) + O_2(g) \longrightarrow CO_2(g)$; $\Delta H = -94$ kcal
$2CO + O_2(g) \longrightarrow 2CO_2(g)$; $\Delta H = -135.2$ kcal
The heat of formation of CO(g) is **[WB JEE]**

(a) − 26.4 kcal (b) 41.2 kcal (c) 26.4 kcal (d) 229.2 kcal

19 In order to decompose 9 g water, 142.5 kJ heat is required. Hence, enthalpy of formation of water is **[KCET]**

(a) −142.5 kJ (b) +142.5 kJ (c) −285 kJ (d) +285 kJ

20 The enthalpy of combustion of $C_6H_6(l)$ is −3250 kJ. When 0.39 g of benzene is burnt in excess of oxygen in an open vessel, the amount of heat liberated is **[KCET]**

(a) 16.25 J (b) 16.25 kJ (c) 32.5 J (d) 32.5 kJ

2012

21 Standard enthalpy of vaporisation $\Delta_{vap} H°$ for water at 100°C is 40.66 kJ/mol. The internal energy of vaporisation of water at 100°C (in kJ/mol) is
(Assume water vapour behave like an ideal gas) **[CBSE AIPMT]**

(a) +37.56 (b) −43.76
(c) + 43.76 (d) + 40.66

22 The enthalpy of dissolution of $BaCl_2(s)$ and $BaCl_2 \cdot 2H_2O(s)$ are 20.6 and 8.8 kJ/mol respectively. The enthalpy of hydration for
$BaCl_2(s) + 2H_2O \longrightarrow BaCl_2 \cdot 2H_2O(s)$ is **[AFMC]**

(a) 29.4 kJ (b) − 29.4 kJ (c) − 11.8 kJ (d) 38.2 kJ

23 If bond dissociation energies of xy, x_2 and y_2 (all diatomic molecules) are in the ratio of 1:1:0.5 and ΔH_f for the formation of xy is –200 kJ mol^{-1}, the bond dissociation energy of x_2 will be **[Manipal]**

(a) 400 kJ/mol (b) 300 kJ/ mol
(c) 200 kJ/ mol (d) 800 kJ/ mol

2011

24 Enthalpy change for the reaction, $4H(g) \longrightarrow 2H_2(g)$ is – 869.5 kJ. The dissociation energy of H—H bond is **[CBSE AIPMT]**

(a) + 217.4 kJ (b) – 434.8 kJ
(c) – 869.6 kJ (d) + 434.8 kJ

25 The enthalpy of solution of sodium chloride is 4 kJ mol^{-1} and its enthalpy of hydration of ions is –784 kJ mol^{-1}. Then, the lattice enthalpy of NaCl (in kJ mol^{-1}) is **[Kerala CEE]**

(a) + 788 (b) + 4
(c) +398 (d) + 780
(e) + 394

26 4 g of graphite is burnt in a bomb calorimeter of heat capacity 30 kJ K^{-1} in excess of oxygen at 1 atm pressure. The temperature rises from 300 to 304 K. What is the enthalpy of combustion of graphite (in kJ mol^{-1})? **[Kerala CEE]**

(a) 360 (b) 144 (c) –360
(d) –1440 (e) –520

2010

27 For an endothermic reaction, energy of activation is E_a and enthalpy of the reaction is ΔH (both of these in kJ/mol). Minimum value of E_a will be **[CBSE AIPMT]**

(a) equal to zero (b) less than ΔH
(c) equal to ΔH (d) more than ΔH

28 Given,

$$NH_3(g) + 3Cl_2(g) \rightleftharpoons NCl_3(g) + 3HCl(g); -\Delta H_1$$
$$N_2(g) + 3H_2(g) \rightleftharpoons 2NH_3(g); -\Delta H_2$$
$$H_2(g) + Cl_2(g) \rightleftharpoons 2HCl(g); \Delta H_3$$

The heat of formation of $NCl_3(g)$ in terms of $\Delta H_1, \Delta H_2$ and ΔH_3 is **[AFMC]**

(a) $\Delta H_f = -\Delta H_1 + \frac{\Delta H_2}{2} - \frac{3}{2}\Delta H_3$

(b) $\Delta H_f = \Delta H_1 + \frac{\Delta H_2}{2} - \frac{3}{2}\Delta H_3$

(c) $\Delta H_f = \Delta H_1 + \frac{\Delta H_2}{2} + \frac{3}{2}\Delta H_3$

(d) None of the above

29 The heat liberated when 1.89 g of benzoic acid is burnt in a bomb calorimeter at 25°C increases the temperature of 18.94 kg of water by 0.632 °C. If the specific heat of water at 25°C is 0.998 cal/g-deg, the value of the heat of combustion of benzoic acid is **[AFMC]**

(a) 881.1 kcal (b) 771.2 kcal
(c) 981.1 kcal (d) 852.7 kcal

30 The heat of combustion of methane, if the heat of formation of CH_4, CO_2 and H_2O are respectively –18.4 kcal, –94.0 kcal, –68.4 kcal is **[UP CPMT]**

(a) –212.4 kcal (b) +212.4 kcal
(c) –249.2 kcal (d) +249.2 kcal

31 The heats of neutralisation of four acids *A*, *B*, *C* and *D* when neutralised against a common base are 13.7, 9.4, 11.2 and 12.4 kcal respectively. The weakest among these acids is **[BVP]**

(a) *A* (b) *B* (c) *C* (d) *D*

32 The bond energies of C—C, C=C, H—H and C—H linkages are 350, 600, 400 and 410 kJ/mol respectively. The heat of hydrogenation of ethylene is **[BVP]**

(a) –170 kJ mol^{-1} (b) – 260 kJ mol^{-1}
(c) – 400 kJ mol^{-1} (d) – 450 kJ mol^{-1}

33 The heat of formation of water is 260 kJ. How much H_2O is decomposed by 130 kJ of heat? **[MHT CET]**

(a) 0.25 mol (b) 1 mol (c) 0.5 mol (d) 2 mol

34 Find the correct equation **[MHT CET]**

(a) $E_2 - E_1 - H_2 + H_1 = n_2RT - n_1RT$
(b) $E_2 - E_1 - H_2 - H_1 = n_2RT - n_1RT$
(c) $H_2 - H_1 + E_2 - E_1 = n_2RT - n_1RT$
(d) $H_2 - H_1 - E_2 + E_1 = n_2RT - n_1RT$

35 Reaction for the formation of NaCl is **[MHT CET]**

(a) $N_2(g) + Cl_2(g) \longrightarrow NaCl(s)$

(b) $Na(s) + \frac{1}{2}Cl_2(g) \longrightarrow NaCl(s)$

(c) $Na(g) + \frac{1}{2}Cl_2(g) \longrightarrow NaCl(s)$

(d) $Na(g) + Cl_2(g) \longrightarrow NaCl(s)$

36 What will be the enthalpy of combustion of ethylene (gas) to form CO_2 (gas) and water at 298 K and 1 atm pressure? The enthalpies of formation of CO_2, H_2O and C_2H_4 are –393.5, –241.8 and + 52.3 kJ/mol respectively. **[Haryana PMT]**

(a) –1332.9 kJ mol^{-1}
(b) –1322.9 kJ mol^{-1}
(c) +1332.9 kJ mol^{-1}
(d) +1322.9 kJ mol^{-1}

37 Thermodynamically, the most stable form of carbon is **[AMU]**

(a) diamond (b) graphite
(c) fullerenes (d) coal

38 The amount of heat evolved when 500 cm^3 of 0.1 M HCl is mixed with 200 cm^3 of 0.2 M NaOH is **[KCET]**

(a) 2.292 kJ (b) 1.292 kJ
(c) 0.292 kJ (d) 3.392 kJ

39 The heat of neutralisation is highest for the reaction between **[JCECE]**

(a) NH_4OH-CH_3COOH (b) HNO_3-NH_4OH
(c) NaOH-CH_3COOH (d) HCl-NaOH

40 For the reaction of one mole of zinc dust with one mole of sulphuric acid in a bomb calorimeter, ΔE and W corresponds to **[CMC]**

(a) $\Delta E < 0, W = 0$ (b) $\Delta E = 0, W < 0$
(c) $\Delta E > 0, W = 0$ (d) $\Delta E = 0, W > 0$

2009

41 Enthalpy of combustion of methane and ethane are –210 kcal/mol and –368 kcal/mol respectively. The enthalpy of combustion of decane is **[AIIMS]**

(a) –158 kcal
(b) –1632 kcal
(c) –1700 kcal
(d) Data is incomplete

42 The difference between heat capacity at constant pressure and heat capacity at constant volume for the combustion of carbon monoxide at 27°C will be **[AFMC]**

(a) –124.7 kJ (b) –1.247 J
(c) –1.247 kJ (d) –124.71 J

43 Consider the following reactions,

I. $C(s) + \frac{1}{2}O_2(g) \longrightarrow CO(g);\ \Delta H_1 = a$

II. $CO(g) + \frac{1}{2}O_2(g) \longrightarrow CO_2(g);\ \Delta H_2 = b$

III. $C(s) + CO_2(g) \longrightarrow 2CO(g);\ \Delta H_3 = c$

Select the correct statement. **[UP CPMT]**

(a) Heat of formation of CO_2 is $(a + b)$
(b) Heat of combustion of C is $(a + b)$
(c) $\Delta H_3 = \Delta H_1 - \Delta H_2$
(d) All the above are correct statements

44 Heat of combustion of methane is –800 kJ. What is the heat of combustion for 4×10^{-4} kg of methane? **[MHT CET]**

(a) –800 kJ (b) -3.2×10^4 kJ
(c) –20 kJ (d) –1600 kJ

45 Kirchhoff's equation is **[MHT CET]**

(a) $\log \frac{k_2}{k_1} = \frac{E_a}{2.303R}\left[\frac{1}{T_1} - \frac{1}{T_2}\right]$

(b) $\log \frac{p_2}{p_1} = \frac{\Delta H_V}{2.303R}\left[\frac{T_2 - T_1}{T_1 \times T_2}\right]$

(c) $\Delta C_p = \frac{\Delta H_2 - \Delta H_1}{T_2 - T_1}$

(d) $\log \frac{k_2}{k_1} = \frac{\Delta H}{2.303R}\left[\frac{1}{T_1} - \frac{1}{T_2}\right]$

46 The heat change for the following reaction at 298 K and constant pressure is +7.3 kcal.

$$A_2B(s) \longrightarrow 2A(s) + \frac{1}{2}B_2(g);\ \Delta H = +7.3 \text{ kcal}$$

The heat change at constant volume would be **[Manipal]**

(a) + 7.3 kcal (b) more than 7.3 kcal
(c) less than 7.3 kcal (d) zero

47 The standard heats of formation of CH_4, H_2O and CH_3OH are –76, –242 and –266 kJ/mol respectively. The enthalpy change for the following reaction is

$CH_3OH(l) + H_2(g) \longrightarrow CH_4(g) + H_2O(l)$ **[OJEE]**

(a) – 4 kJ/mol (b) –556 kJ/mol
(c) – 318 kJ/mol (d) –52 kJ/mol

48 The heat of atomisation of $PH_3(g)$ and $P_2H_4(g)$ are 953 kJ mol^{-1} and 1485 kJ mol^{-1} respectively. The P—P bond energy in (kJ mol^{-1}) is **[Kerala CEE]**

(a) 213 (b) 426 (c) 318 (d) 1272 (e) 107

49 Equal volumes of molar hydrochloric acid and sulphuric acid are neutralised by dilute NaOH solution and x kcal and y kcal of heat are liberated respectively. Which of the following is true? **[WB JEE]**

(a) $x = y$ (b) $x = y/2$
(c) $x = 2y$ (d) None of these

50 Which one of the following is always not negative?
(a) Enthalpy of combustion **[J&K CET]**
(b) Enthalpy of formation
(c) Enthalpy of neutralisation
(d) Lattice enthalpy

51 When 400 mL of 0.2 N solution of a weak acid is neutralised by a dilute aqueous solution of sodium hydroxide under standard conditions, 4.4 kJ of heat is liberated. Therefore, the standard enthalpy of neutralisation of this weak acid (in kJ $equivalent^{-1}$) is **[J&K CET]**

(a) –11 (b) – 44 (c) –55 (d) –22

52 Given that ΔH_f (H) = 218 kJ/mol, express the H—H bond energy in kcal/mol **[EAMCET]**

(a) 52.15 (b) 911 (c) 104 (d) 52153

53 Calculate $\Delta H°$ for the reaction,

$Na_2O(s) + SO_3(g) \longrightarrow Na_2SO_4(s)$

Given the following **[EAMCET]**

I. $Na(s) + H_2O(l) \longrightarrow NaOH(s) + \frac{1}{2}H_2(g);\ \Delta H° = -146$ kJ

II. $Na_2SO_4(s) + H_2O(l) \longrightarrow 2NaOH(s) + SO_3(g);\ \Delta H° = +418$ kJ

III. $2Na_2O(s) + 2H_2(g) \longrightarrow 4Na(s) + 2H_2O(l),\ \Delta H° = +259$ kJ

(a) +823 kJ (b) –581 kJ (c) – 435 kJ (d) +531 kJ

54 The enthalpy of neutralisation of oxalic acid by a strong base is –25 kcal mol^{-1}. The enthalpy of neutralisation of strong acid and strong base is –13.7 kcal $equiv^{-1}$. The enthalpy of dissociation of

$H_2C_2O_4 \rightleftharpoons 2H^+ + C_2O_4^{2-}$ is **[DUMET]**

(a) 1.0 kcal mol^{-1} (b) 2.0 kcal mol^{-1}
(c) 18.55 kcal mol^{-1} (d) 11.7 kcal mol^{-1}

55 An endothermic reaction has a positive internal energy change ΔU. In such a case, what is the minimum value that activation energy can have? **[DUMET]**

(a) ΔU (b) $\Delta U = \Delta H + \Delta nRT$
(c) $\Delta U = \Delta H - \Delta nRT$ (d) $\Delta U = E_a + RT$

56 The enthalpy of formation of NH_3 is –46 kJ mol^{-1}. The enthalpy change for the reaction

$2NH_3(aq) \longrightarrow N_2(g) + 3H_2(g)$ is **[KCET]**

(a) +23 kJ (b) +92 kJ
(c) +46 kJ (d) +184 kJ

2008

57 What will be the heat of formation of methane, if the heat of combustion of carbon is $-x$ kJ, heat of formation of water is $-y$ kJ and heat of combustion of methane is z kJ?

(a) $(-x-y+z)$kJ (b) $(-z-x+2y)$kJ **[AIIMS]**
(c) $(-x-2y-z)$kJ (d) $(-x-2y+z)$kJ

58 **Assertion** (A) For a reaction,

$2NH_3(g) \longrightarrow N_2(g) + 3H_2(g); \Delta H > \Delta E$

Reason (R) Enthalpy change is always greater than internal energy change. **[AIIMS]**

(a) Both A and R are correct and R is the correct explanation of A
(b) Both A and R are correct but R is not the correct explanation of A
(c) A is correct but R is incorrect
(d) Both A and R are incorrect

59 Identify the reaction for which $\Delta H \neq \Delta E$. **[AFMC]**

(a) $S(\text{rhombic}) + O_2(g) \longrightarrow SO_2(g)$
(b) $N_2(g) + O_2(g) \longrightarrow 2NO(g)$
(c) $H_2(g) + Cl_2(g) \longrightarrow 2HCl(g)$
(d) $CO(g) + \frac{1}{2}O_2(g) \longrightarrow CO_2(g)$

60 If ΔE is the heat of reaction for,

$C_2H_5OH(l) + 3O_2(g) \longrightarrow 2CO_2(g) + 3H_2O(l)$

at constant volume, the ΔH (heat of reaction at constant pressure), at constant temperature is **[MHT CET]**

(a) $\Delta H = \Delta E + RT$
(b) $\Delta H = \Delta E - RT$
(c) $\Delta H = \Delta E - 2RT$
(d) $\Delta H = \Delta E + 2RT$

61 Which of the following reaction defines ΔH_f°? **[Manipal]**

(a) $C(\text{diamond}) + O_2(g) \longrightarrow CO_2(g)$
(b) $\frac{1}{2}H_2(g) + \frac{1}{2}F_2(g) \longrightarrow HF(g)$
(c) $N_2(g) + 3H_2(g) \longrightarrow 2NH_3(g)$
(d) $CO(g) + \frac{1}{2}O_2(g) \longrightarrow CO_2(g)$

62 The heat of combustion of solid benzoic acid at constant volume is –321.30 kJ at 27°C. The heat of combustion at constant pressure is **[Manipal]**

(a) – 321.30 – 300 R (b) – 321.30 + 300 R
(c) – 321.30 – 150 R (d) – 321.30 + 900 R

63 Which one of the ions in the table below would have the largest value of enthalpy of hydration? **[Kerala CEE]**

	Ionic radius (in nm)	Charge of ion
(a)	0.065	+2
(b)	0.095	+1
(c)	0.135	+2
(d)	0.169	+1
(e)	0.181	–1

64 ΔH for the reaction,

$C(\text{graphite}) + 2H_2(g) \longrightarrow CH_4(g)$ at 298 K

and 1 atm is –17900 cal. The ΔE for the above conversion would be **[J&K CET]**

(a) – 17900 cal (b) 17900 cal
(c) 17308 cal (d) – 17304 cal

65 100 cm^3 of 0.1 M HCl and 100 cm^3 of 0.1 M NaOH solutions are mixed in a calorimeter. If the heat liberated is "Q" kcal, the heat of neutralisation (ΔH) (in kcal) of HCl (aq) and NaOH (aq) is **[EAMCET]**

(a) $-10Q$ (b) $-100Q$ (c) $-1000Q$ (d) $-Q$

66 If one mole of ammonia and one mole of hydrogen chloride are mixed in a closed container to form ammonium chloride gas, then **[KCET]**

(a) $\Delta H > \Delta U$ (b) $\Delta H = \Delta U$
(c) $\Delta H < \Delta U$ (d) there is no relationship

2007

67 One mole of methanol when burnt in O_2, gives out 723 kJ mol^{-1} heat. If one mole of O_2 is used, what will be the amount of heat evolved? **[AIIMS]**

(a) 723 kJ (b) 924 kJ (c) 482 kJ (d) 241 kJ

68 **Assertion** (A) For the combustion of methane, $\Delta E > \Delta H$.

Reason (R) ΔH is related to ΔE by the expression, $\Delta H = \Delta E + \Delta n_g RT$ **[AIIMS]**

(a) Both A and R are correct and R is the correct explanation of A

(b) Both A and R are correct but R is not the correct explanation of A
(c) A is correct but R is incorrect
(d) Both A and R are incorrect

69 The enthalpy of hydrogenation of cyclohexene is $-119.5 \text{ kJ mol}^{-1}$. If resonance energy of benzene is $-150.4 \text{ kJ mol}^{-1}$, its enthalpy of hydrogenation would be [AIIMS]
(a) $-208.1 \text{ kJ mol}^{-1}$
(b) $-269.9 \text{ kJ mol}^{-1}$
(c) $-358.5 \text{ kJ mol}^{-1}$
(d) $-508.9 \text{ kJ mol}^{-1}$

70 Which of the following is combustion reaction? [UP CPMT]
(a) $C + O_2 \longrightarrow CO_2$
(b) $CH_4 + O_2 \longrightarrow CO_2 + H_2O$
(c) $Mg + O_2 \longrightarrow MgO$
(d) All of these

71 For the reaction, [MHT CET]
$2H_2(g) + O_2(g) \longrightarrow 2H_2O(g); \Delta H° = -573.2 \text{ kJ}$
The heat of decomposition of water per mole is
(a) 286.6 kJ (b) 573.2 kJ
(c) – 28.66 kJ (d) zero

72 The bond energy is the energy required to [MHT CET]
(a) dissociate one mole of the substance
(b) dissociate bond in 1 kg of the substance
(c) break one mole of similar bonds
(d) break bonds in one mole of substance

73 If 150 kJ of energy is needed for muscular work to walk a distance of one km, then how much weight of glucose one has to consume to walk a distance of 5 km, provided only 30% of energy is available for muscular work? (The enthalpy of combustion of glucose is 3000 kJ mol^{-1}) [Kerala CEE]
(a) 75 g (b) 30 g (c) 180 g (d) 150 g
(e) 45 g

74 The quantity of heat measured for a reaction in a bomb calorimeter is equal to [J&K CET]
(a) ΔG (b) ΔH (c) $p\Delta V$ (d) ΔE

75 Heat of combustion of carbon monoxide at constant volume at 17°C is 67,710 cal. The heat of combustion at constant pressure is [J&K CET]
(a) – 68000 cal (b) – 67800 cal
(c) – 67050 cal (d) + 68500 cal

76 Calculate the difference between ΔE and ΔH for the following reaction at 27°C (in kcal)
$C(\text{graphite}) + 2H_2(g) \longrightarrow CH_4(g)$ [EAMCET]
(a) – 0.6 (b) – 1.2
(c) + 0.6 (d) + 1.2

2006

77 The enthalpy change (ΔH) for the reaction,
$$N_2(g) + 3H_2(g) \longrightarrow 2NH_3(g)$$
is – 92.38 kJ at 298 K. The internal energy change ΔU at 298 K is [AIIMS]
(a) – 92.38 kJ (b) – 87.42 kJ (c) –97.34 kJ (d) – 89.9 kJ

78 A cylinder of gas supplied by Bharat petroleum is assumed to contain 14 kg of butane. If a normal family requires 20,000 kJ of energy per day for cooking, butane gas in the cylinder would last for ... days.
(ΔH_c of $C_4H_{10} = -2658$ kJ per mol) [BHU]
(a) 15 days (b) 20 days
(c) 32 days (d) 40 days

79 Calculate ΔH (in J) for, $C_{(\text{graphite})} \longrightarrow C_{(\text{diamond})}$ from the following data [J&K CET]
$C_{(\text{graphite})} + O_2(g) \longrightarrow CO_2(g); \Delta H = -393.5 \text{ kJ}$
$C_{(\text{diamond})} + O_2(g) \longrightarrow CO_2(g); \Delta H = -395.4 \text{ kJ}$
(a) 1900 (b) -788.9×10^3
(c) 190000 (d) $+788.9 \times 10^3$

80 In which of the following reactions, the heat liberated is known as 'heat of combustion'? [J&K CET]
(a) $H^+(aq) + OH^-(aq) \longrightarrow H_2O(l) + \text{Heat}$
(b) $C_{(\text{graphite})} + \frac{1}{2}O_2(g) \longrightarrow CO(g) + \text{Heat}$
(c) $CH_4(g) + 2O_2(g) \longrightarrow CO_2(g) + 2H_2O(l) + \text{Heat}$
(d) $H_2SO_4(aq) + H_2O(l) \longrightarrow H_2SO_4(aq) + \text{Heat}$

81 $\Delta E°$ of combustion of isobutylene is $-X \text{ kJ mol}^{-1}$. The value of $\Delta H°$ is [AMU]
(a) $= \Delta E°$ (b) $> \Delta E°$ (c) $= 0$ (d) $< \Delta E°$

82 For $CaCO_3(s) \rightleftharpoons CaO(s) + CO_2(g)$ at 927°C, $\Delta H = 176$ kJ/mol; then ΔE is [BCECE]
(a) 180 kJ (b) 186.4 kJ (c) 166.0 kJ (d) 160 kJ

83 $S + \frac{3}{2}O_2 \longrightarrow SO_3; \quad \Delta H = 2x,$
$SO_2 + \frac{1}{2}O_2 \longrightarrow SO_3; \quad \Delta H = y,$
then heat of formation of SO_2 is [JCECE]
(a) $2x - y$ (b) $2x + y$ (c) $x + y$ (d) $\frac{2x - y}{2}$

2005

84 The absolute enthalpy of neutralisation of the reaction,
$MgO(s) + 2HCl(aq) \longrightarrow MgCl_2(aq) + H_2O(l)$
will be [CBSE AIPMT]
(a) less than $-57.33 \text{ kJ mol}^{-1}$
(b) $-57.33 \text{ kJ mol}^{-1}$
(c) greater than $-57.33 \text{ kJ mol}^{-1}$
(d) $57.33 \text{ kJ mol}^{-1}$

85 ΔH_f° (298 K) of methanol is given by the chemical equation, **[AIIMS]**

(a) $CH_4(g)+\frac{1}{2}O_2(g) \longrightarrow CH_3OH(g)$

(b) $C_{(graphite)}+\frac{1}{2}O_2(g)+2H_2(g) \longrightarrow CH_3OH(l)$

(c) $C_{(diamond)}+\frac{1}{2}O_2(g)+2H_2(g) \longrightarrow CH_3OH(l)$

(d) $CO(g)+2H_2(g) \longrightarrow CH_3OH(l)$

86 Heat of formation of SO_2 is –298 kJ. What is the heat of combustion of 4 g of S? **[MHT CET]**

(a) + 37 kJ (b) – 37.25 kJ
(c) + 298 kJ (d) 18.6 kJ

87 Heat required to raise the temperature of 1 mole of a substance by 1°C is called **[Manipal]**

(a) specific heat
(b) water equivalent
(c) specific gravity
(d) molar heat capacity

88 The standard enthalpy of formation, ΔH_f° of hypothetical $CaCl(s)$ theoretically found to be –188 kJ mol^{-1} and that of $CaCl_2(s)$ –795 kJ mol^{-1}.

Calculate the value of standard heat of reaction for the following disproportionation reaction.

$2CaCl(s) \longrightarrow CaCl_2(s)+Ca(s)$ **[Kerala CEE]**

(a) – 435 kJ mol^{-1} (b) + 435 kJ mol^{-1}
(c) – 419 kJ mol^{-1} (d) + 419 kJ mol^{-1}
(e) None of the above

89 The enthalpy of the formation of $H_2O(l)$ is –285.77 kJ mol^{-1} and enthalpy of neutralisation of a strong acid and strong base is – 56.07 kJ mol^{-1}. What is the enthalpy of formation of OH^- ion? **[Kerala CEE]**

(a) – 229.70 kJ (b) + 229.70 kJ
(c) + 350.75 kJ (d) – 350.75 kJ
(e) None of these

90 If the value of C_p for nitrogen gas is 7 $JK^{-1}mol^{-1}$, then the value of ΔH on heating 28 g of nitrogen gas from 0°C to 100°C at constant pressure will be **[AMU]**

(a) 1200 J (b) 1300 J (c) 1400 J (d) 1500 J

91 The heat of neutralisation of any strong acid and a strong base is nearly equal to **[BCECE]**

(a) – 75.3 kJ (b) + 57.3 kJ
(c) – 57.3 kJ (d) + 75.3 kJ

92 Given the following thermochemical equations,

$$Zn+\frac{1}{2}O_2 \longrightarrow ZnO+84000 \text{ cal}$$

$$Hg+\frac{1}{2}O_2 \longrightarrow HgO+21700 \text{ cal}$$

Accordingly the heat of reaction for the following reaction, $Zn + HgO \longrightarrow ZnO + Hg + \text{Heat}$ is **[JCECE]**

(a) 105700 cal (b) 61000 cal
(c) 105000 cal (d) 62300 cal

93 Which of the following is not an endothermic reaction? **[J&K CET]**

(a) Dehydrogenation
(b) Ethane to ethene
(c) Combustion of propane
(d) Change of chlorine molecule into chlorine atoms

Answers

1 (c)	2 (d)	3 (a)	4 (d)	5 (d)	6 (b)	7 (b)	8 (b)	9 (e)	10 (a)
11 (b)	12 (a)	13 (b)	14 (b)	15 (b)	16 (c)	17 (a)	18 (a)	19 (d)	20 (b)
21 (a)	22 (b)	23 (d)	24 (d)	25 (a)	26 (a)	27 (d)	28 (d)	29 (b)	30 (a)
31 (b)	32 (a)	33 (c)	34 (d)	35 (b)	36 (b)	37 (b)	38 (a)	39 (d)	40 (a)
41 (b)	42 (c)	43 (d)	44 (c)	45 (c)	46 (c)	47 (d)	48 (a)	49 (b)	50 (b)
51 (c)	52 (c)	53 (b)	54 (b)	55 (a)	56 (b)	57 (d)	58 (c)	59 (d)	60 (b)
61 (b)	62 (c)	63 (a)	64 (d)	65 (b)	66 (c)	67 (c)	68 (a)	69 (a)	70 (d)
71 (a)	72 (d)	73 (d)	74 (d)	75 (a)	76 (c)	77 (b)	78 (c)	79 (a)	80 (c)
81 (d)	82 (c)	83 (a)	84 (a)	85 (b)	86 (b)	87 (d)	88 (c)	89 (a)	90 (*)
91 (c)	92 (d)	93 (c)							

Explanations

1 (*c*) Given,

$$\frac{1}{2}H_2 + \frac{1}{2}Cl_2 \longrightarrow HCl,$$
$$\Delta H_f = -93 \text{ kJ/mol}$$

$\because$ In this reaction, one mole of HCl is formed

$\therefore \Delta H_f$ of the reaction will remain same, i.e. -93 kJ/mol

Let the bond dissociation energy of H — Cl bond be x.

For the given reaction,

$$\Delta H_f = \Sigma B.E_{(reactants)} - \Sigma B.E_{(products)}$$
$$-93 = \frac{1}{2}(434) + \frac{1}{2}(242) - x$$
$$-93 = +338 - x$$
$$x = 431 \text{ kJ/mol}$$

2 (*d*) For any chemical reaction,

$$\Delta H = \Delta E + \Delta n_g RT$$

Where, Δn_g = total number of moles of gaseous products – total number of moles of gaseous reactants

For the given reaction,

$$Fe_2O_3(s) + 3H_2(g) \rightarrow 2Fe(s) + H_2O(l)$$
$$\Delta n_g = 0 - 3 = -3$$
$$\therefore \quad \Delta H = \Delta E + (-3)RT$$
$$\Delta H = \Delta E - 3RT$$

3 (*a*) Relation between heat of reaction $(\Delta_r H)$ and bond energies (BE) of reactants and products is given by

$$\Delta_r H = \Sigma BE_{Reactants} - \Sigma BE_{Products}$$

The reaction of formation for XY is

$$\frac{1}{2}X_2(g) + \frac{1}{2}Y_2(g) \longrightarrow XY(g);$$
$$\Delta H = -200 \text{ kJ mol}^{-1}$$

Given, the bond dissociation energies of X_2, Y_2 and XY are in the ratio 1 : 0.5 : 1. Let the bond dissociation energies of X_2, Y_2 and XY are a kJ mol^{-1}, $0.5a$ kJ mol^{-1} and a kJ mol^{-1}, respectively.

$$\therefore \quad \Delta_r H = \Sigma BE_{Reactants} - \Delta BE_{Products}$$
$$= \left[\frac{1}{2} \times a + \frac{1}{2} \times 0.5a\right] - [1 \times a]$$
$$-200 = \frac{a}{2} + \frac{a}{4} - a$$
$$-200 = \frac{2a + a - 4a}{4} = \frac{-a}{4}$$
$$a = 800 \text{ kJ mol}^{-1}$$

$\therefore$ The bond dissociation energy of

$$X_2 = a \text{kJ mol}^{-1} = 800 \text{ kJ mol}^{-1}$$

4 (*d*) $C + O_2 \rightarrow CO_2; \Delta H = -490 \text{ J}$ ...(i)

$$H_2 + \frac{1}{2}O_2 \rightarrow H_2O; \Delta H = -240 \text{ J} \text{ ...(ii)}$$
$$8C + 9H_2 \rightarrow C_8H_{18}; \Delta H = -160 \text{ J...(iii)}$$

On applying, 8 × Eq. (i) + 9 × Eq. (ii) – Eq. (iii), we get

$$C_8H_{18} + \frac{25}{2}O_2 \longrightarrow 8CO_2 + 9H_2O$$
$$\Delta H_R^0 = [8 \times (-490)] + [9 \times (-240)] + 160$$
$$= -5920 \text{ J mol}^{-1}$$

Hence, energy released when 6 moles of octane is burnt in air is

$$= -5920 \times 6 = -35520 \text{ J} = -35.5 \text{ kJ}$$

5 (*d*) For the reaction,

$$CH_2 = CH_2 + H_2 \longrightarrow CH_3 — CH_3$$
$$\Delta H_R = \Sigma(BE)_{Reactants} - \Sigma(BE)_{Products}$$
$$= [4(BE)_{C—H} + (BE)_{C=C} + (BE)_{H—H}]$$
$$- [6(BE)_{C—H} + (BE)_{C—C}]$$
$$= [4 \times 414 + 615 + 435]$$
$$- [6 \times 414 + 347]$$
$$= [2706 - 2831] \Rightarrow -125 \text{ kJ}$$

6 (*b*) I. $H_2(g) + \frac{1}{2}O_2(g) \rightarrow H_2O(l);$

$$\Delta_{comb} H = -286 \text{ kJ}$$

II. $\underset{18 g}{H_2O(s)} \longrightarrow H_2O(l); \quad \Delta_{fus} H = +6 \text{ kJ}$

On subtracting (II) from (I)

$$H_2(g) + \frac{1}{2}O_2(g) \longrightarrow H_2O(s);$$
$$\Delta H = -286 - 6 = -292 \text{ kJ}$$

$\because$ On formation of 18 g ice, change in enthalpy = –292 kJ

$\therefore$ On formation of 100 g ice, change in enthalpy $= -\frac{292 \times 100}{18} = -1622.2$ kJ

$$= -1622 \text{ kJ}$$

7 (*b*) $\Delta H_{combustion} = -393.5$ kJ/mol,

molar mass of CO_2 = 44 g

i.e. 1 mole of CO_2 on combustion releases = –393.5 kJ

$\frac{35.2}{44}$ mole of CO_2 will release

$$= -\frac{393.5 \times 35.2}{44} = -314.8 \text{ kJ}$$

8 (*b*) $C_{12}H_{22}O_{11} + 12O_2 \rightarrow 12CO_2 + 11H_2O$

12 mole$(12 \times 32 \text{ g})$ = 384 g of oxygen requires 1 mole of sucrose 342 g

Hence, 640 g of O_2 requires $\left(\frac{342}{384} \times 640 \text{g}\right)$ 570 g of sucrose.

640 g O_2= 20 mole O_2 will require $\frac{20}{12}$ mole sucrose.

$$\Delta H \text{ evolved} = -5645 \times \frac{20}{12}$$
$$= -9408.33 \text{ kJ}$$

9 (*e*) $2O_2 + CH_4(g) \rightarrow CO_2(g) + 2H_2O(l)$

$$\Delta H_{combustion} = H_{f(CO_2)} + 2 \times H_{f(H_2O)} - H_{f(CH_4)}$$
$$= -393.5 + 2 \times -285.5 - (-74.8)$$
$$= -889.7 \text{ kJ/mol or} \approx -890.3 \text{ kJ mol}^{-1}$$

10 (*a*) Enthalpy of sublimation of $N_2O_5(s)$ is 53 kJ/mol.

$\Delta H_{reaction} = -110$ kJ for 2 mole of $N_2O_5(g)$

Hence, for $2N_2O_5(g) \longrightarrow 2N_2O_5(s)$

$$\Delta H_{sublimation} = -53 \times 2 = -106 \text{ kJ},$$
$$\Delta H = -110 - 106 = -216 \text{ kJ}$$

11 (*b*) $\Delta H = -nC_p\Delta T$

$$= -2 \times \frac{5}{2}R(225 - 125)$$
$$= -5R(100) = -500R$$

12 (*a*) Given,

$$C + O_2 \longrightarrow CO_2; \Delta H° = -x \text{ kJ} \quad \text{...(i)}$$
$$2CO + O_2 \longrightarrow 2CO_2; \quad \Delta H° = -y \text{ kJ} \quad \text{...(ii)}$$

Required equation is

$$C + \frac{1}{2}O_2 \longrightarrow CO; \Delta H_1° = ?$$

On reversing Eq (ii), we get

$$2CO_2 \longrightarrow 2CO + O_2; \quad \Delta H° = +y \text{ kJ} \text{ ....(iii)}$$

On dividing Eq (iii) by 2 gives

$$CO_2 \longrightarrow CO + \frac{1}{2}O_2; H_3° = \frac{y}{2} \text{kJ ...(iv)}$$

On adding Eqs (i) and (iv), we get (required equation)

$$C + \frac{1}{2}O_2 \longrightarrow CO; \Delta H_1° = \Delta H° + \Delta H_3°$$
$$= \left(-x + \frac{y}{2}\right) = \frac{y - 2x}{2} \text{ kJ}$$

13 (*b*) Number of moles of 1 kg coke

$$= \frac{1000}{12} = 83.33 \text{ mol}$$

(*i*) For the combustion of 1 kg of coke

$C + O_2 \longrightarrow CO_2;\ \Delta H = 393.5\,kJ$

Heat liberated from 1 mole coke

$= 393.5\,kJ$

$\therefore$ Heat liberated from 83.33 mol coke

$(H_1) = (393.5 \times 83.33)\,kJ$

(*ii*) For the burning of water gas

$C + H_2O \longrightarrow \underset{\text{Water gas}}{CO + H_2}$

$CO + H_2 + O_2 \longrightarrow CO_2 + H_2O$

$\Delta H = 285 + 285 = 570\,kJ$

$\therefore$ Heat liberated from burning of water gas $(H_2) = (570 \times 83.33)\,kJ$

Required ratio $= H_1 : H_2$

$= 393.5 : 570$

$= 0.69 : 1$

14 (*b*) $N_2(g) + O_2(g) \rightleftharpoons 2NO(g)$

We know that, $\Delta H = \Delta U + \Delta n_g RT$

Δn_g = change in gaseous moles

$= 2 - 2 = 0$

$\Delta H = \Delta U + 0 \times RT$

$\Delta H = \Delta U$

Reason that all reactants and products are in gaseous state is also true but Reason is not the correct explanation of Assertion.

15 (*b*) $C_{10}H_8(s) + 12O_2(g) \longrightarrow 10CO_2(g) + 4H_2O(l)$

We know that, $\Delta H = \Delta U + \Delta n_g RT$

$\Delta n_g = 10 - 12 = -2,$

$T = 298K,\ R = 2$ cal

$\Delta H = -1228.2 \times 10^3 + (-2)(2)298$

$= -1229392$ cal

or $= -1229.392$ kcal ~ 1229.3 kcal

16 (*c*) Write the chemical reaction and then use the formula

$\Delta H = \Sigma_{f(P)}H - \Sigma_{f(R)}H$

$3C_2H_2(g) \longrightarrow C_6H_6(g);$

$\Delta H = \Sigma_{f(P)}H - \Sigma_{f(R)}H$

Given, H_f of $C_2H_2 = 230$ kJ/mol

H_f of $C_6H_6 = 85$ kJ/mol

$\Delta H = \Sigma_{f(P)}H - \Sigma_{f(R)}H$

$= 85 - (3 \times 230)$

$= -605$ kJ/mol.

17 (*a*) $\Delta n_g = 2 - (3 + 1) = -2$

$\Delta H = \Delta E + \Delta n_g RT$

$= \Delta E - 2RT,\ \Delta H < \Delta E$

18 (*a*) The required reaction is

$C(s) + \frac{1}{2}O_2(g) \longrightarrow CO(g)$

Given, $CO_2(g) \longrightarrow CO(g) + \frac{1}{2}O_2(g);$

$\Delta H = \frac{+135.2}{2}$ kcal ...(i)

$C(s) + O_2(g) \longrightarrow CO_2(g);$

$\Delta H = -94$ kcal ...(ii)

The required equation can be achieved by adding Eq. (i) and (ii).

So, $\Delta H_{f(CO)} = -94 + \frac{135.2}{2}$

$= -26.4$ kcal

19 (*d*) For the decomposition of 9 g of water, heat required = 142.5 kJ

It is known that the molecular weight of H_2O = 18 g/mol

Therefore, heat required for decomposition of 18 g of water

$= \frac{18}{9} \times 142.5 = +285\,kJ$

Therefore, enthalpy of formation of water = + 285 kJ

20 (*b*) The enthalpy of combustion of $C_6H_6(l) = -3250$ kJ

Molecular weight of benzene

= 78 g/mol

On burning, 0.39 g of C_6H_6 liberated heat $= \frac{0.39}{78} \times 3250 = 16.25$ kJ

21 (*a*) $H_2O(l) \xrightarrow{100°C} H_2O(g)$

$\Delta_{vap}H° = \Delta_{vap}U° + \Delta n_g RT$

For above reaction, $\Delta n_g = 1 - 0 = 1$

$\because \quad \Delta H = \Delta U + \Delta n_g RT$

$\therefore \quad 40.66\,kJmol^{-1} = \Delta_{vap}U° + 1 \times 8.314 \times 10^{-3} \times 373$

$\Delta_{vap}E° = 40.66\,kJ\,mol^{-1} - 3.1\,kJ\,mol^{-1}$

$= +37.56$ kJ/mol

22 (*b*) $BaCl_2(s) + (aq) \longrightarrow BaCl_2(aq);$

$\Delta H = -20.6$ kJ ...(i)

$BaCl_2 \cdot 2H_2O(s) + (aq) \longrightarrow BaCl_2(aq);$

$\Delta H = +8.8$ kJ ...(ii)

Eq. (i) can be split into two steps as,

$BaCl_2(s) + 2H_2O(l) \longrightarrow BaCl_2 \cdot 2H_2O(s);\ \Delta H = \Delta H_1$

$BaCl_2 \cdot 2H_2O(s) + (aq) \longrightarrow BaCl_2(aq);\ \Delta H = \Delta H_2$

$\Delta H_1 + \Delta H_2 = -20.6$

$\Delta H_1 + 8.8 = -20.6$

$\Delta H_1 = -29.4$ kJ

23 (*d*) $X_2 + Y_2 \longrightarrow 2XY$

$\Delta H = (BE)_{x-x} + (BE)_{y-y} - 2(BE)_{x-y}$

If BE of $(x — y) = a,$

then BE of $(x — x) = a$

and BE of $(y — y) = \frac{a}{2}$

$\Delta H_f(x — y) = -200$ kJ

$\therefore -400$ kJ (for 2 moles of xy)

$\Rightarrow -400 = -\frac{a}{2}$ or $a = +800$ kJ

The bond dissociation energy of $x_2 = 800$ kJ/mol

24 (*d*) The dissociation energy of H—H bond is $\frac{869.5}{2} = 434.75\,kJ \sim 434.8\,kJ$

25 (*a*) I. $NaCl(s) \longrightarrow Na^+(aq) + Cl^-(aq);$

$\Delta H_1 = 4\,kJ\,mol^{-1}$

II. $Na^+(g) + Cl^-(g) + aq \longrightarrow Na^+(aq) + Cl^-(aq);$

$\Delta H_2 = -784\,kJ\,mol^{-1}$

On subtracting Eq. (ii) from Eq. (i),

$NaCl(s) \longrightarrow Na^+(g) + Cl^-(g)$

$= 788\,kJ\,mol^{-1}$

26 (*a*) $C(s) + O_2(g) \longrightarrow CO_2(g)$

Number of moles of C(*s*) $= \frac{4}{12}$ moles

$\Delta H = C_V dT$

$= 30 \times 4 \times 3\,kJ\,mol^{-1} = 360\,kJ\,mol^{-1}$

Combustion reactions are exothermic in nature.

27 (*d*)

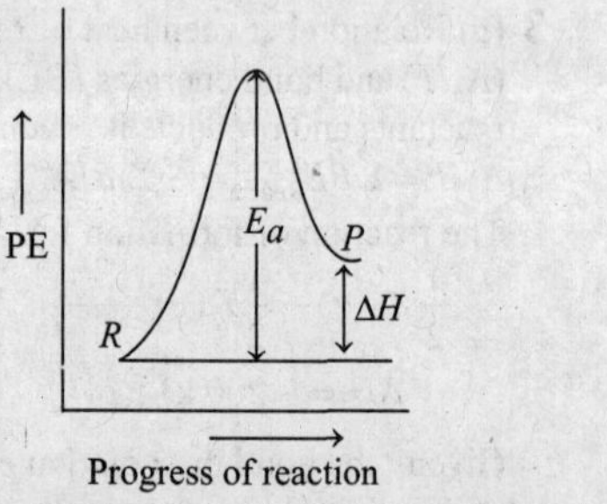

PE

E_a

P

R

ΔH

Progress of reaction

Therefore, minimum value of E_a will be more than ΔH.

28 (*d*) I. $NH_3(g) + 3Cl_2(g) \rightleftharpoons NCl_3(g) + 3HCl(g), -\Delta H_1$ ...(i)

II. $N_2(g) + 3H_2(g) \rightleftharpoons 2NH_3(g),$

$-\Delta H_2$ ...(ii)

III. $H_2(g) + Cl_2(g) \rightleftharpoons 2HCl(g),$

ΔH_3 ...(iii)

On multiplying Eq. (iii) by 3, we get

$3H_2(g) + 3Cl_2(g) \rightleftharpoons 6HCl(g);$

$3 \times \Delta H_3$ ...(iv)

On inverting Eq. (iv), we get

$6HCl(g) \rightleftharpoons 3H_2(g) + 3Cl_2(g);$

$-3 \times \Delta H_3$ ...(v)

On multiplying Eq. (i) with 2, we get

$$2NH_3 + 6Cl_2 \rightleftharpoons 2NCl_3 + 6HCl; \quad -2\times\Delta H_1 \quad ...(vi)$$

On adding Eq. (ii), (v) and (vi), we get

$$N_2 + 3Cl_2 \rightleftharpoons 2NCl_3;$$

$$\Delta H_r = -\Delta H_2 - 3\times\Delta H_3 - 2\times\Delta H_1$$

$$\therefore \Delta H_f = \frac{\Delta H_r}{2} = -\frac{\Delta H_2}{2} - \frac{3}{2}\Delta H_3 - \Delta H_1$$

$$= -\Delta H_1 - \frac{\Delta H_2}{2} - \frac{3}{2}\Delta H_3$$

29 (*b*) Heat capacity,

$$C_V = 18.94 \times 0.998 \times 10^3$$

$$= 18.902 \times 10^3 \text{ cal/deg}$$

$$\text{Moles of benzoic acid} = \frac{1.89}{122}$$

$$C_p = C_V + R = 18.902 \times 10^3 + 2$$

$$= 18904 \text{ cal/deg}$$

$$\text{Heat of combustion} = \frac{C_p \times \Delta t}{\text{moles}}$$

$$= \frac{18904 \times 0.632 \times 122}{1.89}$$

$$= 771.203 \times 10^3 \text{ cal} = 771.2 \text{ kcal}$$

30 (*a*) $CH_4 + 2O_2 \longrightarrow CO_2 + 2H_2O$

$$\Delta H_{\text{comb}} = (\Delta H_{f_{CO_2}} + 2\times\Delta_{f_{H_2O}}) - (\Delta H_{f_{CH_4}} + 2\times\Delta H_{f_{O_2}})$$

$$= [-94.0 + 2\times(-68.4) - (-18.4 + 0)]$$

$$= -212.4 \text{ kcal}$$

31 (*b*) In case of weak acids, some of the heat evolved during neutralisation reaction is utilised to completely ionise the weak acid. Thus, less heat is evolved. Hence, lower the value of heat of neutralisation, weaker is the acid. Thus, *B* is the weakest acid.

32 (*a*) $H_2C{=}CH_2 + H{-}H \longrightarrow H_3C{-}CH_3$

$$\Delta H_{\text{reaction}} = \Sigma BE_{(\text{reactants})} - \Sigma BE_{(\text{products})}$$

$$= [BE\,(4C{-}H) + BE\,(C{=}C) + BE\,(H{-}H)] - [BE\,(6C{-}H) + BE\,(C{-}C)]$$

$$= BE\,(C{=}C) + BE\,(H{-}H) - BE\,(2C{-}H) - BE\,(C{-}C)$$

$$= 600 + 400 - 2\times 410 - 350$$

$$= 1000 - 1170 = -170 \text{ kJ mol}^{-1}$$

33 (*c*) The reaction for the formation of water is as,

$$H_2 + \frac{1}{2}O_2 \longrightarrow H_2O; \quad \Delta H = 260 \text{ kJ} \quad ...(i)$$

Reversing Eq. (i)

$$\underset{1\text{ mol}}{H_2O} \longrightarrow H_2 + \frac{1}{2}O_2; \quad \Delta H = -260 \text{ kJ} \quad ...(ii)$$

$\because$ By 260 kJ of heat, water decomposed $= 1$ mol

$\therefore$ 130 kJ of heat will decompose water

$$= \frac{1\times 130}{260} = 0.5 \text{ mol}$$

34 (*d*) We know that,

$$\Delta H = \Delta E + \Delta n_g RT$$

$$H_2 - H_1 = E_2 - E_1 + (n_2RT - n_1RT)$$

$$\text{or } H_2 - H_1 - E_2 + E_1 = n_2RT - n_1RT$$

35 (*b*) The correct reaction for the formation of NaCl is,

$$Na(s) + \frac{1}{2}Cl_2(g) \longrightarrow NaCl(s)$$

(As the compound is formed from their elements when they are present in their most stable form)

36 (*b*) $C_2H_4(g) + 3O_2(g) \longrightarrow 2CO_2(g) + 2H_2O(g)$

Given, $\Delta_f H^\circ_{(CO_2)} = -393.5 \text{ kJ mol}^{-1}$

$\Delta_f H^\circ_{(H_2O)} = -241.8 \text{ kJ mol}^{-1}$

$\Delta_f H^\circ_{(C_2H_4)} = +52.3 \text{ kJ mol}^{-1}$

$\Delta_r H^\circ$ = [sum of $\Delta_f H^\circ$ values of products] − [sum of $\Delta_f H^\circ$ values of reactants]

$$= [2\times\Delta_f H^\circ_{(CO_2)} + 2\times\Delta_f H^\circ_{(H_2O)}] - [\Delta_f H^\circ_{(C_2H_4)} + 3\times\Delta_f H^\circ_{(O_2)}]$$

$$= [2\times(-393.5) + 2\times(-241.8)] - [(52.3) + 0]$$

($\because$ $\Delta_f H^\circ$ for elementary substance = 0)

$$= [-787.0 - 483.6] - 52.3$$

$$= -1322.9 \text{ kJ mol}^{-1}$$

37 (*b*) Thermodynamically, the most stable form of carbon is graphite.

38 (*a*)

	HCl +	NaOH ⟶	NaCl +	H_2O
Initial moles =	$\frac{500\times 0.1}{1000}$ = 0.05	$\frac{200\times 0.2}{1000}$ = 0.04	0	0
Final moles	0.05 − 0.04 = 0.01	0	0.04	0.04

$\because$ In neutralisation of 1 mole of NaOH by 1 mole HCl, heat evolved = 57.1 kJ

$\therefore$ To neutralise 0.04 mole of NaOH by 0.04 mole of HCl, heat evolved will be

$$= 57.1 \times 0.04$$

$$= 2.284 \sim 2.292 \text{ kJ}$$

39 (*d*) Heat of neutralisation of strong acid by strong base is always greater than the heat of neutralisation of weak acid or weak base because some energy is used to completely ionise weak acid or weak base.

(a) NH_4OH-CH_3COOH — Weak base – Weak acid

(b) HNO_3-NH_4OH — Strong acid – Weak base

(c) NaOH-CH_3COOH — Strong base – Weak acid

(d) HCl-NaOH — Strong acid – Strong base

$\because$ HCl is a strong acid and NaOH is a strong base.

$\therefore$ Their heat of neutralisation will be highest among the given.

40 (*a*) Bomb calorimeter is commonly used to find the heat of combustion of organic substances which consist of a sealed combustion chamber called a bomb. If a process is run in a sealed container then no expansion or compression is allowed, so, $W = 0$ and $\Delta E = q$. Thus, it has $\Delta E < 0, W = 0$.

41 (*b*) Given,

$$CH_4 + 2O_2 \longrightarrow CO_2 + 2H_2O; \quad \Delta H = -210 \text{ kcal/mol} \quad ...(i)$$

$$C_2H_6 + \frac{7}{2}O_2 \longrightarrow 2CO_2 + 3H_2O; \quad \Delta H = -368 \text{ kcal/mol} \quad ...(ii)$$

On subtracting Eq. (i) from Eq. (ii), we get

$$CH_2 + \frac{3}{2}O_2 \longrightarrow CO_2 + H_2O; \quad \Delta H = -158 \text{ kcal/mol} \quad ...(iii)$$

$\therefore$ Enthalpy of combustion of one CH_2 unit = −158 kcal/mol

$$\Delta H_{\text{comb}}(C_{10}H_{22}) = \Delta H_{\text{comb}}(CH_4) + 9\times\Delta H_{\text{comb}}(CH_2)$$

$$= -210 + (9\times -158)$$

$$= -1632 \text{ kcal}$$

42 (c) $\Delta H = \Delta U + \Delta n_g RT$

For the reaction,

$$CO(g) + \frac{1}{2} O_2(g) \longrightarrow CO_2(g)$$

$$\Delta n_g = 1 - 1\frac{1}{2} = -\frac{1}{2}$$

$$\therefore \Delta H - \Delta U = -\frac{1}{2} \times 8.314 \times 300$$

$$= -1247.1 \text{ or } = -1.247 \text{ kJ}$$

43 (d) I. $C(s) + \frac{1}{2} O_2(g) \longrightarrow CO(g);$ $\Delta H_1 = a$

II. $CO(g) + \frac{1}{2} O_2(g) \longrightarrow CO_2(g);$ $\Delta H_2 = b$

III. $C(s) + CO_2(g) \longrightarrow 2CO(g);$ $\Delta H_3 = c$

On adding Eqs. I and II,

$C(s) + O_2(g) \longrightarrow CO_2(g);$

$\Delta H = \Delta H_1 + \Delta H_2 = a + b$

$\therefore$ Heat of formation of $CO_2 = a + b$ and heat of combustion of $C = a + b$

On subtracting Eq. II from Eq. I, we get

$C(s) + CO_2(g) \longrightarrow 2CO(g);$

$\Delta H_3 = \Delta H_1 - \Delta H_2$

44 (c) $\underset{16\text{ g}}{CH_4} + 2O_2 \longrightarrow CO_2 + 2H_2O;$

$\Delta H_c = -800$ kJ

$\because$ Heat of combustion of 16×10^{-3} kg of $CH_4 = -800$ kJ

$\therefore$ Heat of combustion of 4×10^{-4} kg of CH_4 will be

$$= -\frac{800 \times 4 \times 10^{-4}}{16 \times 10^{-3}} = -20 \text{ kJ}$$

45 (c) Equation given in option (a) is Arrhenius equation, in option (b) is Clausius-Clapeyron equation, in option (c) is Kirchhoff's equation, in option (d) is van't Hoff equation.

46 (c) $\Delta H = \Delta U + \Delta n_g RT$

or $\Delta U = \Delta H - \Delta n_g RT$

$$\Delta n_g = \frac{1}{2}$$

$$\Rightarrow \quad \Delta U = 7.3 \times 10^3 - \frac{1}{2} \times 2 \times 298$$

$$= 7300 \text{ cal} - 298$$

$$= 7002 \text{ cal} \approx 7.002 \text{ kcal}$$

47 (d) The given reaction is

$$CH_3OH + H_2 \longrightarrow CH_4 + H_2O$$

$$\Delta H = \Sigma \Delta H_f^\circ(\text{products}) - \Sigma \Delta H_f^\circ(\text{reactants})$$

$$\Delta H = \Delta_f H^\circ_{(CH_4)} + \Delta_f H^\circ_{(H_2O)} - \Delta_f H^\circ_{(CH_3OH)} - \Delta_f H^\circ_{(H_2)}$$

$$= (-242 - 76) - (-266 + 0)$$

$$= -52 \text{ kJ}$$

48 (a) For PH_3, P—H bond energy

$$= \frac{\text{heat of atomisation of } PH_3}{3}$$

$$= \frac{953 \text{ kJ mol}^{-1}}{3} = 317.67 \text{ kJ mol}^{-1}$$

For P_2H_4,

Heat of atomisation

= P—P bond energy + 4 × P—H bond energy

$\therefore$ P—P bond energy

= 1485 – (4 × 317.67)

= 214.3 kJ mol^{-1} ≈ 213 kJ mol^{-1}

49 (b) By equal volumes of molar HCl and H_2SO_4, the ratio of H^+ ions furnished = 1 : 2

$\therefore$ Ratio of heat liberated $= x : \frac{y}{2}$

$$\Rightarrow \quad x = \frac{y}{2}.$$

50 (b) Enthalpy of combustion, lattice enthalpy and enthalpy of neutralisation are exothermic, i.e. – ve while enthalpy of formation may be + ve or –ve.

51 (c) Number of equivalents of a weak acid $= \frac{400}{1000} \times 0.2 = 0.08$

So, amount of heat liberated per equivalent $= \frac{-4.4}{0.08} = -55$ kJ

52 (c) Given, $\Delta H_f(H) = 218$ kJ/mol,

i.e. $\frac{1}{2} H_2 \longrightarrow H;$

or $\Delta H\,(2H) = 436$ kJ/mol

$$= \frac{436}{4.18} = 104.3 \text{ kcal/mol}$$

$$\sim 104 \text{ kcal/mol}$$

Thus, 104 kcal/mol energy is absorbed for breaking one mole of H—H bonds.

Hence, H—H bond energy is 104 kcal/mol.

53 (b) By '$2I + \frac{III}{2} - II$', we get

$$Na_2O + SO_3 \longrightarrow Na_2SO_4;$$

$$\Delta H = -2 \times 146 + \frac{259}{2} - 418$$

or $\Delta H = -580.5 \approx -581$ kJ

54 (b) The enthalpy of neutralisation of strong acid and strong base

= – 13.7 kcal equiv.$^{-1}$

As two equivalents of oxalic acid are neutralised

= – 13.7 × 2

= – 27.4 kcal mol^{-1}

Enthalpy of neutralisation of oxalic acid

= – 25 kcal mol^{-1}

$\therefore$ Enthalpy of dissociation

= – 25 – (–27.4) = 2.4 kcal mol^{-1}

or ≈ 2.0 kcal mol^{-1}

55 (a) Activation energy is the additional amount of energy needed to overcome the potential barrier of reaction.

Hence, $E_a = \Delta U$.

56 (b) The amount of heat absorbed or evolved when 1 mole of the substance is directly obtained from its constituent elements is called heat or enthalpy of formation.

The reaction for the formation of NH_3 is

$$\frac{1}{2} N_2 + \frac{3}{2} H_2 \longrightarrow NH_3;$$

$$\Delta H = -46 \text{ kJ mol}^{-1}$$

Heat of formation of NH_3

= – 46 kJ mol^{-1}

The enthalpy change for the given reaction,

$$2NH_3(g) \longrightarrow N_2(g) + 3H_2(g);$$

$$\Delta H_1 = ?$$

$$\Delta H_1 = -(2 \times \Delta H)$$

$$= -(2 \times -46) = 92 \text{ kJ}$$

57 (d) I. $C + O_2 \longrightarrow CO_2;$ $\Delta H = -x$ kJ

II. $H_2 + \frac{1}{2} O_2 \longrightarrow H_2O;$ $\Delta H = -y$ kJ

III. $CH_4 + 2O_2 \longrightarrow CO_2 + 2H_2O;$ $\Delta H = -z$ kJ

Multiply Eq. II by 2, adding to Eq. I and then, subtract Eq. III from the sum,

$$C + 2H_2 \longrightarrow CH_4,$$

$$\Delta H = (-x - 2y + z) \text{ kJ}$$

58 (c) For the reaction,

$$2NH_3(g) \longrightarrow N_2(g) + 3H_2(g)$$

$$\Delta n_g = (3 + 1) - 2 = 2$$

$$\Delta H = \Delta E + \Delta n_g RT$$

$$= \Delta E + 2RT$$

$$\therefore \quad \Delta H > \Delta E$$

If the value of Δn_g is less than one, then $\Delta H < \Delta E$.

59 (*d*) $\Delta H \neq \Delta E$ for

$$CO(g)+\frac{1}{2}O_2(g) \longrightarrow CO_2(g)$$

as $\Delta n_g \neq 0$

60 (*b*) $C_2H_5OH(l) + 3O_2(g) \longrightarrow 2CO_2(g) + 3H_2O(l)$

$\Delta H = \Delta E + \Delta n_g RT$

$\Delta n = n_p - n_r = 2 - 3 = -1$

$\Delta H = \Delta E - RT$

61 (*b*) ΔH_f° is the enthalpy change when 1 mole of the substance is formed from its elements in the standard state. Hence, reaction (b) represents ΔH_f°.

62 (*c*) $C_6H_5COOH(s)+\frac{15}{2}O_2(g) \longrightarrow 7CO_2(g) + 3H_2O(l)$

$\Delta n_g = n_p - n_r = 7-\frac{15}{2} = \frac{-1}{2}$

$\Rightarrow \quad q_p = q_V + \Delta n_g(RT)$

$= -321.30+\left(-\frac{1}{2}\right)300R$

$= -321.30 - 150R$

63 (*a*) As the size of metal ion decreases, enthalpy of hydration increases. Among these, ionic radius is least for (a), thus its enthalpy of hydration is maximum.

64 (*d*) $C_{(graphite)} + 2H_2(g) \longrightarrow CH_4(g)$;

$\Delta H = -17900$ cal, $\Delta E = ?$

$\Delta n_g = 1-2 = -1$

$\because \quad \Delta H = \Delta E + \Delta n_g RT$

$\therefore \quad \Delta H = \Delta E - 1 \times R \times T$

$\Rightarrow -17900 = \Delta E - 1 \times 298 \times 2$

$\Delta E = -17900 + 596$

$= -17304$ cal

65 (*b*) Number of moles of HCl in 100 cm^3 solution

$= \frac{100}{1000} \times 0.1 = 0.01$ mol

Number of moles of NaOH in 100 cm^3 solution $= \frac{100}{1000} \times 0.1 = 0.01$ mol

$$NaOH + HCl \longrightarrow NaCl + H_2O$$

$\because$ When 0.01 mole of NaOH is neutralised by 0.01 mole of HCl, then heat liberated = $-Q$ kcal

$\therefore$ When 1 mole of NaOH are neutralised by 1 mole of HCl, the heat liberated, i.e. heat of neutralisation (ΔH)

$= -\frac{Q}{0.01} = -100\,Q$ kcal

66 (*c*) $\underset{1\text{ mol}}{NH_3(g)} + \underset{1\text{ mol}}{HCl(g)} \longrightarrow \underset{1\text{ mol}}{NH_4Cl(g)}$;

$\Delta H = \Delta U + \Delta n_g RT$

Δn_g = number of moles of products − number of moles of reactants

$= 1 - 2 = -1$

$\Delta H = \Delta U + \Delta n_g RT = \Delta U + (-1) \times RT$

$\Rightarrow \quad \Delta H = \Delta U - RT$

$\therefore \quad \Delta H < \Delta U$

67 (*c*) $CH_3OH(l)+\frac{3}{2}O_2(g) \longrightarrow CO_2(g) + 2H_2O(l);\ \Delta H = -723$ kJ

By burning with $\frac{3}{2}O_2(g)$ heat evolved

$= -723$ kJ

$\therefore$ By burning with 1 mole

$O_2(g) = \frac{-723 \times 2}{3} = -482$ kJ

68 (*a*) Combustion of methane is

$CH_4(g)+2O_2(g) \rightarrow CO_2(g)+2H_2O(l)$

The relation between ΔH and ΔE is

$\Delta H = \Delta E + \Delta n_g RT$

$\Delta n_g = n_p - n_r = 1 - 3 = -2$

$\Delta H = \Delta E - 2RT$

So, $\quad \Delta H < \Delta E$

Hence, reason is the correct explanation of assertion.

69 (*a*) The enthalpy of hydrogenation of cyclohexene (having one double bond) is -119.5 kJ mol^{-1}. Hence, theoretically enthalpy of hydrogenation of Kekule's structure of benzene should be $3 \times (-119.5)$ kJ mol^{-1}. Since, the resonance energy of benzene is -150.4 kJ mol^{-1}, the actual enthalpy of hydrogenation of benzene will be

$= [3 \times (-119.5) - (-150.4)]$

$= -208.1$ kJ mol^{-1}

70 (*d*) When all substances in a compound combine with oxygen and produces carbon dioxide and water, it is commonly called **burning**.

During combustion, substances reacts with oxidising agent such as O_2 and F_2. Not all combustion reactions release CO_2 and H_2O.

e.g. $Mg + O_2 \longrightarrow MgO + \text{Heat}$

Hence, all the gives reactions are combustion reactions.

71 (*a*) Heat of decomposition of water is

$$H_2O(g) \longrightarrow H_2(g)+\frac{1}{2}O_2(g),$$

$\Delta H = \frac{+573.2}{2} = 286.6$ kJ/mol

72 (*d*) **Bond enthalpy (bond energy)** It is amount of energy released when gaseous atoms combine to form one mole of bonds between them or heat absorbed when one mole of bonds between them are broken to give free gaseous atoms.

$\Delta_r H = \Sigma$ B.E.(Reactants) $- \Sigma$B.E.(Products)

73 (*d*) $\because$ 150 kJ of energy is required for muscular work to walk a distance of one km. (Given)

$\therefore$ 750 kJ energy is required for work to walk of 5 km distance.

Enthalpy of combustion of glucose is 3000 kJ/mol.

Glucose provides 30% energy of its mass., i.e.

$\frac{30}{100} \times 3000 = 900$ kJ/mol

$\therefore$ For 900 kJ of energy, weight of glucose required = 180 g

Thus, for 750 kJ of energy, weight of glucose required

$= \frac{180}{900} \times 750 = 150$ g

74 (*d*) Heat of combustion is usually measured by placing a known mass of a compound in a steel container called a constant volume bomb calorimeter.

$q_{reaction}$ (heat of reaction) $= C_V \Delta T = \Delta E$

75 (*a*) $CO(g)+\frac{1}{2}O_2(g) \longrightarrow CO_2(g)$

$\Delta H = \Delta U + \Delta n_g RT$

$\Delta n_g = 1-\left(1+\frac{1}{2}\right) = -\frac{1}{2}$

$\Delta H = -67710 - \frac{1}{2} \times 2 \times 290$

$= -68000$ cal

76 (*c*) $C_{(graphite)} + 2H_2(g) \longrightarrow CH_4(g)$

$\Delta H = \Delta E + \Delta n_g RT$

$\Delta E - \Delta H = -\Delta n_g RT$

$\Delta n_g = 1 - 2 = -1$

$\Delta E - \Delta H = -(-1) \times 2 \times 300$

$= 600$ cal or $= 0.6$ kcal

77 (*b*) $\Delta H = \Delta U + p\Delta V$

$\Delta H = \Delta U + \Delta n_g RT$

$\Delta U = \Delta H - \Delta n_g RT$

$= -92.38 - (-2)(8.314) \times 10^{-3} \times (298)$

$\Delta U = -92.38 + 4.955$

$= -87.385$ kJ ~ -87.4

78 (*c*) Calorific value of butane

$$= \frac{\Delta H_c}{\text{molecular weight}} = \frac{2658}{58} = 45.8 \text{ kJ/g}$$

Cylinder contains 14 kg of butane means 14000 g of butane.

$\because$ 1g gives = 45.8 kJ

$\therefore$ 14000 g gives

$$= 14000 \times 45.8 = 641200 \text{ kJ}$$

Family needs 20000 kJ/day

So, gas will fulfil the requirement for

$$\frac{641200}{20000} = 32.06 \text{ days} \sim 32 \text{ days}$$

79 (*a*) $C_{(graphite)} + O_2(g) \longrightarrow CO_2(g);$

$$\Delta H = -393.5 \text{ kJ} \quad \ldots\text{(i)}$$

$C_{(diamond)} + O_2(g) \longrightarrow CO_2(g);$

$$\Delta H = -395.4 \text{ kJ} \quad \ldots\text{(ii)}$$

$C_{(graphite)} \longrightarrow C_{(diamond)}; \Delta H = ?$

On subtracting the Eq. (ii) from Eq. (i)

$C_{(graphite)} \longrightarrow C_{(diamond)};$

$$\Delta H = -393.5 - (-395.4)$$
$$= 1.9 \text{ kJ} = 1900 \text{ J}$$

80 (*c*) When 1 mole of the substance is completely oxidised, the amount of heat which is evolved or absorbed is known as "heat of combustion."

e.g. $CH_4(g) + 2O_2(g) \longrightarrow CO_2(g) + 2H_2O(l) + \text{Heat}$

81 (*d*)

$$(CH_3)_2C{=}CH_2(g) + 6O_2(g) \longrightarrow 4CO_2(g) + 4H_2O(l)$$

$\Delta n_g = 4 - 7 = -3$ (i.e. negative)

It is known that, $\Delta H = \Delta E + \Delta n_g RT$

$= \Delta E - |\Delta n_g| RT \quad (\because \Delta n_g = -\text{ve})$

$\therefore \quad \Delta H < \Delta E$

or $\quad \Delta H° < \Delta E°$

82 (*c*) $CaCO_3(s) \longrightarrow CaO(s) + CO_2(g)$

$$(\Delta n_g = 1 - 0 = 1)$$

We know that, $\Delta H = \Delta E + \Delta n_g RT$

$176 = \Delta E + 1 \times 8.31 \times 10^{-3} \times (273 + 927)$

$\therefore \quad \Delta E = 176 - 8.31 \times 10^{-3} \times 1200$

$= 176 - 9.97$

$= 166.03 \text{ kJ} \sim 166 \text{ kJ}$

83 (*a*) Given, $S + \frac{3}{2}O_2 \longrightarrow SO_3;$

$$\Delta H = 2x \quad \ldots\text{(i)}$$

$$SO_2 + \frac{1}{2}O_2 \longrightarrow SO_3; \Delta H = y \ldots\text{(ii)}$$

On adding the Eq. (i) and reverse of Eq (ii)

$$S + \frac{3}{2}O_2 \longrightarrow SO_3 + 2x \quad \ldots\text{(i)}$$
$$SO_3 \longrightarrow SO_2 + \frac{1}{2}O_2 - y \ldots\text{(ii)}$$
$$S + O_2 \longrightarrow SO_2 + (2x - y) \ldots\text{(iii)}$$

So, heat of formation of SO_2 is $2x - y$.

84 (*a*) Heat of neutralisation of strong acid and strong base is –57.1 kJ. MgO is weak base while HCl is a strong acid, so the heat of neutralisation of MgO and HCl is lower than –57.1 kJ because MgO requires some heat in ionisation, then net released amount of heat is decreased.

85 (*b*) Heat of formation is defined as the heat released when one mole of a substance is formed from its constituent elements at STP. In case of allotropes, most stable allotrope is taken into account. Among graphite and diamond, graphite is more stable. Hence, heat of formation of CH_3OH is represented by equation,

$$C_{(graphite)} + \frac{1}{2}O_2(g) + 2H_2(g) \longrightarrow CH_3OH(l)$$

86 (*b*) $S + O_2 \longrightarrow SO_2; \Delta H = -298 \text{ kJ}$

Heat of formation of SO_2 is also the heat of combustion of sulphur.

$\because$ Heat of combustion of 32 g of S $= (-298)$ kJ

$\therefore$ Heat of combustion of 4 g of S

$$= \frac{(-298) \times 4}{32} = -37.25 \text{ kJ}$$

87 (*d*) The amount of heat required to raise the temperature of one mole of a substance through 1°C is called molar heat capacity.

$$C = \frac{q}{T_2 - T_1}$$

88 (*c*) A disproportionation reaction is that in which the same species (in this case, Ca^{2+}) is oxidised as well as reduced.

$$2CaCl(s) \longrightarrow CaCl_2(s) + Ca(s)$$

(Reduction: $2CaCl(s) \to Ca(s)$; Oxidation: $2CaCl(s) \to CaCl_2(s)$)

To determine standard heat of reaction,

$$\Delta H° = \Delta H_f°(\text{products}) - \Delta H_f°(\text{reactants})$$

$\Delta H_f°$ of element = 0

Thus, $\Delta H° = \Delta H_f°(CaCl_2) + \Delta H_f°(Ca) - 2\Delta H_f°(CaCl)$

$= (-795 + 0) - (-2 \times 188)$

$= -419 \text{ kJ mol}^{-1}$.

89 (*a*) $H^+(aq) + OH^-(aq) \longrightarrow H_2O(l);$

$$\Delta H = -56.07 \text{ kJ}$$

$\Delta H = [\Delta H_f(H_2O)] - [\Delta H_f(H^+) + \Delta H_f(OH^-)]$

$-56.07 = -285.77 - (0 + x)$

$x = -285.77 + 56.07 = -229.70 \text{ kJ}$

90 (*) Given that, $C_p = 7 \text{ JK}^{-1} \text{ mol}^{-1}$

Weight of N_2 gas = 28 g

$T_1 = 0°C = 273 + 0 = 273 \text{ K}$

$T_2 = 100°C = 273 + 100 = 373 \text{ K}$

Number of moles

$$= \frac{\text{weight of } N_2}{\text{molecular weight of } N_2} = \frac{28}{28} = 1 \text{ mol}$$

Now, by using $\Delta H = nC_p(T_2 - T_1)$

$= 1 \times 7(373 - 273)$

$= 7 \times 100 = 700 \text{ J}$

None of the given option is correct.

91 (*c*) The heat of neutralisation of strong acid and strong base is constant because it is infact heat of formation of water by H^+ and OH^-. Its value is almost equal to –57.3 kJ.

92 (*d*) Using Hess's law,

$$Zn + \frac{1}{2}O_2 \longrightarrow ZnO + 84000 \text{ cal} \ldots\text{(i)}$$

$$Hg + \frac{1}{2}O_2 \longrightarrow HgO + 21700 \text{ cal} \ldots\text{(ii)}$$

On subtracting Eq. (ii) from Eq. (i)

$$Zn + HgO \longrightarrow ZnO + Hg + 62300 \text{ cal}$$

$\therefore$ Heat of reaction = + 62300 cal

93 (*d*) Combustion of propane is an exothermic reaction because the enthalpy of combustion (i.e. $\Delta_{comb}H$) is always negative.

Topic 4

Entropy, Free Energy Change and Spontaneity

2019

1 In which case change in entropy is negative? **[NEET (National)]**

(a) Expansion of a gas at constant temperature
(b) Sublimation of solid to gas
(c) $2H(g) \longrightarrow H_2(g)$
(d) Evaporation of water

2017

2 For a given reaction, $\Delta H = 35.5\,\text{kJ mol}^{-1}$ and $\Delta S = 83.6\,\text{JK}^{-1}\,\text{mol}^{-1}$. The reaction is spontaneous at : (Assume that ΔH and ΔS do not vary with temperature) **[NEET]**

(a) $T < 425\,\text{K}$ (b) $T > 425\,\text{K}$
(c) all temperatures (d) $T > 298\,\text{K}$

3 When the heat of reaction at constant pressure is -2.5×10^3 cal and entropy change is 7.4 cal deg^{-1} at 25° C, the reaction is predicted as **[JIPMER]**

(a) reversible (b) spontaneous
(c) non-spontaneous (d) irreversible

2016

4 For a sample of perfect gas, when its pressure is changed isothermally from p_i to p_f, the entropy change is given **[NEET Phase II]**

(a) $\Delta S = nR \ln\left(\frac{p_f}{p_i}\right)$ (b) $\Delta S = nR \ln\left(\frac{p_i}{p_f}\right)$

(c) $\Delta S = nRT \ln\left(\frac{p_f}{p_i}\right)$ (d) $\Delta S = RT \ln\left(\frac{p_i}{p_f}\right)$

5 The correct thermodynamic conditions for the spontaneous reaction at all temperatures is **[NEET]**

(a) $\Delta H > 0$ and $\Delta S < 0$ (b) $\Delta H < 0$ and $\Delta S > 0$
(c) $\Delta H < 0$ and $\Delta S < 0$ (d) $\Delta H < 0$ and $\Delta S = 0$

2015

6 Which of the following statements is correct for a reversible process in a state of equilibrium? **[CBSE, AIPMT]**

(a) $\Delta G = -\,2.30\,RT \log \text{K}$
(b) $\Delta G = 2.30\,RT \log K$
(c) $\Delta G° = -\,2.303\,RT \log K$
(d) $\Delta G° = 2.303\,RT \log K$

2014

7 For the reaction, $X_2O_4(l) \longrightarrow 2XO_2(g)$
$\Delta U = 2.1\,\text{kcal}$, $\Delta S = 20\,\text{cal K}^{-1}$ at 300 K. Hence, ΔG is **[CBSE AIPMT]**

(a) 2.7 kcal (b) -2.7 kcal (c) 9.3 kcal (d) -9.3 kcal

8 Which of the following statements is correct for the spontaneous adsorption of a gas? **[CBSE AIPMT]**

(a) ΔS is negative and therefore, ΔH should be highly positive
(b) ΔS is negative and therefore, ΔH should be highly negative
(c) ΔS is positive and therefore, ΔH should be negative
(d) ΔS is positive and therefore, ΔH should also be highly positive

9 For a certain process, $\Delta H = 178\,\text{kJ}$ and $\Delta S = 160\,\text{J/K}$. What is the minimum temperature at which the process is spontaneous (assuming that ΔH and ΔS do not vary with temperature? **[Manipal]**

(a) 2112.3 K (b) 136.7 K
(c) 275.8 K (d) 1112.5 K

10 The values of ΔH and ΔS of a certain reaction are $-400\,\text{kJ mol}^{-1}$ and $-20\,\text{kJ mol}^{-1}\text{K}^{-1}$ respectively. The temperature below which the reaction is spontaneous, is **[WB JEE]**

(a) 100 K (b) 20° C
(c) 20 K (d) 120°C

11 For a spontaneous process, the correct statement (s) is (are) **[WB JEE]**

(a) $(\Delta G_{\text{system}})_{T,p} > 0$
(b) $(\Delta S_{\text{system}}) + (\Delta S_{\text{surroundings}}) > 0$
(c) $(\Delta G_{\text{system}})_{T,p} < 0$
(d) $(\Delta U_{\text{system}})_{T,p} > 0$

12 The enthalpy of vaporisation of a certain liquid at its boiling point of 35°C is 24.64 kJ mol^{-1}. The value of change in entropy for the process is **[WB JEE]**

(a) 704 JK^{-1}mol^{-1} (b) 80 JK^{-1}mol^{-1}
(c) 24.64 JK^{-1}mol^{-1} (d) 7.04 JK^{-1}mol^{-1}

13 Conversion of oxygen into ozone is non-spontaneous at **[KCET]**

(a) all temperature (b) high temperature
(c) room temperature (d) low temperature

2013

14 Which one of the following has ΔS° greater than zero? [AIIMS]

(a) $CaO(s) + CO_2(g) \rightleftharpoons CaCO_3(s)$

(b) $NaCl(aq) \rightleftharpoons NaCl(s)$

(c) $NaNO_3(s) \rightleftharpoons Na^+(aq) + NO_3^-(aq)$

(d) $N_2(g) + 3H_2(g) \rightleftharpoons 2NH_3(g)$

15 When ice melts into water, entropy [WB JEE]

(a) become zero (b) decreases
(c) increases (d) remains the same

16 Calculate the temperature at which $\Delta G = -5.2$ kJ/mol, $\Delta H = 145.6$ kJ/mol and $\Delta S = 216$ J/K mol for a chemical reaction. [WB JEE]

(a) 698.1°C (b) 698.1 K (c) 130 K (d) 130°C

17 For the reaction, $H_2O(s) \rightleftharpoons H_2O(l)$ at 0°C and normal pressure [KCET]

(a) $\Delta H > T\Delta S$ (b) $\Delta H = T\Delta S$ (c) $\Delta H = \Delta G$ (d) $\Delta H < T\Delta S$

2012

18 The enthalpy of fusion of water is 1.435 kcal/mol. The molar entropy change for the melting of ice at 0° C is [CBSE AIPMT]

(a) 10.52 cal/mol K (b) 21.04 cal/mol K
(c) 5.260 cal/mol K (d) 0.526 cal/mol K

19 In which of the following reactions, standard entropy change (ΔS°) is positive and standard Gibbs energy change (ΔG°) decreases sharply with increase in temperature? [CBSE AIPMT]

(a) $C_{(graphite)} + \frac{1}{2}O_2(g) \longrightarrow CO(g)$

(b) $CO(g) + \frac{1}{2}O_2(g) \longrightarrow CO_2(g)$

(c) $Mg(s) + \frac{1}{2}O_2(g) \longrightarrow MgO(s)$

(d) $\frac{1}{2}C_{(graphite)} + \frac{1}{2}O_2(g) \longrightarrow \frac{1}{2}CO_2(g)$

20 The occurrence of reaction is impossible if [AFMC]

(a) ΔH is + ve; ΔS is also + ve

(b) ΔH is – ve; ΔS is also – ve

(c) ΔH is – ve; ΔS is also + ve

(d) ΔH is + ve; ΔS is also – ve

21 Entropy of the universe is [UP CPMT]

(a) constant (b) zero
(c) continuously decreasing (d) continuously increasing

22 Which of the following is correct? [WB JEE]

(a) Evaporation of water causes an increase in disorder of the system

(b) Melting of ice causes a decrease in randomness of the system

(c) Condensation of steam causes an increase in disorder of the system

(d) There is practically no change in the randomness of the system when water is evaporated

23 Identify the correct statement from the following in a chemical reaction. [WB JEE]

(a) The entropy always increases

(b) The change in entropy along with suitable change in enthalpy decides the rate of reaction

(c) The enthalpy always decreases

(d) Both the enthalpy and the entropy remain constant

24 The equilibrium constant of a reaction is 0.008 at 298 K. The standard free energy change of the reaction at the same temperature is [KCET]

(a) –11.96 kJ (b) – 5.43 kJ
(c) – 8.46 kJ (d) +11.96 kJ

2011

25 If the enthalpy change for the transition of liquid water to steam is 300 kJ mol^{-1} at 27°C, the entropy change for the process would be [CBSE AIPMT]

(a) 1000 JK^{-1} mol^{-1} (b) 10 JK^{-1} mol^{-1}
(c) 1.0 JK^{-1} mol^{-1} (d) 0.1 JK^{-1} mol^{-1}

26 A reaction is spontaneous at low temperature but non-spontaneous at high temperature. Which of the following is true for the reaction? [Kerala CEE]

(a) $\Delta H > 0, \Delta S > 0$ (b) $\Delta H < 0, \Delta S > 0$
(c) $\Delta H > 0, \Delta S = 0$ (d) $\Delta H < 0, \Delta S < 0$
(e) $\Delta H = 0, \Delta S < 0$

27 At the sublimation temperature, for the process [Kerala CEE]

$$CO_2(s) \rightleftharpoons CO_2(g)$$

(a) $\Delta H, \Delta S$ and ΔG are all positive

(b) $\Delta H > 0, \Delta S > 0$ and $\Delta G < 0$

(c) $\Delta H < 0, \Delta S > 0$ and $\Delta G < 0$

(d) $\Delta H > 0, \Delta S > 0$ and $\Delta G > 0$

(e) $\Delta H > 0, \Delta S > 0$ and $\Delta G = 0$

28 Which reaction, with the following values of ΔH, ΔS at 400 K is spontaneous and endothermic? [DUMET]

(a) $\Delta H = -48$ kJ, $\Delta S = +135$ J/K

(b) $\Delta H = -48$ kJ; $\Delta S = -135$ J/K

(c) $\Delta H = +48$ kJ, $\Delta S = +135$ J/K

(d) $\Delta H = +48$ kJ, $\Delta S = -135$ J/K

29 The enthalpy of vaporisation of benzene is +35.3 kJ/mol at its boiling point of 80°C. The entropy change in the transition of vapour to liquid at its boiling point is .... (in J mol^{-1} K^{-1}). [KCET]

(a) –100 (b) +100
(c) +342 (d) –342

30 For the reversible reaction,
$A(s)+B(g) \rightleftharpoons C(g)+D(g); \Delta G° = -350$ kJ
Which one of the following statement is true? **[KCET]**
(a) The reaction is thermodynamically non-feasible
(b) The entropy change is negative
(c) Equilibrium constant is greater than one
(d) The reaction should be instantaneous

31 A container of 1.0 L capacity filled with 1.0 mole of an ideal gas is connected to an evacuated vessel of 9.0 L. Calculate the change in entropy. ($R = 1.987$ cal) **[Guj CET]**
(a) 0.188 cal K^{-1} mol^{-1}
(b) 0.4576 cal K^{-1} mol^{-1}
(c) 4.576 cal K^{-1} mol^{-1}
(d) 4.366 cal K^{-1} mol^{-1}

2010

32 Standard entropies of X_2, Y_2 and XY_3 are 60, 40 and 50 $JK^{-1}mol^{-1}$ respectively. For the reaction,
$$\frac{1}{2}X_2 + \frac{3}{2}Y_2 \rightleftharpoons XY_3; \Delta H = -30 \text{ kJ}$$
to be at equilibrium, the temperature should be **[CBSE AIPMT]**
(a) 500 K (b) 750 K (c) 1000 K (d) 1250 K

33 Calculate the free energy change for the following reaction at 300 K.
$$2CuO(s) \longrightarrow Cu_2O(s) + \frac{1}{2}O_2(g)$$
Given, $\Delta H = 145.6$ $kJmol^{-1}$ and $\Delta S = 116$ JK^{-1} mol^{-1} **[Manipal]**
(a) 110.8 kJ mol^{-1} (b) 221.5 kJ mol^{-1}
(c) 55.4 kJ mol^{-1} (d) 145.6 kJ mol^{-1}

34 Which of the following thermodynamic relation is correct? **[WB JEE]**
(a) $dG = Vdp - SdT$
(b) $dE = pdV + TdS$
(c) $dH = -Vdp + TdS$
(d) $dG = Vdp + SdT$

35 Which of the following reactions define ΔG_f°? **[Guj CET]**
(a) $C_{(diamond)} + O_2(g) \longrightarrow CO_2(g)$
(b) $\frac{1}{2}H_2(g) + \frac{1}{2}F_2(g) \longrightarrow HF(g)$
(c) $H_4P_2O_7 + H_2O \longrightarrow 2H_3PO_4$
(d) $SO_2(g) + \frac{1}{2}O_2(g) \longrightarrow SO_3(g)$

36 Which one of the following is correct? **[JCECE]**
(a) $-\Delta G = \Delta H - T\Delta S$ (b) $\Delta H = \Delta G - T\Delta S$
(c) $\Delta S = \frac{1}{T}[\Delta G - \Delta H]$ (d) $\Delta S = \frac{1}{T}[\Delta H - \Delta G]$

2009

37 The value of ΔH and ΔS for the reaction,
$C_{(graphite)} + O_2(g) \longrightarrow CO_2(g)$
are 170 kJ and 170 JK^{-1}, respectively. This reaction will be spontaneous at **[CBSE AIPMT]**
(a) 710 K (b) 910 K (c) 1110 K (d) 510 K

38 **Assertion** (A) The enthalpy of formation of gaseous oxygen molecules at 298 K and under a pressure of one atmosphere is zero.
Reason (R) The entropy of formation of gaseous oxygen molecule under the same conditions is zero.
(a) Both A and R are correct and R is the correct explanation of A **[AIIMS]**
(b) Both A and R are correct but R is not the correct explanation of A
(c) A is correct but R is incorrect
(d) Both A and R are incorrect

39 Predict the sign value of $\Delta S°$ for the following reaction,
$2H_2S(g) + 3O_2(g) \longrightarrow 2H_2O(g) + 2SO_2(g)$ **[OJEE]**
(a) positive (b) negative
(c) zero (d) Cannot be predicted

40 ΔG in $Ag_2O \longrightarrow 2Ag + \frac{1}{2}O_2$ at a certain temperature is -10 kJ/mol. Pick the correct statement. **[OJEE]**
(a) Ag_2O decomposes to Ag and O_2
(b) Ag and O_2 combines to form Ag_2O
(c) Reaction is in equilibrium
(d) Reaction does not take place

41 Under which of the following sets of conditions, ΔG is always negative? **[OJEE]**
(a) $\Delta H = -$ve and $\Delta S = +$ve (b) $\Delta H = -$ve and $\Delta S = -$ve
(c) $\Delta H = +$ve and $\Delta S = +$ve (d) $\Delta H = +$ve and $\Delta S = -$ve

42 Pick out the wrong statement. **[Kerala CEE]**
(a) The standard free energy of formation of all elements is zero
(b) A process accompanied by decrease in entropy is spontaneous under certain conditions
(c) The entropy of a perfectly crystalline substance at absolute zero is zero
(d) A process that leads to increase in free energy will be spontaneous
(e) Enthalpy of combustion is always negative

43 A reaction cannot take place spontaneously at any temperature when **[Kerala CEE]**
(a) Both ΔH and ΔS are positive
(b) Both ΔH and ΔS are negative
(c) ΔH is negative and ΔS is positive
(d) ΔH is zero and ΔS is positive
(e) ΔH is positive and ΔS is negative

44 The equilibrium constant (K) of a reaction may be written as **[WBJEE]**

(a) $K = e^{-\Delta G/RT}$ (b) $K = e^{-\Delta G°/RT}$
(c) $K = e^{-\Delta H/RT}$ (d) $K = e^{-\Delta H°/KT}$

45 Entropy changes for the process,

$$H_2O(l) \longrightarrow H_2O(s)$$

at normal pressure and 274 K are given below $\Delta S_{system} = -22.13$, $\Delta S_{surr} = +22.05$, the process is non-spontaneous because **[AMU]**

(a) ΔS_{system} is –ve (b) ΔS_{surr} is +ve
(c) ΔS_u is –ve (d) $\Delta S_{system} \neq \Delta S_{surr}$

('surr' stands for surroundings and 'u' stands for universe)

2008

46 For the gas phase reaction,

$$PCl_5(g) \rightleftharpoons PCl_3(g) + Cl_2(g)$$

Which of the following conditions are correct? **[CBSE AIPMT]**

(a) $\Delta H = 0$ and $\Delta S < 0$ (b) $\Delta H > 0$ and $\Delta S > 0$
(c) $\Delta H < 0$ and $\Delta S < 0$ (d) $\Delta H > 0$ and $\Delta S < 0$

47 When compared to $\Delta G°$ for the formation of Al_2O_3, the $\Delta G°$ for the formation of Cr_2O_3 is **[J&K CET]**

(a) higher (b) lower (c) same (d) unpredicted

2007

48 Standard enthalpy and standard entropy changes for the oxidation of ammonia at 298 K are –382.64 kJ mol^{-1} and -145.6 JK^{-1} mol^{-1}, respectively. Standard Gibbs energy change for the same reaction at 298 K is **[Manipal]**

(a) –2221.1 kJ mol^{-1} (b) –339.3 kJ mol^{-1}
(c) – 439.3 kJ mol^{-1} (d) –523.2 kJ mol^{-1}

49 The decomposition of limestone,

$$CaCO_3(s) \rightleftharpoons CaO(s) + CO_2(g)$$

is non-spontaneous at 298 K. The $\Delta H°$ and $\Delta S°$ values for the reaction are 176.0 kJ and 160 JK^{-1} respectively. At what temperature the decomposition becomes spontaneous? **[Kerala CEE]**

(a) At 1000 K (b) Below 500°C
(c) At 500°C (d) Between 500°C and 600°C
(e) Above 827°C

50 For a reaction, $\Delta H = +29$ kJ mol^{-1}; $\Delta S = -35$ kJ mol^{-1} At what temperature the reaction will be spontaneous?

(a) 828.7°C **[Haryana PMT]**
(b) 828.7 K
(c) Spontaneous at all temperature
(d) Not possible

51 All naturally occurring processes, proceed in a direction, which leads to **[J&K CET]**

(a) increase of enthalpy (b) increase of free energy
(c) decrease of free energy (d) decrease of entropy

52 2 moles of an ideal gas at 27°C temperature is expanded reversibly from 2L to 20 L. Find entropy change ($R = 2$ cal / mol K) **[Punjab PMET]**

(a) 92.1 (b) 0 (c) 4 (d) 9.2

53 In which of the following process, maximum increase in entropy is observed? **[KCET]**

(a) Melting of ice
(b) Sublimation of naphthalene
(c) Condensation of water
(d) Dissolution of salt in water

54 Considering the reaction,
$C(s) + O_2(g) \longrightarrow CO_2(g) + 393.5$ kJ, the signs of ΔH, ΔS and ΔG respectively are **[KCET]**

(a) +, –, – (b) –, +, + (c) –, –, – (d) –, +, –

55 If $K < 1.0$, what will be the value of $\Delta G°$? **[Guj CET]**

(a) Zero (b) 1.0 (c) Positive (d) Negative

2006

56 **Assertion** (A) Water in liquid state is more stable than ice at room temperature.
Reason (R) Water in liquid form has higher entropy than ice. **[AIIMS]**

(a) Both A and R are correct and R is the correct explanation of A
(b) Both A and R are correct but R is not the correct explanation of A
(c) A is correct but R is incorrect
(d) Both A and R are incorrect

57 Calculate the entropy change for

$$CH_4(g) + H_2O(g) \longrightarrow 3H_2(g) + CO(g),$$

using the following data **[Punjab PMET]**

Substance	$CH_4(g)$	$H_2O(g)$	$H_2(g)$	$CO(g)$
$S°$/JK^{-1} mol^{-1}	186.2	188.7	130.6	197.6

The entropy change is

(a) –46 JK^{-1} mol^{-1} (b) +46 JK^{-1} mol^{-1}
(c) –214.5 JK^{-1} mol^{-1} (d) +214.5 JK^{-1} mol^{-1}

58 For spontaneous reaction or the reaction at equilibrium, which of the following is wrong? **[DUMET]**

(a) $\Delta H < T\Delta S$ reaction is exothermic and $T\Delta S$ is positive
(b) $\Delta H = -$ve, $T\Delta S = 0$
(c) $\Delta H = T\Delta S$
(d) $\Delta H = -$ve, $T\Delta S = -$ve

2005

59 Which of the following pairs of a chemical reaction iscertain to result in a spontaneous reaction? **[CBSE AIPMT]**

(a) Exothermic and decreasing disorder
(b) Endothermic and increasing disorder
(c) Exothermic and increasing disorder
(d) Endothermic and decreasing disorder

60 For $A \rightarrow B$, $\Delta H = 4$ kcal mol^{-1}, $\Delta S = 10$ cal mol^{-1} K^{-1}, reaction is spontaneous when temperature can be
(a) 400 K (b) 300 K **[Punjab PMET]**
(c) 500 K (d) None of these

61 Molar heat of vaporisation of a liquid is 6 kJ mol^{-1}. If the entropy change is 16 J mol^{-1} K^{-1}, the boiling point of the liquid is **[KCET]**
(a) 375°C (b) 375 K (c) 273 K (d) 102°C

Answers

1 (c)	2 (b)	3 (b)	4 (b)	5 (b, d)	6 (c)	7 (b)	8 (b)	9 (d)	10 (c)
11 (b, c)	12 (b)	13 (b)	14 (c)	15 (c)	16 (b)	17 (b)	18 (c)	19 (a)	20 (d)
21 (d)	22 (a)	23 (b)	24 (d)	25 (a)	26 (d)	27 (e)	28 (c)	29 (b)	30 (c)
31 (d)	32 (b)	33 (a)	34 (a)	35 (b)	36 (d)	37 (c)	38 (c)	39 (b)	40 (a)
41 (a)	42 (d)	43 (e)	44 (b)	45 (c)	46 (b)	47 (a)	48 (b)	49 (e)	50 (d)
51 (c)	52 (d)	53 (b)	54 (d)	55 (c)	56 (b)	57 (d)	58 (a)	59 (c)	60 (c)
61 (b)									

Explanations

1 (*c*) The explanation of given statements are :

(a) Entropy is positive in case of expansion of a gas at constant temperature. It is because during expansion of gas, volume increases and hence randomness increases.

(b) Entropy is positive in case of sublimation of solid to gas as gas is much disordered than a solid.

(c) Entropy is negative in case of $2H(g) \longrightarrow H_2(g)$ as the number of moles of gaseous reactants are more that of gaseous products.

(d) Entropy is positive in case of evaporation of water as gas is much disordered than a liquid.

Hence, option (c) is correct.

2 (*b*) According to Gibbs-Helmholtz equation,

Gibb's energy $(\Delta G) = \Delta H - T\Delta S$

where, ΔH = Enthalpy change
ΔS = Entropy change
T = Temperature

For a reaction to be spontaneous
$\Delta G < 0$.

$\therefore$ Gibbs -Helmholtz equation becomes,
$$\Delta G = \Delta H - T\Delta S < 0$$
or, $\Delta H < T\Delta S$
or, $T > \dfrac{\Delta H}{\Delta S}$
$$\frac{\Delta H}{\Delta S} = \frac{35.5 \text{ kJ mol}^{-1}}{83.6 \text{ JK}^{-1}\text{mol}^{-1}}$$
$$\frac{\Delta H}{\Delta S} = \frac{35.5 \times 1000 \text{ J mol}^{-1}}{83.6 \text{ J K}^{-1} \text{ mol}^{-1}}$$
$$= 424.6 \text{ K}$$
$$\sim 425 \text{ K}$$
$$T > 425 \text{ K}$$

3 (*b*) For the reaction at constant pressure,
$$\Delta H = -2.5 \times 10^3 \text{ cal}$$
$$\Delta S = 7.4 \text{ cal deg}^{-1}$$
$$\therefore \quad \Delta G = \Delta H - T\Delta S$$
$$= (-)\, 2.5 \times 10^3 - 298 \times 7.4$$
$$= (-)\, 2.5 \times 10^3 - 2205.2$$
$$\Delta G = -4705 \cdot 2 \text{ cal}$$
$\therefore$ Reaction is spontaneous.

4 (*b*) Entropy change is given as,
$$\Delta S = nC_P \ln \frac{T_f}{T_i} + nR \ln \frac{p_i}{p_f} \quad \ldots\text{(i)}$$
For isothermal process, $T_i = T_f$
$$\because nC_p \ln \frac{T_f}{T_i} = nC_p \ln \frac{T_i}{T_i} = 0 \ [\ln 1 = 0]$$
From Eq. (i), $\Delta S = nR \ln \dfrac{p_i}{p_f}$

5 (*b, d*) We have the Gibbs Helmholtz reaction for spontaneity as
$$\Delta G = \Delta H - T\Delta S$$
For reaction to be spontaneous, ΔG must be negative.
For this, ΔH should be negative and ΔS should be positive.
$$\therefore \quad \Delta H < 0 \text{ and } \Delta S > 0.$$
and also $\Delta S = 0$ shows ΔG a negative quantity.

6 (*c*) Mathematical expression of the thermodynamic equilibrium is
$$\Delta G = \Delta G° + 2.303RT \log Q$$
At equilibrium, when $\Delta G = 0$ and $Q = K$
then, $\Delta G = \Delta G° + 2.303\,RT \log K = 0$
$$\Delta G° = -2.303\,RT \log K$$

7 (*b*) The change in Gibbs free energy is given by
$$\Delta G = \Delta H - T\Delta S$$
where, ΔH = change in enthalpy of the reaction
ΔS = change in entropy of the reaction

Thus, in order to determine ΔG, the value of ΔH must be known. The value of ΔH can be calculated by the equation.
$$\Delta H = \Delta U + \Delta n_g RT$$
where, ΔU = change in internal energy
$$\Delta n_g = 2 - 0 = 2$$
R = gas constant = 2 cal
$$\Delta U = 2.1 \text{ kcal} = 2.1 \times 10^3 \text{ cal}$$
$$[\because 1 \text{ kcal} = 10^3 \text{ cal}]$$
$$\therefore \quad \Delta H = (2.1 \times 10^3) + (2 \times 2 \times 300)$$
$$= 3300 \text{ cal}$$
Hence, $\Delta G = \Delta H - T\Delta S$
$$\Delta G = (3300) - (300 \times 20)$$
$$= -2700 \text{ cal}$$
$$\therefore \quad \Delta G = -2.7 \text{ kcal}$$

8 (*b*) ΔS [change in entropy] and ΔH [change in enthalpy] are related by the equation,
$\Delta G = \Delta H - T\Delta S$
[here, ΔG = change in Gibbs free energy]

For adsorption of a gas, ΔS is negative because randomness decreases.

Thus, in order to make ΔG negative [for spontaneous reaction], ΔH must be highly negative. Hence, for the adsorption of a gas, if ΔS is negative, therefore, ΔH should be highly negative.

Hence, statement (b) is correct while all other statements are incorrect.

9 (*d*) Process is spontaneous, ΔG must be less than 0, i.e. negative

$\therefore\ 0 \geq \Delta H - T\Delta S \Rightarrow T\Delta S \leq \Delta H$

$$\frac{178 \times 10^3}{160} \geq T_{min} \Rightarrow T_{min} \leq 1112.5\,K$$

10 (*c*) Given, $\Delta H = -400\ kJ\ mol^{-1}$

$\Delta S = -20\ kJ\ mol^{-1}K^{-1}$

Gibbs Helmholtz equation is

$$\Delta G = \Delta H - T\Delta S$$

For a reaction to be spontaneous, ΔG must be less than 0, i.e. negative.

$\therefore\quad 0 \geq \Delta H - T\Delta S \Rightarrow T\Delta S \leq \Delta H$

$$T \leq \frac{\Delta H}{\Delta S} \leq \frac{-400}{-20} \leq 20\,K$$

11 (*b, c*) For a process to be spontaneous,

$\Delta S_{system} + \Delta S_{surroundings} > 0$

$(\Delta G_{system})_{T,p} < 0$

$(\Delta U_{system})_{T,V} < 0$

12 (*b*) Entropy of vaporisation (ΔS)

$$= \frac{\text{enthalpy of vaporisation } (\Delta H)}{\text{boiling point (in K)}}$$

Given, $\Delta H = 24.64\ kJ\ mol^{-1}$ and

Boiling point = 35 + 273 = 308 K

$$\therefore\quad \Delta S = \frac{24.64 \times 10^3\,J\,mol^{-1}}{308\ K} = 80\ JK^{-1}mol^{-1}$$

13 (*b*) Ozone is not stable at high temperature so, it decomposes into oxygen at high temperature.

$$2O_3 \longrightarrow 3O_2$$

Thus, the reverse of this reaction is non-spontaneous at high temperature.

14 (*c*) The entropy (ΔS) of a reaction is positive if the products are in more random state as compared to reactants. (order of randomness is : gas > liquid > solid).

$$NaNO_3(s) \rightleftharpoons Na^+(aq) + NO_3^-(aq)$$

This process is accompanied by increase in randomness because Na^+ and NO_3^- ions are free to move in solution whereas they are not free to move in solid $NaNO_3$.

In (a), product (solid) has lesser entropy as compared to reactants. In (b), NaCl (solid) has lesser entropy as compared to NaCl (*aq*) (Na^+ and Cl^-).

In (d), both reactants and products are in gaseous state but number of moles of products are decreasing.

$\therefore$ For reaction given in option (c) has $\Delta S°$ greater than zero.

15 (*c*) The greater the randomness in a system, greater is its entropy. The randomness is greater in liquid state as compared to that in solid state, so the entropy increases when ice melts into water.

16 (*b*) $\Delta G = \Delta H - T\Delta S$

$\Rightarrow T\Delta S = \Delta H - \Delta G$

$$\Rightarrow\quad T = \frac{\Delta H - \Delta G}{\Delta S}$$

$$\text{or}\quad T = \frac{[145.6 - (-5.2)] \times 10^3}{216} = 698.1\,K$$

17 (*b*) $H_2O(s) \rightleftharpoons H_2O(l)$

We know that, $\Delta G = \Delta H - T\Delta S$

At equilibrium, $\Delta G = 0$

Therefore, $\Delta H = T\Delta S$

18 (*c*) Molar entropy change for the melting of ice,

$$\Delta S_{melt} = \frac{\Delta H_{fusion}}{T} = \frac{1.435}{273\,K}\ kcal/mol = 5.26\ cal\ /mol\ K$$

19 (*a*) $C(\text{graphite}) + \frac{1}{2}O_2(g) \longrightarrow CO(g)$

Entropy increases because randomness (disorder) increases. Thus, standard entropy change ($\Delta S°$) is positive.

Moreover, it is a combustion reaction and all the combustion reactions are generally exothermic,

i.e $\Delta H° = -ve$

We know that, $\Delta G° = \Delta H° - T\Delta S°$

$$\Delta G° = -ve - T(+\,ve)$$

Thus, as the temperature increases, the value of $\Delta G°$ decreases.

20 (*d*) The expression for ΔG is given below :

$$\Delta G = \Delta H - T\Delta S$$

For the conditions, $\Delta H = +$ ve, $\Delta S = -$ve, both the energy factor as well as entropy factor are unfavourable for the occurrence of reaction and the reaction would be non-spontaneous.

21 (*d*) According to second law of thermodynamics, the entropy of the universe always increases in the course of every spontaneous (natural) change.

22 (*a*) Water evaporates into steam. In this physical state, its disorder or randomness increases.

When ice melts into water and steam is condensed, randomness increases and decreases, respectively. Hence, statement (a) is correct while all other statements are incorrect.

23 (*b*) $\Delta G_{(T,p)} = \Delta H - T\Delta S$ determines the occurrence of a reaction. The change in enthalpy along with change in entropy, such that the value of ΔG is negative, decides the rate of the reaction.

Enthalpy and entropy in a chemical reaction may increase or decrease, accordingly. Hence, statement (b) is correct while other statements are incorrect.

24 (*d*) Standard free energy change,

$$\Delta G° = -2.303RT \log K_C$$
$$= -2.303 \times 8.314 \times 298 \log 0.008$$
$$= -2.303 \times 8.314 \times 298 \times (-2.097)$$
$$= +11965.16\ J$$
$$= +11.96\ kJ$$

25 (*a*) $$\Delta S_{vap} = \frac{\Delta H_{vap}}{T} = \frac{300\ kJ\ mol^{-1}}{300\ K} = 1000\ JK^{-1}\ mol^{-1}$$

26 (*d*) $\Delta H < 0, \Delta S < 0,\ \Delta G = \Delta H - T\Delta S$

When $\Delta H < 0$ and $\Delta S < 0$, then ΔG will be negative only at low temperature because the value of $T\Delta S$ is positive.

27 (*e*) Since, the process is at equilibrium, $\Delta G = 0$ then from the equation, $\Delta G = \Delta H - T\Delta S;\ \Delta H > 0, \Delta S > 0$.

28 (*c*) $\Delta G = \Delta H - T\Delta S$

$= 48000 - 400 \times 135$

$= 48000 - 54000 = -6000 \text{ J mol}^{-1}$

Negative ΔG indicates that reaction (c) is spontaneous.

29 (*b*) $\Delta S = \frac{\Delta H}{T} = \frac{35300 \text{ J mol}^{-1}}{353 \text{ K}}$

$= +100 \text{ JK}^{-1} \text{ mol}^{-1}$

30 (*c*) If $\Delta G°$ is negative, then equilibrium constant will be greater than one.

$\Delta G° = -2.303RT \log K$

where, K is the equilibrium constant

$\log K = \frac{\Delta G°}{-2.303RT} = \frac{-350}{-2.303RT}$

$\log K = \frac{350}{2.303RT}$ = positive number

This shows that the value of K would be greater than 1. Since, the value of ΔG is negative, the reaction is thermodynamically feasible and the reaction would be spontaneous. The number of moles of gaseous products are more as compared to the number of moles of gaseous reactants. So, the entropy change would be positive.

31 (*d*) $\Delta S = 2.303 \times nR \log (V_2 / V_1)$

$\Delta S = 2.303 \times 1 \times 1.987 \log \frac{9}{1}$

$\Delta S = 2.303 \times 1.987 \times 0.9542$

$= 4.366 \text{ cal K}^{-1} \text{ mol}^{-1}$

32 (*b*) $\frac{1}{2} X_2 + \frac{3}{2} Y_2 \rightleftharpoons XY_3$

$\Delta S° = \Sigma S°_P - \Sigma S°_R = 50 - (30 + 60)$

$\Delta S° = -40 \text{ JK}^{-1} \text{ mol}^{-1}$

$T = \frac{\Delta H°}{\Delta S°} = \frac{-30 \times 10^3 \text{ J mol}^{-1}}{-40 \text{ JK}^{-1} \text{ mol}^{-1}}$

$= 750 \text{ K}$

33 (*a*) $\Delta G = \Delta H - T\Delta S$

$= 145.6 \times 10^3 - 300 \times 116$

$= 145.6 \times 10^3 - 34.8 \times 10^3$

$= 110.8 \times 10^3 \text{ J mol}^{-1} = 110.8 \text{ kJ mol}^{-1}$

34 (*a*) $dG = dH - TdS - SdT$

(as $G = H - TS$)

Again, $H = E + pV$

$\therefore$ $dH = dE + pdV + Vdp$

and $dE = TdS - pdV$

Thus, $dG = (TdS - pdV) + pdV + Vdp - TdS - SdT$

$= Vdp - SdT$

35 (*b*) Standard Gibbs energy of formation ($\Delta G_f°$) of a substance is defined as the Gibbs energy change when one mole of the substance is formed from its elements in their standard states. The following reaction defines $\Delta G_f°$.

$\frac{1}{2} H_2(g) + \frac{1}{2} F_2(g) \longrightarrow HF(g)$

36 (*d*) Gibbs energy change,

$\Delta G = \Delta H - T\Delta S$

$T\Delta S = \Delta H - \Delta G$

$\Rightarrow \quad \Delta S = \frac{1}{T}[\Delta H - \Delta G]$

37 (*c*) $\Delta G = \Delta H - T\Delta S$

At equilibrium, $\Delta G = 0$

$\therefore \Delta H = T\Delta S$

or $T = \frac{\Delta H}{\Delta S}$

or $T = \frac{170 \times 10^3}{170} = 1000 \text{ K}$

$\therefore$ The reaction will be spontaneous above 1000 K, i.e. 1110 K.

38 (*c*) Standard enthalpy of formation of gaseous oxygen molecules is zero. Entropy of formation of even elementary substances at 298 K and one atmosphere is not zero.

39 (*b*) As the number of moles are decreasing on the product side, thus the ΔS will be negative.

40 (*a*) $\Delta G = -$ve means the process is spontaneous. Hence, Ag_2O decomposes to Ag and O_2.

Also, at equilibrium, $\Delta G = 0$

41 (*a*) $\Delta G = \Delta H - T\Delta S$

This shows, whenever $\Delta H = -$ ve and $\Delta S = +$ ve, ΔG is $-$ve.

42 (*d*) For a spontaneous process, Gibbs free energy, $\Delta G < 0$. Thus, only those processes that have a natural tendency to decrease free energy are said to be spontaneous.

43 (*e*) For a spontaneous reaction, ΔS must be positive.

$\Delta G = \Delta H - T\Delta S$

If $\Delta H = +$ve and $\Delta S = -$ve, the value of ΔG is positive and the reaction is non-spontaneous at any temperature.

44 (*b*) $\Delta G° = -RT \ln K$ or $K = e^{-\Delta G°/RT}$

Here, K = Equilibrium constant

$\Delta G°$ = Standard Gibb's free energy change

R = Gas constant

T = Temperature (in Kelvin)

45 (*c*) $\Delta S_{universe}$

$= \Delta S_{system} + \Delta S_{surroundings}$

$= -22.13 + 22.05 = -0.08$

For a spontaneous process, ΔS_u must be positive, i.e.

$\Delta S_{universe} = \Delta S_{system} + \Delta S_{surroundings} > 0$

Thus, the process is non-spontaneous because ΔS_u is negative.

46 (*b*) $\Delta H = \Delta U + \Delta n_g RT$

and $\Delta G = \Delta H - T\Delta S$

For a spontaneous process, ΔG must be negative.

$PCl_5(g) \rightleftharpoons PCl_3(g) + Cl_2(g)$

In this reaction, $\Delta n_g = 2 - 1 = 1$

Thus, ΔH is positive, i.e. > 0

If ΔH is positive, then to maintain the value of ΔG negative, ΔS should be positive, i.e. $\Delta S > 0$.

47 (*a*) Between Al_2O_3 and Cr_2O_3, Al_2O_3 is more stable so, its ease of formation is high, i.e. $\Delta G°$ is negative or less than that of Cr_2O_3.

Hence, $\Delta G°$ of $Cr_2O_3 > \Delta G°$ of Al_2O_3.

48 (*b*) Given that, $\Delta H = -382.64 \text{ kJ mol}^{-1}$

$\Delta S = -145.6 \text{ JK}^{-1} \text{ mol}^{-1}$

or $= -145.6 \times 10^{-3} \text{ kJ K}^{-1}\text{mol}^{-1}$

$\because \quad \Delta G = \Delta H - T\Delta S$

or $\Delta G = -382.64 - (298 \times -145.6 \times 10^{-3})$

$= -339.3 \text{ kJ mol}^{-1}$

49 (*e*) Reaction is non-spontaneous at 298 K (given).

$\Delta G° = \Delta H° - T\Delta S°$

$= 176000 - 298 \times 160$

$= 128320 \text{ J}$ (i.e. $\Delta G° = +$ ve)

For a spontaneous reaction, $\Delta G°$ must be negative.

At equilibrium, $\Delta G = 0$

$\therefore \quad \Delta H° = T\Delta S°$

$T = \frac{\Delta H°}{\Delta S°} = \frac{176000}{160}$

$= 1100\text{K}$

$= (1100 - 273)°\text{C}$

$= 827°\text{C}$

$\therefore$ Above 827°C, the reaction will be spontaneous.

50 (*d*) For spontaneous reaction,

$$\Delta H = \pm \text{ ve}, \Delta S = + \text{ve},$$

But, in the given reaction ΔS is negative and ΔH is positive. Hence, ΔG will be positive. Thus, reaction is not possible.

51 (*c*) For a spontaneous or naturally occurring process, free energy change is always negative, i.e. $\Delta G < 0$

52 (*d*) $\Delta S = 2.303 \; nR \log_{10} \frac{V_2}{V_1}$

$= 2.303 \times 2 \times 2 \times \log_{10} \frac{20}{2}$

$= 2.303 \times 2 \times 2 \times 1$

$= 9.212 \text{ cal K}^{-1} \text{mol}^{-1}$

$\sim 9.2 \text{ cal K}^{-1} \text{mol}^{-1}$

53 (b) The order of entropy in solid, liquid and gas is,

$$\text{gas} > \text{liquid} > \text{solid}$$

Hence, in sublimation of naphthalene, maximum increase in entropy is observed as solid state changes directly to gaseous state.

54 (*d*) $\Delta H = -$ ve (combustion reaction)

$\Delta S = +$ ve (spontaneous at all temperature)

$\Delta G = -$ve (because reaction is spontaneous)

55 (*c*) $\Delta G° = -2.303 RT \log K$

$$\log K = \frac{\Delta G°}{-2.303 RT}$$

$$K = 10^{\frac{-\Delta G°}{2.303RT}}$$

If $K < 1$ then $\Delta G° > 0$ hence, the value of $\Delta G°$ is positive.

56 (*b*) Water in liquid state is more stable than ice at room temperature because water is more dense than ice. Ice has a honeycomb structure with hexagonal channels. Relatively smaller density of ice is due to these holes. It is also true that water in liquid form has higher entropy than ice. So, both the statements are true but reason is not the correct explanation of assertion.

57 (*d*) $\Delta S°_{\text{reaction}}$

$$= \Sigma \Delta S°_{\text{products}} - \Delta S°_{\text{reactants}}$$

Thus, entropy change for,

$CH_4(g) + H_2O(g) \longrightarrow 3H_2(g) + CO(g)$;

$\Delta S°_{\text{reaction}} = [3 \times S°_{H_2(g)} + S°_{CO(g)}]$

$- [S°_{CH_4(g)} + S°_{H_2O(g)}]$

$= [3 \times 130.6 + 197.6] - [186.2 + 188.7]$

$= 589.4 - 374.9$

$= 214.5 \text{ JK}^{-1} \text{ mol}^{-1}$

58 (*a*) For reaction to be spontaneous or the reaction, at equilibrium

$$\Delta H = - \text{ ve}, \Delta S = + \text{ ve}$$

$$\Delta G = \Delta H - T\Delta S = - \text{ ve}$$

So, statement (a) is wrong.

Rest of the statements are correct.

59 (*c*) For spontaneous reaction, ΔG must be negative by considering Gibb's Helmholtz equation

$$\Delta G = \Delta H - T\Delta S$$

If both the energy factor as well as entropy factor are favourable, i.e. ΔH is negative (exothermic reaction) and ΔS is positive (entropy increases), under these conditions, ΔG would certainly be negative and the process will be spontaneous.

60 (*c*) The reaction is spontaneous when value of ΔG is negative.

Given, $\Delta S = 10 \text{ cal mol}^{-1} \text{ K}^{-1}$

$\Delta H = 4 \text{ kcal mol}^{-1} = 4000 \text{ cal mol}^{-1}$

Let, $\Delta G = 0$

$\Delta G = \Delta H - T\Delta S$

$\Rightarrow \quad 0 = 4000 - T \times 10$

or $\quad T = \frac{4000}{10} = 400 \text{ K}$

$\therefore$ Reaction is spontaneous at temperature above 400 K.

The only choice having temperature above = 400 K is (c) 500 K.

61 (*b*) $\Delta S = 16 \text{ J mol}^{-1} \text{ K}^{-1}$,

$\Delta H_V = 6 \text{ kJ mol}^{-1}$

$$T_{bp} = \frac{\Delta H_{\text{vapour}}}{\Delta S_{\text{vapour}}}$$

$$= \frac{6 \times 1000}{16} = 375 \text{ K}$$

07

Equilibrium

Quick Review

Equilibrium represents the state of a process in which the properties like temperature, pressure, concentration of the system do not show any change with the passage of time.

Equilibrium establishes in reversible reactions whereas irreversible reactions never attain equilibrium.

Dynamic Nature of Equilibrium

When there is no change in the concentration of either of the reactants or products, this stage of the system is the dynamic equilibrium.

Equilibrium is classified as follows:

(*i*) **Physical equilibrium** is established between different physical states of a substance at a particular temperature.

(*ii*) **Chemical equilibrium** is the equilibrium that involves only chemical change.

Chemical Equilibrium

In case of reversible reaction, when the rate of forward reaction becomes equal to rate of backward reaction,
then this is called the state of chemical equilibrium.

- At chemical equilibrium,
  rate of forward reaction = rate of backward reaction
- A chemical equilibrium can be **homogeneous** (when all the reactants and products are in same phase) or **heterogeneous** (when reactants and products are in different phase).

Law of Mass Action

- The rate of a chemical reaction at which a substance reacts is directly proportional to its active mass with each concentration term raised to the power of stoichiometric coefficient of that species. Here, active mass means molar concentration.
- Active masses of pure solids and liquids are taken as unity because their concentration remains same throughout the reaction.

Equilibrium Constant

- It is the ratio of the concentrations of the products raised to the power of their stoichiometric coefficients to the concentration of reactants raised to the power of their stoichiometric coefficients at equilibrium state.
- For a homogeneous reversible reaction,

$$aA + bB \rightleftharpoons cC + dD$$

$$K_C = \frac{k_f}{k_b} = \frac{[C]^c [D]^d}{[A]^a [B]^b}$$

k_f and k_b are the rate constants for forward and backward reactions respectively and K = equilibrium constant.

- For gaseous systems, $K_p = \dfrac{p_C^c \cdot p_D^d}{p_A^a \cdot p_B^b}$

where, K_p is equilibrium constant at constant pressure. p_A, p_B, p_C and p_D are the partial pressures due to gases A, B, C and D respectively.

Relationship between K_p and K_C

$$K_p = K_C (RT)^{\Delta n_g}$$

where, Δn_g = moles of gaseous products − moles of gaseous reactants.

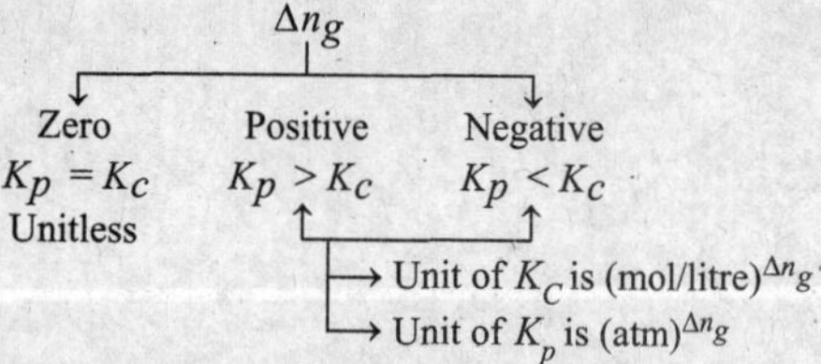

Characteristics of Equilibrium Constant

- A chemical equation when divided by a factor 'n', then new equilibrium constant is nth root of previous value.
$$K'_C = \sqrt[n]{K_C}$$
- A chemical equation when multiplied by a factor 'n', then new equilibrium constant becomes nth power of the previous value.
$$K'_C = (K_C)^n$$
- When a chemical equation is reversed, the new equilibrium constant becomes inverse of the previous value.
$$K'_C = \frac{1}{K_C}$$
- When two chemical equations are added, their equilibrium constant are multiplied.
$$K'_C = K_1 K_2$$
- When two chemical equations are subtracted, their equilibrium constant are divided.
$$K'_C = K_1/K_2$$
- Equilibrium constant changes with change in temperature.
$$\log \frac{K_2}{K_1} = \frac{\Delta H}{2.303R}\left[\frac{1}{T_1} - \frac{1}{T_2}\right]$$

when $\Delta H = 0$ (K remains same at all temperatures)

when $\Delta H > 0$ ($K_2 > K_1$)

when $\Delta H < 0$ ($K_1 > K_2$)

Reaction Quotient (Q)

It is the ratio of molar concentration partial pressure of the product species to that of reactant species at any stage in the reaction. It can be calculated at any point during the reaction.

Generalisations Concerning the Direction of the Reaction

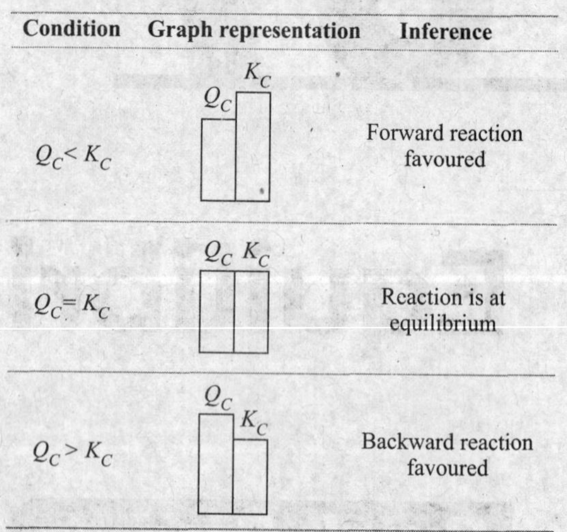

Note The extent of reaction is determined as,

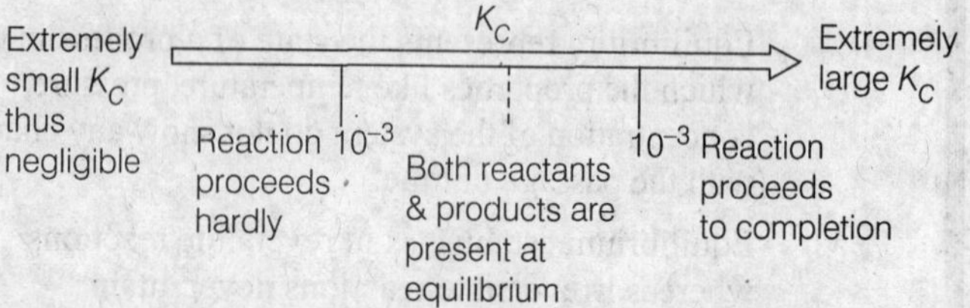

Relationship between Equilibrium Constant (K) and Gibb's Free Energy (G)

At equilibrium, standard Gibb's free energy ($\Delta G°$) and equilibrium constant (K_C) are related as,

$$\Delta G° = -2.303\, RT \log K_C$$

or $$\ln K_C = -\frac{\Delta G°}{RT} \Rightarrow K_C = e^{-\Delta G°/RT}$$

For gaseous reaction,

$$\Delta G° = -2.303\, RT \log K_p$$

or $$K_p = e^{-\Delta G°/RT}$$

Factors Affecting Equilibrium (Le-Chatelier's Principle)

When a change is brought about on a system in equilibrium, the system tends to adjust itself to reduce the effect of change. This is applicable to all physical and chemical equilibria.

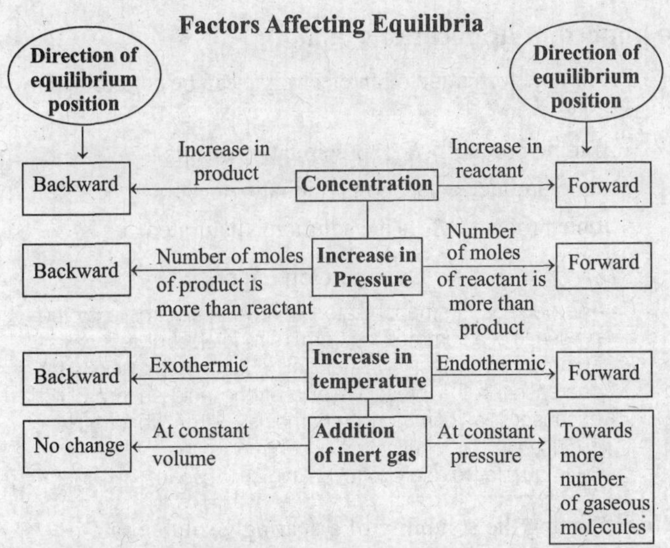

Ionic Equilibrium

Equilibria that involves ion only, are called ionic equilibrium.

- **Non-electrolytes** A solution of substances like urea, glucose etc. that does not dissociate into ions when dissolved in water. They are poor conductors of electricity.
- **Electrolytes** Substances dissociating into ions when dissolved in water. Electrolytes may be **strong** (ionising 100% in solution) or **weak** (partially dissociating into ions).

Arrhenius Theory of Electrolytic Ionisation

It has following postulates:

(i) In aqueous solution, the molecules of an electrolyte undergo spontaneous dissociation into positive ions called **cations** and negative ions called **anions.**

(ii) On passing electricity through a solution of electrolyte, the cations and anions start moving towards their respective electrodes. This movement of ions produces electric current in solution.

(iii) An **ionic equilibrium** is established between ions and the undissociated molecules of an electrolyte.

Degree of Dissociation or Ionisation (α)

- Fraction of total number of molecules undergoing association or dissociation.

  It is given by

$$\alpha = \frac{\text{Amount of the ionised electrolyte}}{\text{Total amount of electrolyte dissolved}}$$

- Degree of dissociation depends upon, nature of solute and solvent, concentration, temperature.

Ostwald's Dilution Law

- The degree of dissociation (α) of weak electrolyte is inversely proportional to the square root of the molar concentration of the solution.

$$K = \frac{C\alpha^2}{1-\alpha}$$

- If α is very small $1-\alpha \approx 1$ (i.e in case of weak electrolytes)

$$\Rightarrow K = C\alpha^2 \text{ or } \alpha = \sqrt{\frac{K}{C}}$$

$$\Rightarrow \quad \text{'}\alpha\text{'} \propto \frac{1}{\sqrt{C}}$$

where, K = dissociation constant

Different Theories Related to Acids and Bases

Concept	Acids	Bases	Examples
Arrhenius concept	Furnish/release H^+ ions in their aqueous solution.	Furnish/release OH^- ions in their aqueous solution.	$\underset{\text{(Acid)}}{HCl} \rightleftharpoons H^+ + Cl^-$; $\underset{\text{(Base)}}{NaOH} \rightleftharpoons Na^+ + OH^-$
Lewis concept	Accept a pair of electrons, i.e. acids are electron deficient compounds.	Donate a pair of electrons to form coordinate bond, i.e. bases are electron rich compounds.	$\underset{\text{(Acid)}}{H^+} + \underset{\text{(Base)}}{OH^-} \longrightarrow H_2O$ **Acids** BF_3, $AlCl_3$, Fe^{3+}, Al^{3+}, Cu^{2+}, SF_6 (vacant *d*-orbitals) **Bases** $H_2\ddot{O}:$, $\ddot{N}H_3$, OH^-
Bronsted-Lowry	Acid is a proton donor.	Base is a proton acceptor.	$\underset{\text{(Base)}}{NH_3} \overset{H^+}{\rightleftharpoons} \underset{\text{(Acid)}}{NH_4^+}$

Note The compounds which have dual character, i.e. behave as an acid as well as base are called **amphoteric**.

Ionisation of Water

- Being a weak electrolyte and a poor conductor of electricity, water undergoes ionisation to a small extent.
- The equilibrium constant for the self-ionisation of water is called ionic product of water and is represented as K_w.

$$K_w = [H^+][OH^-] = 10^{-14}\ M^2$$

where, K_w = ionic product of water

Relative Strength of Acids and Bases

The extent to which the acidic property is shown by an acid is the measure of its strength.

$$\frac{\text{Strength of acid I}}{\text{Strength of acid II}} = \frac{\alpha_1}{\alpha_2} = \sqrt{\frac{K_1/C}{K_2/C}} = \sqrt{\frac{K_1}{K_2}}$$

Polybasic or Polyprotic Acids

These are the acids which have more than one ionisable proton per molecule of the acid.

- The ionisation constants for a dibasic acid (protons) H_2X are given as:

$$K_{a_1} = \frac{[H^+][HX^-]}{[H_2X]} \text{ and } K_{a_2} = \frac{[H^+][X^{2-}]}{[HX^-]}$$

where, K_{a_1} and K_{a_2} are called first and second ionisation constant respectively of the acid H_2X.

- K_{a_1} of a polyprotic acid is greater than K_{a_2} or K_{a_3}, as it is more difficult to remove a positively charged proton from a negative ion due to electrostatic forces.

Relation between Acid Dissociation (K_a) and Base Dissociation Constants (K_b)

$$K_a \times K_b = K_w \Rightarrow 10^{-14}$$

- Taking logarithm on both sides, the above equation becomes, $pK_a + pK_b = pK_w$
  where pK_a and pK_b are the negative logarithm of dissociation constant for acids and bases.
- Greater the value of K_a (or lesser the pK_a), stronger is the acid.

Solubility and Solubility Product

(*i*) **Solubility** The amount of solute dissolved in a given volume of a solvent to form a saturated solution at a given temperature is termed as the solubility of the solute in the solvent at that temperature.

(*ii*) **Solubility Product** (K_{sp}) For the dissolution of a sparingly soluble salt,

$$A_xB_y \rightleftharpoons xA^{y+} + yB^{x-}$$

$$K_{sp} = [A^{y+}]^x [B^{x-}]^y = x^x \cdot y^y \cdot S^{x+y}$$

where, S = solubility of sparingly soluble salt

K_{sp} = solubility product

For salt of the type AB : $K_{sp} = S^2$ or $S = \sqrt{K_{sp}}$

For salt of the type AB_2, $K_{sp} = 4S^3$ or $S = \left(\frac{K_{sp}}{4}\right)^{1/3}$

- For salt of the type AB_3, $K_{sp} = 27S^4$ or $S = \left(\frac{K_{sp}}{27}\right)^{1/4}$

Some Important Applications of K_{sp}

(*i*) Precipitate formation of an electrolyte can be determined by K_{sp} as,

- If ionic product > K_{sp}, precipitation occurs
- Ionic product < K_{sp}, no precipitation occurs
- Ionic product = K_{sp}, the solution is saturated

Common Ion Effect

The decrease in the ionisaton of a weak electrolyte by the presence of a common ion from a strong electrolyte is called common ion effect. e.g. ionisation of a weak acid (*HA*) decreases in the presence of a strong acid such as HCl because H^+ as common ion combines with A^- to form *HA*. It is used in (a) purification of common salt (b) in qualitative analysis (c) salting out of soap

(*ii*) In predicting the solubility of a sparingly soluble salt,

$$\underset{S \text{ mol/L}}{A_xB_y} \rightleftharpoons \underset{xS}{xA^{y+}} + \underset{yS}{yB^{x-}}$$

By knowing the values of K_{sp}, x and y, solubility of the salt can be computed.

pH Scale

It is defined as the negative logarithm of hydrogen ion concentration.

$$pH = -\log[H^+]$$

Similarly, pOH is the negative logarithm of hydroxyl ion concentration.

Relationship between pH and pOH

We know that at 298 K in aqueous solution,

$$[H^+][OH^-] = K_w = 1 \times 10^{-14}$$

Multiplying both sides by − log

$$\Rightarrow \quad -\log[H^+] - \log[OH^-] = -\log(10^{-14})$$

$$pH + pOH = 14$$

(*i*) In case of pure water, $[H^+] = [OH^-]$, thus pH = pOH = 7.

(*ii*) In case of acidic solutions, $[H^+] > [OH^-]$, thus pH < 7 and pOH > 7.

(*iii*) In case of alkaline solution, $[H^+] < [OH^-]$ thus pH > 7 pOH < 7.

- pH of weak acid, $pH = \frac{1}{2}[pK_a - \log C]$
- pH of a weak base, $pH = \frac{1}{2}[pK_b - \log C]$
- pH of a mixture of acids, $[H^+] = \Sigma NV / \Sigma V$

$\therefore \quad pH = -\log[H^+]$

- pH of mixture of base, $[OH^-] = \frac{\Sigma NV}{\Sigma V}$,

$\therefore \quad pH = 14 - pOH$

Hydrolysis of Salts

The process of interaction of an anion or cation of a salt with water accompanied by the cleavage of O—H bond is called **salt hydrolysis.**

Summary of Salt Hydrolysis

Salt of	Example	K_h (hydrolysis constant)	h (degree of hydrolysis)	pH of solution
weak acid and strong base	CH_3COONa	$\frac{K_w}{K_a}$	$\sqrt{\frac{K_w}{K_a \cdot C}}$	$\frac{1}{2}pK_w + \frac{1}{2}pK_a + \frac{1}{2}\log C$
strong acid and weak base	NH_4Cl	$\frac{K_w}{K_b}$	$\sqrt{\frac{K_w}{K_b \cdot C}}$	$\frac{1}{2}pK_w - \frac{1}{2}pK_b - \frac{1}{2}\log C$
weak acid and weak base	CH_3COONH_4	$\frac{K_w}{K_a \cdot K_b}$	$\sqrt{\frac{K_w}{K_a \cdot K_b}}$	$\frac{1}{2}pK_w + \frac{1}{2}pK_a - \frac{1}{2}pK_b$
strong acid and strong base	NaCl	Does not undergo hydrolysis		

Buffer Solution

- A buffer solution is defined as "a solution that resists change in pH when a small amount of an acid or base is added or when solution is diluted."
- A buffer is acidic, basic or neutral.
- The pH of acidic and basic buffer solutions can be calculated by **Henderson-Hasselbalch** equation as,

For acidic buffer, $pH = pK_a + \log \frac{[\text{salt}]}{[\text{acid}]}$

For basic buffer, $pOH = pK_b + \log \frac{[\text{salt}]}{[\text{base}]}$

Buffer Capacity

It is defined as the number of moles of acid or base added in one litre of a buffer solution to change its pH by one unit.

$$\text{Buffer capacity} = \frac{\text{moles of acid or base added to 1 L of buffer}}{\text{change in pH}}$$

Topical Practice Questions

All the exam questions of this chapter have been divided into six topics as listed below.

Topic 1

Chemical Equilibrium Basics, Law of Mass Action and Equilibrium Constant

2019

1 If equilibrium constant is 2.6×10^8 at 298 K then find the value of ΔG° [JIPMER]

(a) -48.014 kJ (b) -63.2 kJ
(c) -23.3 kJ (d) $+40$ kJ

2018

2 The value of K_C for the reaction, $2A \rightleftharpoons B + C$ is 2×10^{-3}. At a given time, the composition of reaction mixture is $[A] = [B] = [C] = 3 \times 10^{-4}$ M. In which direction, the reaction will proceed? [JIPMER]

(a) Forward direction (b) Reverse direction
(c) No net reaction occur (d) None of these

3 At equilibrium, the concentration of

$N_2 = 3.0 \times 10^{-3}$ M
$O_2 = 4.2 \times 10^{-3}$ M
and $NO = 2.8 \times 10^{-3}$ M

in a sealed vessel at 800 K and 1 atm pressure. What will be K_p for the given reaction?

$$N_2(g) + O_2(g) \rightleftharpoons 2NO(g)$$ [AIIMS]

(a) 0.328 atm (b) 0.622 atm
(c) 0.483 atm (d) 0.712 atm

4 The equilibrium constants of the following are [NEET]

$$N_2 + 3H_2 \rightleftharpoons 2NH_3;\ K_1$$
$$N_2 + O_2 \rightleftharpoons 2NO;\ \ K_2$$
$$H_2 + \frac{1}{2}O_2 \longrightarrow H_2O; K_3$$

The equilibrium constant (K) of the reaction

$$2NH_3 + \frac{5}{2}O_2 \overset{K}{\rightleftharpoons} 2NO + 3H_2O,$$ will be

(a) $K_1K_3^3 / K_2$ (b) $K_2K_3^3 / K_1$
(c) K_2K_3 / K_1 (d) $K_2^3K_3 / K_1$

2017

5 For the reaction

$H_2(g) + CO_2(g) \rightleftharpoons CO(g) + H_2O(g)$, If the initial concentration of $[H_2] = [CO_2]$ and x mol/L of hydrogen is consumed at equilibrium, the correct expression of K_p is [AIIMS]

(a) $\dfrac{x^2}{(1-x)^2}$ (b) $\dfrac{x^2}{(2+x)^2}$

(c) $\dfrac{x^2}{1-x^3}$ (d) $\dfrac{(1+x)^2}{(1-x)^2}$

2014

6 The value of equilibrium constant for the reaction, $N_2 + 2O_2 \rightleftharpoons 2NO_2$ is 100. The equilibrium constant for the reaction, $NO_2 \rightleftharpoons \frac{1}{2}N_2 + O_2$ will be [Manipal]

(a) 100 (b) 0.010 (c) 0.10 (d) 1000

7 In the equilibrium, $N_2O_4(g) \rightleftharpoons 2NO_2(g)$, the N_2O_4 is fifty per cent dissociated at 60°C. What will be the value of K_p at this temperature and one atmosphere? [Manipal]

(a) 0.33 atm (b) 1.33 atm (c) 2.33 atm (d) 3.33 atm

8 28 g of N_2 and 6 g of H_2 were mixed. At equilibrium 17 g NH_3 was produced. The weights of N_2 and H_2 at equilibrium are respectively [Manipal]

(a) 11 g, 0 g (b) 1 g, 3 g (c) 14 g, 3 g (d) 11 g, 3 g

9 When 0.1 mole of $N_2O_4(g)$ was placed in a 1.0 L flask at 400 K and closed, the following equilibrium is reached with a total pressure of 6 bar $N_2O_4(g) \rightleftharpoons 2NO_2(g)$. Assuming ideal behaviour of the gases, the partial pressure of $N_2O_4(g)$ at equilibrium in bar is ($R = 0.083$ bar L mol^{-1} K^{-1}) [EAMCET]

(a) 3.32 (b) 9.32 (c) 0.66 (d) 2.68

2013

10 At 490°C, the equilibrium constant for the synthesis of HI is 50, the value of K for the dissociation of HI will be [KCET]

(a) 20.0 (b) 2.0 (c) 0.2 (d) 0.02

11 For which of the following reactions are the numerical value of K_p and K_C the same? [KCET]

(a) $H_2(g) + Cl_2(g) \rightleftharpoons 2HCl(g)$
(b) $2SO_2(g) + O_2(g) \rightleftharpoons 2SO_3(g)$
(c) $2NOCl(g) \rightleftharpoons 2NO(g) + Cl_2(g)$
(d) $N_2(g) + 3H_2(g) \rightleftharpoons 2NH_3(g)$

2012

12 Given that equilibrium constant for the reaction, $2SO_2(g) + O_2(g) \rightleftharpoons 2SO_3(g)$ has a value of 278 at a particular temperature. What is the value of the equilibrium constant for the following reaction at the same temperature?

$$SO_3(g) \rightleftharpoons SO_2(g) + \frac{1}{2}O_2(g)$$ [CBSE AIPMT]

(a) 1.8×10^{-3} (b) 3.6×10^{-3}
(c) 6×10^{-2} (d) 1.3×10^{-5}

13 Given the reaction between two gases represented by A_2 and B_2 to give the compound $AB(g)$

$$A_2(g) + B_2(g) \rightleftharpoons 2AB(g)$$

At equilibrium the concentration of $A_2 = 3.0 \times 10^{-3}$ M, of $B_2 = 4.2 \times 10^{-3}$ M and of $AB = 2.8 \times 10^{-3}$ M. If the reaction takes place in a sealed vessel at 527°C, then the value of K_C will be **[CBSE AIPMT]**

(a) 2.0 (b) 1.9 (c) 0.62 (d) 4.5

14 In the reaction, $H_2(g) + Cl_2(g) \rightleftharpoons 2HCl(g)$ **[UP CPMT]**

(a) $K_p \neq K_C$ (b) $K_p = K_C$
(c) $K_p > K_C$ (d) $K_p < K_C$

15 Reaction which can go fastest for completion should have **[OJEE]**

(a) $K = 100$ (b) $K = 1$ (c) $K = 0.1$ (d) $K = 10^{-2}$

2011

16 For the reaction,

$$N_2(g) + O_2(g) \rightleftharpoons 2NO(g),$$

the equilibrium constant is K_1. The equilibrium constant is K_2 for the reaction,

$$2NO(g) + O_2(g) \rightleftharpoons 2NO_2(g).$$

What is K for the reaction,

$$NO_2(g) \rightleftharpoons \frac{1}{2}N_2(g) + O_2(g)?$$ **[CBSE AIPMT]**

(a) $\dfrac{1}{(K_1K_2)}$ (b) $\dfrac{1}{(2K_1K_2)}$

(c) $\dfrac{1}{(4K_1K_2)}$ (d) $\left[\dfrac{1}{K_1K_2}\right]^{1/2}$

17 For the reaction, $C(s) + CO_2(g) \longrightarrow 2CO(g)$, $K_p = 63$ atm at 1000 K. If at equilibrium $p_{CO} = 10p_{CO_2}$, then the total pressure of the gases at equilibrium is **[Kerala CEE]**

(a) 6.3 atm (b) 6.93 atm
(c) 0.63 atm (d) 0.693 atm
(e) 69.3 atm

18 In the reaction, $AB(g) \rightleftharpoons A(g) + B(g)$ at 30°C, K_p for the dissociation equilibrium is 2.56×10^{-2} atm. If the total pressure at equilibrium is 1 atm, then the percentage dissociation of AB is **[Kerala CEE]**

(a) 87% (b) 13%
(c) 43.5% (d) 6%
(e) 16%

19 For a chemical reaction of the type $A \rightleftharpoons B, K = 2.0$ and $B \rightleftharpoons C, K = 0.01$. Equilibrium constant for the reaction, $2C \rightleftharpoons 2A$ is **[WB JEE]**

(a) 25 (b) 50
(c) 2500 (d) 4×10^{-4}

20 α-D-glucose $\rightleftharpoons$ β-D-glucose, equilibrium constant for this is 1.8. The percentage of α-D-glucose at equilibrium is **[WB JEE]**

(a) 35.7 (b) 55.6 (c) 44.4 (d) 64.3

21 Consider the following gaseous equilibria with equilibrium constants K_1 and K_2 respectively,

$$SO_2(g) + \frac{1}{2}O_2(g) \rightleftharpoons SO_3(g)$$

$$2SO_3(g) \rightleftharpoons 2SO_2(g) + O_2(g)$$

The equilibrium constants are related as **[KCET]**

(a) $2K_1 = K_2^2$ (b) $K_1^2 = \dfrac{1}{K_2}$ (c) $K_2^2 = \dfrac{1}{K_1}$ (d) $K_2 = \dfrac{2}{K_1^2}$

22 Final pressure is higher than initial pressure of a container filled with an ideal gas at constant temperature. What will be the value of equilibrium constant? **[Guj CET]**

(a) $K = 1.0$ (b) $K = 10.0$ (c) $K > 1.0$ (d) $K < 1.0$

2010

23 In which of the following equilibrium, K_C and K_p are not equal? **[CBSE AIPMT]**

(a) $2C(s) + O_2(g) \rightleftharpoons 2CO_2(g)$
(b) $2NO(g) \rightleftharpoons N_2(g) + O_2(g)$
(c) $SO_2(g) + NO_2(g) \rightleftharpoons SO_3(g) + NO(g)$
(d) $H_2(g) + I_2(g) \rightleftharpoons 2HI(g)$

24 The relation between K_p and K_C for the following reaction

$N_2(g) + 3H_2(g) \longrightarrow 2NH_3(g)$ is **[OJEE]**

(a) $K_p = K_C(RT)$ (b) $K_C = K_p(RT)^{-2}$
(c) $K_C = K_p(RT)$ (d) $K_p = K_C(RT)^{-2}$

25 Calculate K_C for the reversible process given below if $K_p = 167$ and $T = 800°$C

$CaCO_3(s) \rightleftharpoons CaO(s) + CO_2(g)$ **[WB JEE]**

(a) 1.95 (b) 1.85
(c) 1.89 (d) 1.60

26 At 450 K, $K_p = 2.0 \times 10^{10}$/bar for the given reaction at equilibrium,

$$2SO_2(g) + O_2(g) \rightleftharpoons 2SO_3(g).$$

What is K_C at this temperature? **[Haryana PMT]**

(a) 73.8×10^{10} (b) 7.38×10^{11}
(c) Both (a) and (b) (d) Zero

27 For the reaction, $AB(g) \rightleftharpoons A(g) + B(g)$, AB is 33% dissociated at a total pressure of p. Therefore, p is related to K_p by one of the following options. **[AMU]**

(a) $p = K_p$ (b) $p = 3K_p$
(c) $p = 4K_p$ (d) $p = 8K_p$

28 Which one of the following reactions has $K_p = K_C$? [JCECE]
(a) $PCl_5 \rightleftharpoons PCl_3 + Cl_2$
(b) $N_2 + O_2 \rightleftharpoons 2NO$
(c) $N_2 + 3H_2 \rightleftharpoons 2NH_3$
(d) $2SO_3 \rightleftharpoons 2SO_2 + O_2$

29 In which one of the following gaseous equilibria, K_p is less than K_C? [CMC]
(a) $N_2O_4 \rightleftharpoons 2NO_2$ (b) $2SO_2 + O_2 \rightleftharpoons 2SO_3$
(c) $2HI \rightleftharpoons H_2 + I_2$ (d) $N_2 + O_2 \rightleftharpoons 2NO$

30 In the equilibrium reaction, $2HI(g) \rightleftharpoons H_2(g) + I_2(g)$. Which of the following expressions is true? [VMMC]
(a) $K_p = K_C$ (b) $K_C = 2K_p$
(c) $K_p = \frac{K_C}{2}$ (d) $K_C = K_p(RT)^2$

31 What is K_C for the following equilibrium when equilibrium concentration of each substance is $[SO_2] = 0.60$ M, $[O_2] = 0.82$ M and $[SO_3] = 1.90$ M?
$2SO_2(g) + O_2(g) \rightleftharpoons 2SO_3(g)$ [VMMC]
(a) 12.229 (b) 21.229 (c) 12.922 (d) 21.046

2009

32 Two moles of each reactant A and B are taken in a reaction flask. They react in the following manner,
$$A(g) + B(g) \rightleftharpoons C(g) + D(g)$$
At equilibrium, it was found that the concentration of C is triple to that of B. The equilibrium constant for the reaction is [AIIMS]
(a) 4.5 (b) 6 (c) 9 (d) $\frac{1}{6}$

33 An equilibrium constant of 10^{-4} for a reaction means, the equilibrium is [OJEE]
(a) largely towards backward direction
(b) largely towards forward direction
(c) equally poised
(d) never established

34 Consider the reaction, where $K_p = 0.497$ at 500 K.
$$PCl_5(g) \rightleftharpoons PCl_3(g) + Cl_2(g)$$
If the three gases are mixed in a rigid container so that the partial pressure of each gas is initially 1 atm. Which is true? [OJEE]
(a) More PCl_5 will be produced
(b) More PCl_3 will be produced
(c) Equilibrium will be established when 50% reaction is complete
(d) None of the above

35 Identify the incorrect statement regarding chemical equilibrium. [OJEE]
(a) It can be attained from either side
(b) $Q_C = K_C$ at equilibrium
(c) Equilibrium is achieved when the reactant and product concentrations become equal
(d) Presence of catalyst influences the positions of equilibrium

36 For the reaction, $SO_2(g) + \frac{1}{2}O_2(g) \rightleftharpoons SO_3(g)$ if we write $K_p = K_C(RT)^x$, then x is equal to [WB JEE]
(a) -1 (b) $-\frac{1}{2}$ (c) $\frac{1}{2}$ (d) 1

37 Standard free energy change for an equilibrium is zero, the value of K_p is [CGPMT, Haryana PMT]
(a) zero (b) 1 (c) 2 (d) 100

38 K_p and K'_p are the equilibrium constants of the two reactions, given below.
$$\frac{1}{2}N_2(g) + \frac{3}{2}H_2(g) \rightleftharpoons NH_3(g)$$
$$N_2(g) + 3H_2(g) \rightleftharpoons 2NH_3(g)$$ [AMU]
Therefore, K_p and K'_p are related by
(a) $K_p = K'^2_p$ (b) $K_p = \sqrt{K'_p}$
(c) $K_p = 2K'_p$ (d) $K_p = K'_p$

39 Reactions that have standard free energy changes less than zero always have equilibrium constant equal to [AMU]
(a) unity (b) greater than unity
(c) less than unity (d) zero

40 5 moles of SO_2 and 5 moles of O_2 are allowed to react. At equilibrium, it was found that 60% of SO_2 is used up. If the partial pressure of the equilibrium mixture is one atmosphere, the partial pressure of O_2 is [KCET]
(a) 0.52 atm (b) 0.21 atm (c) 0.41 atm (d) 0.82 atm

41 $2HI(g) \rightleftharpoons H_2(g) + I_2(g)$
The equilibrium constant of the above reaction is 6.4 at 300 K. If 0.25 mole each of H_2 and I_2 are added to the system, the equilibrium constant will be [KCET]
(a) 0.8 (b) 3.2 (c) 1.6 (d) 6.4

2008

42 If the concentration of OH^- ions in the reaction, $Fe(OH)_3(s) \rightleftharpoons Fe^{3+}(aq) + 3OH^-(aq)$ is decreased by $\frac{1}{4}$ times, then equilibrium concentration of Fe^{3+} will increase by [CBSE AIPMT]
(a) 8 times (b) 16 times
(c) 64 times (d) 4 times

43 The dissociation equilibrium of a gas AB_2 can be represented as
$$2AB_2(g) \rightleftharpoons 2AB(g) + B_2(g).$$
The degree of dissociation is 'x' and is small compared to 1. The expression relating the degree of dissociation (x) with equilibrium constant K_p and total pressure p, is [CBSE AIPMT]
(a) $\left(\frac{2K_p}{p}\right)$ (b) $\left(\frac{2K_p}{p}\right)^{1/3}$
(c) $\left(\frac{2K_p}{p}\right)^{1/2}$ (d) $\left(\frac{K_p}{p}\right)$

44 The values of K_{p_1} and K_{p_2} for the reactions.

$$X \rightleftharpoons Y + Z \quad \ldots(\text{I})$$

and $$A \rightleftharpoons 2B \quad \ldots(\text{II})$$

are in the ratio of 9 : 1. If degree of dissociation of X and A be equal, then total pressure at equilibrium (I) and (II) are in the ratio **[CBSE AIPMT]**

(a) 3 : 1 (b) 1 : 9
(c) 36 : 1 (d) 1 : 1

45 In which of the following reactions, the concentration of the product is higher than the concentration of reactant at equilibrium? (K = equilibrium constant) **[AIIMS]**

(a) $A \rightleftharpoons B, K = 0.001$ (b) $M \rightleftharpoons N, K = 10$
(c) $X \rightleftharpoons Y, K = 0.005$ (d) $R \rightleftharpoons P, K = 0.01$

46 **Assertion** (A) For the reaction,

$N_2(g) + 3H_2(g) \rightleftharpoons 2NH_3(g)$

Unit of $K_C = \text{L}^2\ \text{mol}^{-2}$

Reason (R) For the reaction,

$N_2(g) + 3H_2(g) \rightleftharpoons 2NH_3(g)$

Equilibrium constant, $K_C = \dfrac{[NH_3]^2}{[N_2][H_2]^3}$. **[AIIMS]**

(a) Both A and R are correct and R is the correct explanation of the A
(b) Both A and R are correct but R is not the correct explanation of A
(c) A is correct but R is incorrect
(d) Both A and R are incorrect

47 Formaldehyde polymerises to form glucose according to the reaction, $6HCHO \rightleftharpoons C_6H_{12}O_6$.
The theoretically computed equilibrium constant for this reaction is found to be 6×10^{22}. If 1 M solution of glucose dissociates according to the above equilibrium, the concentration of formaldehyde in the solution will be **[Manipal]**

(a) 1.6×10^{-2} M (b) 1.6×10^{-4} M
(c) 1.6×10^{-6} M (d) 1.6×10^{-8} M

48 Equimolar concentrations of H_2 and I_2 are heated to equilibrium in a 2 L flask. At equilibrium, the forward and backward rate constants are found to be equal. What percentage of initial concentration of H_2 has reacted at equilibrium? **[Kerala CEE]**

(a) 33% (b) 66%
(c) 50% (d) 40%
(e) 20%

49 9.2 g of N_2O_4 is heated in a 1 L vessel till equilibrium state is established,

$$N_2O_4(g) \rightleftharpoons 2NO_2(g).$$

In equilibrium state 50% N_2O_4 was dissociated, equilibrium constant will be
[molecular weight of N_2O_4 = 92] **[MP PMT]**

(a) 0.1 (b) 0.4
(c) 0.3 (d) 0.2

50 In the equilibrium $2NH_3 \rightleftharpoons N_2 + 3H_2$, 6 moles of NH_3 is taken in 10 L flask. If concentration of N_2 at equilibrium is x, then concentration of NH_3 at equilibrium is **[DUMET]**

(a) $0.6 - x$ (b) $0.6 - 2x$
(c) $0.6 - \dfrac{x}{2}$ (d) None is correct

51 Three moles of PCl_5, three moles of PCl_3 and two moles of Cl_2 are taken in a closed vessel. If at equilibrium the vessel has 1.5 moles of PCl_5, the number of moles of PCl_3 present in it is **[KCET]**

(a) 5 (b) 3
(c) 6 (d) 4.5

52 For the reaction,

$$C(s) + CO_2(g) \rightleftharpoons 2CO(g).$$

The partial pressure of CO_2 and CO are 2.0 and 4.0 atm respectively then equilibrium K_p for the reaction will be **[BCECE]**

(a) 0.5 (b) 8.0 (c) 4.0 (d) 32

2007

53 Which of the following is irreversible reaction? **[CBSE AIPMT]**

(a) $2NH_3 \longrightarrow N_2 + 3H_2$
(b) $PCl_5 \longrightarrow PCl_3 + Cl_2$
(c) $KClO_3 \longrightarrow KCl + O_2$
(d) $SO_3 \longrightarrow SO_2 + O_2$

54 The following equilibrium constants are given

$N_2 + 3H_2 \rightleftharpoons 2NH_3,\ K_1$
$N_2 + O_2 \rightleftharpoons 2NO,\ K_2$
$H_2 + \frac{1}{2}O_2 \rightleftharpoons H_2O,\ K_3$

The equilibrium constant for the oxidation of NH_3 by oxygen to give NO is **[UP CPMT]**

(a) $\dfrac{K_2K_3^3}{K_1}$ (b) $\dfrac{K_2K_3^2}{K_1}$
(c) $\dfrac{K_2^2K_3^6}{K_1^2}$ (d) $\dfrac{K_1K_2}{K_3}$

55 The equilibrium constant (K_p) for the decomposition of gaseous,

$$H_2O(g) \rightleftharpoons H_2(g) + \frac{1}{2}O_2(g)$$

is related to degree of dissociation (α) at a total pressure p is given by **[Kerala CEE]**

(a) $K_p = \dfrac{\alpha^3 p^{1/3}}{(1+\alpha)(2+\alpha)^{1/2}}$ (b) $K_p = \dfrac{\alpha^3 p^{3/2}}{(1-\alpha)(2+\alpha)^{1/2}}$
(c) $K_p = \dfrac{\alpha^{3/2} p^2}{(1-\alpha)(2+\alpha)^{1/2}}$ (d) $K_p = \dfrac{\alpha^{3/2} p^{1/2}}{(1-\alpha)(2+\alpha)^{1/2}}$
(e) $K_p = \dfrac{\alpha^2 p}{\sqrt{2}}$

56 For the reaction 1 g moles of $CaCO_3$ is enclosed in 5L container

$$CaCO_3(s) \longrightarrow CaO(s) + CO_2(g)$$

$K_p = 1.16$ at 1073 K, then percentage dissociation of $CaCO_3$ is **[DUMET]**

(a) 65% (b) 100% (c) 6.5% (d) zero

2006

57 The equilibrium constant K_p for the thermal dissociation of PCl_5 at 200°C is 1.6 atm. The pressure (in atm) at which it is 50% dissociated at that temperature is **[Kerala CEE]**

(a) 4.8 (b) 4.2 (c) 3.2 (d) 2.4 (e) 6.4

2005

58 Equilibrium constant, K_1 and K_2 for the following equilibria, **[CBSE AIPMT]**

$$NO(g) + \frac{1}{2}O_2 \overset{K_1}{\rightleftharpoons} NO_2(g)$$

and $$2NO(g) \overset{K_2}{\rightleftharpoons} 2NO(g) + O_2(g)$$

are related as

(a) $K_2 = \frac{1}{K_1}$ (b) $K_2 = K_1^2$ (c) $K_2 = \frac{K_1}{2}$ (d) $K_2 = \frac{1}{K_1^2}$

59 At 600°C, K_p for the following reaction is 1 atm,

$$X(g) \rightleftharpoons Y(g) + Z(g).$$

at equilibrium, 50% of $X(g)$ is dissociated. The total pressure of the equilibrium system is p atm. What is the partial pressure (in atm) of $X(g)$ at equilibrium? **[EAMCET]**

(a) 1 (b) 4 (c) 2 (d) 0.5

60 $NH_4COONH_2(s) \rightleftharpoons 2NH_3(g) + CO_2(g)$.

If equilibrium pressure is 3 atm for the above reaction. K_p for the reaction is **[DUMET]**

(a) 4 (b) 27 (c) $\frac{4}{27}$ (d) $\frac{1}{27}$

61 If in the reaction, $N_2O_4 \rightleftharpoons 2NO_2$, x is that part of N_2O_4 which dissociates, then the number of molecules at equilibrium will be **[KCET]**

(a) 1 (b) 3 (c) $(1+x)$ (d) $(1+x)^2$

Answers

1 (a)	2 (b)	3 (b)	4 (b)	5 (a)	6 (c)	7 (b)	8 (c)	9 (c)	10 (d)
11 (a)	12 (c)	13 (c)	14 (b)	15 (a)	16 (d)	17 (b)	18 (e)	19 (c)	20 (a)
21 (b)	22 (d)	23 (a)	24 (d)	25 (c)	26 (c)	27 (d)	28 (b)	29 (b)	30 (a)
31 (a)	32 (c)	33 (a)	34 (a)	35 (c)	36 (b)	37 (b)	38 (b)	39 (b)	40 (c)
41 (d)	42 (c)	43 (b)	44 (c)	45 (c)	46 (a)	47 (b)	48 (a)	49 (d)	50 (b)
51 (d)	52 (b)	53 (c)	54 (c)	55 (d)	56 (c)	57 (a)	58 (d)	59 (a)	60 (a)
61 (c)									

Explanations

1 (a) ΔG° is related to thermodynamic equilibrium constant as

$= 2.303\, RT \log K.$

$= -2.303 \times 8.314 \times 298 \log(2.6 \times 10^8)$

$= -48014.56$ J

The answer should be 48.014 kJ.

2 (b) For the reaction, the reaction quotient Q_C is given by $Q_C = [B][C]/[A]^2$

Given that,

$$[A] = [B] = [C] = 3 \times 10^{-4}\ M$$

Then, $$Q_C = \frac{(3 \times 10^{-4})\ (3 \times 10^{-4})}{(3 \times 10^{-4})^2} = 1$$

As, $Q_C > K_C$, so the reaction will proceed in the reverse direction.

3 (b) Given, $N_2 = 3.0 \times 10^{-3}M$

$O_2 = 4.2 \times 10^{-3}M$

$NO = 2.8 \times 10^{-3}M$

For the given reaction,

$$N_2(g) + O_2(g) \rightleftharpoons 2\,NO(g)$$

equilibrium constant K_C can be written as

$$K_C = \frac{[NO]^2}{[N_2]\,[O_2]}$$

$$\therefore K_C = \frac{(2.8 \times 10^{-3}M)^2}{(3.0 \times 10^{-3}M)\ (4.2 \times 10^{-3}M)} = 0.622$$

$\because K_p = K_C \cdot (RT)^{\Delta n}$

Δn_g = Number of moles of gaseous products − number of moles of gaseous reactants

$\Delta n = 2 - 2 = 0$

$\therefore\ K_p = K_C \cdot (RT)^\circ$

or $K_p = K_C$

or $K_p = 0.622$ atm

4 (b) Given, $N_2 + 3H_2 \rightleftharpoons 2NH_3$, K_1 ...(i)

$N_2 + O_2 \rightleftharpoons 2NO$, K_2 ...(ii)

$H_2 + \frac{1}{2}O_2 \longrightarrow H_2O$, K_3 ...(iii)

To calculate,

$$2NH_3 + \frac{5}{2}O_2 \overset{K}{\rightleftharpoons} 2NO + 3H_2O,\quad K = ?\ ...(iv)$$

On reversing the equation (i) and multiplying the equation (iii) by 3,

$$2NH_3 \rightleftharpoons N_2 + 3H_2, \frac{1}{K_1}\quad ...(v)$$

$$3H_2 + \frac{3}{2}O_2 \longrightarrow 3H_2O, K_3^3\quad ...(vi)$$

Now, add equation. (ii), (v) and (vi), we get the resultant equation. (iv).

$$2NH_3 + \frac{5}{2}O_2 \overset{K}{\rightleftharpoons} 2NO + 3H_2O$$

$$\therefore\ K = \frac{K_2 K_3^3}{K_1}$$

5 (a) For the reaction,

$$H_2(g) + CO_2(g) \rightleftharpoons CO(g) + H_2O(g)$$

	$H_2(g)$	$CO_2(g)$	$CO(g)$	$H_2O(g)$
Initial con.	1	1	0	0
At equil.	$1-x$	$1-x$	x	x

Thus, $$K_p = \frac{x^2}{(1-x)(1-x)} = \frac{x^2}{(1-x)^2}$$

6 (c) $N_2 + 2O_2 \rightleftharpoons 2NO_2$,

K_C for the reaction, $K_C = \frac{[NO_2]^2}{[N_2][O_2]^2}$

For the reaction,

$$NO_2 \rightleftharpoons \frac{1}{2}N_2 + O_2$$

$$K_{C_1} = \frac{[N_2]^{1/2}[O_2]}{[NO_2]}$$

Hence, $K_{C_1} = \frac{1}{\sqrt{K_C}}$ (given, $K_C = 100$)

So, $K_{C_1} = \frac{1}{\sqrt{100}} = 0.1$

7 (b) $N_2O_4(g) \rightleftharpoons 2NO_2(g)$

At equilibrium $(1-x)$ $(2x)$

Total number of moles $= 1 + x$

Value of $x = 0.5$ (given)

$p = 1$ atm

$$K_p = \frac{(p_{NO_2})^2}{p_{N_2O_4}} = \frac{\left(\frac{2x}{1+x} \times p\right)^2}{\left(\frac{1-x}{1+x} \times p\right)}$$

$$= \frac{1}{0.75} \times 1$$

$\Rightarrow$ $K_p = 1.33$ atm

8 (c) $N_2 + 3H_2 \rightleftharpoons 2NH_3$

	N_2	$3H_2$	$2NH_3$
Initially	28 g	6 g	0
	1 mole	3 mole	2 mole
At equil.	(1 − 0.5)	(3 − 1.5)	17 g NH_3

Concentration of 1 mole of N_2 combines with 3 moles of H_2 to produce 2 moles of NH_3 but, since at equilibrium 1 mole of NH_3 is produced. So, 0.5 moles, i.e. 14 g of N_2 are left at equilibrium.

Similarly, 3 moles of $H_2 \equiv 2$ moles of NH_3.

For 1 mole of $NH_3 \equiv 1.5$ mole of H_2

Hence, 1.5 mole, i.e. 3 g of H_2 are left at equilibrium.

So, 14 g of N_2 and 3 g of H_2 are left at equilibrium.

9 (c) $N_2O_4(g) \rightleftharpoons 2NO_2(g)$

	$N_2O_4(g)$	$2NO_2(g)$
Initially	0.1	0
Conc. at equil.	$0.1 - x$	$2x$

Total pressure = 6 bar

Initially, $pV = nRT$

$$p \times 1 = 0.1 \times 0.083 \times 400$$

$$p = 3.32 \text{ bar}$$

$p \propto n$ (at constant V and T)

$$\Rightarrow \frac{p_{\text{initial}}}{p_{\text{equilibrium}}} = \frac{\text{Total number of moles initially}}{\text{Total number of moles at equilibrium}}$$

$$\frac{3.32}{6} = \frac{0.1}{0.1 + x}$$

$\Rightarrow$ $0.1 + x = 0.18$

$\therefore$ $x = 0.08$ mol

Partial pressure of N_2O_4 at equilibrium

$$= \frac{(0.1 - 0.08)}{(0.1 + 0.08)} \times 6$$

$$= \frac{0.02}{0.18} \times 6 = 0.66 \text{ bar}$$

10 (d) The equilibrium constant K_1 for the synthesis of HI = 50

K_2 for dissociation of HI will be equal to $\frac{1}{K_1}$

$$H_2 + I_2 \rightleftharpoons 2HI$$

$\therefore$ $K_2 = \frac{1}{K_1} = \frac{1}{50} = 0.02$

11 (a) We know that, $K_p = K_C(RT)^{\Delta n_g}$

K_p and K_C are equal when $\Delta n_g = 0$

Hence, $K_p = K_C$ in case

$H_2(g) + Cl_2(g) \longrightarrow 2HCl(g)$

because $\Delta n_g = 2 - (1 + 1) = 0$

12 (c) $2SO_2(g) + O_2(g) \rightleftharpoons 2SO_3(g)$

Equilibrium constant for this reaction,

$$K = \frac{[SO_3]^2}{[SO_2]^2[O_2]} \quad \text{...(i)}$$

$$SO_3(g) \rightleftharpoons SO_2(g) + \frac{1}{2}O_2(g)$$

Equilibrium constant for this reaction is

$$K' = \frac{[SO_2][O_2]^{1/2}}{[SO_3]} \quad \text{...(ii)}$$

On squaring both sides in Eq. (ii),

$$(K')^2 = \frac{[SO_2]^2[O_2]}{[SO_3]^2}$$

$$= \frac{1}{K} = \frac{1}{278} \text{ (as } K = 278)$$

$$K' = \sqrt{\frac{1}{278}} = \sqrt{0.003597}$$

$$= 5.99 \times 10^{-2} \text{ or} \approx 6.0 \times 10^{-2}$$

13 (c) $A_2(g) + B_2(g) \rightleftharpoons 2AB(g)$

The equilibrium constant is given by

$$K_C = \frac{[AB]^2}{[A_2][B_2]} = \frac{(2.8 \times 10^{-3})^2}{(3 \times 10^{-3})(4.2 \times 10^{-3})}$$

$$= \frac{7.84}{12.6} = 0.62$$

14 (b) $H_2(g) + Cl_2(g) \rightleftharpoons 2HCl(g)$

$K_p = K_C(RT)^{\Delta n_g}$

Δn_g = number of moles of gaseous products − number of moles of gaseous reactants = 2 − 2 = 0

$$K_p = K_C(RT)^0 \text{ or } K_p = K_C$$

15 (a) As it is known that greater the value of equilibrium constant, greater will be the tendency of the reaction to go in the forward direction. So, for reaction to be fastest, K must be larger. As, $K = 10^2$ is greater among other values.

Hence in this case, reaction would be fastest for completion

16 (d) $N_2(g) + O_2(g) \rightleftharpoons 2NO(g), K_1$

$2NO(g) + O_2(g) \rightleftharpoons 2NO_2(g), K_2$

$N_2(g) + 2O_2(g) \rightleftharpoons 2NO_2(g)$,

$K = K_1 \times K_2$

$\therefore$ For $NO_2(g) \rightleftharpoons \frac{1}{2}N_2(g) + O_2(g)$,

$$K' = \left[\frac{1}{K_1K_2}\right]^{1/2}$$

17 (b) $K_p = \frac{p^2_{CO}}{p_{CO_2}}$. Given $p_{CO} = 10\ p_{CO_2}$

$$K_p = \frac{(10\ p_{CO_2})^2}{p_{CO_2}} = \frac{100pCO_2^2}{pCO_2}$$

$$63 = 100\ p_{CO_2}$$

Let, $p_{CO_2} = x$,

then, $63 = 100x$ or $x = 0.63$

$p_{CO_2} = 0.63$ atm

and $p_{CO} = 10 \times 0.63 = 6.3$ atm

Total equilibrium pressure

$= (6.3 + 0.63)$ atm $= 6.93$ atm

18 (e) $AB(g) \longrightarrow A(g) + B(g)$

$$K_p = \frac{\alpha^2 p}{1 - \alpha^2} = 2.56 \times 10^{-2} \text{ atm}$$

$$\frac{\alpha^2 \times 1\text{atm}}{1 - \alpha^2} = 2.56 \times 10^{-2} \text{ atm}$$

$$\alpha = 0.16 \text{ or } 16\%$$

19 (c) For $A \rightleftharpoons B, K_1 = 2$

For $B \rightleftharpoons C, K_2 = 0.01$

Multiply these by 2

$2A \rightleftharpoons 2B;\ K_1 = (2)^2 = 4$ ...(i)

$2B \rightleftharpoons 2C;$

$K_2 = (0.01)^2 = 10^{-4}$ ...(ii)

On adding Eqs. (i) and (ii), we get

$$2A \rightleftharpoons 2C, K_1 \cdot K_2 = 4 \times 10^{-4}$$

$$2C \rightleftharpoons 2A, K' = \frac{1}{4 \times 10^{-4}}$$

$$= \frac{10000}{4} = 2500$$

20 (*a*) α-D-glucose $\rightleftharpoons$ β-D-glucose

At equil. $1-x$ $\quad x$

$$K_C = \frac{x}{1-x} = 1.8 \Rightarrow x = 1.8 - 1.8x$$

$$\Rightarrow \quad 2.8x = 1.8$$

$$\therefore \quad x = \frac{1.8}{2.8} = 0.643$$

Moles of α-D-glucose

$$= (1-x) = 1 - 0.643 = 0.357$$

Percentage of α-D-glucose

$$= 0.357 \times 100 = 35.7\%$$

21 (*b*) For the reaction,

$$SO_2(g) + \frac{1}{2}O_2(g) \rightleftharpoons SO_3(g)$$

Equilibrium constant,

$$K_1 = \frac{[SO_3]}{[SO_2][O_2]^{1/2}} \quad \text{...(i)}$$

For the reaction,

$$2SO_3(g) \rightleftharpoons 2SO_2(g) + O_2(g)$$

Equilibrium constant,

$$K_2 = \frac{[SO_2]^2[O_2]}{[SO_3]^2} \quad \text{...(ii)}$$

On squaring both sides in Eq. (i),

$$K_1^2 = \frac{[SO_3]^2}{[SO_2]^2[O_2]} \quad \text{...(iii)}$$

On multiplying Eq. (ii) and Eq. (iii),

$$K_1^2 \times K_2 = 1 \Rightarrow K_2 = \frac{1}{K_1^2} \Rightarrow K_1^2 = \frac{1}{K_2}$$

22 (*d*) $K < 1.0$

Final pressure > initial pressure, i.e. at equilibrium total number of gaseous moles present are more than that taken initially.

But, value of K depends on partial pressure of products and reactants.

23 (*a*) $K_p = K_C(RT)^{\Delta n_g}$

$\Delta n_g \neq 0$ for the reaction,

$$2C(s) + O_2(g) \rightleftharpoons 2CO_2(g)$$

Thus, $\quad K_p \neq K_C$

24 (*d*) $\Delta n = 2 - 4 = -2$

$$K_p = K_C(RT)^{\Delta n_g} = K_C(RT)^{-2}$$

25 (*c*) $K_p = K_C(RT)^{\Delta n_g}$

For equation,

$$CaCO_3(s) \rightleftharpoons CaO(s) + CO_2(g), \quad \Delta n_g = 1,$$

$$T = 800 + 273 = 1073 \text{ K}$$

$$K_C = \frac{K_p}{(RT)^{\Delta n_g}} = \frac{167}{(0.0821 \times 1073)^1}$$

$$= 1.89$$

26 (*c*) For the given reaction,

$$\Delta n_g = 2 - 3 = -1$$

$$K_p = K_C(RT)^{\Delta n_g}$$

$$K_C = K_p(RT)^{-\Delta n_g}$$

$$K_C = K_p(RT)$$

(after putting the value of Δn_g)

$$= (2.0 \times 10^{10} \text{ bar}^{-1})$$

$$(0.0821 \text{ bar L K}^{-1} \text{ mol}^{-1}) \times (450 \text{ K})$$

$$= 73.8 \times 10^{10} \text{ L mol}^{-1}$$

$$K_C = 7.38 \times 10^{11} \text{ L mol}^{-1}$$

27 (*d*) $AB(g) \rightleftharpoons A(g) + B(g)$

	$AB(g)$	$A(g)$	$B(g)$
Initially	1	0	0
	$1-0.33$	0.33	0.33

Final pressure after 33% dissociation = 0.67

Total pressure at equilibrium

$$= 1 - 0.33 + 0.33 + 0.33$$

$$\Rightarrow \quad = 1 + 0.33 = 1.33$$

$$p_A = \frac{0.33}{1.33}p \Rightarrow p_B = \frac{0.33}{1.33}p$$

$$\Rightarrow p_{AB} = \frac{0.67}{1.63}p$$

(where, p_A, p_B and p_{AB} are partial pressures of A, B and AB)

$$K_p = \frac{p_A \cdot p_B}{p_{AB}}$$

$$= \frac{\frac{0.33}{1.33}p \cdot \frac{0.33}{1.33}p}{\frac{0.67}{1.33}p} = \frac{(0.33)^2 p}{1.33 \times 0.67}$$

$$= \frac{0.1089 \times p}{0.8911}$$

$$K_p = 0.122p$$

$$\Rightarrow \quad p = \frac{K_p}{0.122} = 8K_p$$

28 (*b*) $K_p = K_C(RT)^{\Delta n_g}$

$K_p = K_C$ only when $(RT)^{\Delta n_g} = 0$

(a) $PCl_5 \rightleftharpoons PCl_3 + Cl_2$

$$\Delta n_g = n_p - n_r$$

$$\Rightarrow \quad 2 - 1 = 1$$

$$\therefore \quad \Delta K_p \neq K_C$$

(b) $N_2 + O_2 \rightleftharpoons 2NO$

$$\Delta n_g = 2 - 2 = 0$$

$$\therefore \quad K_p = K_C$$

(c) $N_2 + 3H_2 \rightleftharpoons 2NH_3$

$$\Delta n_g = 2 - 4 = -2$$

$$\therefore \quad K_p \neq K_C$$

(d) $2SO_3 \rightleftharpoons 2SO_2 + O_2$

$$\Delta n_g = 3 - 2 = 1$$

$$K_p \neq K_C$$

29 (*b*) $K_p = K_C(RT)^{\Delta n_g}$

$\Delta n_g = -1$ for the reaction,

$$2SO_2 + O_2 \rightleftharpoons 2SO_3$$

Thus, for this reaction, K_p is less than K_C.

30 (*a*) $\quad K_p = K_C(RT)^{\Delta n_g}$

$$\Delta n_g = 2 - 2 = 0$$

$$\therefore \quad K_p = K_C$$

31 (*a*) For equation,

$$2SO_2(g) + O_2(g) \rightleftharpoons 2SO_3(g)$$

$$K_C = \frac{[SO_3]^2}{[SO_2]^2[O_2]}$$

$$= \frac{[1.90 \text{ M}]^2}{[0.60\text{M}]^2 [0.82 \text{ M}]}$$

$$= 12.229 \text{ M}^{-1} \text{ or } 12.229 \text{L mol}^{-1}$$

32 (*c*) $A(g) + B(g) \rightleftharpoons C(g) + D(g)$

	$A(g)$	$B(g)$	$C(g)$	$D(g)$
Initially	2	2	0	0
At equil,	$(2-x)$	$(2-x)$	x	x

At equilibrium given that, $3[B] = [C]$ (given)

$$3(2-x) = x \Rightarrow x = \frac{3}{2}$$

$$K_C = \frac{[C][D]}{[A][B]}$$

$$= \frac{\left(\frac{x}{V}\right)^2}{\left(\frac{2-x}{V}\right)^2} = \frac{\left(\frac{3}{2}\right)^2}{\left(2-\frac{3}{2}\right)^2} = 9$$

33 (*a*) If the value of K_C is less than 10^{-3}, reactants predominate and equilibrium shifts towards backward direction.

As the given value of K_C is less than 10^{-3}, i.e. 10^{-4}, thus the reaction will shift largely towards backward direction.

34 (*a*) $Q_p = \frac{p_{PCl_3} \times p_{Cl_2}}{p_{PCl_5}} = \frac{1\text{atm} \times 1\text{atm}}{1\text{atm}} = 1$

Since, $Q_p > K_p$, the equilibrium shifts towards left.

Hence, more PCl_5 will be produced.

35 (*c*) Equilibrium is achieved when rate of forward reaction = rate of backward reaction.

Rest of the other statements are correct.

36 (*b*) $K_p = K_C(RT)^x$

$$x = \Delta n_g = 1 - \left(1 + \frac{1}{2}\right) = -\frac{1}{2}$$

37 (*b*) Standard free energy change,

$$\Delta G° = -2.303\, RT \log K_p$$

If, $\quad \Delta G° = 0 = 2.303\, RT \log K_p$

$$\log K_p = 0$$

$$\therefore \quad K_p = 1$$

38 (*b*) When a balanced equation having equilibrium constant K_p is multiplied by a certain value n, the equilibrium constant for the new equation will be equal to $(K_p)^n$.

In the given equation, $n = 2$

So, $K'_p = (K_p)^2$ or $K_p = \sqrt{K'_p}$

39 (*b*) $\Delta G° = -2.303\, RT \log K_C$

when $\Delta G° < 0$, i.e. −ve, then $K_C > 1$. In this case, forward reaction is feasible showing thereby a large concentration of products.

40 (*c*) $2SO_2(g) + O_2(g) \rightleftharpoons 2SO_3(g)$

Initially, 5 5 0

As 60% SO_2 is used up.

$\therefore$ 2 moles of SO_2 are left at equilibrium

$\therefore$ 40% of 5 moles) $= \frac{40 \times 5}{100} = 2$

Number of moles of O_2 at equilibrium $= 3.5$ ($\because$ 30% of O_2 is used up)

$\therefore$ Number of moles of SO_3 produced at equilibrium = 3

$$\therefore \quad p_{O_2} = \frac{3.5 \times 1}{8.5} = 0.41 \text{atm}$$

41 (*d*) The value of equilibrium constant varies only with temperature. Its value is independent of the concentration of reactants. Thus, when concentrations of H_2 and I_2 are increased, the equilibrium constant will remain same as given, i.e. 6.4.

42 (*c*) $Fe(OH)_3(s) \rightleftharpoons Fe^{3+}(aq) + 3OH^-(aq)$

$\therefore K = [Fe^{3+}][OH^-]^3 \; [\because Fe(OH)_3(s) = 1]$

Hence, if OH^- ion concentration is decreased by 1/4 times, then equilibrium concentration of Fe^{3+} will increase by 64 times.

43 (*b*) $2AB_2(g) \rightleftharpoons 2AB(g) + B_2(g)$

	$2AB_2(g)$	$2AB(g)$	$B_2(g)$
Initial moles	1	0	0
At equil.	$2(1-x)$	$2x$	x

where, x = degree of dissociation

Total moles at equilibrium

$= 2 - 2x + 2x + x = (2 + x)$

so, $p_{AB_2} = \frac{2(1-x)p}{(2+x)}$ and $p_{AB} = \frac{2xp}{(2+x)}$

$$p_{B_2} = \frac{xp}{(2+x)} \Rightarrow K_p = \frac{(p_{AB})^2(p_{B_2})}{(p_{AB_2})^2}$$

$$= \frac{\left(\frac{2xp}{2+x}\right)^2\left(\frac{x}{2+x}p\right)}{\left(\frac{2(1-x)}{(2+x)}p\right)^2}$$

$$= \frac{4x^3p}{4(2+x)(1-x)^2} = \frac{x^3p}{(2+x)(1-x)^2}$$

$[\because x <<< 1$ and 2, so $(1-x) \approx 1, (2+x) \approx 2]$

$$K_p = \frac{x^3p}{2} \quad \therefore x = \left(\frac{2K_p}{p}\right)^{1/3}$$

44 (*c*) From equation, $X \rightleftharpoons Y + Z$

	X	Y	Z
Initial mole	1	0	0
Mole at equilibrium	$(1-\alpha)$	α	α

$$K_{p_1} = \frac{p_Y \times p_Z}{p_X} = \frac{\left[\frac{\alpha \times p_1}{1+\alpha}\right]\left[\frac{\alpha \times p_1}{1+\alpha}\right]}{\left[\frac{1-\alpha}{1+\alpha}\right]p_1}$$

$$= \frac{\alpha^2 p_1}{1-\alpha^2} \quad \text{...(i)}$$

From equation, $A \rightleftharpoons 2B$

	A	$2B$
Initial mole	1	0
Mole at equilibrium	$(1-\alpha)$	2α

$$K_{p_2} = \frac{\left[\frac{2\alpha}{1+\alpha} \cdot p_2\right]^2}{\left[\frac{1-\alpha}{1+\alpha}\right]p_2} = \frac{4\alpha^2 p_2}{1-\alpha^2} \quad \text{...(ii)}$$

From Eqs. (i) and (ii),

$$\frac{K_{p_1}}{K_{p_2}} = \frac{p_1}{4p_2} \Rightarrow \frac{9}{1} = \frac{p_1}{4p_2}$$

$$\Rightarrow \frac{p_1}{p_2} = \frac{36}{1} \Rightarrow p_1 : p_2 = 36:1$$

45 (*c*) If $K > 10^3$, products predominates over reactants. Thus, concentration of products is greater than that of reactants. But if $K < 10^{-3}$, reactants predominates over products, thus, concentration of reactants is greater than that of products.

(a) $A \rightleftharpoons B, K = 0.001$ or 10^{-3} [products] < [reactants]

(b) $M \rightleftharpoons N, K = 10$, [products] > [reactants]

(c) $X \rightleftharpoons Y, K = 0.005$ or 5×10^{-3} [products] < [reactants]

(d) $R \rightleftharpoons P, K = 0.01$ or 10^{-2} appreciable concentration of both reactants and products are present.

46 (*a*) $N_2 + 3H_2 \rightleftharpoons 2NH_3$

$$K_C = \frac{[NH_3]^2}{[N_2][H_2]^3}$$

So, unit of K_C

$$= \frac{\text{mol}^2 \times \text{L} \times \text{L}^3}{\text{L}^2 \times \text{mol} \times \text{mol}^3} = \text{L}^2\,\text{mol}^{-2}$$

47 (*b*) $6HCHO \rightleftharpoons C_6H_{12}O_6$

A very high value of K for the given equilibrium shows that dissociation of glucose to form HCHO is very-very small. Hence, at equilibrium,

$$[C_6H_{12}O_6] = 1\text{M}$$

$$K = \frac{[C_6H_{12}O_6]}{[HCHO]^6}$$

$$\text{i.e. } 6 \times 10^{22} = \frac{1}{[HCHO]^6}$$

$$\text{or} \quad [HCHO] = \left(\frac{1}{6 \times 10^{22}}\right)^{1/6}$$

$$= 1.6 \times 10^{-4}\text{ M}$$

48 (*a*) $H_2 + I_2 \rightleftharpoons 2HI$

	H_2	I_2	$2HI$
Initially	1	1	0
At equil. (moles)	$1-\alpha$	$1-\alpha$	2α
(mol/L)	$\frac{1-\alpha}{2}$	$\frac{1-\alpha}{2}$	$\frac{2\alpha}{2}$

where, α = degree of dissociation

Since, rate constant of forward reaction = rate constant of backward reaction

$$\because \quad K_C = \frac{[HI]^2}{[H_2][I_2]}$$

$$\therefore \; 1 = \frac{\left(\frac{2\alpha}{2}\right)^2}{\left(\frac{1-\alpha}{2}\right)\left(\frac{1-\alpha}{2}\right)} \quad (\because K_C = 1)$$

$$1 = \frac{(2\alpha)^2}{(1-\alpha)^2} \Rightarrow 1 - \alpha = 2\alpha \Rightarrow \alpha = \frac{1}{3}$$

Percentage dissociation

$$= \frac{1}{3} \times 100 = 33.33\% = 33\%$$

49 (*d*) $N_2O_4(g) \rightleftharpoons 2NO_2(g)$

Molar concentration of

$$[N_2O_4] = \frac{9.2}{92} = 0.1 \text{ mol/L}$$

In equilibrium state when it 50% dissociates,

$$[N_2O_4] = 0.05\text{ M}, \quad [NO_2] = 0.1\text{ M}$$

$$K_C = \frac{[NO_2]^2}{[N_2O_4]} = \frac{0.1 \times 0.1}{0.05} = 0.2 \text{ mol/L}$$

50 (*b*) Concentration of

$$[NH_3] = \frac{\text{number of moles}}{\text{volume (in L)}} = \frac{6}{10} = 0.6$$

$2NH_3 \rightleftharpoons N_2 + 3H_2$

	$2NH_3$	N_2	$3H_2$
Initial mole	0.6	0	0
At equil.	$0.6 - 2x$	x	$3x$

Then, concentration of NH_3 at equilibrium will be $0.6 - 2x$.

51 (*d*) $PCl_5 \rightleftharpoons PCl_3 + Cl_2$

	PCl_5	PCl_3	Cl_2
Initially	3 mol	3 mol	2 mol
At equil.	$(3-x)$ mol	$(3+x)$ mol	$(2+x)$ mol

$\because \quad 3 - x = 1.5$

$\therefore \quad x = 1.5$

Number of moles of $PCl_3 = 3 + x$
$= 3 + 1.5 = 4.5$ mol

52 (*b*) For the reaction,

$C(s) + CO_2(g) \rightleftharpoons 2CO(g)$

$$K_p = \frac{\text{partial pressure of gaseous products}}{\text{partial pressure of gaseous reactants}}$$

$$= \frac{p_{CO}^2}{p_{CO_2}} = \frac{(4)^2}{2} \quad (\because p_C = 1)$$

$= 8$

53 (*c*) $2KClO_3 \xrightarrow{\Delta} 2KCl + 3O_2$

Above reaction is example of thermal decomposition. $KClO_3$ is decomposed into KCl and O_2 but KCl and O_2 cannot be converted into $KClO_3$. Hence, it is an example of irreversible reaction.

54 (*c*) The required equation for the oxidation of NH_3 by oxygen to give NO is

$$4NH_3 + 5O_2 \xrightarrow[800°C]{\text{Pt (gauze)}} 4NO + 6H_2O$$

For this, $K = \dfrac{[NO]^4\,[H_2O]^6}{[NH_3]^4\,[O_2]^5}$

For the Eq. (i), $K_1 = \dfrac{[NH_3]^2}{[N_2][H_2]^3}$

For the Eq. (ii), $K_2 = \dfrac{[NO]^2}{[N_2][O_2]}$

For the Eq. (iii), $K_3 = \dfrac{[H_2O]}{[H_2][O_2]^{1/2}}$

For getting the value of K, the following must be done,.

$$K_1^2 = \frac{[NH_3]^4}{[N_2]^2\,[H_2]^6},$$

$$K_2^2 = \frac{[NO]^4}{[N_2]^2\,[O_2]^2},$$

$$K_3^6 = \frac{[H_2O]^6}{[H_2]^6\,[O_2]^{\frac{6}{2}=3}}, \quad K = \frac{K_2^2 \times K_3^6}{K_1^2}$$

On substituting the values, we get

$$K = \frac{[NO]^4\,[H_2O]^6}{[NH_3]^4\,[O_2]^5}$$

55 (*d*) $H_2O(g) \rightleftharpoons H_2(g) + \frac{1}{2}O_2(g)$

	$H_2O(g)$	$H_2(g)$	$O_2(g)$
Initial	1	0	0
At equil.	$(1-\alpha)$	α	$\alpha/2$

Total moles

$$= (1-\alpha) + \alpha + \frac{\alpha}{2} = 1 + \frac{\alpha}{2}$$

$$\text{Partial pressure of } H_2O = p\left(\frac{1-\alpha}{1+\frac{\alpha}{2}}\right)$$

$$\text{Partial pressure of } H_2 = p\left(\frac{\alpha}{1+\frac{\alpha}{2}}\right)$$

$$\text{Partial pressure of } O_2 = p\left(\frac{\alpha/2}{1+\alpha/2}\right) = p\left(\frac{\alpha}{2+\alpha}\right)$$

$$K_p = \frac{p_{H_2} \cdot p_{O_2}^{1/2}}{p_{H_2O}}$$

$$\Rightarrow \quad K_p = \frac{\alpha^{3/2}\,p^{1/2}}{(1-\alpha)\,(2+\alpha)^{1/2}}$$

56 (*c*) $CaCO_3(s) \longrightarrow CaO(s) + CO_2(g)$,

$K_p = p_{CO_2}$

($\therefore$ only gaseous molecule count)

$K_p = K_C(RT)^{\Delta n}$

Then, moles of $CaCO_3$, dissociated is

x = percentage dissociation

$$1.16 = \frac{x}{5}\,(0.0821 \times 1073)^1$$

$$x = \frac{1.16 \times 5}{0.0821 \times 1073} = \frac{5.8}{88.1} = 0.0658$$

$= 0.0658 \times 100 = 6.58\% = 6.5\%$

57 (*a*) $PCl_5 \rightleftharpoons PCl_3 + Cl_2$

	PCl_5	PCl_3	Cl_2
Initially	1	0	0
At equil.	$(1-\alpha)$	α	α

$$K_p = \frac{p_{PCl_3} \times p_{Cl_2}}{p_{PCl_5}}$$

$$\Rightarrow \quad K_p = \frac{\alpha^2 p}{(1+\alpha)(1-\alpha)}$$

$$1.6 = \frac{0.5 \times 0.5 \times p}{(1+0.5)\,(1-0.5)} = \frac{0.25 \times p}{0.75}$$

$\therefore \quad p = 4.8$ atm

58 (*d*) $NO(g) + \frac{1}{2}O_2(g) \overset{K_1}{\rightleftharpoons} NO_2(g)$

So, $K_1 = \dfrac{[NO_2]}{[NO][O_2]^{1/2}}$ ...(i)

$2NO_2(g) \overset{K_2}{\rightleftharpoons} 2NO + O_2(g)$

So, $K_2 = \dfrac{[NO]^2[O_2]}{[NO_2]^2}$ ...(ii)

From Eq. (i),

$$K_1^2 = \frac{[NO_2]^2}{[NO]^2\,[O_2]}$$

or $\dfrac{1}{K_1^2} = \dfrac{[NO]^2[O_2]}{[NO_2]^2}$ ...(iii)

From Eq. (ii) and (iii),

$$K_2 = \frac{1}{K_1^2}$$

59 (*a*) $X(g) \rightleftharpoons Y(g) + Z(g)$

	$X(g)$	$Y(g)$	$Z(g)$
Initial	1	0	0
At equilibrium	0.5	0.5	0.5
Partial pressure	$\frac{0.5p}{1.5}$	$\frac{0.5p}{1.5}$	$\frac{0.5p}{1.5}$

$$K_p = \frac{p_Y \cdot p_Z}{p_X}$$

$$1 = \frac{p/3 \times p/3}{p/3} \Rightarrow p = 3 \text{ atm}$$

Partial pressure of $X = \dfrac{p}{3} = 1$ atm

60 (*a*) $NH_4COONH_2(s) \rightleftharpoons 2NH_3(g) + CO_2(g)$

$$\therefore \quad K_p = \frac{p_{NH_3}^2 \times p_{CO_2}}{p_{NH_4COONH_2}(s)}$$

But, $p_{NH_4COONH_2} = 1$

(since, p of solids is taken as one)

$\therefore \quad K_p = p_{NH_3}^2 \times p_{CO_2}$

where, $p_{NH_3} = \dfrac{2}{3} \times 3$

and $p_{CO_2} = \dfrac{1}{3} \times 3 = 1$

$\therefore \quad K_p = (2)^2 \times 1 = 4$

61 (*c*) $N_2O_4 \rightleftharpoons 2NO_2$

	N_2O_4	$2NO_2$
Before dissociation	1	0
After dissociation	$(1-x)$	$2x$

Total number of moles at equilibrium
$= 1 - x + 2x = 1 + x$

Topic 2

Le-Chatelier's Principle

2018

1 Assertion (A) K_p can be equal to or less than or even greater than the value of K_C.

Reason (R) $K_p = K_C (RT)^{\Delta n}$

Relation between K_p and K_C depends on the change in the number of moles of gaseous reactants and products. **[AIIMS]**

(a) Both A and R an correct and R is the correct explanation of A
(b) Both A and R are correct but R is not the correct explanation of A
(c) A is correct but R is incorrect
(d) Both A and R are incorrect

2014

2 For a given exothermic reaction, K_p and K'_p are the equilibrium constants at temperatures T_1 and T_2, respectively. Assuming that heat of reaction is constant in temperature range between T_1 and T_2, it is readily observed that **[CBSE AIPMT]**

(a) $K_p > K'_p$ (b) $K_p < K'_p$
(c) $K_p = K'_p$ (d) $K_p = 1/K'_p$

3 For the reversible reaction,

$$N_2(g) + 3H_2(g) \rightleftharpoons 2NH_3(g) + \text{Heat}$$

the equilibrium shifts in forward direction **[CBSE AIPMT]**

(a) by increasing the concentration of $NH_3(g)$
(b) by decreasing the pressure
(c) by decreasing the concentrations of $N_2(g)$ and $H_2(g)$
(d) by increasing pressure and decreasing temperature

4 Predict the effect of increased pressure on the following reaction equilibrium,

$$2SO_2(g) + O_2(g) \rightleftharpoons 2SO_3(g)$$ **[Manipal]**

(a) Equilibrium shift to the right
(b) Equilibrium shift to the left
(c) No effect on equilibrium
(d) Reaction stops

5 In which one of the following equilibria will the point of equilibrium shift to left when the pressure of the system is increased? **[Kerala CEE]**

(a) $H_2(g) + I_2(g) \rightleftharpoons 2HI(g)$
(b) $2NH_3(g) \rightleftharpoons N_2(g) + 3H_2(g)$
(c) $C(s) + O_2(g) \rightleftharpoons CO_2(g)$
(d) $2H_2(g) + O_2(g) \rightleftharpoons 2H_2O(g)$
(e) $2H_2(g) + O_2(g) \rightleftharpoons H_2O(l)$

2013

6 In which of the following equilibrium system is the rate of backward reaction favoured by increase of pressure?

(a) $PCl_5 \rightleftharpoons PCl_3 + Cl_2$ (b) $2SO_2 + O_2 \rightleftharpoons 2SO_3$
(c) $N_2 + 3H_2 \rightleftharpoons 2NH_3$ (d) $N_2 + O_2 \rightleftharpoons 2NO$

2011

7 The value of ΔH for the reaction, $X_2(g) + 4Y_2(g) \rightleftharpoons 2XY_4(g)$ is less than zero. Formation of $XY_4(g)$ will be favoured at **[CBSE AIPMT]**

(a) high pressure and low temperature
(b) high temperature and high pressure
(c) low pressure and low temperature
(d) high temperature and low pressure

8 Given exothermic reaction,

$CoCl_4^{2-}(aq) + 6H_2O(l) \rightleftharpoons [Co(H_2O)_6]^{2+} + 4Cl^-$.

Which one of the following will decrease the equilibrium concentration of $CoCl_4^{2-}$? **[DUMET]**

(a) Addition of HCl (b) Addition of $Co(NO_3)_2$
(c) The solution is diluted with water
(d) The temperature is increased

2010

9 For a reversible chemical reaction where the forward process is exothermic, which of the following is correct?

(a) The backward reaction has higher activation energy than the forward reaction **[WB JEE]**
(b) The backward and the forward processes have the same activation energy
(c) The backward reaction has lower activation energy
(d) No activation energy is required at all since energy is liberated in the process

10 A reversible chemical reaction is having two reactants, in equilibrium. If concentration of the reactants are doubled, then the equilibrium constant will **[JCECE]**

(a) be doubled (b) become one-fourth
(c) be halved (d) remain the same

2009

11 Assertion (A) For the reaction,

$$2NO(g) + O_2(g) \rightleftharpoons 2NO_2(g)$$

Increase in pressure favours the formation of NO_2.

Reason (R) The reaction is exothermic. **[AIIMS]**

(a) Both A and R are correct and R is the correct explanation of A
(b) Both A and R are correct but R is not the correct explanation of A
(c) A is correct but R is incorrect
(d) Both A and R are incorrect

12 Which reaction is not affected by change in pressure? **[AFMC]**

(a) $H_2 + I_2 \rightleftharpoons 2HI$ (b) $2C + O_2 \rightleftharpoons 2CO$
(c) $N_2 + 3H_2 \rightleftharpoons 2NH_3$ (d) $PCl_5 \rightleftharpoons PCl_3 + Cl_2$

13 For the equilibrium,

$$2NO_2(g) \rightleftharpoons N_2O_4(g) + 14.6\,\text{kcal}$$

increase in temperature **[UP CPMT]**

(a) favours the formation of N_2O_4
(b) favours the decomposition of N_2O_4
(c) does not affect equilibrium
(d) stop the reaction

14 For the given equilibrium,

$$2SO_2 + O_2 \rightleftharpoons 2SO_3 + \text{Heat}$$

the equilibrium reaction proceeds in forward direction when **[OJEE]**

(a) oxygen is removed (b) SO_3 is added
(c) heat is added (d) oxygen is added

15 For the equilibrium, $H_2 + I_2 \rightleftharpoons 2HI$, which of the following will affect the equilibrium constant? **[KCET]**

(a) Pressure change
(b) Concentration change
(c) Catalyst
(d) Promoter
(e) Temperature change

16 In which one of the following equilibria, the increase of pressure over the equilibrium will favour the backward reaction? **[J&K CET]**

(a) Decomposition equilibrium of HI
(b) Formation equilibrium of SO_3
(c) Decomposition equilibrium of NH_3
(d) Formation of equilibrium of PCl_5

17 At the equilibrium of the reaction,

$$2X(g) + Y(g) \longrightarrow X_2Y(g)$$

the number of moles of X_2Y at equilibrium is affected by the **[DUMET]**

(a) temperature and pressure
(b) temperature only
(c) pressure only
(d) temperature, pressure and catalyst used

2008

18 The reaction favoured at low pressure is **[BHU]**

(a) $H_2(g) + I_2(g) \rightleftharpoons 2HI(g)$
(b) $PCl_5(g) \rightleftharpoons PCl_3(g) + Cl_2(g)$
(c) $N_2(g) + O_2(g) \rightleftharpoons 2NO(g)$
(d) $N_2(g) + 3H_2(g) \rightleftharpoons 2NH_3(g)$

19 $N_2 + 3H_2 \rightleftharpoons 2NH_3$ + Heat. What is the effect of the increase of temperature on the equilibrium of the reaction? **[KCET]**

(a) Equilibrium is shifted to the left
(b) Equilibrium is shifted to the right
(c) Equilibrium is unaltered
(d) Reaction rate does not change

20 When hydrogen molecules decomposed into its atoms, which condition gives maximum yield of H-atoms? **[BCECE]**

(a) High temperature and low pressure
(b) Low temperature and high pressure
(c) High temperature and high pressure
(d) Low temperature and low pressure

2007

21 Reaction, $BaO_2(s) \rightleftharpoons BaO(s) + O_2(g)$; $\Delta H = +\text{ve}$. In equilibrium condition, pressure of O_2 depends on **[Punjab PMET]**

(a) increased mass of BaO_2
(b) increased mass of BaO
(c) increased temperature of equilibrium
(d) increased mass of BaO_2 and BaO both

2006

22 For the reaction,

$$CH_4(g) + 2O_2(g) \rightleftharpoons CO_2(g) + 2H_2O(l),$$
$$\Delta_r H = -170.8\,\text{kJ mol}^{-1}$$

Which of the following statements is not true?

(a) At equilibrium, the concentration of $CO_2(g)$ and $H_2O(l)$ are not equal **[CBSE AIPMT]**
(b) The equilibrium constant for the reaction is given by $K_p = \dfrac{[CO_2]}{[CH_4][O_2]}$
(c) Addition on $CH_4(g)$ or $O_2(g)$ at equilibrium will cause a shift to the right
(d) The reaction is exothermic

23 For reaction, $3X + Y \rightleftharpoons X_3Y, \Delta H = +\text{ve}$, amount of X_3Y can be changed by **[JCECE]**

(a) changing temperature
(b) changing pressure
(c) changing temperature and pressure
(d) changing temperature, pressure and adding catalyst

2005

24 $CaCO_3 \rightleftharpoons CaO + CO_2$ reaction in lime kiln goes to completion, because **[AFMC]**

(a) CaO does not react to CO_2 to give $CaCO_3$
(b) backward reaction is very low
(c) CO_2 formed escapes out
(d) None of the above

Answers

1 (a)	2 (a)	3 (d)	4 (a)	5 (b)	6 (a)	7 (a)	8 (c)	9 (a)	10 (d)
11 (b)	12 (a)	13 (b)	14 (d)	15 (c)	16 (c)	17 (a)	18 (b)	19 (a)	20 (a)
21 (c)	22 (b)	23 (c)	24 (c)						

Explanations

1 (*a*) Both Assertion and Reason are correct and Reason is the correct explanation of Assertion.

$$K_p = K_C(RT)^{\Delta n}$$

$\Delta n =$ number of moles of gaseous products – number of moles of gaseous reactants

When, $\Delta n > 1$, $K_p > K_C$
When, $\Delta n < 1$, $K_p < K_C$
When, $\Delta n = 0$, $K_p = K_C$

2 (*a*) The equilibrium constant at two different temperatures for a thermodynamic process is given by

$$\log\frac{K_2}{K_1} = \frac{\Delta H°}{2.303R}\left[\frac{1}{T_1} - \frac{1}{T_2}\right]$$

Here, K_1 and K_2 are replaced by K_p and K'_p.

Therefore,

$$\log\frac{K'_p}{K_p} = \frac{\Delta H°}{2.303R}\left[\frac{1}{T_1} - \frac{1}{T_2}\right]$$

For exothermic reaction,

$T_2 > T_1$ and $\Delta H = -$ ve

$\therefore \quad K_p > K'_p$

3 (*d*) Any change in the concentration, pressure and temperature of the reaction results in change in the direction of equilibrium. This change in the direction of equilibrium is governed by Le-Chatelier's principle. According to Le-Chatelier's principle, equilibrium shifts in the opposite direction to undo the change.

$$N_2(g) + 3H_2(g) \rightleftharpoons 2NH_3(g)$$

(a) **Increasing the concentration of $NH_3(g)$** On increasing the concentration of $NH_3(g)$, the equilibrium shifts in the backward direction where concentration of $NH_3(g)$ decreases.

(b) **Decreasing the pressure** Since, $p \propto n$ (number of moles), therefore equilibrium shifts in the backward direction where number of moles are increasing.

(c) **Decreasing the concentration of $N_2(g)$ and $H_2(g)$** Equilibrium shifts in the backward direction when concentration of $N_2(g)$ and $H_2(g)$ decreases.

(d) **Increasing pressure and decreasing temperature** On increasing pressure, equilibrium shifts in the forward direction where number of moles decreases while on decreasing temperature, it will move in forward direction where temperature increases.

4 (*a*) On increasing pressure, volume decreases. Hence, the reaction will move in the direction where there are less number of moles(according to Le-Chatelier's principle).

$$\underset{(2+1)\text{ moles}}{2SO_2 + O_2} \rightleftharpoons \underset{2\text{ moles}}{2SO_3}$$

Hence, the equilibrium will move towards right, to overcome change.

5 (*b*) According to Le-Chatelier's principle, on increasing pressure, volume will decrease. Hence, the reaction will move in the direction where there are less number of moles. In given reaction, in option (b) $2NH_3 \rightleftharpoons N_2 + 3H_2$ equilibrium will shift to the left.

6 (*a*) The rate of backward reaction is favoured by increase of pressure in the reaction,

$$PCl_5 \rightleftharpoons PCl_3 + Cl_2$$

Due to increase in pressure, the reaction takes place in a direction where number of moles decreases.

7 (*a*) According to Le-Chatelier's principle, the reaction (in forward direction) is favourable at high pressure and low temperature because $\Delta n_g =$ negative and reaction is exothermic in forward direction.

8 (*c*) Here, water is reactant so increase in concentration of reactant shifts the equilibrium in the forward direction. Hence, on diluting the solution, the equilibrium shifts in the forward direction which leads to the decrease in concentration of $CoCl_4^{2-}$.

9 (*a*) The energy profile diagram for an exothermic reaction is as,

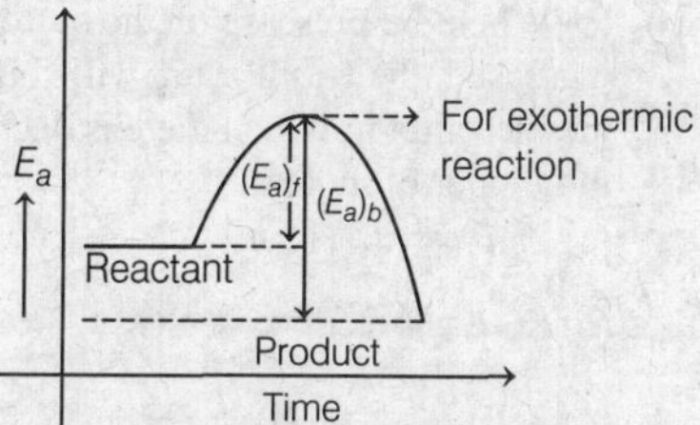

As from graph, it is clear that

$$(E_a)_b > (E_a)_f$$

Thus, option (a) is correct.

10 (*d*) Equilibrium constant depends only upon the temperature, not upon the concentration of reactant.

Thus, on doubling concentration, equilibrium constant remains the same.

11 (*b*) $2NO + O_2 \rightleftharpoons 2NO_2$

In this reaction,
Number of moles of gaseous reactants, $n_r = 3$
Number of moles of gaseous products, $n_p = 2$
Since, n_p is less than n_r, according to Le-Chatelier principle, increase in pressure shifts the equilibrium in forward direction, i.e. more NO_2 is formed.

The reaction given above is exothermic.

12 (*a*) The reaction in which number of gaseous products (n_p) is equal to number of gaseous reactants, is not affected by change in pressure.

For reaction, $H_2 + I_2 \rightleftharpoons 2HI$
Number of gaseous products = 2
Number of gaseous reactants = 2
Hence, it is not affected by change in pressure.

13 (*b*) The given reaction is exothermic and according to Le-Chatelier, principle high temperature shifts the equilibrium in backward direction. In other words, high temperature favours the decomposition of N_2O_4.

14 (*d*) According to Le-Chatelier's principle, when O_2 is added it combines with SO_2 to form SO_3. Hence, the reaction proceeds in forward direction.

15 (*c*) Equilibrium constant depends only upon temperature and nature of reaction but independent of initial concentration of reactants, presence of catalyst and pressure.

16 (*c*) When the pressure on the system is increased, the equilibrium will shift in the direction in which there is decrease in number of moles.

(a) $2HI \rightleftharpoons H_2 + I_2$

(b) $SO_2 + \frac{1}{2}O_2 \rightleftharpoons SO_3$

(c) $2NH_3 \rightleftharpoons N_2 + 3H_2$

(d) $PCl_3 + Cl_2 \rightleftharpoons PCl_5$

So, in reaction (c) the increase in pressure will favour backward reaction.

17 (*a*) For the reaction,

$$2X(g) + Y(g) \rightleftharpoons X_2Y(g)$$

On increasing the pressure, the formation of the product increases.

Increase in temperature also affects the production of X_2Y as this increases kinetic energy of molecule.

18 (*b*) At equilibrium, low pressure favours those reactions which are accompanied by increase in total number of moles and high pressure favours those reactions which take place with decrease in total number of moles. However, pressure has no effect on an equilibrium reaction which proceeds with no change in total number of moles.

Hence, reaction

$$PCl_5(g) \rightleftharpoons PCl_3(g) + Cl_2(g)$$

$$\Delta n_g = n_P - n_R$$

or $\quad = 2 - 1 = 1$

is favoured by low pressure.

19 (*a*) $N_2 + 3H_2 \rightleftharpoons 2NH_3 + \text{Heat}$

It is an exothermic reaction, so high temperature favours backward reaction. Hence, equilibrium is shifted towards the left.

20 (*a*) $\underset{\text{Hydrogen molecule}}{H_2} \xrightarrow[2000°C]{\text{Electric arc}} \underset{\text{Atomic hydrogen}}{2H}$;

$$\Delta H = +104.5\,\text{kcal}$$

The reaction is endothermic. For endothermic reaction, increase in temperature shift the equilibrium in forward direction. To proceed forward, the pressure must be low because for the above reaction, increase of pressure will favour backward reaction. So, for maximum yield, the conditions are high temperature and low pressure.

21 (*c*) $BaO_2(s) \rightleftharpoons BaO(s) + O_2(g)$;

$$\Delta H = +\text{ve}$$

According to law of mass action,

The rate of forward reaction = R_1

$$R_1 \propto [BaO_2] \text{ or } R_1 = k_1[BaO_2]$$

But concentration of solid = 1

Then, $\quad R_1 = k_1$

Similarly, the rate of backward reaction = R_2

$$R_2 \propto [BaO][O_2]$$

or $\quad R_2 = k_2\,[BaO][O_2]$

$\because$ Conc. of $[BaO] = 1$

or $\quad R_2 = k_2[O_2]$

At equilibrium, $R_1 = R_2$

$$k_1 = k_2\,[O_2] \quad \text{or } k_1 = k_2 \cdot p_{O_2}$$

where, p_{O_2} = partial pressure of O_2

or $\quad \frac{k_1}{k_2} = p_{O_2}$ (equilibrium constant)

$\therefore \quad \frac{k_1}{k_2} = K \text{ or } K = p_{O_2}$

So, from the above it is clear that pressure of O_2 does not depend upon concentration of reactants. The given equation is an endothermic reaction. If the temperature of such reaction is increased, then dissociation of BaO_2 would increase and more O_2 is produced.

22 (*b*) For the reaction,

$$CH_4(g) + 2O_2(g) \rightleftharpoons CO_2(g), + 2H_2O(l)$$

$$\Delta H_r = -170.8\,\text{kJ mol}^{-1}$$

$$K_C = \frac{[CO_2]}{[CH_4][O_2]^2}$$

$(\because [\text{liquid}] = 1)$ ...(i)

and $K_p = \frac{p_{CO_2}}{p_{CH_4} \times p^2_{O_2}}$ ...(ii)

Thus, in it the concentration of $CO_2(g)$ and $H_2O(l)$ are not equal at equilibrium as the number of moles of dboth are different.

The equilibrium constant

$(K_p) = \frac{[CO_2]}{[CH_4][O_2]}$ is not correct.

23 (*c*) $3X + Y \rightleftharpoons X_3Y - Q$ cal

According to Le-Chatelier's principle, amount of X_3Y can be changed by changing temperature, because reaction is endothermic and it can also be changed by changing in pressure because number of moles of reactants and products are different. The amount can never change by adding catalyst because the above example is a reversible reaction.

24 (*c*) In the lime kiln, the CO_2 formed during decomposition of calcium carbonate escapes out continuously. Hence, the reaction is not a reversible one and proceeds towards completion. On the other hand, if the reaction takes place in a closed container where none of the reactant or product is allowed to escape, then the reaction soon reaches the equilibrium state.

Topic 3

Ostwald's Dilution Law

(Concept of Acids and Bases and Ionic Equilibrium)

1 Which of the following cannot act both as Bronsted acid and as Bronsted base? **[NEET (Odisha)]**

(a) HCO_3^- (b) NH_3
(c) HCl (d) HSO_4^-

2 Conjugate base for Bronsted acids H_2O and HF are **[NEET (National)]**

(a) H_3O^+ and F^-, respectively
(b) OH^- and F^-, respectively
(c) H_3O^+ and H_2F^+, respectively
(d) OH^- and H_2F^+, respectively

2018

3 Assertion (A) The pH of acid rain is less than 5.6.

Reason (R) Carbon dioxide present in the atmosphere dissolves in rain water and becomes carbonic acid. **[AIIMS]**

(a) Both A and R as correct and R is the correc explanation of A
(b) Both A and R are correct but R is not the correct explantion of A
(c) A is correct but R is incorrect
(d) Both A and R are incorrect

4 Which of the following pair behaves as strong and weak base hydride respectively
NH_3, PH_3, AsH_3, SbH_3, BiH_3 **[JIPMER]**

(a) NH_3, PH_3 (b) NH_3, BiH_3
(c) PH_3, BiH_3 (d) BiH_3, AsH_3

5 In which of the following arrangements, the order is not strictly according to the property written against it? **[AIIMS**

(a) $CO_2 < SiO_2 < SnO_2 < PbO_2$ (oxidising power)
(b) $HF < HCl < HBr < HI$ (acidic strength)
(c) $NH_3 > PH_3 < AsH_3 < SbH_3$ (basic strength)
(d) $B < C < O < N$ (first ionisation enthalpy)

2017

6 Assertion (A) The ionisation of hydrogen sulphide in water is low in the presence of HCl.

Reason (R) H_2S is a weak acid. **[AIIMS]**

(a) Both A and R an correct and R is the correct explanation of A
(b) Both A and R are correct but R is not the correct explanation of A
(c) A is correct but R is incorrect
(d) Both A and R are incorrect

2016

7 Which of the following fluoro-compounds is most likely to behave as a Lewis base? **[NEET]**

(a) BF_3 (b) PF_3
(c) CF_4 (d) SiF_4

2013

8 Which is the strongest acid in the following? **[NEET]**

(a) H_2SO_4 (b) $HClO_3$
(c) $HClO_4$ (d) H_2SO_3

9 The dissociation constant of two acids HA_1 and HA_2 are 3.0×10^{-4} and 1.8×10^{-5}, respectively. The relative strength of the acids is **[UP CPMT, RPMT]**

(a) 1 : 16 (b) 1 : 4 (c) 4 : 1 (d) 16 : 1

10 The dissociation constant value of four acids are as follows. Which of the values stand for strongest acid? **[Manipal]**

(a) 2×10^{-4} (b) 2×10^{-2}
(c) 3×10^{-4} (d) 0.02×10^{-2}

11 For a weak acid, the incorrect statement is **[Manipal]**

(a) its dissociation constant is low
(b) its pK_a is very low
(c) it is partially dissociated
(d) solution of its sodium salt is alkaline in water

12 Which one of the following can be classified as a Bronsted base? **[KCET]**

(a) NO_3^- (b) H_3O^+
(c) CH_3COOH (d) NH_4^+

2012

13 Ammonia gas dissolves in water to form NH_4OH. In this reaction, water acts as **[AIIMS]**

(a) conjugate base (b) a non-polar molecule
(c) an acid (d) a base

14 Which of the following is not a conjugate acid-base pairs? **[Manipal]**

(a) HPO_3^{2-}, PO_3^{3-} (b) $H_2PO_4^-$, HPO_4^{2-}
(c) $H_2PO_4^-$, H_3PO_4 (d) $H_2PO_4^-$, PO_3^{2-}

2011

15 Which of the following is least likely to behave as Lewis base? **[CBSE AIPMT]**

(a) OH^- (b) H_2O (c) NH_3 (d) BF_3

16 A monobasic weak acid solution has a molarity of 0.005 and pH of 5. What is its percentage ionisation in this solution. [Kerala CEE]
(a) 2.0 (b) 0.2 (c) 0.5 (d) 0.25
(d) 20.0

17 Which one of the following species acts only as a base? [DUMET]
(a) H_2S (b) HS^-
(c) S^{2-} (d) H_2O

18 Which one of the following is not acid-base conjugate pair? [DUMET]
(a) $HONO, NO_2^-$
(b) $CH_3NH_3^+, CH_3NH_2$
(c) $C_6H_5—COOH, C_6H_5COO^-$
(d) $H_3O^+; OH^-$

2010

19 Which one of the following molecular hydrides acts as a Lewis acid? [CBSE AIPMT]
(a) CH_4 (b) NH_3 (c) H_2O (d) B_2H_6

20 Conjugate acid-base pair differ by [MHT CET]
(a) electron (b) proton
(c) neutron (d) hydroxyl group

21 How many gram-equivalents of NaOH are required to neutralise 25 cm^3 of a decinormal HCl solution? [MHT CET]
(a) 0.00125 (b) 0.0025
(c) 0.0050 (d) 0.025

22 The conjugate base of $H_2PO_4^-$ is [Manipal]
(a) PO_4^{3-} (b) P_2O_5
(c) H_3PO_4 (d) HPO_4^{2-}

23 The charge balance equation of species in 0.100 M acetic acid solution is given by [AMU]
(a) $[H^+]=[OH^-]$
(b) $[H^+]=[CH_3COO^-]$
(c) $[H^+]=[OH^-]+[CH_3COO^-]$
(d) $2[H^+]=[OH^-]+[CH_3COO^-]$

24 The strongest Bronsted base is [JCECE]
(a) ClO_3^- (b) ClO_2^-
(c) ClO_4^- (d) ClO^-

2009

25 Which of the following molecules acts as Lewis acid? [CBSE AIPMT]
(a) $(CH_3)_3B$ (b) $(CH_3)_2O$
(c) $(CH_3)_3P$ (d) $(CH_3)_3N$

26 Ammonium ion is [AFMC]
(a) a conjugate acid
(b) a conjugate base
(c) Neither an acid nor a base
(d) Both an acid and a base

27 In a solution, 0.02 M acetic acid is 4% dissociated. The $[OH^-]$ in the solution is [MHT CET]
(a) 8×10^{-4} (b) 2×10^{-14} (c) 88×10^{10} (d) 1.25×10^{-11}

28 0.1 M solution of which of the following has almost unity degree of dissociation? [MHT CET]
(a) Ammonium chloride (b) Potassium chloride
(c) Sodium acetate (d) All of these

29 The number of hydroxyl ions in 10 cm^3 of 0.2 M HCl solution is [MHT CET]
(a) 5×10^{-14} (b) 3×10^{8} (c) 3×10^{12} (d) 5×10^{-12}

30 *B*OH is a weak base. Molar concentration of *B*OH that provides a $[OH^-]$ of 1.5×10^{-3} M is ($K_b=(BOH)=1.5\times10^{-5}$) [Manipal]
(a) 1.5×10^{-5} M (b) 0.015M
(c) 0.0015M (d) 0.15M

31 H_3BO_3 is [CG PMT, Haryana PMT]
(a) monobasic acid and weak Lewis acid
(b) monobasic acid and weak Bronsted acid
(c) monobasic and strong Lewis acid
(d) tribasic and weak Bronsted acid

32 Which one of the following is the correct quadratic form of the Ostwald's dilution law equation? [J&K CET]
(a) $\alpha^2C+\alpha K-K=0$ (b) $\alpha^2C-\alpha K-K=0$
(c) $\alpha^2C-\alpha K+K=0$ (d) $\alpha^2C+\alpha K+K=0$

33 Among the following, the strongest conjugate base is [DUMET]
(a) NO_3^- (b) Cl^-
(c) SO_4^{2-} (d) CH_3COO^-

2008

34 Basic strength of
I. $H_3C\overset{\ominus}{C}H_2$ II. $H_2C{=}\overset{\ominus}{C}H$ and III. $H—C{\equiv}\overset{\ominus}{C}$
is in the order of [CBSE AIPMT]
(a) II > I > III (b) III > II > I
(c) I > III > II (d) I > II > III

35 **Assertion** (A) $[Al(H_2O)_6]^{3+}$ is a stronger acid than $[Mg(H_2O)_6]^{2+}$.
Reason (R) Size of $[Al(H_2O)_6]^{3+}$ is smaller than $[Mg(H_3O)_6]^{2+}$ and possesses more effective nuclear charge. [AIIMS]
(a) Both A and R are correct and R is the correct explanation of A
(b) Both A and R are correct but R is not the correct explanation of A
(c) A is correct but R is incorrect
(d) Both A and R are incorrect

36 Which one of the following species acts as both Bronsted acid and base? [MHT CET]
(a) $H_2PO_2^-$ (b) HPO_3^{2-}
(c) HPO_4^{2-} (d) All of these

37 Which of the oxide of manganese is amphoteric? [Manipal]
(a) MnO_2 (b) Mn_2O_3
(c) Mn_2O_7 (d) MnO

38 Identify Bronsted-Lowry acids in the reaction given
$$\underset{A}{[Al(H_2O)_6]^{3+}} + \underset{B}{HCO_3^-} \rightleftharpoons \underset{C}{[Al(H_2O)_5(OH^-)]^{2+}} + \underset{D}{H_2CO_3}$$
The correct answer is [EAMCET]
(a) A and C (b) B and D (c) A and D (d) B and C

39 Strongest Lewis acid among the following is [DUMET]
(a) NF_3 (b) PCl_3 (c) $SnCl_4$ (d) $PbCl_2$

40 Which one of the following compounds is not a protonic acid? [JCECE]
(a) $SO(OH)_2$ (b) $SO_2(OH)_2$
(c) $B(OH)_3$ (d) $PO(OH)_3$

2007

41 The correct order of basic strength is [AIIMS]
(a) $H_2O < OH^- < CH_3OH < CH_3O^-$
(b) $CH_3OH < H_2O < CH_3O^- < OH^-$
(c) $H_2O < CH_3OH < OH^- < CH_3O^-$
(d) $OH^- < H_2O < CH_3O^- < CH_3OH$

2006

42 Which of the following is not Lewis acid? [UP CPMT]
(a) $AlCl_3 \cdot 6H_2O$ (b) $AlCl_3$
(c) $SnCl_4$ (d) $FeCl_3$

43 Degree of dissociation of 0.1N CH_3COOH is ($K_{acid} = 1 \times 10^{-5}$) [UP CPMT]
(a) 10^{-5} (b) 10^{-4}
(c) 10^{-3} (d) 10^{-2}

44 Conjugate acid of $S_2O_8^{2-}$ is [MHT CET]
(a) $H_2S_2O_8$ (b) H_2SO_4 (c) $HS_2O_8^-$ (d) HSO_4^-

45 Which of the following solvents are aprotic? [J&K CET]
I. NH_3 II. SO_2
III. CH_3CN IV. CH_3CO_2H
(a) I, II and III (b) I, III and IV
(c) II and III (d) I and III

46 A monoprotic acid in 1.00 M solution is 0.01% ionised. The dissociation constant of this acid is [BCECE]
(a) 1×10^{-8} (b) 1×10^{-4}
(c) 1×10^{-6} (d) 1×10^{-5}

47 Arrange NH_4^+, H_2O, H_3O^+, HF and OH^- in increasing order of acidic nature. [BCECE]
(a) $H_3O^+ < NH_4^+ < HF < OH^- < H_2O$
(b) $NH_4^+ < HF < H_3O^+ < H_2O < OH^-$
(c) $HO^- < H_2O < NH_4^+ < HF < H_3O^+$
(d) $H_3O^+ > HF > H_2O > NH_4^+ > OH^-$

48 A weak acid, HA has a K_a of 1.00×10^{-5}. If 0.100 mole of this acid is dissolved in 1 L of water, the percentage of acid dissociated at equilibrium is closest to [CBSE AIPMT]
(a) 99.0% (b) 1.00%
(c) 99.9% (d) 0.100%

2005

49 The pair of amphoteric hydroxides is [AIIMS]
(a) $Al(OH)_3$, LiOH
(b) $Be(OH)_2$, $Mg(OH)_2$
(c) $B(OH)_3$, $Be(OH)_2$
(d) $Be(OH)_2$, $Zn(OH)_2$

50 If 0.1 M of a weak acid is taken and its percentage degree of ionisation is 1.34%, then its ionisation constant will be [AFMC]
(a) 0.8×10^{-5} (b) 1.79×10^{-5}
(c) 0.182×10^{-5} (d) None of these

51 The values of dissociation constant of bases are given below. Which is the weakest base? [MHT CET]
(a) 1.8×10^{-5} (b) 4.8×10^{-10}
(c) 7.2×10^{-11} (d) 7.07×10^{-7}

52 Which is Lewis base $I_2 + I^- \longrightarrow I_3^-$? [BCECE]
(a) I_2 (b) I_3^-
(c) I^- (d) None of these

Answers

1 (c)	2 (b)	3 (a)	4 (b)	5 (c)	6 (a)	7 (b)	8 (c)	9 (c)	10 (b)
11 (b)	12 (a)	13 (c)	14 (d)	15 (d)	16 (b)	17 (c)	18 (d)	19 (d)	20 (b)
21 (b)	22 (d)	23 (d)	24 (d)	25 (a)	26 (a)	27 (d)	28 (b)	29 (b)	30 (d)
31 (a)	32 (a)	33 (d)	34 (d)	35 (a)	36 (d)	37 (a)	38 (c)	39 (d)	40 (c)
41 (c)	42 (a)	43 (d)	44 (c)	45 (a)	46 (a)	47 (c)	48 (b)	49 (d)	50 (b)
51 (c)	52 (c)								

Explanations

1 (*c*) Bronsted acid is a substance which has a tendency to donate proton. Bronsted base is a substance which has a tendency to accept proton.

HCl can act as Bronsted acid becuase it can only donate proton.

$$\underset{\text{Acid}}{HCl} + \underset{\text{Base}}{H_2O} \rightleftharpoons H_3O^+ + Cl^-$$

The remaining options contains substances which act both as Bronsted acid and Bronsted base.

$$HCO_3^- + HCO_3^- \rightleftharpoons H_2CO_3 + CO_3^{2-}$$

$$NH_3 + NH_3 \rightleftharpoons NH_4^+ + NH_2^-$$

$$HSO_4^- + HSO_4^- \rightleftharpoons H_2SO_4 + SO_4^{2-}$$

Thus, option (c) is correct.

2 (*b*) An acid on losing a proton produces a species which has the tendency to accept H^+.
It is called conjugate base of that acid.

$$\underset{\text{Acid}}{H_2O} \rightleftharpoons \underset{\substack{\text{Conjugate}\\\text{base}}}{\bar{O}H} + H^+,$$

$$\underset{\text{Acid}}{HF} \rightleftharpoons \underset{\substack{\text{Conjugate}\\\text{base}}}{F^-} + H^+$$

Water (H_2O) is amphoteric in nature and thus act both as an acid and base. e.g.

$$\underset{\text{Acid}}{HF} + \underset{\text{Base}}{H_2O} \rightleftharpoons \underset{\substack{\text{Conjugate}\\\text{base}}}{F^-} + \underset{\substack{\text{Conjugate}\\\text{acid}}}{H_3O^+}$$

3 (*a*) Both assertion and Reason are correct but reason is not the correct explanation of Assertion.

Normally, rain water has a pH of 5.6 due to the presence of H^+ ions formed by the reaction of rain water with carbon dioxide present in the atmosphere.

$$H_2O(l) + CO_2(g) \longrightarrow H_2CO_3(aq)$$

$$H_2CO_3(aq) \rightleftharpoons H^+(aq) + HCO_3^-(aq)$$

When the pH of rain water drops below 5.6, it is called acid rain.

4 (*b*) The basic strength of given hydrides decreases in the order as follows

$$NH_3 > PH_3 > AsH_3 > SbH_3 > BiH_3$$

This is due to the decrease in the availability of the lone pair of electrons which depends on the size of central atom that increase from N to Bi. Therefore, NH_3 and BiH_3 acts as a strong and weak base hydride respectively.

5 (*c*) The correct decreasing order of basic strength is

$$NH_3 > PH_3 > AsH_3 > SbH_3$$

NH_3 is the most basic because of its small size, the electron density of electron pair is concentrated over small region.

As the size increases, the electron density gets diffused over a large surface area. Hence, the ability to donate the electron pair (basicity) decreases.

The other three orders given are correct.

6 (*a*) H_2S is a weak acid and also a weak electrolyte, thus its ionisation is suppressed when small amount of strong electrolyte (like HCl) is added due to common ion effect.

$$H_2S \rightleftharpoons \boxed{2H^+} + S^{2-}$$

$$HCl \rightleftharpoons \boxed{H^+} + Cl^-$$

Common ion

7 (*b*) The molecule with lone pair of electrons at centre atom, will behave as Lewis base.
In the given molecules, only PF_3 has lone pair of electrons at P as shown below :

Thus, PF_3 acts as a Lewis base (electron-pair donor).

8 (*c*) The strength of oxyacids can also be decided with the help of oxidation number of central atom. Higher the oxidation number of central atom, more acidic is the oxyacid.

$$\overset{+6}{H_2SO_4}, \overset{+5}{HClO_3}, \overset{+7}{HClO_4}, \overset{+4}{H_2SO_3}$$

Since, in $HClO_4$, oxidation number of Cl is the highest, so $HClO_4$ is the strongest acid among the given acids.

9 (*c*) $\dfrac{\text{Strength of acid } HA_1}{\text{Strength of acid } HA_2} = \sqrt{\dfrac{K_1}{K_2}}$

Given, dissociation constant for $HA_1 = 3.0 \times 10^{-4}$

and dissociation constant for $HA_2 = 1.8 \times 10^{-5}$

$$\frac{\text{Strength of acid } HA_1}{\text{Strength acid } HA_2} = \sqrt{\frac{16.66}{1}} \approx \frac{4}{1}$$

$\therefore$ Strength of acid HA_1: Strength of acid $HA_2 = 4:1$.

10 (*b*) The strongest acid shows dissociation constant value 2×10^{-2}, because it is the highest value among all the given values. The strongest acid shows highest dissociation constant value.

11 (*b*) A weak acid dissociates partially when dissolved in water. Thus, it has very low value of K_a i.e. dissociation constant. Since, pK_a is the negative logarithm of K_a ($pK_a = -\log K_a$) thus, weak acid has a very high value of pK_a.

Also, the solution of its sodium salt is alkaline in water, e.g. CH_3COONa is alkaline in aqueous solution is incouse. Thus, option (v) is micousect while rest the statement are correct.

12 (*a*) The Bronsted base is NO_3^-, because a Bronsted base is the one that receives a proton.

13 (*c*) $H_2O + NH_3 \rightleftharpoons NH_4^+ + OH^-$

In this reaction, H_2O acts as an acid, because it donates a proton.

14 (*d*) $\text{Acid}_1 + \text{Base}_2 \rightleftharpoons \text{Acid}_2 + \text{Base}_1$

$$HPO_3^{2-} + H_2O \rightleftharpoons H_3O^+ + PO_3^{2-}$$

$$H_2PO_4^- + H_2O \rightleftharpoons H_3O^+ + HPO_4^{2-}$$

$$H_3PO_4 + H_2O \rightleftharpoons H_3O^+ + H_2PO_4^-$$

Therefore, pair paid given in option (d) is not a conjugate acid pair as one species is not formed from the other by donation of proton.

15 (*d*) Electron deficient species behaves as Lewis acids. As, BF_3 is an electron deficient species thus, it behaves as a Lewis acid.

16 (*b*) $C\alpha = [H^+]$

$$\alpha = \frac{10^{-5}}{5 \times 10^{-3}} = \frac{1}{5} \times 10^{-2}$$

$$\text{Percentage} = \frac{1}{5} = 0.2\%$$

17 (*c*) S^{2-} can accept a proton only, thus acts only as a base.

18 (*d*) Conjugate acid-base pair differs by only one proton.

Thus, H_3O^+, OH^-, is not a conjugate acid-base pair.

19 (*d*) B_2H_6 is electron deficient compound, so it acts as a Lewis acid.

20 (*b*) According to Bronsted-Lowry concept, after losing a proton, acids convert into their conjugate base and after gaining a proton, bases convert into their conjugate acids, i.e.

$$\text{Acid} - H^+ \longrightarrow \text{Conjugate base}$$
$$\text{Base} + H^+ \longrightarrow \text{Conjugate acid}$$

Thus, conjugate acid-base pair differs by a proton.

21 (*b*) For acid-base reactions,
g-equivalent of acid (HCl) = g-equivalent of base (NaOH)

$\therefore$ g-equivalent of acid

$$= (25 \times 10^{-3})\text{dm}^3 \times \frac{1}{10}$$
$$= 25 \times 10^{-4}$$
$$= 0.0025 \text{ g}$$

equivalent of NaOH

22 (*d*) $\text{Acid} - H^+ \longrightarrow \text{Conjugate base}$

$\therefore \; H_2PO_4^- - H^+ \longrightarrow HPO_4^{2-}$

So, HPO_4^{2-} is the conjugate base of $H_2PO_4^-$.

23 (*d*)
$$CH_3COOH \rightleftharpoons CH_3COO^- + H^-$$
$$[CH_3COO^-] = [H^+] \quad \ldots\text{(i)}$$
$$H_2O \rightleftharpoons H^+ + OH^-$$
$$[H^+] = [OH^-] \quad \ldots\text{(ii)}$$

From Eqs. (i) and (ii),
$$[H^+] + [H^+] = [CH_3COO^-] + [OH^-]$$
$$2[H^+] = [CH_3COO^-] + [OH^-]$$

24 (*d*) Strongest Bronsted base is that which has weakest conjugate acid.

Base	Conjugate acid (base + H^+)
ClO^-	HClO
ClO_2^-	$HClO_2$
ClO_3^-	$HClO_3$
ClO_4^-	$HClO_4$

Since, HClO is the weakest conjugate acid.

So, ClO^- is the strongest Bronsted base.

25 (*a*) $(CH_3)_3B$ is electron deficient.
So, it acts as a Lewis acid.

26 (*a*) $\underset{\text{Base}}{NH_3} + H^+ \longrightarrow \underset{\text{Conjugate acid}}{NH_4^+}$

Hence, ammonium ion is a conjugate acid of ammonia.

27 (*d*) $[H^+] = \alpha C = 0.04 \times 0.02 = 8 \times 10^{-4}$

$$[H^+][OH^-] = 10^{-14}$$
$$\therefore \quad [OH^-] = \frac{10^{-14}}{8 \times 10^{-4}}$$
$$= 1.25 \times 10^{-11} \text{ M}$$

28 (*b*) Among the given, only potassium chloride (KCl) is a strong electrolyte, so its degree of dissociation is almost unity.

29 (*b*) $[H^+] = 0.2$ M (given, HCl = 0.2M)

$$[H^+] \times [OH^-] = 10^{-14}$$
$$[OH^-] = \frac{10^{-14}}{0.2} = 5 \times 10^{-14} \text{ M}$$

Concentration of hydroxyl ions in 0.2 M HCl = 5×10^{-14} M

or 5×10^{-14} mol L^{-1}

$\therefore$ The number of moles in 10 cm^3 solution $= \frac{5 \times 10^{-14} \times 10}{1000}$ mol

$\therefore$ The number of OH^- ions in 10 cm^3 solution

$$= \frac{5 \times 10^{-14} \times 10}{1000} \times 6.023 \times 10^{23}$$
$$= 30.11 \times 10^7$$
$$= 3.0 \times 10^8$$

30 (*d*) $BOH \rightleftharpoons B^+ + OH^-$

$$K_b = \frac{[B^+][OH^-]}{[BOH]}$$

As $[B^+] = [OH^-]$

$$K_b = \frac{[OH^-]^2}{[BOH]}$$
$$\therefore \quad [BOH] = \frac{[OH^-]^2}{K_b}$$
$$= \frac{(1.5 \times 10^{-3})^2}{1.5 \times 10^{-5}}$$
$$= 1.5 \times 10^{-1} = 0.15 \text{ M}$$

31 (*a*) Orthoboric acid, H_3BO_3 is a weak monobasic acid but its acidic character is not due to liberation of H^+ ion from it. Its acidic character is due to acceptance of electron from H_2O molecule towards boron (due to very small size and high charge density of boron). Therefore, H_3BO_3 due to the acceptance of electrons is a weak Lewis acid.

32 (*a*) According to Ostwald's dilution law,

$$K = \frac{C\alpha^2}{1 - \alpha}$$
$$\Rightarrow \quad K - K\alpha = C\alpha^2$$
$$\Rightarrow \quad C\alpha^2 + K\alpha - K = 0$$

33 (*d*) Weakest acid gives strongest base. Amongst HCl, HNO_2, H_2SO_4 and CH_3COOH, CH_3COOH is the weakest acid. So, it will give strongest conjugate base.

34 (*d*) Stronger the acid, weaker is its conjugate base.
The strength of their conjugate acids are in the order

$$HC{\equiv}CH > H_2C{=}CH_2 > CH_3{-}CH_3$$

Therefore, the correct order of strength of their conjugate base is

$$CH_3\overset{\ominus}{C}H_2 > H_2C{=}\overset{\ominus}{C}H > HC{\equiv}\overset{\ominus}{C}$$

35 (*a*) The size of $[Al(H_2O)_6]^{3+}$ is smaller than that of $[Mg(H_2O)_6]^{2+}$. Also the former possesses more effective nuclear charge and thus, attracts electron pair from donor more effectively.
This gives rise to relatively strong acidic nature of $[Al(H_2O)_6]^{3+}$.

36 (*d*) All can accept and donate proton. Hence, they can act as both Bronsted acid and base.

37 (*a*) Oxide of Mn is in its intermediate oxidation state, i.e. +4 in MnO_2. This is amphoteric in character.

38 (*c*) According to Bronsted-Lowry, acids are the substances which can donate a proton.
A base after gaining a proton (H^+) gives conjugate acid.

$$\underset{\substack{(A)\\ \text{Acid}}}{[Al(H_2O)_6]^{3+}} + \underset{\substack{(B)\\ \text{Base}}}{HCO_3^-} \rightleftharpoons \underset{\substack{(C)\\ \text{Conjugate base}}}{[Al(H_2O)_5(OH^-)]^{2+}} + \underset{\substack{(D)\\ \text{Conjugate acid}}}{H_2CO_3}$$

Hence, in the above reaction *A* and *D* are the acids.

39 (*d*) In $PbCl_2$, lead is most electron deficient due to inert pair effect. Therefore, $PbCl_2$ is the strongest Lewis acid.

40 (*c*) $B(OH)_3$ is not a protonic acid because it does not give proton on ionisation directly while it acts as Lewis acid due to acceptance of OH^- from water and forms a hydrated species.

$$B(OH)_3 + H_2O \longrightarrow [B(OH)_4]^- + H^+$$

41 (*c*) Strong acid has a weak conjugate base and *vice-versa*.

$$H_2O < CH_3OH < OH^- < CH_3O^-$$

Increasing order of basic strength →

42 (*a*) $AlCl_3$ is sp^2-hybridised. When it combines with six H_2O molecules, one of the vacant p-orbitals and five d-orbitals are filled by electron pairs, as a result of which it cannot accept more electrons and so, will not act as electron acceptor that is, Lewis acid.

43 (*d*) $\alpha = \sqrt{\frac{K_a}{C}} = \sqrt{\frac{1.0 \times 10^{-5}}{0.1}}$

$= \sqrt{1.0 \times 10^{-4}} = 1.0 \times 10^{-2}$

44 (*c*) Base $+ H^+ \longrightarrow$ Conjugate acid

$$S_2O_8^{2+} + H^+ \longrightarrow HS_2O_8^-$$

So, $HS_2O_8^-$ is the conjugate acid of $S_2O_8^{2-}$.

45 (*a*) A solvent that has hydrogen atom bound to an oxygen, nitrogen or a fluorine is called protic solvents and these can readily donate protons to reagents.

NH_3, SO_2 and CH_3CN are aprotic solvent while CH_3COOH is protic solvent.

46 (*a*) For weak electrolytes, according to Ostwald's dilution law, $\alpha = \sqrt{KV}$

Here, $\alpha = 0.01\% = 0.0001 = 1 \times 10^{-4}$

$$V = \frac{1}{C} = \frac{1}{1.0} = 1L$$

$$\therefore \quad K_a = \frac{\alpha^2}{V} = \frac{(1 \times 10^{-4})^2}{1} = 1 \times 10^{-8}$$

47 (*c*) Among the given species, correct order of increasing acidic strength is $OH^- < H_2O < NH_4^+ < HF < H_3O^+$.

OH^- is basic (i.e. it tends to gain a proton) and hence is least acidic. H_2O is neutral species. H_3O^+ is most acidic as it readily loses proton.

48 (*b*) $HA \rightleftharpoons H^+ + A^-$

$$K_a = \frac{[H^+][A^-]}{[HA]} = \frac{[H^+]^2}{[HA]}$$

$$[H^+] = \sqrt{K_a[HA]}$$

$$= \sqrt{1 \times 10^{-5} \times 0.1}$$

$$= \sqrt{1 \times 10^{-6}} = 1 \times 10^{-3}$$

$$\alpha = \frac{\text{actual ionisation}}{\text{molar concentration}}$$

$$= \frac{10^{-3}}{0.1} = 10^{-2}$$

% of acid dissociated $= 10^{-2} \times 100 = 1\%$

49 (*d*) $Be(OH)_2$ and $Zn(OH)_2$ are amphoteric hydroxides in nature.

$$Be(OH)_2 + 2HCl \longrightarrow BeCl_2 + 2H_2O$$

$$Be(OH)_2 + 2NaOH \longrightarrow Na_2BeO_2 + 2H_2O$$

$$Zn(OH)_2 + 2HCl \longrightarrow ZnCl_2 + 2H_2O$$

$$Zn(OH)_2 + 2NaOH \longrightarrow Na_2ZnO_2 + 2H_2O$$

50 (*b*) According to Ostwald's dilution law,

$$K_a = \frac{C\alpha^2}{1-\alpha}$$

For very weak acid $\alpha <<<< 1$ or $1 - \alpha \approx 1$,

$$K_a = C\alpha^2$$

$$C = 0.1\text{ M}, \alpha = 1.34\% = 0.0134$$

$$\therefore K_a = 0.1 \times (1.34 \times 10^{-2})^2$$

$$= 1.79 \times 10^{-5}$$

51 (*c*) For a base BOH,

$$BOH \rightleftharpoons B^+ + OH^-$$

Dissociation constant,

$$K_b = \frac{[B^+][OH^-]}{[BOH]}$$

Hence, higher the value of K_b, stronger will be the base (i.e. more ionisation) and *vice-versa*. Therefore, the weakest base is the one with K_b equal to 7.2×10^{-11}.

52 (*c*) Electron donors are Lewis bases. In the reaction,

$I_2 + I^- \longrightarrow I^{3-}$, I^- donates a pair of electrons and I_2 accepts it to form I^{3-}.

So, I^- is Lewis base.

Topic 4

Solubility Product and Common Ion Effect

2019

1 pH of a saturated solution of Ca $(OH)_2$ is 9. The solubility product (K_{sp}) of Ca $(OH)_2$ is [NEET]

(a) 0.25×10^{-10} (b) 0.125×10^{-15}
(c) 0.5×10^{-10} (c) 0.5×10^{-15}

2 The molar solubility of CaF_2 $(K_{sp}=5.3\times 10^{-11})$ in 0.1 M solution of NaF will be [NEET (Odisha)]

(a) 5.3×10^{11} mol L^{-1} (b) 5.3×10^{-8} mol L^{-1}
(c) 5.3×10^{-9} mol L^{-1} (d) 5.3×10^{-10} mol L^{-1}

2018

3 The solubility of $BaSO_4$ in water is 2.42×10^{-3} g L^{-1} at 298 K. The value of its solubility product (K_{sp}) will be (Given molar mass of $BaSO_4 = 233$ g mol^{-1}) [NEET 2018]

(a) 1.08×10^{-14} mol^2L^{-2} (b) 1.08×10^{-12} mol^2L^{-2}
(c) 1.08×10^{-10} mol^2L^{-2} (d) 1.08×10^{-8} mol^2L^{-2}

4 The solubility product of sparingly soluble salt AX_2 is 3.2×10^{-11}. Its solubility (in mol/L) is [AIIMS 2018]

(a) 5.6×10^{-6} (b) 3.1×10^{-4}
(c) 2×10^{-4} (d) 4×10^{-4}

2014

5 When ammonium chloride is added to ammonium hyd roxide solution, the dissociation of ammonium hydroxide is suppressed due to [Kerala CEE]

(a) hydrolysis
(b) oxidation
(c) reduction
(d) increase in dielectric constant
(e) common ion effect

6 A saturated solution of $Ca_3(PO_4)_2$ contains 2.0×10^{-8} M of Ca^{2+} and 1.6×10^{-5} M of PO_4^{3-} at a certain temperature. The solubility product (K_{sp}) of $Ca_3(PO_4)_2$ at that temperature is [EAMCET]

(a) 2.048×10^{-34} (b) 2.048×10^{-33}
(c) 3.20×10^{-34} (d) 8.00×10^{-34}

7 One mole of ammonia was completely absorbed in one litre solution each of

I. 1 M HCl II. 1 M CH_3COOH and
III. 1 M H_2SO_4 at 298 K

The decreasing order for the pH of the resulting solution is (given $K_b(NH_3)=4.74$) [KCET]

(a) II > III > I (b) I > II > III
(c) II > I > III (d) III > II > I

2013

8 Using the Gibbs energy change, $\Delta G° = +63.3$ kJ for the following reactions,

$$Ag_2CO_3(s) \rightleftharpoons 2Ag^+(aq) + CO_3^{2-}(aq)$$

the K_{sp} of $Ag_2CO_3(s)$ in water at 25°C is ($R = 8.314$ JK^{-1} mol^{-1}) [CBSE AIPMT]

(a) 3.2×10^{-26} (b) 8.0×10^{-12}
(c) 2.9×10^{-3} (d) 7.9×10^{-2}

9 The product of molar concentrations of hydrogen ions and hydroxide ions in a 0.01 M aqueous solution of sodium chloride is known as [MHTCET]

(a) hydrolysis constant of salt
(b) dissociation constant of acid
(c) dissociation constant of base
(d) ionic product of water

10 The solubility product of calcium fluoride is 3.2×10^{-11} M^3. Its solubility in saturated solution is [UP CPMT]

(a) 8×10^{-12} mol L^{-1} (b) 2×10^{-4} mol L^{-1}
(c) 4×10^{-12} mol L^{-1} (d) 1×10^{-4} mol L^{-1}

11 The solubility product of a binary weak electrolyte is 4×10^{-10} at 298 K. Its solubility in mol/dm^3 at the same temperature is [KCET]

(a) 4×10^{-5} (b) 2×10^{-5}
(c) 8×10 (d) 16×10^{-20}

2012

12 pH of a saturated solution of $Ba(OH)_2$ is 12. The value of solubility product of K_{sp} of $Ba(OH)_2$ is [CBSE AIPMT]

(a) 3.3×10^{-7} (b) 5.0×10^{-7}
(c) 4.0×10^{-6} (d) 5.0×10^{-6}

13 On adding $AlCl_3$ to water [AFMC]

(a) the ionisation of water increases
(b) the ionisation of water decreases
(c) the ionisation of water remains constant
(d) the ionic product of water increases

14 What is the value of K_{sp} of $Fe(OH)_3$? [OJEE]

(a) s^2 (b) $4s^3$ (c) $27s^4$ (d) $64s^4$

2011

15 At 25°C the solubility product of Hg_2Cl_2 in water is 3.2×10^{-17} mol^3 dm^{-9}. What is the solubility of Hg_2Cl_2 in water at 25°C? [Kerala CEE]

(a) 1.2×10^{-12} M (b) 3.0×10^{-6} M
(c) 2×10^{-6} M (d) 1.2×10^{-16} M

16 A solution is 0.1 M with respect to Ag^+, Ca^{2+}, Mg^{2+} and Al^{3+} which will precipitate at lowest concentration of $[PO_4^{3-}]$ when solution of Na_3PO_4 is added? **[DUMET]**

(a) Ag_3PO_4 ($K_{sp} = 1\times10^{-6}$)
(b) $Ca_3(PO_4)_2$ ($K_{sp} = 1\times10^{-33}$)
(c) $Mg_3(PO_4)_2$ ($K_{sp} = 1\times10^{-24}$)
(d) $AlPO_4$ ($K_{sp} = 1\times10^{-20}$)

17 H_2S is passed into one dm^3 of a solution containing 0.1 mole of Zn^{2+} and 0.01 mole of the Cu^{2+} till the sulphide ion concentration reaches 8.1×10^{-19} moles. Which one of the following statements is true? (K_{sp} of ZnS and CuS are 3×10^{-22} and 8×10^{-36} respectively) **[KCET]**

(a) Only ZnS precipitates
(b) Both CuS and ZnS precipitate
(c) Only CuS precipitates
(d) No precipitation occurs

2010

18 Which is not example of common ion effect? **[MHT CET]**

(a) NaCl + AgCl
(b) H_2S + HCl
(c) CH_3COOH + NaOH
(d) $NH_4OH + NH_4Cl$

19 The concentration of Ag^+ ion in a given saturated solution of AgCl at 25°C is 1.06×10^{-5} g ion per litre. Thus, the solubility product of AgCl is **[Manipal]**

(a) 0.353×10^{-10}
(b) 0.530×10^{-10}
(c) 1.12×10^{-10}
(d) 2.12×10^{-10}

20 The solubility product of $Mg(OH)_2$ is 4×10^{-12} $(mol L^{-1})^3$. Solubility of $Mg(OH)_2$ is **[OJEE]**

(a) 4×10^{-4} mol L^{-1}
(b) 1×10^{-12} mol L^{-1}
(c) 1×10^{-4} mol L^{-1}
(d) 2×10^{-6} mol L^{-1}

21 1 dm^3 solution containing 10^{-5} moles each of Cl^- ions and CrO_4^{2-} ions is treated with 10^{-4} moles of silver nitrate. Which one of the following observations is made?

(K_{sp} of $Ag_2CrO_4 = 4\times10^{-12}$)
(K_{sp} of AgCl $= 1\times10^{-10}$) **[KCET]**

(a) Precipitation does not occur
(b) Silver chromate gets precipitated first
(c) Silver chloride gets precipitated first
(d) Both silver chromate and silver chloride start precipitating simultaneously

2009

22 The solubility product of a salt having formula M_2X_3 is 2.2×10^{-20}. If the solubility of an another salt having formula M_2X is twice the molar solubility of M_2X_3, the solubility product of M_2X is **[AIIMS]**

(a) 3×10^{-12}
(b) 9.16×10^{-5}
(c) 4.58×10^{-5}
(d) 2.76×10^{-18}

23 If the solubility of calcium fluoride in pure water is x mol/L, its solubility product is **[AFMC]**

(a) $\sqrt{2}x$
(b) $2x^2$
(c) $4x^3$
(d) x^2

24 The precipitate of Ag_2CrO_4 ($K_{sp} = 9\times10^{-12}$) is obtained when equal volumes of which of the following are mixed **[Kerala CEE]**

(a) 10^{-5} M Ag^+ and 10^{-3} M CrO_4^{2-}
(b) 10^{-5} M Ag^+ and 10^{-2} M CrO_4^{2-}
(c) 10^{-4} M Ag^+ and 10^{-2} M CrO_4^{2-}
(d) 10^{-7} M Ag^+ and 10^{-3} M CrO_4^{2-}
(e) 10^{-4} M Ag^+ and 10^{-4} M CrO_4^{2-}

25 The solubility product of a sparingly soluble metal hydroxide $M(OH)_2$ at 298 K is 5×10^{-16} mol^3 dm^{-9}. The pH value of its aqueous and saturated solution is **[J&K CET]**

(a) 5
(b) 9
(c) 11.5
(d) 2.5

26 When equal volumes of $AgNO_3$ and NaCl solution are mixed, the precipitation of AgCl ($K_{sp} = 1.81\times10^{-10}$) will occur with **[AMU]**

(a) 10^{-3} M (Ag^+) and 10^{-10} M (Cl^-)
(b) 10^{-5} M (Ag^+) and 10^{-5} M (Cl^-)
(c) 10^{-6} M (Ag^+) and 10^{-5} M (Cl^-)
(d) 10^{-4} M (Ag^+) and 10^{-4} M (Cl^-)

27 Solubility (s) of CaF_2 in terms of its solubility product is given as **[AMU]**

(a) $s = (K_{sp})^{1/3}$
(b) $s = (K_{sp}/2)^{1/3}$
(c) $s = (K_{sp}/4)^{1/3}$
(d) $s = (K_{sp}/2)^{1/2}$

2008

28 On adding 0.1 M solution each of $[Ag^+]$, $[Ba^{2+}]$, $[Ca^{2+}]$ in a Na_2SO_4 solution, species first precipitated is [K_{sp} of $BaSO_4 = 10^{-11}$, K_{sp} of $CaSO_4 = 10^{-6}$, K_{sp} of $Ag_2SO_4 = 10^{-5}$] **[AIIMS]**

(a) Ag_2SO_4
(b) $BaSO_4$
(c) $CaSO_4$
(d) All of these

29 Solubility product of a salt AB is 1×10^{-8} M^2 in a solution in which the concentration of A^+ ions is 10^{-3} M. The salt will precipitate when the concentration of B^- ions is kept **[AFMC]**

(a) between 10^{-8} M to 10^{-7} M
(b) between 10^{-7} M to 10^{-8} M
(c) $> 10^{-5}$ M
(d) $< 10^{-8}$ M

30 An aqueous solution contains Ni^{2+}, Co^{2+} and Pb^{2+} ions at equal concentrations. The solubility product of NiS, PbS and CoS in water at 25°C are 1.4×10^{-24}, 3.4×10^{-26} and 3×10^{-26}, respectively. Indicate which of these ions will be precipitated first and last when sulphide concentration is progressively increased from zero? **[J&K CET]**

(a) NiS and PbS
(b) NiS and CoS
(c) CoS and NiS
(d) PbS and NiS

2007

31 Assertion (A) NaCl is precipitated when HCl gas is passed in a saturated solution of NaCl.

Reason (R) HCl is strong acid. [AIIMS]

(a) Both A and R are correct and R is the correct explanation of the A
(b) Both A and R are correct but R is not the correct explanation of A
(c) A is correct but R is incorrect
(d) Both A and R are incorrect

32 Assertion (A) On mixing 500 mL of 10^{-6} M Ca^{2+} ion and 500 mL of 10^{-6} M F^- ion, the precipitate of CaF_2 will be obtained K_{sp} ($CaF_2 = 10^{-18}$).

Reason (R) If K_{sp} is greater than ionic product, a precipitate will develop. [AIIMS]

(a) Both A and R are correct and R is the correct explanation of the A
(b) Both A and R are correct but R is not the correct explanation of A
(c) A is correct but R is incorrect
(d) Both A and R are incorrect

33 The solubility of AgCl is 1×10^{-5} mol/L. Its solubility in 0.1 molar sodium chloride solution is [MHT CET]

(a) 1×10^{-10} (b) 1×10^{-5}
(c) 1×10^{-9} (d) 1×10^{-4}

34 x mole of $BaCO_3$ are soluble in 1 L, then x is related to its solubility product by the expression [DUMET]

(a) $x = K_{sp}$ (b) $x^2 = \sqrt{K_{sp}}$
(c) $x = \sqrt{K_{sp}}$ (d) $x = \dfrac{K_{sp}}{2}$

35 The solubility product of $BaCl_2$ is 4×10^{-9}. Its solubility in mol/L is [BCECE]

(a) 4×10^{-3} (b) 4×10^{-9}
(c) 1×10^{-3} (d) 1×10^{-9}

2006

36 The solubility of AgI in NaI solution is less than that in pure water, because [Manipal]

(a) the temperature of the solution decreases
(b) solubility product of AgI is less than that of NaI
(c) of common ion effect
(d) AgI forms complex with NaI

37 Some chemists at ISRO wished to prepare a saturated solution of a silver compound and they wanted it to have the highest concentration of silver ion possible. Which of the following compounds, would they use? [BCECE]

K_{sp} (AgCl) $= 1.8\times 10^{-10}$, K_{sp} (AgBr) $= 5.0\times 10^{-13}$

K_{sp} (Ag_2CrO_4) $= 2.4\times 10^{-12}$

(a) AgCl (b) AgBr
(c) Ag_2CrO_4 (d) None of these

2005

38 At 25°C, the dissociation constant of a base, BOH, is 1.0×10^{-12}. The concentration of hydroxyl ions in 0.01 M aqueous solution of the base would be [CBSE AIPMT]

(a) 2.0×10^{-6} mol L^{-1} (b) 1.0×10^{-5} mol L^{-1}
(c) 1.0×10^{-6} mol L^{-1} (d) 1.0×10^{-7} mol L^{-1}

39 If a saturated solution prepared by dissolving Ag_2CO_3 in water has $[Ag^+] = 2.56\times 10^{-4}$. What is the value of K_{sp} for Ag_2CO_3? [Kerala CEE]

(a) 83.9×10^{-12} (b) 8.39×10^{-12}
(c) 93.8×10^{-12} (d) 9.38×10^{-12}

40 The precipitation takes place only when the product of concentrations of ions [J&K CET]

(a) exceeds the solubility product
(b) is less than the solubility product
(c) is negligible
(d) is equal to the solubility product

41 The K_{sp} of $Mg(OH)_2$ is 1×10^{-12}. 0.01 $Mg(OH)_2$ will precipitate at the limited pH [DUMET]

(a) 3 (b) 9 (c) 5 (d) 8

Answers

1 (d)	2 (c)	3 (c)	4 (c)	5 (e)	6 (b)	7 (c)	8 (b)	9 (d)	10 (b)
11 (b)	12 (b)	13 (a)	14 (c)	15 (c)	16 (d)	17 (b)	18 (c)	19 (c)	20 (c)
21 (c)	22 (a)	23 (c)	24 (c)	25 (b)	26 (d)	27 (c)	28 (b)	29 (c)	30 (d)
31 (b)	32 (d)	33 (c)	34 (c)	35 (c)	36 (c)	37 (c)	38 (d)	39 (b)	40 (a)
41 (b)									

Explanations

1 (*d*) For the reaction,

$$Ca(OH)_2(s) \rightleftharpoons \underset{S}{Ca^{2+}}(aq) + \underset{2S}{2\bar{O}H}(aq)$$

[where, S = solubility]

$$K_{sp} = [Ca^{2+}][OH^-]^2 = S(2S)^2 \quad ...(i)$$

Given, pH = 9

We know that, pH + pOH = 14

$\therefore$ pOH = 14 − 9 = 5

$pOH = -\log[\bar{O}H]$

$5 = -\log[OH^-]$

or, $[OH^-] = 10^{-5}$

From above equation,

$[\bar{O}H] = 2S = 10^{-5}$

$\therefore \quad S = \dfrac{10^{-5}}{2}$

On substituting the value of 'S' in Eq. (i), we get

$$K_{sp} = 4S^3 = 4\left(\frac{10^{-5}}{2}\right)^3$$

$= 0.5 \times 10^{-15}$

2 (*c*) Let the solubility of CaF_2 in 0.1 M NaF is 'S' mol L^{-1}

$$CaF_2(s) \rightleftharpoons \underset{S}{Ca^{2+}}(aq) + \underset{2S}{2F^-}(aq)$$

$$NaF(aq) \rightleftharpoons \underset{0.1\text{ M}}{Na^+} + \underset{0.1\text{ M}}{F^-}(aq)$$

$[F^-] = 2S + 0.1$

K_{sp} of $CaF_2 = [Ca^{2+}][F^-]^2$

$= [S][2S + 0.1]^2$

$\Rightarrow 5.3 \times 10^{-11} = [S][2S + 0.1]^2$

$\Rightarrow 5.3 \times 10^{-11} = [S][0.1]^2$

$[\because 2S << 0.1]$

$[S] = \dfrac{5.3 \times 10^{-11}}{(0.1)^2}$

$= 5.3 \times 10^{-9}$ mol L^{-1}

3 (*c*) For a general reaction,

$$A_xB_y \rightleftharpoons xA^{y+} + yB^{x-}$$

Solubility product

$(K_{sp}) = [A^{y+}]^x [B^{x-}]^y$

For $BaSO_4$ (binary solute giving two ions)

$$BaSO_4(s) \rightleftharpoons \underset{S}{Ba^{2+}}(aq) + \underset{S}{SO_4^{2-}}(aq)$$

$\therefore K_{sp} = [Ba^{2+}][SO_4^{2-}]$

$= (S)(S) = S^2 \quad ...(i)$

[where, S = Solubility]

Given, $S = 2.42 \times 10^{-3}$ gL^{-1}

Molar mass of $BaSO_4$ = 233 g mol^{-1}

$\therefore$ Solubility of $BaSO_4$

$(S) = \dfrac{2.42 \times 10^{-3}}{233}$ mol L^{-1}

$= 1.04 \times 10^{-5}$ mol L^{-1}

On substituting the value of S in Eq. (i),

$K_{sp} = (1.04 \times 10^{-5} \text{ mol L}^{-1})^2$

$= 1.08 \times 10^{-10}$ mol^2 L^{-2}

4 (*c*) AX_2 is ionised as follows:

$$\underset{S \text{ mol L}^{-1}}{AX_2} \rightleftharpoons \underset{S}{A^{2+}} + \underset{2S}{2X^-}$$

Solubility product of AX_2

$K_{sp} = [A^{2+}][X^-]^2$

$= [S] \times [2S]^2 = 4S^3$

$\because K_{sp}$ of $AX_2 = 3.2 \times 10^{-11}$

$\therefore \quad 3.2 \times 10^{-11} = 4S^3$

or, $\quad S^3 = 0.8 \times 10^{-11} = 8 \times 10^{-12}$

or, $\quad S = \sqrt[3]{8 \times 10^{-12}}$

$= 2 \times 10^{-4}$ mol/L

Solubility $= 2 \times 10^{-4}$ mol/L

5 (*e*) $NH_4Cl(aq) \rightleftharpoons NH_4^+ + Cl^-$

$NH_4OH(aq) \rightleftharpoons NH_4^+ + OH^-$

NH_4OH is weak electrolyte. Both NH_4Cl and NH_4OH contain NH_4^+ as common ion. Hence, on dissolving simultaneously, the dissociation of ammonium hydroxide is suppressed due to common ion effect.

6 (*b*) $Ca_3(PO_4)_2 \longrightarrow 3Ca^{2+} + 2PO_4^{3-}$

$[Ca^{2+}] = 2 \times 10^{-8}$, $[PO_4^{3-}] = 1.6 \times 10^{-5}$

$K_{sp} = [Ca^{2+}]^3 [PO_4^{3-}]^2$

$= (2 \times 10^{-8})^3 (1.6 \times 10^{-5})^2$

$= 8 \times (1.6)^2 \times 10^{-34}$

$= 20.48 \times 10^{-34} = 2.048 \times 10^{-33}$

7 (*c*) Acids which are weak in water will be highly acidic in NH_3.

(a) $HCl + NH_3 \rightleftharpoons NH_4Cl$

(b) $CH_3COOH + NH_3 \rightleftharpoons CH_3COONH_4$

(c) $H_2SO_4 + 2NH_3 \rightleftharpoons (NH_4)_2SO_4$ (more acidic)

$\therefore$ Effect of ammonia is least in H_2SO_4 and maximum in CH_3COOH.

$\therefore$ Order of pH of resulting solution is $(NH_4)_2SO_4 > NH_4Cl > CH_3COONH_4$

$\therefore$ Order of pH of resulting solution is $CH_3COONH_4 > NH_4Cl > (NH_4)_2SO_4$

Hence, correct option is II > I > III.

8 (*b*) $\Delta G°$ is related to K_{sp} by the equation,

$\Delta G° = -2.303\, RT \log K_{sp}$

Given, $\Delta G° = +63.3$ kJ $= 63.3 \times 10^3$ J

Thus, substitute $\Delta G° = 63.3 \times 10^3$ J,

$R = 8.314$ JK^{-1} mol^{-1}

and $\quad T = 298$ K (25 + 273 K)

into the above equation to get,

$63.3 \times 10^3 = -2.303 \times 8.314 \times 298 \log K_{sp}$

$\therefore \quad \log K_{sp} = -11.09$

K_{sp} = antilog (− 11.09)

$K_{sp} = 8.1 \times 10^{-12} \approx 8.0 \times 10^{-12}$

9 (*d*) Sodium chloride is a salt of strong base NaOH and strong acid HCl. In the aqueous solution, following equilibrium is observed.

$NaCl + H_2O \rightleftharpoons Na^+ + Cl^- + H_2O$

Hence, no hydroglysis takes place in this case, and the solution remains neutral. Thus, here the product of molar concentrations of hydrogen ions and hydroxide ions is ionic product of water.

10 (*b*) Let the solubility of CaF_2 is S mol/L.

$$\underset{\text{Moles after dissolution}}{CaF_2} \longrightarrow \underset{S}{Ca^{2+}} + \underset{2S}{2F^-}$$

$K_{sp} = [Ca^{2+}][F^-]^2 = S \times (2S)^2 = 4S^3$

$K_{sp} = 3.2 \times 10^{-11}$ (given)

$3.2 \times 10^{-11} = 4S^3$

$S = \sqrt[3]{\dfrac{3.2 \times 10^{-11}}{4}}$

$= 2 \times 10^{-4}$ mol/L

11 (*b*) The solubility product of a binary weak electrolyte $= 4 \times 10^{-10}$.

$\therefore$ Solubility $= \sqrt{4 \times 10^{-10}}$

$= 2 \times 10^{-5}$ mol/dm^3

12 (*b*) Given, pH of $Ba(OH)_2 = 12$

pOH = 14 − pH = 14 − 12 = 2

We know that, pOH = − log [OH^-]

2 = − log [OH^-]

$[OH^-] = 10^{-2}$

$Ba(OH)_2$ dissolve S in water as

$$Ba(OH)_2(s) \rightleftharpoons \underset{S}{Ba^{2+}} + \underset{2S}{2OH^-}$$
S mol L^{-1}

$[OH^-] = 2S = 10^{-2}$

$$K_{sp} = [Ba^{2+}][OH^-]^2 = \frac{(10^{-2})}{2} \times (10^{-2})^2$$
$$= 0.5 \times 10^{-6} = 5 \times 10^{-7}$$

13 (*a*) $AlCl_3$ gives Al^{3+} ions which combine with OH^- given by H_2O so that dissociation equilibrium of H_2O shifts in forward direction, i.e. ionisation of water increases.

14 (*c*) $Fe(OH)_3 \rightleftharpoons Fe^{3+} + 3OH^-$

Let solubility of $Fe(OH)_3 = s$ mol/L

$[Fe^{3+}] = s$ mol / L, $[OH^-] = 3s$ mol/L

$$K_{sp} = [Fe^{3+}][OH^-]^3 = S \times (3s)^3$$
$$K_{sp} = 27S^4$$

15 (*c*) $Hg_2Cl_2 \longrightarrow \underset{S}{Hg_2^{2+}} + \underset{2S}{2Cl^-}$

$K_{sp} = 4s^3 = 32 \times 10^{-18}$

$s = 2 \times 10^{-6}$ M

16 (*d*)

(a) $Ag_3PO_4 \rightleftharpoons 3Ag^+ + PO_4^{3-}$

$$[PO_4^{3-}] = \frac{K_{sp}}{(0.1)^3} = \frac{1 \times 10^{-6}}{10^{-3}} = 10^{-3}$$

(b) $Ca_3(PO_4)_2 \rightleftharpoons 3Ca^{2+} + 2PO_4^{3-}$

$4x^2\,(0.1)^3 = K_{sp}$

$$x = \sqrt{\frac{K_{sp}}{4 \times 10^{-3}}} = \sqrt{\frac{10^{-33}}{4 \times 10^{-3}}}$$
$$= \sqrt{2.5 \times 10^{-31}}$$

$PO_4^{3-} = 5 \times 10^{-16}$

(c) $Mg_3(PO_4)_2 \rightleftharpoons \underset{0.1}{3Mg^{2+}} + \underset{2x}{2PO_4^{3-}}$

$(2x)^2\,(0.1)^3 = 10^{-24}$

$$4x^2 = \frac{10^{-24}}{0.001} = 10^{-21}$$
$$x = \sqrt{2.5 \times 10^{-22}} = 1.58 \times 10^{-11}$$

(d) $AlPO_4 \rightleftharpoons \underset{0.1}{Al^{3+}} + \underset{x}{PO_4^{3-}}$

$$x = \frac{K_{sp}}{0.1} = \frac{10^{-20}}{0.1} = 10^{-19}$$

∴ The correct option is (d).

17 (*b*) For precipitation,

ionic product > solubality product (K_{sp})

$[Zn^{2+}][S^{2-}] = 10^{-1} \times 8.1 \times 10^{-19}$

$= 8.1 \times 10^{-20} > K_{sp}$ of ZnS (3×10^{-22})

$[Cu^{2+}][S^{2-}] = 10^{-2} \times 8.1 \times 10^{-19}$

$= 8.1 \times 10^{-21} > K_{sp}$ of CuS (8×10^{-36})

∴ Both ZnS and CuS precipitate.

18 (*c*) Common ion effect is the suppression of degree of dissociation of a weak electrolyte in the presence of a strong electrolyte having common ion. Among the given, CH_3COOH + NaOH has no common ion, thus does not exhibit common ion effect.

19 (*c*) $[Ag^+] = 1.06 \times 10^{-5}$ g - ion/L

$= 1.06 \times 10^{-5}$ mol/L = [Cl^-]

$AgCl(s) \rightleftharpoons Ag^+ + Cl^-$

$K_{sp} = [Ag^+][Cl^-] = (1.06 \times 10^{-5})^2$

$= 1.12 \times 10^{-10}$

20 (*c*) $Mg(OH)_2 \longrightarrow \underset{S}{Mg^{2+}} + \underset{2S}{2OH^-}$

S is the solubility in mol/L.

$K_{sp} = [Mg^{2+}][OH^-]^2$

$= S \times (2S)^2 = 4S^3$

$$S = \left(\frac{K_{sp}}{4}\right)^{1/3} = \left(\frac{4 \times 10^{-12}}{4}\right)^{1/3}$$
$$= 1 \times 10^{-4} \text{ mol/L}$$

21 (*c*) For precipitation,

ionic product > solubility product (K_{sp})

For Ag_2CrO_4,

ionic product = $[Ag^+]^2\,[CrO_4^-]$

$= (10^{-4})^2(10^{-5}) = 10^{-13}$

K_{sp} of $Ag_2CrO_4 = 4 \times 10^{-12}$

Here, K_{sp} > Ionic proeduct

Thus, no precipitate is obtained.

For AgCl,

ionic product = $[Ag^+][Cl^-]$

$= [10^{-4}][10^{-5}] = 10^{-9}$

K_{sp} of (AgCl) $= 1 \times 10^{10}$

Here, Ionic product > K_{sp}

So, precipitate will form.

Thus, silver chloride gets precipitated first.

22 (*a*) $M_2X_3 \rightleftharpoons \underset{2S}{2M^{3+}} + \underset{3S}{3X^{2-}}$

(where, S = solubility)

$K_{sp} = (2S)^2 \cdot (3S)^3 = 108S^5$

or $2.2 \times 10^{-20} = 108S^5$

∴ $S = 4.59 \times 10^{-5}$

For M_2X, $M_2X \rightleftharpoons \underset{2S}{2M^+} + \underset{S}{X^{2-}}$

$K_{sp} = (2S)^2 \cdot (S) \Rightarrow K_{sp} = 4S^3$

$K_{sp} = 4(2 \times 4.59 \times 10^{-5})^3 = 3 \times 10^{-12}$

(∵ solubility of M_2X = 2 × solubility of M_2X_3)

23 (*c*) $\underset{x}{CaF_2} \rightleftharpoons \underset{x}{Ca^{2+}} + \underset{2x}{2F^-}$

$K_{sp} = [Ca^{2+}][2F^-]^2 = (x)(2x)^2 = 4x^3$

24 (*c*) For precipitation,

$[Ag^+]^2\,[CrO_4^{2-}] > K_{sp}$

$$\Rightarrow \left(\frac{10^{-4}}{2}\right)^2 (10^{-2}) > K_{sp}$$
$$\Rightarrow 2.5 \times 10^{-11} > K_{sp}$$

∴ Precipitate of Ag_2CrO_4 is formed when equal volumes of 10^{-4} M Ag^+ and 10^{-2} M CrO_4^{2-} are mixed.

25 (*b*) $M(OH)_2 \rightleftharpoons \underset{S}{M^{2+}} + \underset{2S}{2OH^-}$

$K_{sp} = [S][2S]^2 = 4S^3$

$$\Rightarrow S^3 = \frac{5 \times 10^{-16}}{4}$$
$$\Rightarrow S = 5 \times 10^{-6}$$

$[OH^-] = 2 \times 5 \times 10^{-6} = 10^{-5}$

pOH = − log [OH^-] = − log 10^{-5} = 5

pH = 14 − 5 = 9

26 (*d*) After mixing,

$[Ag^+] = (1/2) \times 10^{-4} = 5 \times 10^{-5}$ M

$[Cl^-] = (1/2) \times 10^{-4} = 5 \times 10^{-5}$ M

$K_{sp} = [Ag^+]\,[Cl^-] = (5 \times 10^{-5})^2$

$= 2.5 \times 10^{-9}$

Since, ionic product is greater than solubility product, hence precipitation will take place.

27 (*c*) It is ternary electrolyte,

$CaF_2 \rightleftharpoons Ca^{2+} + 2F^-$

Let solubility of CaF_2 be s mol L^{-1},

then $CaF_2 \rightleftharpoons \underset{S}{Ca^{2+}} + \underset{2S}{2F^-}$

Let $K_{sp} = [Ca^{2+}][F^-]^2$

$= (S) \times (2S)^2 = 4S^3$

$$S = \sqrt[3]{\frac{K_{sp}}{4}}$$

28 (*b*) Solubility of

$BaSO_4(x) = \sqrt{K_{sp}} = \sqrt{10^{-11}}$

$= 3.16 \times 10^{-6}$ mol/L

Solubility of

$CaSO_4(x) = \sqrt{K_{sp}} = \sqrt{10^{-6}}$

$= 1.0 \times 10^{-3}$ mol/L

Solubility of $Ag_2SO_4 = \sqrt[3]{\frac{K_{sp}}{4}}$

($\because$ for Ag_2SO_4, $4x^3 = K_{sp}$)

$= \sqrt[3]{\frac{10^{-5}}{4}} = 1.3 \times 10^{-2}$ mol/L

Least solubility is of $BaSO_4$, hence it will precipitate first.

29 (*c*) A salt is precipitated only when the product of ionic concentration is more than its solubility product.

$K_{sp} = 1 \times 10^{-8}$

$[A^+] = 10^{-3}$ M

$[B^-] = \frac{1 \times 10^{-8}}{10^{-3}} = 10^{-5}$ M

So, *AB* will be precipitated only when the concentration of $[B^-]$ is more than 10^{-5} M.

30 (*d*) Solubility of NiS $= \sqrt{K_{sp}}$

$= \sqrt{1.4 \times 10^{-24}} = 1.18 \times 10^{-12}$

Solubility of PbS $= \sqrt{K_{sp}}$

$= \sqrt{3.4 \times 10^{-28}} = 1.84 \times 10^{-14}$

Solubility of CoS $= \sqrt{K_{sp}}$

$= \sqrt{3 \times 10^{-26}} = 1.732 \times 10^{-13}$

$\because$ Least and maximum solubilities are of PbS and NiS respectively. Therefore, PbS and NiS will be precipitated first and last respectively.

31 (*b*) Pure NaCl is precipitated when HCl gas is passed in a saturated solution of NaCl.

This is due to the common ion effect. The concentration of Cl^- increases in the solution, due to which the reaction of dissociation of NaCl moves in the backward direction leading to precipitation of NaCl.

32 (*d*) $CaF_2 \rightleftharpoons Ca^{2+} + 2F^-$

$K = (10^{-6})\left(\frac{10^{-6}}{2}\right)^2 = 2.5 \times 10^{-19}$ which is less than K_{sp}.

Hence, no precipitate will develop. Thus, both A and R are incorrect. Hence, pH value decreases.

33 (*c*) K_{sp} of AgCl = (solubility of AgCl)^2

$= (1 \times 10^{-5})^2 = 1 \times 10^{-10}$

Suppose its solubility in 0.1 M NaCl is *x* mol/L.

$$\underset{}{AgCl} \rightleftharpoons \underset{x}{Ag^+} + \underset{x}{Cl^-}$$

$$NaCl \rightleftharpoons \underset{0.1\text{ M}}{Na^+} + \underset{0.1\text{ M}}{Cl^-}$$

$[Cl^-] = (x + 0.1)$ M

K_{sp} of AgCl $= [Ag^+][Cl^-]$

$= x \times (x + 0.1)$

$1 \times 10^{-10} = x^2 + 0.1x$

Higher power of *x* are neglected

$1 \times 10^{-10} = 0.1x \quad x = 1 \times 10^{-9}$ M

34 (*c*) $BaCO_3 \longrightarrow Ba^{2+} + CO_3^{2-}$

If solubility = *x*

$K_{sp} = x^2 \Rightarrow x = \sqrt{K_{sp}}$

35 (*c*) $1BaCl_2 \longrightarrow Ba^{2+} + 2Cl^-$

Let, the solubility of $BaCl_2$ is *x* mol/L

$\therefore \; K_{sp} = [Ba^{2+}][Cl^-]^2 = (x) \times (2x)^2$

$= x \times 4x^2 = 4x^3$

or solubility of $BaCl_2$

$= \left(\frac{\text{solubility product of } BaCl_2}{4}\right)^{1/3}$

$= \left(\frac{4 \times 10^{-9}}{4}\right)^{1/3} = 10^{-3}$ mol/L

36 (*c*) The solubility of AgI in NaI solution is less than that in pure water because of common ion effect of I^- ions suppresses the dissociation of AgI

37 (*c*) For binary salts (like AgCl, AgBr)

$S = \sqrt{K_{sp}}$

$\therefore$ Solubility of AgCl $= \sqrt{1.8 \times 10^{-10}}$

$= 1.34 \times 10^{-5}$ mol/L

Solubility of AgBr $= \sqrt{5.0 \times 10^{-13}}$

$= 7.1 \times 10^{-7}$ mol/L

For Ag_2CrO_4, $K_{sp} = 4S^3$

$\therefore$ Solubility of Ag_2CrO_4

$= \sqrt[3]{\frac{K_{sp}}{4}} = \sqrt[3]{\frac{2.4 \times 10^{-12}}{4}} = \sqrt[3]{600 \times 10^{-15}}$

$= 8.44 \times 10^{-5}$ mol/L

As Ag_2CrO_4 has maximum solubility, it will give maximum Ag^+ ions in solution. Hence, it will be used.

38 (*d*) Base *BOH* is dissociated as follows

$BOH \rightleftharpoons B^+ + OH^-$

So, the dissociation constant of *BOH* base is,

$K_b = \frac{[B^+][OH^-]}{[BOH]}$ ...(i)

At equilibrium, $[B^+] = [OH^-]$

$\therefore \quad K_b = \frac{[OH^-]^2}{[BOH]}$

Given that $K_b = 1.0 \times 10^{-12}$

and $[BOH] = 0.01$ M

Thus, $1.0 \times 10^{-12} = \frac{[OH^-]^2}{0.01}$

$[OH^-]^2 = 1 \times 10^{-14}$

$\Rightarrow \quad [OH^-] = 1.0 \times 10^{-7}$ mol L^{-1}

39 (*b*) $[Ag^+] = 2.5 \times 10^{-4}$

$[CO_3^{2-}] = \frac{2.5 \times 10^{-4}}{2} = 1.28 \times 10^{-4}$

$K_{sp} = [Ag^+]^2[CO_3^{2-}]$

$= (2.5 \times 10^{-4})^2 (1.28 \times 10^{-4})$

$= 8.39 \times 10^{-12}$

40 (*a*) The precipitation takes place only when the product of concentrations of ions exceeds the solubility product. If the product concentration of ions is less than solubility product, it will dissolve.

$AB \rightleftharpoons A^+ + B^-$

If $[A^+][B^-] > K_{sp}$ precipitation takes place.

If $[A^+][B^-] < K_{sp}$ substance will dissolve.

41 (*b*) Given, K_{sp} of $Mg(OH)_2 = 1 \times 10^{-12}$

Concentration of $Mg(OH)_2 = 0.01$ M

$Mg(OH)_2 \rightleftharpoons Mg^{2+} + 2OH^-$

$\therefore \quad K_{sp} = [Mg^{2+}][OH^-]^2$

or $\quad 1 \times 10^{-12} = 0.01 \times [OH^-]^2$

or $\quad [OH^-]^2 = 1 \times 10^{-10}$

or $\quad [OH^-] = 1 \times 10^{-5}$

Again, from $[H^+][OH^-] = 10^{-14}$

or $\quad [H^+][1 \times 10^{-5}] = 10^{-14}$

or $\quad [H^+] = \frac{10^{-14}}{10^{-5}} = 10^{-9}$

$\because \quad pH = -\log[H^+]$

$\therefore \quad pH = -\log 10^{-9} = 9$

$\therefore$ $Mg(OH)_2$ will precipitate at limited pH of 9.

Topic 5

pH, Buffer and Indicator

2019

1 If 50 mL of 0.1 HBr is mixed with 50 mL 0.2 M NaOH, find pH of resulting mixture **[JIPMER]**
(a) 2.7 (b) 12.7
(c) 10.7 (d) 1.3

2 pH of a salt solution of weak acid ($pK_a = 4$) and weak base ($pK_b = 5$) at 25° is **[AIIMS]**
(a) 6.5 (b) 6
(c) 7 (d) 7.5

3 Which will make basic buffer?
(a) 100 mL of 0.1 M CH_3COOH + 100 mL of 0.1 M NaOH **[NEET]**
(b) 100 mL of 0.1 M HCl + 200 mL of 0.1 M NH_4OH
(c) 100 mL of 0.1 M HCl + 100 mL of 0.1 M NaOH
(d) 50 mL of 0.1 M NaOH + 25 mL of 0.1 M CH_3COOH

4 The pH of 0.01 M NaOH (*aq*) solution will be **[NEET (Odisha)]**
(a) 7.01 (b) 2
(c) 12 (d) 9

5 Following solutions were prepared by mixing different volumes of NaOH and HCl of different concentrations

I. $60\text{mL} \frac{M}{10}$ HCl + $40\text{mL} \frac{M}{10}$ NaOH

II. $55\text{mL} \frac{M}{10}$ HCl + $45\text{mL} \frac{M}{10}$ NaOH

III. $75\text{ mL} \frac{M}{5}$ HCl + $25\text{ mL} \frac{M}{5}$ NaOH

IV. $100\text{ mL} \frac{M}{10}$ HCl + $100\text{ mL} \frac{M}{10}$ NaOH

pH of which one of them will be equal to 1?
(a) IV (b) I (c) II (d) III

2017

6 pH of solution of a strong acid is 5.0. What will be the 1 pH of solution obtained after diluting the given solution to 100 times? **[JIPMER]**
(a) 5.8 (b) 6.7
(c) 9.3 (d) 13

7 **Assertion** (A) Buffer solutions are composed of strong acids and strong bases.
Reason (R) It maintain the pH to a constant value of 7.4. **[AIIMS]**
(a) Both A and R are correct and R is the correct explanation of the A
(b) Both A and R are correct bu R′ is not the correct explanation of A
(c) A is correct but R is incorrect
(d) Both A and R are incorrect

2013

8 What is the pH of millimolar solution of ammo hydroxide which is 20% dissociated? **[MHTCET]**
(a) 3.699 (b) 10.301
(c) 4.691 (d) 9.301

9 0.001 mole of strong electrolyte $Zn(OH)_2$ is present in 200 mL of an aqueous solution. The pH of this solution is **[KERALA CEE]**
(a) 2 (b) 4 (c) 12 (d) 10
(e) 7

10 The pH of 10^{-4} M KOH solution will be **[WB JEE]**
(a) 4 (b) 11
(c) 10.5 (d) 10

11 How many litres of water must be added to 1 L of an aqueous solution with a pH of 1 to create an aqueous solution of pH of 3? **[UKPMT]**
(a) 49 L (b) 99 L (c) 79 L (d) 59 L

12 The pH value of $\frac{N}{10}$ NaOH is **[AIIMS]**
(a) 9 (b) 10 (c) 12 (d) 13

13 Solution of 0.1 N NH_4OH and 0.1 NH_4Cl has pH 9.2 Then pK_b of NH_4OH is **[WB JEE, Punjab PMET]**
(a) 9.25 (b) 4.75
(c) 3.75 (d) 8.25

2012

14 pH of a solution produced when an aqueous solution of pH 6 is mixed with an equal volume of an aqueous solution of pH 3 is about
(a) 3.3 (b) 4.3
(c) 4.0 (d) 4.5

15 The pH of a solution obtained by mixing 100 mL of a solution of pH = 3 with 400 mL of a solution of pH = 4 **[Karnataka CET]**
(a) 7 − log 2.8 (b) 4 − log 2.8
(c) 5 − log 2.8 (d) 3 − log 2.8

16 Buffer solutions have constant acidity and alkalinity, because **[CBSE AIPMT]**
(a) these give unionised acid or base on reaction with added acid or alkali
(b) acids and alkalies in these solutions are shielded from attack by other ions
(c) they have large excess of H^+ or OH^- ions
(d) they have fixed value of pH

17 20 mL, 0.1 N acetic acid is mixed with 10 mL 0.1 N solution of NaOH. The pH of the resulting solution is (pK_a of acetic acid is 4.74) [WB JEE]
(a) 3.74 (b) 4.74 (c) 5.74 (d) 6.74

18 The most important buffer in the blood consists of [AMU]
(a) HCl and Cl^- (b) H_2CO_3 and HCO_3^-
(c) H_2CO_3 and Cl^- (d) HCl and HCO_3^-

2011

19 0.023 g of sodium metal is reacted with 100 cm^3 of water. The pH of the resulting solution is [Karnataka CET]
(a) 10 (b) 8 (c) 9 (d) 12

20 pH value of which one of the following is not equal to one? [Karnataka CET]
(a) 0.1 M CH_3COOH
(b) 0.1 M HNO_3
(c) 0.05 M H_2SO_4
(d) 50 cm^3 0.4 M HCl + 50 cm^3 0.2 M NaOH

21 A buffer solution is prepared in which the concentration of NH_3 is 0.30 M and the concentration of NH_4^+ is 0.20 M. If the equilibrium constant, K_b for NH_3 equals 1.8×10^{-5}, what is the pH of this solution? [CBSE AIPMT]
(a) 8.73 (b) 9.08 (c) 9.44 (d) 11.72

22 For preparing a buffer solution of pH = 7.0, which buffer system you will choose? [DUMET]
(a) $H_3PO_4, H_2PO_4^-$ (b) $H_2PO_4^-, HPO_4^{2-}$
(c) HPO_4^{2-}, PO_4^{3-} (d) H_3PO_4, PO_4^{3-}

23 A buffer solution contains 0.1 mole of sodium acetate dissolved in 1000 cm^3 of 0.1 M acetic acid. To the above buffer solution, 0.1 mole of sodium acetate is further added and dissolved. The pH of the resulting buffer is [KCET]
(a) pK_a (b) $pK_a + 2$
(c) $pK_a - \log 2$ (d) $pK_a + \log 2$

2010

24 0.1 M HCl and 0.1 M H_2SO_4 each of volume 2 mL are mixed and the volume is made upto 6 mL by adding 2 mL of 0.01 N NaCl solution. The pH of the resulting mixture is [WB JEE]
(a) 1.17 (b) 1.0
(c) 0.3 (d) $\log 2 - \log 3$

25 Calculate the normality of 250 mL aqueous solution of H_2SO_4 having pH = 0.00. [Guj CET]
(a) 0.25 N (b) 0.50 N
(c) 1 N (d) 2 N

26 If pH of a saturated solution of $Ba(OH)_2$ is 12, the value of its K_{sp} is [CBSE AIPMT]
(a) 5.00×10^{-7} M^3 (b) 4.00×10^{-6} M^3
(c) 4.00×10^{-7} M^3 (d) 5.00×10^{-6} M^3

27 The pH value of 0.01 N NaOH solution is [UP CPMT]
(a) 2 (b) 6
(c) 12 (d) 11

28 The pH of 10^{-3} M solution of NaOH is [OJEE]
(a) 3 (b) 11
(c) 4 (d) 12

29 The concentration of hydronium ions in a cup of black coffee is 1.3×10^{-5} M. What will be the pH of the coffee? [HARYANA PMT]
(a) 4.89 (b) 3.89
(c) 2.20 (d) None of these

30 A weak acid of dissociation constant 10^{-5} is being titrated with aqueous NaOH solution. The pH at the point of one-third neutralisation of the acid will be [WB JEE]
(a) $5 + \log 2 - \log 3$ (b) $5 - \log 2$
(c) $5 - \log 3$ (d) $5 - \log 6$

31 The pH of a solution obtained be mixing equal volume of $\frac{N}{10}$ NaOH and $\frac{N}{20}$ HCl is [AMU (MED)]
(a) 13.4 (b) 12.4
(c) 7.6 (d) 1.6

32 The pH of a solution prepared by mixing 2.0 mL of HCl solution of pH 3.0 and 3.0 mL of NaOH of pH 10.0 is [AMU (MED)]
(a) 2.5 (b) 3.5
(c) 5.5 (d) 6.5

33 A solution contains 10 mL 0.1 N NaOH and 10 mL 0.05 N H_2SO_4. pH of this solution is [JCECE]
(a) less than 7 (b) 7
(c) zero (d) greater than 7

34 What is the pH value of 10^{-2} molar HNO_3 solution? [VMMC]
(a) 1 (b) 2
(c) 3 (d) 4

35 In a buffer solution containing equal concentration of B^- and HB, then K_b for B^- is 10^{-10}. The pH of buffer solution is [CBSE AIPMT]
(a) 4 (b) 10
(c) 7 (d) 6

36 What is $[H^+]$ in mol/L of a solution that is 0.20 M in CH_3COONa and 0.10 M in CH_3COOH? (K_a for $CH_3COOH = 1.8 \times 10^{-5}$) [CBSE AIPMT]
(a) 9.0×10^{-6} (b) 3.5×10^{-4}
(c) 1.1×10^{-5} (d) 1.8×10^{-5}

37 100 mL of HCl + 35 mL of NaOH, colour of methyl orange in the solution will be [AFMC]
(a) red
(b) yellow
(c) can't be predicted
(d) methyl orange is not suitable indicator

38 The pH of an acidic buffer mixture is [Manipal]
(a) 6.8
(b) 7
(c) 7.5
(d) depends upon K_a of the acid

2009

39 When strong acid is titrated using a weak base, the pH at the equivalence point is [OJEE]
(a) 7 (b) > 7 (c) < 7 (d) = 7

40 Two acids A and B have pK_a 4 and 6, then [UP CPMT]
(a) A is 4/6 times stronger than B
(b) A is 10 times stronger than B
(c) A is 6/4 times stronger than B
(d) B is 10 times stronger than A

41 The degree of dissociation of a 0.01 M weak acid is 10^{-3}. Its pOH is [MHT CET]
(a) 5 (b) 3 (c) 9 (d) 11

42 Both HCOOH and CH_3COOH solutions have equal pH. If $\frac{K_1}{K_2}$ (ratio of acid ionisation constants) of these acids is 4, their molar concentration ratio will be [Manipal]
(a) 2 (b) 0.5 (c) 4 (d) 0.25

43 20 mL of 0.1 M acetic acid is mixed with 50 mL of potassium acetate. K_a of acetic acid $= 1.8 \times 10^{-5}$ at 27°C. Calculate the concentration of potassium acetate if pH of the mixture is 4.8. [EAMCET]
(a) 0.1 M (b) 0.04 M (c) 0.4 M (d) 0.02 M

44 If the dissociation constant of 5×10^{-4} M aqueous solution of diethylamine is 2.5×10^{-5}. Its pH value is [AIIMS]
(a) 8 (b) 3.95 (c) 10.04 (d) 2

45 The number of hydroxyl ions in 100 mL of a solution having pH 10 is [AIIMS]
(a) 1×10^4 (b) 3.012×10^4
(c) 6.02×10^{18} (d) 6.023×10^{19}

46 If 20 mL of an acidic solution of pH 3 is diluted to 100 mL the H^+ ion concentration will be [MHT CET]
(a) 1×10^{-3} M (b) 2×10^{-3} M
(c) 2×10^{-4} M
(d) 0.02×10^{-4} M

47 Which one of the following has pH value of 10.5 ? [KERALA CEE]
(a) Lemon juice (b) Blood
(c) Milk (d) Soft drink
(e) Lime water

48 Which of the following will decrease the pH of a 50 mL solution of 0.01 M HCl ? [WB JEE]
(a) Addition of 5 mL of 1 M HCl
(b) Addition of 50 mL of 0.01 M HCl
(c) Addition of 50 mL of 0.001 M HCl
(d) None of the above

49 If pK_a of acetic acid and pK_b of ammonium hydroxide are 4.76 each. The pH of ammomium acetate is [AMU (MED)]
(a) 7 (b) less than 7
(c) more than 7 (d) zero

50 Determine the pH of the solution that results from the addition of 20.00 mL of 0.01 M $Ca(OH)_2$ to 30.00 mL of 0.01 M HCl. [DUMET]
(a) 11.30 (b) 10.55
(c) 2.70 (d) 83.35

51 30 cc of $\frac{M}{3}$ HCl, 20 cc of $\frac{M}{2}$ HNO_3 and 40 cc of $\frac{M}{4}$ NaOH solutions are mixed and the volume was made upto 1 dm^3. The pH of the resulting solution is [KARNATAKA CET]
(a) 2 (b) 1 (c) 3 (d) 8

52 10^{-6} M NaOH is diluted 100 times. The pH of the diluted base is [KARNATAKA CET]
(a) between 5 and 6 (b) between 6 and 7
(c) between 10 and 11 (d) between 7 and 8

53 The dissociation constant for acetic acid and HCN at 25° C are 1.5×10^{-5} and 4.5×10^{-10} respectively.
The equilibrium constant for the equilibrium.
$CN^- + CH_3COOH \rightleftharpoons HCN + CH_3COO^-$ would be [CBSE AIPMT]
(a) 3.0×10^5 (b) 3.0×10^{-5}
(c) 3.0×10^{-4} (d) 3.0×10^4

54 A buffer solution is used in [Manipal]
(a) preparation of potash alum
(b) the removal of PO_4^{3-} ions
(c) increasing the pH value of a solution
(d) precipitation of $Cr(OH)_3$ from $CrCl_3$

55 pH of a buffer solution decreases by 0.02 units when 0.12 g of acetic acid is added to 250 mL of a buffer solution of acetic acid and potassium acetate at 27°C. The buffer capacity of the solution is [EAMCET]
(a) 0.1 (b) 10 (c) 1 (d) 0.4

2008

56 Equal volumes of three acid solutions of pH 3, 4 and 5 are mixed in a vessel. What will be the H^+ ion concentration in the mixture? [CBSE AIPMT]
(a) 1.11×10^{-4} M (b) 3.7×10^{-4} M
(c) 3.7×10^{-3} M (d) 1.11×10^{-8} M

57 Which of the following is correct? [UP CPMT]
(a) The pH of 1 L solution containing 0.49 g of H_2SO_4 is 2.0
(b) The conjugate base of H_2S is S^{2-}
(c) BF_3 is a Lewis base
(d) Phenolphthalein is colourless in basic medium

58 Number of H^+ ions present in 250 mL of lemon juice of pH = 3 is [Kerala CEE]
(a) 1.50×10^{22} (b) 1.50×10^{23}
(c) 1.506×10^{20} (d) 3.01×10^{21}
(e) 2.008×10^{23}

59 Which will have the minimum value of pK_b? [Haryana PMT]
(a) OH^- (b) CH_3COO^-
(c) Cl^- (d) $HCOO^-$

60 Which of the following solutions will have pH = 9 at 298 K? [BCECE]
(a) 1×10^{-9} M HCl solution
(b) 1×10^{-5} M NaOH solution
(c) 1×10^{-9} M KOH solution
(d) Both (a) and (b)

61 The pH of 10^{-8} M HCl solution is
(a) 8
(b) more than 8
(c) between 6 and 7
(d) slightly more than 7

62 Which one of the following solution will have pH close to unity? [BHU, KERALA PMT]
(a) 100 mL of $\frac{M}{10}$ HCl = 100mL of $\frac{M}{10}$ NaOH
(b) 55 mL of $\frac{M}{10}$ HCl − 45 mL of $\frac{M}{10}$ NaOH
(c) 10 mL of $\frac{M}{10}$ HCl + 90 mL of $\frac{M}{10}$ NaOH
(d) 75 mL of $\frac{M}{5}$ HCl − 25 mL of $\frac{M}{5}$ NaOH
(e) 50 mL of $\frac{M}{5}$ HCl + 50 mL of $\frac{M}{5}$ NaOH

63 pH of HCl (conc. 0.1 mol/L) is one. Compute the pH of 0.05 mol/L solution of H_2SO_4. [Haryana PMT]
(a) 0.05 (b) 0.5 (c) 1 (d) 2

64 When 0.1 mole of an acid is added to 2 L of a buffer solution, the pH of the buffer decreases by 0.5. The buffer capacity of the solution is [EAMCET]
(a) 0.6 (b) 0.4 (c) 0.2 (d) 0.1

65 When ammonium chloride is added to ammonia solution, the pH of the resulting solution will be [MHT CET]
(a) increased (b) seven
(c) decreased (d) unchanged

66 100 mL of 0.1 M H_2SO_4 is added to 200 mL of 0.1 M NaOH. What is the pH of the resulting mixture? [EAMCET]
(a) 2 (b) 7 (c) 10 (d) 12

2007

67 pH of the solution containing 1.04×10^{-12} M KOH is [Haryana PMT]
(a) −11.9 (b) +11.9
(c) 7 (d) 2.30

68 What will be the resultant pH when 200 mL of an aqueous solution of HCl (pH = 2) is mixed with 300 mL of an aqueous solution of NaOH (pH = 12)? [Haryana PMT]
(a) 10 (b) 11
(c) 12 (d) 14

69 The rapid changes of pH near the stoichiometric point of an acid base titration is the basis of indicator detection. pH of the solution is related to ratio of the concentrations of the conjugate acid (HIn) and base (In^-) forms of the indicator given by the expression [Manipal]
(a) $\log\frac{[In^-]}{[HIn]} = pK_{In} - pH$ (b) $\log\frac{[HIn]}{[In^-]} = pK_{In} - pH$
(c) $\log\frac{[HIn]}{[In^-]} = pH - pK_{In}$ (d) $\log\frac{[In^-]}{[HIn]} = pH - pK_{In}$

70 What is the pH at equivalence point in the titration of 0.1 M CH_3COOH and 0.1 M NaOH?
(K_a for acetic acid is 1.8×10^{-5}) [MP PMT]
(a) 7 (b) Between 7 and 8
(c) Between 8 and 9 (d) Between 6 and 7

2006

71 The hydrogen ion concentration of a 10^{-8} M HCl aqueous solution at 298 K ($K_w = 10^{-14}$) is [CBSE AIPMT]
(a) 1.0×10^{-6} M (b) 1.0525×10^{-7} M
(c) 9.525×10^{-8} M (d) 1.0×10^{-8} M

72 At 90°C, pure water has H_3O^+ ion concentration of 10^{-6} mol/L. The K_w at 90°C is [AMU]
(a) 10^{-6} (b) 10^{-14} (c) 10^{-12} (d) 10^{-8}

73 pH of 1 L 0.1 M HCl when 5 g of HF is added [DUMET]
(a) 0.53 (b) 1 (c) 0.1 (d) 0.01

74 The pH of 0.1 M solution of the following salts increase in the order [BHU]
(a) NaCl < NH_4Cl < NaCN < HCl
(b) HCl < NH_4Cl < NaCl < NaCN
(c) NaCN < NH_4Cl < NaCl < HCl
(d) HCl < NaCl < NaCl < NH_4Cl

75 Which of the following has highest pH? [Manipal]
(a) $\frac{M}{4}$ KOH (b) $\frac{M}{4}$ NaOH
(c) $\frac{M}{4}$ NH_4OH (d) $\frac{M}{4}$ $Ca(OH)_2$

76 0.005 M acid solution has 5 pH. The percentage ionisation of acid is [RPMT]
(a) 0.8% (b) 0.6% (c) 0.4% (d) 0.2%

77 If the pH value is 4.5 for a solution then what is the value of H^+ concentration? [MP PMT]
(a) 3.162×10^{-5} mol/L (b) 31.62×10^{-5} mol/L
(c) 0.3162×10^{-5} mol/L (d) 3.162×10^{-8} mol/L

78 Which of the following pairs constitutes a buffer? [CBSE AIPMT]
(a) HNO_2 and $NaNO_2$ (b) NaOH and NaCl
(c) HNO_3 and NH_4NO_3 (d) HCl and KCl

79 Consider the following solutions of equal concentrations.
$A = NH_4Cl$ $B = CH_3COONa$
$C = NH_4OH$ $D = CH_3COOH$
A buffer solution can be obtained by mixing equal volumes of **[J&K CET]**
(a) C and D (b) A and B
(c) A and C (d) C and D

80 The pK_b value of NH_3 is 5. Calculate the pH of the buffer solution, 1 L of which contains 0.01 M NH_4Cl and 0.10 M NH_4OH **[Punjab PMET]**
(a) 4 (b) 6 (c) 8 (d) 10

2005

81 pK_a of CH_3COOH is 4.74. The pH of 0.01 M CH_3COONa will be **[KERALA CEE]**
(a) 3.28 (b) 2.38 (c) 8.37 (d) 3.87
(e) 9.25

82 When 10 mL of 0.1 M acetic acid ($pK_a = 5.0$) is titrated against 10 mL of 0.1 M ammonia solution ($pK_b = 5.0$), the equivalence point occurs at pH **[AIIMS]**
(a) 5.0 (b) 6.0 (c) 7.0 (d) 9.0

83 The pK_a of HCN is 9.30. The pH of a solution prepared by mixing 2.5 moles of KCN and 2.5 moles of HCN in water and making total volume upto 500 mL is **[Haryana PMT]**
(a) 9.30 (b) 7.30
(c) 10.30 (d) 8.30

84 A solution has pH = 5, it is diluted 100 times, then it will become **[AFMC]**
(a) neutral (b) basic
(c) unaffected (d) more acidic

85 Given pH of a solution A is 3 and it is mixed with another solution B having pH 2. If both are mixed, then resultant pH of the solution will be **[BHU]**
(a) 3.2 (b) 1.9 (c) 3.4 (d) 3.5
(e) 9.2

86 When 0.10 mole of NH_3 is dissolved in water to make 1.0 L solution, the solution is found to have $[OH]^- = 1.34 \times 10^{-3}$ m. The value of K_b for NH_3 is **[Kerala CEE]**
(a) 1.8×10^{-5} (b) 2.8×10^{-5}
(c) 1.8×10^{-7} (d) 2.8×10^{-7}
(e) None of these

Answers

1 (b)	2 (a)	3 (b)	4 (c)	5 (d)	6 (b)	7 (d)	8 (b)	9 (c)	10 (d)
11 (b)	12 (d)	13 (b)	14 (a)	15 (b)	16 (a)	17 (b)	18 (b)	19 (d)	20 (a)
21 (c)	22 (b)	23 (d)	24 (b)	25 (d)	26 (a)	27 (c)	28 (b)	29 (a)	30 (b)
31 (b)	32 (b)	33 (d)	34 (b)	35 (a)	36 (a)	37 (a)	38 (d)	39 (c)	40 (b)
41 (c)	42 (d)	43 (b)	44 (c)	45 (c)	46 (c)	47 (e)	48 (a)	49 (a)	50 (a)
51 (a)	52 (d)	53 (d)	54 (b)	55 (d)	56 (b)	57 (a)	58 (c)	59 (a)	60 (b)
61 (c)	62 (d)	63 (c)	64 (d)	65 (c)	66 (b)	67 (c)	68 (b)	69 (d)	70 (c)
71 (b)	72 (c)	73 (b)	74 (b)	75 (d)	76 (d)	77 (a)	78 (a)	79 (c)	80 (d)
81 (c)	82 (c)	83 (a)	84 (a)	85 (b)	86 (a)				

Explanations

1 (*b*) $N_{Mix}V_{Mix} = N_1V_1 - N_2V_2$ ... (i)
$\qquad\qquad$ (Base) $\quad$ (Acid)

Given, $M_1 = 0.2M$, $N_1 = 0.2$ N
$M_2 = 0.1$ M, $N_2 = 0.1$ N
$V_1 = 50$ mL, $V_2 = 50$ mL, $V_{mix} = 100$ mL

On substituting the given values in equation. (i)

$$N_{mix} \times 100 = 50 \times 0.2 - 50 \times 0.1$$

$$N_{mix} = \frac{5}{100} = 5 \times 10^{-2}$$

$\therefore$ $[OH^-] = 5 \times 10^{-2}$

Now, $pOH = -\log[OH^-] = -\log[5 \times 10^{-2}]$
$= 2 - \log 5 = 1.3$

Also, pH + pOH = 14
pH = 14 − 1.3 = 12.7

2 (*a*) pH of buffer solution of weak acid and weak base is calculated, using the following formula.

$$pH = \frac{1}{2}[pK_w + pK_a - pK_b]$$

Given : $pK_a = 4$, $pK_b = 5$, $pK_w = 14$

$$\therefore \quad pH = \frac{1}{2}[14 + 4 - 5] = 6.5$$

Hence, option (a) is the correct.

3 (*b*) A buffer solution having pH more than 7 is known as basic buffer. It is obtained by mixing weak base and its salt with strong acid in a fixed proportion.

Let us consider all the options,

(a) 100 mL of 0.1 M CH_3COOH + 100 mL of 0.1M NaOH

	CH_3COOH +	NaOH $\longrightarrow$	$CH_3COONa + H_2O$
Initial Conc.	100 mL × 0.1 M = 10 mmol	100 mL × 0.1 M = 10 mmol	0 mmol
Final conc.	0	0	10 mmol

It is not basic buffer because hydrolysis of salt takes place and final solution contains salt of weak acid with strong base only.

Hence, option (a) is incorrect.

(b) 100 mL of 0.1 M HCl + 200 mL of 0.1 M NH_4OH

	HCl	+ NH_4OH	$\longrightarrow NH_4Cl + H_2O$
Initial conc.	100 mL× 0.1 M HCl = 10 mmol	200 mL × 0.1 M = 20 mmol	0 mmol
Final conc.	0	10 mmol	10 mmol

It is basic buffer because final solution contains weak base and its salt with strong acid. Hence, option (b) is correct.

(c) 100 mL of 0.1 M HCl + 100 mL of 0.1 M NaOH

	HCl +	NaOH	$\longrightarrow$ NaCl + H_2O
Initial conc.	100 mL × 0.1 M = 10 mmol	1 00 mL × 0.1 M = 10 mmol	0 mmol
Final conc.	0	0	10 mmol

It is a neutral solution. Hence, option (c) is incorrect.

(d) 50 mL of 0.1 M NaOH + 25mL of 0.1 M CH_3COOH

	CH_3COOH +	NaOH	$\longrightarrow CH_3COONa + H_2O$
Initial conc.	25 mL × 0.1 M = 2.5 mmol	50 mL × 0.1 M = 5 mmol	0 mmol
Final conc.	0	2.5 mol	2.5 mmol

It is basic solution. Hence, option (d) is incorrect.

4 (c) NaOH is a strong base, thus

$[OH^-] = 0.01\,M = 10^{-2}\,M$

$pOH = -\log[OH^-] = -\log(10^{-2}) = 2$

We know that, pH + pOH = 14

$\therefore \quad pH = 14 - 2 = 12$

Thus, option (c) is correct.

5 (*d*) $75\text{ mL}\frac{M}{5}\text{ HCl} + 25\text{mL}\frac{M}{5}\text{NaOH}$

Milliequivalent of HCl $= 75\text{ mL of}\frac{M}{5}\text{ HCl} = \frac{1}{5}\times 75 = 15$

Milliequivalent of NaOH

$25\text{ mL of}\frac{M}{5}\text{ NaOH} = \frac{1}{5}\times 25 = 5$

$\therefore$ Milliequivalent of HCl left unused = 15 – 5 = 10

Volume of solution = 100 mL

$\therefore$ Molarity of $[H^+]$ in the resulting mixuture $= \frac{10}{100} = \frac{1}{10}$

$\therefore \quad pH = \log\frac{1}{[H^+]} = \log(10) = 1$

6 (*b*) Given, pH = 5,

i.e. $\quad [H^+] = 10^{-5}\text{ mol L}^{-1}$

On diluting the solution to 100 times.

$[H^+] = \frac{10^{-5}}{100} = 10^{-7}\text{ mol L}^{-1}.$

Total $[H^+]$ concentration = H^+ water ions from acid + H^+ ions from water.

$[H^+] = 10^{-7} + 10^{-7} = 2\times 10^{-7}\text{ M}$

$\therefore \quad pH = -\log[2\times 10^{-7}]$

$pH = 7 - 0.3010 = 6.699 \approx 6.7$

7 (*d*) Both (A) and (R) are false as buffer solutions are made by mixing weak acid with its salt of strong base or by mixing weak base with its salt of strong acid. It is never formed by mixing strong acid and strong base.

The pH of buffer solution remain constant but not always equal to 7.4.

8 (*b*) Concentration of NH_4OH solution = 0.001 M

Degree of dissociation $= 20\% = \frac{20}{100} = 0.2$

Concentration of OH^- i.e. $[OH^-]$

= Concentration of solution × degree fo dissociation

$= 0.001 \times 0.2 = 2\times 10^{-4}$

$\therefore [H^+][OH^-] = 1\times 10^{-14}$

$\therefore \quad [H^+] = \frac{1\times 10^{-14}}{2\times 10^{-4}} = \frac{1}{2}\times 10^{-10}$

Again, $\quad pH = -\log[H^+] = 10 + \log 2 = 10.301$

9 (*c*) $pOH = -\log[OH^-]$, where $[OH^-]$ is concentration of OH^-.

Concentration of OH^- is given as,

$[OH^-] = \frac{0.001}{200}\times 1000 = 5\times 10^{-3}\text{ M}$

$pOH = -\log(5\times 10^{-3}) = 3 - \log 5 = 2.30$

pH + pOH = 14

$pH = 14 - 2.30 = 11.7 \approx 12$

10 (*d*) $10^{-4}\text{ M KOH} = 10^{-4}\text{ M}[OH^-]$

We know that,

$[H^+][OH^-] = 1\times 10^{-14}$

$[H^+]\times 10^{-4} = 1\times 10^{-14}$

$[H^+] = \frac{1\times 10^{-14}}{1\times 10^{-4}} = 1\times 10^{-10}\text{ M}$

$pH = -\log[H^+] = -\log(1\times 10^{-10}) = 10$

11 (*b*) pH = 1, i.e. solution contain $[H^+] = 0.1\text{ M}$

pH = 3, i.e. solution contain

$[H^+] = 10^{-3}\text{ M}$

$M_1V_1 = M_2V_2$ (Law of dilution)

$1\times 10^{-1} = 10^{-3}\times V_2 \Rightarrow V_2 = 100\text{ L}$

Water added = 100 – 1 = 99 L

12 (*d*) Normality of NaOH = Molarity $= \frac{M}{10}$

($\because$ NaOH is monoacidic base and molarity = acidity × N)

$[OH^-] = \frac{1}{10} = 0.1\text{ M}$

$[H^+][OH^-] = 10^{-14}$

$[H^+] = \frac{10^{-14}}{0.1} = 10^{-13}$

$pH = -\log[H^+]$

$= -\log 10^{-13} = 13$

13 (*b*) $pOH = pK_b + \log \frac{(\text{salt})}{(\text{base})} = pK_b + 0$

$pK_b = pOH = 14 - pH$
$= 14 - 9.25 = 4.75$

14 (*a*) Aqueous solution of pH 6 means

$[H^+] = 10^{-6}$

Aqueous solution pH 3 means

$[H^+] = 10^{-3}$

Aqueous solution of both pH are mixed in equal volume.

Hence,

$$[H^+] = \frac{10^{-6} + 10^{-3}}{2} = 10^{-6} \times 500.5$$

$pH = -\log[H^+]$
$= 6 - \log 500.5$
$= 6 - 2.6994 = 3.3$

15 (*b*) For solution 1, pH = 3

$[H^+] = 10^{-3}$

Concentration of solution $M_1 = 10^{-3}$ M, $V_1 = 100$ mL

For solution 2, pH = 4

$[H^+] = 10^{-4}$

Concentration of resulting solution

$$M = \frac{M_1V_1 + M_2V_2}{V_1 + V_2} = \frac{10^{-3} \times 100 + 10^{-4} \times 400}{100 + 400}$$

$$M = \frac{0.14}{500} = 2.8 \times 10^{-4}$$

$[H^+] = 2.8 \times 10^{-4}$

pH of resulting solution $= -\log[H^+]$
$= -\log[2.8 \times 10^{-4}]$
$= 4 - \log 2.8$

16 (*a*) If small amount of an acid or alkali is added to a buffer solution, it converts them into unionised acid or base. Thus, its pH remains unaffected or in the other words, its acidity/alkalinity remains constant, e.g.

$$H_3O^+ + A^- \rightleftharpoons H_2O + HA$$
$$OH^- + HA \longrightarrow H_2O + A^-$$

If acid is added, it reacts with A^- to form undissociated HA. Similarly, if base/alkali is added, OH^- combines with HA to give H_2O and A^- and thus maintains the acidity/alkalinity of the buffer solution.

17 (*b*) $CH_3COOH + NaOH \longrightarrow CH_3COONa + H_2O$

Initially, $20 \times 0.1 = 2$ mmol, $10 \times 0.1 = 1$ mmol

After some time, $2 - 1 = 1$ mmol, $1 - 1 = 0$ mmol

$$pH = pK_a + \log \frac{[\text{salt}]}{[\text{base}]} = 4.74 + \log \frac{0.1}{0.1} = 4.74$$

18 (*b*) The most important butter in the blood consists of H_2CO_3 and HCO_3^-. Ratio of dissolved HCO_3^- to H_2CO_3 is helpful in controlling pH of the blood.

19 (*d*) $2Na + 2H_2O \longrightarrow 2NaOH + H_2$

2×23 2×40 g

46 g Na given 80 g NaOH

0.023 g Na gives 0.04 g NaOH

Mass per 1000 cm^3 of NaOH = 0.4 g

Moles of NaOH $= \frac{0.4}{40} = 0.01$

$[OH^-] = 10^{-2}$

$pOH = 2$

$pH = 14 - 2 = 12$

20 (*a*) pH value for weak acids are very high. Thus, CH_3COOH being a weak acid does not have its pH value equal to 1.

21 (*c*) $pOH = pK_b + \log \frac{[\text{salt}]}{[\text{base}]}$

$$= 4.74 + \log \frac{0.20}{0.30} = 4.74 - 0.176 = 4.56$$

$[\because pK_b = \log K_b = \log(1.8 \times 10^{-5}) = 4.74]$

$pH = 14 - 4.56 = 9.44$

22 (*b*) A weak acid $H_2PO_4^-$ and its conjugate base HPO_4^{2-}.

23 (*d*) $pH = pK_a + \log \frac{[CH_3COONa]}{[CH_3COOH]}$

$$= pK_a + \log \frac{0.2}{0.1} = pK_a + \log 2$$

24 (*b*) Millimoles of H^+

$= 0.1 \times 2 + 0.1 \times 2 \times 2 = 0.6$

Total volume in mL = 6

$$pH = -\log[H^+] = -\log\left(\frac{0.6}{6}\right) = -\log 0.1 = 1$$

25 (*b*) $pH = -\log[H^+]$

$\log[H^+] = -pH = 0.00$

$[H^+] = \text{antilog}(0.00)$

$[H^+] = 1.0$ M

$1 M\ H_2SO_4 = 2N\ H_2SO_4$

Hence, normality = 2 N

26 (*a*) pH = 12, so pOH = 2

$\therefore [OH^-] = 10^{-2}$

$Ba(OH)_2 \rightleftharpoons \underset{S}{Ba^{2+}} + 2OH^-$

$2S = 10^{-2}$

$\Rightarrow S = \frac{10^{-2}}{2} = 5 \times 10^{-3}$ M

$K_{sp} = [Ba^{2+}][OH^-]^2$
$= [5 \times 10^{-3}][10^{-2}]^2$

$K_{sp} = 5 \times 10^{-7}\ M^3$

27 (*c*) Given, NaOH = 0.01 N

$[OH^-] = 0.01\ N = 1 \times 10^{-2}$ N

$pOH = -\log[OH^-]$
$= -\log(1 \times 10^{-2}) = 2$

$pH + pOH = 14 \Rightarrow pH + 2 = 14$

$\therefore pH = 12$

28 (*b*) $[OH^-] = 10^{-3}$ M

$pOH = -\log[OH^-] = -\log(10^{-3}) = 3$

$\Rightarrow pH = 14 - pOH = 14 - 3 = 11$

29 (*a*) Given, $[H_3O^+] = 1.3 \times 10^{-5}$

$\because pH = -\log[H_3O^+]$
$= -\log(1.3 \times 10^{-5})$
$= -(\log 1.3 + \log 10^{-5})$
$= 0.1139 + 5$

$\therefore pH = 4.886 = 4.89$

30 (*b*) $K_a = 10^{-5}$

$pK_a = -\log K_a = -\log 10^{-5} = 5$

$HA + NaOH \longrightarrow NaA + H_2O$

	HA		NaA	H_2O
Initial	1 mole	0	0	0
Final	$\left(1 - \frac{1}{3}\right)$ mole $= \frac{2}{3}$ mole		$\frac{1}{3}$ mole	$\frac{1}{3}$ mole

(Assumed weak acid to be monoprotic, since only one dissociation constant value is provided).

$$pH = pK_a + \log \frac{[\text{salt}]}{[\text{acid}]}$$

or $pH = 5 + \log \frac{1/3}{2/3} = 5 + \log \frac{1}{2}$

$\Rightarrow pH = 5 - \log 2$

31 (*b*) Let the volume of NaOH used $= V =$ Volume of HCl used

Concentration in the mixture $[OH^-]$

$$= \frac{0.1\,V - 0.05\,V}{(V + V)}$$

[∴ milliequivalent of NaOH is in excess]

$$= \frac{0.05}{2} = 0.025$$

$$pOH = -\log[OH^-]$$
$$= -\log(0.025) = 1.602$$
$$pH = 14 - 1.602 = 12.4$$

32 (*b*) ∵ pH of HCl solution = 3.0

∴ $[H^+]$ in HCl solution $= 1 \times 10^{-3}$

∵ pH of NaOH solution = 10.0

∴ $[H^+]$ in NaOH solution $= 1 \times 10^{-10}$

$[OH^-]$ in NaOH solution

$$= \frac{1 \times 10^{-14}}{1 \times 10^{-10}} = 10^{-4}$$

Milliequivalents of HCl

$= N_1V_1 = 2.0 \times 1 \times 10^{-3} = 2.0 \times 10^{-3}$

Milliequivalents of NaOH

$= 3.0 \times 1 \times 10^{-4} = 3.0 \times 10^{-4}$

Since, milliequivalents of HCl are in excess, the milliequivalents of $[H^+]$ in mixture

$$= (2.0 \times 10^{-3}) - (3.0 \times 10^{-4})$$
$$= 1.7 \times 10^{-3}$$

Concentration of $[H^+]$ in mixture

$$= \frac{1.7 \times 10^{-3}}{3 + 2} = 3.4 \times 10^{-4}$$

pH of mixture $= -\log[H^+]$

$$= -\log(3.4 \times 10^{-4})$$
$$= 3.46 \sim 3.5$$

33 (*d*) 10 mL of 0.1 N (0.1 M) NaOH $= 10 \times 0.1$ millimole

10 mL of 0.05 N (0.025 M) $H_2SO_4 = 10 \times 0.025 = 0.25$ millimole

$$\underset{1\text{ mol}}{H_2SO_4} + \underset{2\text{ mol}}{2NaOH} \longrightarrow Na_2SO_4 + H_2O$$

0.25 millimole of H_2SO_4 will react with 0.5 millimole of NaOH

∴ NaOH left = 1 − 0.5 = 0.5 mmol

Volume of reaction mixture = 20 mL

Molarity of NaOH in mixture solution

$$= \frac{0.5}{20} = 2.5 \times 10^{-2}\text{ M}$$

$$pOH = -\log[OH^-]$$
$$= -\log(2.5 \times 10^{-2}) = 1.60$$
$$pH = 12.4$$

34 (*b*) HNO_3 completely ionises as,

$$HNO_3 + H_2O \longrightarrow H_3O^+ + NO_3^-$$

∴ $[H_3O^+] = HNO_3 = 10^{-2}$ M (given)

$$pH = -\log[H_3O^+] = -\log 10^{-2}$$
$$= -(-2\log 10) = 2$$

35 (*a*) $pOH = pK_b + \log\frac{[B^-]}{[HB]}$

$pOH = 10$

(∵ concentration of $[B^-] = [HB]$)

∴ $pH = 14 - 10 = 4$

36 (*a*)

$$\underset{C-x}{CH_3COOH} \rightleftharpoons \underset{x}{CH_3COO^-} + \underset{x}{H^+}$$

$$\underset{0.2}{CH_3COONa} \longrightarrow \underset{0.2\text{ M}}{CH_3COO^-} + \underset{0.2\text{ M}}{Na^+}$$

$$K_a = \frac{[CH_3COO^-][H^+]}{[CH_3COOH]}$$

$[CH_3COOH] = C - x \approx C = 0.1$ M

$[CH_3COO^-] = 0.2 + x \approx 0.2$ M

$$\therefore \quad [H^+] = \frac{K_a[CH_3COOH]}{[CH_3COO^-]}$$
$$= \frac{1.8 \times 10^{-5} \times 0.1}{0.2}$$
$$[H^+] = 9 \times 10^{-6}$$

37 (*a*) When 100 mL HCl is added to 35 mL NaOH, 35 mL HCl is utilised to neutralise NaOH, while 65 mL HCl remains as such. Hence, the solution becomes acidic. In acid solution, the colour of methyl orange (indicator) is red due to the presence of Me^+ ions as,

$$\underset{\substack{\text{Methyl orange}\\\text{(yellow)}}}{MeOH} \rightleftharpoons \underset{\text{Red}}{Me^+} + OH^-$$

38 (*d*) The pH of acidic buffer is calculated by following formula

$$pH = -\log K_a + \log\left[\frac{\text{salt}}{\text{acid}}\right]$$

∴ pH of acidic buffer depends on value of K_a and is always less than 7.

39 (*c*) When a strong acid like HCl is treated using a weak base like NH_4OH, HCl will completely ionise in solution while NH_4OH ionises very less. Thus, the resulting solution will contain large amounts of H^+ ions.

Hence, the resulting solution will be acidic with a pH value less than 7.

40 (*b*) $pK_a = -\log K_a$

$$\therefore \quad (pK_a)_A = -\log(K_a)_A$$
$$(K_a)_A = \text{antilog}(-4) = 10^{-4}$$

Similarly, $(K_a)_B = \text{antilog}(-6) = 10^{-6}$

$$\frac{\text{Strength of } A}{\text{Strength of } B} = \sqrt{\frac{K_a}{K_b}} = \sqrt{\frac{10^{-4}}{10^{-6}}} = 10$$

∴ Strength of $A = 10 \times$ strength of B

41 (*c*) $[H^+] = \sqrt{K_a \cdot C}$

or $= \sqrt{\alpha^2C^2} = C\alpha \quad (\because K_a = \alpha^2 C)$

$$= (10^{-3}) \cdot (0.01) = 10^{-5}$$
$$pH = -\log[H^+] = -\log 10^{-5} = 5$$
$$pOH = 14 - 5 = 9$$

42 (*d*) As pH of HCOOH solution = pH of CH_3COOH solution

$[H^+]$ in HCOOH solution $= [H^+]$ in CH_3COOH solution

$$K_1 = \frac{[HCOO^-][H^+]}{[HCOOH]} = \frac{[H^+]^2}{[HCOOH]}$$

$$K_2 = \frac{[CH_3COO^-][H^+]}{[CH_3COOH]}$$
$$= \frac{[H^+]^2}{[CH_3COOH]}$$

$$\Rightarrow K_1[HCOOH] = K_2[CH_3COOH]$$

$$\frac{[HCOOH]}{[CH_3COOH]} = \frac{K_2}{K_1} = \frac{1}{4} = 0.25$$

43 (*b*) Let the concentration of potassium acetate is x.

From Henderson-Hasselbalch equation,

$$pH = pK_a + \log\frac{[\text{salt}]}{[\text{acid}]}$$

$$4.8 = -\log(1.8 \times 10^{-5}) + \log\frac{x \times 50}{20 \times 0.1\text{ M}}$$

$$4.8 = 4.74 + \log 25x$$

or $\log 25x = 0.06$

$$25x = 1.148$$

∴ $x = 0.045\text{ M} \sim 0.04\text{ M}$

44 (*c*) Diethylamine is a weak base and from Ostwald's dilution law, for weak base,

$$K_b = C\alpha^2$$

$$\therefore \quad \alpha = \sqrt{\frac{2.5 \times 10^{-5}}{5 \times 10^{-4}}} = 0.22$$

$$[OH^-] = C\alpha = 5 \times 10^{-4} \times 0.22$$
$$= 1.1 \times 10^{-4}$$

$$\therefore \quad pOH = -\log[OH^-]$$
$$= -\log(1.1 \times 10^{-4}) = 3.96$$

$$\therefore \quad pH = 14 - 3.96 = 10.04$$

45 (*c*) Given, pH = 10

$\therefore$ $[H^+] = 1\times10^{-pH} = 1\times10^{-10}$ mol/L

$\therefore$ $[OH^-] = \dfrac{1\times10^{-14}}{1\times10^{-10}} = 1\times10^{-4}$ mol/L

$\because$ The number of hydroxyl ions present in 1 mole $= 6.023\times10^{23}$

$\therefore$ The number of hydroxyl ion in 1×10^{-4} mol/L

$= 6.023\times10^{23}\times10^{-4}$/L

$= 6.023\times10^{19}$ mol /L

$\because$ In 1000 mL, number of hydroxyl ion $= 6.023\times10^{19}$

$\therefore$ In 100 mL, number of hydroxyl ions

$= \dfrac{6.023\times10^{19}\times100}{1000} = 6.02\times10^{18}$

46 (*c*) pH = 3 (given)

$\therefore$ $[H^+] = 10^{-3}$ M $= 1\times10^{-3}$ N

$N_1V_1 = N_2V_2$

$1\times10^{-3}\times20 + N_2\times100$

$N_2 = 2\times10^{-4}$

$\therefore$ $[H^+] = 2\times10^{-4}$ M

47 (*e*) pH value above 7 shows that the solution is alkaline. Among the given, lemon juice, milk and soft drink are acidic in nature, i.e. have pH < 7, blood is slightly alkaline, i.e. has pH = 7 while lime water is strongly alkaline, i.e. has pH 10.5.

48 (*a*) Addition of 5 mL of 1 M HCl will decrease the pH, because only this will increase the H^+ ion concentration in the solution.

49 (*a*) pH of a salt of weak acid and weak base is

$$pH = 7 + \frac{1}{2}pK_a - \frac{1}{p}K_b$$

$$pH = 7 + \frac{1}{2}\times4.76 - \frac{1}{2}\times4.76 = 7$$

50 (*a*) Millimoles of $H^+ = 30\times0.01 = 0.3$

Millimole of $OH^- = 20\times0.01\times2 = 0.4$

Remaining millimoles of OH^-

$= 0.4 - 0.3 = 0.1$

$\Rightarrow [OH^-] = \dfrac{0.1}{50}$ or 2×10^{-3}

So, pOH = 2.7

pH = 14 − 2.7 = 11.30

51 (*a*) Total milliequivalents of H^+

$= 20\times\dfrac{1}{2} + 30\times\dfrac{1}{3} = 20$

Total milliequivalents of

$OH^- = 40\times\dfrac{1}{4} = 10$

Thus, milliequivalents of H^+ left

$= 20 - 10 = 10$

Total volume of solution = 1 dm^3

= 1000 mL

$\therefore$ $[H^+] = \dfrac{10}{100} = 10^{-2}$

$\Rightarrow$ $pH = -\log[H^+] = -\log[10^{-2}] = 2$

52 (*d*) $[OH^-]$ of 10^{-6} M NaOH $= 10^{-6}$

When, the solution is diluted 100 times,

$$[OH^-] = \frac{10^{-6}}{10^2} = 10^{-8}$$

As $[OH^-]$ is very less, auto-protolysis of water will also be considered.

So, the contribution of OH^- ions from water must also be considered,

$\therefore$ Total $[OH^-] = 10^{-8} + [OH^-]_{water}$

$= 10^{-8} < [OH^-] < 10^{-7}$

$\therefore$ pH is between 7 and 8.

53 (*d*) $CH_3COOH \rightleftharpoons CH_3COO^- + H^+$

$$K_{acetic\ acid} = \frac{[CH_3COO^-][H^+]}{[CH_3COOH]} = 1.5\times10^{-5}$$

$$HCN \rightleftharpoons H^+ + CN^-$$

$$K_{HCN} = 4.5\times10^{-10} = \frac{[H^+][CN^-]}{[HCN]}$$

For equilibrium,

$$CN^- + CH_3COOH \rightleftharpoons HCN + CH_3COO^-$$

$$K = \frac{K_{acetic\ acid}}{K_{HCN}} = \frac{[CH_3COO^-][HCN]}{[CN^-][CH_3COOH]}$$

$$= \frac{1.5\times10^{-5}}{4.5\times10^{-10}} = 3.3\times10^4 \simeq 3.0\times10^4$$

54 (*b*) A buffer solution is used in the removal of PO_4^{3-} ions.

55 (*d*) Buffer capacity, $\beta = \dfrac{dC_{HA}}{d_{pH}}$

Where, dC_{HA} = number of moles of acid added per litre

d_{pH} = change in pH

$$dC_{HA} = \frac{\text{Moles of acetic acid}}{\text{Volume}} = \frac{\frac{0.12/60}{250}}{1000} = \frac{1}{125}$$

$$\beta = \frac{1/125}{0.02} = \frac{1}{2.5} = 0.4$$

56 (*b*) $[H^+]$ in mixture

$$= \frac{[H^+] \text{ of I acid} \times \text{its volume} + [H^+] \text{ of II acid} \times \text{its volume} + [H^+] \text{ of III acid} \times \text{its volume}}{\text{total volume}}$$

$$M = \frac{M_1V_1 + M_2V_2 + M_3V_3}{V}$$

Assume the volume of each solution is 1 L.

$[H_3O^+]$ in solution I (pH = 3) $= 10^{-3}$ M

$[H_3O^+]$ in solution II

(pH = 4) $= 10^{-4}$ M

$[H_3O^+]$ in solution III

(pH = 5) $= 10^{-5}$ M

$$\text{Total } [H_3O^+] = \left(\frac{10^{-3} + 10^{-4} + 10^{-5}}{3}\right)$$

$= 0.00037 = 3.7\times10^{-4}$ M

57 (*a*) $\because$ $N = \dfrac{w\times1000}{E\cdot V}$

[$\because$ $w = 0.49$ g and E of $H_2SO_4 = 49$]

$N = \dfrac{0.49\times1000}{49\times1000}$ or $N = 10^{-2}$

$[H^+] = 0.01$

$\because$ $pH = -\log[H^+]$

$\therefore$ $pH = -\log(1\times10^{-2}) = 2$

The conjugate base of H_2S is HS^-. BF_3 is a Lewis acid as B is electron deficient. Phenolphthalein is pink in basic medium.

58 (*c*) pH of lemon juice = 3

$[H^+] = 1\times10^{-3}$ mol/L

$\because$ 1000 mL lemon juice contains

$[H^+] = 1\times10^{-3}$ mol

250 mL lemon juice contains

$= \dfrac{1\times10^{-3}\times250}{1000} = 2.5\times10^{-4}$ mol

Number of $[H^+]$ ions $= 2.5\times10^{-4}\times N_A$

$= 2.5\times10^{-4}\times6.023\times10^{23}$

$= 1.506\times10^{20}$

59 (*a*) OH^- will have the minimum value of pK_b, because it acts as a strongest base.

60 (*b*) pH of 10^{-9} M HCl $= -\log[H^+]$

Thus, $[H^+] = [H^+]$ from HCl $+ [H^+]$ from H_2O

$= 10^{-9} + 10^{-7}$

$= 1.01\times10^{-7}$ mol L^{-1}

$pH = -\log[H^+]$

$= -\log(1.01\times10^{-7}) = 6.9957$

(b) pOH of 10^{-5} NaOH $= -\log[OH^-]$

$= -\log[1 \times 10^{-5}] = 5$

$\because$ pH + pOH = 14

$\therefore$ pH = 14 − 5 = 9

(c) pH of 10^{-9} M KOH will be slightly greater than 7.

61 (c) From H_2O, $[H^+] = 1 \times 10^{-7}$ M

From HCl, $[H^+] = 1 \times 10^{-8}$ M

Total $[H^+] = (1 \times 10^{-7} + 1 \times 10^{-8})$ m

$= (1 \times 10^7 + 0.1 \times 10^{-7})$ M

$= 1.1 \times 10^{-7}$ M

$pH = -\log(1.1 \times 10^{-7}) = 6.9586$

62 (d) $N_{mixture} = \dfrac{N_1V_1 - N_2V_2}{V_{mixture}}$

For 75 mL of $\frac{M}{5}$ HCl − 25 mL of $\frac{M}{5}$ NaOH

$$N_{mixture} = \frac{75 \times \frac{1}{5} - 25 \times \frac{1}{5}}{100}$$

$$= \frac{10}{100} = 10^{-1}$$

pH = 1

63 (b) Normality of H_2SO_4

$= 0.05 \times 2 = 0.1$ M

$\therefore$ $pH = -\log[H^+] = -\log[10^{-1}] = 1$

64 (d) Buffer capacity

$$= \frac{\text{number of moles of acid added/L}}{\text{change in pH}}$$

$$\text{Buffer capacity} = \frac{0.1/2}{0.5} = \frac{0.1}{1} = 0.1$$

65 (c) Due to common ion effect, rate of ionisation of NH_4OH decreases. So, lower $[OH^-]$ is obtained.

66 (b) 0.1 M H_2SO_4 = 0.2 N H_2SO_4

(Normality = Molarity × Valence factor)

0.1 M NaOH = 0.1 N NaOH

Milliequivalent of acid

$= N_1V_1 = 0.2 \times 100 = 20$

Milliequivalent of base $= N_2V_2$

$= 0.1 \times 200 = 20$

Here, $N_1V_1 = N_2V_2$

Hence, resulting mixture is neutral and its pH is 7.

67 (c) A solution containing 1.04×10^{12} M KOH means that very little amount of KOH is present in solution.

So, pH of solution ≈ 7

68 (b) Moles of H^+ in 200 mL of

$$10^{-2} \text{ M HCl} = \frac{10^{-2}}{10^3} \times 200$$

$$= 2 \times 10^{-3} \text{ mol}$$

Moles of OH^- in 300 mL of, 10^{-2} M

$$\text{NaOH} = \frac{10^{-2}}{10^3} \times 300 = 3 \times 10^{-3} \text{ mol}$$

Moles of OH^- left in 500 mL of solution

$= (3 \times 10^{-3}) - (2 \times 10^{-3}) = 1 \times 10^{-3}$

Number of moles OH^- in 1000 mL

$= 2 \times 10^{-3}$

$[OH^-] = 2 \times 10^{-3}$ M

$\Rightarrow$ pOH = 2.69

pH = 14 − 2.69 = 11.31 ≈ 11

69 (d) Acid indicators are generally weak acids. The dissociation of indicator HIn takes place as follows:

$$HIn \rightleftharpoons H^+ + In^-$$

$$\therefore \quad K_{In} = \frac{[H^+][In^-]}{[HIn]}$$

$$\text{or } [H^+] = K_{In}\frac{[HIn]}{[In^-]}$$

$$\because \quad pH = -\log[H^+]$$

$$\therefore \quad pH = -\log\left(K_{In} \cdot \frac{[HIn]}{[In^-]}\right)$$

$$= -\log K_{In} + \log\frac{[In^-]}{[HIn]}$$

$$= pK_{In} + \log\frac{[In^-]}{[HIn]}$$

$$\text{or } \log\frac{[In^-]}{[HIn]} = pH - pK_{In}$$

70 (c) For weak acid and strong base,

$$pH = 7 + \frac{1}{2}pK_a + \frac{1}{2}\log C$$

$$= 7 + \frac{4.74}{2} + \frac{1}{2}\log 10^{-1} = 8.87$$

71 (b) In aqueous solution of 10^{-8} M HCl, $[H^+]$ is based upon the concentration of H^+ ion of 10^{-8} M HCl andconcentration of H^+ ion of water.

K_w of $H_2O = 10^{-14} = [H^+][OH^-]$

or $[H^+] = 10^{-7}$ M (due to its neutral behaviour)

So, in aqueous solution of 10^{-8} M HCl,

$[H^+] = [H^+]$ of HCl + $[H^+]$ of water

$= 10^{-8} + 10^{-7} = 11 \times 10^{-8}$ M

$\approx 1.10 \times 10^{-7}$ M.

This value is closest to the value given in option (b).

72 (c) $K_w = [H^+][OH^-] = (10^{-6}) \times (10^{-6})$

$= 10^{-12}$ $(\because [H^+] = [OH^-])$

73 (b) pH of mixture of strong and weak acid depends only upon strong acid concentration.

0.1 M HCl = 0.1 N HCl

$\because$ $[H^+] = 0.1$

$$pH = -\log[H^+] = \log\frac{1}{[H^+]}$$

$$\therefore pH = \log\frac{1}{[0.1]} = \log 10 = 1$$

74 (b) pH increases in the following order

HCl < NH_4Cl < NaCl < NaCN

This order, HCl is a strong acid, NH_4Cl is an acidic salt, NaCl is a neutral salt and NaCN is a basic salt.

75 (d) pH of solution $\propto [OH^-]$

$\frac{M}{4}$ $Ca(OH)_2$ solution will give highest concentration of OH^-.

Hence, it has highest pH.

76 (d) We know that, $[H^+] = 10^{-pH} = 10^{-5}$

$$\alpha = \frac{\text{actual concentration}}{\text{molar concentration}}$$

$$= \frac{10^{-5}}{0.005} = 0.2 \times 10^{-2}$$

or % α = 0.2%

73 (a) $[H^+] = 10^{-pH}$

$= 10^{-4.5}$ mol/L $= 10^{0.5} \times 10^{-5}$

$= \sqrt{10} \times 10^{-5} = 3.162 \times 10^{-5}$ mol/L

78 (a) A pair of HNO_2 and $NaNO_2$ constitutes a buffer, because HNO_2 is weak acid and $NaNO_2$ is a salt of weak acid (HNO_2) with strong base (NaOH). Hence, it is an example of acidic buffer solution.

79 (c) A solution with reserve acidity or basicity is known as buffer solution. It is of two types:

(i) **Acidic buffer solution** A mixture of weak acid and its salt with strong base.

e.g. $CH_3COOH + CH_3COONa$

(ii) **Basic buffer solution** A mixture of weak base and its salt with strong acid.

e.g. $NH_4OH + NH_4Cl$

$\therefore$ A and C can form a buffer solution.

80 (*d*) $pOH = pK_b + \log \frac{[salt]}{[base]}$

$\therefore \quad pOH = 5 + \log \frac{0.01}{0.10} = 4$

$\because \; pH + pOH = 14$

$\therefore \; pH = 14 - 4 = 10$

81 (*c*) CH_3COONa^- is the salt of weak acid (CH_3COOH) and strong base and (NaOH) is hydrolysed as,

$$CH_3COO^- + H_2O \longrightarrow CH_3COOH + OH^-$$

Due to OH^- ions, solution is basic.

$$pH = 7 + \frac{pK_a}{2} + \frac{\log C}{2}$$

$$= 7 + \frac{4.74}{2} - \frac{\log 0.01}{2}$$

$$= + 7 + 2.37 - 1 = 8.37$$

82 (*c*) $pK_a = -\log K_a$

and $pK_b = -\log K_b$

$$pH = -\frac{1}{2}[\log K_a + \log K_w - \log K_b]$$

$$= -\frac{1}{2}[-5 + \log 10^{-14} - (-5)]$$

$$= -\frac{1}{2}[-5 - 14 + 5] = 7$$

Thus, the end point or equivalence point is obtained at pH = 7 in neutral medium.

83 (*a*) Concentration of KCN

= Concentration HCN

$$= \frac{2.5}{500/1000} = 5 \text{ M}$$

$$\therefore \quad \log \frac{[KCN]}{[HCN]} = \log \frac{5}{5} = 0$$

Now, from Henderson-Hasselbalch equation

$$pH = pK_a + \log \frac{[salt]}{[acid]} = 9.30 + 0$$

$\Rightarrow \quad pH = 9.30$

84 (*a*) $\quad pH = 5$

$$[H_3O^+] = 10^{-pH} = 10^{-5} \text{ M}$$

$\Rightarrow \quad M_1 = 10^{-5}$

Let $\quad V_1 = x, \; V_2 = 100x$

According to dilution law,

$$M_1V_1 = M_2V_2$$

$\Rightarrow \quad 10^{-5}x = M_2 \times 100x$

$$\frac{10^{-5}x}{100x} = M_2$$

$\Rightarrow \quad M_2 = 10^{-7}$

$$[H_3O^+] = 10^{-7} + 10^{-7} \text{ M}$$

(from water)

$$= 2 \times 10^{-7} \text{ M}$$

$$pH = -\log [H_3O^+]$$

$$= -\log (2 \times 10^{-7}) = 6.69$$

Hence, the solution becomes almost neutral in nature.

85 (*b*)

A	*B*
pH = 3	pH = 2
$\therefore [H^+] = 10^{-3}$	$[H^+] = 10^{-2}$

$$\text{Total } [H^+] = 10^{-3} + 10^{-2} = 11 \times 10^{-3}$$

$$pH = -\log [H^+]$$

$$= -\log (11 \times 10^{-3})$$

$$= 3 - \log 11$$

$$= 3 - 1.04 = 1.96 \approx 1.9$$

86 (*b*)

$$\underset{0.10}{NH_3} + \underset{0.10}{H_2O} \rightleftharpoons \underset{0}{NH_4^+} + \underset{0}{OH^-}$$

$$\left(\begin{array}{c}0.10 - 1.34 \times 10^{-3}\\ \approx 0.10\end{array}\right) \qquad 1.34 \times 10^{-3}$$

Also $[OH^-] = [NH_4^+] = 1.34 \times 10^{-3}$ m

$[NH_3] = 0.10 - 1.34 \times 10^{-3} \approx 0.10$ m

$$K_b = \frac{[NH_4^+][OH^-]}{[NH_3]}$$

$$= \frac{(1.34 \times 10^{-3})^2}{0.1}$$

$$= 1.79 \times 10^{-5} \approx 1.8 \times 10^{-5}$$

Topic 6

Hydrolysis of Salts

2014

1 Which of the following salts will give highest pH in water? [CBSE AIPMT]

(a) KCl (b) NaCl
(c) Na_2CO_3 (d) $CuSO_4$

2 The pK_a of a weak acid H*A* and pK_b of weak base BOH are 4.60 and 4.80 respectively. The pH of 0.1 M solution of the salt, B*A* formed from the acid H*A* and base BOH is [Kerala CEE]

(a) 7.10 (b) 9.40
(c) 6.90 (d) 0.20
(e) 4.80

2012

3 Equimolar solutions of the following substances were prepared separately. Which one will record the highest pH value? [CBSE AIPMT]

(a) $BaCl_2$ (b) $AlCl_3$
(c) LiCl (d) $BeCl_2$

4 A 100 mL, 0.1 M (solution of ammonium acetate is diluted by adding 100 mL of water. The pH of the resulting solution will be

(pK_a of acetic acid is nearly equal to pK_b of NH_4OH) [CBSE AIPMT]

(a) 4.9 (b) 5.0
(c) 7.0 (d) 10.0

5 NH_4Cl is acidic due to [MHT CET]

(a) cationic hydrolysis (b) anionic hydrolysis
(c) its ionic nature (d) pH > 7

6 Ammonium acetate which is 0.01 M is hydrolysed to 0.001 M concentration. Calculate the change in pH in 0.001 M solution, if initially $pH = pK_a$. [MHT CET]

(a) 5 (b) 10
(c) 100 (d) 1

7 The solution of NH_4Cl is [MP PMT]

(a) acidic (b) alkaline
(c) neutral (d) coloured

8 A weak acid HX has the dissociation constant 1×10^{-5} M. It forms a salt NaX on reaction with alkali. The degree of hydrolysis of 0.1 M solution of NaX is **[AIIMS]**
(a) 0.0001% (b) 0.01% (c) 0.1% (d) 0.15%

2009

9 The ionisation constant of ammonium hydroxide is 1.77×10^{-5} at 298 K. Hydrolysis constant of ammonium chloride is **[CBSE AIPMT]**
(a) 5.65×10^{-10} (b) 6.50×10^{-12}
(c) 5.65×10^{-13} (d) 5.65×10^{-12}

10 Which one of the following aqueous solutions of salts has the lowest pH value? **[J&K CET]**
(a) CH_3COONa (b) NaCl
(c) NH_4OOCCH_3 (d) NH_4Cl

2010

11 Hydrolysis of sodium acetate will give **[AFMC]**
(a) acidic solution (b) basic solution
(c) neutral solution (d) normal solution

12 NaH, when dissolved in water, produces **[DUMET]**
(a) acidic medium
(b) basic medium
(c) neutral medium
(d) cannot be predicted

2007

13 The hydrolysis of sodium carbonate involves the reaction between **[MHT CET]**
(a) sodium ion and water (b) Na^+ and OH^-
(c) CO_3^{2-} and water (d) CO_3^{2-} and H^+

14 The aqueous solutions of HCOONa, $C_6H_5NH_3Cl$ and KCN are respectively **[Kerala CEE]**
(a) acidic, acidic, basic (b) acidic, basic, neutral
(c) basic, neutral, neutral (d) basic, neutral, basic
(e) basic, acidic, basic

15 HCl is completely neutralised by NaOH solution. The resulting solution contains the following species. **[MP PMT]**
(a) Na^+, Cl^-, H_3O^+ (b) Na^+, Cl^-, H_2O
(c) Na^+, Cl^-, OH^- (d) H^+, H_3O^+

16 The ionisation of strong electrolytes in acetic acid, compared to water, is **[J&K CET]**
(a) weak, low (b) strong, more
(c) medium, the same (d) no ionisation, 100%

17 Which one of the following salts being dissolved in water gives pH > 7 at 25° C? **[KCET]**
(a) KCN (b) KNO_3
(c) NH_4Cl (d) NH_4CN

18 When KBr is dissolved in water, K^+ ions are **[KCET]**
(a) hydrated (b) hydrolysed
(c) reduced (d) oxidised

2006

19 Which of the following salts does not get hydrolysed in water? **[RPMT]**
(a) $KClO_4$ (b) NH_4Cl
(c) CH_3COONa (d) None of these

20 If at 25° C the ionisation constant of acetic acid is 2×10^{-5}, the hydrolysis constant of sodium acetate will be **[Punjab PMET]**
(a) 5×10^{-8} (b) 5×10^{-9}
(c) 5×10^{-10} (d) 4×10^{-10}

21 A solution of $FeCl_3$ in water acts as acidic solution due to **[BCECE]**
(a) hydrolysis of Fe^{3+}
(b) acidic impurities
(c) dissociation
(d) ionisation

2005

22 Which is a basic salt? **[UP CPMT]**
(a) PbS
(b) $2PbCO_3\cdot Pb(OH)_2$
(c) $PbSO_4$
(d) $PbCO_3$

23 Relation between hydrolysis constant and dissociation constant are given. Which is the correct formula for $MgCl_2$? **[MHT CET]**
(a) $K_h=\dfrac{K_w}{K_a}$ (b) $K_h=\dfrac{K_w}{K_b}$
(c) $K_h=\dfrac{K_w}{K_a\times K_b}$ (d) $K_w=\dfrac{K_h}{K_b}$

Answers

1 (c)	2 (c)	3 (a)	4 (c)	5 (a)	6 (d)	7 (a)	8 (b)	9 (a)	10 (d)
11 (b)	12 (b)	13 (c)	14 (e)	15 (b)	16 (a)	17 (a)	18 (a)	19 (a)	20 (c)
21 (b)	22 (b)	23 (b)							

Explanations

1 (c) The highest pH refers to the basic solution containing OH^- ions. Therefore, the basic salt releasing OH^- ions on hydrolysis will give highest pH in water. Only the salt of strong base and weak acid would release OH^- ion on hydrolysis. Among the given salts, Na_2CO_3 corresponds to the basic salt as it is formed by the neutralisation of NaOH (strong base) and H_2CO_3 (weak acid).

$$CO_3^{2-} + H_2O \rightleftharpoons HCO_3^- + OH^-$$

2 (c) BA is a salt of weak acid and weak base.

$$pH = \frac{1}{2}[pK_w + pK_a - pK_b]$$
$$= \frac{1}{2}[14 + 4.6 - 4.8]$$
$$= \frac{1}{2}[14 - 0.2] = \frac{1}{2} \times 13.8 = 6.9$$

3 (a) $BaCl_2$ is a salt of strong acid, HCl and strong base $Ba(OH)_2$. So, its aqueous solution is neutral with pH 7. All other salts give acidic solution due to cationic hydrolysis. So, their pH is less than 7. Thus, pH value is highest for the solution of $BaCl_2$.

4 (c) Ammonium acetate is a salt of weak acid and weak base. When solutions are of weak acid and weak base, pH of solution is calculated from the following relationship.

$$pH = 7 + \frac{1}{2}pK_a - \frac{1}{2}pK_b$$

or $\quad pK_a \approx pK_b$ (given)

$\therefore\quad$ pH of solution = 7

5 (a)

$$NH_4Cl + H_2O \longrightarrow NH_4OH + HCl$$
or $$NH_4^+ + Cl^- + H_2O \longrightarrow NH_4OH + H^+ + Cl^-$$
or $$\underset{\text{Cation}}{NH_4^+} + H_2O \longrightarrow NH_4OH + H^+$$

Due to the presence of H^+, after cationic hydrolysis, in the solution, the solution of NH_4Cl is acidic.

6 (d) $\underset{0.01\text{ M}}{CH_3COONH_4} + H_2O \longrightarrow CH_3COOH + \underset{0.001\text{ M}}{NH_4OH}$

$$pH = pK_a + \log\frac{[CH_3COONH_4]}{[CH_3COOH]}$$
$$= pK_a + \log\left[\frac{0.01}{0.001}\right]$$
$$= pK_a + \log 10 = pK_a + 1$$

Change in pH =1

7 (a) The solution of NH_4Cl is acidic because it is formed by the combination of a weak base, NH_4OH and strong acid, HCl.

8 (b) $X^- + H_2O \rightleftharpoons HX + OH^-$

$$K_h = \frac{K_w}{K_a} = \frac{10^{-14}}{10^{-5}} = 10^{-9}$$

So, degree of hydrolysis

$$h = \sqrt{\frac{K_h}{C}} = \sqrt{\frac{10^{-9}}{10^{-1}}} = 10^{-4}$$

Percentage of degree of hydrolysis

$$= 10^{-4} \times 100 = 10^{-2}\% = 0.01\%$$

9 (a) For hydrolysis of salt,

Hydrolysis constant, $K_h = \dfrac{K_w}{K_b}$

$$= \frac{1 \times 10^{-14}}{1.77 \times 10^{-5}} = 5.65 \times 10^{-10}$$

10 (d) NH_4Cl is a salt of strong acid and weak base.

11 (b) Hydrolysis of sodium acetate is given by

$$\underset{\text{Sodium acetate}}{CH_3COONa} + H_2O \rightleftharpoons \underset{\text{Acetic acid}}{CH_3COOH} + \underset{\text{Sodium hydroxide}}{NaOH}$$

Sodium acetate gives weak acid and strong base on hydrolysis. Therefore, the aqueous solution of sodium acetate will be basic in nature.

12 (b) $NaH + H_2O \rightleftharpoons NaOH + H_2\uparrow$

NaH, when dissolved in water, produces basic medium, because H^- will act as a proton acceptor.

13 (c) $Na_2CO_3 + 2H_2O \rightleftharpoons 2NaOH + H_2CO_3$

or $2Na^+ + CO_3^{2-} + 2H_2O \rightleftharpoons 2Na^+ + 2OH^- + H_2CO_3$

or $CO_3^{2-} + 2H_2O \rightleftharpoons 2OH^- + H_2CO_3$

It is anionic hydrolysis.

14 (e) Aqueous solution of HCOONa, $C_6H_5NH_3Cl$, KCN are

$$HCOONa + H_2O \rightleftharpoons \underset{\text{Weak acid}}{HCOOH} + \underset{\text{Strong base}}{NaOH}$$
(basic solution)

$$C_6H_5NH_3Cl\,(aq) \rightleftharpoons \underset{\text{Weak base}}{C_6H_5NH_2} + \underset{\text{Strong acid}}{HCl}$$
(acidic solution)

$$KCN + H_2O \rightleftharpoons \underset{\text{Strong base}}{KOH} + \underset{\text{Weak acid}}{HCN}$$
(basic solution)

15 (b) HCl is completely neutralised by NaOH solution and gives NaCl(salt).

$$HCl + NaOH \rightleftharpoons NaCl + H_2O$$
$$HCl \rightleftharpoons H^+ + Cl^-$$
$$NaOH \rightleftharpoons Na^+ + OH^-$$
$$H^+ + OH^- \longrightarrow H_2O$$

Hence, the resulting solution contains Na^+, Cl^- and H_2O.

16 (a) The ionisation of strong electrolytes in acetic acid, compared to water, is weak and low because acetic acid is a non-polar solvent.

17 (a) KCN is a salt of weak acid (HCN) and strong base (KOH). Hence, on being dissolved in water it gives basic solution,

i.e. $\quad$ pH > 7 at 25°C.

18 (a) When KBr is dissolved in water K^+ and Br^- are hydrated.

19 (a) Only salts of (weak acid + strong acid) and (weak acid + weak base) get hydrolysed (i.e. show alkalinity or acidity in water). $KClO_4$ is a salt of strong acid and strong base, therefore, it does not get hydrolysed in water.

$$KClO_4 \rightleftharpoons K^+ + ClO_4^-$$
$$H_2O \rightleftharpoons OH^- + H^+$$
$$\underset{\text{Strong base}}{KOH} \qquad \underset{\text{Strong acid}}{HClO_4}$$

20 (c) Hydrolysis constant of sodium acetate

$$K_h = \frac{K_w}{K_a}$$

$\because K_w = 10^{-14}$ and $K_a = 2 \times 10^{-5}$(given)

$$\therefore K_h = \frac{10^{-14}}{2 \times 10^{-5}} = \frac{10}{2} \times 10^{-10} = 5 \times 10^{-10}$$

21 (b) $FeCl_3$ on hydrolysis gives acidic solution due to the presence of strong acid (HCl) and weak base $[Fe(OH)_3]$ in the solution.

$$FeCl_3 \xrightarrow{3H_2O} \underset{\text{Weak base}}{Fe(OH)_3} + \underset{\text{Strong acid}}{3HCl}$$

Hence, solution is acidic.

22 (b) $PbCO_3 \cdot Pb(OH)_2$ is a salt of strong base and weak acid.

23 (b) For a salt of weak base and strong acid (i.e. $MgCl_2$, NH_4Cl), the relation is

$$K_h = \frac{K_w}{K_b}$$

08

Redox Reactions

Quick Review

Chemical reactions which involve both oxidation as well as reduction process simultaneously are known as **redox reactions** ('red' from reduction and 'ox' from oxidation).

Oxidation and Reduction

According to classical concept, oxidation and reduction are defined as the process that involve :

Oxidation	Reduction
• Addition of oxygen to an element or compound, or the removal of hydrogen from a compound. e.g. $2Mg + O_2 \longrightarrow 2MgO$ $2H_2S + O_2 \longrightarrow 2H_2O + 2S$	• Addition of hydrogen to an element or compound, or the removal of oxygen from a compound. e.g. $H_2S + Cl_2 \longrightarrow 2HCl + S$ $Fe_2O_3 + 3CO \longrightarrow 2Fe + 3CO_2$
• Addition of electronegative element or removal of any other electropositive element. $Zn + S \longrightarrow ZnS$ $2KI + Cl_2 \longrightarrow 2KCl + I_2$	• Addition of electropositive element or removal of any other electronegative element. $2HgCl_2 + SnCl_4 \longrightarrow Hg_2Cl_2 + SnCl_4$ $SiCl_4 + 4Na \longrightarrow Si + 4NaCl$
• Oxidation is the loss of electrons by an atom, ion or molecule. It is also known as de-electronation. $Zn \longrightarrow Zn^{2+} + 2e^-$	• Reduction is the gain of electrons by an atom, ion or molecule. This process is known as electronation. $Cu^{2+} + 2e^- \longrightarrow Cu$
• Oxidation involves increase in oxidation number.	• Reduction involves decrease in oxidation number.
• Oxidation is caused by an oxidising agent.	• Reduction is caused by a reducing agent.

Oxidants and Reductants

- The species which gets reduced is called **oxidant** or **oxidising agent** and it is acceptor of electrons.
- The species which gets oxidised is called **reductant** or **reducing agent** and it is donor of electrons.

Addition of oxygen i.e. oxidation, thus carbon behaves as reducing agent

$$CuO + C \longrightarrow CO + Cu$$

Removal of oxygen i.e. reduction, thus CuO behave as oxidising agent

Oxidation Number (ON)

The oxidation number of an atom in a molecule or in a polyatomic ion is a hypothetical charge the atom would have if the electrons in each bond were located on the more electronegative atom.

Some rules for finding oxidation number are as follows :

(*i*) Oxidation number of elements in their elementary state is 0.

(*ii*) Oxidation number of IA and IIA group elements = their group number.

(*iii*) Fluorine always has -1 oxidation state.

(*iv*) Oxidation number of oxygen is -2 (usually), in peroxides -1, in superoxides $-1/2$ and in OF_2 is $+2$.

(*v*) Oxidation number of H is $+1$ when combined with non-metals and -1 when combined with metals.

(*vi*) In a compound, the more electronegative atom will have negative oxidation number whereas the less electronegative atom will have positive oxidation number.

(*vii*) Algebraic sum of oxidation number of all atoms in a neutral molecule is zero and in an ion is equal to charge on ion.

(*viii*) Oxidation number of any element never exceeds its group number and oxidation number increases across a period.

Exceptional Cases of Oxidation Number

- In bleaching powder [Ca (OCl) Cl], oxidation state of Cl in Cl^- is -1 and in OCl^- is $+1$.
- In Fe_3O_4, two Fe-atoms are in +3 and one Fe-atom is in +2 oxidation state.
- In Caro's acid (H_2SO_5), oxidation number of S is +6.
- In $H_2S_2O_8$; oxidation number of S is +6. In CrO_5, oxidation number of Cr is +6 .
- In $C_3O_2\left(\overset{-2}{O}=\overset{+2}{C}=\overset{0}{C}=\overset{+2}{C}=\overset{-2}{O}\right)$, average oxidation number of carbon is +4 / 3.
- In $S_4O_6^{2-}$ $\left[{}^{-}O-\underset{\underset{O^{-2}}{\|}}{\overset{\overset{O}{\|}}{S^{+5}}}-\overset{0}{S}-\overset{0}{S}-\underset{\underset{O^{-2}}{\|}}{\overset{\overset{O^{-2}}{\|}}{S^{+5}}}-O^{-}\right]$, average oxidation number of sulphur atom is 2.5.
- In Br_3O_8, $\left[\overset{-2}{O}-\underset{\underset{\underset{-2}{O}}{\|}}{\overset{\overset{O^{-2}}{\|}}{Br^{+6}}}-\underset{\underset{\underset{-2}{O}}{\|}}{\overset{\overset{O^{-2}}{\|}}{Br^{+4}}}-\underset{\underset{\underset{-2}{O}}{\|}}{\overset{\overset{O^{-2}}{\|}}{Br^{+6}}}=O^{-2}\right]$, average oxidation number of bromine atom is $\frac{16}{3}$.

Prediction of Oxidising and Reducing Agent

Oxidising agent is the substance whose oxidation number decreases, while reducing agent is the substance whose oxidation number increases.

Stock Notation

The oxidation states of elements exhibiting variable oxidation states are specified by **Roman numerals** such as I, II, III, IV, etc., within parenthesis after the symbol or name of the element. This system was introduced for the first time by German chemist, Alfred **Stock** and is known as **Stock** notation. This may be illustrated as

Formula of the compound	Chemical name	Stock notation
Cu_2O	Cuprous oxide	Copper (I) oxide; Cu_2(I)O
Fe_2O_3	Ferric oxide	Iron (III) oxide; Fe_2(III)O_3
$HgCl_2$	Mercuric chloride	Mercury (II) chloride; Hg(II) Cl_2
$SnCl_2$	Stannous chloride	Stannous (II) chloride, Sn(II) Cl_2

Redox Reactions

The reactions that involve oxidation and reduction as its two half reactions are called **redox reactions.**

e.g. if we consider the following reaction,

Addition of chlorine (an electronegative element)

Oxidation

$$2\,HgCl_2\,(aq) + SnCl_2(aq) \longrightarrow Hg_2Cl_2(s) + SnCl_4(aq)$$

Addition of Hg (an electropositive element)

Reduction

Since, in the above reaction oxidation and reduction occur simultaneously, so it is an example of redox reaction.

Types of Redox Reactions

Redox reactions can be classified as combination reactions, decomposition reactions, displacement reactions and disproportionation reactions.

(*i*) **Combination reactions** are the reactions in which two atoms or molecules combine together to form a third molecule. It may be denoted in the manner

$$A + B \longrightarrow C$$

i.e. $\quad C + O_2 \longrightarrow CO_2$

(*ii*) **Decomposition reactions** are the reactions in which molecule breaks down to form two or more components. In a decomposition reaction, it is essential that one of the products of decomposition must be in elemental state.

$$AB \longrightarrow A + B$$

i.e. $\quad 2H_2O \longrightarrow 2H_2 + O_2$

(*iii*) **Displacement reactions** are the reactions in which an atom (or ion) of a compound is replaced by another ion of same nature.

$$A + BC \longrightarrow AC + B$$

i.e. $2Na(s) + 2H_2O(l) \longrightarrow 2NaOH(aq) + H_2(s)$

(*iv*) **Disproportionation reaction** is a special type of redox reaction in which the same species is simultaneously oxidised as well as reduced.

e.g.

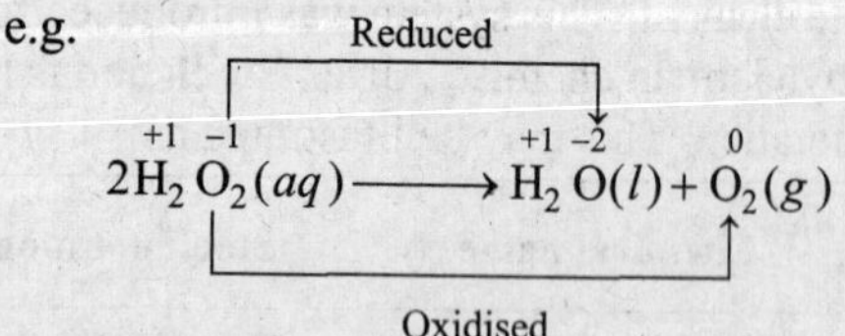

Balancing of Redox Chemical Reactions

The redox reactions can be balanced through an ion electron method and oxidation number method.

1. Ion Electron Method

This method is based upon the splitting of a redox reaction into two half reactions (one is oxidation half reaction and the other is reduction half reaction).

It includes the following steps

Step I. Write the skeleton equation and indicate the oxidation number of all the elements appearing in the skeletal equation above their respective symbols.

Step II. Determine the species which are oxidised and which are reduced.

Step III. Split the redox reaction into its two half reactions, i.e. oxidation half and reduction half.

Step IV. Balance all atoms which have undergone a change in oxidation number except hydrogen (H) and oxygen (O) of each half reaction by using simple multiples.

Step V. For balancing H and O

- **In acidic and neutral solution** Add water molecules to the side deficient in O atoms and H to the side deficient in H-atoms.
- **In alkaline solution** Add one water molecule for each excess of oxygen to the same side and two OH^- on the other side. If the hydrogen is still unbalanced, add one OH^- ion for each excess hydrogen on the same side and one water molecule to the other side.

Step VI. Add electrons to balance the charge in each half equation towards the side having more positive charge.

Step VII. Multiply the half reactions by suitable integer so that the total number of electrons become equal in both the half equations.

Step VIII. Add the two balanced half reactions and cancel any term common to both the sides.

2. Oxidation Number Method

This method is based on the change in the oxidation number of oxidant and reductant.

It involves the following steps.

Step I. Write the skeleton ionic equation representing the chemical change.

Step II. Assign oxidation number to atoms in the equation. Identify which atoms are undergoing oxidation and reduction.

Step III. Balance all atoms other than H and O.

Step IV. Balance the change in oxidation number by cross multiplying oxidant and reductant with suitable integers.

Step V. Finally, balance H and O-atoms by adding H_2O molecules using hit and trial method.

Step VI. In case of ionic reactions.

- **Acidic medium** Balance O-atoms by adding H_2O molecules to whatever side deficient in O-atoms and then balance H-atoms by adding H^+ ions to the side deficient in H-atoms.
- **Basic medium** Balance O-atoms by adding H_2O molecules to the side deficient in O-atoms and twice OH^- ions are added to the opposite side of the equation.

Topical Practice Questions

All the exam questions of this chapter have been divided into three topics as listed below

Topic 1

Oxidation and Reduction

2019

1 Which of the following reaction are disproportionation reaction?

(i) $2Cu^{+} \longrightarrow Cu^{2+} + Cu^{0}$

(ii) $3MnO_4^{2-} + 4H^{+} \longrightarrow 2MnO_4^{-} + MnO_2 + 2H_2O$

(iii) $2KMnO_4 \longrightarrow K_2MnO_4 + MnO_2 + O_2$

(iv) $2MnO_4^{-} + 3Mn^{2+} + 2H_2O \longrightarrow 5MnO_2 + 4H^{+}$

Select the correct option from the following. **[NEET]**

(a) (i), (ii) and (iii) (b) (i), (ii) and (iv)
(c) (i) and (iv) (d) (i) and (ii)

2014

2 Given the reaction for the discharge of a cobalt-cadmium battery

$2Co(OH)_3 + Cd + 2H_2O \longrightarrow 2Co(OH)_2 + Cd(OH)_2$

Which species is oxidised during the discharge of the battery? **[Manipal]**

(a) Co^{3+} (b) Co^{2+}
(c) Cd (d) Cd^{2+}

3 In which of the following reactions, H_2O_2 acts as a reducing agent? **[EAMCET]**

(a) $HOCl + H_2O_2 \xrightarrow{H^+} H_3O^+ + Cl^- + O_2$

(b) $Mn^{2+} + H_2O_2 \xrightarrow{OH^-} Mn^{4+} + 2OH^-$

(c) $2Fe^{2+} + H_2O_2 \xrightarrow{OH^-} 2Fe^{3+} + 2OH^-$

(d) $PbS(s) + 4H_2O_2(aq) \xrightarrow{H^+} PbSO_4(s) + 4H_2O(l)$

4 Observe the following reaction,

$2NO_2(g) + 2OH^-(aq) \longrightarrow NO_3^-(aq) + H_2O(l) + NO_2^-(aq)$ in this reaction, **[EAMCET]**

(a) OH^- is oxidised to H_2O

(b) HO^- is reduced to H_2O

(c) $NO_2(g)$ is reduced to $NO_2^-(aq)$ and oxidised to $NO_3^-(aq)$

(d) $NO_2(g)$ is reduced to $NO_3^-(aq)$ and oxidised to $NO_2^-(aq)$

2013

5 Both oxidation and reduction takes place in **[AIIMS]**

(a) $NaBr + HCl \longrightarrow NaCl + HBr$

(b) $HBr + AgNO_3 \longrightarrow AgBr + HNO_3$

(c) $H_2 + Br_2 \longrightarrow 2HBr$

(d) $CaO + H_2SO_4 \longrightarrow CaSO_4 + H_2O$

6 Which one of the following cannot act as a reducing agent? **[UP CPMT]**

(a) CO_2 (b) SO_2
(c) NO_2 (d) ClO_2

7 The equivalent weight of $MnSO_4$ is equal to its molecular weight when it is converted to **[WB JEE]**

(a) Mn_2O_3 (b) MnO_2 (c) MnO_4^- (d) MnO_4^{2-}

2012

8 In the reaction, $Ag_2O + H_2O_2 \longrightarrow 2Ag + H_2O + O_2$ H_2O_2 acts as a/an. **[Manipal]**

(a) reducing agent (b) oxidising agent
(c) bleaching agent (d) None of these

2011

9 Which change requires an oxidising agent? **[DUMET]**

(a) $2S_2O_3^{2-} \rightleftharpoons S_4O_6^{2-}$ (b) $Zn^{2+} \rightleftharpoons Zn$
(c) $ClO^- \rightleftharpoons Cl^-$ (d) $SO_3 \rightleftharpoons SO_4^{2-}$

10 In the reaction, **[DUMET]**

$2H_2O_2 \longrightarrow 2H_2O + O_2$,

oxygen is

(a) oxidised only (b) reduced only
(c) Neither oxidised nor reduced
(d) Both oxidised and reduced

2010

11 In which of the following reactions, the underlined substance has been oxidised? **[BVP]**

(a) $\underline{Br_2} + H_2S \longrightarrow \underline{2HBr} + S$

(b) $\underline{2HgCl_2} + SnCl_2 \longrightarrow \underline{Hg_2Cl_2} + SnCl_4$

(c) $Cl_2 + \underline{2KI} \longrightarrow 2KCl + \underline{I_2}$

(d) $\underline{2Cu^{2+}} + 4I^- \longrightarrow \underline{Cu_2I_2} + I_2$

12 The equivalent mass of $KMnO_4$ in the following reaction is

$MnO_4^- + 5Fe^{2+} + 8H^+ \longrightarrow Mn^{2+} + 5Fe^{2+} + 4H_2O$

(M = Molecular mass) **[OJEE]**

(a) $\frac{M}{2}$ (b) $\frac{M}{3}$ (c) $\frac{M}{4}$ (d) $\frac{M}{5}$

13 In oxidation process, **[MP PMT]**

(a) oxidation number decreases
(b) number of electrons decreases
(c) oxygen content decreases
(d) number of ions decreases

14 In the reaction, $SO_2 + 2H_2S \longrightarrow 3S + 2H_2O$, the substance oxidised is **[JCECE]**

(a) H_2S (b) SO_2 (c) S (d) H_2O

2009

15 Strongest reducing agent is **[AFMC]**

(a) K (b) Mg (c) Al (d) Ba

16 $I_2 + 2S_2O_3^{2-} \longrightarrow S_4O_6^{2-} + 2I^-$
In the above reaction, **[UP CPMT]**
(a) iodine is reduced; sulphur is reduced
(b) iodine is reduced; sulphur is oxidised
(c) iodine is oxidised; sulphur is reduced
(d) iodine is oxidised; sulphur is oxidised

2008

17 Which of the following molecules can act as an oxidising as well as reducing agent? **[AIIMS]**
(a) H_2S (b) SO_3 (c) H_2O_2 (d) F_2

18 Which of the following substances acts as an oxidising as well as reducing agent? **[DUMET]**
(a) Na_2O (b) $SnCl_2$ (c) $NaNO_3$ (d) $NaNO_2$

2007

19 Which is the best description of behaviour of bromine in the reaction given below?
$H_2O + Br_2 \longrightarrow HBr + HOBr$ **[Manipal]**
(a) Proton accepted only
(b) Both oxidised and reduced
(c) Oxidised only
(d) Reduced only

20 Which of the following is a redox reaction? **[Kerala CEE]**
(a) $2CuSO_4 + 4KI \longrightarrow Cu_2I_2 + 2K_2SO_4 + I_2$
(b) $SO_2 + H_2O \longrightarrow H_2SO_3$
(c) $Na_2SO_4 + BaCl_2 \longrightarrow BaSO_4 + 2NaCl$
(d) $CuSO_4 + 4NH_3 \longrightarrow [Cu(NH_3)_4]SO_4$
(e) $C_{12}H_{22}O_{11} + H_2O \longrightarrow C_6H_{12}O_6 + C_6H_{12}O_6$

2005

21 Which of the following chemical reactions depicts the oxidising behaviour of H_2SO_4? **[RPMT]**
(a) $Ca(OH)_2 + H_2SO_4 \longrightarrow CaSO_4 + 2H_2O$
(b) $NaCl + H_2SO_4 \longrightarrow NaHSO_4 + HCl$
(c) $2HI + H_2SO_4 \longrightarrow I_2 + SO_2 + 2H_2O$
(d) $2PCl_5 + H_2SO_4 \longrightarrow 2POCl_3 + 2HCl + SO_2Cl_2$

22 In one of the following reactions, HNO_3 does not behave as an oxidising agent. Identify it. **[JCECE]**
(a) $I_2 + 10HNO_3 \longrightarrow 2HIO_3 + 10NO_2 + 4H_2O$
(b) $3Cu + 8HNO_3 \longrightarrow 3Cu(NO_3)_2 + 2NO + 4H_2O$
(c) $4Zn + 10HNO_3 \longrightarrow 4Zn(NO_3)_2 + NH_4NO_3 + 3H_2O$
(d) $2HNO_3 + P_2O_5 \longrightarrow 2HPO_3 + N_2O_5$

23 The equivalent mass of potassium permanganate in strong alkaline medium is **[J&K CET]**
(a) $\frac{\text{Molar mass}}{5}$ (b) $\frac{\text{Molar mass}}{3}$
(c) $\frac{\text{Molar mass}}{2}$ (d) Molar mass itself

Answers

1 (d)	2 (c)	3 (a)	4 (c)	5 (c)	6 (a)	7 (a)	8 (a)	9 (a)	10 (d)
11 (c)	12 (d)	13 (b)	14 (a)	15 (a)	16 (b)	17 (c)	18 (d)	19 (b)	20 (a)
21 (c)	22 (d)	23 (b)							

Explanations

1 (*d*) The reaction in which the same species is simultaneously oxidised and reduced are called disproportionation reactions.
Let us, consider the given reaction one by one:

(i) $2Cu^+ \longrightarrow Cu^{2+} + Cu^0$
The above reaction is a disproportionation reaction as Cu(+1) is oxidised to Cu(+2) and reduced to Cu(0).

(ii) $3\overset{+6}{Mn}O_4^{2-} + 4H^+ \longrightarrow 2\overset{+7}{Mn}O_4^- + \overset{+4}{Mn}O_2 + 2H_2O$
The above reaction is a disproportionation reaction as Mn(+6) is oxidised to $MnO_4^-(Mn^{+7})$ and reduced to $\overset{+4}{MnO_2(Mn)}$.

(iii) $2K\overset{+7}{Mn}O_4 \xrightarrow{\Delta} K_2\overset{+6}{Mn}O_4 + \overset{+4}{Mn}O_2 + O_2$
The above reaction is not a disproportionation reaction as Mn (+7) is only reduced to $K_2MnO_4(\overset{+6}{Mn})$ and $MnO_2(\overset{+4}{Mn})$.

(iv) $2\overset{+7}{Mn}O_4^- + 3Mn^{2+} + 2H_2O \longrightarrow 5\overset{+4}{Mn}O_2 + 4H^+$
The above reaction is not a disproportionation reaction as Mn(+7) is only reduced to MnO_2 (Mn^{4+}). Hence, option (d) is correct.

2 (*c*) $2\overset{+3}{Co}(OH)_3 + \overset{0}{Cd} + 2H_2O \longrightarrow 2\overset{+2}{Co}(OH)_2 + \overset{+2}{Cd}(OH)_2$
Increase in ON
Here, oxidation number of Cd increases from 0 to + 2, hence Cd is oxidised.

3 (*a*) In the reaction,
$HOCl + H_2\overset{-1}{O_2} \longrightarrow H_3O^+ + Cl^- + \overset{0}{O_2}$,
Increase in ON
Oxidation number of oxygen increases from − 1 to 0. Hence, H_2O_2 acts as reducing agent.

4 (*c*)
Decrease in ON
$\overset{+4}{N}O_2 + OH^- \longrightarrow \overset{+5}{N}O_3^- + \overset{+3}{N}O_2^- + H_2O$
Increase in ON
$NO_2(g)$ is oxidised to NO_3^- and reduced to NO_2^-.

5 (c) Both oxidation and reduction are taking place in the following reaction,

Oxidised (Reducing agent)

$$\overset{0}{H_2} + \overset{0}{Br_2} \longrightarrow 2\overset{+1\,-1}{HBr}$$

Reduced (Oxidising agent)

H_2-reducing agent; Br_2-oxidising agent. In the other options, neither oxidation nor reduction takes place because oxidation number of elements involved in reaction remain same.

6 (a) Reducing agent is one which donates electrons. The compound which has central atom in its highest oxidation state cannot act as reducing agent because it can accept the electrons but cannot donate electrons. It will infact act as an oxidising agent.

(a) **CO_2** Oxidation state of carbon in CO_2 is + 4 which is the highest oxidation state of carbon.

$\therefore$ CO_2 cannot act as reducing agent.

(b) **SO_2** Oxidation state of sulphur in SO_2 is + 4. The highest oxidation state of sulphur is + 6.

$\therefore$ SO_2 can act as reducing agent.

(c) **NO_2** Oxidation state of nitrogen in NO_2 is + 4. The highest oxidation state of nitrogen is + 5.

$\therefore$ NO_2 can act as reducing agent.

(d) **ClO_2** The oxidation state of chlorine in ClO_2 is + 4. The highest oxidation state of chlorine is + 7.

$\therefore$ ClO_2 can act as reducing agent.

7 (a) In $MnSO_4$, oxidation state of Mn = + 2. In Mn_2O_3, oxidation state of Mn = + 3. There is an increase of oxidation state by 1 when $MnSO_4$ changes to Mn_2O_3.
Hence, its equivalent mass is equal to its molecular mass.

$$\because \text{ Equivalent weight} = \frac{\text{Molecular weight}}{\text{Change in oxidation states}}$$

Decrease in ON (Reduction)

8 (a) $\overset{+1}{Ag_2}O + H_2\overset{-1}{O_2} \longrightarrow 2\overset{0}{Ag} + H_2O + \overset{0}{O_2}$

Increase in ON (Oxidation)

The oxidation number of O in H_2O_2 increases. Hence, H_2O_2 acts as a reducing agent as it is undergoing oxidation.

9 (a) The reaction which involves oxidation, requires an oxidising agent.

$$S_2O_3^{2-} \longrightarrow S_4O_6^{2-}$$

Oxidation state of S changes from 2 to 2.5. Thus, S is undergoing oxidation and hence, requires an oxidising agent.

10 (d) $2H_2\overset{-1}{O_2} \longrightarrow 2H_2\overset{-2}{O} + \overset{0}{O_2}$

Hence, oxygen is both oxidised and reduced.

11 (c) Oxidation is the addition of electronegative element or removal of electropositive element or increase in oxidation number.

$$Cl_2 + \underline{2KI} \longrightarrow 2KCl + I_2$$

In this reaction, the underlined species is oxidised as it involves the removal of electropositive element, i.e. K^+.

Note However, in the option (d), on the basis of applied concept, Cu^{2+} seems to undergo oxidation but in actual, Cu^{2+} is undergoing reduction and reduces to Cu^+. Thus, in the reaction,

$$2Cu^{2+} + 4I^- \longrightarrow \overset{+1}{Cu_2}I_2 + I_2$$

(Reduction, decrease in oxidation number)

12 (d) Here, equivalent weight of salt

$$= \frac{\text{Molecular weight}}{\text{Number of electrons lost or gained}}$$

Number of electrons lost or gained = 5

$$\text{Equivalent mass} = \frac{M}{5}$$

13 (b) In oxidation process, oxidation number increases and number of electrons decreases.

Reduction

14 (a) $\overset{+4}{S}O_2 + 2H_2\overset{-2}{S} \longrightarrow 3\overset{0}{S} + 2H_2O$

Oxidation

$\therefore$ H_2S is oxidised in this reaction.

15 (a) Since, K contains only one electron in its outermost shell, it has higher tendency to donate it, i.e. has higher tendency to get oxidised.
Therefore, it is the strongest reducing agent among the given elements.

Oxidation

16 (b) $\overset{0}{I_2} + 2\overset{+2}{S_2}O_3^{2-} \longrightarrow \overset{+2.5}{S_4}O_6^{2-} + 2I^-$

Reduction

Increase in oxidation number is oxidation while decrease in oxidation number represents reduction. Thus, I_2 is reduced to I^- and $S_2O_3^{2-}$ is oxidised to $S_4O_6^{2-}$.

17 (c) The species in which an element has oxidation number lying in between its minimum and maximum oxidation states, can act as an oxidant and reductant both.

Oxidation state of O in species H_2O_2	Minimum oxidation state of O	Maximum oxidation state of O
–1 in H_2O_2	– 2	0

Thus, hydrogen peroxide (H_2O_2) can act as an oxidising as well as a reducing agent.

H_2O_2 as a reducing agent,

$$Ag_2O + H_2O_2 \longrightarrow 2Ag + H_2O + O_2$$

H_2O_2 as an oxidising agent,

$$PbS + 4H_2O_2 \longrightarrow PbSO_4 + 4H_2O$$

18 (d)

Oxidation state of N in species	Minimum oxidation state of N	Maximum oxidation state of N
+3 in $NaNO_2$	– 3	+ 5

$NaNO_2$ (sodium nitrite) acts both as an oxidising as well as reducing agent.

$NaNO_2$ as an oxidising agent

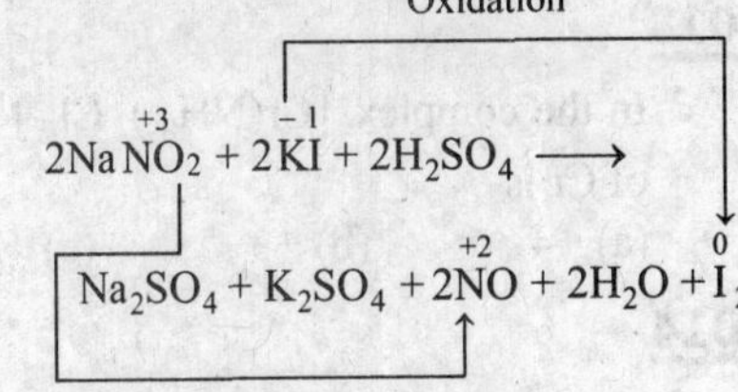

$$2Na\overset{+3}{N}O_2 + 2K\overset{-1}{I} + 2H_2SO_4 \longrightarrow Na_2SO_4 + K_2SO_4 + 2\overset{+2}{N}O + 2H_2O + \overset{0}{I_2}$$

Oxidation / Reduction

$NaNO_2$ as a reducing agent.

Reduction

$$H_2\overset{-1}{O_2} + Na\overset{+3}{N}O_2 \longrightarrow Na\overset{+5}{N}O_3 + H_2\overset{-2}{O}$$

Oxidation

Reduction

19 (b) $H_2O + \overset{0}{Br_2} \longrightarrow H\overset{-1}{Br} + HO\overset{+1}{Br}$

Oxidation

Thus, bromine is oxidised as well as reduced in this reaction.

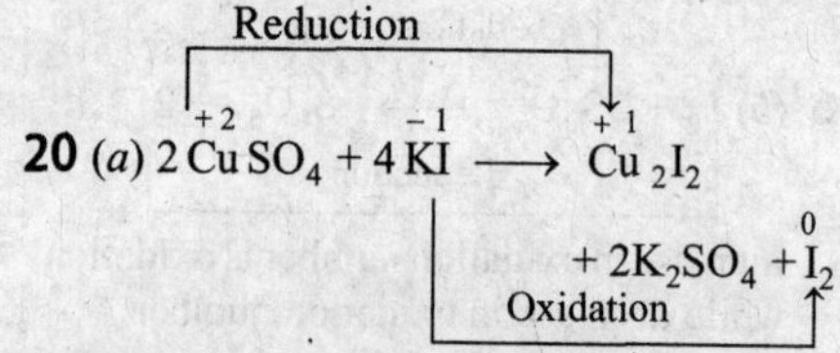

In redox reaction, oxidation and reduction occur simultaneously.

21 (c) $2\overset{-1}{H}I + H_2\overset{+6}{S}O_4 \longrightarrow \overset{0}{I_2} + \overset{+4}{S}O_2 + 2H_2O$

H_2SO_4 is reduced to SO_2 and I^- is oxidised to I_2.

In this reaction, H_2SO_4 behaves as an oxidising agent.

22 (d) (a) $I_2 + 10H\overset{+5}{N}O_3 \longrightarrow 2HIO_3 + 10\overset{+4}{N}O_2 + 4H_2O$

In this reaction, HNO_3 is acting as an oxidising agent because oxidation state of N decreases from + 5 to + 4.

(b) $3Cu + 8H\overset{+5}{N}O_3 \longrightarrow 3Cu(NO_3)_2 + 2\overset{+2}{N}O + 4H_2O$

In this a reaction, HNO_3 is acting as an oxidising agent because oxidation number of nitrogen is decreasing.

(c) $4Zn + 10H\overset{+5}{N}O_3 \longrightarrow 4Zn(NO_3)_2 + \overset{+2}{N}H_4NO_3 + 3H_2O$

As oxidation number of N is decreasing. Therefore, it is also a reaction, in which HNO_3 act as an oxidising agent.

(d) $2H\overset{+5}{N}O_3 + P_2O_5 \longrightarrow 2HPO_3 + \overset{+5}{N_2}O_5$

P_2O_5 is a dehydrating agent. So, in this reaction, HNO_3 does not act as an oxidising agent. Also, there is no change in oxidation number of N.

23 (b) In alkaline medium, following reaction occurs:

$$2KMnO_4 + H_2O \xrightarrow[\text{Medium}]{\text{Alkaline}} 2MnO_2 + 2KOH + 3[O]$$

or $$2\overset{+7}{Mn}O_4^- + H_2O \longrightarrow 2\overset{+4}{Mn}O_2 + 2OH^- + 3[O]$$

Equivalent mass = $\dfrac{\text{Molar mass}}{\text{Change in oxidation number of Mn}} = \dfrac{\text{Molar mass}}{3}$

Topic 2
Oxidation Number

2019

1 The oxidation state of Cr in CrO_5 is **[NEET (Odisha)]**
(a) −6 (b) +12 (c) +6 (d) +4

2 What is the oxidation number of Cr in $Na_2Cr_2O_7$
(a) 2 (b) 6 (c) 10 (d) 16 **[JIPMER]**

2018

3 In the complex, $[Cr(NH_3)_4Cl_2]^+$, the oxidation number of Cr is
(a) +4 (b) +3 (c) +2 (d) +6 **[JIPMER]**

2014

4 In acidic medium, H_2O_2 changes $Cr_2O_7^{2-}$ to CrO_5 which has two (— O — O —) bonds. Oxidation state of Cr in CrO_5 is **[CBSE AIPMT]**
(a) + 5 (b) + 3 (c) + 6 (d) − 10

5 The reaction of aqueous $KMnO_4$ with H_2O_2 in acidic conditions gives **[CBSE AIPMT]**
(a) Mn^{4+} and O_2 (b) Mn^{2+} and O_2
(c) Mn^{2+} and O_3 (d) Mn^{4+} and MnO_2

6 Oxidation number of nitrogen in which among the oxides of nitrogen is the lowest? **[MHT CET]**
(a) Nitric oxide (b) Nitrous oxide
(c) Nitrogen dioxide (d) Nitrogen trioxide

7 What is the oxidation number of vanadium in $Rb_4Na[HV_{10}O_{28}]$? **[Manipal]**
(a) + 8 (b) + 5 (c) + 3 (d) + 1

2013

8 The oxidation number of Cr in $K_2Cr_2O_7$ is **[AIIMS]**
(a) + 2 (b) + 4 (c) + 6 (d) + 7

9 The oxidation state of M^{3+} after removing three electrons is **[UP CPMT]**
(a) zero (b) + 3 (c) + 6 (d) − 6

10 The oxidation number of sulphur in $Na_2S_2O_3$ is **[UP CPMT]**
(a) + 1 (b) + 2 (c) + 3 (d) − 3

11 The oxidation number of P in $Mg_2P_2O_7$ is **[Manipal]**
(a) + 2 (b) + 5
(c) − 3 (d) + 3

12 The oxidation number and the electronic configuration of sulphur in H_2SO_4 is **[KCET]**
(a) + 4, $1s^2, 2s^2, 2p^6, 3s^2$ (b) + 2, $1s^2, 2s^2, 2p^6, 3s^2$
(c) + 3, $1s^2, 2s^2, 2p^6, 3s^2, 3p^1$ (d) + 6, $1s^2, 2s^2, 2p^6$

2012

13 In which of the following compounds, nitrogen exhibits highest oxidation state? **[CBSE AIPMT]**
(a) N_2H_4 (b) NH_3
(c) N_3H (d) NH_2OH

14 A mixture of potassium chlorate, oxalic acid and sulphuric acid is heated. During the reaction, which element undergoes maximum change in oxidation number? **[CBSE AIPMT]**
(a) S (b) H
(c) Cl (d) C

15 The oxidation number of iron in Fe_3O_4 is **[AIIMS]**
(a) +2 (b) +3 (c) $\frac{8}{3}$ (d) $\frac{2}{3}$

2011

16 In chromite ore, the oxidation number of iron and chromium respectively, are **[KCET]**
(a) +3, +2 (b) +3, +6 (c) +2, +6 (d) +2, +3

2010

17 Oxidation states of P in $H_4P_2O_5$, $H_4P_2O_6$, $H_4P_2O_7$, respectively are **[CBSE AIPMT]**
(a) +3, +4, +5 (b) +3, +5, +4
(c) +5, +3, +4 (d) +5, +4, +3

18 Highest oxidation state of Mn is present in **[AFMC]**
(a) $KMnO_4$ (b) K_2MnO_4 (c) Mn_2O_3 (d) MnO_2

19 The oxidation number and covalency of sulphur in sulphur molecule (S_8) are **[BVP]**
(a) 0 and 2 (b) +6 and 8 (c) 0 and 8 (d) +6 and 2

20 Which gives +7 oxidation state? **[MHT CET]**
(a) Mn (25) (b) Cr (24) (c) Cu (29) (d) Fe (26)

21 Oxidation number of N in HNO_3 is **[Manipal]**
(a) −3.5 (b) +3.5 (c) −3, +5 (d) +5

22 When a manganous salt is fused with a mixture of KNO_3 and solid NaOH, the oxidation number of Mn changes from +2 to **[WB JEE]**
(a) +4 (b) +3 (c) +6 (d) +7

23 Chlorine is in +1 oxidation state in **[MP PMT]**
(a) HCl (b) $HClO_4$ (c) ICl (d) Cl_2O

24 Which of the following have been arranged in the decreasing order of oxidation number of sulphur? **[AMU]**
(a) $Na_2S_4O_6 > H_2S_2O_7 > Na_2S_2O_3 > S_8$
(b) $H_2SO_4 > SO_2 > H_2S > H_2S_2O_8$
(c) $SO_2^{2-} > SO_4^{2-} > SO_3^{2-} > HSO_4^-$
(d) $H_2SO_5 > H_2SO_3 > SCl_2 > H_2S$

25 State the oxidation number of carbonyl carbon in methanal and methanoic acid respectively. **[Guj CET]**
(a) 0 and 0 (b) 0 and +2
(c) +1 and +2 (d) +1 and +3

2009

26 Oxidation number of P in PO_4^{3-}, of S in SO_4^{2-} and that of Cr in $Cr_2O_7^{2-}$ respectively, are **[CBSE AIPMT]**
(a) +5, +6 and +6 (b) +3, +6 and +5
(c) +5, +3 and +6 (d) −3, +6 and +6

27 Oxidation number of S in $H_2S_2O_8$ is **[Manipal]**
(a) +2 (b) +4
(c) +3 (d) +6

28 The oxidation states of S-atoms in $S_4O_6^{2-}$ from left to right respectively, are **[OJEE]**

$$^{-}O-\overset{\overset{O}{\|}}{\underset{\underset{O}{\|}}{S}}-S-S-\overset{\overset{O}{\|}}{\underset{\underset{O}{\|}}{S}}-O^{-}$$

(a) +6, 0, 0, +6 (b) +3, 1, +1, +3
(c) +5, 0, 0, +5 (d) +4, +1, +1, +4

29 In which of the following compounds, iron has an oxidation number of +3? **[DUMET]**
(a) $Fe(NO_3)_2$
(b) FeC_2O_4
(c) $[Fe(H_2O)_6]Cl_3$
(d) $(NH_4)_2SO_4 \cdot FeSO_4 \cdot H_2O$

30 In which of the following reactions, there is no change in valency? **[DUMET]**
(a) $SO_2 + 2H_2S \longrightarrow 2H_2O + 3S$
(b) $2Na + O_2 \longrightarrow 2Na_2O_2$
(c) $Na_2O_2 + H_2SO_4 \longrightarrow Na_2SO_4 + H_2O_2$
(d) $4KClO_3 \longrightarrow 3KClO_4 + KCl$

31 The oxidation state of Fe in the brown ring complex $[Fe(H_2O)_5NO]SO_4$ is **[KCET]**
(a) 0 (b) +2 (c) +1 (d) +3

2008

32 In the conversion of Br_2 to BrO_3^-, the oxidation number of Br changes from **[AFMC]**
(a) zero to +5 (b) +1 to +5
(c) zero to −3 (d) +2 to +5

33 Oxidation state of oxygen in F_2O is **[UP CPMT]**
(a) +1 (b) −1
(c) +2 (d) −2

34 Oxidation number of iodine in IO_3^-, IO_4^-, KI and I_2 respectively, are **[Kerala CEE]**
(a) −1, −1, 0, +1 (b) +3, +5, +7, 0
(c) +5, +7, −1, 0 (d) −1, −5, −1, 0
(e) −2, −5, −1, 0

35 When sulphur dioxide is passed in an acidified $K_2Cr_2O_7$ solution, the oxidation state of sulphur is changed from **[KCET]**
(a) +4 to 0 (b) +4 to +2
(c) +4 to +6 (d) +6 to +4

2007

36 Which of the following oxidation states are the most characteristics for lead and tin respectively? **[CBSE AIPMT]**
(a) +4, +2 (b) +2, +4
(c) +4, +4 (d) +2, +2

37 +3 oxidation state is most common in **[AFMC]**
(a) Ni (28) (b) Fe (26) (c) Zn (30) (d) Cu (29)

38 The oxidation state of chlorine in $KClO_4$ is **[AMU]**
(a) -1 (b) $+1$ (c) $+7$ (d) -7

39 Out of the following outer electronic configurations of atoms, the highest oxidation state is achieved by which one of them? **[Guj CET]**
(a) $(n-1)d^8ns^2$ (b) $(n-1)d^5ns^2$
(c) $(n-1)d^3ns^2$ (d) $(n-1)d^5ns^1$

2006

40 Oxidation number of 'N' in N_3H (hydrazoic acid) is **[Manipal]**
(a) $-\frac{1}{3}$ (b) $+3$ (c) 0 (d) -3

41 What is the oxidation state of P in $Ba(H_2PO_2)_2$?
(a) +1 (b) + 2 **[Haryana PMT]**
(c) + 3 (d) -1

42 Oxidation state of nitrogen is correctly given for **[Punjab PMET]**

Compound	Oxidation state
(a) Mg_3N_2	-3
(b) NH_2OH	$+1$
(c) $(N_2H_5)_2SO_4$	$+2$
(d) $[Co(NH_3)_5Cl]Cl_2$	0

43 Oxidation state of phosphorus in pyrophosphoric acid is
(a) + 5 (b) + 3 (c) + 4 (d) + 1 **[JCECE]**

2005

44 The oxidation number of xenon in $XeOF_2$ is **[J&K CET]**
(a) zero (b) 2 (c) 4 (d) 3

45 The oxidation number of cobalt in $K[Co(CO)_4]$ is **[J&K CET]**
(a) +1 (b) +3
(c) -1 (d) -3

Answers

1 (c)	2 (b)	3 (b)	4 (c)	5 (b)	6 (b)	7 (b)	8 (c)	9 (c)	10 (b)
11 (b)	12 (d)	13 (c)	14 (c)	15 (c)	16 (d)	17 (a)	18 (a)	19 (a)	20 (a)
21 (d)	22 (c)	23 (d)	24 (d)	25 (b)	26 (a)	27 (d)	28 (c)	29 (c)	30 (c)
31 (c)	32 (a)	33 (c)	34 (c)	35 (c)	36 (b)	37 (b)	38 (c)	39 (b)	40 (a)
41 (a)	42 (a)	43 (a)	44 (c)	45 (c)					

Explanations

1 (c) The structure of CrO_5 is

O (double bonded to Cr), with two O–O peroxide groups bonded to Cr

Oxidation state of Cr is +6 due to the presence of two peroxide linkages, which can be calculated as in $CrO(O_2)_2$, let the oxidation state of Cr be x.

$$x+(-1)4+(-2)=0$$
$$x-6=0$$
$$x=+6$$

2 (b) Let the oxidation number of Cr in $Na_2Cr_2O_7$ be x.

$$\therefore \quad 2(+1)+2x+7(-2)=0$$
$$2+2x-14=0$$
$$2x=12 \Rightarrow x=6$$

3 (b) Let the oxidation number of Cr is x in the complex $[Cr(NH_3)_4Cl_2]^+$

$$\therefore x+4\times(0)+2\times(-1)=+1$$
$$x-2=+1$$
$$x=+3$$

Thus, oxidation number of Cr is + 3.

4 (c) When H_2O_2 is added to an acidified solution of a dichromate, $Cr_2O_7^{2-}$, a deep blue coloured complex, chromic peroxide, CrO_5 [or $CrO(O_2)_2$] is formed.

$$Cr_2O_7^{2-}+2H^++4H_2O_2 \longrightarrow \underset{\text{Chromic peroxide}}{2CrO(O_2)_2}+5H_2O$$

This deep blue coloured complex has the following structure

O (double bonded to Cr), with two O–O peroxide groups bonded to Cr

Oxidation state of Cr is in CrO_5 + 6 due to the presence of two peroxide linkages, which can be calculated as:
In $CrO(O_2)_2$, let the oxidation state of Cr be x.

$$x+(-1)4+(-2)=0$$
$$x-6=0$$
$$x=+6$$

5 (b) The reaction of aqueous $KMnO_4$ with H_2O_2 in acidic medium is

$$3H_2SO_4+2KMnO_4+5H_2O_2 \longrightarrow 5O_2+2MnSO_4+8H_2O+K_2SO_4$$

In the above reaction, $KMnO_4$ oxidises H_2O_2 to O_2 and itself (MnO_4^-) gets reduced to Mn^{2+} ion as $MnSO_4$.

Hence, aqueous solution of $KMnO_4$ with H_2O_2 yields Mn^{2+} and O_2 in acidic conditions.

6 (b) Let the oxidation state of nitrogen in the given compounds be x.

(a) Nitric oxide (NO)
$$x-2=0 \Rightarrow x=+2$$
(b) Nitrous oxide (N_2O)
$$2x-2=0 \Rightarrow x=+1$$
(c) Nitrogen dioxide (NO_2)
$$x+2(-2)=0 \Rightarrow x=+4$$
(d) Nitrogen trioxide NO_3,
$$x+2(-3)=0 \Rightarrow x=+6$$

Thus, in nitrous oxide, oxidation number of nitrogen is the lowest.

7 (b) Algebraic sum of oxidation number of all the atoms in a neutral molecule is zero.

Let the oxidation number of vanadium be x, then

$$4\times1+1+1+10x+(-2)\times28=0$$
$$10x=56-6$$
$$x=+5$$

8 (*c*) Let the oxidation number of Cr in $K_2Cr_2O_7$ be *x*.

Oxidation number of O = − 2, K = + 1

$$2 \times 1 + 2x + 7(-2) = 0$$
$$2x = 12$$
$$x = +6$$

9 (*c*) Write the balanced equation for the given reaction. The reaction must be balanced with respect to charge.

$$M^{3+} - 3e^- \longrightarrow M^{6+}$$

∴ After removing 3 electrons from M^{3+}, its oxidation state will be + 6.

10 (*b*) The sum of oxidation states of all atoms in a neutral molecule is zero.

Suppose oxidation state of S in $Na_2S_2O_3$ be *x*.

$$\therefore\ 2 \times 1 + 2x + (-2 \times 3) = 0$$
$$2 + 2x - 6 = 0$$
$$2x = +4 \Rightarrow x = +2$$

11 (*b*) The oxidation number of P in $Mg_2P_2O_7$ can be calculated as follows: Suppose the oxidation number of P be *x* then, $2(+2) + 2x + (-14) = 0$

$$4 + 2x - 14 = 0$$
$$2x = 10$$
$$x = +5$$

12 (*d*) Let the oxidation number of sulphur in H_2SO_4 be *x*

then, $(2 \times 1) + x + (4 \times -2) = 0$

$$2 + x + (-8) = 0$$
$$x = 8 - 2 = +6$$

The electronic configuration of sulphur

$_{16}S = 1s^2, 2s^2, 2p^6, 3s^2, 3p^4$

Electronic configuration of S^{+6} in H_2SO_4

$$16 - 6 = 10, 1s^2, 2s^2, 2p^6$$

13 (*c*) Let the oxidation state of nitrogen in the given compounds be *x*.

(a) $\overset{x\ +1}{N_2H_4}$, $2x + (+1)4 = 0$

$$2x = -4$$
$$x = -2$$

(b) $\overset{x\ +1}{NH_3}$, $x + (+1)3 = 0$

$$x = -3$$

(c) $\overset{x\ +1}{N_3H}$, $3x + (+1) = 0$

$$3x = -1$$
$$x = -1/3$$

(d) $\overset{x+1-2+1}{NH_2OH}$,

$$x + (+1)2 + (-2) + (+1) = 0$$
$$x + 2 - 2 + 1 = 0$$
$$x + 1 = 0 \Rightarrow x = -1$$

The oxidation state of nitrogen is highest in N_3H.

14 (*c*) When a mixture of potassium chlorate, oxalic acid and sulphuric acid is heated, the following reaction occurs:

$$\overset{+1+5-2}{KClO_3} + \overset{+1+3-2}{H_2C_2O_4} + \overset{+1+6-2}{H_2SO_4} \xrightarrow{\Delta}$$
$$\overset{+1+6-2}{K_2SO_4} + \overset{+1-1}{KCl} + \overset{+4-2}{CO_2} + \overset{+1-2}{H_2O}$$

Thus, Cl is the element which undergoes maximum change in the oxidation state (+5 to − 1).

15 (*c*) In Fe_3O_4, let the oxidation number of Fe = *x*

$$3x + 4(-2) = 0 \Rightarrow = \frac{8}{3}$$

16 (*d*) Chromite or chrome iron ore is $FeCr_2O_4$. Its actual composition is $FeO \cdot Cr_2O_3$.

In FeO, oxidation state of Fe is calculated as: $x + (-2) = 0$

$$x = +2$$

Similarly, in Cr_2O_3, the oxidation state of Cr is calculated as

$$2 \times x + (-2) \times 3 = 0$$
$$2x = +6 \Rightarrow x = +3$$

17 (*a*) Let the oxidation state of P in the given compounds be *x*.

$H_4P_2O_5$, $2x + 4 - 10 = 0$

$$2x = 6 \Rightarrow x = +3$$

$H_4P_2O_6$, $2x + 4 - 12 = 0$

$$2x = 8$$
$$x = +4$$

$H_4P_2O_7$, $2x + 4 - 14 = 0$

$$2x = 10$$
$$x = +5$$

18 (*a*) Let the oxidation state of Mn be *x*.

(a) $KMnO_4$,

$$+1 + x + (-2) \times 4 = 0$$
$$x - 7 = 0$$
$$x = +7$$

(b) K_2MnO_4,

$$(+1) \times 2 + x + (-2) \times 4 = 0$$
$$x - 6 = 0$$
$$x = +6$$

(c) Mn_2O_3,

$$x \times 2 + (-2) \times 3 = 0$$
$$2x = +6$$
$$x = +3$$

(d) MnO_2, $x + (-2) \times 2 = 0$

$$x = +4$$

Thus, oxidation state of Mn is highest in $KMnO_4$.

19 (*a*) In elemental state, the oxidation number of an element is zero.

Therefore, oxidation number of S in S_8 is zero. Further in the S_8 molecule, each sulphur atom is connected to two other sulphur atoms, therefore its covalency is 2.

20 (*a*) For *d*-block elements,

Oxidation state = *ns* electrons + (*n* − 1) *d* electron (unpaired),

(a) $Mn(25) = [Ar]\,3d^5, 4s^2$

Oxidation state (highest) = 5 + 2 = 7

(b) $Cr(24) = [Ar]\,3d^5, 4s^1$

Oxidation state (highest) = 5 + 1 = 6

(c) $Cu(29) = [Ar]\,3d^{10}, 4s^1$

Oxidation state (highest) = + 2

(d) $Fe(26) = [Ar]\,3d^6, 4s^2$

Oxidation state (highest) = + 3

Thus, only Mn exhibits + 7 oxidation state among the given elements.

21 (*d*) Let the oxidation state of N in $HNO_3 = x$

$$+1 + x + (-2 \times 3) = 0$$

or $x + 1 - 6 = 0 \Rightarrow x = +5$

22 (*c*) $\overset{(+2)}{Mn^{2+}} + 2NO_3^- + 2OH^- \longrightarrow$

$$\overset{(+6)}{MnO_4^{2-}} + 2H_2O + 2NO$$

∴ The oxidation number of Mn changes from + 2 to + 6.

23 (*d*) The oxidation state of chlorine is +1 in Cl_2O. It is shown below in its structure.

$$Cl^{+1} - O^{-2} - Cl^{+1}$$

24 (*d*) (a) $Na_2\overset{2.5}{S_4}O_6$; $H_2\overset{+6}{S_2}O_7$; $Na_2\overset{+2}{S_2}O_3$; $\overset{0}{S_8}$

(b) $H_2\overset{+6}{S}O_4$; $\overset{+4}{S}O_2$; $H_2\overset{-2}{S} > H_2\overset{+6}{S_2}O_8$

(c) $\overset{+2}{SO_2^{2}}$; $\overset{+6}{SO_4^{2}}$; $\overset{+4}{SO_3^{2-}}$; $H\overset{+6}{SO_4^-}$

(d) $H_2\overset{+6}{S}O_5$; $H_2\overset{+4}{S}O_3$; $\overset{+2}{S}Cl_2$; $H_2\overset{-2}{S}$

Thus, in option (d), compounds are arranged in the decreasing order of oxidation number of sulphur.

25 (*b*) Let the oxidation number of carbonyl carbon in methanal (HCHO) and methanoic acid (HCOOH) is *x* and *y* respectively.

In HCHO, $2(+1) + x + (-2) = 0$

$$2 + x - 2 = 0 \Rightarrow x = 0$$

In HCOOH, $2(+1) + y + 2(-2) = 0$

$$2 + y - 4 = 0 \Rightarrow y = +2$$

26 (*a*) (i) Oxidation state of P in PO_4^{3-},

$$x + 4 \times (-2) = -3$$

or $x = +5$

(ii) Oxidation state of S in SO_4^{2-},

$$x + 4 \times (-2) = -2$$

or $x = +6$

(iii) Oxidation state of Cr in $Cr_2O_7^{2-}$,

$$2x + 7 \times (-2) = -2$$

or $2x = 12$ or $x = +6$

27 (*d*) The structure of $H_2S_2O_8$ is as follows:

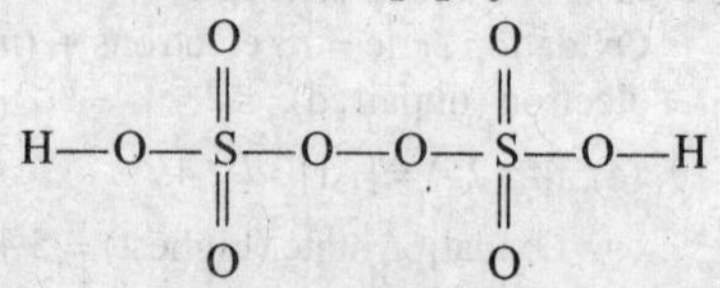

It contains peroxide linkage due to which the oxidation number of these two oxygen atoms will be – 1 each.

Let the oxidation number of S in this compound is x and it is calculated below:

$2 \times (+1) + 2x + 6 \times (-2) + 2(-1) = 0$

$2 + 2x - 12 - 2 = 0$ or $2x = 12$

$\therefore \quad x = +6$

28 (*c*) The tetrathionate anion, $S_4O_6^{2-}$ is a sulphur oxoanion derived from the compound tetrathionic acid, $H_4S_4O_6$. The structure of $S_4O_6^{2-}$

$$^{-}O-\overset{\overset{O^{-2}}{\|}}{\underset{\underset{O^{-2}}{\|}}{S}}{}^{+5}-\overset{0}{S}-\overset{0}{S}-\overset{\overset{O^{-2}}{\|}}{\underset{\underset{O^{-2}}{\|}}{S}}{}^{+5}-O^{-}$$

Since, each of the terminal sulphur atoms is connected to two oxygen atoms by a double bond and to one oxygen atom by a single bond, the oxidation state of these terminal sulphur atoms is +5. Since, two central sulphur atoms are linked to each other by a single bond and each sulphur is further attached to similar species on either side, the electron pair forming S—S bond remains in the centre and hence, each of the two central sulphur atoms has an oxidation state of zero. Thus, the oxidation states of S-atoms in $S_4O_6^{2-}$ from left to right respectively are +5, 0, 0, +5.

29 (*c*) NO_3^- has a –1 charge.

$\therefore$ In $Fe(NO_3)_2$, Fe has oxidation number + 2.

$C_2O_4^{2-}$ has –2 charge.

$\therefore$ In FeC_2O_4, Fe has oxidation number + 2.

In $[Fe(H_2O)_6]Cl_3$, the cation $[Fe(H_2O)_6]^{3+}$ is present and H_2O is neutral.

$\therefore$ Fe has oxidation number + 3.

In Mohr's salt' $FeSO_4$ has SO_4^{2-} ion which has –2 charge.

Therefore, Fe has + 2 oxidation number.

30 (*c*)(a) $\overset{+4}{S}O_2 + 2H_2\overset{-2}{S} \longrightarrow 2H_2O + 3\overset{0}{S}$

(b) $2\overset{0}{Na} + \overset{0}{O_2} \longrightarrow 2\overset{+1}{Na_2}\overset{-1}{O_2}$

(c) $2\overset{+1}{Na_2}\overset{-1}{O_2} + H_2SO_4 \longrightarrow \overset{+1}{Na_2}SO_4 + H_2\overset{-1}{O_2}$

(no change in valency)

(d) $4K\overset{+5}{Cl}O_3 \longrightarrow 3K\overset{+7}{Cl}O_4 + K\overset{-1}{Cl}$

31 (*c*) Let the oxidation state of Fe in $[Fe(H_2O)_5NO]^{2+}$ be x.

Charge on H_2O is zero as it is a neutral ligand.

NO is present as NO^+.

$\therefore \quad x + 0 + 1 = 2 \Rightarrow x = +2 - 1$

$\therefore$ Oxidation state of Fe = + 1.

32 (*a*) Bromine has zero oxidation state in Br_2 because it is in free state.

$\overset{0}{Br_2} \longrightarrow BrO_3^-$

In BrO_3^-, let Br has oxidation state x.

$x + (-2 \times 3) = -1$

$x + (-6) = -1$

$x = +6 - 1 = +5$

So, oxidation number changes from 0 to +5.

33 (*c*) In F_2O, let the oxidation state of O be x.

$2(-1) + x = 0$

($\because$ F is more electronegative)

$-2 + x = 0 \quad \Rightarrow \quad x = +2$

34 (*c*) Oxidation state of I in IO_3^-

$x + (-2)3 = -1 \quad \Rightarrow \quad x = +5$

Oxidation state of I in IO_4^-

$x + (-2)4 = -1 \quad \Rightarrow \quad x = +7$

Oxidation state of I in KI

$+1 + x = 0 \quad \Rightarrow \quad x = -1$

Oxidation state of I in I_2

$x = 0$

Hence, the oxidation number of iodine in IO_3^-, IO_4^-, KI and I_2 are respectively + 5, + 7, – 1 and 0.

35 (*c*) Acidified $K_2Cr_2O_7$ solution oxidises SO_2 into $Cr_2(SO_4)_3$.

$3\overset{+4}{S}O_2 + K_2Cr_2O_7 + H_2SO_4 \longrightarrow K_2SO_4 + Cr_2(\overset{+6}{S}O_4)_3 + H_2O$

Hence, the oxidation state of sulphur changes from + 4 to + 6.

36. (*b*) The most characteristic oxidation state of group 14 elements is +4. But the tendency to form + 2 oxidation state increases on moving down the group due to the inert pair effect.

Most characteristic oxidation state for lead and tin are + 2 and + 4 respectively.

37. (*b*) (a) Ni(III) = $3d^7 4s^0$ =

3d: ⇅ ⇅ ↑ ↑ ↑ 4s: □

(b) Fe(III) = $3d^5 4s^0$ =

3d: ↑ ↑ ↑ ↑ ↑ 4s: □

+ 3 oxidation state of Fe provides the extra stability due to half-filled *d*-orbitals.

(c) Zn(III) = $3d^9 4s^0$ =

3d: ⇅ ⇅ ⇅ ⇅ ↑ 4s: □

(d) Cu(III) = $3d^8 4s^0$ =

3d: ⇅ ⇅ ⇅ ↑ ↑ 4s: □

38 (*c*) $KClO_4$ Let the oxidation state of Cl be x.

$1 + x + 4(-2) = 0$

$1 + x - 8 = 0$

$x - 7 = 0$

$x = +7$

39 (*b*) The highest oxidation state is achieved by $(n-1)d^5ns^2$ electronic configuration. It shows the + 7 (highest among all) oxidation state.

40 (*a*) N_3H (hydrazoic acid)

Let the oxidation state of N be x.

$+3(x) + 1 = 0$

$3x + 1 = 0 \Rightarrow x = -\frac{1}{3}$

41 (*a*) $Ba(H_2PO_2)_2$

Let the oxidation state of P be x.

$(+2) + 2[2(+1) + x + 2(-2)] = 0$

$2 + 2(2 + x - 4) = 0$

$2 + 4 + 2x - 8 = 0$

$2 + 2x - 4 = 0 \Rightarrow 2x = 2 \Rightarrow x = +1$

42 (*a*) The oxidation number of nitrogen in different compounds are

(a) Mg_3N_2	– 3
(b) NH_2OH	– 1
(c) $(N_2H_5)_2SO_4$	– 2
(d) $[Co(NH_3)_5Cl]Cl_2$	– 3

43 (*a*) $H_4P_2O_7$

Let the oxidation number of P be x.

$(+1 \times 4) + 2x + (-2 \times 7) = 0$

$+4 + 2x - 14 = 0$

$2x = 14 - 4 \Rightarrow 2x = 10$

$\therefore \quad x = +5$

44 (*a*) $XeOF_2$

Let the oxidation number of Xe be x.

$x + (-2) + 2(-1) = 0$

$x - 2 - 2 = 0 \quad \therefore \ x = +4$

45 (*c*) $K[Co(CO)_4]$

Let the oxidation number of Co be x.

$1 + x + 0 = 0$ (as CO is neutral)

$x = -1$

Topic 3

Balancing of Chemical Equations

2018

1 For the redox reaction,

$MnO_4^- + C_2O_4^{2-} + H^+ \longrightarrow Mn^{2+} + CO_2 + H_2O$

the correct coefficients of the reactants for the balanced equation are [NEET]

	MnO_4^-	$C_2O_4^{2-}$	H^+		MnO_4^-	$C_2O_4^{2-}$	H^+
(a)	2	16	5	(b)	2	5	16
(c)	16	5	2	(d)	5	16	2

2 Consider the change in oxidation state of bromine corresponding to different emf values as shown in the diagram below. [NEET]

$BrO_4^- \xrightarrow{1.82\text{ V}} BrO_3^- \xrightarrow{1.5\text{ V}} HBrO$

$\xrightarrow{1.595\text{ V}} Br_2 \xrightarrow{1.0652\text{ V}} Br^-$

Then the species undergoing disproportionation is

(a) Br_2 (b) BrO_4^- (c) BrO_3^- (d) HBrO

2010

3 How many moles of iodine are liberated when 1 mole of potassium dichromate reacts with potassium iodide?

(a) 1 (b) 2 (c) 3 (d) 4 [AIIMS]

4 The coefficients of I^-, IO_3^- and H^+ in the redox reaction,

$I^- + IO_3^- + H^+ \longrightarrow I_2 + H_2O$

in the balanced form respectively are [CMC]

(a) 5, 1, 6 (b) 1, 5, 6

(c) 6, 1, 5 (d) 5, 6, 1

2009

5 In the following redox reaction,

$xUO^{2+} + Cr_2O_7^{2-} + yH^+ \longrightarrow aUO_2^{2+} + z\,Cr^{3+} + bH_2O$

the values of coefficients x, y and z respectively, are [AIIMS]

(a) 3, 8, 2 (b) 3, 8, 7

(c) 3, 2, 4 (d) 3, 1, 8

6 For the redox reaction,

$Zn + NO_3^- \longrightarrow Zn^{2+} + NH_4^+$

In basic medium, coefficients of Zn, NO_3^- and OH^- in the balanced reaction respectively, are [Manipal]

(a) 4, 1, 7 (b) 7, 4, 1

(c) 4, 1, 10 (d) 1, 4, 10

7 The number of electrons involved in the reduction of one nitrate ion tohydrazine is [AIIMS]

(a) 8 (b) 5

(c) 3 (d) 7

(e) 4

8 $Cu + xHNO_3 \longrightarrow Cu(NO_3)_2 + yNO_2 + zH_2O$, the above equation balances when, [J&K CET]

(a) $x=2, y=4, z=3$ (b) $x=4, y=2, z=2$

(c) $x=2, y=4, z=2$ (d) $x=4, y=4, z=2$

9 In the redox reaction,

$xKMnO_4 + NH_3 \longrightarrow yKNO_3 + MnO_2 + KOH + H_2O$

x and y are [DUMET]

(a) $x=4, y=6$ (b) $x=3, y=8$

(c) $x=8, y=6$ (d) $x=8, y=3$

2007

10 In the ionic equation,

$BiO_3^- + 6H^+ + xe^- \longrightarrow Bi^{3+} + 3H_2O$,

the value of x is [KCET]

(a) 6 (b) 2 (c) 4 (d) 3

2006

11 In alkaline medium, ClO_2 oxidises H_2O_2 to O_2 and reduced itself to Cl^-, then how many moles of H_2O_2 will be oxidise by one mole of ClO_2? [BHU]

(a) 1.0 (b) 1.5

(c) 2.5 (d) 3.5

Answers

1 (b)	2 (d)	3 (c)	4 (a)	5 (a)	6 (c)	7 (d)	8 (b)	9 (d)	10 (b)
11 (c)									

Explanations

1 (*b*) The given redox reaction is

$$MnO_4^- + C_2O_4^{2-} + H^+ \longrightarrow Mn^{2+} + CO_2 + H_2O$$

The reaction can be balanced by considering the following steps:

***Step* I** Balance the atoms except H and O.

$$MnO_4^- + C_2O_4^{2-} + H^+ \longrightarrow Mn^{2+} + 2CO_2 + H_2O$$

***Step* II** Write the oxidation number of each atom

$$\overset{+7}{MnO_4^-} + \overset{+3}{C_2O_4^{2-}} + H^+ \longrightarrow Mn^{2+} + \overset{+4}{2CO_2} + H_2O$$

Oxidation $(-2e^-)$; Reduction $(+5e^-)$

***Step* III** Cross multiply by change in oxidation number

$$\overset{+7}{MnO_4^-} \longrightarrow Mn^{2+};\ 5e^- \text{ gain}$$

$$\overset{+6}{C_2O_4^{2-}} \longrightarrow \overset{+8}{2CO_2};\ 2e^- \text{ loss}$$

$$2MnO_4^- + 5C_2O_4^- + H^+ \longrightarrow 2Mn^{2+} + 10CO_2 + H_2O$$

***Step* IV** Balance oxygen by adding H_2O on deficient site.

$$2MnO_4^- + 5C_2O_4^{2-} + H^+ \longrightarrow 2Mn^{2+} + 10CO_2 + 8H_2O$$

***Step* V** Balance hydrogen ion

$$2MnO_4^{2-} + 5C_2O_4^{2-} + 16H^+ \longrightarrow 2Mn^{2+} + 10CO_2 + 8H_2O$$

∴ The coefficients of the reactants, MnO_4^-, $C_2O_4^{2-}$ ad H^+ are 2, 5 and 16, respectively.

2 (*d*) The reaction in which same species is oxidised as well as reduced is called disproportionation reaction. Firstly, calculate the value of E°_{cell} of each species undergoing disproportionation reaction. The reaction whose E°_{cell} value is positive will be feasible (spontaneous).

(i) Given, $BrO_3^- \longrightarrow HBrO$;

$$E^\circ_{BrO_3^-/HBrO} = 1.5\ V$$

$$BrO_3^- \longrightarrow BrO_4^-;$$

$$E^\circ_{BrO_3^-/BrO_4^-} = -1.82\ V$$

$$\therefore\ 2\overset{+5}{BrO_3^-} \longrightarrow \overset{+1}{HBrO} + \overset{+7}{BrO_4^-}$$

$$E^\circ_{cell} = E^\circ_{red} + E^\circ_{ox}$$

$$E^\circ_{cell} = E^\circ_{BrO_3^-/HBrO} + E^\circ_{BrO_3^-/BrO_4^-}$$

$$= 1.5 - 1.82 = -0.32\ V$$

[Non-spontaneous]

(ii) $\overset{+1}{HBrO} \longrightarrow \overset{0}{Br_2}$;

$$E^\circ_{HBrO/Br_2} = 1.595\ V$$

$$\overset{+1}{HBrO} \longrightarrow \overset{+5}{BrO_3^-};$$

$$E^\circ_{HBrO/BrO_3^-} = -1.5\ V$$

$$\therefore\ 2\overset{+1}{HBrO} \longrightarrow \overset{0}{Br_2} + \overset{+5}{BrO_3^-}$$

$$E^\circ_{cell} = E^\circ_{HBrO/Br_2} + E^\circ_{HBrO/BrO_3^-}$$

$$= 1.595 - 1.5 = 0.095\ V$$

[Spontaneous]

(iii) $\overset{0}{Br_2} \longrightarrow \overset{-1}{Br^-}$; $E^\circ_{Br_2/Br^-} = 1.0652\ V$

$$\overset{0}{Br_2} \longrightarrow \overset{+1}{HBrO};$$

$$E^\circ_{Br_2/HBrO} = -1.595\ V$$

$$\therefore\ 2\overset{0}{Br_2} \longrightarrow \overset{-1}{Br^-} + \overset{+1}{HBrO}$$

$$E^\circ_{cell} = E^\circ_{Br_2/Br^-} + E^\circ_{Br_2/HBrO}$$

$$= 1.0652 - 1.595$$

$$= -0.5298\ V$$

∴ Among the given options, only HBrO undergoes disproportionation.

3 (*c*) The balanced chemical reaction is

$$14H^+ + Cr_2O_7^{2-} + 6I^- \longrightarrow 2Cr^{3+} + 3I_2 + 7H_2O$$

Thus, 3 moles of I_2 are evolved, when KI reacts with 1 mole of potassium dichromate.

4 (*a*) $I^- + (\overset{+5}{IO_3^-}) + H^+ \longrightarrow \overset{0}{I_2} + H_2O$

Oxidation half reaction :

$$2I^- \longrightarrow I_2 + 2e^- \quad \text{...(i)}$$

Reduction half reaction :

$$10e^- + 2(\overset{+5}{IO_3^-}) \longrightarrow \overset{0}{I_2} \quad \text{...(ii)}$$

In order to cancel the electrons, multiplying Eq. (i) by 5 and then adding to Eq. (ii), we get

$$10I^- + 2IO_3^- \longrightarrow 6I_2$$

To balance O-atom, add $6H_2O$ molecules on RHS and $12H^+$ on LHS, then

$$10I^- + 2IO_3^- + 12H^+ \longrightarrow 6I_2 + 6H_2O$$

or $5I^- + IO_3^- + 6H^+ \longrightarrow 3I_2 + 3H_2O$

5 (*a*) The balanced chemical reaction is given as

$$3UO^{2+} + Cr_2O_7^{2-} + 8H^+ \longrightarrow 3UO_2^{2+} + 2Cr^{3+} + 4H_2O$$

Hence, the value of x, y and z are respectively 3, 8 and 2.

6 (*c*) The balanced reaction is

$$4Zn + NO_3^- + 7H_2O \longrightarrow 4Zn^{2+} + NH_4^+ + 10OH^-$$

Thus, the coefficients of Zn, NO_3^- and $\overline{O}H$ are 4, 1, 10 respectively.

7 (*d*) Given, $NO_3^- \longrightarrow N_2H_4$

The balanced reaction is

$$2NO_3^- + 16H^+ + 14e^- \longrightarrow N_2H_4 + 6H_2O$$

∵ Number of electrons involved in the reduction of two nitrate ions = $14e^-$

∴ One nitrate ion will involve

$$= \frac{14}{2}e^- = 7e^-$$

8 (*b*) The balanced reaction is given as,

$$Cu + 4HNO_3 \longrightarrow Cu(NO_3)_2 + 2NO_2 + 2H_2O$$

Therefore, values of x, y and z are respectively 4, 2 and 2.

9 (*d*) The balanced reaction is as follows:

$$8KMnO_4 + 3NH_3 \longrightarrow 8MnO_2 + 3KNO_3 + 5KOH + 2H_2O$$

∵ x and y are respectively 8 and 3.

10 (*b*) Balanced reaction is

$$BiO_3^- + 6H^+ + 2e^- \longrightarrow Bi^{3+} + 3H_2O$$

∴ Value of x is 2.

11 (*c*) The reaction between ClO_2 and H_2O_2 in alkaline medium can be balanced as follows :

Reduction half reaction

$$ClO_2 \longrightarrow Cl^-$$

$$ClO_2 + 2H_2O + 5e^- \longrightarrow Cl^- + 4OH^-$$

Oxidation half reaction

$$H_2O_2 \longrightarrow O_2$$

$$H_2O_2 + 2OH^- \longrightarrow O_2 + 2H_2O + 2e^-$$

$$[ClO_2 + 2H_2O + 5e^- \longrightarrow Cl^- + 4OH^-] \times 2$$

$$[H_2O_2 + 2OH^- \longrightarrow O_2 + 2H_2O + 2e^-] \times 5$$

$$2ClO_2 + 5H_2O_2 + 2OH^- \longrightarrow 2Cl^- + 5O_2 + 6H_2O$$

$$2ClO_2 \equiv 5H_2O_2$$

$$ClO_2 \equiv 2.5\ H_2O_2$$

Hence, one mole of ClO_2 oxidises 2.5 moles of H_2O_2.

09

Hydrogen

Quick Review

Hydrogen is the lightest and most abundant element in the universe (70% of the total mass of universe). In normal elemental form, it exists as diatomic molecule, i.e. H_2.

Position of Hydrogen in the Periodic Table

Hydrogen resembles with alkali metals (group 1) as well as halogens (group 17). At the same time, it differs from both in certain characteristics. That is why hydrogen is called **"rogue element"**. However, it has been placed in group 1 on the basis of its configuration $1s^1$, which is the basis of modern classification of elements.

Isotopes of Hydrogen

Isotopes are the different forms of the same element having same atomic number but different mass numbers. There are three isotopes of hydrogen namely protium, deuterium and tritium.

Name	Symbol	Atomic number	Relative atomic mass	Density	Relative abundance	Nature
Protium	${}^1_1H$ or H	1	1.0078	0.09	99.98%	Non-radioactive
Deuterium	${}^2_1H$ or D	1	2.0141	0.18	0.0156%	Non-radioactive
Tritium	${}^3_1H$ or T	1	3.016	0.27	10^{-15}%	Radioactive (emits β-rays, $t_{1/2} = 12.33$ year)

Different Forms of Hydrogen

Different forms of hydrogen are as follows :

1. Atomic Hydrogen

- It is obtained from thermal decomposition of molecular hydrogen at high temperature and low pressure.

$$H_2 \xrightarrow{\text{Electric arc}} 2H; \Delta H = 105.4 \text{ kcal mol}^{-1}$$

- It is very reactive and its half-life period is 0.33 s.

2. Nascent Hydrogen

Freshly prepared hydrogen is known as nascent hydrogen and is more reactive than ordinary hydrogen. It causes the reduction of certain compounds which is not possible with ordinary hydrogen. It can never be isolated.

$$Zn + H_2SO_4 \longrightarrow ZnSO_4 + 2[H]$$

Activity of nascent H depends upon the reaction by which it is obtained.

3. *ortho* and *para* Hydrogen

- When hydrogen molecule have nuclear spins in the same direction, it is known as *ortho* hydrogen.
- On the other hand, when the nuclear spins are in the opposite direction, it is known as *para* hydrogen.

At room temperature, hydrogen consists of 75% *ortho* and 25% *para* hydrogen.

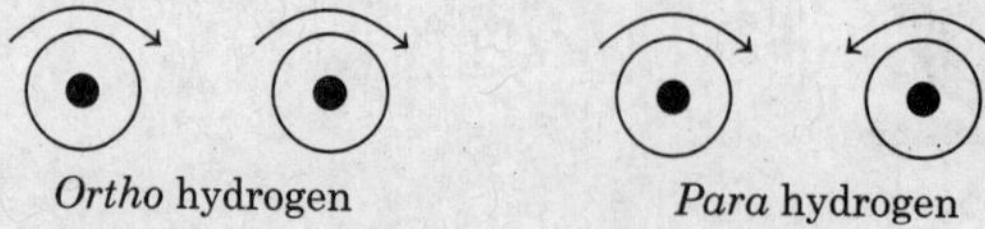

Dihydrogen

Dihydrogen is a colourless, odourless, tasteless, combustible gas. It is lighter than air and insoluble in water. It is neutral to litmus.

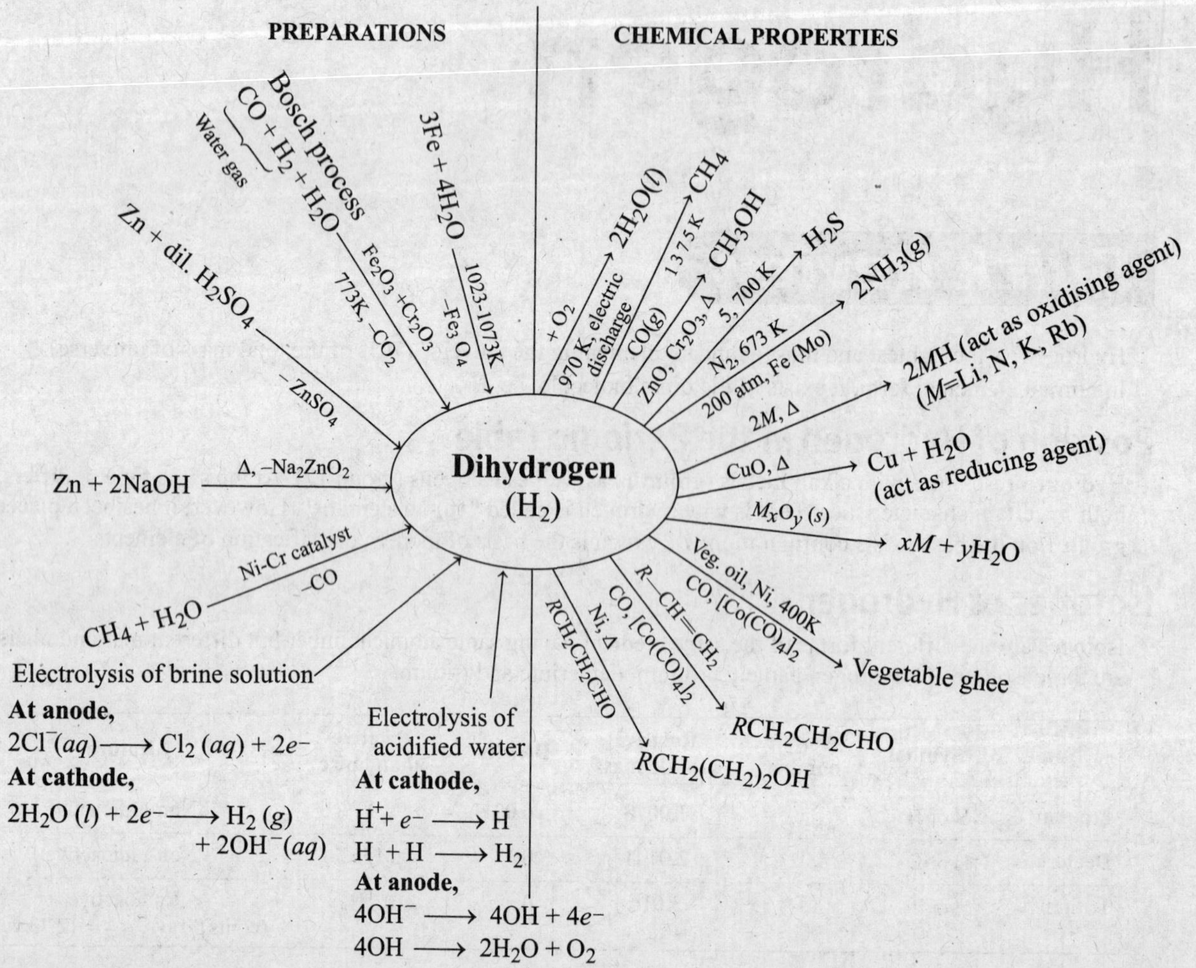

PREPARATIONS

- Bosch process: $\underbrace{CO + H_2}_{\text{Water gas}} + H_2O \xrightarrow[773K,\ -CO_2]{Fe_2O_3 + Cr_2O_3}$ Dihydrogen
- $3Fe + 4H_2O \xrightarrow[-Fe_3O_4]{1023\text{-}1073K}$ Dihydrogen
- $Zn + \text{dil. } H_2SO_4 \xrightarrow{-ZnSO_4}$ Dihydrogen
- $Zn + 2NaOH \xrightarrow{\Delta,\ -Na_2ZnO_2}$ Dihydrogen
- $CH_4 + H_2O \xrightarrow[-CO]{\text{Ni-Cr catalyst}}$ Dihydrogen
- Electrolysis of brine solution
  At anode,
  $2Cl^-(aq) \longrightarrow Cl_2(aq) + 2e^-$
  At cathode,
  $2H_2O(l) + 2e^- \longrightarrow H_2(g) + 2OH^-(aq)$
- Electrolysis of acidified water
  At cathode,
  $H^+ + e^- \longrightarrow H$
  $H + H \longrightarrow H_2$
  At anode,
  $4OH^- \longrightarrow 4OH + 4e^-$
  $4OH \longrightarrow 2H_2O + O_2$

CHEMICAL PROPERTIES

Dihydrogen (H_2)

- $\xrightarrow[\text{970 K, electric discharge}]{+O_2} 2H_2O(l)$
- $\xrightarrow[CO(g)]{1375\text{ K}} CH_4$
- $\xrightarrow{ZnO,\ Cr_2O_3,\ \Delta} CH_3OH$
- $\xrightarrow{S,\ 700\text{ K}} H_2S$
- $\xrightarrow[\text{200 atm, Fe (Mo)}]{N_2,\ 673\text{ K}} 2NH_3(g)$
- $\xrightarrow{2M,\ \Delta}$ 2MH (act as oxidising agent) (M=Li, N, K, Rb)
- $\xrightarrow{CuO,\ \Delta} Cu + H_2O$ (act as reducing agent)
- $\xrightarrow{M_xO_y(s)} xM + yH_2O$
- $\xrightarrow{\text{Veg. oil, Ni, 400K}}$ Vegetable ghee
- $\xrightarrow{R{-}CH{=}CH_2,\ CO,\ [Co(CO)_4]_2} RCH_2CH_2CHO$
- $\xrightarrow{RCH_2CH_2CHO,\ Ni,\ \Delta} RCH_2(CH_2)_2OH$

Uses of Dihydrogen

(*i*) It is used in the manufacture of CH_3OH.

$$CO(g) + 2H_2(g) \xrightarrow{Co} CH_3OH(l)$$

(*ii*) It produces temperature of 2850°C and oxy-atomic hydrogen flame produces a temperature of 4000°C, so it is used in oxy-hydrogen flame.

(*iii*) The largest single use of H_2 is in the synthesis of NH_3 which is used in the manufacture of HNO_3 and fertilizers.

(*iv*) Liquid hydrogen mixed with liquid oxygen is used as rocket fuel in space research.

(*v*) H_2 is used as a reducing agent in extraction of metals.

(*vi*) H_2 is used in fuel cell for generating electrical energy.

(*vii*) Hydrogen is used in the manufacture of synthetic petrol. (By heating H_2 with coal and heavy oils under very high pressure in the presence of catalyst.)

(*viii*) It is used in the preparation of metal hydrides, hydrogen chloride.

(*ix*) It is used in metallurgical processes to reduce heavy metal oxides to metals.

(*x*) Atomic hydrogen and oxy hydrogen torches find use for cutting and welding purposes.

Hydrides

Hydrogen combines with almost all the elements (except noble gases) under certain reaction condition to give binary compounds. These binary compounds are called **hydrides**.

These are generally represented by the formula EH_x (where E is the other element and x is the number of hydrogen atoms (e.g. CaH_2) or E_mH_n [here also E is the elements and m and n show the number of E and H-atoms respectively] e.g. B_2H_6.

Hydrides can be classified into following categories :

1. Ionic or Saline Hydrides

These are formed by elements of group I, II, (except Be and Mg) by heating them in hydrogen. These are white colourless solids (crystalline) having high m.p. and b.p. easily decomposed by water, CO_2 or SO_2.

$$CaH_2 + 2H_2O \longrightarrow Ca(OH)_2 + 2H_2$$

$$CaH_2 + 2CO_2 \longrightarrow (HCOO)_2Ca$$

They are strong reducing agents. Alkali metal hydrides are used for making $LiAlH_4$, $NaBH_4$, etc and for removing last traces of water from organic compounds.

2. Molecular or Covalent Hydrides

These are formed by elements of *p*-block having higher electronegativity than hydrogen. These are further classified according to the relative number of electrons and bonds in their Lewis structures :

(*i*) **Electron Deficient Hydrides** These are the hydrides which do not have sufficient number of electrons needed to form normal covalent bonds, e.g. hydrides of group 13 (BH_3, AlH_3, etc.)

(*ii*) **Electron Precise Hydrides** These are the hydrides which have exact number of electrons needed to form normal covalent bonds, e.g. hydrides of group 14 (CH_4, SiH_4, etc.)

(*iii*) **Electron Rich Hydrides** These are the hydrides which have greater number of electrons than required to form normal covalent bonds, e.g. hydrides of group 15, 16, 17, (NH_3, PH_3, H_2S, HF, HCl, etc). The excess electrons in these hydrides are present as lone pairs of electrons.

3. Metallic or Interstitial or Non-stoichiometric Hydrides

The transition metals and rare earth metals combine with hydrogen to form interstitial hydrides. They exhibit metallic properties and are powerful reducing agents. They are non-stoichiometric hydrides and their composition varies with temperature and pressure. e.g. $LaH_{2.87}$, $TiH_{1.73}$. Metals of group 7, 8 and 9 do not form hydrides and this region of the Periodic Table is called **hydride gap**.

4. Polymeric Hydrides and Complex Hydrides

Polymeric hydrides are formed by elements having electronegativity in the range 1.4 to 2.0, e.g. $(BeH_2)_n$, $(AlH_3)_n$ etc. In **complex hydrides**, H^- acts as ligand and is attached to central metal atom, e.g. $LiAlH_4$, $LiBH_4$, etc.

Water

- It is the most abundant and widely distributed on the earth.
- It occurs in three physical states (solid, liquid and gas).
- It is a covalent molecule in which oxygen is sp^3-hybridised and has bent structure.

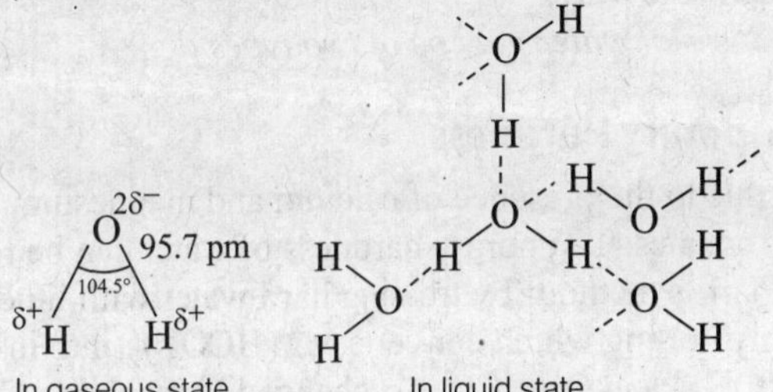

Structure of water in gaseous and liquid state

- In ice, each H_2O molecule is surrounded by three H_2O molecules in hexagonal honeycomb manner, thus giving rise to open-cage like structure. Hence, open spaces are formed in such a structure, therefore small number of molecules are placed. Thus, volume of ice is greater than liquid and thus ice is less dense than its liquid form due to which ice can float on water.

Physical Properties

(*i*) It is colourless, odourless, tasteless liquid.

(*ii*) It is not a good conductor so it is made conductor by adding small amount of acid or alkali.

(*iii*) It is highly polar solvent with high dielectric constant.

(*iv*) It is regarded as a universal solvent because of its tendency to dissolve almost all the substances.

Chemical Properties

Some important chemical reactions are as follows :

(*i*) Water is amphoteric in nature.

$$\underset{\text{base}}{H_2O(l)} + \underset{\text{acid}}{HCl(aq)} \rightleftharpoons \underset{\text{acid}}{H_3O^+(aq)} + \underset{\text{base}}{Cl^-(aq)}$$

$$\underset{\text{acid}}{H_2O(l)} + \underset{\text{base}}{NH_3(aq)} \rightleftharpoons \underset{\text{acid}}{NH_4^+(aq)} + \underset{\text{base}}{OH^-(aq)}$$

Amphoteric nature of water is responsible for its **autoprotolysis**.

(*ii*) In redox reactions, water reacts with both metals and non-metals.

$$2Na(s) + 2H_2O(l) \longrightarrow 2NaOH(aq) + H_2(g)$$

$$2F_2(g) + 2H_2O(l) \longrightarrow 4H^+(aq) + 4F^-(aq) + O_2(g)$$

(*iii*) In **hydrated salts**, water may remain in five types such as coordinated water, hydrogen bonded water, lattice water, clathrate water and zeolite water.

(*iv*) A number of compounds such as calcium hydride, calcium phosphide, etc., undergo hydrolysis with water.

Soft and Hard Water

The water which produces large amount of lather with soap is known as **soft water** and which forms a scum with soap is called **hard water**.

Hardness of water may be of two types :

1. Temporary Hardness

It is due to the presence of calcium and magnesium bicarbonates. Temporary hardness of water can be removed by Clark's method (by treating hard water with lime) or by simply boiling which converts $Mg(HCO_3)_2$ into insoluble $Mg(OH)_2$ and $Ca(HCO_3)_2$ changed to insoluble $CaCO_3$.

2. Permanent Hardness

It is due to the presence of chlorides and sulphates of Ca and Mg. Permanent hardness of water can be removed (or softening of water is done) by treatment with washing soda, $Na_2CO_3 \cdot 10H_2O$ which converts Ca^{2+} and Mg^{2+} bicarbonates into insoluble carbonates or by Calgon's method (treatment with sodium hexametaphosphate, $Na_2[Na_4(PO_3)_6]$ that forms soluble complex).

Ion-exchange method is also employed in which $NaAlSiO_4$ (zeolite) is used which replaces Ca^{2+}/Mg^{2+} ions by Na^+ ion.

Degree of Hardness

Water is measured in ppm by weight of $CaCO_3$ irrespective of its presence and is estimated by simple titration of ethylene diamine tetraacetate (EDTA) solution. EDTA forms stable complexes with Ca^{2+}/Mg^{2+} ions.

Degree of hardness (in ppm)

$$= \frac{\text{Weight of } CaCO_3(g)}{\text{Weight of hard water } (g)} \times 10^6$$

Heavy Water (D_2O)

- It is an oxide of deuterium (heavy hydrogen).
- It is obtained by the multistage electrolysis of ordinary water.

Properties of Heavy Water (D_2O)

- It is colourless, odourless and tasteless liquid.
- It shows following reactions :

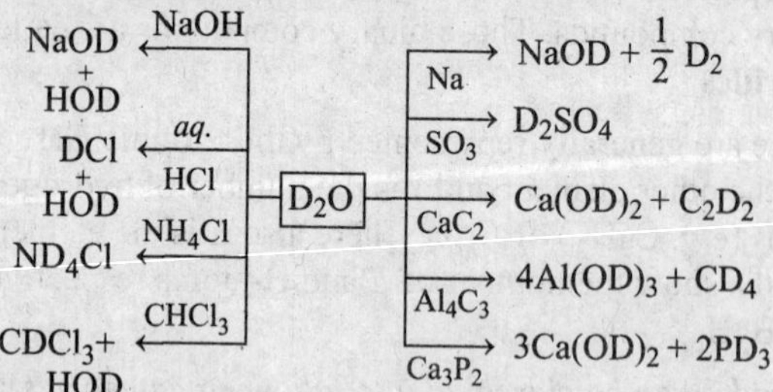

Uses of Heavy Water

- It is used as a moderator in nuclear reactor.
- D_2O is used as a tracer compound in studying reaction mechanism of chemical reactions involving hydrogen and its compounds etc.

Hydrogen Peroxide (H_2O_2)

- It is an important compound used in pollution control treatment of domestic and industrial effluents.
- In structure of H_2O_2, two O—H bonds are in different planes due to repulsion of bonding and anti-bonding orbitals.

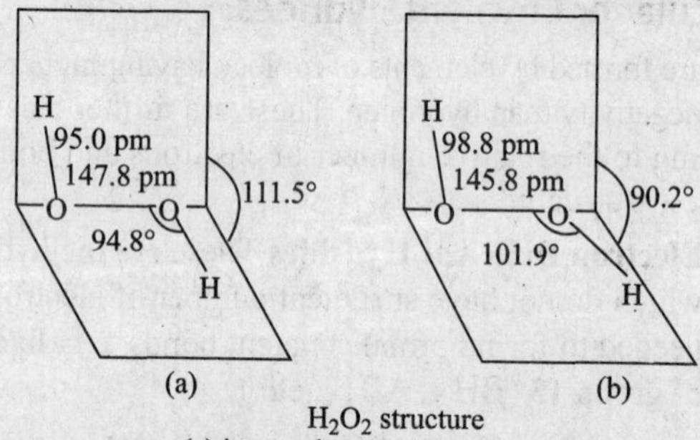

H_2O_2 structure
(a) in gas phase (b) in solid phase

Preparation of H_2O_2

- It is manufactured by the electrolysis of 50% H_2SO_4 using Pt as anode and graphite as cathode or by the auto-oxidation of 2-alkyl anthraquinols. In laboratory, H_2O_2 is prepared by **Merck's process.**

$$Na_2O_2 + H_2SO_4 \longrightarrow Na_2SO_4 + H_2O_2$$

- Hydrous BaO_2 can also be used in place of Na_2O_2. But anhydrous form cannot be used because $BaSO_4$ forms a protective layer around unreacted barium peroxide which slows down reaction.

Physical Properties

(*i*) In the pure state, H_2O_2 is almost colourless (very pale blue) liquid.

(*ii*) It is miscible with water in all proportions and forms a hydrate $H_2O_2 \cdot H_2O$.

Chemical Properties

Some important chemical reactions are as follows :

(*i*) **Acidic nature** It is weakly acidic in nature and pure hydrogen peroxide turns blue litmus red.

(*ii*) **Oxidising agent** It acts as a strong oxidising agent in acidic as well as in basic medium.

$$H_2O_2 + 2H^+ + 2e^- \longrightarrow 2\,H_2O$$
$$H_2O_2 + OH^- + 2e^- \longrightarrow 3\,OH^-$$

e.g. oxidising action of H_2O_2 is

$$2Cr^{3+} + 3H_2O_2 + 10OH^- \longrightarrow 2CrO_4^{2-} + 8H_2O$$
$$Mn^{2+} + H_2O_2 + 2\,OH^- \longrightarrow MnO_2 + 2H_2O$$

(*iii*) **Reducing agent**

(a) In acidic medium,

$$2MnO_4^- + 6H^+ + 5H_2O_2 \longrightarrow 2Mn^{2+} + 8H_2O + 5O_2$$
$$Cr_2O_7^{2-} + 8H^+ + 3H_2O_2 \longrightarrow 2Cr^{3+} + 7H_2O + 3O_2$$

(b) In basic medium,

$$2K_3[Fe(CN)_6] + 2KOH + H_2O_2 \longrightarrow 2K_4[Fe(CN)_6] + 2H_2O + O_2$$

(*iv*) **Bleaching properties** Its bleaching action is due to oxidation by atomic oxygen.

$$H_2O_2 \longrightarrow H_2O + [O]$$
$$\text{dye} + [O] \longrightarrow \text{dye is oxidised and bleached}$$

(*v*) **Addition reactions** H_2O_2 reacts with alkene to give respective glycols.

$$CH_2 = CH_2 + H_2O_2 \longrightarrow CH_2OH—CH_2OH$$

Uses of H_2O_2

- Hydrogen peroxide is used as an oxidant for rocket fuel and in the detection of Ti, V and Cr ions. H_2O_2 reduces ozone into oxygen.
- Blackened oil painting due to formation of PbS can be restored by H_2O_2 which converts it into white $PbSO_4$.

$$\underset{\text{(White)}}{PbO} + H_2S \longrightarrow \underset{\text{(Black)}}{PbS} + H_2O$$
$$PbS + 4H_2O_2 \longrightarrow \underset{\text{(White)}}{PbSO_4} + 4H_2O$$

- 30% H_2O_2 is called perhydroxy which is used as an antiseptic and germicide for washing wounds, teeth and ears.

Strength of H_2O_2

- It is expressed in terms of the volume (in mL) of oxygen liberated at NTP by decomposition of 1 mL of that sample of H_2O_2.
- 10 volume H_2O_2 means, 1 mL of this solution on decomposition liberates 10 mL of O_2 at NTP.
- % strength $= \frac{17}{56} \times$ volume strength
- Strength of H_2O_2 in terms of normality or molarity,

(*i*) $\frac{68 \times x}{22.4} = 17 \times N \Rightarrow x = 5.6 \times N$

(*ii*) $x = 11.2 \times$ molarity

where, x is volume strength, N is normality and M is molarity.

Hydrogen Economy

It is the use of liquid hydrogen as an alternate source of energy. Hydrogen fuel has many advantages over conventional fuels as it is non-polluting and liberates large amount of energy on combustion.

Topical Practice Questions

All the exam questions of this chapter have been divided into three topics as listed below

Topic 1

Preparation and Properties of Hydrogen

2018

1 **Assertion** (A) Among the two O—H bonds in H_2O molecule, the energy required to break the first O—H bond and the other O—H bond is same.
Reason (R) This is because the electronic environment around oxygen is the same even after breakage of one O—H bond. **[AIIMS]**
(a) Both A and R are correct and R is the correct explanation of A
(b) Both A and R are correct but R is not the correct explanation of A
(c) A is correct but R is incorrect
(d) Both A and R are incorrect

2016

2 Which of the following statements about hydrogen is incorrect? **[NEET]**
(a) Hydrogen never acts as cation in ionic salts
(b) Hydronium ion, H_3O^+ exists freely in solution
(c) Dihydrogen does not act as a reducing agent
(d) Hydrogen has three isotopes of which tritium is the most common

2013

3 Which of the following process is used for the manufacture of H_2? **[WB JEE]**
(a) Hoope's process (b) Le-Blanc process
(c) Lane's process (d) Carter's process

4 Smallest among these species is **[KCET]**
(a) lithium (b) lithium ion
(c) hydrogen (d) helium

2011

5 Hydrogen is prepared from H_2O by adding **[DUMET]**
(a) Ca, which acts as reducing agent
(b) Al, which acts as oxidising agent
(c) Ag, which acts as reducing agent
(d) Au, which acts as oxidising agent

2010

6 *Ortho* and *para* hydrogens have **[WB JEE]**
(a) identical chemical properties but different physical properties
(b) identical physical and chemical properties
(c) identical physical properties but different chemical properties
(d) different physical and chemical properties

7 Hydrogen sulphide is acidic while water is neutral. The reason is **[RPMT]**
(a) molecular weight of H_2S is more than H_2O
(b) water molecules associate, while H_2S molecules does not
(c) H—S bond is weaker than H—O bond due to the bigger size of S-atom
(d) S-atoms has less affinity for hydrogen atom than O-atom has for it

2009

8 Which one of the following statements is incorrect with regard to *ortho* and *para* dihydrogen? **[Kerala CEE]**
(a) They are nuclear spin isomers
(b) The *ortho* isomer has zero nuclear spin whereas the *para* isomer has one nuclear spin
(c) The *para* isomer is favoured at low temperatures
(d) The thermal conductivity of the *para* isomer is 50% greater than that of the *ortho* isomer
(e) It is never possible to obtain 100% pure *ortho* isomer

2007

9 Hydrogen can be prepared by the action of dil. H_2SO_4 on **[AIIMS]**
(a) copper (b) iron
(c) lead (d) mercury

10 Radioactive isotope of hydrogen is **[RPMT]**
(a) uranium (b) deuterium
(c) tritium (d) None of these

11 Which one of the following is correct order? **[MP PMT]**
I. $T_2 > D_2 > P_2$ (order of BP)
II. $T_2 > D_2 > P_2$ (order of BE)
III. $T_2 = D_2 = P_2$ (order of BL)
IV. $T_2 < D_2 < P_2$ (order of reactivity with Cl_2)
(a) I, II and III (b) I, II, III and IV
(c) I and II (d) II, III and IV

2006

12 How many neutrons are present in tritium nucleus? **[RPMT]**
(a) 2 (b) 3
(c) 1 (d) 0

Answers

1 (d)	2 (c, d)	3 (c)	4 (c)	5 (a)	6 (a)	7 (c)	8 (b)	9 (b)	10 (c)
11 (b)	12 (a)								

Explanations

1 (*d*) The bond enthalpies of the two O—H bonds in H—O—H are not equal. This is because electronic environment around O is not same after breakage of one O—H bond. Therefore, both Assertion and Reason are incorrect.

2 (*c, d*) Statements (c,d) are incorrect.

- Hydrogen has three isotopes which are protium (^1_1H), deuterium (^2_1H) and tritium (^3_1H). Protium is the most common isotopes of hydrogen with an abundance of 99.98%.
- Dihydrogen acts as a reducing agent.
- For ionic salts, hydrogen never behaves as cation, but behaves as anion (H^-).
- H_3O^+ exists freely in solution.

3 (c) Lane's process → Manufacture of H_2 (by passing steam over spongy iron at 773-1050 K)

$$3Fe + 4H_2O \longrightarrow Fe_3O_4 + 4H_2$$

Hoope's process → Purification of Al

Le-Blanc process → Manufacture of Na_2CO_3

Carter's process → Manufacture of basic lead carbonate

4 (*c*) The smallest species is hydrogen having atomic number 1. It is the lightest known element.

5 (*a*) H_2 can be prepared from H_2O by adding Ca.

$$\underset{\text{Reducing agent}}{Ca} + 2\overset{+1}{H_2}O \longrightarrow Ca(OH)_2 + \overset{0}{H_2} \quad \text{(Reduction)}$$

$$\underset{\text{Reducing agent}}{2Al} + 6\overset{+1}{H_2}O \longrightarrow 2Al(OH)_3 + 3\overset{0}{H_2}$$

6 (*a*) *Ortho* and *para* hydrogen, the allotropic forms of hydrogen differ in the direction of spinning of protons, have same chemical properties but different physical properties.

7 (*c*) Hydrogen sulphide is acidic because H—S bond is weaker than H—O bond due to bigger size of S-atom.

8 (*b*) On the basis of spinning of protons, hydrogen has two allotropes, called *ortho* hydrogen and *para* hydrogen. In *ortho* hydrogen, spins of proton are in same direction, so the nuclear spin $= \frac{1}{2} + \frac{1}{2} = 1$.

While in *para* hydrogen, spins of proton are in opposite direction, so the nuclear spin $= \frac{1}{2} + \left(-\frac{1}{2}\right) = 0$.

All other statements about *ortho* and *para* hydrogens are correct.

9 (*b*) Hydrogen cannot be prepared by action of dil. H_2SO_4 on copper or mercury as these two metals cannot displace hydrogen from acids. Action of dil. H_2SO_4 on Pb stops after some time due to the formation of insoluble $PbSO_4$. Only iron reacts rapidly with dil. H_2SO_4 to give H_2.

10 (*c*) Tritium (^3_1H) is the radioactive isotope of hydrogen.

It has $\frac{n}{p}$ ratio = 2.0, so it is unstable.

11 (*b*) Protium(P), deuterium (D) and tritium (T) are the three isotopes of hydrogen. These isotopes gives the following order in different contexts as shown below :

$T_2 > D_2 > P_2$ [order of boiling point (BP)]

$T_2 > D_2 > P_2$ [order of bond energy(BE)]

$T_2 = D_2 = P_2$ [order of bond length (BL)]

$T_2 < D_2 < P_2$ [order of reactivity with Cl_2]

12 (*a*) Tritium ($_1H^3$) is an isotope of hydrogen. Its composition is as follows:

$n = A - Z = 3 - 1 = 2$

Topic 2
Hydrides and Water

2012

1 When zeolite is treated with hard water, the sodium ions are exchanged with **[AMU]**

(a) H^+ ions
(b) H^+ and Ca^{2+} ions
(c) OH^- and Mg^{2+} ions
(d) Ca^{2+} and Mg^{2+} ions

2011

2 Permanent hardness of water is due to the presence of **[Kerala CEE]**

(a) bicarbonates of sodium and potassium
(b) chlorides and sulphates of sodium and potassium
(c) chlorides and sulphates of calcium and magnesium
(d) bicarbonates of calcium and magnesium
(e) phosphates of sodium and potassium

2010

3 The degree of hardness of water is usually expressed in terms of **[AMU]**

(a) ppm by weight of $MgSO_4$
(b) g/L of $CaCO_3$ and $MgCO_3$ present
(c) ppm by weight of $CaCO_3$ irrespective of whether it is actually present
(d) ppm of $CaCO_3$ actually present in water

2008

4 Which one of the following processes will produce hard water? **[RPMT]**

(a) Saturation of water with $CaCO_3$
(b) Saturation of water with $MgCO_3$
(c) Saturation of water with $CaSO_4$
(d) Addition of Na_2SO_4 to water

5 If 11.1 mg of $CaCl_2$ and 12 mg of $MgSO_4$ are present in 2 L of water, what is its hardness (in gram $CaCO_3$/ppm)? **[EAMCET]**

(a) 5 (b) 10
(c) 15 (d) 203

2007

6 The formula of calgon, used for water softening is **[EAMCET]**

(a) $Na_2[Na_4(PO_3)_6]$ (b) $Na_4[Na_2(PO_3)_6]$
(c) $Na_2[Na_4(PO_4)_5]$ (d) $Na_4[Na_4(PO_4)_6]$

2005

7 The hardness of water is estimated by **[AMU]**

(a) EDTA method
(b) titrimetric method
(c) conductivity method
(d) distillation method

8 Water is oxidised to oxygen by **[JCECE]**

(a) ClO_2 (b) $KMnO_4$
(c) H_2O_2 (d) fluorine

9 The reagent commonly used to determine hardness of water titrimetrically is **[AIIMS]**

(a) oxalic acid
(b) disodium salt of EDTA
(c) sodium citrate
(d) sodium thiosulphate

Answers

1 (d)	2 (c)	3 (c)	4 (c)	5 (b)	6 (a)	7 (a)	8 (d)	9 (b)

1 (*d*) When zeolite is treated with hard water, the sodium ions are exchanged with Ca^{2+} and Mg^{2+} ions.

$$\underset{\text{Zeolite}}{Na_2Z} + M^{2+} \longrightarrow 2Na^+ + MZ \quad (M = \text{Ca or Mg})$$

2 (*c*) Permanent hardness of water is due to chlorides and sulphates of calcium and magnesium. Hardness can be removed by adding Na_2CO_3 or by passing the water through an ion-exchange column.

3 (*c*) Degree of hardness of water is measured in terms of ppm by weight of $CaCO_3$ irrespective of whether it is actually present or not.

4 (*c*) Saturation of water with earth metal salts cause hardness of water. Temporary hardness is caused by soluble Ca and Mg hydrogen carbonates. Calcium and magnesium sulphates and chlorides cause permanent hardness.

5 (*b*)

$$\underset{\substack{40+35.5\times 2\\ =111\times 10^3\text{ mg}}}{CaCl_2} \equiv \underset{\substack{40+12+48\\ =100\times 10^3\text{ mg}}}{CaCO_3}$$

$$\underset{\substack{24+32+64\\ =120\times 10^3\text{ mg}}}{MgSO_4} \equiv \underset{\substack{40+12+48\\ =100\times 10^3\text{ mg}}}{CaCO_3}$$

111×10^3 mg of $CaCl_2 = 100\times 10^3$ mg of $CaCO_3$

$$11.1 \text{ mg of } CaCl_2 = \frac{100\times 10^3 \times 11.1}{111\times 10^3} \text{ mg of } CaCO_3$$

$$= 10 \text{ mg of } CaCO_3$$

Similarly, 120×10^3 mg of $MgSO_4 = 100\times 10^3$ mg of $CaCO_3$

$$12 \text{ mg of } MgSO_4 = \frac{100\times 10^3}{120\times 10^3}\times 12 \text{ mg of } CaCO_3$$

$$= 10 \text{ mg of } CaCO_3$$

In 2 L of water, total weight of $CaCO_3 = 10 + 10 = 20$ mg

$\therefore$ In 1 L of water, total weight of $CaCO_3 = \frac{20}{2}$ mg $= 10$ mg

$\therefore$ In 10^6 mg of water, total weight of $CaCO_3 = 10$ mg

So, in 10^6 part water, hardness of water in terms of $CaCO_3$ = 10 ppm

6 (*a*) Calgon is used for water softening. Its formula is $Na_2[Na_4(PO_3)_6]$. It removes dissolved minerals of water which reduces the cleaning efficiency of water.

7 (*a*) Ethylene diamine tetraacetate (EDTA) when treated with water forms stable complex with metal ions and hence, it is used to measure hardness of water.

8 (*d*) Fluorine being a good oxidising agent, oxidises H_2O to O_2.

$$2F_2 + 2H_2O \longrightarrow O_2 + 4HF$$

$\therefore$ Water is oxidised to O_2 by F_2.

9 (*b*) The hardness of water is estimated by simple titration of ethylene diamine tetraacetate (EDTA) solution, i.e. disodium salt of EDTA. EDTA forms stable complexes with metal ions present in the hard water. Since, stability constants of calcium and magnesium complexes of EDTA are different, even the selective estimation of these ions is possible.

Topic 3

Heavy Water and H_2O_2

2019

1 H_2O_2 is obtained by which of the following? **[AIIMS]**

(a) BaO_2 (b) MnO_2 (c) SeO_2 (d) TeO_2

2014

2 I. $H_2O_2 + O_3 \longrightarrow H_2O + 2O_2$

II. $H_2O_2 + Ag_2O \longrightarrow 2Ag + H_2O + O_2$

Role of hydrogen peroxide in the above reactions is respectively **[CBSE AIPMT]**

(a) oxidising in I and reducing in II

(b) reducing in I and oxidising in II

(c) reducing in I and II

(d) oxidising in I and II

3 The volume of oxygen evolved at STP by decomposition of 0.68 g '20 volume' hydrogen peroxide solution is

(a) 2.24 mL (b) 22.4 mL **[MHT CET]**

(c) 224 mL (d) 2240 mL

4 A commercial sample of H_2O_2 marked as 100 volume hydrogen peroxide, it means that **[Manipal]**

(a) 1 mL H_2O_2 will give 100 mL O_2 at STP

(b) 1 L of H_2O_2 will give 100 mL O_2 at STP

(c) 1 L of H_2O_2 will give 22.4 L O_2 at STP

(d) 1 mL of H_2O_2 will give 1 mole of O_2 at STP

5 Commercial sample of H_2O_2 is labelled as 10 V. Its % strength is nearly **[WB JEE]**

(a) 3 (b) 6 (c) 9 (d) 12

6 The hydrides of the first elements in groups 15-17 namely NH_3, H_2O and HF respectively show abnormally high values for melting and boiling points. This is due to

(a) small size of N, O and F **[WB JEE]**

(b) the ability to form extensive intermolecular H-bonding

(c) the ability to form extensive intramolecular H-bonding

(d) effective van der Waals' interaction

7 30 volume hydrogen peroxide means **[UK PMT]**

(a) 30% of H_2O_2 solution

(b) 30 cm^3 of the solution contains 1 g of H_2O_2

(c) 1 cm^3 of the solution liberates 30 cm^3 of O_2 at STP

(d) 30 cm^3 of the solution contains 1 mole of H_2O_2

8 In which of the following reactions, H_2O_2 acts as a reducing agent? **[EAMCET]**

(a) $HOCl + H_2O_2 \xrightarrow{H^+} H_3O^+ + Cl^- + O_2$

(b) $Mn^{2+} + H_2O_2 \xrightarrow{OH^-} Mn^{4+} + 2OH^-$

(c) $2Fe^{2+} + H_2O_2 \xrightarrow{OH^-} 2Fe^{3+} + 2OH^-$

(d) $PbS(s) + 4H_2O_2(aq) \xrightarrow{H^+} PbSO_4(s) + 4H_2O(l)$

2013

9 **Assertion** (A) Anhydrous BaO_2 (barium peroxide) is used for preparing H_2O_2.

Reason (R) Hydrated BaO_2 is not available. **[AIIMS]**

(a) Both A and R are correct and R is the correct explanation of A

(b) Both A and R are correct but R is not the correct explanation of A

(c) A is correct but R is incorrect

(d) Both A and R are incorrect

10 Strength of H_2O_2 is 15.18 gL^{-1}, then it is equal to **[KCET]**

(a) 1 volume (b) 10 volume

(c) 5 volume (d) 7 volume

11 The laboratory method for the preparation of H_2O_2 is by

(a) H_2SO_4 **[UP CPMT]**

(b) NH_4HSO_4

(c) $Na_2O_2 + H_2SO_4$

(d) All of the above

12 The moderator used in nuclear reactor is **[UP CPMT]**

(a) TEL (b) D_2O

(c) H_2O_2 (d) $R—O—R$

2012

13 **Assertion** (A) In alkaline medium, H_2O_2 reacts with potassium ferricyanide.

Reason (R) H_2O_2 is a strong reducing agent. **[AIIMS]**

(a) Both A and R are correct and R is the correct explanation of A

(b) Both A and R are correct but R is not the correct explanation of A

(c) A is correct but R is incorrect

(d) Both A and R are correct

14 The normality of 20 volume hydrogen peroxide solution is **[AMU]**

(a) 3.57 N (b) 0.68 N

(c) 5.60 N (d) 5.35 N

2010

15 Permanent hardness of water can be removed by adding

(a) Na_2CO_3 (b) K **[AFMC]**

(c) Ca (OCl)Cl (d) Cl_2

16 Semi-water gas is a mixture of **[UP CPMT]**

(a) $CO + H_2$ (b) $CO + N_2$

(c) $CO + H_2 + N_2$ (d) $H_2 + CH_4$

17 Which of the following is responsible for the permanent hardness of water? **[UP CPMT]**
(a) Calcium bicarbonate
(b) Sodium chloride
(c) Magnesium bicarbonate
(d) Calcium sulphate

18 What is the structure of H_2O_2? **[MP PMT]**

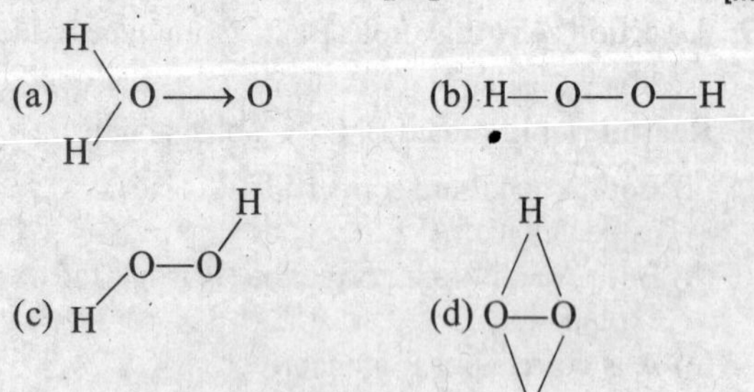

2009

19 Blackened oil painting can be restored into original form by the action of **[WB JEE]**
(a) chlorine (b) BaO_2
(c) H_2O_2 (d) MnO_2

20 Which one of the following is non-reducing? **[J&K CET]**
(a) H_2S (b) H_2Te
(c) H_2Se (d) H_2O

21 How many 'mL' of perhydrol is required to produce sufficient oxygen which can be used to completely convert 2 L of SO_2 gas? **[EAMCET]**
(a) 10 mL (b) 5 mL
(c) 20 mL (d) 30 mL

2008

22 Which of the following is correct regarding the electrolytic preparation of H_2O_2? **[AIIMS]**
(a) Lead is used as cathode
(b) 50% H_2SO_4 is used
(c) Hydrogen is liberated at anode
(d) Sulphuric acid undergoes oxidation

23 Which of the following is incorrect? **[BHU]**
(a) H_2O_2 is a weak acid
(b) H_2O_2 is a weak alkali
(c) H_2O_2 acts as an oxidising agent
(d) H_2O_2 is a reducing agent

24 Match the following Columns. **[UP CPMT]**

Column I	Column II
A. 10 vol H_2O_2	1. Perhydrol
B. 20 vol H_2O_2	2. 5.358 N
C. 30 vol H_2O_2	3. 1.785 M
D. 100 vol H_2O_2	4. 3.03%

The correct match is

	A	B	C	D
(a)	4	3	2	1
(b)	1	2	3	4
(c)	1	3	2	4
(d)	4	2	3	1

25 Which of the following statement is correct? Dielectric constant of H_2O_2 **[Manipal]**
(a) increases with dilution (b) decreases with dilution
(c) is unaffected on dilution (d) None of these

2007

26 Which cannot be oxidised by H_2O_2? **[BCECE]**
(a) Na_2SO_3 (b) PbS (c) KI (d) O_3

2005

27 When CO_2 is bubbled through a solution of barium peroxide in water **[AFMC]**
(a) O_2 is released (b) carbonic acid is formed
(c) H_2O_2 is formed (d) no reaction occurs

28 Hydrogen peroxide when added to a solution of potassium permanganate acidified with sulphuric acid **[JCECE]**
(a) forms water only
(b) acts as an oxidising agent
(c) acts as a reducing agent
(d) reduces sulphuric acid

Answers

1 (a)	2 (a)	3 (c)	4 (a)	5 (a)	6 (b)	7 (c)	8 (a)	9 (d)	10 (c)
11 (c)	12 (b)	13 (a)	14 (a)	15 (a)	16 (c)	17 (d)	18 (c)	19 (c)	20 (d)
21 (a)	22 (b)	23 (b)	24 (a)	25 (a)	26 (d)	27 (c)	28 (c)		

Explanations

1 (*a*) H_2O_2 can be obtained by $BaO_2.8H_2O$ as follows:

$$\underset{\text{Barium peroxide}}{BaO_2.8H_2O(s)} + H_2SO_4(aq) \longrightarrow BaSO_4(s) + \underset{\text{Hydrogen peroxide}}{H_2O_2(aq)} + 8H_2O(l)$$

Anhydrous barium oxide is not used here because the precipitate $BaSO_4$ forms a protective layer on the unreacted barium peroxide and this prevents its further participation in the reaction.

Hence, option (a) is the correct.

2 (*a*) In the reaction,

$$\overset{+1\ -1}{H_2O_2} + \overset{0,\ -2}{O_3} \longrightarrow \overset{+1\ -2}{H_2O} + \overset{0}{2O_2}$$

(Oxidation: $O_3 \rightarrow O_2$; Reduction: $H_2O_2 \rightarrow H_2O$)

Since, H_2O_2 oxidises O_3 into O_2, thus it behaves as an oxidising agent.

Further in the reaction,

$$\overset{+1\ -1}{H_2O_2} + \overset{+1\ -2}{Ag_2O} \longrightarrow \overset{0}{2Ag} + \overset{+1\ -2}{H_2O} + \overset{0}{O_2}$$

(Reduction: $Ag_2O \rightarrow Ag$; Oxidation: $H_2O_2 \rightarrow O_2$)

H_2O_2 reduces Ag_2O into metallic silver (Ag) (as oxidation number is reducing from +1 to 0). Thus, H_2O_2 behaves as a reducing agent.

3 (*c*)
$$\underset{\substack{2\text{ mol}\\ = 2\times 34\\ = 68\text{ g}}}{2H_2O_2} \longrightarrow 2H_2O + \underset{\substack{1\text{ mol}\\ 22400\text{ mL}}}{O_2}$$

$\therefore$ At STP, 68 g H_2O_2 produced $O_2 = 22400$ mL

$\therefore$ At STP, 0.68 g H_2O_2 will produce

$$O_2 = \frac{22400 \times 0.68}{68} = 224\text{ mL}$$

4 (*a*) 100 volume hydrogen peroxide means 1 L of this solution produces 100 L O_2 at STP or 1 mL of this solution produces 100 mL O_2 at STP.

5 (*a*) '10 V H_2O_2' means 1 L of this solution will produce 10 L O_2 at STP.

$$\underset{68\text{ g}}{2H_2O_2} \longrightarrow 2H_2O + \underset{22.4\text{ L at STP}}{O_2}$$

$\because$ 22.4 L of O_2 is obtained from 68 g H_2O_2.

$\therefore$ 10 L of O_2 will be obtained from

$$H_2O_2 = \frac{68}{22.4} \times 10 = 30.36\text{ g}$$

$\therefore$ 1000 mL of the given solution contains 30.36 g H_2O_2 and 100 mL of the given solution contains

$$\frac{30.36 \times 100}{1000} = 3.03\text{ g } H_2O_2$$

Thus, % strength of H_2O_2 is 3.03 ($\approx$ 3).

6 (*b*) Hydrides of N, O and F because of the small size and high electronegativity of elements, have ability to form extensive intermolecular, (i.e. between two molecules) hydrogen bonding. Thus, a large amount of energy is required to break these bonds, i.e. the melting and boiling points of hydrides of these elements are abnormally high.

7 (*c*) 30 volume hydrogen peroxide means 1 cm^3 of this solution produces 30 cm^3 O_2 at STP.

8 (*a*) Due to electron donating property of H_2O_2, it acts as a reducing agent in acidic as well as in alkaline medium and gets oxidised to O_2.

$$HOCl + H_2O_2 \xrightarrow{H^+} H_3O^+ + Cl^- + O_2$$

On the other hand, its reaction with Mn^{2+}, Fe^{2+} and PbS, show its oxidising property in which it reduces to H_2O.

9 (*d*) H_2O_2 is prepared by the action of dil. H_2SO_4 with hydrated barium peroxide ($BaO_2 \cdot 8H_2O$). Anhydrous BaO_2 is not used because its reaction is slow and ceases after sometime due to formation of protective layer of precipitated $BaSO_4$ on it, which in case of solution of $BaO_2 \cdot 8H_2O$ is filtered off frequently.

10 (*c*) Volume strength

$$= \frac{5.6 \times \text{strength in gL}^{-1}}{\text{Eq. wt of } H_2O_2}$$

$$= \frac{5.6 \times 15.18}{17} = 5\text{ volume}$$

11 (*c*) In laboratory, H_2O_2 is prepared by Merck's process. In this reaction, Na_2O_2 and H_2SO_4 are used as reactant. It is shown as below:

$$\underset{\text{Sodium peroxide}}{Na_2O_2} + H_2SO_4 \longrightarrow Na_2SO_4 + \underset{\text{Hydrogen peroxide}}{H_2O_2}$$

12 (*b*) D_2O is used as moderator in nuclear reactor.

Uses of other given options are as follows :

(a) TEL (tetraethyl lead) is used as antiknock agent in petrol engine.

(c) H_2O_2 is used for bleaching delicate articles like wood chair. It is also used as an antiseptic and germicide.

(d) R—O—R (ether) is used as a solvent.

13 (*a*) R is the correct explanation of A. H_2O_2 reduces potassium ferricyanide to potassium ferrocyanide in alkaline medium.

14 (*a*) Volume strength = 5.6 × normality

$$\text{Normality} = \frac{20}{5.6} = 3.57\text{ N}$$

15 (*a*) Washing soda, ($Na_2CO_3 \cdot 10H_2O$) is used to remove permanent hardness of water. It converts Ca^{2+} and Mg^{2+} salts (soluble) to carbonates (insoluble).

$$MgCl_2 + Na_2CO_3 \longrightarrow MgCO_3 \downarrow + 2NaCl$$

$$CaSO_4 + Na_2CO_3 \longrightarrow CaCO_3 \downarrow + Na_2SO_4$$

16 (*c*) Semi-water gas is a mixture of water gas ($CO + H_2$) and producer gas ($CO + N_2$). Its approximate composition is

$$CO = 25.28\%;\ N_2 = 50.55\%;\ H_2 = 10\text{-}12\%;\ CO = 4\text{-}5\%.$$

17 (*d*) Chlorides and sulphates of calcium and magnesium are responsible for the permanent hardness of water.

18 (*c*) In the structure of H_2O_2, the two O—H bonds are in different planes due to the repulsion between different bonding and anti-bonding orbitals.

19 (*c*) For refreshing old oil paintings which becomes black due to the formation of black PbS, H_2O_2 converts it into white $PbSO_4$.

20 (*d*) All hydrides (except of H_2O) act as reducing agents. The reducing nature increases as the atomic number of the central atom increases.

This is due to weakening of M—H bonds as the bond length increases with increase in size of M atom.

21 (*a*) Perhydrol means 30% solution of H_2O_2.

H_2O_2 decomposes as

$$2H_2O_2 \longrightarrow 2H_2O + O_2$$

Volume strength of 30% H_2O_2 solution is 100 that means 1 mL of this solution on decomposition gives 100 mL oxygen.

$$\begin{array}{ccc} SO_2 + \frac{1}{2}O_2 & \longrightarrow & SO_3 \\ 1\text{ L} \quad 1/2\text{ L} & & 1\text{ L} \\ 2\text{ L} \quad 1\text{ L} & & 2\text{ L} \end{array}$$

Since, 100 mL of oxygen is obtained by = 1 mL of H_2O_2.

$\therefore$ 1000 mL of oxygen will be obtained by

$$= \frac{1}{100} \times 1000 \text{ mL of } H_2O_2$$

$$= 10 \text{ mL of } H_2O_2$$

22 (*b*) H_2O_2 can be prepared by electrolysis of 50% H_2SO_4. In this method, hydrogen is liberated at cathode.

$$H_2SO_4 \rightleftharpoons 2H^+ + 2HSO_4^-$$

At anode $2HSO_4^- \longrightarrow H_2S_2O_8 + 2e^-$

$$H_2S_2O_8 + 2H_2O \longrightarrow 2H_2SO_4 + H_2O_2$$

At cathode $2H^+ + 2e^- \longrightarrow H_2 \uparrow$

23 (*b*) Statement (b) is incorrect while all other statements are correct.

- Hydrogen peroxide is weakly acidic.
- It forms two series of salt,

$$H_2O_2 \rightleftharpoons H^+ + HO_2^- \text{ (hydroperoxide ion)}$$

$$H_2O_2 \rightleftharpoons 2H^+ + O_2^{2-} \text{ (peroxide ion)}$$

H_2O_2 behaves as oxidising as well as reducing agent in acidic and alkaline medium.

As oxidising agent,

in acidic medium,

$$H_2O_2 + 2H^+ + 2e^- \longrightarrow 2H_2O$$

in alkaline medium,

$$H_2O_2 + OH^- + 2e^- \longrightarrow 3OH^-$$

As reducing agent,

in acidic medium,

$$H_2O_2 \longrightarrow 2H^+ + O_2 + 2e^-$$

in alkaline medium,

$$H_2O_2 + 2OH^- \longrightarrow 2H_2O + O_2 + 2e^-$$

24 (*a*) (a) % strength $= \frac{17}{56} \times$ volume strength

$$= \frac{17}{56} \times 10 = 3.03$$

(b) Volume strength = 11.2 × molarity

$$\text{Molarity} = \frac{20}{11.2} = 1.785$$

(c) Volume strength = 5.6 × normality

$$\text{Normality} = \frac{30}{5.6} = 5.358$$

(d) % strength $= \frac{17 \times 100}{56} = 30.3$

30.0% H_2O_2 is called perhydrol which is used as an antiseptic.

25 (*a*) Dielectric constant of H_2O_2 increases with dilution. It is 93.7 for pure H_2O_2, 97.3 for 90% H_2O_2 and 120 for 65% H_2O_2.

26 (*d*) O_3 cannot be oxidised by H_2O_2 but it is reduced to O_2 by H_2O_2.

$$H_2O_2 + O_3 \longrightarrow H_2O + 2O_2$$

- Na_2SO_3 is oxidised by H_2O_2 to Na_2SO_4.
- PbS is oxidised by H_2O_2 to $PbSO_4$. KI is oxidised by H_2O_2 to I_2.

27 (*c*) This is Merck's process of preparing hydrogen peroxide. When CO_2 is passed through an aqueous solution of BaO_2, $BaCO_3$ is precipitated and H_2O_2 is formed.

$$BaO_2 + CO_2 + H_2O \longrightarrow BaCO_3 \downarrow + H_2O_2$$

H_2O_2 can also be prepared by reaction of H_2SO_4 with hydrated barium peroxide.

$$BaO_2 \cdot 8H_2O + H_2SO_4 \longrightarrow BaSO_4 + 8H_2O + H_2O_2$$

28 (*c*) $2K\overset{+7}{Mn}O_4 + 3H_2SO_4 + 5H_2O_2 \rightarrow$

$$K_2SO_4 + 2\overset{+2}{Mn}SO_4 + 8H_2O + 5O_2$$

$\therefore$ H_2O_2 is acting as a reducing agent. It reduces $KMnO_4$ to Mn^{2+} ion.

10

s-Block Elements

Quick Review

- In *s*-block elements, the last electron enters in the *s*-orbital.
- As the *s*-orbital can accommodate only two electrons, two groups (1 and 2) belong to the *s*-block.
- The general electronic configuration of *s*-block elements is ns^1 or ns^2.
- *s*-block elements (group I and II) are found only in combined state in nature and never found in their free states.

Alkali Metals or Group I Elements

- Li, Na, K, Rb, Cs and Fr belong to alkali metals.
- These are collectively called alkali metals because their oxides and hydroxides form strong alkalies like NaOH, KOH etc.

Physical Properties

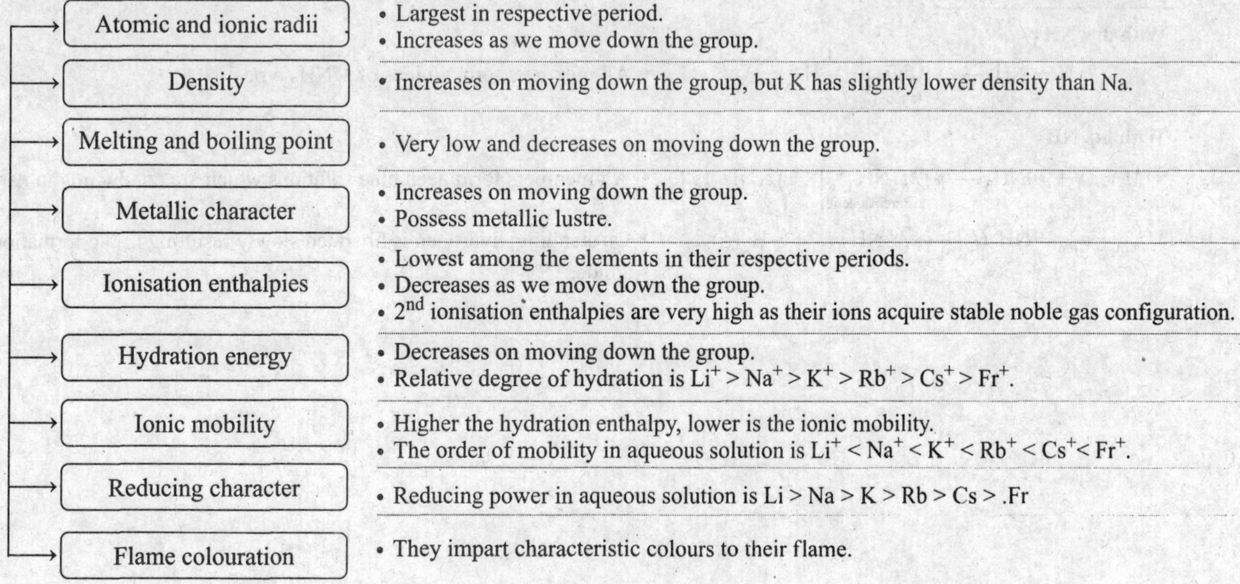

Atomic and ionic radii	• Largest in respective period. • Increases as we move down the group.
Density	• Increases on moving down the group, but K has slightly lower density than Na.
Melting and boiling point	• Very low and decreases on moving down the group.
Metallic character	• Increases on moving down the group. • Possess metallic lustre.
Ionisation enthalpies	• Lowest among the elements in their respective periods. • Decreases as we move down the group. • 2nd ionisation enthalpies are very high as their ions acquire stable noble gas configuration.
Hydration energy	• Decreases on moving down the group. • Relative degree of hydration is $Li^+ > Na^+ > K^+ > Rb^+ > Cs^+ > Fr^+$.
Ionic mobility	• Higher the hydration enthalpy, lower is the ionic mobility. • The order of mobility in aqueous solution is $Li^+ < Na^+ < K^+ < Rb^+ < Cs^+ < Fr^+$.
Reducing character	• Reducing power in aqueous solution is Li > Na > K > Rb > Cs > .Fr
Flame colouration	• They impart characteristic colours to their flame.

Chemical Properties

Reaction with water

$2M + 2H_2O \longrightarrow 2MOH + H_2$

- Hydroxides are strongest of all bases.
- Hydroxides dissolve in water with the evolution of heat on account of hydration.

Reaction with oxygen

$4Li + O_2 \longrightarrow 2Li_2O$ (oxide)

$2Na + O_2 \longrightarrow Na_2O_2$ (peroxide)

$M + O_2 \longrightarrow MO_2$ (superoxide) (M = K, Rb, Cs)

- Basic nature of oxides increases from Li to Cs due to increase in size of cation and increase in metallic character down the group from Li to Cs.
- Solubility in water increases from Li to Cs oxides, due to increase in ionic character of these metal oxides.
- Super oxides are ionic oxides $H^+O_2^-$, stability of super oxides follows the order,

$$KO_2 < RbO_2 < CsO_2$$

Reaction with hydrogen

$2M + H_2 \longrightarrow 2MH$

- Ionic salt like hydrides with high melting points.

Reaction with halogen

$2M + X_2 \longrightarrow 2MX$

- All metals form halides of type M^+X^-.
- Halides formed are highly stable due to high negative standard enthalpies of formation.
- For fluorides, the order of stability is LiF > NaF > KF > RbF > CsF.
- For other halides, the order of stability is $LiX < NaX < KX > RbX < CsX$.

Reaction with carbon dioxide

- No direct reaction
- Metal salt on reaction with NH_4HCO_3 forms respective bicarbonates

$NH_4HCO_3 + MCl \longrightarrow NH_4Cl + MHCO_3$

- The thermal stability of carbonates increases on moving down the group as,

$$Li_2CO_3 < Na_2CO_3 < K_2CO_3 < Rb_2CO_3 < Cs_2CO_3$$

- The solubility of the carbonates and bicarbonates increases on moving down the group due to decrease in lattice enthalpies. Thus, the order of solubility is,

$$LiHCO_3 < NaHCO_3 < KHCO_3 < RbHCO_3 < CsHCO_3$$

- A mixture of Na_2CO_3 and K_2CO_3 is known as **fusion mixture**. K_2CO_3 is known as **pearl ash**.
- Bicarbonates, except $LiHCO_3$ on heating form carbonates.

$$2MHCO_3 \longrightarrow M_2CO_3 + CO_2 + H_2O$$

Reaction with ammonia

With dry NH_3

$$\underset{(dry)}{M + NH_3} \longrightarrow \underset{(amide)}{MNH_2} + \frac{1}{2}H_2$$

- All members form amides of MNH_2 type.

With liq. NH_3

$$M + (x+y)NH_3 \longrightarrow \underset{(Paramagnetic)}{[M(NH_3)_x]^+ + [e(NH_3)_y]^-}$$

- All members form deep blue solutions which are conducting in nature.

$$M^+_{(am)} + e^-_{(am)} + NH_3(l) \longrightarrow MNH_{2(am)} + \frac{1}{2}H_2(g)$$

- On standing, hydrogen is liberated slowly resulting in the formation of amide.

Comparison of Important Compounds of Sodium

Compound	Sodium carbonate or washing soda ($Na_2CO_3.10H_2O$)	Sodium chloride or common salt or table salt or rock salt (NaCl)	Sodium hydroxide or caustic soda (NaOH)	Sodium hydrogen carbonate or baking soda ($NaHCO_3$)
Preparation	It is manufactured by Solvay process also called ammonia soda process. Sodium bicarbonate being sparingly soluble, crystallises out. This is finally calcined to form sodium carbonate. **Reactions involved** • $2NH_3 + H_2O + CO_2 \longrightarrow (NH_4)_2CO_3$ • $(NH_4)_2CO_3 + H_2O + CO_2 \longrightarrow 2NH_4HCO_3$ • $NH_4HCO_3 + NaCl \longrightarrow NH_4Cl + NaHCO_3\downarrow$ • $2NaHCO_3 \longrightarrow Na_2CO_3 + CO_2\uparrow + H_2O$	Salty water on evaporation in open air in fields leaves behind residue of impure sodium chloride as deposits. • Purification is based on fractional crystallisation and done by using difference in solubilities. • Through saturated solution of impure NaCl, HCl gas is passed, where NaCl is precipitated first, owing to least K_{sp}. • Due to high K_{sp}, impurities remain in solution. The crystals are filtered, washed and dried. **Reactions involved** • $NaCl\ (s) \xrightleftharpoons{water} Na^+\ (aq.) + Cl^-\ (aq.)$ • $HCl\ (s) \xrightleftharpoons{water} H^+\ (aq.) + Cl^-\ (aq.)$ Thus, $[Na^+][Cl^-] > K_{sp}$	Electrolysis of sodium chloride in Castner-Kellner cell; brine solution using a mercury cathode and carbon anode. • At cathode : $Na^+ + e^- \xrightarrow{Hg} Na^-$(amalgam) • At anode : $Cl^- \longrightarrow \frac{1}{2}Cl_2 + e^-$ • Amalgam is treated with water to give NaOH and H_2. • 2 Na-amalgam $+ 2H_2O \longrightarrow 2NaOH + 2Hg + H_2$	• Obtained as an intermediate compound in the manufacture of sodium carbonate by Solvay process. $NaCl + NH_3 + CO_2 + H_2O \longrightarrow NaHCO_3 + NH_4Cl$ • Also prepared by saturating solution of Na_2CO_3 (cold) with CO_2. $Na_2CO_3 + H_2O + CO_2 \longrightarrow 2NaHCO_3$
Physical Properties	• White crystalline solid. • Readily dissolves in water. • Solubility decreases with increase in temperature.	• White crystalline ionic solid (melting point 1073 K). • Soluble in water (solubility 36% at 293 K) with absorption of heat. • Aqueous solution of NaCl is neutral.	• Deliquescent, white crystalline solid. • Dissolves readily in water to yield highly alkaline solution which is corrosive, soapy to touch and bitter in taste.	• White crystalline powder • Less soluble than sodium carbonate.
Chemical Properties	$Na_2CO_3.10H_2O \xrightarrow{CO_2} 2NaHCO_3$ $Na_2CO_3.10H_2O \xrightarrow{SiO_2} Na_2SiO_3 + CO_2\uparrow$ $Na_2CO_3.10H_2O \xrightarrow{Ca(OH)_2} CaCO_3 + 2NaOH$ $Na_2CO_3.10H_2O \xrightarrow{\Delta} NaCO_2 + 10H_2O$ $Na_2CO_3.10H_2O \xrightarrow{H_2O} 2NaOH + H_2CO_3$ $Na_2CO_3.10H_2O \xrightarrow{HCl} NaCl + H_2O + CO_2$ $Na_2CO_3.10H_2O \xrightarrow{SO_2} Na_2SO_3 + CO_2$ $Na_2CO_3.10H_2O \xrightarrow{H_2O,\ S} Na_2S_2O_3$	$NaCl \xrightarrow{\text{Electrolysis of aqueous solution}} NaOH + Cl_2 + H_2$ $NaCl \xrightarrow{\text{Electrolysis of fused NaCl containing } CaCl_2 \text{ and KF}} Na$ $NaCl \xrightarrow{H_2SO_4 \text{ Le-Blanc process}} Na_2SO_4 + HCl$; $Na_2SO_4 \xrightarrow{C} Na_2S \xrightarrow{CaCO_3} Na_2CO_3$ $NaCl \xrightarrow{NH_3 + CO_2 \text{ (Solvay process)}} NaHCO_3$	$NaOH \xrightarrow{ZnSO_4} Zn(OH)_2 \xrightarrow{NaOH} Na_2ZnO_2$ $NaOH \xrightarrow{Sn} Na_2SnO_2$ $NaOH \xrightarrow{Al_2O_3 \text{ or } Al(OH)_3} NaAlO_2$ $NaOH \xrightarrow{SiO_2} Na_2SiO_3$ $NaOH \xrightarrow{Zn \text{ or } ZnO_2} Na_2ZnO_2$ $NaOH \xrightarrow{NH_4Cl} NH_3 + NaCl + H_2O$ $NaOH \xrightarrow{X_2 \text{(hot or cold)}} NaX + NaXO_3 + H_2O$ $NaOH \xrightarrow{M=B,\ Al} NaMO_2$ $NaOH \xrightarrow{P_4} NaH_2PO_2 + PH_3$ $NaOH \xrightarrow{S,\ \Delta} Na_2S_2O_3$ $NaOH \xrightarrow{SO_2} Na_2SO_3$ $NaOH \xrightarrow{CO} HCOONa$ $NaOH \xrightarrow{CO_2} Na_2CO_3$ $NaOH \xrightarrow{FeCl_3} Fe(OH)_3 + NaCl$	• On heating decomposes to produce bubbles of CO_2 which make the cakes and pastries fluffy. $2NaHCO_3 \xrightarrow[100°C]{\Delta} Na_2CO_3 + H_2O + CO_2$ • It is amphiprotic i.e. it can donate and accept H^+ as Shown below. $HCO_3^- + H^+ \rightleftharpoons H_2CO_3$; $HCO_3^- \rightleftharpoons H^+ + CO_3^{2-}$
Uses	• In water softening, laundering and cleaning. • In paper, paints and textile industries. • In the manufacture of glass, soap, borax and caustic soda. • As laboratory reagent both in qualitative and quantitative analysis. • Soda ash (Na_2CO_3) is used in petroleum refinery and textile industry.	• An essential constituent of food (common salt or table salt) and a preservative of food articles like meat, fish etc. • Used to prepare sodium compounds, Na_2O_2, NaOH, Na_2CO_3. • To clear blocked drain pipes. • In 'salting out' of soap, and in making freezing mixtures.	• In the manufacture of soap, paper, artificial silk, pure fats, oils and a number of chemicals. • In petroleum refining and textile industries for mercerising cotton fabrics. • In the purification of bauxite. • As a laboratory reagent.	• In pharmaceutical products including antacid. • As a mild antiseptic for skin infections. • In fire extinguishers.

Anomalous Behaviour of Lithium

Due to smallest size of lithium it shows very high ionisation enthalpy and highest electronegativity in the group. It also shows following properties which differ it from other alkali metals.

- It is harder than other alkali metals due to strong metallic bond.
- Unlike other alkali metals, it reacts with nitrogen to form nitride.
- Li_2CO_3, LiF, $LiSO_4$ and Li_3PO_4 are insoluble in water while the corresponding salts of other alkali metals are soluble in water.
- Its melting and boiling points are higher than that of other alkali metals.
- It is least reactive but strongest reducing agent among all alkali metals.
- LiCl is deliquescent and crystallises as $LiCl \cdot 2H_2O$ whereas, other alkali metal chlorides do not form hydrates.
- Li unlike other alkali metals does not form ethynide on reaction with ethyne.
- $LiNO_3$ on heating gives Li_2O while other alkali metal nitrates give nitrites.
- Bicarbonates and carbonates of Li are unstable towards heat and decomposes to give Li_2O.

Diagonal Relationship between Li and Mg

- Li and Mg show diagonal resemblance with each other and this is due to similar polarising power of both these elements.
- Due to diagonal relationship, Li and Mg have similar atomic and ionic radii, electronegativities.

Uses of Alkali Metals

- Lithium metal is used to make useful alloys and it is also used in thermonuclear reactions.
- Na is used to make a Na/Pb alloy needed to make $PbEt_4$ and $PbMe_4$.

Biological Importance of Na and K

Sodium and potassium ions are responsible for transmission of nerve signals and their ionic gradient are maintained by sodium potassium pumps that operate across the cell membranes.

Alkaline Earth Metals or Group II Elements

- Be, Mg, Ca, Sr, Ba and Ra belong to group II or alkaline earth metals.
- These are commonly called alkaline earth metals because their oxides are alkaline in nature and are found in earth's crust.

Physical Properties

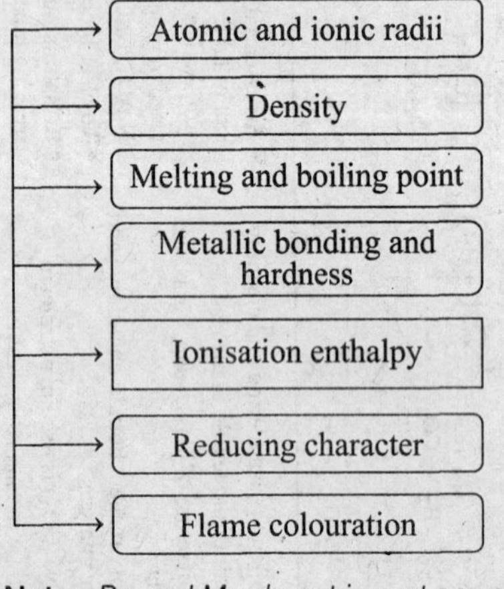

Atomic and ionic radii	• Quite large but smaller than those of corresponding alkali metals.
Density	• Do not show any regular trend but in general these are more dense than alkali metals.
Melting and boiling point	• Not regular in the group. • Higher than those of alkali metals.
Metallic bonding and hardness	• Harder than alkali metals. • Inspite of hardness these can be cut by a sharp knife.
Ionisation enthalpy	• 1st ionisation enthalpy is higher than those of corresponding alkali metals. • 2nd ionisation enthalpy values are higher than their 1st ionisation enthalpy but lower than 2nd ionisation enthalpy values of alkali metals.
Reducing character	• Good reducing agents but less stronger as compared to alkali metals.
Flame colouration	• They impart characteristic colours to the flame. • Ca–brick red, Sr–crimson red, Ba–apple green, Ra–crimson red.

Note *Be and Mg do not impart any characteristic colour to the flame because of their high ionisation enthalpy.*

Chemical Properties

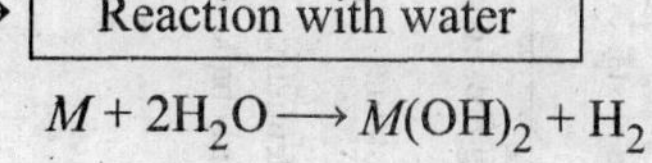

Reaction with water

$M + 2H_2O \longrightarrow M(OH)_2 + H_2$

- Order of reactivity with water is as follows:
  $Be < Mg < Ca < Sr < Ba$
  (Be: No reaction; Mg: Hot water; Ca, Sr, Ba: Cold water)
- From $Mg(OH)_2$ to $Ba(OH)_2$, the solubility, thermal stability and basic character of hydroxides increases with increasing atomic number.
- Hydroxides are less basic and less stable than alkali metal hydroxides.

Reaction with oxygen

with limited amount of O_2

$2M + O_2 \xrightarrow{\Delta} 2MO$

with excess oxygen

$M + O_2 \longrightarrow MO_2$

- Monoxide formed by B, Mg, Ca
- Peroxide formed by Ba, Sr.
- Except BeO, all oxides are basic in nature and basic character decreases from Be to Ba.
- Except Be and Mg, all other oxides are soluble in water.
- Because of high enthalpies of formation, these oxides are very stable towards heat.

Reaction with halogen

$M + X_2 \xrightarrow{\Delta} MX_2$

- All alkaline earth metal halides (except BeX_2) are ionic in nature and ionic character increases from Mg to Ba.
- The tendency to form halide hydrates gradually decreases down the group.

Reaction with hydrogen

$M + H_2 \xrightarrow{\Delta} MH_2$

- All alkaline earth elements form hydrides directly on reaction with H_2 (except Be).
- Order of stability of hydrides is
  $BeH_2 > MgH_2 > CaH_2 > SrH_2 > BaH_2$.

Reaction with liq. NH_3

$M + (x+y)NH_3 \longrightarrow [M(NH_3)_x]^{2+} + 2[e(NH_3)_y]^-$

- BeH_2 and MgH_2 are covalent in nature and exist in polymeric form.
- Alkaline earth metals give deep blue black solutions forming ammoniated ions.

Reaction with acids

$M + 2HCl \xrightarrow{\Delta} MCl_2 + H_2$

- All members react with acids and liberate hydrogen gas.

Comparison of Important Compounds of Calcium

Compounds	**Calcium oxide** or **quick lime or burnt** lime (CaO)	**Calcium hydroxide** or **slaked lime** ($Ca(OH)_2$)	**Calcium carbonate** ($CaCO_3$)	**Plaster of Paris** or **hemihydrate of calcium sulphate** $\left(CaSO_4 \cdot \frac{1}{2} H_2O\right)$
Preparation	• By heating limestone to 1000°C in rotary kiln. $CaCO_3 \underset{}{\overset{1070-1270K}{\rightleftharpoons}} CaO + CO_2$ • Also prepared by heating $Ca(OH)_2$ at high temperature and by heating $CaSO_4$. $Ca(OH)_2 \xrightarrow[\Delta]{1000°C} CaO + H_2O$ $2CaSO_4 \xrightarrow{\Delta} 2CaO(s) + 2SO_2 + O_2$	• By adding water to quick lime $\underset{\text{Quick lime}}{CaO} + H_2O \longrightarrow Ca(OH)_2$ • By adding $CaCl_2$ and NaOH $CaCl_2 + 2NaOH \longrightarrow Ca(OH)_2 + 2NaCl$	• By passing CO_2 through slaked lime. $Ca(OH)_2 + CO_2 \longrightarrow CaCO_3 + H_2O$ • By adding aqueous solution of Na_2CO_3 in $CaCl_2$ solution. $CaCl_2 + Na_2CO_3 \longrightarrow CaCO_3 + 2NaCl$	• It can be prepared by heating gypsum at 150–160°C. $\underset{\text{Gypsum}}{2(CaSO_4.2H_2O)} \xrightarrow{150-160°C} \underset{\text{Plaster of Paris}}{(CaSO_4)_2 . H_2O + 3H_2O}$
Physical Properties	• White amorphous solid having melting point 2870 K. • Basic in nature.	• White amorphous powder. • Sparingly soluble in water. • Aqueous solution is known as lime water • Suspension of slaked lime in water is known as milk of lime.	• $CaCO_3$ is a white fluffy powder. • Insoluble in water. • Dimorphous solid i.e., found in two crystalline forms, calcite and aragonite.	• It is a white powder. • It has a remarkable property of setting with water. • On mixing with an adequate quantity of water it forms a plastic mass that gets into a hard solid in 5-15 min.
Chemical Properties	$CaO \xrightarrow{H_2O} Ca(OH)_2$ $CaO \xrightarrow{CO_2} CaCO_3$ $CaO \xrightarrow{SiO_2} CaSiO_3$ $CaO \xrightarrow{P_4O_{10}} Ca_3(PO_4)_2$	$Ca(OH)_2 \xrightarrow{Cl_2 \text{ Below } 35°C} CaCl_2.Ca(OH)_2.H_2O + Ca(OCl)_2 + 2H_2O$ $Ca(OH)_2 \xrightarrow{\text{Red heat}} CaCl_2 + 2H_2O + O_2$ $Ca(OH)_2 \xrightarrow{Cl_2} CaCl_2 + Ca(OCl)_2 + H_2O$ $Ca(OH)_2 \xrightarrow{Cl_2 \text{ Cold}} $ … $Ca(OH)_2 \xrightarrow{Cl_2, \text{ heat}} CaCl_2 + Ca(ClO_3)_2 + H_2O$ $Ca(OH)_2 \xrightarrow[\Delta]{NH_4Cl} CaCl_2 + NH_3 + H_2O$ $Ca(OH)_2 \xrightarrow{H_2O + CO_2} Ca(HCO_3)_2$ $Ca(OH)_2 \xrightarrow{SO_2} CaSO_3$ $Ca(OH)_2 \xrightarrow{CO_2} CaCO_3$	$CaCO_3 \xrightarrow{1200K} CaO + CO_2$ $CaCO_3 \xrightarrow{2HCl} CaCl_2 + H_2O + CO_2$ $CaCO_3 \xrightarrow{H_2SO_4} CaSO_4 + H_2O + CO_2$	$\underset{\text{Orthorhombic}}{2CaSO_4 \cdot 2H_2O} \xrightarrow{\text{Hardening}} \underset{\text{Monoclinic}}{CaSO_4 \cdot 2H_2O}$ $2(CaSO_4).H_2O \xrightarrow[H_2O]{\text{Setting}} 2CaSO_4 \cdot 2H_2O$ $2(CaSO_4).H_2O \xrightarrow[\Delta]{200°C} \underset{\text{Dead plaster}}{CaSO_4 \cdot (\text{anhy.})}$
Use	• For manufacturing cement. • In the manufacture of sodium carbonate from caustic soda. • In the purification of sugar.In the manufacture of dye stuffs.	• In water softening. • In preparation of washing soda. • In the preparation of mortar, a building material. • In white wash due to disinfectant nature. • For purification of sugar. • In glass making. • In the preparation of bleakhing powder.	• As a building material in the form of marble. • Raw material in Solvay process. • Used as a flux along with magnesium carbonate in the extraction of metals such as iron. • Specially precipitated $CaCO_3$ is extensively used in the manufacture of high quality paper. • As an antacid, mild abrasive in tooth paste, a constituent of chewing gum, and a filler in cosmetics.	• In surgery for setting broken or dislocated bones. • In making casts for statues, toys, surgical instruments etc. • In making casts in dentistry. • In making blackboard chalk. • In plastering walls.

Anomalous Behaviour of Beryllium

Due to small atomic and ionic size, high charge density and absence of vacant *d*-orbitals, Be shows following points of differences :

- It is denser and harder than other members of the family.
- It has high ionisation potential as compared to the rest of the members of this group.
- Be when heated with carbon form Be_2C which on reaction with water gives methane while other alkaline earth metals form acetylene gas.
- It has higher melting and boiling point.
- Be does not react with water even at high temperature while other elements do.
- Be forms covalent compounds because of high charge density and greater polarising power.
- BeO and $Be(OH)_2$ are amphoteric whereas, oxides of other elements are basic.
- Carbides of Be are covalent whereas, carbides of other elements are ionic.
- $BeCO_3$ is unstable to heat and Be_3N_2 is volatile.
- $BeSO_4$ is soluble in water.

Diagonal Relationship Between Be and Al

The main physical and chemical properties of Be with Al are given below :

- Both are stable in air.
- Both of the metals do not decompose water even at 373 K.
- Be and Al react with sodium hydroxide liberating hydrogen.
- Oxides of both Be and Al are amphoteric in nature.

Uses of Alkaline Earth Metals

- Be is used in corrosion resistant alloys.
- Alloys of Mg with Al are used as structural material.
- Strontium carbonate is used for the manufacture of glass for colour TV picture tubes.
- Magnesium perchlorate is used as a drying agent under the name anhydrone.

Biological Importance of Mg and Ca

Biologically, Mg^{2+} acts as co-factor in the enzymes that utilize ATP in phosphate transfer, whereas, Ca is present in bones and teeth as apatite $Ca_3(PO_4)_2$ and in enamel on teeth as fluorapatite, $3Ca_3(PO_4)_2$.

Topical Practice Questions

All the exam questions of this chapter have been divided into four topics as listed below

Topic 1
General Characteristics of Alkali Metals

2019

1 Which of the alkali metal chlorides (MCl) forms its dihydrate salt ($MCl.2H_2O$) easily? **[NEET (Odisha)]**
(a) LiCl (b) CsCl
(c) RbCl (d) KCl

2015

2 The function of "sodium pump" is a biological process operating in each and every cell of all animals. Which of the following biologically important ions is also a constituent of this pump? **[CBSE AIPMT]**
(a) Ca^{2+} (b) Mg^{2+}
(c) K^+ (d) Fe^{2+}

2014

3 The least stable carbonate of alkali metals is **[Kerala CEE]**
(a) Cs_2CO_3 (b) Na_2CO_3
(c) K_2CO_3 (d) Rb_2CO_3
(e) Li_2CO_3

4 In the reaction, $M + O_2 \longrightarrow MO_2$ (superoxide), the metal M is **[EAMCET]**
(a) lithium (b) sodium (c) potassium (d) barium

2013

5 Which of the following metal hydroxides do not dissolve in sodium hydroxide solution? **[KCET]**
(a) $Zn(OH)_2$ (b) $Al(OH)_3$ (c) $Fe(OH)_3$ (d) $Pb(OH)_2$

2012

6 The ease of adsorption of the hydrated alkali metal ions on an ion-exchange resin follows the order: **[CBSE AIPMT]**
(a) $Li^+ < K^+ < Na^+ < Rb^+$
(b) $Rb^+ < K^+ < Na^+ < Li^+$
(c) $K^+ < Na^+ < Rb^+ < Li^+$
(d) $Na^+ < Li^+ < K^+ < Rb^+$

7 **Assertion** (A) CsI is least soluble of all caesium halides in water.
Reason (R) It is due to low hydration energy. **[AIIMS]**
(a) Both A and R are correct and R is the correct explanation of A
(b) Both A and R are correct but R is not the correct explanation of A
(c) A is correct but R is incorrect
(d) Both A and R are incorrect

8 On dissolving moderate amount of sodium metal in liquid NH_3 at low temperature. Which one of the following does not occur? **[AFMC]**
(a) Na^+ ions are formed in the solution
(b) Blue coloured solution is obtained
(c) Liquid NH_3 becomes good conductor of electricity
(d) Liquid NH_3 remains diamagnetic

9 The reaction between sodium and water can be made less vigorous by **[Gujarat CET]**
(a) adding a little alcohol
(b) amalgamated sodium
(c) adding a little acetic acid
(d) lowering the temperature

2011

10 The alkali halide that is soluble in pyridine is **[Kerala CEE]**
(a) NaCl (b) LiCl (c) KCl (d) CsI
(e) NaBr

2010

11 Among the alkali metals, caesium is the most reactive because **[RPMT]**
(a) its incomplete shell is nearest to the nucleus.
(b) it has a single electron in the valence shell.
(c) it is the heaviest alkali metal.
(d) the outermost electron is more loosely bound than the outermost electron of the other alkali metals.

12 The ionic mobility of alkali metal ions in aqueous solution is maximum for **[RPMT]**
(a) K^+ (b) Rb^+
(c) Li^+ (d) Na^+

13 Which of the metal carbonates is decomposed on heating? **[MP PMT]**
(a) $MgCO_3$ (b) Na_2CO_3
(c) K_2CO_3 (d) Rb_2CO_3

14 The yellow coloured flame is of **[MP PMT]**
(a) Na (b) K
(c) Ca (d) Ba

15 For alkali metals, which one of the following trends is incorrect? **[KCET]**
(a) Hydration energy, Li > Na > K > Rb
(b) Ionisation energy, Li > Na > K > Rb
(c) Density, Li < Na < K < Rb
(d) Atomic size, Li < Na < K < Rb

16 In the case of alkali metals, the covalent character decreases in the order: **[CBSE AIPMT]**

(a) $MCl > MI > MBr > MF$
(b) $MF > MCl > MBr > MI$
(c) $MF > MCl > MI > MBr$
(d) $MI > MBr > MCl > MF$

17 **Assertion** (A) Among the alkali metals, lithium salts exhibit the least electrical conductance in aqueous solutions.
Reason (R) Smaller the radius of the hydrated cations, lower is the electrical conductance in aqueous solution. **[AIIMS]**

(a) Both A and R are correct and R is the correct explanation of A
(b) Both A and R are correct but R is not the correct explanation of A
(c) A is correct but R is incorrect
(d) Both A and R are incorrect

18 Which physical property in the alkali metal group increases with atomic number? **[AMU]**

(a) Melting point
(b) Electronegativity
(c) Hydration enthalpy
(d) Density

19 **Assertion** (A) K, Rb and Cs form superoxide.
Reason (R) The stability of the superoxide increases from K to Cs due to decrease in lattice energy. **[EAMCET]**

(a) Both A and R are correct and R is the correct explanation of A
(b) Both A and R are correct but R is not the correct explanation of A
(c) A is correct but R is incorrect
(d) Both A and R are incorrect

20 The characteristic not related to alkali metals is **[KCET]**

(a) their ions are isoelectronic with noble gases
(b) low melting point
(c) low electronegativity
(d) high ionisation energy

2008

21 The alkali metals form salt like hydride by the direct synthesis at elevated temperature. The thermal stability of these hydrides decreases in which of the following orders? **[CBSE AIPMT]**

(a) CsH > RbH > KH > NaH > LiH
(b) KH > NaH > LiH > CsH > RbH
(c) NaH > LiH > KH > RbH > CsH
(d) LiH > NaH > KH > RbH > CsH

22 The correct order of stability for the following superoxides is **[EAMCET]**

(a) $KO_2 > RbO_2 > CsO_2$ (b) $RbO_2 > CsO_2 > KO_2$
(c) $CsO_2 > RbO_2 > KO_2$ (d) $KO_2 > CsO_2 > RbO_2$

2006

23 Which of the following metal in solution forms a precipitate with NaOH, which is not soluble in an excess of the base? **[Kerala CEE]**

(a) Fe (b) Sn
(c) Pb (d) Zn
(e) Al

24 Consider the following abbreviations for hydrated alkali ions.

$X = [Li(H_2O)_n]^+$ $Y = [K(H_2O)_n]^+$
$Z = [Cs(H_2O)_n]^+$

What is the correct order of size of these hydrated alkali ions? **[J&K CET]**

(a) $X > Y > Z$ (b) $Z > Y > X$
(c) $X = Y = Z$ (d) $Z > X > Y$

25 Lower melting point chloride is **[JCECE]**

(a) LiCl (b) NaCl
(c) KCl (d) CsCl

26 The alkali metal that reacts with C directly at 1000°C to form carbide is **[DUMET]**

(a) Li (b) Na
(c) K (d) Cs

Answers

1 (a)	2 (c)	3 (e)	4 (c)	5 (c)	6 (b)	7 (a)	8 (d)	9 (b)	10 (b)
11 (d)	12 (b)	13 (a)	14 (a)	15 (c)	16 (d)	17 (c)	18 (d)	19 (c)	20 (d)
21 (d)	22 (c)	23 (a)	24 (a)	25 (a)	26 (a)				

Explanations

1 (*a*) The size of the ion and its charge determines the extent of hydration. Greater the charge and smaller the size of ion, greater is the extent of hydration and hence, greater is the hydration enthalpy. Thus, Li^+ having maximum hydration tendency forms dihydrate salt ($LiCl.2H_2O$) easily.

2 (*c*) The "sodium pump" is also known as a sodium-potassium pump. This pump is an important contributor to action potential produced by nerve cells. The process of moving sodium and potassium ions across the cell membrane is an active transport process involving the hydrolysis of ATP to provide the necessary energy. This process is responsible for maintaining the large excess of Na^+ outside the cell and the large excess of K^+ ions on the inside of the cell.

3 (*e*) Due to small size of lithium ion, polarisability increases. Hence, Li_2CO_3 is least stable.

This carbonate is thermally unstable and decomposes to give CO_2 and lithium oxide.

4 (*c*) In superoxide, oxygen is in O_2^- form. Since, superoxide is of MO_2 type, it is clear that, it is alkali metal superoxide. As the size of metal ions increases, tendency to form superoxides increases. Hence, it is potassium superoxide (KO_2).

5 (*c*) $Fe(OH)_3$ does not dissolve in NaOH, as it does not produce $[Fe(OH)_4]^-$ in NaOH solution.

6 (*b*) Ease of adsorption of the hydrated alkali metal ions on an ion-exchange resin decreases as the size of alkali metal ions increases.

Since, the order of size of alkali metal ions is $Li^+ < Na^+ < K^+ < Rb^+$, the ease of adsorption follows the order: $Rb^+ < K^+ < Na^+ < Li^+$.

7 (*a*) As the size of an ion increases, its hydration energy decreases due to decrease in polarising power of the ion. Therefore, low solubility of CsI in water is due to smaller hydration energy of its two ions.
Hence, both A and R are correct and R is the correct explanation of A.

8 (*d*) The alkali metals are soluble in liquid NH_3 giving a solution which is paramagnetic, highly conducting, highly reducing and deep blue in colour.

It is due to the following:

$$M + (x+y)NH_3(\text{excess}) \longrightarrow \underset{\text{Ammoniated cation}}{[M^+ \cdot (NH_3)_x]^+} \ \underset{\text{Ammoniated electron}}{[e(NH_3)_y]^-}$$

These ammoniated or solvated electrons are responsible for all the above written properties of solution.

9 (*b*) Reaction of sodium with water is quite vigorous. To reduce its vigorousness, it is amalgamated with mercury (Na-Hg amalgam).

10 (*b*) Pyridine is a non-polar solvent. Covalent compounds are soluble in non-polar solvents. Therefore, Li, being very small in size, is highly polarising in nature and forms covalent compounds. Therefore, LiCl, being covalent, is soluble in pyridine.

11 (*d*) On moving down a group, size of metal increases, i.e. the distance between nucleus and valence shell increases. As, Cs lies towards the bottom of group 1, the outermost shell electron of caesium is more loosely bound than the outermost shell electron of the other alkali metals. That's why, caesium is most reactive among the alkali metals.

12 (*b*) Smaller the size of the ion, more highly it is hydrated due to high polarising power and hence, its hydrated ionic radius will be greater and its ionic mobility is lesser in aqueous solution.
Thus, the order of ionic mobility is,

$$Li^+ < Na^+ < K^+ < Rb^+ < Cs^+$$

13 (*a*) The carbonates of alkali metals (i.e. $Na_2CO_3, K_2CO_3, Rb_2CO_3$) are stable up to 1000°C, whereas, carbonates of alkaline earth metals (i.e $MgCO_3$) decompose on heating to form corresponding metal oxide and CO_2.

$$MgCO_3 \xrightarrow{\Delta} MgO + CO_2$$

14 (*a*) On burning, sodium imparts yellow colour to the flame, potassium imparts pale violet colour, calcium imparts brick red colour and barium imparts grassy green colour.

15 (*c*) In general, density increases on moving down in a group but density of potassium (K) is lesser than that of sodium (Na). This is because of the abnormal increase in atomic size on moving from Na (86 pm) to K (227 pm).
Thus, the correct order of density is

$$Li < K < Na < Rb.$$

16 (*d*) Among metal halides, metal iodide has the maximum covalent character as the polarisability of I^- ion is very large. Therefore, MI is covalent in nature because of large size of anion, whereas MF is ionic in nature due to small size of anion.

∴ The decreasing order of the covalent character is

$$MI > MBr > MCl > MF$$

17 (*c*) Hydration energy varies inversely with size. Hence, as we move from Li to Cs, size of alkali metals increases and thus hydration energy decreases.

Lithium ion being smallest in size among alkali metals, and it is the most extensively hydrated ion and becomes largest hydrated cation. Thus, it has least electrical conductivity among alkali metals.

Electrical conductance

$$\propto \frac{1}{\text{Size of hydrated cation}}$$

Hence, A is correct but R is incorrect.

18 (*d*) Density of the alkali metals almost increases on moving down the group. However, a small decrease in density is observed from Na to K, due to abnormal increase in atomic size from Na to K.

19 (*c*) Superoxides are the species having a O—O bond and O in an oxidation state of $-\frac{1}{2}$ (superoxide ion is O_2^-).

Usually, these are formed by active metals K, Rb and Cs and their formula are respectively, KO_2, RbO_2 and CsO_2.

For the salts of larger anions (like O_2^-), lattice energy increases in a group. Since, lattice energy is the driving force for the formation of an ionic compound and its stability, hence the stability of the superoxides from K to Cs also increases.
Hence, A is correct but R is incorrect.

20 (*d*) The alkali metals have ns^1 outer electronic configuration, thus, on losing this electron, the ion formed will be isoelectronic with noble gases.
The energy binding the atoms in the crystal lattices of these metals is relatively low due to the presence of only one electron in the valence shell. Thus, alkali metals have low melting points.
Alkali metals are highly electropositive thus, they have low electronegativity.
The alkali metals have large size and, thus the outermost electron is far from the nucleus. Hence, they have relatively low ionisation energies.

21 (*d*) Small anion forms stable compounds with small cation.
Since, the size of cation increases as,

$$Li^+ < Na^+ < K^+ < Rb^+ < Cs^+$$

Therefore, the thermal stability of alkali metal hydrides decreases as

$$LiH > NaH > KH > RbH > CsH$$

22 (*c*) With progressive increase in the size of alkali metal ions, the stability of superoxides increases. This is because the size of superoxide ion is large and large cation can be stabilised more by large anion.
Hence, the order of stability of superoxides of alkali metals is,

$$CsO_2 > RbO_2 > KO_2$$

23 (*a*) Iron (Fe) metal in solution forms a red precipitate with NaOH and this precipitate is not soluble in an excess of the base as it does not form $[Fe(OH)_4]^-$ in excess of NaOH solution.

$$FeCl_3 + 3NaOH \longrightarrow \underset{\text{Ferric hydroxide (red ppt.)}}{Fe(OH)_3} + 3NaCl$$

While the precipitate of Sn, Pb, Zn are soluble in the excess of base.

24 (*a*) All alkali metal salts are soluble in water. The degree of hydration depends upon the size of the cation. Smaller the size of a cation, greater is its charge density and hence, greater is its tendency to draw electrons from molecules which are thus, polarised.
Li^+ ion, being smallest in size among alkali metal ions and it is the most extensively hydrated while Cs^+ ion, the largest alkali metal ion is the least hydrated. The size of hydrated alkali ions is as,

$$Li^+ > Na^+ > K^+ > Rb^+ > Cs^+$$

Thus, correct order of size is $X > Y > Z$.

25 (*a*) Alkali metal halides have high melting point. The melting point of alkali metal chlorides decreases from NaCl to CsCl (except Li).

LiCl	NaCl	KCl	RbCl
878 K	1081 K	1043 K	990 K

So, NaCl has the highest melting point and LiCl has the lowest melting point,due to covalent character of LiCl.

26 (*a*) Only Li reacts with C directly at 1000°C to form carbide.

$$2Li + 2C \xrightarrow{1000°C} \underset{\text{Lithium carbide}}{Li_2C_2}$$

Topic 2
Compounds of Alkali Metals

2019

1 Crude sodium chloride obtained by crystallisation of brine solution does not contain. **[NEET (Odisha)]**
(a) $MgSO_4$ (b) Na_2SO_4 (c) $MgCl_2$ (d) $CaSO_4$

2018

2 **Assertion** (A) NaCl reacts with concentrated H_2SO_4 to give colourless fumes with pungent smell. But on adding MnO_2, the fumes become greenish yellow.
Reason (R) MnO_2 oxidises HCl to chlorine gas which is greenish yellow. **[AIIMS]**
(a) Both A and R are correct and R is the correct explanation of A.
(b) Both A and R are correct but R is not the correct explanation of A
(c) A is correct but R is incorrect
(d) Both A and R are incorrect

2017

3 CO_2 gas along with solid (*Y*) is obtained when sodium salt (*X*) is heated. (*X*) is again obtained when CO_2 gas is passed into aqueous solution *Y*. *X* and *Y* respectively are **[HPMT]**
(a) Na_2CO_3, Na_2O (b) Na_2CO_3, NaOH
(c) $NaHCO_3$, Na_2CO_3 (d) Na_2CO_3, $NaHCO_3$

4 Water glass is **[AIIMS]**
(a) Na_2SiO_3 (b) Mg_2Si
(c) $SiCl_4$ (d) $Ca(H_2PO_4)_2$

5 Sodium carbonate is manufactured by **[JIPMER]**
(a) Lawing process (b) Le-blanc process
(c) Solvay process (d) Haber's process

6 When sodium hydroxide reacts with sand, it forms **[WB JEE]**
(a) sodium silicate (b) silicon oxide
(c) silicon hydroxides (d) None of these

7 Which one of the following is true? **[KCET]**
(a) NaOH is used in the concentration of bauxite ore.
(b) NaOH is a primary standard in volumetric analysis.
(c) Manganous hydroxide is soluble in excess of NaOH solution.
(d) NaOH solution does not react with Cl_2

2010

8 Washing soda is **[MP PMT]**
(a) Na_2CO_3 (b) $Na_2CO_3 \cdot H_2O$
(c) $Na_2CO_3 \cdot 5H_2O$ (d) $Na_2CO_3 \cdot 10H_2O$

9 Molecular formula of Glauber's salt is **[JCECE]**
(a) $MgSO_4 \cdot 7H_2O$ (b) $CuSO_4 \cdot 5H_2O$
(c) $FeSO_4 \cdot 7H_2O$ (d) $Na_2SO_4 \cdot 10H_2O$

10 Which of the following compounds does not give a precipitate with excess of NaOH? **[AFMC]**

(a) $ZnSO_4$ (b) $FeSO_4$
(c) $AgNO_3$ (d) $HgCl_2$

11 Excess of sodium hydroxide reacts with zinc to form **[Manipal]**

(a) ZnH_2 (b) Na_2ZnO_2
(c) ZnO (d) $Zn(OH)_2$

2008

12 SiO_2 is reacted with sodium carbonate. What is the gas liberated? **[MP PMT]**

(a) CO (b) O_2
(c) CO_2 (d) O_3

13 Which of the following is formed by the action of water on Na_2O_2? **[BHU]**

(a) H_2 (b) O_2
(c) N_2 (d) CO

14 Potassium superoxide finds use in breathing equipment and safeguards the user to breathe in oxygen generated internally in the apparatus without being exposed to toxic fumes outside. The supply of oxygen is due to

I. slow decomposition of KO_2.
II. reaction of superoxide with moisture in the exhaled air.
III. reaction of KO_2 with CO_2 in the exhaled air.

Select the correct answer using the code given below. **[Kerala CEE]**

(a) I, II and III (b) II and III
(c) Only III (d) I and II
(e) Only II

15 Sodium hypohalite when dissolved in water will turn **[DUMET]**

(a) blue litmus red (b) red litmus blue
(c) red litmus green (d) no change

2006

16 Main process for the manufacture of sodium carbonate is **[MP PMT]**

(a) Nelson process (b) Down's process
(c) Castner process (d) Solvay process

17 Aluminium reacts with caustic soda to form **[AMU]**

(a) aluminium hydroxide (b) aluminium oxide
(c) sodium metaaluminate (d) sodium tetraaluminate

18 Consider the following reactions.

I. $Al + NaOH + H_2O \xrightarrow{\Delta}$
II. $F_2 + NaOH\ (conc.) \longrightarrow$
III. $NaOH + P\ (white) + H_2O \longrightarrow$

The correct set of reactions which give gaseous product is **[EAMCET]**

(a) I, II and III (b) I and II
(c) I and III (d) II and III

19 When sodium nitrate is heated above 600°C then, **[JCECE]**

(a) only Na_2O is formed (b) only N_2 is formed
(c) only O_2 is formed (d) All are formed

20 In photography, sodium thiosulphate is used as **[DUMET]**

(a) complexing agent (b) oxidising agent
(c) reducing agent (d) None of these

Answers

1 (a)	2 (a)	3 (c)	4 (a)	5 (c)	6 (a)	7 (a)	8 (d)	9 (d)	10 (a)
11 (b)	12 (c)	13 (b)	14 (b)	15 (b)	16 (d)	17 (c)	18 (a)	19 (d)	20 (a)

Explanations

1 (*a*) Crude sodium chloride obtained by crystallisation of brine solution contains $CaSO_4$, Na_2SO_4, $CaCl_2$, $MgCl_2$ as impurities. $CaCl_2$ and $MgCl_2$ are deliquescent, i.e. absorb moisture from atmosphere and give wet appearance to the salt. Crude salt is dissolved in water and insoluble impurities are removed by filtration. Hence, $MgSO_4$ is not present in crude sodium chloride.

2 (*a*) Both Assertion and Reason are correct and Reason is the correct explanation of the Assertion.

NaCl reacts with concentrated H_2SO_4 to give colourless fumes with pungent smell. This pungent smell is due to formation of HCl.

$$2NaCl + H_2SO_4 \longrightarrow Na_2SO_4 + 2HCl$$

But on adding MnO_2, the fumes become greenish yellow due to the formation of chlorine gas.

3 (*c*) Here, *X* is $NaHCO_3$ and *Y* is Na_2CO_3.

$$\underset{(X)}{NaHCO_3} \xrightarrow{\Delta} \underset{(Y)}{Na_2CO_3} + H_2O$$

$$\underset{(Y)}{Na_2CO_3} + H_2O + CO_2 \longrightarrow \underset{(X)}{NaHCO_3}$$

4 (*a*) Sodium silicate (Na_2SiO_3) is known as water glass. As plants and trees can be made to grow in the soil to get a natural garden, in the same way, crystals of coloured salts grow in the water glass and look like plants and trees.

5 (*c*) Na_2CO_3 is manufactured by Solvay process. In this process, CO_2 is bubbled through a solution of NaCl saturated with NH_3. The precipitated $NaHCO_3$ is filtered and decomposed to Na_2CO_3 by heating. Lawing process is used for manufacture of NaOH, Le-blanc process is now obsolete. Haber's process is used for the manufacture of NH_3.

6 (*a*) When NaOH reacts with sand (SiO_2), it forms sodium silicate which is generally called glass.

$$2NaOH + SiO_2 \longrightarrow \underset{\text{Sodium silicate (Glass)}}{Na_2SiO_3} + H_2O$$

7 (*a*) NaOH is used in the concentration of bauxite ore as it forms a complex with Al in bauxite ore. Other corrected statements are as follows:

- Manganous hydroxide is insoluble in excess of NaOH solution as it does not form a complex with excess NaOH solution.
- Cl_2 reacts with cold and dilute NaOH to form NaCl, NaClO and H_2O.
- Cl_2 reacts with hot and concentrated NaOH to form NaCl, $NaClO_3$ and $3H_2O$.

8 (*d*) Sodium carbonate decahydrate $(Na_2CO_3 \cdot 10H_2O)$ is known as washing soda or sol soda.

9 (*d*) Sodium sulphate decahydrate $(Na_2SO_4 \cdot 10H_2O)$ is also known as Glauber's salt.

10 (*a*) On adding sodium hydroxide to the $ZnSO_4$ solution, first the white precipitate of zinc hydroxide is obtained, which dissolves in excess of NaOH due to the formation of sodium zincate.

$$ZnSO_4 + 2NaOH \longrightarrow \underset{\text{White (insoluble)}}{Zn(OH)_2} + Na_2SO_4$$

$$Zn(OH)_2 + 2NaOH \longrightarrow \underset{\substack{\text{Sodium zincate}\\ \text{(soluble)}}}{Na_2ZnO_2} + 2H_2O$$

11 (*b*) Excess of sodium hydroxide reacts with zinc to form Na_2ZnO_2.

$$Zn + 2NaOH \longrightarrow Na_2ZnO_2 + H_2\uparrow$$

12 (*c*) When silica is heated with metal carbonate, it forms silicates and releases CO_2 gas.

$$SiO_2 + Na_2CO_3 \xrightarrow{\Delta} Na_2SiO_3 + CO_2\uparrow$$

13 (*b*) Peroxides of alkali metal react with warm water to give oxygen.

$$2Na_2O_2 + \underset{\text{(Warm)}}{2H_2O} \longrightarrow 4NaOH + O_2$$

14 (*b*) Potassium superoxide is used in breathing equipment and safeguards the user to breathe in O_2 generated internally in the apparatus without being exposed to toxic fumes. The supply of O_2 is maintained by the reaction of superoxide with moisture in the exhaled air and also reaction of KO_2 with CO_2 in exhaled air.

15 (*b*) Sodium hypohalite when dissolved in water gives alkaline solution, thus it will turn red litmus into blue.

$$NaClO + H_2O \longrightarrow NaOH + HOCl$$

16 (*d*) Solvay process is used for the manufacture of sodium carbonate.

In this process, CO_2 is bubbled through a solution of NaCl saturated with NH_3. The precipitated $NaHCO_3$ is filtered and decomposed to Na_2CO_3 by heating.

17 (*c*) The reaction of Al with caustic soda (NaOH) gives sodium meta aluminate ($NaAlO_2$).

$$2Al + 2NaOH + 2H_2O \longrightarrow \underset{\substack{\text{Sodium}\\ \text{meta aluminate}}}{2NaAlO_2} + 3H_2\uparrow$$

18 (*a*) Reaction of Al, F_2 and P_4 with NaOH evolves the gases H_2, O_2 and PH_3 respectively as shown below:

$$2Al + 2NaOH + 2H_2O \xrightarrow{\Delta} \underset{\substack{\text{Sodium}\\ \text{meta aluminate}}}{2NaAlO_2} + 3H_2$$

$$2F_2 + 4NaOH\,(\text{conc.}) \longrightarrow O_2 + 4NaF + 2H_2O$$

$$P_4 + 3NaOH + 3H_2O \longrightarrow \underset{\substack{\text{Sodium}\\ \text{hypophosphite}}}{3NaH_2PO_2} + \underset{\text{Phosphine}}{PH_3}$$

So, all the three reactions give gaseous products.

19 (*d*) When $NaNO_3$ is heated above 600°C, Na_2O, O_2 and N_2 are formed as shown below:

$$4NaNO_3 \xrightarrow{600°C} 2Na_2O + 5O_2 + 2N_2$$

20 (*a*) In photography $Na_2S_2O_3$ (hypo or sodium thiosulphate) is used as complexing agent. It dissolves unreduced silver bromide by forming a complex.

$$AgBr + \underset{\text{Hypo}}{2Na_2S_2O_3} \longrightarrow \underset{\substack{\text{Sodium argentothiosulphate}\\ \text{(soluble complex)}}}{Na_3[Ag(S_2O_3)_2]} + NaBr$$

Therefore, $Na_2S_2O_3$ is used as a complexing agent.

Topic 3

General Characteristics of Alkaline Earth Metals

2019

1 Which of the following is an amphoteric hydroxide? **[NEET]**

(a) $Ca(OH)_2$ (b) $Mg(OH)_2$
(c) $Be(OH)_2$ (d) $Sr(OH)_2$

2 Out of BeF_2, MgF_2, CaF_2, SrF_2 which has maximum solubility? **[AIIMS]**

(a) BeF_2 (b) MgF_2
(c) CaF_2 (d) SrF_2

3 Which is least soluble? **[AIIMS]**

(a) Na_2S (b) MgS (c) $MgCl_2$ (d) NaCl

2018

4 If Na^+ ion is larger than Mg^{2+} ions and S^{2-} ion is larger than Cl^- ion, which of the following will be stable salt in water? **[JIPMER]**

(a) Sodium chloride (b) Sodium sulphide
(c) Magnesium sulphide (d) Magnesium chloride

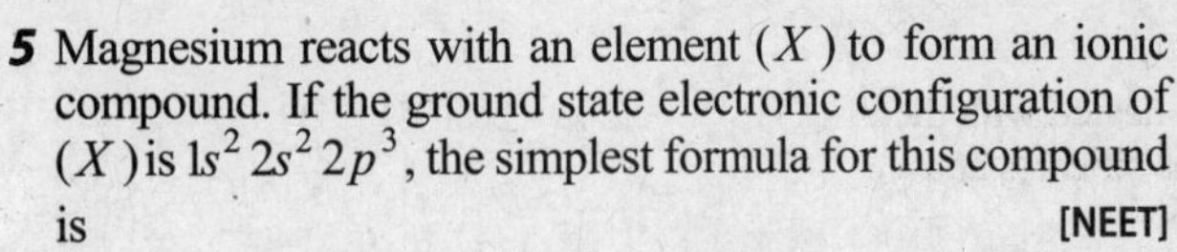

5 Magnesium reacts with an element (X) to form an ionic compound. If the ground state electronic configuration of (X) is $1s^2 2s^2 2p^3$, the simplest formula for this compound is **[NEET]**
(a) Mg_2X (b) MgX_2 (c) Mg_2X_3 (d) Mg_3X_2

2015

6 Solubility of the alkaline earth metal sulphates in water decreases in the sequence **[CBSE]**
(a) Mg > Ca > Sr > Ba (b) Ca > Sr > Ba > Mg
(c) Sr > Ca > Mg > Ba (d) Ba > Mg > Sr > Ca

7 The decreasing order of hydration enthalpies of alkaline earth metal ions is **[EAMCET]**
(a) $Be^{2+} > Ba^{2+} > Ca^{2+} > Sr^{2+}$
(b) $Ba^{2+} > Sr^{2+} > Ca^{2+} > Mg^{2+} > Be^{2+}$
(c) $Be^{2+} > Ca^{2+} > Mg^{2+} > Ba^{2+}$
(d) $Be^{2+} > Mg^{2+} > Ca^{2+} > Sr^{2+} > Ba^{2+}$

2013

8 Assertion (A) $BaCO_3$ is more soluble in HNO_3 than in water.
Reason (R) Carbonate is a weak base and reacts with H^+ from the strong acid, causing the barium salt to dissociate. **[AIIMS]**
(a) Both A and R are correct and R is the correct explanation of A
(b) Both A and R are correct but R is not the correct explanation of A
(c) A is correct but R is incorrect
(d) Both A and R are incorrect

2012

9 The decomposition temperature is lowest for **[AMU]**
(a) $BeCO_3$ (b) $MgCO_3$ (c) $SrCO_3$ (d) $BaCO_3$

2011

10 Which of the following compounds has the lowest melting point? **[CBSE AIPMT]**
(a) CaF_2 (b) $CaCl_2$ (c) $CaBr_2$ (d) CaI_2

2010

11 Property of the alkaline earth metals that increase with their atomic number is **[CBSE AIPMT]**
(a) electronegativity
(b) solubility of their hydroxides in water
(c) solubility of their sulphates in water
(d) ionisation energy

12 Which of the following alkaline earth metal sulphates has hydration enthalpy higher than the lattice enthalpy? **[CBSE AIPMT]**
(a) $SrSO_4$ (b) $CaSO_4$ (c) $BeSO_4$ (d) $BaSO_4$

13 Which of the following alkaline earth metal sulphates is least soluble in water? **[Haryana PET]**
(a) $BaSO_4$ (b) $MgSO_4$ (c) $SrSO_4$ (d) $CaSO_4$

14 The solubilities of Na_2SO_4, $BeSO_4$, $MgSO_4$ and $BaSO_4$ will follow the order **[AMU]**
(a) $BeSO_4 > MgSO_4 > Na_2SO_4 > BaSO_4$
(b) $BeSO_4 > Na_2SO_4 > MgSO_4 > BaSO_4$
(c) $MgSO_4 > BeSO_4 > Na_2SO_4 > BaSO_4$
(d) $Na_2SO_4 > BeSO_4 > MgSO_4 > BaSO_4$

15 Correct order of stability of group II A metal carbonates is **[OJEE]**
(a) $MgCO_3 > CaCO_3 > SrCO_3 > BaCO_3$
(b) $BaCO_3 > SrCO_3 > CaCO_3 > MgCO_3$
(c) $SrCO_3 > BaCO_3 > CaCO_3 > MgCO_3$
(d) $CaCO_3 > MgCO_3 > BaCO_3 > SrCO_3$

16 Which one of the following does not react with water even under hot condition? **[RPMT]**
(a) Na (b) Be (c) Ca (d) K
(e) Sr

17 A sodium salt on treatment with $MgCl_2$ gives white precipitate on heating. The anion of sodium salt is **[CG PMT]**
(a) HCO_3^- (b) CO_3^{2-}. (c) NO_3^- (d) SO_4^{2-}

18 Among the following, the least thermally stable is **[J&K CET]**
(a) K_2CO_3 (b) Na_2CO_3
(c) $BaCO_3$ (d) Li_2CO_3

19 Equimolar solutions of the following were prepared in water separately. Which one of the solutions will record the highest pH? **[CBSE AIPMT]**
(a) $SrCl_2$ (b) $BaCl_2$ (c) $MgCl_2$ (d) $CaCl_2$

20 Select the correct statement(s). **[AIIMS]**
(a) Cyanamide ion (CN_2^{2-}) is isoelectronic with CO_2 and has the same linear structure
(b) Mg_2C_3 reacts with water to form propyne
(c) CaC_2 has NaCl type lattice
(d) All of the above

21 Which of the following on thermal decomposition yields a basic as well as an acidic oxide? **[Kerala CEE]**
(a) $KClO_3$ (b) Na_2CO_3
(c) $NaNO_3$ (d) $CaCO_3$
(e) NH_4NO_3

22 The solubilities of carbonates decrease down the magnesium group due to the decrease in **[RPMT]**
(a) lattice energies of solids
(b) hydration energies of cations
(c) inter-ionic attraction
(d) entropy of solution formation

2007

23 In which of the following the hydration energy is higher than the lattice energy? **[CBSE AIPMT]**
(a) $BaSO_4$ (b) $MgSO_4$
(c) $RaSO_4$ (d) $SrSO_4$

24 Lithophone is [RPMT]
(a) $ZnSO_4 + PbS$ (b) $BaSO_4 + ZnS$
(c) PbO_2 (d) $ZnSO_4$

25 Which of the following statements about alkaline earth metals are correct? [Kerala CEE]
I. Hydration energy of Sr^{2+} is greater than that of Be^{2+}.
II. $CaCO_3$ decomposes at a higher temperature than $BaCO_3$.
III. $Ba(OH)_2$ is a stronger base than $Mg(OH)_2$.
IV. $SrSO_4$ is less soluble in water than $CaSO_4$.
Select the correct answer using the codes given below.
(a) Only IV (b) I and III (c) I and IV
(d) II and III (e) III and IV

26 Lightest alkaline earth metal is [Haryana PMT]
(a) Be (b) Mg
(c) Ca (d) Sr

Answers

1 (c)	2 (a)	3 (b)	4 (c)	5 (d)	6 (a)	7 (d)	8 (a)	9 (a)	10 (d)
11 (b)	12 (c)	13 (a)	14 (d)	15 (b)	16 (b)	17 (a)	18 (d)	19 (b)	20 (d)
21 (d)	22 (b)	23 (b)	24 (b)	25 (e)	26 (c)				

Explanations

1 (c) $Be(OH)_2$ is amphoteric in nature as it reacts with acid and alkali both as:
$$Be(OH)_2 + 2HCl \longrightarrow BeCl_2 + 2H_2O$$
$$Be(OH)_2 + 2NaOH \longrightarrow Na_2[Be(OH)_4]$$
This amphoteric nature of Be is due to small size of Be. The other hydroxides of alkaline earth metals are basic in nature.

2 (a) Solubility of fluorides of alkaline earth metals decreases down the group due to increase in value of lattice enthalpies as compared to hydration-enthalpy.
Thus, the order of solubility of given compounds is as follows:
$BeF_2 > MgF_2 > CaF_2 > SrF_2$
Hence, BeF_2 has maximum solubility.

3 (b) More the covalent nature of compounds lesser will be its solubility. Also, according to Fajan's rule, lesser be the size of cation or more be size of anion, species show more covalent nature.
As, Mg show +2 oxidation state and Na is in +1 oxidation state the size of Mg^{2+} is less than that of Na^+. On the other hand, sulphur is in −2 oxidation state while chlorine is in −1 oxidation state, therefore sulphur anion in larger in size. Thus, among the given species, the combination of magnesium (Mg) and sulphur (S) show maximum covalent nature and therefore is least soluble.
Hence, option (b) is the correct.

4 (c) Higher the lattice energy, lower the solubility and more stable will be the salt in water. Since lattice energy varies directly with charge, among the four combinations given, the lattice energy of MgS is higher than those of Na_2S, $MgCl_2$ and NaCl. Hence, MgS is a stable salt in water and the least soluble salt.

5 (d) Given, electronic configuration of $X = 1s^2 2s^2 2p^3$
∴ The valency of X will be 3.
The valency of Mg is +2.
∴ Magnesium reacts with element X to form an ionic compound with formula Mg_3X_2.

6 (a) The sulphates of alkaline earth metals becomes less soluble on moving down the group, i.e. Mg > Ca > Sr > Ba
This decrease in solubility of alkaline earth metal sulphates is due to increase in size of the metal ion down the group.

7 (d) As the size of metal ion increases, hydration enthalpy decreases. This is due to decrease in polarizing power of the cation with increase in size.
Therefore, the decreasing order of hydration enthalpies is,
$Be^{2+} > Mg^{2+} > Ca^{2+} > Sr^{2+} > Ba^{2+}$

8 (a) $BaCO_3$ is more soluble in HNO_3 than in water because carbonate is a weak base and reacts with H^+ ion of HNO_3 causing barium salt to dissociate.
$$BaCO_3 + 2HNO_3 \longrightarrow Ba(NO_3)_2 + CO_2 + H_2O$$

9 (a) Thermal stability of carbonates of II A group increases down the group due to increase in size of metal cation.
$\underset{523\text{ K}}{BeCO_3} < \underset{813\text{ K}}{MgCO_3} < \underset{1562\text{ K}}{SrCO_3} < \underset{1633\text{ K}}{BaCO_3}$

10 (d) CaI_2 has the lowest melting point as it is more covalent than the other given compounds. Metal iodide has the maximum covalent character among metal halides due to large polarizability of I^- ion.

11 (b) Solubility of alkaline earth metal hydroxides increases with increase in atomic number due to decrease in lattice enthalpy down the group.

12 (c) Hydration energy decreases down the group, whereas lattice energy remains almost constant. Thus, hydration enthalpy is higher than the lattice enthalpy in case of $BeSO_4$.

13 (a) $BaSO_4$ is least soluble in water. The solubility of the alkaline earth metal sulphates in water decreases down the group because of the decrease in hydration energy due to increase in atomic size, i.e.
Be > Mg > Ca > Sr > Ba. In case of sulphates of alkaline earth metals, lattice energy remains almost constant as the size of metal increases, thus solubility is decided only by hydration energy.

14 (d) Alkali metal sulphates are more soluble as compared to alkaline earth metal sulphates. Thus, Na_2SO_4 is most soluble.
Among alkaline earth metal sulphates, $BeSO_4$ is most soluble. This is because on moving downward, the magnitude of lattice energy remains almost constant (due to large sized sulphate ion) but hydration energy decreases.
Hence, the order of solubility is
$Na_2SO_4 > BeSO_4 > MgSO_4 > BaSO_4$

15 (*b*) Mg^{2+} is smallest in size hence, show high polarising power. Thus, $MgCO_3$ is most covalent and least stable. Stability of metal carbonates increases on moving down the group due to decrease in stability of resulting metal oxide. Therefore, the correct order of stability is

$BaCO_3 > SrCO_3 > CaCO_3 > MgCO_3$.

16 (*b*) Be is the element that does not react with water even under hot conditions. Alkaline earth metals being less electropositive, are less reactive towards water as compared to alkali metals. Their reactivity with water increases on moving down the group.

17 (*a*) Since, the sodium salt on treatment with $MgCl_2$ gives white precipitate on heating, the salt must be sodium bicarbonate and the reactions are as follows:

$$\underset{\text{Sodium bicarbonate}}{2NaHCO_3} + MgCl_2 \longrightarrow \underset{\text{Magnesium bicarbonate}}{Mg(HCO_3)_2} + 2NaCl$$

$$Mg(HCO_3)_2 \xrightarrow{\Delta} \underset{\text{(White ppt.)}}{MgCO_3 \downarrow} + H_2O + CO_2$$

Therefore, the anion of sodium salt is HCO_3^-.

18 (*d*) Stability can be explained on the basis of polarisation and covalent character. Since, Li^+ is smallest in size, hence it shows high polarising power. Thus, Li_2CO_3 is least ionic and has least stability.

19 (*b*) $BaCl_2$ will have highest pH. As the basic nature increases, pH increases.

pH of base > 7
pH of acid < 7

In alkaline earth metals on moving downward, the size of cation increases, thus basicity increases. Hence, the increasing order of basicity is as:

$MgCl_2 < CaCl_2 < SrCl_2 < BaCl_2$

20 (*d*) The structures of CN_2^{2-} and CO_2 are given below:

$:\overset{-}{N}=C=\overset{-}{N}:; O=C=O$

Thus, CN_2^{2-} and CO_2 both are isoelectronic and isostructural.

The reaction of Mg_2C_3 with H_2O is shown below.

$$Mg_2C_3 + H_2O \longrightarrow \underset{\text{Propyne}}{CH_3-C\equiv CH} + Mg(OH)_2$$

$(Ca^{2+}C_2^{2-})$ CaC_2 has NaCl type lattice.

21 (*d*) $CaCO_3$ on decomposition yields a basic as well as an acidic oxide.

$$CaCO_3 \xrightarrow{\Delta} \underset{\text{(Basic oxide)}}{CaO} + \underset{\text{(Acidic oxide)}}{CO_2}$$

CaO is a basic oxide as it is the oxide of alkaline earth metal. (Except BeO, all alkaline earth metal oxides are basic in nature) . CO_2 is acidic as it is the oxide of a non metal.

22 (*b*) Solubilities of carbonates decrease down the group because their lattice energy remains almost constant while hydration energy decreases sharply on moving downwards due to increase in size of metal cation. Thus, the solubility decreases.

23 (*b*) Hydration energy of sulphates decreases from top to bottom in a II A group due to increase in size of metal cation. Mg^{2+} is smaller than other ions of the group so, Mg^{2+} is readily hydrated. Thus, $MgSO_4$ has higher hydration energy than lattice energy.

24 (*b*) Lithophone is a mixture of $BaSO_4$ and ZnS. It is used in wall paints and enamel paints. It is quite cheap and possesses good covering power.

25 (*e*)

(I) Hydration energy of Be^{2+} is 2385.45 kJ/mol and that of Sr^{2+} is 1485.67 kJ/mol due to smaller size of Be^{2+}. So, given statement is not correct.

(II) Decomposition temperature of $CaCO_3$ is 900°C whereas decomposition temperature of $BaCO_3$ is 1360°C as the thermal stability of carbonates increases down the group. So, the given statement is also incorrect.

(III) Basic character of hydroxides of IIA group increases from top to bottom. So, $Ba(OH)_2$ is a strongest base.

(IV) Calcium sulphate is soluble in water while $SrSO_4$ is almost insoluble due to decrease in solubility down the group.

26 (*c*) Calcium is the lightest metal among alkaline earth metals. Its density is 1.5 g cm^{-1} (minimum).

Topic 4

Compounds of Alkaline Earth Metals

2019

1 Bordeaux mixture consists of **[JIPMER]**

(a) $CuSO_4 + Ca(OH)_2$
(b) $CuSO_4 + CaCl_2$
(c) $ZnSO_4 + Mg(OH)_2$
(d) $FeSO_4 + Ba(OH)_2$

2018

2 The correct formula for plaster of Paris is **[JIPMER]**

(a) $CaSO_4 \cdot 4H_2O$ (b) $CaSO_4 \cdot 2H_2O$
(c) $CaSO_4 \cdot \frac{1}{2}H_2O$ (d) $CaSO_4 \cdot 1H_2O$

2016

3 The suspension of slaked lime in water is known as **[NEET (Phase II)]**

(a) limewater (b) quicklime
(c) milk of lime (d) aqueous solution of slaked lime

2014

4 Find the wrong statement. **[Manipal]**

(a) Na_2CO_3 is used in glass industry
(b) $KHCO_3$ is acidic salt
(c) K_2CO_3 can be prepared by Solvay process
(d) Na_2CO_3 is used for metal refining.

2012

5 The chief component of cement that has property of setting quickly and acquiring considerable strength within few days is **[AMU]**

(a) tricalcium silicate ($3CaO \cdot SiO_2$)
(b) dicalcium silicate ($2CaO \cdot SiO_2$)
(c) tricalcium aluminate ($3CaO \cdot Al_2O_3$)
(d) All of the above

2011

6 Which one of the following is present as an active ingredient in bleaching powder for bleaching action? **[CBSE AIPMT]**

(a) $CaCl_2$ (b) $CaOCl_2$
(c) $Ca(OCl)_2$ (d) CaO_2Cl_2

2010

7 H_2SO_4 is added to 20% cold aqueous solution of BaO_2. The product formed is **[OJEE]**

(a) H_2O_2 (b) BaO
(c) $Ba(OH)_2$ (d) H_2SO_5

8 A major consitituent of Portland cement (except lime) is **[BVP]**

(a) silica
(b) alumina
(c) iron oxide
(d) magnesia

9 Gypsum on heating to 390 K gives **[RPMT]**

(a) $CaSO_4 \cdot 2H_2O$ (b) $CaSO_4$
(c) $CaSO_4 \cdot \frac{1}{2} H_2O$ (d) SO_3 and CaO

10 Epsom salt is **[RPMT, VMMC]**

(a) $MgSO_4 \cdot 7H_2O$
(b) $CaSO_4 \cdot H_2O$
(c) $MgSO_4 \cdot 2H_2O$
(d) $BaSO_4 \cdot 2H_2O$

2009

11 **Assertion** (A) Bleaching powder is a mixed salt.
Reason (R) In the presence of $CoCl_2$, bleaching powder decomposes to give $CaCl_2$ and O_2. **[AIIMS]**

(a) Both A and R are correct and R is the correct explanation of A
(b) Both A and R are correct but R is not the correct explanation of A
(c) A is correct but R is incorrect
(d) Both A and R are incorrect

12 $\underset{\text{(Dry)}}{Ca(OH)_2} \xrightarrow[-H_2O]{Cl_2} A \xrightarrow{\text{Auto-oxidation}} CaCl_2 + B$

Identify B in the above reaction. **[EAMCET]**

(a) $CaOCl_2$ (b) $Ca(ClO_3)_2$
(c) $Ca(OH)_2$ (d) $Ca(ClO_2)_2$

13 Dead burnt plaster is **[Kerala CEE]**

(a) $CaSO_4 \cdot 2H_2O$ (b) $MgSO_4 \cdot 7H_2O$
(c) $CaSO_4 \cdot \frac{1}{2} H_2O$ (d) $CaSO_4$ (e) $MgSO_4$

14 The product obtained on fusion of $BaSO_4$ and Na_2CO_3 is **[MHTCET]**

(a) $BaCO_3$ (b) BaO
(c) $Ba(OH)_2$ (d) $BaHSO_4$

15 On strong heating $MgCl_2 \cdot 6H_2O$, the product obtained is **[Punjab MET]**

(a) $MgCl_2$ (b) MgO
(c) $MgCl_2 \cdot 2H_2O$ (d) $MgCl_2 \cdot 4H_2O$

16 Initial setting of cement is mainly due to **[JCECE]**

(a) hydration and gel formation
(b) dehydration and gel formation
(c) hydration and hydrolysis
(d) dehydration and dehydrolysis

Answers

1 (a)	2 (c)	3 (c)	4 (c)	5 (d)	6 (c)	7 (a)	8 (a)	9 (c)	10 (a)
11 (b)	12 (b)	13 (d)	14 (a)	15 (b)	16 (a)				

Explanations

1 (a) Bordeaux is a mixture of copper (II) sulphate ($CuSO_4$) and slaked lime $[Ca(OH)_2]$ used as a fungicide. It was invented in the bordeaux region of France in the late 19th century.

If it is applied in large quantities annually for many years, the copper in the mixture eventually becomes a pollutant.

2 (c) Plaster of Paris (POP) is a hemihydrate of calcium sulphate. Its chemical formula is $CaSO_4 \cdot \frac{1}{2} H_2O$ [or $(CaSO_4)_2 \cdot H_2O$].

3 (c) Aqueous solution of slaked lime is called lime water whereas suspension of slaked lime is called milk of lime.

4 (c) $KHCO_3$ is much more soluble than $NaHCO_3$. So, in Solvay process, $KHCO_3$ cannot be precipitated. Therefore, K_2CO_3 cannot be prepared by Solvay process.

5 (d) The chief components of cement are $3CaO.SiO_2$, $2CaO.SiO_2$ and $3CaO.Al_2O_3$. The silicates and aluminates form more than 90% of the cement. Gypsum is added to decrease the setting time of the cement.

6 (c) Active ingredient in bleaching powder for bleaching action is $Ca(OCl)_2$.

7 (a) H_2O_2 is formed when H_2SO_4 is added to 20% cold aqueous solution of BaO_2.

$$BaO_2 + H_2SO_4 \xrightarrow{0°C} BaSO_4 + H_2O_2$$

8 (a) Except lime (50-60%), the major constituent of Portland cement is silica (20-25%).

9 (c) Gypsum on heating to 390K forms plaster of Paris.

$$\underset{\text{Gypsum}}{2CaSO_4 \cdot 2H_2O} \xrightarrow{390\text{ K}} \underset{\text{Plaster of Paris}}{2CaSO_4 \cdot \frac{1}{2} H_2O} + 3H_2O$$

10 (a) Epsom salt is $MgSO_4 \cdot 7H_2O$.

11 (b) Bleaching powder is a mixed salt of calcium hypochloride $[Ca(ClO)_2]$, calcium chloride ($CaCl_2$) and calcium hydroxide $[Ca(OH)_2]$. It is represented by $CaOCl_2$. In the presence of cobalt chloride, it decomposes into $CaCl_2 + O_2$.

$$CaOCl_2 \xrightarrow{CoCl_2} 2CaCl_2 + O_2$$

Therefore, both reaction and reason are correct but reason is not the correct explanation of assertion.

12 (b) Calcium hydroxide or slaked lime $[Ca(OH)_2]$ reacts with Cl_2 to give bleaching powder, $CaOCl_2$. Bleaching powder on auto-oxidation gives calcium chlorate, $[Ca(ClO_3)_2]$.

$$\underset{\text{(Dry)}}{Ca(OH)_2} \xrightarrow[-H_2O]{Cl_2} \underset{\substack{\text{Bleaching powder} \\ (A)}}{CaOCl_2}$$

$$\xrightarrow{\text{Auto-oxidation}} 5CaCl_2 + \underset{\substack{\text{Calcium chlorate} \\ (B)}}{Ca(ClO_3)_2}$$

13 (d) Plaster of Paris or gypsum when heated to about 200°C is converted into anhydrous calcium sulphate which is known as dead burnt plaster because it does not set like plaster of Paris when moistened with water.

$$\underset{\text{Plaster of Paris}}{CaSO_4 \cdot \frac{1}{2} H_2O} \xrightarrow{200°\text{ C}} \underset{\substack{\text{Dead burnt} \\ \text{plaster}}}{CaSO_4} + \frac{1}{2} H_2O$$

14 (a) $BaCO_3$ is formed on fusion of $BaSO_4$ with Na_2CO_3.

$$BaSO_4 + Na_2CO_3 \longrightarrow BaCO_3 + Na_2SO_4$$

15 (b) MgO is formed on strong heating of $MgCl_2.6H_2O$.

$$MgCl_2 \cdot 6H_2O \xrightarrow{\Delta} MgO + 2HCl + 5H_2O$$

16 (a) Initial setting of cement is mainly due to hydration and gel formation.

11

p-Block Elements (I)

Quick Review

- In p-block elements, the last electron enters in the outermost p-orbital.
- There are six groups of p-block elements in the periodic table and their valence shell electronic configuration is $ns^2 np^{1-6}$ (except for He).

Elements of Group 13 (Boron Family)

- 13th group consists of boron (B), aluminium (Al), gallium (Ga), indium (In) and thallium (Tl).
- Their general electronic configuration is [inert gas] $ns^2 np^1$.

Physical Properties

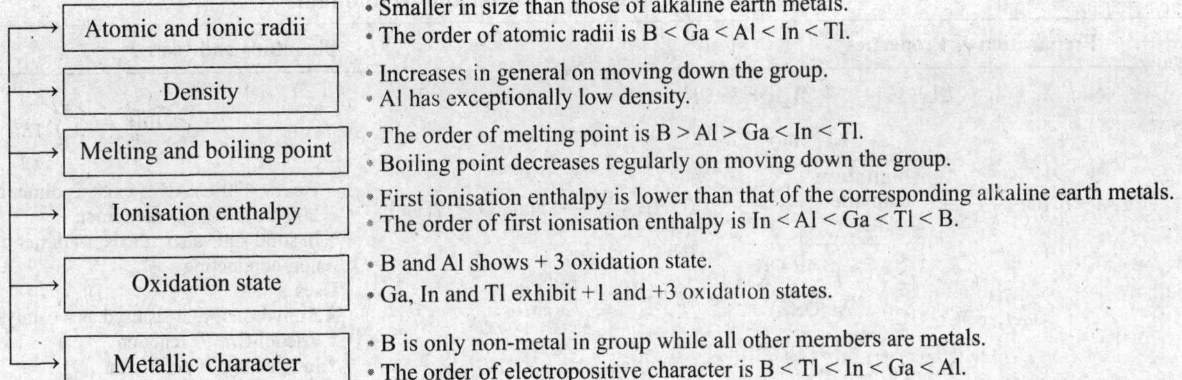

Anomalous Behaviour of Boron

Due to small size, high electron density, high electronegativity and non-availability of d-electrons boron exhibits the following anomalous properties are

- It exhibits allotropy and exists in crystalline as well as amorphous forms.
- Its oxides and hydroxides are acidic in nature while that of other members are amphoteric and basic in nature.
- It forms covalent compounds while other members can form covalent as well as ionic compounds.
- It does not form M^{3+} cation while other members does.
- It obeys octet rule and shows maximum covalency of four.

Chemical Properties

Reaction with oxygen

$$4E(s)+3O_2(g) \xrightarrow{\Delta} 2E_2O_3(s)$$

For thallium, $4Tl + O_2 \longrightarrow 2\,Tl_2O$

- Crystalline boron is unreactive.
- Tl forms thallium (I) oxide, Tl_2O more stable than Tl_2O_3.
- B_2O_3 is acidic, Al and Ga oxide are amphoteric and those of In and Tl are basic.

Reaction with nitrogen

$$2E(s)+N_2(g) \xrightarrow{\Delta} 2EN(s)$$

- All elements readily form nitrides.

Reaction with water

- No reaction occurs with B.
- Aluminium is very reactive even at lower temperature
  $$2Al(s) + 3H_2O(l) \longrightarrow Al_2O_3 + 3H_2(g)\uparrow$$
- Amalgamated Al reacts with H_2O evolving H_2
  $$2Al(Hg) + 6H_2O \longrightarrow 2Al(OH)_3 + 3H_2 + 2Hg$$

- Ga, In and Tl are less reactive.
- They get attacked by the combination of both water and oxygen.
- Individual reaction with water and oxygen do not take place.

Reaction with acids

$$2M + 6HCl \longrightarrow 2M^{3+} + 6Cl^- + 3H_2\uparrow$$
(exception boron)

- Conc. HNO_3 renders Ga and Al passive by forming a protective oxide layer on surface.

Reaction with alkalies

$$2M + 2NaOH + 2H_2O \longrightarrow 2NaMO_2 + 3H_2$$
(exception In and Tl)

- Al reacts with both mineral acids and aqueous alkalies and thus shows amphoteric character.

Reaction with halogen

$$2E(s) + 3X_2(g) \longrightarrow 2EX_3(s)$$
(exception TlI_3)

- Halides of boron are covalent.
- Halides have sp^2 hybridisation, trigonal planar geometry and acts as Lewis acids.

Important Compounds of Boron and Aluminium

Preparation & Properties | **Structure and Uses**

Aluminium chloride ($AlCl_3$)

- $2Al + 3Cl_2 \longrightarrow AlCl_3$
- $2Al + 6HCl \xrightarrow{-H_2} AlCl_3$
- $Al_2O_3 + 3C + 3Cl_2 \xrightarrow[-CO]{100°C} AlCl_3$
- $AlCl_3 \xrightarrow{+3H_2O} Al(OH)_3 + 3HCl$
- $AlCl_3 \xrightarrow{3NaOH} Al(OH)_3\downarrow + 3NaCl \xrightarrow{NaOH} NaAlO_2 + 2H_2O$
- $AlCl_3 \xrightarrow{3NH_4OH} Al(OH)_3 + NH_4Cl$

Structure (dimer): Cl, Cl, Al (221 pm, 101°, 79°), Al (206 pm, 118°), Cl, Cl

- Below 400°C, $AlCl_3$ exist as dimer and above 800°C, it exist as monomer.
- In solid state also, it exist as dimer and is non-conducting.

Uses

- Anhydrous $AlCl_3$ is used as a catalyst in Friedel-Craft's reaction.
- In cracking of petroleum

Borax ($Na_2B_4O_7\cdot10H_2O$)

- $Ca_2B_6O_{11} + 2Na_2CO_3 \xrightarrow[-2NaBO_2,\ -2CaCO_3]{\Delta}$ Borax
- $4NaBO_2 + CO_2 \xrightarrow{-Na_2CO_3}$ Borax
- $Na_2CO_3 + 4H_3BO_3 \xrightarrow[-6H_2O,\ -CO_2]{\Delta}$ Borax
- Borax $\xrightarrow[-H_2O]{\Delta} Na_2B_4O_7 \xrightarrow{\Delta} \underbrace{2NaBO_2 + B_2O_3}_{\text{Transparent glassy bead}}$
- $Na_2B_4O_7 \xrightarrow[2NH_4Cl]{\Delta} 2BN + B_2O_3 + 2NaCl + 4H_2O$
- $Na_2B_4O_7 \xrightarrow[6CaF_2 + 8H_2SO_4]{\Delta} 2NaHSO_4 + 6\,CaSO_4 + 7H_2O + 4BF_3$
- $Na_2B_4O_7 \xrightarrow{7H_2O} 4H_3BO_3 + 2NaOH$
- $Na_2B_4O_7 \xrightarrow{H_2SO_4} Na_2SO_4 + H_2B_4O_7$

Structure: $2Na^+\,[B_4O_5(OH)_4]^{2-}$ (HO–B, B–OH, two B^-–OH units linked by O bridges)

- Two tetrahedral and two triangular units combine together to form the structure.

Uses

- As water softener and cleansing agent.
- In the laboratory for borax bead test.

Note (i) α-form of Al_2O_3 (corundum) is an extremely hard substance used as jeweller's rouge to polish glass.

(ii) When alum contains Al as trivalent cation, it is named after monovalent cation, e.g potash alum.

Preparation & Properties	Structure and Uses

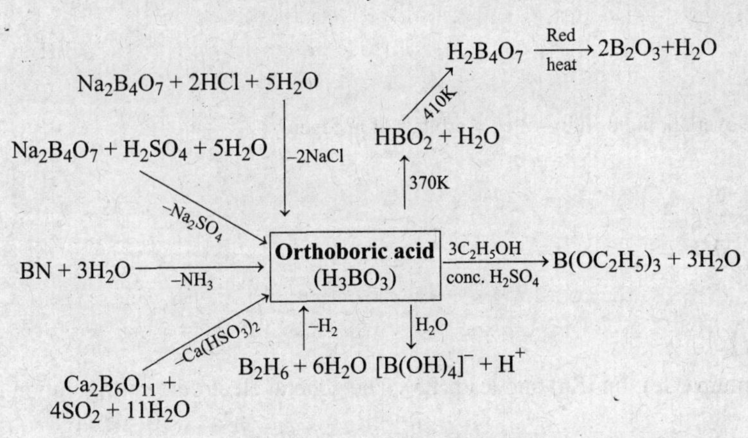

Planar structure in which planar BO_3 units are joined by hydrogen bonds.

Uses

- It is used in the manufacture of heat resistant borosilicate glass.
- The aqueous solution of boric acid is used as a mild antiseptic especially as eye wash under the name boric lotion.

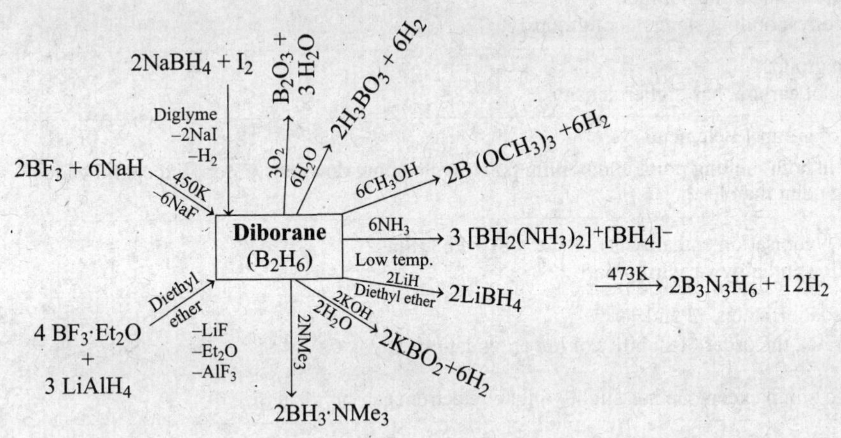

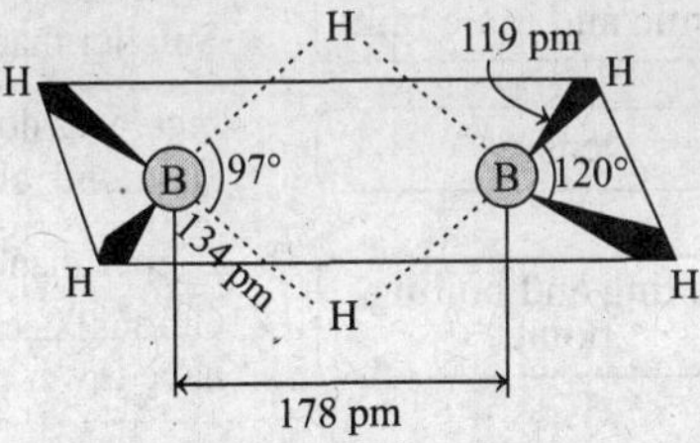

- The terminal B — H bonds are normal 2-centre-2-electron bonds.
- Two bridge bonds are 3-centre-2-electron bonds (banana bonds).

Uses

- For preparing a number of borohydrides such as $LiBH_4$, $NaBH_4$, etc.
- As a reducing agent in organic reactions.

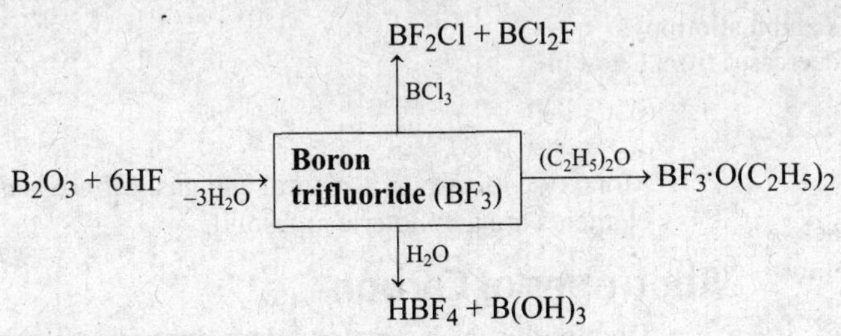

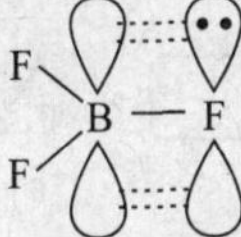

- Two 2*p* orbitals involved in the formation of B—F bond laterally overlap ($p\pi$-$p\pi$ bond).
- Bond acquires double bond character. This type of bond formation is known as back bonding.

Uses

- It acts as a catalyst in organic reactions.
- It is used as an important reagent in organic chemistry as a Lewis acid.

Note (i) Boranes having general formula, B_nH_{n+6} are called **arachno-boranes** while boranes having general formula B_nH_{n+4} are called **nido-boranes**.

(ii) $H_3B_3O_6$ is known as **boroxine**.

BORAZINE - $B_3N_3H_6$
(Borazole or Inorganic benzene)

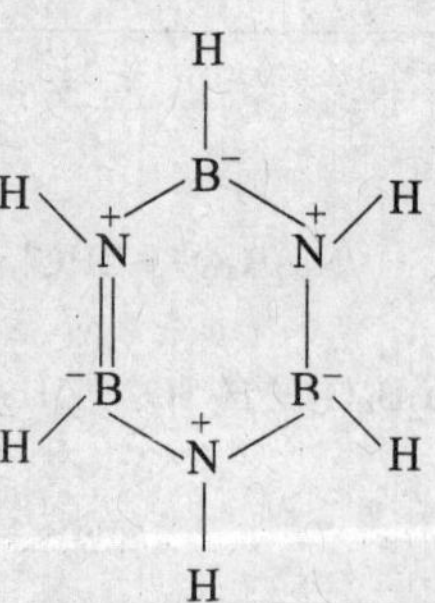

Preparation $2B_2H_6 + 6NH_3 \xrightarrow{450\text{ K}} 2B_3N_3H_6 + 12H_2$

Structure

- It is similar to benzene
- Bonding in borazine is dative and it arises from the sidewise overlapping of fully-filled p-orbitals of nitrogen and empty p-orbitals of boron.

Properties

- Readily undergoes addition reactions.

$$B_3N_3H_6 + 3HX \longrightarrow (H_2N - BHX)_3$$

- Forms metal complexes

Elements of Group 14 (Carbon Family)

- Group 14th includes carbon (C), silicon (Si), germanium (Ge), tin (Sn) and lead (Pb). The general electronic configuration is [inert gas] $ns^2 np^2$. Carbon is a non-metal.
- Silicon and germanium are metalloids while tin and lead are metals.

Physical Properties

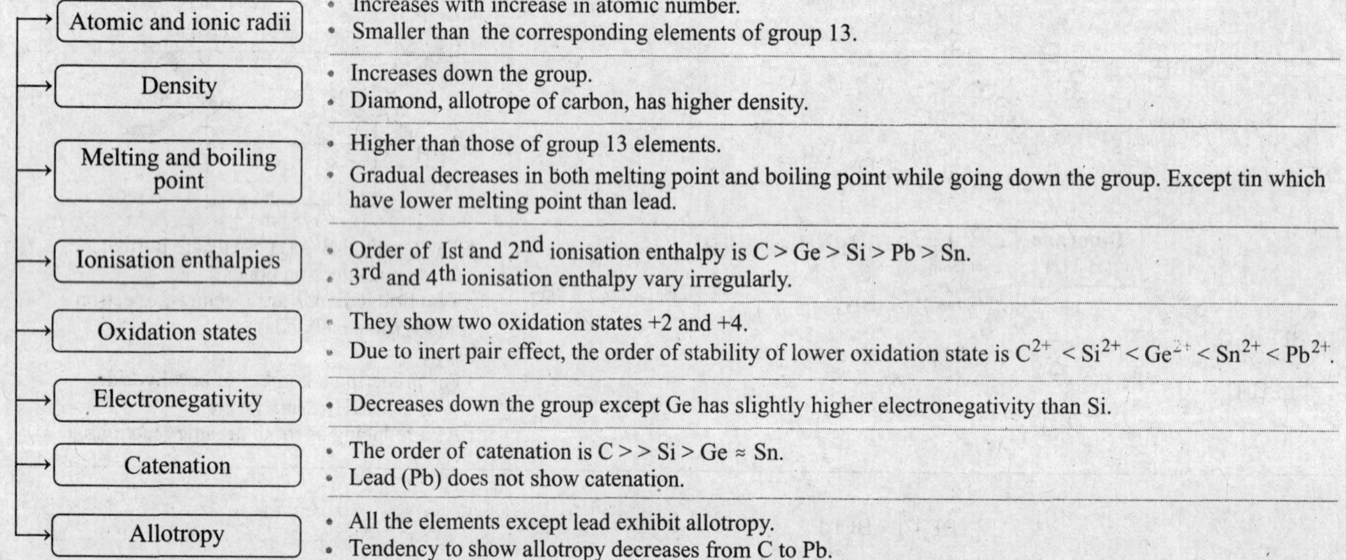

Atomic and ionic radii	• Increases with increase in atomic number. • Smaller than the corresponding elements of group 13.
Density	• Increases down the group. • Diamond, allotrope of carbon, has higher density.
Melting and boiling point	• Higher than those of group 13 elements. • Gradual decreases in both melting point and boiling point while going down the group. Except tin which have lower melting point than lead.
Ionisation enthalpies	• Order of Ist and 2nd ionisation enthalpy is C > Ge > Si > Pb > Sn. • 3rd and 4th ionisation enthalpy vary irregularly.
Oxidation states	• They show two oxidation states +2 and +4. • Due to inert pair effect, the order of stability of lower oxidation state is $C^{2+} < Si^{2+} < Ge^{2+} < Sn^{2+} < Pb^{2+}$.
Electronegativity	• Decreases down the group except Ge has slightly higher electronegativity than Si.
Catenation	• The order of catenation is C >> Si > Ge ≈ Sn. • Lead (Pb) does not show catenation.
Allotropy	• All the elements except lead exhibit allotropy. • Tendency to show allotropy decreases from C to Pb.

Anomalous Behaviour of Carbon

Carbon due to its very small size, high electronegativity and lack of d-orbitals possesses some unique properties that are given below

- It has unusually high tendency of catenation
- Due to high tendency of $p\pi$-$p\pi$ multiple bond formation, carbon forms double and triple bond with its own atoms.
- It does not react with alkalies while other members react with alkalies such as NaOH, KOH etc.
- It is quite hard (diamond) while other members are soft.
- Melting point and boiling point are very high in comparison to other members.
- CO_2 is a gas while dioxides of other members are solid.
- Carbon has highest ionisation energy among group 14 elements.
- Monoxide of carbon is neutral and gas. Monoxides of other elements are amphoteric and solid.

Allotropes of Carbon

- **Diamond** is the hardest and three dimensional polymeric structure in which sp^3-hydridised C-atoms are arranged tetrahedrally. It is a covalent solid and has a melting point of 3650°C.
- **Graphite** is a grey coloured allotrope with two dimensional structure.
  - It has sp^2 hybridisation of each carbon.
  - It is good conductor of heat and electricity due to the presence of free electrons.
- **Buckminster fullerene** contains 60 carbon atoms with sp^2-hybridisation.

Chemical Properties

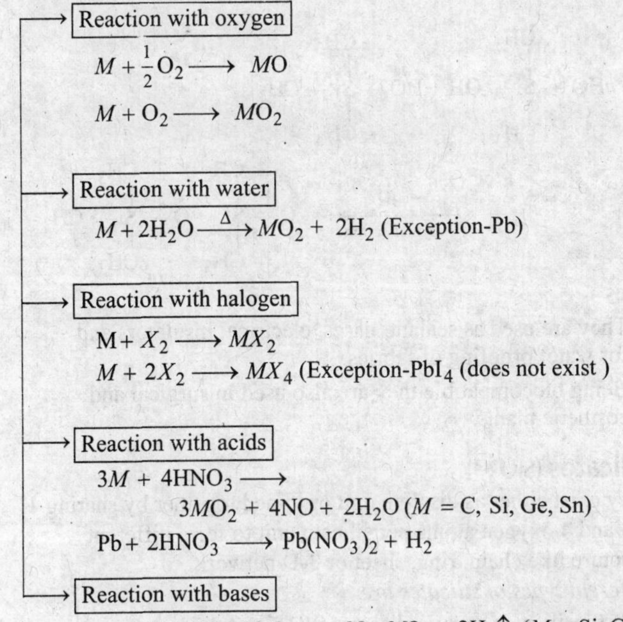

Reaction with oxygen

$M + \frac{1}{2}O_2 \longrightarrow MO$

$M + O_2 \longrightarrow MO_2$

- Forms two types of oxides i.e. monoxide and dioxide.
- Nature of monoxide is CO-neutral, GeO-acidic, SnO and PbO-amphoteric
- Nature of dioxides is $\underbrace{CO_2, SiO_2, GeO_2}_{\text{Acidic}}, \underbrace{SnO_2, \text{and } PbO_2}_{\text{Amphoteric}}$

Reaction with water

$M + 2H_2O \xrightarrow{\Delta} MO_2 + 2H_2$ (Exception-Pb)

- C, Si, Ge are not affected by water.
- Sn decomposes steam to form dioxide and H_2 gas.
- Pb is unaffected by H_2O due to the formation by oxide film.

Reaction with halogen

$M + X_2 \longrightarrow MX_2$

$M + 2X_2 \longrightarrow MX_4$ (Exception-PbI_4 (does not exist))

- MX_4 are covalent in nature (exception SnF_4 and PbF_4).
- Stability of dihalides increases down the group.
- The order of thermal stability of halides is $CX_4 > SiX_4 > GeX_4 > SnX_4 > PbX_4$

Reaction with acids

$3M + 4HNO_3 \longrightarrow 3MO_2 + 4NO + 2H_2O$ (M = C, Si, Ge, Sn)

$Pb + 2HNO_3 \longrightarrow Pb(NO_3)_2 + H_2$

- C, Si, Ge and Sn react to form oxides, while with Pb forms nitrate.
- Carbon in form of graphite reacts with conc. HNO_3 to form benzene hexacarboxylic acid.

Reaction with bases

$M + 2NaOH + H_2O \longrightarrow Na_2MO_3 + 2H_2\uparrow$ (M = Si, Ge)

$M + 2NaOH \longrightarrow Na_2MO_2 + H_2\uparrow$ (M = Sn, Pb)

- Carbon is not affected by alkalies.
- Sn and Pb slowly attacked by cold alkali and rapidly by hot alkali giving stemnates and plumbates.

Important Compounds of Carbon

Preparation & Properties	Structure and Uses
Carbon monoxide (CO) $2C + O_2 \longrightarrow$ CO $HCOOH \xrightarrow[\text{conc. } H_2SO_4]{373\text{ K}, H_2O}$ CO $C + H_2O \xrightarrow{473\text{–}1273\text{K}}$ CO $2C + O_2 + 4N_2 \xrightarrow[-H_2]{473\text{–}1273\text{K}}$ CO CO $\xrightarrow[\Delta]{O_2}$ $2CO_2$ CO $\xrightarrow[\Delta]{Fe_2O_3}$ $Fe(s) + CO_2(g)$ CO $\xrightarrow[\Delta]{ZnO}$ $Zn + CO_2$ CO $\xrightarrow{Fe,\ 180°C}$ $[Fe(CO)_5]$ CO $\xrightarrow{Ni,\ 80°C}$ $[Ni(CO)_4]$	$:C{=}\ddot{O}: \longleftrightarrow :\bar{C}{\equiv}\overset{+}{O}:$ or $:C{\equiv}O:$ • Colourless, odourless toxic gas. • Toxic nature is due to its ability to form a complex with haemoglobin in the blood. **Uses** • As fuel such as water gas ($CO + H_2$), producer gas ($CO + N_2$). • In the manufacture of compounds like petrol, methanol, phosgene gas etc.
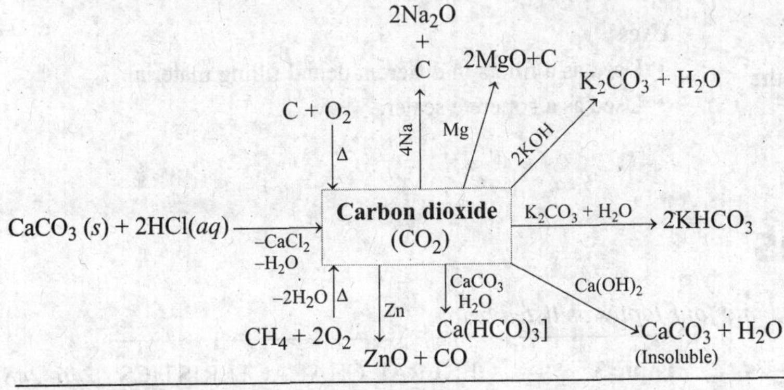 **Carbon dioxide (CO_2)** $C + O_2 \xrightarrow{\Delta} CO_2$ $CaCO_3(s) + 2HCl(aq) \xrightarrow[-H_2O]{-CaCl_2} CO_2$ $CH_4 + 2O_2 \xrightarrow{-2H_2O,\ \Delta} CO_2$ $CO_2 \xrightarrow{4Na} 2Na_2O + C$ $CO_2 \xrightarrow{Mg} 2MgO + C$ $CO_2 \xrightarrow{2KOH} K_2CO_3 + H_2O$ $CO_2 \xrightarrow{K_2CO_3 + H_2O} 2KHCO_3$ $CO_2 \xrightarrow{Zn} ZnO + CO$ $CO_2 \xrightarrow{CaCO_3,\ H_2O} Ca(HCO)_3]$ $CO_2 \xrightarrow{Ca(OH)_2} CaCO_3 + H_2O$ (Insoluble)	$:\ddot{\bar{O}}{-}C{\equiv}\overset{+}{O}: \longleftrightarrow :\ddot{O}{=}C{=}\ddot{O}: \longleftrightarrow :\overset{+}{O}{\equiv}C{-}\ddot{\bar{O}}:$ • Colourless gas with pungent odour. • Three structures of CO_2 are possible *via* resonance. **Uses** • In the manufacture of soda. • As carbogen [mixture of $O_2 + CO_2$ (5-10%)] in artificial respiration especially for pneumonia patients and victims of CO poisoning. • As a fire extinguisher.

Note (*i*) Graphite can be converted into diamond at $\approx 55 \times 10^3$ atmospheric pressure.

(*ii*) Highly lustrous form of carbon is 'Glanzkohlenstoff's which is harder than graphite and has high absorbing power.

Important Compounds of Silicon

1. Silicon dioxide (SiO_2)

- Covalent, three dimensional solid network.
- Almost non-reactive due to high Si—O bond enthalpy
- It is attacked by HF and NaOH.

$SiO_2 + 2NaOH \longrightarrow Na_2SiO_3 + H_2O$

$SiO_2 + 4HF \longrightarrow SiF_4 + 2H_2O$

Uses

- Quartz is extensively used as a piezoelectric material.
- It has made possible to develop extremely accurate clocks, modern radio and television broadcasting and mobile radio communications.
- Silica gel is used as a drying agent and as a support for chromatographic materials and catalysts.
- Kieselghur, an amorphous form of silica is used in filtration plants.

2. Silicones $-(R_2SiO)-$

- Synthetic organosilicon polymers containing repeated R_2SiO units held by Si—O—Si linkage.

$$2CH_3Cl + Si \xrightarrow[570\,K]{\text{Cu powder}} (CH_3)_2SiCl_2 \xrightarrow[-2HCl]{+2H_2O} (CH_3)_2Si(OH)_2$$

$$HO-Si(CH_3)_2-OH + HO-Si(CH_3)_2-OH + HO-Si(CH_3)_2-OH \xrightarrow[-H_2O]{\text{Polymerisation}} -O-[Si(CH_3)_2-O-Si(CH_3)_2]-O- \text{ (Silicone)}$$

- They are water repelling due to non-polar alkyl groups.
- The chain length of the polymer can be controlled by adding $(CH_3)_3SiCl$ which blocks the ends as shown in the following equation.

$$nHO-Si(CH_3)_2-OH + HO-Si(CH_3)_3 \xrightarrow[\text{Polymerisation}]{-H_2O} -O-[Si(CH_3)_2-O]_n-Si(CH_3)_3$$

Uses

- They are used as sealant, gases, electrical insulators and for water proofing of fabrics.
- Being biocompatible they are also used in surgical and cosmetic plants.

3. Silicates (SiO_4^{4-})

They exist either as discrete unit or joined together by sharing 1, 2, 3 and 4 oxygen atoms per silicate unit to form different structure like chain, ring, sheet or 3-D network.

Different types of silicates are

- Orthosilicates contain discrete SiO_4^{4-} tetrahedra.
- Pyrosilicates contain $Si_2O_7^{6-}$ anion.
- Cyclic or ring silicates contain $(SiO_3)_n^{2n-}$ anions.
- Chain silicates contain $(SiO_3)_n^{2n-}$ anions
- Sheet silicates contain $(Si_2O_5^{2-})_n$ anions.
- Three dimensional silicates–Three dimensional network structure.

O = Oxygen
⊙ = Silicon
Discrete SiO_4^{4-} tetrahedron

- Two important non-made silicates are glass and cement.
- Zeolites are 3-D silicates in which some of the Si atoms are replaced by Al^{3+} ions and to balance the negative charge of some cations like Na^+, K^+ or Ca^{2+} are incorporated.
- Zeolites are widely used as a catalyst in petrochemical industries for cracking of hydrocarbons and isomerisation, e.g. ZSM-5 (a type of zeolite) used to convert alcohols directly into gasoline.

Uses

- Used as a fillers in different dental filling material.
- Used as a concrete scaler.

Topical Practice Questions

All the exam questions of this chapter have been divided into four topics as listed below

Topic 1

General Characteristics of Group 13 Elements

2018

1 The correct order of atomic radii in group 13 elements is **[NEET]**

(a) $B < Ga < Al < Tl < In$ (b) $B < Al < Ga < In < Tl$
(c) $B < Al < In < Ga < Tl$ (d) $B < Ga < Al < In < Tl$

2014

2 Which of the following is a least stable compound? **[Manipal]**

(a) BCl_3 (b) $GaCl_3$ (c) $InCl_3$ (d) $TlCl_3$

3 Which species does not exist? **[UK PMT]**

(a) $[BF_6]^{3-}$ (b) $[AlF_6]^{3-}$
(c) $[GaF_6]^{3-}$ (d) $[InF_6]^{3-}$

4 The correct increasing order of the stability of Al^+, Ga^+, In^+, Tl^+ ions are **[EAMCET]**

(a) $Al^+ < Ga^+ < Tl^+ < In^+$
(b) $Al^+ < Ga^+ < In^+ < Tl^+$
(c) $Tl^+ < In^+ < Ga^+ < Al^+$
(d) $Tl^+ < Al^+ < Ga^+ < In^+$

2012

5 Ammonal used in bomb is a mixture of **[AFMC]**

(a) $Al + KNO_3$ (b) $Al + Al_2O_3 + B_2O_3$
(c) $Al + Al(NO_3)_3$ (d) $Al_2O_3 + C$

6 Correct formula of aluminium nitride is **[OJEE]**

(a) Al_2N_2 (b) AlN_3
(c) AlN_2 (d) AlN

2010

7 The tendency of BF_3, BCl_3 and BBr_3 to behave as Lewis acid decreases in the sequence **[CBSE AIPMT]**

(a) $BF_3 > BCl_3 > BBr_3$
(b) $BCl_3 > BF_3 > BBr_3$
(c) $BBr_3 > BCl_3 > BF_3$
(d) $BBr_3 > BF_3 > BCl_3$

8 The composition of duralumin is **[AIIMS]**

(a) Al 94%, Mg 6%
(b) Cu 56%, Zn 24%, Ni 20 %
(c) Cu 95%, Al 5%
(d) Al 95%, Cu 4%, Mn 0.5%, Mg 0.5 %

9 The strongest Lewis acid among boron halides is **[RPMT, AMU]**

(a) BBr_3 (b) BCl_3
(c) BI_3 (d) BF_3

10 BF_3 is **[RPMT]**

(a) electron deficient compound
(b) Lewis base
(c) used as rocket fuel
(d) ionic compound

11 Magnalium contains **[JCECE]**

(a) Mg + Al (b) Mg + Cu
(c) Mg + Fe (d) Mg + Mn

2005

12 Which of the following is the electron deficient molecule? **[AIIMS]**

(a) B_2H_6 (b) C_2H_6
(c) PH_3 (d) SiH_4

Answers

1 (d)	2 (d)	3 (d)	4 (b)	5 (c)	6 (d)	7 (c)	8 (d)	9 (c)	10 (a)
11 (a)	12 (a)								

Explanations

1 (*d*) The atomic radii as well as ionic radii increases on moving down the group 13 elements because of the successive addition of one extra shell of electrons. However, there is an anomaly at gallium in case of atomic radii.
Atomic radii of Ga is lesser than that of Al. Gallium (Ga) with electronic configuration, $[Ar]_{18} 3d^{10} 4s^2 4p^1$ has *d*-electrons, which do not screen the nucleus effectively. Consequently, electrons of Ga are more attracted by nucleus.
Thus, the increasing order of atomic radii of the group 13 elements is B (85 pm) < Ga (135 pm) < Al (143 pm) < In (167 pm) < Tl (170 pm).

2 (*d*) Thallium trihalide is least stable due to inert pair effect. The stability of +3 oxidation state decreases down the group and that of +1 oxidation state increases down the group.

3 (*d*) All central ele nts in given options belong to group 1ɔ.
They show oxidation state of
$x + 6(-1) = -3, \ x = +3.$
Due to inert pair effect, stability of higher oxidation state, i.e. +3 decreases on moving down the group.
Hence, $[InF_6]^{3-}$ is least stable and does not exist.

4 (*b*) Group 13 elements have three electrons in their outermost shell with the valence electronic configuration, ns^2np^1.
The boron family shows oxidation states +3 or +1.
Due to inert pair effect, on moving down the group stability of higher oxidation state (+3) decreases. Thus, the stability of +1 oxidation state increases.
Hence, the correct order is

$$Al^+ < Ga^+ < In^+ < Tl^+.$$

5 (*c*) Mixture of Al powder and $Al(NO_3)_3$ is known as ammonal. It is used in bomb formation material.

6 (*d*) Formula of aluminium nitride is AlN. It is a covalently bonded ceramic. It is an explosive made up of ammonium nitrate and Al powder. It can be synthesised from the element. 'Al' and 'N'. It does not occur naturally.

7 (*c*) On moving from BF_3 to BCl_3, the tendency to form $p\pi$-$p\pi$ bond decreases. Thus, back donation is maximum in BF_3. Hence, Lewis acid character decreases in it. So, the correct order to act as Lewis acid is : $BBr_3 > BCl_3 > BF_3$.

8 (*d*) **Duralumin** is an alloy of Al(95%), Cu(4%), Mn (0.5%) and Mg (0.5%).
Magnalium is an alloy of Al (94%) and Mg (6%).
German silver is an alloy of Cu (56%), Zn (24%) and Ni (20%).
Aluminium bronze is an alloy of Cu (95%) and Al (5%).

9 (*c*) Generally, as the electronegativity increases, acidic character increases, but in case of boron halides, BI_3 is most acidic, i.e. strongest Lewis acid.
This is because there is back donation of electrons from halogen atom to boron in BX_3 (X = F, Cl, Br, I).
This makes the BX_3 less electron deficient. The tendency of back donation decreases as the size of halogen atom increases (due to large energy difference).
Hence, due to large size of I, BI_3 is most electron deficient and thus, the strongest Lewis acid.

10 (*a*) Boron has 3 electrons in outerment shell and fluorine has 7 electrons in outermost shell with 1 unpaired electron. Therefore, boron can accept the electron, and behave as Lewis acid.

11 (*a*) Magnalium is an alloy of Al (94.5%) and Mg (5.5%). It is used to make light instruments.

12 (*a*) In B_2H_6, each B-atom uses sp^3-hybrid orbitals for bonding. Out of 4 sp^3-hybrid orbitals, one orbital is empty.
Here, one half-filled orbital of other B-atom overlaps with one empty orbital of other B-atom and half-filled orbitals of hydrogen atom resulting in 3 centred two e^- bridge bonds. Thus, these bonds are electron deficient.

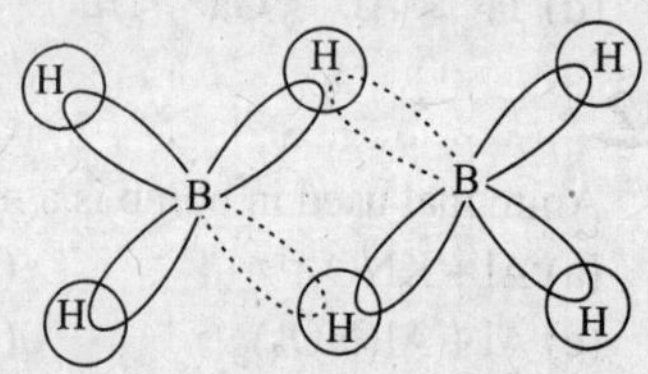

Topic 2

Compounds of Group 13 Elements

2014

1 The ultimate product obtained on heating B_2H_6 with NH_3 is **[Manipal]**
(a) $B_3N_3H_6$
(b) $(B—N)_3$
(c) N_2H_4
(d) BH^{-4}

2013

2 The molecular formula of cryolite is **[Manipal]**
(a) $Na_2F \cdot AlF_6$
(b) Na_3AlF_6
(c) Na_3AlF_5
(d) Na_2AlF_3

2010

3 In which of the following molecules is hydrogen bridge bond present? **[WB JEE]**
(a) Water
(b) Inorganic benzene
(c) Diborane
(d) Methanol

4 Borax is used as a cleansing agent because on dissolving in water, it gives **[RPMT, AMU]**
(a) alkaline solution
(b) acidic solution
(c) bleaching solution
(d) amphoteric solution

5 Inorganic benzene is [Guj CET]
(a) $B_3H_3N_3$ (b) BH_3NH_3 (c) $B_3H_6N_3$ (d) $H_3B_3N_6$

6 The structure of BF_3 is [VMCC]
(a) triangular planar (b) pyramidal
(c) tetrahedral (d) T-shaped

2009

7 **Assertion** (A) Coloured cations can be identified by borax bead test.
Reason (R) Transparent bead ($NaBO_2 + B_2O_3$) forms coloured bead with coloured cation. [AIIMS]
(a) Both A and R are correct and R is the correct explanation of A
(b) Both A and R are correct but R is not the correct explanation of A
(c) A is correct but R is incorrect
(d) Both A and R are incorrect

8 Which among the following is not a borane? [AMU]
(a) B_2H_6 (b) B_3H_6
(c) B_4H_{10} (d) None of these

9 Which of the following reactions will not give the anhydrous $AlCl_3$? [DUMET]
(a) By heating $AlCl_3 \cdot 6H_2O$
(b) By passing dry HCl gas on heated aluminium powder
(c) By passing dry chlorine gas on heated aluminium powder
(d) By passing dry chlorine gas over a heated mixture of alumina and coke

2008

10 A mixture of boron trichloride and hydrogen is subjected to silent electric discharge to form *A* and HCl. *A* reacts with NH_3 and heated to 200°C to form *B*. The formula of *B* is [EAMCET]
(a) H_3BO_3 (b) B_2O_3 (c) $B_3N_3H_6$ (d) B_2H_6

11 For which one of the following minerals, the composition given is incorrect? [Kerala CEE]
(a) Glauber's salt —$Na_2SO_4 \cdot 10H_2O$
(b) Borax—$Na_2B_4O_7 \cdot 7H_2O$
(c) Carnallite — $KCl \cdot MgCl_2 \cdot 6H_2O$
(d) Soda ash—Na_2CO_3
(e) Epsom salt—$MgSO_4 \cdot 7H_2O$

12 In borax bead test which compound is formed? [Punjab PMET]
(a) Orthoborate (b) Metaborate
(c) Double oxide (d) Tetraborate

2006

13 The number of isomers possible for disubstituted borazine, $B_3N_3H_4X_2$ is [Kerala CEE]
(a) 3 (b) 4 (c) 6 (d) 2 (e) 5

14 In diborane, the two H—B—H angles are nearly [AIIMS]
(a) 60°, 120° (b) 97°, 120°
(c) 95°, 150° (d) 120°,180°

15 *X* reacts with aqueous NaOH solution to form *Y* and H_2. Aqueous solution of *Y* is heated to 323-333 K and on passing CO_2 into it, Na_2CO_3 and *Z* were formed. When *Z* is heated to 1200°C, Al_2O_3 is formed. *X, Y* and *Z* respectively are [EAMCET]
(a) Al, $AlCl_3$, $NaAlO_2$
(b) Zn, Na_2ZnO_2, $Al(OH)_3$
(c) Al, $Al(OH)_3$, $AlCl_3$
(d) Al, $NaAlO_2$, $Al(OH)_3$

Answers

1 (a)	2 (b)	3 (c)	4 (a)	5 (c)	6 (a)	7 (a)	8 (b)	9 (a)	10 (c)
11 (b)	12 (b)	13 (a)	14 (b)	15 (d)					

Explanations

1 (*a*) $3B_2H_6 + 6NH_3 \xrightarrow{200°C} 2B_3N_3H_6 + 12H_2$
1 : 2 — Borazine or Borazole

2 (*b*) The molecular formula of cryolite is Na_3AlF_6.

3 (*c*) The hydrogen bridge bonds are present in diborane (B_2H_6)

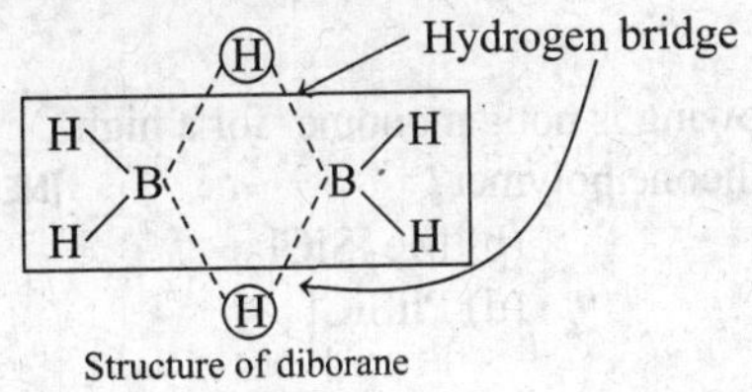

Structure of diborane

4 (*a*) The aqueous solution of borax is alkaline due to hydrolysis and thus, is used as a cleansing agent.

$$\underset{\text{(Borax)}}{Na_2B_4O_7} + 7H_2O \longrightarrow \underset{\text{(Strong alkali)}}{2NaOH} + \underset{\text{(Weak acid)}}{4H_3BO_3}$$

5 (*c*) Borazine, $B_3N_3H_6$ is also known as inorganic benzene due to its resemblance in structure and some physical and chemical properties with benzene.

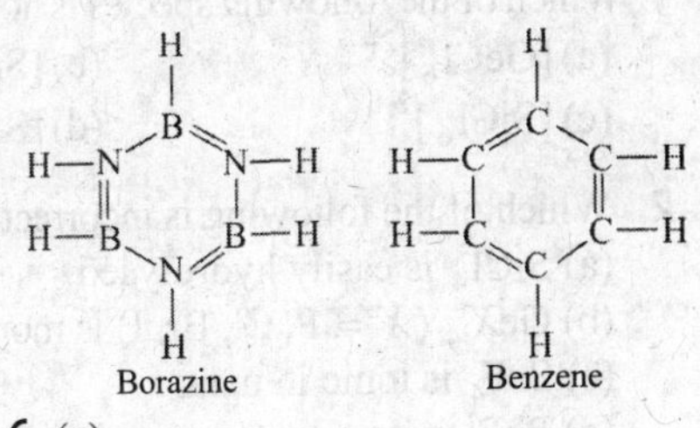

6 (*a*)

$$\begin{array}{c} F \\ | \\ B \\ \diagup \quad \diagdown \\ F \qquad F \end{array}$$

Due to sp^2-hybridisation, the structure of BF_3 is triangular planar.

7 (*a*) Borax, when heated at about 740°C, forms a glassy mass like bead.

$$Na_2B_4O_7 \xrightarrow{740°C} \underbrace{\underset{\text{Sodium metaborate}}{2NaBO_2} + \underset{\text{Boric anhydride}}{B_2O_3}}_{\text{Glassy bead}}$$

This glassy bead gives different colour beads with different cations. Hence, it is used to identify cations in qualitative analysis. This test is called borax bead test.

8 (*b*) Boranes fall into following categories :

(i) $B_nH_{(n+4)}$ (called *nido*-boranes); B_2H_6

(ii) $B_nH_{(n+6)}$ (called *arachno*-boranes); B_4H_{10}

B_3H_6 does not fall into any of the above categories.

9 (*a*) Hydrated aluminium chloride undergoes decomposition to form Al_2O_3 on heating.

$$2AlCl_3 \cdot 6H_2O \xrightarrow{\Delta} 2Al(OH)_3 + 6HCl$$

$$2Al(OH)_3 \xrightarrow{\Delta} Al_2O_3 + 3H_2O$$

10 (*c*) When a mixture of BCl_3 and H_2 is subjected to silent electric discharge, diborane (*A*) and HCl are formed and diborane (*A*) reacts with NH_3 at 200°C to give borazine (inorganic benzene).

$$2BCl_3—6H_2 \xrightarrow[\text{discharge}]{\text{Electric}} \underset{(A)}{B_2H_6} + 6HCl$$

$$\underset{1}{3B_2H_6} + \underset{2}{6NH_3} \xrightarrow{200°C} \underset{(B)}{2B_3N_3H_6} + 12H_2$$

11 (*b*) (a) Glauber's salt — $Na_2SO_4 \cdot 10H_2O$

(b) Borax — $Na_2B_4O_7 \cdot 10H_2O$

(c) Carnallite — $KCl \cdot MgCl_2 \cdot 6H_2O$

(d) Soda ash — Na_2CO_3

(e) Epsom salt — $MgSO_4 \cdot 7H_2O$

12 (*b*) In borax bead test, the coloured metaborates are formed by transition metal salt.

$$Na_2B_4O_7 \cdot 10H_2O \xrightarrow[-10H_2O]{\Delta} Na_2B_4O_7$$

$$\xrightarrow{\Delta} \underset{\text{Sodium metaborate}}{2NaBO_2} + \underset{\text{Boric anhydride}}{B_2O_3}$$

$$B_2O_3 + CuO \longrightarrow \underset{\substack{\text{Cupric metaborate}\\ \text{(Blue bead)}}}{Cu(BO_2)_2}$$

13 (*a*) Borazine is called inorganic benzene. The number of isomers possible for disubstituted borazine ($B_3N_3H_4X_2$) is three.

14 (*b*) Structure of diborane is as follows :

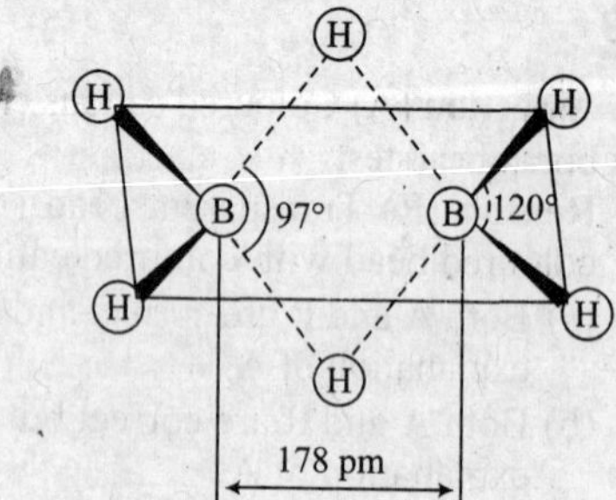

Thus, the H—B—H angles are nearly 97° and 120°.

15 (*c*) The reactions are as follows:

$$\underset{X}{2Al} + 2NaOH + 2H_2O \longrightarrow 2NaAlO_2 + \underset{Y}{3H_2} \uparrow$$

$$2NaAlO_2 + CO_2 + 3H_2O \xrightarrow{\Delta} Na_2CO_3 + \underset{Z}{2Al(OH)_3}$$

$$\underset{Z}{2Al(OH)_3} \xrightarrow{1200°C} Al_2O_3 + 3H_2O$$

Topic 3

General Characteristics of Group 14 Elements

2019

1 Which of the following species is not stable? **[NEET]**

(a) $[GeCl_6]^{2-}$ (b) $[Sn(OH)_6]^{2-}$

(c) $[SiCl_6]^{2-}$ (d) $[SiF_6]^{2-}$

2 Which of the following is incorrect statement? **[NEET]**

(a) $SiCl_4$ is easily hydrolysed

(b) GeX_4 (X = F, Cl, Br, I) is more stable than GeX_2

(c) SnF_4 is ionic in nature

(d) PbF_4 is covalent in nature

3 Which of the following statement is correct for isotope of carbon? **[JIPMER]**

(a) Graphite is conductor of electricity

(b) Diamond have all sp^3 hybridised carbon

(c) Graphite is more stable thermodynamically than diamond

(d) All are correct

2014

4 Which of the following is used as black pigment in black ink? **[EAMCET]**

(a) Carbon black (b) Germanium

(c) Graphite (d) Coke

2013

5 Which of the following is not a monomer for a high molecular mass silicone polymer? **[NEET]**

(a) $MeSiCl_3$ (b) Me_2SiCl_2

(c) Me_3SiCl (d) $PhSiCl_3$

2012

6 Ge (II) compounds are powerful reducing agents whereas Pb (IV) compounds are strong oxidants. It can be because [AFMC]
(a) Pb is more electropositive than Ge
(b) ionisation potential of lead is less than that of Ge
(c) ionic radii of Pb^{2+} and Pb^{4+} are larger than those of Ge^{2+} and Ge^{4+}
(d) more pronounced inert pair effect in lead than Ge

7 Graphite is a soft solid lubricant extremely difficult to melt. The reason for this anomalous behaviour is that graphite [UP CPMT]
(a) is an allotropic form of carbon
(b) is a non-crystalline substance
(c) has carbon atoms arranged in large plates of rings of strongly bonded carbon atoms with weak interplate bonds
(d) has molecule of variable molecular masses like polymers

2010

8 Graphite is a good conductor of electricity. Its electrical conductivity is due to the fact that [UP CPMT]
(a) it is an allotrope of carbon
(b) it has C-atoms arranged in large plates of rings of strongly bound C-atoms
(c) in it C-atoms are sp^2-hybridised
(d) it is a non-crystalline substance

9 Which of the following is not hydrolysed easily? [OJEE]
(a) CCl_4 (b) $SiCl_4$
(c) $GeCl_4$ (d) $SnCl_4$

10 For which element the inertness of the electron pair will not be observed? [WB JEE]
(a) Sn (b) Fe (c) Pb (d) In

2009

11 The number of carbon atoms in Buckminster fullerene is [WB JEE]
(a) 50 (b) 350
(c) 60 (d) 70
(e) 80

12 Which of the following statement is not correct? [WB JEE]
(a) Silicon is extensively used as a semiconductor
(b) Carborundum is SiC
(c) Silicon occurs in free state in nature
(d) Mica contains the element silicon

2008

13 A fibrous mineral which can withstand red hot flames without any damage is [Manipal]
(a) talc (b) glass wool
(c) soap stone (d) asbestos

14 The geometry at which carbon atoms in diamond are bonded to each other is [Kerala CEE]
(a) linear (b) tetrahedral
(c) square planar (d) octahedral
(e) hexagonal

2007

15 Which element is used for making a transistor? [Manipal]
(a) Sn (b) Sb (c) Si (d) Mg

16 Which of the following is not silicate? [DUMET]
(a) Zeolite (b) Feldspar (c) Silica (d) Ultramarine

2005

17 Which of the following waste materials can be used for producing bio-gas? [AMU]
(a) Thermocoal (b) Glass bottle
(c) Tin cans (d) Paper scrap

Answers

1 (c)	2 (d)	3 (d)	4 (a)	5 (c)	6 (d)	7 (c)	8 (c)	9 (a)	10 (b)
11 (c)	12 (c)	13 (d)	14 (b)	15 (c)	16 (c)	17 (d)			

Explanations

1 (*c*) $[SiCl_6]^{2-}$ is not stable and does not exist because
(i) six large chloride ions cannot be accommodated around Si^{4+} due to limitation of its size.
(ii) interaction between lone pair of chloride ion and Si^{4+} is not very strong.

On the other hand, due to presence of *d*-orbital in Si, Ge and Sn they form species like $[SiF_6]^{2-}$, $[GeCl_6]^{2-}$ and $[Sn(OH)_6]^{2-}$. Hence, option (c) is correct.

2 (*d*) All the tetrahalides of group-14 elements are covalent in nature and sp^3-hybridised with tetrahedral geometry. Exceptions are SnF_4 and PbF_4 which are ionic in nature. Thus, statement (d) is incorrect while the remaining statements are correct.

3 (*d*) The explanation of given statements are as follows :
(a) Graphite is conductor of electricity because it has 1 free valence electron which does not participate in bonding. Thus, statement (a) is correct.
(b) Diamond has a three dimensional structure in which sp^3-hybridised C-atoms are arranged tetrahedrally. Thus, statement (b) is correct.
(c) Graphite is thermodynamically more stable than diamond and its free energy of formation is less than that of diamond. However, entropy of graphite is more than that of diamond.

4 (*a*) Carbon black particles are used as black pigments and employed in photocopier, laser printer, other inks and paintings.

5 (c) Me_3SiCl is not a monomer for a high molecular mass silicone polymer because it generates Me_3SiOH when subjected to hydrolysis which contains only one reacting site.

Hence, the polymerisation reaction stops just after first step.

$$Me-\underset{Me}{\overset{Me}{Si}}-OH + HO-\underset{Me}{\overset{Me}{Si}}-Me \xrightarrow{-H_2O} Me-\underset{Me}{\overset{Me}{Si}}-O-\underset{Me}{\overset{Me}{Si}}-Me$$

[Final product (dimer)]

6 (d) Inert pair effect is more pronounced in heavier members like Pb. Hence, Pb (IV) compounds act as strong oxidising agents and are reduced to more stable Pb (II) compounds. Whereas Ge (II) compounds act as powerful reducing agents and itself get oxidised.

7 (c) Graphite is a soft solid lubricant extremely difficult to melt. The reason for this anomalous behaviour is that graphite has carbon atoms arranged in large plates of rings of strongly bound carbon atoms with weak van der Waals' forces (interplate bonds). Thus, these layers can slide over one another. This gives softness, greasiness and lubricating character to graphite.

8 (c) In graphite, each carbon atom is sp^2-hybridised having 3 covalent bonds with 3 other C-atoms in the same plane. The remaining fourth electron of each carbon atom does not participate in bonding and is free to move. These free electrons make the graphite good conductor of electricity.

9 (c) CCl_4, due to the absence of *d*-orbitals, cannot accommodate the electron pair supplied by H_2O in the first step of hydrolysis reaction.

10 (b) Inert pair effect is exhibited only by heavy metals of *p*-block elements and Fe belongs to *d*-block elements. So, inertness of electron pair will not be observed in Fe.

11 (c) Buckminster fullerene is the first discovered fullerene which contains 60 carbon atoms. The molecules has shape of soccer ball in which 12 five membered and 20 six membered rings are present.

12 (c) Silicon occurs in combined state in nature as silica, SiO_2 and silicates. Rest of the given statements are correct.

13 (d) Asbestos can withstand red hot flames without any damage. Asbestos is a hydrous magnesium silicate with the chemical formula of $[Mg_3Si_2O_5(OH)_4]$.

14 (b) In diamond each carbon atom is sp^3-hybridised, so the geometry of diamond is tetrahedral.

15 (c) Si is a semiconductor material, it is used in transistors.

16 (c) (a) Zeolite — $Na_2Al_2SiO_8 \cdot xH_2O$

(b) Feldspar — $KAlSi_3O_8$

(c) Silica — SiO_2

(d) Ultramarine — $Na_8(AlO_2)_6 \cdot (SiO_2)_6S_2$

Except silica, all other three are silicates.

17 (d) Bio-gas can be produced by the fermentation process of paper scrap (this process takes place in a digester tank).

Topic 4

Compounds of Group 14 Elements

2019

1 Which of the following compounds is used in cosmetic surgery? [NEET (Odisha)]

(a) Silica (b) Silicates
(c) Silicones (d) Zeolites

2 Which of the following is not allotrope of carbon? [JIPMER]

(a) Diamond (b) Fullerene
(c) Soot (d) Graphite

3 Silicon carbide is an example of [JIPMER]

(a) molecular solid (b) metallic solid
(c) ionic crystal (d) covalent solid

2013

4 The basic structural unit of silicates are [NEET]

(a) SiO^- (b) SiO_4^{4-} (c) SiO_3^{2-} (d) SiO_4^{2-}

5 Which of the following structure is similar to graphite? [NEET]

(a) $(BN)_x$ (b) B
(c) B_4C (d) B_2H_6

6 **Assertion** (A) PbI_4 is a stable compound.

Reason (R) Iodide stabilises higher oxidation state.

(a) Both A and R are correct and R is correct explanation of A [AIIMS]
(b) Both A and R are correct but R is not the correct explanation of A
(c) A is correct but R is incorrect
(d) Both A and R are incorrect

7 Water gas is produced by [AIIMS]

(a) passing steam over red hot coke
(b) passing steam and air over red hot coke
(c) burning coke in excess of air
(d) burning coke in limited supply of air

8 Sindoor is represented by [UP CPMT]

(a) $Pb(NO_3)_2$
(b) $PbCO_3 \cdot Pb(OH)_2$
(c) $Pb(OH)_2 \cdot 4PbCO_3$
(d) Pb_3O_4

2011

9 Name the type of the structure of silicate in which one oxygen atom of $[SiO_4]^{4-}$ is shared? [CBSE AIPMT]
(a) Three dimensional (b) Linear chain silicate
(c) Sheet silicate (d) Pyrosilicate

2010

10 Chemical formula of phosgene is [AFMC, MP PMT]
(a) $COCl_2$ (b) $CaOCl_2$ (c) $CaCO_3$ (d) COCl

11 Which of the following is not attacked by hot sodium hydroxide solution? [Manipal]
(a) Silicon (b) Carbon (c) Tin (d) Lead

12 The products of the following reaction are [OJEE]

$$SiO_2 + C \xrightarrow{\Delta}$$

(a) SiC and CO_2 (b) SiO and CO
(c) SiC and CO (d) Si and CO_2

13 Atomic orbitals of carbon in carbon dioxide are [RPMT]
(a) *sp*-hybridised (b) sp^3d-hybridised
(c) sp^2-hybridised (d) sp^3-hybridised

14 Which type of silicate is shown in the given figure? [Guj CET]

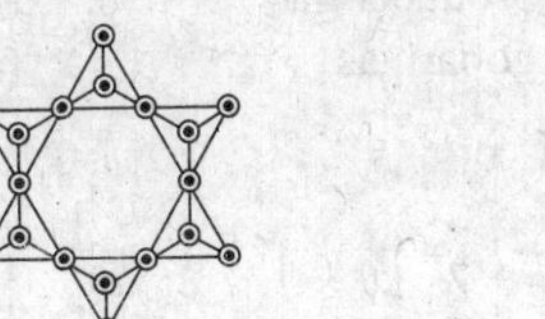

(a) Orthosilicate (b) Pyrosilicate
(c) Metasilicate (d) None of these

2009

15 The lead of the lead pencils melts at [AIIMS]
(a) 2000°C (b) 350°C (c) 3170°C (d) 75°C

16 Darkening of surface painted with white lead is due to [UP CPMT]
(a) H_2S (b) CO_2 (c) Cu (d) O_2

17 The anion $(Si_6O_{18}^{12-})$ is present in [Kerala CEE]
(a) pyroxene (b) beryl (c) mica (d) albite
(e) asbestos

18 The main reason that $SiCl_4$ is easily hydrolysed as compared to CCl_4 is that [Kerala CEE]
(a) Si—Si bond is weaker
(b) $SiCl_4$ can form hydrogen bonds
(c) $SiCl_4$ is covalent
(d) $SiCl_4$ is ionic
(e) Si can extend its coordination number beyond four

19 $SiCl_4$ on hydrolysis forms '*X*' and HCl. Compound '*X*' loses water at 1000°C and gives '*Y*'. Compounds '*X*' and '*Y*' respectively are [EAMCET]
(a) H_2SiCl_6, SiO_2 (b) H_4SiO_4, Si
(c) SiO_2, Si (d) H_4SiO_4, SiO_2

20 Silica is soluble in [CG PMT, Haryana PMT]
(a) HCl (b) HNO_3 (c) H_2SO_4 (d) HF

2008

21 Non-oxide ceramics can be [AIIMS]
(a) B_4C (b) SiC
(c) Si_3N_4 (d) All of these

22 Which of the following is used for making optical instruments? [AFMC]
(a) SiO_2 (b) Si (c) SiH_4 (d) SiC

23 **Assertion** (A) Silica is soluble in HF.

$$SiO_2 + 4HF \longrightarrow SiF_4 + 2H_2O$$ [BHU]

Reason (R) $SiF_4 + 6HF \longrightarrow H_2SiF_6$
(a) Both A and R are correct and R is the correct explanation of A
(b) Both A and R are correct but R is not the correct explanation of A
(c) A is correct but R is incorrect
(d) Both A and R are incorrect

24 Lead pipes can be used safely for carrying [Manipal]
(a) soft water
(b) soft water first heated with limestone
(c) conc. HNO_3
(d) soft as well as hard water

25 Product of the following reaction is

$$Al_4C_3 + D_2O \longrightarrow$$ [Haryana PMT]

(a) $Al(OD)_3 + CD_4$ (b) $Al(OD)_2 + CD_4$
(c) $Al(OD)_4 + CD_4$ (d) $Al(OD)_3 + CD$

2007

26 Which one of the following anions is present in the chain structure silicates? [CBSE AIPMT]
(a) $Si_2O_7^{6-}$ (b) $(Si_2O_5^{2-})_n$ (c) $(SiO_3^{2-})_n$ (d) SiO_4^{4-}

27 Supercritical CO_2 is used as [AIIMS]
(a) dry ice
(b) fire fighting
(c) a solvent for extraction of organic compounds from natural sources
(d) a highly inert medium for carrying out various reactions

28 Carborundum is [BHU]
(a) SiC (b) $AlCl_3$
(c) $Al_2(SO_4)_3$ (d) $Al_2O_3 \cdot 2H_2O$

29 When lead nitrate is heated, it gives [BHU]
(a) NO_2 (b) PbO
(c) Both (a) and (b) (d) NO

30 White lead is [UP CPMT]
(a) Pb_3O_4 (b) PbO
(c) $2PbCO_3 \cdot Pb(OH)_2$ (d) $Pb(CH_3COO)_2 \cdot Pb(OH)_2$

31 Monosilane on coming in contact with air burns with a luminous flame producing vortex rings. These rings are of **[MHT CET]**
(a) SiO_2 (b) SiO
(c) Si (d) H_2SiO_3

32 For prevention of rusting of iron, which paint is used? **[RPMT]**
(a) PbO (b) PbO_2
(c) Pb_3O_4 (d) $PbSO_4$

33 How many O-atoms are shared per SiO_4^{4-} tetrahedral in silicate anion of beryl mineral? **[Haryana PMT]**
(a) 3 (b) 4 (c) 1 (d) 2

34 *A* when added to silicon will give *B*. *A* and *B* are **[DUMET]**
(a) HF, H_2SiF_4 (b) HF, H_2SiF_6
(c) HCl, H_2SiCl_6 (d) HI, H_2SiI_6

2006

35 **Assertion** (A) Silicones are hydrophobic in nature.
Reason (R) Si—O—Si linkages are moisture sensitive. **[AIIMS]**
(a) Both A and R are correct and R is the correct explanation of A
(b) Both A and R are correct but R is not the correct explanation of A
(c) A is correct but R is incorrect
(d) Both A and R are incorrect

36 The composition of the common glass is **[Manipal]**
(a) $Na_2O \cdot CaO \cdot 6SiO_3$ (b) $Na_2O \cdot Al_2O_3 \cdot SiO_2$
(c) $CaO \cdot Al_2O_3 \cdot SiO_2$ (d) $Na_2O \cdot CaO \cdot 6SiO_2$

2005

37 **Assertion** (A) SiF_6^{2-} is known but $SiCl_6^{2-}$ is not.
Reason (R) Size of fluorine is small and its lone pair of electrons interacts with *d*-orbitals of Si strongly. **[AIIMS]**
(a) Both A and R are correct and R is the correct explanation of A
(b) Both A and R are correct but R is not the correct explanation of A
(c) A is correct but R is incorrect
(d) Both A and R are incorrect

38 In the preparation of amorphous silicon, HF acid is used to remove **[MHT CET]**
(a) Mg
(b) SiO_2
(c) Si
(d) None of the above

39 In laboratory burners, we use **[Manipal]**
(a) producer gas (b) oil gas
(c) gobar gas (d) coal gas

Answers

1 (c)	2 (c)	3 (d)	4 (b)	5 (a)	6 (d)	7 (a)	8 (d)	9 (d)	10 (a)
11 (b)	12 (c)	13 (a)	14 (d)	15 (c)	16 (a)	17 (b)	18 (e)	19 (d)	20 (d)
21 (d)	22 (a)	23 (a)	24 (b)	25 (a)	26 (c)	27 (c)	28 (a)	29 (c)	30 (c)
31 (a)	32 (c)	33 (d)	34 (b)	35 (c)	36 (d)	37 (a)	38 (b)	39 (b)	

Explanations

1 (*c*) Silicones are synthetic organo-silicon polymers containing repeated R_2SiO units. It is used in surgical and cosmetic implants. They are also used as low temperature lubricants, in making waterproof clothes and papers, etc.

2 (*c*) The properties of catenation and $p\pi$-$p\pi$ bond formation allow carbon to exist in multiple allotropes. Diamond, graphite and fullerene are crystaline allotrope of carbon. Coal, coke, charcoal, lamp are amorphous allotrope of carbon.

3 (*d*) Silicon carbide (SiC) is an example of covalent solids. Covalent or network solids are crystalline solids of non-metals that result from the formation of covalent bonds between adjacent atoms throughout the crystal. They are insulators and do not conduct electricity.

4 (*b*) The basic building unit of all silicates is the tetrahedral SiO_4^{4-}. It is represented as :

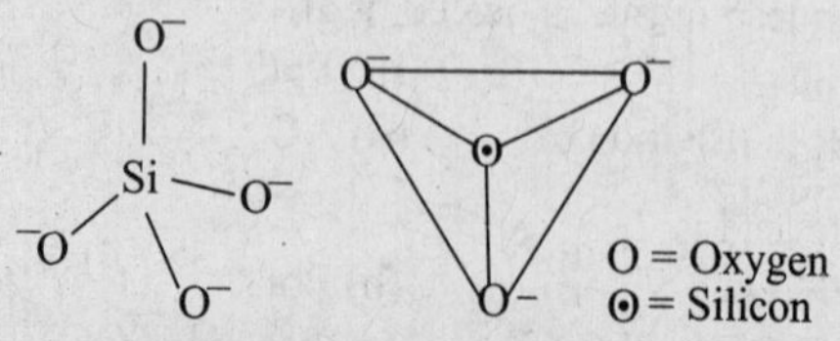

O = Oxygen
⊙ = Silicon

Structure of SiO_4^{4-} ion

5 (*a*) Boron nitride, $(BN)_x$ resembles with graphite in structure as

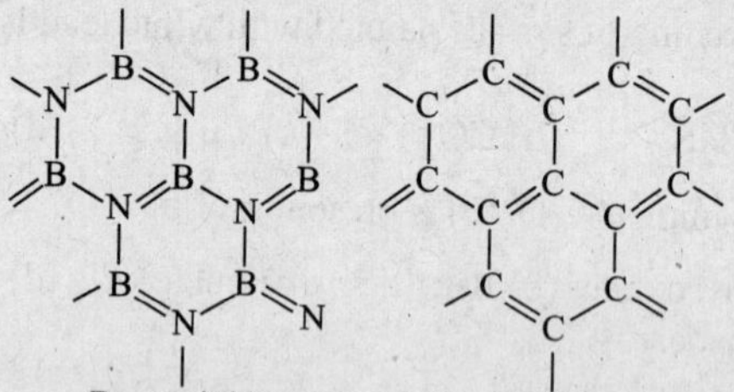

Boron nitride Graphite

6 (*d*) Common oxidation state of IVA group elements is +2 and +4 but as we move down the group, +2 oxidation state becomes more stable. Thus, Pb^{4+} is not possible, i.e. PbI_4 is highly unstable.

7 (*a*) Water gas is produced by passing steam over a bed of red hot coke at 1000-1400°C.

$$\underset{\text{Coke}}{C} + H_2O \longrightarrow \underbrace{CO + H_2}_{\text{Water gas}}; \ \Delta H = +28 \text{ kcal}$$

Water gas consist of 40 volume of CO, 50 volume of H_2, 5 volume of CO_2 and 4-5 volume of N_2.

8 (*d*) Pb_3O_4 is sindoor or red lead or triplumbic tetraoxide. It is used as protective paint in iron, steel and silver mirrors and in glass industry.

9 (*d*) In pyrosilicates, two SiO_4^{4-} tetrahedrons share a corner oxygen atom.

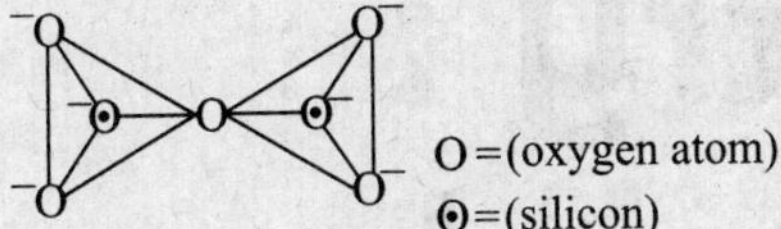

$Si_2O_7^{6-}$ anion of pyrosilicate

10 (*a*) Phosgene is another name of carbonyl chloride ($COCl_2$).

11 (*b*) Carbon remains unaffected by the action of hot sodium hydroxide solution.

12 (*c*) When heated with carbon in an electric furnace, Si is reduced to carborundum or silicon carbide, SiC.

$$SiO_2 + 3C \xrightarrow{\Delta} SiC + 2CO$$

13 (*a*) $\underset{sp}{O{=}C{=}O}$

In CO_2, carbon is in *sp*-hybridised state.

14 (*d*) When two oxygen of each SiO_4^{4-} tetrahedron are shared with others, cyclic or ring structures are obtained. These silicates are known as cyclosilicates or cyclic silicates.

The given figure i.e., $Si_6O_{18}^{12-}$ is an example of cyclosilicate. In this silicate, six SiO_4^{4-} tetrahedral linked together.

15 (*c*) The lead of lead pencils is made up of graphite (an allotrope of carbon), melting point of which is 3160°C.

Hence, lead of lead pencils melts at 3170°C.

16 (*a*) White lead reacts with H_2S of the atmosphere and forms lead sulphide which is black in colour. Due to this reason, the surface painted with white lead becomes dark after sometimes.

17 (*b*) Beryl ($Be_3Al_2Si_6O_{18}$) is a cyclic or ring silicate that consists of discrete units of ($Si_6O_{18}^{12-}$).

18 (*e*) Carbon, due to its smaller size and non-availability of *d*-orbitals, cannot extend its covalency more than four, while Si due to the presence of vacant *d*-orbitals can extend its covalency more than four. Due to this reason, $SiCl_4$ is easily hydrolysed but CCl_4 not.

$$SiCl_4 + 2H_2O \xrightarrow{\Delta} \underset{\text{Silicic acid}}{H_4SiO_4}$$

$$CCl_4 + H_2O \longrightarrow \text{No reaction}$$

19 (*d*) $SiCl_4 + 4H_2O \longrightarrow \underset{(X)}{H_4SiO_4} + 4HCl$

$$\underset{(X)}{H_4SiO_4} \xrightarrow[1000°C]{\Delta} \underset{(Y)}{SiO_2} + 2H_2O$$

20 (*d*) Hydrofluoric acid, HF is the only acid in which silica (SiO_2) is soluble due to the formation of silicon tetrafluoride as,

$$SiO_2 + 4HF \longrightarrow SiF_4 + 2H_2O$$

21 (*d*) The carbides, nitrides or silicides are generally called non-oxide ceramics. They have high proportion of covalent bond. They are made exclusively from synthetic raw materials.

22 (*a*) Silica (SiO_2) is used for making optical instruments.

23 (*a*) Silica is soluble in HF.
SiO_2 reacts with HF to give SiF_4, but if HF is present in excess, it gives fluorosilicic acid (H_2SiF_6).

$$SiO_2 + 4HF \longrightarrow SiF_4 + 2H_2O$$

$$SiF_4 + 6HF \longrightarrow \underset{\text{Hydrofluoro silicic acid}}{H_2SiF_6} + 2H_2$$

24 (*b*) Soft water first heated with limestone ($CaCO_3$) contains some dissolved CO_3^{2-} ions in it which can form a coating of insoluble lead carbonate on the surface of lead pipe and protect it from further action.

25 (*a*) $Al_4C_3 + 12D_2O \longrightarrow 3CD_4 + 4Al(OD)_3$

26 (*c*) $[SiO_3^{2-}]_n$ and $[Si_4O_{11}^{6-}]$ are the building units of chain silicates.
Thus, SiO_3^{2-} is present in chain structure silicates.

27 (*c*) Supercritical CO_2 is used as a solvent for the extraction of organic compound from their natural sources.

28 (*a*) Silicon combines with carbon at 2500 K forming silicon carbide (SiC) which is known as carborundum. It is an extremely hard substance.

29 (*c*) $\underset{\text{Lead nitrate}}{2Pb(NO_3)_2} \xrightarrow{\Delta} \underset{\text{Litharge}}{2PbO} + 4NO_2 + O_2$

30 (*c*) White lead is $2PbCO_3 \cdot Pb(OH)_2$. It is also known as basic lead carbonate. It is useful for the manufacturing of white paints.

31 (*a*) Monosilane (e.g. SiH_4) on coming in contact with air burns with a luminous flame producing vortex ring.

These rings are of silica.

$$SiH_4 + 2O_2 \longrightarrow SiO_2 + 2H_2O$$

32 (*c*) Pb_3O_4 or red lead, when mixed with linseed oil is used for making protective paint for iron, steel and silver mirrors.

33 (*d*) The two oxygen atoms are shared per SiO_4^{4-} tetrahedron in silicate anion of beryl ($Be_3Al_{12}Si_6O_{18}$) mineral.

34 (*b*) $\underset{\substack{\text{Hydrogen fluoride}\\(A)}}{6HF} + \underset{\text{Silicon}}{Si} \longrightarrow \underset{(B)}{H_2SiF_6} + 2H_2$

35 (*c*) Silicones are insoluble in water and hence, do not react with it. So, they are hydrophobic in nature.

The crystal structure of silica has Si—O—Si linkage which is water repellent. It is extremely stable and considerable energy is required to break the silicon oxygen bonds in it.

So, silicones are hard and have high melting point. Thus, the reason is incorrect but Assertion is correct.

36 (*d*) The simplest glass is soda glass which is also called soft glass. Glass is supercooled liquid mixture.

The composition of soft glass is $Na_2O \cdot CaO \cdot 6SiO_2$.

37 (*a*) Both Assertion and Reason are correct and Reason is the correct explanation of Assertion.

SiF_6^{2-} is known, as F has small size and thus, the ion is quite stable unlike $SiCl_6^{2-}$ in which size of Cl-atom is large which destabilise, it.

38 (*b*) Amorphous silicon is prepared by the reduction of silica (rocks). Extra pure silicon is obtained by the removal of SiO_2 by HF.

$$SiO_2 + 4HF \longrightarrow SiF_4 + 2H_2O$$

39 (*b*) In laboratory burners, oil gas is generally used. Oil gas is a mixture of $CH_4 + CO + CO_2 + H_2$.

12

Organic Chemistry : Some Basic Principles and Techniques

Quick Review

Hydrocarbons and their derivatives are called **organic compounds**.

Bonding in Organic Compounds

- Carbon is the essential element of all organic molecules. It always forms covalent bonds.
- Carbon has a unique property of self-linking and it forms single, double and triple bonds.
- A single bond contains only σ bond, whereas there are one σ and one π bond in case of a double bond and one σ and two π bonds in case of a triple bond.

Hybridisation and Shape

- It is the intermixing of orbitals of almost similar energy to form the same number of orbitals of exactly similar energy.
- Depending upon the number of σ bonds formed in its compounds, the carbon atoms show three types of hybridisation:
  (*i*) sp^3 with tetrahedral shape
  (*ii*) sp^2 with trigonal planar shape
  (*iii*) sp with linear shape

Functional Group and Homologous Series

- **Functional group** is an atom or a group of atoms, present in an organic compound which is responsible for its properties. Some functional groups are $-Cl$, $-Br$, $-OH$, $-COOH$, $-CHO$, $-\overset{O}{\overset{\|}{C}}-$, $-\overset{O}{\overset{\|}{C}}-O-$, etc.
- **Homologous series** is a series of group of compounds in which molecular formula of adjacent members differ by a $-CH_2$ unit.
- All the homologous series contain same functional groups and same general formula.

Note In **three dimensional structure** of organic molecule, a dashed wedge represents a bond away from observer, solid wedge represents a bond towards observer, while, bond in plane of paper are represented by single line.

IUPAC Nomenclature of Organic Compounds

Following rules or steps are used to write the IUPAC name of an organic compound :

- ***Step* I** Locate the longest chain with as many possible secondary functional groups alongwith multiple bonds.
- ***Step* II** Select the root word corresponding to the length of longest possible chain.
- ***Step* III** Number the longest possible chain according to the rules to give an identification number to each C-atom of longest possible chain.
- ***Step* IV** Add suitable prefixes and suffixes alongwith numerals to indicate the number and position of each side chain substituent or functional group present in the compound.

- Hence, according to these rules, the IUPAC name of a compound can be written as:

Prefix	+ Root Word	+ Suffix
Tells us about the branches or substituents except in the case of multiple bonds.	Tells us about the length of longest possible chain.	Tells us about the principal functional groups and multiple bonds mostly except in case of halogens.

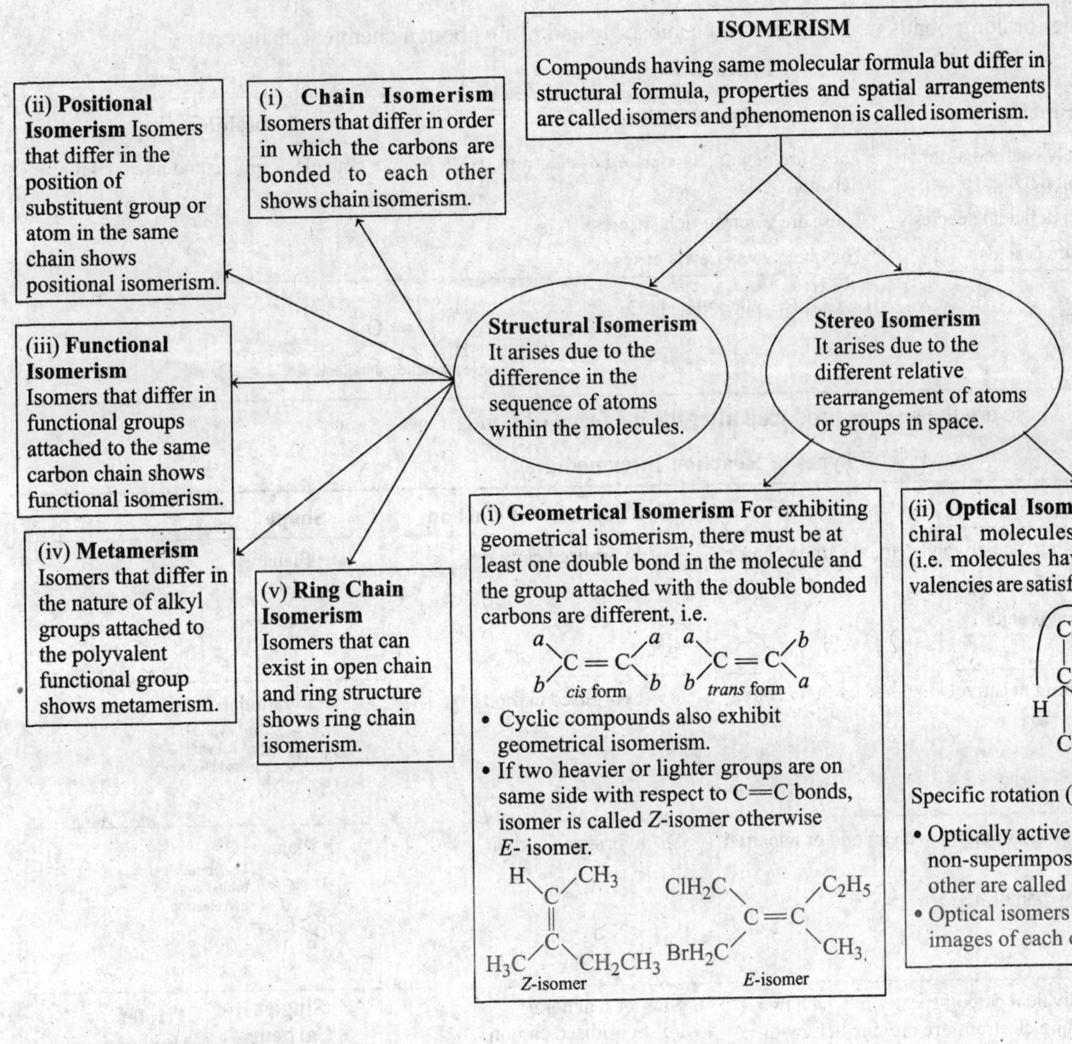

(ii) **Optical Isomerism** It is only exhibited by chiral molecules or asymmetric molecules (i.e. molecules having such a carbon whose four valencies are satisfied by four different groups).

$$\text{Specific rotation } (\alpha) = \frac{\text{observed rotation}}{\text{length} \times \text{density}}$$

- Optically active compounds which are non-superimposable mirror images of each other are called **enantiomers**.
- Optical isomers which are not the mirror images of each other are called **diastereomers**.

R and *S* Configuration

It is given by Cahn, Ingold and Prelog.

The priority sequence rules are as follows:

- Atoms directly attached to the chiral carbon are arranged in decreasing atomic number.
- If the sequence $a \rightarrow b \rightarrow c$ traces a clockwise turn, configuration is '*R*'.
- If the sequence $a \rightarrow b \rightarrow c$ traces an anti-clockwise turn, configuration is '*S*'.

Fission in Organic Reactions

Organic reactions begin with the breakage of covalent bond and this breakage or cleavage are of two types :

(i) Homolytic fission produces free radicals.

$$A—B \longrightarrow \underbrace{A^{\bullet} + B^{\bullet}}_{\text{Free radicals}}$$

(*ii*) Heterolytic fission produces ions (i.e. anion and cation).

$$\underset{}{A—B} \longrightarrow \underset{\text{Electrophile}}{A^+} + \underset{\text{Nucleophile}}{B^-}$$

- Heterolytic fission requires larger energy than homolytic fission. Heterolytic fission is favoured in acid or base catalysed reaction, while homolytic fission is favoured in gas phase reactions.
- Heterolytic cleavage generally takes place in polar covalent molecules but in non-polar molecules, it takes place in the presence of catalyst.

- **Reagents** are the species or compounds which attacks on a substrate and bring about a chemical change.

Types of Reagents

Reagents	Electrophiles	Nucleophiles	Ambiphiles
Definition	• These are positively charged atom or contain an electron deficient atom. • These are electron deficient species. • They behave as Lewis acids.	• These are negatively charged or electron rich atom. • These are electron rich species. • They behave as Lewis bases.	• These have both electrophilic and nucleophilic sites. • They have dual nature.
Examples	• H^+, Cl^+, Br^+, I^+, NO^+, $BeCl_2$, $ZnCl_2$, AlX_3, $SnCl_4$, etc.	H^-, Cl^-, Br^-, I^-, $\ddot{N}H_3$, $H_2\ddot{O}$	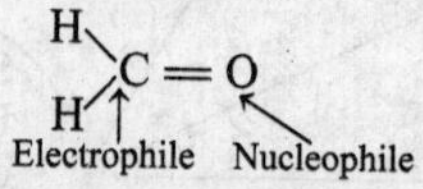 $H_2C=O$ (C: Electrophile, O: Nucleophile)

Reaction Intermediates These are the species produced after the cleavage of bonds.

Types of Reaction Intermediates

Intermediates	Definition	Hybridisation of Carbon	Shape
CARBOCATION	• Ion containing positively charged carbon centre. • Electron deficient species. • Act as Lewis acid.	sp^2 hybridised carbon	• Planar 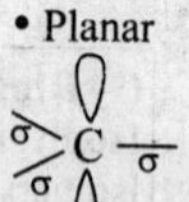
CARBANION	Ion containing negatively charged carbon centre.	sp^3 hybridised carbon	• Pyramidal 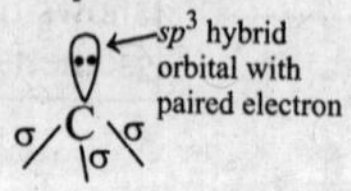 sp^3 hybrid orbital with paired electron
FREE RADICAL	• Atom or group of atoms with an odd or unpaired electron. • Formed by homolysis.	sp^2 hybridised carbon	• Planar 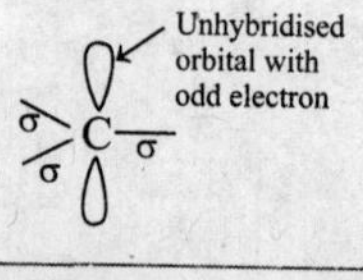 Unhybridised orbital with odd electron
CARBENES	• Neutral divalent carbon species in which two non-bonding electrons are present alongwith 2 bonding pairs.	**Singlet Carbene** sp^2 hybridised carbon. **Triplet Carbene** sp hybridised carbon	**Singlet Carbene**  / **Triplet Carbene** 
NITRENES	• Neutral monovalent nitrogen species in which nitrogen has two unshared pair of electrons with a monovalent atom or group.	Ground state triplet with two degenerate sp-orbitals containing single electron each.	**Singlet Nitrene** 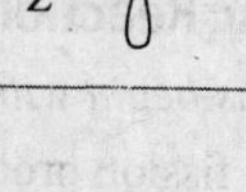 / **Triplet Nitrene** 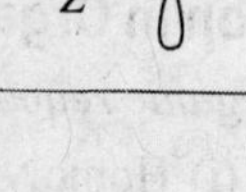

Electron Displacement in Organic Molecules

Effect	Definition	Types and Examples	Applications
Inductive Effect	• It is defined as the polarity produced in a molecule due to the presence of polar bond. • It is a permanent effect. • It operates through σ bonds. • It decreases in magnitude as we move away from the cause of polarity.	• $-I$ effect (electron withdrawing) e.g. R_3N^+, NO_2, SO_3H, —CN, —COCl, —COOR, —OR etc. • $+I$ effect (electron releasing) e.g. :— O^-, — COO^-, — CH_3 etc.	• In determining the stability of free radicals, carbocations and carbanions. 3° > 2° > 1° (stability order for carbocation and free radical). 1° > 2° > 3° (stability order for carbanion). • In determining the strength of acids and bases. (i) Strength of an acid $\propto K_a \propto \frac{1}{pK_a}$ $\propto$ stability of acid anion. Stability of acid anion $\propto -I$ power of group. (ii) Strength of base $\propto +I$ power of group $\propto K_b$.
Electromeric Effect	• It is defined as the polarity produced in a multiple bonded molecule as a reagent approaches it. • It is a temporary effect.	• $+E$ effect (π-electron of double bond are transferred to that atoms of the double bond to which the reagent gets finally attached). $CH_3—CH=CH_2 + H^+ \longrightarrow CH_3\overset{+}{C}HCH_3$ • $-E$ effect (π-electrons of the double bond are transferred to an atom of the double bond other than the one to which the reagent gets finally attached). $>C=O + CN \longrightarrow >C(CN)—O$	• It helps in determining the direction of a reaction. • It is the basis for the nucleophilic addition reactions of carbonyl compound and electrophilic addition in unsaturated hydrocarbons.
Mesomeric Effect	• Polarity produced in a molecule due to conjugation. • It is a permanent effect. • It operates in unsaturated and conjugated compounds.	• $+M$ effect (electron repelling), e.g. —O^-, —NH_2, —OH, —OR, —NHAc. • $-M$ effect (electron releasing), e.g. —NH_3^+, —NO_2, —CX_3, —SO_3H.	• In determining the relative acidity of phenol and alcohol. Phenols are more acidic than alcohols. • Aryl halides are less reactive than alkyl halides towards nucleophilic substitution. This can be explained by $+M$ effect of halogen atom.
Resonance Effect	• When all the properties of a molecule cannot be shown by a single structure and two or more structures are required to show all the properties of that molecule, then those structures are called resonating structures. • This phenomenon is called resonance.	• $+R$ effect (electron donating groups). eg. —OH, —OR, —SH, —SR, —NH_2, —NHR, —NR_2, —Cl, —Br, —I etc. • —R effect (electron withdrawing groups) eg. $>C=O$, —CHO, —COOR, —CN, —NO_2, etc.	• In determining the stability of molecules. • Resonance structures with a greater number of covalent bonds are more stable than those with less number.
Hyper-Conjugation	• It involves delocalisation of σ-electrons of the bond of an alkyl group directly attached to an atom with an unshared *p*-orbital. • It is also called no bond resonance or Baker - Nathan effect.	• (C—H) π - conjugation [occur in alkenes] • (C—H), positive charge conjugation [occur in alkyl carbocation]. • (C—H) odd electron conjugation [occur in free radicals]	• Stability order of carbocations and free radicals. • Stability order of benzyl carbocation. • Stability order of alkene.

Types of Organic Reactions

Substitution Reactions
In these reactions, one atom or group of atoms in a molecule is replaced by a nucleophile or electrophile.

Addition Reactions
These reactions are given by unsaturated compounds. Here, C—C π bond is involved in the reaction with attacking reagent.

Elimination Reactions
In these reactions, two groups from the same or adjacent atoms are lost and electron deficient or unsaturated compounds are formed.

Rearrangement Reactions
These reactions involve the migration of atom or group from one atom to another within the same molecule.

Methods of Purification of Organic Compounds

Methods	Principle	Process	Applications
Filteration	• It is based on the difference in filterability of different components present in a solution.	• A filteration apparatus with a filter paper is used. • Large quantity of material is filtered by Buchner funnel.	• Separation of sand from salt by dissolving in water. • Separation of tea leaves from tea is done by this method.
Crystallisation	• It is based on the difference in the solubilities of the compound and the impurities in the suitable solvent.	• In this method, a hot concentrated solution of the compound is prepared. • This upon filteration and cooling gives the crystals of the pure compound.	• Sugar having common salt as impurity can be crystallised through hot ethanol as it is soluble in hot ethanol but common salt does not.
Sublimation	• Process is employed for those solids which convert from solid into vapour. • On heating, the solid changes to vapour without converting into vapour liquid phase and the vapours upon cooling give back the solid.	• In this process, the impure solid is taken into China dish and is covered with a perforated filter paper. • An inverted funnel is placed over the dish and stem is plugged with cotton. • On heating, solid get converted into vapours.	• Impure samples of naphthalene, anthracene, camphor, benzoic acid, NH_4Cl, dry ice, salicylic acid can be purified by this process. • The vapours on cooling condense to give crystals at the neck of funnel.
Distillation	• It is based upon the difference in the boiling points of two liquids or two components. • It is generally used if an organic liquid contains a non-volatile impurity.	• In this process, a liquid is heated to its boiling point and is converted into vapours. • The vapours on cooling condense to give back the original liquid in its pure form.	• Separation of mixture of hexane (b.pt 342 K) and toluene (b. pt 384 K) • Separation of mixture of chloroform (b.pt 334 K) and aniline (b.pt 457 K)
Fractional Distillation	• This method is based upon the separation of two liquids having nearly equal boiling points.	• The distillation is carried out with the help of specially designed fractionating columns.	• A mixture of acetone and methyl alcohol is separated by this process.
Distillation under Reduced Pressure	• It is used for those liquids which have a tendency to decompose at a temperature below their boiling point.	• Under reduced pressure, the liquid will boil at low temperature.	• At 12 mm of Hg pressure, glycerol boils at 453 K without decomposition.
Steam Distillation	• It is used for steam volatile substances and non-volatile impurities.	• Compound is distilled with steam under reduced pressure at a temperature below its boiling point. • Pure compound comes out with steam and separates on cooling.	• *ortho* and nitro phenols, compounds like aniline, nitrobenzene, terpentine oil are purified by this process.
Differential Extraction	• It is based on the more solubility of solute in a suitable organic compound as compared to water.	• Process involves shaking of solution with a suitable organic solvent in which compound is more soluble as compared to water.	• Benzoic acid is separated from water by using benzene.
Chromatography	• It is based upon the principle of distribution of components of a given organic mixture between two phases. **Types of Chromatography** – Column chromatography – Thin layer chromatography – High performance liquid chromatography – Partition chromatography	• In this process, the stationary phase can either be solid or liquid supported over a solid. • The mobile phase may be a liquid or a gas.	• For separation of sugars and amino acids.

Qualitative and Quantitative Analysis

Element	Qualitative Analysis			Quantitative Analysis
	Method/Detection Test	**Confirmatory Test**	**Chemical Reactions**	**Reactions Involved and Formula**
Carbon and Hydrogen	• Heat the compound with copper (II) oxide	• CO_2 reacts with lime water which develops turbidity. • H_2O reacts with anhyd. $CuSO_4$ that develops blue colour.	• $C + 2CuO \xrightarrow{\Delta} 2Cu + CO_2$ • $CO_2 + Ca(OH)_2 \longrightarrow CaCO_3 + H_2O$ • $2H + CuO \xrightarrow{\Delta} Cu + H_2O$ • $5H_2O + CuSO_4 \xrightarrow{\Delta} CuSO_4 \cdot 5H_2O$	**Liebig's Combustion Method** • $C\% = \frac{12 \times \text{mass of } CO_2 \times 100}{44 \times \text{mass of compound}}$ • $H\% = \frac{2 \times \text{mass of } H_2O \times 100}{18 \times \text{mass of compound}}$
Nitrogen	• Boil Lassaigne's extract with $FeSO_4$ and then acidify with conc. H_2SO_4.	• Formation of prussian blue colour.	• $Na + C + N \xrightarrow{\Delta} NaCN$ • $6\ CN + Fe^{2+} \longrightarrow [Fe(CN)_6]^{4-}$ • $3\ [Fe(CN)_6]^{4-} + 4\ Fe^{3+} \xrightarrow{xH_2O} Fe_4[Fe(CN)_6]_3 + H_2O$	**Duma's Method** • $N\% = \frac{28 \times \text{volume of } N_2 \text{ gas} \times 100}{22400 \times \text{mass of compound}}$ • **Kjeldahl's Method** $N\% = 1.4 N_1V_1$/mass of organic compound
Sulphur	• Add acetic acid and lead acetate in Lassaigne's extract.	• Formation of black precipitate.	• $2Na + S \xrightarrow{\Delta} Na_2S$	• **Carius Method** $S\% = \frac{32 \times \text{mass of } BaSO_4 \times 100}{233 \times \text{mass of compound}}$
	• Add sodium nitroprusside in Lassaigne's extract.	• Formation of violet colour.	• $S^{2-} + Pb^{2+} \longrightarrow PbS$ • $S^{2-} + [Fe(CN)_5NO]^{2-} \longrightarrow [Fe(CN)_5NOS]^{4-}$	
Halogen	• Acidify Lassaigne's extract with HNO_3 and then add $AgNO_3$.	• White ppt. soluble in NH_4OH shows presence of chlorine. • Yellow ppt. sparingly soluble in NH_4OH shows presence of bromine. • A yellow ppt. insoluble in NH_4OH shows presence of iodine.	• $Na + X \xrightarrow{\Delta} NaX$ • $X^- + Ag^+ \longrightarrow AgX$	**Carius Method** • $Cl\% = \frac{35.5 \times \text{mass of AgCl} \times 100}{143.5 \times \text{mass of compound}}$ • $Br\ \% = \frac{80 \times \text{mass of AgBr} \times 100}{188 \times \text{mass of compound}}$ • $I\% = \frac{127 \times \text{mass of AgI} \times 100}{235 \times \text{mass of compound}}$
Phosphorus	• Heat the compound with sodium peroxide. • Then boil the solution with HNO_3 and treat it with $(NH_4)_2MoO_4$.	• Formation of yellow colouration or ppt.	• $Na_3PO_4 + 3HNO_3 \longrightarrow H_3PO_4 + 3NaNO_3$ • $H_3PO_4 + 12\ (NH_4)_2MoO_4 + 21\ HNO_3 \longrightarrow (NH_4)_3PO_4 \cdot 12MoO_3 + 21NH_4NO_3 + 12H_2O$	**Ignition Method** • $P\% = \frac{62 \times \text{mass of } Mg_2P_2O_7 \times 100}{222 \times \text{mass of compound}}$
Oxygen	• No specific method for qualitative analysis of oxygen.			• $O\% = \frac{32 \times \text{mass of } CO_2 \times 100}{88 \times \text{mass of compound}}$

Topical Practice Questions

All the exam questions of this chapter have been divided into eleven topics as listed below:

Topic 1

Nomenclature

2019

1 IUPAC name of (cyclohexene ring bearing OH and CH_3)

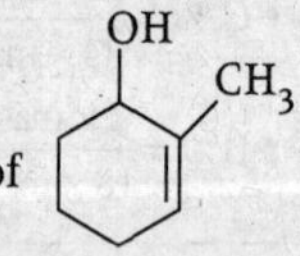

(a) 4-hydroxy-3-methyl cyclohexane **[NEET odisha]**
(b) 2-methyl cyclohex-2-en-1-ol
(c) 3-hydroxy-2-methyl cyclohexane
(d) 1-hydroxy-3-methyl cyclohexane

2018

2 The IUPAC name of the following compound is

$$CH_2=CH-\underset{\underset{CH_2-CH_2-CH_3}{|}}{CH}-CH_2-CH_3$$

[JIPMER]

(a) 3-propylpent-1-ene (b) 3-ethylpent-1-ene
(c) 4-ethylhex-1-ene (d) 3-ethylhex-1-ene

3 The correct IUPAC name of the given compound is (cyclohexenone ring bearing OH) **[AIIMS]**

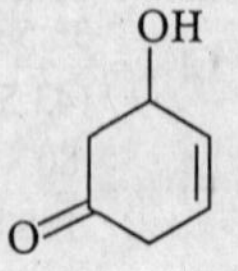

(a) 7-hydroxy cyclohex -5-en-1-one
(b) 3-hydroxy cyclohex-5-en-1-one
(c) 8-hydroxy cyclohex -3-en-1-one
(d) 5-hydroxy cyclohex -3-en-1-one

2017

4 The IUPAC name of the compound **[NEET]**

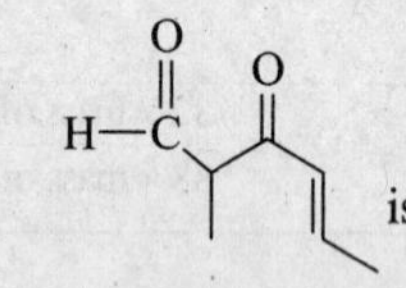

(structure: H–C(=O)– attached to a carbon chain with C=O and C=C) is ....

(a) 3-keto-2-methylhex-4-enal
(b) 5-formylhex-2-en-3-one
(c) 5-methyl-4-oxohex-2-en-5-al
(d) 3-keto-2-methylhex-5-enal

5 The IUPAC nomenclature of **[AIIMS]**

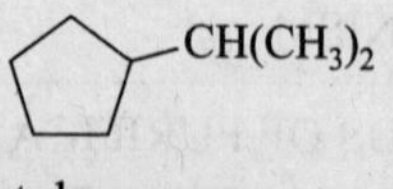

(cyclopentane)–$CH(CH_3)_2$ is

(a) 2-cyclopentylpropane
(b) 1, 1-dimethyl-1-cyclopentylmethane
(c) 1-(1-methyl) ethylcyclopentane
(d) None of the above

6 The IUPAC name of

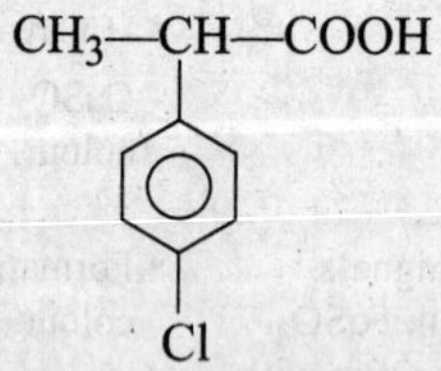

$CH_3-CH-COOH$ is (with the CH bonded to a benzene ring carrying Cl in the para position) **[JIPMER]**

(a) 2-(1-chlorophenyl) propanoic acid
(b) 2-methyl-(2-chlorophenyl) ethanoic acid
(c) 1-methyl-(2-chlorophenyl) ethanoic acid
(d) 2-(4-chlorophenyl) propanoic acid

2014

7 Write IUPAC name of the following compound. **[MHT CET]**

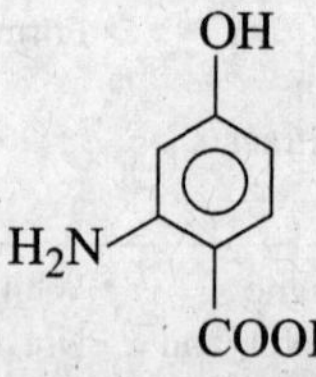

(benzene ring with OH, H_2N and COOH)

(a) 2-amino-4-hydroxybenzoic acid
(b) 6-amino-4-hydroxybenzoic acid
(c) 3-amino-4-carboxyphenol
(d) 2-carboxy-4-hydroxyaniline

8 Which of the following names does not fit a real name?

(a) 3-methyl-3-hexanone
(b) 4-methyl-3-hexanone
(c) 3-methyl-3-hexanol
(d) 2-methyl cyclohexanone

9 The correct IUPAC name of the organic compound

$$CH_3-\underset{\underset{Cl}{|}}{CH}-\underset{\underset{CH_3}{|}}{CH}-\underset{\underset{CH_3}{|}}{CH}-CH_2OH \text{ is}$$

(a) 4-chloro-2, 3-dimethylpentan-1-ol **[Kerala CEE]**
(b) 2-chloro-3-4-dimethylpentan-5-ol
(c) 2,3-dimethyl-4-chloropentan-1-ol
(d) 2-chloro-3, 4-dimethyl *n*-pentyl alcohol
(e) 2,3-dimethyl-4-chloro *n*-pentyl alcohol

10 The IUPAC name of the following molecule is **[WB JEE]**

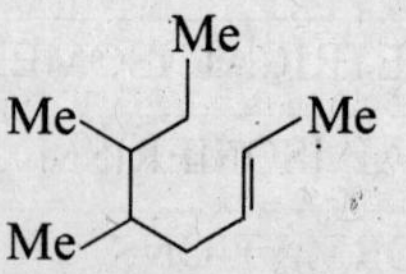

(skeletal structure with substituents Me, Me, Me, Me)

(a) 5,6-dimethyloct-2-ene (b) 2,3-dimethylhept-5-ene
(c) 5,6-dimethylhept-3-ene (d) 5-*iso*-propylhex-2-ene

11 The IUPAC name of the compound is **[UK PMT]**

(Benzene ring with OMe at position 1, Cl at position 2 and CH_3 at position 4)

(a) 2-chloro-4-methyl anisole
(b) 3-chloro-1-methyl anisole
(c) 1-methoxy-2-chloro toluene
(d) 1-methoxy-4-methyl chlorobenzene

2013

12 The structure of *iso*butyl group in an organic compound is **[NEET]**

(a) $(CH_3)_2CH—CH_2—$

(b) $CH_3—CH_2—CH_2—CH_3$

(c) $CH_3—CH_2—CH_2—CH_2—$

(d) $CH_3—C(CH_3)_2—$

13 IUPAC name of CH_3 is **[AIIMS]**

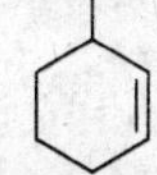

(a) 3-methyl cyclohexene (b) 1-methyl cyclohex-2-ene
(c) 6-methyl cyclohexene (d) 1-methyl cyclohex-5-ene

14 The structure of *neo*-heptyl alcohol is **[WB JEE]**

(a) $CH_3CH_2—C(CH_2CH_3)_2—OH$

(b) $CH_3—C(CH_3)_2—CH_2CH_2CH_2OH$

(c) $CH_3—C(CH_3)_2—CH(OH)—CH_2CH_3$

(d) $n—C_7H_{15}OH$

15 The IUPAC name of **[WB JEE]**

(skeletal structure: $CH_2=CH—CH(OH)—CH(OH)—CH_3$)

(a) pent-1-en-3,4-diol (b) 3, 4-dehydroxy pentene-1
(c) pent-4-en-2, 3-diol (d) 2, 3-dihydroxy pent-4-ene

16 Name of the compound given below **[J&K CET]**

(skeletal structure)

(a) 3-methyl-4-ethyloctane (b) 2, 3-diethyl heptane
(c) 5-ethyl-6-methyloctane (d) 4-ethyl-3-methyloctane

17 The IUPAC name for the formula

$$CH_3—C(CH_3)=C(H)—COOH$$

[Punjab PHET]

(a) 2-methyl-2-butenoic acid
(b) 3-methyl-3-butenoic acid
(c) 3-methyl-2-butenoic acid
(d) 2-methyl-3-butenoic acid

18 The IUPAC name of

$$CH_3—H_2C—C(H)(CH_3)—C(C_4H_9)(CH_3)—CH_3 \text{ is}$$

(a) 3, 4, 4-trimethylheptane **[KCET]**
(b) 3, 4, 4-trimethyloctane
(c) 2-butyl-2-methyl-3-ethyl butane
(d) 2-ethyl -3, 3-dimethyl heptane

2012

19 Which of the following is not in accordance to IUPAC system? **[CBSE AIPMT]**

(a) $Br—CH_2—CH=CH_2$
1-bromoprop-2-ene

(b) $CH_3—CH_2—C(CH_3)(Br)—CH_2—CH(CH_3)CH_3$
4-bromo-2, 4-dimethyl hexane

(c) $CH_3—CH(CH_3)—CH(C_6H_5)—CH_2—CH_3$
2-methyl-3- phenylpentane

(d) $CH_3—C(=O)—CH_2—CH_2CH_2COOH$
5-oxohexanoic acid

20 The IUPAC name of tertiary butyl iodide is **[UP CPMT]**

(a) 4-iodobutane
(b) 2-iodobutane
(c) 1-iodo-3-methyl propane
(d) 2-iodo-2-methyl propane

21 The IUPAC name of [OJEE]

OH O

is

(a) 2-hydroxy-4-pentanone (b) 2-oxo-4-pentanol
(c) 4-keto-2-pentanol (d) 4-hydroxy-2-pentanone

2011

22 The correct IUPAC name of the compound

is [CBSE AIPMT]

(a) 3-(1-ethyl propyl) hex-1-ene
(b) 4-ethyl-3-propyl hex-1-ene
(c) 3-ethyl-4-ethenyl heptane
(d) 3-ethyl-4-propyl hex-5-ene

23 For the given alkane, [DUMET]

The IUPAC name is
(a) 1,1-dimethyl-5-ethyl octane
(b) 6-ethyl-2-methyl nonane
(c) 4-ethyl-8-methyl nonane
(d) 2-methyl-6-propyl octane

24 The IUPAC name of [KCET]

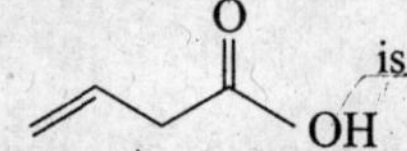

is

(a) but-3-enoic acid (b) but-1-enoic acid
(c) pent-4-enoic acid (d) prop-2-enoic acid

2010

25 IUPAC nomenclature of

$$H_3C-\overset{\overset{CH_3}{|}}{\underset{\underset{CH_3}{|}}{C}}-CH=\overset{\overset{CH_3}{|}}{C}-CH_3$$ is [AFMC]

(a) 2,4,4-trimethylpent-2-ene
(b) 2,4,4-trimethylpent-3-ene
(c) 2,2,4-trimethylpent-3-ene
(d) 2,2,4-trimethylpent-2-ene

26 The IUPAC name of the following compound is
$CH_2=C=CH-CH_3$ [UP CPMT]

(a) but-2,3-diene (b) buta-1,2-diene
(c) but-1-ene-2-yne (d) conjugated butadiene

27 The IUPAC name of $CH_3CH_2CH(CH_3)CH(C_2H_5)_2$ is [BVP]

(a) 4-ethyl-3-methylhexane
(b) 3-ethyl-4-methylhexane
(c) 4-methyl-3-ethylhexane
(d) 2,4-diethylpentane

28 The IUPAC name of the following compound is

$$H_3C-\overset{\overset{C_2H_5}{|}}{CH}-\underset{\underset{CHO}{|}}{CH}-CH_3$$

[MHT CET]

(a) 3-ethyl-2-methybutanal
(b) 2,3-dimethylpentanal
(c) 2-ethyl-3-methylbutanal
(d) 2-ethyl-3-methylbutan-3-al

29 The IUPAC name of the compound having the molecular formula $Cl_3C\cdot CH_2CHO$ is [Manipal]

(a) 3,3,3-trichloropropanal (b) 1,1,1-trichloropropanal
(c) 2,2,2-trichloropropanal (d) chloral

30 The incorrect IUPAC name is [RPMT]

(a) $CH_3\underset{\underset{O}{||}}{C}-\underset{\underset{CH_3}{|}}{CH}-CH_3$
2-methyl-3-butanone

(b) $CH_3\underset{\underset{CH_3}{|}}{CH}-\underset{\underset{CH_2CH_3}{|}}{CH}-CH_3$
2,3-dimethylpentane

(c) $CH_3C\equiv C-CH_2CH_3$
2-pentyne

(d) $CH_3-\underset{\underset{Cl}{|}}{CH}-\underset{\underset{Br}{|}}{CH}-CH_3$
2-bromo-3-chloro-butane

31 The IUPAC name for the hydrocarbon represented by swastik sign is [Haryana PMT]

(a) *neo*-nonane (b) tetraethylcarbon
(c) 2-ethylpentane (d) 3,3-diethylpentane

32 The IUPAC name of

CHO

Br

is [KCET]

(a) 2-methyl-3-bromohexanal
(b) 3-bromo-2-methylbutanal
(c) 2-methyl-3-bromobutanal
(d) 3-bromo-2-methylpentanal

33 The IUPAC name of the compound [JCECE]

$$C_2H_5-\underset{\underset{CH_2}{||}}{C}-CH_2OH$$ is

(a) 2-ethylprop-2-en-1-ol
(b) 2-hydroxymethylbutan-1-ol
(c) 2-methylenebutan-1-ol
(d) 2-ethyl-3-hydroxyprop-1-ene

34 The IUPAC name of the compound [CMC]

OH

is

O

(a) 2-ethenyl-3-methyl cyclohexa-1,3-diene
(b) 2,5-dimethyl hepta-2,6-dienoic acid
(c) 2,6-dimethyl hepta-2,5-dienoic acid
(d) 2,3-dimethyl epoxyethane

35 The IUPAC name of the compound [VMMC]

is

OH

(a) 1,1-dimethyl-3-cyclohexanol
(b) 1,1-dimethyl-3-hydroxycyclohexane
(c) 3,3-dimethyl-1-cyclohexanol
(d) 3,3-dimethyl-1-hydroxycyclohexane

2009

36 The IUPAC name of the compound having the formula $CH \equiv C - CH = CH_2$ is [CBSE AIPMT]

(a) 3-butene-1-yne (b) 1-butyn-3-ene
(c) but-1-yne-3-ene (d) 1-butene-3-yne

37 IUPAC name of the given compound is

$$H_3C-\underset{|}{\overset{CH_3}{C}}=\overset{H}{C}-COOH$$ [AFMC]

(a) 2-methylbut-2-enoic acid
(b) 3-methylbut-2-enoic acid
(c) 3-methybut-3-enoic acid
(d) 2-methylbut-3-enoic acid

38 A compound with molecular formula, C_6H_{14} has two tertiary carbons. Its IUPAC name is [AFMC]

(a) *n*-hexane (b) 2-methyl pentane
(c) 2,3-dimethyl butane (d) 2, 2-dimethyl butane

39 $H_3C-CH=C(-CH_2-CH_2-CH_3)-CH_2-CH_3$ [UP CPMT]

(substituent on C: $CH_3-CH_2-CH_2$)

Correct IUPAC name is
(a) 3-ethylhex-2-ene (b) 3-ethylpent-2-ene
(c) 3-ethylpent-3-ene (d) 3-propylpent-2-ene

40 The IUPAC name of crotonaldehyde is [MHT CET]

(a) butenaldehyde (b) butanal-1
(c) but-2-en-1-al (d) prop-2-en-1-ol

41 The IUPAC name of the molecule

$$CH_3-\overset{O}{\overset{\|}{C}}-\underset{H_3C}{\underset{|}{C}}=\underset{CH_3}{\underset{|}{C}}-\overset{O}{\overset{\|}{C}}-OH$$ is [J&K CET]

(a) 4-oxo-2,3-dimethylpent-2-en-1-oic acid
(b) 2-carboxy-3-methylpent-2-en-3-one
(c) 4-carboxy-3-methylpent-3-en-2-one
(d) 2,3-dimethyl-4-oxo-pent-2-en-1-oic acid

42 IUPAC name of $(CH_3)_3CCl$ is [KCET]

(a) 3-chlorobutane (b) 2-chloro-2-methylpropane
(c) *t*-butyl chloride (d) *n*-butyl chloride

2008

43 The correct structure of 4-bromo-3-methyl but-1-ene is [AIIMS]

(a) $Br-CH=C(CH_3)_2$
(b) $CH_2=CH-CH(CH_3)-CH_2Br$
(c) $CH_2=C(CH_3)CH_2CH_2Br$
(d) $CH_3-C(CH_3)=CHCH_2-Br$

44 The IUPAC name of $H_3C-\underset{OC_3H_7}{\underset{|}{CH}}-C_3H_7$ is [MHT CET]

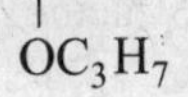

(a) 4-propoxy pentane (b) pentyl-propyl ether
(c) 2-propoxy pentane (d) 2-pentoxy propane

45 Give the IUPAC name of the alkene [Kerala CEE]

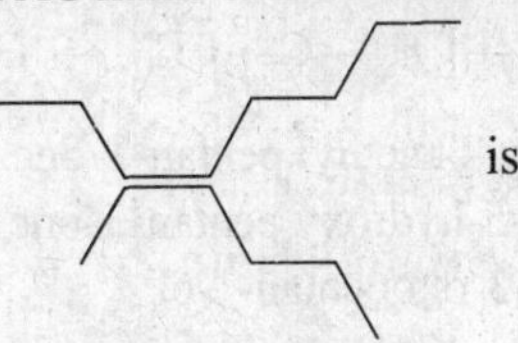

is

(a) *Z*-3methyl-4-propyl-3-octene
(b) *E*-3-methyl-4-propyl-3-octene
(c) *E*-4-butyl-3-methyl-3-heptene
(d) *E*-2-ethyl-3-propyl-2-heptene
(e) *Z*-2-ethyl-3-propyl-2-heptene

46 IUPAC name of [Punjab PMET]

$$CH_3-CH_2-\underset{CH_2-CH_3}{\underset{|}{CH}}-\underset{CH_3}{\underset{|}{C}}=CH_2$$ is

(a) 2-methyl-3-ethyl-1-pentene
(b) 3-ethyl-4-methyl-4-pentene
(c) 3-ethyl-2-methyl-1-pentene
(d) 3-methyl-2-ethyl-1-pentene

47 IUPAC name of the following

$$H_3C-\underset{CH_3}{\underset{|}{N}}-\underset{C_2H_5}{\underset{|}{\overset{CH_3}{\overset{|}{C}}}}-CH_2-CH_3$$ is [DUMET]

(a) 3-dimethylamino-3-methyl pentane
(b) 3 (N, N-trimethyl)-3-amino pentane
(c) 3 N-N-trimethyl pentammine
(d) 3-(N, N-dimethyl) amino-3-methyl pentane

48 Which is the incorrect name of CH_3NC? **[Guj CET]**

(a) Aceto isonitrile
(b) Methyl isocyanide
(c) Methyl carbylamine
(d) Methyl isonitrile

49 What is the correct IUPAC name of **[JCECE]**

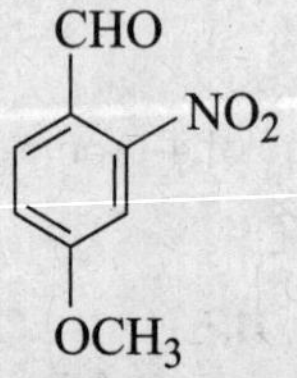

(Benzene ring with CHO, ortho NO_2 and para OCH_3)

(a) 4-methoxy-2-nitrobenzaldehyde
(b) 4-formyl-3-nitro anisole
(c) 4-methoxy-6-nitrobenzaldehyde
(d) 2-formyl-5-methoxy nitrobenzene

2007

50 The IUPAC name of

$CH_3-CH(CH_3)-C(=O)-CH_2-CH_2OH$ is **[AIIMS]**

(a) 1-hydroxy-4-methyl pentan-3-one
(b) 2-methyl-5-hydroxy pentan-3-one
(c) 4-methyl-3-oxopentan-1-ol
(d) hexan-1-ol-3-one

51 The IUPAC name of the following compound **[Manipal]**

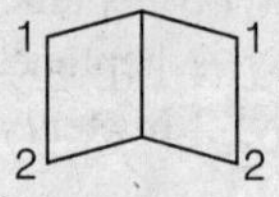

(bicyclic structure with positions labelled 1, 1, 2, 2) is

(a) bicyclo [2.2.0] octane
(b) bicyclo [0.2.2] hexane
(c) bicyclo [2.1.1] hexane
(d) bicyclo [2.2.0] hexane

52 IUPAC name of the following compound **[JCECE]**

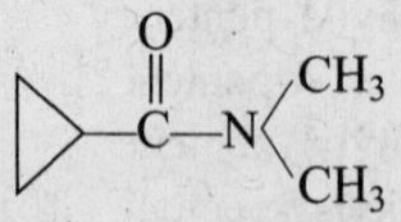

(cyclopropyl–C(=O)–N(CH_3)$_2$) is

(a) N, N-dimethyl cyclopropane carboxamide
(b) N-methylcyclopropanamide
(c) cyclopropionamide
(d) None of the above

2006

53 The IUPAC name of **[CBSE AIPMT]**

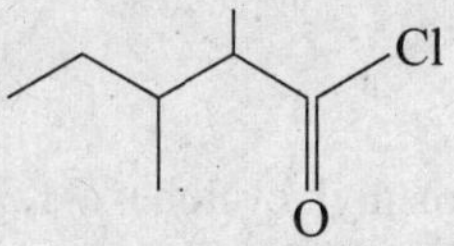

(skeletal structure with Cl and O) is

(a) 3, 4-dimethylpentanoyl chloride
(b) 1-chloro-1-oxo-2, 3-dimethylpentane
(c) 2-ethyl-3-methylbutanoyl chloride
(d) 2, 3-dimethylpentanoyl chloride

54 The IUPAC name of the compound

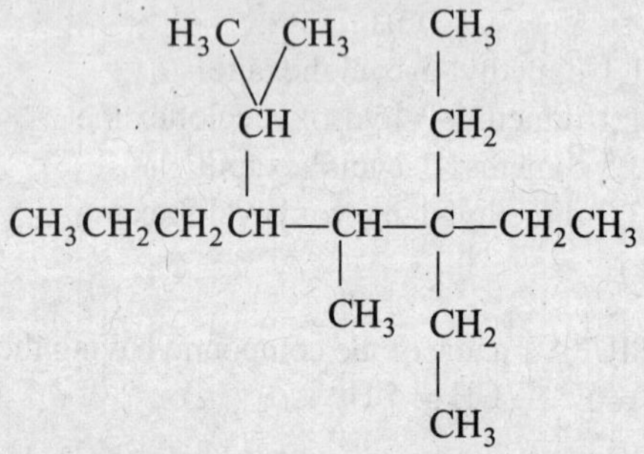

$CH_3CH_2CH_2CH(CH(CH_3)_2)-CH(CH_3)-C(CH_2CH_3)(CH_2CH_3)-CH_2CH_3$

[MHT CET]

(a) 5-methyl-4-isopropyl-6, 6′ diethyloctane
(b) 3, 3-dimethyl-3-ethyl-5-isopropyl octane
(c) 3, 3-diethyl-4-methyl-5 (1, 1-dimethyl) octane
(d) 3, 3-diethyl-4-methyl-5 (1′-methylethyl) octane

55 Consider the following compound IUPAC name of this compound is **[Kerala CEE]**

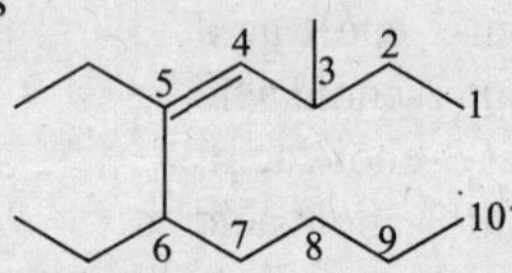

(skeletal structure with carbons numbered 1 to 10)

(a) 5,6-diethyl-3-methyl decane
(b) 5,6-diethyl-3-methyl dec-4-ene
(c) 3,5, 6-trimethyl-dec-6-ene
(d) 3,5,6-triethyl-dec-4-ene
(e) 5,6-diethyl-8-methyl-dec-6-ene

56 The IUPAC name of

$CH_3-CH(CH_2CHO)-CH_2-CHO$ is

(a) 3-(formyl methyl) hexane dial **[Guj CET]**
(b) 3-methyl pentane dial
(c) 3-(formyl methyl) butanal
(d) 2-(formyl methyl) butanal

2005

57 Names of some compounds are given. Which one is not the correct in IUPAC system? **[CBSE AIPMT]**

(a) $CH_3-CH(OH)-CH(CH_3)-CH_3$
3-methyl-2-butanol

(b) $CH_3-C\equiv C-CH(CH_3)_2$
4-methyl-2-pentyne

(c) $CH_3-CH_2-C(=CH_2)-CH(CH_3)-CH_3$
2-ethyl-3-methyl-but-1-ene

(d) $CH_3-CH_2-CH_2-CH(CH_2CH_3)-CH(CH_3)-CH_2CH_3$
3-methyl-4-ethyl heptane

58 Which one of the following contain isopropyl group? **[BHU]**

(a) 2,2,3,3-tetramethylpentane
(b) 2-methylpentane
(c) 2,2,3-trimethylpentane
(d) 3,3-dimethylpentane

Answers

1 (b)	2 (d)	3 (d)	4 (a)	5 (c)	6 (d)	7 (a)	8 (a)	9 (a)	10 (a)
11 (a)	12 (a)	13 (a)	14 (b)	15 (a)	16 (d)	17 (c)	18 (b)	19 (a)	20 (d)
21 (d)	22 (b)	23 (b)	24 (a)	25 (a)	26 (b)	27 (b)	28 (b)	29 (a)	30 (a)
31 (d)	32 (d)	33 (a)	34 (c)	35 (c)	36 (d)	37 (b)	38 (c)	39 (a)	40 (c)
41 (d)	42 (b)	43 (b)	44 (c)	45 (a)	46 (c)	47 (d)	48 (a)	49 (a)	50 (a)
51 (d)	52 (a)	53 (d)	54 (d)	55 (b)	56 (b)	57 (d)	58 (b)		

Explanations

1 (*b*) IUPAC name of given compound is

(structure: cyclohexene ring with OH at C-1 and CH_3 at C-2, numbered 1–6)

2-methylcyclohex-2-en-1-ol

2 (*d*) Given, the correct IUPAC name of the compound is

$\overset{1}{C}H_2=\overset{2}{C}H-\overset{3}{C}H(\overset{4}{C}H_2-\overset{5}{C}H_2-\overset{6}{C}H_3)-CH_2-CH_3$

3-ethylhex-1-ene

Select the longest possible carbon atom chain, number the chain and write the name of compound according to IUPAC rules.

3 (*d*) The correct IUPAC name of the given compound is 5-hydroxy cyclohex -3-en-1-one.

The structure is shown below.

(structure: cyclohexenone ring with C=O at C-1, OH at C-5, double bond between C-3 and C-4)

4 (*a*)

(structure: H–C(=O) at C-1, C-2 bearing methyl, C-3 ketone, C-4=C-5 double bond, C-6)

— CHO group gets higher priority (act as principal group) over $>C=O$ and $C=C$ group in numbering of principal carbon chain.

IUPAC name :
3-keto-2-methylhex-4-enal.

5 (*c*)

(structure: cyclopentyl–$\overset{1}{C}H(CH_3)_2$; Substituent)

1-(1-methyl) ethylcyclopentane

6 (*d*) The IUPAC name of compound is 2-(4-chlorophenyl) propanoic acid.

$\overset{3}{C}H_3-\overset{2}{C}H(C_6H_4Cl)-\overset{1}{C}OOH$

(benzene ring attached at C-1, Cl at C-4)

7 (*a*) Priority order of functional groups is

$-COOH>-OH>-NH_2$

Therefore, IUPAC name of the compound is as follows:

(structure: benzene ring with COOH at C-1, H_2N at C-2, OH at C-4)

2-amino-4-hydroxybenzoic acid

8 (*a*) 3-methyl-3-hexanone does not fit in correct real name because

$\overset{1}{C}H_3-\overset{2}{C}H_2-\overset{3}{C}(=O)-\overset{4}{C}H_2-\overset{5}{C}H_2-\overset{6}{C}H_3$.

Carbon is tetravalent which is full for 3-carbon. There is no space for methyl group to get attached.

9 (*a*) $\overset{5}{C}H_3-\overset{4}{C}H(Cl)-\overset{3}{C}H(CH_3)-\overset{2}{C}H(CH_3)-\overset{1}{C}H_2OH$

Longest chain-5 carbon
1-C atom-alcohol, 4-C atom -chloro, 2, 3-C atom-methyl
IUPAC name: 4-chloro-2, 3 dimethylpentan-1-ol.

10 (*a*)

Me8, Me 7, 6, 5, Me, 4, 3, 2, 1Me

The longest chain contains 8C-atom, so the root word is oct and suffix ene is added for double bond along with its position. Since, two methyl groups are also present at 5 and 6 positions, so the correct IUPAC name of the compound is 5, 6-dimethyloct-2-ene.

11 (*a*) OMe (1), Cl (2), 3, 4, CH_3

The given compound represents the derivative of anisole. Two functional groups are present among which $Cl > CH_3$ in priority. So, Cl will get lower position. Numbering will be in clockwise manner. Hence, IUPAC name is 2-chloro-4-methyl anisole.

12 (*a*) '*iso*' mean one Me group is present in side chain. Hence, the structure of *iso* butyl group in an organic compound is

$$CH_3-\underset{H}{\overset{CH_3}{\overset{|}{\underset{|}{C}}}}-CH_2-$$

'yl' suffix is used to represent one —H less than the parent hydrocarbon.

13 (*a*) CH_3 at 3; ring numbered 1–6 with double bond at 1,2

IUPAC name is 3-methyl cyclohexene or 3-methyl cyclohex-1-ene.

14 (*b*) The prefix *neo* means a carbon atom attached to three alkyl groups and one main chain possessing functional group. Position of alcohol group should be at C. So, the structure of *neo*-heptyl alcohol is

$$CH_3-\underset{CH_3}{\overset{CH_3}{\overset{|}{\underset{|}{C}}}}-CH_2\,CH_2CH_2OH$$

15 (*a*) Compound is a diol, hence

1, 2, 3 OH, 4, 5 OH

Pent-1-en-3, 4-diol

16 (*d*) 1, 2, 3, 4, 5, 6, 7, 8

4-ethyl-3-methyloctane

17 (*c*)
$$\overset{4}{C}H_3-\overset{CH_3}{\overset{|}{C^3}}=\overset{H}{\overset{|}{C^2}}-\overset{1}{C}OOH$$

3-methyl-2-butenoic acid

18 (*b*) The IUPAC name is 3, 4, 4-trimethyloctane

$$\underset{1}{C}H_3-\underset{2}{C}H_2-$$
$$\underset{CH_3}{\overset{H}{\overset{|}{\underset{|}{\overset{3}{C}}}}}-\underset{CH_3}{\overset{\overset{5}{C}H_2-\overset{6}{C}H_2-\overset{7}{C}H_2-\overset{8}{C}H_3}{\overset{|}{\underset{|}{_4C}}}}-CH_3$$

19 (*a*) In IUPAC system of nomenclature, preference is given to multiple bond than halogen substituent, so the correct name of

$$Br-\overset{3}{C}H_2-\overset{2}{C}H=\overset{1}{C}H_2 \text{ is}$$

3-bromo prop-1-ene

20 (*d*)
$$CH_3-\underset{CH_3}{\overset{I}{\overset{|}{\underset{|}{C}}}}-CH_3$$

(*t*-butyl iodide)

IUPAC name ; 2-iodo-2-methyl propane.

21 (*d*) OH O; 5, 4, 3, 2, 1

IUPAC name:
4-hydroxy-2-pentanone

22 (*b*) 1, 2, 3, 4, 5, 6

IUPAC name :
4-ethyl-3-propyl-hex-1-ene

23 (*b*) 1, 2, 3, 4, 5, 6, 7, 8, 9

The correct name is 6-ethyl-2-methyl nonane.

24 (*a*)
$$\underset{4}{C}H_2=\underset{3}{C}H-\underset{2}{C}H_2-\underset{1}{\overset{O}{\overset{||}{C}}}-OH$$

IUPAC name is but-3-enoic acid

25 (*a*)
$$H_3\overset{5}{C}-\underset{CH_3}{\overset{CH_3}{\overset{|}{\underset{|}{\overset{4}{C}}}}}-\overset{3}{C}H=\overset{CH_3}{\overset{2|}{C}}-\overset{1}{C}H_3$$

2,4,4-trimethylpent-2-ene

26 (*b*)
$$\overset{1}{C}H_2=\overset{2}{C}=\overset{3}{C}H-\overset{4}{C}H_3$$

buta-1, 2-diene

27 (*b*)
$$\overset{6}{C}H_3-\overset{5}{C}H_2-\underset{CH_3}{\underset{|}{\overset{4}{C}H}}-\underset{C_2H_5}{\underset{|}{\overset{3}{C}H}}-\overset{2}{C}H_2-\overset{1}{C}H_3$$

3 - ethyl - 4 - methylhexane

28 (*b*)
$$H_3C-\overset{\overset{4}{C}H_2-\overset{5}{C}H_3}{\overset{|}{^3CH}}-\underset{^1CHO}{\underset{|}{\overset{2}{C}H}}-CH_3$$

2, 3-dimethylpentanal

29 (*a*)
$$Cl-\underset{Cl}{\overset{Cl}{\overset{|}{\underset{|}{\overset{3}{C}}}}}-\overset{2}{C}H_2-\overset{1}{C}HO$$

3, 3,3-trichloropropanal

30 (*a*)
$$\overset{1}{C}H_3-\underset{O}{\underset{||}{\overset{2}{C}}}-\underset{CH_3}{\underset{|}{\overset{3}{C}H}}-\overset{4}{C}H_3$$

The correct **IUPAC name** is 3-methyl-2-butanone.

31 (*d*) 2, 1, 3, 4, 5

The IUPAC name for the hydrocarbon is 3, 3-diethylpentane.

32 (*d*) 1 CHO, 2, 3, 4, 5, Br

IUPAC name : 3-bromo-2-methylpentanal

33 (*a*)
$$C_2H_5-\underset{_3CH_2}{\underset{||}{\overset{2}{C}}}-\overset{1}{C}H_2-OH$$

IUPAC name: 2-ethylprop-2-en-1-ol

34 (*c*) 1 OH, 2, 3, 4, 5, O, 6, 7

The IUPAC name is 2,6-dimethylhepta-2,5-dienoic acid

35 (*c*) HO, 1, 2, 3

IUPAC name: 3, 3-dimethyl-1-cyclohexanol

36 (*d*) $\overset{4}{C}H \equiv \overset{3}{C}—\overset{2}{C}H = \overset{1}{C}H_2$.
The IUPAC name of the compound is but-1-en-3-yne (formerly 1-butene-3-yne).

37 (*b*) $H_3\overset{4}{C}—\overset{3}{C}(CH_3) = \overset{2}{C}(H)—\overset{1}{C}OOH$
3-methylbut-2-enoic acid
∵ Order or preference
COOH > (=) > alkyl group.

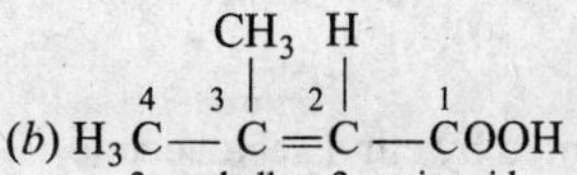

38 (*c*) The possible structures of molecular formula, C_6H_{14} are
(i) *n*-hexane (No tertiary carbon)
(ii) 2-methyl pentane (one 3° carbon)
(iii) 2, 2-dimethyl butane (No 3° carbon)
(iv) 2, 3-dimethyl butane (two, 3° carbon)
Hence, (iv) is the correct option.

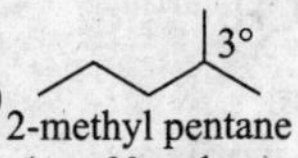

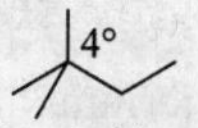

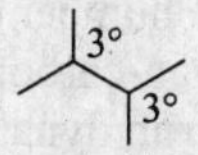

39 (*a*) $H_3\overset{1}{C}—\overset{2}{C}H = \overset{3}{C}(—\overset{4}{C}H_2—\overset{5}{C}H_2—\overset{6}{C}H_3)—CH_2—CH_3$
3-ethyl hex-2-ene

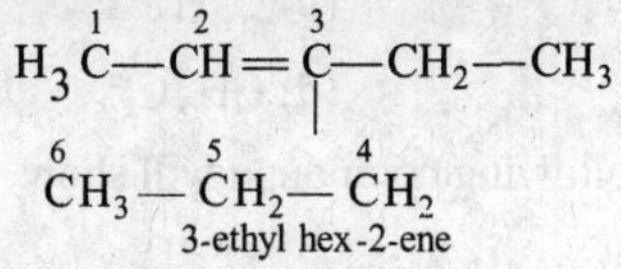

40 (*c*) The structural formula of crotonaldehyde is,
$\overset{4}{C}H_3—\overset{3}{C}H = \overset{2}{C}H—\overset{1}{C}HO$
but-2-en-1-al

41 (*d*) $\overset{5}{C}H_3—\overset{4}{C}(=O)—\overset{3}{C}(CH_3) = \overset{2}{C}(CH_3)—\overset{1}{C}(=O)—OH$
IUPAC name : 2,3-dimethyl-4-oxo-pent-2-en-1-oic acid.

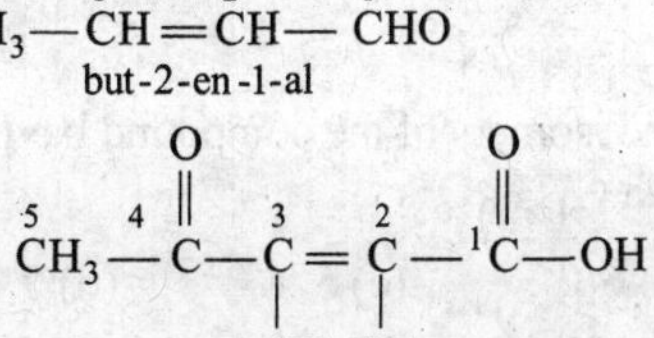

42 (*b*) $H_3C—\overset{2}{C}(\overset{3}{C}H_3)(\overset{1}{C}H_3)—Cl$
IUPAC name : 2-chloro-2-methylpropane

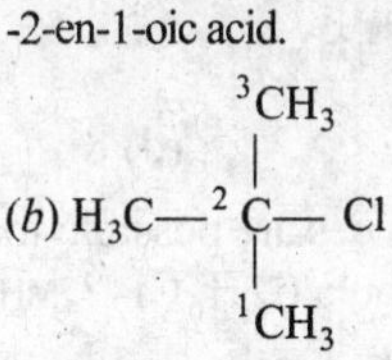

43 (*b*) $\overset{1}{C}H_2 = \overset{2}{C}H—\overset{3}{C}H(CH_3)—\overset{4}{C}H_2Br$
4–bromo-3- methylbut -1- ene

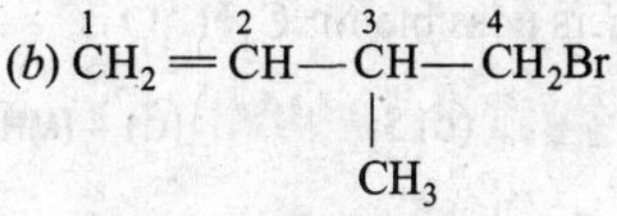

44 (*c*) $\overset{1}{C}H_3—\overset{2}{C}H(O—CH_2—CH_2—CH_3)—\overset{3}{C}H_2—\overset{4}{C}H_2—\overset{5}{C}H_3$
2-propoxy pentane

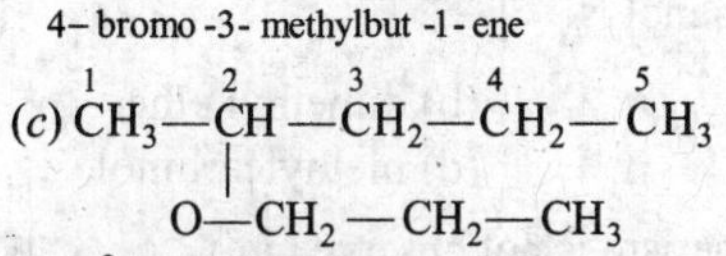

45 (*a*) If the lighter groups (atoms) are present on the same side of double bond, then the isomer is called *Z* and if the lighter groups (atoms) are present on opposite side of double bond, then the isomer is called as *E*.

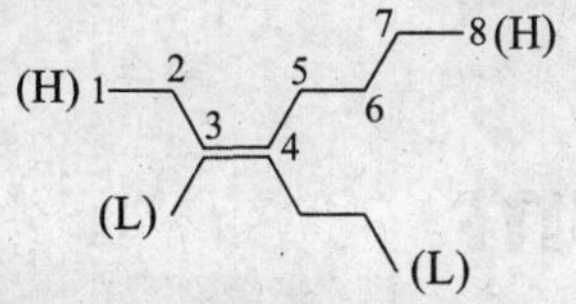

(H) 1–2–3(=4)–5–6–7–8 (H); (L) on C-3, (L) on C-4
Z-3-methyl-4-propyl-3-octene
Or
Z-3-methyl-4-propyl-oct-3-ene

46 (*c*) $\overset{5}{C}H_3—\overset{4}{C}H_2—\overset{3}{C}H(CH_2CH_3)—\overset{2}{C}(CH_3) = \overset{1}{C}H_2$
3-ethyl-2-methyl-1-pentene

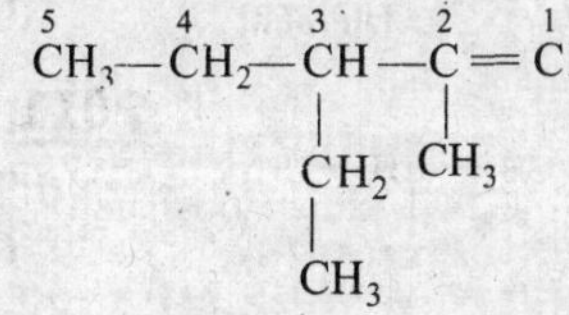

47 (*d*) $CH_3—N(CH_3)—\overset{3}{C}(CH_3)(\overset{4}{C}H_2\overset{5}{C}H_3)—\overset{2}{C}H_2—\overset{1}{C}H_3$
3-(N, N-dimethyl) amino-3-methylpentane

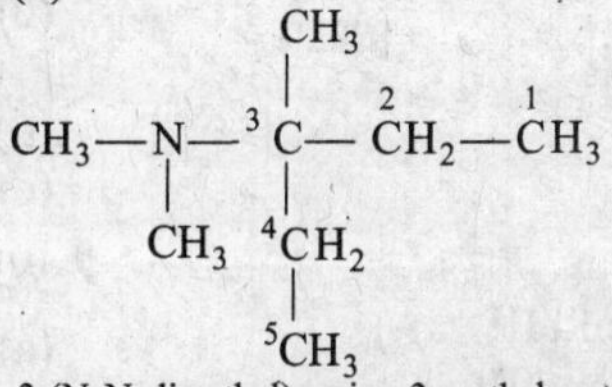

48 (*a*) $H—C(H)(H)—N \equiv C$,
organic compounds obtained by replacement of H-atom of hydrogen isocyanide by alkyl or aryl group are called isocyanides or isonitriles. They are also called carbylamine. Hence, CH_3NC may be called methyl isocyanide, methyl carbylamine or methyl isonitrile but not aceto isonitrile.

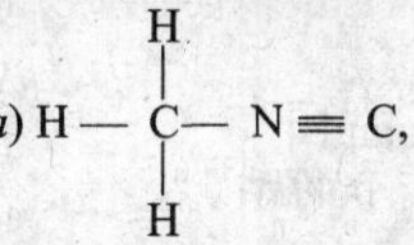

49 (*a*) Benzene ring with CHO at C-1, NO_2 at C-2, OCH_3 at C-4
4-methoxy- 2-nitrobenzaldehyde

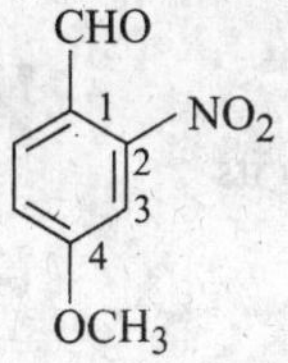

50 (*a*) $\overset{5}{C}H_3—\overset{4}{C}H(CH_3)—\overset{3}{C}(=O)—\overset{2}{C}H_2—\overset{1}{C}H_2OH$
1 - hydroxy - 4 - methylpentan - 3 - one

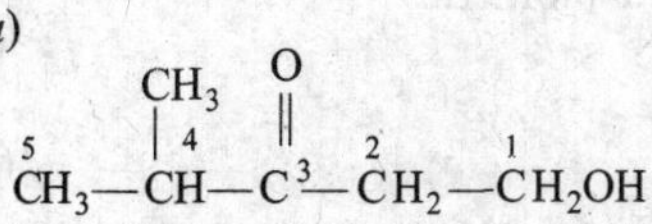

51 (*d*) 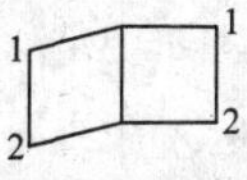
bicyclo [2.2.0] hexane

52 (*a*) Cyclopropyl—C(=O)—N(CH_3)(CH_3)
N,N-dimethyl cyclopropane carboxamide

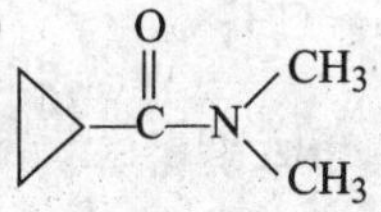

53 (*d*) $\overset{5}{C}H_3—\overset{4}{C}H_2—\overset{3}{C}H(CH_3)—\overset{2}{C}H(CH_3)—\overset{1}{C}(=O)—Cl$
2,3-dimethylpentanoyl chloride

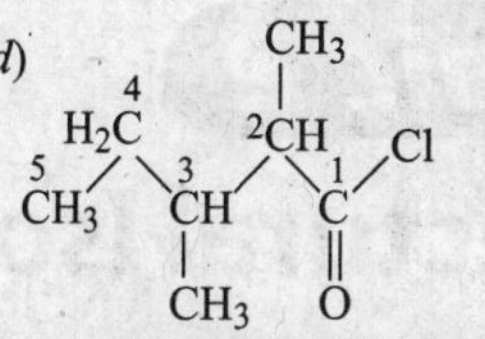

54 (*d*) $\overset{8}{C}H_3\overset{7}{C}H_2\overset{6}{C}H_2\overset{5}{C}H(CH(CH_3)_2)—\overset{4}{C}H(CH_3)—\overset{3}{C}(CH_2CH_3)(CH_2CH_3)—\overset{2}{C}H_2—\overset{1}{C}H_3$
3,3-diethyl-4-methyl-5 (1′-methylethyl) octane

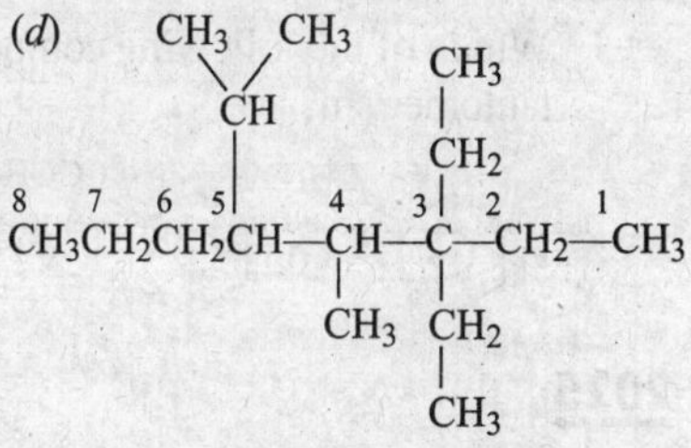

55 (*b*) 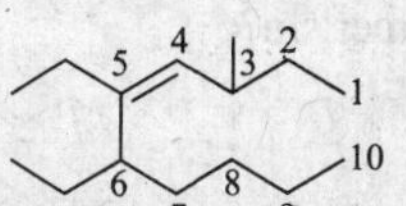
5,6-diethyl-3-methyl dec-4-ene

56 (*b*) $CH_3—\overset{3}{C}H(\overset{4}{C}H_2CHO)—CH_2—CHO$
IUPAC name is 3-methyl pentane dial

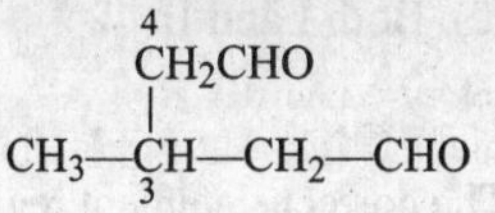

57 (*d*) $\overset{7}{C}H_3—\overset{6}{C}H_2—\overset{5}{C}H_2—\overset{4}{C}H(CH_2—CH_3)—\overset{3}{C}H(CH_3)—\overset{2}{C}H_2—\overset{1}{C}H_3$
4-ethyl-3-methylheptane
Thus, the incorrect option is (d).

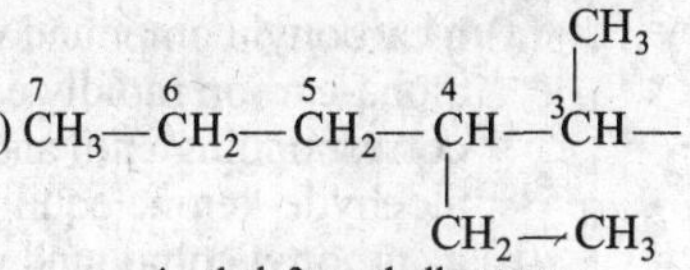

58 (*b*) Isopropyl group means one methyl group is present on 2nd carbon which is linked to the longest chain of carbon atom.
(a) $H_3\overset{5}{C}—\overset{4}{C}H_2\overset{3}{C}(CH_3)_2—\overset{2}{C}(CH_3)_2—\overset{1}{C}H_3$
2,2,3,3-tetramethylpentane
(b) $H_3\overset{5}{C}—\overset{4}{C}H_2—\overset{3}{C}H_2—\overset{2}{C}H(CH_3)—\overset{1}{C}H_3$
2-methyl pentane, it has *iso*-propyl group
(c) $H_3\overset{5}{C}—\overset{4}{C}H_2\overset{3}{C}H(CH_3)—\overset{2}{C}(CH_3)_2—\overset{1}{C}H_3$
2,2,3-trimethyl pentane
(d) $H_3\overset{5}{C}—\overset{4}{C}H_2—\overset{3}{C}(CH_3)_2—\overset{2}{C}H_2—\overset{1}{C}H_3$
3,3-dimethyl pentane
∴ 2-methylpentane has *iso*-propyl group.

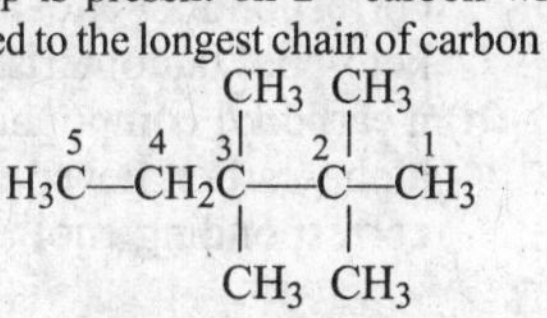

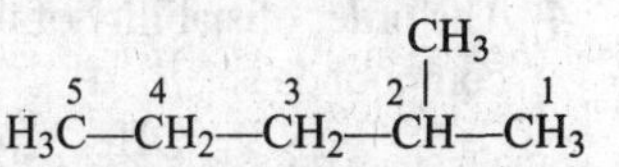

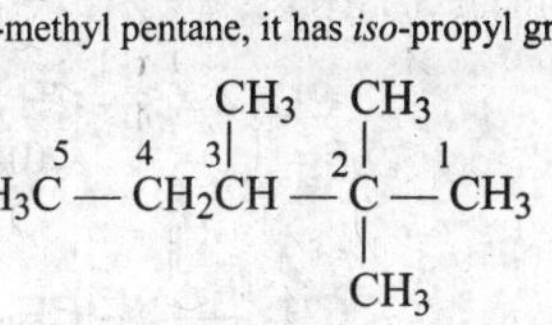

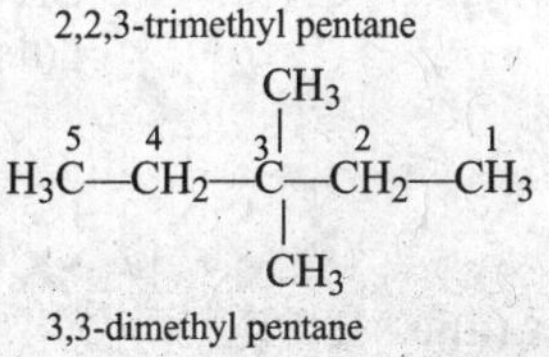

Topic 2

Structural Isomerism

2018

1 Which of the following compound can exhibit tautomerism? **[JIPMER]**

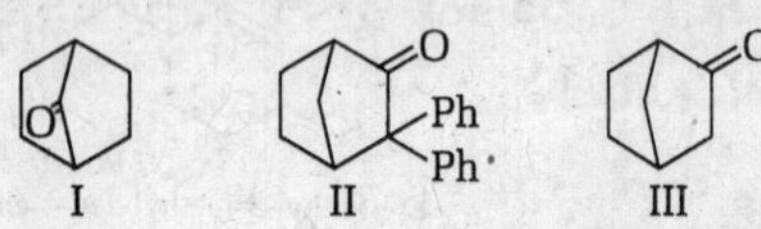

2016

2 Which among the given molecules can exhibit tautomerism? **[NEET]**

I, II (Ph, Ph), III

(a) III Only (b) Both I and III
(c) Both I and II (d) Both II and III

2015

3 The correct statement regarding a carbonyl compound with a hydrogen atom on its alpha-carbon, is **[AIPMT]**

(a) a carbonyl compound with a hydrogen atom on its alpha-carbon rapidly equilibrates with its corresponding enol and this process is known as aldehyde-ketone equilibration
(b) a carbonyl compound with a hydrogen atom on its alpha-carbon rapidly equilibrates with its corresponding enol and this process is known as carbonylation
(c) a carbonyl compound with a hydrogen atom on its alpha-carbon rapidly equilibrates with its corresponding enol and this process is known as keto-enol tautomerism
(d) a carbonyl compound with a hydrogen atom on its alpha-carbon never equilibrates with its corresponding enol

2013

4 The order of stability of the following tautomeric compounds is

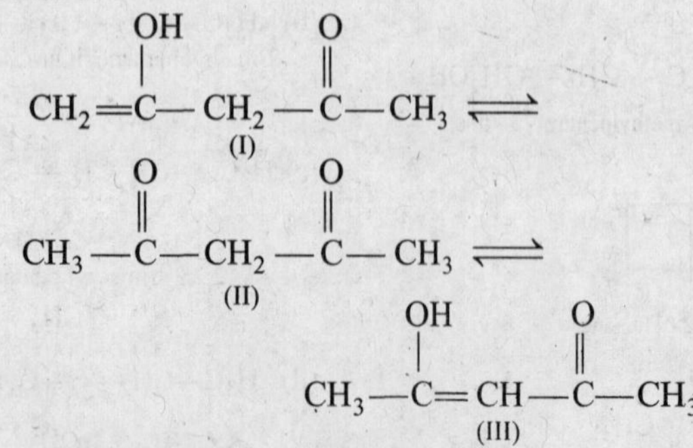

(a) I > II > III (b) III > II > I **[NEET]**
(c) II > I > III (d) II > III > I

5 The isomerism represented by ethyl acetoacetate **[BHU]**

(a) keto-enol isomerism (b) geometrical isomerism
(c) enantiomerism (d) diastereoisomerism

2011

6 The compounds $CH_3CH{=}CHCH_3$ and $CH_3CH_2CH{=}CH_2$ **[Kerala CEE]**

(a) are tautomers
(b) are position isomers
(c) contain same number of sp^3-sp^3 sp^3-sp^2 and sp^2-sp^2 carbon-carbon bonds
(d) exist together in dynamic equilibrium
(e) are optical isomers

7 Which one of the following shows functional isomerism? **[KCET]**

(a) C_2H_4 (b) C_3H_6
(c) C_2H_5OH (d) CH_2Cl_2

8 Which of the following compound will show metamerism? **[JCECE]**

(a) $CH_3—CO—C_2H_5$ (b) $C_2H_5—S—C_2H_5$
(c) $CH_3—O—CH_3$ (d) $CH_3—O—C_2H_5$

2010

9 Number of acyclic isomers of the compound having the molecular formula $C_4H_{10}O$ is **[AFMC]**

(a) 4 (b) 6 (c) 5 (d) 7

10 The total number of isomer of C_4H_7OH is **[UP CPMT]**

(a) 3 (b) 4 (c) 6 (d) 7

11 The total number of isomers for C_4H_8 is **[BVP]**

(a) 5 (b) 6 (c) 7 (d) 8

12 How many isomeric *vicinal*-dihalides are possible for the compound having molecular formula $C_3H_6Cl_2$? **[MHT CET]**

(a) 1 (b) 2 (c) 3 (d) 4

13 The number of metamers possible for $C_4H_{10}O$ is

(a) 1 (b) 2 (c) 3 (d) 4 **[MHT CET]**

14 The isomer of ethanol is **[OJEE]**

(a) acetaldehyde (b) dimethyl ether
(c) acetone (d) methylcarbinol

15 Keto-enol tautomerism is not observed in **[WB JEE]**

(a) $C_6H_5COC_6H_5$ (b) $C_6H_5COCH{=}CH_2$
(c) $C_6H_5COCH_2COCH_3$ (d) $CH_3COCH_2COCH_3$

16 How many primary amines are possible for the formula $C_4H_{11}N$? **[Haryana PMT]**

(a) 1 (b) 2 (c) 3 (d) 4

2009

17 The number of metamers of the compound with molecular formula $C_5H_{10}O$ is **[AFMC]**

(a) 1 (b) 3 (c) 8 (d) 6

18 Ether and alcohol are .... isomers. **[MHT CET]**

(a) chain (b) position
(c) functional (d) not isomer

19 The number of chain isomers possible for the hydrocarbon C_5H_{12} is **[Kerala CEE]**

(a) 1 (b) 2 (c) 3 (d) 4
(e) 5

20 A compound is formed by substitution of two chlorine for two hydrogens in propane. The number of possible isomeric compound is **[WB JEE]**

(a) 4 (b) 3 (c) 5 (d) 2

2008

21 Maximum enol content is in **[AIIMS]**

(a) CH_3COCH_3 (b) $CH_3COCH_2COCH_3$
(c) CH_3COCH_3 (d) CH_3COCH_2CHO

22 The number of isomeric ethers with molecular formula $C_4H_{10}O$ are **[MHT CET]**

(a) one (b) two (c) three (d) four

23 Empirical formula of compound having molar mass 58 is C_2H_5. Number of structural isomers possible, are

(a) 1 (b) 2 (c) 3 (d) 4 **[DUMET]**

24 Methoxy methane and ethanol are **[KCET]**

(a) position isomers (b) chain isomers
(c) functional isomers (d) optical isomers

2007

25 The type of isomerism observed in urea molecule is

(a) chain (b) position **[AIIMS]**
(c) geometrical (d) tautomerism

26 Which one of the following compounds cannot show tautomerism? **[Kerala CEE]**

(a) $CH_3-\underset{\underset{O}{\|}}{C}-CH_3$ (b) $CH_2=CH-OH$

(c) δ-lactone (six-membered ring, C=O adjacent to ring O) (d) unsaturated six-membered lactone (ring with C=C) (e) six-membered lactam (C=O adjacent to NH)

27 The total number of possible isomer of trimethyl benzene is

(a) 2 (b) 3 **[RPMT]**
(c) 4 (d) 6

28 The total number of isomers in $C_6H_3Cl_3$

(a) two (b) three **[Haryana PMT]**
(c) four (d) five

29 *n*-pentane, *iso*-pentane, and *neo*-pentane are examples for isomers of the type **[J&K CET]**

(a) geometrical (b) optical
(c) chain (d) positional

2006

30 Number of primary alcohols of the formula $C_5H_{12}O$ are

(a) 1 (b) 4 (c) 5 (d) 3 **[BHU]**

31 How many isomers are possible for the alkane C_4H_{10}?

(a) 3 (b) 5 **[Manipal]**
(c) 2 (d) 4

32 Which type of isomerism is shown by the propanal and propanone? **[RPMT]**

(a) Functional group (b) Metamerism
(c) Tautomerism (d) Chain isomerism

33 Nitroethane can exhibit one of the following kind of isomerism **[AMU, Haryana PMT]**

(a) metamerism
(b) optical activity
(c) tautomerism
(d) position isomerism

34 2-pentanone and 3-methyl-2-butanone are a pair of .... isomers. **[J&K CET]**

(a) functional (b) chain
(c) positional (d) stereo

35 *n*-pentane and 2-methylbutane are a pair of **[J&K CET]**

(a) enantiomers
(b) stereoisomers
(c) diastereomers
(d) constitutional isomers

2005

36 How many structural isomers are possible for C_4H_9Cl?

(a) 2 (b) 4 **[MHT CET]**
(c) 8 (d) 10

37 The number of isomeric hexanes is **[JCECE]**

(a) 5 (b) 2
(c) 3 (d) 4

Answers

1 (b)	2 (a)	3 (c)	4 (b)	5 (a)	6 (b)	7 (c)	8 (b)	9 (d)	10 (d)
11 (b)	12 (a)	13 (c)	14 (b)	15 (a)	16 (d)	17 (b)	18 (c)	19 (c)	20 (c)
21 (b)	22 (c)	23 (b)	24 (c)	25 (d)	26 (d)	27 (b)	28 (b)	29 (c)	30 (b)
31 (c)	32 (a)	33 (c)	34 (b)	35 (d)	36 (b)	37 (a)			

Explanations

1 (*b*) Presence of α – H atom along with a multibonded functional group is an essential condition for exhibiting tautomerism.

$C_6H_5COCH_3$

Acetophenone satisfies this condition, therefore it exhibits tautomerism.

2 (*a*) In tautomerism, α –hydrogen along with a multibonded functional group must be present in the molecule. Thus, molecule II will not show tautomerism. As at bridge, double bond is highly unstable, thus, molecule I will also not show tautomerism. For III molecule,

(III) Keto form ⇌ Enol form

So only, molecule (III) will show tautomerism. Thus, correct option is (a).

3 (*c*) In keto-enol tautomerism, a carbonyl compound with a hydrogen atom on its alpha-carbon rapidly equilibrates with its corresponding enol.

$$\underset{\text{Ketone}}{R-\overset{O}{\overset{\|}{C}}-}\underset{(\alpha\text{-hydrogen atoms})}{CH_2R'} \rightleftharpoons \underset{\text{Enol}}{R-\overset{OH}{\overset{|}{C}}=CHR'}$$

4 (*b*) The enols of β-dicarbonyl compounds are more stable because of conjugation and intramolecular hydrogen bonding.
Thus, the order of stability is III > II > I.

$$\underset{\text{III}}{CH_3-\overset{OH}{\overset{|}{C}}=CH-\overset{O}{\overset{\|}{C}}-CH_3}$$

(stabilised by conjugation and hydrogen bonding)

$$> \underset{\text{II}}{CH_3-\overset{O}{\overset{\|}{C}}-CH_2-\overset{O}{\overset{\|}{C}}-CH_3}$$

$$> \underset{\text{I}}{CH_2=\overset{OH}{\overset{|}{C}}-CH_2-\overset{O}{\overset{\|}{C}}-CH_3}$$

I is less stable, as (=) bond is not in conjugation with carbonyl group.

5 (*a*) Ethyl acetoacetate represents keto-enol isomerism.

$$\underset{\text{Keto form}}{CH_3-\overset{O}{\overset{\|}{C}}-\overset{H}{\overset{|}{C}}HCOOC_2H_5} \rightleftharpoons \underset{\text{Enolic form}}{CH_3-\overset{OH}{\overset{|}{C}}=CHCOOC_2H_5}$$

6 (*b*) $CH_3CH=CHCH_3$ and $CH_3CH_2CH=CH_2$ are position isomers. The two isomers differ in the position of double bond.

7 (*c*) Ethyl alcohol (C_2H_5OH) shows functional isomerism with dimethyl ether.

$$\underset{\text{Alcohol}}{C_2H_5OH} \qquad \underset{\text{Dimethyl Ether}}{CH_3-O-CH_3}$$

8 (*b*) Compounds having bivalent functional group (like C = O, —O—, —S—, etc) with at least 4 carbon atoms (in case of ether and thioether) or at least 5 carbon atoms (in case of ketones) exhibit metamerism.
Hence, $C_2H_5-S-C_2H_5$ will show metamerism.

9 (*d*) The acyclic isomers of compound having molecular formula $C_4H_{10}O$ are as,

(i) *n*-butanol
(ii) butan-2-ol
(iii) 2-methyl propanol
(iv) diethyl ether (or ethoxy ethane)
(v) 2-methyl propan-2-ol
(vi) methoxy propane
(vii) 2-methoxy propane

Thus, 7 acyclic isomers exist for molecular formula $C_4H_{10}O$.

10 (*d*) The following isomers are possible for C_4H_7OH.

(i) *n*-butanal
(ii) 2-methyl propanal
(iii) butan-2-one
(iv) but-3-en-1-ol
(v) but-2-en-1-ol
(vi) 2-methyl-prop-2-en-1-ol
(vii) but-3-en-2-ol

Thus, 7 isomers are possible for C_4H_7OH.

11 (*b*) The possible isomers of C_4H_8 are as

(i) $CH_3CH_2CH = CH_2$
but-1-ene

(ii) $CH_3 - C(H) = C(H) - CH_3$
trans-but-2-ene

(iii) $CH_3CH = CHCH_3$
cis-but-2-ene

(iv) $CH_3 - C(CH_3) = CH_2$
2-methyl propene

(v) Cyclobutane

(vi) Methyl cyclopropane

Thus, 6 metamers are possible for C_4H_8.

12 (*a*) In *vicinal*-dihaldes, the two —Cl atoms are present at adjacent carbons. In case of $C_3H_6Cl_2$ only one such structure is possible. Hence, only one *vicinal*-dihalide is possible for $C_3H_6Cl_2$.

$CH_3 - CH(Cl) - CH_2(Cl)$
1,2-dichloropropane

13 (*c*) Compound with molecular formula $C_4H_{10}O$ has the following metamers

(i) (ii) (iii)

Thus, three metamers are possible.

14 (*b*) Dimethyl ether is the functional isomer of ethanol.

$CH_3 - CH_2 - OH$
Ethanol

$CH_3 - O - CH_3$
Dimethyl ether

15 (*a*) $C_6H_5COC_6H_5$ does not exhibit tautomerism as it does not contain α-H atom.

16 (*d*) For the formula $C_4H_{11}N$, the possible primary amines are:

(i) $CH_3 - CH_2 - CH_2 - CH_2 - NH_2$

(ii) $CH_3 - CH(CH_3) - CH_2 - NH_2$

(iii) $CH_3 - C(CH_3)_2 - NH_2$

(iv) $H_3C - CH(CH_2CH_3) - NH_2$

Hence, four primary amines are possible for the formula $C_4H_{11}N$.

17 (*b*) Since the compound has $C_nH_{2n}O$ type general formula, it must be a ketone (or aldehyde). It has the following metamers (the isomers having same functional group, but different alkyl group attached with the same functional group) :

(i) $CH_3 - CO - CH_2CH_2CH_3$
pentan-2-one

(ii) $CH_3CH_2 - CO - CH_2CH_3$
pentan-3-one

(iii) $CH_3 - CO - CH(CH_3) - CH_3$
3-methyl-butan-2-one

Hence, it has three metamers.

18 (*c*) The general formula for both ether and alcohol is $C_nH_{2n+2}O$ but the functional group present in ethers is —O— and in alcohols is —OH, so they are functional isomers.

19 (*c*) The possible chain isomers of hydrocarbon C_5H_{12} are :

(i) *n*-pentane (ii) *iso*-pentane

(iii) *neo*-pentane

20 (*c*) The compound is $C_3H_6Cl_2$ and the number of possible isomeric compounds is 5.

$CH_2Cl - CH_2 - CH_2Cl$
1, 3-dichloropropane

$CH_2Cl - C^*HCl - CH_3$ (Asymmetric carbon atom)
(*d*, *l* pair)
1, 2-dichloropropane

$CHCl_2 - CH_2 - CH_3$
1, 1-dichloropropane

$CH_3 - CCl_2 - CH_3$
2, 2-dichloropropane

21 (*b*) $CH_3 - CO - CH_2 - CO - CH_3$
Acetyl acetone
(keto form-24%)

$CH_3 - C(OH) = CH - CO - CH_3 \longleftrightarrow$ (O—H---O)
(Enol form-76%)

$CH_3 - CO - CH = C(OH) - CH_3$ (O---H—O)

In acetyl acetone, the enol form is stabilised by H-bonding, hence it has more enol content than others.

22 (*c*) Possible isomeric ethers of $C_4H_{10}O$ are as follows :

(i) $C_2H_5 - O - C_2H_5$
Diethyl ether

(ii) $CH_3 - O - C_3H_7$
1-methoxypropane

(iii) $CH_3 - O - CH(CH_3)_2$
2-methoxypropane

Hence, three isomeric ethers are possible.

23 (*b*) Empirical formula is C_2H_5.

Empirical formula mass = 29 g/mol

Molar mass = 58 g/mol

$$n = \frac{\text{molar mass}}{\text{empirical mass formula}} = \frac{58}{29} = 2$$

∴ Molecular formula $= (C_2H_5)_2 = C_4H_{10}$

The molecular formula is C_4H_{10} and the isomers are two (chain isomers) in number.

$CH_3 - CH_2 - CH_2 - CH_3$,

$CH_3 - CH(CH_3) - CH_3$

24 (*c*) CH_3OCH_3,

Methoxy methane is an ether. Its molecular formula is C_2H_6O.

C_2H_5OH

Ethanol is an alcohol. Its molecular formula is C_2H_6O.

In both methoxy methane and ethanol molecular formula is same, but functional groups are different, so they are functional isomers.

25 (*d*) Keto-enol tautomerism is observed in urea.

$H_2N-\overset{O}{\overset{\|}{C}}-NH_2 \rightleftharpoons HN=\overset{OH}{\overset{|}{C}}-NH_2$

Keto form — Enol form

26 (*d*) Option (d) cannot show tautomerism.

(a) $CH_3-\underset{O}{\underset{\|}{C}}-CH_3 \xrightleftharpoons{\text{Tautomerism}} CH_3-\underset{OH}{\underset{|}{C}}H=CH_2$

Keto form — Enol form

(b) $CH_2=CH-OH \xrightleftharpoons{\text{Tautomerism}} CH_3-\underset{H}{\underset{|}{C}}=O$

enol form — Keto form

(c) 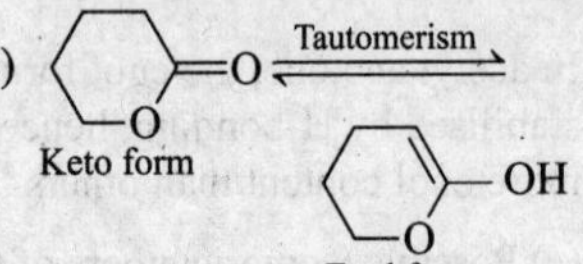 Keto form $\xrightleftharpoons{\text{Tautomerism}}$ Enol form

(d) 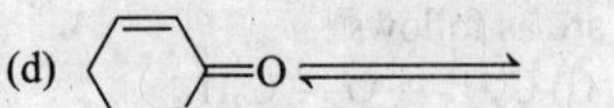 $\rightleftharpoons$ × (no tautomerism)

(e) 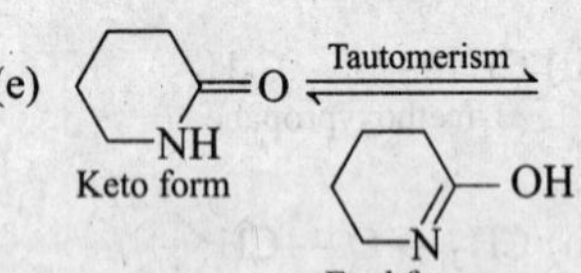 Keto form $\xrightleftharpoons{\text{Tautomerism}}$ Enol form

27 (*b*) The total number of possible isomer of trimethyl benzene are 3.

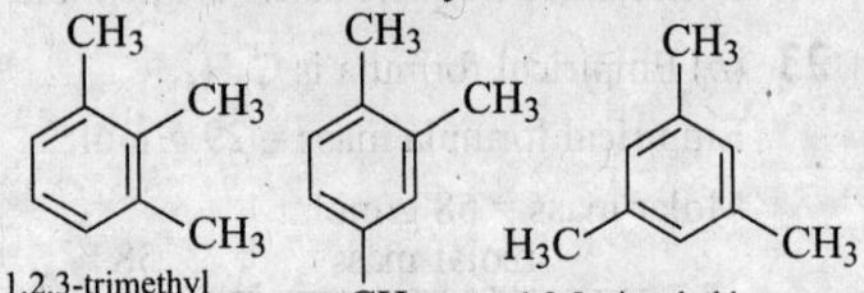

1,2,3-trimethyl benzene (i); 1,2,4-trimethyl benzene (ii); 1,3,5-trimethyl benzene (iii)

28 (*b*) The total number of isomers in $C_6H_3Cl_3$ are three.

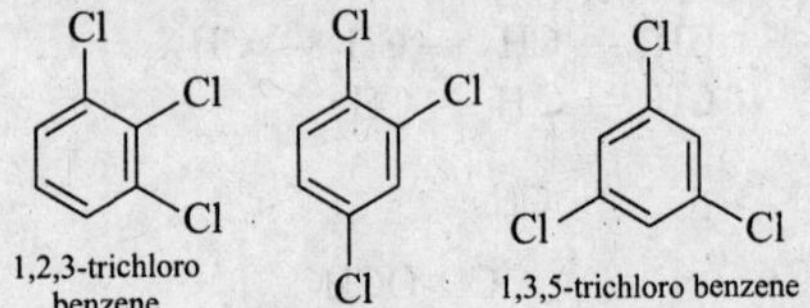

1,2,3-trichloro benzene (i); 1,2,4-trichloro benzene (ii); 1,3,5-trichloro benzene (iii)

Hence, three isomers are possible.

29 (*c*) The compounds which differ in the nature of carbon chain are called chain isomers, e.g.

(i) $CH_3-CH_2-CH_2-CH_2-CH_3$
(*n*-pentane (C_5H_{12}))

(ii) $CH_3-\overset{CH_3}{\overset{|}{C}}H-CH_2CH_3$
iso-pentane (C_5H_{12})

(iii) $H_3C-\overset{CH_3}{\underset{CH_3}{\overset{|}{\underset{|}{C}}}}-CH_3$
neo-pentane (C_5H_{12})

30 (*b*) Four primary alcohols of the formula $C_5H_{12}O$ are possible :

(i) $CH_3CH_2CH_2CH_2CH_2OH$, Pentan-1-ol

(ii) $CH_3-CH_2-\underset{CH_3}{\underset{|}{C}}H-CH_2OH$ 2-methylbutan-1-ol

(iii) $CH_3-\underset{CH_3}{\underset{|}{C}}H-CH_2-CH_2OH$ 3-methylbutan-1-ol

(iv) $CH_3-\overset{CH_3}{\underset{CH_3}{\overset{|}{\underset{|}{C}}}}-CH_2OH$ 2,2-dimethylpropan-1-ol

31 (*c*) The isomers of C_4H_{10} are :

(i) $CH_3-\underset{CH_3}{\underset{|}{C}}H-CH_3$ *iso*-butane

(ii) $CH_3-CH_2-CH_2-CH_3$ *n*-butane

∴ Two isomers are possible.

32 (*a*) When two compounds have similar molecular formula but differ in the functional group, then the isomerism is called functional group isomerism, i.e.

CH_3CH_2CHO (Aldehyde) (C_3H_6O) propanal

$CH_3-\overset{O}{\overset{\|}{C}}-CH_3$ (Ketone) (C_3H_6O) propanone

33 (*c*) Nitro alkanes exhibit tautomerism. In it, α-H-atom is labile and form nitrolic acid.

$H_3C-CH_2-N(=O)\rightarrow O \rightleftharpoons H_3C-CH=N(-OH)\rightarrow O$

34 (*b*) Pentan-2-one and 3-methylbutan-2-one are chain isomers because they differ in carbon skeleton.

$CH_3CH_2CH_2COCH_3$ Pentan-2-one

$CH_3\underset{CH_3}{\underset{|}{C}}H\cdot COCH_3$ 3-methyl-butan-2-one

35 (*d*) *n*-pentane and 2-methylbutane are constutional isomers or chain isomers or skeletal isomers.

$CH_3CH_2CH_2CH_2CH_3$ *n*-pentane

$CH_3\underset{CH_3}{\underset{|}{C}}HCH_2CH_3$ 2-methyl butane

36 (*b*) The possible isomers of C_4H_9Cl are as follows :

(*i*) **Structural isomers**

(a) $CH_3-CH_2-CH_2-CH_2Cl$ 1-chlorobutane

(b) $CH_3-CH_2-\underset{Cl}{\underset{|}{C}}H-CH_3$ 2-chlorobutane

(c) $CH_3-\underset{CH_3}{\underset{|}{C}}H-CH_2Cl$ 1-chloro 2-methyl propane

(d) $CH_3-\overset{Cl}{\underset{CH_3}{\overset{|}{\underset{|}{C}}}}-CH_3$ 2-chloro-2-methyl propane

(*ii*) **Stereoisomers** : 2-chlorobutane show optical isomerism and has two enantiomers.

$CH_3CH_2-\underset{Cl}{\underset{|}{\overset{*}{C}}}H-CH_3$

(*d*-and *l*-isomers)

Thus, there are four structural isomers and 5 isomers in all of C_4H_9Cl.

37 (*a*) C_6H_{14}-hexane.

The isomers of hexane are :

(i) $CH_3-CH_2-CH_2-CH_2-CH_2-CH_3$ hexane

(ii) $CH_3-\overset{CH_3}{\overset{|}{C}}H-CH_2-CH_2-CH_3$ 2-methyl pentane

(iii) $CH_3-CH_2-\overset{CH_3}{\overset{|}{C}}H-CH_2-CH_3$ 3-methyl pentane

(iv) $CH_3-CH_2-\overset{CH_3}{\underset{CH_3}{\overset{|}{\underset{|}{C}}}}-CH_3$ 2,2-dimethyl butane

(v) $CH_3-\overset{CH_3}{\overset{|}{C}}H-\overset{CH_3}{\overset{|}{C}}H-CH_3$ 2, 3-dimethyl butane

∴ Total of five isomeric hexanes are possible.

Topic 3

Geometrical Isomerism

2018

1 The pair of structures given below represents **[JIPMER]**

CH_2OH and CH_3 OH

(a) Chain isomers (b) Position isomers
(c) Tautomers (d) Metamers

2 Among the following complex ions, the one which shows geometrical isomerism will be **[AIIMS]**

(a) $[Cr(H_2O)_4Cl_2]^+$ (b) $[Pt(NH_3)_3Cl]$
(c) $[CO(NH_3)_6]^{3+}$ (d) $[CO(CN)_5(NC)]^{3-}$

2017

3 **Assertion** (A) Complexes of MX_6 and MX_5L type (X and L are unidentate) do not show geometrical isomerism.

Reason (R) Geometrical isomerism is not shown by complexes of coordinate number – 6. **[AIIMS]**

(a) Both A and R are correct and R is the correct explanation of A
(b) Both A and R are correct but R is not the correct explanation of A
(c) A is correct but R is incorrect
(d) Both A and R are incorrect

2017

4 **Assertion** (A) The configuration of given compound is z.

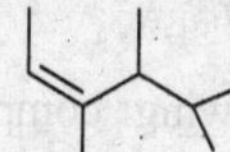

Reason (R) z-configuration shows the presence of bulkier groups at the opposite side of double bond. **[AIIMS]**

(a) Both A and R are correct and R is the correct explanation of A
(b) Both A and R are correct but R is not the correct explanation of A
(c) A is correct but R is incorrect
(d) Both A and R are incorrect

2014

5 Geometrical isomerism is not possible in **[Kerala CEE]**

(a) 2,4-hexadiene (b) benzophenone oxime
(c) but-2-ene (d) 1,2-dichloroethene

2013

6 The *cis* and *trans* isomers are represented by **[UP CPMT]**

(a) pent-1-ene (b) but-2-ene
(c) prop-1-ene (d) but-1-ene

2012

7 Geometrical isomerism is shown by **[UP CPMT]**

(a) $-\overset{|}{C}-\overset{|}{C}-$ (b) $>C=C<$
(c) $-C\equiv C-$ (d) None of these

2011

8 Which one of the following exhibits geometrical isomerism? **[Kerala CEE]**

(a) 1,2-dibromopropene (b) 2,3-dimethylbut-2-ene
(c) 2,3-dibromobut-2-ene (d) 2-methylbut-2-ene
(e) 2,3-dibromobut-1-ene

2011

9 Among the following, the oxime of which shows geometrical isomerism, is **[DUMET]**

(a) acetone (b) diethylketone
(c) formaldehyde (d) benzaldehyde

2010

10 The number of isomers for the compound with the molecular formula $C_2BrCl\cdot FI$ is **[Manipal]**

(a) 3 (b) 4 (c) 5 (d) 6

11 Which of the following can exhibit geometrical isomerism? **[OJEE]**

(a) But-1-ene (b) 2-methylbut-2-ene
(c) 2,3-dimethylbut-2-ene (d) 2-chloro but-2-ene

2009

12 Which of the following compounds will exhibit *cis-trans* (geometrical) isomerism? **[CBSE AIPMT]**

(a) 2-butene (b) Butanol
(c) 2-butyne (d) 2-butenol

13 Which will not show geometrical isomerism? **[AIIMS]**

(a) $CH_3CH=NOH$ (b)
(c) $HO-N=N-OH$ (d) $(CH_3)_2C=NOH$

14 Which among the following will not exhibit geometrical isomerism? **[Kerala CEE]**

(a) 2-methyl-2-butene
(b) 2-butene
(c) 2,3-dichloro-2-butene
(d) 1-chloro-1-pentene
(e) 1,2-dichloroethene

15 Which will exhibit geometrical isomerism? **[CG PMT, Haryana PMT]**

(a) 3-phenyl-1-butene (b) 1-phenyl-2-butene
(c) 2-phenyl-1-butene (d) 1,1-diphenyl-1-propene

16 Which of the following compounds will show geometrical isomerism? **[DUMET]**

(a) Cyclohexene (b) 2-hexene
(c) 3-hexyne (d) 1,1-diphenylethylene

2008

17 C_8H_{16} that can form *cis-trans* geometrical isomers and also has a chiral centre, is **[AIIMS]**

(a) 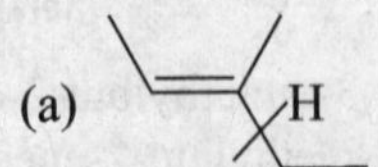

(b) 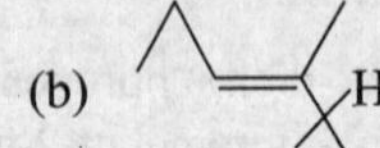

(c) Both 'a' and 'b' (d) None of these

18 Assertion (A) Boiling points of *cis*-isomers are higher than *trans*-isomers.

Reason (R) Dipole moments of *cis*-isomers are higher than *trans*-isomers. **[AIIMS]**

(a) Both A and R are correct and the R is the correct explanation of the A
(b) Both A and R are correct but R is not the correct explanation of the A
(c) A is correct but R is incorrect
(d) Both A and R are incorrect

19 The total number of acyclic isomers including the stereoisomers (geometrical and optical), with the molecular formula C_4H_7Cl is **[Manipal]**

(a) 12 (b) 11 (c) 10 (d) 9

20 The most stable geometrical isomer among the following is **[Kerala CEE]**

(a) 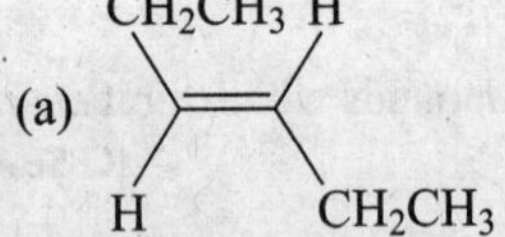

(b) 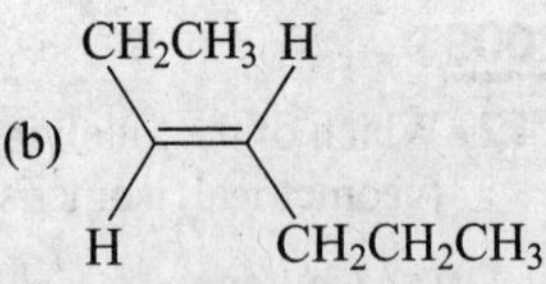

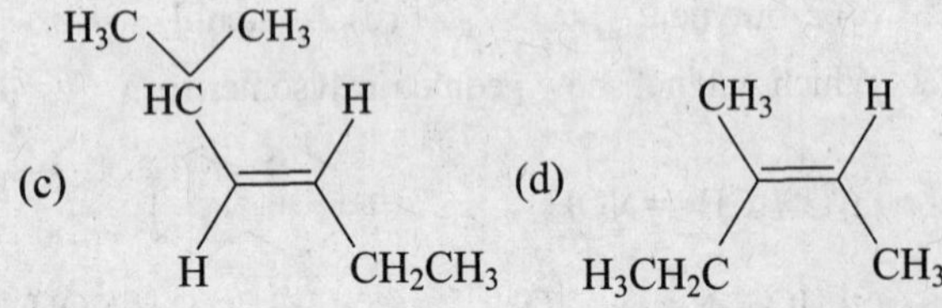

(e) 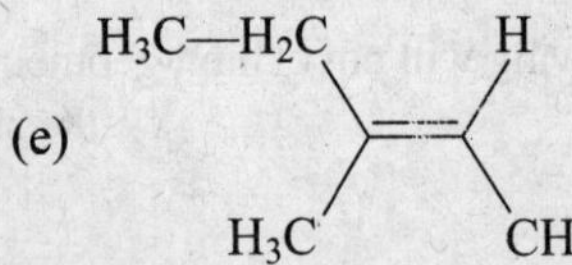

21 Which one of the following alkenes does not exhibit geometrical isomerism? **[J&K CET]**

(a) C_4H_8 (b) C_3H_6
(c) C_5H_{10} (d) C_8H_{16}

22 How many numbers of possible stereoisomers are there of 2,3,4-trichloro pentanoic acid? **[Guj CET]**

(a) 8 (b) 12 (c) 16 (d) 4

23 Which one of the following compounds exhibit geometrical isomerism? **[J&K CET]**

(a) $CH_3CH_2CH_2CH_3$
(b) $CH_3—HC(CH_3)—CH(CH_3)—CH_3$
(c) $CH_3—HC(CH_3)—CH_3$
(d) $CH_3CH=CH—CH_3$

2007

24 Geometrical isomers differ in **[Punjab PMET]**

(a) position of functional group
(b) position of atoms
(c) spatial arrangement of atoms
(d) length of carbon chain

25 The number of geometrical isomers in $CH_3CH=CHCH_2CH=CH_2$ are **[DUMET]**

(a) two (b) three (c) four (d) five

26 The number of isomers of the compound with molecular formula $C_2H_2Br_2$ is **[Manipal]**

(a) 4 (b) 3
(c) 5 (d) 2

27 Which shows geometrical isomerism? **[MP PMT]**

(a) $(H)(H)C=C(I)(Br)$
(b) $(H)(H_3C)C=C(I)(Br)$
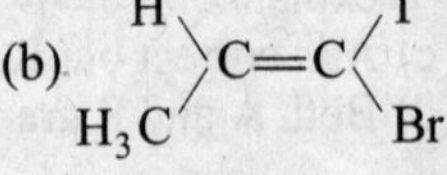
(c) $(H_3C)(H_3C)C=C(Cl)(Br)$
(d) $(H)(H_3C)C=C(Cl)(Cl)$

28 Which of the following compounds will not exhibit *cis-trans* isomerism? **[Punjab PMET]**

(a) (b) Cl
(c) (d)

29 The number of isomeric alkenes with molecular formula C_6H_{12} are **[Punjab PMET]**

(a) 8 (b) 10 (c) 11 (d) 13

2006

30 Number of isomers possible for C_4H_8O is **[AMU]**

(a) 3 (b) 4 (c) 5 (d) 6

31 Among the following the most stable compound is **[AIIMS]**

(a) *cis*-1, 2-cyclohexanediol
(b) *trans*-1, 2-cyclohexanediol
(c) *cis*-1, 3-cyclohexanediol
(d) *trans*-1, 3-cyclohexanediol

32 What kind of isomerism is possible for 1-chloro-2-nitroethene? **[J&K CET]**

(a) Functional group isomerism
(b) Position isomerism
(c) *E/Z*- isomerism
(d) Optical isomerism

33 Which of the following shows geometrical isomerism? **[BCECE]**

(a) C_2H_5Br
(b) $(CH_2)(COOH)_2$
(c) $(CH)_2(COOH)_2$
(d) C_2H_6

Answers

1 (b)	2 (a)	3 (c)	4 (c)	5 (b)	6 (b)	7 (b)	8 (c)	9 (d)	10 (d)
11 (d)	12 (a)	13 (d)	14 (a)	15 (b)	16 (b)	17 (a)	18 (a)	19 (a)	20 (d)
21 (b)	22 (a)	23 (d)	24 (c)	25 (a)	26 (b)	27 (b)	28 (b)	29 (d)	30 (d)
31 (d)	32 (c)	33 (c)							

Explanations

1 (*b*) The pair of the given structures,

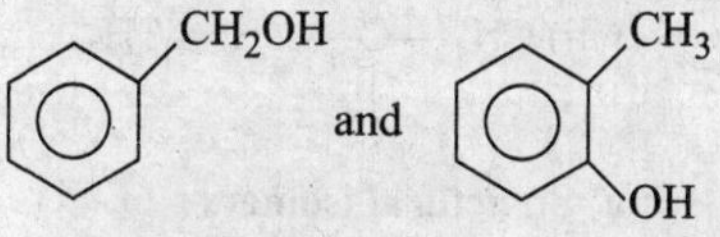

(benzene ring with CH_2OH) and (benzene ring with CH_3 and OH)

represents position isomers. In case of position isomers, the difference lies in the position of substituent groups or atom in the same chain.

2 (*a*) $[Cr(H_2O)_4Cl_2]^+$ shows geometrical isomerism because it is a MA_4B_2 type coordination compound which contains two set of equivalent ligands, four H_2O and 2Cl.

Hence, the possible geometrical isomers are:

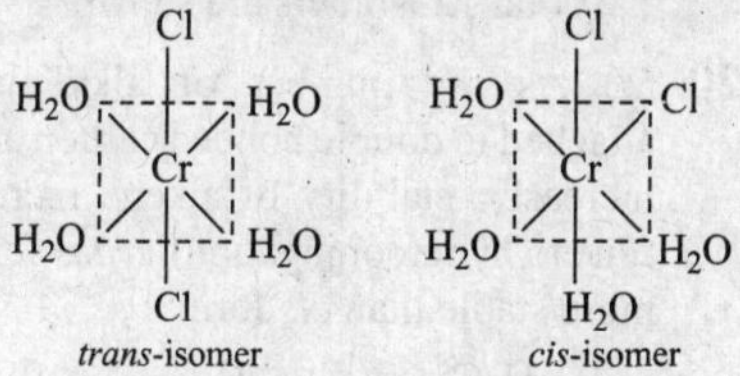

trans-isomer   *cis*-isomer

Hence, correct option is (a).

3 (*c*) MX_6 and MX_5L type complexes do not show geometrical isomerism (due to symmetry) although many coordinated complexes like complex of type MA_3B_3 exhibits geometrical isomerism. Hence, (A) is correct but (R) is incorrect.

4 (*c*) In *z*-configuration, bulkier groups exist on the same side of double bond.

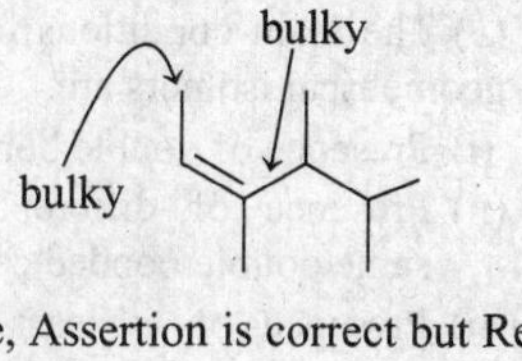

bulky   bulky

Hence, Assertion is correct but Reason is incorrect.

5 (*b*) In option (b) benzophenone oxime, same functional group is present on the double bond.

Hence, it will not show geometrical isomerism.

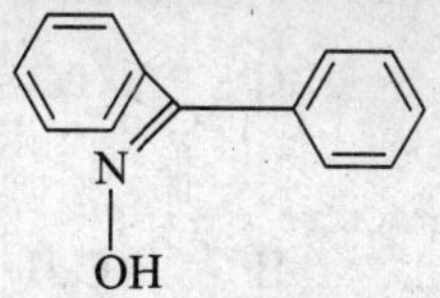

6 (*b*) The geometrical isomers must have :

(*i*) At least one carbon-carbon double bond.

(*ii*) The two groups attached to same carbon atom should be different. Geometrical isomers exists in two structural forms *cis* and *trans*.

In *cis* form the two groups are present on the same side and in *trans* form the two same groups are present on different sides.

The isomers which form *cis* and *trans* form, will show geometrical isomerism.

The possible geometrical isomers are as follows:

(a) $CH_3—CH_2—CH_2—CH=CH_2$ Pent-1-ene

(c) $CH_3—CH=CH_2$ Prop-1-ene

(d) $CH_3—CH_2—CH=CH_2$. but-1-ene.

∵ Choices (a), (c) and (d) have two identical group (hydrogen) attached to same double bonded carbon atoms.

∴ They don't exhibit geometrical isomerism,

But in (b), but-2-ene, the groups attached to the same carbon atom are different.

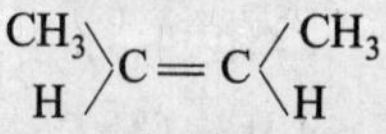

cis-but-2-ene

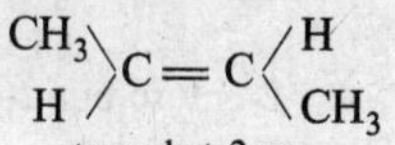

trans-but-2-ene

∴ Choice (b) will show geometrical isomerism.

7 (*b*) Geometrical isomerism is shown by $>C=C<$ only when identical groups are not present on the double bonded carbon atoms.

8 (*c*) 2, 3-dibromobut-2-ene exhibits geometrical isomerism. The isomers are as follows:

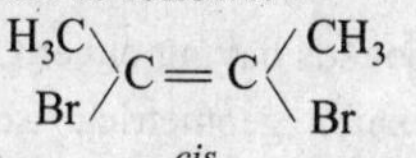

cis 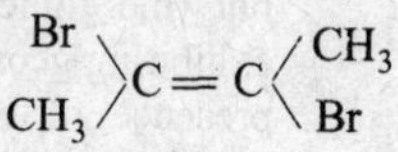   *trans*

9 (*d*) The oxime of benzaldehyde shows geometrical isomerism.

$$C_6H_5—\overset{O}{\overset{\|}{C}}—H + NH_2OH \longrightarrow C_6H_5—\overset{H}{\overset{|}{C}}=NOH$$

Benzaldehyde

The isomers are as follows:

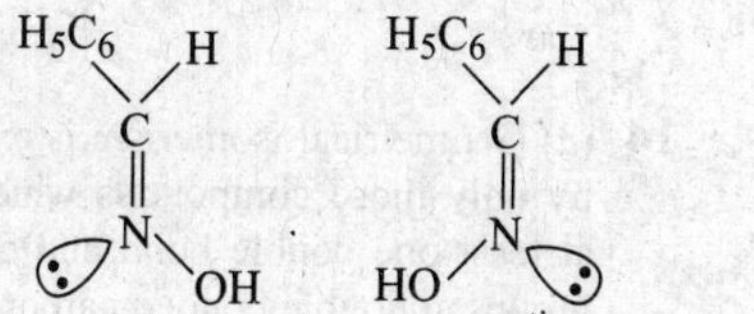

syn   *anti*

10 (*d*) The possible isomers of $C_2BrClFI$ are as

(i) $BrIC=CClF$ (Br, I on one carbon; Cl, F on the other)

(ii) $BrClC=CFI$

(iii) $BrFC=CClI$

(iv) $BrIC=CFCl$

(v) $BrClC=CIF$

(vi) $BrFC=CICl$

11 (*d*) $CH_3-C(Cl)=CH-CH_3$

2-chloro but-2-ene exhibits geometrical isomerism.

12 (*a*) 2-butene can exhibit geometrical isomerism. Its isomers are as follows:

$H_3C(H)C=C(H)CH_3$ — *cis*-form

$H(H_3C)C=C(H)CH_3$ — *trans*-form

13 (*d*) Compounds having either $C=C$ or $C=N$ exhibit geometrical isomerism but the other main condition for exhibiting geometrical isomerism is the presence of two different groups on double bonded carbon atoms.

Since in ketoxime, $(CH_3)_2C=NOH$, two same $(-CH_3)$ groups are present on double bonded carbon atom, its other form is not possible and it doesn't exhibit geometrical isomerism.

Compounds with $N=N$ having two geometrical forms are as follows :

$HO-N=N-OH$ *cis* $\qquad$ $HO-N=N-OH$ *trans*

14 (*a*) Geometrical isomerism is exhibited by only those compounds which have at least one double bond and different groups at double bonded carbon atoms. Since, 2-methyl-2-butene $((CH_3)_2C=CH-CH_3)$ contains same group at double bonded carbon atom, it does not exhibit geometrical isomerism.

15 (*b*) The compound which has at least one double bond and the groups attached with double bonded carbon atoms are different, exhibits geometrical isomerism.

$CH_3CH=CHCH_2C_6H_5$ exhibits geometrical isomerism.

$H_3C(H)C=C(H)CH_2C_6H_5$

1-phenyl-2-butene
cis-form

$H_3C(H)C=C(CH_2C_6H_5)H$

trans-form

16 (*b*) Cyclohexene is unsubstituted alicyclic compound. 2-hexene exhibits geometrical isomerism.

$H_3C(H)C=C(H)C_3H_7$

In 3-hexyne, the triply bonded carbon atoms have only one substituent each.

In 1,1-diphenylethylene, one double bonded carbon atom has two similar groups.

17 (*a*)

(a) *Chiral carbon $\qquad$ (b)

Compound (a) will exhibit geometrical isomerism and have chiral centre, while compound (b) exhibit geometrical isomerism but it does not have a chiral centre.

18 (*a*) Boiling points of isomeric compounds depends on dipole-dipole interactions and *cis*-isomers have greater dipole moments (more polar) than *trans*-isomers (less polar).

Thus, both A and R are correct and R is the correct explanation of A.

19 (*a*) **Geometrical isomers**

(*i*) $H_3CH_2C(H)C=C(Cl)H$

(*ii*) $H_3CH_2C(H)C=C(H)Cl$

(*iii*) $H_3C(H)C=C(CH_3)Cl$

(iv) $H_3C(H)C=C(Cl)CH_3$

(v) $H_3C(H)C=C(CH_2Cl)H$

(vi) $H_3C(H)C=C(H)CH_2Cl$

(b) **Optical isomers**

(vii) $CH_3-\overset{*}{C}(Cl)(H)-CH=CH_2$

(viii) $CH_3-\overset{*}{C}(H)(Cl)-CH=CH_2$

(c) **Structural isomers**

(ix) $CH_3CH_2-C(H)=CHCl$

(x) $CH_3-C(CH_3)=CHCl$

(xi) $CH_3-C(CH_2Cl)=CH_2$

(xii) $ClCH_2-CH_2-CH=CH_2$

∴ Total 12 isomers are shown.

20 (*d*) As the number of alkyl group attached to double bonded carbon atoms increases, stability of alkene increases (due to hyperconjugation). *trans* form is more stable than *cis* form:

$H_3C(H_3C-CH_2)C=C(H)CH_3$ *trans*-form (more stable) $>$ $H_3C-CH_2(H_3C)C=C(H)CH_3$ *cis*-form (less stable)

21 (*b*) The main conditions for exhibiting geometrical isomers are:

(i) Presence of double bond.

(ii) Presence of different groups on same double bonded carbon.

(iii) Presence of at least one similar group on adjacent double bonded carbon atoms.

$\therefore$ C_3H_6 ($\overset{3}{C}H_3-\overset{2}{C}H=\overset{1}{C}H_2$) does not exhibit geometrical isomerism due to presence of same group on double bonded carbon atom (C_1).

22 (*a*) The structural formula of 2, 3, 4-trichloropentanoic acid is given below:

$$HOOC-\overset{*}{C}H(Cl)-\overset{*}{C}H(Cl)-\overset{*}{C}H(Cl)-CH_3$$

Number of optical active isomers = 2^n

where, n = number of asymmetric carbon atom.

2,3,4-trichloro pentanoic acid has three asymmetric carbon atoms. So, number of optically active isomers = $2^3 = 8$

Since, there is no double bond in between C-atoms, therefore geometrical isomerism will not be shown.

Thus, total number of stereoisomers = 8

23 (*d*) The structures of given compounds are shown below.

(a) $CH_3-CH_2-CH_2-CH_3$

(b) $CH_3-CH(CH_3)-CH(CH_3)-CH_3$

(c) $CH_3-CH(CH_3)-CH_3$

(d) $H_3C(H)C=C(H)CH_3$ — *cis* (H and H on same side, H_3C and CH_3 on same side)

$H_3C(H)C=C(H)CH_3$ — *trans* (H_3C and CH_3 on opposite sides)

Therefore, only compound (d) exhibits geometrical isomerism due to the presence of double bond.

24 (*c*) $(a)(b)C=C(a)(b)$ — *cis*; $(a)(b)C=C(b)(a)$ — *trans*

Thus, geometrical isomers differ in spatial arrangement of atoms only.

25 (*a*) $CH_3CH=CHCH_2CH=CH_2$ exhibits two geometrical isomers :

$H_3C(H)C=C(H)CH_2CH=CH_2$ — *cis*-isomer (H_3C and $CH_2CH=CH_2$ on same side)

$H_3C(H)C=C(H)CH_2CH=CH_2$ — *trans*-isomer (H_3C and $CH_2CH=CH_2$ on opposite sides)

26 (*b*) Three isomers are possible having molecular formula $C_2H_2Br_2$. The isomers are as follows:

(i) $H_2C=CBr_2$

(ii) $H(Br)C=C(H)Br$ — *cis*-isomer II (H, H same side)

(iii) $H(Br)C=C(Br)H$ — *trans*-isomer III

27 (*b*) $H(H_3C)C=C(I)Br$ shows the geometrical isomerism as

$H_3C(H)C=C(I)Br$ (*Z*) (H_3C and I on same side); $H_3C(Br)C=C(I)H$ (*E*)

28 (*b*) $CH_3-CH_2-CH_2-C(CH_3)=CH_2$

It does not show *cis-trans* (i.e. geometrical isomerism) due to presence of same group on double bonded carbon atom.

29 (*d*) The isomers having molecular formula C_6H_{12} are as follows:

(i) $CH_2=CH-CH_2-CH_2-CH_2-CH_3$

(ii) $CH_3-CH=CH-CH_2-CH_2-CH_3$ (*cis and trans*)

(iii) $CH_3-CH_2-CH=CH-CH_2-CH_3$ (*cis* and *trans*)

(iv) $CH_2=CH-CH(CH_3)-CH_2-CH_3$

(v) $CH_2=C(CH_3)-CH_2-CH_2-CH_3$

(vi) $CH_2=CH-CH_2-CH(CH_3)-CH_3$

(vii) $CH_3-CH=CH-CH(CH_3)-CH_3$ (*cis* and *trans*)

(viii) $CH_3-C(CH_3)=CH-CH_2-CH_3$

(ix) $CH_3-CH=C(CH_3)-CH_2-CH_3$ (*cis and trans*)

Thus, number of isomeric alkenes with molecular formula C_6H_{12} are 13.

30 (*d*) There are 6 isomers possible for the compounds having molecular formula C_4H_8O, which are as follows :

(i) $CH_3CH_2-CO-CH_3$

(ii) $CH_3CH_2CH_2\ CHO$

(iii) $(H_3C)_2CH\cdot CHO$

(iv) $H_3C(H)C=C(H)CH_2OH$ — *cis*

(v) $H_3C(H)C=C(H)CH_2OH$ — *trans*

(vi) $CH_2=CH-CH_2CH_2OH$

31 (*d*) Among 1, 2 and 1, 3 configurations, 1, 3 is more stable due to less repulsion. Further among *cis* and *trans* configurations, the *trans* is more stable due to less crowding. Hence, *trans*-1, 3-cyclohexanediol is the most stable among the given compounds.

32 (*c*) The structure of 1-chloro-2-nitroethene is as :

$NO_2(H)C=C(H)Cl$

In this compound E/Z isomerism is possible because it is highly substituted alkene. The E-Z system of nomenclature is developed by Cahn-Ingold and Prelog.

33 (*c*) The compounds must fulfill two conditions to show geometrical isomerism:

(i) The compounds should have at least one C=C.

(ii) The two groups attached to same carbon atom must be different.

Out of given choice, only (c) fulfills both condition and shows geometrical isomerism.

$H-C-COOH \,\|\, H-C-COOH$

But-2-ene-1,4-dioic acid

Topic 4

Optical Isomerism

2017

1 Total number of optically active forms in molecules with 'n' number of asymmetric C-atoms and which are not divisible into two equal halves is **[AIIMS]**

(a) 2^n

(b) 2^{n-1}

(c) $2^{\frac{(n-1)}{2}}$

(d) $2^{\left(\frac{n}{2}-1\right)}$

2 Assertion (A) The following molecule is non-superimposable on its mirror image, hence it is chiral.

$$H-\underset{C_2H_5}{\overset{CH_3}{C}}-OH$$

Reason (R) All chiral molecules have chiral centres. **[AIIMS]**

(a) Both A and R are correct and R is the correct explanation of A

(b) Both A and R are correct but R is not the correct explanation of A

(c) A is correct but R is incorrect

(d) Both A and R are incorrect

2016

3 Which of the following biphenyls is optically active?

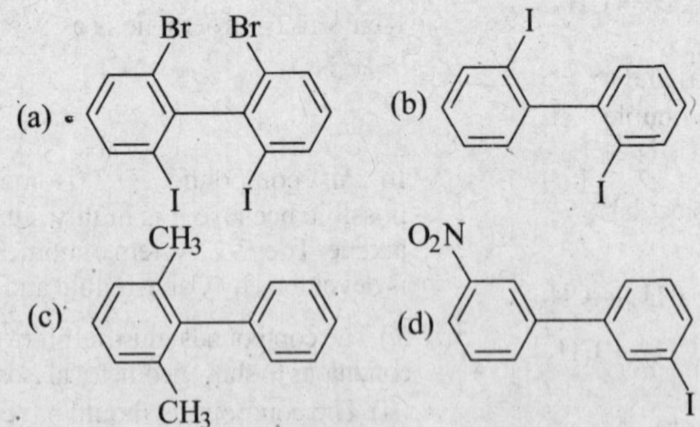

2014

4 The organic compound with two asymmetric carbon atoms is **[Kerala CEE]**

(a) 3,4-dimethylheptane

(b) 3-methyl-1-pentene

(c) 2-chlorohexane

(d) 5-ethyl-2,3-dimethylheptane

2013

5 The absolute configuration of the following is **[AIIMS]**

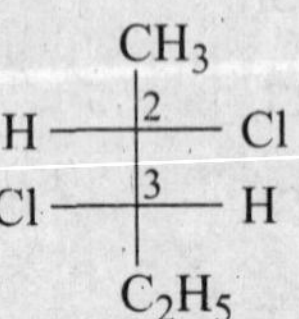

(a) $2S, 3R$ (b) $2S, 3S$ (c) $2R, 3S$ (d) $2R, 3R$

6 Which of the following pairs of compounds are enantiomers? **[WB JEE]**

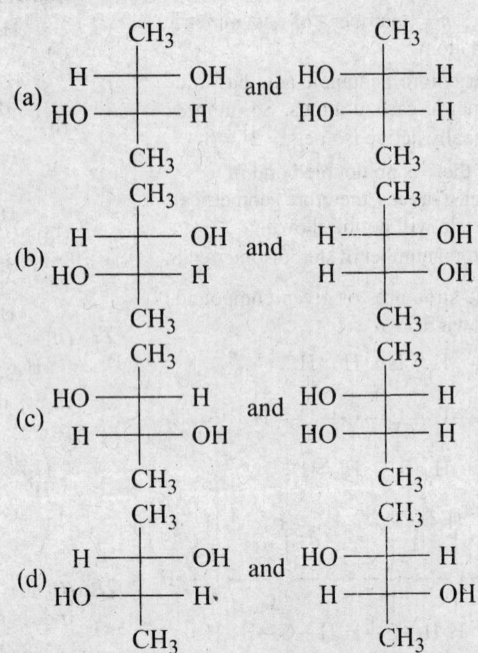

2012

7 Which of the following acids does not exhibit optical isomerism? **[CBSE AIPMT]**

(a) Maleic acid (b) α-amino acid

(c) Lactic acid (d) Tartaric acid

8 In which of the following compounds, one of the structural isomers is also capable of showing enantiomorphism **[AFMC]**

(a) C_3H_8 (b) $C_3H_6Br_2$

(c) C_5H_{12} (d) C_6H_{14}

9 The amino acid which is not optically active is **[UP CPMT]**

(a) lactic acid (b) serine (c) alanine (d) glycine

10 Which of the following shows optical isomerism? **[OJEE]**

(a) Butan-1-ol (b) Butan-2-ol

(c) Butene (d) But-2-enol

2011

11 Among the following, the optically active compound is **[Kerala CEE]**

(a) CH_3CH_2OH (b) $CH_3CH{=}CHCH_3$
(c) CH_3CHDOH (d) $CH_3CH_2COCH_3$
(e) CH_3CHO

12 The well known compounds, (+) lactic acid and (−) lactic acid, have the same formula, $C_3H_6O_3$. The correct relationship between them is **[WB JEE]**

(a) constitutional isomers (b) geometrical isomers
(c) identical (d) optical isomers

13 The maximum number of possible optical isomers in 1-bromo-2-methyl cyclobutane is **[KCET]**

(a) 4 (b) 2 (c) 8 (d) 16

14 Which of the compounds when brominated turns to *meso* 2,3-dibromobutane? **[Guj CET]**

(a) *cis*-2-butene
(b) *iso*-butane
(c) Butane
(d) *trans*-2-butene

2010

15 α-hydroxypropanoic acid has ……… asymmetric carbon atoms. **[MHT CET]**

(a) 4 (b) 3 (c) 2 (d) 1

16 Which of the following is optically active? **[Manipal]**

(a) $CH_3—CH(OH)—CH(OH)—CH_3$ (b) $CH_3—CHOH—CH_3$

(c) $CH_3—C(=O)—CBr_2—COOH$ (d) $CH_3—CH_2—C(=O)—OH$

2009

17 The first Nobel prize in Chemistry was given to **[AFMC]**

(a) JH van't Hoff (b) Cannizzaro
(c) Mendeleev's (d) Moseley

18 Which of the following compounds is optically active? **[MHT CET]**

(a) Butanal (b) Butanol
(c) Butan-2-ol (d) 2-methyl propan-2-ol

19 Optical isomerism arises from the presence of **[Manipal]**

(a) a centre of symmetry
(b) a line of symmetry
(c) an asymmetric carbon atom
(d) All of the above

20 *meso*-tartaric acid is optically inactive due to the presence of **[Manipal]**

(a) molecular symmetry
(b) molecular asymmetry
(c) external compensation
(d) None of these

21 Diastereomerism will not be exhibited by **[Kerala CEE]**

(a) 2,3-dichlorobutane
(b) 2-hydroxy propanoic acid
(c) tartaric acid
(d) 2,3-butane diol
(e) threonine

22 The two structures written below represent **[WB JEE]**

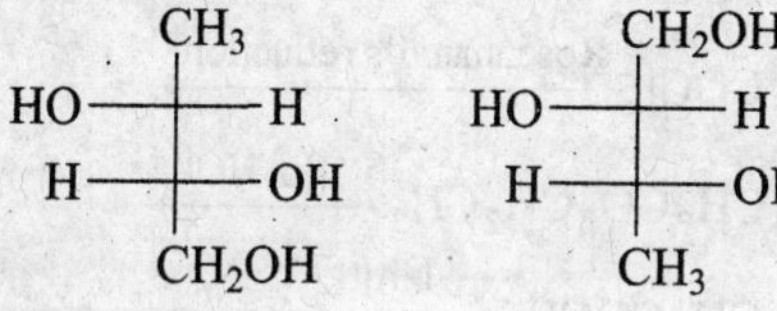

(a) pair of diastereomers
(b) pair of enantiomers
(c) same molecule
(d) both are optically inactive

23 The optical rotation of an optically active compound is

(a) directly proportional to the length of the polarimeter tube only **[J&K CET]**
(b) directly proportional to the molar concentration of the compound
(c) independent of the length of the polarimeter tube and concentration of the compound
(d) inversely proportional to both the length of the polarimeter tube and molar concentration of the compound

24 The absolute configuration of the C_2 and C_3 atoms in the molecule with the structure is **[J&K CET]**

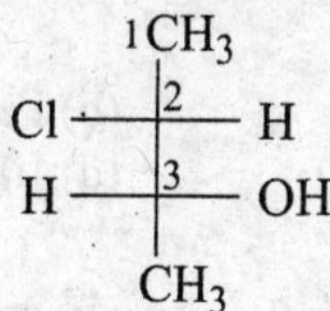

(a) 2*S*, 3*S* (b) 2*R*, 3*S* (c) 2*S*, 3*R* (d) 2*R*, 3*R*

25 The total number of acyclic structural and optical isomers possible for a hydrocarbon of molecular formulae C_7H_{16} is **[J&K CET]**

(a) 12 (b) 8
(c) 10 (d) 6

26 The concentration of an organic compound in chloroform is 6.15 g per 100 mL of solution. A portion of this solution in a 5 cm polarimeter tube causes an observed rotation of −1.2°. What is the specific rotation of the compound? **[EAMCET]**

(a) + 12° (b) − 3.9°
(c) − 39° (d) + 61.5°

27 The configuration of the chiral centre and the geometry of the double bond in the following molecule can be described by **[DUMET]**

$$\mathrm{HOOC{-}\underset{\underset{\displaystyle Me\diagdown C{=}C\diagup Me \atop \qquad\quad H}{|}}{\overset{F}{\overset{|}{C}}}{-}OH}$$

(a) R and E (b) S and E
(c) R and Z (d) S and Z

28 In which of the following reactions, the product obtained is chiral? **[DUMET]**

(a) $CH_3COCH_3 \xrightarrow{NaBH_4}$
(b) $CH_3COCl \xrightarrow{\text{Rosenmund's reduction}}$
(c) $CH_3CH_2CO_2CH_2CH_3 \xrightarrow{Sn, HCl}$
(d) $CH_3CH_2COCH_3 \xrightarrow{LiAlH_4}$

2008

29 Which of the following compounds is not chiral? **[MHT CET]**

(a) 1-chloro-2-methyl pentane
(b) 2-chloropentane
(c) 1-chloropentane
(d) 3-chloro-2-methyl pentane

30 The R-isomers among the following are **[Kerala CEE]**

(I) Fischer projection: top CHO, left H, right OH, bottom CH_2OH
(II) Fischer projection: top H, left D, right OH, bottom CH_3
(III) Fischer projection: top CH_3, left H, right OH, bottom CH_2CH_3
(IV) Fischer projection: top COOH, left H_3C, right NH_2, bottom H

Codes

(a) I and II (b) I and III
(c) II and III (d) III and IV
(e) I, II and IV

31 Which among the following compound will exhibit optical isomerism? **[Kerala CEE]**

(a) *tert*-butyamine
(b) *sec*-butylamine
(c) *iso*-butylamine
(d) *n*-butylamine
(e) *neo*-pentylamine

32 Among the following four structures I to IV,

(I) $C_2H_5-\underset{}{\overset{CH_3}{\overset{|}{CH}}}-C_3H_7$

(II) $CH_3-\overset{O}{\overset{\|}{C}}-\overset{CH_3}{\overset{|}{CH}}-C_2H_5$

(III) $H-\underset{H}{\underset{|}{\overset{H}{\overset{|}{C^{\oplus}}}}}$

(IV) $C_2H_5-\overset{CH_3}{\overset{|}{CH}}-C_2H_5$

[RPMT]

Which is/are chiral compounds?

(a) All four (b) I and II
(c) Only II (d) II and IV

33 Which of the following is chiral? **[DUMET]**

(a) $Cl-CH_2-CH_2-CH_2-CH_2-CH_3$
(b) $CH_3-CH_2-\underset{Cl}{\underset{|}{CH}}-CH_2-CH_3$
(c) $Cl-CH=CH-CH_2-CH_2-CH_3$
(d) $H-\underset{Cl}{\underset{|}{C}}=C=CH-CH_2-CH_3$

34 How many optically active stereomers are possible for butan-2, 3-diol? **[KCET]**

(a) 1 (b) 2 (c) 3 (d) 4

35 Optical isomerism is shown by **[BCECE]**

(a) propanol-2 (b) butanol-2
(c) ethanol (d) methanol

2007

36 $CH_3-CHCl-CH_2-CH_3$ has a chiral centre. Which one of the following represents its R configuration? **[CBSE AIPMT]**

(a) $H_3C-\underset{H}{\underset{|}{\overset{C_2H_5}{\overset{|}{C}}}}-Cl$ (b) $H-\underset{Cl}{\underset{|}{\overset{C_2H_5}{\overset{|}{C}}}}-CH_3$

(c) $Cl-\underset{H}{\underset{|}{\overset{C_2H_5}{\overset{|}{C}}}}-CH_3$ (d) $H-\underset{C_2H_5}{\underset{|}{\overset{CH_3}{\overset{|}{C}}}}-Cl$

37 If there is no rotation of plane polarised light by a compound in a specific solvent, thought to be chiral, it may mean that **[CBSE AIPMT]**

(a) the compound is certainly *a* chiral
(b) the compound is certainly *meso*
(c) there is no compound in the solvent
(d) the compound may be a racemic mixture

38 Which of the following will have a *meso* isomer also? **[AFMC]**

(a) 2,3-dichloropentane
(b) 2,3-dichlorobutane
(c) 2-chlorobutane
(d) 2-hydroxy propanoic acid

39 Which of the following molecules will not show optical activity? **[Kerala CEE]**

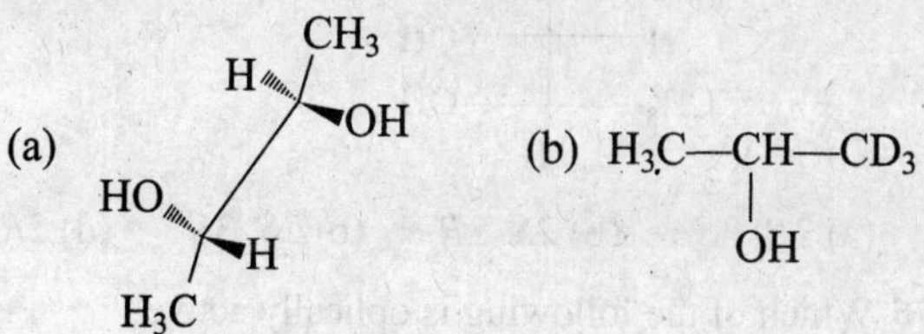

(c) HOOC(H)C(OH)–C(H)(H)COOH (d) Br, H / H, Br substituted cyclopropane

(e) $H_3C—CH(OH)—CH_2CH_3$

40 The correct statement about the compounds I, II and III is

I: $COOCH_3$ (top); H–C–OH; H–C–OH; COOH (bottom)

II: COOH (top); HO–C–H; H–C–OH; $COOCH_3$ (bottom)

III: COOH (top); H–C–OH; HO–C–H; $COOCH_3$ (bottom)

[Kerala CEE]

Codes

(a) I and II are identical (b) I and II are diastereomers
(c) I and III are enantiomers (d) I and II are enantiomers
(e) II and III are enantiomers

41 Which one of the following molecules has *S*-configuration? **[Kerala CEE]**

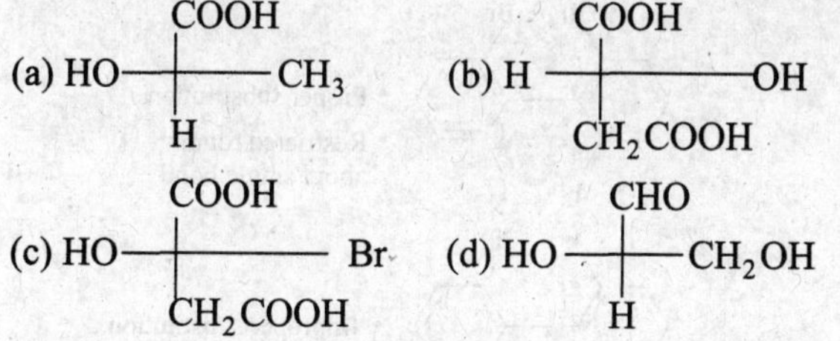

(e) COOH (top); CH_3–C–CH_2OH; C_6H_5 (bottom)

42 How many chiral carbon atoms are present in 2, 3, 4-trichloropentane? **[KCET]**

(a) 4 (b) 1 (c) 2 (d) 3

43 The number of optical isomers of 2, 3-dihydroxy butanal is/are **[Guj CET]**

(a) two (b) three (c) four (d) one

2006

44 Which of the following is not a chiral? **[CBSE AIPMT]**

(a) 2-butanol (b) 2, 3-dibromopentane
(c) 3-bromopentane (d) 2-hydroxy propanoic acid

45 Among the following which one can have a *meso* form? **[AIIMS]**

(a) $CH_3CH(OH)CH(Cl)C_2H_5$
(b) $CH_3CH(OH)CH(OH)CH_3$
(c) $C_2H_5CH(OH)CH(OH)CH_3$
(d) $HOCH_2CH(Cl)CH_3$

46 **Assertion** (A) Diastereoisomers have different physical properties.

Reason (R) They are non-superimposable mirror images. **[AIIMS]**

(a) Both A and R are correct and the R is the correct explanation of the A
(b) Both A and R are correct but R is not the correct explanation of the A
(c) A is correct but R is incorrect
(d) Both A and R are incorrect

47 The number of *meso* forms in the following compound is

$HOOC\cdot CH(CH_3)\cdot CH(OH)\cdot CH(Cl)\cdot CH(OH)CH(CH_3)\cdot COOH$ **[MHT CET]**

(a) 3 (b) 4 (c) 8 (d) 16

48 Consider the structure given below

$(H_3C)(H)C=C=C(H)(CH_3)$ $(H)(H_3C)C=C=C(CH_3)(H)$

They are **[Kerala CEE]**

(a) enantiomers (b) homomers
(c) *meso*-isomers (d) diastereoisomers
(e) geometrical isomers

49 Consider the following representation

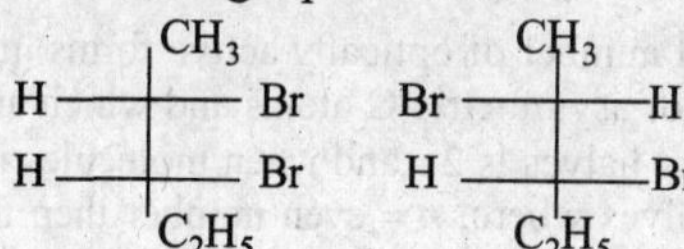

They are **[Kerala CEE]**

(a) enantiomers
(b) diastereomers
(c) conformational isomers
(d) identical
(e) *cis-trans* isomers

50 Compound $(H_3C)_2C=CH–CH(CH_3)COOH$

can exhibit **[J&K CET]**

(a) geometrical isomerism
(b) tautomerism
(c) optical isomerism
(d) geometrical and optical isomerism

51 Which of the following molecules is achiral? **[Punjab PMET]**

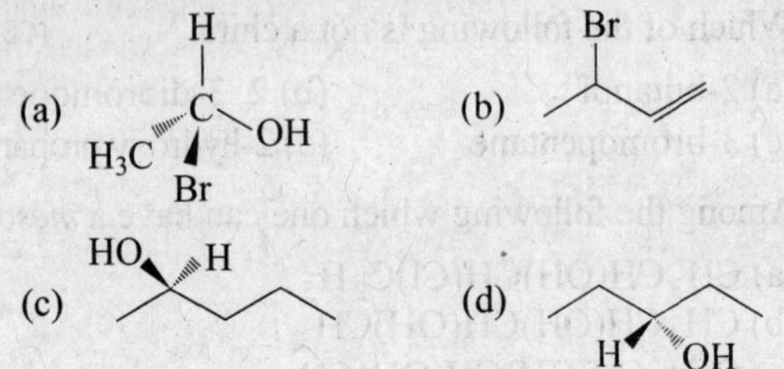

52 A compound has 3 chiral carbon atoms. The number of possible optical isomers it can have **[AMU]**

(a) 3 (b) 3 (c) 8 (d) 4

53 A compound has two different asymmetric carbon then the number of stereomers **[DUMET]**

(a) 4 (b) 2 (c) 3 (d) 1

2005

54 The chirality of the compound **[CBSE AIPMT]**

Br, H_3C, C, H, Cl is

(a) *R* (b) *S* (c) *Z* (d) *E*

55 Correct configuration of the following is

CH_3
H — — OH
CH_3 — — OH
H

[AIIMS]

(a) 2*R*, 3*S* (b) 2*S*, 3*R* (c) 2*S*, 3*S* (d) 2*R*, 3*R*

56 Which of the following is optically active? **[BHU]**

(a) Butane
(b) 4-methylheptane
(c) 3-methylheptane
(d) 2-methylheptane

57

COOH | COOH
H — — OH | HO — — H
H — — OH | HO — — H
COOMe | COOMe
I. | II.

I and II are **[DUMET]**

(a) enantiomers
(b) diastereomers
(c) *meso* compound
(d) identical

Answers

1 (c)	2 (c)	3 (a)	4 (a)	5 (b)	6 (d)	7 (a)	8 (b)	9 (d)	10 (b)
11 (c)	12 (d)	13 (a)	14 (d)	15 (d)	16 (a)	17 (a)	18 (c)	19 (c)	20 (a)
21 (b)	22 (c)	23 (d)	24 (d)	25 (c)	26 (c)	27 (c)	28 (d)	29 (c)	30 (a)
31 (b)	32 (b)	33 (d)	34 (b)	35 (b)	36 (c)	37 (d)	38 (b)	39 (a)	40 (e)
41 (e)	42 (c)	43 (c)	44 (c)	45 (b)	46 (c)	47 (b)	48 (a)	49 (b)	50 (c)
51 (d)	52 (c)	53 (a)	54 (b)	55 (c)	56 (c)	57 (a)			

Explanations

1 (*c*) Total number of optically active forms in molecules with '*n*' number of asymmetric C-atoms and which are not divisible into two equal halves is 2^n and when molecules is divisible into two equal halves where, n = even number then number of optically active forms is 2^{n-1}.

However, when n = odd number then number of optically active forms is $2^{\left(\frac{n-1}{2}\right)}$.

2 (*c*) Molecules having perpendicular disymmetric plane are supposed to have chirality without having chiral centre. e.g.

CH_3, H, C, H, CH_3 and NO_2 COOH, HOOC NO_2 (biphenyl)

Hence, (A) is correct but (R) is incorrect.

3 (*a*) The biphenyl compounds having proper substitution at *ortho*-position of benzene rings result in steric hindrance. This steric hindrance makes the biphenyl system non-planar and, hence optically active compounds.

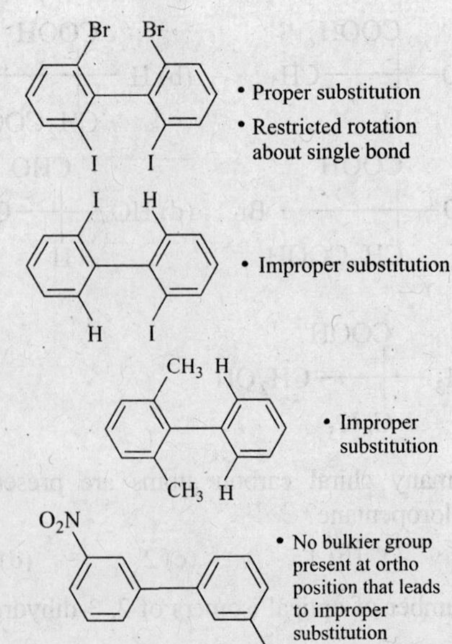

4 (*a*) Optical isomerism is exhibited by chiral molecule or asymmetric molecules i.e. molecules having a carbon whose four valencies are satisfied by four different groups.

(a) $H_3C—CH_2—C^*(CH_3)(H)—C^*(H)(CH_3)—CH_2—CH_2—CH_3$

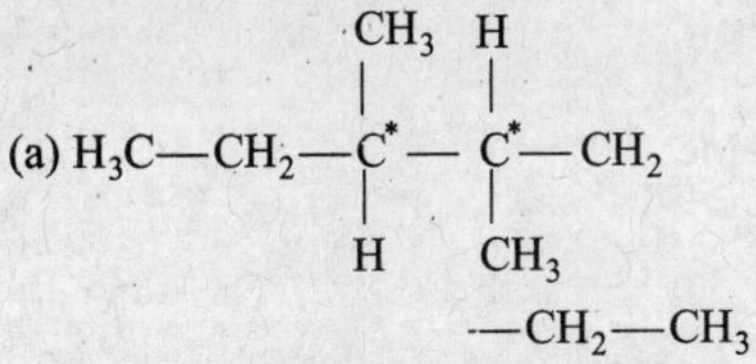

IUPAC name: 3, 4-dimethyl heptane

The starred carbon is attached with four different groups.

5 (*b*)

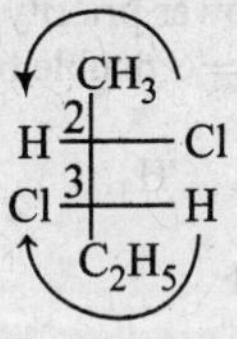

Fischer projection: CH_3 (top); C-2: H—C—Cl; C-3: Cl—C—H; C_2H_5 (bottom)

Absolute configuration (2*S*, 3*S*) or sinister (left) is used for counterclockwise configuration, whereas *R* or rectus (right) is used for clockwise configuration.

6 (*d*) A pair of molecules which cannot be superimposed on its mirror image i.e. asymmetrical and related to each other as an object and its mirror image are known as enantiomers. So,

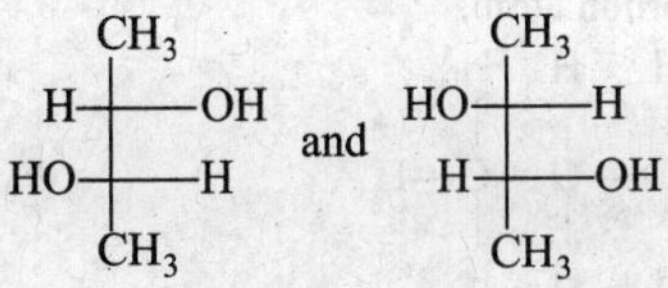

CH_3; H—C—OH; HO—C—H; CH_3 and CH_3; HO—C—H; H—C—OH; CH_3

are enantiomers.

7 (*a*) Only those compounds exhibit optical isomerism which have chiral centre or absence of symmetry elements. A chiral carbon is the carbon, where all the four valencies of it are satisfied by four different groups.

(a) CHCOOH ‖ CHCOOH
Maleic acid
(no chiral centre, so, optically inactive)

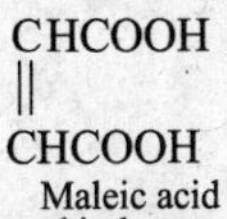

(b) $R—\overset{*}{C}H(NH_2)—COOH$
α-amino acid
(one chiral centre, so, optically active)

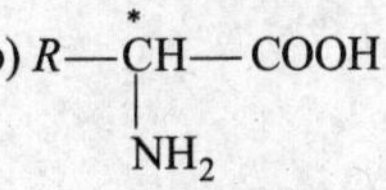

(c) $CH_3\overset{*}{C}H(OH)COOH$
Lactic acid
(one chiral centre, so, optically active)

(d) CH(OH)COOH | CH(OH)COOH
Tartaric acid
(two chiral carbon, so, optically active)

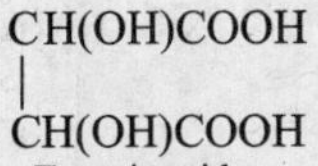

Thus, maleic acid does not exhibit optical isomerism.

Note If *R* =H, the α-amino acid is achiral.

8 (*b*) Structural isomer of $C_3H_6Br_2$ are :

(i) $Br \cdot CH_2CH_2CH_2Br$ (I)

(ii) $BrCH_2CHBrCH_3$ (II)

(iii) $Br_2CHCH_2CH_3$ (III)

(iv) $CH_3—CBr_2CH_3$ (IV)

Out of these four structural isomers, isomer (ii) has a chiral carbon atom and hence, shows enantiomorphism (i.e. optical isomerism)

9 (*d*) Glycine is optically inactive amino acid due to the absence of chiral carbon atom.

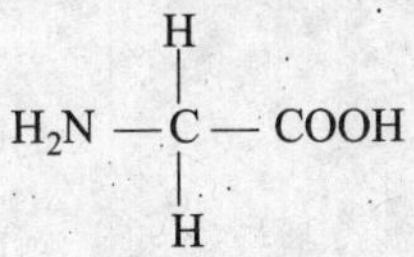

$H_2N—C(H)(H)—COOH$
(optically inactive)

10 (*b*) For optical isomerism, there must be a chiral C-atom. Butan-2-ol have one chiral C-atom.

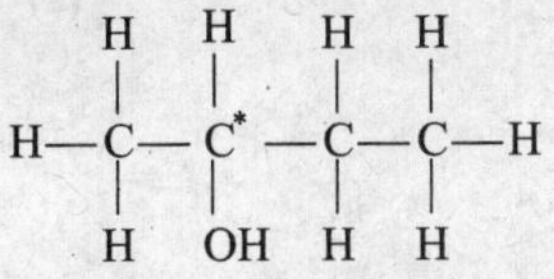

$H—C(H)(H)—C^*(H)(OH)—C(H)(H)—C(H)(H)—H$

(C^* = chiral C-atom)

11 (*c*) CH_3CHDOH contains a chiral carbon. Hence, it is optically active.

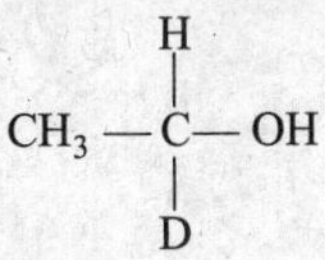

$CH_3—C(H)(D)—OH$

12 (*d*) (+) lactic acid and (–) lactic acid are optical isomers because they rotate the plane of polarised light in opposite direction.

13 (*a*)

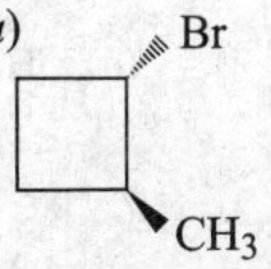

Cyclobutane with Br (wedge/hashed) and CH_3 on adjacent carbons

trans-1-bromo-2-methylcyclobutane has 2 optical isomers.

Cyclobutane with Br and CH_3 on adjacent carbons

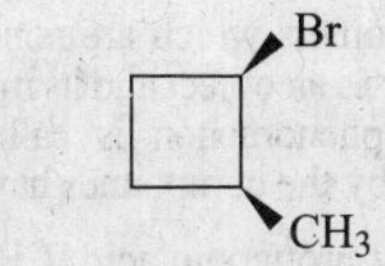

cis-1-bromo-2-methyl cyclobutane has 2 optical isomers.

Total isomers = 2 + 2 = 4

14 (*d*) On bromination, *trans*-2-butene turns to *meso* 2,3-dibromobutane.

15 (*d*) Asymmetric carbon atom is the carbon, four valencies of which are satisfied by four different groups. The structure of α-hydroxypropanoic acid is

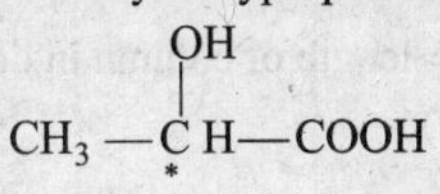

$CH_3—\overset{*}{C}H(OH)—COOH$

(C* = asymmetric carbon atom)

Thus, α-hydroxy propanoic acid has one asymmetric carbon atom.

16 (*a*) Optically active compounds have at least one asymmetric or chiral carbon atom. Compound given in option (a) contains two chiral carbon atoms as,

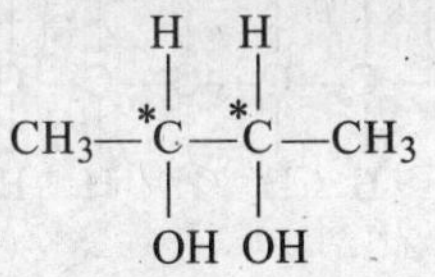

$CH_3—\overset{*}{C}(H)(OH)—\overset{*}{C}(H)(OH)—CH_3$

∴ It is optically active.

17 (*a*) JH van't Hoff was the scientist who got first nobel prize in Chemistry.

He predicted in 1874 that the four bonds of a carbon atom are directed towards the four corners of a regular tetrahedron and the angle between any two adjacent bonds is 109°28′. This tetrahedron arrangement of four bonds of carbon laid the foundation of the present day fascinating field of 'stereochemistry'.

18 (*c*) Only chiral or asymmetric carbon (the carbon, four valencies of which are satisfied by four different groups) containing compounds are optically active.

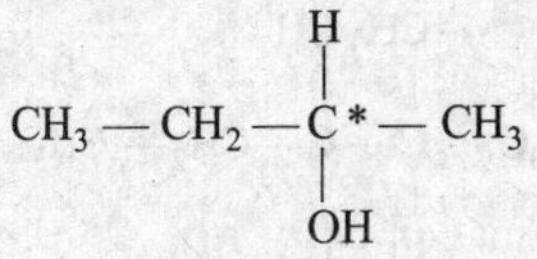

$CH_3—CH_2—C^*(H)(OH)—CH_3$
Butan-2-ol
(C* = chiral carbon atom)

So, butan-2-ol is optically active.

19 (*c*) A compound could be optically active only when it contains at least one asymmetric carbon atom or a chiral centre.

20 (*a*) *meso*-tartaric acid is optically inactive due to presence of molecular symmetry.

21 (*b*) The isomers which are non-superimposable and not related to each other as an object and its mirror image are called diastereomers and this phenomenon is called diastereomerism. It is usually exhibited by the compounds having two or more chiral centres.

2-hydroxy propanoic acid [$CH_3\overset{*}{C}H(OH)COOH$], contains only one chiral carbon (C*), so it does not exhibit diastereomerism. In other organic compounds, two chiral centres are present. Thus, they exhibit diastereomerism.

22 (*c*) The two structures given in question represents same molecule as they are superimposable on each other.

23 (*d*) The optical rotation of an optically active compound is inversely proportional to both the length of the polarimeter tube and molar concentration of the compound.

$$[\alpha]_D^T = \frac{\alpha}{ld} \text{ where, } \alpha = \text{observed rotation,}$$

l = length of column in dm, d = density

24 (*d*)

Fischer projection: CH_3 (top); C-2: Cl (left), H (right); C-3: H (left), OH (right); CH_3 (bottom)

Absolute configuration is (2*R*, 3*R*)

25 (*c*) Total number of acyclic structural and optical isomers possible for hydrocarbon C_7H_{16} is 10.

(i) $H-\underset{H}{\overset{H}{C}}-\underset{H}{\overset{H}{C}}-\underset{H}{\overset{H}{C}}-\underset{H}{\overset{H}{C}}-\underset{H}{\overset{H}{C}}-\underset{H}{\overset{H}{C}}-\underset{H}{\overset{H}{C}}-H$,

(ii) $H_3C-H_2C-H_2C-H_2C-\underset{H}{\overset{CH_3}{C}}-CH_3$,

(iii) $H_3C-CH_2-CH_2-\overset{CH_3}{CH}-CH_2-CH_3$,
(Optically active-2 isomers)

(iv) $H_3C-H_2C-H_2C-\underset{CH_3}{\overset{CH_3}{C}}-CH_3$,

(v) $H_3C-H_2C-\underset{CH_3}{\overset{CH_3}{C}}-CH_2-CH_3$,

(vi) $H_3C-\underset{H}{\overset{CH_3}{C}}-\underset{H}{\overset{CH_3}{C}}-CH_2-CH_3$,

(vii) $H_3C-\underset{H}{\overset{CH_3}{C}}-CH_2-\underset{H}{\overset{CH_3}{C}}-CH_3$

(viii) $C_2H_5-\underset{C_3H_7}{\overset{H}{C^*}}-CH_3$
(Optically active-2-isomers)

26 (*c*) $$[\alpha] = \frac{[\alpha]_{\text{observed}}}{l \times C} = \frac{-1.2}{0.5\ \text{dm} \times \frac{6.15\ \text{g}}{100\text{mL}}} = -39°$$

27 (*c*)

$HOOC^{3}-\overset{*}{C}(^{1}F)(^{2}OH)-C^{4}H(a)=C(Me)(Me)$ — C* bears F (1), OH (2), HOOC (3) and C4 (4); C4 bears Me (*b*); the other alkene carbon bears Me (*a*) and H (*b*).

In the above compound, the configuration about the chiral carbon (C*) is *R*.

Since, the groups with higher priority marked as (a) are on the same side of the double bond and those with lower priority are on the other side, thus the geometry about the C=C double bond is *Z*.

28 (*d*) (a) $CH_3COCH_3 \xrightarrow{NaBH_4} CH_3\underset{OH}{CH}CH_3$, Achiral

(b) $CH_3COCl \xrightarrow[\text{reduction}]{\text{Rosenmund's}} CH_3CHO + HCl$, Achiral

(c) $CH_3CH_2CO_2CH_2CH_3 \xrightarrow{Sn,\ HCl} CH_3CH_2CH_2OH + CH_3CH_2OH$ Achiral

(d) $CH_3CH_2COCH_3 \xrightarrow{LiAlH_4} CH_3CH_2\underset{OH}{\overset{*}{C}}HCH_3$ Chiral

29 (*c*) To be optically active, compound or structure should possess a chiral or asymmetric carbon atom.

(a) $H-\underset{H}{\overset{Cl}{C}}-\underset{H}{\overset{CH_3}{C^*}}-\underset{H}{\overset{H}{C}}-\underset{H}{\overset{H}{C}}-\underset{H}{\overset{H}{C}}-H$
1-chloro-2-methyl pentane

(b) $H-\underset{H}{\overset{H}{C}}-\underset{H}{\overset{Cl}{C^*}}-\underset{H}{\overset{H}{C}}-\underset{H}{\overset{H}{C}}-\underset{H}{\overset{H}{C}}-H$
2-chloropentane

(c) $H-\underset{H}{\overset{Cl}{C}}-\underset{H}{\overset{H}{C}}-\underset{H}{\overset{H}{C}}-\underset{H}{\overset{H}{C}}-\underset{H}{\overset{H}{C}}-H$
1-chloropentane

(d) $H-\underset{H}{\overset{H}{C}}-\underset{H}{\overset{CH_3}{C^*}}-\overset{Cl}{C}-\underset{H}{\overset{H}{C}}-\underset{H}{\overset{H}{C}}-H$
3-chloro-2-methyl pentane

(C^* = asymmetric C-atom)

Hence, 1-chloropentane is not chiral.

30 (*a*)

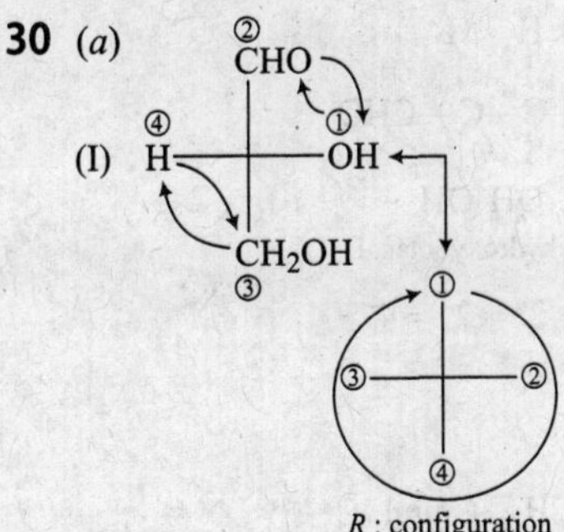

R : configuration

(II) D, H, OH, CH_3

R : configuration

(III) H, CH_3, OH, CH_2CH_3

S : configuration

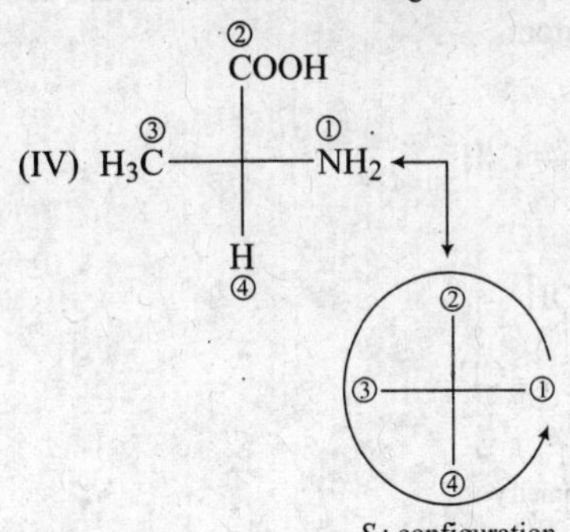

S : configuration

Hence, only (I) and (II) are *R*-isomers.

31 (*b*) $CH_3-\overset{*}{C}H-CH_2-CH_3$ with NH_2 on the starred carbon

sec-butylamine

$\overset{*}{C}$ = asymmetric carbon atom

This compound contains asymmetric or chiral carbon atom, hence exhibits optical isomerism.

32 (*b*) Chiral compounds are those which have one chiral centre i.e. all four atoms or groups attached to carbon are different. In structure (I) and (II) chiral carbon is present, represented by C^*.

$C_2H_5-\overset{*}{C}H(CH_3)-C_3H_7$ (I)

$CH_3-C(=O)-\overset{*}{C}H(CH_3)-C_2H_5$ (II)

33 (*d*) A molecule is said to be chiral or asymmetric, if it does not possess any element of symmetry and not superimposable on its mirror image and this property of the molecule to show non-superimposability is called chirality.

(a) $Cl-CH_2-CH_2-CH_2-CH_2-CH_3$

Achiral molecule, absence of asymmetrical carbon atom.

(b) $CH_3-CH_2-CH(Cl)-CH_2-CH_3$

Achiral molecule, absence of asymmetrical carbon atom.

(c) $Cl-CH=CH-CH_2-CH_2-CH_3$

Achiral molecule

(d) $(H)(Cl)C=C=C(C_2H_5-CH_3)(H)$

Allenes exhibit optical isomerism (chiral), provided that the two groups attached to each terminal carbon atoms are different.

34 (*b*) $CH_3-\overset{*}{C}H(OH)-\overset{*}{C}H(OH)-CH_3$

Butane-2,3-diol

where, C^* = asymmteric C-atom

It is symmetrical molecule, so the number of optically active stereomers $= 2^{n-1}$.(n = number of asymmetric C atom)

$= 2^{2-1} = 2^1 = 2$

35 (*b*) (a) $CH_3-CH(OH)-CH_3$

Propan-2-ol

(b) $CH_3-CH_2-\overset{*}{C}H(OH)-CH_3$

Butan-2-ol

(c) CH_3-CH_2-OH

Ethanol

(d) CH_3OH

Methanol

Butanol-2 contains chiral carbon (C^*) therefore, butan-2-ol shows optical isomerism.

36 (*c*) $CH_3-CHCl-CH_2-CH_3$.

Priority order is

$-Cl > -C_2H_5 > -CH_3 > -H$

(a) $H_3C-C(C_2H_5)(H)-Cl$ (Cl ①, C_2H_5 ②, CH_3 ③, H ④)

Anticlockwise (*S*)

(b) $H-C(C_2H_5)(Cl)-CH_3$ (Cl ①, C_2H_5 ②, CH_3 ③, H ④)

Interchange

$Cl-C(CH_3)(H)-C_2H_5$

Anticlockwise (*S*)

(c) $Cl-C(C_2H_5)(H)-CH_3$ (Cl ①, C_2H_5 ②, CH_3 ③, H ④)

Clockwise (*R*)

(d) $H-C(CH_3)(C_2H_5)-Cl$ (Cl ①, C_2H_5 ②, CH_3 ③, H ④)

Interchange

$C_2H_5-C(Cl)(H)-CH_3$

Anticlockwise (*S*)

37 (*d*) An optically active compound rotates plane polarised light. But due to some external compensation (heat, light, catalyst, solvent etc), the optically active compound loses, its optical activity. The compound then exists as racemic mixture, i.e. both *d* and *l* form are present in solution due to some intramolecular rearrangement. So, there is no rotation of plane polarised light and compound does not have an asymmetric centre and when it again forms the symmetric centre, both *d* and *l*-forms are obtained in equal amounts.

38 (*b*)

(a)
CH_3
H—C—Cl
H—C—Cl
H—C—H
CH_3
(2,3-dichloropentane)

(b)
CH_3
H—C—Cl
H—C—Cl
CH_3
(2,3-dichlorobutane)

(Absence of plane of symmetry) (Presence of plane of symmetry)

(c)
CH_3
Cl—H
H—H
CH_3
2-chlorobutane
(Absence of plane of symmetry

(d) $H_3C—C(OH)(H)—COOH$
(2-hydroxy propanoic acid)
(Absence of plane of symmetry)

Hence, compound (b) is *meso* isomer due to the presence of plane of symmetry.

39 (*a*) Compound (a) has plane of symmetry, so it will not show optical activity.

40 (*e*)

COOH
HO—H
H—OH
$COOCH_3$
(II)

COOH
H—OH
HO—H
$COOCH_3$
(III)

(II) and (III) are enantiomers (non-superimposable mirror images).

41 (*e*)

$\overset{1}{COOH}$; $\overset{4}{CH_3}$—$\overset{2}{CH_2OH}$; $\underset{3}{C_6H_5}$ $\xrightarrow[3,4,2\ \&\ 1]{\text{Interchange}}$ $^{2}CH_2OH$; $\overset{3}{C_6H_5}$—$\overset{1}{COOH}$; $_4CH_3$

Anticlockwise rotation (*S*-configuration)

42 (*c*) The structure of 2, 3, 4-trichloropentane is,

H H H H H
H—C—C*—C—C*—C—H
H Cl Cl Cl H

Hence, two chiral carbon atoms are present in 2,3,4-trichloropentane.

43 (*c*)

$CH_3—\overset{*}{C}H(OH)—\overset{*}{C}H(OH)—CHO$
2,3-dihydroxybutanal

Number of optical isomers $= 2^n = 2^2 = 4$

44 (*c*) (a) 2-butanol

$CH_3—C^*H(OH)—CH_2—CH_3$ Chiral 'C*'

(b) 2,3-dibromopentane

$CH_3—C^*H(Br)—C^*H(Br)—CH_2—CH_3$

(c) 3-bromopentane

$CH_3—CH_2—CH(Br)—CH_2—CH_3$

No chiral 'C*' atom is present.

(d) 2-hydroxy propanoic acid

$CH_3—C^*H(OH)—COOH$

Hence, in these 3-bromopentane is not a chiral molecule due to absence of chiral 'C*' atom.

45 (*b*) (a) $CH_3—CH(OH)—CH(Cl)—C_2H_5$

(b) $CH_3—CH(OH)—CH(OH)—CH_3$
Plane of symmetry

(c) $C_2H_5—CH(OH)—CH(OH)—CH_3$

(d) $H—CH(OH)—CH(Cl)—CH_3$

Since, (b) has plane of symmetry, thus it has a *meso* form.

46 (*c*) The optical isomers which are not related to each other as object and mirror images are known as diastereoisomers. They may differ in physical and chemical properties. So, Assertion is correct but Reason is incorrect.

47 (*b*) HOOC—C*(H)(CH₃)—C*(H)(OH)—C*(H)(Cl)—C*(H)(OH)—C*(H)(CH₃)—COOH

The number of chiral carbon = 5 which is an odd number. Further it is symmetrical molecule.

So, number of *meso* forms $= 2^{\left(\frac{n}{2}-\frac{1}{2}\right)} = 2^{\left(\frac{5}{2}-\frac{1}{2}\right)} = 2^2 = 4$

48 (*a*) $(H_3C)(H)C{=}C{=}C(H)(CH_3)$ and $(H)(H_3C)C{=}C{=}C(CH_3)(H)$

These molecules do not contain any asymmetric carbon atom but these molecules are enantiomers. The two forms are non-superimposable mirror images and are optically active.

49 (*b*) [Fischer projections: CH₃ / H—Br / H—Br / C₂H₅] and [CH₃ / Br—H / H—Br / C₂H₅]

are diastereomers because these stereoisomers are not mirror images of each other.

50 (*c*) $(H_3C)_2C{=}C(H)—C^*(CH_3)(H)—COOH$

Since, it contains one asymmetric carbon atom, i.e. chiral centre, therefore, it will show optical isomerism.

51 (*d*) If a molecule has an asymmetric carbon atom and is not superimposable on its mirror image then it is chiral, while if it is superimposable on its mirror image, it is achiral.

Therefore, (d) is achiral.

52 (*c*) The number of possible optical isomers $= 2^n$

(where, '*n*' is the number of chiral C-atoms) $= 2^3 = 8$

53 (*a*) For asymmetric compound, number of stereomers are 2^n.

So, $2^2 = 4$.

54 (*b*) [Structure: C with ¹Br, ²Cl, ³H₃C, ⁴H] $\equiv$ Interchange → [Fischer projection: ③ top, ① left, ② right, ④ bottom] Anticlockwise

The chirality of the compound is *S*.

55 (*c*) [Fischer projection: ① CH₃ top; H—C—OH (2*S*); CH₃—C—OH (3*S*); H bottom]

56 (*c*) (a) H—C(H)(H)—C(H)(H)—C(H)(H)—C(H)(H)—H

Butane

(b) H—C(H)(H)—C(H)(H)—C(H)(H)—C(H)(CH₃)—C(H)(H)—C(H)(H)—C(H)(H)—H

4-methyl heptane

(c) H—C(H)(H)—C(H)(H)—C(H)(H)—C(H)(H)—C*(H)(CH₃)—C(H)(H)—C(H)(H)—H

3-methyl heptane

(d) H—C(H)(H)—C(H)(H)—C(H)(H)—C(H)(H)—C(H)(H)—C(H)(CH₃)—CH₃

2-methyl heptane

∵ Choice (c) has one asymmetric carbon (C*) atom.

∴ It is optically active.

57 (*a*) Since, it is a pair of optical isomers which are related as non-superimposable mirror images of each other, therefore (I) and (II) are enantiomers.

[Fischer projections: COOH / H—OH / H—OH / COOMe (I); COOH / HO—H / HO—H / COOMe (II)]

Topic 5
Conformations

2017

1 With respect to the conformers of ethane, which of the following statement(s) is/are true?
(a) Bond angle remains same but bond length changes
(b) Bond angle changes but bond length remains same
(c) Both bond angle and bond length change
(d) Both bond angle and bond length remain same

2014

2 Match the following Columns. **[Kerala CEE]**

Column I	Column II
A. Acetaldehyde and vinylalcohol	1. Enantiomers
B. Eclipsed and staggered ethane	2. Tautomers
C. (+)-2-butanol and (–)-2-butanol	3. Chain isomers
D. methyl-*n*-propylamine and diethylamine	4. Conformational isomers
	5. Metamers

Codes

	A	B	C	D		A	B	C	D
(a)	2	4	4	5	(b)	1	2	3	4
(c)	5	1	4	2	(d)	5	1	3	2
(e)	2	4	1	5					

2011

3 Which of the following is the most energetic conformation of cyclohexane? **[KCET]**
(a) Boat (b) Twisted boat
(c) Chair (d) Half-chair

4 Which of the following compounds exhibit rotamers? **[Guj CET]**
(a) 2-butene (b) Maleic acid
(c) Butane (d) Fumeric acid

2010

5 In the following the most stable conformation of *n*-butane is **[CBSE AIPMT]**

(a) 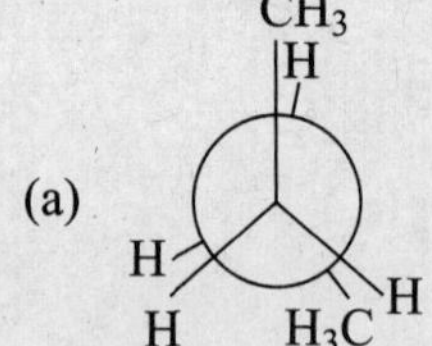

(b) Newman projection: front CH_3 (top), H, H; rear CH_3, H, H (bottom)

(c) Newman projection: CH_3 (top), H, H, H, H, CH_3 (bottom)

(d) Newman projection: CH_3 eclipsed with CH_3 (top), H, H, H, H

6 At room temperature, the eclipsed and staggered forms of ethane cannot be isolated because **[AFMC]**
(a) they interconvert rapidly.
(b) both the conformers are equally stable.
(c) the energy difference between the conformers is large.
(d) there is a large energy barrier of rotation about the σ-bond.

2009

7 The most stable conformation of *n*-butane is **[CG PMT, Haryana PMT]**
(a) skew (b) eclipsed
(c) staggered (d) None of these

2008

8 Least stable conformer of cyclohexane is **[J&K CET]**
(a) chair (b) boat
(c) twist boat (d) planar hexagon

9 The correct order of stability of conformations of cyclohexane is **[KCET]**
(a) chair > twist boat > boat > half chair
(b) chair > half chair > boat > twist boat
(c) boat > half boat > chair > half chair
(d) boat > chair > twist boat > half chair

2007

10 Different structures generated due to rotation about, C—C axis, of an organic molecule, are the examples of **[J&K CET]**
(a) geometrical isomerism
(b) conformational isomerism
(c) optical isomerism
(d) structural isomerism

2005

11 Given below are conformations of butane. Which conformation is the most stable? **[Kerala CEE]**
(a) Staggered-*anti*
(b) Methyl-hydrogen eclipse
(c) Hydrogen-hydrogen eclipse
(d) Staggered-*gauche*
(e) Methyl-methyl eclipsed

Answers

1 (d)	2 (e)	3 (d)	4 (c)	5 (c)	6 (a)	7 (c)	8 (d)	9 (a)	10 (b)
11 (a)									

Explanations

1 (*d*) Spatial arrangements of atoms which can be converted into one another by rotation around a C—C single bond are called conformations. In ethane, an infinite number of conformations are possible. There are two extreme forms, the staggered conformation which is the most stable and the eclipsed conformation which is least stable. Among the conformers of ethane, bond angle and bond length remain same, while their energy, stability and dihedral angle are different.

2 (*e*) The correct match is :

$A \rightarrow 2$, $B \rightarrow 4$, $C \rightarrow 1$, $D \rightarrow 5$

A. Acetaldehyde and vinyl alcohol show tautomerism.

$$CH_3-\overset{\overset{\displaystyle O}{\|}}{C}-H \rightleftharpoons CH_2=\overset{\overset{\displaystyle OH}{|}}{C}H$$

B. Eclipsed and staggered ethane are conformational isomers.

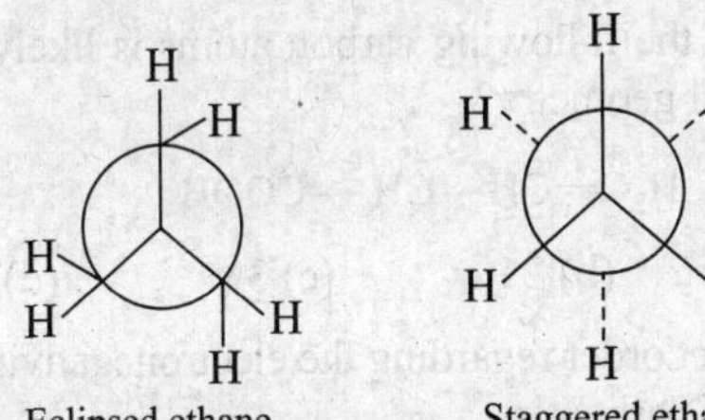

Eclipsed ethane   Staggered ethane

C. (+)-2-butanol and (−)-2-butanol exhibit optical isomerism. They are mirror images.

D. $C_3H_7NHCH_3$ (methyl *n*-propylamine) and diethylamine $C_2H_5NHC_2H_5$ are metamers as, they differ in alkyl groups on both sides of the functional group.

3 (*d*) Half-chair conformation is the most energetic conformation of cyclohexane. Order of increasing energy (or decreasing stability) of conformations of cyclohexane is

chair < twist boat < boat < half-chair.

Increasing stability ← → Increasing energy

4 (*c*) Rotamer — One of a set of conformational isomers that differ from each other by restricted rotation about one or more single bonds. Butane exhibits rotamers.

5 (*c*) Staggered conformation is most stable.

Hence, option (c) is correct.

6 (*a*) Since, the energy difference between two conformations of ethane is not so large, so the eclipsed and staggered conformations interconvert rapidly. Thus, it is impossible to isolate these forms at room temperature.

7 (*c*)

Staggered or *anti* form (most stable)   Skew form   Eclipsed (least stable)

Since, in staggered conformation, the groups are present as far apart as possible, it is the most stable conformation of *n*-butane.

8 (*d*) Planar hexagon conformer has considerable angle strain due to the fact that its bonds are not present at 109.5°. It also has torsional strain. Due to presence of these strains, planar hexagon conformer of cyclohexane is least stable.

9 (*a*) The stability order of conformation of cyclohexane is.

chair > twist boat > boat > half chair.

The chair form is most stable because it does not have angle strain or eclipsing strain. The twist boat form is less stable than chair form as it has slight angle strain, small eclipsing strain and small steric strain.

The boat form is less stable than twist boat as it possesses steric crowding at two hydrogen atoms. The half chair form is the least stable form due to torsional angle strain.

10 (*b*) The different arrangement of atoms in space that results from the carbon-carbon single bond free rotation by 360° are called conformations or conformational isomers and this phenomenon is called **conformational isomerism.**

11 (*a*) In the given alternates of conformation of butane, staggered-*anti* conformation is the most stable.

Topic 6
Cleavage of Bonds and Electronic Displacement

2014

1 The effect that makes 2,3-dimethyl-2-butene more stable than 2-butene is **[Kerala CEE]**

(a) resonance
(b) hyperconjugation
(c) electromeric effect
(d) inductive effect
(e) steric effect

2 Among the following structure the one which is not a resonating structure of other is

Me, O, O, $\bar{}$, Me — I

Me, O, O^-, O, Me — II

Me, O, O, O^-, Me — III

Me, O, O, O, $\bar{}$ — IV **[WB JEE]**

(a) I (b) II (c) III (d) IV

2012

3 The correct order of decreasing acid strength of trichloroacetic acid (A), trifluoroacetic acid (B), acetic acid (C) and formic acid (D) is **[CBSE AIPMT]**

(a) $B > A > D > C$ (b) $B > D > C > A$
(c) $A > B > C > D$ (d) $A > C > B > D$

4 Which of the following does not show electromeric effect?

(a) Alkene (b) Ether **[AFMC]**
(c) Aldehyde (d) Ketone

5 The stability of $Me_2C{=}CH_2$ is more than that of $MeCH_2CH{=}CH_2$ due to **[WB JEE]**

(a) inductive effect of the Me group
(b) resonance effect of the Me group
(c) hyperconjugative effect of the Me group
(d) resonance as well as inductive effect of the group

2011

6 Formic acid is a stronger acid than acetic acid. This can be explained using **[KCET]**

(a) $+M$ effect (b) $-I$ effect
(c) $+I$ effect (d) $-M$ effect

2010

7 Given are cyclohexanol (I), acetic acid (II), 2,4,6-trinitrophenol (III) and phenol (IV). In these the order of decreasing acidic character will be **[CBSE AIPMT]**

(a) III > IV > II > I (b) III > II > IV > I
(c) II > III > I > IV (d) II > III > IV > I

8 The correct order of acidity of the following compound is **[UP CPMT]**

(a) $RCOOH > C_2H_2 > H_2O > ROH$
(b) $RCOOH > ROH > H_2O > C_2H_2$
(c) $RCOOH > ROH > C_2H_2 > H_2O$
(d) $RCOOH > H_2O > ROH > C_2H_2$

9 Which of the following has minimum -*I*-effect? **[Manipal]**

(a) $-NO_2$ (b) $-COOH$
(c) $-F$ (d) $-\overset{+}{N}R_3$

10 Which of the following carbon atoms is likely to possess tetrahedral geometry?

$$\overset{4}{H_2C}{=}\overset{3}{C}H{-}\overset{2}{C}H_2{-}\overset{1}{C}OOH$$ **[RPMT]**

(a) 1 (b) 2 (c) 3 (d) 4

11 The correct order regarding the electronegativity of hybrid orbitals of carbon is **[RPMT]**

(a) $sp < sp^3 < sp^2$ (b) $sp < sp^2 < sp^3$
(c) $sp^2 > sp < sp^3$ (d) $sp > sp^2 > sp^3$

12 The arrangement of $(CH_3)_3C-$, $(CH_3)_2CH-$, CH_3CH_2- when attached to benzene or unsaturated group in increasing order of inductive effect is **[J&K CET]**

(a) $(CH_3)_3C- < (CH_3)_2CH- < CH_3CH_2-$
(b) $CH_3CH_2- < (CH_3)_2CH- < (CH_3)_3C-$
(c) $(CH_3)_2CH- < (CH_3)_3C- < CH_3CH_2-$
(d) $(CH_3)_3C- < CH_3CH_2- < (CH_3)_2CH-$

13 $\overset{-}{\ddot{C}}H_2-\underset{\underset{\ddot{O}:}{\|}}{C}-CH_3$ and $CH_2=\underset{\underset{:\ddot{O}:^-}{|}}{C}-CH_3$ are **[Punjab PHET]**

(a) resonating structures (b) tautomers
(c) geometrical isomers (d) optical isomers

14 Chloroacetic acid is a stronger acid than acetic acid. This can be explained using **[KCET]**

(a) $-M$ effect (b) $-I$ effect
(c) $+M$ effect (d) $+I$ effect

2009

15 Assertion (A) A compound with delocalised electron is more stable than that compound would be if all its electrons were localised.

Reason (R) The extra stability, a compound gains as a result of having delocalised electrons, is called delocalisation energy. **[AIIMS]**

(a) Both A and R are correct and R is the correct explanation of A
(b) Both A and R are correct but R is not the correct explanation of A
(c) A is correct but R is incorrect
(d) Both A and R are incorrect

16 The C—H bond distance is the longest in **[AFMC]**

(a) C_2H_2 (b) C_2H_4
(c) $C_2H_4Br_2$ (d) C_6H_6

17 Which is the strongest acid? **[UP CPMT]**

(a) C_6H_6 (b) C_6H_6
(c) $CH \equiv CH$ (d) CH_3OH

18 Negative inductive effect is shown by **[MHT CET]**

(a) $—CH_3$ (b) $—CH_2CH_3$
(c) $—\overset{\oplus}{N}H_3$ (d) $(CH_3)_2CH—$

19 Hyperconjugation effect is also known as **[AMU]**

(a) Baker-Nathan effect (b) no bond resonance
(c) Both (a) and (b) (d) None of the above

20 Which of the groups has highest $+I$-effect? **[AMU]**

(a) H_3C (b) CH_3CH_2
(c) $(CH_3)_2CH$ (d) $(CH_3)_3C$

21 Which kind of fission is favoured by sunlight? **[VMMC]**

(a) Heterolytic fission (b) Homolytic fission
(c) Both 'a' and 'b' (d) None of the above

2008

22 Inductive effect involves **[AFMC]**

(a) displacement of σ-electrons
(b) delocalisation of π-electrons
(c) delocalisation of σ-electrons
(d) displacement of π-electrons

23 Which among the following statements are true with respect to electronic displacement in a covalent bond?

I. Inductive effect operates through π-bond.
II. Resonance effect operates through σ-bond.
III. Inductive effect operates through σ-bond.
IV. Resonance effect operates through π-bond.
V. Resonance and inductive effects operate through σ-bond.

(a) III and IV (b) I and II **[Kerala CEE]**
(c) II and IV (d) I and III
(e) II and III

24 Mesomeric effect involves delocalisation of **[KCET]**

(a) π-electrons (b) σ-electrons
(c) protons (d) None of these

25 CH_3CH_2Cl undergoes homolytic fission, produces **[BCECE]**

(a) $CH_3\dot{C}H_2$ and $\dot{C}l$ (b) $CH_3\overset{\oplus}{C}H_2$ and Cl^-
(c) $CH_3\overset{\oplus}{C}H_2$ and $\overset{\oplus}{Cl}$ (d) $CH_3\dot{C}H_2$ and Cl^-

26 The highest electrical conductivity among the following aqueous solutions, is of **[JCECE]**

(a) 0.1 M difluoroacetic acid (b) 0.1 M fluoroacetic acid
(c) 0.1 M chloroacetic acid (d) 0.1 M acetic acid

2007

27 Which of the following represents the correct order of the acidity in the given compounds? **[CBSE AIPMT]**

(a) $CH_3COOH > BrCH_2COOH > ClCH_2COOH > FCH_2COOH$
(b) $FCH_2COOH > CH_3COOH > BrCH_2COOH > ClCH_2COOH$
(c) $BrCH_2COOH > ClCH_2COOH > FCH_2COOH > CH_3COOH$
(d) $FCH_2COOH > ClCH_2COOH > BrCH_2COOH > CH_3COOH$

28 Which of the following is most basic? **[UP CPMT]**

(a) Benzamide (b) Butamine
(c) Nitrobenzene (d) Benzene

29 The rate of reaction,

$$R—C_6H_4—CH_2Br + C_5H_5\ddot{N} \longrightarrow \left[R—C_6H_4—CH_2—\overset{+}{N}C_5H_5\right]Br^-$$

is influenced by the hyperconjugation effect of group *R*. If *R* sequentially is

I. $CH_3—$ II. $CH_3—CH_2—$
III. $H_3C—\underset{CH_3}{\underset{|}{C}H}—$ IV. $H_3C—\underset{CH_3}{\underset{|}{\overset{CH_3}{\overset{|}{C}}}}—$

The increasing order of speed of the above reaction is **[Kerala CEE]**

(a) IV, III, II, I
(b) I, II, III, IV (c) I, IV, III, II
(d) III, II, I, IV (e) II, III, I, IV

30 Correct order of basic nature is **[RPMT]**

(a) $NH_3 > CH_3NH_2 > C_6H_5NH_2$
(b) $C_6H_5NH_2 > NH_3 > CH_3NH_2$
(c) $CH_3NH_2 > NH_3 > C_6H_5NH_2$
(d) None of the above

31 Which of the following is maximum basic? **[MP PMT]**

(a) $(C_2H_5)_2NH$ (b) $(CH_3)_2NH$
(c) $(C_2H_5)_3N$ (d) $C_2H_5NH_2$

32 Among the following compounds, the most basic is **[J&K CET]**

(a) aniline (b) acetanilide
(c) *p*-nitroaniline (d) benzylamine

33 Which one of the following, is most acidic? **[J&K CET]**

(a) o-nitrophenol (NO_2 and OH on benzene ring, ortho) (b) m-nitrophenol (O_2N and OH on benzene ring)

(c) O_2N—C_6H_4—OH (para) (d) O_2N—C_6H_4—OH (meta)

34 Carbon-oxygen bond length of CH_2O (I); $CH_2\bar{O}$ (II), CH_3OH (III) follows the order **[DUMET]**

(a) I > II > III (b) II > I > III (c) III > II > I (d) III > I > II

2006

35 Which species are more resonance stabilised in the following pairs? **[Kerala CEE]**

$[C_6H_5Cl, C_6H_5CH_3]$, $[CH_2=CHCl, CH_2=CHCH_2Cl]$, $[C_6H_5Br, C_6H_5CH_2Br]$ $[CH_3COOH, CH_3COO^-]$,

(a) $C_6H_5Cl, CH_2=CHCH_2Cl, C_6H_5CH_2Br, CH_3COO^-$
(b) $C_6H_5CH_3, CH_2=CHCH_2Cl, C_6H_5CH_2Br, CH_3COO^-$
(c) $C_6H_5CH_3, CH_2=CHCH_2Cl, C_6H_5CH_2Br$ CH_3COOH
(d) $C_6H_5Cl, CH_2=CHCl, C_6H_5Br, CH_3COOH$
(e) $C_6H_5Cl, CH_2=CHCl, C_6H_5Br, CH_3COO^-$

36 Chlorobenzene is *o,p*-directing in electrophilic substitution reaction. The directing influence is explained by **[J&K CET]**

(a) $+M$ of Ph (b) $+I$ of Cl (c) $+M$ of Cl (d) $-I$ of Ph

37 The correct order for homolytic bond dissociation energies (ΔH in kcal/mol) for $CH_4(A)$, $C_2H_6(B)$ and $CH_3Br(C)$, under identical experimental conditions **[J&K CET]**

(a) $C > B > A$ (b) $B > C > A$
(c) $C > A > B$ (d) $A > B > C$

2005

38 Most acidic is **[UP CPMT]**

(a) Phenol (OH on benzene ring) (b) p-nitrophenol (OH, NO_2 para)

(c) o-nitrophenol (OH, NO_2 ortho) (d) Benzoic acid (COOH on benzene ring)

Answers

1 (b)	2 (d)	3 (a)	4 (b)	5 (c)	6 (c)	7 (b)	8 (d)	9 (c)	10 (b)
11 (d)	12 (a)	13 (a)	14 (b)	15 (b)	16 (c)	17 (d)	18 (c)	19 (c)	20 (d)
21 (b)	22 (c)	23 (a)	24 (a)	25 (a)	26 (a)	27 (d)	28 (b)	29 (a)	30 (c)
31 (a)	32 (d)	33 (c)	34 (c)	35 (e)	36 (c)	37 (*)	38 (d)		

Explanations

1 (*b*) $H_3C—C(CH_3)=C(CH_3)—CH_3$ is more stable than
2,3-dimethyl but-2-ene

$CH_3—CH=CH—CH_3$
But-2-ene

Due to presence of methyl group, 2,3-dimethyl -2-butene shows hyperconjugation, which increases its stability.

2 (*d*) Resonating structures involve movement of electrons, but they do not involve movement of atom or group of atoms.

Me–O–C(=O)–$\bar{C}$H–C(=O)–Me (I) ⟷ Me–O–C(–O^-)=CH–C(=O)–Me (II) ⟷ Me–O–C(=O)–CH=C(O^-)–Me (III)

The structure IV is not a resonating structure of others.

3 (*a*) If an electron withdrawing group (–*I* showing group) is present in carboxylic acid, it makes the removal of proton more easy by stabilising the remaining carboxylate ion and thus, makes acid more acidic. The order of acidity of given compounds is

$F_3C\leftarrow COOH > Cl_3C\leftarrow COOH > HCOOH$
Trifluoroacetic acid (*B*) Trichloroacetic acid (*A*) Formic acid (*D*)

$> H_3C\rightarrow COOH$
Acetic acid (*C*)

C is least acidic
It has an electron donating group (—CH_3) which decreases the acidic character.

4 (*b*) Electromeric effect implies complete transfer of π-electrons in presence of a reagent. Since, simple ethers do not contain any multiple bond, hence they do not show electromeric effect.

5 (*c*) $Me_2C{=}CH_2$ (Me, Me / H, H)

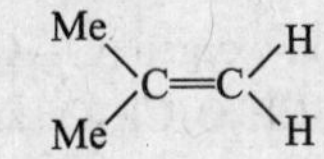

has 6- hyperconjugate forms while

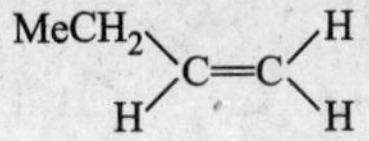

$MeCH_2CH{=}CH_2$

has 2- hyperconjugate forms

Therefore, $Me_2C{=}CH_2$ is more stable than $MeCH_2CH{=}CH_2$.

6 (*c*) Due to $+I$ effect, electron density increases, which results in decrease in acidic character. Acetic acid, CH_3-COOH has $-CH_3$ group that shows $+I$ effect, whereas no such group is present in formic acid. Therefore, formic acid is a stronger acid than acetic acid.

7 (*b*)

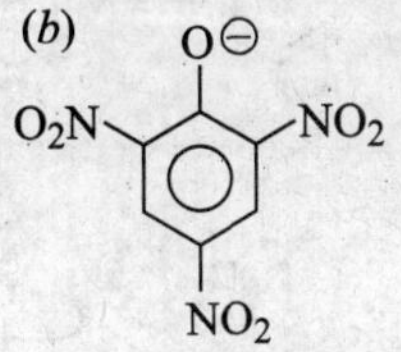

O_2N–(ring with $O^{\ominus}$)–NO_2, NO_2

2, 4, 6-trinitrophenol has maximum resonance stabilisation and has maximum $-I$ and $-M$ effect due to the presence of three $-NO_2$ groups. Therefore, it is more acidic than CH_3COOH. Thus, the decreasing order of acidic strength III > II > IV > I.

8 (*d*) Higher the tendency to lose a proton, more will be the acidic character and also higher the stability of conjugate base, more will be acidic character. Among the given option, carboxylate ion ($RCOO^-$) is stabilised by resonance, thus it is more stable and hence, $RCOOH$ is the most acidic. C_2H_2, on the other hand, gives $HC{\equiv}C^-$ ion which is not so stable, thus it is a weak acid. Alcohols are more acidic as compared to ethyne but less acidic as compared to water.

Thus, the order of acidic character is $RCOOH > H_2O > ROH > C_2H_2$.

9 (*c*) The correct decreasing order of $-I$ effect is as follows :

$$-\overset{+}{N}R_3 > -NO_2 > -COOH > -F$$

Therefore, F has the minimum $-I$ effect.

10 (*b*)

$$\underset{sp^2}{\overset{4}{H_2C}}{=}\underset{sp^2}{\overset{3}{CH}}-\underset{sp^3}{\overset{2}{CH_2}}-\underset{sp^2}{\overset{O}{\overset{\|}{C}}}-O-H$$

sp^3-hybridised carbon (i.e. 2–C) atom is likely to possess tetrahedral geometry.

11 (*d*) The electronegativity of the hybrid orbitals decreases as the percentage of *s*-character decreases. Hence, the correct order is $sp > sp^2 > sp^3$.

12 (*a*) The inductive effect of the alkyl group on a saturated carbon chain follows the order

$(CH_3)_3C- > (CH_3)_2CH- > CH_3CH_2-$

However, when an alkyl group is attached to an unsaturated system such as double bond or a benzene ring, the order of inductive effect is actually reversed.

This effect is called hyperconjugation effect or Baker-Nathan effect. Now, the reactivity order is

$$(CH_3)_3C- < (CH_3)_2CH- < CH_3-CH_2-$$

13 (*a*)

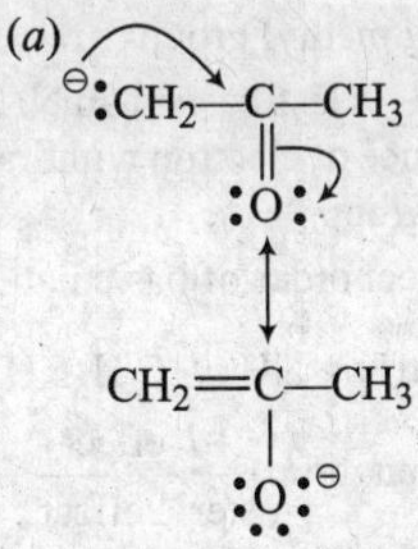

$$^{\ominus}{:}CH_2-\underset{\underset{:O:}{\|}}{C}-CH_3 \longleftrightarrow CH_2{=}\underset{\underset{:\ddot{O}:^{\ominus}}{|}}{C}-CH_3$$

Hence, these are resonating structures.

14 (*b*) —Cl is an electron withdrawing (i.e. $-I$) group. It withdraws electron when attached to the carboxylic acid and decreases the electron density on the oxygen atom. This will facilitate the release of H^+ by making O—H bond more polar and thus —Cl increases the acidity of acetic acid when attached at α position because of $-I$ effect.

15 (*b*) Delocalisation of electrons provide more stability to the compounds. The extra stability which is acquired by a compound as a result of resonance (delocalisation of electrons) is called resonance energy or delocalisation energy. Hence, statement I and II both are correct but statement II is not the correct explanation of I.

16 (*c*) As the *s*-character or number of π-electrons increases, bond length decreases.

$$H-\underset{sp}{C}\overset{2\pi}{\equiv}\underset{sp}{C}-H;\quad H_2\underset{sp^2}{C}\overset{\pi}{\underset{\sigma}{=}}\underset{sp^2}{C}H_2$$

$$H_2(Br)\underset{sp^3}{C}\overset{}{\underset{\sigma}{-}}\underset{sp^3}{C}H_2(Br);\quad \text{benzene (}\sigma, \pi, sp^2\text{)}$$

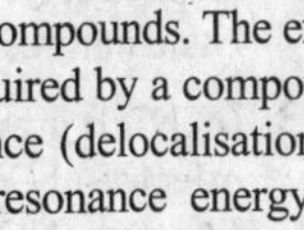

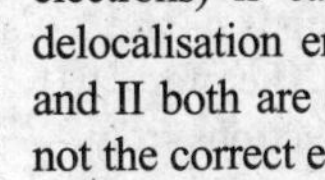

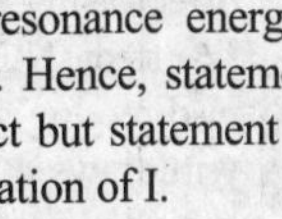

Therefore, $C_2H_4Br_2$ due to the absence of π-electrons or due to the presence of lesser *s*-character (25%), has the longest C—H bond distance.

17 (*d*) CH_3OH (methyl alcohol) among the given compounds, has the highest tendency to donate a proton, hence it is the strongest acid.

$$\underset{\text{Methanol}}{CH_3OH} \rightleftharpoons \underset{\text{Methoxide ion}}{CH_3O^-} + H^+$$

18 (*c*) Among the given, $-CH_3$, $-CH_2CH_3$ and $(CH_3)_2CH-$ being electron releasing, increase the electron density, so exhibit positve inductive effect, while $-\overset{\oplus}{N}H_3$ exhibits negative inductive effect.

19 (*c*) Hyperconjugation effect is also known as no bond resonance and Baker-Nathan effect.

20 (*d*) Greater is the number of alkyl groups greater is the $+I$ effect. Thus, $(CH_3)_3C$ exhibits highest $+I$-effect.

21 (*b*) If a covalent bond breaks in such a way that each atom takes away one electron of the shared pair, it is called homolytic or symmetrical fission. It is carried out in the presence of sunlight or high temperature.

$$A{-}B \xrightarrow{\text{Homolytic fission}} \underset{\text{Free radicals}}{A^{\bullet} + B^{\bullet}}$$

22 (*c*) During inductive effect shifting (delocalisation) of σ-electrons takes place due to which partial charges are developed on the atom

$$\overset{+\delta''}{CH_3}\!\to\!\!\to\!\!\to\overset{+\delta'}{CH_2}\!\to\!\!\to\overset{+\delta}{CH_2}\!\to\overset{-\delta}{Cl}$$

23 (*a*) Inductive effect is a permanent effect that operates through σ-electrons while resonance involves delocalisation of π electrons.

24 (*a*) Mesomeric effect involves complete transfer of π or lone pair of electrons to the adjacent atom or covalent bond. Hence, it involves delocalisation of pi (π)-electrons.

25 (*a*) Homolytic cleavage results in the formation of free radical.

$$CH_3CH_2-Cl \xrightarrow[\text{fission}]{\text{Homolytic}} CH_3\dot{C}H_2 + {}^{\bullet}Cl$$

26 (*a*) Fluoro group causes negative inductive effect, thus increasing ionisation, hence 0.1 M difluoroacetic acid has highest electrical conductivity.

$$F \leftarrow \overset{H}{\underset{F}{C}} \leftarrow \overset{O}{\overset{\|}{C}} \leftarrow O \leftarrow H$$

27 (*d*) The acidity of halogenated acid increases with the increase in electronegativity of the halogen present. So, the correct order is ;

$FCH_2COOH > ClCH_2COOH > BrCH_2COOH > CH_3COOH$

28 (*b*) Basicity increases with $+I$ (inductive) effect and also with presence of lone pairs, which are available for protonation.

(b) Butamine

$CH_3 - CH_2 - CH_2 - CH_2 - NH_2$

Aliphatic primary amine

i.e. $R \longrightarrow NH_2$

R-group due to $+I$ effect intensifies the electron density on nitrogen. Therefore, it is highly basic in nature.

(a) Benzamide

$C_6H_5-\overset{O}{\overset{\|}{C}}-\ddot{N}H_2$

Aromatic amide

It does not show basic character because lone pair on nitrogen is delocalised by resonance with the carbonyl group which makes it less available for protonation.

(c) Nitrobenzene

$C_6H_5NO_2$

Due to the presence of $-NO_2$ group, it shows $-I$ effect. Therefore, it makes the ring electron deficient. Hence, it is acidic in nature.

(d) Benzene

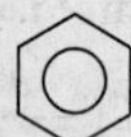

It is neutral.

Thus, option 'b' is correct.

29 (*a*) The rate of reaction is influenced by the hyperconjugation effect of *R* group. It depends on the electron donating power of alkyl group (*R*). The electron releasing power of *R* group depends on the number of hydrogen present on α carbon.

The increasing order of hyperconjugational *R* group in the given reaction is

$(CH_3)_3C- < (CH_3)_2CH- < CH_3-CH_2- < CH_3-$

i.e. IV < III < II < I

30 (*c*) (*i*) CH_3NH_2 is more basic than NH_3 due to presence of electron donating methyl group.

(*ii*) $C_6H_5NH_2$ is less basic than NH_3 due to presence of electron withdrawing phenyl group.

∴ Correct order of basic nature is

$$CH_3NH_2 > NH_3 > C_6H_5NH_2$$

31 (*b*) Basic strength $\propto \frac{+I \text{ effect}}{\text{steric effect}}$

$(C_2H_5)_2NH$ is maximum basic due to $+I$-effect, but $(C_2H_5)_3N$ is less basic than $(C_2H_5)_2NH$ due to less steric effect on the latter.

32 (*d*) Benzylamine is most basic because basic strength depends upon the availability of lone pair at the donor atom. In acetanilide and aniline, the lone pair of electrons involves in conjugation and resonance respectively, thereby, decreasing their basic nature.

33 (*c*) Nitro group shows both $-R$ and $-I$ effect. But $-R$ effect predominates over $-I$-effect. NO_2 group is *o*- and *m*-directing group. Therefore, it withdraws more electrons from *o*/*p*-position than *m*-position. Further, *p*-nitrophenol is more acidic due to intramolecular hydrogen bonding in *o*-nitrophenol which makes loss of proton little more difficult. Thus, *p*-nitrophenol is most acidic.

34 (*c*) Carbon-oxygen (C—O) bond length of CH_2O, CH_2O^- and CH_3OH is in order.

$CH_3OH > CH_2O^- > CH_2O$

35 (*e*) C_6H_5Cl, $CH_2{=}CHCl$, C_6H_5Br and CH_3COO^- are more resonance stabilised than $C_6H_5CH_3$, $CH_2{=}CH{\cdot}CH_2Cl$, $C_6H_5CH_2Br$ and CH_3COOH respectively.

36 (*c*) Chlorobenzene is *o*, *p*-directing in electrophilic substitution reaction. The directing influence is explained by $+M$ of Cl atom.

+*M* effect of chlorine atom

37 (*) In C_2H_6, maximum number of homolytic bonds are present. Therefore, it has maximum bond dissociation energy while in CH_3Br, minimun number of homolytic bonds are present. Therefore, its bonds dissociation energy is least. Thus, the order of ΔH is $B > A > C$.

38 (*d*)

- Carboxylic acids are more acidic than phenol.
- Phenols are acidic and their acidity increases by the presence of electron withdrawing group. The effect of group is more at *o*-position due to less distance.

Thus,

C_6H_5-COOH is most acidic.

Topic 7
Reaction Intermediate

2019

1 The most stable carbocation, among the following is **[NEET Odisha]**

(a) $(CH_3)_3C-\overset{\oplus}{C}H-CH_3$

(b) $CH_3-CH_2-\overset{\oplus}{C}H-CH_2-CH_3$

(c) $CH_3-\overset{\oplus}{C}H-CH_2-CH_2-CH_3$

(d) $CH_3-CH_2-\overset{\oplus}{C}H_2$

2 Compare stability of free radicals. **[AIIMS, MBBS]**

(I) $CH_3-\dot{C}H-CH_3$

(II) $C_6H_5-\dot{C}H_2$

(III) $CH_2-\dot{C}H(CH_3)_2$

(IV) $\dot{C}H_2-CH_3$

(a) II > I > III > IV (b) II > I > IV > III

(c) I > II > III > IV (d) IV > III > I > II

2018

3 Relative stabilites of the following carbocations will be in the order

$\overset{\oplus}{C}H_3$ CH_3 $\overset{\oplus}{C}H_2$ $\overset{\oplus}{C}H_2$ OCH_3
(A) (B) (C)

(a) $C > B > A$ (b) $C < B < A$

(c) $B > C > A$ (d) $C > A > B$

4 The correct order of decreasing stability of the following carbocations is

$CH_3-\overset{\oplus}{C}H-CH_3$ (I) $CH_3-\overset{\oplus}{C}H-OCH_3$ (II)

$CH_3-\overset{\oplus}{C}H-CH_2-OCH_3$

(a) II > I > III (b) II > III > I

(c) III > I > II (d) I > II > III

2017

5 Predict the correct intermediate and product in the following reaction. **[NEET]**

$$H_3C-C\equiv CH \xrightarrow[HgSO_4]{H_2O,\,H_2SO_4} \underset{(A)}{\text{Intermediate}} \longrightarrow \underset{(B)}{\text{Product}}$$

(a) $A \Rightarrow H_3C-\underset{SO_4}{\underset{|}{C}}=CH_2$; $B \Rightarrow H_3C-\underset{O}{\underset{||}{C}}-CH_3$

(b) $A \Rightarrow H_3C-\underset{OH}{\underset{|}{C}}=CH_2$; $B \Rightarrow H_3C-\underset{SO_4}{\underset{|}{C}}=CH_2$

(c) $A \Rightarrow H_3C-\underset{O}{\underset{||}{C}}-CH_3$; $B \Rightarrow H_3C-C\equiv CH$

(d) $A \Rightarrow H_3C-\underset{OH}{\underset{|}{C}}=CH_2$; $B \Rightarrow H_3C-\underset{O}{\underset{||}{C}}-CH_3$

6 The most stable carbocation is **[AIIMS]**

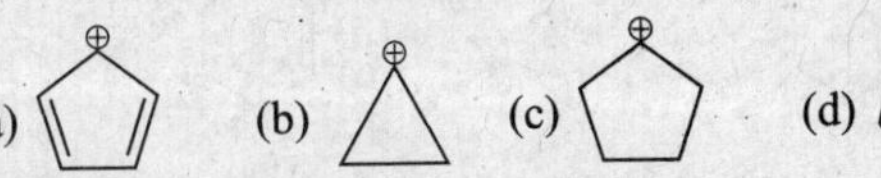

2014

7 The correct order of decreasing length of the bond as indicated by the arrow in the following structures is **[WB JEE]**

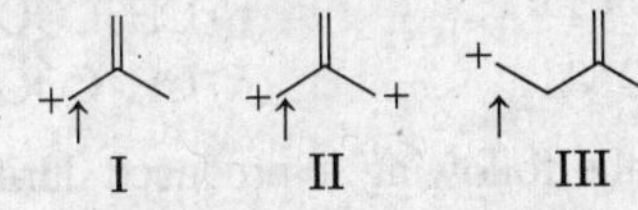

(a) I > II > III (b) II > I > III (c) III > II > I (d) I > III > II

2012

8 **Assertion** (A) Allyl and benzyl carbonium ions are more stable than propyl carbonium ions. **[AIIMS]**

Reason (R) Electron releasing group stabilises carbonium ion.

(a) Both A and R are correct and R is the correct explanation of the A

(b) Both A and R are correct but R is not the correct explanation of A

(c) A is correct but R is incorrect

(d) Both A and R are incorrect

9 Among the following carbocations $Ph_2C^+CH_2Me$ (I), $PhCH_2CH_2CH^+Ph$ (II), $Ph_2CHCH_2^+$ (III), $Ph_2C(Me)\dot{}CH_2^{\oplus}$ (IV) the order of stability is **[WB JEE]**

(a) IV > II > I > III (b) I > II > III > IV

(c) II > I > IV > III (d) I > IV > III > II

2011

10 Which one of the following is an intermediate in the reaction of benzene with CH_3Cl in the presence of anhydrous $AlCl_3$? **[KCET]**

(a) Cl^+ (b) $\overset{+}{C}H_3$

(c) CH_3^+ (d) $C_6H_5^+$ (phenyl cation)

11 Which one of the nitrogen atoms in

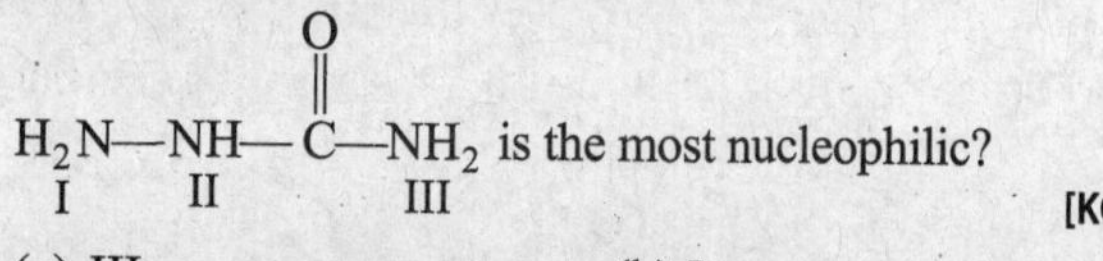

is the most nucleophilic? **[KCET]**

(a) III (b) I
(c) II
(d) All three nitrogen atoms are equally strong nucleophilic centres.

12 Most stable carbocation is **[DUMET]**

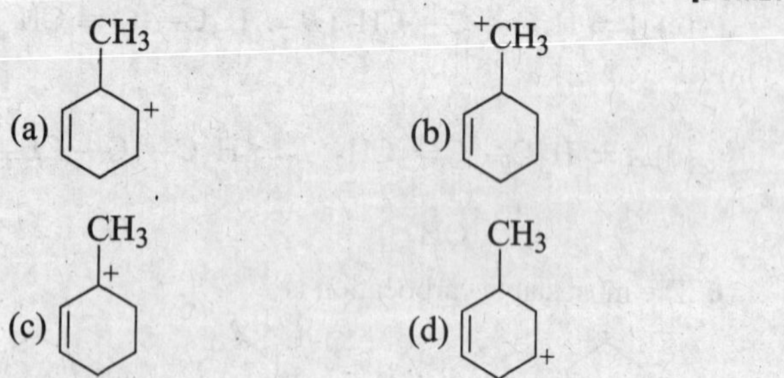

2010

13 Among the given compounds, the most susceptible to nucleophilic attack at the carbonyl group is **[CBSE AIPMT]**

(a) CH_3COCl (b) CH_3COOCH_3
(c) CH_3CONH_2 (d) $CH_3COOCOCH_3$

14 Which of the following is produced during nucleophilic reaction? **[UP CPMT]**

(a) Atoms (b) Anion
(c) Free radical (d) Cation

15 Which of the following is the most stable carbocation? **[UP CPMT]**

(a) $C_6H_5CH_2^+$ (b) $CH_3CH_2^+$
(c) $(CH_3)_2\overset{+}{C}H$ (d) $(CH_3)_3C^+$

16 Which of the following is a nucleophile? **[MHT CET]**

(a) BH_3 (b) NH_3
(c) $AlCl_3$ (d) All of these

17 Chlorine (Cl^{17}) free radical contains how many electrons around the nucleus? **[MHT CET]**

(a) 16 (b) 17 (c) 18 (d) 19

18 The effective electrophile in aromatic sulphonation is **[Manipal, KCET]**

(a) HSO_4^- (b) SO_2
(c) SO_2^+ (d) SO_3

19 The most stable carbonium ion among the following is **[Manipal]**

(a) $C_6H_5\overset{\oplus}{C}HC_6H_5$ (b) $C_6H_5\overset{\oplus}{C}H_2$
(c) $CH_3CH_2^{\oplus}$ (d) $C_6H_5CH_2\overset{\oplus}{C}H_2$

20 An example of electrophile is **[Kerala CEE]**

(a) NO_2 (b) NH_3
(c) $^+NO_2$ (d) H_2O
(e) —OH

21 Which among the following free radicals is most stable? **[Kerala CEE]**

(a) [cyclohexene ring with CH_3 and radical dot] (b) [cyclohexene ring with $\dot{C}H_2$]
(c) $\dot{C}H_3$ (d) $\dot{C}H_2$—CH=CH_2

22 Which of the following carbocations will be most stable? **[WB JEE]**

(a) Ph_3C^+ (b) $CH_3—\overset{+}{C}H_2$
(c) $(CH_3)_2\overset{+}{C}H$ (d) $CH_2=CH—\overset{+}{C}H_2$

23 Which has the highest nucleophilicity? **[CG PMT, Haryana PMT]**

(a) F^- (b) OH^-
(c) CH_3^- (d) NH_2^-

24 The ascending order of stability of the carbanion $\overset{-}{C}H_3(P), C_6H_5\overset{-}{C}H_2(Q), (CH_3)_2\overset{-}{C}H(R)$ and $H_2\overset{-}{C}—CH=CH_2(S)$ is **[J&K CET]**

(a) $P < R < S < Q$ (b) $R < P < S < Q$
(c) $R < P < Q < S$ (d) $P < R < Q < S$

25 The descending order of stability of the carbonium ions

$C_6H_5\overset{+}{C}H_2$, (I) p-$(CH_3O)C_6H_4\overset{+}{C}H_2$, (II)

p-$(NO_2)C_6H_4\overset{+}{C}H_2$ (III) and p-$(CH_3)C_6H_4\overset{+}{C}H_2$ (IV) is **[J&K CET]**

(a) IV > II > I > III (b) II > IV > III > I
(c) II > IV > I > III (d) IV > II > III > I

26 Which one of the following species is involved in the sulphonation of aromatic hydrocarbons? **[AMU]**

(a) HSO_4^- (b) Dil. H_2SO_4
(c) SO_2 (d) SO_3

27 Arrange the following free radicals in order of decreasing stability.

Methyl (I), Vinyl (II), Allyl (III), Benzyl (IV) **[DUMET]**

Codes

(a) I > II > III > IV (b) III > II > I > IV
(c) II > I > IV > III (d) IV > III > I > II

28 Most stable carbonium ion is **[JCECE]**

(a) $\overset{+}{C_2}H_5$ (b) $(CH_3)_3\overset{+}{C}$
(c) $(C_6H_5)_3\overset{+}{C}$ (d) $C_6H_5\overset{+}{C}H_2$

29 Which of the following species is paramagnetic in nature? **[CMC]**

(a) Carbonium ion
(b) Free radical
(c) Carbene
(d) Nitrene

2008

30 The stability of carbanions in the following

I. $R\text{C}\equiv\bar{\text{C}}$ II.

III. $R_2\text{C}=\bar{\text{C}}\text{H}$ IV. $R_3\text{C}-\bar{\text{C}}\text{H}_2$

is in the order of **[CBSE AIPMT]**

Codes

(a) I > II > III > IV (b) II > III > IV > I
(c) IV > II > III > I (d) I > III > II > IV

31 Which reaction, intermediate is formed during the condensation reaction between acetaldehyde and formaldehyde? **[MHT CET]**

(a) $:\bar{\text{C}}\text{H}_2\text{CHO}$ (b) $\overset{+}{\text{C}}\text{H}_2\text{CHO}$
(c) $\overset{+}{\text{C}}\text{H}_2\text{OH}$ (d) $:\bar{\text{C}}\text{HCHO}$

32 Most stable carbocation among the following is **[DUMET]**

(a) 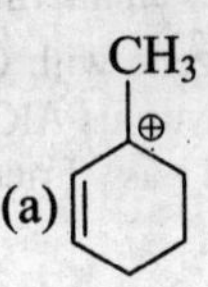

(b) 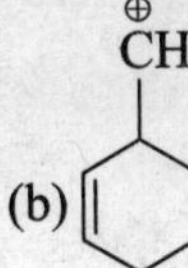

(c) CH_3 ⊕

(d) All are equally stable

33 Due to presence of an unpaired electron, free radicals are **[JCECE]**

(a) cations (b) anions
(c) chemically inactive (d) chemically reactive

2007

34 For the following, I. I^- II. Cl^- III. Br^- the increasing order of nucleophilicity would be **[CBSE AIPMT]**

(a) $I^- < Br^- < Cl^-$ (b) $Cl^- < Br^- < I^-$
(c) $I^- < Cl^- < Br^-$ (d) $Br^- < Cl^- < I^-$

35 The decreasing order of the stability of the ions **[AIIMS]**

$\text{CH}_3-\overset{+}{\text{C}}\text{H}-\text{CH}_3$ (I) $\text{CH}_3-\overset{+}{\text{C}}\text{H}-\text{OCH}_3$ (II)

$\text{CH}_3-\overset{+}{\text{C}}\text{H}-\text{COCH}_3$ (III)

(a) I > II > III (b) III > II > I
(c) II > III > I (d) II > I > III

36 Which of the following free radicals is the most stable? **[AFMC]**

(a) Primary (b) Methyl (c) Secondary (d) Tertiary

2006

37 Consider the following carbocations,

I. $\text{C}_6\text{H}_5\overset{+}{\text{C}}\text{H}_2$ II. $\text{C}_6\text{H}_5\text{CH}_2\overset{+}{\text{C}}\text{H}_2$

III. $\text{C}_6\text{H}_5\overset{+}{\text{C}}\text{HCH}_3$ IV. $\text{C}_6\text{H}_5\overset{+}{\text{C}}(\text{CH}_3)_2$

The correct sequence of the stability of these is **[MHT CET]**

(a) II < I < III < IV (b) II < III < I < IV
(c) III < I < II < IV (d) IV < III < I < II

38 Which of the following carbocations is most stable? **[DUMET]**

(a) 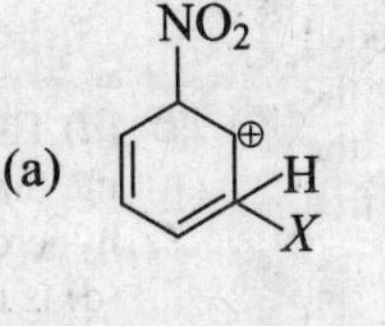

(b) 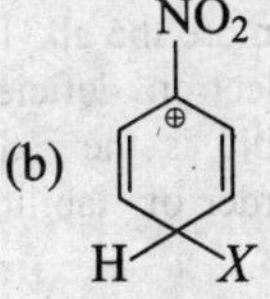

(c) O_2N, H, X, ⊕

(d) NO_2, ⊕, H, X

39 Order of stability of vinyl, allyl, tertiary radicals is **[DUMET]**

(a) tertiary, vinyl, allyl
(b) vinyl, tertiary, allyl
(c) tertiary, allyl, vinyl
(d) allyl, tertiary, vinyl

2005

40 Among the following the strongest nucleophile is **[AIIMS]**

(a) C_2H_5SH (b) CH_3COO^- (c) CH_3NH_2 (d) $NC\bar{C}H_2$

41 Consider the following carbocations **[Kerala CEE]**

I. Cl_3C^+ II. Cl_2CH^+

III. $\text{Cl}\overset{+}{\text{C}}\text{H}_2$ IV. CH_3^+

The stability sequence follows the order

(a) IV > I < II < III (b) I < II < III < IV
(c) IV < I < III < II (d) IV < II < I < III
(e) IV < I < III < II

42 Which of the following is an electrophile? **[WB JEE]**

(a) H_2O (b) SO_3
(c) NH_3 (d) $R-O-R$

Answers

1 (c)	2 (b)	3 (a)	4 (a)	5 (d)	6 (d)	7 (c)	8 (b)	9 (b)	10 (c)
11 (b)	12 (c)	13 (a)	14 (b)	15 (d)	16 (b)	17 (b)	18 (d)	19 (a)	20 (c)
21 (a)	22 (a)	23 (c)	24 (b)	25 (c)	26 (d)	27 (d)	28 (c)	29 (b)	30 (a)
31 (a)	32 (a)	33 (d)	34 (b)	35 (d)	36 (d)	37 (a)	38 (a)	39 (d)	40 (a)
41 (b)	42 (b)								

Explanations

1 (c) $CH_3\overset{+}{C}HCH_2CH_2CH_3$ is the most stable carbocation among the given carbocations. It is because the number of α-H atom attached to carbocation is maximum in $CH_3\overset{+}{C}HCH_2CH_2CH_3$. Thus, it has maximum number of hyperconjugating structure hence, it is most stable.

2 (b) Among the given free radicals, $C_6H_5-\dot{C}H_2$ is most stable due to resonance. In the remaining free radicals, more the alkyl groups bonded to the electron deficient carbon, the more stable is the radical. Thus, the correct order of stability of given free radicals is

$$\underset{\text{(II)}}{C_6H_5-\dot{C}H_2} > \underset{\text{(I)}}{CH_3\dot{C}HCH_3} > \underset{\text{(IV)}}{\dot{C}H_2-CH_3} > \underset{\text{(III)}}{(\dot{C}H_3)}$$

3 (a) The dispersal of the charge stabilises the carbocation. More the number of alkyl groups, the greater is the dispersal of positive charge and therefore more is the stability of cabocation. Thus, the correct order is

$$\underset{(C)}{\overset{\oplus}{C}H_2OCH_3} > \underset{(B)}{CH_3\overset{\oplus}{C}H_2} > \underset{(A)}{\overset{\oplus}{C}H_3}$$

4 (a) Stability of the given cations can be understood by the following structures

$$CH_3 \rightarrow \overset{+}{C}H_2 \leftarrow CH_3; \quad \text{I}$$

+I-effect of two methyl groups stabilises the cobocation (I)

$$CH_3 \longrightarrow \overset{+}{C}H-\ddot{O}-CH_3; \quad \text{II}$$

Strong +R-effect of —CH_3 group stabilises the carbocation (II)

$$CH_3-\overset{+}{C}H-CH_2 \rightarrow OCH_3 \quad \text{III}$$

−I-effect of —OCH_3 groups destabilises the cobocation (III)

Thus, the stability of carbocation decreases in the order, II > I > III.

5 (d)

$$CH_3-C\equiv CH \xrightarrow[HgSO_4]{H_2O, H_2SO_4} \underset{\substack{\text{Intermediate}\\ \text{(Enol) }(A)}}{CH_3-\overset{OH}{\overset{|}{C}}=CH_2} \overset{\text{Tautomerisation}}{\rightleftharpoons} \underset{\text{(Acetone) }(B)}{CH_3-\overset{O}{\overset{\|}{C}}-CH_3}$$

Therefore, $A = CH_3-\overset{OH}{\overset{|}{C}}=CH_2$

$B = CH_3-\overset{O}{\overset{\|}{C}}-CH_3$

6 (d) The carbocation, which shows maximum conjugation and hyperconjugation is most stable. Thus, (d) is the most stable carbocation.

7 (c) The length of carbon-carbon single bond is always greater than that of the carbon-carbon double bond.

In III, positive charge is not in conjugation with double bond. However, chances of acquiring double bond character (of the indicated bond) is much more in I than that in case of II.

Thus, the correct order of decreasing bond length is

III > II >

III: No double bond character

II: Both the positive charge have equal tendency to impart double bond character

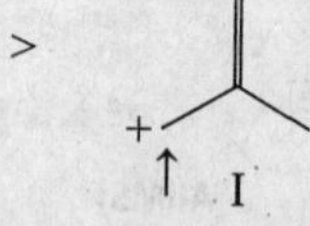

I: Readily acquire double bond character

8 (b) The stability of carbonium ions is influenced by both resonance and inductive effects. Allyl and benzyl carbonium ions can be stabilised by resonance but propyl carbonium ion ($CH_3CH_2CH_2^+$) has no resonating forms.

9 (b) The order of stability of carbocation is 3° benzylic > 2° benzylic > 3° > 2° > 1°

Thus, the correct order of stability will be

$$\underset{\text{(I)}}{Ph-\overset{Ph}{\overset{|}{\underset{+}{C}}}-CH_2CH_3} > \underset{\text{(II)}}{PhCH_2CH_2-\overset{H}{\overset{|}{\underset{+}{C}}}-Ph} > \underset{\text{(III)}}{Ph_2CH-\overset{H}{\overset{|}{\underset{H}{\underset{|}{C^+}}}}} > \underset{\text{(IV)}}{Ph-\overset{Me}{\overset{|}{\underset{Ph}{\underset{|}{C}}}}-\overset{+}{C}H_2}$$

10 (c) $\overset{+}{C}H_3$ group acts as an intermediate in the reaction of benzene with CH_3Cl in the presence of anhydrous $AlCl_3$. This reaction is called as Friedel-Craft alkylation.

11 (b) $\underset{\text{(I)}}{H_2\ddot{N}}-\underset{\text{(II)}}{\ddot{N}H}-\overset{O}{\overset{\|}{C}}-\underset{\text{(III)}}{\ddot{N}H_2} \longleftrightarrow H_2\ddot{N}-\ddot{N}H-\overset{O^-}{\overset{|}{C}}=\overset{+}{N}H_2 \longleftrightarrow H_2\ddot{N}-\overset{+}{N}H=\overset{O^-}{\overset{|}{C}}-\ddot{N}H_2$

The —NH_2 group (I) away from $-\overset{O}{\overset{\|}{C}}-$ group is not involved in resonance. Hence, its lone pair is readily available.

12 (c) 1-methylcyclohex-2-enyl cation (CH_3, ⊕)

Being 3° allyl carbocation is the most stable carbocation as the order of stability follows the trend : *tert*-allyl carbocation > 2° allyl > 1° allyl > 3° > 2° > 1°.

13 (a) Cl^- is the weakest base, therefore good leaving group and thus, CH_3COCl is most susceptible to nucleophilic attack at the carbonyl group.

14 (*b*) Anions are formed during nucleophilic reaction as

$$>C=O + HCN \xrightarrow[-H^+]{} >C<^{O^-}_{CN}$$

$$R_3C—Br \xrightarrow{S_N1} R_3C^+ + \underset{\text{Anion}}{Br^-}$$

15 (*d*) As the number of electron releasing groups ($+I$ showing groups such as $—CH_3$, $—C_2H_5$ etc), attached with positively charged carbon increases, stability of carbocations increases. Further, more the number of alkyl groups attached with C^+, more will be the hyperconjugative forms and higher will be the stability. Benzyl carbocation being resonance stabilised, is almost as stable as secondary alkyl carbocation. Therefore, the order of stability of given carbocations is as

$$\underset{\text{9 hyperconjugative structures}}{(CH_3)_3C^+} > \underset{\text{resonance stabilised}}{C_6H_5\overset{+}{C}H_2} > \underset{\text{6 hyperconjugative structure}}{(CH_3)_2\overset{+}{C}H} > \underset{\text{3 hyperconjugative structures}}{CH_3\overset{+}{C}H_2}$$

Hence, $(CH_3)_3C^+$ is the most stable carbocation among the given.

16 (*b*) Nucleophiles are the species that have at least one lone pair of electrons for donation, i.e. they can also be called Lewis bases. Among the given, BH_3 and $AlCl_3$, being electron deficient, behave like electrophiles while $\ddot{N}H_3$, due to the presence of a lone pair over N, is a nucleophile.

17 (*b*) In free radicals, the number of electrons are same as that in isolated neutral atom.

$\because$ In Cl atom, the number of electrons $= 17$

$\therefore$ In Cl free radical, the number of electrons $= 17$

18 (*d*) $2H_2SO_4 \rightleftharpoons \underset{\text{(Electrophile of aromatic sulphonation)}}{SO_3} + HSO_4^- + H_3O^+$

19 (*a*) $C_6H_5\overset{+}{C}HC_6H_5$ is most stable since the positive charge can be delocalised over both the phenyl rings.

20 (*c*) Electrophiles are electron deficient species. Hence, among the given species, nitronium ion ($\overset{+}{N}O_2$) due to lack of electrons act as electrophile while all other given species due to the presence of lone pair of electrons, act as nucleophile.

21 (*a*) Among the given free radicals, allyl free radical is stabilised by resonance, hence is more stable.

1-methylcyclohexenyl radical, CH_3 (3° allyl free radical)

and $H_2\dot{C}—CH=CH_2$

(1° allyl free radical)

both are allyl free radicals but the former is more stable due to hyperconjugation.

22 (*a*) Due te presence of 3 phenyl groups around the carbon, Ph_3C^+ is the most resonance stabilised and the order of stability is

$$Ph_3C^+ > CH_2=CH—\overset{\oplus}{C}H_2 > (CH_3)_2\overset{+}{C}H > CH_3—\overset{\oplus}{C}H_2$$

23 (*c*) Electronegativity $\propto \dfrac{1}{\text{nucleophilicity}}$

$\therefore$ CH_3^- has the highest nucleophilicity.

24 (*b*) Stability of carbanions is enhanced by

(*i*) presence of conjugation

(*ii*) presence of group exerting $-I$effect

So correct order is

$$C_6H_5\,\bar{C}H_2(Q) > H_2\bar{C}—CH=CH_2(S) > \bar{C}H_3(P) > (CH_3)_2\,\bar{C}H(R)$$

25 (*c*) Stability of carbocations is enhanced by

(i) presence of conjugation

(ii) presence of groups having $+I$ effect.

So, the correct order is

$p\text{-}OCH_3C_6H_4\overset{+}{C}H_2$ (II) $>$ $p\text{-}CH_3C_6H_4\overset{+}{C}H_2$ (IV) $>$ $C_6H_5\overset{+}{C}H_2$ (I) $>$ $p\text{-}NO_2C_6H_4\overset{+}{C}H_2$ (III)

26 (*d*) In sulphonation,

$$2H_2SO_4 \rightleftharpoons \underset{\text{Sulphur trioxide (electrophile)}}{SO_3} + H_3O^+ + HSO_4^-$$

27 (*d*) Among the alkyl free radicals, tertiary alkyl free radicals are most stable and methyl free radical is least stable.

Benzyl and allyl free radicals are resonance stabilized and are more stable than alkyl free radicals. Vinyl radical is least stable as the odd electron is present on sp^3 C-atom.

$C_6H_5\dot{C}H_2 \longleftrightarrow$ (ortho radical)$=CH_2 \longleftrightarrow$ (para radical)$=CH_2 \longleftrightarrow$ (ortho radical)$=CH_2$

Resonance in benzyl radical

$$CH_2=CH—\dot{C}H_2 \longleftrightarrow \dot{C}H_2—CH=CH_2$$

Resonance in allyl radical

$\therefore$ Order is

benzyl (IV) > allyl (III) > methyl (I) > vinyl (II).

28 (*c*) $\overset{+}{C}_2H_5$ and $CH_3—\overset{\oplus}{C}(CH_3)—CH_3$ are stabilised by hyperconjugation.

In $C_6H_5\overset{\oplus}{C}H_2$ benzyl group is resonance stabilised. In the triphenylmethyl carbonium ion, the π-electrons of all the three benzene rings are delocalised with the vacant *p*-orbital of central carbon atom. So, it is resonance stabilised.

Therefore, it is most stable among the given carbonium ions. More the number of resonating structures, more will be the stability.

29 (*b*) Species with odd number of electrons is paramagnetic in nature.

Species	Valence Electrons	Magnetic Behaviour
Carbonium ion	6	Diamagnetic
Free radical	7	Paramagnetic
Carbene	6	Diamagnetic
Nitrene	6	Diamagnetic

30 (*a*) When *s*-character increases, then electrons become more closer to the nucleus and structure becomes more stable. The stability order of carbanions is as :

$$RC\equiv\bar{C} > —\bar{C}_6H_5 > R_2C=\bar{C}H > R_3C—\bar{C}H_2$$

31 (a) The α-hydrogen atoms of acetaldehyde due to −E effect of C=O group is slightly acidic in nature. In crossed aldol condensation between formaldehyde and acetaldehyde in the first step, OH^- ion (from the base added) abstracts one of these acidic-hydrogens to form carbanion or enolate ion which is stabilised by resonance.

Slow step :

$$HO^- + H-CH_2-\overset{O}{\overset{\|}{C}}-H \longrightarrow H_2O + \overset{-}{:CH_2}-\overset{O}{\overset{\|}{C}}-H$$

32 (a) The stability of carbocation increases with increasing number of alkyl groups attached to positively charged carbon atom or with increasing number of hyperconjugative structures. Thus, order of stability is 1° carbocation < 2° carbocation < 3° carbocation.

Allyl and benzyl carbocation are stabilised by resonance.

[Structure: cyclohexenyl carbocation with CH_3 and ⊕]

Hence, it is most stable due to resonance, which is absent in other carbocations.

33 (d) Free radicals have unpaired electrons, so are neutral and very reactive species.

$$\dot{C}H_3 + \dot{C}H_3 \longrightarrow CH_3-CH_3$$

34 (b) Halogens are the most reactive elements. High reactivity is due to their low dissociation energy. More the ability of leaving group, more is the nucleophilicity. So, the correct order of nucleophilicity would be $I^- > Br^- > Cl^-$.

35 (d) $CH_3-\overset{+}{C}H-OCH_3$ is most stable due to resonance.

$$CH_3-\overset{+}{C}H-\ddot{\underset{\cdot\cdot}{O}}-CH_3 \longleftrightarrow \underset{(II)}{CH_3-CH=\overset{+}{\underset{\cdot\cdot}{O}}-CH_3}$$

Carbocation $CH_3-\overset{+}{C}H-COCH_3$(III) is least stable due to electron withdrawing nature of carbonyl group. Carbocation $CH_3-\overset{+}{C}H-CH_3$(I) is less stable than $CH_3-\overset{+}{C}H-OCH_3$ because it is stabilised only by the +I effect of the two methyl groups

$CH_3 > \overset{+}{C}H < CH_3$.

Therefore, correct order of decreasing stability is II > I > III.

36 (d) Stability order of free radical is as;

$$\underset{\text{tertiary free radical}}{(CH_3)_3\dot{C}} > \underset{\text{secondary free radical}}{(H_3C)_2\dot{C}H} > \underset{\text{primary free radical}}{CH_3-\dot{C}H_2} > \underset{\text{methyl free radical}}{\dot{C}H_3}$$

Greater the number of alkyl groups attached to the carbon atom carrying the odd electrons, greater is the delocalisation of odd electron and hence, more stable is the free radical.

37 (a) The correct order for stability of carbocation is II < I < III < IV.

$$\underset{\text{Resonance and more +I effect}}{H_3C\rightarrow\overset{\oplus}{C}(C_6H_5)\leftarrow CH_3} > \underset{\text{Resonance and less +I effect}}{H-\overset{+}{C}(C_6H_5)\leftarrow CH_3} > \underset{\text{Only resonance}}{C_6H_5\overset{+}{C}H_2} > \underset{\text{No resonance}}{C_6H_5CH_2\overset{+}{C}H_2}$$

38 (a) [Structure: arenium ion with NO_2, ⊕, H and X]

is most stable because electron withdrawing group (−I group) $-NO_2$ is attached to it and positive charge of arenium ion do not appear on to the carbon directly attached to NO_2 group.

39 (d) The stability of alkyl free radicals is not influenced by inductive effect because they have no charge (difference from carbonium and carbanions). So, they are stabilised by hyperconjugation (no bond resonance).

The relative order of stability of given free radicals is,

allyl > *tert*. > vinyl.

40 (a) Nucleophile is a species which has high electron density in it and it attack on the site of less electron density. More the electron density on a species better nucleophile it is. Nucleophiles may be neutral (but with an atom with lone pairs of electron) or it can be negatively charged. C_2H_5SH is the weakest acid so it readily loses a proton to form strong conjugate base $C_2H_5S^-$ which is a strong nucleophile

(+I effect of C_2H_5 group).

41 (b) Electron withdrawing groups like $-NO_2$, $-X$ etc., decrease the stability of carbonium ion.

So, the stability order is :

Cl_3C^+ (I) < Cl_2CH^+ (II) < $ClCH_2^+$ (III) < CH_3^+(IV)

42 (b) The species which are electron deficient and accept a pair of electron are called electrophiles.

Hence, SO_3 is an electrophile as it contains an electron deficient centre. While H_2O, NH_3 and $R-O-R$ are nucleophiles.

Topic 8

Types of Reaction Mechanism

1 Which of the following compounds shall not produce propene by reaction with HBr followed by elimination or only direct elimination reaction? **[NEET]**

(a) H_2C-CH_2 / C / H_2 (cyclopropane) (b) $H_3C-\overset{H_2}{C}-CH_2OH$

(c) $H_2C=C=O$ (d) $H_3C-\overset{H_2}{C}-CH_2Br$

2014

2 Which one is most reactive towards nucleophilic addition reaction? **[CBSE AIPMT]**

(a) C_6H_5-CHO (b) $C_6H_5-COCH_3$

(c) p-$CH_3C_6H_4-CHO$ (d) p-$NO_2C_6H_4-CHO$

3 An incorrect statement with respect to S_N1 and S_N2 mechanisms for alkyl halide is **[KCET]**

(a) A strong nucleophile in an aprotic solvent increases the rate or favours S_N2 reaction
(b) Competing reaction for an S_N2 reaction is rearrangement
(c) S_N1 reaction can be catalysed by some Lewis acids
(d) A weak nucleophile and a protic solvent increases the rate or favours S_N1 reaction

4 The boiling points of four saturated hydrocarbons are given below which boiling point suggests maximum number of carbon atoms in its molecule? **[AIIMS]**

(a) $-162°C$ (b) $-88.6°C$ (c) $-0.5°C$ (d) $-42.2°C$

2012

5 Among the following compounds the one that is most reactive toward electrophilic nitration is **[CBSE AIPMT]**

(a) benzoic acid (b) nitrobenzene
(c) toluene (d) benzene

6 Consider the reaction,

$RCHO + NH_2NH_2 \longrightarrow RCH=N-NH_2.$

What type of reaction is it? **[CBSE AIPMT]**

(a) Electrophilic addition elimination reaction
(b) Free radical addition elimination reaction
(c) Electrophilic substitution elimination reaction
(d) Nucleophilic addition elimination reaction.

7 Which of the following does not show S_N2 reaction?

(a) Vinylic halide $>C=CH-X$ **[AIIMS]**
(b) Allyl chloride $CH_2=CHCH_2Cl$
(c) Chlorobenzene
(d) All of the above

8 Which of the following applies in the reaction? **[AIIMS]**

$$CH_3CHBrCH_2CH_3 \xrightarrow{\text{Alc. KOH}} ?$$

I. $CH_3CH=CHCH_3$ major product +
II. $CH_2=CHCH_2CH_3$ minor product

(a) Hofmann's rule
(b) Saytzeff's rule
(c) Kharasch effect
(d) Markovnikoff's rule

9 Under identical conditions, S_N1 reaction will occur most efficient with **[WB JEE]**

(a) *tert*-butyl chloride
(b) 1-chlorobutane
(c) 2-methyl-1-chloropropane
(d) 2-chlorobutane

10 The following reaction,

$$CH_3-\underset{CH_3}{\overset{H}{C}}-\underset{X}{\overset{CH_3}{C}}-CH_3 \xrightarrow[-H_2O,\ -KBr]{\text{Alcoholic KOH}} CH_3-\underset{CH_3}{C}=\overset{CH_3}{C}-CH_3$$

is an example of **[AMU]**

(a) α-elimination
(b) β-elimination
(c) Hofmann elimination
(d) None of these

11 Which one of the following undergoes S_N2 reaction faster? **[AMU]**

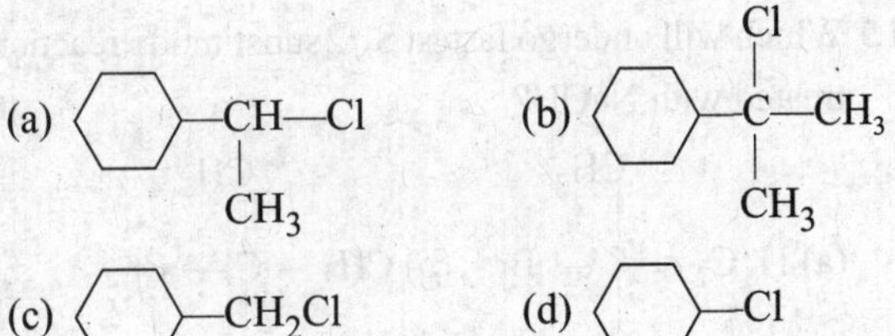

2011

12 Which of the following is the most reactive towards electrophilic reagent? **[CBSE AIPMT]**

(a) benzene ring with CH_3 and CH_2OH (ortho) (b) benzene ring with CH_3 and OCH_3 (ortho)

(c) benzene ring with CH_3 and OH (ortho) (d) benzene ring with CH_3 and $NHCOCH_3$ (ortho)

13 Which one is a nucleophilic substitution reaction among the following? **[CBSE AIPMT]**

(a) $CH_3CHO + HCN \longrightarrow CH_3CH(OH)CN$

(b) $CH_3-CH=CH_2 + H_2O \xrightarrow{H^+} CH_3-CH(OH)-CH_3$

(c) $RCHO + R'MgX \longrightarrow R-CH(OH)-R'$

(d) $CH_3-CH_2-CH(CH_3)-CH_2Br + NH_3 \longrightarrow CH_3-CH_2-CH(CH_3)-CH_2NH_2$

14 The compound that does not undergo hydrolysis by S_N1 mechanism is **[Kerala CEE]**

(a) $CH_2=CHCH_2Cl$
(b) C_6H_5Cl
(c) $C_6H_5CH_2Cl$
(d) $C_6H_5CH(CH_3)Cl$
(e) $C_6H_5CH(C_6H_5)Cl$

15 Which one of the following alkylbromides undergoes most rapid solvolysis in methanol solution to give corresponding methyl ether? **[DUMET]**

(a) $(CH_3)_2C=CH-CH_2-Br$ (b) $(CH_3)_2CH-CH_2-CH_2-Br$

(c) $(CH_3)_2CH-CH_2-CH(CH_3)-Br$ (d) 1-bromo-1,2-dimethylcyclopentane (Br on ring carbon)

16 Which will undergo fastest S_N2 substitution reaction when treated with NaOH? **[DUMET]**

(a) $H_5C_2-C(CH_3)(H)-Br$ (b) $CH_3-C(CH_3)(CH_3)-Br$

(c) $H-C(CH_3)(C_2H_5)-Br$ (d) $H-C(H)(Br)-CH_2-CH_2-CH_3$

17 Which of the following is nucleophilic addition reaction? **[Guj CET]**

(a) Hydrolysis of ethyl chloride by NaOH
(b) Purification of acetaldehyde by $NaHSO_3$
(c) Alkylation of anisole
(d) Decarboxylation of acetic acid

2011

18 The correct order of increasing reactivity of C—X bond towards nucleophile in the following compound is **[CBSE AIPMT]**

(I) C_6H_5X (II) 2,4-dinitrophenyl-X (X with NO_2 at ortho and para) (III) $(CH_3)_3C-X$ (IV) $(CH_3)_2CH-X$

(a) III < II < I < IV (b) I < II < IV < III
(c) II < III < I < IV (d) IV < III < I < II

19 Ethanolic KOH gives **[MHT CET]**

(a) dehalogenation reactions
(b) dehydrogenation reactions
(c) dehydrohalogenation reactions
(d) substitution reactions

20 The S_N1 reactivity of the following halides will be in the order **[Manipal]**

I. $(CH_3)_3CBr$ II. $(C_6H_5)_2CHBr$
III. $(C_6H_5)_2C(CH_3)Br$ IV. $(CH_3)_2CHBr$
V. C_2H_5Br

Codes

(a) II > I > III > V > IV (b) I > III > V > II > IV
(c) V > I > II > IV > III (d) III > II > I > IV > V

21 S_N1 reaction of alkyl halides leads to **[Manipal]**

(a) retention of configuration (b) racemisation
(c) inversion of configuration (d) None of the above

22 In the following halogen compounds, which compound undergoes fastest S_N1 reaction? **[RPMT]**

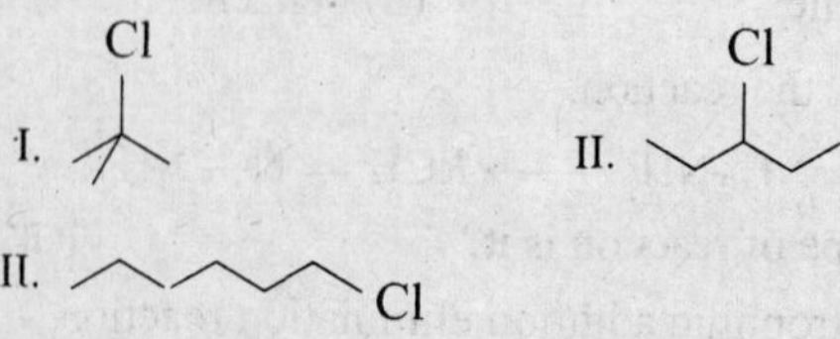

(a) I (b) II
(c) III (d) None of these

23 The following reaction is described as **[CMC]**

$$CH_3(CH_2)_5(H_3C)(H)C—Br \xrightarrow{OH^-} HO—C(H)(CH_3)(CH_2)_5CH_3$$

(a) S_E2 (b) S_N2 (c) S_N1 (d) S_N0

24 Assertion (A) In S_N1 reaction on 2-bromobutane, product formed is a racemic mixture.

Reason (R) Carbocation is the intermediate of S_N1 reaction. **[VMMC]**

(a) Both A and R are correct and R is the correct explanation of A
(b) Both A and R are correct but R is not the correct explanation of A
(c) A is correct but R is incorrect
(d) Both A and R are incorrect

2009

25 Which of the following reactions is an example of nucleophilic substitution reaction? **[CBSE AIPMT]**

(a) $RX + KOH \longrightarrow ROH + KX$
(b) $2RX + 2Na \longrightarrow R—R + 2NaX$
(c) $RX + H_2 \longrightarrow RH + HX$
(d) $RX + Mg \longrightarrow RMgX$

26 The product of which of the following reactions has the highest ease to undergo electrophilic substitution? **[AIIMS]**

(a) $C_6H_5COCl \xrightarrow{Pd/BaSO_4}$ (b) $C_6H_6 \xrightarrow{Cl_2/FeCl_3}$
(c) $C_6H_6 \xrightarrow{CH_3Cl/\text{Anhy. }AlCl_3}$ (d) $C_2H_5OH \xrightarrow{\text{Conc. }H_2SO_4}$

27 Find the major product (considering E as an electrophile) when the following substrate is subjected to electrophilic aromatic substitution. **[OJEE]**

$$C_6H_5—\overset{O}{\overset{\|}{C}}—O—C_6H_5$$

(a) $C_6H_5—CO—O—C_6H_4$ (E at meta position of the O-bonded ring)
(b) $C_6H_4(E)—CO—O—C_6H_5$ (E at meta position of the C=O-bonded ring)
(c) $C_6H_5—CO—O—C_6H_4—E$ (E at para position)
(d) $C_6H_5—CO—O—C_6H_4$ (E at ortho position of the O-bonded ring)

28 Correct order of reactivity towards electrophilic substitution on the following substrate is **[OJEE]**

I. C_6H_5Cl II. $C_6H_5CH_3$ III. $C_6H_5NO_2$ IV. C_6H_6

(a) I > IV > II > III (b) II > I > III > IV
(c) II > IV > I > III (d) I > II > III > IV

29 Order of reactivity towards nucleophilic substitution reaction of the compounds **[AMU]**

I. 4-Cl-C_6H_4-NMe_2 (Cl with NMe_2 para) II. 4-Cl-C_6H_4-NO_2 (Cl with NO_2 para) III. Cl with NO_2 at ortho and para positions IV. Cl with O_2N, NO_2 at both ortho positions and NO_2 at para position

(a) I > II > III > IV (b) II > I > III > IV
(c) IV > III > II > I (d) III > IV > II > I

2008

30 Which one of the following is the most reactive towards electrophilic attack? **[CBSE AIPMT]**

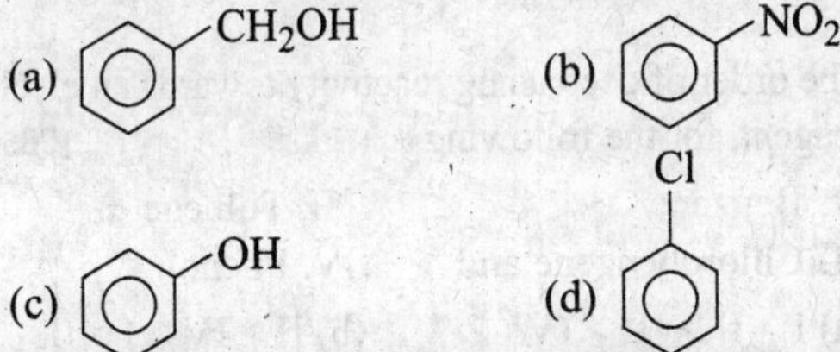

31 In S_N2 substitution reaction of the type

$$R—Br + Cl^- \xrightarrow{DMF} R—Cl + Br^-$$

Which one of the following has the highest relative rate? **[CBSE AIPMT]**

(a) $CH_3—CH_2—CH_2Br$ (b) $CH_3—CH(CH_3)—CH_2Br$
(c) $CH_3—C(CH_3)_2—CH_2Br$ (d) CH_3CH_2Br

32 The hydrolysis of 2-bromo-3-methylbutane by S_N1 mechanism gives mainly **[Kerala CEE]**

(a) 3-methyl-2-butanol (b) 2-methyl-2-butanol
(c) 2,2-dimethyl-1-propanol (d) 2-methyl-1-butanol
(e) 1-pentanol

33 Dehydration of alcohol is an example of which type of reaction? **[J&K CET]**

(a) Substitution (b) Elimination
(c) Addition (d) Rearrangement

34 Conversion of chlorobenzene to phenol involves **[J&K CET]**
(a) electrophilic substitution
(b) nucleophilic substitution
(c) free radical substitution
(d) electrophilic addition

35 Most reactive compound towards electrophilic substitution is **[DUMET]**

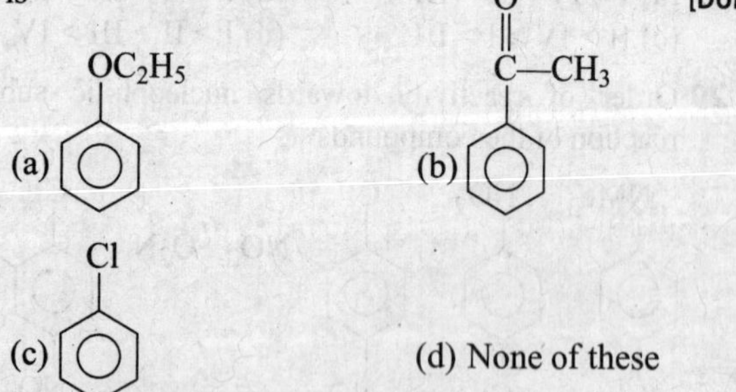

(d) None of these

36 The formation of cyanohydrin from acetone is which type of reaction? **[Guj CET]**
(a) Electrophilic substitution reaction
(b) Electrophilic addition reaction
(c) Nucleophilic addition reaction
(d) Nucleophilic substitution reaction

2007

37 The order of decreasing reactivity towards an electrophilic reagent, for the following **[CBSE AIPMT]**
I. Benzene II. Toluene
III. Chlorobenzene and IV. Phenol
(a) I > II > III > IV (b) II > IV > I > III
(c) IV > III > II > I (d) IV > II > I > III

38 Williamson's synthesis involves **[MHT CET]**
(a) S_N1 mechanism (b) nucleophilic addition
(c) S_N2 mechanism (d) S_E mechanism

39 Which of the following is least reactive in nucleophilic substitution reaction? **[Manipal]**
(a) $(CH_3)_3C-Cl$ (b) $CH_2{=}CHCl$
(c) CH_3CH_2Cl (d) $CH_2{=}CHCH_2Cl$

2006

40 Assertion (A) The presence of nitro group facilitates nucleophilic substitution reactions in aryl halides.
Reason (R) The intermediate carbanion is stabilised due to the presence of nitro group. **[AIIMS]**
(a) Both A and R are correct and R is the correct explanation of A
(b) Both A and R are correct but R is not the correct explanation of R
(c) A is correct but R is incorrect
(d) Both A and R are incorrect

41 *neo*-pentyl bromide undergoes dehydrohalogenation to give alkene even though it has no β-hydrogen. This is due to **[Kerala CEE]**
(a) E_2 mechanism
(b) E_1 mechanism
(c) due to rearrangement of carbocation by E_1 mechanism
(d) E_1CB mechanism
(e) Hofmann elmination

42 In the solvolysis of 3-methyl-3-bromo hexane, which of the following statements is not correct? **[Kerala CEE]**
(a) It involves carbocation intermediate
(b) The intermediate involves sp^2 carbon
(c) Polar solvents accelerates the reaction
(d) The rate of the reaction depends upon 3-methyl-3-bromo hexane concentration
(e) It involves inversion of configuration

2005

43 Assertion (A) Rate of hydrolysis of methyl chloride to methanol is higher in DMF than in water.
Reason (R) Hydrolysis of methyl chloride follows second order kinetics. **[AIIMS]**
(a) Both A and R are correct and R is the correct explanation of A
(b) Both A and R are correct but R is not the correct explanation of A
(c) A is correct, but R is incorrect
(d) Both A and R are incorrect

44 Which gives nucleophilic addition most easily? **[UP CPMT]**
(a) CH_3CHO (b) CH_3CH_2CHO
(c) $CH_3-\underset{\displaystyle CH_3}{\underset{|}{C}}HCHO$ (d) HCHO

45 Consider the parallel reactions in the electrophilic addition of HBr to propene *via* the alternative pathways shown below

$$\text{Propene + HBr} \xrightarrow[\text{Path 2 (without peroxide)}]{\text{Path 1 (with peroxide)}} \underset{(A)}{\text{1-bromopropane}} + \underset{(B)}{\text{2-bromopropane}}$$

Identify the wrong statement with reference to the above **[Kerala CEE]**
(a) Path 1 has predominance of (*A*) over (*B*)
(b) Path 2 has predominance of (*B*) over (*A*)
(c) Path 1 is in accordance with anti-Markovnikoff's rule
(d) Path 2 follows Markovnikov's rule
(e) Both the paths afford 50% yield of (*A*) and (*B*)

46 Which of the following compound does not show anti-Markovnikov's addition? **[BCECE]**
(a) Propene (b) 1-butene (c) 2-butene (d) 2-pentene

Answers

1 (c)	2 (d)	3 (b)	4 (c)	5 (c)	6 (d)	7 (d)	8 (b)	9 (a)	10 (b)
11 (c)	12 (c)	13 (d)	14 (b)	15 (a)	16 (d)	17 (b)	18 (b)	19 (c)	20 (d)
21 (b)	22 (a)	23 (b)	24 (a)	25 (a)	26 (c)	27 (c)	28 (c)	29 (c)	30 (c)
31 (d)	32 (b)	33 (b)	34 (b)	35 (a)	36 (c)	37 (d)	38 (c)	39 (b)	40 (a)
41 (b)	42 (e)	43 (a)	44 (d)	45 (e)	46 (c)				

Explanations

1 (c) $H_2C{=}C{=}O$ will not produce propene by reaction with HBr followed by elimination or only direct elimination reaction.

The reaction of compounds are as follows :

(a) $H_2C{-}CH_2$ (cyclopropane, CH_2) $\xrightarrow{HBr} CH_3CH_2CH_2Br \xrightarrow{\text{Elimination}} H_3CCH{=}CH_2$

(b) $CH_3CH_2CH_2OH \xrightarrow{HBr} CH_3CH_2CH_2Br \xrightarrow{\text{Elimination}} CH_3{-}CH{=}CH_2$

(c) $H_2C{=}C{=}O \xrightarrow{HBr} H_2C{=}C(Br){-}OH \rightleftharpoons H_3C{-}C(O^{\ominus}){-}Br$

(Enol form) (Keto form)

(d) $CH_3CH_2CH_2Br \xrightarrow{\text{Elimination}} CH_3CH{=}CH_2$

2 (d) Reactivity of carbonyl compounds towards nucleophilic addition reactions depends on the presence of substituted group. Electron withdrawing $(-I, -M)$ groups increases reactivity towards nucleophilic addition reactions.

p-nitrobenzaldehyde $(-I, -M)$ > benzaldehyde > p-methylbenzaldehyde (CH_3, $(+I)$) > acetophenone ($C(=O){-}CH_3$, $(+R)$)

3 (b) S_N1 reaction occurs through the formation of carbocation as intermediate. Hence, rearrangement occur in S_N1 reaction and not in S_N2 reaction. S_N1 reaction is favoured in presence of a polar protic solvent and a weak nucleophile.

A strong nucleophile in an aprotic solvent increases the rate of S_N2 reaction. Hence, option (b) is incorrect.

4 (c) Boiling point of any hydrocarbon is proportional to the number of carbon atoms. Hence, compound with boiling point $-0.5°C$ has maximum number of C-atoms and compound with boiling point $-162°C$ has minimum number of C-atoms.

5 (c) Presence of electron releasing group like $-R$, $-OH$ etc increases the electron density at o/p position and thus, makes the benzene ring more reactive (at o/p positions) towards electrophilic substitution. On the other hand, electron withdrawing groups like $-COOH$, $-NO_2$ etc, if present reduces electron density and thus, reduces the activity of benzene nucleus towards electrophile.

Hence, the order of the given compounds towards electrophilic nitration is

Nitro benzene (NO_2) < Benzoic acid ($COOH$) < Benzene < Toluene (CH_3—electron releasing group)

Thus, toluene is most reactive towards electrophilic nitration.

6 (d) $RCHO + \ddot{N}H_2\ddot{N}H_2 \longrightarrow RCH{=}N{-}NH_2 + H_2O.$

In this reaction, $-NH_2$ acts as nucleophilic species which adds on carbon. Therefore, this is the case of nucleophilic addition reaction. Simultaneously, a mole of H_2O is also eliminataed. Therefore, overall this reaction is nucleophilic addition elimination reaction.

7 (d) Allyl chloride show formation of very stable $CH_2{=}CH{-}\overset{+}{C}H_2$ ion and rest two also have partial double bond character in their $C{-}X$ bond. Thus, all the given compounds do not undergo S_N2 reaction.

8 (b) $CH_3{-}CH(Br){-}CH_2CH_3 \xrightarrow{\text{Alc. KOH}}$

$CH_3CH{=}CHCH_3$ (Major) $+ CH_2{=}CH{-}CH_2CH_3$ (Minor)

The reaction is governed by Saytzeff's rule. According to this rule, the elimination of β-hydrogen atom takes place from the carbon having the less number of H-atoms or in other words, a stable alkene is to be formed (more substituted alkene is more stable).

9 (a) S_N1 reaction is most effective in 3° carbon because of higher stability of 3° carbocation.

$(CH_3)_3{-}C{-}Cl$, tert-butyl chloride (3°); $CH_3CH_2CH_2Cl$, 1-chlorobutane (1°)

$Cl{-}CH_2{-}CH(CH_3){-}CH_3$, 2-methyl-1-chloropropane (1°); $CH_3CH_2CH(Cl){-}CH_3$, 2-chlorobutane (2°)

Thus option (a) is correct.

10 (b) $CH_3{-}C^{\beta}H(CH_3){-}C^{\alpha}X(CH_3){-}CH_3 \xrightarrow[-H_2O,\,-KBr]{\text{Alc. KOH}} CH_3{-}C(CH_3){=}C(CH_3){-}CH_3$

When a haloalkane with β-hydrogen atom is heated with alc. KOH solution, there is elimination of hydrogen atom from β-carbon and a halogen atom from α-carbon atom (β-elimination).

11 (c) (cyclohexyl)$-CH_2Cl$ is a primary halide and therefore undergoes faster S_N2 reaction.

12 (c) + R-effect of OH > OCH_3

Hence, [2-methylphenol structure: benzene ring with CH_3 and OH on adjacent carbons]

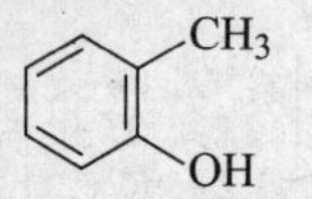

2-methylphenol is more reactive towards electrophilic reagent.

13 (d) $CH_3-CH_2-\underset{}{\overset{CH_3}{\overset{|}{C}}}H-CH_2Br + NH_3 \longrightarrow$

$$CH_3-CH_2-\overset{CH_3}{\overset{|}{C}}H-CH_2NH_2$$

It is an example of nucleophilic substitution reaction.

14 (b) In S_N1 reaction, formation of carbocation takes place. As in C_6H_5Cl, the C — Cl bond acquires double bond character thus, carbocation does not form easily. Hence, it doesn't undergo hydrolysis by S_N1 mechanism. Thus, option 'b' is correct.

15 (a) 1-bromo-3-methylbut-2-ene reacts most readily by S_N1 because the bromine is allylic. CH_3OH is a weak nucleophile and weak nucleophile favours S_N1.

$$(CH_3)_2C{=}CH{-}CH_2Br + CH_3OH \longrightarrow (H_3C)_2C{=}CH{-}CH_2OCH_3$$

16 (d) Primary alkyl halides undergo bimolecular nucleophilic substitution most readily. Thus, $CH_3CH_2CH_2CH_2Br$ undergoes fastest S_N2 substitution reaction with NaOH.

17 (b) Addition of sodium hydrogen sulphite to acetaldehyde is an example of nucleophilic addition reaction.

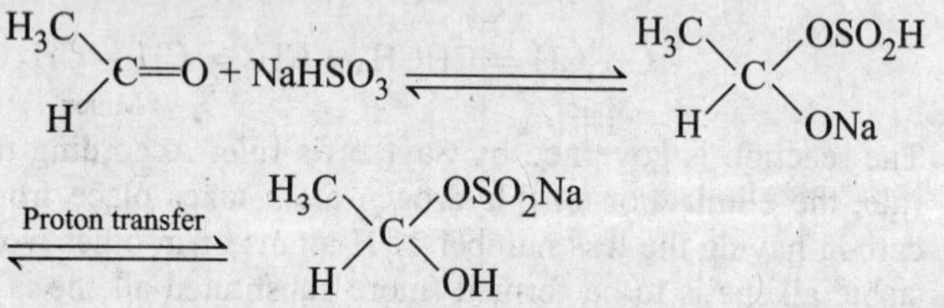

$$\begin{matrix}H_3C\\H\end{matrix}\!\!>C{=}O + NaHSO_3 \rightleftharpoons \begin{matrix}H_3C\\H\end{matrix}\!\!>C<\!\!\begin{matrix}OSO_2H\\ONa\end{matrix} \xrightleftharpoons{\text{Proton transfer}} \begin{matrix}H_3C\\H\end{matrix}\!\!>C<\!\!\begin{matrix}OSO_2Na\\OH\end{matrix}$$

Bisulphite addition compound (crystalline)

18 (b) Alkyl halides (3° > 2°) are more reactive than aryl halides towards nucleophilic substitution. Among I and II compounds, II has more reactivity due to $-I$ effect of two —NO_2 groups.

Hence, the correct order is

I < II < IV < III

19 (c) Ethanolic KOH removes hydrogen and halogen atoms from a haloalkane, thus it is a dehydrohalogenating reagent and gives the same type of reactions.

20 (d) In S_N1 (unimolecular nucleophilic substitution) reactions,

$$\text{Rate} \propto [\text{substrate}]$$

Rate determining step is the formation of carbocation and depends on the stability of carbocation formed. The stability of carbocations follow the order

$$(C_6H_5)_2C^+(CH_3) > (C_6H_5)_2\overset{+}{C}H > (CH_3)_3C^+ > (CH_3)_2\overset{+}{C}H > CH_3CH_2^+$$

Thus, the order of reactivity towards S_N1 reaction is

(III) > (II) > (I) > (IV) > (V).

21 (b) S_N1 reactions involve racemisation, i.e. when an optically active *d* (act as reactant) form is subjected to S_N1 reaction, the product obtained is a racemic mixture of *d* and *l* (forms).

22 (a) The order of reactivity depends upon the stability of carbocation. Greater the stability of the carbocation, faster will be the rate of reaction. Hence, the order of reactivity will be
3° alkyl halide > 2° alkyl halide > 1° alkyl halide > methyl halide.

23 (b)

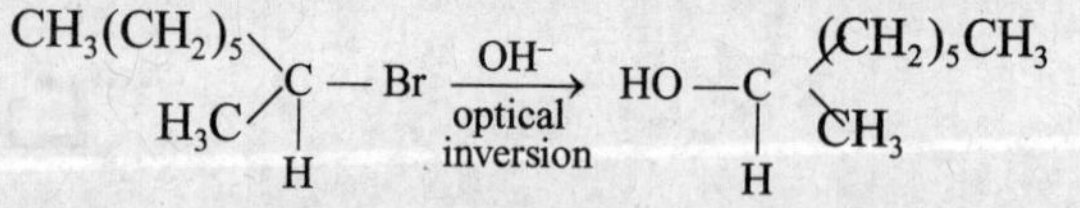

$$\begin{matrix}CH_3(CH_2)_5\\H_3C\end{matrix}\!\!>\underset{H}{\overset{}{C}}-Br \xrightarrow[\text{optical inversion}]{OH^-} HO-\underset{H}{C}<\!\!\begin{matrix}(CH_2)_5CH_3\\CH_3\end{matrix}$$

In this reactions, inversion takes place. Hence, it is an example of S_N2 reaction. In this mechanism, the attack of OH^- ion takes place from the back side, while the Br^- ion leaves from the front side.

24 (a) 2-bromobutane is an optically active alkyl halide. When it undergoes S_N1 reaction, the intermediate carbocation is formed which is a planar species, therefore the attack of nucleophile can take place with equal ease from both the faces.

Thus, the product formed is a racemic mixture (±) which is optically inactive. Hence, Reason is the correct explanation of Assertion.

25 (a) Reaction of alkyl halide with aqueous KOH is an example of nucleophilic substitution reaction.

$$R\boxed{X + K^+}\,OH^- \longrightarrow ROH + KX$$

Here, OH^- ion acts as a nucleophile and halide ion acts as a leaving group.

26 (c) Product of reaction given in option (c) is, as

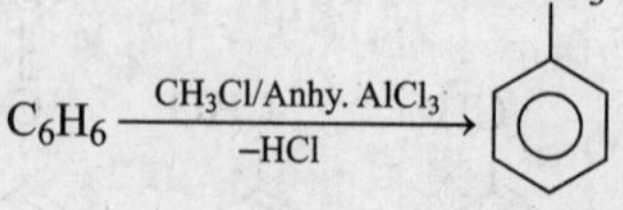

$$C_6H_6 \xrightarrow[-HCl]{CH_3Cl/\text{Anhy. }AlCl_3} C_6H_5CH_3$$

Toluene

— CH_3 group present in toluene, activate the benzene nucleus towards electrophilic substitution due to its electron releasing nature.

27 (c)

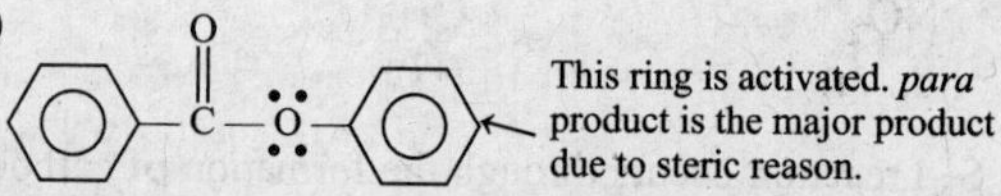

$$C_6H_5-\overset{O}{\overset{\|}{C}}-\ddot{O}-C_6H_5$$

This ring is activated. *para* product is the major product due to steric reason.

Hence, option (c) is the correct answer.

28 (c) —Cl and — NO_2 both are deactivating groups but —NO_2 is more deactivating than — Cl and —CH_3 is an activating group. So, correct order is II > IV > I > III.

29 (c) Nucleophile will preferentially attack on the compound which has lower electron density. Out of the given options, (IV) has four electron withdrawing groups and is the most preferred substrate. As, the number of electrons withdrawing groups decreases or the number of electron donating groups increases, the electron density of the compound increases. Hence, the reactivity towards nucleophilic substitution reaction decreases.

So, the order is (IV) > (III) > (II) > (I)

30 (c) Electron releasing groups stabilise the intermediate cation whereas electron withdrawing groups destabilise it.

The order of stability of electron withdrawing group is:

$NO_2 > Cl > C_6H_5 > OH$.

Hence, (phenol, C_6H_5OH) is most reactive towards electrophilic substitution because —OH group least destabilise the carbocation. Further, —OH group is strongly activating group while $—NO_2$ and —Cl are deactivating groups.

31 (*d*) The relative reactivity of alkyl halides toward S_N2 reactions is as follows :

Primary > secondary > tertiary

CH_3CH_2Br is the least hindered, hence it has the highest relative rate towards S_N2 reaction.

32 (*b*)
$$CH_3-\underset{\underset{Br}{|}}{CH}-\underset{\underset{CH_3}{|}}{CH}-CH_3 \xrightarrow[-HBr]{H^+} CH_3-\overset{\oplus}{CH}-\underset{\underset{CH_3}{|}}{\overset{\overset{H}{|}}{C}}-CH_3 \quad \text{2° carbocation}$$
$$\xrightarrow{H^+ \text{ rearrangement}} CH_3-CH_2-\underset{\underset{CH_3}{|}}{\overset{\oplus}{C}}-CH_3 \quad \text{3° (carbocation) (more stable)}$$
$$\xrightarrow{OH^-} \overset{4}{CH_3}-\overset{3}{CH_2}-\underset{\underset{OH}{|}}{\overset{\overset{CH_3}{|}}{\overset{2}{C}}}-CH_3 \quad \text{2-methyl-2-butanol}$$

33 (*b*) Dehydration of alcohol involves the loss of two atoms or groups from the adjacent carbon atoms, hence it is an example of β-elimination reaction.

34 (*b*)
$$\text{Chlorobenzene } (C_6H_5Cl) \xrightarrow{NaOH} \text{Phenol } (C_6H_5OH)$$

In this process one group is replaced by other, hence it is a substitution process and both the leaving and attacking groups are nucleophilic, therefore it is an example of nucleophilic substitution reaction.

35 (*a*) During electrophilic substitution, the substituent already present in the benzene ring directs the incoming group either to *ortho* and *para* or to *meta* position and the reaction may be faster or slower as compared to benzene. All groups which activate the ring, i.e. increase the reaction rate are *o,p*-directing.

Activating groups increase the electron density in the benzene nucleus either due to inductive effect (+*I* effect) or resonance or both. Therefore, electrophile will attack on benzene nucleus easily.

Halogens are exceptions in the sense that they deactivate the ring, but are *o,p*-directing.

Hence, $—OC_2H_5$ is the most activating group while —Cl, $—COCH_3$ are deactivating groups.

36 (*c*) Ketone undergoes nucleophilic addition reaction because, if nucleophiles attack first followed by electrophiles, anion is formed as intermediate and if electrophiles attack first followed by nucleophiles, cation is formed as intermediate. The stability of anion is more than that of cation.

So, probable mechanism will be,

$$\overset{+\delta}{>C}=\overset{-\delta}{O} + \ddot{N}u \longrightarrow >\underset{\underset{Nu}{|}}{C}-\ddot{O} + E^+ \longrightarrow >\overset{\overset{Nu}{|}}{C}-OE$$
Anion → Product

e.g.
$$(H_3C)_2\overset{+\delta}{C}=\overset{-\delta}{O} + \ddot{C}N \longrightarrow (H_3C)_2\overset{+\delta}{C}(CN)-\ddot{O} \xrightarrow[\text{from } H_2O \text{ or } HCN]{H^+} (H_3C)_2C(OH)(CN)$$
Cyanohydrin

37 (*d*) Benzene having any activating group i.e. OH, *R*, etc. undergoes electrophilic substitution very easily as compared to benzene itself. Thus, toluene ($C_6H_5CH_3$), phenol (C_6H_5OH) undergo electrophilic substitution very readily than benzene. Chlorine with +*E* and +*M* effect deactivates the ring due to strong –*I* effect. So, it is difficult to carry out the substitution in chlorobenzene than in benzene. Thus the correct order is,

$$\underset{IV}{\text{phenol}} > \underset{II}{\text{toluene}} > \underset{I}{\text{benzene}} > \underset{III}{\text{chlorobenzene}}$$

38 (*c*) When sodium or potassium alkoxide is heated with an alkyl halide to give ether, this reaction is known as Williamson's synthesis.

$$RONa + R'X \longrightarrow R-O-R' + NaX$$

This is an example of nucleophilic substitution and follow S_N2 mechanism.

39 (*b*) Chlorine of vinyl chloride ($CH_2=CHCl$) is non-reactive (less reactive) towards nucleophile in nucleophilic substitution reaction because it shows the following resonating structures due to +*M*-effect of — Cl atom.

$$\underset{I}{CH_2=CH-\ddot{\underset{..}{Cl}}:} \longleftrightarrow \underset{II}{\overset{\delta-}{CH_2}-CH=\overset{\delta+}{Cl}}$$

In structure II, Cl-atom has positive charge and partial double bond character with C of vinyl group, so it is more strongly attracted towards the nucleus and it does not get replaced by nucleophile in S_N reaction.

40 (*a*) Nitro group is an electron-withdrawing group (–*I* groups). It stabilises the carbanion because it disperses the negative charge on the carbon by attracting electrons or negative charge. So, both the statements are true and Reason is the correct explanation.

41 (*b*) Neopentyl bromide undergoes dehydrohalogenation to give alkene even through it has no β-hydrogen atom. This is due to rearrangement of carbocation by E_1 mechanism.

$$CH_3-\underset{\underset{CH_3}{|}}{\overset{\overset{CH_3}{|}}{C}}-CH_2Br \xrightarrow{-Br^-} CH_3-\underset{\underset{CH_3}{|}}{\overset{\overset{CH_3}{|}}{C}}-\overset{\oplus}{CH_2} \xrightarrow{\text{Rearrangement}}$$

$$\underset{\text{2-methyl but-2-ene}}{CH_3-\overset{\overset{CH_3}{|}}{C}=CH\cdot CH_3} + H_2O \xleftarrow{OH^-} CH_3-\overset{\overset{CH_3}{|}}{\underset{+}{C}}-\underset{\underset{H}{|}}{CH}-CH_3 \quad OH^-$$

42 (*e*) $H_3C-H_2C-\overset{*}{C}(CH_3)(Br)-CH_2-CH_2-CH_3$

3-methyl 3-bromohexane is an optically active alkyl halide. In case of optically active alkyl halides, S_N1 reactions are accompanied by racemisation. Rest of the statements are correct.

43 (*a*) Primary alkyl halide (here CH_3Cl) undergo S_N2 mechanism and not S_N1 mechanism. Hence, hydrolysis of CH_3Cl is favoured by non-polar medium or polar non-protic solvent (in which proton is not generated) like DMF whereas S_N1 mechanism are favoured by polar solvents like water.

44 (*d*) Aldehydes undergo nucleophilic addition reaction. Among carbonyl compounds, reactivity decreases with increase in number of alkyl groups as these groups decrease the polarity of $>C=O$ bond.

(a) $CH_3-\overset{O}{\overset{\|}{C}}-H$ (b) $CH_3-CH_2-\overset{O}{\overset{\|}{C}}-H$

(c) $CH_3-CH(CH_3)-\overset{O}{\overset{\|}{C}}-H$ (d) $H-\overset{O}{\overset{\|}{C}}-H$

∵ Formaldehyde (HCHO) has least (no.) number of alkyl groups.
∴ It gives nucleophilic addition most easily.

45 (*e*) $CH_2=CH-CH_3 + HBr$

Path I with peroxide → $CH_3-CH_2-CH_2Br$ (1-bromo propane)

Path II without peroxide → $CH_3-CH(Br)-CH_3$ (2-bromo propane)

In the above reaction, all the statements given in the question are correct except that both the paths afford 50% yield of (*A*) and (*B*). In path I, *A* is the major product while in path II, *B* is the major product.

46 (*c*) Anti-Markownikoff's addition is shown when unsymmetrical reagent reacts with unsymmetrical double or triple bond containing compound.

$CH_3-CH=CH_2$ Propene (a) $CH_3-CH_2-CH=CH_2$ But-1-ene (b)

$CH_3-CH=CH-CH_3$ But-2-ene (c) $CH_3-CH_2-CH=CH-CH_3$ Pent-2-ene (d)

∵ Choice (c) 2-butene is symmetrical alkene.∴ It does not show anti-Markownikoff addition.

Topic 9

Methods of Purification

2017

1 The most suitable method of separation of 1 : 1 mixture of *ortho* and *para*-nitrophenols is **[NEET]**

(a) sublimation (b) chromatography
(c) crystallisation (d) steam distillation

2014

2 A liquid which decomposes at its boiling point can be purified by **[Manipal]**

(a) distillation at atmospheric pressure
(b) distillation under reduced pressure
(c) fractional distillation
(d) steam distillation

3 Which one of the following methods can be used to separate a mixture of *ortho* and *para*-nitrophenols? **[EAMCET]**

(a) Crystallisation
(b) Solubility
(c) Sublimation
(d) Steam distillation

2010

4 Sublimation is a process in which a solid **[KCET]**

(a) changes into vapour form
(b) changes into another allotropic form
(c) changes into liquid form
(d) None of the above

2008

5 **Assertion** (A) Oils are purified by steam distillation.
Reason (R) The compounds which decompose at their boiling points can be purified by steam distillation.

(a) Both A and R are correct and R is the correct explanation of A **[AIIMS]**
(b) Both A and R are correct but R is not the correct explanation of A
(c) A is correct but R is incorrect
(d) Both A and R are incorrect

6 Which one of the following can be purified by sublimation? **[MHT CET]**

(a) F_2 (b) Cl_2 (c) Br_2 (d) I_2

2007

7 For the purification, isolation and separation of organic compounds, the latest technique followed is **[Kerala CEE]**

(a) chromatography (b) steam distillation
(c) fractional crystallisation (d) sublimation
(e) vacuum distillation

8 Fractional distillation is a process by which the separation of different fractions from mixture of solution is carried by making use of the following property of the fractions

(a) freezing point (b) boiling point **[J&K CET]**
(c) melting point (d) solubility

2006

9 Styrene can be purified by **[AFMC]**

(a) simple distillation
(b) fractional distillation
(c) steam distillation
(d) vacuum distillation

10 A mixture of camphor and benzoic acid can be separated by

(a) sublimation **[Manipal]**
(b) extraction with a solvent
(c) chemical method
(d) fractional crystallisation

11 Which of the following reagents will be fruitful for separating a mixture of nitrobenzene and aniline? **[MHT CET]**

(a) Aqueous $NaHCO_3$ (b) H_2O
(c) Aqueous HCl (d) Aqueous NaOH

2005

12 The best method for the separation of naphthalene and benzoic acid from their mixture is **[CBSE AIPMT]**

(a) chromatography (b) crystallisation
(c) distillation (d) solvent extraction

13 How will you separate a solution (miscible) of benzene and $CHCl_3$? **[AFMC]**

(a) Sublimation (b) Filtration
(c) Distillation (d) Crystallisation

Answers

1 (d)	2 (b)	3 (d)	4 (a)	5 (c)	6 (d)	7 (a)	8 (b)	9 (d)	10 (c)
11 (c)	12 (d)	13 (c)							

Explanations

1 (*d*) Steam distillation is used to purify the substances which

(i) are volatile in steam but are immiscible with water.
(ii) possess sufficiently high vapour pressure at the boiling point of water.
(iii) contain non- volatile impurities.

The process of steam distillation can also be used to separate a mixture of two organic compounds one of which is steam volatile while the other is not. In *ortho* and *para*-nitrophenols, the latter is non-volatile, hence they are separated by steam distillation.

2 (*b*) A liquid which decomposes at its normal boiling point can be purified by vacuum distillation i.e. distillation under reduced pressure.

3 (*d*) *para*-nitrophenols, on account of larger distance between the groups (—OH and —NO_2) does not show any intramolecular hydrogen bonding. As a result of intermolecular hydrogen bonding the *para* derivative undergoes association, resulting in an increase in molar mass due to formation of long chain of molecules and hence, an increase in boiling point.

In *ortho* derivative, on account of intramolecular hydrogen bonding, no such association of molecules is possible therefore, no formation of long chains and no increase in boiling point and melting point takes place. Consequently, the *ortho* derivative is more volatile in steam, the *para* nitrophenol is completely non-volatile. Hence, steam distillation method is used to separate them.

4 (*a*) Sublimation is a process in which a solid changes into the vapour form on heating without passing through the intermediate liquid state and *vice-versa* on cooling.

5 (*c*) Steam distillation is carried out only when a solid or liquid is insoluble in water and volatile with steam but the impurities are non-volatile. The compound to be purified is distilled with steam under reduced pressure at a temperature below its boiling point. Compounds like aniline, wood oil, terpentine oil are purified by this method. Hence, A is correct but R is incorrect.

6 (*d*) In the sublimation, the solid substance converts into vapours directly. Iodine is found in solid state, while F_2 and Cl_2 are found in gaseous state and Br_2 is found in liquid state. So, iodine can be purified by sublimation.

7 (*a*) Chromatography is a modern technique used for the separation of mixtures into its components, purification of compounds and also to test the purity of compounds.

8 (*b*) Distillation is used to purify liquids and it is based on difference in their boiling points. When the boiling points of liquids are very close to each other, then fractional distillation is used.

9 (*d*) Styrene can be purified by vacuum distillation. i.e distillation under reduced pressure.

10 (*c*) Aqueous solution of $NaHCO_3$ (a chemical method) can be used to separate benzoic acid from its mixture with camphor. Benzoic acid forms water soluble sodium benzoate with $NaHCO_3$.

11 (*c*) Aqueous HCl can be used to separate a mixture of nitrobenzene and aniline.

$$\text{Aniline} + aq.\ \text{HCl} \longrightarrow \text{Salt,}$$
which is water soluble
$$\text{Nitrobenzene} + aq.\ \text{HCl} \longrightarrow \text{No reaction}$$

12 (*d*) Both naphthalene and benzoic acid sublimes on heating and are soluble in diethyl ether. When NaOH dissolved in water is poured to ether mixture, benzoic acid forms sodium benzoate which is more soluble in water than ether and moves out of mixture.

13 (*c*) Fractional distillation is the method used to separate a mixture of two miscible liquids having slight difference in their boiling points. The more volatile liquid distills over first and is collected in a receiver. The two fractions are redistilled separately a number of times to ensure complete purity of the liquids.

Topic 10

Qualitative Analysis

2014

1 In which of the following compounds presence of nitrogen cannot be detected by Lassaigne's method? [MHT CET]

(a) Hydrazine (b) Aniline
(c) *p*-toluidine (d) Picric acid

2 Lassaigne's test is used in qualitative analysis to detect [UK PMT]

(a) nitrogen (b) sulphur
(c) chlorine (d) All of these

2012

3 Kjeldahl's method cannot be used for the estimation of nitrogen in [AFMC]

(a) pyridine (b) nitro compounds
(c) azo compounds (d) All of these

4 Presence of halogen in organic compounds can be detected by using [UP CPMT]

(a) Leibig's test (b) Duma's test
(c) Kjeldahl's test (d) Beilstein test

2011

5 The Lassaigne's extract is boiled with conc. HNO_3 while testing for halogens. By doing so it [CBSE AIPMT]

(a) increase the concentration of NO_3^- ions
(b) decomposes Na_2S and NaCN, if formed
(c) helps in the precipitation of AgCl
(d) increases the solubility product of AgCl

2010

6 In an organic compound, phosphorus is estimated as [AFMC]

(a) $Mg_2P_2O_7$ (b) $Mg_3(PO_4)_2$
(c) H_3PO_4 (d) P_2O_5

7 Violet coloured complex obtained in the detection of sulphur is [AFMC]

(a) $Na_2[Fe(NO)(CN)_5]$
(b) $Na_3[Fe(ONS)(CN)_5]$
(c) $Na_4[Fe(CN)_5NOS]$
(d) Both (b) and (c)

8 Chemical formula of prussian blue is [AFMC]

(a) $Na_4[Fe(CN)_6]$ (b) $K_4[Fe(CN)_6]$
(c) $Fe_4[Fe(CN)_6]_3$ (d) None of these

9 The compound formed in the positive test for nitrogen with the Lassaigne solution of an organic compound is [RPMT]

(a) $Fe_4[Fe(CN)_6]_3$
(b) $Na_3[Fe(CN)_6]$
(c) $Fe(CN)_3$
(d) $Na_4[Fe(CN)_5COS]$

2009

10 Which of the following compounds gives blood red colouration when its Lassaigne's extract is treated with alkali and ferric chloride? [OJEE]

(a) Thiourea (b) Diphenyl sulphide
(c) Phenyl hydrazine (d) Benzamide

2008

11 The prussian blue colour obtained in the Lassaigne's test for nitrogen is due to the formation of [Kerala CEE]

(a) iron (II) hexacyanoferrate (II)
(b) iron (III) hexacyanoferrate (II)
(c) iron (III) hexacyanoferrate (III)
(d) iron (II) hexacyanoferrate (III)
(e) sodium hexacyanoferrate (III)

2007

12 **Assertion** (A) During the test for nitrogen with Lassaigne extract, on adding $FeCl_3$ solution sometimes a red precipitate is obtained.
Reason (R) Sulphur is also present. [AIIMS]

(a) Both A and R are correct and R is the correct explanation of A
(b) Both A and R are correct but R is not the correct explanation of A
(c) A is correct but R is incorrect
(d) Both A and R are correct

13 During Lassaigne's test N and S present in an organic compound changes into **[BHU]**

(a) Na_2S and NaCN (b) NaSCN
(c) Na_2SO_4 and NaCN (d) Na_2S and NaCN

2006

14 During the fusion of an organic compound with sodium metal, nitrogen of the compound is converted into **[KCET]**

(a) $NaNO_2$ (b) $NaNH_2$ (c) NaCN (d) NaNC

2005

15 Which of the following statement is wrong? **[JCECE]**

(a) Using Lassaigne's test nitrogen and sulphur present in organic compound can be tested.
(b) Using Beilstein's test the presence of halogen in a compound can be tested.
(c) In Lassaigne's filtrate, the nitrogen present in an organic compound is converted into NaCN.
(d) In the estimation of carbon, an organic compound is heated with CaO in a combustion tube.

Answers

1 (a)	2 (d)	3 (d)	4 (d)	5 (b)	6 (a)	7 (c)	8 (c)	9 (a)	10 (a)
11 (b)	12 (a)	13 (b)	14 (c)	15 (d)					

Explanations

1 (*a*) Lassaigne's method is used to detect the presence of elements like N, S, F, Cl, Br, I etc in an organic sample.

(a) $NH_2—NH_2$ Hydrazine (b) Aniline (NH_2 on benzene ring)

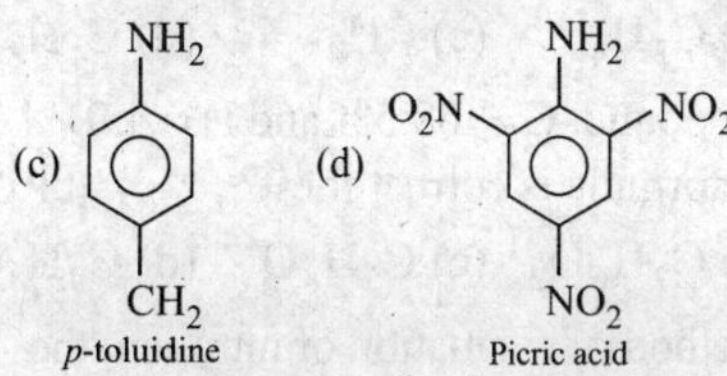

Since, hydrazine is not an organic compound, thus presence of nitrogen in it cannot be detected by Lassaigne's method.

2 (*d*) Presence of extra elements (such as N, S and halogens) is detected by Lassaigne's test.

3 (*d*) Kjeldahl's method cannot be used for the estimation of nitro and azo compounds and other compounds containing nitrogen in the ring (like pyridine) because these compounds are not converted into $(NH_4)_2SO_4$ during reaction.

4 (*d*) Presence of halogens in organic compounds can be detected by Beilstein test.

5 (*b*) Lassaigne's extract is boiled with conc. HNO_3 to decompose Na_2S and NaCN formed before testing for halogens. These ions would otherwise interfere with silver nitrate test for halogens.

6 (*a*) In Carius method, the weighed organic compound (containing phosphorus) is heated with conc. HNO_3 followed by $MgCl_2$ in the presence of NH_4Cl and NH_4OH. By this process, magnesium ammonium phosphate $MgNH_4PO_4$ is formed which on ignition gives magnesium pyrophosphate ($Mg_2P_2O_7$). From the amount of magnesium pyrophosphate, the percentage of phosphorus is calculated as

$$\% \text{ of P} = \frac{62}{222} \times \frac{\text{weight of } Mg_2P_2O_7}{\text{weight of substance taken}} \times 100$$

7 (*c*) Sulphur in organic compounds is detected by using sodium nitroprusside. With it sulphur forms a violet colour complex, called sodium thionitroprusside.

$$\underset{\text{Sodium nitroprusside}}{Na_2S + Na_2[Fe(CN)_5NO]} \longrightarrow \underset{\text{Sodium thionitroprusside}}{Na_4[Fe(CN)_5NOS]}$$

8 (*c*) The colour of ferric ferrocyanide is prussian blue. Its chemical formula is $Fe_4[Fe(CN)_6]_3$.

9 (*a*) $3Na_4[Fe(CN)_6] + 4Fe^{3+} \longrightarrow \underset{\substack{\text{Iron (III) hexacyanoferrate (II)} \\ \text{(Prussian blue)}}}{Fe_4[Fe(CN)_6]_3} + 12Na^+$

Appearance of blue or green colour by using Lassaigne's extract indicates the presence of nitrogen.

10 (*a*) Thiourea contains both S and N and hence gives blood red colouration when its Lassaigne's extract is treated with alkali and $FeCl_3$.

$$3NaSCN + FeCl_3 \longrightarrow \underset{\substack{\text{Ferric isothiocyanate} \\ \text{(Blood red)}}}{Fe(SCN)_3} + 3NaCl$$

11 (*b*) **Lassaigne's test for nitrogen in sodium extract** : Add fresh and saturated solution of $FeSO_4$ followed by NaOH. Now, boil and cool the contents. A few drops of $FeCl_3$ solution is added and then acidified with conc HCl. Formation of prussian blue colour shows the presence of nitrogen.

$$FeSO_4 + 2NaOH \longrightarrow Fe(OH)_2 \downarrow + Na_2SO_4$$

$$Fe(OH)_2 + \underset{\substack{\text{From sodium} \\ \text{extract}}}{4\,NaCN} \longrightarrow Na_4[Fe(CN)_6]$$

$$3\,Na_4[Fe(CN)_6] + 4\,FeCl_3 \longrightarrow \underset{\substack{\text{Iron (III) hexacyano-} \\ \text{ferrate (II)}}}{Fe_4[Fe(CN)_6]_3} + 12\,NaCl$$

12 (a) During test for nitrogen with Lassaigne extract, on adding $FeCl_3$ solution a red precipitate is obtained when both nitrogen and sulphur are present.

13 (*b*) If both N and S are present, it may result in the formation of NaSCN during fusion with sodium metal

$$Na + C + N + S \longrightarrow NaSCN$$

If sodium metal is present in excess, the sodium sulphocyanide formed decomposes into sodium cyanide and sodium sulphide.

$$NaSCN + 2\,Na \longrightarrow NaCN + Na_2S$$

14 (*c*) When organic compound is fused with sodium metal, nitrogen of the compound is converted into sodium cyanide as

$$Na + C + N \longrightarrow NaCN$$

15 (*d*) In the estimation of carbon, an organic compound is heated over CuO not CaO. The other given statements are correct.

Topic 11

Quantitative Analysis and Empirical Formula

2019

1 Which method is used to find halogen in organic compound? **[JIPMER]**

(a) Duma's method (b) Leibig's method
(c) Kjeldahl method (d) Carius method

2018

2 In Kjeldahl's method, the nitrogen present in an organic compound is quantitatively converted into **[JIPMER]**

(a) gaseous ammonia (b) ammonium sulphate
(c) ammonium phosphate (d) ammonia

2017

3 A primary alcohol with a vapour density of 29 contained C = 62.1%, H = 10.3% and reacted with bromine to give a derivative which contains C = 16.5%, H = 2.7% and Br_2 = 73.4%. The structural formula of the compound is **[AIIMS]**

(a) $CH_3CH_2CH_2OH$
(b) $CH_3CH{=}CHOH$
(c) $CH_2{=}CH{-}CH_2OH$
(d) ▷—OH

2014

4 In the Kjeldahl's method for estimation of nitrogen present in a soil sample, ammonia evolved from 0.75 g of sample neutralised 10 mL of 1 M H_2SO_4. The percentage of nitrogen in the soil is **[CBSE AIPMT]**

(a) 37.33 (b) 45.33 (c) 35.33 (d) 45.33

2013

5 A hydrocarbon contains 20% of hydrogen and 80% of carbon. The empirical formula is **[Manipal]**

(a) CH_4 (b) CH_3 (c) CH_2 (d) CH

2011

6 In Dumas' method of estimation of nitrogen 0.35 g of an organic compound gave 55 mL of nitrogen collected at 300 K temperature and 715 mm pressure. The percentage composition of nitrogen in the compound would be (aqueous tension at 300 K = 15 mm) **[CBSE AIPMT]**

(a) 14.45 (b) 15.45 (c) 16.45 (d) 17.45

7 1.2 g of organic compound of Kjeldahlisation liberates ammonia which consumes 30 cm^3 of 1 N HCl. The percentage of nitrogen in the organic compound is **[KCET]**

(a) 30 (b) 35 (c) 46.67 (d) 20.8

8 In Carius method of estimation of halogens, 0.099 g organic compound gave 0.287 g AgCl. The percentage of chlorine in the compound will be **[Haryana PMT]**

(a) 28.6 (b) 71.7 (c) 35.4 (d) 64.2

9 0.765 g of an acid gives 0.535 g of CO_2 and 0.138 g of H_2O. Then, the ratio of the percentage of carbon and hydrogen is **[JCECE]**

(a) 19 : 2 (b) 18 : 11 (c) 20 : 17 (d) 1 : 7

10 In Kjeldahl's method, ammonia from 5 g of food neutralises 30 cm^3 of 0.1 N acid. The percentage of nitrogen in the food is **[KCET]**

(a) 0.84 (b) 8.4 (c) 16.8 (d) 1.68

2009

11 A hydrocarbon has carbon and hydrogen. Its molecular weight is 28. Its possible formula would be **[AFMC]**

(a) C_3H_6 (b) C_2H_4 (c) CH_4 (d) C_4H_8

12 In an organic compound, C = 68.5% and H = 4.91%. Which empirical formula is correct for it? **[UP CPMT]**

(a) C_6H_{10} (b) $C_7H_6O_2$ (c) C_5H_8O (d) C_9H_3O

13 In the Duma's method of estimation of nitrogen, the nitrogen in the organic compound is finally converted into **[Kerala CEE]**

(a) NO_2 (b) N_2
(c) NH_3 (d) $(NH_4)_2SO_4$
(e) HNO_3

14 The masses of carbon, hydrogen and oxygen in an organic compound are in the ratio 6 : 1 : 8 respectively. Which of the following pairs of formulae correspond to the above information? **[Kerala CEE]**

(a) CH_2O and CH_3CHO (b) CH_2O and C_3H_6O
(c) C_3H_6O and $C_2H_6O_2$ (d) $C_3H_6O_3$ and HCHO
(e) C_2H_4O and $C_4H_8O_2$

15 One percent composition of an organic compound *A* is carbon 85.71% and hydrogen 14.20%. Its vapour density is 14. Consider the following reaction sequence,

$$A \xrightarrow{Cl_2/H_2O} B \xrightarrow[(ii)\ H_3O^+]{(i)\ KCN/EtOH} C.$$ Identify *C* **[EAMCET]**

(a) $CH_3{-}CH(OH){-}CO_2H$
(b) $HO{-}CH_2{-}CH_2{-}CO_2H$
(c) $HO{-}CH_2{-}CO_2H$
(d) $CH_3{-}CH_2{-}CO_2H$

2008

16 If two compounds have the same empirical formula but different molecular formula, they must have **[Manipal]**
(a) different percentage composition.
(b) different molecular weights.
(c) same viscosity.
(d) same vapour density.

17 An organic compound whose empirical and molecular formulae are same, contains 20% carbon, 6.7% hydrogen, 46.7% nitrogen and the rest oxygen. On heating it yields ammonia, leaving a solid residue. The solid residue gives a violet colour with dilute solution of alkaline copper sulphate. The organic compound is **[Kerala CEE]**
(a) NH_2COONH_4 (b) CH_3COONH_4
(c) NH_2NHCHO (d) $HCOONH_4$
(e) NH_2CONH_2

18 The ratio of carbon, hydrogen and oxygen in 3-methyl benzoic acid is **[Punjab PMET]**
(a) 4 : 2 : 2 (b) 2 : 4 : 1
(c) 4 : 4 : 1 (d) 4 : 4 : 2

19 In a compound C, H and N are present in 9 : 1 : 3.5 by weight. If molecular weight of the compound is 108, then the molecular formula of the compound is **[BCECE]**
(a) $C_2H_6N_2$ (b) C_3H_4N
(c) $C_6H_8N_2$ (d) $C_9H_{12}N_3$

2007

20 An organic compound weighing 0.31g gave 0.444 g of magnesium pyrophosphate in the estimation of phosphorus by Carius method. The percentage of *P* in the compound is **[Kerala CEE]**
(a) 20 (b) 60
(c) 15 (d) 30
(e) 40

21 Following is estimated by Liebig method **[RPMT]**
(a) C and H (b) nitrogen
(c) chlorine (d) bromine

22 An unknown compound has molar mass 240 g/mol. Its empirical formula is CH_2O then its molecular formula will be **[MP PMT]**
(a) $C_4H_8O_4$ (b) $C_{12}H_{22}O_{12}$
(c) $C_6H_{12}O_6$ (d) $C_8H_{16}O_8$

2006

23 Two organic compounds (*A*) and (*B*) both containing only carbon and hydrogen, on quantitative analysis gave the same percentage composition by weight.
$$C=\left(\frac{12}{13}\right)\times 100\%,\ H=\left(\frac{1}{13}\right)\times 100\%$$
A decolourises bromine water but *B* does not, *A* and *B* respectively are **[MHT CET]**
(a) C_2H_2 and C_6H_6
(b) C_6H_6 and C_2H_2
(c) C_2H_4 and C_2H_6
(d) C_2H_2 and C_2H_6

24 An organic compound has an empirical formula CH_2O, its vapour density is 45. The molecular formula of the compound is **[Manipal]**
(a) CH_2O (b) C_2H_5O
(c) C_2H_2O (d) $C_3H_6O_3$

2005

25 An alkaloid contains 17.28% of nitrogen and it's molecular mass is 162. The number of nitrogen atoms present in one molecule of alkaloid is **[Kerala CEE]**
(a) five (b) four
(c) three (d) two
(e) one

26 4 g of hydrocarbon (C_xH_y) on complete combustion gave 12 g of CO_2. What is the empirical formula of the hydrocarbon? (C = 12, H = 1) **[EAMCET]**
(a) CH_3 (b) C_4H_9 (c) CH (d) C_3H_8

Answers

1 (d)	2 (b)	3 (c)	4 (a)	5 (b)	6 (c)	7 (b)	8 (b)	9 (a)	10 (a)
11 (b)	12 (b)	13 (b)	14 (d)	15 (b)	16 (b)	17 (e)	18 (c)	19 (c)	20 (e)
21 (a)	22 (d)	23 (a)	24 (d)	25 (d)	26 (d)				

Explanations

1 (*d*) Carius method is used to find halogen in organic compound. Here, the weighed amount of organic compound is heated in a sealed tube with fuming HNO_3 in the presence of $AgNO_3$. As a result, halogen present in organic compound is converted into AgX which is weighed. The percentage of halogens can be calculated with the help of direct formula as

$$\% \text{ of chlorine} = \frac{35.5}{143.5} \times \frac{\text{weight of AgCl} \times 100}{\text{weight of compound}}$$

$$\% \text{ of bromine} = \frac{80}{188} \times \frac{\text{weight of AgBr} \times 100}{\text{weight of compound}}$$

$$\% \text{ of iodine} = \frac{127}{235} \times \frac{\text{weight of AgI} \times 100}{\text{weight of compound}}$$

2 (*b*) In Kjeldahl's method, the nitrogen is quantitatively converted into ammonium sulphate by heating with NaOH.

$$\underset{\text{from organic compound}}{C + H + N} \xrightarrow{\Delta} (NH_4)_2SO_4 + CO_2 + H_2O$$

3 (*c*)

Element	C	H	O
% of element	62.1%	10.3%	27.6%
Atomic mass of element	12	1	16
Moles = %atomic mass	$\frac{62.1}{12} = 5.17$	$\frac{10.3}{1} = 10.3$	$\frac{27.6}{16} = 1.72$
Simplest mole ratio	$\frac{5.17}{1.72} = 3.00$	$\frac{10.3}{1.72} = 5.98$	$\frac{1.72}{1.72} = 1$
Simplest whole mole ratio	3	6	1

Empirical formula is C_3H_6O.

We know that $2 \times V \cdot D =$ molecular mass

$2 \times 29 =$ molecular mass of organic primary alcohol

molecular mass = 58 g/mol

We know, $n = \frac{\text{Molecular mass}}{\text{Empirical formula mass}} = \frac{58}{58} = 1$

So, molecular formula of compound is C_3H_6O.

As, this alcohol reacted with Br_2 to give a derivative whose molecular formula can be deduced as :

Element	C	H	Br	O
% of element	16.5%	2.7%	73.4%	7.4%
Atomic mass of element	12	1	79.8≈80	16
Moles =% atomic mass	1.375	2.7	0.92	0.46
Simplest mole ratio	2.98	5.87	2	1
Simplest whole mole ratio	3	6	2	1

So, the structural formula of derivative is $C_3H_6Br_2O$. As, among the given compound, $CH_2 = CH — CH_2OH$ would give an addition product with Br_2 readily thus, option (c) is correct. Compound given in option (b) undergoes tautomerism to form keto product which gives addition reaction. Also, compound given in option (d) does not give feasible addition reaction.

4 (*a*) In Kjeldahl's method, percentage of N is given by

$$\% \text{ N} = \frac{1.4 \times \text{Normality of acid} \times \text{volume of acid}}{\text{Weight of compound}}$$

$1 \text{ M } H_2SO_4 \equiv 2 \text{ N } H_2SO_4$, V = 10 mL

$$\therefore \quad \% \text{ N} = \frac{1.4 \times 2 \times 10}{0.75} = 37.33\%$$

5 (*b*)

Element	H	C
Percentage	20	80
Atomic Mass	1	12
Relative number of atoms	20	6.66
Simplest ratio	20/6.66 = 3	6.66/6.66 = 1

$\therefore$ Empirical formula = CH_3

6 (*c*) $\frac{p_1V_1}{T_1} = \frac{p_2V_2}{T_2}$, $V_1 = 55$ mL, V_2 at NTP = ?

$p_1 = 715 - 15 = 700$ mm, $p_2 = 760$ mm,

$T_1 = 300$ K, $T_2 = 273$K

$$\therefore V_2 = \frac{p_1V_1T_2}{p_2T_1} = \frac{700 \times 55 \times 273}{760 \times 300} = 46.09 \text{ mL}$$

$$\% \text{ of N} = \frac{28 \times 46.09 \times 100}{22400 \times 0.35} = 16.46 \approx 16.45$$

7 (*b*) Percentage of nitrogen $= \frac{1.4 \times N \times V}{w}$

$$= \frac{1.4 \times 1 \times 30}{1.2} = 35\%$$

8 (*b*) $\% \text{ of chlorine} = \frac{35.5}{143.5} \times \frac{\text{mass of AgCl}}{\text{mass of the compound}} \times 100$

$$= \frac{35.5}{143.5} \times \frac{0.287}{0.099} \times 100 = 71.71\%$$

9 (*a*) $\% \text{ of C} = \frac{12}{44} \times \frac{0.535}{0.765} \times 100 = 19.07$

$$\% \text{ of H} = \frac{2}{18} \times \frac{0.138}{0.765} \times 100 = 2.004$$

Ratio of % of C : H = 19 : 2 (approx)

10 (*a*) From Kjeldahl's method,

$$\text{Percentage of nitrogen} = \frac{1.4 \times N \times V}{w} = \frac{1.4 \times 0.1 \times 30}{5}$$

$$= 0.84\%$$

11 (*b*)

Compound	Molecular weight
C_3H_6	12 × 3 + 6 = 42
C_2H_4	12 × 2 + 4 = 28
CH_4	12 + 4 = 16
C_4H_8	12 × 4 + 8 = 56

Hence, the formula of the given compound is C_2H_4.

12 (*b*)

Element	C	H	O
At. wt.	12	1	16
Per. composition	68.5	4.91	(100 − 68.5 − 4.91) = 26.59
No. of moles	$\frac{68.5}{12}$ = 5.708	$\frac{4.91}{1}$ = 4.91	$\frac{26.59}{16}$ = 1.66
Simple mole ratio	$\frac{5.708}{1.66}$ = 3.44 × 2 ≈ 7	$\frac{4.91}{1.66}$ = 2.96 × 2 ≈ 6	$\frac{1.66}{1.66}$ = 1 × 2 ≈ 2

Hence, the empirical formula of the compound is $C_7H_6O_2$.

13 (*b*) Duma's method involves the conversion of elemental nitrogen into molecular nitrogen (N_2) by a suitable reagent such as CuO, Cu etc.

$$2N + CuO \longrightarrow N_2 + \text{oxides of nitrogen}$$

$$\text{Oxides of nitrogen} + Cu \longrightarrow N_2 + CuO$$

From the volume (V) of nitrogen gas (N_2) formed, the N% can be calculated as $\%\,N = \frac{28}{22400} \times \frac{V}{\text{weight of substance}} \times 100$

14 (*d*)

Element	Relative mass (*x*)	Atomic mass (*y*)	*x/y*	Simple ratio
C	6	12	$\frac{6}{12} = 0.5$	$\frac{0.5}{0.5} = 1$
H	1	1	$\frac{1}{1} = 1$	$\frac{1}{0.5} = 2$
O	8	16	$\frac{8}{16} = 0.5$	$\frac{0.5}{0.5} = 1$

Hence, the empirical formula of the compound must be CH_2O. The formula of other compounds having CH_2O empirical formula are $(CH_2O)_2$ or $C_2H_4O_2$, $(CH_2O)_3$ or $C_3H_6O_3$ and so on.

15 (*b*) First calculate the molecular formula of *A* from the given data :

Element	Percentage	Atomic mass	Relative number of atoms	Simple ratio
C	85.71	12	$\frac{85.71}{12} = 7.14$	$\frac{7.14}{7.14} = 1$
H	14.20	1	$\frac{14.20}{1} = 14.20$	$\frac{14.20}{7.14} = 1.98 \simeq 2$

∴ Empirical formula = CH_2

Empirical formula mass = 12 + 2 = 14

Now, molecular mass of the compound

$$= 2 \times \text{vapour density} = 2 \times 14 = 28$$

$$n = \frac{\text{molecular mass}}{\text{empirical formula mass}} = \frac{28}{14} = 2$$

Hence, molecular formula of the compound = $(CH_2)_2 = C_2H_4$

The reactions for the given sequence is as follows:

$$C_2H_4 + Cl_2 \longrightarrow \underset{(A)}{} \; \underset{(B)}{\begin{array}{l} CH_2-Cl \\ | \\ CH_2-Cl \end{array}} + H_2O \longrightarrow \begin{array}{l} CH_2-OH \\ | \\ CH_2-OH \end{array}$$

$$\begin{array}{l} CH_2-OH \\ | \\ CH_2-CN \end{array} \xleftarrow{\text{KCN}} \quad ; \quad \underset{(C)}{\begin{array}{l} CH_2-OH \\ | \\ CH_2-COOH \end{array}} \xleftarrow{H_2O} \begin{array}{l} CH_2-OH \\ | \\ CH_2-CN \end{array}$$

16 (*b*) Since, the molecular formula is *n* times the empirical formula, therefore, different compounds having the same empirical formula must have different molecular weights.

17 (*e*)

Element	Percentage	At. wt.	Relative no. of atoms	Simple ratio of atoms
C	20	12	$\frac{20}{12} = 1.67$	$\frac{1.67}{1.66} = 1$
H	6.7	1	$\frac{6.7}{1} = 6.7$	$\frac{6.7}{1.66} \approx 4$
N	46.7	14	$\frac{46.7}{14} = 3.33$	$\frac{3.33}{1.66} = 2$
O	26.6	16	$\frac{26.6}{16} = 1.66$	$\frac{1.66}{1.66} = 1$

Thus, the empirical formula of compound is CH_4N_2O.

∴ Molecular formula = CH_4N_2O

This formula suggests the compound may be NH_2CONH_2 or NH_2NHCHO.

The compound on heating gives NH_3 and a solid residue. The solid residue gives violet colour with alkaline $CuSO_4$.

This suggests the compound is urea NH_2CONH_2, not NH_2NHCHO.

$$NH_2CONH_2 + NH_2CONH_2 \xrightarrow{\Delta} \underset{\text{Biuret (solid residue)}}{NH_2CONHCONH_2} + NH_3 \uparrow$$

$$\text{Biuret} + \text{alkaline } CuSO_4 \longrightarrow \text{Blue colour}$$

18 (*c*) 3-methyl benzoic acid is $(CH_3)C_6H_4$—COOH

Number of carbon, hydrogen and oxygen atoms are 8, 8, 2

So, C : H : O is 4 : 4 : 1.

19 (*c*)

Element	Percentage	Atomic weight	Relative no. of atoms	Simplest ratio of atoms
C	9	12	0.75	$\frac{0.75}{0.25} = 3$
H	1	1	1	$\frac{1.00}{0.25} = 4$
N	3.5	14	0.25	$\frac{0.25}{0.25} = 1$

So, empirical formula = C_3H_4N

Empirical formula weight = 36 + 4 + 14 = 54

$$n = \frac{\text{molecular weight}}{\text{empirical formula weight}} = \frac{108}{54} = 2$$

∴ Molecular formula = $(C_3H_4N)_2 = C_6H_8N_2$

20 (*e*) Percentage of P $= \frac{62}{222} \times \frac{\text{mass of } Mg_2P_2O_7 \text{ formed}}{\text{mass of substance taken}} \times 100$

$= \frac{62}{222} \times \frac{0.444}{0.31} \times 100 = 40\%$

21 (*a*) (*i*) Carbon and hydrogen are estimated by Leibig's method. In this method carbon and hydrogen are quantitatively converted into CO_2 and H_2O. By knowing the weights of CO_2 and H_2O formed, percentage of carbon and hydrogen in the compound can be calculated.

(*ii*) Nitrogen is estimated by Duma's and Kjeldahl's method.

(*iii*) Chlorine and bromine are estimated by Carius method.

22 (*d*) Empirical formula is CH_2O

$\therefore$ Empirical formula weight = 30 $\Rightarrow n = \frac{240}{30} = 8$

Molecular formula = (Empirical formula)$_n$

$= (CH_2O)_8 = C_8H_{16}O_8$

23 (*a*) % of C $= \frac{12}{13} \times 100 = 92.3,$

% of H $= \frac{1}{13} \times 100 = 7.69$

Ratio of C and H $= \frac{92.3}{12} : \frac{7.69}{1} = 1 : 1$

Hence, empirical formula = CH. Thus, molecular formula can be C_2H_2, C_3H_3, C_4H_4 and C_6H_6 etc.

Since, *A* decolourises Br_2 water, while *B* does not so, '*A*' is C_2H_2 and *B* is C_6H_6.

24 (*d*) Molecular weight = 2 × vapour density = 2 × 45 = 90 g/mol

Empirical formula weight = 30 (12 + 2×1 + 16) g/mol

$\therefore \quad n = \frac{\text{molecular weight}}{\text{empirical formula weight}} = \frac{90}{30} = 3$

$\therefore$ Molecular formula of the compound $= (CH_2O)_3 = C_3H_6O_3$

25 (*d*) $\because$ 100 g alkaloid contains nitrogen = 17.28 g

$\therefore$ 162 g alkaloid contain nitrogen $= \frac{17.28 \times 162}{100} = 27.9 \approx 28$ g.

$\because$ Atomic weight of nitrogen = 14 g

$\therefore$ Number of atoms of nitrogen present in one molecule of alkaloid $= \frac{28}{14} = 2$

26 (*d*) Percentage of carbon in compound

$= \frac{12}{44} \times \frac{\text{weight of } CO_2}{\text{weight of compound}} \times 100 = \frac{12}{44} \times \frac{12}{4} \times 100 = 81.81\%$

% of H = 100 − 81.81 = 18.19%

Element	%	Atomic weight	Relative no. of atoms	Simplest ratio of atoms	Simple ratio
C	81.81	12	$\frac{81.81}{12} \approx 6.82$	$\frac{6.82}{6.82} = 1$	$1.0 \times 3 = 3$
H	18.19	1	$\frac{18.19}{1} = 18.19$	$\frac{18.19}{6.82} \approx 2.67$	$2.67 \times 3 = 8$

Hence, empirical formula of the compound $= C_3H_8$

13

Hydrocarbons

Quick Review

- Organic compounds composed of only C and H are called **hydrocarbons.**
- Hydrocarbons are mainly obtained from petroleum, which is the major source of commercial energy.

Classification of Hydrocarbons

Any two carbon atoms of a hydrocarbon may combine through single (—), double (═) or triple (≡) bonds. Depending upon the manner of attachment of carbon atoms, hydrocarbons can be classified in three major classes that are shown in the chart given below :

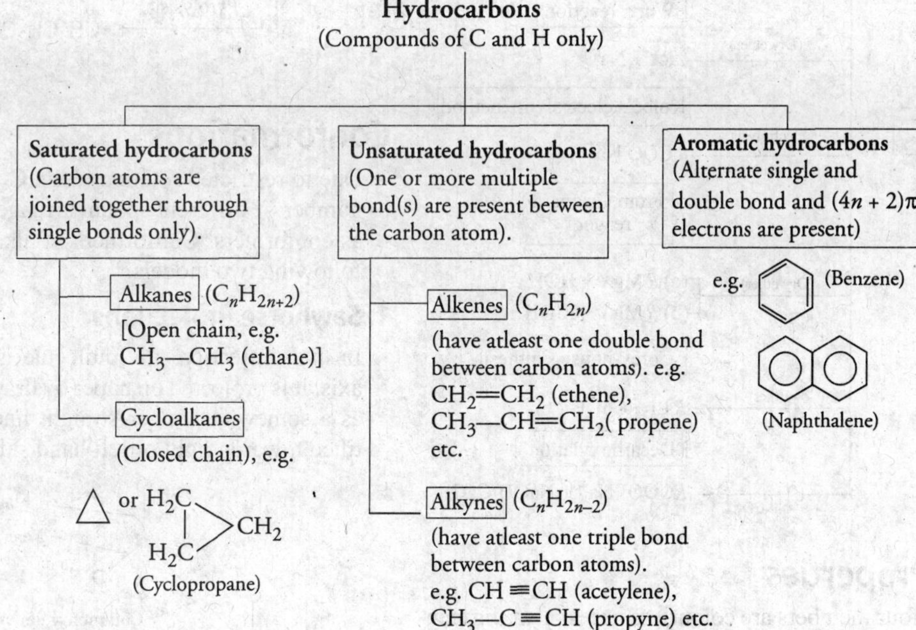

Alkanes (or Paraffins)

- These are the simplest organic compounds made up of carbon and hydrogen only containing carbon-carbon single bonds.
- The general formula for alkanes is C_nH_{2n+2}.
- These are named by adding suffix 'ane' to the root word.
- Alkanes exhibit chain and position isomerism.

Structure

All the carbon-carbon bonds in alkanes are sp^3-sp^3 hybridised where σ-bond is quite strong. They have three dimensional structures where all the four bonds are tetrahedrally arranged making a normal angle of 109°28′, e.g. methane (CH_4).

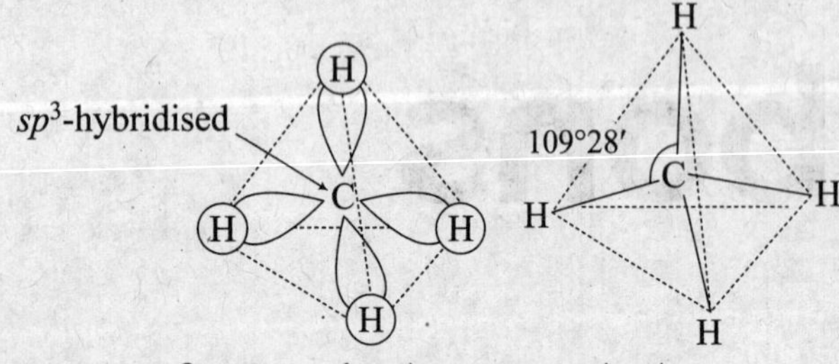

Structures of methane (CH_4) molecule

Preparation

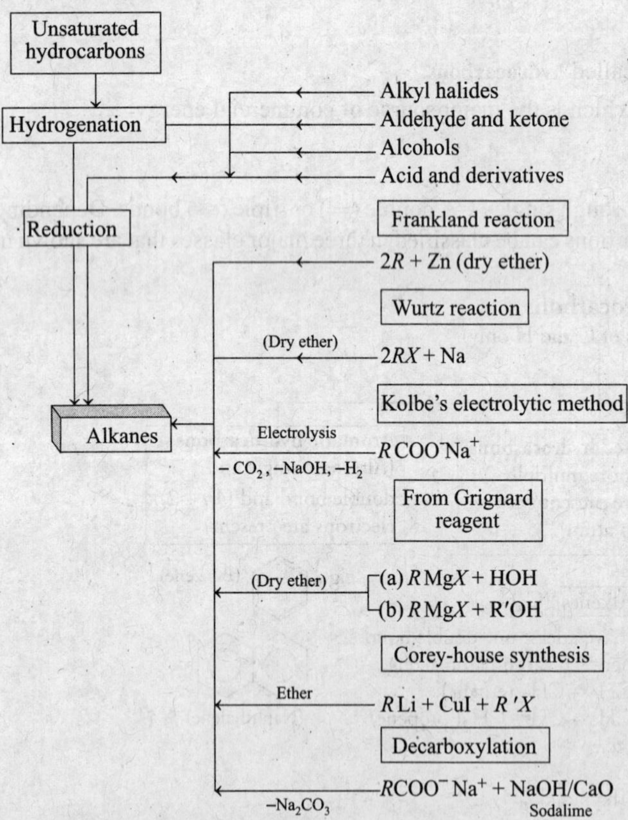

Physical Properties

- The first four members are colourless gases, next thirteen members are colourless liquids and next higher members are colourless solids.
  (It can be explained on the basis of magnitude of attractive forces.)
- Boiling point of alkanes decreases on branching.
  BP ∝ VAF (van der Waals' forces)
  AF ∝ molecular mass or VAF ∝ SA (Surface area)

So, boiling point order can be given as :

n-octane > *iso*-octane > 2, 2, 3, 3-tetramethylbutane

- Alkanes with even number of carbon atoms have higher melting points as compared to next higher or lower alkanes with odd number of carbon atoms.
- Alkanes being non-polar in nature, soluble in non-polar solvents but insoluble in polar solvent such as water.

Chemical Properties

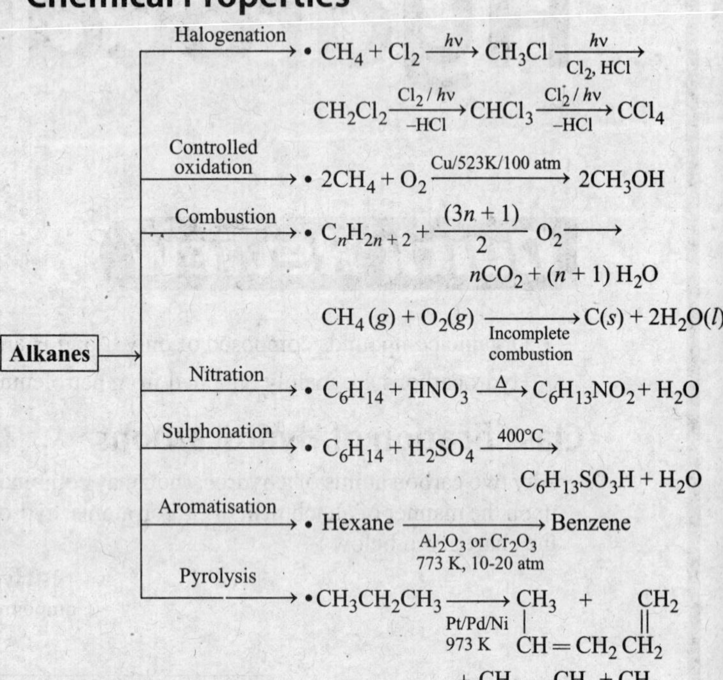

Conformations

Due to restricted rotation along C—C single bond, an infinite number of different spatial arrangements are possible, known as conformers. Conformers of alkanes can be represented by following two models.

1. Sawhorse Projections

In this projection, the molecule is seen along the molecular axis. It is projected on paper by drawing the central C—C bond as a somewhat longer straight line. Upper end of the end is tilted towards right or left hand side.

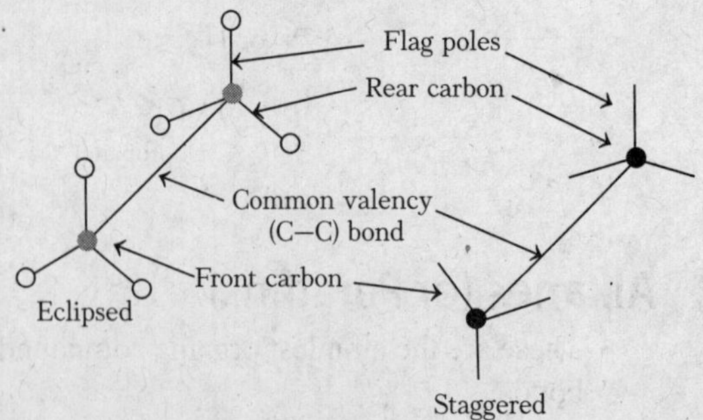

Note *n*-alkanes on heating in the presence of anhyd. $AlCl_3$ and HCl gas isomerise to branched chain alkanes.

2. Newman Projections

In this projection, bond connecting two carbon atoms is such that C—C bond appears to be head observer. The carbon atom nearer to eye is represented by a point.

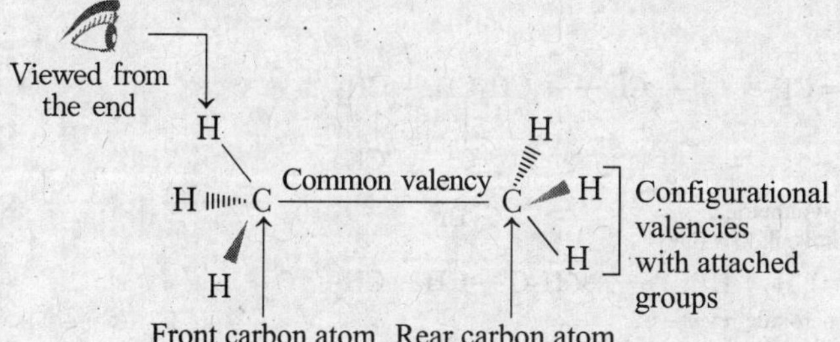

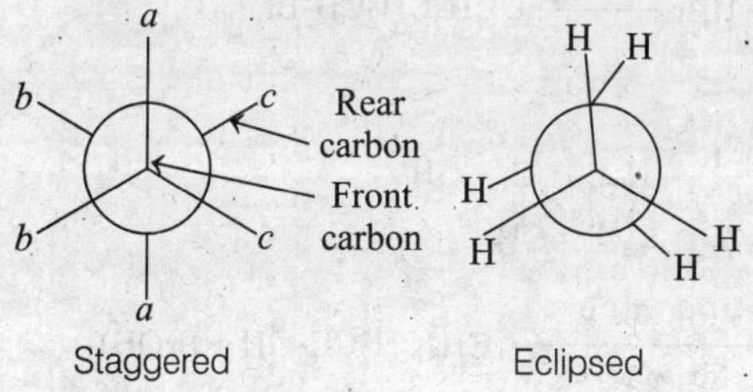

- Intermediate conformation between **eclipsed** and **staggered** are known as **skew** (gauche) **conformations**.
- Eclipsed form is least stable and staggered form is most stable due to greater distance between the bond pairs or lesser torsional strain.
- The energy difference between the two extreme forms is of the order of 12.5 kJ mol^{-1}.

Alkenes

- These are unsaturated hydrocarbons which have sp^2-hybridisation with 120° bond angle containing at least one double bond.
- These are also called olefins due to high reactivity.
- Alkenes with two double bonds are called dienes.
  Isolated dienes have —C=C—C—C=C— structure
  Conjugated dienes have —C=C—C=C— structure
  Commulated dienes have —C=C=C— structure
- These are named by adding suffix 'ene' to the root word.

Structure

In alkenes, double bond between two carbon atoms consists of the one strong σ-bond formed by the head on overlapping of sp^2-hybrid orbitals and one weak π-bond formed by sideways overlapping of two 2*p*-orbitals of two C-atoms.

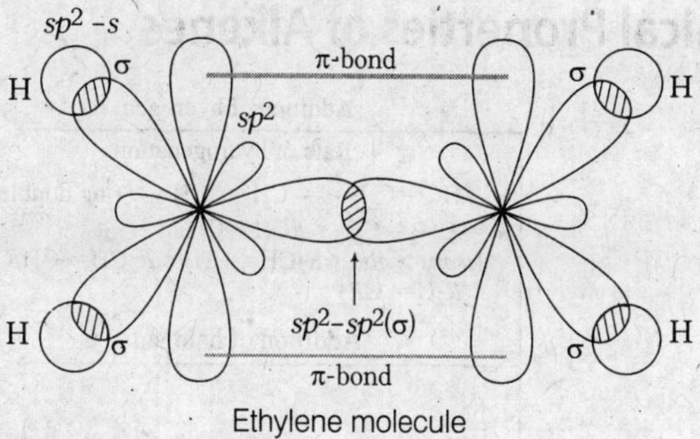

Ethylene molecule

Isomerism

- Alkene show both structural and geometrical isomerism. Structural isomerism exhibited by alkenes are chain and position isomerism.
- Alkenes also exhibit stereoisomerism as geometrical (*cis-trans*) isomerism. *cis*-form of alkene is found to be more polar than *trans*-form because dipole moment of *trans*-form is almost zero.

H_3C and CH_3 on the same side, H and H on the same side: $C=C$ (μ = 0.33D) [*cis*-but-2-ene]

$H_3C^{\delta+}$, H / H, $CH_3^{\delta+}$ across: $C^{\delta-}=C^{\delta-}$ (μ = 0) [*trans*-but-2-ene]

Preparation

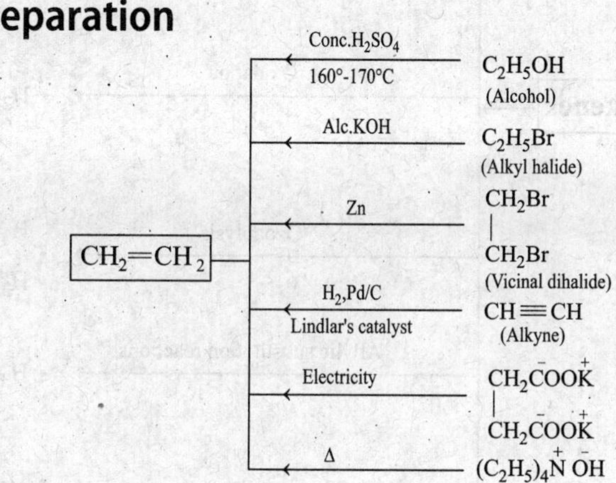

Physical Properties

- Alkene resemble alkanes in physical properties except in type of isomerism and in polar nature.
- *Cis*-alkenes have higher boiling point than *trans*-isomers.
- *trans*-isomers have almost zero dipole moment and exhibit weak intermolecular interaction.
- These are insoluble in water but soluble in non-polar solvents.

Chemical Properties

These generally undergo electrophilic addition reactions because of the presence of a double bond. In polar solvents, addition proceeds by ionic mechanism whereas in light or non-polar solvents, the addition occurs by free radical mechanism.

Chemical Properties of Alkenes

Alkenes →

- **Addition of hydrogen**
  - $H_2C{=}CH_2 \xrightarrow[523\text{-}573K]{H_2/Ni,\ Pt\ or\ Pd} H_3C{-}CH_3$
  - Rate of hydrogenation
    - $-HC{=}CH_2 > -CH{=}CH-$ > ring double bond
    - $-CH_2{=}CH_2 < RCH{=}CHR$ (*trans* > *cis*) $< R_2CH{=}CH_2 < R_2CH{=}CHR < R_2C{=}CR_2$

- **Addition of halogen**
  - $H_3CCH{=}CH_2 + Cl{-}Cl \xrightarrow{CCl_4} CH_3CH(Cl){-}CH_2(Cl)$

- **Addition of hydrogen halides**
  - (For unsymmetrical alkene-Markownikoff's rule)
  - $H_3CCH{=}CH_2 + HBr \longrightarrow H_3C{-}CH(Br){-}CH_3$
  - (In presence of peroxide-reverse of Markownikoff's rule)
  - $H_3CCH{=}CH_2 + HBr \xrightarrow{Peroxide} CH_3CH_2CH_2Br$

- **Addition of water**
  - $(CH_3)_2C{=}CH_2 + H_2O \xrightarrow{H^+} (H_3C)_2C(OH){-}CH_3$

- **Hydroboration-oxidation**
  - $CH_3CH{=}CH_2 \xrightarrow[(ii)\ H_2O_2,\ OH^-]{(i)\ (BH_3)_2} CH_3CH_2CH_2OH + B(OH)_3$

- **Oxymercuration-demercuration**
  - $(CH_3)_3CCH{=}CH_2 \xrightarrow[(ii)\ NaBH_4/NaOH]{(i)\ Hg(OCOCH_3)_2} (CH_3)_3C\cdot CH(OH)CH_3$

- **Oxidation**
  - $H_2C{=}CH_2 + H_2O + [O] \xrightarrow[273K]{Dil.\ KMnO_4} CH_2(OH){-}CH_2(OH)$

- **Ozonolysis**
  - $(H_3C)_2C{=}CH_2 + O_3 \xrightarrow{Zn/H_2O} (H_3C)_2C{=}O + HCHO + H_2O_2$

- **Allylic substitution reactions**
  - $H_3C{-}CH{=}CH_2 + Cl_2 \xrightarrow[or\ h\nu]{500\text{-}600°C} CH_2{=}CHCH_2Cl + HCl$
  - $H_3C{-}CH{=}CH_2 \xrightarrow[Benzoyl\ peroxide]{NBS,\ h\nu} CH_2{=}CH{-}CH_2Br$ + succinimide ($CH_2{-}C(=O)$, $CH_2{-}C(=O)$ joined by NH)

- **Polymerisation reaction**
  - $nCH_2{=}CH_2 \xrightarrow{\text{High temperature/ pressure, catalyst}} {-}[CH_2{-}CH_2]_n{-}$

- **Wacker process**
  - $H_2C{=}CH_2 + PdCl_2 + H_2O \xrightarrow{323K} CH_3CHO + Pd + 2HCl$

- **Diels-Alder reaction**
  - $CH_2{=}CH{-}CH{=}CH_2 + CH_2{=}CH_2 \xrightarrow{h\nu}$ cyclohexene (CH_2, CH_2, CH_2, CH_2, $CH{=}CH$ ring as drawn)

Alkynes

- These are unsaturated hydrocarbons having at least one triple bond between two C-atoms with general formula C_nH_{2n-2}.
- These are named by adding suffix 'yne' to the root word.
- These also exhibit electrophilic addition reactions but these are less reactive than alkenes.

Structure

- Ethyne is the simplest molecule of alkyne series where each carbon atom of ethyne has two *sp*-hybridised orbitals.
- H—C≡C—H contains 3σ and 2π-bonds with bond length 120 pm and bond angle 180°.

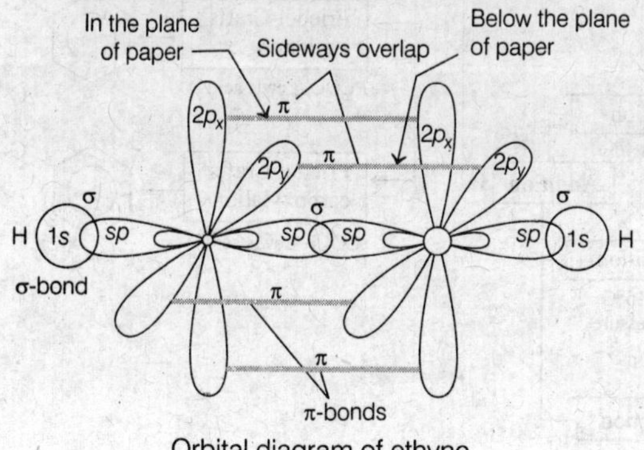

Orbital diagram of ethyne

Preparation

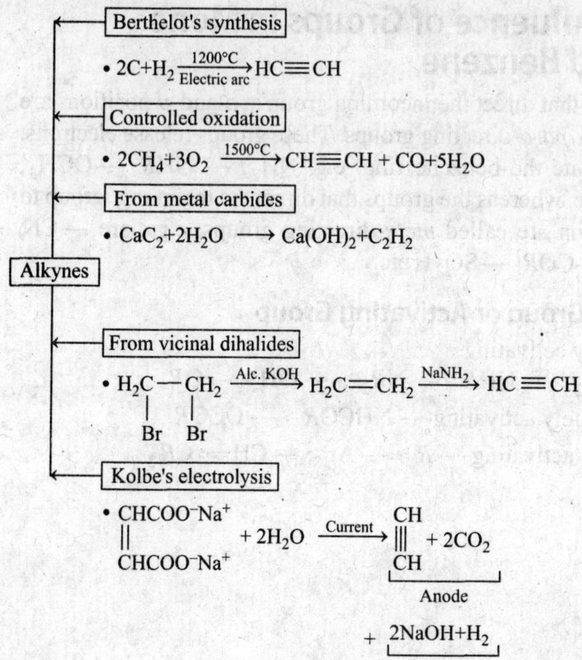

Physical Properties

- These are insoluble in water but soluble in organic solvents like ethers, CCl_4 and benzene.
- Melting point, boiling point and density increases with increase in molar mass.

Chemical Properties

Alkyne exhibit the following characteristic reactions :

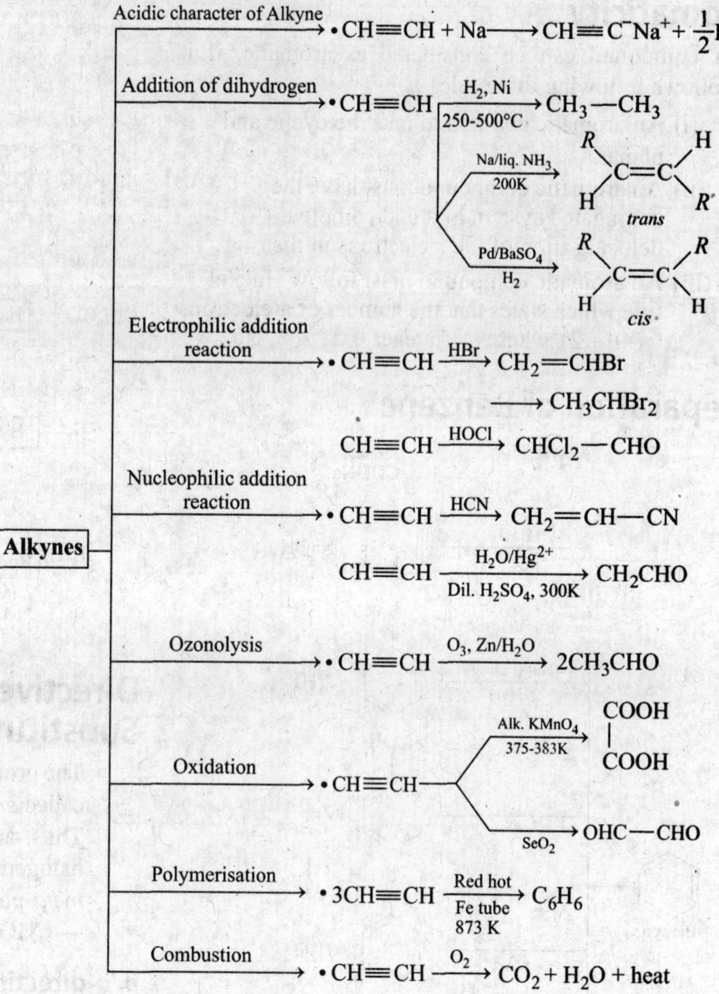

Aromatic Hydrocarbons or Arenes

- These are specialised cyclic compounds known for their characteristic smell.
- Aromatic compound containing benzene ring are known as benzenoids and those which do not contain a benzene ring are called non-benzenoids.
- **Benzene** It is a parent member of the family of aromatic hydrocarbons.

- It is resonance stabilised due to delocalisation of π-electrons and the structure may be represented as,

- Bond length in benzene rings lies between the single bond and double bond lengths, i.e. 1.39 Å.

Aromaticity

A compound can be considered as aromatic, if it follows following three rules :

(i) An aromatic compound must be cyclic and planar.

(ii) An aromatic compound must have the conjugated system in it and complete delocalisation of the π electrons in the ring.

(iii) An aromatic compound must follow Huckel rule which states that the number of π-electrons $= (4n + 2)$, where $n =$ integer 0, 1, 2, 3, etc.

Preparation of Benzene

Benzene ← (CaO, Δ) — Sodium benzoate ($\overset{-}{C}OO\overset{+}{N}a$) + NaOH

Benzene ← (Ni-Al alloy, NaOH) — Chlorobenzene + 2[H]

Benzene ← (Δ) — Phenol (OH) + Zn

Benzene ← (Δ) — Benzenesulphonic acid (SO_3H) + H_2O

Benzene ← (Δ) — Benzenediazonium chloride ($\overset{+}{N_2}Cl^-$) + CH_3CH_2OH

Benzene ← (Red hot tube) — $3CH{\equiv}CH$

Chemical Properties

Chemical reaction of benzene may be summarised as

BENZENE → Electrophilic substitution:

- Halogenation (Cl_2/Fe or $FeCl_3$ or $AlCl_3$; Br_2/Fe or $FeCl_3$ or $AlCl_3$) → Chlorobenzene (Cl)
- Dark nitration (HNO_3/H_2SO_4, 323-333 K) → Nitrobenzene (NO_2)
- Sulphonation (H_2SO_4/Δ) → Benzenesulphonic acid (SO_3H)
- Friedel-Crafts' alkylation (*RX*/Lewis acid) → Alkylbenzene (R)
- Friedel-Crafts' acylation (*R*COCl/Lewis acid) → C_6H_5—C(=O)—R
- Friedel-Crafts' carboxylation ($COCl_2$/Lewis acid) → C_6H_5—C(=O)—Cl

BENZENE → Oxidation:

- Ozonolysis (O_3/Zn) → CHO—CHO (Glyoxal)
- Vapour phase oxidation (V_2O_5/450°C) → Maleic anhydride

BENZENE → Addition:

- Halogenation (Cl_2 or Br_2/$h\nu$) → $C_6H_6Cl_6$
- Hydrogenation (H_2/Ni, 15°C under pressure) → Cyclohexane
- Birch reduction (Metal-alcohol Liquid NH_3) → 1,4-cyclohexadiene

Directive Influence of Groups in Mono Substituted Benzene

- The groups that direct the incoming group at *o*-and *p*-positions are called *ortho* /*para*-directing groups. These groups release electrons. Thus, activate the benzene ring, e.g. NH_2, — NH*R*, —OCH_3, halogens etc. whereas the groups that direct the incoming group to *meta*-position are called *meta*-directing groups. e.gs. are —CN, —CHO, —CO*R*, —SO_3H etc.

o/p-directing Group or Activating Group

(i) Strongly activating
$-NH_2 > -NHR > -NR_2 > -OH > -OR$

(ii) Moderately activating — NHCO*R* > — OCO*R*

(iii) Weakly activating — *R* > — Ar > — CH$=$CR_2

m-directing or deactivating

(i) Weakly deactivating — F > — Cl > — Br > — I

(ii) Moderately deactivating — CHO > — COR > — COOR > — COOH

(iii) Strongly deactivating — CN <— SO_3 < $\overset{+}{N}H_3$ < $\overset{+}{N}H_2R_2$ < $\overset{+}{N}HR_2$ < $\overset{+}{N}R_3$ <— NO_2

Carcinogenecity and Toxicity

Benzene and polynuclear hydrocarbons containing more than two benzene rings together are toxic and said to possess cancer producing (carcinogenic) property, e.g.

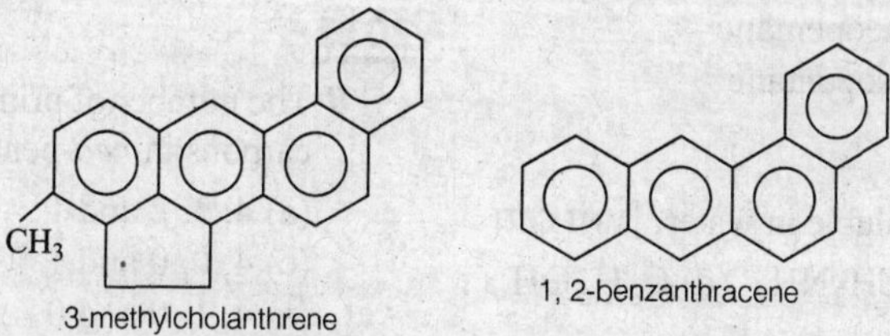

3-methylcholanthrene

1, 2-benzanthracene

Alicyclic Compounds

- Organic compound that can be both aliphatic and cyclic group are called alicylic compounds. They contain one or more aliphatic side chains.
- The simplest alicyclic compounds are the monocyclic cycloalkanes (cyclopropane, cyclobutane etc).
- Bicyclic alkanes include bicycloundecane, decalin etc.
- Polycyclic alkanes include cubane, basketane etc.

Topical Practice Questions

All the exam questions of this chapter have been divided into six topics as listed below :

Topic 1

Alkanes

2019

1 The alkane that gives only one mono-chloro product on chlorination with Cl_2 in presence of diffused sunlight is **[NEET (Odisha)]**

(a) 2, 2-dimethylbutane (b) neopentane
(c) *n*-pentane (d) isopentane

2017

2 Which of the following is least soluble in water? **[MHT CET]**

(a) C_2H_6 (b) CH_3OH (c) CH_3NH_2 (d) C_6H_5OH

2014

3 Select the alkane that is expected to have lowest boiling point. **[MHT CET]**

(a) Hexane (b) 2-methylpentane
(c) 3-methylpentane (d) 2, 2-dimethylbutane

4 '*X*' is an optically active alkane having lowest molecular mass, predict the structure of the major product obtained on monochlorination of '*X*' **[MHT CET]**

(a) $CH_3—CH_2—CH_2—C(CH_3)(Cl)—CH_2—CH_3$

(b) $CH_3—CH_2—CH_2—CH(CH_3)—CH(Cl)—CH_3$

(c) $CH_3—CH_2—CH_2—CH(CH_3)—CH_2—CH_2—Cl$

(d) $Cl—CH_2—CH_2—CH_2—CH(CH_3)—CH_2—CH_3$

5 C—H and C—C bond lengths (in pm) in ethane are **[EAMCET]**

(a) 133, 154 (b) 110, 136
(c) 112, 154 (d) 110, 154

2013

6 Assertion (A) CH_4 does not react with Cl_2 in dark.
Reason (R) Chlorination of CH_4 takes place in sunlight. **[Manipal]**

(a) Both A and R are correct and R is correct explanation of A
(b) Both A and R are correct but R is not correct explanation of A
(c) A is correct but R is incorrect
(d) Both A and R are incorrect

7 Wurtz reaction involves the interaction of alkyl halides in dry ether with **[WB JEE]**

(a) sodium (b) zinc
(c) copper (d) platinum

2011

8 The number of primary, secondary, tertiary and quaternary carbons in *neo*-pentane are respectively, **[Kerala CEE]**

(a) 4, 3, 2 and 1 (b) 5, 0, 0 and 1
(c) 4, 0, 0 and 1 (d) 4, 0, 1 and 1
(e) 4, 1, 0 and 0

9 Which one of the following has the lowest boiling point? **[Kerala CEE]**

(a) 2-methylbutane (b) 2-methylpropane
(c) 2,2-dimethylpropane (d) *n*-pentane
(e) *n*-butane

2010

10 Which compound cannot be formed from Wurtz reaction? **[UP CPMT]**

(a) Propane (b) Butane
(c) Ethane (d) Methane

11 On mixing an alkane with chlorine and irradiating with ultraviolet light, it forms only one monochloroalkane. The alkane is **[WB JEE]**

(a) propane (b) pentane
(c) *iso*-pentane (d) *neo*-pentane

12 Which of the following can be used for the preparation of propane? **[CMC]**

(a) $CH_3CH{=}CH_2 \xrightarrow[\text{2. } AgNO_3/NaOH]{\text{1. } B_2H_6}$

(b) $CH_3CH_2CH_2Cl \xrightarrow[\text{2. } H_2O_2]{\text{1. Mg/ether}}$

(c) $CH_3CH_2CH_2I \xrightarrow{\text{HI/Red P, } \Delta\, 150^\circ C}$

(d) $CH_3CH_2COONa \xrightarrow[\Delta]{NaOH\ (CaO)}$

13 The compound with highest boiling point is **[JCECE]**

(a) *n*-hexane
(b) *n*-pentane
(c) 2,2-dimethylpropane
(d) 2-methylbutane

14 The compound with an isopropyl group is **[RPMT]**

(a) 2,2,3,3-tetramethylpentane
(b) 2,2-dimethylpentane
(c) 2,2,3-trimethylpentane
(d) 2-methylpentane

2009

15 The number of primary, secondary and tertiary carbons in 3,4-dimethylheptane are respectively [Kerala CEE]

(a) 4, 3 and 2 (b) 2, 3 and 4
(c) 4, 2 and 3 (d) 3, 4 and 2
(e) 3, 3 and 3

16 Which of the following is a 3-methylbutyl group? [Kerala CEE]

(a) $CH_3CH_2CH_2CH_2CH_2$—
(b) $(CH_3CH_2)_2CH$—
(c) $(CH_3)_3CCH_2$—
(d) $(CH_3)_2CHCH_2CH_2$—
(e) $CH_3CH_2CH(CH_3)CH_2$—

17 Which isomer of hexane has only two different sets of structurally equivalent hydrogen atoms? [DUMET]

(a) 2,2-dimethylbutane (b) 2-methylpentane
(c) 3-methylpentane (d) 2,3-dimethylbutane

2008

18 The compounds formed at anode in the electrolysis of an aqueous solution of potassium acetate, are [UP CPMT]

(a) C_2H_6 and CO_2 (b) C_2H_4 and CO_2
(c) CH_4 and H_2 (d) CH_4 and CO_2

19 Which of the following reagents converts both acetaldehyde and acetone to alkanes? [UP CPMT]

(a) Ni / H_2 (b) $LiAlH_4$
(c) I_2 / NaOH (d) Zn-Hg/conc. HCl

20 When 2-chloro-2-methylbutane is heated with alcoholic KOH, the possible product/s is/are [Kerala CEE]

I. $(CH_3)_2C{=}CHCH_3$
II. $CH_2{=}C(CH_3)CH_2CH_3$
III. $(CH_3)_2CHCH{=}CH_2$

(a) I, II and III (b) I and III
(c) II and III (d) Only I
(e) I and II

21 When 1,1-dichloropropane and 2,2-dichloropropane are reacted separately with aqueous potassium hydroxide solution, compounds '*A*' and '*B*' are formed. Both '*A*' and '*B*' gave the same product '*C*' on reduction using amalgamated zinc and HCl. Identify '*C*'. [EAMCET]

(a) propyl alcohol (b) isopropyl alcohol
(c) propyl chloride (d) propane

2007

22 By which one of the following compounds both CH_4 and $CH_3—CH_3$ can be prepared in one step? [Manipal]

(a) CH_3I (b) CH_3OH
(c) CH_3CH_2I (d) C_2H_5OH

2006

23 Aromatisation of *n*-heptane by passing over $(Al_2O_3 + Cr_2O_3)$ catalyst at 773 K gives [Haryana PMT]

(a) benzene (b) toluene
(c) mixture of both (d) heptylene

24 Methyl bromide is converted into ethane by heating it in ether medium with [KCET]

(a) Al (b) Zn
(c) Na (d) Cu

25 By Wurtz reaction a mixture of methyl iodide and ethyl iodide gives [BCECE]

(a) butane
(b) ethane
(c) propane
(d) a mixture of the above three

2005

26 *X* is heated with soda lime and gives ethane, *X* is [AFMC]

(a) ethanoic acid (b) methanoic acid
(c) propanoic acid (d) Either (a) or (c)

27 When a mixture of CS_2 and steam (H_2O) or H_2S is passed over red hot copper, the product obtained is [Kerala CEE]

(a) CH_4 (b) C_2H_6
(c) Both (a) and (b) (d) C_2H_2
(e) None of these

28 Which of the following gas has the highest heat of combustion? [Haryana PMT]

(a) Methane (b) Ethane
(c) Ethene (d) Ethyne

29 Which of the following is called marsh gas? [AMU]

(a) C_2H_4 (b) C_2H_6 (c) C_2H_2 (d) CH_4

30 Household gaseous fuel (LPG) mainly contains [KCET]

(a) CH_4 (b) C_2H_2
(c) C_2H_4 (d) C_4H_{10}

Answers

1 (b)	2 (a)	3 (d)	4 (a)	5 (d)	6 (b)	7 (a)	8 (c)	9 (b)	10 (d)
11 (d)	12 (c)	13 (a)	14 (d)	15 (a)	16 (d)	17 (d)	18 (a)	19 (d)	20 (e)
21 (d)	22 (a)	23 (b)	24 (c)	25 (d)	26 (a)	27 (a)	28 (b)	29 (d)	30 (d)

Explanations

1 (*b*) Alkanes which contain all equivalent hydrogen atoms form only one monochloro derivative on halogenation.

$$neo\text{-pentane, } H_3C-\underset{CH_3}{\overset{CH_3}{\overset{|}{\underset{|}{C}}}}-CH_3$$

contains all equivalent hydrogen atoms. So, it will give only one monochloro derivative on halogenation.

2 (*a*) The solubility of a compound is governed by the principle that like dissolves like. Therefore, alkanes being non-polar are almost insoluble in water but readily soluble in ethanol and ether. Among the given options, C_2H_6 (ethane) is alkane. Thus, option (a) is least soluble in water.

3 (*d*) As the number of carbon atom increases, the boiling point of alkane increases because van der Waals' forces increases. However, branching results in decrease in boiling point due to decreased surface area which results in weaker van der Waals' forces. Hence, order of boiling points of given alkanes is

$$\underset{\text{Hexane}}{CH_3-CH_2-CH_2-CH_2-CH_2-CH_3}$$

$$> \underset{\text{3-methylpentane}}{CH_3-CH_2-\overset{CH_3}{\overset{|}{CH}}-CH_2-CH_3} >$$

$$\underset{\text{2-methylpentane}}{CH_3-CH_2-CH_2-\overset{CH_3}{\overset{|}{CH}}-CH_3} >$$

$$\underset{\text{2, 2-dimethylbutane}}{CH_3-\overset{CH_3}{\overset{|}{CH}}-\overset{CH_3}{\overset{|}{CH}}-CH_3}$$

Thus, 2, 2-dimethylbutane has lowest boiling point as it has maximum branching and least surface area among all the compounds.

4 (*a*) 3-methylhexane is an optically active alkane having lowest molecular mass among the given options.

$$\underset{(X)}{CH_3-CH_2-CH_2-\underset{H}{\underset{|}{\overset{CH_3}{\overset{|}{C^*}}}}-CH_2-CH_3}$$

$$\xrightarrow[hv]{Cl_2} CH_3-CH_2-CH_2-\underset{Cl}{\underset{|}{\overset{CH_3}{\overset{|}{C^*}}}}-CH_2-CH_3$$

Major product

5 (*d*) Bond distance is the average distance between nuclei of two bonded atoms in a molecule.

C—H bond length is 1.09 Å (109 pm) ≈ (110 pm) and

C—C bond length is 1.54 Å (154 pm) (approx). So, the correct option is (d).

6 (*b*) Chlorination of CH_4 does not take place in dark free radicals can be generated only in the presence of sunlight as this reaction follows free radical mechanism and which is necessary for the reaction to proceed further.

Hence, both A and R are correct. But R is not the correct explanation of A.

7 (*a*) Wurtz reaction is condensation reaction of two molecules of alkyl halides with sodium metal in the presence of dry ether.

$$RBr + 2Na + RBr \xrightarrow[\text{Dry ether}]{\Delta} R-R + 2NaBr$$

8 (*c*) $\underset{(P)}{H_3C}-\underset{CH_3^{(P)}}{\underset{|}{\overset{\overset{(P)}{CH_3}}{\overset{|}{\underset{(Q)}{C}}}}}-\underset{(P)}{CH_3}$

neo-pentane

Here, P = Primary carbon atom

Q = Quaternary carbon atom

Thus, *neo*-pentane has four primary carbon atoms, 0-secondary, 0-tertiary and 1 quaternary carbon atom.

9 (*b*) For the compounds with same molecular mass, boiling point decreases with increase in branching. Thus, the order for the boiling point of given alkanes is 2-methyl propane < *n*-butane < 2,2-dimethyl propane < 2-methyl butane < *n*- pentane. Hence, 2-methypropane has lowest boiling point.

10 (*d*) Compounds containing two or more carbon atoms are prepared by Wurtz reaction. Thus, methane, CH_4 cannot be prepared by this reaction.

11 (*d*) Alkanes which contain all equivalent hydrogen atoms forms only one monochloroderivative on halogenation. *neo*-pentane it contains all equivalent hydrogen atoms.

So, it will give only one monochloroderivative on halogenation.

$$\underset{neo\text{-pentane}}{H_3C-\underset{CH_3\,(1°)}{\underset{|}{\overset{CH_3\,(1°)}{\overset{|}{C}}}}-CH_3\,(1°)}$$

12 (*c*) Alkyl halides undergo reduction with red phosphorus and hydrogen iodide and result in the formation of alkane.

$$\underset{\text{Propyl iodide}}{CH_3CH_2CH_2I} \xrightarrow[150°C]{\text{Red P/HI}} \underset{\text{Propane}}{CH_3CH_2CH_3}$$

The products obtained in the other reactions are as follows:

(a) $CH_3-CH=CH_2 \xrightarrow[2.\ AgNO_3/NaOH]{1.\ B_2H_6} CH_3-CH_2-CH_2OH$

(b) $CH_3CH_2CH_2-Cl \xrightarrow[2.\ H_2O_2]{1.\ Mg/ether} CH_3CH_2CH_2OH$

(c) $CH_3CH_2CO\overset{-}{O}\overset{+}{Na} \xrightarrow[\Delta]{NaOH(CaO)} CH_3-CH_3$

13 (*a*) Boiling point ∝ molecular mass

$$\propto \frac{1}{\text{branching}} \quad (\because \text{Surface area decreases})$$

∴ *n*-hexane (straight chain) has the highest boiling point among the given alkanes.

14 (*d*) *iso* word is used for those alkanes which have a methyl group attached to the second last carbon atom of the continuous chain. Hence, 2-methylpentane is a compound with an *iso*-propyl group.

$$\underset{CH_3}{\underset{|}{\boxed{CH_3-CH}}}-CH_2-CH_2-CH_3$$

iso-propyl group

15 (*a*) In a compound, the carbon atoms present, may be primary (1°), secondary (2°), tertiary (3°) or quaternary (4°) depending upon whether these are attached with one, two, three or four carbon atoms. The structure of 3,4-dimethylheptane is given as :

$$\overset{P}{CH_3}-\overset{S}{CH_2}-\underset{T}{CH}(\overset{P}{CH_3})-\underset{T}{CH}(CH_2\overset{P}{CH_3})-\overset{S}{CH_2}-\overset{S}{CH_2}-\overset{P}{CH_3}$$

Here, P = primary carbon atom
S = secondary carbon atom
T = tertiary carbon atom

Hence, the number of primary, secondary and tertiary carbons present in 3,4-dimethylheptane are 4, 3 and 2 respectively.

16 (*d*) When a hydrogen is removed from butane, butyl group is obtained.

Hence, the structure of 3-methylbutyl group is $CH_3-\underset{CH_3}{\underset{|}{CH}}CH_2CH_2-$

or

$(CH_3)_2CHCH_2CH_2-$

17 (*d*) Only 2, 3-dimethyl butane has only two different sets of structurally equivalent hydrogen atoms.

$$\overset{P}{CH_3}-\underset{T}{CH}(\overset{P}{CH_3})-\underset{T}{CH}(\overset{P}{CH_3})-\overset{P}{CH_3}$$

2, 3-dimethyl butane

It has 12 primary and 2 tertiary H-atoms.

Other given options are explained below :

(a) 2, 2-dimethylbutane

$$\overset{P}{CH_3}-\overset{Q}{C}(\overset{P}{CH_3})_2-\overset{S}{CH_2}-\overset{P}{CH_3}$$

It has 3 sets of structurally different H-atoms, i.e. 12 primary, 2 secondary H-atoms and 1 quaternary H-atom.

(b) $$\overset{P}{CH_3}-\underset{T}{CH}(\overset{P}{CH_3})-\overset{S}{CH_2}-\overset{S}{CH_2}-\overset{P}{CH_3}$$

2-methylpentane

It has 3 sets of structurally different H-atoms, i.e. 9 primary, 4 secondary and 1 tertiary H-atoms.

(c) $$\overset{P}{CH_3}-\overset{S}{CH_2}-\underset{T}{CH}(\overset{P}{CH_3})-\overset{S}{CH_3}-\overset{P}{CH_3}$$

3-methyl pentane

It has 3 sets of structurally different H-atoms, i.e. 9 primary, 4 secondary and 1tertiary H-atoms.

18 (*a*) This is an example of Kolbe's electrolysis.

$$2CH_3\,CO\overset{-}{O}\overset{+}{K} \xrightarrow{\text{Electrolysis}} 2CH_3COO^- + 2K^+$$

At cathode

$$2K^+ + 2H_2O \longrightarrow 2KOH + H_2\uparrow$$

At anode

$$2CH_3COO^- \longrightarrow 2CH_3COO^\bullet + 2e^-$$

$$\downarrow -2CO_2$$

$$2CH_3^\bullet + 2CO_2\uparrow$$

$$\downarrow$$

$$C_2H_6\uparrow$$

19 (*d*) Carbonyl compounds like aldehydes [e.g. acetaldehyde, propanal, formaldehydes and ketones [e.g. acetone, propanone] can be converted into alkanes by either Clemmensen reduction [Zn-Hg/conc. HCl] or Wolff-Kishner reduction [$NH_2-NH_2 / C_2H_5ONa^+$]. Thus, both acetaldehyde and acetone can be converted into alkane by Zn-Hg/conc. HCl.

$$\begin{matrix}H\\CH_3\end{matrix}\!\!>C=O \xrightarrow[4[H]]{\text{Zn-Hg/conc.HCl}} \begin{matrix}H\\CH_3\end{matrix}\!\!>CH_2 + H_2O + H_2O$$

$$CH_3-\overset{O}{\overset{\|}{C}}-CH_3 \xrightarrow[4[H]]{\text{Zn-Hg/conc. HCl}} CH_3-CH_2-CH_3 + H_2O$$

20 (*e*) $$CH_3-\underset{Cl}{\underset{|}{\overset{CH_3}{\overset{|}{C}}}}-CH_2-CH_3 \xrightarrow[\Delta]{\text{Alc. KOH}} \underset{\substack{\text{(Major)}\\(A)}}{CH_3-\overset{CH_3}{\overset{|}{C}}=CH-CH_3} + \underset{\substack{\text{(Minor)}\\(B)}}{CH_2=\overset{CH_3}{\overset{|}{C}}-CH_2-CH_3}$$

21 (*d*) (i) $$\underset{\text{1,1-dichloropropane}}{CH_3-CH_2-CH\!<\!\begin{matrix}Cl\\Cl\end{matrix}} \xrightarrow{aq.\ KOH} \underset{\text{Unstable}}{CH_3-CH_2-CH\!<\!\begin{matrix}OH\\OH\end{matrix}} \xrightarrow{-H_2O} \underset{\substack{\text{Propanal}\\(A)}}{CH_3CH_2\overset{O}{\overset{\|}{C}}H}$$

$$\underset{(A)}{CH_3CH_2-\overset{H}{\overset{|}{C}}=O} \xrightarrow[\text{conc. HCl}]{\text{Zn-Hg}} \underset{\substack{\text{Propane}\\(C)}}{CH_3CH_2CH_3}$$

(ii) $$\underset{\text{2,2-dichloropropane}}{CH_3-\underset{Cl}{\underset{|}{\overset{Cl}{\overset{|}{C}}}}-CH_3} \xrightarrow{\text{aq. KOH}} \underset{\text{Unstable}}{CH_3-\underset{OH}{\underset{|}{\overset{OH}{\overset{|}{C}}}}-CH_3} \xrightarrow{-H_2O} \underset{\substack{\text{Acetone}\\(B)}}{CH_3-\underset{O}{\underset{\|}{C}}-CH_3}$$

$$\underset{(B)}{CH_3-\underset{O}{\underset{\|}{C}}-CH_3} \xrightarrow{\text{Zn-Hg/conc. HCl}} \underset{\substack{\text{Propane}\\(C)}}{CH_3-CH_2-CH_3}$$

Hence, compound (C) is propane.

22 (*a*) Methane and Ethane can be prepared in one step from CH_3I by reduction with Zn – Cu / H_2O and Wurtz reaction [Which double the number of C-atoms] respectively.

• $\underset{\text{Methyl iodide}}{CH_3I} + 2[H] \xrightarrow[H_2O]{\text{Zn–Cu (Reduction)}} \underset{\text{Methane}}{CH_4} + HI$

$CH_3I + 2Na + CH_3I \xrightarrow[\text{ether}]{\text{Wurtz reaction}} \underset{\text{Ethane}}{CH_3 - CH_3} + 2NaI$

23 (*b*) *n*-heptane ($CH_3-CH_2-CH_2-CH_2-CH_2-CH_2-CH_3$) $\xrightarrow[773\ K]{Al_2O_3/Cr_2O_3}$ toluene

24 (*c*) When alkyl halides are treated with sodium metal in dry ether, it results in the formation of an alkane having double number of carbon atoms as that are present in parent halide. This reaction is called **Wurtz reaction.**

e.g. $\underset{\text{Methyl bromide}}{CH_3Br} + 2Na + Br—CH_3 \xrightarrow{\text{Ether}} \underset{\text{Ethane}}{CH_3—CH_3} + 2NaBr$

25 (*d*) A single product, is obtained as symmetrical alkane, if alkyl halides are of single type during Wurtz reaction. But if different alkyl halides are used, the product is non-separable mixture of alkanes.

Methyl iodide and ethyl iodide, on treatment with sodium in ethereal solution, gives a mixture of propane, ethane and butane, as follows :

$CH_3I + 2Na + I — CH_2CH_3 \xrightarrow{\text{Ether}} \underset{\text{Propane}}{CH_3CH_2CH_3} + 2NaI$

$CH_3I + 2Na + I — CH_3 \longrightarrow \underset{\text{Ethane}}{CH_3 — CH_3} + 2NaI$

$C_2H_5I + 2Na + I — C_2H_5 \longrightarrow \underset{\text{Butane}}{C_2H_5C_2H_5} + 2NaI$

26 (*a*) Sodium salt of any carboxylic acid with hot soda lime undergoes decarboxylation to form alkane which has one carbon atom less than the parent molecule.

$\underset{\text{Propanoic acid}}{C_2H_5COOH} \xrightarrow[\Delta]{NaOH/CaO} \underset{\text{Ethane}}{C_2H_6} \uparrow + Na_2CO_3$

27 (*a*) $CS_2 + 2H_2O + 6Cu \longrightarrow 2Cu_2S + 2CuO + CH_4$

$CS_2 + 2H_2S + 8Cu \longrightarrow 4Cu_2S + CH_4$

28 (*b*) Ethane has seven sigma bonds, hence it has highest heat of combustion among the given compounds.

29 (*d*) Methane is called marsh gas because it is found in swamps or marshy places and can be obtained by bacterial decomposition of fossils of plants and animals.

30 (*d*) LPG is chiefly a mixture of butane and *iso*-butane. Their molecular formula is C_4H_{10}. The gas is used for cooking purpose.

Topic 2

Alkenes

2019

1 Correct order for reaction with alcoholic KOH

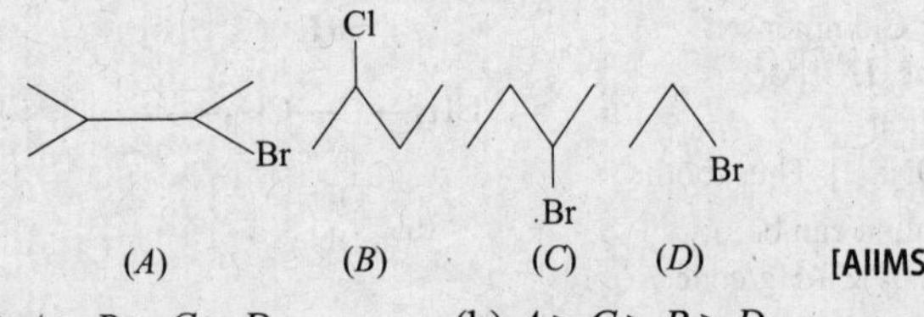

[AIIMS]

(a) $A > B > C > D$ (b) $A > C > B > D$
(c) $D > B > C > A$ (d) $A > D > B > C$

2 $CH_3 — CH_2 — CH_2 — Br \xrightarrow{\text{Alc. KOH}}$ Final product is [JIPMER]

(a) propene (b) propanol
(c) cyclopropane (d) propan-1, 2-diol

3 The most suitable reagent for the following conversion, is

$H_3C—C{\equiv}C—CH_3 \longrightarrow$ *cis*-2-butene ($H_3C(H)C{=}C(H)CH_3$) [NEET]

(a) H_2, Pd/C, quinoline (b) Zn/HCl
(c) $Hg^{2+}/H^+, H_2O$ (d) Na/liquid NH_3

4 Among the following rules, the one which is applied in the given reaction is [AIIMS]

$CH_3CHBrCH_2CH_3 \xrightarrow{\text{Alc. KOH}}$

I. $CH_3CH = CHCH_3$ (major product)
II. $CH_2 = CHCH_2CH_3$ (minor product)

(a) Saytzeff 's rule (b) Hofmann 's rule
(c) Markownikoff's rule (d) Kharasch effect

2018

5 $Y \xleftarrow{H_3O^+}$ (cyclohexylidene)$=CH_2 \xrightarrow[\text{(ii) } H_2O_2/OH^-]{\text{(i) } B_2H_6/THF} X$

X and *Y* respectively are

(a) Both cyclohexyl–CH_2OH (b) Both 1-methylcyclohexanol (ring with CH_3 and OH)
(c) cyclohexyl–CH_2OH ; 1-methylcyclohexanol (CH_3, OH)
(d) 1-methylcyclohexanol (CH_3, OH) ; cyclohexyl–CH_2OH

2014

6 The compound that yields only ketonic compound/s on ozonolysis is **[MHT CET]**

(a) but-2-ene
(b) pent-2-ene
(c) 2, 3-dimethylbut-2-ene
(d) 2-methylbut-2-ene

7 Major product A of the reaction is

$(CH_3)_2C{=}CH_2 \xrightarrow{ICl} A$ **[Manipal]**

(a) 2-chloro-1-iodo-2-methyl propane
(b) 1-chloro-2-iodo-2-methyl propane
(c) 1, 2-dichloro-2-methyl propane
(d) 1, 2-diiodo-2-methyl propane

8 The correct order of decreasing H—C—H angle in the following molecule is **[WB JEE]**

I: cyclopropane CH_2 (H, C, H); II: $=CH_2$ (H, C, H); III: CH_4 type (H, H, C, H, H)

(a) I > II > III (b) II > I > III
(c) III > II > I (d) I > III > II

9 What are Y and Z in the following reaction sequence?

$$CH_2 = CHBr \xrightarrow{NaNH_2} Y \xrightarrow[H_2O]{Hg^{2+}/H^+} Z$$

(a)	Ethyne	Acetic acid
(b)	Ethyne	Ethanal
(c)	Ethylamine	Ethanal
(d)	Ethane	Ethanol

2013

10 In the following reaction,

$$CH_3-\underset{CH_3}{\overset{CH_3}{\underset{|}{\overset{|}{C}}}}-CH{=}CH_2 \xrightarrow{H_2O/H^+} \underset{\text{Major product}}{A} + \underset{\text{Minor product}}{B}$$

The major product is **[CBSE AIPMT]**

(a) $CH_3-\underset{OH}{\overset{CH_3}{\underset{|}{\overset{|}{C}}}}-\underset{CH_3}{\underset{|}{CH}}-CH_3$

(b) $\underset{OH}{\underset{|}{CH_2}}-\underset{CH_3}{\overset{CH_3}{\underset{|}{\overset{|}{C}}}}-CH_2-CH_3$

(c) $CH_3-\underset{CH_3}{\overset{CH_3}{\underset{|}{\overset{|}{C}}}}-\underset{OH}{\underset{|}{CH}}-CH_3$

(d) $CH_3-\underset{CH_3}{\overset{CH_3}{\underset{|}{\overset{|}{C}}}}-CH_2-\underset{OH}{\underset{|}{CH_2}}$

2012

11 Which one of the following has the minimum boiling point? **[AIIMS]**

(a) *n*-butane (b) 1-butyne (c) 1-butene (d) *iso*-butene

12 When one mole of an alkene (detan) on ozonolysis produces 2 moles of propanone, the alkane is **[Kerala CEE]**

(a) 3-methyl-1-butene (b) 2,3-dimethyl-1-butene
(c) 2, 3-dimethyl-2-pentene (d) 2,3-dimethyl-2-butene

13 Reaction of propene with diborane followed by alkaline hydrolysis in the presence of hydrogen peroxide gives **[AMU]**

(a) 1-propanol (b) 2-propanol
(c) 1, 2-dihydroxypropane (d) *n*-propane

14 2-phenyl propene on acidic hydration gives **[JIPMER]**

(a) 2-phenyl propen-2-ol (b) 2-phenyl propen-1-ol
(c) 3-phenyl propan-1-ol (d) 2-phenyl propan-1-ol

2011

15 Identify B and D in the following sequence of reactions. **[KCET]**

$$CH_2{=}CH_2 \xrightarrow[H_2SO_4]{Conc.} A \xrightarrow[H_2O]{\Delta} B \xrightarrow[[D]]{} \underset{[C]}{C_2H_4}$$

(a) Methanol and bromoethane
(b) Ethyl hydrogen sulphate and alcoholic KOH
(c) Ethyl hydrogen sulphate and aqueous KOH
(d) Ethanol and alcoholic KOH

2010

16 Ethylene combine with sulphur monochloride to form **[BVP]**

(a) phosgene (b) mustard gas
(c) methyl isocyanate (MIC) (d) lewisite

17 Aqueous solution of sodium succinate on electrolysis gives **[OJEE]**

(a) CH_3-CH_3 (b) $CH_2{=}CH_2$
(c) $CH{\equiv}CH$ (d) CO_2

18 Which alkene on ozonolysis gives CH_3CH_2CHO and CH_3COCH_3 ? **[RPMT]**

(a) $CH_3CH_2CH{=}C(CH_3)_2$
(b) $CH_3CH_2CH{=}CHCH_2CH_3$
(c) $CH_3CH_2CH{=}CHCH_3$
(d) $(CH_3)_2C{=}CHCH_3$

19 In the following sequence of reactions, the alkene gives the compound *B*.

$$CH_3-CH=CH-CH_3 \xrightarrow{O_3} A \xrightarrow{H_2\,O/Zn} B$$

B is **[Haryana PMT]**

(a) CH_3CH_2CHO (b) CH_3CH_3
(c) $CH_3CH_2COCH_3$ (d) CH_3CHO

20 When subjected to acid catalysed hydration, the order of reactivity of the alkenes is; **[AMU]**

I. $(CH_3)_2C{=}CH_2$, II. $CH_3CH{=}CH_2$ and
III. $CH_2{=}CH_2$ is

(a) III > II > I (b) I > III > II
(c) I > II > III (d) II > I > III

21 Which of the following is the predominant product in the reaction of HOBr with propene? **[JCECE]**

(a) 2-bromo-1-propanol (b) 3-bromo-1-propanol
(c) 2-bromo-2-propanol (d) 1-bromo-2-propanol

22 An alkene, on ozonolysis gives formaldehyde and acetaldehyde. The alkene is **[VMMC]**

(a) ethene (b) propene (c) but-1-ene (d) but-2-ene

2009

23 The compound which is obtained by treating chloropropane with alcoholic KOH, when reacts with BH_3 / THF followed by acetic acid gives **[AIIMS]**

(a) $CH_3CH_2CH_2OH$ (b) $CH_3CH_2CH_3$
(c) $CH_3CH(OH)CH_3$ (d) $CH_3CH_2CHOHCH_3$

24 Formation of alcohol by oxymercuration- demercuration of alkenes **[AIIMS]**

(a) involves carbocations and rearrangement
(b) involves carbanions and rearrangement
(c) is stereospecific
(d) does not involve rearrangement and carbocation

25 Three products are obtained by the ozonolysis of penta-1, 3-diene. Out of these, if two products are formaldehyde and acetaldehyde, the name of the third one is **[AFMC]**

(a) formaldehyde (b) ethanal
(c) glyoxal (d) propanaldehyde

26 $CH_2{=}CH{-}CH_2{-}CH{=}CH_2$ represents a/an **[AFMC]**

(a) conjugated system (b) cumulative system
(c) isolated system (d) All of these

27 Ethylene can be separated from acetylene by passing the mixture through **[WB JEE]**

(a) fuming H_2SO_4
(b) pyrogallol
(c) ammoniacal Cu_2Cl_2
(d) charcoal powder

28 The addition of HBr to 2-pentene gives **[WB JEE]**

(a) 2-bromopentane only
(b) 3-bromopentane only
(c) 2-bromopentane and 3-bromopentane
(d) 1-bromopentane and 3-bromopentane

29 Among the following, the alkene on ozonolysis giving rise to only one aldehyde as the product is **[J&K CET]**

(a) 1-butene (b) propane
(c) 2-butene (d) 2-methylprop-1-ene

30 Products of the following reaction,

$$Me_2C=CHCH_3 \xrightarrow[\text{(ii) }(CH_3)_2S]{\text{(i) }O_3} \text{? are}$$ **[AMU]**

(a) $CH_3CHO + CH_3COOH$ (b) $Me_2CO + CH_3CHO$
(c) $Me_2CO + CH_3COOH$ (d) $2Me_2CO$

31 One mole of alkene *X* on ozonolysis gave one mole of acetaldehyde and one mole of acetone. The IUPAC name of *X* is **[EAMCET]**

(a) 2-methyl-2-butene (b) 2-methyl-1-butene
(c) 2-butene (d) 1-butene

2008

32 $H_3C-\underset{\underset{CH_3}{|}}{CH}-CH{=}CH_2 + HBr \longrightarrow A$

A (predominantly) is **[CBSE AIPMT]**

(a) $CH_3-\underset{\underset{CH_3}{|}}{CH}-CH_2-CH_2Br$

(b) $CH_3-\overset{\overset{Br}{|}}{\underset{\underset{CH_3}{|}}{C}}-CH_2CH_3$

(c) $CH_3-\underset{\underset{Br}{|}}{CH}-\underset{\underset{CH_3}{|}}{CH}-CH_3$

(d) $CH_3-\underset{\underset{CH_3}{|}}{CH}-\underset{\underset{Br}{|}}{CH}-CH_3$

33 An alkene on vigorous oxidation with $KMnO_4$ gives only acetic acid. The alkene is **[Manipal]**

(a) $CH_3CH_2CH{=}CH_2$ (b) $CH_3CH{=}CHCH_3$
(c) $(CH_3)_2C{=}CH_2$ (d) $CH_3CH{=}CH_2$

34 What will be the product in the following reaction? **[AMU]**

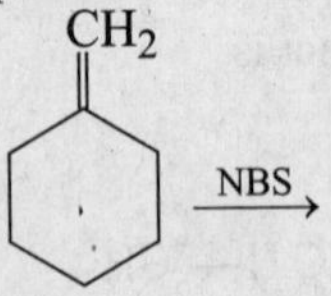

Methylenecyclohexane (CH_2 on ring) $\xrightarrow{NBS}$

(a) ring with $=CH_2$ and adjacent Br
(b) ring with CH_3 and Br (1,4-positions)
(c) ring with CH_2Br
(d) ring with CH_3 and Br (1,3-positions)

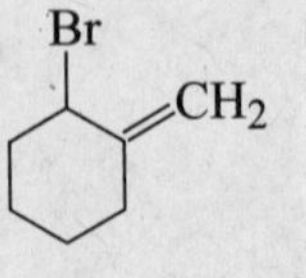

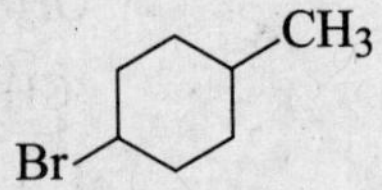

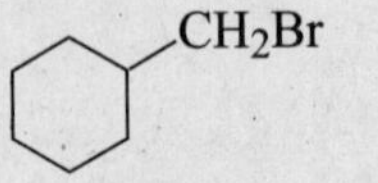

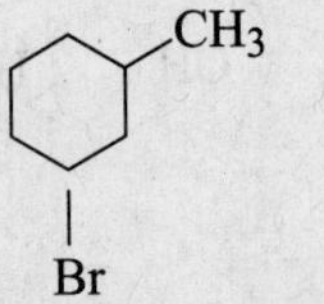

35 Which one of the following reactions yield 2*E*-butene as the major product? **[EAMCET]**

(a) $CH_3—C{\equiv}C—CH_3 + Na/NH_3$ (liq.)
(b) $CH_3—CH{=}CH—CH_3 + Li/NH_3$ (liq.)
(c) $CH_3—C{=}C—CH_3 + Na/NH_4OH$
(d) $CH_3—C{\equiv}C—CH_3 + Pd/BaSO_4$

36 Acid catalysed hydration of alkenes except ethene leads to the formation of **[JCECE]**

(a) mixture of secondary and tertiary alcohols
(b) mixture of primary and secondary alcohols
(c) secondary or tertiary alcohol
(d) primary alcohol

2007

37 Predict the product *C* obtained in the following reaction of butyne-1. **[CBSE AIPMT]**

$$CH_3CH_2—C{\equiv}CH + HCl \longrightarrow B \xrightarrow{HI} C$$

(a) $CH_3—CH(Cl)—CH_2CH_2I$
(b) $CH_3—CH_2—CH_2—C(I)(Cl)—H$
(c) $CH_3—CH_2—CH(I)—CH_2Cl$
(d) $CH_3CH_2—C(I)(Cl)—CH_3$

38 For synthesis of 1-butene, CH_3MgI should be treated with **[MHT CET]**

(a) propene (b) 2-chloropropene
(c) allyl chloride (d) ethyl chloride

39 Reaction of HBr with propene in the presence of peroxide gives **[Manipal]**

(a) isopropyl bromide (b) 3-bromo propane
(c) allyl bromide (d) *n*-propyl bromide

40 Oxidation of an alkene *X* gives a diol; further oxidation gives a diketone. Which one of the following could be *X* ? **[Kerala CEE]**

(a) $(CH_3)_2C{=}C(CH_3)_2$ (b) $CH_3CH{=}C(CH_3)_2$
(c) $(CH_3)_2CHCH{=}CH_2$ (d) $C_6H_5CH{=}CHC_6H_5$
(e) $(C_6H_5)_2C{=}CHCH_3$

2006

41 **Assertion** (A) Addition of HBr on 2-butene gives two isomeric products.
Reason (R) Addition of HBr on 2-butene follows Markownikoff's rule. **[AIIMS]**

(a) Both A and R are correct and R is the correct explanation of A
(b) Both A and R are correct but R is not the correct explanation of A
(c) A is correct but R is incorrect
(d) Both A and R are incorrect

42 In the following reaction, *A* and *B*, respectively are

$$A \xrightarrow{HBr} C_2H_5Br \xrightarrow{B} A$$ **[J&K CET]**

(a) C_2H_4, alc. KOH/Δ (b) C_2H_5Cl, *aq* KOH/Δ
(c) CH_3OH, *aq*. KOH/Δ (d) C_2H_2, PBr_3

43 Which of the following compounds is generally used for hydrogenation of alkenes? **[Punjab PMET]**

(a) $Ni(CO)_4$ (b) $[(C_6H_5)_3P]_3RhCl$
(c) $(CH_3)_3Al$ (d) $(C_2H_5)_2Fe$

44 $C_6H_9Br \xrightarrow[-(CH_3)_3COH]{(CH_3)_3CO^-K^+} X \xrightarrow{CH_2{=}CHCOCH_3} B$

conversion of *X* to *B* is **[DUMET]**

(a) Claisen reaction (b) Perkin reaction
(c) Diels-Alder reaction (d) Mannich reaction

2005

45 Which one of the following alkenes will react faster with H_2 under catalytic hydrogenation conditions? (R = Alkyl substituent) **[CBSE AIPMT]**

(a) 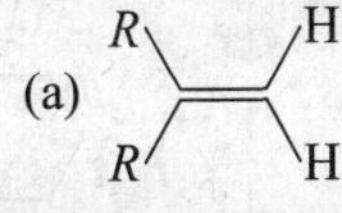

(b) 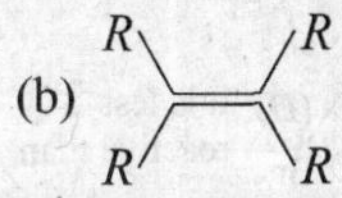

(c) 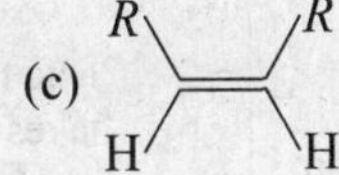

(d) $R_2C{=}CRH$

46 3-phenylpropene on reaction with HBr gives (as a major product) **[AIIMS]**

(a) $C_6H_5CH_2CH(Br)CH_3$
(b) $C_6H_5CH(Br)CH_2CH_3$
(c) $C_6H_5CH_2CH_2CH_2Br$
(d) $C_6H_5CH(Br)CH{=}CH_2$

47 $R—CH{=}CH_2 \xrightarrow[C_2H_5OH]{Na/NH_3(l)} RCH_2CH_3$ **[Haryana PMT]**

This reaction is called

(a) Arndt-Eistert reaction (b) Birch reduction
(c) Clemmensen reduction (d) Fisher-Spier reaction

48 Which of the following has the smallest heat of hydrogenation per mole? **[Haryana PMT]**

(a) 1-butene (b) *trans*-2-butene
(c) *cis*-2-butene (d) 1,3-butadiene

49 The most stable alkene is **[Punjab PMET]**

(a) $R_2C{=}CR_2$ (b) $RCH{=}CHR$
(c) $CH_2{=}CH_2$ (d) $RCH{=}CR_2$

Answers

1 (b)	2 (a)	3 (a)	4 (a)	5 (c)	6 (c)	7 (a)	8 (b)	9 (b)	10 (a)
11 (d)	12 (d)	13 (a)	14 (a)	15 (d)	16 (b)	17 (b)	18 (a)	19 (d)	20 (c)
21 (d)	22 (b)	23 (b)	24 (a)	25 (c)	26 (c)	27 (c)	28 (c)	29 (c)	30 (b)
31 (a)	32 (b)	33 (b)	34 (a)	35 (a)	36 (c)	37 (d)	38 (c)	39 (d)	40 (d)
41 (d)	42 (a)	43 (b)	44 (c)	45 (a)	46 (a)	47 (b)	48 (b)	49 (a)	

Explanations

1 (*b*) When alcoholic KOH react with haloalkanes, the reaction (rate) depends on the following factor:

(i) Size of halogen

(ii) Degree of C-atom, to which the halogen atom is bonded, i.e. more the degree of haloalkane, more is its reactivity.

As, bromine atom is large in size, thus

(*A*) [skeletal structure with Br] and (*C*) [skeletal structure with Br] are more reactive than (*B*) [skeletal structure with Cl] but, due to lesser degree of (*D*) [skeletal structure with Br], it is less reactive than [skeletal structure with Cl]

Hence, correct order is $A > C > B > D$.

Thus, option (b) is the correct.

2 (*a*) When haloalkane with β-hydrogen atom is heated with alc. KOH solution, then alkene is formed

$$CH_3CH_2CH_2Br \xrightarrow{\text{alc. KOH}} \underset{\text{Propene}}{CH_3CH = CH_2}$$

Carbon and the halogen is lost from α-carbon atom. As a result, an alkene is formed as a product.

Due to the involvement of elimination of β-hydrogen atom, the process is often called β -elimination.

3 (*a*) Hydrogenation of alkynes in the presence of Pd/C, quinoline proceeds through *syn* addition of hydrogen and the alkene thus formed has *cis*-configuration.

$$\underset{\text{But-2-yne}}{H_3C{-}C{\equiv}C{-}CH_3} \xrightarrow[\text{Quinoline}]{H_2,\ Pd/C} \underset{\substack{cis\text{-2-butene} \\ (syn\ \text{addition})}}{(H_3C)(H)C{=}C(H)(CH_3)}$$

4 (*a*) Alkyl halide on heating with alcoholic KOH undergoes dehydrohalogenation to yield alkene. If in reaction, more than one alkene is formed, then according to Saytzeff rule, the most highly substituted alkene formed is the major product.

$$CH_3-\underset{Br}{CH}-\overset{H}{CH}-CH_3 \xrightarrow[\text{Alc. KOH}]{-H_2O} \underset{\text{(Major product)}}{CH_3CH{=}CHCH_3} + Br^-$$

5 (*c*)

$$\underset{(X)}{C_6H_{11}{-}CH_2OH} \xleftarrow[\text{(ii) } H_2O_2, OH^-]{\text{(i) } B_2H_6/THF} C_6H_{10}{=}CH_2 \xrightarrow{H_3O^+} \underset{(Y)}{C_6H_{10}(CH_3)(OH)}$$

Due to hydration, addition of H_2O takes place by Markownikoff's rule and by hydroboration-oxidation, addition of H_2O takes place by anti-Markownikoff's rule.

6 (*c*)

(a) $\underset{\text{But-2-ene}}{(CH_3)(H)C{=}C(CH_3)(H)} \xrightarrow[Zn/H_2O]{O_3} \underset{\text{Acetaldehyde}}{2CH_3CHO} + H_2O_2$

(b) $\underset{\text{Pent-2-ene}}{(C_2H_5)(H)C{=}C(CH_3)(H)} \xrightarrow[Zn/H_2O]{O_3} \underset{\text{Propanaldehyde}}{C_2H_5CHO} + \underset{\text{Acetaldehyde}}{CH_3CHO} + H_2O_2$

(c) $\underset{\text{2, 3-dimethyl but-2-ene}}{(CH_3)_2C{=}C(CH_3)_2} \xrightarrow[Zn/H_2O]{O_3} 2\underset{\text{Propanone}}{(CH_3)_2C{=}O} + H_2O_2$

(d) $\underset{\text{2-methylbut-2-ene}}{(CH_3)(H)C{=}C(CH_3)_2} \xrightarrow{O_3 / H_2O} \underset{\text{Acetaldehyde}}{CH_3CHO} + \underset{\text{Acetone}}{(CH_3)_2C{=}O} + H_2O_2$

Hence, 2, 3-dimethylbut - 2-ene yields only ketonic products.

7 (*a*) I—Cl is polarised and undergoes heterolytic fission [as Cl being more electronegative than I] to generate iodonium ion (I^+) and chloride ion (Cl^-).

$$I{-}Cl \longrightarrow I^+ + Cl^-$$

The reaction proceeds through the formation of a bridged iodonium ion which is more stable than carbocation followed by the attack of chloride ion

$$CH_3-\overset{CH_3}{C}=CH_2 \longrightarrow CH_3-\overset{CH_3}{\overset{+}{C}}-CH_2 + I{-}Cl \text{ (more electronegative)}$$

$$\longrightarrow CH_3-\underset{Cl}{\overset{CH_3}{C}}-CH_2^{\ominus}$$

Hence, A is $CH_3-\underset{CH_3}{\overset{Cl}{C}}-CH_2I$

i.e. 2-chloro-1-iodo-2-methylpropane

8 (*b*) H—C—H bond angle is about 120°, when C is bonded through a double bond but in case of CH_4, the H—C—H bond angle is only 109° 28′. Cyclic compounds have a H—C—H bond angle greater than 109° 28′ due to ring strain.

Thus, the correct order of H—C—H bond angle is II > I > III.

9 (*b*) $CH_2{=}CHBr \xrightarrow{NaNH_2} CH{\equiv}CH \xrightarrow[H_2O]{Hg^{2+}/H^+}$ (Ethyne)

$H_2C{=}C(H)(O{-}H) \xrightleftharpoons{\text{Tautomerism}} CH_3{-}CHO$ (Ethanal)

10 (*a*) $CH_3{-}C(CH_3)_2{-}CH{=}CH_2 \xrightarrow{H^+/H_2O}$

$CH_3{-}C(CH_3)_2{-}\overset{\oplus}{C}H{-}CH_3 \xrightarrow{\text{(1,2-methyl shift)}}$

2° carbocation

$CH_3{-}\overset{+}{C}(CH_3){-}CH(CH_3){-}CH_3 \xrightarrow{H_2\ddot{O}:}$

3°carbocation (more stable)

$CH_3{-}C(CH_3)(\overset{+}{O}H_2){-}CH(CH_3){-}CH_3 \xrightarrow{-H^+} CH_3{-}C(CH_3)(OH){-}CH(CH_3){-}CH_3$

2,3-dimethylbutan-2-ol (major product) '*A*'

From 2° carbocation minor product will form

$CH_3{-}C(CH_3)_2{-}\overset{+}{C}H\,CH_3 \xrightarrow[(ii)\,-H^+]{(i)\,H_2\ddot{O}:} H_3C{-}C(CH_3)_2{-}CH(OH)CH_3$

2°carbocation

(Minor product '*B*')

11 (*d*) *iso*-butene ($CH_3{-}C(CH_3){=}CH_2$) possesses branching, thus, minimum van der Waals' force of attraction are present in it.

Hence, possesses minimum boiling point.

12 (*d*) $CH_3{-}C(CH_3){=}C(CH_3){-}CH_3 \xrightarrow[O_3;Zn/H_2O]{\text{Ozonolysis}} 2CH_3{-}\overset{O}{\overset{\|}{C}}{-}CH_3$

2,3-dimethylbut-2-ene — Propanone

Products obtained by other alkenes are as follows:

(a) $CH_2{=}CH{-}CH(CH_3){-}CH_3 \xrightarrow{\text{Ozonolysis}} \overset{O}{\overset{\|}{C}}H_2 + CH_3{-}CH(CH_3){-}CHO$

(b) $CH_2{=}C(CH_3){-}CH(CH_3){-}CH_3 \xrightarrow{\text{Ozonolysis}} \overset{O}{\overset{\|}{C}}H_2 + CH_3{-}\overset{O}{\overset{\|}{C}}{-}CH(CH_3){-}CH_3$

(c) $CH_3{-}C(CH_3){=}C(CH_3){-}CH_2CH_3 \xrightarrow{\text{Ozonolysis}} CH_3{-}\overset{O}{\overset{\|}{C}}{-}CH_3 + CH_3{-}\overset{O}{\overset{\|}{C}}{-}CH_2CH_3$

13 (*a*) $CH_3CH{=}CH_2 + (H{-}BH_2)_2 \longrightarrow CH_3{-}CH_2{-}CH_2{-}BH_2$

$\xrightarrow{CH_3CH=CH_2} (CH_3{-}CH_2{-}CH_2)_2BH$

$\xrightarrow{CH_3CH=CH_2} (CH_3CH_2CH_2)_3B \xrightarrow[OH^-]{3H_2O_2} 3\,CH_2CH_2CH_2(OH) + B(OH)_3$

1-propanol — Boric acid

14 (*a*) 2-phenylpropane on acidic hydrogen gives 2-phenyl propan-2-ol. Overall reaction is as follows :

$C_6H_5{-}C(CH_3){=}CH_2 \xrightarrow{H^+} C_6H_5{-}\overset{+}{C}(CH_3)_2 \xrightarrow{H_2O} C_6H_5{-}C(CH_3)_2{-}\overset{+}{O}H_2 \xrightarrow{-H^+} C_6H_5{-}C(CH_3)_2{-}OH$

15 (*d*) $CH_2{=}CH_2 \xrightarrow{\text{Conc. }H_2SO_4} \underset{(A)}{CH_3CH_2OSO_3H} \xrightarrow[H_2O]{\Delta} \underset{(B)}{C_2H_5OH} \xrightarrow{\text{Alc. KOH }(D)} \underset{(C)}{C_2H_4}$

16 (*b*) $CH_2{=}CH_2 + S_2Cl_2 \longrightarrow S(CH_2CH_2Cl)_2 + S$

Sulphur mono chloride — Mustard gas (war gas)

17 (*b*) $\begin{matrix} CH_2{-}CO\bar{O}\overset{+}{N}a \\ | \\ CH_2{-}CO\bar{O}\overset{+}{N}a \end{matrix} + 2H_2O \xrightarrow{\text{Electrolysis}} \underbrace{CH_2{=}CH_2 + 2CO_2}_{\text{At anode}} + \underbrace{2NaOH + H_2}_{\text{At cathode}}$

18 (a) $CH_3CH_2CH{=}C(CH_3)_2 \xrightarrow{O_3}$ [ozonide: $CH_3CH_2HC(O{-}O)(O)C(CH_3)_2$] $\xrightarrow{Zn,\,H_2O} CH_3CH_2CHO + CH_3COCH_3$

(b) $CH_3CH_2CH{=}CHCH_2CH_3 \xrightarrow[(ii)\,Zn/H_2O]{(i)\,O_3} 2CH_3CH_2CHO$

(c) $CH_3CH_2CH{=}CHCH_3 \xrightarrow[(ii)\,Zn/H_2O]{(i)\,O_3} CH_3CH_2CHO + CH_3CHO$

(d) $CH_3{-}C(CH_3){=}CH{-}CH_3 \xrightarrow[(ii)\,Zn/H_2O]{(i)\,O_3} CH_3COCH_3 + CH_3{-}CHO$

Hence, option (a) is correct.

19 (*d*)

$$CH_3—CH=CH—CH_3 \xrightarrow[\text{(Ozonolysis)}]{O_3}$$
but-2-ene

$$CH_3HC \overset{O}{\frown} CH—CH_3$$ (O—O bridged)
Ozonide (*A*)

$$\downarrow -H_2O_2 \mid H_2O/Zn$$

$$2CH_3CHO$$
Acetaldehyde (*B*)

Hence, the given alkene on ozonolysis gives only acetaldehyde.

20 (*c*) Acid catalysed hydration of alkenes involve formation of carbocation intermediate. Higher the stability of carbocation intermediate, more is the reactivity towards acid catalysed hydration. The order of stability of carbocation (formed) is

$$(CH_3)_2\overset{+}{C}CH_3 > CH_3\overset{+}{C}HCH_3 > \overset{+}{C}H_2—CH_3$$

Thus, the order of reactivity towards acid catalysed hydration is

$$\underset{I}{(CH_3)_2C=CH_2} > \underset{II}{CH_3CH=CH_2} > \underset{III}{CH_2=CH_2}$$

21 (*d*) $CH_3CH=CH_2 + \overset{\delta-}{HO}\overset{\delta+}{Br} \longrightarrow CH_3\underset{OH}{\underset{|}{CH}}—CH_2Br$
Propene; 1-bromo-2-propanol

The addition takes place according to Markownikoff's rule.

22 (*b*) $CH_3—CH=CH—H \xrightarrow[\text{(Ozonolysis)}]{O_3}$
Propene

$$CH_3HC \overset{O}{\frown} CH—H$$ (O—O bridged)
Ozonide (*A*)

$$\downarrow -H_2O_2 \mid H_2O/Zn$$

$$CH_3—CHO + HCHO$$
Acetaldehyde Formaldehyde

23 (*b*) $CH_3CH_2CH_2Cl \xrightarrow[-KCl;\ -H_2O]{\text{Alc. KOH}}$
Chloropropane

$$CH_3CH=CH_2 \xrightarrow{BH_3/THF}$$
Propene

$$(CH_3CH_2CH_2)_3B \xrightarrow{CH_3COOH} CH_3CH_2CH_3$$
Propane

24 (*a*) Oxymercuration-demercuration takes place in the following steps:

(*i*) Generation of an electrophile (mercurinium ion).

$$CH_3—COO—Hg—OCOCH_3 \longrightarrow \underset{\text{(electrophile)}}{CH_3COO—Hg^+} + CH_3COO^-$$

(*ii*) Attack of electrophile on double bond of alkene

$$\overset{OCOCH_3}{\overset{|}{Hg^+}}—\overset{|}{C}=\overset{|}{C}— \longrightarrow \overset{HgOCOCH_3}{\overset{|}{—C}}—\overset{+}{C}—$$
Carbocation (less stable)

$$\longleftrightarrow \ —\overset{\overset{OCOCH_3}{|}}{\underset{/+\backslash}{Hg}}\ \ —C—C—$$
Bridged mercurinium ion (intermediate) (more stable)

(*iii*) Addition of water

$$—C—C— \text{(bridged by } \overset{+}{Hg}OCOCH_3) + :\ddot{O}—H \ (\text{with } H) \longrightarrow \ >C—C< \text{ with } HgOCOCH_3 \text{ and } \overset{+}{O}(H)—H$$

(*iv*) Reduction of C — $HgOCOCH_3$ bond

$$>C—C< (HgOCOCH_3,\ \overset{+}{O}(H)—H) \xrightarrow{\text{Reduction}} \ >C—C< (H,\ HO) + Hg$$

Hence, oxymercuration-demercuration process involves reduction and bridged mercurinium ion formation.

25 (*c*) $CH_2=CH—CH=CH—CH_3 \xrightarrow{O_3}$
Penta-1,3-diene

$$H_2C \overset{O}{\frown} CH—HC \overset{O}{\frown} CH—CH_3$$ (two O—O bridged ozonide rings)

$$\xrightarrow{Zn/H_2O} \underset{\text{Formaldehyde}}{HCHO} + \underset{\text{Glyoxal}}{\overset{CHO}{\underset{CHO}{|}}} + \underset{\text{Acetaldehyde}}{CH_3CHO}$$

26 (*c*) In conjugated system, double bonds are present at alternate positions, in cumulative system, double bonds are present at adjacent positions while in isolated system, there is a large difference, between the positions of double bond.

Hence, $CH_2=CH—CH_2—CH=CH_2$ represents an isolated system.

27 (*c*) Due to the presence of acidic hydrogen, ammoniacal Cu_2Cl_2 will give red copper acetylide ppt. with C_2H_2, whereas C_2H_4 will be neutral to ammoniacal Cu_2Cl_2.

28 (*c*) The given alkene forms two types of carbocations having same nature, i.e. both are secondary carbocations.

$$\underset{\text{Pent-2-ene}}{CH_3—CH_2—CH=CH—CH_3} \xrightarrow{H^+} CH_3—CH_2—CH_2—\overset{+}{C}H—CH_3$$

and $CH_3—CH_2—\overset{+}{C}H—CH_2—CH_3$

Hence, two different types of products, i.e. 2-bromopentane and 3-bromopentane are formed when Br^- is added to these carbocations.

29 (*c*) Symmetrical alkene form only one type of aldehyde on ozonolysis. Thus, among the following, only 2-butene gives only one aldehyde as a product on ozonolysis.

$$\underset{\text{But-2-ene}}{CH_3—CH=CHCH_3} \xrightarrow{O_3\text{-}Zn/H_2O} \underset{\text{Acetaldehyde}}{2CH_3CHO}$$

30 (*b*) In presence of Me_2S, ozonide decomposes by reduction, so

$$Me_2C=CHCH_3 \xrightarrow[\text{(ii) }(CH_3)_2S]{\text{(i) }O_3} Me_2C=O + CH_3CHO$$

31 (*a*) To decide the structure of alkene that undergoes ozonolysis, bring the products together in such a way that O-atoms are face to face, and replace O by double (=) bond. Thus,

$$\underset{\text{Acetaldehyde}}{\overset{H_3C}{\underset{H}{>}}C=O} + \underset{\text{Acetone}}{O=C\overset{CH_3}{\underset{CH_3}{<}}}$$

$$\xrightarrow[\text{by double bond}]{\text{Replacement of O}} \underset{\text{2-methyl-2-butene}}{\overset{4}{H_3C}\underset{H}{>}\overset{3}{C}=\overset{2}{C}\overset{\overset{1}{CH_3}}{\underset{CH_3}{<}}}$$

32 (b)
$$CH_3-\underset{H}{\overset{CH_3}{C}}-CH=CH_2 + HBr \xrightarrow[-Br]{} H_3C-\underset{H}{\overset{CH_3}{C}}-\overset{+}{C}HCH_3$$
2° carbocation (less stable)
$$\xrightarrow[\text{1,2-H}^- \text{ shift}]{} H_3C-\overset{CH_3}{\underset{\oplus}{C}}-CH_2-CH_3$$
3° carbocation (more stable)
$$\xrightarrow{Br^-} H_3C-\underset{Br}{\overset{CH_3}{C}}-CH_2-CH_3$$

33 (b) Since, the alkene on oxidation gives only acetic acid, therefore, the alkene must be symmetrical containing two carbon-atoms on either side of the double bond, i.e. 2-butene.
$$CH_3CH=CHCH_3 \xrightarrow{\text{alk. }KMnO_4} 2CH_3COOH$$

34 (a) NBS is a selective brominating reagent. Since, it normally brominates the ethylenic compounds in the allylic position. Thus, the reaction would be

Methylenecyclohexane ($=CH_2$) $\xrightarrow{NBS}$ 2-bromo-1-methylenecyclohexane (Br, $=CH_2$)

35 (a) When alkynes are reduced with Li or Na metal in NH_3, at low temperature, an anti-addition of hydrogen atoms takes place and trans or E product is obtained.
$$H_3C-C\equiv C-CH_3 + Na \xrightarrow{\text{Liq. }NH_3} H_3C-\overset{H}{C}=\underset{H}{C}-CH_3$$
2E-butene or *trans*-2-butene

36 (c) (i) $CH_2=CH_2 \xrightarrow{H_2O/H^+} CH_3CH_2OH$ (1° alcohol)

(ii) $CH_3-CH=CH_2 \xrightarrow{H_2O/H^+} CH_3\underset{OH}{CH}CH_3$

2° alcohol through 2° carbocation $(CH_3\overset{\oplus}{C}HCH_3)$

(iii) $CH_3-\underset{CH_3}{C}=CH_2 \xrightarrow{H_2O/H^+} (CH_3)_3COH$

3°alcohol through 3° carbocation $[(CH_3)_3\overset{\oplus}{C}]$.

(iv) $CH_3-\overset{CH_3}{CH}-CH=CH_2 \xrightarrow{H_2O/H^+} CH_3\overset{CH_3}{CH}-\underset{\oplus}{CH}-CH_3$

2° carbocation
$$\xrightarrow{\text{Rearrangement}} CH_3-\overset{CH_3}{\underset{\oplus}{C}}-CH_2CH_3$$
3° carbocation
$$\xrightarrow{H_2O/OH^-} CH_3-\overset{CH_3}{\underset{OH}{C}}-CH_2CH_3$$
3° alcohol

Thus, correct option is (c).

37 (d) $CH_3-CH_2-C\equiv CH + HCl \longrightarrow CH_3-CH_2-\underset{Cl}{C}=CH_2$ (B)
$$\xrightarrow{HI} CH_3-CH_2-\overset{I}{\underset{Cl}{C}}-CH_3$$
2-chloro-2-iodobutane (C)

38 (c) $CH_2=CH-CH_2Cl + CH_3MgI \rightarrow$ (Allyl chloride)
$CH_2=CH-CH_2CH_3 + Mg\langle^{I}_{Cl}$ (1-butene)

39 (d) Reaction of HBr with propene in the presence of peroxide gives *n*-propyl bromide.

This addition reaction is an example of anti-Markownikoff addition reaction.
$$CH_3-CH=CH_2 \xrightarrow{H^+Br^-} CH_3-CH_2-CH_2Br$$
Propene → *n*-propyl bromide

40 (d) $C_6H_5CH=CHC_6H_5 \xrightarrow{[O]}$ Alkene (X)
$$C_6H_5-\underset{OH}{CH}-\underset{OH}{CH}-C_6H_5 \text{ (Diol)} \xrightarrow{[O]} C_6H_5-\underset{O}{\underset{\|}{C}}-\underset{O}{\underset{\|}{C}}-C_6H_5$$
Diketone

41 (d) As 2-butene is a symmetrical molecule, thus it does not give any isomer and also Markownikoff's rule is not applicable in this case. (applicable for unsymmetrical alkene).

Hence, both A and R are incorrect.

42 (a) $\underset{(A)}{H_2C=CH_2} \xrightarrow{HBr} \underset{(B)}{CH_3CH_2Br}$
$$\xrightarrow[\Delta]{\text{Alc. KOH}(B)} \underset{(A)}{H_2C=CH_2}$$
Hence, $A = C_2H_4 \quad B = \text{alc. KOH}/\Delta$.

43 (b) $[(C_6H_5)_3P]_3\,RhCl$ is Wilkinson's catalyst, the most widely used catalysts for homogeneous hydrogenation.

44 (c) Bromo-substituted triene (Br) $\xrightarrow[-(CH_3)_3COH]{(CH_3)_3CO^-K^+}$ $\overset{\oplus}{K}$ anion (Br)

(X) ($\overset{\oplus}{K}$, Br) + $\underset{CH_2}{\overset{COCH_3}{CH}}$ $\longrightarrow$ benzene ring with $COCH_3$ and C_2H_5Br (B)

The conversion of X to B is Diels-Alder reaction because it consists of the addition of a conjugated diene to an unsaturated molecule, generally called as a dienophile, resulting in the formation of a cyclic compound, commonly known as adduct.

45 (*a*) Stability of alkene

$$\propto \frac{1}{\text{heat of hydrogenation of alkene}}$$

Greater the number of alkyl groups attached to the doubly bonded carbon atoms, more stable is the alkene. Hence, given alkene follow the following order of stability.

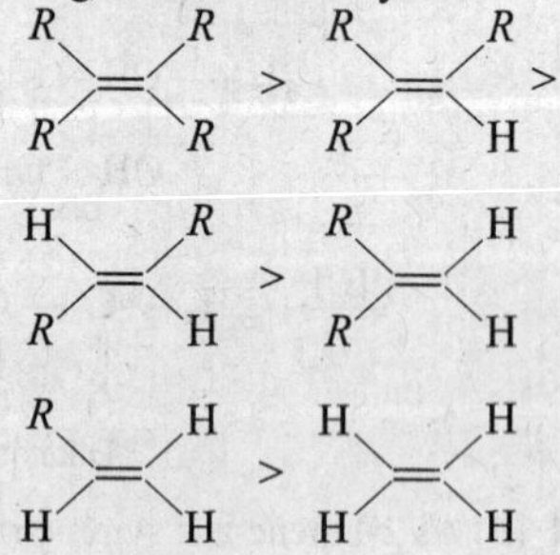

Thus, least stable alkene undergoes hydrogenation faster than stable one. Hence, the alkene which reacts faster with H_2 under catalytic hydrogenation conditions is

$R_2C=CH_2$ (R, R / H, H)

46 (*a*) The addition of HBr on unsymmetrical alkene takes place on the basis of Markownikoff's addition — "The negative part of the addendum is added to that carbon atom which has lesser number of H-atom."

$$\underset{\text{3 -phenylpropene}}{C_6H_5CH_2CH=CH_2} + \overset{+\ -}{HBr} \longrightarrow \underset{\text{2-bromo-1-phenylpropane}}{C_6H_5CH_2\underset{|}{\overset{Br}{CH}}CH_3}$$

47 (*b*) Reduction of alkene using sodium in liquid ammonia to give corresponding alkane is called Birch reduction.

48 (*b*) *trans*-2-butene is the most stable alkene among given alkenes, hence it has lowest heat of hydrogenation.

49 (*a*) Alkylated alkenes are most stable than other. Greater the alkylation of an alkene, i.e. greater the number of alkyl groups in an alkene, greater is its stability, thus the stability order is

$$\underset{\substack{\text{Most stable} \\ \text{(tetra alkylated ethylene)}}}{R-\underset{R}{\underset{|}{C}}=\underset{R}{\underset{|}{C}}-R} > R_2C=CHR > RCH=CHR$$

$$\approx R_2C=CH_2 > R-CH=CH_2 > \underset{\text{Least stable}}{CH_2=CH_2}$$

Topic 3

Alkynes

2017

1 1-butyne on oxidation with hot alkaline $KMnO_4$ would yield which of the following as end product? **[AIIMS]**

(a) $CH_3CH_2CH_2COOH$
(b) CH_3CH_2COOH
(c) $CH_3CH_2COOH + CO_2 + H_2O$
(d) $CH_3CH_2COOH + HCOOH$

2 Which one is the correct order of acidity? **[NEET]**

(a) $CH_2=CH_2 > CH_3-CH=CH_2 > CH_3-C\equiv CH > CH\equiv CH$
(b) $CH\equiv CH > CH_3-C\equiv CH > CH_2=CH_2 > CH_3-CH_3$
(c) $CH\equiv CH > CH_2=CH_2 > CH_3-C\equiv CH > CH_3-CH_3$
(d) $CH_3-CH_3 > CH_2=CH_2 > CH_3-C\equiv CH > CH\equiv CH$

2014

3 Which of the following organic compounds has same hybridisation as its combustion product — (CO_2)? **[Manipal]**

(a) Ethane (b) Ethyne
(c) Ethene (d) Ethanol

4 Arrange the following molecules in the correct order of decreasing C—C bond length. **[Kerala CEE]**

$$C_2H_6, C_2H_4, C_2H_2, C_6H_6$$

(a) $C_2H_6 > C_6H_6 > C_2H_4 > C_2H_2$
(b) $C_2H_6 > C_2H_4 > C_6H_6 > C_2H_2$
(c) $C_2H_4 > C_2H_2 > C_2H_6 > C_6H_6$
(d) $C_2H_2 > C_6H_6 > C_2H_4 > C_2H_6$
(e) $C_6H_6 > C_2H_4 > C_2H_6 > C_2H_2$

5 In the given reaction the compound (*A*) is **[WB JEE]**

Cyclopentyl–C≡CH $\xrightarrow[H_2SO_4]{H_2O, HgSO_4} A$

(a) cyclopentyl–CH₂–CHO (C=O, H)
(b) cyclopentyl–C(=O)–CH₃
(c) cyclopentyl–CH=CH(HSO₄) (H, HSO₄, H)
(d) cyclopentene

6 The reagents to carry out the following conversion are

Me–C≡CH ⟶ Me–CH₂–C(=O)–Me **[WB JEE]**

(a) $HgSO_4/\text{dil.} H_2SO_4$
(b) $BH_3, H_2SO_2/NaOH$
(c) OsO_4, HIO_4
(d) $NaNH_2/CH_3I, HgSO_4/\text{dil.} H_2SO_4$

2013

7 With ammonical cuprous chloride solution, a reddish brown precipitiate is obtained on treating with **[AIIMS]**

(a) CH_4 (b) C_2H_4
(c) C_2H_2 (d) C_3H_6

8 $CH \equiv CH + H_2O \xrightarrow{H_2SO_4 + HgSO_4} X$,
X is identified as **[Manipal]**

(a) ketone
(b) ethanol
(c) acetaldehyde
(d) propionaldehyde

2012

9 Which of the following reagents will be able to distinguish between 1-butyne and 2-butyne **[CBSE AIPMT]**

(a) $NaNH_2$ (b) HCl
(c) O_2 (d) Br_2

10 $CaC_2 + H_2O \longrightarrow (A) \xrightarrow{H_2SO_4/HgSO_4} (B)$ A and B are respectively **[UP CPMT]**

(a) C_2H_2 and CH_3CHO (b) CH_4 and $HCOOH$
(c) C_2H_4 and CH_3COOH (d) C_2H_2 and CH_3COOH

11 Propyne on ozonolysis gives **[OJEE]**

(a) $CH_3COOH + HCOOH$
(b) $CH_3COOH + HCHO$
(c) $CH_3CHO + HCHO$
(d) $CH_3CHO + HCOOH$

2010

12 Among the given compounds, one which can be distinguished by $AgNO_3$ is **[AFMC]**

(a) ethane (b) ethylene
(c) acetylene (d) diethyl ether

13 Consider the following (BVP) reaction

$$CaC_2 + H_2O \longrightarrow A \xrightarrow{H_2SO_4/HgSO_4} B$$

Identify A and B

(a) C_2H_2 and CH_3CHO (b) CH_4 and $HCOOH$
(c) C_2H_4 and CH_3COOH (d) C_2H_2 and CH_3COOH

14 Which of the following compounds reacts with an aqueous solution of $[Ag(NH_3)_2]OH$? **[CMC]**

(a) Ethane (b) Ethene
(c) 1-butyne (d) 2-butyne

2009

15 Assertion (A) Alkynes are more reactive towards nucleophilic addition reaction as compared to alkenes.
Reason (R) Alkynes contain two pi bonds, while alkenes have only one bond. **[AIIMS]**

(a) Both A and R are correct and R is the correct explanation of A
(b) Both A and R are correct but R is not the correct explanation of A
(c) A is correct but R is incorrect
(d) Both A and R are incorrect

2008

16 Ethylidene dichloride is obtained by the reaction of excess of HCl with **[MHT CET]**

(a) ethylene (b) acetylene
(c) propene (d) methane

17 Treatment of calcium carbide with water gives **[Kerala CEE]**

(a) ethene (b) ethyne
(c) ethane (d) benzene
(e) methane

18 From which one of the following, both ethylene and acetylene could be prepared in a single step reaction? **[Kerala CEE]**

(a) CH_3CH_2OH (b) $Br—CH_2—CH_2—Br$
(c) CH_3CH_2Br (d) $Br—CH_2—CH_2—OH$
(e) CH_3COOH

19 Which of the following will give H_2 gas with Na? **[Haryana PMT]**

(a) CH_4 (b) C_2H_6
(c) C_2H_4 (d) C_2H_2

20 Hydration of which one of the following yields ketone? **[J&K CET]**

(a) Propyne (b) Ethene
(c) Propene (d) Ethyne

21 1-butyne on hydration gives **[J&K CET]**

(a) butan-1,2-diol (b) butan-1-ol
(c) butan-2-ol (d) butan-2-one

22 Which one of the following compounds does not form an ozonide? **[AMU]**

(a) Ethene (b) Propyne
(c) Propene (d) Propane

23 Identify the alkyne in the following sequence of reactions.

$$\text{Alkyne} \xrightarrow[\text{Lindlar's catalyst}]{H_2} A \xrightarrow[\text{Only}]{\text{Ozonolysis}} B \xleftarrow[\text{process}]{\text{Wacker}} CH_2{=}CH_2$$

[EAMCET]

(a) $H_3C—C{\equiv}C—CH_3$
(b) $H_3C—CH_2—C{\equiv}CH$
(c) $H_2C{=}CH—C{\equiv}C$
(d) $HC{\equiv}C—CH_2—C{\equiv}CH$

24 The reagent used to convert an alkyne to alkene is **[KCET]**

(a) Zn/HCl (b) Sn/HCl (c) Zn-Hg/HCl (d) Pd / H_2

25 In the following reaction,

$$C_2H_2 \xrightarrow[HgSO_4/H_2SO_4]{H_2O} X \rightleftharpoons CH_3CHO.$$

What is X? **[BCECE]**

(a) CH_3CH_2OH (b) $CH_3—O—CH_3$
(c) CH_3CH_2CHO (d) $CH_2{=}CHOH$

26 What is the product formed when acetylene reacts with hypochlorous acid? **[MHT CET]**

(a) CH_3COCl (b) $ClCH_2CHO$
(c) Cl_2CHCHO (d) $ClCH_2COOH$

2007

27 A hydrocarbon of molecular formula C_6H_{10} reacts with sodamide and the same on ozonolysis followed by hydrogen peroxide oxidation gives two molecules of carboxylic acids, one being optically active. Then the hydrocarbon may be **[Kerala CEE]**

(a) 1-hexyne (b) 2-hexyne
(c) 3-hexyne (d) 3-methyl-1-pentyne
(e) 3, 3-dimethyl-1-butyne

28 Which of the following does not give a white precipitate with $AgNO_3$ solution? **[MP PMT]**

(a) Propyne (b) 1-butyne (c) 2-butyne (d) 1-pentyne

29 Match the following Columns. **[EAMCET]**

	Column I		Column II
A.	$C_2H_5OH \xrightarrow[170°C]{\text{Conc. } H_2SO_4}$	1.	Methane
B.	$CHI_3 \xrightarrow[\text{Ag (Powder)}]{\Delta}$	2.	Ethylene
C.	$CH_3COONa\ (aq) \xrightarrow{\text{Electrolysis}}$	3.	Benzene
D.	$CH_3COONa \xrightarrow[\text{CaO}, \Delta]{\text{NaOH}}$	4.	Acetylene
		5.	Ethane

Codes

	A	B	C	D		A	B	C	D
(a)	2	4	5	1	(b)	2	4	5	3
(c)	4	2	5	1	(d)	4	2	5	3

30 In the reactions, $B \xleftarrow{\text{Lindlar catalyst} + H_2}$

$RC{\equiv}CR \xrightarrow{Na/NH_3} A$, A and B are geometrical isomers. Thus, **[EAMCET]**

(a) A is *cis* and B is *trans* (b) A is *trans* and B is *cis*
(c) A and B are *cis* (d) A and B are trans

2006

31 Which among the following will give a precipitate with ammoniacal silver nitrate? **[Kerala CEE]**

(a) 2-butene (b) 2-butyne
(c) Chlorobenzene (d) 3-methyl-1-butyne
(e) 1,3-butadiene

32 The test for unsaturation is confirmed by the decolourisation of which of the following ? **[RPMT]**

(a) Iodine water (b) $CuSO_4$ solution
(c) Bromine water (d) All of these

33 The major product in the reaction of 2-butyne with Li/liq. NH_3 is **[J&K CET]**

(a) 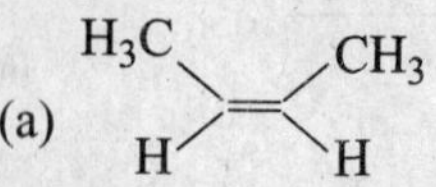

(b) 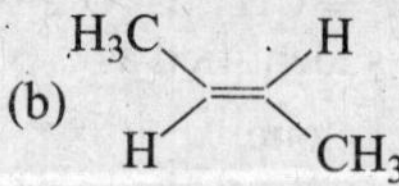

(c) $CH_3CH_2CH_2CH_3$ (d) $H_2C{=}CH{-}CH_2CH_3$

2005

34 Products of the following reaction,

$CH_3C{\equiv}C{\cdot}CH_2CH_3 \xrightarrow[\text{(ii) Hydrolysis}]{\text{(i) } O_3}$ are **[CBSE AIPMT]**

(a) $CH_3CHO + CH_3CH_2CHO$
(b) $CH_3COOH + CH_3COCH_3$
(c) $CH_3COOH + HOOC{\cdot}CH_2CH_3$
(d) $CH_3COOH + CO_2$

35 Which of the following gives propyne on hydrolysis ? **[AIIMS]**

(a) Al_4C_3 (b) Mg_2C_3 (c) B_4C (d) La_4C_3

36 $\begin{matrix} CH \\ \| \! | \\ CH \end{matrix}$ reacts with acetic acid in the presence of Hg^{2+} to give **[BHU]**

(a) $\begin{matrix} CH_3 \\ | \\ CH(CH_3COO)_2 \end{matrix}$ (b) $\begin{matrix} CH(CH_3COO)_2 \\ | \\ CH(CH_3COO)_2 \end{matrix}$

(c) $\begin{matrix} CH_3 \\ | \\ CH_2(CH_3COO) \end{matrix}$ (d) None of these

37 The silver salt of an unknown monoacidic alkyne contains 67.08% silver. The structure of the alkyne is **[Kerala CEE]**

(a) $H_3C{-}CH_2{-}C{\equiv}CH$ (b) $H_3C{-}C{\equiv}CH$
(c) $HC{\equiv}CH$ (d) $H_3C{-}C{\equiv}CH{-}CH_3$
(e) Either (c) or (d)

38 A salt producing hydrocarbon among these compounds **[RPMT]**

(a) ethane (b) ethene
(c) ethyne (d) methane

39 Which of the following is most acidic? **[J&K CET]**

(a) Methane (b) Acetylene
(c) 1-butene (d) *neo*-pentane

40 Which of the following reacts with $KMnO_4$ but does not react with $AgNO_3$? **[BCECE]**

(a) C_2H_6 (b) CH_4 (c) C_2H_4 (d) C_2H_2

Answers

1 (c)	2 (b)	3 (b)	4 (a)	5 (b)	6 (d)	7 (c)	8 (c)	9 (a)	10 (a)
11 (a)	12 (c)	13 (a)	14 (c)	15 (a)	16 (b)	17 (b)	18 (b)	19 (d)	20 (a)
21 (d)	22 (d)	23 (a)	24 (d)	25 (d)	26 (c)	27 (d)	28 (c)	29 (a)	30 (b)
31 (d)	32 (c)	33 (b)	34 (c)	35 (b)	36 (a)	37 (a)	38 (c)	39 (b)	40 (c)

Explanations

1 (*c*) 1-butyne or oxidation with alk. $KMnO_4$

$$CH_3CH_2\cdot C\equiv CH \xrightarrow{\text{Hot } KMnO_4\text{(alk).}} CH_3CH_2COOH + CO_2 + H_2O$$

2 (*b*) Greater the *s*-character of C-atom in hydrocarbons, greater the electronegativity of that carbon and thus greater is the acidic nature of the H attached to electronegative carbon.

Presence of alkyl group (EDG) decreases the acidity of alkyne.

	$CH\equiv CH$	$CH_2=CH_2$	CH_3-CH_3
Hybridisation:	sp	sp^2	sp^3
% *s*-character:	50%	33%	25%
Electronegativity:	Max. ⟵		
Acidic character of terminal H	Max. ⟵		

Thus, $CH\equiv CH > CH_3C\equiv CH > CH_2=CH_2 > CH_3-CH_3$

3 (*b*) Hybridisation of carbon $= sp^{3-\text{number of }\pi\text{-bonds}}$

In CO_2 ($O=C=O$) hybridisation of carbon $= sp^{3-2} = sp$

In ethyne or acetylene,

C_2H_2, ($H-\overset{2\pi}{C\equiv C}-H$) hybridisation of carbon $= sp^{3-2} = sp$

4 (*a*) As number of bonds increases between two carbon atoms, bond length decreases.
C_2H_6-single bond, C_6H_6-double bond and single bond (bond length is between double and single bond) C_2H_4-double bond, C_2H_2-triple bond.
Thus, the correct order of decreasing $C-C$ bond length is,
$C_2H_6 > C_6H_6 > C_2H_4 > C_2H_2$

5 (*b*) (Cyclopentyl)$-C\equiv CH$ $\xrightarrow[H_2SO_4]{H_2O,\ HgSO_4}$ (Cyclopentyl)$-\overset{O}{\overset{\|}{C}}-CH_3$
(*A*)

6 (*d*) $Me-\!\!\equiv + NaNH_2 \xrightarrow{-NH_3} Me-\equiv\overset{-}{C}-\overset{+}{Na}$

$\xrightarrow{CH_3I} Me-\equiv C-CH_3$

$\xrightarrow[\text{(addition of Water)}]{HgSO_4/\text{dil. } H_2SO_4} Me-\overset{H}{\overset{|}{C}}=\overset{OH}{\overset{|}{C}}-CH_3$

$\Updownarrow$ Tautomerisation

$Me-\equiv C-CH_3 \xrightarrow[\text{(addition of water)}]{HgSO_4 \text{ dil } H_2SO_4}$ $Me-CH_2-\underset{\underset{O}{\|}}{C}-CH_3$

or Me—(C=O)—Me

[Here, Me means methyl group]

Thus, the correct set of reagents is : $NaNH_2 / CH_3I$, $HgSO_4$ / dil. H_2SO_4.

7 (*c*) All terminal alkynes behave as very weak acids. They react with $NaNH_2$, Na, Tollen's reagent, ammonical cuprous chloride solution.

$$R-C\equiv CH + [Cu(NH_3)_2]^+OH^- \longrightarrow \underset{\substack{\text{Copper alkynide}\\\text{(red ppt)}}}{R-C\equiv C\cdot Cu}\downarrow + H_2O + 2NH_3$$

This reaction show the acidic nature of alkynes. C_2H_2 being an alkyne gives this reaction.

8 (*c*)

$$CH\equiv CH + H_2O \xrightarrow{HgSO_4 + H_2SO_4} \underset{CHOH}{\overset{CH_2}{\|}} \xrightleftharpoons{\text{Tautomerism}} \underset{X}{CH_3CHO}$$

9 (*a*) $NaNH_2$ is used to distinguish between 1-butyne and 2-butyne

$$CH_3CH_2C\equiv CH \xrightarrow{NaNH_2} CH_3CH_2C\equiv\overset{-}{C}\overset{+}{Na} + \frac{1}{2}H_2\uparrow$$

$$CH_3-C\equiv C-CH_3 \xrightarrow{NaNH_2} \text{No reaction}$$

10 (*a*) $CaC_2 + 2H_2O \longrightarrow \underset{(A)}{C_2H_2} + Ca(OH)_2$

$$\underset{CH}{\overset{CH}{\|}} \xrightarrow[HgSO_4]{\text{Dil } H_2SO_4} \underset{CHOH}{\overset{CH_2}{\|}} \xrightleftharpoons{\text{Tautomerisation}} \underset{\substack{\text{Acetaldehyde}\\(B)}}{CH_3CHO}$$

11 (*a*) $\underset{\text{Propyne}}{CH_3-C\equiv CH} + O_3 \xrightarrow{\text{ozonolysis}}$ CH_3-C(ozonide ring with O—O)CH (Unstable)

$$\xrightarrow[-H_2O_2]{H_2O} CH_3COOH + HCOOH$$

12 (*c*) Only acetylene reacts with $AgNO_3$ and gives white precipitate of silver acetylide among the given compounds.

$$HC\equiv CH \xrightarrow[+NH_4OH]{AgNO_3} \underset{\text{White ppt.}}{\overset{+}{Ag}\overset{-}{C}\equiv\overset{-}{C}\overset{+}{Ag}}$$

Thus, it is distinguished by $AgNO_3$.

13 (*a*) The complete reaction is as follows :

$$CaC_2 + H_2O \longrightarrow Ca(OH)_2 + \underset{(A)}{C_2H_2} \xrightarrow[HgSO_4]{H_2SO_4} \underset{(B)}{CH_3CHO}$$

14 (*c*) Due to the acidic nature of the hydrogen atoms attached to a triple bonded carbon atoms, acetylene and terminal alkynes form metal acetylides.

Reaction with ammonical $AgNO_3$ solution $[Ag(NH_3)_2]OH$ is as follows:

$$\underset{\text{1-butyne}}{CH_3CH_2C \equiv CH} + AgNO_3 + NH_4OH \longrightarrow \underset{\text{Silver butylide}}{CH_3CH_2C \equiv \bar{C}\overset{+}{A}g} + NH_4NO_3 + H_2O$$

15 (*a*) $\underset{\text{alkene}}{>C \overset{\pi}{\underset{\sigma}{=}} C<}$ $\underset{\text{alkyne}}{-C \overset{2\pi}{\underset{\sigma}{\equiv}} C-}$

Although there are more π-electrons associated with the triple bond, the *sp* hybridised carbon exert a strong attraction for these π-electrons which are consequently bonded more tightly to the functional group than the π-electrons of a double bond. Hence, a nucleophile attack occur more readily on triple bonded carbon atom.

16 (*b*) Alkynes due to presence of two pi-bonds, form dichloroderivative.

$$\underset{\text{Acetylene}}{CH \equiv CH} + HCl \longrightarrow \underset{\text{Vinyl chloride}}{CH_2 = CHCl} \xrightarrow{HCl} \underset{\text{Ethylene dichloride}}{CH_3CHCl_2}$$

17 (*b*) Calcium carbide when reacts with water, gives acetylene, IUPAC name of which is ethyne

$$CaC_2 + 2H_2O \longrightarrow \underset{\text{Calcium hydroxide}}{Ca(OH)_2} + \underset{\text{Ethyne}}{C_2H_2}$$

18 (*b*) From 1,2-dibromoethane, both acetylene and ethylene can be prepared in a single step.

$$CH_2Br-CH_2Br \xrightarrow[\Delta]{\text{Zn dust}} \underset{\text{Ethylene}}{CH_2=CH_2} + ZnBr_2$$

$$CH_2Br-CH_2Br \xrightarrow[\Delta]{\text{Alc. KOH}} \underset{\text{Acetylene}}{CH \equiv CH} + 2HBr$$

19 (*d*) Acetylene being a terminal alkyne have 2 acidic hydrogens thus, liberates H_2 on reaction with Na.

$$CH \equiv CH + 2Na \rightarrow NaC \equiv C{\cdot}Na + H_2\uparrow$$

20 (*b*) $H_3C-C \equiv CH + HOH \xrightarrow[HgSO_4]{H_2SO_4(\text{dil.})}$ $\underset{\text{Enolic form}}{\left[CH_3-\underset{OH}{\underset{|}{C}}=CH_2\right]} \xrightleftharpoons{\text{Tautomerism}} \underset{\text{(Ketone)}}{CH_3-\underset{O}{\underset{\|}{C}}-CH_3}$

21 (*d*) $\underset{\text{1-butyne}}{CH_3CH_2C \equiv CH} + H_2O \xrightarrow{HgSO_4/H_2SO_4} CH_3CH_2\overset{OH}{\overset{|}{C}} = CH_2 \xrightarrow{+H_2O} \underset{\text{(unstable)}}{CH_3CH_2-\overset{OH}{\overset{|}{\underset{OH}{\underset{|}{C}}}}-CH_3}$

$$\xrightleftharpoons{\text{Tautomerism}} \underset{\text{Butane-2-one}}{CH_3CH_2-\underset{O}{\underset{\|}{C}}-CH_3}$$

22 (*d*) As propane is a saturated compound. Thus, it does not form an ozonide. Ozonide is formed only by unsaturated compounds, i.e. alkenes or alkynes.

$$CH_2=CH_2 + O_3 \longrightarrow \underset{\text{Ethene ozonide}}{CH_2\text{—}CH_2 \text{ (ozonide ring: } -O- \text{ bridge, } O-O)}$$

$$CH_3-C \equiv CH + O_3 \longrightarrow CH_3-C\text{—}CH \text{ (ozonide ring)}$$

$$CH_3-HC=CH_2 + O_3 \longrightarrow CH_3-CH\text{—}CH_2 \text{ (ozonide ring)}$$

23 (*a*) In Wacker process, alkene is oxidised into aldehyde.

$$CH_2 = CH_2 + \frac{1}{2}O_2 \xrightarrow[H_2O]{PdCl_2\,CuCl_2} \underset{(B)}{CH_3CHO}$$

Since, on ozonolysis only alkenes produce aldehydes, '*A*' must be an alkene.

To decide the structure of alkene that undergoes ozonolysis, bring the products together in such a way that O-atoms are face to face and replace O by double bond. Thus,

$$\underset{(B)}{\overset{H_3C}{\underset{H}{>}}C=O} + \underset{(B)}{O=C\overset{CH_3}{\underset{H}{<}}} \xrightarrow{\text{Replacement of by double bond}} \underset{(B)}{\overset{H_3C}{\underset{H}{>}}C=C\overset{CH_3}{\underset{H}{<}}}$$

Thus, alkyne must be

$$\underset{\text{(Alkyne)}}{CH_3-C \equiv C-CH_3} \xrightarrow[\text{Lindlar's catalyst}]{H_2} \underset{(A)}{\overset{H_3C}{\underset{H}{>}}C=C\overset{CH_3}{\underset{H}{<}}}$$

24 (*d*) Alkynes are converted into alkenes by using Lindlar's catalyst (H_2 / Pd).

$$\underset{\text{Alkyne}}{R-C \equiv C-R} \xrightarrow{H_2/Pd} \underset{\textit{cis}\text{ alkene}}{R-\underset{H}{\underset{|}{C}}=\underset{H}{\underset{|}{C}}-R}$$

25 (*d*) $HC \equiv CH \xrightarrow[HgSO_4/H_2SO_4,\ 60°C]{H_2O} [CH_2=CHOH] \underset{\text{Tautomerisation}}{\overset{X}{\rightleftharpoons}} CH_3CHO$

26 (*c*) $\underset{CH}{\overset{CH}{|||}} \xrightarrow{HOCl} \underset{CHCl}{\overset{CHOH}{\|}} \xrightarrow{HOCl} \left[\underset{CHCl_2}{\overset{CH(OH)_2}{|}}\right] \xrightarrow{-H_2O} \underset{CHCl_2}{\overset{CHO}{|}}$

27 (*d*)

$$\underset{\text{3-methyl-1-pentyne}}{CH_3-CH_2-\overset{CH_3}{\overset{|}{CH}}-C \equiv CH} \xrightarrow[+O_3]{+NaNH_2} \underset{\text{Ozonide}}{CH_3-CH_2-\overset{CH_3}{\overset{|}{CH}}-C\text{—}CH \text{ (ozonide ring)}} \xrightarrow[H_2O_2]{[O]}$$

$$\underset{\text{Optically active carboxylic acid}}{CH_3-CH_2-\overset{CH_3}{\overset{|}{CH}}-COOH} + HCOOH$$

28 (*c*) Terminal alkynes gives white precipitate with ammoniacal $AgNO_3$ solution, due to the presence of terminal hydrogen, whereas internal alkynes does not react so. Thus, 2-butyne do not give a white ppt. with $AgNO_3$ solution.

29 (*a*) The correct match is :
A → 2, B → 4, C → 5, D → 1

Column I	Column II
$C_2H_5OH \xrightarrow[170°C]{\text{Conc. } H_2SO_4}$	Ethylene
$CHI_3 \xrightarrow[\text{Ag powder}]{\Delta}$	Acetylene

Column I	Column II
$CH_3COONa(aq) \xrightarrow{\text{Electrolysis}}$	Ethane
$CH_3COONa \xrightarrow[+CaO, \Delta]{NaOH}$	Methane

30 (b) $R-C\equiv C-R$ (Alkyne) $\xrightarrow[+H_2]{\text{Lindlar catalyst}}$ $RCH=CHR$ *cis*-alkene (B)

$R-C\equiv C-R$ (Alkyne) $\xrightarrow{\text{Na in liq. } NH_3}$ $RCH=CHR$ *trans*-alkene (A)

31 (d) C_2H_2 and all terminal-alkynes give white precipitate with ammoniacal silver nitrate. Therefore, 3-methyl-1-butyne will give a white precipitate with ammoniacal silver nitrate.

$$\underset{\text{3-methyl-1-butyne}}{CH_3-CH(CH_3)-C\equiv CH} \xrightarrow[AgNO_3]{NH_4OH} \underset{\text{White ppt}}{CH_3-CH(CH_3)-C\equiv \overset{-}{C}\overset{+}{Ag}}$$

32 (c) By adding bromine water to a solution, if the colour of bromine water decolourise then the compound is unsaturated. This is a confirmatory test for unsaturation.

33 (b) Reaction of a non-terminal alkyne with a solution of an alkali metal (usually Na or Li or K) in liquid ammonia gives a *trans*-alkene.

$$CH_3-C\equiv C-CH_3+2[H] \xrightarrow{\text{Li/liq. } NH_3} \underset{H}{\overset{H_3C}{}}\!>C=C<\!\underset{CH_3}{\overset{H}{}}$$

34 (c)

$$CH_3-C\equiv C-CH_2-CH_3 \xrightarrow{O_3} \text{(ozonide)}\ CH_3-C(O)(O-O)C-CH_2-CH_3$$

$$\xrightarrow{2H_2O} \underset{\text{Acetic acid}}{CH_3COOH} + \underset{\text{Propionic acid}}{CH_3CH_2COOH}$$

35 (b) Magnesium carbide on hydrolysis gives propyne,

$$Mg_2C_3+4H_2O \longrightarrow \underset{\text{Propyne}}{CH_3C\equiv CH} + 2Mg(OH)_2$$

36 (a)

$$CH\equiv CH + CH_3COOH \xrightarrow{Hg^{2+}} \underset{\text{Vinyl acetate}}{CH_2=CHOOCCH_3}$$

$$\xrightarrow[Hg(OOCCH_3)_2]{CH_3COOH} \underset{\text{Ethylidene diacetate}}{CH_3-CH(OOC\cdot CH_3)_2}$$

37 (a) Mono acidic alkyne is that having one hydrogen attached to the triple bonded carbon. In $CH_3-CH_2-C\equiv CH$ molecular weight of Ag salt of above compound will be 161.

∵ 161 g of compound contains Ag = 108

∴ 100 g of compound contains

$$Ag=\frac{108}{161}\times 100 = 67.08$$

So, the correct answer is

$$CH_3-CH_2-C\equiv CH.$$

38 (c) Ethyne have most acidic hydrogen, thus it reacts with metals to form salt.

39 (b) In C_2H_2 each C-atom is *sp*-hybridised which contains 50% *s*-character. The greater the *s*-character of an orbital, the bonding electron pair will be more inclined towards the nucleus as a result carbon would acquire a negative charge and hydrogen a positive charge. Hence, it is acidic in nature.

$$H-\underset{sp}{C}\equiv\underset{sp}{C}-H$$

40 (c) Alkene and alkynes both react with $KMnO_4$ and decolourise it. Only alkynes react with $AgNO_3$ to give white precipitate.

(a) C_2H_6 (Alkane): H_3C-CH_3 (b) CH_4 (Alkane) (c) C_2H_4 (Alkene): $H_2C=CH_2$ (d) C_2H_2 (Alkyne): $H-C\equiv C-H$

∴ C_2H_4 (an alkene) reacts with $KMnO_4$ and decolourises it but does not react with $AgNO_3$. where, as C_2H_6 and CH_4 are alkanes they do not react with both $KMnO_4$ and $AgNO_3$.

Topic 4

Aromaticity

2014

1 The most likely protonation site in the following molecule is [WB JEE]

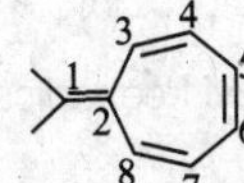

(a) C − 1 (b) C − 2
(c) C − 3 (d) C − 6

2013

2 The radical is aromatic because it has [NEET]

$C_6H_5-\dot{C}H_2$

(a) 6*p*-orbitals and 6 unpaired electrons
(b) 7*p*-orbitals and 6 unpaired electrons
(c) 7*p*-orbitals and 7 unpaired electrons
(d) 6*p*-orbitals and 7 unpaired electrons

2011

3 Which one of the following is a non-benzenoid aromatic compound? **[Kerala CEE]**

(a) Aniline (b) Benzoic acid
(c) Naphthalene (d) Tropolone
(e) Anthracene

2009

4 Which of the following is an aromatic compound? **[AFMC]**

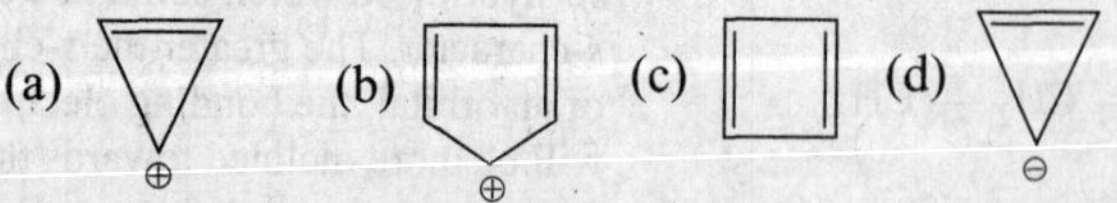

5 Which one of the following is aromatic? **[J&K CET]**

(a) Cyclopentadienyl cation
(b) Cyclo-octatetraene
(c) Cycloheptatriene
(d) Cycloheptatrienyl cation

6 Which of the following is aromatic? **[OJEE]**

(a) (b) (c) + (d) −

7 Assertion (A) Tropylium cation is aromatic in nature.
Reason (R) The only property that determines its aromatic behaviour is planar structure. **[AIIMS]**

(a) Both A and R are correct and R is the correct explanation of A
(b) Both A and R are correct but R is not the correct explanation of A
(c) A is correct but R is incorrect
(d) Both A and R are incorrect

8 Which of the following is aromatic? **[BCECE]**

(a) (b) OH

(c) O (d) C_6H_5 $C^{\oplus}$ $HC{=}CC_6H_5$

2006

9 Which of the following compound shows aromatic properties? **[RPMT]**

(a) Valine (b) Leucine (c) Serine (d) Tyrosine

2005

10 Assertion (A) Cyclopentadienyl anion is much more stable than allyl anion.
Reason (R) Cyclopentadienyl anion is aromatic in character. **[AIIMS]**

(a) Both A and R are correct and R is the correct explanation of A
(b) Both A and R are correct, but R is not the correct explanation of A
(c) A is correct, but R is incorrect
(d) Both A and R are incorrect

11 An aromatic compound among other things should have a π-electron cloud containing $(4n + 2)$ π-electrons where n can't be **[J&K CET]**

(a) $\frac{1}{2}$ (b) 3 (c) 2 (d) 1

Answers

1 (a)	2 (c)	3 (d)	4 (a)	5 (d)	6 (c)	7 (c)	8 (d)	9 (d)	10 (a)
11 (a)									

Explanations

1 (*a*) Addition of a proton at C^1 results in the formation of tropylium carbocation (an aromatic species with more stability due to delocalisation of π electrons) thus, it is the most reactive site towards protonation.

Addition of proton at any other carbon atom, interrupt in the delocalisation of π electrons by disturbing planarity of molecules and hence, makes it less stable. Thus, rest all are less reactivesites toward protonation.

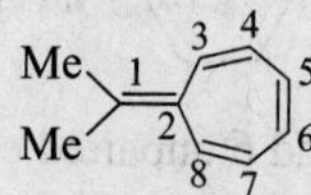

2 (*c*) Because of the presence of $7p$-orbitals and 7 unpaired electrons, it is aromatic is nature as these unpaired electrons delocalise in p-orbitals.

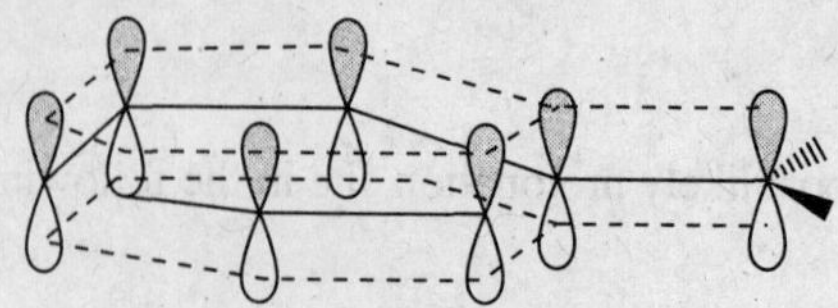

Benzyl free radical

3 (*d*) Non-benzenoid aromatic compound are chemical compounds with conjugated pi-electron system with 5-7 membered ring. Tropolone is a non-benzenoid arromatic compound as it has 7 carbon atom.

Tropolone

4 (*a*) The main condition for a compound is be aromatic is presence of $(4n+2)\pi$ electrons. (Huckel rule)

(a) $= 2\pi e^-$ (b) $= 4\pi e^-$

(c) $= 4\pi e^-$ (d) $= 4\pi e^-$

∴ due to the presence of

$(4n+2)\pi e^- = 2, n = 0$.

As it follows Huckel' rule.

Thus, it is aromatic in nature.

5 (*d*) To be aromatic, a compound should

(*i*) have $(4n+2)$ π-electrons in conjugation.

(*ii*) be planar

has $(3 \times 2)\ \pi e^-$

Cycloheptarienyl cation

It follows Huckel's rule,

$(4n+2)\pi = 6\pi$

$n = 1.$

It is in conjugation due to presence of alternate double and single bond. It is planar. Hence, it is aromatic.

6 (*c*) is aromatic because compound is cyclic and obeys the Huckel's rule.

$(4n+2)$ π-electrons and planar structure are the essential conditions for aromaticity.

7 (*c*) is aromatic, because it contains $(4n+2)\pi$ electrons. $(4n+2)\pi$ electrons and planar structure are essential conditions for aromaticity. Thus, A is correct but R is incorrect.

8 (*d*) $HC = C - C_6H_5$, $\overset{\oplus}{C}$, C_6H_5

is aromatic because the compound is cyclic and number of π-electrons are 2, which is in accordance with the Huckel's rule, $(4n+2)\pi$. When $n = 0$, according to this rule, number of π-electrons is $4 \times 0 + 2 = 2$.

9 (*d*) The aromatic properties can only be represented by tyrosine. Tyrosine is α-amino β (*p*-hydroxyphenyl) propionic acid. It has aromatic nucleus. It is aromatic amino acid.

10 (*a*) Cyclopentadienyl anion is more stable than allyl anion as the former is aromatic and is stabilised by resonance.

6π electrons (Huckel's rule)

$\overset{-}{C}H_2 - CH = CH_2 \longleftrightarrow CH_2 = CH - \overset{-}{C}H_2$

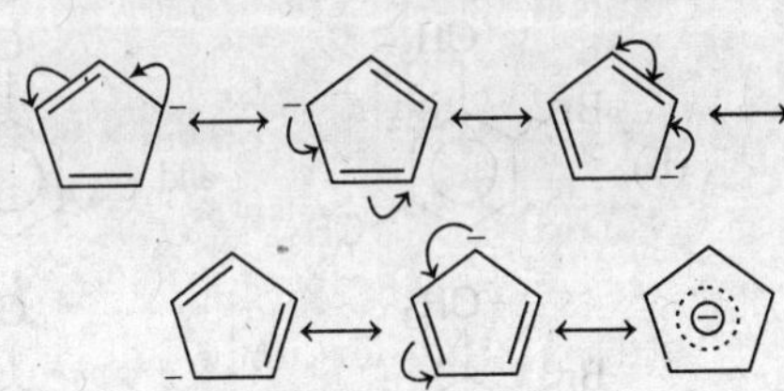

Thus, A and R are correct and R is correct explanation of A.

11 (*a*) According to Huckel's rule, an aromatic compound should have $(4n+2)$π-electrons where, *n* is an integer, i.e. 0, 1, 3, 4, ... and possesses unusual stability due to the delocalisation of π-electrons.

Topic 5

Benzene and its Alkyl Derivatives

2019

1 Correct order of electrophillic substitution reaction is

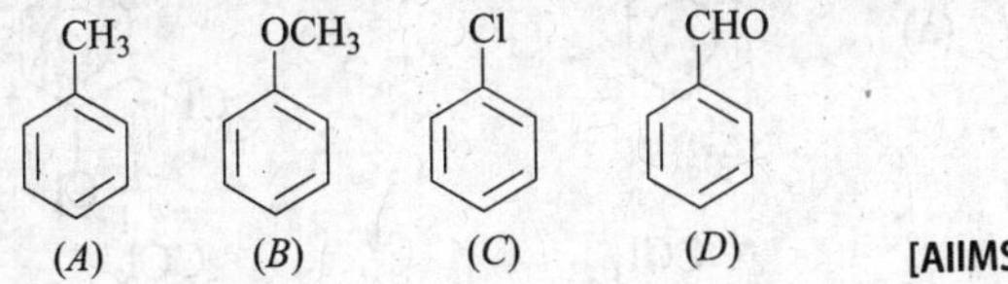

[AIIMS]

(a) $A > B > C > D$ (b) $D > B > A > C$
(c) $B > A > C > D$ (d) $B > A > D > C$

2 During nitration of benzene, the attacking electrophile is [JIPMER]

(a) NO_3^- (b) NO_2^-
(c) NO_2^+ (d) HNO_3

3 A reactant (*X*) pass through hot red tube at 1600-1800°C and produces benzene. Hence (*X*) is [AIIMS]

(a) acetylene
(b) ethene
(c) ethane
(d) cyclohexane

4 Assertion (A) Nitration of benzene with nitric acid requires the use of concentrated sulphuric acid.

Reason (R) The mixture of concentrated sulphuric acid and concentrated nitric acid produces the electrophile, NO_2^+. [AIIMS]

(a) Both A and R are correct and R is the correct explanation of A
(b) Both A and R are correct but R is not the correct explanation of A
(c) A is true but R is incorrect
(d) Both A and R are incorrect

5 What products are formed when the following compound is treated with Br_2 in the presence of $FeBr_3$? **[CBSE AIPMT]**

CH_3, CH_3

(a) CH_3, Br, CH_3 and CH_3, CH_3, Br

(b) CH_3, Br, CH_3 and CH_3, Br, CH_3

(c) CH_3, Br, CH_3 and CH_3, CH_3, Br

(d) CH_3, CH_3, Br and CH_3, Br, CH_3

6 Benzene can be conveniently converted into *n*-propyl benzene by **[MHT CET]**
(a) Friedel-Craft alkylation with *n*-propyl chloride
(b) Friedel-Craft acylation with propionyl chloride followed by Wolff-Kishner reduction
(c) Friedel-Craft acylation with propionyl chloride followed by catalytic hydrogenation
(d) Friedel-Craft acylation with propionyl chloride followed by reduction with $LiAlH_4$

7 Which of the following compounds undergoes nitration more readily? **[Manipal]**
(a) Benzene (b) Benzoic acid
(c) Nitrobenzene (d) Toluene

8 The correct sequence of reactions to be performed to convert benzene into *m*-bromoaniline is? **[KCET]**
(a) nitration, reduction, bromination
(b) bromination, nitration, reduction
(c) nitration, bromination, reduction
(d) reduction, nitration, bromination

2013

9 The treatment of benzene with *iso*-butene in the presence of sulphuric acid gives. **[AIIMS]**
(a) *iso*-butyl benzene (b) *tert*-butyl benzene
(c) *n*-butyl benzene (d) No reaction

10 Which of the following compounds will not undergo Friedel-Craft's reaction easily? **[NEET]**
(a) Cumene (b) Xylene
(c) Nitrobenzene (d) Toluene

11 Some *meta*-directing substituents in aromatic substitution are given. Which one is the most deactivating **[NEET]**
(a) $-C\equiv N$ (b) $-SO_3H$
(c) $-COOH$ (d) $-NO_2$

12 To get DDT, chlorobenzene has to react with which of the following compound in the presence of concentrated sulphuric acid. **[KCET]**
(a) trichloroethane (b) dichloro acetone
(c) dichloro acetaldehyde (d) trichloro acetaldehyde

13 Which of the following is not used in Friedel-Craft's reaction? **[KCET]**
(a) Phenyl acetanilide (b) Bromobenzene
(c) Benzene (d) Chlorobenzene

2012

14 Identify '*C*' in the following reaction, **[AFMC]**

$$C_6H_6 + CH_2{=}CHCH_2Cl \xrightarrow{AlCl_3} A \xrightarrow[\text{(ii) } H_2O_2,\, OH^-]{\text{(i) } BH_3,\, THC} B \xrightarrow[\Delta]{HF} C$$

(a)

(b) 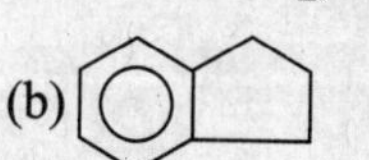

(c) 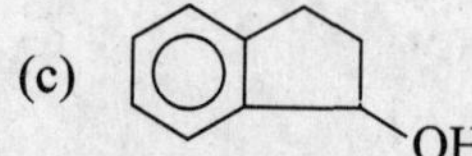

(d) 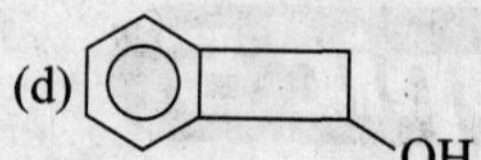

15 By passing excess Cl_2 in boiling toluene, which one of the following compound is exclusively formed? **[WB JEE]**

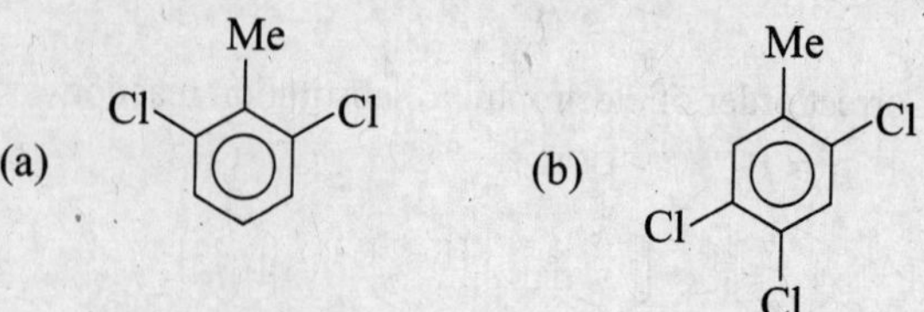

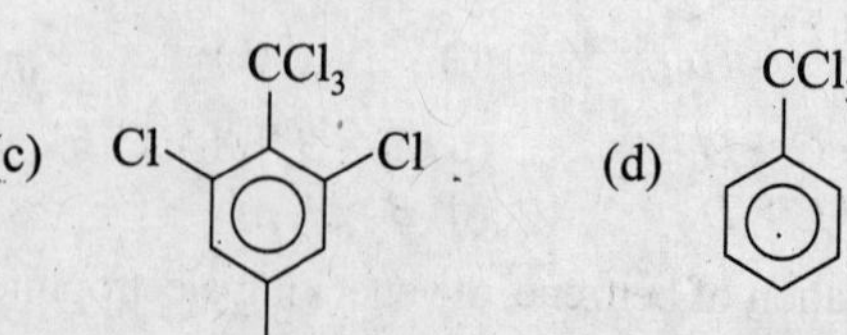

16 Acylation of benzene to produce aliphatic aromatic ketone is known as **[AMU]**

(a) Benzoin condensation
(b) Hydroformylation
(c) Clemmensen reduction
(d) Friedel-Craft's reaction

2011

17 Ethyl benzene cannot be prepared by **[KCET]**

(a) Wurtz reaction (b) Wurtz-Fittig reaction
(c) Friedel-Craft's reaction (d) Clemmensen reduction

2010

18 Which one is the most reactive towards electrophilic reagent? **[CBSE AIPMT]**

(a) Benzene ring with CH_3 and $-OCH_3$ (ortho)
(b) Benzene ring with CH_3 and $-OH$ (ortho)
(c) Benzene ring with CH_3 and $-CH_2OH$ (ortho)
(d) Benzene ring with CH_3 and $-NHCOCH_3$ (ortho)

19 In the following reaction, the product '*R*' is **[AFMC]**

$$CaC_2 \xrightarrow{H_2O} P \xrightarrow[\text{tube}]{\text{Hot iron}} Q \xrightarrow[AlCl_3]{CH_3Cl} R$$

(a) Benzene (b) Ethylbenzene
(c) Toluene (d) *N*-propylbenzene

20 Benzene does not undergo addition reactions easily because **[BVP]**

(a) it has a cyclic structure
(b) double bonds in it are very strong
(c) resonance stabilised system is to be preserved
(d) it has six hydrogen atoms

21 The characteristic reactions shown by benzene is **[OJEE]**

(a) electrophilic addition reactions
(b) electrophilic substitution reactions
(c) nucleophilic addition reactions
(d) nucleophilic substitution reactions

22 The final product formed in the this reaction is **[OJEE]**

$$C_6H_5CH_3 \xrightarrow[KOH]{KMnO_4} \xrightarrow{H_3O^+}$$

(a) C_6H_5CHO (b) $C_6H_5COO^-K^+$
(c) $C_6H_5CH_2OH$ (d) C_6H_5COOH

23 In Friedel-Craft's alkylation besides $AlCl_3$ the other reactants are : **[UP CPMT, Haryana PMT]**

(a) $C_6H_6 + NH_3$
(b) $C_6H_6 + CH_3COCl$
(c) $C_6H_6 + CH_3Cl$
(d) $C_6H_6 + CH_4$

24 What is the ratio of π and σ-bonds in benzene? **[Haryana PMT]**

(a) 1:4 (b) 2:1
(c) 1:1 (d) 2:2

25 Which one of these is not true for benzene? **[KCET]**

(a) It forms only one type of monosubstituted product
(b) There are three carbon-carbon single bonds and three carbon-carbon double bonds
(c) The heat of hydrogenation of benzene is less than the theoretical value
(d) The bond angle between the carbon-carbon bonds is 120°

26 Which order is correct for the decreasing reactivity towards monobromination of the following compounds? **[VMMC]**

$\underset{I}{C_6H_5CH_3}$, $\underset{II}{C_6H_5COOH}$, $\underset{III}{C_6H_6}$, $\underset{IV}{C_6H_5NO_2}$

(a) I > II > III > IV (b) I > III > II > IV
(c) II > III > IV > I (d) III > I > II > IV

Answers

1 (c)	2 (c)	3 (a)	4 (a)	5 (c)	6 (a, b)	7 (d)	8 (c)	9 (b)	10 (c)
11 (d)	12 (d)	13 (a)	14 (b)	15 (d)	16 (d)	17 (a)	18 (b)	19 (c)	20 (c)
21 (b)	22 (d)	23 (c)	24 (a)	25 (b)	26 (b)				

Explanations

1 (c) Electron donating group when bonded with benzene ring will activate the ring due to $(+I)$ effect and show better electrophilic substitution reaction, whereas electron withdrawing groups show $(-I)$ effect, will decreases the nature of electrophilic substitution

(a) Here, alkyl group (i.e. $—CH_3$) show $(+I)$ effect, but lesser than $—OCH_3$ due to presence of oxygen atom, thus $C_6H_5—OCH_3$ show better electrophilic substitution than that of $C_6H_5—CH_3$.

(b) Chlorine, i.e. Cl show $-I$ and $+R$ effect due to presence of lone pair of electrons, while $—CHO$ group is of $(-R)$ nature. Thus, C_6H_5Cl show more electrophilic substitution than that of $C_6H_5—CHO$.

Groups showing $(+I)$ and $(+R)$ effect have more electrophilic substitution tendency than those that show either or $(-I)$ and $(+R)$ effect.

Hence, correct order is $B > A > C > D$ and option (c) is the correct.

2 (c) During nitration of benzene the attacking electrophile is NO_2^+. It is formed by the reaction between HNO_3 and H_2SO_4.

$$HNO_3 + H_2SO_4 \longrightarrow H—\overset{+}{\underset{|}{O}}(H)—NO_2 + HSO_4^-$$

$$H—\overset{+}{\underset{|}{O}}(H)—NO_2 \rightleftharpoons H_2O + \underset{\text{Nitronium ion}}{NO_2^+}$$

3 (a) Reactant (X) in the reaction is acetylene overall reaction is as follows :

$$\underset{(X)}{3HC\equiv CH} \xrightarrow[1600\text{-}1800°C]{\text{Red hot tube}} \text{Benzene}$$

4 (a) Both Assertion and Reason are correct and Reason is the correct explanation of Assertion.

In nitration of benzene with nitric acid, sulphuric acid acts as catalyst. It helps in the formation of electrophile, i.e. nitronium ion NO_2^+.

The reaction is shown below:

$$HNO_3 + H_2SO_4 \longrightarrow NO_2^+ + 2HSO_4^- + H_3O^+$$

$$C_6H_6 \xrightarrow[H_2SO_4]{HNO_3} C_6H_5NO_2 + H_2O$$

5 (c) $—CH_3$ (an alkyl group) is an *ortho* and *para* directing group, thus 2 isomeric products are formed. Out of these 2 products. *ortho* one is a minor product while *para* product is a major one.

Thus, the complete reaction can be represented as :

$$m\text{-}CH_3C_6H_4CH_3 \xrightarrow[\text{Electrophilic substitution}]{Br_2/FeBr_3} \text{(Br ortho to one } CH_3\text{)} + \text{(Br ortho to other } CH_3\text{)}$$

$$m\text{-}CH_3C_6H_4CH_3 \xrightarrow[\text{Electrophilic substitution}]{Br_2/FeBr_3} \text{(Br between both } CH_3\text{)}$$

[Not possible due to steric hinderance]

6 (a, b) Benzene can be converted into *n*-propyl benzene either by Friedel-Craft alkylation reaction with *n*-propyl chloride or Friedel-Craft acylation with propionyl chloride, followed by Wolf-Kishner reduction. Thus, *n*-propyl benzene can be prepared from both mentioned reaction.

(i) $$C_6H_6 + \underset{n\text{-propyl chloride}}{CH_3\,CH_2\,CH_2Cl} \xrightarrow{\text{Anhy-}AlCl_3} \underset{n\text{-propyl chloride}}{C_6H_5CH_2CH_2CH_3}$$

(ii) $$\underset{\text{Benzene}}{C_6H_6} + \underset{\text{Propionyl chloride}}{CH_3—CH_2—\overset{O}{\overset{\|}{C}}—Cl} \xrightarrow[\text{acylation}]{\text{Friedel-Craft}} C_6H_5—\overset{O}{\overset{\|}{C}}—CH_2—CH_3$$

$$\xrightarrow[\text{Wolf-Kishner reduction}]{NH_2—NH_2\,(-H_2O)} C_6H_5—C(=N—NH_2)—CH_2—CH_3 \xrightarrow{\text{KOH/ethylene glycol}} \underset{n\text{-propyl benzene}}{C_6H_5—CH_2—CH_2—CH_3}$$

7 (d) $—CH_3$ group activates the benzene ring, whereas, $—COOH$ and $—NO_2$ deactivates the ring. Hence, toluene $(C_6H_5—CH_3)$ undergoes nitration easily.

8 (c) Conversion of benzene into *m*-bromoaniline can be done by successive nitration, bromination and reduction using following reagent.

Nitration $\rightarrow$ conc. HNO_3/conc. H_2SO_4

Bromination $\rightarrow$ Br_2/H_2O Reduction $\rightarrow$ Sn/HCl

Formation of nitrobenzene in the first step, direct incoming of electrophile towards *meta* position on the further step and reduction of nitro compound produces *m*-bromoaniline very easily. Complete sequence of the chemical reaction can be shown as.

$$C_6H_6 \xrightarrow[H_2SO_4]{HNO_3^+} C_6H_5NO_2 \xrightarrow{Br_2/H_2O} m\text{-}BrC_6H_4NO_2 \xrightarrow{Sn/HCl} m\text{-}BrC_6H_4NH_2$$

9 (*b*) Benzene reacts with *iso*-butene in the presence of H_2SO_4 to produce *t*-butyl benzene. The reaction takes place as follows :

$$C_6H_6 + CH_3-\underset{|}{\overset{CH_3}{C}}H=CH_2 \xrightarrow{H_2SO_4} C_6H_5-C(CH_3)_3$$

10 (*c*) Nitro group being electron withdrawing, deactivates the benzene nucleus to such an extent so that it becomes incapable to give Friedel-Craft's reaction.
Nitrobenzene because of its unreactivity towards Friedel-Craft's reaction is used as a solvent for this reaction.

11 (*d*) The deactivating tendency of given groups follows the order

$$-NO_2 > -SO_3H > -C\equiv N > -\overset{O}{\overset{\|}{C}}-O-H$$

So, the most deactivating group is $-NO_2$ group.

12 (*d*) DDT is dichloro-diphenyl trichloro ethane. It can be prepared by treating chlorobenzene with chloral or trichloro acetaldehyde.

$$2C_6H_5Cl + \underset{\text{Trichloro acetaldehyde}}{CCl_3CHO} \xrightarrow{\text{Conc. } H_2SO_4} \underset{\text{DDT}}{CCl_3CH(C_6H_4Cl)_2}$$

13 (*a*) Friedel-Craft's reaction involves the introduction of an alkyl or acyl group into the benzene ring in presence of catalyst. The presence of an electron withdrawing group in the ring hinders the reaction. Therefore, phenyl acetanilide is not used.

14 (*b*)

$$C_6H_6 + CH_2=CHCH_2Cl \xrightarrow{AlCl_3} \underset{(A)}{C_6H_5-CH_2-CH=CH_2}$$

$$\xrightarrow[\text{(ii) } H_2O_2, OH^-]{\text{(i) } BH_3, THC} \underset{(B)}{C_6H_5-CH_2-CH_2-CH_2OH} \xrightarrow[\Delta]{HF} \underset{(C)}{\text{Indane}}$$

15 (*d*)

$$C_6H_5CH_3 \xrightarrow[\text{(excess)}]{Cl_2} C_6H_5CH_2Cl \xrightarrow[\text{(excess)}]{Cl_2} C_6H_5CHCl_2 \xrightarrow[\text{(excess)}]{Cl_2} C_6H_5CCl_3$$

16 (d)

$$C_6H_6 + CH_3COCl \xrightarrow[\Delta]{\text{Anhy. } AlCl_3} \underset{\text{Acetophenone}}{C_6H_5COCH_3} + HCl$$

This reaction is known as Friedel craft's reaction.

17 (*a*) Ethyl benzene cannot be prepared by Wurtz reaction. (Wurtz reaction. is used to prepare alkanes).

18 (*b*) Electron withdrawing substituent deactivates the benzene nucleus towards electrophilic substitution while electron releasing substituent activates the ring towards electrophilic substitution.

Among the given option, —OH has the higher electron donating tendency and thus, activates the ring more towards electrophilic substitution, hence

$$o\text{-}CH_3C_6H_4OH$$

is more reactive towards electrophilic reagents.

19 (*c*)

$$CaC_2 \xrightarrow[-Ca(OH)_2]{H_2O} \underset{\text{Acetylene 'P'}}{CH\equiv CH} \xrightarrow[\text{tube}]{\text{Hot iron}} \underset{\text{Benzene 'Q'}}{C_6H_6}$$

$$\xrightarrow[\text{(Friedel-Craft's alkylation)}]{CH_3Cl,\ AlCl_3} \underset{\text{Toluene 'R'}}{C_6H_5CH_3}$$

20 (*c*) In benzene, the π-electrons are delocalised and makes the structure more stable. (Delocalisation of πe^- is called resonance). Thus, benzene does not give addition reactions because of resonance stabilisation.

21 (*b*) Benzene shows electrophilic substitution reactions rather than addition to preserve the delocalisation and stability in benzene ring.

22 (*d*)

$$C_6H_5CH_3 \xrightarrow[KOH]{KMnO_4} C_6H_5\overset{-}{COO}\overset{+}{K} \xrightarrow{H_3O^+} C_6H_5COOH$$

23 (*c*) When benzene or benzene derivatives react with alkyl halide in the presence of anhydrous $AlCl_3$, alkylation of benzene ring takes place. This reaction is called Friedel-Craft's alkylation.

$$C_6H_6 + CH_3Cl \xrightarrow[-HCl]{\text{Anhy. } AlCl_3} C_6H_5CH_3$$

Thus, C_6H_6 and CH_3Cl are the other reactants besides $AlCl_3$.

24 (*a*)

(Benzene)

3π-and 12σ-bonds are present in benzene. Hence, the ratio of π and σ-bonds in benzene is 3 : 12 or 1 : 4.

25 (*b*) The structure of benzene is

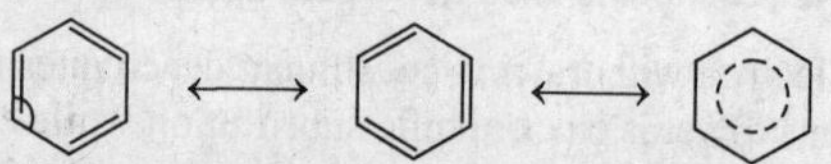

$$\text{Bond order} = \frac{\text{total number of bonds between two carbon atoms}}{\text{total number of resonating structure}} = \frac{2+1}{2} = 1.5$$

Since, the bond order is in between single and double bond, thus it contains delocalised π-bonds. Hence, it is not possible to obtain number of single and double bonds in benzene. Therefore, statement (b) is not true.

26 (*b*) Monobromination of the aromatic compound is an electrophilic substitution reaction. The electron donating group (like —CH_3) will increase the reactivity of ring while electron withdrawing groups decreases the reactivity of the ring. Hence, among the given aromatic compounds, the reactivity of $C_6H_5CH_3$ is highest. Between C_6H_5COOH and $C_6H_5NO_2$, electron withdrawing power of —NO_2 group is higher than —COOH so the reactivity of C_6H_5COOH is higher than $C_6H_5NO_2$. Thus, the decreasing reactivity order of ring towards monobromination is

$$\underset{(I)}{C_6H_5CH_3} > \underset{(III)}{C_6H_6} > \underset{(II)}{C_6H_5COOH} > \underset{(IV)}{C_6H_5NO_2}$$

Topic 6

Petroleum

2012

1 Liquid hydrocarbons can be converted to a mixture of gaseous hydrocarbons by **[CBSE AIPMT]**

(a) hydrolysis (b) oxidation
(c) cracking
(d) distillation under reduced pressure

2 Petrochemicals can be used to prepare **[Manipal]**

(a) synthetic fibres (b) pesticides
(c) plastics (d) All of the above

3 Power alcohol is a mixture of **[KCET]**

(a) 80% petrol + 20% ethanol + small quantity of benzene
(b) 80% ethanol + 20% benzene + small quantity of petrol
(c) 50% petrol + 50% ethanol + small quantity of benzene
(d) 80% petrol + 20% benzene + small quantity of ethanol

2008

4 Which of the following isomer will have the higher octane number? **[Kerala CEE]**

(a) *n*-octane (b) 2-methyl heptane
(c) 2-methyl pentane (d) 2,2,4-trimethyl pentane
(e) 2-methyl hexane

2007

5 Which of the following has highest knocking property? **[AIIMS]**

(a) Aromatic hydrocarbons (b) Olefins
(c) Branched chain paraffins (d) Straight chain paraffins

6 Which of the following substance is used as an anti-knocking compound? **[BHU]**

(a) Tetraethyl lead (b) Lead tetrachloride
(c) Lead acetate (d) Ethyl acetate

7 Indane is **[RPMT]**

(a) commercial butane, *iso*-butane and propane mixture
(b) butane, ethane mixture
(c) commercial propane
(d) methane, propane mixture

2006

8 Which of the following fraction of coal tar distillation is obtained at 270° – 360°C ? **[MHT CET]**

(a) Light oil (b) Middle oil
(c) Green oil (d) Heavy oil

9 A sample of gasoline contains 80% *iso*-octane and 20% *n*-heptane. Its octane number will be **[MP PMT]**

(a) 62 (b) 100 (c) 20 (d) 80

10 Octane number can be changed by **[AMU]**

(a) isomerisation (b) alkylation
(c) cyclisation (d) All of these

2005

11 Cetane is a compound which has very good ignition property. Chemically it is **[MP PMT]**

(a) $CH_3(CH_2)_{14}CH_3$ (b) $(CH_3)_3C(CH_2)_{11}CH_3$
(c) $C_{17}H_{34}$ (d) None of these

Answers

1 (c)	2 (d)	3 (a)	4 (d)	5 (d)	6 (a)	7 (a)	8 (c)	9 (d)	10 (d)
11 (a)									

Explanations

1 (*c*) Liquid hydrocarbon can be converted into a gaseous mixture of hydrocarbon by cracking. It is the process of breaking a heavier hydrocarbon into two or more smaller hydrocarbons.

2 (*d*) Petrochemicals can be used to prepare synthetic fibres, pesticides and plastics etc.

3 (*a*) Ethanol in the presence of small quantity of benzene when mixed with petrol (i.e. 80% petrol + 20% ethanol + small quantity of benzene) is termed as power alcohol. It is used as a vehicle fuel.

4 (*d*) Octane number represents the relative anti-knock tendency of a fuel. It is lowest (i.e. zero) for *n*-heptane and highest (i.e. 100) for 2,2,4-trimethylpentane (*iso*-octane).

$$H_3C-\underset{CH_3}{\overset{CH_3}{C}}-CH_2-\overset{CH_3}{CH}-CH_3$$

2,2,4-trimethylpentane
(octane number 100)

5 (*d*) Knocking character of fuel increases with decrease in octane number of a fuel. The octane number increases in the following order : straight chain alkanes < branched chain alkanes < olefins < cycloalkanes < aromatic compounds. Since, straight chain alkane (paraffin) has minimum octane number hence, it produces maximum knocking.

6 (*a*) Tetraethyl lead $Pb(C_2H_5)_4$ is an anti-knocking compound. It decomposes to produce radicals which combine with the radical produced due to irregular combustion. As a result, the reaction chains are broken and smooth burning of fuel occurs. It prevents knocking.

7 (*a*) Indane is a mixture of butane, *iso*-butane and propane. It is generally called LPG gas.

8 (*c*) Green oil (anthracene oil) is obtained at 270-360°C by distillation of coal tar. It has mainly anthracene and phenanthrene.

9 (*d*) A petrol is said to have an octane number of 80, if it behaves as a mixture of 80% *iso*-octane and 20% *n*-heptane in a standard test engine.

10 (*d*) The octane number of fuel can be improved by increasing the percentage of branched chain alkanes, alkenes and aromatic hydrocarbon.

Thus, octane number can be changed by isomerisation, alkylation and aromatisation (cyclisation).

11 (*a*) Cetane is chemically hexadecane $CH_3(CH_2)_{14}CH_3$ or $C_{16}H_{34}$. It is colourless liquid and straight chain hydrocarbon used in rating of diesel.

Topic 7

Cyclic Hydrocarbons

2014

1 Consider the following reaction **[WB JEE]**

(Octane) $\xrightarrow{X}$ 'Y' $\xrightarrow{'Z'}$ Ethyl benzene

(a) $Al_2O_3 + Cr_2O_3/600°C$, (Me-cyclohexane) Al/600°C

(b) $Al_2O_3 + Cr_2O_3/600°C$, (Me-cyclohexane) Pt/600°C

(c) $Al_2O_3/600°C$, (cyclohexane) Pt/600°C

(c) $Al_2O_3/600°C$, (cyclohexane) Pt/600°C

2 The order of decreasing ease of abstraction of hydrogen atoms in the following molecule **[WB JEE]**

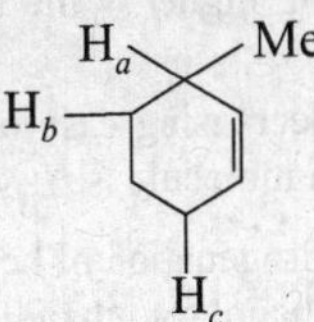

(a) $H_a > H_b > H_c$ (b) $H_a > H_c > H_b$
(c) $H_b > H_a > H_c$ (d) $H_c > H_b > H_a$

3 The correct statement is **[KCET]**

(a) cyclohexadiene and cyclohexene cannot be isolated with ease during controlled hydrogenation of benzene
(b) one mole each of benzene and hydrogen when reacted gives 1/3 mole of cyclohexane and 2/3 mole unreacted hydrogen
(c) hydrogenation of benzene to cyclohexane is an endothermic process
(d) it is easier to hydrogenate benzene as compared to cyclohexene

4 The final product in the given reaction **[Guj. CET]**

cyclohexene $\xrightarrow[H_2SO_4, \Delta]{KMnO_4}$ is

(a) OH, OH (b) CHO, CHO

(c) O (d) COOH, COOH

2010

5 In the following reaction, the major product is **[AMU]**

CH_3 (methylcyclopentane) $\xrightarrow[h\nu]{Br_2}$

(a) CH_2Br (b) CH_3, Br (c) CH_3, Br (d) CH_3, Br

6 A dibromo derivative of an alkane reacts with sodium metal to form an alicyclic hydrocarbon. The derivative is **[KCET]**

(a) 1,1-dibromopropane (b) 2,2-dibromobutane
(c) 1,2-dibromoethane (d) 1,4-dibromobutane

7 Cycloalkanes are isomeric with **[Guj CET]**

(a) alkanes (b) alkenes (c) alkynes (d) arenes

8 The molecule which is free from angular strain is **[BCECE]**

(a) Cyclopropane (b) Cyclobutane
(c) Cyclopentane (d) Cyclohexane
(e) Cycloheptane

Answers

1 (a)	2 (b)	3 (a)	4 (d)	5 (c)	6 (d)	7 (b)	8 (d)

Explanations

1 (*a*) Correct option is (a), Reaction involved is as follows :

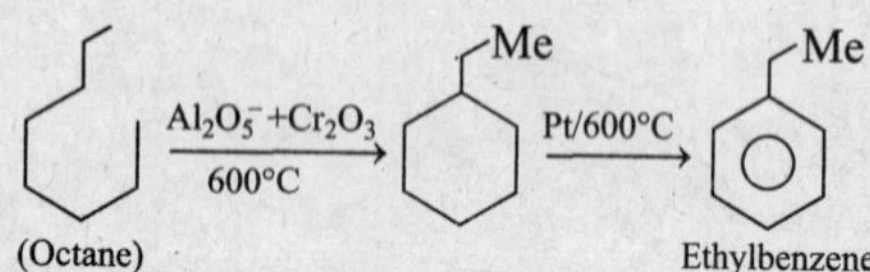

2 (*b*) Abstraction of (H_a) hydrogen atom results in the formation of 3° allylic carbocation whereas abstraction of H_c gives 2° allylic carbocation (which is less stable as compared to former one). However, abstraction of H_b gives only a 2° carbocation which is less stable as compared to former two. More the stability of generated carbocation, higher is the tendency of abstraction of hydrogen.

Thus, the order of decreasing ease of abstraction of hydrogen atoms from the given molecule is $H_a > H_c > H_b$.

3 (*a*) On controlled hydrogenation of benzene with group I metal (like Na, Li) and methanol (or ethanol) in liquid NH_3, it reduces into cyclohexadiene and cyclohexene, which cannot be isolated.

Benzene $\xrightarrow[CH_3OH]{Na, liq. NH_3}$ Cyclohexadiene + Cyclohexene

Corrected statements are:

(i) One mole of benzene reacts with three moles of hydrogen to give one mole of cyclohexane.

(ii) Hydrogenatom of benzene to cyclohexane is an exothermic process (– 208. $kmol^{-1}$)

(iii) It is easier to hydrogenate cyclohexane ($\Delta H° = -119.5\ kJmol^{-1}$) as compared to benzene ($\Delta H° = -208\ kmol^{-1}$)

4 (*d*) In acidic medium, $KMnO_4$ is very powerful oxidising agent.

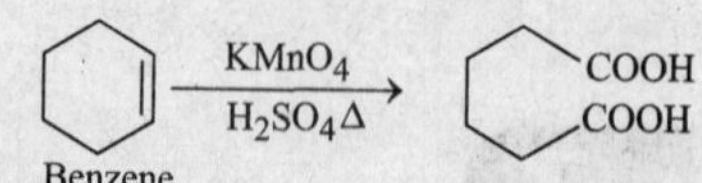

5 (*c*) $Br_2 + h\nu \longrightarrow Br^\bullet + Br^\bullet$

CH_3 (methylcyclopentane) + $Br^\bullet \longrightarrow$ CH_3 (tertiary radical, major) + $\dot{C}H_2$ (cyclopentyl)

(major)

CH_3 (radical) + $Br_2 \longrightarrow$ CH_3, Br

6 (*d*) ω-dihalides when reacts with sodium metal, gives cyclic hydrocarbons. This is an example of intramolecular Wurtz reaction.

$$\underset{Br}{CH_2}\text{—}CH_2CH_2\text{—}\underset{Br}{CH_2} \xrightarrow[-2NaBr]{Na} \text{Cyclobutane}$$

7 (*b*) Cycloalkanes are isomeric with alkenes because they have same general formula C_nH_{2n} (i.e. same molecular formula) but possessing different structures. They show ring chain isomerism.

8 (*d*) Cyclohexane adopts a conformation in which all the bond angles between carbon atoms are close to tetrahedral angle, i.e., 109.5°, called chair conformation. This conformation is free from angular strain as well as torsional strain.

Chain conformation

14

Environmental Chemistry

Quick Review

Environmental chemistry is the branch of chemistry which is concerned with the chemical phenomenon occurring in the environment. Atmosphere is one of the major component of environment.

Atmosphere

Earth is surrounded by a covering of various gases called atmosphere.

It can be divided into following regions

(*i*) **Troposphere** It is the lower layer of atmosphere which extends upto the height of ~ 10 to ~ 18 km from the sea level. It contains water vapours and is greatly affected by air pollution.

(*ii*) **Stratosphere** It is the region of the earth's atmosphere present above the troposphere. Ozone layer is present in this region.

(*iii*) **Mesosphere** It is the region of the earth's atmosphere present above the stratosphere. It is the coldest region of atmosphere.

(*iv*) **Thermosphere** It is the upper region of the atmosphere present above mesosphere. It is the hottest region of atmosphere.

(*v*) **Enosphere** It is the uppermost region of atmosphere. It contains atomic and ionic O_2, H_2 and CO_2.

Environmental Pollution

- The effect of undesirable changes in our surroundings which have adverse effect on plants, animals and human beings termed as environmental pollution.
- The main causes of pollution are rapid growth in population, urbanisation, proliferation of industries, craze for development of materials for our comforts, development of new weapons for mass destruction etc.

Pollutants

Any substance produced either by a natural source or by human activity which causes adverse effect on the environment is called pollutant.

Pollutants can be of following types depending upon the following factors :

- *Classification on the basis of their occurrence in nature*

  (*i*) **Primary Pollutants** These are simple molecules that persist in the environment in the form they are formed, e.g. oxides of carbon, nitrogen, sulphur such as, CO, NO_2, SO_2.

  (*ii*) **Secondary Pollutants** These are products derived from primary pollutants by chemical reactions, e.g. PAN (peroxyacetyl nitrate).

- *Classification on the basis of their existence in nature*

  (i) **Quantitative Pollutants** These are naturally present in nature and also added by man. These become pollutants when their concentration reaches beyond a threshold value in the environment, e.g. CO_2, nitrogen oxide etc.

(ii) **Qualitative Pollutants** These are not present in the nature but are added by nature only due to human activities, e.g. pesticides, fungicides, herbicides etc.

- *Classification on the basis of their degradation*

(i) **Biodegradable Pollutants** Pollutants capable of being degraded by biological or microbial actions are called biodegradable pollutants, e.g. domestic sewage.

(ii) **Non-biodegradable Pollutants** The substances which are normally not acted upon by microbes are called non-biodegradable pollutants. These undergo biological magnification.

Atmospheric or Air Pollution

- Presence of undesirable gaseous or particulate substance in atmosphere is called atmospheric or air pollution.
- It affects both plants and animals directly and indirectly.

Gaseous or Air Pollutants

Various gaseous or air pollutants, their source and harmful effects are given below :

(*i*) **Oxides of Carbon** The two main oxides of carbon that cause pollution are carbon monoxide (CO) and carbon dioxide (CO_2).

(a) **Carbon monoxide** is produced by incomplete combustion of gasoline in motor vehicles, wood, coal, forest fires etc.

It induces headache, block the normal transport of oxygen from the lungs to other parts of body by combining with haemoglobin of the blood.

(b) **Carbon dioxide** causes mild narcotic effects.

(*ii*) **Oxides of Sulphur** These are produced by petrol combustion, petrol refining and smelting operation. It obstruct the movement of air in and out of lungs.

Taj Mahal is reported to be affected by SO_2 and other pollutants released by oil refinery of Mathura.

(*iii*) **Oxides of Nitrogen** (NO_2 and NO) These are obtained by combustion of coal, gasoline, natural gas, tobacco smoke etc.

Breathing NO_2 causes chlorosis in plants and chronic lung condition in human being. These oxides destroy ozone layer.

(iv) **Hydrocarbons** These are formed by incomplete combustion of fuel and also carcinogenic. They harm plants by causing ageing, breakdown of tissues and shedding of leaves.

Particulate Pollutants

These are minute solid particles or liquid droplets in air. These may be viable and non-viable.

- **Viable particulates** are minute living organisms that dispersed in the atmosphere.
- **Non-viable particulates** *may be classified as follows* :

(*i*) **Smoke** The vaporised matter with suspended particles of carbon, that arises as a result of burning or combustion is called smoke.

(*ii*) **Dust** The air borne solid particles having size $0.1\,\mu$-$25\,\mu$ are called dust.

As a result of smoke and dust, coal miners suffer from black lung disease and textile workers suffer from white lung disease.

Consequences of Air Pollutants

The main consequences of air pollutants are as follows

Green House Effect and Global Warming

- The phenomenon of heating of earth and its objects because of trapping of IR radiations coming from the sun and prevent them from escaping into outer space is called **green house effect.**

  The major green house gases are CO_2, CH_4, N_2O, water vapour, O_3 and CFC's.
- When concentration of green house gases increases, these trap excess IR-rays and increases the temperature of earth too much. This is termed as **global warming**. It has drastic effect on climatic conditions.

Acid Rain

- When the pH of rainwater drops below 5.6 due to the presence of certain acids like H_2SO_4, HNO_3, it is called acid rain.
- Oxide of nitrogen and sulphur released into the atmosphere from thermal power plants, industries and automobiles are the main sources of acid rain.

$$2SO_2(g) + O_2(g) + 2H_2O(l) \longrightarrow 2H_2SO_4(aq)$$
$$4NO_2(g) + O_2(g) \longrightarrow 4HNO_3(aq)$$

- Acid rain damages buildings, corrodes metal pipes, causes respiratory diseases.

Smog

It is the mixture of smoke (composed of tiny particles of carbon, ash and oil etc., from coal combustion) and fog in suspended droplets from.

It is of two types

London Smog or Classical Smog	Photochemical Smog or Los Angeles Smog
• It occurs in cool humid climate when carbon soot particles combine with gaseous oxides of sulphur present in atmosphere.	• It occurs in warm, dry and sunny climate by the action of sunlight or unsaturated hydrocarbons and nitrogen oxides.
• It is reducing in nature.	• It is oxidising in nature.
• It causes bronchial irritation	• It causes irritation to eyes, lungs, nose and damage to plant life.

Ozone Layer

- The upper layer of the atmosphere enveloped by ozone (16 km - 40 km) is commonly known as ozonosphere, ozone layer, stratospheric ozone layer, protective layer or ozone umbrella.
- Ozone layer acts as a protective shield in the biospheric ecosystem against their exposure to harmful ultraviolet (UV) radiations.

Depletion of Ozone Layer

- The main cause of ozone depletion is the wide spread use of chlorofluorocarbons (CFCs).
- Ozone depletion is also taking place due to NO_x, SO_2, CH_4, photochemical smog and green house effect.
- The UV radiations damage the cornea and lens of the eyes and also causes skin cancer.

Ozone Hole

It is formed over Antarctica and some parts of non-polar regions also. In other parts of stratosphere NO_2, CH_4 react with $ClO^{\bullet}$ and $Cl^{\bullet}$ respectively and act as natural sink for $ClO^{\bullet}$ and $Cl^{\bullet}$

$$ClO^{\bullet}(g) + NO_2(g) \longrightarrow ClONO_2(g)$$
$$Cl^{\bullet}(g) + CH_4(g) \longrightarrow {}^{\bullet}CH_3(g) + HCl(g)$$

These reactions consume $Cl^{\bullet}$ and $ClO^{\bullet}$ and initiate to ozone depletion.

Water Pollution

- The contamination of water by foreign substances which would cause health problems and make it unfit for all purposes is known as water pollution.
- Detergents, toxic metals, pesticides, acids, alkalis, salts, sediments, medical wastages etc., are the main sources of water and soil pollution.
- The degree of water pollution is measured in terms of BOD and COD.

  (*i*) **Biochemical Oxygen Demand** (BOD) is defined as the total amount (in milligram) required by microbes to decompose the organic matter present in 1 L of water sample. While the term BOD refers to the total amount of oxygen required.
  In darkness under incubation at 20°C for five days by microbes to decompose the organic matter.

  $$\text{BOD} = \frac{\text{Number of mg of } O_2 \text{ required}}{\text{Number of litres of samples}}$$

  For clean water, the BOD value is less than 5 ppm while highly polluted water could have a BOD value of 17 ppm or more.

  (*ii*) **Chemical Oxygen Demand** (COD) is the total amount of oxygen in ppm that would be consumed by the pollutants, in a given water sample. For pure water, COD value is 4 ppm.

Chemical Pollutants

The toxic chemicals that destroy microbes and kill aquatic animals by poisoning are known as chemical pollutants.

Some chemical pollutants present in water are as follows :

(*i*) Excess nitrate (NO_3^-) in drinking water causes methemoglobinemia or blue baby syndrome.

(*ii*) Excess mercury (Hg) in drinking water causes minamata disease, which is characterised by diarrhoea, haemolysis, meningitis and finally death.

(*iii*) Excess cadmium (Cd) in drinking water causes itai-itai disease, characterised by high blood pressure and kidney malfunctioning.

(*iv*) Excess of lead (upper limit concentration = 50 ppb) in drinking water can cause kidney, liver and reproductive system etc.

(v) Excess of sulphate (>500 pm) causes laxative effect.

Note The process of enrichment of water by plant nutrients (like phosphates and nitrates) to support a dense plant pollution, which affect the fish population and also kills other aquatic animals by depriving them from oxygen is called **eutrophication**.

Soil Pollution

- The addition of substances, in an indefinite proportion changes the productivity of the soil. This is called soil pollution.
- Chemicals like insecticides (DDT, BHC), pesticides ($NaClO_3$, Na_3AsO_3), industrial wastes, radioactive wastes from research centres etc., are the main sources of soil pollution.

Prevention of Pollution

Pollution may be prevented by using

(*i*) zoning.

(*ii*) installation of controlling devices and equipments.

(*iii*) by providing means of equipments to discharge, pollutants at higher altitudes.

(*iv*) by planting trees and growing vegetation.

(*v*) by public awareness.

Green Chemistry

- It is the branch of chemistry in which chemicals of daily needs are produced by using such reactions or processes that neither use toxic chemicals nor emit harmful chemicals into the atmosphere.
- Some examples of such chemicals are use of H_2O_2 for bleaching purposes, use of identified CO_2 with suitable detergents for dry cleaning clothes which replaces tetrachloro ethene, a major pollutant.

Topical Practice Questions

All the exam questions of this chapter have been divided into two topics as listed below

Topic 1

Atmospheric Pollution

2019

1 Among the following, the one that is not a green house gas is **[NEET]**

(a) methane (b) ozone

(c) sulphur dioxide (d) nitrous oxide

2018

2 Which of the following chemicals are used to manufacture methyl isocyanate that caused "Bhopal tragedy"?

(i) Methylamine (ii) Phosgene **[JIPMER]**

(iii) Phosphine (iv) Dimethylamine

(a) (i) and (ii) (b) (iii) and (iv)

(c) (i) and (iii) (d) (ii) and (iv)

3 Which oxide of nitrogen is not a common pollutant introduced into the atmosphere both due to natural and human activity? **[NEET]**

(a) N_2O (b) NO_2 (c) N_2O_5 (d) NO

2017

4 **Assertion** (A) London smog is produced when carbon soot particles combine with gaseous oxides of sulphur.

Reason (R) Presence of carbon particles and SO_2 makes it reducing in nature. **[AIIMS]**

(a) Both A and R are correct and R is the correct explanation of A

(b) Both A and R are correct but R is not the correct explanation of A

(c) A is correct but R is incorrect

(d) Both A and R are incorrect

2014

5 Which one of the following is not a common component of photochemical smog? **[CBSE AIPMT]**

(a) Ozone (b) Acrolein

(c) Peroxyacetyl nitrate (d) Chlorofluorocarbons

6 Ozone is present as a chief constituent, in which region of the atmosphere? **[MHT CET]**

(a) Troposphere

(b) Stratosphere

(c) Mesosphere

(d) Thermosphere

7 Among the following, the one which is not a 'green house gas', is **[Kerala CEE]**

(a) N_2O (b) CO_2

(c) CH_4 (d) O_2

2013

8 **Assertion** (A) Nitrogen oxides are one of the components of photochemical smog.

Reason (R) Vehicular pollution is a major source of nitrogen oxides. **[AIIMS]**

(a) Both A and R are correct and R is the correct explanation of A

(b) Both A and R are correct but R is not the correct explanation of A

(c) A is correct but R is incorrect

(d) Both A and R are incorrect

2012

9 Which one of the following statements regarding photochemical smog is not correct? **[CBSE AIPMT]**

(a) Carbon monoxide does not play any role in formation of photochemical smog.

(b) Photochemical smog is an oxidising agent by character.

(c) Photochemical smog is formed through photochemical reaction involving solar energy.

(d) Photochemical smog does not cause irritation in eyes and throat.

10 Assertion (A) CO and NO combine with haemoglobin.
Reason (R) Both have equal affinity for haemoglobin. [AIIMS]

(a) Both A and R are correct and the R is the correct explanation of the A
(b) Both A and R are correct but the R is not the correct explanation of the A
(c) A is correct but R is incorrect
(d) Both A and R is incorrect

2010

11 Pollution is [MHT CET]

(a) removal of top soil
(b) release of toxic and undesirable materials in environment
(c) conservation of energy
(d) All of the above

12 UV radiations brings about [RPMT]

(a) skin cancer (b) mouth cancer
(c) lung cancer (d) liver cancer

13 Gas released during Bhopal Gas Tragedy was [RPMT]

(a) methyl isocyanate (b) potassium isocyanate
(c) sodium isocyanate (d) ethyl isothiocyanate

14 Green house effect is caused by [JCECE]

(a) NO_2 (b) CO (c) NO (d) CO_2

2009

15 Assertion (A) London smog is oxidising in nature.
Reason (R) London smog contains O_3, NO_2 and hydrocarbons. [AIIMS]

(a) Both A and R are correct and R is the correct explanation of A
(b) Both A and R are correct but R is not the correct explanation of A
(c) A is correct but R is incorrect
(d) Both A and R are incorrect

16 Photochemical smog is caused due to the presence of [Kerala CEE]

(a) oxides of sulphur (b) oxides of nitrogen
(c) oxides of carbon (d) lead
(e) chlorofluorocarbons

17 Antidote for carbon monoxide is/are [CG PMT, Haryana PMT]

(a) carborundum (b) dry ice
(c) carbonic acid (d) pure oxygen and carbogen

18 The chemical entities present in thermosphere of the atmosphere [EAMCET]

(a) O_2^+, O^+, NO^+ (b) O_3
(c) N_2, O_2, CO_2, H_2O (d) O_3, O_2^+, O_2

2008

19 Which one of the following compounds helps in achieving equilibrium between O_2 and CO_2 in atmosphere? [EAMCET]

(a) Chlorophyll
(b) Vitamin-B_{12}
(c) Porphyrin
(d) Acetyl salicylic acid

20 Which of the following is responsible for depletion of the ozone layer in the upper strata of the atmosphere?

(a) Polyhalogens (b) Ferrocenes [JCECE]
(c) Fullerenes (d) Freons

2007

21 Which of the following is secondary pollutant? [Manipal]

(a) CO_2 (b) N_2O (c) PAN (d) SO_2

22 The brown haze of photochemical smog is largely attributable to [Punjab PMET]

(a) NO (b) NO_2
(c) $CH_3—\underset{\underset{O}{\|}}{C}OONO_2$ (d) $CH_2{=}CHCH{=}O$

2006

23 Match the Column I and Column II and pick the correct matching from the codes given below. [Kerala CEE]

Column I	Column II
A. Peroxyacetyl nitrate	1. Waste incineration
B. Polycyclic aromatic	2. Global warming
C. Dioxins	3. Photochemical smog
D. Indigo	4. Carcinogens
E. IR active molecules	5. Vat dye

Codes

	A	B	C	D	E
(a)	3	4	1	5	2
(b)	1	2	3	4	5
(c)	3	5	1	2	4
(d)	5	3	1	2	4
(e)	2	3	5	4	1

2005

24 The basic components of the smog are [AMU]

(a) PAN (b) PBN
(c) NO_2 (d) All of these

25 Use of chlorofluorocarbon is not encouraged because [KCET]

(a) they are harmful to the eyes of people
(b) they damage the refrigerators and air conditioners
(c) they eat away the ozone in the atmosphere
(d) they destroy the oxygen layer

Answers

1. (c)	2. (a)	3. (c)	4. (a)	5. (d)	6. (b)	7. (d)	8. (b)	9. (d)	10. (a)
11. (b)	12. (a)	13. (a)	14. (d)	15. (d)	16. (b)	17. (d)	18. (a)	19. (a)	20. (d)
21. (c)	22. (b)	23. (a)	24. (d)	25. (c)					

Explanations

1 (*c*) Sulphur dioxide (SO_2) is not a green house gas. Carbon dioxide (CO_2), methane (CH_4), water vapour, nitrous oxide (N_2O), CFCs and ozone (O_3) are the green house gases.

These gases are responsible for global warming.

2 (*a*) Methyl isocyanate (CH_3NCO) is industrially prepared by the reaction of methyl amine and phosgene (carbonyl chloride).

$$\underset{\text{Methyl amine}}{CH_3NH_2} + \underset{\text{Phosgene}}{COCl_2} \xrightarrow{-HCl} [CH_3NH—CO—Cl] \xrightarrow{\Delta, -HCl} \underset{\text{Methyl isocyanate}}{CH_3N{=}C{=}O}$$

3 (*c*) Nitrous oxide (N_2O), nitrogen dioxide (NO_2) and nitric oxide (NO) are the common pollutants whereas N_2O_5 is not a common pollutant introduced into the atmosphere.

N_2O occurs naturally in environment. NO and NO_2 causes considerable amount of air pollution.

They are given off in car exhaust fumes and when fossil fuels are burnt as well as produced during thunderstorms. In each case, NO is formed first and then NO_2.

4 (*a*) Both Assertion and Reason are correct and Reason is the correct explanation of Assertion.

London smog occurs in cold humid climate, when carbon soot particles combine with gaseous oxides of sulphur, present in atmosphere. Due to presence of carbon particles and SO_2 it is reducing in nature. This smog causes lung and throat irritation and in high concentration it leads to death.

5 (*d*) Among the given components, chlorofluorocarbons are responsible for ozone depletion which degrades ozone into molecular oxygen. It is not a component of photochemical smog. While other given compounds are the main components of photochemical smog, inorganic gases and organic hydroperoxides, like PAN, PBN, PPN etc.

6 (*b*) Ozone is mainly found in the lower portion of the atmosphere in higher concentrations within the stratosphere. It is present at about 20 km to 40 km height from the sea level.

7 (*d*) The gases N_2O, CO_2 and CH_4 have the ability to trap thermal radiations but O_2 does not. That's why it is not a green house gas.

Note O_2 is a gas, which is essential for life and in its absence life is not possible.

8 (*b*) It is correct that nitrogen oxides are one of the component of photochemical smog (other components) and vehicular pollution is major source of nitrogen oxides. Thus, both A and R are correct but R is not the correct explanation of A.

9 (*d*) Photochemical smog is formed in warm and sunny climate during day time by the action of sunlight on primary pollutants. It contains nitrogen oxides, ozone, PAN, etc which are oxidising in nature. So, photochemical smog is an oxidising agent in character. It causes irritation in eyes and throat.

10 (*a*) CO and NO both have equal affinity for haemoglobin. Hence, both sentences are correct and reason is correct explanation of assertion.

11 (*b*) The addition of any toxic and undesirable material in environment is called a pollution and the added material is known as pollutant.

12 (*a*) UV radiation causes skin cancer.

13 (*a*) Gas released during Bhopal Gas Tragedy was methyl isocyanate (MIC).

14 (*d*) Green house effect is caused by CO_2.

15 (*d*) London smog is formed at low temperature, i.e. in early hours of winter months and contains SO_2, smoke and dust particles. Hence, it is reducing in nature.

16 (*b*) Photochemical smog (or Los Angeles smog) is formed by the action of sunlight on unsaturated hydrocarbons and oxides of nitrogen are present in the atmosphere. Due to the presence of oxides of nitrogen and ozone, it is oxidising in nature.

17 (*d*) Carbon monoxide binds tightly to haemoglobin to form carboxy-haemoglobin. It lowers oxygen saturation of blood and also causes haemoglobin to bind more tightly to oxygen. Therefore, carbon poisoning basically blocks oxygen transport to tissues.

The antidote for carbon monoxide poisoning involves having the patient breathe 100% oxygen or carbogen with 95% O_2, 5% CO_2. So, more oxygen will be available to displace the carbon monoxide from haemoglobin. Hence, both carbogen and pure O_2 act as an antidote for carbon monoxide.

18 (*a*) The thermosphere is the fourth layer of the earth's atmosphere. It includes the region of the atmosphere, called the **ionosphere**.

The ionosphere is the region of the atmosphere that is filled with charged particles such as O_2^+, O^+, NO^+. The high temperature in the thermosphere can cause molecules to ionise.

19 (*a*) In atmosphere, the equilibrium between oxygen (O_2) and carbon dioxide (CO_2) is maintained by photosynthesis and chlorophyll is the necessary green pigment (present in plants) for photosynthesis. Thus, chlorophyll helps in achieving equilibrium between O_2 and CO_2 in atmosphere.

20 (*d*) Freons or chlorofluorocarbons (CFCs) are responsible for depletion of ozone layer in the upper strata of the atmosphere. They absorb UV radiation and break down CFCs liberating free atomic chlorine which causes decomposition of ozone through free radical reaction. This results in the depletion of the ozone layer.

21 (*c*) Pollutants which are formed by reaction amongst the primary pollutants (persist in the environment in the form they are passed into it) are called as secondary pollutants, e.g. peroxyacyl nitrates (PAN) are formed through the reaction between nitrogen oxides and hydrocarbons in the presence of sunlight.

22 (*b*) Photochemical smog is initiated by the photochemical dissociation of NO_2 that results in the formation of NO. This NO rapidly reacts with O_3 [formed by molecular oxygen with O-atoms] to give NO_2 [a brown gas], responsible for causing haze, if its concentration is very high.

$$NO_2(g) \xrightarrow{h\nu} NO\,(g) + \underset{\substack{\text{Nascent oxygen} \\ \text{(very reactive)}}}{[O]}$$

$$[O] + O_2 \longrightarrow O_3 \text{ [reacts rapidly with NO]}$$

$$O_3 + NO \longrightarrow \underset{\substack{\text{(Brown gas)} \\ \text{[in high concentration} \\ \text{from haze]}}}{NO_2} + O_2$$

23 (*a*) The correct match is A→3, B→4, C→1, D→5, E→2.

- Peroxyacetyl nitrate is the main component formed in photochemical smog.
- Polycyclic aromatic hydrocarbons act as carcinogens. Dioxins are used to burn the waste into ashes.
- Indigo is called as vat dye because the dyeing with indigotin was carried out in wooden vats in the form of water soluble indigotin-white.
- IR active molecules are responsible for global warming.

24 (*d*) Peroxyacetyl nitrate (PAN), peroxybenzoyl nitrate (PBN), nitrogen dioxide (NO_2) and hydrogen peroxide (H_2O_2) are the main components of smog.

25 (*c*) Chlorofluorocarbon is used in air conditioners and in domestic refrigerators for cooling purposes. Its main drawback is that, it is responsible for ozone depletion. Basically, it eats away the ozone layer in atmosphere by generating free chlorine radicals which reacts with ozone and cause its depletion.

$$CF_2Cl_2 + Cl_2 \xrightarrow{h\nu} \dot{C}F_2Cl$$

$$Cl^{\bullet} + O_3 \longrightarrow ClO^{\bullet} + O_2$$

$$ClO^{\bullet} + O \longrightarrow \underset{\text{Chlorine free radical}}{Cl^{\bullet}} + O_2$$

Topic 2

Water and Soil Pollution

2011

1 Which one of the following statement is not true? **[CBSE-AIPMT]**

(a) Oxides of sulphur, nitrogen and carbon are the most widespread air pollutant
(b) pH of drinking water should be between 5.5-9.5
(c) Concentration of DO below 6 ppm is good for the growth of fish
(d) Clean water would have a BOD value of less than 5 ppm

2 Excess nitrate in drinking water can cause **[Kerala CEE]**

(a) methemoglobinemia
(b) kidney damage
(c) liver damage
(d) laxative effect
(e) leucoderma

2008

3 The process of 'eutrophication' is due to the **[Kerala CEE]**

(a) increase in concentration of insecticide in water
(b) increase in concentration of fluoride ion in water
(c) reduction in concentration of the dissolved oxygen in water due to phosphate pollution in water
(d) attack of younger leaves of a plant by peroxyacetyl nitrate
(e) increase in concentration of radioactive substances in water

4 5 L aqueous solution is kept in the presence of oxygen and suitable microorganism for five days at 20°C. If the O_2 consumed is 0.2 g, the BOD value of the sample is **[EAMCET]**

(a) 4 ppm
(b) 0.4 mg L^{-1}
(c) 40 ppm
(d) 20 mg L^{-1}

2006

5 The water pollutants mainly responsible for eutrophication are **[Punjab PMET]**

(a) Cd, Pb and Hg present in industrial waste
(b) heavy metals present in mining waste
(c) detergents and fertilisers containing phosphate anion
(d) polychlorinated biphenyls

Answers

1. (c)	2. (a)	3. (c)	4. (c)	5. (c)

Explanations

1 (*c*) Statement (c) is not true. The fish growth is inhibited, if the dissolved concentration of oxygen in water is below 6 ppm.

2 (*a*) Excess of nitrate in drinking water causes methemoglobinemia.

3 (*c*) The process by which the aquatic life gets deprived oxygen results in subsequent loss of biodiversity is known as eutrophication. It is due to the reduction in concentration of the dissolved oxygen in water due to phosphate pollution in water.

4 (*c*) Water pollution is measured by BOD.

$$BOD = \frac{\text{weight of oxygen (in mg)}}{\text{volume of water sample (in L)}}$$

Given, weight of oxygen = 0.2 g = 200 mg

Volume of solution = 5 L

$$BOD = \frac{200}{5} \text{ mg / L} = 40 \text{ mg / L} = 40 \text{ ppm}$$

5 (*c*) Detergents and fertilisers contain phosphates as additives. The addition of phosphorus to water, in the form of the phosphate anion (PO_4^{3-}) encourages the formation of algae, which reduces the dissolved oxygen concentration of water. This process is known as eutrophication.

15

Solid State

Quick Review

- The constituent particles of solids are closely packed and held together by strong interparticle forces.
- On the basis of the arrangement of their constituent particles, solids are classified into two categories :

(i) **Crystalline solids** have systematic and regular arrangement of particles. They are anisotropic in nature. They have long range order and possess a sharp melting point.

Types of Crystalline Solids

Character	**Ionic solids**	**Covalent solids**	**Molecular solids**	**Metallic solids**
Constituent particles	Positive and negative ions	Atoms	Molecules	Positive metals ions (kernels) and free electrons
Binding forces	Electrostatic attraction	Covalent	van der Waals', dipole- dipole	Electrostatic attraction between positive and negative ions/species
Melting point and boiling point	High	Very high	Low	Moderate to high
Physical nature	Hard and brittle	Very hard except graphite	Very soft	Hard and soft
Conductivity	Conductor in aqueous solution or in molten state	Non-conductor except graphite	Insulator	Good conductor
Examples	NaCl, CaF_2, MgO, ZnS	Diamond, silica, SiC	H_2O, CO_2, CCl_4, HCl, SO_2	Cu, Fe, Ag, Mg.

(*ii*) **Amorphous solids** have unsystematic and irregular arrangement of particles. They are isotropic in nature. They have short range order. They melt over a range of temperature.

Crystal Lattice and Unit Cell

- There are 14 possible three-dimensional lattices called **Bravais lattice**.
- The smallest portion of a crystal lattice, when repeated in different directions generate the entiré lattice and is called **unit cell.**
- Unit cell can be of the following types :

(*i*) Simple or primitive unit cell have 1 atom per unit cell.

(*ii*) Body centred cubic unit cell have 2 atoms per unit cell.

(*iii*) Face centred cubic unit cell have 4 atoms per unit cell.

Seven Crystal Systems and their Unit Cell Parameters

S.No.	Crystal systems	Bravais lattices	Unit cell parameters: Edge lengths	Unit cell parameters: Axial angles	Examples
1.	Cubic	Primitive, face centred, body centred	$a = b = c$	$\alpha = \beta = \gamma = 90°$	NaCl, KCl, diamond, copper, zinc blende etc.
2.	Rhombohedral (Trigonal)	Primitive	$a = b = c$	$\alpha = \beta = \gamma \neq 90°$	$NaNO_3$, $CaCO_3$, HgS, etc.
3.	Orthorhombic	Primitive, face centred, body centred, end centred	$a \neq b \neq c$	$\alpha = \beta = \gamma = 90°$	Rhombic sulphur, $BaSO_4$, $PbCO_3$ etc.
4.	Triclinic (most asymmetric)	Primitive	$a \neq b \neq c$	$\alpha \neq \beta \neq \gamma \neq 90°$	$K_2Cr_2O_7$, H_3BO_3, $CuSO_4 \cdot 5H_2O$ etc.
5.	Monoclinic	Primitive, end centred	$a \neq b \neq c$	$\alpha = \gamma = 90°, \beta \neq 90°$	$Na_2SO_4 \cdot 10H_2O$, $Na_2B_4O_7 \cdot 10H_2O$, monoclinic S etc.
6.	Tetragonal	Primitive, body centred	$a = b \neq c$	$\alpha = \beta = \gamma = 90°$	Cassiterite, white tin, rutile etc.
7.	Hexagonal	Primitive	$a = b \neq c$	$\alpha = \beta = 90°, \gamma = 120°$	Mg, beryl, ZnO (zincite) PbI_2, graphite etc.

Number of Particles (or Atoms) in a Unit Cell

Each type of crystal system has characteristic number of particles per unit cell. Contribution of different atoms per unit cell is given in following table:

Type of crystal	Type of lattice point	Contribution to one unit cell
Cubic	Corner	1/8
	Edge	1/4
	Face centred	1/2
	Body centred	1
Hexagonal	Corner	1/6
	Face centred	1/2
	Body centred	3

Packing in Solids

- In solid, each atom is surrounded by certain number of atoms leaving the minimum vacant space. It is expressed in terms of **packing fraction.**
- Packing in solids can be summarised as:

Type	Arrangement	Coordination no.	Packing efficiency	Unit cell
(*i*) Square closed packing	*AAA*	4	52.4%	Primitive
(*ii*) Hexagonal closed packing	*AB AB*......	12	74%	Non-cubic
(*iii*) Cubic or face centred cubic packing	*ABC ABC*......	12	74%	F.C.C.
(*iv*) Body centred cubic packing	*AB AB*......	8	68%	B.C.C.

Voids

- In two dimensional packing, void can be triangular while in three dimensional packing, voids can be of two types : Tetrahedral voids (holes surrounded by four spheres present at the corners of a tetrahedron) and octahedral voids (holes surrounded by six spheres located on a regular octahedron).
- Number of tetrahedral voids = Number of atoms in ccp $\times 2 = 2N$
- Number of octahedral voids = Number of atoms in ccp $= N$
- Increasing order of void size : Trigonal < Tetrahedral < Octahedral

Radius Ratio

- The ionic radius ratios play a very important role in giving clue to the nature of crystal structure of the ionic substance.
- This can be made clear from the table given below :

Radius Ratio and Crystal Structure

S. No.	Radius ratio (r^+/r^-)	Coordination number	Geometry	Crystal structure	Example
1.	< 0.225	2 or 3	Linear or triangular	Linear or triangular	B_2O_3
2.	0.225–0.414	4	Tetrahedral	ZnS type (sphalerite)	CuCl, CuBr, HgS, BaS
3.	0.414–0.732	6	Octahedral	NaCl type	MgO, NaBr, CaS, KBr, CaO, AgCl
4.	0.732 or more	8	Cubic	CsCl type	CsI, CsBr, NH_4Br, TlBr

Calculations Involving Unit Cell Parameters

- Density of solid can be calculated as :

$$\text{Density } (d) = \frac{Z \times M}{a^3 \times N_A} \text{ or } \frac{Z \times M}{V \times N_A}$$

where, Z = number of atoms per unit cell
M = atomic mass
a = edge length
V = volume
N_A = Avogadro's number

- Relation between edge length and radius of sphere for different unit cells is given as :

(*i*) Radius of sphere, for scc structure $= \frac{a}{2}$

for fcc structure $= \frac{a}{2\sqrt{2}}$

for bcc structure $= \frac{\sqrt{3}}{4} a$

Here, a = edge length

(*ii*) **Ionic radius,** for fcc structure,

$$r_c + r_a = \frac{a}{2}$$

for bcc structure, $r_c + r_a = \frac{\sqrt{3}a}{2}$

where, r_c and r_a = radius of cation and anion respectively.

- Bragg's equation is a fundamental equation which gives a relation between wavelength of X-rays, the interplanar distance in the crystal and the angle of diffraction,

$$n\lambda = 2d \sin \theta$$

where, n = order of diffraction
λ = wavelength of X-rays used
d = distance between two diffracted planes
θ = angle of diffraction

Imperfections in Solids

- In a crystalline solid, the atoms, ions and molecules are arranged in a definite repeating pattern, but some defects may occur in the pattern.
- The defects are of two types, namely point defects and line defects.

Point Defects and Line Defects

The irregularities or deviation from ideal arrangement around a point or an atom in a crystalline solid is called point defects whereas the line defects are the irregularities or deviations from ideal arrangement in entire row of lattice points.

Types of Point Defects

Point defects are of following three types:

1. These are the point defects that do not disturb the stoichiometry of a solid. This is also known as **intrinsic** or **thermodynamic defects.**

In non-ionic solids, this defect is of two types:

- When some of the lattice sites are vacant, the crystal is said to have **vacancy defect**. It results in decrease in density of the substance. This defect can arise when substance is heated.
- When some constituent particles occupy an interstitial site the crystal is said to have **interstitial defect** and due to this defect, the density of the substance increases.
- In ionic solids, this defect is of two types. The differences between these two types are given below :

	Schottky defect	Frenkel defect
(*i*)	It is due to equal number of cations and anions missing from the lattice sites.	It is due to the missing of ions (usually cations) from the lattice sites and they occupy the interstitial sites.
(*ii*)	This results in the decrease in density of crystal.	It has no effect on the density of crystal.
(*iii*)	This type of defect is found in highly ionic compounds with high coordination number, e.g. NaCl, CsCl, etc.	This type of defect is found in crystal, where the difference in the size of cations and anions is very large, e.g. AgCl, ZnS, etc.

2. Those imperfections in the crystal, which lead to change in the composition of solids are called **non-stoichiometric defects**. They contain constituent elements in non-stoichiometric ratio due to defects in their crystal structures. Non-stoichiometric defects are of two types; metal excess defect and metal deficiency defect.
   - **Metal excess defect due to anionic vacancies :** Arises when metal halides are heated in metal vapours like NaCl, KCl.
   - **Metal excess defect due to presence of extra cations :** Arises on heating metal oxides, e.g. ZnO.
   - **Metal deficiency defect :** Arises due to absence of metal ion from its lattice site, e.g. $Fe_{0.95}O$.

   Note F-centres Anionic site occupied by unpaired electrons are called F-centres or Farbecenter. These impart colour to crystals like alkali halides.

3. These are the point defects arises when foreign atoms or ions are present in the lattice site or in the interstitial sites.

Properties of Solids

There are different types of properties constituted by solids which are as follows :

1. Electrical Properties

Solids are classified into three groups on the basis of conduction power. These are as follows:

Type of solid	Conductivity (ohm^{-1} m^{-1})	Reason of conductivity	Examples
Conductors	$10^4 - 10^7$ (Very high)	Motion of electrons	Metals like Ag, Al
Insulators	10^{-20} to 10^{-10} (Very low)	Do not permit electricity to pass	Wood, rubber, bakelite
Semiconductors	$10^{-6} - 10^4$ (Moderate)	Motion of interstitial electrons or holes or both	Si, Ge, etc.

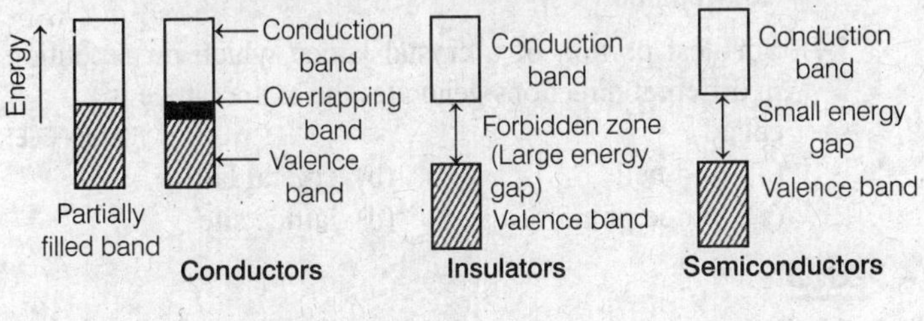

Conduction of Electricity in Semiconductors

- Gap between valence band and conduction band is small. Electrons can jump to the conduction band with rise in temperature. Such type of behaviour is shown by Si and Ge and are called **intrinsic semiconductors.**
- Conductivity of intrinsic semiconductor is increased by adding appropriate amount of impurity and this process is called **doping**. Two such type of impurities are electron-rich impurities and electron deficient impurities.

(a) **Electron rich impurities**: Si or Ge is doped with group 15 elements (known as *n*-type semiconductor).

(b) **Electron-deficit impurities**: Si or Ge is doped with group 13 elements (known as *p*-type semiconductor).

2. Magnetic Properties

- Solids can be divided into different classes depending on their response to magnetic field.

These classes are as follows :

(*i*) **Diamagnetic** substances are weakly repelled by the magnetic field and do not have any unpaired electron.
e.g. TiO_2, V_2O_5, C_6H_6, NaCl, etc.

(*ii*) **Paramagnetic** substances are weakly attracted by the magnetic field and have unpaired electrons. These lose magnetism in the absence of magnetic field.
e.g. O_2, Cu^{2+}, Fe^{3+}, etc.

(*iii*) **Ferromagnetic** substances are strongly attracted by the magnetic field and show permanent magnetism even in the absence of magnetic field, e.g. Fe, Co and Ni, etc.

(*iv*) **Antiferromagnetic** substances have net magnetic moment zero due to compensatory alignment of magnetic moments,
e.g. MnO, MnO_2, Mn_2O_3, FeO, etc.

(*v*) **Ferrimagnetic** substances have a net dipole moment due to unequal parallel and antiparallel alignment of magnetic moments, e.g. Fe_3O_4, ferrites, etc.

Topical Practice Questions

All the exam questions of this chapter have been divided into four topics as listed below

Topic 1

Classification and Basic Terminology Related to Solids

2019

1 Silicon carbide is example of [JIPMER]
(a) molecular solid
(b) metallic solid
(c) ionic crystal
(d) covalent solid

2 Quartz is crystalline silica and silica glass is [AIIMS]
(a) amorphous
(b) crystalline
(c) Both (a) and (b)
(d) None of the above

2018

3 Which of the following is an example of network solid? [AIIMS]
(a) SO_2 (solid) (b) I_2
(c) Diamond (d) H_2O (ice)

2014

4 Solid SO_2 and NH_3 are the examples of which of the following types of solids? [CBSE AIPMT]
(a) Polar molecular solids
(b) Non-polar molecular solids
(c) Hydrogen bonded molecular solids
(d) None of the above

5 Which of the following can be regarded as molecular solid? [EAMCET]
(a) AlN (b) SiC
(c) I_2 (d) Diamond

2013

6 Which of the following does not show electrical conduction in its physical states? [CBSE AIPMT]
(a) Sodium (b) Diamond
(c) Graphite (d) Calcium

2012

7 Which of the following exists as covalent crystals in the solid state? [CBSE AIPMT]
(a) Iodine (b) Silicon
(c) Sulphur (d) Phosphorus

2011

8 Which one of the following is a covalent crystal? [KCET]
(a) Rock salt (b) Ice
(c) Quartz (d) Dry ice

2010

9 Match the following columns.

	Column I		Column II
A.	Ionic solid	1.	NaCl
B.	Metallic solid	2.	Fe
C.	Covalent solid	3.	C(graphite)
D.	Molecular solid	4.	Dry ice

Codes [OJEE]

	A	B	C	D
(a)	2	1	4	3
(b)	1	2	3	4
(c)	3	2	1	4
(d)	2	4	1	3

10 The property of crystalline solid is not [OJEE]
(a) anisotropic (b) isotropic
(c) hard (d) dense

11 Bravais lattices are of [RPMT]
(a) 8 types (b) 9 types
(c) 12 types (d) 14 types

12 Which one of the following is a molecular crystal? [KCET]
(a) Rock salt (b) Quartz
(c) Dry ice (d) Diamond

2009

13 Which one of the following forms a molecular solid when solidified? [Kerala CEE]
(a) Silicon carbide (b) Calcium fluoride
(c) Rock salt (d) Silica
(e) Methane

14 Smallest portion of a crystal lattice which on repetition in different directions generates the entire lattice is called [Kerala CEE]
(a) unit cell (b) crystal lattice
(c) lattice point (d) lattice site

2008

15 When constituent particles are present only on the corner positions of a unit cell, it is called [CBSE AIPMT]
(a) primitive unit cell (b) centred unit cell
(c) body-centred unit cell (d) face-centred unit cell

16 Which of the following crystal system has cinnabar as an example? [CBSE AIPMT]
(a) Cubic (b) Monoclinic
(c) Trigonal (d) Triclinic

2007

17 The axial angles in triclinic crystal system are [AFMC]
(a) $\alpha = \beta = \gamma = 90°$ (b) $\alpha = \gamma = 90°, \beta \neq 90°$
(c) $\alpha \neq \beta \neq \gamma \neq 90°$ (d) $\alpha = \beta = \gamma \neq 90°$

18 Coordination number of a body centred cubic is [DUMET]
(a) 6 (b) 8 (c) 10 (d) 12

2006

19 **Assertion** (A) Graphite is an example of tetragonal crystal system.
Reason (R) For a tetragonal system, $a = b \neq c$, $\alpha = \beta = 90°, \gamma = 120°$. [AIIMS]
(a) Both A and R are correct and R is the correct explanation of A
(b) Both A and R are correct but R is not the correct explanation of A
(c) A is correct but R is incorrect
(d) Both A and R are incorrect

20 A particular solid is very hard and has a high melting point. In solid state, it is a non-conductor and its melt is a conductor of electricity.
Classify the solid. [Kerala CEE]
(a) Metallic
(b) Molecular
(c) Network
(d) Ionic
(e) Amorphous

2005

21 Which crystal system has no rotation of symmetry? [MHCET]
(a) Hexagonal
(b) Orthorhombic
(c) Cubic
(d) Triclinic

Answers

1 (d)	2 (a)	3 (c)	4 (a)	5 (c)	6 (b)	7 (b)	8 (c)	9 (b)	10 (b)
11 (d)	12 (c)	13 (e)	14 (a)	15 (a)	16 (c)	17 (c)	18 (b)	19 (d)	20 (d)
21 (d)									

Explanations

1. *(d)* Silicon carbide (SiC) is an example of covalent solids.
Covalent or network solids are crystalline solids of non-metals that result from the formation of covalent bonds between adjacent atoms throughout the crystal. They are insulators and do not conduct electricity.

2. *(a)* Silica glass is an amorphous solid.

3. *(c)* Diamond is a giant molecule in which constituent atoms are held together by covalent bonds. Hence, it is a network solid.
Note SO_2 (solid), H_2O (ice) and I_2 are examples of molecular solid.

4. *(a)* Solid SO_2 and solid NH_3 are polar molecules, so form polar molecular solids.

5. *(c)* Diamond, AlN and SiC are covalent solids because of the presence of covalent bonds between constituent atoms, whereas I_2 is a molecular solid as in it London forces exist between the I_2 molecules.

6. *(b)* Graphite contains free electrons and, hence, shows electrical conduction in its natural physical state.

7. *(b)* In silicon, constituent particles are bonded together by covalent bonds, therefore it exists as covalent crystals in the solid state.

8. *(c)* Rock salt (NaCl) is ionic solid. Ice and dry ice are molecular solids and quartz (SiO_2) is covalent or network solids.

9. *(b)* Ionic solid-NaCl; metallic solid-Fe; covalent solid-C (graphite); molecular solid-dry ice.

10. *(b)* Crystalline solids are anisotropic, hard and dense in nature. They are not isotropic in nature.

11. *(d)* Unit cells of 14 types of lattices are called **Bravais lattices**. These are:
(i) Three cubic lattices (simple, body centred and face centred) all sides of same length, angles between faces are 90°.
(ii) Two tetragonal lattices (primitive and body centred) one side different in length to the other, two angles between faces are 90°.
(iii) Four orthorhombic lattices (primitive, end centred, body centred and face centred) unequal sides, angles between faces are 90°.
(iv) Two monoclinic lattices (primitive and end centred) unequal sides two faces have angles different from 90°.
(v) Hexagonal lattice one side different in length to the other two.
(vi) Rhombohedral (all equal sides angle < 90°) and triclinic (unequal sides and angle ≠ 90°).

12. *(c)* Rock salt (NaCl) is ionic solid. Quartz and diamond are covalent or network solids. In dry ice (solid CO_2), constituents are molecules. The various molecules are held together through weak forces like dipole-induced dipole interaction etc. Thus, it is a molecular crystal.

13. *(e)* Molecular solids are formed when the constituent particles are molecules/atoms and the interparticle forces are van der Waals' forces.
Thus, methane (CH_4) is a molecular solid. Calcium fluoride (CaF_2) and rock salt (NaCl), due to the presence of ions as constituent particles, are ionic solids while silica (SiO_2) and silicon carbide (SiC), due to the presence of covalent bonds between atoms, form covalent solids.

14. *(a)* Smallest portion of a cystal lattice which on repetition in different directions generates the entire lattice is called unit cell.

15. *(a)* When constitutent particles are present only on the corner positions of unit cell it is called primitive unit cell.

16. (c) Cinnabar $a = b = c$ and $\alpha = \beta = \gamma \neq 90°$.

So, it is an example of trigonal (rhombohedral) crystal system.

17. (c) In triclinic crystal system, $\alpha \neq \beta \neq \gamma \neq 90°$.

18. (b) Coordination number of body centred cubic (bcc) is 8.

19. (d) Like quartz and ice, graphite is an example of hexagonal system. For this $\alpha = \beta = 90°$ and $\gamma = 120°$ and $a = b \neq c$.

For a tetragonal system $\alpha, \beta = \gamma = 90°$ and $a = b \neq c$

So, both (A) and (R) are incorrect.

20. (d) A particular solid is very hard and has high melting point. In solid state, it is a non-conductor and in molten state it is a conductor of electricity. Therefore, it is an ionic solid.

21. (d) Triclinic system is totally asymmetric, i.e. $a \neq b \neq c$ and $\alpha \neq \beta \neq \gamma = 90°$. So, it has no rotation of symmetry.

Topic 2

Structure Related Calculations

2019

1 Formula of nickel oxide with metal deficiency defect in its crystal is $Ni_{0.98}O$. The crystal contains Ni^{2+} and Ni^{3+} ions. The fraction of nickel existing as Ni^{2+} ions in the crystal is **[NEET (Odisha)]**

(a) 0.96 (b) 0.04 (c) 0.50 (d) 0.31

2 The tetrahedral voids present in 0.5 mole of hcp crystal structure are **[AIIMS]**

(a) 3.6×10^{23} (b) 9×10^{23}
(c) 3.6×10^{24} (d) 6.02×10^{23}

3 A compound is formed by cation C and anion A. The anions form hexagonal close packed (hcp) lattice and the cations occupy 75% of octahedral voids. The formula of the compound is **[NEET]**

(a) C_3A_2 (b) C_3A_4 (c) C_4A_3 (d) C_2A_3

2018

4 Niobium crystallises in body centred cubic structure. If density is $8.55 g cm^{-3}$, then the atomic radius of niobium is (atomic mass of niobium = 93u) **[AIIMS]**

(a) 163 pm (b) 143 pm (c) 182 Å (d) 152 Å

5 An atom forms face centred cubic crystal with density $d = 8.92 g/mL$ and edge length $a = 3.6 \times 10^{-8}$ cm. The molecular mass of atom in amu is **[JIPMER]**

(a) 98 (b) 63 (c) 32 (d) 93

6 In a crystalline solid, having formula XY_2O_4, oxide ions are arranged in cubic close packed lattice while, cations X are present in tetrahedral voids and cations Y are present in octahedral voids. The percentage of tetrahedral voids occupied by X is **[JIPMER]**

(a) 12.5% (b) 25% (c) 50% (d) 75%

7 A solid has a structure in which W atoms are located at the corners of a cubic lattice. O atoms at the centre of edges and Na atom at centre of the cube. The formula for the compound is **[AIIMS]**

(a) $NaWO_2$ (b) $NaWO_3$ (c) Na_2WO_3 (d) $NaWO_4$

2016

8 Lithium has a bcc structure. Its density is 530 kg m^{-3} and its atomic mass is 6.94g mol^{-1}. The edge length of a unit cell of lithium metal will be **[NEET]**
($N = 6.02 \times 10^{23} mol^{-1}$)

(a) 352 pm (b) 527 pm
(c) 264 pm (d) 154 pm

2015

9 A given metal crystallises out with a cubic structure having edge length of 361 pm. If there are four metal atoms in one unit cell, what is the radius of one atom?

(a) 40 pm (b) 127 pm
(c) 80 pm (d) 108 pm

2014

10 The number of tetrahedral and octahedral voids in a CCP array of 100 atoms are respectively **[Kerala CEE]**

(a) 200 and 100 (b) 100 and 200
(c) 200 and 200 (d) 100 and 100
(e) 50 and 50

11 Copper crystallises in face centred cubic lattice with a unit cell length of 361 pm. What is the radius of copper atom in pm? **[Manipal]**

(a) 157 (b) 181 (c) 108 (d) 128

12 A solid AB has NaCl structure. If the radius of cation A^+ is 170 pm. Calculate the maximum possible radius of the anion B^- **[WB JEE]**

(a) 210.3 pm (b) 397.4 pm
(c) 410.6 pm (d) 347.9 pm

13 The diffraction of a crystal of barium with X-rays of wavelength 2.29 Å gives a first order reflection at 27°8′. What is the distance between the diffracting planes? [sin 27°8′ = 0.4561] **[WB JEE]**

(a) 1.46 Å (b) 1.59 Å
(c) 2.51 Å (d) 5.46 Å

14 Volume occupied by single CsCl ion pair in a crystal is 7.014×10^{-23} cm^3. The smallest Cs—Cs internuclear distance is equal to length of the side of the cube corresponding to volume of one CsCl ion pair. The smallest Cs to Cs internuclear distance is nearly **[KCET]**
(a) 4.4 Å (b) 4.3 Å (c) 4 Å (d) 4.5 Å

2013

15 The metal has a fcc lattice. The edge length of the unit cell is 404 pm. The density of the metal is 2.72 g/cm^3. The molar mass of the metal is
(N_A = Avogadro's constant = 6.02×10^{23} mol^{-1}) **[NEET]**
(a) 40 g/mol (b) 30 g/mol (c) 27 g/mol (d) 20 g/mol

2012

16 The metal crystallises with a face-centred cubic lattice. The edge of the unit cell is 408 pm. The diameter of the metal atom is **[CBSE AIPMT]**
(a) 288 pm (b) 408 pm (c) 144 pm (d) 204 pm

17 Structure of a mixed oxide is cubic close packed (ccp). The cubic unit cell of mixed oxide is composed of oxide ions. One fourth of the tetrahedral voids are occupied by divalent metal *A* and the octahedral voids are occupied by a monovalent metal *B*. The formula of oxide is **[CBSE AIPMT]**
(a) ABO_2 (b) A_2BO_2 (c) $A_2B_3O_4$ (d) AB_2O_2

2011

18 If in a crystal lattice of a compound, each corner of a cube is occupied by sodium, each edge of a cube has oxygen and centre of cube is occupied by tungsten (W), then give its formula **[Guj CET]**
(a) Na_2WO_4 (b) $NaWO_3$ (c) Na_3WO_3 (d) Na_2WO_3

19 The first order reflection ($n = 1$) from a crystal of the X-ray from a copper anode tube ($\lambda = 1.54$ Å) occurs at an angle of 45°. What is the distance between the set of plane causing the diffraction? **[Guj CET]**
(a) 0.1089 cm (b) 0.1089 m
(c) 1.089 Å (d) 1.089×10^{-9} m

2010

20 *AB* crystallises in a body-centred cubic lattice with edge '*a*' equal to 387 pm. The distance between two oppositely charged ions in the lattice is **[CBSE AIPMT]**
(a) 300 pm (b) 335 pm (c) 250 pm (d) 200 pm

21 Number of unit cells in 4 g of *X* (atomic mass = 40) which crystallises in bcc pattern is (N_A = Avogadro's number)
(a) $0.1 N_A$ (b) $2 \times 0.1 N_A$ **[OJEE]**
(c) $\frac{0.1 N_A}{2}$ (d) $2 \times N_A$

22 Total number of voids in 0.5 mole of a compound forming hexagonal closed packed structure are **[AMU]**
(a) 6.022×10^{23} (b) 3.011×10^{23}
(c) 9.033×10^{23} (d) 4.516×10^{23}

23 A solid is formed by two elements *P* and *Q*. The element *Q* forms cubic close packing and atoms of *P* occupy one third of tetrahedral voids. The formula of the compound is
(a) PQ_3 (b) P_3Q (c) P_2Q_3 (d) P_3Q_2 **[AMU]**

24 If the radius of K$^+$ and F$^-$ are 133 pm and 136 pm respectively, the distance between K$^+$ and F$^-$ in KF is
(a) 269 pm (b) 134.5 pm **[JCECE]**
(c) 136 pm (d) 3 pm

2009

25 Sodium crystallises in bcc arrangement with the interfacial separation between the atoms at the edge 53 pm. The density of the solid is **[AIIMS]**
(a) 1.23 g/cc (b) 485 g/cc (c) 4.85 g/cc (d) 123 g/cc

26 For tetrahedral coordination, the radius ratio $\left(\frac{r_+}{r_-}\right)$ should be
(a) 0.414 - 0.732 (b) > 0.732 **[Manipal]**
(c) 0.156 - 0.225 (d) 0.225 - 0.414

27 Aluminium has fcc structure. The length of the unit cell is 404 pm. If the density of the metal is 2.7 g cm^{-3}, the molar mass of Al atom is **[Manipal]**
(a) 28 g mol^{-1} (b) 30 g mol^{-1}
(c) 26.80 g mol^{-1} (d) 25 g mol^{-1}

28 The unit cell of a binary alloy composed of *A* and *B* metals, has a ccp structure with *A* atoms occupying the corners and *B* atoms occupying centres of each face of the cube. If during the crystallisation of this alloy, in the unit cell two *A* atoms are missed, the overall composition per unit cell is
(a) AB_6 (b) AB_2 **[J&K CET]**
(c) AB_8 (d) A_6B_{24}

29 Three elements *A*, *B* and *C* crystallise into a cubic solid lattice. Atom *A* occupy the corners, *B* atom, the cube centres and *C* atom, the edge. The formula of the compound is **[AMU]**
(a) ABC (b) ABC_2 (c) ABC_3 (d) ABC_4

30 The cubic unit cell of a metal (molar mass = 63.55 g mol^{-1}) has an edge length of 362 pm. Its density is 8.92 g cm^{-3}. The type of unit cell is **[EAMCET]**
(a) primitive (b) face centred
(c) body centred (d) end centred

31 A compound contains two types of atoms *X* and *Y*. It crystallises in a cubic lattice with atoms *X* at the corners of the unit cell and atoms *Y* at the body centre. The simplest possible formula of this compound is **[DUMET]**
(a) X_8Y (b) X_2Y (c) XY (b) XY_8

32 A compound of '*A*' and '*B*' crystallises in a cubic lattice in which the '*A*' atoms occupy the lattice points at the corners of the cube. The '*B*' atoms occupy the centre of each face of the cube. The probable empirical formula of the compound is **[KCET]**
(a) A_3B (b) AB (c) AB_3 (d) AB_2

2008

33 Percentage of free space in a body centred cubic unit cell is [CBSE AIPMT]
(a) 30% (b) 32%
(c) 34% (d) 28%

34 Edge length of a cube is 400 pm, its body diagonal would be [AFMC]
(a) 566 pm (b) 600 pm (c) 500 pm (d) 693 pm

35 In the calcium fluoride structure, the coordination number of the cation and anion are respectively, [AMU]
(a) 6, 6 (b) 8, 4 (c) 4, 4 (d) 4, 8

36 AB is an ionic solid. If the ratio of ionic radius of A^+ and B^- is 0.52, what is the coordination number of B^-? [EAMCET]
(a) 2 (b) 3
(c) 6 (d) 8

37 In a closed packed structure [DUMET]
(a) tetrahedral voids are bigger than octahedral
(b) tetrahedral voids are smaller than octahedral
(c) tetrahedral voids are equal in size as octahedral
(d) None of the above

38 Total volume of atoms present in a face centred cubic unit cell of a metal is (r = radius of atom) [BCECE]
(a) $\frac{20}{3}\pi r^3$ (b) $\frac{24}{3}\pi r^3$ (c) $\frac{12}{3}\pi r^3$ (d) $\frac{16}{3}\pi r^3$

2007

39 The fraction of total volume occupied by the atoms present in a simple cube is [CBSE AIPMT]
(a) $\frac{\pi}{6}$ (b) $\frac{\pi}{3\sqrt{2}}$ (c) $\frac{\pi}{4\sqrt{2}}$ (d) $\frac{\pi}{4}$

40 If AgI crystallises in zinc blende structure with I^- ions at lattice points. What fraction of tetrahedral voids is occupied by Ag^+ ions? [AIIMS]
(a) 25% (b) 50%
(c) 100% (d) 75%

41 Ag crystallises as fcc. If radius of Ag is 144 pm then its density will be [DUMET]
(a) $10\,g\,cm^{-3}$ (b) $5\,g\,cm^{-3}$
(c) $15\,g\,cm^{-3}$ (d) $6.5\,g\,cm^{-3}$

2006

42 CsBr crystallises in a body-centred cubic lattice. The unit cell length is 436.6 pm. Given that the atomic mass of Cs = 133 u and that of Br = 80 u and Avogadro's number being $6.02\times10^{23}\,mol^{-1}$, the density of CsBr is [CBSE AIPMT]
(a) $42.5\,g/cm^3$ (b) $0.425\,g/cm^3$
(c) $8.25\,g/cm^3$ (d) $4.25\,g/cm^3$

43 The Ca^{2+} and F^- are located in CaF_2 crystal, respectively at body centred cubic lattice points and in [AIIMS]
(a) tetrahedral voids (b) half of tetrahedral voids
(c) octahedral voids (d) half of octahedral voids

44 Na and Mg crystallise in bcc and fcc type crystals respectively, then the number of atoms of Na and Mg present in the unit cell of their respective crystal is [BHU]
(a) 4 and 2 (b) 9 and 14
(c) 14 and 9 (d) 2 and 4

45 A metallic element has a cubic lattice. Each edge of the unit cell is 2 Å. The density of the metal is $2.5\,g\,cm^{-3}$. The unit cells in 200 g of metal are [MHT CET]
(a) 1×10^{24} (b) 1×10^{20} (c) 1×10^{22} (d) 1×10^{25}

46 If Z is the number of atoms in the unit cell that represents the closest packing sequence ... $ABC\,ABC$ ..., the number of tetrahedral voids in the unit cells is equal to [AIIMS]
(a) Z (b) $2Z$ (c) $\frac{Z}{2}$ (d) $\frac{Z}{4}$

2005

47 The radius of Na^+ and Cl^- ions are 95 pm and 181 pm respectively. The edge length of NaCl unit cell is [KCET]
(a) 276 pm (b) 138 pm (c) 552 pm (d) 415 pm

48 Which of the following is correct order of packing efficiency? [AIIMS]
(a) hcp = fcc > bcc > sc (b) sc > bcc > hcp = fcc
(c) bcc > sc > hcp < fcc (d) fcc = hcp > sc > bcc

49 If a is the length of the side of a cube, the distance between the body-centred atom and one corner atom in the cube will be [CBSE AIPMT]
(a) $\frac{2}{\sqrt{3}}a$ (b) $\frac{4}{\sqrt{3}}a$ (c) $\frac{\sqrt{3}}{4}a$ (d) $\frac{\sqrt{3}}{2}a$

50 The percentages of void space for simple cubic, body centred cubic and hexagonal close packed arranged respectively are [EAMCET]
(a) 48, 32, 26 (b) 48, 26, 32
(c) 26, 48, 32 (d) 32, 48, 26

51 The number of carbon atoms per unit cell of the diamond unit cell is [NEET]
(a) 4 (b) 8 (c) 6 (d) 1

52 The number of octahedral void (s) per atom present in a cubic close packed structure is [CBSE AIPMT]
(a) 1 (b) 3 (c) 2 (d) 4

53 The number of atoms per unit cell of bcc structure is [Kerala CEE]
(a) 1 (b) 2 (c) 4 (d) 6 (e) 8

54 Which of the following statements is not correct? [CBSE AIPMT]
(a) The fraction of the total volume occupied by the atoms in a primitive cell is 0.48
(b) Molecular solids are generally volatile
(c) The number of carbon atoms in a unit cell of diamond is 4
(d) The number of Bravais lattices in which a crystal can be categorised is 14

55 If 'a' stands for the edge length of the cubic systems : simple cubic, body centred cubic and face centred cubic, then the ratio of radius of the spheres in these systems will be respectively, [CBSE AIPMT]

(a) $\frac{1}{2}a:\frac{\sqrt{3}}{4}a:\frac{1}{2\sqrt{2}}a$ (b) $\frac{1}{2}a:\sqrt{3}a:\frac{1}{\sqrt{2}}a$

(c) $\frac{1}{2}a:\frac{\sqrt{3}}{2}a:\frac{\sqrt{2}}{2}a$ (d) $1a:\sqrt{3}a:\sqrt{2}a$

56 A fcc unit cell of aluminium contains the equivalent of how many atoms? [AFMC]

(a) 1 (b) 2
(c) 3 (d) 4

57 Which of the following unit cell having maximum number of atoms? [MHT CET]

(a) bcc (b) hcp
(c) fcc (d) Cubic

Answers

1 (a)	2 (d)	3 (b)	4 (b)	5 (b)	6 (a)	7 (b)	8 (a)	9 (b)	10 (a)
11 (d)	12 (c)	13 (c)	14 (c)	15 (c)	16 (a)	17 (d)	18 (b)	19 (c)	20 (b)
21 (c)	22 (c)	23 (c)	24 (a)	25 (a)	26 (d)	27 (c)	28 (d)	29 (c)	30 (b)
31 (c)	32 (c)	33 (b)	34 (d)	35 (b)	36 (c)	37 (b)	38 (d)	39 (a)	40 (b)
41 (a)	42 (d)	43 (a)	44 (d)	45 (d)	46 (b)	47 (c)	48 (a)	49 (d)	50 (a)
51 (b)	52 (a)	53 (b)	54 (a)	55 (a)	56 (d)	57 (c)			

1. (*a*) Let, in the given crystal $Ni_{0.98}O$

$Ni^{2+} = x$ and $Ni^{3+} = 0.98 - x$

Total charge on M^{2+} and M^{3+}

$= (+2)x + (+3)(0.98 - x)$

$= 2x + 2.94 - 3x = 2.94 - x$

As metal oxide is neutral. Therefore, total charge on cations = total charge on anions.

$2.94 - x = 2$

[$\because$ Charge of oxygen atom = −2]

$x = 2.94 - 2 = 0.94$

So, the fraction of Ni^{2+} ions in the crystal

$= \frac{0.94}{0.98} = 0.959 \sim 0.96$

2. (*d*) Number of particles or atoms present in 1 mole $= 6.022 \times 10^{23}$

$\therefore$ Number of particles or atoms present in 0.5 mole $= 0.5 \times 6.022 \times 10^{23}$

$= 3.011 \times 10^{23}$

Number of tetrahedral voids

= 2 × number of atoms in close packaging

$= 2 \times 3.011 \times 10^{23} = 6.022 \times 10^{23}$

$= 6.02 \times 10^{23}$ voids

3. (*b*) Anions (A) form hexagonal close packed (hcp) lattice, so

number of anions (A) = 6

number of octahedral voids = number of atoms in the close packed structure = 6.

Cations (C) occupy 75% of octahedral voids, so number of cations (C)

$= 6 \times \frac{75}{100} = 6 \times 3/4 = 9/2$

$\therefore$ The formula of compound $= C_{9/2}A_6$

$= C_9A_{12} = C_3A_4$

Thus, option (b) is correct.

4. (*b*) Given, ρ (density) = 8.55 g cm^{-3}

Atomic mass of niobium = 93u

As we know that,

$$\text{density } (\rho) = \frac{MZ}{a^3 N_A} \quad \text{...(i)}$$

where, M = atomic mass

Z = number of unit cell

a = edge length

N_A = Avogadro's number

For bcc, $Z = 2$

Putting the values in equation (i)

$$8.55 = \frac{93 \times 2}{a^3 \times 6.02 \times 10^{23}}$$

or, $a^3 = 3.6137 \times 10^{-23} cm^3$

or, $a = 3.306 \times 10^{-8} cm$

For body centred cube, radius $= \frac{\sqrt{3}}{4}a$

or, $r_{bcc} = \frac{\sqrt{3}}{4} \times 3.306 \times 10^{-8}$

or, $r_{bcc} = 1.43 \times 10^{-8} cm$

$= 1.43 \times 10^{-10} m$

= 143 pm

5. (*b*) Given:

Density (d) = 8.92 g/mL

Edge length (a) $= 3.6 \times 10^{-8}$ cm

$Z = 4$ (fcc)

The molecular mass of atom in a lattice can be caluculated by using the formula,

$$d = \frac{Z \times M}{N_A a^3}$$

$$\therefore \quad M = \frac{dN_A a^3}{Z}$$

$$M = \frac{8.92 \times 6.023 \times 10^{23} \times (3.6)^3 \times (10^{-8})^3}{4}$$

$M = 62.66 \approx 63$ amu

6. (*a*) In a cubic close packed lattice of oxide ions, there would be two tetrahedral and one octahedral void per oxide ion.

Since, the formula shows the presence of 4 oxide ions, the number of tetrahedral voids is eight and that of octahedral voids is four. Out of the eight tetrahedral voids, one is occupied by X.

$\therefore$ Percentage of tetrahedral voids occupied $= \frac{1}{8} \times 100 = 12.5\%$

7. (*b*) In a unit cell,

W atoms at the corner $= \frac{1}{8} \times 8 = 1$

O atoms at the centre of edges

$= \frac{1}{4} \times 12 = 3$

Na atoms at the centre of the cube = 1

$\therefore$ W : O : Na = 1 : 3 : 1

Hence, formula of compound is $NaWO_3$.

8. (*a*) Given, Li has a bcc structure.

Density (d) = 530 kg m^{-3}

Atomic mass (M) = 6.94 g mol^{-1}

Avogadro's number (N_A)
$= 6.02 \times 10^{23}$ mol^{-1}

We know that, number of atoms per unit cell in bcc (Z) = 2

$\therefore$ The formula for density is, $d = \dfrac{ZM}{N_A a^3}$

where, a = edge-length of a unit cell.

or $a = \sqrt[3]{\dfrac{ZM}{dN_A}}$

$= \sqrt[3]{\dfrac{2 \times 6.94 \text{ g mol}^{-1}}{0.53\text{gcm}^{-3} \times 6.02 \times 10^{23} \text{ mol}^{-1}}}$

$= \sqrt[3]{4.35 \times 10^{-23}}$ cm

$= 3.517 \times 10^{-8}$ cm

$\therefore\ a = 352$ pm

9. (*b*) Given, edge length = 361 pm

Four metal atoms in one unit cell i.e. effective number in unit cell (Z) = 4 (given)

$\therefore$ It is a FCC Structure,

$\therefore$ Face diagonal = $4r$

$\sqrt{2}a = 4r$

$\Rightarrow \quad r = \dfrac{\sqrt{2} \times 361}{4} = 127$ pm

10. (*a*) The close packed structure has both octahedral and tetrahedral voids. For n atoms, there are $2n$ tetrahedral voids and n octahedral voids.

For 100 atoms, there will be 200 tetrahedral voids and 100 octahedral voids.

11. (*d*) For fcc, radius of atom

$r = \dfrac{a}{2\sqrt{2}}$

$a = 361$ pm (given)

$r = \dfrac{361}{2\sqrt{2}} = 127.6 \text{ pm} \approx 128$ pm

12. (*c*) For closed packed NaCl type structure,

$\dfrac{r_{A^+}}{r_{B^-}} = 0.414 - 0.732$

For maximum possible radius of B^-,

$\dfrac{r_{A^+}}{r_{B^-}} = 0.414$

$r_{B^-} = \dfrac{170}{0.414} = 410.6$ pm

13. (*c*) According to Bragg's equation

$n\lambda = 2d \sin \theta$

$1 \times 2.29 = 2d \times 0.4561$

$d = 2.51$ Å

14. (*c*) $\because$ Volume, $V = 7.014 \times 10^{-23}$ cm^3

$\therefore \quad a^3 = 7.014 \times 10^{-23}$ cm^3

or $\quad a = \sqrt[3]{7.014 \times 10^{-23} \text{ cm}^3}$

$= \sqrt[3]{70.14 \times 10^{-24} \text{ cm}^3}$

$= 4.124 \times 10^{-8}$ cm

$= 4.12 \text{ Å} \approx 4$ Å

15. (*c*) Given cell is fcc. So, $Z = 4$

Edge length, $a = 404$ pm

$= 4.04 \times 10^{-8}$ cm

Density of metal $d = 2.72$ g/cm^3

$N_A = 6.02 \times 10^{23}$ mol^{-1}

Molar mass of the metal, M = ?

We know that,

density (d) $= \dfrac{Z \times M}{a^3 \cdot N_A} \Rightarrow M = \dfrac{d \cdot a^3 N_A}{Z}$

$= \dfrac{2.7 \times (4.04 \times 10^{-8})^3 \times 6.02 \times 10^{23}}{4}$

$= 26.79$ g/mol

~ 27 g/mol

16. (*a*) For fcc lattice, $4r = \sqrt{2}a$

$r = \dfrac{\sqrt{2}a}{4} = \dfrac{a}{2\sqrt{2}} = \dfrac{408}{2\sqrt{2}}$

$= 144.2 \text{ pm} \sim 144$ pm

Diameter, $d = 2r = 2 \times 144$ pm
$= 288$ pm

17. (*d*) From ccp arrangement, number of O^{2-} ions = 4

(number of octahedral voids)

Thus, number of tetrahedral voids
$= 4 \times 2 = 8$

Number of A^{2+} ions $= \dfrac{1}{4} \times 8 = 2$

Again, B^+ ions occupied all octahedral voids.

$\therefore$ Number of B^+ ions = 4

$A : B : O = 2 : 4 : 4 = 1 : 2 : 2$

$\therefore$ Structure of oxide = AB_2O_2

18. (*b*) Sodium atom

$= 8 \text{ corners} \times \dfrac{1}{8}$ per corner

$= 8 \times \dfrac{1}{8} = 1$

Oxygen atom = 12 edges $\times \dfrac{1}{4}$ per edge

$= 12 \times \dfrac{1}{4} = 3$

Tungsten atom is in the centre of cube = 1.

Hence, chemical formula = $NaWO_3$.

19. (*c*) $n\lambda = 2d \sin \theta$

$1 \times 1.54 = 2\,d \sin 45$

$1 \times 1.54 = 2\,d \times \dfrac{1}{\sqrt{2}} = 1.089$ Å

20. (*b*) For a body centred cubic lattice,

$2(r^+ + r^-) = \sqrt{3}a$

$(r^+ + r^-) = \dfrac{\sqrt{3}a}{2}$

$= \dfrac{\sqrt{3} \times 387}{2}$

$= 335.15 \text{ pm} \sim 335$ pm

21. (*c*) Number of atoms = Number of moles $\times N_A$

$= \dfrac{4}{40} \times N_A = 0.1 \times N_A$

As, 2 atoms form 1 unit cell in bcc crystal

$\therefore$ $0.1 \times N_A$ atoms will form

$= \dfrac{0.1 \times N_A}{2}$ unit cells

22. (*c*) In hexagonal close packed structure, there are 6 atoms per unit cell.

$\therefore$ Number of octahedral voids = 6

$\therefore$ Number of tetrahedral voids
$= 2 \times 6 = 12$

Total number of voids = 6 + 12 = 18

$\therefore$ Total number of voids per atom
$= \dfrac{18}{6} = 3$

$\because$ In 1 mole of a compound, the total number of voids $= 3 \times 6.023 \times 10^{23}$

$\therefore$ In 0.5 mole compound, the total number of voids

$= 3 \times 0.5 \times 6.022 \times 10^{23} = 9.033 \times 10^{23}$

23. (*c*) Let the number of atoms in cubic close packing be x.

$\therefore$ Number of tetrahedral voids $= 2x$

Since, Q forms cubic close packing, the number of Q atoms $= x$

P occupy one third of tetrahedral voids,

the number of P atoms $= \dfrac{1}{3} \times 2x = \dfrac{2}{3}x$

$\dfrac{\text{Number of } P \text{ atoms}}{\text{Number of } Q \text{ atoms}} = \dfrac{2x}{3x} = \dfrac{2}{3}$

Therefore, the formula of the compound is P_2Q_3.

24. (*a*) Distance between K^+ and F^- in KF

$= r_{K^+} + r_{F^-} = 133 + 136 = 269$ pm

25. (*a*) Given, $a - 2r = 53$ pm

In bcc structure, atom at the centre touches the other two atoms which are diagonally arranged.

For bcc structure,

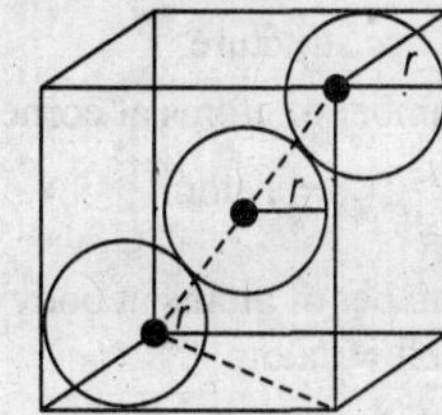

$4r = \sqrt{3}a$ or $2r = \frac{\sqrt{3}}{2}a$

$\Rightarrow \quad a - \frac{\sqrt{3}}{2}a = 53$

$\therefore \quad a = 395.5$ pm

Density $(d) = \frac{ZM}{N_A \times a^3}$

$d = \frac{2 \times 23}{6.023 \times 10^{23} \times (395.5)^3 \times 10^{-30}}$

$= 1.23$ g/cc.

26. (*d*) For tetrahedral coordination, the radius ratio $\left(\frac{r_+}{r_-}\right)$ should be 0.225-0.414.

For other, the radius ratio are as follows:

0.414-0.732 → Octahedral coordination;

0.732-1 → Cubic or body centred;

0.156-0.225 → Planar triangular

27. (*c*) $\because Z = 4$ for fcc, $M = \frac{da^3 N_A}{Z}$

$= \frac{2.7 \times (404 \times 10^{-10})^3 \times 6.023 \times 10^{23}}{4}$

$= 26.80$ g mol^{-1}

28. (*d*) Permitted coordination number for ccp is 8, but 2*A* atoms are missing.

$\therefore$ Contribution of $A = 6 \times \frac{1}{8} = \frac{6}{8}$

Contribution of $B = 6 \times \frac{1}{2} = 3$

So, $A_{6/8}B_3$ or A_6B_{24} or AB_4

29. (*c*) Number of atoms of *A* per unit cell

$= 8 \times \frac{1}{8}$ (at the corners) = 1

Number of atoms of *B* per unit cell = 1 (at the centre) = 1

Number of atoms of *C* per unit cell

$= 12 \times \frac{1}{4}$ (at the edge centre) = 3

So, formula of compound is ABC_3.

30. (*b*) Density $(d) = \frac{Z \times M}{N_A \times a^3}$

Given, $a = 362 \times 10^{-10}$ cm,

$M = 63.55$ g mol^{-1}, $d = 8.92$ g cm^{-3}, $Z = ?$

$\therefore \quad Z = \frac{d \times N_A \times a^3}{M}$

$= \frac{8.92 \times 6.023 \times 10^{23} \times (362 \times 10^{-10})^3}{63.55}$

$= 4.01 \sim 4$

i.e. the metal crystallises in face centred cell.

31. (*c*) Contribution of *X* (at the corner)

$= 1/8 \times 8 = 1$

Contribution of *Y* (at the body centre) = 1

So, formula is *XY*.

32. (*c*) $\because$ *A* atoms occupy the corners of the cube.

$\therefore$ Numbers of atoms of $A = \frac{1}{8} \times 8 = 1$

$\because$ *B* atoms occupy the centre of each face of cube.

$\therefore$ Number of atoms of $B = \left(\frac{1}{2}\right) \times 6 = 3$

Thus, probable empirical formula of the compound is AB_3.

33. (*b*) Packing efficiency

$= \frac{\text{volume occupied by two atoms in a unit cell}}{\text{volume of the unit cell}} \times 100$

For bcc, packing efficiency

$= \frac{2 \times \frac{4}{3}\pi r^3}{\left(\frac{4r}{\sqrt{3}}\right)^3} \times 100 = \frac{\sqrt{3}\pi}{8} \times 100 = 68\%$

$\therefore$ Volume occupied = 68% and volume vacant = 100 − 68 = 32%

34. (*d*) Length of body diagonal $= a\sqrt{3}$

$= 400\sqrt{3} = 692.82$ pm ≈ 693 pm

35. (*b*) In calcium fluoride structure, the Ca^{2+} ions are arranged in ccp/fcc (cubic closed packed) arrangement, i.e. Ca^{2+} ions are present at all corners and the centre of each face of the cube. The fluoride ions occupy all the tetrahedral sites. This is 8 : 4 arrangement, i.e. each Ca^{2+} ion is surrounded by 8F^- ions and each F^- ion by four Ca^{2+} ions.

36. (*c*)

Radius ratio (r_+/r_-)	Coordination number
0.155 - 0.225	3
0.225 - 0.414	4
0.414 - 0.732	6
0.732 - 1.00	8

Hence, if the ratio of ionic radius is 0.52, then the coordination number of B^- is 6.

37. (*b*) Radius ratio as for a tetrahedral void $(r_+/r_-) = 0.2247$ to 0.414.

For an octahedral void $(r_+/r_-) = 0.414$ to 0.732.

Therefore, in a closed packed structure, tetrahedral voids are smaller than octahedral voids.

38. (*d*) Volume of an atom $= \frac{4}{3}\pi r^3$

In fcc, number of atoms per unit cell = 4

$\therefore$ Volume of total atoms

$= 4 \times \frac{4}{3}\pi r^3 = \frac{16}{3}\pi r^3$

39. (*a*) For simple cubic cell,

radius $(r) = \frac{a}{2}$

Volume of the atom $= \frac{4}{3}\pi r^3 = \frac{4}{3}\pi\left(\frac{a}{2}\right)^3$

$\therefore$ Packing fraction $= \frac{\frac{4}{3}\pi\left(\frac{a}{2}\right)^3}{a^3} = \frac{\pi}{6}$

40. (*b*) In AgI crystal, number of Ag^+ ions is equal to I^- ions. However, the number of tetrahedral voids are twice the number of atoms forming the cubic lattice.

$\therefore$ Number of tetrahedral voids occupied by Ag^+ ion = 50%

41. (*a*) For fcc,

Radius of Ag$(r) = 144 \times 10^{-10}$ cm,

$\therefore \quad a = 2\sqrt{2}r$

$= 2\sqrt{2} \times 144 \times 10^{-10}$

$= 4.0729 \times 10^{-8}$ cm

$= 407.29 \times 10^{-10}$ cm

Density $(\rho) = \frac{Z \times M}{a^3 \times N_A}$

$= \frac{4 \times 108}{(407.29 \times 10^{-10})^3 \times 6.02 \times 10^{23}}$

$= \frac{432}{6.76 \times 10^{-23} \times 6.02 \times 10^{23}}$

$= \frac{432}{40.7} = 10.6 \approx 10$ g cm^{-3}

42. (*d*) Density of CsBr $(d) = \frac{Z \times M}{a^3 \times N_A}$;

$Z = 1$ ($\because$ CsBr contains one formula unit per unit cell)

$M = 133 + 80 = 213$ u

$a = 436.6 \text{ pm} = 436.6 \times 10^{-10}$ cm

$\therefore$ Density (d)

$$= \frac{1 \times (133 + 80)}{(436.6 \times 10^{-10})^3 \times 6.02 \times 10^{23}}$$

$$= 4.25 \text{ g/cm}^3$$

43. (*a*) In CaF_2, radius ratio = 0.73
It crystal structure is said to be body centred cubic. In this, each Ca^{2+} ion is surrounded by eight F^- ions, i.e. for calcium, coordination number is eight and for fluorine it is 4.

In fluoride, the Ca^{2+} ions are too small to touch each other, hence the structure is not strictly close packed structure. Relative positions of Ca^{2+} ions are like ions in a cubic close packed structure in which all the tetrahedral holes are occupied by the F^- ions.

44. (*d*) The bcc cell consists of 8 atoms at the corners and one atom at body centre

$\therefore \quad n = \left(8 \times \frac{1}{8}\right) + 1 = 2$

The fcc cell consists of 8 atoms at the eight corners and one atom at each of the six faces. This atom at the face is shared by two unit cells.

$\therefore n = 8 \times \frac{1}{8} + \left(6 \times \frac{1}{2}\right) = 4$

45. (*d*) Edge length of the unit cell = 2 Å
$= 2 \times 10^{-8}$ cm

Volume of unit cell $= (2 \times 10^{-8})^3$
$= 8 \times 10^{-24}$ cm^3

Mass of one unit cell
= volume × density $= 8 \times 10^{-24} \times 2.5$

Number of unit cells in 200 g of metal

$$= \frac{\text{mass of the metal}}{\text{mass of one unit cell}}$$

$$= \frac{200}{8 \times 10^{-24} \times 2.5}$$

$= 1 \times 10^{25}$ unit cells

46. (*b*) *ABC ABC* ...... arrangement of layers` is found in cubic closed pack system (ccp system). In this, atoms are at the corner as well as centre of the unit cell.

$\therefore$ Number of atoms per unit cell

$$= 8 \times \frac{1}{8} + 1 = 2$$

$\therefore$ Number of tetrahedral voids in a unit cell = $2Z$.

47. (*c*) NaCl has fcc structure.
In fcc lattice, $r_+ + r_- = \frac{a}{2}$

$\therefore$ Edge length, $a = 2r^+ + 2r^-$
$= (2 \times 95 + 2 \times 181)$ pm
$= 190 + 362 = 552$ pm

48. (*a*) Packing efficiency for :
Hexagonal close packing (hcp) = 74%
Face-centred cubic (fcc) close packing = 74%
Body centered cubic (bcc) close packing = 68%
and simple cubic (sc) = 52%
Thus, correct order of packing efficiency is hcp = fcc > bcc > sc
Hence, option (a) is the correct.

49. (*d*) In bcc, 2 atoms are present. One atom lies at the centre of cube while, other lies at the corner of the cube. Hence, the distance between the body centred and one corner atom is half of the body diagonal, i.e. $\frac{\sqrt{3}}{2}a$.

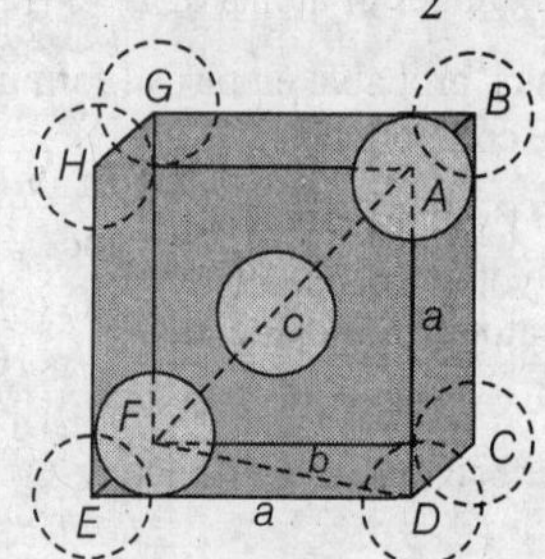

50. (*a*)

Packing	Fraction	Space
Simple cubic unit cell	52%	48%
Body centred cubic unit cell	68%	32%
Face centred cubic unit cell	74%	26%

51. (*b*) Carbon as diamond crystallises in a face centred cubic structure and possesses four more carbon atoms that are found to be present in the alternate tetrahedral voids.

Thus, Z_{eff} [number of C-atoms] in diamond
$= Z_{eff}$ in fcc unit cell + Z_{eff} in alternate tetrahedral voids

$$\therefore Z_{eff} = \underbrace{\left[\frac{1}{8}\times 8 + \frac{1}{2}\times 6\right]}_{\text{fcc unit cell}} + \underbrace{[1\times 4]}_{\text{Alternate tetrahedral voids}} = 8$$

Hence, the number of carbon atoms per unit cell of the diamond unit cell is 8.

52. (*a*) Number of octahedral voids
= Number of atoms in the close packed structure

Since, number of atom = 1
So, number of octahedral void = 1

53. (*b*) In bcc structure,
the number of atoms at corners per unit cell $= \frac{1}{8} \times 8 = 1$ atom

the number of atoms at body centre per unit cell = 1 atom

$\therefore$ Total number of atoms per unit cell
$= 1 + 1 = 2$ atoms

54. (*a*) Packing fraction of lattice structure or fraction of total volume occupied

$$= \frac{\text{Volume occupied by atoms in a unit cell}}{\text{Volume of the unit cell}}$$

Packing fraction of simple cubic unit cell

$$= \frac{Z \times \frac{4}{3}\pi r^3}{a^3} = \frac{1 \times \frac{4}{3}\pi r^3}{(2r)^3}$$

($\because$ For primitive cell, $a = 2r$)

$= 0.52$

$\therefore$ Volume occupied = 0.52
The other given statements are correct.

55. (*a*) For simple cubic, $a = 2r$

$\therefore \quad r = a/2$

For body centred cubic, $a = \frac{4r}{\sqrt{3}}$

$\therefore \quad r = \frac{\sqrt{3}a}{4}$

For face centred cubic, $a = 2\sqrt{2}\,r$

$\therefore \quad r = \frac{1}{2\sqrt{2}}a$

Therefore, the ratio of radius of scc, bcc and fcc.

$$= \frac{1}{2}a : \frac{\sqrt{3}}{4}a : \frac{1}{2\sqrt{2}}a$$

$$= \frac{1}{2} : \frac{\sqrt{3}}{4} : \frac{1}{2\sqrt{2}}$$

56. (*d*) For fcc, number of atoms at corner
$= \frac{1}{8} \times 8 = 1$

Number of atoms at face centre
$= \frac{1}{2} \times 6 = 3$

$\therefore$ Total number of atoms = 1 + 3 = 4

57. (*c*) In face centred cubic cell (fcc), there are four atoms per unit cell which is maximum.

Number of atoms per unit cell

$$= \left(6 \times \frac{1}{2}\right) + 8 \times \frac{1}{8} = 3 + 1 = 4$$

Topic 3

Imperfections in Solids

2019

1 Which type of defect present in NaCl? [JIPMER]
(a) Frenkel defect (b) Schottky defect
(c) F-centre defect (d) None of these

2 Frenkel defect is present in which of the following? [JIPMER]
(a) NaOH (b) NaI
(c) AgBr (d) None of these

3 **Assertion** (A) ZnO becomes yellow when it is heated.
Reason (R) The anionic sites (*F*-centres) occupied by unpaired electrons. [AIIMS]
(a) Both A and R are correct and R is the correct explanation of A
(b) Both A and R are correct but R is not the correct explanation of A
(c) A is correct but R is incorrect
(d) Both A and R are incorrect

2013

4 Which one of the following defects in the crystal lowers its density? [KCET]
(a) F-centres (b) Interstitial defect
(c) Frenkel defect (d) Schottky defect

2010

5 Schottky defect in crystals is observed when [RPMT]
(a) density of crystal is increased
(b) an ion leaves its normal site and occupies an interstitial site
(c) equal number of cations and anions are missing from the lattice
(d) unequal number of cations and anions are missing from the lattice

6 Which of the following compounds shows both Frenkel and Schottky defects? [AMU]
(a) NaCl (b) AgCl
(c) AgBr (d) KCl

7 Which kind of defect is shown by the given crystal?

K^+ Cl^- K^+ Cl^- K^+ Cl^-
Cl^- □ Cl^- K^+ □ K^+
K^+ Cl^- □ Cl^- K^+ Cl^-
Cl^- K^+ Cl^- K^+ □ K^+

(a) Schottky defect [Guj CET]
(b) Frenkel defect
(c) Schottky and Frenkel defects
(d) Substitution disorder

8 **Assertion** (A) In any ionic solid (*MX*) with Schottky defect, the number of positive and negative ions are same.
Reason (R) Unequal numbers of cation and anion vacancies are present. [VMMC]
(a) Both A and R are correct and R is the correct explanation of A
(b) Both A and R are correct but R is not the correct explanation of A
(c) A is correct but R is incorrect
(d) Both A and R are incorrect

2009

9 With which one of the following elements silicon should be doped so as to give *p*-type of semiconductor?
(a) Germanium (b) Arsenic [CBSE AIPMT]
(c) Selenium (d) Boron

10 In a solid lattice, the cation has left a lattice site and is located at an interstitial position. The lattice defect is [BHU]
(a) interstitial defect (b) vacancy defect
(c) Frenkel defect (d) Schottky defect

11 Schottky defect is observed in the crystal of [Punjab PMET]
(a) NaCl (b) TiCl
(c) AgCl (d) $MgCl_2$

12 **Assertion** (A) No compound has both Schottky and Frenkel defects.
Reason (R) Both defects change the density of the solid.
(a) Both A and R are correct and R is the correct explanation of A [AIIMS]
(b) Both A and R are correct but R is not the correct explanation of A
(c) A is correct but R is incorrect
(d) Both A and R are incorrect

2007

13 If NaCl is doped with 10^{-4} mole % of $SrCl_2$, the concentration of cation vacancies will be
($N_A = 6.02 \times 10^{23}$ mol^{-1}) [CBSE AIPMT]
(a) 6.023×10^{15} mol^{-1} (b) 6.023×10^{16} mol^{-1}
(c) 6.023×10^{17} mol^{-1} (d) 6.023×10^{14} mol^{-1}

2005

14 When electrons are trapped into the crystal in anion vacancy, the defect is known as [BHU]
(a) Schottky defect (b) Frenkel defect
(c) stoichiometric defect (d) *F*-centres

Answers

1 (b)	2 (c)	3 (a)	4 (d)	5 (c)	6 (c)	7 (a)	8 (c)	9 (d)	10 (c)
11 (a)	12 (d)	13 (c)	14 (d)						

Explanations

1. (*b*) Schottky defect is a vacancy defect in ionic solids. It is shown by those ionic substances in which the cations and anions are of almost similar sizes.

Schottky defect is present in sodium chloride (NaCl). This defect arises when equal number of cations and anions are missing from their lattice sites such that electrical neutrality is maintained.

e.g. CsCl, NaCl, KCl, AgBr, etc.

2. (*c*) Frenkel defect is generally found in ionic crystals where anion is much larger in size than the cation. It is also known as dislocation defect.

Frenkel defect is present in AgBr. This defect arises when the smaller ion (usually cation) is dislocated from its normal site. It creates a vacancy defect at its original site and an interstitial defect at its new location.

e.g. AgBr, AgCl, AgI, ZnS.

3. (*a*) Zinc oxide which is white in colour on heating loses oxygen and turns yellow.

$$ZnO \xrightarrow{\text{Heating}} Zn^{2+} + \frac{1}{2}O_2 + 2e^-$$

It is due to metal excess defect in which excess ions (cation and electron) occupy interstitial site.

A negative ion missing from its lattice site leaves a hole which is occupied by an extra electron to maintain electrical neutrality. Thus, anionic site is called *F*-centre.

Hence, both Assertion and Reason are correct and Reason is the correct explanation of Assertion.

4. (*d*)

(a) *F*-centres imparts colours in the crystals.

(b) Interstitial defects contain some free electrons, so material act as semiconductors.

(c) Due to Frenkel defect density of the solid remain unchanged.

(d) Schottky defect lowers the density of a crystal. It is a vacancy defect in ionic solids. This defect arises when equal number of cations and anions are missing from the lattice and thus, electrical neutrality is maintained, e.g.CsCl, NaCl, KCl, AgBr in which cations and anions are of almost same size.

5. (*c*) When the equal number of cations and anions are missing from their position, the defect, that arises in a crystal is known as Schottky defect. (For further detail, refer to answer 1).

6. (*c*) NaCl and KCl exhibit Schottky defect, AgCl exhibits Frenkel defect. AgBr is the compound that exhibits, Frenkel as well as Schottky defects.

7. (*a*) In the given crystal, equal number of cations and anions are missing (two K^+ and two Cl^-) from their normal lattice sites and the crystal maintains electrical neutrality. Hence, this is Schottky defect.

K^+	Cl^-	K^+	Cl^-	K^+	Cl^-
Cl^-	□	Cl^-	K^+	□	K^+
K^+	Cl^-	□	Cl^-	K^+	Cl^-
Cl^-	K^+	Cl^-	K^+	□	K^+

Number of missing cations

= Number of missing anions =2

8. (*c*) In any ionic solid (*MX*) with Schottky defect, equal number of positive and negative ions are missing from their normal lattice sites and, thus equal number of cations and anion vacancies are present.

Hence assertion is correct but reason is incorrect.

9. (*d*) *p*-type semiconductors are obtained when Si or Ge are doped with traces of elements of group 13, i.e. indium (In), boron (B).

While *n*-type semiconductors are obtained when Si or Ge are doped with elements of group 15, e.g. arsenic (As).

10. (*c*) If an ion is missing from its lattice site and it occupies the interstitial site, this type of defect is called Frenkel defect.

11. (*a*) Schottky defect is generally shown by ionic solids having high coordination number and in which cations and anions are of equal sizes. e.g. NaCl, CsCl. AgCl and $MgCl_2$ show Frenkel defect and TiCl shows non-stoichiometric defects.

12. (*d*) Certain ionic solids (e.g. AgBr) have both Schottky and Frenkel defects. Only Schottky defects change the density of solids because anions or cations are missing while Frenkel defects have no change in density because they have same number of cations or anions, only the position of ions is changed.

Hence, both A and R are incorrect.

13. (*c*) Due to the addition of $SrCl_2$, each Sr^{2+} ion replaces $2Na^+$ ions. This creates cation vacancy. Doping of NaCl with 10^{-4} mole % of $SrCl_2$ means, 100 moles of NaCl are doped with 10^{-4} mole of $SrCl_2$.

∴ 1 mole of NaCl is doped with $SrCl_2$

$$= \frac{10^{-4}}{100} = 10^{-6}\text{ mol}$$

As each mole of Sr^{2+} ion introduces one cation vacancy, therefore, total number of cation vacancies,

$$= 10^{-6} \times N_A$$

$$= 10^{-6} \times 6.023 \times 10^{23}\text{ mol}^{-1}$$

$$= 6.023 \times 10^{17}\text{ mol}^{-1}$$

14. (*d*)

(a) **Schottky Defect** When equal number of cations and anions are missing from an ionic crystal, it is called Schottky defect.

(b) **Frenkel Defect** When an ion is missing from its position in lattice and occupies the interstitial site, electrical neutrality and stoichiometry of compound is maintained. It is called Frenkel defect.

(c) **Stoichiometric Defect** These are imperfections in crystals in which the ratio of cations and anions remain same as represented by molecular formula.

(d) ***F*-centres** When an anion is missing from its site and its position is taken by electron to maintain electrical balance, the electron thus trapped in anion vacancy is called F-centres. Thus, F-centres are responsible for imparting colours to crystal.

Topic 4

Electrical and Magnetic Properties

2014

1 Which one of the following is used as a piezoelectric material? **[Kerala CEE]**

(a) Silicones (b) Graphite
(c) Silica gel (d) Kieselghur
(e) Quartz

2010

2 The electrical conductivity of semiconductor is **[AIIMS]**

(a) 10^8 ohm^{-1}cm^{-1}
(b) in the range of 10^{-9} to 10^2 ohm^{-1}cm^{-1}
(c) 10^{-22} ohm^{-1}cm^{-1}
(d) 10^2 ohm^{-1}cm^{-1}

2009

3 To get *n*-type semiconductor from silicon, it should be doped with a substance with valency. **[CBSE AIPMT]**

(a) 5 (b) 2 (c) 3 (d) 1

2006

4 Some of the polar crystals when heated produces small electrical current. This phenomenon is called **[Guj CET]**

(a) ferroelectricity (b) pyroelectricity
(c) piezoelectricity (d) anti-ferroelectricity

5 Which one of the given magnetic properties possess zero dipole moment? **[KERALA CEE]**

(a) Ferrimagnetism
(b) Anti-ferromagnetism
(c) Ferromagnetism
(d) Diamagnetism

6 At 850 K, the ferrimagnetic Fe_3O_4 changes to **[AIIMS]**

(a) paramagnetic
(b) diamagnetic
(c) antiferromagnetic
(d) ferromagnetic

Answers

1 (e)	2 (b)	3 (a)	4 (b)	5 (b)	6 (a)

Explanations

1. (*e*) Piezoelectric effect is the ability of some materials to create an electric potential in response to applied mechanical stress. The commonly used piezoelectric materials are quartz (SiO_2), zinc oxide etc.

2. (*b*) Electrical conductivity of semiconductors lies in the range of 10^{-9} to 10^2 ohm^{-1}cm^{-1}.

3. (*a*) Group 14 elements doped with group 15 elements, form *n*-type semiconductors and group 15 elements have 1 electron excess to Si or Ge, after forming 4 covalent bonds with group 14 elements. So, their valency is 5.

4. (*b*) (a) **Ferroelectricity** The dipoles are permanently polarised even in absence of the electric field.

(b) **Pyroelectricity** Some of the polar crystals when heated produce small electrical current.

(c) **Piezoelectricity** When mechanical stress is applied on crystal to deform and electricity is produced.

(d) **Anti-ferroelectricity** Dipoles align themselves alternatively so, that net dipole moment is zero.

5. (*b*) In anti-ferromagnetism, the number of parallel and antiparallel magnetic dipoles are equal and hence they cancel out each other resulting in zero dipole moment.

6. (*a*) The magnetic behaviour of Fe_3O_4 changes from ferrimagnetic to paramagnetic at 850 K due to randomisation of spins.

16

Solutions

Quick Review

- Solution is a homogeneous mixture of two or more substances in same or different physical phases.
- Generally, a solution contains two components (solute and solvent). **Solvent** is that component of solution which is usually present in large quantity while **solute** is the component which is usually present in small quantity.

Types of Solutions

On the basis of physical states of components, there are three types of solution which are tabulated below:

Types of Solutions	Solute	Solvent	Examples
Solid Solutions	Solid	Solid	Alloys (copper dissolved in gold)
	Liquid	Solid	Hydrated salts, amalgam of Hg with Na
	Gas	Solid	Solution of hydrogen in palladium
Liquid Solutions	Solid	Liquid	Salt/sugar solution in water
	Liquid	Liquid	Alcohol in water
	Gas	Liquid	Aerated drinks, O_2 in water
Gaseous Solutions	Solid	Gas	Iodine vapour in air
	Liquid	Gas	Water vapour in air
	Gas	Gas	Air ($O_2 + N_2$)

- *On the basis of amount of solute dissolved in a solvent, we have following types of solutions :*
  (*i*) **Unsaturated Solution** A solution in which more solute can be dissolved without raising temperature is called an unsaturated solution.
  (*ii*) **Saturated Solution** A solution in which no solute can be dissolved further at a given temperature is called a saturated solution.
  (*iii*) **Supersaturated Solution** A solution which contains more solute than that would be necessary to saturate it at a given temperature is called a supersaturated solution.

Expressing Concentration of Solutions

The amount of solute present in the given quantity of the solution is called concentration of solution.

There are several methods to express the concentration of the solution. *These are as follows:*

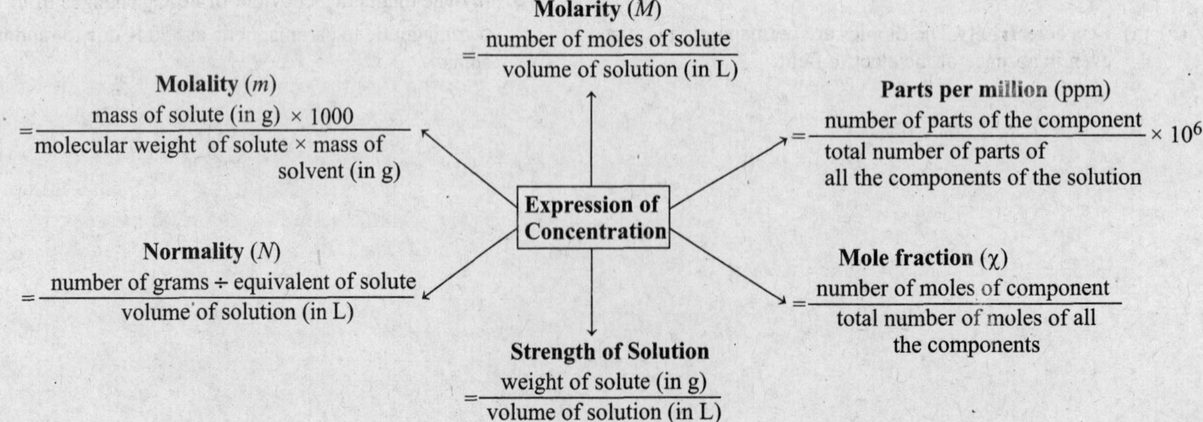

Note • Molarity equation, $M_1V_1 = M_2V_2$
• Normality equation, $N_1 V_1 = N_2V_2$
• Molarity, mole fraction, mass fraction etc., are preferred over molarity, normality etc. because the former are temperature independent entities.

Solubility

The maximum amount of solute that may be dissolved in a given amount of solvent at a given temperature is termed as solubility.

- All gases are soluble in water as well as in other liquids to a small extent.
- Solubility of gas in liquid varying with change in pressure is governed by the Henry's law.

Henry's Law

- This law states that 'the solubility of a gas in a liquid is directly proportional to the pressure of the gas'. If 'p' is the partial pressure of the gas in solution and χ is the mole fraction, then, $p \propto \chi$ and $p = K_H \cdot \chi$ where, K_H is Henry's law constant.
- K_H depends on the nature of the gas. Generally, higher the value of K_H at a particular temperature, lower is the solubility of gas in the liquid.

Effect of Temperature on Solubility

The solubility of a solid in a liquid is significantly affected by temperature change.

(i) In general, if in a saturated solution, the dissolution process is endothermic (i.e. $\Delta_{sol} H > 0$), the solubility should increase with increase in temperature e.g. $NaNO_3$, KNO_3, NaCl, KCl, etc.

(ii) If it is exothermic (i.e. $\Delta_{sol} H < 0$), the solubility should decrease in accordance with Le-Chatelier's principle (e.g. Li_2CO_3, $Na_2CO_3 \cdot H_2O$).

(iii) Some substances do not show a continuous decrease or increase of solubility. These on heating change from one polymorphic form to another.

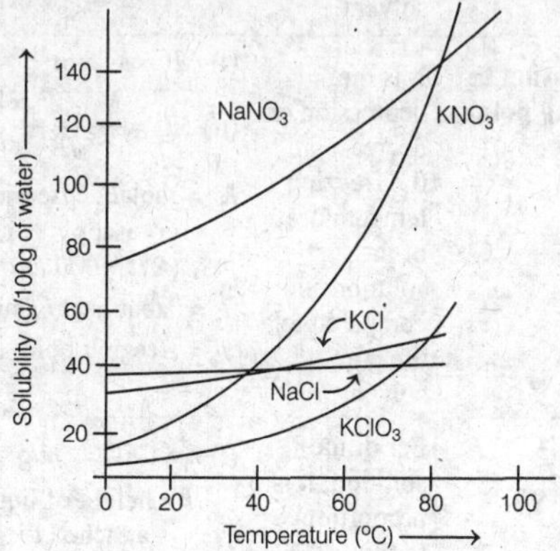

Continuous solubility curve

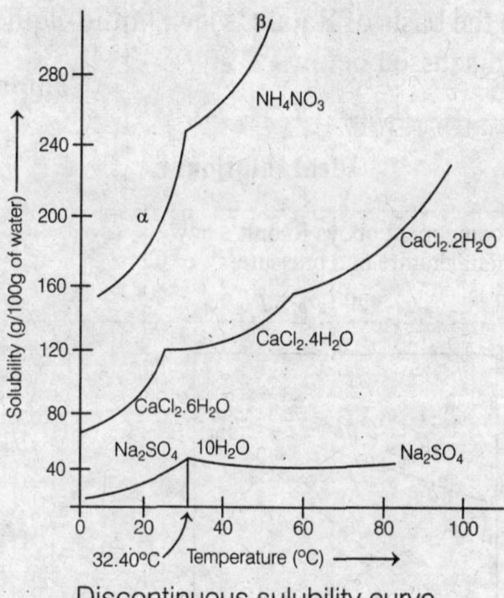

Discontinuous sulubility curve

Vapour Pressure

The pressure exerted by the vapours above the liquid surface in equilibrium with liquid at a given temperature is called vapour pressure.

Raoult's Law

According to Raoult's law, 'at a given temperature, for a solution of volatile liquids, the partial vapour pressure of each component of the solution is directly proportional to its mole fraction present in the solution'.

For a solution containing two liquids A and B, the partial pressure of liquid A is

$$p_A \propto \chi_A$$

$$\Rightarrow \quad p_A = p_A^\circ \chi_A$$

where, $\chi_A = \dfrac{n_A}{n_A + n_B}$,

where, χ_A is the mole fraction of liquid A

p_A° = vapour pressure of pure liquid.

- In case of binary solution of two volatile liquids, total vapour pressure, $p = p_A + p_B = p_A^\circ \chi_A + p_B^\circ \chi_B$
- Raoult's law is not applicable, if the total number of particles of solute changes in the solution due to association or dissociation.
- When concentration of a salt solution is increased, boiling point of salt solution increases while vapour pressure decreases.

- On the basis of Raoult's law, liquid-liquid solutions can be divided into two types of solutions i.e. ideal and non-ideal solutions as discussed below

Comparison between Ideal and Non-Ideal Solutions

Ideal solutions	Non-ideal solutions	
	Positive deviation from Raoult's law	**Negative deviation from Raoult's law**
Each component obeys Raoult's law at all temperature and pressure, i.e. $p_A = p_A^\circ \chi_A$ and $p_B = p_B^\circ \chi_B$	Their components do not obey Raoult's law. i.e. $p_A > p_A^\circ \chi_A$ and $p_B > p_A^\circ \chi_B$	Their components do not obey Raoult's law, i.e. $p_A < p_A^\circ \chi_A$ and $p_B < p_B^\circ \chi_B$
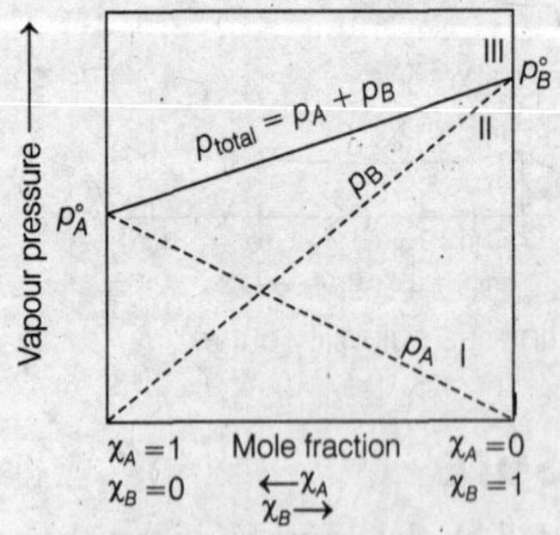	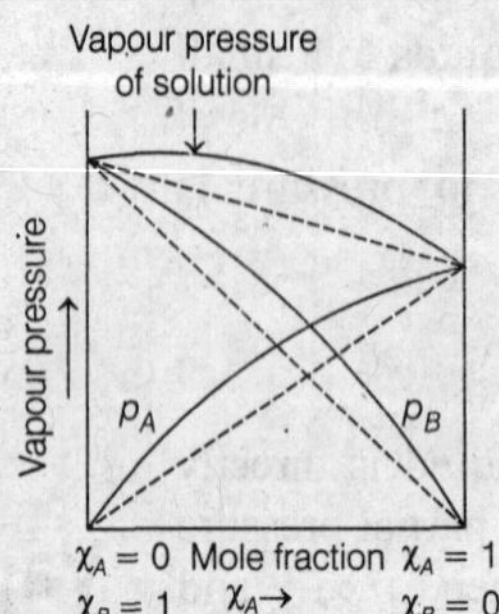	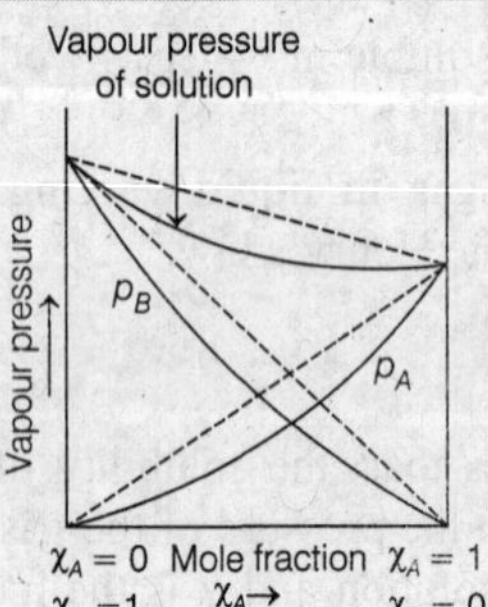
$\Delta_{mix} V = 0$, $\Delta_{mix} H = 0$	$\Delta_{mix} V > 0$, $\Delta_{mix} H > 0$ (endothermic)	$\Delta_{mix} V < 0$, $\Delta_{mix} H < 0$ (exothermic)
Intermolecular interactions, i.e. *A—B* interactions are same as present in pure components, i.e. *A—A* or *B—B*.	Intermolecular interactions, i.e. *A—B* interactions are weaker than in pure components, i.e. between *A—A* or *B—B*	Intermolecular interactions, i.e. *A—B* interactions are stronger than in pure components, i.e. between *A—A* or *B—B*.
Examples : Benzene + toluene, *n*-hexane + *n*-heptane; chlorobenzene + bromobenzene; ethyl bromide + ethyl iodide; *n*-butyl chloride + *n*-butyl bromide.	**Examples :** Ethanol + water, ether + acetone, acetone + benzene, carbon disulphide + acetone, carbon tetrachloride + methanol, cyclohexane + ethanol, water + methanol, carbon tetrachloride + benzene.	**Examples** : Acetic acid + methanol, acetic acid + pyridine, acetone + aniline, acetone + chloroform, benzene + chloroform, water + hydrochloric acid, water + nitric acid.

Azeotropic Mixture

An azeotropic mixture boils at a constant temperature and distills over without undergoing any change in its composition. These are formed by non-ideal solutions. There are two types of azeotropes called as **minimum boiling azeotropes** and **maximum boiling azeotropes**.

Colligative Properties

The properties of dilute solution which depend only upon the number of particles present in a solution and their concentration are called colligative properties. The four types of colligative properties are discussed below:

A Summary of Colligative Properties of Solutions

Colligative properties	Definition	Formulae
Relative lowering of vapour pressure	It is equal to the mole fraction of the solute present in the solution.	(*i*) $\frac{p^\circ - p_s}{p^\circ} = \chi_B = \frac{n_B}{n_A + n_B}$ where, p° = vapour pressure of pure solvent p_s = vapour pressure of solution χ_B = mole fraction of solute (*ii*) $MW_B = \frac{W_B \times MW_A}{W_A\left(\frac{p^\circ - p_s}{p^\circ}\right)}$ where, MW_B = molecular weight of solute W_B = weight of solute MW_A = molecular weight of solvent W_A = weight of solvent
Elevation in boiling point (Ebullioscopy)	It is an elevation or increase in the boiling temperature of the solution as compared to the pure solvent.	(*i*) $\Delta T_b = K_b m$ (*ii*) $\Delta T_b = \frac{K_b \times W_B \times 1000}{MW_B \times W_A}$ ΔT_b = elevation in boiling point. k_b = molal elevation constant or ebullioscopic constant $(RT_0^2/1000\Delta H_v)$
Depression in freezing point (Cryoscopy)	It is the depression or decrease in the freezing temperature of the solution as compared to the pure solvent.	(*i*) $\Delta T_f = K_f \times m$ (*ii*) $\Delta T_f = \frac{K_f \times W_B \times 1000}{MW_B \times W_A}$ K_f = molal depression constant or cryoscopic constant $(RT_0^2/1000\ l_f)$ l_f = latent heat of fusion T_o = freezing point of pure solvent
Osmotic pressure	For dilute solution, it is proportional to the molarity (*C*) of the solution of given temperature (*T*).	(*i*) $\pi = CRT = hdg$ h = height of liquid raised on capillary attached to solution chamber d = density of solution g = acceleration due to gravity $C = \frac{\text{number of moles of solute}}{\text{volume of solution}}$ (*ii*) $\pi = \frac{W_B RT}{MW_B \times V}$

Osmosis

- Spontaneous flow of solvent from dilute solution into the concentrated solution through a semipermeable membrane is called **osmosis**.
- The pressure required to prevent osmosis is called osmotic pressure.
- Two or more solutions having equal osmotic pressure under given conditions are called **isotonic solutions.**
- A solution having lower or higher osmotic pressure than the other is said to be **hypotonic** or **hypertonic respectively.**

Abnormal Molar Mass

Some compounds dissociate into ions or associate when used as a solute, e.g. ionic compounds dissociate into cations and anions when dissolved in water while molecules of few organic compounds associate in benzene.

These association or dissociation results in new apparent molar mass which is either lower or higher than the expected normal values and this is called **abnormal molar mass.**

van't Hoff Factor (*i*)

It is the ratio of normal molar mass to the abnormal molar mass.

$$i = \frac{\text{normal molar mass}}{\text{abnormal molar mass}}$$

If solutes undergo either association or dissociation, each colligative property is multiplied by a factor, called van't Hoff factor (*i*)

$$i = \frac{\text{observed value of colligative property}}{\text{theoretical value of colligative property}}$$

Modified Forms of Colligative Properties

Due to inclusion of van't Hoff factor, the modified forms of colligative properties are:

Relative lowering of vapour pressure, $\frac{\Delta p}{p^\circ} = i\chi_2$

or $\frac{p_1^\circ - p_1}{p_1^\circ} = i \cdot \frac{n_2}{n_1 + n_2}$

Elevation in boiling point, $\Delta T_b = iK_b m$

Depression in freezing point, $\Delta T_f = iK_f m$

Osmotic pressure, $\pi = iCRT$ or $\frac{in_2RT}{V}$

Relation Between Degree of Dissociation / Association (α) and van't Hoff Factor (*i*)

- van't Hoff factor $(i) = 1 + (y-1)\alpha$

  Here, y = number of particles after dissociation/association
  α = degree of dissociation/association
- Degree of dissociation $(\alpha) = \frac{i-1}{n-1}$

  (n = number of particles per molecule)
- Degree of association $(\alpha) = \frac{i-1}{\left(\frac{1}{n} - 1\right)}$

  $i = 1$, for non-electrolytes
  $i > 1$, for dissociation
  $i < 1$, for association

Some Important Facts

(*i*) Intramolecular H-bonding lowers boiling point.

(*ii*) Phenylacetic acid dimerises in benzene.

(*iii*) When egg is kept in saturated solution after removing the hard shell in dil. HCl, egg will shrink due to osmosis.

(*iv*) $CaCl_2$ with ice forms brine rapidly which lowers the freezing point of water and melts snow quickly. So property of $CaCl_2$ used to prevent block of roads in polar region.

(*v*) Camphor is used in molecular mass determination due to its volatile nature.

(*vi*) To increase the solubility of CO_2 in soft drinks, the bottle is sealed under high pressure.

(*vii*) Helium-oxygen mixture is used by deep sea divers because of its very low solubility in blood.

(*viii*) Nernst gave distribution law, which governs the distribution of solute between two non-miscible solvents.

Topical Practice Questions

All the exam questions of this chapter have been divided into four topics as listed below

Topic 1

Expressions of Concentration

2014

1 What is the molality of a solution containing 200 mg of urea (molar mass 60 g mol^{-1}) dissolved in 40 g of water? **[MHT CET]**

(a) 0.0833 (b) 0.825
(c) 0.498 (d) 0.0013

2 The volume of ethyl alcohol (density 1.15 g/cc) that has to be added to prepare 100 cc of 0.5 M ethyl alcohol solution in water is **[WB JEE]**

(a) 1.15 cc (b) 2 cc (c) 2.15 cc (d) 2.30 cc

2013

3 6.02×10^{20} molecules of urea are present in 100 mL of its solution. The concentration of solution is **[NEET]**

(a) 0.02 M (b) 0.01 M
(c) 0.001 M (d) 0.1 M

4 How many gram of concentrated nitric acid solution should be used to prepare 250 mL of 2.0 M HNO_3. The concentrated acid is 70% HNO_3? **[NEET]**

(a) 45.0 g conc. HNO_3 (b) 90.0 g conc. HNO_3
(c) 70.0 g conc. HNO_3 (d) 50.0 g conc. HNO_3

5 The normality of orthophosphoric acid having purity of 70% by weight and specific gravity 1.54 is **[AIIMS]**

(a) 11 N (b) 22 N (c) 33 N (d) 44 N

6 The molarity of H_2SO_4 solution, which has a density 1.84 g/cc at 35°C and contains 98% by weight is **[AIIMS]**

(a) 1.84 M (b) 18.4 M
(c) 20.6 M (d) 24.5 M

2012

7 138 g ethyl alcohol is mixed with 72 g of water. The ratio of mole fraction of alcohol to water is **[Manipal]**

(a) 3 : 4 (b) 1 : 2 (c) 1 : 4 (d) 1 : 1

2011

8 Mole fraction of the solute in a 1.00 molal aqueous solution is **[CBSE AIPMT]**

(a) 1.7700 (b) 0.1770
(c) 0.0177 (d) 0.0344

9 How many grams of sulphuric acid is to be dissolved to prepare 200 mL aqueous solution having concentration of $[H_3O^+]$ ions 1 M at 25°C temperature?
(H = 1, O = 16, S = 32 g mol^{-1}) **[Guj CET]**

(a) 4.9 g (b) 19.6 g
(c) 9.8 g (d) 0.98 g

2010

10 25.3 g of sodium carbonate, Na_2CO_3 is dissolved in enough water to make 250 mL of solution. If sodium carbonate dissociates completely, molar concentration of sodium ion, Na^+ and carbonate ions, CO_3^{2-} are respectively (Molar mass of Na_2CO_3 = 106 g mol^{-1}) **[CBSE AIPMT]**

(a) 0.477 M and 0.477 M
(b) 0.955 M and 1.910 M
(c) 1.910 M and 0.955 M
(d) 1.90 M and 1.910 M

11 450 mg of glucose is dissolved in 100 g of solvent. What is the molality of solution? **[MHT CET]**

(a) 0.0025 m (b) 0.025 m
(c) 0.25 m (d) 2.5 m

12 2.5 cm^3 of 0.2 M H_2SO_4 solution is diluted to 0.5 dm^3. Find normality of the diluted solution. **[MHT CET]**

(a) 0.2 N (b) 0.02 N (c) 0.002 N (d) 0.04 N

13 4.0 g of NaOH is dissolved in 100 mL solution. The normality of the solution is **[Manipal]**

(a) 0.1 N (b) 0.5 N (c) 4.0 N (d) 1.0 N

14 Calculate the mass of urea (NH_2CONH_2) required in making 2.5 kg of 0.25 molal aqueous solution. **[Haryana PMT]**

(a) 37.5 g (b) 73.5 g
(c) 53.7 g (d) 75.3 g

15 What is the mole fraction of benzene in solution containing 30% by mass in carbon tetrachloride? **[Haryana PMT]**

(a) 1.459 (b) 0.459
(c) 4.159 (d) None of these

16 What is the molarity of K^+ in aqueous solution that contains 17.4 ppm of K_2SO_4 (molar mass = 174 g mol^{-1})?

(a) 2×10^{-2} M (b) 2×10^{-3} M
(c) 4×10^{-4} M (d) 2×10^{-4} M

17 50 cm^3 of 0.2 N HCl is titrated against 0.1 N NaOH solution. The titration is discontinued after adding 50 cm^3 of NaOH. The remaining titration is completed by adding 0.5 N KOH. The volume of KOH required for completing the titration is **[KCET]**

(a) 12 cm^3 (b) 10 cm^3
(c) 25 cm^3 (d) 10.5 cm^3

18 What is the molarity of 0.2 N Na_2CO_3 solution? **[JCECE]**

(a) 0.1 M (b) 0 M
(c) 0.4 M (d) 0.2 M

2009

19 **Assertion** (A) 1.575 g $H_2C_2O_4 \cdot 2H_2O$ in 250 mL solution makes it 0.1N.

Reason (R) $H_2C_2O_4 \cdot 2H_2O$ is a dihydrate organic acid. [AIIMS]

(a) Both A and R are correct and R is the correct explanation of A

(b) Both A and R are correct, but R is not the correct explanation of A

(c) A is correct, but R is incorrect

(d) Both A and R are incorrect

20 The molarity of a solution containing 5.0 g of NaOH in 250 mL solution is [AFMC]

(a) 0.1M (b) 0.5M (c) 1.0M (d) 2.0M

21 The percentage (by weight) of sodium hydroxide in a 1.25 molal NaOH solution is [MHT CET]

(a) 4.76% (b) 1.25% (c) 5% (d) 40%

22 0.126 g of an acid is titrated with 0.1 N 20 mL of a base. The equivalent weight of the acid is [UP CPMT]

(a) 63 (b) 50 (c) 53 (d) 23

23 60 mL of $\frac{N}{5}$ H_2SO_4, 10 mL of $\frac{N}{2}$ HNO_3 and 30 mL of $\frac{N}{10}$ HCl are mixed together. The strength of the resulting mixture is [UP CPMT]

(a) 0.10 N (b) 0.2 N (c) 0.3 N (d) 0.4 N

24 25 g of a solute of molar mass 250 g mol^{-1} is dissolved in 100 mL of water to obtain a solution whose density is 1.25 g mL^{-1}. The molarity and molality of the solution are respectively [J&K CET]

(a) 0.75 and 1 (b) 0.8 and 1 (c) 1 and 0.8 (d) 1 and 0.75

25 The molarity of a solution obtained by mixing 800 mL of 0.5 M HCl with 200 mL of 1 M HCl will be [AMU]

(a) 0.8 M (b) 0.6 M (c) 0.4 M (d) 0.2 M

2008

26 **Assertion** (A) One molal aqueous solution of glucose contains 180 g of glucose in 1 kg water.

Reason (R) Solution containing one mole of solute in 1000 g of solvent is called one molal solution. [AIIMS]

(a) Both A and R are correct and R is the correct explanation of A

(b) Both A and R are correct, but R is not the correct explanation of A

(c) A is correct, but R is incorrect

(d) Both A and R are incorrect

27 Which of the following concentration factors affected by change in temperature? [MHT CET]

(a) Molarity (b) Molality

(c) Mole fraction (d) Weight fraction

28 Two bottles *A* and *B* contains 1 M and 1 m aqueous solution of sulphuric acid respectively. [Manipal]

(a) *A* is more concentrated than *B*

(b) *B* is more concentrated than *A*

(c) concentration of *A* is equal to concentration of *B*

(d) it is not possible to compare the concentration

29 An aqueous solution of 6.3 g of oxalic acid dihydrate is made up to 250 mL. The volume of 0.1 N NaOH required to completely neutralise 10 mL of this solution is [RPMT]

(a) 40 mL (b) 20 mL (c) 10 mL (d) 4 mL

30 10 cm^3 of 0.1 N monobasic acid requires 15 cm^3 of sodium hydroxide solution whose normality is [KCET]

(a) 1.5 N (b) 0.15 N (c) 0.066 N (d) 0.66 N

31 The volume of water to be added to 100 cm^3 of 0.5 N H_2SO_4 to get decinormal concentration is [BCECE]

(a) 400 cm^3 (b) 450 cm^3 (c) 500 cm^3 (d) 100 cm^3

2007

32 Concentrated aqueous sulphuric acid is 98% H_2SO_4 by mass and has a density of 1.80 g mL^{-1}. Volume of acid required to make 1 L of 0.1 M H_2SO_4 solution is [CBSE AIPMT]

(a) 11.10 mL (b) 16.65 mL

(c) 22.20 mL (d) 5.55 mL

33 An aqueous solution of glucose is 10% in strength. The volume in which 1 g mole of it is dissolved will be [AFMC]

(a) 18 L (b) 9 L (c) 0.9 L (d) 1.8 L

34 A mixture has 18 g water and 414 g ethanol. The mole fraction of water in mixture is (assume ideal behaviour of the mixture) [MP PMT]

(a) 0.1 (b) 0.4 (c) 0.7 (d) 0.9

35 The volume of 10 N and 4 N HCl required to make 1 L of 7 N HCl are [KCET]

(a) 0.50 L of 10 N HCl and 0.50 L of 4 N HCl

(b) 0.60 L of 10 N HCl and 0.40 L of 4 N HCl

(c) 0.80 L of 10 N HCl and 0.20 L of 4 N HCl

(d) 0.75 L of 10 N HCl and 0.25 L of 4 N HCl

2005

36 To prepare a solution of concentration of 0.03 g/mL of $AgNO_3$, what amount of $AgNO_3$ should be added in 60 mL of solution? [AFMC]

(a) 1.8 g (b) 0.8 g

(c) 0.18 g (d) None of these

37 5 L of a solution contains 25 mg of $CaCO_3$. What is its concentration in ppm? (Molecular weight of $CaCO_3$ is 100.) [J&K CET]

(a) 25 (b) 1 (c) 5 (d) 2500

2006

38 The volume strength of 1.5 N H_2O_2 solution is [EAMCET]

(a) 4.8 (b) 8.4 (c) 3.0 (d) 8.0

39 How much volume of 1 M H_2SO_4 is required to neutralise 20 mL of 1 M NaOH? [JCECE]

(a) 10 mL (b) 20 mL (c) 5 mL (d) 15 mL

Answers

1 (a)	2 (b)	3 (b)	4 (a)	5 (c)	6 (b)	7 (a)	8 (c)	9 (c)	10 (c)
11 (b)	12 (c)	13 (d)	14 (a)	15 (b)	16 (d)	17 (b)	18 (a)	19 (a)	20 (b)
21 (a)	22 (a)	23 (b)	24 (c)	25 (b)	26 (a)	27 (a)	28 (a)	29 (a)	30 (c)
31 (a)	32 (d)	33 (d)	34 (a)	35 (a)	36 (a)	37 (c)	38 (b)	39 (a)	

Explanations

1 (*a*) Molality

$$(m) = \frac{\text{mass of solute (in g)} \times 1000}{\text{molecular weight of solute} \times \text{mass of solvent (in g)}}$$

$$= \frac{200 \times 10^{-3} \times 1000}{60 \times 40}$$

$$= 0.0833 \text{ m}$$

2 (*a*) Molarity

$$= \frac{\text{mass of solute} \times 1000}{\text{molecular weight of solute} \times \text{volume of solution}}$$

Molecular weight of ethyl alcohol,

$$C_2H_5OH = 12 \times 2 + 5 + 16 + 1$$

$$= 24 + 22$$

$$= 46 \text{ g mol}^{-1}$$

On substituting the values, we get

$$0.5 \text{ M} = \frac{\text{mass of ethyl alcohol} \times 1000}{46 \times 100}$$

$$\text{Mass of ethyl alcohol} = \frac{0.5 \times 46}{10} = 2.3\text{g}$$

$\therefore$ Volume of ethyl alcohol required,

$$V = \frac{\text{mass of ethyl alcohol}}{\text{density of ethyl alcohol}}$$

$$= \frac{2.3 \text{ g}}{1.15 \text{ g/cc}} = 2 \text{ cc}$$

3 (*b*) Given, number of molecules of urea

$$= 6.02 \times 10^{20}$$

$$\therefore \text{Number of moles} = \frac{6.02 \times 10^{20}}{6.02 \times 10^{23}}$$

$$= 1 \times 10^{-3} \text{ mol}$$

Volume of the solution = 100 mL

$$= \frac{100}{1000} \text{ L} = 0.1 \text{ L}$$

Concentration of urea solution

$$(\text{in mol L}^{-1}) = \frac{\text{number of moles}}{\text{volume (L)}}$$

$$= \frac{1 \times 10^{-3} \text{ mol}}{0.1 \text{ L}}$$

$$= 1 \times 10^{-2} \text{ mol L}^{-1}$$

$$= 0.01 \text{ mol/L or M}$$

4 (*a*) Given, molarity of solution = 2

Volume of solution = 250 mL

$$= \frac{250}{1000} = \frac{1}{4} \text{ L}$$

$$\text{Molar mass of } HNO_3 = 1 + 14 + 3 \times 16$$

$$= 63 \text{ g mol}^{-1}$$

$$\text{Molarity} = \frac{\text{Weight of } HNO_3}{\text{molecular mass of } HNO_3 \times \text{volume of solution (in L)}}$$

$$\text{Weight of } HNO_3 = \text{molarity} \times \text{molecular mass} \times \text{volume (in L)}$$

$$= \left(2 \times 63 \times \frac{1}{4}\right) \text{g} = 31.5 \text{ g}$$

31.5 g is the weight of 100% HNO_3.

But the given acid is 70% HNO_3.

$$\therefore \text{ Its weight} = 31.5 \times \frac{100}{70} \text{ g} = 45 \text{ g}$$

5 (*c*) 70% by weight means 70 g of orthophosphoric acid is present in 100 g of acid.

$$N = \frac{w}{\text{Eq. wt.}} \times \frac{1000}{V_{(\text{cc})}} \Rightarrow w = 70 \text{ g},$$

Orthophosphoric acid is H_3PO_4

Eq. wt.

$$= \frac{\text{molecular mass}}{\text{number of replaceable H - atom}}$$

$$= 98/3$$

$$V = \frac{\text{mass}}{\text{density}} = \frac{100}{1.54}$$

Putting values in Eq. (i)

$$N = \frac{70 \times 3 \times 1000 \times 1.54}{98 \times 100} = 33 \text{ N}$$

6 (*b*) 98% by mass means 98 g H_2SO_4 is present in 100 g of acid.

$$M = \frac{\text{given mass} \times 1000}{\text{molecular mass} \times V_{(\text{cc})}}$$

Given, mass = 98 g,

molecular mass = 98 g

$$V = \frac{\text{mass}}{\text{density}} = \frac{100}{1.84}$$

($\because$ density of H_2SO_4 is 1.84)

Putting the values,

$$M = \frac{98 \times 1000 \times 1.84}{98 \times 100} = 18.4 \text{ M}$$

7 (*a*) Number of moles of C_2H_5OH

$$= \frac{138}{46} = 3 \; (M_{C_2H_5OH} = 46 \text{ g/mol})$$

$$\text{Number of moles of } H_2O = \frac{72}{18} = 4$$

$$(\because M_{H_2O} = 18 \text{ g/mol})$$

$$\text{Mole fraction, } \chi_{C_2H_5OH} = \frac{3}{3+4} = \frac{3}{7}$$

$$\chi_{H_2O} = \frac{4}{3+4} = \frac{4}{7}$$

$$\frac{\chi_{C_2H_5OH}}{\chi_{H_2O}} = \frac{3/7}{4/7}$$

$$= 3/4 = 3:4$$

8 (*c*) 1 molal solution means 1 mole of the solute is present in 1000 g of water.

Moles of water = 1000/18 = 55.55

Mole of solute = 1

$\therefore$ Mole fraction of solute

$$= 1/56.55 = 0.0177$$

9 (*c*) 2 M $[H_3O^+]$ ions are obtained from 1 M H_2SO_4.

1 M $[H_3O^+]$ ions are obtained from 0.5 M H_2SO_4.

Molarity,

$$M = \frac{m(H_2SO_4) \times 1000}{M \text{ (molar mass) } H_2SO_4 \times \text{volume of solution (mL)}}$$

$$0.5 = \frac{m \times 1000}{98 \times 200}$$

$$m = \frac{0.5 \times 98 \times 200}{1000} = 9.8 \text{ g}$$

10 (*c*) Molarity $= \dfrac{m(Na_2CO_3) \times 1000}{M \text{(molar mass) } Na_2CO_3 \times \text{volume of solution (mL)}}$

$$\text{Molarity} = \frac{25.3 \times 1000}{106 \times 250} = 0.955 \text{ M}$$

$$Na_2CO_3 \longrightarrow 2Na^+ + CO_3^{2-}$$

Molar concentration of sodium ion, $Na^+ = 2 \times 0.955\ M = 1.910\ M$

Molar concentration of carbonate ion, $CO_3^{-2} = 0.955\ M$

11 (*b*) Molality $= \dfrac{\text{moles of solute} \times 1000}{\text{weight of solvent (in g)}}$

or $= \dfrac{\text{weight of solute} \times 1000}{\text{molecular weight of solute} \times \text{weight of solvent (in g)}}$

$= \dfrac{450 \times 10^{-3} \times 1000}{180 \times 100} = 0.025\ m$

[∵ Molecular mass of glucose $(C_6H_{12}O_6) = 180$]

12 (*c*) Given, volume of H_2SO_4 before dilution,

$V_1 = 2.5\ cm^3 = 2.5 \times 10^{-3}\ dm^3$

Volume of H_2SO_4 after dilution,

$V_2 = 0.5\ dm^3$

Concentration of H_2SO_4 before dilution,

$= 0.2\ M = 0.4\ N$

[∵ For H_2SO_4 1 N = 2 M]

Concentration (normality) of H_2SO_4 after dilution, $N_2 = ?$

Normality equation is

$N_1V_1 = N_2V_2$
(before dilution) (after dilution)

$2.5 \times 10^{-3} \times 0.4 = N_2 \times 0.5$

$N_2 = \dfrac{2.5 \times 10^{-3} \times 0.4}{0.5}$

$= 2 \times 10^{-3} = 0.002\ N$

13 (*d*) Given, mass of solute = 4.0 g

Normality $= \dfrac{\text{gram equivalent of solute}}{\text{volume of solution (in L)}}$

Molecular mass of NaOH = 23 + 16 + 1 = 40

Volume of solution

$= 100\ mL = 100/1000\ L = 0.1\ L$

∴ Normality $= \dfrac{4/40}{0.1} = 1.0\ N$

14 (*a*) Molality $= \dfrac{\text{moles of solute}}{\text{mass of solvent (in kg)}}$

∵ Moles of solute

$= \dfrac{\text{mass of solute}}{\text{molar mass of solute}}$

So, molality $= \dfrac{\dfrac{\text{mass}}{\text{molar mass}}}{\text{mass of solvent (in kg)}}$

⇒ $0.25 = \dfrac{\text{mass}/60}{2.5}$

(∵ Molar mass of urea $NH_2CONH_2 = 60$)

or mass $= 0.25 \times 2.5 \times 60 = 37.5$ g

15 (*b*) Mole fraction of a component

$= \dfrac{\text{number of moles of the component}}{\text{total number of moles of all components}}$

Given, mass of benzene = 30 g

So, moles of benzene $= \dfrac{30}{78} = 0.385$

(∵ Molecular mass of $C_6H_6 = 78$)

Mass of CCl_4 = 70 g

Moles of $CCl_4 = \dfrac{70}{154} = 0.454$

(∵ Molecular mass of $CCl_4 = 154$)

∴ Mole fraction of benzene

$\chi_{C_6H_6} = \dfrac{0.385}{0.385 + 0.454} = 0.459$

16 (*d*) K_2SO_4 is 17.4 ppm i.e. 10^6 g has 17.4 g K_2SO_4.

1 L (10^3 mL) has K_2SO_4

$= 17.4 \times 10^3 / 10^6 = 0.0174$ g/L

⇒ $\dfrac{0.0174}{174}$ mol/L

∴ $[K_2SO_4] = 1 \times 10^{-4}$ M

$K_2SO_4 \rightleftharpoons 2K^+ + SO_4^{2-}$

∴ $[K^+] = 2 \times 10^{-4}$ M

17 (*b*) When 0.1 N NaOH is used,

$N_1V_1 = N_2V_2$
(For HCl) (For NaOH)

$0.2\ N \times V_1 = 50 \times 0.1\ N$

$V_1 = \dfrac{50 \times 0.1}{0.2} = 25\ cm^3$

When 0.5 N KOH is used,

$N_1V_1 = N_3V_3$
(For remaining HCl) (For KOH)

$0.2\ N \times 25 = 0.5\ N \times V_3$

$V_3 = \dfrac{0.2 \times 25}{0.5} = 10\ cm^3$

18 (*a*) Molarity

$=$ normality $\times \dfrac{\text{equivalent weight}}{\text{molecular weight}}$

Given, normality of Na_2CO_3 solution = 0.2 N

Equivalent weight = *M*

Molecular weight = 2*M*

(∵ Na_2CO_3 is dipositive)

∴ Molarity $= 0.2 \times \dfrac{M}{2M} = 0.1$ M

19 (*a*) $w = \dfrac{ENV}{1000}$

where, *E* = equivalent weight

N = normality

V = volume

⇒ $N = \dfrac{1.575 \times 1000}{63 \times 250}$

$\left[∵ E \text{ of } H_2C_2O_4 \cdot 2H_2O = \dfrac{126}{2} = 63\right]$

$= 0.1$ N

$H_2C_2O_4 \cdot 2H_2O$ is a dihydrate organic acid, since it contains 2 molecules of water of crystallisation.

Hence, both (A) and (R) are correct and R is the correct explaration of A.

20 (*b*) Molarity

$= \dfrac{\text{number of moles of solute}}{\text{volume of solution}}$

$= \dfrac{5 \times 1000}{40 \times 250} = 0.5$ M

$\left[∵ \text{Moles of NaOH} = \dfrac{5}{40}\right]$

21 (*a*) 1.25 molal NaOH solution means, 1.25 moles of NaOH are present in 1000 g of water

Weight of NaOH $= 1.25 \times 40 = 50$ g

Weight of solution

∴ $= 1000 + 50 = 1050$ g

∵ Molecular weight of NaOH = 40

% (by weight) of NaOH

$= \dfrac{\text{weight of solute}}{\text{weight of solution}} \times 100$

$= 50/1050 \times 100 = 4.76\%$

22 (*a*) $w = ENV/1000$

∴ Equivalent weight of acid $= \dfrac{w \times 1000}{NV}$

$= \dfrac{0.126 \times 1000}{0.1 \times 20} = 63$ g eq^{-1}

23 (*b*) Strength of resulting mixture,

$N = \dfrac{N_1V_1 + N_2V_2 + N_3V_3}{V_1 + V_2 + V_3}$

$= \dfrac{60 \times \dfrac{N}{5} + 10 \times \dfrac{N}{2} + 30 \times \dfrac{N}{10}}{60 + 10 + 30}$

$= 0.2$ N

24 (*c*) Number of moles of solute

$= \dfrac{25}{250} = 0.1$ mol

Molarity $= \dfrac{\text{number of moles of solute}}{\text{volume of solution (in L)}}$

$= \dfrac{0.1}{100/1000} = 1$ M

Molality $= \dfrac{\text{number of moles of solute}}{\text{mass of solvent in kg}}$

$$\text{Mass} = d \times V$$
$$= 1.25 \times 100 = 125 \text{ g}$$
$$\text{Molality} = \frac{0.1}{125/1000} = 0.8 \text{ m}$$

25 (*b*) $M_1V_1 + M_2V_2 = M_3V_3$
(Initial) (Final)
$$V_3 = V_1 + V_2 = 800 + 200 = 1000$$
$$M_3 \times 1000 = 0.5 \times 800 + 1 \times 200$$
$$M_3 = \frac{600}{1000} = 0.6 \text{ M}$$

26 (*a*) Molality
$$= \frac{\text{number of moles of solute}}{\text{weight of solvent (in kg)}}$$
If number of moles of solute = 1
Weight of solvent = 1 kg
Then, molality = 1, i.e. one molal
For glucose ($C_6H_{12}O_6$),
Molecular weight = 180
Number of moles = 180 / 180 = 1
Weight of water = 1kg
Hence, molality of the solution is one.

27 (*a*) Molarity gets affected with temperature as it is the number of moles per unit volume (volume increases with increase of temperature).

28 (*a*) 1 M H_2SO_4 means 1 mole H_2SO_4 present in 1000 cc of solution whereas 1 m means 1 mole H_2SO_4 present in 1000 g of water (= 1000 cc of water). Total volume of 1 m solution will be > 1000 cc due to extra 1 mole H_2SO_4. Hence, number of moles in 1M H_2SO_4 solution is more than the number of moles in 1m H_2SO_4 solution. Thus, 1 M is more concentrated than 1 m.
∴ Option (a) is correct.

29 (*a*) Equivalent weight of oxalic acid
$$= \frac{126}{2} = 63, \ (C_2O_4H_2 \cdot H_2O = 126)$$
(∵ Basicity of oxalic acid = 2)
$$\because \quad w = \frac{NEV}{1000}$$
$$\therefore \quad N = \frac{w \times 1000}{E \times V} = \frac{6.3 \times 1000}{63 \times 250} = 0.4 \text{ N}$$
$$\because N_1V_1 = N_2V_2$$
(Acid) (Base)
$$\therefore \ 0.4 \times 10 = 0.1 \times V_2 = V_2 = 40 \text{ mL}$$

30 (*c*) $N_1V_1 = N_2V_2$
(For monobasic acid) (For NaOH)
$$10 \times 0.1 \text{ N} = 15 \times N_2$$
$$N_2 = 1 \text{ N}/15 = 0.066 \text{ N}$$

31 (*a*) $N_1V_1 = N_2V_2$,
$$0.5 \times 100 = 0.1 \times V_2, \ V_2 = 500 \text{ cm}^3$$
∴Water to be added to 100 cm^3 solution
$$= 500 - 100 = 400 \text{ cm}^3$$

32 (*d*) Normality
$$= \frac{\text{weight \% } \times \text{density} \times 10}{\text{eq. wt.}}$$
$$= \frac{98 \times 1.8 \times 10}{49} = 36 \text{ N}$$
$$\because \quad N_1V_1 = N_2V_2$$
$$\therefore \ 36 \times V = 0.2 \times 1000$$
$$V = \frac{0.2 \times 1000}{36} = 5.55 \text{ mL}$$

33 (*d*) 10% glucose solution = 10 g
= 10 / 180 mol in 100 cc i.e. 0.1 L
Hence, 1 mole of glucose will be present in
$$= \frac{0.1 \times 180}{10} = 1.8 \text{ L}$$

34 (*a*) Mole fraction
$$= \frac{\text{moles of water}}{\text{moles of water + moles of ethanol}}$$
$$= \frac{w/m}{w/m + W/M}$$
Molecular weight of $H_2O = 18$, molecular weight of $C_2H_5OH = 46$
Mole fraction of water
$$= \frac{18/18}{18/18 + 414/46} = \frac{1}{1+9} = \frac{1}{10} = 0.1$$

35 (*a*) Let V L of 10 N HCl be mixed with $(1-V)$ L of 4 N HCl to give 1L of 7N HCl as given below
$(V + 1 - V) = 1$ L of 7 N HCl.
$$N_1V_1 + N_2V_2 = NV$$
$$10V + 4(1-V) = 7 \times 1$$
$$10V + 4 - 4V = 7$$
$$\Rightarrow \quad 6V = 7 - 4$$
$$\Rightarrow \quad V = 3/6 = 0.50 \text{ L}$$
Volume of 10 N HCl = 0.50 L
Volume of 4 N HCl = 1 − 0.50 = 0.50 L

36 (*a*) Concentration in terms of g/mL is given as:
$$0.03 = \frac{\text{mass of AgNO}_3}{60}$$
Mass of $AgNO_3$ = 60 × 0.03 = 1.8 g

37 (*c*) $\text{ppm} = \dfrac{\text{weight of solute} \times 10^6}{\text{weight of solution}}$
$$= \frac{25 \times 10^{-3} \times 10^6}{5000} = 5 \text{ ppm}$$

38 (*b*) ∵ Strength = normality × eq. wt.
$$= 1.5 \times 17$$
$$= 25.5 \text{ gL}^{-1}$$
(∵ Equivalent weight of H_2O_2 = 17)
$$\underset{68 \text{ g}}{2H_2O_2} \longrightarrow 2H_2O + \underset{22400 \text{ mL}}{O_2}$$
∵ 68 g of H_2O_2 gives 22400 mL O_2 at STP
∴ 25.5 g of H_2O_2 gives
$$\frac{22400 \times 25.5}{68} = 8400 \text{ mL } O_2 \text{ at STP}$$
and 1 mL H_2O_2 solution will give
= 8.4 mL of O_2
∴ Volume strength of 1.5 N H_2O_2 solution = 8.4

39 (*a*) **For H_2SO_4,**
$$\because \quad N = M \times \text{basicity}$$
$$N = 1 \times 2 = 2\text{N}$$
For NaOH, $N = M \times \text{acidity}$
$$N = 1 \times 1 = 1 \text{ N}$$
Now from normality equation
$$(N_1V_1)\ H_2SO_4 = (N_2V_2)\ \text{NaOH}$$
$$2 \times V_1 = 1 \times 20$$
$$V_1 = \frac{20}{2} = 10 \text{ mL of } H_2SO_4$$

Topic 2

Henry's Law and Raoult's Law
(Ideal and Non-Ideal Solutions)

2019

1 Which of the following statements is correct regarding a solution of two compounds A and B exhibiting positive deviation from ideal behaviour? **[NEET (Odisha)]**

(a) Intermolecular attractive forces between A—A and B—B are stronger than those between A—B.
(b) $\Delta_{mix} H = 0$ at constant T and p
(c) $\Delta_{mix} V = 0$ at constant T and p
(d) Intermolecular attractive forces between A—A and B—B are equal to those between A—B.

2 For an ideal solution, the correct option is **[NEET]**

(a) $\Delta_{mix} V \neq 0$ at constant T and p
(b) $\Delta_{mix} H = 0$ at constant T and p
(c) $\Delta_{mix} G = 0$ at constant T and p
(d) $\Delta_{mix} S = 0$ at constant T and p

3 The mixture that forms maximum boiling azeotrope is **[NEET]**

(a) ethanol + water
(b) acetone + carbon disulphide
(c) heptane + octane
(d) water + nitric acid

4 Moles of $N_2 = 0.4$ and moles of $O_2 = 0.1$ find p_{N_2} (Partial pressure) = ? at atmospheric pressure **[JIPMER]**

(a) 0.2 atm (b) 0.8 atm (c) 0.6 atm (d) 0.4 atm

2017

5 **Assertion** (A) ΔH_{mixing} and ΔV_{mixing} for non-ideal solution with positive deviation is zero. **[AIIMS]**

Reason (R) A—B interaction is more than that between A—A and B—B components.

(a) Both Assertion and Reason are true and Reason is the correct explanation of Assertion.
(b) Both Assertion and Reason are true but Reason is not the correct explanation of Assertion
(c) Assertion is true but Reason is false.
(d) Both Assertion and Reason are false.

6 **Assertion** (A) Both vapour pressure and boiling point depends on surface area of the liquid. **[AIIMS]**

Reason (R) Higher the surface area, lower be the boiling point whereas higher will be the vapour pressure.

(a) Both Assertion and Reason are true and Reason is the correct explanation of Assertion.
(b) Both Assertion and Reason are true but Reason is not the correct explanation of Assertion.
(c) Assertion is true but Reason is false.
(d) Both Assertion and Reason are false.

2016

7 Which one of the following is incorrect for ideal solution? **[NEET]**

(a) $\Delta H_{mix} = 0$
(b) $\Delta U_{mix} = 0$
(c) $\Delta p = p_{obs} - p_{\text{calculated by Raoult's law}} = 0$
(d) $\Delta G_{mix} = 0$

8 Which of the following statements about the composition of the vapour over an ideal 1 : 1 molar mixture of benzene and toluene is correct? Asssume that the temperature is constant at 25°C.

(Given, vapour pressure data at 25°C, benzene = 12.8kPa, toluene = 3.85 kPa)

(a) The vapour will contain a higher percentage of toluene
(b) The vapour will contain equal amounts of benzene and toluene
(c) Not enough information is given to make a prediction
(d) The vapour will contain a higher percentage of benzene

2015

9 Which one is not equal to zero for an ideal solution? **[CBSE AIPMT]**

(a) ΔH_{mix}
(b) ΔS_{mix}
(c) ΔV_{mix}
(d) $\Delta p = p_{observed} - p_{\text{calculated by Raoult's law}}$

2012

10 p_A and p_B are the vapour pressure of pure liquid components A and B respectively of an ideal binary solution. If χ_A represents the mole fraction of component A, the total pressure of the solution will be **[CBSE AIPMT]**

(a) $p_A + \chi_A (p_B - p_A)$ (b) $p_A + \chi_A (p_A - p_B)$
(c) $p_B + \chi_A (p_B - p_A)$ (d) $p_B + \chi_A (p_A - p_B)$

11 Vapour pressure of chloroform ($CHCl_3$) and dichloro methane (CH_2Cl_2) at 25°C are 200 mm Hg and 41.5 mm Hg respectively. Vapour pressure of the solution obtained by mixing 25.5 g of $CHCl_3$ and 40 g of CH_2Cl_2 at the same temperature will be
(Molecular mass of $CHCl_3$ = 119.5 u and molecular mass of CH_2Cl_2 = 85 u) **[CBSE AIPMT]**

(a) 173.9 mm Hg (b) 615.0 mm Hg
(c) 347.9 mm Hg (d) 90.63 mm Hg

12 In which case Raoult's law is not applicable? **[AIIMS]**

(a) 1 M NaCl (b) 1 M urea
(c) 1 M glucose (d) 1 M sucrose

13 Which of the following will show a negative deviation from Raoult's law? **[WB JEE]**
(a) Acetone-benzene (b) Acetone-ethanol
(c) Benzene-methanol (d) Acetone-chloroform

2011

14 The system that forms maximum boiling azeotrope is **[Kerala CEE]**
(a) carbon disulphide - acetone
(b) benzene - toluene
(c) acetone - chloroform
(d) *n*-hexane - *n*-heptane
(e) ethanol - acetone

15 A solution of two liquids boil at a temperature more than the boiling point of either of them. Hence, the binary solution shows **[KCET]**
(a) negative deviation from Raoult's law
(b) positive deviation from Raoult's law
(c) no deviation from Raoult's law
(d) positive or negative deviation from Raoult's law depending upon the composition

16 Choose the correct statement. **[Guj CET]**
When concentration of a salt solution is increased
(a) boiling point increases while vapour pressure decreases
(b) boiling point decreases while vapour pressure increases
(c) Both freezing point and vapour pressure increases
(d) Both freezing point and vapour pressure decreases

17 Which one of the following gases has the lowest value of Henry's law constant? **[Kerala CEE]**
(a) N_2 (b) He (c) CO_2 (d) O_2

2010

18 An aqueous solution is 1.00 molal in KI. Which change will cause the vapour pressure of the solution to increase? **[CBSE AIPMT]**
(a) Addition of water (b) Addition of NaCl
(c) Addition of Na_2SO_4 (d) Addition of 1.00 molal KI

19 Ratio of loss in weight of solvent to gain in weight of $CaCl_2$ tube is **[MHT CET]**
(a) $\frac{p^\circ}{p}$ (b) $\frac{p}{p^\circ}$ (c) $\frac{p^\circ - p}{p^\circ}$ (d) $\frac{p - p^\circ}{p}$

20 Which of the following gas mixture ions is used by the divers inside the sea? **[RPMT]**
(a) $O_2 + He$ (b) $O_2 + Xe$ (c) $O_2 + Ar$ (d) $O_2 + N_2$

21 Which of the following is the expression of Raoult's law? (p = vapour pressure of pure solvent, p_s = vapour pressure of the solution) **[RPMT]**
(a) $\frac{p - p_s}{p} = \frac{n}{n + N}$ (b) $\frac{p_s - p}{p} = \frac{N}{N + n}$
(c) $\frac{p - p_s}{p_s} = \frac{N}{N - n}$ (d) $\frac{p_s - p}{p_s} = \frac{N - n}{N}$

22 The vapour pressure of pure solvent is 0.8 mm of Hg at a particular temperature. On addition of a non-volatile solute '*A*' the vapour pressure of solution becomes 0.6 mm of Hg. The mole fraction of component '*A*' is **[OJEE]**
(a) 0.25 (b) 0.75 (c) 0.5 (d) 0.35

23 The value of Henry's law constant for argon (Ar), carbon dioxide (CO_2), methane (CH_4) and formaldehyde (HCHO) are respectively 40.3 kbar, 1.67 kbar, 0.413 kbar and 1.83×10^{-5} kbar at 298 K. The correct order of their solubility is
(a) $Ar < CH_4 < CO_2 < HCHO$
(b) $HCHO < CH_4 < CO_2 < Ar$
(c) $Ar < CO_2 < CH_4 < HCHO$
(d) $Ar < CO_2 < HCHO < CH_4$

24 At a constant temperature, which of the following aqueous solutions will have the maximum vapour pressure? (Molecular weight NaCl = 58.5, $H_2SO_4 = 98.0$ g mol^{-1}) **[Guj CET]**
(a) 1 molal NaCl (*aq*) (b) 1 molar NaCl (*aq*)
(c) 1 molal H_2SO_4 (*aq*) (d) 1 molar H_2SO_4 (*aq*)

2009

25 Which of the following azeotropic solutions has the boiling point less than boiling point of the constituents *A* and *B*? **[AIIMS]**
(a) $CHCl_3$ and CH_3COCH_3
(b) CS_2 and CH_3COCH_3
(c) CH_3CH_2OH and CH_3COCH_3
(d) CH_3CHO and CS_2

26 Lowering of vapour pressure of an aqueous solution of a non-volatile, non-electrolyte 1 m aqueous solution at 100°C is **[Manipal]**
(a) 14.12 torr (b) 312 torr (c) 13.45 torr (d) 352 torr

27 At 300 K, the vapour pressure of an ideal solution containing 1 mole of liquid *A* and 2 moles of liquid *B* is 500 mm of Hg. The vapour pressure of the solution increases by 25 mm of Hg, if one more mole of *B* is added to the above ideal solution at 300 K. Then the vapour pressure of *A* in its pure state is **[Kerala CEE]**
(a) 300 mm of Hg (b) 400 mm of Hg
(c) 500 mm of Hg (d) 600 mm of Hg
(e) 200 mm of Hg

28 Henry's law constant of oxygen is 1.4×10^{-3} mol L^{-1}atm^{-1} at 298 K. How much of oxygen is dissolved in 100 mL at 298 K when the partial pressure of oxygen is 0.5 atm? **[Kerala CEE]**
(a) 1.4 g (b) 3.2 g (c) 22.4 mg (d) 2.24 mg
(e) 3.2 mg

29 At 300 K two pure liquids *A* and *B* have vapour pressures respectively 150 mm Hg and 100 mm Hg. In an equimolar liquid mixture of *A* and *B*, the mole fraction of *B* in the vapour mixture at this temperature is **[J&K CET]**
(a) 0.6 (b) 0.5 (c) 0.8 (d) 0.4

30 Vapour pressure of pure 'A' is 70 mm of Hg at 25°C. It forms an ideal solution with 'B' in which mole fraction of A is 0.8. If the vapour pressure of the solution is 84 mm of Hg at 25°C, the vapour pressure of pure 'B' at 25°C is **[KCET]**
(a) 56 mm (b) 70 mm
(c) 140 mm (d) 28 mm

2008

31 Which of the following liquid pairs shows a positive deviation from Raoult's law? **[Haryana PMT]**
(a) Water—nitric acid (b) Benzene—methanol
(c) Water—hydrochloric acid (d) Acetone—chloroform

2007

32 An aqueous solution of methanol in water has vapour pressure **[MP PMT]**
(a) equal to that of water (b) equal to that of methanol
(c) more than that of water (d) less than that of water

33 A solution containing components A and B follows Raoult's law if **[Punjab PMET]**
(a) $A—B$ attraction force is greater than $A—A$ and $B—B$
(b) $A—B$ attraction force is less than $A—A$ and $B—B$
(c) $A—B$ attraction force remains same as $A—A$ and $B—B$
(d) volume of solution is different from sum of volumes of solute and solvent

2006

34 At 25°C, the total pressure of an ideal solution obtained by mixing 3 moles of 'A' and 2 moles of 'B', is 184 torr. What is the vapour pressure (in torr) of pure 'B' at the same temperature? (Vapour pressure of pure 'A' at 25°C, is 200 torr). **[J&K CET]**
(a) 180 (b) 160 (c) 16 (d) 100

35 A non-ideal solution was prepared by mixing 30 mL chloroform and 50 mL acetone. The volume of mixture will be **[J&K CET]**
(a) > 80 mL (b) < 80 mL
(c) = 80 mL (d) ≥ 80 mL

2005

36 If two substances A and B have $p_A^\circ : p_B^\circ = 1:2$ and have mole fraction in solution 1 : 2 then mole fraction of A in vapours is **[DUMET]**
(a) 0.33 (b) 0.25
(c) 0.52 (d) 0.2

37 An azeotropic solution of the two liquids has boiling point lower than either of the two liquids when it :
(a) shows no deviation from Raoult's law
(b) shows a negative deviation from Raoult's law
(c) shows a positive deviation from Raoult's law
(d) is saturated

Answers

1 (a)	2 (b)	3 (d)	4 (b)	5 (d)	6 (d)	7 (d)	8 (d)	9 (b)	10 (d)
11 (d)	12 (a)	13 (d)	14 (c)	15 (a)	16 (a,d)	17 (c)	18 (a)	19 (c)	20 (a)
21 (a)	22 (a)	23 (a)	24 (a)	25 (b,c)	26 (c)	27 (a)	28 (d)	29 (d)	30 (c)
31 (b)	32 (c)	33 (c)	34 (b)	35 (b)	36 (d)	37 (c)			

Explanations

1 (*a*) Solution exhibits positive deviation from ideal behaviour if the intermolecular interactions, i.e. $A—B$ interactions are weaker than in pure components, i.e. between $A—A$ or $B—B$. Thus. option (a) is correct. The remaining options are valid only for ideal solutions.

2 (*b*) Ideal solutions are those which obey Raoult's law over all concentration ranges at a given temperature, e.g. benzene-toluene, *n*-hexane-*n*-heptane, etc. For an ideal solution,

$$\Delta V_{\text{mix}} = 0, \Delta H_{\text{mix}} = 0,$$
$$\Delta G_{\text{mix}} < 0, \Delta S_{\text{mix}} > 0.$$

Hence, option (b) is correct.

3 (*d*) The binary liquid mixtures having the same composition in liquid and vapour phase and boil at constant temperature are called azeotropic mixtures or azeotropes.
The solutions that show large negative deviation from Raoult's law forms maximum boiling azeotrope. For, e.g. nitric acid and water. The remaining option containing different mixtures forms minimum boiling azeotrope.

4 (*b*) According to Raoult's law, "at a given temperature, for a solution of volatile liquids, the partial vapour pressure of each component of the solution is directly proportional to its mole fraction present in solution.

According to Raoult's law,

$$p_A = X_A p_T = \frac{n_A}{n_A + n_B} p_T$$

where, p_A = partial pressure
p_T = total pressure
n_A and n_B = moles
Given, $n_{N_2} = 0.4$, $n_{O_2} = 0.1$, $p_T = 1$ atm

$$\therefore p_{N_2} = \frac{n_{N_2}}{n_{N_2} + n_{O_2}} p_T$$
$$= \frac{0.4}{0.4 + 0.1} \times 1\text{ atm} = \frac{0.4}{0.5} = 0.8\text{ atm}$$

5 (*d*) Both (A) and (R) are false as, in the positive deviation, ΔV and ΔH both increases because interaction between $A-B$ is less than that between $A-A$ and $B-B$ components.

6 (*d*) Both vapour pressure and boiling point are independent of surface area.

Vapour pressure is the pressure exerted by the vapours of the liquid on its own surface, when it is in equilibrium with its liquid at given temperature whereas boiling point is the temperature at which vapour pressure becomes equal to the external pressure (for a given liquid).

Hence, (A) and (R) both are false.

7 (*d*) For this problem, the following expression can be used:

$$\Delta G_{mix} = \Delta H_{mix} - T\Delta S_{mix} \quad ...(i)$$

For an ideal solution, $\Delta H_{mix} = 0$, $\Delta U_{mix} = 0, \Delta S_{mix} \neq 0$

Putting all these values in the expression (i)

$$\Delta G_{mix} = \Delta H_{mix} - T\Delta S_{mix}$$

$$\Delta G_{mix} = 0 - T\Delta S_{mix}$$

$$\therefore \quad \Delta G_{mix} \neq 0$$

Hence, option(d) is not correct.

Also, for an ideal solution Δp is equal to zero because ΔV_{mix} is zero.

8 (*d*) Component having higher vapour pressure will have higher percentage in vapour phase. Benzene has vapour pressure 12.8kPa which is greater than that of toluene 3.85 kPa.

Therefore, the vapour will contain a higher percentage of benzene.

Rest of the statements are not correct.

9 (*b*) For an ideal solution

(i) There will be no change in volume on mixing the two components, i.e. $\Delta V_{mixing} = 0$ and as a result $\Delta p = 0$.

(ii) There will be no change in enthalpies on mixing the two components, i.e. $\Delta H_{mixing} = 0$

(iii) $\Delta S_{mix} \neq 0$ for an ideal solution.

10 (*d*) Total pressure for an ideal binary solution, $p_T = p'_A + p'_B \quad ...(i)$

We know that, $p'_A = p_A \chi_A$

and $p'_B = p_B \chi_B$

Substituting the values of p'_A and p'_B in Eq. (i)

$$p_T = p_A \chi_A + p_B \chi_B$$

Also, $\chi_A + \chi_B = 1$

$$\Rightarrow \quad \chi_A = 1 - \chi_B \quad \text{or} \quad \chi_B = 1 - \chi_A$$

$$\therefore \quad p_T = p_A \chi_A + p_B (1 - \chi_A)$$

$$= p_A \chi_A + p_B - p_B \chi_A$$

$$p_T = p_B + \chi_A (p_A - p_B)$$

11 (*d*) Number of moles of $CHCl_3$,

$$n_A = \frac{w}{M} = \frac{25.5}{119.5} = 0.213$$

Number of moles of CH_2Cl_2,

$$n_B = \frac{40}{85} = 0.47$$

Mole fraction of $CHCl_3$,

$$\chi_A = \frac{n_A}{n_A + n_B} = \frac{0.213}{0.684} = 0.31$$

Mole fraction of CH_2Cl_2

$$\chi_B = 1 - x_A = 1 - 0.31 = 0.69$$

$$p_{total} = p_A \chi_A + p_B \chi_B$$

$$= 200 \times 0.31 + 41.5 \times 0.69$$

$$= 62 + 28.63 = 90.63 \text{ mm Hg}$$

12 (*a*) Raoult's law is not applicable, if the total number of particles of solute changes in the solution due to association or dissociation. Among the given compounds, NaCl undergoes dissociation and forms Na^+ and Cl^- ions, thus Raoult's law is not applicable to NaCl.

13 (*d*) When the intermolecular interaction between the components are greater than the pure components, then the solution shows negative deviation

$$\underset{\text{Acetone}}{CH_3-\overset{\overset{O}{\|}}{C}-CH_3} \qquad \underset{\text{Chloroform}}{CHCl_3}$$

Acetone and chloroform will show a negative deviation due to their association after mixing.

14 (c) Solution which show negative deviation from Raoult's law are also called maximum boiling azeotrope. Carbon disulphide-acetone and ethanol-acetone show positive deviation.

Benzene, toluene and *n*-heptane-*n*-hexane are nearly ideal solutions. Acetone and chloroform shows negative deviation. Hence, acetone-chloroform forms maximum boiling azeotrope.

15 (*a*) A solution of two liquids boil at a temperature more than the boiling point of either of them. It indicates that the vapour pressure of the solution is lower than that of either of two liquids. Hence, the solution shows negative deviation from Raoult's law.

16 (*d*) The vapour pressure of the solution is lower than that of the pure solvent. When concentration of a salt solution increases, vapour pressure decreases, boiling point increases and freezing point decreases.

17 (c) The values of Henry's law constant are 76.48, 144.97, 34.86 for N_2, He and O_2 at 293 K respectively. For CO_2, it is 1.67.

18 (*a*) With the addition of water, concentration decreases thus vapour pressure increases.

19 (*c*) $\because$ Loss in the weight of solvent $= p^\circ - p$

and gain in the weight of $CaCl_2$ tube $= p^\circ$

$$= \frac{\text{loss in the weight of solvent}}{\text{gain in the weight of } CaCl_2 \text{ tube}}$$

$$= \frac{p^\circ - p}{p^\circ}$$

20 (*a*) Helium-oxygen mixture is used by deep sea divers because of its very low solubility in blood.

21 (*a*) According to Raoult's law, for non-volatile solute the relative lowering of vapour pressure of a solution is equal to the mole fraction of the solute.

$$\frac{p - p_s}{p} = \frac{n}{n + N}$$

22 (*a*) $\dfrac{p^\circ - p_s}{p^\circ} = \chi_{solute}$

$$\Rightarrow \quad \frac{0.8 - 0.6}{0.8} = \chi_{solute} = 0.25$$

23 (*a*) Higher the value of Henry's law constant, lower is the solubility of gas in water (or in liquid solvent)

The order of K_H value is :

Ar		CO_2		CH_4		HCHO
40.3	>	1.67	>	0.413	>	1.83×10^{-5}

Thus, order of solubility is

$$Ar < CO_2 < CH_4 < HCHO$$

24 (*a*) One molar (1 M) aqueous solution is more concentrated than one molal aqueous solution of the same solute. In solution, H_2SO_4 provides three ions, while NaCl provides two ions.

Hence, vapour pressure of solution of NaCl is higher (as it gives less ions). Therefore, 1 molal NaCl will have the maximum vapour pressure.

25 (*b,c*) When the intermolecular interaction is weaker than those in the pure constituents, the boiling point of the resultant solution is less than that of the constituents. Such condition is found in case of non-ideal solution showing positive deviation from Raoult's law.

Among the given, solution of CH_3CH_2OH and CH_3COCH_3 and solution of CS_2 and CH_3COCH_3 are non-ideal and show positive deviation. Hence, they have lesser boiling point or higher vapour pressure.

26 (*c*) $p^\circ = 760$ torr,

1 m aqueous solution contains 1 mole of solute in 1000 g (55.5 mol) of water.

$$\chi_B = \frac{1}{1 + 55.5} = \frac{1}{56.5}$$

$$\frac{\Delta p}{p^\circ} = \chi_B, \Delta p = p^\circ \chi_B$$

$$= \frac{760 \times 1}{56.5} = 13.45 \text{ torr}$$

27 (*a*) $p_t = p_A\chi_A + p_B\chi_B$

In Ist case, $500 = \frac{1}{3} p_A + \frac{2}{3} p_B$

or $1500 = p_A + 2p_B$ ...(i)

In IInd case, (when one more mole of B is added)

$$500 + 25 = \frac{1}{4} p_A + \frac{3}{4} p_B$$

$$2100 = p_A + 3p_B \quad \text{...(ii)}$$

From Eqs. (i) and (ii)

$$p_B = 600 \text{ mm of Hg}$$

and $p_A = 300$ mm of Hg

28 (*d*) $C = K_H \cdot p, C = 1.4 \times 10^{-3} \times 0.5$

$= 7 \times 10^{-4}$ mol / L

∴ Number of moles of oxygen dissolved in 1000 mL $= 7 \times 10^{-4}$

∴ Number of moles of oxygen dissolved in 100 mL

$$= \frac{7 \times 10^{-4} \times 100}{1000} = 7 \times 10^{-5}$$

∴ Weight of oxygen in 100 mL

$= 7 \times 10^{-5} \times 32$

$= 2.24 \times 10^{-3}$ g $= 2.24$ mg

29 (*d*) In equimolar liquid mixture

$X_A = 0.5$, $X_B = 0.5$

So, $p = 0.5 \times 150 + 0.5 \times 100$

$= 125$ mmHg

Now, let Y_B be the mole fraction of vapour B then

$$Y_B = \frac{X_B p_B^\circ}{p} = \frac{0.5 \times 100}{125} = 0.4$$

30 (*c*) Given, $p_A^\circ = 70$ mm

∵ $\chi_A = 0.8$

∴ $\chi_B = 0.2$ and $p = 84$ mm

According to Raoult's law,

$$p = p_A^\circ\chi_A + p_B^\circ\chi_B$$

$$84 = 0.8 \times 70 + 0.2 \times p_B^\circ$$

$$p_B^\circ = \frac{28}{0.2} = 140 \text{ mm}$$

31 (*b*) Benzene-methanol attraction are smaller than the average of benzene-benzene and methanol-methanol attraction. So, benzene-methanol liquid pair shows a positive deviation from Raoult's law, whereas water-nitric acid, water-hydrochloric acid and acetone-chloroform shows negative deviation.

32 (*c*) Methanol is a volatile substance, therefore aqueous solution of methanol in water has more vapour pressure than that of water.

33 (*c*) Raoult's law is valid for ideal solution only. In these solutions two components A and B follows the condition of Raoult's law, if the force of attraction between A and B is equal to the force of attraction between A—A and B—B.

34 (*b*) $p = p_A^\circ\left(\frac{n_A}{n_A + n_B}\right) + p_B^\circ\left(\frac{n_B}{n_A + n_B}\right)$

$$184 = 200\left(\frac{3}{3+2}\right) + p_B^\circ\left(\frac{2}{3+2}\right)$$

$$184 = 200 \times \frac{3}{5} + p_B^\circ \times \frac{2}{5}$$

$$184 = 120 + p_B^\circ \frac{2}{5}, \; 64 = p_B^\circ \frac{2}{5}$$

$$p_B^\circ = \frac{64 \times 5}{2} = 160 \text{ torr}$$

35 (*b*) Chloroform and acetone form a non-ideal solution in which $A-B$ type interaction are more than $A-A$ and $B-B$ type interaction due to H-bonding. Hence, the solution shows negative deviation from Raoult's law, i.e. $\Delta V_{mix} = -$ ve; $\Delta H_{mix} = -$ ve

∴ Total volume of solution = less than (30+ 50 mL) or < 80 mL

36 (*d*) Mole fraction of component 'A' in vapour phase

$$= \frac{\text{partial pressure of '}A\text{'}}{\text{total vapour pressure}} = \frac{p_A}{p_A + p_B}$$

but $p_A = p_A^\circ\chi_A$ and $p_B = p_B^\circ\chi_B$

∴ Mole fraction of A in vapour phase.

$$= \frac{p_A^\circ\chi_A}{p_A^\circ\chi_A + p_B^\circ\chi_B}$$

Given, $p_A^\circ = 1, \chi_A = 1, p_B^\circ = 2, \chi_B = 2$

On substituting the values, we get

Mole fraction of component 'A' in apour phase

$$= \frac{1 \times 1}{1 \times 1 + 2 \times 2} = \frac{1}{1+4} = \frac{1}{5} = 0.2$$

37 (*c*) Azeotropes are constant boiling mixtures. Minimum boiling azeotropes are formed from non-ideal solutions showing large positive deviations and such solution have boiling point lower than either of their two components. Whereas, maximum boiling azeotropes are formed from non-ideal solutions showing large negative deviations and such solutions have boiling point higher than either of their two components.

Topic 3

Colligative Properties

2019

1 The vapour pressure of pure $CHCl_3$ and CH_2Cl_2 are 200 and 41.5 atm respectively. The weight of $CHCl_3$ and CH_2Cl_2 are respectively 11.9 g and 17 g. The vapour pressure of solution will be **[AIIMS]**

(a) 80.5 (b) 79.5 (c) 94.3 (d) 105.5

2 If boiling point of water is 100°C. How much gram of NaCl is added in 500 g of water to increase its boiling point by approx 1°C $(K_b)_{H_2O} = 0.52\,K \times kg/mole$. **[AIIMS]**

(a) 2.812 g (b) 28.12 g (c) 14.06 g (d) 7.03 g

2018

3 If osmotic pressure of 4% (*w/V*) solution of sucrose is same as 2% (*w/V*) solution of '*X*', then the molecular mass of *X* (g/mol) is **[JIPMER]**

(a) 171 (b) 205.2 (c) 570 (d) None of these

2017

4 If molality of the dilute solution is doubled, the value of molal depression constant (K_f) will be **[NEET]**

(a) doubled (b) halved (c) tripled (d) unchanged

2014

5 To observe an elevation of boiling point of 0.05°C, the amount of a solute (molecular weight = 100) to be added to 100 g of water $(K_b = 0.5)$ is **[WB JEE]**

(a) 2 g (b) 0.05 g (c) 1 g (d) 0.75 g

6 The unit of ebullioscopic constant is **[UK PMT]**

(a) $K\ kg\ mol^{-1}$ (b) $mol\ kg\ K^{-1}$
(c) $kg\ mol^{-1}\ K^{-1}$ (d) $K\ mol\ kg^{-1}$

2013

7 The colligative property is not represented by **[AIIMS]**

(a) elevation in boiling point
(b) osmotic pressure
(c) optical activity
(d) relative lowering of vapour pressure

8 Which one of the following statements given below concerning properties of solution, describes a colligative effect? **[AIIMS]**

(a) Boiling point of pure water decreases by the addition of ethanol
(b) Vapour pressure of pure water decreases by the addition of nitric acid
(c) Vapour pressure of pure benzene decreases by the addition of naphthalene
(d) Boiling point of pure benzene increases by the addition of toluene

2012

9 The vapour pressure lowering caused by the addition of 100 g of sucrose (molecular mass = 342) to 1000 g of water, if the vapour pressure of water at 25°C is 23.8 mm Hg is **[AFMC]**

(a) 0.12 mm Hg (b) 0.125 mm Hg
(c) 1.15 mm Hg (d) 1.25 mm Hg

10 A solution has higher osmotic pressure than its standard solution. Which of the following term will be used for this solution? **[OJEE]**

(a) Isotonic (b) Hypertonic
(c) Dilute (d) Hypotonic

11 The mass of non-volatile solute of molar mass 40 g/mol that should be dissolved in 114 g of octane to lower its vapour pressure by 20% is **[KCET]**

(a) 11.4 g (b) 9.8 g (c) 12.8 g (d) 10 g

2011

12 The empirical formula of a non-electrolyte is CH_2O. A solution containing 3 g of the compound exerts the same osmotic pressure as that of 0.05 M glucose solution. The molecular formula of the compound is **[KCET]**

(a) CH_2O (b) $C_2H_4O_2$ (c) $C_4H_8O_4$ (d) $C_3H_6O_3$

2010

13 A solution of sucrose (molar mass = $342\,g\,mol^{-1}$) has been prepared by dissolving 68.5 g of sucrose in 1000 g of water. The freezing point of the solution obtained will be ((K_f for water = $1.86\,K\,Kg\,mol^{-1}$) **[AFMC]**

(a) −0.570° C (b) −0.372° C
(c) −0.520° C (d) + 0.372° C

14 Dissolution of 1.5 g of a non-volatile solute (molecular weight = 60) in 250 g of a solvent reduces its freezing point by 0.01°C. Find the molal depression constant of the solvent. **[MHT CET]**

(a) 0.01 (b) 0.001 (c) 0.0001 (d) 0.1

15 If the elevation in boiling point of a solution of 10 g of solute (molecular weight = 100) in 100 g of water is ΔT_b, the ebullioscopic constant of water is **[Manipal]**

(a) 10 (b) $100T_b$ (c) ΔT_b (d) $\frac{\Delta T_b}{10}$

16 What happens to freezing point of benzene when naphthalene is added? **[OJEE]**

(a) Increases
(b) Decreases
(c) Remains unchanged
(d) First decreases and then increases

17 What happens when an egg is kept in saturated solution of NaCl after removing its hard shell in dilute HCl? **[RPMT]**
(a) Egg will swell (b) Egg will shrink
(c) Egg will remain same
(d) Egg will first shrink and then swell

18 The boiling point of water is 100°C. What will be the boiling point of an aqueous solution containing 0.6 g of urea (molar mass = 60) in 100 g of water?
(k_b for water $= 0.52$ K / m) **[RPMT]**
(a) 100.052°C (b) 101.052°C
(c) 120.52°C (d) None of these

19 Isotonic solutions are the solutions having the same
(a) surface tension (b) vapour pressure **[RPMT]**
(c) osmotic pressure (d) viscosity

20 0.1 M NaCl and 0.05 M $BaCl_2$ solutions are separated by a semipermeable membrane in a container. For this system, choose the correct answer. **[AMU]**
(a) There is no movement of any solution across the membrane
(b) Water flows from $BaCl_2$ solution towards NaCl solution
(c) Water flows from NaCl solution towards $BaCl_2$ solution
(d) Osmotic pressure of 0.1 M NaCl is lower than the osmotic pressure of 0.05M $BaCl_2$ (assume complete dissociation)

21 The osmotic pressure is expressed in the unit of **[VMMC]**
(a) MeV (b) calorie
(c) cm/s (d) atm

22 The relative lowering of vapour pressure is equal to the ratio between the number of **[BVP]**
(a) solute molecules to the solvent molecules
(b) solute molecules to the total molecules in the solution
(c) solvent molecules to the total molecules in the solution
(d) solvent molecules to the total number of ions of the solute

2009

23 The order of boiling points of four equimolar aqueous solutions is $C < B < A < D$. The correct order of their freezing points is **[AIIMS]**
(a) $D < C < B < A$ (b) $D > C < B < A$
(c) $D < B > A < C$ (d) $D > A > B > C$

24 The concentration (in mol/L) of the solution having osmotic pressure 0.0821 atm at 300 K will be **[AFMC]**
(a) 0.33 (b) 0.066
(c) 0.3×10^{-2} (d) 3

25 20 g of a non-volatile solute is added to 500 g of solvent. Freezing point of solvent = 5.48° C and solution = 4.47°C, $k_f = 1.93$° C / m. Molecular mass of the solute is **[OJEE]**
(a) 77.2 (b) 76.4
(c) 73.2 (d) 70.6

26 During the depression of freezing point experiment an equilibrium is established between the molecules of **[EAMCET, CG PMT, Haryana PMT]**
(a) liquid solvent and solid solvent
(b) liquid solute and solid solvent
(c) liquid solute and solid solute
(d) liquid solvent and solid solute

27 A 6% solution of urea is isotonic with **[KCET]**
(a) 0.05 M solution of glucose
(b) 6% solution of glucose
(c) 25% solution of glucose
(d) 1 M solution of glucose

2008

28 The vapour pressure of benzene at a certain temperature is 640 mm of Hg. A non-volatile and non-electrolyte solid weighing 2.175 g is added to 39.08 g of benzene. If the vapour pressure of the solution is 600 mm of Hg. What is the molecular weight of solid substance? **[MHT CET]**
(a) 49.50 (b) 59.60 (c) 69.60 (d) 79.89

29 The temperature at which 10% aqueous solution (w/V) of glucose will exhibit the osmotic pressure of 16.4 atm, is ($R = 0.082$ dm^3 atm K^{-1} mol^{-1}) **[Kerala CEE]**
(a) 360° (b) 180 K (c) 90 K
(d) 300 K (e) 360 K

30 A solution containing 4 g of polyvinyl chloride polymer in 1 L of dioxane was found to have an osmotic pressure of 4.1×10^{-4} atm at 27°C. The approximate molecular weight of the polymer is **[J&K CET]**
(a) 1500 (b) 10000 (c) 2.4×10^5 (d) 2×10^{12}

31 Which of the following can be measured by the Ostwald-Walker dynamic method? **[KCET]**
(a) Relative lowering of vapour pressure
(b) Lowering of vapour pressure
(c) Vapour pressure of the solvent
(d) All of the above

2007

32 A solution contains non-volatile solute of molecular mass M_2. Which of the following formulae can be used to calculate the molecular mass of solute in terms of osmotic pressure? **[Punjab PMET]**
(a) $M_2 = \left[\frac{m_2}{\pi}\right] VRT$ (b) $M_2 = \left[\frac{m_2}{V}\right]\frac{RT}{\pi}$
(c) $M_2 = \left[\frac{m_2}{V}\right]\pi RT$ (d) $M_2 = \left[\frac{m_2}{V}\right]\frac{\pi}{RT}$

33 A 5% solution (by mass) of cane sugar in water has freezing point of 271 K and freezing point of pure water is 273.15 k. The freezing point of a 5% solution (by mass) of glucose in water is **[AIPMT]**
(a) 271 K (b) 269.0 K (c) 273.15 K (d) 272.23 K

2006

34 A solution containing 10 g per dm^3 of urea (molecular mass = 60 g mol^{-1}) is isotonic with a 5% solution of a non-volatile solute. The molecular mass of this non-volatile solute is **[CBSE AIPMT]**

(a) 250 g mol^{-1} (b) 300 g mol^{-1}
(c) 350 g mol^{-1} (d) 200 g mol^{-1}

35 Assertion (A) If red blood cells were removed from the body and placed in pure water, pressure inside the cells increases.

Reason (R) The concentration of salt content in the cells increases. **[AIIMS]**

(a) Both A and R are correct and R is the correct explanation of A
(b) Both A and R are correct, but R is not the correct explanation of A
(c) A is correct but R is incorrect
(d) Both A and R are incorrect

36 Assertion (A) The water pouch of instant cold pack for treating athletic injuries breaks when squeezed and NH_4NO_3 dissolves lowering the temperature.

Reason (R) Addition of non-volatile solute into solvent results into depression of freezing point of the solvent.

(a) Both A and R are correct and R is the correct explanation of A **[AIIMS]**
(b) Both A and R are correct, but R is not the correct explanation of A
(c) A is correct but R is incorrect
(d) Both A and R are incorrect

37 Which of the following colligative properties can provide molar mass of proteins (or polymers or colloids) with greater precision? **[BHU]**

(a) Relative lowering of vapour pressure
(b) Elevation in boiling point
(c) Depression in freezing point
(d) Osmotic pressure

38 The freezing point of 1% solution of lead nitrate in water will be **[Manipal]**

(a) 2°C (b) 1°C (c) 0°C (d) below 0°C

39 The mass of glucose that should be dissolved in 50 g of water in order to produce the same lowering of vapour pressure as is produced by dissolving 1 g of urea in the same quantity of water is **[KCET]**

(a) 1 g (b) 3 g
(c) 6 g (d) 18 g

2005

40 A solution of urea (molecular mass 56 g mol^{-1}) boils at 100.18°C at the atmospheric pressure. If K_f and K_b for water are 1.86 and 0.512 K kg mol^{-1} respectively. The above solution will freeze at **[CBSE AIPMT]**

(a) – 6.54°C (b) 6.54°C
(c) 0.654°C (d) – 0.654°C

41 Assertion (A) The molecular weight of acetic acid determined by depression in freezing point method in benzene and water was found to be different.

Reason (R) Water is polar and benzene is non-polar.

(a) Both A and R are correct and R is the correct explanation of A **[AIIMS]**
(b) Both A and R are correct but R is not the correct explanation of A
(c) A is correct but R is incorrect
(d) Both A and R are incorrect

42 Relative lowering of vapour pressure of a dilute solution is 0.2. What is the mole fraction of the non-volatile solute ? **[Kerala CEE]**

(a) 0.8 (b) 0.5
(c) 0.3 (d) 0.2

43 Latent heat of vaporisation of water is 9.72 kcal mol^{-1} at 373.15 K. Calculate molal boiling point elevation constant of water. **[Kerala CEE]**

(a) 5.2° (b) 0.052°
(c) 52.2° (d) 0.52°
(e) None of these

44 If at certain temperature, the vapour pressure of pure water is 25 mm Hg and that of a very dilute aqueous urea solution is 24.5 mm Hg, the molality of solution is **[Kerala CEE]**

(a) 0.02 (b) 1.2
(c) 1.11 (d) 0.08
(e) 0.06

Answers

1 (c)	2 (b)	3 (a)	4 (d)	5 (c)	6 (a)	7 (c)	8 (c)	9 (b)	10 (b)
11 (d)	12 (b)	13 (b)	14 (d)	15 (c)	16 (b)	17 (b)	18 (a)	19 (c)	20 (b)
21 (d)	22 (b)	23 (c)	24 (c)	25 (b)	26 (a)	27 (d)	28 (c)	29 (e)	30 (c)
31 (d)	32 (b)	33 (b)	34 (b)	35 (c)	36 (a)	37 (d)	38 (d)	39 (b)	40 (d)
41 (a)	42 (d)	43 (d)	44 (c)						

Explanations

1 (c) Given,

Vapour pressure of pure $CHCl_3[p_1]$ and $CH_2Cl_2[p_2]$ = 200 atm and 41.5 atm respectively. Weight (w_1) of $CHCl_3$ and $CH_2Cl_2(w_2)$ = 11.9 g and 17g respectively. Molar mass of $CHCl_3(M_1)$ and $CH_2Cl_2(M_2) = 119\ g\ mol^{-1}$ and $85\ g\ mol^{-1}$ respectively. Thus, number of moles (n) of $CHCl_3 = \frac{11.9}{119} = 0.1$ mol

Number of moles of

$$CH_2Cl_2 = \frac{17}{85} = 0.2\ \text{mol}$$

As we know, $p_{total} = p_1\chi_1 + p_2\chi_2$

$$\chi_1 = \frac{n_1}{n_T} = \frac{0.1}{0.3} = 0.33$$

$$\chi_2 = \frac{n_2}{n_T} = \frac{0.2}{0.3} = 0.66$$

$$\therefore p_{Total} = 200 \times 0.33 + 41.5 \times 0.66 = 94.33$$

Hence, option (c) is the correct.

2 (b) For the solutes, which can undergo association or dissociation in a given solvent,

Elevation in boiling point

$$(\Delta T_b) = iK_b \times m,$$

where, K_b = molal elevation constant

m = molality, i = van't Hoff factor

Given,

$\Delta T_b = 1°\ C$ and M (NaCl) = 58.5

$K_b(H_2O) = 0.52\ K\ kg\ mol^{-1}$

for NaCl = n = (2) and $w_{solvent}$ = 500 g

Thus,

$$\Delta T_b = i \times K_b \times \frac{w(\text{solute})}{M(\text{solute})} \times \frac{1000}{w(\text{solvent})}$$

$$1° = 2 \times 0.52 \times \frac{w}{58.5} \times \frac{1000}{500}$$

$$w = \frac{58.5 \times 500}{2 \times 0.52 \times 1000} = 28.125\ g$$

Hence, option (b) is the correct.

3 (a) 4% solution of sucrose (w/v) means 4g of sucrose is dissolved in 40 mL of solution. Similarly, 2% (w/v) solution of 'X' means 2g of X present in 40 mL of solution.

As we know that, osmotic pressure

$$(\pi) = CRT \text{ or } \pi = \frac{n}{V}RT.$$

where, n = number of moles of solute.

Since, π_1 (for sucrose solution) = π_2 (for X solution)

$$\therefore \frac{n_1}{V_1}RT = \frac{n_2}{V_2}RT$$

$$\Rightarrow \frac{4}{342} = \frac{2}{\text{Molecular weight}}$$

$$\left[\because n = \frac{\text{Mass of solute}}{\text{Molar mass of solute}}\right]$$

$$\Rightarrow \text{Molecular weight} = \frac{2}{4} \times 342$$

Molecular weight = $171\ g\ mol^{-1}$

4 (d) For a dilute solution, the depression in freezing point (ΔT_f) is directly proportional to molality (m) of the solution.

$$\Delta T_f \propto m \text{ or } \Delta T_f = K_f m$$

where, K_f is called molal depression constant or freezing point depression constant or cryoscopic constant.

The value of K_f depends only on nature of the solvent and independent of composition of solute particles, i.e. does not depend on the concentration of solution.

5 (c) Elevation of boiling point,

$$\Delta T_b = \frac{w \times K_b \times 1000}{M \times W(\text{g})}$$

(Here, w and W = weights of solute and solvent respectively.)

M = molecular weight of solute and

K_b = Molar elevation constant.

On substituting values, we get

$$0.05 = \frac{w \times 0.5 \times 1000}{100 \times 100}$$

or $$w = \frac{0.05 \times 100 \times 100}{0.5 \times 1000} = 1\text{g}$$

6 (a) Ebullioscopic constant,

$$K_b = \frac{\Delta T_b}{\text{molality}}$$

Unit will be $K\ kg\ mol^{-1}$.

7 (c) Colligative properties are defined as properties of dilute solutions of non-volatile solutes whose values depend upon the concentration and number of solute particles in the solution but not on the individual identity of the solute. Various colligative properties are :

(i) Relative lowering of vapour pressure

(ii) Elevation in boiling point

(iii) Depression in freezing point

(iv) Osmotic pressure

So, optical activity is not a colligative property.

8 (c) The colligative properties are the properties of dilute solution of non-volatile solutes whose value depend on concentration of solute particles in the solution. Naphthalene is a non-volatile solid whereas, all other solutes are volatile. Hence, addition of naphthalene in benzene decreases the vapour pressure of benzene.

9 (a) Number of moles of $C_{12}H_{22}O_{11}$

$$= \frac{100}{342}$$

$$= 0.292\ \text{mol}$$

$$\text{Number of moles of } H_2O = \frac{1000}{18}$$

$$= 55.5\ \text{mol}$$

($\because$ Molecular mass of sucrose = 342),

(Molecular mass of H_2O = 18)

Vapour pressure of pure water

$$p° = 23.8\ \text{mm Hg}$$

According to Raoult's law, $\frac{\Delta p}{p°} = \frac{n}{n+N}$

$$\Rightarrow \frac{\Delta p}{23.8} = \frac{0.292}{0.292 + 55.5}$$

$$\Delta p = \frac{23.8 \times 0.292}{55.79} = 0.125\ \text{mm Hg}$$

10 (b) A solution having lower or higher osmotic pressure than the other is said to be hypotonic or hypertonic respectively.

11 (d) Given, $p° = 100$, $p = 100 - 20 = 80$, $M_2 = 40\ g\ mol^{-1}$,

M_1 (octane) = $C_8H_{18} = 12 \times 8 + 18 = 114$

$w_2 = ?$, w_1(octane) = 114 g

$$\frac{p° - p}{p} = \frac{w_2}{M_2} \times \frac{M_1}{w_1},$$

$$\frac{100 - 80}{80} = \frac{w_2}{40} \times \frac{114}{114}$$

or $$\frac{20}{80} = \frac{w_2}{40} = 10\text{g}$$

12 (b) For isotonic solution, $\pi_1 = \pi_2$

So, $$\frac{w_1}{m_1} = \frac{w_2}{m_2}$$

Mass of 0.05 M glucose

$$= 0.05 \times 180 = 9\ g$$

[$\because$ Molecular mass of glucose $(C_6H_{12}O_6)$ = 180]

$$\frac{3}{m_1} = \frac{9}{180} \Rightarrow m_1 = 60\ g$$

$n = \frac{\text{molecular weight}}{\text{empirical formula weight}} = \frac{60}{30} = 2$

The molecular formula of the compound $= (CH_2O)_2 = C_2H_4O_2$

13 (b) $\Delta T_f = \frac{1000 \times K_f \times w_2}{M_2 \times w_1}$

$= \frac{1000 \times 1.86 \times 68.5}{342 \times 1000} = 0.372°C$

$\therefore T_f = T_f^\circ - \Delta T_f$

$= 0 - 0.372 = -0.372°C$

14 (d) Depression in freezing point,

$\Delta T_f = K_f \times m$

where, m = molality

$= \frac{\text{weight of solute} \times 1000}{\text{molecular weight of solute} \times \text{weight of solvent}}$

$= \frac{1.5 \times 1000}{60 \times 250} = 0.1$

$\Delta T_f = K_f \times 0.1 \Rightarrow 0.01 = K_f \times 0.1$

$\therefore K_f = \frac{0.01}{0.1} = 0.1$

15 (c) $\Delta T_b = \frac{1000 \times K_b \times w}{W \times M}$

Where, K_b = molal boiling elevation constant

Given, $w = 10$ and $W = 100$ g

$\therefore \Delta T_b = \frac{1000 \times K_b \times 10}{100 \times 100}, \Delta T_b = K_b$

16 (b) Freezing point of a pure solvent decreases on addition of solute, as the vapour pressure of the solvent decreases in the presence of non-volatile solute.

17 (b) When an egg is kept in saturated solution after removing its hard shell in dil. HCl, egg will shrink. This is because osmosis occur from higher concentration of solvent to lower concentration of solvent.

18 (a) $\Delta T_b = \frac{K_b \times w_B \times 1000}{M_B \times w_A}$,

$K_b = 0.52 \text{ K m}^{-1}, w_B = 0.6$ g,

$M_b = 60, w_A = 100$ g

$\therefore \Delta T_b = \frac{0.52 \times 0.6 \times 1000}{60 \times 100}$

$= 0.052°C$

Thus, boiling point of the solution

$= 100 + 0.052 = 100.052°C$

19 (c) The solution having same osmotic pressure are called isotonic solution.

20 (b) The concentration of $BaCl_2$ solution is lower, thus solvent (water) moves from the $BaCl_2$ solution towards NaCl solution, when both the solutions are separated by a semipermeable membrane. Therefore, option (b) is correct.

21 (d) The osmotic pressure is expressed in the unit of atmosphere (atm).

22 (b) According to Raoult's law, relative lowering in vapour pressure is directly proportional to the mole fraction of solute, i.e. $\frac{p^\circ - p}{p^\circ} = \chi_s$

where,

$\chi_s = \frac{n_s}{n_s + N} = \frac{\text{moles of solute}}{\text{total number of moles}}$

$\therefore$ Relative lowering of vapour pressure

$= \frac{n_2}{n_1 + n_2} = \frac{\text{solute molecules}}{\text{total molecules in the solution}}$

23 (c) Elevation in boiling point and depression in freezing point, both are the colligative properties, i.e. depend only upon the number of particles. In other words, as the number of particles increases, boiling point increases while freezing point decreases. Since, the order of boiling point is

$C < B < A < D$

$\therefore$ The order of freezing point is

$D < A < B < C$ or $D < B > A < C$

24 (c) $\pi = CRT$

where, C = concentration,

π = osmotic pressure,

R = gas constant, T = temperature

$C = \frac{\pi}{RT} = \frac{0.0821}{0.0821 \times 300}$

$= 0.3 \times 10^{-2}$ mol / L

25 (b) $\Delta T_f = 5.48 - 4.47 = 1.01$,

$\Delta T_f = K_f \times m$

$\therefore 1.01 = 1.93 \times \frac{20}{M} \times \frac{1000}{500} \Rightarrow M = 76.4$

26 (a) Freezing point of a substance is the temperature at which the solid and the liquid forms of the substance are in equilibrium. When freezing starts, liquid solvent is in equilibrium with the solid solvent (and both have the same vapour pressure).

27. (d) When a solution of urea (6%) is isotonic with a solution of glucose

$\pi_{\text{glucose}} = \pi_{\text{urea}}, C_{\text{glucose}} = C_{\text{urea}}$

$\therefore \left(\frac{w_g \times 1000}{m_g \times 100}\right) = \left(\frac{w_u \times 1000}{m_u \times 100}\right)$

where, w_g = mass of glucose = x g

m_g = molecular mass of glucose = 180

w_u = mass of urea = 6 g

m_u = molecular mass of urea = 60

$\therefore \frac{x \times 1000}{180 \times 100} = \frac{6 \times 1000}{60 \times 100} \Rightarrow x = 18$ g

Thus, 18 g of glucose are present in 100 mL of solution. In other words, 1 M solution of glucose (18 g in 100 mL) is isotonic with 6% solution of urea.

28 (c) According to Raoult's law,

$\frac{p^\circ - p}{p^\circ} = \frac{w \times M}{m \times W}$

$\Rightarrow \frac{640 - 600}{640} = \frac{2.175 \times 78}{m \times 39.08}$

$\Rightarrow \frac{40}{640} = \frac{2.175 \times 78}{m \times 39.08}$

$\Rightarrow m = \frac{16 \times 2.175 \times 78}{39.08}$

$= 69.46 \approx 69.60$ g/mol

29 (e) $\pi = CRT = \frac{w \times R \times T}{m \times V}$

$16.4 = \frac{10 \times 1000}{180 \times 100} \times 0.082 \times T$

$\therefore T = \frac{16.4 \times 180}{0.082 \times 100} = 360$ K

30 (c) $\because \pi = CRT \Rightarrow \pi = \frac{n}{V}RT$

$\pi \times V = nRT$

$\Rightarrow \pi \times V = \frac{w}{m}RT \quad \left(\because n = \frac{w}{m}\right)$

$m = \frac{wRT}{\pi \times V}$

$= \frac{4 \times 0.0821 \times (27 + 273)}{4 \times 10^{-4} \times 1}$

$= 2.4 \times 10^5$ g

31 (d) By Ostwald-Walker dynamic method, the relative lowering of vapour pressure, lowering of vapour pressure and vapour pressure of the solvent, all can be measured. In this method, the apparatus used, contains two bulbs, bulb A contains solution and bulb B contains solvent. The loss of weight in bulb B gives the lowering of vapour pressure and total loss of weight in both the tubes gives the vapour pressure of the solvent and relative lowering of vapour pressure

$= \frac{\text{lowering of vapour pressure}}{\text{vapour pressure of solvent}}$

32 (*b*) For dilute solution, $pV = nRT$

or $\pi V = nRT$ or $\pi = \frac{n}{V}RT$

$$\pi V = \frac{m_2}{M_2}RT, M_2 = \frac{m_2 RT}{\pi V}$$

where, π = osmotic pressure
V = volume of solution
n = number of moles of solute
m_2 = mass of solute
M_2 = molecular mass of solute

33 (*b*) $\Delta T_f = K_f \times \frac{w}{m} \times \frac{1000}{W}$

$$\frac{\Delta T_{f_2}}{\Delta T_{f_1}} = \frac{m_1}{m_2}$$

where, ΔT_{f_1} = depression in freezing point of cane sugar.
ΔT_{f_2} = depression in freezing point of glucose.

Here, m_1(cane sugar $C_{12}H_{22}O_{11}$) = 342
m_2 (glucose $C_6H_{12}O_6$) = 180

$$\Delta T_{f_1} = 273.15 - 271 = 2.15 \text{ K}$$

$$\frac{\Delta T_{f_2}}{2.15} = \frac{342}{180}$$

$\Rightarrow \Delta T_{f_2} = 4.085$ K

So, freezing point of glucose in water
$= 273.15 - 4.085 = 269.0$ K

34 (*b*) Molar concentration of urea solution

$$= \frac{10 \text{ g / dm}^3}{\text{molecular weight of urea}}$$

$$= \frac{10}{60} \text{ M} = \frac{1}{6} \text{ M}$$

Molar concentration of 5% non-volatile solute

$$= \frac{50 \text{ g / dm}^3}{\text{molecular weight of non-volatile solute}}$$

$$= \frac{50}{m} \text{M}$$

Both solutions are isotonic to each other, therefore

$$\frac{1}{6} = \frac{50}{m}$$

or $m = 50 \times 6 = 300 \text{ g mol}^{-1}$

35 (*c*) When a solution is separated from the pure solvent by means of a semipermeable membrane, the pure solvent passes through the membrane and goes to solution and a hydrostatic pressure is set up which is called as the osmotic pressure of the solution.

So, when red blood cells are placed in pure water, the concentration of water is increased in the cell due to osmosis and the concentration of salt content would increase in the solution, or decrease in cell so, the assertion is true but reason is false.

36 (*a*) The water pouch of instant cold pack for treating athletic injuries breaks when squeezed and NH_4NO_3 dissolves lowering the temperature because addition of non-volatile solute into solvent results into depression of freezing point of the solvent.
Hence, A and R are correct and R is the correct explanation of A.

37 (*d*) Osmotic pressure method is especially suitable for the determination of molecular masses of macromolecules such as proteins and polymers because for these substances the value of other colligative properties such as elevation in boiling point or depression in freezing point are too small to be measured.

38 (*d*) Aqueous solution of any substance (non-volatile) freezes below 0°C because the vapour pressure of the solution becomes lower than that of pure solvent.

39 (*b*) $\frac{p° - p_s}{p°} = \frac{w_1 M_2}{w_2 M_1}$.

To produce same lowering of vapour pressure, $\frac{p° - p_s}{p°}$ will be same for both cases.

So, $\frac{w_{(\text{glucose})} \times 18}{50 \times 180} = \frac{w_{(\text{urea})} \times 18}{50 \times 60}$

[$w_{(\text{glucose})}$ = weight of glucose
$w_{(\text{urea})}$ = weight of urea]

or $\frac{w_{(\text{glucose})} \times 18}{50 \times 180} = \frac{1 \times 18}{50 \times 60}$

$$w_{(\text{glucose})} = 3\text{g}$$

40 (*d*) $\Delta T_f = K_f \times$ molality of solution
$\Delta T_b = K_b \times$ molality of solution

molality of solution or $\frac{\Delta T_f}{\Delta T_b} = \frac{K_f}{K_b}$

Given, $\Delta T_b = T_b - T_b°$
$= 100.18 - 100 = 0.18$
K_f for water = 1.86 K kg mol^{-1}
K_b for water = 0.512 K kg mol^{-1}

$\therefore \frac{\Delta T_f}{0.18} = \frac{1.86}{0.512}$

$\Rightarrow \Delta T_f = \frac{1.86 \times 0.18}{0.512}$
$= 0.6539 \sim 0.654$
$\Delta T_f = T_f° - T_f$
$\Rightarrow 0.654 = 0°\text{C} - T_2$
$\therefore T_f = -0.654°\text{C}$

($T_f \rightarrow$ Freezing point of aqueous urea solution)

41 (*a*) In benzene, acetic acid dimerises but in water it does not. This is because benzene is non-polar whereas water is polar. The number of particles become different in both the solvents.
Depression in freezing point is a colligative property, i.e. it depends upon the number of particles in solution. Hence, molecular mass determined by depression in freezing point method comes out to be different.

42 (*d*) According to Raoult's law, the relative lowering in vapour pressure of an ideal solution containing the non-volatile solute is equal to the mole fraction of the solute.
$\because$ Relative lowering of vapour pressure = 0.2
$\therefore$ Mole fraction of the solute = 0.2

43 (*d*) $K_b = \frac{RT_0^2}{1000 l_v}$

(where, l_v = latent heat of vaporisation per gram of the solvent)

$$= \frac{M_1 RT_0^2}{1000 \Delta_{\text{vap}} H}$$

(where, M_1 = molecular mass of solvent
$\Delta_{\text{vap}} H$ = latent heat of vaporisation per mole of the solvent)

$$K_b = \frac{18 \times 0.002 \times (375.15)^2}{1000 \times 9.72}$$

$$= 0.52°\text{C kg mol}^{-1}$$

44 (*c*) By using the relation, molality

$$= \frac{p° - p_s}{p°} \times \frac{1000}{M}$$

Molality (m) $= \frac{25 - 24.5}{24.5} \times \frac{1000}{18}$

$$= \frac{0.5}{24.5} \times \frac{1000}{18}$$

$$= 1.11$$

$\therefore$ Molality of solution = 1.13 m
Since, this value is close to 1.11.
Hence, option 'c' is correct.

Topic 4

Abnormal Molecular Masses and Distribution Law

2018

1 Benzoic acid undergoes dimerisation in benzene solution. The van't Hoff factor (i) is related to the degree of association 'x' of the acid as [NEET]

(a) $i=(1-x)$ (b) $i=(1+x)$

(c) $i=\left(1-\frac{x}{2}\right)$ (d) $i=\left(1+\frac{x}{2}\right)$

2017

2 Which of the following aqueous solution should have highest boiling point? [JIPMER]

(a) 1.0 M NaOH (b) 1.0 M Na_2SO_4

(c) 1.0 M NH_4NO_3 (d) 1.0 M KNO_3

2016

3 The boiling point of 0.2 mol kg^{-1} solution of X in water is greater than equimolal solution of Y in water. Which one of the following statements is true in this case? [NEET]

(a) X is undergoing dissociation in water.

(b) Molecular mass of X is greater than the molecular mass of Y.

(c) Molecular mass of X is less than the molecular mass of Y.

(d) Y is undergoing dissociation in water while X undergoes no change.

2015

4 Which one of the following electrolytes has the same value of van't Hoff's factor (i) as that of $Al_2(SO_4)_3$ (if all are 100% ionised)? [CBSE]

(a) K_2SO_4 (b) $K_3[Fe(CN)_6]$

(c) $Al(NO_3)_3$ (d) $K_4[Fe(CN)_6]$

2014

5 Of the following 0.10 m aqueous solutions, which one will exhibit the largest freezing point depression? [CBSE AIPMT]

(a) KCl (b) $C_6H_{12}O_6$ (c) $Al_2(SO_4)_3$ (d) K_2SO_4

6 If α is the degree of dissociation of Na_2SO_4 the van't Hoff factor (i) used for calculating the molecular mass is [UK PMT]

(a) $1+\alpha$ (b) $1-\alpha$

(c) $1+2\alpha$ (d) $1-2\alpha$

7 van't Hoff factor, (i), of a 0.5% (w/W) aqueous solution of KCl which freezes at $-0.24°C$ is (k_f of water = 1.86 K kg mol^{-1}, molecular weight of KCl = 74.5) [EAMCET]

(a) 1.52 (b) 2.32

(c) 1.92 (d) 1.32

8 A solution of 1.25 of 'P' in 50 g of water lowers freezing point by 0.3°C. Molar mass of 'P' is 94. $K_{f(\text{water})}=1.86$ K kg mol^{-1}. The degree of association of 'P' in water is [KCET]

(a) 80% (b) 60%

(c) 65% (d) 75%

9 Distribution law was given by [OJEE]

(a) Ostwald (b) Nernst

(c) Henry (d) vant't Hoff

2012

10 The freezing point of one molal NaCl assuming NaCl to be 100% dissociated in water is (molal depression constant is 1.86). [Manipal]

(a) $-2.72°C$ (b) $-3.72°C$

(c) $2.72°C$ (d) $3.72°C$

11 58.5 g of NaCl and 180 g of glucose were separately dissolved in 1000 mL of water. Identify the correct statement regarding the elevation of boiling point of the resulting solution. [WB JEE]

(a) NaCl solution will show higher elevation of boiling point

(b) Glucose solution will show higher elevation of boiling point

(c) Both the solution will show equal elevation of boiling point

(d) The boiling point elevation will be shown by neither of the solutions

2011

12 The freezing point depression constant for water is 1.86° K kg mol^{-1}. If 5.00 g Na_2SO_4 is dissolved in 45.0 g H_2O, the freezing point is changed by $-3.82°C$. Calculate the van't Hoff factor for Na_2SO_4 [CBSE AIPMT]

(a) 0.381

(b) 2.05

(c) 2.63

(d) 3.11

13 The van't Hoff factor (i) for a compound which undergoes dissociation in one solvent and association in other solvent is respectively [CBSE AIPMT]

(a) greater than one and greater than one

(b) less than one and greater than one

(c) less than one and less than one

(d) greater than one and less than one

14 Which one of the following statements is false? **[Kerala CEE]**

(a) Raoult's law states that the vapour pressure of a component over a binary solution of volatile liquids is directly proportional to its mole fraction
(b) Two sucrose solutions of the same molality prepared in different solvents will have the same depression of freezing point
(c) The correct order of osmotic pressures of 0.01 M solution of each compound is $BaCl_2 > KCl > CH_3COOH >$ glucose
(d) In the equation osmotic pressure $\pi = MRT$, M is the molarity of the solution
(e) The molecular weight of NaCl determined by colligative property measurement is less than its theoretical molecular weight

15 1×10^{-3} m solution of $Pt(NH_3)_4Cl_4$ in H_2O shows depression in freezing point by 0.0054°C. The structure of the compound will be (given K_{sp} (H_2O) = 1.860 km^{-1}) **[DUMET]**

(a) $[Pt(NH_3)_4]Cl_4$ (b) $[Pt(NH_3)_3Cl]Cl_3$
(c) $[Pt(NH_3)_2Cl_2]Cl_2$ (d) $[Pt(NH_3)Cl_3]Cl$

2010

16 Pure benzene freezes at 5.3°C. A solution of 0.223 g of phenylacetic acid ($C_6H_5CH_2COOH$) in 4.4 g of benzene (k_f = 5.12 K kg mol^-) freezes at 4.47°C. From the observation, one can conclude that **[AFMC]**

(a) phenylacetic acid exists as such in benzene
(b) phenylacetic acid undergoes partial ionisation in benzene
(c) phenylacetic acid undergoes complete ionisation in benzene
(d) phenylacetic acid dimerises in benzene

17 Four solutions of K_2SO_4 with the following concentration 0.1 m, 0.01 m, 0.001 m and 0.0001 m are available. The maximum value of van't Hoff factor, *i*, corresponds to **[AMU]**

(a) 0.0001 m solution
(b) 0.001 m solution
(c) 0.01 m solution
(d) 0.1 m solution

18 What is the freezing point of a solution containing 8.1 g HBr in 100 g water assuming the acid to be 90% ionised? (K_f for water = 1.86 K kg mol^{-1}) **[JCECE]**

(a) 0.85°C (b) –3.53°C
(c) 0°C (d) –0.35°C

19 The molal elevation constant of water is 0.52°cm^{-1}. The boiling point of 1.0 molal aqueous KCl solution (assuming complete dissociation of KCl), therefore, should be **[CMC]**

(a) 98.96°C (b) 100.52°C
(c) 101.04°C (d) 107.01°C

2009

20 A 0.0020 m aqueous solution of an ionic compound $[Co(NH_3)_5(NO_2)]Cl$ freezes at –0.00732°C. Number of moles of ions which one mole of ionic compound produces on being dissolved in water will be (K_f = 1.86° C / m) **[CBSE AIPMT]**

(a) 2 (b) 3
(c) 4 (d) 1

21 0.2 molal acid *HX* ionises 20%. K_f for acid is 1.86 molality. Freezing point is **[CG PMT, Haryana PMT]**

(a) –0.45 (b) –0.50
(c) – 0.31 (d) –0.53

22 The molar mass of the solute sodium hydroxide obtained from the measurement of the osmotic pressure of its aqueous solution at 27°C is 25 g mol^{-1}. Therefore, its ionisation percentage in this solution is **[J&K CET]**

(a) 75 (b) 60
(c) 80 (d) 70

23 Which of the following pair of solutions are expected to be isotonic at the same temperature? **[AMU]**

(a) 0.2 M urea and 0.2 M NaCl
(b) 0.1 M urea and 0.2 M $MgCl_2$
(c) 0.1M NaCl and 0.1 M Na_2SO_4
(d) 0.1 M $Ca(NO_3)_2$ and 0.1 M Na_2SO_4

2008

24 0.01 M solution of KCl and $BaCl_2$ are prepared in water. The freezing point of KCl is found to be –2°C. What is the freezing point of $BaCl_2$ to be completely ionised? **[AIIMS]**

(a) –3°C (b) +3°C
(c) –2°C (d) – 4°C

25 van't Hoff factor more than unity indicates that the solute in solution is **[Manipal]**

(a) dissociated (b) associated
(c) Both (a) and (b) (d) cannot say anything

26 Solutions *A, B, C* and *D* are respectively 0.1 M glucose, 0.05 M NaCl, 0.05 M $BaCl_2$ and 0.1 M $AlCl_3$. Which one of the above pairs is isotonic? **[MHT CET]**

(a) *A* and *B* (b) *B* and *C*
(c) *A* and *D* (d) *A* and *C*

27 Maximum lowering of vapour pressure is observed in the case of **[J&K CET]**

(a) 0.1 M glucose (b) 0.1 M $BaCl_2$
(c) 0.1 M $MgSO_4$ (d) 0.1 M NaCl

28 Benzoic acid is dissolved in benzene, van't Hoff factor will be **[BHU]**

(a) 1 (b) 0.5
(c) 1.5 (d) 2

2007

29 Camphor is often used in molecular mass determination because **[Manipal]**

(a) it is readily available
(b) it has a very high cryoscopic constant
(c) it is volatile in nature
(d) it is solvent for organic substances

30 Consider the following aqueous solutions and assume 100% ionisation in electrolytes **[Kerala CEE]**

I. 0.1 m urea II. 0.04 m $Al_2(SO_4)_3$
III. 0.05 m $CaCl_2$ IV. 0.005 m NaCl

Correct statement regarding the above solutions is

(a) freezing point will be lowest for solution I
(b) freezing point will be highest for solution IV
(c) boiling point will be highest for solution IV
(d) vapour pressure will be highest for solution II
(e) osmotic pressure will be highest for solution III

31 The degree of dissociation of *XY* in case of the following reaction is found to be 0.4 from vapour density measurement. If the observed vapour density of *XY* be 100 then its molecular weight (in g/mol) is ($XY \rightarrow X + Y$) **[MP PMT]**

(a) 140
(b) 70
(c) 280
(d) 210

2006

32 KBr is 80% dissociated in aqueous solution of 0.5 m concentration. (Given, K_f for water = 1.86 K kg mol^{-1}). The solution freezes at **[Kerala CEE]**

(a) 271.326 K
(b) 272 K
(c) 270.5 K
(d) 268.5 K
(e) 269 K

Answers

1 (c)	2 (b)	3 (a)	4 (d)	5 (c)	6 (c)	7 (c)	8 (a)	9 (b)	10 (b)
11 (a)	12 (c)	13 (d)	14 (b)	15 (c)	16 (d)	17 (a)	18 (b)	19 (c)	20 (a)
21 (a)	22 (b)	23 (d)	24 (a)	25 (a)	26 (a)	27 (b)	28 (b)	29 (c)	30 (b)
31 (c)	32 (a)								

Explanations

1 (*c*) $2C_6H_5COOH \longrightarrow (C_6H_5COOH)_2$

Before ass.	2	–
	2–2*x*	*x*
After ass.	$1-x$	$x/2$

$$\text{Total} = 1 - x + \frac{x}{2} = 1 - \frac{x}{2}$$

$$\therefore \quad i = \frac{1 - x/2}{1} \text{ or } i = 1 - \frac{x}{2}$$

2 (*b*) More be the value of van't Hoff factor more will be the boiling point.

As, *i* is maximum for Na_2SO_4 (= 3)

Therefore, it has maximum boiling point.

3 (*a*) Boiling point depends upon the number of non-volatile solute particles present in the solution as greater is the number of solute particles, more will be its boiling point. Boiling point of solution *X* is greater than solution *Y* which can be achieved by the following three ways :

(i) *X* is undergoing dissociation.
(ii) *Y* is undergoing association.
(iii) Number of solute particles in solution *X* are greater than the solution *Y*.
(iv) Can be neglected as this is not given any in option.
(v) Can be neglected as both the solution are equimolal.

Therefore, the only way to achieve higher boiling point of solution *X* than *Y* is that *X* must be undergoing dissociation, which can be verified as follows,

$\Delta T_b = iK_b m$ or $\Delta T_b \propto i$

As, ΔT_b of solution $X > \Delta T_b$ of solution *Y*

$\therefore$ *i* of solution $X >$ *i* of solution *Y*

or solution *X* is undergoing dissociation.

4 (*d*) $Al_2(SO_4)_3 \rightleftharpoons 2\,Al^{3+} + 3\,SO_4^{2-}$

Value of van't Hoff's factor (*i*) = 5

(a) $K_2SO_4 \rightleftharpoons 2K^+ + SO_4^{2-}$ $(i = 3)$

(b) $K_3[Fe(CN)_6] \rightleftharpoons 3\,K^+ + [Fe(CN)_6]^{3-}$ $(i = 4)$

(c) $Al(NO_3)_3 \rightleftharpoons Al^{3+} + 3\,NO_3^-$ $(i = 4)$

(d) $K_4[Fe(CN)_6] \rightleftharpoons 4\,K^+ + [Fe(CN)_6]^{3-}$ $(i = 5)$

Therefore, $K_4[Fe(CN)_6]$ has same value of *i* as that of $Al_2(SO_4)_3$, i.e. $i = 5$.

5 (*c*) Freezing point depression (ΔT_f) is a colligative property and depends upon the van't Hoff factor (*i*), i.e. number of ions given by the electrolyte in aqueous solution.

$$\Delta T_f = i \times K_f \times m$$

where, K_f = molal freezing point depression constant

m = molality of the solution

$\therefore$ K_f and *m* are constant

$\therefore$ $\Delta T_f \propto i$

(a) $KCl(aq) \rightleftharpoons K^+(aq) + Cl^-(aq)$
(Total ions = 2 thus, *i* = 2)

(b) $C_6H_{12}O_6 \rightleftharpoons$ no ions $[i = 0]$

(c) $Al_2(SO_4)_3(aq) \rightleftharpoons 2\,Al^{3+} + 3SO_4^{2-}$
(Total ions = 5, thus, *i* = 5)

(d) $K_2SO_4(aq) \rightleftharpoons 2K^+ + SO_4^{2-}$
(Total ions = 3, thus, $i = 3$)

Hence, $Al_2(SO_4)_3$ will exhibit largest freezing point depression due to the highest value of i.

6 (c) Degree of dissociation $(\alpha) = \dfrac{i-1}{n-1}$

n = number of particles per molecule.

$$Na_2SO_4 \rightleftharpoons 2Na^+ + SO_4^{-2}$$

$$n = 3 \text{ for } Na_2SO_4\ \alpha = \frac{i-1}{3-1}$$

$$\Rightarrow \quad i = 1 + 2\alpha$$

7 (c) Depression in freezing point

$$\Delta T_f = K_f \times \text{molality} \times i$$

$$i = \frac{\Delta T_f}{K_f \times \text{molality}}$$

$$\text{Molality } (m) = \frac{\text{Mass of solute}}{\text{Molar weight of solute} \times \text{mass of solvent}} \times 1000$$

$$\text{Molality} = \frac{0.5 \times 1000}{74.5 \times 100} = 0.067 \text{ m}$$

($\because$ Molar weight of KCl = 74.5)

$$\text{van't Hoff factor } (i) = \frac{0.24}{1.86 \times 0.067} = 1.92$$

8 (a) **Step I** Calculation of van't Hoff factor of '*P*'

$$\Delta T_f = i \times K_f \times m$$

$$= i \times K_f \times \frac{w_1 \times 1000}{w_2 \times M_1}$$

where, i = van't Hoff factor
K_b = molal depression constant
m = molality

$$0.3 = i \times 1.86 \times \frac{1.25 \times 1000}{50 \times 94}$$

$$\Rightarrow \quad i = \frac{0.3 \times 50 \times 94}{1.86 \times 1.25 \times 1000} = 0.6064$$

Step II Calculation of degree of association of '*P*'

Degree of association

$$\alpha = \frac{i-1}{\frac{1}{n}-1} = \frac{0.6064-1}{\frac{1}{2}-1} = \frac{-0.3936}{-0.5}$$

$$= 0.7872$$

$$= 78.72\% \approx 80\%$$

9 (b) Nernst gave the distribution law. According to this law, 'if a solute X distributes itself between non-miscible solvents A and B, at constant temperature and X is in the same molecular condition in both the solvents, then,

$$\frac{\text{concentration of } X \text{ in } A}{\text{concentration of } X \text{ in } B} = K_d$$

where, K_d is called distribution coefficient.

10 (b) For NaCl, $i = 2$

$$\Delta T_f = i\, K_f\, m = 2 \times 1.86 \times 1 = 3.72$$

$$T_{\text{solution}} = T_f^\circ - \Delta T_f = (0 - 3.72)°\text{C} = -3.72°\text{C}$$

11 (a) Elevation in boiling point

$$\Delta T_b = i \times K_b \times m$$

Molality of NaCl solution = $n/w \times 1000$,

$$m_{\text{NaCl}} = 58.5$$

$$\text{Similarly,} \quad = \frac{58.5/58.5}{w_{H_2O}} \times 1000 = \frac{1000}{w_{H_2O}}$$

$$m_{\text{glucose}} = 180$$

Molality of $C_6H_{12}O_6$ solution

$$= \frac{\frac{180}{180} \times 1000}{w_{H_2O}} = \frac{1000}{w_{H_2O}}$$

Both solutions have same molality but values of i, (van't Hoff factor) for NaCl and glucose are 2 and 1 respectively. Hence, NaCl will show higher elevation.

12 (c) Using, $\Delta T_f = i \times K_f \times m$,

$$m = \frac{n_B}{w_A} \times 1000$$

$$i = \frac{\Delta T_f \times w_A}{K_f \times n_B \times 1000}$$

$$= \frac{3.82 \times 45}{1.86 \times \left(\frac{5}{142}\right) \times 1000} = 2.63$$

13 (d) In case of dissociation, van't Hoff factor $i > 1$.
In case of association, vant't Hoff factor $i < 1$.

14 (b) Two sucrose solutions of the same molality prepared in different solvents will have the different depression of freezing point.

$$\Delta T_f = K_f \times m$$

K_f values are different for different solvents.
Rest of the given statements are correct.

15 (c) $\Delta T_f = i K_f m = 0.0054$

$$= i \times 1.86 \times 0.001$$

$$\Rightarrow i = \frac{5.4}{1.86} = 3$$

So, structure of compound is
$[Pt(NH_3)_2Cl_2]Cl_2$
Since, it gives 3 moles on dissociation.
$[Pt(NH_3)_2\ Cl_2]^{+2}$ = 1 and 2 Cl^- ions

16 (d) Depression in freezing point,
$\Delta T_f = K_f m$ (where, m = molality)

$$= 5.12 \times \frac{0.223 \times 1000}{4.4 \times 136}$$

$$= 5.12 \times 0.372 = 1.91°\text{C}$$

$\therefore$ Theoretical $\Delta T_f = 1.91$

Actual $\Delta T_f = 5.3°\text{C} - 4.47°\text{C} = 0.83°\text{C}$

$\therefore \quad i = 0.83/1.91 = 0.43$

$\because \quad i < 1$

$\therefore$ Association will take place.

Thus, it can be said that phenylacetic acid dimerises in benzene.

17 (a) van't Hoff factor,

$$i \propto \frac{1}{\text{concentration, } (C)}$$

$\therefore$ 0.0001 m solution has the maximum van't Hoff factor.

18 (b) $\Delta T_f = i \times K_f \times m$

After ionisation

	HBr	$\longrightarrow$	H^+	+ Br^-
	$1-\alpha$		α	α
Initial moles	1		0	0

Total ions = $1 - \alpha + \alpha + \alpha = 1 + \alpha$

$\therefore \quad i = 1 + \alpha$

Given, $K_f = 1.86$ K kg mol^{-1}
mass of HBr = 8.1 g, mass of H_2O = 100 g

α = degree of ionisation = 90%

$$i = 1 + \alpha = 1 + 90/100 = 1.9$$

Also, m (molality)

$$= \frac{\text{mass of solute/mol. wt. of solute}}{\text{mass of solvent in kg}}$$

$$= \frac{8.1/81}{100/1000}$$

$$\therefore \Delta T_f = i \times K_f \times m$$

$$= 1.9 \times 1.86 \times \frac{8.1/81}{100/1000}$$

$$= 3.534°\text{C}$$

ΔT_f (depression in freezing point)
= freezing point of water − freezing point of solution

3.534 = 0 − freezing point of solution

$\therefore$ Freezing point of solution
= − 3.534°C.

19 (c) Total number of ions

$$KCl \longrightarrow K^+ + Cl^-$$

$\therefore\ i = 2$

$$\Delta T_b = imK_b$$
$$= 2 \times 1 \times 0.52 = 1.04$$
$$\therefore T_b = T_b^0 + \Delta T_b = 100 + 1.04$$
$$= 101.04°C$$

20 (a) $\Delta T_f = iK_f m$ or $i = \dfrac{\Delta T_f}{K_f \times m}$

$$= \frac{0.00732}{1.86 \times 0.0020} = 1.9 \simeq 2.$$

21 (a) Since, HX is 20% ionised, van't Hoff factor, $i = 1 + (y-1)\,\alpha$

($\because$ $y = 2$, as two particles are produced)

$$= 1 + (2-1)\,0.2 = 1.2$$
$$\Delta T_f = iK_f \cdot m = 1.2 \times 1.86 \times 0.2$$
$$= 0.45°C$$
$$\Delta T_f = T_f - T_{f°}$$
$$T_f = 0°C - 0.45°C = -0.45°C$$

22 (b) In case of ionisation of binary electrolyte

$$\text{Abnormal molecular mass} = \frac{M_{\text{normal}}}{1+\alpha}$$

Abnormal molecular mass (given) = 25

So, $\quad 25 = \dfrac{40}{1+\alpha} \Rightarrow \alpha = 0.6$

$\therefore$ Ionisation percentage

$$= 0.6 \times 100 = 60\%$$

23 (d) Both the solvents will furnish equal number of ions in solution. So, if value of 'i' is same, the solutions will exert equal osmotic pressure.

$$Ca(NO_3)_2 \rightleftharpoons Ca^{2+} + 2NO_3^-;\ i = 3$$
$$Na_2SO_4 \rightleftharpoons 2Na^+ + SO_4^{2-};\ i = 3$$

24 (a) i for KCl = 2, $KCl \longrightarrow K^+ + Cl^-$

i for $BaCl_2 = 3$

$BaCl_2 \longrightarrow Ba^{+2} + 2Cl^-$

$\because \quad \Delta T_f \propto i$

$$\frac{\Delta T_f\,(KCl)}{\Delta T_f\,(BaCl_2)} = \frac{2}{3}$$

$$\Delta T_f\,(BaCl_2) = \frac{3}{2} \times 2 = 3°C$$

$\therefore$ Freezing point of KCl

$$= 0°C - 3°C = -3°C$$

25 (a) van't Hoff factor (i)

$i = 1$, for non-electrolytes

$i > 1$, for dissociation

$i < 1$, for association

26 (a) Isotonic solutions have same molar concentration of solute particles in solution. Molar concentration of solute particles in solution are 0.1 M in glucose, 2×0.05 M in NaCl, 3×0.05 in $BaCl_2$ and 4×0.1 in $AlCl_3$. Therefore, 0.1 M glucose and 0.05 M NaCl solutions are isotonic.

27 (b) Lowering of vapour pressure is a colligative property, i.e. depends only upon the number of particles of solute and not on the nature of solute.

0.1 M glucose $\longrightarrow$ remains undissociated

0.1 M $BaCl_2 \longrightarrow Ba^{2+} + 2Cl^-$ $\Rightarrow$ 3 ions

0.1 M $MgSO_4 \longrightarrow Mg^{2+} + SO_4^{2-}$ $\Rightarrow$ 2 ions

0.1 M NaCl $\longrightarrow Na^+ + Cl^-$ $\Rightarrow$ 2 ions

$\because$ 0.1 M $BaCl_2$ gives maximum number of particles, hence it exhibits maximum lowering of vapour pressure.

28 (b) When benzoic acid dissolves in benzene it will be dimerise due to the intermolecular hydrogen bonding

$$2C_6H_5COOH \xrightarrow{\text{Benzene}} (C_6H_5COOH)_2$$

van't Hoff factor

$$= \frac{\text{number of particles after association or dissociation}}{\text{number of particles before association or dissociation}}$$

$$= \frac{1}{2} = 0.5$$

29 (c) Camphor is used in molecular mass determination due to its volatile nature. The method is called Rast's camphor method. Camphor acts as a solid solvent which is volatile, hence can be removed easily.

30 (b) Since, colligative property depends upon number of particles obtained after dissociation. Therefore, according to colligative property, freezing point will be highest for solution IV due to least concentration of NaCl.

31 (c) The degree of dissociation

$$(\alpha) = \frac{D_T - D_0}{D_0}$$

where, D_T and D_0 are the theoretical and observed values of vapour densities respectively

$$0.4 = \frac{D_T - 100}{100}$$
$$D_T = 40 + 100 = 140$$
$$\therefore \quad D_T = \frac{\text{molecular weight}}{2}$$

$$\text{Molecular weight} = D_T \times 2 = 140 \times 2$$
$$= 280 \text{ g/mol}$$

32 (a) $\Delta T_f = i \times K_f \times \text{molality } (m)$

Here, degree of dissociation = 80%

$$\because \quad i = \frac{1 - \alpha + n\alpha}{1}$$

$$KBr \rightleftharpoons K^+ + Br^-$$

$$i = \frac{1 - 0.8 + 2 \times 0.8}{1} = 1.8$$

$\therefore \quad \Delta T_f = 1.8 \times 1.86 \times 0.5$

$\Rightarrow \quad \Delta T_f = 1.674$ K

$$\Delta T_f = T_f^\circ - T_f$$

T_f° = Freezing point of pure solvent (water)

Freezing point of solution

$$1.674 = 273 - T_f$$
$$T_f = 273 - 1.674$$

$\Rightarrow \quad T_f = 271.326$ K

17

Electrochemistry

Quick Review

- Electrochemistry studies production of electricity from energy released during chemical reaction. It is related to the electrical conductance of a solution and chemical changes associated with it.
- The reactions which involve oxidation and reduction as their two half-reactions are called **redox reactions.** They are responsible for the flow of electrons in various solutions.

Types of Conductors

- On the basis of species that conduct electricity (current), *conductors are of two types* :
  (i) **Metallic or electronic conductors** conduct electricity by transfer of electrons.
  (ii) **Electrolytes or electrolytic conductors** conduct electricity by the mobility of ions.
- Acids, bases and their salts all are the examples of electrolytes. An electrolyte can be **strong** or **weak.** **Strong electrolytes** (e.g. NaCl, HCl, KCl, H_2SO_4, $ZnCl_2$ etc.) have the ability to dissociate completely, while **weak electrolytes** (e.g. H_2CO_3, CH_3COOH, etc.) does not dissociate completely.

Conductance of Electrolytic Solutions

- The property that describes the case with which electric current flows through a medium is called **conductance** (*G*).
- It is the reciprocal of resistance,

i.e. $$G=\frac{1}{R}$$

Its unit is mho or Ω^{-1} or Seimens (S).

- The conductance of a solution of length 1 cm and area of cross-section 1 cm^2 is called **conductivity** or **specific conductance** (κ). It is the inverse of resistivity.

$$\kappa=\frac{1}{\rho}$$

where, ρ = resistivity

$$\therefore \quad \kappa=G\times\frac{l}{a} \quad \left[\because \rho=R\times\frac{a}{l}\Rightarrow\frac{1}{\rho}=\frac{1}{R}\times\frac{l}{A}\right]$$

where, $\frac{l}{a}$ = cell constant

Its unit is $ohm^{-1}cm^{-1}$ or S cm^{-1}.

- The conductance provided by 1 mole of electrolyte kept between two electrodes 1 cm apart, is called **molar conductivity** (Λ_m).

$$\Lambda_m=\frac{\kappa\times1000}{\text{molarity}}$$

Its unit is $ohm^{-1}cm^2mol^{-1}$ or Scm^2mol^{-1}.

- The conductance of all the ions produced from 1 gm equivalent of the electrolyte kept between two electrodes 1 cm apart is called **equivalent conductivity** (Λ_{eq}).

$$\Lambda_{eq}=\frac{\kappa\times1000}{\text{Normality}}$$

Its unit is ohm^{-1} cm^2 $(g\ eq)^{-1}$ or Scm^2 $(g\ eq)^{-1}$.

- On dilution, equivalent and molar conductivities increases and specific conductivity decreases.

- Molar conductivity and equivalent conductivity are related as,

$$\Lambda_m = n \times \Lambda_{eq}$$

Here, n is the valence factor,

$$n = \frac{\text{atomic weight}}{\text{equivalent weight}}$$

Variation in Conductivity with Concentration

- In case of strong electrolytes, there is no rapid increase in their equivalent or molar conductivity on dilution, while in case of weak electrolytes, there is rapid increase in equivalent or molar conductivity with dilution.
- The variation of molar conductivity for strong electrolytes is represented by Debye-Huckel Onsager equation.

$$\Lambda_m = \Lambda^\circ_m - A\sqrt{C}$$

where, Λ°_m = molar conductivity at infinite dilution
C = concentration
A = constant

A plot of Λ_m against $\sqrt{C}$ is a straight line with slope as $-$'A' and intercept as Λ°_m. Value of constant A depends on the type of electrolyte.

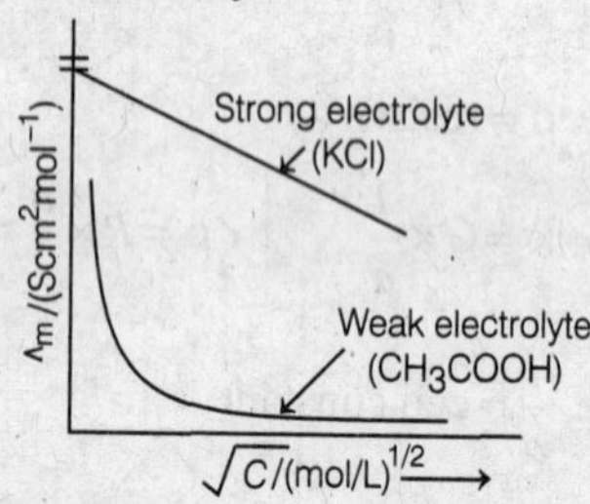

- **Kohlrausch's Law** It states that the limiting molar conductivity for any electrolyte is the sum of contribution of cations and anions of the electrolyte.

e.g. $\Lambda^\circ_{m(CH_3COOH)} = \Lambda^\circ_{m(CH_3COO^-)} + \Lambda^\circ_{m(H^+)}$

Degree of Dissociation

The ratio of molar conductivity (Λ_m) at a specific concentration (C) to the molar conductivity at infinite dilution, i.e. limiting molar conductivity, Λ°_m is known as degree of dissociation.

At any concentration C, if α is the degree of dissociation, then for a weak electrolyte, $\alpha = \frac{\Lambda_m}{\Lambda^\circ_m}$

Since, for a weak electrolyte, $K_a = \frac{C\alpha^2}{(1-\alpha)}$

$$= \frac{C\Lambda^2_m}{(\Lambda^\circ_m)^2\left(1 - \frac{\Lambda_m}{\Lambda^\circ_m}\right)} = \frac{C\Lambda^2_m}{\Lambda^\circ_m(\Lambda^\circ_m - \Lambda_m)}$$

Electrolysis

- The decomposition of an electrolyte by the passage of electricity through its aqueous solution or molten state is called electrolysis.
- In this process, anions react at anode and release their electrons, while cations react at the cathode and take up electrons.

Products of Electrolysis

- **Molten NaCl**

Cathode : $Na^+(aq) + e^- \longrightarrow Na(s)\downarrow$ (Na is deposited)

Anode : $Cl^-(aq) \longrightarrow \frac{1}{2}Cl_2(g)\uparrow + e^-$ (Cl_2 is liberated)

- **Aqueous NaCl**

Cathode : $H_2O(l) + e^- \longrightarrow \frac{1}{2}H_2(g) + OH^-(aq)$ (H_2 is liberated)

Anode : $Cl^-(aq) \longrightarrow \frac{1}{2}Cl_2(g) + e^-$ (Cl_2 is liberated)

Faraday's Law of Electrolysis

The two laws given by Faraday are as follows :

(*i*) **Faraday's First Law of Electrolysis** It states that "the amount of chemical reaction occurring at any electrode by passing current is directly proportional to the quantity of electricity passed through the electrolyte (in solution or in molten state)". Thus, w g of the substance gets deposited on passing Q Coulomb of electricity.

$$w \propto Q \text{ or } w = ZQ$$

$$w = Z \times it \qquad (\because Q = it)$$

where, Q = quantity of electricity, i = current (in A), t = time (in s), Z = constant of proportionality called electrochemical equivalent.

(*ii*) **Faraday's Second Law of Electrolysis** It states that "when the same quantity of electricity is passed through different electrolytes, the amounts of different substances formed are directly proportional to their equivalent weights.

$$\frac{w_A}{w_B} = \frac{E_A}{E_B}$$

where, w_A and w_B are the deposited masses of substance A and B, and E_A and E_B are the equivalent masses of A and B respectively.

Cells

Cell are the devices that involves the interconversion of electrical energy and chemical energy.

These are classified as follows :

(*i*) **Electrolytic Cell** Convert electrical energy into chemical energy.

(*ii*) **Electrochemical Cell** Convert chemical energy into electrical energy.

These are further classified as follows :

(a) **Chemical Cell** It involves the chemical change inside the cell which is responsible for the flow of current.

(b) **Concentration Cell** Flow of current is due to the difference in concentration. *It is further divided into two types :*

- Electrode concentration cell
- Electrolyte concentration cell.

Some Important Terms Related to Cells

(*i*) **Electrode Potential** The potential difference developed between an electrode and the electrolyte in which it is placed, is called electrode potential.

(*ii*) **Standard Electrode Potential** In standard state (i.e. 1 bar pressure at 298 K, that is, at 25°C temperature and 1 M concentration, the electrode potential is called standard electrode potential.

(*iii*) **Cell Potential** The potential difference between two electrodes (anode and cathode) of cell is called cell potential.

(*iv*) **Electromotive Force** (EMF) **of a Cell** The potential difference between the electrodes of cell, wher no current is drawn from the cell is called emf of the cell.

Electrochemical Series

The arrangement of elements in the order of increasing reduction potential values is called electrochemical series.

Element	Electrode reaction (reduction)	Standard electrode reduction potential, $E°$ (volt)
Li	$Li^+ + e^- \longrightarrow Li$	− 3.05
K	$K^+ + e^- \longrightarrow K$	− 2.925
Ca	$Ca^{2+} + 2e^- \longrightarrow Ca$	− 2.87
Na	$Na^+ + e^- \longrightarrow Na$	− 2.714
Mg	$Mg^{2+} + 2e^- \longrightarrow Mg$	− 2.37
Al	$Al^{3+} + 3e^- \longrightarrow Al$	− 1.66
Zn	$Zn^{2+} + 2e^- \longrightarrow Zn$	− 0.7628
Cr	$Cr^{3+} + 3e^- \longrightarrow Cr$	− 0.74
Fe	$Fe^{2+} + 2e^- \longrightarrow Fe$	− 0.44
Cd	$Cd^{2+} + 2e^- \longrightarrow Cd$	− 0.403
Ni	$Ni^{2+} + 2e^- \longrightarrow Ni$	− 0.25
Sn	$Sn^{2+} + 2e^- \longrightarrow Sn$	− 0.14
H_2	$2H^+ + 2e^- \longrightarrow H_2$	0.00
Cu	$Cu^{2+} + 2e^- \longrightarrow Cu$	+ 0.337
I_2	$I_2 + 2e^- \longrightarrow 2I^-$	+ 0.535
Ag	$Ag^+ + e^- \longrightarrow Ag$	+ 0.799
Hg	$Hg^{2+} + 2e^- \longrightarrow Hg$	+ 0.885
Br_2	$Br_2 + 2e^- \longrightarrow 2Br^-$	+ 1.08
Cl_2	$Cl_2 + 2e^- \longrightarrow 2Cl^-$	+ 1.36
Au	$Au^{3+} + 3e^- \longrightarrow Au$	+ 1.50
F_2	$F_2 + 2e^- \longrightarrow 2F^-$	+ 2.87

(Arrows beside the table: Increasing tendency for reduction ↑; Increasing strength of oxidising agent ↑; Increasing strength of reducing agent ↓; Increasing tendency for oxidation ↓)

- Electrochemical series is used for prediciting the product of electrolysis; i.e. the ion which is the stronger oxidising agent out of the given cations and the ion which is the stronger reducing agent out of the given anion will be discharged at cathode and anode respectively.
- It is also helpful in predicitng the feasibility of a reaction.

Electrochemical Cell (or Voltaic or Galvanic Cell)

- In this device, the Gibb's energy of the spontaneous redox reaction is converted into electrical energy, e.g. Daniell cell.
- Daniell cell converts the chemical energy liberated during the redox reaction to electrical energy.

$$Zn(s) + Cu^{2}(aq) \longrightarrow Zn^{2+}(aq) + Cu(s)$$

- The two electrodes, i.e. anode made up of Zn rod and cathode made up of copper are connected by a salt-bridge.
- General representation of an electrochemical cell is given as:

$$\underset{\text{Anode}}{M_1(s)} \,\Big|\, \underset{\text{Oxidation half-cell}}{M_1^{n+}(aq)} \,\Big\|\, \underset{\text{Reduction half-cell}}{M_2^{n+}(aq)} \,\Big|\, \underset{\text{Cathode}}{M_2(s)}$$

Electrons flow this way →

- The difference in potentials of the two half-cells of a cell is known as **electromotive force** (emf) or **cell potential.**

At equilibrium,

$$E^\circ_{cell} = E^\circ_{oxi} + E^\circ_{red}$$

or $E^\circ_{cell} = E^\circ_{ox} + E^\circ_{red}$ or $E^\circ_{cell} = E^\circ_{cathode} - E^\circ_{anode}$

where, E°_{cell} = standard electrode potential.

Nernst Equation

- The relationship between electrode potential and concentration of solution is given by **Nernst equation.**

$$E_{cell} \text{ or EMF} = E^\circ_{cell} - \frac{2.303\,RT}{nF} \log Q$$

where, n = total number of electrons gained or lost

$1F = 96500\,C$, T = temperature

R = gas constant

Q = reaction quotient of overall reaction

At 298 K,

$$E_{cell} = E^\circ_{cell} - \frac{0.0591}{n} \log Q$$

- Nernst equation is used to find equilibrium constant and Gibb's free energy change by using the formula's :

(*i*) $E^\circ_{cell} = \dfrac{0.0591}{n} \log K$ [∵ At equilibrium $E_{cell} = 0$]

where, K = equilibrium constant

(*ii*) $\Delta G^\circ = -nFE^\circ_{cell}$

where, ΔG° = standard Gibb's free energy change

(*iii*) Relation between cell potential, free energy and equilibrium constant is,

$$\Delta_r G^\circ = -2.303\,RT \log K_C$$

- If two half reactions having potentials E°_1, E°_2 are combined to give a third half reaction having a potential E°_3, then, $\Delta G^\circ_3 = \Delta G^\circ_1 + \Delta G^\circ_2$ or $E^\circ_3 = \dfrac{n_1 E^\circ_1 + n_2 E^\circ_2}{n_3}$

Batteries

The arrangement in which a number of cells are arranged in a series is called a **battery**.

These are of two types

(*i*) **Primary Battery** Redox reaction occurs only once and cell become dead after sometime. These cannot be recharged or used again.

(*ii*) **Secondary Battery** It can be recharged by passing an electric current. These can be used over again and again.

	Primary Cell		Secondary Cell	
Cell	**Dry cell**	**Mercury cell**	**Lead storage cell**	**Nickel-cadmium cell**
Definition	• It consist of zinc container that also act as anode and cathode is a carbon (graphite) rod. • Filled with moist paste of NH_4Cl	• It consist of Zn-Hg amalgam as anode and paste of HgO and C as the cathode. • Electrolyte is a paste of KOH and ZnO	• It consist of lead anode and a grid of lead packed with PbO_2 as cathode. • 38% solution of H_2SO_4 is used as an electrolyte.	• Cadmium metal acts as anode, nickel (III) compound like NiO_2 act as cathode. • KOH act as an electrolyte.
Figure	Carbon rod (cathode); Zinc cup (anode); MnO_2 + carbon black + NH_4Cl paste	Anode; Anode cap; Gasket; Separator; Cathode; Cell can	Anode; Cathode; Negative plates (lead grids filled with spongy lead); Positive plates (lead grids filled with PbO_2); 38% sulphuric acid solution	Positive plate; Separator; Negative plate
Reactions involved				
Anode	$Zn(s) \longrightarrow Zn^{2+} + 2e^-$	$Zn(Hg) + 2OH^-(aq) \longrightarrow ZnO(s) + H_2O(l) + 2e^-$	$PbO_2(s) + SO_4^{2-}(aq) \longrightarrow PbSO_4(s) + 2e^-$	$Cd(s) + 2OH^-(aq) \longrightarrow Cd(OH)_2(s) + 2e^-(aq)$
Cathode	$MnO_2(s) + NH_4^+(aq) + e^- \longrightarrow MnO(OH)(s) + NH_3(g)$	$HgO(s) + H_2O(l) + 2e^- \longrightarrow Hg(l) + 2OH^-(aq)$	$PbO_2 + SO_4^{2-}(aq) + 4H^+(aq) + 2e^- \longrightarrow PbSO_4(s) + 2H_2O(l)$	$NiO_2(s) + 2H_2O(l) + 2e^- \longrightarrow Ni(OH)_2(s) + 2OH^-(aq)$

Note In lead storage battery, the reaction get reversed during charging.

Fuel Cells

- The galvanic cells in which chemical energy from combustion of fuels like hydrogen, methane etc. is converted into electrical energy are called fuel cells.
- Energy can be obtained indefinitely from a fuel cell as long as outside supply of fuel is maintained, e.g. $H_2 - O_2$ fuel cell.

The half-reactions are,

At anode, $2H_2(g) + 4OH^-(aq) \longrightarrow 4H_2O(l) + 4e^-$

At cathode, $O_2(g) + 2H_2O(l) + 4e^- \longrightarrow 4OH^-(aq)$

Overall cell reaction, $2H_2(g) + O_2(g) \longrightarrow 2H_2O(l)$

- **Efficiency of fuel cell** is given by the formula,

$$\eta = \frac{\Delta G}{\Delta H} \times 100$$

where, η = Thermodynamic efficiency of fuel cell

ΔH = Heat of combustion

ΔG = Useful work done as electricity $= -nFE^\circ_{cell}$

Corrosion

It is the oxidative deterioration of a metal such as iron into rust. It is basically an electrochemical phenomenon.

Corrosion may be prevented by:

(*i*) Shielding of the metal surface from oxygen and moisture.

(*ii*) Coating or paint

(*iii*) Cathodic protection

Topical Practice Questions

All the exam questions of this chapter have been divided into four topics as listed below

Topic 1

Electrolytes and Electrolytic Conductance

2019

1 Following limiting molar conductivities are given as, **[NEET Odisha]**

$\Lambda^\circ_{m(H_2SO_4)} = x \text{ S cm}^2\text{ mol}^{-1}$

$\Lambda^\circ_{m(K_2SO_4)} = y \text{ S cm}^2\text{ mol}^{-1}$

$\Lambda^\circ_{m(CH_3COOK)} = z \text{ S cm}^2\text{ mol}^{-1}$

$\Lambda^\circ_{m(\text{in S cm}^2\text{ mol}^{-1})}$ for CH_3COOH will be

(a) $x-y+2z$ (b) $x+y-z$ (c) $x-y+z$ (d) $\frac{(x-y)}{2}+z$

2018

2 At 25°C, the molar conductance at infinite dilution for the strong electrolytes NaOH, NaCl and $BaCl_2$ are 248×10^{-4}, 126×10^{-4} and 280×10^{-4} $\text{Sm}^2\text{mol}^{-1}$ respectively. λ°_m $Ba(OH)_2$ in $\text{Sm}^2\text{mol}^{-1}$ is **[AIIMS]**

(a) 362×10^{-4} (b) 402×10^{-4}

(c) 524×10^{-4} (d) 568×10^{-4}

3 If molar conductivity of Ca^{2+} and Cl^- ions are 119 and 71 S cm^2mol^{-1} respectively, then the molar conductivity of $CaCl_2$ at infinite dilution is **[JIPMER]**

(a) 215 S cm^2mol^{-1} (b) 340 S cm^2mol^{-1}

(c) 126 S cm^2mol^{-1} (d) 261 S cm^2mol^{-1}

2016

4 The molar conductivity of a 0.5 mol/dm^3 solution of $AgNO_3$ with electrolytic conductivity of 5.76×10^{-3} S cm^{-1} at 298 K is **[NEET (Phase II)]**

(a) 2.88 S cm^2/mol (b) 11.52 S cm^2/mol

(c) 0.086 S cm^2/mol (d) 28.8 S cm^2/mol

2014

5 How is electrical conductance of a conductor related with length and area of cross-section of the conductor? **[MHT CET]**

(a) $G = l\cdot A\cdot\kappa^{-1}$ (b) $G=\kappa\cdot l\cdot A^{-1}$

(c) $G=\kappa\cdot A\cdot l^{-1}$ (d) $G=\kappa\cdot l\cdot A^{-2}$

6 At 25° C, the molar conductance of 0.007 M hydrofluoric acid is 150 mho cm^2 mol^{-1} and its Λ°_m = 500 mho $cm^2 mol^{-1}$. The value of the dissociation constant of the acid at the given concentration at 25° C is **[WB JEE]**

(a) 7×10^{-4} M (b) 7×10^{-5} M

(c) 9×10^{-3} M (d) 9×10^{-4} M

7 Conductivity of a saturated solution of a sparingly soluble salt *AB* at 298 K is 1.85×10^{-6} Sm^{-1}. Solubility product of the salt *AB* at 298 K is **[KCET]**

[given, $\Lambda^\circ_m(AB) = 140\times10^{-4}$ Sm^{-2} mol^{-1}]

(a) 5.7×10^{-12} (b) 1.32×10^{-12}

(c) 7.5×10^{-12} (d) 1.74×10^{-2}

2013

8 At 25° C, molar conductance of 0.1 molar aqueous solution of ammonium hydroxide is 9.54 $\Omega^{-1}cm^2$ mol^{-1} and at infinite dilution, its molar conductance is 238 $ohm^{-1}cm^2mol^{-1}$. The degree of ionisation of ammonium hydroxide at the same concentration and temperature is **[NEET]**

(a) 2.080%

(b) 20.800%

(c) 4.008%

(d) 40.80%

2012

9 Limiting molar conductivity of NH_4OH i.e. $\Lambda^\circ_{m(NH_4OH)}$ is equal to **[CBSE AIPMT]**

(a) $\Lambda^\circ_{m(NH_4Cl)} + \Lambda^\circ_{m(NaCl)} + \Lambda^\circ_{m(NaOH)}$

(b) $\Lambda^\circ_{m(NaOH)} + \Lambda^\circ_{m(Na_4Cl)} - \Lambda^\circ_{m(NH_4Cl)}$

(c) $\Lambda^\circ_{m(NH_4OH)} + \Lambda^\circ_{m(NH_4Cl)} - \Lambda^\circ_{m(HCl)}$

(d) $\Lambda^\circ_{m(NH_4Cl)} + \Lambda^\circ_{m(NaOH)} - \Lambda^\circ_{m(NaCl)}$

10 Molar conductivities (Λ°_m) at infinite dilution of NaCl, HCl and CH_3COONa are 126.4, 425.9 and 91.0 S cm^2 mol^{-1} respectively. Λ°_m for CH_3COOH will be **[CBSE AIPMT]**

(a) 425.5 S cm^{2}mol^{-1} (b) 180.5 S cm^2 mol^{-1}

(c) 290.85 S cm^2 mol^{-1} (d) 390.5 S cm^2 mol^{-1}

11 Read the following statement and predict the corresponding law.

"At infinite dilution, when dissociation is complete, each ion makes a definite contribution towards total equivalent conductance of the electrolyte irrespective of the nature of the ion." **[OJEE]**

(a) Ostwald's dilution law (b) Kohlrausch's law

(c) Nernst equation (d) Ohm's law

2011

12 Which one of the following has the highest molar conductivity? **[Kerala CEE]**

(a) Diamminedichloroplatinum (II)

(b) Tetraamminedichlorocobalt (III) chloride

(c) Potassiumhexacyanoferrate (II)

(d) Hexaaquachromium (III) chloride

(e) Potassiumhexacyanoferrate (III)

2010

13 An increase in equivalent conductance of a strong electrolyte with dilution is mainly due to **[CBSE AIPMT]**

(a) increase in number of ions

(b) increase in ionic mobility of ions

(c) 100% ionisation of electrolyte at normal dilution

(d) increase in both i.e. number of ions and ionic mobility of ions

14 At 18°C, the conductance of H^+ and CH_3COO^- at infinite dilution are 315 and 35 mho cm^2 eq^{-1} respectively. The equivalent conductivity of CH_3COOH at infinite dilution is ...... mho cm^2 eq^{-1}. **[AFMC]**

(a) 350 (b) 280 (c) 30 (d) 315

15 Unit of ionic mobility is **[OJEE]**

(a) m^2 V^{-1}s^{-1} (b) m s^{-1}

(c) m s^{-1} V (d) m s^{-1} V^{-1}

16 Conductivity of 0.01 M NaCl solution is 0.00147 ohm^{-1} cm^{-1}. What happens to this conductivity, if extra 100 mL of H_2O will be added to the above solution? **[OJEE]**

(a) Increases

(b) Decreases

(c) Remains unchanged

(d) First increases and then decreases

17 The unit of conductivity is **[RPMT]**

(a) ohm^{-1} (b) ohm^{-1}cm^{-1}

(c) ohm^{-2}cm^2 equiv^{-1} (d) ohm^{-1}cm^2

18 The conductivity of 0.20 M KCl solution at 298 K is 0.0248 S cm^{-1}. What will be its molar conductivity?

(a) 124 S cm^2 (b) 124 cm^{-1} **[Haryana PMT]**

(c) 124 ohm^{-1} cm^2 equiv^{-1} (d) 124 S cm^2 mol^{-1}

19 The compound exhibiting maximum value of equivalent conductance in a fused state is **[AMU]**

(a) $SrCl_2$ (b) $CaCl_2$ (c) $MgCl_2$ (d) $BeCl_2$

20 The resistance of 1 N solution of acetic acid is 250 Ω, when measured in a cell having a cell constant of 1.15 cm^{-1}. The equivalent conductance (in Ω^{-1} cm^2 equiv^{-1}) of 1 N acetic acid is **[Guj CET]**

(a) 2.3 (b) 4.6 (c) 9.2 (d) 18.42009

21 The equivalent conductance of $M/32$ solution of a weak monobasic acid is 8.0 mho cm^2 and at infinite dilution is 400 mho cm^2. The dissociation constant of this acid is

(a) 1.25×10^{-5} (b) 1.25×10^{-6} **[CBSE AIPMT]**

(c) 6.25×10^{-4} (d) 1.25×10^{-4}

22 **Assertion** (A) On dilution, the equivalent as well as molar conductivity of solution increases.

Reason (R) With dilution, the number of current carrying particles per cm^3 increases. **[AIIMS]**

(a) Both A and R are correct and R is the correct explanation of A

(b) Both A and R are correct but R is not the correct explanation of A

(c) A is correct but R is incorrect

(d) Both A and R are incorrect

23 The correct expression in SI system relating the equivalent conductance (Λ_c), specific conductance (κ) and equivalent concentration (C) is

[where, C is the number of gram equivalents in one litre of the solution]. **[J&K CET]**

(a) $\Lambda_C = \dfrac{\kappa}{C}$ (b) $\Lambda_C = \dfrac{\kappa\times 1000}{C}$

(c) $\Lambda_C = \dfrac{\kappa\times 10^{-3}}{C}$ (d) $\Lambda_C = \dfrac{\kappa\times 10^{-6}}{C}$

24 An aqueous solution containing 6.5 g of NaCl of 90% purity was subjected to electrolysis. After the complete electrolysis, the solution was evaporated to get solid NaOH. The volume of 1 M acetic acid required to neutralise NaOH obtained above is [KCET]

(a) 2000 cm^3 (b) 100 cm^3
(c) 200 cm^3 (d) 1000 cm^3

25 The one which decreases with dilution is [KCET]

(a) conductance (b) specific conductance
(c) equivalent conductance (d) molar conductance

2008

26 Kohlrausch's law states that at [CBSE AIPMT]

(a) finite dilution, each ion makes definite contribution to the equivalent conductance of an electrolyte, whatever be the nature of the other ion of the electrolyte
(b) infinite dilution, each ion makes definite contribution to equivalent conductance of an electrolyte depending on the nature of the other ion of the electrolyte
(c) infinite dilution, each ion makes definite contribution to conductance of an electrolyte whatever be the nature of the other ion of the electrolyte
(d) infinite dilution, each ion makes definite contribution to equivalent conductance of an electrolyte, whatever be the nature of the other ion of the electrolyte

27 Which one of the following solutions will have the highest conductivity? [EAMCET]

(a) 0.1 M CH_3COOH (b) 0.1 M NaCl
(c) 0.1 M KNO_3 (d) 0.1 M HCl

28 Which of the following electrolytic solutions has the least specific conductance? [KCET]

(a) 0.02 N (b) 0.2 N (c) 2 N (d) 0.002 N

2007

29 **Assertion** (A) According to Kohlrausch's law the molar conductivity of a strong electrolyte at infinite dilution is sum of molar conductivities of its ions.
Reason (R) The current carried by cation and anion is always equal. [AIIMS]

(a) Both A and R are correct and R is the correct explanation of A
(b) Both A and R are correct but R is not the correct explanation of A
(c) A is correct but R is incorrect
(d) Both A and R are incorrect

30 Which of the following is not a non-electrolyte? [AFMC]

(a) Acetic acid (b) Glucose
(c) Ethanol (d) Urea

31 Which of the following is a good conductor of electricity? [BHU]

(a) Diamond (b) Graphite
(c) Solid NaCl (d) Wood

32 The resistance of $N/10$ solution is found to be $2.5 \times 10^3\ \Omega$. The equivalent conductance of the solution is [Cell constant = $1.25\ cm^{-1}$] [Kerala CEE]

(a) $2.5 \Omega^{-1}\ cm^2\ equiv^{-1}$
(b) $5.0 \Omega^{-1}\ cm^2\ equiv^{-1}$
(c) $2.5 \Omega^{-1}\ cm^{-2}\ equiv^{-1}$
(d) $5.0\ W^{-1}\ cm^{-2}\ equiv^{-1}$

33 The electrolyte $[Co(NH_3)_5Cl]Cl_2$ is which of the following type? [Haryana PMT]

(a) 1 : 2 (b) 1 : 3
(c) 2 : 3 (d) 4 : 1

34 The specific conductance (κ) of an electrolyte of 0.1 N concentration is related to equivalent conductance (Λ) by the following formula [J&K CET]

(a) $\Lambda = \kappa$ (b) $\Lambda = 10\,\kappa$
(c) $\Lambda = 100\,\kappa$ (d) $\Lambda = 10000\,\kappa$

35 Pure water does not conduct electricity because it is [J&K CET]

(a) basic
(b) almost not ionised
(c) decomposed easily
(d) acidic

2006

36 The ionic conductance of Ba^{2+} and Cl^- are respectively 127 and 76 $\Omega^{-1}\ cm^2$ at infinite dilution. The equivalent conductance (in $\Omega^{-1}\ cm^{-1}$) of $BaCl_2$ at infinite dilution will be [MHT CET]

(a) 139.5 (b) 203
(c) 279 (d) 101.5

37 Which of the following does not conduct electricity? [AFMC]

(a) Fused NaCl
(b) Solid NaCl
(c) Brine solution
(d) Copper

Answers

1 (d)	2 (c)	3 (d)	4 (b)	5 (c)	6 (d)	7 (d)	8 (c)	9 (d)	10 (d)
11 (b)	12 (c)	13 (b)	14 (a)	15 (a)	16 (b)	17 (b)	18 (d)	19 (a)	20 (b)
21 (a)	22 (c)	23 (b)	24 (b)	25 (b)	26 (d)	27 (b)	28 (d)	29 (c)	30 (a)
31 (b)	32 (b)	33 (a)	34 (d)	35 (b)	36 (c)	37 (b)			

Explanations

1 (*d*) According to Kohlrausch's law,
Λ°_m for $A_xB_y = x\Lambda^\circ_{(A)^{y+}} + y\Lambda^\circ_{(B)^{x-}}$

where, Λ°_m = limiting molar conductivity of electrolyte and $\Lambda^\circ_{(A)^{y+}}$ and $\Lambda^\circ_{(B)^{x-}}$ are the limiting molar conductivities of cation (A^{y+}) and anion (B^{x-}), respectively.

Given $\Lambda^\circ_{m(H_2SO_4)} = 2\Lambda^\circ_{H^+} + \Lambda^\circ_{SO_4^{2-}}$
$= x \text{ S cm}^2\text{mol}^{-1}$ ...(i)

$\Lambda^\circ_{m(K_2SO_4)} = 2\Lambda^\circ_{K^+} + \Lambda^\circ_{SO_4^{2-}}$
$= y \text{ S cm}^2\text{mol}^{-1}$ ...(ii)

$\Lambda^\circ_m(CH_3COOK) = \Lambda^\circ_{CH_3COO^-} + \Lambda^\circ_{K^+}$
$= z \text{ S cm}^2\text{mol}^{-1}$ ...(iii)

To find :
$\Lambda^\circ_{m(CH_3COOH)} = \Lambda^\circ_{CH_3COO^-} + \Lambda^\circ_{H^+}$

The above equation can be obtained by
Eq. (iii) + $\frac{\text{Eq. (i)}}{2} - \frac{\text{Eq. (ii)}}{2}$

$$\therefore \Lambda^\circ_{m(CH_3COOH)} = \Lambda^\circ_{m(CH_3COOK)} + \frac{\Lambda^\circ_{m(H_2SO_4)}}{2} - \frac{\Lambda^\circ_{m(K_2SO_4)}}{2}$$

$$= \left(z + \frac{x}{2} - \frac{y}{2}\right) \text{S cm}^2 \text{ mol}^{-1}$$

$$= \left(\frac{x-y}{2} + z\right) \text{S cm}^2 \text{ mol}^{-1}$$

2 (*c*) Given,
$\Lambda^\circ_m(NaOH) = 248 \times 10^{-4}\text{Sm}^2\text{mol}^{-1}$
$\Lambda^\circ_m(NaCl) = 126 \times 10^{-4}\text{Sm}^2\text{mol}^{-1}$
$\Lambda^\circ_m(BaCl_2) = 280 \times 10^{-4}\text{Sm}^2\text{mol}^{-1}$

The reaction for the formation of $Ba(OH)_2$ can be written as,
$BaCl_2 + 2NaOH \longrightarrow Ba(OH)_2 + 2NaCl$

$$\because \Lambda^\circ_{m\ Ba(OH)_2} = \Lambda^\circ_{m\ BaCl_2} + 2\Lambda^\circ_{m\ NaOH} - 2\Lambda^\circ_{m\ NaCl}$$

$$\therefore \Lambda^\circ_{m\ Ba(OH)_2} = (280 \times 10^{-4}) + (2 \times 248 \times 10^{-4}) - (2 \times 126 \times 10^{-4})$$
$$= (280 + 496 - 252) \times 10^{-4}$$
$$= 524 \times 10^{-4}\text{Sm}^2\text{mol}^{-1}$$

3 (*d*) Given, $\Lambda^\circ_{Ca^{2+}} = 119 \text{ S cm}^2 \text{ mol}^{-1}$
$\Lambda^\circ_{Cl^-} = 71 \text{ S cm}^2 \text{ mol}^{-1}$

As we know that,
$$\Lambda^\circ_{CaCl_2} = \Lambda^\circ_{Ca^{2+}} + 2 \times \Lambda^\circ_{Cl^-}$$
$$\therefore \Lambda^\circ_{CaCl_2} = 119 + 2 \times 71$$
$$\Lambda^\circ_{CaCl_2} = 261 \text{ S cm}^2 \text{ mol}^{-1}$$

4 (*b*) The relation between molar conductivity (Λ_m) and electrolytic conductivity (κ) is given as,

$$\Lambda_m = \frac{\kappa \times 1000}{M}$$

where, M is molarity of solution.
Given,
Concentration of solution,
$$M = 0.5 \text{ mol / dm}^3$$
Electrolytic conductivity,
$$\kappa = 5.76 \times 10^{-3} \text{ S cm}^{-1}$$
$\therefore$ Temperature, $T = 298$ K

$$\lambda_m = \frac{\kappa \times 1000}{M} = \frac{5.76 \times 10^{-3} \times 1000}{0.5}$$
$$= 11.52 \text{ S cm}^2/\text{mol}$$

5 (*c*) Specific conductance, $\kappa = G \times l / A$
where, G = electrical conductance or
$$G = \kappa \times A / l$$
thus, electrical conductance is given by,
$$G = \kappa \cdot A \cdot l^{-1}$$

6 (*d*) Degree of dissociation,
$$\alpha = \frac{\Lambda_m}{\Lambda^0_m} = \frac{150}{500} = 0.3$$
where, Λ_m = Molar conductance
Λ°_m = equivalent conductivity at infinite dilution

Given, $C = 0.007$ M

Hydrofluoric acid dissociates in the following manner.

	HF $\longrightarrow$	H^+	+ F^-
Initial	C	0	0
At time, t	$C(1-\alpha)$	$C\alpha$	$C\alpha$

Dissociation constant,
$$K_a = \frac{[H^+][F^-]}{[HF]} = \frac{C\alpha \cdot C\alpha}{C(1-\alpha)} = \frac{C\alpha^2}{(1-\alpha)}$$

On substituting values
$$K_a = \frac{0.007 \times (0.3)^2}{(1-0.3)} = \frac{63 \times 10^{-3} \times 10^{-2}}{0.7}$$
$$= 9 \times 10^{-4} \text{ M}$$

7 (*d*) $\Lambda^\circ_m = \frac{\kappa \times 1000}{S}$

where, Λ°_m = molar conductivity at infinite dilution.

$$S = \frac{\kappa \times 1000}{\Lambda^\circ_m} = \frac{1.85 \times 10^{-6} \times 1000}{140 \times 10^{-4}}$$
$$= (0.1321) \text{ M}$$

$$AB \rightleftharpoons A^+ + B^-$$
$$K_{sp} = [A^+][B^-] = S^2 = (0.1321)^2$$
$$= 1.74 \times 10^{-2} \text{ mol}^2 \text{ L}^{-2}$$

8 (*c*) Given, molar conductance at 0.1 M concentration,
$$\Lambda_m = 9.54\ \Omega^{-1} \text{ cm}^2\text{mol}^{-1}$$
Molar conductance at infinite dilution
$$\Lambda^\infty_m = 238\ \Omega^{-1} \text{ cm}^2\text{mol}^{-1}$$
We know that, degree of ionisation,
$$\alpha = \frac{\Lambda_m}{\Lambda^\circ_m} \times 100 = \frac{9.54}{238} \times 100 = 4.008\%$$

9 (*d*) According to Kohlrausch's law, limiting molar conductivity of NH_4OH,
$$\Lambda^\circ_{m\ (NH_4OH)} = \Lambda^\circ_{m\ (NH_4Cl)} + \Lambda^\circ_{m\ (NaOH)} - \Lambda^\circ_{m\ (NaCl)}$$

10 (*d*) $CH_3COONa + HCl \longrightarrow NaCl + CH_3COOH$

$$\Lambda^\circ_{m(CH_3COOH)} = \Lambda^\circ_{m\ (CH_3COONa)} + \Lambda^\circ_{m\ (HCl)} - \Lambda^\circ_{m\ (NaCl)}$$
$$\Lambda^\circ_{m(CH_3COOH)} = (91.0 + 425.9 - 126.4) \text{ Scm}^2\text{mol}^{-1}$$
$$\Lambda^\circ_{m(CH_3COOH)} = 390.5 \text{ S cm}^2\text{mol}^{-1}$$

11 (*b*) The given statement is termed as Kohlrausch's law. According to this law, the limiting molar conductivity of an electrolyte is the sum of cation and anions of the electrolyte.

12 (*c*) Maximum number of ions (5) is obtained from potassium hexacyanoferrate(II), i.e. $K_4[Fe(CN)_6]$ and higher number of ions, higher the molar conductivity.

13 (*b*) In strong electrolyte, number of ions remains constant on dilution. So, equivalent conductance increases due to increase in ionic mobility.

14 (*a*) $\Lambda^\circ_{(CH_3COOH)} = \Lambda^\circ_{(H^+)} + \Lambda^\circ_{(CH_3COO^-)}$
$$= (315 + 35) \text{ mho cm}^2 \text{ eq}^{-1}$$
$$= 350 \text{ mho cm}^2 \text{ eq}^{-1}$$

15 (*a*) Ionic mobility,
$$u = \frac{v}{\frac{dv}{dx}}$$
$$= \frac{\text{m s}^{-1}}{\text{Vm}^{-1}} = \text{m}^2 \text{ V}^{-1} \text{ s}^{-1},$$

Here, V = Volt
where, $\frac{dv}{dx}$ = potential gradient (Vm^{-1})
v = velocity (ms^{-1})

16 (*b*) The given conductivity is specific conductivity. On dilution, the number of ions per unit volume decreases, so it decreases with dilution.

17 (*b*) $\kappa = \frac{l}{A} \times G$

The unit of conductivity (specific conductivity) is $ohm^{-1}\ cm^{-1}$ or $S\ cm^{-1}$.

18 (*d*) Molar conductivity, $\Lambda_m = \frac{\kappa \times 1000}{C}$

Given, $\kappa = 0.0248\ S\ cm^{-1}, C = 0.20\ M$

$$\therefore \quad \Lambda_m = \frac{0.0248 \times 1000}{0.20}$$
$$= 124\ S\ cm^2\ mol^{-1}$$

19 (*a*) On moving downward in a group, atomic size increases, and, hence ionic character increases. Thus, $SrCl_2$ is most ionic among the given compounds, i.e. it will give ion readily in fused state. Hence, $SrCl_2$ exhibit the maximum value of equivalent conductance in fused state.

20 (*b*) Equivalent conductivity

$$(\Lambda_{eq}) = \frac{\kappa \times 1000}{C}$$

$$\text{Conductivity } (\kappa) = \frac{\text{cell constant}}{\text{resistance}}$$
$$= \frac{1.15}{250}\ S\ cm^{-1}$$
$$\therefore \quad \Lambda_{eq} = \frac{1.15 \times 1000}{250 \times 1}$$

[$\because M = N \times$ valence factor for acetic acid]

$$\Lambda_{eq} = 4.6\ \Omega^{-1}\ cm^2\ eq^{-1}$$

21 (*a*) Given, concentration, $C = \frac{M}{32} = \frac{1}{32} M$

$$\Lambda_m = 8.0\ mho\ cm^2$$
$$\Lambda_m^\circ = 400\ mho\ cm^2$$

Degree of dissociation,

$$(\alpha) = \frac{\Lambda_m^C}{\Lambda_m^\circ} = \frac{8}{400} = 0.02$$

For a weak electrolyte, dissociation constant,

$$K_C = \frac{C\alpha^2}{1-\alpha} = \frac{1}{32} \times 0.02 \times 0.02 \quad [\because 1-\alpha \simeq 1]$$
$$= 1.25 \times 10^{-5}$$

22 (*c*) On dilution, the interionic attractions decreases, so dissociation increases. Thus, equivalent as well as molar conductivities increases. This is because the total V of a solution containing 1g equivalent or 1 mole of electrolyte also increases.

However, the number of current carrying particles per cm^3 decreases on diluting the solution.

Hence, Assertion is correct but Reason is incorrect.

23 (*b*) Equivalent conductance is related to specific conductance as

$$\Lambda_C = \frac{\kappa \times 1000}{C}$$

where, C is the number of gram equivalents of solute dissolved in one litre of the solution.

24 (*b*) Weight of NaCl $= 6.5 \times \frac{90}{100} = 5.85$ g

Number of equivalent (mole) of NaCl

$$= \frac{\text{weight of NaCl}}{\text{molecular mass of NaCl}} = \frac{5.85}{58.5} = 0.1$$

Number of equivalents of NaOH obtained = 0.1

[$\because$ 1 mole of NaCl gives 1 mole of NaOH]

$$\therefore \quad N_{NaOH} \times V_{NaOH} = N_{CH_3COOH} \times V_{CH_3COOH}$$
$$0.1 \times 1000 = 1 \times V_{CH_3COOH}$$
$$V_{CH_3COOH} = 100\ cm^3$$

25 (*b*) On dilution, number of ions carrying current in the solution decreases per unit volume, thus the value of specific conductance decreases.

26 (*d*) According to Kohlrausch's law at infinite dilution, when the dissociation is complete, each ion makes a definite contribution towards equivalent conductivity of the electrolyte irrespective of the nature of the other ion with which it is associated.

Or

Equivalent conductivity of an electrolyte at infinite dilution is the sum of the equivalent conductivities of the cations and anions.

27 (*b*) The conductivity of an electrolyte depends upon the nature of electrolyte as the conductivity of strong electrolytes is higher than that of weak electrolytes. NaCl is much stronger electrolyte than HCl and KNO_3, while CH_3COOH is a weak acid. Hence, NaCl has greatest conductivity than the given electrolytes.

28 (*d*) Specific conductance $\propto$ (concentration of electrolytes). Hence, specific conductance is least for the solution of 0.002 N concentration.

29 (*c*) The correct reason is the current carried by cation and anion is equal to their transport number. Hence, Assertion is correct but Reason is incorrect.

30 (*a*) The substance whose aqueous solution allows the passage of electric current and is chemically decomposed, is termed as electrolyte. Electrolytic substances are classified as strong or weak, according to acid base concept. Acetic acid is a weak electrolyte while glucose, ethanol and urea are non-electrolytes.

31 (*b*) Graphite is a good conductor of electricity because it has weak van der Waals' forces and has a delocalised π-electron cloud.

32 (*b*) Resistance of $N/10$ solution

$$= 2.5 \times 10^3\ \Omega$$
$$\kappa = \frac{1}{\text{resistance}} \times \text{cell constant}$$
$$= \frac{1}{2.5 \times 10^3} \times 1.25$$
$$= \frac{1.25 \times 10^{-3}}{2.5}$$
$$= 5 \times 10^{-4}\ \Omega^{-1}\ cm^{-1}$$

Equivalent conductance

$$= \frac{\kappa \times 1000}{C} = \frac{5 \times 10^{-4} \times 1000}{\frac{1}{10}}$$
$$= 5\ \Omega^{-1}\ cm^2\ equiv^{-1}$$

33 (*a*) $[Co(NH_3)_5Cl]Cl_2$ can be dissociated as

$$[Co(NH_3)_5Cl]Cl_2 \xrightleftharpoons{H_2O} [Co(NH_3)_5Cl]^{2+} + 2Cl^-$$

As $[Co(NH_3)_5Cl]Cl_2$ gives three ions, one $[Co(NH_3)_5Cl]^{2+}$ and two Cl^- ions.

Thus, the ratio would be 1 : 2.

34 (*d*) $\Lambda_{eq} = \kappa \times \frac{1000}{C_{eq}}$ (here, $C_{eq} = 0.1$ N)

$$\therefore \Lambda_{eq} = 10000\ \kappa$$

35 (*b*) Pure water does not contains any mineral ions, that is, it is almost not ionised. Thus, it does not conduct electricity.

36. (*c*) $\because BaCl_2 \rightleftharpoons Ba^{2+} + 2Cl^-$

$$\therefore \Lambda^\circ_{BaCl_2} = \Lambda^\circ_{Ba^{2+}} + 2\Lambda^\circ_{Cl^-}$$
$$= 127 + 2 \times 76$$
$$= 279.5\Omega^{-1}\ cm^{-1}$$

37 (*b*) Solid NaCl does not conduct electricity due to the absence of free ions.

Topic 2

Electrolysis and its Quantitative Aspects

2016

1 During the electrolysis of molten sodium chloride, the time required to produce 0.10 mole of chlorine gas using a current of 3 A is [NEET PHASE II]

(a) 55 mins (b) 110 mins (c) 220 mins (d) 330 mins

2 The number of electrons delivered at the cathode during electrolysis by a current of 1A in 60 sec is (charge on electron = 1.60×10^{-19} C) [NEET PHASE II]

(a) 6×10^{23} (b) 6×10^{20}
(c) 3.75×10^{20} (d) 7.48×10^{23}

2014

3 When 0.1 mole of MnO_4^{2-} is oxidised, the quantity of electricity required to completely oxidise MnO_4^{2-} to MnO_4^- is [CBSE AIPMT]

(a) 96500 C (b) 2×96500 C
(c) 9650 C (d) 96.50 C

4 The weight of silver (atomic weight = 108) displaced by a quantity of electricity which displaces 5600 mL of O_2 at STP will be [AFMC]

(a) 5.4 g (b) 10.8 g (c) 54.0 g (d) 108.0 g

5 The quantity of electricity needed to separately electrolyse 1 M solution of $ZnSO_4$, $AlCl_3$ and $AgNO_3$ completely is in the ratio of [WB JEE]

(a) 2:3:1 (b) 2:1:1
(c) 2:1:3 (d) 2:2:1

6 When molten magnesium oxide was electrolysed for a certain period, 150 mg of Mg was deposited on the cathode. The volume of oxygen gas in cm^3 at STP conditions liberated at the anode during the same period is [atomic mass of Mg = 24 g mol^{-1}] [Kerala CEE]

(a) 140 (b) 280
(c) 70 (d) 120
(e) 240

7 In the electrolysis of aqueous solution of copper sulphate using copper strips as anode and cathode, the anode reaction is [Kerala CEE]

(a) $Cu^{2+} + 2e^- \longrightarrow Cu$
(b) $Cu \longrightarrow Cu^{2+} + 2e^-$
(c) $2HO^- \longrightarrow H_2 + \frac{1}{2}O_2 + 2e^-$
(d) $SO_4^{2-} \longrightarrow SO_4 + 2e^-$
(e) $2HSO_4^- \longrightarrow H_2S_2O_8 + 2e^-$

8 Impure copper containing Fe, Au, Ag as impurities is electrolytically refined. A current of 140 A for 482.5 secs decreased the mass of the anode by 22.26 g and increased the mass of cathode by 22.011 g. Percentage of iron in impure copper is,

[given molar mass of Fe = 55.5 g mol^{-1}, molar mass of Cu = 63.54 g mol^{-1}] [KCET]

(a) 0.95 (b) 0.85 (c) 0.97 (d) 0.90

9 Which of the following reactions takes place at the cathode in the electrolytic cell used for extraction of aluminium from alumina? [WB JEE]

(a) $12F^- \longrightarrow 12F + 12e^-$
(b) $Al^{3+} + 3e^- \longrightarrow Al$
(c) $2C(s) + O_2 \longrightarrow 2CO(g)$
(d) $2Al_2O_3 + 12F \longrightarrow 4Al^{3+} + 3O_2 + 12F$

10 When 9.65 Coulomb of electricity is passed through a solution of silver nitrate (atomic mass of Ag = 108 mol^{-1}). The amount of silver deposited is [KCET]

(a) 16.2 mg (b) 21.2 mg
(c) 10.8 mg (d) 6.4 mg

2012

11 What is the time required (in seconds) for depositing all the silver present in 125 mL of 1M $AgNO_3$ solution by passing a current of 241.25 A? [1F = 96500 C] [UP CPMT]

(a) 10 (b) 50 (c) 1000 (d) 100

12 On passing 3 A of electricity for 50 min, 1.8 g metal deposits. The equivalent mass of metal is [Manipal]

(a) 9.3 (b) 19.3
(c) 38.3 (d) 39.9

13 The approximate time duration in hour to electroplate 30 g of calcium from molten calcium chloride using a current of 5 A is [Atomic mass of Ca = 40] [KCET]

(a) 80 (b) 10 (c) 16 (d) 8

2011

14 Which pair of electrolytes could not be distinguished by the products of electrolysis using inert electrodes? [Kerala CEE]

(a) 1 M $CuSO_4$ solution, 1 M $CuCl_2$ solution
(b) 1 M KCl solution, 1 M KI solution.
(c) 1 M $AgNO_3$ solution, 1 M $Cu(NO_3)_2$ solution
(d) 1 M KCl solution, 1 M NaCl solution
(e) 1 M $CuBr_2$ solution, 1 M $CuSO_4$ solution

15 A current is passed through two cells connected in series. The first cell contains $X(NO_3)_3(aq)$ and the second cell contains $Y(NO_3)_2(aq)$. The relative atomic mass of X and Y are in the ratio 1 : 2. What is the ratio of liberated mass of X to that of Y? **[Kerala CEE]**

(a) 3 : 2 (b) 1 : 2 (c) 1 : 3 (d) 3 : 1 (e) 2 : 1

16 One gram of silver gets distributed between 10 cm^3 of molten zinc and 100 cm^3 of molten lead at 800°C. The percentage of silver still left in the lead layer is approximately **[KCET]**

(a) 2 (b) 5 (c) 3 (d) 1

17 9.65 C of electric current is passed through fused anhydrous $MgCl_2$. The magnesium metal thus, obtained is completely converted into a Grignard reagent. The number of moles of Grignard reagent obtained is **[KCET]**

(a) 5×10^{-4} (b) 1×10^{-4} (c) 5×10^{-5} (d) 1×10^{-5}

18 Two different electrolytic cells filled with molten $Cu(NO_3)_2$ and molten $Al(NO_3)_3$ respectively are connected in series. When electricity is passed, 2.7 g Al is deposited on electrode. Calculate the weight of Cu deposited on cathode. [Cu = 63.5; Al = 27.0 g mol^{-1}] **[Guj CET]**

(a) 190.5 g (b) 9.525 g
(c) 63.5 g (d) 31.75 g

2010

19 In electrolysis of dil. H_2SO_4 using platinum electrodes **[BVP]**

(a) H_2 is evolved at cathode
(b) SO_2 is produced at anode
(c) O_2 is obtained at cathode
(d) SO_2 is produced at cathode

20 1 C electricity deposits **[MHT CET]**

(a) 10.8 g of Ag
(b) 96500 g of Ag
(c) electrochemical equivalent of Ag
(d) half of electrochemical equivalent of Ag

21 When same quantity of electricity is passed for half an hour, the amount of Cu and Cr deposited are respectively 0.375 g and 0.30 g. Ratio of electrochemical equivalent of Cu and Cr is **[OJEE]**

(a) 0.8 (b) 1.25 (c) 2.5 (d) 1.62

22 How many coulombs are required to deposit 50 g of aluminium when the electrode reaction is **[RPMT]**

$$Al^{3+} + 3e^- \longrightarrow Al$$

(a) 536111 C (b) 536.111 C
(c) 96500 C (d) 38600 C

23 Give the products available on the cathode and the anode respectively during the electrolysis of an aqueous solution of $MgSO_4$ between inert electrodes. **[Guj CET]**

(a) $H_2(g)$ and $O_2(g)$ (b) $O_2(g)$ and $H_2(g)$
(c) $O_2(g)$ and $Mg(s)$ (d) $O_2(g)$ and $SO_2(g)$

2009

24 Al_2O_3 is reduced by electrolysis at low potential and high current. If 4.0×10^4 A of current is passed through molten Al_2O_3 for 6 hours, what mass of aluminium is produced? [Assume 100% current efficiency, atomic mass of Al = 27] **[CBSE AIPMT]**

(a) 9.0×10^3 g (b) 8.1×10^4 g
(c) 2.4×10^3 g (d) 1.3×10^4 g

25 Copper is a divalent metal. The value of its electrochemical equivalent is 3.29×10^{-4} g. Its atomic mass is **[MHT CET]**

(a) 31.74 g (b) 63.5 g
(c) 126.9 g (d) 15.87 g

26 4.5 g of aluminium (atomic mass 27 u) is deposited at cathode from a molten electrolyte containing Al^{3+} ions by a certain quantity of electric charge. The volume of hydrogen produced at STP from H^+ ions in a solution by the same quantity of electric charge will be **[Manipal]**

(a) 44.8 L (b) 11.2 L
(c) 22.4 L (d) 5.6 L

27 How many Coulombs of electricity are required for the reduction of 1 mole of MnO_4^- to Mn^{2+}? **[Manipal]**

(a) 96500 C (b) 9.65×10^6 C
(c) 4.83×10^5 C (d) 1.93×10^5 C

28 In the electrolytic cell, electron flows from

(a) cathode to anode in solution **[CG PMT, Haryana PMT]**
(b) cathode to anode through external circuit
(c) cathode to anode through internal circuit
(d) anode to cathode through external circuit

29 In the electrolysis of acidulated water, it is desired to obtained 1.12 cc of hydrogen per second under STP condition. The current to be passed is **[KCET]**

(a) 9.65 A (b) 19.3 A (c) 0.965 A (d) 1.93 A

2008

30 On passing 3A of electricity for 50 min, 1.8 g of metal deposits. The equivalent mass of metal is

(a) 9.3 (b) 19.3 **[AFMC]**
(c) 38.3 (d) 39.9

31 Which one of the following reaction occurs at the cathode?

(a) $2OH^- \longrightarrow H_2O + \frac{1}{2}O_2 + 2e^-$ **[MHT CET]**
(b) $Ag \longrightarrow Ag^+ + e^-$
(c) $Fe^{2+} \longrightarrow Fe^{3+} + e^-$
(d) $Cu^{2+} + 2e^- \longrightarrow Cu$

32 A direct current deposits 54 g of silver (atomic mass = 108) during the electrolysis reaction. How much aluminium (atomic mass = 27) would be deposited from aluminium chloride solution by the same amount of electricity?

(a) 4.5 g (b) 5.4 g (c) 54 g **[Kerala CEE]**
(d) 2.7 g (e) 27 g

33 What will be the proportion of moles of metal (Cu : Ni : Ag) at cathode, according to the second law of Faraday? **[Guj CET]**

(a) 1 : 2 : 1 (b) 2 : 2 : 1
(c) 1 : 2 : 2 (d) 1 : 1 : 2

2007

34 A current of 96.5 A is passed for 18 min between nickel electrodes in 500 mL solution of 2M $Ni(NO_3)_2$. The molarity of solution after electrolysis would be **[AIIMS]**

(a) 0.46 M
(b) 0.92 M
(c) 0.625 M
(d) 1.25 M

35 **Assertion** (A) In the electrolysis of aqueous NaCl, Na is preferentially discharged at mercury cathode forming sodium amalgam.

Reason (R) It is due to the fact that hydrogen has a high over voltage at mercury cathode. **[AIIMS]**

(a) Both A and R are correct and R is the correct explanation of A
(b) Both A and R are correct but R is not the correct explanation of A
(c) A is true but R is incorrect
(d) Both A and R are incorrect

36 In electrolytic cell, cathode acts as an/a **[UP CPMT]**

(a) oxidising agent (b) reducing agent
(c) Either of the two (d) Neither (a) nor (b)

37 How many atoms of calcium will be deposited from a solution of $CaCl_2$ by a current of 25 mA flowing for 60 s? **[MP PMT]**

(a) 4.68×10^{18} (b) 4.68×10^{15}
(c) 4.68×10^{12} (d) 4.68×10^{9}

38 When 3.86 A current is passed through an electrolyte for 50 min, 2.4 g of a divalent metal is deposited. The gram atomic weight of the metal (in grams) is **[EAMCET]**

(a) 24 (b) 12 (c) 64 (d) 40

2006

39 If the aqueous solutions of the following salts are electrolysed for 1 h with 10 A current, which solution will deposit the maximum mass of the metal at the cathode? The atomic weights are $Fe^{2+} = 56$, $Zn^{2+} = 65$, $Ag^{+} = 108$, $Hf^{3+} = 178$ and $W^{3+} = 184$ **[Kerala CEE]**

(a) $ZnSO_4$ (b) $FeCl_3$ (c) $HfCl_4$ (d) WCl_6
(e) $AgNO_3$

40 In the electrolysis of water, one Faraday of electrical energy would evolve **[AMU]**

(a) one mole of oxygen (b) one gram atom of oxygen
(c) 8 g of oxygen (d) 22.4 L of oxygen

41 The charge required to liberate one gram equivalent of an element is **[BCECE]**

(a) 96500 F (b) 1 F
(c) 1 C (d) None of these

2005

42 A current of strength 2.5 A was passed through $CuSO_4$ solution for 6 min 26 s. The amount of copper deposited is [Atomic weight of Cu = 63.5, 1 F = 96500 C]

(a) 0.3175 g (b) 3.175 g **[Punjab PMET]**
(c) 0.635 g (d) 6.35 g

43 What is the electrochemical equivalent (in g C^{-1}) of silver? [Ag = 108; F = Faraday] **[EAMCET]**

(a) $108F$ (b) $\frac{108}{F}$ (c) $\frac{F}{108}$ (d) $\frac{1}{108F}$

Answers

1 (b)	2 (c)	3 (c)	4 (d)	5 (a)	6 (c)	7 (b)	8 (d)	9 (b)	10 (c)
11 (b)	12 (b)	13 (d)	14 (d)	15 (c)	16 (c)	17 (c)	18 (b)	19 (a)	20 (c)
21 (b)	22 (a)	23 (a)	24 (b)	25 (b)	26 (d)	27 (c)	28 (d)	29 (a)	30 (b)
31 (d)	32 (a)	33 (d)	34 (b)	35 (a)	36 (a)	37 (a)	38 (d)	39 (e)	40 (c)
41 (b)	42 (a)	43 (b)							

Explanations

1 (*b*) This problem is based on Faraday's first law of electrolysis which states that when an electric current is passed through an electrolytic solution, the amount of substance (*w*), deposited at the electrode, is proportional to the electric charge (*q*) passed through the electrolytic solution.

The formula used in the problem is

$$w = \frac{Eit}{96500} \quad \ldots(i)$$

where, E = gram-equivalent mass of Cl^-

i = current, t = time, it = q

Given, $n = 0.1$ mol

$\therefore \quad w = (0.10 \times 71)$ g,

$i = 3$ A, $E = 35.5$ g-eq.

The following reactions occured,

At cathode : $2H_2O \xrightarrow{+2e^-} H_2 + 2OH^-$

At anode : $\underset{35.5g}{2Cl^-} \xrightarrow{-2e^-} \underset{71\,g}{Cl_2}$

Putting all values in expression (i)

$$(0.10 \times 71) = \frac{35.5}{96500} \times 3 \times t$$

or $t = 6433.3 \sim 6433$ s

or $t = \frac{6433}{60}$ min $= 107.22$ min

[1s = 1/60 min]

The value of time is closest to the option (b), ie 110 mins.

∴ Option (b) is correct.

2 (*c*) From Faraday's first law of electrolysis,

$$\frac{w}{E} = \frac{it}{96500} \quad ...(i)$$

Given, $i = 1$ A; $t = 60$ s

Putting these values in eq. (i)

$$\frac{w}{E} = \frac{1 \times 60}{96500}$$

or $\frac{w}{E} = \frac{6}{9650}$

= Number of moles of electrons

∴ Number of electrons

$$= \frac{6}{9650} \times 6.022 \times 10^{23}$$

$$= 3.75 \times 10^{20}$$

3 (*c*) $\underset{(+6)}{MnO_4^{2-}} \xrightleftharpoons{1 \text{ mole } e^- [=1F]} \underset{(+7)}{MnO_4^-}$

As per the equation, for 1 mole of MnO_4^{2-}, 1 F of electricity is required. Thus, for 0.1 mole of MnO_4^{2-}, 0.1 F of electricity is required.

Since, 1 F = 96500 C

∴ 0.1 F = 0.1 × 96500 C = 9650 C

Hence, 9650 C of electricity is required to completely oxidise MnO_4^{2-} to MnO_4^-.

4 (*d*) Since, 22400 mL volume is occupied by 1 mole of O_2 at STP,

thus, 5600 mL O_2 means

$$= \frac{5600}{22400} \text{ mol } O_2 = \frac{1}{4} \text{ mol } O_2$$

∴ Weight of $O_2 = \frac{1}{4} \times 32 = 8$ g

According to problem,

equivalents of Ag = equivalents of O_2

$$\Rightarrow \frac{\text{weight of Ag}}{\text{equivalent weight of Ag}} = \frac{w_{O_2}}{\text{equivalent weight of } O_2}$$

$$\Rightarrow \frac{w_{Ag}}{\frac{M_{Ag}}{1}} = \frac{w_{O_2}}{\frac{M_{O_2}}{4}} \quad [\because 2H_2O \longrightarrow O_2 + 4H^+ + 4e^-]$$

$$\therefore \frac{w_{Ag}}{108} \times 1 = \frac{8}{32} \times 4$$

$$\Rightarrow w_{Ag} = 108 \text{ g}$$

5 (*a*) From the Faraday's second law

$$w \propto zit, \; w \propto \frac{E}{96500} it$$

or $it \propto \frac{1}{E}$ or electricity

$$\propto \frac{1}{E} \propto \frac{\text{valency}}{\text{atomic weight}}$$

Thus, the amount of electricity required for $ZnSO_4$, $AlCl_3$ and $AgNO_3$ is in the ratio of 2 : 3 : 1. (Here, 2, 3 and 1 are the valencies of metal atom in the given compounds).

Alternatively,

In $ZnSO_4$,

$$\underset{1 \text{ mole}}{Zn^{2+}} + \underset{\substack{2 \text{ mol or} \\ 2 \text{ Faraday}}}{2e^-} \longrightarrow Zn$$

In $AlCl_3$, $\underset{1 \text{ mol}}{Al^{3+}} + \underset{3 \text{ F}}{3e^-} \longrightarrow Al$

In $AgNO_3$, $\underset{1 \text{ mol}}{Ag^+} + \underset{1 \text{ F}}{e^-} \longrightarrow Ag$

Thus, the ratio of the amount of electricity required is 2 : 3 : 1.

6 (*c*) $2MgO \longrightarrow 2Mg + O_2$

2 moles of Mg is equivalent to 1 mole of O_2 in reaction. Hence, 150 mg i.e. $\frac{150}{24}$ milli mole Mg is equivalent is

$$= \frac{150}{24} \times \frac{1}{2} \text{ millimole } O_2$$

1 mole O_2 has volume of 22400 cc at STP.

Hence, $\frac{150}{24} \times \frac{1}{2} \times 10^{-3}$ mole has volume

$$= \frac{150}{24} \times \frac{1}{2} \times 10^{-3} \times 22400 \text{ cc}$$

$$= 70 \text{ cc } O_2 \text{ at STP.}$$

7 (*b*) In the electrolysis of aqueous solution of copper sulphate using copper strips as anode and cathode, the anode reaction is

$$Cu \longrightarrow Cu^{2+} + 2e^-$$

as oxidation takes place at anode.

8 (*d*) Amount of impurity

= decreased mass of anode – increased mass of cathode

= 22.26 – 22.011 = 0.249 g

Amount of pure Cu deposited,

$$w = zit = \frac{E}{96500} \times it$$

$$= \frac{63.54}{2 \times 96500} \times 140 \times 482.5$$

$$= 22.239 \text{ g}$$

But increased mass of cathode

= 22.011 g

∴ Amount of impurity (Fe)

= 22.239 – 22.011 = 0.228 g

Now, from Faraday's second law of electrolysis,

$$\frac{\text{weight of Fe deposited}}{\text{weight of Cu deposited}} = \frac{\text{equivalent weight of Fe}}{\text{equivalent weight of Cu}}$$

(≈ amount of impurity)

$$\therefore \frac{\text{weight of Fe deposited}}{0.228} = \frac{27.55}{31.77}$$

$$\therefore \text{Weight of Fe} = \frac{27.75 \times 0.228}{31.77} = 0.199$$

∴ % of iron in impure copper

$$= \frac{0.199}{22.26} \times 100$$

$$= 0.89 \approx 0.90$$

9 (*b*) At cathode, the reaction in which reduction takes place is,

$$Al^{3+} + 3e^- \longrightarrow Al$$

10 (*c*) Electricity passed = 9.65 Coulomb

The amount of silver deposited = ?

We know that, 96500 Coulomb electricity deposits

Ag = 108 mol^{-1}

∴ 9.65 coulomb electricity deposits Ag

$$= \frac{9.65}{96500} \times 108 = 108 \times 10^{-4} \text{g}$$

$$= 10.8 \text{ mg}$$

11 (*b*) 1000 mL of $AgNO_3$ solution contains 108 g Ag

∴ 125 mL of $AgNO_3$ solution will contain $= \frac{108 \times 125}{1000} = 13.5$g of Ag

$$Ag^+ + \underset{(1F = 96500)}{e^-} \longrightarrow \underset{108\text{g}}{Ag}$$

108 g of Ag is deposited by 96500 C

∴ 13.5 g of Ag is deposited by

$$= \frac{96500}{108} \times 13.5 = 12062.5 \text{ C}$$

$$Q = it$$

$$t = \frac{Q}{i} = \frac{12062.5}{241.25} = 50 \text{ s}$$

12 (*b*) $w_{\text{metal}} = \frac{Eit}{96500} = \frac{E \times 3 \times 50 \times 60}{96500}$

$$E = \frac{96500 \times w}{3 \times 50 \times 60}$$

$$\Rightarrow E = \frac{96500 \times 1.8}{3 \times 50 \times 60} = 19.3 \text{ equiv}$$

13 (*d*) $Ca^{2+} + 2e^- \longrightarrow Ca$ (at cathode)
2F 40 g

Total charge $= 2 \times 96500$ C
40 g Ca is deposited by 2×96500 C charge.

$\therefore$ 30 g Ca will be deposited by

$$= \frac{2 \times 96500 \times 30}{40} \text{ C charge}$$

$$Q = it = \frac{2 \times 96500 \times 30}{40} = 5 \times t$$

$$t = \frac{2 \times 96500 \times 30}{40 \times 5} = 28950 \text{ s}$$

$$= \frac{28950}{60 \times 60} = 8.04 \text{ h} \sim 8\text{h}$$

14 (*d*) Electrolysis of both KCl and NaCl liberates H_2 at the cathode and Cl_2 at the anode. But the products of electrolysis of remaining solutions will be different.

15 (*c*) $X(NO_3)_3$ and $Y(NO_3)_2$ suggests that X is trivalent, X^{3+} and Y is divalent, Y^{2+}.

Atomic mass **Equivalent mass**

$$X^{3+} + 3e^- \rightarrow X \quad A_x \quad E_x = \frac{A_x}{3}$$

$$Y^{2+} + 2e^- \rightarrow Y \quad A_y \quad E_y = \frac{A_y}{2}$$

As mass is deposited in the ratio of equivalent mass, thus,

$$\frac{E_x}{E_y} = \frac{A_x}{3} \times \frac{2}{A_y} = \frac{2A_x}{3A_y} = \frac{2}{3} \times \frac{1}{2} = \frac{1}{3}$$

$[\because A_x : A_y = 1:2]$

Thus, the ratio of liberated mass of X to that of Y is 1 : 3.

16 (*c*) Concentration of Ag in zinc $= \dfrac{x}{10}$

$\therefore$ Concentration of Ag in Pb $= \dfrac{1-x}{100}$

$$= \frac{x/10}{1 - x/100} = 300$$

On solving, we get $x = 97\%$

$\therefore$ The percentage of silver in lead layer $= 100 - 97 = 3$

17 (*c*) $Mg^{2+} + 2e^- \longrightarrow Mg$

Equivalent mass of Mg $= \dfrac{24}{2} = 12$ g eq

$\because$ 96500 C current produces 12 g Mg.

$\therefore$ 9.65 C current produces 1.2×10^{-3} g of Mg

Thus, moles of Mg $= \dfrac{1.2 \times 10^{-3}}{24}$

$= 5 \times 10^{-5}$ mol

Now,

$$R{-}X + Mg \longrightarrow RMgX$$

$\therefore 5 \times 10^{-5}$ mol $\quad 5 \times 10^{-5}$ mol

18 (*b*) According to Faraday second law,

$$\frac{w_1}{E_1} = \frac{w_2}{E_2}$$

$$\frac{2.7 \times 3}{27} = \frac{w_2 \times 2}{63.5}$$

$(E_{Al} = 27/3$ and $E_{Cu} = 63.5/2)$

$w_2 = 9.525$ g

19 (*a*) Dilute sulphuric acid contains H^+, SO_4^{2-} and OH^- ions.

At cathode

H^+ ions undergo reduction by taking up electrons to form H_2.

$$2H^+(aq) + e^- \longrightarrow H_2(g)$$

At anode:

The concentration of OH^- ions is too low to maintain a reaction and sulphate ions are not oxidised but remain in the solution at the end. Thus, OH^- ions are discharged in preference over SO_4^{2-} giving off O_2 gas.

$$4OH^-(aq) \longrightarrow O_2(g) + 2H_2O(l) + 4e^-$$

20 (*c*) From Faraday's first law,

mass $w = z \cdot Q$

when, $Q = 1$ C

$w = z =$ electrochemical equivalent.

21 (*b*) $\dfrac{w_1}{w_2} = \dfrac{E_1}{E_2} = \dfrac{Z_1}{Z_2}$

$$\frac{0.375}{0.3} = \frac{Z_1}{Z_2} = 1.25$$

22 (*a*) $Al^{3+} + 3e^- \longrightarrow Al$

1 mole of Al requires 3 moles of electrons or 3×96500 C of electricity

As 1 mole of Al = 27 g

$\therefore$ 27 g of Al require $= 3 \times 96500$ C

Hence, 50 g of Al require

$$= \frac{3 \times 96500 \text{ C} \times 50}{27} \simeq 536111 \text{ C}$$

23 (*a*) The reactions, which might occur when an aqueous $MgSO_4$ solution is electrolysed are given below :

At cathode

$$2H_2O(l) + 2e^- \longrightarrow 2OH^-(aq) + H_2(g)$$

$$Mg^{2+} + (aq) + 2e^- \longrightarrow Mg(s)$$

At anode

$$SO_4^{2-} \longrightarrow SO_2 + O_2 + 2e^-$$

$$2H_2O(l) \longrightarrow O_2(g) + 4H^+ + 4e^-$$

But reactions that actually take place are as follows:

At cathode

$$2H_2O(l) + 2e^- \longrightarrow H_2(g) + 2OH^-(aq)$$

At anode

$$2H_2O(l) \longrightarrow O_2(g) + 4H^+ + 4e^-$$

The above anode reaction takes place because SO_4^{2-} ions are resistant to oxidation and cathode reaction takes place because H_2O is easier to reduce than Mg^{2+}.

24 (*b*) The reaction is $Al^{3+} + 3e^- \longrightarrow Al$

$$\therefore \quad E_{Al} = \frac{\text{atomic weight}}{3} = \frac{27}{3} = 9 \text{ g eq}$$

Now, $w = \dfrac{E \cdot i \cdot t}{96500}$

$$= \frac{9 \times 4 \times 10^4 \times 6 \times 60 \times 60}{96500}$$

$$= 8.05 \times 10^4 \simeq 8.1 \times 10^4 \text{ g}$$

25 (*b*) Electrochemical equivalent,

$$Z = \frac{E}{96500}$$

or $\quad 3.29 \times 10^{-4} = \dfrac{E}{96500}$

$\therefore \quad E = 31.74$

Atomic mass $= 2 \times E$

$[\because$ Cu is divalent$]$

$= 2 \times 31.74 = 63.48$ g ≈ 63.5 g

26 (*d*) Equivalent mass of Al $= \dfrac{27}{3} = 9$ g eq

Equivalent mass of H = 1

$$\therefore \quad \frac{w_{Al}}{w_{H_2}} = \frac{\text{equivalent mass of Al}}{\text{equivalent mass of } H_2}$$

$$\Rightarrow \quad \frac{4.5}{w_{H_2}} = \frac{9}{1} \Rightarrow w_{H_2} = 0.5 \text{ g}$$

$\because$ 2 g of H_2 at STP occupies volume $= 22.4$ L

$\therefore$ 0.5 g of H_2 at STP will occupy

volume $= \dfrac{22.4 \times 0.5}{2} = 5.6$ L

27 (*c*) $MnO_4^- + 8H^+ + 5e^- \longrightarrow Mn^{2+} + 4H_2O$
1 mole 5 mol

i.e. 5 F of electricity is required.

Hence, electricity required

$= 5 \times 96500$ C $= 482500$ C

$= 4.83 \times 10^5$ C

28 (*d*) In an electrolytic cell, electrons are forced through the circuit (i.e. from anode to cathode) by an external source. In this cell, cathode is the site of reduction (negative electrode) and anode is the site of oxidation (positive electrode).

29 (a) $22400\ dm^3$ of H_2 = 1 mole of H_2

$\therefore 1.12\,dm^3$ of $H_2 = \frac{1.12}{22400}$ mole of H_2

$[\because 1\ dm^3 = 1\ cc]$

$\therefore$ Number of equivalents of hydrogen

$= \frac{1.12 \times 2}{22400} = 10^{-4}$

Number of Faraday required $= 10^{-4}$

$\therefore$ Current to be passed in 1 s

$= 96500 \times 10^{-4} = 9.65$ A

30 (b) $w_{metal} = \frac{E \times i \times T}{96500}$

$\therefore \quad E = \frac{96500 \times w}{3 \times 50 \times 60}$

$= \frac{E \times 3 \times 50 \times 60}{96500}$

$= \frac{96500 \times 1.8}{3 \times 50 \times 60} = 19.3$

31 (d) At cathode, reduction (i.e. gain of electron) takes place, while at anode, oxidation (loss of electron) takes place.

Thus, $Cu^{2+} + 2e^- \longrightarrow Cu$ occurs at cathode.

32 (a) According to second law of electrolysis,

$\frac{\text{weight of Ag}}{\text{weight of Al}} = \frac{\text{equivalent weight of Ag}}{\text{equivalent weight of Al}}$

Equivalent weight of Ag

$= \frac{\text{atomic mass}}{\text{valency}} = \frac{108}{1} = 108$ g eq.

Equivalent weight of Al $= \frac{27}{3} = 9$ g eq.

$\frac{54}{w_{Al}} = \frac{108}{9}$ or $w_{Al} = \frac{54 \times 9}{108} = 4.5$ g

33 (d) According to Faraday's second law of electrolysis, when the same quantity of electricity is passed through the solutions of different electrolytes connected in series, the weights of substances produced at the electrodes are directly proportional to their equivalent weight.

If M stands for atomic weight of substances,

Equivalent weight of Cu $= \frac{M}{2}$

Equivalent weight of Ni $= \frac{M}{2}$

Equivalent weight of Ag $= \frac{M}{1}$

So, the proportion of moles of metals

$\frac{M}{2} : \frac{M}{2} : \frac{M}{1}$

$\therefore \quad 1 : 1 : 2$

34 (b) Moles of $Ni(NO_3)_2$ in 500 mL of 2 M

$Ni(NO_3)_2$ is $\frac{2 \times 500}{1000} = 1$ mol

Charge $= it = 96.5 \times 18 \times 60 = 104220$ C

$Ni^{2+} + 2e^- \longrightarrow Ni$

$\because$ 2×96500 C deposits 1 mole of $Ni(NO_3)_2$

$\therefore$ 104220 C will deposit $= \frac{104220}{2 \times 96500}$

$= 0.54$ mol

So, moles of $Ni(NO_3)_2$ left

$= 1.0 - 0.54 = 0.46$ mol

Thus, molarity of $Ni(NO_3)_2$ solution

$= 2 \times 0.46 = 0.92$ mol/L

35 (a) In the electrolysis of aqueous NaCl, sodium is preferentially discharged at the mercury cathode forming sodium amalgam (Na-Hg) due to the fact that hydrogen has a high over voltage at mercury cathode.

36 (a) In electrolytic cell, reduction takes place at cathode. Therefore, in electrolytic cell, cathode acts as a oxidising agent. e.g.

At cathode,

$2Na^+ + 2e^- \longrightarrow 2Na$ (reduction)

At anode,

$2Cl^- \longrightarrow Cl_2 + e^-$ (oxidation)

Overall reaction

$2Na^+ + 2Cl^- \longrightarrow \underset{\text{Cathode}}{2Na} + \underset{\text{Anode}}{Cl_2}$

37 (a) Charge, $Q = i \times t = \frac{25}{1000} \times 60 = 1.5$ C

$\underset{2 \times 96500\ C}{Ca^{2+}} + 2e^- \longrightarrow \underset{6.02 \times 10^{23}}{Ca}$

$\because$ At 2×96500 C, the deposited Ca-atoms $= 6.02 \times 10^{23}$

$\therefore$ At 1.5 C, the deposited Ca-atoms

$= \frac{6.02 \times 10^{23} \times 1.5}{2 \times 96500} = 4.68 \times 10^{18}$

38 (d) $w = zit$

or $\quad w = \frac{\text{equivalent weight}}{96500} \times i \times t$

or $\quad w = \frac{\text{atomic weight}}{\text{valency} \times 96500} \times i \times t$

or Atomic weight

$= \frac{w \times \text{valency} \times 96500}{i \times t}$

$= \frac{2.4 \times 2 \times 96500}{3.86 \times 50 \times 60} = 40$ g

39 (e) According to Faraday, first law of electrolysis,

$w = \frac{E}{96500} \times i \times t$

Here, i and t are same

$\therefore \quad w \propto E$

Now, equivalent weight $= \frac{\text{atomic weight}}{\text{valency}}$

As the equivalent weight of Ag is maximum among these ions hence, $AgNO_3$ solution will deposit the maximum mass of the metal at the cathode on electrolysis.

40 (c) Hydrolysis of water is given as,

$2H_2O \rightleftharpoons O_2 + 4H^+ + 4e^-$

$\because$ 4 F of charge liberate $O_2 = 32$ g

$\therefore$ 1 F of charge liberate $O_2 = \frac{32}{4} = 8$ g

41 (b) The charge required to liberate one gram equivalent of an element is always equal to 1 F (i.e. 96500 C).

42. (a) Number of coulombs passed $= i \times t$

$t = 6 \times 60 + 26$

$= 360 + 26$

$= 386$ s

$\because \quad Q = i \times t$

$\therefore \quad Q = 2.5 \times 386$

$= 965$ C

2×96500 C charge deposits $= 63.5$ g

1 C charge deposits $= \frac{63.5}{2 \times 96500}$

$\therefore$ 965 C charge deposits $= \frac{63.5 \times 965}{2 \times 96500}$

$= 0.3175$ g

43. (b) Electrochemical equivalent

$(z) = \frac{E}{F}$

$= \frac{108}{F}\ g \cdot C^{-1}$

(Equivalent weight of Ag = 108)

Topic 3

Electrochemical Series, Electrode Potential and EMF

2019

1 For the cell reaction,

$2Fe^{3+}(aq)+2I^-(aq) \longrightarrow 2Fe^{2+}(aq)+I_2(aq)$

$E^\ominus_{cell}=0.24$ V at 298 K. The standard Gibb's energy $(\Delta_r G^\ominus)$ of the cell reaction is **[NEET]**

[Given that Faraday constant $F=96500$ C mol^{-1}]

(a) -23.16 kJ mol^{-1} (b) 46.32 kJ mol^{-1}
(c) 23.16 kJ mol^{-1} (d) -46.32 kJ mol^{-1}

2 For a cell involving one electron, $E^\circ_{cell}=0.59$ V at 298 K, the equilibrium constant for the cell reaction is **[NEET]**

$\left[\text{Given that, } \frac{2.303\,RT}{F}=0.059 \text{ V at } T=298 \text{ K}\right]$

(a) 1.0×10^{5} (b) 1.0×10^{10}
(c) 1.0×10^{30} (d) 1.0×10^{2}

3 Cell notation, $M|\underset{0.01}{M^{2+}}||\underset{0.0001}{M^{2+}}|M$. If value of E°_{cell} is 4 volt (Given, $\frac{RT}{F}\log 10=0.06$) **[AIIMS]**

(a) 3.94 V (b) 4.06 V
(c) 2.03 V (d) 8.18 V

4 The standard electrode potential (E^-) values of $(Al^{3+}/Al, Ag^+/Ag, K^+/K$ and Cr^{3+}/Cr are -1.66 V, 0.80V, 2.93 V and -0.74 V, respectively. The correct decreasing order of reducing power of the metal is **[NEET (Odisha)]**

(a) Ag > Cr > Al > K (b) K > Al > Cr > Ag
(c) K > Al > Ag > Cr (d) Al > K > Ag > Cr

5 Given, $E^\circ_{Cr^{3+}/Cr}=-0.72$ V, $E^\circ_{Fe^{2+}/Fe}=-0.42V$,

The potential for the cell

$Cr|Cr^{3+}$ (0.1 M) $||$ Fe^{2+} (0.01 M) | Fe is **[JIPMER]**

(a) -0.339 V (b) -0.26 V
(c) 0.26 V (d) 0.3 V

2018

6 For a Ag-Zn button cell, net reaction is

$Zn(s)+Ag_2O(s) \longrightarrow ZnO(s)+2Ag(s)$

$\Delta G^\circ_f(Ag_2O)=-11.21$ kJ mol^{-1}

$\Delta G^\circ_f(ZnO)=-318.3$ kJ mol^{-1}

Then, E°_{cell} of the button cell is **[AIIMS]**

(a) 3.182 V (b) -1.621 V
(c) 1.591 V (d) -1.591 V

7 The emf of a Daniell cell at 298 K is E_1,

$Zn\,|\,\underset{(0.01M)}{ZnSO_4}\,||\,\underset{(1.0M)}{CuSO_4}\,|\,Cu$

When the concentration of $ZnSO_4$ is 1.0 M and that of $CuSO_4$ is 0.01 M, the emf changed to E_2. What is the relationship between E_1 and E_2?

(a) $E_1=E_2$ (b) $E_1<E_2$
(c) $E_2=0, E_1\neq 0$ (d) $E_1>E_2$

8 If $E^\circ(Zn^{2+}, Zn)=-0.763$ V and $E^\circ(Fe^{2+}, Fe)=-0.44$ V, then the emf of the cell

$Zn|\,Zn^{2+}(a=0.001)||\,Fe^{2+}(a=0.005)|$ Fe is **[JIPMER]**

(a) equal to 0.323 V (b) less than 0.323 V
(c) greater than 0.323 V (d) equal to 1.103 V

9 For the electrochemical cell,

$Ag^+|AgCl|KCl\,||AgNO_3|\,Ag^+$, the overall cell reaction is **[JIPMER]**

(a) $Ag^+ + KCl \longrightarrow AgCl(s)+K^+$
(b) $Ag+AgCl \longrightarrow 2Ag+\frac{1}{2}Cl_2$
(c) $AgCl(s) \longrightarrow Ag^+ + Cl^-$
(d) $Ag^+ + Cl^- \longrightarrow AgCl(s)$

2017

10 **Assertion** (A) E_{cell} increases with increase in concentration of Ag^+ ions for the following reaction

$Ag^+ + e^- \longrightarrow Ag$

Reason (R) E_{cell} has positive value. **[AIIMS]**

(a) Both A and R are correct and R is the correct explanation of A
(b) Both A and R are correct but R is not the correct explanation of A
(c) A is correct but R is incorrect
(d) Both A and R are incorrect

11 The value of reaction quotient (Q), for the following cell

Zn(s) | Zn^{2+} (0.01 M) || Ag^+ (1.25 M) | Ag(s) is **[JIPMER]**

(a) 156 (b) 125 (c) 1.25×10^{-2} (d) 6.4×10^{-3}

12 The standard reduction potential for Zn^{2+}/Zn, Ni^{2+}/Ni and Fe^{2+}/Fe are -0.76, -0.23 and -0.44 V, respectively. The reaction $X+Y^{2+} \longrightarrow X^{2+}+Y$ will be spontaneous when **[JIPMER]**

(a) $X=Ni, Y=Fe$ (b) $X=Ni, Y=Zn$
(c) $X=Fe, Y=Zn$ (d) $X=Zn, Y=Ni$

2016

13 The pressure of H_2 required to make the potential of H_2-electrode zero in pure water at 298 K is **[NEET]**

(a) 10^{-12} atm (b) 10^{-10} atm (c) 10^{-4} atm (d) 10^{-14} atm

14 If the E°_{cell} for a given reaction has a negative value, which of the following gives correct relationship for the values of ΔG° and K_{eq}? **[NEET Phase II] [CBSE AIPMT 2011]**

(a) $\Delta G^\circ > 0;\ K_{eq} < 1$ (b) $\Delta G^\circ > 0;\ K_{eq} > 1$
(c) $\Delta G^\circ < 0;\ K_{eq} > 1$ (d) $\Delta G^\circ < 0;\ K_{eq} < 1$

15 Zinc can be coated on iron to produce galvanised iron but the reverse is not possible. It is because **[NEET Phase II]**

(a) zinc is lighter than iron
(b) zinc has lower melting point than iron
(c) zinc has lower negative electrode potential than iron
(d) zinc has higher negative electrode potential than iron

16 The formal potential of Fe^{3+}/Fe^{2+} in a sulphuric acid and phosphoric acid mixture ($E^\circ = +0.16$ V) is much lower than the standard potential ($E^\circ = +0.77$ V). This is due to

(a) formation of the species $[FeHPO_4]^+$ **[Manipal]**
(b) lowering of potential upon complexation
(c) formation of the species $[FeSO_4]^+$
(d) high acidic of the medium

17 Given, $E^\circ_{Cr^{3+}/Cr} = -0.72$ V, $E^\circ_{Fe^{2+}/Fe} = -0.42$ V. The potential for the cell **[UK PMT]**

Cr/Cr^{3+} (0.1 M) $\|$ Fe^{2+} (0.01 M)/ Fe is

(a) −0.339 V (b) −0.26 V
(c) 0.26 V (d) 0.3 V

18 For $Cr_2O_7^{2-} + 14H^+ + 6e^- \longrightarrow 2Cr^{3+} + 7H_2O;$ $E^\circ = +1.33$ V. At $[Cr_2O_7^{2-}] = 4.5$ millimoles, $[Cr^{3+}] = 15$ millimoles, E is 1.067 V. The pH of the solution is nearly equal to **[KCET]**

(a) 2 (b) 3 (c) 5 (d) 4

19 The emf of a galvanic cell with electrode potential of zinc $= -0.76$ V and that of copper $= 0.34$ V is **[KCET]**

(a) 0.76 V (b) 1.1 V (c) −1.1 V (d) 1.6 V

20 Standard electrode potential data are useful for understanding the suitability of an oxidant in a redox titration. Some half-cell reactions and their standard potentials are given below

$MnO_4^-(aq) + 8H^+(aq) + 5e^- \longrightarrow Mn^{2+}(aq) + 4H_2O(l);\ E^\circ = 1.51$ V

$Cr_2O_7^{2-}(aq) + 14H^+(aq) + 6e^- \longrightarrow 2Cr^{3+}(aq) + 7H_2O(l);$ $E^\circ = 1.38$ V

$Fe^{3+}(aq) + e^- \longrightarrow Fe^{2+}(aq);\ E^\circ = 0.77$ V

$Cl_2(g) + 2e^- \longrightarrow 2Cl^-(aq);\ E^\circ = 1.4$ V

Identify the only incorrect statement regarding the quantitative estimation of aqueous $Fe(NO_3)_2$ **[WB JEE]**

(a) MnO_4^- can be used in aqueous HCl
(b) $Cr_2O_7^-$ can be used in aqueous HCl
(c) MnO_4^- can be used in aqueous H_2SO_4
(d) $Cr_2O_7^{2-}$ can be used in aqueous H_2SO_4

2013

21 A hydrogen gas electrode is made by dipping platinum wire in a solution of HCl and pH = 10 and by passing hydrogen gas around the platinum wire at 1 atm pressure. The oxidation potential of electrode would be **[NEET]**

(a) 0.059 V (b) 0.59 V
(c) 0.118 V (d) 1.18 V

22 A button cell used in watches, functions as following

$Zn(s) + Ag_2O(s) + H_2O(l) \rightleftharpoons 2Ag(s) + Zn^{2+}(aq) + 2OH^-(aq)$

If half-cell potentials are

$Zn^{2+}(aq) + 2e^- \longrightarrow Zn(s), E^\circ = -0.76$ V

$Ag_2O(s) + H_2O(l) + 2e^- \longrightarrow 2Ag(s) + 2OH^-,\ E^\circ = 0.34$ V

The cell potential will be **[NEET]**

(a) 1.1 V (b) 0.42 V
(c) 0.84 V (d) 1.34 V

23 Aluminium displaces hydrogen from acids, but copper does not. A galvanic cell prepared by combining Cu/Cu^{2+} and Al/Al^{3+} has an emf of 2.0 V at 298 K. If the potential of copper electrode is 0.34 V, then that of aluminium electrode is **[KCET]**

(a) −2.3 V (b) +2.34 V
(c) −1.66 V (d) +1.66 V

2012

24 The Gibbs energy for the decomposition of Al_2O_3 at 500°C is as follows

$$\frac{2}{3}Al_2O_3 \longrightarrow \frac{4}{3}Al + O_2;\quad \Delta_r G = +960\ \text{kJ mol}^{-1}$$

The potential difference needed for the electrolytic reduction of aluminium oxide (Al_2O_3) at 500°C is at least **[CBSE AIPMT]**

(a) 4.5 V (b) 3.0 V
(c) 2.5 V (d) 5.0 V

25 The standard emf for the given cell reaction, $Zn + Cu^{2+} \longrightarrow Cu + Zn^{2+}$ is 1.10 V at 25°C. The emf for the cell reaction, when 0.1 M Cu^{2+} and 0.1 M Zn^{2+} solutions are used at 25°C is **[AIIMS]**

(a) 1.10 V (b) −1.10 V
(c) 2.20 V (d) −2.20 V

26 The equilibrium constant of the reaction,

$Cu(s) + 2Ag^+(aq) \longrightarrow Cu^{2+}(aq) + 2Ag(s)$

$E° = 0.46$ V at 298 K is **[AFMC]**

(a) 2.4×10^{10} (b) 2.0×10^{10}
(c) 4.0×10^{10} (d) 4.0×10^{15}

27 Li occupies higher position in the electrochemical series of metals as compared to Cu. Since, **[WB JEE]**

(a) the standard reduction potential of Li^+/Li is lower than that of Cu^{2+}/Cu.
(b) the standard reduction potential of Cu^{2+}/Cu is lower than that of Li^+/Li.
(c) the standard oxidation potential of Li/Li^+ is lower than that of Cu/Cu^{2+}.
(d) Li is smaller in size as compared to Cu.

2011

28 The electrode potentials for

$Cu^{2+}(aq) + e^- \longrightarrow Cu^+(aq)$

and $Cu^+(aq) + e^- \longrightarrow Cu(s)$ are + 0.15 V and + 0.50 V respectively. The value of $E°_{Cu^{2+}/Cu}$ will be **[CBSE AIPMT]**

(a) 0.150 V (b) 0.500 V
(c) 0.325 V (d) 0.650 V

29 Standard electrode potential of three metals *X*, *Y* and *Z* are −1.2 V, + 0.5 V and − 3.0 V respectively. The reducing power of these metals will be **[CBSE AIPMT]**

(a) $X > Y > Z$ (b) $Y > Z > X$
(c) $Y > X > Z$ (d) $Z > X > Y$

30 Standard electrode potential for Sn^{4+}/Sn^{2+} couple is + 0.15 V and that for the Cr^{3+}/Cr couple is − 0.74 V. These two couples in their standard state are connected to make a cell. The cell potential will be **[CBSE AIPMT]**

(a) + 1.83 V (b) + 1.19 V
(c) + 0.89 V (d) + 0.18 V

31 Given, the following reactions involving, *A*, *B*, *C* and *D*.

I. $C + B^+ \longrightarrow C^+ + B$
II. $A^- + D \longrightarrow$ No reaction
III. $C^+ + A \longrightarrow$ No reaction
IV. $D + B^+ \longrightarrow D^+ + B$

The correct arrangement of *A*, *B*, *C*, *D* in order of their decreasing ability as reducing agent. **[DPMT]**

(a) $D > B > C > A$ (b) $A > C > D > B$
(c) $C > A > B > D$ (d) $C > A > D > B$

32 Which of the following reactions is correct for a given electrochemical cell at 25°C? **[Guj CET]**

$Pt \mid Br_2(g) \mid Br^-(aq) \| Cl^-(aq) \mid Cl_2(g) \mid Pt$

(a) $2Br^-(aq) + Cl_2(g) \longrightarrow 2Cl^-(aq) + Br_2(g)$
(b) $Br_2(g) + 2Cl^-(aq) \longrightarrow 2Br^-(aq) + Cl_2(g)$
(c) $Br_2(g) + Cl_2(g) \longrightarrow 2Br^-(aq) + 2Cl^-(aq)$
(d) $2Br^-(aq) + 2Cl^-(aq) \longrightarrow Br_2(g) + Cl_2(g)$

33 Saturated solution of KNO_3 is used to make salt bridge because **[Manipal]**

(a) velocity of K^+ is greater than that of NO_3^-
(b) velocity of NO_3^- is greater than that of K^+
(c) velocity of both K^+ and NO_3^- are nearly same
(d) KNO_3 is soluble in water

34 The standard emf of a galvanic cell involving 2 moles of electrons in its redox reaction is 0.59 V. The equilibrium constant for the redox reaction of the cell is **[KCET]**

(a) 10^{20} (b) 10^5
(c) 10 (d) 10^{10}

35 E_1, E_2 and E_3 are the emf of the following three galvanic cells respectively.

I. $Zn(s) \mid Zn^{2+}$ (0.1 M) $\|$ Cu^{2+} (1 M) $\mid Cu(s)$
II. $Zn(s) \mid Zn^{2+}$ (1 M) $\|$ Cu^{2+} (1 M) $\mid Cu(s)$
III. $Zn(s) \mid Zn^{2+}$ (1 M) $\|$ Cu^{2+} (0.1 M) $\mid Cu(s)$

Which one of the following is true? **[KCET]**

(a) $E_2 > E_1 > E_3$ (b) $E_1 > E_2 > E_3$
(c) $E_3 > E_1 > E_2$ (d) $E_3 > E_2 > E_1$

2010

36 The $E°_{M^{3+}/M^{2+}}$ values for Cr, Mn, Fe and Co are − 0.41, + 1.57, + 0.77 and + 1.97 V respectively. For which one of these metals, the change in oxidation state from + 2 to + 3 is easiest? **[Manipal]**

(a) Cr (b) Mn (c) Fe (d) Co

37 The potential of a hydrogen electrode at pH = 10 is **[WB JEE]**

(a) 0.59 V (b) 0.00 V
(c) − 0.59 V (d) − 0.059

38 Oxidation potential of unimoles of calomel is **[MHT CET]**

(a) + 0.25 V (b) 0.00 V
(c) + 0.287 V (d) − 0.28 V

39 Which of the following statements is true for the electrochemical Daniell cell? **[Manipal]**

(a) Electrons flow from copper electrode to zinc electrode
(b) Current flows from zinc electrode to copper electrode
(c) Cations move towards copper electrode
(d) Cations move towards zinc electrode

40 For the reduction of silver ions with copper metal, the standard cell potential was found to be + 0.46 V at 25°C. The value of standard Gibbs energy, $\Delta G°$ will be ($F = 96500$ C mol^{-1}) **[CBSE AIPMT]**

(a) − 98.0 kJ (b) − 89.0 kJ
(c) − 89.0 J (d) − 44.5 kJ

41 The logarithm of the equilibrium constant of the cell reaction corresponding to the cell $X(s)|X^{2+}(aq)||Y^{+}(aq)|Y(s)$ with standard cell potential, $E^\circ_{cell} = 1.2$ V is given by **[AMU]**

(a) 12.5 (b) 21.5
(c) 40.6 (d) 47.2

42 If the half-cell reactions are given as

I. $Fe^{2+}(aq)+2e^- \longrightarrow Fe(s), E^\circ=-0.44$ V

II. $2H^+(aq)+\frac{1}{2}O_2(g)+2e^- \longrightarrow H_2O(l),$ $E^\circ=+1.23$ V

then E° for the reaction,

$$Fe(s)+2H^+ +\frac{1}{2}O_2(g) \longrightarrow Fe^{2+}(aq)+H_2O(l)$$ **[AMU]**

(a) + 1.67 V (b) − 1.67 V
(c) + 0.79 V (d) − 0.79 V

43 At 25°C temperature, the cell potential of a given electrochemical cell is 1.92 V. Find the value of x.

$$Mg(s)|Mg^{2+}(aq)x\text{ M}||Fe^{2+}(aq)0.01\text{ M}|Fe(s)$$

$$E^\circ_{Mg/Mg^{2+}(aq)}=2.37\text{ V}, E^\circ_{Fe/Fe^{2+}(aq)}=0.45\text{ V}$$ **[Guj CET]**

(a) $x=0.01$ M (b) $x<0.01$ M
(c) $x>0.01$ M (d) x cannot be predicted

2009

44 Given, I. $Cu^{2+}+2e^- \longrightarrow Cu; E^\circ=0.337$ V

II. $Cu^{2+}+e^- \longrightarrow Cu^+; E^\circ=0.153$ V

Electrode potential, E° for the reaction,

$Cu^+ + e^- \longrightarrow Cu$, will be **[CBSE AIPMT, AMU]**

(a) 0.52 V (b) 0.90 V
(c) 0.30 V (d) 0.38 V

45 The reduction potential at pH = 14 for the Cu^{2+}/Cu couples is [Given, $E^\circ_{Cu^{2+}/Cu}=0.34$ V, $K_{sp}[Cu(OH)_2]=1\times10^{-19}$] **[AIIMS]**

(a) 0.34 V (b) −0.34 V
(c) 0.22 V (d) −0.22 V

46 E° for $Mg^{2+}/Mg=-2.37$ V, $Zn^{2+}/Zn=-0.76$ V and $Fe^{2+}/Fe=-0.44$ V. Which statement is correct? **[UP CPMT]**

(a) Zn reduces Fe^{2+} (b) Zn reduces Mg^{2+}
(c) Mg oxidises Fe (d) Zn oxidises Fe

47 The standard emf of a cell involving one electron charge is found to be 0.591 V at 25°C. The equilibrium constant of the reaction is

[$1\text{ F}=96500\text{ C mol}^{-1}$, $R=8.314\text{ JK}^{-1}\text{mol}^{-1}$]

(a) 1.0×10^1 (b) 1.0×10^{30} **[Manipal]**
(c) 1.0×10^{10} (d) 1.0×10^5

48 A solution of nickel sulphate in which nickel rod is dipped is diluted 10 times. The reduction potential of Ni at 298 K **[Kerala CEE]**

(a) decreases by 60 mV (b) decreases by 30 mV
(c) decreases by 30 V (d) increases by 30 mV
(e) increases by 30 V

49 The standard reduction potentials for Cu^{2+}/Cu; Zn^{2+}/Zn; Li^+/Li; Ag^+/Ag and H^+/H_2 are + 0.34 V, − 0.762 V, − 3.05 V, + 0.80 V and 0.00 V respectively. Choose the strongest reducing agent among the following. **[Kerala CEE]**

(a) Zn (b) H_2 (c) Ag (d) Li (e) Cu

50 The standard reduction electrode potentials of the three electrodes P, Q and R are respectively − 1.76 V, 0.34 V and 0.8 V. Then **[J&K CET]**

(a) metal Q will displace the cation of P from its aqueous solution and deposit the metal P
(b) both metals Q and R will displace the cation of P from its aqueous solution and deposit the metal P
(c) metal R will displace the cation of P from its aqueous solution and deposit the metal R
(d) metal P will displace the cation of R from its aqueous solution and deposit the metal R

51 A gas X at 1 atm is bubbled through a solution containing a mixture of 1 M Y^- and 1 M Z^- at 25°C. If the order of reduction potential of Z, Y and X is $Z>Y>X$, then **[AMU]**

(a) Y will oxidise X but not Z
(b) Y will oxidise both X and Z
(c) Y will oxidise Z but not X
(d) Y will reduce both X and Z

52 The potential of standard hydrogen electrode is zero. This implies that **[AMU]**

(a) $\Delta G^\circ_f(H^+, aq)=0$ (b) $\Delta H^\circ_f(H^+, aq)=0$
(c) $\Delta G^\circ_f(H^+, aq)<0$ (d) $\Delta G^\circ_f(H^+, aq)>0$

53 For the following cell reaction,

$$Ag|Ag^+|AgCl|Cl^-|Cl_2, Pt$$
$$\Delta G^\circ_f(AgCl)=-109\text{ kJ/mol}$$
$$\Delta G^\circ_f(Cl^-)=-129\text{ kJ/mol}$$
$$\Delta G^\circ_f(Ag^+)=78\text{ kJ/mol}$$

E° of the cell is **[EAMCET]**

(a) − 0.60 V (b) 0.60 V
(c) 6.0 V (d) None of these

54 The standard electrode potential for the half-cell reactions are

$$Zn^{2+}+2e^- \longrightarrow Zn; E^\circ=-0.76\text{ V}$$
$$Fe^{2+}+2e^- \longrightarrow Fe; E^\circ=-0.44\text{ V}$$

The emf of the cell reaction,

$$Fe^{2+}+Zn \longrightarrow Zn^{2+}+Fe \text{ is}$$ **[KCET]**

(a) − 1.20 V (b) + 1.20 V (c) + 0.32 V (d) − 0.32 V

2008

55 Galvanic cell is a device in which [J&K CET]

(a) chemical energy is converted into electrical energy
(b) electrical energy is converted into chemical energy
(c) chemical energy is seen in the form of heat
(d) thermal energy from an outside source is used to drive the cell reaction

56 On the basis of the following $E°$ values, the strongest oxidising agent is

$[Fe(CN)_6]^{4-} \longrightarrow [Fe(CN)_6]^{3-} + e^-; E° = -0.35$ V

$Fe^{2+} \longrightarrow Fe^{3+} + e^-; E° = -0.77$ V [CBSE AIPMT]

(a) $[Fe(CN)_6]^{4-}$ (b) Fe^{2+}
(c) Fe^{3+} (d) $[Fe(CN)_6]^{3-}$

57 $Cu^+(aq)$ is unstable in solution and undergoes simultaneous oxidation and reduction, according to the reaction,

$$2Cu^+(aq) \rightleftharpoons Cu^{2+}(aq) + Cu(s)$$

Choose the correct $E°$ for the above reaction if

$$E°_{Cu^2/Cu} = 0.49 \text{ V and } E°_{Cu^{2+}/Cu^+} = 0.15 \text{ V}$$

[MHT CET]

(a) −0.34 V (b) +0.49 V
(c) +0.34 V (d) −0.19 V

58 The equilibrium constant for the following redox reaction at 298 K is 1×10^8.

$$2Fe^{3+}(aq) + 2I^-(aq) \rightleftharpoons 2Fe^{2+}(aq) + I_2(s)$$

If the standard reduction potential of iodine becoming iodide is +0.54 V, what is the standard reduction potential of Fe^{3+}/Fe^{2+}? [Kerala CEE]

(a) +1.006 V (b) −1.006 V (c) +0.77 V (d) −0.77 V
(e) −0.652 V

59 What is the electrode potential (in volt) of the following electrode at 25°C ?

$$Ni^{2+}(0.1 \text{ M}) | Ni(s)$$

[Standard reduction potential of $Ni^{2+}|Ni$ is −0.25 V, $\frac{2.303RT}{F} = 0.06$] [Punjab PMET]

(a) −0.28 V (b) −0.34 V
(c) −0.82 V (d) −0.22 V

60 The cell potential of the following cell at 25°C (in volts) is

$$|(Pt)\ \underset{(1\ atm)}{H_2}\ |\ \underset{(0.01\ M)}{H^+}\ ||\ \underset{(0.1\ M)}{Cu^{2+}}\ |\ Cu\ (E°_{Cu^{2+}|Cu} = 0.337\ V)$$

[EAMCET]

(a) 0.308 (b) 0.427 (c) −0.308 (d) 0.337

61 $Zn(s) + Cl_2\ (1atm) \longrightarrow Zn^{2+} + 2Cl^-$; $E°_{cell}$ of the cell is 2.12 V. To increase E [DUMET]

(a) $[Zn^{2+}]$ should be increased
(b) $[Zn^{2+}]$ should be decreased
(c) $[Cl^-]$ should be increased
(d) p_{Cl_2} should be decreased

62 Hydrogen gas is not liberated when the following metal is added to dil. HCl [KCET]

(a) Ag (b) Zn (c) Mg (d) Sn

63 EMF of hydrogen electrode in terms of pH is (at 1 atm pressure) [MHT CET]

(a) $E_{H_2} = \frac{RT}{F}$ pH (b) $E_{H_2} = \frac{RT}{F} \frac{1}{\text{pH}}$

(c) $E_{H_2} = \frac{2.303RT}{F}$ pH (d) $E_{H_2} = -0.0591$ pH

64 Standard free energies of formation (in kJ/mol) at 298 K are −237.2, −394.4 and −8.2 for $H_2O(l)$, $CO_2(g)$ and pentane (*g*), respectively. The value of $E°_{cell}$ for the pentane-oxygen fuel cell is [CBSE AIPMT]

(a) 1.968 V (b) 2.0968 V
(c) 1.0968 V (d) 0.0968 V

2007

65 The standard electrode potential of hydrogen electrode at 1 M concentration and hydrogen gas at 1 atm pressure is [J&K CET]

(a) 1 V (b) 6 V (c) 8 V (d) 0 V

66 In the silver plating of copper, $K[Ag(CN)_2]$ is used instead of $AgNO_3$. The reason is [Punjab PMET]

(a) a thin layer of Ag is formed on Cu
(b) more voltage is required
(c) Ag^+ ions are completely removed from solution
(d) less availability of Ag^+ ions, as Cu cannot displace Ag from $[Ag(CN)_2]^-$ ion

67 Zn gives H_2 gas with H_2SO_4 and HCl but not with HNO_3 because [Punjab PMET]

(a) Zn act as oxidising agent when react with HNO_3
(b) HNO_3 is weaker acid than H_2SO_4 and HCl
(c) in electrochemical series, Zn is above hydrogen
(d) NO_3^- is reduced in preference to hydronium ion

2006

68 What is the cell reaction occurring in Daniell cell (galvanic cell)? [J&K CET]

(a) $Cu(s) + ZnSO_4(aq) \longrightarrow CuSO_4(aq) + Zn(s)$
(b) $Zn(s) + CuSO_4(aq) \longrightarrow Cu(s) + ZnSO_4(aq)$
(c) $Ni(s) + ZnSO_4(aq) \longrightarrow NiSO_4(aq) + Zn(s)$
(d) $2Na(s) + CdSO_4(aq) \longrightarrow Na_2SO_4(aq) + Cd(s)$

69 A hypothetical electrochemical cell is shown below

$$A|A^+(x\text{M})||B^+(y\text{M})|B$$

The emf measured is + 0.20 V. The cell reaction is [CBSE AIPMT]

(a) $A^+ + B \longrightarrow A + B^+$
(b) $A^+ + e^- \longrightarrow A;\ B^+ + e^- \longrightarrow B$
(c) the cell reaction cannot be predicted
(d) $A + B^+ \longrightarrow A^+ + B$

70 **Assertion** (A) $E°$ for Mn^{3+}/Mn^{2+} is more positive than Cr^{3+}/Cr^{2+}.

Reason (R) The third ionisation energy of Mn is larger than that of Cr. **[AIIMS]**

(a) Both A and R are correct and R is the correct explanation of A
(b) Both A and R are correct but R is not the correct explanation of A
(c) A is correct but R is incorrect
(d) Both A and R are incorrect

71 For the electrochemical cell, $M \mid M^+ \parallel X^- \mid X$, $E°_{(M^+/M)} = 0.44$ V and $E°_{(X/X^-)} = 0.33$ V. From this data, one can deduce that **[BHU]**

(a) $M + X \longrightarrow M^+ + X^-$ is the spontaneous reaction
(b) $M^+ + X^- \longrightarrow M + X$ is the spontaneous reaction
(c) $E_{cell} = 0.77$ V
(d) $E_{cell} = -\ 0.77$ V

72 The reduction electro[illegible] of 0.1 M solution of M^+ ions ($E°$ [illegible] V) is **[MHT CET]**

(a) −4.82 V
(b) −2.41 V
(c) + 2.41 V
(d) None of the above

73 The metal used to recover copper from a solution of $CuSO_4$ is **[RPMT]**

(a) Fe (b) He (c) Na (d) Ag

74 $E° = \frac{RT}{nF} \ln K_{eq}$. This equation is called **[MP PMT]**

(a) Gibbs equation
(b) Nernst equation
(c) Gibbs-Helmholtz equation
(d) van der Waals' equation

75 Two concentration cells of Ag with Ag electrode are dipped in solution of $AgNO_3$. In first cell, concentration of one electrode is 1 M and other electrode is 0.1 and emf is 0.06 V. In second cell, concentration of one electrode is 1 M and other electrode is 0.01 M. Calculate the emf of second cell. **[DUMET]**

(a) 0.12 V (b) 0.06 V
(c) 0.09 V (d) 0.16 V

76 During electrochemical process, **[Guj CET]**

(a) Gibbs free energy increases
(b) Gibbs free energy remains constant
(c) no prediction can be made about Gibbs free energy
(d) Gibbs free energy decreases

77 Which will reduce zinc oxide to zinc? **[BCECE]**

(a) Mg (b) Pb
(c) Cu (d) Fe

2005

78 The chemical reaction,

$$2AgCl(s) + H_2(g) \longrightarrow 2HCl(aq) + 2Ag(s)$$

taking place in a galvanic cell is represented by the notation. **[AIIMS]**

(a) $Pt(s) \mid H_2(g)$, 1 bar $\mid$ 1 M $KCl(aq) \mid AgCl(s) \mid Ag(s)$
(b) $Pt(s) \mid H_2(g)$, 1 bar $\mid$ 1 M $HCl(aq) \mid$ 1 M $Ag^+(aq) \mid Ag(s)$
(c) $Pt(s) \mid H_2(g)$, 1 bar $\mid$ 1 M $HCl(aq) \mid AgCl(s) \mid Ag(s)$
(d) $Pt(s) \mid H_2(g)$, 1 bar $\mid$ 1 M $HCl(aq) \mid Ag(s) \mid AgCl(s)$

79 Na is used in reduction of Zn salt because **[MHT CET]**

(a) $E°_{Zn\,(oxi)} > E°_{Na\,(oxi)}$ (b) $E°_{Zn\,(red)} < E°_{Na\,(red)}$
(c) $E°_{Zn\,(oxi)} < E°_{Na\,(oxi)}$ (d) Both (a) and (b)

80 Reduction potentials of A, B, C and D are 0.8 V, 0.79 V, 0.34 V and –2.37 V respectively. Which element displace all the other three elements? **[MHT CET]**

(a) B (b) A
(c) D (d) C

81 The standard emf of Daniell cell is 1.10 V. The maximum electrical work obtained from the cell is **[Haryana PMT]**

(a) 212.3 kJ (b) 175.4 kJ
(c) 106.15 kJ (d) 350.8 kJ

82 If hydrogen electrode dipped in two solutions of pH = 3 and pH = 6 and salt bridge is connected. The emf of resulting cell is **[DUMET]**

(a) 0.177 V (b) 0.3 V
(c) 0.052 V (d) 0.104 V

83 The standard electrode potential is measured by **[KCET]**

(a) electrometer
(b) voltmeter
(c) pyrometer
(d) galvanometer

84 Alkali metals have high oxidation potential and hence, they behave as **[JCECE]**

(a) oxidising agents (b) Lewis bases
(c) reducing agents (d) electrolytes

85 What is the potential of platinum wire dipped into a solution of 0.1 M in Sn^{2+} and 0.01 M in Sn^{4+}? **[JCECE]**

(a) $E°$ (b) $E° + 0.059$
(c) $E° + \frac{0.059}{2}$ (d) $E° - \frac{0.059}{2}$

Answers

1 (d)	2 (b)	3 (b)	4 (b)	5 (c)	6 (c)	7 (d)	8 (c)	9 (c)	10 (b)
11 (d)	12 (d)	13 (d)	14 (a)	15 (d)	16 (b)	17 (d)	18 (a)	19 (b)	20 (a)
21 (b)	22 (a)	23 (c)	24 (c)	25 (a)	26 (d)	27 (a)	28 (c)	29 (d)	30 (c)
31 (d)	32 (b)	33 (c)	34 (a)	35 (b)	36 (a)	37 (c)	38 (d)	39 (c)	40 (b)
41 (c)	42 (a)	43 (a)	44 (a)	45 (d)	46 (a)	47 (c)	48 (b)	49 (d)	50 (d)
51 (a)	52 (a)	53 (a)	54 (c)	55 (a)	56 (c)	57 (c)	58 (c)	59 (a)	60 (b)
61 (b)	62 (a)	63 (d)	64 (c)	65 (d)	66 (d)	67 (d)	68 (b)	69 (d)	70 (b)
71 (b)	72 (b)	73 (a)	74 (b)	75 (a)	76 (d)	77 (a)	78 (b)	79 (c)	80 (c)
81 (a)	82 (a)	83 (b)	84 (c)	85 (c)					

Explanations

1 (*d*) The relation between E°_{cell} and $\Delta_r G^\circ$ is as follows:

$$\Delta_r G^\circ = -nFE^\circ_{cell}$$

For the cell reaction,

$$2Fe^{3+}(aq) + 2I^-(aq) \longrightarrow 2Fe^{2+}(aq) + I_2(aq)$$

$$n = 2$$

Given, $F = 96500 \text{ C mol}^{-1}$,

$$E^\circ_{cell} = 0.24 \text{ V}$$

Now, we know that

$$\Delta_r G^\circ = -n FE^\circ_{cell}$$

On substituting the given values in above equation,

$$\Delta_r G^\circ = -2 \text{ mol} \times 96500 \text{ C mol}^{-1} \times 0.24 \text{ J mol}^{-1}$$

$$= -46320 \text{ J mol}^{-1}$$

$$= -46.32 \text{ kJ mol}^{-1}$$

Hence, option (d) is correct.

2 (*b*) We know that

$$E_{cell} = E^\circ_{cell} - \frac{2.303\, RT}{nF} \log Q$$

At equilibirum,

$$Q = K_{eq} \text{ and } E_{cell} = 0$$

$$\therefore E^\circ_{cell} = \frac{2.303RT}{nF} \log K_{eq} \quad \text{... (i)}$$

Given, $E^\circ_{cell} = 0.59$ V

Also, at 298 K, $\frac{2.303RT}{F} = 0.059$ V,

$$T = 298\text{K}, n = 1$$

On substituting the given values in Eqn. (i)

$$0.59 = \frac{0.059}{1} \log K_{eq}$$

$$\therefore \log K_{eq} = \frac{0.59}{0.059} = 10$$

$$K_{eq} = 10^{10} = 1 \times 10^{10}$$

Thus, option (b) is correct.

3 (*b*) According to Nernst equation,

$$E_{cell} = E^\circ_{cell} - \frac{2.303}{nF} RT \log \frac{[M_p]^{n+}}{[M_r]^{n+}}$$

where, $[M_p]^{n+}$ and $[M_r]^{n+}$ are the concentrations of products and reactants respectively.

For the given cell, emf can be calculated as follows:

$$E_{emf} = E^\circ_{cell} - \frac{2.303RT}{nF} \log \frac{[M_p]^{n+}_{(aq)}}{[M_r]^{n+}_{(aq)}}$$

For the reaction at 25° C

$$E_{emf} = E^\circ_{cell} - \frac{0.059}{n} \log \frac{[M_p^{n-1}]}{[M_r^{n+}]}$$

$$\therefore E^\circ_{cell} = 4 \text{ V}$$

(Given) and $n = 2$

$$E_{emf} = 4 - \frac{0.059}{2} \log \frac{10^{-4}}{10^{-2}}$$

$$E_{emf} = 4 - 0.03 \log 10^{-2}$$

$$E_{emf} = 4 + 0.06 = 4.06 \text{ V}$$

Hence, option (b) is correct.

4 (*b*) More negative the value of standard reduction potential, higher is the reduction power.

i.e. Reducing power $\propto \frac{1}{\text{standard reduction potential}}$

Thus, the correct decreasing order of reducing power of the metal is

K > Al > Cr > Ag

$(E^\circ_{K^+/K} = -2.93\text{V})$ $(E^\circ_{Al^{3+}/Al} = -1.66\text{V})$ $(E^\circ_{Cr^{3+}/Cr} = -0.74\text{V})$ $(E^\circ_{Ag^+}/Ag = 0.80\text{V})$

5 (*c*) $E^0_{cell} = E_{cathode} - E_{anode}$

$$= -0.42 - (-0.72) = 0.3 \text{ V}$$

At anode $\text{Cr} \longrightarrow Cr^{3+} + 3e^-] \times 2$

At cathode $Fe^{2+} + 2e^- \longrightarrow Fe] \times 3$

$$2Cr + 3Fe^{2+} \rightarrow 2Cr^{3+} + 3Fe$$

$$\therefore E = E^0_{cell} - \frac{0.0591}{6} \log \frac{[Cr^{3+}]^2}{[Fe^{2+}]^3}$$

$$= 0.3 - \frac{0.0591}{6} \log \frac{(0.1)^2}{(0.01)^3}$$

$$= 0.26 \text{ V}$$

6 (*c*) Given,

$$\Delta G^\circ_f(Ag_2O) = -11.21 \text{ kJ mol}^{-1}$$

$$\Delta G^\circ_f(ZnO) = -318.3 \text{ kJ mol}^{-1}$$

As we know that,

$$\Delta G^\circ = \Delta G^\circ_f(ZnO) - \Delta G^\circ_f(Ag_2O)$$

Putting the values in the above given equation

$$\therefore \quad \Delta G^\circ = (-318.30 + 11.21) \text{ kJ mol}^{-1}$$

$$= -307.09 \text{kJ}$$

$$= -307.09 \times 10^3 \text{J}$$

$$\because \quad \Delta G^\circ = -nFE^\circ_{cell}$$

$$\therefore -307.09 \times 10^3 = -2 \times 96500 \times E^\circ_{cell}$$

or $$E^\circ_{cell} = 1.591 \text{ V}$$

7 (*d*) $E_1 = E_0 - \frac{0.0591}{n} \log \frac{[Zn^{2+}]}{[Cu^{2+}]}$

$$= E_0 + \frac{0.0591}{2} \log \frac{0.01}{1}$$

$$E_2 = E_0 - \frac{0.0591}{n} \log \frac{[Zn^{2+}]}{[Cu^{2+}]}$$

$$= E_0 - \frac{0.0591}{2} \log \frac{1}{0.01}$$

$$\therefore E_1 > E_2$$

8 (*c*) The cell reaction is

$Zn + Fe^{2+} \longrightarrow Zn^{2+} + Fe$

From Nernst equation

$$E_{cell} = E°_{cell} - \frac{0.0591}{n}\log\frac{a_{Zn^{2+}}}{a_{Fe^{2+}}}$$

$$= (0.763 - 0.44) - \frac{0.0591}{2}\log\frac{0.001}{0.005}$$

$$= 0.344 \text{ V}$$

9 (*c*) For the electrochemical cell,

$Ag^+|AgCl|KCl\|AgNO_3|Ag^+$

The cell reaction is,

$AgCl(s) + e^- \longrightarrow Ag + Cl^-(aq)$

$Ag \longrightarrow Ag^+(aq) + e^-$

Overall reaction,

$AgCl(s) \longrightarrow Ag^+ + Cl^-$

10 (*b*) (*A*) and (*R*) both are correct but (*R*) is not the explanation of (*A*).

$\because \quad E_{cell} = E° - \frac{0.0591}{n}\log\frac{1}{[M^{n+}]}$

or, $\quad E_{cell} = E° + \frac{0.0591}{1}\log[Ag^+]$

Thus, $\quad E \propto [Ag^+]$

Hence, E increases with the increase in concentration of Ag^+.

11 (*d*) The cell reaction is

$Zn(s) \longrightarrow Zn^{2+}(0.01\text{ M}) + 2e^-$

$[Ag^+(1.25\text{ M}) + e^- \longrightarrow Ag(s)] \times 2$

$Zn(s) + 2Ag^+(1.25\text{ M}) \longrightarrow Zn^{2+}(0.01\text{ M}) + 2Ag(s)$

$$\therefore \quad Q = \frac{[Zn^{2+}]}{[Ag^+]^2} = \frac{0.01}{(1.25)^2} = 6.4 \times 10^{-3}$$

$\therefore \quad$ Value of $Q = 6.4 \times 10^{-3}$

12 (*d*) The reaction is spontaneous when $\Delta G° < 0$ and $E_{cell} > 0$.

$\because \quad \Delta G° = -nFE°$ and $E° > 0$

Also $\quad E°_{cell} = E°_{oxi} + E°_{red}$

or $\quad E°_{cell} = E°_{cathode} - E°_{anode}$

Here, (Reduction)

$X + Y^{2+} \longrightarrow X^{2+} + Y$

(Oxidation)

Thus, $E°_{cell}$ for

(a) – 0.21 V, i.e. $E°_{cell} < 0$

(b) – 0.53 V, i.e. $E°_{cell} < 0$

(c) – 0.32 V, i.e. $E°_{cell} < 0$

(d) 0.53 V, i.e. $E° > 0$

13 (*d*) From the question, we have an equation

$2H^+ + 2e^- \longrightarrow H_2(g)$

According to Nernst equation,

$$E = E° - \frac{0.0591}{2}\log\frac{p_{H_2}}{[H^+]^2}$$

$$= 0 - \frac{0.0591}{2}\log\frac{p_{H_2}}{(10^{-7})^2}$$

$[\because [H^+] = 10^{-7}]$

$\therefore$ For potential of H_2 electrode to be zero, p_{H_2} should be equal to $[H^+]^2$, i.e. 10^{-14} atm.

$$\therefore \quad \log\frac{10^{-14}}{(10^{-7})^2} = 0$$

14 (*a*) Given, $E°_{cell}$ = –ve

Now, the relation between $\Delta G°$ and $E°_{cell}$ is given as,

$$\Delta G° = -nFE°_{cell} \quad \text{... (i)}$$

as $E°_{cell}$ is negative, so $\Delta G°$ comes out to be positive. Again, relation between $\Delta G°$ and K_{eq} is given as

$$\Delta G° = -2.303nRT\log K_{eq} \quad \text{...(ii)}$$

From Eq. (i) we get that $\Delta G°$ is positive. Now, if $\Delta G°$ is positive then K_{eq} comes out to be negative from eq (ii).

i.e. $\quad \Delta G° > 1$ and $K_{eq} < 1$

Short trick As $E°_{cell}$ is negative so reaction is non-spontaneous or you can say reaction is moving in backward direction. For non-spontaneous reaction, $\Delta G°$ is always positive and K_{eq} is always less than 1.

15 (*d*) The metal with higher negative standard reduction potential, has higher tendency to get reduced.

$Zn^{2+} + 2e^- \longrightarrow Zn; \quad E° = -0.76$ V

$Fe^{2+} + 2e^- \longrightarrow Fe; \quad E° = -0.44$ V

Here, in galvanised iron, Zn has higher negative reduction potential means Zn takes electrons given by iron and itself gets reduced. Thus, Zn works as anode and protects iron from rusting by making iron as cathode.

16 (*b*) Since, H_2SO_4 and H_3PO_4 both are strong acids so, their presence makes the medium more acidic. The Fe^{3+} ions form complex, $[FeHPO_4]^+$ with these acids and hence, the concentration of Fe^{3+} ion reduces which results in lowering in the formal reduction potential.

17 (*d*) $E°_{cell} = E°_{cathode} - E°_{anode}$

$= -0.42 - (-0.72)$

$= -0.42 + 0.72 = 0.3$ V

18. (*a*) $Cr_2O_7^{2-} + 14H^+ + 6e^- \longrightarrow 2Cr^{3+} + 7H_2O$

$$E = E° - \frac{0.059}{n}\log\frac{[Cr^{3+}]^2[H_2O]^7}{[Cr_2O_7^{2-}][H^+]^{14}}$$

$$1.067 = 1.33 - \frac{0.059}{6}\log\frac{(15\times10^{-3})^2(1)^7}{(4.5\times10^{-3})[H^+]^{14}}$$

$$\frac{0.059}{6}\log\left[\frac{225\times10^{-6}}{(4.5\times10^{-3})\times[H^+]^{14}}\right] = 0.263$$

$$\Rightarrow \frac{0.263\times6}{0.059} = \log\left[\frac{50\times10^{-3}}{[H^+]^{14}}\right]$$

$\log(50\times10^{-3}) - \log(H^+)^{14} = 26.74$

$-1.3010 - 14\log[H^+] = 26.74$

$-14\log[H^+] = 26.74 + 1.30101$

or $+14\,pH = 28.041$

$[\because pH = -\log[H^+]]$

$$pH = \frac{28.041}{14} = 2$$

19 (*b*) The emf of a galvanic cell = electrode potential of copper – electrode potential of zinc,

$Zn|Zn^{+2}\|Cu^{+2}|Cu$

$= 0.34 - (-0.76) = 1.1$ V

20 (*a*) MnO_4^- will oxidise Cl^- ion according to following equation.

$2MnO_4^- + 16H^+ + 10Cl^- \longrightarrow 2Mn^{2+} + 8H_2O + 5Cl_2$

The cell corresponding to this reaction is as follows,

Pt, Cl_2 (1 atm) $|Cl^-\|MnO_4^-, Mn^{2+}, H^+|Pt$

$E°_{cell} = 1.51 - 1.40 = 0.11$ V

As $E°_{cell}$ is positive, the above reaction is feasible. Thus, MnO_4^- will not oxidise Fe^{2+} ion but also Cl^- ion simultaneously.

21 (*b*) For hydrogen electrode, oxidation half-reaction is,

$\underset{(1\text{ atm})}{H_2} \longrightarrow \underset{(\text{at pH }10)}{2H^+} + 2e^-$

If pH = 10,

$[H^+] = 1\times10^{-pH} = 1\times10^{-10}$

From Nernst equation,

$$E = E° - \frac{0.0591}{2}\log\frac{[H^+]^2}{p_{H_2}}$$

For hydrogen electrode, $E° = 0$

p_{H_2} = Pressure of hydrogen

$$E = -\frac{0.0591}{2}\log\frac{(10^{-10})^2}{1}$$

$$= \frac{0.0591 \times 2}{2}\log(10)$$

$$= 0.0591 \times \log 10^{10} = 0.59\ V$$

22 (*a*) Anode is always a site of oxidation and cathode is a site of reduction.

Thus, anode half-cell is,

$$Zn^{2+}(aq) + 2e^- \longrightarrow Zn(s) \quad E° = -0.76\ V$$

Cathode half-cell is,

$$Ag_2O(s) + H_2O(l) + 2e^- \longrightarrow 2Ag(s) + 2OH^-(aq) \quad E° = 0.34\ V$$

$$E°_{cell} = E°_{cathode} - E°_{anode}$$

$$= 0.34 - (-0.76) = 1.1\ V$$

23 (*c*) $\because$ $E_R = Cu^{2+}/Cu$

$E_L = Al^{3+}/Al$

We know that, $E_{cell} = E_R - E_L$

$2 = +0.34 - x$

$x = 0.34 - 2 = -1.66\ V$

24 (*c*) $4Al^{3+} \longrightarrow 4Al + 12e^-$

$12e^- + 6O^{2-} \longrightarrow 3O_2$

or $\frac{4}{3}Al^{3+} \longrightarrow \frac{4}{3}Al + 4e^-$

$4e^- + 2O^{2-} \longrightarrow O_2$

$\Delta G° = -nFE°$

$\Delta G = +960\ kJ\ mol^{-1}$

$= 960 \times 1000\ J\ mol^{-1}$

$nF = 4F = 4 \times 96500\ C$

$\therefore\ 960 \times 1000 = -4 \times 96500 \times E°$

$$E° = \frac{960000}{4 \times 96500} = -2.48\ V$$

Potential difference ≈ 2.5 V

25 (*a*) $E_{cell} = E°_{cell} - \frac{0.059}{2}\log\frac{[Zn^{2+}]}{[Cu^{2+}]}$

$$= 1.10 - \frac{0.059}{2}\log\frac{0.1}{0.1},\ E_{cell} = 1.10\ V$$

26 (*d*) $Cu(s) + 2Ag^+(aq) \longrightarrow Cu^{2+}(aq) + 2Ag(s)$

$E° = 0.46$ V at 298 K

$$E° = \frac{0.059}{2}\log K_C, \text{ at 298 K}$$

$$0.46 = \frac{0.059}{2}\log K_C$$

$\log K_C = 15.59$

$K_C = \text{antilog } 15.59$

$K_C = 3.89 \times 10^{15} \approx 4 \times 10^{15}$

27 (*a*) In the electrochemical series, metals are arranged in the increasing order of their standard reduction potential. The standard reduction potentials of Li^+/Li and Cu^{2+}/Cu are – 3.05 V and + 0.034 V respectively. Therefore, Li occupies higher position in series as compared to Cu.

28 (*c*) $\Delta G_3 = \Delta G_1 + \Delta G_2$

$\Delta G° = -nFE°$

$-2FE° = -1\ F \times 0.15 + (-1\ F \times 0.50)$

$-2FE° = -0.15\ F - 0.50\ F$

$-2FE° = -F(0.15 + 0.50)$

$$\therefore\ E° = \frac{0.65}{2} = 0.325\ V$$

29 (*d*) $Z > X > Y$; higher the reduction potential, lesser is the reduction power.

30 (*c*) $E°_{cell} = E°_{cathode} - E°_{anode}$

$= 0.15 - (-0.74) = +0.89\ V$

31 (*d*) $C + B^+ \longrightarrow C^+ + B$ So, reducing power of $C > B$

$A^+ + D \longrightarrow$ No reaction So, reducing power of $A > D$

$C^+ + A \longrightarrow$ No reaction So, reducing power of $C > A$

$D + B^+ \longrightarrow D^+ + B$ So, reducing power of $D > B$

Hence, $C > A > D > B$.

32 (*b*) Correct reaction for a given electrochemical cell is,

$$Br_2 + 2Cl^- \longrightarrow 2Br^- + Cl_2$$

33 (*c*) Saturated solution of KNO_3 is used to make salt bridge because the ions have same ionic mobility.

34 (*a*) $nFE° = 2.303RT\log K$

$$\log K = \frac{nFE°}{2.303\ RT}$$

$$\log K = \frac{2 \times 96500 \times 0.59}{2.303 \times 8.314 \times 298} = 19.9 \sim 20.0$$

$K = \text{antilog } 20.0 = 1 \times 10^{20}$

35 (*b*) $E_{cell} = E°_{cell} + \frac{0.0591}{n}\log\frac{[Cu^{2+}]}{[Zn^{2+}]}$

$$E_1 = E°_{cell} + \frac{0.0591}{2}\log\frac{1}{0.1}$$

$E_1 = E°_{cell} + 0.02955$

$$E_2 = E°_{cell} + \frac{0.0591}{2}\log\frac{1}{1}$$

$\therefore\ E_2 = E°_{cell}$

$$E_3 = E°_{cell} + \frac{0.0591}{2}\log\frac{0.1}{1}$$

$E_3 = E°_{cell} - 0.02955$

$\therefore\ E_1 > E_2 > E_3$

36 (*a*) More the negative value of standard reduction potential, higher is the reduction power and higher is the tendency to get oxidised. The $E°$ value most negative is for Cr among the given, hence it has higher tendency to change from +2 to +3 state.

37 (*c*) H^+ (pH = 10) | H_2 (1 atm) | Pt(*s*)

Reaction $2H^+(pH = 10) + 2e^- \longrightarrow H_2$ (1 atm)

$$E = E° - \frac{0.0591}{2}\log\left(\frac{p_{H_2}}{[H^+]^2}\right)$$

$$= 0 - \frac{0.0591}{2}\log\frac{1}{(10^{-10})^2}$$

$$= -\frac{0.0591}{2} \times \log 10^{20}$$

$$= -0.0591 \times 10 = -0.591\ V$$

i.e. $E = -0.59$ V

38 (*d*) Calomel is used as a secondary reference electrode. Since, Hg is less reactive than H, its standard reduction potential is positive. Hence, its standard oxidation potential must be negative, i.e. – 0.28 V. [As standard reduction potential = – standard oxidation potential]

39 (*c*) In Daniell cell, following reaction occurs.

$$Zn + Cu^{2+} \longrightarrow Zn^{2+} + Cu$$

At cathode : $Cu^{2+} + 2e^- \longrightarrow Cu$

At anode : $Zn \longrightarrow Zn^{2+} + 2e^-$

Electrons moves from anode (Zn) to cathode (Cu) and electricity flows from Cu to Zn. Here, cations move towards cathode (copper) electrode.

40 (*b*) $Cu + 2Ag^+ \longrightarrow Cu^{2+} + 2Ag$

$\Delta G° = -nFE° = -2 \times 96500 \times 0.46$

$= -88780\ J \approx -89\ kJ$

41 (*c*) $X(s) \longrightarrow X^{2+} + 2e^-$

$[Y^+ + e^- \longrightarrow Y] \times 2$

$2Y^+ + 2e^- \longrightarrow 2Y$

Overall reaction :

$$X(s) + 2Y^+ \longrightarrow X^{2+} + 2Y$$

Thus, $n = 2$

$$E^\circ_{cell} = \frac{0.0591}{n} \log K_C,$$

$$1.2 = \frac{0.0591}{2} \log K_C$$

$$\log K_C = \frac{1.2 \times 2}{0.0591} = 40.6$$

42 (a) $E^\circ_{cell} = E^\circ_{cathode} - E^\circ_{anode}$

$= +1.23 - (-0.44)$

$= +1.67$ V

43 (a) $E^\circ_{cell} = E^\circ_{cathode} - E^\circ_{anode}$

$= -0.45 - (-2.37) = 1.92$ V

$Mg(s) \mid Mg^{2+}(aq)\, x\,M \parallel Fe^{2+}(aq)$ 0.01 M $\mid Fe(s)$

The cell reaction is

$$Mg + Fe^{2+} \longrightarrow Mg^{2+} + Fe$$

$$E_{cell} = E^\circ_{cell} - \frac{0.059}{2} \log \frac{[Mg^{2+}]}{[Fe^{2+}]}$$

$$1.92 = 1.92 - \frac{0.059}{2} \log \frac{x}{0.01}$$

$$0 = \frac{-0.059}{2} \log \frac{x}{0.01}$$

$\therefore \quad x = 0.01$ M

44 (a) Given, (i) $Cu^{2+} + 2e^- \longrightarrow Cu$;

$E^\circ = 0.337$ V

$\Delta G^\circ_1 = -2 \times F \times 0.337$ J

(ii) $Cu^{2+} + e^- \longrightarrow Cu^+$;

$E^\circ = 0.153$ V

$\Delta G^\circ_2 = -1 \times F \times 0.153$ J

Eqs. (i) – (ii) gives the required results,

i.e. $\Delta G^\circ_3 = \Delta G^\circ_1 - \Delta G^\circ_2 = -0.521\,F$

$\therefore \quad -nFE^\circ_{Cu^+/Cu} = -0.521\,F$

or $\quad E^\circ_{Cu^+/Cu} = 0.52$ V $\quad (\because n = 1)$

45 (d) Given, pH = 14; pOH = 0 and $[OH^-] = 1$ M

$$[Cu^{2+}][OH^-]^2 = K_{sp} = 1.0 \times 10^{-19}$$

$\therefore \quad [Cu^{2+}] = 1.0 \times 10^{-19}$ M

For the half-cell reaction,

$$Cu^{2+} + 2e^- \longrightarrow Cu$$

$$E_{Cu^{2+}/Cu} = E^\circ_{Cu^{2+}/Cu} - \frac{0.0591}{2} \log \frac{1}{[Cu^{2+}]}$$

$$= 0.34 - \frac{0.0591}{2} \log 10^{19} = -0.22 \text{ V}$$

46 (a) Higher the negative value of reduction potential, higher will be the reducing power. Hence, Mg reduces both Zn^{2+} and Fe^{2+}. Zn can reduce Fe^{2+} but not Mg^{2+}. Similarly, Fe^{2+} can oxidise Zn and Mg both.

47 (c) At 298 K, $E^\circ = \frac{0.0591}{n} \log K_C$

$$0.591 = \frac{0.0591}{1} \log K_C$$

$$\log K_C = \frac{0.5910}{0.0591}$$

$$\log K_C = 10 \Rightarrow K_C = 10^{10}$$

48 (b) Ni^{2+} (From nickel sulphate) $+ 2e^- \rightleftharpoons Ni$

From Nernst equation,

$$E = E^\circ_{cell} - \frac{0.0591}{2} \log \frac{1}{[Ni^{2+}]}$$

$$E_1 = E^\circ_{cell} - \frac{0.0591}{2} \log \frac{1}{C} \quad \ldots(i)$$

[Let $[Ni^{2+}] = C$]

When the solution is diluted,

$$E^\circ_2 = E^\circ_{cell} - \frac{0.0591}{2} \log \frac{10}{C} \quad \ldots(ii)$$

Eqs. (i) - (ii) gives,

$$E_1 - E_2 = \frac{0.0591}{2} \log 10$$

$$= 0.0295 \text{ V} \approx 0.03 \text{ V} = 30 \text{ mV}$$

Hence, reduction potential of Ni decreases by 30 mV.

49 (d) Higher the negative value of reduction potential, stronger will be the reducing agent.

Hence, the correct order of reducing power is

Li^+/Li (−3.05 V) $> Zn^{2+}/Zn$ (− 0.762 V) $> H^+/H_2$ (0.00 V) $> Cu^{2+}/Cu$ (+ 0.34 V) $> Ag^+/Ag$ (+ 0.80 V)

Thus, Li is the strongest reducing agent among the given options.

50 (d) The metal having low standard reduction potential will displace the metal from its salt's solution which has higher value of standard reduction potential. Hence, metal P will displace the cation of R from its aqueous solution and deposit the metal R.

51 (a) Reducing nature depends on the tendency of losing electron or electrons. Lesser is the negative value of reduction potential, more is the tendency to lose electrons. Then, reducing nature decreases from top to bottom. So, Y cannot reduce X but can reduce Z, or Y will oxidise X but not Z.

52 (a) As $\Delta G^\circ_f = -nFE^\circ$

if $\quad E^\circ = 0$

then, $\Delta G^\circ_f = 0$

53 (a) For the given cell,

$$Ag \mid Ag^+ \mid AgCl \mid Cl^- \mid Cl_2, Pt$$

The cell reactions are as follows

At anode $\quad Ag \longrightarrow Ag^+ + e^-$

At cathode $AgCl + e^- \longrightarrow Ag(s) + Cl^-$

Net cell reaction

$$AgCl \longrightarrow Ag^+ + Cl^-$$

$$\therefore \quad \Delta G^\circ_{reaction} = \Sigma \Delta G^\circ_p - \Sigma \Delta G^\circ_R$$

$$= (78 - 129) - (-109)$$

$$= +58 \text{ kJ/mol}$$

$$\Delta G^\circ = -nFE^\circ$$

$$58 \times 10^3 \text{ J} = -1 \times 96500 \times E^\circ_{cell}$$

$$E^\circ_{cell} = \frac{-58 \times 1000}{96500} = -0.60 \text{ V}$$

54 (c) Given, cell reaction is,

$$Zn + Fe^{2+} \longrightarrow Zn^{2+} + Fe$$

In the above reaction, Zn is being oxidised and Fe^{2+} is being reduced, thus the cell can be represented as,

$$Zn \mid Zn^{2+} \parallel Fe^{2+} \mid Fe$$

$$E_{cell} = E_{Right} - E_{Left}$$

$$= E_{Fe^{2+}/Fe} - E_{Zn^{2+}/Zn}$$

$$= (-0.44) - (-0.76)$$

$$= 0.32 \text{ V}$$

55 (a) Galvanic cell is an electrochemical cell that converts the chemical energy of a spontaneous reaction into electrical energy.

56 (c) Substance which has higher reduction potential is a stronger oxidising agent.

$[Fe(CN)_6]^{3-} + e^- \longrightarrow [Fe(CN)_6]^{4-}$; $\quad E^\circ = 0.35$ V

$Fe^{3+} + e^- \longrightarrow Fe^{2+}$; $E^\circ = 0.77$ V

The reduction potential of Fe^{3+}/Fe^{2+} is higher, hence, Fe^{3+} is the strongest oxidising agent.

57 (c) Reaction,

$2Cu^+(aq) \rightleftharpoons Cu^{2+}(aq) + Cu(s)$

$E^\circ = ?$

So, $\quad Cu^+(aq) + e^- \rightleftharpoons Cu(s)$; $\quad E^\circ = +0.49$ V

$Cu^+(aq) \rightleftharpoons Cu^{2+}(aq) + e^-$; $\quad E^\circ = -0.15$ V

On addition,

$2Cu^+(aq) \rightleftharpoons Cu^{2+}(aq) + Cu(s)$; $\quad E^\circ = +0.34$ V

58 (c) Given, $K_C = 1 \times 10^8$

$E^\circ_{(I_2/I^-)} = +0.54$ V, $E^\circ_{(Fe^{3+}/Fe^{2+})} = ?$

$$2Fe^{3+}(aq) + 2I^-(aq) \rightleftharpoons 2Fe^{2+}(aq) + I_2(s)$$

Number of electrons involved $(n) = 2$

$$E^\circ_{cell} = \frac{0.0591}{n} \log K_C$$
$$= \frac{0.0591}{2} \log 1 \times 10^8$$
$$= 0.0591 \times 4$$
$$= 0.2364 \text{ V}$$
$$E^\circ_{cell} = E^\circ_{(Fe^{3+}/Fe^{2+})} - E^\circ_{(I_2/I^-)}$$
$$0.23 = E^\circ_{(Fe^{3+}/Fe^{2+})} - (+0.54)$$
$$E^\circ_{(Fe^{3+}/Fe^{2+})} = 0.23 + 0.54$$
$$= +0.77 \text{ V}$$

59 (*a*) $E_{cell} = E^\circ_{cell} - \frac{2.303RT}{nF} \log\left[\frac{[Ni]}{[Ni^{2+}]}\right]$

$$= -0.25 - \frac{0.06}{2} \log\left(\frac{1}{0.1}\right)$$

$(\because n = 2)$

$$= -0.25 - 0.03 \times 1$$
$$E_{cell} = -0.28 \text{ V}$$

60 (*b*) $(Pt)H_2 \begin{vmatrix} H^+ \\ (1 \text{ atm}) \end{vmatrix} (0.01 \text{ M}) \begin{Vmatrix} Cu^{2+} \\ (0.1 \text{ M}) \end{Vmatrix} Cu$

For the above cell, the cell reaction is

$$H_2 + Cu^{2+} \longrightarrow 2H^+ + Cu$$

According to the Nernst equation,

$$E_{cell} = E^\circ_{(Cu^{2+}/Cu)} - \frac{0.0591}{n} \log \frac{[H^+]^2}{[Cu^{2+}]}$$
$$= 0.337 - \frac{0.0591}{2} \log \frac{(0.01)^2}{(0.1)}$$
$$= 0.337 - 0.02955 \log 10^{-3}$$
$$= 0.337 + 0.08865$$
$$= 0.42565 \approx 0.427$$

61 (*b*) According to Nernst equation,

$$E_{cell} = E^\circ_{cell} - \frac{2.303RT}{nF} \log \frac{C_1}{C_2}$$

For, $Zn(s) + Cl_2(1 \text{ atm}) \longrightarrow Zn^{2+} + 2Cl^-$

$$E_{cell} = E^\circ_{cell} - \frac{2.303RT}{nF} \log \frac{[Zn^{2+}][Cl^-]^2}{p_{Cl_2}}$$

Hence, to increase E, C_1 should be decreased and C_2 should be increased, i.e. $[Zn^{2+}]$ and $[Cl^-]$ should be decreased and p_{Cl_2} should be increased.

62 (*a*) Among the given metals, only Ag is present below hydrogen in electrochemical series, so it does not evolve hydrogen with dil. HCl.

$$Ag + \text{dil. HCl} \longrightarrow \text{No reaction}$$

63 (*d*) $2H^+ + 2e^- \longrightarrow H_2$

According to Nernst equation,

$$E_{H^+/H_2} = E^\circ_{H^+/H_2} - \frac{0.0591}{n} \log \frac{1}{[H^+]^2}$$
$$= 0 - \frac{0.0591}{2} (-\log [H^+]^2)$$
$$= -0.0591 (-\log [H^+])$$
$$= -0.0591 \text{ pH}$$
$$(\because -\log [H^+] = \text{pH})$$

64 (*c*) Given, $\Delta G^\circ_{H_2O(l)} = -237.2$ kJ/mol

$$\Delta G^\circ_{CO_2(g)} = -394.4 \text{ kJ/mol}$$
$$\Delta G^\circ_{C_5H_{12}(g)} = -8.2 \text{ kJ/mol}$$

Combustion of pentane-oxygen fuel cell occurs as,

$$C_5H_{12} + 8O_2 \longrightarrow 5CO_2 + 6H_2O$$
$$\Delta G^\circ = 5 \times \Delta G^\circ_{CO_2} + 6 \times \Delta G^\circ_{H_2O} - (\Delta G^\circ_{C_5H_{12}} + \Delta G^\circ_{O_2})$$
$$= 5 \times (-394.4) + 6 \times (-237.2) - (-8.2) + 0$$
$$= -3387 \text{ kJ/mol}$$

In pentane oxygen fuel cell, 32 electrons are involved.

$$\Delta G^\circ = -nFE^\circ$$
$$-3387 \times 10^3 = -32 \times 96500 \times E^\circ$$
$$(\because 16(O) + 32e^- \longrightarrow 16O^{2-})$$

or $$E^\circ = \frac{3387 \times 10^3}{32 \times 96500} = 1.0968 \text{ V}$$

65 (*d*) Standard electrode potential of hydrogen electrode at 1 M concentration and 1 atm pressure is zero volts.

66 (*d*) In the silver plating of copper, $K[Ag(CN)_2]$ is used instead of $AgNO_3$. The reason is less availability of Ag^+ ions, as Cu cannot displace Ag from $K[Ag(CN)_2]$ ion due to lower electrode potential of Cu than Ag.

67 (*d*) Zn is present above H_2 in electrochemical series. So, it liberates hydrogen gas from dilute HCl/H_2SO_4. But HNO_3 is an oxidising agent. The hydrogen obtained in this reaction is converted into H_2O. In HNO_3, NO_3^- ion is reduced and give NH_4NO_3, N_2O, NO and NO_2 (based upon the concentration of HNO_3).

$$[Zn + \underset{\text{(Nearly 6\%)}}{2HNO_3} \longrightarrow Zn(NO_3)_2 + 2H^+] \times 4$$
$$HNO_3 + 8H^+ \longrightarrow NH_3 + 3H_2O$$
$$NH_3 + HNO_3 \longrightarrow NH_4NO_3$$
$$\overline{4Zn + 10HNO_3 \longrightarrow 4Zn(NO_3)_2 + NH_4NO_3 + 3H_2O}$$

68 (*b*) In galvanic cell (Daniell cell), the electrical energy is produced from chemical reactions.

At anode

$$Zn \longrightarrow Zn^{2+} + 2e^- \quad \text{(oxidation)}$$

At cathode

$$Cu^{2+} + 2e^- \longrightarrow Cu \quad \text{(reduction)}$$

Cell reaction,

$$Zn + Cu^{2+} \longrightarrow Zn^{2+} + Cu$$

or $$Zn(s) + CuSO_4(aq) \longrightarrow Cu(s) + ZnSO_4(aq)$$

69 (*d*) Electrochemical cell

$$A \mid A^+(x \text{ M}) \parallel B^+(y \text{ M}) \mid B$$

The emf of cell is +0.20 V. So, cell reaction is spontaneous. The half-cell reaction are given as follows :

(i) At negative pole

$$A \longrightarrow A^+ + e^- \quad \text{(oxidation)}$$

(ii) At positive pole

$$B^+ + e^- \longrightarrow B \text{ (reduction)}$$

Hence, cell reaction is

$$A + B^+ \longrightarrow A^+ + B;$$
$$E^\circ_{cell} = +0.20 \text{ V}$$

70 (*b*) Mn has more oxidation potential than Cr. It is present below Cr in electrochemical series. So, its reduction potential is less than Cr.

The third ionisation energy for Mn is 3258 kJ mol^{-1} and for Cr is 2994 kJ mol^{-1}. So, both the statements are true but not correct explanation.

71 (*b*) For the given cell, $M \mid M^+ \parallel X^- \mid X$, the cell reaction is derived as follows

RHS : reduction, $X + e^- \longrightarrow X^-$ ...(i)

LHS : oxidation, $M \longrightarrow M^+ + e^-$ ...(ii)

Add (i) and (ii)

$$M + X \longrightarrow M^+ + X^-$$
$$\therefore \quad F_{cell} = 0.33 - 0.44 \text{ V}$$
$$= -0.11 \text{ V}$$

Hence, the cell potential = – 0.11 V

Since, E_{cell} = – ve, the cell reaction derived above is not spontaneous. In fact, the reverse reaction will occur spontaneously.

72 (*b*) $E = E^\circ_{RP} + \frac{0.0591}{n} \log [M^+]$

Given, $E^\circ_{RP} = -2.36$ V, $[M^+] = 0.1$ M

$n = 1$ (for $M^+ \rightarrow M$)

$$E = E^\circ_{RP} + \frac{0.0591}{n} \log [M^+]$$

$$= -2.36 + \frac{0.0591}{1} \log 0.1$$

$$= -2.36 + 0.0591 \times (-1)$$

$$= -2.36 - 0.0591$$

$$= -2.419 \text{ V}$$

$$\approx -2.41 \text{ V}$$

73 (*a*) From a solution of $CuSO_4$, Cu can be recovered by Fe metal. Because the electrode potential of Fe is more negative than that of Cu, thus, Fe is more reactive than Cu and it can displace Cu easily.

74 (*b*) $E^\circ = \frac{RT}{nF} \ln K_{eq}$.

It is Nernst equation. It gives the relation between emf of a cell and equilibrium constant of the reaction.

75 (*a*) $E_{cell} = E^\circ - \frac{0.059}{n} \log \frac{[\text{Product}]}{[\text{Reactant}]}$

$$(E_{cell})_1 = 0 - \frac{0.059}{1} \log \frac{0.1}{1}$$

$$0.06 = -\frac{0.059}{1} \log \frac{1}{10} \quad \ldots \text{(i)}$$

$$(E_{cell})_2 = 0 - \frac{0.059}{1} \log \frac{0.01}{1}$$

$$(E_{cell})_2 = -\frac{0.059}{1} \log \frac{1}{100} \quad \ldots \text{(ii)}$$

Dividing Eq. (i) by Eq. (ii)

$$\frac{0.06}{(E_{cell})_2} = \frac{\log 1 - \log 10}{\log 1 - \log 100}$$

$$\frac{0.06}{(E_{cell})_2} = \frac{0 - 1}{0 - 2 \log 10}$$

$$\frac{0.06}{(E_{cell})_2} = \frac{-1}{-2} = \frac{1}{2}$$

$$(E_{cell})_2 = 2 \times 0.06$$

$$= 0.12 \text{ V}$$

76 (*d*) In a cell reaction, electrical energy is produced. The electrical work is done by the system and it results in decrease in the free energy of the system.

77 (*a*) Magnesium is more electropositive than zinc, hence it can reduce Zn^{2+} (magnesium is placed above zinc in electrochemical series).

$$Mg + ZnO \longrightarrow MgO + Zn$$

78 (*b*) $2AgCl(s) + H_2(g)(1 \text{ bar}) \longrightarrow 2HCl(aq) + 2Ag(s)$

The cell with this cell reaction can be represented as,

$$\underset{\text{(anode)}}{Pt(s)} \mid H_2(g)(1 \text{ bar}) \mid 1M\,HCl(aq), \; \| \underset{\text{(cathode)}}{Ag^+(aq) \| Ag(s)}$$

Silver is undergoing reduction ($Ag^+ \longrightarrow Ag$) in this reaction, hence, it will act as cathode in the cell. Option (a) has KCl which is not present in the cell, so it is incorrect. Option (c) has AgCl(*s*) and AgCl do not ionise, it is also incorrect. Option (d) at cathode Ag is being oxidised to Ag^+ but at cathode, oxidation does not take place hence, it is also incorrect. Hence, option (b) is correct.

79 (*c*) Metals having higher oxidation potential (or lesser E°_{red}) can displace metals having lesser oxidation potential. The oxidation potential of Na is more than that of Zn.

Hence, Na is used to reduce Zn salts.

80 (*c*) The element having lower reduction potential can displace metal having higher reduction potential. Reduction potential of *D* is least among the given elements. Hence, it can displace all other metals.

81 (*a*) To obtain maximum work done from a galvanic cell, charge has to be passed reversibly. The reversible work done by a galvanic cell is equal to the decrease in its Gibbs energy.

Thus, maximum work $= nFE^\circ_{cell}$.

$$\text{Electrical work} = nFE^\circ_{cell}$$

$$= 2 \times 96500 \times 1.1$$

$$= 212300 \text{ J}$$

$$= 212.3 \text{ kJ}$$

82 (*a*) For concentration cells,

$$E^\circ_{cell} = \frac{0.0591}{1} \log \left[\frac{\text{anode}}{\text{cathode}}\right]$$

Given, pH = 3 for first solution and pH = 6 for second solution.

$\therefore [H^+]$ for first solution $= 10^{-pH}$ $= 10^{-3}$ mol/L and $[H^+]$ for second solution $= 10^{-pH} = 10^{-6}$ mol/L

$$\therefore \quad E^\circ_{cell} = -\frac{0.0591}{1} \log \left[\frac{10^{-6}}{10^{-3}}\right]$$

$$= -0.0591 \log 10^{-3}$$

$$= -0.0591 \times (-3 \log 10)$$

$$= -0.0591 \times (-3 \times 1)$$

$$= -0.0591 (-3)$$

$$\therefore \quad E^\circ_{cell} = 0.1773 \text{ V} \sim 0.177 \text{V}$$

83 (*b*) Standard electrode potential is measured by voltmeter.

84 (*c*) Alkali metals get oxidised easily as they have high value of oxidation potential, hence they behave as good reducing agents.

85 (*c*) $E_{cell} = E^\circ_{cell} - n\frac{0.059}{n} \log \left[\frac{\text{product}}{\text{reactant}}\right]$

$$Sn^{2+} \longrightarrow Sn^{4+} + 2e^-$$

$\therefore \; n = 2$

Given, $[Sn^{2+}] = 0.1$M, $[Sn^{4+}] = 0.01$M

$$E_{cell} = E^\circ_{cell} - \frac{0.059}{2} \log \left[\frac{Sn^{4+}}{Sn^{2+}}\right]$$

$$= E^\circ_{cell} - \frac{0.059}{2} \log \left[\frac{0.01}{0.1}\right]$$

$$= E^\circ_{cell} - \frac{0.059}{2} \log 0.1$$

$$= E^\circ_{cell} + \frac{0.059}{2} \times -1$$

$$= E^\circ_{cell} + \frac{0.059}{2}$$

Topic 4

Batteries, Fuel Cells and Corrosion

2017

1 When a lead storage battery is discharged **[JIPMER]**

(a) SO_2 is evolved
(b) lead sulphate is consumed
(c) lead is formed
(d) sulphuric acid is consumed

2 A device that converts energy of combustion of fuels like hydrogen and methane, directly into electrical energy is known as **[CBSE AIPMT]**

(a) fuel cell (b) electrolytic cell
(c) dynamo (d) Ni-Cd cell

3 For hydrogen-oxygen fuel cell at 1 atm and 298 K

$$H_2(g) + \frac{1}{2}O_2(g) \longrightarrow H_2O(l),\ \Delta G^\circ = -240\ \text{kJ}$$

E° for the cell is approximately, [Given F = 96500 C] **[KCET]**

(a) 2.48 V (b) 1.25 V (c) 2.5 V (d) 1.26 V

2013

4 Which of the following reaction is used to make a fuel cell? **[AIIMS]**

(a) $Cd(s) + 2Ni(OH)_3(s) \longrightarrow CdO(s) + 2Ni(OH)_2(s) + H_2O(l)$
(b) $Pb(s) + PbO_2(s) + 2H_2SO_4(aq) \longrightarrow 2PbSO_4(s) + 2H_2O(l)$
(c) $2H_2(g) + O_2(g) \longrightarrow 2H_2O(l)$
(d) $2Fe(s) + O_2(g) + 4H^+(aq) \longrightarrow 2Fe^{2+}(aq) + 2H_2O(l)$

2012

5 Which of the following is used widely in the manufacture of lead storage battery? **[Manipal]**

(a) Arsenic (b) Lithium
(c) Bismuth (d) Antimony

2010

6 Chemical formula of rust is **[OJEE]**

(a) $Fe_2O_3 \cdot H_2O$ (b) $Fe_2O_3 \cdot 5H_2O$
(c) $Fe_2O_3 \cdot xH_2O$ (d) None of these

7 When iron is rusted, it is **[MP PMT]**

(a) reduced
(b) decomposed
(c) oxidised
(d) changed in the fine powder

2009

8 The rusting of iron is catalysed by **[CG PMT, Haryana PMT]**

(a) Fe
(b) O_2
(c) H^+
(d) Zn

2008

9 **Assertion** (A) The cell potential of mercury cell is 1.35 V, which remains constant.
Reason (R) In mercury cell, the electrolyte is a paste of KOH and ZnO. **[AIIMS]**

(a) Both A and R are correct and R is the correct explanation of A
(b) Both A and R are correct but R is not the correct explanation of A
(c) A is correct but R is incorrect
(d) Both A and R are incorrect

2007

10 The efficiency of a fuel cell is given by **[CBSE AIPMT]**

(a) $\frac{\Delta H}{\Delta G}$ (b) $\frac{\Delta G}{\Delta S}$
(c) $\frac{\Delta G}{\Delta H}$ (d) $\frac{\Delta S}{\Delta G}$

11 When lead storage battery is charged **[AFMC]**

(a) lead dioxide dissolves
(b) sulphuric acid is regenerated
(c) the lead electrode becomes coated with lead sulphate
(d) the amount of sulphuric acid decreases

2005

12 **Assertion** (A) Galvanised iron does not rust.
Reason (R) Zinc has a more negative electrode potential than iron. **[AIIMS]**

(a) Both A and R are correct and R is the correct explanation of A
(b) Both A and R are correct but R is not the correct explanation of A
(c) A is correct but R is incorrect
(d) Both A and R are incorrect

13 When an acid cell is charged then **[AFMC]**

(a) voltage of cell increases
(b) electrolyte of cell dilutes
(c) resistance of cell increases
(d) None of the above

Answers

1 (d)	2 (a)	3 (b)	4 (c)	5 (d)	6 (c)	7 (c)	8 (c)	9 (b)	10 (c)
11 (b)	12 (a)	13 (a)							

Explanations

1 (*d*) H_2SO_4 is consumed during discharging of lead storage battery as, Pb changes to $PbSO_4$, and PbO_2 changes to $PbSO_4$.

2 (*a*) Fuel cell is a device that converts energy of combustion of fuels like hydrogen and methane, directly into electrical energy. Electrolytic cell converts electrical energy into chemical energy. Dynamo is an electrical generator that produces direct current with the use of a commutator.

Ni-Cd cell is a type of rechargeable battery which consists of a cadmium anode and a metal grid containing NiO_2 acting as a cathode.

3 (*b*) From $\Delta G° = -nFE°$

where, n = number of moles of electrons transferred = 2

$\Rightarrow \quad F = 96500$ C

$$\Delta G° = -240 \text{ kJ} = -240 \times 1000 \text{ J}$$

$$\therefore \quad E° = \frac{-240000}{-2 \times 96500} = 1.25 \text{ V}$$

4 (*c*) Cell which converts chemical energy of a fuel directly into electrical energy is called fuel cell, e.g. $H_2—O_2$ fuel cell, also called Bacon cell. The net reaction taking place in Bacon cell is

$$2H_2(g) + O_2(g) \longrightarrow 2H_2O(l)$$

Other fuel cells are

Propane-oxygen fuel cell

$$C_3H_8 + 5O_2 \longrightarrow 3CO_2 + 4H_2O$$

Methane oxygen fuel cell

$$CH_4 + 2O_2 \longrightarrow CO_2 + 2H_2O$$

Methanol-oxygen fuel cell

$$2CH_3OH + 3O_2 \longrightarrow 2CO_2 + 4H_2O$$

Note Efficiency of fuel cell is 70 – 75% which is much higher than connected cells (40% only)

5 (*d*) Antimony is used in making lead storage batteries because lead containing antimony is harder and more resistant towards the action of acids than ordinary lead.

6 (*c*) The chemical formula of rust is $Fe_2O_3 \cdot xH_2O$.

7 (*c*) When iron is rusted, it is oxidised to hydrated ferric oxide.

$$4Fe + 3O_2 + xH_2O \longrightarrow \underset{\text{Hydrated ferric oxide (rust)}}{2Fe_2O_3 \cdot xH_2O}$$

8 (*c*) The reaction occurring during rusting process are as follows,

At anode

$$Fe(s) \longrightarrow Fe^{2+}(aq) + 2e^-$$

At cathode

$$O_2(g) + 4H^+(aq) + 4e^- \longrightarrow 2H_2O$$

The Fe^{2+} ions, formed, are further oxidised by atmospheric oxygen to Fe^{3+} (as Fe_2O_3) and comes out as rust ($Fe_2O_3 \cdot xH_2O$). The H^+, formed in the rust formation, catalysed the process of rusting.

9 (*b*) $Zn(l) + HgO(s) \longrightarrow ZnO(s) + Hg(l)$

The cell potential of a mercury cell remains constant during its life as the overall reaction does not involve any ion in solution whose concentration changes during its life time. Moreover, a paste of KOH and ZnO is used as an electrolyte in the mercury cell. Thus, both A and R are correct but R is not the correct explanation of A.

10 (*c*) The efficiency of fuel cell is given by

$$\eta = \frac{\Delta G}{\Delta H}$$

11 (*b*) During the charging of a lead storage battery, the reactions at the anode and cathode are :

At anode

$$PbSO_4 + 2e^- \longrightarrow Pb + SO_4^{2-}$$

At cathode

$$PbSO_4 + 2H_2O \longrightarrow PbO_2 + 4H^+ + SO_4^{2-} + 2e^-$$

In both the reactions, H_2SO_4 is regenerated.

12 (*a*) Galvanised iron, i.e. iron coated with zinc does not rust easily as zinc has more negative electrode potential (– 0.76 V) than iron (– 0.41 V) i.e. zinc is less reactive than iron.

13 (*a*) The discharged acid cell (lead storage battery or cell) can be recharged by passing a direct current through in opposite direction. During recharging of cell, the electrode material are restored in their original forms.

Due to formation of H^+ and SO_4^{2-} ions, the specific gravity of sulphuric acid increases and it attains the original value (1.3 g/cm^3) and also its voltage increases.

18

Chemical Kinetics

Quick Review

The branch of chemistry which studies the rate of reaction and factors affecting it is called **chemical kinetics**.

Rate of Reaction

The rate (or speed or velocity) of a reaction is the rate of change of concentration of reactants or products in unit time. It is always positive.

It can be classified in the following two ways:

- On the basis of rate of reaction, chemical reactions can be **instantaneous** or fast reactions, **extremely slow reactions** and **moderately slow reactions**.
- On the basis of number of steps, chemical reactions can be **elementary reactions** and **complex reactions**.

Average and Instantaneous Rate

If the rate of appearance of product or disappearance of reactants takes place in a long period of time, then it is expressed as **average rate of reaction**. The rate of a reaction expressed at a particular moment of time is called **instantaneous rate of reaction**.

For a reaction, $aA + bB \longrightarrow cC + dD$

$$r_{av} = \frac{-1}{a}\frac{\Delta[A]}{\Delta t} = \frac{-1}{b}\frac{\Delta[B]}{\Delta t} = \frac{1}{c}\frac{\Delta[C]}{\Delta t} = \frac{1}{d}\frac{\Delta[D]}{\Delta t}$$

For a reaction, $aA + bB \rightarrow cC + dD$

$$r_{inst} = -\frac{1}{a}\frac{d[A]}{dt} = -\frac{1}{b}\frac{d[B]}{dt} = \frac{1}{c}\frac{d[C]}{dt} = \frac{1}{d}\frac{d[D]}{dt}$$

Graphical Interpretation of Rate of a Reaction

Rate of a reaction can be determined from the slope of the graph between the concentration of any of the reactants or products and time as given below:

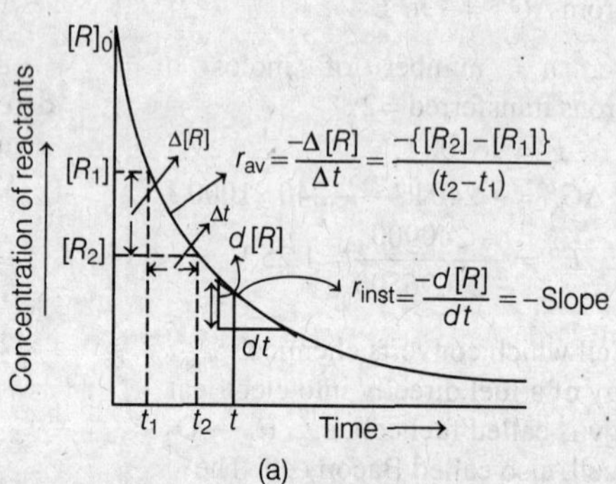

(a)

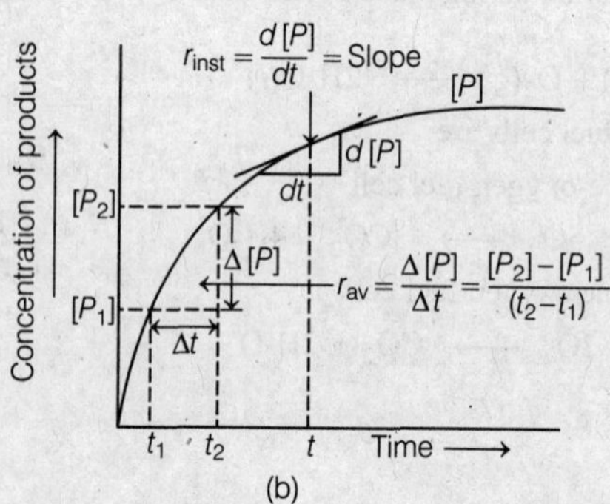

(b)

Determination of instantaneous and average rate of a reaction

Note The unit of rate of reaction is mol $L^{-1}s^{-1}$ or atm s^{-1} for gaseous reactants.

Rate Expression and Rate Constant
(Specific Rate Constant)

The representation of rate of reaction in terms of concentration of the reactants is called **rate law** or **rate expression**.

In a general reaction, $aA + bB \longrightarrow$ Product

The rate expression is shown below:

$$\text{Rate} \propto [A]^x [B]^y$$

Here, x and y are determined experimentally and may be or may not be equal to stoichiometric coefficient (*a* and *b*).

$$\text{Rate} = k[A]^x [B]^y$$

$$\frac{-d[R]}{dt} = k[A]^x [B]^y$$

This form of rate expression is called **differential rate equation**. The above expression is also known as **rate law**. *k* is called **rate constant** or **specific rate constant** and is defined as the rate of chemical reaction when concentration of each reactant is unity.

Factors Affecting Rate of Reaction

There are various factors that affect the rate of a reaction such as:

(*i*) **Concentration of Reactants** Higher the concentration, of reactants faster will be the reaction.

(*ii*) **Catalyst** Rate increases by lowering the energy barrier in the presence of catalyst.

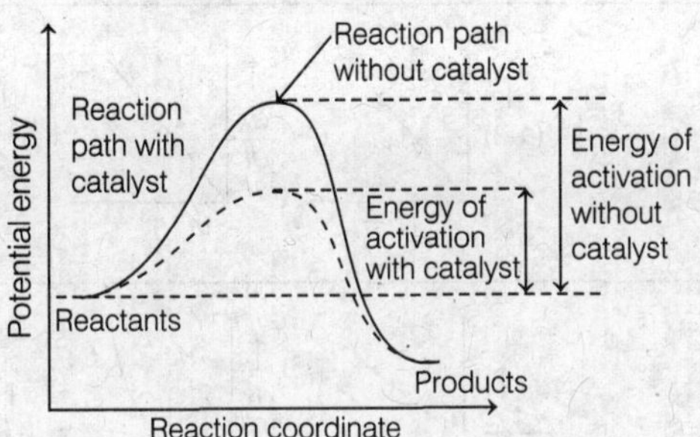

(iii) **Temperature** The rate of a reaction increases with an increase in temperature. The rate of the reaction nearly doubles for every 10°C rise in temperature.

$$\frac{K_{(T+10)}}{K_T} = 2 \text{ to } 3$$

Arrhenius Equation

The temperature dependence of the rate of a reaction can be accurately explained by the Arrhenius equation,

$$K = Ae^{-E_a/RT}$$

where, E_a = activation energy
= threshold energy − energy of reactants
A = pre-exponential factor or frequency factor

or, $$\log k = \log A - \frac{E_a}{2.303RT}$$

(i) If E_a is high, reaction is slow.

(ii) If E_a is low, reaction is fast.

or, $$\log \frac{k_2}{k_1} = \frac{E_a}{2.303R}\left[\frac{T_2 - T_1}{T_1 T_2}\right]$$

where, k_1 and k_2 = rate constants at temperatures T_1 and T_2 respectively.

As the value of activation energy (E_a) increases, the value of *k* decreases and therefore, rate of reaction decreases.

Molecularity of a Reaction

It can be defined as the number of reacting species (atoms, ions or molecules) taking part in an elementary reaction which must collide simultaneously in order to bring about a chemical reaction.

(*i*) If one reactant is involved, the reaction is called **unimolecular reaction**.

e.g. $NH_4NO_2 \longrightarrow N_2 + 2H_2O$

(*ii*) Reaction involving simultaneous collision between two species are called **bimolecular reactions.**

e.g. $2HI \longrightarrow H_2 + I_2$

(*iii*) Reactions involving simultaneous collision between three reacting species are called **trimolecular reactions.**

e.g. $2FeCl_3 + SnCl_2 \longrightarrow 2FeCl_2 + SnCl_4$

The probability that more than three molecules can collide and react simultaneously is very small. Thus, the molecularity greater than three is not observed.

Note Reactions having molecularity more than 3 are rare because chances for larger number of molecules to come simultaneously for collision are less.

Characteristics

- It cannot be zero, fractional or more than three.
- In case of complex reactions, the atoms, molecules or ions participating in rate determining step decide the molecularity. Among several steps, the slowest step is the rate determining step, e.g. if two molecules participate in the rate determining step, then molecularity is two.
- It does not provide the information about mechanism of the reaction.

Order of a Chemical Reaction

The order of reaction is defined as "the sum of the power to which the concentration terms in the rate law equation are raised to express the observed rate of the reaction."

$$\text{rate} = k[A]^c [B]^d \qquad \text{...(i)}$$

For the rate expression (i) the sum of *c* and *d* is the order of the reaction.

Characteristics

- Order of reaction is purely an experimental quantity. It may be a whole number, zero or fraction.
- Depending upon whether $(c + d)$ is equal to zero, 1, 2 or 3, the reactions are said to be zero order, first order, second order or third order respectively.

Rate Equations Unit and Plot of Various Order of Reactions

Reaction	Order	Differential equation	Integral equation	Unit of k	$t_{1/2}$	Plot
$A \longrightarrow$ Product (a) a = initial concentration of reactants	0	$\frac{dx}{dt} = k$	$k = \frac{x}{t}$	mol $L^{-1}s^{-1}$	$\frac{a}{2k}$	x vs $t \longrightarrow$; $\frac{dx}{dt}$ vs $(a-x) \longrightarrow$; $t_{1/2}$ vs $(a-x) \longrightarrow$
$A \longrightarrow P$	1	$\frac{dx}{dt} = k(a-x)$	$k = \frac{2.303}{t}\log\frac{a}{a-x}$	s^{-1}	$\frac{0.693}{k}$	log $(a-x)$ vs $t \longrightarrow$; $\frac{dx}{dt}$ vs $(a-x) \longrightarrow$; $t_{1/2}$ vs $(a-x) \longrightarrow$
$2A \longrightarrow P$	2	$\frac{dx}{dt} = k(a-x)^2$	$k = \frac{1}{t}\left[\frac{1}{a-x} - \frac{1}{a}\right]$	L $mol^{-1}s^{-1}$	$\frac{1}{ka}$	$\frac{x}{a-x}$ vs $t \longrightarrow$; $\frac{dx}{dt}$ vs $(a-x)^2 \longrightarrow$; $t_{1/2}$ vs $a \longrightarrow$ Regular hyperbola
$A + B \longrightarrow P$	2	$\frac{dx}{dt} = k(a-x)(b-x)$	$k = \frac{2.303}{t(a-b)} \times \log\frac{b(a-x)}{a(b-x)}$			$\frac{1}{a-x}$ vs $t \longrightarrow$; $\frac{dx}{dt}$ vs $(a-x) \longrightarrow$ Parabola; $t_{1/2}$ vs $a^{-1} \longrightarrow$
$3A \longrightarrow P$	3	$\frac{dx}{dt} = k(a-x)^3$	$k = \frac{1}{2t}\left(\frac{1}{(a-x)^2} - \frac{1}{a^2}\right)$	$L^2mol^{-1}s^{-1}$	$\frac{3}{(a-x)^2}$	$(a-x)^2$ vs $t \longrightarrow$; $\frac{dx}{dt}$ vs $(a-x)^3 \longrightarrow$; $t_{1/2}$ vs $a^{-2} \longrightarrow$
						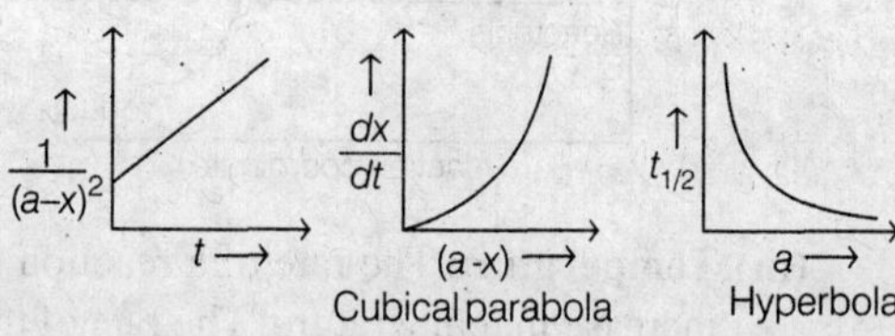 $\frac{1}{(a-x)^2}$ vs $t \longrightarrow$; $\frac{dx}{dt}$ vs $(a-x) \longrightarrow$ Cubical parabola; $t_{1/2}$ vs $a \longrightarrow$ Hyperbola

Pseudo First Order Reaction

- The reactions which are not actually of first order but behave so due to altered conditions are called **pseudo first order reactions**, for example hydrolysis of ethyl acetate.

$$\underset{\text{Ethyl acetate}}{CH_3COOC_2H_5} + H_2O \xrightarrow{H^+} CH_3COOH + C_2H_5OH$$

- The concentration of water is not considered in calculation as its concentration does not get altered much with time.

Note

(i) For any reaction, half-life period, $t_{1/2} \propto \left(\frac{1}{a}\right)^{n-1} \Rightarrow \frac{(t_{1/2})_1}{(t_{1/2})_2} = \left(\frac{a_2}{a_1}\right)^{n-1}$

(ii) $\frac{(\text{Rate})_1}{(\text{Rate})_2} = \left(\frac{a_1}{a_2}\right)^n$

where, a_1 and a_2 = initial concentrations, n = order of reaction.

(iii) For number of half-lives, $C = C_0\left(\frac{1}{2}\right)^y$

where, $y = \frac{\text{total time } (t)}{t_{1/2}}$

C = final concentration, C_0 = initial concentration

Collision Theory

According to this theory, for a reaction to occur, reaction species like, molecules, atoms or ions must collide first. Increased concentrations of reacting species result in greater number of collisions per unit time.

However, not all collisions result in reaction, i.e. not all collisions are effective collisions.

Factors Affecting Effective Collisions

(*i*) For a collision to be effective, the reacting species must

- possess atleast a certain minimum energy, i.e. threshold energy which is defined as the minimum amount of energy which the colliding molecules must possess so as to make the chemical reaction to take place.
- have proper orientation towards each other at the time of collision. If colliding molecules have improper orientations, they do not react even though they may possess sufficient energy.

(*ii*) The minimum additional energy required by the molecule to attain threshold energy is called **activation energy**, which is required by the species during collision as a result of interchange of energies.

$$E_a = E_{\text{(threshold energy)}} - E_{\text{(reactants)}}$$

The fraction of collisions (f) with an energy equal to or greater than the activation energy (E_a) is given as,

$$f = e^{-E_a/RT}$$

where, $e^{-E_a/RT}$ is called **Boltzmann factor.**

The fraction of collisions having proper orientation for conversion of reactants to products is called the **steric factor**, P.

Topical Practice Questions

All the exam questions of this chapter have been divided into three topics as listed below.

Topic 1

Rate of Reaction : Its Definition, Expression and Characteristics

2019

1 For the chemical reaction, $N_2(g) + 3H_2(g) \rightleftharpoons 2NH_3(g)$

The correct option is **[NEET]**

(a) $-\dfrac{d[N_2]}{dt} = 2\dfrac{d[NH_3]}{dt}$

(b) $-\dfrac{d[N_2]}{dt} = \dfrac{1}{2}\dfrac{d[NH_3]}{dt}$

(c) $3\dfrac{d[H_2]}{dt} = 2\dfrac{d[NH_3]}{dt}$

(d) $-\dfrac{1}{3}\dfrac{d[H_2]}{dt} = -\dfrac{1}{2}\dfrac{d[NH_3]}{dt}$

2018

2 In the reversible reaction, $2NO_2 \underset{k_2}{\overset{k_1}{\rightleftharpoons}} N_2O_4$

the rate of disappearance of NO_2 is equal to **[JIPMER]**

(a) $\dfrac{2k_1}{k_2}[NO_2]^2$

(b) $2k_1[NO_2]^2 - 2k_2[N_2O_4]$

(c) $2k_1[NO_2]^2 - k_2[N_2O_4]$

(d) $(2k_1 - k_2)[NO_2]$

2014

3 For the set of reactions

(i) $A + B \underset{k_2}{\overset{k_1}{\rightleftharpoons}} C$, (ii) $C + B \xrightarrow{k_3} D$

$k_1 [A][B] - k_2 [C] - k_3 [C][B]$ is equal to **[Manipal]**

(a) $\frac{-d[A]}{dt}$ (b) $\frac{-d[B]}{dt}$

(c) $\frac{d[C]}{dt}$ (d) $\frac{d[D]}{dt}$

2010

4 For the reaction, $N_2O_5(g) \longrightarrow 2NO_2(g) + \frac{1}{2}O_2(g)$ the value of the rate of disappearance of N_2O_5 is given as 6.25×10^{-3} mol L^{-1} s^{-1}. The rate of formation of NO_2 and O_2 is given respectively as **[CBSE AIPMT]**

(a) 1.25×10^{-2} mol L^{-1} s^{-1} and 6.25×10^{-3} mol L^{-1} s^{-1}

(b) 6.25×10^{-3} mol L^{-1} s^{-1} and 6.25×10^{-3} mol L^{-1} s^{-1}

(c) 1.25×10^{-2} mol L^{-1} s^{-1} and 3.125×10^{-3} mol L^{-1} s^{-1}

(d) 6.25×10^{-3} mol L^{-1} s^{-1} and 3.125×10^{-3} mol L^{-1} s^{-1}

5 Consider the decomposition of N_2O_5 as

$$N_2O_5 \longrightarrow 2NO_2 + \frac{1}{2}O_2$$

The rate of reaction is given by

$$\frac{-d[N_2O_5]}{dt} = \frac{1}{2}\frac{d[NO_2]}{dt} = 2\frac{d[O_2]}{dt} = k_1[N_2O_5]$$

Therefore, $\frac{-d[N_2O_5]}{dt} = k_1[N_2O_5]$

$$\frac{+d[NO_2]}{dt} = 2k_1[N_2O_5] = k_1'[N_2O_5]$$

$$\frac{+d[O_2]}{dt} = \frac{1}{2}k_1[N_2O_5] = k_1''[N_2O_5]$$

Choose the correct option. **[AMU]**

(a) $k_1 = k_1' = k_1''$ (b) $k_1 = 2k_1' = k_1''$

(c) $4k_1 = k_1' = 2k_1''$ (d) $2k_1 = k_1' = 4k_1''$

2009

6 For the reaction, $N_2 + 3H_2 \longrightarrow 2NH_3$, if $\frac{d[NH_3]}{dt} = 2 \times 10^{-4}$ mol L^{-1} s^{-1}, the value of $\frac{-d[H_2]}{dt}$ would be **[CBSE AIPMT]**

(a) 3×10^{-4} mol L^{-1} s^{-1}

(b) 4×10^{-4} mol L^{-1} s^{-1}

(c) 6×10^{-4} mol L^{-1} s^{-1}

(d) 1×10^{-4} mol L^{-1} s^{-1}

7 In the synthesis of ammonia from nitrogen and hydrogen gases, if 6×10^{-2} mole of hydrogen disappears in 10 min, the number of moles of ammonia formed in 0.3 min is **[J&K CET]**

(a) 1.8×10^{-2} (b) 1.2×10^{-3}

(c) 4×10^{-2} (d) 3.6×10^{-2}

2007

8 For the reaction, $Cl_2 + 2I^- \longrightarrow I_2 + 2Cl^-$, the initial concentration of I^- was 0.20 mol L^{-1} and the concentration after 20 min was 0.18 mol L^{-1}. Then, the rate of formation of I_2 in mol L^{-1} min^{-1} would be **[Kerala CEE]**

(a) 1×10^{-3} (b) 5×10^{-4}

(c) 1×10^{-4} (d) 2×10^{-3}

(e) 5×10^{-3}

2006

9 A gaseous hypothetical chemical equation $2A \rightleftharpoons 4B + C$ is carried out in a closed vessel. The concentration of B is found to increase by 5×10^{-3} mol L^{-1} in 10 s. The rate of appearance of B is **[BHU]**

(a) 5×10^{-4} mol L^{-1} s^{-1}

(b) 5×10^{-5} mol L^{-1} s^{-1}

(c) 6×10^{-5} mol L^{-1} s^{-1}

(d) 4×10^{-4} mol L^{-1} s^{-1}

Answers

1. (b)	2. (b)	3. (d)	4. (c)	5. (d)	6. (a)	7. (b)	8. (b)	9. (a)

Explanations

1 (*b*) Rate of reaction,

$$= \frac{\text{Decrease in the concentration of reactants or increase in the concentration of products}}{\text{Time taken}}$$

For the given reaction,

$$N_2(g) + 3H_2(g) \rightleftharpoons 2NH_3(g)$$

$$\text{Rate of reaction} = \frac{-d[N_2]}{dt} = -\frac{1}{3}\frac{d[H_2]}{dt} = +\frac{1}{2}\frac{d[NH_3]}{dt}$$

Hence, option (b) is correct.

2 (*b*) $2NO_2 \underset{k_2}{\overset{k_1}{\rightleftharpoons}} N_2O_4$

$$\text{Rate of reaction} = -\frac{1}{2}\frac{d[NO_2]}{dt} = k_1[NO_2]^2 - k_2[N_2O_4]$$

$\therefore$ Rate of disappearance of NO_2

i.e. $\frac{-d[NO_2]}{dt} = 2k_1[NO_2]^2 - 2k_2[N_2O_4]$

3 (*d*) For equilibrium reaction (i),

Rate of forward reaction $= k_1\,[A][B]$

Rate of backward reaction $= k_2\,[C]$

Hence, $k_1\,[A][B] - k_2\,[C]$; represent the production of $[C]$.

For reaction (ii), $\frac{d[D]}{dt} = k_3\,[C][B]$

Production of $[D]$ is governed by production of reactant $[C]$ in reaction (i).

Hence, $k_1\,[A][B] - k_2\,[C] - k_3\,[C][B] = \frac{d[D]}{dt}$

4 (*c*) $N_2O_5(g) \longrightarrow 2NO_2(g) + \frac{1}{2}O_2(g)$

$$-\frac{d[N_2O_5]}{dt} = \frac{1}{2}\frac{d[NO_2]}{dt} = \frac{2d[O_2]}{dt}$$

$$\frac{d[NO_2]}{dt} = \frac{-2d[N_2O_5]}{dt}$$

$$= 2 \times 6.25 \times 10^{-3} = 1.25 \times 10^{-2} \text{ mol L}^{-1}\text{ s}^{-1}$$

$$\frac{d[O_2]}{dt} = -\frac{1}{2}\frac{d[N_2O_5]}{dt}$$

$$= \frac{1}{2} \times 6.25 \times 10^{-3} = 3.125 \times 10^{-3} \text{ mol L}^{-1}\text{ s}^{-1}$$

5 (*d*) Given, $\frac{-d[N_2O_5]}{dt} = \frac{1}{2}\frac{d[NO_2]}{dt}$

$$= \frac{2d[O_2]}{dt} = k_1[N_2O_5]$$

$$\therefore \quad k_1[N_2O_5] = \frac{k_1'}{2}[N_2O_5] = 2k_1''[N_2O_5]$$

or $\quad 2k_1 = k_1' = 4k_1''$

6 (*a*) For the reaction, $N_2 + 3H_2 \longrightarrow 2NH_3$

Rate of reaction

$$= -\frac{d[N_2]}{dt} = -\frac{1}{3}\frac{d[H_2]}{dt} = \frac{1}{2}\frac{d[NH_3]}{dt}$$

or $-\frac{d[H_2]}{dt} = \frac{3}{2}\frac{d[NH_3]}{dt}\left(\because \frac{d[NH_3]}{dt} = 2 \times 10^{-4}\text{ mol L}^{-1}\text{ s}^{-1}\right)$

$$= 3 \times 10^{-4} \text{ mol L}^{-1}\text{ s}^{-1}$$

7 (*b*) $N_2 + 3H_2 \longrightarrow 2NH_3$

$$-\frac{1}{3}\frac{\Delta[H_2]}{\Delta t} = \frac{1}{2}\frac{\Delta[NH_3]}{\Delta t}$$

$$-\frac{\Delta[H_2]}{\Delta t} = \frac{3}{2}\frac{\Delta[NH_3]}{\Delta t}$$

or $\frac{\Delta[NH_3]}{\Delta t} = -\frac{2}{3}\frac{\Delta[H_2]}{\Delta t}$

$$= \frac{2}{3} \times \frac{6 \times 10^{-2}}{10} = 4 \times 10^{-3}$$

$$\Delta[NH_3] = 4 \times 10^{-3} \times 10 = 4 \times 10^{-2}$$

In 10 min number of moles of $NH_3 = 4 \times 10^{-2}$

Then, in 0.3 min $= \frac{4 \times 10^{-2} \times 0.3}{10} = 1.2 \times 10^{-3}$

8 (*b*) Rate of formation of I_2 is given below:

$$I_2 = \frac{dI_2}{dt} = -\frac{1}{2}\frac{d[I^-]}{dt}$$

$$= \frac{-1}{2} \times \frac{0.18 - 0.20}{20}$$

$$= \frac{-1}{2} \times \frac{-0.02}{20}$$

$$= 5 \times 10^{-4} \text{ mol L}^{-1}\text{ min}^{-1}$$

9. (*a*) Increase in concentration of $B = 5 \times 10^{-3}$ mol L^{-1}

Time = 10 s

Rate of appearance of $B = \frac{\text{increase in conc. of } B}{\text{time taken}}$

$$= \frac{5 \times 10^{-3}}{10} = 5 \times 10^{-4} \text{ mol L}^{-1}\text{ s}^{-1}$$

Topic 2

Rate Expression, Order and Molecularity

2019

1 A first order reaction has a rate constant of $2.303 \times 10^{-3}\ s^{-1}$. The time required for 40 g of this reactant to reduce to 10 g will be [Given that: $\log_{10} 2 = 0.3010$] [NEET (Odisha)]

(a) 230.3 s (b) 301 s
(c) 2000 s (d) 602 s

2 If the rate constant for a first order reaction is k, the time (t) required for the completion of 99% of the reaction is given by [NEET]

(a) $t = 6.909/k$ (b) $t = 4.606/k$
(c) $t = 2.303/k$ (d) $t = 0.693/k$

3 Formula for half- life of a zero order reaction is [JIPMER]

(a) $\frac{C_0}{k}$ (b) $\frac{C_0}{2k}$ (c) $\frac{2C_0}{k}$ (d) $\frac{2C_0}{2k}$

4 If half-life of a substance is 36 minutes. Find amount left after 2 hrs. Initial amount is 10 g [JIPMER]

(a) 1 g (b) 2 g (c) 3 g (d) 4 g

5 Find out time period of Ist order reaction when reaction complete 2/3 rd, if the value of rate constant is $4.3 \times 10^{-4}\ s^{-1}$ [JIPMER]

(a) 0.0025×10^3 sec (b) 0.25×10^3 sec
(c) 0.025×10^3 sec (d) 2.5×10^3 sec

2018

6 Among the following statements, the correct statement about the half-life period for a first order reaction is [AIIMS]

(a) independent of concentration
(b) proportional to concentration
(c) inversely proportional to concentration
(d) inversely proportional to the square of the concentration

7 The correct difference between first and second order reactions is that [NEET]

(a) a first-order reaction can be catalysed; a second-order reaction cannot be catalysed
(b) the half-life of a first-order reaction does not depend on $[A]_0$; the half-life of a second-order reaction does depend on $[A]_0$
(c) the rate of a first-order reaction does not depend on reactant concentrations; the rate of a second-order reaction does depend on reactant concentrations
(d) the rate of a first-order reaction does depend on reactant concentrations; the rate of a second-order reaction does not depend on reactant concentrations

8 When initial concentration of the reactant is doubled, the half-life period of a zero order reaction [NEET]

(a) is tripled (b) is doubled
(c) is halved (d) remains unchanged

2017

9 For the chemical reaction, $2O_3 \rightleftharpoons 3O_2$

The reaction proceed as follows:

$$O_3 \rightleftharpoons O_2 + O\text{(fast)}$$
$$O + O_3 \longrightarrow 2O_2 \text{ (slow)}$$

The order of reaction in rate law expression will be [JIPMER]

(a) 2 (b) 1
(c) 2 (d) Unpredictable

10 A first order reaction is 50% completed in 1.26×10^{14} s. How much time would it take for 100% completion?

(a) 1.26×10^{15} s (b) 2.52×10^{14} s [JIPMER]
(c) 2.52×10^{28} s (d) Infinite

11 Mechanism of a hypothetical reaction, $X_2 + Y_2 \longrightarrow 2XY$ is given below

(i) $X_2 \rightleftharpoons X + X$(fast)
(ii) $X + Y_2 \longrightarrow XY + Y$(slow)
(iii) $X + Y \longrightarrow XY$ (fast)

The overall order of the reaction will be [NEET]

(a) 1 (b) 2 (c) 0 (d) 1.5

12 A first order reaction has a specific reaction rate constant of $10^{-2}\ s^{-1}$. How much time will it take for 20 g of the reactant to reduce to 5 g? [NEET]

(a) 238.6 s (b) 138.6 s (c) 346.5 s (d) 693.0 s

2016

13 The decomposition of phosphine (PH_3) on tungsten at low pressure is a first-order reaction. It is because the [NEET]

(a) rate is proportional to the surface coverage
(b) rate is inversely proportional to the surface coverage
(c) rate is independent of the surface coverage
(d) rate of decomposition is very slow

14 The rate of a first-order reaction is 0.04 mol $L^{-1}\ s^{-1}$ at 10 sec and 0.03 mol $L^{-1}\ s^{-1}$ at 20 sec after initiation of the reaction. The half-life period of the reaction is [NEET]

(a) 34.1 s (b) 44.1 s (c) 54.1 s (d) 24.1 s

2015

15 When initial concentration of a reactant is doubled in a reaction, its half-life period is not affected. The order of the reaction is [CBSE AIPMT]

(a) zero
(b) first
(c) second
(d) more than zero but less than first

2014

16 Rate law for the reaction, $A+2B \rightarrow C$ is found to be, Rate $= k[A][B]$.
Concentration of reactant 'B' is doubled, keeping the concentration of 'A' constant, the value of rate constant will be **[UK PMT]**
(a) same (b) doubled (c) quadrupled (d) halved

17 Rate law for the reaction, $A+B \longrightarrow$ product is rate $= k[A]^2[B]$. What is the rate constant, if rate of reaction at a given temperature is 0.22 Ms^{-1}, when $[A]=1$ M and $[B]=0.25$ M? **[MHT CET]**
(a) 3.52 $M^{-2}s^{-1}$ (b) 0.88 $M^{-2}s^{-1}$
(c) 1.136 $M^{-2}s^{-1}$ (d) 0.05 $M^{-2}s^{-1}$

18 For reaction, $2N_2O_5 \rightarrow 4NO_2 + O_2$, the rate is directly proportional to $[N_2O_5]$. At 45° C, 90% of the N_2O_5 reacts in 3600 seconds. The value of the rate constant is **[Manipal]**
(a) $3.2\times10^{-4}s^{-1}$ (b) $6.4\times10^{-4}s^{-1}$
(c) $8.5\times10^{-4}s^{-1}$ (d) $12.8\times10^{-4}s^{-1}$

19 The $t_{1/2}$ for a zero order reaction at the initial concentration of 6×10^{-3} M is one minute at 27° C. The rate constant at 27° C in mol $dm^{-3}s^{-1}$ is **[Kerala]**
(a) 3×10^{-4} (b) 6×10^{-4} (c) 5×10^{-5} (d) 5×10^{-4}
(e) 3×10^{-5}

20 The inversion of cane sugar is first order in [sugar] and proceeds with half-life of 600 minutes at pH = 4 for a given concentration of sugar. However, if pH = 5, the half-life changes to 60 minutes. The rate law expression for the sugar inversion can be written as **[Kerala]**
(a) rate $= k[\text{sugar}]^1[H^+]^2$ (b) rate $= k[\text{sugar}]^1[H^+]^1$
(c) rate $= k[\text{sugar}]^1[H^+]^4$ (d) rate $= k[\text{sugar}]^1[H^+]^0$
(e) rate $= k[\text{sugar}]^1[H^+]^5$

21 In an attempt to compare the half-lives of two radioactive elements A and B, a scientist set aside 400 g of each. After 3 months, the scientist found 25 g of A and 200 g of B. Which one of the following statements is correct? **[Kerala]**
(a) Half-life of B is twice that of A
(b) Half-life of B is four times that of A
(c) Half-life of A is twice that of B
(d) Half-life of A is four times that of B
(e) Half-life of B is eight times that of A

22 The rate of a certain reaction is given by, rate $= k[H^+]^n$. The rate increases 100 times when the pH changes from 3 to 1. The order (n) of the reaction is **[WB JEE]**
(a) 2 (b) 0 (c) 1 (d) 1.5

23 If 60% of first order reaction was completed in 60 min, 50% of the same reaction would be completed in approximately **[UK PMT]**
(a) 45 min (b) 60 min (c) 40 min (d) 50 min

24 $A(g) \xrightarrow{\Delta} P(g)+Q(g)+R(g)$, follows first order kinetics with a half-life of 69.3 s at 500°C. Starting from the gas 'A' enclosed in a container at 500°C and at a pressure of 0.4 atm, the total pressure of the system after 230 s will be **[Karnataka]**
(a) 1.15 atm (b) 1.32 atm (c) 1.22 atm (d) 1.12 atm

25 The value of rate constant for a first order reaction is $2.303\times10^{-2}s^{-1}$. What will be the time required to reduce the concentration to $\frac{1}{10}$th of its initial concentration? **[GCET]**
(a) 100 s (b) 10 s
(c) 2303 s (d) 23.03 s

2013

26 75% of a first order reaction is completed in 30 minutes, what is the time required for completion of 93.75% of the reaction (in minutes)? **[KCET]**
(a) 45 (b) 120 (c) 90 (d) 60

27 For a given reaction, $t_{1/2} = \frac{1}{ka}$, the order of the reaction is
(a) 1 (b) 0 (c) 3 (d) 2 **[KCET]**

2012

28 In a reaction, $A + B \rightarrow$ product, rate is doubled when the concentration of B is doubled, and rate increases by a factor of 8 when the concentrations of both the reactants (A and B) are doubled. Rate law for the reaction can be written as **[CBSE AIPMT]**
(a) Rate $= k[A][B]^2$ (b) Rate $= k[A]^2[B]^2$
(c) Rate $= k[A][B]$ (d) Rate $= k[A]^2[B]$

29 **Assertion** (A) The order of reaction may be defined as the sum of the powers which the concentration terms are raised in order to determine the rate of reaction gives the total order of reaction.

Reason (R) The number of molecules whose concentrations determine the rate of reaction at a given temperature is called order of reaction. **[AIIMS]**
(a) Both A and R are correct and the R is the correct explanation of the A
(b) Both A and R are correct but the R is not the correct explanation of the A
(c) A is correct but R is incorrect
(d) Both A and R are incorrect

30 **Assertion** (A) Acid catalysed hydrolysis of ethyl acetate is a first order reaction. **[AIIMS]**

Reason (R) Water does not take part in the reaction.
(a) Both A and R are correct and the R is the correct explanation of the A
(b) Both A and R are correct but the R is not the correct explanation of the A
(c) A is correct but R is incorrect
(d) Both A and R are incorrect

31 Half-life of a reaction is found to be inversely proportional to the cube of initial concentration. The order of reaction is

(a) 5 (b) 2 (c) 4 (d) 3 **[AFMC]**

32 Units of specific reaction rate for second order reaction

(a) s^{-1} (b) $mol\ L^{-1}\ s^{-1}$ **[UP CPMT]**
(c) $L^2\ mol^{-2}\ s^{-1}$ (d) $L\ mol^{-1}\ s^{-1}$

33 For a reaction, $A + B \rightarrow$ products the rate of the reaction at various concentrations are given below.

Exp. No.	$[A]$	$[B]$	Rate (mol $dm^3 s^{-1}$)
1	0.2	0.2	2
2	0.2	0.4	4
3	0.6	0.4	36

The rate law for the above reaction is **[KCET]**

(a) $r = k[A][B]^2$ (b) $r = k[A]^3[B]$
(c) $r = k[A]^2[B]^2$ (d) $r = k[A]^2[B]$

2011

34 Which one of the following statements for the order of a reaction is incorrect? **[CBSE AIPMT]**

(a) Order of reaction is always whole number
(b) Order can be determined only experimentally
(c) Order is not influenced by stoichiometric coefficient of the reactants
(d) Order of reaction is sum of power to the concentration terms of reactants to express the rate of reaction

35 The rate law for the reaction, $xA + yB \longrightarrow mP + nQ$ is rate $= k[A]^c[B]^d$. What is the total order of the reaction?

(a) $(x + y)$ (b) $(m + n)$ (c) $(c + d)$ (d) x/y
(e) Two **[Kerala CEE]**

36 The initial rates of reaction, $3A + 2B + C \longrightarrow$ Products, at different initial concentrations are given below.

Initial rate, Ms^{-1}	$[A]_0, M$	$[B]_0$, M	$[C]_0, M$
5.0×10^{-3}	0.010	0.005	0.010
5.0×10^{-3}	0.010	0.005	0.015
1.0×10^{-2}	0.010	0.010	0.010
1.25×10^{-3}	0.005	0.005	0.010

The order with respect to the reactants *A*, *B* and *C* are respectively **[Kerala CEE]**

(a) 3, 2, 0 (b) 3, 2, 1 (c) 2, 2, 0 (d) 2, 2, 1
(e) 2, 1, 0

37 For a first order reaction, the time taken to reduce the initial concentration by a factor of 1/4 is 20 min. The time required to reduce initial concentration by a factor of 1/16 is **[Kerala CEE]**

(a) 20 min (b) 10 min (c) 80 min (d) 40 min
(e) 5 min

38 Which one of the following is wrong about molecularity of a reaction? **[WB JEE]**

(a) It may be whole number or fractional
(b) It is calculated from reaction mechanism
(c) It is the number of molecules of the reactants taking part in a single step chemical reaction
(d) It is always equal to the order of elementary reaction

39 A chemical reaction proceeds into the following steps:

Step I, $2A \rightleftharpoons X$, fast
Step II, $X + B \rightleftharpoons Y$, slow
Step III, $Y + B \rightleftharpoons$ Product, fast

The rate law for the overall reaction is **[DUMET]**

(a) rate $= k[A]^2$ (b) rate $= k[B]^2$
(c) rate $= k[A][B]$ (d) rate $= k[A]^2[B]$

40 The time required for 100% completion of a zero order reaction is **[KCET]**

(a) ak (b) $\frac{a}{2k}$ (c) $\frac{a}{k}$ (d) $\frac{2k}{a}$

41 The following data were obtained during the first order decomposition of $2A(g) \longrightarrow B(g) + C(s)$ at a constant volume and at a particular temperature.

S.No.	Time	Total pressure in Pascal
1	At the end of 10 min	300
2	After completion	200

The rate constant in min^{-1} is **[KCET]**

(a) 0.0693 (b) 69.3
(c) 6.93 (d) 6.93×10^{-4}

42 Give relation between half reaction time ($t_{1/2}$) and initial concentration of reactant for $(n-1)$ order reaction **[Guj CET]**

(a) $t_{1/2} \propto [R]_0$ (b) $t_{1/2} \propto [R]_0^{2-n}$
(c) $t_{1/2} \propto [R]_0^{n+1}$ (d) $t_{1/2} \propto [R]_0^{n-2}$

43 For a first order reaction, the initial concentration of a reactant is 0.05 M. After 45 min, it is decreased by 0.015 M. Calculate the half reaction time ($t_{1/2}$). **[Guj CET]**

(a) 88.96 min (b) 25.90 min
(c) 78.72 min (d) 77.20 min

2010

44 During the kinetic study of the reaction $2A + B \longrightarrow C + D$, following results were obtained

S.No.	$[A]$/mol L^{-1}	$[B]$/mol L^{-1}	Rate of formation of D/mol L^{-1} min^{-1}
I.	0.1	0.1	6.0×10^{-3}
II.	0.3	0.2	7.2×10^{-2}
III.	0.3	0.4	2.88×10^{-1}
IV.	0.4	0.1	2.40×10^{-2}

Based on the above data, which one of the following is correct? [CBSE AIPMT]
(a) Rate $= k[A][B]^2$ (b) Rate $= k[A]^2[B]$
(c) Rate $= k[A][B]$ (d) Rate $= k[A]^2[B]^2$

45 The rate constant for the reaction,
$2N_2O_5 \longrightarrow 4NO_2 + O_2$ is $3.0\times 10^{-5}\ s^{-1}$.
If the rate is 2.40×10^{-5} mol $L^{-1}\ s^{-1}$, then the concentration of N_2O_5 (in mol L^{-1}) is [BVP]
(a) 1.4 (b) 1.2 (c) 0.04 (d) 0.8

46 For a reaction between gaseous compounds,
$2A + B \longrightarrow C + D$
the reaction rate $= k[A][B]$. If the volume of the container is made 1/4 of the initial, then what will be the rate of reaction as compared to the initial rate? [Guj CET]
(a) 16 times (b) 4 times (c) $\frac{1}{8}$ times (d) $\frac{1}{16}$ times

47 The reaction, N_2O_5 in CCl_4 (solution) $\longrightarrow$
$$2NO_2\ (\text{solution}) + \frac{1}{2}O_2(g)$$
is of first order in N_2O_5 with rate constant $6.2\times 10^{-4}\ s^{-1}$. What is the value of rate of reaction when $[N_2O_5] = 1.25$ mol L^{-1}? [AFMC]
(a) 5.15×10^{-5} mol $L^{-1}\ s^{-1}$ (b) 6.35×10^{-3} mol $L^{-1}\ s^{-1}$
(c) 7.75×10^{-4} mol $L^{-1}\ s^{-1}$ (d) 3.85×10^{-4} mol $L^{-1}\ s^{-1}$

48 The first order integrated rate equation is [MHT CET]
(a) $k = \frac{x}{t}$ (b) $k = -\frac{2.303}{t}\log\frac{a}{a-x}$
(c) $k = \frac{1}{t}\ln\frac{a}{a-x}$ (d) $k = \frac{1}{t}\frac{x}{a(a-x)}$

49 The unit of rate constant depends upon [OJEE]
(a) rate of reaction (b) order of reaction
(c) molecularity of reaction (d) All of these

50 In the hydrolysis of an organic chloride in the presence of large excess of water,
$RCl + H_2O \longrightarrow ROH + HCl$. [WB JEE]
(a) molecularity and order of reaction both are 2
(b) molecularity is 2 but order of reaction is 1
(c) molecularity is 1 but order of reaction is 2
(d) molecularity is 1 and order of reaction is also 1

51 The rate constant for a first order reaction is $60\,s^{-1}$. How much time it will take to reduce the concentration of the reactant to 1/10th of its initial value? [Haryana PMT]
(a) 3.8×10^{-2} s (b) 1.26×10^{13} s
(c) 2.01×10^{13} s (d) 1.097×10^{3} s

52 The order of a reaction with rate equal to $kC_A^{3/2}C_B^{-1/2}$ is
(a) 1 (b) $-\frac{1}{2}$ (c) $-\frac{3}{2}$ (d) 2 [JCECE]

2009

53 Rate of the given reaction,
I. $A + B \xrightarrow{r_1 = 0.05} X$
II. $X + B \xrightarrow{r_2 = 0.89} Y$
III. $Y + A \xrightarrow{r_3 = 0.001} (AY)$
IV. $AY + B \xrightarrow{r_4 = 0.10} AYB$
will be determined by [AMU]
(a) *step* I : because the reaction starts with the formation of X
(b) *step* II : because it is the fastest step
(c) *step* III : because it is the slowest step
(d) *step* IV : because it ends the reaction

54 For the reaction $A + B \longrightarrow$ products, it is observed that
I. On doubling the initial concentration of A only, the rate of reaction is also doubled.
II. On doubling the initial concentration of both A and B, there is a change by a factor of 8 in the rate of reaction.
The rate of this reaction is given by [CBSE AIPMT]
(a) rate $= k[A]^2[B]$ (b) rate $= k[A][B]^2$
(c) rate $= k[A]^2[B]^2$ (d) rate $= k[A][B]$

55 For a reaction, the dimensions of rate constant are same as that of rate, hence order of reaction is [AFMC]
(a) 0 (b) 1 (c) 2 (d) 3

56 $t_{1/2}$ for a first order reaction is 10 min. Starting with 10 M, the rate after 20 min is [Manipal]
(a) 0.0693 M min^{-1} (b) 0.0693×5 M min^{-1}
(c) 0.0693×2.5 M min^{-1} (d) 0.0693×10 M min^{-1}

57 The decomposition of
$$N_2O_5(g) \longrightarrow NO_2(g) + NO_3(g)$$
proceeds as a first order reaction with a half-life period of 30 s at a certain temperature. If the initial concentration $[N_2O_5] = 0.4$ M, what is the rate constant of the reaction? [OJEE]
(a) $0.00924\ s^{-1}$ (b) $0.0231\,s^{-1}$
(c) $75\,s^{-1}$ (d) $12\,s^{-1}$

58 Cyclopropane rearranges to form propene
$$\triangleright \longrightarrow CH_3 - CH = CH_2$$
This follows first order kinetics. The rate constant is $2.714\times 10^{-3}\,s^{-1}$. The initial concentration of cyclopropane is 0.29 M. What will be the concentration of cyclopropane after 100 s?
(a) 0.035 M (b) 0.22 M [OJEE]
(c) 0.145 M (d) 0.0018 M

59 The half-life of a reaction is inversely proportional to the square of the initial concentration of the reactant. Then, the order of the reaction is [Kerala CEE]
(a) 0 (b) 1 (c) 2 (d) 3
(e) 0.5

60 For a first order reaction the rate constant is 6.909 min^{-1}. The time taken for 75% conversion in minutes is
(a) $\frac{3}{2}\log 2$ (b) $\frac{2}{3}\log 3$ (c) $\frac{2}{3}\log 2$ (d) $\frac{3}{2}\log\frac{3}{4}$
(e) $\frac{2}{3}\log\frac{4}{3}$ [Kerala CEE]

61. The unit, mol L^{-1} s^{-1} is meant for the rate constant of the reaction having the order [Kerala CEE]
(a) 0 (b) 2 (c) 1 (d) 3
(e) 4

62 The following graph shows how $t_{1/2}$ (half-life) of a reactant R changes with the initial reactant concentration a_0. The order of the reaction will be [WB JEE]

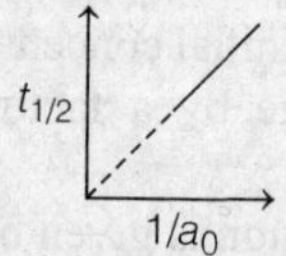

(a) 0 (b) 1 (c) 2 (d) 3

63 In first order reaction, the concentration of reactant decreases from 800 mol cm^{-3} to 50 mol cm^{-3} in 2×10^4 s. The rate constant is [CG PMT, Haryana PMT]
(a) $2\times 10^4\ s^{-1}$ (b) $3.45\times 10^{-5}\ s^{-1}$
(c) $1.386\times 10^{-4}\ s^{-1}$ (d) $2\times 10^{-4}\ s^{-1}$

64 Which of the following is the correct statement? [AMU]
(a) Order of a reaction has always an integral value
(b) Mechanism of a reaction proposed is always final
(c) Zero order reactions are multi step reactions
(d) Order of reaction can be predicted even without knowing the rate law

65 For a first order reaction at 27°C, the ratio of time required for 75% completion to 25% completion of reaction is
(a) 3.0 (b) 2.303 [EAMCET]
(c) 4.8 (d) 0.477

66 For a first order reaction, the time required for 99.9% of the reaction to take place is nearly [DUMET]
(a) 10 times that required for half of the reaction
(b) 100 times that required for two-thirds of the reaction
(c) 10 times that required for one-fourth of the reaction
(d) 20 times that required for half of the reaction

67 For a chemical reaction $A \rightarrow B$, the rate of the reaction is 2×10^{-3} mol dm^{-3} s^{-1}, when the initial concentration is 0.05 mol dm^{-3}. The rate of the same reaction is 1.6×10^{-2} mol dm^{-3} s^{-1}, when the initial concentration is 0.1 mol dm^{-3}. The order of the reaction is [KCET]
(a) 0 (b) 3 (c) 1 (d) 2

68 For the decomposition of a compound AB at 600 K, the following data were obtained.

$[AB]$ mol dm^{-3}	Rate of decomposition of AB in mol dm^{-3} s^{-1}
0.20	2.75×10^{-8}
0.40	11.0×10^{-8}
0.60	24.75×10^{-8}

The order for the decomposition of AB is [KCET]
(a) 0 (b) 1 (c) 2 (d) 1.5

69 The rate equation for a reaction, $A \rightarrow B$ is $r = k[A]^0$. If the initial concentration of the reactant is a mol dm^{-3}, the half period of the reaction is [KCET]
(a) k/a (b) a/k (c) $2a/k$ (d) $a/2k$

2008

70 The bromination of acetone that occurs in acid solution is represented by this equation

$$CH_3COCH_3(aq) + Br_2(aq) \longrightarrow CH_3COCH_2Br(aq) + H^+(aq) + Br^-(aq)$$

These kinetic data were obtained for given reaction concentrations.

Initial Concentrations, M			
$[CH_3COCH_3]$	$[Br_2]$	$[H^+]$	Initial rate, disappearance of Br_2, Ms^{-1}
0.30	0.05	0.05	5.7×10^{-5}
0.30	0.10	0.05	5.7×10^{-5}
0.30	0.10	0.10	1.2×10^{-4}
0.40	0.05	0.20	3.1×10^{-4}

Based on these data, the rate equation is [CBSE AIPMT]
(a) Rate $= k[CH_3COCH_3][H^+]$
(b) Rate $= k[CH_3COCH_3][Br_2]$
(c) Rate $= k[CH_3COCH_3][Br_2][H^+]^2$
(d) Rate $= k[CH_3COCH_3][Br_2][H^+]$

71 The reaction $2NO(g) + O_2(g) \rightleftharpoons 2NO_2(g)$ is of first order. If volume of reaction vessel is reduced to 1/3 the rate of reaction would be [AMU]
(a) $\frac{1}{3}$ times (b) $\frac{2}{3}$ times (c) 3 times (d) 6 times

72 The rate law for a reaction between the substances A and B is given by rate $= k[A]^n[B]^m$. On doubling the concentration of A and halving the concentration of B, the ratio of the new rate to the earlier rate of the reaction will be as [JCECE]
(a) $\frac{1}{2^{m+n}}$ (b) $(m+n)$
(c) $(n-m)$ (d) $2^{(n-m)}$

73 For a first order reaction, to obtain a positive slope, we need to plot {where $[A]$ is the concentration of reactant A}

(a) $-\log_{10}[A]$ *vs* t (b) $-\log_e[A]$ *vs* t **[AIIMS]**
(c) $\log_{10}[A]$ *vs* $\log t$ (d) $[A]$ *vs* t

74 Assertion (A) The order of a reaction can have fractional value.

Reason (R) The order of a reaction cannot be written from balanced equation of a reaction. **[AIIMS]**

(a) Both A and R are correct and R is the correct explanation of A
(b) Both A and R are correct but R is not the correct explanation of A
(c) A is correct but R is incorrect
(d) Both A and R are incorrect

75 A hypothetical reaction, $A_2 + B_2 \longrightarrow 2AB$ follows the mechanism as given below,

$$A_2 \rightleftharpoons A + A \text{ (fast)}$$
$$A + B_2 \longrightarrow AB + B \text{ (slow)}$$
$$A + B \longrightarrow AB \text{ (fast)}$$

The order of the overall reaction is **[Manipal]**

(a) 2 (b) 1 (c) $1\frac{1}{2}$ (d) 0

76 Consider the following statements:
The rate law for the acid catalysed hydrolysis of an ester being given as
Rate $= k[\text{H}^+][\text{ester}] = k'[\text{ester}]$. If the acid concentration is doubled at constant ester concentration

I. The second order rate constant, k is doubled.
II. The pesudo first order rate constant, k is doubled.
III. The rate of the reaction is doubled.

Which of the above statements are correct? **[Manipal]**

(a) I and II (b) II and III
(c) I and III (d) I, II and III

77 Which among the following plots are linear?

I. $(a-x)$ *vs* t, for a first order reaction.
II. $(a-x)$ *vs* t, for a zero order reaction.
III. $(a-x)$ *vs* t, for a second order reaction.
IV. $\frac{1}{(a-x)}$ *vs* t, for a second order reaction.

Here, $(a-x)$ is the concentration of reactant remaining after time, t **[Kerala CEE]**

(a) I and II (b) I and III (c) II and III (d) II and IV
(e) I and IV

78 The integrated rate equation is $kt = \log C_0 - \log C_t$. The straight line graph is obtained by plotting **[Haryana PMT]**

(a) $\log C_t$ *vs* time (b) $\frac{1}{\text{time}}$ *vs* C_t
(c) time *vs* C_t (d) $\frac{1}{\text{time}}$ *vs* $\frac{1}{C_t}$

79 A reaction involving A, B and C as reactants is found to obey the rate law, rate $= k[A]^x[B]^y[C]^z$. When the concentrations of A, B and C are doubled separately, the rate is also found to increase two, zero and four times, respectively. The overall order of the reaction is **[J&K CET]**

(a) 1 (b) 2 (c) 3 (d) 4

80 $A(g) \longrightarrow B(g)$ is a first order reaction. The initial concentration of A is 0.2 mol L^{-1}. After 10 min, the concentration of B is found to be 0.18 mol L^{-1}. The rate constant (in min^{-1}) for the reaction is **[EAMCET]**

(a) 0.2303 (b) 2.303
(c) 0.693 (d) 0.01

81 When plotted a graph of concentration versus time for zero order reaction, then the value of slope is **[Guj CET]**

(a) $-\frac{k}{2.303}$ (b) $-2.303\,xk$ (c) $-k$ (d) $-\frac{E_a}{2.303R}$

82 The order of a reaction for an esterification process is **[Guj CET]**

(a) zero (b) first
(c) second order (d) pseudo first order

83 The following data are for the decomposition of ammonium nitrite in aqueous solution.

Vol. of N_2 in cc	Time (min)
6.25	10
9.00	15
11.40	20
13.65	25
35.05	Infinity

The order of reaction is **[BCECE]**

(a) zero (b) one (c) two (d) three

2007

84 The reaction follows the mechanism,

$$A + B \underset{k_{-1}}{\overset{k_1}{\rightleftharpoons}} AB \text{ (fast)}$$
$$AB + B \xrightarrow{k_2} A + B_2 \text{ (slow)}$$

then order of reaction according to rate law is **[Haryana PMT]**

(a) 1 (b) 2
(c) 3 (d) 4

85 In a first order reaction $A \longrightarrow B$, if k is rate constant and initial concentration of the reactant A is 0.5 M then the half-life is **[CBSE AIPMT]**

(a) $\frac{0.693}{0.5k}$ (b) $\frac{\log 2}{k}$
(c) $\frac{\log 2}{k\sqrt{0.5}}$ (d) $\frac{\ln 2}{k}$

86 The reaction of hydrogen and iodine monochloride is given as :

$$H_2(g) + 2ICl(g) \longrightarrow 2HCl(g) + I_2(g)$$

This reaction is of first order with respect to $H_2(g)$ and $ICl(g)$, following mechanisms were proposed.

Mechanism I.

$$H_2(g) + 2ICl(g) \longrightarrow 2HCl(g) + I_2(g)$$

Mechanism II.

$$H_2(g) + ICl(g) \longrightarrow HCl(g) + HI(g); \text{(slow)}$$
$$HI(g) + ICl(g) \longrightarrow HCl(g) + I_2(g); \text{(fast)}$$

Which of the above mechanism(s) can be consistent with the given information about the reaction? **[CBSE AIPMT]**

(a) Only II (b) Both I and II
(c) Neither I nor II (d) Only I

87 Assertion (A) The hydrolysis of methyl acetate by dilute HCl is a pseudo first order reaction.

Reason (R) HCl acts as a catalyst for the hydrolysis. **[AIIMS]**

(a) Both A and R are correct and R is the correct explanation of A
(b) Both A and R are correct but R is not the correct explanation of A
(c) A is correct but R is incorrect.
(d) Both A and R are incorrect

2006

88 On increasing the pressure three fold, the rate of reaction of $2H_2S + O_2 \longrightarrow$ products, would increase **[EAMCET]**

(a) 3 times (b) 9 times (c) 12 times (d) 27 times

89 For the following homogeneous reaction, the unit of rate constant is **[Manipal]**

$$A + B \xrightarrow{k} C$$

(a) $mol^{-1} L s^{-1}$ (b) s^{-1} (c) s (d) s^{-1} mol L^{-1}

90 In a chemical reaction two reactants take part. The rate of reaction is directly proportional to the concentration of one of them and inversely proportional to the concentration of the other. The order of reaction is **[RPMT]**

(a) zero (b) 1 (c) 2 (d) 4

91 What is the two third life of a first order reaction having $k = 5.48 \times 10^{-14}\ s^{-1}$? **[J&K CET]**

(a) 2.01×10^{11} s (b) 2.01×10^{13} s
(c) 8.08×10^{13} s (d) 16.04×10^{11} s

92 For a reaction,

$$X(g) \longrightarrow Y(g) + Z(g)$$

the half-life period is 10 min. In what period of time would the concentration of X be reduced to 10% of original concentration? **[AMU]**

(a) 20 min (b) 33 min (c) 15 min (d) 25 min

93 Rate constant of a reaction (k) is 300 $L^2\ mol^{-2}\ s^{-1}$. What is the order of reaction? **[Guj CET]**

(a) First (b) Second (c) Third (d) Zero

2005

94 According to law of mass action, rate of a chemical reaction is proportional to **[AFMC]**

(a) concentration of reactants
(b) molar concentration of reactants
(c) concentration of products
(d) molar concentration of products

95 For reaction, $aA \longrightarrow xP$, when $[A] = 2.2$ mM, the rate was found to be 2.4 mM s^{-1}. On reducing concentration of A to half, the rate changes to 0.6 mM s^{-1}. The order of reaction with respect to A is **[AIIMS]**

(a) 1.5 (b) 2.0
(c) 2.5 (d) 3.0

96 Which of the following graphs represent relation between initial concentration of reactants and half-life for third order reaction? **[AIIMS]**

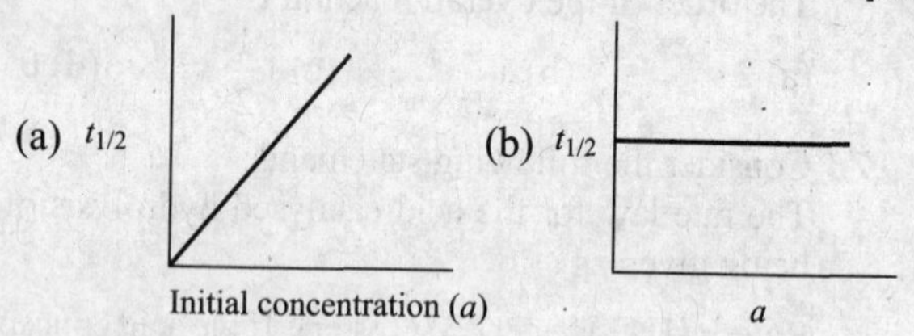

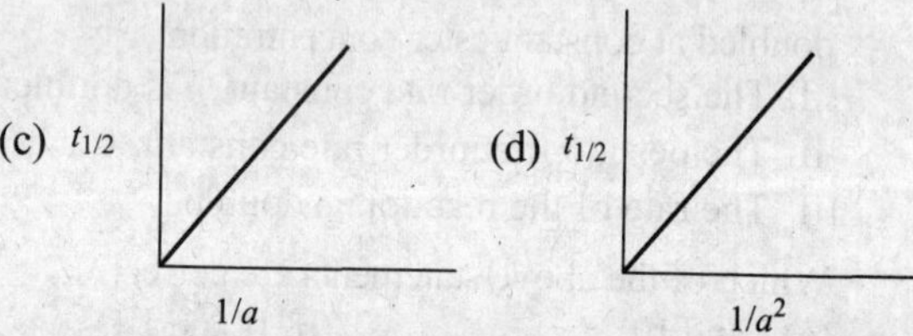

97 The half-life period of decomposition of a compound is 50 min. If the initial concentration is made 4 times, the half-life period reduces to half, i.e. 25 min. What is the order of reaction? **[Haryana PMT]**

(a) 0 (b) $\frac{1}{2}$
(c) $\frac{3}{2}$ (d) 2

98 Which of the following statement is not correct? **[JCECE]**

(a) In zero order reaction, the rate of the reaction remains constant throughout
(b) A second order reaction would become a pseudo first order reaction when one of the reactants is taken in large excess
(c) The value of first order rate constant depends on the units of the concentration terms used
(d) In a first order reaction the plot of log $(a - x)$ *vs* time gives a straight line

Answers

1 (d)	2 (b)	3 (b)	4 (a)	5 (d)	6 (a)	7 (b)	8 (b)	9 (b)	10 (d)
11 (d)	12 (b)	13 (a)	14 (d)	15 (b)	16 (a)	17 (b)	18 (b)	19 (c)	20 (d)
21 (b)	22 (c)	23 (a)	24 (d)	25 (a)	26 (d)	27 (d)	28 (d)	29 (c)	30 (d)
31 (c)	32 (d)	33 (d)	34 (a)	35 (c)	36 (e)	37 (d)	38 (a)	39 (d)	40 (c)
41 (a)	42 (b)	43 (a)	44 (a)	45 (d)	46 (a)	47 (c)	48 (c)	49 (b)	50 (b)
51 (a)	52 (a)	53 (c)	54 (b)	55 (a)	56 (c)	57 (b)	58 (b)	59 (d)	60 (c)
61 (a)	62 (c)	63 (c)	64 (d)	65 (c)	66 (a)	67 (b)	68 (c)	69 (d)	70 (a)
71 (c)	72 (d)	73 (b)	74 (b)	75 (c)	76 (b)	77 (d)	78 (a)	79 (c)	80 (a)
81 (c)	82 (c)	83 (b)	84 (c)	85 (d)	86 (b)	87 (c)	88 (d)	89 (a)	90 (a)
91 (b)	92 (b)	93 (c)	94 (b)	95 (b)	96 (d)	97 (c)	98 (c)		

Explanations

1 (*d*) For first order reaction,

$$t=\frac{2.303}{k}\log\frac{a}{a-x} \quad \ldots(i)$$

Given: $k=2.303\times10^{-3}\text{ s}^{-1}$

$a=40\text{ g}$

$a-x=10\text{ g}$

On substituting the given values in Eq. (i),

$$t=\frac{2.303}{2.303\times10^{-3}}\log\frac{40}{10}$$

$$=10^3\log2^2=2\times10^3\times\log2$$

$$=2\times10^3\times0.3010=602\text{ s}$$

Alternative method

For first order reaction,

$$t_{1/2}=\frac{0.693}{k}$$

$$t_{1/2}(t_{50\%})=\frac{0.693}{2.303\times10^{-3}}=301\text{s}$$

Also, $t_{75\%}=2t_{50\%}$

$\therefore \quad t_{75\%}=2\times301=602\text{ s}$

2 (*b*) For first order reaction,

$$t=\frac{2.303}{k}\log\frac{a}{a-x}$$

where, a = initial concentration,

$a-x$ = final concentration.

Let the initial concentration $(a)=100$

After time t, final concentration $(a-x)=100-99=1$

We know that,

$$t=\frac{2.303}{k}\log\frac{a}{a-x}$$

On substituting the given values in above Eq.

$$t=\frac{2.303}{k}\log\frac{100}{1}=\frac{2.303}{k}\log10^2$$

$$=\frac{2.303}{k}\times2\log10=\frac{4.606}{k}$$

Thus, option (b) is correct.

3 (*b*) For zero order reaction, if concentration of product is $[C_0]$ at time t_1 and $\frac{[C_0]}{2}$ at time t_2, then

$$k=\frac{\left[\frac{C_0}{2}\right]-[C_0]}{t_2-t_1}=\frac{[C_0]-\left[\frac{C_0}{2}\right]}{t_{1/2}}$$

$$\therefore \quad t_{1/2}=\frac{[C_0]}{2k}$$

Thus, $t_{1/2}$ for zero order reaction is directly proportional to the initial concentration of the reactant.

4 (*a*) Given, $t_{1/2}=36$ min

$t=2\text{hrs}=120\text{ min}, [A_0]=10\text{g}$

For first order reaction, $k=\frac{0.693}{t_{1/2}}$

$$\therefore \quad k=\frac{0.693}{36}=0.01925$$

$$t=\frac{2.303}{k}\log\frac{[A]_0}{[A]}\text{g}$$

where, $[A]_0$ = initial amount = 10 g

$[A]$ = final amount

$$\therefore \quad 120=\frac{2.303}{0.01925}\log\frac{10}{[A]}$$

$$\log10-\log[A]=1$$

$$1-\log[A]=1$$

$$\log[A]=0$$

$$[A]=1\text{g}$$

5 (*d*) For a first order reaction,

$$t=\frac{2.303}{k}\log\frac{a}{a-x}$$

where, a = initial concentration

$a-x$ = final concentration

Given, rate constant $(k)=4.3\times10^{-4}\text{s}^{-1}$

Let, the initial concentration = a

$\therefore$ Final concentration $(a-x)$

$$=a-\frac{2}{3}a=\frac{a}{3}$$

For first order reaction,

$$t=\frac{2.303}{k}\log\frac{a}{a-x}$$

$$=\frac{2.303}{4.3\times10^{-4}}\log\frac{a}{a/3}$$

$$=2.5\times10^3\text{ sec}$$

Thus, option (d) is correct.

6 (*a*) For a first order reaction, the integrated rate law is written as,

$$k=\frac{2.303}{t}\log\frac{a}{a-x}$$

where, k = rate constant

a = initial concentration

$a-x$ = concentration after time 't'

For half-life, $t=t_{1/2}$, $x=\frac{a}{2}$

On substituting the values,

$$k=\frac{2.303}{t_{1/2}}\log\frac{a}{a-\frac{a}{2}}=\frac{2.303}{t_{1/2}}\log2$$

$$\therefore \quad k=\frac{0.693}{t_{1/2}}$$

Thus, $t_{1/2}$ of a first order reaction does not depend upon the concentration.

7 (*b*) For first order reactions, the rate of reaction is proportional to the first power of the concentration of the reactant.

For, $\quad A\rightarrow B$

$$\text{Rate}=-\frac{d[A]}{dt}=k[A]$$

[where, k = constant]

$$\text{Half-life }(t_{1/2})=\frac{0.693}{k}$$

$\therefore$ Rate of first order reaction depends upon reactant concentrations and half life does not depend upon initial concentration of reactant, $[A]_0$.

For second order reactions, the rate of reaction is proportional to the second power of the concentration of the reactant.

For, $2A \rightarrow B$

Rate $= k[A]^2$

Half-life $(t_{1/2}) = \frac{1}{k[A]_0}$

$\therefore$ Rate of second order reaction depends upon reactant concentration and half-life also does depend on $[A]_0$.

8 (*b*) For zero order reaction, $t_{1/2} = \frac{[R]_0}{2k}$

where, $[R]_0$ = Initial concentration of the reactant.

k = Rate constant.

Thus, $t_{1/2}$ for zero order reaction is directly proportional to the initial concentration of the reactant.

$$t_{1/2} \propto [R]_0$$

$\therefore$ For zero order reaction, when the concentration of reactant is doubled, the half-life $(t_{1/2})$ will also get doubled.

9 (*b*) As slowest step is the rate determining step. Hence, from slow reaction,

$$r = k[O][O_3] \quad ...(i)$$

From fast reaction, $K_C = \frac{[O_2][O]}{[O_3]}$

$$[O] = \frac{K_C \cdot [O_3]}{[O_2]}, \text{ i.e.}$$

$$r = \frac{kK_C[O_3]}{[O_2]} \cdot [O_3] \Rightarrow kK_C \cdot [O_3]^2 [O_2]^{-1}$$

$\therefore$ Rate $(r) = k'[O_3]^2 \cdot [O_2]^{-1}$

$(k' = K_C \cdot k)$

Hence, the order of reaction in rate law expression will be 1.

10 (*d*) k for first order reaction can be found out by using the formula,

$$k = \frac{0.693}{t_{1/2}} = \frac{0.693}{1.26 \times 10^{14}}$$

$$\because \quad t = \frac{2.303}{k} \log \frac{a}{a-x}$$

Thus, for 100% completion,

$$t = \frac{2.303 \times 1.26 \times 10^{14}}{0.693} \log \frac{100}{0}$$

$$\therefore \quad t = \infty$$

11 (*d*) It is known that, slowest step is the rate determining step.

$\therefore$ Rate $(r) = k_1[X][Y_2] \quad ...(i)$

Now, from equation. (i), i.e.

$X_2 \rightleftharpoons 2X$ [fast]

$$K_{eq} = \frac{[X]^2}{[X_2]}$$

$$\Rightarrow [X] = \{K_{eq}[X_2]\}^{1/2} \quad ...(ii)$$

Now, substitute the value of $[X]$ from equation. (ii) in equation. (i),

$$\text{Rate } (r) = k_1(K_{eq})^{1/2}[X_2]^{1/2}[Y_2]$$

$$= k[X_2]^{1/2}[Y_2]$$

$\therefore$ Order of reaction $= \frac{1}{2} + 1 = \frac{3}{2} = 1.5$

12 (*b*) For a first order reaction,

$$\text{Rate constant } (k) = \frac{2.303}{t} \log \frac{a}{a-x}$$

where, a = initial concentration

$a - x$ = concentration after time 't'

t = time in sec.

Given, $a = 20$ g, $a - x = 5$ g, $k = 10^{-2}\text{s}^{-1}$

$$\therefore \quad t = \frac{2.303}{10^{-2}} \log \frac{20}{5} = 138.6 \text{ s}$$

Alternatively,

Half-life for the first order reaction,

$$t_{1/2} = \frac{0.693}{k} = \frac{0.693}{10^{-2}} = 69.3 \text{ s}$$

Two half-lives are required for the reduction of 20 g of reactant into 5 g.

$$20 \text{ g} \xrightarrow{t_{1/2}} 10 \text{ g} \xrightarrow{t_{1/2}} 5 \text{ g}.$$

$\therefore$ Total time $= 2t_{1/2} = 2 \times 69.3 = 138.6$ s

13 (*a*) $PH_3 \xrightarrow{W} P + \frac{3}{2}H_2$

This is an example of surface catalysed unimolecular decomposition.

For the above reaction, rate is given by using Langmuir adsorption isotherm.

$$\text{Rate} = \frac{k\alpha p}{1 + \alpha p}$$

where, p = partial pressure of adsorbing substrate, α is a constant

At low pressure, $\alpha p << 1$

or rate $= k\alpha p$

So, $(\alpha p + 1)$ can be neglected.

Thus, the decomposition is predicted to be first order and is proportional to the surface coverage.

14 (*d*) Given, order of reaction = 1

Rate of reaction at 10 s = 0.04 mol L^{-1} s^{-1}

Rate of reaction at 20 s = 0.03 mol L^{-1} s^{-1}

$\therefore$ Half-life period $(t_{1/2})$ = ?

The equation for rate-constant 'k' for first order reaction is,

$$k = \frac{2.303}{t} \log \frac{A_0}{A_t} = \frac{2.303}{10} \log \frac{0.04}{0.03}$$

$$= \frac{2.303}{10} \times 0.124$$

$$\Rightarrow \quad k = 0.0287 \text{ s}^{-1}$$

The half-life is calculated as,

$$t_{1/2} = \frac{0.693}{k} = \frac{0.693}{0.0287 \text{ s}^{-1}}$$

$$= 24.14 \text{ s} \approx 24.1 \text{ s}$$

15 (*b*) For a zero order reaction $t_{1/2}$ is directly proportional to the initial concentration of the reactant $[R]_0$

$$t_{1/2} \propto [R]_0,$$

For a first order reaction

$$k = \frac{2.303}{t} \log \frac{[R]_0}{[R]}$$

at $t_{1/2}, [R] = \frac{[R]_0}{2}$

So, the above equation becomes

$$k = \frac{2.303}{t_{1/2}} \log \frac{[R]_0}{[R]_0/2}$$

$$t_{1/2} = \frac{2.303}{k} \times \log 2$$

$$= \frac{2.303}{k} \times 0.3010$$

$$t_{1/2} = \frac{0.693}{k}$$

i.e. half-life period is independent of initial concentration of a reactant.

16 (*a*) Rate $= k[A][B] = r_1 \quad ...(i)$

when, $[B] = [2B]$, then,

new rate $= k[A][2B] = r_2 \quad ...(ii)$

Divide Eq. (ii) by (i) to get,

$$\frac{r_2}{r_1} = \frac{k[A][2B]}{k[A][B]} \Rightarrow \frac{r_2}{r_1} = 2$$

$$r_2 = 2r_1$$

This shows that a change in concentration of reactants leads to a change in rate of the reaction, but the value of rate constant remains unchanged. At a fixed temperature, the value of rate constant remains the same and is characteristic of a reaction.

17 (*b*) For reaction, $A + B \longrightarrow$ Product

$$\frac{dr}{dt} = k[A]^2[B]$$

$$\Rightarrow \quad 0.22 = k(1)^2(0.25)$$

$$\therefore \quad k = \frac{0.22}{0.25} = 0.88 \text{ M}^{-2}\text{s}^{-1}$$

18 (*b*) Reaction is of first order as given rate is proportional to $[N_2O_5]$ only.

So, $\quad \ln\left(\frac{a}{a-x}\right) = kt$

where, a = initial concentration

$a = 100$ (Let)

$\Rightarrow (a - x) = 10 \quad (\because x = 90\%)$

$a - x$ = concentration at an instant

$$\ln\left(\frac{100}{10}\right) = k \times 3600 \quad (t = 3600 \text{ s})$$

$$2.303 \log 10 = k \times 3600 \quad (\log 10 = 1)$$

$$k = \frac{2.303}{3600} = 6.4 \times 10^{-4} \text{ s}^{-1}$$

19 (*c*) For zero order reaction, $C_0 - C_A = kt$

C_0 = initial concentration = 6×10^{-3} M (given)

C_A = final concentration

$t_{1/2} = 1$ min

As $t_{1/2}$ of the reaction is that time in which the concentration of the reactant reduces to half of its initial value.

Hence, $C_A = \frac{C_0}{2}$

$$\Rightarrow C_0 - \frac{C_0}{2} = k \times 60 \text{ (1 min = 60 s)}$$

$$\frac{6 \times 10^{-3}}{2 \times 60} = k$$

$$\Rightarrow k = 0.5 \times 10^{-4} \text{ or } 5 \times 10^{-5}$$

20 (*d*) Rate = $k[A]^a[B]^b$

Overall order of reaction = $a + b$.

Inversion of cane sugar is first order reaction (given) and medium is acidic as pH is less than seven (given).

Hence, rate = $k\,[\text{sugar}]^x[H^+]^y$ and $x + y = 1$

In option given, only (d) has a value of $x + y = 1$.

21 (*b*) For *A*, $\underset{(A)}{400\text{g}} \longrightarrow \underset{\text{1 half-life}}{200\text{g}} \longrightarrow \underset{2t_{1/2}}{100\text{g}} \longrightarrow \underset{3t_{1/2}}{50\text{g}} \longrightarrow \underset{4t_{1/2}}{25\text{g}}$

$\therefore$ *A* undergoes 4 half-lives.

For *B*, $\underset{(B)}{400\text{g}} \longrightarrow \underset{\text{half-life}}{200\text{g}}$

$\therefore$ *B* undergoes 1 half-life.

Thus, $t_{1/2}$ of $B = 4t_{1/2}$ of *A*.

22 (*c*) Given, rate = $k[H^+]^n$

Initial pH = 3, so $[H^+] = 1 \times 10^{-3}$,

initial rate = r_1

Final pH = 1, so $[H^+] = 1 \times 10^{-1}$,

Final rate = $r_2 = 100r_1$

On substituting values,

$$r_1 = k[1 \times 10^{-3}]^n \quad \text{...(i)}$$

$$r_2 = 100r_1 = k[10^{-1}]^n \quad \text{...(ii)}$$

On dividing Eq. (i) by Eq. (ii),

$$\frac{r_1}{100r_1} = \left[\frac{1 \times 10^{-3}}{1 \times 10^{-1}}\right]^n$$

$$\Rightarrow \frac{1}{100} = \left[\frac{10^{-2}}{1}\right]^n$$

$$\Rightarrow \left[\frac{1}{100}\right]^1 = \left[\frac{1}{100}\right]^n$$

$$\therefore \quad n = 1$$

Thus, the reaction is of first order.

23 (*a*) The reaction is of first order,

$$k = \frac{2.303}{t} \log \frac{[R]_0}{[R]}$$

Where, $[R]_0$ = initial concentration

$[R]$ = concentration at time *t*.

Given, $t = 60$ min

Let $[R]_0 = 100$

$[R] = 100 - 60 = 40$ (as 60% is completed)

Thus, $k = \frac{2.303}{60} \log \frac{[100]}{[40]}$

$$k = \frac{2.303}{60} \times 0.398 \quad \text{....(i)}$$

Later on 50% of the reaction would be completed, thus,

$$k = \frac{2.303}{t} \log \frac{100}{50} \quad \text{...(ii)}$$

From (i) and (ii)

we have, $\frac{2.303}{60} \times 0.398 = \frac{2.303}{t} \log \frac{100}{50}$

$$\Rightarrow \frac{0.398}{60} = \frac{0.3010}{t}$$

$$\Rightarrow t = \frac{0.3010 \times 60}{0.398} \text{ or } t = 45 \text{ min}$$

24 (*d*) $A(g) \longrightarrow P(g) + Q(g) + R(g)$

	$A(g)$	$P(g)$	$Q(g)$	$R(g)$
At $t = 0$	0.4 atm	0	0	0
At time, t	$(0.4 - x)$	x	x	x

$$p_t = (0.4 - x) + x + x + x$$

$$p_t = 0.4 + 2x \text{ or } x = \frac{p_t - 0.4}{2}$$

$$\therefore p_A = 0.4 - x = 0.4 - \frac{p_t - 0.4}{2}$$

$$= \frac{2 \times 0.4 - p_t + 0.4}{2} = \frac{1.2 - p_t}{2}$$

From $k = \frac{2.303}{t} \log\left(\frac{p_0}{p_A}\right)$

$$\frac{0.693}{t_{1/2}} = \frac{2.303}{230} \log\left(\frac{0.4 \times 2}{1.2 - p_t}\right)$$

$$\frac{0.693}{69.3} = \frac{2.303}{230} \log\left(\frac{0.8}{1.2 - p_t}\right)$$

$$\log\left(\frac{0.8}{1.2 - p_t}\right) = \frac{0.693 \times 230}{69.3 \times 2.303}$$

$$\Rightarrow \log\left(\frac{0.8}{1.2 - p_t}\right) = 0.9987$$

$$\Rightarrow \frac{0.8}{1.2 - p_t} = \text{antilog } (0.9987)$$

$$\Rightarrow \frac{0.8}{1.2 - p_t} \approx 10$$

$$\Rightarrow 12 - 10p_t = 0.8$$

$$\therefore p_t = 1.12 \text{ atm}$$

25 (*a*) Given, rate constant for a first order reaction,

$$k = 2.303 \times 10^{-2} \text{s}^{-1}$$

Let the initial concentration be *a*

Then, final concentration

$$(a - x) = \frac{1}{10} \text{ of } a = \frac{a}{10}$$

Integrated rate law expression for first order reaction is

$$k = \frac{2.303}{t} \log \frac{a}{a - x}$$

or $t = \frac{2.303}{k} \log \frac{a}{(a - x)}$

On substituting values,

$$t = \frac{2.303}{2.303 \times 10^{-2}} \log \frac{a}{a/10}$$

or $t = 10^2 \log 10$

$t = 100$ s $\quad (\because \log 10 = 1)$

26 (*d*) For first order reaction,

$$k = \frac{2.303}{t} \log \frac{a}{a - x}$$

For completion of 75% reaction in 30 min,

$$k = \frac{2.303}{30} \log \frac{100}{(100 - 75)}$$

or $k = \frac{2.303}{30} \log 4$

$$k = \frac{2.303}{30} \times 0.602$$

For completion of 93.75% reaction, *t* is given by

$$t = \frac{2.303}{k} \log \frac{100}{(100 - 93.75)}$$

$$t = \frac{2.303 \times 30}{2.303 \times 0.602} \log 16$$

$$t = \frac{30}{0.602} \times 1.204 \Rightarrow t = 60 \text{ min}$$

27 (*d*) In general, $t_{1/2} \propto \frac{1}{(a)^{n-1}}$ ...(i)

Here, *n* = order of reaction

Given, $t_{1/2} \propto \frac{1}{a}$ ...(ii)

On comparing (i) and (ii)

$$(a)^{n-1} = a \Rightarrow n - 1 = 1$$

$$\therefore \quad n = 2$$

28 (*d*) Let the order of reaction with respect to A and B is x and y, respectively.

So, the rate law can be given as

$$R = k.[A]^x[B]^y \quad ...(i)$$

When the concentration of only B is doubled the rate is doubled. So,

$$R_1 = k\,[A]^x\,[2B]^y = 2R \quad ...(ii)$$

If concentrations of both the reactants A and B are doubled the rate increases by a factor 8. So,

$$R_2 = k\,[2A]^x\,[2B]^y = 8R \quad ...(iii)$$

Divide Eq. (iii) by (ii) to get,

$$\frac{8R}{2R} = \frac{k[2A]^x[2B]^y}{k[A]^x[2B]^y}$$

$$4 = (2)^x \Rightarrow (2)^2 = (2)^x \Rightarrow x = 2$$

Now, divide Eq. (ii) by (i) to get,

$$\frac{2R}{R} = \frac{k[A]^x[2B]^y}{k[A]^x[B]^y}$$

$$\Rightarrow (2)^1 = (2)^y \Rightarrow y = 1$$

Substitution of values of x and y in Eq. (i) gives

$$R = k\,[A]^2[B]$$

29 (*c*) It is true that order of reaction is defined as the sum of powers of concentrations present in the rate law.

$$\text{Rate} = k\,[A]^m[B]^n$$

Order of reaction $= m + n$

30 (*d*) It is a pseudo first order reaction. In this reaction, water takes part in large amount, so the concentration change in water is not measurable.

31 (*c*) If $t_{1/2} \propto \frac{1}{a^{n-1}}$, then

order of reaction $= n$

Given that, $t_{1/2} \propto \frac{1}{a^3}$

$$n - 1 = 3$$

$\therefore$ Order of reaction $(n) = 3 + 1 = 4$

32 (*d*) For second order reaction,

$$\frac{dx}{dt} = k\,[R]^2$$

$$k = \frac{\text{conc.}}{\text{time} \times (\text{conc.})^2} = \text{conc}^{-1}\ \text{time}^{-1}$$

$$k = \text{L mol}^{-1}\ \text{s}^{-1}$$

33 (*d*) Let order of reaction w.r.t A and B is x and y respectively. Then,

$$\text{rate} = k\,[A]^x\,[B]^y$$

$$2 = k\,[0.2]^x[0.2]^y \quad ...(i)$$

$$4 = k\,[0.2]^x[0.4]^y \quad ...(ii)$$

$$36 = k\,[0.6]^x[0.4]^y \quad ...(iii)$$

On comparing Eqs. (i) and (ii), we get

$$\frac{4}{2} = \frac{(0.4)^y}{(0.2)^y}$$

$$\Rightarrow \quad (2)^1 = 2^y \quad \Rightarrow \quad y = 1$$

On comparing Eqs. (ii) and (iii), we get

$$\frac{36}{4} = \frac{(0.6)^x}{(0.2)^x} \Rightarrow 9 = 3^2 = 3^x$$

$$\Rightarrow \quad x = 2$$

$\therefore$ Rate law, $r = k\,[A]^2[B]$

34 (*a*) The sum of the coefficient (or powers) of the reacting species that are involved in the rate law expression for the reaction represents the order of a reaction. It can be 0, 1, 2, 3 or even a fractional number. It can only be determined by experiments.

35 (*c*) Order of reaction is the sum of the powers to which the concentration terms are raised in the rate equation. Thus, the order for the given rate equation is $(c + d)$.

36 (*e*) 1st and 2nd set of data – No change in rate with the change in concentration of 'C'. Thus, the order with respect to reactant 'C' is zero.

1st and 3rd set of data – On doubling the concentration of 'B', rate becomes double. Thus, the order with respect to reactant 'B' is 1.

4th and 1st set of data – On doubling the concentration of 'A', rate becomes four times. Thus, the order with respect to reactant 'A' is 2.

37 (*d*) For number of half-lives,

$$C = C_0\left(\frac{1}{2}\right)^y$$

where, $\quad y = \dfrac{\text{total time } (t)}{t_{1/2}}$

Here, $\quad C$ = final concentration

C_0 = initial concentration

$t_{1/2}$ = half-life period

For Ist case

$$C = \frac{1}{4}C_0$$

$$t = 20\text{ min}$$

$$\therefore \quad \frac{1}{4}C_0 = C_0\left(\frac{1}{2}\right)^y \Rightarrow \left(\frac{1}{2}\right)^2 = \left(\frac{1}{2}\right)^y$$

$$y = 2 = \frac{20}{t_{1/2}} \Rightarrow t_{1/2} = 10\text{min}$$

For IInd case

$$C = \frac{1}{16}C_0 \Rightarrow t = ?$$

$$\therefore \quad \frac{1}{16}C_0 = C_0\left(\frac{1}{2}\right)^y$$

$$\Rightarrow \quad \left(\frac{1}{2}\right)^4 = \left(\frac{1}{2}\right)^y$$

$$\Rightarrow \quad y = 4 = \frac{t}{10\text{min}}$$

$\therefore$ Total time $= 40$ min

Alternatively

$$1 \xrightarrow{1} \frac{1}{2} \xrightarrow{2} \frac{1}{4} \xrightarrow{3} \frac{1}{8} \xrightarrow{4} \frac{1}{16}$$

$\frac{1}{16}$ of initial concentration occurs at 4 half-lives and $\frac{1}{4}$ of initial concentration occurs after 2 half-lives.

For 2 half-lives, $t = 20$min

$\therefore$ For 1 half-lives, $t = 10$min

Hence, for 4 half-lives, $t = 40$min

38 (*a*) Molecularity is defined as the number of ions or molecules or atoms taking part in an elementary process of the reaction mechanism. It can never be a fraction. It is always a whole number.

39 (*d*) Rate law is given for only slowest step of the reaction. Thus, on taking slowest step,

$$\frac{dx}{dt} = k'[X][B]$$

From ***step*** **I** $K_{eq} = \dfrac{[X]}{[A]^2}$

$$\Rightarrow \quad [X] = K_{eq}\,[A]^2$$

$$\frac{dx}{dt} = k' \cdot K_{eq}\,[A]^2[B] = k[A]^2[B]$$

where $k = k' \cdot K_{eq}$

40 (*c*) For a zero order reaction, $\frac{dx}{dt} = k$,

$$dx = k\,dt \qquad [\textstyle\int dx = \int k\,dt]$$

$$x = kt$$

For 100% completion of the reaction, $x = a$

Therefore, $a = kt$ or $t = \dfrac{a}{k}$

41 (*a*)

$$2A(g) \longrightarrow B(g) + C(s)$$

At $t = 0$, $\quad 2 \qquad 0$

At $t = t$ min, $\quad (2 - 2x) \qquad x$

Solids do not have any pressure

At the end of the reaction, only 1 mole of gas is present whose pressure is 200 Pa. Thus, at the beginning of the reaction 2 moles of gas should have a pressure of 400 Pa.

After time, 10 minutes, number of moles present,

$$(2-2x)+x=2-x$$

The pressure of 2 moles is 400 pascals,

Thus, $400-x=300 \Rightarrow x=100$

Hence, pressure due to $(2-2x)$ moles of

$$A=400-200=200$$

Therefore, p_0(at the beginning) $=400$

p_{10} (after 10 min) $=200$

$$k=\frac{2.303}{t}\log\frac{p_0}{p_{10}}$$

$$k=\frac{2.303}{10}\log\frac{400}{200}; \quad [\because \log 2=0.30]$$

$$k=\frac{2.303\times 0.30}{10}=0.0693 \text{ min}^{-1}$$

42 (*b*) $t_{1/2}\propto\left(\frac{1}{[R]_0}\right)^{x-1}$

where, x = order of reaction

$[R]_0$ = initial concentration

If, $x=n-1$

$$\therefore\ t_{1/2}\propto\left(\frac{1}{[R]_0}\right)^{n-2} \text{ or } t_{1/2}\propto[R]_0^{2-n}$$

43 (*a*) $k=\frac{2.303}{45}\log\frac{0.05}{0.035}$

$$k=\frac{2.303}{45}\times 0.155=0.0079$$

$$\Rightarrow t_{1/2}=\frac{0.693}{0.0079}\approx 88 \text{ min}$$

44 (*a*) Let the order of A and B be a and b respectively.

Thus, rate $=k[A]^a[B]^b$

$r_2=k[0.3]^a[0.2]^b=7.2\times10^{-2}$ ...(i)

$r_3=k[0.3]^a[0.4]^b=2.88\times10^{-1}$ ...(ii)

Divide (i) by (ii) to get,

$$\frac{7.2\times10^{-2}}{2.88\times10^{-1}}=\frac{[0.2]^b[0.3]^a}{[0.4]^b[0.3]^a}$$

$$\therefore \quad \frac{1}{4}=\frac{1}{2^b}\Rightarrow 2^2=2^b$$

$$\Rightarrow \quad b=2$$

Similarly, $r_1=k[0.1]^a[0.1]^b$

$=6.0\times10^{-3}$ ...(iii)

$r_4=k[0.4]^a[0.1]^b$

$=2.4\times10^{-2}$ ...(iv)

Divide (iii) by (iv) to get,

$$\Rightarrow \frac{6\times10^{-3}}{2.4\times10^{-2}}=\frac{[0.1]^a[0.1]^b}{[0.4]^a[0.1]^b}$$

$$\Rightarrow \frac{1}{4}=\frac{1}{4^a}\Rightarrow 4^1=4^a$$

$$\therefore \quad a=1$$

Thus, rate $=k[A][B]^2$

45 (*d*) For a first order reaction,

$$\text{rate}=k[N_2O_5]$$

$$2.4\times10^{-5}=3.0\times10^{-5}[N_2O_5]$$

$$[N_2O_5]=\frac{2.4\times10^{-5}}{3.0\times10^{-5}}=0.8 \text{ mol L}^{-1}$$

Note The order of reaction is found from the given units of k. For first order reaction, unit of k is s^{-1}.

46 (*a*) When volume is reduced to one fourth, concentrations become four times [as concentration $\propto\frac{1}{\text{volume}}$].

Hence, the rate of reaction becomes 16 times as compared to the initial rate.

47 (*c*) For first order reaction,

Rate $=k[N_2O_5]$

$=6.2\times10^{-4} \text{ s}^{-1}\times1.25 \text{ mol L}^{-1}$

$=7.75\times10^{-4} \text{ mol L}^{-1}\text{ s}^{-1}$

48 (*c*) For first order, rate $=\frac{d[R]}{dt}=-k[R]$

or $\quad \frac{d[R]}{[R]}=-k\,dt$ ...(i)

On integrating Eq. (i),

$$\int\frac{d[R]}{[R]}=-k\int dt$$

$\ln[R]=-kt+C$ ...(ii)

At $\quad t=0,[R]=[R]_0$

(where, R = final concentration, i.e. $a-x$ and R_0 is the initial concentration, i.e. a.)

$$\ln[R]_0=C$$

On putting the value of C in Eq. (ii),

$$\ln[R]=-kt+\ln[R]_0$$

$$-kt=\ln[R]-\ln[R]_0$$

$$kt=\ln[R]_0-\ln[R]$$

$$k=\frac{1}{t}\ln\frac{[R]_0}{[R]}$$

$$\therefore \quad k=\frac{1}{t}\ln\frac{a}{a-x}$$

49 (*b*) $r=k[A]^x[B]^y$

$$\frac{dx}{dt}=k[A]^x[B]^y$$

$$\frac{\text{mol L}^{-1}}{\text{sec}}=k(\text{mol L}^{-1})^x(\text{mol L}^{-1})^y$$

$$k=(\text{mol L}^{-1})^{1-(x+y)}\text{ s}^{-1}$$

where, $(x+y)$ is the order.

50 (*b*) As water used is in large excess thus, order depends only upon the concentration of RCl. However, molecularity is the number of reactants taking part in a reaction, thus, here molecularity is equal to 2.

51 (*a*) For a first order reaction,

$$t=\frac{2.303}{k}\log\frac{[A]_0}{[A]}$$

Here, A_0 = initial concentration

A = final concentration

Given, $\quad k=60 \text{ s}^{-1},\ [A]=\frac{[A]_0}{10}$

Now, $\quad t=\frac{2.303}{60}\log\frac{[A]_0}{[A]_0/10}$

$$=\frac{2.303}{60}\log 10$$

$$=0.038 \text{ s or } 3.8\times10^{-2}\text{ s}$$

52 (*a*) Given, $r=kC_A^{3/2}C_B^{-1/2}$

$$\therefore \text{ Order of reaction}=\frac{3}{2}+\left(-\frac{1}{2}\right)$$

$$=\frac{3-1}{2}=1$$

53 (*c*) Slowest step is the rate determining step. In comparison of the values of rate step III have lowest value.

54 (*b*) On doubling the initial concentration of A only, the rate of reaction is doubled. Thus, the order of reaction with respect to A is 1.

On the other hand, on doubling the initial concentration of both A and B, there is a change by a factor of 8. Thus, rate of reaction with respect to B is 2.

$\therefore$ Overall rate $=k[A][B]^2$

55 (*a*) We know that,

rate, $\quad r=k[A]^x$

Given, $\quad r=k$

(as their dimensions are same)

$$\therefore \quad r=r[A]^x=r^0=[A]^x$$

$$\therefore \quad x=0$$

56 (*c*) Given, $t_{1/2}=10$ min, $t=20$ min, $N_0=10$ M

$$\Rightarrow \quad t=nt_{1/2}\Rightarrow 20=n\times10$$

$$\therefore \quad n=2$$

$$\Rightarrow \quad \frac{N}{N_0}=\left(\frac{1}{2}\right)^n$$

$$\Rightarrow \quad \frac{N}{10}=\left(\frac{1}{2}\right)^2\Rightarrow\frac{N}{10}=\frac{1}{4}$$

$$\therefore \quad N=\frac{10}{4}=2.5 \text{ M}$$

$$\therefore \quad \text{Rate}=k[A]=\frac{0.693}{10}\times2.5$$

$$=0.0693\times2.5 \text{ M min}^{-1}$$

$$\left[\because k=\frac{0.693}{t_{1/2}}\right]$$

57 (*b*) For a first order reaction,

$$k = \frac{0.693}{t_{1/2}} = \frac{0.693}{30} = 0.0231\ s^{-1}$$

58 (*b*) $k = \frac{2.303}{t}\log\frac{a}{(a-x)}$

$(a-x)$ is the concentration left after 100 s.

$$2.714 \times 10^{-3} = \frac{2.303}{100}\log\frac{0.29}{(a-x)}$$

$$\Rightarrow \frac{0.27}{2.303} = \log\frac{0.29}{(a-x)}$$

$$0.117 = \log\frac{0.29}{(a-x)}$$

$$\Rightarrow \text{Antilog } 0.117 = \frac{0.29}{(a-x)}$$

$$\therefore \quad (a-x) = 0.22\ M$$

59 (*d*) For *n*th order reaction, $t_{1/2} \propto \frac{1}{a^{n-1}}$

Given, $t_{1/2} \propto \frac{1}{a^2}$

On comparing, $a^{n-1} = a^2 \Rightarrow n-1 = 2$

$\therefore \quad n = 3$

Hence, the order of reaction is 3.

60 (*c*) For first order reaction,

$$k = \frac{2.303}{t}\log\frac{a}{a-x}$$

$$6.909 = \frac{2.303}{t}\log\frac{100}{100-75}$$

$$t = \frac{2.303}{6.909}\log 4$$

$$= \frac{1}{3}\log 2^2 = \frac{2}{3}\log 2$$

61 (*a*) General unit for rate constant

$$= \left(\frac{mol}{L}\right)^{1-n} s^{-1}$$

(where, n = order of reaction)

Given, unit for rate constant $= \left(\frac{mol}{L}\right) s^{-1}$

On comparing, $\left(\frac{mol}{L}\right)^{1-n} s^{-1} = \left(\frac{mol}{L}\right) s^{-1}$

$$1 - n = 1 \Rightarrow n = 0$$

Hence, the order of reaction is zero.

62 (*c*) $t_{1/2} \propto \frac{1}{a_0^{n-1}}$; $a_0^{n-1} = a_0$ (given)

$\therefore \quad n - 1 = 1 \Rightarrow n = 2.$

63 (*c*) For first order reaction,

Rate constant, $k = \frac{2.303}{t}\log\frac{a}{a-x}$

$$\left(\because \begin{array}{l} a = 800\ mol/cm^3 \\ a - x = 50\ mol/cm^3 \end{array}\right)$$

$$t = 2 \times 10^4\ s$$

$$k = \frac{2.303}{2 \times 10^4}\log\frac{800}{50} = 1.386 \times 10^{-4}\ s^{-1}$$

64 (*d*)

(a) Order of a reaction may be zero, negative or fractional.

(b) Mechanism of a reaction proposed is not always final.

(c) Zero order reactions are single step reactions.

(d) Order of a reaction is determined experimentally, i.e. it can be predicted even without knowing the rate law.

Thus, the correct statement among the given options is (d).

65 (*c*) For a first order reaction,

$$t = \frac{2.303}{k}\log_{10}\frac{a}{a-x}$$

Let initial amount of reactant is 100.

$$\frac{t_1}{t_2} = \frac{\log\frac{100}{100-75}}{\log\frac{100}{100-25}}$$

($\because$ k remains constant)

$$\frac{t_1}{t_2} = \frac{\log\frac{100}{25}}{\log\frac{100}{75}} = \frac{\log 4}{\log 4/3}$$

$$= \frac{\log 4}{\log 4 - \log 3}$$

$$= \frac{2 \times 0.3010}{2 \times 0.3010 - 0.4771}$$

$$= \frac{0.6020}{0.1249} = 4.819 \approx 4.8$$

66 (*a*) Time required to complete 99.9% of reaction is given as:

$$t_{99.9} = \frac{2.303}{k}\log\frac{100}{100-99.9}$$

$$= \frac{2.303}{k}\log 1000 = \frac{6.909}{k}$$

($\because$ $\log 10^3 = 3$)

and $t_{1/2} = \frac{2.303}{k}\log\frac{100}{100-50}$

$$= \frac{2.303}{k}\log 2 = \frac{0.693}{k}$$

So, $t_{99.9}$ is 10 times that required for half of the reaction.

67 (*b*) Let the rate equation for the reaction be,

$$\text{Rate} = k[A]^n$$

where, k = rate constant,

n = order of reaction,

$[A]$ = concentration of reactant

Given : $\text{Rate}_I = 2 \times 10^{-3}\ mol\ dm^{-3}\ s^{-1}$

$[A]_0 = 0.05\ mol\ dm^{-3}$

$\text{Rate}_{II} = 1.6 \times 10^{-2}\ mol\ dm^{-3}\ s^{-1}$

$[A]_0 = 0.1\ mol\ dm^{-3}$

$$\therefore \quad 2 \times 10^{-3} = k\,[0.05]^n \quad \text{...(i)}$$

$$1.6 \times 10^{-2} = k\,[0.1]^n \quad \text{...(ii)}$$

Dividing Eq. (i) by Eq. (ii),

$$\frac{2 \times 10^{-3}}{1.6 \times 10^{-2}} = \frac{[0.05]^n}{[0.1]^n} = \frac{[0.05]^n}{2^n[0.05]^n}$$

$$\Rightarrow \frac{1}{2^n} = \frac{1}{8} \Rightarrow \frac{1}{2^n} = \frac{1}{2^3}$$

$$\Rightarrow n = 3$$

$\therefore$ Order of reaction = 3

68 (*c*) Let rate equation be,

$$\text{rate} = k[AB]^n$$

Case (i) $2.75 \times 10^{-8} = k[0.2]^n$ ...(i)

Case (ii) $11 \times 10^{-8} = k[0.40]^n$ ...(ii)

Case (iii) $24.75 \times 10^{-8} = k[0.6]^n$ ...(iii)

Dividing Eq. (ii) by Eq. (i),

$$\frac{11 \times 10^{-8}}{2.75 \times 10^{-8}} = \frac{[0.40]^n}{[0.2]^n}$$

$$\Rightarrow \quad 2^n = 4 \text{ or } = 2^2 \Rightarrow n = 2$$

$\therefore$ Order of reaction is 2.

69 (*d*) According to the rate equation given, the reaction is of zero order.

For a zero order reaction, $t_{1/2} \propto a$

$$\therefore \quad t_{1/2} = a/2k$$

70 (*a*) Let the order of the reaction w.r.t. $[CH_3COCH_3]$, $[Br_2]$ and $[H^+]$ are x, y and z, respectively. Thus,

$$\text{Rate} \propto [CH_3COCH_3]^x[Br_2]^y[H^+]^z$$

$$5.7 \times 10^{-5} = k[0.30]^x[0.05]^y[0.05]^z \quad \text{...(i)}$$

$$5.7 \times 10^{-5} = k[0.30]^x[0.10]^y[0.05]^z \quad \text{...(ii)}$$

$$1.2 \times 10^{-4} = k[0.30]^x[0.10]^y[0.10]^z \quad \text{...(iii)}$$

$$3.1 \times 10^{-4} = k[0.40]^x[0.05]^y[0.20]^z \quad \text{...(iv)}$$

From Eqs. (i) and (ii), $y = 0$

From Eqs. (ii) and (iii), $z = 1$

From Eqs. (i) and (iv), $x = 1$

Thus, rate law $\propto [CH_3COCH_3][H^+]$

$= k[CH_3COCH_3][H^+]$

71 (*c*) $2NO(g) + O_2(g) \rightleftharpoons 2NO_2(g)$

When the volume of vessel is reduced to 1/3, then concentration of reactant become three times, as concentration $\propto \frac{1}{\text{volume}}$. The rate of reaction for first order reaction is directly proportional to concentration. Therefore, rate of reaction will increase three times.

72 (*d*) Initial rate $= k[A]^n[B]^m$ ....(i)

When $[A]=[2A]$ and $[B]=\left[\frac{1}{2}B\right]$,

then, new rate is given as:

New rate $= k[2A]^n[1/2B]^m$ ....(ii)

Divide (ii) by (i) to get,

$$\frac{\text{new rate}}{\text{initial rate}} = \frac{k[2A]^n[1/2B]^m}{k[A]^n[B]^m}$$

$$\frac{\text{new rate}}{\text{initial rate}} = (2)^n(1/2)^m$$

$$= (2)^n(2)^{-m} = (2)^{n-m}$$

Hence, the ratio of the new rate to the earlier rate of the reaction is $(2)^{n-m}$.

73 (*b*) For a first order reaction to obtain a positive slope, a graph is plotted between $-\log_e[A]$ *vs t*.

74 (*b*) Order is an experimentally determined value and depends upon the concentration change of reactant. It changes with pressure, temperature and concentration and it can have fractional values also.

75 (*c*) From slow step, rate $= k[B_2][A]$

From 1st equation, $K_{eq} = \frac{[A]^2}{[A_2]}$

or $[A] = \sqrt{K_{eq}[A_2]} = K_{eq}^{1/2}A_2^{1/2}$

Hence, rate

$= k[B_2]K_{eq}^{1/2}[A_2]^{1/2} = k'[A_2]^{1/2}[B_2]$.

where $k' = kK_{eq}^{1/2}$

Hence, order $= 1\frac{1}{2}$

76 (*b*) Pseudo first order rate constant is doubled as well as rate of reaction is doubled. It may be noted that in presence of acid, hydrolysis of ethyl acetate is a pseudo-unimolecular reaction but the actual value of *k* depends upon the concentration of H^+ ions, otherwise rate constant of a reaction is constant at constant temperature.

Thus, 'II' and 'III' are the correct statements.

77 (*d*) The plot of conc. $(a-x)$ *vs t* for different order of reactions are shown below.

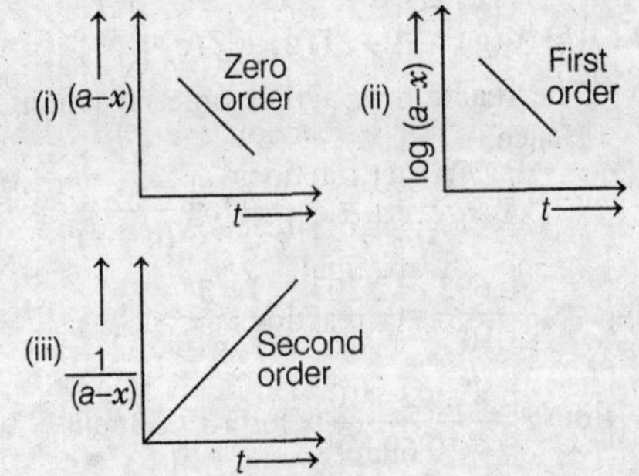

Hence, for zero order reaction, plot of $(a-x)$ *vs t* is linear and for second order reaction, plot of $\frac{1}{a-x}$ *vs t* is linear.

78 (*a*) For first order reaction, the integrated rate equation is given by

$$kt = \log C_o - \log C_t$$

The straight line graph is obtained by plotting $\log C_t$ *versus* time.

79 (*c*) $\because$ On doubling the concentration of *A*, the rate of reaction becomes two times.

$\therefore$ The order of reaction w.r.t. *A* is 1.

$\because$ On doubling the concentration of *B*, the rate of reaction does not change.

$\therefore$ The order of reaction with respect to *B* is 0.

$\because$ On doubling the concentration of *C*, the rate of reaction becomes four times.

$\therefore$ The order of reaction with respect to *C* is 2.

$\therefore$ The overall order of reaction $= 1 + 0 + 2 = 3$

80 (*a*) Given, $A(g) \longrightarrow B(g)$ (first order reaction)

Initial concentration of $A = 0.2 \text{ mol L}^{-1}$

Concentration of $B = 0.18 \text{ mol L}^{-1}$

$\therefore$ Concentration of *A* after 10 min $= 0.2 - 0.18 = 0.02 \text{ mol L}^{-1}$

Time $(t) = 10$ min

$\because$ Rate constant for first order reaction,

$$k = \frac{2.303}{t}\log\frac{a}{a-x}$$

$$= \frac{2.303}{10}\log\frac{0.2}{0.02} = 0.2303 \text{ min}^{-1}$$

81 (*c*) Expression of rate constant for zero order reaction is

$$k = \frac{1}{t}\{[A]_0 - [A]\}$$

$$kt = [A]_0 - [A]$$

$$\Rightarrow [A] = -kt + [A]_0$$

It is an equation of straight line $[y = mx + c]$. The plot of $[A]$ *versus t* will be a straight line with slope $= -k$ and intercept on the concentration axis $= [A]_0$.

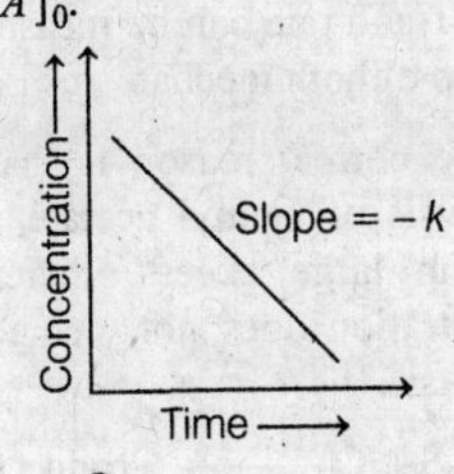

82 (*c*) $R\text{—}\overset{\overset{\large O}{\|}}{C}\text{—}OH + HO\text{—}R' \xrightarrow{H^+} R\text{—}\overset{\overset{\large O}{\|}}{C}\text{—}OR' + H_2O$

(Carboxylic acid, Alcohol → Ester)

Rate of reaction $= k$ [carboxylic acid] [alcohol]

So, order of reaction = 2

83 (*b*) For first order reaction,

$$k = \frac{2.303}{t}\log\frac{a}{a-x}$$

$a \propto V_\infty$ (= 35.05) and $x \propto V_t$

Constant values of *k* calculated for different times, shows first order reaction.

84 (*c*) Mechanism, $A + B \underset{k_{-1}}{\overset{k_1}{\rightleftharpoons}} AB$ (fast)

$$AB + B \xrightarrow{k_2} A + B_2 \text{ (slow)}$$

As slowest step is the rate determining step, thus, rate law $= k_2[AB][B]$.

For fast reaction (steady state step)

$$k_1[A][B] = k_{-1}[AB]$$

$$\Rightarrow [AB] = \frac{k_1[A][B]}{k_{-1}}$$

Substitute the value of $[AB]$ in rate law expression.

$$\text{Rate law} = \frac{k_2k_1}{k_{-1}}[A][B]^2$$

$\therefore$ Rate law $= k[A][B]^2$

where, $k = \frac{k_2k_1}{k_{-1}}$

$\therefore$ Order of reaction according to rate law is 3.

85 (*d*) For first order reaction,

$$k = \frac{2.303}{t}\log\frac{a}{(a-x)}$$

$$t_{1/2} = \frac{2.303}{k}\log\frac{a}{a-\frac{a}{2}}$$

$$t_{1/2} = \frac{2.303}{k}\log 2 = \frac{\ln 2}{k}$$

86 (*b*) Rate of reaction always depends on the slowest step of the reaction. $H_2(g)+2ICl(g) \longrightarrow 2HCl(g)+I_2(g)$ is first order reaction with respect to H_2 and IC1 and rate can be measured with the help of both mechanisms I and II.

87 (*c*) The correct reason is that during hydrolysis of methyl acetate, water is taken in large excess, therefore, its concentration does not change during hydrolysis.

88 (*d*) $2H_2S + O_2 \longrightarrow$ Product

$$\text{Rate} = k\, p_{H_2S}^2 \times p_{O_2} = x$$

On increasing the pressure three fold,

$$\text{Rate} = k\,[3p_{H_2S}]^2 \times [3p_{O_2}]$$

$$= k \times 9p_{H_2S}^2 \times 3p_{O_2}$$

$$= k \times 27 \times p_{H_2S}^2 \times p_{O_2} = 27x$$

Hence, rate will increase 27 times.

89 (*a*) For the homogeneous gaseous reaction,

$$A + B \xrightarrow{k} C,$$

the rate law is, $\frac{dx}{dt} = k[A][B]$

$$\Rightarrow k = \frac{dx}{dt \times [A][B]}$$

$$\Rightarrow \quad = \frac{\text{mol L}^{-1}}{\text{s} \times \text{mol L}^{-1} \times \text{mol L}^{-1}}$$

$$= \text{mol}^{-1}\text{ L s}^{-1}$$

90 (*a*) Suppose the following reaction takes place:

$$A + B \longrightarrow \text{Product}$$

$\because$ Rate $= k[A][B]^{-1}$

$\therefore$ Order $= 1 + (-1) = 0$

Hence, the order of reaction is zero.

91 (*b*) For two-third of a reaction :

$$[A]_0 = a, \quad [A] = a - \frac{2}{3}a = \frac{a}{3}$$

$$t_{2/3} = \frac{2.303}{k}\log\frac{[A]_0}{[A]}$$

$$= \frac{2.303}{k}\log\frac{a}{a/3} = \frac{2.303}{k}\log 3$$

$$t_{2/3} = \frac{2.303 \times 0.4771}{5.48 \times 10^{-14}} = 2.01 \times 10^{13}\text{ s}$$

$[\because \log 3 = 0.4771]$

92 (*b*) $X(g) \longrightarrow Y(g) + Z(g)$

The reaction is a first order reaction. Hence,

$$k = \frac{0.693}{t_{1/2}} = \frac{2.303}{t}\log\frac{a}{(a-x)}$$

$$\Rightarrow \frac{0.693}{10} = \frac{2.303}{t}\log\frac{a}{a/10}$$

$$\text{or} \quad t = \frac{2.303 \times 10}{0.693} \times \log 10 = 33\text{ min}$$

$[\because \log 10 = 1]$

93 (*c*) Order of reaction can be identified by unit of rate constant. For *n*th order of reaction,

$$\frac{dx}{dt} = k(\text{conc.})^n$$

$$k = \frac{dx}{dt}\frac{1}{(\text{conc.})^n} = \frac{\text{conc.}}{\text{time}} \times \frac{1}{(\text{conc.})^n}$$

$$= \frac{1}{\text{time} \times (\text{conc.})^{n-1}} = \frac{1}{\text{s}} \times \frac{\text{L}^{n-1}}{\text{mol}^{n-1}}$$

$$= (\text{L})^{n-1}\,(\text{mol})^{1-n}\text{s}^{-1}$$

For, $n = 3$

unit of $k = \text{L}^2\text{ mol}^{-2}\text{ s}^{-1}$

94 (*b*) **Guldberg** and **Waage** (1864) suggested relationship between rate of reaction and the concentration of the reacting species known as **law of mass action**. According to this "at constant temperature, the rate of a chemical reaction is directly proportional to the product of the molar concentrations of reacting species, with each concentration term raised to the power equal to the numerical coefficient of that species in that chemical equation".

For any general reaction,

$$aA + bB \longrightarrow \text{Products}$$

$$\text{Rate} = k[A]^a[B]^b$$

i.e. $\quad \text{Rate} \propto [A]^a[B]^b$

95 (*b*) $aA \longrightarrow xP$

$$\text{Rate} \propto [A]^a = k[A]^a$$

Initially $[A]_1 = 2.2$ mM,

$r_1 = 2.4$ mM/s

If $[A]_2 = \frac{2.2}{2} = 1.1$ mM,

$r_2 = 0.6$ mM/s

We have, $\frac{r_1}{r_2} = \frac{[A]_1^a}{[A]_2^a}$ (*a* is the order)

$$\frac{2.4}{0.6} = \frac{(2.2)^a}{(1.1)^a}$$

$$\Rightarrow \frac{2.4}{0.6} = (2)^a$$

$$\text{or} \quad 4 = 2^a$$

$$\Rightarrow 2^2 = 2^a \Rightarrow a = 2$$

The reaction is of second order.

96 (*d*) $\because t_{1/2} \propto \frac{1}{a^{n-1}}$,

Graph between $t_{1/2}$ and initial concentration represents for

(a) zero order reaction

(b) first order reaction

(c) second order reaction

(d) third order reaction

Thus, plot given in option (d) represents for third order reaction.

97 (*c*) We know that, $t_{1/2} \propto C^{1-n}$

(where, *n* is the order of reaction)

$$\therefore \frac{(t_{1/2})_1}{(t_{1/2})_2} = \left(\frac{C_1}{C_2}\right)^{1-n} \Rightarrow \frac{50}{25} = \left(\frac{C}{4C}\right)^{1-n}$$

$$2 = \left(\frac{1}{4}\right)^{1-n} \Rightarrow 2 = (2)^{2n-2}$$

$$2n - 2 = 1 \Rightarrow n = 3/2$$

Hence, the order of reaction = 3/2.

98 (*c*) The incorrect statement is that the value of first order rate constant depends upon the units of concentration terms used.

In actual case, unit of rate constant of first order is independent of unit of concentration. The unit of *k* is s^{-1}.

The rest of the given statements are correct.

Topic 3

Factors Affecting Rate of Reaction and Temperature Dependence of Rate Constant

2019

1 For a reaction, activation energy $E_a = 0$ and the rate constant at 200 K is $1.6 \times 10^6 \, s^{-1}$. The rate constant at 400K will be
[Given that gas constant $R = 8.314 \, JK^{-1} mol^{-1}$] **[NEET]**

(a) $3.2 \times 10^4 \, s^{-1}$ (b) $1.6 \times 10^6 \, s^{-1}$
(c) $1.6 \times 10^3 \, s^{-1}$ (d) $3.2 \times 10^6 \, s^{-1}$

2 What is the activation energy (kJ/mol) for a reaction, if its rate constant doubles when the temperature is raised from 300 K to 400 K ($R = 8.314 \, Jmol^{-1} K^{-1}$) **[AIIMS]**

(a) 68.8 (b) 6.88
(c) 34.4 (d) 3.44

2018

3 A chemical reaction was carried out at 300 K and 280 K. The rate constant were found to be k_1 and k_2 respectively, then **[JIPMER]**

(a) $k_2 = 4k_1$ (b) $k_2 = 0.25k_1$
(c) $k_2 = 2k_1$ (d) $k_2 = 0.5k_1$

4 The rate constant for the first order decomposition of a certain reaction is described by the equation

$$\ln k \, (s^{-1}) = 14.34 - \frac{1.25 \times 10^4 \text{ K}}{T}.$$

The energy of activation for this reaction is **[AIIMS]**

(a) $1.26 \times 10^4 \, cal \, mol^{-1}$
(b) $4.29 \times 10^4 \, cal \, mol^{-1}$
(c) $3.12 \times 10^4 \, cal \, mol^{-1}$
(d) $2.50 \times 10^4 \, cal \, mol^{-1}$

5 Assertion (A) The reaction
$2NO + O_2 \longrightarrow 2NO_2$ and $2CO + O_2 \longrightarrow 2CO_2$
proceeds at the same rate because they are similar.

Reason (R) Both the reactions have same activation energy. **[AIIMS]**

(a) Both (A) and (R) are true and (R) is the correct explanation of (A).
(b) Both (A) and (R) is true but (R) is not the correct explanation of (A).
(c) (A) is true but (R) is false.
(d) Both (A) and (R) are false.

2017

6 Consider the figure given below. **[AIIMS]**

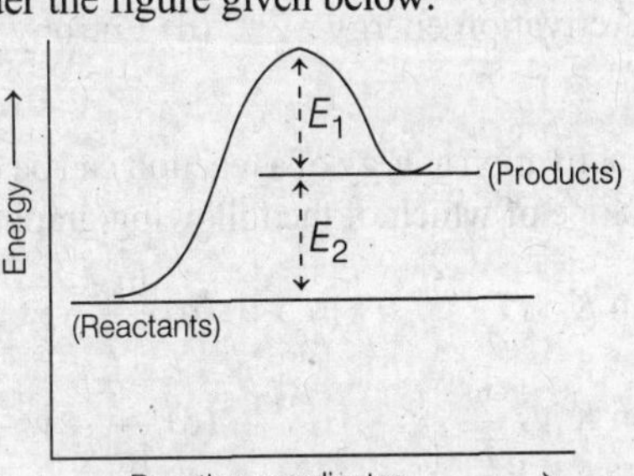

The correct option for the above presentation is
(a) activation energy of forward reaction is $E_1 + E_2$ and product is less stable than reactant
(b) activation energy of forward reaction is $E_1 + E_2$ and product is more stable than reactant
(c) activation energy for both forward and backward reaction is $E_1 + E_2$ and reactant is more stable than product
(d) activation energy for the backward direction is E_1 and product is more stable than reactant

7 Rate constant (k) varies with temperature as given by equation $\log k \, (\text{min}^{-1}) = 5 - \frac{2000}{T}$ **[AIIMS]**

Consider the following about this equation :
I. Pre-exponential factor is 10^5.
II. E_a is 9.212 kcal.
III. Variation of $\log k$ with $\frac{1}{T}$ is linear.

Select the correct statement.
(a) I, II and III (b) Both I and II
(c) Both II and III (d) Both I and III

2017

8 In the following graph. **[JIPMER]**

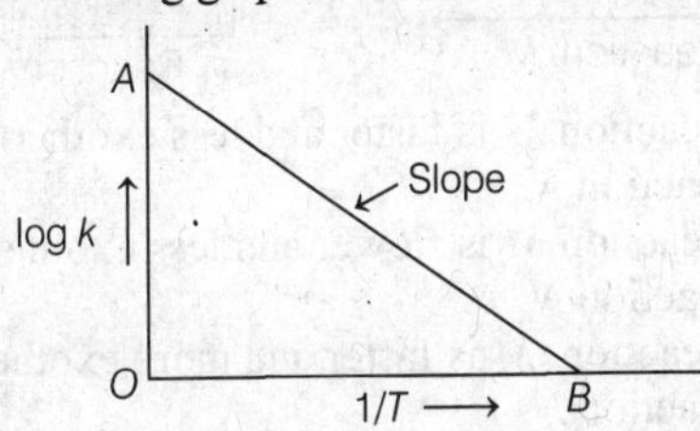

The slope of line AB gives the information of the

(a) value of $\frac{E_a}{2.303}$ (b) value of $\frac{2.303}{E_a}$

(c) value of $-\frac{E_a}{2.303\,R}$ (d) value of $-\frac{E_a}{2.303\,RT}$

2016

9 The addition of a catalyst during a chemical reaction alters which of the following quantities? **[NEET]**

(a) Internal energy (b) Enthalpy
(c) Activation energy (d) Entropy

2015

10 The activation energy of a reaction can be determined from the slope of which of the following graphs? **[CBSE AIPMT]**

(a) $\ln K$ *vs* T (b) $\frac{\ln K}{T}$ *vs* T

(c) $\ln K$ *vs* $\frac{1}{T}$ (d) $\frac{T}{\ln K}$ *vs* $\frac{1}{T}$

2014

11 The potential energy diagram for a reaction $R \rightarrow P$ is given below.

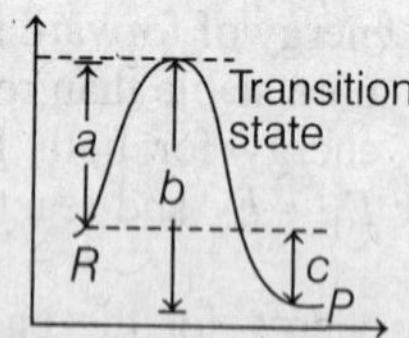

$\Delta H°$ of the reaction corresponding to the energy **[AIIMS]**

(a) a (b) b (c) c (d) $a+b$

12 A plot of $\frac{1}{T}$ *vs* $\ln k$ for a reaction gives the slope -1×10^4 K. The energy of activation for the reaction is (Given, $R = 8.314$ JK^{-1} mol^{-1}) **[KCET]**

(a) 8314 J mol^{-1} (b) 1.202 kJ mol^{-1}
(c) 12.02 J mol^{-1} (d) 83.14 kJ mol^{-1}

13 The correct statement regarding the following energy diagrams is. **[WB JEE]**

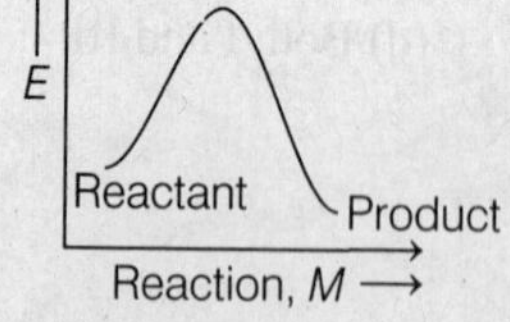

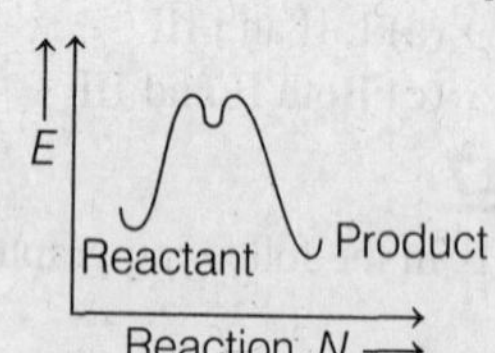

(a) Reaction M is faster and less exothermic than reaction N
(b) Reaction M is slower and less exothermic than reaction N
(c) Reaction M is faster and more exothermic than reaction N
(d) Reaction M is slower and more exothermic than reaction N

14 According to Arrhenius equation, the slope of $\log k \longrightarrow \frac{1}{T}$ plot is **[GCET]**

(a) $\frac{-E_a}{2.303R}$ (b) $\frac{-E_a}{2.303}$ (c) $\frac{-E_a}{2.303RT}$ (d) $\frac{E_a}{2.303RT}$

2013

15 What is the activation energy for a reaction if its rate doubles when the temperature is raised from 20°C to 35°C ($R = 8.314$ J mol^{-1} K^{-1}) **[NEET]**

(a) 342 kJ mol^{-1} (b) 269 kJ mol^{-1}
(c) 34.7 kJ mol^{-1} (d) 51.1 kJ mol^{-1}

16 A reaction having equal energies of activation for forward and reverse reactions has **[NEET]**

(a) $\Delta S = 0$ (b) $\Delta G = 0$
(c) $\Delta H = 0$ (d) $\Delta H = \Delta G = \Delta S = 0$

2012

17 In a zero order reaction for every 10° rise of temperature, the rate is doubled. If the temperature is increased from 10°C to 100°C, the rate of reaction will become

(a) 256 times (b) 512 times **[CBSE AIPMT]**
(c) 64 times (d) 128 times

18 Activation energy (E_a) and rate constant (k_1 and k_2) of a chemical reaction at two different temperatures (T_1 and T_2) are related by **[CBSE AIPMT]**

(a) $\ln\frac{k_2}{k_1} = -\frac{E_a}{R}\left(\frac{1}{T_1} - \frac{1}{T_2}\right)$ (b) $\ln\frac{k_2}{k_1} = -\frac{E_a}{R}\left(\frac{1}{T_2} - \frac{1}{T_1}\right)$

(c) $\ln\frac{k_2}{k_1} = \frac{E_a}{R}\left(\frac{1}{T_2} + \frac{1}{T_1}\right)$ (d) $\ln\frac{k_2}{k_1} = \frac{E_a}{R}\left(\frac{1}{T_1} - \frac{1}{T_2}\right)$

19 For the first order reaction rate constant depends upon **[OJEE]**

(a) temperature
(b) reactant's initial concentration
(c) time
(d) extent of reaction

20. A given sample of milk turns sour at room temperature (27°C) in 5h. In a refrigerator at −3°C, its can be stored 10 times longer. The energy of activation for the souring of milk is **[KCET]**

(a) $2.303\times 5R$ kJ mol^{-1}
(b) $2.303\times 3R$ kJ mol^{-1}
(c) $2.303\times 2.7R$ kJ mol^{-1}
(d) $2.303\times 10R$ kJ mol^{-1}

2011

21 The activation energy of a reaction at a given temperature is found to be 2.303 RT J mol^{-1}. The ratio of rate constant to the Arrhenius factor is **[KCET]**

(a) 0.01 (b) 0.1
(c) 0.02 (d) 0.001

2010

22 Rate of a reaction [Manipal]

(a) decreases with increase in temperature
(b) increases with increase in temperature
(c) may increase or decrease with increase in temperature
(d) does not depend on temperature

23 By increase in temperature by 10 K, the rate of reaction becomes double. How many times the rate of reaction will be, if the temperature is increased from 303 K to 353 K? [Guj CET]

(a) 4 (b) 8
(c) 16 (d) 32

24 The first order rate constant for the decomposition of ethyl iodide is given by the reaction

$$C_2H_5I(g) \longrightarrow C_2H_4(g) + HI(g)$$

at 600 K is $1.60 \times 10^{-5}\ s^{-1}$. Its energy of activation is 209 kJ mol^{-1}. What is the rate constant of the reaction at 700 K? [VMMC]

(a) $6.36 \times 10^{3}\ s^{-1}$ (b) $6.36 \times 10^{-3}\ s^{-1}$
(c) 6.36×10^{3} s (d) 6.36×10^{-3} s

2009

25 In the presence of a catalyst, activation energy of a reaction is lowered by 2 kcal at 27°C. Hence, rate will be [AFMC]

(a) 20 times
(b) 28 times
(c) 14 times
(d) remain the same

26 When we increase temperature, the rate of reaction increases because of [Manipal]

(a) more number of collisions
(b) decrease in mean free path
(c) more number of energetic collisions
(d) less number of energetic collisions

27 Pick the appropriate choice about collision theory of reaction rates.

I. It explains the effect of temperature on rate of reaction.
II. It assumes that the reactants must be in correct orientation to react.
III. It says rate depends upon the frequency at which reactants collide.
IV. The collisions having energy higher than the threshold value will give successful reactions.

The correct points are [OJEE]

(a) I, III, IV
(b) II, IV
(c) I, IV
(d) I, II, III, IV

2008

28 The rate constant k_1 and k_2 for two different reactions are $10^{16} \cdot e^{-2000/T}$ and $10^{15} \cdot e^{-1000/T}$, respectively. The temperature at which $k_1 = k_2$ is [CBSE AIPMT]

(a) 1000 K (b) $\frac{2000}{2.303}$ K
(c) 2000 K (d) $\frac{1000}{2.303}$ K

29 The rate constant of a first order reaction at 27°C is $10^{-3}\ min^{-1}$. The temperature coefficient of this reaction is 2. What is the rate constant (in min^{-1}) at 17°C for this reaction? [AFMC]

(a) 10^{-3} (b) 5×10^{-4}
(c) 2×10^{-3} (d) 10^{-2}

30 Assertion (A) Rate of reaction increases with increase in temperature.

Reason (R) Number of collisions increases with increase in temperature. [BHU]

(a) Both A and R are correct and R is the correct explanation of A
(b) Both A and R are correct but R is not the correct explanation of A
(c) A is correct but R is incorrect
(d) Both A and R are incorrect

31 For a reaction taking place in three steps, the rate constants are k_1, k_2 and k_3. The overall rate constant $k = \frac{k_1 k_2}{k_3}$. If the energy of activation values for the first, second and third stages are respectively 40, 50 and 60 kJ mol^{-1}, then the overall energy of activation in kJ mol^{-1} is [Kerala CEE]

(a) 30 (b) 40 (c) 60 (d) 50
(e) 150

32 Which equation is true to calculate the energy of activation, if the rate of reaction is doubled by increasing temperature from T_1 K to T_2 K? [Guj. CET]

(a) $\log_{10}\frac{k_1}{k_2} = \frac{E_a}{2.303R}\left[\frac{1}{T_1} - \frac{1}{T_2}\right]$

(b) $\log_{10}\frac{k_2}{k_1} = \frac{E_a}{2.303R}\left[\frac{1}{T_2} - \frac{1}{T_1}\right]$

(c) $\log_{10}\frac{1}{2} = \frac{E_a}{2.303}\left[\frac{1}{T_2} - \frac{1}{T_1}\right]$

(d) $\log_{10} 2 = \frac{E_a}{2.303R}\left[\frac{1}{T_1} - \frac{1}{T_2}\right]$

2006

33 The potential energy diagrams for four reactions are given below.

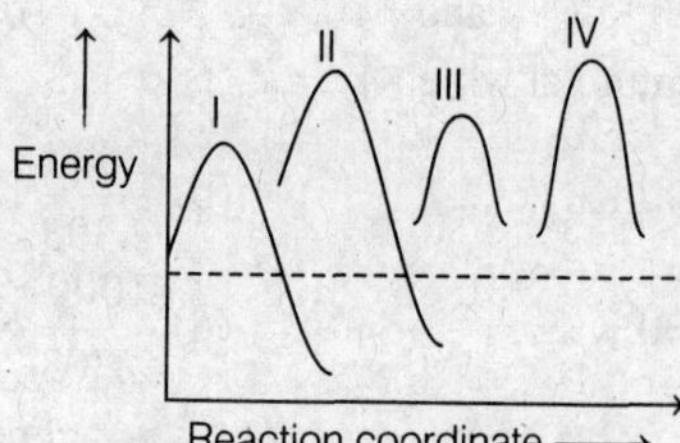

Which one of the following statements about these diagrams is incorrect? **[Kerala CEE]**

(a) I has the largest rate constant for an exothermic reaction

(b) II has the smallest rate constant for the reverse reaction

(c) III will have the most rapid establishment of equilibrium

(d) IV has the largest rate constant for an endothermic reaction

(e) The magnitude of the enthalpy of reaction I is greater than that of III

34 The temperature dependence of rate constant (k) of a chemical reaction is written in terms of Arrhenius equation $k = Ae^{-E_a/RT}$. Activation energy (E_a) of the reaction can be calculated by plotting **[AIIMS]**

(a) $\log k$ vs T

(b) $\log k$ vs $\frac{1}{T}$

(c) k vs T

(d) k vs $\frac{1}{\log T}$

35 $N_2(g) + 3H_2(g) \rightleftharpoons 2NH_3(g) + 22$ kcal, the activation energy for the forward reaction is 50 kcal. What is the activation energy for the backward reaction? **[EAMCET]**

(a) – 72 kcal

(b) – 28 kcal

(c) + 28 kcal

(d) + 72 kcal

2006

36 Assertion (A) According to transition state theory, for the formation of an activated complex, one of the vibrational degree of freedom is converted into a translational degree of freedom.

Reason (R) Energy of the activated complex is higher than energy of reactant molecules. **[AIIMS]**

(a) Both A and R are correct and R is the correct explanation of A

(b) Both A and R are correct but R is not the correct explanation of A

(c) A is correct but R is incorrect

(d) Both A and R are incorrect

37 The rate constant for a first order reaction becomes six times when the temperature is raised from 350 K to 400 K. Calculate the activation energy for the reaction. ($R = 8.314\ JK^{-1}\ mol^{-1}$) **[Kerala CEE]**

(a) 41.7 kJ mol^{-1} (b) 4.17 kJ mol^{-1}

(c) 417 kJ mol^{-1} (d) 0.417 kJ mol^{-1}

(e) 4170 kJ mol^{-1}

38 An endothermic reaction with high activation energy for the forward reaction is given by the diagram **[AIIMS]**

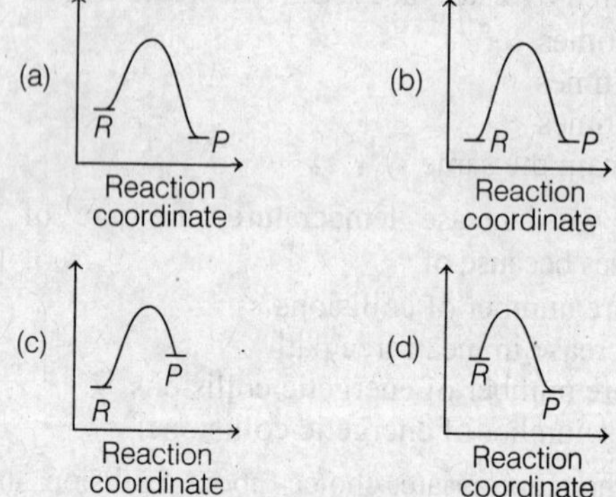

39 Which of these does not influence the rate of reaction? **[KCET]**

(a) Nature of the reactants

(b) Concentration of the reactants

(c) Temperature of the reaction

(d) Molecularity of the reaction

Answers

1 (b)	2 (b)	3 (b)	4 (d)	5 (d)	6 (a)	7 (a)	8 (c)	9 (c)	10 (c)
11 (c)	12 (d)	13 (c)	14 (a)	15 (c)	16 (c)	17 (b)	18 (b, d)	19 (a)	20 (c)
21 (b)	22 (c)	23 (d)	24 (b)	25 (b)	26 (c)	27 (d)	28 (d)	29 (b)	30 (a)
31 (a)	32 (d)	33 (d)	34 (b)	35 (d)	36 (b)	37 (a)	38 (c)	39 (d)	

Explanations

1 (*b*) Rate constants at two different temperatures is given by Arrhenius equation as follows:

$$\log \frac{k_2}{k_1} = \frac{E_a}{2.303R}\left[\frac{1}{T_1} - \frac{1}{T_2}\right]$$

$$T_2 > T_1$$

Given, $E_a = 0$, $T_1 = 200\text{ K}$

$k_1 = 1.6 \times 10^6 \text{s}^{-1}$, $T_2 = 400\text{ K}$

$R = 8.314 \text{ JK}^{-1}\text{ mol}^{-1}$

On substituting the given values in above equation

$$\log \frac{k_2}{1.6 \times 10^6} = \frac{0}{2.303 \times 8.314}\left[\frac{1}{200} - \frac{1}{400}\right]$$

$$\log\left(\frac{k_2}{1.6 \times 10^6}\right) = 0$$

$$\frac{k_2}{1.6 \times 10^6} = 10^0 = 1$$

$$k_2 = 1.6 \times 10^6 \text{s}^{-1} \text{ at 400K}$$

Thus, option (b) is correct.

2 (*b*) $\log \frac{k_2}{k_1} = \frac{E_a}{2.303R}\left[\frac{1}{T_1} - \frac{1}{T_2}\right]$

where T_1 and T_2 are initial and final temperature and k_1 and k_2 are initial and final rate constants, E_a = activation energy and R = gas constant.

Given, $T_1 = 300\text{ K}$,

$T_2 = 400\text{ K}$

$R = 8.314 \text{ J mol}^{-1}\text{ K}^{-1}$

$$\frac{k_2}{k_1} = \frac{2}{1}$$

$$\log \frac{k_2}{k_1} = \frac{E_a}{2.303 \times R}\left[\frac{1}{T_1} - \frac{1}{T_2}\right]$$

Thus, $\log \frac{2}{1} = \frac{E_a}{2.303 \times 8.314}\left[\frac{1}{300} - \frac{1}{400}\right]$

$E_a = 0.30 \times 2.303 \times 8.314 \times 3 \times 400$

$E_a = 6.88 \text{ kJ mol}^{-1}$

3 (*b*) For every 10°C rise, rate constant gets doubled. Hence, for every 20° C rise, rate constant will be 4 times. Therefore, according to the given statement,

Temperature	280K	300K
Rate constant	k_2	$k_1(4k_2)$

Thus, $k_1 = 4k_2 \Rightarrow k_2 = 0.25k_1$

4 (*d*) Given that,

$$\ln k(\text{s}^{-1}) = 14.34 - \frac{1.25 \times 10^4}{T}\text{ K} \quad \ldots(\text{i})$$

We know that,

$$\ln k(\text{s}^{-1}) = \ln A - \frac{E_a}{RT} \quad \ldots(\text{ii})$$

On comparing equation (i) and (ii), we get

$$\frac{E_a}{R} = 1.25 \times 10^4\text{ K}$$

$\therefore \quad E_a = 1.25 \times 10^4 \text{ K} \times R\text{cal K}^{-1}\text{ mol}^{-1}$

$= 1.25 \times 10^4 \text{ K} \times 2\text{cal K}^{-1}\text{ mol}^{-1}$

$[\because R = 2 \text{ cal K}^{-1}\text{ mol}^{-1}]$

$= 2.50 \times 10^4 \text{cal mol}^{-1}$

5 (*d*) Both Assertion and Reason are false.

The reaction $2NO + O_2 \longrightarrow 2NO_2$ and $2CO + O_2 \longrightarrow 2CO_2$ proceeds at the different rates. Both the reactions have different activation energies.

6 (*a*) Activation energy for backward direction $= E_1$

Activation energy for forward direction $= E_1 + E_2$

As energy $\propto \frac{1}{\text{Stability}}$

Thus, product is less stable than reactant.

7 (*a*) Given,

$$\log k(\text{min}^{-1}) = 5 - \frac{2000}{T} \quad \ldots(\text{i})$$

$$\because \log_{10} k = \log_{10} A - \frac{E_a}{2.303\, RT} \quad \ldots(\text{ii})$$

On comparing equations (i) and (ii)

I. $\log A = 5$ or $A = 10^5$

Thus, (I) is true

II. $\frac{E_a}{2.303R} = 2000$

$\Rightarrow E_a = 2.303 \times 2000 \times 0.002\text{ kcal}$

$\therefore E_a = 9.212\text{ kcal}$

Thus (II) is true.

III. From Eq. (ii), it is clear that ,

$$\log k \propto \frac{1}{T}$$

$\therefore$ Thus (III) is also true.

8 (*c*) $\because \ln k = \ln A - \frac{E_a}{RT}$

$$\ln k = \ln A - \frac{E_a}{R} \cdot \frac{1}{T}$$

Thus, $\log_{10} k = \log A - \frac{E_a}{2.303\, RT}$

or $\quad \log k = \log A - \frac{E_a}{2.303R} \cdot \frac{1}{T}$

On comparing the above equation with equation of straight line, i.e. $y = mx + c$, a slope $= \frac{-E_a}{2.303R}$ is obtained.

9 (*c*) A catalyst is a substance which alters the reaction rate but itself remains unchanged in amount and chemical composition at the end of the reaction.

It provides a new reaction path with a lower energy barrier (lowering activation energy).

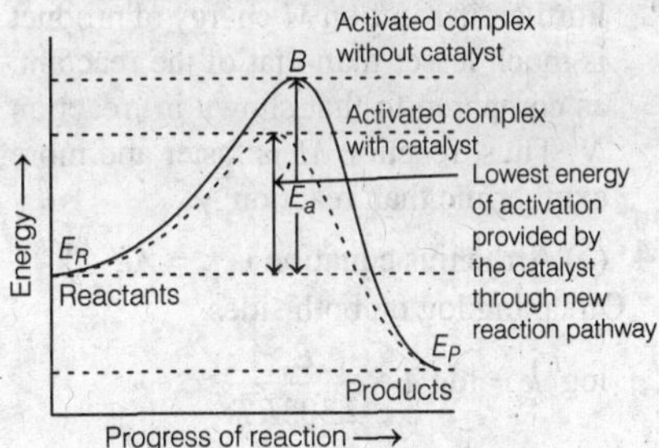

10 (*c*) By Arrhenius equation,

$$K = Ae^{-E_a/RT}$$

where, E_a = energy of activation

Applying natural log on both the sides,

$$\ln K = \ln A - \frac{E_a}{RT} \quad \ldots(\text{i})$$

or $\ln K = -\frac{E_a}{RT} + \ln A \quad \ldots(\text{ii})$

This equation is of the form of $y = mx + c$ i.e. the equation of a straight line. Thus, if a plot of $\ln K$ *vs* $\frac{1}{T}$ is a straight line, the validity of the equation is confirmed.

Slope of the line $= -\frac{E_a}{R}$

Thus, measuring the slope of the line, the value of E_a can be calculated.

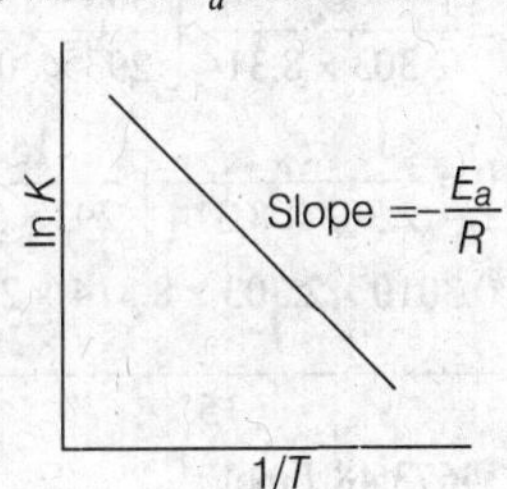

11 (c) Activation energy of forward reaction = a

Activation energy of backward reaction = b

$\because$ Reaction is exothermic

$\therefore$ Heat of reaction = $b - a = c\ (b > a)$.

12 (d) If a plot is drawn between $1/T$ and $\ln k$, then according to Arrhenius equation, $\ln k = \ln A - \dfrac{E_a}{RT}$

Here, slope $= -\dfrac{E_a}{R}$

$\Rightarrow -1 \times 10^4 = -\dfrac{E_a}{8.314}$

$\therefore \quad E_a = 8.314 \times 10^4 \text{ J mol}^{-1}$

or $\quad = 83.14 \text{ kJ mol}^{-1}$

13 (c) In reaction M, there is only an intermediate step, so it is a fast reaction. Further, in reaction M energy of product is much lesser than that of the reactant, as compared to that shown in reaction N. Thus, reaction M is faster and more exothermic than reaction N.

14 (a) Arrhenius equation is $k = Ae^{-Ea/RT}$

On taking log on both sides,

$$\log k = \log A - \frac{E_a}{2.303RT}$$

When $\log k$ is plotted with $1/T$, the slope of the reaction will be $-E_a/2.303R$ and intercept is given by $\log A$.

15 (c) Given, initial temperature

$T_1 = 20 + 273 = 293$ K

Final temperature,

$T_2 = 35 + 273 = 308$ K

$R = 8.314 \text{ J mol}^{-1} \text{ K}^{-1}$

Since, rate becomes double on raising temperature,

$r_2 = 2r_1 \Rightarrow \dfrac{r_2}{r_1} = 2$

As rate constant $k \propto r \Rightarrow \dfrac{k_2}{k_1} = 2$

From Arrhenius equation, we know that

$$\log \frac{k_2}{k_1} = \frac{E_a}{2.303\,R}\left(\frac{T_2 - T_1}{T_1 T_2}\right)$$

$$\log 2 = \frac{E_a}{2.303 \times 8.314}\left[\frac{308 - 293}{293 \times 308}\right]$$

$$0.3010 = \frac{E_a}{2.303 \times 8.314}\left[\frac{15}{293 \times 308}\right]$$

$$E_a = \frac{0.3010 \times 2.303 \times 8.314 \times 293 \times 308}{15}$$

$= 34673.48 \text{ J mol}^{-1}$

$= 34.7 \text{ kJ mol}^{-1}$

16 (c) Energy profile diagram for a reaction is shown below:

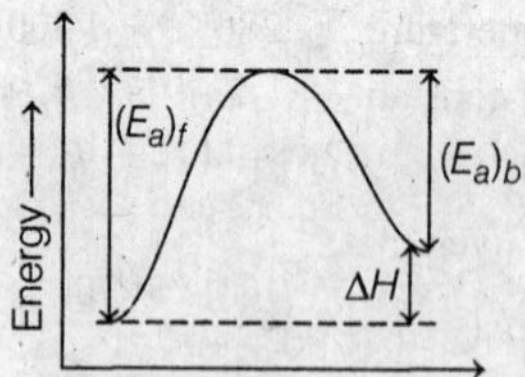

As from the figure, it is clear that

$$\Delta H = (E_a)_f - (E_a)_b$$

[Here, $(E_a)_b$ = activation energy of backward reaction and $(E_a)_f$ = activation energy of forward reaction]

If $\quad (E_a)_b = (E_a)_f$

Then, $\quad \Delta H = 0$

17 (b) For 10° rise in temperature, $n = 1$

So, rate $= 2^n = 2^1 = 2$

When temperature is increased from 10°C to 100°C, change in temperature $= 100 - 10 = 90$°C

$n = 9$

So, $\quad$ rate $= 2^9$

$= 512$ times

18 (b, d) According to Arrhenius equation, activation energy (E_a) and rate constants (k_1 and k_2) of a chemical reaction at two different temperatures (T_1 and T_2) are related as

$$\ln \frac{k_2}{k_1} = \frac{E_a}{R}\left(\frac{1}{T_1} - \frac{1}{T_2}\right)$$

Or $$\ln \frac{k_2}{k_1} = -\frac{E_a}{R}\left(\frac{1}{T_2} - \frac{1}{T_1}\right)$$

19 (a) According to Arrhenius equation,

$$k = Ae^{-E_a/RT}$$

Rate constant is dependent upon temperature only.

20 (c) $\log \dfrac{k_2}{k_1} = \dfrac{E_a}{2.303R}\left(\dfrac{T_2 - T_1}{T_1 \times T_2}\right)$

Here, $\dfrac{k_1}{k_2} = 10$,

$T_1 = 27°\text{C} = 300$ K

$\Rightarrow \quad T_2 = -3°\text{C} = 270$ K

$$\log \frac{1}{10} = \frac{E_a}{2.303\,R}\left[\frac{270 - 300}{300 \times 270}\right]$$

$$-1 = -\frac{E_a}{2.303\,R} \times \frac{30}{300 \times 270}$$

$E_a = +\,2.303\,R \times 2700 \text{ J mol}^{-1}$

$E_a = 2.303 \times 2.7\,R \text{ kJ mol}^{-1}$

21 (b) $\log k = \log A - \dfrac{E_a}{2.303\,RT}$

$\log k - \log A = -\dfrac{E_a}{2.303\,RT}$

$\Rightarrow \quad \log\left(\dfrac{k}{A}\right) = -\dfrac{2.303RT}{2.303RT} = -1$

$\dfrac{k}{A} = \text{antilog}(-1.0) = 1 \times 10^{-1} = 0.1$

22 (c) The rate of exothermic reaction decreases with the increase in temperature and that of endothermic reaction increases with increase in temperature. Thus, it can be said that rate may increase or decrease with increase in temperature.

23 (d) By increasing 10 K temperature, the rate of reaction becomes double. When temperature is increased from 303 K to 353 K, the rate increases in steps of 10 K that has been made 5 times. Hence, the rate of reaction should increase 2^5 times, i.e. 32 times.

24 (b)

$E_a = 209 \text{ kJ mol}^{-1} = 209 \times 10^3 \text{ J mol}^{-1}$

$k_1 = 1.60 \times 10^{-5} \text{ s}^{-1}, T_1 = 600$ K

$k_2 = ? \quad T_2 = 700$ K

$$\log \frac{k_2}{k_1} = \frac{E_a}{2.303R}\left(\frac{T_2 - T_1}{T_1 T_2}\right)$$

On substituting the values,

$$\log \frac{k_2}{1.60 \times 10^{-5}} = \frac{209 \times 10^3}{2.303 \times 8.314}\left[\frac{700 - 600}{700 \times 600}\right]$$

$$\log \frac{k_2}{1.60 \times 10^{-5}} = 2.599$$

$\Rightarrow \quad \dfrac{k_2}{1.60 \times 10^{-5}} = 397.19$

$\therefore \quad k_2 = 397.19 \times 1.60 \times 10^{-5}$

$= 6.36 \times 10^{-3} \text{ s}^{-1}$

25 (b) Arrhenius equation is

$$k = Ae^{-E_a/RT} \quad \ldots\text{(i)}$$

In the presence of catalyst,

rate constant $k' = Ae^{-E_a'/RT} \quad \ldots$(ii)

On dividing Eq. (ii) by Eq. (i), we get

$$\frac{k'}{k} = e^{(E_a - E_a')/RT}$$

$$\frac{k'}{k} = e^{\left(\frac{2000}{2 \times 300}\right)} = e^{3.33}$$

[$\because E_a - E_a' = 2000$cal (given)]

$\because$ On taking log both sides,

$$\log \frac{k'}{k} = \frac{3.33}{2.303}$$

$$\frac{k'}{k} = \text{antilog } 1.446 = 27.92 \approx 28$$

We know that, rate $(R) \propto k$

$\therefore \quad R'/R = k'/k = 28$

$\therefore \quad R' = 28R$

26 (*c*) Rate of reaction increases with increase in temperature because the number of energetic collision increases.

27 (*d*) All the given statements are correct.

28 (*d*) Arrhenius equation,

$$k = Ae^{-E_a/RT}$$

$$\therefore \quad k_1 = 10^{16} e^{-2000/T}$$

$$\text{and} \quad k_2 = 10^{15} e^{-1000/T}$$

On taking log on both sides,

$$\log k_1 = \log 10^{16} - \frac{2000}{2.303T} \quad \ldots\text{(i)}$$

$$\log k_2 = \log 10^{15} - \frac{1000}{2.303T} \quad \ldots\text{(ii)}$$

$\because \quad k_1 = k_2$

Hence, from Eqs. (i) and (ii),

$$T = \frac{1000}{2.303} \text{ K}$$

29 (*b*) Temperature coefficient $= \dfrac{k_t + 10}{k_t}$

$$\Rightarrow 2 = \frac{10^{-3}}{k_t}$$

$$k_t = \frac{10^{-3}}{2} = \frac{10 \times 10^{-4}}{2} = 5 \times 10^{-4} \text{ min}^{-1}$$

30 (*a*) Rate of reaction increases with increase in temperature. On increase of temperature, number of collisions increases. But the increase in the rate of reaction with increase in temperature is mainly due to increase in the number of effective collisions.

Therefore, both assertion and reason are correct and the reason is the correct explanation for assertion.

31 (*a*) Given, $k = k_1 k_2 / k_3$

On taking log on both sides,

$$\log k = \log k_1 + \log k_2 - \log k_3 \quad \ldots\text{(i)}$$

We know that,

$$\log k = \log A - \frac{E_a}{2.303RT}$$

On putting values of $\log k, \log k_1, \log k_2$ and $\log k_3$ in Eq. (i) and solving

$$E_a = E_{a_1} + E_{a_2} - E_{a_3}$$
$$= 40 + 50 - 60$$
$$= 30 \text{ kJ mol}^{-1}$$

32 (*d*) If rate of reaction is doubled by increasing temperature from T_1 K to T_2 K.

At $T_1 \quad k_1 = k$ (say)

and $T_2 \quad k_2 = 2k$

$$\log_{10} \frac{k_2}{k_1} = \frac{E_a}{2.303R}\left[\frac{1}{T_1} - \frac{1}{T_2}\right]$$

On applying the values of k_1 and k_2 in the above equation,

$$\log_{10} \frac{2k}{k} = \frac{E_a}{2.303R}\left[\frac{1}{T_1} - \frac{1}{T_2}\right]$$

$$\log_{10} 2 = \frac{E_a}{2.303R}\left[\frac{1}{T_1} - \frac{1}{T_2}\right]$$

33 (*d*) From the potential energy diagrams, the statement (d) is not correct, i.e. diagram (IV) does not have the largest rate constant for an endothermic reaction.

34 (*b*) $\quad k = Ae^{-E_a/RT}$

$$\therefore \quad \log k = \log A - \frac{E_a}{2.303RT}$$

Comparing this equation with straight line

$$y = mx + c$$

$$\Rightarrow \quad y = \log k \text{ and } x = 1/T$$

$\therefore$ E_a is calculated with the help of slope by plotting the curve between $\log k$ and $\dfrac{1}{T}$.

35 (*d*) $N_2(g) + 3H_2(g) \rightleftharpoons 2NH_3(g) + 22 \text{ kcal}$

$\because$ The activation energy for the forward reaction = 50 kcal

$\therefore$ The activation energy for the backward reaction

= 50 + 22 = 72 kcal.

36 (*b*) The formation of an activated complex takes place when vibrational degree of freedom converts into a translational degree of freedom. This statement is given by transition state theory. Also, the energy of activated complex is higher than the energy of reactant molecule, is true but it is not the correct explanation of the assertion.

37 (*a*) $\log \dfrac{k_2}{k_1} = \dfrac{E_a}{2.303R}\left[\dfrac{T_2 - T_1}{T_1 \cdot T_2}\right]$

$$\frac{k_2}{k_1} = 6, \quad T_1 = 350 \text{ K}, \quad T_2 = 400 \text{ K}$$

$$\log 6 = \frac{E_a}{2.303 \times 8.314}\left[\frac{400 - 350}{400 \times 350}\right]$$

$$0.7782 = \frac{E_a}{2.303 \times 8.314} \times \frac{50}{400 \times 350}$$

$$E_a = 41721 \text{ J mol}^{-1}$$
$$= 41.721 \text{ kJ mol}^{-1}$$
$$= 41.7 \text{ kJ mol}^{-1}$$

38 (*c*) Reactions involving the absorption of heat energy are called **endothermic reactions.**

For such reactions, $\quad \Sigma H_P < \Sigma H_R$

In graph (c), the heat of products is less than the heat of reactants. Thus, this graph represents endothermic reaction. But in graph (b) Only small amount of energy is absorbed, i.e. less, that is there is difference between energy of reactants and products.

Hence, graph (c) represent is endothermic reaction with maximum activation energy.

39 (*d*) Nature and concentration of the reactants and temperature of the reaction influence the rate of reaction. But molecularity does not affect the rate of reaction as it includes the number of atoms, ions or molecules that must collide with one another to result into a chemical reaction.

19

Surface Chemistry

Quick Review

Adsorption

The process in which molecular species are accumulated at the surface rather than in the bulk of a solid or liquid phase is termed as adsorption, e.g. water vapours on silica gel, H_2, O_2 and NH_3 on activated charcoal.

Terminology Related with Adsorption

(*i*) **Adsorbent** The solid/liquid that takes up a gas or vapour or a solute from solution, is called the adsorbent. Some important adsorbents are charcoal (both vegetable and animal), silica gel (obtained by heating a mixture of sodium silicate and 10% hydrochloric acid at $\approx 50°C$), metals such as Ni, Cu, Ag, Au, Pt colloids, etc.

Note Colloids, on account of their extremely small dimensions, have larger surface area per unit mass and these are good adsorbents.

(*ii*) **Adsorbate** The gas or the solute, which is held to the surface of the solid is called the adsorbate.

(*iii*) **Desorption** The removal of the adsorbed substance from a surface is called desorption. When equilibrium is reached,

Rate of adsorption = Rate of desorption

(*iv*) **Capillary condensation** : If adsorbent is porous, the adsorbate gets condensed into its pores. This process is called capillary condensation.

(*v*) **Positive and negative adsorption** : When concentration of adsorbate is more at the surface of adsorbent than its bulk (or interior phase), the adsorption is called positive adsorption and when concentration of adsorbate is less at the surface of adsorbent than its bulk (or interior), the adsorption is called negative adsorption. E.g. in some cases conc. of solute is more in bulk.

(*vi*) **Sorption** : When adsorption and absorption take place simultaneously and it is difficult to determine the relative extent of adsorption and absorption, the term **sorption** is used. This term was introduced by MC Bain.

Thermodynamics of Adsorption

During adsorption, following thermodynamical changes appear.

(*i*) Heat is evolved, i.e. adsorption is an exothermic process and for an exothermic process, ΔH is negative.

(*ii*) When adsorbate is adsorbed, freedom of movement of its molecules gets restricted. It results in decrease in entropy of adsorbate i.e. ΔS is negative for adsorption.

(*iii*) From Gibbs Helmholtz equation,

$$\Delta G = \Delta H - T\Delta S$$

If $\Delta H = -\text{ve}$ and $\Delta S = -\text{ve}$

$\therefore$ $\Delta G = -\text{ve} - [T(-\text{ve})] = -\text{ve} + T$

i.e. ΔG is negative only when ΔH has sufficiently high negative value, and temperature is not very high.

(*iv*) $\Delta G = -\text{ve}$ means, Gibbs free energy decreases and when ΔG becomes zero, a state of adsorption equilibrium is established.

Types of Adsorption

There are mainly two types of adsorption of gases on solid :

1. Physisorption

- It arises when the adsorbate molecules accumulate on the surface of adsorbent on account of weak van der Waals' forces. It occurs at low temperature.

- Heat of adsorption is low and it is in the range of 20-40 kJ/mol.
- It is a reversible process.
- Multilayer adsorption and adsorbed layer formed is several molecules thick.
- It decreases with increase in temperature.

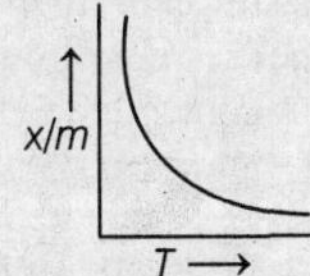

2. Chemisorption

- It arises when the adsorbate molecules accumulate on the surface of adsorbent on account of chemical bonds.
- It occurs at high temperature.
- Heat of adsorption is high and it is in the range of 80-240 kJ/mol.
- It is an irreversible process.
- Monolayer adsorption and adsorbed layer formed is only unimolecular in thickness.
- It increases with increase in temperature.

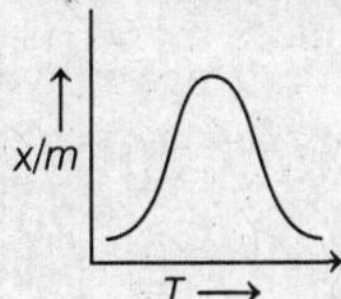

Factors Affecting Adsorption of Gases on Solids

Adsorption depends upon the following factors :

- A gas is adsorbed in different amounts on different adsorbents.
- Greater the surface area, greater is the extent of adsorption.
- With increase of temperature, adsorption decreases and *vice-versa*.
- Adsorption increases with pressure at constant temperature.

Adsorption Isotherms

The variation in the amount of gas adsorbed by the adsorbent with pressure at constant temperature can be expressed by means of a curve called as **adsorption isotherm.**

There are several adsorption isotherms, two important of them are as follows :

1. Freundlich Adsorption Isotherm

$$\frac{x}{m} = k \cdot p^{1/n}, \text{ or } \log \frac{x}{m} = \log k + \frac{1}{n} \log p$$

where, $\frac{x}{m}$ = amount of gas adsorbed per unit mass of the adsorbent at pressure. p, k and n are constants, $n \geq 1$.

At low pressure, $\frac{x}{m} = kp$; At high pressure, $\frac{x}{m} = kp^\circ$

- Plot of $\frac{x}{m}$ *vs* p
- Plot of $\log \frac{x}{m}$ *vs* $\log p$ is shown below

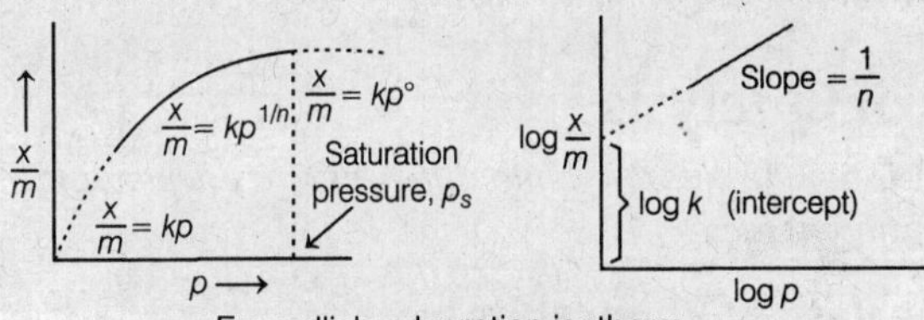

Freundlich adsorption isotherm

Note For solution phase, $\frac{x}{m} = kC^{1/n}$ $(n > 1)$;

where, C = equilibrium concentration

2. Langmuir Adsorption Isotherm

$$\frac{x}{m} = \frac{ap}{1 + bp}$$

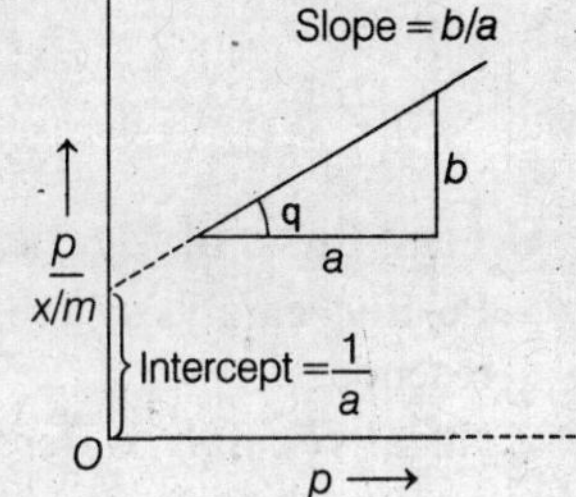

where, a and b

= Langmuir parameters

At high pressure,

$$\frac{x}{m} = \frac{a}{b} = \text{constant}$$

At low pressure, $\frac{x}{m} = ap$, i.e. $\frac{x}{m} \propto p$

Applications of Adsorption

Some of the important applications of adsorption are as follows :

(*i*) Activated charcoal is used in gas masks (to remove poisonous gases) and to generate high vacuum.

(*ii*) Animal charcoal, fuller's earth etc., are used to adsorb colouring impurities during the production of sugar, vinegar etc.

(*iii*) In froth floatation process of concentration of ore, the sulphide ores are wetted with oil and are adsorbed on the froth.

(*iv*) Ion exchange resins (used to remove hardness of water) also works on the principle of adsorption.

(*v*) Silica gel and alumina are used to remove moisture (i.e. as drying agents).

(*vi*) Heterogeneous catalysis and chromatographic analysis are based on the principle of adsorption.

(*vii*) All types of chromatographic techniques are based upon selective adsorption of different types of substances on a given adsorbent.

(*viii*) In analytical chemistry.

(*ix*) In medicines etc.

Catalysis

Substance that alters the rate of reaction without being consumed in the reaction is called catalyst and the phenomenon is known as catalysis.

Types of Catalysis

Catalysis can be classified into different types depending upon different factors.

1. On the Basis of Physical State

- **Homogeneous catalysis** Reactants and catalyst should be in same phase.

  e.g. $2SO_2(g) + O_2(g) \xrightarrow{NO(g)} 2SO_3(g)$

- **Heterogeneous catalysis** Reactants and catalyst are in different phase.

  e.g. $N_2(g) + 3H_2(g) \xrightarrow[\text{divided } Fe(s)]{\text{Finely}} 2NH_3(g)$

2. On the Basis of Mechanism of Catalysis

- **Positive catalysis** Here, catalyst enhances the rate of reaction.
- **Negative catalysis** Here, catalyst retards the rate of reaction.
- **Autocatalysis** One of the product formed during the reaction act as catalyst for the reaction,
  e.g. $2KMnO_4 + 5H_2C_2O_4 + 3H_2SO_4 \longrightarrow K_2SO_4 + 2MnSO_4 + 8H_2O + 10CO_2$
- **Induced catalysis** Here, one reaction induces the rate of other reaction.

Important Features of Solid Catalyst

Solid catalyst exhibits following two important characteristics.

- **Activity** of catalyst depends upon the strength of chemisorption to a larger extent.
- **Selectivity** means a given substance can act as catalyst only in a particular reaction and not for all reactions.

Enzyme Catalysis

Enzymes are biochemical catalysts. They are proteins and extremely specific in nature. A number of reactions that occur in the body of living organisms are catalysed by enzymes. Enzymes are known as biochemical catalysts.

e.g. $NH_2CONH_2 + H_2O \xrightarrow{\text{Urease}} 2NH_3 + CO_2$

Common steps for all enzyme catalysed reactions are :

(*i*) Enzyme + substrate $\longrightarrow$ Enzyme substrate complex (fast reversible)

(*ii*) Enzyme substrate complex $\longrightarrow$ Enzyme + product (slow rate determining)

Colloidal State

A colloid is a heterogeneous system in which one substance is dispersed (dispersed phase) as very fine particles in another substance (dispersion medium).

On the basis of size of dispersed particle, solutions can be classified into following three categories :

(*i*) True Solution	(*ii*) Colloidal Solution	(*iii*) Suspension
Particle size < 10 Å (1 nm)	10 Å – 1000 Å (1 nm – 100 nm)	> 1000 Å (100 nm)
Pass through filter paper as well as animal membrane.	Pass through filter paper but not through animal membrane.	Pass through neither of the two.
Do not settle.	Do not settle.	Settle on standing.
Particles are invisible.	Particles scatter light.	Particles are visible.
Diffuse quickly.	Diffuse slowly.	Do not diffuse.
Clear and transparent.	Translucent.	Opaque.

Colloids

Finely divided particles of any substance with diameter lying with 1 to 1000 nm range dispersed in any medium constitute colloidal system or colloids.

Classification of Colloids are as follows :

Based on Affinity of Phase

- Lyophilic (solvent attracting) or hydrophilic (if dispersion medium is water) colloids.
- Lyophobic (solvent repelling) or hydrophobic (if dispersion medium is water) colloids.

Based on Molecular Size

- **Multimolecular colloids** It contains aggregates of atoms or small molecules (diameter < 1 nm), e.g. gold sol, sulphur sol.
- **Macromolecular colloids** Particle size >> that of colloidal particles (most lyophilic sols belong to this category).
- **Associated colloids or micelles** When in low concentration, a substance behave as normal strong electrolyte and when in high concentration, exhibit colloidal properties (also called micelles).

Based on Physical State (Different colloidal system)

Colloidal system	Dispersed phase	Dispersion medium	Examples
Foam	Gas	Liquid	Soda water, froth, shaving cream
Solid foam	Gas	Solid	Foam rubber, cork
Aerosol	Liquid	Gas	Fog, mist, clouds
Emulsion	Liquid	Liquid	Milk, hair cream
Solid emulsion (gel)	Liquid	Solid	Butter, cheese
Aerosol of solids	Solid	Gas	Dust in air, smoke
Sol	Solid	Liquid	Paint, ink, colloidal gold,
Solid sol	Solid	Solid	Ruby glass, some gem stones

Preparation of Colloids

Colloidal solution can be prepared by two methods

(*i*) **Dispersion method** (Bredig's arc method and peptisation).

(*ii*) **Chemical or condensation method** (douple decomposition, hydrolysis, oxidation).

Note The methods used to purify colloids are dialysis, electrodialysis, ultrafiltration and ultracentrifugation.

Properties of Colloidal Solutions

The important properties of the colloidal solutions are given below:

- Colloidal particles are always in a state of rapid random motion, which is termed as **Brownian movement**.
- When a strong and converging beam of light is passed through a colloidal solution, its path becomes visible due to scattering of light by particles. It is called **Tyndall effect**.
- The phenomenon, involving the migration of colloidal particles under the influence of electric field towards the oppositely charged electrode, is called **electrophoresis**.
- The precipitation of particles of the dispersed phase in a sol is known as **coagulation**.
- Flocculation value $\propto \dfrac{1}{\text{coagulating power}}$

Hardy-Schulze Rule

Higher the valency of the active ion, the greater will be its power to precipitate the sol.

e.g. order of coagulating power is

$$Al^{3+} > Ba^{2+} > Na^{+} \Rightarrow PO_4^{3-} > SO_4^{2-} > Cl^{-}$$

Note Protective power of colloids $\propto \dfrac{1}{\text{Gold number}}$

Emulsions

If a pair of immiscible liquids such as olive oil and water are mixed and shaken vigorously, a dispersion of very fine droplets of one liquid in the other will result. Such a dispersion is termed as emulsion.

Some important characteristics of emulsions are given below :

(*i*) One of the components in emulsion is water and the other is an oily substance immiscible in water.

(*ii*) Emulsion droplets are bigger than sol particles ($\approx 10^{-6}$ m) and can be seen under an ordinary microscope or sometimes even with a magnifying glass.

(*iii*) Emulsions resemble lyophobic sols in some of the properties.

Types of Emulsions

Depending on the nature of the dispersed phase, the emulsions are classified as follows :

	Property	Oil in water type emulsion	Water in oil type emulsion
(*i*)	Electrical conductivity	High	Low
(*ii*)	Viscosity	More viscous in nature	Less viscous in nature
(*iii*)	Dye test	Dye remains insoluble when oil soluble dye is added	On adding oil soluble dye; it dissolves giving a bright colour.
(*iv*)	Dilution test	It is soluble on adding more water to it, e.g. milk	It is soluble on adding more oil to it, e.g. stiff greases.

Topical Practice Questions

All the exam questions of this chapter have been divided into three topics as listed below

Topic 1

Adsorption and Absorption Isotherms

2019

1 The correct option representing a Freundlich adsorption isotherm is **[NEET (Odisha)]**

(a) $\frac{x}{m} = kp^{0.3}$ (b) $\frac{x}{m} = kp^{2.5}$

(c) $\frac{x}{m} = kp^{-0.5}$ (d) $\frac{x}{m} = kp^{-1}$

2017

2 Which of the following curve best explains the Freundlich adsorption isotherm? **[AIIMS]**

(a)
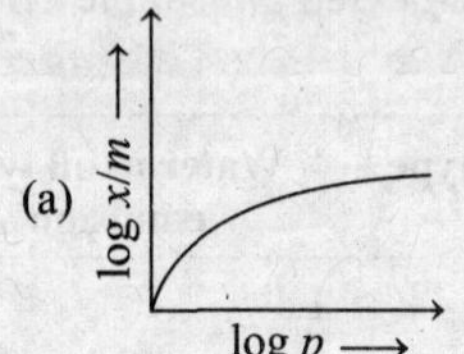

(c)
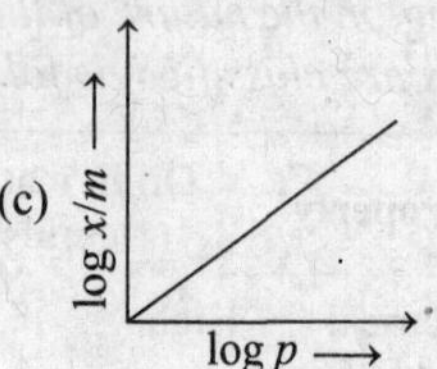

(b)
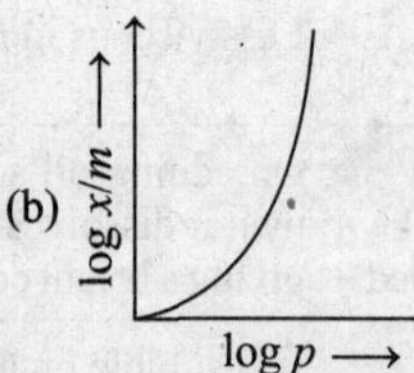

(d)
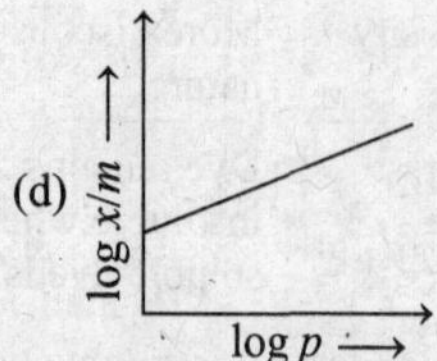

2014

3 Which one of the following is not explained by adsorption? **[Kerala CEE]**

(a) When acetic acid solution is shaken with charcoal, the concentration of the acid decreases

(b) The white precipitate of $Mg(OH)_2$ attains blue colour when precipitated in the presence of magneson reagent

(c) The air becomes dry in the presence of silica gel

(d) An aqueous solution of NaOH attains pink colour with a drop of phenolphthalein

(e) When animal charcoal is shaken with coloured methylene blue solution, the solution turns colourless

4 For Freundlich isotherm a graph of $\log x/m$ is plotted against $\log p$. The slope of the line and its Y-axis intercept, respectively corresponds to **[KCET]**

(a) $\frac{1}{n}, k$ (b) $\log \frac{1}{n}, k$

(c) $\frac{1}{n}, \log k$ (d) $\log \frac{1}{n}, \log k$

5 Which of the following statement is incorrect for physical adsorption? **[Guj CET]**

(a) It is instantaneous

(b) Monomolecular layer forms on the adsorbent

(c) Less activation energy is required for it

(d) Generally, it results at low temperature and adsorption decreases with increase in temperature

2013

6 In adsorption of oxalic acid on activated charcoal, the activated charcoal is called **[UP CPMT]**

(a) adsorber (b) adsorbate (c) adsorbent (d) occlusion

2012

7 In Freundlich adsorption isotherm, the value of $\frac{1}{n}$ is **[CBSE AIPMT]**

(a) between 0 and 1 in all cases

(b) between 2 and 4 in all cases

(c) 1 in case of physical adsorption

(d) 1 in case of chemisorption

8 Adsorption is accompanied by the evolution of heat, so according to Le-Chatelier's principle, the amount of substance adsorbed should **[AIIMS]**

(a) increase with decrease in T

(b) increase with increase in T

(c) decrease with decrease in T

(d) decrease with increase in T

9 Which among the following statements is false? **[UP CPMT]**

(a) The adsorption may be monolayered or multilayered

(b) Particle size of adsorbent will not affect the amount of adsorption

(c) Increase of pressure increases amount of adsorption

(d) All of the above

10 The gas that is adsorbed to a larger extent on charcoal is

(a) H_2 (b) CO_2 (c) CO (d) NH_3 **[AMU]**

2011

11 If x is the amount of adsorbate and m is the amount of adsorbent, which of the following relations is not related to adsorption process? **[CBSE AIPMT]**

(a) $\frac{x}{m} = p \times T$

(b) $\frac{x}{m} = f(p)$ at constant T

(c) $\frac{x}{m} = f(T)$ at constant p

(d) $p = f(T)$ at constant (x/m)

12 Choose the incorrect statement in respect of physisorption. **[Kerala CEE]**
(a) It is not specific in nature
(b) It arises because of van der Waals' forces
(c) It is reversible in nature
(d) No appreciable activation energy is needed
(e) Enthalpy of adsorption is in the range 80-240 kJ mol^{-1}

2010

13 Pieces of wood burn faster than a log of wood of the same mass because **[RPMT]**
(a) surface area of log of wood is larger and needs more time to burn
(b) pieces of wood have large surface area
(c) all pieces of wood catch fire at the same time
(d) block of wood has higher density than pieces of the same wood

14 During the adsorption of krypton on activated charcoal at low temperature **[KCET]**
(a) $\Delta H > 0$ and $\Delta S < 0$ (b) $\Delta H < 0$ and $\Delta S < 0$
(c) $\Delta H > 0$ and $\Delta S > 0$ (d) $\Delta H < 0$ and $\Delta S > 0$

15 Which of the following is a wrong statement for physisorption? **[Guj CET]**
(a) It is a reversible reaction
(b) Reaction requires an energy of activation
(c) The value of adsorption enthalpy is low
(d) It generally occurs at a low temperature

2009

16 Select the incorrect statement. **[AIIMS]**
(a) Physical adsorption is reversible, while chemical adsorption is irreversible
(b) High pressure favours physical adsorption while low pressure favours chemical adsorption
(c) Physical adsorption is not specific while chemical adsorption is highly specific
(d) High activation energy is involved in chemical adsorption

17 The gas which is least adsorbed on charcoal (under identical conditions) is **[Kerala CEE]**
(a) HCl (b) O_2 (c) CO_2 (d) NH_3
(e) SO_2

18 Adsorption of gases on solid surface is exothermic since **[CG PMT, Haryana PMT]**
(a) enthalpy is positive
(b) entropy is negative
(c) entropy increases
(d) free energy increases

19 In the Freundlich adsorption isotherm equation $\log \frac{x}{m} = \log k + \frac{1}{n} \log P$, the value of n is **[J&K CET]**
(a) any value from 0 to 1
(b) a negative integer
(c) a positive integer
(d) a positive or a negative fractional number

20 Which characteristic is not associated with chemical adsorption? **[AMU]**
(a) Is irreversible
(b) Forms monolayer
(c) Not very specific
(d) Heat of adsorption > 50 kJ mol^{-1}

21 Rate of physical adsorption increases with **[KCET]**
(a) decrease in temperature
(b) decrease in pressure
(c) increase in temperature
(d) decrease in surface area

2008

22 Identify the correct statement for the adsorption of a real gas on charcoal at 1 atm and 15°C. **[J&K CET]**
(a) gases which are small in molecular size are adsorbed more
(b) decrease in pressure increases the extent of adsorption
(c) gases which are easily liquefiable are adsorbed more in quantity
(d) gas which has a behaviour similar to an inert gas is adsorbed more

23 Which type of graph gives straight line in Langmuir adsorption isotherm? **[Guj CET]**
(a) $\frac{x}{m} \to \frac{1}{p}$ (b) $\frac{m}{x} \to \frac{1}{p}$
(c) $\log_{10} \frac{x}{m} \to \frac{1}{p}$ (d) $\log_{10} \frac{x}{m} \to p$

24 Which type of phenomenon is seen when coloured dye is removed from the solution of sugar by charcoal ? **[Guj CET]**
(a) Absorption
(b) Adsorption
(c) Both (a) and (b)
(d) None of the above

2007

25 The Langmuir adsorption isotherm is deduced using the assumption **[CBSE AIPMT]**
(a) the adsorption sites are equivalent in their ability to adsorb the particles
(b) the adsorption takes place in multilayers
(c) the heat of adsorption varies with coverage
(d) the adsorbed molecules interact with each other

26 At the high pressure, Langmuir adsorption isotherm takes the form **[AIIMS]**
(a) $x/m = ap/1+bp$ (b) $x/m = a/b$
(c) $x/m = ap$ (d) $m/x = b/a + 1/ap$

27 Freundlich adsorption isotherm is **[MHT CET]**
(a) $\frac{x}{m} = k\,p^{1/n}$ (b) $x = mk\,p^{1/n}$
(c) $\frac{x}{m} = k\,p^{-n}$ (d) All of these

28 Which among the following statements are correct with respect to adsorption of gases on a solid? **[Kerala CEE]**

I. The extent of adsorption is equal to kp^n according to Freundlich isotherm.

II. The extent of adsorption is equal to $kp^{1/n}$ according to Freundlich isotherm.

III. The extent of adsorption is equal to $\frac{(1+bp)}{ap}$ according to Langmuir isotherm.

IV. The extent of adsorption is equal to $\frac{ap}{(1+bp)}$ according to Langmuir isotherm.

V. Frendluich adsorption isotherm fails at-low pressure, where k, a and b are constants and p is pressure.

(a) I and II (b) I and IV (c) II and III (d) II and IV (e) II and V

2006

29 A plot of $\log x/m$ *versus* $\log p$ for the adsorption of a gas on a solid gives a straight line with slope equal to

(a) $-\log k$ (b) n **[CBSE AIPMT]**
(c) $1/n$ (d) $\log k$

Answers

1 (a)	2 (d)	3 (d)	4 (c)	5 (b)	6 (c)	7 (a)	8 (a, d)	9 (b)	10 (d)
11 (a)	12 (e)	13 (b)	14 (b)	15 (b)	16 (b)	17 (b)	18 (b)	19 (c)	20 (c)
21 (a)	22 (c)	23 (b)	24 (b)	25 (a)	26 (b)	27 (d)	28 (d)	29 (c)	

Explanations

1 (*a*) According to Freundlich adsorption isotherm,

$$\frac{x}{m} = kp^{1/n}$$

where, $\frac{x}{m}$ = amount of the gas adsorbed per unit mass of adsorbent

p = pressure, k and n = constants.

The value of n lies in between 0 and 1.

Thus, $\frac{x}{m} = kp^{0.3}$ and option (a) is correct.

2 (*d*) Curve (d) is in accordance with Freundlich adsorption isotherm as :

$$\frac{x}{m} = k \cdot p^{1/n}$$

or $$\log \frac{x}{m} = \log k + \frac{1}{n} \log p.$$

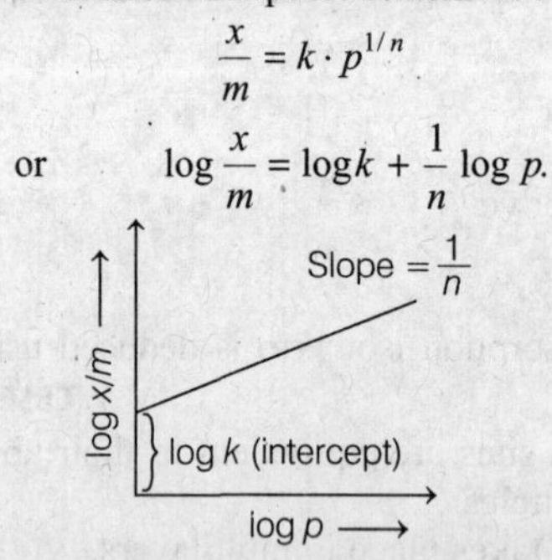

3 (*d*) An aqueous solution of NaOH attains pink colour with a drop of phenolphthalein due to its basic nature and presence of OH^- ions. This change in colour is due to presence of indicator. This is not explained by adsorption.

4 (*c*) According to Freundlich adsorption isotherm,

$$\frac{x}{m} = kp^{1/n}$$

where, $\frac{x}{m}$ is the amount of the gas adsorbed per gram of the adsorbent (x/m) and k and n are the constants depending upon nature of the adsorbate and adsorbent at a particular temperature. The factor $1/n$ has values between 0 and 1 (probable range is 0.1 to 0.5)

On taking log on both sides, we get

$$\log \frac{x}{m} = \frac{1}{n} \log p + \log k$$

Slope = $\frac{1}{n}$

$\log \frac{x}{m}$ ↑

Intercept = $\log k$

⟶ log p

A graph between $\log x/m$ against $\log p$ should therefore give a straight line with slope equal to $1/n$ and intercept equal to $\log k$.

5 (*b*) Physical adsorption is an instantaneous process in which van der Waals' forces exist between the adsorbate and adsorbent. Thus, activation energy of such adsorption is low and it results in the formation of multimolecular layer. Physisorption occurs at low temperature and decreases with rise in temperature.

6 (*c*) **Adsorption** is the phenomenon of attracting and retaining the molecules of a substance on the surface of solid or liquid resulting into higher concentration of molecules on the surface. The substance thus adsorbed on the surface is called **absorbate** and the substance on which it is adsorbed is called **adsorbent.**

So, activated charcoal is adsorbent because oxalic acid is adsorbed on its surface.

7 (*a*) In Freundlich adsorption isotherm

$$\frac{x}{m} = kp^{1/n}$$

The constant n is a positive integer and thus, its value is always greater than 1. The factor $1/n$ has values between 0 and 1 (probably 0.1 to 0.5). So, the value of $1/n$ lies between 0 and 1 in all cases.

8 (*a, d*) As the adsorption process is exothermic, the adsorption occurs readily at low temperature and decreases with increasing temperature (in accordance to Le-chatelier's principle, exothermic process favours backward reaction, thus adsorption decreases with increase in temperature) except chemisorption. In other words, adsorption increases with decrease in temperature.

9 (*b*) Adsorption in some cases form monolayer, but van der Waals' adsorption may be multilayered. The magnitude of adsorption increases with an increase in pressure. An increase in the surface area of adsorbent increases the adsorption. So, the option (b) is not correct among all.

10 (*d*) It is seen that, higher the critical temperature of the gas, more easily it can be liquefied, i.e. greater the intermolecular forces of attraction of gaseous molecules on the surface of adsorbent, greater will be the adsorption.

Gas	Critical temperature (k)
H_2	33
CO_2	304
CO	134
NH_3	406

Hence, NH_3 is adsorbed to a larger extent on charcoal.

11 (*a*) The amount adsorbed (x/m) is a function of pressure (p) and temperature (T).
$x/m = f(p, T)$
x/m is not equal to $p \times T$.
Therefore, $x/m = p \times T$ is the incorrect relation.

12 (*e*) No doubt, physiosorption is an exothermic process but its enthalpy of adsorption is quite low (20-40 $kJ mol^{-1}$). This is because physisorption involves only van der Waals' forces of attraction and no chemical change. Rest all the other statements are correct.

13 (*b*) Large surface area of adsorbent adsorbs more O_2. Pieces of wood burn faster than a log of wood because pieces of wood have large surface area.

14 (*b*) Adsorption is an exothermic process, thus ΔH is negative (i.e. $\Delta H < 0$). Moreover, adsorption results in more ordered arrangements of molecules, thus entropy decreases (i.e. $\Delta S < 0$).

$$\Delta G = \Delta H - T\Delta S$$

Hence, low temperature favours the reaction.

15 (*b*) When the particles of the adsorbate are held to the surface of the adsorbent by the physical forces, the adsorption is called physical adsorption or physisorption. It is a reversible process and usually occurs at low temperature. The value of adsorption enthalpy is low in this process. It forms multimolecular layers. As this type of adsorption involves no chemical reaction, no activation energy is required for the adsorption to occur.

16 (*b*) Both physical as well as chemical adsorptions are favoured by high pressure. However, the point of difference is that decrease in pressure causes desorption in case of physical adsorption but not in the case of chemical adsorption. Rest all the given statements are correct.

17 (*b*) Permanent gases such as O_2, H_2 are adsorbed to a lesser extent than the easily liquefiable gases such as NH_3, HCl, CO_2 and SO_2 due to lower value of critical temperatures.

18 (*b*) During adsorption, the molecules of adsorbate (i.e. gaseous molecules) are held on the surface of the adsorbent leading to the decrease in randomness. Therefore, entropy decreases, i.e. ΔS is negative.

19 (*c*) n is a positive integer, and it is the constant depending upon the nature of adsorbate and adsorbent at a particular temperature. The factor $\frac{1}{n}$ has values between 0 and 1.

20 (*c*) Chemisorption is highly specific and it will only occur if there is some possibility of chemical bonding. E.g. Oxygen is adsorbed on metals by virtue of oxide formation and hydrogen is adsorbed by transition metals with unpaired *d*-orbital leading to hydride formation.

21 (*a*) Low temperature favours physical adsorption. It increases with decrease of temperature and vice-versa while decrease of pressure causes desorption. Further, physical adsorption varies directly with surface area, i.e. higher the surface area, more will be the adsorption.

22 (*c*) Gases which have high critical temperature, have strong van der Waals' forces of attraction and are easily liquefied and hence, are adsorbed to a greater extent on solid surfaces like charcoal.

23 (*b*) $\frac{x}{m} = \frac{ap}{1 + bp}$

This equation is known as Langmuir adsorption isotherm.

where, x = mass of gas adsorbed
m = grams of the adsorbent and a and b are constants.
p = pressure of gas

Taking reciprocal on both sides, we have

$$\frac{m}{x} = \frac{1 + bp}{ap} \Rightarrow \frac{m}{x} = \frac{1}{ap} + \frac{b}{a}$$

Thus, a plot of $\frac{m}{x}$ *versus* $\frac{1}{p}$ will be a straight line.

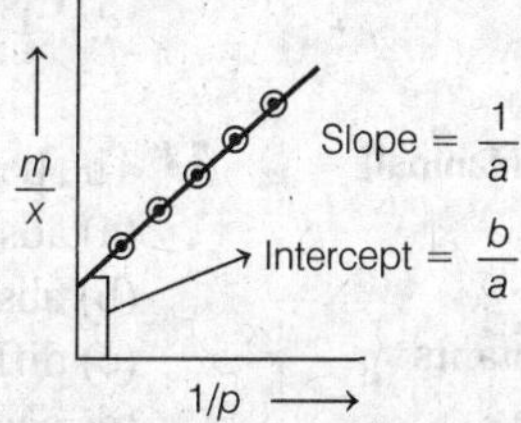

24 (*b*) On adding charcoal in cane sugar, some amount of coloured dye has been adsorbed by charcoal. This phenomenon is known as adsorption.

25 (*a*) The main points of Langmuir's theory of adsorption are as follows :

(*i*) Adsorption takes place on the surface of the solid only till the whole of the surface is completely covered with a unimolecular layer of the adsorbed gas. This suggests all the adsorption sites present on solids surface are equivalent in their ability to adsorb the particles.

(*ii*) Adsorption consists of two opposing processes (a) condensation and (b) evaporation.

(*iii*) The rate of condensation depends upon the uncovered surface of the adsorbent available for condensation.

Thus, option (a) is correct.

26 (*b*) Langmuir adsorption isotherm, is

$$\frac{x}{m} = \frac{ap}{1 + bp}$$

At high pressure, $1 + bp \sim bp$

or $\frac{x}{m} = \frac{ap}{bp} = \frac{a}{b}$

27 (*d*) Freundlich adsorption isotherm is represented by, $\frac{x}{m} = kp^{1/n}$

The above expression can be rearranged as, $x = mkp^{1/n}$ or $\frac{x}{m} = kp^{-n}$

Here, k and n are constant and p is pressure and $\frac{x}{m}$ is the amount of gas adsorbed.

28 (*d*) According to Freundlich adsorption isotherm the extent of adsorption, is $\frac{x}{m} = kp^{1/n}$. Moreover, at low pressure, $\frac{x}{m} = kp^{1/n}$.

On the other hand, according to Langmuir adsorption isotherm, the extent of adsorption $\left(\frac{x}{m}\right) = \frac{ap}{1+bp}$ where, a, b are constants and p is pressure.

Thus, statements II and IV are correct.

29 (*c*) $\frac{x}{m} = kp^{1/n} \Rightarrow \log\frac{x}{m} = \log k + \frac{1}{n}\log p$

In a graph plotted between log x/m against log p, a straight line with slope equal to $1/n$ and ordinate intercept equal to log k is obtained.

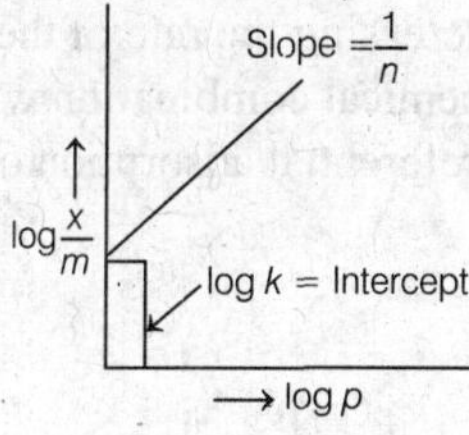

Topic 2

Catalyst

2017

1 Which one of the following statement(s) is/are not correct? **[NEET]**

(a) Catalyst does not initiate any reaction

(b) The value of equilibrium constant is changed in the presence of a catalyst in the reaction equilibrium

(c) Enzymes catalyse mainly biochemical reaction

(d) Coenzymes increase the catalytic activity of enzyme

2014

2 *Zeigler-Natta* catalyst is **[Kerala CEE]**

(a) $ZnCl_2$ (b) $Et_3Al + TiCl_4$

(c) $Cu/ZnO\text{-}Cr_2O_3$ (d) Pt

(e) V_2O_5

2011

3 For the following reaction,

$$C_6H_{12}O_6(aq) + H_2(g) \rightleftharpoons C_6H_{14}O_6(aq)$$

Which one of the following is not affected by the addition of catalyst? **[UP CPMT]**

(a) Rate of forward reaction

(b) Rate of backward reaction

(c) Time required to reach the equilibrium

(d) Spontaneity

4 Match the following.

	Catalyst		Industrial product
A.	V_2O_5	1.	High density polyethylene
B.	*Ziegler-Natta*	2.	Polyacrylonitrile
C.	Peroxide	3.	NH_3
D.	Finely divided Fe	4.	H_2SO_4

Codes **[Kerala CEE]**

	A	B	C	D		A	B	C	D
(a)	4	1	2	3	(b)	4	3	2	1
(c)	3	1	2	4	(d)	4	2	1	3
(e)	4	1	3	2					

2010

5 Catalytic poisons act by **[Manipal]**

(a) making the products chemically inactive

(b) increasing the rate of the backward reactions

(c) chemical combination with any one of the rectants

(d) preferential adsorption on the catalyst surface

6 Which one of the following is an example for homogeneous catalysis? **[KCET]**

(a) Manufacture of sulphuric acid by contact process

(b) Manufacture of ammonia by Haber's process

(c) Hydrolysis of sucrose in the presence of dilute hydrochloric acid

(d) Hydrogenation of oil

2009

7 Following reaction is catalysed by $Br^-(aq)$.

$$2H_2O_2(aq) \longrightarrow 2H_2O(l) + O_2(g)$$

This is an example of **[UP CPMT]**

(a) homogeneous catalysis

(b) heterogeneous catalysis

(c) autocatalysis

(d) enzyme catalysis

8 Which type of metal form effective catalyst?

(a) Alkali metal **[UP CPMT, Haryana PMT]**

(b) Transition metal

(c) Alkaline earth metal

(d) Radioactive metal

2008

9 Shape-selective catalysis is a reaction catalysed by

(a) zeolites **[Kerala CEE]**

(b) enzymes

(c) platinum

(d) *Zeigler-Natta* catalyst

(e) acids or basis

10 Which one of the following reactions is an example of auto-catalysis? **[EAMCET]**

(a) $2AsH_3(s) \longrightarrow 2As(s) + 3H_2(g)$

(b) $N_2(g) + 3H_2(g) \xrightarrow{Fe(s)} 2NH_3(g)$

(c) $2SO_2(g) + O_2(g) \xrightarrow{NO(g)} 2SO_3(g)$

(d) $C_{12}H_{22}O_{11}(l) + H_2O(l) \xrightarrow{H^+(l)} C_6H_{12}O_6(l) + C_6H_{12}O_6(l)$

11 The best condition for heterogeneous catalysis is

(a) adsorption **[DUMET]**

(b) absorption

(c) diffusion

(d) occlusion

2007

12 According to the adsorption theory of catalysis, the speed of the reaction increases because [AIIMS]

(a) adsorption produces heat which increases the speed of the reaction
(b) adsorption lowers the activation energy of the reaction
(c) the concentration of reactant molecules at the active centres of the catalyst becomes high due to adsorption
(d) in the process of adsorption, the activation energy of the molecules is large

13 What is the role of a catalyst in a reaction? [AMU]

(a) Lowers the activation energy
(b) Increase the activation energy
(c) Affects the free energy change
(d) Affects the enthalpy change

14 $2SO_2(g) + O_2(g) \xrightleftharpoons{V_2O_5}$ is an example for [KCET]

(a) neutralisation reaction
(b) homogeneous catalysis
(c) heterogeneous catalysis
(d) irreversible reaction

2006

15 Given below, catalyst and corresponding process/ reaction are matched. The mismatch is [AIIMS]

(a) $[RhCl(PPh_3)_2]$: Hydrogenation
(b) $TiCl_4 + Al(C_2H_5)_3$: Polymerisation
(c) V_2O_5 : Haber-Bosch process
(d) Nickel : Hydrogenation

16 Which enzyme converts sucrose into ethanol? [BHU]

(a) Diastase
(b) Invertase
(c) Zymase
(d) Both (b) and (c)

17 Which acts as auto catalyst during titration of $KMnO_4$ and oxalic acid in the presence of H_2SO_4? [BHU]

(a) H_2SO_4 (b) $KMnSO_4$
(c) Oxalic acid (d) $MnSO_4$

18 Which of the following factors are responsible for the increase in the rate of surface catalysed reaction?

I. A catalyst provides proper orientation for the reactant molecules to react.
II. Heat of adsorption of reactants on a catalyst helps reactant molecules to overcome activation energy.
III. The catalyst increases the activation energy of the reaction.
IV. Adsorption increases the local concentration of reactant molecules on the surface of the catalyst.

Select the correct answer using the codes given below. [Kerala CEE]

(a) I and II (b) I and III
(c) II and IV (d) I, II and III
(e) I, II and IV

19 The efficiency of an enzyme to catalyse a reaction is due to its capacity to [Kerala CEE]

(a) reduce the activation energy of the reaction
(b) form strong enzyme-substrate complex
(c) decrease the bond energy of all substrate molecules
(d) increase the free energy of the catalyst-substrate reaction
(e) alter the substrate geometry to fit into the shape of the enzyme molecule

20 In which of these process platinum is used as a catalyst? [Haryana PMT]

(a) Oxidation of ammonia to form HNO_3
(b) Hardening of oils
(c) Production of synthetic rubber
(d) Synthesis of methanol

2005

21 The addition of 1% alcohol to chloroform acts as [AMU]

(a) auto-catalyst (b) bio-catalyst
(c) positive catalyst (d) negative catalyst

22 Hydrolysis of ethyl acetate is catalysed by aqueous [EAMCET]

(a) Na_2SO_4 (b) K_2SO_4
(c) H_2SO_4 (d) $BaSO_4$

23 In Ostwald process of manufacturing of HNO_3, catalyst used is [BCECE]

(a) Mo (b) Fe
(c) Mn (d) Pt

Answers

1 (b)	2 (b)	3 (d)	4 (a)	5 (d)	6 (c)	7 (a)	8 (b)	9 (a)	10 (a)
11 (a)	12 (a)	13 (a)	14 (c)	15 (c)	16 (d)	17 (d)	18 (e)	19 (a)	20 (a)
21 (d)	22 (c)	23 (d)							

Explanations

1 (*b*) For a reversible reaction, catalyst accelerates the speed of forward as well as backward reaction to the same extent. Hence, it does not disturb the equilibrium, i.e. does not change the equilibrium constant of the reaction but helps to attain the equilibrium faster.

2 (*b*) Combination of $TiCl_4$ and triethyl aluminium represents *Ziegler-Natta* catalyst which acts as a catalyst in polymerisation of ethene.

3 (*d*) A catalyst catalyses both forward and backward reactions to the same extent in a reversible reaction and thus, helps in the achievement of equilibrium quicker. Thus, it does not have any effect on spontaneity of a reaction.

4 (*a*) The correct match is :
$A \rightarrow 4, B \rightarrow 1, C \rightarrow 2, D \rightarrow 3$
V_2O_5 – H_2SO_4
Ziegler-Natta — HDPE
Peroxide — Polyacrylonitrile
Finely divided Fe — NH_3

5 (*d*) The catalytic poisons decreases the activity of catalyst due to strong preferential adsorption of the poison on the surface of the catalyst.

6 (*c*) In homogeneous catalysis, reactants and catalyst are in the same phase.

$$SO_2(g) + O_2(g) \underset{}{\overset{Pt(s)}{\rightleftharpoons}} SO_3(g)$$

(Contact process)

Manufacture of sulphuric acid by contact process an example of heterogeneous catalysis.

$$N_2(g) + 3H_2(g) \overset{Fe\,(s)}{\rightleftharpoons} 2NH_3(g)$$

(Haber's process)

It is an example of heterogeneous catalysis.

$$C_{12}H_{22}O_{11}(aq) + H_2O(aq) \overset{HCl(aq)}{\rightleftharpoons} C_6H_{12}O_6 + C_6H_{12}O_6$$

It is an example of homogeneous catalysis.

$$Oil(l) + H_2(g) \xrightarrow[Pt(s)]{(Hardening)} fat$$

Thus, it is also an example of heterogeneous catalysis.

7 (*a*) When the reactants and the catalyst are in same phase, the catalysis is homogeneous.

Reactant : H_2O_2; Phase : (*aq*)

Catalyst : Br^-; Phase (*aq*)

Hence, it is an example of homogeneous catalysis.

8 (*b*) Transition metals, due to their variable valency, are able to form unstable intermediate compounds very readily.

Moreover, these provide a large surface area for the reactant to be absorbed. Due to both of these properties, transition metals have good catalytic property.

9 (*a*) Zeolites are shape selective catalysts. Their general formula is

$$M_{x/n}[(AlO_2)_x \cdot (SiO_2)_y] \cdot mH_2O$$

where, $M = Na^+, K^+$ or Ca^{2+}

n = charge on cation

m = number of molecules of water of crystallisation

The reaction selectivity of zeolites depends upon the size of cavities and pores in the structure.

10 (*a*) The reactions which are catalysed by one of the product formed, are called autocatalysis reactions and the process is called autocatalysis, e.g.

$$2AsH_3(s) \longrightarrow 2As(s) + 3H_2(g)$$

11 (*a*) In heterogeneous catalysis, the reactant molecules are adsorbed on the surface of the catalyst and the reaction takes place on that surface. The adsorbed molecules are held to the surface of the catalyst by bonds similar in strength to those in chemical compounds. Now some bonds of adsorbed molecule may be stretched, weakened and ultimately cleaved to form products.

12 (*a*) A catalyst lowers the activation energy of the reaction and hence accelerates the speed of the reaction. In other words,

$$\because \text{Rate of reaction} \propto \frac{1}{\text{Activation energy}}$$

Further, as adsorption is exothermic, the heat released further helps to speed up-the reaction.

13 (*a*) All substances have average energy and before the reaction occurs, energy of the reactant should be higher than the average energy. The catalyst lowers the activation energy. Therefore, rate of reaction is increased.

14 (*c*) $2SO_2(g) + O_2(g) \underset{(solid)}{\overset{V_2O_5}{\rightleftharpoons}} 2SO_3(g)$

In this reaction, reactants as well as the catalyst are present in more than one phase, hence it is an example of heterogeneous catalysis.

15 (*c*) In Haber-Bosch process, i.e. for the manufacture of NH_3, finely divided iron + molybdenum as promotor is used as catalyst.

$$N_2 + 3H_2 \underset{Mo}{\overset{Fe}{\rightleftharpoons}} 2NH_3$$

16 (*d*) Inversion of cane sugar

$$\underset{\text{Sucrose}}{C_{12}H_{22}O_{11}} + H_2O \xrightarrow{\text{Invertase}} \underset{\text{Glucose}}{C_6H_{12}O_6} + \underset{\text{Fructose}}{C_6H_{12}O_6}$$

$$\underset{\text{Glucose}}{C_6H_{12}O_6} \xrightarrow{\text{Zymase}} \underset{\text{Ethanol}}{2C_2H_5OH} + 2CO_2$$

17 (*d*) $MnSO_4$ acts as auto catalyst during the titration of $KMnO_4$ and oxalic acid in presence of $H_2SO_4 \cdot MnSO_4$ is formed during the reaction

$$5H_2C_2O_4 + 2KMnO_4 + 3H_2SO_4 \longrightarrow 2MnSO_4 + K_2SO_4 + 10CO_2 + 8H_2O$$

18 (*e*) The factors which are responsible for the increase in the rate of surface catalysed reaction are as :

(*i*) A catalyst provides proper orientation for the reactant molecules to react.

(*ii*) Heat of adsorption of reactants on the catalyst helps reactant molecules to overcome activation energy.

(*iv*) Adsorption increases the local concentration of reactant molecules on the surface of the catalyst.

19 (*a*) The efficiency of an enzyme to catalyse a reaction is due to its capacity to reduce the activation energy of the reaction.

20 (*a*) Platinum acts as catalyst in the oxidation of ammonia to form nitric oxide. This reaction is used in the Ostwald's method of nitric acid preparation.

$$4NH_3 + 5O_2 \xrightarrow[800°C]{Pt} 4NO + 6H_2O$$

$$2NO + O_2 \longrightarrow 2NO_2$$

$$4NO_2 + O_2 + 2H_2O \longrightarrow 4HNO_3$$

21 (*d*) The addition of 1% alcohol to chloroform reduces rate of reaction. Hence, it acts as negative catalyst or inhibitor.

22 (*c*) Hydrolysis of ethyl acetate is catalysed by aqueous H_2SO_4.

$$\underset{\text{Ethyl acetate}}{CH_3COOC_2H_5(l)} + H_2O(l) \xrightarrow{H^+(aq)} \underset{\text{Acetic acid}}{CH_3COOH(l)} + \underset{\text{Ethyl alcohol}}{C_2H_5OH(l)}$$

23 (*d*) **Ostwald process**

$$4NH_3 + 5O_2 \xrightarrow[800°C]{Pt} 4NO + 6H_2O + \text{Heat}$$

$$2NO + O_2 \xrightarrow{300°C} 2NO_2(g)$$

$$4NO_2 + 2H_2O + O_2 \longrightarrow 4HNO_3$$

So, Pt is catalyst in Ostwald process..

Topic 3

Colloids, Micelles and Emulsions

2019

1 Butter is a colloidal solution of **[JIPMER]**

(a) solid-solid (b) liquid-solid
(c) solid-liquid (d) gas-solid

2018

2 When an excess and a very dilute aqueous solution of KI is added to very dilute aqueous solution of silver nitrate. The colloidal particles of silver iodide which are associated with the Helmholtz double layer in the form of **[AIIMS]**

(a) $AgI / Ag^+ : I^-$ (b) $AgI / K^+ : NO_3^-$
(c) $AgI / NO_3^- : Ag^+$ (d) $AgI / I^- : K^+$

3 Assertion (A) Micelles are formed by surfactant molecules above the critical micelle concentration (CMC).

Reason (R) The conductivity of a solution having surfactant molecules decreases sharply at the CMC. **[AIIMS]**

(a) Both Assertion and Reason are true and Reason is the correct explanation of the Assertion
(b) Both Assertion and Reason are true but Reason is not the correct explanation of the Assertion.
(c) Assertion is true but Reason is false.
(d) Both Assertion and Reason are false.

4 On which of the following properties does the coagulating power of an ion depend? **[NEET]**

(a) Both magnitude and sign of the charge on the ion
(b) Size of the ion alone
(c) The magnitude of the charge on the ion alone
(d) The sign of charge on the ion alone

5 Bleeding due to a cut can be stopped by applying ferric chloride solution in the laboratory. This is due to **[JIPMER]**

(a) coagulation of negatively charged blood particles by Fe^{3+} ions.
(b) coagulation of positively charged blood particles by Cl^- ions.
(c) reaction taking place between ferric ions and the haemoglobin forming a complex.
(d) common element, iron, in both $FeCl_3$ and haemoglobin.

2016

6 The coagulation values in millimoles per litre of the electrolytes used for the coagulation of As_2S_3 are given below **[NEET]**

I. $(NaCl) = 52$
II. $(BaCl_2) = 0.69$
III. $(MgSO_4) = 0.22$

The correct order of their coagulating power is

(a) I > II > III (b) II > I > III
(c) III > II > I (d) III > I > II

7 Fog is a colloidal solution of **[NEET]**

(a) gas in liquid (b) solid in gas
(c) gas in gas (d) liquid in gas

2015

8 Which property of colloidal solution is independent of charge on the colloidal particles? **[CBSE AIPMT; 2014]**

(a) Coagulation (b) Electrophoresis
(c) Electroosmosis (d) Tyndall effect

2014

9 The amount of electrolytes required to coagulate a given amount of AgI colloidal solution (-ve charge) will be in the order. **[WB JEE]**

(a) $NaNO_3 > Al(NO_3)_3 > Ba(NO_3)_2$
(b) $Al(NO_3)_3 > Ba(NO_3)_2 > NaNO_3$
(c) $Al(NO_3)_3 > NaNO_3 > Ba(NO_3)_2$
(d) $NaNO_3 > Ba(NO_3)_2 > Al(NO_3)_3$

10 Protective sols are **[UK PMT]**

(a) lyophilic (b) lyophobic
(c) Both (a) and (b) (d) None of these

11 Gold sol is not **[KCET]**

(a) a macromolecular colloid
(b) a lyophobic colloid
(c) a multimolecular colloid
(d) negatively charged colloid

2013

12 The colloid is [AIIMS]
(a) urea (b) blood
(c) cane sugar (d) NaCl

13 Which of the following colloid is formed by the aggregation of large number of atoms? [UP CPMT]
(a) Polystyrene (b) Sulphur sol
(c) Sodium stearate (d) Nylon

14 A colloidal solution is subjected to an electric field. The colloidal particles move towards anode. The coagulation of the same solution studied by using NaCl, $BaCl_2$ and $AlCl_3$ solutions. The coagulation power is in the order of [Manipal]
(a) $BaCl_2 > NaCl > AlCl_3$
(b) $NaCl > BaCl_2 > AlCl_3$
(c) $AlCl_3 > BaCl_2 > NaCl$
(d) $NaCl > AlCl_3 > BaCl_2$

15 The random motion of colloidal particles in the dispersion medium is known as [Manipal]
(a) Tyndall effect (b) coagulation
(c) adsorption (d) Brownian movement

16 Amount of protective colloid in milligram is called [WB JEE]
(a) gold number (b) congo rubin number
(c) coagulating power (d) None of these

17 Which of the following ions can cause coagulation of proteins? [KCET]
(a) Ag^+ (b) Na^+ (c) Mg^{2+} (d) Ca^{2+}

2012

18 The protecting power of lyophilic colloidal sol is expressed in terms of [CBSE AIPMT]
(a) coagulation value
(b) gold number
(c) critical micelle concentration
(d) oxidation number

19 Cow milk is an example of natural emulsion stabilised by [AFMC]
(a) fat (b) water
(c) casein (d) Mg^{2+} ions

20 The simplest way to check whether a system is collidal is [UP CPMT]
(a) electrodialysis (b) finding out particle size
(c) Tyndall effect (d) Brownian movement

21 Which of the following is not correct? [Manipal]
(a) Milk is a naturally occurring emulsion
(b) Gold sol is a lyophilic sol
(c) Physical adsorption decreases with rise in temperature
(d) Chemical adsorption is unlayered

22 Milk is a kind of [OJEE]
(a) sol (b) gel
(c) emulsion (d) mixture

23 All colloidal dispersion have [KCET]
(a) low osmotic pressure
(b) no osmotic pressure
(c) high osmotic pressure
(d) very high osmotic pressure

2011

24 Which one of the following is correctly matched? [Kerala CEE]
(a) Emulsion – smoke (b) Gel – butter
(c) Aerosol – hair cream (d) Sol – whipped cream
(e) Foam – mist

25 Which one of the following does not involve coagulation? [KCET]
(a) Clotting of blood by the use of ferric chloride
(b) Formation of delta region
(c) Treatment of drinking water by potash alum
(d) Peptisation

26 Which of the following has maximum coagulation power with ferric hydroxide sol? [Guj CET]
(a) Cryolite (b) $K_2C_2O_4$
(c) $K_3[Fe(CN)_6]$ (d) $K_4[Fe(CN)_6]$

2010

27 Which substance is not used for preparing lyophilic sols? [Manipal]
(a) Starch (b) Gum
(c) Gelatin (d) Metal sulphide

28 The colloidal system in which the disperse phase and dispersion medium both are liquids is known as [RPMT]
(a) a gel (b) an aerosol (c) an emulsion (d) a foam

29 Tyndall effect is observed [MP PMT]
(a) in the solution (b) in the precipitate
(c) in sols (d) in vapour

30 Gold number of protective colloids *A*, *B*, *C* and *D* are 0.50, 0.01, 0.10 and 0.005, respectively. The correct order of their protective power is [Haryana PMT]
(a) $D < A < C < B$ (b) $C < B < D < A$
(c) $A < C < B < D$ (d) $B < D < A < C$

31 The size of colloidal particles is in between [JCECE]
(a) 10^{-7} - 10^{-9} cm (b) 10^{-9} - 10^{-11} cm
(c) 10^{-4} - 10^{-7} cm (d) 10^{-2} - 10^{-3} cm

32 Gold number is associated with [VMMC]
(a) electrophoresis
(b) purple of cassius
(c) protective colloid
(d) amount of pure gold

33 100 mL of a colloidal solution is completely precipitated by addition of 5 mL of 1 M NaCl solution. What is the coagulation value of NaCl? [VMMC]
(a) 50 (b) 40
(c) 30 (d) None of these

2009

34 Four different colloids have the following gold number. Which one has its most effective action? **[AFMC]**
(a) 10 (b) 30 (c) 20 (d) 40

35 Which of the following metal sols cannot be prepared by Bredig's arc method? **[Manipal]**
(a) Copper (b) Potassium (c) Gold (d) Platinum

36 The process of separation of colloids by passing through semi-permeable membrane is called **[Manipal]**
(a) filtration (b) electrophoresis
(c) dialysis (d) ultrafiltration

37 Hair cream is an example of **[Kerala CEE]**
(a) gel (b) sol
(c) aerosol (d) foam
(e) emulsion

38 Which one of the following is most effective in causing the coagulation of an As_2S_3 sol? **[EAMCET]**
(a) KCl (b) $AlCl_3$
(c) $MgSO_4$ (d) $K_3Fe(CN)_6$

2008

39 The dispersed phase, dispersion medium and nature of colloidal solution (lyophilic or lyophobic) of 'gold sol' respectively, are **[AFMC]**
(a) solid, solid, lyophobic (b) liquid, liquid, lyophobic
(c) solid, liquid, lyophobic (d) solid, liquid, lyophilic

40 Which of the following electrolytes will have maximum flocculation value for $Fe(OH)_3$ sol? **[AFMC]**
(a) NaCl (b) Na_2S
(c) $(NH_4)_3PO_4$ (d) K_2SO_4

41 Which of the following is incorrect match? **[BHU]**

	Name of colloidal solution	Examples	Dispersed phase	Dispersion medium
(a)	Foam	Soap lather, soda water	Gas	Liquid
(b)	Solid foam	Rubber, bread	Gas	Solid
(c)	Aerosol	Mist, fog, cloud	Liquid	Solid
(d)	Emulsion	Milk, cod liver oil	Liquid	Liquid

42 **Statement** 'To stop bleeding from an injury ferric chloride can be applied.' Which comment about the statement is justified? **[Kerala CEE]**
(a) It is not true, ferric chloride is a poison
(b) It is true; Fe^{3+} ions coagulate blood which is a negatively charged sol
(c) It is not true, Cl^- ions form positively charged sol; profuse bleeding takes place
(d) It is true, coagulation takes place because of formation of negatively charged sol with Cl^-
(e) It is not true, ferric chloride is ionic and gets into the blood stream

43 In an electrical field, the particles of a colloidal system move towards cathode. The coagulation of the same sol is studied using K_2SO_4 (I), Na_3PO_4 (II), $K_4[Fe(CN)_6]$(III) and NaCl (IV). Their coagulating power should be **[Kerala CEE]**
(a) I > II > III > IV (b) III > II > I > IV
(c) III > I > II > IV (d) IV > III > I > II
(e) IV > I > II > III

44 The phenomenon observed when a beam of light is passed through a colloidal solution, is **[J&K CET]**
(a) cataphoresis (b) deelectrophoresis
(c) coagulation (d) Tyndall effect

45 The colour of sky is due to **[KCET]**
(a) transmission of light
(b) wavelength of scattered light
(c) absorption of light by atmospheric gases
(d) All of the above

46 The basic principle of Cottrell's precipitator is **[KCET]**
(a) Le-Chatelier's principle
(b) peptisation
(c) neutralisation of charge on colloidal particles
(d) scattering of light

47 Which has least gold number? **[BCECE]**
(a) Gelatin (b) Starch
(c) Albumin (d) Blood

2007

48 **Assertion** (A) The conversion of fresh precipitate to colloidal state is called peptisation.
Reason (R) It is caused by addition of common ions. **[AIIMS]**
(a) Both A and R are correct and R is the correct explanation of A
(b) Both A and R are correct but R is not the correct explanation of A
(c) A is correct but R is incorrect
(d) Both A and R are incorrect

49 Example of intrinsic colloid is **[AFMC]**
(a) glue (b) sulphur
(c) Fe (d) As_2S_3

50 Peptisation denotes **[MHT CET]**
(a) digestion of food
(b) hydrolysis of proteins
(c) breaking and dispersion into colloidal state
(d) precipitation of solid from colloidal dispersion

51 Blue colour of water in sea is due to **[MHT CET]**
(a) refraction of blue light by impurities
(b) refraction of blue sky by water
(c) scattering of light by water
(d) None of the above

52 Which of the following forms cationic micelles above certain concentration? **[Manipal]**
(a) Sodium ethyl sulphate
(b) Sodium acetate
(c) Urea
(d) Cetyltrimethylammonium bromide

53 The presence of electric charge on colloidal particles is indicated by the property **[J&K CET]**
(a) dialysis (b) solubility
(c) electrophoresis (d) osmosis

54 When a sulphur sol is evaporated, sulphur is obtained. On mixing with water sulphur sol is not formed. The sol is **[KCET]**
(a) lyophilic (b) reversible
(c) hydrophobic (d) hydrophilic

55 Which of the following acts as best semi-permeable membrane? **[Guj CET]**
(a) $Cu_2[Fe(CN)_6]$ (b) Parchment paper
(c) Cellophane (d) Plant cell wall

56 The physical states of dispersed phase and dispersion medium in colloid like pesticide spray respectively are **[Guj CET]**
(a) gas, liquid (b) solid, gas
(c) liquid, solid (d) liquid, gas

2006

57 **Assertion** (A) Fe^{3+} can be used for coagulation of As_2S_3 sol.
Reason (R) Fe^{3+} reacts with As_2S_3 to give Fe_2S_3. **[AIIMS]**
(a) Both A and R are correct and R is the correct explanation of A
(b) Both A and R are correct but R is not the correct explanation of A
(c) A is correct but R is incorrect
(d) Both A and R are incorrect

58 "The greater the charge on an ion, the greater its coagulating power" is a statement of **[BHU]**
(a) Tyndall's effect
(b) Faraday's law
(c) Moseley's law
(d) Hardy-Schulze law

59 The coagulation of 200 mL of a positive colloid took place when 0.73 g HCl was added to it without changing the volume much. The flocculation value of HCl for the colloid is **[Kerala CEE]**
(a) 0.365 (b) 36.5 (c) 100 (d) 150
(e) 200

60 Which of the following is a use of alum? **[RPMT]**
(a) Making explosive (b) Bleaching clothes
(c) Water softening (d) All of these

61 Which of the following is not a method of preparation of colloidal solution? **[J&K CET]**
(a) Electrical dispersion
(b) Peptisation
(c) Coagulation
(d) Mechanical dispersion

62 Cod liver oil is **[DUMET]**
(a) solution (b) an emulsion
(c) colloidal solution (d) suspension

63 When dilute aqueous solution of $AgNO_3$ (excess) is added to KI solution, positively charged sol of AgI is formed due to adsorption of **[BCECE]**
(a) NO_3^- (b) O_2^- (c) Ag^+ (d) K^+

2005

64 Sulphur colloid is prepared by **[MHT CET]**
(a) mechanical dispersion (b) oxidation
(c) electrical dispersion (d) reduction

65 10^{-4} g of gelatin is required to be added to 100 cm^3 of a standard gold solution to just prevent its precipitation by the addition of 1 cm^3 of 10% NaCl solution to it. Hence, the gold number of gelatin (in mg) is **[Kerala CEE]**
(a) 10 (b) 1.0 (c) 0.1 (d) 0.01
(e) 0.001

66 A emulsifier is a substance which **[KCET]**
(a) stabilises the emulsion
(b) homogenises the emulsion
(c) coagulates the emulsion
(d) accelerates the dispersion of liquid in liquid

Answers

1 (b)	2 (d)	3 (b)	4 (a)	5 (a)	6 (c)	7 (d)	8 (d)	9 (b)	10 (a)
11 (a)	12 (b)	13 (b)	14 (c)	15 (d)	16 (a)	17 (d)	18 (b)	19 (c)	20 (c)
21 (b)	22 (c)	23 (b)	24 (b)	25 (d)	26 (d)	27 (d)	28 (c)	29 (c)	30 (c)
31 (c)	32 (c)	33 (a)	34 (a)	35 (b)	36 (c)	37 (e)	38 (b)	39 (c)	40 (a)
41 (c)	42 (b)	43 (b)	44 (d)	45 (b)	46 (c)	47 (a)	48 (b)	49 (a)	50 (*)
51 (c)	52 (b)	53 (c)	54 (c)	55 (c)	56 (d)	57 (a)	58 (d)	59 (c)	60 (c)
61 (c)	62 (b)	63 (c)	64 (b)	65 (d)	66 (a)				

Explanations

1 (*b*) In butter, the dispersed phase is liquid and dispersion medium is solid. This type of colloid is called gel. It is called liquid-solid emulsion.

2 (*d*) When excess KI solution is added to $AgNO_3$ solution, negatively charged solution results due to adsorption of I^- from dispersion medium forming AgI / I^-. Having acquired a negative charge, this layer attracts counter ions from the medium forming a second layer as $AgI / I^- : K^+$.

3 (*b*) Both assertion and reason are true but reason is not the correct explanation of assertion.

At a certain concentration, surfactant molecule aggregates and forms micelle. This concentration is called critical micelle concentration (CMC). Aggregation of surfactant molecules (ions; $RCOO^-$), i.e. micelle formation causes effective fall in number of free ions to conduct electricity, thus conductivity decreases at CMC.

4 (*a*) The process of settling of colloidal particles due to the neutralisation of their charge by any means is called coagulation.

Coagulation power of an ion depends on both **magnitude and sign of the charge** (positive or negative) **on the ion**. This fact can be explained by **Hardy-Schulze rule**.

According to this rule "greater the valency of the coagulating ion/flocculating ion (oppositely charged ion) added, the greater is its power to cause coagulation.

To coagulate a positively charged sol, the order of coagulating power of negative ion is

$$I^- < SO_4^{2-} < PO_4^{3-} < [Fe(CN)_6]^{4-}.$$

Similarly, to coagulate a negatively charged sol, the order of coagulating power of positive ions is

$$Ag^+ < Pb^{2+} < Fe^{3+} < Si^{4+}$$

5 (*a*) Bleeding due to a cut can be stopped by applying $FeCl_3$ or alum solution. This is due to coagulation of negatively charged colloidal blood particles (albuminoid substance) by positively charged Fe^{3+} ions. These substances are used as styptic (which check the flow of blood).

6 (*c*) Lower the coagulating power, higher is the coagulation value in millimoles per litre, i.e. coagulating power is inversely proportional to coagulation values. Thus, correct order of coagulating power is

$MgSO_4 > BaCl_2 > NaCl$ or III > II > I

7 (*d*) Fog is a colloidal solution of liquid in a gas, in which liquid is the dispersed phase whereas gas is the dispersion medium. Examples of other options are as follows:

Gas in liquid : Shaving cream, soda water froth

Solid in gas : Dust in air

Gas in gas : Atmospheric air.

8 (*d*)
- Tyndall effect property of colloidal solution is independent of charge on the colloidal particles while coagulation, electrophoresis and electro-osmosis depend on charge on colloidal particle.
- Coagulation is generally brought about by the addition of electrolytes. When an electrolyte is added to a colloidal solution, the particles of the sol take up the ions which are oppositely charged. As a result, their charge gets neutralised.
- Electrophoresis is the movement of colloidal particles under an applied electric potential.
- Electroosmosis may be defined as a phenomenon in which the molecules of the dispersion medium are allowed to move under the influence of an electric field whereas colloidal particles are not allowed to move.
- Tyndall effect is the scattering of light by sol particles, which cannot be affected by charge on them.

Thus, 'option d' is correct.

9 (*b*) Since, AgI is a negatively charged sol, so according to Hardy-Schulze law, higher the positive charge on the metal atoms, more is the tendency of metal atom to cause coagulation of negatively charged colloid.

The order of positive charge is :

$$Na^+ < Ba^{2+} < Al^{3+}$$

Hence, the order for coagulating the AgI solution is

$$Al(NO_3)_3 > Ba(NO_3)_2 > NaNO_3$$

10 (*a*) Lyophobic colloids are readily coagulated but it is difficult to coagulate lyophilic colloid. When lyophilic colloid is added to lyophobic one, the lyophobic colloid gets enveloped by lyophilic colloid. Therefore, former remains protected against action of electrolytes.

11 (*a*) Gold sol contain particles of various sizes having several atoms of gold. Thus, it is a multimolecular colloid instead of macromolecular colloid.

12 (*b*) Blood is an example of colloid. Particles which range between 1 nm-1000 mm forms colloidal solution. It is a heterogeneous solution.

Urea, cane sugar and NaCl are crystalloids, i.e. forms true solution.

13 (*b*) Sulphur sol is a multimolecular colloid. These colloids are formed by the aggregation of large number of atoms that have diameters less than 1 nm. Polystyrene and nylon are macromolecular colloids whereas sodium stearate is an associated colloid.

14 (*c*) The correct order for coagulation power is $AlCl_3 > BaCl_2 > NaCl$.

The reason for this is that greater the valency of an ion, greater is its coagulating power according to Hardy-Schulze law.

15 (*d*) The random motion of colloidal particles in the dispersion medium is known as Brownian movement.

16 (*a*) The amount of protective colloid in milligrams that prevents the coagulation of 10mL of a given sol on adding 1 mL of 10% solution of sodium chloride is known as gold number.

17 (*d*) On heating or on treatment with mineral acids the colloidal proteins are precipitated. This change is irreversible and is known as coagulation. It is due to Ca^{2+} ions.

18 (*b*) Lyophobic sols are unstable, so they are stabilised by adding some lyophilic colloids which protect them from precipitation. Thus, lyophilic colloids are called protecting colloids. Their protecting power is expressed in terms of gold number.

19 (*c*) Cow milk is a natural emulsion stabilised by casein, milk protein.

20 (*c*) The simplest way to check whether a system is colloidal or not is to pass a beam of light through the colloidal solution, then the solution is colloidal in nature. If the path becomes visible as a bright streak, than the solution is colloidal in nature. This is known as Tyndall effect.

21 (*b*) Gold sol is a lyophobic sol lyophobic sols are unstable and can be precipitated easily by the addition of an electrolyte.

22 (*c*) Milk is an emulsion of liquid which is dispersed in water. If a mixture of two immiscible or partially miscible liquids is shaken, a coarse dispersion of one liquid in the other is obtained which is termed as emulsion, e.g. milk, vanishing cream, etc.

23 (*b*) Colloidal particles are bigger aggregates. Thus, the number of particles in the colloidal solution is comparatively lesser than that in true solution. Hence, the values of colligative properties such osmotic pressure are of small order (or no value) as compared to values shown by true solution at the same concentration.

24 (*b*) Smoke — Aerosols
Butter — Gel
Hair cream — Emulsion
Whipped cream — Foam
Mist — Aerosols
Butter is an example for gel.

25 (*d*) Peptisation is the process of converting a precipitate into colloidal sol by shaking it with dispersion medium in the presence of a small amount of electrolyte. It is the method of preparation of colloids.

26 (*d*) Ferric hydroxide is a positively charged solution. Thus, a negative ion causes the precipitation of positively charged sol and *vice-versa*. "According to Hardy-Schulze rule, greater is the valency of the coagulating or flocculating ion, greater is its power to bring about coagulation. Thus, in coagulation of a positively charged solution of ferric hydroxide, the flocculating power is maximum for $[Fe(CN)_6]^{4-}$ ion. Thus, $K_4[Fe(CN)_6]$ possesses the maximum coagulating power for Fe $(OH)_3$ solution.

27 (*d*) Metal sulphides are not used to prepare lyophilic sols as lyophilic sols are prepared by just dissolving substance into water, e.g. sols of starch, gum and gelatin are prepared by dissolving them in water. Thus, they are lyophilic.

28 (*c*)

Dispersed phase	Dispersion medium	Name	Example
Liquid	Solid	Gel	Cheese butter
Liquid	Gas	Aerosol	Fog, mist
Liquid	Liquid	Emulsion	Milk, hair cream
Gas	Liquid	Foam	Froth, whipped cream

29 (*c*) Tyndall effect is the characterstic feature of colloidal solutions (i.e. sols).

30 (*c*) Smaller the value of gold number, greater will be protective power of the protective colloid.

Protective power of a colloid
$$\propto \frac{1}{\text{Gold number}}$$

Hence, the correct order is
$$A < C < B < D.$$

31 (*c*) The size of colloidal particles is in the range of 1000 nm to 1 nm or 10^{-4} cm to 10^{-7} cm.

32 (*c*) Gold number is used to describe the protective power of different colloids.

33 (*a*) Coagulation value is the millimoles of an electrolyte that must be added to 1 L of a colloidal solution for complete coagulation.

$$\because 5 \text{ mL of } 1 \text{ M NaCl} = \frac{1}{1000} \times 5$$
$$= 0.005 \text{ mol or } 5 \text{ mmol.}$$

$\because$ 100 mL of colloidal solution require NaCl for complete coagulation
$$= 5 \text{ mmol}$$

$\therefore$ 1 L of colloidal solution require NaCl for complete coagulation
$$= 50 \text{ mmol}$$

$\therefore$ Coagulation value of NaCl $= 50$

34 (*a*) Higher the gold number of colloid, lesser will be its protective power (gold number is the measure of protective power). Hence, colloid with gold number 10 is most effective amongst the given.

35 (*b*) Potassium sol cannot be prepared by Bredig's arc method because it reacts vigorously with water.

36 (*c*) The process of separation of colloids by passing through semi-permeable membrane is called dialysis.

37 (*e*) In hair cream both the dispersion medium and dispersed phase are liquids, hence it is an example of emulsion.

38 (*b*) As_2S_3 is a negative sol. It is obvious that cations are effective in coagulating negative sols. According to Hardy Schulze rule, greater the valency of the coagulating ion, greater is its coagulating power.

Thus, out of the given $AlCl_3(Al^{3+})$ is the most effective for causing coagulation of As_2S_3 sol.

39 (*c*) Colloidal solution of gold is obtained when dispersed phase is solid and dispersion medium is liquid.

Substances like metals (e.g. gold, silver) cannot be brought into the colloidal state simply by bringing them in contact with water or solvent and therefore, special methods are used for the purpose. Hence, they are known as hydrophobic or lyophobic colloids.

40 (*a*) Flocculation value
$$\propto \frac{1}{\text{Coagulating power}}$$

$Fe(OH)_3$ is a positively charged sol. To coagulate $Fe(OH)_3$, negatively charged electrolyte is used and greater the value of negative charge, coagulating power will be strong.

Among the given electrolytes, NaCl has lowest coagulating power, so its flocculation value will be maximum.

41 (*c*)

Name of colloidal solution	Dispersed phase	Dispersion medium	Examples
Foam	Gas	Liquid	Soap lather
Solid foam	Gas	Solid	Rubber, bread
Aerosol	Liquid	Gas	Fog, mist, cloud
Emulsion	Liquid	Liquid	Milk, cod liver oil

Thus, option 'c' corresponds to incorrect match.

42 (*b*) Blood is a negatively charged solution, so it can be coagulated by the addition of a positively charged ion, i.e. Fe^{3+} ion (from $FeCl_3$). Hence, addition of ferric chloride to blood causes coagulation of blood and stops bleeding. Thus, only option 'b' justifies the given statement.

43 (*b*) Since, in an electrical field, the particles of a colloidal system move towards cathode, so they are positively charged and coagulated by negatively charged ions. According to Hardy-Schulze rule "Greater the valency of coagulating ion added, the greater is its power to cause coagulation."

Thus, the order of coagulating power is

$$\underset{\text{III}}{[Fe(CN)_6]^{4-}} > \underset{\text{II}}{PO_4^{3-}} > \underset{\text{I}}{SO_4^{2-}} > \underset{\text{IV}}{Cl^-}$$

44 (*d*) On passing a beam of light through a colloidal solution, the colloidal particles absorb light energy and then emit it in all the possible directions. This phenomenon is called scattering of light or Tyndall effect.

Note Tyndall effect is not observed in true solutions.

45 (*b*) The blue colour of sky is due to Tyndall effect, i.e. the colloidal particles absorb light, causes the sky to be luminous and then scatter light of different wavelengths in all possible directions.

46 (*c*) In Cottrell's precipitator, the charged particles are attracted towards the walls of precipitator, where they lose their charge and coagulate. Hence, the basic principle of Cottrell's precipitator is the neutralisation of charge on colloidal particles.

47 (*a*) The gold number of the given compounds is :

Gelatin	— 0.005 to 0.1
Starch	— 25
Albumin	— 0.2
Blood or haemoglobin	— 0.03

So, gelatin has the least gold number.

48 (*b*) Correct reason to assertion is that common ion adsorb on the surface of precipitate.
Due to repulsion between adsorbed ions, the precipitate undergo fragmentation resulting in colloidal state.

49 (*a*) On shaking with the dispersion medium, colloids directly form the colloidal solution. Hence, they are called intrinsic colloid, i.e. glue.

50 (*) The dispersal of a precipitated material into colloidal solution by the action of an electrolyte in solution is called peptisation and the electrolyte is called a peptising agent.

51 (*c*) The colour of water in sea is blue due to the scattering of light by water. The colour of a colloidal solution depends on the wavelength of the light scattered by the dispersed particles, which in turn depends on the size and the nature of particle.

52 (*b*) Sodium acetate forms cationic micelles above a certain concentration. In the molecule of detergents and soap, the negative ions aggregate to form a micelle of colloidal size. In polar medium (like water), the negative ion has a long hydrocarbon chain and a polar group ($—COO^-$) at one end and on other end it has Na^+ ions, thus cationic micelle is formed.

53 (*c*) Colloidal particles possess some type of electric charge. The migration of colloidal particles under the influence of an electric field is known as electrophoresis.

54 (*c*) Hydrophobic sols are irreversible in nature. They have no affinity between the dispersed phase and the dispersion medium (H_2O). Further once precipitated, they do not form the colloidal sol by simple addition of water.

55 (*c*) Cellophane acts as best semi-permeable membrane.

56 (*d*) The physical states of dispersed phase and dispersion medium in colloid like pesticide spray are liquid and gas, respectively.

57 (*a*) Fe^{3+} can be used for coagulation of As_2S_3 sol because As_2S_3 is negatively charged sol and hence, it can be coagulated by Fe^{3+} which is positively charged.

58 (*d*) According to Hardy-Schulze law "The greater the charge on an ion, the greater its coagulating power."

59 (*c*) Molarity $= \dfrac{0.73}{36.5} \times \dfrac{1000}{200}$

$= 0.1$ M

This means that a minimum of 0.1 mole or $0.1 \times 1000 = 100$ millimoles are required for coagulating 1 L of colloid.

$\therefore$ Flocculation value of HCl for the colloid = 100.

60 (*c*) Alums are used as water-sofener and act as coagulant. These are also used in tanning of leather, as mordant in dyeing and to stop bleeding.

61 (*c*) Colloidal solution is prepared by electrical dispersion, peptisation and mechanical dispersion. It is not prepared by coagulation because coagulation is the phenomenon of the precipitation of colloidal solution by the addition of the electrolyte.

62 (*b*) "Emulsions are the colloidal solutions in which both the dispersed phase and the dispersion medium are liquids."
Example — Milk, cod liver oil, butter and cold cream.

63 (*c*) When aqueous solution of $AgNO_3$ is added to KI solution, positively charged sol of AgI is obtained due to the adsorption of Ag^+ ions on KI molecules.

$$\underset{\text{Excess}}{AgNO_3} + KI \longrightarrow AgI + KNO_3$$

$$AgI \xrightarrow{Ag^+} \underset{\substack{\text{Positively} \\ \text{charged sol}}}{[AgI]Ag^+}$$

64 (*b*) Sulphur sol is prepared by the oxidation of H_2S by bromine.

$$Br_2 + H_2S \longrightarrow 2HBr + \underset{\text{(sol)}}{S}$$

65 (*d*) $\because$ 100 cc gold sol + 1 cc of 10%
Amount of NaCl solution that prevents coagulation when gelatin is added $= 10^{-4}$ g

$\therefore$ 10 cc gold solution + 1 cc of 10%
Amount of NaCl solution that prevents coagulation when gelatin is added

$$= \frac{10^{-4}}{100} \times 10 = 10^{-5} \text{ g}$$

So, gold number of gelatin in milligram

$= 10^{-5} \times 1000$
$= 10^{-2} = 0.01$ mg

66 (*a*) The substance which is added to stabilise the emulsion is known as emulsifier or emulsifying agent.

Emulsions are of two types :

(i) Water in oil
(ii) Oil in water

20

General Principles and Processes of Isolation of Elements

Quick Review

- **Minerals** The naturally occurring substances in the form of which the metals occurs in the earth crust along with impurities are called minerals.
- **Ores** These are the minerals from which metals are extracted conveniently and economically.
- **Gangue or matrix** These are the impurities associated with ores.

Metallurgy

The complete scientific and technological process of extraction of a metals in its pure form from its ore is called metallurgy. It depends upon the nature of ore as well as associated impurities.

Depending upon the methods employed for extraction, metallurgical processes may be of following three types

(*i*) **Hydrometallurgy** It is used when aqueous solution is involved to extract an element. It is generally used in case of gold, silver etc.

(*ii*) **Pyrometallurgy** Shows the use of heat to extract an element. It is used when an ore is roasted or calcined or smelted e.g. sulphides, carbonates and oxides ores.

(*iii*) **Electrometallurgy** Indicates the involvement of process of electrolysis in the extraction of a metal. It is used in case of extraction of highly electropositive metals like sodium (Na), potassium (K), magnesium (Mg), calcium (Ca), aluminium (Al) etc.

Steps Involved in Metallurgy

The whole process of metallurgy can be understood by following chart:

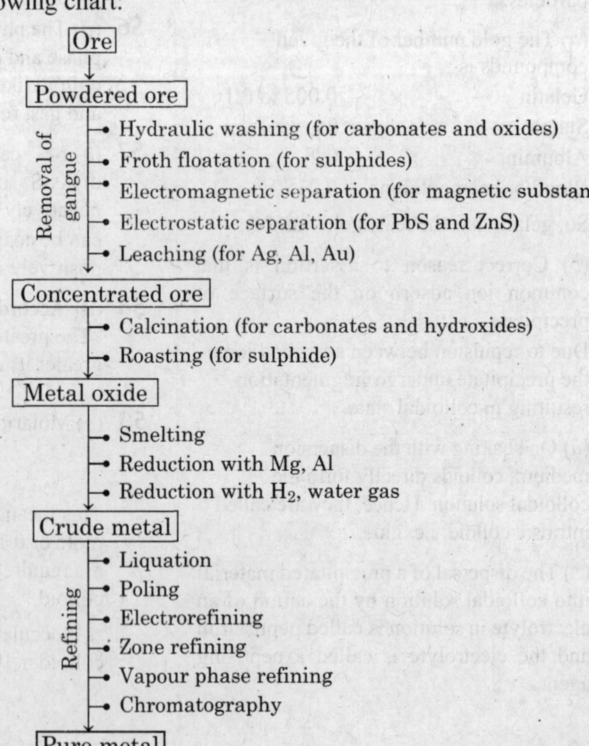

Concentration of Ore or Benefication

The various methods adopted for the concentration of ore are as follows

(*i*) **Gravity Separation or Hydraulic Washing** It is based on the difference in the specific gravities of the ore and gangue. Cassiterite or tin-stone, chromite and pitch-blende are concentrated by this method.

(*ii*) **Magnetic Separation** It is based on the difference in magnetic properties of minerals. Magnetite, haematite and ilmenite are separated from non-magnetic impurities.

(*iii*) **Froth Floatation Process** It is used to concentrate sulphide ores. It is based on the difference in wettability of different minerals.

(*iv*) **Leaching** It is useful in case of which ore is soluble in a suitable solvent. Pure Al_2O_3 is obtained from the bauxite ore in the Baeyer's process by leaching.

Some Important Ores

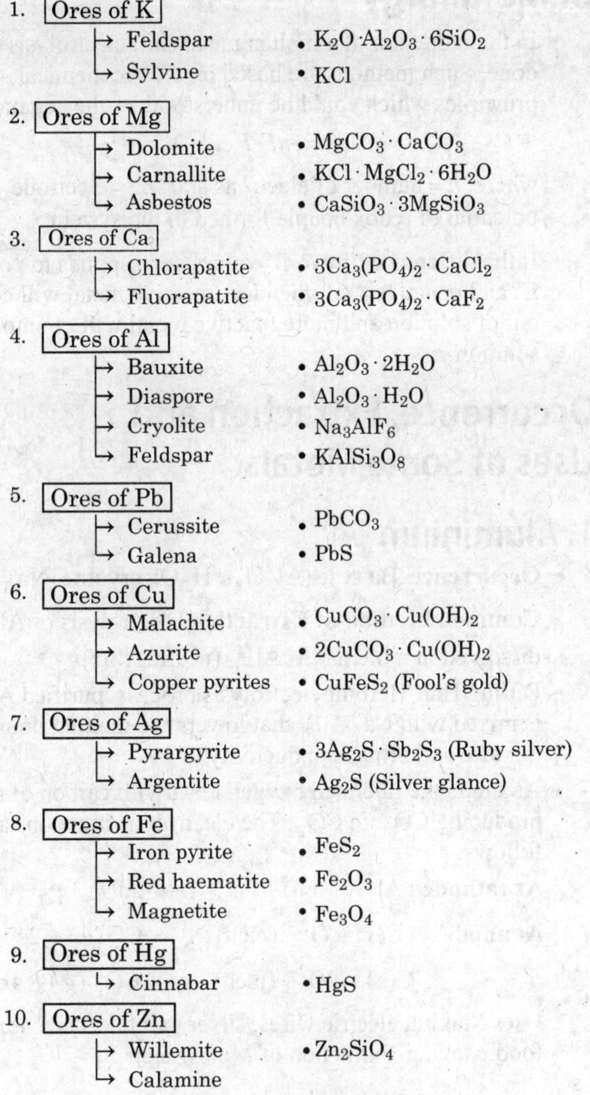

Conversion of Concentrated Ore into Oxide

It is done by following methods:

(*i*) **Calcination** This method is used when concentrated ore is in the form of hydroxide or carbonate; volatile matter is burnt away. It is done in a reverberatory furnace.

(*ii*) **Roasting** In this, sulphide ore is heated in a regular supply of air at a temperature below the melting point of the metal. It converts sulphide into oxide or sulphate.

Reduction of Oxides

(*i*) **Smelting** It is the process of reduction of metal oxides (like oxides of less electropositive metals such as Zn, Fe, Pb etc.) by using coke, coal or CO as reductant at high temperature.

(*ii*) **Reduction by Aluminium** (or Gold Schmidt aluminothermic process) is the process of reduction of oxides of chromium, iron, manganese etc by using aluminium metal as reductant.

(*iii*) **Auto-reduction** It is the process of reduction of metal oxides on their own without the use of any external reducing agent.

(*iv*) **Electrolytic Reduction Method** In this method, highly electropositive metals like elements of group 1 and 2 are themselves good reductant so these metals are extracted by electrolysis of their salts in fused state.

Refining of Crude Metal

Depending upon the nature of metals and associated impurities, different methods are employed to purify metals.

(*i*) **Distillation** This method is used in cases where metals are easily volatile as compared to impurities. e.g. zinc, mercury and cadmium.

(*ii*) **Liquation** In this method, a low melting metal like tin, bismuth, lead, mercury etc. can be made to flow on a sloping surface and thus separated from higher melting impurities.

(*iii*) **Electrolysis** It is used for metals like copper, gold, silver, lead, zinc, aluminium. Impure metal is made anode and the pure metal is cathode. The net result is the transfer of pure metal from anode to cathode.

(*iv*) **Zone Refining** In this method, metal of high purity are obtained. Silicon, germanium, boron, gallium, indium are purified (which are used in semiconductors). It is based on the fact that impurities are more soluble in the melt than in the pure metal.

(*v*) **Vapour Phase Refining** It involve conversion of metal to volatile compound and decomposition of compound to pure metal. Ni and Ti are extracted by this method.

Thermodynamics of Metallurgy

- The free energy change (ΔG) occurring during the reduction processes help in deciding the suitable method for reduction of metal oxide to free metal.
- For the spontaneous reduction of an oxide, halide or sulphide by an element, the essential condition is that there is a decrease in the free energy of the system (–ve ΔG).
- More the negative value of ΔG, the higher is the reducing power of an element.
- Gibbs equation; $\Delta G^\circ = \Delta H^\circ - T\Delta S^\circ$ and $\Delta G^\circ = -2.303\, RT \log K$
- If reactants and products of two reactions (i.e. reduction of metal oxide and oxidation of reducing agent) are put together and the net ΔG° of reactions is negative (–ve), the overall reaction will occur.

Ellingham Diagram

HJT Ellingham plots Gibbs free energy change (ΔG) values for formation of oxides against temperature and the plots obtained are called Ellingham diagram.

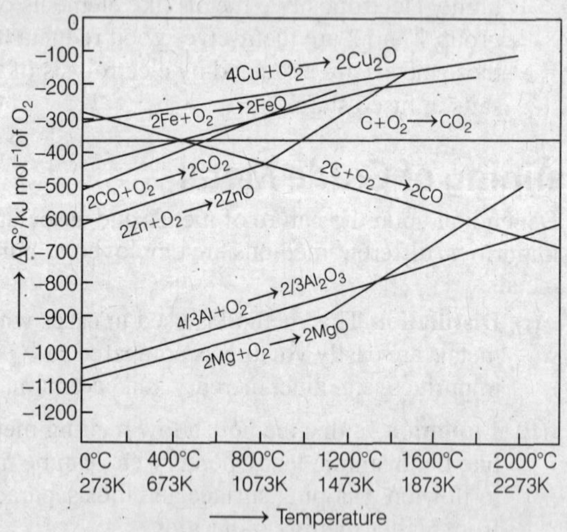

Characteristics of Ellingham Diagram

(*i*) All the slope are upwards since, ΔG° becomes more positive when temperature increases, i.e. stability of oxides decreases.

(*ii*) A metal will reduce the oxide of other metals which lie above it in Ellingham diagram, i.e. the metals for which the free energy of formation (ΔG_f°) of their oxides is more negative can reduce those metal oxides which has less negative ΔG_f°.

(*iii*) The decreasing order of the negative values of ΔG_f° of metal oxides is

Ca > Mg (below 1773 K) > Al > Ti > Cr > C > Fe > Ni > Hg > Ag

Thus, Al reduces FeO, CrO and NiO in thermite reduction but it will not reduce MgO at temperature below 1773 K.

Mg can reduce Al_2O_3 below 162 K but above 1023 K, Al can reduce MgO.

(*iv*) CO is more effective reducing agent below 1073 K and above 1073 K, coke is more effective reducing agent, e.g. CO reduces Fe_2O_3 below 1073 K but above it, coke reduces Fe_2O_3. Coke reduces ZnO above 1270 K.

Electrochemical Principles of Metallurgy

- In the reduction of a molten metal salt, electrolysis is done. Such methods are based on electrochemical principles which could be understood by the equation

$$\Delta G^\circ = -nE^\circ F$$

where, n = number of electrons and E° = electrode potential of redox couple formed in the system.

- If the difference of two E° values corresponds to positive E° and negative ΔG°, then less reactive metal will come out of solution and more reactive metal will go into solution.

Occurrence, Extraction and Uses of Some Metals

1. Aluminium (Al)

- **Occurrence** Bauxite ($Al_2O_3 \cdot xH_2O$), cryolite (Na_3AlF_6)
- **Common Method of Extraction** Electrolysis of Al_2O_3 dissolved in molten Na_3AlF_6 (neutral flux).
- During Hall-Heroult electrolysis process, purified Al_2O_3 is mixed with Na_3AlF_6 that lowers the melting point of mixture and brings conductivity.
- At anode the liberated oxygen react with carbon of anode producing CO and CO_2. The electrolytic reactions are as follows:

At cathode : $Al^{3+}(\text{Melt}) + 3e^- \longrightarrow Al(l)$

At anode : $C(s) + O^{2-}(\text{melt}) \longrightarrow CO(g) + 2e^-$

$C(s) + 2O^{2-}(\text{melt}) \longrightarrow CO_2(g) + 4e^-$

- **Uses** Making electric wires, silver paint, kitchen utensils, food packing, extraction of Mo, Cr etc.

2. Iron (Fe)

- **Occurrence** Haematite (Fe_2O_3), magnetite (Fe_3O_4)
- **Common Method of Extraction** Reduction of the oxide with CO and coke in blast furnace. The iron obtained from blast furnace contains about 4% carbon and many impurities in smaller amount (e.g. S, P, Si, Mn) and is known as **pig iron.**
- **Cast iron** is made by melting pig iron with scrap iron and coke using hot air blast. It has slightly lower carbon content (about 3%) and is extremely hard and brittle.
- **Wrought iron** or **malleable iron** is the purest form of commercial iron and is prepared from cast iron by oxidising impurities in a reverberatory furnace lined with haematite. This haematite oxidises carbon to carbon monoxide.

$$Fe_2O_3 + 3C \longrightarrow 2Fe + 3CO$$

Ore → Concentration of ore done by gravity separation and negative separator → **Concentrated ore** → Calcination (to remove moisture) decomposes carbonate ore to oxide → **Calcined ore**

- $Fe_2O_3 \cdot 3H_2O \xrightarrow{\Delta} Fe_2O_3 \cdot 2H_2O$
- $FeCO_3 \xrightarrow{\Delta} FeO + CO_2$

Calcined ore → Roasting with coal → **Roasted mass** → Smelting is done in blast furnace in presence of coke and lime stone

Cast iron 93-94% Fe (iron) with 3% carbon, 0.5% impurities P, Si, Mn etc → Puddling process [In reverberatory lined with haematite, cast iron is fused.] → **Wrought iron** is the purest form of iron

After pouring into shapes of moulds → Cast iron

Molten iron in the lowest zone is called pig iron [92-93% Fe, 3-4% carbon and Si, P, S etc impurities]

In reductive zone

$3Fe_2O_3 + CO \longrightarrow 2Fe_3O_4 + CO_2$

$Fe_3O_4 + CO \longrightarrow 3FeO + CO_2\uparrow$

$FeO + CO \longrightarrow FeCO_2$

$CaCO_3 \xrightarrow{\Delta} CO_2 + CaO$

In central zone

$FeO + CO \longrightarrow CO_2 + Fe$

$CaO + SiO_2 \longrightarrow \underset{\text{Slag}}{CaSiO_3}$

In fusion zone

$CO_2 + C \xrightarrow{\Delta} 2CO, \Delta H = +ve$

In combustion zone

$C + O_2 \xrightarrow{\Delta} CO_2, \Delta H = -ve$

- **Uses** Makin g wrought iron and different varieties of steel.

3. Copper (Cu)

- **Occurrence** Copper pyrites ($CuFeS_2$), Copper glance (Cu_2S)
- **Common Method of Extraction** Roasting of sulphide partially and reduction. $Cu_2S + FeS$ is called **matte**. Blister copper contains 96-98% copper with small amounts of Ag and Au as impurity.

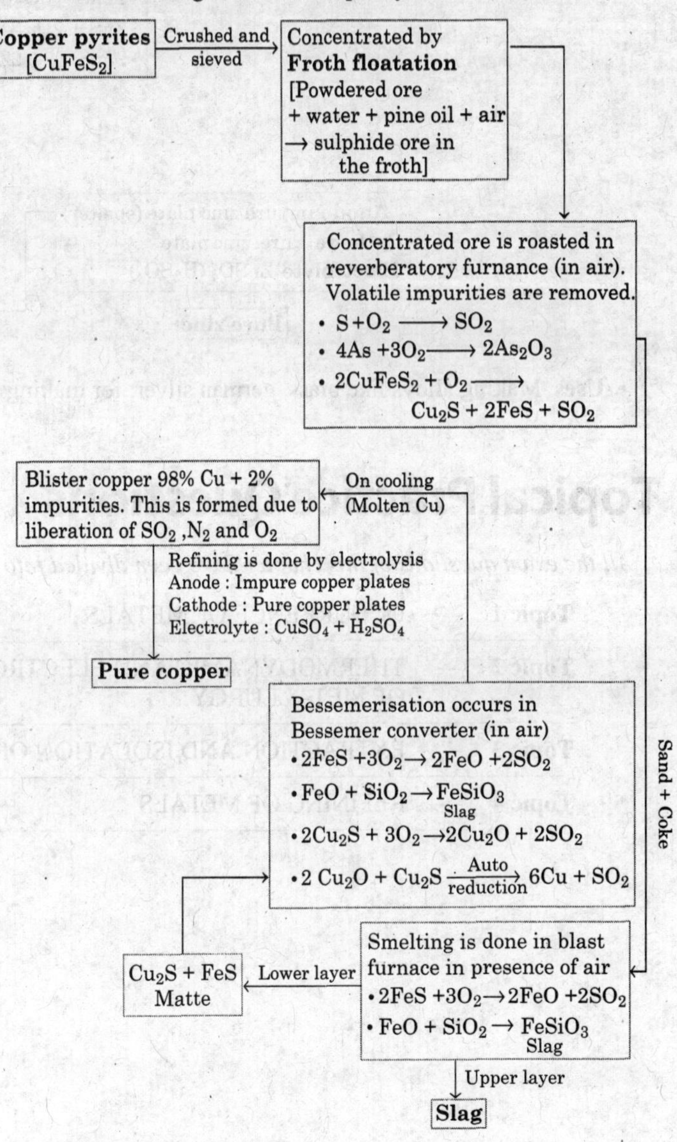

- **Uses** For the preparation of steam pipes, in making electrical wires, calorimeters, alloys like brass, bronze, etc.

4. Zinc (Zn)

- **Occurrence** Zinc blende or sphalerite (ZnS), calamine ($ZnCO_3$), zincite (ZnO).
- **Common method of extraction** Roasting followed by reduction with coke.

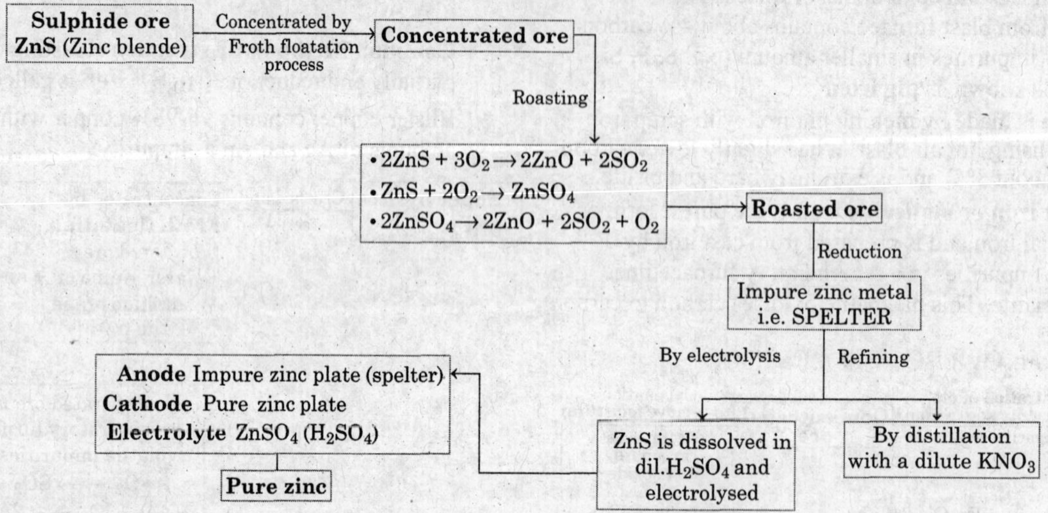

- **Uses** Making alloys like brass, german silver, for making dry cell, for galvanisation of iron, etc.

Topical Practice Questions

All the exam questions of this chapter have been divided into four topics as listed below:

Topic 1

Occurrence of Metals

2015

1 Identify the incorrect statement. [NEET (Odisha)]
(a) The scientific and technological process used for isolation of the metal from its ore known as metallurgy
(b) Minerals are naturally occurring chemical substance in the earth's crust.
(c) Ores are minerals that may contain a metal
(d) Gangue is an ore contaminated with undesired materials

2 Which one is malachite from the following? [NEET]
(a) $Cu(OH)_2$ (b) Fe_3O_4
(c) $CuCO_3 \cdot Cu(OH)_2$ (d) $CuFeS_2$

3 "Metals are usually not found as nitrates in their ores". Out of the following two (I and II) reasons which is/are true for the above observation?
I. Metal nitrates are highly unstable.
II. Metal nitrates are highly soluble in water. [CBSE AIPMT]
(a) I and II are true (b) I and II are false
(c) I is false but II is true (d) I is true but II is false

2013

4 The ore of aluminium is [UP CPMT]
(a) carnallite (b) malachite
(c) galena (d) bauxite

5 The formula of malachite ore is [Manipal]
(a) Fe_3O_4 (b) Mn_3O_4
(c) NiAs (d) $Cu(OH)_2 \cdot CuCO_3$

6 Azurite is an ore of [WB JEE]
(a) gold (b) silver
(c) copper (d) zinc

7 Brass is an alloy of [WB JEE]
(a) Al and Zn (b) Cu and Al
(c) Ni and Zn (d) Cu and Zn

2012

8 Which one of the following is a mineral of iron? [AIPMT]
(a) Malachite (b) Cassiterite
(c) Pyrolusite (d) Magnetite

9 Identify the ore not containing iron. [UP CPMT]
(a) Limonite (b) Siderite
(c) Carnallite (d) Chalcopyrite

10 Which of the following is an oxide ore? [OJEE]
(a) Malachite (b) Haematite
(c) Copper glance (d) Zinc blende

2011

11 Which one of the following does not occur as sulphide ore? [Kerala CEE]
(a) Zn (b) Cr
(c) Ag (d) Fe (e) Hg

2010

12 Which of the following metals has the largest abundance in the earth's crust? [WB JEE]
(a) Aluminium (b) Calcium
(c) Magnesium (d) Sodium

13 Which of the following is not an ore of magnesium? [RPMT]
(a) Gypsum (b) Dolomite
(c) Magnesite (d) Carnallite

14 Solder is an alloy of [CMC Ludhiana]
(a) Pb + Sn (b) Pb + Sn + Zn
(c) Pb + Zn (d) Sn + Zn

15 Calcium ammonium nitrate is known as [VMMC]
(a) Nangal fertiliser (b) Chile saltpetre
(c) Thomas slag (d) Sindri

2009

16 German silver is an alloy of [UP CPMT]
(a) Cu and Zn (b) Cu and Ag
(c) Cu and Sn (d) Cu, Zn and Ni

17 Willemite is [MHT CET]
(a) Zn_2SiO_4 (b) H_2PtCl_6
(c) ZnO (d) $ZnOFe_2O_3$

18 Cerussite is an ore of [Manipal]
(a) Na (b) Cu (c) Pb (d) Fe

19 The approximate percentage of iron in misch metal is [Kerala CEE]
(a) 10 (b) 20
(c) 50 (d) 95 (e) 5

20 Elektron is an alloy of [WB JEE]
(a) Mg and Zn (b) Fe and Mg
(c) Ni and Zn (d) Al and Zn

21 The composition of bell metal is [J&K CET]
(a) Cu (80%), Zn (20%)
(b) Cu (60%), Ni (40%)
(c) Cu (90%), Sn (10%)
(d) Cu (80%), Sn (20%)

22 The percentage of carbon in cast iron is [J&K CET]
(a) 5-10 (b) 0.250-2.5
(c) 2.5-4.5 (d) 0.12-0.2

23 Match the following Columns.

	Column I		Column II
A.	Feldspar	1.	Ag_3SbS_3
B.	Asbestos	2.	$Al_2O_3 \cdot H_2O$
C.	Pyrargyrite	3.	$MgSO_4 \cdot H_2O$
D.	Diaspore	4.	$KAlSi_3O_8$
		5.	$CaMg_3(SiO_3)_4$

Codes [EAMCET]

	A	B	C	D		A	B	C	D
(a)	4	5	2	1	(b)	4	5	1	2
(c)	4	1	3	2	(d)	2	5	4	1

2008

24 What are the metal ions present in carnallite ? [AFMC]
(a) Mg, K (b) Al, Na
(c) Na, Mg (d) Zn, Mg

25 Calamine is [MHT CET]
(a) $CaCO_3$ (b) $MgCO_3$
(c) $ZnCO_3$ (d) $CaCO_3 + CaO$

2007

26 Which of the following does not contain silicon? [MHT CET]
(a) Kaolin (b) Agate
(c) Ruby (d) Quartz

27 Argentite is a mineral of [AMU]
(a) Copper (b) Silver
(c) Platinum (d) Aluminium

28 Which of the following ore is not an ore of Al? [Guj CET]
(a) Mica (b) Anglesite
(c) Orthoclase (d) Beryl

2006

29 Cinnabar is [BHU]
(a) HgS (b) PbS
(c) SnO_2 (d) $PbCO_3$

30 Apatite is an ore of [MHT CET]
(a) fluorine (b) chlorine
(c) bromine (d) iodine

31 Which of the following ores is an ore of copper ? [J&K CET]
(a) Argentite (b) Haematite
(c) Malachite (d) Calamine

32 The chief impurity present in red bauxite is [AMU]
(a) SiO_2
(b) Fe_2O_3
(c) K_2SO_4
(d) NaF

2005

33 The most important ore of tin is [AFMC]
(a) cassiterite
(b) cryolite
(c) cerussite
(d) None of these

34 Formula for agate is [MHT CET]
(a) Na_2SiO_3
(b) $K_2O \cdot SiO_2 \cdot Al_2O_3$
(c) SiO_2
(d) CaF_2

35 Match the following columns. [Kerala CEE]

	Column I (Metal)		Column II (Ore)
A.	Aluminium	1.	Bauxite
B.	Copper	2.	Dolomite
C.	Potassium	3.	Pyrites
D.	Magnesium	4.	Pitchblende
E.	Radium	5.	Sylvine

Codes

	A	B	C	D	E		A	B	C	D	E
(a)	1	3	4	5	2	(b)	1	3	4	2	5
(c)	4	5	2	1	3	(d)	4	2	1	5	3
(e)	1	3	5	2	4						

36 Which of the following is the chief ore of copper ? [AMU]
(a) Cu_2S (b) Cu_2O
(c) $CuFeS_2$ (d) $CuCO_3 \cdot Cu(OH)_2$

37 Important ore of Mg is [BCECE]
(a) gypsum (b) carnallite (c) magnatite (d) carnolite

Answers

1 (d)	2 (c)	3 (c)	4 (d)	5 (d)	6 (c)	7 (d)	8 (d)	9 (c)	10 (b)
11 (b)	12 (a)	13 (a)	14 (a)	15 (a)	16 (d)	17 (a)	18 (c)	19 (e)	20 (a)
21 (d)	22 (c)	23 (b)	24 (a)	25 (c)	26 (c)	27 (b)	28 (b)	29 (a)	30 (a)
31 (c)	32 (b)	33 (a)	34 (c)	35 (e)	36 (c)	37 (b)			

Explanations

1 (*d*) The earthly impurities like sand, clay, mica, etc., associated with ores are called gangue or matrix. In other words, contaminated undesired materials present in an ore is called gangue. Thus, statement (d) is incorrect while other options contain correct statements.

2 (*c*) Malachite is an ore of copper and its composition is $CuCO_3 \cdot Cu(OH)_2$.
Azurite ($Cu(OH)_2$) and copper pyrites ($CuFeS_2$) are also the ores of copper (Cu).
Mgnetite (Fe_3O_4) is an ore of iron (Fe).
Hence, option (c) is correct.

3 (*c*) Metals are usually not found as nitrates in their ores, because metal nitrates are highly soluble in water. For example, KNO_3 (salt peter) would be classified as completely soluble. Thus, KNO_3 could be expected to dissociate completely in aqueous solution to give K^+ and NO_3^- ions.

$$KNO_3 \rightleftharpoons K^+(aq) + NO_3^-(aq)$$

The nitrate anion has three equivalent oxygen surrounding a central nitrogen atom. This tends to spread the single negative charge and make it easier for water (using hydrogen bonds) to separate the ions in solution.

4 (*d*) (a) Carnallite $KCl \cdot MgCl_2 \cdot 6H_2O$
(b) Malachite $CuCO_3 \cdot Cu(OH)_2$
(c) Galena PbS
(d) Bauxite $Al_2O_3 \cdot 2H_2O$
$\therefore$ Ore of aluminium is bauxite.

5 (*d*) Malachite is an ore of copper. The molecular formula of malachite ore is $Cu(OH)_2 \cdot CuCO_3$.

6 (*c*) The composition of an azurite is $Cu(OH)_2 \cdot 2CuCO_3$ hence, it is an ore of copper.

7 (*d*) Brass is an alloy of copper (60%) and zinc (40%). It is used for making utensils, condenser tubes, wires.

8 (*d*) Magnetite, Fe_3O_4 is a mineral of iron.

9 (*c*) Limonite : $Fe_2O_3 \cdot 3H_2O$-ore of iron

Siderite	$FeCO_3$-ore of iron
Carnallite	$KCl \cdot MgCl_2 \cdot 6H_2O$-ore of magnesium
Chalcopyrite	$CuFeS_2$-ore of copper

Hence, carnallite is not an iron containing ore.

10 (*b*)

Ore	Formula	Nature
(a) Malachite	$CuCO_3 \cdot Cu(OH)_2$	Carbonate ore
(b) Haematite	Fe_2O_3	Oxide ore
(c) Copper glance	Cu_2S	Sulphide ore
(d) Zinc blende	ZnS	Sulphide ore

11 (*b*) Chromium does not exist as sulphide ore.

12 (*a*) Aluminium is the most abundant metal and third most abundant element in earth's crust.

13 (*a*) Dolomite ($MgCO_3 \cdot CaCO_3$), magnesite ($MgCO_3$) and carnallite ($KCl \cdot MgCl_2 \cdot 6H_2O$) are ores of magnesium. Whereas gypsum ($CaSO_4 \cdot 2H_2O$) is an ore of calcium.

14 (*a*) Solder is an alloy of lead (Pb) with tin (Sn).

15 (*a*) Calcium ammonium nitrate (CAN), $Ca(NO_3)_2 \cdot NH_4NO_3$ is known as nitrolime stone or Nangal fertiliser.

16 (*d*) German silver, an alloy of copper, contains copper, zinc and nickel in the ratio of 2 : 1 : 1. It is used in utensils and resistance coils etc.

17 (*a*) Willemite, a rare zinc silicate mineral, is Zn_2SiO_4. It has trigonal symmetry and is strongly fluorescent under short wave ultraviolet light..

18 (*c*) Cerussite is an ore of lead (Pb). Its chemical formula is $PbCO_3$.

19 (*e*) Misch metal is a pyrophoric alloy which contains 95% lanthanide elements such as, Nd and Ce and 5% Fe.

20 (*a*) Electron is an alloy of Mg (95%), Zn (4 -5%) and Cu (0·5%). It is used in the construction of aircrafts.

21 (*d*) The composition of bell metal is Cu (80%) and Sn (20%).

22 (*c*) Cast iron has 2.5-4.5 per cent of carbon.

23 (*b*) Feldspar (orthosilicate) ($KAlSi_3O_8$)
It is used in the manufacture of porcelain.
Asbestos $[CaMg_3(SiO_3)_4]$
It is used for fireproof sheets, cloths etc.
Pyrargyrite (Ruby silver) ($Ag_3 \cdot SbS_3$)
It is an ore of silver.
Diaspore ($Al_2O_3 \cdot H_2O$)
It is an ore of aluminium.

24 (*a*) Formula of carnallite is $KCl \cdot MgCl_2 \cdot 6H_2O$, so carnallite contains K and Mg.

25 (*c*) Calamine ($ZnCO_3$) is the carbonate ore of zinc.

26 (*c*) Ruby is an mineral of aluminium, i.e. Al_2O_3.
It does not contain silicon.

27 (*b*) The chemical formula of argentite or silver glance is Ag_2S. Hence, argentite is a mineral of silver.

28 (*b*) Anglesite ($PbSO_4$) is not an ore of aluminium. It is an ore of lead.

29 (*a*) Cinnabar (HgS) is an ore of mercury.

30 (*a*) Apatite is $[CaF_2 \cdot 3Ca_3(PO_4)_2]$, i.e. it is an ore of fluorine with calcium.

31 (c) Argentite — Ag_2S
Haematite — Fe_2O_3
Malachite — $Cu(OH)_2 \cdot CuCO_3$
Calamine — $ZnCO_3$

32 (b) The main impurity found in red bauxite is that of ferrite (Fe_2O_3) while silica is the chief impurity in white bauxite.

33 (a) The chief ore of tin is cassiterite or tin stone, SnO_2.

34 (c) Quartz is found in many varieties which have different colour due to impurities, e.g. amethyst (purple), opal (white) carnelian (brownish red) and agate. Hence, agate is SiO_2.

35 (e)

Metal	Ore
A. Aluminium	1. Bauxite ($Al_2O_3 \cdot 2H_2O$)
B. Copper	3. Pyrites ($CuFeS_2$)
C. Potassium	5. Sylvine (KCl)
D. Magnesium	2. Dolomite ($MgCO_3 \cdot CaCO_3$)
E. Radium	4. Pitch blende

36 (c) Copper pyrite ($CuFeS_2$) is the chief ore of copper.

37 (b) Carnallite is $KCl \cdot MgCl_2 \cdot 6H_2O$. It is an ore of Mg.

Topic 2

Thermodynamic and Electrochemical Principle of Metallurgy

2018

1 Considering Ellingham diagram, which of the following metals can be used to reduce alumina? **[NEET]**
(a) Mg (b) Zn (c) Fe (d) Cu

2011

2 Carbon cannot reduce Fe_2O_3 to Fe at a temperature below 983 K because **[KCET]**
(a) free energy change for the formation of CO is more negative than that of Fe_2O_3
(b) CO is thermodynamically more stable than Fe_2O_3
(c) carbon has higher affinity towards oxygen than iron
(d) iron has higher affinity towards oxygen than carbon

2010

3 Carbon can reduce ferric oxide to iron at a temperature above 983 K because **[KCET]**
(a) carbon monoxide formed is thermodynamically less stable than ferric oxide
(b) carbon has a higher affinity towards oxygen than iron
(c) free energy change for the formation of carbon dioxide is less negative than that for ferric oxide
(d) iron has a higher affinity towards oxygen than carbon

2009

4 The minimum voltage required to electrolyse alumina in the Hall-Heroult process is
(Given, $\Delta G_f^\circ(Al_2O_3) = -1520$ kJ mol^{-1};
$\Delta G_f^\circ(CO_2) = -394$ kJ mol^{-1}) **[AIIMS]**
(a) 1.575 V (b) 1.60 V
(c) 1.312 V (d) – 2.62 V

5 In aluminium extraction by the Baeyer's process, alumina is extracted from bauxite by sodium hydroxide at high temperature and pressures.

$$Al_2O_3(s) + 2OH^-(aq) \longrightarrow 2Al_2O_2^-(aq) + H_2O(l)$$

Solid impurities such as Fe_2O_3 and SiO_2 are removed and then $Al(OH)_4^-$ is reprecipitated.

$$2Al(OH)_4^- \longrightarrow Al_2O_3 \cdot 3H_2O(s) + 2OH^-(aq)$$

In the industrial world **[WB JEE]**
(a) carbon dioxide is added to precipitate the alumina
(b) temperature and pressure are dropped and the supersaturated solution seeded
(c) Both (a) and (b) are practised
(d) the water is evaporated

6 The temperature of the slag zone in the metallurgy of iron using blast furnace is **[KCET]**
(a) 1500-1600°C (b) 400-700°C
(c) 800-1000°C (d) 1200-1500°C

2006

7 Consider the following reaction at 1000°C

(A) $Zn(s) + \frac{1}{2}O_2(g) \longrightarrow ZnO(s)$; $\Delta G^\circ = -360$ kJ mol^{-1}

(B) $C\text{ (graphite)} + \frac{1}{2}O_2(g) \longrightarrow CO(g)$; $\Delta G^\circ = -460$ kJ mol^{-1}

Choose the correct statement at 1000°C. **[Kerala CEE]**
(a) Zinc can be oxidised by carbon monoxide.
(b) Zinc oxide can be reduced by graphite.
(c) Both statements (a) and (b) are true.
(d) Both statements (a) and (b) are false.
(e) Carbon monoxide can be reduced by zinc.

8 Which of the following taking place in the blast furnace is endothermic ? **[KCET]**

(a) $CaCO_3 \longrightarrow CaO + CO_2$

(b) $2C + O_2 \longrightarrow 2CO$

(c) $C + O_2 \longrightarrow CO_2$

(d) $Fe_2O_3 + 3CO \longrightarrow 2Fe + 3CO_2 3$

2005

9 Assertion (A) Extraction of iron metal from iron oxide ore is carried out by heating with coke.

Reason (R) The reaction,

$$Fe_2O_3(s) \longrightarrow Fe(s) + \frac{3}{2}O_2(g)$$

is a spontaneous process. **[AIIMS]**

(a) Both A and R are correct and R is the correct explanation of A

(b) Both A and R are correct but R is not the correct explanation of A

(c) A is correct but R is incorrect

(d) Both A and R are incorrect

Answers

1 (a)	2 (d)	3 (b)	4 (b)	5 (c)	6 (c)	7 (b)	8 (a)	9 (c)

Explanations

1 (*a*) Ellingham diagrams help us in predicting the feasibility of thermal reduction of an ore. The criterion of feasibility is that at a given temperature, Gibbs energy of the reaction must be negative.

Gibbs energy ΔG° *vs* T plots (schematic) for formation of some oxides (Ellingham diagram) is given below :

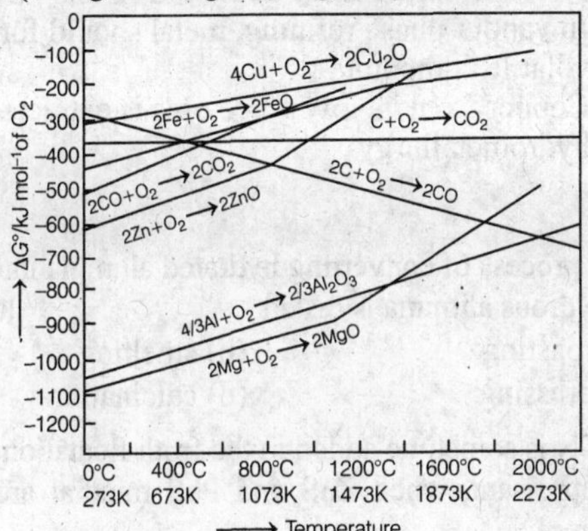

Gibbs energy ΔG° *vs* T plots (schematic) for formation of some oxides (Ellingham diagram).

According to Ellingham diagram, the temperature at which two lines intersect shows that the metal will reduce the oxide of other metals which lie above it in Ellingham diagram.

In other words, the metal oxide having more negative value of ΔG_f° can reduce the oxide having less negative ΔG_f°. As, Mg has more $-\Delta G^\circ$ value than alumina, so it will be in lower part of Ellingham diagram. Hence, Mg will be used to reduce alumina.

2 (*d*) Iron has higher affinity towards oxygen than carbon. So, it cannot reduce Fe_2O_3 to Fe at a temperature below 983 K.

3 (*b*) Above 983 K, free energy change for the formation of CO_2 is more negative than that for ferric oxide. Thus, above this temperature, carbon has a higher affinity towards oxygen than iron.

4 (*b*) In Hall-Heroult process, the following reactions occur

$$3C + 2Al_2O_3 \longrightarrow 4Al + 3CO_2$$

$$4Al^{3+} + 12e^- \longrightarrow 4Al$$

$$\therefore \Delta G^\circ = 3\Delta G_f^\circ(CO_2) - 2\Delta G_f^\circ(Al_2O_3)$$

$$= 3(-394) - 2(-1520) = 1858 \text{ kJ}$$

$$\Delta G^\circ = -nFE^\circ_{cell}$$

$$-E^\circ_{cell} = \frac{1858 \times 1000}{12 \times 96500} = 1.60 \text{ V}$$

5 (*c*) Both (a) and (b) are practised.

6 (*c*) Slag formation zone is the central zone in the blast furnace where the temperature varies from 800 – 1000°C. Here, limestone decomposes into CaO and CO_2.

$$CaCO_3 \xrightarrow{1000^\circ C} CaO + CO_2$$

7 (*b*) At 1000°C zinc oxide can be reduced by graphite.

$$ZnO + C \longrightarrow Zn + CO$$

8 (*a*) Bond breaking processes or decomposition processes are endothermic process. Thus, decomposition of $CaCO_3$ is an endothermic process.

9 (*c*) Iron is obtained from Fe_2O_3 by heating Fe with a mixture of coke and $CaCO_3$ in a blast furnace in which CO formed reduce Fe_2O_3 to Fe.

$$Fe_2O_3 + CO \longrightarrow Fe + CO_2$$

$$Fe_2O_3(s) \longrightarrow Fe(s) + \frac{3}{2}O_2(g)$$

Topic 3

Extraction and Isolation of Metals

2019

1 Which of the following has maximum iron content ? **[AIIMS]**

(a) Cast iron (b) Wrought iron
(c) Pig iron (d) Stainless steel

2018

2 In the extraction of copper from its sulphide ore, the metal is formed by the reduction of Cu_2O with **[JIPMER]**

(a) FeS (b) CO (c) Cu_2S (d) SO_2

3 Lead is extracted from galena (PbS), either by following ways. **[JIPMER]**

(i) $PbS \xrightarrow[-SO_2]{\text{Roasted in air}} PbO \xrightarrow[-CO_2]{\text{Heated with C}} Pb$

(ii) $PbS \xrightarrow[-SO_2]{\text{Roasted in air}} PbO \xrightarrow{\text{Heated with PbS}} Pb + SO_2$

Auto-reduction process is **[JIPMER]**

(a) I (b) II
(c) Both (a) and (b) (d) None of these

2017

4 In cyanide extraction process of silver from argentite ore, the oxidising and reducing agents are respectively. **[JIPMER]**

(a) O_2 and CO_2 (b) O_2 and Zn dust
(c) HNO_3 and Zn dust (d) HNO_3 and CO

5 Flux is used to **[JIPMER]**

(a) remove all type of impurities
(b) reduce metal oxide
(c) remove carbonate and sulphate
(d) remove silica and undesirable metal oxides

6 Extraction of gold and silver involves leaching with CN^- ion. Silver is later recovered by **[NEET]**

(a) liquation
(b) distillation
(c) zone-refining
(d) displacement with Zn

2016

7 Match items of Column I with the items of Column II and assign the correct code. **[NEET]**

Column I	Column II
A. Cyanide process	1. Ultrapure Ge
B. Froth floatation process	2. Dressing of ZnS
C. Electrolytic reduction	3. Extraction of Al
D. Zone refining	4. Extraction of Au
	5. Purification of Ni

Codes

	A	B	C	D
(a)	2	3	1	5
(b)	1	2	3	4
(c)	3	4	5	1
(d)	4	2	3	1

2014

8 Sphalerite is concentrated by **[Kerala CEE]**

(a) gravity separation (b) froth floatation
(c) magnetic separation (d) hydraulic washing
(e) leaching

9 Which one of the following methods is used in the concentration of sulphide ore? **[EAMCET]**

(a) Froth floatation (b) Smelting
(c) Roasting (d) Leaching

10 Which of the following statement is incorrect? **[KCET]**

(a) A furnace lined with haematite is used to convert cast iron to wrought iron
(b) Collectors enhance the wettability of mineral particles during froth floatation
(c) In vapour phase refining, metal should form a volatile compound
(d) Copper from its low grade ores is extracted by hydrometallurgy

2013

11 The process of converting hydrated alumina into anhydrous alumina is called **[CBSE AIPMT]**

(a) roasting (b) smelting
(c) dressing (d) calcination

12 NaCN is sometime added in the froth floatation process as a depressant, when ZnS and PbS mineral are extracted because **[AIIMS]**

(a) ZnS forms soluble complex $Na_2[Zn(CN)_4]$ while PbS forms froth
(b) $Pb(CN)_2$ is precipitated while no effect on ZnS
(c) PbS forms soluble complex $Na_2[Pb(CN)_4]$ while ZnS forms froth
(d) NaCN is never added in froth floatation process

13 Auto reduction process is used in the extraction of **[AFMC]**

(a) Cu and Hg (b) Zn and Hg
(c) Cu and Al (d) Fe and Pb

2011

14 Which of the following elements is present as the impurity to the maximum extent in the pig iron? **[CBSE AIPMT]**

(a) Phosphorus (b) Manganese
(c) Carbon (d) Silicon

15 Which one of the following statements is false? [KCET]
(a) During roasting, moisture is removed from the ore
(b) The ore is freed from almost all non-metallic impurities
(c) Calcination of ore is carried out in the absence of any blast of air
(d) The concentrated zinc blende is subjected to calcination during its extraction by pyrometallurgy

2010

16 In the equation; $4M + 8CN^- + 2H_2O + O_2 \longrightarrow 4[M(CN)_2]^- + 4OH^-$, identify the metal M. [AFMC]
(a) Copper (b) Iron
(c) Gold (d) Zinc

17 These are the extraction processes of silver except [Manipal]
(a) as a side product in electrolytic refining of copper
(b) Parke's process in which Zn is used to extract silver by solvent extraction from molten lead
(c) by reaction of silver sulphide with KCN and then reaction of soluble complex with Zn
(d) by heating $Na[Ag(CN)_2]$

18 When AgCl is treated with KCN, [WB JEE]
(a) Ag is precipitated
(b) a complex ion is formed
(c) double decompostion takes place
(d) no reaction takes place

19 Impurities present in the ore react to form a fusible substance known as [OJEE]
(a) flux (b) slag
(c) nugget (d) mineral

20 During smelting an additional substance is added which combines with impurities to form a fusible product which is known as [RPMT]
(a) mud (b) slag (c) flux (d) gangue

2009

21 Mark the wrong statement.
(a) K boils at the melting point of KCl
(b) K is insoluble in molten KCl
(c) K is extracted by the elecrolysis of fused KOH
(d) K is extracted by the reduction of molten KCl by metallic Na

22 Gravity separation process is used for the concentration of
(a) calamine (b) haematite [AFMC]
(c) chalcopyrite (d) bauxite

23 Hydro-metallurgical process of extraction of metals is based on [OJEE]
(a) complex formation (b) hydrolysis
(c) dehydration (d) dehydrogenation

24 Which one of the following ores is concentrated by chemical leaching method? [Kerala CEE]
(a) Galena (b) Copper pyrite
(c) Cinnabar (d) Argentite
(e) Copper glance

25 The slag formed in the extraction of copper is [CG PMT, Haryana PMT]
(a) $CuFeS_2$ (b) $Cu_2O + FeS$
(c) $Cu_2S + FeO$ (d) $FeSiO_3$

26 Which of the following statement is incorrect?
(a) Hydrogen is used to reduce NiO [J&K CET]
(b) Zirconium is refined by van-Arkel method
(c) The sulphide ore galena is concentrated by froth floatation
(d) In the metallurgy of iron, the flux used is SiO_2

27 The ore that is concentrated by froth floatation process is
(a) cinnabar (b) bauxite [KCET]
(c) malachite (d) zincite

28 The auto-reduction process is not used in the metallurgy of
(a) Hg (b) Cu [KCET]
(c) Fe (d) Pb

2008

29 $(Ag + Pb) \text{ alloy} \xrightarrow[\text{zinc is added}]{\text{Melt and}} (Ag + Pb + Zn) \text{ melt} \xrightarrow{\text{Cool}} \begin{matrix}\text{Layer } X \\ \text{Layer } Y\end{matrix}$

Select the correct statement based on the above reaction.
(a) Layer X contains Zn and Ag. [AIIMS]
(b) Layer Y contains Pb and Ag but amount of silver in this layer is smaller than in layer X.
(c) X and Y are immiscible layer.
(d) All the above statements are correct.

30 Steel is heated to below red heat and then, cooled slowly. The process refers to [UP CPMT, MP PMT, RPMT]
(a) hardening
(b) annealing
(c) tempering
(d) nitriding

31 Impurities of Cu and Ag from gold are removed by
(a) boiling impure gold with dil. H_2SO_4 [Manipal]
(b) boiling impure gold with conc. H_2SO_4
(c) electrolytically
(d) Both (b) and (c)

32 Silica is a/an [Manipal]
(a) acidic flux only
(b) gangue only
(c) basic flux only
(d) Both gangue and acidic flux

33 Roasted tin stone ore after washing with water is known as
(a) block tin (b) white tin [Manipal]
(c) black tin (d) granulated tin

34 The metallurgical process in which a metal is obtained in a fused state is called [J&K CET]
(a) smelting
(b) roasting
(c) calcination
(d) froth floatation

35 Which one of the following metals is extracted by a carbon reduction process? [J&K CET]
(a) Copper (b) Iron
(c) Aluminium (d) Magnesium

2007

36 Sulphide ores of metals are usually concentrated by froth floatation process. Which one of the following sulphide ores offers an exception and is concentrated by chemical leaching? [CBSE AIPMT]
(a) Argentite (b) Galena
(c) Copper pyrite (d) Sphalerite

37 Reagent used to extract silver from Ag_2S is [RPMT]
(a) NaCN
(b) NaCN in the presence of O_2
(c) NaCl
(d) $AgNO_3$

38 In Hall's process, the main reagent is mixed with [AMU]
(a) NaF (b) Na_3AlF_6
(c) AlF_3 (d) None of these

39 In aluminothermite process 'Al' acts as a/an [BHU]
(a) flux
(b) oxidising agent
(c) reducing agent
(d) solder

2006

40 Copper pyrites ore is concentrated by [MP PMT]
(a) electromagnetic method (b) gravity method
(c) froth floatation process (d) All of these

2005

41 Heating of ore in the presence of air to remove sulphur impurities is called [AFMC]
(a) calcination (b) roasting
(c) smelting (d) None of these

42 In Mac-Arthur Forrest method, silver is extracted from the solution of $Na[Ag(CN)_2]$ by the use of [MP PMT]
(a) Fe (b) Mg (c) Cu (d) Zn

43 Slag is represented by [Punjab PMET]
(a) $CaSiO_3$ (b) SiO_3 (c) $Ca(OH)_2$ (d) CaO

44 In blast furnace, iron oxide is reduced by [KCET]
(a) hot blast of air (b) carbon monoxide
(c) carbon (d) silica

45 Railway wagon axles are made by heating iron rods embedded in charcoal powder. This process is known as [AMU]
(a) tempering (b) annealing
(c) sherardsing (d) case hardening

Answers

1 (b)	2 (c)	3 (b)	4 (b)	5 (d)	6 (d)	7 (d)	8 (b)	9 (a)	10 (b)
11 (d)	12 (a)	13 (a)	14 (c)	15 (d)	16 (c)	17 (d)	18 (b)	19 (b)	20 (b)
21 (b)	22 (b)	23 (a)	24 (d)	25 (d)	26 (d)	27 (a)	28 (c)	29 (d)	30 (b)
31 (d)	32 (d)	33 (c)	34 (a)	35 (b)	36 (d)	37 (b)	38 (b)	39 (c)	40 (c)
41 (b)	42 (d)	43 (a)	44 (b)	45 (d)					

Explanations

1 (*b*) The percentage of other elements in iron are as follows:
(a) Cast iron = about 2.1%
(b) Wrought iron = about 0.08%
(c) Pig iron = about 4%
(d) Stainless steel = about 1.7%

On the basis of above information wrought iron has maximum iron content.

Hence, option (b) is the correct.

2 (*c*) In the extraction of copper from its sulphide ore, the metal is formed by the reduction of Cu_2O with Cu_2S. This reaction completes with the process of auto-reduction. Chemical reaction occuring in this reaction is as follows

$$2Cu_2S + 3O_2 \longrightarrow 2Cu_2O + 2SO_2 \uparrow$$

$$Cu_2O + \frac{1}{2}Cu_2S \longrightarrow 3Cu + \frac{1}{2}SO_2$$

The molten copper is allowed to cool. During cooling, dissolved SO_2 comes out in the form of blisters, so it is called blister copper.

3 (*b*) In auto-reduction, no external reducing agent is required. In such reduction reaction, the product formed acts as a reducing agent and reduces the oxide to metal. Thus, only reaction II is called auto-reduction.

$$2\,PbS + 3O_2 \xrightarrow{\text{Roasted in air}} 2PbO + 2SO_2$$

$$2\,PbO + PbS \longrightarrow 3Pb + SO_2$$

(Act as a reducing agent)

4 (*b*) The extraction of silver involves cyanide process

(*i*) $Ag_2S + 2CN^- + O_2 \longrightarrow 2[Ag(CN)_2]^- + SO_2$

(*ii*) $2[Ag(CN)_2]^- + Zn \longrightarrow [Zn(CN)_4]^{2-} + 2Ag$

Thus, in (i) O_2-act as oxidising agent (oxidise sulphide to SO_2) and in (ii) Zn act as reducing agent (reduce Ag^+ to Ag).

5 (*d*) Flux removes silica and undesirable metal oxides such as silicates, etc.

6 (*d*) Extraction of gold and silver involves leaching with CN^- ion. Silver is later recovered by displacement with Zn.

In the metallurgy of silver or gold, the respective metal is leached with a dilute solution of NaCN or KCN in the presence of air to obtain the metal in solution as complex. From the complex, metal is obtained later by replacement.

In general,

$$4M(s)+8CN^-(aq)+2H_2O(aq)+O_2(g) \longrightarrow 4[M(CN)_2]^-(aq)+4OH^-(aq)$$

$$2[M(CN)_2]^-(aq)+Zn(s) \longrightarrow [Zn(CN)_4]^{2-}(aq)+2M(s)$$

M = Ag or Au

This method is known as Mac-Arthur Forest cyanide process.

7 (*d*) A – 4, B – 2, C – 3, D – 1

- **Cyanide process** It is a metallurgical technique for extracting Au (gold) from low grade ore by converting the Au to a water-soluble coordination complex.
- **Froth floatation process** This process is used for dressing of sulphide ore, i.e. ZnS.
- **Electrolytic reduction** This process is used for extraction of Al which is carried out in a steel tank lined inside with graphite. Here, graphite serves as cathode. The electrolyte consists of alumina dissolved in fused cryolite (Na_3AlF_6) and fluorspar (CaF_2).
- **Zone refining** This process is used for ultra pure Ge element. An ingot of Ge is first purified by zone refining. Then a small amount of antimony is placed in the molten zone which is passed through the pure Ge with the proper choice of rate of heating and other variables.

8 (*b*) Sphalerite also known as blende or zinc blende is a major ore of zinc (ZnS). It is sulphide ore. Hence, can be concentrated by froth floatation.

9 (*a*) Froth floatation process is widely used for the concentration of sulphide ore. This method is based upon the fact that the surface of sulphide ores is preferentially wetted by oil while that of gangue is preferentially wetted by water.

10 (*b*) In froth floatation method, the substances like pine oil, xanthates and fatty acids are added as collectors. These substances attach themselves by polar groups to drain the minerals which then become water repellant and thus pass into the froth. Thus, in other words, collectors enhance the non wettability of mineral acids.

11 (*d*) Calcination is a process in which ore is heated in the absence of air to expel water from a hydrated oxide or carbon dioxide from a carbonate.

12 (*a*) In froth floatation process, depressant prevents the formation of froth. It is used to separate two sulphide ores by preventing the formation of froth of one sulphide ore with air bubbles and allowing the other to form the froth, e.g. NaCN is used as a depressant to separate lead sulphide (PbS) ore from zinc sulphide (ZnS) ore. This is due to the reason that NaCN forms a zinc complex, $Na_2[Zn(CN)_4]$ on the surface of ZnS thereby preventing it from the formation of froth. Under these conditions only PbS forms a froth and hence can be separated from ZnS.

13 (*a*) Auto reduction process is used in the extraction of Cu and Hg.

$$2Cu_2S+3O_2 \longrightarrow 2Cu_2O+2SO_2$$

$$2Cu_2O+Cu_2S \longrightarrow 6Cu+SO_2$$

$$2HgS+3O_2 \longrightarrow 2HgO+3SO_2$$

$$2HgO \xrightarrow{\Delta} 2Hg+O_2$$

14 (*c*) Carbon is present as an impurity in the pig iron (4%). Many other impurities such as S, P, Si and Mn are present in smaller amount.

15 (*d*) Zinc blende is heated in a regular supply of air in a furnace at a temperature below the melting point of the metal (roasting).

$$2ZnS+3O_2 \longrightarrow 2ZnO+2SO_2$$

16 (*c*) Least reactive metals like silver (Ag) and gold (Au) are obtained by cyanide process. In this process, the impure metal is treated with NaCN (solution) and air is passed. Metal is converted into soluble complex as

$$4Au+8CN^-+2H_2O+O_2 \longrightarrow \underset{\text{Soluble}}{4[Au(CN)_2]^-}+4OH^-$$

From this soluble complex, metal is displaced by using more electropositive metal like Zn.

$$2[Au(CN)_2]^-+Zn \longrightarrow \underset{\text{Soluble}}{[Zn(CN)_4]^{2-}}+\underset{\text{ppt}}{2Au\downarrow}$$

17 (*d*) Silver is not obtained by heating $Na[Ag(CN)_2]$. It is obtained by treating $Na[Ag(CN)_2]$ with more electropositive metal Zn, which replaces Ag from it.

$$2Na[Ag(CN)_2]+Zn \longrightarrow Na_2[Zn(CN)_4]+2Ag\downarrow$$

18 (*b*) $AgCl+2KCN \longrightarrow K[Ag(CN)_2]+KCl$

19 (*b*) Flux + Gangue $\longrightarrow$ Slag

20 (*b*) During smelting an additional substance is added which combines with impurities to form an easily fusible product which is known as slag.

$$\underset{\text{(present in the ore)}}{\text{Impurities}}+\text{flux} \longrightarrow \underset{\text{(slag)}}{\text{fusible product}}$$

21 (*b*) Potassium is highly soluble in molten KCl, thus it is not prepared by the electrolysis of molten KCl. All other given statements are correct.

22 (*b*) Gravity separation method is used when there is large difference between the densities of gangue and the ore particles.

Hence, heavy oxide ores like haematite is concentrated by this process.

23 (*a*) Hydrometallurgical process of extraction of metals is based on complex formation. For example, Ag_2S is converted into $Na[Ag(CN)_2]$. When Zn is added, Ag is displaced.

24 (*d*) Gold and silver ores are concentrated by leaching. In this method, the ore is treated with a suitable reagent in which ore is soluble but impurities do not. Thus, impurities are removed by filtration.

Among galena (PbS), copper pyrites ($CuFeS_2$), cinnabar (HgS), argentite (Ag_2S) and copper glance (Cu_2S), argentite being silver ore is concentrated by chemical leaching method as

$$\underset{\text{Argentite}}{Ag_2S}+4NaCN \longrightarrow \underset{\text{Soluble}}{2Na[Ag(CN)_2]}+\underset{\text{Insoluble}}{Na_2S}$$

25 (*d*) In the extraction of copper, the impurities of iron oxide combine with silica (flux) and form insoluble slag.

$$FeO+SiO_2 \longrightarrow \underset{\text{Slag}}{FeSiO_3}$$

26 (*d*) In the metallurgy of iron, CaO acts as a flux as it combines with silica present as an impurity (gangue) to form a fusible slag, $CaSiO_3$.

27 (*a*) Froth floatation is used for the concentration of sulphide ores only. Thus, cinnabar, i.e. HgS is concentrated by this method. Bauxite ($Al_2O_3 \cdot 2H_2O$), malachite ($CuCO_3 \cdot Cu(OH)_2$) and zincite ($ZnCO_3$) cannot be concentrated by this method.

28 (*c*) The auto-reduction process is used for less electropositive metals.

$$2HgS + 3O_2 \longrightarrow 2HgO + 2SO_2$$
$$2HgO + HgS \longrightarrow 3Hg + SO_2$$
$$2Cu_2S + 3O_2 \longrightarrow 2Cu_2O + 2SO_2$$
$$Cu_2S + 2Cu_2O \longrightarrow 6Cu + SO_2$$
$$2PbS + 3O_2 \longrightarrow 2PbO + 2SO_2$$
$$2PbO + PbS \longrightarrow 3Pb + SO_2$$

Hence, this process is not used in the extraction of Fe.

29 (*d*) Zn and Pb in molten state are immiscible and form separate layers. Zinc being lighter forms upper layer. Ag is soluble in both. Hence, all statements are correct.

30 (*b*) The process of heating the steel to a temperature much below to redness and cooling it slowly, is called annealing.

31 (*d*) Impurities of Cu and Ag from gold are removed by boiling impure gold with conc. H_2SO_4 and also by electrolytic method.

32 (*d*) When SiO_2 (silica) is present as earthly impurity in an ore, it is called gangue and when it is added to remove basic impurities like CaO, FeO, etc; it is called an acidic flux.

33 (*c*) Tin stone (SnO_2) after roasting and washing is called black tin.

34 (*a*) The process in which metal is obtained in fused state is called smelting. During roasting and calcination metal oxides are formed while froth floatation process is used to concentrate the ore.

35 (*b*) The less electropositive metals such as Fe, Zn, Sn, etc. are extracted from their oxides by reduction with carbon or coal.

$$Fe_2O_3 + 3C \longrightarrow 2Fe + 3CO$$
$$Fe_2O_3 + 3CO \longrightarrow \underset{\text{iron}}{2Fe} + 3CO_2$$

36 (*d*) Galena (PbS), copper pyrite ($CuFeS_2$) and argentite (Ag_2S) are concentrated by froth floatation process but sphalerite (ZnS) is concentrated by chemical leaching.

37 (*b*) The reaction is based on the fact that silver and its compounds form soluble complex with NaCN. This reaction is reversible and accumulation of Na_2S must be prevented. A free excess of air (O_2) is continuously passed through the solution which oxidises Na_2S to $Na_2S_2O_3$.

$$Ag_2S + 4NaCN \rightleftharpoons 2Na[Ag(CN)_2] + Na_2S$$
$$2Na_2S + 2O_2 + H_2O \longrightarrow Na_2S_2O_3 + 2NaOH$$

Silver is recovered from solution by precipitating with zinc.

$$2Na[Ag(CN)_2] + 4NaOH + Zn \longrightarrow Na_2ZnO_2 + 4NaCN + 2H_2O + 2Ag$$

38 (*b*) Pure alumina is a bad conductor of electricity and the fusion temperature of pure alumina is about 2000°C.

At this temperature, when the electrolysis is carried of fused mass, the metal formed vaporises as the boiling point of Al is 1800°C. To overcome this difficulty, Na_3AlF_6 and CaF_2 are mixed with alumina.

Hence, Na_3AlF_6 and CaF_2 are the main reagent which are mixed with aluminium in Hall's process.

39 (*c*) In aluminothermite process, aluminium acts as a reducing agent.

In thermite process, mixture of 3 parts (by weight) Fe_2O_3 and 1 part (by weight) aluminium powder is used.

$$2Al + FeO_3 \longrightarrow Al_2O_3 + Fe$$
$$Al \longrightarrow Al^3 + 3e^- \text{ (oxidation)}$$

Therefore, aluminium metal act as reducing agent.

40 (*c*) Sulphide ores are concentrated by froth floatation method. Thus, copper pyrites ($CuFeS_2$) is concentrated by froth floatation process.

41 (*b*) Roasting is the process of heating the ore in excess supply of air below its melting point. This process is employed when oxidation of ore is required. During roasting moisture is drawn away.

This process in mainly employed for sulphide ore.

42 (*d*) In Mac-Arthur Forrest method silver is extracted from the solution of sodium argentocyanide by using zinc.

$$2Na[Ag(CN)_2] + Zn \longrightarrow Na_2[Zn(CN)_4] + 2Ag\downarrow$$

43 (*a*) Slag is the product of the reaction between flux and infusible impurities and it floats on the surface of the metal.

$$\underset{\text{Gangue}}{SiO_2} + \underset{\text{Flux}}{CaO} \longrightarrow \underset{\text{Slag}}{CaSiO_3}$$

44 (*b*) In the blast furnace iron oxide is reduced as :

$$3Fe_2O_3 + CO \xrightarrow{300\text{–}400°C} 2Fe_3O_4 + CO_2$$
$$Fe_3O_4 + CO \xrightarrow{500\text{–}600°C} 3FeO + CO_2$$
$$FeO + CO \xrightarrow{700°C} Fe + CO_2$$

45 (*d*) In case hardening technique, iron rods embedded in charcoal powder are heated repeatedly and thus, this technique is used in making axles of railway wagon.

Topic 4

Refining of Metals

2014

1 Which among the following metals is refined by electrolytic method ? **[MHT CET]**

(a) Aluminium (b) Bismuth
(c) Tin (d) Lead

2 The following set of reactions are used in refining zirconium.

$$Zr\,(impure) + 2I_2 \xrightarrow{523\,K} ZrI_4 \xrightarrow{1800\,K} Zr\,(pure) + 2I_2$$

This method is known as **[Kerala CEE]**

(a) distillation (b) liquation
(c) Hall-Heroult method (d) van-Arkel method
(e) Mond's process

2013

3 Which of the following pairs of metals is purified by van Arkel method? **[CBSE AIPMT]**

(a) Ni and Fe (b) Ga and In
(c) Zr and Ti (d) Ag and Au

2010

4 In which process, fused sodium hydroxide is electrolysed for the extraction of sodium? **[AFMC]**

(a) Castner's process
(b) Cyanide process
(c) Down's process
(d) Both (b) and (c)

5 In the electrolytic refining of zinc **[KCET]**

(a) graphite is at the anode
(b) the impure metal is at the cathode
(c) the metal ion gets reduced at the anode
(d) acidified zinc sulphate is the electrolyte

6 In zone refining method, the molten zone **[AIIMS]**

(a) contains impurities
(b) contains purified metal only
(c) contains more impurity than the original metal
(d) moves to either side

2009

7 Which of the following is the purest commercial form of iron ? **[UP CPMT]**

(a) Cast iron (b) Steel
(c) Wrought iron (d) Pig iron

2008

8 The purest zinc is made by **[MHT CET]**

(a) electrolytic refining (b) zone refining
(c) van-Arkel method (d) Mond's process

9 One of the following metals form a volatile compound and this property is taken advantage for its extraction. This metal is **[Manipal]**

(a) iron (b) nickel (c) cobalt (d) tungsten

10 Which of the following metal is not manufactured by electrolysis? **[Kerala CEE]**

(a) Na (b) Mg (c) Al (d) Fe
(e) Li

11 The method not used in metallurgy to refine the impure metal is **[Kerala CEE]**

(a) Mond's process (b) van-Arkel process
(c) amalgamation process (d) liquation
(e) zone-refining

12 Metallic silver may be obtained from AgCl by **[J&K CET]**

(a) heating it in the current by H_2
(b) fusing it with sand
(c) treating with carbon monoxide
(d) fusing it with Na_2CO_3

2007

13 Blister copper is **[CPMT]**

(a) impure Cu (b) Cu alloy
(c) pure Cu (d) Cu having 1% impurity

2006

14 Which of the following metal can be obtained by the electrolysis of the aqueous solution of their salts ? **[J&K CET]**

(a) Cu (b) Na
(c) Mg (d) K

15 Which of the following statements is incorrect ? **[Punjab PMET]**

(a) Pure aluminium oxide is obtained by heating aluminium hydroxide
(b) Cryolite lowers down the melting temperature of bauxite in the electrolytic cell for extraction of aluminium
(c) Carbonate ores are converted into oxides by roasting ore in air
(d) Mercury cannot be produced by roasting the ore cinnabar in air

2005

16 The mass of carbon anode consumed (giving only carbon dioxide) in the production of 270 g of aluminium metal from bauxite by the Hall process is **[CBSE AIPMT]**

(a) 180 g (b) 270 g (c) 540 g (d) 90 g

Answers

1 (a)	2 (d)	3 (c)	4 (a)	5 (d)	6 (c)	7 (c)	8 (b)	9 (b)	10 (d)
11 (c)	12 (d)	13 (d)	14 (a)	15 (d)	16 (d)				

Explanations

1 (*a*) Metals like Na, K, Mg, Ca, Al, etc., are reduced by electrolytic method.

2 (*d*) van-Arkel process was the first industrial process used for the commercial production of zirconium. It primarily involves the formation of the metal iodides and their subsequent decomposition to yield pure metal.

3 (*c*) Zr and Ti are purified by van Arkel method. This method is very useful for removing all the oxygen and nitrogen present in the form of impurity in certain metals like Zr and Ti.

$$Zr + 2I_2 \xrightarrow{600°C} ZrI_4 \xrightarrow{1800°C} Zr + 2I_2$$

4 (*a*) In Castner's process, fused caustic soda (or sodium hydroxide) is electrolysed to get Na. The reactions of the process are as follows :

$$NaOH \rightleftharpoons Na^+ + OH^-$$

$$Na^+ + e^- \longrightarrow Na \text{ (At cathode)}$$

$$4OH^- \longrightarrow O_2 + 2H_2O + 4e^- \text{ (At anode)}$$

5 (*d*) In the electrolytic refining of zinc, anode is made up of impure zinc while a strip of pure zinc acts as cathode. An acidified solution of zinc sulphate acts as electrolyte.

When electricity is passed, following reactions occur :

At cathode $Zn^{2+} + 2e^- \longrightarrow \underset{\text{Pure}}{Zn}$

At anode $\underset{\text{Impure}}{Zn} \longrightarrow Zn^{2+} + 2e^-$

6 (*c*) Zone refining process is based upon the fact that impurities are more soluble in melt than in the original metal. Hence, molten zone contains more impurities than the original metal.

7 (*c*) Wrought iron is the purest form of iron as it contains minimum amount of carbon (0.12 – 0.25%).

8 (*b*) The purest zinc is made by zone refining.

9 (*b*) Ni combines with CO to form volatile $Ni(CO)_4$ which decomposes to give pure Ni metal and CO on heating.

10 (*d*) The reduction potential of Fe is less negative than that of H_2O, so it is not manufactured by electrolysis.

11 (*c*) Impure metal can be refined by the following methods:

(*i*) Distillation (*ii*) Electrolysis
(*iii*) Liquation (*iv*) Zone-refining
(*v*) Vapour phase refining

Thus, amalgamation process is not used for refining impure metal.

12 (*d*) On fusing AgCl with Na_2CO_3, metallic silver is obtained.

$$2AgCl + Na_2CO_3 \xrightarrow{\text{Fuse}} \underset{\substack{\text{Metallic}\\ \text{silver}}}{2Ag\downarrow} + 2NaCl + CO_2 + \frac{1}{2}O_2$$

13 (*d*) Blister copper is obtained by the process of bessemerisation from the copper matte in the metallurgy of Cu. It is impure. Blister copper contain about 98 to 99% pure copper and 1 to 2% impurities like Ag, Au, Zn, Ni, etc.

14 (*a*) Copper metal (Cu) is obtained by the electrolysis of the aqueous solution of their salts.

15 (*d*) Roasting process is commonly used for sulphide ores.

Cinnabar is HgS. Thus, mercury can be produced by roasting the cinnabar in air.

Rest of the other statements are correct.

16 (*d*) In Hall and Heroult process :

$$2Al_2O_3 \longrightarrow 4Al + 3O_2$$

$$4C + 3O_2 \longrightarrow 2CO_2 + 2CO\uparrow$$

$$2Al_2O_3 + 4C \longrightarrow 4Al + 2CO_2 + 2CO$$

Only for the removal of CO_2, following equation is possible :

$$2Al_2O_3 + \underset{3\times 12 = 36}{3C} \longrightarrow \underset{4\times 27 = 108}{4Al} + 3CO_2$$

$\because$ For 108 g of Al, 36 g of C is required in the above reaction

$\therefore$ For 270 g of Al, require amount of C $= \frac{36}{108} \times 270 = 90$ g

21

p-Block Elements (II)

Quick Review

Group 15 Elements

- The group 15 includes nitrogen (N), phosphorus (P), arsenic (As), antimony (Sb) and bismuth (Bi).
- The elements in this group are collectively called 'pnictogens, pnicogens or pnictides' derived from Greek synonym because N does not support combustion.

General Introduction of Group 15 Elements

- **Electronic configuration** The general configuration of these elements is $ns^2 np^3$.
- **Occurrence** Nitrogen constitutes about 78% of atmosphere. In combined state, it is found as nitrates or in proteins and amino acids. Phosphorus is found as phosphate. The rest elements occur as sulphides or oxides.
- **Oxidation states** Common oxidation states of these elements are +5 and +3. Out of which +3 stabilises on moving down the group due to inert pair effect.

Trends in Physical Properties

- On moving down the group, the metallic character increases as well as the boiling point increases.
- The melting point of group 15 elements first increases from N to As and then decreases to Sb and Bi.

Trends in Chemical Properties

1. Reactivity Towards Hydrogen

- Elements of group 15 form hydrides of the type MH_3, (where, M = N, P, As, Sb, Bi).
- The correct order of boiling point and melting point of hydrides are as follows :
  $PH_3 < AsH_3 < NH_3 < SbH_3 < BiH_3$ (boiling point).
  $PH_3 < AsH_3 < SbH_3 < NH_3$ (melting point).
- Reducing nature of these hydrides increases on moving down the group. The correct order is
  $NH_3 < PH_3 < AsH_3 < SbH_3 < BiH_3$.
- The bond angle and basic strength of the hydrides decreases on moving down the group.

2. Reactivity Towards Halogens

- Group 15 elements form trihalides (MX_3) and pentahalides (MX_5).
- The bond angle of trihalides increases in the order :
  $PF_3 < PCl_3 < PBr_3 < PI_3$
- The ease of hydrolysis of trihalides follows the order :
  $NCl_3 > PCl_3 > AsCl_3 > SbCl_3 > BiCl_3$.
- The correct order of Lewis acid strength is,
  $PCl_3 > AsCl_3 > SbCl_3$
  $PF_3 > PCl_3 > PBr_3 > PI_3$

3. Reactivity Towards Oxygen

These elements form different oxides on reaction with oxygen. N has the strongest tendency to form $p\pi - p\pi$ multiple bonds with O.

Oxides of Nitrogen

Oxides	Structure
N_2O (nitrous oxide)	$N \equiv N \rightarrow \ddot{O}:$ (Colourless gas)
NO (nitric oxide)	$:\dot{N} = \ddot{O}:$ (Colourless gas)
N_2O_3 (dinitrogen trioxide)	$:\ddot{O}=N-N(\rightarrow \ddot{O}:)(=\ddot{O})$ (Blue solid)

Oxides	Structure
N_2O_4 (dinitrogen tetraoxide)	O_2N-NO_2 (Colourless liquid)
NO_2 (nitrogen dioxide)	$O=\dot{N}-O$ (Brown gas)
N_2O_5 (dinitrogen pentoxide)	$O_2N-O-NO_2$ (Colourless gas)

Some Important Compounds of Nitrogen

1. **Dinitrogen** It is a colourless, odourless, tasteless and non-toxic gas. In laboraties, it is prepared by treating an aqueous solution of ammonium chloride with sodium nitrite.

$$NH_4Cl(aq.) + NaNO_2(aq.) \longrightarrow N_2(g) + 2H_2O(l) + NaCl(aq.)$$

Dinitrogen is used in the manufacture of ammonia. Liquid dinitrogen is used as a refrigerant to pressure biological materials, food items etc.

2. **Ammonia** (NH_3) It is a colourless, pungent smelling gas. It is prepared by Haber's process.

$$N_2 + 3H_2 \rightleftharpoons 2NH_3$$

NH_3 act as a reducing agent and reduces metallic oxides and gives a yellow brown colour with Nesseler's reagent. On reaction with conc. HCl, it gives white fumes of NH_4Cl.

3. **Nitric Acid** (HNO_3) It is a colourless fuming liquid which boils at 83°C. It can be prepared by heating $NaNO_3$ with conc. H_2SO_4 or by Ostwald's process.

$$4NH_3 + 5O_2 \xrightarrow[500\,K,\,9\,bar]{Pb/Rh,\,gauge\,catalyst} 4NO + 6H_2O$$

$$2NO + O_2 \longrightarrow 2NO_2$$

$$4NO_2 + O_2 + 2H_2O \longrightarrow 4HNO_3$$

It is a strong oxidising agent and gives nitrate on reaction with active metals like Zn, Fe, Cu and Ag.

Phosphorus

Common allotropes of phosphorus are white P, red P, α-black P and β-black P.

Important Compounds of Phosphorus

Some important compounds of phosphorus are as follows

1. Phosphine (PH_3)

- It is highly toxic and reactive gas. It can be obtained by heating phosphorus acid.

$$4H_3PO_3 \xrightarrow{473\,K} 3H_3PO_4 + \underset{\text{Phosphine}}{PH_3\uparrow}$$

- When heated in air it decomposes to give red phosphorus and hydrogen gas. In contact with HNO_3, it begins to burn.

2. Phosphorus Trichloride (PCl_3) and Pentachloride (PCl_5)

- PCl_3 can be obtained when Cl_2 is passed over red or white phosphorus.

$$P_4 + 3Cl_2 \longrightarrow 4PCl_3$$

It is violently hydrolysed by water.

- PCl_5 can be obtained by passed Cl_2 over PCl_3.

$$PCl_3 + Cl_2 \longrightarrow PCl_5$$

- It is also violently hydrolysed by water to give $POCl_3$ and H_3PO_4.

3. Oxoacids of Phosphorus

Phosphorus forms a number of oxoacids which are as follows:

Oxoacids	Structure	Basicity
H_3PO_2 (hypophosphorous acid)	$HO-P(=O)(H)-H$	Monobasic
H_3PO_3 (orthophosphorous acid)	$H-P(=O)(OH)-OH$	Dibasic
H_3PO_4 (phosphoric acid)	$HO-P(=O)(OH)-OH$	Tribasic
$H_4P_2O_5$ (pyrophosphoric acid)	$H-P(=O)(OH)-O-P(=O)(OH)-H$	Dibasic
$H_4P_2O_6$ (hypophosphoric acid)	$HO-P(=O)(HO)-O-P(=O)(OH)-OH$	Tetrabasic

Group 16 Elements

- The elements of group 16 includes oxygen (O), sulphur (S), selenium (Se), tellurium (Te) and polonium (Po).
- They are collectively called as '**chalcogens**' which means, ore forming (oxides, sulphides, selenides, tellunides).

General Introduction of Group 16 Elements

- **General electronic configuration** The general configuration of these elements is ns^2np^4.
- **Occurrence** Oxygen is the most abundant element. It can occur in free state, whereas all other elements are found in combined state.
- **Oxidation states** Oxygen can exhibit +2, –2, +1, –1/2 and –1 oxidation states, whereas other elements show +2, +4 and +6 state.

Trends in Physical Properties

On moving down the group, the metallic character of group 16 elements increases.
The melting and boiling point also increases regularly down the group. Oxygen exist as a diatomic gas, while all others exist as octaatomic solid. O can form $p\pi$-$p\pi$ bonds, while others form $p\pi$-$d\pi$ bonds.

Trends in Chemical Properties

(i) **Reactivity towards hydrogen** • Elements of group 16 form hydrides of type H_2X. The bond angle of these hydrides decreases from H_2O to H_2Te whereas reducing character increases.

- The correct order of bond angle and thermal stability of hydrides is, $H_2O > H_2S > H_2Se > H_2Te$.
- The correct order of acidic strength and reducing nature is, $H_2O < H_2S < H_2Se < H_2Te$.

(ii) **Reactivity towards halogens** Elements of group 16 form number of halides in the oxidation state +1, +2, +4 and +6. The correct stability order is, $SF_6 > SeF_6 > TeF_6$.

(iii) **Reactivity towards oxygen** All the elements of this group form oxides of type MO_2 and MO_3.

Some Important Compounds of Oxygen

- **Ozone** It is formed in the upper layer of atmosphere by the action of UV rays from sun on oxygen, $3O_2 \xrightarrow{\text{UV light}} 2O_3$
  It is a pale blue gas with a characteristic pungent odour. It is thermodynamically unstable and is a powerful oxidising agent. It is used as a disinfectant and in purifying water.
- **Dioxygen** It can prepared by decomposition of oxygen rich compounds like $KClO_3$, $KMnO_4$ and KNO_3.
  $$2KClO_3 \xrightarrow{\Delta} 2KCl + 3O_2$$
  It can also be prepared by the action of water on sodium peroxide. It forms different oxides with active metals like, Na, Ca etc. at room temperature. On reaction with dihydrogen, it forms water.
- **Sulphur** It is found in free as well as in combined states.
- **Common allotropes of sulphur** are rhombic sulphur, monoclinic sulphur and colloidal sulphur.

Some Important Compounds of Sulphur

Some important compounds of sulphur are as follows :

1. Sulphur Dioxide (SO_2)

- It is a colourless gas with pungent odour. SO_2 is formed together with a little (6 – 8%) sulphur trioxide when sulphur is burnt in air.
  $$S + O_2 \longrightarrow SO_2$$
- It is acidic in nature and have both oxidising and reducing properties. It also acts as a mild bleaching agent.

2. Sulphuric Acid (H_2SO_4)

- It is colourless, viscous liquid which is soluble in water. H_2SO_4 can be manufactured by lead chamber and contact process.
- When heated it undergoes dissociation into steam and SO_3.
- It behaves as a strong dibasic acid and is a powerful oxidising agent. It also works as a dehydrating agent. It helps in purification of petroleum.

3. Oxoacids of Sulphur *Sulphur forms a number of oxoacids which are given in table:*

Oxoacids	Sulphurous acid (H_2SO_3)	Sulphuric acid (H_2SO_4)	Caro's acid (H_2SO_5)	Marshall's acid ($H_2S_2O_8$)
Structure	S; HO; O; OH	O; S; HO; O; OH	O; S; O; O—OH; OH	O; S; O; O—O; OH; O; S; O; OH
Oxidation state of sulphur	+4	+6	+6	+6
Basicity	Dibasic	Dibasic	Monobasic	Dibasic
Types of salt	Sulphate and bisulphate	Sulphates and bisulphates	Peroxo monosulphates	Peroxy disulphates
Properties	• It exists only in solution. • It acts both as reducing and oxidising agent.	• Highly corrosive. • It acts both as oxidising and dehydrating agent.	• It is crystalline white and hygroscopic solid. • Powerful oxidising agent.	• It is colourless, crystalline and hygroscopic solid. • Strong oxidising agent.

Group 17 Elements (Halogen Family)

The elements of group 17 consists of fluorine ($_9F$), chlorine ($_{17}Cl$), bromine ($_{35}Br$), iodine ($_{53}I$) and astatine ($_{85}At$). They are collectively known as '**halogens.**'

General Introduction of Group 17 Elements

- **Electronic configuration** The general electronic configuration of these elements ns^2np^5.
- **Occurrence** They do not occur free in nature but in combined form. At is radioactive and occurs very sparsely.
- **Oxidation states** Common oxidation state of these elements is −1.

Trends in Physical Properties

- On moving down the group, there is an increase in melting and boiling point.
- On moving down the group, the non-metallic character of halogens decreases.
- Halogens are insoluble in water.
- The oxidising power decreases from F_2 to I_2.
- The bond dissociation enthalpy decreases in the order : $Cl_2 > Br_2 > F_2 > I_2$.

The lower value of bond dissociation enthalpy of fluorine is due to high repulsion between the non-bonding electrons in 2*p*-orbitals of fluorine.

Trends in Chemical Properties

1. Reaction with Water

F_2 decomposes with water even at low temperatures. Cl_2 and Br_2 decompose with water in presence of sunlight, whereas I_2 does not decompose.

2. Reaction with Hydrogen

Halogens react with hydrogen to form hydrides of type *HX*. The order of bond length, acidic strength and reducing nature of these hydrides is,

$$HF < HCl < HBr < HI.$$

Dipole moment and thermal stability follows the order :

$$HF > HCl > HBr > HI$$

3. Reaction with Oxygen

Halogens form binary compounds with O_2, but most of them are unstable. F forms OF_2 and O_2F_2.

Cl forms Cl_2O, ClO_2, Cl_2O_6, ClO_3 and Cl_2O_7. Br forms Br_2O and BrO_2. I forms I_2O_4 and I_2O_5.

Some Important Compounds of Halogens

1. Chlorine (Cl_2)

- Cl_2 is a greenish yellow gas with pungent and suffocating odour.
- It can be prepared by heating concentrated hydrochloric acid with an oxidising agent. It can also prepared by Deacon's and electrolytic process.
- **Deacon's process** $4HCl + O_2 \xrightarrow{CuCl_2} 2Cl_2 + 2H_2O$
- It can react with metals, non-metals and metalloids. It has oxidising and bleaching property.

2. Hydrochloric Acid (HCl)

- It is a colourless pungent smelling gas. HCl can be manufactured by salt cake process.

$$NaCl + H_2SO_4 \xrightarrow{420\,K} NaHSO_4 + HCl$$

- It is an oxidising agent . It forms insoluble chlorides with soluble salt of Ag, Pb and Hg. It is used in the manufacturing of dyes, in sugar industry and as a laboratory reagent.

3. Oxoacids of Halogens

Halogens form four series of oxoacids. These are illustrated in following table :

HOX (Hypohalous acid)	HXO_2 (Halous acid)	HXO_3 (Halic acid)	HXO_4 (Perhalic acid)	H_5XO_6 (para perhalic acid)
HOF	-	-	-	-
HOCl	$HClO_2$	$HClO_3$	$HClO_4$	-
HOBr	-	$HBrO_3$	$HBrO_4$	-
HOI	-	HIO_3	HIO_4	H_5IO_6

The oxidising power of these haloacids follows the order :

$$HClO > HClO_2 > HClO_3 > HClO_4$$

The correct order of acidic strength is,

$$HClO < HClO_2 < HClO_3 < HClO_4$$
$$HOCl > HOBr > HOI$$
$$HClO_4 > HBrO_4 > HIO_4$$

The structure of oxoacids of chlorine are shown below:

Oxoacids	Structure	Oxoacids	Structure
HOCl (hypochlorous acid)	H–O–Cl (with lone pairs)	$HClO_3$ (chloric acid)	H–O–Cl(=O)=O (with lone pair)
$HClO_2$ (chlorous acid)	H–O–Cl=O (with lone pairs)	$HClO_4$ (perchloric acid)	H–O–Cl(=O)(=O)=O

Interhalogen Compounds

- Halogens react with each other to produce a number of interhalogen compounds of the type XX', XX'_3, XX'_5, XX'_7 where, X is halogen of larger size.
- The stability of interhalogen compounds increases as the size of central atom increases. F cannot form any interhalogen compound as central atom.

Some of the important interhalogen compounds with their properties are tabulated below:

Types of Interhalogen Compounds	Formula and Name	Physical State and Colour at Ordinary Temperatures	Structure and Shape
XX'	ClF-chlorine fluoride	Gas, colourless	$X-X'$ (Linear)
	BrF-bromine fluoride	Liquid below 293 K. Pale-brown gas above 293 K	
	BrCl-bromine chloride	Liquid, reddish yellow	
	ICl-iodine chloride	Solid, rubby red	
	IBr-iodine bromide	Solid, brown like iodine	
XX'_3	ClF_3-chlorine trifluoride	Liquid below 261 K, colourless gas above 261 K	(Bent T-shaped)
	BrF_3-bromine trifluoride	Liquid, yellow green	
	$BrCl_3$-bromine trichloride	Solid, orange	
	IF_3-iodine trifluoride	Yellow powder	
XX'_5	ClF_5-chlorine pentafluoride	Gas, colourless but solid below 77 K	(Square pyramidal)
	BrF_5-bromine pentafluoride	Liquid, colourless	
	IF_5-iodine pentafluoride	Liquid, colourless	
XX'_7	IF_7-iodine heptafluoride	Gas, colourless	(Pentagonal bipyramidal)

Group 18 Elements

The 18th or zero group includes helium (He), neon (Ne), argon (Ar), krypton (Kr), xenon (Xe) and radon (Rn). Rn is radioactive. These are known as rare gas or inert gases. Noble gases are monoatomic.

General Introduction of Group 18 Elements

- **Electronic configuration** The general electronic configuration of these elements is $ns^2 np^6$.
- **Occurrence** All the gases except Rn are present in atmosphere. The total abundance of these elements in dry air is ~ 1%.

Trends in Physical Properties

Noble gases have low boiling point. On moving down the group from He to Xe, the melting point, adsorption and polarisability increases. They have high ionisation enthalpy and zero electron affinity.

Uses of Noble Gases

Helium is used in deep sea breathing. Neon lamps are used in botanical garden and radon is used in radiotherapy for the treatment of cancer. Xe and Kr mixtures are used in high intensity short exposure photographic flash tubes.

Some Important Compounds of Xe

Some important compounds of Xe *are given below :*

Compounds	XeF_2 (xenon difluoride)	XeF_4 (xenon tetrafluoride)	XeO_3 (xenon trioxide)	$XeOF_2$ (xenon oxydifluoride)	XeO_2F_2 (xenon dioxydifluoride)
Structure	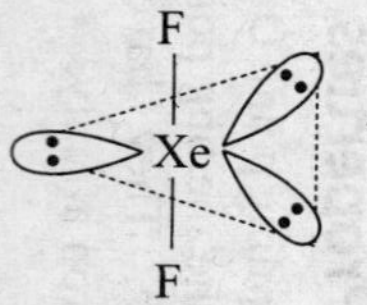 sp^3d, linear	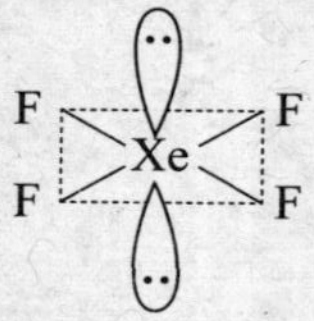 sp^3d^2, square planar	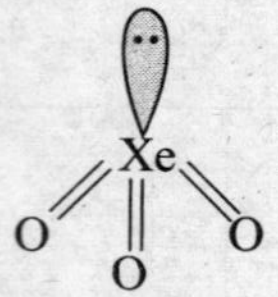 sp^3, pyramidal	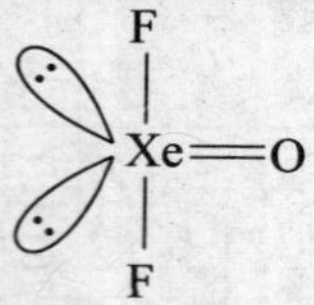 sp^3d, T-shaped	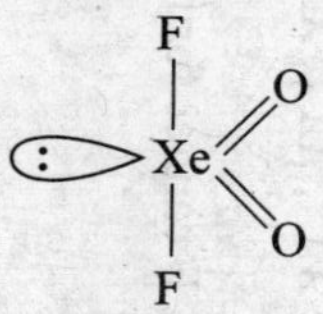 sp^3d, *see-saw* shape
Preparation	(a) By action of F_2 on Xe $Xe + F_2 \xrightarrow[400°C/atm]{Ni} XeF_2$ $Xe + F_2 \xrightarrow[Light]{Hg\text{-}arc} XeF_2$ (b) By action of O_2F_2 on Xe $Xe + O_2F_2 \xrightarrow{118°C} XeF_2 + O_2 \uparrow$	(a) By action of F_2 on Xe $Xe + 2F_2 \xrightarrow[7\ atm]{Ni/600°C} XeF_4$ (b) From XeF_2 $XeF_2 + F_2 \longrightarrow XeF_4$	(a) By action of F_2 on Xe $Xe + F_2 \xrightarrow[60\ atm]{300°C} XeF_6$ (b) By hydrolysis of xenon fluorides $XeF_6 + 3H_2O \longrightarrow XeO_3 + 6HF$ $6XeF_4 + 12H_2O \longrightarrow 2XeO_3 + 24HF + 4Xe + 3O_2$	By partial hydrolysis of XeF_4 $XeF_4 + H_2O \longrightarrow XeOF_2 + 2HF$	• By partial hydrolysis of $XeOF_4$ or XeF_6. $XeOF_4 + H_2O \longrightarrow XeO_2F_2 + 2HF$ $XeF_6 + 2H_2O \longrightarrow XeO_2F_2 + 4HF$ • Action of SiO_2 on $XeOF_4$. $2XeOF_4 + SiO_2 \longrightarrow 2XeO_2F_2 + SiF_4$
Physical Properties	• Colourless, crystalline solid. • Stable can be stored in Ni vessel. • Dissolves in HF without any chemical reaction.	• Colourless, crystalline volatile solid which sublimes on heating in a current of N_2 giving colourless vapours.	• Colourless, highly explosive. • Powerful oxidising agent.	—	• Colourless solid
Chemical Properties	• $XeF_2 \xrightarrow{H_2} Xe + 2HF$ • $XeF_2 \xrightarrow[\overline{O}H]{H_2O} Xe + 2HF + \frac{1}{2}O_2$ • $XeF_2 \xrightarrow[BF_3]{I_2} 2IF + Xe$ • $XeF_2 \xrightarrow{2HCl} Xe + 2HF + Cl_2$ • Used as fluorinating agent	$XeF_4 + 2H_2 \longrightarrow Xe + 4HF$ • Undergoes disproportionation in water $6XeF_4 + 12H_2O \longrightarrow 4Xe + 2XeO_3 + 24HF + 3O_2$ • Forms adduct $XeF_4 + SbF_5 \longrightarrow [XeF_3]^+[SbF_6]^-$ • Dissolves in only HF and used as fluorinating agent.	• With water forms xemic acid. $XeO_3 + H_2O \longrightarrow H_2XeO_4$ • Undergoes disproportionation when dissolved in alkali. • $2XeO_3 + 4OH^- \longrightarrow Xe + O_2 + XeO_6^{4-} + 2H_2O$	Unstable	• Undergoes hydrolysis easily. • $XeO_2F_2 + H_2O \longrightarrow XeO_3 + 2HF$

Topical Practice Questions

All the exam questions of this chapter have been divided into 4 topics as listed below:

Topic 1

Chemistry of Group 15 Elements

2019

1 Identify the incorrect statement related to PCl_5 from the following: **[NEET]**

(a) Two axial P—Cl bonds make an angle of 180° with each other.
(b) Axial P—Cl bonds are longer than equatorial P—Cl bonds.
(c) PCl_5 molecule is non-reactive.
(d) Three equatorial P—Cl bonds make an angle of 120° with each other.

2 A compound 'X' upon reaction with H_2O produced a colourless gas 'Y' with rotten fish smell. Gas 'Y' is absorbed in a solution of $CuSO_4$ to give Cu_3P_2 as one of the products. Predict the compound 'X' **[NEET (Odisha)]**

(a) Ca_3P_2 (b) NH_4Cl (c) As_2O_3 (d) $Ca_3(PO_4)_2$

3 Which of the following oxoacids of phosphorus has strongest reducing property? **[NEET (Odisha)]**

(a) $H_4P_2O_7$ (b) H_3PO_3 (c) H_3PO_2 (d) H_3PO_4

4 In which of the following, oxidation state of phosphorus is +3? **[JIPMER]**

(a) Orthophosphoric acid (b) Pyrophosphoric acid
(c) Orthophosphorous acid (d) Meta phosphoric acid

2018

5 In which of the following arrangements, the order is not strictly according to the property written against it? **[AIIMS]**

(a) $CO_2 < SiO_2 < SnO_2 < PbO_2$ (oxidising power)
(b) $HF < HCl < HBr < HI$ (acidic strength)
(c) $NH_3 > PH_3 < AsH_3 < SbH_3$ (basic strength)
(d) $B < C < O < N$ (first ionisation enthalpy)

6 Which of the following products will be obtained when copper metal is reacted with HNO_3? **[AIIMS]**

(a) NO and N_2O_5 (b) NO and NO_2
(c) NO_2 and N_2O_5 (d) HNO_2 and N_2

7 Which of the following oxyacid does not contain P—O—P bond? **[AIIMS]**

(a) Isohypophosphoric acid (b) Pyrophosphorus acid
(c) Diphosphoric acid (d) Hypophosphoric acid

8 The correct order of N-compounds in its decreasing order of oxidation states is **[NEET]**

(a) HNO_3, NH_4Cl, NO, N_2 (b) HNO_3, NO, NH_4Cl, N_2
(c) HNO_3, NO, N_2, NH_4Cl (d) NH_4Cl, N_2, NO, HNO_3

9 Which of the following chemicals are used to manufacture methyl isocyanate that caused "Bhopal Gas Tragedy"? **[JIPMER]**

(i) Methylamine (ii) Phosgene
(iii) Phosphine (iv) Dimethylamine
(a) (i) and (ii) (b) (iii) and (iv)
(c) (i) and (iii) (d) (ii) and (iv)

10 Which of the following pair behaves as strong and weak base hydride respectively? **[JIPMER]**

NH_3, PH_3, AsH_3, SbH_3, BiH_3

(a) NH_3, PH_3 (b) NH_3, BiH_3
(c) PH_3, BiH_3 (d) BiH_3, AsH_3

2017

11 Which of the following oxide is most acidic? **[JIPMER]**

(a) As_2O_3 (b) P_2O_5 (c) Sb_2O_3 (d) Bi_2O_3

12 Among the following compounds, which will produce $POCl_3$ with PCl_5? **[JIPMER]**

(a) Only O_2 (b) O_2 and CO_2
(c) CO_2, O_2 and P_4O_{10} (d) SO_2, H_2O, H_2SO_4, P_4O_{10}

2014

13 The statement that is not correct is **[KCET]**

(a) hypophosphorus acid reduces silver nitrate to silver
(b) in solid state PCl_5 exists as $[PCl_4]^+$ $[PCl_6]^-$
(c) pure phosphine is non-inflammable
(d) phosphorous acid on heating disproportionates to give metaphosphoric acid and phosphine

14 The species that is not hydrolysed in water is **[KCET]**

(a) P_4O_{10} (b) BaO_2 (c) Mg_3N_2 (d) CaC_2

15 The correct arrangement of following acids of phosphorus in the increasing order of oxidation state of phosphorus is **[Guj CET]**

(a) hypophosphorus acid (<) orthophosphorus acid < pyrophosphoric acid
(b) hypophosphorus acid (<) pyrophosphoric acid = orthophosphorus acid

(c) pyrophosphoric acid (<) hypophosphorus acid < orthophosphorus acid
(d) pyrophosphoric acid (<) orthophosphorus acid < hypophosphorus acid

2013

16 The mixture of concentrated HCl and HNO_3 made in 3 : 1 ratio contains [AIIMS]
(a) ClO_2 (b) NOCl (c) NCl_3 (d) N_2O_4

17 In pyrophosphoric acid the number of hydroxyl groups are [UP CPMT]
(a) 2 (b) 3 (c) 4 (d) 5

2012

18 Which acid is the hydride of nitrogen ? [AIIMS]
(a) NH_3 (b) N_3H (c) N_2H_2 (d) N_2H_4

19 When conc. H_2SO_4 is heated with P_2O_5, the acid is converted to [UP CPMT]
(a) sulphur trioxide (b) sulphur dioxide
(c) sulphur
(d) a mixture of sulphur dioxide and sulphur trioxide

20 Which of the following statements is not valid for oxoacids of phosphorus? [Manipal]
(a) Orthophosphoric acid is used in the manufacture of triple super phosphate
(b) Hypophosphorous acid is a diprotic acid
(c) All oxoacids contain tetrahedral four coordinated phosphorus
(d) All oxo-acids contain at least one P$=$O unit and one P—OH group

2011

21 The oxidation state of phosphorus in cyclotrimetaphosphoric acid is [WB JEE]
(a) + 3 (b) + 5 (c) – 3 (d) + 2

22 The basicity of pyrophosphorus acid is [WB JEE]
(a) 2 (b) 4 (c) 1 (d) 5

2010

23 Ammonia, on reaction with excess of chlorine, gives [AFMC]
(a) NCl_3 and HCl (b) N_4 and NH_4Cl
(c) NCl_3 and NH_4Cl (d) N_2 and HCl

24 The number of P—O bonds in P_4O_{10} is [UP CPMT]
(a) 16 (b) 12 (c) 8 (d) 4

25 Gaseous product obtained on thermal decomposition of $(NH_4)_2Cr_2O_7$ is [OJEE]
(a) NH_3 (b) N_2 (c) O_2 (d) NO

26 P_4O_{10} is the anhydride of [WB JEE]
(a) H_3PO_2 (b) H_3PO_3 (c) H_3PO_4 (d) $H_4P_2O_7$

27 The nitrogen atom has 7 protons and 7 electrons. The nitride ion will have [RPMT]
(a) 7 protons and 10 electrons
(b) 4 protons and 7 electrons
(c) 4 protons and 10 electrons
(d) 10 protons and 7 electrons

28 On heating NH_4NO_3 strongly, which is obtained? [MP PMT]
(a) NO_2 (b) NH_3
(c) N_2 (d) N_2O

29 Nitrous oxide is [MP PMT]
(a) acidic (b) basic (c) amphoteric (d) neutral

30 The maximum number of P—H bonds are contained in which of the following molecules? [AMU]
(a) H_3PO_2 (b) H_3PO_3 (c) H_3PO_4 (d) $H_4P_2O_7$

31 The hydrolysis of NCl_3 by water produces [AMU]
(a) NH_2OH and HOCl (b) NH_2NH_2 and HCl
(c) NH_4OH and HOCl (d) NH_2Cl and HOCl

32 Phosphorus pentoxide is widely used as [Guj CET]
(a) bleaching agent (b) dehydrating agent
(c) oxidising agent (d) reducing agent

33 Given oxo acids are H_3PO_2, H_3PO_3, H_3PO_4 and $H_4P_2O_7$. Which of the above oxoacids results into two series of salts? [Guj CET]
(a) H_3PO_2 (b) H_3PO_3 (c) H_3PO_4 (d) $H_4P_2O_7$

34 Which of the following is not correct? White phosphorus (P_4) has [Haryana PMT]
(a) six P—P single bond (b) four P—P single bonds
(c) four lone pair of electrons (d) P—P—P angle is 60°

35 For H_3PO_3, the correct choice is [VMMC]
(a) dibasic and reducing (b) dibasic and non-reducing
(c) tribasic and reducing (d) tribasic and non-reducing

2009

36 When nitric acid reacts with nitric oxide, a gas is released, which converts H_2S into [AIIMS]
(a) SO_4^{2-} (b) S^{2-} (c) S (d) $S_2O_5^{2-}$

37 By which of the following processes, pure nitrogen gas is prepared? [AFMC]
(a) $(NH_4)_2Cr_2O_7 \xrightarrow{\Delta}$ (b) $NH_4Cl + NaNO_2 \xrightarrow{\Delta}$
(c) $Ba(N_3)_2 \xrightarrow{\Delta}$ (d) $N_2O + Cu \xrightarrow{\Delta}$

38 Products formed on heating $Pb(NO_3)_2$ are [OJEE]
(a) PbO, N_2, O_3 (b) $Pb(NO_2)_2$, O_2
(c) PbO, NO_2, O_2 (d) Pb, N_2, O_2

39 The reaction of elemental P_4 in aqueous NaOH gives [OJEE]
(a) PH_3, NaH_2PO_2 (b) PH_3, Na_2PO_4
(c) $NaHPO_4$, Na_2PO_4 (d) Na_3P, Na_3PO_4

40 One of the product of the following reaction is [OJEE]
$KCNO + (NH_4)_2SO_4 \xrightarrow{\Delta}$
(a) NH_4NO_3 (b) NH_2CONH_2
(c) N_2 (d) NO_2

41 Atoms in a P_4 molecule of white phosphorus are arranged regularly in the following way **[WB JEE]**
(a) at the corners of a cube
(b) at the corners of an octahedron
(c) at the corners of a tetrahedron
(d) at the centre and corners of a tetrahedron

42 The products of following reactions respectively are

I. $CuSO_4 + PH_3 \longrightarrow A + H_2SO_4$

II. $HgCl_2 + PH_3 \longrightarrow B + HCl$

	A	B		A	B
(a)	CuP_3	HgP	(b)	Cu_3P_2	Hg_3P_2
(c)	CuP_3	Hg_3P_2	(d)	CuP	HgP

43 When PbO_2 reacts with conc. HNO_3, the gas evolved is **[CG PMT, Haryana PMT]**
(a) NO_2 (b) O_2 (c) N_2 (d) N_2O

44 Thermodynamically, most stable form of phosphorus is **[AFMC, CG PMT, Haryana PMT]**
(a) red (b) black (c) white (d) yellow

2008

45 Pick out the strongest reducing agent among the following oxy-acids of phosphorus. **[Kerala CEE]**
(a) Hypophosphorus acid (b) Phosphorus acid
(c) Hypophosphoric acid (d) Pyrophosphorus acid

2007

46 Which of the following oxides of nitrogen is an anhydride of nitrous acid? **[AFMC]**
(a) NO (b) N_2O_3 (c) N_2O_4 (d) N_2O_5

47 When heated NH_3 is passed over CuO, gas evolved is **[BCECE]**
(a) N_2 (b) N_2O
(c) HNO_3 (d) NO_2

48 Sodium pyrophosphate is represented by which of the following formula? **[Manipal]**
(a) $Na_2P_2O_4$ (b) $Na_4P_2O_5$ (c) $Na_4P_2O_7$ (d) $Na_2P_2O_5$

49 Which of the following is the correct order of increasing enthalpy of vaporisation? **[Kerala CEE]**
(a) $NH_3 < PH_3 < AsH_3$ (b) $AsH_3 < PH_3 < NH_3$
(c) $PH_3 < AsH_3 < NH_3$ (d) $NH_3 < AsH_3 < PH_3$

50 Which of the following oxide of nitrogen is most thermally stable? **[RPMT]**
(a) N_2O_5 (b) N_2O (c) NO (d) N_2O_3

51 Which of the following has the highest proton affinity? **[Guj CET]**
(a) Arsine (AsH_3) (b) Stibine (SbH_3)
(c) Ammonia (NH_3) (d) Phosphine (PH_3)

52 The correct formula of salt formed by the neutralisation of hypophosphorus acid with NaOH is **[Guj CET]**
(a) Na_3PO_3 (b) Na_3PO_2 (c) Na_2HPO_2 (d) NaH_2PO_2

53 Zinc and cold dil. HNO_3 reacts to produce **[BCECE]**
(a) NO (b) NO_2 (c) NH_4NO_3 (d) $ZnNO_3$

2006

54 Which of the following acts as a pickling agent? **[UP CPMT]**
(a) HNO_3 (b) HCl (c) H_2SO_4 (d) HNO_2

55 Pnicogens are the elements of group **[OJEE]**
(a) 15 (b) 13 (c) VIII (d) zero

56 Which of the following forms vortex ring? **[OJEE]**
(a) P_2O_5 (b) PH_3 (c) NH_3 (d) P_4O_{10}

57 As the number of —OH groups increases in hypophosphorus acid, phosphorus acid and phosphoric acid, the acidic strength **[Manipal]**
(a) increases (b) decreases
(c) remain nearly same (d) remain appropriately same

58 Which of the following metals, Fe, Zn, Pb, Ag and Pt, do not give a metal nitrate on treatment with concentrated HNO_3? **[Kerala CEE]**
(a) Fe and Zn (b) Fe and Pt
(c) Pb, Ag and Pt (d) Fe, Ag and Pt
(e) Fe, Zn and Pt

59 The decreasing order of boiling point of the following hydrides. **[Kerala CEE]**
I NH_3 II PH_3 III AsH_3 IV SbH_3 V H_2O
(a) V > IV > I > III > II (b) V > I > II > III > IV
(c) II > IV > III > I > V (d) IV > III > I > II > V
(e) V > IV > III > II > I

60 Which phosphorus reacts with KOH solution to produce phosphine gas? **[RPMT]**
(a) White phosphorus (b) Red phosphorus
(c) Both (a) and (b) (d) None of the above

61 Iron is dropped in dil. HNO_3, it gives **[AMU]**
(a) ferric nitrate
(b) ferric nitrate and NO_2
(c) ferrous nitrate and ammonium nitrate
(d) ferrous nitrate and nitric oxide

62 When tin is treated with concentrated nitric acid **[AMU]**
(a) it is converted into stannous nitrate
(b) it is converted into stannic nitrate
(c) it is converted into metastannic acid
(d) it becomes passive

2005

63 Nausadar is **[UP CPMT]**
(a) NH_4NO_3 (b) NH_4Cl (c) $(NH_4)_2SO_4$ (d) NH_4OH

64 When plants and animals decay, the organic nitrogen is converted into inorganic nitrogen. The inorganic nitrogen is in the form of **[KCET]**
(a) ammonia (b) elements of nitrogen
(c) nitrates (d) nitrides

65 Which of the following is kept in water? **[BCECE]**
(a) White phosphorus (b) Sodium
(c) Potassium (d) Calcium

Answers

1 (c)	2 (a)	3 (c)	4 (c)	5 (c)	6 (b)	7 (d)	8 (c)	9 (a)	10 (b)
11 (b)	12 (d)	13 (c)	14 (a)	15 (a)	16 (b)	17 (c)	18 (b)	19 (a)	20 (b)
21 (b)	22 (a)	23 (a)	24 (a)	25 (b)	26 (c)	27 (a)	28 (d)	29 (d)	30 (a)
31 (c)	32 (b)	33 (b)	34 (b)	35 (a)	36 (c)	37 (b)	38 (c)	39 (a)	40 (b)
41 (c)	42 (c)	43 (b)	44 (b)	45 (a)	46 (b)	47 (a)	48 (c)	49 (c)	50 (c)
51 (c)	52 (d)	53 (c)	54 (c)	55 (a)	56 (b)	57 (c)	58 (b)	59 (a)	60 (a)
61 (c)	62 (c)	63 (b)	64 (a)	65 (a)					

Explanations

1 (*c*) In gaseous and liquid phases, PCl_5 has a trigonal bipyramidal structure with sp^3d-hybridisation.

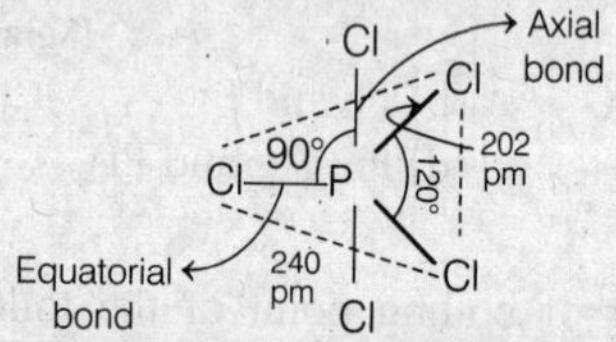

Axial bond; Equatorial bond; 90°; 120°; 202 pm; 240 pm

Due to presence of longer and weaker axial bonds, PCl_5 is a reactive molecule.

Hence, statement in option (c) is incorrect while the remaining options contain correct statements.

2 (*a*) The road map of given problem is

'X' + H_2O ⟶ 'Y' (colourless) Rotten fish smell

$\downarrow CuSO_4$

Cu_3P_2 + Product

As compound 'X' produces a colourless gas 'Y' with rotten fish smell, X can be Ca_3P_2 (calcium phosphide). The reaction takes palce as follows :

$Ca_3P_2 + H_2O \longrightarrow Ca(OH)_2 + PH_3$

Colourless gas with rotten fish smell. 'Y'

$CuSO_4 + \underset{'Y'}{PH_3} \longrightarrow Cu_3P_2 + H_2SO_4$

3 (*c*) P—H bonds found in phosphorus acids have reducing properties.

Thus, reducing property is directly proportional to number of P—H bonds.

The structures of given oxoacids of phosphorus are as follows:

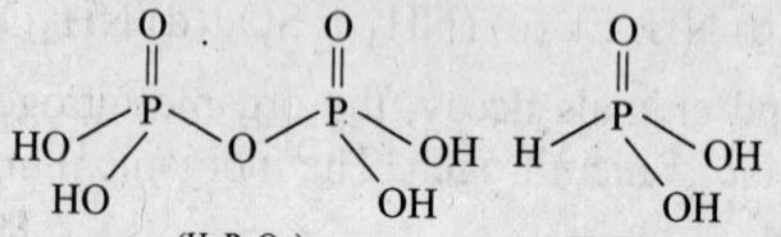

($H_4P_2O_7$) (H_3PO_3) 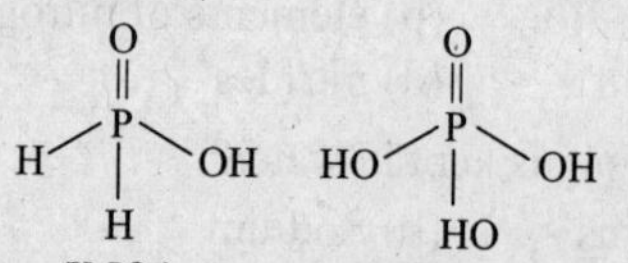 (H_3PO_2) (H_3PO_4)

H_3PO_2 contains 2P—H bonds which is maximum among the given options. Thus, H_3PO_2 has strongest reducing property.

4 (*c*) The structure and oxidation state of oxoacids of phosphorus are as follows :

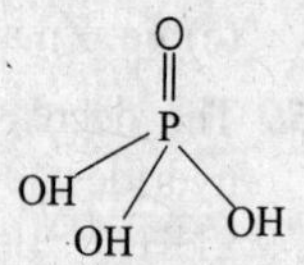

Orthophosphoric acid (H_3PO_4) (+5)

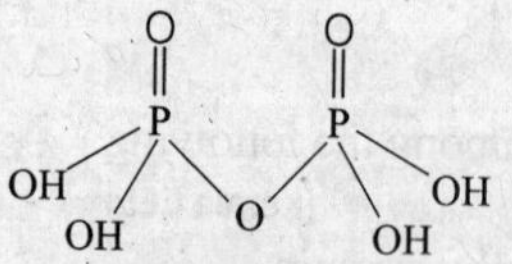

Pyrophosphoric acid (+5)

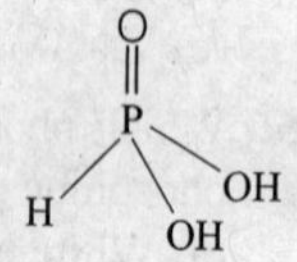

Orthophosphorous acid (H_3PO_3) (+3)

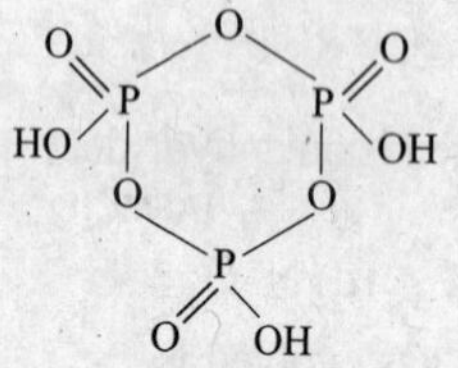

Metaphosphoric acid $(HPO_3)_3$ (+5)

Thus, oxidation state of orthophosphorous acids is +3.

5 (*c*) The correct decreasing order of basic strength is

$$NH_3 > PH_3 > AsH_3 > SbH_3$$

NH_3 is the most basic because of its small size, the electron density of electron pair is concentrated over small region. As the size increases, the electron density gets diffused over a large surface area.

Hence, the ability to donate the electron pair (basicity) decreases. The other three statements given are correct.

6 (*b*) The products of the reaction of copper with HNO_3 depends upon the concentration of HNO_3 used.

Copper metal reacts with dilute HNO_3 to form nitrogen (II) oxide (NO).

$$3Cu + 8HNO_3(dil.) \longrightarrow 3Cu(NO_3)_2 + 2NO + 4H_2O$$

Copper metal reacts with conc. HNO_3 to form nitrogen (IV) oxide or nitrogen dioxide (NO_2).

$$Cu + 4HNO_3 (conc.) \longrightarrow Cu(NO_3)_2 + 2NO_2 + 2H_2O$$

7 (*d*) Hypophosphoric acid ($H_4P_2O_6$) does not contain P–O–P bond whereas, isohypophosphoric acid ($H_4P_2O_6$), diphosphorus acid ($H_4P_2O_5$) and diphosphoric acid ($H_4P_2O_7$) all contain P–O–P bonds.

The structures of the following oxyacids of phosphorus is shown below:

(a) Isohypophosphoric acid

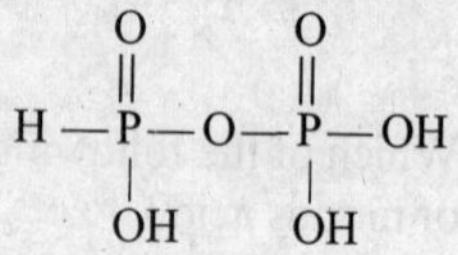

(b) Pyrophosphorus acid

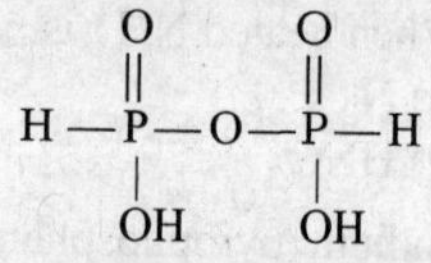

(c) Diphosphoric acid

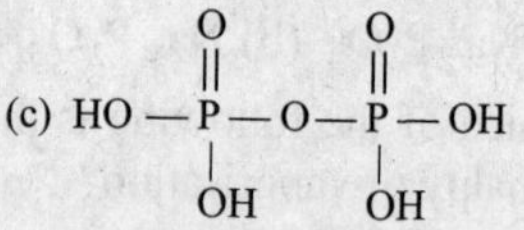

(d) Hypophosphoric acid

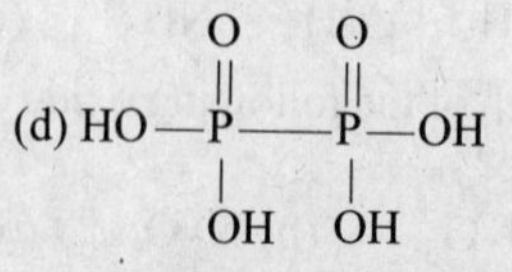

8 (*c*) Let the oxidation state of nitrogen in each of the given N-compounds be *x*.

(i) $HNO_3 : +1 + x + 3(-2) = 0$

$x = +5$

$\therefore$ Oxidation state of N in HNO_3 is +5.

(ii) $NO : x + 1(-2) = 0$

$x = +2$

$\therefore$ Oxidation state of N in NO is +2.

(iii) $NH_4Cl: x + 4(+1) + 1(-1) = 0$

$x = -3$

$\therefore$ Oxidation state of N in NH_4Cl is -3.

(iv) $N_2: x = 0$

[$\because N_2$ is present in elemental state]

$\therefore$ Oxidation state of N in N_2 is 0.

Thus, the correct decreasing order of oxidation states of given N- compounds will be $\overset{+5}{HNO_3} > \overset{+2}{NO} > \overset{0}{N_2} > \overset{-3}{NH_4Cl}$

9 (*a*) Methyl isocyanate (CH_3NCO) is industrially prepared by the reaction of methylamine and phosgene (carbonyl chloride).

$$\underset{\text{Methyl amine}}{CH_3NH_2} + \underset{\text{Phosgene}}{COCl_2} \xrightarrow{-HCl} [CH_3NH-CO-Cl] \xrightarrow{\Delta, -HCl} \underset{\text{Methyl isocyanate}}{CH_3N=C=O}$$

10 (*b*) The basic strength of given hydrides decreases in the order as follows :

$NH_3 > PH_3 > AsH_3 > SbH_3 > BiH_3$

This is due to the decrease in the availability of the lone pair of electrons which depends on the size of central atom that increases from N to Bi. Therefore, NH_3 and BiH_3 acts as a strong and weak base hydride respectively.

11 (*b*) More be the positive oxidation state of a non-metallic oxide, more be its acidic nature.

$\therefore P_2O_5$ (oxidation state of P is +5) is most acidic.

12 (*d*) PCl_5 on reaction with the given compounds produces $POCl_3$.

$$2PCl_5 + SO_2 \longrightarrow POCl_3 + SOCl_2$$

$$PCl_5 + H_2O \longrightarrow POCl_3 + 2HCl$$

$$2PCl_5 + H_2SO_4 \longrightarrow SO_2Cl_2 + 2POCl_3 + 2HCl$$

$$6PCl_5 + P_4O_{10} \longrightarrow 10POCl_3$$

13 (*c*) Pure phosphine gas is stable in air and not inflammable at normal temperature but on heating upto 150°C, it catches fire and produces phosphorus pentaoxide.

$$2PH_3 + 4O_2 \xrightarrow{150°C} P_2O_5 + 3H_2O$$

14 (*a*) Chemical reactions that occur when P_4O_{10}, Mg_3N_2, CaC_2 and BaO_2 reacts with water are as shown below:

$$P_4O_{10} + 6H_2O \longrightarrow 4H_3PO_4$$

$$Mg_3N_2 + 6H_2O \longrightarrow 3Mg(OH)_2 + 2NH_3$$

$$CaC_2 + 2H_2O \longrightarrow Ca(OH)_2 + C_2H_2$$

$$BaO_2 + 2H_2O \longrightarrow Ba(OH)_2 + H_2O_2$$

15 (*a*)

Hypophosphorous acid H_3PO_2 (structure: P with =O, two H and one OH)

$+3 + x + 2(-2) = 0$

$x = +1$

Orthophosphorous acid H_3PO_3 (structure: P with =O, one H and two OH)

$+3 + x + 3(-2) = 0$

$x = +3$

Pyrophosphoric acid $H_4P_2O_7$ (structure: two P=O units bridged by O, with HO, OH OH, OH)

$+4 + 2x + 7(-2) = 0$

$x = +5$

Thus, correct order of acids of phosphorus in the increasing order of oxidation state of phosphorus is

hypophosphorus acid < orthophosphorus acid < pyrophosphoric acid

16 (*b*) The mixture of one part of conc. HNO_3 and three parts of conc. HCl is known as aqua-regia. It contains NOCl.

$$HNO_3 + 3HCl \longrightarrow 2H_2O + NOCl + 2[Cl]$$

The enhanced ability to dissolve metals shown by *aquaregia* arises from the oxidising power of HNO_3 coupled with the ability of Cl^- to form complexes with the metal ions.

17 (*c*) Draw the structure of pyrophosphoric acid and count —OH groups in it.

($H_4P_2O_7$): two P atoms, each with =O and two OH, bridged by O.

$\therefore$ Pyrophosphoric acid has 4—OH groups.

18 (*b*) Hydrazoic acid (N_3H) is a weak acid. Its weak acidic character is due to the formation of azide ion (N_3^-) after the loss of a proton. Azide ion is more stabilised by resonance as compared to hydrazoic acid itself.

$$[N\equiv N^+-N^-]^- \longleftrightarrow [N^--\overset{+}{N}\equiv N]^-$$

19 (*a*) $2H_2SO_4 + 2P_2O_5 \longrightarrow \underset{\text{Sulphur trioxide}}{2SO_3} + 4HPO_3$

20 (*b*) Hypophosphorous acid H_3PO_2 has the following structure.

H—P(=O)(H)—OH

As, it contains only one replaceable H-atom (that is attached with O, not with P directly) so it is a monoprotic acid.

All other given statements are true.

21 (*b*) The structure of cyclotrimetaphosphoric acid is

(six-membered ring of alternating P and O; each P bears =O and OH)

and oxidation state of P = + 5

22 (*a*) The structure of pyrophosphorous acid ($H_4P_2O_5$) is

HO—P(=O)(H)—O—P(=O)(H)—OH

Here, 2 hydrogen atoms are replaceable. So, basicity is 2.

23 (*a*) $NH_3 + \underset{\text{Excess}}{3Cl_2} \longrightarrow \underset{\text{Explosive}}{NCl_3} + 3HCl$

24 (*a*) The structure of P_4O_{10} is

(four P atoms each bearing =O, linked by six bridging O atoms)

Number of P—O single bonds = 12

Number of P=O bonds = 4

Total number of P—O bonds

= 12 + 4 = 16

25 (*b*) $(NH_4)_2Cr_2O_7 \xrightarrow{\Delta} N_2 + Cr_2O_3 + 4H_2O$

26 (*c*) P_4O_{10} is an anhydride of H_3PO_4. Reaction is given as follows:

$$4H_3PO_4 \xrightarrow{\Delta} P_4O_{10} + 6H_2O$$

27 (*a*) In N^{3-} (nitride) ion,

Number of protons = Atomic number = 7

and number of electrons = Atomic number ± charge on the ion

$\therefore$ Number of electrons = 7 + 3 = 10

Hence, N^{3-} ion have 7 protons and 10 electrons.

28 (*d*) On heating ammonium nitrate, nitrous oxide or nitrogen(I) oxide is formed.

$$NH_4NO_3 \xrightarrow{475\text{-}530°C} \underset{\text{Nitrous oxide}}{N_2O} + 2H_2O$$

Nitrous oxide is called laughing gas.

29 (*d*) Nitrous oxide is a neutral gas.

30 (*a*) The structures of the given oxyacids of phosphorus are as follows :

(a) HO–P(=O)(H)–H, H_3PO_2 (2 P—H bonds)
(b) HO–P(=O)(H)–OH, H_3PO_3 (1 P—H bond)
(c) HO–P(=O)(OH)–OH, H_3PO_4 (no P—H bond)
(d) HO–P(=O)(HO)–O–P(=O)(OH)–OH, $H_4P_2O_7$ (no P—H bond)

Thus, H_3PO_2 contains the maximum number of P—H bonds, i.e. 2.

31 (*c*) $2NCl_3 + 8H_2O \longrightarrow 2NH_4OH + 6HOCl$

32 (*b*) Phosphorus pentoxide acts as a powerful dehydrating agent. It dehydrates HNO_3 to N_2O_5, H_2SO_4 to SO_3, $HClO_4$ to Cl_2O_7 etc.

$$4HNO_3 + P_4O_{10} \longrightarrow 2N_2O_5 + 4HPO_3$$
$$4H_2SO_4 + P_4O_{10} \longrightarrow 2SO_3 + 4HPO_3$$
$$4HClO_4 + P_4O_{10} \longrightarrow 2Cl_2O_7 + 4HPO_3$$

33 (*b*) Phosphorous acid (H_3PO_3) is a diprotic acid. It forms two series of salts such as NaH_2PO_3 and Na_2HPO_3 but none of the type Na_3PO_3 with NaOH. Its structure is as follows :

H–P(=O)(OH)–OH

34 (*b*)

P_4 White phosphorus (P–P–P angle 60°)

Hence, the white phosphorus has six P—P single bonds, four lone pairs of electrons and the P—P—P angle is 60°. Hence, option (b) is correct.

35 (*a*)

HO–P(=O)(H)–OH

(H_3PO_3)

H_3PO_3 is dibasic because it has two P—OH bonds and reducing due to the presence of one P—H bond.

36 (*c*) When nitric acid (HNO_3) reacts with nitric oxide (NO), NO_2 gas is released which oxidises H_2S into sulphur. The reactions are as follows :

$$2HNO_3 + NO \longrightarrow H_2O + 3NO_2$$
$$NO_2 + H_2S \longrightarrow H_2O + S + NO$$

37 (*c*) Very pure nitrogen can be obtained by the thermal decomposition of barium azide as.

$$Ba(N_3)_2 \longrightarrow Ba + 3N_2$$

In other reactions, impurities are also obtained. Hence, option (c) is correct.

38 (*c*) $2Pb(NO_3)_2 \longrightarrow 2PbO + 4NO_2 + O_2$

39 (*a*) $P_4 + 3NaOH + 3H_2O \longrightarrow 3NaH_2PO_2 + PH_3$

40 (*b*) $KCNO + (NH_4)_2SO_4 \longrightarrow NH_2CONH_2$

41 (*c*) From this structure, P–atom placed at the corners of a tetrahedron.

42 (*b*) $3CuSO_4 + 2PH_3 \longrightarrow Cu_3P_2 + 3H_2SO_4$

$$3HgCl_2 + 2PH_3 \longrightarrow Hg_3P_2 + 6HCl$$

43 (*b*) PbO_2 being a powerful oxidising agent, liberates O_2, when treated with conc. HNO_3.

$$2PbO_2 + 4HNO_3 \longrightarrow 2Pb(NO_3)_2 + 2H_2O + O_2$$

44 (*b*) Black phosphorus has a highly polymeric layer type structure. Hence, thermodynamically, it is the most stable form of phosphorus.

45 (*a*) Among the given oxyacids of phosphorus, hypophosphorous acid is the strongest reducing agent because in it, oxidation state of phosphorus is least (i.e. +1) and it contains two hydrogen atoms linked directly to the phosphorus.

46 (*b*) Nitrous acid gives dinitrogen trioxide on dehydration.

$$2HNO_2 \xrightarrow{\Delta} H_2O + N_2O_3$$

(anhydride of nitrous acid)

47 (*a*) $3CuO + 2NH_3 \longrightarrow 3Cu + N_2\uparrow + 3H_2O$

48 (*c*) Sodium pyrophosphate is represented by $Na_4P_2O_7$. It is sodium salt of pyrophosphoric acid ($H_4P_2O_7$), which may be considered to be made up by two molecules of ortho phosphoric acid (H_3PO_4), eliminating one molecule of H_2O.

$$2H_3PO_4 \xrightarrow{-H_2O} H_4P_2O_7$$

Pyrophosphoric acid

NaO–P(=O)(ONa)–O–P(=O)(ONa)–ONa

49 (*c*) The enthalpy of NH_3 is higher due to the H-bonding. In PH_3 and AsH_3, the intermolecular forces are dipole-dipole interactions which are relatively stronger in AsH_3. Therefore, order of increasing enthalpy of vaporisation is

$$PH_3 < AsH_3 < NH_3.$$

50 (*c*) Nitric oxide (NO) is decomposed at 900°C. So, it is the most thermally stable oxide of nitrogen.

$$2NO \xrightarrow{900°C} N_2 + O_2$$

51 (*c*) Ammonia has the highest proton affinity.

$$NH_3 + H^+ \longrightarrow NH_4^+$$

52 (*d*) NaOH (Sodium hydroxide) + H_3PO_2 (Hypophosphorous acid) $\longrightarrow$ NaH_2PO_2 (Sodium hypophosphite) + H_2O

53 (*c*) $4Zn + 10HNO_3$ (Cold and diluted) $\longrightarrow 4Zn(NO_3)_2 + NH_4NO_3$ (Ammonium nitrate) $+ 3H_2O$

54 (*c*) H_2SO_4 acts as a pickling agent. Pickling is an industrial process for removing layers of basic oxides from metals like Fe and Cu before electroplating, enameling, galvanising and soldering.

55 (*a*) Nitrogen ($_7N$), phosphorus ($_{15}P$), arsenic ($_{33}As$), antimony ($_{51}Sb$) and bismuth ($_{83}Bi$) constitute group 15 or VA of the periodic table. Collectively, these elements are called pnicogens and their compounds are pnictides.

56 (*b*) When phosphine comes in contact with air, it forms vortex rings of P_2O_5 in the form of white smoke so it is used to prepare smoke screens in warfare.

$$2PH_3 + 4O_2 \longrightarrow P_2O_5 + 3H_2O$$

57 (c) H_3PO_2 has 1 — OH group, H_3PO_3 has 2 — OH groups and H_3PO_4 has 3 — OH groups. In these acid although the number of —OH groups (ionisable hydrogen) increases, yet the acidity does not increase very much.

This is due to the fact that the number of unprotonated oxygen, responsible for the enhancement of acidity due to inductive effect, remains the same with the result dissociation constant also remain nearly same.

58 (b) Fe and Pt metals do not give a metal nitrate on treatment with concentrated HNO_3 because Pt has no action with HNO_3 of any concentration and Fe becomes passive on treatment with highly concentrated HNO_3. It is due to the deposition of oxide layer on the metal surface.

59 (a) The decreasing order of boiling point of NH_3, PH_3, AsH_3, SbH_3 and H_2O is $H_2O > SbH_3 > NH_3 > AsH_3 > PH_3$.

The boiling point generally increases as the molecular mass increases, but in NH_3 and H_2O the boiling point increases also due to the presence of hydrogen bonding, hence they have higher boiling points.

60 (a) White phosphorus on heating with aqueous solution of KOH produce phosphine (PH_3) gas.

$$\underset{\text{White phosphorus}}{P_4} + 3KOH + 3H_2O \longrightarrow \underset{\text{Potassium hypophosphite}}{3KH_2PO_2} + \underset{\text{Phosphine}}{PH_3}$$

61 (c) $$4Fe + \underset{\text{(dil.)}}{10HNO_3} \longrightarrow \underset{\text{Ferrous nitrate}}{4Fe(NO_3)_2} + \underset{\text{Ammonium nitrate}}{NH_4NO_3} + 3H_2O$$

62 (c) $$Sn + \underset{\text{(conc.)}}{4HNO_3} \longrightarrow \underset{\text{Metastannic acid}}{H_2SnO_3} + 4NO_2 + H_2O$$

63 (b) NH_4Cl is called nausadar. It is used in dry cell.

64 (a) The inorganic nitrogen exists in the form of ammonia, which may be lost as gas to atmosphere, may be acted upon by nitrifying bacteria, or may be taken up directly by plants.

65 (a) White phosphorus readily catches fire in air to produce dense white fumes of P_2O_5. Therefore, it is kept in water.

Topic 2

Chemistry of Group 16 Elements

2019

1 Which is the correct order of thermal stability for H_2E (E = O, S, Se, Te and Po)? **[NEET]**

(a) $H_2O < H_2S < H_2Se < H_2Te < H_2Po$
(b) $H_2Po < H_2Te < H_2Se < H_2S < H_2O$
(c) $H_2Se < H_2Te < H_2Po < H_2O < H_2S$
(d) $H_2S < H_2O < H_2Se < H_2Te < H_2Po$

2 Which of the following statement is correct for oleum? **[AIIMS]**

(a) It is prepared by absorption of SO_3 in conc. H_2SO_4
(b) It contains O— O groups
(c) It has six OH groups
(d) None of the above

3 Identify the correct formula of oleum from the following : **[NEET (Odisha)]**

(a) $H_2S_2O_7$ (b) H_2SO_3
(c) H_2SO_4 (d) $H_2S_2O_8$

2018

4 Conversion of oxygen into ozone is non-spontaneous at **[AIIPMT]**

(a) low temperature (b) all temperature
(c) high temperature (d) room temperature

5 Among the following, the correct formula of Marshall's acid is **[JIPMER]**

(a) $H_2S_2O_6$ (b) $H_2S_2O_8$
(c) H_2SO_4 (d) H_2SO_5

2017

6 In which of the following compounds, sulphur show maximum oxidation number? **[JYPMER]**

(a) H_2SO_4
(b) SO_3
(c) $H_2S_2O_7$
(d) All have same oxidation number for sulphur

7 Name the gas that can readily decolourise acidified $KMnO_4$ solution. **[NEET]**

(a) CO_2 (b) SO_2 (c) NO_2 (d) P_2O_5

2015

8 Nitrogen dioxide and sulphur dioxide have some properties in common. Which property is shown by one of these compounds, but not by the other? **[CBSE AIPMT]**

(a) Forms acid-rain
(b) Is a reducing agent
(c) Is soluble in water
(d) Is used as a food-preservative

2014

9 Acidity of diprotic acids in aqueous solutions increases in the order **[CBSE AIPMT]**

(a) $H_2S < H_2Se < H_2Te$
(b) $H_2Se < H_2S < H_2Te$
(c) $H_2Te < H_2S < H_2Se$
(d) $H_2Se < H_2Te < H_2S$

10 Which among the following group 16 elements exists in more than two allotropic states? [JCECE]
(a) Polonium (b) Tellurium
(c) Selenium (d) Oxygen

2013

11 Aqueous solutions of hydrogen sulphide and sulphur-dioxide when mixed together, yield [KCET]
(a) sulphur trioxide and water
(b) hydrogen and sulphurous acid
(c) sulphur and water
(d) hydrogen peroxide and sulphur

2011

12 Which is not the correct statement? [AIIMS]
(a) The S_8 ring is not planar
(b) Oxygen is more electronegative than sulphur
(c) SF_4 exists but OF_4 does exist
(d) SO_3 and SO_3^{2-} both have trigonal planar geometry

2010

13 If the supply of oxygen is limited, H_2S reacts with O_2 to form [AFMC]
(a) $H_2O + SO_3$ (b) $H_2O + S$
(c) $H_2SO_4 + S$ (d) $H_2O + SO_2$

14 Bromine water reacts with SO_2 to form [AFMC]
(a) HBr and S (b) H_2O and HBr
(c) S and H_2O (d) H_2SO_4 and HBr

15 O_2 and O_3 are [UP CPMT]
(a) allotropes (b) isotopes
(c) isomorphs (d) polymorphs

16 Sulphuric acid reacts with PCl_5 to give [Manipal]
(a) thionyl chloride (b) sulphur monochloride
(c) sulphuryl chloride (d) sulphur tetrachloride

17 Sulphur trioxide gas when dissolved in H_2SO_4, the product obtained is [OJEE]
(a) H_2SO_3 (b) H_2SO_5
(c) $H_2S_2O_7$ (d) $H_2S_2O_8$

18 α-and β-forms of sulphur are at equilibrium at a temperature known as [OJEE]
(a) critical temperature (b) transition temperature
(c) Boyle's temperature (d) inversion temperature

19 Which of the following statements regarding ozone is not correct? [WB JEE]
(a) The ozone molecule is angular in shape
(b) The ozone is a resonance hybrid of two structures
(c) The oxygen-oxygen bond length in ozone is identical with that of molecular oxygen
(d) Ozone is used as *germicide* and disinfectant for the purification of air

20 Ozone can be tested by [Haryana PMT]
(a) Ag (b) Hg (c) Zn (d) Au

21 Caro's acid is [VMMC]
(a) $H_2S_2O_3$ (b) H_2SO_5
(c) $H_2S_2O_8$ (d) $H_2S_2O_7$

2009

22 The acid having O—O bond is [CG PMT, Haryana PMT]
(a) $H_2S_2O_3$ (b) $H_2S_2O_6$
(c) $H_2S_2O_8$ (d) $H_2S_4O_6$

23 The type of bonds present in sulphuric anhydride [EAMCET]
(a) 3σ and three $p\pi$-$d\pi$
(b) 3σ, one $p\pi$-$p\pi$ and two $p\pi$-$d\pi$
(c) 2σ and three $p\pi$-$d\pi$
(d) 2σ and two $p\pi$-$d\pi$

2008

24 Perdisulphuric acid has the following bond [AIIMS]
(a) O ⟵ O=O (b) ⟵ O=O⟶
(c) >O ⟶ O< (d) —O—O—

25 S^{2-} and SO_3^{2-} can be distinguished by using [AIIMS]
(a) $(CH_3COO)_2Pb$ (b) $Na_2[Fe(CN)_5NO]$
(c) Both (a) and (b) (d) None of these

26 **Assertion** (A) The S—S—S bond angle in S_8 molecule is 107°.
Reason (R) S_8 has V-shape. [AIIMS]
(a) Both A and R are correct and R is the correct explanation of A
(b) Both A and R are correct but R is not the correct explanation of A
(c) A is correct but R is incorrect
(d) Both A and R are incorrect

27 Which of the following salt would give SO_2 with hot and dil. H_2SO_4 and also decolourises Br_2 water? [Manipal]
(a) Na_2SO_3 (b) $NaHSO_4$
(c) Na_2SO_4 (d) Na_2S

28 Ozone is used for purifying water because [BCECE]
(a) it dissociates and release oxygen
(b) do not leave any foul smell like chlorine
(c) kills bacteria, cyst, fungi and acts as a biocide
(d) All of the above

2007

29 H_2S is not a / an [UP CPMT]
(a) reducing agent (b) acidic
(c) oxidising agent (d) None of these

2006

30 The incorrect statement among the following is [AIIMS]
(a) C_{60} is an allotropic form of carbon
(b) O_3 is an allotropic form of oxygen
(c) S_8 is only allotropic form of sulphur
(d) red phosphorus is more stable in air than white phosphorus

31 **Assertion** (A) Molecular nitrogen is less reactive than molecular oxygen.
Reason (R) The bond length of N_2 is shorter than that of oxygen. **[AIIMS]**
(a) Both A and R are correct and R is the correct explanation of A
(b) Both A and R are correct but R is not the correct explanation of A
(c) A is correct but R is incorrect
(d) Both A and R are incorrect

32 Bleaching action of SO_2 is due to its **[RPMT]**
(a) oxidising property
(b) acidic property
(c) basic property
(d) reducing property

33 The molecular formula of dithionic acid is **[J&K CET]**
(a) $H_2S_2O_4$ (b) $H_2S_2O_6$
(c) $H_2S_2O_5$ (d) $H_2S_2O_7$

34 The acidity of hydrides of O, S, Se, Te varies in the order **[Punjab PMET]**
(a) $H_2O > H_2S > H_2Se > H_2Te$
(b) $H_2O < H_2S < H_2Se < H_2Te$
(c) $H_2S > H_2O > H_2Se > H_2Te$
(d) $H_2Se > H_2S > H_2O > H_2Te$

35 Catalyst used in making H_2SO_4 in contact process is **[JCECE]**
(a) V_2O_5 (b) Fe_2O_3
(c) Cr_2O_3 (d) CrO_3

2005

36 What is the correct relationship between the pHs of isomolar solutions of sodium oxide (pH_1), sodium sulphide (pH_2), sodium selenide (pH_3) and sodium telluride (pH_4)? **[CBSE AIPMT]**
(a) $pH_1 > pH_2 \approx pH_3 > pH_4$
(b) $pH_1 < pH_2 < pH_3 < pH_4$
(c) $pH_1 < pH_2 < pH_3 \approx pH_4$
(d) $pH_1 > pH_2 > pH_3 > pH_4$

37 **Assertion** (A) Reaction of SO_2 and H_2S in the presence of Fe_2O_3 catalyst gives elemental sulphur.
Reason (R) SO_2 is a reducing agent. **[AIIMS]**
(a) Both A and R are correct and R is the correct explanation of A
(b) Both A and R are correct but R is not the correct explanation of A
(c) A is correct but R is incorrect
(d) Both A and R are incorrect

38 **Assertion** (A) Ozone is powerful oxidising agent in comparison to O_2.
Reason (R) Ozone is diamagnetic but O_2 is paramagnetic. **[AIIMS]**
(a) Both A and R are correct and R is the correct explanation of A
(b) Both A and R are correct but R is not the correct explanation of A
(c) A is correct but R is incorrect
(d) Both A and R are incorrect

39 Carbogen is a mixture of **[RPMT]**
(a) $CO_2 + N_2$ (b) $CO + O_2$
(c) $CO_2 + O_2$ (d) $C + H_2 + N_2$

40 $H_2S_2O_8$ is **[MP PMT]**
(a) pyrosulphuric acid (b) Marshall's acid
(c) oleum (d) All of these

41 The oxidation states of the most electronegative element in the products of the reaction between BaO_2 and H_2SO_4 are **[Haryana PMT]**
(a) 0 and –1 (b) – 1 and – 2
(c) – 2 and – 3 (d) – 2 and 0

42 Fuming sulphuric acid is **[Punjab PMET]**
(a) $H_2SO_4 + SO_3$ (b) $H_2SO_4 + SO_2$
(c) H_2SO_4 (d) $H_2SO_4 + SO_4$

43 Which of the following pairs are correctly matched?

I. Haber process	Manufacture of ammonia
II. Le Blanc process	Manufacture of sulphuric acid
III. Birkeland-Eyde process	Manufacture of nitric acid
IV. Solvay process	Manufacture of sodium carbonate

Select the correct answer using the codes given below : **[JCECE]**
(a) II and III and IV
(b) I, II, III and IV
(c) I and II
(d) I, III and IV

44 Consider the following compounds. **[JCECE]**
I. Sulphur dioxide
II. Hydrogen peroxide
III. Ozone
Among these compounds identify those that can act as bleaching agent.
(a) I and III (b) II and III
(c) I and II (d) All of the above

Answers

1 (b)	2 (a)	3 (a)	4 (c)	5 (b)	6 (d)	7 (b)	8 (d)	9 (a)	10 (c)
11 (c)	12 (d)	13 (b)	14 (d)	15 (a)	16 (c)	17 (c)	18 (b)	19 (c)	20 (b)
21 (b)	22 (c)	23 (b)	24 (d)	25 (c)	26 (c)	27 (a)	28 (c)	29 (c)	30 (c)
31 (a)	32 (d)	33 (b)	34 (b)	35 (a)	36 (d)	37 (c)	38 (b)	39 (c)	40 (b)
41 (b)	42 (a)	43 (d)	44 (d)						

Explanations

1 (*b*) For group 16 elements, the hydrides with higher molar mass (e.g. H_2PO) are less thermally stable than hydride with lower molar mass (e.g. H_2O). This is due to the increase in size of central atom which results to the weakening of M—H bond due to increased bond length.

Thus, the correct order of thermal stability for $H_2E(E = O, S, Se, Te$ and Po) is as follows:

$H_2Po < H_2Te < H_2Se < H_2S < H_2O$

2 (*a*) Oleum, i.e. $H_2S_2O_7$ can be prepared by absorption of SO_3 in conc. H_2SO_4 as follows:

$$SO_3 + H_2SO_4 \longrightarrow \underset{\text{Oleum}}{H_2S_2O_7}$$

It's structure is as follows:

$$HO{-}\overset{\overset{O}{\|}}{\underset{\underset{O}{\|}}{S}}{-}O{-}\overset{\overset{O}{\|}}{\underset{\underset{O}{\|}}{S}}{-}OH$$

Thus, it has no O— O bond and has 2 —OH groups.

Thus, option (a) is the correct.

3 (*a*) The correct formula of oleum is $H_2S_2O_7$ which is also known as pyrosulphuric acid.

$$HO{-}\overset{\overset{O}{\|}}{\underset{\underset{O}{\|}}{S}}{-}O{-}\overset{\overset{O}{\|}}{\underset{\underset{O}{\|}}{S}}{-}OH$$

4 (*c*) Ozone is not stable at high temperature.

So, it decomposes into oxygen at high temperature.

$$2O_3 \longrightarrow 3O_2$$

Thus, the reverse of this reaction is non-spontaneous at high temperature.

5 (*b*) The correct formula of Marshall's acid is $H_2S_2O_8$. It is known as peroxodisulphuric acid having sulphur (S) in +6 oxidation state. The structure of this acid is shown below:

$$HO{-}\overset{\overset{O}{\|}}{\underset{\underset{O}{\|}}{S}}{-}O{-}O{-}\overset{\overset{O}{\|}}{\underset{\underset{O}{\|}}{S}}{-}OH$$

$(H_2S_2O_8)$

6 (*d*) All have same oxidation number for sulphate, i.e + 6.

(a) Oxidation number of S is

$H_2SO_4 = +2 + x - 8 = 0$

$\therefore \quad x = +6$

(b) Oxidation number of S in SO_3

$= x - 6 = 0$

$\therefore \quad x = +6$

(c) Oxidation number of S in $H_2S_2O_7$

$= 2 + 2x - 14 = 0$

$\therefore \quad 2x = +12$

$x = +6$

[where, x = Oxidation number of sulphur (*S*)]

7 (*b*) SO_2 gas can readily oxidise acidified $KMnO_4$ solution because $KMnO_4$ is an oxidising agent that easily oxidises SO_2.

$$2MnO_4^- + 5SO_2 + 2H_2O \longrightarrow 2Mn^{2+} + 5SO_4^{2-} + 4H^+$$

While other options such as NO_2 (strong oxidising agent), CO_2 (neither oxidising agent nor reducing agent) cannot decolourise acidified $KMnO_4$ solution.

8 (*d*) Nitrogen dioxide and sulphur dioxide forms acid rain. 'Acid rain' is the rain water containing sulphuric acid and nitric acid.

(a) $3NO_2 + H_2O \longrightarrow 2HNO_3 + NO$

$2SO_2 + 2H_2O + O_2 \longrightarrow 2H_2SO_4$

(b) NO_2 and SO_2 act as a good reducing agents e.g. SO_2 reduces halogens to halogen acid.

$$Cl_2 + 2H_2O + SO_2 \longrightarrow 2HCl + H_2SO_4$$

(c) NO_2 and SO_2 both are soluble in water.

(d) SO_2 is used in the manufacture of sodium bisulphite ($NaHSO_3$) which is used as a preservative for jams, jellies and squashes. But NO_2 is not used as a preservative.

9 (*a*) Acidic strength of hydrides increases as the size of central atom increases which weakens the M—H bond. Since, the size increases from S to Te, thus acidic strength follows the order :

$$H_2S < H_2Se < H_2Te$$

or as we go down the group, acidic strength of hydride increases.

10 (*c*)

	Element	Allotropes
(a)	Polonium	α- and β-polonium
(b)	Tellurium	None
(c)	Selenium	Trigonal, rhombohedral, three deep red monoclinic forms (α, β and γ-amorphous red, black vitrous selenium).
(d)	Oxygen	Dioxygen and ozone

11 (*c*) On mixing aqueous solution of H_2S and SO_2, colloidal sulphur and water are obtained.

$$2H_2S + SO_2 \longrightarrow 3S + 2H_2O$$

12 (*d*) SO_3 is trigonal planar due to sp^2 hybridised sulphur. SO_3^{2-} is sp^3 hybridised, but pyramidal due to presence of lone pair of electron.

13 (*b*) In limited supply of oxygen, H_2S burns with blue flame and S and H_2O are the main products

$$2H_2S + O_2 \longrightarrow 2H_2O + 2S$$

Note In excess of oxygen, H_2S gives SO_2 and water as main product.

14 (*d*) When bromine water reacts with SO_2, it oxidises SO_2 to sulphuric acid and itself gets reduced to HBr.

$$\underbrace{Br_2 + 2H_2O}_{\text{Bromine water}} + SO_2 \longrightarrow 2HBr + H_2SO_4$$

15 (*a*) Since, in O_2 and O_3, different number of same element, i.e. oxygen is present, hence these are allotropes.

Note Different crystalline structure, different number of atoms and different nuclear spins all result in allotropy.

16 (*c*) $H_2SO_4 + 2PCl_5 \longrightarrow \underset{\text{Sulphuryl chloride}}{SO_2Cl_2} + 2POCl_3 + 2HCl$

17 (*c*) $SO_3 + H_2SO_4 \longrightarrow \underset{\text{Oleum}}{H_2S_2O_7}$

18 (*b*) The temperature at which both the allotropic forms of sulphur coexist, is called transition temperature.

$$\alpha\text{-sulphur} \underset{< 369\text{ K}}{\overset{> 369\text{ K}}{\rightleftharpoons}} \beta\text{-sulphur}$$

19 (*c*) Due to resonance, the bond order in ozone is 1.5 where in O_2, bond order is 2. Hence O — O bond length in O_3 is greater than O—O bond length in O_2.

20 (*b*) Ozone can be tested by Hg (mercury).

$$2Hg + O_3 \longrightarrow \underset{\text{Mercurous oxide}}{Hg_2O} + O_2$$

During this reaction, mercury loses its meniscus and starts sticking to the side of the glass. This is known as tailing of mercury.

21 (*b*) H_2SO_5 (peroxomonosulphuric acid) is known as Caro's acid.

22 (*c*) (a) $H_2S_2O_3$ = HO—S(=S)(=O)—OH

(b) $H_2S_2O_6$ = HO—S(=O)(=O)—S(=O)(=O)—OH

(c) $H_2S_2O_8$ = HO—S(=O)(=O)—O—O—S(=O)(=O)—OH

(d) $H_2S_4O_6$ = HO—S(=O)(=O)—S—S—S(=O)(=O)—OH

Hence, $H_2S_2O_8$ has a O—O (peroxide) linkage.

23 (*a*) Sulphuric anhydride is SO_3 and its structure is as follows :

SO_3: S bonded to three O atoms; labels: σ, $d\pi$-$p\pi$, $p\pi$-$p\pi$, σ, σ, $d\pi$-$p\pi$

24 (*d*) The structure of perdisulphuric acid ($H_2S_2O_8$) is

HO—S(=O)(=O)—O—O—S(=O)(=O)—OH (Peroxide linkage)

Thus, peroxodisulphuric acid contains peroxide (—O—O—) bond.

25 (*c*) $S^{2-} + (CH_3COO)_2Pb \longrightarrow \underset{\text{Black ppt.}}{PbS\downarrow} + 2\,CH_3COO^-$

$S^{2-} + Na_2[Fe(CN)_5NO] \longrightarrow \underset{\text{Violet ppt.}}{[Fe(CN)_5NOS]^{4-}} + 2Na^+$

Hence, they are distinguished by both the reagents as only S^{2-} gives precipitate with these reagents, while SO_3^{2-} does not.

26 (*c*) S-atoms in S_8 molecule are sp^3 hybridised and contain two lone pairs of electrons on each and exist as staggered eight atom ring. Tetrahedral angle is 109° but due to lone pair of electrons, it reduces to 105°. S_8 ring is puckered and has a crown shape.

Hence, A is correct but R is incorrect.

27 (*a*) Na_2SO_3 reacts with hot and diluted H_2SO_4 to give SO_2 gas which decolourises bromine water.

$$Na_2SO_3 + H_2SO_4 \longrightarrow Na_2SO_4 + SO_2 + H_2O$$

$$Br_2 + H_2O \longrightarrow 2HBr + [O]$$

Decolourisation of bromine water.

$$SO_2 + [O] \longrightarrow SO_3$$

28 (*c*) Ozone is used for purifying water because ozone kills the bacteria, cysts, fungi, mold, parasites, viruses, contaminates, etc. It is one of the effective way of eliminating microorganisms present in the water. Ozone is very good biocide. Ozone also absorbs UV radiation.

29 (*c*) H_2S acts as a reducing agent, because it can reduce PbO into PbS.

$$PbO + H_2S \longrightarrow PbS + H_2O$$

It is acidic in nature. In chalcogens, the acidic nature of hydride increases from H_2O to H_2Te. It is not an oxidising agent.

30 (*c*) There are five allotropic forms of sulphur is

1. rhombic, octahedral or α-sulphur
2. monoclinic, prismatic or β-sulphur
3. plastic or γ-sulphur
4. milk of sulphur
5. colloidal or δ-sulphur.

31 (*a*) Molecular nitrogen is less reactive than that of oxygen because nitrogen has high dissociation energy in comparison to oxygen so, its reactivity is less. Also, bond length of nitrogen is shorter than oxygen because of presence of triple bond between nitrogen atoms. Hence, both A and R are correct and R is the correct explanation of A.

32 (*d*) SO_2 act as bleaching agent due to its reducing property.

$$SO_2 + 2H_2O \longrightarrow H_2SO_4 + 2H$$

Coloured matter + [H] ⟶ colourless matter

33 (*b*)

(a) $H_2S_2O_4$ — Dithionous acid
(b) $H_2S_2O_6$ — Dithionic acid
(c) $H_2S_2O_5$ — Disulphurous acid
(d) $H_2S_2O_7$ — Disulphuric acid

Hence, the molecular formula of dithionic acid is $H_2S_2O_6$.

34 (*b*) The acidic nature increases from H_2O to H_2Te. The increase in acidic character of hydrides on moving down the group may be explained in terms of bond length of H—*M* bond, larger is bond length, lesser is bond dissociation energy and thus easier is ionisation of H—*M* bond or easier is proton donating nature.

Hence, $H_2O < H_2S < H_2Se < H_2Te$

35 (*a*) Even at 400-500°C, the rate of reaction is very low. Therefore, to increase the reaction velocity a suitable catalyst is used. Now a days, most of the sulphuric acid plants use V_2O_5 as a catalyst.

36 (*d*) The correct order of pH of isomolar solution of sodium oxide (pH_1), sodium sulphide (pH_2), sodium selenide (pH_3) and sodium telluride (pH_4) is $pH_1 > pH_2 > pH_3 > pH_4$ because in aqueous solution, they are hydrolysed as follows :

$$Na_2O + 2H_2O \longrightarrow \underset{\text{Strong base}}{2NaOH} + H_2O$$

$$Na_2S + 2H_2O \longrightarrow \underset{\text{Strong base}}{2NaOH} + \underset{\text{Weak acid}}{H_2S}$$

$$Na_2Se + 2H_2O \longrightarrow \underset{\text{Strong base}}{2NaOH} + \underset{\text{Weak acid}}{H_2Se}$$

$$Na_2Te + 2H_2O \longrightarrow \underset{\text{Strong base}}{2NaOH} + \underset{\text{Weak acid}}{H_2Te}$$

Order of acidic strength

$H_2Te > H_2Se > H_2S > H_2O$

Order of neutralisation of NaOH

$H_2Te > H_2Se > H_2S > H_2O$

Hence, their aqueous solution have the following order of basic character due to neutralisation of NaOH with H_2O, H_2S, H_2Se and H_2Te.

$Na_2O > Na_2S > Na_2Se > Na_2Te$

(∵ pH of basic solutions is higher than that of acidic or least basic solutions).

37 (*c*) H_2S and SO_2 react as follows:

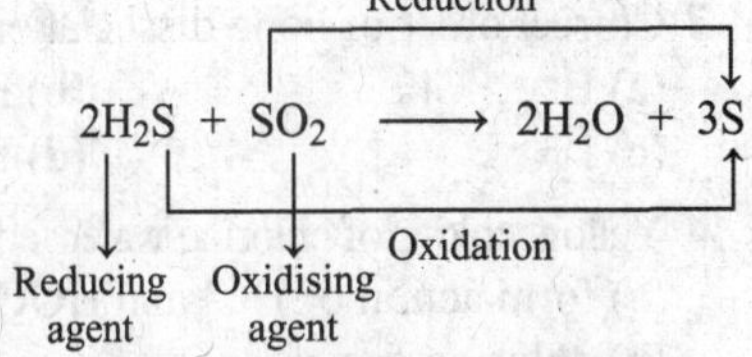

In this reaction, SO_2 is oxidising agent and H_2S is reducing agent.

Thus, A is correct but R is incorrect.

38 (*b*) Ozone is a powerful oxidising agent next to fluorine. It is much stronger oxidising agent than oxygen because on easy decomposition it forms nascent oxygen.

$$O_3 \longrightarrow O_2 + [O]$$

It is also true that O_3 is diamagnetic while O_2 is paramagnetic.

Hence, both A and R are correct but R is not the correct explanation of A.

39 (*c*) Carbogen is a mixture of 90% oxygen and 10% carbon dioxide.

40 (*b*) $H_2S_2O_8$ is peroxodisulphuric acid. It is also called Marshall's acid.

41 (*b*) $BaO_2 + H_2SO_4 \longrightarrow Ba\overset{-2}{SO_4} + H_2\overset{-1}{O_2}$

42 (*a*) Fuming sulphuric acid is oleum ($H_2S_2O_7$).

$$H_2SO_4 + SO_3 \longrightarrow \underset{\text{Pyrosulphuric acid}}{H_2S_2O_7}$$

SO_3 is absorbed in concentrated H_2SO_4 to give oleum.

43 (*d*) Le Blanc process is used in the manufacturing of sodium carbonate. So, II is incorrect pair among all.

44 (*d*) $SO_2 + 2H_2O \longrightarrow H_2SO_4 + 2\,[H]$

$$H_2O_2 \longrightarrow H_2O + [O]$$

$$O_3 \longrightarrow O_2 + [O]$$

The nascent [H] and [O] produced in the above reaction bleach the coloured articles. Thus, all the compounds act as bleaching agent.

Topic 3

Chemistry of Group 17 Elements

2019

1 The correct structure of tribromooctaoxide is **[NEET]**

(a) O=Br—Br—Br—O⁻ (with =O, =O and O⁻ substituents)

(b) 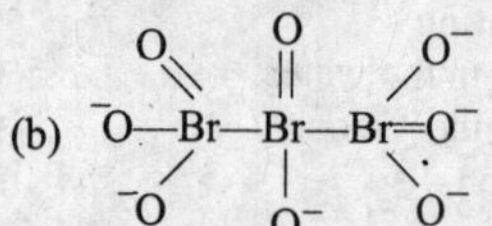

(c) 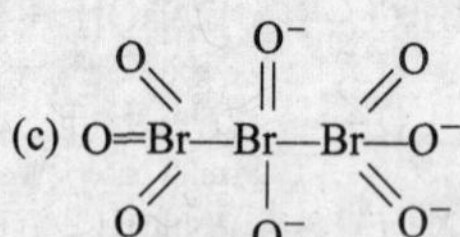

(d) 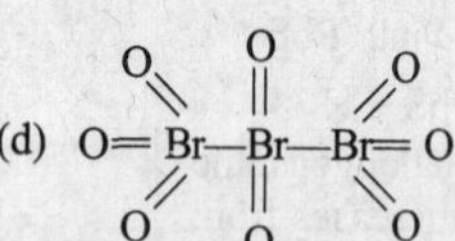

2 Match the following : **[NEET]**

A. Pure nitrogen	(i) Chlorine
B. Haber's process	(ii) Sulphuric acid
C. Contact process	(iii) Ammonia
D. Deacon's process	(iv) Sodium azide or barium azide

Which of the following is the correct option?

	A	B	C	D
(a)	(ii)	(iv)	(i)	(iii)
(b)	(iii)	(iv)	(ii)	(i)
(c)	(iv)	(iii)	(ii)	(i)
(d)	(i)	(ii)	(iii)	(iv)

3 Correct order of bond dissociation energy is **[AIIMS]**

(a) $Br_2 > Cl_2$ (b) $F_2 > Cl_2$
(c) $I_2 > F_2$ (d) $F_2 > I_2$

4 Yellow colour of chlorine water fades because of **[AIIMS]**

(a) form action of HCl and HOCl
(b) chlorine gas escapes
(c) $ClO_2 + H_2$
(d) Cl_2O

5 Affinity for hydrogen decreases in the group from fluorine to iodine. Which of the halogen acids should have highest bond dissociation enthalpy? **[AIIMS]**

(a) HF (b) HCl (c) HBr (d) HI

6 $\underset{\text{(Excess)}}{8NH_3} + 3Cl_2 \longrightarrow X$

$NH_3 + \underset{\text{(Excess)}}{3Cl_2} \longrightarrow Y$

What is X and Y in the above reaction? **[AIIMS]**

(a) $X = 6NH_4Cl + N_2$; $Y = NCl_3 + 3HCl$
(b) $X = NCl_3 + 3HCl$; $Y = 6NH_4Cl + N_2$
(c) $X = NCl_3 + N_2$; $Y = 6\,NH_4Cl + 3HCl$
(d) $X = 6NH_4Cl + 3HCl$; $Y = NCl_3 + N_2$

7 A green yellow gas reacts with an alkali metal hydroxide to form a halate which can be used in fireworks and safety matches. The gas and halate are, respectively **[AAIIMS]**

(a) Br_2, $KBrO_3$ (b) Cl_2, $KClO_3$
(c) I_2, $NaIO_3$ (d) Cl_2, $NaClO_3$

8 Which of the following statements is not true for halogens? **[NEET]**

(a) All but fluorine show positive oxidation states
(b) All are oxidising agents
(c) All form monobasic oxyacids
(d) Chlorine has the highest electron-gain enthalpy

2017

9 $HgCl_2$ and I_2 both when dissolved in water containing I^- ions, the pair of species formed is **[NEET]**

(a) HgI_4^{2-}, I_3^- (b) HgI_2, I_3^- (c) HgI_4^{2-}. I_3^- (d) Hg_2I_2, I_3^-

2016

10 AlF_3 is soluble in HF only in presence of KF. It is due to the formation of **[NEET (Phase II)]**

(a) $K_3[AlF_3H_3]$ (b) $K_3[AlF_6]$
(c) AlH_3 (d) $K[AlF_3H]$

2014

11 The gaseous product formed when HOCl reacts with H_2O_2 in acidic medium is **[Kerala CEE]**
(a) H_2 (b) Cl_2 (c) O_2 (d) $HClO_2$
(e) $HClO_3$

2013

12 The correct order of relative acidity is **[UP CPMT]**
(a) $HClO > HClO_2 > HClO_3 > HClO_4$
(b) $HClO_4 > HClO_3 > HClO_2 > HClO$
(c) $HClO > HClO_4 > HClO_2 > HClO_3$
(d) $HClO_3 > HClO_2 > HClO_4 > HClO$

13 The increasing order of reducing power of halogen acid is **[Manipal]**
(a) $HCl < HBr < HF < HI$ (b) $HF < HCl < HBr < HI$
(c) $HI < HBr < HCl < HF$ (d) $HBr < HCl < HF < HI$

14 The compound represents phosgene is **[Manipal]**
(a) phosphine (b) phosphorus trichloride
(c) carbonyl chloride (d) phosphorus oxychloride

15 Which of the following statement is incorrect? **[WB JEE]**
(a) ICl is a good conductor of electricity in fused state
(b) Cl_2O_7 is anhydride of perchloric acid
(c) Melting and boiling points of HBr is less than HCl
(d) F_2 forms only one oxoacid

16 Sea weeds are an important source of **[WB JEE]**
(a) chlorine (b) bromine (c) iodine (d) zinc

17 Bleaching powder loses its power on keeping for a long time because **[KCET]**
(a) it changes into calcium hypochlorate
(b) it changes into calcium chloride and calcium hydroxide
(c) it absorbs moisture
(d) it changes into calcium chloride and calcium chlorate

2012

18 When Cl_2 gas reacts with hot and concentrated sodium hydroxide solution, the oxidation number of chlorine changes from **[CBSE AIPMT]**
(a) zero to +1 and zero to − 5
(b) zero to − 1 and zero to + 5
(c) zero to − 1and zero + 3
(d) zero to + 1and zero to − 3

19 When a colourless gas is passed through bromine water, only decolourisation takes place. The gas is **[AFMC]**
(a) SO_2 (b) HBr
(c) HCl (d) H_2S

20 Which of the following is not a peroxyl acid? **[Manipal]**
(a) Perphosphoric acid (b) Pernitric acid
(c) Perdisulphuric acid (d) Perchloric acid

21 Which of the following is not a pseudohalide? **[OJEE]**
(a) $RCOO^-$ (b) N_3^-
(c) CNO^- (d) CN^-

2011

22 When Br_2 is treated with aqueous solutions of NaF, NaCl and NaI separately **[Kerala CEE]**
(a) F_2, Cl_2 and I_2 are liberated.
(b) only F_2 and Cl_2 are liberated.
(c) only I_2 is liberated.
(d) only Cl_2 is liberated.
(e) only Cl_2 and I_2 are liberated.

23 Which element undergoes disproportionation in water? **[DUMET]**
(a) Cl_2 (b) F_2 (c) K (d) Cs

2010

24 Least volatile hydrogen halide is **[AFMC]**
(a) HF (b) HCl
(c) HI (d) HBr

25 To make a painting over glass, we use **[UP CPMT]**
(a) fluorine (b) chlorine
(c) bromine (d) hydrogen chloride

26 Which of the following has *germicidal* effect? **[UP CPMT]**
(a) KCl (b) KBr (c) KI (d) NaCl

27 Fluorine is not prepared by general methods because **[BVP]**
(a) HF can be easily oxidised.
(b) HF cannot be easily oxidised.
(c) HF is highly poisonous.
(d) HF is a good conductor of electricity.

28 Fluorine react with water to give **[BVP]**
(a) HF and O_2 (b) HF and OF_2
(c) HF and O_3 (d) HF, O_2 and O_3

29 Chlorine shows bleaching action in **[OJEE]**
(a) dry condition (b) presence of HCl only
(c) moist condition (d) None of these

30 The correct order of increasing hydration energy of the following conjugate bases of oxyacids of chlorine is **[AMU]**
(a) $ClO^- < ClO_2^- < ClO_3^- < ClO_4^-$
(b) $ClO_4^- < ClO_3^- < ClO_2^- < ClO^-$
(c) $ClO_4^- < ClO_3^- < ClO^- < ClO_2^-$
(d) $ClO_3^- < ClO_4^- < ClO_2^- < ClO^-$

31 Which of the following compounds give chlorine dioxide when it reacts with SO_2 in the presence of acid? **[Guj CET]**
(a) Sodium chloride
(b) Sodium chlorate
(c) Sodium perchlorate
(d) Sodium chlorite

32 In the manufacture of bromine from sea water, the mother liquor containing bromide is treated with **[JCECE]**
(a) carbon dioxide (b) chlorine
(c) iodine (d) sulphur dioxide

33 Which one of the following halogens has the highest bond dissociation energy? **[VMMC]**
(a) F_2 (b) Cl_2 (c) Br_2 (d) I_2

34 **Assertion** (A) F_2 has high reactivity.

Reason (R) F—F bond has low bond dissociation enthalpy. [VMMC]

(a) Both A and R are correct and R is the correct explanation of A
(b) Both A and R are correct but R is not the correct explanation of A
(c) A is correct but R is incorrect
(d) Both A and R are incorrect

2009

35 Hypochlorite disproportionates to give [OJEE]

(a) Cl^- and ClO_4^- (b) ClO_4^- and ClO_3^-
(c) ClO_3^- and Cl^- (d) ClO_2^- and Cl^-

36 The reaction of Cl_2 with X gives bleaching powder. X is [OJEE]

(a) CaO (b) $Ca(OH)_2$
(c) $Ca(OCl)_2$ (d) $Ca(ClO_3)_2$

37 Fluorine reacts with dilute NaOH and forms a gaseous product A. The bond angle in the molecule of A is [EAMCET]

(a) 104°40′ (b) 103°
(c) 107° (d) 109°28′

38 Which of the following halogens does not exhibit a positive oxidation number in their compounds? [DUMET]

(a) I (b) Br (c) Cl (d) F

39 Anhydrous ferric chloride is prepared by [CG PMT]

(a) heating $FeCl_3$ at high temperature in steam of air.
(b) heating iron in stream of dry chlorine.
(c) heating ferric oxide with hydrochloric acid.
(d) reacting iron with hydrochloric acid.

2008

40 Which of the following dissolves in water but does not give any oxyacid solution? [UP CPMT]

(a) SO_2 (b) OF_2 (c) SCl_4 (d) SO_3

41 When chlorine reacts with dil. NaOH under cold conditions, the oxidation state of chlorine changes from zero to [J&K CET]

(a) –1 and +5 (b) +1 and +4
(c) +5 and +3 (d) –1 and +1

42 One gas bleaches the colour of flowers by reduction and another gas by oxidation. The gases respectively, are [Punjab PMET]

(a) SO_2 and Cl_2 (b) CO and Cl_2
(c) NH_3 and SO_2 (d) H_2S and Br_2

43 NaCl, NaBr and NaI mixture on heating with conc. H_2SO_4 gives gases, respectively [JCECE]

(a) HCl, HBr, HI (b) HCl, Br_2, I_2
(c) Cl_2, Br_2, I_2 (d) Cl_2, HBr, HI

2007

44 Which one of the following is the true covalent oxide of iodine? [AIIMS]

(a) I_2O_4 (b) I_2O_5 (c) I_2O_7 (d) I_2O_9

45 Which one below is a pseudohalide? [AFMC]

(a) CN^- (b) ICl (c) IF_5 (d) I_3^-

46 Chlorine reacts with excess of ammonia to form [Kerala CEE]

(a) NH_4Cl (b) N_2 + HCl
(c) $N_2 + NH_4Cl$ (d) $N_2 + NCl_3$
(e) NCl_3 + HCl

47 The bleaching action of chlorine is due to the liberation of the following [J&K CET]

(a) HOCl (b) HCl (c) [O] (d) O_2

48 Which reaction is not feasible? [Punjab PMET]

(a) $2KI + Br_2 \longrightarrow 3KBr + I_2$
(b) $2KBr + I_2 \longrightarrow 2KI + Br_2$
(c) $2KBr + Cl_2 \longrightarrow 2KCl + Br_2$
(d) $2H_2O + 2F_2 \longrightarrow 4HF + O_2$

49 Which of the following is not correct? [EAMCET]

(a) In Nelson method of NaOH preparation, Cl_2 is liberated at anode
(b) With hot and conc. NaOH, Cl_2 gas gives NaOCl
(c) NaOH reacts with white phosphorus to give phosphine
(d) NaOH is used in rayon industry

50 Least stable oxide of chlorine is [BCECE]

(a) Cl_2O (b) ClO_2
(c) Cl_2O_7 (d) ClO_3

2006

51 Which two of the following salts are used for preparing iodised salt?

I. KIO_3 II. KI III. I_2 IV. HI [AIIMS]

(a) I and II (b) I and III
(c) II and IV (d) III and IV

52 Solubility of iodine in water may be increased by adding [Manipal]

(a) chloroform (b) potassium iodide
(c) carbon disulphide (d) sodium thiosulphate

53 Which of the following is anhydride of perchloric acid? [RPMT]

(a) Cl_2O_7 (b) Cl_2O_5
(c) Cl_2O_3 (d) HClO

54 Fluorine is the best oxidising agent because it has [RPMT]

(a) highest electron affinity (b) highest E°_{red}
(c) highest E°_{oxid} (d) lowest electron affinity

55 What is X in the following reaction?

$KHSO_4 + F_2 \longrightarrow HF + X$ [EAMCET]

(a) K_2SO_4 (b) $K_2S_2O_4$
(c) $K_2S_2O_2$ (d) $K_2S_2O_8$

56 Tincture of iodine is [Punjab PMET]

(a) CHI_3 in alcohol (b) I_2 in alcohol
(c) I_2 in KI (d) CHI_3 in KI

57 Colour of the solution when KI reacts with Br_2 is **[JCECE]**
(a) blue (b) black
(c) red (d) no change

2005

58 Which one of the following oxides is expected to exhibit paramagnetic behaviour? **[CBSE AIPMT]**
(a) CO_2 (b) SO_2 (c) ClO_2 (d) SiO_2

59 When F_2 react with hot and concentrated alkali, then following will be obtained **[MHT CET]**
I. OF_2 II. O_2
III. H_2O IV. NaF
(a) I, III and IV (b) II, III only
(c) II, III and IV (d) All of these

60 The mixture of conc. HCl and HNO_3 made in 3 : 1 ratio contains **[Kerala CEE]**
(a) ClO_2 (b) NOCl (c) NCl_3 (d) N_2O_4
(e) N_2O

61 I_2 dissolves in KI solution due to the formation of **[MP PMT]**
(a) KI_2 and I^-
(b) K^+, I^- and I_2
(c) KI_3
(d) None of the above

62 Which of the following is the strongest acid? **[Haryana PMT]**
(a) $ClO_3(OH)$ (b) $ClO_2(OH)$
(c) $SO(OH)_2$ (d) $SO_2(OH)_2$

63 S_2Cl_2 hydrolyses slowly to form HCl, SO_2 and X. Which of the following is X? **[EAMCET]**
(a) SO_3 (b) H_2
(c) O_2 (d) S

64 Which of the following is used during the preparation of fluorine by Whytlaw-Gray method? **[EAMCET]**
(a) Aqueous KF (b) Aqueous HF
(c) Molten KHF_2 (d) NH_4F

Answers

1 (d)	2 (c)	3 (d)	4 (a)	5 (a)	6 (a)	7 (b)	8 (a)	9 (c)	10 (b)
11 (c)	12 (b)	13 (b)	14 (b)	15 (c)	16 (c)	17 (d)	18 (b)	19 (a)	20 (d)
21 (a)	22 (c)	23 (a)	24 (a)	25 (a)	26 (c)	27 (b)	28 (d)	29 (c)	30 (a)
31 (b)	32 (b)	33 (b)	34 (a)	35 (c)	36 (b)	37 (b)	38 (d)	39 (b)	40 (b)
41 (d)	42 (a)	43 (b)	44 (b)	45 (a)	46 (c)	47 (c)	48 (b)	49 (b)	50 (a)
51 (a)	52 (b)	53 (a)	54 (b)	55 (d)	56 (b)	57 (b)	58 (c)	59 (c)	60 (b)
61 (c)	62 (a)	63 (d)	64 (c)						

Explanations

1 (*d*) The correct structure of tribromooctaoxide is

$$\begin{array}{ccccc} O & & O & & O \\ & \diagdown\!\!\diagdown & \| & /\!\!/ & \\ O{=} & Br & {-}Br{-} & Br & {=}O \\ & /\!\!/ & \| & \diagdown\!\!\diagdown & \\ O & & O & & O \end{array}$$

In this compound, Br exhibits variable oxidation state. The oxidation state of Br from left to right are + 6, + 4 and + 6, respectively.

2 (*c*) The correct match is as follows :

(A) **Pure nitrogen** Pure nitrogen can be obtained by thermal decomposition of sodium or barium azide.

$$Ba(N_3)_2 \xrightarrow{\Delta} Ba + 3N_2$$
$$2NaN_3 \xrightarrow{\Delta} 2Na + 3N_2$$

(B) **Haber's process** On large scale, ammonia is manufactured by Haber's process.

$$N_2(g) + 3H_2(g) \underset{723-773\ K}{\overset{Fe,\ (MO),\ 200 bar}{\rightleftharpoons}} 2NH_3(g)$$

(C) **Contact process** Sulphuric acid is manufactured by the contact process.

(D) **Deacon's process** Chlorine is prepared by Deacon's process.

$$4HCl + O_2 \xrightarrow{CuCl_2} 2Cl_2 + 2H_2O$$

Hence, the correct match is
(A) → (iv), (B) → (iii), (C) → (ii), (D) → (i)

3 (*d*) In general, bond enthalpy or bond dissociation energy of halogen molecules (X_2) decreases down the group from Cl_2 to I_2.

$$Cl_2 > Br_2 > F_2 > I_2$$

The decrease in bond enthalpy from Cl_2 to I_2 is due to increase in atomic size that increases the distance between two atoms. Hence, it becomes easier to break them apart. The exceptionally low bond dissociation energy of fluorine molecule is due to very small size of fluorine atom. This brings the non-bonding electrons on fluorine nearer to each other, resulting in a much greater lone pair-lone pair repulsion, which weakens the covalent bond and lowers its dissociation energy.

Hence, option (d) is correct.

4 (*a*) Chlorine water on standing loses yellow colour due to formation of HCl and HOCl which in turn provides nascent oxygen.

$$Cl_2 + H_2O \longrightarrow HCl + HOCl$$
$$HClO \longrightarrow HCl + \underset{\text{Nascent oxygen}}{[O]}$$

5 (*a*) As the size of the halogen atom increases from F to I, H—X bond length in halogen acids also increases from H—F to HI. (HF < HCl < HBr < HI). The increase in HX bond length decreases the strength of HX bond from HF to HI (HF > HCl > HBr > HI).

Due to successive decrease in the strength of HX bonds, bond dissociation enthalpy decreases from HF to HI.

HX :	HF	>	HCl	>	HBr	>	HI
Bond dissociation enthalpy (kJ / mol)	574.0		428.1		362.5		294.6

6 (*a*) $8NH_3 + 3Cl_2 \longrightarrow 6NH_4Cl + N_2\uparrow$
(Excess)

$NH_3 + 3Cl_2 \longrightarrow NCl_3 + 3HCl$
(Excess)

Hence, $X = 6NH_4Cl + N_2\uparrow$,

$Y = NCl_3 + 3HCl$

7 (*b*) A halate will be formed from halogen and the greenish yellow gas is Cl_2. The halate which is used in fireworks and safety matches is $KClO_3$. The reaction is as follows :

$$3Cl_2 + 6KOH \longrightarrow KClO_3 + 5KCl + 3H_2O$$

8 (*a*)

(a) Fluorine is the most electronegative element and cannot exhibit any positive oxidation state. Other halogens have *d*-orbitals and therefore, can expand their octets and show +1, +3, +5 and +7 oxidation states. Thus, option (a) is incorrect.

Note Fluorine can form an oxoacid, HOF in which oxidation state of F is +1. But HOF is highly unstable compound.

(b) All halogens are strong oxidising agents as they have strong tendency to accept an electron. Thus, option (b) is correct.

(c) All halogens form monobasic oxyacids. Thus, option (c) is also correct.

(d) Electron gain enthalpy of halogens become less negative down the group. However, the negative electron gain enthalpy of fluorine is less than chlorine due to small size of fluorine atom. Thus, option (d) is also correct.

9 (*c*) $HgCl_2$ and I_2 both when dissolved in water containing I^- ions, the pair of species formed is HgI_4^{2-} and I_3^-.

In aqueous solution, I_2 reacts with I^- and maintains the following equilibrium.

$$I_2 + I^- \rightleftharpoons I_3^-$$

Hg^{2+} gives ppt. of HgI_2 on reaction with I^-.

But HgI_2 is soluble in excess of I^-

$$Hg^{2+} + 2I^- \longrightarrow \underset{\text{Red ppt.}}{HgI_2\downarrow} + 2Cl^-$$

$$HgI_2 + 2I^- \rightleftharpoons [HgI_4]^{2-}$$

10 (*b*) Al^{3+} shows maximum coordination number 6, thus it will form AlF_6^{3-}.

AlF_3 forms $K_3[AlF_6]$ when dissolved in HF in the presence of KF as shown below:

$$AlF_3 + 3KF \xrightarrow{HF} K_3[AlF_6]$$

11 (*c*) When HOCl is treated with H_2O_2 in acidic medium it gets reduced to Cl^- with the evolution of oxygen gas.

$$HOCl(aq) + H_2O_2(aq) \longrightarrow HCl(aq) + H_2O(l) + O_2(g)$$

So, the correct answer is (c) i.e. O_2

12 (*b*) Acidic strength of oxyacids increases with increase in oxidation state of central atom.

Find the oxidation state of chlorine in all the oxyacids to decide the decreasing acidic strength order among oxyacids.

(i) $HClO_4 = +1 + x + (-2 \times 4) = 0$

$\therefore \quad x = +7$

(ii) $HClO_3 = +1 + x + (-2 \times 3) = 0$

$\therefore \quad x = +5$

(iii) $HClO_2 = 1 + x + (-2 \times 2) = 0$

$\therefore \quad x = +3$

(iv) $HClO = +1 + x + (-2 \times 1) = 0$

$\therefore \quad x = +1$

$HClO_4$ is the strongest acid and HClO is the weakest acid.

$\therefore$ Correct order of acidic strength is

$$HClO_4 > HClO_3 > HClO_2 > HClO$$

13 (*b*) The increasing order of reducing power of halogen acid is

$$HF < HCl < HBr < HI$$

The reason is that, by increasing the size of halogen atom, the bond strength of H—*X* decreases. Thus, the ease of hydrogen donation increases and hence, reducing power increases.

14 (*b*) Phosgene is a poisonous gas. It is also known as carbonyl chloride, $(COCl_2)$ as shown below :

$$Cl-\overset{\overset{\displaystyle O}{\|}}{C}-Cl$$

15 (*c*) Melting and boiling points of HCl is the lowest amongst H*X* due to weak intermolecular H—bonding in H— Cl.

16 (*c*) Sea weeds contain iodine.

Hence, option (c) is correct.

17 (*d*) Bleaching powder loses its power on keeping for a long time because it changes into calcium chloride and calcium chlorate.

18 (*b*) When chlorine gas reacts with hot and concentrated NaOH solution, it disproportionates into chloride (Cl^-) and chlorate (ClO_3^-) ions.

$$\overset{0}{3Cl_2} + \underset{\text{(hot and conc.)}}{6NaOH} \longrightarrow 5Na\overset{-1}{Cl} + Na\overset{+5}{Cl}O_3 + 3H_2O$$

In this process, oxidation number of chlorine changes from 0 to – 1 and 0 to +5.

Note In disproportionation reaction, the same element undergoes oxidation as well as reduction.

19 (*a*) Bromine water is an oxidising agent It oxidises SO_2 to SO_3 and itself gets reduced to colourless HBr.

$$\underset{\text{Orange red}}{Br_2} + H_2O \longrightarrow \underset{\text{Colourless}}{2HBr} + [O]$$

$$SO_2 + [O] \longrightarrow SO_3$$
$$H_2O + SO_3 \longrightarrow H_2SO_4$$

H_2S is also oxidised by bromine water but in this case, decolourisation is also accompanied by the formation of sulphur.

$$H_2S + [O] \longrightarrow H_2O + S$$

20 (*d*) A peroxyl acid is one that contain peroxide [—O—O—] linkage. As perchloric acid $(HClO_4)$ doesn't contain a peroxide linkage, it is not a peroxyl acid, whereas others having a peroxide linkage are peroxyl acid.

Structure of $HClO_4$

21 (*a*) Pseudohalides are the combinations of more than one electronegative atoms which have one unit negative charge, e.g. CN^-, CNO^- N_3^-, etc., $RCOO^-$ is not a pseudohalide.

22 (*c*) Only I_2 is liberated. Br_2 liberates I_2 from NaI, because iodine lies below bromine in electrochemical series and can be easily displaced by more reactive element (lie above in electrochemical series).

23 (*a*) Chlorine undergo disproportionation on reaction with water and gives HCl and HClO.

$$Cl_2 + H_2O \longrightarrow H\overset{-1}{Cl} + H\overset{+1}{Cl}O$$

Other options does not give disproportionation reaction.

24 (*a*) Except HF (least volatile), all hydrogen halides are gases. HF is a liquid with boiling point 19.5°C. This behaviour is due to association of HF molecules through hydrogen bonding.

$$\overset{\delta^+}{H}-\overset{\delta^-}{F}\cdots\overset{\delta^+}{H}-\overset{\delta^-}{F}\cdots\overset{\delta^+}{H}-\overset{\delta^-}{F}\cdots\overset{\delta^+}{H}-\overset{\delta^-}{F}$$

25 (*a*) Fluorine attacks on glass but very slowly. Thus, it is used to make painting over glass.

26 (*c*) Among the given options only potassium iodide (KI) is used as a germicide.

27 (*b*) Fluorine is not prepared by general methods as used for the preparation of Cl_2 and Br_2 because HF cannot be easily oxidised to F_2. (Fluorine is the most electronegative element)

28 (*d*) Fluorine react with water to give HF, O_2 and O_3.

$$2H_2O + 2F_2 \xrightarrow{\text{Cold}} 4HF + O_2$$

$$3H_2O + 3F_2 \xrightarrow{\text{Hot}} 6HF + O_3$$

29 (*c*) In moist condition, Cl_2 releases nascent oxygen that can act as a bleaching agent. Reactions involved are as follows :

$$Cl_2 + H_2O \longrightarrow HCl + HOCl$$

$$HOCl \longrightarrow HCl + \underset{\text{Nascent oxygen}}{[O]}$$

$$\text{Coloured substance} + [O] \longrightarrow \text{Colourless substance}$$

30 (*a*) Hydration energy varies inversely with size. Among the given oxyacids, ClO_4^- has the smallest size because of the presence of Cl^{7+} followed by ClO_3^- (with Cl^{5+}) and ClO_2^- (with Cl^{3+}). ClO^- has the largest size with Cl^+ ion. Hence, the order of increasing hydration energy is

$$ClO^- < ClO_2^- < ClO_3^- < ClO_4^-.$$

31 (*b*) Commercially, chlorine dioxide is prepared by passing SO_2 gas into a mixture of sodium chlorate and H_2SO_4 having NaCl in traces.

$$\underset{\text{Sodium chlorate}}{2NaClO_3} + SO_2 + H_2SO_4 \xrightarrow[\text{NaCl}]{\text{Trace}} \underset{\text{Chlorine dioxide}}{2ClO_2} + 2NaHSO_4$$

32 (*b*) Sea water contains KBr, $MgBr_2$ etc. apart from NaCl. The mother liquor containing bromide ions is treated with chlorine gas such that bromine gas is liberated. This bromine gas dissolves in water. This solution is further treated by passing hot air, then passing through hot aqueous Na_2CO_3 and further treating with H_2SO_4 to obtain Br_2.

33 (*b*) As the size of atom increases, bond length increases, thus bond dissociation energy decreases.

Molecule	Bond dissociation energy (kJ mol^{-1})
F_2	158.8
Cl_2	242.6
Br_2	192.8
I_2	151.1

However, the dissociation energy of fluorine is lesser than that of chlorine because of its small size.

Hence, Cl_2 has the highest bond dissociation energy.

34 (*a*) Fluorine is the most reactive among all the halogens due to its low bond dissociation enthalpy.

Hence, both A and R are correct and Reason is the correct explanation of Assertion.

35 (*c*) Hypochlorite disproportionates to give ClO_3^- and Cl^-

$$\underset{\text{Hypochlorite}}{2ClO} \longrightarrow \underset{\text{Chlorate}}{ClO_3^-} + \underset{\text{Chloride}}{Cl^-}$$

36 (*b*) $$\underset{(X)}{Ca(OH)_2} + Cl_2 \longrightarrow \underset{\text{Bleaching powder}}{Ca(OCl)Cl} + H_2O$$

37 (*b*) $$2F_2 + \underset{\text{(dil.)}}{2NaOH} \longrightarrow 2NaF + \underset{(A)}{OF_2}\uparrow + H_2O$$

The structure of *A* (OF_2) is bent or V shape as,

(O with two lone pairs bonded to F and F; angle 103.2°)

σ-bond made by O = 2

Lone pairs of electrons on O = 2

Number of orbitals used by O for hybridisation = 2 + 2 = 4

Hybridisation of (b) in OF_2 is sp^3.

38 (*d*) F is the most electronegative atom. So, it cannot exhibit positive oxidation state.

39 (*b*) Anhydrous $FeCl_3$ is prepared by passing dry chlorine over heated iron.

$$2Fe + \underset{\text{(Dry)}}{3Cl_2} \longrightarrow \underset{\text{Deliquescent salt}}{2FeCl_3}$$

40 (*b*) OF_2 dissolves in water but does not give any oxyacid solution. While SO_2, SCl_4 and SO_3 give oxyacid in water.

$$SO_2 + H_2O \longrightarrow \underset{\text{Sulphurous acid}}{H_2SO_3}$$

$$SCl_4 + 3H_2O \longrightarrow \underset{\text{Sulphurous acid}}{H_2SO_3} + 4HCl$$

$$SO_3 + H_2O \longrightarrow \underset{\text{Sulphuric acid}}{H_2SO_4}$$

41 (*d*) $$\underset{\text{dil. and cold}}{2NaOH + Cl_2} \longrightarrow \underset{\text{soduim chloride}}{NaCl} + \underset{\text{Sodium hypochlorite}}{NaClO} + H_2O$$

Let oxidation state of Cl in NaCl is *x*.

$$+1 + x = 0$$

$$x = -1$$

Let oxidation state of Cl in NaClO is *x*.

$$+1 + x - 2 = 0$$

$$x - 1 = 0$$

$$x = +1$$

42 (*a*) The bleaching action of SO_2 is due to reduction while the bleaching action of Cl_2 is due to oxidation.

$$SO_2 + 2H_2O \longrightarrow H_2SO_4 + 2[H]$$

$$Cl_2 + H_2O \longrightarrow 2HCl + [O]$$

43 (*b*) $$NaCl + H_2SO_4 \xrightarrow{\Delta} NaHSO_4 + HCl\uparrow$$

$$HCl + H_2SO_4 \xrightarrow{\Delta} \text{No reaction}$$

$$NaBr + H_2SO_4 \xrightarrow{\Delta} NaHSO_4 + HBr$$

$$2HBr + H_2SO_4 \xrightarrow{\Delta} Br_2\uparrow + SO_2 + 2H_2O$$

$$NaI + H_2SO_4 \xrightarrow{\Delta} NaHSO_4 + HI$$

$$2HI + H_2SO_4 \xrightarrow{\Delta} I_2\uparrow + SO_2 + 2H_2O$$

Hence, the gases released are HCl, Br_2 and I_2.

44 (*b*) In general, higher the oxidation state, more is the covalent character of the oxide. I_2O_7 and I_2O_9 do not exist. I_2O_4 is ionic in nature. It is infact iodyl iodates $[IO]^+ [IO_3]^-$. The only covalent oxide of iodine is I_2O_5.

45 (*a*) **Pseudohalide ions and pseudohalogens** There are certain monovalent negative ions made up of two or more electronegative atoms which exhibit properties similar to those of halide ions. Such ions are known as pseudo halide ions. Just as halide ions, pseudohalide ions have also corresponding dimeric molecules. These are called pseudohalogens and have properties similar to those of halogens.

Pseudohalides	Pseudohalogens
cyanide CN^-	cyanogen $(CN)_2$
thiocyanate SCN^-	thiocyanogen $(SCN)_2$

46 (*c*) Chlorine gives nitrogen and ammonium chloride with excess ammonia.

$$\underset{\text{Excess}}{3Cl_2 + 8NH_3} \longrightarrow 6NH_4Cl + N_2\uparrow$$

47 (*c*) Chlorine reacts slowly with H_2O to form HCl and HOCl. The HOCl then decomposes into HCl and [O] radicals.

$$Cl_2 + H_2O \rightleftharpoons HCl + HOCl$$

$$HOCl \longrightarrow HCl + \underset{\text{mascent oxygen}}{[O]}$$

This nascent oxygen is very strong oxidising as well as effective bleaching agent in aqueous solution of Cl_2 or hypochlorite salt.

48 (*b*) $2KBr + I_2 \longrightarrow 2KI + Br_2$

Above reaction is not possible because Br^- ion is not oxidised to Br_2 with I_2 due to lower electrode potential of I_2 than bromine.

49 (*b*) Statement (c) is incorrect. NaOH on reaction with Cl_2 gives NaCl and $NaClO_3$.

$$\underset{\text{Hot + conc.}}{6NaOH} + 3Cl_2 \longrightarrow 5NaCl + \underset{\text{Sodium chlorate}}{NaClO_3} + 3H_2O$$

50 (*a*) The stability of oxides increases with increase in oxidation state of halogen.

Oxide	Oxidation state of halogen
Cl_2O	+1
ClO_2	+4
ClO_3	+6
Cl_2O_7	+7

Hence, Cl_2O is the least stable oxide of chlorine.

51 (*a*) To prepare iodised salt KIO_3 and KI are used.

52 (*b*) The solubility of I_2 in water increases by the addition of KI due to formation of polyhalide ion, i.e. I_3^-.

$$KI + I_2 \longrightarrow KI_3$$

53 (*a*) Chlorine heptoxide (Cl_2O_7) is the anhydride of perchloric acid.

$$2HClO_4 \xrightarrow{\Delta} Cl_2O_7 + H_2O$$

54 (*b*) Fluorine has the highest E°_{red} (equal to +2.9 V) due to which it can easily accept an electron and hence it is the best oxidising agent.

55 (*d*) $2KHSO_4 + F_2 \longrightarrow 2HF + \underset{X}{K_2S_2O_8}$

56 (*b*) 2-7% I_2 in a mixture of alcohol and water is known as tincture of iodine.

It is used as an antiseptic.

57 (*b*) Bromine liberates iodine from KI solution because of its oxidising property. Colour of iodine is grey black so, black colour is obtained.

$$2KI + Br_2 \longrightarrow 2KBr + \underset{\text{Black or grey}}{I_2\downarrow}$$

58 (*c*) ClO_2 shows paramagnetic character due to presence of unpaired electron in its structure.

O=Cl=O (with unpaired electron on Cl)

59 (*c*) $2F_2 + 4NaOH \longrightarrow 4NaF + O_2 + 2H_2O$

60 (*b*) The mixture of one part of concentrated HNO_3 and three parts of concentrated HCl is known as aquaregia. It contains NOCl.

$$HNO_3 + 3HCl \longrightarrow 2H_2O + NOCl + \underset{\text{Nascent chloride}}{2[Cl]}$$

61 (*c*) I_2 forms complex ion I_3^- in KI solution due to which it dissolves in it.

$$KI + I_2 \longrightarrow KI_3$$

62 (*a*) Perchloric acid $(HClO_4)$ is the strongest acid among the given compounds due to highest oxidation state of Cl (+7).

63 (*d*) $2S_2Cl_2 + 2H_2O \longrightarrow \underset{(X)}{3S} + SO_2 + 4HCl$

64 (*c*) In Whytlaw-Gray method, fluorine is obtained by electrolysis of molten KHF_2 in a cell made of Cu, Ni or monel-metal.

$$2KHF_2 \rightleftharpoons 2K^+ + 2H^+ + 4F^-$$

$$4F^- \longrightarrow 2F_2 + 4e^-$$

Topic 4

Chemistry of Group 18 Elements

2019

1 Match the xenon compounds in Column I with its structure in Column II and assign the correct code: **[NEET]**

Column I	Column II
A. XeF_4	(i) Pyramidal
B. XeF_6	(ii) Square planar
C. $XeOF_4$	(iii) Distorted octahedral
D. XeO_3	(iv) Square pyramidal

Codes

	A	B	C	D
(a)	(ii)	(iii)	(iv)	(i)
(b)	(ii)	(iii)	(i)	(iv)
(c)	(iii)	(iv)	(i)	(ii)
(d)	(i)	(ii)	(iii)	(iv)

2 Which of the following inert gas participate in chemical reaction? **[AIIMS]**

(a) Xe
(b) He
(c) Ne
(d) None of the above

3 In how many of the following number of lone pairs at central atom is zero
$XeO_3, XeO_2F_2, XeO_4, XeO_3F_2, XeF_6$? [AIIMS]
(a) 2 (b) 3
(c) 4 (d) Zero

4 Which of the following rare gas is the abundant in air? [JIPMER]
(a) He (b) Ne
(c) Ar (d) Kr

2018

5 A gas '*X*' is used in filling balloons for meteorological observations. It is also used in gas-cooled nuclear reactors. Here, the gas *X* is [AIIMS]
(a) neon (b) argon
(c) krypton (d) helium

6 Xenon hexafluoride reacts with silica to form a xenon compound *X*. The oxidation state of xenon in *X* is [JIPMER]
(a) + 2 (b) + 4 (c) + 6 (d) 0

2017

7 Consider the following reactions

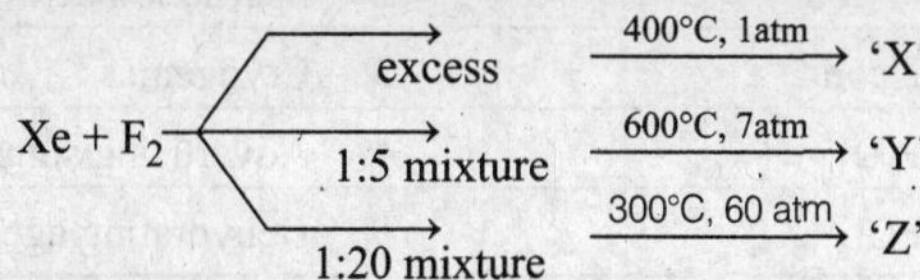

Here, X, Y and Z respectively, are [AIIMS]
(a) XeF_2, XeF_6, XeF_4 (b) XeF_2, XeF_4, XeF_6
(c) XeF_4, XeF_2, XeF_6 (d) XeF_6, XeF_4, XeF_2

2014

8 Among the following inert gas elements, the element that shows highest chemical reactivity is [EAMCET]
(a) Ne (b) Ar (c) He (d) Xe

2011

9 In Ramsay and Rayleigh's isolation of noble gases from air, the nitrogen of the air is finally converted into [KCET]
(a) $NaNO_2$ only (b) NO and NO_2
(c) $NaNO_3$ only (d) $NaNO_2$ and $NaNO_3$

10 Number of non-bonding electron pair on Xe in XeF_6, XeF_4 and XeF_2 respectively will be [Guj CET]
(a) 6, 4, 2 (b) 1, 2, 3 (c) 3, 2, 1 (d) 0, 3, 2

2010

11 Argon possesses [MHT CET]
(a) translational motion only
(b) translational + rotational motion
(c) translational + vibrational motion
(d) translational + rotational + vibrational motion

12 The noble gas was first time discovered by [Manipal]
(a) Cavendish (b) William Ramsay
(c) Rayleigh (d) Frankland

13 The geometry of $XeOF_2$ is [RPMT]
(a) pyramidal (b) T-shaped
(c) octahedral (d) tetrahedral

14 The noble gas compound prepared by Bartlett was [RPMT]
(a) XeO_3 (b) $XePtF_6$
(c) KrF_2 (d) XeF_2

15 The noble gas which can diffuse through rubber and glass easily is [RPMT]
(a) Xe (b) Ne (c) Ar (d) He

16 Which is monoatomic? [MP PMT]
(a) Sulphur (b) Helium
(c) Phosphorus (d) Chlorine

17 Molecules of a noble gas do not possess vibrational energy because noble gases [KCET]
(a) are monoatomic
(b) is chemically inert
(c) has completely filled shells
(d) is diamagnetic

18 Which one has the highest boiling point? [JCECE]
(a) H_2 (b) Xe (c) CH_4 (d) He

19 Argon was discovered by [CMC]
(a) Rayleigh (b) Ramsay
(c) Both (a) and (b) (d) Frankland and Lockeyer

2009

20 The coloured discharged tubes for a advertisement mainly contain [Manipal]
(a) xenon (b) helium (c) neon (d) argon

21 The forces acting between noble gas atoms are [Manipal]
(a) van der Waals' forces (b) ion-dipole forces
(c) London-dispersion forces (d) magnetic forces

22 The number of $p\pi$-$d\pi$ 'pi' bonds present in XeO_3 and XeO_4 molecules, respectively [EAMCET]
(a) 3, 4 (b) 4, 2 (c) 2, 3 (d) 3, 2

23 Argon is used [KCET]
(a) to obtain low temperature
(b) in high temperature welding
(c) in radiotherapy for the treatment of cancer
(d) in filling airships

2008

24 What is the correct order of occurrence (% by weight) in air of Ne, Ar and Kr? [AFMC]
(a) Ne > Ar > Kr (b) Ar > Ne > Kr
(c) Ar > Kr > Ne (d) Ne > Kr > Ar

25 In the separation of noble gas mixture from air by Ramsay Rayleigh's first method, the substances used for the removal of N_2 and O_2 respectively, are [Punjab PMET]
(a) Cu and Mg (b) Mg and Cu
(c) C and CaC_2 (d) KOH solution

26 Which of the following statements about noble gases are correct?

I. XeO_3 is an explosive tetrahedral molecule.
II. In Fisher Ringe's method, a mixture of $CaCl_2$ and CaC_2 is used to remove N_2 and O_2.
III. He and Ne are chemically inert due to lack of *d*-orbitals and high ionisation potential.
IV. At 173 K, He and Ne are adsorbed on activated charcoal.

The correct answer is. **[EAMCET]**

(a) I and II (b) II and III
(c) II, III and IV (d) I, II, III and IV

27 Helium is used in balloons in place of hydrogen because it is **[KCET]**

(a) incombustible (b) lighter than hydrogen
(c) radioactive (d) more abundant than hydrogen

2007

28 Which of the following gas mixture is used by the divers inside the sea? **[AFMC]**

(a) O_2 + He (b) O_2 + Xe (c) O_2 + Ar (d) $O_2 + N_2$

29 Which of the following radioactive elements is inert gas?

(a) Ra (b) Rn (c) Pu (d) Po **[BHU]**

30 Noble gases are adsorbed by **[AMU]**

(a) anhydrous calcium chloride.
(b) ferric hydroxide.
(c) conc. H_2SO_4.
(d) activated coconut charcoal.

31 The noble gas mixture is cooled in a coconut bulb at 173 K. The gases that are not adsorbed are **[KCET]**

(a) Ne and Xe (b) He and Xe
(c) Ar and Kr (d) He and Ne

2006

32 Which of the following is not obtained by direct reaction of constituent elements? **[BHU]**

(a) XeF_2 (b) XeF_4 (c) XeO_3 (d) XeF_6

33 Which inert gas show abnormal behaviour on liquefication? **[UP CPMT]**

(a) Xe (b) He (c) Ar (d) Kr

34 In clatherates of xenon with water, the nature of bonding between xenon and water molecule is **[MHT CET]**

(a) dipole-induced dipole interaction
(b) coordinate
(c) hydrogen bonding (d) covalent

35 The formation of $O_2^+[PtF_6]^-$ is the basis for the formation of xenon fluorides. This is because **[KCET]**

I. O_2 and Xe have comparable sizes.
II. Both O_2 and Xe are gases.
III. O_2 and Xe have comparable ionisation energies.
IV. O_2 and Xe have comparable electronegativities.

(a) I and II (b) I and III (c) II and III (d) II and IV

36 XeF_4 reacts with water at – 80°C to give **[Guj CET]**

(a) $XeOF_2$ (b) $XeOF_4$
(c) XeO_3 (d) XeO_2F_2e

2005

37 Which of the following is planar? **[J&K CET]**

(a) XeF_2 (b) XeO_3F
(c) XeO_2F_2 (d) XeF_4

38 Match the following Columns. **[Kerala CEE]**

Column I (Substance)	Column II (Application)
A. Helium	1. Chlorinating agent
B. Argon	2. Inert atmosphere (metallurgy)
C. Neon	3. Cryogenics
D. P_4O_{10}	4. Advertising signs
E. PCl_5	5. Dehydrating agent

	A	B	C	D	E
(a)	3	2	1	4	5
(b)	3	4	1	5	2
(c)	3	2	4	5	1
(d)	5	4	1	2	3
(e)	5	2	1	3	4

39 D_3 line observed in the yellow region of the Sun's spectrum is due to **[Haryana PMT]**

(a) sodium (b) neon
(c) krypton (d) helium

40 Which of the following is not correct? **[EAMCET]**

(a) XeO_3 has four σ and four π-bonds.
(b) The hybridisation of Xe in XeF_4 is sp^3d^2
(c) Among noble gases, the occurrence (per cent by weight) of argon is highest in air
(d) Liquid helium is used as cryogenic liquid

41 Which of the following is the most polarised? **[DUMET]**

(a) Kr (b) He (c) Ar (d) Xe

Answers

1 (a)	2 (a)	3 (a)	4 (c)	5 (d)	6 (c)	7 (b)	8 (d)	9 (d)	10 (b)
11 (a)	12 (b)	13 (b)	14 (b)	15 (d)	16 (b)	17 (a)	18 (b)	19 (c)	20 (c)
21 (a)	22 (a)	23 (b)	24 (b)	25 (b)	26 (b)	27 (a)	28 (a)	29 (b)	30 (d)
31 (d)	32 (c)	33 (b)	34 (a)	35 (b)	36 (a)	37 (d)	38 (c)	39 (d)	40 (a)
41 (d)									

Explanations

1 (*a*) The given xenon compounds with its structures are as follows:

(A) XeF_4 —

(Square planar)

(B) XeF_6 —

(Distorted octahedral)

(C) $XeOF_4$—

(Square pyramidal)

(D) XeO_3 —

(Pyramidal)

Hence, the correct match is

(A) → (ii), (B) → (iii), (C) → (iv), (D) → (i)

2 (*a*) Neil Bartlett prepared a red compound,

$O_2^+[PtF_6]^-$ by reacting platinum hexafluoride (PtF_6) with oxygen.

He found that, ionisation energy of Xe(1170 kJ mol^{-1}) is nearly equal to that of molecular oxygen (1175 kJ mol^{-1}) available.

Therefore, he was able to form compound of xenon.

$Xe + PtF_6 \longrightarrow Xe^+[PtF_6]$,

On the other hand, He and Ne has very high values of ionisation energy.

Therefore, only Xe can participate in chemical reactions and form compounds.

Hence, option (a) is correct.

3 (*a*) Structures of XeO_4 and XeO_3F_2 do not have any lone pair at central-atom. i.e.

(XeO_4) (XeO_3F_2)

While in XeO_3, XeO_2F_2 and XeF_6 one lone pair of electrons is present on central atom of each compound.

(XeO_3, one lone pair of electrons) (XeO_2F_2, one lone pair of electrons)

(XeF_6, one lone pair of electrons)

Thus, option (a) is the correct.

4 (*c*) The % by volume of rare gases are :

	% by volume	% by weight
He	0.0005	0.000037
Ne	0.0015	0.001
Ar	0.932	1.285
Kr	0.0001	0.00028
Xe	0.0001	0.00004

So, Ar is most abundant in air.

5 (*d*) Helium is used in filling balloons for meteorological observations. It is also used in gas-cooled nuclear reactors. Liquid helium is used as cryogenic agent for carrying out various experiments at low temperature.

6 (*c*) Xenon hexafluoride reacts with silica to form $XeOF_4$ as

$$2XeF_6 + SiO_2 \longrightarrow 2XeOF_4 + SiF_4$$

The oxidation state of xenon in $XeOF_4$ is + 6 as calculated below:

Let the oxidation state of Xe is a.

$\therefore \quad a + 1 \times (-2) + 4 \times (-1) = 0$

$a - 2 - 4 = 0 \quad a = +6$

7 (b) Xenon reacts with fluorine under different conditions to form binary fluorides, i.e., XeF_2, XeF_4 and XeF_6. In these compounds, Xe is present in + 2, + 4 and + 6 oxidation state respectively. The products formed depends on ratio of Xe and F.

$Xe + F_2 \xrightarrow[\text{in excess}]{} \xrightarrow{400°C,\ 1atm} XeF_2$

$Xe + F_2 \xrightarrow[\text{1:5 mixture}]{} \xrightarrow{600°C,\ 7atm} XeF_4$

$Xe + F_2 \xrightarrow[\text{1:20 mixture}]{} \xrightarrow{300°C,\ 60\ atm} XeF_6$

8 (*d*) Xe, because of its low ionisation energy forms many compounds. However, no true compounds of He, Ne and Ar are known. Xe forms most of the compounds with F and O, like XeF_2, XeF_4, XeF_6 and XeO_3 etc.

9 (*d*) In Ramsay and Rayleigh's isolation of noble gases from air, the nitrogen of air is finally converted into $NaNO_2$ and $NaNO_3$.

10 (*b*) The structure of XeF_6, XeF_4 and XeF_2 are as follows :

XeF_6 XeF_4

XeF_2

Hence, number of non-bonding pair of electrons on Xe in XeF_6, XeF_4 and XeF_2 respectively will be 1, 2, 3.

11 (*a*) Argon is a monoatomic gas, thus its molecules can move in any direction in space. Hence, it can have three independent motions (all translational). Therefore, argon possesses only translational motion.

12 (*b*) William Ramsay was the scientist who discovered noble gas for the first time.

13 (*b*)

$XeOF_2$

(The geometry of $XeOF_2$ is T-shaped).

14 (*b*) Bartlett reacted xenon and platinum hexafluoride in gas phase and an orange yellow solid of $XePtF_6$ was obtained.

$$Xe(g) + PtF_6(g) \longrightarrow \underset{\text{Orange yellow}}{Xe^+[PtF_6]^-(s)}$$

15 (*d*) Helium has an unusual property of diffusing through commonly used laboratory material such as rubber and glass.

16 (*b*) Helium (He) is a noble and monoatomic gas.

17 (*a*) Since, noble gases are monoatomic, these do not possess vibrational energy as monoatomic molecules do not vibrate.

18 (*b*) Boiling point $\propto$ van der Waals' force $\propto$ atomic mass (or molecular mass)

Atomic mass of Xe is the highest among H_2, He, CH_4 and Xe.

19 (*c*) Argon was discovered by both Rayleigh and Ramsay.

20 (*c*) Neon gives brilliant orange red glow in discharged tube and is widely used for advertisement purposes.

21 (*a*) Atoms of noble gases are held together by weak van der Waals' forces of attraction.

22 (*a*) **Structure of XeO_3**

Hence, $3p\pi$-$d\pi$ bonds are present.

Structure of XeO_4

Hence, 4 $p\pi$-$d\pi$ bonds are present.

23 (*b*) Argon is used in producing inert atmosphere during welding and extraction of various metals.

24 (*b*) The correct order of occurrence in air is

$$Ar > Ne > Kr$$

25 (*b*) In the separation of noble gas mixture from air by Ramsay-Rayleigh's method, magnesium and copper are used for the removal of N_2 and O_2 respectively.

$$3Mg + N_2 \longrightarrow Mg_3N_2$$

$$2Cu + O_2 \longrightarrow 2CuO$$

26 (*b*) XeO_3 is an explosive pyramidal molecule due to presence of one lone pair of electron on Xe atom.

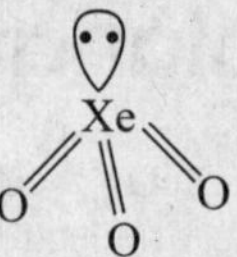

Pyramidal structure

In Fisher Ringe's method, the oxygen and nitrogen of air are removed by passing it over a mixture of calcium carbide and calcium chloride.

He and Ne both have high ionisation energy and lack of *d*-orbitals, so they are chemically inert.

Except He, all inert gases are adsorbed on activated charcoal and the extent of adsorption increases on moving down the group.

Thus, correct statements are II and III.

27 (*a*) Helium (He) is a non-flammable (incombustible) gas and its lifting power is 93% as compared to flammable hydrogen gas. Due to these reasons it is used in filling balloons and other lighter aircrafts.

28 (*a*) Helium is not soluble in blood even under high pressure, hence a mixture of 80% helium and 20% oxygen is used instead of ordinary air by sea divers for respiration.

29 (*b*) Radon is an inert gas. Its atomic number is 86. It has stable electronic configuration. It is an element of 18th group. It is a radioactive element.

30 (*d*) Noble gases are adsorbed by coconut charcoal. The adsorption of different noble gases occur at different temperatures. Hence, charcoal is used to separate these gases. Helium is not adsorbed by charcoal as it is very difficult to liquefy the gas.

31 (*d*) When the mixture of noble gas is cooled in a coconut bulb at 173K then Ar, Kr and Xe are adsorbed on charcoal while He and Ne are not adsorbed.

32 (*c*) XeF_2, XeF_4 and XeF_6 can be directly prepared.

$$Xe + F_2 \xrightarrow[\text{673 K, 1 bar}]{\text{Ni tube}} XeF_2$$

$$Xe + 2F_2 \xrightarrow[\text{7 bar}]{\text{873 K}} XeF_4$$

$$Xe + 3F_2 \xrightarrow[\text{60-70 bar}]{\text{523-573 K}} XeF_6$$

XeO_3 is obtained by the hydrolysis of XeF_6.

$$XeF_6 + 3H_2O \longrightarrow XeO_3 + 6HF$$

33 (*b*) On liquefication, He shows abnormal behaviour because it shows behaviour of liquid with gas properties i.e. of a degenerate gas. Its interatomic forces are so weak that it does not liquefy.

34 (*a*) Clatherate formation involves dipole induced dipole attraction ($\because$ water is polar molecule and Xe is non-polar).

35 (*b*) The first ionisation energy of xenon (1170 kJ mol^{-1}) is quite close to that of oxygen (1175 kJ mol^{-1}) and the molecular diameter of xenon and oxygen are almost identical. Based on the above facts, it is suggested that since oxygen combines with PtF_6, so xenon should also form similar compound with PtF_6.

36 (*a*) $XeF_4 + H_2O \xrightarrow{-80^\circ C} \underset{\text{Xenon oxyfluoride}}{XeOF_2} + 2HF$

37 (*d*) XeF_4 has square planar structure. It involves sp^3d^2 hybridisation of xenon which possesses octahedral geometry in which two positions are occupied by lone pairs.

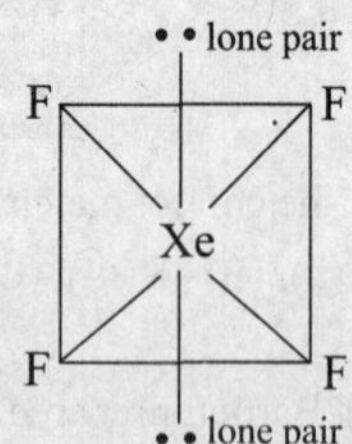

38 (*c*) Argon provides inert atmosphere in the welding of metals or alloys that are easily oxidised.

Helium is used in gas filled electric lamps i.e. cryogenics.

Neon is used in electric sign i.e. advertising sign.

P_4O_{10} is used as a valuable drying and dehydrating agent.

PCl_5 is used in organic reaction for the replacement of hydroxyl group by chlorine atom.

39 (*d*) D_3 line in the yellow region of Sun's spectrum is due to helium.

40 (*a*) XeO_3 has the following structure

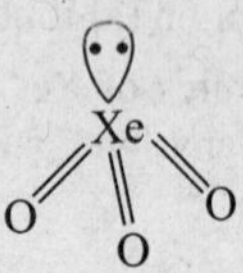

Pyramidal

Number of σ-bonds = 3

Number of π-bonds = 3

41 (*d*) Most polarised atom will have largest size. Size of Xe is the largest among given choices. Hence, Xe is the most polarised atom.

22

d- and f-Block Elements

Quick Review

d-Block Elements (Transition Elements)

These elements occupies the large middle section of *s* and *p*-block in the periodic table. Hence, they are also known as **transition elements.** These elements have incompletely filled *d*-orbitals in its ground state or in their most common oxidation state. Exceptions are Zn, Cd and Hg.

Electronic Configuration

- General electronic configuration of transition metals is $(n-1)d^{1-10}ns^{1-2}$.
- Some of the exceptions observed in 3*d*-series are

Cr : $3d^5 4s^1$ instead of $3d^4 4s^2$ Cu : $3d^{10} 4s^1$ instead of $3d^9 4s^2$

General Characteristics

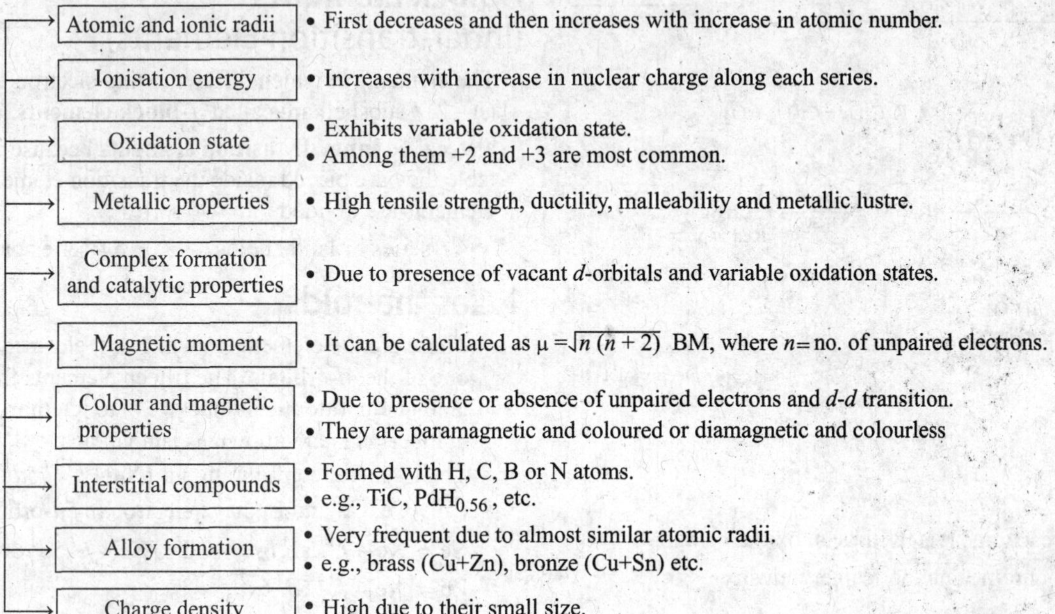

Note Cu^{2+} is more stable than Cu^+ because Cu^{2+} has lower reduction potential and high negative hydration enthalpy to nullify lattice enthalpy.

Oxides and Halides of Transition Metals

- The oxides of transition metals in their lower oxidation states are basic and in their higher oxidation states, they are acidic, whereas in the intermediate oxidation states, the oxides are 'amphoteric' in nature.

  Basic oxides Sc_2O_3, TiO, Ti_2O_3, VO, V_2O_3, MnO, FeO, CuO, CoO, NiO, Cu_2O, CrO

  Acidic oxides Mn_2O_7, CrO_3, OsO_4

  Amphoteric oxides TiO_2, ZnO, Cr_2O_3, Mn_2O_3, MnO_2, V_2O_5, Mn_3O_4, Fe_3O_4
- Transition metal halides in lower oxidation state are ionic and in higher oxidation state are covalent.

Some Important Compounds of Transition Elements

Potassium dichromate and potassium permanganate are important compounds of transition elements which are discussed below

1. Potassium Dichromate

Its chemical formula is $K_2Cr_2O_7$. It contains ionic as well as covalent bonds.

Preparation

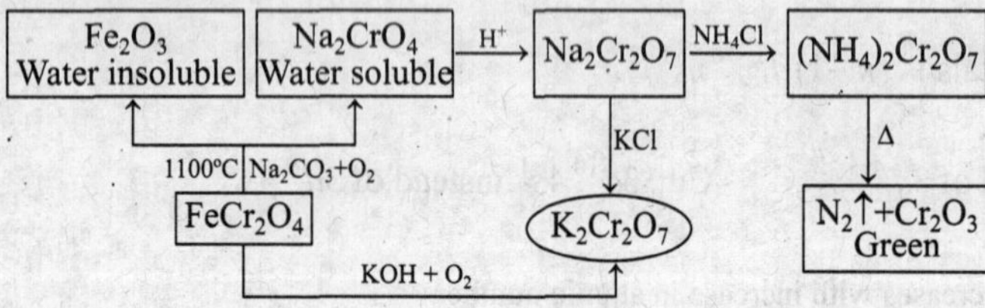

Properties

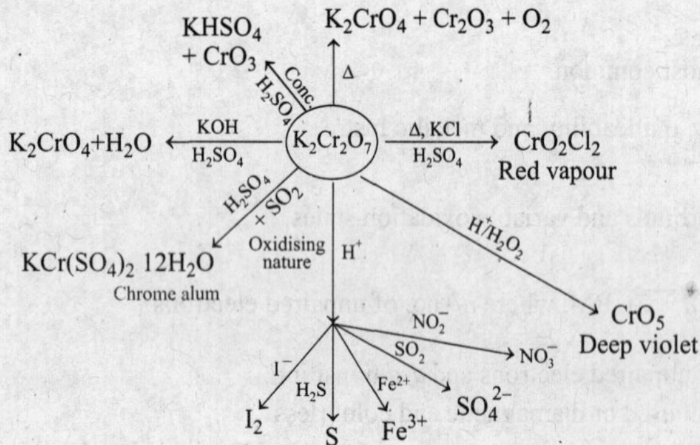

Uses

- In organic reactions, it is used as an oxidising agent.
- It is used in chrome tanning leather industry.

2. Potassium Permanganate

Its chemical formula is $KMnO_4$. It is salt of permanganic acid $HMnO_4$, which is an unstable acid and exists only in solution.

Preparation

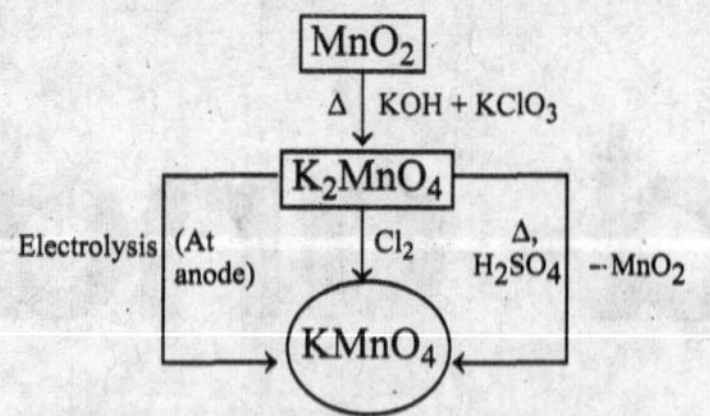

Properties

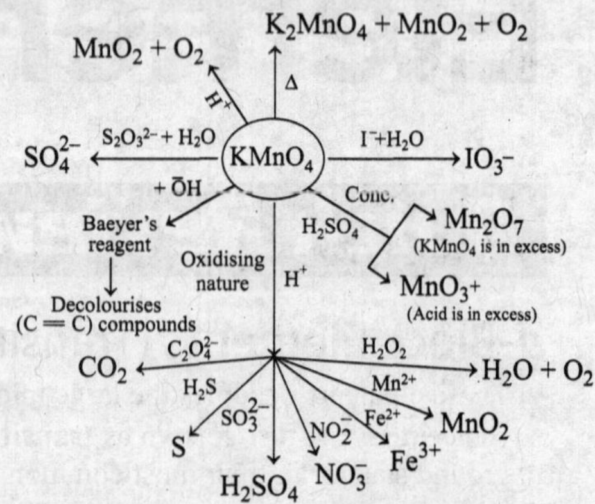

Uses

- $KMnO_4$ is also widely used as a disinfectant and germicide.
- A very dilute solution of $KMnO_4$ is used for washing wounds and gargling of mouth sore.

f-Block Elements (Inner-transition Elements)

The elements in which differentiating electron enters in $(n-2)f$ subshell are called ***f*-block elements**. They are also called **inner-transition elements** because in periodic table they are placed inside the transition elements. These elements are divided into two series :

- 4*f*-series or lanthanoids
- 5*f*-series or actinoids.

1. Lanthanoids

- These are the elements in which last electron enters in one of the 4*f*-orbitals. The fifteen elements from lanthanum (atomic number = 57) to lutetium (atomic number = 71) are known as lanthanoids.
- Their general configuration is $[Xe]4f^{1-14}5d^{0-1}6s^2$
- Only Ce, Gd and Lu have electron in 5*d*-orbital

  $Ce = [Xe]4f^1 5d^1 6s^2$, $Gd = [Xe]4f^7 5d^1 6s^2$

  $Lu = [Xe]4f^{14} 5d^1 6s^2$

- Their common **oxidation state** is +3. However +2 and+ 4 are also exhibited by some elements.
- All lanthanoid ions (except La^{3+}, Lu^{3+} Ce^{4+}) are paramagnetic in nature.
- Lanthanide ions have very less tendency to form complexes because of their low charge density. The higher the charge on the metal ion, smaller is the ionic size and more is the complex formation ability.

Chemical reactions of lanthanoids are as follows :

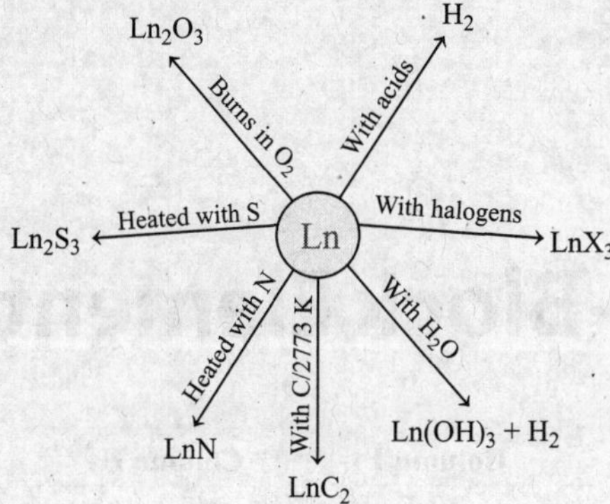

Lanthanoid Contraction and its Consequences

- It is a regular decrease in atomic and ionic radii of lanthanoid with increasing atomic number.
- This is due to poor shielding effect of 4*f*-electrons, the attraction between the electrons and the nucleus increases and hence radius decreases.

Some of the consequences of lanthanoid contractions are :

(*i*) Separation of lanthanoids in the pure state is difficult.
(*ii*) Similarity in size of elements belonging to same group of second and third transition series.
(*iii*) The basicity of lanthanoid hydroxides decreases as the size decreases from La^{3+} to Lu^{3+}.

Uses

- They are used in the production of alloys like mischmetal. Their oxides are lessed in glass industry for polishing, for colouring.

2. Actinoids

- These are the elements in which the last electron enters in one of the 5*f*-orbital. The fourteen elements from actinium (atomic number = 89) to lawrencium (atomic number = 103) are known as actinoids.
- General configuration is [Rn] $5f^{1\text{-}14}\,6d^{0\text{-}2}\,7s^2$.
- The irregularities in configuration is due to stabilities of f^0, f^7 and f^{14} occupancies of $5f$ orbital.
- Actinoids have high values of melting point and boiling points but there is no regular trend.
- These elements have more tendency to form complexes because they have higher nuclear charge and small size.
- These are very reactive in nature and combine with oxygen and halogen like lanthanoids.

Chemical reactions of actinoids are as follows

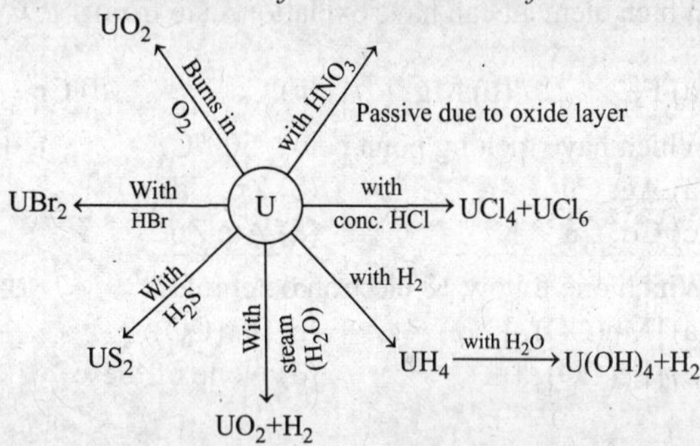

Uses

- The most useful actinides are thorium, uranium and plutonium. Thorium is used in atomic reactors and in the treatment of cancer, uranium is used as nuclear fuel.

Difference between Lanthanoids and Actinoids

	Lanthanoids	Actinoids
Properties		
• Oxidation states	They show mainly + 3 oxidation state. + 2 and + 4 oxidation states also exist.	In addition to + 3 oxidation state, actinoids also show higher oxidation states like + 4, + 5, + 6 and + 7.
• Binding energies	Binding energies of 4 *f* are higher.	Binding energies of 5 *f* are lower.
• Shielding effect	They have poor shielding effect.	They have even poor shielding effect than lanthanoids.
• Magnetic properties	They are paramagnetic and their magnetic properties can be easily explained.	They are also paramagnetic, but their magnetic properties cannot be easily explained.
Chemical Reactivities		
• Tendency to form complexes	Less	More
• Radioactivity	Except promethium, these are non-radioactive substances.	These are radioactive substances.
• Basic character	These are less basic.	These are more basic.

Topical Practice Questions

All the exam questions of this chapter have been divided into three topics as listed below

Topic 1

General Characteristics of *d*-Block Elements

2019

1 Which element can have oxidation state from 4 to 6? [AIIMS]

(a) Fe (b) Mg (c) Co (d) Cr

2 Which have melting point below 500°C? [AIIMS]

(a) Ag, Cu (b) Zn, Cd
(c) Cd, Cu (d) Ag, Zn

3 Which one follow 18 electron octet rule? [JIPMER]

(a) $[Mn(CO)_5]$ (b) $[Cr(CO)_5]$
(c) $[Fe(CO)_5]$ (d) None of these

2018

4 The correct order of spin only magnetic moment (in BM) for Mn^{2+}, Cr^{2+} and Ti^{2+} ions is [AIIMS]

(a) $Mn^{2+} > Ti^{2+} > Cr^{2+}$
(b) $Ti^{2+} > Cr^{2+} > Mn^{2+}$
(c) $Mn^{2+} > Cr^{2+} > Ti^{2+}$
(d) $Cr^{2+} > Ti^{2+} > Mn^{2+}$

5 Which one of the following species is paramagnetic in nature? [JIPMER]

(a) V^{4+} (b) Sc^{3+}
(c) V^{5+} (d) Zn^{2+}

6 Among the following species, the one which become paramagnetic on heating at 850 K is [JIPMER]

(a) Fe_3O_4
(b) MnO
(c) $ZnFe_2O_4$
(d) Both (a) and (c)

7 Match the metal ions given in Column I with the spin magnetic moments of the ions given in Column II and assign the correct code. [NEET]

Column I	Column II
1. Co^{3+}	(i) $\sqrt{8}$ BM
2. Cr^{3+}	(ii) $\sqrt{35}$ BM
3. Fe^{3+}	(iii) $\sqrt{3}$ BM
4. Ni^{2+}	(iv) $\sqrt{24}$ BM
	(v) $\sqrt{15}$ BM

	1	2	3	4		1	2	3	4
(a)	(iv)	(i)	(ii)	(iii)	(b)	(i)	(ii)	(iii)	(iv)
(c)	(iv)	(v)	(ii)	(i)	(d)	(iii)	(v)	(i)	(ii)

2017

8 Which of the following compound is not coloured? [JIPMER]

(a) Na_2CuCl (b) $Na_2Cd\cdot Cl_4$
(c) $FeSO_4$ (d) VI_3

9 Regarding the ions Zn^{2+}, Ni^{2+} and Cr^{3+} (atomic number of Zn = 30, Ni = 28, Cr = 24), which of the following statement is correct? [Gujarat CET]

(a) All three are coloured
(b) All three are colourless
(c) Only Zn^{2+} is colourless and Ni^{2+}, Cr^{3+} are coloured
(d) Only Ni^{2+} is coloured and Zn^{2+}, Cr^{3+} are colourless

10 Which of the following has maximum number of unpaired *d*-electrons? [AIIMS]

(a) Fe^{2+} (b) Cu^{+} (c) Zn (d) Ni^{3+}

2016

11 When copper is heated with conc. HNO_3 it produces [NEET]

(a) $Cu(NO_3)_2$ and NO (b) $Cu(NO_3)_2$, NO and NO_2
(c) $Cu(NO_3)_2$ and N_2O (d) $Cu(NO_3)_2$ and NO_2

2015

12 Ground state configuration of element having atomic number = 24 is $3d^5 4s^1$. This is because **[UP PMT]**
(a) the energy of 3*d* and 4*s* orbitals is very low.
(b) 3*d* and 4*s* orbitals are of comparable energy.
(c) Energy of 3*d*-orbital is lower than the energy of 4*s*-orbital.
(d) None of the above

13 Which of the following processes does not involve oxidation of iron? **[CBSE AIPMT]**
(a) Rusting of iron sheets
(b) Decolourisation of blue $CuSO_4$ solution by iron
(c) Formation of $Fe(CO)_5$ from Fe
(d) Liberation of H_2 from steam by iron at a high temperature

14 Magnetic moment 2.84 BM is given by **[Kerala CEE]**
(At. no. Ni = 28, Ti = 22, Cr = 24, Co = 27)
(a) Ni^{2+} (b) Ti^{3+} (c) Cr^{3+} (d) Co^{2+}

15 In which of the following metallic bond is strongest?
(a) V (b) Fe **[RPMT]**
(c) Cr (d) Sc

16 Magnetic moment 2.83 BM is given by which of the following ions? [Atomic number Ti = 22, Cr = 24, Mn = 25 and Ni = 28] **[CBSE AIPMT]**
(a) Ti^{3+} (b) Ni^{2+} (c) Cr^{3+} (d) Mn^{2+}

17 Which one of the following transition metal ions is colourless in aqueous solutions? **[Kerala CEE]**
(a) Ti^{4+} (b) V^{4+} (c) Mn^{2+} (d) Fe^{3+}
(e) Ni^{2+}

18 Metal ion responsible for the minimata disease is **[WB JEE]**
(a) Co^{2+} (b) Hg^{2+} (c) Cu^{2+} (d) Zn^{2+}

19 Cupric compounds are more stable than their cuprous counter parts in solid state. This is because **[WB JEE]**
(a) the endothermic characteristics of the 2nd IP of Cu is not so high.
(b) size of Cu^{2+} is less than Cu^+.
(c) Cu^+ has stable electronic configuration as compared to Cu.
(d) the lattice energy released for cupric compounds is much higher than Cu^+.

2013

20 Which of the following statements about the interstitial compounds is incorrect? **[NEET]**
(a) They retain metallic conductivity
(b) They are chemically reactive
(c) They are much harder than the pure metal
(d) They have higher melting points than the pure metal

21 Which of the following does not give oxygen on heating? **[NEET]**
(a) $KClO_3$ (b) $Zn(ClO_3)_2$
(c) $K_2Cr_2O_7$ (d) $(NH_4)_2Cr_2O_7$

22 The number of water molecules in Mohr's salts is **[AIIMS]**
(a) 2 (b) 4
(c) 6 (d) 8

23 The correct configuration for *d*-orbital element is **[UP CPMT]**
(a) $(n-1)d^{1-9}ns^1$ (b) $(n-1)d^{1-10}ns^{1-2}$
(c) $(n-1)d^{1-5}$ (d) $(n-1)d^{1-10}ns^2$

24 Transition elements do not show **[Manipal]**
(a) paramagnetism (b) colour
(c) fixed valency (d) All of the above

25 Cuprous ion is colourless while cupric ion is coloured because **[KCET]**
(a) both have half-filled *p* and *d*-orbitals
(b) cuprous ion has incomplete *d*-orbital and cupric ion has a complete *d*-orbital
(c) both have unpaired electrons in the *d*-orbitals
(d) cuprous ion has completely filled *d*-orbitals and cupric ion has an incompletely filled *d*-orbital

2012

26 Which one of the following does not correctly represent the correct order of the property indicated against it? **[CBSE AIPMT]**
(a) Ti < V < Cr < Mn increasing number of oxidation states
(b) $Ti^{3+} < V^{3+} < Cr^{3+} < Mn^{3+}$ increasing magnetic moment
(c) Ti < V < Cr < Mn increasing melting points
(d) Ti < V < Mn < Cr increasing 2nd ionisation enthalpy

27 Four successive members of the first series of the transition metals are listed below. For which one of them, the standard potential ($E^\circ_{M^{2+}/M}$) value has a positive sign?
(a) Co (*Z* = 27) (b) Ni (*Z* = 28) **[CBSE AIPMT]**
(c) Cu (*Z* = 29) (d) Fe (*Z* = 26)

28 Stainless steel contains **[KCET]**
(a) Fe + Cr + Cu (b) Fe + C + Ni
(c) Fe + Cr + Ni (d) Fe + Ni + Cu

2011

29 For the four successive transition elements (Cr, Mn, Fe and Co), the stability of +2 oxidation state will be there in which of the following order? [Atomic number Cr = 24, Mn = 25, Fe = 26 and Co = 27] **[CBSE AIPMT]**
(a) Cr > Mn > Co > Fe
(b) Mn > Fe > Cr > Co
(c) Fe > Mn > Co > Cr
(d) Co > Mn > Fe > Cr

30 Which of the following species is/are paramagnetic?
$Fe^{2+}, Zn^0, Hg^{2+}, Ti^{4+}$ **[Kerala CEE]**
(a) Only Fe^{2+} (b) Zn^0 and Ti^{4+}
(c) Fe^{2+} and Hg^{2+} (d) Zn^0 and Hg^{2+}
(e) Fe^{2+} and Ti^{4+}

31 Ammonia will not form complex with **[Kerala CEE]**
(a) Ag^{2+} (b) Pb^{2+} (c) Cu^{2+} (d) Cd^{2+}
(e) Fe^{2+}

32 The titanium (atomic number 22) compound that does not exist is **[Kerala CEE]**
(a) TiO (b) TiO_2 (c) K_2TiF_6 (d) $TiCl_3$
(e) K_2TiO_4

33 The spin only magnetic moment of Fe^{3+} ion (in BM) is approximately **[KCET]**
(a) 4 (b) 7 (c) 5 (d) 6

34 Copper exhibits only +2 oxidation state in its stable compounds. Why? **[Guj CET]**
(a) Copper is transition metal in +2 state
(b) +2 state compounds of copper are formed by exothermic reactions
(c) Electron configuration of copper in +2 state is $[Ar]\,3d^9, 4s^0$
(d) Copper gives coloured compounds in +2 state

35 German silver alloy contains **[Guj CET]**
(a) zinc, silver and copper
(b) nickel, silver and copper
(c) germanium, silver and copper
(d) zinc, nickel and copper

36 Experimental value of magnetic moment of Mn^{2+} complex is 5.96 BM. This indicates **[Guj CET]**
(a) axial and orbital motion of electron in same direction
(b) axial and orbital motion of electron in opposite direction
(c) electron does not exhibit orbital motion, it only exhibits axial motion
(d) electron does not exhibit axial motion, it only exhibits orbital motion

2010

37 Magnetic moment of $[Ti(H_2O)_6]^{3+}$ is **[AIIMS]**
(a) 1.73 BM (b) 2.83 BM
(c) 3.87 BM (d) 4.90 BM

38 Which of the following ions will exhibit colour in aqueous solutions? **[CBSE AIPMT]**
(a) $Sc^{3+} (Z = 21)$ (b) $La^{3+} (Z = 57)$
(c) $Ti^{3+} (Z = 22)$ (d) $Lu^{3+} (Z = 71)$

39 When Zn is treated with excess of NaOH, the product obtained is **[BVP]**
(a) $Zn(OH)_2$ (b) ZnOH
(c) Na_2ZnO_2 (d) None of these

40 Which of the following statements concerning transition elements is false? **[Manipal, JCECE]**
(a) They are all metals
(b) They easily form complex coordination compounds
(c) They form compounds containing unpaired electrons and their ions are mostly coloured
(d) They show multiple oxidation states always differing by units of two

41 In Cu how many electrons have spin in one direction and in other direction? (Atomic number = 29) **[RPMT]**
(a) 13 electrons have spin in one direction and 16 electrons in other direction
(b) 14 electrons have spin in one direction and 15 electrons in other direction
(c) one electron can have spin only in the clockwise direction
(d) None of the above is correct

42 The colour of zinc sulphide is **[MP PMT]**
(a) white (b) black (c) brown (d) red

43 The formula of mercurous ion is **[MP PMT]**
(a) Hg^+ (b) Hg_2^+ (c) Hg_2^{2+} (d) None

44 Choose the correct reaction to prepare mercurous chloride (calomel). **[Guj CET]**
(a) $HgCl_2 + Hg \xrightarrow{\Delta}$ (b) $Hg + Cl_2 \longrightarrow$
(c) $HgCl_2 + SnCl_2 \longrightarrow$ (d) Both options (a) and (c)

45 A transition element X has the configuration $[Ar]\,d^4$ in its +3 oxidation state. Its atomic number is **[JCECE]**
(a) 25 (b) 26 (c) 22 (d) 19

46 Which of the following is magnetite? **[VMMC]**
(a) Fe_2CO_3 (b) Fe_2O_3
(c) Fe_3O_4 (d) $Fe_2O_3 \cdot 3H_2O$

2009

47 Out of TiF_6^{2-}, CoF_6^{3-}, Cu_2Cl_2 and $NiCl_4^{2-}$ (Z of Ti = 22, Co = 27, Cu = 29, Ni = 28), the colourless species are **[CBSE AIPMT, AMU]**
(a) TiF_6^{2-} and CoF_6^{3-} (b) Cu_2Cl_2 and $NiCl_4^{2-}$
(c) TiF_6^{2-} and Cu_2Cl_2 (d) CoF_6^{3-} and $NiCl_4^{2-}$

48 For which of the following pairs, magnetic moment is same? **[AIIMS]**
(a) $MnCl_2, CuSO_4$ (b) $CuCl_2, TiCl_3$
(c) $TiO_2, CuSO_4$ (d) $TiCl_3, NiCl_2$

49 Transition metals show paramagnetic behaviour. This is because of their **[AFMC]**
(a) high lattice energy
(b) variable oxidation state
(c) characteristic configuration
(d) unpaired electrons

50 Which compound is expected to be coloured? **[UP CPMT]**
(a) CuCl (b) CuF_2 (c) Ag_2SO_4 (d) MgF_2

51 The solid product formed on heating $AgNO_3$ strongly to 980 K is **[Kerala CEE]**
(a) silver carbonate (b) silver nitride
(c) silver oxide (d) silver metal
(e) silver nitrite

52 The maximum oxidation state shown by Mn in its compounds is **[Kerala CEE]**
(a) + 4 (b) + 5 (c) + 6 (d) + 7
(e) + 8

53 The ion of least magnetic moment among the following is [J&K CET]
(a) Ti^{3+} (b) Ni^{2+}
(c) Co^{2+} (d) Mn^{2+}

54 Which of the following is useful in battery industries? [UP PMT]
(a) MNO_2 (b) Zn
(c) Ni/Cd (d) All of these

55 The amphoteric oxide among the following is [J&K CET]
(a) Cr_2O_3 (b) Mn_2O_7 (c) V_2O_3 (d) CrO

56 Which one of the following is a *d*-block element? [J&K CET]
(a) Gd (b) Hs (c) Es (d) Cs

57 The magnetic moment of a transition metal ion is $\sqrt{15}$ BM. Therefore, the number of unpaired electrons present in it is
(a) 4 (b) 1 (c) 2 (d) 3 [KCET]

58 Which one of the following sets correctly represent the increase in the paramagnetic property of the ions? [EAMCET]
(a) $Cu^{2+} < V^{2+} < Cr^{2+} < Mn^{2+}$
(b) $Cu^{2+} < Cr^{2+} < V^{2+} < Mn^{2+}$
(c) $Cu^{2+} > V^{2+} > Cr^{2+} > Mn^{2+}$
(d) $V^{2+} < Cu^{2+} < Cr^{2+} < Mn^{2+}$

2008

59 Which of the following compounds is coloured? [AIIMS]
(a) $TiCl_3$ (b) $FeCl_3$
(c) $CoCl_2$ (d) All of these

60 The true statement about Mn_2O_7 is/are [RPMT]
(a) it is an ionic oxide
(b) it includes a Mn–O–Mn bridge
(c) Mn is tetrahedrally surrounded by oxygen
(d) All of the above

61 A transition metal *A* has 'spin-only' magnetic moment value of 1.8 BM. When it is reacted with dilute sulphuric acid in the presence of air, a compound *B* is formed. *B* reacts with compound *C* to give compound *D* with liberation of iodine. Then, the metal *A* and compounds *B*, *C* and *D* are respectively [Kerala CEE]
(a) Ti, $TiSO_4$, KI and TiI_2
(b) Zn, $ZnSO_4$, KI and Zn_2I_2
(c) Cu, $CuSO_4$, KI and Cu_2I_2
(d) Cu, $CuSO_4$, Cu_2I_2 and CuI_2
(e) Cu, $CuSO_4$, KI and CuI_2

62 Which of the following pairs of transition metal ions are the stronger oxidising agents in aqueous solutions? [Kerala CEE]
(a) V^{2+} and Cr^{2+} (b) Ti^{2+} and Cr^{2+}
(c) Mn^{3+} and Co^{3+} (d) V^{2+} and Fe^{2+}
(e) Ni^{2+} and Fe^{2+}

63 Which of the following group of transition metals is called coinage metals? [RPMT]
(a) Cu, Ag, Au (b) Ru, Rh, Pd
(c) Fe, Co, Ni (d) Os, Ir, Pt

64 The highest oxidation state exhibited by transition metals is [J&K CET]
(a) +7 (b) +8 (c) +6 (d) +5

65 Which one of the following statements is not true with regard to transition elements? [J&K CET]
(a) They readily form complex compounds.
(b) They show variable oxidation states.
(c) All their ions are colourless.
(d) Their ions contain partially filled *d*-electrons.

66 Mercury is a liquid metal because [KCET]
(a) it has a completely filled *s*-orbital
(b) it has a small atomic size
(c) it has a completely filled *d*-orbital that prevents *d-d* overlapping of orbitals
(d) it has a completely filled *d*-orbital that causes *d-d* overlapping

67 An aqueous solution of $CoCl_2$ on addition of excess of conc. HCl turns blue due to the formation of [DUMET]
(a) $[Co(H_2O)]Cl_2$ (b) $[Co(H_2O)_2Cl_4]^{2-}$
(c) $[CoCl_4]^{2-}$ (d) $[Co(H_2O)_2Cl_2]$

68 Transition metals form alloys easily. The reas on for this is [RPMT]
(a) their occurrence (b) similar size
(c) magnetic nature (d) None of these

69 Calomel on reaction with ammonium hydroxide gives [JCECE]
(a) HgO (b) Hg_2O
(c) NH_2—Hg—Hg—Cl (d) $HgNH_2Cl$

2007

70 Which one of the following ions is the most stable in aqueous solution?
[Atomic number Ti = 22, V = 23, Cr = 24 and Mn = 25] [CBSE AIPMT]
(a) Cr^{3+} (b) V^{3+}
(c) Ti^{3+} (d) Mn^{3+}

71 **Assertion** (A) Mercury vapour is shining silvery in appearance.
Reason (R) Mercury is a metal with shining silvery appearance. [AIIMS]
(a) Both A and R are correct and R is the correct explanation of A
(b) Both A and R are correct but R is not the correct explanation of A
(c) A is correct but R is incorrect
(d) Both A and R are incorrect

72 The courect statement about ionisation energies of Cu and Zn is/are [PbPMT]
(a) IE_1 of Cu is less than that of Zn
(b) IE_2 of Cu is more than that of Zn
(c) IE_2 of Zn is more than that of Cu
(d) Both (a) and (b)

73 Among the following series of transition metal ions, the one in which all metal ions have $3d^2$, $3p^6$ electronic configuration is [atomic number Ti = 22, V = 23, Cr = 24 and Mn = 25] **[Manipal]**
(a) $Ti^{3+}, V^{2+}, Cr^{3+}, Mn^{4+}$ (b) $Ti^{+}, V^{4+}, Cr^{6+}, Mn^{7+}$
(c) $Ti^{4+}, V^{3+}, Cr^{2+}, Mn^{3+}$ (d) $Ti^{2+}, V^{3+}, Cr^{4+}, Mn^{5+}$

74 Among K, Ca, Fe and Zn, the element which can form more than one binary compound with chlorine is **[Manipal]**
(a) Fe (b) Zn (c) K (d) Ca

75 The dark blue colour of the solution formed when excess of ammonia is added to a solution of copper(II) sulphate is due to the presence of the ion **[Kerala CEE]**
(a) $[Cu(OH)_4(H_2O)_2]^{2-}$ (b) $[Cu(H_2O)_6]^{2+}$
(c) $[Cu(NH_3)_2(H_2O)_4]^{4+}$ (d) $[Cu(NH_3)_2(H_2O)_4]^{2+}$
(e) $[Cu(NH_3)_4(H_2O)_2]^{2+}$

76 Blue vitriol is **[RPMT]**
(a) $MgSO_4 \cdot 7H_2O$ (b) $CuSO_4 \cdot 5H_2O$
(c) $CaSO_4 \cdot 2H_2O$ (d) $ZnSO_4 \cdot 7H_2O$

77 Reason of passivity of iron is **[RPMT]**
(a) Fe_2O_3 (b) Fe_3O_4
(c) FeO (d) $Fe_2O_4 \cdot 3H_2O$

78 $CuSO_4$ when reacts with KCN forms CuCN which is insoluble in water. It is soluble in excess of KCN, due to formation of the following complex **[Punjab PMET]**
(a) $K_2[Cu(CN)_4]$
(b) $K_3[Cu(CN)_4]$
(c) $CuCN_2$
(d) $Cu[KCu(CN)_4]$

79 Formula of ammonium manganate is **[DUMET]**
(a) NH_4MnO_4 (b) $(NH_4)_2MnO_4$
(c) $NH_4(MnO_4)_2$ (d) $NH_4Mn_2O_4$

80 In which of the following ions, *d-d* transition is not possible? **[Guj CET]**
(a) Cr^{3+} (b) Ti^{4+}
(c) Cu^{2+} (d) Mn^{2+}

2006

81 The following is known as 'bordeaux mixture'. **[Kerala CEE]**
(a) Borax and copper sulphate
(b) Orthoboric acid and ferrous sulphate
(c) Sodium borate and zinc sulphate
(d) Copper sulphate and lime
(e) Borax and manganous sulphate

82 Which of the following metals form amphoteric oxide? **[MP PMT]**
(a) Fe (b) Cu
(c) Zn (d) Ca

83 The coordination number in a/an ...... complex may increase to 8. **[J&K CET]**
(a) cobalt (b) osmium
(c) nickel (d) iron

84 Which of the following is used as indelible ink? **[J&K CET]**
(a) Aqueous $CuSO_4$ solution
(b) Aqueous $AgNO_3$ solution
(c) Aqueous NaCl solution
(d) Aqueous NaOH solution

85 A transition metal ion exists in its highest oxidation state. It is expected to behave as **[KCET]**
(a) a chelating agent
(b) a central metal in a coordination compound
(c) an oxidising agent
(d) a reducing agent

86 The stability of ferric ion is due to **[BCECE]**
(a) half-filled *f*-orbitals
(b) half-filled *d*-orbitals
(c) completely filled *f*-orbitals
(d) completely filled *d*-orbitals

87 Which of the following is red in colour? **[JCECE]**
(a) Cu_2O (b) CuF (c) ZnF_2 (d) $ZnCl_2$

88 Fenton's reagent is **[JCECE]**
(a) $SnCl_2 + HCl$ (b) $AgNO_3 + NH_4OH$
(c) $CuSO_4 + NaOH$ (d) $FeSO_4 + H_2O_2$

2005

89 Four successive members of the first row transition elements are listed below with their atomic numbers. Which one of them is expected to have the highest third ionisation enthalpy? **[CBSE AIPMT]**
(a) Vanadium ($Z = 23$) (b) Chromium ($Z = 24$)
(c) Iron ($Z = 26$) (d) Manganese ($Z = 25$)

90 Which of the following is a highly corrosive salt? **[AFMC]**
(a) $FeCl_2$ (b) $PbCl_2$ (c) Hg_2Cl_2 (d) $HgCl_2$

91 Green vitriol is formed by **[Punjab PMET]**
(a) $FeS_2 + H_2O + O_2$ (b) $FeS_2 + H_2O + CO_2$
(c) $FeS_2 + CO + CO_2$ (d) $FeS_2 + CO$

92 Which of the following is obtained when auric chloride reacts with sodium chloride? **[AMU]**
(a) Na[AuCl] (b) $Na[AuCl_2]$
(c) $Na[AuCl_3]$ (d) $Na[AuCl_4]$

93 Which of the following pairs of elements cannot form an alloy? **[KCET]**
(a) Zn, Cu (b) Fe, Hg (c) Fe, C (d) Hg, Na

94 **Assertion** (A) The spin only magnetic moment of Sc^{3+} is 1.73 BM.
Reason (R) The spin only magnetic moment (in BM) of an ion is equal to $\sqrt{n(n+2)}$, where *n* is the number of unpaired electrons present in the ion. **[EAMCET]**
(a) Both A and R are correct and R is the correct explanation of A
(b) Both A and R are correct and R is not the correct explanation of A
(c) A is correct but R is incorrect
(d) A is incorrect but R is correct

Answers

1 (d)	2 (b)	3 (c)	4 (c)	5 (a)	6 (d)	7 (c)	8 (b)	9 (c)	10 (a)
11 (d)	12 (b)	13 (c)	14 (a)	15 (c)	16 (b)	17 (a)	18 (b)	19 (d)	20 (a)
21 (d)	22 (c)	23 (b)	24 (c)	25 (d)	26 (c)	27 (c)	28 (c)	29 (b)	30 (a)
31 (b)	32 (c)	33 (d)	34 (b)	35 (d)	36 (a)	37 (a)	38 (c)	39 (c)	40 (d)
41 (b)	42 (a)	43 (c)	44 (d)	45 (a)	46 (c)	47 (c)	48 (b)	49 (d)	50 (b)
51 (d)	52 (d)	53 (a)	54 (d)	55 (a)	56 (b)	57 (d)	58 (a)	59 (d)	60 (c)
61 (c)	62 (c)	63 (a)	64 (b)	65 (c)	66 (c)	67 (c)	68 (b)	69 (d)	70 (d)
71 (d)	72 (d)	73 (d)	74 (a)	75 (e)	76 (b)	77 (b)	78 (b)	79 (b)	80 (b)
81 (d)	82 (c)	83 (b)	84 (b)	85 (c)	86 (b)	87 (a)	88 (d)	89 (d)	90 (d)
91 (a)	92 (d)	93 (b)	94 (d)						

Explanations

1 (*d*) Oxidation state of *d*-block elements can vary, i.e. of Fe, Co and Cr as follows:

(a) (c) Oxidation state of Co = (+)2 to (+) 5 and oxidation state of Fe = (+) 2 to (+) 6, but (+) 6 is less stable. Also (+) 4 and + 5 oxidationi states of Fe are very rare.

(d) Oxidation state of Cr = (+) 2 to (+) 6, where (+) 6 state is more stable.

(b) Oxidation state of alkaline earth metals (i.e. Mg) is fixed and equal to (+)2.

Hence, option (d) is the correct.

2 (*b*) Since, Zn and Cd both have completely filled outermost shells, i.e. have no unpaired electrons.

Thus, they cannot form covalent and metallic bonds strongly and show boiling point less than 500°C [Zn (146°C) and Cd (321°C)]

Hence, option (b) is the correct.

3 (*c*) The compound which contains 18 valence electrons are said to follow 18 electrons octet rule.

(a) $[Mn(CO)_5]$ – Mn{$[Ar]_{18}3d^54s^2$}=7 valence electrons + 10e⁻s from 5 CO ligands

(b) $[Cr(CO)_5]$ – Cr{$[Ar]_{18}3d^54s^1$} = 6 valence electrons + 10e⁻s from 5 CO ligands

(c) $[Fe(CO)_5]$ – Fe{$[Ar]_{18}3d^64s^2$} = 8 valence electrons + 10e⁻s from 5 CO ligands

∴ $[Fe(CO)_5]$ follow 18 electron octet rule

4 (*c*) Spin only magnetic moment depends upon the number of unpaired electrons. Magnetic moment,

$$\mu = \sqrt{n(n+2)}$$

where, n = number of unpaired electrons

The electronic configuration for the given ions is as follows:

(i) For $Mn^{2+}[Z = 25] = 1s^2, 2s^2 2p^6, 3s^2 3p^6, 3d^5 4s^0$

$3d^5$: | 1 | 1 | 1 | 1 | 1 |

$$\mu = \sqrt{5(5+2)} = \sqrt{35}$$

(ii) For $Cr^{2+}[Z = 24] = 1s^2, 2s^2 2p^6, 3s^2 3p^6, 3d^4, 4s^0$

$3d^4$: | 1 | 1 | 1 | 1 | |

$$\mu = \sqrt{4(4+2)} = \sqrt{24}$$

(iii) For $Ti^{2+}[Z = 22] = 1s^2, 2s^2 2p^6, 3s^2 3p^6, 3d^2, 4s^0$

$3d^2$: | 1 | 1 | | | |

$$\mu = \sqrt{2(2+2)} = \sqrt{8}$$

∴ Correct order of spin only magnetic moment is $Mn^{2+} > Cr^{2+} > Ti^{2+}$.

5 (*a*) The number of unpaired electrons and electronic configuration of the given species is shown below :

(a) V^{4+} $[Z = 23] = [Ar]_{18}3d^1$

No. of unpaired electron = 1

(b) Sc^{3+} $[Z = 21] = [Ar]_{18}3d^0$

No. of unpaired electron = 0

(c) V^{5+} $[Z = 23] = [Ar]_{18}3d^0$

No. of unpaired electron = 0

(d) Zn^{2+} $[Z = 30] = [Ar]_{18}3d^{10}$

No. of unpaired electron = 0

∴ The correct option is (a).

6 (*d*) All magnetically ordered solids, i.e. ferromagnetic; antiferromagnetic; ferrimagnetic changes to paramagnetic state at high temperature because of the randomisation of spins.

Ferrimagnetic species such as Fe_3O_4 (magnetite) and ferrites, i.e. $MgFe_2O_4$ and $ZnFe_2O_4$ loses ferrimagnetism on heating and transforms to paramagnetic species.

7 (*c*) Spin magnetic moment can be calculated as

$$\mu = \sqrt{n(n+2)}\ \text{BM}$$

where, μ = magnetic moment,

BM = Bohr Magneton (unit of μ)

and n = number of unpaired electrons in *d*-orbital.

1. The electronic configuration of Co^{3+} is $[Ar]\,3d^6$.

Here, $n = 4$

$$\mu = \sqrt{4(4+2)} = \sqrt{24}\ \text{BM}$$

2. The electronic configuration of Cr^{3+} is $[Ar]3d^3$.

Here, $n = 3$

$$\mu = \sqrt{3(3+2)} = \sqrt{15}\ \text{BM}$$

3. The electronic configuration of Fe^{3+} is $[Ar]3d^5$. Here, $n = 5$

$$\mu = \sqrt{5(5+2)} = \sqrt{35}\ \text{BM}$$

4. The electronic configuration of Ni^{2+} is $[Ar]\,3d^8$. Here, $n = 2$

$$\mu = \sqrt{2(2+2)} = \sqrt{8}\ \text{BM}$$

So, the correct option is (c).

8 (*b*) In $Na_2Cd \cdot Cl_4$, Cd^{2+} has no unpaired electron due to presence of d^{10} electronic configuration. Hence, $Na_2Cd.Cl_4$ is a colourless compound.

9 (*c*) $Ni^{2+}(3d^6 4s^0)$ and $Cr^{3+}(3d^3 4s^0)$ are coloured due to the presence of unpaired electrons. But Zn^{2+} is colourless because of the absence of unpaired electrons.

10 (*a*) (a) $Fe^{2+} = [Ar]\, 3d^6 4s^0$

$\Rightarrow$ 4 unpaired electrons.

(b) $Cu^+ = [Ar]\, 3d^{10} 4s^0$

$\Rightarrow$ No unpaired electron

(c) $Zn = [Ar]\, 3d^{10} 4s^2$

$\Rightarrow$ No unpaired electron

(d) $Ni^{3+} = [Ar]\, 3d^7 4s^0$

$\Rightarrow$ 3 unpaired electrons

11 (*d*) Nitric acid acts as an oxidising agent while reacting with copper. When dil. HNO_3 reacts with Cu, reaction proceeds as:

$$3Cu + 8HNO_3(\text{dil.}) \longrightarrow 3Cu(NO_3)_2 + 2NO + 4H_2O$$

and when conc. HNO_3 is used, reaction proceeds as :

$$Cu + 4HNO_3(\text{conc.}) \longrightarrow Cu(NO_3)_2 + 2NO_2 + 2H_2O$$

12 (*b*) One electron in case of atomic number 24 moves from 4*s* to 3*d* orbital to achieve the state of more stability. This is because energy of 3*d* and 4*s*-orbitals are comparable.

13 (*c*) (a) $\overset{0}{Fe} + \underbrace{H_2O + O_2}_{\text{from air}} \longrightarrow \overset{III}{Fe_2}O_3 \cdot x\,H_2O$

(b) $\overset{0}{Fe} + CuSO_4 \longrightarrow \overset{II}{Fe}SO_4 + Cu$

(c) $\overset{0}{Fe} + 5CO \longrightarrow \overset{0}{Fe}(CO)_5$

(d) $\overset{0}{Fe} + \underset{\text{Steam}}{H_2O} \longrightarrow \overset{III}{Fe_2}O_3 + H_2$

Formation of $Fe(CO)_5$ from Fe does not involve oxidation of iron because there is no change in oxidation state.

14 (*a*) Magnetic moment, $\mu = \sqrt{n(n+2)}$ BM where, n = number of unpaired electrons

$\mu = 2.84$ (given)

$$2.84 = \sqrt{n(n+2)} \text{ BM}$$
$$(2.84)^2 = n(n+2)$$
$$8 = n^2 + 2n \Rightarrow n^2 + 2n - 8 = 0$$
$$n^2 + 4n - 2n - 8 = 0$$
$$n(n+4) - 2(n+4) = 0$$
$$(n+4)(n-2) = 0 \Rightarrow n = 2 \quad [\because n \neq -4]$$

(a) $Ni^{2+} = [Ar]3d^8 4s^0$

(two unpaired electrons)

(b) $Ti^{3+} = [Ar]3d^1 4s^0$

(one unpaired electron)

(c) $Cr^{3+} = [Ar]3d^3$,

(three unpaired electrons)

(d) $Co^{2+} = [Ar], 3d^7, 4s^0$

(three unpaired electrons)

So, only Ni^{2+} has 2 unpaired electrons.

15 (*c*) Strength of metallic bond depends upon number of unpaired electrons. As number of unpaired electrons increases the bond strength increases. So, Cr shows strongest metallic bonding due to maximum number of unpaired electrons.

16 (*b*) Magnetic moment is given by

$$\mu = \sqrt{n(n+2)}$$

Here, n = number of unpaired electrons.

$$\Rightarrow \quad 2.83 = \sqrt{n(n+2)}$$
$$\Rightarrow \quad (2.83)^2 = n(n+2)$$
$$\Rightarrow \quad 8.00 = n^2 + 2n$$
$$\Rightarrow \quad n^2 + 2n - 8 = 0$$
$$\Rightarrow \quad n^2 + 4n - 2n - 8 = 0$$
$$\Rightarrow \quad (n+4)(n-2) = 0$$
$$n = 2 \quad [\because n \neq -4]$$

Among the given ions,

(a) $_{22}Ti^{3+} \longrightarrow 3d^1$

1				

$\Rightarrow$ one unpaired electron

(b) $_{28}Ni^{2+} \longrightarrow 3d^8$

⥮	⥮	⥮	1	1

$\Rightarrow$ two unpaired electrons

(c) $_{24}Cr^{3+} \longrightarrow 3d^3$

1	1	1		

$\Rightarrow$ three unpaired electrons

(d) $_{25}Mn^{2+} \longrightarrow 3d^5$

1	1	1	1	1

$\Rightarrow$ five unpaired electrons

Hence, Ni^{2+} possesses a magnetic moment of 2.83 BM.

Short Trick

(Relation between spin only magnetic moment (BM) and number of unpaired electrons).

If number of unpaired electrons (n)

$n = 1$, BM $(\mu) \approx 1.73 \ (= \sqrt{3})$

$n = 2$, BM $(\mu) \approx 2.83 \ (= \sqrt{8})$

$n = 3$, BM $(\mu) \approx 3.87 \ (= \sqrt{15})$

$n = 4$, BM $(\mu) \approx 4.90 \ (= \sqrt{24})$

$n = 5$, BM $(\mu) \approx 5.91 \ (= \sqrt{35})$

i.e. number of unpaired electrons = whole number value of the magnetic moment i.e. (BM).

17 (*a*) (a) $Ti^{4+} (22 - 4 = 18) = [Ar]3d^0$

(no unpaired electron)

(b) $V^{4+} (23 - 4 = 19) = [Ar]3d^1$

(one unpaired electron)

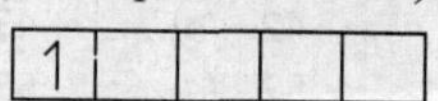

(c) $Mn^{2+} (25 - 2 = 23) = [Ar]3d^5$

(five unpaired electrons)

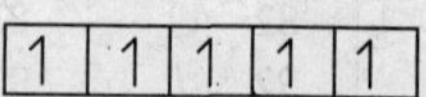

(d) $Fe^{3+} (26 - 3 = 23)$ = same as Mn^{2+}

(five unpaired electrons)

(e) $Ni^{2+} (28 - 2 = 26) = [Ar]3d^8$

(two unpaired electrons)

⥮	⥮	⥮	1	1

Since, Ti^{4+} does not have any unpaired electron.

So, *d-d* transition is not possible and, hence its aqueous solution is colourless.

18 (*b*) Eating animals flesh, poisoned with mercury (Hg^{2+}) cause deformity. This condition is known as minamata (minimata) disease which is characterised by diarrhoea, haemolysis, impairment of various senses, meningitis and death.

19 (*d*) Electronic configuration of cuprous (Cu^+) and cupric (Cu^{2+}) ions are as follows:

$$Cu^+ = [Ar]3d^{10}, 4s^0$$
$$Cu^{2+} = [Ar]3d^9, 4s^0$$

It seems to be that electronic configuration of Cu^+ is more stable but it is less stable than Cu^{2+}. Due to the small size of Cu^{2+} ions, its nuclear charge is sufficient to hold 25 electrons but in Cu^+ such a condition is not true. Further, 2nd ionisation potential of copper is large but lattice energy released for Cu^{2+} compounds is much more negative than that for Cu^+ compounds. Hence, option (d) is the correct answer.

20 (*a*) Interstitial compounds are obtained when small atoms like H, B, C, N fit into the interstitial sites of the lattice. These compounds retain their metallic conductivity but are chemically inert.

21 (*d*) All compounds give O_2 on heating except $(NH_4)_2Cr_2O_7$.

$$2KClO_3 \xrightarrow{\Delta} 2KCl + 3O_2$$

$$Zn(ClO_3)_2 \xrightarrow{\Delta} ZnCl_2 + 3O_2$$
$$K_2Cr_2O_7 \xrightarrow{\Delta} 2CrO_2 + K_2O + O_2$$
$$(NH_4)_2Cr_2O_7 \xrightarrow{\Delta} Cr_2O_3 + N_2\uparrow + 4H_2O$$

On heating '$(NH_4)_2Cr_2O_7$, the products formed are N_2, Cr_2O_3 and H_2O.' Oxygen is not formed in the reaction.

22 (c) Formula for Mohr's salt is $[(NH_4)_2Fe(SO_4)_2.6H_2O]$. Thus, it has 6 water molecules.

23 (b) The general electronic configuration of d-block element is $(n-1)d^{1-10}, ns^{1-2}$ (because the last electron here enters into penultimate d-orbital).

24 (c) Transition elements show variable valencies. As it depends only upon stability of metal ions, so valency varies.
e.g. $Fe^{2+}, Fe^{3+}, Co^{2+}, Co^{3+}$, etc.

25 (d) Cuprous ion is colourless while cupric ion is coloured because cuprous ion has completely filled d-orbitals, i.e. $3d^{10}, 4s^0$ configuration and cupric ion has incompletely filled d-orbital due to $3d^9, 4s^0$ configuration.

26 (c) The correct order of melting points is Ti < V < Cr > Mn. The melting point of transition elements first increase to a maximum extent and then fall as atomic number increases. Mn, however has abnormally low melting point, due to stable configuration and weak intermetallic bonding.

27 (c) In electrochemical series, metals with positive standard potential are placed below hydrogen. Out of given transition metals, only Cu is lower than hydrogen in electrochemical series. Therefore, it must have positive sign for standard potential. $[E^o_{M^{2+}/M}]$.

28 (c) Stainless steel contains
Fe + Cr + Ni.

29 (b) This can be understood on the basis of E° values for M^{2+}/M.

E°/V	Cr	Mn⁻	Fe	Co
M^{2+}/M	–0.90	–1.18	–0.44	–0.28

E° value for Mn is more negative than expected from general trend due to extra stability of half-filled electronic configuration of Mn^{2+} ion.

Thus, the correct order should be
Mn > Cr > Fe > Co

An examination of E° values for redox couple M^{3+}/M^{2+} shows that Cr^{2+} is strong reducing agent ($E_{M^{3+}/M^{2+}} = 0.41$ V) and liberates H_2 from dilute acids.

$$2Cr^{2+}(aq) + 2H^+(aq) \longrightarrow 2Cr^{3+}(aq) + H_2\uparrow(g)$$

The correct order is Mn > Fe > Cr > Co.

30 (a) Species with unpaired electrons are paramagnetic in nature.

(i) $Fe^{2+} = 3d^6, 4s^0 \Rightarrow$ [↿⇂ | ↿ | ↿ | ↿ | ↿]
(four unpaired electrons)

(ii) $Zn = 3d^{10}, 4s^2 \Rightarrow$ [↿⇂ | ↿⇂ | ↿⇂ | ↿⇂ | ↿⇂]
(zero unpaired electron)

(iii) $Hg^{2+} = 5d^{10}, 6s^2$ (no unpaired electron)

(iv) $Ti^{4+} = 3d^0, 4s^0$ (no unpaired electron)

Hence, only Fe^{2+} is paramagnetic.

31 (b) Generally, d-block element form complexes and lead is a p-block element. So, ammonia does not form complex with Pb^{2+}.

32 (c) The oxidation states exhibited by Ti in its complexes are + 2, + 3 and + 4. Thus, K_2TiO_4 does not exist. Ti possesses +6 oxidation state in this compound which is not possible.

33 (d) The electronic configuration of Fe is

$$_{26}Fe = [Ar]\,3d^6\,4s^2$$
$$Fe^{3+} = [Ar]\,3d^5$$

Thus, five unpaired electrons are present.

∴ Spin only magnetic moment,

$$\mu = \sqrt{n(n+2)}$$

Here, $n = 5$

$$\mu = \sqrt{5(5+2)} = \sqrt{35} = 5.91 \approx 6 \text{ BM}$$

34 (b) Compounds of copper in +2 oxidation state are more stable than that of +1 state because lattice enthalpy released by Cu^{2+} compounds is much more negative than that for Cu^+ compounds.
Since, release of energy is exothermic process, thus more stable Cu^{2+} compounds are formed by exothermic process.

35 (d) German silver is an alloy of zinc, nickel and copper.

36 (a) It shows axial and orbital motion of electrons in the same direction because it has 5 unpaired electrons with same spin.

37 (a) $[Te(H_2O)_6]^{3+}$

$Ti(22) = [Ar]\,4s^2 3d^2$

$Ti^{3+} = [Ar]\,4s^0 3d^1$

$\therefore \mu = \sqrt{n(n+2)} = \sqrt{1(1+2)} = 1.73$ BM

38 (c) Electronic configuration of Ti^{3+} is $3d^1$. Thus, Ti^{3+} contains an unpaired electron, so it will exhibit colour in aqueous solution due to d-d transition.

39 (c) On treating zinc with excess of NaOH, sodium zincate is obtained as major product.

$$Zn + 2NaOH \longrightarrow \underset{\text{Sodium zincate}}{Na_2ZnO_2} + H_2$$

40 (d) The false statement about transition elements is that they show multiple oxidation states always differing by units of two, because they show variable oxidation state but not always have a difference of two units, e.g. Mn exhibit oxidation state from +1 to +7.

41 (b) Cu (atomic number = 29)
$= 1s^2, 2s^2, 2p^6, 3s^2, 3p^6, 3d^{10}, 4s^1$
∵ In an orbital, the two electrons must have the opposite spin.
∴ In Cu, 14 electrons have spin in one direction and 15 electrons in other direction.

42 (a) Zinc sulphide (ZnS) is white to yellow coloured powder or crystal. Because Zn has +2 state in ZnS in which all d-orbitals are completely filled.

43 (c) The formula of mercurous ion is Hg_2^{2+}.

44 (d) Mercurous chloride (calomel) is prepared by heating $HgCl_2$ and Hg in iron vessel.

(a) $HgCl_2 + Hg \xrightarrow{\Delta} Hg_2Cl_2$

It can also be prepared by the reduction of mercury (II) chloride by tin (II) chloride in a limited quantity.

(c) $2HgCl_2 + SnCl_2 \longrightarrow Hg_2Cl_2 + SnCl_4$

Hence, both the options (a) and (c) are correct.

45 (a) Given, $X = [Ar]\,d^4$
∴ The complete configuration of the ion,

$$X^{3+} = 1s^2, 2s^2, 2p^6, 3s^2, 3p^6, 3d^4$$
$$\therefore X = 1s^2, 2s^2, 2p^6, 3s^2, 3p^6, 3d^5, 4s^2$$

∴ The atomic number of the element is 25 and the element is Mn.

46 (*c*) Fe_3O_4 (lodestone or magnetic oxide of iron) is called magnetite. It is a mixed oxide and, thus known as ferrosoferric oxide.

47 (*c*) Oxidation state of Ti in $TiF_6^{2-} = Ti^{4+}$
$= [Ne]\,3s^2, 3p^6$ (no unpaired electron)
Oxidation state of Cu in $Cu_2Cl_2 = Cu^+$
$= [Ar]\,3d^{10}$ (no unpaired electron)
$\therefore$ As both the species have paired electrons, hence both are colourless species.

48 (*b*) Species having the same number of unpaired electrons, have same magnetic moment.
(a) $MnCl_2 \Rightarrow Mn^{2+} = [Ar]\,3d^5, 4s^0$
(five unpaired electrons)
$CuSO_4 \Rightarrow Cu^{2+} = [Ar]\,3d^9, 4s^0$
(one unpaired electron)
(b) $CuCl_2 \Rightarrow Cu^{2+} = [Ar]\,3d^9, 4s^0$
(one unpaired electron)
$TiCl_3 \Rightarrow Ti^{3+} = [Ar]\,3d^1, 4s^0$
(one unpaired electron)
(c) $TiO_2 \Rightarrow Ti^{4+} = [Ar]\,3d^0, 4s^0$
(no unpaired electron)
$CuSO_4 \Rightarrow Cu^{2+} = [Ar]\,3d^9, 4s^0$
(one unpaired electron)
(d) $TiCl_3 \Rightarrow Ti^{3+} = [Ar]\,3d^1, 4s^0$
(one unpaired electron)
$NiCl_2 \Rightarrow Ni^{2+} = [Ar]\,3d^8, 4s^0$
(two unpaired electrons)
$\therefore$ $CuCl_2$ and $TiCl_3$ will have same magnetic moment.
$\mu = \sqrt{1(1+2)} = \sqrt{3} = 1.73$ BM

49 (*d*) Magnetic moment, $\mu = \sqrt{n(n+2)}$ BM, where n=number of unpaired electrons. Hence, paramagnetic behaviour of transition metals is due to the presence of unpaired electrons.

50 (*b*) Those compounds which have unpaired electrons will be coloured. In CuF_2, Cu is present as Cu^{2+}.
$Cu^{2+} = [Ar]\,3d^9, 4s^0$
Since, in it unpaired electron is present, thus it is coloured.

51 (*d*) $AgNO_3$ when heated above its melting point, i.e. above 212°C, decomposed to give silver nitrite and oxygen but when heated at high temperature (i.e. 980 K), it gives silver metal (Ag).

$$2AgNO_3 \xrightarrow[\Delta]{>212°C} 2AgNO_2 + O_2$$
$$2AgNO_3 \xrightarrow{980\text{ K}, \Delta} 2Ag\downarrow + 2NO_2 + O_2$$

52 (*d*) The electronic configuration of Mn is $Mn(25) = [Ar]\,3d^5, 4s^2, 4p^0$
In excited state,

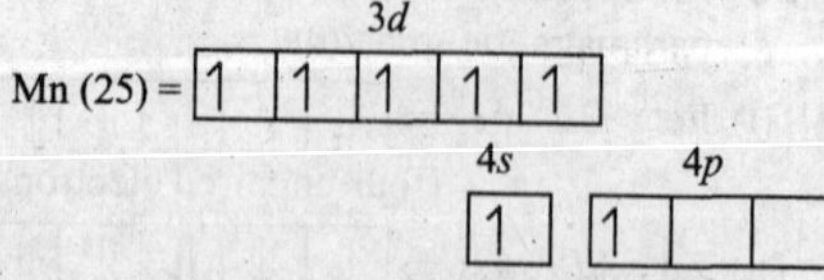

(seven unpaired electrons)

Hence, maximum oxidation state exhibited by Mn is +7 which is found in $KMnO_4$.

53 (*a*)

Metal ion	Configuration	Number of unpaired electrons	Magnetic moment
Ti^{3+}	$3d^1$	1	1.75
Ni^{2+}	$3d^8$	2	2.76
Co^{3+}	$3d^7$	3	3.86
Mn^{2+}	$3d^5$	5	5.96

54 (*d*) MnO_2 is used in dry battery cell. Zn and Ni/Cd is used in battery industry.

55 (*a*) (i) The oxides with lower oxidation states are basic in nature.
(ii) The oxides with intermediate oxidation states are amphoteric.
(iii) The oxides with higher oxidation states are acidic in nature.
Thus, Cr_2O_3 is an amphoteric oxide.

56 (*b*) *d*-block elements have incompletely filled *d*-orbitals in their ground state or in their most common oxidation state. The general electronic configuration of *d*-block elements is $(n-1)\,d^{1-10}ns^{1-2}$.
Among the given element, Hs ($Z = 108$) belongs to 6*d* series with electronic configuration $[Rn]\,5f^{14}, 6d^6, 7s^2$. Thus, it is a *d*-block element.

57 (*d*) Magnetic moment, $\mu = \sqrt{n(n+2)}$
where, n = number of unpaired electrons.
Given, $\mu = \sqrt{15}$
$\therefore \sqrt{15} = \sqrt{n(n+2)} \Rightarrow 15 = n(n+2)$
This is possible only, when $n = 3$.

58 (*a*) Paramagnetic property depends upon the number of unpaired electrons. Higher the number of unpaired electrons, higher will be the paramagnetic property.
(i) $Cu^{2+} = [Ar]\,3d^9$, number of unpaired electron $= 1$
(ii) $V^{2+} = [Ar]\,3d^3$, number of unpaired electrons $= 3$
(iii) $Cr^{2+} = [Ar]\,3d^4$, number of unpaired electrons $= 4$
(iv) $Mn^{2+} = [Ar]\,3d^5$, number of unpaired electrons $= 5$
Hence, correct order is
$Cu^{2+} < V^{2+} < Cr^{2+} < Mn^{2+}$.

59 (*d*) The compounds having metal ions with unpaired electrons, are coloured. Thus,
(a) in $TiCl_3$, $Ti^{3+} = [Ar]3d^1$
(one unpaired electron)
(b) In $FeCl_3$, $Fe^{3+} = [Ar]3d^5$
(five unpaired electrons)
(c) In $CoCl_2$, $Co^{2+} = [Ar]3d^7$
(three unpaired electrons)
Hence, all compounds are coloured.

60 (*c*) Mn_2O_7 is a covalent oxide and have a Mn—O—Mn bridge. Here, Mn is tetrahedrally surrounded by O—atoms.

$$O_3Mn{-}O{-}MnO_3$$

61 (*c*) The spin only magnetic moment is given by $\mu = \sqrt{n(n+2)}$,
where n = number of unpaired electron.
Thus, $\sqrt{n(n+2)} = 1.8$
Squaring both sides, we get
$n(n+2) = 3.24$
$\Rightarrow n^2 + 2n = 3 \quad (\because 3.24 \approx 3)$
$\therefore n^2 + 2n - 3 = 0$
$\Rightarrow n^2 + 3n - n - 3 = 0$
$\Rightarrow (n-1)(n+3) = 0$
$\Rightarrow n = 1$ but $n \neq -3$ is not possible
Thus, $n = 1$
It means one unpaired electron is present, i.e. it is copper.
Thus,
$$\underset{(A)}{2Cu} + 2H_2SO_4 + O_2 \longrightarrow \underset{(B)}{2CuSO_4} + 2H_2O$$
$$\underset{(B)}{2CuSO_4} + \underset{(C)}{4KI} \longrightarrow 2K_2SO_4 + \underset{\text{Unstable}}{2CuI_2}$$
$$2CuI_2 \longrightarrow \underset{(D)}{Cu_2I_2} + I_2$$

62 (*c*) The electronic configuration of Mn^{3+} and Co^{3+} are given below

$Mn^{3+} = [Ar]3d^4$

$Co^{3+} = [Ar]3d^6$

Hence, they can easily accept electrons (undergoes reduction) to get stable configuration, and behave as good oxidising agent in aqueous solution.

63 (*a*) Cu, Ag and Au elements are called coinage metals because in the early times, they were used in making coins.

64 (*b*) Maximum oxidation state of transition metals = number of electrons in $(n-1)d$ orbital + number of electrons in *ns*-orbital.

The electronic configuration of

$Os = [Xe]4f^{14}, 5d^6, 6s^2$

∴ Maximum oxidation state $= 6+2 = 8$

∴ The highest oxidation state exhibited by transition metal is +8, e.g. OsO_4.

65 (*c*) Most of the transition metal ions due to the presence of unpaired *d*-electrons are coloured. Rest all the given options are true.

66 (*c*) The electronic configuration of mercury (80) is $[Xe]4f^{10}, 5d^{10}, 6s^2$. Its *d*-subshell is completely filled, thus it prevents the overlapping of *d*-orbitals (*d*-*d* overlapping). Hence, it is liquid metal at room temperature.

67 (*c*) $CoCl_2$, a weak Lewis acid, reacts with chloride ion to produce salt containing the tetrahedral $[CoCl_4]^{2-}$ ion. It is blue when anhydrous and a deep magenta colour when hydrated, and for this reason it is widely used as an indicator in water.

68 (*b*) Transition metals are quite similar in atomic size. Therefore, the atoms of one metal can substitute the atom of other metal in its crystal lattice. Thus, on cooling solution of two or more transition metals, i.e. smooth alloy is formed.

69 (*d*) $Hg_2Cl_2 + 2NH_4OH$

$\downarrow$

$HgNH_2Cl + Hg + NH_4Cl + H_2O$
Black ppt.

70 (*d*) Stability of transition metal ion is directly proportional to the unpaired electrons.

The exactly half-filled and completely filled *d*-orbitals are extra stable.

(a) Cr^{3+} (24) $= 3d^3, 4s^0$ (three unpaired electrons)

(b) V^{3+} (23) $= 3d^2, 4s^0$ (two unpaired electrons)

(c) Ti^{3+} (22) $= 3d^1, 4s^0$ (one unpaired electron)

(d) Mn^{3+} (25) $= 3d^4, 4s^0$ (four unpaired electrons)

So, Mn^{3+} ion is the most stable in aqueous solution.

71 (*d*) Mercury vapours are invisible as no metallic bonding is possible in vapour state. So, both A and R are incorrect.

72 (*d*) IE_1 of $Cu(3d^{10}4s^1)$ is less than that of $Zn(3d^{10}4s^2)$ because its is easy to remove an electron from a half filled *s*-orbital as compared to fully filled *s*-orbital teowever in case of IE_2, the electron is lost from 3*d* orbital of Cu and 4*s* orbital of Zn and loss of electron from 4*s* orbital is easier as compared to fully filled 3*d* orbital.

73 (*d*)

(i) $Ti^{2+} = 1s^2, 2s^2, 2p^6, 3s^2, 3p^6, 3d^2, 4s^0$

(ii) $V^{3+} = 1s^2, 2s^2, 2p^6, 3s^2, 3p^6, 3d^2, 4s^0$

(iii) $Cr^{4+} = 1s^2, 2s^2, 2p^6, 3s^2, 3p^6, 3d^2, 4s^0$

(iv) $Mn^{5+} = 1s^2, 2s^2, 2p^6, 3s^2, 3p^6, 3d^2, 4s^0$

74 (*a*) A binary compound is that compound which is formed by two different elements. Metals or elements which show variable oxidation states can form more than one binary compound. In the given elements Fe shows +2 and +3 oxidation states. So, it can form two binary compounds with chlorine as $FeCl_2$ and $FeCl_3$.

75 (*e*) $CuSO_4 + 4NH_4OH \longrightarrow [Cu(NH_3)_4(H_2O)_2]SO_4 + 2H_2O$
Dark blue colour

76 (*b*) $CuSO_4 \cdot 5H_2O$ is blue vitriol. It is a blue crystalline substance soluble in water.

77 (*b*) Iron is rendered passive due to the formation of layer of ferro-ferric oxide ($FeO \cdot Fe_2O_3$ or Fe_3O_4).

78 (*b*) $CuSO_4 + 2KCN \longrightarrow K_2SO_4 + Cu(CN)_2$

$2Cu(CN)_2 \longrightarrow 2CuCN$ (Insoluble) $+ CN—CN$ (Cyanogen)

$CuCN + 3KCN \longrightarrow K_3[Cu(CN)_4]$ (Soluble)

79 (*b*) Formula of ammonium manganate is $(NH_4)_2MnO_4$.

80 (*b*) The electronic configuration of Ti^{4+} is

$Ti^{4+} = 1s^2, 2s^2, 2p^6, 3s^2, 3p^6, 3d^0$

In Ti^{4+}, *d*-orbitals are empty, hence *d*-*d* transition is not possible.

81 (*d*) "Bordeaux mixture" consists of copper sulphate and lime. It is used as fungicide.

82 (*c*) Zinc metal forms amphoteric oxide.

$ZnO + H_2SO_4 \longrightarrow ZnSO_4 + H_2O$

$ZnO + 2NaOH \longrightarrow Na_2ZnO_2 + H_2O$

83 (*b*) $Os(Z = 76) = [Xe]4f^{14}, 5d^6, 6s^2$
Hence, the coordination number in an osmium complex may increase to +8.

84 (*b*) Aqueous silver nitrate ($AgNO_3$) solution is used as indelible ink.

85 (*c*) If a transition metal ion exists in its highest oxidation state, it is expected to behave as an oxidising agent.

86 (*b*) Fe^{3+} ion has the following configuration.

$Fe^{3+} = 1s^2, 2s^2, 2p^6, 3s^2, 3p^6, 3d^5$

Thus, ferric ion is quite stable due to half-filled *d*-orbitals ($3d^5$).

87 (*a*) Most of the cuprous compounds are usually colourless and diamagnetic as 3*d*-orbital is completely filled ($3d^{10}$). Cu_2O is exception and is red of colour.

88 (*d*) A solution of H_2O_2 with Fe^{2+} (ferrous) salt is known as Fenton's reagent ($FeSO_4 + H_2O_2$).

89 (*d*)

(a) In $_{23}V = 1s^2, 2s^2, 2p^6, 3s^2, 3p^6, 3d^3, 4s^2$

Third electron which is removed in third ionisation potential belongs to $3d^3$-subshell.

(b) $_{24}Cr = 1s^2, 2s^2, 2p^6, 3s^2, 3p^6, 3d^5, 4s^1$

Third electron which is removed in third ionisation potential belongs to $3d^5$-subshell.

(c) $_{26}Fe = 1s^2, 2s^2, 2p^6, 3s^2, 3p^6, 3d^6, 4s^2$

Third electron which is removed in third ionisation potential belongs to $3d^6$-subshell.

(d) $_{25}Mn = 1s^2, 2s^2, 2p^6, 3s^2, 3p^6, 3d^5, 4s^2$

Third electron which is removed in third ionisation potential belongs to $3d^5$-subshell.
In all elements shell and subshells are same. Required amount of energy (enthalpy) is based upon the stability of d-subshell.

The $3d^5$-subshell has the highest stability in an ion because it is half-filled subshell (while other are incomplete).
So, Mn shows highest third ionisation potential or enthalpy.

90 (*d*) Mercuric chloride ($HgCl_2$) is also known as corrosive sublimate as it is highly poisonous and corrosive. It is used (9% solution) for sterlisation of surgical instruments, washing hands, preservative for wood. It is antidote for white of an egg. It is commercially prepared as follows

$$HgSO_4 + 2NaCl \longrightarrow HgCl_2 + Na_2SO_4$$

91 (*a*) $\underset{\text{Pyrites}}{2FeS_2} + 2H_2O + 7O_2 \longrightarrow \underset{\text{Green vitriol}}{2FeSO_4} + 2H_2SO_4$

92 (*d*) $AuCl_3 + NaCl \longrightarrow \underset{\text{Sodium chloroaurate}}{Na[AuCl_4]}$

93 (*b*) Alloy is a homogeneous mixture of two or more metals. Mercury forms amalgams (alloy) with gold, silver and tin. But it does not react with iron or platinum. Thus, Fe and Hg cannot form alloy.

94 (*d*) $_{21}Sc^{3+} = 1s^2, 2s^2, 2p^6, 3s^2, 3p^6$
Number of unpaired electrons $(n) = 0$
Hence, spin only magnetic moment, i.e.

$$\mu = \sqrt{n(n+2)} = 0$$

Hence, A is incorrect but R is correct

Topic 2

Some Important Compounds of Transition Elements

2019

1 When neutral or faintly alkaline $KMnO_4$ is treated with potassium iodide, iodide ion is converted into '*A*', '*A*' is

(a) I_2 (b) IO_4^- (c) IO_3^- (d) IO^- **[NEET (Odisha)]**

2 Which of the following can react with $K_2Cr_2O_7$? **[AIIMS, 2019]**

(a) SO_3^{-2} (b) CO_3^{-2} (c) SO_4^{-2} (d) NO_3^-

3 The manganate and permanganate ions are tetrahedral, due to **[NEET]**

(a) there is no π-bonding
(b) the π-bonding involves overlap of p-orbitals of oxygen with p-orbitals of manganese
(c) the π-bonding involves overlap of d-orbitals of oxygen with d-orbitals of manganese
(d) the π-bonding involves overlap of p-orbitals of oxygen with d-orbitals of manganese

2018

4 Assertion (A) NaCl reacts with concentrated H_2SO_4 to give colourless fumes with pungent smell. But on adding MnO_2 the fumes become greenish yellow.
Reason (R) MnO_2 oxidises HCl to chlorine gas which is greenish yellow. **[AIIMS]**

(a) Both A and R are correct and R is the correct explanation of A
(b) Both A and R are correct and R is not the correct explanation of A
(c) A is correct but R is incorrect
(d) A is incorrect but R is correct

5 When hydrogen peroxide is added to acidified solution of dichromate $Cr_2O_7^{2-}$, a deep blue coloured complex of chromic peroxide CrO_5 is formed. Oxidation state of Cr in CrO_5 is **[JIPMER]**

(a) +5 (b) +3 (c) +6 (d) −10

6 Which one of the following ions exhibits d-d transition and paramagnetism as well? **[NEET]**

(a) MnO_4^- (b) $Cr_2O_7^{2-}$ (c) CrO_4^{2-} (d) MnO_4^{2-}

2016

7 Which one of the following statements is correct when SO_2 is passed through acidified $K_2Cr_2O_7$ solution? **[NEET]**

(a) The solution is decolourised
(b) SO_2 is reduced
(c) Green $Cr_2(SO_4)_3$ is formed
(d) The solution turns blue

2013

8 $KMnO_4$ can be prepared from K_2MnO_4 as per the reaction,

$$3MnO_4^{2-} + 2H_2O \rightleftharpoons 2MnO_4^- + MnO_2 + 4OH^-$$

The reaction can go for completion by removing OH^- ions or by adding **[NEET]**

(a) HCl
(b) KOH
(c) CO_2
(d) SO_2

9 Assertion (A) Solution of Na_2CrO_4 in water is intensely coloured.
Reason (R) Oxidation state of Cr in Na_2CrO_4 is (+ VI). [AIIMS]
(a) Both A and R are correct and R is correct explanation of A
(b) Both A and R are correct but R in not the correct explanation of A
(c) A is correct but R is incorrect
(d) Both A and R are incorrect

2012

10 Which of the following statements is not true? [CBSE AIPMT]
(a) On passing H_2S through acidified $K_2Cr_2O_7$ solution, a milky colour is observed
(b) $Na_2Cr_2O_7$ is preferred over $K_2Cr_2O_7$ in volumetric analysis
(c) $K_2Cr_2O_7$ solution in acidic medium is orange
(d) $K_2Cr_2O_7$ solution becomes yellow on increasing the pH beyond 7

11 The oxidation state of chromium in the final product formed by the reaction between KI and acidified potassium dichromate solution is [AIIMS]
(a) + 3 (b) + 2 (c) + 6 (d) + 4

12 When H_2O_2 is shaken with an acidified solution of $K_2Cr_2O_7$ in the presence of ether, the ethereal layer turns blue due to the formation of [WB JEE]
(a) Cr_2O_3 (b) CrO_4^{2-} (c) $Cr_2(SO_3)_3$ (d) CrO_5

13 Acidified $K_2Cr_2O_7$ solution turns green when Na_2SO_3 is added to it. This is due to the formation of [CBSE AIPMT]
(a) $CrSO_4$ (b) $Cr_2(SO_4)_3$ (c) CrO_4^{2-} (d) $Cr_2(SO_3)_3$

2011

14 The acidic, basic or amphoteric nature of Mn_2O_7, V_2O_5 and CrO are respectively, [Kerala CEE]
(a) acidic, acidic and basic
(b) basic, amphoteric and acidic
(c) acidic, amphoteric and basic
(d) acidic, basic and amphoteric
(e) acidic, basic and basic

15 Which is the correct statement about $Cr_2O_7^{2-}$ structure? [DUMET]
(a) It has neither Cr—Cr bonds nor O—O bonds
(b) It has one Cr—Cr bond and six O—O bonds
(c) It has no Cr—Cr bond and has six O—O bonds
(d) It has one Cr—Cr bond and seven Cr—O bonds

16 When dil. H_2SO_4 is added to aqueous solution of potassium chromate, yellow colour of solution turns to orange colour. It indicates [Guj CET]
(a) chromate ions are reduced
(b) chromate ions are oxidised
(c) monocentric complex is converted into dicentric complex
(d) oxygen gets removed from chromate ions

2006

17 $4K_2Cr_2O_7 \xrightarrow{\text{Heat}} 4K_2CrO_4 + 3O_2 + X$.
In the above reaction X is [AMU]
(a) CrO_3 (b) Cr_2O_7
(c) Cr_2O_3 (d) CrO_5

2005

18 CrO_3 dissolves in aqueous NaOH to give [J&K CET]
(a) CrO_4^{2-} (b) $Cr(OH)_3^-$
(c) $Cr_2O_7^{2-}$ (d) $Cr(OH)_2$

19 Which of the following is the green coloured powder produced when ammonium dichromate is used in fire works? [J&K CET]
(a) Cr (b) CrO_3
(c) Cr_2O_3 (d) $CrO(O_2)$

20 Potassium dichromate is used [Guj CET]
(a) in electroplating
(b) as a reducing agent
(c) oxidise ferrous ions into ferric ions in acidic medium as an oxidising agent
(d) as an insecticide

21 Acidified potassium permanganate solution is decolourised by [AFMC]
(a) bleaching powder (b) white vitriol
(c) Mohr's salt (d) microcosmic salt

Answers

1 (c)	2 (a)	3 (d)	4 (a)	5 (c)	6 (d)	7 (c)	8 (c)	9 (b)	10 (b)
11 (a)	12 (d)	13 (b)	14 (c)	15 (a)	16 (c)	17 (c)	18 (a)	19 (c)	20 (c)
21 (c)									

Explanations

1 (*c*) When neutral or faintly alkaline $KMnO_4$ is treated with potassium iodide, $KMnO_4$ is converted into MnO_2 while iodide (I^-) ion is converted into IO_3^- (iodate). The reaction takes place as follows :

$$KMnO_4 + I^- + \bar{O}H \longrightarrow MnO_2 + IO_3^- + H_2O$$

2 (*a*) Among the given options, oxidation state of .

(a) sulphur in $SO_3^{-2} = +4$

(b) carbon in $CO_3^{-2} = +4$

(c) sulphur in $SO_4^{-2} = +6$

(d) nitrogen in $NO_3^- = +5$

Since, $K_2Cr_2O_7$ is a strong oxidising agent it can oxidise the species, which is not in its most possible positive oxidising state.

Thus, SO_3^{-2} can react with $K_2Cr_2O_7$ as follows:

$$Cr_2O_7^{2-}(aq) + 3SO_3^{2-}(aq) + 8H^+(aq) \longrightarrow 2Cr^{3+}(aq) + 3SO_4^{2-}(aq) + 4H_2O(l)$$

3 (*d*) The structures of manganate and permanganate ions are as follows:

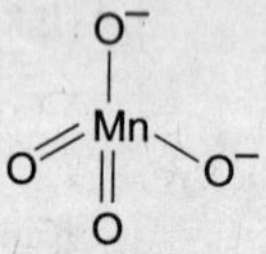

[Structures: Manganate (MnO_4^{2-}) and Permanganate (MnO_4^-)]

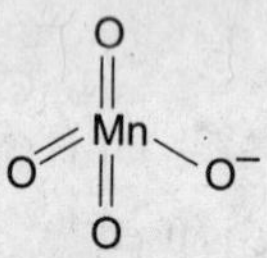

The manganate and permanganate ions are tetrahedral and contain π-bonds of $d\pi$ - $p\pi$-type, oxygen does not have any d-orbital.

Hence, the π-bonding takes place by overlap of p-orbitals of oxygen and d-orbitals of manganese.

4 (*a*) Both Assertion and Reason are correct and Reason is the correct explanation of the Assertion.

NaCl reacts with concentrated H_2SO_4 to give colourless fumes with pungent smell. This pungent smell is due to formation of HCl.

$$NaCl + H_2SO_4 \longrightarrow Na_2SO_4 + 2HCl$$

But on adding MnO_2, the fumes become greenish yellow due to formation of chlorine gas.

5 (*c*) When H_2O_2 is added to an acidified solution of dichromate $Cr_2O_7^{2-}$, a deep blue complex chromic peroxide, CrO_5 is formed.

$$Cr_2O_7^{2-} + 2H^+ + 4H_2O_2 \longrightarrow 2CrO(O_2)_2 + 5H_2O$$

This deep blue coloured complex has the following structure

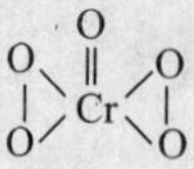

[Structure of $CrO(O_2)_2$]

In $CrO(O_2)_2$, let the oxidation state of Cr be x.

$$\therefore \quad x + (-1)4 + (-2) = 0$$

$$x - 6 = 0 \Rightarrow x = +6$$

6 (*d*) In d-d transition, an electron in a d-orbital of the metal is excited by a photon to another d-orbital of higher energy. The complex compound which contains unpaired electrons shows paramagnetism while which contains paired electrons shows diamagnetism. The complex which contains unpaired electrons exhibit d-d transition and paramagnetism.

(a) In MnO_4^-,

the electronic configuration of Mn^{7+} is $[Ar]3d^0$.

Number of unpaired electrons = 0

Therefore, it will be diamagnetic and will not show d-d transition.

(b) In $Cr_2O_7^{2-}$,

the electronic configuration of Cr^{6+} is $[Ar]3d^0$.

Number of unpaired electrons = 0

Therefore, it will be diamagnetic and will not show d-d transition.

(c) In CrO_4^{2-},

the electronic configuration of Cr^{6+} is $[Ar]3d^0$.

Number of unpaired electrons = 0

Therefore, it is also diamagnetic and will not show d-d transition.

(d) In MnO_4^{2-},

the electronic configuration of Mn^{6+} is $[Ar]3d^1$.

Number of unpaired electrons = 1.

Since, it contains one unpaired electron, so it will exhibit both d-d transition and paramagnetism.

7 (*c*) When SO_2 is passed through acidified $K_2Cr_2O_7$ solution, green chromium sulphate is formed. In this reaction, oxidation state of Cr changes from +6 to +3.

$$\underset{\text{OS of Cr}=+6}{K_2Cr_2O_7} + H_2SO_4 + 3SO_2 \longrightarrow K_2SO_4 + \underset{\substack{\text{OS of Cr}=+3\\ \text{Green}}}{Cr_2(SO_4)_3} + H_2O$$

The appearance of green colour is due to the reduction of chromium metal.

8 (*c*) $3MnO_4^{2-} + 2H_2O \rightleftharpoons 2MnO_4^- + MnO_2 + 4OH^-$

The reaction can go for completion by removing OH^- ions or by adding CO_2 as it reacts with OH^- ions to form CO_3^{2-} ions.

$$4OH^- + 2CO_2 \longrightarrow 2CO_3^{2-} + 2H_2O$$

9 (*b*) In Na_2CrO_4, Cr is in +6 oxidation state with d^0 configuration. The CrO_4^{2-} ions in aqueous solution give yellow colour which is not due to d-d transition but due to charge transfer, i.e. momentary transfer of charge from O-atom to metal atom, thereby changing O^{2-} ion momentarily to O^- ion and reducing the oxidation state of Cr from +6 to +5.

Hence, both A and R are correct but R is not the correct explanation of A.

10 (*b*) Being hygroscopic or deliquescent, sodium dichromate, $Na_2Cr_2O_7$ cannot be used in volumetric analysis. So, other statements are true.

11 (*a*) $Cr_2O_7^{2-} + 14H^+ + 6I^- \longrightarrow 2Cr^{3+} + 7H_2O + 3I_2$

Thus, final oxidation state of Cr is +3.

12 (*d*) Acidified $K_2Cr_2O_7$ solution reacts with H_2O_2 to give a deep blue solution due to the formation of peroxo compound, $CrO(O_2)_2$ or CrO_5.

$$Cr_2O_7^{2-} + 2H^+ + 4H_2O_2 \longrightarrow 2CrO_5 + 5H_2O$$

Note The blue colour fades away gradually due to the decomposition of CrO_5 into Cr^{3+} ions and oxygen.

13 (*b*) $K_2Cr_2O_7 + 3Na_2SO_3 + 4H_2SO_4 \longrightarrow 3Na_2SO_4 + K_2SO_4 + 4H_2O + Cr_2(SO_4)_3$

14 (*c*) In general, the oxides in lower oxidation states of the metals are basic and in their higher oxidation states they are acidic, whereas in the intermediate oxidation states the oxides are amphoteric.

(i) In Mn_2O_7, Mn exhibits its highest oxidation state of +7, thus it is highly acidic and dissolves in water to give an acid, $HMnO_4$.

(ii) In case of vanadium, though V in V_2O_5 exhibits its highest oxidation state of +5 but it is amphoteric in nature.

(iii) Similarly, CrO is basic in nature as Cr exhibits its lower oxidation state of +2.

Thus, Mn_2O_7 is acidic, V_2O_5 is amphoteric CrO is basic in nature.

15 (*a*) The structure of $Cr_2O_7^{2-}$ ion is

$$^{-}O-Cr(=O)_2-O-Cr(=O)_2-O^{-}$$

Thus, it has no Cr— Cr bonds and no O—O bonds.

16 (*c*) On acidification of potassium chromate solution, yellow colour changes to orange colour due to reformation of dichromate. This suggests that potassium chromate is a monocentric complex. This potassium monochromate converts into dicentric complex, i.e. potassium dichromate solution.

$$\underset{\text{Potassium chromate}}{2K_2CrO_4} + H_2SO_4 \longrightarrow \underset{\text{Potassium dichromate}}{K_2Cr_2O_7} + K_2SO_4 + H_2O$$

17 (*c*) $4K_2Cr_2O_7 \xrightarrow{\Delta} 4K_2CrO_4 + 3O_2 + \underset{X}{2Cr_2O_3}$

18 (*a*) CrO_3 dissolves in aqueous NaOH to give sodium chromate.

$$CrO_3 + 2NaOH \longrightarrow \underset{\text{Sodium chromate}}{Na_2CrO_4} + H_2O$$

19 (*c*) Ammonium dichromate on heating gives green coloured powder of Cr_2O_3. which is used in fire works.

$$(NH_4)_2Cr_2O_7 \xrightarrow{\Delta} \underset{\text{Chromic oxide}}{Cr_2O_3} + 4H_2O + N_2$$

20 (*c*) Potassium dichromate is an oxidising agent, thus it oxidises ferrous ions into ferric ion in acidic medium.

$$Cr_2O_7^{2-} + 14H^+ + 6e^- \longrightarrow 2Cr^{3+} + 7H_2O$$
$$[Fe^{2+} \longrightarrow Fe^{3+} + e^-] \times 6$$
$$Cr_2O_7^{2-} + 6Fe^{2+} + 14H^+ \longrightarrow 2Cr^{3+} + 6Fe^{3+} + 7H_2O$$

21 (*c*) Mohr's salt is $[FeSO_4 \cdot (NH_4)_2SO_4 \cdot 6H_2O]$

$$\underset{\text{Purple}}{2\overset{+7}{K}MnO_4} + 8H_2SO_4 + \underset{\text{From Mohr's salt}}{10FeSO_4} \longrightarrow K_2SO_4 + \underset{\text{Colourless}}{2\overset{+2}{Mn}SO_4} + 5Fe_2(SO_4)_3 + 8H_2O$$

Hence, Mohr's salt decolourises $KMnO_4$ by reducing Mn^{7+} ion to Mn^{2+} ions.

Topic 3

Inner Transition Elements : Lanthanides and Actinides

2019

1 Assertion Yb^{2+} is more stable in compare to Gd^{+2}.
Reason The electronic configuration of Gd is $[Xe]4f^7 5d^2 6s^2$. [AIIMS]
(a) If both Assertion and Reason are true and Reason is the correct explanation of Assertion
(b) If both the Assertion and Reason are true, but Reason is not the correct explanation of Assertion
(c) If Assertion is true, but Reason is false
(d) If both Assertion and Reason are false

2018

2 If *M* is element of actinoids series, the degree of complex formation decreases in the order [JIPMER]
(a) $M^{4+} > M^{3+} > MO_2^{2+} > MO_2^{+}$
(b) $M^{4+} > MO_2^{2+} > M^{3+} > MO_2^{+}$
(c) $MO_2^{+} > MO_2^{2+} > M^{3+} > M^{4+}$
(d) $MO_2^{2+} > MO_2^{+} > M^{4+} > M^{3+}$

2017

3 Assertion (A) Separation of Zr and Hf is difficult.
Reason (R) Zr and Hf lie in the same group of the periodic table. [AIIMS]
(a) Both Assertion and Reason are correct and Reason is the correct explanation of the Assertion.
(b) Both Assertion and Reason are correct but Reason is not the correct explanation of Assertion.
(c) Assertion is correct but Reason is incorrect.
(d) Assertion is incorrect but Reason is correct.

4 The reason for greater range of oxidation states in actinoids is attributed to [NEET]
(a) the radioactive nature of actinoids
(b) actinoid contraction
(c) $5f$, $6d$ and $7s$ levels having comparable energies
(d) $4f$ and $5d$ levels being close in energies

5 The correct increasing order of ionic radii of the following Ce^{3+}, La^{3+}, Pm^{3+} and Yb^{3+} is [JIPMER]
(a) $Yb^{3+} < Pm^{3+} < Ce^{3+} < La^{3+}$
(b) $Ce^{3+} < Yb^{3+} < Pm^{3+} < La^{3+}$
(c) $Yb^{3+} < Pm^{3+} < La^{3+} < Ce^{3+}$
(d) $Pm^{3+} < La^{3+} < Ce^{3+} < Yb^{3+}$

2016

6 Which one of the following statements related to lanthanoids is incorrect? [NEET (Phase II)]
(a) Europium shows + 2 oxidation state.
(b) The basicity decreases as the ionic radius decreases from Pr to Lu.
(c) All the lanthanons are much more reactive than aluminium.
(d) Ce (+4) solution are widely used as oxidising agent in volumetric analysis.

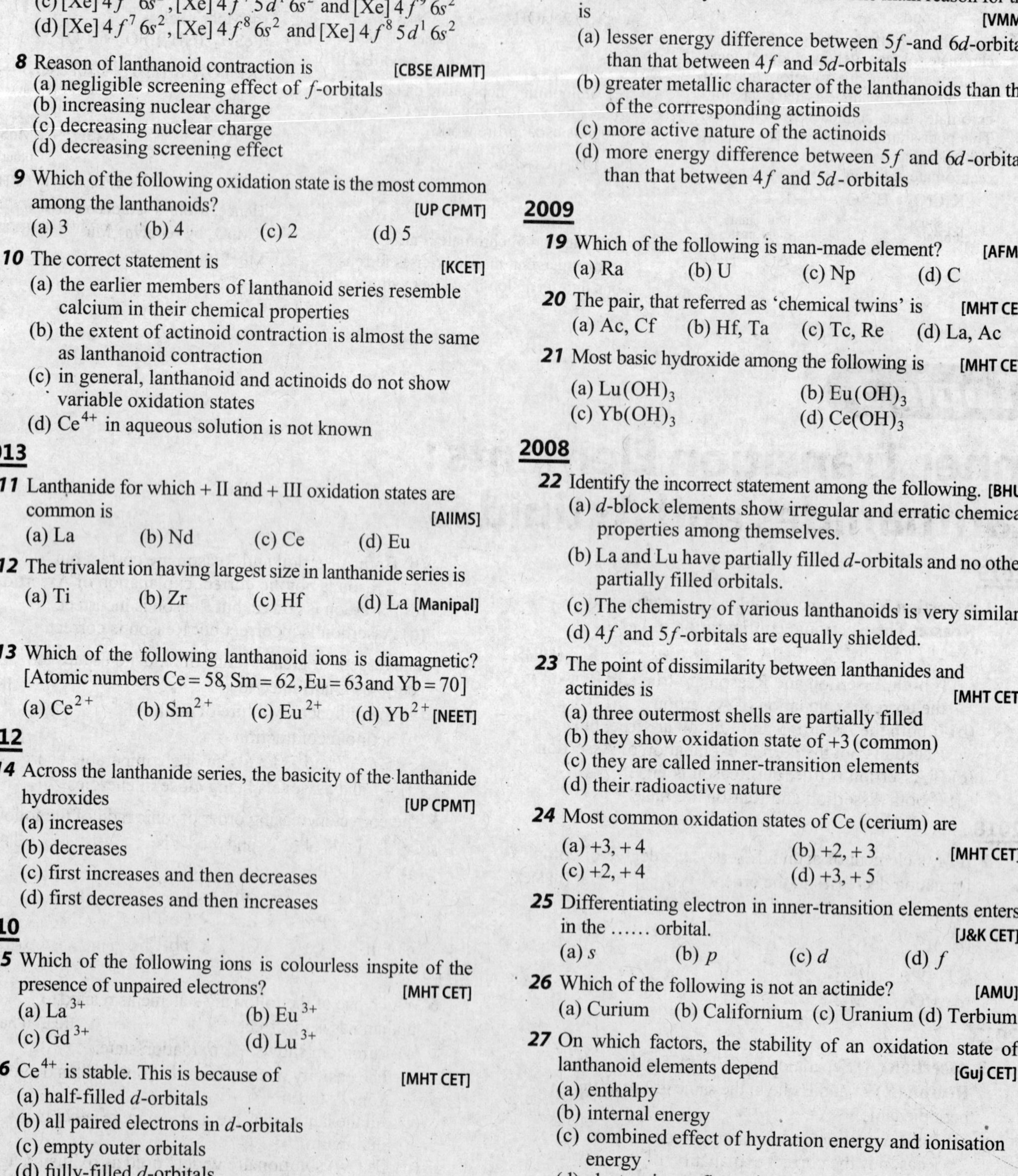

7 The electronic configurations of Eu (Atomic no. 63), Gd (Atomic no. 64) and Tb (Atomic no. 65) are **[NEET]**

(a) $[Xe]4f^6 5d^1 6s^2$, $[Xe]4f^7 5d^1 6s^2$ and $[Xe]4f^9 6s^2$

(b) $[Xe]4f^6 5d^1 6s^2$, $[Xe]4f^7 5d^1 6s^2$ and $[Xe]4f^8 5d^1 6s^2$

(c) $[Xe]4f^7 6s^2$, $[Xe]4f^7 5d^1 6s^2$ and $[Xe]4f^9 6s^2$

(d) $[Xe]4f^7 6s^2$, $[Xe]4f^8 6s^2$ and $[Xe]4f^8 5d^1 6s^2$

8 Reason of lanthanoid contraction is **[CBSE AIPMT]**

(a) negligible screening effect of f-orbitals
(b) increasing nuclear charge
(c) decreasing nuclear charge
(d) decreasing screening effect

9 Which of the following oxidation state is the most common among the lanthanoids? **[UP CPMT]**

(a) 3 (b) 4 (c) 2 (d) 5

10 The correct statement is **[KCET]**

(a) the earlier members of lanthanoid series resemble calcium in their chemical properties
(b) the extent of actinoid contraction is almost the same as lanthanoid contraction
(c) in general, lanthanoid and actinoids do not show variable oxidation states
(d) Ce^{4+} in aqueous solution is not known

2013

11 Lanthanide for which + II and + III oxidation states are common is **[AIIMS]**

(a) La (b) Nd (c) Ce (d) Eu

12 The trivalent ion having largest size in lanthanide series is

(a) Ti (b) Zr (c) Hf (d) La **[Manipal]**

13 Which of the following lanthanoid ions is diamagnetic? [Atomic numbers Ce = 58, Sm = 62, Eu = 63 and Yb = 70]

(a) Ce^{2+} (b) Sm^{2+} (c) Eu^{2+} (d) Yb^{2+} **[NEET]**

2012

14 Across the lanthanide series, the basicity of the lanthanide hydroxides **[UP CPMT]**

(a) increases
(b) decreases
(c) first increases and then decreases
(d) first decreases and then increases

2010

15 Which of the following ions is colourless inspite of the presence of unpaired electrons? **[MHT CET]**

(a) La^{3+} (b) Eu^{3+}
(c) Gd^{3+} (d) Lu^{3+}

16 Ce^{4+} is stable. This is because of **[MHT CET]**

(a) half-filled d-orbitals
(b) all paired electrons in d-orbitals
(c) empty outer orbitals
(d) fully-filled d-orbitals

17 The lanthanoid contraction relates to **[CMC]**

(a) atomic radius (b) atomic as well as M^{3+} radii
(c) valence electrons (d) oxidation states

18 More number of oxidation states are exhibited by the actinoids than by the lanthanoids. The main reason for this is **[VMMC]**

(a) lesser energy difference between $5f$-and $6d$-orbitals than that between $4f$ and $5d$-orbitals
(b) greater metallic character of the lanthanoids than that of the corrresponding actinoids
(c) more active nature of the actinoids
(d) more energy difference between $5f$ and $6d$-orbitals than that between $4f$ and $5d$-orbitals

2009

19 Which of the following is man-made element? **[AFMC]**

(a) Ra (b) U (c) Np (d) C

20 The pair, that referred as 'chemical twins' is **[MHT CET]**

(a) Ac, Cf (b) Hf, Ta (c) Tc, Re (d) La, Ac

21 Most basic hydroxide among the following is **[MHT CET]**

(a) $Lu(OH)_3$ (b) $Eu(OH)_3$
(c) $Yb(OH)_3$ (d) $Ce(OH)_3$

2008

22 Identify the incorrect statement among the following. **[BHU]**

(a) d-block elements show irregular and erratic chemical properties among themselves.
(b) La and Lu have partially filled d-orbitals and no other partially filled orbitals.
(c) The chemistry of various lanthanoids is very similar.
(d) $4f$ and $5f$-orbitals are equally shielded.

23 The point of dissimilarity between lanthanides and actinides is **[MHT CET]**

(a) three outermost shells are partially filled
(b) they show oxidation state of +3 (common)
(c) they are called inner-transition elements
(d) their radioactive nature

24 Most common oxidation states of Ce (cerium) are **[MHT CET]**

(a) +3, + 4 (b) +2, + 3
(c) +2, + 4 (d) +3, + 5

25 Differentiating electron in inner-transition elements enters in the ...... orbital. **[J&K CET]**

(a) s (b) p (c) d (d) f

26 Which of the following is not an actinide? **[AMU]**

(a) Curium (b) Californium (c) Uranium (d) Terbium

27 On which factors, the stability of an oxidation state of lanthanoid elements depend **[Guj CET]**

(a) enthalpy
(b) internal energy
(c) combined effect of hydration energy and ionisation energy
(d) electronic configuration

2007

28 Identify the incorrect statement among the following. [CBSE AIPMT]

(a) There is a decrease in the radii of the atoms or ions as one proceeds from La to Lu.

(b) Lanthanoid contraction is the accumulation of successive shrinkages.

(c) As a result of lanthanoid contraction, the properties of 4*d*-series of the transition elements have no similarities with the 5*d*-series of elements.

(d) Shielding power of 4f-electrons is quite weak.

29 Lanthanides are [Manipal]

(a) 14 elements in the sixth period (atomic number = 90 to 103) that are filling 4f sub-level

(b) 14 elements in the seventh period (atomic number = 90 to 103) that are filling 5f sub-level

(c) 14 elements in the sixth period (atomic number = 58 to 71) that are filling 4f sub-level

(d) 14 elements in the seventh period (atomic number = 58 to 71) that are filling 4f sub-level

30 General electronic configuration of lanthanides are [Punjab PMET]

(a) $(n-2)f^{1-14}(n-1)d^{0-1}ns^2$

(b) $(n-2)f^{10-14}(n-1)d^{0-1}ns^2$

(c) $(n-2)f^{0-14}(n-1)d^{10}ns^2$

(d) $(n-2)d^{0-1}(n-1)f^{1-14}ns^2$

2006

31 Which of the following is not an actinoid? [DUMET]

(a) Am (b) Cm (c) Fm (d) Tm

32 The lanthanoid contraction is responsible for the fact that [Guj CET]

(a) Zr and Y have about the same radius

(b) Zr and Nb have similar oxidation state

(c) Zr and Hf have about the same radius

(d) Zr and Zn have the same oxidation state

2005

33 Europium is [DUMET]

(a) s-block element (b) p-block element

(c) d-block element (d) f-block element

34 Which belongs to the actinide series? [J&K CET]

(a) Ce (b) Cf

(c) Ca (d) Cs

35 Because of lanthanoid contraction, which of the following pairs of elements have nearly same atomic radii? (Numbers in the parenthesis are atomic numbers). [CBSE AIPMT]

(a) Ti (22) and Zr (40)

(b) Zr (40) and Nb (41)

(c) Zr (40) and Hf (72)

(d) Zr (40) and Ta (73)

36 Which of the following pairs has the same size? [CBSE AIPMT]

(a) Zn^{2+}, Hf^{4+} (b) Fe^{2+}, Ni^{2+}

(c) Zr^{4+}, Ti^{4+} (d) Zr^{4+}, Hf^{4+}

37 The atom of which one of the following elements has the highest number of unpaired electrons? [J&K CET]

(a) $_{25}Mn$ (b) $_{24}Cr$

(c) $_{96}Cm$ (d) $_{26}Fe$

Answers

1 (c)	2 (b)	3 (b)	4 (c)	5 (b)	6 (c)	7 (c)	8 (a)	9 (a)	10 (a)
11 (d)	12 (d)	13 (d)	14 (b)	15 (c)	16 (c)	17 (b)	18 (a)	19 (c)	20 (c)
21 (d)	22 (d)	23 (d)	24 (a)	25 (d)	26 (d)	27 (c)	28 (c)	29 (c)	30 (a)
31 (a)	32 (c)	33 (d)	34 (b)	35 (c)	36 (c)	37 (c)			

Explanations

1 (*c*) The electronic configuration of

$Yb^{+2} = [Xe], 4f^{14}, 5d^0, 6s^0$

$Gd^{+2} = [Xe], 4f^7, 5d^1 6s^0$

Since, Yb^{2+} has full-filled (f^{14}) configuration. It is more stable than that of Gd^{2+}.

Thus, Assertion is correct but Reason is incorrect

Hence, option (c) is the correct.

2 (*b*) The higher the charge on the metal ion, smaller is the ionic size and more is the complex forming ability.

Thus, the degree of complex formation decreases in the order :

$$M^{4+} > MO_2^{2+} > M^{3+} > MO_2^{+}$$

Note : MO_2^{2+} and MO_2^{+} also have even higher charges than M^{4+} and M^{3+} respectively but in these ions, (MO_2^{2+}, MO_2^{+}) metal has larger size as it is present in bonded state.

3 (*b*) Assertion and Reason are true but Reason is not correct explanation of Assertion.

Separation of Zr and Hf is difficult, it is not because of they lie in the same group of the periodic table. This is due to the lanthanide contraction which causes almost similar radii of both of them.

4 (*c*) The reason for greater range of oxidation states in actinoid is attributed to the 5f, 6d and 7s levels having comparable energies. The 5f-orbitals extend into space beyond the 7s and 6p-orbitals and participate in bonding.

This is in direct contrast to the lanthanides where the 4 f-orbitals are buried deep inside the atom, totally shielded by outer orbitals and, thus unable to take part in bonding.

5 (a) Due to lanthanide contraction, size of + 3 ions decreases from La^{3+} to Lu^{3+}. As the atomic number increases in order

$Yb^{3+} < Pm^{3+} < Ce^{3+} < La^{3+}$. Thus, the correct order of ionic radii will be $Yb^{3+} < Pm^{3+} < Ce^{3+} < La^{3+}$.

6 (c) $Eu(63) = 4f^7 \cdot 5d^0, 6s^2, Eu^{2+} = 4f^7$

In lanthanoid series, ionic radius decreases and covalent character increases, thus basicity decreases. Lanthanoids are less reactive than aluminium due to high ionisation potential. The reason for this high ionisation potential is lanthanoid contraction.

Ce^{4+} is a good oxidising agent ∵ it is easily converted to Ce^{3+}.

7 (c) Electronic configuration of $_{63}Eu$
$= [Xe]_{54}\, 4f^7 6s^2$

Electronic configuration of $_{64}Gd$
$= [Xe]_{54}\, 4f^7 5d^1 6s^2$

Electronic configuration of $_{65}Tb$
$= [Xe]_{54}\, 4f^9 6s^2$

8 (a) Lanthanoid contraction is the regular decrease in atomic and ionic radii of lanthanides. This is due to the imperfect shielding (or poor screening effect) of f-orbitals due to their diffused shape, which unable to counter balance the effect of the increased nuclear charge.
Hence, the net result is a contraction in size of lanthanoids.

9 (a) In lanthanoids, the most common oxidation state is 3. For most of the lanthanides, the ionisation energy to lose a fourth electron will be so large that it cannot be compensated by bond formation, this is due to the 4 f-electrons which are shielded.

10 (a) The earlier members of lanthanoid series resemble calcium in some of their chemical properties, e.g. hydroxides of both of them are ionic and basic.

11 (d) Lanthanoids are f-block elements starting from Ce (58) to Lu (71).

Elements	Atomic number	Oxidation state
La	57	+ 3
Ce	58	+ 3, + 4
Nd	60	+ 2, + 3, + 4
Eu	63	+ 2, + 3

Thus, for Eu common oxidation states are + 2 and + 3. Nd also exhibits +2 and +3 oxidation state. But +3 is its common oxidation state.

12 (d) The trivalent ion having largest size in lanthanide series is lanthanum (La). This is due to lanthanide contraction.

13 (d) Lanthanoid ion with no unpaired electron is diamagnetic in nature.

(a) $Ce_{58} = [Xe]\,4f^2, 5d^0, 6s^2$
$Ce^{2+} = [Xe]\,4f^2$
(two unpaired electrons)

(b) $Sm_{62} = [Xe]\,6f^6, 5d^0, 6s^2$
$Sm^{2+} = [Xe]\,6f^6, 5d^0$
(six unpaired electrons)

(c) $Eu_{63} = [Xe]\,6f^7, 5d^0, 6s^2$
$Eu^{2+} = [Xe]\,6f^7, 5d^0$
(seven unpaired electrons)

(d) $Yb_{70} = [Xe]\,6f^{14}, 5d^2$
$Yb^{2+} = [Xe]\,6f^{14}, 5d^0$
(no unpaired electron)

Since, Yb^{2+} has no unpaired electron, so it is a diamagnetic ion.

14 (b) Across lanthanide series, due to lanthanoid contraction, size of cation decreases, which results in increase in covalent character and decrease in ionic character. So, the basicity of hydroxides decreases.

15 (c) Gadolinium (Gd^{3+}) does not absorb light in the visible region of the spectrum, hence it is colourless inspite of the presence of 7 unpaired electrons. Being colourless, gadolinium is sometimes used as a support for luminescence objects for the knowledge that it will not quench their intense colour.

16 (c) The electronic configuration of Ce is

$Ce^{58} = [Xe]\,4f^1, 5d^1, 6s^2$ (predicted)

or $= [Xe]\,4f^2, 5d^0, 6s^2$ (observed)

$Ce^{4+} = [Xe]\,4f^0, 5d^0, 6s^0$

Since, in + 4 oxidation state, all (i.e. $4f$, $5d$ and $6s$) orbitals are empty and Ce gains the stable configuration of nearest inert gas xenon, thus, Ce^{4+} is most stable.

17 (b) Lanthanoid contraction relates to decrease in atomic as well as ionic size of M^{3+} ions.

18 (a) The energy difference between $5f$ and $6d$-orbitals is less than that between $4f$ and $5d$-orbitals. Therefore, actinoids (having valence electrons in $5f$ and $6d$) exhibit more number of oxidation states.

19 (c) The elements present after uranium in the periodic table are synthesised artificially by nuclear reactions. Hence, these are called synthetic or man-made elements. Hence, Np is a man-made element.

20 (c) Due to lanthanoid contraction, the atomic radius of elements of second transition series (i.e. Nb, Mo, Tc, etc) is similar to that of corresponding third transition series elements (i.e. Ta, W, Re). Hence, Nb-Ta; Mo-W or Tc-Re are called chemical twins.

21 (d) Due to lanthanide contraction, the size of M^{3+} ions [i.e. Lu^{3+}, Eu^{3+}, Yb^{3+} and Ce^{3+}] decreases and thus, the basic strength of their hydroxides decreases. The order of size of given M^{3+} ion is

$$Ce^{3+} > Eu^{3+} > Yb^{3+} > Lu^{3+}$$

∴ The order of basic strength of hydroxides is

$$\underset{\text{(Most basic)}}{Ce(OH)_3} > Eu(OH)_3 > Yb(OH)_3 > Lu(OH)_3$$

22 (d) $4f$ and $5f$-orbitals belong to different shell, thus experience different amount of shielding. All the other given options are correct.

23 (d) Except promethium, all lanthanides are non-radioactive while all actinides are radioactive.

24 (a) Cerium $Ce_{58} = [Xe]\,4f^1, 5d^1, 6s^2$
Its most stable oxidation state is +3 but +4 is also existing.

25 (d) In inner-transition elements, the differentiating electrons enter into $(n-2)f$-orbital. Therefore, these elements are also known as f-block elements.

26 (d) Terbium is a lanthanide as it belongs to $4f$-series having configuration $[Xe]4f^9, 6s^2$. However, the remaining members belongs to $5f$-series of actinides.

27 (*c*) Stability of oxidation state of lanthanides depends upon the combined effect of ionisation energy and hydration energy.
For stability, element should have low value of ionisation energy and ions should have high value of hydration energy.

28 (*c*) The regular decrease in the radii of lanthanoid ions from La^{3+} to Lu^{3+} is known as lanthanoid contraction. It is due to the greater effect of the increased nuclear charge than that of screening effect (shielding effect).
As a result of lanthanoid contraction, the atomic radii of elements of 4*d* and 5*d* becomes closer and so the properties of 4*d* and 5*d* transition element show the similarities.

29 (*c*) Lanthanides are the 14 elements of III B group and sixth period (atomic number = 58 to 71) that are filling 4 *f*-subshell of antipenultimate shell from 1 to 14. Actually, they are placed below the periodic table in horizontal row as lanthanide series.

30 (*a*) In lanthanides (atomic number = 58 to 71), the electronic configuration of three outermost shell is $(n-2)f^{1-14}(n-1)d^{0-1}ns^2$.

31 (*d*) Tm ⟶ Thulium—Atomic number 69. It is a lanthanide because lanthanides are present in sixth period of periodic table from atomic number 57 (lanthanum) to atomic number 71 (lutetium).

32 (*c*) Zr and Hf have about the same radius and are called twins of periodic table due to lanthanoid contraction. On going down the group, lanthanoid contraction occurs and radius becomes nearly same.

33 (*d*) Europium (atomic number 53) belongs to lanthanide series of *f*-block. Its electronic configuration is $[Xe]\, 4f^7, 5d^0, 6s^2$.

34 (*b*) The fourteen elements which follow actinium from thorium ($Z = 90$) to lawrencium ($Z = 103$) are called actinoids. They involve the filling of 5 *f*-subshell. Californium (Cf) has the atomic number 98 and its configuration is

$$Cf_{98} = [Rn]\, 5f^{10}, 6d^0, 7s^2$$

Hence, it is a member of actinide series.

35 (*c*) Because of the lanthanoid contraction, Zr (atomic radii 160 pm) and Hf (atomic radii 158 pm) have nearly same atomic radii.
Lanthanoids include the elements from lanthanum, La ($Z = 57$) to lutetium, Lu ($Z = 71$). Zirconium Zr (40) belong to the second transition series (4*d*) and Hf (72) belongs to third transition series (5*d*). Lanthanoid contraction is associated with the intervention of the 4 *f*-orbitals which are filled before the 5*d*-series of elements starts. The filling of 4 *f*-orbitals before 5*d*-orbitals results in regular decrease in atomic radii which compensates the expected increase in atomic size with increasing atomic number. As a result of this lanthanoid contraction, the elements of second and third transition series have almost similar atomic radii.

36 (*d*) Zr^{4+} and Hf^{4+} have similar ionic radius due to lanthanoid contraction.

37 (*c*)

Metal ion	Configuration	Number of unpaired electrons	Magnetic moment
Ti^{3+}	$3d^1$	1	1.75
Ni^{2+}	$3d^8$	2	2.76
Co^{3+}	$3d^7$	3	3.86
Mn^{2+}	$3d^5$	5	5.96

23 Coordination Compounds

Quick Review

The complex compounds which are formed by the transition metals in which the metal atoms are bonded to the number of anions or neutral molecules through the coordinate bonds are called **coordination compounds.**

$$K_4[Fe(CN)_6] + H_2O \longrightarrow 4K^+ + [Fe(CN)_6]^{4-}$$

Definitions of Some Important Terms Used in Coordination Compounds

(a) **Coordination entity** It constitutes a central metal atom or ion bonded to a fixed number of ions or molecules. E.g. $[Ni(CO)_4]$, $[PtCl_2(NH_3)_2]$, $[Fe(CN)_6]^{4-}$ etc.

(b) **Central atom/ion** The atom/ion to which a fixed number of ions/groups are bound in a definite geometrical arrangement around it in a coordination entity. E.g. $[NiCl_2(H_2O)_4]$, $[CoCl(NH_3)_5]^{2+}$ and $[Fe(CN)_6]^{3-}$ are Ni^{2+}, Co^{3+} and Fe^{3+} respectively.

(c) **Ligands** The molecules or ions that bind to the central atom/ion in the coordination entity. e.g. H_2O, Cl^-, NH_3, $C_2O_4^{2-}$ etc.

(d) **Coordination number** The number of ligand donor atoms to which the metal is directly bonded. E.g. in the complex ions, $[PtCl_6]^{2-}$ and $[Ni(NH_3)_4]^{2+}$, Pt and Ni have 6 and 4 coordination numbers.

(e) **Coordination sphere** The central atom/ion and the ligands attached to it are enclosed in square bracket. They are collectively termed as coordination sphere. E.g. $K_4[Fe(CN)_6]$. Here, $[Fe(CN)_6]^{4-}$ is the coordination sphere.

(f) **Oxidation number of central atom** It is defined as the charge it would carry if all the ligands are removed along with electron pairs that are shared with central atom.

(g) **Homoleptic and heteroleptic complexes** In homoleptic complexes, metal is bound to only one kind of donor groups while in heterolytic complexes, metal is bound to more than one kind of donor groups.

Nomenclature of Coordination Compounds

Naming of complex compound is done as per the rules set by IUPAC. These rules are as follows :

(*i*) In both positively and negatively charged coordination entities, the cation is named first.

(*ii*) Before the name of the central atom/ion, the ligands are named in an alphabetical order.

(*iii*) Neutral and cationic ligands remain same except *aqua* for H_2O, ammine for NH_3, carbonyl for CO and nitrosyl for NO while names of the anionic ligands end in –O.

(*iv*) After writing the formula, coordination entity are enclosed in brackets [ ].

(*v*) Prefixes mono, di, tri etc., are used to indicate the number of individual ligands in the coordination entity.

(*vi*) When name of ligands include a numerical prefix, then the terms, *bis, tris*, *tetrakis* are used.

(*vii*) Oxidation state of the metal in cation, anion or neutral coordination entity is indicated by roman numeral in parenthesis.

(*viii*) If the complex ion is a cation, then metal is named same as the element.

Isomerism in Coordination Compounds

The isomerism in coordination compounds is discussed as follows :

Type of Isomerism	Definition	Examples
1. STRUCTURAL ISOMERISM	Isomers have same chemical formula but different chemical bonds.	
(a) **Linkage isomerism**	• It arises in a coordination compound containing ambidentate ligand.	• Thiocyanate (NCS^-) ligand that can bind through nitrogen gives $M—NCS$ or through sulphur to give $M—SCN$
(b) **Coordination isomerism**	• It arises from the interchange of ligands between cationic and anionic entities of different metal ions present in a complex.	• $[Co(NH_3)_6][Cr(CN)_6]$ and $[Cr(NH_3)_6][Co(CN)_6]$
(c) **Ionisation isomerism**	• It arises when the counter ion in a complex salt is itself a potential ligand and can displace a ligand which can then become the counter ion.	• $[Co(NH_3)_5SO_4]Br$ and $[Co(NH_3)_5Br]SO_4$
(d) **Solvate isomerism**	• It is also known as hydrate isomerism. • These complexes differ in number of water molecules present as ligands (inside the coordination sphere) and as free molecules (outside the coordination sphere)	• $[Cr(H_2O)_6]Cl_3$ and $[Cr(H_2O)_5Cl]Cl_2 \cdot H_2O$
2. STEREO ISOMERISM	Isomers have same chemical formula and chemical bonds but different spatial arrangements.	
(a) **Geometrical isomerism**	• This type of isomerism arises in heteroleptic complexes. • It arises due to different possible geometric arrangements of ligands. • It is found in complexes with coordination number 4 and 6. • In MX_2L_2 or $MX_2(L—L)$ two ligands X are arranged as *cis* and *trans*. • $MABXL$ shows three isomers, two *cis* and one *trans*. • Ma_3b_3 shows *facial* and *meridional* isomer.	• MX_2L_2 (square planar complex) *cis* *trans* • $MABXL$ (square planar complex) • Ma_3b_3 (octahedral complexes) *fac–* *mer–*
(b) **Optical isomerism**	• It occurs in compounds having mirror images. • These are common in octahedral complexes involving didentate ligands. • These generally occur in two forms, i.e. *dextro* and *laevo*.	• $[M(aa)_3]^{3+}$ *dextro* Mirror *laevo* • $[M(aa)_2b_2]$ Mirror

Bonding in Coordination Complexes

Bonding in coordination complexes are explained through Werner's theory, valence bond theory and crystal field theory which are discussed below :

Werner's Theory

In 1898, Alfred Werner's proposed a theory about the structures of coordination compounds.

The main postulates of Werner's theory are as follows :

(i) Each metal ion shows two types of valencies; primary and secondary valency.

(ii) **Primary valency** is ionisable and corresponds to oxidation number. It is satisfied by anions and is non-directional in nature.

(iii) **Secondary valency** is non-ionisable and corresponds to coordination number. It is satisfied by neutral or anionic ligands and is directional in nature.

(iv) Metal ion should satisfy both primary and secondary valencies. Some negative ions may satisfy primary as well as secondary valencies and are said to have dual nature.

e.g. in the complex $[Co(NH_3)_6]Cl_3$, primary valency of Co is three and secondary valency is six.

Valence Bond Theory (VBT)

The main points of this theory are as follows :

(a) Central atom/ion makes available required number of empty orbitals.

(b) These orbitals undergo hybridisation under the influence of ligands to give same number of hybrid orbitals of equal energy and definite geometry.

(c) The hybridised orbitals are allowed to overlap with ligand orbitals that can donate electron pairs for bonding.

This can be illustrated by the following examples given in the table :

Type of hybridisation	sp	sp^2	sp^3	dsp^2	dsp^3	sp^3d	d^2sp^3	sp^3d^2
Coordination number	2	3	4	4	5	5	6	6
Geometry	Linear	Trigonal planar	Tetrahedral	Square planar	Square pyramidal	Trigonal bipyramidal	Octahedral (inner orbital)	Octahedral (outer orbital)
Examples	$[Ag(NH_3)_2]^+$ $[Ag(CN)_2]^-$	$[HgI_3]^-$	$Ni[CO)_4$ $[NiX_4]^{2-}$ $[ZnCl_4]^{2-}$ $[CuX_4]^{2-}$	$[Ni(CN)_4]^{2-}$ $[Cu(NH_3)_4]^{2+}$ $[Ni(NH_3)_4]^{2+}$	$Fe(CO)_5$, $[CuCl_5]^{3-}$	$[SbF_5]^{2-}$	$[Cr(NH_3)_6]^{3+}$ $[Fe(CN)_6]^{3-}$	$[FeF_6]^{3-}$ $[Fe(H_2O)_6]^{2+}$ $[Ni(NH_3)_6]^{2-}$

Inner and Outer Orbital Complexes

- When complex involves inner $(n-1)$ d-orbitals and hybridisation comes out to be d^2sp^3 or dsp^2 it is called **inner orbital complex**, e.g. $Ni(CN)_4^{2-}$. These are also called **low spin** or **spin paired complexes**.
- When complex involves outer $(n-1)$ d-orbitals and hybridisation is sp^3d^2, it is called **outer orbital complex** or **high spin** or **spin free complexes**, e.g. $[CoF_6]^{3-}$ and $[CoCl_4]^{2-}$.
- If no unpaired electron is present, the complex is diamagnetic. If unpaired electron/s is/are present, complex is paramagnetic and its magnetic moment $\mu = \sqrt{n(n+2)}$ B.M. where, n is the number of unpaired electrons present.

Crystal Field Theory

It is a more appropriate theory than VBT. According to CFT, under the influence of ligand, degeneracy of the d-orbital is destroyed and it splits into two or more energy levels.

Some assumptions of crystal field theory are as follows :

(i) Ligands are considered as point charges and anionic ligands as negative point charges.

(ii) The interaction between metal ion and ligand is purely electrostatic. Therefore, metal ion and ligands do not mix their orbitals, i.e. no overlap of orbitals occur.

(iii) The d-orbitals present in metal ion are degenerate. This degeneracy is lost in presence of ligands as the field produced by ligands is not symmetrical.

(iv) Due to this loss in degeneracy, d-orbitals split into t_{2g} and e_g sets of orbitals.

(v) t_{2g} orbitals (d_{xy}, d_{yz}, d_{xz}) are triply degenerate while e_g orbitals ($d_{x^2-y^2}$ and d_{z^2}) are doubly degenerate.

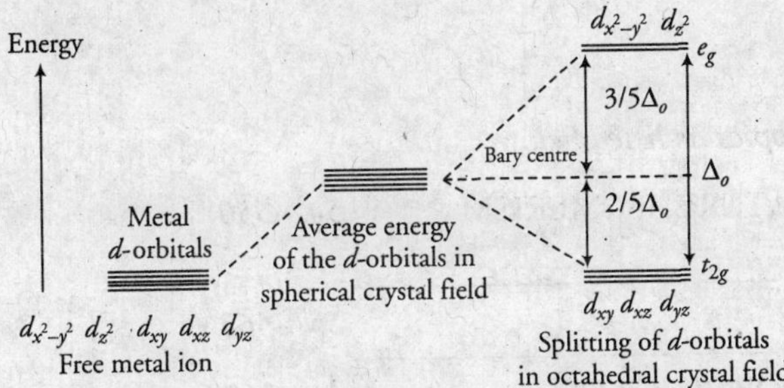

d-orbital splitting in an octahedral crystal field

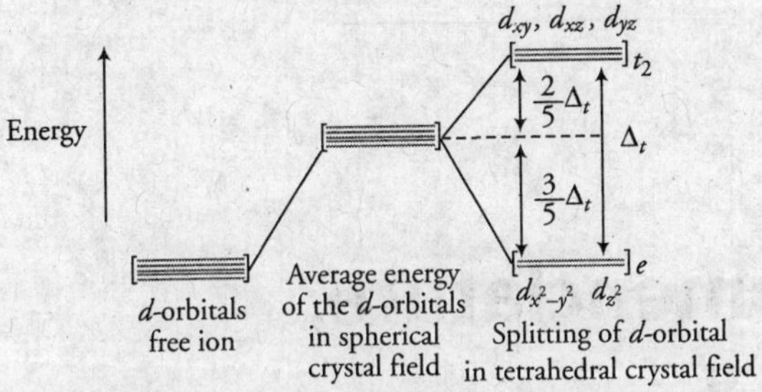

d-orbital splitting in a tetrahedral crystal field

Crystal Field Splitting Energy

- The extent of splitting depends on the strength of ligand. Strong ligand causes large splitting, while a weak ligand causes smaller splitting.
- The difference of energy between the two sets of *d*-orbital (in octahedral complexes) is called **crystal field splitting energy** (CFSE) or Δ.

Spectrochemical Series

- The magnitude of Δ_o depends upon the nature of the ligands. The increasing order of ligands in order of Δ_o is given below :

$I^- < Br^- < S^{2-} < SCN^- < Cl^- < F^- < OH^- < C_2O_4^{2-}$
$< H_2O < NCS^- < NH_3 < en < NO_2^- < CN^- < CO$

This series is called spectrochemical series.

Calculation of CFSE

- CFSE value for octahedral coordination entity can be calculated as:

$$CFSE = [-0.4x + 0.6y]\Delta_o$$

where, Δ_o = CFSE in octahedral complex
x = number of electrons in t_{2g} orbitals.
y = number of unpaired electrons in e_g orbitals

- CFSE value for tetrahedral coordination entity can be calculated as:

$$CFSE = [-0.6x + 0.4y]\Delta_t$$

where, Δ_t = CFSE in tetrahedral complex
x = number of electrons in e_2-orbitals.
y = number of electrons in t_2-orbitals.

Also, $\Delta_t = \frac{4}{9}\Delta_o$.

Stability of Coordination Compounds

The stability of a complex or coordination compound refers to the extent upto which it exists in a solution as coordination sphere. Factors affecting the stability of complex are :

(*i*) **Charge on the central metal ion** Greater the charge on the central metal ion, greater the stability of complex.

(*ii*) **Nature of the metal ion** Groups 3 and 6 and inner transition elements form stable complexes when donor atoms of the ligands are N, O and F. The elements after group 6 of the transition metals form stable complexes when the donor atoms of the ligands are the heavier members of N, O and F family.

(*iii*) **Basic nature of the ligands** Greater the basic strength, greater is the stability of the complex.

(*iv*) **Presence of chelate rings** Its presence increases the stability of the complex. It is called chelate effect. It is maximum for the 5 and 6 membered rings.

(*v*) **Effect of multidentate cyclic ligands** If the ligands are π multidentate and cyclic without any steric effect, the stability of the complex get increased.

Importance of Coordination Compounds

Important applications in qualitative analysis and biological system of these compounds are discussed below :

(*i*) Haemoglobin, the oxygen carrier in blood, is a coordination compound of Fe^{2+} with porphyrin.

(*ii*) The pigment chlorophyll in plants, responsible for photosynthesis, is a coordination compound of Mg^{2+} with porphyrin.

(*iii*) Estimation of hardness of water.

(*iv*) Ni^{2+} is detected by the formation of a red complex with dimethyl glyoxime (DMG).

(*v*) The platinum complex *cis*-$[Pt(NH_3)_2Cl_2]$, commonly known as *cis*-platin, is used in the treatment of cancer.

Organometallic Compounds

Organometallic compounds are those compounds which contain metal-carbon bond. The first organometallic compound of *d*-block elements was prepared by W.C. Zeise.

Some examples of organometallic compounds are $[Pt(C_2H_4)Cl_3]^-$, $Ni(CO)_4$, $[Fe(C_5H_5)_2]$ (also known as ferrocene.) etc

Metal Carbonyls

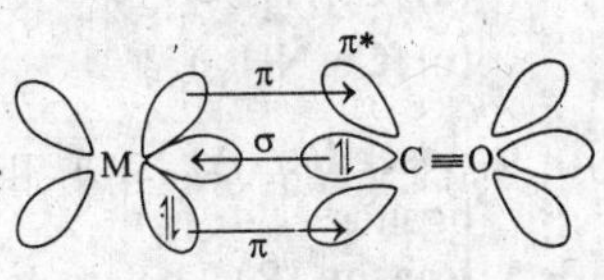

Many transition metals form metal carbonyl compounds. In these compounds, CO acts as donor ligand and donates lone pairs of electrons of carbonyl carbon into vacant orbital of metal forming σ-bond. It also behaves as an acceptor ligand and forms π-bond by back donation of electrons from filled *d*-orbital of metal to vacant antibonding π^*-orbital of CO. This backbonding stabilises the metal-ligand interaction. It is also called synergic bonding.

Topical Practice Questions

All the exam questions of this chapter have been divided into three topics as listed below

Topic 1

Coordination Compounds : Nomenclature, Isomerism and Werner's Theory

2018

1 The type of isomerism shown by the complex $[CoCl_2(en)_2]$ is **[NEET]**

(a) ionisation isomerism (b) coordination isomerism
(c) geometrical isomerism (d) linkage isomerism

2 In the complex, $[Cr(NH_3)_4Cl_2]^+$, the oxidation number of Cr is **[JIPMER]**

(a) +4 (b) +3 (c) +2 (d) +6

3 Which of the following compound has same oxidation state of the central metal atom in the cationic and anionic part? **[AIIMS]**

(a) $[Pt(NH_3)_4][PtCl_6]$ (b) $[Pt(NH_3)_4Cl_2][PtCl_4]$
(c) $[Pt(Py)_4][PtCl_4]$ (d) $K_4[Ni(CN)_6]$

4 The IUPAC name of the complex $[Pt(NH_3)_3Br(NO_2)Cl]Cl$ is **[AIIMS]**

(a) triammine chloridobromidonitro platinum (IV) chloride
(b) triammine bromidochloridonitro platinum (IV) chloride
(c) triammine bromidochloridonitro platinum (II) chloride
(d) triammine chloridobromidonitro platinum (II) chloride

5 Among the following complex ions, the one which shows geometrical isomerism will be **[AIIMS]**

(a) $[Cr(H_2O)_4Cl_2]^+$ (b) $[Pt(NH_3)_3Cl]$
(c) $[Co(NH_3)_6]^{3+}$ (d) $[Co(CN)_5(NC)]^{3-}$

6 **Assertion** (A) Toxic metal ions are removed by the chelating ligands.
Reason (R) Chelate complexes tend to be more stable. **[AIIMS]**

(a) Both A and R are correct and R is the correct explanation of A
(b) Both A and R are correct and R is not the correct explanation of A
(c) A is correct but R is incorrect
(d) Both A and R are incorrect

2017

7 Which of the following coordination compounds would exhibit optical isomerism? **[JIPMER]**

(a) Pentamminenitrocobalt (III) iodide
(b) *Tris*-(ethylenediamine) cobalt (III) bromide
(c) *Trans*-dicyanobis (ethylenediamine)
(d) Diamminedinitroplatinum (II)

8 **Assertion** (A) Complexes of MX_6 and MX_5L type (X and L are unidentate) do not show geometrical isomerism.

Reason (R) Geometrical isomerism is not shown by complexes of coordination number-6. **[AIIMS]**

(a) Both A and R are correct and R is the correct explanation of A
(b) Both A and R are correct and R is not the correct explanation of A
(c) A is correct but R is incorrect
(d) Both A and R are incorrect

9 The correct order of the stoichiometries of AgCl formed when $AgNO_3$ in excess is treated with the complexes: $CoCl_3 \cdot 6NH_3$, $CoCl_3 \cdot 5NH_3$, $CoCl_3 \cdot 4NH_3$ respectively is **[NEET]**

(a) 1 AgCl, 3 AgCl, 2 AgCl
(b) 3 AgCl, 1 AgCl, 2 AgCl
(c) 3 AgCl, 2 AgCl, 1 AgCl
(d) 2 AgCl, 3 AgCl, 1 AgCl

2014

10 The pair of compounds that can exist together is **[CBSE AIPMT]**

(a) $FeCl_3$, $SnCl_2$ (b) $HgCl_2$, $SnCl_2$
(c) $FeCl_2$, $SnCl_2$ (d) $FeCl_3$, KI

11 Which of the following complexes have lowest molar conductance? [MHT CET]

(a) $CoCl_3 \cdot 3NH_3$ (b) $CoCl_3 \cdot 4NH_3$
(c) $CoCl_3 \cdot 5NH_3$ (d) $CoCl_3 \cdot 6NH_3$

12 Which of the following compounds show optical isomerism ?

I. *cis*-$[Co(NH_3)_4Cl_2]^+$ II. *trans*-$[Co(en)_2Cl_2]^+$
III. *cis*-$[Co(en)_2Cl_2]^+$ IV. $[Co(en)_3]^{3+}$

Choose the correct answer from the codes given below.

(a) I and II (b) II and III [Kerala CEE]
(c) III and IV (d) I, III and IV
(e) I, II, III and IV

13 How many isomers are possible in $[Co(en)_2Cl_2]$?

(a) 2 (b) 4 (c) 6 (d) 1 [UK PMT]

14 In which one of the pairs of ion given, there is an ion that forms a coordination compound with both aqueous sodium hydroxide and ammonia and an other ion that forms a coordination compound only with aqueous sodium hydroxide? [KCET]

(a) Pb^{2+}, Cu^{2+} (b) Zn^{2+}, Al^{3+} (c) Cu^{2+}, Zn^{2+} (d) Al^{3+}, Cu^{2+}

15 The IUPAC name of the complex ion formed when gold dissolves in *aqua-regia* is [KCET]

(a) tetrachloridoaurate (III) (b) tetrachloridoaurate (I)
(c) tetrachloridoaurate (II) (d) dicoloridoaurate (III)

2013

16 The coordination number of platinum in $[Pt(NH_3)_4Cl_2]^{2+}$ ion is [UP CPMT]

(a) 2 (b) 4 (c) 6 (d) 8

17 Which of the following ligands is not a chelating agent?

(a) EDTA (b) en [WB JEE]
(c) Oxalate (d) Pyridine

18 The oxidation number of Co in $[Co(NH_3)_3(NO_2)_3]$ is

(a) +3 (b) 0 (c) −3 (d) + 6 [WB JEE]

19 IUPAC name of $K_3[Fe(CN)_6]$ is [KCET]

(a) potassium ferricyanide
(b) potassium hexacyanoferrate (I)
(c) potassium hexacyanoferrate (III)
(d) potassium hexacyanoferrate (II)

2012

20 Compounds $[PtCl_2(NH_3)_4]Br_2$ and $[PtBr_2(NH_3)_4]Cl_2$, shows the following type of isomerism. [AFMC, AMU]

(a) Hydrate isomerism
(b) Ionisation isomerism
(c) Linkage isomerism
(d) Coordination position isomerism

21 The IUPAC name of $K_2[Ni(CN)_4]$ is [AFMC, KCET]

(a) potassium tetracyanonickelate (II)
(b) potassium tetracyanatonickelate (III)
(c) potassium tetracyanatonickel (II)
(d) potassium tetracyanonickel (III)

22 Which of the following compounds shows optical isomerism? [Manipal]

(a) $[Co(CN)_6]^{3-}$ (b) $[Cr(C_2O_4)_3]^{3+}$
(c) $[ZnCl_4]^{2-}$ (d) $[Cu(NH_3)_4]^{2+}$

23 In the brown ring complex $[Fe(H_2O)_5(NO)]SO_4$, nitric oxide behaves as [WB JEE]

(a) NO^+ (b) neutral, no molecule
(c) NO^- (d) NO^{2-}

2011

24 The complexes $[Co(NH_3)_6][Cr(CN)_6]$ and $[Cr(NH_3)_6][Co(CN)_6]$ are the examples of which type of isomerism? [CBSE AIPMT]

(a) Geometrical isomerism (b) Linkage isomerism
(c) Ionisation isomerism (d) Coordination isomerism

25 The complex, $[Pt(py)(NH_3)BrCl]$ will have how many geometrical isomers? [CBSE AIPMT]

(a) 2 (b) 3 (c) 4 (d) 0

26 The ligand $N(CHCH_2NH_2)_3$ is [Kerala CEE]

(a) tridentate (b) pentadentate
(c) tetradentate (d) bidentate
(e) hexadentate

27 Which can exist both as diastereoisomer and enantiomer? [DUMET]

(a) $[Pt(en)_3]^{4+}$ (b) $[Pt(en)_2ClBr]^{2+}$
(c) $[Ru(NH_3)_4Cl_2]^0$ (d) $[PtCl_2Br_2]^0$

28 Number of isomeric forms (constitutional and stereoisomers) for $[Rh(en)_2(NO_2)(SCN)]^+$ are [DUMET]

(a) three (b) six (c) nine (d) twelve

29 Excess of silver nitrate solution is added to 100 mL of 0.01 M pentaaquachlorochromium (III) chloride solution. The mass of silver chloride obtained (in gram) is [Atomic mass of silver is 108] [KCET]

(a) 287×10^{-3} (b) 143.5×10^{-3}
(c) 143.5×10^{-2} (d) 287×10^{-2}

30 The IUPAC name of the complex $[Co(NH_3)_4Cl_2]Cl$ is [KCET]

(a) dichlorotetraamminecobalt (III) chloride
(b) tetraamminedichlorocobalt (III) chloride
(c) tetraamminedichlorocobalt (II) chloride
(d) tetraamminedichlorocobalt (IV) chloride

31 Ammonia gas does not evolve from the complex $FeCl_3 \cdot 4NH_3$ but it gives white precipitate with aqueous solution of $AgNO_3$. Coordination number of central metal ion in the above complex is six. Give IUPAC name of the complex. [Guj CET]

(a) Ammoniumtrichlorotriammineferric (III)
(b) Tetraammineferric (III) chloride
(c) Dichlorotetraammineferrate (II) chloride
(d) Tetraamminedichloro iron (III) chloride.

2010

32 The existence of two different coloured complexes with the composition $[Co(NH_3)_4Cl_2]^+$ is due to **[CBSE AIPMT]**
(a) Ionisation isomerism (b) Linkage isomerism
(c) Geometrical isomerism (d) Coordination isomerism

33 In the complex ion $[Co(NH_3)_6]^{3+}$, the NH_3 molecules are linked to the central metal ion by **[AFMC]**
(a) ionic bonds (b) covalent bonds
(c) coordinate bonds (d) hydrogen bonds

34 $[Co(NH_3)_4Cl_2]NO_2$ and $[Co(NH_3)_4ClNO_2]Cl$ exhibit which type of isomerism? **[Manipal]**
(a) Geometrical (b) Optical (c) Linkage (d) Ionisation

35 The name of the complex $[Pt(NH_3)_6]Cl_4$ is **[Manipal]**
(a) hexaammineplatinum (IV) chloride
(b) hexammineplatinum (II) chloride
(c) tetrachlorohexammineplatinum (IV)
(d) tetrachlorohexammineplatinum (II)

36 The effective atomic number of Cr (atomic no. 24) in $[Cr(NH_3)_6]Cl_3$ is **[Manipal]**
(a) 35 (b) 27 (c) 33 (d) 36

37 How many ions are produced from $[Co(NH_3)_6]Cl_3$ in solution? **[RPMT]**
(a) 6 (b) 4 (c) 3 (d) 2

38 EDTA has coordination number **[RPMT]**
(a) 3 (b) 4 (c) 5 (d) 6

39 The IUPAC name of the complex $[Pt(NH_3)_3Br(NO_2)Cl]Cl$ is **[Haryana PMT]**
(a) triamminechlorobromonitroplatinum (IV) chloride
(b) triamminebromonitrochloroplatinum (IV) chloride
(c) triamminebromochloronitroplatinum (IV) chloride
(d) triamminenitrochlorobromoplatinum (IV) chloride

40 AgCl is dissolved in excess of each of NH_3, KCN and $Na_2S_2O_3$. The complex ions produced in each case are **[AMU]**
(a) $[Ag(NH_3)_2]^+$, $[Ag(CN)_2]^+$ and $[Ag(S_2O_3)_2]^{3-}$
(b) $[Ag(NH_3)_2]^{2+}$, $[Ag(CN)_2]^{3-}$ and $[Ag(S_2O_3)_2]^{2-}$
(c) $[Ag(NH_3)_4]^{2+}$, $[Ag(CN)_2]^{3-}$ and $[Ag_2(S_2O_3)_2]^{2-}$
(d) $[Ag(NH_3)_2]^+$, $[Ag(CN)_2]^-$ and $[Ag(S_2O_3)_2]^{3-}$

41 Which of the following 0.1 M complex compound solutions will have the minimum electrical conductivity? **[Guj CET]**
(a) Hexaammine platinum (IV) chloride
(b) Chloropentaammineplatinum (IV) chloride
(c) Dichlorotetraammineplatinum (IV) chloride
(d) Trichlorotriammineplatinum (IV) chloride

2009

42 Which of the following does not show optical isomerism? (en = ethylenediammine) **[CBSE AIPMT]**
(a) $[Co(en)_2Cl_2]^+$ (b) $[Co(NH_3)_3Cl_3]^0$
(c) $[Co(en)Cl_2(NH_3)_2]^+$ (d) $[Co(en)_3]^{3+}$

43 The IUPAC name of $K[Ag(CN)_2]$ is **[Manipal]**
(a) dicyanopotassiumargentate (I)
(b) dicyanopotassiumargentate (II)
(c) potassiumdicyanoargentate (I)
(d) potassiumdicyanoargentate (II)

44 On heating $K_4[Fe(CN)_6]$ with conc. H_2SO_4, it gives the gas **[OJEE]**
(a) SO_2 (b) CO_2 (c) CO (d) NO_2

45 Facial and meridional isomerism will be exhibited by **[Kerala CEE]**
(a) $[Co(NH_3)_3Cl_3]$ (b) $[Co(NH_3)_4Cl_2]Cl$
(c) $[Co(en)_3]Cl_3$ (d) $[Co(NH_3)_5Cl]Cl_2$
(e) $K_3[Co(CN)_4Cl_2]$

46 In solid $CuSO_4 \cdot 5H_2O$ copper is coordinated to number of water molecules equal to **[CG PMT, Haryana PMT]**
(a) 5 (b) 4 (c) 1 (d) 2

47 The coordination compound of which, one of the following compositions will produce two equivalents of AgCl on reaction with aqueous silver nitrate solution? **[J&K CET]**
(a) $CoCl_3 \cdot 3NH_3$ (b) $CoCl_3 \cdot 6NH_3$
(c) $CoCl_3 \cdot 4NH_3$ (d) $CoCl_3 \cdot 5NH_3$

48 The optically active coordination complex ion among the following is **[J&K CET]**
(a) *trans*-$[Co(en)_2Cl_2]^+$ (b) *cis*-$[Co(en)(NH_3)_2Cl_2]^+$
(c) $[Co(NH_3)_6]^{3+}$ (d) $[Fe(CN)_6]^{3-}$

49 $[Fe(CN)_6]^{3-}$ ion is **[AMU]**
(a) hexacyanoferrate (II) ion
(b) hexacyanoferrate (III) ion
(c) hexacyanide iron (III) ion
(d) iron (III) hexacyanide ion

50 The IUPAC name of $[Co(NH_3)_5ONO]^{2+}$ ion is **[KCET]**
(a) pentaamminenitritocobalt (III) ion
(b) pentaamminenitrocobalt (III) ion
(c) pentaamminenitrocobalt (IV) ion
(d) pentaamminenitritocobalt (II) ion

51 Aluminium reacts with NaOH and forms compound '*X*'. If the coordination number of aluminium in '*X*' is 6, the correct formula of *X* is **[EAMCET]**
(a) $[Al(H_2O)_4(OH)_2]^+$ (b) $[Al(H_2O)_3(OH)_3]$
(c) $[Al(H_2O)_2(OH)_4]^-$ (d) $[Al(H_2O)_6](OH)_3$

2008

52 For the square planar complex $[M(a)(b)(c)(d)]$ (where, M = central metal and *a*, *b*, *c* and *d* are monodentate ligands), the number of possible geometrical isomers are
(a) 1 (b) 2 (c) 3 (d) 4 **[Manipal]**

53 Among the following which are ambidentate ligands? **[Kerala CEE]**
I. NO_2^- II. NO_3^-
III. $EDTA^{4-}$ IV. $C_2O_4^{2-}$
V. SCN^- VI. $H_2NCH_2CH_2NH_2$
(a) I and II (b) III and IV (c) I and VI (d) III and VI
(e) I and V

54 In the complex with formula $MCl_3 \cdot 4H_2O$, the coordination number of the metal M is six and there is no molecule of hydration in it. The volume, if 0.1 M $AgNO_3$ solution needed to precipitate the free chloride ions in 200 mL of 0.01 M solution of the complex, is **[Kerala CEE]**

(a) 40 mL (b) 20 mL (c) 60 mL (d) 80 mL
(e) 10 mL

55 The number of ions formed when hexaamminecopper (II) sulphate is dissolved in water is **[J&K CET]**

(a) 1 (b) 2 (c) 4 (d) 6

56 When $AgNO_3$ solution is added in excess to 1 M solution of $CoCl_3 \cdot xNH_3$, one mole of AgCl is formed. What is the value of x? **[Punjab PMET]**

(a) 1 (b) 2 (c) 3 (d) 4

57 A ligand can also be regarded as **[KCET]**

(a) Lewis acid (b) Bronsted base
(c) Lewis base (d) Bronsted acid

2007

58 Which of the following will give a pair of enantiomorphs? ($en = NH_2CH_2CH_2NH_2$) **[CBSE AIPMT]**

(a) $[Co(NH_3)_4Cl_2]NO_2$ (b) $[Cr(NH_3)_6][Co(CN)_6]$
(c) $[Co(en)_2Cl_2]Cl$ (d) $[Pt(NH_3)_4][PtCl_6]$

59 Which of the following coordination compounds would exhibit optical isomerism? **[Manipal]**

(a) Pentamminenitrocobalt (III) iodide
(b) Diamminedinitroplatinum (II)
(c) *trans*-dicyano *bis*-(ethylenediamine)
(d) *tris*-(ethylenediamine) cobalt (III) bromide

60 Which one of the following is tridentate ligand? **[Kerala CEE]**

(a) NO_2^- (b) Oxalate ion
(c) Glycinate ion (d) Dien
(e) EDTA

61 Pick out the wrong match. **[MP PMT]**

(a) $[Cr(NH_3)_4Cl_2]Br$ –Ionisation isomerism
(b) $[Co(C_2O_4)_3]^{3-}$ –Geometrical isomerism
(c) $[Fe(en)_2Cl_2]^+$ –Optical isomerism
(d) $[Co(en)_3][Cr(ox)_3]$ – Coordination isomerism

62 Which one amongst the following, exhibit geometrical isomerism? **[J&K CET]**

(a) $[Co^{III}(NH_3)_5Br]SO_4$
(b) $Co^{III}[EDTA]^{1-}$
(c) $[Cr^{III}(SCN)_6]^{3-}$
(d) $[Pt^{II}(NH_3)_2Cl_2]$

63 Benzoylacetonato beryllium exhibit isomerism of the type **[J&K CET]**

(a) structural (b) geometrical
(c) optical (d) conformational

64 The hypothetical complex chlorodiaquatriammine cobalt (III) chloride can be represented as **[Punjab PMET]**

(a) $[CoCl(NH_3)_3(H_2O)_2]Cl_2$
(b) $[Co(NH_3)_3(H_2O)Cl_3]$
(c) $[Co(NH_3)_3(H_2O)_2Cl]$
(d) $[Co(NH_3)_3(H_2O)_3]Cl_3$

65 Which complex cannot ionise in solution? **[KCET]**

(a) $[CoCl_3(NH_3)_3]$ (b) $K_4[Fe(CN)_6]$
(c) $K_2[Pt(F_6)]$ (d) $[Pt(NH_3)_6]Cl_4$

2006

66 The number of possible isomers of an octahedral complex $[Co(C_2O_4)_2(NH_3)_2]^-$ is **[AIIMS]**

(a) 1 (b) 2
(c) 3 (d) 4

67 The example of coordination isomerism is **[Punjab PMET]**

(a) $[Co(NH_3)_6][Cr(CN)_6]$ and $[Cr(NH_3)_6][Co(CN)_6]$
(b) $[Co(NH_3)_5Br]SO_4$ and $[Co(NH_3)_5SO_4]Br$
(c) $[Co(NH_3)_5NO_3]SO_4$ and $[Co(NH_3)_5SO_4]NO_3$
(d) $[Pt(NH_3)_4Cl_2]Br_2$ and $[Pt(NH_3)_4Br_2]Cl_2$

68 How many ions will be furnished by $CoCl_3 \cdot 6NH_3$? **[DUMET]**

(a) 3 (b) 4
(c) Either (a) or (b) (d) 2

69 Which of the following can participate in linkage isomerism? **[KCET]**

(a) NO_2^- (b) $H_2\ddot{N}CH_2CH_2\ddot{N}H_2$
(c) H_2O (d) $:NH_3$

2005

70 The number of chloride ions produced by complex tetramminedichloroplatinum (IV) chloride in an aqueous solution is **[Kerala CEE]**

(a) four (b) two (c) one (d) three
(e) None of these

Answers

1. (c)	2. (b)	3. (c)	4. (b)	5. (a)	6. (a)	7. (b)	8. (c)	9. (c)	10. (c)
11. (a)	12. (c)	13. (b)	14. (b)	15. (a)	16. (c)	17. (d)	18. (a)	19. (c)	20. (b)
21. (a)	22. (b)	23. (a)	24. (d)	25. (b)	26. (c)	27. (b)	28. (d)	29. (a)	30. (b)
31. (d)	32. (c)	33. (c)	34. (d)	35. (a)	36. (c)	37. (b)	38. (d)	39. (c)	40. (d)
41. (d)	42. (b)	43. (c)	44. (c)	45. (a)	46. (b)	47. (d)	48. (b)	49. (b)	50. (a)
51. (c)	52. (c)	53. (e)	54. (b)	55. (b)	56. (d)	57. (c)	58. (c)	59. (d)	60. (d)
61. (b)	62. (d)	63. (c)	64. (a)	65. (a)	66. (c)	67. (a)	68. (c)	69. (a)	70. (b)

Explanations

1. (c) Isomers in which the atoms or ligands occupy different positions around central metal/ion are called geometrical isomers. Complexes having coordination number six of central atom/ion 6 with formula $M(AA)_2B_2$ exhibit geometrical isomerism [where, AA is a bidentate ligand].
In $[CoCl_2(en)_2]$, coordination number of Co is 6 with octahedral geometry.

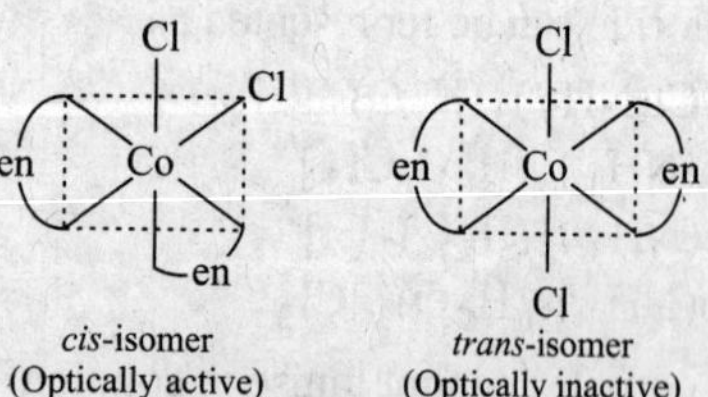

cis-isomer (Optically active) *trans*-isomer (Optically inactive)

Thus, $[CoCl_2(en)_2]$ show geometrical isomerism.

2. (b) Let the oxidation number of Cr be x in the complex $[Cr(NH_3)_4Cl_2]^+$

$$\therefore \quad x + 4 \times (0) + 2 \times (-1) = +1$$
$$x - 2 = +1$$
$$x = +3$$

Thus, the oxidation number of Cr is +3.

3. (c) $[Pt(Py)_4]\,[PtCl_4]$

Let the oxidation state of Pt be x.

$$x + 0\times 4 + x + (-1)\times 4 = 0$$

or, $\quad 2x = +4 \quad$ or, $\quad x = +2$

Thus, it is the complex in which the central metal atom in cationic and anionic parts have same oxidation state.

4. (b) The oxidation state of central atom (Pt) is calculated as
Let the oxidation state of Pt $= x$, then

$$(x\times 1) + 3\times(0) + (1\times -1) + (1\times -1) + (1\times -1) = +1$$
$$x - 3 = +1$$
$$x = +4$$

Thus, the IUPAC name of the complex $[Pt(NH)_3Br(NO_2)Cl]$ Cl is triamminebromidochloridonitroplatinum (IV) chloride as the names of the different ligands are arranged alphabetically.

5. (a) $[Cr(H_2O)_4Cl_2]^+$ shows geometrical isomerism because it is a MA_4B_2 type coordination compound which contains two set of equivalent ligands, four H_2O and 2Cl.
Hence, the possible geometrical isomers are:

trans-isomer *cis*-isomer

Hence, correct option is (a).

6. (a) Assertion and reason both are correct and reason is the correct explanation of the assertion.
Toxic metal ions are removed by chelating ligands. When a solution of chelating ligand is added to solution containing toxic metal, ligands chelate the metal ions by formation of stable complex.

7. (b) *Tris*-(ethylenediamine) cobalt (III) bromide, i.e. $[Co(en)_3]Br_3$ exhibits optical isomerism.

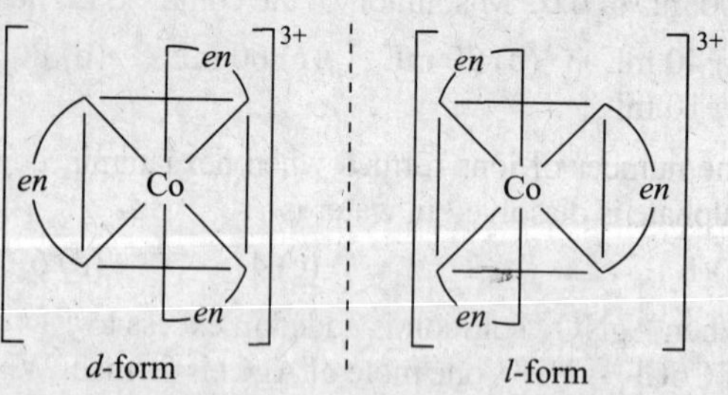

d-form *l*-form

8. (c) MX_6 and MX_5L type complexes do not show geometrical isomerism (due to symmetry) although many coordinated complexes like complex of type MA_3B_3 exhibits geometrical isomerism. Hence (A) is true but (R) is false.

9. (c) According to Werner's theory,

$$CoCl_3\cdot 6NH_3 \longrightarrow [Co(NH_3)_6]^{3+}\,3Cl^-$$
$$CoCl_3\cdot 5NH_3 \longrightarrow [Co(NH_3)_5Cl]^{2+}\,2Cl^-$$
$$CoCl_3\cdot 4NH_3 \longrightarrow [Co(NH_3)_4Cl_2]^{+}\,Cl^-$$

When $AgNO_3$ in excess is treated with these complexes then following reactions take place :

$$[Co(NH_3)_6]^{3+}\,3Cl^- + \underset{(Excess)}{AgNO_3} \longrightarrow 3AgCl + [Co(NH_3)_6]^{3+}$$
$$[Co(NH_3)_5Cl]^{2+}\,2Cl^- + \underset{(Excess)}{AgNO_3} \longrightarrow 2AgCl + [Co(NH_3)_5Cl]^{2+}$$
$$[Co(NH_3)_4Cl_2]^{+}\,Cl^- + \underset{(Excess)}{AgNO_3} \longrightarrow AgCl + [Co(NH_3)_4\,Cl_2]^{+}$$

10. (c) The compounds with lower oxidation number and those which cannot be reduced by one another can exist together. Thus, $FeCl_2$ and $SnCl_2$ can exist together as Fe^{2+} cannot be reduced by Sn^{2+}.

11. (a) Molar conductance is the conducting power of all the ions produced by dissolving 1 g-mole of an electrolyte. Therefore, molar conductance $\propto$ number of ions produced.

Werner complex	Modern-notation	Ionisation
(a) $CoCl_3\cdot 3NH_3$	$[Co(NH_3)_3Cl_3]$	$[Co(NH_3)_3Cl_3]$ (No ionisation)
(b) $CoCl_3\cdot 4NH_3$	$[Co(NH_3)_4Cl_2]Cl$	$[Co(NH_3)_4Cl_2]^+ + Cl^-$ (2 ions)
(c) $CoCl_3\cdot 5NH_3$	$[Co(NH_3)_5Cl]\,Cl_2$	$[Co(NH_3)_5Cl]^{2+} + 2Cl^-$ (3 ions)
(d) $CoCl_3\cdot 6NH_3$	$[Co(NH_3)_6]Cl_3$	$[Co(NH_3)_6]^{3+} + 3Cl^-$ (4 ions)

From the above table it is clear that, molar conductance of the complexes will be in the following order : $a < b < c < d$. So, the complex having lowest molar conductance is $CoCl_3.3NH_3$.

12. *(c)* Only those complex exhibit optical isomerism which have atleast one or more bidentate or polydentate group (s) and absence of plane of symmetry (symmetry elements). Among the given complex II, III and IV have bidentate ligand (en) but in case of (II) symmetry is present, so it does not exhibit optical isomerism.

trans-$[Co(en)_2Cl_2]^+$

Thus, only *cis* - $[Co(en)_2Cl_2]^+$ and $[Co(en)_3]^{3+}$ can exhibit optical isomerism.

13. *(b)* $[Co(en)_2Cl_2]$ will form *cis* and *trans*-isomers. Its *cis*-isomer will show optical isomerism.

Cis-isomer *Trans*-isomer

Dextro Enantiomers *leavo*

Although *cis*-isomer and *dextro*-isomer are same but these are aligned to different properties, that's why these are counted separately. Hence, 4 isomers are possible.

14. *(b)* Zn^{2+}, Al^{3+}

I. $Zn(OH)_2 + 2NaOH \longrightarrow Na[Zn(OH)_4]^{2-} + 2Na^+$

$ZnCl_2 + 4NH_3 \longrightarrow [Zn(NH_3)_4]Cl_2$
Anhydrous — Tetrammine zinc chloride

II. $Al(OH)_3 + NaOH \longrightarrow [Al(OH)_4]^-$

$Al^{3+} + 3NH_3 \longrightarrow Al(NH_3)_3$

15. *(a)* *Aqua-regia* is a solution containing conc HCl and conc HNO_3 in the ratio 3 : 1.

It dissolves noble metals like Au, Pt etc.

$$Au(s) + 3NO_3^- + 6H^+(aq) \rightleftharpoons Au^{3+}(aq) + 3NO_2(g) + 3H_2O$$

$$Au^{3+}(aq) + 4Cl^-(aq) \rightleftharpoons AuCl_4^-(aq)$$

16. *(c)* Coordination number = number of monodentate ligands.

In $[Pt(NH_3)_4Cl_2]^{2+}$

Number of monodentate ligands = $4NH_3 + 2Cl^- = 6$

17. *(d)* Pyridine is a monodentate ligand. It coordinates with a metal only from one site, i.e. the lone pair on N.

Thus, it is not a chelating agent. While the other three are chelating ligands, i.e. these are attached to a central metal ion by bonds from two or more donor atoms.

18. *(a)* Oxidation state of $NH_3 = 0$ and $NO_2 = -1$

So, $[Co(NH_3)_3(NO_2)_3]$

$x + (0)3 + (-1)3 = 0 \Rightarrow x - 3 = 0$

$\Rightarrow x = +3$

19. *(c)* The IUPAC name of $K_3[Fe(CN)_6]$ is potassium hexacyanoferrate (III).

20. *(b)* Since, the complexes $[PtCl_2(NH_3)_4]Br_2$ and $[PtBr_2(NH_3)_4]Cl_2$ have the same molecular formula but on ionisation they give different ions, they exhibit ionisation isomerism.

$[PtCl_2(NH_3)_4]Br_2 \rightleftharpoons [PtCl_2(NH_3)_4]^{2+} + 2Br^-$

$[PtBr_2(NH_3)_4]Cl_2 \rightleftharpoons [PtBr_2(NH_3)_4]^{2+} + 2Cl^-$

21. *(a)* The IUPAC name of $K_2[Ni(CN)_4]$ is potassium tetracyanonickelate (II).

22. *(b)* $[Cr(C_2O_4)_3]^{3+}$ shows optical isomerism because its mirror image is not superimposable.

23. *(a)* In Fe-complexes, NO behaves as NO^+.

24. *(d)* When the cation and anion both are complex ions, the coordination compound exhibits coordination isomerism. Thus, the given example is of coordination isomerism.

25. *(b)* $M(ABCD)$ type complex has three geometrical isomers as

26. *(c)* $N(CH_2CH_2NH_2)_3$ is a tetradentate ligand as it contains four coordinating sites.

27. *(b)* $[Pt(en)_2ClBr]^{2+}$ can exist both as diastereoisomer and enantiomer.

cis (+) (−) , *trans*

The (+) and (−) forms of *cis* $[Pt(en)_2ClBr]^{2+}$ are enantiomers. The *cis* and *trans* forms of $[Pt(en)_2ClBr]^{2+}$ are diastereoisomers.

28. *(d)* Ambidentate ligand NO_2 and SCN will give two different isomers.

I to IV each will have two isomers (*d* and *l*) each

total isomeric forms - 12

29. *(a)* $[CrCl(H_2O)_5]Cl_2 \longrightarrow [CrCl(H_2O)_5]^{2+} + 2Cl^-$

$\frac{100 \times 0.01}{1000} = 0.001$ mol $= 0.001 \times 2$ mol of Cl^-

$$\underset{0.002 \text{ mol}}{Ag^+ + Cl^-} \longrightarrow \underset{0.002 \text{ mol}}{AgCl}$$

0.001 mol of $[Cr \cdot Cl(H_2O)_5]Cl_2$ gives 0.002 mol of AgCl

$\therefore$ Mass of silver chloride $= 143.5 \times 0.002 = 0.287$ g $= 287 \times 10^{-3}$ g

30. *(b)* The IUPAC name of the complex $[Co(NH_3)_4Cl_2]Cl$ is tetraamminedichlorocobalt (III) chloride.

31. *(d)* The IUPAC name of complex is tetraamminedichloroiron (III) chloride having formula $[Fe(NH_3)_4Cl_2]Cl$.

32. *(c)* The existence of two different coloured complexes is due to geometrical isomerism as *cis* and *trans* forms are present.

33. *(c)* A complex is formed, when ligand(s) donates its (their) electrons to the vacant *d*-orbital of transition metals. Since, the electrons are given by only ligands and used up by metals as well as ligands, the bond formed is called coordinate bond.

34. *(d)* $[Co(NH_3)_4Cl_2]NO_2$ and $[Co(NH_3)_4ClNO_2]Cl$ give different ions when subjected to ionisation. Thus, these are ionisation isomers and they exhibit ionisation isomerism.

$$[Co(NH_3)_4Cl_2]NO_2 \longrightarrow [Co(NH_3)_4Cl_2]^+ + NO_2^-$$
$$[Co(NH_3)_4ClNO_2]Cl \longrightarrow [Co(NH_3)_4ClNO_2]^+ + Cl^-$$

35. *(a)* The IUPAC name of $[Pt(NH_3)_6]Cl_4$ is hexaammineplatinum (IV) chloride.

36. *(c)* Effective atomic number, EAN
= number of electrons in Cr + 2 × number of ligands − charge
$= 24 + 2 \times 6 - 3 = 33$

37. *(b)* $[Co(NH_3)_6]Cl_3 \rightleftharpoons [Co(NH_3)_6]^{3+} + 3Cl^-$
Hence, four ions are produced in the solution.

38. *(d)* Coordination number of the central atom or ion is determined by the number of sigma bonds formed by the ligand with the central atom or ion.

$\therefore$ (Ethylene diamminetetraacetate) EDTA has C.N = 6.

$$\begin{matrix} ^-OOC\cdot H_2C \\ ^-OOC\cdot H_2C \end{matrix} \rangle \ddot{N} - CH_2CH_2 - \ddot{N} \langle \begin{matrix} CH_2\cdot COO^- \\ CH_2\cdot COO^- \end{matrix}$$

EDTA

39. *(c)* The IUPAC name of the complex $[Pt(NH_3)_3Br(NO_2)Cl]Cl$ is triamminebromochloronitroplatinum (IV) chloride. The names of the different ligands are arranged alphabetically in the given complex.

40. *(d)* On dissolving AgCl in excess of NH_3, KCN and $Na_2S_2O_3$, following complex ions are produced.

$$AgCl + 2NH_3 \longrightarrow [Ag(NH_3)_2]^+ Cl^-$$
$$AgCl + 2KCN \longrightarrow K^+ [Ag(CN)_2]^- + KCl$$
$$AgCl + Na_2S_2O_3 \longrightarrow [Ag(S_2O_3)_2]^{3-}$$

41. *(d)* The formula of given complexes are as follows :

(a) Hexaammineplatinum (IV) chloride $[Pt(NH_3)_6]Cl_4$

(b) Chloropentaammineplatinum (IV) chloride $[Pt(NH_3)_5Cl]Cl_3$

(c) Dichlorotetraammineplatinum (IV) chloride $[Pt(NH_3)_4Cl_2]Cl_2$

(d) Trichlorotriammineplatinum (IV) chloride $[Pt(NH_3)_3Cl_3]Cl$

In aqueous solution, the complexes ionise as follows :

$$[Pt(NH_3)_6]Cl_4 \rightleftharpoons \underbrace{[Pt(NH_3)_6]^{4+} + 4Cl^-}_{5 \text{ ions}}$$
$$[Pt(NH_3)_5Cl]Cl_3 \rightleftharpoons \underbrace{[Pt(NH_3)_5Cl]^{3+} + 3Cl^-}_{4 \text{ ions}}$$
$$[Pt(NH_3)_4Cl_2]Cl_2 \rightleftharpoons \underbrace{[Pt(NH_3)_4Cl_2]^{2+} + 2Cl^-}_{3 \text{ ions}}$$
$$[Pt(NH_3)_3Cl_3]Cl \rightleftharpoons \underbrace{[Pt(NH_3)_3Cl_3]^{+} + Cl^-}_{2 \text{ ions}}$$

Trichlorotriammineplatinum (IV) chloride gives the minimum number of ions in the solution.

Hence, it has the minimum electrical conductivity.

42. *(b)* Octahedral complexes of $[M(AA)_2B_2]$ type, e.g. $[Co(en)_2Cl_2]^+$, $[M(AA)B_2C_2]$ type, e.g. $[Co(en)Cl_2(NH_3)_2]^+$ and $[M(AA)_3]$ type, e.g. $[Co(en)_3]^{3+}$ show optical isomerism, whereas complexes of $[MA_3B_3]$ type, e.g. $[Co(NH_3)_3Cl_3]^0$ do not show optical isomerism.

43. *(c)* The IUPAC name of $K[Ag(CN)_2]$ is potassiumdicyanoargentate (I).

44. *(c)* $K_4[Fe(CN)_6] + 6H_2SO_4 + 6H_2O \longrightarrow 2K_2SO_4 + FeSO_4 + 3(NH_4)_2SO_4 + 6CO$

45. *(a)* Facial (*fac*) and meridional (*mer*) isomerism, a type of geometrical isomerism, is shown by octahedral complexes having Ma_3b_3 general formula. Where, *M* is central metal and *a* and *b* are monodentate ligands. Hence, $[Co(NH_3)_3Cl_3]$ exhibits *fac-mer* isomerism as

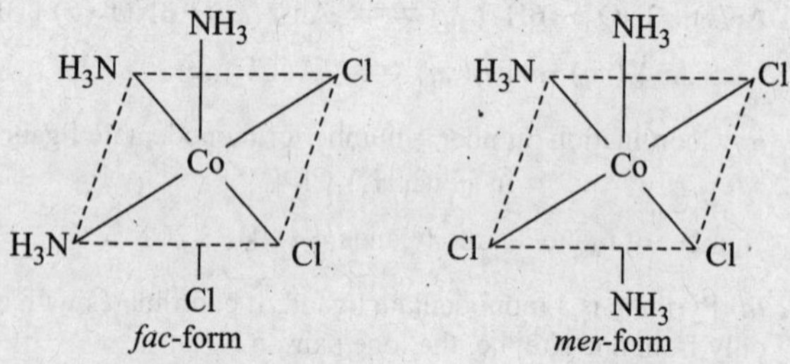

46. *(b)* In solid $CuSO_4 \cdot 5H_2O$, four water molecules are coordinated with copper as

$$CuSO_4 \cdot 5H_2O \longrightarrow [Cu(H_2O)_4]SO_4 \cdot H_2O$$

Water molecules form coordinate bonds.

47. *(d)* The chloride ions which are present outside the coordination sphere get precipitated as AgCl on reaction with $AgNO_3$. Thus, depending on the number of chloride ions present outside the coordination sphere, the number of equivalents of AgCl produced can be determined.

$$[Co(NH_3)_5Cl]Cl_2 + 2AgNO_3 \longrightarrow [Co(NH_3)_5Cl](NO_3)_2 + 2AgCl$$

48. *(b)* Octahedral complexes of the type $[M(AA)_2b_2]^{n\pm}$ and $[M(AA)a_2b_2]^{n\pm}$ exhibit geometrical isomerism.

Option (a), i.e. *trans*-$[Co(en)_2Cl_2]^+$ which belongs to the 1st category is optically inactive owing to the presence of an element of symmetry. However (b), *cis* $[Co(en)(NH_3)_2Cl_2]^+$ exists in optically active forms.

Complex given in options (c) and (d) are optically inactive as all the ligands are same.

49. *(b)* $[Fe(CN)_6]^{3-}$

Let the oxidation number of Fe in $[Fe(CN)_6]^{3-}$ be x.

$$x + (-1) \times 6 = -3$$

$$x - 6 = -3 \Rightarrow x = +3$$

IUPAC name is hexacyanoferrate (III) ion.

50. *(a)* The IUPAC name of $[Co(NH_3)_5ONO]^{2+}$ is pentaamminenitrito cobalt (III) ion.

51. *(c)* $2Al + 2NaOH + 2H_2O \longrightarrow \underset{\text{Sodium meta aluminate}}{2NaAlO_2} + 3H_2$

$$NaAlO_2 + 2H_2O \longrightarrow Al(OH)_3 \downarrow + NaOH$$

$$Al(OH)_3 + NaOH \longrightarrow Na^+[Al(H_2O)_2(OH)_4]^-$$

Sodium metaaluminate, thus formed is soluble in water and changes into the complex $[Al(H_2O)_2(OH)_4]^-$, in which coordination number of Al is 6.

52. *(c)* For $[M\,(a)\,(b)\,(c)\,(d)]$ square planar complex, the number of possible geometrical isomers is three which is obtained by fixing the position of one of the ligands say a while the other ligands b, c and d are placed *trans* to it.

53. *(e)* The ligands that can ligate through two different atoms are called ambidentate ligand, e.g. SCN^-, NO_2^-.

54. *(b)* The coordination number of metal $M = 6$

Number of molecules of hydration = 0

Thus, the formula of complex = $[M(H_2O)_4Cl_2]Cl$

$$[M(H_2O)_4Cl_2]Cl + AgNO_3 \longrightarrow [M(H_2O)_4Cl_2]NO_3 + AgCl$$

$$Cl^- + AgNO_3 \longrightarrow NO_3^- + AgCl$$

Let the volume of $AgNO_3$ used = V

$\because \quad \underset{\text{for } AgNO_3}{M_1V_1} = \underset{\text{for } Cl^-}{M_2V_2}$

$\therefore \quad 0.1 \times V = 200 \times 0.01$ or $V = 20$ mL

55. *(b)* The formula of hexaamminecopper (II) sulphate is $[Cu(NH_3)_6]SO_4$.

It dissolves in water as,

$$[Cu(NH_3)_6]SO_4 \rightleftharpoons \underbrace{[Cu(NH_3)_6]^{2+} + SO_4^{2-}}_{2 \text{ ions}}$$

56. *(d)* When $AgNO_3$ is added to $CoCl_3 \cdot xNH_3$, one mole of AgCl is formed, hence the value of x is 4.

$$[Co(NH_3)_4Cl_2]Cl \rightleftharpoons [Co(NH_3)_4Cl_2]^+ + \underset{\text{can be precipitated}}{Cl^-}$$

57. *(c)* A ligand is a species that is capable of donating an electron pair(s) to the central metal ion. The substances which are capable of donating an electron pair are called Lewis base, so a ligand is also a Lewis base.

58. *(c)* A pair of molecules related to each other as an object and its mirror image are known as enantiomorphs or enantiomers. These are not superimposable on their mirror image.

$[Co(en)_2Cl_2]^+$ Dichloro *bis*-(ethylenediamine) cobalt (III) would give enantiomorphs.

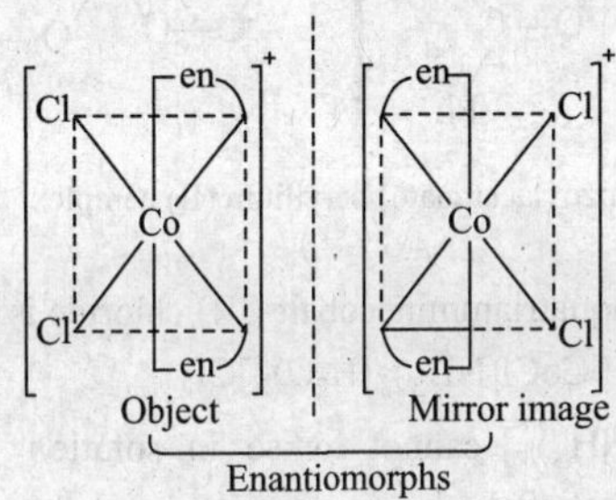

Enantiomorphs

59. *(d)* *tris*-(ethylenediamine) cobalt (III) bromide ($[Co(en)_3]Br_3$) is of type $M(AA)_3B_3$ and, hence, exhibits optical isomerism.

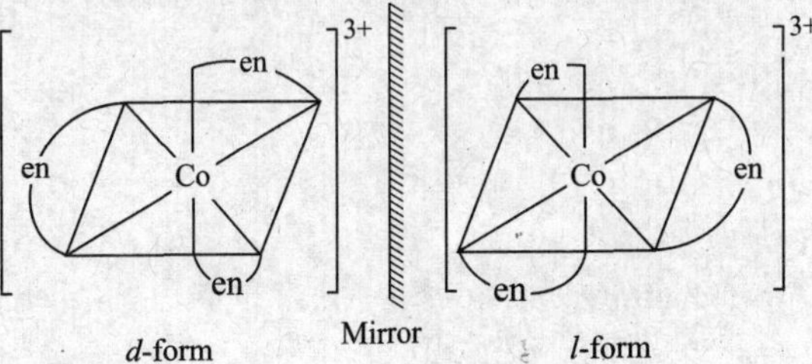

60. *(d)* Dien (diethylenetriamine) is a tridentate ligand.

$$H_2\ddot{N}(CH_2)_2—\ddot{N}H—(CH_2)_2—\ddot{N}H_2$$

61. *(b)* $[Co(C_2O_4)_3]^{3-}$ shows optical isomerism.

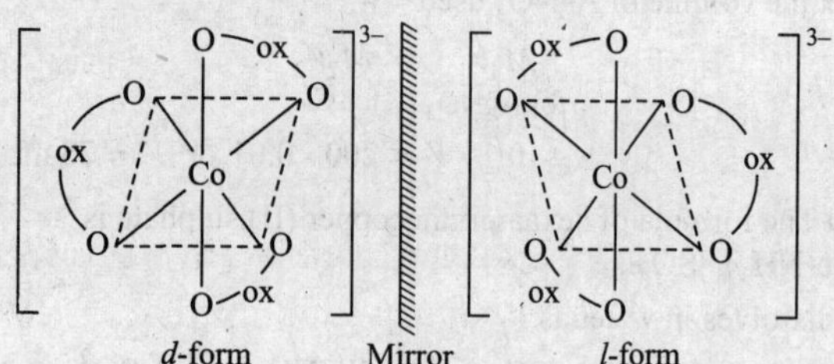

62. *(d)* $[Pt^{II}(NH_3)_2Cl_2]$ shows geometrical isomerism.

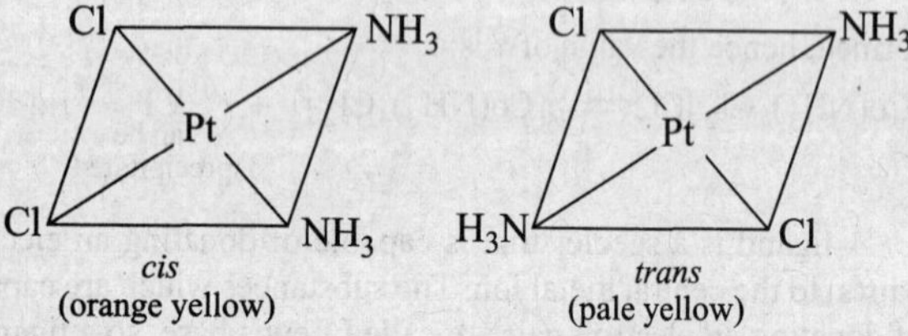

63. *(c)* Benzoylacetonato beryllium exhibitd optical isomerism as follows:

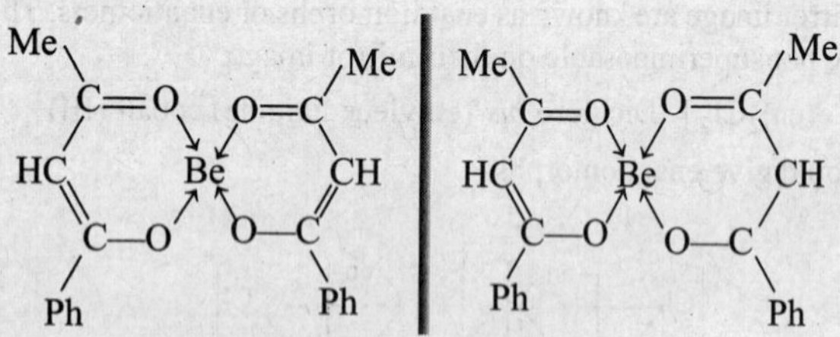

bis (benzoylacetonato) beryllium (II) complex

64. *(a)* Chlorodiaquatriamminecobalt (III) chloride is represented as

$$[CoCl(NH_3)_3(H_2O)_2]Cl_2.$$

65. *(a)* $[CoCl_3(NH_3)_3]$ cannot ionise in solution because three chloride ions satisfy both primary and secondary valencies. It will not be precipitated by the addition of $AgNO_3$.

66. *(c)* $[Co(C_2O_4)_2(NH_3)_2]^-$ has 3 isomers,

(1) *cis*-isomer-also exists in two optically active isomeric forms.
(2) *trans*-isomers

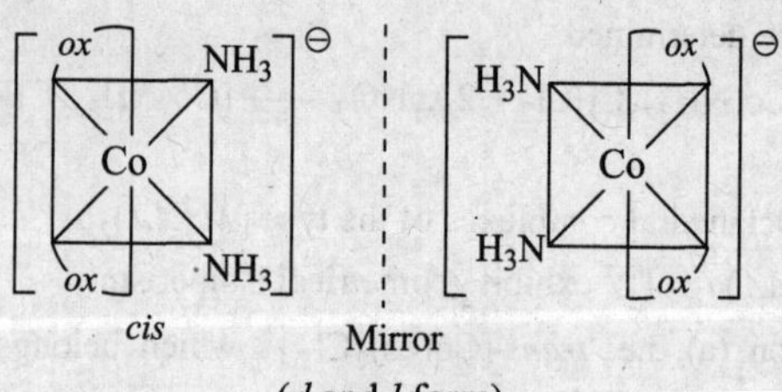

(*d* and *l* form)

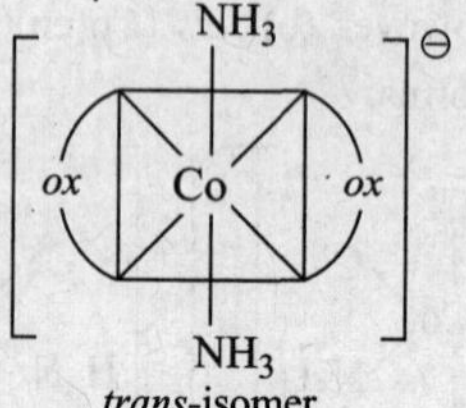

trans-isomer

67. *(a)* Coordination isomerism is caused by interchange of ligands with the metal atoms. Therefore, it is found in

$[Co(NH_3)_6][Cr(CN)_6]$ and $[Cr(NH_3)_6][Co(CN)_6]$.

68. *(c)* $CoCl_3 \cdot 6NH_3$ forms the compounds $[Co(NH_3)_6]Cl_3$ or $[Co(NH_3)_5Cl]Cl_2$. So, the above compound can form 4 or 3 ions in the solution.

69. *(a)* NO_2^- can participate in linkage isomerism because it may be bonded to metal through nitrogen or through oxygen, e.g.

$[Co(NH_3)_5NO_2]Cl_2$ Pentamminenitrito-N-cobalt (III) chloride and $[Co(NH_3)_5ONO]Cl_2$ Pentamminenitrito-O-cobalt (III) chloride

70. *(b)* Formula of tetramminedichloroplatinum (IV) chloride is

$$[Pt(NH_3)_4Cl_2]Cl_2$$

In aqueous solution, the above compound ionises as

$$[Pt(NH_3)_4Cl_2]Cl_2 \rightleftharpoons [Pt(NH_3)_4Cl_2]^{2+} + 2Cl^-$$

So, number of chloride ions is 2.

Topic 2

Bonding in Coordination Compounds

2019

1 Aluminium chloride in acidified aqueous solution forms a complex '*A*', in which hybridisation state of Al is '*B*'. What are '*A*' and '*B*', respectively? **[NEET (Odisha)]**

(a) $[Al(H_2O)_6]^{3+}, sp^3d^2$ (b) $[Al(H_2O)_4]^{3+}, sp^3$

(c) $[Al(H_2O)_4]^{3+}, dsp^2$ (d) $[Al(H_2O)_6]^{3+}, d^2sp^3$

2 The Crystal Field Stabilisation Energy (CFSE) for $[CoCl_6]^{4-}$ is $18000\ cm^{-1}$. The CFSE for $[CoCl_4]^{2-}$ will be **[NEET (Odisha)]**

(a) $6000\ cm^{-1}$ (b) $16000\ cm^{-1}$

(c) $18000\ cm^{-1}$ (d) $8000\ cm^{-1}$

3 $[Co(C_2O_4)_3]^{3-}$ is a **[AIIMS]**

(a) low spin complex (b) paramagnetic

(c) high spin (d) sp^3d^2-hybridised

4 Correct increasing order for the wavelength of absorption in the visible region for the complexes of Co^{3+} is **[AIIMS]**

(a) $[Co(CN)_6]^{3-}, [Co(NH_3)_6]^{3+}$, $[Co(NH_3)_5(H_2O)]^{3+}, [Co(NH_3)_5Cl]^{+2}$

(b) $[Co(CN)_6]^{3-}, [Co(NH_3)_5(H_2O)]^{3+}$ $[Co(NH_3)_5Cl]^{2+}, [Co(NH_3)_6]^{3+}$

(c) $[Co(NH_3)_6]^{3+}, [Co(CN)_6]^{3-}$, $[Co(NH_3)_5(H_2O)]^{3+}, [Co(NH_3)Cl]^{+2}$

(d) $[Co(NH_3)_5Cl]^{+2}, [Co(NH_3)_5(H_2O)]^{3+}$, $[Co(NH_3)_6]^{3+}, [Co(CN)_6]^{3-}$

5 What is the correct electronic configuration of the central atom in $K_4[Fe(CN)_6]$ based on crystal field theory? **[NEET]**

(a) $t_{2g}^6 e_g^0$ (b) $e^3 t_2^3$

(c) $e^4 t_2^2$ (d) $t_{2g}^4 e_g^2$

2018

6 The geometry and magnetic behaviour of the complex $[Ni(CO)_4]$ are **[NEET]**

(a) square planar geometry and paramagnetic
(b) tetrahedral geometry and diamagnetic
(c) square planar geometry and diamagnetic
(d) tetrahedral geometry and paramagnetic

7 The electronic configuration of central metal atom/ion in $[Co(CN)_6]^{3-}$ is **[AIIMS]**

(a) $t_{2g}^5 e_g^0$ (b) $t_{2g}^4 e_g^2$

(c) $t_{2g}^4 e_g^3$ (d) $t_{2g}^6 e_g^0$

8 The spin only magnetic moment of $[MnBr_4]^{2-}$ is 5.9 BM. The geometry of this complex ion is **[AIIMS]**

(a) tetrahedral (b) octahedral

(c) trigonal pyramidal (d) square planar

2017

9 Which of the following is not expected to show paramagnetism? **[JIPMER]**

(a) $[Ni(H_2O)]^{2+}$ (b) $Ni(CO)_4$

(c) $[Ni(NH_3)_4]^{2+}$ (d) $[Co(NH_3)_6]^{2+}$

10 Correct increasing order for the wavelengths of absorption in the visible region for the complexes of Co^{3+} is **[NEET]**

(a) $[Co(en)_3]^{3+}, [Co(NH_3)_6]^{3+}, [Co(H_2O)_6]^{3+}$

(b) $[Co(H_2O)_6]^{3+}, [Co(en)_3]^{3+}, [Co(NH_3)_6]^{3+}$

(c) $[Co(H_2O)_6]^{3+}, [Co(NH_3)_6]^{3+}, [Co(en)_3]^{3+}$

(d) $[Co(NH_3)_6]^{3+}, [Co(en)_3]^{3+}, [Co(H_2O)_6]^{3+}$

11 Pick out the correct statement with respect to $[Mn(CN)_6]^{3-}$. **[NEET]**

(a) It is sp^3d^2 hybridised and octahedral
(b) It is sp^3d^2 hybridised and tetrahedral
(c) It is d^2sp^3 hybridised and octahedral
(d) It is dsp^2 hybridised and square planar

2016

12 Jahn-Teller effect is not observed in high spin complexes of **[NEET Phase II]**

(a) d^7 (b) d^8 (c) d^4 (d) d^9

2015

13 Which of these statements about $[Co(CN)_6]^{3-}$ is true? **[CBSE AIPMT]**

(a) $[Co(CN)_6]^{3-}$ has no unpaired electrons and will be in a low-spin configuration
(b) $[Co(CN)_6]^{3-}$ has four unpaired electrons and will be in a low-spin configuration
(c) $[Co(CN)_6]^{3-}$ has four unpaired electrons and will be in a high-spin configuration
(d) $[Co(CN)_6]^{3-}$ has no unpaired electrons and will be in a high-spin configuration

14 Among the following complexes, the one which show zero crystal field stabilisation energy (CFSE) is **[CBSE AIPMT]**

(a) $[Mn(H_2O)_6]^{3+}$ (b) $[Fe(H_2O)_6]^{3+}$

(c) $[Co(H_2O)_6]^{2+}$ (d) $[Co(H_2O)_6]^{3+}$

15 Select the diamagnetic complex ion amongst the following complexes (Atomic number of Fe = 26, Co = 27) [MHT CET]

(a) $K_3[Fe(CN)_6]$ (b) $[Co(NH_3)_6]Cl_3$
(c) $K_3[FeF_6]$ (d) $K_3[CoF_6]$

16 The hybridisation of central metal ion in $K_2[Ni(CN)_4]$ and $K_2[NiCl_4]$ are respectively [Kerala CEE]

(a) dsp^2, sp^3 (b) sp^3, sp^3
(c) dsp^2, dsp^3 (d) sp^3, sp^3d^2
(e) sp^3d^2, d^2sp^2

17 Incorrect statement is [KCET]

(a) $[Co(NH_3)_6]^{2+}$ is paramagnetic
(b) $[MnBr_4]^{2-}$ is tetrahedral
(c) $[CoBr_2(en)_2]^-$ exhibits linkage isomerism
(d) $[Ni(NH_3)_6]^{2+}$ is not an inner orbital complex

18 In $[CoF_6]^{3-}$, Co^{3+} uses outer *d*-orbitals (4*d*) in sp^3d^2 hybridisation. The number of unpaired electrons present in complex ion is [EAMCET]

(a) 0 (b) 4 (c) 2 (d) 3

19 Crystal field theory does not explain which of the following property of coordination compounds? [EAMCET]

(a) The covalent character of the bond between metal and the ligand
(b) Magnetic property
(c) Colour
(d) Structure of coordination compounds

2013

20 A magnetic moment of 1.73 BM will be shown by one among the following. [NEET]

(a) $[Cu(NH_3)_4]^{2+}$ (b) $[Ni(CN)_4]^{2-}$
(c) $TiCl_4$ (d) $[CoCl_6]^{4-}$

21 Which of the following salts is colourless? [WB JEE]

(a) $CdCl_2$ (b) $CuSO_4 \cdot 5H_2O$
(c) $MnSO_4 \cdot 7H_2O$ (d) $NiSO_4 \cdot 7H_2O$

2012

22 Which one of the following is an outer orbital complex and exhibits paramagnetic behaviour? [CBSE AIPMT]

(a) $[Ni(NH_3)_6]^{2+}$ (b) $[Zn(NH_3)_6]^{2+}$
(c) $[Cr(NH_3)_6]^{3+}$ (d) $[Co(NH_3)_6]^{3+}$

23 Red precipitate is obtained when ethanol solution of dimethylglyoxime is added to ammoniacal Ni(II). Which of the following statements is not true? [CBSE AIPMT]

Dimethylglyoxime = $H_3C—C{=}N—OH$ / $H_3C—C{=}N—OH$ (the two C atoms bonded)

(a) Red complex has a square planar geometry
(b) Complex has symmetrical H-bonding
(c) Red complex has a tetrahedral geometry
(d) Dimethylglyoxime functions as bidentate ligand

2011

24 The *d*-electron configuration of Cr^{2+}, Mn^{2+}, Fe^{2+} and Co^{2+} are d^4, d^5, d^6 and d^7 respectively. Which one of the following will exhibit minimum paramagnetic behaviour? (Atomic number of Cr = 24, Mn = 25, Fe = 26, Co = 27) [CBSE AIPMT]

(a) $[Cr(H_2O)_6]^{2+}$ (b) $[Mn(H_2O)_6]^{2+}$
(c) $[Fe(H_2O)_6]^{2+}$ (d) $[Co(H_2O)_6]^{2+}$

25 Which of the following complex ions is diamagnetic in nature? [CBSE AIPMT]

(a) $[CoF_6]^{3-}$ (b) $[NiCl_4]^{2-}$
(c) $[Ni(CN)_4]^{2-}$ (d) $[CuCl_2]^{2-}$

26 Four transition metal octahedral complexes, (the choice given below) low spin electronic configurations arises only for [DPMT]

(a) d^1 to d^3 complexes (b) d^4 to d^7 complexes
(c) d^7 to d^9 complexes (d) d^1, d^2 and d^8 complexes

2010

27 Crystal field stabilisation energy for high spin d^4 octahedral complex is [CBSE AIPMT]

(a) $-0.6\Delta_o$ (b) $-1.8\Delta_o$ (c) $-1.6\Delta_o + P$ (d) $-1.2\Delta_o$

28 Which of the following complex ion is not expected to absorb visible light? [CBSE AIPMT]

(a) $[Ni(H_2O)_6]^{2+}$ (b) $[Ni(CN)_4]^{2-}$
(c) $[Cr(NH_3)_6]^{3+}$ (d) $[Fe(H_2O)_6]^{2+}$

29 In which of the following the magnetic character is not correct? [RPMT]

(a) $CuCl_4^{2-}$ — 1 unpaired electron
(b) $[Fe(H_2O)_6]^{2+}$ — 5 unpaired electrons
(c) $[Zn(NH_3)_2]^{2+}$ — Diamagnetic
(d) $[CoF_6]^{3-}$ — 4 unpaired electrons

30 The most stable complex among the following is [AMU]

(a) $[Pd(CN)_4]^{4-}$ (b) $[Fe(CO)_5]$
(c) $[Ni(CN)_4]^{4-}$ (d) $[Ni(CN)_4]^{3-}$

31 Choose the correct statement. [AMU]

(a) $[Co(NH_3)_6]^{2+}$ is oxidised to diamagnetic $[Co(NH_3)_6]^{3+}$ by the oxygen in air
(b) Tetrahedral complexes are more stable than octahedral complexes
(c) $[Fe(CN)_6]^{3-}$ is stable but $[FeF_6]^{3-}$ is unstable
(d) The $[Cu(NH_3)_4]^{2+}$ ion has a tetrahedral geometry and is diamagnetic

32 Which one of the following is wrongly matched? **[KCET]**

(a) $[Cu(NH_3)_4]^{2+}$ — Square planar
(b) $[Ni(CO)_4]$ — Neutral ligand
(c) $[Fe(CN)_6]^{3-}$ — sp^3d^2
(d) $[Co(en)_3]^{3+}$ — Follows EAN rule

33 The correct order of magnetic moments (spin only values in BM) among the following is
(Atomic number of Mn = 25, Fe = 26, Co = 27) **[KCET]**

(a) $[MnCl_4]^{2-} > [CoCl_4]^{2-} > [Fe(CN)_6]^{4-}$
(b) $[MnCl_4]^{2-} > [Fe(CN)_6]^{4-} > [CoCl_4]^{2-}$
(c) $[Fe(CN)_6]^{4-} > [MnCl_4]^{2-} > [CoCl_4]^{2-}$
(d) $[Fe(CN)_6]^{4-} > [CoCl_4]^{2-} > [MnCl_4]^{2-}$

34 Show the coordination number of the metal ion, its oxidation number, the number of electrons in *d*-orbitals and the number of unpaired electrons in *d*-orbitals respectively in complex $[Co(H_2O)_4SO_3]Cl$. **[Guj CET]**

(a) 6, 3, 6, 4 (b) 6, 3, 6, 0
(c) 5, 3, 6, 4 (d) 5, 3, 6, 0

35 $[Sc(H_2O)_6]^{3+}$ ion is **[JCECE]**

(a) colourless and diamagnetic
(b) coloured and octahedral
(c) colourless and paramagnetic
(d) coloured and paramagnetic

2009

36 Which of the following complex ion is expected to absorb visible light? **[CBSE AIPMT]**

(a) $[Sc(H_2O)_3(NH_3)_3]^{3+}$ (b) $[Ti(en)_2(NH_3)_2]^{4+}$
(c) $[Cr(NH_3)_6]^{3+}$ (d) $[Zn(NH_3)_6]^{2+}$

37 Which of the following coordination entities should be expected to absorb light of lowest frequency? **[AIIMS]**

(a) $[Cr(en)_3]^{3+}$ (b) $[CrCl_6]^{3-}$
(c) $[Cr(NH_3)_6]^{3+}$ (d) $[Cr(CN)_6]^{3-}$

38 **Assertion** (A) If β_4 for $[Cu(NH_3)_4]^{2+}$ is 2.1×10^{13}, its instability constant is 4.76×10^{-14}.

Reason (R) Overall dissociation equilibrium constant varies inversely with formation constant. **[AIIMS]**

(a) Both A and R are correct and R is the correct explanation of A
(b) Both A and R are correct and R is not the correct explanation of A
(c) A is correct but R is incorrect
(d) Both A and R are incorrect

39 **Assertion** (A) $K_4[Fe(CN)_6]$ is diamagnetic and $[Fe(H_2O)_6]Cl_3$ is paramagnetic.

Reason (R) Hybridisation of central metal in $K_4[Fe(CN)_6]$ is sp^3d^2, while in $[Fe(H_2O)_6]Cl_3$ is d^2sp^3. **[AIIMS]**

(a) Both A and R are correct and R is the correct explanation of A
(b) Both A and R are correct and R is not the correct explanation of A
(c) A is correct but R is incorrect
(d) Both A and R are incorrect

40 Magnetic moment of $(NH_4)_2[MnBr_4]$ is ...... BM. **[OJEE]**

(a) 5.91 (b) 4.91 (c) 3.91 (d) 2.46

41 The crystal field splitting energy for octahedral (Δ_o) and tetrahedral (Δ_t) complexes is related as **[Kerala CEE]**

(a) $\Delta_t = -\frac{1}{2}\Delta_o$ (b) $\Delta_t = -\frac{4}{9}\Delta_o$
(c) $\Delta_t = -\frac{3}{5}\Delta_o$ (d) $\Delta_t = -\frac{2}{5}\Delta_o$
(e) $\Delta_t = -\frac{9}{4}\Delta_o$

42 The species having tetrahedral shape is **[CG PMT, Haryana PMT]**

(a) $[PdCl_4]^{2-}$ (b) $[Ni(CN)_4]^{2-}$
(c) $[Pd(CN)_4]^{2-}$ (d) $[NiCl_4]^{2-}$

43 Which one of the following complex ion has the highest magnetic moment? **[J&K CET]**

(a) $[Cr(NH_3)_6]^{3+}$ (b) $[Fe(CN)_6]^{3-}$
(c) $[Fe(CN)_6]^{4-}$ (d) $[Zn(NH_3)_6]^{2+}$

44 What is (are) number(s) of unpaired electrons in the square planar $[Pt(CN)_4]^{2-}$ ion? **[AMU]**

(a) zero (b) 1 (c) 4 (d) 6

45 The magnitude of crystal field stabilisation energy in tetrahedral complexes (CFSE of Δ_t) is considerably less than that in the octahedral field because **[DUMET]**

(a) there are only four ligands instead of six so the ligand field is only 2/3 the size, hence the Δ_t is 2/3
(b) the direction of the orbitals does not coincide with the direction of the ligands. This reduce the crystal field stabilisation energy (Δ) by further 2/3
(c) Both points (a) and (b) are correct
(d) Both points (a) and (b) are incorrect

46 The crystal field stabilisation energy (CFSE) is highest for **[DUMET]**

(a) $[CoF_4]^{2-}$ (b) $[Co(NCS)_4]^{2-}$
(c) $[Co(NH_3)_6]^{3+}$ (d) $[CoCl_4]^{2-}$

2008

47 Which of the following complexes exhibit the highest paramagnetic behaviour? (where, gly = glycine, en = ethylenediammine and bpy = bipyridyl moities)
(Atomic number of Ti = 22, V = 23, Fe = 26, Co = 27) **[CBSE AIPMT]**

(a) $[V(gly)_2(OH)_2(NH_3)_2]^+$
(b) $[Fe(en)(bpy)(NH_3)_2]^{2+}$
(c) $[Co(ox)_2(OH)_2]^-$ (d) $[Ti(NH_3)_6]^{3+}$

48 In which of the following coordination entities the magnitude of Δ_o (CFSE in octahedral field) will be maximum? (Atomic number of Co = 27) **[CBSE AIPMT]**

(a) $[Co(H_2O)_6]^{3+}$ (b) $[Co(NH_3)_6]^{3+}$
(c) $[Co(CN)_6]^{3-}$ (d) $[Co(C_2O_4)_3]^{3-}$

49 **Assertion** (A) $[CoF_6]^{3-}$ is paramagnetic.
Reason (R) Co^{3+} has $3d^6$ outer electronic configuration. The unpaired electrons do not pair up because of weak field provided by F^-. **[BHU]**

(a) Both A and R are correct and R is the correct explanation of A
(b) Both A and R are correct and R is not the correct explanation of A
(c) A is correct but R is incorrect
(d) Both A and R are incorrect

50 Which of the following is false for tetrahedral complexes? **[DUMET]**

(a) Low spin (b) High spin
(c) *d-d* transition (d) Coloured

51 An octahedral complex is formed when hybrid orbitals of the following type are involved **[KCET]**

(a) sp^3 (b) dsp^2 (c) d^2sp^3 (d) sp^2d^2

52 How many electrons are present in 3*d* orbital of tetrahedral $K_2[NiCl_4]$ complex? **[Guj CET]**

(a) 8 electrons (b) 10 electrons
(c) 7 electrons (d) 6 electrons

2007

53 Among $[Ni(CO)_4]$, $[Ni(CN)_4]^{2-}$, $[NiCl_4]^{2-}$ species, the hybridisation states of Ni atom are, respectively. (Atomic number of Ni = 28) **[Manipal]**

(a) sp^3, dsp^2, dsp^2 (b) sp^3, dsp^2, sp^3
(c) sp^3, sp^3, dsp^2 (d) dsp^2, sp^3, sp

54 The geometry of $[Ni(CO)_4]$ and $[Ni(PPh_3)_2Cl_2]$ are **[Manipal]**

(a) both square planar
(b) tetrahedral and square planar respectively
(c) both tetrahedral
(d) square planar and tetrahedral respectively

55 The increasing order of the crystal field splitting power of some common ligands is **[Kerala CEE]**

(a) $H_2O < OH^- < Cl^- < F^- < CN^-$
(b) $H_2O < Cl^- < OH^- < CN^- < F^-$
(c) $CN^- < H_2O < OH^- < F^- < Cl^-$
(d) $F^- < CN^- < OH^- < Cl^- < H_2O$
(e) $Cl^- < F^- < OH^- < H_2O < CN^-$

56 Atomic number of Cr and Fe are 24 and 26 respectively. Which of the following is paramagnetic with the spin of electron? **[Punjab PMET]**

(a) $[Cr(CO)_6]$ (b) $[Fe(CO)_5]$
(c) $[Fe(CN)_6]^{4-}$ (d) $[Cr(NH_3)_6]^{3+}$

57 What will be the theoretical value of magnetic momentum (μ), when CN^- ligands join Fe^{3+} ion to yield complex? **[Guj CET]**

(a) 3.87 BM (b) 2.83 BM
(c) 1.73 BM (d) 5.92 BM

2006

58 $[Cr(H_2O)_6]Cl_3$ (at. no. of Cr = 24) has a magnetic moment of 3.83 BM, the correct distribution of 3*d*-electrons in the chromium of the complex is **[CBSE AIPMT]**

(a) $3d^1_{x^2-y^2}, 3d^1_{z^2}, 3d^1_{xz}$ (b) $3d^1_{xy}, 3d^1_{x^2-y^2}, 3d^1_{yz}$
(c) $3d^1_{xy}, 3d^1_{zy}, 3d^1_{zx}$ (d) $3d^1_{xy}, 3d^1_{yz}, 3d^1_{z^2}$

59 The pair in which both species have same magnetic moment (spin only value) is **[AIIMS]**

(a) $[Cr(H_2O)_6]^{2+}, [CoCl_4]^{2-}$
(b) $[Cr(H_2O)_6]^{2+}, [Fe(H_2O)_6]^{2+}$
(c) $[Mn(H_2O)_6]^{2+}, [Cr(H_2O)_6]^{2+}$
(d) $[CoCl_4]^{2-}, [Fe(H_2O)_6]^{2+}$

60 Among the following, the species having square planar geometry for central atom are **[AIIMS]**

I. XeF_4 II. SF_4
III. $[NiCl_4]^{2-}$ IV. $[PtCl_4]^{2-}$

(a) I and IV (b) I and II (c) II and III (d) III and IV

61 Among the following complexes, which has a magnetic moment 5.9 BM?
$Ni(CO)_4$, $[Fe(H_2O)_6]^{2+}$, $[Co(NH_3)_6]^{3+}$, $[MnBr_4]^{2-}$, $[Zn(NH_3)_4]^{2+}$ **[Kerala CEE]**

(a) $Ni(CO)_4$ (b) $[Fe(H_2O)_6]^{2+}$
(c) $[Co(NH_3)_6]^{3+}$ (d) $[MnBr_4]^{2-}$
(e) $[Zn(NH_3)_4]^{2+}$

62 The metal ion in complex *A* has EAN identical to the atomic number of krypton. *A* is (atomic number of Cr = 24, Fe = 26, Pd = 46) **[J&K CET]**

(a) $[Pd(NH_3)_6]Cl_4$ (b) $[Cr(NH_3)_5Cl]SO_4$
(c) $Na_4[Fe(CN)_6]$ (d) $K_3[Fe(CN)_6]$

2005

63 The correct order for the wavelength of absorption in the visible region is **[AIIMS]**

(a) $[Ni(NO_2)_6]^{4-} < [Ni(NH_3)_6]^{2+} < [Ni(H_2O)_6]^{2+}$
(b) $[Ni(NO_2)_6]^{4-} < [Ni(H_2O)_6]^{2+} < [Ni(NH_3)_6]^{2+}$
(c) $[Ni(H_2O)_6]^{2+} < [Ni(NH_3)_6]^{2+} < [Ni(NO_2)_6]^{4-}$
(d) $[Ni(NH_3)_6]^{2+} < [Ni(H_2O)_6]^{2+} < [Ni(NO_2)_6]^{4-}$

64 **Assertion** (A) Potassium ferrocyanide is diamagnetic, whereas potassium ferricyanide is paramagnetic.
Reason (R) Crystal field splitting in ferrocyanide ion is greater than that of ferricyanide ion. **[AIIMS]**

(a) Both A and R are correct and the R is the correct explanation of the A
(b) Both A and R are correct but the R is not the correct explanation of the A
(c) A is correct but R is incorrect
(d) Both A and R are incorrect

65 Match the following columns. [Kerala CEE]

Column I (Complex)	Column II (Structure and magnetic moment)
A. $[Ag(NH_3)_2]^+$	1. Square planar and 1.73 BM
B. $[Co(NH_3)_6]^{3+}$	2. Linear and 0
C. $[Fe(CN)_6]^{3-}$	3. Octahedral and 0
D. $[Cu(NH_3)_4]^{2+}$	4. Octahedral and 0
E. $[Fe(CN)_6]^{4-}$	5. Octahedral and 1.73 BM

Codes

	A	B	C	D	E
(a)	1	2	3	4	5
(b)	1	3	2	5	4
(c)	2	4	5	1	3
(d)	5	4	3	2	1
(e)	4	2	5	3	1

Answers

1. (a)	2. (d)	3. (a)	4. (a)	5. (a)	6. (b)	7. (d)	8. (a)	9. (b)	10. (a)
11. (c)	12. (b)	13. (a)	14. (b)	15. (b)	16. (a)	17. (c)	18. (b)	19. (a)	20. (a)
21. (a)	22. (a)	23. (c)	24. (d)	25. (c)	26. (b)	27. (a)	28. (b)	29. (b)	30. (b)
31. (a)	32. (c)	33. (a)	34. (a)	35. (a)	36. (c)	37. (b)	38. (a)	39. (c)	40. (a)
41. (b)	42. (d)	43. (a)	44. (a)	45. (c)	46. (c)	47. (c)	48. (c)	49. (a)	50. (a)
51. (c)	52. (a)	53. (b)	54. (c)	55. (e)	56. (d)	57. (c)	58. (c)	59. (c)	60. (a)
61. (d)	62. (c)	63. (a)	64. (c)	65. (c)					

Explanations

1. *(a)* Aluminium chloride in acidified aqueous solution forms an octahedral complex. Aqueous solution is mostly water and when the compound is dissolved in acidified aqueous solution, the water fills its vacancies and an octahedral complex, '*A*' which is $[Al(H_2O)_6]^{3+}$ is formed.

$$Al(13) = 1s^2, 2s^2, 2p^6, 3s^2, 3p^1$$

$$Al^{3+} = 1s^2, 2s^2, 2p^6.$$

Al^{3+} = 2s [↿⇂] 2p [↿⇂][↿⇂][↿⇂]

$[Al(H_2O)_6]^{3+}$ = 2s [↿⇂] 2p [↿⇂][↿⇂][↿⇂]

3s [××] 3p [××][××][××] 3d [××][××][ ][ ][ ]

sp^3d^2 hybridisation

$\therefore$ $[Al(H_2O)_6]^{3+}$ has sp^3d^2 hybridisation.

2. *(d)* $[CoCl_6]^{4-}$ is octahedral while $[CoCl_4]^{2-}$ is a tetrahedral complex.

$$\Delta_{octahedral} = 18000\ cm^{-1}$$

We know that,

$$\Delta_{tetrahedral} = \frac{4}{9}\Delta_{octahedral}$$

$$= \frac{4}{9} \times 18000\ cm^{-1} = 8000\ cm^{-1}$$

Hence, option (d) is correct.

3. *(a)* Oxalate $(C_2O_4^{2-})$ is a bidentate strong field ligand, thus it can use six orbitals of Co^{3+} ion having d^2sp^3-hybridisation. In $[Co(C_2O_4)_3]^{3-}$, Co^{3+} has all the paired electrons, therefore it is a low spin complex.

Hence, option (a) is correct.

4. *(a)* The wavelength of absorption in visible region for a complex (e.g. Co^{3+}) depends on the nature of ligand, i.e. stronger be the ligand (i.e. higher the value of Δ_o) lower is the wavelength.

$$\text{Wavelength } (\lambda) \propto \frac{1}{\infty}$$

$\therefore$ Strength of ligands in the spectrochemical series are in order:

$$CN^- > NH_3 > H_2O > Cl^-.$$

Therefore, the correct increasing order for wavelength of absorption is, $[Co(CN)_6]^{3-}, [Co(NH_3)_6]^{3+}, [Co(NH_3)_5(H_2O)]^{3+}, [Co(NH_3)_5Cl]^{2+}$

Thus, option (a) is the correct.

5. *(a)* In $K_4[Fe(CN)_6]$,

$$Fe^{2+} = [Ar]3d^6 4s^0.$$

CN^- is a strong field ligand and as it approaches the metal ion, the electrons must pair up.

The splitting of the *d*-orbitals in two sets orbitals in an octahedral complex, $K_4[Fe(CN)_6]$ may be represented as :

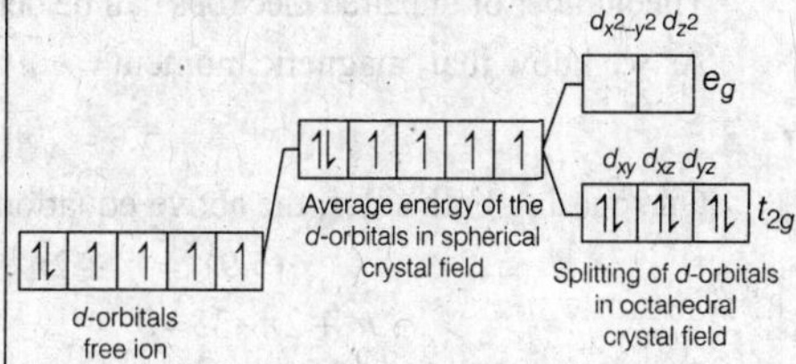

Hence, the electronic configuration of the central atom in $K_4[Fe(CN)_6]$ is $t_{2g}^6 e_g^0$.

6. *(b)* The complexes having sp^3-hybridisation are tetrahedral while having dsp^2-hybridisation are square planar. The magnetic behaviour of complexes can be paramagnetic or diamagnetic based on the presence or absence of unpaired electrons, respectively.

Electronic configuration of Ni ($Z = 28$) is $[Ar]_{18}\ 3d^8 4s^2$. Due to presence of CO (neutral ligand), oxidation state of Ni in $[Ni(CO)_4]$ is 0.

Ni-atom = 3d: ⥮ ⥮ ⥮ 1 1 | 4s: ⥮ | 4p: ☐ ☐ ☐

Since, CO is a strong field ligand, it pairs up the unpaired electrons of Ni.

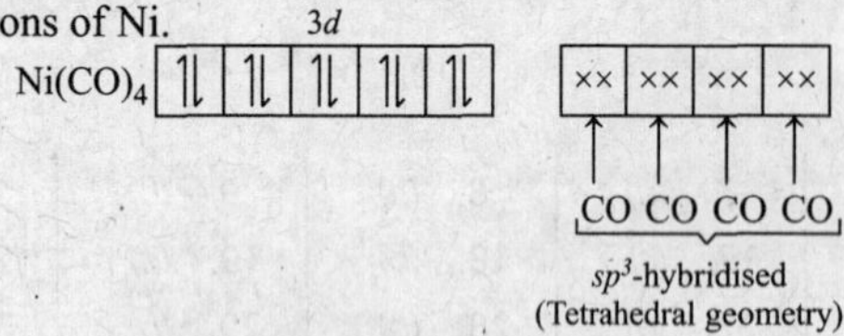

Since, all the electrons are paired, $[Ni(CO)_4]$ is diamagnetic in nature.

7. *(d)* $[Co(CN)_6]^{3-}$ contains Co^{3+} as central metal ion.

The electronic configuration of Co^{3+} ion $= [Ar]_{18}\ 3d^6$

$$Co^{3+} = 3d^6 \text{ (or } t_{2g}^6\, e_g^0)$$

The splitting in octahedral field is shown below:

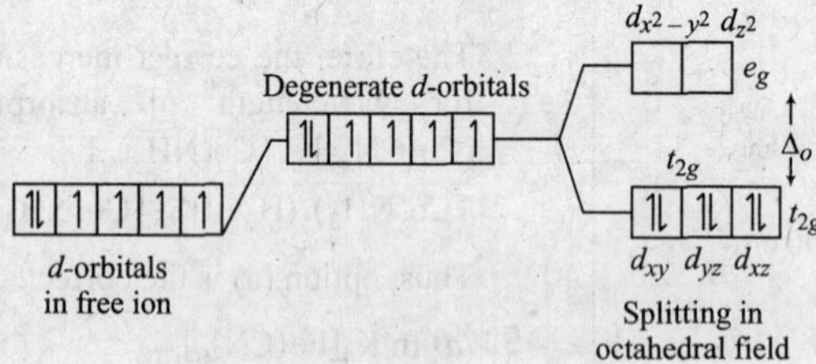

8. *(a)* Since, the coordination number of Mn^{2+} ion in the complex ion is 4, it will have either tetrahedral (sp^3-hybridisation) or square planar (dsp^2-hybridisation) geometry. But the fact that the magnetic moment of the complex ion is 5.9BM suggests that it should have tetrahedral geometry rather than square planar because of the presence of five unpaired electrons in the *d*-orbitals.

The number of unpaired electrons can be determined as follows:

As we know that, magnetic moment $= \sqrt{n(n+2)}$

$$5.9 = \sqrt{n(n+2)}$$

On squaring both sides, the above equation becomes

$$(5.9)^2 = n^2 + 2n$$

$$n^2 + 2n - 35 = 0$$

On solving the above equation, we get $n=5$

9. *(b)* $Ni(CO)_4$ due to absence of unpaired electrons does not show paramagnetism.

$$Ni \rightarrow [Ar]_{18}\ 3d^8 4s^2$$

10. *(a)* Wavelength (λ) of absorption is inversely proportional to CFSE (Δ_o value) of ligands attached with the central metal ion

i.e. $$\lambda \propto \frac{1}{\Delta_o}$$

According to spectrochemical series,

$I^- < Br^- < S^{2-} < SCN^- < Cl^- < F^- < OH^-$
$< C_2O_4^{2-} < O^{2-} < H_2O < NCS^- < NH_3 < en < NO_2^- < CN^-$

Weak field ligands ⟶ Increasing order of Δ_0 ⟶ Strong field ligands

The CFSE of ligands attached with Co^{3+} ion is in the order en > NH_3 > H_2O (From spectrochemical series).

$\because$ Wavelength of absorbed light $(\lambda) \propto \frac{1}{\Delta_o}$

$\therefore$ The order of wavelength of absorption in the visible region will be : en < NH_3 < H_2O

or, $[Co(en)_3]^{3+} < [Co(NH_3)_6]^{3+} < [Co(H_2O)_6]^{3+}$

11. *(c)* $[Mn(CN)_6]^{3-}$ is d^2sp^3-hybridised and octahedral. In $[Mn(CN)_6]^{3-}$, Mn is in +3 oxidation state.

$Mn^{3+} = 3d^4\ 4s^0$

Orbitals of Mn^{3+} ion = 3d: 1 1 1 1 ☐ | 4s: ☐ | 4p: ☐ ☐ ☐

$[Mn(CN)_6]^{3-}$ = 3d: ⥮ 1 1 | ×× ×× ×× ×× ×× ××

d^2sp^3-hybridised (Octahedral)

12. *(b)* Jahn-Teller distortion is observed in those octahedral complexes in which *d*-electrons are filled unsymmetrically.

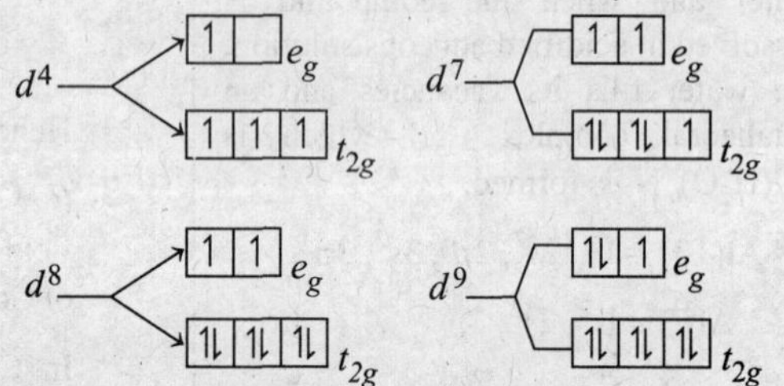

Except d^8, all are unsymmetrically filled, thus d^8 complex will not show Jahn-Teller distortion.

13. *(a)* $[Co(CN)_6]^{3-}$, $\quad Co^{3+} = 1s^2\ 2s^2\ 2p^6\ 3s^2\ 3p^6\ 3d^6$

CN^- is a strong field ligand and as it approaches the metal ion, the electrons must pair up. As the ligand approach to the metal ion, the *d*-orbitals split into two sets of orbitals in an octahedral complex. $[Co(CN)_6]^{3-}$ may be represented as here, for d^6 ions, three electrons first enter orbitals with parallel spin and the remaining may pair up in t_{2g} orbital giving rise to low spin complex (strong ligand) field.

$\therefore [Co(CN)_6]^{3-}$ has no unpaired electron and will be in a low spin configuration.

14. *(b)* CFSE for octahedral complex $[Fe(H_2O)_6]^{3+}$ is given by

For Fe^{3+}, $[3d^5] \rightarrow t_{2g}^3 e_g^2$

$$CFSE = [-0.4 t_{2g} + 0.6 e_g]$$

$$CFSE = [(-0.4 \times 3) + (2 \times 0.6)] = 0$$

15. *(b)* Coordination compound/ion having unpaired electron is paramagnetic in nature while if it has all the electrons paired, it is diamagnetic.

(a) $K_3[Fe(CN)_6]$, i.e. $[Fe(CN)_6]^{3-}$ ion

$_{26}Fe = [Ar]3d^6, 4s^2 \Rightarrow Fe^{3+} = [Ar]3d^5, 4s^0$

$3d^5$ $4s^0$ $4p^0$

Fe^{3+} = | 1 | 1 | 1 | 1 | 1 | | | | | |

$3d$

$[Fe(CN)_6]^{3-}$ = | 1l | 1l | 1 | ×× | ×× | ×× | ×× | ×× | ×× |

CN^- CN^- CN^- CN^- CN^- CN^-

d^2sp^3-hybridised

(b) $[Co(NH_3)_6]Cl_3$, i.e. $[Co(NH_3)_6]^{3+}$ ion

$_{27}Co = [Ar]3d^7, 4s^2$

$\Rightarrow$ $Co^{3+} = [Ar]3d^6, 4s^0$

$3d^6$ $4s^0$ $4p^0$

Co^{3+} = | 1l | 1 | 1 | 1 | 1 | | | | |

$3d$

$[Co(NH_3)_6]^{3+}$ = | 1l | 1l | 1l | ×× | ×× | ×× | ×× | ×× | ×× |

NH_3 NH_3 NH_3 NH_3 NH_3 NH_3

d^2sp^3-hybridised

(c) $K_3[FeF_6]$, i.e. FeF_6^{3-} ion

$_{26}Fe = [Ar]3d^6, 4s^2 \Rightarrow Fe^{3+} = [Ar]3d^5, 4s^0$

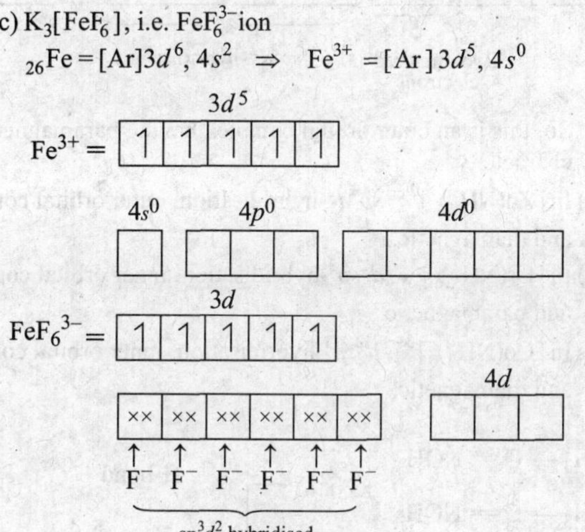

(d) $K_3[CoF_6]$, i.e. CoF_6^{3-} ion

$_{27}Co = [Ar]3d^7, 4s^2 \Rightarrow Co^{3+} = [Ar]3d^6 4s^0$

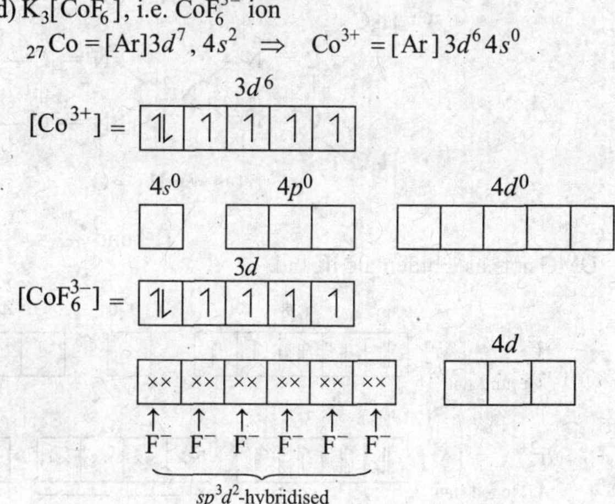

Therefore, $[Co(NH_3)_6]Cl_3$ is diamagnetic in nature.

16. *(a)* In both the complexes Ni is present as Ni^{2+}.

$Ni^{2+} = [Ar]3d^8, 4s^0, 4p^0$

$3d^8$ $4s^0$ $4p^0$

Ni^{2+} = | 1l | 1l | 1l | 1 | 1 | | | | |

CN^- being strong field ligand, pair up the unpaired electrons of Ni^{2+} and hence $4CN^-$ ions will occupy one $3d$, one $4s$ and two $4p$ orbitals, i.e. hybridisation is dsp^2.

But Cl^- is a weak field ligand and is not capable to pair up the unpaired electrons of Ni^{2+}. Hence, the orbitals available for it are one $4s$ and three $4p$, i.e. hybridisation of the complex is sp^3.

17. *(c)*

(a) In $[Co(NH_3)_6]^{2+}$ ion, Co is present as Co^{2+}. NH_3 being strong field ligand, pair up the unpaired electrons.

Electronic configuration of $Co^{2+} = 3d^7, 4s^0, 4p^0$

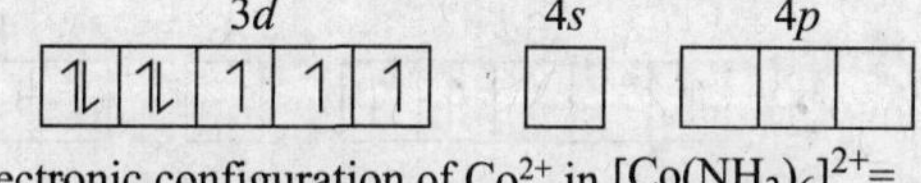

Electronic configuration of Co^{2+} in $[Co(NH_3)_6]^{2+}$=

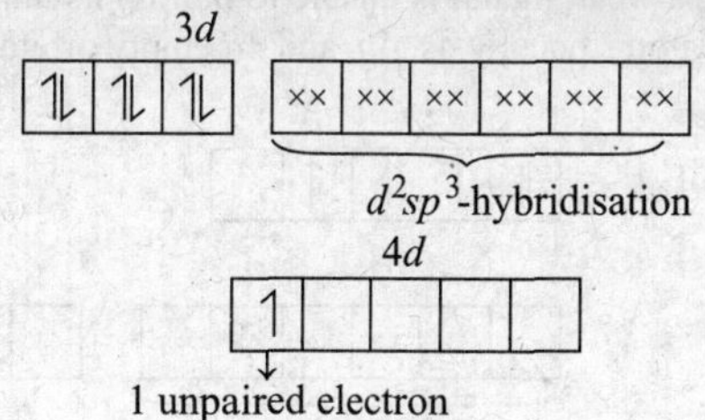

Due to the presence of one unpaired electron, $[Co(NH_3)_6]^{2+}$ is paramagnetic.

(b) In $[MnBr_4]^{2-}$ ion, Mn is present as Mn^{2+}. Br, being weak field ligand, leave unpaired electrons of the metal ion as such. Electronic configuration of $Mn^{2+} = 3d^5, 4s^0, 4p^0$.

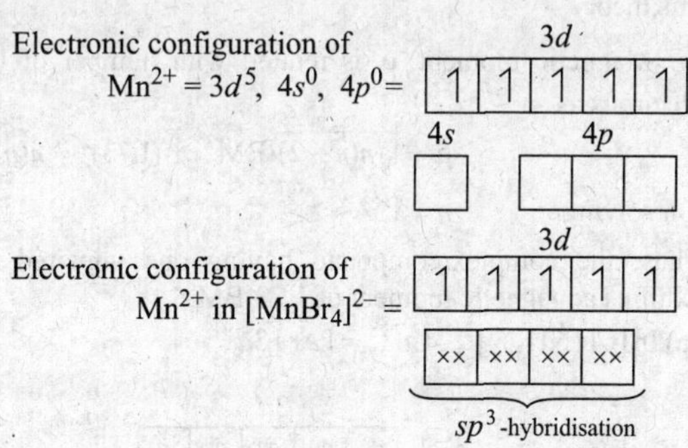

Due to sp^3-hybridisation, shape of $[MnBr_4]^{2-}$ is tetrahedral.

(c) Linkage isomerism occurs when two or more different atoms in a monodentate ligand may function as a donor.

Therefore, $[CoBr_2(en)_2]^-$ does not exhibit linkage isomerism.

(d) In $[Ni(NH_3)_6]^{2+}$ ion, Ni is present as Ni^{2+}.

Electronic configuration of $Ni^{2+} = [Ar]3d^8, 4s^0$

$3d$ $4s$

Ni^{2+} = | 1l | 1l | 1l | 1 | 1 | |

NH_3 is a strong field ligand, but cannot pair up electrons as if it pair up electron then hybridisation comes out to be dsp^3d which is not possible. Hence, here no pairing of e^- takes places.

Electronic configuration of Ni in $[Ni(NH_3)_6]^{2+}$

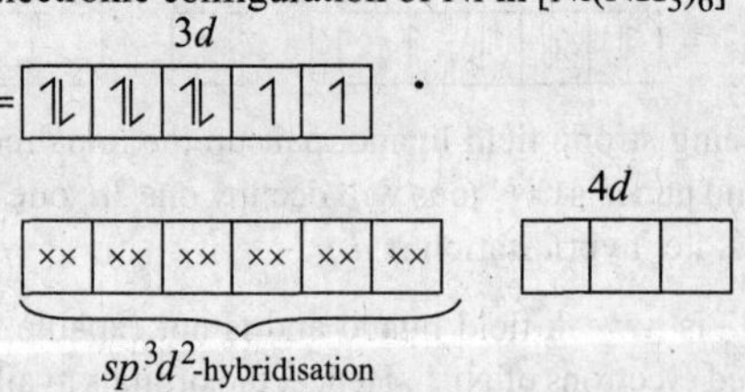

Since, $(n-1)\,d$, i.e. $3d$ orbital does not take part in hybridisation, it is not an inner orbital complex. It is an outer orbital complex.

18. *(b)* $[CoF_6]^{3-}$

Here, Co is present in + 3 oxidation state

$$_{27}Co = [Ar]3d^7, 4s^2 \Rightarrow Co^{3+} = [Ar]\,3d^6, 4s^0$$

Co^{3+} = 3d [⇅ | ↑ | ↑ | ↑ | ↑] 4s [ ] 4p [| |]

F being a weak ligand is unable to pair up its unpaired electrons thus, F atoms occupy $4s$, $4p$, and $4d$ empty orbitals as

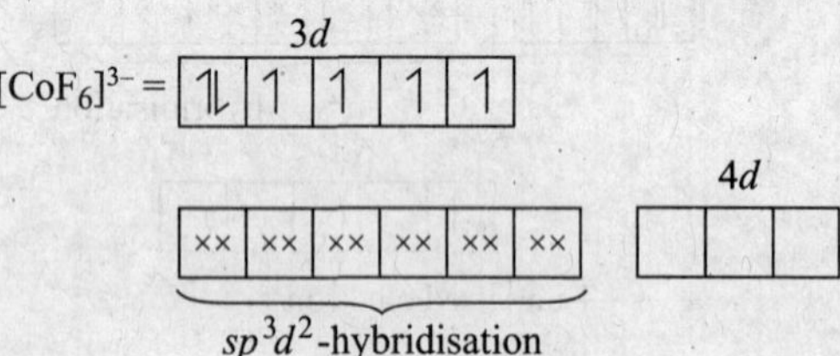

Hence, number of unpaired electrons in complex ion is 4.

19. *(a)* The crystal field theory can explain the spectra, i.e. colour magnetic property and structure of coordination compounds. However, the position of intensities of spectral bands (or covalent character of covalent bonds) cannot be explained on the basis of this theory.

20. *(a)* Magnetic moment, μ is related with number of unpaired electrons as

$$\mu = \sqrt{n(n+2)}\text{ BM} \Rightarrow (1.73)^2 = n(n+2)$$

On solving, $n = 1$

Thus, the complex/compound having one unpaired electron exhibits a magnetic moment of 1.73 BM.

(a) In $[Cu(NH_3)_4]^{2+}$, $Cu^{2+} = [Ar]\,3d^9$

Cu^{2+} = 3d [⇅ | ⇅ | ⇅ | ⇅ | ↑]

(Although in the presence of strong field ligand NH_3, the unpaired electrons get excited to higher energy level but it still remains unpaired).

(b) In $[Ni(CN)_4]^{2-}$, $Ni^{2+} = [Ar]\,3d^8$

Ni^{2+} = 3d [⇅ | ⇅ | ⇅ | ↑ | ↑]

But CN^- being strong field ligand pair up the unpaired electrons and hence, in this complex, number of unpaired electrons = 0

(c) In $[TiCl_4]$, $Ti^{+4} = [Ar]$ no unpaired electron.

(d) In $[CoCl_6]^{4-}$, $Co^{2+} = [Ar]3d^7$

Co^{2+} = 3d [⇅ | ⇅ | ↑ | ↑ | ↑]

It contains three unpaired electrons.

Thus, $[Cu(NH_3)_4]^{2+}$ is the complex that exhibits a magnetic moment of 1.73 BM.

21. *(a)* $CdCl_2$ has Cd^{2+} ion $(4d^{10})$ which is colourless. Here, d^{10} configuration suggests that it has completely filled d-orbital. And, hence there will be no d-d transition. As a result, it is colourless.

22. *(a)* Outer orbital complex utilises d-orbitals for bonding and exhibits paramagnetic behaviour, only if it has unpaired electrons.

(a) In $[Ni(NH_3)_6]^{2+}$, $Ni^{2+} = [Ar]\,3d^8\,4s^0$

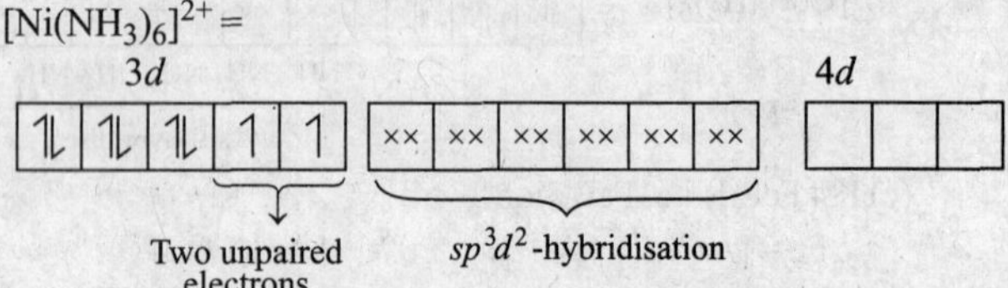

So, this is an outer orbital complex having paramagnetic character.

(b) In $[Zn(NH_3)_6]^{2+}$, sp^3d^2-hybridisation, outer orbital complex and diamagnetic.

(c) In $[Cr(NH_3)_6]^{3+}$, d^2sp^3-hybridisation, inner orbital complex and paramagnetic.

(d) In $[Co(NH_3)_6]^{3+}$, d^2sp^3-hybridisation, inner orbital complex and diamagnetic.

23. *(c)*

$CH_3—C{=}NOH$ / $CH_3—C{=}NOH$ $+ Ni^{2+}$ → (H-bond, O······H—O, H_3C, C=N, Ni^{2+}, N=C—CH_3, $^-$O······H—O, H-bond)

DMG acts as a bidentate ligand.

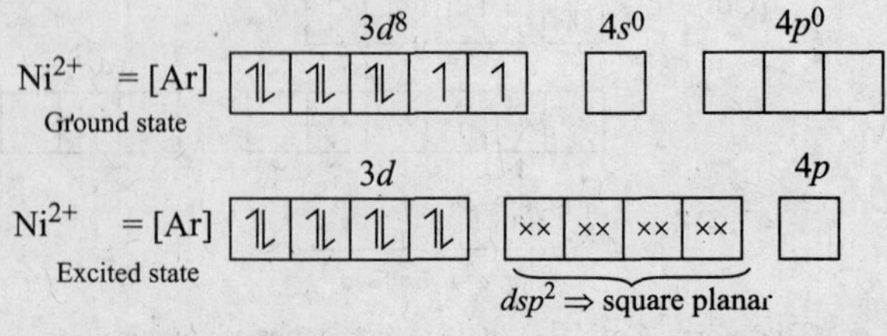

24. *(d)* Smaller the number of unpaired electrons, smaller is the paramagnetic behaviour.

$$Co^{2+} \longrightarrow 3d^7, 4s^0$$

3d

Co^{2+} = ⇅ ⇅ 1 1 1, having minimum number of unpaired electrons.

Thus, Co^{2+} has minimum paramagnetic behaviour.

25. *(c)* Ni has dsp^2-hybridisation where CN^- is a strong field ligand.

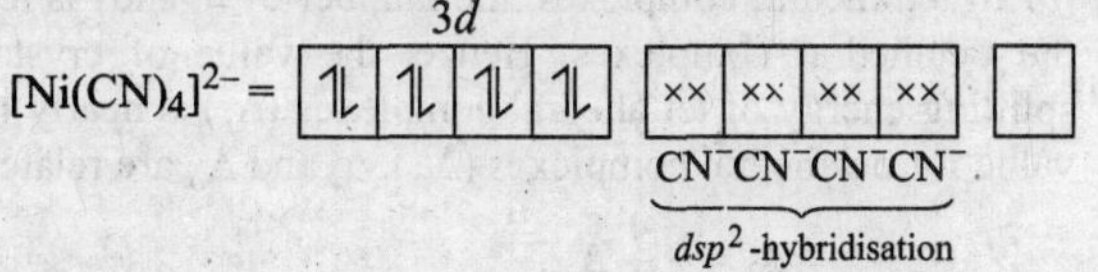

Since, all the electrons are paired, it is diamagnetic.

26. *(b)* The distribution of electrons of d^1, d^2, d^3, d^8, d^9 in t_{2g} and e_g sets both for strong and weak ligands field is same.

But for d^4, d^5, d^6 and d^7 there is difference in the arrangement of electrons in weak and strong field ligands. A weak ligand will have greater number of unpaired electrons.

27. *(a)* For high spin d^4 complex, $t_{2g}^{\ 3} e_g^{\ 1}$

$$CFSE = 3(-0.4) + 1(0.6) = -0.6\Delta_O$$

28. *(b)* $[Ni(CN)_4]^{2-}$ does not contain unpaired electrons, so cannot absorb visible light.

29. *(b)* In $[Fe(H_2O)_6]^{2+}$, the Fe(II) ion has $3d^6$ electronic configuration and pairing of electrons in 3*d*-orbital does not take place due to the presence of weak field ligand, H_2O.

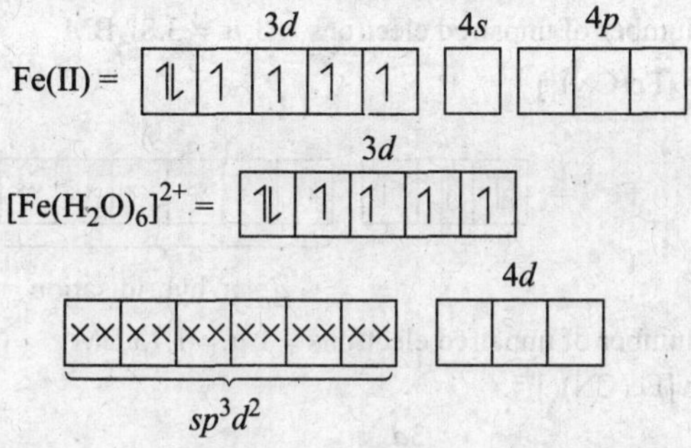

Hence, there are four unpaired electrons in $[Fe(H_2O)_6]^{2+}$ ion.

30. *(b)* Stability of a complex depends upon the strength of ligand and charge of the central metal ion.

Stability of complex ∝ strength of ligand

∝ charge of central metal ion.

Among the given complexes, in $[Ni(CN)_4]^{3-}$ the charge of central metal ion is highest, i.e. + 1 while CO is the strongest field ligand. Hence, $[Fe(CO)_5]$ is the most stable complex among the given complexes.

31. *(a)* (a) $[Co(NH_3)_6]^{2+} = [Ar]\,3d^7$

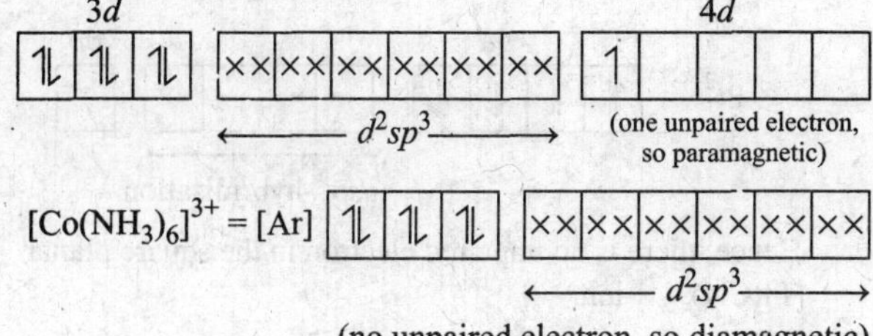

(b) Tetrahedral complexes are less stable than octahedral complexes.

(c) $[Fe(CN)_6]^{3-}$ and $[FeF_6]^{3-}$ both are stable but former is more stable, since it forms inner orbital complex.

(d) $[Cu(NH_3)_4]^{2+}$ has square planar geometry and is paramagnetic.

32. *(c)* (a) In $[Cu(NH_3)_4]^{2+}$, Cu is present as Cu^{2+}.

$$Cu^{2+} = [Ar]\,3d^9, 4s^0$$

3d 4p

$[Cu(NH_3)_4]^{2+}$ = [Ar] ⇅ ⇅ ⇅ ⇅ | ×× ×× ×× ×× | 1

dsp^2-hybridisation ⇒ square planar geometry

(NH_3 being a strong field ligand shifts one electron from 3*d*-orbital to 4*p*-orbital.)

(b) In $[Ni(CO)_4]$, CO is a neutral ligand.

(c) In $[Fe(CN)_6]^{3-}$, Fe is present as Fe^{3+}.

$$Fe^{3+} = [Ar]\,3d^5, 4s^0 \Rightarrow [Fe(CN)_6]^{3-}$$

$3d^5$

[Ar] = ⇅ ⇅ 1 | ×× ×× ×× ×× ×× ××

d^2sp^3-hybridisation

Thus, its hybridisation is d^2sp^3, not sp^3d^2, i.e. it is an inner-orbital complex.

(d) $[Co(en)_3]^{3+}$ contains total 36 electrons, i.e. follows EAN rule.

33. *(a)* As the number of unpaired electrons in the central atom increases, magnetic moment of the complex increases.

3d

In $[MnCl_4]^{2-} \Rightarrow Mn_4^{2+}$ = [Ar] 1 1 1 1 1 (Mn = 25)

(five unpaired electrons)

3d

In $[CoCl_4]^{2-} \Rightarrow Co^{2+}$ = [Ar] ⇅ ⇅ 1 1 1 (Co = 27)

(three unpaired electrons)

3d

In $[Fe(CN)_6]^{4-} \Rightarrow Fe^{2+}$ = [Ar] ⇅ ⇅ ⇅ (Fe = 26)

(no unpaired electrons)

∴ The order of magnetic moments is :

$$[MnCl_4]^{2-} > [CoCl_4]^{2-} > [Fe(CN)_6]^{4-}.$$

34. *(a)* Coordination number is the number of monodentate ligands in the coordination sphere. Hence, the coordination number of cobalt ion in $[Co(H_2O)_4SO_3]Cl$ is 6.

Let, the oxidation number of Co be *x*

$$x + 4(0) + (-2) + (-1) = 0$$

$$x + 0 - 2 - 1 = 0 \Rightarrow x = 3$$

Number of electrons in *d*-orbital are six.

$3d^6$

Co^{3+} = ⇅ 1 1 1 1

Number of unpaired electrons in d-orbital are 4 because H_2O is a weak ligand and therefore, pairing of d-electrons in d-orbital is not possible. So, correct sequence is 6, 3, 6, 4.

35. *(a)* In $[Sc(H_2O)_6]^{3+}$, Sc (21) $3d^1, 4s^2$

oxidation state of Sc is + 3.

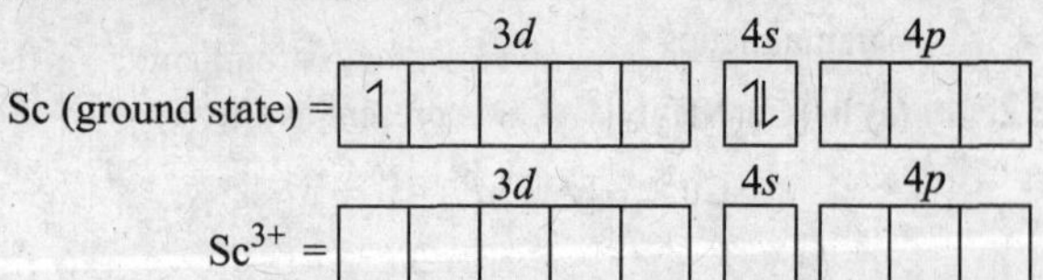

$\because$ Sc^{3+} has no unpaired electrons.

$\therefore$ $[Sc(H_2O)_6]^{3+}$ is diamagnetic and colourless.

36. *(c)* The oxidation state of Cr in $[Cr(NH_3)_6]^{+3}$ is +3. Its electronic configuration will be $3d^3$.

3d

$[Cr(NH_3)_6]^{3+}$ = | 1 | 1 | 1 | | | xx | xx | xx | xx | xx | xx |

d^2sp^3 (electrons donated by NH_3 ligand)

Since, $[Cr(NH_3)_6]^{3+}$ has three unpaired electrons so, it will absorb visible light. All the other complex ions do not have any unpaired electrons. That's why they do not absorb visible light.

37. *(b)* The coordination entity, for which crystal field splitting is smallest, absorbs light of lowest frequency. Weaker the ligand field strength, smallest will be the crystal field splitting. The order of field strength of various ligands is as,

$$CN^- > en > NH_3 > Cl^-$$

Hence, $[CrCl_6]^{3-}$ due to the presence of weak field Cl^- ligand absorbs light of lowest frequency.

38. *(a)* Formation constant, $\beta_4 = \dfrac{1}{\text{dissociation constant}}$

Dissociation constant is also called instability constant.

$$= \frac{1}{4.76 \times 10^{-14}} = 2.1 \times 10^{13}.$$

39. *(c)* In $K_4[Fe(CN)_6]$, Fe is present as Fe^{2+}.

$Fe = [Ar]\,3d^6, 4s^2$, $Fe^{2+} = [Ar]\,3d^6, 4s^0$

3d

$[Fe(CN)_6]^{4-}$ = [Ar] | ⥮ | ⥮ | ⥮ | | | xx | xx | xx | xx | xx | xx |

d^2sp^3-hybridisation

Since, all elecrons are paired, it is diamagnetic in nature.

In $[Fe(H_2O)_6]Cl_3$, Fe is present as Fe^{3+}

$$Fe^{3+} = [Ar]\,3d^5, 4s^0$$

$[Fe(H_2O)_6]^{3+}$ =

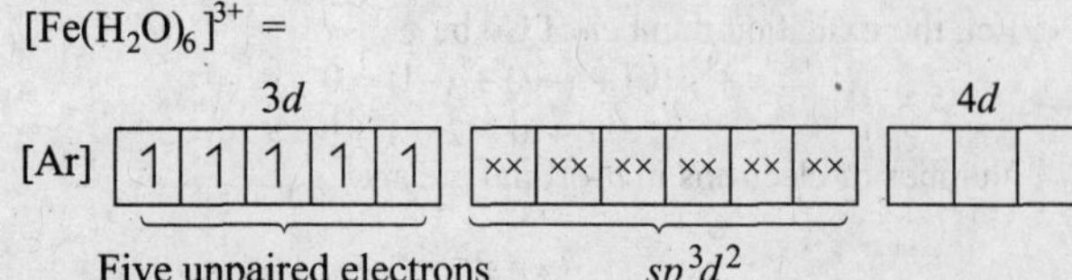

Since, it contains five unpaired electrons, it is paramagnetic in nature.

40. *(a)* $[MnBr_4]^{2-}$ has Mn in + 2 state (d^5 ion) and in sp^3-hybridised form.

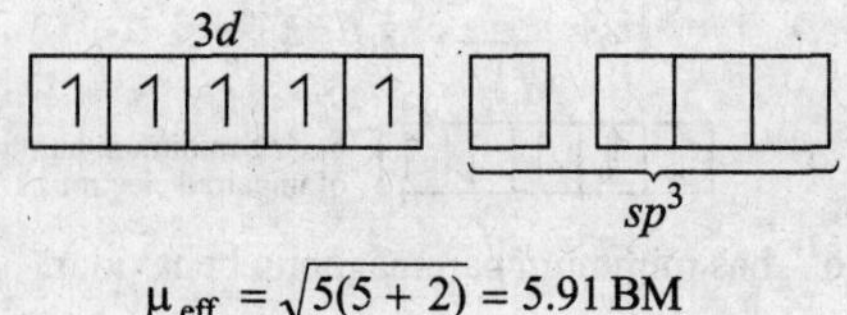

$$\mu_{eff} = \sqrt{5(5+2)} = 5.91 \text{ BM}$$

41. *(b)* In tetrahedral complexes, the number of ligands is less than the octahedral complexes. Hence, the value of crystal field splitting energy of tetrahedral complexes (Δ_t) is nearly half the value for octahedral complexes (Δ_o). Δ_t and Δ_o are related as

$$\Delta_t = -\frac{4}{9}\Delta_o$$

42. *(d)* The complex, in which ligand is weak field, has tetrahedral shape and sp^3-hybridisation.

$$Ni^{2+} = [Ar]\,3d^8, 4s^0$$

3d

$[NiCl_4]^{2-}$ = [Ar] | ⥮ | ⥮ | ⥮ | 1 | 1 | | | xx | xx | xx | xx |

Cl Cl Cl Cl

$sp^3 \Rightarrow$ tetrahedral

43. *(a)* $[Cr(NH_3)_6]^{3+}$

3d

Cr^{3+} = | 1 | 1 | 1 | | | xx | xx | xx | xx | xx | xx |

d^2sp^3-hybridisation

Number of unpaired electrons = 3; μ = 3.87 BM

In $[Fe(CN)_6]^{3-}$

3d

Fe^{3+} = | ⥮ | ⥮ | 1 | | | xx | xx | xx | xx | xx | xx |

d^2sp^3-hybridisation

Number of unpaired electrons = 1; μ = 1.73 BM

In $[Fe(CN)_6]^{4-}$

3d

Fe^{2+} = | ⥮ | ⥮ | ⥮ | | | xx | xx | xx | xx | xx | xx |

d^2sp^3-hybridisation

Number of unpaired electrons = 0, μ = 0

In $[Zn(NH_3)_6]^{2+} \longrightarrow Zn^{2+} \longrightarrow 3d^{10}$

Number of unpaired electrons = 0; μ = 0

44. *(a)* Outer electronic configuration of Pt is $5d^9, 6s^1$.

Outer electronic configuration of Pt^{2+} is $5d^8$.

As CN^- is strong field ligand, so pairing will take place.

5d 6p

Pt^{2+} = | ⥮ | ⥮ | ⥮ | ⥮ | | | xx | xx | xx | xx | | | |

dsp^2-hybridisation

Hence, there is no unpaired electron in the square planar $[Pt(CN)_4]^{2-}$ ion.

45. *(c)* Both (a) and (b) statements are correct.

(a) There are only four ligands instead of six. So, the ligand field is only 2/3 the size, hence the Δ_t is 2/3.

(b) The direction of the orbital does not coincide with the direction of the ligands. This reduces the crystal field stabilisation energy (Δ) by further 2/3.

46. *(c)* Higher the oxidation state of the metal, greater the crystal field splitting. In options (a), (b) and (d), Co is present in +2 oxidation state and in (c) it is present in + 3 oxidation state and hence, $[Co(NH_3)_6]^{3+}$ has a higher value of CFSE.

47. *(c)* Greater the number of unpaired electrons, larger is the paramagnetism.

$[V(gly)_2(OH)_2(NH_3)_2]^+$

$V_{23} = [Ar]3d^3, 4s^2 \Rightarrow V^{5+} = [Ar]3d^0$

$3d^0$

V^{5+} = | | | | | |

(no unpaired electrons)

$[Fe(en)(bpy)(NH_3)_2]^{2+}$

$Fe_{26} = [Ar]3d^6, 4s^2$

$Fe^{2+} = [Ar]3d^6$

$3d^6$

Fe^{2+} = | ⥮ | 1 | 1 | 1 | 1 |

(four unpaired electrons)

But en, bpy and NH_3 all are strong field ligands, so pairing occurs, thus no unpaired electrons.

$[Co(ox)_2(OH)_2]^-$ $\quad Co_{27} = [Ar]3d^7, 4s^2$

$Co^{5+} = [Ar]3d^4$

$3d^4$

Co^{5+} = | 1 | 1 | 1 | 1 | |

(four unpaired electrons)

$[Ti(NH_3)_6]^{3+}$ $\quad Ti_{22} = [Ar]3d^2, 4s^2$

$Ti^{3+} = [Ar]3d^1$

$3d^1$

Ti^{3+} = | 1 | | | | |

(one unpaired electron)

Hence, $[Co(ox)_2(OH)_2]^-$ has highest paramagnetic behaviour.

48. *(c)* The magnitude of Δ_o (the orbital splitting energy) is decided by the nature of ligand. Strong field ligand has highest Δ_o. The increasing field strength is as

$I^- < Br^- < Cl^- < F^- < OH^- < H_2O < C_2O_4^{2-} < NH_3 <$ en

$< NO_2^- < CN^-$

The CN^- is the strongest ligand among these, hence the magnitude of Δ_o will be maximum in $[Co(CN)_6]^{3-}$.

49. *(a)* In complex $[CoF_6]^{3-}$,

Oxidation number of Co = +3

Electronic configuration of $Co^{3+} = 1s^2, 2s^22p^6, 3s^23p^63d^6$

In Co^{3+},

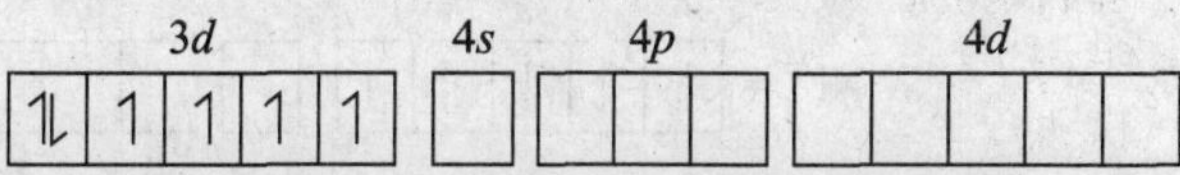

In Co^{3+}, number of unpaired electrons is four, and F^- is the weak field ligand. Hence, it does not pair up the electrons of *d*-orbital.

In $[CoF_6]^{3-}$,

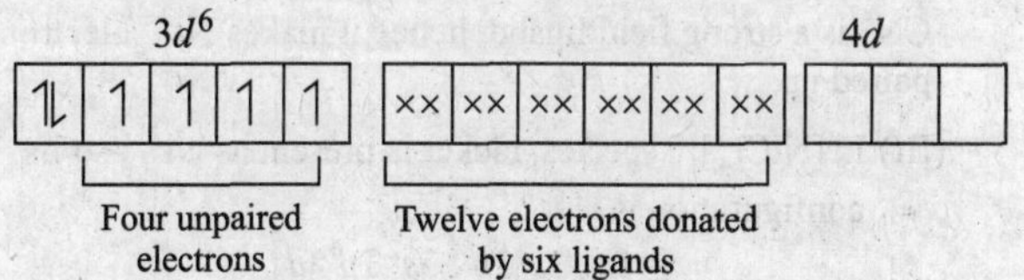

Co^{3+} has $3d^6$ outer electronic configuration and have four unpaired electrons which do not pair up because of weak field provided by F^-. So, $[CoF_6]^{3-}$ is paramagnetic.

50. *(a)* Tetrahedral complexes show sp^3-hybridisation, so low spin (pairing of electrons in the *d*-orbitals) is false for tetrahedral complexes. Tetrahedral complexes show *d-d* transition due to high spin of *d*-orbitals. Tetrahedral complexes are coloured due to the absence of symmetry and presence of unpaired electron in *d*-orbitals.

51. *(c)*

Hybridisation	Geometry of complex
sp^3	Tetrahedral
dsp^2	Square planar
d^2sp^3	Octahedral
sp^2d^2	Does not exist

52. *(a)* For complex $K_2[NiCl_4]$

Oxidation number of Ni = +2

Electronic configuration of $_{28}Ni^{2+} = 1s^2, 2s^22p^6, 3s^23p^63d^8$

$3d^8$

Ni^{2+} = | ⥮ | ⥮ | ⥮ | 1 | 1 |

Thus, it has 2 unpaired electrons and a total of 8 electrons.

53. *(b)*

(a) In $[Ni(CO)_4]$, nickel is sp^3-hybridised because in it oxidation state of Ni is zero. So, its electronic configuration is

$_{28}Ni = 1s^2, 2s^22p^6, 3s^23p^63d^8, 4s^2$

$3d^8$ $\quad 4s \quad 4p$

Ni = | ⥮ | ⥮ | ⥮ | 1 | 1 | ⥮ | | | |

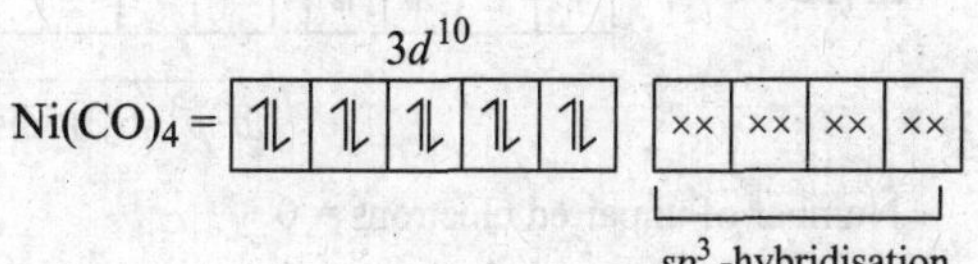

(b) In $[Ni(CN)_4]^{2-}$, nickel is present as Ni^{2+} so its configuration is $= 1s^2, 2s^2 2p^6, 3s^2 3p^6 3d^8$

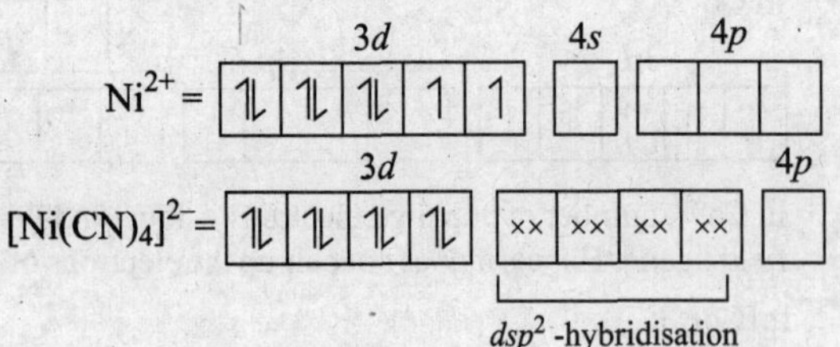

dsp^2 -hybridisation

CN^- is a strong field ligand, hence it makes Ni^{2+} electrons to be paired up.

(III) In $[NiCl_4]^{2-}$ species, nickel is present as Ni^{2+}, so its configuration is

$= 1s^2, 2s^2 2p^6, 3s^2 3p^6 3d^8$

3d 4s 4p

| ⥮ | ⥮ | ⥮ | 1 | 1 | | | | |

3d

$[NiCl_4]^{2-}$ = | ⥮ | ⥮ | ⥮ | 1 | 1 | ×× | ×× | ×× | ×× |

sp^3-hybridisation

Cl^- is a weak field ligand, hence Ni^{2+} electrons are not paired.

54. *(c)* $[Ni(CO)_4]$ and $[Ni(PPh_3)_2Cl_2]$ are tetrahedral in geometrical shape, because coordination number of Ni is 4 in both cases and both use $3s$ and $3p$-orbitals of the central metal to give sp^3-hybridisation.

55. *(e)* Increasing order of crystal field splitting power

$Cl^- < F^- < OH^- < H_2O < CN^-$

Weak field ligand — Strong field ligand

56. *(d)* Atoms, ions or molecules having unpaired electrons are paramagnetic.

(a) In $[Cr(CO)_6]$, (oxidation number of Cr = 0)

$_{24}Cr$ (Ground state) $= 1s^2, 2s^2 2p^6, 3s^2 3p^6 3d^5, 4s^1$

3d

In $[Cr(CO)_6]$ = | ⥮ | ⥮ | ⥮ | ×× | ×× | ×× | ×× | ×× | ×× |

d^2sp^3 -hybridisation

Number of unpaired electrons = 0

(b) In $[Fe(CO)_5]$, (oxidation number of Fe = 0)

$_{26}Fe$ (Ground state) $= 1s^2, 2s^2 2p^6, 3s^2 3p^6 3d^6, 4s^2$

3d

In $[Fe(CO)_5]$ = | ⥮ | ⥮ | ⥮ | ⥮ | ×× | ×× | ×× | ×× | ×× |

dsp^3 -hybridisation

Number of unpaired electrons = 0

(c) In $[Fe(CN)_6]^{4-}$, (oxidation number of Fe = +2)

$_{26}Fe^{2+}$ (Ground state) $= 1s^2, 2s^2 2p^6, 3s^2 3p^6 3d^6$

3d

In $[Fe(CN)_6]^{4-}$ = | ⥮ | ⥮ | ⥮ | ×× | ×× | ×× | ×× | ×× | ×× |

d^2sp^3 -hybridisation

Number of unpaired electrons = 0

(d) In $[Cr(NH_3)_6]^{3+}$, (oxidation number of Cr = + 3)

So,electronic configuration is

$_{24}Cr$ (Ground state) $= 1s^2, 2s^2 2p^6, 3s^2 3p^6 3d^5, 4s^1$

$Cr^{3+} = 1s^2, 2s^2 2p^6, 3s^2 3p^6 3d^3$

Number of unpaired electrons = 3

Hence, complex (d) has paramagnetic character as it contains three unpaired electrons.

57. *(c)* $[Fe(CN)_6]^{3-}$

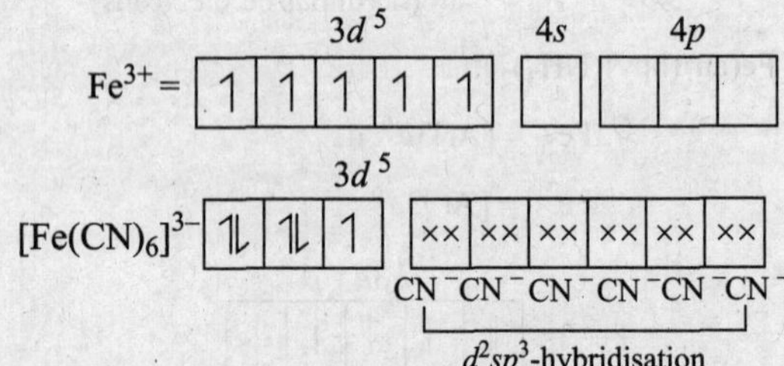

∵ Number of unpaired electrons is one

$$\mu = \sqrt{n(n+2)} = \sqrt{1(1+2)} = \sqrt{3} = 1.73 \text{ BM}$$

58. *(c)* Magnetic moment $(\mu) = \sqrt{n(n+2)}$ BM

or $3.83 = \sqrt{n(n+2)}$

or $3.83 \times 3.83 = n^2 + 2n \Rightarrow 14.6689 = n^2 + 2n$

On solving this, we get $n = 3$

Hence, number of unpaired electrons in d-subshell of chromium (Cr = 24) = 3.

So, the configuration of chromium ion is

$Cr^{3+} = 1s^2, 2s^2 2p^6, 3s^2 3p^6 3d^3$

(In $[Cr(H_2O)_6]Cl_3$ oxidation state of Cr is +3)

Hence, in $3d^3$ the distribution of electrons

$$3d_{xy}^1, 3d_{yz}^1, 3d_{zx}^1, 3d_{x^2-y^2}^0, 3d_{z^2}^0$$

59. *(c)* Species having same number of unpaired electrons have same magnetic moment.

Magnetic moment $(\mu) = \sqrt{n(n+2)}$ BM

$[Cr(H_2O)_6]^{2+} = Cr^{2+} = 3d^4 = 4$ unpaired electrons

$[CoCl_4]^{2-} = Co^{2+} = 3d^7 = 3$ unpaired electrons

$[Fe(H_2O)_6]^{2+} = Fe^{2+} = 3d^6 = 4$ unpaired electrons

$[Mn(H_2O)_6]^{2+} = Mn^{2+} = 3d^5 = 5$ unpaired electrons

So, $[Cr(H_2O)_6]^{2+}$ and $[Fe(H_2O)_6]^{2+}$ have same magnetic moment.

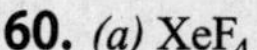

60. *(a)* XeF_4

In ground state,

5s 5p 5d

Xe = [⇅] [⇅ ⇅ ⇅] [ ]

In excited state,

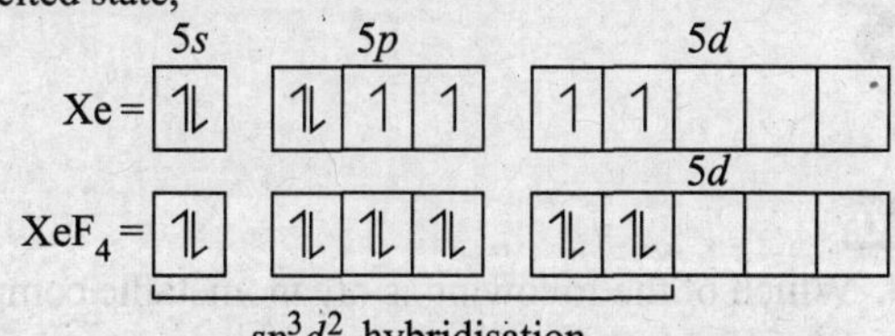

sp^3d^2-hybridisation

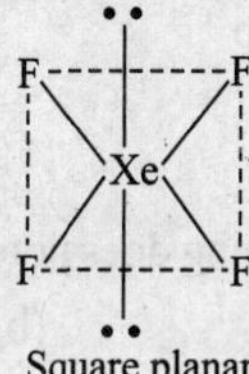

Square planar

SF_4 has *see-saw* structure.

F, F, S, F, F

$[NiCl_4]^{2-}$ has sp^3-hybridisation and tetrahedral structure.

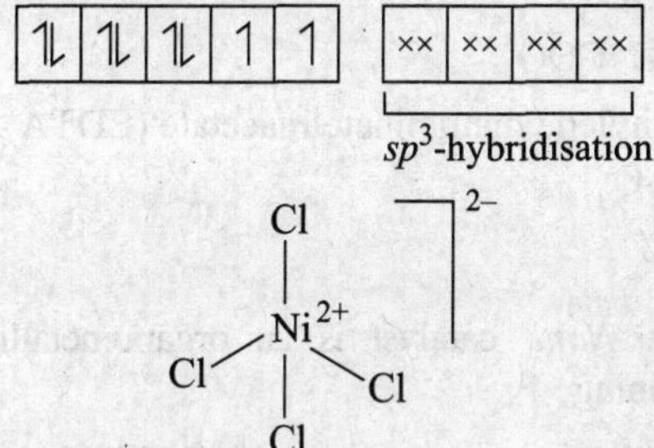

sp^3-hybridisation

$[PtCl_4]^{2-}$ has square planar structure.

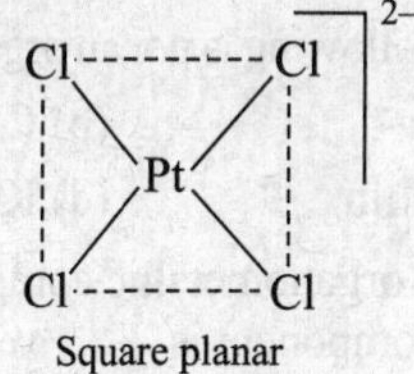

Square planar

61. *(d)* $\because \quad \mu = \sqrt{n(n+2)}$

where, n = number of unpaired electron

$$5.9 = \sqrt{n(n+2)} \Rightarrow 35 = n^2 + 2n$$

$$n^2 + 2n - 35 = 0 \Rightarrow n^2 + 7n - 5n - 35 = 0$$

$$n(n+7) - 5(n+7) = 0$$

$$(n+7)(n-5) = 0$$

$$\therefore \qquad n = 5$$

Hence, required complex must possess 5 unpaired electrons.

In $[MnBr_4]^{2-}$, Mn is present in +2 oxidation state as :

$$x + 4(-1) = -2$$

$$x = -2 + 4 \Rightarrow x = 2$$

Mn^{2+} [$Z = 25$] : [Ar] $3d^5$: 5 unpaired electrons.

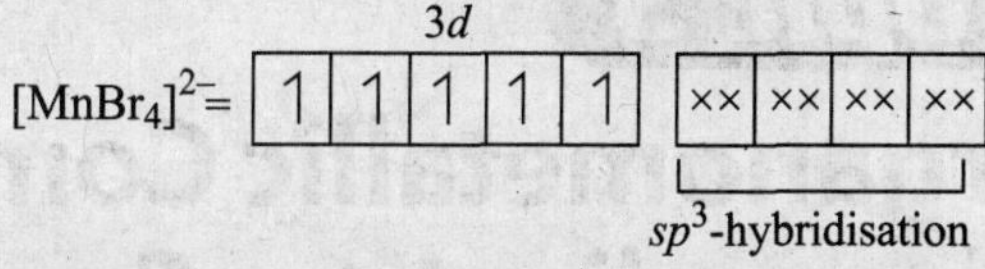

sp^3-hybridisation

In $[MnBr_4]^{2-}$, five unpaired electrons are present, thus it has magnetic moment 5.9 BM.

62. *(c)* EAN = $Z -$ (O.N) + 2(C.N)

where, O.N = oxidation number

C.N = coordination number

Z = atomic number

$$[Fe(CN)_6]^{4-} : \text{EAN} = 26 - (2) + 2(6)$$

$$= 26 - 2 + 12 = 36$$

So, the complex A is $Na_4[Fe(CN)_6]$.

63. *(a)* When central metal ion is same (here Ni^{2+}), the absorption of colour depends on the ligand. According to spectrochemical series, various ligands are as follows:

$$I^- < Br^- < Cl^- < NO_3^- < F^- < H_2O < NH_3 < NO_2^- < CN^- < CO$$

Thus, H_2O is the weakest ligand among these, therefore, the absorbed energy will be lowest in $[Ni(H_2O)_6]^{2+}$, so it will absorb highest wavelength (red light) $\left(\because \; E \propto \frac{1}{\lambda}\right)$

$\therefore$ The order of increasing wavelength is,

$$[Ni(NO_2)_6]^{4-} < [Ni(NH_3)_6]^{2+} < [Ni(H_2O)_6]^{2+}$$

64. *(c)* $K_3[\overset{3+}{Fe}(CN)_6]$ (Potassium ferricyanide)

3d

Fe^{3+} in the presence of CN^- [⇅ ⇅ 1] [×× ×× ×× ×× ×× ××]

$n = 1$ paramagnetic, d^2sp^3 -hybridisation

$K_4[\overset{2+}{Fe}(CN)_6]$ (Potassium ferrocyanide)

3d

Fe^{2+} in the presence of CN^- [⇅ ⇅ ⇅] [×× ×× ×× ×× ×× ××]

$n = 0$ diamagnetic, d^2sp^3 -hybridisation

Crystal field splitting in ferrocyanide is less than that of ferricyanide ion because higher the oxidation state of the metal, greater the crystal field splitting.

65. *(c)*

(a) $[Ag(NH_3)_2]^+$ has coordination number 2. It has linear structure and because of no unpaired electron, its dipole moment is zero.

(b) $[Co(NH_3)_6]^{3+}$ has d^2sp^3-hybridisation and octahedral structure. Because of no unpaired electron, it is diamagnetic, i.e. dipole moment = zero.

(c) $[Fe(CN)_6]^{3-}$ has d^2sp^3-hybridisation and octahedral structure. It has one unpaired electron. So, it is paramagnetic and has dipole moment = 1.73 BM.

(d) $[Cu(NH_3)_4]^{2+}$ is square planar and has one unpaired electron. So, it is paramagnetic and has dipole moment = 1.73 BM.

(e) $[Fe(CN)_6]^{4-}$ has d^2sp^3-hybridisation and octahedral structure. It has no unpaired electron, hence dipole moment is zero.

Topic 3

Organometallic Compounds and Importance of Coordination Compounds

2018

1. Iron carbonyl, $Fe(CO)_5$ is **[NEET]**

(a) trinuclear (b) mononuclear
(c) tetranuclear (d) dinuclear

2016

2. Which of the following has longest C—O bond length? (Free C—O bond length in CO is 1.128 Å.) **[NEET]**

(a) $[Co(CO)_4]^-$ (b) $[Fe(CO)_4]^{2-}$
(c) $[Mn(CO)_6]^+$ (d) $Ni(CO)_4$

2014

3. *Zeigler-Natta* catalyst is **[Kerala CEE]**

(a) $ZnCl_2$ (b) $Et_3Al + TiCl_4$
(c) $Cu / ZnO\text{-}Cr_2O_3$ (d) Pt
(e) V_2O_5

2013

4. The complex used as an anticancer agent is **[AIIMS]**

(a) *meso*-$[Co(NH_3)_3Cl_3]$ (b) *cis*-$[PtCl_2(NH_3)_2]$
(c) *cis*-$K_2[PtCl_2Br_2]$ (d) Na_2CoCl_4

5. What is the oxidation number of Fe in $Fe(CO)_5$? **[UP CPMT]**

(a) + 3 (b) Zero (c) + 2 (d) + 5

6. The non-existant metal carbonyl among the following is **[J&K CET]**

(a) $Cr(CO)_6$ (b) $Mn(CO)_5$
(c) $Ni(CO)_4$ (d) $Fe(CO)_5$

2009

7. Assertion (A) CO and CN are referred as π acid ligands.
Reason (R) In CO and CN vacant π type orbitals are present. **[AIIMS]**

(a) Both A and R are correct and R is the correct explanation of A.
(b) Both A and R are correct and R is not the correct explanation of A.
(c) A is correct but R is incorrect.
(d) Both A and R are incorrect.

2007

8. Which of the following is organometallic compound? **[BHU]**

(a) CH_3MgBr
(b) $(CH_3COO)_2Pb$
(c) CH_3COONa
(d) All of these

9. Which of the following does not have a metal-carbon bond? **[Manipal]**

(a) $Al(OC_2H_5)_3$ (b) C_2H_5MgBr
(c) $K[Pt(C_2H_4)Cl_3]$ (d) $Ni(CO)_4$

2006

10. Which ligand is useful for removal of the toxic effect of lead metal in body in chelate therapy treatment? **[Guj CET]**

(a) $\begin{matrix} COO^- \\ | \\ COO^- \end{matrix}$
(b) CH_3COO^-
(c) Ethylene diamminetetraacetate $(EDTA)^{2-}$
(d) AsO_4^{3-}

2005

11. *Ziegler-Natta* catalyst is an organometallic compound containing **[J&K CET]**

(a) iron (b) titanium
(c) rhodium (d) zirconium

12. Which of the following is not an organometallic compound? **[J&K CET]**

(a) C_2H_5ONa (b) CH_3MgI
(c) Tetraethyl tin (d) KC_4H_9

13. The π-bonded organometallic compound which has ethene as one of its component is **[J&K CET]**

(a) Zeise's salt
(b) ferrocene
(c) dibenzene chromium
(d) tetraethyl tin

Answers

1. (b)	2. (b)	3. (b)	4. (b)	5. (b)	6. (b)	7. (a)	8. (a)	9. (a)	10. (c)
11. (b)	12. (a)	13. (a)							

Explanations

1. *(b)* Compounds of transition metal with carbonyls (carbon monoxide) are known as metal carbonyls. These are classified into mononuclear, dinuclear, trinuclear and so on based on the number of central metal atoms/ions present in a complex.

Since, there is only one central metal atom present in iron carbonyl, $Fe(CO)_5$, thus it is mononuclear. The structure of $Fe(CO)_5$ is shown below:

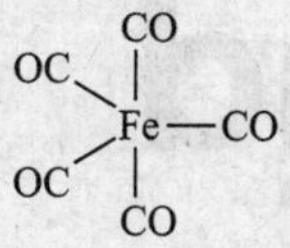

CO, OC, Fe—CO, OC, CO

The examples of dinuclear, trinuclear complexes are $Co_2(CO)_{18}$, $Fe_3(CO)_{12}$ respectively.

2. *(b)* As negative charge on metal carbonyl complex increases, back π-bonding increases and hence bond length of C — O bond increases while bond length of metal-carbon bond decreases.

Hence, $[Fe(CO)_4]^{2-}$ has longest C — O bond length among the given complexes.

The correct order of bond length of the given complexes is

$[Mn(CO)_6]^+ < [Ni(CO)_4] < [Co(CO)_4]^- < [Fe(CO)_4]^{2-}$

3. *(b)* A mixture of triethyl aluminium, (Et_3Al) and titanium tetrachloride, $(TiCl_4)$ is called *Zeigler-Natta* catalyst. It is used for the polymerisation of ethene.

4. *(b)* *cis*-platin, i.e. *cis*-$[PtCl_2(NH_3)_2]$ is anticancer agent. It destroys cancer cells. So, used as antitumour agent.

5. *(b)* Let the oxidation state of Fe in $Fe(CO)_5$ be x.

$Fe(CO)_5$ (∵ oxidation state of CO = 0)

$x + 0 \times 5 = 0 \Rightarrow x = 0$

In metal carbonyls, oxidation state of metal is always zero.

6. *(b)* By applying the EAN rule, the stability of metal carbonyls can be predicted. All the given metal carbonyls except $Mn(CO)_5$ follows the EAN rule and thus, it exists as dimer $Mn_2(CO)_{10}$.

7. *(a)* The ligands having vacant π-type orbitals have a tendency to receive back donated π-electrons, thus these are called π-acid ligands or π-acceptor ligands, e.g. CO and CN have lone pair as well as π electrons or $\overset{*}{\pi}$-orbitals which take part in the formation of π-bond with central metal atom as observed in case of carbonyls.

8. *(a)* Compound containing at least one metal-carbon bond may be called organometallic compound. Thus, CH_3MgBr is an organometallic compound.

9. *(a)* $Al(OC_2H_5)_3$ does not have metal-carbon bond, i.e. it is not an example of organometallic compound. Its structure is

$H_3C—CH_2—O—Al(—O—CH_2—CH_3)_2$

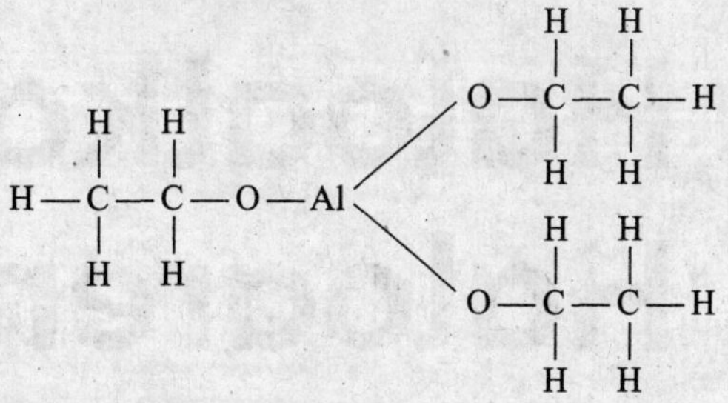

10. *(c)* (Ethylene diamminetetraacetate) $EDTA^{2-}$ ion is used for the removal of the toxic effect of lead metal in body in chelate therapy treatment because it forms complex with lead.

11. *(b)* *Ziegler-Natta* catalyst is an organometallic compound containing titanium. It is $TiCl_4$ and $(C_2H_5)_3Al$. It is used in the preparation of polyethylene.

$$\underset{\text{Ethylene}}{nCH_2{=}CH_2} \xrightarrow[TiCl_4+(C_2H_5)_3Al]{330-350\text{ K},\ 1\text{-}2\text{ atm}} \underset{\text{Polyethylene}}{+CH_2—CH_2+_n}$$

12. *(a)* $C_2H_5\overset{-}{O}\overset{+}{Na}$ does not have metal-carbon bond, therefore, it is not an organometallic compound.

$H_3C—CH_2—\overset{-}{O}—\overset{+}{Na}$

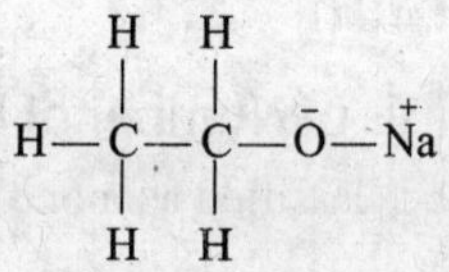

13. *(a)* Zeise's salt, $K[PtCl_3(C_2H_4)]$ is a π-bonded organometallic compound. Its structure is as

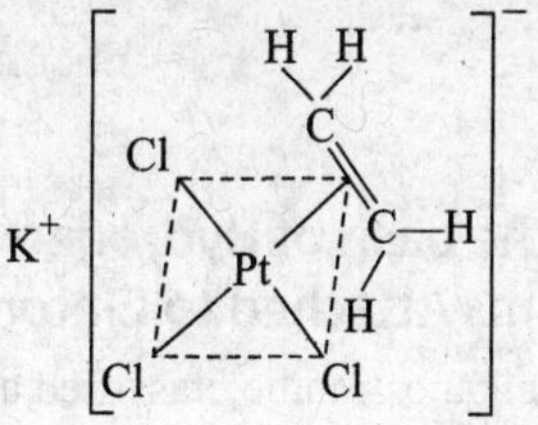

$K^+[PtCl_3(\eta^2\text{-}C_2H_4)]^-$

24

Haloalkanes and Haloarenes

Quick Review

The replacement of hydrogen atoms in hydrocarbons (aliphatic or aromatic) by halogen atoms results in the formation of alkyl halide **(haloalkanes)** and aryl halide **(haloarenes)** respectively.

Classification

A. On the Basis of Number of Halogen Atoms

They may be classified as mono, di or polyhalogen compounds.

C_2H_5X — Mono haloalkane

$CH_2X{-}CH_2X$ — Di haloalkane

$CH_2X{-}CHX{-}CH_2X$ — Tri haloalkane

B. On the basis of Hydrogen Atoms Attached to C-atom

Haloalkanes can be classified as primary, secondary and tertiary depending upon the fact that halogen is attached to primary, secondary or tertiary C-atom.

$H_3C{-}CH_2Br$ — Primary (1°)

$H_3C{-}CH(CH_3){-}Br$ — Secondary (2°)

$H_3C{-}C(CH_3)_2{-}Br$ — Tertiary (3°)

C. On the Basis of Hybridisation of Carbon Atom of C—*X* Bond

Compounds Containing $C_{sp^3}{-}X$ Bond

- **Alkyl Halides** Halogen atom is bonded to an alkyl group. These are further classified as primary, secondary and tertiary.

$R'{-}CH_2{-}X$ — Primary; $R''{-}CHR'{-}X$ — Secondary; $R''{-}CR'R''{-}X$ — Tertiary

- **Allylic Halides** Halogen atom is bonded to sp^3 - hybridised carbon atom next to C—C double bond.

$CH_2{=}CH{-}CH_2X$, 3-halocyclohexene

- **Benzylic Halides** Halogen atom is bonded to a sp^3-hybridised carbon atom next to an aromatic ring.

e.g. $C_6H_5{-}CH_2X$

Compounds Containing $C_{sp^2}{-}X$ Bond

- **Vinylic Halides** Halogen atom is bonded to sp^2-hybridised carbon atom of C—C double bond.

$CH_2{=}CH{-}X$

- **Aryl Halides** In aryl halides, the halogen is attached to carbon atom of an aromatic ring.

X

Nomenclature

- In IUPAC system, these are written by prefixing the word 'halo' to the name of the longest straight chain alkane.
- Since, halogen atoms are more electronegative than carbon, the carbon-halogen (C—X) bond of alkyl halide is polarised.

Preparation

***Method of preparation** of haloalkanes are discussed below:*

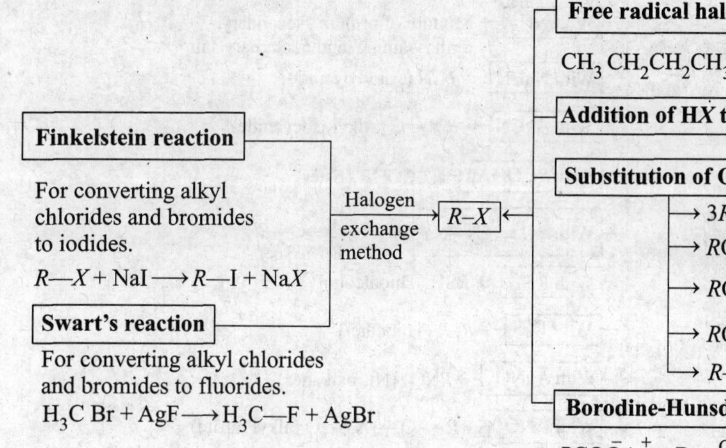

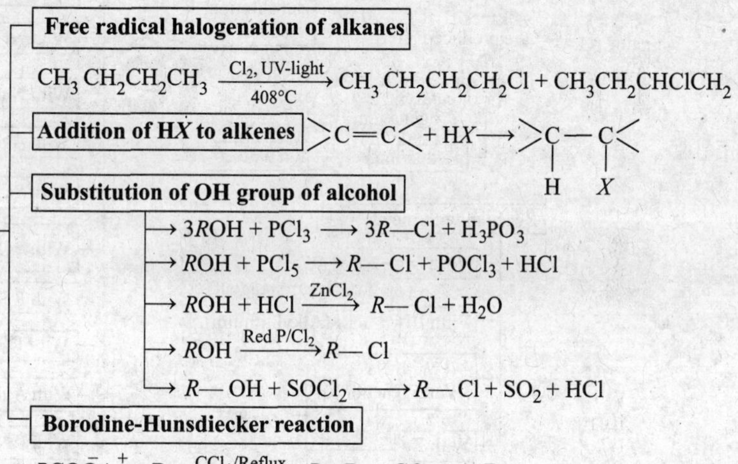

Physical Properties

Boiling points of chlorides, bromides and iodides are higher than those of hydrocarbons of comparable molecular mass.

(*i*) Alkyl halide are colourless when pure but develop colour when exposed to light. They also have sweet smell.

(*ii*) Boiling point order of different alkyl halides are

$$R—I > R—Br > R—Cl > R—F$$

(*iii*) Bond strength of haloalkanes decreases as the size of the halogen atom increases. Thus, the order of bond strength is,

$$CH_3F > CH_3Cl > CH_3Br > CH_3I$$

(*iv*) Dipole moment and polarity of C—X bond decreases as the electronegativity of the halogen decreases.

Chemical Properties

Haloalkanes undergoes substitution and elimination reactions.

Nucleophilic Substitution Reactions

It involves substitution that begins with nucleophilic attack. These are of following types:

1. S_N1 (Unimolecular Nucleophilic Substitution)

- *It proceeds via two steps* :
  (*i*) Formation of carbocation
  (*ii*) and attack of nucleophile on carbocation.
- The S_N1 reaction follows first order kinetics, i.e. rate of reaction depends on the concentration of the alkyl halide only.
- The reactivity of alkyl halide depends upon the formation of stable carbocation.
- Thus, order of reactivity of alkyl halide towards S_N1 reaction is as follows:
  Benzylic halide > 3° > 2° > 1° halide > methyl halide.
- In these reactions, racemisation occurs due to the possibility of frontal as well as backside attack on planar carbocation.

2. S_N2 (Biomolecular Nucleophilic Substitution)

- These reactions proceed in one step and it is a second order reaction. This means that the rate of reaction depends on the concentration of both the alkyl halide and the incoming nucleophile.
- The order of reactivity of alkyl halides for S_N2 reaction is 3° < 2° < 1° < methyl halide.
- Rate of reaction in S_N2 mechanism depends on the strength of the attacking nucleophile, which follows the order.

$$CN^- > : I^- > : OR^- > : OH^- > CH_3COO^- > H_2O > F^-$$

- In these reactions, inversion of configuration takes place.

Elimination Reactions

Dehydrohalogenation of alkyl halide is a β-elimination reaction in which halogen atom is lost from α-carbon atom and the hydrogen from the β-carbon (according to Saytzeff rule).

Important reactions of alkyl halides (haloalkanes) are shown below :

- 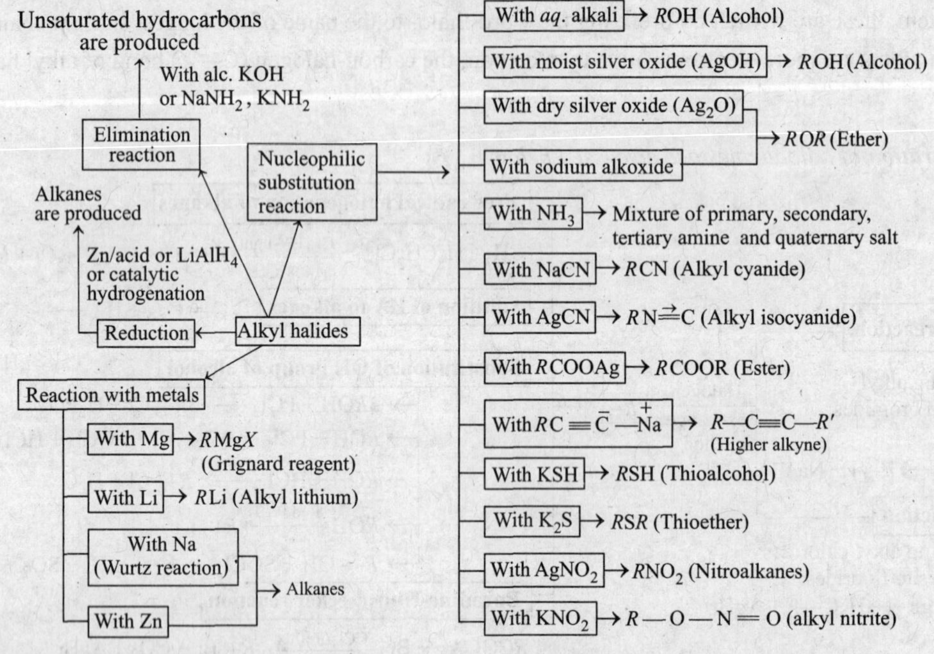

Haloarenes

- These are aromatic compounds in which halogen replaces hydrogen atom (s) of benzene ring.
- In haloarenes, the carbon atom to which halogen is attached is sp^2-hybridised.
- C-X bond in aryl halide or haloarenes have partial double bond character due to conjugation between lone-pair of halogen and benzene.

Preparation

Method	Chemical reaction
Halogenation	$C_6H_6 + X_2 \xrightarrow[\text{or anhyd. } AlCl_3]{Fe} C_6H_5X + HCl$
From benzene diazonium salts	• Sandmeyer's reaction $C_6H_5\overset{+}{N_2}\bar{Cl} \xrightarrow[X = Cl, Br]{Cu_2X_2} C_6H_5X + N_2\uparrow$ • Gattermann reaction $C_6H_5\overset{+}{N_2}\bar{Cl} \xrightarrow[\Delta]{Cu/HCl} C_6H_5Cl + N_2$ • Balz-Schiemann reaction $C_6H_5\overset{+}{N_2}\bar{X} \xrightarrow{HBF_4} C_6H_5\overset{+}{N_2}BF_4^- \xrightarrow{\Delta} C_6H_5F + N_2\uparrow + BF_3$
Borodine Hunsdiecker reaction	$C_6H_5—CO\bar{O}\overset{+}{Ag} + Br_2 \xrightarrow[CCl_4]{\Delta} C_6H_5—Br + AgBr + CO_2$
Decarboxylation of halogenated acids	$XC_6H_4CO\bar{O}\overset{+}{Na} + NaOH \xrightarrow[\Delta]{CaCO_3} C_6H_5X + Na_2CO_3 + CO_2$
From phenol	$C_6H_5OH + PCl_5 \xrightarrow{\text{High temp.}} C_6H_5Cl + POCl_3 + HCl$
Raschig process	$C_6H_6 + HCl + \frac{1}{2}O_2 \xrightarrow[Heat]{CuCl_2} C_6H_5—Cl + H_2O$

Physical Properties

- Haloarenes are crystalline solids, less polar compounds, insoluble in water (due to incapability of forming H-bonds) but soluble in organic solvents, like ethanol and ether.
- For the same aryl group, the boiling point increases as the size of the halogen atom increases.

  Similarly, for the halogen atom, boiling point increases as the size of aryl group increases.
- When aryl group is same, melting point increases as the size of the halogen atom increases. When halogen atom is same, melting point increases as the size of aryl group increases.
- The dipole moment of haloarenes increases in the order: Fluorobenzene < chlorobenzene < bromobenzene < iodobenzene.
- Stability of haloarenes having the same aryl group decreases in the order:

  Arylfluorides > aryl chlorides > arylbromides > aryl iodides

Chemical Properties

- These are less reactive towards nucleophilic substitution reaction due to partial double bond character of C—*X* bonds; stabilisation of the molecule by delocalisation of electrons; instability of phenyl carbocation.
- Aryl halides having electron withdrawing groups (like $—NO_2$, $—SO_3H$ etc.) at *ortho* and *para* positions undergo **nucleophilic substitution reaction** easily.
- Haloarenes undergo typical **electrophilic aromatic substitution** reaction, like nitration, sulphonation, halogenation etc. Here, halogen affects the reactivity, as it is deactivating due to *–I*-effect, still it is *ortho* and *para* directing.

  So, haloarenes are less reactive than benzene towards electrophilic substitution reaction.

Nucleophilic Substitution Reactions

C_6H_5X —(*aq.*NaOH, 300°C)→ C_6H_5OH

C_6H_5X —(CuCN, 470 K, pressure)→ C_6H_5CN

C_6H_5X —(*aq.*NH_3, 200°C, Cu_2O)→ $C_6H_5NH_2$

Electrophilic Substitution Reactions

Chlorobenzene —(conc.HNO_3, conc. H_2SO_4 (nitration))→ 1-Chloro-2-nitrobenzene (Cl, NO_2) + 1-Chloro-4-nitrobenzene (Cl, NO_2)

Chlorobenzene —(Cl_2, Fe, Halogenation)→ 1,2-Dichlorobenzene (Cl, Cl) + 1,4-Dichlorobenzene (Cl, Cl)

Chlorobenzene —(H_2SO_4, Sulphonation)→ 2-Chlorobenzenesulphonic acid (Cl, SO_3H) + 4-Chlorobenzenesulphonic acid (Cl, SO_3H)

Chlorobenzene —(CH_3Cl in presence of $AlCl_3$ (Friedel Craft's alkylation))→ 1-Chloro-2-methylbenzene (Cl, CH_3) + 1-Chloro-4-methylbenzene (Cl, CH_3)

Chlorobenzene —(CH_3COCl + $AlCl_3$, Friedel Craft's acylation)→ 2-Chloroacetophenone (Cl, $COCH_3$) + 4-Chloroacetophenone (Cl, $COCH_3$)

Reaction with Metals

- **Reaction with Mg**

  $C_6H_5Br + Mg \xrightarrow[\Delta]{\text{Dry ether}} C_6H_5MgBr$

- **Ullmann reaction**

  $2C_6H_5I + 2Cu \xrightarrow{\Delta} C_6H_5–C_6H_5 + Cu_2I_2$

- **Wurtz-Fitti g reaction**

  $C_6H_5Cl + CH_3Cl + 2Na \xrightarrow{\text{Ether}} C_6H_5–CH_3$

- **Fittig reaction**

  $2C_6H_5Cl + 2Na \xrightarrow{\text{Ether}} C_6H_5–C_6H_5$

Polyhalogen Compounds

Carbon compounds containing more than one halogen atom are usually referred to as polyhalogen compounds.

Some polyhalogen compounds are as follows :

- **Dichloromethane** (methylene chloride, CH_2Cl_2) It is used as solvent, as propellant in aerosols, as metal cleaning and finishing solvent. Its exposure leads to nausea, numbness and causes mild redness of the skin.
- **Trichloromethane** (chloroform, $CHCl_3$) It is used as a solvent for fats, alkaloids and other substances. Its exposure may cause damage to liver and kidneys.
- **Triiodomethane** (iodoform, CHI_3) It was used as an antiseptic but due to its objectionable smell, it has been replaced.
- **Tetrachloromethane** (carbon tetrachloride, CCl_4) It is used as cleansing fluid. Its exposure causes liver cancer and permanent damage to nerve cell.
- **Freons** (CCl_2F_2) It is used in refrigeration. It is able to initiate radical chain reactions that can upset the natural ozone balance.
- **DDT** (*p*, *p*′-dichloro diphenyltrichloroethane) It is a powerful insecticide but not easily degradable. It slowly changes to DDE. Its long term effect is potentially dangerous.

CCl_3
Cl—⟨C₆H₄⟩—CH—⟨C₆H₄⟩—Cl

Structure of DDT

Topical Practice Questions

All the exam questions of this chapter have been divided into three topics as listed below:

Topic 1

Monohalogen Derivatives of Alkyl Halides

2019

1 Correct order for reaction with alcoholic KOH. **[AIIMS]**

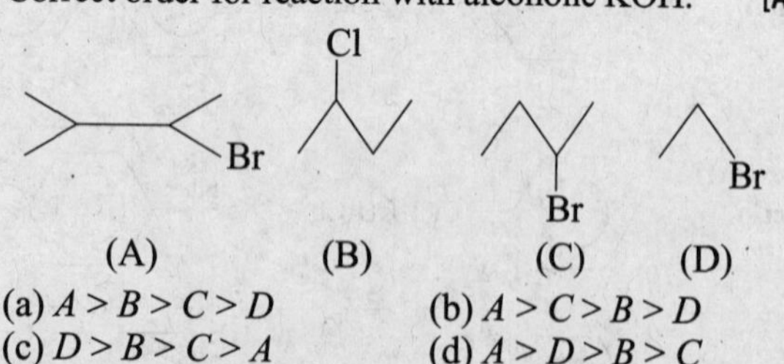

(a) $A > B > C > D$ (b) $A > C > B > D$
(c) $D > B > C > A$ (d) $A > D > B > C$

2 The alkane that gives only one mono-chloro product on chlorination with Cl_2 in presence of diffused sunlight is

(a) 2, 2-dimethylbutane (b) *neo*pentane **[NEET (Odisha)]**
(c) *n*-pentane (d) *iso*pentane

3 If ☐ react with Cl_2 in presence of light and then react with Na metal in dry ether, final product is **[JIPMER]**

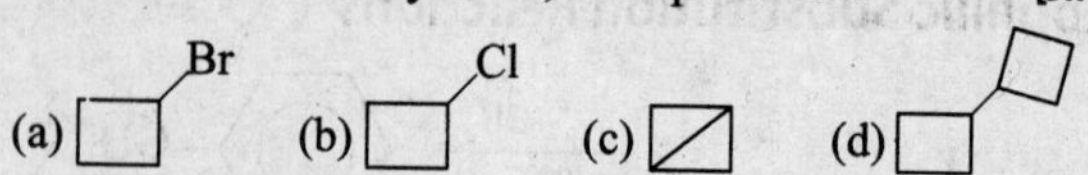

4 Which of the following is not correct? **[JIPMER]**

(a) $PhCH_2Br > PhCHBrCH_3 > PhCBr(CH_3)_2 (S_N1)$
(b) $R—I > R—Br > R—Cl (S_N2)$
(c) $CH_2{=}CH—Cl < CH_2{=}CH—CH_2—Cl < PhCH_2—Cl (S_N1)$
(d) $R—Cl < R—Br < R—I (S_N1)$

5 Which cannot behave as a nucleophile for S_N2 reaction ?

(a) H_2O (b) CN^- (c) NH_2^- (d) I^- **[JIPMER]**

6 $CH_3-CH_2-CH_2-Br \xrightarrow{\text{Alc. KOH}}$ Final product is [JIPMER]

(a) propene (b) propanol
(c) cyclopropane (d) propane-1, 2-diol

2018

7 Neopentyl chloride reacts with benzene in presence of a Lewis acid ($AlCl_3$) to form [JIPMER]

(a) $C_6H_5-CH_2C(CH_3)_3$ (b) $C_6H_5-C(CH_3)_2(CH_2CH_3)$
(c) $C_6H_5-C(CH_3)_3$ (d) $C_6H_5-CH_2CH(CH_3)_2$

8 Identify the major product that is obtained on treatment of $CH_3CH_2CH(F)CH_3$ with CH_3O^-/CH_3OH is [JIPMER]

(a) $CH_3CH_2CH(OCH_3)CH_3$
(b) $CH_3CH=CHCH_3$
(c) $CH_3CH_2CH=CH_2$
(d) $CH_3CH_2CH_2CH_2OCH_3$

9 $CH_3-Br \xrightarrow{\text{Mg/ether}} \xrightarrow[\text{(ii) } H_2O]{\text{(i) } CO_2} \xrightarrow[\Delta]{CH_3OH/H^+} P$

What is the product 'P' in the above reaction? [JIPMER]

(a) Methyl ethanoate (b) Ethanoic acid
(c) Propanal (d) Methyl propanoate

10 Among the following, the suitable reagent for Wurtz reaction is [JIPMER]

(a) Na/alcohol (b) Na/ether
(c) Zn/ether (d) Zn/alcohol

11 Hydrocarbon (A) reacts with bromine by substitution to form an alkyl bromide which by Wurtz reaction is converted to gaseous hydrocarbon containing less than four carbon atoms. A is [NEET]

(a) CH_3-CH_3 (b) $CH_2=CH_2$
(c) $CH\equiv CH$ (d) CH_4

12 A bromoalkane 'X' reacts with magnesium in dry ether to form compound 'Y'. The reaction of 'Y' with methanal followed by hydrolysis yield an alcohol having molecular formula, $C_4H_{10}O$. The compound 'X' is [AIIMS]

(a) bromomethane (b) bromoethane
(c) 1-bromopropane (d) 2-bromopropane

13 **Assertion** (A) The boiling points of alkyl halides decreases in the order RI> RBr> RCl> RF.

Reason (R) The boiling points of alkyl chlorides, bromides and iodides are considerably higher than that of the hydrocarbon of comparable molecular mass. [AIIMS]

(a) Both Assertion and Reason are true and Reason is the correct explanation of assertion
(b) Both Asseertion and Reason are true but Reason is not the correct explanation of Assertion
(c) Assertion is true but Reason is false
(d) Both Assertion and Reason are false

2016

14 For the following reactions,

(i) $CH_3CH_2CH_2Br + KOH \longrightarrow CH_3CH=CH_2 + KBr + H_2O$

(ii) $(CH_3)_2CHBr + KOH \longrightarrow (CH_3)_2CHOH + KBr$

(iii) cyclohexene $+ Br_2 \longrightarrow$ 1,2-dibromocyclohexane

Which of the following statements is correct? [NEET]

(a) (i) is elimination reaction, (ii) is substitution and (iii) is addition reaction.
(b) (i) is elimination, (ii) and (iii) are substitution reactions.
(c) (i) is substitution, (ii) and (iii) are addition reactions
(d) (i) and (ii) are elimination reactions and (iii) is addition reaction.

2015

15 Consider the reaction

$CH_3CH_2CH_2Br + NaCN \rightarrow CH_3CH_2CH_2CN + NaBr$

This reaction will be the fastest in [NEET Phase II]

(a) ethanol (b) methanol
(c) N,N'-dimethylformamide (DMF) (d) water

2014

16 Identify the compound D in the following series of reactions: [MHT CET]

$CH_3-CH(CH_3)-CH_2-CH_2-Br \xrightarrow[\Delta]{\text{Alc. KOH}} A$

$\xrightarrow[\text{(ii) } H_2O,\ \Delta]{\text{(i) Conc. } H_2SO_4} B$ (Major product) $+ C$ (Minor product)

$B \xrightarrow[-H_2O]{\text{HI, }\Delta} D$ (Major product) $+ E$ (Minor product)

(a) $CH_3-CH(CH_3)-CH(I)-CH_3$

(b) $CH_3-C(CH_3)(I)-CH_2-CH_3$

(c) $CH_3-CH(CH_3)-CH_2-CH_2-I$

(d) $CH_3-CH_2-CH(CH_3)-CH_2-I$

17 An incorrect statement with respect to S_N1 and S_N2 mechanisms for alkyl halide is **[KCET]**
(a) a strong nucleophile in an aprotic solvent increases the rate or favours S_N2 reaction
(b) competing reaction for an S_N2 reaction is rearrangement
(c) S_N1 reactions can be catalysed by some Lewis acids
(d) a weak nucleophile and aprotic solvent increases the rate of S_N1 reaction

18 What is the name of the following reaction? **[EAMCET]**

$$CH_3CH_2CH_2Br \xrightarrow[\text{Dry acetone}]{\text{NaI}} CH_3CH_2CH_2I$$

(a) Sandmeyer reaction (b) Gattermann reaction
(c) Finkelstein reaction (d) Swarts reaction

2013

19 Which of the following alkyl halide is used as a methylating agent? **[KCET]**
(a) C_2H_5Br (b) C_6H_5Cl (c) CH_3Cl (d) C_2H_5Cl

2012

20 In the following sequence of reaction,

$$CH_3—Br \xrightarrow{\text{KCN}} A \xrightarrow{H_3O^+} B \xrightarrow[\text{ether}]{\text{LiAlH}_4} C,$$

C is **[CBSE AIPMT]**
(a) acetone (b) methane
(c) acetaldehyde (d) ethyl alcohol

21 In alkaline hydrolysis of a tertiary halide by aqueous solution of alkali if concentration of alkali is doubled, then the reaction **[AIIMS]**
(a) will be doubled (b) will be halved
(c) will remain constant (d) None of these

22 When alkyl halide is heated with dry Ag_2O, it produces
(a) ester (b) ether **[Manipal]**
(c) ketone (d) alcohol

23 An alkyl halide with molecular formula $C_6H_{13}Br$ on dehydrohalogenation gave two isomeric alkenes X and Y with molecular formula C_6H_{12}. On reductive ozonolysis, X and Y gave four compounds CH_3COCH_3, CH_3CHO, CH_3CH_2CHO and $(CH_3)_2CHCHO$. The alkyl halide is
(a) 2-bromohexane **[Kerala CEE]**
(b) 2,2-dimethyl-1-bromobutane
(c) 4-bromo-2-methylpentane
(d) 2-bromo-2,3-dimethylbutane
(e) 3-bromo-2-methylpentane

2011

24 Given reaction, 'Y' in the reaction is

$$\text{(cyclohexyl)}—Br \xrightarrow[\text{Mg}]{\text{Ether}} X \xrightarrow[H_2O]{\text{HCl}} Y \text{ (main product)}$$

(a) hexane **[DUMET]**
(b) cyclohexane
(c) cyclohexylcyclohexane
(d) cyclohexyl ether

25 Which one of the following is not true for the hydrolysis of *t*-butyl bromide with aqueous NaOH? **[KCET]**
(a) Reaction occurs through the S_N1 mechanism
(b) The intermediate formed is a carbocation
(c) Rate of the reaction doubles when the concentration of alkali is doubled
(d) Rate of the reaction doubles when the concentration of *t*-butyl bromide is doubled

26 Following is the substitution reaction in which —CN replaces —Cl

$$R—Cl + \underset{\text{(alcoholic)}}{KCN} \xrightarrow{\Delta} R—CN + KCl$$

To obtain propanenitrile, R—Cl should be **[KCET]**
(a) chloroethane (b) 1-chloropropane
(c) chloromethane (d) 2-chloropropane

27 Which of the following alkyl halides is hydrolysed by S_N2 mechanism? **[BVP]**
(a) $C_6H_5CH_2Br$ (b) CH_3Br
(c) $CH_2{=}CHCH_2Br$ (d) $(CH_3)_3CBr$

28 $CH_3CH_2CH_2Br \xrightarrow[\text{alcohol}]{\text{KOH}} CH_3CH{=}CH_2$
The above reaction is an example of .... reaction.
(a) substitution (b) elimination **[OJEE]**
(c) addition (d) rearrangement

2010

29 *iso*-propyl bromide on Wurtz reaction gives **[RPMT]**
(a) hexane (b) propane
(c) 2, 3-dimethylbutane (d) *neo*-hexane

30 The reaction,

$$RX + 2Na + RX \xrightarrow{\text{Dry ether}} R—R + 2NaX$$

is called **[Haryana PMT]**
(a) Sandmeyer's reaction (b) Wurtz reaction
(c) Fittig reaction (d) Williamson's synthesis

31 $CH_3CH_2Br \xrightarrow[\Delta]{aq.\ KOH} A \xrightarrow[\Delta]{KMnO_4/H^+}$
$B \xrightarrow[\Delta]{NH_3} C \xrightarrow[\text{alkali}]{Br_2} D$, D is **[KCET]**
(a) CH_3Br (b) CH_3CONH_2
(c) CH_3NH_2 (d) $CHBr_3$

32 Reaction of methyl bromide with aqueous sodium hydroxide involves **[KCET]**
(a) racemisation
(b) S_N1 mechanism
(c) retention of configuration
(d) S_N2 mechanism

33 The reactivities of CH_3Cl, $CH_3CH_2CH_2Cl$ and C_6H_5Cl are in the order [CMC]
(a) $CH_3Cl > CH_3CH_2CH_2Cl > C_6H_5Cl$
(b) $CH_3CH_2CH_2Cl > CH_3Cl > C_6H_5Cl$
(c) $C_6H_5Cl > CH_3CH_2CH_2Cl > CH_3Cl$
(d) $CH_3Cl > C_6H_5Cl > CH_3CH_2CH_2Cl$

34 Identify Z, in the following series.

$$C_2H_5I \xrightarrow{\text{alc. KOH}} X \xrightarrow{Br_2} Y \xrightarrow{KCN} Z$$ [VMMC]

(a) CH_3CH_2CN (b) $NCCH_2—CH_2CN$
(c) $BrCH_2—CH_2CN$. (d) $BrCH=CHCN$

2009

35 Identify the reagents A and B in the given reaction sequence. [KCET]

$$CH_3—CH_2—C(Cl)(CH_3)—CH_3 \xrightarrow{A} CH_3—CH_2—C(OH)(CH_3)—CH_3 \xrightarrow{B} CH_3—CH=C(CH_3)—CH_3$$

(a) alc. KOH, aq. KOH (b) alc. KOH, H_3O^+
(c) aq. KOH, conc. HNO_3 (d) aq. KOH, alc. KOH

36 $CH_3—CH_2—Br$ on treatment with $LiAlH_4$ gives ethane gas while $(CH_3)_3C—Br$ on same treatment gives H_2 gas because [OJEE]
(a) the former is S_N2 and latter is E_2 reaction
(b) the former is E_2 and latter is S_N2 reaction
(c) the former is S_N1 and latter is E_2 reaction
(d) the former is E_2 and latter is S_N2 reaction

37 Which one of the following gives only one monochloro derivative? [Kerala CEE]
(a) *n*-hexane (b) 2-methylpentane
(c) 2, 3-dimethylpentane (d) 3-methylpentane
(e) *neo*-pentane

38 When *neo*-pentyl bromide is subjected to Wurtz reaction, the product formed is [Kerala CEE]
(a) 2, 2, 4, 4-tetramethylhexane
(b) 2, 2, 4, 4-tetramethylpentane
(c) 2, 2, 5, 5-tetramethylhexane
(d) 2, 2, 3, 3-tetramethylhexane
(e) 2, 2, 3, 3-tetramethylpentane

39 Which one of the following species will be most reactive in S_N2 reaction? [AMU]
(a) CH_3CH_2Cl (b) $(CH_3)_3CCH_2Cl$
(c) chlorocyclohexane (Cl on ring) (d) 1-chloro-2,2-dimethylcyclohexane (Cl on ring)

40 Consider the following reactions,

$$C_2H_5Cl + AgCN \xrightarrow{EtOH/H_2O} \underset{(Major)}{X}$$

Which one of the following statements is true for X?
I. It gives propanoic acid on hydrolysis.
II. It has an ester functional group.
III. It has a nitrogen linked to ethyl carbon.
IV. It has a cyanide group. [EAMCET]
(a) IV (b) III
(c) II (d) I

2008

41 The catalyst used in the preparation of an alkyl chloride by the action of dry HCl on an alcohol is [AFMC]
(a) anhydrous $AlCl_3$ (b) $FeCl_3$
(c) anhydrous $ZnCl_2$ (d) Cu

42 Which of the following can give a Grignard reagent when reacted with magnesium in dry ether? [UP CPMT]
(a) C_2H_6 (b) C_2H_5Cl
(c) C_2H_5OH (d) C_2H_5CN

43 The alkyl halides that can be made by free radical halogenation of alkanes are [Manipal]
(a) RCl and RBr but not RF or RI
(b) RF, RCl and RBr but not RI
(c) RF, RCl, RBr, RI
(d) RF, RCl and RI but not RBr

44 A mixture of 1-chlorobutane and 2-chlorobutane when treated with alcoholic KOH gives [Manipal]
(a) 1-butene
(b) 2-butene
(c) *iso*-butylene
(d) mixture of 1-butene + 2-butene

45 $$C_2H_5Cl \xrightarrow[Ag_2O]{Moist} A \xrightarrow[360°C]{Al_2O_3} B \xrightarrow{S_2Cl_2} C$$

In the above sequence of reactions, identify C. [Punjab PMET]
(a) Chloretone (b) Chloropicrin
(c) Mustard gas (d) Lewisite gas

46 Alkyl halides react with dialkyl copper reagents to give [JCECE]
(a) alkenyl halides (b) alkanes
(c) alkyl copper halides (d) alkenes

2007

47 Ethyl bromide is industrially prepared from [UP CPMT]
(a) ethyl alcohol + HBr (b) ethanol + Br_2
(c) alcohol + HBr (d) None of these

48 Which of the following is most polar? [MP PMT]
(a) CH_3Cl (b) CH_3F
(c) CH_3Br (d) CH_3I

49 In a group of isomeric alkyl halides, the order of boiling points is [J&K CET]
(a) primary < secondary < tertiary
(b) primary > secondary < tertiary
(c) primary < secondary > tertiary
(d) primary > secondary > tertiary

50 Reactivity order of halides for dehydrohalogenation is [Punjab PMET]
(a) $R—F > R—Cl > R—Br > R—I$
(b) $R—I > R—Br > R—Cl > R—F$
(c) $R—I > R—Cl > R—Br > R—F$
(d) $R—F > R—I > R—Br > R—Cl$

51 Ethyl chloride on reduction with $LiAlH_4$ gives compound X as important product. X on chlorination with one mole of Cl_2 in the presence of light at ordinary temperature gives Y. What is Y? [EAMCET]
(a) C_2H_6 (b) C_2H_4 (c) C_2H_5Cl (d) C_2H_5OH

2006

52 The major product formed in the following reaction
$CH_3CH(Cl)CH_2—CH_2OH \xrightarrow{aq.\ KOH}$ is [AIIMS]
(a) $CH_3CH{=}CH—CH_2OH$
(b) $CH_2{=}CH—CH_2—CH_2OH$
(c) $CH_3—CH—CH_2$ (with CH and CH_2 joined through O—CH_2 ring)
(d) $CH_3—CH(OH)—CH_2—CH_2OH$

53 Alcoholic solution of KOH is used for [BHU]
(a) dehydration (b) dehydrogenation
(c) dehydrohalogenation (d) dehalogenation

54 A secondary halide with molecular formula C_4H_9Cl reacts with Na in dry ether to form compound A. The compound A is [Punjab PMET]
(a) 2, 5-dimethylhexane
(b) octane
(c) 3, 4-dimethylhexane
(d) 2, 2, 4, 4-tetramethylbutane

55 In the reaction,
$R—X \xrightarrow{alc.\ KCN} A \xrightarrow{dil.\ HCl} B$, the product B is [KCET]
(a) alkyl chloride (b) aldehyde
(c) carboxylic acid (d) ketone

56 The major product formed in the following reaction is
$CH_3—C(CH_3)(H)—CH_2Br \xrightarrow[CH_3OH]{CH_3O^-}$ [AIIMS]
(a) $CH_3—C(CH_3)(H)—CH_2OCH_3$ (b) $CH_3—CH(OCH_3)—CH_2CH_3$
(c) $CH_3—C(CH_3){=}CH_2$ (d) $CH_3—C(CH_3)(OCH_3)—CH_3$

2005

57 Which of the following is liquid at room temperature? [AFMC]
(a) CH_3I–66°C, 42°C (b) CH_3Br–94°C, 3°C
(c) C_2H_5Cl–139°C, 12°C (d) CH_3F–115°C, –78°C

58 C—Cl bond is stronger than C—I bond, because [MHT CET]
(a) C—Cl bond is more polar than C—I
(b) C—Cl bond is polar covalent bond
(c) C—Cl bond is more covalent than C—Cl
(d) C—Cl bond length is longer than C—I

59 Which of the following does not give a precipitate with silver nitrate solution? [J&K CET]
(a) Ethyl bromide (b) Sodium bromide
(c) Calcium chloride (d) Sodium chloride

60 KCN reacts readily to give a cyanide with [J&K CET]
(a) ethyl alcohol (b) ethyl bromide
(c) bromobenzene (d) chlorobenzene

61 The order of reactivities of methyl halide in the formation of Grignard reagent is [AMU]
(a) $CH_3Cl > CH_3Br > CH_3I$
(b) $CH_3I > CH_3Br > CH_3Cl$
(c) $CH_3Br > CH_3I > CH_3Cl$
(d) $CH_3Br > CH_3Cl > CH_3I$

62 What are the reagent and reaction conditions used for converting ethyl chloride to ethyl nitrite (as the major product)? [EAMCET]
(a) KNO_2, C_2H_5OH, Δ
(b) $NaNO_2$, HCl, 0°C
(c) KCN, H_2O, Δ
(d) $AgNO_2, C_2H_5OH, H_2O, \Delta$

63 Ethyl chloride on heating with AgCN forms a compound X. The functional isomer of X is [KCET]
(a) C_2H_5NC (b) $C_2H_5NH_2$
(c) C_2H_5CN (d) None of these

Answers

1 (b)	2 (b)	3 (d)	4 (a)	5 (a)	6 (a)	7 (b)	8 (b)	9 (a)	10 (b)
11 (d)	12 (c)	13 (b)	14 (a)	15 (c)	16 (a)	17 (b)	18 (c)	19 (c)	20 (d)
21 (c)	22 (b)	23 (e)	24 (b)	25 (c)	26 (a)	27 (b)	28 (b)	29 (c)	30 (b)
31 (c)	32 (d)	33 (a)	34 (b)	35 (d)	36 (a)	37 (e)	38 (c)	39 (a)	40 (b)
41 (c)	42 (b)	43 (a)	44 (d)	45 (c)	46 (b)	47 (a)	48 (a)	49 (d)	50 (b)
51 (c)	52 (d)	53 (c)	54 (c)	55 (c)	56 (c)	57 (a)	58 (a)	59 (a)	60 (b)
61 (b)	62 (a)	63 (c)							

Explanations

1 (b) When alcoholic KOH reacts with haloalkanes, the reaction (rate) depends on the following factors:

(i) Size of halogen

(ii) Degree of C - atom, to which the halogen atom is bonded, i.e. more be the degree of haloalkanes, more is its reactivity on the above basis.

As, bromine atom is large in size, thus

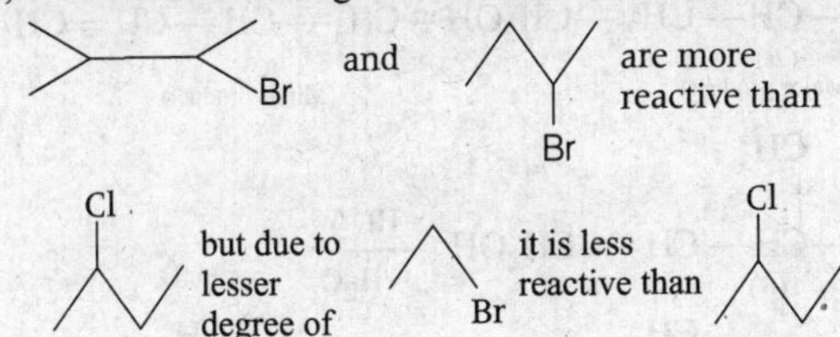

Hence, correct order is $A > C > B > D$.

Thus, option (b) is correct.

2 (b) Alkanes which contain all equivalent hydrogen atoms forms only one monochloro derivative on halogenation.

neo-pentane, $H_3C—\underset{CH_3}{\overset{CH_3}{C}}—CH_3$ contains all equivalent hydrogen atoms. So, it will give only one monochloro derivative on halogenation.

3 (d) When cyclobutane reacts with Cl_2 in presence of light, substitution reaction takes place.

$$\square + Cl_2 \xrightarrow{UV} \square\!-\!Cl + HCl$$

The reaction of product with Na metal in dry ether takes place as,

$$2\,\square\!-\!Cl + 2Na \xrightarrow{\text{dry ether}} \square\!-\!\square$$

4 (a) In S_N1 reactions, carbocations are the intermediates. Greater the stability of carbocation, more easily it is formed and, hence faster will be the rate of reaction.

The stability of carbocation decreases in the order:

3° carbocation > 2° carbocation > 1° carbocation.

$$\therefore \quad \underset{3°}{Ph\overset{+}{C}(CH_3)_2} > \underset{2°}{Ph\overset{+}{C}H\,CH_3} > \underset{1°}{Ph\overset{+}{C}H_2}$$

Thus, option (a) is incorrect, while trends in other options are correct.

5 (a) In S_N2 reaction, nucleophile transfer electron pair to carbon of substrate, leading to the formation of transition state.

$$\ddot{N}u + H_2HC—X \longrightarrow \left[\overset{\delta-}{Nu}\cdots\overset{H}{\underset{H\ H}{C}}\cdots\overset{\delta+}{X}\right] \longrightarrow Nu—CH_3 + X^-$$

H_2O is a neutral nucleophile, while CN^-, NH_2^- and I^- are negatively charged nucleophiles.

Thus, H_2O cannot behave as a nucleophile for S_N2 reaction.

6 (a) When haloalkanes containing β-hydrogen atom is heated with alc. KOH solution, then alkene is formed.

$$CH_3CH_2CH_2Br \xrightarrow{\text{alc. KOH}} \underset{\text{Propene}}{CH_3CH=CH_2}$$

In this reaction, hydrogen is eliminated from β-carbon and the halogen is lost from α-carbon atom of 1-bromopropane. As a result, an alkene is formed as a product. Due to the involvement of elimination of β-hydrogen atom, the process is often called β-elimination.

7 (b)

$$\underset{\text{Neopentyl chloride}}{CH_3—\underset{CH_3}{\overset{CH_3}{C}}—CH_2Cl} \xrightarrow{\text{Anhy. }AlCl_3} \underset{1°\text{ carbocation}}{CH_3—\underset{CH_3}{\overset{CH_3}{C}}—\overset{\oplus}{C}H_2}$$

$$\xrightarrow{\text{Rearrangement of carbocation}} \underset{3°\text{ carbocation (most stable)}}{CH_3—\underset{CH_3}{\overset{\oplus}{C}}—CH_2—CH_3} \xrightarrow{C_6H_5—H} C_6H_5—\overset{CH_2CH_3}{C}(CH_3)_2$$

8 (b) According to Saytzeff's rule, dehydrohalogenation occurs in such a way that the major product is highly substituted.

$$CH_3CH_2CH(F)CH_3 \xrightarrow[CH_3OH]{CH_3O^-} \underset{\text{(Major)}}{CH_3CH=CHCH_3} + \underset{\text{(Minor)}}{CH_3CH_2CH=CH_2}$$

9 (a) The reaction is as follows:

$$\underset{\text{Methyl bromide}}{CH_3-Br} \xrightarrow{\text{Mg / ether}} CH_3-MgBr \xrightarrow[\text{(ii) } H_2O]{\text{(i) } CO_2} \underset{\text{Ethanoic acid}}{CH_3-\overset{O}{\overset{\|}{C}}-OH}$$

$$\xrightarrow[\Delta]{CH_3OH/H^+} \underset{\text{Methyl ethanoate}}{CH_3-\overset{O}{\overset{\|}{C}}-OCH_3}$$

Hence, the product 'P' is methyl ethanoate.

10 (b) The suitable reagent for Wurtz reaction is Na/ether. An ethereal solution of an alkyl halide is treated with sodium to produce higher alkanes. This reaction involves the formation of new C—C bond. e.g.

$$\underset{\text{Ethyl bromide}}{2CH_3CH_2Br} + 2Na \xrightarrow{\text{Ether}} \underset{\text{Butane}}{CH_3CH_2CH_2CH_3}$$

11 (d) The given reaction takes place as follows :

$$\underset{(A)}{CH_4} \xrightarrow[\text{Step 1}]{Br_2/h\nu} CH_3Br \xrightarrow[\text{Wurtz reaction (Step 2)}]{\text{Na / dry ether}} CH_3-CH_3$$

***Step* I** Alkyl halide is formed by free radical halogenation of alkane in the presence of UV-light.

***Step* II** The formed alkyl halide reacts with sodium in the presence of dry ether to form alkane containing double number of carbon atoms present in alkyl halide.

This reaction is known as Wurtz reaction.

From the above reaction, it is concluded that option (d) is correct as in all other cases the hydrocarbon formed in step 2 will have four carbon atoms.

12 (c)
$$\underset{\substack{\text{1-bromopropane} \\ (X)}}{CH_3CH_2CH_2Br} + Mg \xrightarrow{\text{Dry ether}} \underset{(Y)}{CH_3CH_2CH_2MgBr}$$

$$\xrightarrow{HCHO} CH_3CH_2CH_2CH_2-O-MgBr$$

$$\xrightarrow{H_2O} \underset{\text{1-butanol}}{CH_3CH_2CH_2CH_2OH} + Mg\begin{smallmatrix} Br \\ OH \end{smallmatrix}$$

13 (b) Assertion and reason both are correct statements but reason is not the correct explanation of assertion. For the same hydrocarbon part, boiling point depends upon the atomic mass of halogen atom. Higher the mass of the halogen atom, higher will be the boiling point. So, boiling point decreases with decrease in atomic mass of halogen atom. Thus, the decreasing order of boiling point is,

$$RI > RBr > RCl > RF$$

14 (a) (i) $CH_3CH_2CH_2Br + KOH \rightarrow CH_3CH{=}CH_2 + KBr + H_2O$

Elimination reaction

(ii) $H_3C-CH(Br)-CH_3 + KOH \longrightarrow H_3C-CH(OH)-CH_3 + KBr$

Substitution reaction

(iii) Cyclohexene $+ Br_2 \longrightarrow$ 1,2-dibromocyclohexane

Addition reaction

15 (c) The given reaction follows S_N2 mechanism and S_N2 reactions are favoured in polar aprotic medium like DMSO, DMF... etc.

$$CH_3CH_2CH_2Br + NaCN \xrightarrow{DMF} CH_3CH_2CH_2CN + NaBr$$

So, the correct option is (c).

16 (a)
$$CH_3-\underset{}{\overset{CH_3}{\overset{|}{CH}}}-CH_2-CH_2-Br \xrightarrow[\Delta]{\text{alc. KOH}} \underset{(A)}{CH_3-\overset{CH_3}{\overset{|}{CH}}-CH{=}CH_2} + H_2O$$

$$\underset{(A)}{CH_3-\overset{CH_3}{\overset{|}{CH}}-CH{=}CH_2} \xrightarrow{\text{Conc. } H_2SO_4}$$

$$CH_3-\overset{CH_3}{\overset{|}{CH}}-CH_2-CH_2\cdot HSO_4 \xrightarrow[\Delta]{H_2O}$$

$$\underset{\substack{(B) \\ \text{(Major product)}}}{CH_3-\overset{CH_3}{\overset{|}{CH}}-CH_2-CH_2OH} + \underset{\substack{(C) \\ \text{(Minor product)}}}{CH_3-\overset{CH_3}{\overset{|}{CH}}-CH{=}CH_2}$$

$$\underset{(B)}{CH_3-\overset{CH_3}{\overset{|}{CH}}-CH_2-CH_2OH} \xrightarrow[-H_2O]{HI,\ \Delta}$$

$$\underset{\substack{(D) \\ \text{(Major product)}}}{CH_3-\overset{CH_3}{\overset{|}{CH}}-\underset{I}{\underset{|}{CH}}-CH_3} + \underset{\substack{(E) \\ \text{(Minor product)}}}{CH_3-\overset{CH_3}{\overset{|}{CH}}-CH_2-CH_2I}$$

17 (b) This problem includes concept of S_N1 and S_N2 reaction and factors affecting S_N1 and S_N2 reaction.

During S_N2 reaction of alkyl halide, inversion of configuration takes place instead of rearrangement.

While S_N1 reaction occurs through the formation of carbocation intermediate which is favoured by the presence of Lewis acid and aprotic solvent. Rearrangement of carbocation is also possible in this case.

Thus, statement (b) is incorrect and all other statements are correct.

18 (c) Alkyl bromide reacts with sodium iodide(in acetone or methanol) to form alkyl iodides. This is called Finkelstein reaction.

$$CH_3CH_2CH_2Br \xrightarrow[\text{Dry acetone}]{NaI} CH_3CH_2CH_2I + NaBr$$

19 (c) CH_3Cl is used as methylating agent. The methylating agent is one which is used for the introduction of methyl groups.

20 (d)
$$\underset{\text{Methyl bromide}}{CH_3Br} \xrightarrow[-KBr]{KCN} \underset{\substack{\text{Methyl cyanide} \\ (A)}}{CH_3CN} \xrightarrow{H_3O^+} \underset{\substack{\text{Ethanoic acid} \\ (B)}}{CH_3COOH}$$

$$\xrightarrow[\text{ether}]{LiAlH_4} \underset{(C)}{CH_3CH_2OH}$$

21 (c) In alkaline hydrolysis of a tertiary halide by aqueous alkali, if concentration of alkali is doubled, then the reaction will remain constant because t-alkyl halides with aqueous alkali give S_N1 reaction and rate of S_N1 reaction is not based upon concentration of nucleophile, (i.e. alkali).

22 (b) Alkyl halide on reaction with dry silver oxide (Ag_2O) gives ether

$$\underset{\text{Alkyl halide}}{2RX} + Ag_2O \longrightarrow \underset{\text{Ether}}{R—O—R} + 2AgX$$

23 (e) $CH_3—CH(CH_3)—CH(Br)—CH_2—CH_3 \xrightarrow{\text{Alc. KOH}}$
3-bromo-2-methylpentane

$$\underset{(X)}{CH_3—C(CH_3)=CH—CH_2CH_3} + \underset{(Y)}{CH_3—CH(CH_3)—CH=CHCH_3}$$

$$\underset{(X)}{CH_3—C(CH_3)=CH—CH_2CH_3} \xrightarrow[Zn/H_2O_2]{O_3} CH_3—C(CH_3)=O + CH_3CH_2CHO$$

$$\underset{(Y)}{CH_3—CH(CH_3)—CH=CHCH_3} \xrightarrow[Zn/H_2O_2]{O_3} CH_3—CH(CH_3)—CHO + CH_3CHO$$

24 (b) $C_6H_{11}—Br + Mg \xrightarrow{\text{Ether}} \underset{(X)}{C_6H_{11}—MgBr} \xrightarrow[H_2O]{HCl} \underset{\substack{\text{Cyclohexane}\\(C_6H_{12})\\(Y)}}{C_6H_{12}} + Mg(OH)Br$

25 (c) Statement (c) is not true because hydrolysis of t-butyl bromide takes place through S_N1 mechanism, i.e. rate depends only upon the concentration of alkyl halide.

26 (a) Chloroethane reacts with KCN in the presence of heat to form propanenitrile.

$$\underset{\text{Chloroethane}}{CH_3CH_2Cl} + \underset{\text{Alcoholic}}{KCN} \xrightarrow{\Delta} \underset{\text{Propane nitrile}}{CH_3CH_2CN} + KCl$$

27 (b) S_N2 mechanism involves the back side attack and formation of a transition state, thus less hindered alkyl halide readily undergoes S_N2 mechanism. Among the given, CH_3Br (methyl bromide) is less hindered, thus it is hydrolysed by S_N2 mechanism.

28 (b) The given reaction is an example of elimination reaction, in which one molecule of HBr is eliminated from alkyl halide to give alkene.

29 (c) $\underset{\text{iso-propyl bromide}}{(H_3C)_2CH—Br} + 2Na + Br—CH(CH_3)_2 \xrightarrow{\text{Dry ether}} \underset{\text{2,3-dimethylbutane}}{(H_3C)_2CH—CH(CH_3)_2}$

30 (b) When two molecules of alkyl halides (same or different) react with metallic sodium in the presence of ether to form alkane, this reaction is called Wurtz reaction.

31 (c) $CH_3CH_2Br \xrightarrow[\Delta]{aq.\ KOH} \underset{(A)}{CH_3CH_2OH} \xrightarrow[\Delta]{KMnO_4/H^+}$

$$\underset{\substack{\text{Acetic acid}\\(B)}}{CH_3COOH} \xrightarrow{NH_3} CH_3CO\overset{-}{O}\overset{+}{N}H_4 \xrightarrow{\Delta} \underset{\substack{\text{Acetamide}\\(C)}}{CH_3CONH_2} \xrightarrow[\text{(Hofmann bromamide reaction)}]{Br_2/\text{alkali}} \underset{\substack{\text{Methyl amine}\\(D)}}{CH_3NH_2}$$

32 (d) Since, the reaction rate depends upon the concentration of both reactant and nucleophile, it follows S_N2 mechanism. It involves inversion of configuration.

$$\overset{\ominus}{O}H + H_3C—Br \xrightarrow{\text{Backside attack}} \left[HO\overset{-\delta}{---}CH_3\overset{\delta-}{---}Br\right]_{\text{Transition state}} \longrightarrow HO—CH_3 + Br^-$$

33 (a) Bulky group causes steric hindrance in the formation of transition state. Therefore, higher homologous are less reactive than lower homologous.

∴ The correct order is $CH_3Cl > CH_3\ CH_2CH_2Cl > C_6H_5Cl$

34 (b) $C_2H_5I \xrightarrow[-HI]{\text{alc. KOH}} \underset{(X)}{CH_2=CH_2} \xrightarrow{Br_2} \underset{(Y)}{BrCH_2—CH_2Br} \xrightarrow{KCN} \underset{(Z)}{NCCH_2—CH_2CN}$

35 (d) The reaction is completed as shown below :

$$CH_3—CH_2—C(Cl)(CH_3)—CH_3 \xrightarrow{aq.\ KOH} CH_3—CH_2—C(OH)(CH_3)—CH_3$$

$$\xrightarrow{aq.\ KOH} CH_3—CH=C(CH_3)—CH_3$$

∵ The reagents (A) and (B) are aq. KOH and alc. KOH respectively and the correct option is (d).

36 (a) $CH_3—CH_2—Br$ (attacked by H^-) — S_N2 mechanism; $H—C(H)(H)—C(CH_3)(CH_3)—Br$ (with H^-) — E-2 mechanism

Primary alkyl halide undergoes reduction to form ethane *via* S_N2 mechanism where as, tertiary alkyl halide undergoes elimination, liberating H_2 gas *via* E-2 mechanism.

37 *(e)* Compound having only one kind of hydrogen, gives only one monochloro derivative.

(a) *n*-hexane — 3 types of hydrogen, i.e. three monochloro derivatives.

(b) 2-methylpentane — 5 types of hydrogens, i.e. five monochloro derivatives.

(c) 2,3-dimethylpentane — 7 types of hydrogens, i.e. seven monochloro derivatives

(d) 3-methylpentane — 4 types of hydrogens, i.e. four monochloro derivatives.

(e) *neo*-pentane — Only one type of hydrogen hence one monochloro derivative, i.e. $(CH_3)_3C{-}CH_2{-}Cl$

38 *(c)* In Wurtz reaction, an alkane with double the number of carbon atoms, as parent alkyl halide has, is obtained.

$$\underset{neo\text{-pentylbromide}}{CH_3{-}C(CH_3)_2{-}CH_2{-}Br} + 2Na + Br{-}CH_2{-}C(CH_3)_2{-}CH_3 \xrightarrow[-2NaBr]{\text{Dry ether}} \underset{2,2,5,5\text{-tetramethylhexane}}{\overset{1}{C}H_3{-}\overset{2}{C}(CH_3)_2{-}\overset{3}{C}H_2{-}\overset{4}{C}H_2{-}\overset{5}{C}(CH_3)_2{-}\overset{6}{C}H_3}$$

39 *(a)* S_N2 is an inversion reaction, so will be favoured by least sterically hindered carbon atom or a primary carbon atom. Hence, CH_3CH_2Cl will be most reactive in S_N2 reaction.

40 *(b)* $C_2H_5{-}Cl + AgCN \xrightarrow[H_2O]{EtOH/} C_2H_5{-}NC + AgCl$

Nitrogen linked to ethyl carbon.

41 *(c)* —OH group is converted into —Cl group by $SOCl_2$ or anhydride $ZnCl_2$/concentrated HCl or HCl etc.

42 *(b)* C_2H_5Cl gives Grignard reagent when reacted with Mg in dry ether.

$$RX + Mg\,(\text{dry}) \xrightarrow{\text{Dry ether}} RMgX$$

$$C_2H_5Cl + Mg \xrightarrow{\text{Dry ether}} \underset{\text{Ethyl magnesium chloride}}{C_2H_5MgCl}$$

43 *(a)* *R*Cl and *R*Br can be prepared by free radical halogenation of alkanes while *R*F and *R*I cannot be prepared. With F_2, the reaction is not only explosive but also brings cleavage of C—C bonds while with I_2, the reaction is too slow that it does not have any practical value.

44 *(d)* On treatment with alcoholic KOH, 1-chlorobutane gives 1-butene while 2-chlorobutane gives 2-butene (major) + 1-butene (minor). Therefore, a mixture of 1-butene + 2-butene is formed.

45 *(c)*

$$\underset{\text{Ethyl chloride}}{C_2H_5Cl} \xrightarrow[Ag_2O]{\text{Moist}} \underset{\text{Ethanol}}{C_2H_5OH} \xrightarrow[360°C]{Al_2O_3} \underset{\text{Ethene}}{CH_2{=}CH_2} \xrightarrow{S_2Cl_2} \underset{\text{Mustard gas}}{S(CH_2CH_2Cl)_2} + S$$

46 *(b)* It is Corey-House synthesis of alkanes.

$$R-X + Li \longrightarrow R-Li + CuI \rightarrow R_2CuLi$$

$$R_2CuLi + R'-X \rightarrow R-R' \text{ (alkane)}$$

($R'-X$ should be 1° or methyl halide)

This synthesis is important because it affords a synthesis of a larger alkane from two smaller alkyl halides.

47 *(a)* Ethyl bromide is industrially prepared by refluxing ethyl alcohol with constant boiling HBr (48%) in presence of a little amount of concentrated sulphuric acid.

$$\underset{\text{Ethyl alcohol}}{C_2H_5OH} + HBr \xrightarrow[\text{Reflux}]{H_2SO_4\text{ (conc.)}} \underset{\text{Ethyl bromide}}{C_2H_5Br} + H_2O$$

48 *(a)* CH_3Cl has higher dipole moment than CH_3F due to much longer C—Cl bond length than C—F bond length.

49 *(d)* Alkyl halides with branched and more spherical shapes have lower boiling point as a result of their smaller surface area.

So, order of boiling points is

primary > secondary > tertiary

50 *(b)* F, Cl, Br and I are the elements of group 17 of the modern periodic table. In a group, atomic radii increases from top to bottom and the bond dissociation energy of *R*—*X* bond decreases in the order,

$$R{-}F > R{-}Cl > R{-}Br > R{-}I$$

So, during dehydrohalogenation, *R*—I bond breaks more easily than *R*—F bond. Hence, order of reactivity will be

$$R{-}I > R{-}Br > R{-}Cl > R{-}F$$

51 *(c)*

$$\underset{\text{Ethyl chloride}}{C_2H_5Cl} + 2H \xrightarrow{LiAlH_4} \underset{\text{Ethane }(X)}{C_2H_6} \xrightarrow[\text{Chlorination, } h\nu]{Cl_2} \underset{\text{Ethyl chloride }(Y)}{C_2H_5Cl}$$

52 *(d)* It is an example of nucleophilic substitution reaction.

$$R{-}X + KOH \longrightarrow R{-}OH + KX$$

$$\text{So, } CH_3CH(Cl)CH_2{-}CH_2OH \xrightarrow{aq.\ KOH} CH_3{-}CH(OH){-}CH_2{-}CH_2OH$$

53 *(c)*

$$CH_3{-}CH_2Br + KOH(\text{alc.}) \xrightarrow{\text{Dehydrohalogenation}} CH_2{=}CH_2 + KBr + H_2O$$

In alcohol ROH, alkoxide ion (RO^-) is present which is a strong base. It abstracts proton from β-carbon of alkyl halide and favours elimination reaction.

$$\underset{\text{Alcohol}}{ROH} + KOH \longrightarrow \underset{\text{Potassium alkoxide}}{ROK} + H_2O$$

$$ROK \longrightarrow \underset{\text{Alkoxide ion}}{RO^-} + K^+$$

$$RO^- + H-\overset{\beta}{C}H_2-\overset{\alpha}{C}H_2Br \longrightarrow ROH + CH_2{=}CH_2 + Br^-$$

54 (c) The isomers of C_4H_9Cl are

$CH_3CH_2CH_2CH_2Cl$ (Primary halide)

$CH_3-CH(CH_2Cl)-CH_3$ (Primary halide)

$CH_3-CH(Cl)-CH_2CH_3$ (Secondary halide)

$CH_3-C(CH_3)_2-CH_3$ (Tertiary halide)

The reaction of secondary halide with Na in dry ether is given below.

$$2CH_3-CH(Cl)-CH_2CH_3 + 2Na \xrightarrow{\text{dry ether}} \underset{(A)}{CH_3-CH_2-CH(CH_3)-CH(CH_3)-CH_2-CH_3}$$

∴ The compound A is 3, 4-dimethylhexane and the correct option is (c).

55 (c) $R-X \xrightarrow{\text{alc. KCN}} \underset{\text{Alkyl cyanide}}{R-CN} \xrightarrow{\text{dil. HCl}} \underset{\text{Carboxylic acid}}{R-COOH}$

56 (c) Branching at β-carbon increases the rate of E-2 reaction because of the increased stability of the alkene product. The mechanism of the reaction is as follows:

$$CH_3-\overset{CH_3}{\underset{H}{\overset{|\beta}{C}}}-\overset{\alpha}{C}H_2-Br \xrightarrow[\text{(E-2 reaction)}]{-Br^-} CH_3-\overset{CH_3}{\overset{|}{C}}{=}CH_2$$

CH_3O^-

57 (a) CH_3Br (b·p· = 3°C), CH_3F (b·p· = – 78°C) and C_2H_5Cl (bp = 12°C) are all gases at room temperature as their boiling point is much less than room temperature, i.e. they boil (vaporise) at a temperature much less than room temperature. But CH_3I has boiling point 42° C which is above the room temperature so, it is liquid at room temperature and solidifies at around – 66° C.

58 (a) μ_D for C—Cl bond = 1.56 D

μ_D for C—I bond = 1.29 D

C—Cl bond is more polar than C—I bond. Among different alkyl halides C—X bond length increases as the size of halogen atom increases. As bond length is inversely proportional to bond strength therefore, C—Cl bond is stronger than C—I bond.

59 (a) Ethyl bromide does not give a precipitate with $AgNO_3$ solution because it does not give free Br^- ions to react with $AgNO_3$ solution.

60 (b) Ethyl bromide reacts with KCN to give ethyl cyanide.

$$\underset{\text{Ethyl bromide}}{C_2H_5Br} + KCN(\text{alc.}) \longrightarrow \underset{\text{Ethyl cyanide}}{C_2H_5CN} + KBr$$

61 (b) Order of reactivities of alkyl halides depends upon C—X bond length. As, on going down the group, the size of halogen atom increases. Therefore, C—X bond becomes weaker.

Hence, the order of reactivities of methyl halide in the formation of Grignard reagent is, $CH_3I > CH_3Br > CH_3Cl$.

62 (a) Potassium nitrite converts ethyl chloride into ethyl nitrite.

$$C_2H_5Cl + KNO_2 \xrightarrow[\Delta]{C_2H_5OH} \underset{\text{Ethyl nitrite}}{C_2H_5ONO}$$

63 (c) $C_2H_5Cl + AgCN \longrightarrow \underset{(X)}{C_2H_5NC} + AgCl$

Functional isomer of X is C_2H_5CN.

Topic 2

Di and Polyhalogen Derivatives of Alkyl Halides

2019

1 Diethylcarbonate is obtained by the reaction of **[MP PMT]**
(a) ethanol (b) methanol
(c) ethanol (d) methanal

2018

2 **Assertion** (A) CH_4 does not react with Cl_2 in dark.
Reason (R) Chlorination of CH_4 takes place in sunlight. **[AIIMS]**
(a) Both Assertion and Reason are true and Reason is the correct explanation of Assertion.
(b) Both Assertion and Reason are true and Reason is not the correct explanation of Assertion.
(c) Assertion is true but Reason is false.
(d) Both Assertion and Reason are false.

2010

3 Hydrolysis of trichloromethane with aqueous KOH gives **[AFMC]**
(a) methanol (b) acetic acid
(c) ethanol (d) formic acid

4 If 1,3-dibromopropane reacts with zinc and NaI, the product obtained is **[AFMC]**
(a) propene (b) propane
(c) cyclopropane (d) hexane

5 Reaction of chloroform with KOH in the presence of a primary aromatic amine is called **[Manipal]**
(a) carbylamine reaction (b) reduction
(c) hydrolysis (d) Wurtz reaction

6 In the reaction, $CH_3NH_2 + X + KOH \longrightarrow CH_3NC$ the compound X is **[MP PMT]**
(a) CH_2Cl_2 (b) $CHCl_3$
(c) CH_3Cl (d) CCl_4

7 **Assertion** (A) $CHCl_3$ is stored in closed, dark coloured bottles completely filled so that air is kept out.
Reason (R) 1° amines on reaction with ethanolic KOH and $CHCl_3$ gives carbylamine. **[VMMC]**
(a) Both A and R are correct and R is the correct explanation of A
(b) Both A and R are correct and R is not the correct explanation of A
(c) A is correct but R is incorrect
(d) Both A and R are incorrect

2009

8 Ethylidene dibromide $\xrightarrow{A}$ $CH \equiv CH$, A is **[UP CPMT]**
(a) *aq*. KOH (b) alc. KOH
(c) conc. H_2SO_4 (d) All of these

9 A dihaloalkane X, having formula $C_3H_6Cl_2$, on hydrolysis gives a compound, that can reduce Tollen's reagent. The compound X is **[MHT CET]**
(a) 1, 2-dichloropropane (b) 1, 1-dichloropropane
(c) 1, 3-dichloropropane (d) 2, 2-dichloropropane

10 Chloroform on reduction with zinc dust and water gives **[MHT CET]**
(a) methyl chloride (b) dichloromethane
(c) chloromethane (d) methane

11 An organic compound on heating with CuO produces CO_2 but no water. The organic compound may be **[KCET]**
(a) chloroform (b) methane
(c) ethyl iodide (d) carbon tetrachloride

2008

12 The chemical formula of 'tear gas' is **[AIIMS]**
(a) $COCl_2$ (b) CO_2 (c) Cl_2 (d) CCl_3NO_2

13 Which of the following is added to chloroform to slow down its aerial oxidation in presence of light? **[AFMC]**
(a) Carbonyl chloride (b) Ethyl alcohol
(c) Sodium hydroxide (d) Nitric acid

14 Iodoform gives a precipitate with $AgNO_3$ on heating but chloroform does not because **[UP CPMT]**
(a) C—I bond in iodoform is weak and C—Cl bond in chloroform is strong
(b) chloroform is covalent
(c) iodoform is ionic
(d) None of the above

15 CCl_4 is a well known fire extinguisher. However after using it to extinguish fire, the room should be well ventilated. This is because **[Kerala CEE]**
(a) it is flammable at higher temperature
(b) it is toxic
(c) it produces phosgene by reaction with water vapour at higher temperatures
(d) it is corrosive
(e) it is anaesthetic

16 Which of the following has highest chlorine content? [Haryana PMT]
(a) Pyrene (b) DDT
(c) Chloral (d) BHC

17 $AgNO_3$ does not give precipitate with $CHCl_3$ because [BCECE]
(a) $CHCl_3$ does not ionise in water
(b) $AgNO_3$ is chemically inert
(c) $CHCl_3$ is chemically inert
(d) None of the above

2007

18 When ethyl alcohol reacts with Cl_2 in the presence of NaOH, the product will be [BHU]
(a) CH_3Cl (b) C_2H_5Cl (c) $CCl_3 \cdot CHO$ (d) $CHCl_3$

19 2,2-dichloropropane on hydrolysis yields [MHT CET]
(a) acetone (b) 2,2-propane diol
(c) isopropyl alcohol (d) acetaldehyde

20 Chloropicrin is obtained by the reaction of [Manipal]
(a) steam on carbon tetrachloride
(b) nitric acid on chlorobenzene
(c) chlorine on picric acid
(d) nitric acid on chloroform

21 Chloroform gives a trichloro derivative of an alcohol on reaction with [Kerala CEE]
(a) concentrated nitric acid (b) aqueous alkali
(c) acetone and alkali (d) sodium ethoxide
(e) a primary amine and an alkali

22 Which one of the following is not correct order of boiling points of the alkyl/aryl halides? [Kerala CEE]
(a) $CHCl_3 > CH_2Cl_2$
(b) $CH_3(CH_2)_3Cl > CH_3(CH_2)_2Cl$
(c) $(CH_3)_3CCl > (CH_3)_2CHCH_2Cl$
(d) $CH_3(CH_2)_3Cl > CH_3CH_2CHClCH_3$
(e) $C_6H_5Br > C_6H_5Cl$

23 When $CH_3CH_2CHCl_2$ is treated with $NaNH_2$, the product formed is [Punjab PMET]
(a) $CH_3—CH{=}CH_2$ (b) $CH_3—C{\equiv}CH$
(c) $CH_3CH_2CH(NH_2)_2$ (d) $CH_3CH_2CH(Cl)(NH_2)$

2006

24 Freon used as refrigerant is [AFMC]
(a) $CF_2{=}CF_2$ (b) CH_2F_2
(c) CCl_2F_2 (d) CF_4

25 Which of the following gas is used in warfare? [UP CPMT]
(a) N_2O (b) $CCl_3 \cdot NO_2$
(c) CO_2 (d) O_2

26 The reaction conditions used for converting 1,2-dibromopropane to propylene are [J&K CET]
(a) Excess KOH, alcohol/Δ
(b) KOH, water/Δ
(c) Zn, alcohol/Δ
(d) Na, alcohol/Δ

27 The raw materials for the commercial manufacture of DDT are [Kerala CEE]
(a) chlorobenzene and chloroform
(b) chlorobenzene and chloromethane
(c) chlorobenzene and chloral
(d) chlorobenzene and iodoform
(e) chlorobenzene and BHC

2005

28 1,2-dibromoethane reacts with alcoholic KOH to yield a product *X*. The hybridisation state of the carbons present in *X* respectively are [EAMCET]
(a) *sp*, *sp* (b) sp^3, sp^3
(c) sp^2, sp^2 (d) sp^3, sp^2

Answers

1 (c)	2 (a)	3 (d)	4 (c)	5 (a)	6 (b)	7 (b)	8 (b)	9 (b)	10 (d)
11 (d)	12 (d)	13 (b)	14 (a)	15 (c)	16 (a)	17 (a)	18 (d)	19 (a)	20 (d)
21 (c)	22 (c)	23 (b)	24 (c)	25 (b)	26 (a)	27 (c)	28 (a)		

Explanations

1 (*b*) Diethylcarbonate is obtained by the reaction of phosgene with ethanol.

$$COCl_2 + 2C_2H_5OH \longrightarrow O{=}C\begin{matrix} OC_2H_5 \\ OC_2H_5 \end{matrix} + 2HCl$$

$\therefore$ The correct option is (c).

2 (*a*) Both Assertion and Reason are correct and Reason is the correct explanation of the Assertion. Chlorination of CH_4 does not take place in dark as this reaction follows free radical mechanism and free radicals are generated only in the presence of sunlight.

3 (*d*) Trichloromethane on hydrolysis with aqueous KOH give formic acid.

$$\underset{\text{Trichloromethane}}{CH\begin{matrix} Cl \\ Cl \\ Cl \end{matrix}} + 3KOH \longrightarrow \underset{\text{Highly unstable}}{CH\begin{matrix} OH \\ OH \\ OH \end{matrix}} \xrightarrow{-H_2O} \underset{\text{Formic acid}}{H{-}\overset{\overset{\large O}{\|}}{C}{-}OH}$$

4 (*c*) $$\underset{\substack{| \\ Br}}{CH_2}{-}CH_2{-}\underset{\substack{| \\ Br}}{CH_2} \xrightarrow[-ZnBr_2]{\text{Zn or NaI}} \underset{\text{Cyclopropane}}{\triangle}$$

5 (*a*) Aliphatic as well as aromatic amines when treated with chloroform in an alkaline medium, gives an offensive melting compound, called carbylamine. Hence, the reaction is known as carbylamine reaction.

$$C_6H_5NH_2 + 3KOH + CHCl_3 \longrightarrow C_6H_5NC + 3KCl + 3H_2O$$

6 (*b*) Primary amines when warmed with chloroform and alc. KOH produce isocyanides or carbylamines which have very unpleasant odours.

$$CH_3NH_2 + \underset{\substack{\text{Chloroform} \\ 'X'}}{CHCl_3} + 3KOH \rightarrow \underset{\substack{\text{Methyl} \\ \text{isocyanide}}}{CH_3NC} + 3KCl + 3H_2O$$

This is called carbylamine reaction or isocyanide reaction.

7 (*b*) Both A and R are correct and R is not the correct explanation of A.

$CHCl_3$ is stored in dark coloured bottles and properly closed to keep out air because in the presence of air or light, it gets slowly oxidised to poisonous gas phosgene (carbonyl chloride).

$$CHCl_3 + \frac{1}{2}O_2 \xrightarrow[\text{light}]{\text{Air or}} \underset{\text{(Phosgene)}}{COCl_2} + HCl$$

The reaction of 1° amine with ethanolic KOH and $CHCl_3$ is shown below.

$$RNH_2 + \text{alc. KOH} + CHCl_3 \longrightarrow \underset{\text{Carbylamine}}{RNC}$$

8 (*b*) $$\underset{\substack{\text{Ethylidene} \\ \text{dibromide}}}{CH_3CHBr_2} \xrightarrow[-2KBr;\ -2H_2O]{\text{Alc. KOH}} \underset{\text{Acetylene}}{CH{\equiv}CH}$$

Hence, A = Alc. KOH. (a dehydrohalogenating reagent).

9 (*b*) Since, the obtained compound reduces Tollen's reagent, it must be an aldehyde. Thus, it is obvious that both the —Cl atoms are present at C_1. Hence, the compound '*X*' is 1,1-dichloropropane and the reactions are as follows

$$\underset{\substack{\text{1,1-dichloropropane} \\ 'X'}}{CH_3CH_2CHCl_2} \xrightarrow{\text{Hydrolysis}} \underset{\text{Unstable}}{CH_3CH_2CH\begin{matrix} OH \\ OH \end{matrix}}$$

$$\xrightarrow{-H_2O} \underset{\text{Propanal}}{CH_3CH_2CHO} \xrightarrow{\text{Tollen's reagent}} \underset{\text{Propanoic acid}}{CH_3CH_2COOH} + Ag\downarrow$$

10 (*d*) $$\underset{\text{Chloroform}}{CHCl_3} \xrightarrow[-HCl,\ -ZnCl_2]{6[H];\ Zn/H_2O} \underset{\text{Methane}}{CH_4}$$

Chloroform on reduction with Zn and H_2O gives methane CH_4.

11 (*d*) Since the compound on heating produces only CO_2 and no water, thus the compound does not contain any hydrogen atom, hence it is CCl_4.

12 (*d*) Chloropicrin is also known as tear gas. It is obtained by the reaction of chloroform with nitric acid.

$$CHCl_3 + HNO_3 \longrightarrow \underset{\substack{\text{Chloropicrin} \\ \text{(tear gas)}}}{CCl_3NO_2} + H_2O$$

13 (*b*) Chloroform is oxidised to a poisonous gas, by aerial oxidation.

$$CHCl_3 + [O] \longrightarrow \underset{\text{Phosgene}}{COCl_2} + HCl$$

Ethyl alcohol is used as a negative catalyst for the aerial oxidation of chloroform in presence of light. It converts $COCl_2$ to non-poisonous ethyl carbonate.

$$COCl_2 + 2C_2H_5OH \longrightarrow O{=}C(OC_2H_5)_2 + 2HCl$$

14 (*a*) On heating, C—I bond in CHI_3 breaks but C—Cl bond in $CHCl_3$ does not break. This is due to less bond strength of C—I bond than C—Cl bond. Thus, $AgNO_3$ gives precipitate of AgI with iodoform.

15 (*c*) CCl_4 at high temperature reacts with water to give phosgene.

$$CCl_4 + H_2O \xrightarrow{500°C} \underset{\text{Phosgene}}{COCl_2} + 2HCl$$

Phosgene is highly poisonous, so after the use of CCl_4 to extinguish fire, the room should be well ventilated.

16 (*a*) CCl_4 is called pyrene. It has highest chlorine content.

17 (*a*) $AgNO_3$ does not give precipitate with chloroform ($CHCl_3$) because $CHCl_3$ does not ionise in water.

18 (*d*) When ethyl alcohol reacts with chlorine gas in the presence of NaOH, the product will be chloroform.

$$C_2H_5OH + 4Cl_2 + 6NaOH \xrightarrow{\Delta}$$

$$\underset{\text{Chloroform}}{CHCl_3} + HCOONa + 5NaCl + 5H_2O$$

19 (a) 2, 2-dichloropropane on hydrolysis gives acetone.

$$CH_3-\underset{Cl}{\overset{Cl}{C}}-CH_3 \xrightarrow{\text{Hydrolysis}} CH_3-\underset{OH}{\overset{OH}{C}}-CH_3$$

2,2-dichloro propane; Unstable

$$\xrightarrow{-H_2O} CH_3-\underset{\underset{O}{\|}}{C}-CH_3$$

Acetone

20 (d) Chloroform on reaction with nitric acid give chloropicrin (nitro chloroform) according to following reaction.

$$CHCl_3 + HNO_3 \longrightarrow C(NO_2)Cl_3 + H_2O$$

Nitrochloroform (chloropicrin)

21 (c) $CHCl_3 + O{=}C(CH_3)_2 \xrightarrow{NaOH} (HO)(Cl_3C)C(CH_3)_2$

Acetone; (1,1,1-trichloro-2-methyl-propan-2-ol)

22 (c) The boiling point of $(CH_3)_2CHCH_2Cl$ is higher than $(CH_3)_3CCl$, because $(CH_3)_2CHCH_2Cl_2$ has less branching as compared to $(CH_3)_3CCl$.

23 (b) $CH_3-CH_2-CHCl_2 \xrightarrow[\Delta]{NaNH_2} CH_3-CH{=}CHCl$

$$\xrightarrow[\Delta]{NaNH_2} CH_3-C{\equiv}CH$$

Final product

24 (c) Freon used as refrigerant is CCl_2F_2.

$$CCl_4 + 2HF \xrightarrow{Sb_2F_5} CF_2Cl_2 + 2HCl$$

Freon (dichlorodifluoro methane)

25 (b) $CCl_3 \cdot NO_2$ is tear gas and used in warfare. Other gases used in warfare are phosgene ($COCl_2$), mustard gas ($ClC_2H_4-S-C_2H_4Cl$) and lewisite ($CHCl{=}CHAsCl_2$).

26 (a) 1,2-dihalogen (vicinal) derivatives of the alkanes on reaction with excess of KOH and alcohol produces alkynes by the elimination of 2HBr molecules.

$$CH_3-\underset{Br}{CH}-\underset{Br}{CH_2} + \underset{\text{Excess}}{KOH} \xrightarrow{\text{Alcohol}/\Delta} CH_3-C{\equiv}CH$$

1,2-dibromopropane; Propylene

27 (c) The raw materials for the manufacturing of DDT are chlorobenzene and chloral.

$$CCl_3 \cdot CH{=}O + 2\,H-C_6H_4-Cl \xrightarrow{-H_2O,\ H_2SO_4} CCl_3 \cdot CH(C_6H_4-Cl)_2$$

(DDT)

p, p'- dichlorodiphenyltrichloroethane

28 (a) Alkyl halides give elimination reaction with alcoholic KOH and yield an alkene or alkyne (from dihalides) e.g.

$$Br-CH_2-CH_2-Br \xrightarrow[\Delta]{\text{Alc. KOH}} \overset{sp}{CH}{\equiv}\overset{sp}{CH}$$

1,2-dibromoethane; Acetylene

Hence, product has both carbons in *sp*-hybridised state.

Topic 3

Aromatic Halides

2019

1 Among the following, the reaction that proceeds through an electrophilic substitution is **[NEET]**

(a) $C_6H_6 + Cl_2 \xrightarrow{AlCl_3} C_6H_5-Cl + HCl$

(b) $C_6H_6 + Cl_2 \xrightarrow{\text{UV light}} C_6H_6Cl_6$ (hexachlorocyclohexane)

(c) $C_6H_5-CH_2OH + HCl \xrightarrow{\text{Heat}} C_6H_5-CH_2Cl + H_2O$

(d) $C_6H_5-\overset{+}{N_2}Cl^- \xrightarrow{Cu_2Cl_2} C_6H_5-Cl + N_2$

2 The hydrolysis reaction that takes place at the slowest rate, among the following is **[NEET (Odisha)]**

(a) $CH_3-C_6H_4-Cl$ (o-chlorotoluene) $\xrightarrow{aq.NaOH}$ $CH_3-C_6H_4-\overset{\ominus}{O}\overset{\oplus}{Na}$

(b) $H_3C—CH_2—Cl \xrightarrow{aq.\ NaOH} H_3C—CH_2—OH$

(c) $H_2C=CH—CH_2Cl \xrightarrow{aq.\ NaOH} H_2C=CH—CH_2OH$

(d) $C_6H_5—CH_2Cl \xrightarrow{aq.NaOH} C_6H_5—CH_2OH$

2018

3 Which of the following represents Wurtz-Fittig reaction? **[AIIMS]**

(a) $C_6H_5I + 2Na + CH_3I \longrightarrow C_6H_5CH_3 + 2NaI$

(b) $2C_6H_5I + 2Na \longrightarrow C_6H_5C_6H_5 + 2NaI$

(c) $2CH_3CH_2I + 2Na \longrightarrow CH_3CH_2CH_2CH_3 + 2NaI$

(d) $CH_3Br + AgF \longrightarrow CH_3F + AgBr$

4 The compound C_7H_8 undergoes the following reactions

$$C_7H_8 \xrightarrow{3Cl_2/\Delta} A \xrightarrow{Br_2/Fe} B \xrightarrow{Zn/HCl} C$$

The product 'C' is **[NEET]**

(a) 3-bromo-2, 4, 6-trichlorotoluene

(b) *o*-bromotoluene

(c) *m*-bromotoluene

(d) *p*-bromotoluene

2017

5 Identify A and predict the type of reaction, **[NEET]**

$$\text{(3-bromoanisole: } OCH_3 \text{, Br)} \xrightarrow{NaNH_2} A$$

(a) OCH_3, NH_2 (meta) and substitution reaction

(b) OCH_3, NH_2 (ortho) and elimination addition reaction

(c) OCH_3, Br (ortho) and cine substitution reaction

(d) OCH_3 and cine substitution reaction

6 Assertion (A) Presence of nitro group facilitates nucleophilic substitution reactions in aryl halides. **[AIIMS]**

Reason (R) The intermediate carbocation is stable due to presence of nitro group.

(a) Both Assertion and Reason are true and Reason is the correct explanation of Assertion.

(b) Both Assertion and Reason are true but Reason is not the correct explaation of Assertion.

(c) Assertion is true but Reason is false.

(d) Both Assertion and Reason are false.

7 Assertion (A) Aryl halides undergo nucleophilic substitution with ease. **[AIIMS]**

Reason (R) Hybridisation of C-atom attached to halide is sp^3-hybrid.

(a) Both Assertion and Reason are true and Reason is the correct explanation of Assertion.

(b) Both Assertion and Reason are true but Reason is not the correct explanation of Assertion.

(c) Assertion is true but Reason is false.

(d) Both Assertion and Reason are false.

2016

8 Which of the following can be used as the halide component for Friedel-Crafts reaction? **[NEET Phase II]**

(a) Chlorobenzene (b) Bromobenzene

(c) Chloroethene (d) Isopropyl chloride

2014

9 The major product of the reaction of $C_6H_5—CF_3$ with electrophile, E^+, is **[Manipal]**

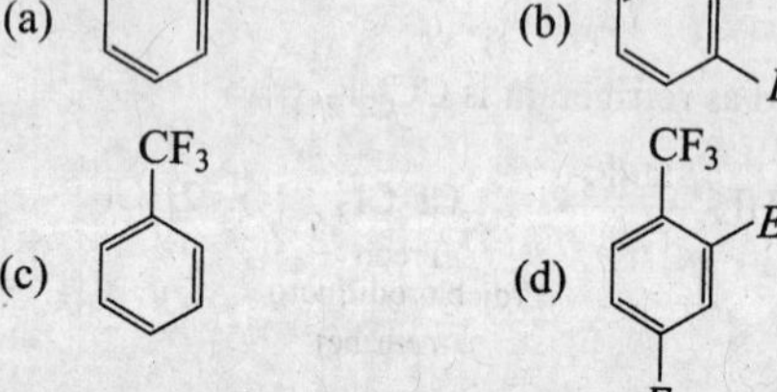

10 Which of the following organic halogen compounds undergoes hydrolysis with aqueous NaOH predominantly by S_N1 mechanism? **[Kerala CEE]**

(a) Ethyl iodide (b) Methyl chloride

(c) *Iso*propyl chloride (d) Chlorobenzene

(e) Benzyl chloride

11 The compound that reacts the fastest with sodium methoxide is **[KCET]**

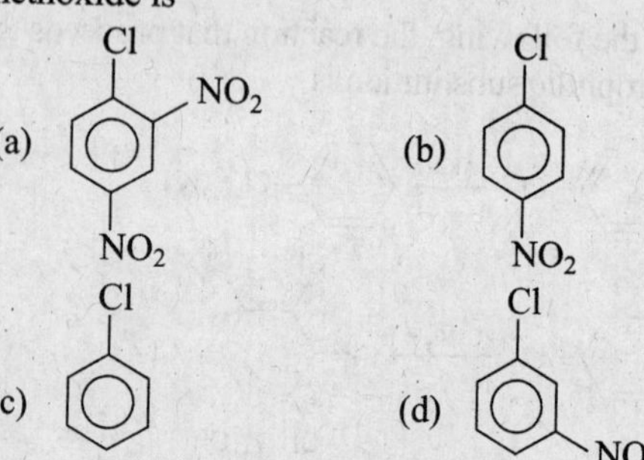

12 Which one is least reactive towards nucleophilic substitution reaction? **[Manipal]**

(a) *o*-aminochlorobenzene (b) Chlorobenzene
(c) *o*-nitrochlorobenzene (d) 2, 4-dinitrochlorobenzene

13 Which one of the following is most reactive towards nucleophilic substitution reaction? **[Manipal]**

(a) 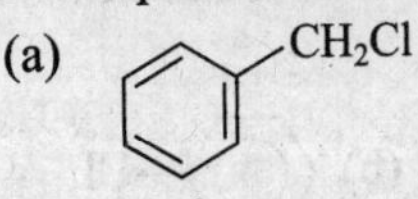

(b) Cl

(c) Cl

(d) Cl

2013

14 **Assertion** (A) Alkyl benzene is not prepared by Friedel-Crafts alkylation of benzene.
Reason (R) Alkyl halides are less reactive than acyl halide in S_N reaction. **[AIIMS]**

(a) Both A and R are correct and R is the correct explanation of A
(b) Both A and R are correct and R is not the correct explanation of A
(c) A is correct but R is incorrect
(d) Both A and R are incorrect

15 Which one of the following is not formed when a mixture of methyl bromide and bromobenzene is heated with sodium metal in the presence of dry ether? **[KCET]**

(a) Diphenyl (b) Propane (c) Toluene (d) Ethane

2011

16 Chlorobenzene on treatment with sodium in dry ether gives diphenyl. The name of the reaction is **[Kerala CEE]**

(a) Fittig reaction (b) Wurtz-Fittig reaction
(c) Sandmeyer reaction (d) Gattermann reaction
(e) Wurtz reaction

2010

17 The reaction of toluene with Cl_2 in the presence of $FeCl_3$ gives *X* and reaction in presence of light gives *Y*. Thus, *X* and *Y* are **[CBSE AIPMT]**

(a) X = benzyl chloride, Y = *m*-chlorotoluene
(b) X = benzal chloride, Y = *o*-chlorotoluene
(c) X = *m*-chlorotoluene, Y = *p*-chlorotoluene
(d) X = *o* and *p*-chlorotoluene, Y = trichloromethyl benzene

18 Which one is the most reactive towards S_N1 reaction? **[BHU]**

(a) $C_6H_5CH_2Br$
(b) $C_6H_5CH(C_6H_5)Br$
(c) $C_6H_5CH(CH_3)Br$
(d) $C_6H_5C(CH_3)(C_6H_5)Br$

19 The raw material for Raschig process is **[MHT CET]**

(a) chlorobenzene (b) phenol
(c) benzene (d) anisole

20 Toluene is nitrated and the resulting product is reduced with tin and hydrochloric acid. The product so obtained is diazotised and then heated with cuprous bromide. The reaction mixture so formed contains **[Haryana PMT]**

(a) mixture of *o*-and-*p*-bromotoluenes
(b) mixture of *o*-and *p*-dibromobenzene
(c) mixture of *o*-and *p*-bromoaniline
(d) mixture of *o*-and *m*-bromotoluenes

2009

21 Trichloroacetaldehyde, CCl_3CHO reacts with chlorobenzene in the presence of sulphuric acid and produces **[CBSE AIPMT]**

(a) $Cl-C_6H_4-C(Cl)(CH_2Cl)-C_6H_4-Cl$

(b) $Cl-C_6H_4-C(H)(C_6H_4Cl)-C_6H_4-Cl$

(c) $Cl-C_6H_4-C(OH)(Cl)-C_6H_4-Cl$

(d) $Cl-C_6H_4-CH(CCl_3)-C_6H_4-Cl$

22 In Dow's process, the starting raw material is **[MHT CET]**

(a) phenol (b) chlorobenzene
(c) aniline (d) diazobenzene

23 Chlorobenzene reacts with Mg in dry ether to give a compound *A*, which further reacts with ethanol to give **[Manipal]**

(a) phenol (b) benzene
(c) ethylbenzene (d) phenyl ether

24 Friedel-Crafts reaction of bromobenzene with methyl iodide gives **[Manipal]**

(a) *o*-bromotoluene
(b) *p*-bromotoluene
(c) *o* and *p*-bromotoluene
(d) *m*-bromotoluene

25 Which of the following will give yellow precipitate on shaking with an aqueous solution of NaOH followed by acidification with dil. HNO_3 and addition of $AgNO_3$ solution? [OJEE]

(a) 1-bromo-4-chlorobenzene (Br and Cl on ring) (b) $C_6H_5-CH_2-Cl$

(c) 4-Br-$C_6H_4-CH_2-I$ (d) 2-chlorotoluene (CH_3, Cl on ring)

26 Find the major product in the following reaction [OJEE]

$$C_6H_5CCl_3 \xrightarrow[FeCl_3]{Cl_2}$$

(a) o-$ClC_6H_4CCl_3$ (b) m-$ClC_6H_4CCl_3$

(c) p-$ClC_6H_4CCl_3$ (d) benzene

27 Chlorination of toluene in the presence of light and heat followed by treatment with aqueous KOH gives [Kerala CEE]

(a) *o*-cresol (b) *m*-cresol
(c) *p*-cresol (d) benzyl alcohol
(e) 2-chloro-4-hydroxytoluene

28 The most easily hydrolysed molecule under S_N1 conditions is [J&K CET]

(a) allyl chloride (b) ethyl chloride
(c) *iso*-propyl chloride (d) benzyl chloride

29 Predict the main product in [AMU]

$$C_6H_5-Cl \xrightarrow{NH_3/Cu_2O} \text{......}$$

(a) phenyl cyanide (b) nitrophenol
(c) aniline (d) hydroxylamine

30 Chlorobenzene is .... reactive than benzene towards electrophilic substitution and directs the incoming electrophile to the .... position. [DUMET]

(a) more, *ortho/para*
(b) less, *ortho/para*
(c) more, *meta*
(d) less, *meta*

2008

31 Among the following, which one has the weakest carbon-halogen bond? [Manipal]

(a) Benzyl bromide (b) Bromobenzene
(c) Vinyl bromide (d) Benzyl chloride

32 Which one of the following chlorohydrocarbons readily undergoes solvolysis? [J&K CET]

(a) $CH_2{=}CHCl$ (b) C_6H_5-Cl
(c) $C_6H_5-CH_2Cl$ (d) $C_6H_5-CH_2CH_2Cl$

2007

33 Chlorobenzene is prepared commercially by [BHU]

(a) Dow's process (b) Dacon's process
(c) Raschig process (d) Etard's process

34 Match the following Columns. [Kerala CEE]

Column I (Haloalkane/arene)	Column II (Applications)
A. Iodoform	1. CF_4
B. BHC	2. Antiseptic
C. Freon-14	3. Moth repellent
D. Halothanes	4. Inhalative anaesthetic
E. *p*-dichlorobenzene	5. Termite pesticide

Codes

	A	B	C	D	E		A	B	C	D	E
(a)	2	4	5	3	1	(b)	2	5	1	4	3
(c)	3	4	2	1	5	(d)	1	3	5	2	4
(e)	3	4	3	2	1						

2006

35 The hybridisation of the *ipso*-carbon in chlorobenzene is [J&K CET]

(a) *sp*-hybridised (b) sp^2-hybridised
(c) sp^2d-hybridised (d) sp^3-hybridised

36 An organic compound which produces a bluish green coloured flame on heating in the presence of copper is [KCET]

(a) chlorobenzene (b) benzaldehyde
(c) aniline (d) benzoic acid

37 Gammaxane is chemically known as [Kerala CEE]

(a) benzene hexachloride
(b) hexachloro benzene
(c) benzene hexabromide
(d) hexabromo benzene
(e) None of these

38 The increasing order of hydrolysis of the following compounds is [AIIMS]

I: bromobenzene; II: 3-bromocyclohexene; III: bromocyclohexane; IV: $(CH_3)_3C—Br$

(a) I < III < II < IV (b) I < IV < III < II
(c) IV < II < III < I (d) I < III < IV < II

39 Write the IUPAC name of given structure: [JIPMER]

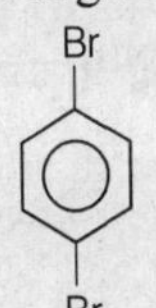

(a) *para*-dibromobenzene
(b) 1,4-dibromobenzene
(c) Both (a) and (b) are correct
(d) *meta*-dibromo benzene

Answers

1 (a)	2 (a)	3 (a)	4 (c)	5 (a)	6 (a)	7 (d)	8 (d)	9 (b)	10 (e)
11 (a)	12 (a)	13 (a)	14 (d)	15 (b)	16 (a)	17 (d)	18 (d)	19 (c)	20 (a)
21 (d)	22 (b)	23 (b)	24 (c)	25 (c)	26 (b)	27 (d)	28 (d)	29 (c)	30 (b)
31 (a)	32 (c)	33 (c)	34 (b)	35 (b)	36 (a)	37 (a)	38 (d)	39 (c)	

Explanations

1 *(a)* Halogenation of benzene is an example of electrophilic substitution reaction.

$$C_6H_6 + Cl_2 \xrightarrow{AlCl_3} C_6H_5Cl + HCl$$

Chlorobenzene

Reaction given in option (b) is an example of addition reaction, reaction in option (c) is an example of nucleophilic substitution reaction and option (d) is an example of substitution reaction.

2 *(a)* In (2-chlorotoluene: ring with Cl and CH_3) Cl atom is directly attached to C atom of benzene ring.

Thus, there is a partial double bond character between sp^2-hybridised C atom on the aromatic ring and Cl. It is most difficult to break this bond and hence, it undergoes hydrolysis reaction with slowest rate.

3 *(a)* The Wurtz-Fittig reaction is the reaction of an aryl halide with alkyl halide and sodium metal to give substituted aromatic compound.

Thus, Wurtz-Fittig reaction is

$$C_6H_5I + 2Na + CH_3I \longrightarrow C_6H_5CH_3 + 2NaI$$

4 *(c)* Given, $C_7H_8 \xrightarrow{3Cl_2/\Delta} A \xrightarrow{Br_2/Fe} B \xrightarrow{Zn/HCl} C$

The reaction in the above road map can be explained by the following steps.

***Step* I** Toluene (*A*) undergoes side chain halogenation with excess of chlorine to give benzotrichloride (*A*).

$$C_6H_5CH_3 \xrightarrow[\Delta]{3Cl_2} C_6H_5CCl_3$$

C_7H_8 (Toluene) → (*A*) (Benzotrichloride)

***Step* II** In compound (*A*), the substituent CCl_3 is an electron withdrawing group, so the electrophile will attack at *m*-position. Thus, benzotrichloride reacts with bromine in presence of Fe- catalyst to give *m*-bromobenzotrichloride (*B*).

$$C_6H_5CCl_3 \xrightarrow{Br_2/Fe} m\text{-}BrC_6H_4CCl_3$$

(*A*) → (*B*) *m*-bromobenzotrichloride

***Step* III** *m*-bromobenzotrichloride undergoes reduction with Zn in presence of HCl to give *m*-bromotoluene (*C*).

$$m\text{-}BrC_6H_4CCl_3 \xrightarrow[Zn/HCl]{Reduction} m\text{-}BrC_6H_4CH_3$$

(*B*) → (*C*) *m*-bromotoluene

5. *(a)* 3-bromoanisole (OCH_3, Br) $\xrightarrow{NaNH_2}$ 3-methoxyaniline (OCH_3, NH_2) (Direct substitution) + 2-methoxyaniline (OCH_3, NH_2) (Cine substitution)

If nucleophile occupies same position of the leaving group, product is called direct substitution product. If nucleophile occupies adjacent position of the leaving group, product is called cine substitution product. Intermediate is benzyne.

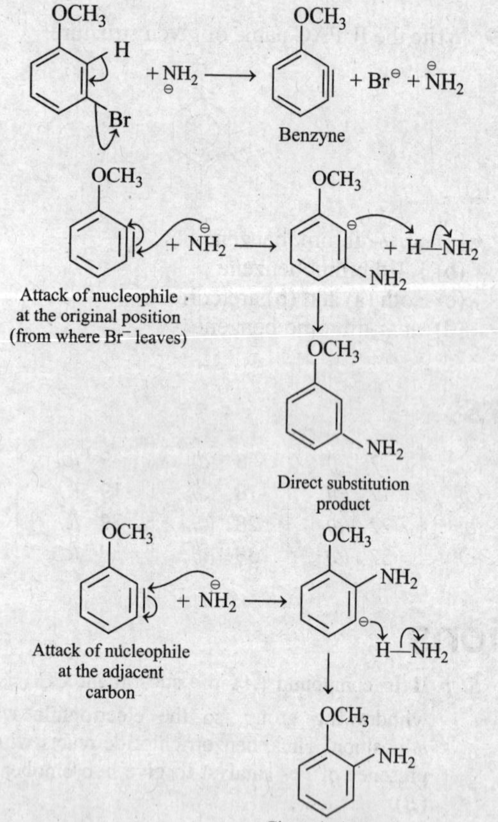

Benzyne

Attack of nucleophile at the original position (from where Br^- leaves)

Direct substitution product

Attack of nucleophile at the adjacent carbon

Cine substitution product

6 (a) Nitro group is an electron withdrawing ($-I$) group, it stabilises the carbocation because it disperses the negative charge on the carbon by attracting electrons.

Hence, both (A) and (R) are correct and (R) is the correct explanation of (A).

7 (d) Both (A) and (R) are false as, aryl halides undergo nucleophilic substitution with great difficulty due to partial double bond character between C-atom of ring and halide atom. Also, hybridisation of C-atom attached to halogen is sp^2-hybridisation.

8 (d) In chlorobenzene, bromobenzene and chloroethene, lone pair of halogen is delocalised with π-bonds so it attains double bond character. Thus, these are not suitable as a halide component for Friedel-Crafts reaction.

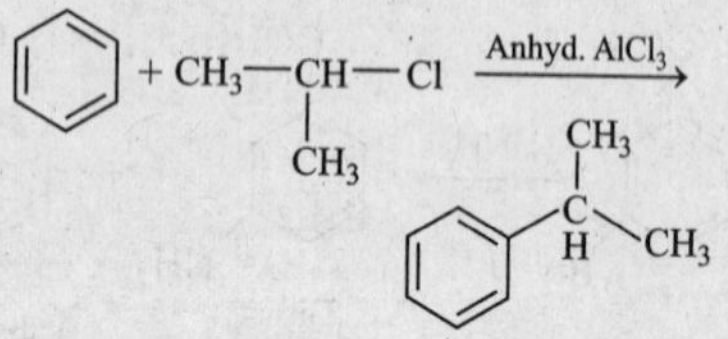

Other halides, i.e. chloro and bromobenzene along with chloroethene have carbon halogen bond as,

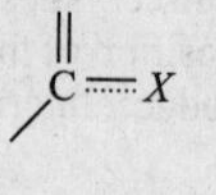

$$>C{=}X$$

9 (b) — CF_3 group given in reactant is electron withdrawing group that deactivates the aromatic ring by decreasing the electron density on the ring through resonance.

The resonance only decreases the electron density at the *ortho*-and *para*-position hence these sites are less nucleophilic, and so the system tends to react with electrophiles at the meta sites.

Hence, CX_3 (CF_3) groups attached to benzene ring are *meta* directors for electrophiles and form compound (b).

10 (e) Nucleophilic substitution of haloalkane by hydroxide ion is done by two different mechanisms —S_N1 and S_N2. S_N2 mechanism is most likely to be followed by primary haloalkane. Reactivity of S_N1 reactions depends on the stability of carbocation formed. Benzyl chloride undergoes hydrolysis with aq. NaOH predominantly by S_N1 mechanism because the carbocation produced is stabilised by resonance.

11 (a) The compound X—Cl (where X aryl, alkyl or their derivatives), on reaction with sodium methoxide (NaOMe) produces X—OMe and NaCl in accordance with following chemical equation.

$$X\text{—Cl} + \text{MeO}^{\ominus}\text{Na}^{\oplus} \longrightarrow X\text{—OMe} + \text{NaCl}$$

The above reaction is a type of nucleophilic substitution reaction in which nucleophile [here OMe] replaces halogen atom of X — Cl.

Reactivity of such organic halides in nucleophilic substitution reaction depends upon polarity of C—Cl bond. Higher the polarity of C—Cl bond easier will be the nucleophilic substitution reaction, hence, faster will be the reaction. Here C—Cl bond of aryl halide has partial double bond character due to conjugation of lone pair of Cl with π electrons of benzene ring.

Due to partial double bond character, breaking of C—Cl bond of aryl halide become impossible. Among the given four substrates, the compound having most polar C—Cl bond will undergo faster nucleophilic substitution reaction. Greater the number of electron withdrawing groups, higher will be the polarity of C—Cl bond.

(a) has two electron withdrawing groups hence, (a) has the most polar C—Cl bond and (a) will undergo fastest reaction.

12 (a) In nucleophilic substitution, for aromatic compounds like benzene, nucleophile displaces a good leaving group like halide on aromatic ring. Electron withdrawing groups also activate the ring towards nucleophilic attack. For e.g. nitro group at *ortho* and *para*-position, halide in 2, 4-dinitrochlorobenzene.
In 2, 4-dinitrochlorobenzene, nitro group is present at *ortho* and *para*-position and activates the ring.

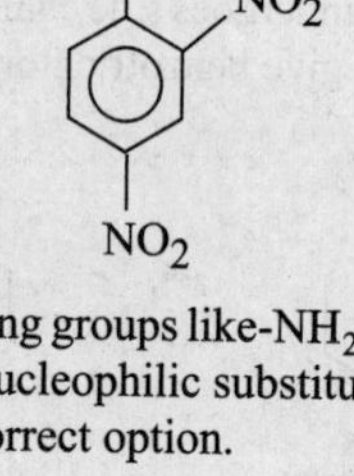

But electron donating groups like-NH_2 (if at ortho, *para*-position) will decrease the nucleophilic substitution reaction.
Hence, (a) is the correct option.

13 *(a)* The carbocation formed should be stable for faster nucleophilic substitution. In this benzyl carbocation is most stable due to resonance.

14 *(d)* Alkyl benzene can be prepared by Friedel-Crafts alkylation of benzene.

$$C_6H_6 + CH_3Cl \xrightarrow{AlCl_3} C_6H_5CH_3$$

In S_N reaction, acyl halides are less reactive than alkyl halides.

15 *(b)* This is an example of Wurtz-Fittig reaction.

(i) $$C_6H_5Br + 2Na + BrCH_3 \xrightarrow{Ether} C_6H_5CH_3 \text{ (Toluene)} + 2NaBr$$

(ii) $$C_6H_5Br + 2Na + C_6H_5Br \xrightarrow{Ether} C_6H_5\text{–}C_6H_5 \text{ (Diphenyl)} + 2NaBr$$

(iii) $$CH_3Br + 2Na + BrCH_3 \longrightarrow CH_3CH_3 \text{ (Ethane)} + 2NaBr$$

Propane cannot be prepared by this reaction.

16 *(a)* Reaction of aryl halides with sodium in ether to form diaryl is known as Fittig reaction.

17 *(d)* Cl_2 in presence of $FeCl_3 \rightarrow$ Ring substitution.

Cl_2 in presence of light $\rightarrow$ Side chain substitution.

$$\text{Toluene} \xrightarrow[FeCl_3]{Cl_2} o\text{-chlorotoluene} + p\text{-chlorotoluene}$$

$$\text{Toluene} \xrightarrow[\text{light}]{Cl_2} \text{Trichloromethylbenzene } (C_6H_5CCl_3)$$

18 *(d)* Reactivity towards S_N1 mechanism depends on the stability of carbocation.

As $C_6H_5\text{—}\overset{+}{C}(CH_3)(C_6H_5)$ carbocation is tertiary and is most stable,

$C_6H_5C(CH_3)(C_6H_5)Br$ readily undergoes S_N1 reaction.

19 *(c)* Raschig process is the commercial method for the preparation of chlorobenzene from benzene.

$$\text{Benzene} + 2HCl + O_2 \xrightarrow[500\text{ K}]{CuCl_2} 2\,\text{Chlorobenzene} + 2H_2O$$

20 *(a)*

$$\text{Toluene} \xrightarrow{\text{Conc. } HNO_3/H_2SO_4} o\text{-nitrotoluene} + p\text{-nitrotoluene}$$

$$\xrightarrow{Sn/HCl} o\text{-toluidine } (CH_3, NH_2) + p\text{-toluidine } (CH_3, NH_2)$$

$$\xrightarrow{\text{(i) } NaNO_2/HCl, 0\text{–}5°C \quad \text{(ii) } CuBr} o\text{-bromotoluene} + p\text{-bromotoluene}$$

Hence, the reaction mixture formed contains mixture of *o* and *p*-bromotoluenes.

21 *(d)* Trichloroacetaldehyde on reaction with chlorobenzene in the presence of sulphuric acid, produces *p,p′*-dichlorodiphenyltrichloroethane (DDT).

$$2\,Cl\text{–}C_6H_4\text{–}H \text{ (Chlorobenzene)} + O{=}CH\text{—}CCl_3 \text{ (Chloral)} \xrightarrow[\Delta, -H_2O]{\text{Conc. } H_2SO_4} (Cl\text{–}C_6H_4)_2CH\text{—}CCl_3$$

p, p′–dichlorodiphenyltrichloro ethane
DDT

22 *(b)* In Dow's process, firstly sodium phenoxide is obtained by the reaction of chlorobenzene with NaOH at 573 – 623 K and 200 atm, which on acid hydrolysis forms phenol.

$$\text{Chlorobenzene} + NaOH \xrightarrow[\text{200 atm, } -HCl]{\text{573–623 K}} \text{Sodium phenoxide} \xrightarrow[-NaCl]{HCl} \text{Phenol}$$

23 *(b)*

$$\text{Chlorobenzene} + Mg \xrightarrow[\text{ether}]{\text{Dry}} \underset{(A)}{C_6H_5MgCl} \xrightarrow{CH_3CH_2OH} \text{Benzene} + C_2H_5OMgCl$$

24 *(c)*

$$\text{Bromobenzene} + CH_3I \xrightarrow[\text{Friedel-Craft's reaction}]{\text{Anhy. } AlCl_3} \text{o- and p-bromotoluene}$$

25 *(c)* (p-bromobenzyl iodide) can give S_N2 reaction under the prevailing condition because alkyl halides are more reactive than aryl halides for undergoing S_N2 reaction. Further, C—I bond is weakest or highly reactive among all C—*X* bonds present in other compounds. Therefore, I^- is released into the solution.

Dil. HNO_3 neutralises excess NaOH. Thus, $AgNO_3$ gives yellow precipitate of AgI.

26 *(b)* CCl_3 is an electron withdrawing group.

It deactivates aromatic ring.

In other words, it decreases the electron density at *ortho* and *para*-position, so $—CCl_3$ is a *meta* directing group.

$$C_6H_5CCl_3 \xrightarrow[FeCl_3]{Cl_2} m\text{-}ClC_6H_4CCl_3$$

27 *(d)* In the presence of light, toluene undergoes free radical substitution and gives benzyl chloride on chlorination. Benzyl chloride with aqueous KOH, gives benzyl alcohol.

$$\underset{\text{Toluene}}{C_6H_5CH_3} \xrightarrow{Cl_2,\ h\nu} \underset{\text{Benzyl chloride}}{C_6H_5CH_2Cl} \xrightarrow{aq.\ KOH} \underset{\text{Benzyl alcohol}}{C_6H_5CH_2OH}$$

28 *(d)* Hydrolysis of alkyl halides by S_N1 mechanism depends on the stability of carbocation and stability order of carbocations is:

Benzyl > Allyl > 2° > 1°.

Therefore, benzyl chloride can be most easily hydrolysed under S_N1 conditions.

29 *(c)*

$$2\,C_6H_5Cl + 2NH_3 + Cu_2O \xrightarrow[\text{60 atm}]{200°C} 2\,\underset{\text{Aniline}}{C_6H_5NH_2} + Cu_2Cl_2 + H_2O$$

30 *(b) ortho-para* directing groups activate the benzene ring towards electrophilic substitution while *meta* directing groups deactivate the benzene ring towards electrophilic substitution. —F, —Cl, —Br and —I (i.e. halogens) are exceptions to the above rule. These groups are *o-*, *p*-directing but deactivate the benzene ring.

31 *(a)* C—*X* bond in benzyl bromide is much weaker than in vinyl bromide and bromobenzene since the benzyl cation left after the removal of the bromide ion is stabilised by resonance. Further, C—Br bond is weaker than C—Cl bond due to larger size of —Br. Therefore, $C_6H_5CH_2Br$ has the weakest C—*X* bond.

32 *(c)* Solvolysis of haloalkanes follows first order kinetics. During this process, an intermediate carbocation is formed. Therefore, the halohydrocarbon which gives more stable carbocation, undergoes solvolysis readily. Thus, benzyl chloride readily undergoes solvolysis.

33 *(c)* Chlorobenzene is prepared commercially by Raschig process.

$$\underset{\text{Benzene}}{2C_6H_6} + 2HCl + O_2 \xrightarrow[\text{500 K}]{Cu_2Cl_2/FeCl_3} \underset{\text{Chlorobenzene}}{2C_6H_5Cl} + 2H_2O$$

34 *(b)*

	Column I (Haloalkane/arene)	Column II (Applications)
A.	Iodoform	Antiseptic
B.	BHC	Termite pesticide
C.	Freon-14	CF_4
D.	Halothanes	Inhalative anaesthetic
E.	*p*-dichlorobenzene	Moth repellent

35 *(b)* The position at which substituent is present is called *ipso*-position.

Cl *ipso*-carbon

Chlorobenzene

The hybridisation of *ipso*-carbon in chlorobenzene is sp^2.

36 *(a)* Halogen containing compounds (C_6H_5Cl) when placed in a flame, reveal the presence of halogen by producing a green to blue flame.

37 *(a)* Gammaxane is chemically known as benzene hexachloride (BHC) though the latter name is incorrect but the older name (BHC) is still in use.

$$C_6H_6 + 3Cl_2 \xrightarrow{\text{Sunlight}} C_6H_6Cl_6$$

BHC

38 *(d)* Cyclic and tertiary halides undergo hydrolysis by S_N1 mechanism and involve the formation of carbocation intermediate. Greater the stability of carbocation intermediate, higher is the ease of halides to undergo hydrolysis. The order of stability of carbocations is given as :

cyclohexyl carbocation $< (CH_3)_3\overset{+}{C} <$ cyclohexenyl (allylic) carbocation

However, C—Br bond in bromobenzene acquires some double bond character, hence it has least tendency to undergo hydrolysis. Therefore, the increasing order of hydrolysis of the given compounds is,

I (bromobenzene) < III (bromocyclohexane) $< (CH_3)_3C—Br <$ II (3-bromocyclohexene)

I III IV II

39 *(c)* The IUPAC name of the given structure

(Benzene ring with Br at positions 1 and 4)

is 1, 4-dibromobenzene or *para* dibromobenzene.

25

Alcohols, Phenols and Ethers

Quick Review

Alcohols

- An alcohol contains one or more hydroxyl group(s) (—OH) directly attached to carbon atom(s) of an aliphatic system.

Classification of Alcohols

I. *On the basis of nature of* C—OH *group*, alcohols are usually classified as primary ($R—CH_2OH$); secondary $\left(\begin{matrix}R\\R\end{matrix}\right\rangle CHOH\right)$ and tertiary $\left(\begin{matrix}R\\R\\R\end{matrix}\!\!>C—OH\right)$ alcohols.

II. *On the basis of number of* —OH *groups present in the molecule, alcohols are classifieds as*

(*i*) **Monohydric alcohols** Alcohols that have one —OH group are said to be monohydric alcohols,

e.g. $\underset{\text{Methanol}}{CH_3OH}$, $\underset{\text{Ethanol}}{C_2H_5OH}$

(*ii*) **Dihydric alcohols** Alcohols that have two —OH groups are said to be dihydric alcohols,

e.g.

$$\begin{matrix}CH_2OH\\|\\CH_2OH\end{matrix}$$

Ethylene glycol

(*iii*) **Trihydric alcohols** Alcohols that have three —OH groups are said to be trihydric alcohols,

e.g.

$$\begin{matrix}CH_2OH\\|\\CHOH\\|\\CH_2OH\end{matrix}$$

Glycerol

Nomenclature

- In IUPAC system, the name of an alcohol is derived from the name of the alkane by replacing 'e' of alkane with the suffix 'ol'. e.g. CH_3CH_2OH - ethanol.

Preparation of Alcohols

The important methods used to prepare alcohols are as follows :

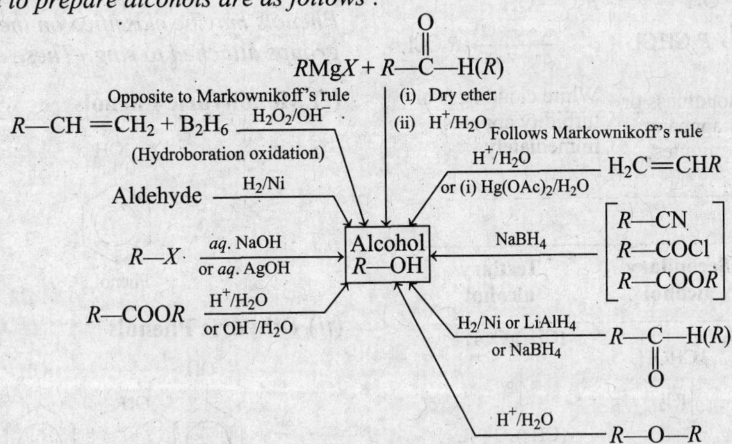

Properties of Alcohols

(*i*) ***Physical properties*** *of alcohols are as follows :*

- Alcohols have higher boiling point than haloalkanes of comparable molecular mass. The boiling point decreases with increase of branching in carbon chain.
- The solubility decreases with increase in number of carbon atoms.

(*ii*) ***Chemical properties*** *of alcohols are as follows :*

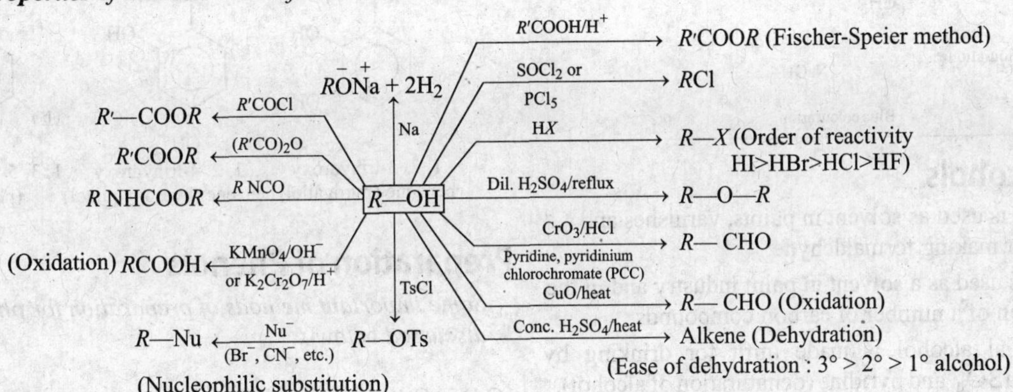

Commercially Important Alcohols

(*i*) **Methanol** Also known as 'wood spirit'. It is produced by destructive distillation of wood. *It is also prepared as follows*

$$CO + 2H_2 \xrightarrow[\substack{200\text{-}300\text{atm} \\ 573-673\text{K}}]{ZnO.Cr_2O_3} CH_3OH$$

It is used as solvent in paints, varnishes and for making aldehyde.

(*ii*) **Ethanol** It is obtained commercially by fermentation. It can be prepared by using following method.

$$C_{12}H_{22}O_{11} + H_2O \xrightarrow{\text{Invertase}} \underset{\text{Glucose}}{C_6H_{12}O_6} + \underset{\text{Fructose}}{C_6H_{12}O_6}$$

$$C_6H_{12}O_6 \xrightarrow{\text{Zymase}} 2C_2H_5OH + 2CO_2$$

Note
- Rectified spirit is 95% ethanol.
- Absolute spirit is 100% ethanol.
- Power alcohol is 20 : 80 mixture of absolute alcohol and gasoline.

Identification of Primary, Secondary and Tertiary Alcohols

- **In Lucas Reagent**

Primary alcohols	Secondary alcohols	Tertiary alcohols
$CH_2OH \xrightarrow[\text{Anhy. } ZnCl_2]{\text{Conc HCl}} X$	$R_2CH—OH \xrightarrow[\text{Anhy. } ZnCl_2]{\text{Conc. HCl}} R_2CHCl$	$R_3C—OH \xrightarrow[\text{Anhy. } ZnCl_2]{\text{Conc. HCl}} R_3CCl$
No reaction and hence, no white cloudiness or turbidity at room temperature.	White cloudiness or turbidity appears within 5 minutes.	White cloudiness or turbidity appears immediately.

- **In Vector Meyer's Test**

Primary alcohol	Secondary alcohol	Tertiary alcohol
CH_3CH_2OH	$(CH_3)_2CHOH$	$(CH_3)_3COH$
↓ P/I_2	↓ P/I_2	↓ P/I_2
CH_3CH_2I	$(CH_3)_2CH—I$	$(CH_3)_3C—I$
↓ $AgNO_2$	↓ $AgNO_2$	↓ $AgNO_2$
$CH_3CH_2NO_2$	$(CH_3)_2CHNO_2$	$(CH_3)_3C—NO_2$
↓ HNO_2	↓ HNO_2	↓ HNO_2
$R—C(=N—OH)—NO_2$ (Nitrolic acid)	$(CH_3)_2C(NO_2)—N=O$	(No reaction) No colour
↓ NaOH	↓ NaOH	
Blood red colouration	Blue colouration	

Uses of Alcohols

- Methanol is used as solvent in paints, varnishes and mainly for making formaldehyde.
- Ethanol is used as a solvent in paint industry and in the preparation of a number of carbon compounds.
- Commercial alcohol is made unfit for drinking by mixing $CuSO_4$ and pyridine (denaturation of alcohol).

Phenols

- A phenol contains — OH group(s) directly attached to carbon atom(s) of an aromatic system.
- The simplest hydroxy derivative of benzene is phenol. It is its common name and also accepted **IUPAC name.**
- All the substituted phenols are termed as derivatives of phenols, i.e. *ortho* (1, 2-disubstituted), *meta* (1, 3-disubstituted) and *para* (1, 4-disubstituted) that are often used in the common names.

Classification of Phenols

Phenols may be classified on the basis of number of —OH groups attached to ring. These are as follows

(*i*) Monohydric Phenols

Phenol; *o*-cresol

(*ii*) Dihydric Phenols

1,2-dihydroxy benzene (catechol); 1, 3-dihydroxy benzene (resorcinol); 1, 4-dihydroxybenzene (quinol)

(*iii*) Trihydric Phenols

1, 2, 3-trihydroxy benzene (pyrogallol); 1, 2, 4-trihydroxy benzene (hydroxyquinol); 1, 3, 5-trihydroxybenzene (phloroglucinol)

Preparation of Phenols

Some important methods of preparation for phenols are discussed below :

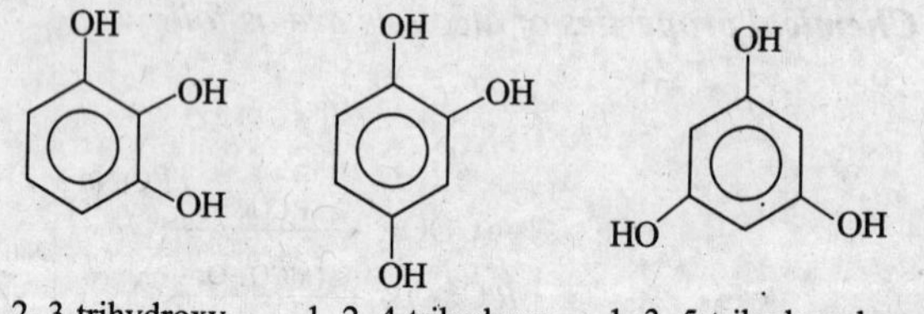

Properties of Phenols

(*i*) ***Physical properties*** *of phenols are as follows*

- Phenols have higher boiling point and soluble in water due to its ability to form hydrogen bond with water.
- Phenol possess high dipole moments.
- Phenols are acidic on nature, even more than alcohols. This is due to conjugation between lone pair of oxygen and benzene nucleus, i.e.

Presence of electron withdrawing groups (such as —Cl, —Br, —NO_2 etc.) increase the acidic strength of phenols while presence of electron releasing groups (such as alkyl group, —OCH_3 etc.) decrease the acidic strength of phenols.

(*ii*) ***Chemical properties*** *of phenols are discussed below :*

Phenol (OH):

- Phthalic anhydride, Conc. H_2SO_4/Δ → Phenolphthalein
- *aq.* NaOH, C_6H_5COCl → $C_6H_5OCOC_6H_5$ (Schotten-Baumann reaction)
- (*i*) NaOH (*ii*) CH_3I → Anisole (OCH_3)
- PCl_5 → $(C_6H_5)_3PO_4$ Triphenylphosphate
- $K_2S_2O_8$, KOH → OH/OH (Major) + OH/OH (Minor)
- Conc. H_2SO_4 + Conc. HNO_3 → (NO_2, OH, NO_2, O_2N) 2, 4, 6-trinitrophenol or picric acid
- Zn, Δ → Benzene
- Br_2 water → (OH, Br, Br, Br) 2, 4, 6-tribromophenol (white precipitate)
- (*i*) $CHCl_3$, NaOH (*ii*) HCl (Reimer-Tiemann's reaction) → (OH, CHO) Salicylaldehyde
- (*i*) CCl_4, NaOH (*ii*) HCl → (OH, COOH) Salicylic acid
- NaOH; CO_2 4-7 atm (Kolbe's reaction) → (OH, COOH) Salicylic acid
- (*i*) $(CH_3)_2SO_4$ (*ii*) $CH_3Cl/AlCl_3$ (*iii*) $AlCl_3/C_2H_5SH$ → (OH, CH_3) (minor) + (OH, CH_3, CH_3) (major)

Note Litmus test, reaction with $FeCl_3$, coupling reaction and bromine water test is given by phenol and not by alcohol. So, these reactions are used to distinguish alcohols and phenols.

Uses of Phenols

- Phenols are used in the manufacture of bakelite, soaps, lotions, etc. and also used in the manufacture of drugs like aspirin, salol etc.
- It is an active ingredient in some oral analgesics such as chloroseptic sprays.
- It is used in manufacture of azodyes, phenolphthalein etc.

Ethers

- The substitution of a hydrogen atom in a hydrocarbon (aliphatic/aromatic) by an alkoxy (O*R*)/aryloxy (OAr) group yield ethers.
- In the **IUPAC system**, ethers are named as 'alkoxy alkanes' in which the ethereal oxygen is taken along with smaller alkyl group while the larger alkyl group is considered as a part of alkane e.g., $CH_3OCH_2CH_2CH_3$-(1-methoxypropane).

Classification of Ethers

On the basis of type of attached groups :

(*i*) **Aliphatic ethers** Both the attached groups (R and R') are alkyl groups. They have the general formula as $C_nH_{2n+2}O$.

e.g. $CH_3CH_2OCH_2CH_3$; $CH_3-O-\underset{CH_3}{\overset{CH_3}{\underset{|}{\overset{|}{C}}}}-CH_3$

Diethyl ether; Methyl *tert*-butyl ether

(*ii*) **Aromatic ethers** Either one or both of the attached groups (R and R') is/are aryl groups

e.g. $C_6H_5-O-C_6H_5$; $C_6H_5-O-C_2H_5$

Diphenyl ether; Ethyl phenyl ether

Preparation of Ethers

General methods used to synthesis ethers are as follows

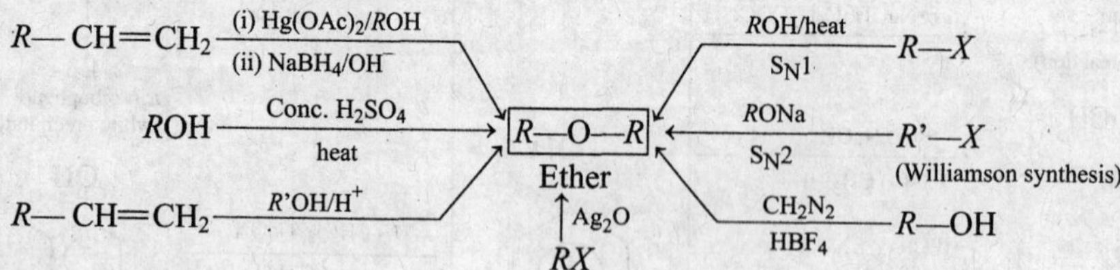

Properties of Ethers

(*i*) ***Physical properties*** *of ethers are as follows* :

- The C—O bonds in ethers are polar and thus, have a net dipole moment
- Ethers are insoluble in H_2O and have lower boiling point than alcohols because they do not form hydrogen bond with water.

(*ii*) ***Chemical properties*** *of ethers are as follows* :

$$2R-Cl \xleftarrow[\Delta]{PCl_5} R-O-R \text{ (Ether)} \xrightarrow[\text{Boil}]{H^+/H_2O} 2R-OH$$

$$2ROH \xleftarrow[H_2O]{\text{Dil. } H_2SO_4} R-O-R \xrightarrow{BF_3} \underset{R}{\overset{R}{>}}\ddot{O} \rightarrow BF_3 \text{ (Boron-triflouride etherate)}$$

$$2R-X + H_2O \xleftarrow[\text{(excess)}]{HX} R-O-R \xrightarrow[\text{in air}]{\text{Oxidation}} \underset{R}{\overset{R}{>}}\ddot{O} \rightarrow O \text{ (Peroxide)}$$

- Order of reactivity of hydrogen halides is HI > HBr > HCl.

Uses of Ethers

- Ethers are used as a solvent for oils, fats and Grignard reagent, etc.
- Diethylether is used as general anaesthetic.

Topical Practice Questions

All the exam questions of this chapter have been divided into four topics as listed below:

Topic 1

Primary Aliphatic Alcohols

2019

1 $CH_3—CH_2—CH=CH_2 \xrightarrow{'X'} CH_3CH_2—CH_2—CH_2OH$

What is suitable reagent 'X' is? **[JIPMER]**

(a) $H_2 | Pt$
(b) $B_2H_6 | THF, \; H_2O_2 | OH^-$
(c) $Br_2 | HCl$
(d) $HBr | H_2O_2$

2018

2 **Assertion** (A) CH_3CH_2OH can be distinguished by haloform test.

Reason (R) Haloform test is given by 2° alcohol.

(a) Both Assertion and Reason are true and Reason is the correct explanation of Assertion
(b) Both Assertion and Reason are true, but Reason is not the correct explanation of Assertion
(c) Assertion is true, but Reason is false
(d) Both Assertion and Reason are false **[AIIMS]**

2017

3 $CH_3—CHO \xrightarrow[\text{(ii) } H_2O]{\text{(i) } CH_3MgBr} (A) \xrightarrow{H_2SO_4,\, \Delta}$

$(B) \xrightarrow{\text{Hydroboration oxidation}} (C)$ **[AIIMS]**

In the above reaction, (A) and (C) are

(a) identical (b) positional isomers
(c) functional isomers (d) optical isomers

2014

4 What reagent(s) can be used to convert 2-methyl pentan-1-ol into 2-methyl pentanal? **[Manipal]**

(a) $Na_2Cr_2O_7$ (b) $LiAlH_4$
(c) CrO_3-pyridine (d) $KMnO_4$

5 0.44 g of a monohydric alcohol when added to methyl magnesium iodide in ether liberates at STP, 112 cm^3 of methane. With PCC the same alcohol forms a carbonyl compound that gives positive silver mirror test. The monohydric alcohol is **[KCET]**

(a) $H_3C—CH(OH)—CH_2—CH_3$
(b) $(CH_3)_3C—CH_2OH$
(c) $H_3C—CH(OH)—CH_2—CH_2—CH_3$
(d) $(CH_3)_2CH—CH_2OH$

2013

6 Conversion of ethyl alcohol into acetaldehyde is an example of **[Manipal]**

(a) hydrolysis (b) oxidation
(c) reduction (d) molecular rearrangement

7 Which of the following combination can be used to synthesize ethanol? **[KCET]**

(a) CH_3MgI and CH_2COCH_3
(b) CH_3MgI and C_2H_5OH
(c) CH_3MgI and $CH_3COOC_2H_5$
(d) CH_3MgI and $HCOOC_2H_5$

2012

8 Which of the following compounds can be used as an antifreeze in an automobile radiator? **[CBSE AIPMT]**

(a) Methyl alcohol (b) Glycol
(c) Nitrophenol (d) Ethyl alcohol

9 The most suitable reagent for the conversion of $RCH_2OH \longrightarrow RCHO$ is **[AFMC]**

(a) $KMnO_4$ (b) $K_2Cr_2O_7$ (c) PCC (d) CrO_3

10 HCHO was treated with reagent X. The product formed upon hydrolysis in the presence of an acid gave C_2H_5OH. The reagent X is **[KCET]**

(a) alcoholic KOH (b) alcoholic KCN
(c) CH_3MgI (d) aqueous KOH

2011

11 Which of the following alcohols give the best yield of dialkyl ether on being heated with a trace of sulphuric acid? **[Kerala CEE]**

(a) 2-pentanol (b) Cyclopentanol
(c) 2-methyl-2-butanol (d) 2-propanol
(e) 1-pentanol

12 Decreasing order of reactivity of hydrogen halide acid in the conversion of $ROH \longrightarrow RX$ is **[DUMET]**

(a) $HCl > HBr > HI > HF$ (b) $HI > HBr > HCl > HF$
(c) $HF > HCl > HBr > HI$ (d) $HF > HBr > HI > HCl$

2010

13 1 mole alcohol reacts with Na to give what weight of hydrogen? **[MHT CET]**

(a) 1 g (b) 2 g (c) 3 g (d) 3.5 g

14 The correct order of dehydration of alcohols is **[MHT CET]**

(a) 1° > 2° > 3° (b) 3° > 2° > 1°
(c) 2° > 1° > 3° (d) 1° > 3° > 2°

15 Boiling point of ethyl alcohol is greater than ether due to [OJEE]
(a) van der Waals' forces
(b) London force
(c) polarity
(d) hydrogen bonding

16 $CO + H_2 \xrightarrow[X \text{ (catalyst)}]{300°C/300 \text{ atm}} CH_3OH.$
The catalyst X is [OJEE]
(a) Fe (b) Cr_2O_3/ZnO
(c) V_2O_5 (d) Al_2O_3

17 Boiling point of alcohol is comparatively higher than that of corresponding alkane due to [VMMC]
(a) intermolecular hydrogen bonding
(b) intramolecular hydrogen bonding
(c) volatile nature
(d) none of the above

2009

18 $CH_2OH \cdot CH_2OH$ on heating with periodic acid gives [CBSE AIPMT]
(a) $2CO_2$ (b) $2HCOOH$ (c) $\begin{array}{l} CHO \\ | \\ CHO \end{array}$ (d) $\begin{array}{l} H \\ \quad \rangle C{=}O \\ H \end{array}$

19 Consider the following reaction,
$$Z \xrightarrow[\text{Ethanol}]{PBr_3} X \xrightarrow{\text{Alc. KOH}} Y \xrightarrow[(ii)\ H_2O,\ \text{heat}]{(i)\ H_2SO_4,\ \text{room temperature}} Z$$
The product Z is, [CBSE AIPMT]
(a) $CH_2{=}CH_2$
(b) $CH_3CH_2{-}O{-}CH_2CH_3$
(c) $CH_3CH_2{-}O{-}SO_3H$
(d) CH_3CH_2OH

20 The best combination of reagent for carrying out the conversion,
$RCH_2CH_2OH \longrightarrow RCH_2CH_2COOH$ is [Kerala CEE]
(a) PBr_3, KCN, H_3O^+ (b) PBr_3, KCN, H_2/Pt
(c) KCN, H_3O^+ (d) PBr_3, H_3O^+

21 Reaction of ROH with $R'MgX$ produces [WB JEE]
(a) RH (b) $R'H$
(c) $R{-}R$ (d) $R'{-}R'$

22 When phenyl magnesium bromide is reacted with ethyl alcohol, product is [CG PMT, Haryana PMT]
(a) benzaldehyde (b) *t*-butyl benzene
(c) benzene (d) *t*-butyl phenyl ether

23 What are X and Y in the following reaction sequence,
$$C_2H_5OH \xrightarrow{Cl_2} X \xrightarrow{Cl_2} Y?$$ [EAMCET]
(a) C_2H_5Cl, CH_3CHO (b) CH_3CHO, CH_3CO_2H
(c) CH_3CHO, CCl_3CHO (d) C_2H_5Cl, CCl_3CHO

2008

24 Methyl alcohol when reacted with carbon monoxide using cobalt or rhodium as catalyst, compound A is formed. On heating A with HI in the presence of red phosphorus as catalyst, B is formed. Identify B. [UP CPMT]
(a) CH_3COOH (b) CH_3CHO
(c) CH_3CH_2I (d) CH_3CH_3

25 Catalytic dehydrogenation of a primary alcohol gives a/an [KCET]
(a) secondary alcohol (b) aldehyde
(c) ketone (d) ester

26 $C_2H_5OH + SOCl_2 \xrightarrow{\text{Pyridine}} X + Y + Z,$
In the reaction X, Y and Z respectively, are [EAMCET]
(a) $C_2H_4Cl_2, SO_2, HCl$ (b) C_2H_5Cl, SO_2, HCl
(c) $C_2H_5Cl, SOCl, HCl$ (d) C_2H_4, SO_2, Cl_2

27 Oxidation of organic compound A with $Na_2Cr_2O_7$ and H_2SO_4 gives compound B, which on reduction with H_2 in the presence of Ni catalyst gives ethyl alcohol. Give the name of compound A. [Guj CET]
(a) Ethanal (b) Ethanol (c) Ethanoic acid (d) Ethene

2007

28 The major product of the following reaction is [AIIMS]
$$H_3C{-}\underset{\underset{OH}{|}}{\overset{\overset{CH_3}{|}}{C}}{-}CH_2{-}OH \xrightarrow{H_2SO_4}$$
(a) $(CH_3)_2C{=}CH_2$ (b) butan-2-one
(c) $(CH_3)_2\overset{\overset{OH}{|}}{C}{-}CHO$ (d) *iso*-butyraldehyde

29 In the following reaction, A is [AFMC]
$$C_2H_5MgBr + H_2C{-}CH_2 \text{ (epoxide, bridging O)} \xrightarrow{H_2O} A$$
(a) $C_2H_5CH_2CHO$ (b) $C_2H_5CH_2CH_2OH$
(c) $C_2H_5CH_2OH$ (d) C_2H_5CHO

30 The product obtained, on heating ethanol with conc. H_2SO_4 at 165-170°C, is [BHU]
(a) $(C_2H_5)_2SO_4$ (b) CH_3COOH
(c) $CH_2{=}CH_2$ (d) $C_2H_5HSO_4$

31 Which one of the following will most readily be dehydrated in acidic conditions? [RPMT]

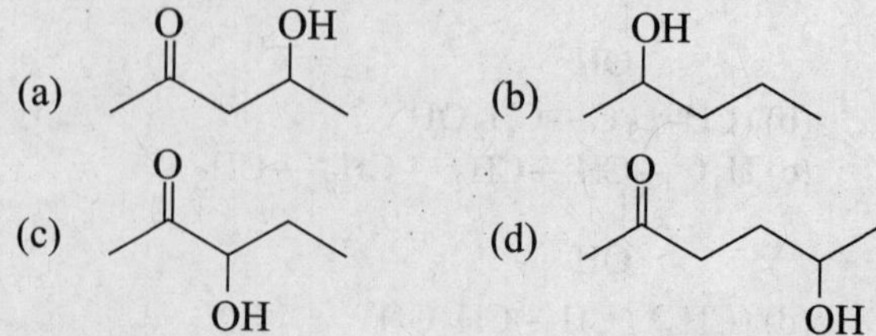

32 Denatured alcohol is **[KCET]**

(a) ethanol + methanol
(b) rectified spirit + methanol + naphtha
(c) undistilled ethanol
(d) rectified spirit

33 Which observation will be given by the compound

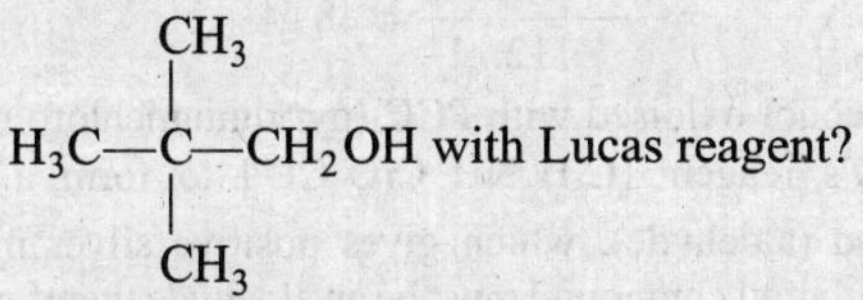

with Lucas reagent? **[Guj CET]**

(a) Solution becomes milky
(b) Oily drops are separated
(c) Coloured layer
(d) Reaction does not take place

34 A fruity smell is obtained by the reaction of ethanol with **[BCECE]**

(a) CH_3COCH_3 (b) PCl_5
(c) CH_3COOH (d) CH_3CHO

35 Which one can differentiate between C_2H_5OH and CH_3OH? **[BCECE]**

(a) H_2O (b) $Na_2CO_3 + I_2$
(c) NH_3 (d) HCl

2006

36 **Assertion** (A) Change in colour of acidic solution of potassium dichromate by breath is used to test drunk drivers.

Reason (R) Change in colour is due to the complexation of alcohol with potassium dichromate. **[AIIMS]**

(a) Both A and R are correct and R is the correct explanation of A
(b) Both A and R are correct but R is not the correct explanation of A
(c) A is correct but R is incorrect
(d) Both A and R are incorrect

37 The product of following reaction is **[AFMC]**

$2CH_3MgBr + CH_2O \longrightarrow$

(a) CH_3OH (b) C_2H_5OH
(c) CH_4 (d) C_2H_6

38 Match the following columns.

	Column I		Column II
A.	Propane-1,2,3-triol	1.	Cyclic ether
B.	Ethane-1,2-diol	2.	Absolute ethanol + petrol
C.	Tetrahydrofuran	3.	Dynamite
D.	Power alcohol	4.	Denatured alcohol
E.	Methylated spirit	5.	Terylene

Codes **[Kerala CEE]**

	A	B	C	D	E		A	B	C	D	E
(a)	1	2	3	4	5	(b)	1	3	5	4	2
(c)	3	2	4	5	1	(d)	3	5	1	2	4
(e)	4	1	5	2	3						

39 In the following reaction, *X* and *Y* respectively are,

$$C_2H_5OH \xrightarrow{KMnO_4/H^+} X \xrightarrow[H_2SO_4/\Delta]{Y} CH_3CO_2C_2H_5$$ **[J&K CET]**

(a) CH_3OH, C_2H_5OH (b) CH_3CHO, CH_3OH
(c) CH_3CO_2H, C_2H_5OH (d) C_2H_4, CH_3CO_2H

40 Starch is converted to ethanol by fermentation. The sequence of enzymes used are **[DUMET]**

(a) amylase, maltase, zymase (b) diastase, maltase, zymase
(c) amylase, invertase, zymase (d) amylase, zymase, maltase

2005

41 When alcohol reacts with conc. H_2SO_4, intermediate compound formed is **[AFMC]**

(a) carbonium ion (b) alkoxy ion
(c) alkyl hydrogen sulphate (d) None of the above

42 The only alcohol that cannot be prepared by the indirect hydration of alkene is **[AFMC]**

(a) ethyl alcohol (b) propyl alcohol
(c) *iso*-butyl alcohol (d) methyl alcohol

43 Identify *B* in the following scheme,

$$CH_3CH_2CH_2OH \xrightarrow{PCl_5} A \xrightarrow{\text{Alc. KOH}} B$$ **[Kerala CEE]**

(a) propyne (b) propene
(c) propanol (d) propanone
(e) $(CH_3)_2CHOH$

44 Which of the following compounds is most acidic? **[AFMC]**

(a) CH_4 (b) C_2H_6 (c) $CH\equiv CH$ (d) C_2H_5OH

Answers

1 (b)	2 (b)	3 (b)	4 (c)	5 (b)	6 (b)	7 (c)	8 (b)	9 (c)	10 (c)
11 (e)	12 (b)	13 (a)	14 (b)	15 (d)	16 (b)	17 (a)	18 (d)	19 (d)	20 (a)
21 (b)	22 (c)	23 (c)	24 (d)	25 (b)	26 (b)	27 (b)	28 (d)	29 (b)	30 (c)
31 (a)	32 (b)	33 (a)	34 (c)	35 (b)	36 (c)	37 (b)	38 (d)	39 (c)	40 (b)
41 (a)	42 (d)	43 (b)	44 (d)						

Explanations

1 (*b*) The suitable reagent X for the conversion is $B_2H_6 \mid THF$, $H_2O_2 \mid OH$.

$$\underset{\text{Butene}}{CH_3CH_2CH=CH_2} \xrightarrow[(ii)\ H_2O_2/OH^-]{(i)\ B_2H_6/THF} \underset{\text{Butanol}}{CH_3CH_2CH_2CH_2OH}$$

Alkenes react with diborane (B_2H_6) in presence of THF or diglyme to form alkyl borane (by hydroboration) which on oxidation gives alcohol. The reaction is known as hydroboration-oxidation reaction.

2 (*b*) Haloform test is used to identify the compound (alcohol or carbonyl compound). In this reaction, alcohols (or aldehydes and ketones) on heating with X_2 (Cl_2, Br_2 and I_2) and OH^- form CHX_3 (haloform). The alcohols containing the CH_3CHOH-group, linked to carbon or hydrogen atom can be distinguished from other alcohols by this test. Thus, ethanol gives positive haloform test.

Therefore, both Assertion and Reason is correct but Reason is not the correct explanation of the Assertion.

3 (*b*) (i)

$$(CH_3)(H)C=O + CH_3MgBr \longrightarrow (CH_3)(H)C(\overset{-}{O}\overset{+}{M}gBr)(CH_3) \xrightarrow{H_2O} \underset{\text{(Propan-2-ol)}\ (A)}{(CH_3)(H)C(OH)(CH_3)}$$

(ii)

$$\underset{\text{Propan-2-ol}}{(CH_3)(H)C(OH)(CH_3)} \xrightarrow[-H_2O]{H_2SO_4,\ \Delta} \underset{\text{Propene}\ (B)}{CH_3-CH=CH_2}$$

(iii)

$$6\times\underset{(B)}{CH_3-CH=CH_2} + B_2H_6 \xrightarrow[\text{oxidation}]{\text{Hydroboration}} 2(CH_3CH_2CH_3)_3B \xrightarrow[-2H_3BO_3]{H_2O_2} \underset{\text{(Propan-1-ol)}\ (C)}{6CH_3CH_2CH_2OH}$$

Hence, (*A*) and (*C*) are positional isomers.

4 (*c*) Reagents used to convert alcohol to aldehyde is CrO_3-pyridine

$$\underset{\text{2-methylpentan-1-ol}}{CH_3CH_2-CH_2-CH(CH_3)-CH_2OH} \xrightarrow[\text{pyridine}]{CrO_3/HCl} \underset{\text{2-methylpentanal}}{CH_3CH_2CH_2-CH(CH_3)-CHO}$$

5 (*b*)

$$\underset{\substack{0.44\text{ g}\\ \text{At STP}}}{ROH} + CH_3MgI \xrightarrow{\text{Ether}} \underset{\substack{112\text{ cm}^3\\ 22400\text{ cm}^3}}{CH_4} + Mg(I)(OR)$$

$\therefore$ Molecular mass of alcohol

$$= \frac{0.44 \times 22400}{112} = 88\text{ g}$$

Since, alcohol oxidised with PCC (pyridiniumchloro chromate) or Corey's reagent $[C_5H_5NH^+CrO_3Cl^-]$ to form a carbonyl compound (aldehyde), which gives positive silver mirror test hence, carbonyl compound must be an aldehyde therefore, it must be a primary alcohol.

$$\underset{m\,=\,88}{(CH_3)_3C-CH_2OH} \xrightarrow{PCC} (CH_3)_3C-CHO$$

$$\underset{m\,=\,74}{(CH_3)_2CH-CH_2OH} \xrightarrow{PCC} (CH_3)_2CH-CHO$$

In the given options, (b) and (d) are primary alcohols having molecular masses 88 and 74, respectively.

Hence, only (b) will be the correct choice.

6 (*b*) Ethyl alcohol is oxidised to produce acetaldehyde

$$\underset{\text{Ethyl alcohol}}{CH_3CH_2OH} \xrightarrow{[O]} \underset{\text{Acetaldehyde}}{CH_3CHO} + H_2O$$

Thus, the conversion of ethyl alcohol into acetaldehyde is an example of oxidation.

7 (*c*) When ethyl acetate is treated with excess CH_3MgI, it gives 2-butanol along with the formation of ethanol.

$$CH_3-\overset{O}{\overset{\|}{C}}-OC_2H_5 + CH_3MgI \longrightarrow CH_3-C(OMgI)(CH_3)-OC_2H_5 \xrightarrow[\text{Hydrolysis}]{H_2O} \underset{\text{Acetone}}{CH_3-\overset{O}{\overset{\|}{C}}-CH_3} + Mg(OH)I + \underset{\text{Ethanol}}{C_2H_5OH}$$

Acetone formed further reacts with CH_3MgI to form tertiary alcohol

$$CH_3-C(CH_3)=O + CH_3MgI \longrightarrow CH_3-C(CH_3)_2-OMgI \xrightarrow[\text{Hydrolysis}]{H_2O} \underset{\text{2-methylpropan-2-ol (3° Alcohol)}}{CH_3-C(CH_3)_2-OH} + Mg(OH)I$$

8 (*b*) Glycol is widely used as an antifreeze in an automobile radiators.

9 (*c*) Pyridinium chlorochromate (PCC) prevents further oxidation of aldehydes to carboxylic acid and steps the reaction at aldehydic stage.

$$RCH_2OH \xrightarrow[CH_2Cl_2 \text{ (Solvent)}]{PCC} RCHO + H_2O$$

10. (*c*) $\underset{\text{Formaldehyde}}{H_2C{=}O} + CH_3MgI \longrightarrow (H)(H)C(CH_3)(OMgI) \xrightarrow{HOH} \underset{\text{Ethanol}}{CH_3CH_2OH} + Mg(OH)I$

11 (*e*) 1° alcohols readily form ethers when heated with conc. H_2SO_4. Thus, 1-pentanol gives the best yield of dialkyl ether when heated with a trace of sulphuric acid.

$$2CH_3CH_2CH_2CH_2CH_2OH \xrightarrow[413K]{H_2SO_4} \underset{\text{Dialkyl ether}}{CH_3CH_2CH_2CH_2CH_2OCH_2CH_2CH_2CH_2CH_3}$$

Note In this reaction, 2° and 3° alcohols readily give alkene.

12 (*b*) HI > HBr > HCl > HF.

This is due to the fact that, nucleophilicity of a halide ion increases with increase in size. As the size of halide ion increases from $F^{\ominus}$ to $I^{\ominus}$, thus, I^- ion will be a better nucleophile followed by Br^-, Cl^- and F^-.

13 (*a*) In general, 2 moles of *R*OH (alcohol) reacts with Na metal to evolve 1 mole of H_2 gas in the presence of dry ether.

$$2ROH + 2Na \xrightarrow{\text{Dry ether}} \underset{\text{(Sodium alkoxide)}}{2R\overset{-}{O}\overset{+}{Na}} + H_2\uparrow$$

$$2 \text{ mol } ROH \longrightarrow 1 \text{ mole } H_2$$

$$\therefore \quad 1 \text{ mol } ROH \longrightarrow \frac{1}{2} \text{ mole } H_2$$

Thus, $\frac{1}{2}$ mole $H_2 = \frac{1}{2} \times 2$ g $H_2 = 1$ g H_2

Hence, 1 mole of alcohol reacts with Na to evolve lg of H_2.

14 (*b*) Dehydration of alcohols involve the formation of carbocation intermediates. More the stability of carbocation, more will be the ease of alcohol towards dehydration.

∵ The order of stability of carbocations is 3° > 2° > 1°.

∴ The order of ease of dehydration of alcohols is 3° > 2° > 1°.

15 (*d*) The boiling point of ethanol is higher than ether due to extensive intermolecular hydrogen bonding.

16 (*b*) In the presence of Cr_2O_3 / ZnO catayst, carbon monoxide and H_2 at 300°C temp. and 300 atm pressure reacts and forms methanol.

$$\underset{\text{Synthesis gas}}{CO + H_2} \xrightarrow[Cr_2O_3/ZnO]{300°C/300 \text{ atm}} CH_3OH$$

17 (*a*) Because of intermolecular hydrogen bonding in alcohols, they exist as associated molecules. Consequently, a large amount of energy is required to break these bonds and therefore, their boiling points are higher than that of the corresponding hydrocarbons (hydrogen bonding is absent in hydrocarbons).

18 (*d*) Upon treatment with HIO_4, (periodic acid) compounds containing two or more —OH groups attached to the adjacent carbon atoms like in ethylene glycol undergoes oxidation with cleavage of carbon-carbon bonds.

$$\begin{matrix} CH_2OH \\ | \\ CH_2OH \end{matrix} + HIO_4 \longrightarrow \underset{\text{Formaldelyde}}{HCHO + HCHO} + HIO_3 + H_2O$$

Note Products are same as obtained by ozonolysis of alkenes.

19 (*d*) $\underset{\text{Ethanol }(Z)}{3CH_3CH_2OH} \xrightarrow[-H_3PO_3]{PBr_3} \underset{X}{3CH_3CH_2Br} \xrightarrow[-3HBr]{\text{Alc. KOH}} \underset{Y}{3CH_2{=}CH_2}$

$$\xrightarrow[\text{(ii) } H_2O, \text{ heat}]{\text{(i) } H_2SO_4, \text{ room temperature}} \underset{\text{Ethanol } Z}{3CH_3CH_2OH}$$

20 (*a*) The best combination of reagent is PBr_3, KCN, H_3O^+.

$$RCH_2CH_2{-}OH \xrightarrow[-H_3PO_3]{PBr_3} RCH_2CH_2Br$$

$$RCH_2CH_2Br \xrightarrow[-KBr]{KCN} RCH_2CH_2CN$$

$$RCH_2CH_2CN \xrightarrow{H_3O^+} RCH_2CH_2COOH$$

21 (*b*) $Mg\langle^{R'}_{X} + HOR \longrightarrow Mg\langle^{OR}_{X} + R'H$

22 (*c*) Alkyl/Aryl group of Grignard reagent has a tendency to give alkane/arene by accepting an acidic hydrogen.

$$\underset{\text{Grignard reagent}}{C_6H_5MgBr} + \underset{\text{Acidic hydrogen}}{C_2H_5OH} \longrightarrow \underset{\text{Benzene}}{C_6H_6} + Mg\langle^{Br}_{OC_2H_5}$$

23 (*c*) Chlorine reacts with ethanol through haloform reaction to give CH_3CHO and CCl_3CHO.

$$2Cl_2 + CH_3CH_2OH \longrightarrow \underset{X}{CH_3CHO} + 2HCl$$

$$3Cl_2 + CH_3CHO \longrightarrow \underset{Y}{CCl_3CHO} + 3HCl$$

Note This reaction takes place in the presence of base like NaOH, KOH. Further, *Y* reacts with NaOH to give chloroform.

24 (*d*) $\underset{\text{Methyl alcohol}}{CH_3OH} + CO \xrightarrow{\text{Rh catalyst}} \underset{\text{Acetic acid}}{\underset{A}{CH_3COOH}} \xrightarrow[\text{Red P}]{H^+} \underset{\text{Ethane}}{\underset{B}{CH_3{-}CH_3}}$

25 (*b*) Primary alcohols get dehydrogenated with reduced copper at 573 K, to give corresponding aldehydes.

$$\underset{\text{Primary alcohol}}{R{-}CH_2OH} \xrightarrow{\text{Cu, 573 K}} \underset{\text{Aldehyde}}{RCHO} + H_2\uparrow$$

26 (*b*) $C_2H_5OH + SOCl_2 \xrightarrow{\text{Pyridine}} \underset{X}{C_2H_5Cl} + \underset{Y}{SO_2} + \underset{Z}{HCl}$

This method is known as **Darzen's method** of preparation of alkyl chloride.

27 (*b*) $A \xrightarrow[\text{[O]}]{Na_2Cr_2O_7/H_2SO_4} B \xrightarrow{H_2/Ni}$ Ethyl alcohol

Compound *B* on reduction with H_2 in the presence of Ni gives ethyl alcohol, it means compound *B* is ethanal because aldehyde or acid on reduction gives primary alcohol.

Again, compound *B* is obtained by the oxidation of *A*, it means *A* is ethanol, because primary alcohol on oxidation gives aldehyde or acid.

$$\underset{A}{CH_3-CH_2-OH} \xrightarrow[\text{[O]}]{Na_2Cr_2O_7/H_2SO_4} CH_3-\overset{O}{\overset{\|}{C}}-H$$

$$\xrightarrow{\text{[O]}} \underset{B}{CH_3-\overset{O}{\overset{\|}{C}}-OH}$$

$$\xrightarrow{H_2/Ni} \underset{\text{Ethyl alcohol or ethanol}}{CH_3-CH_2-OH}$$

28 (*d*) $CH_3-\underset{OH}{\overset{CH_3}{C}}-CH_2-OH \xrightarrow{H^+} CH_3-\underset{\underset{\oplus}{OH_2}}{\overset{CH_3}{C}}-CH_2-OH$

$$\xrightarrow{-H_2O} CH_3-\underset{\oplus}{\overset{CH_3}{C}}-CH_2OH \xrightarrow{\text{+ Hydride ion}}$$

$$CH_3-\overset{CH_3}{CH}-\overset{\oplus}{C}HOH \xrightarrow[-H^+]{} \underset{\textit{Iso}\text{-butyraldehyde}}{CH_3-\overset{CH_3}{CH}-CHO}$$

29 (*b*) $C_2H_5MgBr + \underset{O}{H_2C-CH_2} \xrightarrow{H_2O} \underset{n\text{-butyl alcohol}}{C_2H_5CH_2CH_2OH} + Mg\langle^{OH}_{Br}$

30 (*c*) On heating ethanol with conc. H_2SO_4 at 165°–170°C ethylene is formed.

$$C_2H_5OH \xrightarrow[170°C]{\text{Conc. } H_2SO_4} \underset{\text{Ethylene}}{CH_2=CH_2} + H_2O$$

31 (*a*)

Dehydration of alkene [4-hydroxypentan-2-one] gives more stable conjugated compound

and thus, it is most readily hydrated in acidic conditions.

[4-hydroxypentan-2-one] $\xrightarrow{H^+}$ [pent-3-en-2-one]

32 (*b*) Ethyl alcohol is made unfit for drinking purpose by adding some poisonous substances such as methanol, naphthalene (naphtha), pyridine, rubber etc. It is called denatured alcohol.

33 (*a*) $CH_3-\underset{CH_3}{\overset{CH_3}{C}}-CH_2OH \underset{H^+}{\overset{ZnCl_2}{\rightleftharpoons}} CH_3-\underset{CH_3}{\overset{CH_3}{C}}-CH_2\overset{+}{O}H_2 \xrightarrow[-H_2O]{S_N1}$

$$\underset{1°\text{-carbocation}}{CH_3-\underset{CH_3}{\overset{CH_3}{C}}-\overset{+}{C}H_2} \xrightarrow{\text{1,2-methyl shift}} \underset{3°\text{-carbocation}}{CH_3-\underset{\oplus}{\overset{CH_3}{C}}-CH_2CH_3}$$

$$\xrightarrow{Cl^-} \underset{\text{White ppt.}}{CH_3-\underset{Cl}{\overset{CH_3}{C}}-CH_2CH_3}$$

(Branched chain primary alkyl halides undergo S_N1 reaction with Lucas reagent):

34 (*c*) $\underset{ROH}{\text{Alcohol}} + \underset{RCOOH}{\text{Acid}} \rightleftharpoons \underset{(RCOOR)}{\text{Ester}}$ (fruity smelling)

Alcohols (C_2H_5OH) when react with acids, they produce esters that have fruity smell.

$$\underset{\text{Ethyl alcohol}}{C_2H_5OH} + \underset{\text{Acetic acid}}{CH_3COOH} \longrightarrow \underset{\substack{\text{Ethyl acetate}\\ \text{Fruity smell of ester}}}{C_2H_5COOCH_3} + H_2O$$

35 (*b*) CH_3OH and C_2H_5OH can be differentiated by using Na_2CO_3 and I_2. C_2H_5OH gives yellow precipitate of CHI_3 whereas CH_3OH does not react with it.

$$C_2H_5OH + 4I_2 + Na_2CO_3 \longrightarrow \underset{\substack{\text{Iodoform}\\ \text{(yellow ppt.)}}}{CHI_3\downarrow} + CH_3CH_2\overset{O}{\overset{\|}{C}}O^-Na^+$$

$$CH_3OH + I_2 + Na_2CO_3 \longrightarrow \text{No reaction}$$

36 (*c*) Potassium dichromate reacts with alcohol and the reduction of potassium dichromate takes place from dichromate (orange red) to Cr^{3+} (green).

$$Cr_2O_7^{2-} + 16H^+ + 6e^- \longrightarrow 2Cr^{3+} + 7H_2O$$

So, the reason is false.

37 (*b*) $CH_3MgBr + HCHO \longrightarrow H-\underset{H}{\overset{CH_3}{C}}-OMgBr$

$$\xrightarrow{H_2O/H^+} \underset{\text{Ethanol}}{CH_3CH_2OH} + MgBr(OH)$$

38 (*d*) The correct match is A → 3, B → 5, C → 1, D → 2, E → 4

Column I	Column II
A. Propane-1,2,3-triol	Dynamite
B. Ethane-1,2-diol	Terylene
C. Tetrahydrofuran	Cyclic ether
D. Power alcohol	Absolute ethanol + petrol
E. Methylated spirit	Denatured alcohol

39 (*c*) $\underset{\text{Ethanol}}{C_2H_5OH} + [O] \xrightarrow{KMnO_4/H^+} \underset{\substack{(X)\\ \text{Ethanoic acid}}}{CH_3COOH}$

$$\xrightarrow[\substack{H_2SO_4/\Delta\\ \text{(Esterification)}}]{C_2H_5OH\,(Y)} \underset{\text{Ethylethanoate}}{CH_3COOC_2H_5}$$

40 (*b*) The manufacture of ethyl alcohol from starch consists of the following steps :

(i) **Hydrolysis of starch**

$$2(C_6H_{10}O_5)_n + nH_2O \xrightarrow[50\text{-}60°C]{\text{Diastase}} \underset{\text{Maltose}}{nC_{12}H_{22}O_{11}}$$

This step is called saccharification.

(ii) **Fermentation**

$$\underset{\text{Maltose}}{C_{12}H_{22}O_{11}} + H_2O \xrightarrow{\text{Maltase}} \underset{\text{Glucose}}{2C_6H_{12}O_6} \xrightarrow{\text{Zymase}} \underset{\text{Ethanol}}{2C_2H_5OH} + 2CO_2$$

41 (*a*) Conc. H_2SO_4 is an excellent dehydrating agent. Upon reaction with an alcohol, it forms an alkene and water molecule is given out. First step involves protonation of alcohol.

$$-\overset{|}{\underset{|}{{}^{\beta}C}}-\overset{|}{\underset{|}{C^{\alpha}}}-OH + H^+ \longrightarrow \underset{\text{Unstable}}{\left[-\overset{|}{\underset{|}{C}}-\overset{|}{\underset{|}{C}}-\overset{+}{O}H_2\right]} \xrightarrow{-H_2O} \underset{\text{Carbonium ion}}{-\overset{|}{\underset{|}{{}^{\beta}C}}-{}^{\alpha}\overset{|}{C^+}}$$

42 (*d*) Methyl alcohol cannot be prepared by hydration of alkene as simplest alkene has two carbon atoms so alcohol of atleast two carbon atoms can be formed by this method.

• $H_2C{=}CH_2 \xrightarrow[(H_2SO_4)]{H^+} H_3C{-}CH_2^+ \xrightarrow{HSO_4^-} CH_3{-}CH_2OSO_3H \xrightarrow{HOH} H_2SO_4 + \underset{\text{Ethanol}}{CH_3CH_2OH}$

• $H_2C{=}CH{-}CH_3 \xrightarrow[\substack{H_2SO_4 \\ \text{(Markownikoff's rule)}}]{HOH} \underset{\text{Major product}}{H_3C{-}\underset{OH}{\underset{|}{CH}}{-}CH_3} + \underset{\text{Minor product}}{HO{-}CH_2{-}CH_2CH_3}$

43 (*b*) $CH_3CH_2CH_2OH \xrightarrow{PCl_5} \underset{A}{CH_3CH_2CH_2Cl} \xrightarrow{\text{Alc. KOH}} \underset{\substack{\text{Propene} \\ B}}{CH_3{-}CH = CH_2}$

44 (*d*) Among given choices, C_2H_5OH can give proton (H^+) most easily.

$\therefore C_2H_5OH$ is most acidic among C_2H_6, CH_4 and $CH \equiv CH$.

Topic 2

Secondary and Tertiary Aliphatic Alcohols

2019

1 When vapours of a secondary alcohol is passed over heated copper at 573 K, the product formed is **[NEET (Odisha)]**

(a) a carboxylic (b) an aldehyde
(c) a ketone (d) an alkene

2013

2 Glycerol on oxidation with bismuth nitrate produces **[UP CPMT]**

(a) glyceric acid (b) glyoxalic acid
(c) oxalic acid (d) *meso*-oxalic acid

3 **Assertion** (A) Glycerol is purified by distillation under reduced pressure.

Reason (R) Glycerol is a trihydric alcohol. **[AIIMS]**

(a) Both A and R are correct and R is correct explanation of A
(b) Both A and R are correct but R is not the correct explanation of A
(c) A is correct but R is incorrect
(d) Both A and R are incorrect

2012

4 The alcohol that produce turbidity immediately with Lucas reagent at room temperatures is **[AIIMS]**

(a) 1-hydroxybutane
(b) 2-hydroxybutane
(c) 2-hydroxy-2-methylpropane
(d) 1-hydroxy-2-methylpropane

5 The best reagent to convert pent-3-en-2-ol into pent-3-en-2-one is

(a) pyridinium chlorochromate
(b) chromic anhydride in glacial acetic acid
(c) acidic dichromate
(d) acidic permanganate

2011

6 In the following reactions,

$$\text{I. } CH_3{-}\overset{\overset{CH_3}{|}}{CH}{-}\underset{\underset{OH}{|}}{CH}CH_3 \xrightarrow{H^+/\text{Heat}} \underset{\text{(Major product)}}{A} + \underset{\text{(Minor product)}}{B}$$

II. $A \xrightarrow[\text{in absence of peroxide}]{\text{HBr, dark}} \underset{\text{(Major product)}}{C} + \underset{\text{(Minor product)}}{D}$

The major products (A) and (C) are respectively, **[CBSE AIPMT]**

(a) $CH_2{=}C(CH_3){-}CH_2CH_3$ and $CH_3{-}C(CH_3)(Br){-}CH_2CH_3$

(b) $CH_2{=}C(CH_3){-}CH_2CH_3$ and $CH_2(CH_3){-}CH(Br){-}CH_2CH_3$

(c) $CH_3{-}C(CH_3){=}CH{-}CH_3$ and $CH_3{-}C(CH_3)(Br){-}CH_2CH_3$

(d) $CH_3{-}C(CH_3){=}CHCH_3$ and $CH_3{-}CH(CH_3){-}CH(Br){-}CH_3$

7 The compound that undergoes dehydration very easily is **[Kerala CEE]**

(a) 2-methylpropan-2-ol (b) ethyl alcohol
(c) 3-methyl-2-butanol (d) propyl alcohol
(e) methanol

2010

8 When vapours of *iso*-propyl alcohol are passed over heated copper, the major product obtained is **[Manipal]**

(a) propane (b) propylene
(c) acetaldehyde (d) acetone

9 Lucas reagent reacts fastest with **[WB JEE]**

(a) 1-butanol (b) 2-butanol
(c) 2-methyl-2-propanol (d) 2-methyl-1-propanol

10 When glycerol is heated with $KHSO_4$ it gives **[MP PMT]**

(a) $CH_2{=}CH{-}CH_3$
(b) $CH_2{=}CH{-}CH_2OH$
(c) $CH_2{=}CH{-}CHO$
(d) $CH_2{=}C{=}CH_2$

11 The density of glycerol is higher than propanol due to **[Guj CET]**

(a) van der Waals' attraction
(b) hydrogen bonding
(c) ionic bonding
(d) more number of covalent bonds

2009

12 Which alcohol of molecular formula C_4H_9OH cannot be obtained by the reduction of carbonyl compound? **[MHT CET]**

(a) 2-methylpropan-1-ol
(b) 2-methylpropan-2-ol
(c) Butanol
(d) Butan-2-ol

13 In the reaction given below, X is

neo-pentyl alcohol $\xrightarrow{H_2SO_4} X$ **[DUMET]**

(a) 2-methylpentane (b) 2-methylpent-2-ene
(c) 2-methylbut-2-ene (d) *neo*-pentane

2008

14 Which of the following is incorrect? **[BHU]**

(a) Primary alcohols are easily oxidised to aldehydes, which are oxidised to acids with the same number of C-atoms
(b) Secondary alcohols are easily oxidised to ketones, which are oxidised to acids with the same number of C-atoms
(c) Secondary alcohols are easily oxidised to ketones, which are oxidised to acids with lesser number of C-atoms
(d) Secondary and tertiary alcohols on oxidation form acids with lesser number of C-atoms

15 The correct order of boiling point for primary (1°), secondary (2°) and tertiary (3°) alcohols is **[MHT CET]**

(a) 1° > 2° > 3° (b) 3° > 2° > 1°
(c) 2° > 1° > 3° (d) 2° > 3° > 1°

16 The alcohol which easily reacts with conc. HCl is **[AMU]**

(a) $CH_3{-}CHOH{-}CH_2{-}CH_3$
(b) $(CH_3)_3{-}C{-}OH$
(c) $CH_3{-}CH_2{-}CH_2{-}CH_2{-}OH$
(d) $(CH_3)_2{-}CH{-}CH_2OH$

2007

17 Glycerol has **[BHU]**

(a) 1 primary—OH, 2 secondary—OH
(b) 2 primary—OH, 1 secondary—OH
(c) 3 primary—OH
(d) 1 primary—OH, 1 secondary—OH, 1 tertiary—OH

18 The major product formed when a 3,3-dimethylbutan-2-ol is heated with concentrated sulphuric acid is **[Kerala CEE]**

(a) 2,3-dimethyl-2-butene
(b) 2,3-dimethyl-1-butene
(c) 3,3-dimethyl-1-butene
(d) *cis* and *trans* isomers of 2,3-dimethyl-1-butene
(e) *cis* and *trans* isomers of 3,3-dimethyl-2-butene

19 Which among the following compounds will give a secondary alcohol on reacting with Grignard reagent followed by acid hydrolysis?

I. HCHO II. C_2H_5CHO
III. CH_3COCH_3 IV. $HCOOC_2H_5$

Select the correct answer using the codes given below. **[Kerala CEE]**

(a) Only II (b) Only III (c) I and IV (d) II and III
(e) II and IV

20 Which one of the following alcohols, is used as an antifreeze reagent and for making explosives? **[J&K CET]**

(a) Glycerol (b) Glycol (c) Ethanol (d) Phenol

21 *n*-propyl alcohol and *iso*-propyl alcohol can be chemically distinguished by which reagent **[Punjab PMET]**

(a) PCl_5
(b) reduction
(c) oxidation with potassium dichromate
(d) ozonolysis

2006

22 In the Victor-Meyer's test, the colours given by 1°, 2° and 3° alcohols are respectively, **[Kerala CEE]**

(a) red, colourless, blue (b) red, blue, colourless
(c) colourless, red, blue (d) red, blue, violet
(e) blue, red, violet

2005

23 $Z \xrightarrow{PCl_5} X \xrightarrow{\text{Alc. KOH}} Y \xrightarrow[2H_2O/\Delta]{\text{Conc. } H_2SO_4} Z.$

Here, Z is **[RPMT]**

(a) $CH_3—CH_2—CH_2OH$
(b) $(CH_3)_3—C—OH$
(c) $CH_3—CH(OH)—CH_3$
(d) None of these

24 The order of reactivity of the following alcohols towards conc. HCl is

I. $FCH_2—CH(OH)—CH_3$ (OH on the carbon next to FCH_2)
II. $FCH_2—CH_2—CH(OH)—CH_3$ (OH on the third carbon)
III. $CH_3—CH(OH)—CH_3$
IV. $Ph—CH_2—OH$

[Haryana PMT]

(a) I > II > III > IV (b) I > III > II > IV
(c) IV > III > II > I (d) IV > I > II > III

Answers

1 (c)	2 (d)	3 (b)	4 (c)	5 (b)	6 (c)	7 (a)	8 (d)	9 (c)	10 (c)
11 (b)	12 (b)	13 (c)	14 (b)	15 (a)	16 (b)	17 (b)	18 (a)	19 (e)	20 (a)
21 (c)	22 (b)	23 (c)	24 (c)						

Explanations

1 (*c*) When vapours of alcohols are passed over heated copper at 573 K, primary and secondary alcohols undergo dehydrogenation to give aldehydes and ketones, respectively. While tertiary alcohols undergo dehydration to give alkenes.

$$\underset{\substack{\text{Propan-2-ol} \\ \text{(Alcohol)}}}{(H_3C)_2C(H)OH} \xrightarrow{\text{Cu/573 K}} \underset{\substack{\text{Propanone} \\ \text{(Ketone)}}}{(H_3C)_2C{=}O} + H_2$$

Thus, option (c) is correct.

2 (*d*) Glycerol gives different products on oxidation with different oxidising agents. On oxidation with bismuth nitrate glycerol gives *meso*-oxalic acid.

$$\underset{\text{Glycerol}}{CH_2OH—CHOH—CH_2OH} \xrightarrow[\text{nitrate}]{\text{Bismuth}} \underset{\textit{meso}\text{-oxalic acid}}{COOH—CO—COOH}$$

3 (*b*) Glycerol is a trihydric alcohol. It is purified by its distillation under reduced pressure because it decomposes below its boiling point to form a foul smelling compound acrolein.

$$CH_2OH—CH\,OH—CH_2OH \xrightarrow[-2H_2O]{\Delta} \underset{\text{Acrolein}}{CH_2{=}CH—CHO}$$

4 (*c*) Tertiary alcohol gives turbidity immediately with Lucas reagent. 2-hydroxy-2-methylpropane is a tertiary alcohol.

5 (*b*)

$$CH_3-\underset{OH}{\underset{|}{CH}}-CH{=}CH-CH_3 \rightarrow CH_3-\underset{O}{\underset{\|}{C}}-CH{=}CHCH_3$$

Only suitable reagent is chromic anhydride in glacial acetic acid. Other reagents will also affect (C=C) bond.

6 (*c*)

$$CH_3-\underset{OH}{\underset{|}{CH}}-\overset{CH_3}{\overset{|}{CH}}-CH_3 \xrightarrow[\Delta]{H^{\oplus}} \underset{(A)\ \text{Major}}{CH_3-\overset{CH_3}{\overset{|}{C}}{=}CH-CH_3} + \underset{(B)\ \text{Minor}}{CH_3-\overset{CH_3}{\overset{|}{CH}}-CH{=}CH_2}$$

$$\underset{\text{Major}\ (A)}{H_3C-\overset{CH_3}{\overset{|}{C}}{=}CH-CH_3} \xrightarrow{\text{HBr (dark)}} \underset{\text{Major}\ (C)}{CH_3-\overset{CH_3}{\overset{|}{\underset{Br}{\underset{|}{C}}}}-CH_2-CH_3} + \underset{\text{Minor}\ (D)}{CH_3-\overset{CH_3}{\overset{|}{\underset{H}{\underset{|}{C}}}}-\underset{Br}{\underset{|}{CH}}-CH_3}$$

7 (*a*) 2-methylpropan-2-ol undergoes dehydration very easily as it is a 3° alcohol. The relative ease of dehydration of alcohols follows the following order:

tertiary alcohol > secondary alcohol > primary alcohol

8 (*d*)

$$\underset{iso\text{-propyl alcohol}}{CH_3\underset{OH}{\underset{|}{CH}}-CH_3} \xrightarrow[\Delta]{Cu,\ 300^\circ C} \underset{\text{Propanone or acetone}}{CH_3-\underset{O}{\underset{\|}{C}}-CH_3}$$

9 (*c*) The reactivity order of alcohol with Lucas reagent is 3° > 2° > 1°.

(a) $CH_3CH_2CH_2CH_2-OH$ (1-butanol) 1° alcohol

(b) $CH_3CH_2\underset{OH}{\underset{|}{CH}}CH_3$ (2-butanol) 2° alcohol

(c) $CH_3-\overset{OH}{\overset{|}{\underset{CH_3}{\underset{|}{C}}}}-CH_3$ (2-methyl-2-propanol) 3° alcohol

(d) $CH_3\underset{CH_3}{\underset{|}{CH}}-CH_2OH$ (2-methyl-1-propanol) 1° alcohol

Hence, 2-methyl-2-propanol reacts fastest with Lucas reagent.

10 (*c*) When glycerol is heated with $KHSO_4$, acrolein is produced.

$$\begin{array}{l} CH_2-OH \\ | \\ CH-OH \\ | \\ CH_2OH \end{array} \xrightarrow[\Delta]{KHSO_4} \underset{\text{Acrolein}}{CH_2{=}CH-\overset{O}{\overset{\|}{CH}}} + 2H_2O$$

11 (*b*) The density of glycerol is higher than propanol due to extensive intermolecular hydrogen bonding. Glycerol contains three —OH groups while, propanol contains only one —OH group.

12 (*b*) The structures of possible alcohols having formula C_4H_9OH are as :

(i) Butanol (ii) Butan-2-ol (iii) 2-methylpropan-1-ol (iv) 2-methylpropan-2-ol

Among these, 2-methylpropan-2-ol cannot be prepared by the reduction of carbonyl compounds because it contains 3°–C–atom and corresponding carbonyl compound has no H–atom.

13 (*c*)

$$\underset{neo\text{-pentyl alcohol}}{H_3C-\overset{CH_3}{\overset{|}{\underset{CH_3}{\underset{|}{C}}}}-CH_2-OH} \xrightarrow[-H_2O]{H^+} H_3C-\overset{CH_3}{\overset{|}{\underset{CH_3}{\underset{|}{C}}}}-\overset{+}{C}H_2 \xrightarrow{1,2\text{-methyl shift}} CH_3-\overset{CH_3}{\overset{|}{\underset{+}{C}}}-CH_2-CH_3 \xrightarrow{-H^+} \underset{\substack{\text{2-methylbut-2-ene} \\ \text{(Major product)}}}{CH_3-\overset{CH_3}{\overset{|}{C}}{=}CH-CH_3}$$

14 (*b*) Secondary alcohols are easily oxidised to ketone with same number of carbon atoms, but ketones are oxidised to carboxylic acid containing lesser number of carbon atoms than original alcohol.

$$\underset{\substack{iso\text{-propyl alcohol} \\ \text{(3-carbon)}}}{(H_3C)_2CHOH} \xrightarrow[-H_2O]{K_2Cr_2O_7/H_2SO_4} \underset{\substack{\text{Acetone} \\ \text{(3-carbon)}}}{(H_3C)_2C{=}O} \xrightarrow{K_2Cr_2O_7/H_2SO_4} \underset{\substack{\text{Acetic acid} \\ \text{(2-carbon)}}}{CH_3COOH} + CO_2 + H_2O$$

15 (*a*) Alcohols with same molecular weight are expected to have almost same boiling point, however two more factors other than molecular weight are important; they are namely H-bonding and surface area of molecule. Both these factors are least in 3° alcohols and maximum in 1° alcohols. Hence, 3° alcohols have least boiling point while 1° alcohols have maximum boiling point.

Hence, the correct order of boiling point is 1°>2°>3°.

16 (*b*) Tertiary alcohol readily reacts with halogen acid.

$$\underset{\text{3° alcohols}}{CH_3-\underset{CH_3}{\overset{CH_3}{|}}{C}-OH} \longrightarrow \underset{\text{Carbonium ion}}{CH_3-\underset{CH_3}{\overset{CH_3}{|}}{C^+}} + OH^-$$

Presence of three alkyl groups increases electron density on 3° carbon atom. Hence, —OH group is easily removed. After removal of —OH group, 3° carbonium ion is formed which is most stable.

17 (*b*) Structure of glycerol is as follows :

$$\begin{array}{c} ^{1°}CH_2OH \\ | \\ ^{2°}CHOH \\ | \\ ^{1°}CH_2OH \end{array}$$

It has two types of —OH groups. Two —OH groups are primary (1°) but one —OH group (2°) is secondary.

18 (*a*) $H_2SO_4 \rightleftharpoons HSO_4^- + H^+$

$$\underset{\text{3,3-dimethyl butan-2-ol}}{{}^4CH_3-{}^3\underset{CH_3}{\overset{CH_3}{C}}-{}^2\underset{OH}{CH}-{}^1CH_3} \underset{}{\overset{H^+}{\rightleftharpoons}} CH_3-\underset{CH_3}{\overset{CH_3}{C}}-\underset{^+OH_2}{CH}-CH_3$$

$$\xrightarrow[\text{slow}]{-H_2O} \underset{\text{(2° carbocation)}}{CH_3-\underset{CH_3}{\overset{CH_3}{C}}-\overset{\oplus}{C}H-CH_3} \overset{\text{2, 3–}\overline{CH_3}\text{ shift}}{\rightleftharpoons} \underset{\text{(3° carbocation)}}{CH_3-\underset{\oplus}{\overset{CH_3}{C}}-\overset{CH_3}{CH}-CH_3}$$

$$\xrightarrow{-H^+} \underset{\text{(Major product)}}{\underset{\text{2, 3-dimethylbut -2-ene}}{CH_3-\overset{CH_3}{C}=\overset{CH_3}{C}-CH_3}}$$

$$\text{(2° carbocation)} \xrightarrow{-H^+} \underset{\text{(Minor product)}}{\underset{\text{3, 3-dimethylbut-1-ene}}{CH_3-\underset{CH_3}{\overset{CH_3}{C}}-CH=CH_2}}$$

19 (*e*) $\underset{\text{Grignard reagent}}{C_2H_5CHO + RMgX} \longrightarrow C_2H_5-\underset{R}{\overset{H}{C}}-OMgX \xrightarrow{H_3O^+} \underset{\text{2° alcohol}}{C_2H_5CHOHR} + Mg\begin{smallmatrix} OH \\ X \end{smallmatrix}$

$$HCOOC_2H_5 + RMgX \longrightarrow H-\underset{R}{\overset{OC_2H_5}{C}}-OMgX$$

$$\xrightarrow[(-C_2H_5OH)]{H_3O^{\oplus}} \underset{R}{\overset{R}{C}}=O + Mg\begin{smallmatrix} OH \\ X \end{smallmatrix} \xrightarrow[\text{(ii) } H_3O^+]{\text{(i) } RMgX} \underset{\text{2° alcohol}}{H-\underset{R}{\overset{R}{C}}-OH}$$

20 (*a*) Glycerol is generally used as an antifreeze reagent and for making explosives.

21 (*c*) *n*-propyl alcohol and *iso*-propyl alcohol give different products on oxidation with $K_2Cr_2O_7$.

$$\underset{n\text{-propyl alcohol}}{CH_3CH_2-CH_2OH} \xrightarrow[K_2Cr_2O_7/H_2SO_4]{[O]} \underset{\text{Propanal}}{CH_3-CH_2-CHO}$$

$$\underset{iso\text{-propyl alcohol}}{CH_3-\underset{OH}{CH}-CH_3} \xrightarrow[K_2Cr_2O_7/H_2SO_4]{[O]} \underset{\text{Acetone}}{CH_3-\underset{O}{\overset{\|}{C}}-CH_3}$$

22 (*b*) In the Victor-Meyer's test, the primary and secondary alcohols give red and blue colour respectively while tertiary alcohols give colourless solution.

23 (*c*) $\underset{(Z)}{\underset{\text{Propan-2-ol}}{CH_3-\underset{OH}{CH}-CH_3}} \xrightarrow{PCl_5} \underset{(X)}{\underset{\text{2-chloropropane}}{CH_3-\underset{Cl}{CH}-CH_3}}$

$$\xrightarrow{\text{Alc. KOH}} \underset{(Y)}{\underset{\text{Propene}}{CH_3-CH=CH_2}}$$

$$\xrightarrow[2H_2O/\Delta]{\text{Conc. } H_2SO_4} \underset{(Z)}{\underset{\text{Propan-2-ol}}{CH_3-\underset{OH}{CH}-CH_3}}$$

24 (*c*) Reaction of alcohols towards conc. HCl is a nucleophilic substitution reaction. Hence, more stable the carbocation, more reactive will be the alcohol. The order of stability of carbocations is

$$Ph\overset{+}{C}H_2 > CH_3-\overset{+}{C}H-CH_3 > FCH_2-CH_2-\overset{+}{C}H-CH_3 > FCH_2-\overset{+}{C}H-CH_3$$

Hence, order of reactivity of alcohols towards conc. HCl is IV > III > II > I.

Topic 3

Phenols

2019

1 Order of acidic nature

(A) p-nitrophenol; (B) o-nitrophenol; (C) p-cresol; (D) phenol **[AIIMS]**

(a) $A > C > D > B$ (b) $A > B > D > C$
(c) $A > B > C > D$ (d) $D > C > B > A$

2 The compound that is most difficult to protonate is **[NEET]**

(a) $H_3C—O—H$ (b) $H_3C—O—CH_3$
(c) $Ph—O—H$ (d) $H—O—H$

3 The structure of intermediate *A* in the following reaction, is

$$C_6H_5CH(CH_3)_2 \xrightarrow{O_2} A \xrightarrow[H_2O]{H^+} C_6H_5OH + H_3C—CO—CH_3$$

[NEET]

(a) $H_3C—C(CH_3)(C_6H_5)—O—O—H$ (b) $C_6H_5—O—O—CH(CH_3)_2$
(c) $C_6H_5—CH(CH_3)—CH_2—O—O—H$ (d) $C_6H_5—O—CH(CH_3)_2$

2018

4 In the reaction **[NEET]**

$$C_6H_5OH + CHCl_3 + NaOH \longrightarrow o\text{-}(O^-Na^+)C_6H_4CHO$$

the electrophile involved is
(a) dichloromethyl anion ($\bar{C}HCl_2$)
(b) formyl cation ($\overset{+}{C}HO$)
(c) dichloromethyl cation ($\overset{+}{C}HCl_2$)
(d) dichlorocarbene ($:CCl_2$)

5 When phenol is treated with $CHCl_3$ and NaOH followed by acidification, salicylaldehyde is obtained. Which of the following species is involved in the above mentioned reaction as intermediates? **[JIPMER]**

(a) cyclohexadienone with $\overset{\ominus}{C}Cl_2$ and H at ring carbon (b) OH-substituted ring with $CHCl_2$
(c) cyclohexanone with CCl_2, H and OH (d) OH-substituted ring with $=C(H)Cl$

6 Compound *A*, $C_8H_{10}O$, is found to react with NaOI (produced by reacting *Y* with NaOH) and yields a yellow precipitate with characteristic smell.
A and *Y* are respectively. **[NEET]**

(a) $C_6H_5—CH(OH)—CH_3$ and I_2
(b) $C_6H_5—CH_2—CH_2—OH$ and I_2
(c) $H_3C—C_6H_4—CH_2—OH$ and I_2
(d) $CH_3—C_6H_3(CH_3)—OH$ and I_2

7 Identify the major products *P*, *Q* and *R* in the following sequence of reactions : **[NEET]**

$$C_6H_6 + CH_3CH_2CH_2Cl \xrightarrow[AlCl_3]{Anhy.} P \xrightarrow[(ii)\ H_3O^+/\Delta]{(i)\ O_2} Q + R$$

	P	Q	R
(a)	$C_6H_5CH(CH_3)_2$	C_6H_5OH	$CH_3CH(OH)CH_3$
(b)	$C_6H_5CH_2CH_2CH_3$	C_6H_5CHO	C_6H_5COOH
(c)	$C_6H_5CH_2CH_2CH_3$	C_6H_5CHO	$CH_3CH_2—OH$
(d)	$C_6H_5CH(CH_3)_2$	C_6H_5OH	$CH_3—CO—CH_3$

2017

8 Which one is the most acidic compound? [NEET]

(a) p-cresol (OH and CH_3 para) (b) p-nitrophenol (OH and NO_2 para)

(c) phenol (d) 2,4,6-trinitrophenol (OH with O_2N, NO_2, NO_2)

9 Phenol $\xrightarrow[\text{(ii) } CO_2/140°C]{\text{(i) NaOH}} A \xrightarrow{H^+/H_2O} B \xrightarrow{Ac_2O} C$

In the above reaction, end product 'C' is [JIPMER]

(a) salicylaldehyde (b) salicylic acid

(c) phenyl acetate (d) aspirin

2014

10 Among the following sets of reactants which one produces anisole? [CBSE AIPMT]

(a) CH_3CHO, $RMgX$ (b) C_6H_5OH, NaOH, CH_3I

(c) C_6H_5OH, neutral $FeCl_3$

(d) $C_6H_5—CH_3$, CH_3COCl, $AlCl_3$

11 Butylated hydroxy toluene is used in [MHT CET]

(a) preventing oxidative rancidity of fats

(b) preserving food grains

(c) killing bacteria living tissues

(d) reducing stress and anxiety

12 When phenol is treated with D_2SO_4/D_2O, some of the hydrogens get exchanged. The final product in this exchange reaction is [Manipal]

(a) OD; D, D (ortho); H, H (meta); D (para)

(b) OD; D, H (ortho); H, H (meta); D (para)

(c) OD; D, H (ortho); H, D (meta); H (para)

(d) OD; H, H (ortho); D, D (meta); H (para)

13 Phenol (OH) $\xrightarrow{C_6H_5COCl/\text{base}} X \xrightarrow{\text{Nitration}} Y$ (major product). Y is

(a) C_6H_5—COO—C_6H_4—NO_2

(b) OH—C_6H_4—COO—C_6H_4—NO_2

(c) O_2N—C_6H_4—COO—C_6H_5

(d) O_2N—C_6H_4—COO—C_6H_4—NO_2 [RPMT]

14 The main product obtained from phenol with PCl_5 is [Manipal]

(a) BHC (b) hexachlorobenzene

(c) chlorobenzene (d) triphenyl phosphate

15 Phenol is treated with bromine water and shaken well. The white precipitate formed during the process is [KCET]

(a) *m*-bromophenol

(b) 2, 4, 6- tribromophenol

(c) 2, 4- dibromophenol

(d) a mixture of *o*- and *p*- bromophenol

2012

16 Which one of the following properties is exhibited by phenol? [Manipal]

(a) It is soluble in *aq* NaOH and evolves CO_2 with *aq* $NaHCO_3$

(b) It is soluble in *aq*. NaOH and does not evolve CO_2 with *aq*. $NaHCO_3$

(c) It is not soluble in *aq* NaOH but evolves CO_2 with *aq* $NaHCO_3$

(d) It is insoluble in *aq* NaOH but does not evolve CO_2 with *aq*. $NaHCO_3$

2011

17 The conversion of *m*-nitrophenol to resorcinol involves respectively [KCET]

(a) hydrolysis, diazotisation and reduction

(b) diazotisation, reduction and hydrolysis

(c) hydrolysis, reduction and diazotisation

(d) reduction, diazotisation and hydrolysis

18 Chlorobenzene $\xrightarrow[X]{\text{Reaction}}$ phenol $\xrightarrow[Y]{\text{Reaction}}$ salicylaldehyde

X and Y reactions are respectively, [Guj CET]

(a) Fries rearrangement and Kolbe-Schmidt

(b) Cumene and Reimer-Tiemann

(c) Dow's process and Reimer-Tiemann

(d) Dow's process and Friedel-Craft

19 Phenol is heated with phthalic anhydride in the presence of conc. H_2SO_4. The product gives pink colour with alkali. The product is [BVP]

(a) phenolphthalein (b) bakelite

(c) salicylic acid (d) fluorescein

2010

20 Which one of the following compounds has the most acidic nature? **[CBSE AIPMT]**

(a) cyclohexyl–CH(OH)–cyclohexyl (b) C_6H_5–CH_2OH

(c) C_6H_5–OH (d) cyclohexyl–OH

21 Which of the following does not give iodoform test?

(a) C_2H_5OH (b) C_6H_5OH **[UP CPMT]**
(c) $(CH_3)_2$ CHOH (d) All of these

22 $C_6H_5OH \xrightarrow{K_2S_2O_8,\ KOH}$?

The major product in the above reaction is **[Manipal]**

(a) *p*-benzoquinone (b) *p*-benzoic acid
(c) aniline (d) None of the above

23 The product of the following reaction is **[OJEE]**

$C_6H_5OH \xrightarrow[\text{Conc. } H_2SO_4]{\text{Conc. } HNO_3}$?

(a) *o*-nitrophenol (b) *m*-nitrophenol
(c) 2,4-dinitrophenol (d) 2,4,6-trinitrophenol

24 Phenol $\xrightarrow{X}$ forms a tribromo derivative. *X* is **[KCET]**

(a) bromine in benzene
(b) bromine in water
(c) potassium bromide solution
(d) bromine in carbon tetrachloride at 0°C

25 Phenol reacts with NH_3 to give **[VMMC]**

(a) benzamide (b) benzoic acid
(c) aniline (d) None of the above

2009

26 Consider the following reaction,

phenol $\xrightarrow{\text{Zn dust}} X \xrightarrow[\text{Anhy. } AlCl_3]{CH_3Cl} Y \xrightarrow{\text{Alk. } KMnO_4} Z.$

The product *Z* is **[CBSE AIPMT]**

(a) toluene (b) benzaldehyde
(c) benzoic acid (d) benzene

27 Phenol is heated with $CHCl_3$ and alcoholic KOH, salicylaldehyde is produced. This reaction is known as **[Manipal]**

(a) Rosenmund's reaction
(b) Reimer-Tiemann reaction
(c) Friedel-Crafts reaction
(d) Sommelet reaction

28 Sulphonation of phenol with conc. H_2SO_4 at 288-293 K gives **[Manipal]**

(a) *o*-phenolsulphonic acid (b) sulphanilic acid
(c) *p*-phenolsulphonic acid (d) sulphone

29 Which of the following is most acidic? **[Manipal]**

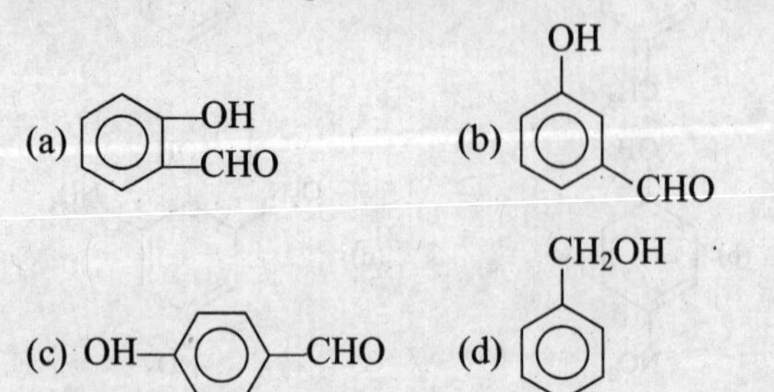

30 Most acidic amongst the following is **[OJEE]**

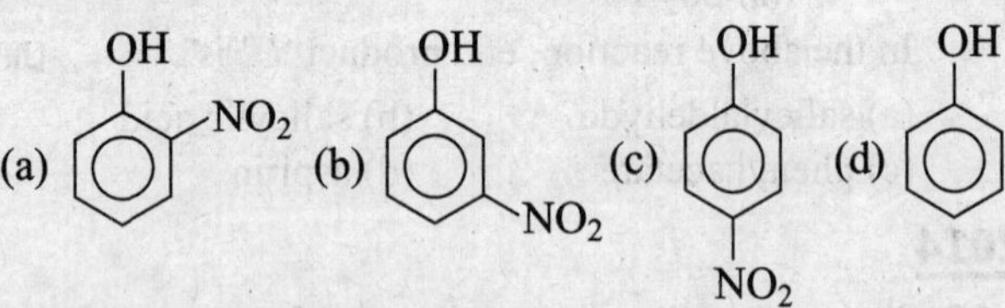

31 Which of the following statements is incorrect? **[WB JEE]**

(a) Phenol is a weak acid.
(b) Phenol is an aromatic compound.
(c) Phenol liberates CO_2 from Na_2CO_3 solution.
(d) Phenol is soluble in NaOH.

32 The most acidic among the following is **[J&K CET]**

(a) *p*-cresol (b) *o*-cresol
(c) *p*-nitrophenol (d) *p*-chlorophenol

33 Which of the following reactions involves carbon- carbon bond formation? **[DUMET]**

(a) Reimer-Tiemann reaction
(b) Hydroboration-oxidation
(c) Cannizzaro reaction
(d) Reaction of primary alcohol with PCC

2008

34 Assertion (A) The ease of dehydration of the following alcohols is

OH (cyclohexadienol) < OH (cyclohexanol) < OH (cyclohexenol) < OH (cyclohexenol)

Reason (R) Alcohols leading to conjugated alkenes are dehydrated to a greater extent. **[AIIMS]**

(a) Both A and R are correct and R is the correct explanation of A
(b) Both A and R are correct but R is not the correct explanation of A
(c) A is correct but R is incorrect
(d) Both A and R are incorrect

35 In which of the following compounds —OH group is least reactive? **[Manipal]**

(a) OH, CHO (b) OH, CHO

(c) HO—⟨⟩—CHO (d) All are equally reactive

36 When *o*-or *p*-phenolsulphonic acid is treated with bromine water, the product formed is **[Manipal]**

(a) 2,4-dibromophenol
(b) 2,4,6-tribromophenol
(c) 3-bromophenol boric acid
(d) 3,5-dibromophenol

37 Among the following, which is least acidic? **[KCET]**

(a) Phenol
(b) *o*-cresol
(c) *p*-nitrophenol
(d) *p*-chlorophenol

38 The following reaction is known as

$$\text{C}_6\text{H}_5\text{OH} + \text{HCl} + \text{HCN} \xrightarrow[\text{ZnCl}_2]{\text{Anhy.}} o\text{-OHC-C}_6\text{H}_4\text{-OH}$$

(a) Perkin reaction **[BCECE]**
(b) Gattermann reaction
(c) Kolbe reaction
(d) Gattermann-aldehyde reaction

2007

39 The reaction,

$$\text{C}_6\text{H}_4(\text{OH})_2 \xrightarrow[\text{NaOH}]{\text{CH}_2\text{I}_2} \text{C}_6\text{H}_4\text{O}_2\text{CH}_2$$

is an example of **[Kerala CEE]**

(a) Wurtz reaction
(b) Wittig reaction
(c) Ullmann reaction
(d) Williamson reaction
(e) Wurtz-Fittig reaction

40 On reacting with neutral ferric chloride, phenol gives **[J&K CET]**

(a) red colour (b) blue colour
(c) violet colour (d) green colour

41 At low temperature, phenol reacts with Br_2 in CS_2 to form **[AMU]**

(a) *m*-bromophenol
(b) *o* and *p*-bromophenol
(c) *p*-bromophenol
(d) 2,4,6-tribromophenol

2006

42 *Iso*-propylbenzene on air oxidation in the presence of dilute acid gives **[AIIMS]**

(a) C_6H_5COOH (b) $C_6H_5COCH_3$
(c) C_6H_5CHO (d) C_6H_5OH

43 What amount of bromine will be required to convert 2 g of phenol into 2,4,6-tribromophenol? **[MHT CET]**

(a) 4.00 (b) 6.00 (c) 10.22 (d) 20.44

44 Which is used to obtain salicylic acid from phenol? **[MP PMT]**

(a) HNO_3 (b) $CHCl_3$ (c) CH_3Br (d) CCl_4

45 Select the structural formula of resorcinol. **[Guj CET]**

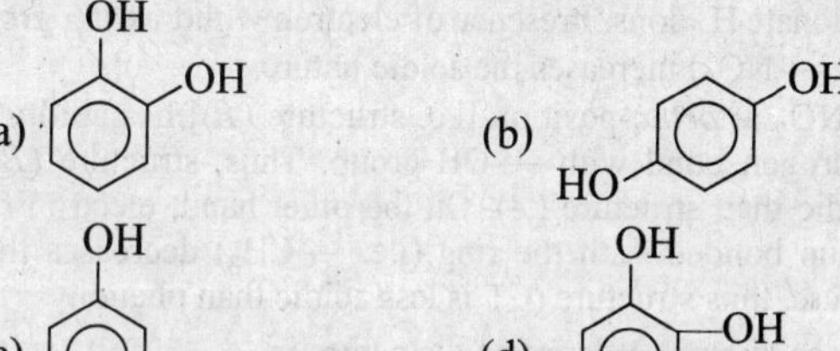

2005

46 Which one of the following compounds is most acidic? **[CBSE AIPMT]**

(a) $Cl—CH_2—CH_2OH$ (b) OH, NO_2

(c) OH (d) OH, CH_3

47 Choose the correct acidity order of the following phenols. **[Kerala CEE]**

(a) *o*-nitrophenol > *p*-chlorophenol > *p*-cresol > phenol
(b) *p*-nitrophenol > *p*-cresol > *p*-chlorophenol > phenol
(c) *o*-nitrophenol > *p*-chlorophenol > phenol > *p*-cresol
(d) *p*-nitrophenol > phenol > *p*-chlorophenol > *p*-cresol
(e) *p*-nitrophenol > *p*-cresol > phenol > *p*-chlorophenol

48 Hydrogenation of phenol gives **[MP PMT]**

(a) salicylic acid (b) *p*-benzoquinone
(c) cyclohexanol (d) None of these

49 Which of the following statements is not correct? **[J&K CET]**

(a) Phenol is more acidic than acetic acid
(b) Ethanol is less acidic than phenol
(c) Ethanol has lower boiling point than ethanoic acid
(d) Ethane is a non-linear molecule

50 Reaction of phenol with chloroform/sodium hydroxide to give *o*-hydroxybenzaldehyde involves the formation of **[J&K CET]**

(a) dichlorocarbene (b) trichlorocarbene
(c) chlorine atoms (d) chlorine molecules

Answers

1. (b)	2. (c)	3. (a)	4. (d)	5. (a)	6. (a)	7. (d)	8. (d)	9. (d)	10. (b)
11. (a)	12. (a)	13. (a)	14. (d)	15. (b)	16. (b)	17. (d)	18. (c)	19. (a)	20. (c)
21. (b)	22. (a)	23. (d)	24. (b)	25. (c)	26. (c)	27. (b)	28. (a)	29. (c)	30. (c)
31. (c)	32. (c)	33. (a)	34. (a)	35. (a)	36. (b)	37. (b)	38. (b)	39. (d)	40. (c)
41. (c)	42. (d)	43. (c)	44. (d)	45. (c)	46. (a)	47. (c)	48. (c)	49. (a)	50. (a)

Explanations

1 (*b*) Acidic nature of aromatic compounds depend on the ability to donate H^+ ions. Presence of electron withdrawing group (i.e. $—NO_2$) increases the acidic nature.

$—NO_2$ at *ortho*-position [i.e. structure (*B*)] has ability to form hydrogen bond with —OH group. Thus, structure (*B*) is less acidic than structure (*A*). On the other hand, electron releasing group bonded with the ring (i.e. $—CH_3$) decreases the acidic nature, thus structure (C) is less acidic than phenol.

Hence, correct order of acidic nature is

p-nitrophenol (*A*) > o-nitrophenol (*B*) > phenol (*D*) > p-cresol (*C*)

and option (b) is the correct.

2 (*c*) In CH_3OH and CH_3OCH_3, — CH_3 group shows + *I*-effect due to which oxygen acquires partial negative charge in both the compounds.

$H_3C \rightarrow \overset{\delta-}{O} — H$ (+*I*-effect); $CH_3 \rightarrow \overset{\delta\delta-}{O} \leftarrow CH_3$ (+*I*-effect) (+*I*-effect)

On the other hand in Ph—OH, —Ph shows –*I* effect due to which oxygen acquire partial positive charge.

$Ph \leftarrow \overset{\delta+}{O} — H$

Along with, the lone pair of oxygen also show conjugation with benzene ring which increases the positive charge on oxygen as:

(resonance structure: $\overset{\delta+}{O}—H$ with $\delta-$ at ortho and para positions of the ring)

Thus, further decreasing the process of protonation.

Therefore, incoming proton will not be able to attack easily on partial positive 'O' atom. Hence, phenol is most difficult to protonate. Thus, option (c) is correct.

3 (*a*) The given reaction is of cumene process for phenol production and intermediate (*A*) is cumene hydroperoxide. In the process, cumene (isopropylbenzene) is oxidised in the presence of air to cumene hydroperoxide which is then converted to phenol and acetone by treating with dilute acid. Acetone, a by-product of this reaction is also obtained in large quantities by this method. The reaction takes place as follows:

$$\text{Cumene} \xrightarrow{O_2} \underset{\text{Cumene hydroperoxide } (A)}{C_6H_5C(CH_3)_2OOH} \xrightarrow[H_2O]{H^+} \underset{\text{Phenol}}{C_6H_5OH} + \underset{\text{Acetone}}{CH_3COCH_3}$$

4 (*d*)

$$C_6H_5OH + CHCl_3 + NaOH \longrightarrow o\text{-}(CHO)C_6H_4O^{\ominus}Na^+$$

The above given reaction is known as Riemer-Tiemann reaction. In this reaction, electrophile involved is dichlorocarbene ($:CCl_2$) which is formed in the I[st] step of mechanism.

Mechanism

***Step* I** Generation of electrophile

$$CHCl_3 + OH^- \rightleftharpoons {}^-CCl_3 + H_2O$$

$${}^-CCl_3 \longrightarrow \underset{\substack{\text{(Electrophile)}\\ \text{Dichlorocarbene}}}{:CCl_2} + Cl^-$$

***Step* II** Reaction of electrophile with phenoxide

$$C_6H_5O^- + :CCl_2 \longrightarrow \text{(cyclohexadienone intermediate with H and } \bar{C}Cl_2) \longrightarrow \underset{o\text{-dichloromethyl phenoxide}}{o\text{-}(CHCl_2)C_6H_4O^-}$$

***Step* III** Hydrolysis

$$o\text{-}(CHCl_2)C_6H_4O^- \xrightarrow{2\,OH^-} o\text{-}(CH(OH)_2)C_6H_4O^-$$

$$\xrightarrow{-H_2O} o\text{-}(CHO)C_6H_4O^- \xrightarrow{H^+} \underset{\text{Salicylaldehyde}}{o\text{-}(CHO)C_6H_4OH}$$

5 (*a*) On refluxing alkaline solution of phenol with $CHCl_3$ at 330 K and on subsequent acidification, *o*-hydroxy benzaldehyde (salicylaldehyde) is obtained. This reaction is known as Riemer-Tiemann reaction.

Mechanism

$$CHCl_3 + OH^- \rightleftharpoons CCl_3^- + H_2O$$

$$CCl_3^- \longrightarrow :CCl_2 + Cl^-$$

∴ The correct option is (a).

6 (*a*) Iodoform reaction with sodium hypoiodite (NaOI) is used for the detection of CH_3CO group. Also compounds containing $CH_3CH(OH)$ group shows positive iodoform test as it produces CH_3CO group on oxidation. Since, among the compounds, $CH_3CH(OH)$ group is given only in the substrate of option (a) hence, it is correct.

The reaction of compound *A* with NaOI is given as follows :

$$2NaOH + I_2 \longrightarrow NaOI + NaI + H_2O$$

(*A*) Acetophenone

Iodoform (yellow ppt.)

Sodium benzoate

7 (*d*) The given reaction takes place as follows :

Cumene (*P*) Phenol (*Q*) Acetone (*R*)

Mechanism

***Step* I** Formation of carbocation

$$CH_3CH_2CH_2-Cl + \underset{\text{(Anhy.)}}{AlCl_3} \longrightarrow CH_3CH_2\overset{+}{C}H_2 + \overset{-}{AlCl_4}$$

$$\underset{\text{Carbocation (1°)}}{CH_3CH_2\overset{+}{C}H_2} \xrightarrow{\text{1, 2 H}^- \text{shift}} \underset{\text{Carbocation (2°)}}{CH_3\overset{+}{C}H-CH_3}$$

***Step* II** Electrophilic substitution reaction

(*P*)

***Step* III** Formation of peroxide

***Step* IV** Hydrolysis of oxidised product formed in step III.

Migration of phenyl to oxygen, $-H_2O$

Acetone Phenol

8 (*d*) This problem is based on the acidic character of phenol. Electron withdrawing group at *o* and *p*-position w.r.t. — OH group of phenol, increases the acidic strength.

Picric acid (2,4,6-trinitrophenol) is most acidic compounds than other given compounds, because its pK_a value is close to zero and also due to the presence of three strong electron withdrawing groups (—NO_2 group) at *ortho* and *para*-positions, picric acid is most acidic compound.

9 (*d*)

Phenol

(i) NaOH (ii) CO_2/140°C; H^+/H_2O; Ac_2O

(Aspirin) Acetyl salicylic acid

10 (*b*) Phenol + NaOH ⟶ Sodium phenoxide ($C_6H_5\bar{O}\overset{+}{N}a$) $\xrightarrow[S_N2]{CH_3I}$ Anisole ($C_6H_5OCH_3$)

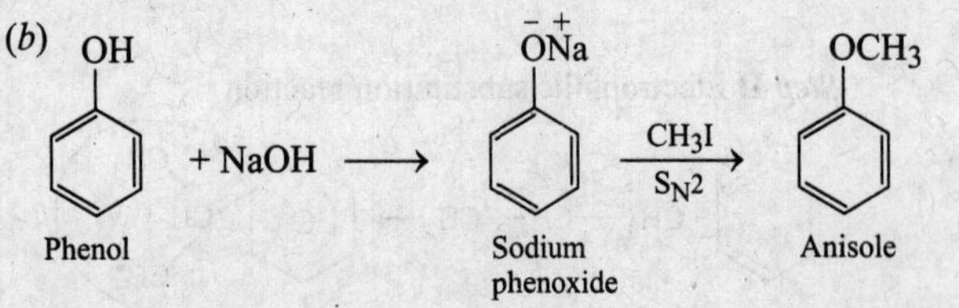

11 (*a*) Butylated hydroxy toluene (BHT) is used as an antioxidant. It retards the action of oxygen on the food material and thereby helps in preventing oxidative rancidity of fats.

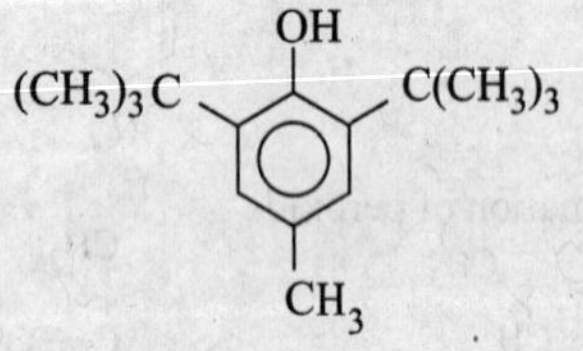

OH, $(CH_3)_3C$, $C(CH_3)_3$, CH_3

BHT

12 (*a*) In acidic medium, phenol exists in the following resonating structures.

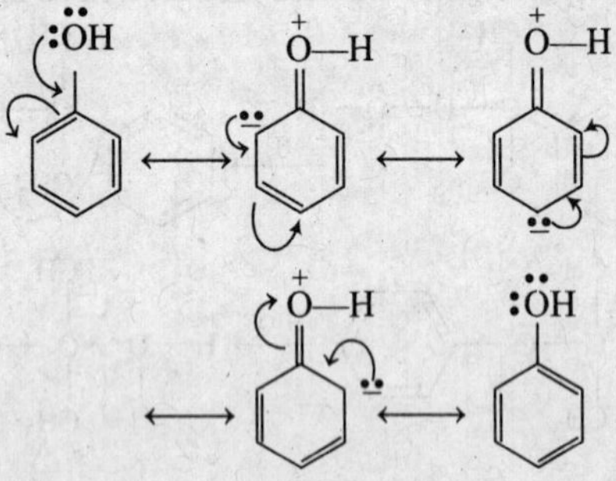

Since, *o*/*p* positions are electron rich sites, so electrophile will attack on these sites, i.e. hydrogen of these sites get exchanged by D (deuterium). Hence, the final product of the reaction is

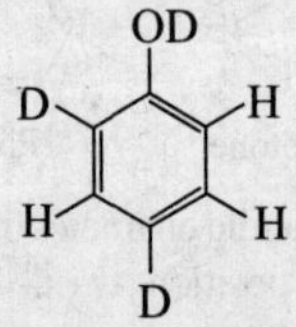

(OD, D, H, H, H, D) which is formed as

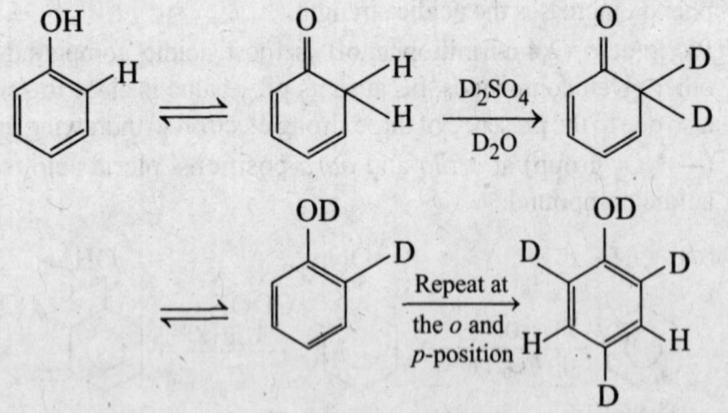

$\xrightarrow[D_2O]{D_2SO_4}$ ⇌ $\xrightarrow{\text{Repeat at the } o \text{ and } p\text{-position}}$ (OD, D, D, H, H, D)

13 (*a*) Phenol on reaction with benzoyl chloride produces phenyl benzoate by means of nucleophilic substitution reaction which on further nitration using HNO_3 / H_2SO_4 produces the desired product.

The complete sequence of above reaction can be shown as :

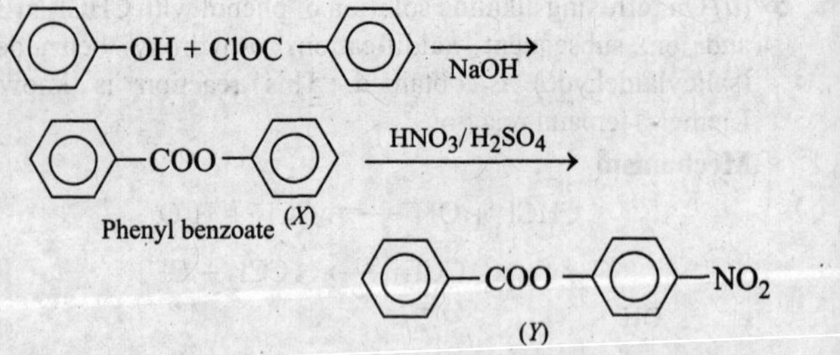

$C_6H_5OH + ClOCC_6H_5 \xrightarrow{NaOH}$ $C_6H_5COOC_6H_5$ Phenyl benzoate (*X*) $\xrightarrow{HNO_3/H_2SO_4}$ $C_6H_5COOC_6H_4NO_2$ (*Y*)

14 (*d*) $C_6H_5OH + PCl_5 \longrightarrow C_6H_5Cl + POCl_3 + HCl$

Chlorobenzene (minor product)

$3C_6H_5OH + POCl_3 \longrightarrow (C_6H_5)_3PO_4 + 3HCl$

Triphenyl phosphate

The yield of chlorobenzene in the above reaction is very poor. The main product of the reaction is triphenyl phosphate $(C_6H_5)_3PO_4$.

15 (*b*) Phenol on treatment with bromine water produces a white precipitate of 2, 4, 6-tribromophenol.

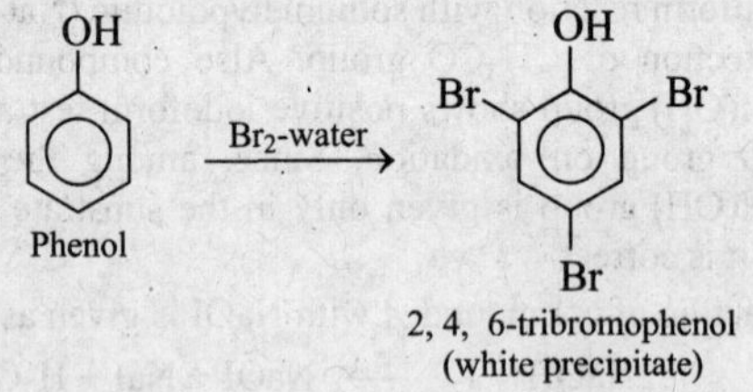

Phenol $\xrightarrow{Br_2\text{-water}}$ 2, 4, 6-tribromophenol (white precipitate)

16 (*b*) Phenol is a weak acid. It reacts with NaOH to produce salt.

$C_6H_5OH + NaOH \longrightarrow C_6H_5\bar{O}\overset{+}{N}a + H_2O$

Sodium phenoxide

But it is not sufficiently acidic to evolve CO_2 from $NaHCO_3$ solution.

17 (*d*) *m*-nitrophenol (OH, NO_2) $\xrightarrow[\text{Sn/HCl (Reduction)}]{[H]}$ *m*-aminophenol (OH, NH_2) $\xrightarrow[0°C]{NaO_2/HCl}$ (Diazotisation) (OH, $\overset{+}{N}\equiv N—Cl^-$) $\xrightarrow[\Delta]{H^+/H_2O}$ Resorcinol (OH, OH)

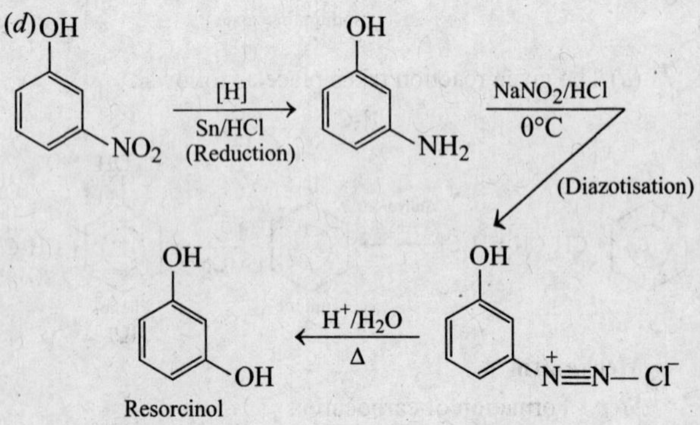

18 (c) Chlorobenzene $\xrightarrow[\text{Dow's process }(X)]{\text{(i) NaOH, (ii) }H^+}$ Phenol $\xrightarrow[\text{(ii) }H^+\text{ (Reimer-Tiemann reaction) }(Y)]{\text{(i) }CHCl_3 + \text{aq. NaOH}}$ Salicylaldehyde

X—Dow's process, Y—Reimer-Tiemann reaction.

19 (a) 2 Phenol + Phthalic anhydride $\xrightarrow[\text{Heat }(-H_2O)]{\text{Conc. }H_2SO_4}$ Phenolphthalein (colourless) $\xrightarrow{\text{NaOH}}$ Pink colour

20 (c) Phenoxide ions are more resonance stabilised, therefore phenol is more acidic.

21 (b) Compounds containing either $CH_3\underset{|}{C}HOH$ or $CH_3-\overset{O}{\overset{\|}{C}}-$ group when react with NaOH and I_2, form yellow coloured iodoform. This test is called **iodoform test**. C_6H_5OH contains neither $CH_3\underset{\underset{OH}{|}}{C}H-$ nor $CH_3-\overset{O}{\overset{\|}{C}}-$ group, thus it does not give iodoform test.

Note The I_2 converts C_2H_5OH into CH_3CHO. That's why it gives iodoform test.

22 (a) Phenol $\xrightarrow[\text{KOH, }\Delta]{K_2S_2O_8}$ p-benzenediol or quinol + o-benzenediol or catechol

23 (d) —OH is a very strong activator.

Phenol $\xrightarrow[\text{Conc. }H_2SO_4]{\text{Conc. }HNO_3 +}$ 2, 4, 6-trinitrophenol (picric acid)

24 (b) Here, X is bromine in water i.e. Br_2/H_2O

Phenol $\xrightarrow[\Delta]{2Br_2/H_2O\ (X)}$ 2,4,6-tribromophenol

25 (c) Phenol reacts with ammonia in the presence of anhydrous $ZnCl_2$ to give aniline.

Phenol $+ NH_3 \xrightarrow[\text{675 K}]{\text{Anhyd. }ZnCl_2}$ Aniline $+ H_2O$

26 (c) Phenol $\xrightarrow[-ZnO]{\text{Zn dust}}$ Benzene (X) $\xrightarrow[\text{Anhydrous }AlCl_3]{CH_3Cl}$ Toluene (Y) $\xrightarrow{\text{Alkaline }KMnO_4}$ Benzoic acid (Z)

27 (b) Phenol reacts with chloroform and alcoholic KOH to give salicylaldehyde. This reaction is called as Reimer-Tiemann reaction.

Phenol $+ CHCl_3 \xrightarrow{\text{Alc. KOH}}$ Salicylaldehyde

28 (a) Sulphonation of phenol with conc. H_2SO_4 at 288-293 K gives o-phenolsulphonic acid.

Phenol $+ H_2SO_4 \xrightarrow[-H_2O]{\text{288-293 K}}$ o-phenolsulphonic acid

29 (*c*) The phenoxide ion left from *o*-hydroxybenzaldehyde and *p*-hydroxybenzaldehyde are stabilised by $-I$ and $-R$ effect of the —CHO group. But in *o*-isomer due to chelation, it is difficult to remove the H-atom. Hence, *p*-hydroxybenzaldehyde is the strongest acid.

30 (*c*) Nitro group shows both $-R$ effect and $-I$ effect but the $-R$ effect predominates over $-I$-effect.

—NO_2 group at *o*-and *p*-position withdraws electrons of O—H bond towards it by the stronger *R*-effect while —NO_2 group at *m*-position withdraws electrons of O—H bond by the weaker *I*-effect.

Thus, *o* and *p*-nitrophenols are more acidic than *m*-nitrophenol. However, *o*-nitrophenol is little less acidic than *p*-nitrophenol due to intermolecular H-bonding which makes a loss of a proton little more difficult.

$$H-O-C_6H_4-N^+(=O)O^- \longrightarrow H^+ + O=C_6H_4=N^+(O^-)O^-$$

p-nitrophenol

$$\text{o-nitrophenol} \longrightarrow H^+ + \text{(quinonoid form)}$$

o-nitrophenol

H-bonding in *o*-nitrophenol

31 (*c*) Phenol is not sufficient acidic to liberate CO_2 from Na_2CO_3 solution.

32 (*c*) Electron withdrawing group increases acidic strength and electron donating group decreases acidic strength of phenol. Thus, *p*-nitrophenol is most acidic among the given options.

33 (*a*) (a) **Reimer-Tiemann reaction**

$$C_6H_5OH \xrightarrow[NaOH(aq)]{CHCl_3} C_6H_4(O^-Na^+)CHO \xrightarrow{H^+, H_2O} C_6H_4(OH)CHO$$

∴ C—C bond is formed.

(b) **Hydroboration-oxidation**

$$RCH{=}CH_2 \xrightarrow[\text{(ii) } H_2O_2,\ OH^-]{\text{(i) } B_2H_6} R{-}CH_2{-}CH_2OH$$

∴ C—O bond is formed.

(c) **Cannizzaro reaction**

$$2RCHO + 50\%\ NaOH \longrightarrow RCH_2OH + RCO\bar{O}\overset{+}{Na}$$

∴ C—OH and C=O bonds are formed.

(d) **Reaction of 1° alcohol by PCC**

$$RCH_2OH \xrightarrow[{[O]}]{PCC} RCHO$$

∴ C=O bond is formed.

34 (*a*) Phenol is least reactive towards dehydration due to resonance stabilisation. 2-cyclohexenol undergoes dehydration more readily as it gives conjugated alkene. (Alcohols leading to conjugated alkenes are dehydrated more readily).

Thus, both (A) and (R) are correct and (R) is the correct explanation of the (A).

35 (*a*) In salicylaldehyde, the —OH group is less reactive than in *m*-and *p*-isomers due to chelation.

36 (*b*) Bromination of *o*-or *p*-phenolsulphonic acid occurs with simultaneous replacement of SO_3H-group by Br-atom to ultimately give 2,4,6-tribromophenol.

37 (*b*) When an electron withdrawing group (like $-NO_2$) is attached to the phenol ring, it stabilises the negative charge on the oxygen of phenoxide ion. Due to this reason acidic character of phenol increases. But when an electron donating group (like $-CH_3$) is attached to the phenol ring, it destabilises the ring and hence acidic character of phenol decreases.

Thus, the correct order of acidic character is :

p-nitrophenol > *p*-chlorophenol > phenol > *o*-cresol

38 (*b*) In the presence of anhydrous $ZnCl_2$, phenol forms salicylaldehyde. It is known as Gattermann reaction.

39 (*d*) This reaction is called Williamson reaction.

40 (*c*) Phenol reacts with neutral $FeCl_3$ solution to give violet colour complex which is soluble in water.

$$6C_6H_5OH + FeCl_3 \longrightarrow \underset{\text{Violet colour complex}}{[Fe(OC_6H_5)_6]^{3-}} + 3H^+ + 3HCl$$

41 (*c*)

$$C_6H_5OH + Br_2 \xrightarrow[0°C]{CS_2} \underset{\substack{p\text{-bromophenol} \\ \text{(major)}}}{p\text{-}BrC_6H_4OH}$$

In the presence of non-polar solvent (CS_2), the ionisation of phenol is suppressed. The ring is slightly activated and hence, mono substitution occurs. Low temperature favours the formation of *p*-product.

42 (*d*) *iso*-propylbenzene is cumene. Its air oxidation followed by acidic hydrolysis produces phenol.

$$\underset{\text{Cumene}}{H_5C_6{-}CH(CH_3)_2} + O{=}O \longrightarrow \underset{\text{Cumene hydroperoxide}}{C_6H_5{-}C(CH_3)_2{-}O{-}O{-}H} \xrightarrow{\text{Dil. } H_2SO_4} \underset{\text{Phenol}}{C_6H_5OH} + \underset{\text{Propanone}}{CH_3COCH_3}$$

43 (*c*)

$$\underset{94\text{ g}}{C_6H_5OH} + \underset{480\text{ g}}{3Br_2} \longrightarrow \text{2,4,6-}Br_3C_6H_2OH$$

∵ 94 g of phenol requires = 480 g Br_2.

∴ 2 g of phenol will require $= \frac{480}{94} \times 2 = 10.22$ g

44 (*d*) Carbon tetrachloride is used to obtain salicylic acid from phenol.

$$\text{Phenol} + CCl_4 \xrightarrow[\Delta]{KOH} \text{(o-}CCl_3\text{ phenol)} \xrightarrow[\Delta, -3HCl]{3HOH} \text{Unstable (o-}C(OH)_3\text{ phenol)} \xrightarrow{-H_2O} \text{Salicylic acid}$$

Phenol Unstable Salicylic acid

45 (*c*) Catechol Quinol Resorcinol Pyrogallol

46 (*a*) Phenols are much more acidic than alcohols due to stabilisation of phenoxide ion by resonance.

$$\text{Phenol} \rightleftharpoons \text{Phenoxide ion} + H^+$$

Phenoxide ion is stabilised due to the following resonating structures

I ⟷ II ⟷ III ⟷ IV ⟷ V

While in alcohols

$$R—\ddot{O}—H \rightleftharpoons R—\ddot{O}:^{\ominus} + H^+$$

Alcohol (Not stabilised due to absence of resonance)

ortho nitrophenol is most acidic because in it $—NO_2$, an electron withdrawing group is attached at *ortho* position which helps in stabilising of negative charge on the oxygen of phenoxide ion.

Due to this reason acidic character of phenol is increased, while on attachment of $—CH_3$ group (electron donating group), acidic strength of phenol is decreased in cresol due to destabilisation of phenoxide ion.

47 (c) Electron withdrawing substituents like $-X$ or $-NO_2$ increases the acidity of phenol and electron releasing substituents like $-CH_3$ decreases the acidity.

So, *o*-nitrophenol is the strongest acid in the given compounds. The correct order of acidity is

o-nitrophenol > *p*-chlorophenol > phenol > *p*-cresol.

48 (c) Hydrogenation of phenol gives cyclohexanol.

$$\text{Phenol} + 3H_2 \longrightarrow \text{Cyclohexanol}$$

49 (*a*) Phenol is less acidic than acetic acid, because carboxylate ion is relatively more stable as compared to phenoxide ion.

50 (*a*) Phenol reacts with chloroform and NaOH to give *o*-hydroxy benzaldehyde or salicylaldehyde. In this reaction, dichlorocarbene ($:CCl_2$) electrophile is generated.

This reaction is called Reimer-Tiemann reaction.

$$OH^- + CHCl_3 \longrightarrow :CCl_3^- + HOH$$

$$:CCl_3^- \longrightarrow \underset{\text{Dichlorocarbene}}{:CCl_2} + Cl^-$$

Topic 4

Ethers

2019

1 The major products *C* and *D* formed in the following reactions respectively are

$$H_3C—CH_2—CH_2—OC(CH_3)_3 \xrightarrow[\Delta]{\text{Excess HI}} C + D$$ [NEET]

(a) $H_3C—CH_2—CH_2—I$ and $I—C(CH_3)_3$
(b) $H_3C—CH_2—CH_2—OH$ and $I—C(CH_3)_3$
(c) $H_3C—CH_2—CH_2—I$ and $HO—C(CH_3)_3$
(d) $H_3C—CH_2—CH_2—OH$ and $HO—C(CH_3)_3$

2 **Assertion** Phenol reacts with CH_3I in presence of NaOH to form methoxybenzene.

Reason Phenoxide is better nucleophile than phenol.

(a) Both Assertion and Reason are true and Reason is the correct explanation of Assertion
(b) Both Assertion and Reason are true, but Reason is not the correct explanation of Assertion
(c) Assertion is true, but Reason is false
(d) Both Assertion and Reason are false

3 **Assertion** *tert*-butyl methyl ether react with HBr to form *tert* butyl bromide, $(CH_3)_3$ C—Br and CH_3—OH, methanal.

Reason It follows S_N1 mechanism.

(a) Both Assertion and Reason are true and Reason is the correct explanation of Assertion
(b) Both Assertion and Reason are true, but Reason is not the correct explanation of Assertion
(c) Assertion is true, but Reason is false
(d) Both Assertion and Reason are false

2018

4 **Assertion** (A) IUPAC name of the compound $CH_3—CH(CH_3)—O—CH_2—CH_2—CH_3$ is 1-(2-propoxy) propane

Reason (R) In IUPAC nomenclature, ether is regarded as hydrocarbon derivative in which a hydrogen atom is replaced by-*OR* or-*OAr* group [where, *R*=alkyl group and *Ar* = aryl group]. **[AIIMS]**

(a) Both Assertion and Reason are correct and Reason is the correct explanation of Assertion
(b) Both Assertion and Reason are correct but Reason is not correct Explanation of Assertion
(c) Assertion is correct but Reason is incorrect
(d) Both Assertion and Reason are incorrect

5 The compound *A* on treatment with Na gives *B*, and with PCl_5 gives *C*. *B* and *C* react together to give diethyl ether. *A*, *B* and *C* are in the order **[NEET]**

(a) C_2H_5Cl, C_2H_6, C_2H_5OH
(b) C_2H_5OH, C_2H_5Cl, C_2H_5ONa
(c) C_2H_5OH, C_2H_6, C_2H_5Cl
(d) C_2H_5OH, C_2H_5ONa, C_2H_5Cl

2017

6 In the presence of light, perchlorodiethyl ether is obtained from diethyl ether.

$$(C_2H_5)_2O \xrightarrow{Cl_2} (C_2Cl_5)_2O$$ **[AIIMS]**

The mechanism through which this reaction proceed is
(a) Addition mechanism
(b) Substitution mechanism
(c) Free radical mechanism
(d) Elimination mechanism

7 *Iso*-propyl chloride + $A \xrightarrow{\Delta}$ 2-ethoxy propane + NaCl.
The compound (*A*) is **[JIPMER]**
(a) C_2H_5Cl (b) C_2H_5ONa (c) CH_2N_2 (d) CH_3ONa

8 $C_6H_5\overset{-}{O}\overset{+}{Na}$ + $C_2H_5Cl \longrightarrow$ Product (*P*)

The product (*P*) is **[JIPMER]**

(a) C_6H_5—O—C_2H_5 (b) benzene ring with C_2H_5 at top and OH at para position (c) benzene ring with ONa at top and C_2H_5 at para position (d) benzene ring with ONa at top, C_2H_5 at ortho and C_2H_5 at para position

9 The heating of phenyl-methyl ethers with HI produces **[NEET]**
(a) ethyl chlorides (b) iodobenzene
(c) phenol (d) benzene

2016

10 The reaction

$$\text{cyclopentyl—OH} \xrightarrow{NaH} \text{cyclopentyl—}O^{\ominus}Na^{+} \xrightarrow{MeI} \text{cyclopentyl—O—Me}$$

can be classified as **[NEET]**
(a) alcohol formation reaction
(b) dehydration reaction
(c) Williamson alcohol synthesis reaction
(d) Williamson ether synthesis reaction

2014

11 Select the ether among following that yields methanol as one of the products on reaction with cold hydroiodic acid **[MHT CET]**
(a) 1-methoxybutane
(b) 1-methoxy-2-methylpropane
(c) 2-methoxy-2-methylpropane
(d) methoxybenzene

12 Williamson's synthesis of preparing dimethyl ether is a/an **[Kerala CEE]**
(a) electrophilic substitution
(b) S_N1 reaction (c) electrophilic addition
(d) S_N2 reaction (e) free radical substitution

13 When $CH_2=CH—O—CH_2—CH_3$ reacts with one mole of HI, one of the products formed is **[KCET]**
(a) ethane (b) ethanol (c) iodoethene (d) ethanal

2013

14 Among the following ethers, which one will produce methyl alcohol on treatment with hot concentrated HI? **[NEET]**
(a) $CH_3—CH_2—CH_2—CH_2—O—CH_3$
(b) $CH_3—CH_2—CH(CH_3)—O—CH_3$
(c) $CH_3—C(CH_3)_2—O—CH_3$
(d) $CH_3—CH(CH_3)—CH_2—O—CH_3$

2010

15 One mole of an organic compound A with the formula C_3H_8O reacts completely with two moles of HI to form X and Y. When Y is boiled with aqueous alkali it forms Z. Z gives the iodoform test. The compound A is **[KCET]**

(a) propane-2-ol (b) propane-1-ol
(c) ethoxyethane (d) methoxyethane

16 Which of the following is an approximate set of reactants for the preparation of 1-methoxy- 4-nitrobenzene? **[AMU]**

(A) Br–C_6H_4–NO_2 (p-bromonitrobenzene) + CH_3ONa (B) NaO–C_6H_4–NO_2 (sodium p-nitrophenoxide) + CH_3Br

(a) A (b) B
(c) Both A and B (d) None of these

17 A simple method to remove peroxides from ethers is to treat them with an aqueous solution of **[JCECE]**

(a) KI (b) KCNS
(c) $Na_2S_2O_3$ (d) Br_2

18 Which of the following is not isomeric with diethyl ether? **[CMC]**

(a) Methyl-n-propylether (b) Butan-1-ol
(c) 2-methylpropan-2-ol (d) Butan-2-one

2009

19 Dehydration of methyl alcohol with conc. H_2SO_4 yields **[UP CPMT]**

(a) methane (b) ethane
(c) dimethyl ether (d) acetone

20 In the following reaction,

$$\underset{\text{(in excess)}}{\text{Ethyl alcohol}} + \underset{\text{(from } H_2SO_4)}{H^+} \xrightarrow{413\text{ K}} \text{Product}$$

The product is **[MHT CET]**

(a) ethene (b) ethyl hydrogen sulphate
(c) diethyl ether (d) acetylene

21 The major product of the reaction between *tert*-butyl chloride and sodium ethoxide is **[Kerala CEE]**

(a) 2-methylprop-1-ene (b) 1-butene
(c) 2-butene (d) ethene
(e) 2-ethoxy-2-methylpropane

2008

22 In which of the following reactions, the product obtained is *tert*-butyl methyl ether? **[AIIMS]**

(a) $CH_3OH + HO—CH_2—CH_3 \xrightarrow{\text{Conc. } H_2SO_4}$

(b) $CH_3—C(CH_3)_2—Br + CH_3OH \xrightarrow{HO^-Na^+}$

(c) $CH_3Br + Na^+O^-—C(CH_3)_2—CH_3 \longrightarrow$

(d) $CH_3—O^-Na^+ + CH_3—C(CH_3)_2—Br \longrightarrow$

23 In the reaction, $2A$ + dry silver oxide $\xrightarrow{\Delta}$ ether + $2AgX$, A is a/an **[MHT CET]**

(a) primary alcohol (b) acid
(c) alkyl halide (d) alcohol

24 An organic compound, C_3H_6O does not give a precipitate with 2,4-dinitrophenyl hydrazine reagent and does not react with metallic sodium. It could be **[Manipal]**

(a) $CH_3—CH_2—CHO$
(b) $CH_2{=}CH—CH_2OH$
(c) $CH_3—CO—CH_3$
(d) $CH_2{=}CH—O—CH_3$

25 *Tert*-butyl methyl ether on heating with anhydrous HI in ether gives **[Manipal]**

(a) $CH_3OH + (CH_3)_3CI$ (b) $CH_3I + (CH_3)_3COH$
(c) $CH_3I + (CH_3)_3CI$ (d) None of these

26 Anisole $\xrightarrow{(CH_3)_3CCl} \xrightarrow{Cl_2/FeCl_3} \xrightarrow[\text{heat}]{HBr} X$.

The product X in the above series of reaction is **[Kerala CEE]**

(a) OCH_3, Br, $C(CH_3)_3$ substituted benzene (b) Br, Cl, $C(CH_3)_3$ substituted benzene (c) Br, Br, $C(CH_3)_3$ substituted benzene (d) OH, Cl, $C(CH_3)_3$ substituted benzene

(e) 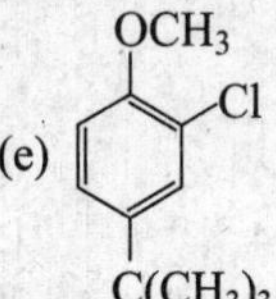

27 A reacts with C_2H_5I giving B and NaI. Here A and B respectively, are **[Punjab PMET]**

(a) CH_3COONa, CH_3OCH_3
(b) $C_2H_5OC_2H_5, C_2H_5COOC_2H_5$
(c) $C_2H_5ONa, C_2H_5OC_2H_5$
(d) $C_2H_5OH, C_2H_5OC_2H_5$

28 Anisole can be prepared by the action of methyl iodide on sodium phenate. The reaction is called **[KCET]**

(a) Wurtz's reaction (b) Williamson's reaction
(c) Fittig's reaction (d) Etard's reaction

2007

29 The reaction,

$$CH_3-\underset{\displaystyle|}{\overset{\displaystyle CH_3}{CH}}-CH_2-O-CH_2-CH_3+HI\xrightarrow{\text{Heated}}\dots$$

Which of the following compounds will be formed? [CBSE AIPMT]

(a) $CH_3-\overset{CH_3}{CH}-CH_2-I+CH_3CH_2OH$

(b) $CH_3-CH-CH_3+CH_3CH_2OH$ (with CH_3 on CH)

(c) $CH_3-\overset{CH_3}{CH}-CH_2OH+CH_3CH_3$

(d) $CH_3-\overset{CH_3}{CH}-CH_2OH+CH_3-CH_2-I$

30 **Assertion** (A) Alcohols have higher boiling points than ethers of comparable molecular masses.
Reason (R) Alcohols and ethers are isomeric in nature. [AIIMS]

(a) Both A and R are correct and R is the correct explanation of A
(b) Both A and R are correct but R is not the correct explanation of A
(c) A is correct but R is incorrect
(d) Both A and R are incorrect

31 In Williamson's synthesis, ethoxyethane is prepared by [Manipal]

(a) passing ethanol over heated alumina
(b) heating sodium ethoxide with ethyl bromide
(c) treating ethyl alcohol with excess of H_2SO_4 at 430-440 K
(d) heating ethanol with dry Ag_2O

2006

32 Which product is formed during the reaction between sodium phenoxide and ethyl iodide on heating? [Guj CET]

(a) Benzyl alcohol (b) Phenol
(c) Phenetol (d) Cresol

2005

33 **Assertion** (A) *t*-butyl methyl ether is not prepared by the reaction of *t*-butyl bromide with sodium methoxide.
Reason (R) Sodium methoxide is a strong nucleophile. [AIIMS]

(a) Both A and R are correct and R is the correct explanation of A
(b) Both A and R are correct but R is not the correct explanation of A
(c) A is correct but R is incorrect
(d) Both A and R are incorrect

34 Methylphenyl ether can be obtained by reacting [J&K CET]

(a) phenolate ion and methyl iodide
(b) methoxide ion and bromobenzene
(c) methanol and phenol
(d) bromobenzene and methyl bromide

35 Match the following Column I and Column II.

Column I	Column II
A. Ethylene	1. Natalite
B. Acetylene	2. Preservative
C. Ethanol	3. Hawker's lamp
D. Diethyl ether	4. Drug

The correct answer is [EAMCET]

Code

	A	B	C	D		A	B	C	D
(a)	4	3	2	1	(b)	4	3	1	2
(c)	1	4	3	2	(d)	2	3	1	4

Answers

1 (a)	2 (a)	3 (a)	4 (a)	5 (d)	6 (c)	7 (b)	8 (a)	9 (c)	10 (d)
11 (c)	12 (d)	13 (d)	14 (c)	15 (d)	16 (c)	17 (a)	18 (d)	19 (c)	20 (c)
21 (a)	22 (c)	23 (c)	24 (d)	25 (b)	26 (d)	27 (c)	28 (b)	29 (d)	30 (b)
31 (b)	32 (c)	33 (b)	34 (a)	35 (d)					

Explanations

1 (*a*) Ethers are readily cleaved by heating in presence of halogen acids to form alcohol and an alkyl halide. In case of unsymmetrical ethers, halogen goes preferentially with smaller alkyl group or more stable carbocation.

If excess of acid is used then only alkyl halide is formed because alcohol formed reacts further with halogen acid to form corresponding alkyl halide.

$$CH_3CH_2CH_2OC(CH_3)_3\xrightarrow[\Delta]{HI}CH_3CH_2CH_2OH+\underset{'D'}{(CH_3)_3I}$$

$$CH_3CH_2CH_2OH\xrightarrow[\Delta]{\text{Excess HI}}\underset{'C'}{CH_3CH_2CH_2I}$$

2 (*a*) When phenol reacts with CH_3I in presence of NaOH, it gives methoxybenzene due to formation of phenoxide ion, which is a better nucleophile than phenol.
The reaction takes place as follows:

$$\underset{\text{Phenol}}{C_6H_5OH} + NaOH \longrightarrow \underset{\text{Sodium phenoxide}}{C_6H_5\overset{-}{O}\overset{+}{Na}} \xrightarrow[S_N2]{CH_3I} \underset{\text{Anisole}}{C_6H_5OCH_3}$$

Thus, given assertion and reason, both are correct and reason is the correct explanation of the assertion.
Hence, option (a) is the correct.

3 (*a*) Ethers are readily cleaved by halogen acids at 373 K to form an alcohol and an alkyl halide.

$$\underset{\textit{tert}\text{-butyl methylether}}{(CH_3)_3COCH_3} + HBr \longrightarrow \underset{\textit{Tert}\text{-butyl bromide}}{(CH_3)_3CBr} + \underset{\text{Methanol}}{CH_3OH}$$

S_N1 mechanism is followed as $(CH_3)_3C^+$ is most stable carbocation and I^- is attached to it.

4 (*a*) IUPAC name of the given compound is correct, i.e. 1-(2-propoxy) propane. In this compound, hydrogen atom is replaced by—*OR* group and thus named ether. Therefore, both assertion and reason is correct and reason is the correct explanation of the assertion.

5 (*d*) According to given question and options, (*A*) must be C_2H_5OH, as it reacts with Na to give C_2H_5ONa. The reaction sequence is as follows :

$$\text{(i)}\ \underset{\substack{\text{Ethanol}\\(A)}}{C_2H_5OH} \xrightarrow{Na} \underset{\substack{\text{Sodium ethoxide}\\(B)}}{C_2H_5\overset{-}{O}\overset{+}{Na}} \xrightarrow{PCl_5} \underset{\substack{\text{Ethyl chloride}\\(C)}}{C_2H_5Cl}$$

$$\text{(ii)}\ C_2H_5\overset{-}{O}\overset{+}{Na} + C_2H_5Cl \xrightarrow{S_N2} \underset{\text{Diethyl ether}}{C_2H_5—O—C_2H_5} + NaCl$$

The above reaction is known as Williamson's ether synthesis. It involves nucleophilic attack of alkoxide ion on alkyl halide according to S_N2 mechanism.

$$\underset{\substack{\text{Nucleophile}\\\text{(Alkoxide ion)}}}{C_2H_5O^-} + \underset{\substack{\text{Substrate}\\\text{(Alkyl halide)}}}{CH_3—CH_2Cl} \xrightarrow{\text{Slow}} C_2H_5—O\ldots\overset{+}{\underset{CH_3}{CH_2}}\ldots Cl^- \xrightarrow{\text{Fast}} C_2H_5—O—C_2H_5 + Cl^-$$

6 (*c*) The given reaction is,

$$(C_2H_5)_2O \xrightarrow{Cl_2} (C_2Cl_5)_2O$$

The reaction proceeds by a free-radical mechanism and α-substitution occurs readily because of resonance stabilisation of the intermediate.

$$Cl_2 \xrightarrow{h\nu} Cl^\bullet + Cl^\bullet$$

$$R\ddot{O}—CH_2R' \xrightarrow{Cl^\bullet} R\ddot{O}—\dot{C}HR'$$

$$R\ddot{O}—\dot{C}HR' \longleftrightarrow R\dot{O}=CHR'$$

$$R\dot{O}=CHR' \xrightarrow{Cl_2} R\ddot{O}—CHClR' + Cl^\bullet$$

7 (*b*)

$$\begin{matrix}CH_3\\CH_3\end{matrix}\!\!>CH.Cl + \underset{(A)}{C_2H_5\overset{-}{O}\overset{+}{Na}} \xrightarrow{\Delta} \underset{\text{(2-ethoxypropane)}}{CH_3—\underset{CH_3}{\underset{|}{CH}}—O—C_2H_5} + NaCl$$

8 (*a*)

$$C_6H_5\overset{-}{O}\overset{+}{Na} + C_2H_5Cl \longrightarrow \underset{(P)}{C_6H_5OC_2H_5}$$

This is an example of Williamson's synthesis.

9 (*c*) **Thinking Process** This problem is based on the resonance stabilisation. In anisole, methyl phenyl oxonium ion is formed by protonation of ether.
The bond between O — CH_3 is weaker than the bond between O — C_6H_5, because the carbon of phenyl group is sp^2 -hybridised and there is a partial double bond character. Thus, the reaction yields phenol and alkyl halide.

$$\underset{\text{Anisole}}{C_6H_5\ddot{O}CH_3} \xrightarrow{H—I} C_6H_5\overset{\oplus}{O}(H)CH_3 \xrightarrow{I^\ominus} \underset{\text{Phenol}}{C_6H_5OH} + CH_3I$$

10 (*d*) The formation of ether from alcohol in the presence of base followed by alkylation is known as Williamson's ether synthesis reaction.

$$C_5H_9—OH \xrightarrow[-H_2]{NaH} C_5H_9—O^\ominus Na^+ \xrightarrow[\text{MeI}]{\text{Alkylation}} C_5H_9—O—Me + NaI$$

11 (*c*) According to Zeisel method, when an ether reacts with cold HI, alkyl iodide and alcohol are formed. In case of asymmetrical ether, the alkyl halide is always formed from the smaller alkyl group provided no tertiary (3°) alkyl group is present and if any 3° alkyl group is present, the halogen gets attached with it. In case of alkyl aryl ethers, the products are always phenol and an alkyl halide.

$$\text{(a)}\ CH_3—O—C_4H_9 + HI \xrightarrow{\text{Cold}} CH_3I + C_4H_9OH$$

$$\text{(b)}\ CH_3—O—CH_2—\underset{CH_3}{\underset{|}{CH}}—CH_3 + HI \xrightarrow{\text{Cold}} CH_3I + CH_3—\underset{CH_3}{\underset{|}{CH}}—CH_2—OH$$

$$\text{(c)}\ CH_3—\underset{CH_3}{\overset{OCH_3}{\overset{|}{\underset{|}{C}}}}—CH_3 + HI \xrightarrow{\text{Cold}} CH_3OH + CH_3—\underset{CH_3}{\overset{CH_3}{\overset{|}{\underset{|}{C}}}}—I$$

(d) Anisole ($C_6H_5OCH_3$) + HI $\xrightarrow{\text{Cold}}$ Phenol (C_6H_5OH) + CH_3I

12 (*d*) $R—X \xrightarrow{\overset{-\ +}{RONa}} R—O—R$

The above reaction represents a Williamson ether synthesis. It involves S_N2 attack of an alkoxide ion on primary alkyl halide.

13 (*d*) Allyl ethyl ether on reaction with HI produces ethanal and ethyl iodide by means of nucleophilic substitution reaction as shown below

$$CH_2{=}CH—O—CH_2—CH_3 \xrightarrow{H^+I^-} CH_3CH_2I + CH_3CHO$$

14 (*c*) The ether which gives more stable carbocation gives CH_3OH as one of the product with hot concentrated HI.

The order of stability of carbocation is 3° > 2° > 1°.

Thus, $(CH_3)_3C—OCH_3$ gives CH_3OH as one of the product.

The reaction proceeds as

$$(CH_3)_3C—O—CH_3 + H^+ \longrightarrow (CH_3)_3C—\overset{+}{O}(H)—CH_3$$

$$\longrightarrow \underset{\text{3° carbocation}}{(CH_3)_3C^+} + CH_3OH \xrightarrow{+I^-} (CH_3)_3C—I + \underset{\text{Methanol}}{CH_3OH}$$

15 (*d*) Molecular formula $C_3H_8O(C_nH_{2n+2}O)$ suggests that the organic compound is either alcohol or ether.

Since, the compound on reaction with HI gives two different compounds, it must be an unsymmetrical ether and its formula must be $CH_3OC_2H_5$ (methoxyethane)

The reactions are as follows :

$$\underset{\text{Methoxyethane}}{CH_3OC_2H_5} + 2HI \longrightarrow \underset{X}{CH_3I} + \underset{Y}{C_2H_5I} + H_2O$$

$$\underset{Y}{C_2H_5I} + \underset{\text{Aqueous}}{2NaOH} \longrightarrow \underset{Z}{C_2H_5OH} + NaI$$

$$\underset{Z}{C_2H_5OH} + \underset{\text{(Aqueous)}}{NaOH} + I_2 \longrightarrow \underset{\text{Iodoform}}{CHI_3}\downarrow + HCOO\overset{-\ +}{Na} + H_2O + NaI$$

16 (*c*) When the alkyl halide is primary, alkoxide (or aryloxide) attacks on it and ether is obtained as a major product.

$$p\text{-}O_2NC_6H_4\overset{-\ +}{ONa} + CH_3Br \longrightarrow \underset{\text{1-methoxy-4-nitrobenzene}}{p\text{-}O_2NC_6H_4OCH_3}$$

Aryl halides generally do not react with sodium alkoxide but presence of strong electron withdrawing group like $—NO_2$ at *ortho/para* position facilitates the reaction.

Thus, reaction given in option (a) also gives 1-methoxy-4-nitrobenzene.

$$p\text{-}O_2NC_6H_4Br + CH_3\overset{-\ +}{ONa} \longrightarrow p\text{-}O_2NC_6H_4OCH_3$$

17 (*a*) Ether peroxide oxidises KI into I_2 and itself gets reduced to ether. Therefore, KI is added to remove peroxides from ethers.

$$2I^- \longrightarrow I_2 + 2e^-$$

$$\text{Ether peroxide} + 2e^- \longrightarrow \text{Ether} + O_2$$

18 (*d*) Butan-2-one, $CH_3—\overset{O}{\overset{\|}{C}}—CH_2—CH_3(C_4H_8O)$ is not isomeric with diethyl ether, $CH_3CH_2—O—CH_2—CH_3$ $(C_4H_{10}O)$, because both have different molecular formula.

19 (*c*)

$$CH_3OH + \underset{\text{(From acid)}}{H^+} \rightleftharpoons \underset{\text{Protonated alcohol}}{CH_3—\overset{\oplus}{\ddot{O}}(H)—H} \xrightarrow{-H_2O}$$

$$\underset{\text{Methyl carbocation}}{\overset{+}{C}H_3} \xrightarrow{CH_3\ddot{O}—H} CH_3—\overset{+}{\ddot{O}}(H)—CH_3 \xrightarrow{-H^+} \underset{\text{Dimethyl ether}}{CH_3—\ddot{O}—CH_3} + H^+$$

20 (*c*)

$$\underset{\text{Ethyl alcohol}}{CH_3CH_2—\ddot{O}—H} + \underset{(\text{From } H_2SO_4)}{H^+} \rightleftharpoons \underset{\text{Protonated ethyl alcohol}}{CH_3—CH_2—\overset{+}{O}H_2} + :\ddot{O}(H)—CH_2CH_3$$

$$\xrightarrow[-H_2O]{413\text{ K}} CH_3CH_2—\overset{+}{O}(H)—CH_2CH_3 \xrightarrow[-H^+]{\text{Fast}} \underset{\text{Diethyl ether}}{C_2H_5OC_2H_5}$$

If temperature is high (i.e. 463 K), ethene is obtained.

21 (*a*) Sodium ethoxide is a strong base, so it causes dehydrohalogenation of 3° alkyl halide and gives alkene.

$$\underset{\textit{tert}\text{-butyl chloride}}{(CH_3)_3C—Cl} + C_2H_5\overset{-\ +}{ONa} \xrightarrow[-C_2H_5OH]{-NaCl} \underset{\text{2-methylprop-1-ene}}{\overset{3}{C}H_3—\overset{2}{C}(CH_3){=}\overset{1}{C}H_2}$$

22 (*c*) *tert*-butyl methyl ether is a mixed ether and for the preparation of mixed ethers in high yield, the essential condition is the use of primary alkyl halide. Thus,

$$CH_3Br + \overset{+}{Na}\overset{-}{O}-\underset{CH_3}{\overset{CH_3}{C}}-CH_3 \xrightarrow{-NaBr} CH_3-O-\underset{CH_3}{\overset{CH_3}{C}}-CH_3$$
t-butyl-methyl ether

This reaction is Williamson's ether synthesis.

23 (*c*) An alkyl halide on heating with dry silver oxide gives ether.

$$\underset{\text{Alkyl halide}}{2R-X} + Ag_2O \xrightarrow[\text{Dry}]{\Delta} \underset{\text{Ether}}{R-O-R} + 2AgX$$

24 (*d*) Since, the compound does not give a precipitate with 2,4-dinitrophenylhydrazine, it cannot be an aldehyde or a ketone. Further since it does not react with metallic sodium, therefore, it cannot be an alcohol.

Thus, the compound C_3H_6O must be an ether, i.e. $CH_2{=}CH-O-CH_3$.

25 (*b*) Here, ether is the solvent. Being less polar, it favours S_N2 reaction and the nucleophile I^- attacks 1° carbon of CH_3.

$$H_3C-\underset{CH_3}{\overset{CH_3}{C}}-O-CH_3 \xrightarrow{H+} H_3C-\underset{CH_3}{\overset{CH_3}{C}}-\overset{+}{\underset{H}{O}}\ CH_3$$

$$I^- + CH_3\overset{\oplus}{\underset{H}{O}}-\underset{CH_3}{\overset{CH_3}{C}}-CH_3 \xrightarrow{S_N2} CH_3I + CH_3-\underset{CH_3}{\overset{CH_3}{C}}-OH$$

26 (*d*)

$$\underset{\text{Anisole}}{C_6H_5OCH_3} \xrightarrow[\text{Anhy. } AlCl_3]{(CH_3)_3CCl} \text{4-}C(CH_3)_3C_6H_4OCH_3 \xrightarrow[FeCl_3]{Cl_2} \text{2-Cl-4-}C(CH_3)_3C_6H_3OCH_3 \xrightarrow[\Delta]{HBr} \underset{X}{\text{2-Cl-4-}C(CH_3)_3C_6H_3OH}$$

27 (*c*) $$\underset{\substack{\text{Sodium}\\ \text{ethoxide}\\ (A)}}{CH_3\overset{-}{O}\overset{+}{Na}} + \underset{\substack{\text{Ethyl}\\ \text{iodide}}}{C_2H_5I} \xrightarrow[\text{synthesis}]{\text{Williamson's}} \underset{\substack{\text{Diethyl ether}\\ (B)}}{C_2H_5OC_2H_5} + NaI$$

28 (*b*) The reaction of alkyl halide with sodium alkoxide to give ether (alkoxy alkane), is known as Williamson's synthesis. In this reaction, an ether (anisole) is prepared by the action of alkyl halide (methyl iodide) on sodium alkoxide (sodium phenate), so it is an example of Williamson's synthesis.

$$\underset{\text{Sodium phenoxide}}{C_6H_5O^-Na^+} + \underset{\substack{\text{Methyl}\\ \text{iodide}}}{CH_3-I} \xrightarrow[\substack{S_N2\\ (-NaI)}]{\Delta} \underset{\text{Anisole}}{C_6H_5OCH_3}$$

29 (*d*) When conc. HI or HBr reacts with ether, the corresponding alcohol and iodide are formed. In a case of mixed ethers, the halogen atom attaches to the smaller alkyl group, due to steric effect

$$CH_3-\overset{CH_3}{CH}-CH_2-O-CH_2-CH_3 + HI \xrightarrow{\Delta} CH_3-\overset{CH_3}{CH}-CH_2OH + CH_3CH_2I$$

30 (*b*) Alcohols have higher boiling points than ethers because intermolecular H-bonding is present in alcohols and not in ethers. Further, alcohols are isomeric with ethers but it is not the correct reason for assertion.

31 (*b*) $$\underset{\text{Sodium ethoxide}}{CH_3CH_2\overset{-}{O}\overset{+}{Na}} + \underset{\substack{\text{Bromo}\\ \text{ethane}}}{C_2H_5Br} \xrightarrow[\text{synthesis}]{\text{Williamson's}} \underset{\text{Ethoxyethane}}{CH_3CH_2OCH_2CH_3} + NaBr$$

32 (*c*) $$\underset{\substack{\text{Sodium}\\ \text{phenoxide}}}{CH_3\overset{-}{O}\overset{+}{Na}} + \underset{\substack{\text{Ethyl}\\ \text{iodide}}}{C_2H_5I} \longrightarrow \underset{\substack{\text{Ethylphenyl ether}\\ \text{(Phenetol)}}}{C_6H_5OC_2H_5} + NaI$$

33 (*b*) *t*-butyl methyl ether cannot be prepared by the reaction of *t*-butyl bromide with sodium methoxide, because sodium methoxide is a strong base hence, *t*-halide undergoes elimination reaction instead of nucleophilic substitution reaction.

$$CH_3-\underset{CH_3}{\overset{CH_3}{C}}-Br + CH_3\overset{-}{O}\overset{+}{Na} \longrightarrow \underset{\text{2-methylpropene}}{CH_3-\underset{CH_3}{C}{=}CH_2} + NaBr + CH_3OH$$

Also, CH_3ONa is a strong nucleophile.

34 (*a*) Methyl phenyl ether is obtained by the reaction of phenolate ion and methyl iodide.

$$\underset{\text{Phenolate ion}}{C_6H_5O^-} + CH_3I \longrightarrow \underset{\text{Methyl phenyl ether}}{C_6H_5OCH_3} + I^-$$

35 (*d*) A → 2, B → 3, C → 1, D → 4,

Ethylene — Preservative
Acetylene — Hawker's lamp
Ethanol — Natalite
Diethyl ether — Drug (anaesthetic)

26

Aldehydes, Ketones and Carboxylic Acids

Quick Review

The organic compounds which contain $-\overset{O}{\overset{||}{C}}-$ functional group are called carbonyl compounds. These are classified as aldehydes and ketones.

Aldehydes and Ketones

- In aldehydes, the carbonyl group is bonded to carbon and hydrogen, while in the ketones, it is bonded to two carbon atoms.

$$R-\underset{\underset{O}{||}}{C}-\boxed{H} \qquad R-\underset{\underset{O}{||}}{C}-\boxed{R'}$$

Aldehyde Ketone

- Ketones may be classified as simple ketone (if two groups R and R' are same) and mixed ketone (if R and R' are different).
- In IUPAC system, aldehydes are named by replacing the terminal suffix 'e' by the suffix 'al' while ketones with suffix 'one'.

Structure

Carbonyl carbon atom in aldehydes and ketones are sp^2-hybridised. It is attached to three atoms which lie in same plane while the π-electron cloud lies above and below the plane. The bond angle formed between the bond pairs is about 120°.

120° 120° 120°

The double bond between carbon and oxygen is similar to alkene double bond but it is shorter and stronger than double bond of alkene (C=C).

Nature of Carbonyl Group

The carbon and oxygen atom of the carbonyl group are sp^2-hybridised and the carbonyl double bond contains one σ-bond and one π-bond.

$$>C=\ddot{O}: \;(120°) \longleftrightarrow >\overset{+}{C}-\overset{-}{\ddot{O}}: \text{ or } >\overset{\delta+}{C}=\overset{\delta-}{\ddot{O}}:$$

The electronegativity of oxygen is much higher than that of the carbon, so their electron cloud is shifted towards the oxygen. Therefore, C—O bond is polar in nature.

Preparation of Aldehydes and Ketones

Some important methods of preparation of aldehydes and ketones are as follows :

- **Oxidation of Alcohols**

$$\underset{1°\text{alcohol}}{R-CH_2OH} \xrightarrow{CrO_3} RCHO + H_2O; \quad \underset{2°\text{alcohol}}{R_2CH-OH} \xrightarrow{CrO_3} R_2C=O + H_2O$$

- **Catalytic Dehydrogenation of Alcohols**

$$\underset{1°\text{alcohol}}{RCH_2OH} \xrightarrow[520\text{-}570K]{Cu,\Delta} RCHO + H_2, \quad \underset{2°\text{alcohol}}{R_2CHOH} \xrightarrow[572K]{Cu,\Delta} R_2C=O$$

- **Ozonolysis of Alkenes**

$$(CH_3)_2C=CH-CH_3 \xrightarrow{O_3} \text{(ozonide)} \xrightarrow{Zn/H_2O} (CH_3)_2C=O + CH_3CHO$$

- **Wacker's Process**

$$R/CH=CH_2 + \frac{1}{2}O_2 \xrightarrow[H_2O]{PdCl_2/CuCl_2} CH_3-\overset{O}{\overset{\|}{C}}-H/R$$

- **Hydration of Alkynes**

$$CH\equiv CH \xrightarrow[HgSO_4,333K]{H_2SO_4} CH_3CHO; CH_3C\equiv CH \xrightarrow[333K]{H_2O,\,Hg^{2+}/H^+} CH_3\underset{OH}{\underset{|}{C}}=CH_2 \overset{\text{Isomerisation}}{\rightleftharpoons} CH_3\underset{O}{\underset{\|}{C}}CH_3$$

- **Hydrolysis of *gem*-Dihalides**

$$CH_3CH_2CHCl_2 + 2NaOH \longrightarrow \underset{(\text{Unstable})}{CH_3CH_2CH(OH)_2} \longrightarrow CH_3CH_2CHO,$$

- **Hydroboration Oxidation**

  - $$CH_3-CCl_2-CH_3 \xrightarrow{OH^-} CH_3C(OH)_2CH_3 \xrightarrow{-H_2O} CH_3COCH_3$$
  - $$CH_3C\equiv CH \xrightarrow{BH_3\cdot THF} \left(CH_3CH=\underset{H}{\underset{|}{C}}-\right)_3 B \xrightarrow[OH^-]{H_2O_2}$$

$$CH_3CH=CHOH \overset{\text{Tautomerism}}{\rightleftharpoons} CH_3CH_2CHO$$

  - Internal alkynes form ketone and terminal alkynes form aldehydes.

- **By Calcium Salts of Dicarboxylic Acid**

  - $$(RCOO)_2Ca + (HCOO)_2Ca \xrightarrow{\Delta} 2R-\overset{O}{\overset{\|}{C}}-H + CaCO_3$$
  - $$2(RCOO)_2Ca \xrightarrow{\Delta} 2R\overset{O}{\overset{\|}{C}}R + 2CaCO_3$$

- **From Grignard Reagent**
  - Reaction with nitriles

$$H-C\equiv N \xrightarrow[H_3O^+]{\triangleright-MgBr} \triangleright-CHO$$

  - Reaction with esters

$$H\overset{O}{\overset{\|}{C}}OC_2H_5 + RMgX \xrightarrow{H_3O^+} RCHO + (C_2H_5O^-)MgX$$

Preparation of Aldehydes

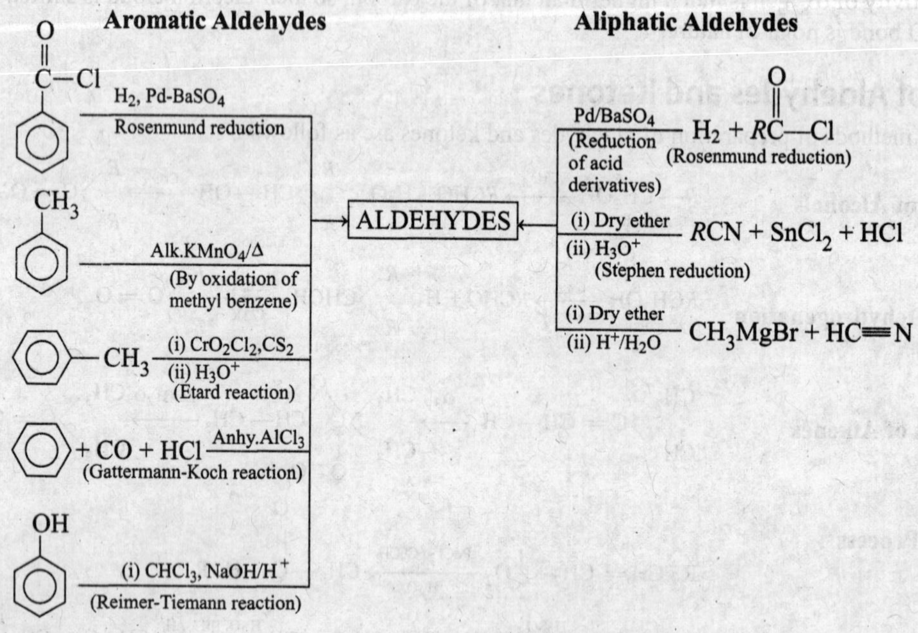

Preparation of Ketones

KETONES ←

- Dry ether — $R'\underset{O}{\underset{\|}{C}}Cl + R_2Cd$
- (i) Ether, (ii) H_3O^+ — $R'\underset{Br}{\underset{|}{Mg}} + RC\equiv N$
- (Friedel-Craft's acylation) Anhy.$AlCl_3$ — $Ar/R\overset{O}{\overset{\|}{C}}Cl + C_6H_6$
- (Oppeneuer oxidation) Al $[(CH_3)_3CO]_3$ — $R_2CHOH + (CH_3)_2C{=}O$

Physical Properties

- Boiling points of carbonyl compounds are higher than those of non-polar compounds, hydrocarbons and ethers due to dipole-dipole interactions.
- Lower aldehyde and ketones are soluble in water in all proportions because they form hydrogen bonds with water.
- The acidity of α-hydrogen atoms of carbonyl compounds is due to the strong electron withdrawing effect of the carbonyl group and resonance stabilisation of the conjugate base.

Chemical Properties

- Carbonyl compounds, due to the presence of polar $>C=O$ group show nucleophilic addition reactions.
- As the number of carbon atoms/number of alkyl groups increases, reactivity decreases due to steric hindrance. Hence, the order of reactivity is: $HCHO > CH_3CHO > CH_3COCH_3 > C_2H_5COC_2H_5$.

Important chemical reactions of aldehydes and ketones are given below.

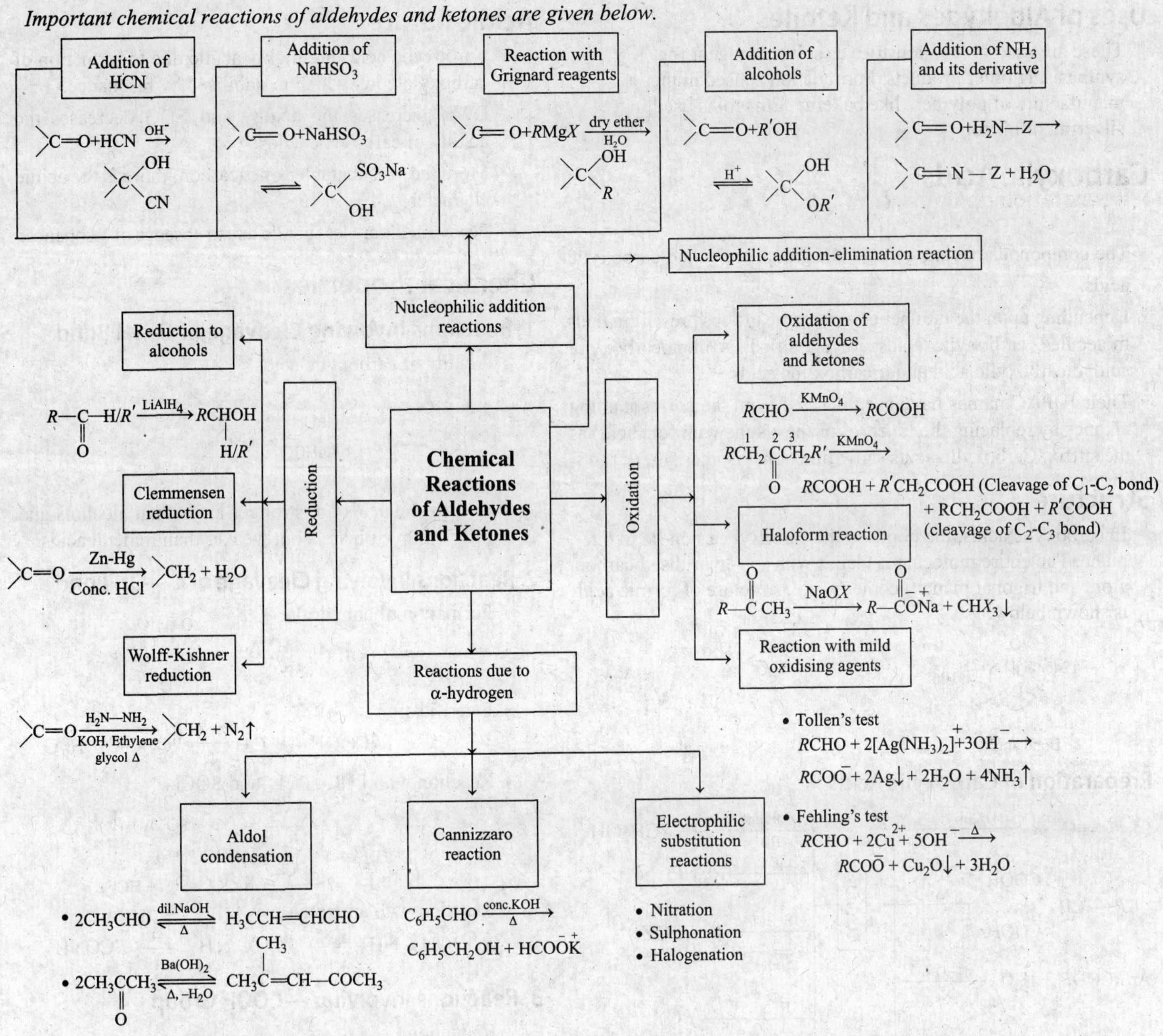

Note When both the aldehydes or ketones are different and also contain α-hydrogen atoms, the reaction gives a mixture of four products. This reaction is called cross-aldol condensation.

$$\begin{matrix} CH_3CHO \\ + \\ CH_3CH_2CHO \end{matrix} \xrightarrow[\text{(ii) }\Delta]{\text{(i) NaOH}} \underset{\substack{\text{But-2-enal} \\ \text{(From two molecules} \\ \text{of ethanal)}}}{CH_3{-}CH{=}CH{-}CHO} + \underset{\substack{\text{2-methylpent-2-enal} \\ \text{(From two molecules of propanal)}}}{CH_3CH_2{-}CH{=}\underset{CH_3}{\underset{|}{C}}{-}CHO}$$

Simple or self aldol products

+

$$\underset{\text{2-methylbut-2-enal}}{CH_3{-}CH{=}\underset{CH_3}{\underset{|}{C}}{-}CHO} + \underset{\text{Pent-2-enal}}{CH_3CH_2{-}CH{=}CHCHO}$$

(From one molecule of ethanal and one molecule of propanal)

Cross-aldol products

Uses of Aldehydes and Ketones

These are used in the industries as solvent reagent for synthesising other products. Formylation is used in the manufacture of polymers like bakelite. Ethanol is used in silvering of mirror.

Carboxylic Acids

- The compounds having $-\overset{O}{\overset{\|}{C}}-$ OH group, are called carboxylic acids.
- Depending upon the number of carboxylic groups present in their molecules, carboxylic acids are classified as monocarboxylic acid, dicarboxylic acid and tricarboxylic acids.
- Their IUPAC names have been derived from the corresponding alkanes by replacing the letter 'e' of the alkane with 'oic acid' as the suffix. Carboxylic acids show functional isomerism.

Structure

In carboxylic acids, the bonds to the carboxyl carbon lie in one plane. The entire molecule is planar with sp^2-hybridised carbon atom and trigonal planar geometry. e.g. structure of formic acid is shown below.

124°, 125°, 106°, 111°

Bond angles

1.23Å, 1.32Å, 1.10Å, 0.97Å

Bond lengths

Preparation of Carboxylic Acids

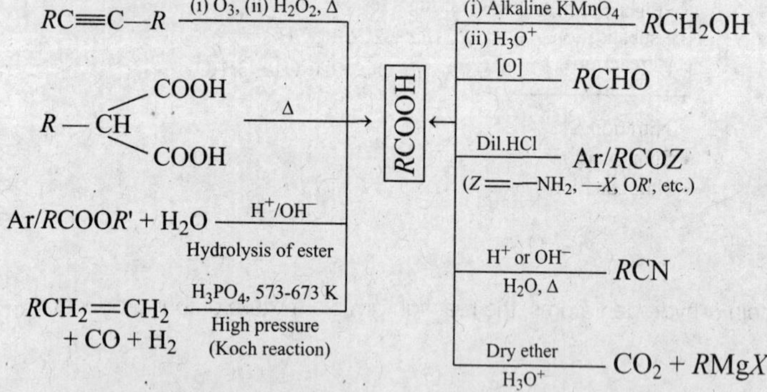

Physical Properties

- Carboxylic acids are polar due to presence of $-\overset{O}{\overset{\|}{C}}-$ and —OH group. Thus, form H-bonds.
- They exist in dimeric forms due to intermolecular hydrogen bonding.
- Acids have high melting points.
- Monocarboxylic acid have higher boiling points as compared to the alcohols of comparable molecular masses due to the presence of strong intermolecular hydrogen bonding.

Acidic nature

- Carboxylic acids are highly acidic due to formation of carboxylate ion which is stabilised by resonance.
- EWG increases the acidity and EDG decreases the acidity of carboxylic acids.
- More the % s-character of α-carbon, more is the acidic character.
- Peroxy acids are less acidic due to absence of resonance.

Chemical Properties

1. Reactions Involving Cleavage of O—H Bond

- Acidity of carboxylic acids

$$R\text{—COOH} \xrightarrow{2Na} 2RCO\bar{O}\overset{+}{Na} + H_2$$
$$R\text{—COOH} \xrightarrow{NaOH} RCO\bar{O}\overset{+}{Na} + H_2$$
$$R\text{—COOH} \xrightarrow{NaHCO_3} RCO\bar{O}\overset{+}{Na} + H_2O + CO_2$$

- Carboxylic acids are stronger acids than alcohols and many simple phenols but weaker than mineral acids.

2. Reactions Involving Cleavage of C—OH Bond

- Formation of anhydride

$$2R\text{—COOH} + \xrightarrow[\text{or } P_2O_5,\ \Delta]{H^+,\ \Delta} R\text{—}\overset{O}{\overset{\|}{C}}\text{—O—}\overset{O}{\overset{\|}{C}}\text{—}R$$

- Esterification

$$RCOOH + R'OH \overset{H^+}{\rightleftharpoons} RCOOR' + H_2O$$

- Reaction with PCl_5, PCl_3 and $SOCl_2$

$$R\text{—COOH} \xrightarrow{PCl_5} RCOCl + POCl_3 + HCl$$
$$R\text{—COOH} \xrightarrow{PCl_3} 3RCOCl + H_3PO_3$$
$$R\text{—COOH} \xrightarrow{SOCl_2} RCOCl + SO_2 + HCl$$

- Reaction with ammonia

$$RCOOH + NH_3 \longrightarrow RCO\overset{-}{O}\overset{+}{N}H_4 \xrightarrow[-H_2O]{\Delta} RCONH_2$$

3. Reactions Involving —COOH Group

- Reduction

$$RCOOH \xrightarrow[\Delta]{N_3H, H_2SO_4} RNH_2 + CO_2 + N_2\uparrow$$
$$RCOOH \xrightarrow[\Delta]{\text{Red P/HI}} RCH_3 + 2H_2O + 3I_2$$
$$RCOOH \xrightarrow{LiAlH_4} RCH_2OH$$

- Decarboxylation

$$RCO\overset{-}{O}\overset{+}{Na} \xrightarrow[\text{Heat}]{NaOH + CaO} R\text{—}H + Na_2CO_3$$

4. Substitution Reactions in the Hydrocarbon Part

- Hell-Volhard Zelinsky Reaction

$$RCH_2COOH \xrightarrow[\text{(ii) } H_2O]{\text{(i) } X_2/\text{Red P}} R\text{—}\underset{X}{\underset{|}{CH}}COOH$$

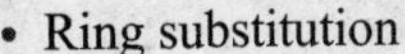

- Ring substitution

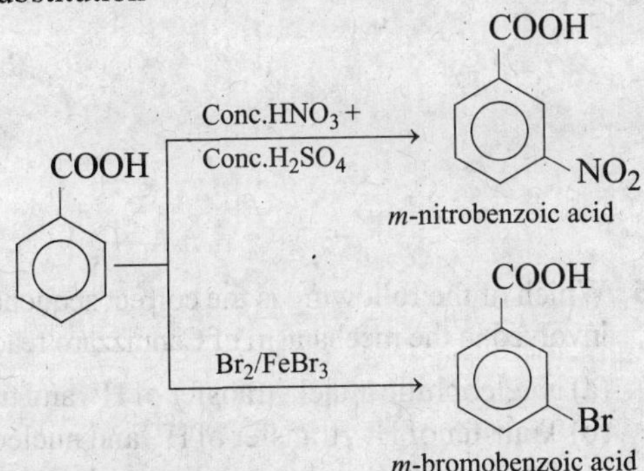

Uses of Carboxylic Acids

Formic acid is used in leather, textile, dyeing industries. Acetic acid is used in the manufacture of rayon and in plasic, in cooking and in vinegar etc.

Acid Derivatives

These are obtained when —OH group of carboxylic acid is replaced by Cl, NH_2, O*R*′ and OCO*R* and are called acid chloride, acid amide, ester and acid anhydride respectively.

Preparation of Acid Derivatives

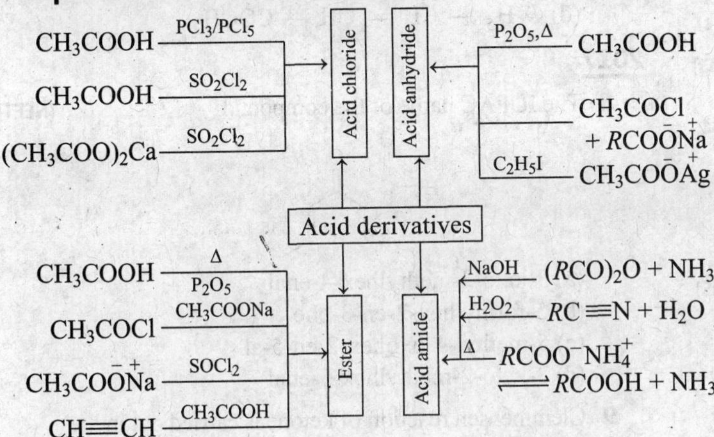

Chemical Properties of Acid Derivatives

- Chemical reactions of acid chloride

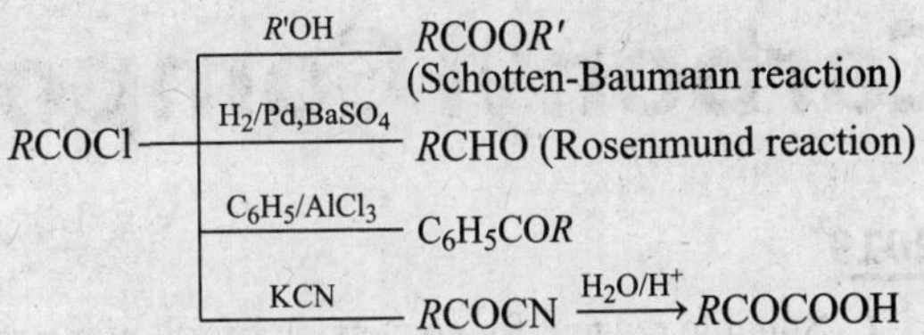

- Chemical reactions of acid amide

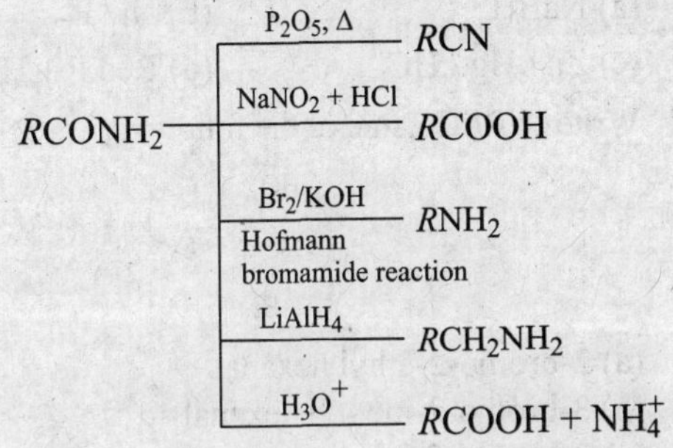

- Chemical reactions of ester

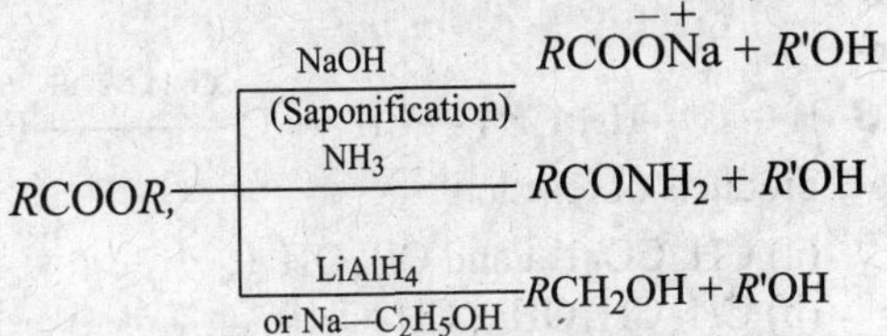

- Chemical reactions of anhydrides

$(RCO)_2O$ —
- R′OH → RCOOR′ + RCOOH
- $C_6H_6/AlCl_3$ → C_6H_5COR + RCOOH
- $C_2H_5NH_2$ → $RCONC_2H_5$ + RCOOH

Topical Practice Questions

All the exam questions of this chapter have been divided into three topics as listed below :

Topic 1

Carbonyl Compounds

2019

1 Suitable reagent for conversion of following reaction

$CH_2=CH-CHO \xrightarrow{?} CH_2=CH-CH_2-OH$?

(a) $NaBH_4$ (b) Ni/H_2 **[JIPMER]**

(c) $Zn/Hg/HCl$ (d) Red P + HI

2 Write IUPAC name of the following **[JIPMER]**

[Structure: ^{1}CHO on C-2, chain 2-3-4-5-6, Br on C-3, methyl on C-2]

(a) 2-bromo-2-ethyl hexanal

(b) 3-bromo-2-methyl hexanal

(c) 2-methyl-3-bromo hexanal

(d) 3-bromo-2-formyl hexane

3 $H-\overset{O}{\overset{\|}{C}}-H + CH_3-CH=O \xrightarrow{Conc.NaOH}$ Find out the products of reaction **[AIIMS]**

(a) CH_3CO_2Na and CH_3OH

(b) $CH_3CH_2OH + CH_3OH$

(c) CH_3CH_2OH and HCO_2Na

(d) $CH_3CO_2Na + HCO_2Na$

2018

4 The correct IUPAC name of the given compound is **[AIIMS]**

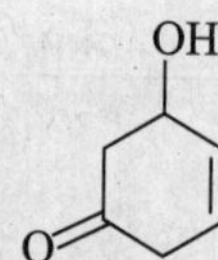

(a) 7-hydroxy cyclohex -5-en-1-one

(b) 3-hydroxy cyclohex-5-en-1-one

(c) 8-hydroxy cyclohex -3-en-1-one

(d) 5-hydroxy cyclohex -3-en-1-one

5 Which of the following compound does not undergo aldol condensation? **[AIIMS]**

(a) $CH_3-\underset{CH_3}{\overset{CH_3}{\overset{|}{\underset{|}{C}}}}-CHO$ (b) CH_3-CHO

(c) $CH_3-\overset{O}{\overset{\|}{C}}-CH_3$ (d) CH_3CH_2CHO

6 Which of the following is the correct sequence of step involved in the mechanism of Cannizzaro reaction? **[JIPMER]**

(a) Nucleophilic attack, transfer of H^- and transfer of H^+

(b) Transfer of H^-, transfer of H^+ and nucleophilic attack

(c) Transfer of H^+, nucleophilic attack and transfer of H^-

(d) Electrophilic attack by OH^-, transfer of H^+ and transfer of H^-

7 In the reaction, **[JIPMER]**

$C_6H_5-CH=O \xrightarrow[CH_3COONa]{CH_3COOCOCH_3} A,$

The major product formed is

(a) $C_6H_5-CH_2-CHO$

(b) C_6H_5-COOH

(c) $C_6H_5-CH=CH-COOH$

(d) $C_6H_5-CH=CH-COCH_3$

2017

8 The IUPAC name of the compound **[NEET]**

[Structure: $H-\overset{O}{\overset{\|}{C}}-CH(CH_3)-C(=O)-CH=CH-CH_3$] is ....

(a) 3-keto-2-methylhex-4-enal

(b) 5-formylhex-2-en-3-one

(c) 5-methyl-4-oxohex-2-en-5-al

(d) 3-keto-2-methylhex-5-enal

9 Clemmensen reaction of ketone is carried out in the presence of **[JIPMER]**

(a) $LiAlH_4$ (b) Zn-Hg with HCl

(c) glycol with KOH (d) H_2 with Pt as catalyst

10 Of the following which is the product formed when cyclohexanone undergoes aldol condensation followed by heating? **[NEET]**

(a) 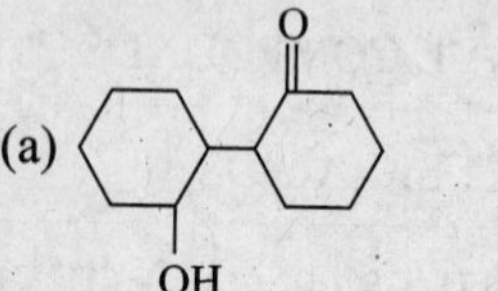

(b) 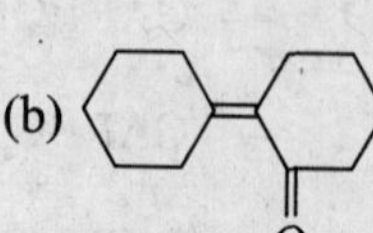

(c) 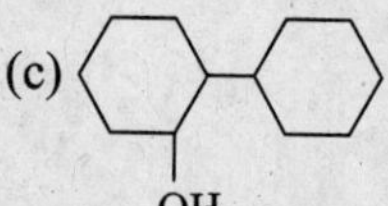

(d) 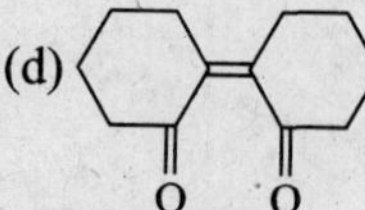

11 Cannizzaro reaction is not shown by **[JIPMER]**

(a) C_6H_5–CHO (b) 1-methylcyclohexane-1-carbaldehyde (ring carbon bearing CHO and CH_3)

(c) CH_3CHO (d) HCHO

12 Consider the following equation **[AIIMS]**

Cyclohexene $\xrightarrow{NBS}$ $\xrightarrow{Mg/ether}$ $\xrightarrow[(ii)\ H_3O^+]{(i)\ CH_3CN}$

The end product for the given sequence of reaction is

(a) 1-cyclohexenyl–$COCH_3$ (b) 3-cyclohexenyl–$COCH_3$

(c) 3-cyclohexenyl–CN (d) 3-cyclohexenyl–COOH

2016

13 Which of the following reagents would distinguish *cis*-cyclopenta-1, 2-diol from the *trans*-isomer? **[NEET]**

(a) Ozone
(b) MnO_2
(c) Aluminium isopropoxide
(d) Acetone

14 The correct structure of the product *A* formed in the reaction **[NEET Phase-II]**

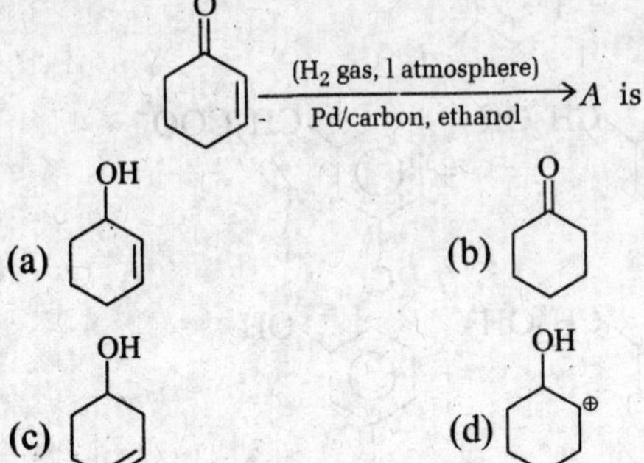

2015

15 Treatment of cyclopentanone (cyclopentyl=O) with methyl lithium gives which of the following intermediate? **[CBSE AIPMT]**

(a) Cyclopentanonyl anion
(b) Cyclopentanonyl cation
(c) Cyclopentanonyl radical
(d) Cyclopentanonyl biradical

16 An organic compound *X* having molecular formula $C_5H_{10}O$ yields phenyl hydrazone and gives negative response to the iodoform test and Tollen's test. It produces *n*-pentane on reduction. *X* could be **[CBSE AIPMT]**

(a) pentanal (b) 2-pentanone
(c) 3-pentanone (d) *n*-amyl alcohol

2014

17 Which one is most reactive towards nucleophilic addition reaction? **[CBSE AIPMT]**

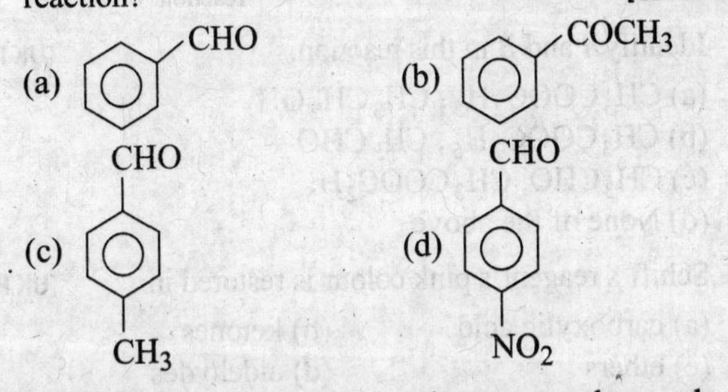

18 In which of the following reactions new carbon-carbon bond is not formed? **[Kerala CEE]**

(a) Cannizzaro reaction (b) Wurtz reaction
(c) Aldol condensation (d) Friedel-Craft's reaction
(e) Kolbe's reaction

19 The reagents to carry out the following conversion are

$Me-C\equiv CH \longrightarrow Me-CO-Me$ **[WB JEE]**

(a) $HgSO_4$ / dil. H_2SO_4
(b) BH_3; H_2O_2 / NaOH
(c) OsO_4; HIO_4
(d) $NaNH_2$ / CH_3I; $HgSO_4$ / dil. H_2SO_4

20 In the following reaction, the product *E* is **[WB JEE]**

$$\underset{CHO}{\overset{CHO}{|}} \xrightarrow[(ii)\ H^+]{(i)\ NaOH} E$$

(a) $\underset{CHO}{\overset{CH_2OH}{|}}$ (b) $\underset{CO_2H}{\overset{CHO}{|}}$ (c) $\underset{CO_2H}{\overset{CH_2OH}{|}}$ (d) $\underset{CO_2H}{\overset{CO_2H}{|}}$

21 The intermediate *J* in the following Wittig reaction is

Cyclopentyl–$\overset{+}{P}Ph_3Br^-$ $\xrightarrow[(ii)\ CH_2=O]{(i)\ n\text{-BuLi}}$ [*J*] $\longrightarrow$ methylenecyclopentane **[WB JEE]**

(a) spiro structure: cyclopentane C bearing PPh_3, with CH_2–O ring
(b) spiro structure: cyclopentane C bearing PPh_3 and O, with CH_2 ring
(c) cyclopentane C bearing O⁻ and CH_2PPh_3
(d) cyclopentane C bearing O^- and $CH_2\overset{+}{P}Ph_3$

22 Which of the following reactions cannot be used to increase the number of carbon atoms in a organic compound? **[UK PMT]**
(a) Grignard reaction
(b) Cannizzaro's reaction
(c) Aldol condensation
(d) All of these

23 $CH_3COC_2H_5 \xrightarrow{C_6H_5CO_3H} A \xleftarrow[\text{reaction}]{\text{Tishchenko}} B$

Identify A and B in this reaction. **[UK PMT]**
(a) $CH_3COOC_2H_5$, CH_3CH_2OH
(b) $CH_3COOC_2H_5$, CH_3CHO
(c) CH_3CHO, $CH_3COOC_2H_5$
(d) None of the above

24 Schiff's reagent's pink colour is restored in **[UK PMT]**
(a) carboxylic acid (b) ketones
(c) ethers (d) aldehydes

25 $X \xrightarrow[\text{(Reductive)}]{\text{Ozonolysis}} Y + Z$

Y can be obtained by Etard's reaction, Z undergoes disproportionation reaction with concentrated alkali. X could be **[KCET]**
(a) $C_6H_5-C\equiv CH$
(b) $C_6H_5-CH=CH_2$
(c) $C_6H_5-CH=CH-CH_3$
(d) $C_6H_5-CH=C(CH_3)_2$

26 $P \xrightarrow[\text{(ii) } H_3O^+]{\text{(i) } CH_3MgBr} R \xrightarrow[\text{(ii) } \Delta]{\text{(i) Dil·NaOH}}$ 4-methylpent-3-en-2-one

compound P is **[KCET]**
(a) propanone
(b) ethanamine
(c) ethane nitrile
(d) ethanal

27 Which one of the following compounds do not give a primary alcohol on reduction? **[Guj CET]**
(a) Propanal
(b) Propanoic acid
(c) Methyl propanoate
(d) Propan-2-one

28 Name the catalyst $[X]$ for the reaction,

$CO(g) + H_2(g) \xrightarrow{X} HCHO(g)$ **[Guj CET]**
(a) Cu (b) Ni
(c) Cu/ZnO (d) Cu/Cr_2O_3

2013

29 Reaction by which benzaldehyde cannot be prepared is **[NEET]**
(a) $C_6H_5CH_3$ + CrO_2Cl_2 in CS_2 followed by H_3O^+
(b) C_6H_5COCl + H_2 in the presence of Pd-$BaSO_4$
(c) C_6H_6 + CO + HCl in the presence of anhyd. $AlCl_3$
(d) C_6H_5COOH + Zn/Hg and conc. HCl

30 Aldehydes and ketones can be distinguished by **[AIIMS]**
(a) ammonia
(b) H_2SO_4
(c) alkaline $KMnO_4$
(d) Fehling solution

31 Which of the following organic compounds answers both iodoform test and Fehling's test? **[KCET]**
(a) Methanal (b) Ethanol
(c) Propane (d) Ethanal

2012

32 Predict the products in the given reaction, **[CBSE AIPMT]**

m-Chlorobenzaldehyde (CHO, Cl at meta) $\xrightarrow{50\%\ KOH}$

(a) m-$ClC_6H_4CH_2OH$ + m-$ClC_6H_4CH_2COO^-$
(b) m-$HOC_6H_4CH_2OH$ + m-HOC_6H_4OH
(c) m-$ClC_6H_4CH_2OH$ + m-$ClC_6H_4COO^-$
(d) m-$HOC_6H_4CH_2OH$ + m-$HOC_6H_4COO^-$

33 Consider the following reaction,

$$C_6H_5COCl \xrightarrow[\text{Pd-BaSO}_4]{H_2} A$$

The product A is [CBSE AIPMT/AMU]

(a) C_6H_5CHO (b) C_6H_5OH
(c) $C_6H_5COCH_3$ (d) C_6H_5Cl

34 Which of the following compounds undergoes both Cannizzaro and aldol reaction? [AFMC]

(a) $(CH_3)_2CH{\cdot}CHO$ (b) HCHO
(c) C_6H_5CHO (d) CH_3CHO

35 The product formed when acetone reacts with nitro methane in the presence of a base is [AFMC]

(a) $CH_3—C(CH_3)_2—CH_2NO_2$

(b) $CH_3—C(CH_3)(OH)—CH(OH)—NO_2$

(c) $(H_3C)_2C{=}CHNO_2$

(d) $CH_3COCH{=}CHNO_2$

36 The reagent used in Clemmensen's reduction is

(a) conc. H_2SO_4 (b) Zn—Hg / conc. HCl
(c) *aq.* KOH (d) alc. KOH [UP CPMT]

37 Which of the following does not give cannizzaro's reaction? [OJEE]

(a) CCl_3CHO (b) C_6H_5CHO
(c) HCHO (d) CH_3CHO

38 Upon treatment with $Al(OEt)_3$ followed by usual reactions (work up), CH_3CHO will produce. [WB JEE]

(a) Only $CH_3COOCH_2CH_3$
(b) A mixture of CH_3COOH and EtOH
(c) Only CH_3COOH
(d) Only EtOH

39 An organic compound A burns with a sooty flame. It is negative towards Tollen's reagent test and positive for Brady's reagent test. The compound A is [KCET]

(a) acetophenone (b) acetone
(c) salicylic acid (d) benzaldehyde

2011

40 Which of the following pairs can be distinguished by sodium hypoiodide? [Kerala CEE]

(a) CH_3CHO and CH_3COCH_3
(b) CH_3CH_2CHO and CH_3COCH_3
(c) CH_3CH_2OH and $CH_3CH_2CHOHCH_3$
(d) CH_3OH and CH_3CH_2CHO
(e) CH_3OH and $CH_3CH_2CH_2OH$

41 The compound that neither forms semicarbazone nor oxime is [Kerala CEE]

(a) HCHO (b) CH_3COCH_2Cl
(c) CH_3CHO (d) $CH_3CONHCH_3$
(e) $(CH_3)_2CHCHO$

42 The reagent with which both acetaldehyde and acetone react is [KCET]

(a) Fehling's solution (b) I_2 / NaOH
(c) Tollen's reagent (d) Carbonic acid

43 Which of the following gives an aldehyde on dry distillation? [KCET]

(a) Calcium formate + calcium acetate
(b) Calcium acetate + calcium benzoate
(c) Calcium acetate
(d) Calcium benzoate

44 Which of the following reactions convert acetone into hydrocarbon having same number of carbon atoms? [Guj CET]

(a) Wolff-Kishner reaction
(b) Hofmann reaction
(c) Grignard reaction
(d) Reduction with $LiAlH_4$

45 In Tollen's test, aldehyde [DUMET]

(a) are oxidised
(b) are reduced to alcohol
(c) neither reduced nor oxidised
(d) precipitate Ag^+ as AgCl

46 In the conversion of

$$C_6H_5—CH{=}CH—CH_2—\overset{O}{\overset{\|}{C}}—CH_3 \xrightarrow{X} C_6H_5—CH{=}CH—CH_2—CH(OH)—CH_3$$

[DUMET]

X is

(a) H_2 / Pt (b) Zn—Hg / HCl
(c) Li / NH_3 (d) $NaBH_4$

2010

47 The major organic product formed from the following reaction, **[AFMC]**

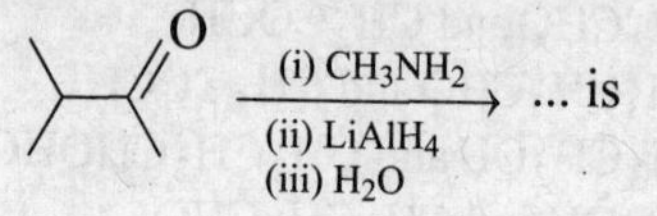

(Structure: ketone) $\xrightarrow[\text{(ii) LiAlH}_4 \text{ (iii) H}_2\text{O}]{\text{(i) CH}_3\text{NH}_2}$ ... is

(a) 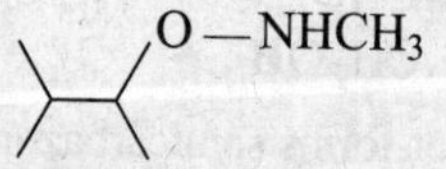 (structure with O—NHCH$_3$) (b) 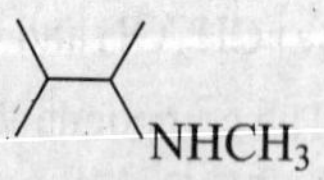 (structure with NHCH$_3$)

(c) 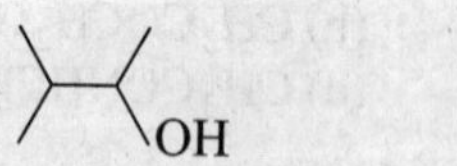 (structure with OH) (d) 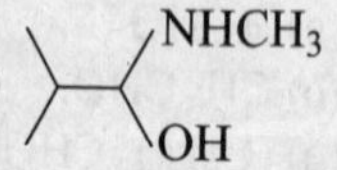 (structure with NHCH$_3$ and OH)

48 Aldehydes and ketones are differentiated by using **[UP CPMT]**

(a) $NaOH / I_2$ (b) $NaHSO_3$
(c) $AgNO_3 / NH_4OH$ (d) $NH_2 \cdot NH_2$

49 Benzophenone can be converted into benzene using **[BVP]**

(a) fused alkali
(b) anhydrous $AlCl_3$
(c) sodium amalgam in water
(d) acidified dichromate

50 Oxidation of acetaldehyde with selenium dioxide produces **[BVP]**

(a) ethanoic acid (b) methanoic acid
(c) glyoxal (d) oxalic acid

51 In the following reaction sequence,

$$CH_3CHO \xrightarrow[\text{Ca(OH)}_2]{\text{Cl}_2} X \xrightarrow[\text{Alc. KOH}]{\text{C}_6\text{H}_5\text{NH}_2} Y$$

Y is **[MHT CET]**

(a) $CH_3CH{=}NHC_6H_5$ (b) $C_6H_5NHCH_3$
(c) C_6H_5NC (d) C_6H_5NCO

52 Ethyl methyl ketone is obtained by heating calcium salts of **[MHT CET]**

(a) formic acid + propionic acid
(b) acetic acid + propionic acid
(c) acetic acid only
(d) acetic acid + methanoic acid

53 Fehling *A* and Fehling *B* are **[OJEE]**

(a) $CuSO_4$ solution and NH_4OH solution
(b) $CuSO_4$ solution and alkaline solution of sodium potassium tartarate
(c) $CuSO_4$ solution and alkaline solution of sodium citrate
(d) $CuSO_4$ solution and NaOH

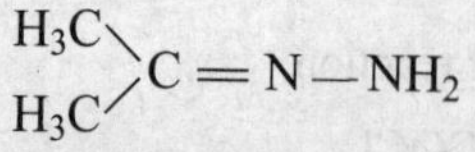

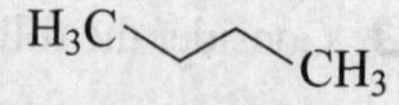

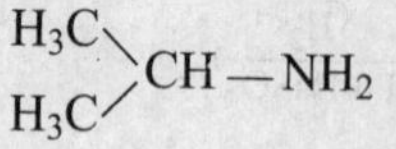

54 The product of this reaction is **[OJEE]**

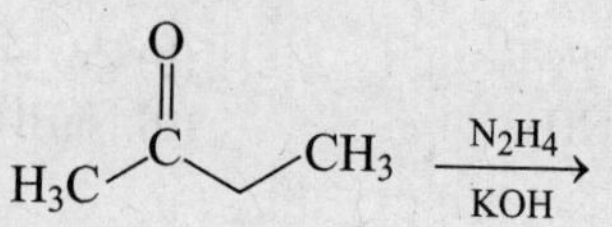

$$H_3C{-}\overset{O}{\overset{\|}{C}}{-}CH_2{-}CH_3 \xrightarrow[\text{KOH}]{\text{N}_2\text{H}_4}$$

(a) $(H_3C)_2C{=}N{-}NH_2$ (b) $H_3C{-}CH_2{-}CH_2{-}CH_3$

(c) $(H_3C)_2CH{-}NH_2$ (d) 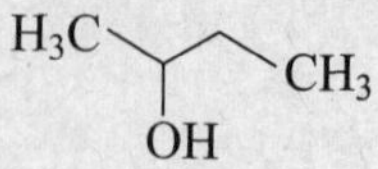 $H_3C{-}CH(OH){-}CH_2{-}CH_3$

55 One of the following named reaction is an example of "disproportionation reaction". Identify it. **[OJEE]**

(a) Birch reduction
(b) Aldol condensation
(c) Reimer-Tiemann reaction
(d) Cannizzaro reaction

56 Which one of the following is produced when acetone is saturated with HCl gas? **[WB JEE]**

(a) Acetone alcohol (b) Phorone
(c) Mesityl oxide (d) Benzene

57 Keto-enol tautomerism is not observed in **[WB JEE]**

(a) $C_6H_5COC_6H_5$ (b) $C_6H_5COCH{=}CH_2$
(c) $C_6H_5COCH_2COCH_3$ (d) $CH_3COCH_2COCH_3$

58 Name the reagent used to bring about the following transformation : But-2-ene to ethanal **[AMU]**

(a) $K_2Cr_2O_7$ in acidic medium
(b) CrO_2Cl_2 / H_3O^+
(c) PCC
(d) O_3 / H_2O—Zn dust

59 Arrange the following compounds in increasing order of their reactivity in nucleophilic addition reactions. Ethanal (I), propanal (II), propanone (III), butanone (IV) **[AMU]**

(a) III < II < I < IV (b) II < I < III < IV
(c) IV < III < II < I (d) I < II < III < IV

60 The compound obtained when acetaldehyde reacts with dilute aqueous sodium hydroxide exhibits **[KCET]**

(a) geometrical isomerism
(b) optical isomerism
(c) Neither optical nor geometrical isomerism
(d) Both optical and geometrical isomerism

61 Identify the reaction which is used to obtain β-hydroxy ketone. **[Guj CET]**

(a) Condensation reaction (b) Aldol condensation
(c) Cross aldol condensation (d) Cannizaro reaction

62 The most reactive compound towards formation of cyanohydrin on treatment with HCN followed by acidification is **[JCECE]**

(a) benzaldehyde (b) *p*-nitrobenzaldehyde
(c) phenylacetaldehyde (d) *p*-hydroxybenzaldehyde

63 Benzaldehyde reacts with ammonia to form **[JCECE]**

(a) benzaldehyde ammonia (b) urotropine
(c) hydrobenzamide (d) ammonium chloride

2009

64 **Assertion** (A) 2-butenal lacks enolisable H-atom, α to carbonyl group, still it has sufficient acidic character.
Reason (R) The conjugate base of 2-butenal is stabilised by resonance. **[AIIMS]**
(a) Both A and R are correct and R is the correct explanation of A
(b) Both A and R are correct but R is not the correct explanation of A
(c) A is correct but R is incorrect
(d) Both A and R are incorrect

65 If heavy water is taken as solvent instead of normal water while performing Cannizzaro reaction, the products of the reaction are **[AIIMS]**
(a) $RCOO^- + RCH_2OH$ (b) $RCOO^- + RCH_2OD$
(c) $RCOOD + RCD_2OD$ (d) $RCOO^- + RCD_2OD$

66 The compound, with which ethanal does not react, is **[AFMC]**
(a) HCl (b) Cl_2
(c) PCl_5 (d) *aq.* $NaHSO_3$

67 The reaction by which benzaldehyde is converted in benzyl alcohol, is **[AFMC]**
(a) Fittig reaction (b) Cannizzaro reaction
(c) Wurtz reaction (d) aldol condensation

68 Pentan-3-one is not obtained from **[MHT CET]**
(a) 2,2-dichloropentane (b) 3,3-dichloropentane
(c) pentan-3-ol (d) pent-2-yne

69 Which of the following will respond to Cannizzaro's reaction? **[Manipal]**
(a) 2,2-dimethylpropanal (b) Acetaldehyde
(c) Propionaldehyde (d) Cinnamaldehyde

70 The rate determining step in Cannizzaro's reaction is **[OJEE]**
(a) attack of OH^- on $>C{=}O$ group
(b) transfer of H^- to $>C{=}O$ group
(c) abstraction of H^+ from —COOH group
(d) lose of H^+ from —COOH group

71 H_3C–(cyclopentyl)–$C(=O)$–CH_3 $\xrightarrow[\text{(ii) NaOH}]{\text{(i) } CF_3COOH}$

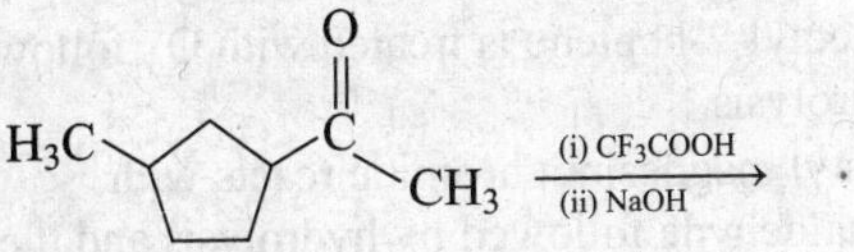

Find the organic acid produced from the above reaction. **[OJEE]**
(a) $CH_3COO^-Na^+$
(b) H_3C–(cyclopentyl)–COO^-Na^+
(c) H_3C–(cyclopentyl)–$CH_2COO^-Na^+$
(d) None of the above

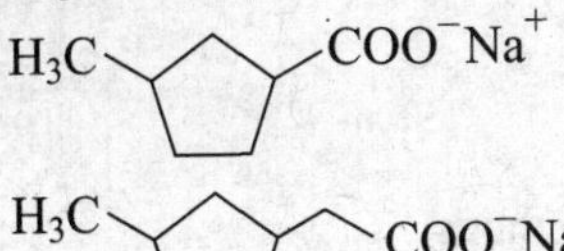

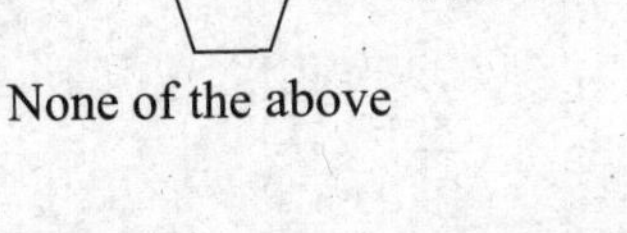

72 Identify the final product, **[OJEE]**

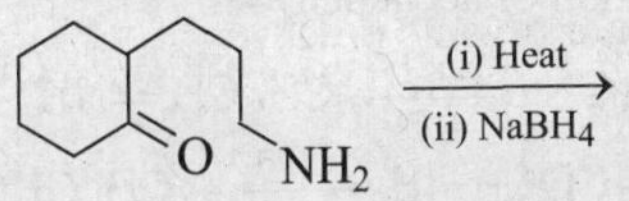

2-(3-aminopropyl)cyclohexanone ($C{=}O$, NH_2) $\xrightarrow[\text{(ii) } NaBH_4]{\text{(i) Heat}}$

(a) octahydrochromene (bicyclic with ring O)
(b) 2-allylcyclohexanol (OH, CH_2)
(c) decalin with NH_2
(d) decahydroquinoline (N–H)

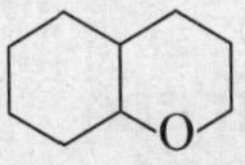

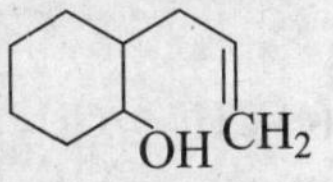

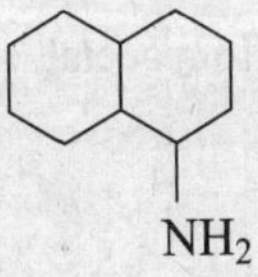

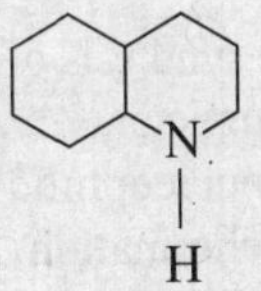

73 C_3H_6O did not give a silver mirror with Tollen's reagent, but gave an oxime with hydroxylamine. It can give positive **[OJEE]**
(a) iodoform test (b) Fehling's test
(c) Schiff's test (d) carbylamine test

74 For making distinction between 2-pentanone and 3-pentanone the reagent to be employed is **[WB JEE]**
(a) $K_2Cr_2O_7 / H_2SO_4$
(b) Zn — Hg / HCl
(c) SeO_2
(d) iodine/NaOH

75 Which is necessary for the conversion of butan-2-one into propanoic acid? **[CG PMT, Haryana PMT]**
(a) Tollen reagent (b) Fehling solution
(c) $NaOH/I_2 / H^+$ (d) $NaOH / NaI / H^+$

76 Which one of the following does not form sodium bisulphite addition product with sodium bisulphite solution? **[J&K CET]**
(a) CH_2O (b) $C_6H_5COCH_3$
(c) C_6H_5CHO (d) CH_3CHO

77 The most reactive of the following is **[J&K CET]**
(a) acetone (b) benzophenone
(c) benzaldehyde (d) acetaldehyde

78 Arrange the following compounds in decreasing order of their boiling points. **[AMU]**
$CH_3CHO, CH_3CH_2OH, CH_3OCH_3, CH_3CH_2CH_3$
(a) $CH_3CH_2CH_3 < CH_3OCH_3 < CH_3CHO < CH_3CH_2OH$
(b) $CH_3CH_2CH_3 < CH_3CHO < CH_3OCH_3 < CH_3CH_2OH$
(c) $CH_3CH_2CH_3 > CH_3CHO > CH_3OCH_3 > CH_3CH_2OH$
(d) $CH_3CH_2OH > CH_3CHO > CH_3OCH_3 > CH_3CH_2CH_3$

79 Which of the following is the industrial method of preparation of acetaldehyde? [AMU]

(a) $CH_3CN \xrightarrow[HCl]{SnCl_2} CH_3CH{=}NH \xrightarrow{H_3O^+} CH_3CHO$

(b) $CH_3COCl + H_2 \xrightarrow[BaSO_4]{Pd} CH_3CHO + HCl$

(c) $CH_2{=}CH_2 + H_2O \xrightarrow{Pd^{2+}} H_3CHO$

(d) None of the above

80 The synthesis of crotonaldehyde from acetaldehyde is an example of .... reaction. [EAMCET]

(a) nucleophilic addition
(b) elimination
(c) electrophilic addition
(d) nucleophilic addition-elimination

81 Aldol condensation does not occur between [DUMET]

(a) two different aldehydes
(b) two different ketone
(c) an aldehyde and ketone
(d) an aldehyde and an ester

82 Compound *A* undergoes Cannizzaro reaction and *B* undergoes positive iodoform test. Therefore [DUMET]

(a) A = Acetaldehyde; B = 1-pentanal
(b) $A = C_6H_5CH_2CHO$; B = 3-pentanone
(c) A = Formaldehyde; B = 2-pentanone
(d) A = Propionaldehyde; B = 1-pentanol

83 The compound which is not formed during the dry distillation of a mixture of calcium formate and calcium acetate is [KCET]

(a) propanal (b) propanone (c) ethanal (d) methanal

84 The compound which forms acetaldehyde when heated with dilute NaOH is [KCET]

(a) 1,1,1-trichloroethane (b) 1-chloroethane
(c) 1,2-dichloroethane (d) 1,1-dichloroethane

85 *A* and *B* in the following reactions, are [VMMCI]

$$R{-}\underset{\underset{O}{\|}}{C}{-}R' \xrightarrow[KCN]{HCN} A \xrightarrow{B} R'{-}\underset{\underset{R}{|}}{C}{<}^{OH}_{CH_2NH_2}$$

	A	*B*
(a)	$RR'CH_2CN$	NaOH
(b)	$RR'C{<}^{OH}_{COOH}$	CH_3NH_2
(c)	$RR'C{<}^{CN}_{COOH}$	CH_3NH_2
(d)	$RR'C{<}^{CN}_{OH}$	$LiAlH_4$

2008

86 Acetophenone when reacted with a base C_2H_5ONa, yields a stable compound which has the structure [CBSE AIPMT]

(a) $C_6H_5{-}\underset{\underset{CH_3}{|}}{C}{=}CH{-}\underset{\underset{O}{\|}}{C}{-}C_6H_5$

(b) $C_6H_5{-}\underset{\underset{CH_3}{|}}{CH}{-}CH_2{-}\underset{\underset{O}{\|}}{C}{-}C_6H_5$

(c) $C_6H_5{-}\overset{\overset{CH_3}{|}}{\underset{\underset{OH}{|}}{C}}{-}\overset{\overset{CH_3}{|}}{\underset{\underset{OH}{|}}{C}}{-}C_6H_5$

(d) $C_6H_5{-}\underset{\underset{OH}{|}}{CH}{-}\underset{\underset{OH}{|}}{CH}{-}C_6H_5$

87 A strong base can abstract an α-hydrogen from [CBSE AIPMT]

(a) alkene (b) amine
(c) ketone (d) alkane

88 3-hydroxybutanal is formed when *X* reacts with *Y* in dilute *Z* solution. What are *X*, *Y* and *Z*? [AIIMS]

	X	*Y*	*Z*
(a)	CH_3CHO,	$(CH_3)_2CO$,	dil. NaOH
(b)	CH_3CHO,	CH_3CHO,	dil. NaCl
(c)	$(CH_3)_2CO$,	$(CH_3)_2CO$,	dil. HCl
(d)	CH_3CHO,	CH_3CHO,	dil. NaOH

89 An organic compound *X* on treatment with pyridinium chloro chromate in dichloromethane gives compound *Y*. Compound *Y* reacts with I_2 and alkali to form triiodomethane. The compound X is [AIIMS]

(a) C_2H_5OH (b) CH_3CHO
(c) CH_3COCH_3 (d) CH_3COOH

90 Which of the following pathways produces 2-hexanone?

I. 1-hexyne is treated with H_2SO_4, $HgSO_4$ and water.
II. 3-methyl-2-heptene is treated with O_3 followed by hydrolysis.
III. *n*-butyl magnesium bromide reacts with acetaldehyde followed by hydrolysis and then chromic acid oxidation.
IV. Hydroboration-oxidation of 1-hexyne. [Kerala CEE]

(a) I, II and III
(b) I and II
(c) I, II and IV
(d) I and III
(e) All the four methods

91 In the given compound, which of the following hydrogen is most acidic?

$$\underset{A}{CH_3}-\underset{B}{CH_2}-\underset{C}{\overset{\overset{O}{\|}}{C}}-CH_3$$ [DUMET]

(a) Only A (b) Only B (c) Only C (d) Both B and C

92 In this reaction,

$CH_3CHO + HCN \longrightarrow CH_3CH(OH)CN$

$\xrightarrow{HOH} CH_3CH(OH)COOH$

an asymmetric centre is generated. The acid obtained would be [JCECE]

(a) 50% D + 50% L-isomer (b) 20% D + 80% L-isomer
(c) D-isomer (d) L-isomer

2007

93 Which of the compounds with molecular formula C_5H_{10} yields acetone on ozonolysis? [CBSE AIPMT]

(a) 2-methyl-2-butene (b) 3-methyl-1-butene
(c) Cyclopentane (d) 2-methyl-1-butene

94 Formalin is the commercial name of [MHT CET]

(a) formic acid
(b) fluoroform
(c) 40% aqueous solution of methanal
(d) *para* formaldehyde

95 Acetone on distillation with conc. H_2SO_4 forms [RPMT]

(a) phorone (b) acrolein
(c) mesitylene (d) mesityl oxide

96 The product formed when hydroxylamine condenses with a carbonyl compound is called [KCET]

(a) hydrazide (b) oxime (c) hydrazine (d) hydrazon

2006

97 A carbonyl compound reacts with hydrogen cyanide to form cyanohydrin which on hydrolysis forms a racemic mixture of α-hydroxy acid. The carbonyl compound is [CBSE AIPMT]

(a) acetaldehyde (b) acetone
(c) diethyl ketone (d) formaldehyde

98 When dihydroxy acetone reacts with HIO_4, the product is/are [AFMC]

(a) HCHO (b) HCOOH
(c) HCHO and HCOOH (d) HCHO and CO_2

99 Acetaldehyde reacts with excess chlorine to give [BHU]

(a) CCl_4 (b) $CHCl_3$
(c) $CCl_3 \cdot COCH_3$ (d) $CCl_3 \cdot CHO$

100 Benzaldehyde condenses with N,N-dimethylaniline in presence of anhydrous $ZnCl_2$ to give [BHU]

(a) Michler's ketone (b) azo-dye
(c) malachite green (d) buffer yellow

101 $A \xrightarrow[\text{(ii) } CH_3COCH_3 \text{ (iii) } \Delta]{\text{(i) Dil. NaOH}} (CH_3)_2C{=}CHCOCH{=}C(CH_3)_2$

What is A? [Kerala CEE]

(a) Acetone (d) Acetaldehyde
(c) Propionaldehyde (b) Formaldehyde
(e) Ethyl alcohol

102 The diketone

$$CH_3-\overset{\overset{O}{\|}}{C}-(CH_2)_2-\overset{\overset{O}{\|}}{C}-CH_3$$

on intramolecular aldol condensation gives the final product [Kerala CEE]

(a) 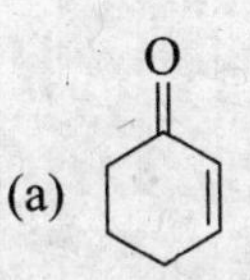

(b) 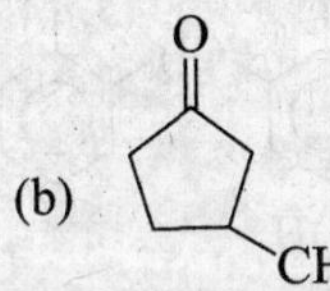

(c) 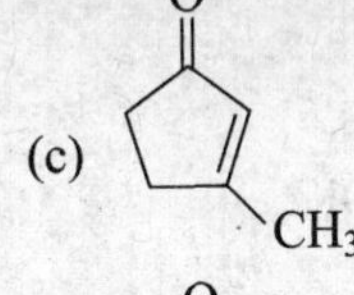

(d) 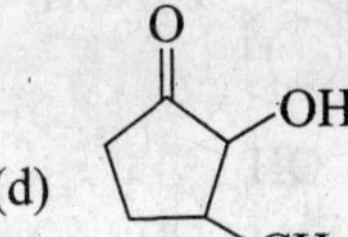

(e) 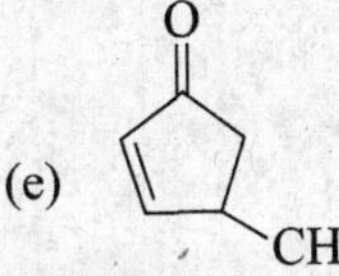

103 The reagent used in Gattermann Koch aldehyde synthesis is [RPMT]

(a) Pb / $BaSO_4$ (b) alkaline $KMnO_4$
(c) acidic $KMnO_4$ (d) CO + HCl

104 Acetylene and HCHO react in presence of copper acetylide catalyst to form [EAMCET]

(a) 1-butyne-1, 4-diol (b) 2-butyne-1, 2-diol
(c) 2-butyne-1, 4-diol (d) None of these

105 Compound A (molecular formula C_3H_8O) is treated with acidified potassium dichromate to form a product B (molecular formula C_3H_6O). B forms a shining silver mirror on warming with ammoniacal silver nitrate. B when treated with an aqueous solution of $H_2NCONHNH_2$, HCl and sodium acetate gives a product C. Identify the structure of C. [EAMCET]

(a) $CH_3CH_2CH{=}NNHCONH_2$
(b) $(CH_3)_2C{=}NNHCONH_2$
(c) $(CH_3)_2C{=}NCONHNH_2$
(d) $CH_3CH_2CH{=}NCONHNH_2$

106 When a mixture of calcium benzoate and calcium acetate is dry distilled, the resulting compound is [KCET]

(a) acetophenone (b) benzaldehyde
(c) benzophenone (d) acetaldehyde

107 Reduction with aluminium isopropoxide in excess of *iso*-propyl alcohol is called Meerwein-Ponndorf-Verley reduction (MPV). What will be the final product when cyclohex-2-enone is selectively reduced in MPV reaction? **[JCECE]**

(a) Cyclohexanol (b) Cyclohex-2-enol
(c) Cyclohexanone (d) Benzene

108 The final product of this reaction is/are **[Punjab PMET]**

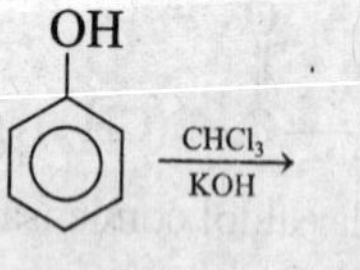

Phenol $\xrightarrow[KOH]{CHCl_3}$

(a) 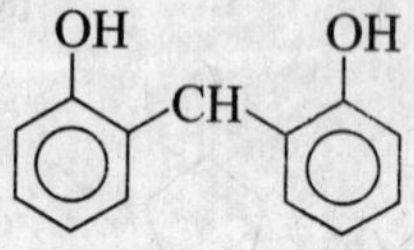 (2-hydroxyphenyl)–CH–(2-hydroxyphenyl)

(b) 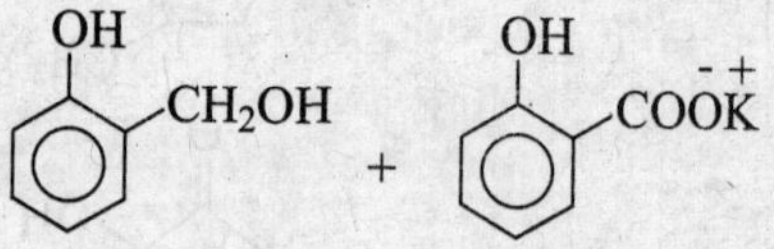 o-HOC$_6$H$_4$CH$_2$OH + o-HOC$_6$H$_4$COO$^-$K$^+$

(c) 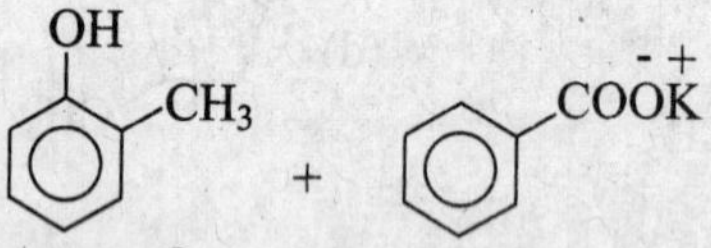 o-HOC$_6$H$_4$CH$_3$ + C$_6$H$_5$COO$^-$K$^+$

(d) 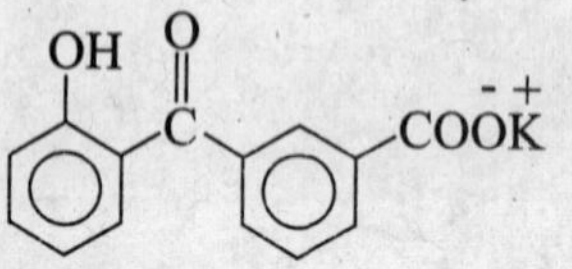 o-HOC$_6$H$_4$–CO–C$_6$H$_4$–COO$^-$K$^+$

2005

109 Ketones react with Mg—Hg over water gives **[AFMC]**

(a) pinacolone (b) pinacols
(c) alcohols (d) None of these

110 By combining the two calcium salts of carboxylic acids, we are preparing 2-butanone. Find the correct pair of the following. **[MHT CET]**

(a) Calcium formate + Calcium propanoate
(b) Calcium acetate + Calcium propanoate
(c) Calcium acetate + Calcium acetate
(d) Calcium formate + Calcium acetate

111 $CH_3CHO + HCHO \xrightarrow[heat]{Dil.\ NaOH} A \xrightarrow[H_3O^+]{HCN} B,$

the structure of compound B is **[Kerala CEE]**

(a) $CH_2{=}CH{-}CH(OH){-}COOH$

(b) $CH_2{=}CH{-}CH(CN){-}OH$

(c) $CH_3CH_2{-}CH(OH){-}COOH$

(d) $CH_3{-}CH(OH){-}COOH$ (e) $CH_3{-}C(CN)(OH){-}COOH$

112 Benzaldehyde on refluxing with aqueous alcoholic KCN produces **[Kerala CEE]**

(a) cyanobenzene (b) cyanohydrin
(c) benzoyl chloride (d) benzoin
(e) None of the above

113 The product obtained in the following reaction is

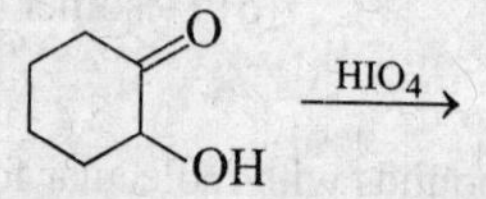

2-hydroxycyclohexanone $\xrightarrow{HIO_4}$ **[Haryana PMT]**

(a) 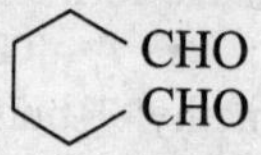 CHO / CHO (b)  COOH / CHO
(c)  COOH / COOH (d) 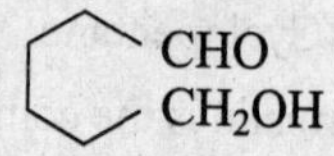 CHO / CH$_2$OH

114 Identify X and Y in the following sequence of reactions,

$$CH_3CHO \xrightarrow{HNO_3} X \xrightarrow[\Delta]{P_4O_{10}} Y$$

	X	Y
(a)	C_2H_5OH,	C_2H_4
(b)	CH_3CO_2H,	$(CH_3CO)_2O$
(c)	CH_3CO_2H,	$CH_3CO_2CH_3$
(d)	C_2H_5OH,	CH_3CO_2H

[EAMCET]

115 A compound A ($C_5H_{10}Cl_2$) on hydrolysis gives $C_5H_{10}O$ which reacts with NH_2OH, forms iodoform, but does not give Fehling test. A is **[DUMET]**

(a) $CH_3{-}CCl_2{-}CH_2{-}CH_2{-}CH_3$

(b) $CH_3{-}CH_2{-}CCl_2{-}CH_2{-}CH_3$

(c) $CH_3{-}CH_2{-}CH_2{-}CH_2{-}CHCl_2$

(d) $CH_3{-}CHCl{-}CHCl{-}CH_2{-}CH_3$

116 If the enolate ion combines with carbonyl group of ester, we get [DUMET]
(a) aldol (b) α, β-unsaturated ester
(c) β-keto ester (d) acid

117 Acetals are [BCECE]
(a) ketones (b) diethers
(c) aldehyde (d) hydroxy aldehydes

118 Conversion of benzaldehyde to 3-phenyl-prop-2- en-1-oic acid is [JCECE]
(a) Perkin condensation
(b) Claisen condensation
(c) Oxidative addition
(d) Aldol condensation

Answers

1 (a)	2 (b)	3 (c)	4 (d)	5 (a)	6 (a)	7 (c)	8 (a)	9 (b)	10 (b)
11 (c)	12 (b)	13 (d)	14 (b)	15 (a)	16 (c)	17 (d)	18 (a)	19 (d)	20 (c)
21 (a)	22 (b)	23 (b)	24 (d)	25 (b)	26 (c)	27 (d)	28 (a)	29 (d)	30 (d)
31 (d)	32 (c)	33 (a)	34 (a)	35 (c)	36 (b)	37 (d)	38 (a)	39 (a)	40 (b)
41 (d)	42 (b)	43 (a)	44 (a)	45 (a)	46 (d)	47 (b)	48 (c)	49 (a)	50 (c)
51 (c)	52 (b)	53 (b)	54 (b)	55 (d)	56 (c)	57 (a)	58 (d)	59 (c)	60 (b)
61 (b)	62 (b)	63 (c)	64 (a)	65 (b)	66 (a)	67 (b)	68 (a)	69 (a)	70 (b)
71 (a)	72 (d)	73 (a)	74 (d)	75 (c)	76 (b)	77 (d)	78 (b)	79 (c)	80 (d)
81 (d)	82 (c)	83 (a)	84 (d)	85 (d)	86 (a)	87 (c)	88 (d)	89 (a)	90 (a)
91 (b)	92 (a)	93 (a)	94 (c)	95 (c)	96 (b)	97 (a)	98 (c)	99 (d)	100 (c)
101 (a)	102 (c)	103 (d)	104 (c)	105 (a)	106 (a)	107 (b)	108 (b)	109 (b)	110 (b)
111 (a)	112 (d)	113 (b)	114 (b)	115 (a)	116 (c)	117 (b)	118 (a)		

Explanations

1 (*a*) The suitable reagent for the conversion

$$CH_2{=}CH{-}CHO \xrightarrow{?} CH_2{=}CH{-}CH_2{-}OH$$

is $NaBH_4$. It is a selective reagent that reduces $>C{=}O$ group to —OH and does not reduce carbon-carbon double bond. Thus, unsaturated alcohols can be prepared.

2 (*b*) The priority order of functional group is —CHO > Br
Therefore, IUPAC name of the given compound is as follows

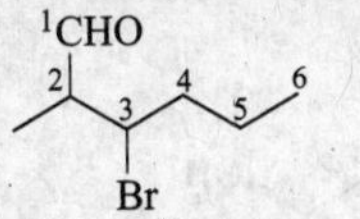

(3-bromo-2-methyl hexanal)

3 (*c*) The given reaction (as per the options) is crossed Cannizzaro reaction. A simple Cannizzaro reaction is shown by those aldehydes in which α-hydrogen is absent. These aldehydes in the presence of a strong base like NaOH show disproportionation, i.e. simultaneous oxidation and reduction of the same molecule. Thus, the product includes an acid alongwith an alcohol.

In crossed Cannizzaro reaction however, two different molecules can participate, out of which the one more prone to nucleophilic attack will show oxidation, while the other show reduction.

Here, out of the given two substrates, HCHO is more prone to nucleophilic attack hence, this will undergo oxidation while CH_3CHO will undergo reduction. Hence, the possible products are $HCOO^-Na^+ + CH_3CH_2OH$. Reaction involved is as follows :

$$HCHO + CH_3CHO \xrightarrow[NaOH]{Conc.} HCO\overset{-}{O}\overset{+}{Na} + CH_3CH_2OH$$

Note Same combination of substrates give crossed aldol as well, in the presence of NaOH to form $CH_3{-}CH(OH){-}CH_2CHO$

But as, it is not among the options as the product, hence we are considering option (c) as the most appropriate option.

4 (*d*) The correct IUPAC name of the given compound is 5-hydroxy cyclohex -3-en-1-one.
The structure is shown below

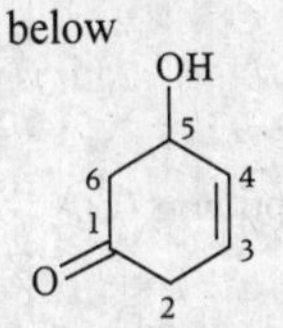

5 (*a*) Necessary condition for aldol condensation is the presence of atleast one α-H atom. Thus, among the given options, $(CH_3)_3C{-}CHO$ does not undergo aldol condensation as it does not contain any α-hydrogen atom.

6 (*a*) Consider the following Cannizzaro reaction,

$$HCHO + HCHO \xrightarrow{KOH\ (conc.)} \underset{\text{Methyl alcohol}}{CH_3OH} + \underset{\text{Potassium formate}}{HCOOK^+}$$

The mechanism of Cannizzaro reaction is as

***Step* I** Attack of nucleophile (OH^-) to the carbonyl carbon.

$$H-\overset{O}{\overset{\|}{C}}-H + \overset{-}{O}H \underset{}{\overset{\text{Fast}}{\rightleftharpoons}} H-\underset{OH}{\underset{|}{\overset{O^{\ominus}}{\overset{|}{C}}}}-H$$

(Anion I)

***Step* II** The transfer of hydride ion from anion (I) to second molecule of aldehyde and finally rapid transfer of proton takes place.

$$H-\underset{OH}{\underset{|}{\overset{O^{\ominus}}{\overset{|}{C}H}}} + H-\overset{O}{\overset{\|}{C}}-H \xrightarrow[\text{transfer}]{\text{Hydride }(H^-)}$$

$$\underset{\text{(Acid)}}{H-\overset{O}{\overset{\|}{C}}-OH} + \underset{\text{(Methoxide ion)}}{H-\underset{H}{\underset{|}{\overset{O^-}{\overset{|}{C}}}}-H} \xrightarrow{\text{Proton exchange}} \underset{\text{(Acid salt)}}{H-\overset{O}{\overset{\|}{C}}-O^-} + \underset{\text{(Methyl alcohol)}}{CH_3OH}$$

7 (*c*) The given reaction is an example of Perkin condensation. In this reaction, aromatic aldehydes react with acid anhydride of an aliphatic acid in presence of sodium salt of same acid to form α, β-unsaturated acid. The steps involved in the process are as follows :

$$\underset{\text{Benzaldehyde}}{C_6H_5CHO} + \underset{\text{Acetic anhydride}}{CH_3-\overset{O}{\overset{\|}{C}}-O-\overset{O}{\overset{\|}{C}}-CH_3} \xrightarrow{CH_3COO^-Na^+} \underset{\text{Cinnamic acid}}{C_6H_5\overset{\beta}{C}H=\overset{\alpha}{C}HCOOH} + CH_3COOH$$

Thus, the correct option is (c).

8 (*a*)

$$H-\overset{O}{\overset{\|}{\underset{1}{C}}}-\underset{2}{CH}(CH_3)-\overset{O}{\overset{\|}{\underset{3}{C}}}-\underset{4}{CH}=\underset{5}{CH}-\underset{6}{CH_3}$$

— CHO group gets higher priority over —C= O and C=C group in numbering of principal carbon chain.

∴IUPAC name = 3-keto-2-methylhex-4-enal.

9 (*b*) Zn-Hg with HCl reduces ketone to respective alkane, i.e. $\rangle C=O$ of ketone reduce to $\rangle CH_2$ group. The reaction is called Clemmensen reduction.

10 (*b*) Aldehydes and ketones containing α—H atoms undergo aldol condensation in presence of dilute alkali as catalyst and gives α, β unsaturated compound with the elimination of H_2O molecule on heating.

2 Cyclohexanone $\xrightarrow{\overset{\ominus}{O}H}$ enolate + cyclohexanone → aldol adduct (O^-) $\xrightarrow[-\overset{\ominus}{O}H]{H_2O}$ β-hydroxy ketone (OH) $\xrightarrow[\Delta]{-H_2O}$

(α, β-unsaturated compound)

11 (*c*) The aldehyde/ketone, which do not contain α-H atom shows Cannizzaro reaction.

In CH_3CHO, carbonyl group is attached to C-atom having α-H; Hence, CH_3CHO does not show Cannizzaro reaction.

12 (*b*)

Cyclohexene $\xrightarrow[\text{Allylic substitution}]{\text{NBS}}$ 3-bromocyclohexene $\xrightarrow{\text{Mg/ether}}$ 3-cyclohexenyl-MgBr $\xrightarrow[\text{(ii) }H_3O^+]{\text{(i) }CH_3CN}$ 3-cyclohexenyl-$\overset{O}{\overset{\|}{C}}CH_3$

13 (*d*) *cis*-cyclopenta-1, 2-diol on reaction with acetone, forms cyclic ketal whereas *trans*-isomer of cyclopenta-1, 2-diol cannot form cyclic ketal.

$$\underset{\textit{cis}\text{-cyclopenta-1, 2-diol}}{\text{C}_5\text{H}_8(OH)_2} + \underset{\text{Acetone}}{O=C(CH_3)_2} \longrightarrow \text{Cyclic ketal}$$

But,

$$\underset{\textit{Trans}\text{-cyclopenta -1, 2-diol}}{\text{C}_5\text{H}_8(OH)_2} + O=C(CH_3)_2 \longrightarrow \text{No reaction}$$

14 (*b*) In presence of Pd-catalyst, hydrogenation of only carbon-carbon double bond takes place. Thus, product '*A*' is cyclohexanone.

$$\text{Cyclohex-2-enone} \xrightarrow[\text{Pd/ Carbon, Ethanol}]{H_2\text{ (gas 1, atmosphere)}} \text{Cyclohexanone}$$

15 (*a*)

$$\underset{\text{Cyclopentanone}}{C_5H_8O} + \underset{\text{Methyl lithium}}{\overset{\ominus}{C}H_3\overset{\oplus}{Li}} \longrightarrow \underset{\text{Lithium cyclopentanonyl anion (Intermediate)}}{C_5H_7O^{\ominus}\overset{\oplus}{Li}} + CH_4$$

16 (c) Since, the compound X yields phenyl hydrazone and gives negative response to the iodoform test and Tollen's test, it must be a ketone and it should not contain $CH_3-\overset{O}{\overset{\|}{C}}-$ group. As among the given compounds, 3-pentanone fulfills all conditions thus, compound X having molecular formula $C_5H_{10}O$ is 3-pentanone.

$$\underset{\text{3-pentanone}}{CH_3-CH_2-\overset{O}{\overset{\|}{C}}-CH_2-CH_3}$$

17 (d) Reactivity of carbonyl compounds toward nucleophilic addition reactions depends on the presence of substituted group. Electron withdrawing ($-I, -M$) groups increases reactivity towards nucleophilic addition reactions. Since, $-NO_2$ is an electron withdrawing group, it withdraws electron density from the compound. ∴ The correct option is (d).

18 (a) (i) When aldehydes having no α-H atom, reacts with concentrated alkali, its one molecule is reduced to respective alcohol and other molecule is oxidised to sodium salt of respective acid. This reaction is called Cannizzaro reaction. It involves two successive additions, first OH^- and second H^-.

e.g. $$2HCHO \xrightarrow{\text{Conc. NaOH}} CH_3OH + HCO\overset{-}{O}\overset{+}{N}a$$

Here, no new C—C bond is formed.

(ii) When alkyl halide is treated with sodium metal in the presence of dry ether, it gives a hydrocarbon having double the number of carbon atoms that present in parent alkyl halide. This reaction is called Wurtz reaction, e.g.

$$2CH_3X + Na \xrightarrow{\text{Dry ether}} CH_3-CH_3 + 2NaX$$

i.e. it involves the formation of a new C—C bond.

(iii) Aldehydes having atleast one α-H atom, undergoes aldol condensation when treated with dilute alkali solution, e.g.

$$2CH_3CHO + \underset{\text{(Dilute)}}{NaOH} \longrightarrow \underset{\text{(Aldol)}}{CH_3CH(OH)CH_2CHO}$$

Here, also a new C—C bond is formed.

(iv) When benzene is treated with alkyl halide or acyl halide in the presence of anhydrous $AlCl_3$, an alkyl group or acyl group is introduced in the benzene ring. This reaction is called Friedel-Craft reaction, e.g.

$$C_6H_6 + CH_3X \xrightarrow[-HX]{\text{Anhyd. } AlCl_3} \underset{\text{Toluene}}{C_6H_5CH_3}$$

This reaction also involves formation of a new C—C bond.

(v) When phenol is treated with NaOH and further with carbon dioxide at a temperature of 140-200°C, the $-COO^-$ group is introduced in the benzene nucleus at *ortho* position (mainly) resulting in the formation of salicylic acid.

$$C_6H_5OH \xrightarrow{NaOH} C_6H_5ONa + CO_2 \xrightarrow[H^+]{140\text{–}200°C} \underset{\text{Major}}{o\text{-}HOC_6H_4COOH} + \underset{\text{Minor}}{p\text{-}HOC_6H_4COOH}$$

Here, also a new C—C bond is formed.

19 (d) $$Me-\!\equiv + NaNH_2 \xrightarrow{-NH_3} Me-\!\equiv\!C-Na \xrightarrow{CH_3I} Me-\!\equiv\!C-CH_3 \xrightarrow[\text{(addition of water)}]{HgSO_4,\ \text{Dil. } H_2SO_4}$$

$$Me-\overset{H}{\overset{|}{C}}=\overset{OH}{\overset{|}{C}}-CH_3 \xrightarrow{\text{Tautomerisation}} Me-CH_2-\underset{O}{\underset{\|}{C}}-CH_3 \text{ or } Me\diagdown\!\!\underset{O}{\underset{\|}{\wedge}}\!\!\diagup Me$$

(Here, Me means methyl group) Thus, the correct set of reagents is $NaNH_2/CH_3I$; $HgSO_4$/dil. H_2SO_4.

20 (c) Aldehydes lacking α-H atom, undergo Cannizzaro reaction, if treated with concentrated alkali (NaOH), i.e. one mole of the aldehyde is reduced to alcohol and other mole is oxidised to salt of acid. Thus, the given aldehyde (glyoxal) undergoes intramolecular Cannizaro reaction, i.e. its half part is oxidised and half is reduced.

$$\begin{array}{c}CHO\\|\\CHO\end{array} \xrightarrow{\text{(i) NaOH}} \begin{array}{c}CH_2OH\\|\\CO\overset{-}{O}\overset{+}{N}a\end{array} \xrightarrow{\text{(ii) }H^+} \begin{array}{c}CH_2OH\\|\\CO_2H\end{array}$$

21 (a) In Wittig reaction, an alkene is formed by the reaction of an aldehyde or ketone *via* generation of a phosphonium intermediate.

$$\text{Cyclopentyl}(H)\overset{+}{P}Ph_3 \xrightarrow{Bu^-} \text{Cyclopentylidene}=\overset{+}{P}Ph_3\ (\text{ylide}) \xrightarrow{CH_2=O} \text{Spiro oxaphosphetane } (PPh_3, O) \longrightarrow \text{Cyclopentylidene}=CH_2 + O=PPh_3$$

Hence, the intermediate J is .

$$\underset{(J)}{\text{Spiro oxaphosphetane } (PPh_3, O)}$$

22 (b) Cannizzaro reaction cannot be used to increase the number of carbon atoms in an organic compound.

- Reaction of ethanal with **Grignard reagent** is given below:

$$\overset{H_3C}{\underset{H}{}}\!\!>C=O + CH_3MgBr \longrightarrow H_3C-\overset{\overset{-}{O}\overset{+}{M}gBr}{\overset{|}{CH}}-CH_3 \xrightarrow{H_2O} H_3C-\overset{OH}{\overset{|}{CH}}-CH_3$$

Here, number of carbon atoms in the product are increased.

- **Cannizzaro's reaction**

$$HCHO + HCHO \xrightarrow{OH^-} CH_2OH + HCO\overset{\ominus}{O}\overset{\oplus}{K}$$

In this reaction, number of carbon atoms in product molecules are same as that in reactant. So, it cannot be used to increase the number of carbon atoms in an organic compound.

- **Aldol condensation**

$$H_3C{-}CHO + CH_3CHO \xrightarrow{OH^-} CH_3{-}\underset{}{\overset{OH}{\overset{|}{C}H}}{-}CH_2{-}CHO$$

$$\xrightarrow[-H_2O]{\Delta} H_3C{-}CH{=}CH{-}CHO$$

Again, number of carbon atoms in the products are increased. So, it is also not the correct option.

23 (*b*) Tishchenko reaction is a disproportionation reaction that allows the preparation of esters from two equivalents of an aldehyde. In actual, aldehydes with or without α-hydrogens can be made to undergo Cannizzaro reaction on treatment with aluminium alkoxide. However, under these conditions, the alcohol and acid produced combine together to form esters. Thus, Tishchenko reaction is a modified form of Cannizzaro reaction.

$$\underset{(B)}{H_3C{-}CHO + H_3C{-}CHO} \xrightarrow{Al(OR)_3} \underset{\text{Acid}}{CH_3COOH} + \underset{\text{Alcohol}}{CH_3CH_2OH}$$

$$\longrightarrow \underset{\text{Ester }(A)}{CH_3{-}\overset{O}{\overset{||}{C}}{-}OCH_2CH_3} + H_2O$$

So, here the compound A is $CH_3COOC_2H_5$ and compound B is CH_3CHO.

Other given reaction is given as below:

$$CH_3COC_2H_5 \xrightarrow[\text{(Per acid)}]{C_6H_5CO_3H} \underset{(A)}{CH_3{-}\overset{O}{\overset{||}{C}}{-}O{-}C_2H_5}$$

24 (*d*) Schiff's reagent is an aqueous solution of pink coloured rosaniline hydrochloride which has been decolourised by passing SO_2. When aldehydes are treated with decolourised solution of Schiff's reagent, its pink colour is restored.

25 (*b*) The substrate containing C=C double bond on ozonolysis using O_3 followed by reductive cleavage using Zn/H_2O produces two carbonyl compounds.

Carbonyl compound obtained after reductive ozonolysis of (b), (c) and (d) are as follows

(b) $C_6H_5{-}CH{=}CH_2 \xrightarrow[Zn/H_2O]{O_3} \underset{\text{Benzaldehyde}}{C_6H_5{-}\overset{H}{\overset{|}{C}}{=}O} + \underset{\text{Formaldehyde}}{O{=}C(H)H}$

(c) $C_6H_5{-}CH{=}CH{-}CH_3 \xrightarrow[Zn/H_2O]{O_3} C_6H_5{-}\overset{H}{\overset{|}{C}}{=}O + \underset{\text{Acetaldehyde}}{CH_3CHO}$

(d) $C_6H_5{-}CH{=}C(CH_3)CH_3 \xrightarrow[Zn/H_2O]{O_3} C_6H_5{-}CHO + \underset{\text{Acetone}}{CH_3{-}\overset{O}{\overset{||}{C}}{-}CH_3}$

In each case, benzaldehyde is produced as one of the product but on the other hand formaldehyde, acetaldehyde and acetone are produced as other products. Thus, in order to select the correct choice, the concept of Cannizzaro reaction (disproportionation reaction) is applied. This reaction is a characteristic reaction of carbonyl compounds having absence of α-hydrogen atom. Hence, correct substrate is $C_6H_5{-}CH{=}CH_2$ as both products are devoid of α-H-atom and easily undergoes Cannizzaro reaction easily.

Chemical reaction occurring in the compound can be sequentially written as

$$\underset{X}{C_6H_5{-}CH{=}CH_2} \xrightarrow[H_2O/Zn]{O_3} \underset{Y}{C_6H_5{-}\overset{H}{C}{=}O} + \underset{Z}{O{=}C(H)H}$$

In Etard reaction, toluene is oxidised to benzaldehyde with a solution of chromyl chloride in CS_2 or CCl_4 as

$$C_6H_5{-}CH_3 \xrightarrow[H_3O^+]{CrO_2Cl_2/CS_2} \underset{Y}{C_6H_5{-}CHO}$$

Cannizzaro reaction shown by HCHO (Z) can be represented as

$$2\,\underset{H}{\overset{H}{>}}C{=}O \xrightarrow{\text{Conc. NaOH}} CH_3OH + HCOO^-Na^+$$

26 (*c*) As the product formed in a given series is alkenone, i.e. aldol condensation product, this suggests that R would be a ketone which undergoes aldol condensation. The end product contains total six C-atoms thus, R would be a ketone of three carbon atoms i.e. acetone (propanone).

This propanone is produced from ethane nitrile through Grignard reagent. Thus, ethane nitrile (P) on reaction with CH_3MgBr followed by hydrolysis produced acetone R which on reaction with dil.NaOH undergo aldol condensation to produce 4-methylpent-3-ene-2-one as shown below.

$$\underset{\text{Ethane nitrile }(P)}{CH_3{-}C{\equiv}N} \xrightarrow{CH_3MgBr} (H_3C)(H_3C)C{=}NMgBr$$

$$\xrightarrow{H_3O^+} \left[(H_3C)(H_3C)C{=}NH + MgBr(OH)\right]$$

$$\xrightarrow{H_3O^+} (H_3C)(H_3C)C{=}O + NH_3$$

$$(H_3C)(H_3C)C{=}O + CH_3{-}\overset{O}{\overset{||}{C}}{-}CH_3 \xrightarrow[\text{Aldol condensation}]{\text{Dil. NaOH}}$$

$$\underset{\text{(ketol)}}{CH_3{-}\overset{OH}{\overset{|}{\underset{CH_3}{\underset{|}{C}}}}{-}CH_2{-}\overset{O}{\overset{||}{C}}{-}CH_3} \xrightarrow[H^+]{\Delta} \underset{\text{4-methylpent-3-en-2-one}}{CH_3{-}\underset{CH_3}{\underset{|}{C}}{=}CH{-}\overset{O}{\overset{||}{C}}{-}CH_3}$$

27 (*d*) Ketones always produce secondary or tertiary alcohols on reduction. Thus, propan-2-one does not give a primary alcohol on reduction whereas all the other compounds produce primary alcohols on reduction.

(a) $CH_3CH_2CHO \xrightarrow[2[H]]{LiAlH_4} CH_3CH_2CH_2OH$
Propanal → Propanol (1°alcohol)

(b) $CH_3CH_2COOH \xrightarrow[4[H]]{LiAlH_4} CH_3CH_2CH_2OH$
(Propanoic acid) → Propanol (1°alcohol)

(c) $CH_3CH_2COOCH_3 \xrightarrow{LiAlH_4} CH_3CH_2CH_2OH + CH_3OH$
Methyl propanoate → (Propanol) 1° alcohol + (Methanol 1° alcohol)

(d) $CH_3-\underset{\underset{O}{\|}}{C}-CH_3 \xrightarrow{LiAlH_4} CH_3\underset{\underset{OH}{|}}{CH}CH_3$
Propan-2-one → Propan-2-ol (2° alcohol)

28 (*a*) $CO(g) + H_2(g) \xrightarrow{[X]} HCHO(g)$

Here, *X* is copper (Cu) which acts as a good reductant and gives formaldehyde in this reaction. The reaction infact occurs in the following manner.

$CO(g) + H_2(g) \longrightarrow CH_3OH \xrightarrow{Cu(X)} HCHO(g)$

29 (*d*) Reaction (d) cannot be used to prepare benzaldehyde.

(d) $C_6H_5COOH + Zn/Hg \xrightarrow{Conc.\ HCl} C_6H_5COCl + H_2O$

Other reactions are given below:

(a) $C_6H_5CH_3 \xrightarrow[CS_2]{2CrO_2Cl_2} C_6H_5CH(OCrOHCl_2)_2 \xrightarrow{H_3O^+} C_6H_5CHO$
Brown (addition product) → Benzaldehyde

This reaction is known as **Etard reaction**.

(b) $C_6H_5COCl \xrightarrow[(Boiling\ xylene)]{Pd/BaSO_4/H_2} C_6H_5CHO + HCl$

This reaction is known as **Rosenmund reduction**.

(c) $C_6H_6 + CO + HCl \xrightarrow{Anhy.\ AlCl_3} C_6H_5CHO + HCl$

This reaction is known as **Gattermann-Koch** aldehyde synthesis.

30 (*d*) Aldehydes and ketones can be distinguished by Fehling's reagent [alkaline solution of $CuSO_4$ containing Rochelle salt (sodium potassium tartarate), mild oxidising agent].

$$\text{Aldehydes} \xrightarrow{\text{Fehling reagent}} \text{Red-brown ppt.}$$

$$\text{Ketones} \xrightarrow{\text{Fehling reagent}} \text{No reaction}$$

Besides this, Tollen's reagent and Benedict's reagent can also be used as they give positive test with aldehydes but not with ketones.

31 (*d*) Iodoform test is given by those compounds which contains $CH_3-\underset{\underset{O}{\|}}{C}-$ group or $CH_3-\underset{\underset{OH}{|}}{CH}$ group while Fehling's test is given by only aldehydic group. Thus, iodoform test and Fehling's test are performed by only ethanal.

$CH_3CHO + 2Cu^{2+} + 5OH^- \xrightarrow[dest]{fehling's} CH_3COO^- + 3H_2O + Cu_2O$
Ethanal, Fehling's solution → Acetate ion, Cuprous oxide (red ppt.)

$CH_3CHO \xrightarrow{NaOH} H-\overset{\overset{O}{\|}}{C}-\overset{-}{O}\overset{+}{Na} + CHI_3\downarrow$

32 (*c*) When benzaldehyde is treated with 50% alkali, it undergoes oxidation to give an acid salt as well as reduction to give an alcohol. This reaction is called Cannizzaro's reaction.

$m\text{-}ClC_6H_4CHO \xrightarrow{50\%\ KOH} m\text{-}ClC_6H_4CH_2OH + m\text{-}ClC_6H_4COO^-$

33 (*a*) Acid chloride reacts with H_2 in the presence of $Pd/BaSO_4$ to yield aldehyde. This reaction is called **Rosenmund's reduction**.

$C_6H_5COCl \xrightarrow[Pd\text{-}BaSO_4]{H_2} C_6H_5CHO + HCl$
Benzoyl chloride → Benzaldehyde

34 (*a*) 2-methylpropanal contains one α-H-atom. Hence, it undergoes aldol condensation. It also undergoes Cannizzaro's reaction. Aldol reaction proceeds *via* formation of carbanion. In 2-methylpropanal, due to + *I*-effect of the two alkyl groups attached to alpha-carbon, the carbanion of 2-methylpropanal is not stable. Thus, it prefers to undergo nucleophilic attack by OH^- ion at the aldehyde leading to the formation of Cannizzaro products.

$$CH_3-\underset{\underset{CH_3}{|}}{\overset{\overset{H}{|}}{C}}-CHO + H-\underset{\underset{CH_3}{|}}{\overset{\overset{CH_3}{|}}{C}}-CHO \xrightarrow{Dil.\ NaOH} CH_3-\underset{\underset{CH_3}{|}}{CH}-\overset{\overset{OH}{|}}{CH}-\underset{\underset{CH_3}{|}}{\overset{\overset{CH_3}{|}}{C}}-CHO$$
(Aldol)

$2(CH_3)_2CH\cdot CHO \xrightarrow[473\ K]{Conc.\ NaOH} (CH_3)_2CHCO\overset{-}{O}\overset{+}{Na} + (CH_3)_2CHCH_2OH$

35 (*c*) $H-CH_2-\overset{+}{N}(=O)-O^- \xrightarrow[\text{Enolisation}]{OH^-} H-CH=\overset{+}{N}(-O^-)-O^-$ (Enolate ion)

CH_3COCH_3 (Acetone) $+ \overset{-}{C}H_2-\overset{+}{N}(=O)O^- \longrightarrow CH_3-C(O^-)(CH_3)-CH_2-NO_2$

$\xrightarrow{H^+} CH_3-C(OH)(CH_3)-CH_2-NO_2$

$\xrightarrow[\text{Pyridine}\ (-H_2O)]{Ac_2O} CH_3-\underset{\underset{CH_3}{|}}{C}=CH-NO_2$

Hence, the product formed when acetone reacts with nitromethane in the presence of a base is

$$(H_3C)_2C=CHNO_2$$

36 (*b*) Clemmensen's reduction is the reduction of carbonyl group into alkane in the presence of zinc amalgam and HCl.

$$\underset{\text{Carbonyl compound}}{>C=O} + 4[H] \xrightarrow{\text{Zn-Hg / conc. HCl}} \underset{\text{Alkane}}{>CH_2} + H_2O$$

37 (*d*) In Cannizzaro's reaction, aldehydes which have no α-hydrogen atom undergo disproportionation in the presence of strong base to form equal amounts of corresponding alcohol and salt of carboxylic acid.

$$\underset{(d)}{2CH_3CHO+NaOH} \xrightarrow[\text{condensation (due to α-atom)}]{\text{Aldol}} \underset{\text{Aldol}}{CH_3-\overset{\overset{OH}{|}}{CH}-CH_2-CHO}$$

Cannizzaro reaction:

$$\underset{(a)}{2CCl_3CHO}+NaOH \rightarrow CCl_3CO\overset{-}{O}\overset{+}{N}a+CCl_3CH_2OH$$

$$\underset{(b)}{2C_6H_5CHO}+NaOH \rightarrow C_6H_5CO\overset{-}{O}\overset{+}{N}a+C_6H_5CH_2OH$$

$$\underset{(c)}{2HCHO}+NaOH \rightarrow HCO\overset{-}{O}\overset{+}{N}a+CH_3OH$$

Acetaldehyde due to the presence of 3α-H-atoms does not perform this reaction. It undergoes aldol condensation.

38 (*a*) $\underset{\text{Acetaldehyde}}{2CH_3CHO} \xrightarrow{Al(OC_2H_5)_3} \underset{\text{Ethyl acetate}}{CH_3COOCH_2CH_3}$

39 (*a*)

(a) $C_6H_5COCH_3$ (Acetophenone) (b) CH_3COCH_3 (Acetone)

(c) o-HOC_6H_4COOH (Salicylic acid) (d) C_6H_5CHO (Benzaldehyde)

Since, the given compound *A* burns with sooty flame, thus, it must be aromatic compound. Again when it reacts with Brady's reagent (2,4- dinitrophenyl hydrazine solution), it yields orange precipitate but gives no precipitate or silver mirror with Tollen's reagent. Therefore, *A* must be an aromatic ketone.

Hence, *A* is acetophenone.

40 (*b*) CH_3CH_2CHO and CH_3COCH_3 can be distinguished by sodium hypoiodide, i.e. iodoform reaction as CH_3COCH_3 contains $CH_3CO—$ group.

CH_3COCH_3 gives yellow precipitate of iodoform when heated with NaOI whereas CH_3CH_2CHO does not give iodoform.

41 (*d*) $CH_3CONHCH_3$ is an amide. Aldehydes and ketones give semicarbazone and oxime, whereas amides do not.

42 (*b*) Aldehydes and ketones containing $CH_3—CO$ group on treatment with an excess of I_2 in the presence of NaOH produce a haloform [iodoform].

$$CH_3—CHO + 3I_2 \xrightarrow{NaOH} CI_3CHO + 3HI$$

$$\xrightarrow{NaOH} \underset{\text{(Iodoform yellow ppt.)}}{CHI_3\downarrow} + HCOONa$$

$$CH_3COCH_3 + 3I_2 \xrightarrow{NaOH} CI_3COCH_3 + 3HI$$

$$\xrightarrow{NaOH} CHI_3\downarrow + CH_3COONa$$

43 (*a*) Calcium formate and calcium acetate gives aldehyde on dry distillation.

$$(CH_3COO)_2Ca + (HCOO)_2Ca \xrightarrow{\Delta} 2CH_3—\overset{\overset{O}{||}}{C}—H + 2CaCO_3$$

44 (*a*) $\underset{\text{Acetone}}{(H_3C)_2C=O} + \underset{\text{Hydrazine}}{NH_2NH_2} \xrightarrow{-H_2O} (H_3C)_2C=N\cdot NH_2$

$$\xrightarrow{\text{KOH /ethylene glycol}} \underset{\text{Propane}}{CH_3CH_2CH_3} + N_2$$

The reaction is known as Wolff-Kishner reduction.

Hofmann reaction is given by amides to yield amines.Grignard reaction is used to increase the number of C-atoms and to yield alcohols. $LiAlH_4$ reduces aldehydes or ketones into alcohols.

45 (*a*) When aldehydes are treated with Tollen's reagent (ammoniacal solution of silver nitrate), these are oxidised to carboxylate ion while Tollen's reagent reduces to metallic silver which gives a shiny appearence of silver mirror.

$$\underset{\text{(Aldehyde)}}{RCHO} + \underset{\text{Tollen's reagent}}{2[Ag(NH_3)_2]^+} + 3OH^- \xrightarrow{\Delta}$$

$$\underset{\text{Carboxylate ion}}{RCOO^-} + \underset{\text{Silver mirror}}{2Ag\downarrow} + 4NH_3 + 2H_2O$$

46 (*d*) $NaBH_4$ does not reduce olefin (alkene) double bond, it only reduces C=O group. Thus, the reagent (X) is $NaBH_4$.

47 (*b*) (CH₃)₂CH–CO–CH₃ $\xrightarrow[\text{(Nucleophilic addition reaction)}]{\text{(i) } CH_3NH_2}$ (CH₃)₂CH–C(=NCH₃)–CH₃ (Imine) $\xrightarrow[\text{(iii) } H_2O]{\text{(ii) } LiAlH_4}$ (CH₃)₂CH–CH(NHCH₃)–CH₃

48 (*c*) With $NaOH / I_2$, $NaHSO_3$ and $NH_2 \cdot NH_2$ (hydrazine), aldehydes as well as ketones can react while with $AgNO_3 / NH_4OH$, (i.e. ammoniacal silver nitrate or Tollen's reagent) only aldehydes react. Thus, $AgNO_3 / NH_4OH$ is used to distinguish aldehydes and ketones.

$$RCHO + 2[Ag(NH_3)_2]^+ + 3OH^- \xrightarrow{\Delta} RCOO^- + 2Ag\downarrow + 4NH_3 + 2H_2O$$

49 (*a*)

$$C_6H_5COC_6H_5 \text{ (Benzophenone)} + \underset{\text{Alkali}}{KOH} \xrightarrow{\text{Fuse}} \underset{\text{Benzene}}{C_6H_6} + \underset{\text{Potassium benzoate}}{C_6H_5COO^-K^+}$$

50 (*c*) Aldehydes and ketones with a methyl or methylene group adjacent to C=O group, on oxidation with SeO_2 give α-dicarbonyl compounds.

Thus, SeO_2 converts —CH_2 group adjacent to the carbonyl group into C=O group.

$$\underset{\text{Acetaldehyde}}{CH_3-CHO} \xrightarrow{SeO_2} \underset{\text{Glyoxal}}{CHO-CHO} + Se + H_2O$$

51 (*c*)

$$\underset{\text{Acetaldehyde}}{CH_3CHO} + \xrightarrow[-3HCl]{Cl_2} \underset{\text{Chloral}}{CCl_3CHO} \xrightarrow[\text{hydrolysis}]{Ca(OH)_2} \underset{\underset{(X)}{\text{Chloroform}}}{CHCl_3} + HCO\overset{-}{O}\overset{+}{Na}$$

$$\underset{(X)}{CHCl_3} + C_6H_5NH_2 \xrightarrow{\text{Alc. KOH}} \underset{\underset{(Y)}{\text{Phenyl isocyanide}}}{C_6H_5NC}$$

52 (*b*) Ethyl methyl ketone is an unsymmetric ketone, so two different acids (in the form of calcium salts) are used. The structure of ethyl methyl ketone is $C_2H_5COCH_3$. The structure shows the presence of four carbon atoms, thus the calcium salts must be of acetic acid and propionic acid to form $C_2H_5COCH_3$.

$$(C_2H_5COO)_2Ca + (CH_3COO)_2Ca \xrightarrow{\text{Distill}} 2C_2H_5COCH_3 + 2CaCO_3$$

53 (*b*) Fehling solution *A* is $CuSO_4$ solution and Fehling solution *B* is alkaline solution of sodium potassium tartarate.

54 (*b*) This is an example of Wolff-Kishner reduction (CO-group reduces to CH_2 group).

$$H_3C-CO-CH_2CH_3 \xrightarrow[KOH]{N_2H_4} CH_3CH_2CH_2CH_3$$

55 (*d*) In Cannizzaro reaction, an aldehyde or ketone, that does not contain α-H, undergoes disproportionation to form a salt of carboxylic acid and an alcohol.

$$HCHO + HCHO \xrightarrow[\text{Cannizzaro reaction}]{OH^-} CH_3OH + HCOOH$$

(Oxidation → HCOOH; Reduction → CH_3OH)

56 (*c*) When acetone is saturated with HCl gas, 2 molecules of acetone combine with the elimination of one molecule of water to form mesityl oxide.

$$\underset{\text{Acetone}}{(H_3C)_2C=O} + \underset{\text{Acetone}}{H_2CHCOCH_3} \xrightarrow[-H_2O]{HCl} \underset{\underset{[4\text{-methylpent-3-en-2-one}]}{\text{Mesityl oxide}}}{(H_3C)_2C=CH-CO-CH_3}$$

Note Small amounts of phorone [2,6-dimethylhepta-2,5-dien-4-one] is also obtained by the further reaction of mesityloxide with another molecule of acetone.

$$(H_3C)_2C=CH-CO-CH\,H_2 + O=C(CH_3)_2 \xrightarrow[-H_2O]{HCl} \underset{\text{Phorone}}{(H_3C)_2C=CH-CO-CH=C(CH_3)_2}$$

57 (*a*) Keto-enol tautomerism is shown by those ketones which possesses α-hydrogen atoms. Thus, compound (a) $C_6H_5COC_6H_5$ does not show this type of tautomerism as it has no α-H-atom.

58 (*d*)

$$\underset{\text{But-2-ene}}{CH_3-CH=CH-CH_3} \xrightarrow[\text{Ozonolysis}]{\text{(i) } O_3} \underset{\text{Ozonide}}{CH_3-CH(-O-)(O-O)CH-CH_3} \xrightarrow[\text{Zn dust}]{\text{(ii) } H_2O} \underset{\text{Ethanal}}{2CH_3-CHO}$$

59 (*c*) Carbonyl group is polar ($\overset{\delta+}{C} = \overset{\delta-}{O}$) because of the presence of partial positive charge at carbon and partial negative charge at oxygen. Presence of electron releasing substituent increases the electron density at carbon, thus, reduces the magnitude of positive charge and hence, the polar nature. Thus, it can be said that as the number of alkyl group or size of alkyl group increases, reactivity decreases. Thus, the order of reactivity is

$$\underset{(IV)}{\text{Butanone}} < \underset{(III)}{\text{Propanone}} < \underset{(II)}{\text{Propanal}} < \underset{(I)}{\text{Ethanal}}$$

(aldehydes are more reactive as compared to ketones.)

60 (*b*) When acetaldehyde is treated with aqueous sodium hydroxide solution, it undergoes aldol condensation (because of the presence of α-H atom) as,

$$CH_3CHO + HCH_2CHO \xrightarrow{\text{Dil. NaOH}} \underset{\underset{\text{(shows optical isomerism)}}{\text{Aldol}}}{CH_3\overset{*}{C}H(OH)CH_2CHO}$$

Since, the aldol formed contains one asymmetric carbon atom, it will show optical isomerism.

61 (*b*) Aldehydes and ketones containing α-hydrogen atom undergo self condensation in the presence of a dilute alkali to form β-hydroxy aldehyde or β-hydroxy ketone. This reaction is called aldol condensation.

$$CH_3-\overset{O}{\overset{\|}{C}}(CH_3) + H-CH_2-\overset{O}{\overset{\|}{C}}-CH_3 \xrightarrow{Ba(OH)_2}$$

$$\overset{\ominus}{C}H_2-\overset{O}{\overset{\|}{C}}-CH_3 + CH_3-\overset{O}{\overset{\|}{C}}-CH_3 \xrightarrow{H^+}$$

$$CH_3-\underset{CH_3}{\overset{OH}{C}}-CH_2-\overset{O}{\overset{\|}{C}}-CH_3$$

β-hydroxy ketone
(4-hydroxy-4-methyl pentan-2-one)

62 (*b*) Addition of HCN to a carbonyl compound is a nucleophilic addition reaction. $-NO_2$ group being electron withdrawing increases the polarity (or electron deficiency) of carbonyl carbon and thus, makes the $C=O$ group of *p*-nitrobenzaldehyde more reactive towards HCN.

63 (*c*) Benzaldehyde reacts with ammonia to form a complex product called hydrobenzamide.

$$\underset{\text{Benzaldehyde}}{C_6H_5CH{=}O} + \underset{\text{Ammonia}}{H_2NH} + \underset{\text{Benzaldehyde}}{O{=}CHC_6H_5}$$

$$\downarrow$$

$$\underset{\text{Hydrobenzamide}}{\begin{matrix} C_6H_5CH=N \\ C_6H_5CH=N \end{matrix} \rangle CHC_6H_5} + 3H_2O$$

64 (*a*) 2-butenal contains γ-H-atoms and the conjugate base obtained after the removal of γ-H-atom, is stabilised by resonance. Hence, 2-butenal is sufficiently acidic. However, it lacks enolisable H-atom, α to carbonyl group.

$$\overset{\gamma}{H}-CH_2-\overset{\beta}{HC}=\overset{\alpha}{C}H-CHO \underset{}{\overset{-H^+}{\rightleftharpoons}} \bar{C}H_2-CH=CHCHO$$

$$[CH_2=CH-CH=\overset{O^-}{C}-H \longleftrightarrow CH_2=CH-\bar{C}H-\overset{O}{\overset{\|}{C}}-H]$$

65 (*b*) If D_2O (heavy water) is taken instead of H_2O, as solvent, the reaction takes place in the following manner.

$$R-\underset{H}{C}=O \xrightarrow[\text{in } D_2O]{OD^-} R-\underset{H}{\overset{OD}{C}}-O^-$$

$$\xrightarrow[\text{(Slow)}]{R-\overset{H}{C}=O} R-\overset{OD}{C}=O + R-\underset{H}{\overset{H}{C}}-O^- \rightarrow RCOO^- + RCH_2OD$$

66 (*a*) HCl is a strong inorganic acid, hence it does not react with ethanal whereas, with other given reagents, it reacts in the following manner.

$$\underset{\text{Ethanal}}{CH_3CHO} + Cl_2 \longrightarrow \underset{\text{Chloral}}{CCl_3CHO}$$

$$CH_3CHO + PCl_5 \longrightarrow CH_3CHCl_2 + POCl_3$$

$$CH_3CHO + NaHSO_3 \longrightarrow CH_3CH\langle^{OH}_{SO_3Na}$$

67 (*b*) The reaction is called Cannizzaro reaction and involves oxidation and reduction of same compound.

68 (*a*) 2, 2-dichloropentane gives pentan-2-one and not pentan-3-one

$$CH_3CH_2CH_2\underset{Cl}{\overset{Cl}{C}}-CH_3 \xrightarrow{\text{Hydrolysis}} CH_3CH_2CH_2\underset{OH}{\overset{OH}{C}}-CH_3$$

$$\xrightarrow{-H_2O} \underset{\text{Pentan-2-one}}{CH_3CH_2CH_2\underset{O}{\underset{\|}{C}}-CH_3}$$

69 (*a*) The aldehydes which do not contain α-hydrogen atom, give Cannizzaro's reaction. 2,2-dimethylpropanal does not contain any α-hydrogen atom and hence, undergoes Cannizzaro's reaction.

70 (*b*) During Cannizzaro reaction, hydride transfer takes place from enolate ion to carbonyl group (or carbonyl carbon). This step is the slowest-step of the reaction and hence, it is the rate determining step.

71 (*a*) The complete reaction can be represented as

$$H_3C\text{-cyclopentyl-}\overset{O}{\overset{\|}{C}}-CH_3 \xrightarrow[\text{(Insertion of oxygen)}]{\text{(i) } CF_3COOH} H_3C\text{-cyclopentyl-}O-\overset{}{\underset{O}{\underset{\|}{C}}}-CH_3$$

$$\xrightarrow[\text{(ii) NaOH}]{\text{Hydrolysis}} H_3C\text{-cyclopentyl-}OH + CH_3CO\overset{-}{O}\overset{+}{Na}$$

Hence, the final product would be $CH_3CO\overset{-}{O}\overset{+}{N}a$.

72 (*d*)

$$\text{2-(3-aminopropyl)cyclohexanone} \xrightarrow[(-H_2O)]{\text{(i) Heat, cyclisation}} \underset{\text{(Imine)}}{\text{bicyclic imine}} \xrightarrow[\text{Reduction of imine}]{\text{(ii) } NaBH_4} \text{decahydroquinoline (N–H)}$$

73 (*a*) The compound must be ketone, $CH_3-\overset{O}{\overset{\|}{C}}-CH_3$ since, it does not give silver mirror with Tollen's reagent but gives an oxime with hydroxylamine. Ketones containing acetyl group (CH_3CO) gives iodoform test.

74 (*d*) Due to the presence of active keto-methyl group, or CH_3CO, 2-pentanone will respond to iodoform test, but 3-pentanone does not.

75 (*c*) Methyl ketones when treated with $NaOH/I_2/H^+$ gives iodoform and an acid (with one carbon less than the parent ketone).

$$\underset{\text{Butan-2-one (methyl ketone)}}{CH_3CH_2-\overset{O}{\overset{\|}{C}}-CH_3} + NaOH + I_2 \xrightarrow[-H_2O]{-NaI}$$

$$\underset{\text{(Yellow ppt.)}}{CHI_3\downarrow} + CH_3CH_2CO\overset{-}{O}\overset{+}{N}a \xrightarrow{H^+} \underset{\text{Propanoic acid}}{CH_3CH_2COOH}$$

76 (*b*) When aldehydes are added with saturated solution of sodium bisulphite with constant stirring, a crystalline solid derivative is observed, but due to high nucleophilic nature of sodium bisulphite, ketones do not give this test. Only aliphatic methyl ketones form addition product with sodium bisulphite. Thus, $C_6H_5COCH_3$ will not form bisulphite addition product.

77 (*d*) Relative reactivity of aldehydes and ketones depend upon (i) inductive effect (ii) steric effect.

Large number of alkyl groups on carbonyl carbon atom decreases their reactivity due to both +*I*-effect (these groups decreases polarity of carbonyl group) and steric effect. As ketones possess large number of alkyl groups, therefore they are less reactive than aldehydes.

Aromatic aldehydes are less reactive than corresponding aliphatic aldehydes and ketones because of the resonance effect (+*R*-effect) of the benzene ring which increases electron density on carbonyl carbon, thereby, repelling nucleophiles and hence, reactivity decreases.

Hence, among the given, acetaldehyde is the most reactive compound.

78 (*b*) Among these only CH_3CH_2OH undergoes H-bonding. So, it will have the highest boiling point. In the case of remaining compounds, CH_3COCH_3 has slightly higher boiling point, than H_3CCHO and $H_3CCH_2CH_3$. This is due to higher molecular weight of CH_3OCH_3 than $CH_3CH_2CH_3$ and CH_3CHO. CH_3CHO has higher boiling point than alkane due to appreciable intermolecular attraction (dipole-dipole interaction). Thus, the correct order is

$CH_3CH_2CH_3 < CH_3CHO < CH_3OCH_3 < CH_3CH_2OH$

79 (*c*) The industrial method of preparation of acetaldehyde is wacker process.

Reaction involved is as follows:

$$H_2C=CH_2 + PdCl_2 + H_2O \xrightarrow[\text{air or } O_2]{CuCl_2} H_3CCHO + Pd + 2HCl$$

80 (*d*) Crotonaldehyde is produced by the aldol condensation of acetaldehyde. Aldol condensation is nucleophilic addition-elimination reaction.

$$\underset{\text{Acetaldehyde}}{CH_3-\overset{H}{\overset{|}{C}}{}^{\delta+}=O^{\delta-}} + \underset{\text{Acetaldehyde}}{H-\overset{H}{\overset{|}{\underset{H}{\underset{|}{C}}}}-CHO} \xrightarrow[\text{(nucleophilic addition)}]{\text{Dil. NaOH}}$$

$$\underset{\text{Aldol}}{CH_3-\overset{H}{\overset{|}{\underset{OH}{\underset{|}{C}}}}-\overset{H}{\overset{|}{\underset{H}{\underset{|}{C}}}}-CHO} \xrightarrow[\substack{-H_2O\\ \text{(elimination)}}]{\Delta} \underset{\text{Crotonaldehyde}}{CH_3CH=CHCHO}$$

81 (*d*) In aldol condensation, two or more molecules of same or different carbonyl compounds containing α-H-atom unite together in presence of dil. NaOH, $Ba(OH)_2$, etc., to form a condensation product called aldol. This reaction may occur between (i) same or different aldehydes (ii) an aldehyde and ketone and (iii) same or different ketones.

82 (*c*) Aldehydes having no α-H atom, on heating with conc. alkali undergo disproportionation, known as Cannizzaro reaction. Ketones do not give this reaction.

Compounds containing CH_3CO- group or

$CH_3-\overset{|}{C}H-OH$ group give positive iodoform test. Among the given options, only option (c) i.e. HCHO and $CH_3CH_2CH_2COCH_3$ respond to the respective reactions.

83 (*a*) The following compounds are obtained when a mixture of calcium formate and calcium acetate are subjected to dry distillation.

$$(HCOO)_2Ca + (CH_3COO)_2Ca \xrightarrow{\Delta}$$

$$\underset{\text{Ethanal}}{2CH_3CHO} + 2CaCO_3 + \underset{\text{Propanone}}{CH_3COCH_3} + \underset{\text{Methanal}}{HCHO}$$

Thus, only propanal is not formed.

84 (*d*) Aldehydes are obtained by alkaline hydrolysis of those *geminal* dihalides in which the halogens are attached to the terminal carbon. Thus, reaction of 1,1-dichloroethane with NaOH gives acetaldehyde.

$$\underset{\text{1,1-dichloroethane}}{CH_3-\overset{Cl}{\overset{|}{C}}H-Cl} \xrightarrow{NaOH} \underset{\text{Unstable}}{CH_3-\overset{OH}{\overset{|}{C}}H-OH} \xrightarrow{-H_2O} \underset{\text{Acetaldehyde}}{CH_3-CHO}$$

85 (*d*)

$$R-\underset{O}{\underset{\|}{C}}-R' \xrightarrow[KCN]{HCN} \underset{\substack{(A)\\ \text{Cyanohydrin}}}{R-\overset{OH}{\overset{|}{\underset{CN}{\underset{|}{C}}}}-R'} \xrightarrow{LiAlH_4(B)} R-\overset{OH}{\overset{|}{\underset{CH_2NH_2}{\underset{|}{C}}}}-R'$$

86 (*a*) Aldehydes or ketones with α-H-atoms, in presence of dilute base, undergoes aldol condensation to give β-hydroxy aldehyde or β-hydroxy ketone. On heating, aldol eliminates water molecule to form α, β-unsaturated compound.

$$C_6H_5-\overset{O}{\overset{\|}{C}}-CH_3 + HCH_2-\overset{O}{\overset{\|}{C}}-C_6H_5$$

Acetophenone

$$\xrightarrow[\text{base}]{C_2H_5ONa} C_6H_5-\overset{OH}{\overset{|}{\underset{CH_3}{\underset{|}{C}}}}-CH_2-\underset{O}{\underset{\|}{C}}-C_6H_5 \xrightarrow{-H_2O} C_6H_5-\underset{CH_3}{\underset{|}{C}}=CH-\underset{O}{\underset{\|}{C}}-C_6H_5$$

87 (*c*) The carbon which is more electrophilic in nature, loses an α-H with a base more readily. Among the given compounds, carbonyl carbon (C=O), i.e. ketone's carbon is more electrophilic in nature, thus it loses an α-H with a base. E.g. in aldol condensation reaction, α-hydrogen atom of aldehyde or ketone is abstracted by a strong base.

$$OH^- + H-CH_2-\overset{O}{\overset{\|}{C}}-CH_3 \underset{-H_2O}{\rightleftharpoons} \left[\ddot{C}H_2-\overset{O}{\overset{\|}{C}}-CH_3 \longleftrightarrow CH_2=\overset{O^-}{\overset{|}{C}}-CH_3\right]$$

$$CH_3-\overset{O^{\delta-}}{\overset{\|}{\underset{\delta+}{C}}}-CH_3 + :\overset{\ominus}{C}H_2-\overset{O}{\overset{\|}{C}}-CH_3 \longrightarrow CH_3-\overset{O^{\ominus}}{\overset{|}{\underset{CH_3}{\underset{|}{C}}}}-CH_2-\overset{O}{\overset{\|}{C}}-CH_3 \xrightarrow{H_2O} CH_3-\overset{OH}{\overset{|}{\underset{CH_3}{\underset{|}{C}}}}-CH_2-\overset{O}{\overset{\|}{C}}-CH_3 + OH^-$$

88 (*d*) Aldehyde having α-H-atoms undergoes aldol condensation in the presence of dil. NaOH and yields β-hydroxy aldehydes.

$$\underset{X}{CH_3CHO} + \underset{Y}{CH_3CHO} \xrightarrow[Z]{\text{Dil. NaOH}} CH_3-\overset{OH}{\overset{|}{CH}}-CH_2CHO$$

3-hydroxybutanal

89 (*a*) $\underset{X}{C_2H_5OH} + [O] \xrightarrow[\text{in } CH_2Cl_2]{PCC} \underset{Y}{CH_3CHO}$

$$\underset{Y}{CH_3CHO} + 4NaOH + 3I_2 \longrightarrow \underset{\substack{\text{Yellow ppt.}\\ \text{(triiodomethane)}}}{CHI_3\downarrow} + HCO\overset{-}{O}\overset{+}{Na} + 3H_2O + 3NaI$$

90 (*a*) I. $\underset{\text{1-hexyne}}{CH_3CH_2CH_2CH_2C\equiv CH} + H_2O \xrightarrow[\text{dil. } H_2SO_4]{HgSO_4} \underset{\text{2-hexanone}}{CH_3CH_2CH_2CH_2\overset{O}{\overset{\|}{C}}-CH_3}$

II. $\underset{\text{3-methyl-2-heptene}}{CH_3CH_2CH_2CH_2-\overset{CH_3}{\overset{|}{C}}=CH-CH_3} \xrightarrow[\text{(ii) } Zn/H_2O]{\text{(i) } O_3} \underset{\text{2-hexanone}}{CH_3CH_2CH_2CH_2-\overset{O}{\overset{\|}{C}}-CH_3} + \underset{\text{Acetaldehyde}}{CH_3CHO}$

III. $\underset{n\text{-butyl magnesium bromide}}{CH_3CH_2CH_2CH_2MgBr} \xrightarrow[\text{(ii) } H_2O/H^+]{\text{(i) } CH_3CHO} \underset{\text{2-hexanol}}{CH_3CH_2CH_2CH_2-\underset{OH}{\underset{|}{CH}}-CH_3} \xrightarrow{[O]} \underset{\text{2-hexanone}}{CH_3CH_2CH_2CH_2-\underset{O}{\underset{\|}{C}}-CH_3}$

IV. $\underset{\text{1-hexyne}}{CH_3CH_2CH_2CH_2C\equiv CH} \xrightarrow{B_2H_6/H_2O_2} \underset{\text{Hexanal}}{CH_3CH_2CH_2CH_2CH_2CHO}$

Hence, from path I, II and III, 2-hexanone can be produced.

91 (*b*) $\underset{A}{CH_3}-\underset{B}{CH_2}-\underset{C}{\overset{O}{\overset{\|}{C}}}-CH_3$

This compound undergoes enolisation by the following mechanism.

$$\underset{A}{CH_3}-\underset{B}{CH_2}-\underset{C}{\overset{O}{\overset{\|}{C}}}-CH_3 \underset{}{\overset{H^+}{\rightleftharpoons}} \underset{A}{CH_3}-\underset{B}{\overset{H}{\overset{|}{\overset{\ominus}{C}}}}-\underset{C}{\overset{OH}{\overset{|}{\overset{\oplus}{C}}}}-CH_3 \xrightarrow[-H^+]{H_2O} \underset{A}{CH_3}-\underset{B}{\overset{\ominus}{C}H}-\underset{C}{\overset{OH}{\overset{|}{\overset{\oplus}{C}}}}-CH_3 \longrightarrow \underset{A}{CH_3}\underset{B}{CH}=\underset{C}{\overset{OH}{\overset{|}{C}}}-CH_3$$

Thus, hydrogen (*B*) is most acidic as it is attached with the active methylene group.

92 (*a*)

$$CH_3-\overset{O}{\overset{\|}{CH}} \xrightarrow{H-CN} CH_3-\overset{OH}{\overset{|}{\underset{CN}{\underset{|}{C}}}}-H \xrightarrow{H_2O/H^+} \underset{\text{(50\% L-isomer)}}{CH_3-\overset{OH}{\overset{|}{\underset{COOH}{\underset{|}{C}}}}-H} + \underset{\text{(50\% D-isomer)}}{H_3C-\overset{OH}{\overset{|}{\underset{COOH}{\underset{|}{C}}}}-H}$$

93 (*a*)

(a) $CH_3-\overset{CH_3}{\overset{|}{C}}=CH-CH_3 + O_3 \xrightarrow[196\ K]{CHCl_3 \text{ or } CCl_4}$ (ozonide) $\xrightarrow{H_2O/Zn\text{-dust}} CH_3-\overset{O}{\overset{||}{C}}-CH_3 + CH_3CHO$

2-methyl-2-butene; Acetone; Ethanal

(b) $CH_2=CH-\overset{CH_3}{\overset{|}{CH}}-CH_3 + O_3 \xrightarrow[196K]{CHCl_3 \text{ or } CCl_4}$ (ozonide) $\xrightarrow{H_2O/Zn\text{-dust}} HCHO + CH_3-\overset{CH_3}{\overset{|}{CH}}-CHO$

3-methyl-1-butene; Methanal; 2-methyl propanal

(c) Cyclopentane $\xrightarrow{O_3}$ No reaction (absence of unsaturation)

(d) $CH_2=\overset{CH_3}{\overset{|}{C}}-CH_2-CH_3 + O_3 \xrightarrow[196K]{CHCl_3 \text{ or } CCl_4}$ (ozonide) $\xrightarrow{H_2O/Zn\text{-dust}} HCHO + CH_3-\overset{O}{\overset{||}{C}}-CH_2-CH_3$

2-methyl-1-butene; Methanal; Butanone

Hence, 2-methyl-2-butene with molecular formula C_5H_{10} yields acetone on ozonolysis.

94 (*c*) 40% aqueous solution of formaldehyde (methanal) is called as formalin.

95 (*c*) When distilled with conc. H_2SO_4, acetone gives mesitylene, i.e. 1,3,5-trimethyl benzene.

$$3CH_3-\overset{O}{\overset{||}{C}}-CH_3 \xrightarrow[-3H_2O]{\text{Conc. } H_2SO_4} \text{1,3,5-trimethylbenzene or Mesitylene}$$

Acetone (three molecules)

96 (*b*) $>C=O + H_2NOH \longrightarrow >C=NOH + H_2O$

Carbonyl compound; Hydroxyl amine; Oxime

97 (*a*) $>C=O + HCN \longrightarrow >C(OH)(CN) \xrightarrow{H_2O} >C(OH)(COOH)$

(It is α-hydroxy acid)

Central C-atom must be asymmetric to form a racemic mixture of *X*-hydroxy acid.

$$(H_3C)(H)C=O + HCN \longrightarrow (H_3C)(H)C(OH)(CN) \xrightarrow{H_2O} H-\overset{CH_3}{\overset{|}{C}}(COOH)-OH + HO-\overset{CH_3}{\overset{|}{C}}(COOH)-H$$

Acetaldehyde; *d*-form; *l*-form — Racemic mixture

$$(H_3C)_2C=O + HCN \longrightarrow (H_3C)_2C(OH)(CN) \xrightarrow{H_2O} (H_3C)_2C(OH)(COOH)$$

Acetone — It is not optical active

$$(H_5C_2)_2C=O + HCN \longrightarrow (H_5C_2)_2C(OH)(CN) \xrightarrow{H_2O} (H_5C_2)_2C(OH)(COOH)$$

Diethyl ketone — It is not optical active

$$(H)_2C=O + HCN \longrightarrow (H)_2C(OH)(CN) \xrightarrow{H_2O} (H)_2C(OH)(COOH)$$

Formaldehyde — It is not optical active

98 (*c*) $CH_2OH-C(=O)-CH_2OH \xrightarrow{HIO_4} 2HCHO + HCOOH$

99 (*d*) $CH_3CHO + 3Cl_2 \xrightarrow[\text{Excess}]{\text{Chlorination}} CCl_3 \cdot CHO$

100 (*c*) $C_6H_5CH=O + 2\ H-C_6H_4-N(CH_3)_2 \xrightarrow{\text{Anhyd. } ZnCl_2} C_6H_5CH[C_6H_4N(CH_3)_2]_2$

Benzaldehyde; N,N-dimethylaniline 2(molecules); Malachite green

101 (*a*)

$$\underset{(A)}{(H_3C)_2C{=}O} + H{-}CH_2{-}COCH_3 \xrightarrow{\text{Dil. NaOH}} (H_3C)_2\underset{OH}{C}{-}CH_2COCH_3 \xrightarrow{CH_3COCH_3}$$

$$(H_3C)_2\underset{OH}{C}{-}CH_2COCH_2{-}\underset{OH}{C}(CH_3)_2 \xrightarrow{\Delta} (CH_3)_2C{=}CHCOCH{=}C(CH_3)_2$$

102 (*c*)

$$H_3C{-}CO{-}CH_2{-}CH_2{-}CO{-}CH_3 \xrightarrow[\text{condensation}]{\text{Aldol}} \text{HO(CH}_3\text{)C}{-}CH_2{-}CH_2{-}CH_2{-}C{=}O \text{ (ring)} \xrightarrow{-H_2O} \text{3-methylcyclopent-2-enone}$$

103 (*d*) Gattermann-Koch aldehyde synthesis is used for the preparation of benzaldehyde.

$$\underset{\text{Benzene}}{C_6H_6} + CO + HCl \xrightarrow[AlCl_3]{\text{Anhyd.}} \underset{\text{Benzaldehyde}}{C_6H_5CHO} + HCl$$

Hence, the reagent used in Gattermann-Koch aldehyde synthesis is CO + HCl.

104 (*c*) $\underset{\text{Acetylene}}{CH{\equiv}CH} + 2HCHO \xrightarrow{C_2Cu_2} \underset{\text{2-butyne-1, 4-diol}}{CH_2OH{-}C{\equiv}C{-}CH_2OH}$

105 (*a*) $\underset{A}{C_3H_8O} \xrightarrow[H_2SO_4]{K_2Cr_2O_7} \underset{B}{C_3H_6O} \xrightarrow[AgNO_3]{\text{Ammoniacal}}$ Silver mirror

$B \xrightarrow{H_2NCONHNH_2} C$

Since, *B* reduces ammoniacal silver nitrate, it should be an aldehyde and hence, *A* is primary alcohol which should be $C_2H_5CH_2OH$. Thus, *B* would be CH_3CH_2CHO.

Hence, the series of reactions can be shown as

$$\underset{(A)}{CH_3CH_2CH_2OH} \longrightarrow \underset{(B)}{CH_3CH_2CHO} \xrightarrow[-H_2O]{H_2NCONHNH_2} \underset{(C)}{CH_3CH_2CH{=}NNHCONH_2}$$

106 (*a*)

$$\underset{\text{Calcium benzoate}}{(C_6H_5COO)_2Ca} + \underset{\text{Calcium acetate}}{Ca(OOCCH_3)_2} \xrightarrow{\Delta} \underset{\text{Acetophenone}}{2C_6H_5{-}\overset{O}{\overset{\|}{C}}{-}CH_3} + 2CaCO_3$$

107 (*b*) Aluminium isopropoxide $[Al[OCH(Me)_2]_3]$ in the presence of excess of isopropyl alcohol reduces $>C{=}O$ group into $>\underset{H}{C}{-}OH$ group and the reaction is called Meerwein-Ponndorf-Verley (MPV) reduction. Reaction involved is as follows :

$$\text{cyclohexenol} \underset{}{\overset{Al[OCH(Me)_2]}{\rightleftharpoons}} \text{cyclohexenol}$$

108 (*b*)

$$\underset{\text{Phenol}}{C_6H_5OH} \xrightarrow[KOH]{CHCl_3} \underset{\text{Salicylaldehyde}}{o\text{-}HOC_6H_4CHO} \xrightarrow[\text{(Cannizzaro's reaction)}]{50\%\ KOH} o\text{-}HOC_6H_4CH_2OH + o\text{-}HOC_6H_4\overset{-}{CO}\overset{+}{OK}$$

109 (*b*)

$$2\underset{\text{Ketone}}{(H_3C)_2C{=}O} \xrightarrow{Mg/Hg} \left[H_3C{-}\underset{O}{\overset{H_3C}{C}}{-}\underset{O}{\overset{CH_3}{C}}{-}CH_3\right] (\text{O–Mg–O}) \xrightarrow{H_3O^+} \underset{\text{Pinacol}}{H_3C{-}\underset{OH}{\overset{CH_3}{C}}{-}\underset{OH}{\overset{CH_3}{C}}{-}CH_3}$$

110 (*b*) $\underset{\text{Calcium acetate}}{(CH_3COO)_2Ca} + \underset{\text{Calcium propanoate}}{(CH_3CH_2COO)_2Ca} \longrightarrow \underset{\text{2-butanone}}{2CH_3{-}\overset{O}{\overset{\|}{C}}{-}CH_2{-}CH_3} + 2CaCO_3$

Calcium acetate and calcium propionate will give 2-butanone

$$\underset{\text{Calcium formate}}{(HCOO)_2Ca} + \underset{\text{Calcium propanoate}}{(CH_3CH_2COO)_2Ca} \longrightarrow \underset{\text{Propanal}}{2CH_3CH_2{-}\overset{O}{\overset{\|}{C}}{-}H} + 2CaCO_3$$

$$\underset{\text{Calcium acetate}}{(CH_3COO)_2Ca} + \underset{\text{Calcium acetate}}{(CH_3COO)_2Ca} \longrightarrow \underset{\text{Acetone}}{2CH_3{-}\overset{O}{\overset{\|}{C}}{-}CH_3} + 2CaCO_3$$

$$\underset{\text{Calcium formate}}{(HCOO)_2Ca} + \underset{\text{Calcium acetate}}{(CH_3COO)_2Ca} \longrightarrow \underset{\text{Ethanal}}{2CH_3{-}\overset{O}{\overset{\|}{C}}{-}H} + 2CaCO_3$$

111 (*a*) $HCHO + CH_3CHO \xrightarrow[\text{Heat}]{OH^-} \underset{A}{CH_2{=}CH{-}CHO}$

$\xrightarrow{HCN} CH_2{=}CH{-}CH\begin{matrix}OH\\CN\end{matrix}$

$\xrightarrow{H_3O^+} \underset{(B)}{CH_2{=}CH{-}\underset{\displaystyle OH}{\underset{|}{CH}}{-}COOH}$

112 (*d*) On heating (or refluxing) with an aqueous alcoholic solution of KCN, two molecules of an aromatic aldehyde undergo condensation to form benzoin. This reaction is called **benzoin condensation.**

$$\underset{\text{Benzaldehyde}}{C_6H_5{-}\overset{O}{\overset{||}{C}}{-}H} + \underset{\text{Benzaldehyde}}{\overset{O}{\overset{||}{C}}(H){-}C_6H_5} \xrightarrow[\Delta]{\text{Alc. KCN}} \underset{\text{Benzoin}}{C_6H_5{-}\overset{O}{\overset{||}{C}}{-}\overset{OH}{\overset{|}{CH}}{-}C_6H_5}$$

113 (*b*)

$$\text{2-hydroxycyclohexanone} \xrightarrow{HIO_4} \text{OHC}{-}(CH_2)_4{-}COOH$$

114 (*b*) $CH_3CHO \xrightarrow{HNO_3} \underset{X}{CH_3COOH} \xrightarrow[\Delta]{P_4O_{10}} \underset{Y}{(CH_3CO)_2O}$

115 (*a*) (*i*) $\underset{\text{Compound } A}{C_5H_{10}Cl_2} \xrightarrow{\text{Hydrolysis}} \underset{\text{Does not give Fehling test}}{C_5H_{10}O} \longrightarrow \underset{\text{Iodoform}}{\text{Forms}}$

$\xrightarrow{NH_2OH} \text{Oxime}$

$C_5H_{10}O$ must be aldehyde or ketone because it reacts with NH_2OH.

(*ii*) It must be a ketone as it does not give Fehling test.

(*iii*) It must have CH_3CO group because it gives iodoform test.

$$\underset{(A)}{CH_3{-}\overset{Cl}{\overset{|}{\underset{Cl}{\underset{|}{C}}}}{-}CH_2CH_2CH_3} \xrightarrow{\text{Hydrolysis}} \underset{\text{(Unstable)}}{H_3C{-}\overset{Cl}{\overset{|}{\underset{OH}{\underset{|}{C}}}}{-}CH_2CH_2CH_3}$$

$$\xrightarrow{-HCl} CH_3{-}\overset{O}{\overset{||}{C}}{-}CH_2CH_2CH_3$$

$\downarrow +NH_2OH$: $\underset{\text{Oxime}}{CH_3{-}\overset{NOH}{\overset{||}{C}}{-}CH_2CH_2CH_3}$

$\downarrow NaOH/I_2$: $\underset{\text{(Iodoform)}}{CHI_3}$

116 (*c*) Enolate ion on combination with carbonyl group of ester gives β-keto ester.

$$H{-}CH_2{-}\overset{O}{\overset{||}{C}}{-}CH_3 \underset{}{\overset{CH_3O^-}{\rightleftharpoons}} \underset{\text{Enolate ion}}{\ddot{C}H_2{-}\overset{O}{\overset{||}{C}}{-}CH_3} + CH_3OH$$

$$\underset{\text{Enolate ion}}{CH_3{-}\overset{O}{\overset{||}{C}}{-}\ddot{C}H_2^-} + \underset{\text{Ester}}{CH_3{-}\overset{O}{\overset{||}{C}}{-}OCH_3} \rightleftharpoons CH_3{-}\overset{O}{\overset{||}{C}}{-}CH_2{-}\overset{O^-}{\overset{|}{\underset{CH_3}{\underset{|}{C}}}}{-}OCH_3$$

$$\xrightarrow{-OCH_3} \underset{\beta\text{-ketoester}}{CH_3{-}\overset{O}{\overset{||}{C}}{-}CH_2{-}\overset{O}{\overset{||}{C}}{-}CH_3}$$

117 (*b*) Aldehydes and ketones condense with alcohol to give acetal and ketals respectively, e.g.

$$CH_3CHO + 2C_2H_5OH \xrightarrow{-H_2O} \underset{\text{Acetal}}{CH_3CH\begin{matrix}OC_2H_5\\OC_2H_5\end{matrix}}$$

Thus, acetates are diethers.

118 (*a*) Conversion of benzaldehyde to 3-phenylprop-2-en-1-oic acid is **Perkin condensation**

$$\underset{\text{Benzaldehyde}}{C_6H_5CHO} + \underset{\text{Acetic anhydride}}{(CH_3CO)_2O} \xrightarrow[-H_2O,\ \Delta]{CH_3CO\bar{O}\overset{+}{Na}}$$

$$\underset{\text{3-phenylprop-2-en-1-oic acid}}{C_6H_5CH{=}CHCOOH} + CH_3COOH$$

Topic 2

Carboxylic Acids

2019

1 The reaction that does not give benzoic acid as the major product is **[NEET (Odisha)]**

(a) $C_6H_5CH_2OH \xrightarrow{K_2Cr_2O_7}$

(b) $C_6H_5COCH_3 \xrightarrow[\text{(ii) } H_3O^+]{\text{(i) NaOCl}}$

(c) $C_6H_5CH_2OH \xrightarrow[\text{(Pyridinium chloro chromate)}]{\text{PCC}}$

(d) $C_6H_5CH_2OH \xrightarrow{KMnO_4/H^+}$

2 Consider the following acids :

(i) $F_3C—COOH$, (ii) CH_3COOH,
(iii) C_6H_5COOH, (iv) CH_3CH_2COOH

Correct order of pK_a value is **[AIIMS]**

(a) (i) > (iii) > (ii) > (iv) (b) (iv) > (ii) > (iii) > (i)
(c) (iv) > (iii) > (ii) > (i) (d) (i) > (ii) > (iv) > (iii)

2018

3 Carboxylic acids have higher boiling points than aldehydes, ketones and even alcohols of comparable molecular mass. It is due to their **[NEET]**

(a) more extensive association of carboxylic acid *via* van der Waals' force of attraction
(b) formation of carboxylate ion
(c) formation of intramolecular H-bonding
(d) formation of intermolecular H-bonding

2017

4 Which of the following reagents is used to distinguish phenol and benzoic acid? **[AIIMS]**

(a) *aq*. NaOH (b) Tollen's reagent
(c) Molisch reagent (d) Neutral $FeCl_3$

5 The product of acid hydrolysis of (*P*) and (*Q*) can be distinguished by **[JIPMER]**

$P \Rightarrow H_2C{=}C(O—COCH_3)(CH_3)$

$Q \Rightarrow CH_3—CH{=}CH—OCOCH_3$

(a) Lucas reagent (b) 2, 4-DNP
(c) Fehling's solution (d) $NaHSO_3$

2016

6 The correct order of strengths of the carboxylic acids

(I: cyclohexane with COOH; II: tetrahydropyran with COOH at position 3; III: tetrahydropyran with COOH at position 4)

is **[NEET Phase II]**

(a) I > II > III (b) II > III > I
(c) III > II > I (d) II > I > III

2014

7 Write the IUPAC name of the following compounds. **[MHCET]**

(Benzene ring bearing COOH, with NH_2 ortho and OH para to COOH)

(a) 2-amino-4-hydroxy benzoic acid
(b) 6-amino-4-hydroxy benzoic acid
(c) 3-amino-4-carboxyphenol
(d) 2-carboxy-4-hydroxyaniline

8 Cyclohexene $\xrightarrow{HBr} A \xrightarrow{KCN} B \xrightarrow{H_3O^+} C \xrightarrow[\text{(ii) } H_2O]{\text{(i) } Br_2 \text{ / red P}} D$

Identify the compound *D* in the above mentioned series of reactions. **[MHCET]**

(a) $C_6H_{11}—C(=O)—Br$ (b) 1-bromocyclohexane-1-carboxylic acid ($C_6H_{10}(Br)—C(=O)—OH$)

(c) $Br—C_6H_{10}—C(=O)—OH$ (4-bromo) (d) 3-bromocyclohexane $—C(=O)—OH$

9 $C_6H_5COOH \xrightarrow[\text{(ii) } \Delta]{\text{(i) } NH_3} P \xrightarrow{NaOBr} Q \xrightarrow[\text{(ii) Heat to 460 K}]{\text{(i) Conc. } H_2SO_4} R$

R is **[KCET]**

(a) *o*-bromo sulphanilic acid
(b) sulphanilamide
(c) sulphanilic acid
(d) *p*-bromo sulphanilamide

10 Which of the following is the correct order of acidic strength? **[Guj CET]**

(a) $Cl_3CCOOH > Cl_2CHCOOH > ClCH_2COOH > CH_3COOH$

(b) $CH_3COOH > ClCH_2COOH > Cl_2CHCOOH > Cl_3CCOOH$

(c) $CH_3COOH > Cl_3CCOOH > Cl_2CHCOOH > ClCH_2COOH$

(d) $CH_3COOH > ClCH_2COOH > Cl_2CHCOOH > Cl_3CCOOH$

2013

11 The carboxylic acid which reduces Tollen's reagent is **[UP CPMT]**

(a) HCOOH (b) CH_3COOH

(c) CH_3CH_2COOH (d) $CH_3CH_2CH_2COOH$

12 Glacial acetic acid is obtained by **[WB JEE]**

(a) distilling vinegar

(b) crystallising, separating and melting of acetic acid

(c) treating vinegar with dehydrating agents

(d) chemically separating acetic acid

13 When salicylic acid is distilled with Zn-dust, the product obtained is **[KCET]**

(a) zinc salicylate (b) salicyl aldehyde

(c) phenol (d) benzoic acid

2012

14 $CH_3COOH \xrightarrow{LiAlH_4} A + CH_3COOH \xrightarrow{H_3O^+} B + H_2O$

In the above reaction A and B respectively are **[Manipal]**

(a) $CH_3COOC_2H_5, C_2H_5OH$

(b) CH_3CHO, C_2H_5OH

(c) C_2H_5OH, CH_3CHO

(d) $C_2H_5OH, CH_3COOC_2H_5$

15 Identify the method by which Me_3CCO_2H can be prepared **[WB JEE]**

(a) treating 1 mole of MeCOMe with 2 moles of Me MgI

(b) treating 1 mole of $MeCO_2Me$ with 3 moles of Me MgI

(c) treating 1 mole of MeCHO with 3 moles of MeMgI

(d) treating 1 mole of dry ice with 1 mole of Me_3CMgI

2011

16 In a set of reactions *m*-bromobenzoic acid gave a product *D*. Identify the product *D*.

(A) m-bromobenzoic acid (COOH, Br) $\xrightarrow{SOCl_2} B \xrightarrow{NH_3} C \xrightarrow[Br_2]{NaOH} D$

(a) benzene ring with $CONH_2$ and Br (meta)

(b) benzene ring with SO_2NH_2 and Br (meta)

(c) benzene ring with COOH and NH_2 (meta)

(d) benzene ring with NH_2 and Br (meta)

17 Which is correct statement? **[DUMET]**

(a) *o*-nitrobenzoic acid is stronger acid than 3, 5- dinitrobenzoic acid in H_2O.

(b) Branched carboxylic acids are more acidic than unbranched acids.

(c) $H_3C-CO-CH_2-CH_2-CO-CH_3 \xrightarrow[\text{condensation}]{\text{Aldol}}$ (cyclic aldol: C=O, H_2C, CH_2, HO–C(CH_3)–CH_2) $\xrightarrow{-H_2O}$ 3-methylcyclopent-2-en-1-one (H_3C, C=O)

(d) Butanoic acid is stronger acid than succinic acid.

18 In the conversion,

cyclohexane-COOH $\longrightarrow$ cyclohexane-NH_2

The sequence of the reagent used are **[DUMET]**

(a) (i) $SOCl_2$ (ii) N_3^- (iii) H_2O, heat

(b) (i) $SOCl_2$ (ii) NH_3

(c) (i) $SOCl_2$ (ii) NH_3 (iii) Heat

(d) (i) $SOCl_2$ (ii) KCN (iii) $LiAlH_4$

2010

19 In a set of reactions, ethyl benzene yields a product *D*.

$C_6H_5CH_2CH_3 \xrightarrow[KOH]{KMnO_4} B \xrightarrow[FeCl_3]{Br_2} C \xrightarrow[H^+]{C_2H_5OH} D$

D would be **[CBSE AIPMT]**

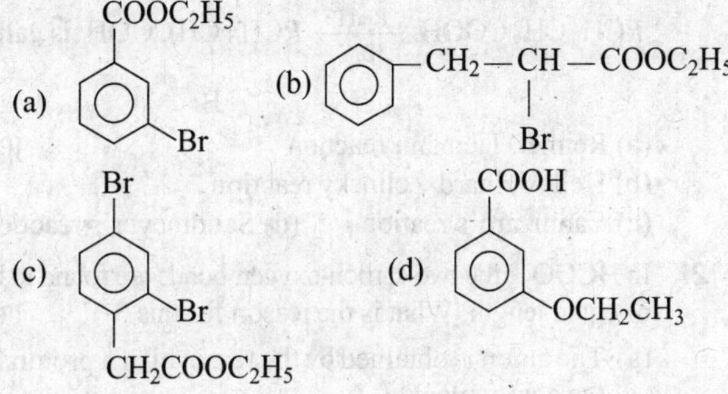

20 Oxalic acid on heating with conc. H_2SO_4 gives [AFMC]

(a) Only CO (b) Only CO_2
(c) $CO_2 + H_2O$ (d) $CO + CO_2 + H_2O$

21 Which of the following carboxylic acid undergoes decarboxylation easily? [BVP]

(a) $C_6H_5—CO—CH_2—COOH$
(b) $C_6H_5—CO—COOH$
(c) $C_6H_5—CH(OH)—COOH$
(d) $C_6H_5—CH(NH_2)—COOH$

22 The correct order of acidity for the following is [OJEE]

(a) HCN > $ClCH_2COOH$ > HCOOH > CH_3COOH
(b) HCN > HCOOH > $ClCH_2COOH$ > CH_3COOH
(c) $ClCH_2COOH$ > HCOOH > CH_3COOH > HCN
(d) $ClCH_2COOH$ > HCN > HCOOH > CH_3COOH

23 $X \xrightarrow{PCl_5} C_2H_5Cl$, $Y \xrightarrow{PCl_5} CH_3COCl$

X and Y are [WB JEE]

(a) $(C_2H_5)_2O$ and CH_3CO_2H
(b) C_2H_5I and C_2H_5CHO
(c) C_2H_5OH and CH_3CO_2H
(d) C_2H_5OH and C_2H_5CHO

24 In the reaction,

$CH_3CH_2COOH \xrightarrow{Cl_2,\ P} X \xrightarrow{\text{Alc. KOH}} Y$, Y is [RPMT]

(a) $CH_3CH_2CH_2OH$ (b) $CH_2{=}CHCOOH$
(c) CH_3CH_2CN (d) $CH_2C(Cl){=}COOH$

25 The product formed as a result of reaction of CH_3MgBr and CO_2, on further hydrolysis gives [RPMT]

(a) CH_3COOH (b) HCOOH
(c) oxalic acid (d) acetic acid

26 The reaction,

$RCH_2CH_2COOH \xrightarrow[Br_2]{\text{Red P}} RCH_2CH(Br)COOH$ is called

(a) Reimer-Tiemann reaction [RPMT]
(b) Hell-Volhard-Zelinsky reaction
(c) Cannizaro's reation (d) Sandmeyer's reaction

27 In $HCOO^-$, the two carbon-oxygen bonds are found to be of equal length. What is the reason for this? [RPMT]

(a) The anion is obtained by the removal of a proton from the acid molecule
(b) Electronic orbitals of carbon atoms are hybridised
(c) The C=O bond is weaker than C—O bond
(d) The anion $HCOO^-$ has two resonating structures

28 In a set of reactions, acetic acid yielded product D.

$CH_3COOH \xrightarrow{SOCl_2} A \xrightarrow[\text{Anhy. } AlCl_3]{\text{Benzene}} B \xrightarrow{HCN} C \xrightarrow{HOH} D.$

The structure of D would be [RPMT]

(a) 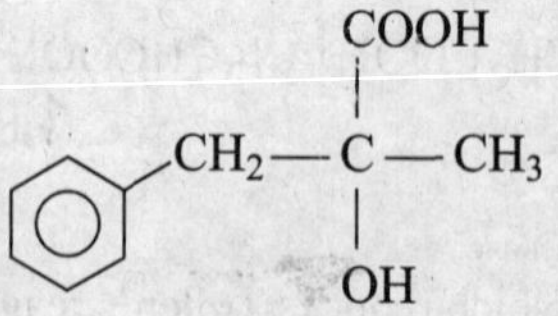 $C_6H_5—CH_2—C(COOH)(OH)—CH_3$
(b) $C_6H_5—C(CN)(OH)—CH_3$
(c) $C_6H_5—CH_2—C(OH)(CN)—CH_3$
(d) 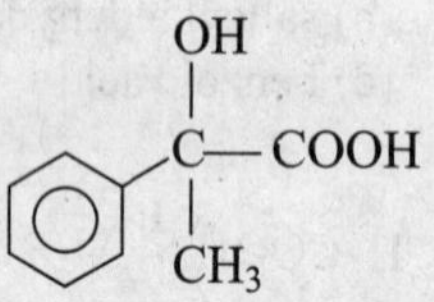 $C_6H_5—C(OH)(CH_3)—COOH$

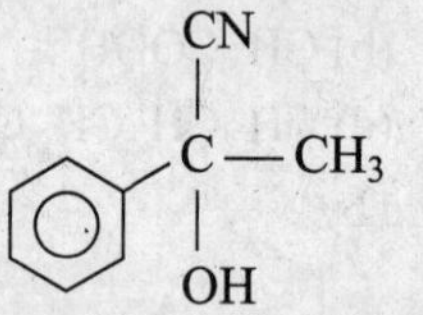

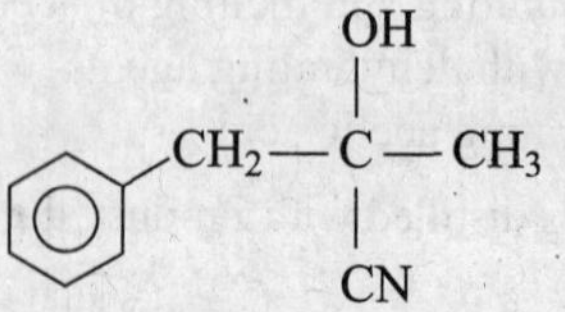

29 Which of the following compound is most acidic? [Haryana PMT]

(a) $BrCH_2COOH$ (b) $ClCH_2COOH$
(c) FCH_2COOH (d) ICH_2COOH

30 An oxygen containing organic compound upon oxidation forms a carboxylic acid as the only organic product with its molecular mass higher by 14 units. The organic compound is [KCET]

(a) an aldehyde (b) a primary alcohol
(c) a secondary alcohol (d) a ketone

31 Phenol and benzoic acid may be distinguished by [VMMC]

(a) $NaHCO_3$ (b) NaOH
(c) Na (d) Both (a) and (c)

2009

32 Propionic acid with Br_2/ Red P yields a dibromo product. Its structure would be [CBSE AIPMT]

(a) $CH_2Br—CHBr—COOH$
(b) $CHBr_2—CH_2—COOH$
(c) $CH_2Br—CH_2—COBr$
(d) $CH_3—CBr_2—COOH$

33 The correct set of reagents for the following conversion is **[AIIMS]**

$(CH_3)_2CHCOOH \longrightarrow$ (cyclic anhydride of tetramethylsuccinic acid)

(a) P_4 / I_2, Na, conc. H_2SO_4
(b) P_2O_5, $LiAlH_4$
(c) $P_2O_5/\Delta, H_2O, P_4/I_2$, Na
(d) P_4 / I_2, Na, P_2O_5/Δ

34

$X \xrightarrow{\text{Fehling solution}} Cu_2O$

$X \xrightarrow{SOCl_2/\text{Pyridine}} RCOCl$

Here, the compound X can be **[AFMC]**
(a) acetic acid (b) formaldehyde
(c) formic acid (d) propionic acid

35 Identify Z in the following sequence of reactions.

$CH_3COOH \xrightarrow{NH_3} X \xrightarrow{\Delta} Y \xrightarrow{P_2O_5} Z$ **[UP CPMT]**

(a) CH_4 (b) CH_3CHO
(c) CH_3CN (d) $CH_3COO^-NH_4^+$

36 The compound from which formic acid cannot be prepared is **[MHT CET]**
(a) methyl alcohol
(b) carbon monoxide + NaOH
(c) glycerol
(d) methyl magnesium bromide

37 The acidic nature of carboxylic acids
$RCOOH \longrightarrow RCOO^- + H^+$ is due to **[Manipal]**
(a) high degree of ionisation of carboxylic acids
(b) greater resonance stabilisation of the carboxylic acid over the carboxylate ion
(c) greater resonance stabilisation of the carboxylate ion over carboxylic acid
(d) solubility of carboxylic acids in water

38 When propionic acid is treated with aqueous sodium bicarbonate, CO_2 is liberated. The 'C' of CO_2 comes from **[Manipal]**
(a) methyl group (b) carboxylic acid group
(c) methylene group (d) bicarbonate

39 In the following sequence of reaction, find the product Y. **[OJEE]**

(cyclopentane-1,2-dione) $\xrightarrow[(ii)\ H^+]{(i)\ OH^-} X \xrightarrow{SOCl_2\ (2\ eq)} Y$

(a) cyclopentane with OH and COCl on the same carbon
(b) cyclobutane with COCl and OH on the same carbon
(c) cyclobutane with COCl and Cl on the same carbon
(d) cyclopentane with COCl and Cl on the same carbon

40 The carboxylic acid of least acidic strength among the following is **[J&K CET]**
(a) p-nitrobenzoic acid (b) p-methylbenzoic acid
(c) p-chlorobenzoic acid (d) p-methoxybenzoic acid

41 Consider the following reactions,

I. $H_3CCl_3 \xrightarrow{OH^\ominus}$ II. $H_3CCHO \xrightarrow{[Ag(NH_3)_2]^+OH^\ominus}$

III. $H_3CCO_2C_2H_5 \xrightarrow{OH^\ominus}$

Carboxylic acid is the final product only in the reaction(s). **[AMU]**
(a) I and II (b) II and III (c) Only II (d) Only III

42 What are A, B, C in the following reactions?

I. $(CH_3CO_2)_2Ca \xrightarrow{\Delta} A$ II. $CH_3CO_2H \xrightarrow[\text{Red P}]{HI} B$

III. $2CH_3CO_2H \xrightarrow{P_4O_{10}} C$ **[EAMCET]**

	A	B	C
(a)	C_2H_6	CH_3COCH_3	$(CH_3CO)_2O$
(b)	$(CH_3CO)_2O$	C_2H_6	CH_3COCH_3
(c)	CH_3COCH_3	C_2H_6	$(CH_3CO)_2O$
(d)	CH_3COCH_3	$(CH_3CO)_2O$	C_2H_6

43 $CH_3COOH \xrightarrow{LiAlH_4} X \xrightarrow[300°C]{Cu} Y \xrightarrow[NaOH]{Dilute} Z$
In the above reaction Z is **[KCET]**
(a) aldol (b) ketol (c) acetol (d) butanol

2008

44 Adipic acid on heating form **[UP CPMT]**
(a) $\begin{array}{l} CH_2—CH_2 \\ | \\ CH_2—CH_2 \end{array}\!\!\!\!\!>C=O$ (b) $\begin{array}{l} CH_2\,CH_2 \\ | \\ CH_2CH_2 \end{array}\!\!\!\!>O$
(c) $\begin{array}{l} CH_2\,CH_2CO \\ | \\ CH_2\,CH_2CO \end{array}\!\!\!\!>O$ (d) $\begin{array}{l} CH_2\,CH_2COOH \\ | \\ CH_2CH_2COOH \end{array}$

45 The end product C in the following sequence of chemical reactions is **[Manipal]**

$CH_3COOH \xrightarrow{CaCO_3} A \xrightarrow{\Delta} B \xrightarrow{NH_2OH} C$

(a) acetaldehyde oxime
(b) formaldehyde oxime
(c) methyl nitrate
(d) acetoxime

46 Carboxylic acids readily dissolve in aqueous sodium bicarbonate, liberating carbon dioxide. Which one of the following is correct? [Manipal]

(a) The free carboxylic acid and its conjugate base are of comparable stability
(b) The free carboxylic acid is more stable than its conjugate base
(c) The conjugate base of the carboxylic acid is more stable than the free carboxylic acid
(d) None of the above

47 When $CH_2 = CH— COOH$ is reduced with $LiAlH_4$, the compound obtained will be [RPMT]

(a) $CH_3 — CH_2 — COOH$ (b) $CH_2 = CH— CH_2OH$
(c) $CH_3 —CH_2—CH_2OH$ (d) $CH_3 —CH_2—CHO$

48 Which of the following diacid readily gives anhydride on heating? [J&K CET]

(a) Fumaric acid (b) Maleic acid
(c) Malic acid (d) Terephthalic acid

49 [DUMET]

$C_6H_5COOH + SOCl_2 \xrightarrow{C_2H_5OH} A$. Product A is

(a) $C_6H_5COOC_2H_5$ (b) $C_6H_5-\overset{O}{\overset{\|}{C}}-Cl$
(c) m-$C_2H_5O-C_6H_4-COOH$ (d) None of these

50 $CH_3CH_2CH_2CH_2CH_2COOH \longrightarrow CH_3CH_2CH_2CH_2—\underset{}{\overset{NH_2}{\overset{|}{CH}}}—COOH$

The reagents used in the conversion are [DUMET]

(a) (i) PBr_3/(ii) NH_3
(b) (i) red P, Br_2/(ii) alc. NH_3 (excess)
(c) (i) PBr_3, NaCN/(ii) $LiAlH_4$
(d) None of the above

51 In a set of the given reactions, acetic acid yielded a product C.

$CH_3COOH + PCl_5 \longrightarrow A \xrightarrow[\text{anhy. } AlCl_3]{C_6H_6} B \xrightarrow[\text{ether}]{C_2H_5MgBr} C$

Product C would be [JCECE]

(a) $CH_3CH(OH)C_6H_5$ (b) $CH_3 — \overset{C_2H_5}{\overset{|}{C}}(OH)C_6H_5$
(c) $CH_3CH(OH)C_2H_5$ (d) $CH_3COC_6H_5$

52 Consider the acidity of the carboxylic acids,

I. PhCOOH II. o-$NO_2C_6H_4COOH$
III. p - $NO_2C_6H_4COOH$ IV. m - $NO_2C_6H_4COOH$

Which of the following order is correct? [JCECE]

(a) I > II > III > IV (b) II > IV > III > I
(c) II > IV > I > III (d) II > III > IV > I

2007

53 Oleic, stearic, palmitic acids are [BHU]

(a) nucleic acids (b) amino acids
(c) fatty acids (d) None of these

54 Corrosive sublimate, $HgCl_2$ can be used to distinguish between [MHT CET]

(a) formic acid and acetic acid
(b) acetaldehyde and butanone
(c) formaldehyde and propanone
(d) All of the above

55 A pure dextrorotatory monocarboxylic acid is treated with racemic mixture of an alcohol containing one chiral carbon. The ester formed will be [Kerala CEE]

(a) pure dextrorotatory (b) racemic mixture
(c) *meso* compound
(d) optically active mixture containing excess dextrorotatory compound
(e) optically active mixture containing excess laevorotatory compound

56 CH_3COOH is a weaker acid than H_2SO_4. It is due to [RPMT]

(a) more ionisation (b) less ionisation
(c) covalent bond (d) electrovalent bond

57 $C_6H_5MgBr \xrightarrow[\text{(ii) } H_3O^+]{\text{(i) } CO_2} P$

In the above reaction, product P is [Punjab PMET]

(a) 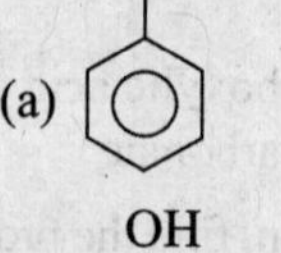 (b) C_6H_5COOH

(c) 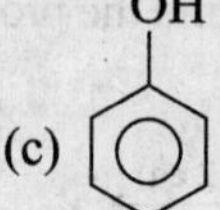 (d) $C_6H_5—\overset{O}{\overset{\|}{C}}—C_6H_5$

2006

58 Saturated fatty acids are represented by which of the formula? **[RPMT]**

(a) $C_nH_nO_2$ (b) $C_nH_{3n}O_2$
(c) C_nH_{2n+1} (d) $C_nH_{2n}O_2$

59 The ratio of carbon, hydrogen and oxygen in 2-methyl benzoic acid is **[EAMCET]**

(a) 4 : 2 : 2 (b) 2 : 4 : 1 (c) 4 : 4 : 1 (d) 4 : 4 : 2

60 Dichlorobenzoic acid $\xrightarrow{\text{Mononitration}}$ Product (only one). The structure of reactant can be **[DUMET]**

(a) 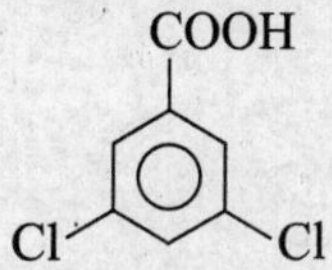 COOH, Cl, Cl
(b) 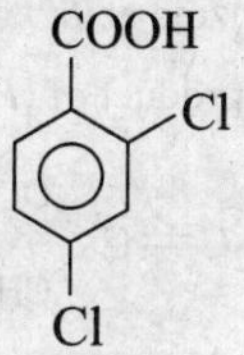 COOH, Cl, Cl
(c) 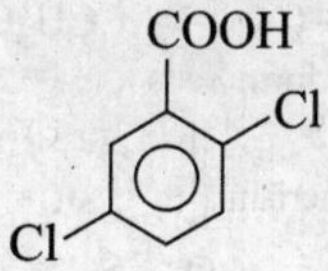 COOH, Cl, Cl
(d) 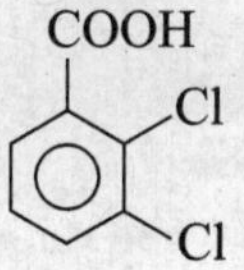 COOH, Cl, Cl

61 Match the following Columns.

Column I	Column II
A. Alkane	1. Molasses
B. Ethers	2. Hell-Volhard-Zelinsky reaction
C. α-halogenation	3. Williamson synthesis
D. Ethyl alcohol	4. Wurtz reaction
	5. Aldol condensation

The correct answer is **[EAMCET]**

	A	B	C	D		A	B	C	D
(a)	4	3	2	1	(b)	3	4	2	5
(c)	2	5	3	4	(d)	5	2	1	4

62 Which of the following does not give benzoic acid on hydrolysis? **[KCET]**

(a) Phenyl cyanide
(b) Benzoyl chloride
(c) Benzyl chloride
(d) Methyl benzoate

63 $D(+)$ lactic acid is obtained from **[Guj CET]**

(a) fermentation of cane sugar
(b) green vegetables
(c) muscles
(d) fermentation of milk sugar

64 When CH_3COOH reacts with $CH_3—MgX$ **[BCECE]**

(a) CH_3COX is formed
(b) hydrocarbon is formed
(c) acetone is formed
(d) alcohol is formed

65 Which reagent can convert acetic acid into ethanol? **[BCECE]**

(a) Na + alcohol (b) $LiAlH_4$ + ether
(c) H_2 + Pt (d) Sn + HCl

2005

66 A compound, containing only carbon, hydrogen and oxygen, has a molecular weight of 44. On complete oxidation it is converted into a compound of molecular weight 60. The original compound is **[KCET]**

(a) an aldehyde (b) an acid
(c) an alcohol (d) an ether

67 An example for a saturated fatty acid, present in nature is **[KCET]**

(a) oleic acid
(b) linoleic acid
(c) linolenic acid
(d) palmitic acid

Answers

1 (c)	2 (b)	3 (d)	4 (d)	5 (c)	6 (b)	7 (a)	8 (b)	9 (c)	10 (a)
11 (a)	12 (b)	13 (d)	14 (d)	15 (d)	16 (d)	17 (a)	18 (a)	19 (a)	20 (d)
21 (a)	22 (c)	23 (c)	24 (b)	25 (a)	26 (b)	27 (d)	28 (d)	29 (c)	30 (b)
31 (a)	32 (d)	33 (d)	34 (c)	35 (c)	36 (d)	37 (c)	38 (d)	39 (c)	40 (d)
41 (b)	42 (c)	43 (a)	44 (a)	45 (d)	46 (c)	47 (b)	48 (b)	49 (a)	50 (b)
51 (b)	52 (d)	53 (c)	54 (a)	55 (d)	56 (b)	57 (b)	58 (d)	59 (c)	60 (b)
61 (a)	62 (c)	63 (c)	64 (b)	65 (b)	66 (a)	67 (d)			

Explanations

1 (*c*) Primary aromatic alcohols on reaction with pyridinium chlorochromate (PCC) (a mild oxidising agent) forms aromatic aldehydes.

$$C_6H_5CH_2OH \xrightarrow[\text{(Pyridinium chlorochromate)}]{\text{PCC}} C_6H_5CHO \text{ (Benzaldehyde)}$$

In the remaining options, benzoic acid is formed as follows:

$$C_6H_5CH_2OH \xrightarrow{K_2Cr_2O_7} C_6H_5COOH \text{ (Benzoic acid)}$$

$$C_6H_5COCH_3 \xrightarrow[\text{(ii) } H_3O^+]{\text{(i) NaOCl}} C_6H_5COOH + CHCl_3 \text{ (Benzoic acid)}$$

$$C_6H_5CH_2OH \xrightarrow{KMnO_4/H^+} C_6H_5COOH \text{ (Benzoic acid)}$$

Thus, option (c) is correct.

2 (*b*) Higher the pK_a value or smaller is the K_a value, weaker is the acid.

$\therefore \quad pK_a = -\log[K_a]$

In structure (i), fluorine (F) show $(-I)$ effect, thus is most acidic.
In structure (ii), CH_3COOH, —CH_3 show $(+I)$ effect, and also hyperconjugation, so is weaker acid than (i).
In structure (iii), i.e. C_6H_5—COOH, the —COOH group is in resonance with the benzene ring. Thus, its carbocation is stable, therefore it is more acidic than (ii) and (iv) but is less acidic than (i).
In structure (iv), larger alkyl group bonded with —COOH group, which show stronger $(+I)$ effect, thus is the weakest acid.

Therefore, order of acidic nature is
(i) > (iii) > (ii) > (iv).

Hence, correct order of pK_a values
(iv) > (ii) > (iii) > (i)

Thus, option (b) is correct.

3 (*d*) Carboxylic acids have higher boiling points than aldehydes, ketones and even alcohols of comparable molecular mass, because of the extent of intermolecular-hydrogen bonding with water, due to which they exist as associated molecules.

(Structure: carboxylic acid molecules R—C(=O)—O—H hydrogen bonded with water molecules, showing δ^+ on H and δ^- on O.)

The hydrogen bonds are not completely broken in the vapour state. In fact, most carboxylic acids exist as dimer in the vapour state or in aprotic solvents.

(Structure: carboxylic acid dimer R—C(=O$^{\delta-}$)—O—H$^{\delta+}$ ··· linked by H-bonds.)

4 (*d*) Neutral $FeCl_3$ is used to distinguish phenol and benzoic acid. It gives violet colour with phenol and buff-coloured precipitates with benzoic acid.

5 (*c*) The product of (*P*) and (*Q*) are

$$P \Rightarrow H_2C{=}C(OCOCH_3)CH_3 \xrightarrow{H_2O/H^+} H_2C{=}C(OH)CH_3 \text{ (Enol form)} + CH_3COOH$$

$\Updownarrow$ Tautomerism

$$CH_3{-}\overset{O}{\overset{\|}{C}}{-}CH_3 \text{ (Acetone)}$$

$$Q \Rightarrow CH_3{-}CH{=}CH{-}OCOCH_3 \xrightarrow{H_2O/H^+} CH_3{-}CH{=}CH{-}OH \text{ (Enol-form)} + CH_3COOH$$

$\Updownarrow$ Tautomerism

$$CH_3{-}CH_2{-}\overset{O}{\overset{\|}{C}}{-}H \text{ (Aldehyde)}$$

∵ Fehling solution cannot be reduced with acetone.
Thus, it can be used to differentiate ketone (acetone) and aldehyde.

6 (*b*) Order of strengths of the given carboxylic acids can be determined by the concept of *I*-effect.
The oxygen atom present in the ring shows –*I*-effect. As the distance between oxygen and —COOH group increases, –*I*-effect of oxygen decreases.
Thus, corresponding carboxylic acid will show less acidic nature.
The correct order of strengths of the carboxylic acids is,

II > III > I

II: More -*I*-effect (Most acidic); III: Less -*I*-effect (Moderately acidic); I: No -*I*-effect (Least acidic)

7 (*a*) Priority order of functional group is
—COOH > —OH > —NH_2

∴ IUPAC name of the compound is
2-amino-4-hydroxy benzoic acid.

8 (*b*) The complete series of reaction can be represented as :

Cyclohexene + HBr ⟶ Bromocyclohexane (*A*) $\xrightarrow{KCN}$ Cyclohexyl cyanide (*B*) $\xrightarrow{H_3O^+}$ Cyclohexanecarboxylic acid (*C*) $\xrightarrow[\text{HVZ reaction}]{Br_2/\text{Red P}}$ 1-bromocyclohexanecarboxylic acid (*D*)

9 (*c*) The complete series of given reactions can be represented as,

C_6H_5COOH or Benzoic acid $\xrightarrow{NH_3}$ Ammonium benzoate ($C_6H_5COONH_4$) $\xrightarrow{\Delta}$ Benzamide ($C_6H_5CONH_2$) (*P*) $\xrightarrow{NaOBr}$ Aniline (*Q*) $\xrightarrow{\text{Conc. } H_2SO_4}$ Anilinium hydrogen sulphate ($\overset{+}{N}H_3\ HSO_4^-$) $\xrightarrow[-H_2O]{460\text{ K}}$ $C_6H_5NHSO_3H$ $\xrightarrow{\text{Rearrangement}}$ (*R*) Sulphanilic acid (NH_2, SO_3H para)

10 (*a*) Presence of an electron withdrawing group, (*–I*-effect showing group) like-Cl facilitates the removal of proton from carboxylic acid by dispersing the negative charge of the carboxylate ion formed. Thus, the acidity of the carboxylic acids is increased. Greater the number of *–I*-effect showing groups, more will be the acidity of carboxylic acid. Thus, the order of the acidic strength is

$$Cl_3CCOOH > Cl_2CHCOOH > ClCH_2COOH > CH_3COOH$$

11 (*a*) Tollen's reagent is ammoniacal silver nitrate ($AgNO_3$). It is reduced to silver by compounds having $-\overset{O}{\overset{\|}{C}}-H$ group.

Since, $H-\overset{O}{\overset{\|}{C}}-OH$ (Formic acid) has $-\overset{O}{\overset{\|}{C}}-H$ group, so, it reduces Tollen's reagent.

$$2[Ag(NH_3)_2]^+ + H-\overset{O}{\overset{\|}{C}}-OH \longrightarrow \underset{\text{Silver}}{2Ag\downarrow} + CO_2 + 2NH_4^+$$

12 (*b*) Below 16.6°C, pure acetic acid is converted into ice-like solid hence, it is called 'glacial acetic acid'. So, it is obtained by crystallisation, separating and melting of acetic acid.

13 (*d*) When salicylic acid is treated with zinc dust, benzoic acid is obtained as the product.

Salicylic acid $\xrightarrow{\text{Zn dust}}$ Benzoic acid + ZnO

14 (*d*) $CH_3COOH + 4[H] \xrightarrow{LiAlH_4} \underset{A}{CH_3CH_2OH} + H_2O$

$$\underset{A}{CH_3CH_2OH} + CH_3COOH \xrightarrow{H_3O^+} \underset{B}{CH_3COOC_2H_5} + H_2O$$

15 (*d*)

$O=C=O$ (Dry ice [1 mole]) + $Me_3C—MgI$ (2-methylpropyl magnesium iodide [1 mole]) $\xrightarrow{\text{Dry ether}}$ $O=C(\overset{-}{O}\overset{+}{Mg}I)—CMe_3$

$\xrightarrow{H_3O^+}$ $O=C(OH)—CMe_3$ + Mg(OH)I or Me_3CCO_2H

16 (*d*) *m*-Bromobenzoic acid (COOH) (*A*) $\xrightarrow{SOCl_2}$ *m*-Bromobenzoyl chloride (COCl) (*B*) $\xrightarrow[NH_3]{-HCl}$ *m*-Bromobenzamide ($CONH_2$) (*C*) $\xrightarrow[Br_2]{NaOH}$ *m*-Bromoaniline (NH_2) (*D*)

17 (*a*) Due to *ortho* effect, *o*-nitrobenzoic acid is stronger acid than 3,5-dinitrobenzoic acid in H_2O.

18 (*a*) For the conversion of carboxylic acids into primary amines, Curtius degradation method is employed.

Cyclohexyl$-\overset{O}{\overset{\|}{C}}-OH \xrightarrow{SOCl_2}$ Cyclohexyl$-\overset{O}{\overset{\|}{C}}-Cl$ (Acyl chloride) $\xrightarrow{NaN_3}$ Cyclohexyl$-\overset{O}{\overset{\|}{C}}-N=\overset{+}{N}=N$ (Acyl azide)

$$\text{Cyclohexyl-}C(=O)-N=\overset{+}{N}=\overset{-}{N} \xrightarrow{-N_2} \text{Cyclohexyl-}C(=O)-\ddot{N}: \xrightarrow{\text{Intramolecular shift}} \text{Cyclohexyl-}N=C=O \xrightarrow[\Delta]{H_2O} \text{Cyclohexyl-}NH_2 + CO_2$$

19 (*a*)

$$C_6H_5CH_2CH_3 \xrightarrow[\text{[oxidation]}]{KMnO_4,\ KOH} \underset{B}{C_6H_5COOH} \xrightarrow[\text{[bromination]}]{Br_2,\ FeCl_3}$$

$$\underset{C}{m\text{-}BrC_6H_4COOH} \xrightarrow[\text{[esterification]}]{C_2H_5OH,\ H^+} \underset{D}{m\text{-}BrC_6H_4COOC_2H_5}$$

20 (*d*) $\underset{COOH}{\overset{COOH}{|}}$ + Conc. $H_2SO_4 \xrightarrow{\Delta} H_2O + CO_2 + CO$

($\because$ Conc. H_2SO_4 is a strong dehydrating agent, i.e. removes water readily)

21 (*a*) β-keto carboxylic acids readily undergo decarboxylation. They get decarboxylated just by heating as,

$$H_5C_6-C(=\ddot{O})-CH_2-C(=O)-O-H \xrightarrow[\Delta]{-CO_2} H_5C_6-C(OH)=CH_2 \xrightarrow{\text{Tautomerisation}} H_5C_6-C(=O)-CH_3$$

22 (*c*) Carboxylic acids are much stronger than hydrocyanic acids, i.e. HCN. On the other hand, acidity of carboxylic acids is influenced by the presence of $-I$-effect showing groups as these groups stablises the carboxyanion. Greater the number of $-I$-effect groups linked to carboxylate carbon, larger would be the acidity of carboxylic acids.

However, the presence of $+I$-effect showing group decreases the acidity of carboxylic acids by increasing the electron density on carboxylate carbon, therefore destablising it.

Hence, the correct order would be,

$$ClCH_2COOH > HCOOH > CH_3COOH > HCN$$

23 (*c*) $C_2H_5OH\ (X) \xrightarrow{PCl_5} C_2H_5Cl + POCl_3 + HCl$

$$CH_3CO_2H\ (Y) \xrightarrow{PCl_5} CH_3COCl + POCl_3 + HCl$$

24 (*b*) $CH_3CH_2COOH \xrightarrow{Cl_2, P} \underset{\text{2-chloropropanoic acid } (X)}{CH_3-\underset{Cl}{\underset{|}{CH}}-COOH} \xrightarrow[-H_2O]{\text{Alc. KOH}} \underset{(Y)}{CH_2=CH-COOH}$

25 (*a*) $\overset{-}{C}H_3\overset{+}{Mg}Br + O=C=O \longrightarrow O=\underset{CH_3}{\underset{|}{C}}-OMgBr \xrightarrow{H_2O} CH_3COOH + Mg(OH)Br$

26 (*b*) The reaction in which α-H is replaced by halogen atom on reaction of the carboxylic acid with red phosphorus and Cl_2 or Br_2 is called Hell-Volhard Zelinsky reaction (or HVZ reaction).

$$RCH_2CH_2COOH \xrightarrow[Br_2]{\text{Red P}} RCH_2\underset{Br}{\underset{|}{C}H}COOH$$

27 (*d*) $H-\overset{O}{\overset{\|}{C}}-\overset{-}{O} \longleftrightarrow H-\overset{O^{\ominus}}{\overset{|}{C}}=O$

In $HCOO^-$, the two carbon oxygen bonds are of equal length because the anion $HCOO^-$ has two resonating structures, and due to resonance, partial double bond character is created which results in equal bond lengths of C — O bond.

28 (*d*) $CH_3COOH \xrightarrow{SOCl_2} \underset{A}{CH_3COCl} \xrightarrow[\text{(Friedel-Craft's acylation)}]{\text{Benzene, Anhy. } AlCl_3}$

$$\underset{B}{C_6H_5-C(=O)-CH_3} \xrightarrow{HCN} \underset{C}{HO-\underset{C_6H_5}{\underset{|}{\overset{CN}{\overset{|}{C}}}}-CH_3} \xrightarrow{H_2O} \underset{D}{HO-\underset{C_6H_5}{\underset{|}{\overset{COOH}{\overset{|}{C}}}}-CH_3}$$

29 (*c*) Greater the electron withdrawing nature of the halogen atom, stronger will be the acid.

Hence, FCH_2COOH is most acidic due to the most electron withdrawing power of the fluorine atom.

30 (*b*) Because the difference in mass between —CH_2OH group and —COOH group is 14, thus the compound which undergoes oxidation is a primary alcohol (—CH_2OH is the functional group of primary alcohols.)

$$\underset{\substack{(R+31)\\ \text{Primary alcohol}}}{RCH_2OH} \xrightarrow{[O]} \underset{\substack{(R+45)\\ \text{Acid}}}{RCOOH}$$

31 (*a*) Benzoic acid reacts with $NaHCO_3$ to give effervescence due to the evolution of CO_2.

$$C_6H_5COOH + NaHCO_3 \longrightarrow C_6H_5CO\overset{-}{O}\overset{+}{Na} + H_2O + CO_2$$

Phenol does not give effervescence. Phenol and benzoic acid cannot be distinguished by NaOH and Na because both can react with NaOH and Na.

32 (*d*) Carboxylic acids react with Cl_2 or Br_2 in the presence of red P to give exclusively α-chloro or α-bromo acids. This reaction is called Hell-Volhard-Zelinsky (HVZ) reaction.

$$\underset{\text{Propionic acid}}{\overset{\beta}{C}H_3\overset{\alpha}{C}H_2COOH} \xrightarrow[-HBr]{Br_2,\ \text{red P}} \underset{\alpha\text{-bromopropionic acid}}{CH_3\overset{\alpha}{C}BrCOOH} \xrightarrow[-HBr]{Br_2,\ \text{red P}} \underset{\alpha,\alpha\text{-dibromopropionic acid}}{CH_3\overset{\alpha}{C}Br_2COOH}$$

33 (d)

$$2CH_3-\underset{}{\overset{CH_3}{\overset{|}{C}}}H-COOH \xrightarrow{P_4/I_2} 2CH_3-\overset{CH_3}{\overset{|}{\underset{I}{\underset{|}{C}}}}-COOH$$

$$\xrightarrow[\text{(Wurtz reaction)}]{2Na/\Delta,\ -2NaI} \begin{matrix} CH_3-\overset{CH_3}{\overset{|}{C}}-COOH \\ | \\ CH_3-\underset{CH_3}{\underset{|}{C}}-COOH \end{matrix} \xrightarrow[P_2O_5,\ \Delta]{-H_2O}$$

(cyclic anhydride: tetramethylsuccinic anhydride, drawn with H_3C groups) or (skeletal form)

34 (c) Only carboxylic acids give acyl chloride with $SOCl_2$/ pyridine. Among acids, only HCOOH (formic acid) due to the presence of aldehyde group, reduces Fehling solution.

$$\underset{(X)}{HCOOH} \xrightarrow[\text{Fehling solution}]{Cu(OH)_2} H_2O + CO_2 + \underset{\text{Red ppt.}}{Cu_2O\downarrow}$$

$$\underset{(X)}{HCOOH} + SOCl_2 \xrightarrow{\text{Pyridine}} \underset{\text{Unstable}}{HCOCl} + HCl$$

$$HCOCl \longrightarrow HCl + CO$$

35 (c) $CH_3COOH \xrightarrow{NH_3} \underset{X}{CH_3CO\overset{-}{O}\overset{+}{N}H_4} \xrightarrow[-H_2O]{\Delta}$

$$\underset{Y}{CH_3CONH_2} \xrightarrow[-H_2O]{P_2O_5} \underset{\text{(Methyl cyanide)}}{\underset{Z}{CH_3CN}}$$

36 (d) Formic acid (HCOOH) cannot be prepared from methyl magnesium bromide (CH_3MgBr) while from all other reagents, it is obtained as

$$\underset{\text{Methyl alcohol}}{CH_3OH} \xrightarrow{[O]} HCHO \xrightarrow{[O]} HCOOH$$

$$\underset{\text{Carbon monoxide}}{CO} + NaOH \longrightarrow HCO\overset{-}{O}\overset{+}{N}a \xrightarrow[\Delta]{NaHSO_4} HCOOH + Na_2SO_4$$

$$\text{Glycerol} + \text{Oxalic acid} \xrightarrow[H_2O]{383\ K} HCOOH + \text{Glycerol}$$

37 (c) The acidic nature of carboxylic acids is due to greater resonance stabilisation of the carboxylate ion over carboxylic acid. The high degree of ionisation or the solubility of carboxylic acids in water is not the correct Reason for the acidic nature of carboxylic acids.

38 (d) $CH_3COOH + \underset{\text{Sodium bicarbonate}}{Na^+O^--\overset{O}{\overset{||}{C}}-OH} \longrightarrow CH_3-\overset{O}{\overset{||}{C}}-\overset{-}{O}\overset{+}{N}a$

$$+ \left[H-O-\overset{O}{\overset{||}{C}}-OH\right] \longrightarrow CO_2 + H_2O$$

Hence, carbon of CO_2 comes from bicarbonate.

39 (c) Cyclopentane-1,2-dione $\xrightarrow[\text{Benzilic acid rearrangement}]{OH^-}$ 1-hydroxycyclobutane-1-carboxylate (OH, COO^-) $\xrightarrow{H^+}$ (X) 1-hydroxycyclobutane-1-carboxylic acid (OH, $COOH$) $\xrightarrow{SOCl_2}$ (Y) (Cl, $COCl$)

40 (d) Electron donating groups decrease acidic strength of benzoic acid and electron withdrawing groups increase acidic strength. Order of $+I$ effect is —OMe > — Me. So, *p*-methoxybenzoic acid is weaker acid than *p*-methylbenzoic acid.

41 (b) Reaction II and III will give carboxylic acid

- $CH_3CHO + \underset{\text{(Tollen's reagent)}}{2[Ag(NH_3)_2]^+} + 3OH^-$
$$\longrightarrow CH_3COO^- + 2Ag\downarrow + 4NH_3 + 2H_2O$$
- $H_3CCO_2C_2H_5 \xrightarrow[\text{(Base hydrolysis of ester)}]{OH^-} H_3CCOO^- + C_2H_5OH$

CH_3COO^- upon hydrolysis will give CH_3COOH.

42 (c) I. $\begin{matrix}CH_3COO \\ CH_3COO\end{matrix}\!\!>Ca \xrightarrow[-CaCO_3]{\Delta} CH_3COCH_3\ (A)$

II. $CH_3COOH + 6HI \xrightarrow{\text{Red P}} \underset{(B)}{CH_3CH_3} + 3I_2 + 2H_2O$

III. $\begin{matrix}CH_3COOH \\ + \\ CH_3COOH\end{matrix} \xrightarrow{\Delta,\ P_4O_{10}} \underset{(C)}{\begin{matrix}CH_3CO \\ CH_3CO\end{matrix}\!\!>O} + H_2O$

43 (a) $CH_3COOH \xrightarrow{LiAlH_4} \underset{X}{CH_3CH_2OH} \xrightarrow[300°C]{Cu} \underset{Y}{CH_3CHO}$

$$\xrightarrow[CH_3CHO]{\text{Dil. NaOH}} \underset{Z\ \text{(aldol)}}{CH_3-\underset{OH}{\underset{|}{C}}H-CH_2CHO}$$

Acetaldehyde (*Y*) undergoes aldol condensation in the presence of dilute caustic alkali to form aldol.

44 (a) $\underset{\text{Adipic acid}}{HOOC-(CH_2)_4-COOH} \xrightarrow{\Delta} \underset{\text{Cyclopentanone}}{\begin{matrix}CH_2-CH_2 \\ | \\ CH_2-CH_2\end{matrix}\!\!>C=O}$

45 (d) $CH_3COOH \xrightarrow{CaCO_3} \underset{A}{(CH_3COO)_2Ca} \xrightarrow[-CaCO_3]{\Delta}$

$$\underset{(B)}{(CH_3)_2CO} \xrightarrow[-H_2O]{NH_2OH} \underset{\text{Acetoxime (C)}}{(CH_3)_2C=NOH}$$

46 (c) $RCOOH + NaHCO_3 \rightleftharpoons RCO\overset{-}{O}\overset{+}{N}a + H_2O + CO_2$

or $RCOOH + HCO_3^- \rightleftharpoons RCOO^- + H_2O + CO_2$

Conjugate base, $RCOO^-$ is more stable than the free carboxylic acid due to resonance. That is why equilibrium shifts in the forward direction.

47 (b) $LiAlH_4$ reduces —COOH to —CH_2OH without affecting C=C bond.

$$CH_2=CH-COOH + 4[H] \xrightarrow[-H_2O]{LiAlH_4} CH_2=CH-CH_2OH$$

48 (b)

$$\begin{array}{c} H \diagdown \quad \diagup COOH \\ C \\ \| \\ C \\ H \diagup \quad \diagdown COOH \end{array} \xrightarrow[-H_2O]{\Delta} \begin{array}{c} HC - CO \\ \| \quad\quad \diagdown \\ \quad\quad\quad O \\ \| \quad\quad \diagup \\ HC - CO \end{array}$$

Maleic acid → Maleic anhydride

49 (a)

$$C_6H_5COOH + SOCl_2 \xrightarrow[-HCl]{-SO_2} C_6H_5COCl \xrightarrow[C_2H_5OH]{-HCl} C_6H_5COOC_2H_5$$

50 (b) The given hexanoic acid can be converted into 2-amino hexanoic acid in two steps:

(i) Hexanoic acid is converted into α-bromo hexanoic acid through Hell-Volhard Zelinsky reaction (HVZ).

$$CH_3CH_2CH_2CH_2CH_2COOH \xrightarrow[\text{HVZ reaction}]{Br_2/\text{red P}} CH_3CH_2CH_2CH_2\underset{|}{\overset{Br}{C}}HCOOH$$

2(α)-bromohexanoic acid

(ii) This α-bromo hexanoic acid is converted into 2-aminohexanoic acid by heating it with an alcoholic solution of ammonia, and this process is called ammonolysis (cleavage of C — X bond by ammonia).

$$CH_3CH_2CH_2CH_2\overset{Br}{\overset{|}{C}}H-COOH \xrightarrow[-HBr]{+NH_3 \text{ alc. (excess)}} CH_3CH_2CH_2CH_2\overset{NH_2}{\overset{|}{C}}H-COOH$$

51 (b)

$$CH_3COOH + PCl_5 \xrightarrow[-HCl]{-POCl_3} \underset{(A)}{CH_3COCl} \xrightarrow[\text{Anhy. AlCl}_3 \text{ [Friedel-Crafts acylation]}]{C_6H_6 \text{ or } \bigcirc}$$

$$\underset{(B)}{C_6H_5COCH_3} \xrightarrow[\text{ether}]{C_2H_5MgBr} C_6H_5-\overset{OMgBr}{\overset{|}{\underset{C_2H_5}{\underset{|}{C}}}}-CH_3$$

$$\xrightarrow{H_3O^+} C_6H_5-\overset{OH}{\overset{|}{\underset{C_2H_5}{\underset{|}{C}}}}-CH_3 \text{ or } C_6H_5-\overset{C_2H_5}{\overset{|}{\underset{OH}{\underset{|}{C}}}}-CH_3$$

(C)

52 (d) Acidic strength of carboxylic acids depend upon the stability of carboxylate ion. —NO_2 group at any position shows electron withdrawing effect, thus acid strength is increased, but *o*-nitrobenzoate ion is stabilised by intramolecular H-bonding, hence its acidic strength is maximum. Further, –*I*-effect is more pronounced at *p*-position.

Thus, the order of acidic strength is

(II) > (III) > (IV) > (I).

53 (c) Oleic acid, stearic acids and palmitic acids are fatty acids.

$C_{17}H_{33}COOH$ — Oleic acid (unsaturated fatty acid)

$C_{15}H_{31}COOH$ — Palmitic acid }
$C_{17}H_{35}COOH$ — Stearic acid } (saturated fatty acid)

54 (a) $2HCOOH + 2HgCl_2 \longrightarrow Hg_2Cl_2 + CO_2 + 2H_2O$

$CH_3COOH + HgCl_2 \longrightarrow$ No reaction

55 (d) Pure dextrorotatory monocarboxylic acid is treated with racemic mixture (*d* and *l*) of an alcohol containing one chiral carbon. The ester formed will be optically active mixture containing excess dextrorotatory compound.

56 (b) CH_3COOH is weaker acid than H_2SO_4. The reason is that CH_3COOH is weakly ionised in comparison to H_2SO_4.

57 (b)

$$\underset{\text{(Grignard reagent)}}{C_6H_5MgBr} \xrightarrow{\text{(i) } CO_2} C_6H_5\overset{O}{\overset{\|}{C}}-OMgBr \xrightarrow{\text{(ii) } H_3O^+} C_6H_5\overset{O}{\overset{\|}{C}}-OH + Mg\begin{array}{l}\diagup Br \\ \diagdown OH\end{array}$$

58 (d) The general formula of saturated acid is $C_nH_{2n+1}COOH$ or $C_nH_{2n}O_2$.

59 (c) 2-methylbenzoic acid is

(benzene ring with CH_3 and $COOH$ at adjacent positions)

Number of carbon, hydrogen and oxygen atoms are 8 : 8 : 2.

So, C : H : O
4 : 4 : 1

60 (b) Carboxyl group of benzoic acid is *meta* activating group.

2,4-dichlorobenzoic acid (COOH, Cl ortho, Cl para) $\xrightarrow{\text{Mononitration}}$ product with O_2N at position 5 (COOH, Cl, Cl, NO_2)

As the position is *ortho* and *para* with respect to chlorine atoms, hence, the nitro occupies *meta* position near to *p*-chloro position to avoid steric hinderance.

61 The correct match is A → 4, B → 3, C → 2, D → 1

(a) **Wurtz reaction** Alkyl halide when heated with metallic sodium in ether gives alkane by joining two alkyl groups.

$$2RX + 2Na \xrightarrow{\text{Ether}} R \cdot R + 2NaX$$

Williamson Synthesis It is the laboratory preparation of ether.

$$\underset{\text{Sodium alkoxide}}{RONa} + \underset{\text{Alkyl halide}}{R'X} \xrightarrow{\Delta} \underset{\text{Ether}}{ROR'} + NaX$$

Hell-Volhard-Zelinsky reaction α-chloro or α-bromo acids are usually prepared by first converting the acid into its chloride or bromide and then carrying out chlorination or bromination. This is called HVZ reaction. So, it is used for α-halogenation.

$$\underset{\text{Acid}}{RCH_2COOH} \xrightarrow{\text{red P} + Br_2} \underset{\alpha\text{-bromo acid}}{RCHBr-COOH} + HBr$$

Molasses : Ethyl alcohol is obtained from molasses. It is obtained as a by-product from sugar industry.

Hence, correct option is (a).

62 (*c*) Benzyl chloride on hydrolysis gives benzyl alcohol. All other compounds yield benzoic acid on hydrolysis.

$$\underset{\text{Benzyl chloride}}{C_6H_5CH_2Cl} \xrightarrow[\text{boil}]{\text{Aq. NaOH}} \underset{\text{Benzyl alcohol}}{C_6H_5CH_2OH} + NaCl$$

63 (*c*) *d*(+) lactic acid is obtained from meat extract. This is also known as sarcolactic acid.

64 (*b*) $CH_3COOH + CH_3MgX \longrightarrow CH_3CO\overset{-}{O}\overset{+}{Mg}X + \underset{\text{Methane}}{CH_4}$

65 (*b*) Lithium aluminium hydride is a powerful reducing agent. It reduces acetic acid into ethanol.

$$CH_3COOH \xrightarrow[\text{ether}]{LiAlH_4} CH_3CH_2OH$$

66 (*a*) On complete oxidation, the obtained compound shows increment in molecular weight of only 16.

It means only one oxygen atom is added here. This condition is fulfilled by only aldehyde which on oxidation gives acid.

$$RCHO \xrightarrow{[O]} RCOOH$$

Hence, original compound must be

$$\underset{\text{Mol. wt. 44}}{CH_3CHO} \xrightarrow{[O]} \underset{\text{Mol. wt. 60}}{CH_3COOH}$$

67 (*d*) Saturated monocarboxylic acids form a homologous series which has a general formula $C_nH_{2n+1}COOH$. Out of all the options only palmitic acid follows this.

Palmitic acid = $C_{15}H_{31}COOH$. All other acids are unsaturated fatty acids.

Topic 3

Derivatives of Carboxylic Acids

2019

1 The major product of the following reaction is **[NEET]**

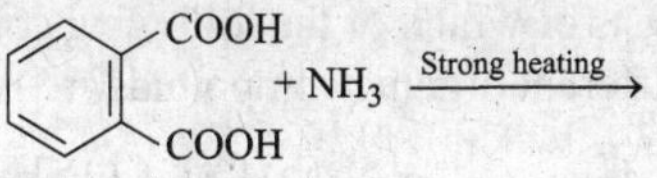

(Benzene ring with two ortho COOH groups) $+ NH_3 \xrightarrow{\text{Strong heating}}$

(a) (phthalimide: ring with two C=O and NH) (b) (benzene ring with COOH and NH_2)

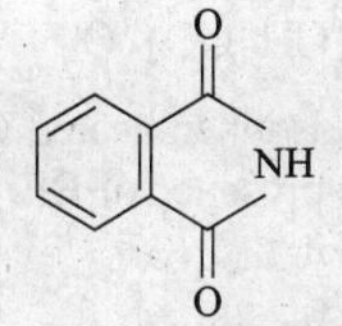

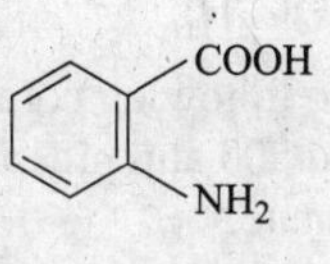

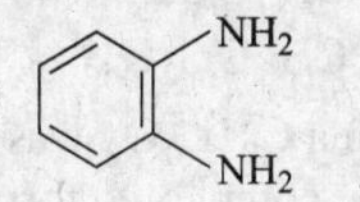

(c) (benzene ring with two NH_2) (d) (benzene ring with COOH and $CONH_2$)

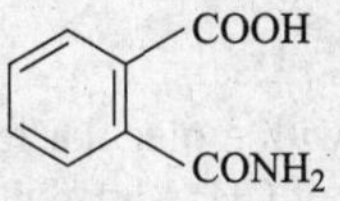

2018

2 The relative reactivities of acyl compounds towards nucleophilic substitution are in the order of **[AIIMS]**

(a) acyl chloride > acid anhydride > ester > amide
(b) ester > acyl chloride > amide > acid anhydride
(c) acid anhydride > amide > ester > acyl chloride
(d) acid chloride > ester > acid anhydride > amide

2017

3 Which of the following is the correct IUPAC name? **[JIPMER]**

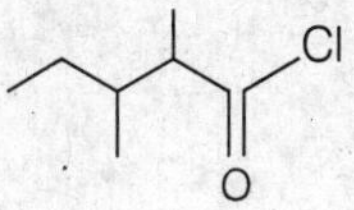

(skeletal structure with Cl and O)

(a) 3, 4-dimethyl pentanoyl chloride
(b) 1-chloro-1-oxo-2, 3-dimethyl pentane
(c) 2-ethyl-3-methyl butanoyl chloride
(d) 2, 3-dimethyl pentanoyl chloride

2014

4 Among the following compounds, the one(s) that gives (give) effervescence with aqueous $NaHCO_3$ solution is (are)

$$\underset{\text{I}}{(CH_3CO)_2O}, \underset{\text{II}}{CH_3COOH}, \underset{\text{III}}{PhOH}, \underset{\text{IV}}{CH_3COCHO}$$ **[WB JEE]**

(a) I and II (b) I and III
(c) Only II (d) I and IV

5 The acid strength of active methylene group in

I. $CH_3COCH_2COOC_2H_5$
II. $CH_3COCH_2COCH_3$
III. $C_2H_5OOCCH_2COOC_2H_5$

decreases as **[KCET]**

(a) I > III > II (b) I > II > III
(c) II > I > III (d) III > I > II

2013

6 At higher temperature, iodoform reaction is given by the dilute solution of **[AIIMS]**

(a) $CH_3CO_2CH_3$ (b) $CH_3CO_2C_2H_5$
(c) $C_6H_5CO_2CH_3$ (d) $CH_3CO_2C_6H_5$

2012

7 The main product obtained in the reaction of acetamide and HNO_2 is **[AIIMS]**

(a) CH_3CN (b) CH_3NC
(c) CH_3NH_2 (d) CH_3COOH

2011

8 Give IUPAC name of the product, when acetamide is heated with anhydrous phosphorus pentoxide. **[Guj CET]**

(a) Ethylamine (b) Propane nitrile
(c) Cyano methane (d) Methyl nitrile

2010

9 In the following reaction,

$$C_6H_5COOCH_3 \xrightarrow[H_2O/H^+]{LiAlH_4} A + B$$

A and B are respectively. **[UP CPMT]**

(a) $C_6H_5CH_2OH + HCOOH$
(b) $C_6H_5CH_2OH + CH_3OH$
(c) $C_6H_5OH + CH_3COOH$
(d) $C_6H_5COOH + CH_3OH$

10 CH_3COOH when reacts with C_2H_5OH give a product. The same product is obtained by which reaction? **[MHT CET]**

(a) Acetic acid + Methanol
(b) Acetic anhydride + Water
(c) Acetic anhydride + Ethanol
(d) Acetamide + Methanol

11 Methyl acetate will be obtained by reacting CH_3OH with

(a) CH_3COOH (b) CH_3COCl **[Manipal]**
(c) $(CH_3CO)_2O$ (d) All of these

12 Which of the following is phenyl ethanoate? **[Guj CET]**

(a) C_6H_5—$COOCH_3$ (b) 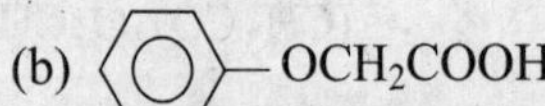

(c) 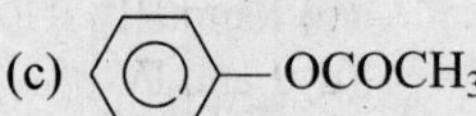 (d) C_6H_5—$COOC_2H_5$

13 Acetic anhydride reacts with diethyl ether in the presence of anhydrous $AlCl_3$ to give **[JCECE]**

(a) CH_3CH_2COOH
(b) $CH_3CH_2COOCH_2CH_3$
(c) CH_3COOCH_3
(d) $CH_3COOC_2H_5$

14 What product is formed on heating two molecules of urea?

(a) Uric acid (b) Biuret **[VMMC]**
(c) Nitrogen (d) Carbon dioxide

2009

15 In the following reaction,

$$C_2H_5OH + CH_3COOH \xrightarrow[-H_2O]{Conc.\ H_2SO_4} CH_3COOC_2H_5$$

C_2H_5OH acts as **[AFMC]**

(a) electrophile (b) nucleophile
(c) dehydrating agent (d) All of these

16 Ethyl butyrate has the flavour of which fruit? **[MHT CET]**

(a) Apple (b) Pineapple
(c) Orange (d) Banana

17 When acetyl chloride reacts with sodium propionate, the product formed is **[DUMET]**

(a) acetic anhydride
(b) acetic propionic anhydride
(c) *n*-propyl acetate (d) pent-2,4-dione

18 The reaction involved in the oil of winter green test is

salicylic acid $\xrightarrow[Conc.\ H_2SO_4]{\Delta}$ products. The product is

treated with Na_2CO_3 solution. The missing reagent in the above reaction is **[KCET]**

(a) NaOH (b) ethanol (c) methanol (d) phenol

2008

19 Acid hydrolysis of which of the following compounds yields two different organic compounds? **[AIIMS]**

(a) CH_3COOH (b) CH_3CONH_2
(c) $CH_3COOC_2H_5$ (d) $(CH_3CO)_2O$

20 Which of the following compounds when heated with CO at 150°C and 500 atm pressure in presence of BF_3 forms ethyl propionate? **[AFMC]**

(a) C_2H_5OH (b) CH_3OCH_3
(c) $C_2H_5OC_2H_5$ (d) $CH_3OC_2H_5$

21 An ester A with molecular formula $C_9H_{10}O_2$ was treated with excess of CH_3MgBr and the complex so formed was treated with H_2SO_4 to give an olefin B. Ozonolysis of B gave a ketone with molecular formula C_8H_8O which shows positive iodoform test. The structure of A is **[MHT CET]**

(a) $C_6H_5COOC_2H_5$ (b) $C_6H_5COOC_6H_5$
(c) $C_6H_5COOCH_3$ (d) p-$H_3COC_6H_4COCH_3$

22 Ethyl acetate is obtained when methyl magnesium bromide reacts with **[Manipal]**

(a) ethyl formate (b) ethyl chloroformate
(c) acetyl chloride (d) carbon dioxide

23 The major product in the reaction of N-phenyl benzamide with Br_2 / Fe is [Kerala CEE]

(a) —CONH— (Br on the benzoyl ring)

(b) —CONH— —Br

(c) —CONH— (Br on the anilide ring)

(d) Br— —CONH—

(e) —CONH— —Br (with Br also on the benzoyl ring)

24 Hydroxamic acid test is employed to detect [J&K CET]

(a) ketones (b) aldehydes (c) esters (d) amides

25 Benzamide can be converted into benzonitrile with [J&K CET]

(a) H_3O^+ (b) OH^- / H_2O

(c) KCN (d) P_2O_5, Δ

26 Identify *C*, in the following reaction,

$$C_2H_2 \xrightarrow[\text{acid}]{\text{Chromic}} A \xrightarrow{NH_3} B \xrightarrow[-H_2O]{\Delta} C$$ [EAMCET]

(a) $CH_3—H_2—NH_2$ (b) $CH_3—CN$

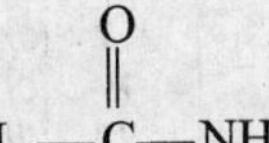

(c) $CH_3CH_2—NH—CH_3$ (d) $CH_3—\overset{O}{\overset{\|}{C}}—NH_2$

27 Waxes are esters of [KCET]

(a) glycerol
(b) long chain alcohols
(c) glycerol and fatty acid
(d) long chain alcohols and long chain fatty acids

2007

28 Methyl acetate and ethyl acetate can be distinguished by [AIIMS]

(a) hot alkaline $KMnO_4$ (b) neutral $FeCl_3$

(c) iodoform test (d) None of the above

29 The reagent which does not give acid chloride on treating with a carboxylic acid is [AFMC]

(a) PCl_5 (b) Cl_2 (c) $SOCl_2$ (d) PCl_3

30 Claisen condensation is not given by [UP CPMT]

(a) —COO—

(b) CH_3CH_2COO—

(c) —$COOCH_3$

(d) —$COOCH_2CH_2CH_3$

31 $CH_3—\overset{O}{CH—CH}CH_3$ is the epoxide of [MHT CET]

(a) 1, 2-butanediol (b) 2, 2-butanediol

(c) 2,3-butanediol (d) 1, 1-butanediol

32 Acetamide and $NaOBr/OH^-$ produce [MP PMT]

(a) ethanamide (b) methanamine

(c) ethanamine (d) formic acid

33 Amides are formed by the reaction of acid chloride with [J&K CET]

(a) NH_2NH_2 (b) NH_3

(c) NH_2OH (d) $C_6H_5NHNH_2$

34 In the reaction,

$$CH_3CH_2COONH_4 \xrightarrow{P_2O_5} A \xrightarrow{H^+ / H_2O} B$$

A and *B* are [DUMET]

(a) $CH_3CH_2CONH_2, CH_3CH_2COO^-$
(b) $CH_3CH_2COONH_2, CH_3CH_2COOH$
(c) $CH_3CH_2CN, CH_3CH_2COO^-$
(d) CH_3CH_2CN, CH_3CH_2COOH

2006

35 Self condensation of two moles of ethyl acetate in the presence of sodium ethoxide yields [CBSE AIPMT]

(a) ethyl butyrate (b) acetoacetic ester

(c) methyl acetoacetate (d) ethyl propionate

36 The following sequence of reactions of *A* gives [AIIMS]

CH_2CONH_2, $COOCH_3$ $\xrightarrow[\text{(ii) Heat}]{\text{(i) Br}_2\text{/NaOH}}$

(a) 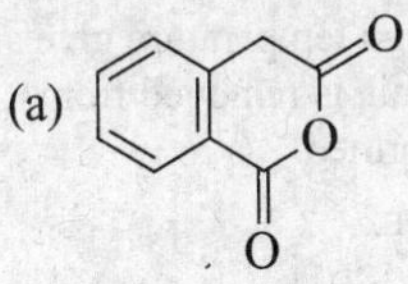 (b) 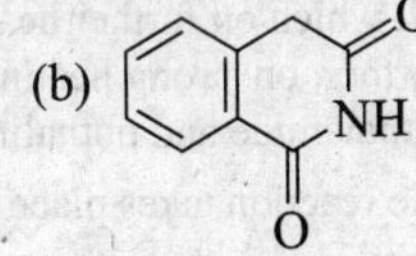

(c) 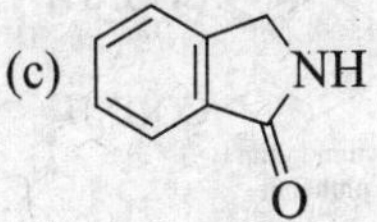 (d)

37 Sodium formate on heating gives [AFMC]

(a) oxalic acid and H_2
(b) sodium oxalate and H_2
(c) sodium oxalate
(d) CO_2 and caustic soda

38 Identify the wrong statement. **[MHT CET]**

(a) Salicylic acid is a monobasic acid
(b) Methyl salicylate is an ester
(c) Salicylic acid gives violet colour with neutral ferric chloride as well as brisk effervescence with sodium bicarbonate
(d) Methyl salicylate does not occur in mineral oils

39 Which reaction is used for the preparation of acetophenone? **[RPMT]**

(a) Reimer-Tiemann reaction
(b) Wurtz-fitting reaction
(c) Friedel-Craft's reaction
(d) Cannizzaro's reaction

40 Match the following columns.

Column I	Column II
A. $PhCO_2CH_3$	1. 2, 4-DNP
B. $C_6H_5CH_2CO_2H$	2. Arndt-Eister synthesis
C. C_6H_5CHO	3. Hydrolysis

Correct answer is **[J&K CET]**

	A	B	C		A	B	C
(a)	1	2	3	(b)	2	3	1
(c)	3	2	1	(d)	2	1	3

41 Which of the following represents soap? **[AMU]**

(a) $C_{17}H_{35}COOK$ (b) $C_{17}H_{35}COOH$
(c) $C_{15}H_{31}COOH$ (d) $(C_{17}H_{35}COO)_2Ca$

42 CH_3COCl does not react with **[JCECE]**

(a) diethyl ether (b) phenol (c) ethanol (d) aniline

2005

43 Among the following which one does not act as an intermediate in Hofmann rearrangement? **[AIIMS]**

(a) $RNCO$ (b) $RCON$ (c) $RCO\ddot{N}HBr$ (d) RNC

44 $CH_3CO_2C_2H_5$ on reaction with sodium ethoxide in ethanol gives *A*, which on heating in the presence of an acid gives *B*. Compound *B* is **[AIIMS]**

(a) CH_3COCH_2COOH (b) CH_3COCH_3
(c) $CH_2{=}$ (cyclic structure with O and $=O$) (d) $CH_2=C(OC_2H_5)_2$

45 Order of hydrolysis for the following

I. $RCOCl$ II. $RCOOR$
III. $RCONH_2$ IV. $(RCO)_2O$ **[DUMET]**

(a) I > IV > II > III (b) I > II > III > IV
(c) I > III > II > IV (d) IV > III > II > I

Answers

1 (a)	2 (a)	3 (d)	4 (a)	5 (c)	6 (b)	7 (d)	8 (d)	9 (b)	10 (c)
11 (d)	12 (c)	13 (d)	14 (b)	15 (b)	16 (b)	17 (b)	18 (c)	19 (c)	20 (c)
21 (a)	22 (b)	23 (b)	24 (c)	25 (d)	26 (d)	27 (d)	28 (c)	29 (b)	30 (a)
31 (c)	32 (b)	33 (b)	34 (d)	35 (b)	36 (c)	37 (b)	38 (d)	39 (c)	40 (b)
41 (a)	42 (b)	43 (d)	44 (a)	45 (a)					

Explanations

1 (*a*) Carboxylic acids react with ammonia to give ammonium salt which on further heating at high temperature give amides. Further, on strong heating, ammonia is removed from phthalamide and phthalimide is formed.

The reaction takes place as follows:

Phthalic acid + NH_3 ⇌ Ammonium phthalate ($C_6H_4(COO^-NH_4^+)_2$)

Ammonium phthalate $\xrightarrow{\Delta,\ -2H_2O}$ Phthalamide ($C_6H_4(CONH_2)_2$)

Phthalamide $\xrightarrow[-NH_3]{\text{Strong heating}}$ Phthalimide

2 (*a*) The ease of nucleophilic substitution depends upon the nature of leaving group. When the leaving tendency of a group in a compound is high, then the compound is more reactive towards nucleophilic substitution. The nucleophilic acyl substitution is completed in two steps as shown below.

$R-C(=O)-A + :Z^- \longrightarrow [R-C(O^{\delta-})(A)\cdots Z]$ (Transition state) $\longrightarrow R-C(=O)-Z + A^-$

The reactivity of the compound may be explained on the basicity of the leaving group. A weaker base is a better leaving group. The relative basic strength of leaving group decreases as,

Hence, the order of leaving tendency is

$$Cl^- > RCOO^- > RO^- > NH_2^-$$

and therefore, the order of reactivity of acyl compound is as

$$\underset{\text{(Acyl chloride)}}{RCOCl} > \underset{\text{(Acid anhydride)}}{(RCO)_2O} > \underset{\text{(Ester)}}{RCOOR} > \underset{\text{(Amide)}}{RCONH_2}$$

3 (*d*)

$$\overset{5}{H_3C}-\overset{4}{CH_2}-\overset{3}{CH}(CH_3)-\overset{2}{CH}(CH_3)-\overset{1}{C}(=O)-Cl$$

2, 3-dimethyl pentanoyl chloride

4 (*a*) Only carboxylic acids and their derivatives like anhydride are able to give effervescence with aqueous $NaHCO_3$ solution, because they are more acidic as compared to H_2CO_3 (carbonic acid).

$$\underset{\text{Acetic acid}}{CH_3COOH} + \underset{\text{Sodium bicarbonate}}{NaHCO_3} \longrightarrow \underset{\text{Sodium acetate}}{CH_3CO\overset{-}{O}\overset{+}{Na}} + H_2O + CO_2$$

$$\underset{\text{Acetic anhydride}}{(CH_3CO)_2O} + \underset{\text{Sodium bicarbonate}}{2NaHCO_3} \longrightarrow \underset{\text{Sodium acetate}}{2CH_3CO\overset{-}{O}\overset{+}{Na}} + H_2O + CO_2$$

5 (*c*) Acidic strength in active methylene compounds can be decided by two factors.

(*i*) Presence of electron withdrawing group.

(*ii*) Stability of enolate anion obtained after removal of H^+.

Higher the electron withdrawing ability of substituents attached to electron withdrawing groups, higher will be acidic strength of methylene group.

Electron withdrawing ability of $CH_3CO—$ is greater than $CH_3CH_2O—\overset{O}{\overset{\|}{C}}—$. Thus, $CH_3—\overset{O}{\overset{\|}{C}}—$ increases acidic strength of active methylene compound to a greater extent than $CH_3CH_2O—\overset{O}{\overset{\|}{C}}—$.

Compounds	No. of $CH_3—\overset{O}{\overset{\|}{C}}—$ group	No. of $\overset{O}{\overset{\|}{C}}O—CH_2CH_3$ group
II $CH_3\overset{O}{\overset{\|}{C}}—CH_2—\overset{O}{\overset{\|}{C}}—CH_3$	2	0
I $CH_3—\overset{O}{\overset{\|}{C}}—CH_2—\overset{O}{\overset{\|}{C}}—O—C_2H_5$	1	1
III $CH_3CH_2O—\overset{O}{\overset{\|}{C}}—CH_2—\overset{O}{\overset{\|}{C}}—OC_2H_5$	0	2

On the other hand, stability of enolate anion obtained after the removal of H^+ can be explained as keto group stabilises enolate anion to more extent than ester. Ketone group stabilises enolate ion by resonance which can be shown as,

$$CH_2(COCH_3)_2 \longrightarrow \overset{\ominus}{C}H(COCH_3)_2 \equiv CH(C(=O)CH_3)(C(-O^{\ominus})=CH_3 \ldots)$$

In $C_2H_5—O—\overset{O}{\overset{\|}{C^1}}—CH_2—\overset{O}{\overset{\|}{C^2}}—CH_3$ lesser tautomerism will be seen due to lesser availability of C^1 atom for tautomerisation as at this C-atom, $C=O$ bond is in conjugation with the lone pair of neighbouring oxygen attached and, hence cross conjugation lowers the stability.

Further, in $C_2H_5—O—\overset{O}{\overset{\|}{C}}—CH_2—\overset{O}{\overset{\|}{C}}—O—C_2H_5$ as both the C-atoms of $C=O$ bond have similar situations hence, tautomerism decreases further. That's why correct order of acidity can be arranged as II > I > III.

6 (*b*) Iodoform test is used for the identification of functional groups like $CH_3—\overset{O}{\overset{\|}{C}}—$ and $CH_3—\overset{OH}{\overset{|}{C}H}—$ in organic compounds. $CH_3COOC_2H_5$ upon hydrolysis at higher temperature yields CH_3COOH and C_2H_5OH. Iodoform test is given by C_2H_5OH. Thus, dilute solution of $CH_3CO_2C_2H_5$ gives positive iodoform test.

$$\underset{\text{Ethyl ethanoate}}{CH_3COOC_2H_5} \xrightarrow[\Delta]{H_2O} \underset{\text{Ethanoic acid}}{CH_3COOH} + \underset{\text{Ethanol}}{C_2H_5OH}$$

$$C_2H_5OH + 4I_2 + 3Na_2CO_3 \longrightarrow \underset{\substack{\text{Iodoform}\\\text{(yellow)}}}{CHI_3}\downarrow + 5NaI + \underset{\text{Sodium formate}}{HCO\overset{-}{O}\overset{+}{Na}} + 3CO_2 + 2H_2O$$

7 (*d*) $CH_3—\overset{O}{\overset{\|}{C}}—NH_2 + HNO_2 \longrightarrow CH_3—\overset{O}{\overset{\|}{C}}—OH + H_2O + N_2\uparrow$

8 (*d*) Acetamide, CH_3CONH_2 on heating with anhydrous P_2O_5 gives methyl cyanide.

$$CH_3CONH_2 \xrightarrow{P_2O_5, \Delta} CH_3CN$$

9 (*b*) $C_6H_5COOCH_3 \xrightarrow[H_2O/H^+]{LiAlH_4} \underset{A}{C_6H_5CH_2OH} + \underset{B}{CH_3OH}$

10 (*c*) Acids react with alcohols to form ester. Thus,

$$CH_3COOH + C_2H_5OH \longrightarrow \underset{\text{Ethyl ethanoate}}{CH_3COOC_2H_5} + H_2O$$

Acetic anhydride reacts with ethanol to give the same product, i.e. ethyl ethanoate.

$$\underset{\text{Acetic anhydride}}{(CH_3CO)_2O} + C_2H_5OH \longrightarrow CH_3COOC_2H_5 + CH_3COOH$$

11 (*d*) When alcohols react with acids or acid derivatives, esters are formed. Thus,

$$CH_3OH + CH_3COOH \longrightarrow \underset{\text{Methyl acetate}}{CH_3COOCH_3} + H_2O$$

$$CH_3OH + CH_3COCl \longrightarrow \underset{\text{Methyl acetate}}{CH_3COOCH_3} + HCl$$

$$CH_3OH + (CH_3CO)_2O \longrightarrow \underset{\text{Methyl acetate}}{CH_3COOCH_3} + CH_3COOH$$

12 (*c*) Esters are named by prefixing the name of the alkyl or aryl group (of *OR′* part) before the name of the parent acid and changing the suffix-'ic' acid to '-ate'. Hence, the structure of phenyl ethanoate is

$$C_6H_5-OCO\cdot CH_3\;;\; CH_3-\overset{O}{\overset{\|}{C}}-O-C_6H_5$$

13 (*d*) $\underset{\text{Diethyl ether}}{C_2H_5OC_2H_5} + \underset{\text{Acetic anhydride}}{(CH_3CO)_2O} \xrightarrow{\text{Anhy. AlCl}_3} \underset{\text{Ethyl acetate}}{2CH_3COOC_2H_5}$

14 (*b*) On heating two molecules of urea at 150°C, a white solid biuret is formed with the evolution of ammonia.

$$NH_2CONHH + H_2NCONH_2 \xrightarrow{150°C} \underset{\text{Biuret}}{NH_2CONH\cdot CONH_2} + \underset{\text{Ammonia}}{NH_3}$$

15 (*b*) Since, in the given reaction, *RO* — H bond breaks, C_2H_5OH acts as nucleophile.

16 (*b*) Ethyl butyrate has a flavour of pineapple, so it is used to impart pineapple flavour in alcoholic beverages.

17 (*b*) Acetyl chloride reacts with sodium salt of carboxylic acid to form anhydride.

$$\underset{\text{Acetyl chloride}}{CH_3COCl} + \underset{\text{Sodium propionate}}{CH_3CH_2COONa} \longrightarrow \underset{\text{Acetic propionic anhydride}}{CH_3COOCOCH_2CH_3}$$

18 (*c*) The direct esterification of methanol with salicylic acid in the presence of conc. H_2SO_4 gives methyl salicylate or oil of winter green.

19 (*c*) Acid hydrolysis of an ester gives two different organic compounds.

$$CH_3COOC_2H_5 + H_2O \longrightarrow \underset{\text{Both organic compounds}}{CH_3COOH + C_2H_5OH}$$

Acid hydrolysis of a symmetrical anhydride gives two molecules of the same organic compound.

$$(CH_2CO)_2O + H_2O \longrightarrow 2CH_3COOH$$

While the acid hydrolysis of an amide gives one organic and one inorganic product as,

$$CH_3CONH_2 + H_2O \longrightarrow \underset{\text{Organic compound}}{CH_3COOH} + \underset{\text{Inorganic compound}}{NH_3}$$

20 (*c*) $C_2H_5OC_2H_5 + CO \xrightarrow[500\text{ atm}]{150°C,\,\Delta,\,BF_3} \underset{\text{Ethyl propionate}}{C_2H_5COOC_2H_5}$

21 (*a*)

$$\underset{(A)}{C_6H_5COOC_2H_5} \xrightarrow{CH_3MgBr} C_6H_5-\overset{\overset{-\;+}{OMgBr}}{\underset{CH_3}{C}}-OC_2H_5 \xrightarrow{-(C_2H_5O)MgBr}$$

$$C_6H_5-\overset{O}{\overset{\|}{C}}-CH_3 \xrightarrow{CH_3MgBr} C_6H_5-\overset{\overset{-\;+}{OMgBr}}{\underset{CH_3}{C}}-CH_3$$

$$\xrightarrow{H_2O} C_6H_5-\overset{OH}{\underset{CH_3}{C}}-CH_3 \xrightarrow[-H_2O]{\text{Conc. }H_2SO_4} \underset{(B)}{C_6H_5-\underset{CH_3}{C}=CH_2}$$

$$C_6H_5-\underset{CH_3}{C}=CH_2 \xrightarrow{O_3/H_2O} \underset{[C_8H_8O]}{C_6H_5-\overset{}{\underset{O}{\underset{\|}{C}}}-CH_3} + HCHO$$

$$C_6H_5-\underset{O}{\underset{\|}{C}}-CH_3 \xrightarrow{I_2/NaOH} \underset{\text{Iodoform}}{CHI_3\downarrow} + C_6H_5CO\overset{-}{O}\overset{+}{Na}$$

22 (*b*) Ethyl acetate is obtained when methyl magnesium bromide reacts with ethyl chloroformate.

$$CH_3MgBr + \underset{\text{Ethyl chloro formate}}{Cl-\overset{O}{\overset{\|}{C}}-OC_2H_5} \longrightarrow \left[Cl-\overset{\overset{-\;+}{OMgBr}}{\underset{CH_3}{C}}-OC_2H_5\right]$$

$$\longrightarrow MgBrCl + \underset{\text{Ethyl acetate}}{CH_3-\overset{O}{\overset{\|}{C}}-O-C_2H_5}$$

23 (*b*) $\underset{\text{N-phenyl benzamide}}{C_6H_5-CONH-C_6H_5} \xrightarrow{Br_2/Fe} C_6H_5-CONH-C_6H_4-Br$

24 (*c*) Hydroxamic acid test is used to detect the presence of esters.

25 (*d*) $\underset{\text{Benzamide}}{C_6H_5CONH_2} \xrightarrow{P_2O_5,\,\Delta} \underset{\text{Benzonitrile}}{C_6H_5CN}$

26 (*d*) $HC\equiv CH \xrightarrow[\text{acid}]{\text{Chromic}} \underset{\substack{(A)\\ \text{Acetic acid}}}{CH_3COOH} \xrightarrow{NH_3}$

$$\underset{\substack{(B)\\ \text{Ammonium acetate}}}{CH_3COO\overset{+}{N}H_4} \xrightarrow[-H_2O]{\Delta} \underset{\substack{(C)\\ \text{Acetamide}}}{CH_3-\overset{O}{\overset{\|}{C}}-NH_2}$$

27 (*d*) Waxes are the esters of long chains fatty acids with long chains monohydric alcohols such as mericyl and cetyl alcohols.

28 (*c*) Iodoform test is carried out in hot alkaline medium. Under these conditions, the esters will hydrolyse to give corresponding alcohols.

$$CH_3-\overset{O}{\overset{\|}{C}}-OCH_3 + NaOH \longrightarrow CH_3\overset{O}{\overset{\|}{C}}-\overset{-}{O}\overset{+}{Na} + \underset{\text{Methanol}}{CH_3OH}$$

$$CH_3-\overset{O}{\overset{\|}{C}}-OC_2H_5 + NaOH \longrightarrow CH_3-\overset{O}{\overset{\|}{C}}-\overset{-}{O}\overset{+}{Na} + \underset{\text{Ethanol}}{C_2H_5OH}$$

Now, ethanol will respond to iodoform test to give yellow ppt. of iodoform while, methanol will not give iodoform test.

Thus, iodoform test can be used to distinguish methyl acetate and ethyl acetate.

29 (*b*) Cl_2 does not give acid chloride on treating with a carboxylic acid.

$$CH_3COOH + PCl_5 \longrightarrow \underset{\text{Acetyl chloride}}{CH_3COCl} + POCl_3 + HCl$$

$$CH_3COOH + Cl_2 \longrightarrow CH_2ClCOOH + HCl$$

$$3CH_3COOH + SOCl_2 \longrightarrow CH_3COCl + SO_2 + HCl$$

$$CH_3COOH + PCl_3 \longrightarrow 3CH_3COCl + H_3PO_3$$

Hence, acetic acid reacts with chlorine gas to give monochloro acetic acid and it does not give acetyl chloride.

30 (*a*) Claisen condensation is a carbon-carbon bond forming reaction between two esters or one ester and another carbonyl compound (containg α-hydrogen atoms) in presence of strong base to form β-keto ester or β-diketone. Hence, phenyl benzoate cannot give this reaction.

31 (*c*) $$\underset{\text{2,3-butane diol}}{CH_3\overset{OH}{\overset{|}{C}H}-\overset{OH}{\overset{|}{C}H}CH_3} \xrightarrow[-H_2O]{\text{Dehydration}} CH_3\,CH\overset{O}{-}CH\,CH_3 + H_2O$$

Hence, $CH_3-CH\overset{O}{-}CH-CH_3$ is epoxide of 2, 3-butane diol.

32 (*b*) $$CH_3CONH_2 \xrightarrow{NaOBr/OH^-} \underset{\text{Methyl amine or methanamine}}{CH_3NH_2}$$

33 (*b*) $$\underset{\text{Acid chloride}}{R-COCl} + NH_3 \longrightarrow \underset{\text{Amide}}{R-CONH_2} + HCl$$

34 (*d*) $$CH_3CH_2COONH_4 \xrightarrow[-2H_2O]{P_2O_5,\,\Delta} CH_3CH_2CN \xrightarrow{H^+/H_2O} \underset{\text{Propionic acid}}{CH_3CH_2COOH}$$

35 (*b*) $$\underset{\text{Ethyl acetate}}{CH_3-\overset{O}{\overset{\|}{C}}-O-C_2H_5} + H-\underset{\text{Ethyl acetate}}{CH_2COOC_2H_5} \xrightarrow{NaOC_2H_5} \underset{\text{Ethyl aceto-acetate (ester)}}{CH_3\overset{O}{\overset{\|}{C}}CH_2COOC_2H_5} + C_2H_5OH$$

36 (*c*) $$C_6H_4(CH_2CONH_2)(COOCH_3) \xrightarrow[\text{(ii) Heat}]{\text{(i) } Br_2/NaOH} C_6H_4(CH_2NH_2)(COOCH_3) \xrightarrow{-CH_3OH} \text{cyclic lactam (C=O, NH)}$$

37 (*b*) $$\begin{matrix}HCO\overset{-}{O}\overset{+}{Na}\\+\\HCO\overset{-}{O}\overset{+}{Na}\end{matrix} \xrightarrow{\Delta} \begin{matrix}CO\overset{-}{O}\overset{+}{Na}\\|\\CO\overset{-}{O}\overset{+}{Na}\end{matrix} + H_2\uparrow$$

38 (*d*) Methyl salicylate is found in essential oils of winter green. Rest of the statements are correct.

39 (*c*) Acetophenone can be prepared by Friedel-Crafts acylation reaction. By treating benzene with acetyl chloride in the presence of anhydrous aluminium chloride; acetophenone is obtained.

$$\underset{\text{Benzene}}{C_6H_5H} + \underset{\text{Acetyl chloride}}{ClCOCH_3} \xrightarrow{\text{Anhyd. }AlCl_3} \underset{\text{Acetophenone}}{C_6H_5COCH_3} + HCl$$

40 (*b*) The correct match is A→2, B→3, C→1

Column I	Column II
$PhCO_2CH_3$	Arndt-Eister synthesis
$C_6H_5CH_2CO_2H$	Hydrolysis
C_6H_5CHO	2, 4-DNP

41 (*a*) Soaps are the sodium or potassium salts of higher fatty acids, e.g., $C_{17}H_{35}CO\overset{-}{O}\overset{+}{K}$ (potassium stearate).

42 (*b*) Acetyl chloride does not react directly with phenol. Firstly phenol reacts with alkali to form sodium phenoxide which reacts with acetyl chloride to give phenyl acetate.

43 (*d*) Hofmann bromamide reaction takes place as follows.

$$R-\overset{O}{\overset{\|}{C}}-\ddot{N}H-H \xrightarrow[-H^+]{\overset{\ominus}{O}H} R-\overset{O}{\overset{\|}{C}}-\overset{\ominus}{N}H \xrightarrow[-Br^-]{\overset{+\delta}{Br}-\overset{\delta-}{Br}} \underset{(RCO\ddot{N}HBr)}{R-\overset{O}{\overset{\|}{C}}-\ddot{N}H-Br} \xrightarrow{\overset{\ominus}{O}H}$$

$$-Br^{\ominus}\left[R-\overset{O^\ominus}{\overset{|}{C}}=\ddot{N}-Br \leftrightarrow R-\overset{O^\ominus}{\overset{|}{C}}=\ddot{N}-Br\right] \longrightarrow \left[R-\overset{O}{\overset{\|}{C}}-\ddot{N}:\right]\,(RCON) \xrightarrow{\text{Rearrangement}} \underset{(RNCO)}{[R-N=C=O]} \xrightarrow{H_2O/\overset{\ominus}{O}H} \left[R-\underset{H}{\underset{|}{N}}-\overset{O}{\overset{\|}{C}}-O^{\ominus}\right] \longrightarrow RNH_2 + CO_2$$

Thus, *RNC* is not an intermediate.

44 (*a*) The reaction is known as Claisen condensation.

$$CH_3CO\,OC_2H_5 + H\,CH_2COOC_2H_5 \xrightarrow{C_2H_5\overset{-}{O}\overset{+}{Na}} \underset{\substack{\text{Ethyl acetoacetate}\\(A)}}{CH_3COCH_2COOC_2H_5} + \underset{\text{Ethanol}}{C_2H_5OH}$$

$$\underset{(A)}{CH_3COCH_2COOC_2H_5} \xrightarrow{H_3O^+} \underset{(B)}{CH_3COCH_2COOH} + C_2H_5OH$$

45 (*a*) Acid chlorides are most reactive and are easily hydrolysed by water as follows

$$CH_3COCl + H_2O \xrightarrow{H^+} CH_3COOH + HCl$$

Acid anhydrides are less reactive than acid chlorides. They are hydrolysed slowly by water than acid chloride.

$$(CH_3CO)_2O + H_2O \xrightarrow{H^+} 2CH_3COOH$$

Esters are hydrolysed by water only in presence of acid or alkali.

$$RCOOR + H_2O \overset{H^+}{\rightleftharpoons} RCOOH + ROH$$

Amides are hydrolysed by water in the presence of an acid

$$R-\overset{O}{\overset{\|}{C}}-NH_2 + H_2O \xrightarrow{H^+} RCOOH + NH_3$$

Hence, the correct order of hydrolysis is

$$RCOCl > (RCO)_2\,O > RCOOR > RCONH_2$$

27

Organic Compounds Containing Nitrogen

Quick Review

Amines

Amines are the derivatives of ammonia obtained by the replacement of one, two or three hydrogen atoms by alkyl/aryl group.

$$NH_3 \xrightarrow[+R]{-H} \underset{(1^\circ \text{ amine})}{RNH_2} \xrightarrow[+R]{-H} \underset{(2^\circ \text{ amine})}{R_2NH} \xrightarrow[+R]{-H} \underset{(3^\circ \text{ amine})}{R_3N}$$

R-alkyl or aryl group.

Classification of Amines

Amines can be classified as primary (1°), secondary (2°) and tertiary (3°) amines depending upon the number of alkyl groups attached to it.

RNH_2 Primary (1°) $R(R')N—H$ Secondary (2°) $R(R'')N—R'$ Tertiary (3°)

Amines can also be classified as **simple** or **mixed** amines depending on whether the alkyl or aryl group attached are same or different.

Structure of Amines

The nitrogen atom in amine is sp^3-hybridised. The three alkyl groups are at the corners of a tetrahedron and their shape is pyramidal. The bond angle become lesser than 109.5° due to the bond pair-lone pair repulsion (e.g. bond angle for trimethylamine is 108°).

Unshared electron pair
sp^3-hybridised
N
108°
H H H
Pyramidal

Nomenclature

In IUPAC system, amines are named as alkanamines, derived by replacement of '*e*' of alkane by word amine.

In case of more than one amino group is present then by assigning number, their positions are specified to the carbon atoms, bearing —NH_2 group.

Isomerism

Amines show metamerism. It is present in those molecules that have same molecular formula but differ with respect to the alkyl groups attached on either sides of the nitrogen atom.

e.g. $\underset{\text{N-ethylethanamine}}{C_2H_5NHC_2H_5}$, $\underset{\text{N-methylpropan-2-amine}}{CH_3—NHCH(CH_3)_2}$

Methods of Preparation

Following methods can be used for the preparation of aliphatic amines :

S.No.	Method	Reaction Involved
I.	**For Primary Amines**	
1.	By reduction of (i) alkyl nitrile	$R—C{\equiv}N \xrightarrow{LiAlH_4} RCH_2NH_2$; $R—C{\equiv}N \xrightarrow{Na/Alcohol} RCH_2NH_2$ (Mendius reaction)
	(ii) nitroalkanes	$RNO_2 + 3H_2 \xrightarrow[\text{or } LiAlH_4/\text{ or } H_2/Pt]{\text{Raney Ni}/250°C} RNH_2$
	(iii) oximes	$R—CH{=}NOH \xrightarrow[Ether]{LiAlH_4} RCH_2NH_2 + H_2\uparrow$
	(iv) amides	$R\overset{O}{\overset{\|}{C}}NH_2 \xrightarrow{LiAlH_4} RCH_2NH_2 + H_2O$
2.	Gabriel phthalimide synthesis	Phthalimide $\xrightarrow{\text{(i) KOH, (ii) } RX, \text{(iii) } H_2O/OH^-}$ Phthalic acid ($C_6H_4(COOH)_2$) $+ RNH_2$
3.	Reductive amination of carbonyl group	$RCHO \xrightarrow[-H_2O]{NH_3} \underset{\text{Imine}}{R—\overset{H}{\overset{\|}{C}}{=}NH} \xrightarrow[\text{Ni or } NaBH_3CN]{H_2} RCH_2NH_2$
4.	Curtius method	$RCOCl \xrightarrow[-N_2]{NaN_3} R—\underset{:\ddot{N}:}{\underset{\|}{C}}{=}O \xrightarrow{\text{Intramolecular alkyl shift}} R—N{=}C{=}O \xrightarrow{2NaOH} RNH_2$
5.	Hofmann bromamide degradation	$RCONH_2 + Br_2 + 4KOH \xrightarrow{\Delta} RNH_2 + 2KBr + K_2CO_3 + 2H_2O$
6.	Schmidt rearrangement	$R—\overset{O}{\overset{\|}{C}}—OH + N_3H \xrightarrow[\Delta]{\text{Conc. } H_2SO_4} RNH_2 + CO_2 + N_2\uparrow$

S.No.	Method	Reaction Involved
II.	**For Secondary Amines**	
1.	Reaction of RX with 1° amine	$RNH_2 + RX \xrightarrow{NaOH} R_2NH + NaX + H_2O$
2.	By reduction of (i) Isonitriles	$RN \rightleftarrows C + 2H_2 \xrightarrow{\text{Ni or Pt}} RNHCH_3$
	(ii) N-substituted amides	$RCONHR' \xrightarrow[Ether]{LiAlH_4} RCH_2NHR'$
3.	Reductive amination of carbonyl compounds	$RCHO \xrightarrow{R'NH_2} [R—CH = NR'] \xrightarrow[Ni]{H_2} R—CH_2—NH—R'$
III.	**For Tertiary Amines**	
1.	Reaction of excess RX with NH_3	$3RX + NH_3 \longrightarrow [R_3\overset{+}{N}H] X^- \xrightarrow{NaOH} R_3N + NaX + H_2O$
2.	Reduction of N, N-disubstituted amides	$R—\overset{O}{\overset{\|}{C}}—NR_2' \xrightarrow[Ether]{LiAlH_4} RCH_2NR_2'$
3.	Decomoposition of tetra alkyl ammonium hydroxide	$R_4\overset{+}{N}\overset{-}{O}H \xrightarrow{\Delta} R_3N + H_2O + CH_2{=}CH_2$
IV.	**For mixture of amines**	
1.	Hofmann ammonolysis method	$R—H \xrightarrow[-HI]{NH_3/393\text{ K}} R\ddot{N}H_2 \xrightarrow[-HI]{RI} R_2\ddot{N}H \xrightarrow[-HI]{RI} R_3\ddot{N} \xrightarrow[-HI]{RI} [R_4\overset{+}{N}]I^-$
2.	By reductive amination of aldehydes and ketones	$RCHO + NH_3 \xrightarrow{\Delta} \underset{\text{Imine}}{RCH = NH} \xrightarrow{H_2,Ni} \underset{1°\text{amine}}{RCH_2NH_2}$

Physical Properties

Pure amines are colourless but develop colour on keeping in air. Lower aliphatic amines can form hydrogen bonds and hence are soluble in water. They have high boiling point. The increasing order of solubility and boiling points of amine is

$$3^\circ \text{ amine} < 2^\circ \text{ amine} < 1^\circ \text{ amine}.$$

Basicity of Amines

- The order of basic strength of methyl substituted amines in aqueous solution is
$$(CH_3)_2NH > CH_3NH_2 > (CH_3)_3N > NH_3.$$
- In gaseous phase: $(CH_3)_3N > (CH_3)_2NH > CH_3NH_2 > NH_3.$
- Aliphatic amines are more basic than aryl amines.

Chemical Properties

Important reactions of aliphatic amines are shown below :

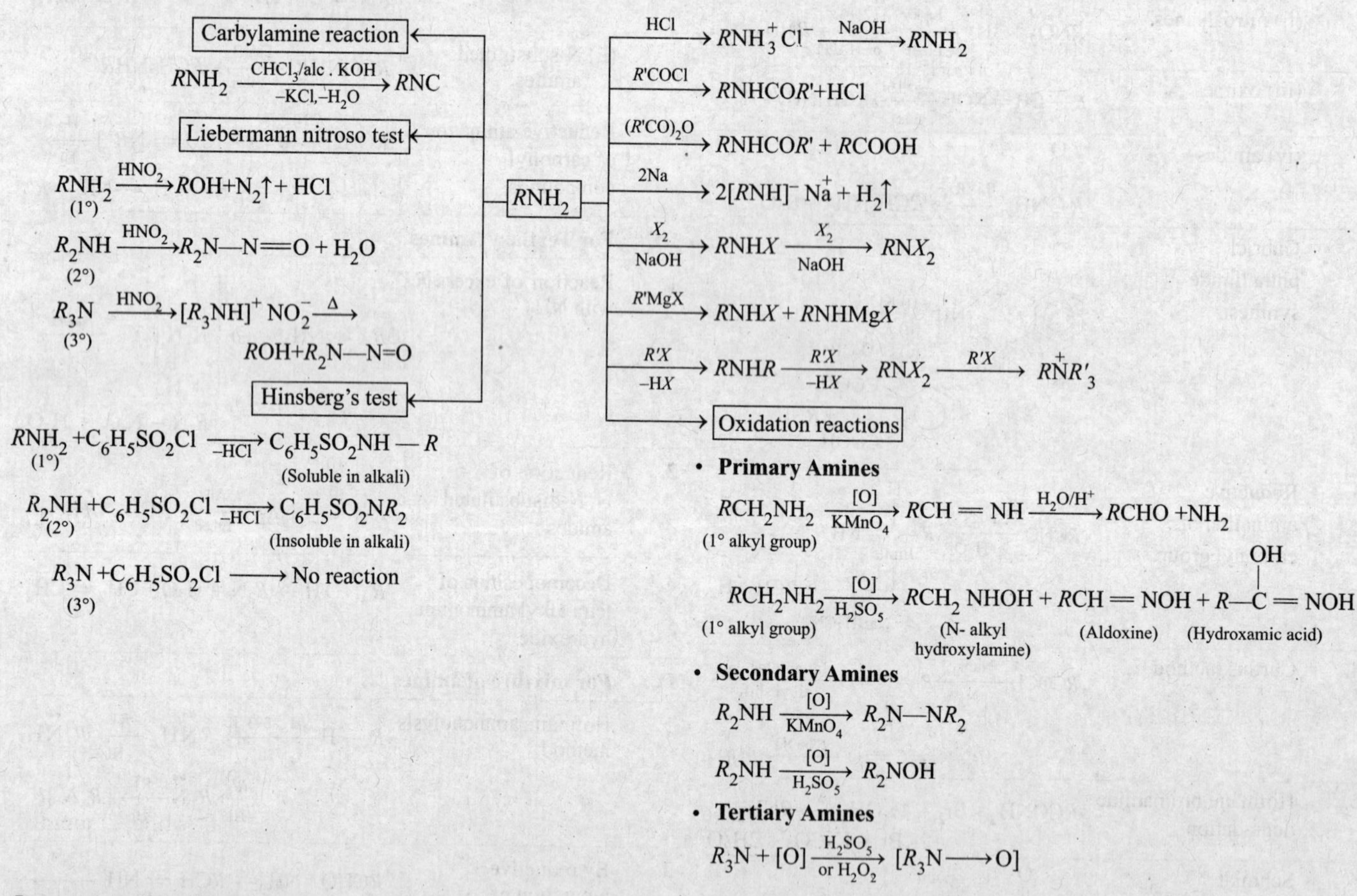

- **Primary Amines**

$RCH_2NH_2 \xrightarrow[KMnO_4]{[O]} RCH{=}NH \xrightarrow{H_2O/H^+} RCHO + NH_2$ (1° alkyl group)

$RCH_2NH_2 \xrightarrow[H_2SO_5]{[O]} RCH_2NHOH + RCH{=}NOH + R{-}\underset{}{\overset{OH}{\overset{|}{C}}}{=}NOH$
(1° alkyl group) (N-alkyl hydroxylamine) (Aldoxine) (Hydroxamic acid)

- **Secondary Amines**

$R_2NH \xrightarrow[KMnO_4]{[O]} R_2N{-}NR_2$

$R_2NH \xrightarrow[H_2SO_5]{[O]} R_2NOH$

- **Tertiary Amines**

$R_3N + [O] \xrightarrow[\text{or } H_2O_2]{H_2SO_5} [R_3N \longrightarrow O]$

Aromatic Amines

Amine in which NH_2 group of amines is directly attached to the benzene ring are called **aromatic amines.**

Nomenclature and Isomerism

- In IUPAC system, the names of aromatic amines are obained by replacing the terminal 'e' from the name of the corresponding arene by the suffix 'amine'.
- Aromatic amines show position isomerism due to the presence of group at *o, m* and *p*-position on benzene ring.

Preparation

Aromatic amines may be prepared by following methods :

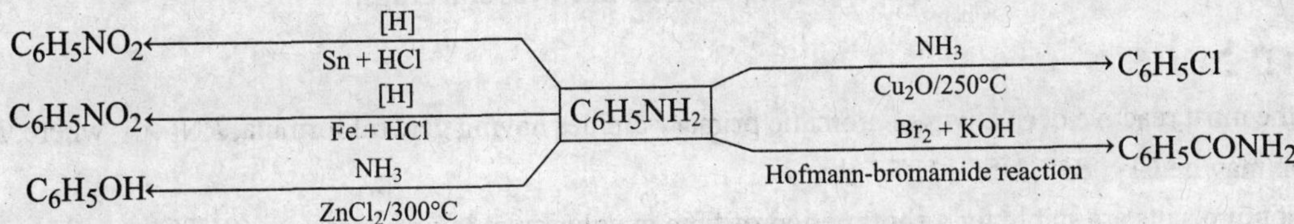

Chemical Properties

Important reactions of aromatic amines are shown below:

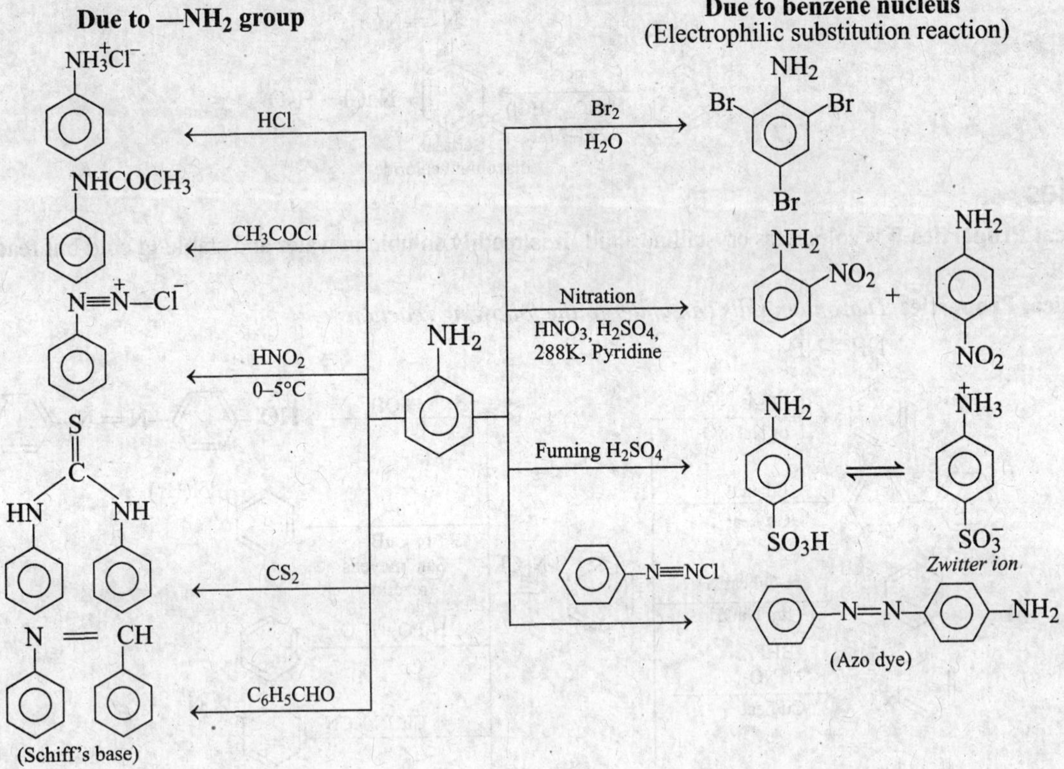

Identification of Amines

1°, 2° and 3° amines can be identified by the following tests :

(*i*) **Carbylamine Test** Only 1° amines give foul smelling isocyanide whereas, 2° and 3° amine do not give this test.

(*ii*) **Reaction with Nitrous Acid** Aliphatic 1° amine gives alcohol, aromatic 1° amine gives diazonium salt while, 2° amine gives a yellow green oily layer of N-nitrosoamine.

(*iii*) **Hinsberg test** Primary amine gives monoalkyl sulphonamide which is soluble in alkali. 2° amine gives dialkyl sulphonamide which is insoluble in KOH whereas, 3° and aromatic amines does not give this test.

(*iv*) **Mustard Oil Test** Only 1° amine gives this test which produces alkyl isothiocyanate.

(*v*) **Azo Dye Test** This test is only given by primary aromatic amines.

(*iv*) **Hofmann Test** 1° amines form solid dialkyl oxamide whereas 2° amine forms liquid dialkyl oxamic ester and 3° amine does not give this reaction.

Uses of Amines

- Aliphatic amines are used as solvents and intermediates in the manufacture of drugs.
- Aromatic compounds are used for the formation of polymers like dyes and drugs.

Diazonium Salts

- These are the most reactive derivatives of aromatic primary amines having general formula, $RN_2^+X^-$ where, R is an aryl group and X^- ion may be Cl^-, Br^-, HSO_4^-, BF_4^- etc.
- Arene diazonium salts are stable for a short period of time in solution at low temperature (0-5°C).

Preparation of Diazonium Salt

Benzene diazonium chloride is prepared by the reaction of aniline with nitrous acid at 273–278 K.

$$C_6H_5NH_2 \xrightarrow[273\text{–}278K]{HNO_2\ (NaNO_2 + HCl)} C_6H_5N^+{\equiv}NCl^- + NaCl + H_2O$$

Benzene diazonium chloride

Properties

- **Physical Properties** It is colourless crystalline solid. It is readily soluble in water and stable in cold but reacts with water on heating.
- **Chemical Properties** *Diazonium salts can undergo the following reactions :*

$C_6H_5\overset{+}{N}_2Cl^-$:

- $\xrightarrow{SnCl_2/HCl \text{ or } NaHSO_3}$ $C_6H_5NH{-}NH_2$
- $\xrightarrow{\text{Ethanol, Cu/heat}}$ $C_6H_5{-}C_6H_5$
- $\xrightarrow{H_2O/\text{heat or } aq.\ NaOH}$ C_6H_5OH
- $\xrightarrow{BHF_4,\ NaNO_2,\ \text{Cu/heat}}$ $C_6H_5NO_2$
- $\xrightarrow{HBF_4,\ \Delta}$ C_6H_5F
- $\xrightarrow{PhOH}$ $HO{-}C_6H_4{-}N{=}N{-}C_6H_5$
- $\xrightarrow{Cu_2Cl_2 \text{ or } CuBr}$ $C_6H_5Cl(Br)$ (Sandmeyer's reaction)
- $\xrightarrow{H_3PO_2+H_2O,\ Cu^+}$ C_6H_6
- $\xrightarrow{CuCN/KCN}$ C_6H_5CN
- $\xrightarrow{Cu/HCl}$ C_6H_5Cl (Gattermann reaction)

Importance of Diazonium Salt

- They are very good intermediates for the introduction of F, Cl, OH, NO_2 etc. in aromatic ring.
- Cyanobenzene can be prepared from them through direct nucleophilic substitution reactions.

Cyanides and Isocyanides

Both cyanides and isocyanides are derived from HCN by replacement of H by an alkyl or aryl group. Cyanides are also known as nitriles having general formula $R{-}C{\equiv}N$. Isocyanides are also known as isonitriles having formula $R{-}N{\equiv}C$.

- *Preparation and properties of cyanide are as follows:*

Preparations

- $R{-}I \xrightarrow{KCN} RCN$
- $R\overset{-}{COO}\overset{+}{N}H_4 \xrightarrow{P_2O_5 \text{ or } POCl_3} RCN$
- $RCH_2NH_2 \xrightarrow{Ni,\ 500°C} RCN$

Properties

- $RCN \xrightarrow{H_2O,\ HCl} R{-}COOH$
- $RCN \xrightarrow{Ni/H_2,\ \text{Pt or } LiAlH_4} RCH_2NH_2$
- $RCN \xrightarrow{SnCl_2 + HCl/H_2O} RCHO$ (Stephen's reaction)
- $RCN \xrightarrow{CH_3MgBr} R{-}C(CH_3){=}O$

- *Preparation and properties of isocyanides are as follows :*

Preparation $C_2H_5NH_2 + CHCl_3 + 3KOH \xrightarrow{\Delta} C_2H_5NC + 3KCl + 3H_2O$ (carbylamine reaction)

Properties

$RNC \xrightarrow{Ni/H_2,\ 4[H] \text{ or } LiAlH_4} RNHCH_3$

$RNC \xrightarrow{Br_2} R—N{=}C(Br)—Br$

$RNC \xrightarrow{[O],\ HgO} RNCO + Hg$

$RNC \xrightarrow{250°C} RC{\equiv}N$

Nitro Compounds

These compounds have general formula RNO_2 where, R can be alkyl or aryl group. They are obtained by replacing one H of hydrocarbon by $—NO_2$ group. They can be classified as 1°, 2° and 3° nitrocompounds.

Preparations

- Aliphatic nitro compounds can be prepared from the corresponding alkyl halides by heating with alcoholic solution of $AgNO_3$.

$$R—X + AgNO_3 \xrightarrow{\Delta} R—NO_2 + AgX.$$

- Aromatic nitro compounds can be prepared by the nitration of benzene in presence of nitrating mixture (conc. HNO_3 + conc. H_2SO_4).

$$C_6H_6 \text{ (Benzene)} + HNO_3 \xrightarrow{H_2SO_4} C_6H_5NO_2 \text{ (Nitrobenzene)} + H_2O$$

Chemical Properties

- *Aliphatic nitro compounds give the following reactions :*

$RNO_2 \xrightarrow{LiAlH_4} RNH_2$

$RNO_2 \xrightarrow{Sn/HCl,\ 6[H]} RNH_2$

$RNO_2 \xrightarrow{Zn/NH_4Cl \text{ or } Al\text{-}Hg,\ H_2O} RNHOH$

$RNO_2 \xrightarrow{H_2O/H^+} RCOOH + NH_2OH$

- *Aromatic nitro compounds given following reaction :*

Due to —NO₂ group (from nitrobenzene)

- $\xrightarrow{Zn,\ CH_3OH,\ NaOH,\ \Delta}$ azobenzene ($C_6H_5N{=}NC_6H_5$)
- $\xrightarrow{[H],\ Sn/HCl}$ aniline ($C_6H_5NH_2$)
- $\xrightarrow{[H],\ Zn—NH_4Cl \text{ or } Zn—Cu + H_2O}$ phenylhydroxylamine (C_6H_5NHOH)
- $\xrightarrow{[H],\ Zn—NaOH}$ hydrazobenzene ($C_6H_5NH—NHC_6H_5$)
- $\xrightarrow{\text{Electrolytic reduction}}$ NH_2-substituted product

Due to benzene nucleus

- $\xrightarrow{Cl_2,\ FeCl_3}$ m-chloronitrobenzene
- $\xrightarrow{\text{Conc. } HNO_3 + \text{Conc. } H_2SO_4,\ 100°C}$ 1,3,5-trinitrobenzene
- $\xrightarrow{\text{Fuming } H_2SO_4,\ 100°C}$ m-nitrobenzenesulphonic acid (SO_3H)
- $\xrightarrow{[H],\ Na_3AsO_3/NaOH,\ \Delta}$ azoxybenzene ($C_6H_5N(\rightarrow O){=}NC_6H_5$)

Topical Practice Questions

All the exam questions of this chapter have been divided into four topics as listed below :

Topic 1
Amines

2019

1 The amine that reacts will Hinsberg's reagent to give an alkali insoluble product is **[NEET Odisha]**

(a) $CH_3-\underset{CH_3}{\underset{|}{CH}}-NH-\underset{CH_3}{\underset{|}{CH}}CH_3$

(b) $CH_3-CH_2-\overset{CH_2CH_3}{\overset{|}{N}}-CH_2CH_3$

(c) $CH_3-\overset{NH_2}{\overset{|}{\underset{CH_3}{\underset{|}{C}}}}-CH_2CH_2CH_3$

(d) $CH_3-\overset{CH_3}{\overset{|}{\underset{CH_3}{\underset{|}{C}}}}-\underset{CH_3}{\underset{|}{CH}}-NH_2$

2 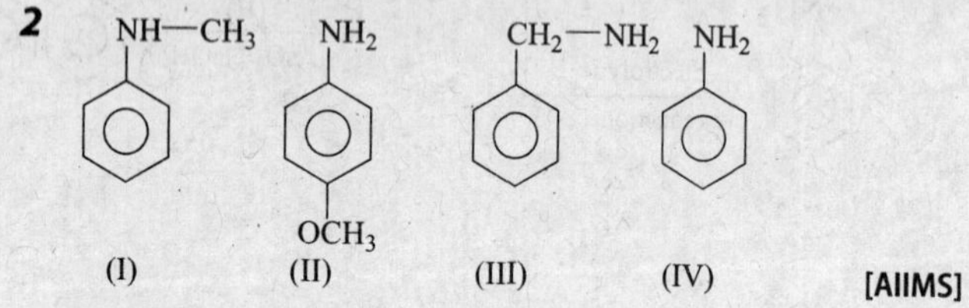

[AIIMS]

Correct order of basic strength is

(a) III > II > IV > I (b) IV > III > II > I
(c) III > II > I > IV (d) III > I > II > IV

3 The correct order of the basic strength of methyl substituted amines in aqueous solution is **[NEET]**

(a) $(CH_3)_3N > CH_3NH_2 > (CH_3)_2NH$
(b) $(CH_3)_3N > (CH_3)_2NH > CH_3NH_2$
(c) $CH_3NH_2 > (CH_3)_2NH > (CH_3)_3N$
(d) $(CH_3)_2NH > CH_3NH_2 > (CH_3)_3N$

2018

4 Nitration of aniline in strong acidic medium also gives *m*-nitroaniline because **[NEET]**

(a) in absence of substituents nitro group always goes to *m*-position
(b) in electrophilic substitution reactions amino group is *meta* directive
(c) in spite of substituents, nitro group always goes to only *m*-position
(d) in acidic (strong) medium, aniline is present as anilinium ion

2017

5 The main product formed in the following reaction is

[JIPMER]

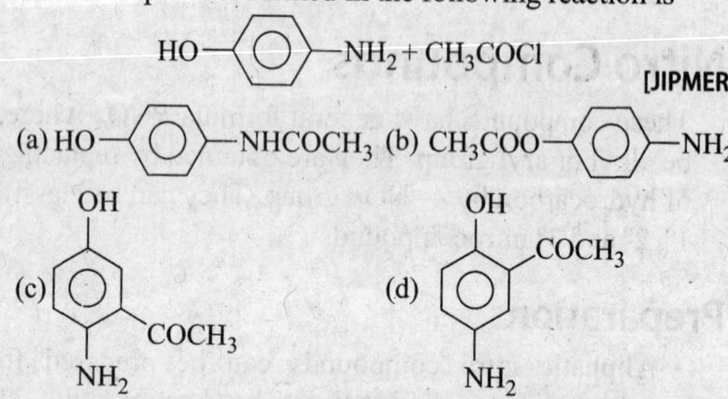

6 The correct order of basic strength of the following are **[JIPMER]**

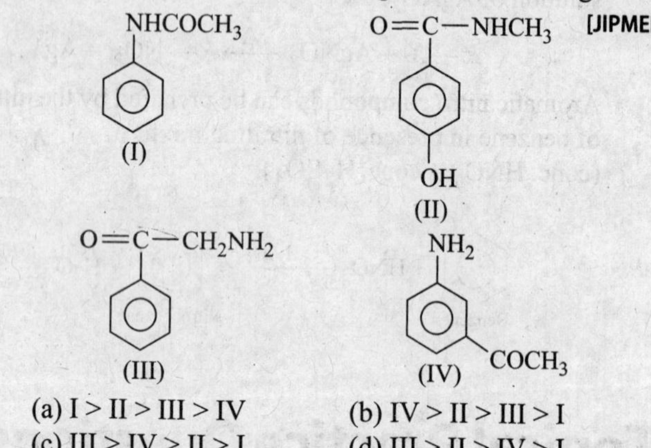

(a) I > II > III > IV (b) IV > II > III > I
(c) III > IV > II > I (d) III > II > IV > I

7 Consider the following reaction, **[JIPMER]**

$$X \xrightarrow{\text{Bromination}} Y \xrightarrow[+\ HCl]{NaNO_2} Z$$

$$Z \xrightarrow[C_2H_5OH]{\text{Boiling}} \text{Tribromobenzene. } X \text{ is}$$

(a) benzoic acid
(b) salicylic acid
(c) phenol
(d) aniline

8 The correct increasing order of basic strength for the following compounds is **[NEET]**

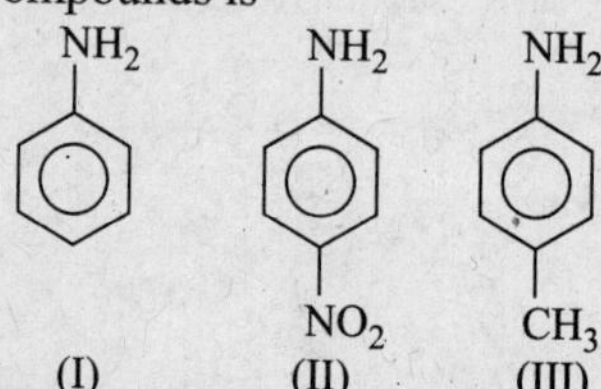

(a) II < III < I (b) III < I < II
(c) III < II < I (d) II < I < III

9 Which of the following reactions is appropriate for converting acetamide to methanamine? **[NEET]**

(a) Carbylamine reaction
(b) Hofmann hypobromamide reaction
(c) Stephen's reaction
(d) Gabriel phthalimide synthesis

10 **Assertion** (A) Aniline on reaction with $NaNO_2/HCl$ at 0° C followed by coupling with β-naphthol gives a dark blue coloured precipitate.

Reason (R) The colour of the compound formed in the reaction of aniline with $NaNO_2/HCl$ at 0° C followed by coupling with β-naphthol is due to the extended conjugation.

(a) Both A and R are correct and R is the correct explanation of A **[AIIMS]**
(b) Both A and R are correct but R is not the correct explanation of A
(c) A is correct but R is incorrect
(d) Both A and R are incorrect

2016

11 In pyrrole **[NEET Phase-II]**

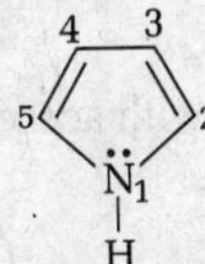

the electron density is maximum on

(a) 2 and 3 (b) 3 and 4 (c) 2 and 4 (d) 2 and 5

12 The correct statement regarding the basicity of arylamines is **[NEET]**

(a) Arylamines are generally more basic than alkylamines because the lone pair of electrons on nitrogen is not delocalized by interaction with the aromatic ring π-electron system
(b) Arylamines are generally more basic than alkylamines because of aryl group
(c) Arylamines are generally more basic than alkylamines, because the nitrogen atom in arylamines is *sp*-hybridised
(d) Arylamines are generally less basic than alkylamines because the lone pair of electron on nitrogen is delocalised by interaction with the aromatic ring π-electron system.

2014

13 Identify the alkene that is produced in the following series of reactions. **[MHT CET]**

$\overset{+}{N}(CH_3)_3\,\overset{-}{I}$ $\xrightarrow{\text{Moist}/Ag_2O}$ $X \xrightarrow{\Delta}$ alkene + tert amine + H_2O

(a) (b)

(c) (d)

14 An organic compound X having molecular formula $C_4H_{11}N$ reacts with *p*-toluene sulphonyl chloride to form a compound Y that is soluble in aqueous KOH. Compound X is optically active and reacts with acetyl chloride to form compound Z. Identify the compound Z. **[MHT CET]**

(a) $CH_3CH_2CH_2CH_2NHCOCH_3$
(b) $CH_3CH_2\underset{|}{\overset{CH_3}{C}}HNHCOCH_3$
(c) $CH_3—\overset{CH_3}{\overset{|}{C}}HCH_2NHCOCH_3$
(d) $CH_3—\underset{\underset{CH_3}{|}}{\overset{\overset{CH_3}{|}}{C}}—NHCOCH_3$

15 Carbylamine test is not answered by **[Kerala CEE]**

(a) $C_6H_5NH_2$
(b) $(CH_3)_3C—CH_2—NH_2$
(c) $C_6H_5CH_2NH_2$
(d) $(CH_3)_3N$
(e) CH_3NH_2

16 The reagent that is used to distinguish between secondary amine and tertiary amine is **[Kerala CEE]**

(a) *p*-toluene sulphonyl chloride
(b) Lucas reagent
(c) $CHCl_3$ and alc. KOH
(d) Borsch's reagent
(e) Bromine water

17 Which one of the following isomeric amines has the highest boiling point? **[Kerala CEE]**

(a) $CH_3—CH_2—CH_2—NH—CH_3$
(b) $CH_3—CH_2—NH—CH_2—CH_3$
(c) $(CH_3)_2N—CH_2—CH_3$
(d) $CH_3—CH_2—CH_2—CH_2—NH_2$
(e) $(CH_3)_2CH—NH—CH_3$

18 Which one of the following reagent will convert acetamide into ethanamine? **[Kerala CEE]**

(a) Phosphorus pentoxide
(b) Lithium aluminium hydride
(c) Potassium cyanide
(d) Thionyl chloride
(e) Bromine and sodium hydroxide

19 An amine C_3H_9N reacts with benzene sulphonyl chloride to form a white precipitate which is insoluble in *aq.* NaOH. The amine is **[WE JEE]**

(a) Me_2N-Me (trimethylamine: N with Me, Me, Me) (b) $Me-NH-CH_2-Me$ (N with Me, H and ethyl)

(c) $Me-CH_2-CH_2-NH_2$ (d) $(Me)_2CH-NH_2$

20 The reaction of aniline with chloroform under alkaline conditions leads to the formation of [WB JEE]

(a) phenyl cyanide (b) phenyl isonitrile
(c) phenyl cyanate (d) phenyl isocyanate

21 The source of nitrogen in Gabriel synthesis of amines is [UK PMT]

(a) NaN_3 (b) $NaNO_2$
(c) KCN (d) $C_6H_5(CO)_2N^-K^+$

22 Hofmann bromamide degradation is shown by [UK PMT]

(a) $ArNH_2$ (b) $ArCONH_2$
(c) $ArNO_2$ (d) $ArCH_2NH_2$

23 An aromatic compound 'A' (C_7H_9N) on reacting with $NaNO_2$/HCl at 0° C forms benzyl alcohol and nitrogen gas. The number of isomers possible for the compound 'A' is [KCET]

(a) 5 (b) 7 (c) 3 (d) 6

24 The correct sequence of reaction to be performed to convert benzene into *m*-bromoaniline is [KCET]

(a) nitration, reduction, bromination
(b) bromination, nitration, reduction
(c) nitration, bromination, reduction
(d) reduction, nitration, bromination

25 Identify the compounds from the following which form primary amines under suitable reduction conditions. [EAMCET]

I. C_2H_5NC II. C_2H_6
III. $C_2H_5CONH_2$ IV. $C_6H_5NO_2$

(a) I, IV (b) III, IV
(c) I, III, IV (d) II, III, IV

2013

26 The product formed by the reaction of acetamide with bromine in the presence of NaOH is [AIIMS]

(a) CH_3CN (b) CH_3CHO
(c) CH_3CH_2OH (d) CH_3NH_2

27 $C_6H_5NH_2 \xrightarrow{NaNO_2/H^+} X \xrightarrow[H_2O/H^+]{Cu_2(CN)_2} Y \xrightarrow{H_2O/H^+} Z,$
Z is defined as [Manipal]

(a) $C_6H_5-NH-CH_3$
(b) C_6H_5-COOH
(c) $C_6H_5-CH_2NH_2$
(d) $C_6H_5-CH_2-COOH$

28 $RCONH_2 + 4NaOH + Br_2 \longrightarrow RNH_2 + 2NaBr + Na_2CO_3 + 2H_2O$

Reaction is said [WB JEE]

(a) Hofmann bromamide reaction
(b) Schmidt reaction
(c) Curtius reaction
(d) Beckmann reaction

2012

29 An organic compound (C_3H_9N) (A), when treated with nitrous acid, gave an alcohol and N_2 gas was evolved. (A) on warming with $CHCl_3$ and caustic potash gave (C) which on reduction gave iso-propylmethyl amine. Predict the structure of (A). [CBSE AIPMT]

(a) $(H_3C)_2CH-NH_2$ (b) $CH_3CH_2-NH-CH_3$
(c) $CH_3-N(CH_3)-CH_3$ (d) $CH_3CH_2CH_2-NH_2$

30 Reaction of aniline with acetyl chloride in the presence of NaOH gives [Manipal]

(a) acetanilide (b) *p*-chloroaniline
(c) a red dye (d) aniline hydrochloride

31 Aniline + excess of $Br_2 \longrightarrow$? [OJEE]

(a) tribromobenzene
(b) *m*-bromoaniline
(c) 3, 4, 5-tribromoaniline
(d) 2, 4, 6-tribromoaniline

2011

32 The strongest base in aqueous solution among the following amines is [Kerala CEE]

(a) N-N-diethylethanamine
(b) N-ethylethanamine
(c) N-methylmethanamine
(d) ethanamine
(e) phenylmethanamine

33 Aniline is treated with bromine water to give an organic compound 'X' which when treated with $NaNO_2$ and HCl at 0°C gives a water soluble compound 'Y'. Compound 'Y' on treatment with Cu_2Cl_2 and HCl gives compound 'Z'. Compound 'Z' is [Kerala CEE]

(a) *o*-bromochlorobenzene
(b) *p*-bromochlorobenzene
(c) 2,4,6-tribromophenol
(d) 2,4,6-tribromochlorobenzene
(e) 2,4-dibromophenol

34 Anilinium hydrogen sulphate on heating with sulphuric acid at 453-473 K produces **[Kerala CEE]**
(a) benzene sulphonic acid
(b) anthranilic acid
(c) aniline
(d) *m*-aminobenzene sulphonic acid
(e) sulphanilic acid

35 Compare boiling points of isomeric alkyl amines. **[Guj CET]**
(a) $1° > 2° > 3°$ (b) $1° > 2° < 3°$
(c) $1° < 2° < 3°$ (d) $1° < 2° > 3°$

2010

36 Aniline in a set of the following reactions yielded a coloured product *Y*,

$$C_6H_5NH_2 \xrightarrow[(273\text{–}278\ K)]{NaNO_2/HCl} X \xrightarrow{N,N\text{-dimethylaniline}} Y$$

The structure of *Y* would be **[CBSE AIPMT]**
(a) CH_3–NH–C_6H_4–N=N–C_6H_4–NH–CH_3
(b) C_6H_5–N=N–C_6H_4–$N(CH_3)_2$
(c) CH_3–NH–C_6H_4–NH–C_6H_4–NH–CH_3
(d) H_3C–C_6H_4–N=N–C_6H_4–NH_2

37 Which of the following statements about primary amines is incorrect? **[CBSE AIPMT]**
(a) Alkyl amines are stronger bases than ammonia
(b) Alkyl amines are stronger bases than aryl amines
(c) Alkyl amines react with nitrous acid to produce alcohols
(d) Aryl amines react with nitrous acid to produce phenols

38 Acetamide is treated with the following reagents separately. Which one of these would yield methyl amine? **[CBSE AIPMT]**
(a) PCl_5 (b) NaOH + Br_2
(c) Sodalime (d) Hot conc. H_2SO_4

39 Arrange the following in the increasing order of their basic strength.
CH_3NH_2 (I); $(CH_3)_2NH$(II);
$(CH_3)_3N$(III); $C_6H_5CH_2NH_2$ (IV) **[AMU]**
(a) IV < III < II < I (b) IV < III < I < II
(c) I < II < III < IV (d) IV < III < I = II

40 N_2 gas will not be evolved upon reaction of HNO_2 with which of the following amines? **[AFMC]**
(a) 1° (b) 2° (c) 3° (d) Both (b) and (c)

41 Primary, secondary and tertiary amines can be distinguished by **[AFMC]**
(a) Schiff's test (b) Fehling's test
(c) Tollen's test (d) Hinsberg's test

42 Amines are basic in character because they have **[BVP]**
(a) a lone pair of electrons on the nitrogen atom
(b) a hydroxyl group in the molecule
(c) replaceable hydrogen atom
(d) tetrahedral structure

43 Which of the following amines gives yellow oily liquid with HNO_2? **[MHT CET]**
(a) Ethyl methylamine
(b) Aniline
(c) 3-methylamine benzyl
(d) Methylamine

44 $C_2H_5NH_2 \xrightarrow{HNO_2} A \xrightarrow{PCl_3} B \xrightarrow{NH_3} C$
recognize the compound *C* from the following **[Guj CET, MHT CET]**
(a) propane nitrile (b) methylamine
(c) ethyl amine (d) acetamide

45 Acetamide and ethylamine can be distinguished by reacting with **[Manipal]**
(a) aqueous HCl and heat (b) aqueous NaOH and heat
(c) acidified $KMnO_4$ (d) bromine water

46 The strongest base among the following is **[Manipal]**
(a) $C_6H_5NH_2$ (b) $(C_6H_5)_2NH$
(c) NH_3 (d) $(C_2H_5)_2NH$

47 The product of the following reaction is **[OJEE]**

$$C_6H_5NH_2 \xrightarrow[\text{Inert solvent}]{COCl_2/\text{Pyridine}}$$

(a) C_6H_5–C(=O)–NH_2 (b) 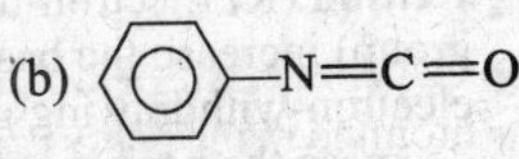
(c) 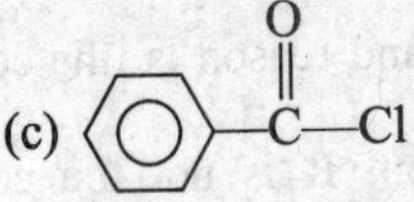 (d) 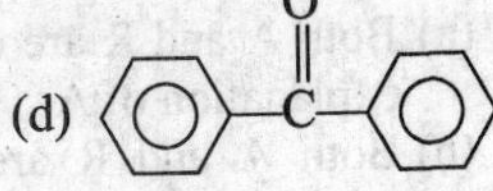

48 Which of the following will not give a primary amine? **[RPMT]**
(a) $CH_3CONH_2 \xrightarrow{Br_2,\ KOH}$
(b) $CH_3CN \xrightarrow{LiAlH_4}$
(c) $CH_3NC \xrightarrow{LiAlH_4}$
(d) $CH_3CONH_2 \xrightarrow{LiAlH_4}$

49 The main product of the reaction
$CH_3CONH_2 + NaOBr \longrightarrow ......$ is **[MP PMT]**
(a) CH_3Br (b) CH_4
(c) CH_3OBr (d) CH_3NH_2

50 Which one of the following has the most nucleophilic nitrogen? **[KCET]**

(a) 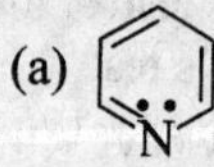 (b) 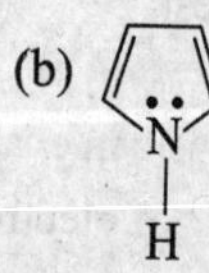

(c) C_6H_5–NHCOCH$_3$ (d) C_6H_5–NH$_2$

51 Why do 2° and 3° amines fail to undergo the carbylamine test? **[Guj CET]**
(a) They combine with chloroform to give a stable compound
(b) They react with alcoholic KOH
(c) The nitrogen atom of the amine group does not have the required number of hydrogen atoms
(d) All of the above

52 Which of the following statements are correct? **[CMC Ludhiyana]**
(a) Aniline is a stronger base than ethyl amine
(b) Aniline is a stronger base than *p*-methoxyaniline
(c) Aniline must be acetylated before nitration with an acid derivative
(d) Aniline is soluble in an ammonium hydroxide solution

53 In aqueous solutions, the basic strength of amines decreases in the order **[JCECE]**
(a) $CH_3NH_2 > (CH_3)_2NH > (CH_3)_3N$
(b) $(CH_3)_2NH > (CH_3)_3N > CH_3NH_2$
(c) $(CH_3)_3N > (CH_3)_2NH > CH_3NH_2$
(d) $(CH_3)_2NH > CH_3NH_2 > (CH_3)_3N$

54 **Assertion** (A) Basicity of $CH_3CH_2NH_2$ (I), NH_3 (II) and $C_6H_5NH_2$ (III) is in the order I > II > III.
Reason (R) Electron-donating groups (such as alkyl group) increase the basicity of amines, and electron-withdrawing groups (such as aryl group) decrease the basicity of amines. **[VMMC]**
(a) Both A and R are correct and reason is the correct explanation of A
(b) Both A and R are true but R is not the correct explanation of A
(c) A is correct but R is incorrect
(d) Both A and R are incorrect

2009

55 Predict the product **[CBSE AIPMT]**

C_6H_5–NHCOCH$_3$ is not shown; reactant: C_6H_5–NHCH$_3$ $+ NaNO_2 + HCl \longrightarrow$ product

(a) C_6H_5–N(CH$_3$)–N=O (b) C_6H_5–N(CH$_3$)–NO$_2$
(c) o-NO–C_6H_4–NHCH$_3$ + p-NO–C_6H_4–NHCH$_3$ (d) C_6H_5–N(OH)–CH$_3$

56 **Assertion** (A) In benzimidazole (N^{I} and N^{II}–H)

both the nitrogens (N^{I} and N^{II}) are basic.
Reason (R) Lone pair of electrons present on N^{I} are involved in delocalisation. **[AIIMS]**
(a) Both A and R are correct and R is the correct explanation of A
(b) Both A and R are correct but R is not the correct explanation of A
(c) A is correct but R is incorrect
(d) Both A and R are incorrect

57 The incorrect order with respect to the acidic strength is
(a) formic acid > acetic acid > propionic acid **[AFMC]**
(b) cyclohexanol < phenol < benzoic acid
(c) benzamide < aniline < cyclohexylamine
(d) $FCH_2COOH > ClCH_2COOH > BrCH_2COOH$

58 Which of the following is soluble in sodium hydroxide? **[AMU]**
(a) H_3C–C_6H_4–SO_2NHCH_3
(b) H_3C–C_6H_4–$SO_2N(CH_3)_2$
(c) H_3C–C_6H_4–NH_2
(d) H_3C–C_6H_4–$NHCH_3$

59 *m*-bromoaniline can be prepared by **[DUMET]**
(a) $C_6H_6 \xrightarrow[H_2SO_4]{HNO_3} \xrightarrow[\text{(ii) NaOH, } H_2O]{\text{(i) Sn – HCl}} \xrightarrow[H_2O]{Br_2}$
(b) $C_6H_6 \xrightarrow[FeBr_3]{Br_2} \xrightarrow[H_2SO_4]{HNO_3} \xrightarrow[Pt]{H_2}$
(c) $m\text{-}BrC_6H_4COOH \xrightarrow{SOCl_2} \xrightarrow{NH_3} \xrightarrow[H^+]{Br_2, NaOH}$
(d) $C_6H_5NH_2 \xrightarrow[Cu_2Br_2]{NaNO_2, HCl} \xrightarrow{NaNH_2}$

60 Which of the following compounds does liberate CO_2 from $NaHCO_3$? **[UP CPMT]**

(a) CH_3OH (b) CH_3NH_2

(c) $(CH_3)_4N^+OH^-$ (d) $CH_3\ NH_3^+Cl^-$

61 Reaction of nitrous acid with aliphatic primary amine in cold gives **[Manipal]**

(a) a diazonium salt (b) an alcohol

(c) a nitrite (d) a dye

62 Most basic amongst the following is **[OJEE]**

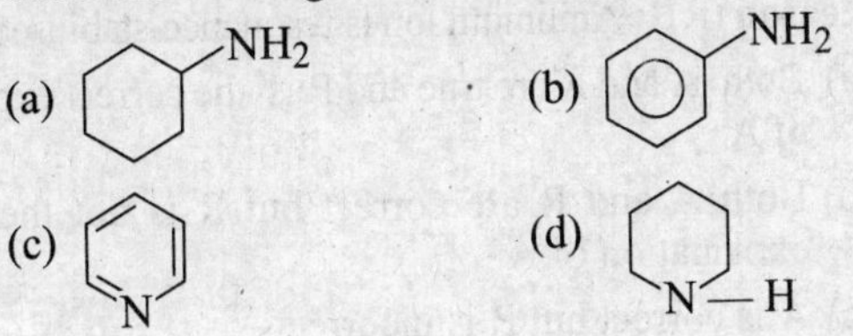

(a) NH_2 (b) NH_2

(c) N (d) N—H

63 The final product in the following sequence of reaction is **[OJEE]**

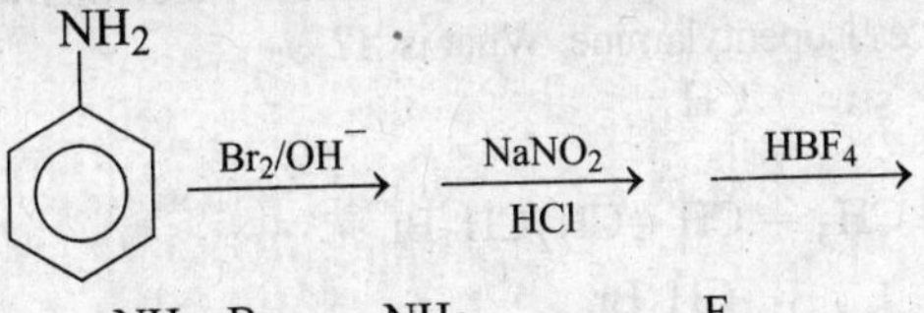

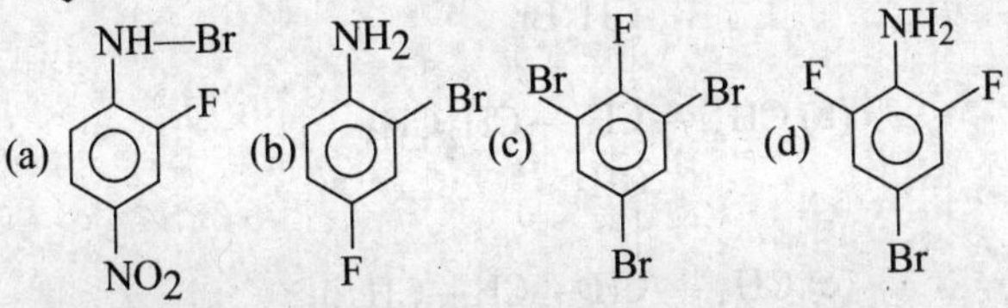

NH_2 $\xrightarrow{Br_2/OH^-}$ $\xrightarrow[HCl]{NaNO_2}$ $\xrightarrow{HBF_4}$

(a) NH—Br, F, NO_2 (b) NH_2, Br, F (c) F, Br, Br, Br (d) NH_2, F, F, Br

64 A primary amine that can be obtained both by the reduction of cyanides and amides is **[Kerala CEE]**

(a) methylamine (b) benzylamine

(c) aniline (d) *iso*-propylamine

(e) tertiary butylamine

65 The amine of highest basic strength among the following is **[J&K CET]**

(a) N-methylaniline (b) benzylamine

(c) *p*-toluidine (d) N, N-dimethylaniline

66 A secondary amine could be prepared readily from the starting material **[J&K CET]**

(a) alkyl isocyanide

(b) alkyl cyanide

(c) alkanamide

(d) phthalimide and alkyl halide

2008

67 During acetylation of amines, what is replaced by acetyl group? **[UP CPMT]**

(a) Hydrogen atom attached to nitrogen atom

(b) One or more hydrogen atoms attached to carbon atom

(c) One or more hydrogen atoms attached to nitrogen atom

(d) Hydrogen atoms attached to either carbon atom or nitrogen atom

68 Nitration of aniline is achieved by **[Punjab PMET]**

(a) direct treatment with nitration mixture under reflux

(b) using fuming HNO_3

(c) acetylation followed by nitration and subsequent hydrolysis

(d) KNO_3 + conc. HNO_3

69 The reaction between aniline and nitrous acid at low temperature yields **[JCECE]**

(a) N-nitrosamine (b) diazonium salt

(c) nitrile (d) amine-nitrite salt

2007

70 Which one of the following on reduction with lithium aluminium hydride yields a secondary amine? **[CBSE AIPMT]**

(a) Nitroethane (b) Methylisocyanide

(c) Acetamide (d) Methyl cyanide

71 An aliphatic amine on treatment with alcoholic carbon disulphide and mercuric chloride forms ethyl isothiocyanate, the reaction is known as **[AIIMS]**

(a) Hofmann's reaction

(b) Hofmann's rearrangement

(c) Hofmann's mustard oil reaction

(d) Hofmann's bromamide degradation reaction

72 **Assertion** (A) Amines are more basic than esters and ethers.

Reason (R) Nitrogen is less electronegative than oxygen. It is in better position to accommodate the positive charge on the proton. **[AIIMS]**

(a) Both A and R are correct and R is the correct explanation of A

(b) Both A and R are correct but R is not the correct explanation of A

(c) A is correct but R is incorrect

(d) Both A and R are incorrect

73 Aniline reacts with acetaldehyde to form **[AFMC]**

(a) Schiff's base (b) carbylamine

(c) immine (d) None of these

74 A mixture of ethyl amine and alcoholic KOH on heating gives **[MHT CET]**

(a) alkyl cyanide (b) ethyl cyanate

(c) ethyl isocyanide (d) ethyl isocyanate

75 Isopropyl amine with excess of acetyl chloride will give **[MHT CET]**

(a) $(CH_3CO)_2N—CH—(CH_3)_2$

(b) $(CH_3)_2CH—N(H)—COCH_3$

(c) $(CH_3)_2CHN(COCH_3)_2$

(d) $CH_3CH_2CH_2—N(H)—COCH_3$

76 Treatment of cyclobutylmethyl amine with nitrous acid does not give [Kerala CEE]

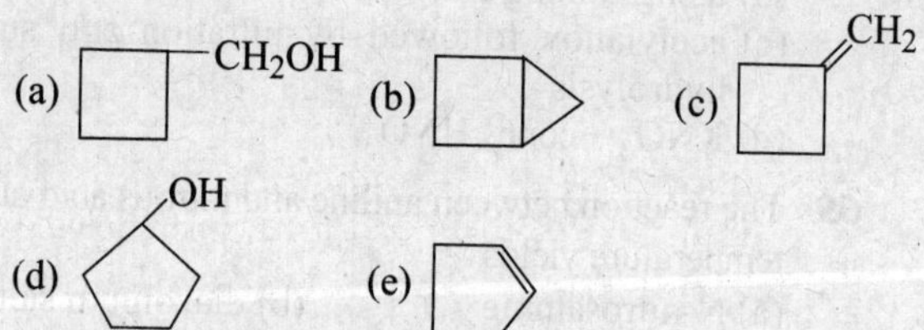

77 In the following reaction sequence,

$$p\text{-}CH_3C_6H_4NH_2 \xrightarrow{\text{Excess } Br_2} X \xrightarrow[\text{(ii) } H_3PO_2]{\text{(i) } NaNO_2/HCl} Y$$

The compounds X and Y are respectively, [Kerala CEE]

(a) 4-methyl-3-bromoaniline (NH_2, Br, CH_3) and 3-bromotoluene (Br, CH_3)

(b) 2,6-dibromo-4-methylaniline (NH_2, Br, Br, CH_3) and 3,5-dibromotoluene (Br, Br, CH_3)

(c) 2,4,6-tribromoaniline (NH_2, Br, Br, Br) and 1,3,5-tribromobenzene (Br, Br, Br)

(d) 2-bromo-4-methylaniline (NH_2, Br, CH_3) and 3-bromotoluene (Br, CH_3)

(e) 2,6-dibromo-4-methylaniline (NH_2, Br, Br, CH_3) and 2,6-dibromo-4-methylphenol (OH, Br, Br, CH_3)

78 Which of the following will be obtained on acetylation of aniline? [Guj CET]

(a) N-acetylamino benzene (b) paracetamol
(c) *p*-amino acetophenone (d) *o*-amino acetophenone

2006

79 Which of the following is more basic than aniline? [CBSE AIPMT]

(a) Diphenylamine
(b) Triphenylamine
(c) *p*-nitroaniline
(d) benzylamine

80 **Assertion** (A) Anilinium chloride is more acidic than ammonium chloride.
Reason (R) Anilinium ion is resonance-stabilised. [AIIMS]

(a) Both A and R are true and R is the correct explanation of A
(b) Both A and R are correct but R is not the correct explanation of A
(c) A is correct but R is incorrect
(d) Both A and R are incorrect

81 Potassium phthalimide reacts with A which on hydrolysis gives isopentylamine. What is A? [DUMET]

(a) $CH_3-CH(CH_3)-CH_2CH_2Br$
(b) $CH_3-CH(CH_2Br)-CH_2CH_3$
(c) $CH_3-CH(CH_3)-CH(Br)-CH_3$
(d) $CH_3-C(CH_3)(Br)-CH_2-CH_3$

82 Aniline reacts with acetic anhydride to give [DUMET]

(a) $CH_3COOH + C_6H_5-NH-\overset{O}{\overset{\|}{C}}-CH_3$
(b) $HCOOH + C_6H_5-NH-\overset{O}{\overset{\|}{C}}-CH_3$
(c) $CH_4 + C_6H_5-NH-\overset{O}{\overset{\|}{C}}-CH_3$
(d) $C_2H_6 + C_6H_5-NH-\overset{O}{\overset{\|}{C}}-CH_3$

83 Match the following Columns.

Columns I (Reactants)	Columns II (Products)
A. $RX + KCN \xrightarrow{\text{Ethanol}}$	1. C_6H_5—NH_2
B. $RX + CH_3COOAg \longrightarrow$	2. RCN
C. $H_3CC{\equiv}N \xrightarrow{LiAlH_4}$	3. CH_3COOR
D. C_6H_5—$CONH_2 \xrightarrow[\text{degradation}]{\text{Hofmann's}}$	4. $CH_3CH_2NH_2$
E. R—$NH_2 \xrightarrow[CHCl_3/KOH]{\text{Carbylamine reaction}}$	5. RNC

Codes [Kerala CEE]

	A	B	C	D	E		A	B	C	D	E
(a)	3	1	2	5	4	(b)	2	3	4	1	5
(c)	3	2	1	5	4	(d)	5	3	2	4	1
(e)	4	2	3	5	1						

84 In the following reaction

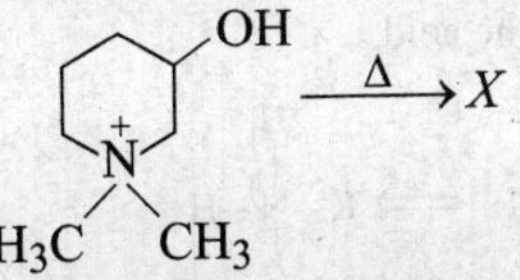

The organic product X has the structure [Kerala CEE]

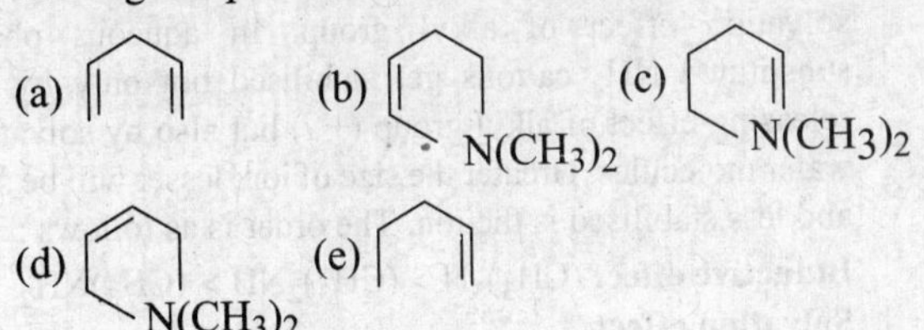

85 Urea is a [MP PMT]

(a) monobasic acid (b) dibasic acid
(c) neutral compound (d) monoacid base

86 Aniline on oxidation with $Na_2Cr_2O_7$ and H_2SO_4 gives [J&K CET]

(a) benzoic acid (b) *m*-amino benzoic acid
(c) Schiff's base (d) *p*-benzoquinone

87 *n*-propylamine yields a volatile compound X on warming with alc. alkali and chloroform. X has an offensive odour. The structure of X is [J&K CET]

(a) $CH_3CH_2CH_2CN$ (b) $(CH_3)_2CHCN$
(c) $CH_3CH_2CH_2NC$ (d) $(CH_3)_2CHNC$

88 In the reaction sequence

$C_6H_5NH_2 \xrightarrow[0°C]{NaNO_2,\ HCl} A \xrightarrow{CuCN} B \xrightarrow{LiAlH_4} C$

the product 'C' is [Punjab PMET]

(a) benzonitrile (b) benzaldehyde
(c) benzoic acid (d) benzylamine

89 Diethyl oxalate is used for distinguishing primary, secondary and tertiary [Punjab PMET]

(a) alcohols (b) amines
(c) alkyl halides (d) hydrogens in hydrocarbons

90 The basicity of aniline is less than that of cyclohexylamine. This is due to [KCET]

(a) $+R$-effect of —NH_2 group
(b) $-I$-effect of —NH_2 group
(c) $-R$-effect of —NH_2 group
(d) None of the above

2005

91 Pyridine is less basic than triethylamine because [AIIMS]

(a) pyridine has aromatic character
(b) nitrogen in pyridine is sp^2-hybridised
(c) pyridine is a cyclic system
(d) in pyridine lone pair of nitrogen is delocalised

92 In order to convert aniline into chlorobenzene, the reagent used is [AMU]

(a) $NaNO_2$ / HCl, CuCl (b) Cl_2 / CCl_4
(c) $Cl_2 / AlCl_3$ (d) $CuCl_2$

93 R—NH—COH $\xrightarrow[\text{pyridine}]{POCl_3}$ product

In the given reaction, what will be the product? [BHU]

(a) R—N=C=O (b) $R—\overset{+}{N}{\equiv}C^-$
(c) R—C≡N (d) None of these

94 Methyl amine reacts with methyl iodide. For completion of reaction, how many moles of methyl iodide are required? [MHT CET]

(a) 1 (b) 2
(c) 3 (d) 4

95 Acetaldoxime on reduction with Na / C_2H_5OH gives [MHT CET]

(a) 2-propanol (b) ethylamine
(c) acetaldehyde (d) ethanol

96 Which one of the following can produce hydrogen when treated with metallic sodium? [RPMT]

(a) $(CH_3)_2NH$ (b) CH_3NH_2
(c) $C_6H_5NH_2$ (d) CH_3CONH_2

Answers

1 (a)	2 (c)	3 (d)	4 (d)	5 (a)	6 (d)	7 (d)	8 (d)	9 (b)	10 (a)
11 (d)	12 (d)	13 (a)	14 (b)	15 (d)	16 (a)	17 (d)	18 (b)	19 (b)	20 (a)
21 (d)	22 (b)	23 (a)	24 (c)	25 (b)	26 (d)	27 (b)	28 (a)	29 (a)	30 (a)
31 (d)	32 (b)	33 (d)	34 (e)	35 (a)	36 (b)	37 (c)	38 (b)	39 (b)	40 (a)
41 (d)	42 (a)	43 (a)	44 (c)	45 (b)	46 (d)	47 (b)	48 (c)	49 (d)	50 (a)
51 (c)	52 (c)	53 (d)	54 (a)	55 (a)	56 (a)	57 (c)	58 (a)	59 (c)	60 (d)
61 (b)	62 (d)	63 (c)	64 (b)	65 (b)	66 (a)	67 (c)	68 (c)	69 (b)	70 (b)
71 (c)	72 (a)	73 (a)	74 (c)	75 (c)	76 (b)	77 (b)	78 (a)	79 (d)	80 (c)
81 (a)	82 (a)	83 (b)	84 (c)	85 (a)	86 (d)	87 (c)	88 (d)	89 (b)	90 (a)
91 (d)	92 (a)	93 (b)	94 (c)	95 (b)	96 (d)				

Explanations

1 (*a*) Secondary amines on reaction with Hinsberg's reagent (benzene sulphonyl chloride) forms N,N-dialkyl benzene sulphonamide. The product formed is not acidic as no H-atom is attached to N thus, it is insoluble in alkali.

The reaction of 2° amine given in option (a) takes place as follows:

$$C_6H_5-SO_2-Cl + \underset{\substack{|\\CH_3}}{CH_3-CH}-NH-\underset{\substack{|\\CH_3}}{CH}-CH_3 \longrightarrow$$

2° amine

$$C_6H_5-SO_2-\overset{H_3C-CH-CH_3}{\overset{|}{N}}-\underset{\substack{|\\CH_3}}{CH}-CH_3$$

On the other hand, 1° amines react with Hinsberg's reagent to yield N-alkyl benzene sulphonamide which is soluble in alkali and 3° amines do not react with $C_6H_5SO_2Cl$. The remaining options contain 1° and 3° amines.

$$CH_3CH_2-\overset{CH_2CH_3}{\overset{|}{N}}-CH_2CH_3,\quad CH_3-\overset{NH_2}{\overset{|}{\underset{\substack{|\\CH_3}}{C}}}-CH_2CH_2CH_3,$$

3° amine   1° amine

$$CH_3-\overset{CH_3}{\overset{|}{\underset{\substack{|\\CH_3}}{C}}}-\underset{\substack{|\\CH_3}}{CH}-NH_2$$

1° amine

Thus, option (a) is correct.

2 (*c*) Basic nature depends on the ability to donate lone pair of electrons by the atoms present in the species. Structure (III) is most basic as in that, $-NH_2$ group is not directly bonded with the benzene ring.

Structure (II) is 2nd most basic due to presence of $-NH_2$ and $-OCH_3$ groups together.

Structure (I) is next basic species which is less basic than (III) and (II) but more basic than structure (I) due to presence of electron releasing ($-CH_3$) group attached to $-NH$ group. Structure IV is least basic, because $-NH_2$ group is directly bonded with the benzene ring, thus lone pair of electrons on N - atom is involved in resonance. Hence correct order is,

(III) > (II) > (I) > (IV) and option (c) is the correct.

3 (*d*) Basic strength of methyl substituted amines in aqueous solution depends upon the ease of formation of cation by accepting a proton from the acid.

$$R-\underset{\substack{|\\H}}{\overset{\substack{H\\|}}{N}}: + H^+ \rightleftharpoons R-\underset{\substack{|\\H}}{\overset{\substack{H\\|}}{N^+}}-H$$

The basic strength can be decided by both inductive effect and solvation effect of alkyl group. In aqueous phase, the substituted $\overset{+}{N}H_4$ cations get stabilised not only by electron releasing effect of alkyl group (+ *I*) but also by solvation with water molecules. Greater the size of ion, lesser will be solvation and less stabilised is the ion. The order is as follows :

Inductive effect $(CH_3)_3N > (CH_3)_2NH > (CH_3)NH_2$

Solvation effect

$$H_3C-\underset{\substack{|\\H\\ \vdots\\OH_2}}{\overset{\substack{H\\|}}{N^+}}-H\text{----}OH_2 \;>\; (H_3C)_2\overset{+}{N}(H\text{----}OH_2)_2 \;>\; (H_3C)_2\underset{\substack{|\\CH_3}}{\overset{+}{N}}-H\text{----}OH_2$$

(1°)   (2°)   (3°)

Strong +*I*-effect and hydrogen bonding favours higher basic strength of 2° amine. Thus, the correct order of basic strength in aqueous media will be $(CH_3)_2NH > CH_3NH_2 > (CH_3)_3N$.

4 (*d*) In strongly acidic medium, aniline is protonated to form the anilinium ion.

$$\text{Aniline } (C_6H_5NH_2) \underset{}{\overset{H^+}{\rightleftharpoons}} \text{Anilinium ion } (C_6H_5\overset{+}{N}H_3)$$

Since, anilinium ion so formed is *meta* directing, thus besides *ortho* and *para* derivatives, significant amount of *meta* derivative is also formed.

$$\text{Aniline} \xrightarrow[288K]{HNO_3, H_2SO_4} \text{p-nitroaniline (51\%)} + \text{m-nitroaniline (47\%)} + \text{o-nitroaniline (2\%)}$$

5 (*a*) As, —NH_2 group is more reactive than —OH group, CH_3COCl will attack on —NH_2 group and gives the following product,

$$HO-C_6H_4-NHCOCH_3.$$

Reaction is given as follows

$$HO-C_6H_4-NH_2 + CH_3COCl\ (1\,\text{equivalent}) \longrightarrow HO-C_6H_4-NHCOCH_3$$

6 (*d*) Electron releasing group—OH in compound (I) increases the basic strength while electron withdrawing group (—$COCH_3$ in compound I and IV) decreases the basic strength of amines. In compound IV, —NH_2 is directly attached to benzene ring, it results in conjugation of unshared pair of electrons with benzene ring and thus making it less available for protonation. Therefore, correct order is III > II > IV > I.

7 (*d*)

$$\text{Aniline} \xrightarrow{\text{Bromination}} \text{2,4,6-tribromoaniline} \xrightarrow[+HCl]{NaNO_2} \text{2,4,6-tribromobenzenediazonium chloride } (\overset{+}{N_2}\overset{-}{Cl}) \xrightarrow{\text{Boiling } (C_2H_5OH)} \text{1,3,5-tribromobenzene}$$

(Tribromobenzene)

8 (*d*)

$$\underset{(I)}{C_6H_5NH_2} \qquad \underset{(II)}{p\text{-}NO_2C_6H_4NH_2} \qquad \underset{(III)}{p\text{-}CH_3C_6H_4NH_2}$$

In structure III, —CH_3 group is an electron donating and *o*/*p* directing group which increases the electron density on benzene ring at *ortho or para* position while in structure II, —NO_2 group is an electron withdrawing group which decreases the electron density on benzene ring.

Hence, the compound III is more basic than II. In structure I, no substituent is attached. Due to this, I is more basic than II and less basic than III.

Therefore, the correct order of basic strength of given compounds is II < I < III.

9 (*b*) The conversion of amide with no substituent on nitrogen to an amine containing one carbon less by the action of alkaline hypobromide is called Hofmann hypobromamide reaction.

It involves the migration of alkyl or aryl group with its electron pair to electron deficient N from adjacent carbon. The reaction involves the intermediate of isocyanate.

$$\underset{\text{Acetamide}}{CH_3-\overset{O}{\overset{\|}{C}}-NH_2} + Br_2 + 4NaOH \xrightarrow{\Delta} \underset{\text{Methanamine}}{CH_3NH_2} + 2NaBr + 2Na_2CO_3 + H_2O$$

Step I : $CH_3-\overset{O}{\overset{\|}{C}}-NH_2 + Br_2 \xrightarrow{HBr} CH_3-\overset{O}{\overset{\|}{C}}-\underset{H}{\underset{|}{N}}-Br$

Step II : $CH_3-\overset{O}{\overset{\|}{C}}-\underset{H}{\underset{|}{N}}-Br + OH^- \longrightarrow CH_3-\overset{O}{\overset{\|}{C}}-\overset{\ominus}{N}-Br + H_2O$

Step III : $CH_3-\overset{O}{\overset{\|}{C}}-\ddot{\overset{-}{N}}-Br \rightarrow CH_3-\overset{O}{\overset{\|}{C}}-\ddot{N}\!: + \overset{\ominus}{Br}$

Step IV: $CH_3-\overset{O}{\overset{\|}{C}}-\ddot{N}\!: \xrightarrow[\text{alkyl migration}]{\text{Intermolecular}} CH_3NCO$

Step V: $CH_3NCO + 2OH^- \xrightarrow{\Delta} CH_3NH_2 + CO_3^{2-}$

10 (*a*) Both (A) are (R) are true and (R) is the correct explanation for (A).

Aniline on reaction with $NaNO_2$/ HCl at 0°C followed by coupling with β-naphthol gives a dark blue coloured precipitate due to extended conjugation.

11 (*d*) The conjugation (delocalisation) of electrons in pyrrole can be visualised as:

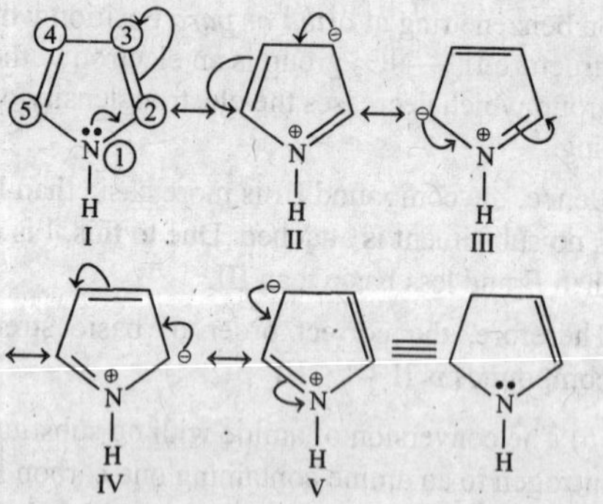

I, II, III, IV, V

As resonating structures III and IV are more stable than II and V. Thus, maximum electron density will be found on carbon 2 and 5.

12 (*d*)

Aryl amine (less basic) $R-\ddot{N}H_2$ Alkyl amine (more basic)

Due to delocalisation of lone pair of electrons of N-atom to the benzene ring, it loses its basicity and becomes less basic than alkyl amine.

On the other hand, alkyl amine has free lone pair of electrons as well as +*I*-effect of alkyl group which increases electron density on N-atom thus, enhancing its basic nature.

13 (*a*) Quaternary ammonium salt of alkyl amines, when reacts with silver oxide yield quaternary ammonium hydroxide. On strong heating, it decomposes into alkene, *tert* amine and water. This reaction is known as Hofmann elimination reaction.

Here elimination of H takes place from β -carbon having more hydrogen atoms.

$$2CH_3-CH_2-CH_2-\underset{\displaystyle CH_3}{\overset{|}{CH}}-CH_2-\overset{+}{N}(CH_3)_3I^- + Ag_2O + H_2O \longrightarrow$$

$$\underset{(X)}{2CH_3-CH_2-CH_2-\underset{\displaystyle CH_3}{\overset{|}{CH}}-CH_2-\overset{+}{N}(CH_3)_3OH^-} \xrightarrow{\Delta}$$

$$\underset{\text{2-methylpent-1-ene (option 'a')}}{2CH_3-CH_2-CH_2-\overset{CH_3}{C}=CH_2} + \underset{\textit{tert}\text{-amine}}{N(CH_3)_3} + H_2O$$

14 (*b*) Since, $X(C_4H_{11}N)$ reacts with *p*-toluene sulphonyl chloride (Hinsberg reagent) to form a compound which is soluble in KOH, therefore, *X* must be a primary amine.

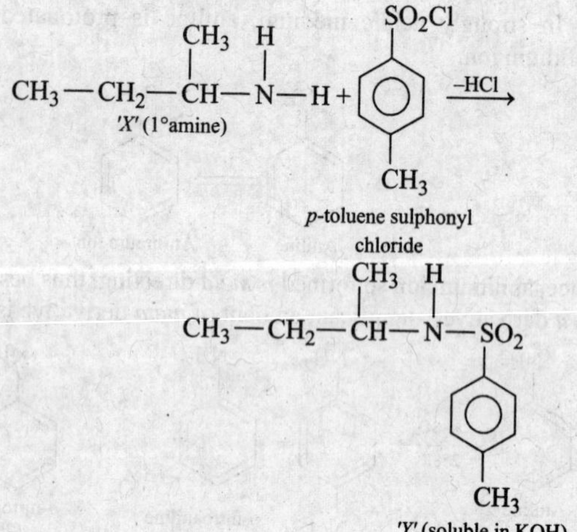

$$\underset{'X'\text{ (1° amine)}}{CH_3-CH_2-\overset{CH_3}{CH}-\overset{H}{N}-H} + \underset{p\text{-toluene sulphonyl chloride}}{CH_3C_6H_4SO_2Cl} \xrightarrow{-HCl} \underset{'Y'\text{ (soluble in KOH)}}{CH_3-CH_2-\overset{CH_3}{CH}-\overset{H}{N}-SO_2-C_6H_4-CH_3}$$

$$\underset{\text{(optically active compound)}}{CH_3-CH_2-\overset{CH_3}{CH}-NH_2} + \underset{\text{Acetyl chloride}}{CH_3COCl} \xrightarrow{-HCl} \underset{(Z)}{CH_3-CH_2-\overset{CH_3}{CH}-NH-COCH_3}$$

15 (*d*) Only primary amines (aromatic as well as aliphatic), i.e. the compounds containing $-NH_2$ group, answer carbylamine test, i.e. form a foul smelling poisonous compound carbylamine when treated with chloroform in alkaline medium.

$$RNH_2 + CHCl_3 + 3KOH \xrightarrow{\Delta} R-N \overset{\rightarrow}{=} C + 3KCl + 3H_2O$$

$(CH_3)_3N$ is a teritary (3°) amine, that's why it does not give carbylamine test.

16 (*a*) Secondary amines form N, N-dialkyl derivative with *p*-toluene sulphonyl chloride which does not dissolve in NaOH whereas tertiary amines do not react with it at all. Hence, secondary and tertiary amines can be distinguished by using *p*-toluene sulphonyl chloride.

17 (*d*) More the tendency to form H-bonding (i.e. more the number of H-atoms attached directly with N atom), higher in the boiling point of amine. Thus, $CH_3CH_2CH_2CH_2NH_2$ has the highest boiling point among the given amines.

18 (*b*) Lithium aluminium hydride ($LiAlH_4$) converts $\rangle C=O$ group into $\rangle CH_2$ group thus, it can be used to convert acetamide into ethanamine.

$$\underset{\text{Acetamide}}{CH_3CONH_2} + 4[H] \xrightarrow{LiAlH_4} \underset{\text{Ethanamine}}{CH_3CH_2NH_2} + H_2O$$

19 (*b*) Since, the amine gives white precipitate with benzene sulphonyl chloride which is insoluble in *aq*. NaOH, so it must be a secondary amine (i.e. amine having *R*NH*R* group.)

Among the given compound, only (b) is a secondary amine, so it represents the structure of given amine.

20 (*a*) Aniline is a primary amine (contains —NH_2 group). When it is treated with chloroform under alkaline condition, it results in the formation of a foul smelling compound, known by the name isonitrile or carbylamine. This reaction is known as carbylamine reaction

$$C_6H_5-NH_2 + CHCl_3 + 3KOH\text{ (alc.)} \longrightarrow C_6H_5-N \overset{\rightarrow}{=} C + 3KCl + 3H_3O^+$$

Aniline → Phenyl isocyanide

21 (*d*) The source of nitrogen in this reaction is $C_6H_4(CO)_2N^-K^+$.

$$C_6H_4(CO)_2NH + KOH\text{ (alc.)} \xrightarrow{-H_2O} C_6H_4(CO)_2N^-K^+ \xrightarrow[-KI]{C_2H_5I,\ \Delta}$$

Phthalimide → Phthalimide

$$C_6H_4(CO)_2N-C_2H_5 \xrightarrow{H^+/H_2O} C_6H_4(COOH)_2 + C_2H_5NH_2$$

Phthalimide → Phthalic acid + Ethylamine

22 (*b*) Hofmann developed a method for the preparation of primary amines by treating an amide with bromine in an aqueous or ethanolic solution of sodium hydroxide. The amine so formed contains one carbon less than that present in the amide.

$$R-\overset{O}{\overset{\|}{C}}-NH_2 + Br_2 + 4NaOH \longrightarrow R-NH_2 + Na_2CO_3 + 2NaBr + 2H_2O$$

23 (*a*) Compound *A* (C_7H_9N) is benzyl amine ($C_6H_5CH_2NH_2$). It reacts with $NaNO_2$/HCl to 0°C to form benzyl alcohol and N_2 gas.

$$C_6H_5CH_2NH_2\ (A) \xrightarrow[0°C]{NaNO_2/HCl} C_6H_5CH_2OH + N_2\uparrow$$

Benzyl amine shows following five isomers:

(I) $C_6H_5CH_2NH_2$ (II) o-$CH_3C_6H_4NH_2$ (III) m-$CH_3C_6H_4NH_2$ (IV) p-$CH_3C_6H_4NH_2$ (V) $C_6H_5NHCH_3$

24 (*c*) Conversion of benzene into *m*-bromoaniline can be done by successive nitration, bromination and reduction using following reagents:

Nitration → conc. HNO_3 / conc. H_2SO_4

Bromination → Br_2 / H_2O

Reduction → Sn / HCl

Formation of nitrobenzene in the first step directs incoming of electrophile towards *meta* position in the second step. Then, reduction of nitro compound produces *m*-bromoaniline very easily. Complete sequence of the chemical reaction can be shown as,

$$\text{Benzene} \xrightarrow[(333\ K)\ (-H_2O)]{\text{Conc. } HNO_3,\ \text{conc. } H_2SO_4} \text{Nitrobenzene} \xrightarrow{Br_2/H_2O} m\text{-nitrobenzene} \xrightarrow{Sn/HCl} m\text{-bromo aniline}$$

25 (*b*) Primary amines may be formed from Hofmann bromamide degradation reaction. The reaction is as follows :

$$RCONH_2 + Br_2 + 4KOH \xrightarrow{\Delta} RNH_2 + 2KBr + K_2CO_3 + 2H_2O$$

$$C_2H_5CONH_2 + Br_2 + 4KOH \longrightarrow C_2H_5NH_2 + 2KBr + K_2CO_3 + 2H_2O$$

Primary amines may also be formed by reduction of nitroalkanes, nitrobenzene, etc.

$$RNO_2 + 3H_2 \xrightarrow[\text{or } LiAlH_4 \text{ or } H_2/Pt \text{ or Metal / Acid}]{Ni/250°C} RNH_2 + 2H_2O$$

$$C_6H_5NO_2 + 3H_2 \xrightarrow{LiAlH_4/\text{ether}} C_6H_5NH_2 + 2H_2O$$

26 (*d*) This reaction is known as Hofmann bromamide reaction and is used for the conversion of amides to amines with one carbon atom less than parent amide.

$$\underset{\text{Acetamide}}{CH_3CONH_2} + Br_2 + 4NaOH \longrightarrow \underset{\text{Methyl amine}}{CH_3NH_2} + Na_2CO_3 + 2KBr + 2H_2O$$

27 (*b*) $C_6H_5NH_2 \xrightarrow{NaNO_2/HCl} \underset{\text{Benzene diazonium chloride}(X)}{C_6H_5\overset{+}{N_2}Cl^-} \xrightarrow{Cu_2(CN)_2} \underset{\text{Benzonitrile }(Y)}{C_6H_5CN} \xrightarrow{H_2O/H^+} \underset{\text{Benzoic acid }(Z)}{C_6H_5-COOH}$

Thus, product *Z* is identified as C_6H_5— COOH.

28 (*a*) $R-\overset{O}{\overset{\|}{C}}-NH_2 + Br_2 \xrightarrow[-HBr]{KOH} R-\overset{O}{\overset{\|}{C}}-\ddot{N}-Br$

$$R-\overset{O}{\overset{\|}{C}}-\bar{N}-Br \xrightarrow[\text{Rearrangement}]{-Br^-} R-\ddot{N}=C=O \xrightarrow{KOH/H_2O} RNH_2 + CO_2$$

The above reaction is known as Hofmann bromamide reaction.

29 (*a*) On treating with nitrous acid, primary amine gives an alcohol and N_2 gas. So, '*A*' should be primary amine having *iso*-propyl.

$$\underset{(A)}{C_3H_7NH_2} + HNO_2 \longrightarrow C_3H_7OH + N_2\uparrow + H_2O$$

$$\underset{'A'}{(H_3C)_2CH—NH_2} \xrightarrow[\text{(Carbylamine test)}]{CHCl_3 + KOH} \underset{'C'}{(H_3C)_2CH—NC} \xrightarrow{\text{Reduction}} \underset{iso\text{-propylmethyl amine}}{(H_3C)_2CH—NH—CH_3}$$

30 (*a*) $C_6H_5NH_2 + CH_3COCl \xrightarrow[-HCl]{NaOH} \underset{\text{Acetanilide}}{C_6H_5NHCOCH_3} + HCl$

31 (*d*) $\underset{\text{Aniline}}{C_6H_5NH_2} + 3Br_2 \longrightarrow$ 2, 4, 6-tribromoaniline

32 (*b*) $(C_2H_5)_2NH$, i.e. N-ethylethanamine is the most basic amine among the given compounds.

33 (*d*) Aniline $\xrightarrow{Br_2/H_2O}$ 2,4,6-tribromoaniline (*X*) $\xrightarrow[0°C]{NaNO_2/HCl}$ 2,4,6-tribromobenzenediazonium chloride $(\overset{+}{N_2}\bar{Cl})$ (*Y*) $\xrightarrow[HCl]{Cu_2Cl_2}$ 2,4,6-tribromochlorobenzene (*Z*)

34 (*e*) $\underset{\text{Anilinium hydrogen sulphate}}{C_6H_5\overset{+}{N}H_3H\overset{-}{S}O_4} \xrightarrow[\text{(Conc.)}]{\Delta(453\text{-}473\ K),\ H_2SO_4}$ Sulphanilic acid (NH_2 and SO_3H para on benzene ring)

35 (*a*) Intermolecular association (due to H— bonding) is more in primary amines than in secondary amines as there are two H-atoms available for hydrogen bond formation in primary amines. Tertiary amines do not have intermolecular association due to the absence of H-atom for hydrogen bond formation. Hence, the order of boiling point of isomeric alkyl amines is as 1° > 2° > 3°.

36 (*b*) Aniline $\xrightarrow[(273\text{–}278\ K)]{NaNO_2/HCl}$ $\underset{(X)}{C_6H_5\overset{+}{N_2}Cl^-}$ $\xrightarrow{\text{N,N-dimethylaniline}}$ $\underset{(Y)}{C_6H_5—N{=}N—C_6H_4—N(CH_3)_2}$

37 (*c*) Statement (c) is incorrect as aryl amines react with nitrous acid to form diazonium salt. Rest all statements are correct.

38 (*b*) The given reaction is the example of Hofmann-bromamide reaction.

$$\underset{\text{Acetamide}}{CH_3CONH_2} \xrightarrow{NaOH + Br_2} \underset{\text{Methyl amine}}{CH_3NH_2}$$

39 (*b*) Basic character depends upon the availability of lone pair of electrons over nitrogen for donation. Presence of electron releasing group like —CH_3 increases the electron density over nitrogen, thus, lone pair of nitrogen are more available for donation. Hence, basic character increases.

But 3° methyl amines are less basic as compared to 2° and 1° amines due to steric hindrance. Thus, the order of basic strength of the given compounds is

$$\underset{(IV)}{C_6H_5CH_2NH_2} < \underset{\substack{3°\ \text{amine} \\ (III)}}{(CH_3)_3N} < \underset{\substack{1°\ \text{amine} \\ (I)}}{CH_3NH_2} < \underset{\substack{2°\ \text{amine} \\ (II)}}{(CH_3)_2NH}$$

40 (*a*) Only 1° amines evolve nitrogen when reacts with nitrous acid (HNO_2).

$$\underset{\text{1-amine}}{\overset{1°}{R—NH_2}} + HNO_2 \longrightarrow ROH + N_2\uparrow + H_2O$$

41 (*d*) Hinsberg's reagent (benzene sulphonyl chloride) is used to distinguish 1°, 2° and 3° amines. With Hinsberg's reagent, 1° amines give a sulphonamide, soluble in alkali; 2° amines form a sulphonamide, insoluble in alkali while, 3° amines do not react at all.

42 (*a*) According to Lewis, species having a tendency of donating an electron pair are called bases. In amines, a lone pair of electrons is present over nitrogen. Since, it is available for donation, thus, it provides basic character to the amines.

43 (*a*) Secondary amines, (containing —NH-group) when treated with HNO_2 give nitrosoamines which separate as yellow oily liquids. The structures of the given compounds are:

$\underset{\text{Ethylmethylamine (2°)}}{C_2H_5—NH—CH_3}$; $\underset{\text{Aniline (1°)}}{C_6H_5NH_2}$; $\underset{\text{3-methylbenzylamine (1°)}}{CH_2NH_2\text{ and }CH_3\text{ on benzene ring}}$; $\underset{\text{Methylamine (1°)}}{CH_3NH_2}$

Among the given compounds, only ethyl methyl amine is a secondary amine, thus, it gives a yellow oil liquid with HNO_2.

44 (c) $C_2H_5NH_2 \xrightarrow[-H_2O]{HNO_2, -N_2} C_2H_5OH \xrightarrow{PCl_3} C_2H_5Cl \xrightarrow{NH_3} C_2H_5NH_2$

Ethyl amine → Ethanol (A) → Ethyl chloride (B) → Ethylamine (C)

45 (b) Acetamide and ethylamine can be distinguished by heating with NaOH solution when acetamide liberates NH_3 but ethylamine does not.

$$CH_3CONH_2 + NaOH \xrightarrow{\Delta} CH_3CO\overset{-}{O}\overset{+}{Na} + NH_3$$

$$CH_3CH_2NH_2 + NaOH \xrightarrow{\Delta} \text{No reaction}$$

46 (d) Basic nature of amines is due to the presence of lone pair of electrons on nitrogen atom which is available for the bond formation with Lewis acid. Due to the $+I$-effect, 2° amine is more basic than 1° amine and NH_3. In case of aromatic amines, the lone pair on nitrogen atom are involved in resonance, therefore not available for bond formation, so aromatic amines are less basic.

Hence, $(C_2H_5)_2NH$ is the strongest base among the given options.

47 (b) This reaction illustrates the electrophilic character of $COCl_2$ and nucleophilic character of Ar—NH_2.

$$C_6H_5\ddot{N}H_2 \xrightarrow[-HCl]{COCl_2} [C_6H_5-NHCOCl] \xrightarrow[-HCl]{Pyridine} C_6H_5-N=C=O$$

Phenyl isocyanate

48 (c) Reaction (c) will not give primary amine. All the given reactions are as follows:

$$CH_3CONH_2 \xrightarrow{Br_2, KOH} CH_3NH_2 \text{ (1° amine)}$$

$$CH_3CN \xrightarrow{LiAlH_4} CH_3CH_2NH_2 \text{ (1° amine)}$$

$$CH_3NC \xrightarrow{LiAlH_4} CH_3NHCH_3 \text{ (2° amine)}$$

$$CH_3CONH_2 \xrightarrow{LiAlH_4} CH_3CH_2NH_2 \text{ (1° amine)}$$

Thus, from the above reactions, it is clear that reduction of methyl isocyanide does not give primary amine.

49 (d) When acid amide is treated with alkaline sodium hypobromite (NaOBr or NaOH + Br_2), it is converted to a primary amine, which has one carbon less than the original amide.

This is known as 'Hofmann bromamide reaction".

$$CH_3CONH_2 + 4NaOH + Br_2 \longrightarrow CH_3NH_2 + Na_2CO_3 + 2NaBr + 2H_2O$$

50 (a) Nucleophiles are the species which have excess of electrons. Among the given species, the lone pair of nitrogen on pyrrole is involved in delocalisation of the ring, thus, are not available for donation. In aniline, the lone pair is involved in conjugation with the π-electrons of the ring while in pyridine, these are relatively free for donation because these lone pairs are not the part of aromatic sextet. Thus, nitrogen of pyridine (pyridine structure) is most nucleophilic.

(phenyl and —$COCH_3$ both are electron withdrawing groups, thus, decreases the nucleophilicity of nitrogen).

51 (c) Secondary and tertiary amines fail to undergo the carbylamine test because the nitrogen atom of amine group does not have the required number of hydrogen atoms to give a stable complex.

52 (c) Only statement (c) is correct, whereas statement (a, b and d) are incorrect. Basic character depends upon the availability of lone pair of electrons for donation. Aliphatic amines are generally more basic than aromatic amines because lone pair takes part in delocalisation in case of aromatic amines. Presence of electron releasing group at benzene nucleus increases the basic character of amine. Amino group strongly activates the ring through delocalisation of lone pair of electrons of N-atom over the aromatic ring. Thus, electron density increases more at o- and p- positions as compared to m-position.

53 (d) Basicity of amines depend upon the availability of lone pair of electrons of nitrogen for donation. Electron releasing group increases the electron density over nitrogen, thus, increases the basic character. 3° methyl amine although contains three electron releasing groups but is least basic because of steric hindrance. Hence, the order of basic character is

$$(CH_3)_2NH > CH_3NH_2 > (CH_3)_3N$$

54 (a) Reason is the correct explanation of Assertion.

Presence of electron releasing group at benzene nucleus increases the basic character whereas electron withdrawing group decrease the basic character. Hence, correct order of basicity is

$$\underset{(I)}{CH_3CH_2NH_2} > \underset{(II)}{NH_3} > \underset{(III)}{C_6H_5NH_2}$$

55 (a) Both aliphatic and aromatic secondary amines react with HNO_2 ($NaNO_2$ + HCl) to give N-nitrosoamines which are insoluble in dilute mineral acids and separate out as neutral yellow oily compounds,

$$C_6H_5-N(CH_3)H + HNO_2 \longrightarrow C_6H_5-N(CH_3)-N=O + H_2O$$

N-methylaniline → N-nitroso-N-methylaniline (yellow oil)

56 (a) In benzimidazole, lone pair of electrons on ^{I}N is fully available for donation i.e. not involved in delocalisation, hence it is basic. The lone pair of ^{II}N takes part in delocalisation, hence not available for donation. Thus, ^{II}N is non-basic.

Benzimidazole

Resonating structures of benzimidazole

57 (c) Usually presence of electron withdrawing groups such as F, Cl, CHO etc., increase the acidic strength and presence of electron releasing groups such as —R, —OCH_3 etc., decrease the acidic strength.

Aromatic compounds are more acidic than their corresponding aliphatic compounds due to resonance stabilisation. Hence, the correct order of acidic strength is

Benzamide > Aniline > Cyclohexylamine

58 (*a*) Only N-alkylbenzene sulphonamide is soluble in NaOH due to the presence of acidic hydrogen on N-atom. These N-alkyl benzene sulphonamides are formed by primary amines on reaction with benzene sulphonyl chloride.

$C_6H_5-SO_2-Cl + RNH_2 \longrightarrow C_6H_5-SO_2-NH-R + HCl$

Benzenesulphonyl chloride; 1° amine; N-alkyl sulphonamide (precipitate)

59 (*c*) m-bromobenzoic acid $\xrightarrow{SOCl_2}$ m-bromobenzoyl chloride $\xrightarrow{NH_3}$ m-bromobenzamide $\xrightarrow[H^+]{Br_2, NaOH}$ m-bromoaniline

60 (*d*) $CH_3NH_3^+Cl^-$ is a salt of methyl amine (weak base) and HCl (strong acid). Hence, it is some what acidic in nature and liberates CO_2 from $NaHCO_3$.

61 (*b*) Aliphatic primary amine reacts with nitrous acid in cold to give alcohol.

$$RNH_2 + HNO_2 \longrightarrow R-OH + N_2\uparrow + H_2O$$

62 (*d*) Secondary amines are more basic than both aliphatic and aromatic primary amines but amongst (c) and (d), (c) is less basic than (d), because the lone pair of electrons present on N-atom are involved in delocalisation i.e. (d) is most basic amine.

63 (*c*) Aniline $\xrightarrow[OH^-]{Br_2}$ 2,4,6-tribromoaniline $\xrightarrow[HCl]{NaNO_2}$ 2,4,6-tribromobenzene diazonium chloride ($\overset{+}{N}\equiv NCl^-$) $\xrightarrow{HBF_4}$ 2,4,6-tribromofluorobenzene

64 (*b*) $C_6H_5CN \xrightarrow[4[H]]{LiAlH_4} C_6H_5CH_2NH_2$

Benzene cyanide → Benzylamine

$C_6H_5CONH_2 \xrightarrow[4[H]]{LiAlH_4} C_6H_5CH_2NH_2 + H_2O$

Benzamide → Benzylamine

65 (*b*) Aliphatic amines are more basic than aromatic amines because in aromatic amines, the lone pair of electrons of N-atom are involved in delocalisation of electrons with the aromatic ring. Amongst the given amines, only benzylamine is aliphatic amine, thus it is most basic.

However, within the aromatic amines, electron donating groups increase the basic strength while, electron withdrawing groups decrease the basic strength of amines.

66 (*a*) Secondary amines are formed when isonitriles are reduced with hydrogen in presence of Pt catalyst.

$$R-N\rightleftarrows C + 4[H] \xrightarrow{Pt} RNHCH_3$$

Reduction of alkyl cyanide, alkanamide, phthalimide and alkylhalide yield primary amines.

67 (*c*) During acetylation of amines, one or more hydrogen atoms attached to nitrogen atom are replaced by acetyl group.

$$R-NH_2 \xrightarrow[-HCl]{CH_3COCl} R-NH-\underset{\underset{O}{\|}}{C}-CH_3 \xrightarrow[-HCl]{CH_3COCl} R-\underset{\underset{COCH_3}{|}}{N}-COCH_3$$

68 (*c*) Direct nitration of aniline with HNO_3 gives a complex mixture of mono, di and tri-nitrocompounds and oxidation products. If—NH_2 group is protected by acetylation and then nitrated, *p*-isomer is obtained as the major product.

$C_6H_5NH_2 \xrightarrow{CH_3COCl} C_6H_5NHCOCH_3 \xrightarrow[conc.\ H_2SO_4]{conc.\ HNO_3} p\text{-}NO_2C_6H_4NHCOCH_3 \xrightarrow{NaOH/H^+} p\text{-}NO_2C_6H_4NH_2$

69 (*b*) Aniline reacts with nitrous acid to give benzene diazonium chloride at low temperature

$$C_6H_5NH_2 + HNO_2 \xrightarrow{0\text{-}5°C} C_6H_5\overset{\oplus}{N}\equiv N\overset{\ominus}{Cl}$$

Aniline; Nitrous acid; Benzene diazonium chloride

70 (*b*) On catalytic reduction or with nascent hydrogen or with lithium aluminium hydride ($LiAlH_4$), alkyl isocyanide yields secondary amine.

$$\underset{\text{Methylisocyanide}}{CH_3—N \rightleftharpoons C} + 4[H] \longrightarrow \underset{\text{secondary amine}}{CH_3—NH—CH_3}$$

71 (*c*) This reaction is known as **Hofmann's mustard oil reaction.**

$$C_2H_5—NH_2 + \underset{\text{(alc.)}}{S=C=S} \longrightarrow C_2H_5—NH—\overset{S}{\overset{\|}{C}}—SH \xrightarrow{HgCl_2} HgS + 2HCl + \underset{\text{Ethyl isothiocyanate (Smellsimilar)}}{C_2H_5—N=C=S}$$

72 (*a*) Amines are more basic than esters and ethers because the nitrogen atom is less electronegative than oxygen, thus, it is in better position to accommodate the positive charge on the proton. Hence, both A and R are correct and R is the correct explanation of A.

73 (*a*) Aniline reacts with acetaldehyde to form anil (Schiff's base).

$$C_6H_5NH_2 + CH_3CHO \longrightarrow \underset{\text{Anil or Schiff's base}}{C_6H_5N=CH—CH_3} + 2H_2O$$

74 (*c*) $\underset{\text{Ethylamine}}{C_2H_5NH_2} + CHCl_3 + \underset{\text{(alc.)}}{3KOH} \longrightarrow \underset{\text{Ethyl isocyanide}}{C_2H_5NC} + 3KCl + 3H_2O$

This reaction is also known as carbylamine reaction.

75 (*c*) $\underset{\text{Isopropyl amine (primary-amine)}}{(CH_3)_2CH \cdot NH_2} + 2CH_3COCl \xrightarrow{-HCl} \underset{\text{Acetylated product}}{(CH_3)_2CH—N(COCH_3)_2}$

76 (*b*)

Cyclobutyl methylamine (cyclobutyl–CH_2NH_2) $\xrightarrow{HNO_2}$ cyclobutyl–CH_2OH $\xrightarrow{-H_2O}$ methylenecyclobutane ($=CH_2$)

Cyclobutyl methylamine $\xrightarrow[-N_2,\,-H_2O]{HNO_2}$ cyclopentanol (OH) $\xrightarrow{-H_2O}$ cyclopentene

Thus, cyclobutyl methyl amine when treated with HNO_2 does not give bicyclo[2.1.0] (cyclobutane fused with cyclopropane).

77 (*b*)

p-toluidine (NH_2, CH_3) $\xrightarrow{\text{Excess } Br_2}$ 2,6-dibromo-4-methylaniline (*X*) $\xrightarrow[0\text{-}5°C]{\text{(i) } NaNO_2/HCl}$ (Br, Br, N_2Cl, CH_3) $\xrightarrow{\text{(ii) } H_3PO_2}$ 3,5-dibromotoluene (Br, Br, CH_3) (*Y*)

78 (*a*) Aniline gives N-acetylamino benzene on acetylation.

$$\underset{\text{Aniline}}{C_6H_5—NH_2} + \underset{\text{Acetyl chloride}}{CH_3COCl} \xrightarrow{\text{Pyridine}} \underset{\text{N-acetylamino benzene}}{C_6H_5—\underset{H}{\underset{|}{N}}—\overset{O}{\overset{\|}{C}}—CH_3} + HCl$$

79 (*d*) Benzylamine, $C_6H_5CH_2—\ddot{N}H_2$ is more basic than aniline, because benzyl group $C_6H_5CH_2—$ is electron donating group due to $+I$-effect. So, it is able to increase the electron density of N atoms of $—NH_2$ group. Thus, due to higher electron density rate of donation of lone pair of electron is increased, i.e. basic character increases.

Phenyl and nitro groups are electron withdrawing groups, so, they decreases the electron density of N atom of $—\ddot{N}H_2$ group. Hence, they are less basic than aniline.

80 (*c*) Anilinium chloride is more acidic than ammonium chloride because it forms salt with water and liberates amine when treated with strong base.

$$C_6H_5NH_3^+Cl^- + NaOH \longrightarrow C_6H_5NH_2 + H_2O + NaCl$$

Anilinium ion does not show resonance because charge dispersion at ring may involve pentavalent nitrogen structure. Hence, A is correct and R is incorrect.

81 (*a*) In the given reaction, '*A*' is 1-bromo-3-methylbutane.

$$\underset{\text{Potassium phthalimide}}{C_6H_4(CO)_2N^-K^+} + \underset{\textit{iso}\text{-pentylbromide } (A)}{BrCH_2—CH_2—\overset{CH_3}{\overset{|}{C}H}—CH_3} \xrightarrow{-KBr} C_6H_4(CO)_2N—CH_2CH_2—\overset{CH_3}{\overset{|}{C}H}—CH_3$$

$$\xrightarrow{H^+/2H_2O} \underset{\text{Phthalic acid}}{C_6H_4(COOH)_2} + \underset{\textit{iso}\text{-pentylamine}}{NH_2—CH_2—CH_2—\overset{CH_3}{\overset{|}{C}H}—CH_3}$$

82 (a) Aniline + Acetic anhydride $(CH_3CO)_2O \longrightarrow CH_3COOH$ (Acetic acid) + $C_6H_5-NH-CO-CH_3$ (Acetanilide)

83 (b) The correct match is A → 2, B → 3, C → 4, D → 1, E → 5

- $RX + KCN \xrightarrow{\text{Ethanol}} RCN$
- $RX + CH_3COOAg \longrightarrow CH_3COOR$
- $CH_3C{\equiv}N \xrightarrow{LiAlH_4} CH_3CH_2NH_2$
- $C_6H_5CONH_2 \xrightarrow[\text{degradation}]{\text{Hofmann's}} C_6H_5NH_2$
- $R-NH_2 \xrightarrow[CHCl_3/KOH]{\text{Carbylamine reaction}} RNC$

84 (c) 3-Hydroxy-N,N-dimethylpiperidinium (H_3C, CH_3 on N^+, OH) $\xrightarrow{\Delta}$ $N(CH_3)_2$ alkene (X) $+ H_2O$

85 (a) Urea (NH_2CONH_2) is a monobasic acid.

86 (d) Aniline on oxidation with $Na_2Cr_2O_7$ and H_2SO_4 gives p-benzoquinone.

Aniline $\xrightarrow{Na_2Cr_2O_7/H_2SO_4}$ p-benzoquinone (quinone)

87 (c) $CH_3CH_2CH_2NH_2 + CHCl_3 + 3KOH$ (Alc.) $\longrightarrow CH_3CH_2CH_2NC + 3KCl + 3H_2O$

n-propylamine → Propyl isocyanide

88 (d) $C_6H_5NH_2 \xrightarrow[0°C]{NaNO_2,\ HCl} C_6H_5\overset{\oplus}{N}{\equiv}N\overset{\ominus}{Cl}$ (A) $\xrightarrow{CuCN} C_6H_5CN$ (B) $\xrightarrow{LiAlH_4} C_6H_5CH_2NH_2$ Benzylamine (C)

89 (b) Diethyl oxalate is used for distinguishing primary, secondary and tertiary amines (Hofmann's method).

(i) The primary (1°) amine forms the corresponding substituted oxamide which is usually a crystalline solid.

$$\begin{matrix}COOC_2H_5\\|\\COOC_2H_5\end{matrix} + \begin{matrix}H-NHR\\H-NHR\end{matrix} \longrightarrow \begin{matrix}CONHR\\|\\CONHR\end{matrix} + 2C_2H_5OH$$

(ii) The secondary amine forms a diethyl oxamic ester which is generally a liquid.

$$\begin{matrix}COOC_2H_5\\|\\COOC_2H_5\end{matrix} + HNR_2 \longrightarrow \begin{matrix}CONR_2\\|\\COOC_2H_5\end{matrix} + C_2H_5OH$$

(iii) The tertiary amine under these conditions does not react at all since, it does not contain a replaceable hydrogen atom.

90 (a) $-NH_2$ shows $+R$-effect in aniline i.e. it donates electrons to the benzene ring. As a result, the lone pair of electron on the N-atom gets delocalised over the benzene ring and thus, it is less readily available for protonation.

Hence, aniline is a weaker base than cyclohexylamine.

Resonating structures of aniline

91 (d) Both pyridine and triethylamine are tertiary amines. Triethylamine is highly basic (gaseous or non-polar medium) due to $+I$-effect of $-C_2H_5$ which increases electron density over N atom whereas in pyridine electron density over N atom is less due to resonance.

Pyridine; $(C_2H_5)_3\ddot{N}$ Triethylamine

92 (a) Aniline $\xrightarrow[276\ K]{NaNO_2/HCl}$ $C_6H_5N_2^+Cl^-$ (Benzene diazonium chloride) $\xrightarrow{CuCl/HCl}$ C_6H_5Cl (Chlorobenzene)

93 (b) $R-NH-COH \xrightarrow[\text{Pyridine}]{POCl_3} R-\overset{+}{N}{\equiv}C^-$

94 (c) In reaction of methylamine with methyl iodide, 3 moles of methyl iodide are required for reaction to complete.

$CH_3-NH_2 + 3CH_3I \longrightarrow (CH_3)_4N^+I^-$

Methyl amine → Quaternary ammonium salt

95 (b) Oximes are reduced by Na/ C_2H_5OH to give amines

$CH_3CH{=}NOH \xrightarrow{Na/C_2H_5OH} CH_3-CH_2NH_2 + H_2O$

Acetaldoxime → Ethylamine

96 (d) CH_3CONH_2 on treatment with metallic sodium produces hydrogen

$$CH_3CONH_2 + Na \longrightarrow CH_3CONH^-Na^+ + \frac{1}{2}H_2\uparrow$$

Topic 2
Diazonium Compounds

2016

1 A given nitrogen-containing aromatic compound A reacts with Sn/HCl, followed by HNO_2 to give an unstable compound B. B, on treatment with phenol, forms a beautiful coloured compound C with the molecular formula $C_{12}H_{10}N_2O$. The structure of compound A is **[NEET Phase-II]**

(a) 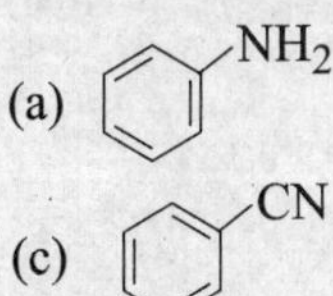

(b) 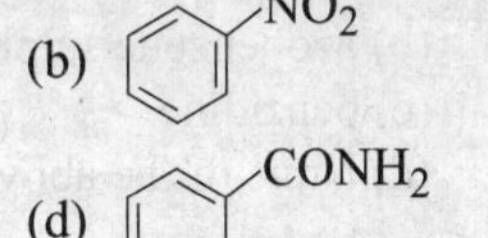

(c) C_6H_5–CN

(d) C_6H_5–$CONH_2$

2014

2 Which of the following will be most stable? **[CBSE AIPMT]**

(a) $CH_2N_2^+X$ (b) $C_6H_5N_2^+X^-$
(c) $CH_3CH_2N_2^+X^-$ (d) $C_6H_5CH_2N_2^+X^-$

2013

3 In the reaction A is **[NEET]**

$$\text{4-}N_2^+Cl^-\text{, 3-Br-nitrobenzene} \xrightarrow{A} \text{3-Br-nitrobenzene } (NO_2, Br)$$

(a) $HgSO_4/H_2SO_4$ (b) Cu_2Cl
(c) H_3PO_2 and H_2O (d) H^+/H_2O

2010

4 Fluorobenzene can be synthesised in the laboratory **[RPMT]**

(a) from aniline by diazotisation followed by heating the diazonium salt with HBF_4
(b) by direct fluorination of benzene with F_2 gas
(c) by reacting bromobenzene with NaF solution
(d) by heating phenol with HF and KF

5 Benzene diazonium chloride on reaction with phenol in weakly basic medium gives **[CMC]**

(a) diphenyl ether (b) *p*-hydroxyazobenzene
(c) chlorobenzene (d) benzene

2009

6 Benzenediazonium chloride on treatment with water gives

(a) benzene (b) *o*-chlorophenol
(c) anisole (d) chlorobenzene
(e) phenol

[Kerala CEE]

7 In Gattermann reaction, a diazonium group is replaced by X using Y. X and Y are **[EAMCET]**

	X	Y
(a)	Cl^-	Cu / HCl
(b)	Cl^+	$CuCl_2$ / HCl
(c)	Cl^-	$CuCl_2$ / HCl
(d)	Cl_2	Cu_2O/ HCl

2008

8 Which one is not a Sandmeyer reagent? **[Guj CET]**

(a) $Cu_2Br_2 + HBr$ (b) $Cu_2Cl_2 + HCl$
(c) $Cu_2I_2 + KI$ (d) $Cu_2(CN)_2 + KCN$

2007

9 $HO-C_6H_4 + C_6H_5-\overset{+}{N_2}\overset{-}{Cl} \xrightarrow{\text{Base}} X$

X is **[AFMC]**

(a) $C_6H_5-N=N-C_6H_4-OH$
(b) $C_6H_5-O-C_6H_5$
(c) $C_6H_5-C_6H_5$
(d) $C_6H_5-C_6H_4-OH$

10 In the reaction,

$$\text{(}NO_2\text{, Br, }\overset{+}{N_2}\overset{-}{Cl}\text{)-benzene} \xrightarrow{A} \text{(}NO_2\text{, Br)-benzene}$$

, A is **[DUMET]**

(a) H_3PO_2 (b) Cu_2Cl_2
(c) $HgSO_4$ / H_2SO_4 (d) H^+ / H_2O

11 Decomposition of benzene diazonium chloride by using Cu_2Cl_2/HCl to form chlorobenzene is **[KCET]**

(a) Raschig's reaction (b) Sandmeyer's reaction
(c) Kolbe's reaction (d) Cannizaro's reaction

2006

12 Benzene diazonium chloride on treatment with hypo phosphorus acid and water in the presence of Cu^+ catalyst produces ..... as main product. **[MHT CET]**

(a) benzene (b) toluene
(c) aniline (d) chlorobenzene

2005

13 Aniline in a following set of reactions yielded a product *D*.

$$C_6H_5NH_2 \xrightarrow[HCl]{NaNO_2} A \xrightarrow{CuCN} B \xrightarrow[Ni]{H_2} C \xrightarrow{HNO_2} D$$

The structure of the product *D* would be **[CBSE AIPMT]**

(a) $C_6H_5CH_2NH_2$
(b) C_6H_5 $NHCH_2CH_3$
(c) C_6H_5 NHOH
(d) $C_6H_5CH_2OH$

14 The reaction of *o*-chloroaniline with a mixture of HCl and $NaNO_2$ followed by cuprous bromide will give **[Kerala CEE]**

(a) chlorobenzene (Cl on benzene ring)
(b) 1-chloro-2-nitrobenzene (NO_2, Cl)
(c) 1-bromo-2-chlorobenzene (Cl, Br)
(d) Cl, Br, Br substituted benzene
(e) H_2N, Cl, Br substituted benzene

15 Hydrazobenzene on treatment with H_2SO_4 forms **[Haryana PMT]**

(a) azobenzene
(b) azobenzene sulphonic acid
(c) benzidine
(d) None of the above

Answers

1 (b)	2 (b)	3 (c)	4 (a)	5 (b)	6 (e)	7 (a)	8 (c)	9 (a)	10 (a)
11 (b)	12 (a)	13 (d)	14 (c)	15 (c)					

Explanations

1 (*b*) The complete road map of the reaction can be seen as :

$$\underset{\text{Nitrobenzene}}{\underset{(A)}{C_6H_5NO_2}} \xrightarrow[\text{Reduction}]{Sn/HCl} \underset{\text{Aniline}}{C_6H_5NH_2} \xrightarrow{HNO_2} \underset{\text{Benzene diazonium chloride (unstable)}}{\underset{(B)}{C_6H_5\overset{+}{N_2}\overset{-}{Cl}}} \xrightarrow{Ph—OH} \underset{\text{Red colour dye}}{C_6H_5—N{=}N—C_6H_4—OH}$$

2 (*b*) Diazonium salt containing aryl group ($C_6H_5\overset{+}{N_2}\overset{-}{X}$) directly attached to the nitrogen atom is most stable due to resonance stabilisation between the benzene nucleus and 'N' atom.

(Resonance structures: $\overset{+}{N}\equiv N:$ ⟷ $\overset{+}{N}=\overset{..}{N}:^-$ ⟷ $\overset{+}{N}\equiv \overset{..}{N}:^-$ ⟷ $\overset{+}{N}=\overset{..}{N}:$ ⟷ $\overset{+}{N}\equiv N$)

3 (*c*) When diazonium salt is treated with H_3PO_2 followed by hydrolysis, it's diazonium group is replaced by —H resulting to the formation of hydrocarbon. Thus, *A*, must be H_3PO_2 and H_2O.

4 (*a*) Aniline reacts with nitrous acid at 0-5°C temperature and gives diazonium salt and the reaction is called diazotisation. When diazonium salt is further treated with fluoroboric acid (HBF_4), the fluorobenzene is obtained. This reaction is called Balz-Schiemann reaction.

$$C_6H_5NH_2 \xrightarrow[0\text{-}5°C]{NaNO_2+HCl} C_6H_5\overset{+}{N_2}Cl^- + \underset{\text{Fluoroboric acid}}{HBF_4} \longrightarrow C_6H_5\overset{+}{N_2}BF_4^- \xrightarrow{\text{Heat}} \underset{\text{Fluorobenzene}}{C_6H_5F}$$

5 (*b*)

$$\underset{\text{Benzene di azonium chloride}}{C_6H_5\overset{\oplus}{N}\equiv N\overset{\ominus}{Cl}} \xrightarrow[\text{Weakly basic medium}]{C_6H_5OH} \underset{p\text{-hydroxy azobenzene}}{C_6H_5—N{=}N—C_6H_4—OH}$$

6 (*e*) When benzene diazonium chloride is treated with water, the diazonium group is replaced by —OH and phenol is obtained.

$$C_6H_5N_2^+Cl^- \xrightarrow{H_2O} C_6H_5OH + N_2\uparrow + HCl$$

Benzene diazonium chloride → Phenol

7 (*a*)

$$o\text{-}CH_3C_6H_4N_2^+Cl^- \xrightarrow[\text{Gattermann reaction}]{Cu/HCl\ (Y)} o\text{-}CH_3C_6H_4Cl\ (X) + N_2\uparrow$$

Benzene diazonium chloride

8 (*c*) $Cu_2I_2 + KI$ is not a Sandmeyer reagent because the replacement of diazonium group by iodine does not require cuprous iodide as catalyst.

It is simply achieved by treating a diazonium salt with potassium iodide.

$$C_6H_5\overset{+}{N}\equiv NCl^- + KI \xrightarrow{\Delta} C_6H_5I + N_2\uparrow + KCl$$

9 (*a*)

$$C_6H_5N_2^+Cl^- + C_6H_5OH \xrightarrow[-HCl]{base} C_6H_5-N=N-C_6H_4-OH$$

Benzene diazonium chloride salt; Phenol; *X* *p*-hydroxy azobenzene (orange dye)

10 (*a*) Mild reducing agents like hypophosphorous acid reduce diazonium salts to arenes.

$$\text{(3-bromo-4-diazonium nitrobenzene) } (NO_2, Br, \overset{+}{N_2}\overset{-}{Cl}) \xrightarrow{H_3PO_2} \text{(3-bromonitrobenzene) } (NO_2, Br) + N_2\uparrow + HCl$$

11 (*b*)

$$C_6H_5N_2^+Cl^- \xrightarrow{Cu_2Cl_2/HCl} C_6H_5Cl + N_2\uparrow$$

Benzene diazonium chloride → Chlorobenzene

This reaction is known as Sandmeyer's reaction.

12 (*a*)

$$C_6H_5\overset{+}{N_2}\overset{-}{Cl} + H_3PO_2 + H_2O \xrightarrow{Cu^+} C_6H_6 + N_2\uparrow + HCl$$

Benzene diazonium chloride; Hypophosphorus acid; Benzene

13 (*d*)

$$C_6H_5NH_2 \xrightarrow[\text{(Diazotisation)}]{NaNO_2 + HCl} C_6H_5N_2^+Cl^- \xrightarrow[\text{(Sandmeyer's reaction)}]{CuCN}$$

'*A*' Benzene diazonium chloride

$$C_6H_5CN \xrightarrow[\text{Reduction}]{H_2/Ni} C_6H_5CH_2NH_2 \xrightarrow{HNO_2} C_6H_5CH_2OH$$

'*B*' Cyanobenzene; '*C*' Benzyl amine; '*D*' Benzyl alcohol

14 (*c*)

$$o\text{-}ClC_6H_4NH_2 \xrightarrow[0°C]{NaNO_2/HCl} o\text{-}ClC_6H_4\overset{+}{N}=N-Cl^- \xrightarrow{CuBr} o\text{-}ClC_6H_4Br$$

o-chloroaniline

15 (*c*) Hydrazobenzene rearranges to benzidine in acidic medium.

$$C_6H_5-NH-NH-C_6H_5 \xrightarrow{H^+} H_2N-C_6H_4-C_6H_4-NH_2$$

Hydrazobenzene → Benzidine

Topic 3

Cyanides and Isocyanides

2018

1 Which of the following chemicals are used to manufacture methyl isocyanate that caused "Bhopal gas tragedy"?

I. Methylamine II. Phosgene **[JIPMER]**

III. Phosphine IV. Dimethyl amine

(a) I and III (b) III and IV

(c) I and II (d) II and IV

2016

2 Consider the reaction $CH_3CH_2CH_2Br + NaCN \longrightarrow CH_3CH_2CH_2CN + NaBr$ **[NEET Phase-II]**

This reaction will be the fastest in

(a) ethanol

(b) methanol

(c) N, N'-dimethylformamide (DMF)

(d) water

2013

3 Unpleasant smell of carbylamine is obtained when chloroform and alcoholic KOH are heated with **[KCET]**

(a) any aliphatic amine (b) any amine

(c) any primary amine (d) any aromatic amine

(e) any secondary amine

2012

4 When CH_3CONH_2 is heated with P_2O_5, the product is

(a) $CH_3CCl_2NH_2$ (b) CH_3CN **[UP CPMT]**

(c) CH_3COCl (d) CCl_3CONH_2

2010

5 Hydrolysis of HCN gives **[Haryana PMT]**

(a) acetic acid (b) alcohol

(c) formaldehyde (d) formic acid

6

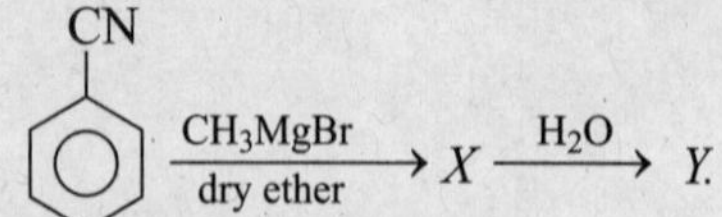

Identify Y **[Haryana PMT]**

(a) benzophenone

(b) acetophenone

(c) benzoic acid

(d) phenol

7 Which one of the following forms propane nitrile as the major product? **[KCET]**

(a) Ethyl bromide + alcoholic KCN

(b) Propyl bromide + alcoholic KCN

(c) Propyl bromide + alcoholic AgCN

(d) Ethyl bromide + alcoholic AgCN

8 Identify Z in the sequence,

$$CH_3COONH_4 \xrightarrow{\Delta} X \xrightarrow[\Delta]{P_2O_5} Y \xrightarrow{H_2O/H^+} Z.$$

(a) $CH_3CH_2CONH_2$ (b) CH_3CN **[JCECE]**

(c) CH_3COOH (d) $(CH_3CO)_2O$

9 The formation of aldehyde from alkyl cyanide is related with the name **[CMC]**

(a) Stephen (b) Rosenmund

(c) Wurtz (d) HVZ reaction

10 Isocyanide can be prepared by alkyl halide on treatment with **[VMMC]**

(a) AgCN (b) AgNC

(c) KCN (d) None of these

2009

11 Commonly used catalyst in the preparation of acrylonitrile from propylene, ammonia and oxygen is **[Kerala CEE]**

(a) silver (b) bismuth molybdates

(c) caesium chloride (d) nickel

(e) organochromium compounds

12 Benzamide on reaction with $POCl_3$ gives **[CG PET, Haryana PMT]**

(a) aniline (b) chlorobenzene

(c) phenylamine (d) phenyl nitrile

2008

13 $CH_3 - CH_2C{\equiv}N \xrightarrow{X} CH_3CH_2CHO$

The compound X is **[AIIMS]**

(a) $SnCl_2/HCl, H_2O$/ boil (b) $H_2/Pd\text{-}BaSO_4$

(c) $LiAlH_4$/ether (d) $NaBH_4$/ether/ H_3O^+

14 Ethyl isocyanide on hydrolysis in acidic medium generates **[RPMT]**

(a) ethylamine salt and methanoic acid

(b) propanoic acid and ammonium salt

(c) ethanoic acid and ammonium salt

(d) methylamine salt and ethanoic acid

15 The compound with foul odour among the following is **[J&K CET]**

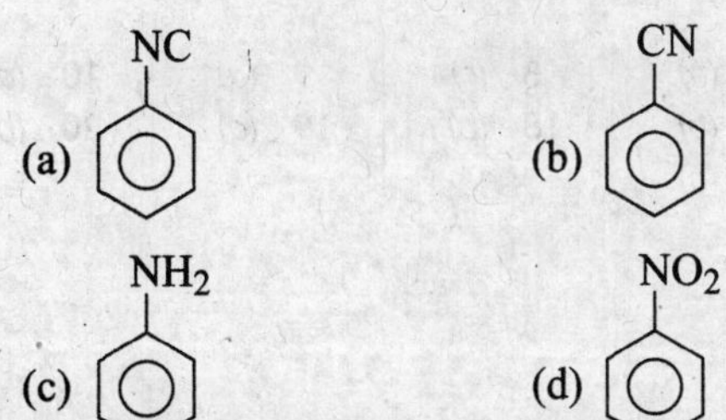

16 $CH_3CN + H_2O \xrightarrow{H^+} A \xrightarrow[\text{Red P}]{\text{Excess } Cl_2} B$

In the above reaction, A and B are respectively **[EAMCET]**

(a) CH_3COOH, CCl_3COOH
(b) CH_3CH_2OH, CH_3CH_2Cl
(c) CH_3CHO, CCl_3CHO
(d) CH_3COCH_3, CCl_3COCH_3

2007

17 Hydrolysis of acetonitrile in acidic medium gives **[BHU]**

(a) $CH_3CH_2NH_2$ (b) CH_3COOH
(c) CH_3CONH_2 (d) CH_3CHO

18 Reduction of alkyl nitrile produces **[J&K CET]**

(a) secondary amine
(b) primary amine
(c) tertiary amine
(d) amide

19 Aliphatic nitriles are prepared by the treatment of alkyl halides with **[J&K CET]**

(a) sodium cyanide (b) sodium isocyanide
(c) sodium isocyanate (d) cyanamide

20 (benzene ring with $C\equiv N$ and meta-OCH_3) $+ CH_3MgBr \longrightarrow P$

Product 'P' in the above reaction is **[Punjab PMET]**

(a) $CH(OH)-CH_3$ with meta-OCH_3 on the benzene ring
(b) $C(=O)-CH_3$ with meta-OCH_3 on the benzene ring
(c) CHO with meta-OCH_3 on the benzene ring
(d) $COOH$ with meta-OCH_3 on the benzene ring

21 $CH_3CH_2Cl \xrightarrow{NaCN} X \xrightarrow{Ni/H_2} Y \xrightarrow{\text{Acetic anhydride}} Z$

In the above reaction sequence, Z is **[Punjab PMET]**

(a) $CH_3CH_2CH_2NHCOCH_3$
(b) $CH_3CH_2CH_2NH_2$
(c) $CH_3CH_2CH_2CONHCH_3$
(d) $CH_3CH_2CH_2CONHCOCH_3$

22 Which of the following compound is obtained when benzene nitrile undergoes hydrolysis? **[Guj CET]**

(a) Benzamide (b) Benzoic acid
(c) Benzoyl chloride (d) Benzophenone

2006

23 Hydrolysis of phenyl isocyanide forms **[AFMC]**

(a) benzoic acid (b) formic acid
(c) acetic acid (d) None of these

24 Hydrolysis of cyanogen gives **[BHU]**

(a) oxalic acid + NH_3 (b) oxalic acid
(c) NH_3 (d) None of these

25 Which one of the following statements about CH_3CN is incorrect? **[Kerala CEE]**

(a) Its IUPAC name is ethanenitrile
(b) The bond between C and N is a triple bond
(c) The C—C—N bond angle is 180°
(d) The carbon-carbon bond is longer than the carbon-nitrogen bond
(e) It has a relatively high boiling point due to hydrogen bonding

26 An organic compound 'A' having molecular formula C_2H_3N on reduction gives another compound 'B', upon treatment with nitrous acid 'B' gives ethyl alcohol. On warming with chloroform and alcoholic KOH, it forms an offensive smelling compound 'C'. The compound 'C' is **[MHT CET]**

(a) $CH_3CH_2NH_2$ (b) $CH_3CH_2N \overset{\rightarrow}{=} C$
(c) $CH_3C\equiv N$ (d) CH_3CH_2OH

2005

27 **Assertion** (A) Alkyl isocyanides in acidified water give alkyl formamides.

Reason (R) In isocyanides, carbon first acts as a nucleophile and then acts as an electrophile. **[AIIMS]**

(a) Both A and R are correct and R is the correct explanation of A
(b) Both A and R are correct but R is not the correct explanation of A
(c) A is correct but R is incorrect
(d) Both A and R are incorrect

Answers

1 (c)	2 (c)	3 (c)	4 (b)	5 (d)	6 (b)	7 (a)	8 (c)	9 (a)	10 (a)
11 (b)	12 (d)	13 (a)	14 (a)	15 (a)	16 (a)	17 (b)	18 (b)	19 (a)	20 (b)
21 (a)	22 (b)	23 (b)	24 (a)	25 (e)	26 (b)	27 (a)			

Explanations

1 (*c*) Methyl isocyanate, MIC (CH_3NCO) is industrially prepared by the reaction of methyl amine and phosgene (carbonyl chloride).

$$\underset{\text{Methylamine}}{CH_3NH_2} + \underset{\text{Phosgene}}{COCl_2} \xrightarrow{-HCl} [CH_3NH—CO—Cl] \xrightarrow[-HCl]{\Delta} \underset{\text{Methyl isocyanate}}{CH_3N{=}C{=}O}$$

On the night of December 2,1984 a major gas tragedy struck Bhopal due to leakage of MIC from storage tank of Union Carbide Ltd. Plant. MIC was used in the manufacture of insecticide.

2 (*c*) The given reaction follows S_N2 mechanism and S_N2 reactions are favourable in polar aprotic medium like DMSO, DMF... etc.

$$CH_3CH_2CH_2Br + NaCN \xrightarrow{DMF} CH_3CH_2CH_2CN + NaBr$$

So, the correct option is (c).

3 (*c*) Primary amine on heating with chloroform and alcoholic KOH produce foul smelling carbylamine (isocyanide).

$$\underset{\text{Primary amine}}{R—NH_2} + CHCl_3 + 3KOH \longrightarrow \underset{\substack{\text{Foul smell}\\ \text{(isocyanide)}}}{R—NC} + 3KCl + 3H_2O$$

4 (*b*) Heating CH_3CONH_2 with P_2O_5 produces methyl cyanide (CH_3CN).

$$CH_3CONH_2 \xrightarrow[\Delta]{P_2O_5} \underset{\text{Methyl cyanide}}{CH_3CN} + H_2O$$

5 (*d*) Hydrolysis of HCN gives formic acid.

$$HCN \xrightarrow{H_2O^+/H^+} \underset{\text{Formic acid}}{HCOOH}$$

6 (*b*)

$$\underset{\text{Benzonitrile}}{C_6H_5CN} \xrightarrow[\text{Dry ether}]{CH_3MgBr} \underset{(X)}{C_6H_5—C(CH_3){=}\overset{-}{N}\overset{+}{Mg}Br} \xrightarrow[2H_2O]{-Mg(OH)Br,\ -NH_3} Mg\begin{matrix}NH_2\\Br\end{matrix} + \underset{\substack{\text{Acetophenone}\\ (Y)}}{C_6H_5—C(CH_3){=}O}$$

7 (*a*) When ethyl bromide reacts with potassium cyanide in dilute alcoholic solution, propane nitrile is obtained as a main product.

$$C_2H_5Br + KCN(\text{alc.}) \xrightarrow{\Delta} \underset{\text{Propane nitrile}}{C_2H_5CN} + KBr$$

8 (*c*)

$$\underset{\text{Ammonum acetate}}{CH_3CO\overset{-}{O}\overset{+}{N}H_4} \xrightarrow{\Delta} \underset{\substack{\text{Acetamide}\\ (X)}}{CH_3CONH_2} \xrightarrow[\Delta,\ (-H_2O)]{P_2O_5} \underset{\substack{\text{Methyl cyanide}\\ (Y)}}{CH_3CN} \xrightarrow{H_2O/H^+} \underset{\substack{\text{Acetic acid}\\ (Z)}}{CH_3COOH}$$

9 (*a*) The formation of aldehyde from alkyl cyanide takes place as :

$$\underset{\text{Alkyl cyanide}}{R—C{\equiv}N} + 2H \xrightarrow[\text{Dry ether+ HCl}]{SnCl_2} \underset{\text{Aldimine hydrochloride}}{RCH{=}NH\cdot HCl} \xrightarrow{\text{Boiling, }H_2O} \underset{\text{Aldehyde}}{RCHO} + NH_4Cl$$

This reaction is known as Stephen's reaction.

10 (*a*)

$$R—X + KCN \longrightarrow \underset{\text{Alkyl cyanide}}{RCN} \quad \text{(attack occurs through C)}$$

$$R—X + AgCN \longrightarrow \underset{\substack{\text{Alkyl}\\ \text{isocyanide}}}{R—NC} \quad \text{(attack occurs through N)}$$

AgCN is predominantly covalent, therefore, in this case only N-atom is free to donate electron pair.

11 (*b*) Acrylonitrile is manufactured by using Sohio technology involving ammoxidation of propylene.

In this technique, propylene, ammonia and oxygen are allowed to react over bismuth molybdates. HCN and acetonitrile are also obtained along with acrylonitrile which are removed by distillation.

$$CH_3CH{=}CH_2 + NH_3 + \frac{3}{2}O_2 \xrightarrow{Bi_2O_3\cdot nMoO_3} \underset{\text{Acrylonitrile}}{CH_2{=}CH—CN} + 3H_2O + HCN + CH_3CN + CO_2 + CO$$

12 (*d*) Benzamide undergoes dehydration on reaction with $POCl_3$ and phenyl nitrile is formed.

$$\underset{\text{Benzamide}}{C_6H_5CONH_2} \xrightarrow[\text{Dehydration}]{POCl_3} \underset{\text{Phenyl nitrile}}{C_6H_5CN}$$

13 (*a*) It is Stephen's reaction.

$$CH_3CH_2C\equiv N \xrightarrow{HCl} [CH_3CH_2C\equiv NH]^+Cl^-$$
$$\xrightarrow{SnCl_2/HCl} [CH_3-CH_2CH=NH_2]^+SnCl_6^{2-}$$
$$\xrightarrow{H_2O/\text{boil}} CH_3CH_2CHO + NH_4Cl$$

14 (*a*) $\underset{\text{Ethyl isocyanide}}{C_2H_5NC} + H_2O \xrightarrow{H^+} \underset{\text{Methanoic acid}}{HCOOH} + \underset{\text{Ethylamine}}{C_2H_5NH_2}$

15 (*a*) Isocyanides (carbylamines) are foul odour compounds

Hence, (benzene ring with NC) benzene isocyanide has foul odour.

16 (*a*) $CH_3CN + H_2O \xrightarrow{H^+} \underset{(A)}{CH_3COOH} + NH_3$

$$\underset{(A)}{CH_3COOH} \xrightarrow[\text{HVZ reaction}]{\text{Excess } Cl_2/P} \underset{(B)}{CCl_3COOH}$$

17 (*b*) $\underset{\text{Acetonitrile}}{CH_3-CN} + H_2O \xrightarrow{HCl} CH_3CONH_2$

$$\xrightarrow{H_2O/HCl} \underset{\text{Acetic acid}}{CH_3COOH} + NH_4Cl$$

18 (*b*) $\underset{\text{Alkyl nitrile}}{R-CN} + 4[H] \xrightarrow{LiAlH_4} \underset{\text{Primary amine}}{R-CH_2NH_2}$

19 (*a*) $\underset{\text{Alkyl halide}}{R-X} + \underset{\text{Sodium cyanide}}{NaCN} \longrightarrow \underset{\text{Aliphatic cyanide}}{R-CN} + NaX$

20 (*b*)

(3-methoxybenzonitrile, $C\equiv N$) $+ \overset{\delta-}{CH_3}\overset{\delta+}{MgBr} \longrightarrow$ (3-methoxyphenyl $C(CH_3)=NMgBr$)

$$\xrightarrow[-NH_3,\ -Mg(OH)Br]{2H_3O^+} \text{(3-methoxyphenyl } C(=O)-CH_3\text{) } 'P'$$

21 (*a*) $CH_3CH_2Cl \xrightarrow{NaCN} \underset{'X'}{CH_3-CH_2-CN} \xrightarrow{Ni/H_2}$

$$\underset{'Y'}{CH_3-CH_2\ CH_2NH_2} \xrightarrow{\text{Acetic anhydride}} \underset{'Z'}{CH_3-CH_2-CH_2-NHCOCH_3}$$

22 (*b*) $\underset{\text{Benzene nitrile}}{C_6H_5CN} + 2H_2O \xrightarrow{H^+} \underset{\text{Benzoic acid}}{C_6H_5COOH} + NH_3$

23 (*b*) Hydrolysis of phenyl isocyanide forms formic acid and aniline.

$$\underset{\text{Phenly isocyanide}}{C_6H_5NC} \xrightarrow[H^+]{H_2O} \underset{\text{Formic acid}}{HCOOH} + \underset{\text{Aniline}}{C_6H_5NH_2}$$

24 (*a*) Cyanogen gives oxalic acid and NH_3

$$\underset{\text{Cyanogen}}{\begin{matrix} CN \\ | \\ CN \end{matrix}} + 4H_2O \xrightarrow{H^+} \underset{\text{Oxalic acid}}{\begin{matrix} COOH \\ | \\ COOH \end{matrix}} + 2NH_3$$

25 (*e*) Statement (e) is incorrect for CH_3CN.

It has relatively high boiling point because — CN group is highly polar hence, cyanides has high dipole moment resulting in strong intermolecular attraction between their molecules. Other statements are correct.

26 (*b*) Isonitriles have offensive foul odour. Thus, on proceeding backward from the known compound-ethyl alcohol one can easily get compound 'C' as :

$$\underset{(C)}{CH_3CH_2N\overset{\rightarrow}{=}C} \xleftarrow[KOH]{CHCl_3} CH_3CH_2OH \xleftarrow{HONO} \underset{(B)}{CH_3CH_2NH_2} \xleftarrow{\text{Reduction}} \underset{(A)}{CH_3C\equiv N}$$

27 (*a*) In an isocyanide, first an electrophile and then a nucleophile is added to the carbon to form a species which undergoes further transformation

$$R-\overset{+}{N}\equiv\overset{-}{C} + E^+ \longrightarrow R\overset{+}{N}\equiv CE \xrightarrow{Nu^-} RN=C(Nu)E$$

$$R-\overset{+}{N}\equiv C^- + H_2O \longrightarrow RN=CHOH \longrightarrow \underset{\text{Alkyl formamide}}{RNHCHO}$$

Hence, in the above reaction, carbon first acts as a nucleophile and then, acts as electrophile.

Topic 4
Nitro Compounds

2018

1 Which of the following carbocations is expected to be most stable? **[NEET]**

(a) 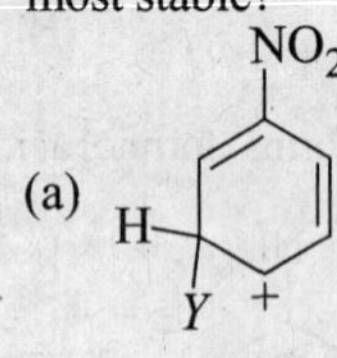

(b) Cyclohexadienyl cation with NO_2 on the positively charged carbon; Y and H on the sp^3 carbon

(c) Cyclohexadienyl cation with NO_2 at the top, ⊕ on the ring; Y and H on the sp^3 carbon

(d) Cyclohexadienyl cation with NO_2 on the ⊕ carbon; H and Y on the adjacent sp^3 carbon

2016

2 Which one of the following nitro-compounds does not react with nitrous acid? **[NEET Phase-II]**

(a) $H_3C—CH_2—CH_2—NO_2$
(b) $(H_3C)_2CH—CH_2—NO_2$
(c) $(H_3C)_3C—NO_2$
(d) $H_3C—C(=O)—CH(CH_3)—NO_2$

2015

3 The electrolytic reduction of nitrobenzene in strongly acidic medium produces **[CBSE AIPMT]**

(a) *p*-aminophenol (b) azoxybenzene
(c) azobenzene (d) aniline

2013

4 Reduction of nitrobenzene with Sn / HCl produce **[AIIMS]**

(a) azobenzene (b) azoxybenzene
(c) nitrobenzene (d) aniline

5 Nitrobenzene gives N-phenylhydroxylamine by **[AIIMS]**

(a) Sn / HCl (b) H_2 / Pd-C
(c) Zn/NaOH (d) Zn / NH_4Cl

6 Nitrobenzene on reaction with conc. HNO_3 / H_2SO_4 at 80–100°C forms which one of the following products? **[NEET]**

(a) 1, 2-dinitrobenzene
(b) 1, 3-dinitrobenzene
(c) 1, 4-dinitrobenzene
(d) 1, 2, 4-trinitrobenzene

2012

7 Nitration of nitrobenzene at 125° C with mixed acids gives **[AFMC]**

(a) *meta*-dinitrobenzene (b) *ortho*-dinitrobenzene
(c) *para*-dinitrobenzene (d) 1, 3, 5-trinitrobenzene

2011

8 What is the product obtained in the following reaction?

$$C_6H_5NO_2 \xrightarrow[NH_4Cl]{Zn} \text{......... ?}$$

[CBSE AIPMT]

(a) $C_6H_5NH_2$ (b) C_6H_5NHOH
(c) $C_6H_5—N=N—C_6H_5$ (d) $C_6H_5—N=\overset{+}{N}(O^-)—C_6H_5$

2010

9 Identify the product (E) in the following sequence of reactions **[AMU]**

$$p\text{-}CH_3C_6H_4NO_2 \xrightarrow{Br_2} A \xrightarrow{Sn/HCl} B \xrightarrow[273–278\text{ K}]{NaNO_2/HCl} C \xrightarrow{H_2O/H_3PO_2} D \xrightarrow[OH^-]{KMnO_4} E$$

(a) C_6H_5COOH (benzoic acid)
(b) COOH with Br at ortho position (2-bromobenzoic acid)
(c) CH_3 with Br (bromotoluene)
(d) Benzene ring with CH_3, Br and O_2N

10 The correct sequence of reactions to convert *p*-nitrophenol into quinol involves **[KCET]**

(a) reduction, diazotisation and hydrolysis
(b) hydrolysis, diazotisation and reduction
(c) hydrolysis, reduction and diazotisation
(d) diazotization, reduction and hydrolysis

11 Benzene on treatment with a mixture of conc. HNO_3 and conc. H_2SO_4 at 100°C gives **[JCECE]**
(a) nitrobenzene (b) *m*-dinitrobenzene
(c) *p*-dinitrobenzene (d) *o*-dinitrobenzene

12 What is obtained when nitrobenzene is treated sequentially with (i) NH_4Cl / Zn dust and (ii) $H_2SO_4 / Na_2Cr_2O_7$? **[WB JEE]**
(a) *meta*-chloronitrobenzene
(b) *para*-chloronitrobenzene
(c) Nitrosobenzene
(d) Benzene

2009

13 Nitrobenzene can be prepared from benzene by using a mixture of conc. HNO_3 and conc. H_2SO_4. In the mixture, nitric acid acts as a/an **[CBSE AIPMT]**
(a) reducing agent (b) acid
(c) base (d) catalyst

14 The product '*Y*' in the following reaction sequence is **[AIIMS]**

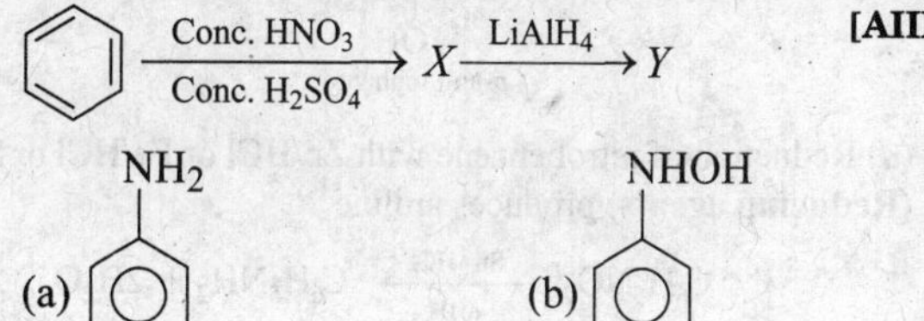

(c) $C_6H_5-N=N-C_6H_5$

(d) None of the above

15 In electrophilic aromatic substitution reaction, the nitro group is *meta* directing because it **[KCET]**
(a) decreases electron density at *meta* position
(b) increases electron density at *meta* position
(c) increases electron density at *ortho* and *para* positions
(d) decreases electron density at *ortho* and *para* positions

16 Nitrobenzene is reduced to azoxybenzene using **[Kerala CEE]**
(a) Sn/HCl (b) Zn/NH_4Cl
(c) As_2O_3 / NaOH (d) Zn/NaOH
(e) H_2 / Pd - C/ C_2H_5OH

17 Which one of the following nitro compounds when reacted with nitrous acid followed by the treatment with alkali produces blue colour? **[J&K CET]**
(a) 2-methyl-2-nitropropane (b) 2-methyl-1-nitropropane
(c) 2-nitropropane (d) nitrobenzene

18 Electrolytic reduction of nitrobenzene in strongly acidic medium gives the product **[J&K CET]**
(a) hydrobenzene (b) azobenzene
(c) phenylhydroxyl amine (d) *p*-aminophenol

2008

19 Which of the following reaction can produce aniline as main product? **[AFMC]**
(a) $C_6H_5NO_2$ + Zn / KOH
(b) $C_6H_5NO_2$ + Zn / NH_4Cl
(c) $C_6H_5NO_2$ + $LiAlH_4$
(d) $C_6H_5NO_2$ + Zn / HCl

20 **Assertion** (A) Nitrobenzene is used as a solvent in Friedel-Craft's reaction.
Reason (R) Fusion of nitrobenzene with solid KOH gives a low yield of a mixture of *o*- and *p*-nitrophenols. **[AIIMS]**
(a) Both A and R are correct and R is the correct explanation of A
(b) Both A and R are correct but R is not the correct explanation of A
(c) A is correct but R is incorrect
(d) Both A and R are incorrect

21 Nitrobenzene undergoes reduction with Zn/alc. KOH to form a compound *A*. The number of sigma and pi bonds in *A*, respectively, are **[EAMCET]**
(a) 17, 6 (b) 27, 6 (c) 27, 8 (d) 17, 8

2006

22 Reactivity order of the following towards NaOEt, EtOH

I. (benzene ring with Cl and NO_2 at *meta*) II. (benzene ring with Cl and NO_2 at *para*) III. (benzene ring with Cl, NO_2 at *ortho* and NO_2 at *para*) **[DUMET]**

(a) III > II > I (b) II > I > III
(c) I > II > III (d) III > I > II

2005

23 **Assertion** (A) *p*-$O_2N-C_6H_4COCH_3$ is prepared by Friedel-Craft's acylation of nitrobenzene.
Reason (R) Nitrobenzene easily undergoes electrophilic substitution reaction. **[AIIMS]**
(a) Both A and R are correct and R is the correct explanation of A
(b) Both A and R are correct but R is not the correct explanation of A
(c) A is correct but R is incorrect
(d) Both A and R are incorrect

24 Which of the following is not a nitro-derivative? **[Manipal]**
(a) $C_6H_5NO_2$ (b) CH_3CH_2ONO
(c) $CH_3CH(CH_3)-NO_2$ (d) $C_6H_4(OH)NO_2$

Answers

1 (a)	2 (c)	3 (a)	4 (d)	5 (d)	6 (b)	7 (a)	8 (b)	9 (b)	10 (a)
11 (b)	12 (c)	13 (c)	14 (c)	15 (d)	16 (c)	17 (c)	18 (d)	19 (d)	20 (c)
21 (b)	22 (a)	23 (d)	24 (b)						

Explanations

1 (*a*) —NO_2 group is an electron withdrawing group and exhibits –*I*-effect. This effect increases with decrease in the distance of positive charge present on C-atom and hence lesser is the stability of carbocation. In option (a), the positive charge is at maximum distance to —NO_2 group, so –*I*-effect due to —NO_2 group will be minimum and stability will be maximum.

(a)

In option (b) and (d), the positive charges is at minimum distance to —NO_2 group hence, the stability will be minimum.

(b) (d)

Also, in option (c) the distance of positive charge to —NO_2 group is more than *ortho* but less than *para*, so it will be less stable as compared to option (a).

(c)

2 (*c*) 1° and 2° nitro compounds react with HNO_2 while 3°-nitro compound does not.

The reactions of given compounds are :

(a) $CH_3CH_2CH_2NO_2$ (1°-nitro compound) $\xrightarrow[-H_2O]{HON=O}$ $CH_3—CH_2—C(=N—OH)—NO_2$ (b)

(b) $(H_3C)(CH_2)CH—NO_2$ (1°-nitro compound) $\xrightarrow[-H_2O]{HO—N=O}$ $CH_3—CH(CH_3)—C(=N—OH)—NO_2$

(c) $(H_3C)_3C—NO_2$ (3°-nitro compound) $\xrightarrow{HO—N=O}$ No reaction

(d) $CH_3—C(=O)—CH(CH_3)—NO_2$ (2°-nitro compound) $\xrightarrow[-H_2O]{HO—N=O}$ $CH_3—C(=O)—C(CH_3)(N=O)—NO_2$

Thus, option (c) does not react with nitrous acid.

3 (*a*) Under weakly acidic conditions, nitrobenzene on electrolytic reduction gives aniline but under strongly acidic conditions give *p*-aminophenol.

Nitrobenzene ($C_6H_5NO_2$) $\xrightarrow[4H^+]{4e^-}$ C_6H_5NHOH $\xrightarrow[\text{weakly acidic}]{2H^+}$ Aniline ($C_6H_5NH_2$)

C_6H_5NHOH $\xrightarrow{H^+ \text{ strongly acidic}}$ *p*-aminophenol ($HO—C_6H_4—NH_2$)

4 (*d*) Reduction of nitrobenzene with Zn/HCl or Fe/HCl or Sn/HCl **(Reducing agents)** produces aniline.

$$C_6H_5NO_2 \xrightarrow[6[H]]{Sn/HCl} C_6H_5NH_2 + 2H_2O$$

5 (*d*) N-phenylhydroxyl amine (C_6H_5NHOH) can be obtained by nitrobenzene as follows :

$$C_6H_5NO_2 \xrightarrow{Zn/NH_4Cl} C_6H_5NHOH + H_2O$$

6 (*b*) —NO_2 group being electron withdrawing reduces electron density at *o*/*p* positions. Hence, the *meta*-position becomes electron rich on which the electrophile (nitronium ion) attacks during nitration. Thus, 1, 3-dinitrobenzene is obtained.

$$HNO_3 + H_2SO_4 \longrightarrow H_2NO_3^+ + HSO_4^- + H_2O + \underset{\text{Electrophile}}{NO_2^+}$$

Nitrobenzene $\xrightarrow{NO_2^+}$ 1,3-dinitrobenzene

7 (*a*) —NO_2 group is *meta* directing and gives *meta*-dinitro benzene on nitration

$$C_6H_5NO_2 \xrightarrow[\text{conc. } HNO_3 + \text{conc. } H_2SO_4]{125°C} m\text{-}C_6H_4(NO_2)_2$$

8 (*b*)

$$\underset{\text{(Nitrobenzene)}}{C_6H_5NO_2} + 4[H] \xrightarrow[\text{(neutral medium)}]{Zn, NH_4Cl} \underset{\text{(N-phenylhydroxylamine)}}{C_6H_5NHOH} + H_2O$$

9 (*b*)

$$\text{p-}CH_3C_6H_4NO_2 \xrightarrow{Br_2} \underset{(A)}{CH_3C_6H_3(Br)NO_2} \xrightarrow{Sn/HCl} \underset{(B)}{CH_3C_6H_3(Br)NH_2}$$

$$\xrightarrow[273-278\,K]{NaNO_2/HCl} \underset{(C)}{CH_3C_6H_3(Br)\overset{+}{N}\equiv N\overset{-}{Cl}} \xrightarrow[-N_2;\ -HCl]{H_2O/H_3PO_2} \underset{(D)}{CH_3C_6H_4Br} \xrightarrow{KMnO_4,\ \overline{O}H} \underset{(E)}{C_6H_4(Br)COOH}$$

10 (*a*)

$$\underset{p\text{-nitrophenol}}{HOC_6H_4NO_2} \xrightarrow[\text{(Reduction)}]{Sn/HCl} HOC_6H_4NH_2 \xrightarrow[\text{(Diazotisation)}]{NaNO_2/HCl} HOC_6H_4\overset{+}{N}\equiv N\overset{-}{Cl} \xrightarrow[H^+/H_2O]{\text{Hydrolysis}} \underset{\text{Quinol}}{HOC_6H_4OH}$$

11 (*b*) At 60°C (low temperature) mononitration occurs and nitrobenzene is obtained but at 100°C, nitrobenzene further undergoes electrophilic substitution and gives *m*-dinitrobenzene (as —NO_2 is a *meta*-directing group).

$$\underset{\text{Benzene}}{C_6H_6} \xrightarrow[100°C]{\text{Conc. } HNO_3 + \text{Conc. } H_2SO_4} \underset{m\text{-dinitrobenzene}}{C_6H_4(NO_2)_2}$$

12 (*c*)

$$C_6H_5NO_2 \xrightarrow{NH_4Cl/Zn} \underset{\text{N-phenyl hydroxylamine}}{C_6H_5NH—OH} \xrightarrow[[O]]{H_2SO_4/Na_2Cr_2O_7} \underset{\text{Nitrosobenzene}}{C_6H_5NO}$$

13 (*c*) In the preparation of nitrobenzene from benzene by using a mixture of conc. H_2SO_4 and conc. HNO_3, the nitric acid acts as a base or proton acceptor.

$$H\ddot{O}—NO_2 + H—SO_4H \underset{}{\overset{\text{Fast}}{\rightleftharpoons}} HSO_4^- + H_2O^+—NO_2$$

$$\overset{\text{Slow}}{\rightleftharpoons} \underset{\text{Nitronium ion}}{NO_2^+} + H_2O$$

14 (*c*)

$$\underset{\text{Benzene}}{C_6H_6} \xrightarrow[\text{(Nitration)}]{\text{Conc. } HNO_3 + \text{Conc. } H_2SO_4} 2\underset{\text{Nitrobenzene 'X'}}{C_6H_5NO_2} \xrightarrow{LiAlH_4} \underset{\text{Azobenzene 'Y'}}{C_6H_5—N=N—C_6H_5}$$

15 (*d*) The directive influence of —NO_2 as an electrophile in electrophilic aromatic substitution is due to the $-I$-effect or electron withdrawing effect of —NO_2 and can be explained on the basis of the resonating structures obtained by the attack of the group on the benzene ring.

The substituent, i.e. —NO_2 withdraws electrons from *o*- and *p*-positions. Thus, decreases electron density at *ortho* and *para* positions.

16 (*c*) Nitrobenzene on reduction with As_2O_3 in alkaline medium gives azoxybenzene.

$$C_6H_5NO_2 + As_2O_3 + NaOH \xrightarrow{6[H]} \underset{\text{Azoxybenzene}}{C_6H_5—N=\overset{O\uparrow}{N}—C_6H_5} + 3H_2O$$

17 (*c*) Nitro group attached to secondary carbon atom will give pseudonitrol with HNO_2 which on further treatment with alkali gives blue colour.

$$\underset{\text{2-nitropropane}}{(CH_3)_2CH—NO_2} \xrightarrow{HONO} \underset{\text{Pseudonitrol}}{H_3C—C(CH_3)(N=O)—NO_2} \xrightarrow{NaOH} \text{Blue colour}$$

18 (*d*) In strongly acidic solution, phenylhydroxyl amine is formed firstly which undergoes intramolecular rearrangement forming *p*-aminophenol.

$$C_6H_5NO_2 \xrightarrow[\text{(strongly acidic medium)}]{\text{Electrolytic reduction}} \underset{\text{Phenyl hydroxyl amine}}{C_6H_5NHOH} \xrightarrow[\text{change}]{\text{Intramolecular rearrangement}} \underset{p\text{-aminophenol}}{HO-C_6H_4-NH_2}$$

19 (*d*) Reduction of nitrobenzene in acidic medium forms aniline.

$$\underset{\text{Nitrobenzene}}{C_6H_5NO_2} + 6[H] \xrightarrow{\text{Zn/HCl}} \underset{\text{Aniline}}{C_6H_5NH_2}$$

20 (*c*) Due to strong deactivation of benzene ring by—NO_2 group, nitrobenzene is often used as a solvent in Friedel-Crafts reaction.

∴ A is correct but R is incorrect.

21 (*b*) Nitrobenzene on reduction with Zn/alc. KOH gives hydrazobenzene (*A*).

$$\underset{\text{Nitrobenzene}}{C_6H_5NO_2} \xrightarrow{\text{Zn/alc. KOH}} \underset{\text{Hydrazobenzene } (A)}{C_6H_5-NH-NH-C_6H_5}$$

Thus, hydrazobenzene contains 27 σ and 6 π-bonds.

22 (*a*) Nucleophilic substitution of aryl halides is favoured by electron withdrawing substituents attached at *ortho* and *para* positions to the halide atom. So, reactivity order of given compounds towards NaOEt and EtOH is

2,4-dinitrochlorobenzene (III) > *p*-nitrochlorobenzene (II) > *m*-nitrochlorobenzene (I)

23 (*d*) —NO_2 group is electron withdrawing group, hence deactivate the benzene ring by decreasing the electron density from it. Hence, nitrobenzene does not undergo Friedel-Craft acylation and electrophilic substitution reactions.

24 (*b*) $CH_3CH_2—O—N=O$ is a nitrite derivative, hence, it is not a nitro derivative.

28

Biomolecules

Quick Review

- **Biomolecules** are the complex lifeless organic chemical substances. These are the carbon compounds mainly produced by the living tissues for the regulation or maintenance of physiological reaction inside the living body.
- These molecules include carbohydrates, proteins, enzymes, lipids, hormones, vitamins, nucleic acids etc.

Carbohydrates

- These are simply polyhydroxy aldehydes or ketones. Those substances which yield, such products on hydrolysis are also carbohydrates.
- These are also known as **saccharides.**

Classification of Carbohydrates

Group	Definition	Examples
1. On the basis of their behaviour on hydrolysis.		
Monosaccharides	• These cannot be hydrolysed to give simpler unit of polyhydroxy aldehyde or ketone. • These contain single unit of saccharide.	• Glucose, fructose, ribose etc.
Disaccharides	• These yield two to ten monosaccharide units on hydrolysis. • These are further classified as disaccharides, trisaccharides, tetrasaccharides etc.	• Disaccharide-sucrose, maltose • Trisaccharide-raffinose • Polysaccharide-stachyose
Polysaccharides	• These yield a large number of monosaccharides. • These are not sweet in taste.	• Starch, cellulose, glycogen, gums etc.
2. On the basis of reducing property.		
Reducing sugars	• These carbohydrates reduce Fehling's solution and Tollen's reagent. • These sugars contain free ketone or aldehyde part.	• Monosaccharides like glucose, fructose, ribose etc.
Non-reducing sugars	• These carbohydrates are not capable of reducing Fehling's solution or Tollen's reagent.	• Disaccharides like sucrose and polysaccharides like starch, cellulose etc.

Monosaccharides

Based on number of carbon atoms and the functional group present in them, monosaccharides are classified as aldose (monosaccharide that contain aldehyde group) and ketose (monosaccharide that contain a keto group).

Some monosaccharides are discussed below:

1. Glucose

Glucose is an aldohexose and is also known as **dextrose**. It exits, as a six membered ring. The existence of glucose can be represented by **Fischer projection** as shown below:

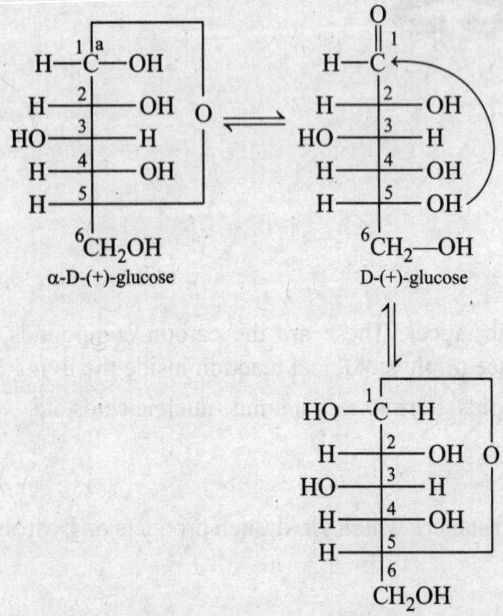

α-D-(+)-glucose ⇌ D-(+)-glucose ⇌ β-D-(+)-glucose

The six membered cyclic structure of glucose is called pyranose structure (α– and β–). It is represented by **Haworth structure** as shown below:

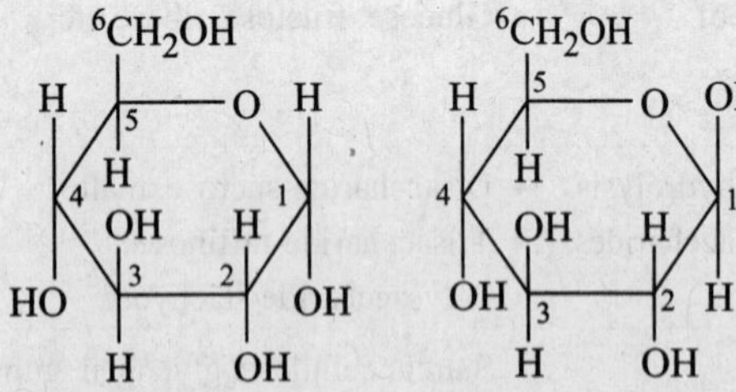

α-D-(+)-glucopyranose β-D-(+)-glucopyranose

Anomers

2. Fructose

- Fructose is a ketohexose and is also known as **laevulose**.
- Most of the chemical properties of fructose are similar to those of glucose. E.g. oxidation of fructose with HNO_3 gives glycolic and tartaric acid.
- It is a five membered ring and is named as furanose.

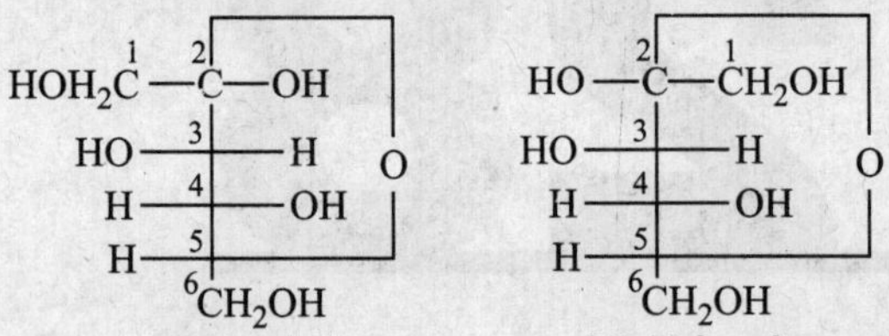

α-D-(–)-fructofuranose β-D-(–)-fructofuranose

- The cyclic structures of two anomers of fructose are represented by Haworth structure as given below:

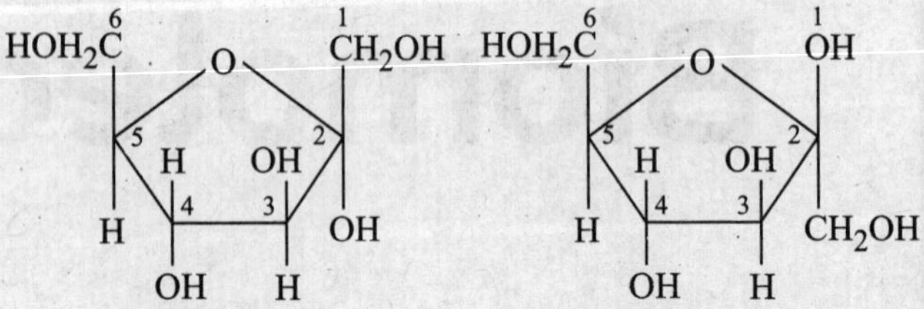

α-D-(–)-fructofuranose β-D-(–)-fructofuranose

Oligosaccharides

The carbohydrates that yield two to ten monosaccharide units on hydrolysis are known as oligosaccharides.

The various oligosaccharides are as follows

1. Sucrose ($C_{12}H_{22}O_{11}$)

Sucrose is also known as invert sugar. It is due to the fact that on hydrolysis, (+)-sucrose gets inverted to give a mixture of D-(+)-glucose and D-(–) - fructose. The structure of sucrose is given below:

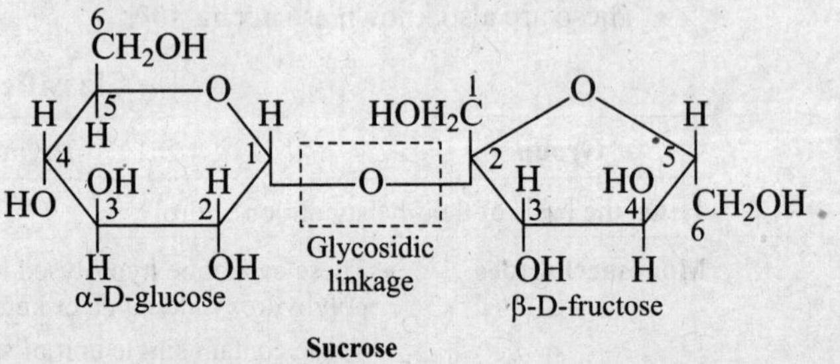

α-D-glucose — Glycosidic linkage — β-D-fructose

Sucrose

2. Maltose ($C_{12}H_{22}O_{11}$)

Maltose on hydrolysis with dilute acid or by enzyme maltase yields two molecules of D-(+) - glucose. The structure of maltose is given below:

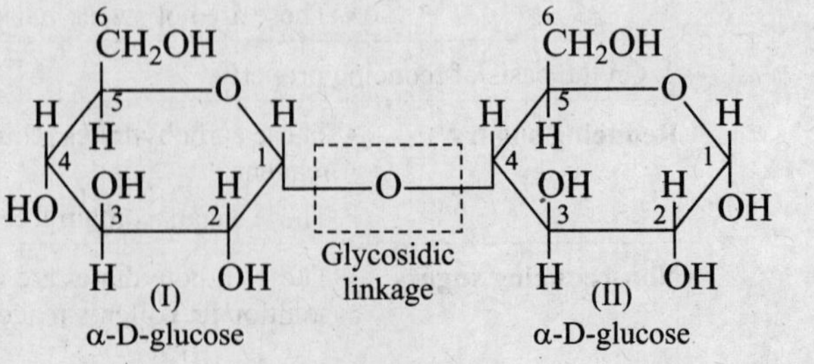

(I) α-D-glucose — Glycosidic linkage — (II) α-D-glucose

Maltose

3. Lactose ($C_{12}H_{22}O_{11}$)

Lactose on hydrolysis by dilute acid or by lactase enzyme yields equimolar mixture of D-(+)-glucose and D-(+)-galactose.

The structure of lactose is given below:

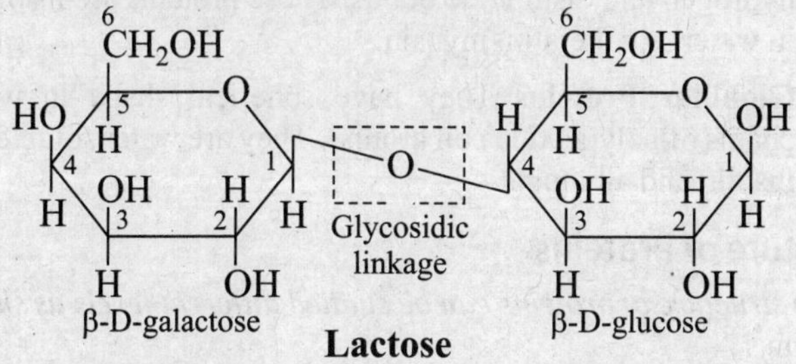

β-D-galactose **Lactose** β-D-glucose

Polysaccharides

Carbohydrates which yield a large number of monosaccharide units on hydrolysis are called polysaccharides, e.g. starch, cellulose, glycogen, gums (acidic) etc. They mainly act as the food storage or structural materials.

The different types of polysaccharides are as follows :

1. Starch

It is a polymer of α-D-glucose units and consists of two components- amylose and amylopectin.

The structure of amylose and amylopectin are as follows:

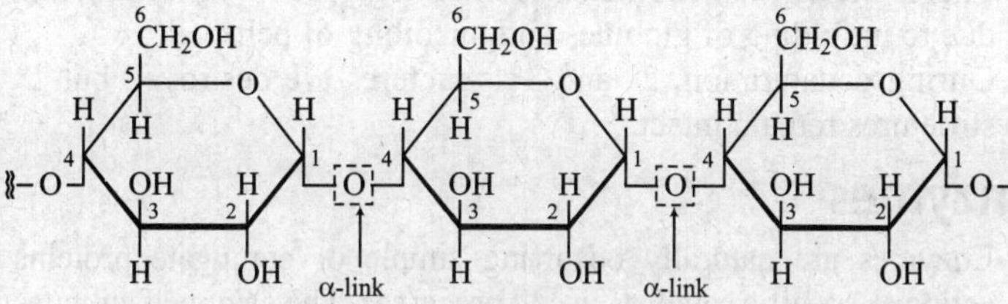

Amylose

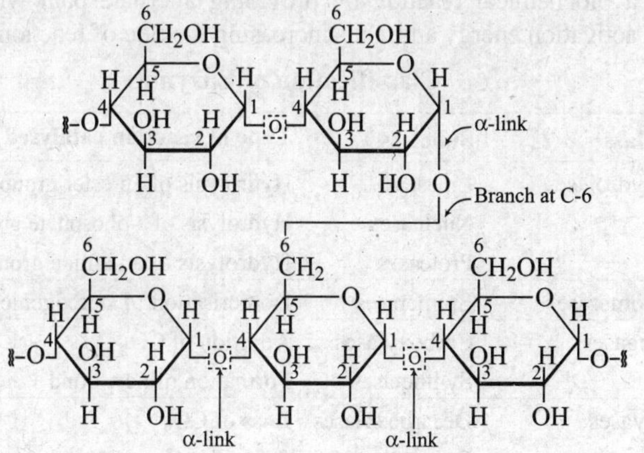

Amylopectin

2. Cellulose

It is a straight chain polysaccharide composed of only β-D-glucose units which are joined by β-1, 4 glycosidic linkages.

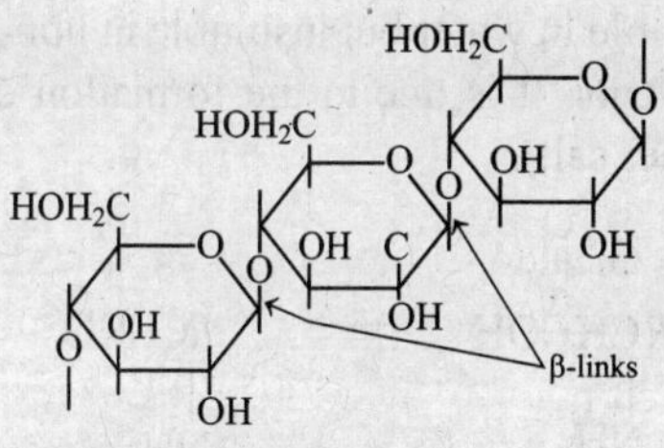

Cellulose

3. Glycogen

It is the condensation polymer of α-D-glucose which is stored in animal body. It is also known as animal starch. It is also found in yeast and fungi.

Importance of Carbohydrates

Carbohydrates are very important and essential for life in both plants and animals.

Few important roles of carbohydrates are listed below

(*i*) They are used as storage materials, like starch in plants and glycogen in animals.

(*ii*) Cellulose in the form of wood is used to build furniture and clothes in the form of cotton fibres.

(*iii*) They provide raw materials for many industries, like textiles, papers and lacquers.

(*iv*) In living systems, carbohydrates are also found in combination with many proteins and lipids such as glycoproteins and glycolipids.

Proteins and Amino Acids

Proteins are polymers of α-amino acids.

On the basis of their synthesis, amino acids are classified into two classes:

(*i*) **Essential amino acids** cannot be synthesised in the body, e.g.valine, lysine, etc.

(*ii*) **Non-essential amino acids** can be synthesised in the body, e.g. alanine, aspartic acid, etc.

These are also classified as acidic, basic or neutral depending upon the relative number of amino and carboxyl groups in their molecule.

These are as follows:

- **Neutral** Equal number of amino and carboxyl groups.
- **Basic** More number of amino groups than carboxyl groups.
- **Acidic** More carboxyl groups than amino groups.

Physical Properties of Amino Acids

(*i*) Amino acids are generally colourless, crystalline solids having melting point above 475 K.

(*ii*) Soluble in water but insoluble in non-polar organic solvents. It is due to the formation of *Zwitter* ion (inner salt).

$$RCH(NH_2)COOH \rightleftharpoons RCH(\overset{\oplus}{N}H_3)CO_2^{\ominus}$$

Zwitter ion

(*iii*) With the exception of glycine, all naturally occurring α-amino acids having asymmetric α-carbon atom and are called **chiral molecules**.

Some examples of chiral amino acids are as follows:

L-serine (*S*): $CO_2^{\ominus}$ at top, $H_3\overset{\oplus}{N}$ left, H right, CH_2OH at bottom.

D-serine (*R*): $CO_2^{\ominus}$ at top, H left, $\overset{\oplus}{N}H_3$ right, CH_2OH at bottom.

These exist in both 'D' and 'L' forms. Most naturally occurring amino acids have L-configuration.

Peptide Bond

In proteins, amino acids are joined together by an amide linkage called **peptide linkage** (— CO—NH).

Characteristics of Peptide Bond

(*i*) Peptide bond is formed by the linkage of carboxyl (—C(=O)—OH) group of one amino acid with amino ($—NH_2$) group of another amino acid along with removal of a water molecule.

(*ii*) A peptide bond has about 40% double bond character because of resonance.

(*iii*) Steric hindrance causes the *trans* configuration to be more stable than the *cis*-configuration, so the α-carbons of adjacent amino acids are *trans* to each other.

(*iv*) As a consequence of the partial double bond character of the peptide bond, free rotation is not possible around this bond.

$$—CH(R)—C(=O)—\ddot{N}(H)—CH(R)— \longleftrightarrow —CH(R)—C(O^{\ominus})=\overset{\oplus}{N}(H)—CH(R)—$$

Classification of Proteins

Proteins can be classified into two types:

1. **Fibrous Proteins** They have thread like structures in which polypeptide chains run parallel and are held together by hydrogen and disulphide bonds. These proteins are insoluble in water. e.g. keratin, myosin.
2. **Globular Proteins** They have spherical shape in which chains of polypeptide coil around. They are water soluble e.g. insulin and albumins.

Structure of Proteins

The structure of proteins can be studied different levels as shown below :

(*i*) **Primary Structure** It simply reveals the sequence of amino acids.

(*ii*) **Secondary Structure** α-helix structure is maintained by hydrogen bonds or β-pleated sheet structure when *R* is small group.

(*iii*) **Tertiary Structure** The folding and superimposition of polypeptide chains form a compact globular shape termed as tertiary structure. It is stabilised by covalent, ionic, hydrogen and disulphide bonds. The precise arrangement constitutes the quaternary structure.

Denaturation of Proteins

This is the phenomenon of loss in biological activity of proteins due to unfolding of globules and uncoiling of helix.

During denaturation, 2° and 3° structures are destroyed but 1° structures remain intact.

Enzymes

Enzymes are naturally occurring simple or conjugate proteins acting as specific catalysts in cell processes. The enzyme facilitates a biochemical reaction by providing alternate path with lower activation energy and, thus increasing the rate of reaction.

Classification of Enzymes

Class	Subclass	Type of reaction catalysed
Hydrolases	Lipases	Hydrolysis of an ester group
	Nucleases	Hydrolysis of a phosphate group
	Proteases	Hydrolysis of an amide group
Isomerases	Epimerases	Isomerisation of stereogenic centre
Ligases	Carboxylases	Addition of CO_2
	Synthetases	Formation of new bond
Lyases	Decarboxylases	Loss of CO_2
	Dehydrases	Loss of H_2O
Oxidoreductases	Dehydrogenases	Introduction of double bond by removal of H_2
	Oxidases	Oxidation
	Reductases	Reduction
Transferases	Kinases	Transfer of a phosphate group
	Transaminases	Transfer of an amino group

Hormones

The chemical substances secreted into blood by ductless glands are called hormones. They participate in different specific biochemical reactions and, hence control specific physiological processes. Based on their chemical compositions, hormones are divided into two main **classes.** (i) Based on their structure –**steroid hormones** and **non-steroid hormones** (ii) Based on activity in the cell.

Vitamins

It may be defined as a group of biomolecules (other than fats, carbohydrates and proteins) which are required in small amounts for normal metabolic processes and for the life, growth and health.

Types of Vitamins

Vitamins are broadly classified into two types :

(*i*) **Water soluble vitamins** (e.g vitamin B and C). (*ii*) **Fat soluble vitamins** (e.g. Vitamins A, D, E and K).

Some Important Vitamins, their Sources and their Deficiency Diseases

Name of vitamins	Sources	Deficiency diseases
Vitamin-A (Retinol)	Fish liver oil, carrots, butter and milk	Xerophthalmia (hardening of cornea of eye) or night blindness
Vitamin-B_1 (Thiamine)	Yeast, milk, green vegetables	*Beri-beri* (loss of appetite)
Vitamin-B_2 (Riboflavin)	Milk, egg white, liver, kidney	Cheilosis (fissuring at corners of mouth and lips)
Vitamin-B_6 (Pyridoxine)	Yeast, milk, egg yolk, cereals	Convulsions, nervousness
Vitamin-B_{12} (Cyanocobalamine)	Meat, fish, egg and curd	Pernicious anaemia (RBC deficient in haemoglobin)
Vitamin-C (Ascorbic acid)	Citrus fruits, amla and green leafy vegetables	Scurvy (bleeding gums)
Vitamin-D	Exposure to sunlight, fish and egg yolk	Rickets and osteomalacia
Vitamin-E	Wheat, germ oil, sunflower oil	Increased fragility of RBC and muscular weakness
Vitamin-K	Green leafy vegetables	Increased blood clotting time

Nucleic Acids

The nucleic acids are the chemical carriers of a cell's genetic information. The chemical composition of nucleic acids acts as coded information.

Chemical Composition of Nucleic Acids

Complete hydrolysis of nucleic acid gives following three different compounds:

(*i*) **Pentose Sugar** DNA molecules contain β-D-2-deoxyribose, a sugar moiety, whereas RNA molecules contain β-D-ribose.

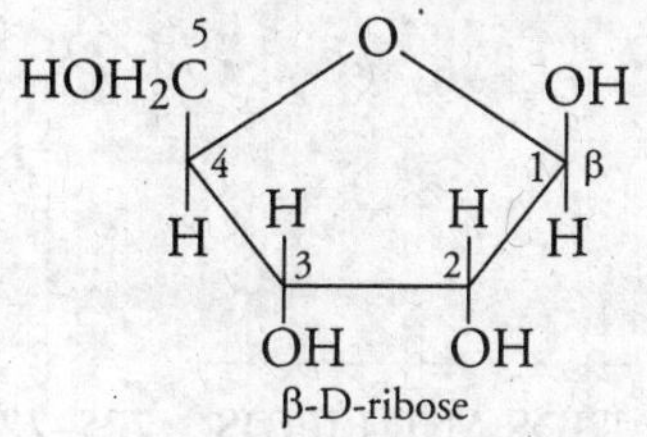

β-D-ribose 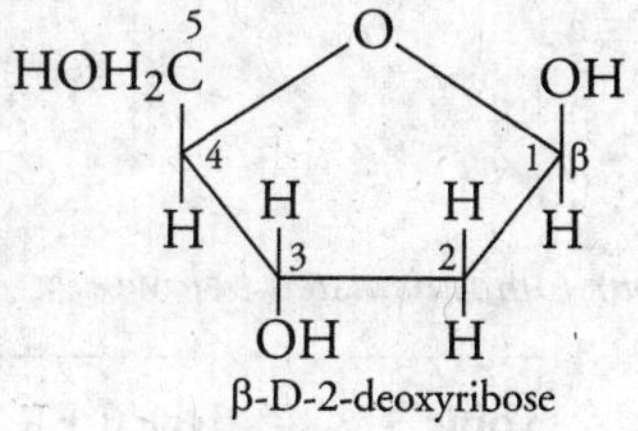 β-D-2-deoxyribose

(*ii*) **Phosphoric Acid** It is the common product for both DNA and RNA hydrolysis.

(*iii*) **Nitrogenous Base** Nitrogen containing heterocyclic compounds are called nitrogenous base.

Nitrogenous bases are of two types:

(a) **Purines**: Adenine (A) and Guanine (G).

(b) **Pyrimidines**: Uracil (U), thymine (T) and cytosine (C).

DNA and RNA both contain three common bases; adenine (A), guanine (G) and cytosine (C). Thymine (T) is present in DNA but in place of thymine, RNA contains uracil (U).

So, there are four bases in each DNA and RNA.

i.e. DNA = A, G, C, T

or RNA = A, G, C, U

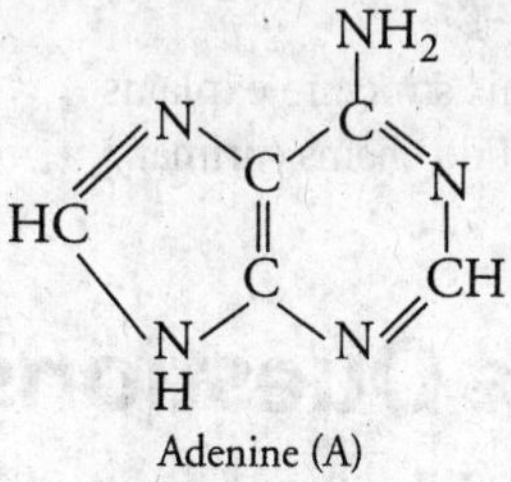

Adenine (A) 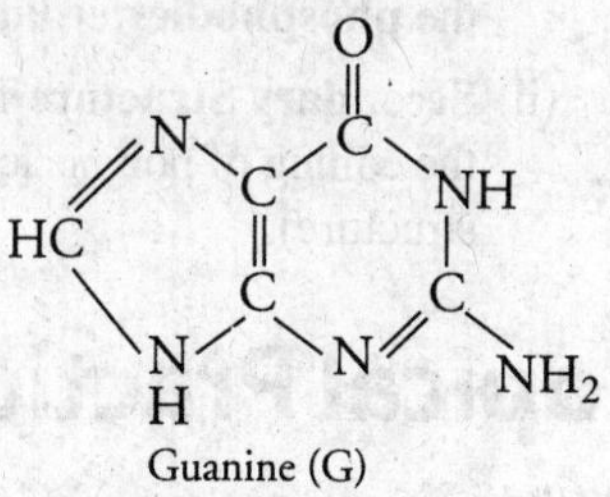 Guanine (G)

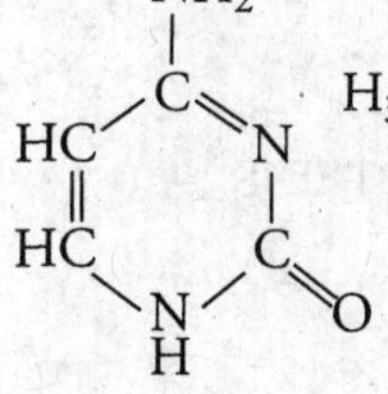

Cytosine (C) 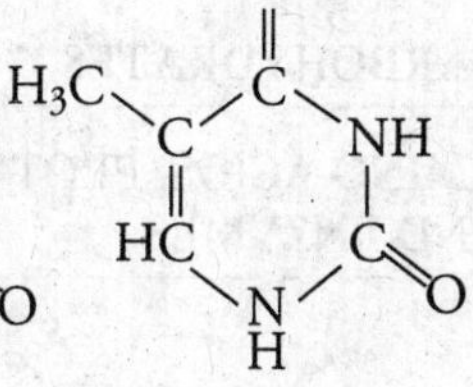 Thymine (T) 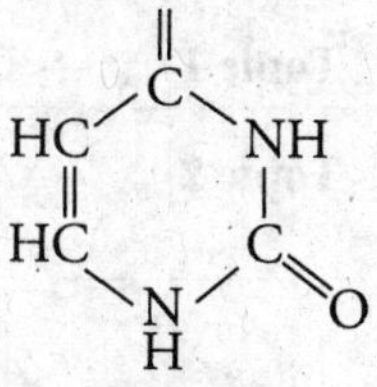 Uracil (U)

Structure of Nucleic Acids

1. Nucleoside

- It is formed by the attachment of a base to 1' position of sugar.

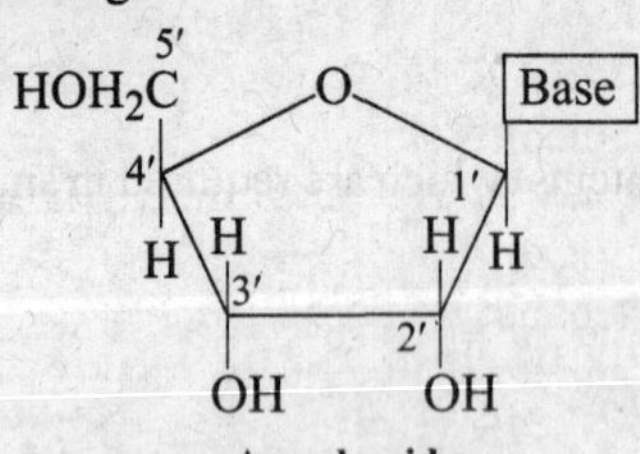

A nucleoside

- Sugar can be deoxyribose (in DNA) or ribose (in RNA).

2. Nucleotide

It is formed when nucleoside is linked to phosphoric acid at 5′ position of sugar moiety.

Phosphate group

A nucleotide

The structure of nucleic acid can be divided into following two categories (with special reference to DNA):

(i) **Primary Structure** It gives information about the sequence of nucleotides in the chain of nucleic acid. This structure is formed by linkage of one nucleotide with other through the **phosphodiester linkage**.

(ii) **Secondary Structure** This structure explains the coiling of polynucleotide chains (primary structure).

Watson and Crick proposed the secondary structure for DNA. This structure is called **double stranded helical structure.** Here, two separate polynucleotide chains (or strands) are helically coiled with each other. These two strands are held together by H-bonds. The direction (with reference to sugar base) is opposite to each other (3′ or 5′).

The two strands are complementary to each other as adenine (A) of one strand is bonded to thymine (T) of the other one, (with 2 H-bonds), while guanine (G) is bonded to cytosine (C) of the other one (with 3 H-bonds) and *vice-versa*.

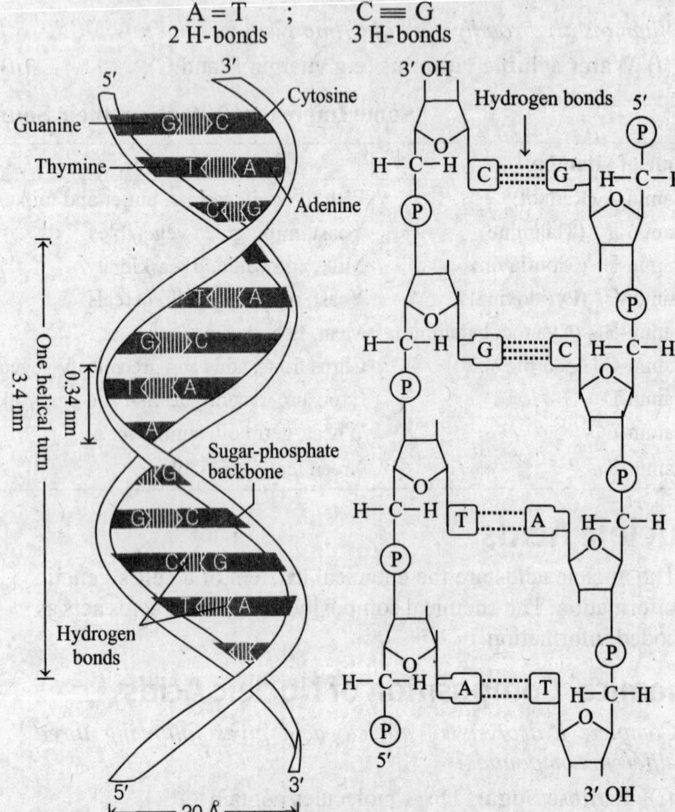

Double helix structure of DNA

Topical Practice Questions

All the exam questions of this chapter have been divided into four topics as listed below:

Topic 1

Carbohydrates

2019

1 Assertion Glucose does not give 2, 4- DNP test.
Reason Glucose exists in cyclic hemiacetal form. **[AIIMS]**
(a) Both A and R are correct and R is the correct explanation of A
(b) Both A and R are correct but R is not the correct explanation of A
(c) A is correct but R is incorrect
(d) Both A and R are incorrect

2 Assertion Two sugar units are joined by 1, 2-glycosidic bond in sucrose. **[AIIMS]**
Reason It contains C_1-glucose and C_2-fructose glycosidic bond.
(a) Both A and R are correct and R is the correct explanation of A
(b) Both A and R are correct but R is not the correct explanation of A
(c) A is correct but R is incorrect
(d) Both A and R are incorrect

3 Invert sugar is mixture of **[JIPMER]**
(a) D-glucose+D-fructose
(b) L-glucose+D-fructose
(c) L-glucose+D-glucose
(d) L-glucose+L-glucose

2018

4 Which one of the following represents the correct structure of cellulose? **[JIPMER]**
(a) Branched, α (1, 4) and β (1, 6) - glucose
(b) Unbranched, α (1, 6) - glucose
(c) Branched, α (1, 4) - glucose
(d) Unbranched, β (1, 4) - glucose

5 Hydrolysis of sucrose with dilute aqueous sulphuric acid yields **[AIIMS]**
(a) 1:2 D-(+)- glucose; D-(–)- fructose
(b) 1:2 D-(–)-glucose; D-(+)-fructose
(c) 1:1 D-(–)- glucose; D-(+)-fructose
(d) 1:1 D-(+)-glucose; D-(–)-fructose

6 The difference between amylose and amylopectin is **[NEET]**
(a) amylopectin have (1, 4) α-linkage and 1, 6 β - linkage
(b) amylose have (1, 4) α-linkage and 1, 6 β - linkage
(c) amylopectin have (1, 4) α-linkage and 1, 6 α-linkage
(d) amylose is made up of glucose and galactose

2017

7 Assertion (A) Glucose gives reddish brown precipitate with Fehling solution.
Reason (R) Reaction of glucose with Fehling solution gives CuO and gluconic acid. **[AIIMS]**
(a) Both A and R are correct and R is the correct explanation of A.
(b) Both A and R are correct but R is not the correct explanation of A.
(c) A is correct but R is incorrect.
(d) Both A and R are incorrect.

8 On hydrolysis of starch, we finally get **[JIPMER]**
(a) glucose (b) fructose
(c) Both (a) and (b) (d) sucrose

2016

9 The correct corresponding order of names of four aldoses with configuration given below :

CHO	CHO	CHO	CHO
H—+—OH	HO—+—H	HO—+—H	H—+—OH
H—+—OH	H—+—OH	HO—+—H	HO—+—H
CH_2OH	CH_2OH	CH_2OH	CH_2OH

respectively, is **[NEET, Phase II]**
(a) L-erythrose, L-threose, L-erythrose, D-threose
(b) D-threose, D-erythrose, L-threose, L-erythrose
(c) L-erythrose, L-threose, D-erythrose, D-threose
(d) D-erythrose, D-threose, L-erythrose, L-threose

10 Which one given below is a non-reducing sugar? **[NEET]**
(a) Lactose (b) Glucose (c) Sucrose (d) Maltose

2014

11 D-(+)- glucose reacts with hydroxyl amine and yields an oxime. The structure of the oxime would be **[CBSE AIPMT]**

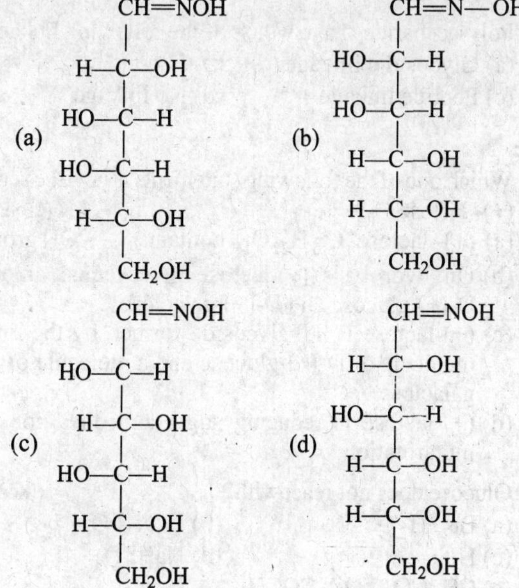

12 One mole of stachyose on hydrolysis yields [MHT CET]
(a) 1 mole of glucose +1 mole of fructose +2 moles of galactose
(b) 2 moles of glucose +1 mole of fructose +1 mole of galactose
(c) 1 mole of glucose +2 moles of fructose +1 mole of galactose
(d) 2 moles of glucose +2 moles of fructose

2013

13 Sucrose on treatment with conc. HCl produce [AIIMS]
(a) glucose (b) fructose
(c) glucose + fructose (d) laevunilic acid

14 Maltose on hydrolysis produces
(a) glucose (b) fructose (c) mannose (d) galactose

15 Which of the following reaction estabilishes difference between glucose and fructose? [WB JEE]
(a) Tollen's reagent reaction (b) Phenyl hydrazine
(c) P/HI (d) Conc. HNO_3

16 Which of the following is an aldohexose? [KCET]
(a) Cellulose (b) Sucrose
(c) Glucose (d) Raffinose

17 A certain compound gives negative test with ninhydrin and positive test with Benedict's solution, it is [KCET]
(a) an amino acid (b) a monosaccharide
(c) a lipid (d) a protein

2012

18 Glucose and mannose are [AIIMS]
(a) anomers (b) epimers
(c) ketohexoses (d) disaccharides

19 Which one of the following is an example of non-reducing sugar? [UP CPMT]
(a) Sucrose (b) Lactose (c) Maltose (d) Cellobiose

20 Polysaccharides have which of the following linkage?
(a) Glycosidic linkage (b) H-bond [OJEE]
(c) Peptide linkage (d) No linkage

2011

21 Which one of the following statements is not true regarding (+)- lactose? [CBSE AIPMT]
(a) (+)- lactose, $C_{12}H_{22}O_{11}$ contains 8 —OH groups
(b) On hydrolysis (+)-lactose gives equal amount of D-(+) glucose and D-(+) galactose
(c) (+)-lactose is a β-glycoside formed by the union of molecule of D-(+)-glucose and a molecule of D-(+)-galactose
(d) (+)-lactose is reducing sugar and does not exhibit mutarotation

22 Glucose does not react with [Kerala CEE]
(a) Br_2/H_2O (b) $H_2N—OH$
(c) HI (d) $NaHSO_3$
(e) $CH_3CO—O—COCH_3$

23 The linkage between the two monosaccharide units in lactose is [Kerala CEE]
(a) C-1 of β-D-glucose and C-4 of β-D-galactose
(b) C-1 of β-D-galactose and C-4 of β-D-glucose
(c) C-1 of α-D-galactose and C-4 of β-D-glucose
(d) C-1 of β-D-galactose and C-4 of α-D-glucose
(e) C-1 of α-D-glucose and C-4 of α-D-glucose

24 α-maltose consists of [KCET]
(a) one α-D-glucopyranose unit and one β-D-glucopyranose unit with 1,2-glycosidic linkage
(b) two α-D-glucopyranose units with 1,2-glycosidic linkage
(c) two β-D-glucopyranose units with 1,4-glycosidic linkage
(d) two α-D-glucopyranose units with 1,4-glycosidic linkage

25 What is the nature of glucose-glucose linkage in starch that makes it so susceptible to acid hydrolysis? [DUMET]
(a) Starch is a hemiacetal
(b) Starch is an acetal
(c) Starch is a polymer
(d) Starch contains only few molecules of glucose

26 How glucose is related with fructose? [Guj CET]
(a) Functional group isomerism
(b) Rotamers
(c) Positions isomerism
(d) Geometrical isomerism

27 How can you say that glucose is cyclic compound?
(a) Glucose undergoes Tollen's reaction [Guj CET]
(b) Glucose reacts with phenyl hydrazine
(c) Glucose fails to react with sodium hydrogen sulphite
(d) Glucose reacts with nitric acid

2010

28 Which of the following does not exhibit the phenomenon of mutarotation? [CBSE AIPMT]
(a) (–)-fructose (b) (+)-sucrose
(c) (+)-lactose (d) (+)-maltose

29 Hydrolysis of sucrose is called [AFMC]
(a) inversion (b) esterification
(c) hydration (d) saponification

30 The change in optical rotation of freshly prepared solution of cane sugar with time is known as [Manipal]
(a) mutarotation (b) inversion
(c) specific rotation (d) rotatory motion

31 Which of the following cannot be hydrolysed into aldose and ketose? [OJEE]
(a) Disaccharide (b) Monosaccharide
(c) Polysaccharide (d) Oligosaccharide

32 The monomer units of starch are [RPMT]
(a) α-glucose (b) β-glucose
(c) pyranose (d) galactose

33 Glucose reacts with X number of molecules of phenyl hydrazine to yield osazone. The value of X is **[RPMT]**
(a) three (b) two (c) one (d) four

34 Water hydrolysis of sucrose produces **[MP PMT]**
(a) two molecules of glucose
(b) two molecules of fructose
(c) one molecule of each glucose and fructose
(d) one molecule and each glucose and mannose

35 The letter 'D' in D-glucose signifies **[KCET]**
(a) configuration at all chiral carbons
(b) dextrorotatory
(c) that it is a monosaccharide
(d) configuration at a particular chiral carbon

36 Which of the following is the correct order of priority of group in D-glyceraldehyde? **[Guj CET]**
(a) OH(1), CHO(2), CH_2OH(3) and H(4)
(b) OH(1), CH_2OH(2), CHO(3) and H(4)
(c) CH_2OH(1), CHO(2), OH(3) and H(4)
(d) CHO(1), OH(2), CH_2OH(3) and H(4)

37 Which of the following compounds, when heated at 483 K turns to caramel? **[Guj CET]**
(a) Glucose (b) Sucrose (c) Fructose (d) Lactose

38 Glucose on reaction with Fehling's solution gives **[MHT CET]**
(a) cupric oxide (b) cuprous oxide
(c) saccharic acid (d) Both (b) and (c)

39 Which of the following is a trisaccharide? **[MHT CET]**
(a) Stachyse (b) Sucrose (c) Raffinose (d) Ribose

40 Glucose + Tollen's reagent $\longrightarrow$ Silver mirror, the above process shows **[VMMC]**
(a) presence of — COOH group
(b) presence of keto group
(c) presence of —CHO group
(d) presence of — $CONH_2$ group

2009

41 When sucrose is heated with conc. HNO_3, the product formed is **[Manipal]**
(a) sucrose nitrate (b) adipic acid
(c) oxalic acid (d) citric acid

42 Glucose forms many derivatives. The derivative which will help to prove the furanose structure is **[Manipal]**
(a) osazone (b) benzoyl
(c) acetyl (d) isopropylidene

43 Carbohydrate is treated with α-naphthol and conc. H_2SO_4, colour developed at the junction of the two liquids is **[OJEE]**
(a) blue (b) violet
(c) green (d) red

44 Which one of the following has maximum laevorotatory nature? **[J&K CET]**
(a) D-glucose (b) D-fructose
(c) Sucrose (d) Invert sugar

45 In the following structure, anomeric carbon is **[AMU]**

$HOCH_2$, O, OH, 4, OH, 1, 2, HO 3, OH

(a) 1 (b) 2 (c) 3 (d) 4

46 A diabetic person carries a packet of glucose with him always, because **[KCET]**
(a) glucose increases the blood sugar level slowly
(b) glucose reduces the blood sugar level
(c) glucose increases the blood sugar level almost instantaneously
(d) glucose reduces the blood sugar level slowly

47 Stachyose is a **[MHT CET]**
(a) monosaccharide (b) disaccharide
(c) trisaccharide (d) tetrasaccharide

2008

48 The beta and alpha glucose have different specific rotations. When either is dissolved in water, their rotation changes until the same fixed value results. This is called **[AIIMS]**
(a) epimerisation (b) racemisation
(c) anomerisation (d) mutarotation

49 Which of the following is incorrect? **[BHU]**
(a) Functional isomerism is shown by $CH_3—CH_2—OH$ and $CH_3—O—CH_3$
(b) $H—\underset{H}{\overset{H}{C}}—\underset{OH}{\overset{H}{C}}—H \xrightarrow{\text{Conc. } H_2SO_4} H—\overset{H}{C}=\overset{H}{C}—H + H_2O$
(c) Glucose is a monosaccharide sugar
(d) Fructose is a disaccharide sugar

50 Which of the following does not form an oxime? **[Manipal]**
(a) Glucose (b) Glucose pentaacetate
(c) Arabinose (d) Galactose

51 Pick out the incorrect statement(s) from the following.
I. Glucose exists in two different crystalline forms, α-D-glucose and β-D-glucose.
II. α-D-glucose and β-D-glucose are anomers.
III. α-D-glucose and β-D-glucose are enantiomers.
IV. Cellulose is a straight chain polysaccharide made up of only β-D-glucose units.
V. Starch is a mixture of amylose and amylopectin, both contain unbranched chain of α-D-glucose units.

(a) I and II (b) II and III **[Kerala CEE]**
(c) III and IV (d) III and V
(e) IV and V

52 Complete hydrolysis of cellulose gives [RPMT]
(a) D-fructose (b) D-ribose
(c) D-glucose (d) L-glucose

53 Which one of the following statements is incorrect for the sucrose? [Guj CET]
(a) It is obtained from cane sugar
(b) It is non-reducing sugar
(c) On hydrolysis, it gives equal quantities of D-glucose and D-fructose
(d) It gives aspartame when it is heated at 210°C

2007

54 Number of chiral carbon atoms in β-D(+)-glucose is [Manipal]
(a) five (b) six
(c) three (d) four

55 Cellulose is soluble in [Guj CET]
(a) ammoniacal cupric hydroxide solution
(b) water
(c) organic solvent
(d) None of the above

56 Which of the following is incorrect for glucose? [Guj CET]
(a) It contains one ketone group
(b) It contains four —CHOH groups
(c) It contains one —CHO group
(d) It contains one —CH_2OH group

57 Which of the following does not reduce Fehling's solution? [JCECE]
(a) Benzaldehyde (b) Formic acid
(c) Glucose (d) Fructose

58 Glucose gives silver mirror with ammoniacal silver nitrate because it has [MHT CET]
(a) aldehydic group (b) ester group
(c) ketone group (d) alcoholic silver nitrate

2006

59 Methyl α-D-glucoside and methyl β-D-glucoside are [AIIMS]
(a) epimers
(b) anomers
(c) enantiomers
(d) conformational diastereomers

60 The number of chiral centres in D-(+)-glucose are [J&K CET]
(a) 4 (b) 3 (c) 2 (d) 1

61 Which of the following compounds is found abundantly in nature? [AMU]
(a) Fructose (b) Starch
(c) Glucose (d) Cellulose

2005

62 **Assertion** (A) Maltose is a reducing sugar which gives two moles of D-glucose on hydrolysis.
Reason (R) Maltose has a 1, 4-β-glycosidic linkage. [AIIMS]
(a) Both A and R are correct and R is the correct explanation of A
(b) Both A and R are correct but R is not the correct explanation of A
(c) A is correct but R is incorrect
(d) Both A and R are incorrect

63 Glucose has difference from fructose in that it [BHU]
(a) does not undergo hydrolysis
(b) gives silver mirror with Tollen's reagent
(c) monosaccharide
(d) None of the above

64 Which of the following is/are true? [Kerala CEE]
I. Sucrose is a non-reducing sugar.
II. Glucose is oxidised by bromine water.
III. Glucose rotates plane polarised light in clockwise direction.
IV. Fructose is oxidised by bromine water.
Select the correct answer using the codes given below.
(a) I, II and III (b) I and II
(c) II and III (d) I and IV
(e) I, II, III and IV

65 Hexoses and pentoses are [AMU]
(a) disaccharides (b) monosaccharides
(c) polysaccharides (d) oligosaccharides

66 Sucrose molecule is made up of [KCET]
(a) a gluco pyranose and a fructo pyranose
(b) a gluco pyranose and a fructo furanose
(c) a gluco furanose and a fructo pyranose
(d) a gluco furanose and a fructo furanose

67 Water insoluble component of starch is [KCET]
(a) amylopectin (b) amylose
(c) cellulose (d) None of these

Answers

1 (a)	2 (a)	3 (a)	4 (d)	5 (d)	6 (c)	7 (c)	8 (a)	9 (d)	10 (c)
11 (d)	12 (a)	13 (d)	14 (a)	15 (d)	16 (c)	17 (b)	18 (b)	19 (a)	20 (a)
21 (d)	22 (d)	23 (b)	24 (d)	25 (b)	26 (a)	27 (c)	28 (b)	29 (a)	30 (b)
31 (b)	32 (a)	33 (a)	34 (c)	35 (d)	36 (a)	37 (b)	38 (b)	39 (c)	40 (c)
41 (c)	42 (d)	43 (b)	44 (b)	45 (a)	46 (c)	47 (d)	48 (d)	49 (d)	50 (b)
51 (d)	52 (c)	53 (d)	54 (a)	55 (a)	56 (a)	57 (d)	58 (a)	59 (b)	60 (a)
61 (d)	62 (c)	63 (b)	64 (a)	65 (b)	66 (b)	67 (a)			

Explanations

1 (*a*) In nature, glucose exists in cyclic hemiacetal form and has no free —CHO group, thus it does not give 2, 4-DNP test.

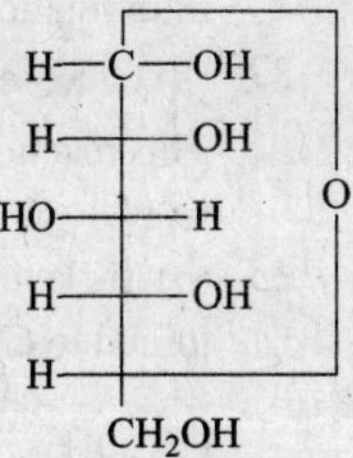

Cyclic structure

Therefore, Assertion and Reason both are correct and Reason is the correct explanation of the given Assertion.

Hence, option (a) is the correct.

2 (*a*) Sucrose on hydrolysis gives equimolar mixture of D-(+)-glucose and D-(−)-fructose. These two monosaccharides are held together by a glycosidic linkage between C-1 of α-glucose and C-2 of β-fructose. Therefore, both, Assertion and Reason are true and Reason is the correct explanation of the given Assertion.

Hence, option (a) is the correct.

α-(D)-glucose Glycosidic linkage β-(D)-fructose

3 (*a*) Invert sugar is a mixture of D-glucose and D-fructose. Solution of sucrose is dextrorotatory. When sucrose is hydrolysed it forms equimolar quantity of D-glucose and D-fructose. The solution of formed products is found to be laevorotatory. This change in optical properties of sucrose is called inversion of cane sugar. The equimolar product formed, i.e D-glucose and D-fructose is called invert sugar.

4 (*d*) Cellulose has a straight chain polysaccharide composed only of β-D glucose units. These β-D glucose units are linked together by C_1-C_4 glycosidic linkage. The structure is shown below:

β-glycosidic linkage

Structure of cellulose

5 (*d*) On hydrolysis with dilute aqueous sulphuric acid, sucrose forms an equimolar mixture of D-(+)-glucose and D-(−)-fructose. The reaction for the hydrolysis of sucrose is as follows :

$$\underset{\text{Sucrose}}{C_{12}H_{22}O_{11}} + H_2O \xrightarrow{H_2SO_4} \underset{\text{D-(+)-glucose}}{C_6H_{12}O_6} + \underset{\text{D-(−)-fructose}}{C_6H_{12}O_6}$$

Solution of sucrose is dextrorotatory (specific rotation = + 66.5°) but after hydrolysis gives dextrorotatory glucose and laevorotatory fructose.

The solution of formed product is found to be laevorotatory (specific rotation = −20.0°)

6 (*c*) Starch consists of two components amylose and amylopectin. Chemically, amylose is a long unbranched chain with 200-1000 α-D- (+)-glucose units held by C_1-C_4 glycosidic linkage.

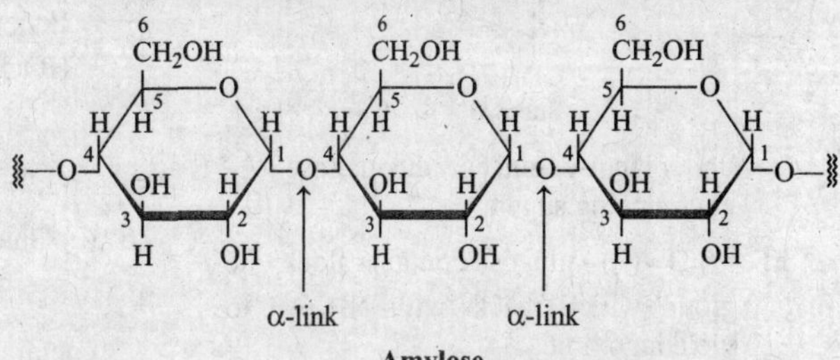

Amylose

Amylopectin is a branched chain polymer of α -D-glucose units in which straight chain is formed by C_1-C_4 glycosidic linkage and branching occurs by C_1-C_6 glycosidic linkage.

α-link
Branching at C_6
α-link α-link

Amylopectin

7 (*c*) Glucose give reddish brown precipitate with Fehling solution and solution consists of Cu^{2+} which gets reduced to Cu^+ (Cu_2O).

$$\underset{\text{Glucose}}{C_6H_{12}O_6} + 2CuO \xrightarrow{OH^-} \underset{\text{Gluconic acid}}{C_5H_{11}O_5COOH} + Cu_2O$$

8 (*a*) Starch is a polymer of D-glucose units, thus on hydrolysis it gives glucose only.

9 (*d*) The correct name of aldoses are as follows:

D-erythrose D-threose L-erythrose L-threose

10 (*c*) Sucrose is non-reducing sugar because reducing part of glucose ($-\overset{O}{\overset{\|}{C}}-H$) and fructose (>C═O) are involved in glycosidic linkage.

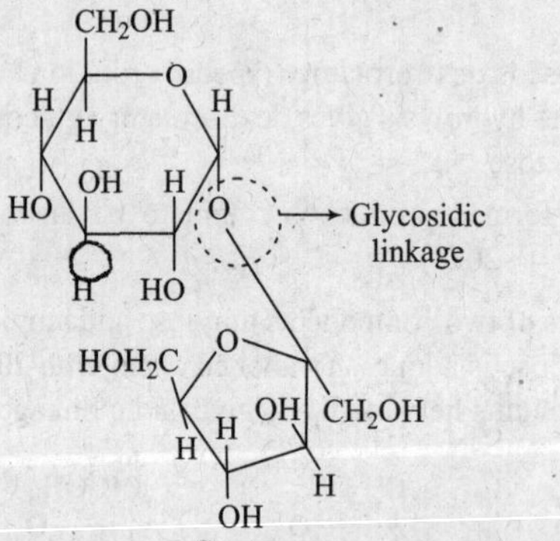

CH₂OH, HO, OH, H, O → Glycosidic linkage; HOH₂C, OH, CH₂OH, OH

Sucrose

While, lactose, glucose and maltose are reducing sugars.

11 (*d*) D-(+)-glucose contains aldehydic group which reacts with NH_2OH to yield an oxime.

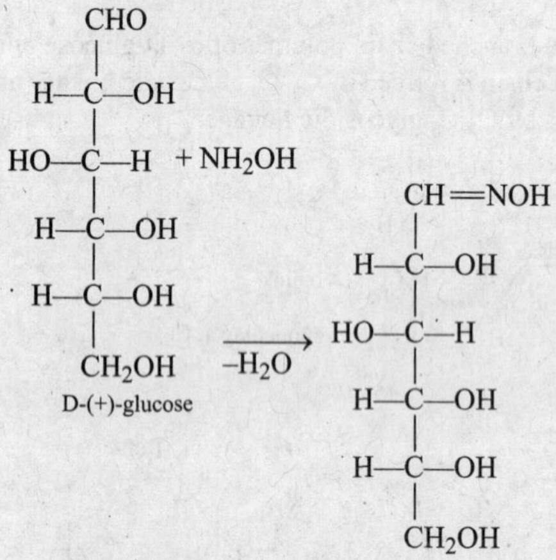

$$\text{D-(+)-glucose: CHO–(H–C–OH)–(HO–C–H)–(H–C–OH)–(H–C–OH)–}CH_2OH + NH_2OH \xrightarrow{-H_2O} \text{CH=NOH–(H–C–OH)–(HO–C–H)–(H–C–OH)–(H–C–OH)–}CH_2OH \text{ (Oxime)}$$

12 (*a*) One mole of stachyose on hydrolysis gives 1 mole of glucose, 1 mole of fructose and 2 moles of galactose.

13 (*d*) Sucrose on reaction with conc. HCl forms laevunilic acid.

$$\underset{\text{Sucrose}}{C_{12}H_{22}O_{11}} \xrightarrow[\text{HCl}]{\text{Conc.}} \underset{\text{Laevunilic acid}}{CH_3COCH_2CH_2COOH}$$

$$C_{12}H_{22}O_{11} \xrightarrow[\text{Enzymes or with HCl (dil.)}]{\text{Inversion}} \underset{\text{Glucose}}{C_6H_{12}O_6} + \underset{\text{Fructose}}{C_6H_{12}O_6}$$

14 (*a*) As we know, disaccharides upon hydrolysis gives two molecules of monosaccharides.

So, maltose is a disaccharide which upon hydrolysis gives two molecules of glucose (a monosaccharides).

$$C_{12}H_{22}O_{11} + H_2O \xrightarrow[\text{Maltase}]{H_2SO_4} \underset{\text{Glucose}}{2C_6H_{12}O_6}$$

15 (*d*) Glucose/fructose both give positive Tollen's test, form same osazone, on reaction with phenyl hydrazine and form *n*-hexane on reaction with P/HI (reduction) but with conc. HNO_3. both give different products.

$$\text{Glucose} \xrightarrow{\text{Conc. } HNO_3} \underset{\text{Saccharie acid}}{COOH—(CHOH)_4—COOH}$$

$$\text{Fructose} \xrightarrow{\text{Conc. } HNO_3} \underset{\text{Tartaric acid}}{HOOC—(CHOH)_2—COOH} + \underset{\text{Glycolic acid}}{HOCH_2—COOH}$$

16 (*c*) Glucose is an aldohexose, because it contains six C-atoms with $—\overset{O}{\overset{\|}{C}}—H$ group.

17 (*b*) Monosaccharides give positive test with Benedict's solution because they are reducing sugars but they give negative test with ninhydrin because this test is performed by proteins, peptides and amino acids.

18 (*b*) Glucose and mannose are isomers that differ in configuration at C_2. The isomers whose configuration is different at C_2 are known as 'epimers'.

19 (*a*) All polysaccharides including sucrose are called non-reducing sugars, because these cannot reduce Fehling's solution and Tollen's reagent.

20 (*a*) In polysaccharides, different monosaccharide unit are linked to one another by glycosidic linkages.

E.g. amylose and amylopectin are composed of α-D-glucose units linked by glycosidic linkages.

21 (*d*) The molecule of (+)-lactose is composed of D-(+) glucose unit and D-(+)-galactose unit. The units are joined by the β-glycosidic linkage (at C-4 of glucose and C-1 of galactose.) The structure is shown below:

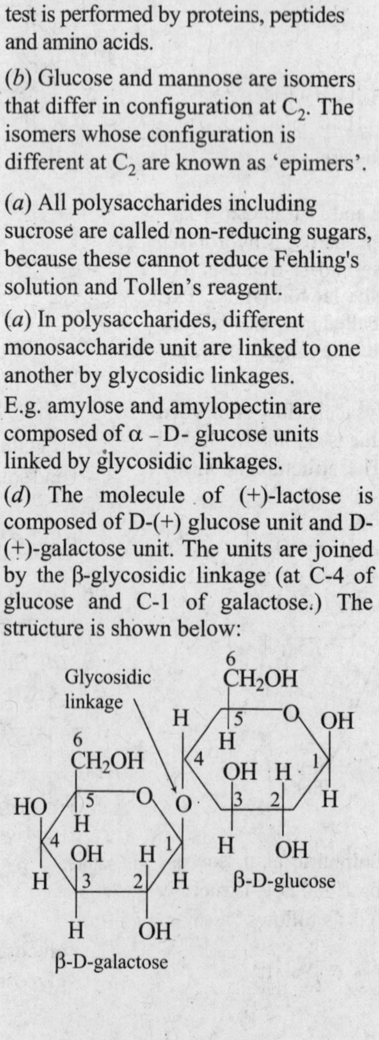

Glycosidic linkage; β-D-galactose (6 CH₂OH, HO, H, OH, H, H, OH) –O– β-D-glucose (6 CH₂OH, H, OH, OH, H, H, OH)

Due to reducing functional group present at C-1 of glucose unit, lactose is a reducing sugar. It also undergoes mutarotation.

22 (*d*) Glucose does not react with $NaHSO_3$. This reaction shows that glucose exist as a cyclic structure.

23 (*b*) In lactose C-1 of β-D-galactose is joined to C-4 of β-D-glucose.

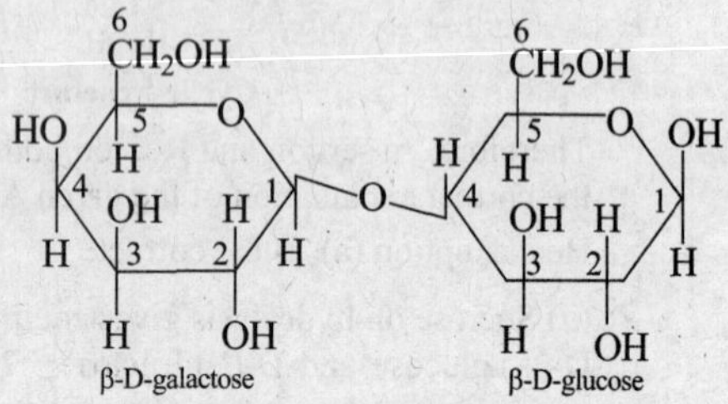

β-D-galactose (6 CH₂OH, HO, H, OH, H, H, OH) –O– β-D-glucose (6 CH₂OH, OH, H, OH, H, H, OH)

24 (*d*) Maltose is composed of two α-D-glucopyranose units in which C-1 of one glucose is linked to C-4 of another glucose unit.

25 (*b*) Starch is an acetal. Monosaccharides are hemiacetals. Acetals and hemiacetals get readily hydrolysed by acids to give alcohols.

26 (*a*) Glucose and fructose are functional isomers. Both differ from each other in their functional group. Hence, they exhibit functional group isomerism.

27 (*c*) Despite having the aldehydic group, glucose does not give 2,4-DNP test, Schiff's test and it does not form the hydrogen sulphite addition product with $NaHSO_3$. It indicates that glucose forms cyclic ring.

28 (*b*) During mutarotation, the ring opens up to give the open chain form which then recloses either in the inverted position or in the original position giving an equilibrium mixture of two anomers with a small amount of the open chain form. Thus, all reducing monosaccharides and disaccharides (except sucrose due to the absence of hemiacetal linkage) undergo mutarotation in aqueous solutions.

29 (*a*) On hydrolysis, sucrose gives an equimolar mixutre of D-(+)-glucose and D-(–)-fructose.

$$\underset{\text{(+)-sucrose}}{C_{12}H_{22}O_{11}} + H_2O \longrightarrow \underset{\text{D-(+)-glucose}}{C_6H_{12}O_6} + \underset{\text{D-(–)-fructose}}{C_6H_{12}O_6}$$

Here, the configuration of sucrose changes (gets inverted) after hydrolysis, thus its hydrolysis is called inversion.

30 (*b*) Inversion is the change in specific rotation of an optically active compound in solution with time to an equilibrium value.

31 (*b*) Monosaccharides are the simplest carbohydrates which cannot be hydrolysed to smaller molecules.

32 (*a*) Starch is a mixture of amylose (15-20%) and amylopectin (80-85%). Both, amylose and amylopectin are polymers of α-D-glucose.

33 (*a*)

$$\underset{\text{Glucose}}{\begin{array}{l}CHO\\|\\CHOH\\|\\(CHOH)_3\\|\\CH_2OH\end{array}} \xrightarrow[-2H_2O,\,-NH_3,\,-C_6H_5NH_2]{3C_6H_5NHNH_2} \underset{\text{Osazone (glucosazone)}}{\begin{array}{l}CH{=}NNHC_6H_5\\|\\C{=}NNHC_6H_5\\|\\(CHOH)_3\\|\\CH_2OH\end{array}}$$

Hence, three molecules of phenyl hydrazine is used to form osazone.

34 (*c*) On hydrolysis with dilute acid or enzyme, sucrose produces an equimolar mixture of D-glucose and D-fructose.

$$\underset{\text{Sucrose}}{C_{12}H_{22}O_{11}} + H_2O \xrightarrow{HCl} \underset{\text{D-glucose}}{C_6H_{12}O_6} + \underset{\text{D-fructose}}{C_6H_{12}O_6}$$

35 (*d*) Letter 'D' before the name of monosaccharide reveals that the—OH group at the second carbon atom is towards the right, i.e. it only shows the configuration at a particular chiral carbon (w.r.t. glyceraldehyde.)

36 (*a*) The structure of D-glyceraldehyde is as

$$\begin{array}{c} {}^2CHO \\ {}_4H - \!\!\!-\!\!\!\!\!\!\!\!\!\!\!\!\!\quad\;\; - OH\,{}_1 \\ {}_3CH_2OH \end{array}$$

The priority of groups is decided by the following rules

(i) Atom having higher atomic number gets higher priority.

(ii) If the priority cannot be decided by rule 1 then the next atoms are considered for priority order.

(iii) Where there is a = bond or ≡ bond, both atoms are considered to be duplicated or triplicated.

$$(\overset{\displaystyle H}{\overset{|}{-C}}{=}O$$ has higher priority than $-CH_2OH$).

Hence, the correct order of priority of group in D-glyceraldehyde is as follows:

OH(1), CHO(2), CH_2OH(3) and H(4)

37 (*b*) On heating slowly, sucrose melts and if allowed to cool, it solidifies to pale-yellow glassy mass called **barley sugar**. At 483 K, it loses water and forms a brown amorphous mass called caramel.

38 (*b*)

$$\underset{\text{Glucose}}{C_5H_{11}O_5CHO} + \underset{\text{(from Fehling solution)}}{2CuO} \xrightarrow{OH^-} \underset{\text{Gluconic acid}}{C_5H_{11}O_5COOH} + \underset{\text{Cuprous oxide (red ppt.)}}{Cu_2O}$$

39 (*c*) On hydrolysis, stachyose gives four, sucrose gives two, raffinose gives three and ribose gives no molecule of monosaccharides. Thus, only raffinose is a trisaccharide.

$$\underset{\text{Raffinose}}{C_{18}H_{32}O_{16}} + H_2O \longrightarrow \underset{\text{Three molecules of glucose}}{3C_6H_{12}O_6}$$

40 (*c*)

$$\underset{\text{Glucose}}{\begin{array}{l}CHO\\|\\(CHOH)_4\\|\\CH_2OH\end{array}} + \underset{\text{Tollen's reagent}}{2[Ag(NH_3)_2]OH} \longrightarrow \begin{array}{l}COONH_4\\|\\(CHOH)_4\\|\\CH_2OH\end{array} + \underset{\text{Silver mirror}}{2Ag\downarrow} + 3NH_3 + H_2O$$

This reaction indicates the presence of —CHO group in glucose.

41 (*c*) Sucrose reacts with conc. HNO_3 to give oxalic acid.

$$C_{12}H_{22}O_{11} + 18[O] \xrightarrow{\text{Conc. }HNO_3} 6\begin{array}{l}COOH\\|\\COOH\end{array} + 5H_2O$$

In this reaction, sucrose oxidises into oxalic acid.

42 (*d*) Formation of isopropylidene derivative requires the presence of two adjacent free —OH groups in *cis*-orientation which is present only in the furanose form and hence, isopropylidene formation proves the presence of furanose form.

43 (*b*) Carbohydrate reacts with α-naphthol and conc. H_2SO_4 to give violet colour. This is known as Molish test for carbohydrates.

44 (*b*) Naturally occurring fructose is laevorotatory. Its specific rotation is –92.4°.

45 (*a*) C-1 is an anomeric carbon and due to this, the given structure exists in two forms, α and β.

46 (*c*) The sugar level in the blood of a diabetic person may suddenly fall. Immediate intake of glucose increases the blood sugar level almost instantaneously, that's why glucose is also called instant energy.

47 (*d*) Stachyose is a tetrasaccharide consisting of two α-D-galactose units, one α-D-glucose unit and one β-D-fructose unit sequentially linked as gal (α1→ 6) gal (α1→ 6) glu (α1→ 2β) fru.

48 (*d*) The β and α-glucose have different rotations. When either is dissolved in water, their rotation changes until the same fixed value results. This is called mutarotation.

$$\underset{\text{Specific rotation} = +111°}{\alpha\text{-D-glucose}} \rightleftharpoons \underset{\text{Specific rotation} = +52.5°}{\text{Open chain form of equilibrium mixture}} \rightleftharpoons \underset{\text{Specific rotation} = +19.2°}{\beta\text{-D-glucose}}$$

49 (*d*) Fructose is a monosaccharide sugar because it does not get hydrolysed further. Rest all the other given statements are correct.

50 (*b*) Glucose pentaacetate does not form an oxime because the glycosidic —OH group is not free because it is involved in ring formation. As a result, it cannot get converted into the open chain form required for the formation of oxime.

51 (*d*) α-D-glucose and β-D-glucose differ in the orientation of H and OH-groups around first carbon atom. Such isomers are called anomers, not enantiomers. Starch is a mixture of amylose and amylopectin but amylose is a straight chain polymer of α-D-glucose while amylopectin is a branched chain polymer of α-D-glucose. Thus statements III & V are incorrect while other statements given are correct.

52 (*c*) Cellulose is a straight chain or polysaccharide composed of D-glucose units which are joined by β-glycosidic linkages. Hence, cellulose on hydrolysis produces only D-glucose units.

53 (*d*) Sucrose is obtained from cane sugar. On hydrolysis of sucrose, it gives equimolar mixture of D-(+)-glucose and D-(–)-fructose. Sucrose is a non-reducing sugar.

$$\text{Sucrose} \xrightarrow[\text{or invertase}]{H^+} \text{D-(+)-glucose} + \text{D-(–)-fructose}$$

Sucrose on heating gets decomposed.

It does not give aspartame when heated at 210°C. Thus, option (d) is incorrect.

54 (*a*) The number of chiral carbon atoms in β-D (+)- glucose is five.

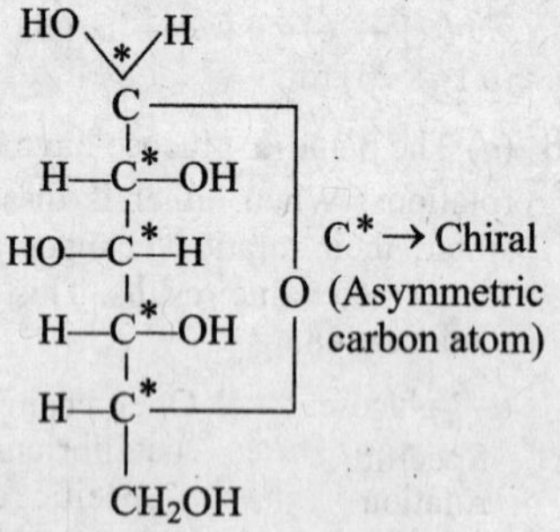

```
HO\*/H
   C ─────────┐
   |          |
H─C*─OH       |
   |          |   C* → Chiral
HO─C*─H       O   (Asymmetric
   |          |    carbon atom)
H─C*─OH       |
   |          |
H─C* ─────────┘
   |
  CH2OH
```

55 (*a*) Cellulose is soluble in ammoniacal cupric hydroxide solution.

56 (*a*) Glucose does not contain ketonic group. It contains one —CHO, four >CHOH and one —CH_2OH group. Its structure is as follows.

```
  CHO
   |
 (CHOH)4
   |
  CH2OH
```

57 (*d*) Fructose does not reduce Fehling's solution, because it contains ketonic group.

58 (*a*) Glucose gives silver mirror with ammoniacal silver nitrate due to the presence of —CHO group (aldehyde group) in the structure of glucose.

$$\underset{\text{Fructose}}{CH_2OH(CHOH)_4CHO} + Ag_2O \xrightarrow{NH_3} \underset{\text{Ammonium salt of gluconic acid}}{CH_2OH(CHOH)_4—COO^-NH_4^+} + \underset{\text{Silver mirror}}{2Ag\downarrow}$$

59 (*b*) The isomers which differ in configuration at asymmetric carbon C_1 produced due to ring formations are known as anomers.

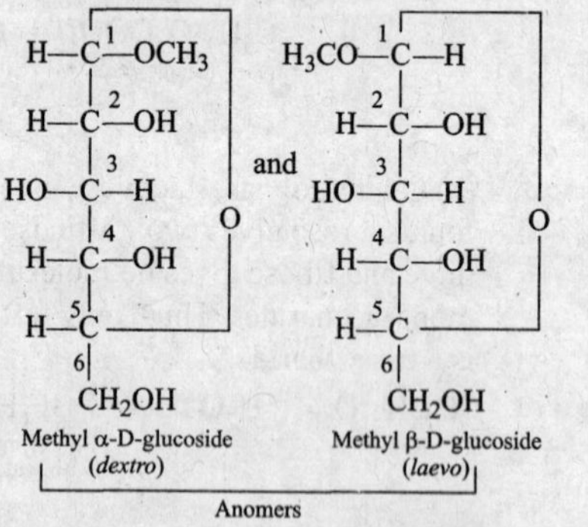

```
     1                          1
H─C─OCH3 ──┐        H3CO─C─H ──┐
  |2        |                |2    |
H─C─OH      |           H─C─OH     |
  |3        |    and       |3      |
HO─C─H      O          HO─C─H      O
  |4        |               |4     |
H─C─OH      |           H─C─OH     |
  |5        |               |5     |
H─C ────────┘           H─C ───────┘
  |6                        |6
 CH2OH                     CH2OH
Methyl α-D-glucoside    Methyl β-D-glucoside
   (dextro)                 (laevo)
              Anomers
```

60 (*a*) A carbon atom which is attached by four different groups is called chiral centre or asymmetric carbon atom. D-(+)-glucose has four chiral centres.

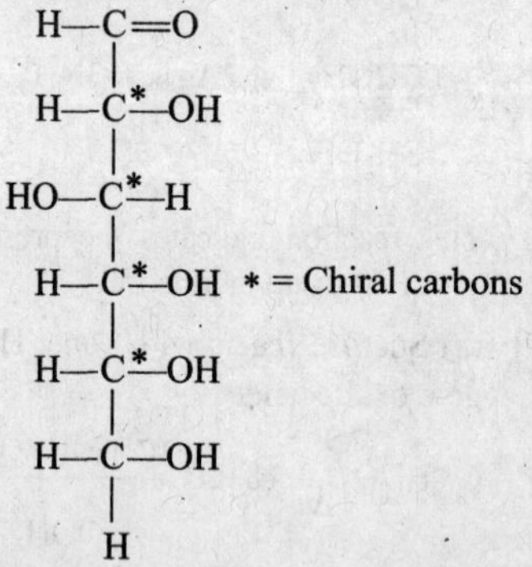

```
H─C═O
  |
H─C*─OH
  |
HO─C*─H
  |
H─C*─OH    * = Chiral carbons
  |
H─C*─OH
  |
H─C─OH
  |
  H
```

61 (*d*) Cellulose is the most abundant polysaccharide. It is the essential constituent of the cell-wall of all green-plants.

62 (*c*) Maltose, a disaccharide ($C_{12}H_{22}O_{11}$) is a reducing sugar, which upon hydrolysis yields 2 moles of D-(+)- glucose. In it, the two D-glucose units are linked through α-glycosidic linkage between C-1 of one glucose unit and C-4 of the other.

63 (*b*) Glucose and fructose both of them do not undergo hydrolysis and both of them are monosaccharides.

∵ Glucose has aldehyde group, it reduces Tollen's reagent to silver mirror. Fructose has ketonic group, it does not form silver mirror with Tollen's reagent.

64 (*a*) Sucrose is a non-reducing sugar. Glucose is oxidised by Br_2-water to give gluconic acid.

$$C_6H_{12}O_6 + [O] \xrightarrow{Br_2 \text{ water}} \underset{\text{Gluconic acid}}{\begin{matrix} COOH \\ | \\ (CHOH)_4 \\ | \\ CH_2OH \end{matrix}}$$

Glucose rotates plane polarised light in clockwise direction.

Fructose is not oxidised by Br_2 water. Thus, statements I, II and III are correct.

65 (*b*) Those sugars which contain 2, 3, 5, 6 carbon atoms and which cannot be hydrolysed further into simpler units are known as monosaccharides.

Hence, hexoses and pentoses are monosaccharides.

66 (*b*) Sucrose molecule is made up of a gluco pyranose and a fructo furanose. On hydrolysis, sucrose gives a mixture of D-glucose and D-fructose.

67 (*a*) Amylopectin consists of D-glucose units and is a branched chain polymer of α-D-glucose. So, it is insoluble in H_2O.

Topic 2

Amino Acids, Proteins and Enzymes

2019

1 Assertion Tryptophan is an example of non-essential amino acids.
Reason The amino acids that are not synthesised in human body are non-essential amino acids. **[AIIMS]**

(a) Both A and R are correct and R is the correct explanation of A
(b) Both A and R are correct but R is not the correct explanation of A
(c) A is correct but R is in correct
(d) Both A and R are incorrect

2 Which structure(s) of proteins remains(s) intact during denaturation process? **[NEET (Odisha)]**

(a) Both secondary and tertiary structures
(b) Primary structure only
(c) Secondary structure only
(d) Tertiary structure only

3 The non-essential amino acid among the following is **[NEET]**

(a) leucine (b) alanine (c) lysine (d) valine

4 Which of the following amino acid is optically inactive? **[JIPMER]**

(a) Glycine (b) Valine (c) Alanine (d) Histidine

2018

5 Which of the following compounds can form a *Zwitter* ion? **[NEET]**

(a) Benzoic acid (b) Acetanilide
(c) Aniline (d) Glycine

2016

6 In a protein molecule various amino acids are linked together by **[NEET]**

(a) β-glycosidic bond (b) peptide bond
(c) dative bond (d) α-glycosidic bond

2014

7 Which one of the following is an essential amino acid? **[Kerala CEE]**

(a) Methionine (b) Tyrosine
(c) Proline (d) Glycine
(e) Alanine

8 The one letter code for the amino acid tryptophan is **[Kerala CEE]**

(a) G (b) V (c) W
(d) H (e) A

2013

9 Subunit present in haemoglobin are **[AIIMS]**

(a) 2 (b) 3 (c) 4 (d) 5

10 Assertion (A) Haemoglobin is an oxygen carrier
Reason (R) Oxygen binds as O_2^- to Fe of haemoglobin.

(a) Both A and R are correct and R is correct explanation of A **[AIIMS]**
(b) Both A and R are correct but R is not the correct explanation of A
(c) A is correct but R is incorrect
(d) Both A and R are incorrect

11 Assertion (A) Glycosides are hydrolysed in acidic conditions.
Reason (R) Glycosides are acetals. **[AIIMS]**

(a) Both A and R are correct and R is correct explanation of A
(b) Both A and R are correct but R are not the correct explanation of A
(c) A is correct but R is incorrect
(d) Both A and R are incorrect

12 The linkage present in proteins and peptides is **[UP CPMT]**

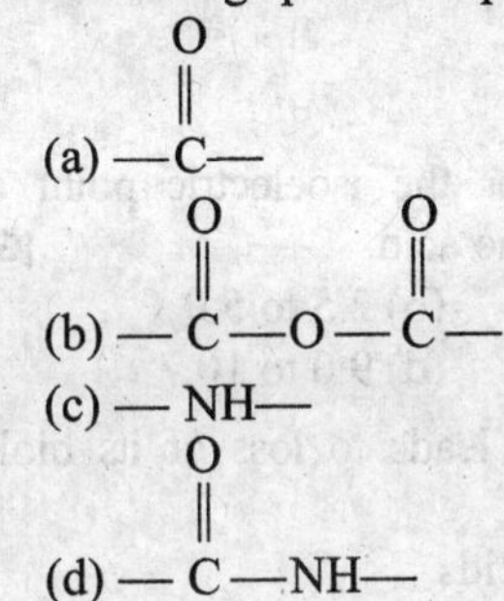

2012

13 Interferon is **[WB JEE]**

(a) the commercial name given to a tonic containing iron
(b) an alloy of iron and chromium used in space vessels
(c) a protein derived from the body against viruses
(d) a trade name of a potent insecticide

14 Which one of the following statements is incorrect about enzyme catalysts? **[CBSE AIPMT]**

(a) Enzymes are mostly protein as in nature
(b) Enzyme action is specific
(c) Enzymes are denatured by ultraviolet rays and at high temperature
(d) Enzymes are least reactive at optimum temperature

15 The enzymes which have control site in addition to active site are called **[AFMC]**

(a) holozymes (b) coenzymes
(c) apoenzymes (d) allosteric enzymes

2011

16 In an alkaline medium, glycine predominantly exists as/in a/an **[KCET]**
(a) cation (b) anion
(c) Zwitter ion (d) covalent form

17 Which one of the following does not correctly match with each other? **[Kerala CEE]**
(a) Silk-polyamide
(b) Lipase-enzyme
(c) Butter-fat
(d) Oxytocin-enzyme

18 Which of the following enzymes is present in animals like cow, buffaloes, etc. to digest compound like paper, cloth, etc.? **[Guj CET]**
(a) Ureaze (b) Cellulase
(c) Silicons (d) Sucrase

2010

19 The pK_{a_1} and pK_{a_2} of an amino acid are 2.3 and 9.7 respectively. The isoelectric point of the amino acid is **[AMU]**
(a) 12.0 (b) 7.4
(c) 6.0 (d) 3.7

20 In alkaline medium, alanine exists predominantly as **[KCET]**
(a) anion
(b) Zwitter ion
(c) cation
(d) covalent form

21 Give the pOH range for the isoelectric point of the amphoteric ion of an amino acid **[Guj CET]**
(a) 5.5 to 6.3 (b) 2.5 to 5.0
(c) 7.7 to 8.5 (d) 9.0 to 10.7

22 Denaturation of proteins leads to loss of its biological activity by **[JCECE]**
(a) formation of amino acids
(b) loss of primary structure
(c) loss of both primary and secondary structures
(d) loss of both secondary and tertiary structures

2009

23 Sanger's reagent is used for the identification of **[OJEE, Manipal]**
(a) C-terminal amino acid of peptide chain
(b) N-terminal amino acid of peptide chain
(c) molecular mass of protein
(d) secondary structure of protein

24 The structural feature that distinguishes proline from other amino acids are **[OJEE]**
(a) it is a secondary amine
(b) it contains an anhydride group
(c) it is a tertiary amine
(d) it exists as cyclic amide

25 The end product in the following sequence of reaction, **[OJEE]**

(pyrrolidine ring: NH, CHOH) $\xrightarrow{LiAlH_4}$ $\xrightarrow{PCl_5}$ $\xrightarrow{NaCN}$ $\xrightarrow{H_3O^+}$

(a) (pyrrolidine ring: NH, CHOH–COOH)
(b) (pyrrolidine ring: NH, –CH₂CH₂–COOH)
(c) (pyrrolidine ring: NH, –CH₂–COOH)
(d) (pyrrolidine ring: NH, CHCl–COOH)

26 A peptide hormone is **[Kerala CEE]**
(a) estrogen (b) testosterone (c) insulin (d) corticoid
(e) progesterone

27 How many tripeptides can be prepared by linking the amino acids glycine, alanine and phenyl alanine? **[EAMCET]**
(a) One (b) Three
(c) Six (d) Twelve

28 There are 20 naturally occurring amino acids. The maximum number of tripeptides that can be obtained are **[KCET]**
(a) 6470 (b) 7465 (c) 5360 (d) 8000

2008

29 Assertion (A) Disruption of the natural structure of a protein is called denaturation.
Reason (R) The change in colour and appearance of precipitates during cooking of an egg is due to denaturation. **[AIIMS]**
(a) Both A and R are correct and R is the correct explanation of A
(b) Both A and R are correct but R is not the correct explanation of A.
(c) A is correct but R is incorrect
(d) Both A and R are incorrect

30 Which of the following exists as *Zwitter* ion? **[Kerala CEE]**
(a) *p*-aminophenol (b) Sulphanilic acid
(c) Salicylic acid (d) Ethanolamine
(e) *p*-amino acetophenone

31 The α-amino acid which does not give purple colour in the ninhydrin test is **[J&K CET]**
(a) proline (b) glycine
(c) lysine (d) aspartic acid

32 Proteins when heated with conc. HNO_3 give a yellow colour. This is **[AMU]**
(a) oxidising test (b) xanthoprotic test
(c) Hoppe's test (d) acid-base test

33 Functionality of protein depends on **[DUMET]**
(a) its shape and structure (b) pH of medium
(c) temperature (d) All of these

34 The number of disulphide linkages present in insulin are **[KCET]**
(a) 1 (b) 2
(c) 3 (d) 4

35 The compound which give a positive ninhydrin test and a negative Benedict's solution test is **[MHT CET]**
(a) a monosaccharide (b) a disaccharide
(c) a lipid (d) a protein

2007

36 Which of the following does not exist as a *Zwitter* ion? **[AIIMS]**
(a) Glycine (b) Glutamic acid
(c) Sulphanilic acid (d) *p*-amino benzoic acid

37 Which one of the following structures represents the peptide chain? **[Manipal]**

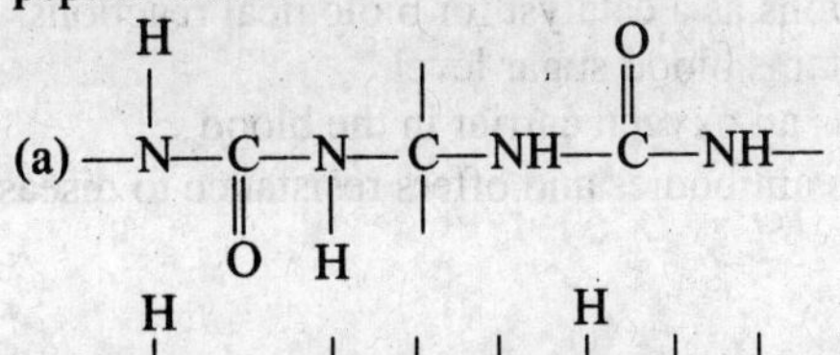

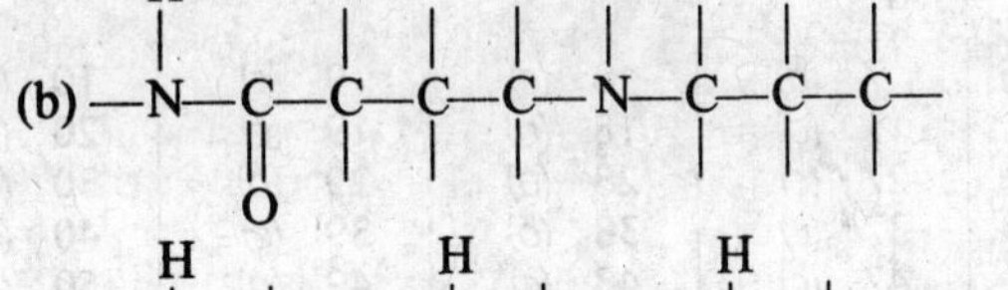

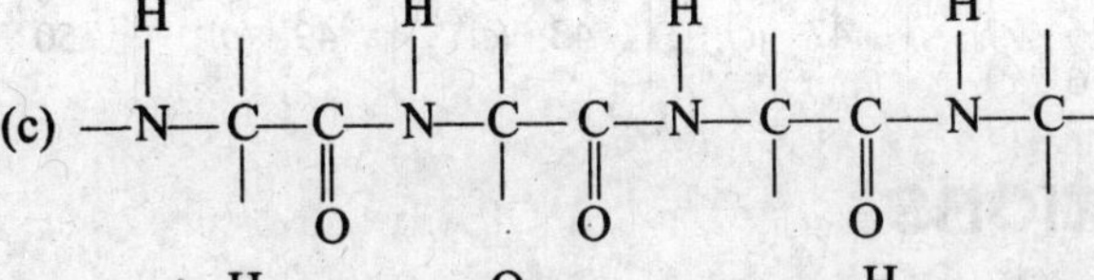

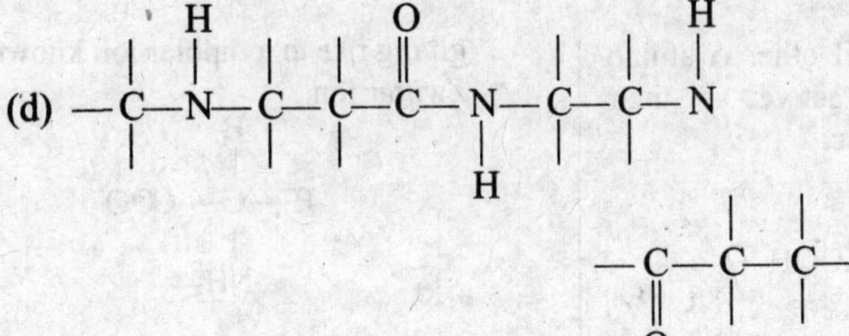

38 The helical structure of protein is stabilised by **[Manipal]**
(a) dipeptide bonds (b) hydrogen bonds
(c) ether bonds (d) peptide bonds

39 Which one of the following statements about amino acids is not true? **[Kerala CEE]**
(a) They are constituents of all proteins
(b) They are all high melting solids
(c) Most naturally occurring amino acids have D-configuration
(d) They are characterised by isoelectric point
(e) Glycine is the only naturally occurring amino acid which is optically inactive

40 The only amino acid which is non chiral, is **[Haryana PMT]**
(a) lysine (b) proline
(c) glycine (d) histidine

41 Polypeptides having molecular weights, above 10000 are known as **[J&K CET]**
(a) amino acids (b) hormones
(c) proteins (d) terminal amino acide

42 Enzymes are made up of **[Punjab PMET]**
(a) edible proteins
(b) proteins with specific structure
(c) nitrogen containing carbohydrates
(d) carbohydrates

43 Which is not a true statement? **[Punjab PMET]**
(a) α-carbon of α-amino acid is asymmetric
(b) All proteins are found in L-form
(c) Human body can synthesise all proteins they need
(d) At pH = 7, both amino acid and carboxylic groups exist in ionised form

44 Which one of the following is a conjugated protein?
(a) Phosphoprotein (b) Glycoprotein **[BCECE]**
(c) Chromoprotein (d) All of these

45 Protein gives blue colour with **[MHT CET]**
(a) Benedict reagent (b) iodine solution
(c) ninhydrin (d) biuret

2006

46 During the process of digestion, the proteins present in food materials are hydrolysed to amino acids. The two enzymes *A* and *B*, involved in the process

$$\text{Proteins} \xrightarrow{\text{Enzyme }(A)} \text{Polypeptides} \xrightarrow{\text{Enzyme }(B)} \text{Amino acids,}$$

are respectively **[CBSE AIPMT]**
(a) amylase and maltase (b) diastase and lipase
(c) pepsin and trypsin (d) invertase and zymase

47 Among the following, L-serine is **[AIIMS]**

(a) Fischer projection: top CO_2H; left H_2N; right CH_2OH; bottom H

(b) Fischer projection: top CO_2H; left HOH_2C; right H; bottom NH_2

(c) Fischer projection: top NH_2; left H; right CO_2H; bottom CH_2OH

(d) Fischer projection: top CH_2OH; left H_2N; right H; bottom CO_2H

48 Lysine is least soluble in water in the pH range **[AIIMS]**
(a) 3-4 (b) 5-6 (c) 6-7 (d) 8-9

49 On treatment with ninhydrin which of the following give, blue colour? **[UP CPMT]**
(a) Proteins (b) Peptides
(c) α-amino acids (d) All of these

50 Among the following amino acids which can be synthesised in the body is **[Kerala CEE]**
(a) lysine (b) leucine
(c) valine (d) phenyl alanine
(e) alanine

2005

51 Which functional group participates in disulphide bond formation in proteins? **[CBSE AIPMT]**
(a) Thiolactone (b) Thiol
(c) Thioether (d) Thioester

52 Which of the following test is not used for testing of proteins? **[AMU]**
(a) Millon's test (b) Molisch's test
(c) Biuret test (d) Ninhydrin test

53 An example of a sulphur containing amino acid is **[KCET]**
(a) lysine (b) serine
(c) cysteine (d) tyrosine

54 Which of the following is an amphoteric acid? **[KCET]**
(a) Glycine
(b) Salicylic acid
(c) Benzoic acid
(d) Citric acid

55 The product formed in the reaction of glycine with benzoyl chloride + aq. NaOH is **[V&K CET]**
(a) $PhCOCH_2NH_2$
(b) $PhCH_2NH_2$
(c) $PhCONHCH_3$
(d) $PhCONHCH_2CO_2H$

56 The correct statement in respect of protein haemoglobin is that it **[Manipal]**
(a) functions as a catalyst for biological reactions
(b) maintains blood sugar level
(c) acts as an oxygen carrier in the blood
(d) forms antibodies and offers resistance to diseases

Answers

1 (d)	2 (b)	3 (b)	4 (a)	5 (d)	6 (b)	7 (a)	8 (c)	9 (c)	10 (c)
11 (d)	12 (d)	13 (c)	14 (d)	15 (b)	16 (b)	17 (d)	18 (b)	19 (c)	20 (a)
21 (c)	22 (d)	23 (b)	24 (a)	25 (c)	26 (c)	27 (c)	28 (d)	29 (b)	30 (b)
31 (a)	32 (b)	33 (d)	34 (b)	35 (d)	36 (d)	37 (c)	38 (b)	39 (c)	40 (c)
41 (c)	42 (b)	43 (b)	44 (d)	45 (c)	46 (c)	47 (c)	48 (c)	49 (a)	50 (e)
51 (b)	52 (b)	53 (c)	54 (a)	55 (d)	56 (c)				

Explanations

1 (*d*) The amino acids that are not synthesised in human body and must be obtained from our diet are essential amino acids. Tryptophan is an example of essential amino acids.
Therefore, both Assertion and Reason are incorrect.

2 (*b*) The loss in biological activity of proteins due to unfolding of globules and uncoiling of helix is called denaturation of proteins. During the denaturation, primary structure remains intact but secondary and tertiary structures are destroyed. E.g. the coagulation of egg white on boiling, curdling of milk caused by bacteria due to formation of lactic acid.

3 (*b*) Alanine is a non-essential amino acid while leucine, lysine and valine are essential amino acid. Non-essential amino acids are synthesised in the body.

4 (*a*) Except glycine, all other α-amino acids are optically active as their α-carbon is asymmetric.

$$H-\overset{\displaystyle H}{\underset{\displaystyle NH_2}{\overset{|}{\underset{|}{C}}}}-COOH$$

Glycine

Thus, glycine is optically inactive.

5 (*d*) Ion containing positive as well as negative charge is called *Zwitter* ion. Among the given options, only glycine (H_2N-CH_2-COOH) is an amino acid which contains both acidic (acquiring negative charge) and basic group (acquiring positive charge). Therefore, glycine can form a *Zwitter* ion. It is because glycine behave like salt rather than simple amines or carboxylic acids. In aqueous solution, the carboxyl group can lose a proton and amino group can accept a proton giving rise to a dipolar ion known as *Zwitter* ion.

$$H-\overset{\displaystyle H}{\underset{\displaystyle \overset{+}{NH_3}}{\overset{|}{\underset{|}{C}}}}-COO^-$$

Zwitter ion

Zwitter ion is a cation in acidic medium and migrates to cathode on passing electric current. It is an anion in basic medium and migrates to anode on passing electric current.

$$\underset{\text{Anion in basic medium}}{H-\underset{\displaystyle NH_2}{\underset{|}{CH}}-COO^-} \xleftarrow{\overline{O}H} H-\underset{\displaystyle \overset{+}{NH_3}}{\underset{|}{CH}}-COO^- \xrightarrow{H^+} \underset{\text{Cation in acidic medium}}{H-\underset{\displaystyle \overset{+}{NH_3}}{\underset{|}{CH}}-COOH}$$

6 (*b*) Two amino acids in a protein are linked by a peptide bond.

E.g. glycylalanine is formed when carboxyl group of glycine combines with the amino group of alanine.

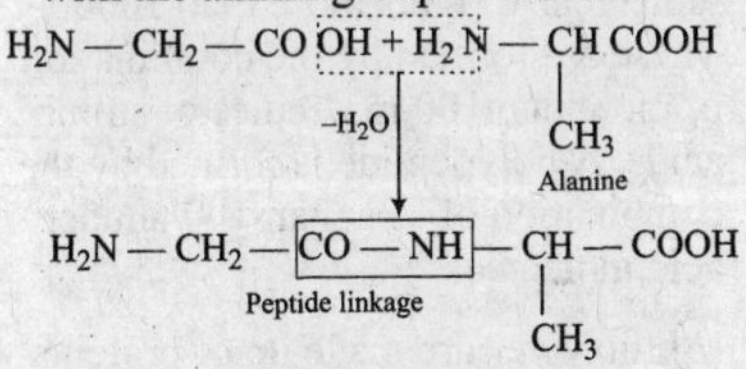

$$H_2N-CH_2-CO\,OH + H_2N-\underset{\underset{\text{Alanine}}{CH_3}}{CH}\,COOH \xrightarrow{-H_2O} H_2N-CH_2-\underbrace{CO-NH}_{\text{Peptide linkage}}-\underset{CH_3}{CH}-COOH$$

Glycylalanine (Gly-ala)

7 (*a*) Among the given amino acids, methionine $[CH_3SCH_2CH_2CH(NH_2)COOH]$ is an essential amino acid because it cannot be synthesised by our body and hence, its presence is necessary in our diet.

8 (*c*)

Letter code	Amino acid
G	Glycine
V	Valine
W	Tryptophan
H	Histidine
A	Alanine

Thus, W is the letter code of tryptophan. The structure of tryptophan is as follows:

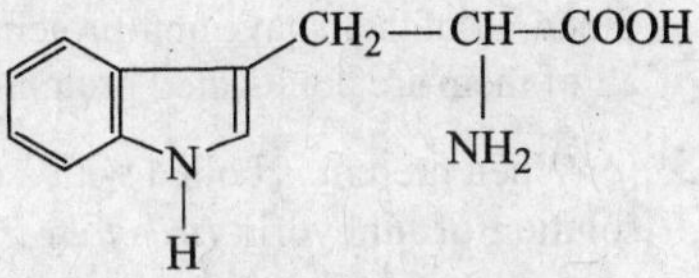

(Indole ring with N–H) $-CH_2-\underset{NH_2}{CH}-COOH$

9 (*c*) One molecule of haemoglobin has four heme groups and each of them can take up one molecule of oxygen. Thus, one molecule of haemoglobin can combine with four molecules of O_2 to form oxyhaemoglobin.

10 (*c*) Haemoglobin is an O_2-carrier, so assertion is right, but the reason that O_2 binds as O_2^- to Fe is wrong, because O_2 binds to Fe of haem part to form oxyhaemoglobin. One molecule of haemoglobin (Hb) binds with four molecules of O_2.

11 (*d*) Glycosides are formed by treating glucose with methanol in the presence of dry HCl gas. They cannot be hydrolysed in acidic medium. Also, they are hemiacetals and not acetals.

Hence both, Assertion and Reason are false.

12 (*d*) The bond formed between adjacent carboxyl (— COOH) and amino $(-NH_2)$ groups with the elimination of water molecule is called a 'peptide bond'. All proteins and peptides contain peptide linkage.

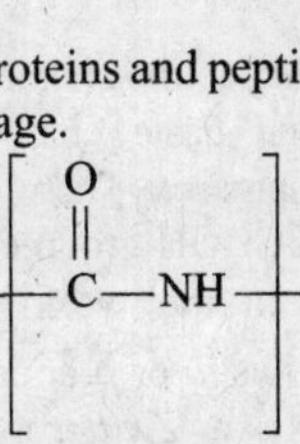

$$\left[\begin{array}{c} O \\ \| \\ -C-NH- \end{array}\right]$$

The reaction of formation of a peptide bond is shown below.

$$\underset{\text{Amino acid}}{H_2NCH(R)-COOH} + \underset{\text{Amino acid}}{H-NH-CH_2COOH} \xrightarrow{-H_2O} -H_2NCH(R)-\underbrace{CO-NH}_{\text{Peptide bond}}-CH_2COOH$$

13 (*c*) Interferon is a protein which is derived from the body against viruses.

14 (*d*) Most of the enzymes are protein in nature. They are highly specific and get denatured at high temperature, or by UV-rays. At optimum temperature, which is generally in between 25°C – 35°C, enzyme activity is maximum.

15 (*b*) A coenzyme is a substance that works with an enzyme to initiate or aid the function of enzyme. They act as control site and active sites.

16 (*b*) In alkaline medium, glycine predominently exists as an anion.

$$\overset{+}{H_3N}-CH_2-COO^- + OH^- \longrightarrow \underset{\text{Anion}}{H_2\ddot{N}-CH_2-COO^-} + H_2O$$

17 (*d*) Oxytocin-enzyme is not a correct match. Oxytocin is a hormone. It is not an enzyme.

18 (*b*) Chemically paper and cloth consists of cellulose. In plant eating animals, digestion of cellulose takes place in presence of enzyme cellulase.

19 (*c*) Isoelectric point of amino acid

$$= \frac{pK_{a_1} + pK_{a_2}}{2} = \frac{2.3 + 9.7}{2} = \frac{12}{2} = 6.0$$

20 (*a*) In alkaline medium, alanine exists as anion.

$$\underset{\text{Alanine}}{CH_3-\underset{COOH}{CH}-NH_2} \xrightarrow[\text{(pH > 7)}]{\text{Basic medium}} CH_3\underset{COO^-}{CH}-NH_2$$

21 (*c*) The pH at which a particular amino acid does not migrate under the influence of an electric field is called isoelectric point of that amino acid. The pH range for the isoelectric point is from 5.5 to 6.3 or the pOH range for the isoelectric point is from 7.7 to 8.5.

22 (*d*) Upon heating, the proteins get coagulated. This process is called denaturation of proteins. During this process, the secondary and tertiary structures get destroyed but primary structure remains intact.

23 (*b*) The Sanger's reagent is FDNB.

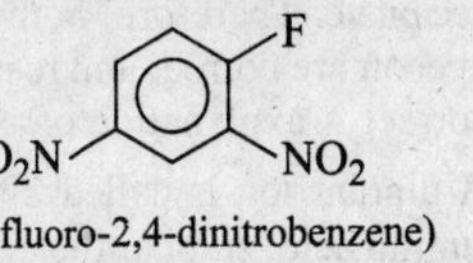

(Benzene ring with F, O_2N and NO_2 substituents)

(1-fluoro-2,4-dinitrobenzene)

It reacts with N-terminal amino acid of peptide chain.

24 (*a*)

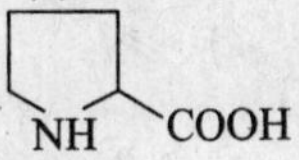

(Pyrrolidine ring, NH, with COOH) , from this structure, it is a secondary amine.

Proline

25 (*c*)

(Pyrrolidine NH)–COOH $\xrightarrow{LiAlH_4}$ (Pyrrolidine NH)–CH_2OH $\xrightarrow{PCl_5}$ (Pyrrolidine NH)–CH_2Cl $\xrightarrow[-Cl]{NaCN}$ (Pyrrolidine NH)–CH_2CN $\xrightarrow{H_3O^+}$ (Pyrrolidine NH)–CH_2COOH

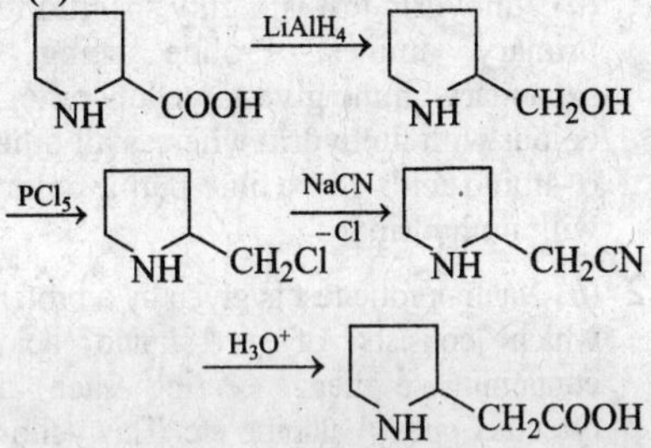

26 (*c*) Insulin contains two polypeptide chains with 21 and 30 amino acids which are joined together by sulphur bridges. Hence, it is a peptide hormone. All other given hormones are examples of steroid hormones.

27 (*c*) Tripeptides are amino acid polymers in which three individual amino acid units, called residues, are linked together by amide bonds. In these, an amino group from one residue forms an amide bond with the carboxyl group of a second residue, the amino group of the second forms an amide bond with the carboxyl group of the third.

Therefore, glycine (NH_2-CH_2-COOH), alanine $(CH_3-\underset{NH_2}{CH}-COOH)$ and phenyl alanine $\left(C_6H_5-CH_2-\underset{NH_2}{CH}COOH\right)$ can be linked in six different ways.

28 (*d*) Since, there are 20 naturally occurring amino acids.

Hence, maximum number of tripeptides that can be obtained are = $(20)^3 = 8000$.

29 (*b*) Due to denaturation, a protein loses its biological activity. In this process, the protein molecule uncoils and forms a more random conformation and precipitates from the solution. Egg is a protein. On heating, it changes colour and appearance of precipitate. Therefore, both assertion and reason are correct and reason is not the correct A explanation of assertion.

30 (*b*) A dipolar ion is called *Zwitter* ion, e.g. amino acid, sulphanilic acid, etc.

$$\text{Sulphanilic acid } (H_2N-C_6H_4-SO_3H) \rightleftharpoons \text{Zwitter ion } (H_3N^+-C_6H_4-SO_3^-)$$

31 (*a*) Ninhydrin test is highly specific for primary amines. Proline being a secondary amine gives a yellow orange colour with ninhydrin whereas all other α-amino acids give a blue-purple colour with ninhydrin.

32 (*b*) Xanthoprotic test is given by a protein which consists of α-amino acids containing a benzene ring such as tyrosine, phenyl alanine etc. This yellow colour is due to nitration of benzene ring and this colour is same as that which forms on skin when conc. HNO_3 comes in contact.

$$\text{Protein} + \text{conc. } HNO_3 \longrightarrow \text{Yellow colour}$$

33 (*d*) Functionality of protein depends on the shape and structure, pH of medium and temperature.

34 (*b*) Insulin is composed of two peptide chains referred to as the chain *A* and chain *B*. Chain *A* consists of 21 residues and chain *B* of 30 residues are cross-linked by two disulphide bridges.

35 (*d*) Only, proteins give positive ninhydrin test. They give blue colour with ninhydrin. Proteins do not respond to Benedict's test.

36 (*d*) *o* and *p*-aminobenzoic acids do not exist as a *Zwitter* ion. The lone pair of electrons on the $-NH_2$ group is delocalised over the benzene ring due to resonance effect.

As a result, acidic character of —COOH group and basic character of $-NH_2$ group decreases. Therefore, the weakly acidic —COOH group cannot transfer a H^+ ion to the weakly basic $-NH_2$ group. Thus, *o* or *p*-aminobenzoic acids do not exist as *Zwitter* ion.

o-amino benzoic acid (COOH and NH_2 on adjacent ring carbons); *p*-amino benzoic acid (COOH and NH_2 on opposite ring carbons)

37 (*c*) The peptide linkage (—NH—CO—) is formed by the condensation of amino acid molecules.

$$\text{HNH}-\underset{R}{\text{CH}}-\underset{\|O}{\text{C}}-\text{OH} + \text{H}-\text{NH}-\underset{R}{\text{CH}}-\underset{\|O}{\text{C}}-\text{OH} \longrightarrow$$

$$-\text{HN}-\underset{R}{\text{CH}}-\underbrace{\underset{\|O}{\text{C}}-\text{NH}}_{\text{Peptide linkage}}-\underset{R}{\text{CH}}-\underset{\|O}{\text{C}}-$$

Hence, following structure represents the peptide chain.

$$-\overset{H}{N}-\overset{H}{C}-\underset{\|O}{C}-\overset{H}{N}-C-\underset{\|O}{C}-\overset{H}{N}$$

$$-C-\overset{O}{\overset{\|}{C}}-\underset{H}{N}-C-$$

38 (*b*) The helical structure of protein is stabilised by hydrogen bonds between amide group of the same peptide chain. These bonds are formed by —NH— group of one unit and oxygen of carbonyl group of the third unit. This H-bonding is responsible for holding helix in a position.

39 (*c*) Amino acids are constituents of all proteins and are high melting solids. They are characterised by isoelectric point. All amino acids are optically active except glycine. Most naturally occurring amino acids have L-configuration.

40 (*c*) Glycine (NH_2-CH_2-COOH) has no chiral carbon atom, so it is optically inactive.

41 (*c*) Proteins are polypeptides with molecular weights more than 10000. These are formed by the combination of more than 100 molecules of amino acids. A polypeptide is formed by the combination of less than 100 amino acid molecules.

42 (*b*) Enzymes are made up of proteins with specific structure and act as a catalyst for biochemical reactions.

43 (*b*) All proteins are not found in *l*-form but they may be present in the form of *d* or *l*. Rest all the other given statements are correct.

44 (*d*) Conjugated proteins on hydrolysis give a non-protein portion alongwith α-amino acid. The non-protein portion is called prosthetic group.

Protein	Prosthetic Group
Phosphoprotein	Lipid (e.g. lecithin)
Glycoprotein	Sugar
Chromoprotein	Colouring matter such as red coloured protophyrin

Since, all of them have non-protein part, all of them are conjugated proteins.

45 (*c*) When protein is boiled with a dilute solution of ninhydrin (*triketohydrin*), a blue colour is produced.

$$\text{Protein} + \text{Ninhydrin solution} \xrightarrow{\Delta} \text{Blue colour}$$

46 (*c*) In the process of digestion, the proteins present in food material are hydrolysed to amino acids. In this process, two enzymes pepsin and trypsin are involved as follows

$$\text{Proteins} \xrightarrow[\text{(Enzyme } A)]{\text{Pepsin}} \text{Polypeptide} \xrightarrow[\text{(Enzyme } B)]{\text{Trypsin}} \text{Amino acid}$$

47 (*c*) Serine is an amino acid and its structure is,

$$HO-CH_2-\underset{NH_2}{CH}-COOH$$

As per exchange rule

$$\text{L-serine is } H-\overset{NH_2}{\underset{CH_2OH}{+}}-COOH$$

48 (*c*) Lysine is α, ∈-diaminocaproic acid.

$$H_2N—CH_2—CH_2—CH_2—CH_2 \\ CH(NH_2)\cdot COOH$$

It is least soluble in water in the pH range 6–7.

49 (*a*) Proteins, peptides and α-amino acids give a characteristic blue colour on treatment with ninhydrin.

50 (*e*) Amino acids which can be synthesised in the body are called non-essential amino acids, e.g. alanine, glycine, proline etc. Amino acids which cannot be synthesised in the body are called essential amino acids, e.g. lysine, valine, leucine, phenyl alanine etc.

So, (e) is the correct answer.

51 (*b*) Disulphide bond may be reduced to thiol by means of reagents such as $NaBH_4$, which shows the presence of thiol group in disulphide bond formation.

52 (*b*) Molisch's test is used for testing the presence of carbohydrate and is not used in testing of protein.

53 (*c*) Structure of cysteine is

$$HSCH_2CH\begin{matrix} NH_2 \\ COOH \end{matrix}$$

∴ It is an example of sulphur containing amino acid.

54 (*a*) Glycine (NH_2CH_2COOH) is an amphoteric acid as it contains both acidic (carboxylate) and basic (amino) groups.

55 (*d*)

$$\underset{\text{Glycine}}{HOOC\cdot CH_2NH_2} + \underset{\text{Benzoyl chloride}}{PhCOCl} \xrightarrow[\Delta]{aq.\ NaOH} \underset{\text{Benzoyl glycine (Hippuric acid)}}{PhCONHCH_2COOH} + HCl$$

56 (*c*) Haemoglobin acts as an oxygen carrier in the blood because four Fe^{2+} ions of each haemoglobin can bind with four molecules of O_2 and form oxyhaemoglobin.

$$4Hb + 4O_2 \longrightarrow \underset{\text{Oxyhaemoglobin}}{Hb_4O_8}$$

Topic 3

Nucleic Acids and Lipids

2017

1 The nitrogen base which is present in RNA and absent in DNA is **[AIIMS]**

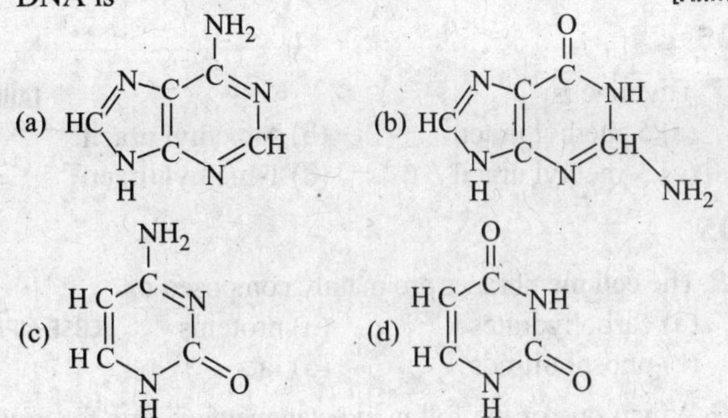

2016

2 The central dogma of molecular genetics states that the genetic information flows from **[NEET, Phase II]**

(a) amino acids → proteins → DNA
(b) DNA → carbohydrates → proteins
(c) DNA → RNA → proteins
(d) DNA → RNA → carbohydrates

3 The correct statement regarding RNA and DNA, respectively is **[NEET]**

(a) The sugar component in RNA is ribose and the sugar component in DNA is 2′-deoxyribose
(b) The sugar component in RNA is arabinose and the sugar component in DNA is ribose
(c) The sugar component in RNA is 2′-deoxyribose and the sugar component in DNA is arabinose
(d) The sugar component in RNA is arabinose and the sugar component in DNA is 2′-deoxyribose

2014

4 Thymine is held by two H-bonds with the base **[UK PMT]**

(a) guanine (b) cytosine
(c) thymine (d) adenine

5 The pair of nitrogenous of bases in DNA are held together by **[Manipal]**

(a) ionic bonds
(b) H-bond
(c) phosphate group
(d) deoxyribose group

2012

6 A codon has a sequence of *A* and specifies a particular *B* that is to be incorporated into *C*. What are *A*, *B*, *C*? **[Manipal]**

	A	*B*	*C*
(a)	3 bases	Amino acid	Carbohydrate
(b)	3 acids	Carbohydrate	Protein
(c)	3 bases	Protein	Amino acid
(d)	3 bases	Amino acid	Protein

2011

7 Which is not the correct statement about RNA and DNA? **[DUMET]**

(a) DNA is active in virus whereas RNA never appears in virus
(b) DNA exists as dimer while RNA is usually single-stranded
(c) DNA contains deoxyribose as its sugar and RNA contains ribose
(d) RNA contains uracil in place of thymine (found in DNA) as a base

2010

8 The digestion of fats in the intestine is aided by [BVP]
(a) diffusion (b) protection
(c) peptisation (d) emulsification

9 Drying oil invariably contains [Manipal]
(a) linoleic acid (b) lauric acid
(c) stearic acid (d) butyric acid

10 Iodine value is related to [AFNC]
(a) fats and oils (b) alcohols
(c) esters (d) hydrocarbons

11 In the following which is not glyceride? [MP PMT]
(a) Fats (b) Oils (c) Phospholipids (d) Soaps

12 The transfer RNA anticodon for the messenger RNA codon G—C—A is [AMU]
(a) C—G—U (b) G—C—U
(c) U—G—C (d) G—U—C

13 Which one of the following statements is true? [KCET]
(a) Saponification of oil yields a diol
(b) Drying of oil involves hydrolysis
(c) Addition of antioxidant to oil minimises rancidity
(d) Refining of oil involves hydrogenation

14 From which group the fats belong? [MHT CET]
(a) Carboxylic acids (b) Carbonyl
(c) Ester (d) Fatty acids

15 Among the following, the formula of saturated fatty acid is [MHT CET]
(a) $C_{17}H_{29}COOH$ (b) $C_{17}H_{35}COOH$
(c) $C_{17}H_{31}COOH$ (d) $C_{17}H_{33}COOH$

16 The common names of the lower fatty acids are obtained from [MHT CET]
(a) their parent hydrocarbon
(b) their reduction product
(c) the sources from which they are obtained
(d) IUPAC system

2009

17 The segment of DNA which acts as the instrumental manual for the synthesis of proteins [CBSE AIPMT]
(a) nucleotides (b) ribose
(c) gene (d) nucleoside

18 The base found only in the nucleotides of RNA, is [AFMC]
(a) adenine (b) uracil (c) guanine (d) cytosine

19 Which of the following contributes to the double helical structure of DNA? [WB JEE]
(a) Hydrogen bond (b) Covalent bond
(c) Disulphide bond (d) van der Waals' force

20 The one which has least iodine value is [KCET]
(a) ginger oil (b) ghee
(c) groundnut oil (d) sunflower oil

21 Hardening of oil is done by [MHT CET]
(a) dehydrogenation (b) hydrogenation
(c) dehydrohalogenation (d) dehydration

2008

22 In DNA, the complementary bases are [CBSE AIPMT]
(a) adenine and thymine; guanine and cytosine
(b) adenine and thymine; guanine and uracil
(c) adenine and guanine, thymine and cytosine
(d) uracil and adenine; cytosine and guanine

23 If one strand of DNA has the sequence ATGCTTGA, the sequence in the compleme ntary strand would be
(a) TCCGAACT (b) TACGTAGT [Kerala CEE]
(c) TACGAACT (d) TACGTAGT
(e) TACGAATC

24 Which of the following is not present in a nucleotide?
(a) Cytosine (b) Guanine [DUMET]
(c) Adenine (d) Tyrosine

25 A base-sugar phosphate unit in nucleic acid is called
(a) nucleoside (b) phosphotide [Guj CET]
(c) nucleotide (d) None of the above

2007

26 A sequence of how many nucleotides in messenger RNA makes a codon for an amino acid? [Manipal]
(a) Three (b) Four (c) One (d) Two

2006

27 Thymine is [AIIMS]
(a) 5-methyl uracil (b) 4-methyl uracil
(c) 3-methyl uracil (d) 1-methyl uracil

2005

28 The cell membranes are mainly composed of
(a) carbohydrates (b) proteins [CBSE AIPMT]
(c) phospholipids (d) fats

29 Which one of the following statements is true for protein synthesis (translation)? [AIIMS]
(a) Amino acids are directly recognised by *m*-RNA
(b) The third base of the codon is less specific
(c) Only one codon codes for an amino acid
(d) Every *t*RNA molecule has more than one amino acid attachment

30 The phenomenon of mutation is [RPMT]
(a) chemical change in DNA molecule
(b) production of macromolecules
(c) synthesis of micromolecules
(d) invasion of foreign microorganism

31 The process used in conversion of triolein to tristearin is
(a) hydrolysis (b) hydration [MHT CET]
(c) hydrogenation (d) dehydrogenation

Answers

1 (d)	2 (c)	3 (a)	4 (d)	5 (b)	6 (d)	7 (a)	8 (d)	9 (a)	10 (a)
11 (d)	12 (a)	13 (c)	14 (c)	15 (b)	16 (c)	17 (c)	18 (b)	19 (a)	20 (b)
21 (b)	22 (a)	23 (c)	24 (d)	25 (c)	26 (a)	27 (a)	28 (c)	29 (b)	30 (a)
31 (c)									

Explanations

1 (*d*) The four bases present in DNA are adenine (A), guanine (G), cytosine (C) and thymine (T). In RNA, uracil (U) is present in place of thymine (T). Structure of all these, bases are given below :

Adenine (A) Guanine (G)

Cytosine (C) Thymine (T)

Uracil (U)

2 (*c*) The central dogma of molecular genetics states that

$$DNA \xrightarrow{\text{Transcription}} RNA \xrightarrow{\text{Translation}} \text{Proteins}$$

3 (*a*) In DNA, two helically twisted strands are connected together by hydrogen bonding. Each strand consists of alternating molecules of deoxyribose at 2′-position and phosphate groups.

∴ The sugar component is 2′-deoxyribose.

On the other hand, in RNA, the pentose sugar has an identical structure with deoxyribose sugar except that there is an —OH group present instead of —H on carbon atom 2′.

Hence, it is only called ribose.

4 (*d*) Two nucleic acid chains are bound about each other and held together by H-bonds between pair of bases. Adenine forms two H-bonds with thymine, whereas cytosine forms three H-bonds with guanine.

i.e. $\underset{\text{2H-bonds}}{A = T}$; $\underset{\text{3H-bonds}}{C \equiv G}$

5 (*b*) The pair of nitrogenous bases in DNA are held with each other by H-bond.

6 (*d*) A codon is a specific sequence of **three adjacent bases** on a strand of DNA or RNA that provides genetic code information for a particular **amino acid**, that is to be incorporated into **protein**.

7 (*a*) A retrovirus is a RNA virus that is duplicated in a host cell.

∴ Statement (a) is incorrect and rest all statement are correct.

8 (*d*) Emulsification aids the digestion of fats in intestine.

9 (*a*) Unsaturated fatty acids such as linoleic acid, are present in drying oil.

10 (*a*) Iodine value is used to find degree of unsaturation in fats and oils. (Higher the iodine value, more unsaturated is the oil or fat).

11 (*d*) The fats and oils are triesters of glycerol with higher fatty acids like palmitic acid, stearic acid, oleic acid etc. and thus, known as glycerides. Phospholipids are phosphorus containing lipids similar to glycerides. Whereas, soaps are sodium and potassium salts of higher fatty acids like stearic acid, palmitic acid, oleic acid etc.

12 (*a*) The transfer RNA anticodon for the messenger RNA codon G—C—A is C—G—U.

∵ C (cytosine) forms triple bond with G (guanine) and A (adenine) forms double bond with U (uracil).

13 (*c*) Saponification of oils yields a triol (glycerol). Drying (hardening) of oil involves hydrogenation. Refining of oil is done by distillation or other such processes but not by hydrogenation. Antioxidants are added to prevent the oxidation of oil, thus they minimise rancidity.

14 (*c*) Fats are obtained by the reaction of glycerol (an alcohol) with different long chain carboxylic acids. Hence, chemically these are carboxylic esters or simply esters and also known as glycerides.

15 (*b*) The general formula for saturated fatty acids is $C_nH_{2n+1}COOH$. Among the given acids, only $C_{17}H_{35}COOH$ satisfies this formula.

Hence, it is a saturated fatty acid.

16 (*c*) The common names of lower fatty acids are obtained from the sources from which they are obtained, e.g. formic acid (HCOOH) gets its name from red ant (Latin *formica*), from which it is obtained.

17 (*c*) Each segment of a DNA molecule, which codes for a specific protein or polypeptide is called a gene and every protein in a cell has a corresponding gene. The relationship between the nucleotide triplets and the amino acids is called the genetic code.

18 (*b*) Nucleotide contains sugar + base + phosphate. The bases present in RNA are adenine, guanine, uracil and cytosine while the bases present in DNA are adenine, guanine, thymine and cytosine. Hence, uracil is the base which is found only in the nucleotide of RNA.

19 (*a*) In double helical structure of DNA, the complementary base pairs (A=T and G≡C) are linked through hydrogen bond.

20 (*b*) The degree of unsaturation of a fat or oil is measured by its iodine number which is defined as the number of grams of iodine that would add to carbon-carbon double bonds (C=C) present in 100 g of the fat or oil. Hence, greater the number of double bonds in the acid residues of a triglyceride, greater will be the iodine number. Because a saturated fatty acidhas no double bonds, it takes up no iodine, thus its iodine number is zero.

Among the given options, ghee has the least iodine value as it is saturated whereas the other compounds contain some degree of unsaturation.

21 (*b*) $\underset{\text{(Unsaturated)}}{\text{Oil}} \xrightarrow{\text{Hydrogenation}} \underset{\text{(Saturated)}}{\text{Ghee}}$

This is called hardening of oil.

22 (*a*) Deoxyribonucleic acid (DNA) has the purine bases adenine and guanine and pyrimidine bases thymine and cytosine. According to base pairing rule, adenine pairs with thymine (A=T) and cytosine pairs with guanine (C≡G).

23 (*c*) In DNA, adenine (A) and thymine (T) are joined by two hydrogen bonds while guanine (G) and cytosine (C) are joined by three hydrogen bonds. No other combination of four bases is possible. Hence, the sequence of complementary strand is TACGAACT.

24 (*d*) Nucleotide contains nitrogenous bases like adenine, guanine, thymine, cytosine and uracil, so tyrosine is not present in nucleotide.

25 (*c*) Only two basic components of nucleic acid (pentose sugar, and a nitrogenous base) are present in nucleoside and all the three basic components of nucleic acid (a phosphoric acid group, a pentose sugar and a nitrogeneous base) are present in nucleotide.

26 (*a*) A sequence of three nucleotides in messenger RNA makes a codon for an amino acid because four bases in messenger RNA i.e. adenine, cytosine, guanine and uracil have been shown to act in the form of triplet.

27 (*a*) Thymine is an amino acid. It is found when C-5 position of uracil is substituted by methyl group so, it is 5-methyl uracil.

28 (*c*) The cell membranes are mainly composed of phospholipids.

29 (*b*) The triplet of nucleotide having a specific sequence of bases is known as codon. Each codon specifies one amino acid. More than one codon can specify same amino acids. According to Wobble hypothesis proposed by FHC Crick, third base of a codon is not very important and specificity of a codon is particularly determined by first two bases. *m*RNA is involved in copying sequences of bases from DNA strand to RNA molecule.

30 (*a*) The mutation is a chemical change in a DNA molecule responsible for the synthesis of proteins with different amino acid sequences.

31 (*c*) Triolein is unsaturated triglyceride while tristearin is saturated glyceride. Thus, hydrogenation (addition of hydrogen) of triolein converts it into tristearin.

Topic 4

Vitamins and Hormones

2017

1 Which of the following statement(s) is/are not correct? **[NEET]**

(a) Insulin maintains sugar level in the blood of a human body
(b) Ovalbumin is a simple food reserve in egg white
(c) Blood proteins thrombin and fibrinogen are involved in blood clotting
(d) Denaturation makes the proteins more active

2014

2 Cheilosis and digestive disorders are due to the deficiency of **[Kerala CET]**

(a) Vitamin A (b) Thiamine
(c) Riboflavin (d) Ascorbic acid
(e) Pyridoxine

3 Metal ion responsible for the minamata disease is **[WB JEE]**

(a) Co^{2+} (b) Hg^{2+} (c) Cu^{2+} (d) Zn^{2+}

4 Which one of the following sets of vitamins is fat soluble? **[EAMCET]**

(a) C, D, B_6, B_{12} (b) A, D, E, K
(c) A, D, B_1, B_2 (d) D, B_1, B_2, E

2010

5 The human body does not produce **[WB JEE]**

(a) enzymes (b) vitamins
(c) proteins (d) nucleic acids

6 Vitamin C is **[WB JEE, AFMC]**

(a) citric acid (b) lactic acid
(c) paracetamol (d) ascorbic acid

7 Insulin, a hormone, chemically is **[Manipal]**

(a) fat (b) steroid (c) protein (d) carbohydrate

8 The only vitamin with metal atom in it, is **[RPMT]**

(a) vitamin A (b) vitamin K
(c) vitamin B_{12} (d) vitamin E

9 The night blindness is developed due to shortage of which vitamin? **[MP PMT]**

(a) Vitamin B_6 (b) Vitamin C
(c) Vitamin B_{12} (d) Vitamin A

10 Identify the vitamin whose deficiency causes pernicious anaemia in humans. **[Haryana PMT]**

(a) vitmain B_1 (b) vitamin B_{12}
(c) vitamin B_2 (d) vitamin K

11 Compare vitamin (column I) with its deficiency disease (column II). **[Guj CET]**

Column I	Column II
A. Vitamin B_{12}	1. Sterility
B. Vitamin B_6	2. Haemorrhagic condition
C. Vitamin E	3. Pernicious anaemia
D. Vitamin K	4. Skin disease

Codes

	A	B	C	D		A	B	C	D
(a)	1	2	3	4	(b)	2	3	4	1
(c)	3	4	2	1	(d)	3	4	1	2

12 The chemical name of vitamin B_1 is **[JCECE]**

(a) ascorbic acid (b) riboflavin
(c) pyridoxine (d) thiamine

2009

13 Which of the following hormones contains iodine? [CBSE AIPMT]
(a) Insulin (b) Testosterone
(c) Adrenaline (d) Thyroxine

14 The hormone that controls the processes like burning of fats, proteins and carbohydrates to liberate energy in the body, is [AIIMS]
(a) cortisone (b) thyroxine
(c) adrenaline (d) insulin

15 Select the incorrect statement, among the following. [AIIMS]
(a) Haemoglobin is soluble in water
(b) α-keratin is soluble in water
(c) Cellulose is a polymer of glucose
(d) Chlorophyll is responsible for the synthesis of carbohydrates in plants

16 The substance with the highest calorific value is [AFMC]
(a) milk (b) rice (c) ghee (d) egg

17 Which of the following statements is not true? [DUMET]
(a) Pheromones are secreted outside the body by the insects
(b) Aspirin is analgesic and antipyretic
(c) Sucrose is a dipeptide commonly known as aspartame
(d) The DNA assists in the synthesis of RNA molecules

18 Which of the following statements is not correct? [DUMET]
(a) Allergic conditions are cured by anti-histamines
(b) Hormones are continuously produced but not stored in the body
(c) The function of the white blood cells is to protect the body against infections
(d) Catabolism involves degradation of molecules

2008

19 Which one of the following is an amine hormone? [CBSE AIPMT]
(a) Thyroxine (b) Oxypurin
(c) Insulin (d) Progesterone

20 The statement which is not correct, is [AIIMS]
(a) chlorophyll is responsible for the synthesis of carbohydrates in plants
(b) the compound formed by the addition of oxygen to haemoglobin is called oxyhaemoglobin
(c) acetyl salicylic acid is known as aspirin
(d) the metal ion present in vitamin B_{12} is Mg^{2+}

21 When oxyhaemoglobin changes to deoxyhaemoglobin, Fe^{2+} ion changes from [Punjab PMET]
(a) diamagnetic to paramagnetic
(b) paramagnetic to diamagnetic
(c) diamagnetic to ferromagnetic
(d) paramagnetic to ferromagnetic

22 Match the following columns.

Column I (Vitamins)		Column II (Chemical name)
A.	B_1	1. Riboflavin
B.	B_2	2. Pantothenic acid
C.	B_3	3. Niacin
D.	B_4	4. Thiamine

[EAMCET]

Codes

	A	B	C	D		A	B	C	D
(a)	4	1	3	2	(b)	4	3	1	2
(c)	3	4	2	1	(d)	4	1	2	3

23 What is the chemical name of the vitamin B_{12}? [Guj CET]
(a) Riboflavin (b) Thiamine
(c) Cyanocobalamine (d) Pyridoxin

24 Which of the following stereoisomers is very active towards the construction of blood vessels? [Guj CET]
(a) (+) adrenaline (b) (–) nicotine
(c) (–) thyroxine (d) S-ibuprofen

2007

25 The hormone that helps in the conversion of glucose to glycogen is [Manipal]
(a) cortisone (b) bile acids
(c) adrenaline (d) insulin

26 Scurvy is caused by the deficiency of which vitamin? [Manipal]
(a) Vitamin K
(b) Vitamin B_1
(c) Vitamin C
(d) Vitamin B_6

27 The vitamin which is neither soluble in water nor in fat is [Kerala CEE]
(a) biotin (b) phylloquinone
(c) thiamine (d) ergocalciferal
(e) pyridoxine

2006

28 Which one of the following is a peptide hormone? [CBSE AIPMT]
(a) Glucagon (b) Testosterone
(c) Thyroxine (d) Adrenaline

29 The pair in which both species have iron is [AIIMS]
(a) nitrogenase, cytochromes
(b) carboxypeptidase, haemoglobin
(c) haemocyanin, nitrogenase
(d) haemoglobin, cytochromes

2005

30 Which of the following biomolecules contain non-transition metal ion? [KCET]
(a) Vitamin B_{12} (b) Chlorophyll
(c) Haemoglobin (d) Insulin

Answers

1 (d)	2 (c)	3 (b)	4 (b)	5 (b)	6 (d)	7 (c)	8 (c)	9 (d)	10 (b)
11 (d)	12 (d)	13 (d)	14 (d)	15 (b)	16 (c)	17 (c)	18 (b)	19 (a)	20 (d)
21 (a)	22 (d)	23 (c)	24 (c)	25 (d)	26 (c)	27 (a)	28 (a)	29 (d)	30 (b)

Explanations

1 (*d*) When protein is subjected to physical change like change in temperature or chemical change like change in pH, the hydrogen bonds are disturbed. As a result, globules unfold and helix get uncoiled and protein loses its biological activity.

Hence, the denaturation of protein makes the protein inactive.

2 (*c*) Cheilosis is a disease of developing sores, caused by nutritional deficiency of riboflavin.

3 (*b*) Eating animals poisoned with mercury (Hg^{2+}) causes deformity, known as minamata (minimata) disease which is characterised by diarrhoea, haemolysis, impairment of various senses, meningitis and death.

4 (*b*) Fat soluble vitamins are A, D, E, and K. These are stored in body for long periods of time. They are found mainly in fatty foods like animal fats.

5 (*b*) Vitamins are naturally occurring organic substances which are needed in minute amount to maintain various metabolic reactions. They are not synthesised in animal body.

6 (*d*) Vitamin C is chemically ascorbic acid.

7 (*c*) Insulin is a hormone, secreted by pancreas. It is chemically protein as it contains polypeptide bonds.

8 (*c*) Vitamin B_{12} contains cobalt and its chemical name is cyanocobalamine. Deficiency of vitamin B_{12} causes pernicious anaemia.

9 (*d*) The night blindness is caused due to the deficiency of vitamin A.

10 (*b*) The deficiency of vitamin B_{12} (cyanocobalamine) causes pernicious anaemia (RBC deficiency in haemoglobin) in humans.

11 (*d*) The correct match is $A \rightarrow 3, B \rightarrow 4, C \rightarrow 1, D \rightarrow 2$

Vitamin	Deficiency disease
Vitamin B_{12}	Pernicious anaemia
Vitamin B_6	Skin disease
Vitamin E	Sterility
Vitamin K	Haemorrhogic condition

12 (*d*) The chemical name of vitamin B_1 is thiamine. Except vitamin A, D, E and K, all vitamins are water soluble.

13 (*d*) Iodine containing hormone is thyroxine.

14 (*d*) Since, insulin maintains the blood glucose level so, it is the hormone that controls the processes of burning of fats, proteins and carbohydrates or in other words it controls catabolism.

15 (*b*) • Haemoglobin is soluble in water.
• α-keratin is in soluble in water.
• Cellulose is a polymer of glucose.
• Chlorophyll is responsible for the synthesis of carbohydrates in plants

Thus, statement (b) is incorrect.

16 (*c*) Milk and egg mainly contain protein, rice is rich in carbohydrate while ghee is a fat. The order of calorific value for carbohydrates, proteins and fats is fats > carbohydrates > proteins

∴ Ghee has the highest calorific value among given options.

17 (*c*) Sucrose is a disaccharide having α-D-glucopyranose and β-D-fructofuranose units.

Rest all other given statements are correct.

18 (*b*) Hormones are not continuously produced, rather they are produced in a controlled manner according to the requirement of the body.
Other given statements are correct.

19 (*a*) The hormone which is proteinaceous in nature are said to be amine hormones because proteins are the polymers of polypeptides and polypeptides are made up of amino acids. Amino acid contains amino group as well as carboxylic acid groups.
Thyroxine is an amine hormone. It is secreted by thyroid gland. Its function is to control the metabolism of carbohydrates, proteins and lipids.

20 (*d*) Vitmain B_{12} or cyanocobalamine contains cobalt, not magnesium.
Only statement (d) is in correct, all other given statements are correct.

21 (*a*) When oxyhaemoglobin changes to deoxyhaemoglobin, Fe^{2+} ion changes from diamagnetic to paramagnetic.

22 (*d*) The correct match is $A \rightarrow 4, B \rightarrow 1, C \rightarrow 2, D \rightarrow 3$

Vitamin (A)	Chemical name
B_1 (A)	Thiamine
B_2 (also called vit. G)	Riboflavin
B_3	Pantothenic acid
B_4	Nicotinic acid or niacin

23 (*c*) The chemical name of vitamin B_{12} is cyanocobalamine.

24 (*c*) (–) thyroxine is very active towards construction of blood vessels.

25 (*d*) Insulin hormone helps in the conversion of glucose into glycogen in the liver and skeletal muscle. Insulin is secreted by pancreas that lower blood glucose level.

26 (*c*) Scurvy is caused by the deficiency of vitamin C.

27 (*a*) Biotin (vitamin H) is neither soluble in water nor in fat.

28 (*a*) Glucagon is a peptide hormone because peptide linkage is present in it.

29 (*d*)
• Nitrogenase contains nitrogen.
• Cytochromes contain iron.
• Carboxypeptidase contains carbon and nitrogen.
• Haemoglobin contains iron.
• Haemocyanin contains copper.

So, haemoglobin and cytochrome contains iron.

30 (*b*)

Biomolecules	Metal ions
Vitamin B_{12}	Co (transition metal)
Chlorophyll	Mg (non-transition metal ion)
Haemoglobin	Fe (transition metal)
Insulin	S (non-metal)

∴ Chlorophyll contains non-transition metal ion.

29

Polymers

Quick Review

Polymers are the chemical substances of high molecular mass formed by the combination of a large number of simple molecules, called **monomers**. The process of formation of polymers from respective monomers is known as **polymerisation**.

Classification of Polymers

- *On the basis of source of origin*
  - *(i)* **Natural Polymers** The polymers which occur in nature, i.e. in plants or animals e.g. starch, cellulose, proteins, natural rubber etc.
  - *(ii)* **Synthetic Polymers** The polymers which are prepared in the laboratory. e.g. polythene, PVC, teflon etc.
  - *(iii)* **Semisynthetic Polymers** These are obtained by making some modification in natural polymers by artificial means. e.g. cellulose acetate, vulcanised rubber etc.
- *On the basis of structure*
  - *(i)* **Linear Polymers** It consist of long chains of atom and are also termed as one dimensional polymers e.g. high density polyethene, nylon, polyesters.
  - *(ii)* **Branched Polymers** The monomer units are linked to form long chains with some branched chains of different lengths attached to the main linear chain, e.g. polyethene, starch etc.
  - *(iii)* **Network or Cross-linked Polymers** The monomer units are linked together to form three dimensional network. e.g. bakelite, glyptal, malamine-formaldehyde etc.
- *On the basis of molecular forces*

Type	Molecular forces	Examples
Elastomers	Weakest intermolecular forces	Natural rubber, buna-S, buna-N etc.
Fibres	Strong intermolecular forces (H-bonding)	Nylon–6, 6, terylene, PAN
Thermo-plastics	Weak van der Waals' forces	Polyethene, poly styrene
Thermosetting plastics	Extensive cross-links between polymeric chains	Bakelite, malamine formaldehyde resin and urea-formaldehyde resin

Note The strength of forces present in different types of polymers follows the order:
Elastomers < thermoplastic polymers < fibres < thermosetting polymers.

- *On the basis of mode of polymerisation*
  - *(i)* **Addition Polymers** These are formed by the repeated addition of monomer molecules possessing double or triple bonds. Addition polymers formed by the polymerisation of single monomeric species are known as **homopolymers.** e.g. polythene while polymers formed from two different monomers are known as **copolymers**. e.g. Buna-S, buna-N etc.
  - *(ii)* **Condensation Polymers** These are formed by repeated condensation reaction between two different bifunctional or trifunctional monomeric units. e.g. Nylon 6,6.

Molecular Mass of a Polymer

There are two ways of expressing molecular mass of a polymer:

(i) **Number Average Molecular Mass** $(\overline{M}_n) = \dfrac{\Sigma N_i M_i}{\Sigma N_i}$

(ii) **Weight Average Molecular Mass** $(\overline{M}_w) = \dfrac{\Sigma N_i M_i^2}{\Sigma N_i M_i}$

where, N_i = number of molecules,
M_i = molecular mass

Types of Polymerisation Reactions

- There are broadly two types of polymerisation reactions, i.e. addition polymerisation and condensation polymerisation, based on the mode of operation.
- A third type known as **copolymerisation**, has also been discussed here, which involves polymerisation reaction between two or more different monomers and proceeding through either addition or condensation mode.

1. Addition Polymerisation or Chain Growth Polymerisation

- It proceeds by chain growth mechanism characterised by initiation, chain propagation and chain termination.
- Only one repeating unit is added at a time.
- Reaction mixture contain only monomers, polymers and the growing chain.

2. Condensation Polymerisation or Step Growth Polymerisation

- It proceeds by step growth mechanism. The step growth process is usually much slower than chain growth polymerisation.
- Any two species present can react with elimination of some by product.
- All the molecular species are present at every stage of polymerisation.

Some Important Polymers

Polymers	Monomers	Synthesis	Uses
(*i*) **Polythene**			
(a) **LDP** • Highly branched polymer and transparent. • Low density and low melting point. • Chemically inert, tough but flexible.	Ethene	Free radical polymerisation $n[CH_2 = CH_2] \xrightarrow[\text{Peroxide}]{350\text{–}570K,\ 1000\text{-}2000\ atm} \!\left[CH_2—CH_2 \right]_n$	In the insulation of electricity carrying wires, toys, flexible pipes.
(b) **HDP** • Linear molecules, closely packed, translucent. • High density and high melting point • Chemically inert, quite hard and high tensile strength.	Ethane	Coordination polymerisation $n(CH_2 = CH_2) \xrightarrow[\textit{Ziegler-Natta}\text{ catalyst}]{333\text{–}343K,\ 6\text{-}7\ atm} \!\left(CH_2 —CH_2 \right)_n$	For making containers, housewares, bottles, electrical insulation etc.
(*ii*) **Polyvinyl chloride** (PVC)	Vinyl chloride	$n\begin{pmatrix} CH_2 = \underset{\mid \atop Cl}{CH} \end{pmatrix} \xrightarrow[\text{peroxide}]{\text{Dibenzoyl}} \left(—CH_2—\underset{\mid \atop Cl}{CH}— \right)_n$	For making rain coats, toys, electrical insulation.
(*iii*) **Polytetrafluoroethane** (teflon)	Tetrafluoro ethene	$n(CF_2 = CF_2) \xrightarrow[\text{High pressure}]{\text{Catalyst}} \!\left[CF_2—CF_2 \right]_n$	In making oil seals, gaskets and also for non-stick surface coated utensils.
(*iv*) **Poly acrylonitrile** (PAN)	Acrylonitrile	$n(CH_2 = CHCN) \xrightarrow[\text{Peroxide catalyst}]{\text{Polymerisation}} \left[—CH_2—\overset{CN \atop \mid}{CH}— \right]_n$	As a substitute for wool in making of commercial fibres known as orlon.

Polymers	Monomers	Synthesis	Uses
(*v*) **Polyamides** (a) **Nylon-6, 6**	Hexamethylene diamine and adipic acid	$nH_2N(CH_2)_6NH_2 + nHO-\overset{O}{\overset{\parallel}{C}}-(CH_2)_4-\overset{O}{\overset{\parallel}{C}}-OH \xrightarrow[553K,\ high\ pressure]{-nH_2O} \left(\overset{H}{\overset{\mid}{N}}-(CH_2)_6-\overset{H}{\overset{\mid}{N}}-\overset{O}{\overset{\parallel}{C}}-(CH_2)_4-\overset{O}{\overset{\parallel}{C}} \right)_n$	In bristle for brushes and in textile.
(b) **Nylon-6**	Caprolactum	Caprolactum $\xrightarrow[Heat]{H_2O} H_2N(CH_2)_5COOH \xrightarrow{\Delta} \left[HN-(CH_2)_5-\overset{O}{\overset{\parallel}{C}} \right]_n$	For manufacturing fabrics, tyre cords etc.
(*vi*) **Bakelite**	Phenol and formaldehyde	n (o-hydroxymethylphenol, OH, CH_2OH) $+ n$ (p-hydroxymethylphenol, OH, CH_2OH) $\xrightarrow[-H_2O]{Polymerisation}$ cross-linked network of phenol rings (OH) joined by $-CH_2-$ bridges ($\sim H_2C-$ … $-CH_2\sim$)	For making combs, phonograph records, electrical switches, wooden planks, lacquers.
(*vii*) **Polyesters** (a) Dacron (terylene)	Ethylene glycol and terephthalic acid	$nHO-CH_2CH_2-O\boxed{H + nHO}-\overset{O}{\overset{\parallel}{C}}-C_6H_4-\overset{O}{\overset{\parallel}{C}}-OH \xrightarrow{Polymerisation} \left[O-CH_2CH_2-O-\overset{O}{\overset{\parallel}{C}}-C_6H_4-\overset{O}{\overset{\parallel}{C}} \right]_n$	For making fibre, safety belts, tents etc.
(b) Polymethyl methacrylate (PMMA)	Methyl methacrylate	$\left(CH_2=\overset{CH_3}{\overset{\mid}{C}}-COOCH_3 \right) \xrightarrow{Organic\ peroxide} \left(CH_2-\overset{CH_3}{\overset{\mid}{C}} \right)_n -\underset{O}{\underset{\parallel}{C}}-OCH_3$	In the manufacture of unbreakable lights, protective coatings, dentures, in making windows for aircrafts.

Rubber

Rubber is an elastic polymer, which reforms its original shape after it has been stretched.

Natural Rubber

- It is manufactured from rubber latex which is colloidal dispersion of rubber in water.
- It is linear polymer of isoprene (2-methyl-1,3-butadiene and also called as *cis* 1,4-polyisoprene).

$$\sim H_2C-C(CH_3)=CH-CH_2-CH_2-C(CH_3)=CH-CH_2-CH_2-C(CH_3)=CH-CH_2\sim$$

- It is held together by weak van der Waals' interactions and has coiled structure.
- It becomes soft at high temperature and brittle at low temperatures. To improve the quality, vulcanisation is carried out.

Vulcanisation

- The properties of natural rubber can be modified by introducing —S—S— polysulphide cross links in its structure at 110°C. ZnO accelerates the rate of vulcanisation.
- Rubber, vulcanised with 3-10% is used for manufacturing tyres while vulcanised with 1-3% is used to make rubber bands.

Synthetic Rubber

It is vulcanisable rubber like polymer, which is capable of getting stretched to twice its length.

Synthetic rubbers are of two types :

1. **Neoprene**

$$nCH_2=C(Cl)-CH=CH_2 \xrightarrow{\text{Polymerisation}} \left[-CH_2-C(Cl)=CH-CH_2-\right]_n$$

2. **Buna-N**

$$nCH_2=CH-CH=CH_2 + nCH_2=CH(CN) \xrightarrow{\text{Copolymerisation}} \underset{\text{Buna-N}}{\left[-CH_2-CH=CH-CH_2-CH_2-CH(CN)-\right]_n}$$

Biodegradable and Non-biodegradable Polymers

1. **Biodegradable Polymers** The polymers which decompose or hydrolyse in the presence of different enzymes are called biodegradable polymers. *There are as follows*

(i) **PHBV**

(Poly- β-hydroxybutyrate-co-β-hydroxyvalerate)

It is copolymer of 3-hydroxybutanoic acid and 3-hydroxypentanoic acid.

$$\underset{\text{3-hydroxy butanoic acid}}{CH_3-CH(OH)-CH_2COOH} + \underset{\text{3-hydroxy pentanoic acid}}{CH_3-CH_2-CH(OH)-CH_2COOH} \longrightarrow$$

$$\underset{\text{PHBV}}{\left[-O-CH(CH_3)-CH_2-C(=O)-O-CH(C_2H_5)-CH_2-C(=O)-\right]_n}$$

(ii) **Nylon-2-Nylon-6**

It is an alternating polyamide copolymer of glycine (H_2N-CH_2-COOH) and amino caproic acid [$H_2N(CH_2)_5COOH$].

2. **Non-biodegradable Polymers** Synthetic polymers do not decompose in the presence of different enzymes and thus, these are non-biodegradable polymers. e.g. polyethene, polyvinyl chloride etc.

Topical Practice Questions

All the exam questions of this chapter have been divided into four topics as listed below

Topic 1

Classification of Polymers

2018

1 Arrange the following polymers in increasing order of their intermolecular forces.
Nylon-6, 6, buna-S, polythene, neoprene **[JIPMER]**
(a) Neoprene < buna-S < nylon-6, 6, < polythene
(b) Neoprene < buna-S < polythene < nylon-6, 6
(c) Polythene < nylon-6, 6 < buna-S < neoprene
(d) Polythene < buna-S < nylon-6, 6 < neoprene

2017

2 Which of the following sets contain only addition polymers? **[AIIMS]**
(a) Polyethylene, polypropylene, terylene
(b) Polyethylene, PVC, teflon
(c) Buna-S, nylon, polybutadiene
(d) Bakelite, PVC, polyethylene

2014

3 Which one of the following is an example of a thermosetting polymer? **[CBSE AIPMT]**
(a) $-\!\!\left(CH_2-\underset{\displaystyle Cl}{\underset{|}{C}}=CH-CH_2\right)\!\!-_n$
(b) $-\!\!\left(CH_2-\underset{\displaystyle Cl}{\underset{|}{CH}}\right)\!\!-_n$
(c) $-\!\!\left(\overset{\displaystyle H}{\overset{|}{N}}-(CH_2)_6-\overset{\displaystyle H}{\overset{|}{N}}-\overset{\displaystyle O}{\overset{||}{C}}-(CH_2)_4-\overset{\displaystyle O}{\overset{||}{C}}\right)\!\!-_n$
(d) $\left(\text{C}_6\text{H}_3(\text{OH})-CH_2-\text{C}_6\text{H}_3(\text{OH})-CH_2\right)_n$

4 Terylene is not a **[KCET]**
(a) copolymer
(b) polyester fibre
(c) chain growth polymer
(d) step growth polymer

2013

5 A condensation polymer among the following polymers is **[KCET]**
(a) teflon
(b) polystyrene
(c) PVC
(d) dacron

2012

6 Which one of the following is not a condensation polymer? **[CBSE AIPMT]**
(a) Melamine
(b) Glyptal
(c) Dacron
(d) Neoprene

7 Which of the following is a polymer? **[AFMC]**
(a) Carnuaba wax
(b) Carbowax
(c) Bees wax
(d) Paraffin wax

2011

8 Out of the following which one is classified as polyester polymer? **[CBSE AIPMT]**
(a) Nylon-6,6
(b) Terylene
(c) Bakelite
(d) Melamine

2010

9 Natural polymer amongst the following is **[OJEE]**
(a) cellulose (b) kodel (c) nylon (d) terylene

10 Which one of the following is an example of copolymer? **[WB JEE]**
(a) Buna-S
(b) Teflon
(c) PVC
(d) Polypropylene

11 Which of the following type of forces are present in nylon-6, 6? **[J&K CET]**
(a) van der Waals' forces of attraction
(b) Hydrogen bonding
(c) Three dimensional network of bonds
(d) Metallic bonding

12 Arrange the following in increasing order of their intermolecular forces : Nylon-6, 6 (I), Buna-S (II), Polythene (III) **[AMU]**
(a) II, I, III (b) III, II I (c) I, II, III (d) II, III, I

2009

13 Which is an example of thermosetting polymer? **[AFMC]**
(a) Polythene
(b) PVC
(c) Neoprene
(d) Bakelite

14 The condensation polymer among the following is **[KCET]**
(a) proteins (b) PVC (c) polythene (d) rubber

2008

15 Which one of the following is a homopolymer? **[Guj CET]**
(a) Butyl rubber
(b) Dacron
(c) Buna-S
(d) Bakelite

2007

16 Three dimensional molecules with cross-links are formed in the case of a **[AFMC]**
(a) thermoplastic
(b) thermosetting plastic
(c) Both (a) and (b)
(d) None of the above

17 Which of the following is not a synthetic rubber? **[MP PMT]**
(a) Neoprene (b) SBR (c) Thiokol (d) Orlon

18 Which of the following is not a thermoplastic? **[JCECE]**
(a) Polystyrene
(b) Teflon
(c) Polyvinyl chloride
(d) Nylon-6, 6

Answers

1 (*b*)	2 (*b*)	3 (*d*)	4 (*c*)	5 (*d*)	6 (*d*)	7 (*b*)	8 (*b*)	9 (*a*)	10 (*a*)
11 (*b*)	12 (*d*)	13 (*d*)	14 (*a*)	15 (*a*)	16 (*b*)	17 (*d*)	18 (*d*)		

Explanations

1 (*b*) The increasing order of intermolecular forces in different polymers is elastomers < plastics < fibres. So, in order to solve such problem, first classify the given polymer into the above classes and then arrange them in increasing order of forces. Neoprene (synthetic rubber) is an elastomer, buna-S is also an elastomer, polythene is plastic and nylon-6, 6 is a fibre. So, the increasing order of intermolecular forces of the given polymer is :

Neoprene < buna-S < polythene < nylon-6, 6

2 (*b*) Polyethylene $-\!\!(CH_2-CH_2)\!\!-_n$, PVC $-\!\!(CH_2-\underset{\large Cl}{\underset{|}{CH}})\!\!-_n$ and teflon $-\!\!(CF_2-CF_2)\!\!-_n$ are addition polymers because all these contain C=C unit in their respective monomers and are formed by the repeated addition of monomer molecules.

3 (*d*) Other options are explained as below :

$$\left(\text{C}_6\text{H}_3(\text{OH})-CH_2-\text{C}_6\text{H}_3(\text{OH})-CH_2\right)_n$$

is a linear polymer called novolac. It is a thermosetting polymer formed by the condensation reaction of phenol and formaldehyde.

(a) $-\!\!(CH_2-\underset{\large Cl}{\underset{|}{C}}=CH-CH_2)\!\!-_n$

is neoprene (synthetic rubber) which is a thermoplastic polymer.

(b) $-\!\!(CH_2-\underset{\large Cl}{\underset{|}{CH}})\!\!-_n$ is polyvinyl chloride which is also a thermoplastic polymer.

(c) $-\!\!(\overset{H}{\overset{|}{N}}-(CH_2)_6-\overset{H}{\overset{|}{N}}-\overset{O}{\overset{\|}{C}}-(CH_2)_4-\overset{O}{\overset{\|}{C}})\!\!-_n$

is nylon 6, 6 which is a polyamide commonly known as fibre.

4 (*c*) Terylene is a copolymer of terephthalic acid and ethylene glycol. It is a polyester fibre.

$$\underset{\text{Terephthalic acid}}{n\text{HOOC}-\text{C}_6\text{H}_4-\text{COOH}} + \underset{\text{Ethylene glycol}}{n\text{HOCH}_2\text{CH}_2\text{OH}} \xrightarrow{-nH_2O} \underset{\text{Terylene (glycol)}}{\left[\text{OC}-\text{C}_6\text{H}_4-\text{COO}-CH_2-CH_2-O\right]_n}$$

Since, it is a product of condensation polymerisation, in which molecular mass of polymer is not a whole number of monomer (due to loss of H_2O molecules). It is also called step growth polymer. it does not involve chain growth polymerisation. Hence, it is not a chain growth polymer.

Note Unsaturated monomers mainly undergo addition polymerisation.

5 (*d*) The polymer formed by the condensation polymerisation is known as condensation polymer. Dacron (Terylene) is a condensation polymer. It is formed by the condensation polymerisation of terephthalic acid and ethylene glycol.

6 (*d*) Condensation polymers are obtained from bi-functional molecules (monomers) with the elimination of smaller molecules. Neoprene is a polymer of chloroprene ($CH_2=C(Cl)-CH=CH_2$).

It is an addition polymer and not a condensation polymer. Addition polymers are obtained from multiple bond containing monomers.

7 (*b*) Carbowax is a polymer of ethylene oxide whereas carnuaba wax and bees wax are esters of higher fatty acids with higher alcohols. Paraffin wax is a mixture of hydrocarbons containing 20 or more C-atoms.

8 (*b*) Terylene is a polyester polymer because it is formed by the condensation polymerisation of the monomer units terephthalic acid (an acid) and ethylene glycol (an alcohol).

9 (*a*) Cellulose is a natural polymer. It is the building block of jute, coir, pineapple leaf fibres, straw and many more such things.

10 (*a*) Copolymers contain two or more different monomer units. Buna-S is a polymer of buta-1,3-diene and styrene. Thus, it is a copolymer.

$$\underset{\text{Buta-1,3-diene}}{nCH_2=CH-CH=CH_2} + \underset{\text{Styrene}}{nCH_2=CH-Ph} \xrightarrow[\text{Co-polymerisation}]{\text{Addition}} \underset{\text{Buna -S}}{-\!\!(CH_2-CH=CH-CH_2-CH_2-\underset{\large Ph}{\underset{|}{CH}})\!\!-_n}$$

11 (*b*) Nylon -6, 6 is a fibre in which intermolecular forces like hydrogen bonds are present between the chains.

12 (*d*) Nylon-6, 6 is a fibre and has hydrogen bonding as intermolecular force. Buna-S is an elastomer and has weak van der Waals' forces. Polythene is thermoplastic and has intermediate intermolecular forces (i.e. stronger than elastomer but weaker than fibre).

Thus, the increasing order of intermolecular forces is shown below :

$$\underset{\text{(II)}}{\text{Buna-S}} < \underset{\text{(III)}}{\text{polythene}} < \underset{\text{(I)}}{\text{nylon-6, 6}}$$

13 (*d*) Bakelite has highly cross-linked structure. It is hard and infusible polymer and does not soften on heating. Hence, it is an example of thermosetting polymer.

14 (*a*) Condensation polymers are formed by the combination of monomers with the elimination of simple molecules like water or alcohol, e.g. proteins, polyesters and polyamides.

Thus, out of the given options, proteins are condensation polymers of amino acids.

15 (*a*) The polymer which contains only single type of monomer units is called homopolymer.

Thus, butyl rubber is a homopolymer of 2-methylpropene or *iso*-butylene.

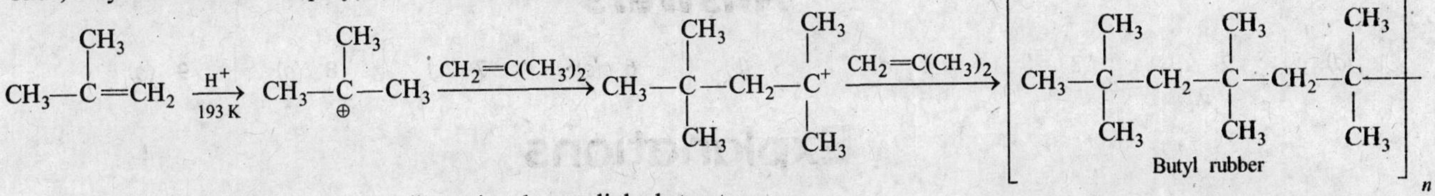

$$CH_3-\underset{}{\overset{CH_3}{\overset{|}{C}}}=CH_2 \xrightarrow[193\,K]{H^+} CH_3-\overset{CH_3}{\overset{|}{\underset{\oplus}{C}}}-CH_3 \xrightarrow{CH_2=C(CH_3)_2} CH_3-\overset{CH_3}{\overset{|}{\underset{CH_3}{\underset{|}{C}}}}-CH_2-\overset{CH_3}{\overset{|}{\underset{CH_3}{\underset{|}{C^+}}}} \xrightarrow{CH_2=C(CH_3)_2} \left[CH_3-\overset{CH_3}{\overset{|}{\underset{CH_3}{\underset{|}{C}}}}-CH_2-\overset{CH_3}{\overset{|}{\underset{CH_3}{\underset{|}{C}}}}-CH_2-\overset{CH_3}{\overset{|}{\underset{CH_3}{\underset{|}{C}}}}-\right]_n$$

Butyl rubber

16 (*b*) Thermosetting plastics have three dimensional cross linked structure.

17 (*d*) Orlon is not a synthetic rubber. It is an acrylic fibre. While neoprene, SBR and thiokol are the examples of synthetic rubber.

18 (*d*) Thermoplastics can be remoulded while nylon 6, 6 cannot be remoulded as it is a fibre. Hence, nylon 6, 6 is not a thermoplastic.

Topic 2

Types of Polymerisation

2018

1 Regarding cross-linked or network polymers, which of the following statements is incorrect? **[NEET]**

(a) Examples are bakelite and melamine

(b) They are formed from bi- and tri-functional monomers

(c) They contain strong covalent bonds between various linear polymer chains

(d) They contain strong covalent bonds in their polymer chains

2017

2 Polymer formation from monomers starts by **[JIPMER]**

(a) condensation reaction between monomers

(b) coordination reaction between monomers

(c) conversion of one monomer into other monomer

(d) hydrolysis of monomers

2016

3 Natural rubber has **[NEET]**

(a) all *trans*-configuration

(b) alternate *cis* - and *trans*-configuration

(c) random *cis* - and *trans*-configuration

(d) all *cis*-configuration

2014

4 Identify from the following, the monomers which undergo condensation polymerisation. **[EAMCET]**

I. $H_2C=CH-CH=CH_2$

II. 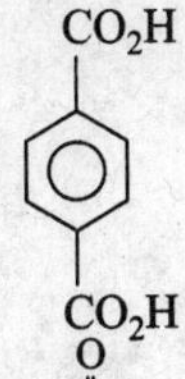 $HO_2C-C_6H_4-CO_2H$ (benzene ring with CO_2H at para positions)

III. $H_2C=CHCl$

IV. 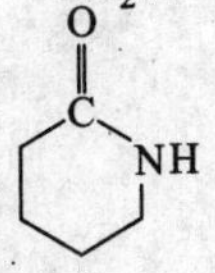 (six-membered ring lactam: $C=O$ and NH in ring)

V. $F_2C=CF_2$

VI $(H_3C)_2C=CH_2$

(a) III, V (b) I, III (c) I, VI (d) II, IV

2009

5 The first step in bakelite formation is **[OJEE]**

(a) aromatic nucleophilic substitution

(b) aromatic electrophilic substitution

(c) condensation

(d) electrophilic addition

2008

6 Which of the following alkenes is most reactive towards cationic polymerisation? **[Manipal]**

(a) $CH_2=CHCH_3$ (b) $H_2C=CHCl$

(c) $H_2C=CHC_6H_5$ (d) $H_2C=CHCO_2CH_3$

7 In case of condensation of polymers **[J&K CET]**

(a) high molecular weight polymers are formed all at once

(b) lower molecular weight polymers are formed all at once

(c) molecular weight of polymer rises throughout the reaction

(d) have no specific relation to their molecular weight

2007

8 Which one of the following polymers is prepared by condensation polymerisation? **[CBSE AIPMT]**

(a) Nylon-6, 6 (b) Teflon (c) Rubber (d) Styrene

2005

9 The monomer of the polymer, **[CBSE AIPMT]**

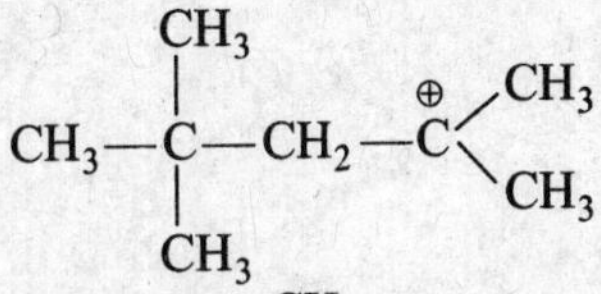

$$CH_3-\overset{CH_3}{\overset{|}{\underset{CH_3}{\underset{|}{C}}}}-CH_2-\overset{\oplus}{C}\begin{matrix}CH_3\\CH_3\end{matrix}$$ is

(a) $H_2C=C(CH_3)_2$ (b) $(CH_3)_2C=C(CH_3)_2$

(c) $CH_3CH=CH\cdot CH_3$ (d) $CH_3CH=CH_2$

Answers

1 (d)	2 (a)	3 (d)	4 (d)	5 (b)	6 (c)	7 (c)	8 (a)	9 (a)

Explanations

1 (*d*) Cross-linked or network polymers are formed from bi-functional and tri-functional monomers and contain strong covalent bonds between various linear polymer chains. These are hard, rigid and brittle due to cross-links, e.g. bakelite, melamine etc. Thus, option (d) is incorrect.

2 (*a*) Polymers are obtained by condensation reaction between monomers. This reaction involves the loss of simple molecules such as water, alcohol etc.

3 (*d*) The repeating unit in natural rubber has all *cis*-configuration with chain extensions on the same side of the ethylene double bond, which is essential for elasticity. If the configuration is *trans*, the polymer is either a hard plastic or a substance like *gutta-percha*.

$$\sim H_2C\text{—}C(CH_3){=}CH\text{—}CH_2\text{—}CH_2\text{—}C(CH_3){=}CH\text{—}CH_2\text{—}CH_2\text{—}C(CH_3){=}CH\text{—}CH_2\sim$$

Natural rubber (all *cis*-configuration)

4 (*d*) In condensation polymerisation, molecules of same or different monomers are combined in a controlled stepwise manner with elimination of small molecules such as water, ammonia, alcohols, etc.

$$\underset{\text{Terephthalic acid}}{nHOOC\text{—}C_6H_4\text{—}COOH} + \underset{\text{Ethylene glycol}}{nHOCH_2CH_2OH} \xrightarrow[-nH_2O]{\text{Condensation polymerisation}} \underset{\text{Terylene or dacron}}{\text{+}OC\text{—}C_6H_4\text{—}COO\text{—}CH_2CH_2O\text{+}_n}$$

$$\underset{\text{Caprolactam}}{\text{Caprolactam (cyclic }C(=O)\text{—}NH)} \xrightarrow[-nH_2O]{\text{Condensation polymerisation}} \underset{\text{Nylon-6 or perlon}}{\text{+}NH\text{—}(CH_2)_5\text{—}\overset{O}{\overset{\|}{C}}\text{+}_n}$$

5 (*b*)

$$\underset{\text{Phenol}}{C_6H_5OH} \xrightarrow[\text{(Aromatic electrophilic substitution)}]{HCHO} o\text{-}HOC_6H_4CH_2OH \text{ and } p\text{-}HOC_6H_4CH_2OH$$

Polymerise to give bakelite

6 (*c*) In cationic polymerisation, carbocations are formed. Greater the stability of the carbocation, more reactive is the alkene. Since, the stability of the intermediate carbocation follows the order :

$$CH_3\text{—}\overset{+}{C}HC_6H_5 > CH_3\text{—}\overset{+}{C}HCH_3 > CH_3\text{—}\overset{+}{C}H\text{—}Cl > CH_3\text{—}\overset{+}{C}HCO_2CH_3$$

Therefore, reactivity decreases in the same order. Thus, styrene $[H_2C{=}CHC_6H_5]$ is most reactive.

7 (*c*) The process of condensation polymerisation takes place in the following manner :

$$\underset{\text{Monomers}}{A + B} \xrightarrow{\text{Condensation}} \underset{\text{Dimer}}{A - B}$$

$$A - B + A \xrightarrow{\text{Condensation}} A - B - A$$

$$A - B - A + B \longrightarrow A - B - A - B$$

In this process, no initiator is required and it is also called step growth polymerisation. Thus, the molecular weight of the polymerises throughout the reaction.

8 (*a*) Polymers which are formed by the combination of monomers with elimination of small molecules like NH_3, H_2O, HCl, CH_3OH etc., are known as condensation polymers. Nylon-6, 6 is prepared by condensation polymerisation.

$$\underset{\text{Hexamethylene diamine}}{nH_2N\text{—}(CH_2)_6\text{—}NH_2} + \underset{\text{Adipic acid}}{nHOOC\text{—}(CH_2)_4\text{—}COOH} \xrightarrow{-nH_2O} \underset{\text{Polyhexamethylene adepate polyamide [nylon 6,6]}}{\left[HN\text{—}(CH_2)_6\text{—}NH\text{—}\overset{O}{\overset{\|}{C}}\text{—}(CH_2)_4\text{—}\overset{O}{\overset{\|}{C}}\right]_n}$$

9 (*a*) The monomer of polymer

$$CH_3\text{—}\underset{CH_3}{\overset{CH_3}{C}}\text{—}CH_2\text{—}\overset{\oplus}{C}(CH_3)_2 \text{ is } CH_2{=}C(CH_3)_2$$

because it shows cationic polymerisation.

Topic 3

Biodegradable and Non-biodegradable Polymers

2019

1 The biodegradable polymer is **[NEET]**

(a) nylon-2-nylon-6 (b) nylon-6
(c) buna-S (d) nylon-6, 6

2018

2 **Assertion** (A) Most of the synthetic polymers are non-biodegradable.

Reason (R) Polymerisation always induces toxic effect in environment. **[AIIMS]**

(a) Both A and R are correct and R is correct explanation of A.
(b) Both A and R are correct but R is not the correct explanation of A.
(c) A is correct but R is incorrect.
(d) Both A and R are incorrect.

2016

3 Biodegradable polymer which can be produced from glycine and aminocaproic acid is **[CBSE AIPMT]**

(a) Nylon-2-nylon 6
(b) PHBV
(c) Buna-N
(d) Nylon-6, 6

2014

4 Which one of the following is an example for biodegradable polyester? **[Kerala CEE]**

(a) PHBV (b) PET (c) Nylon 6 (d) Bakelite
(e) Glyptal

2012

5 Which one of the following sets forms the biodegradable polymer? **[CBSE AIPMT]**

(a) $CH_2=CH—CN$ and $CH_2=CH—CH=CH_2$
(b) $H_2N—CH_2—COOH$ and $H_2N—(CH_2)_5—COOH$
(c) $HO—CH_2CH_2—OH$ and $HOOC—C_6H_4—COOH$
(d) $C_6H_5—CH=CH_2$ and $CH_2=CH—CH=CH_2$

6 Which of the following is a biodegradable polymer? **[Manipal]**

(a) Polythene (b) Bakelite
(c) PHBV (d) PVC

7 Which of the following is a biodegradable polymer? **[JCECE]**

(a) Cellulose (b) Polythene
(c) Polyvinyl chloride (d) Nylon-6

Answers

1 (a)	2 (c)	3 (a)	4 (a)	5 (b)	6 (c)	7 (a)

Explanations

1 (a) Nylon-2-nylon-6 $\left[HN—CH_2CONH(CH_2)_5\overset{O}{\overset{\|}{C}}\right]_n$ is a biodegradable polymer. It is an alternating polyamide copolymer of glycine ($H_2N—CH_2—COOH$) and amino caproic acid [$H_2N(CH_2)_5COOH$].

The remaining polymers, i.e. nylon-6,6, $\left[NH(CH_2)_6NHCO(CH_2)_4CO\right]_n$, nylon-6- $\left[CO(CH_2)_5NH\right]_n$ and buna-S

$$\left[CH_2—CH=CH—CH_2—\underset{C_6H_5}{\overset{|}{CH}}\right]_n$$ are non-biodegradable polymers.

Hence, option (a) is correct.

2 (c) Assertion is correct but reason is incorrect. Most of the synthetic polymers are not biodegradable because they are not easily broken by soil organisms (micro-organism) and are hazardous to the environment. Polymerisation does not always causes toxic effect in the environment.

3 (a) Nylon-2-nylon-6 is an alternating polyamide of glycine (containing two carbon atoms) and amino caproic acid or 6-aminohexanoic acid (containing six carbon atoms).

$$\underset{\text{Glycine}}{nH_2N—CH_2—COOH} + \underset{\text{Amino caproic acid}}{nH_2N—(CH_2)_5—COOH} \longrightarrow \underset{\text{Nylon - 2 - nylon - 6}}{\left[NH—CH_2—\underset{\|}{\overset{}{C}}—NH—(CH_2)_5—\underset{\|}{C}\right]_n}$$

(both C atoms bear =O)

It is a biodegradable step-growth copolymer.

4 (a) PHBV(poly β-hydroxy butyrate-co-β-hydroxyvalerate) a polyester, is a copolymer of 3-hydroxybutanoic acid and 3-hydroxy pentanoic acid.

$$nCH_3-\underset{\substack{|\\OH}}{CH}-CH_2-\overset{\substack{O\\||}}{C}-OH + nCH_3-CH_2-\overset{\substack{OH\\|}}{CH}-CH_2-\overset{\substack{O\\||}}{C}-OH$$

3-hydroxybutanoic acid, 3-hydroxypentanoic acid

$$\longrightarrow \left[O-\underset{\substack{|\\CH_3}}{CH}-CH_2-\overset{\substack{O\\||}}{C}-O-\underset{\substack{|\\CH_2CH_3}}{CH}-CH_2-\overset{\substack{O\\||}}{C}\right]_n$$

PHBV

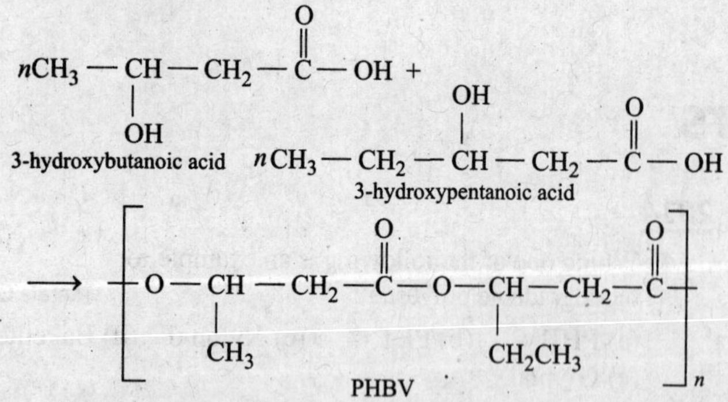

It is a biodegradable polyester, i.e. degraded by microorganisms.

5 (b) Biodegradable polymers, have a tendency to break down and lose their initial integrity, e.g.

$$H_2N-CH_2-COOH + HNH-(CH_2)_5-COOH \xrightarrow[-H_2O]{\Delta} \left[HN-CH_2-CO-NH-(CH_2)_5-CO\right]_n$$

Nylon-2-nylon-6

6 (c) The poly-β-hydroxy butyrate-co-β-hydroxy valerate (PHBV) is a biodegradable polymer.

7 (a) Cellulose is a biodegradable polymer. Different enzymes found in bacteria acts on it and degrade it.

Synthetic polymers like polythene, PVC, nylon-6 etc., are not acted upon by bacteria, hence are non-biodegradable.

Topic 4

Some Important Polymers

2019

1 The polymer that is used as a substitute for wool in making commercial fibres is **[NEET (Odisha)]**

(a) melamine (b) nylon-6, 6
(c) polyacrylonitrile (d) buna-N

2 Match the following Columns :

Polymer		Monomer
(i) Buna -S	(P)	Styrene
(ii) Ethylene glycol	(Q)	Terylene
(iii) Elastomer	(R)	Chloroprene

Correct set of answer: **[AIIMS]**

(a) (i) → (P), (ii) → (Q), (iii) → (R)
(b) (i) → (R), (ii) → (P), (iii) → (Q)
(c) (i) → (Q), (ii) → (R), (iii) → (P)
(d) (i) → (P), (ii) → (R), (iii) → (Q)

2017

3 Which of the following fibres is made of polyamides? **[JIPMER]**

(a) Dacron (b) Orlon (c) Nylon (d) Rayon

2016

4 Which one of the following structures represents nylon 6, 6 polymer? **[NEET, Phase II]**

(a) 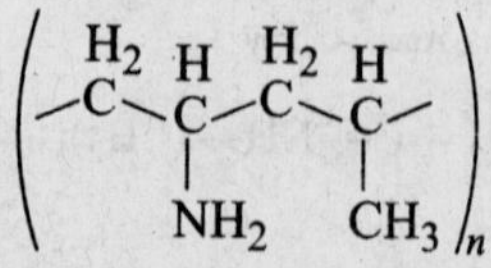 $\left(-\overset{H_2}{C}-\underset{\substack{|\\NH_2}}{\overset{H}{C}}-\overset{H_2}{C}-\underset{\substack{|\\CH_3}}{\overset{H}{C}}-\right)_n$

(b) $\left(-\overset{H_2}{C}-\underset{\substack{|\\NH_2}}{\overset{H}{C}}-\overset{H_2}{C}-\underset{\substack{|\\NH_2}}{\overset{H}{C}}-\right)_n$

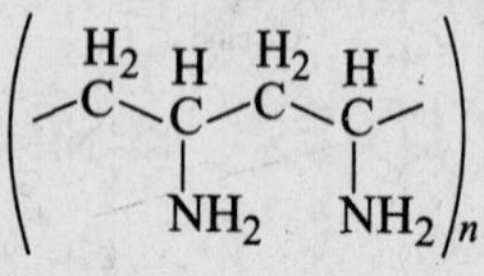

(c) $\left(-\overset{H_2}{C}-\underset{\substack{|\\NH_2}}{\overset{H}{C}}-\overset{H_2}{C}-\underset{\substack{|\\Cl}}{\overset{H}{C}}-\right)_6\left(-\overset{H_2}{C}-\underset{\substack{|\\CH_3}}{\overset{H}{C}}-\overset{H_2}{C}-\underset{\substack{|\\COOH}}{\overset{H}{C}}-\right)_n$

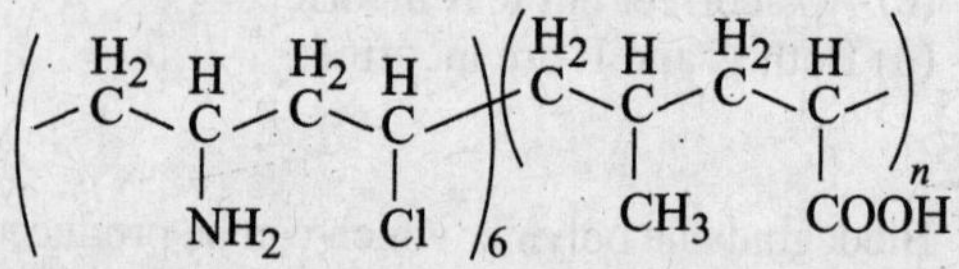

(d) 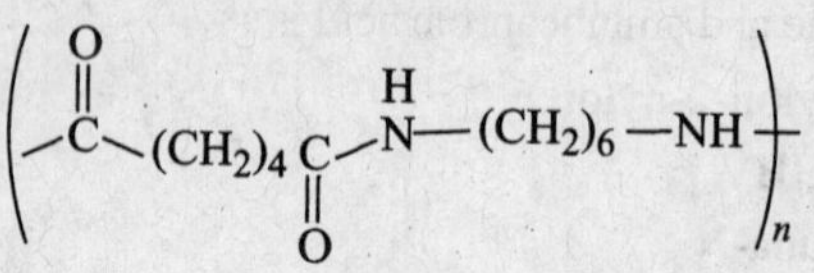 $\left(-\overset{\substack{O\\||}}{C}-(CH_2)_4-\underset{\substack{||\\O}}{C}-\overset{H}{N}-(CH_2)_6-NH-\right)_n$

2014

5 Which of the following organic compounds polymerises to form the polyester dacron? **[CBSE AIPMT]**

(a) Propylene and *para* HO$-(C_6H_4)-$OH
(b) Benzoic acid and ethanol
(c) Terephthalic acid and ethylene glycol
(d) Benzoic acid and *para* HO$-(C_6H_4)-$OH

6 Which of the following polymer is stored in liver of animals? **[UP CPMT]**

(a) Amylose
(b) Cellulose
(c) Amylopectin
(d) Glycogen

7 The two monomers used in the preparation of dextron are **[MHT CET]**

(a) 3-hydroxybutanoic acid and 3-hydroxy pentanoic acid
(b) amino caproic acid and glycine
(c) isobutylene and isoprene
(d) lactic acid and glycolic acid

2013

8 Which is the monomer of neoprene in the following? [NEET]

(a) $CH_2=CH-C\equiv CH$

(b) $CH_2=C(CH_3)-CH=CH_2$

(c) $CH_2=C(Cl)-CH=CH_2$

(d) $CH_2=CH-CH=CH_2$

9 Nylon is an example of [NEET]

(a) polyster (b) polysaccharide
(c) polyamide (d) polythene

10 Natural rubber is a polymer of [Manipal]

(a) *cis*-isoprene (b) *trans*-isoprene
(c) Both (a) and (b) (d) None of these

11 Acrilan is a hard, horny and a high melting material. Its structure is [WB JEE]

(a) $\left[-CH_2-C(CH_3)(COOCH_3)-\right]_n$ (b) $\left[-CH_2-CH(COOC_2H_5)-\right]_n$

(c) $\left[-CH_2-CH(Cl)-\right]_n$ (d) $\left[-CH_2-CH(CN)-\right]_n$

2011

12 Natural rubber is not used in making footwears for polar regions because [Guj CET]

(a) natural rubber becomes soft at temperature lower than 10°C
(b) natural rubber becomes brittle at temperature lower than 10°C
(c) natural rubber melts at temperature lower than 10°C
(d) natural rubber becomes stronger at temperature lower than 10°C

2010

13 Which of the following structure represents neoprene polymer? [CBSE AIPMT]

(a) $\left[-CH(C_6H_5)-CH_2-\right]_n$

(b) $\left[-CH_2-C(Cl)=CH-CH_2-\right]_n$

(b) $\left[-CH_2-CH(CN)-\right]_n$

(d) $\left[-CH_2-CH(Cl)-\right]_n$

14 Teflon is a polymer of [UP CPMT, Guj CET]

(a) vinylchloride (b) tetrachloroethylene
(c) tetrafluoroethylene (d) buta-1,3-diene

15 Which polymer is used for coating cookwares to make them non-sticky? [UP CPMT]

(a) PET (b) PAN (c) Teflon (d) Perlon

16 Which compound/set of compounds is used in the manufacture of nylon-6,6? [BVP]

(a) $HOOC(CH_2)_4COOH + H_2N(CH_2)_6NH_2$
(b) $CH_2=CH-C(CH_3)=CH_2$
(c) $CH_2=CH_2$
(d) $HOOC-C_6H_4-COOH + HOCH_2-CH_2OH$

17 Polymer used in bullet proof glass is [RPMT]

(a) PMMA (b) lexan (c) nomex (d) kevlar

18 Glyptal polymer is obtained from glycol by reacting it with [JCECE]

(a) malonic acid (b) phthalic acid
(c) maleic acid (d) terephthalic acid

19 Esterification of terephthalic acid with glycol produces [VMMC]

(a) nylon (b) buna rubber
(c) polyurethane (d) terylene

2009

20 Structures of some common polymers are given. Which one is not correctly represented? [CBSE AIPMT]

(a) Teflon $\rightarrow \left(CF_2-CF_2\right)_n$

(b) Neoprene $\rightarrow \left(CH_2-C(Cl)=CH-CH_2-CH_2\right)_n$

(c) Terylene $\rightarrow \left(OC-C_6H_4-COOCH_2-CH_2O\right)_n$

(d) Nylon-6, 6 $\rightarrow \left(NH(CH_2)_6NHCO(CH_2)_4-CO\right)_n$

21 The rubber, used for manufacturing tyres, is vulcanised with **[AIIMS]**
(a) 3% S
(b) 7% S
(c) 1% S
(d) All of the above can be used

22 A petrol pump hose pipe, for delivery of petrol, is made up of **[UP CPMT]**
(a) natural rubber (b) vulcanised rubber
(c) neoprene (d) butadiene rubber

23 Adipic acid is used in the preparation of **[MHT CET]**
(a) nylon-6 (b) dacron
(c) nylon-6, 6 (d) novalac

24 The monomer (s) used to prepare polyvinyl polythene is **[Kerala CEE]**
(a) vinyl chloride and ethane
(b) ethene
(c) isoprene
(d) 1,3-butadiene and acrylonitrile
(e) 1,3-butadiene

25 The polymer used in orthopaedic devices and in controlled drug release is **[Kerala CEE]**
(a) orlon (b) PTFE (c) SBR (d) PHBV
(e) PVC

26 The catalyst used for olefin polymerisation is **[WB JEE]**
(a) *Ziegler-Natta* catalyst (b) Wilkinson catalyst
(c) Raney nickel catalyst (d) Merrifield resin

27 The monomer used to produce orlon is **[WB JEE]**
(a) $CH_2{=}CHF$ (b) $CH_2{=}CCl_2$
(c) $CH_2{=}CHCl$ (d) $CH_2{=}CH{-}CN$

28 Which of the following polymers is prepared from caprolactam? **[AMU]**
(a) Nylon-6, 6 (b) Nylon-6, 10
(c) Nylon-6 (d) Nylon-1, 1

2008

29 Which one of the following statements is not true? **[CBSE AIPMT]**
(a) In vulcanisation, the formation of sulphur bridges between different chains make rubber harder and stronger
(b) Natural rubber has the *trans*-configuration at every double bond
(c) Buna-S is a copolymer of butadiene and styrene
(d) Natural rubber is a 1,4-polymer of isoprene

30 Which of the following is a polymer containing nitrogen? **[AIIMS]**
(a) Polyvinyl chloride (b) Bakelite
(c) Nylon (d) Terylene

31 Nylon-6, 6 is **[BHU]**
(a) polyamide (b) polyester
(c) polystyrene (d) polyvinyl

32 The monomers of buna-S rubber are **[KCET]**
(a) vinyl chloride and sulphur
(b) butadiene
(c) styrene and butadiene
(d) isoprene and butadiene

2007

33 Plexi glass is a commercial name of **[AIIMS]**
(a) glyptal
(b) polyacrylonitrile
(c) polymethylmethacrylate
(d) polyethyl acrylate

34 Which one of the following is not a correct match? **[Kerala CEE]**

	Polymer	Monomer(s)
(a)	Teflon	Tetrafluoroethylene
(b)	Plexi glass	Methylmethacrylate
(c)	Orlon	Glycerol, phthalicanhydride
(d)	Buna-S	Styrene, 1,3-butadiene
(e)	Thiokol	Ethylenedichloride, sodium tetrasulphide

35 Monomer of 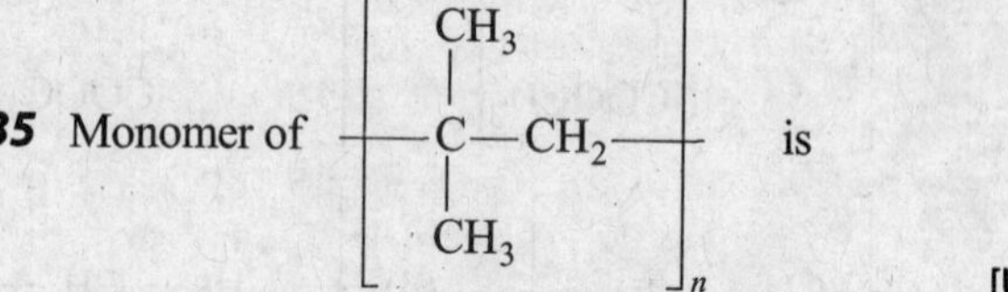 is **[UK PMT]**
(a) 2-methylpropene (b) styrene
(c) propylene (d) ethene

2006

36 **Assertion** (A) 1,3-butadiene is the monomer for natural rubber.
Reason (R) Natural rubber is formed through anionic addition polymerisation. **[AIIMS]**
(a) Both A and R are correct and R is the correct explanation of A.
(b) Both A and R are correct but R is not the correct explanation of A.
(c) A is correct but R is incorrect.
(d) Both A and R are incorrect.

37 In a polymer sample, 30% of molecules have a molecular mass 20000, 40% have 30000 and the rest have 60000. What is the weight average molecular mass of the polymer? **[Kerala CEE]**
(a) 40300 (b) 30600
(c) 43333 (d) 50400
(e) 33333

38 Which of the following polymers can be used for lubrication and as an insulator? **[Guj CET]**
(a) PVC (b) PTFE (c) SBR (d) PMMA

2005

39 The vulcanised rubber has **[Kerala CEE]**

(a) high water absorption, resistant to oxidation and good elasticity.
(b) high water absorption, susceptible to oxidation and no elasticity
(c) high water absorption, susceptible to oxidation and good elasticity
(d) low water absorption, resistance to oxidation and good elasticity
(e) low water absorption, susceptible to oxidation and no elasticity

Answers

1 (c)	2 (a)	3 (c)	4 (d)	5 (c)	6 (d)	7 (d)	8 (c)	9 (c)	10 (a)
11 (d)	12 (b)	13 (b)	14 (c)	15 (c)	16 (a)	17 (b)	18 (b)	19 (d)	20 (b)
21 (b)	22 (d)	23 (c)	24 (e)	25 (d)	26 (a)	27 (d	28 (c)	29 (b)	30 (c)
31 (a)	32 (c)	33 (c)	34 (c)	35 (a)	36 (d)	37 (c)	38 (b)	39 (d)	

Explanations

1 (*c*) Polyacrylonitrile or orlon or acrilan, $-\!\!\left(CH_2-\underset{}{\overset{CN}{\overset{|}{C}}}H\right)\!\!-_n$ is an addition homopolymer of monomer $CH_2 = CH\,CN$ (vinyl cyanide). It is used in making synthetic fibres and synthetic wool. Thus, it is a substitute for wool in making commercial fibres.

2 (*a*) (i) Buna - S → (P) styrene, it is one of the monomer of buna - S, i.e. $[C_6H_5-CH = CH_2]$

(ii) Ethylene glycol → (Q).

Terylene is made by the monomers, ethylene glycol

$$\left[\begin{array}{cc} CH_2- & CH_2 \\ | & | \\ OH & OH \end{array}\right]$$ and terephthalic acid

(iii) Elastomer → (R), Chloroprene is an example of elastomer.

Hence, the correct match is: (i) - P, (ii) - Q, (iii) - R .

3 (*c*) Nylon is a polyamide, e.g. nylon-6,6, nylon-6, etc.

The structures are as follows :

$$\left[-\overset{H}{\overset{|}{N}}-(CH_2)_6-\overset{H}{\overset{|}{N}}-\overset{O}{\overset{\|}{C}}(CH_2)_6-\overset{O}{\overset{\|}{C}}-\right]$$

Nylon 6, 6

$$\left[-\overset{O}{\overset{\|}{C}}-(CH_2)_5-\overset{H}{\overset{|}{N}}-\right]$$

Nylon 6

4 (*d*) Nylon-6, 6 polymer is formed as :

$$\underset{\text{Adipic acid}}{HOOC-(CH_2)_4-COOH} + \underset{\text{Hexamethylene diamine}}{H_2N-(CH_2)_6-NH_2} \xrightarrow{\text{Polymerisation}} \underset{\text{Nylon-6,6}}{\left[-\overset{O}{\overset{\|}{C}}-(CH_2)_4-\overset{O}{\overset{\|}{C}}-NH-(CH_2)_6-NH-\right]_n}$$

5 (*c*) Dacron, commonly known as terylene, is obtained by heating mixture of terephthalic acid and ethylene glycol at 420-460 K in the presence of catalyst like zinc acetate and antimony trioxide.

$$\underset{\text{Terephthalic acid}}{nHOOC-C_6H_4-COOH} + \underset{\text{Ethylene glycol}}{nHOCH_2CH_2OH} \xrightarrow[-HCl]{\Delta} \underset{\text{Dacron}}{\left[-O-CH_2-CH_2-O-CO-C_6H_4-CO-\right]_n}$$

6 (*d*) Glycogen is a multibranched polysaccharide of glucose that serves as a form of energy storage in animals. It is the analogue of starch, a glucose polymer in plants, having a similar structure of amylopectin, but more extensively branched and compact than starch. It is also known as animal starch.

7 (*d*) The monomers of dextron are lactic acid and glycalic acid. It is a copolymer and has ester linkage. It is used in lubricants to reduce surface friction.

8 (*c*) Neoprene is a synthetic rubber and is a homopolymer of chloroprene which is chemically 2-chlorobut-1, 3-diene. It is obtained by free radical polymerisation of chloroprene.

$$\underset{\substack{\text{2-chloro-1, 3-butadiene} \\ \text{(Chloroprene)}}}{nCH_2=\underset{Cl}{\underset{|}{C}}-CH=CH_2} \longrightarrow \underset{\text{Neoprene}}{\left[-CH_2-\underset{Cl}{\underset{|}{C}}=CH-CH_2-\right]_n}$$

9 (*c*) Nylon is an example of polyamide containing amide linkages $-\!\!(CONH)\!\!-$.

These are prepared by condensation copolymerisation of diamines with dicarboxylic acids or by condensation polymerisation of lactam.

$$\left[-R-\overset{O}{\overset{\|}{C}}-\underset{H}{\underset{|}{N}}-R-\right]_n$$

Amide linkage

10 (*a*) Natural rubber is a polymer of *cis*-isoprene, [2-methyl-1, 3-butadiene].

$$CH_2=\overset{CH_3}{\overset{|}{C}}-CH=CH_2$$

2-methyl-1, 3-butadiene

11 (*d*) Acrilan is a cyanide compound. Its structure is shown below :

$$\left[\!\!-CH_2-\underset{\underset{CN}{|}}{CH}-\!\!\right]_n$$

12 (*b*) Natural rubber becomes soft at high temperatures (> 335 K) and brittle at low temperatures (< 283 K). Hence, it is not used in making footwears for polar regions.

13 (*b*) Neoprene is [illegible]thetic rubber, a polymer of chloroprene (which is [illegible]y called 2-chlorobuta-1,3-diene).

$$\text{[illegible]}=CH_2 \xrightarrow{\text{Polymerisation}} \left[CH_2-\underset{\underset{Cl}{|}}{C}=CH-CH_2\right]_n$$

Chloroprene   Neoprene

14 (*c*) Teflon (polytetrafluoroethylene) is a polymer of tetrafluoroethylene ($CF_2{=}CF_2$).

$$nCF_2=CF_2 \xrightarrow{\text{Polymerisation}} \underset{\text{Teflon}}{\left[CF_2-CF_2\right]_n}$$

15 (*c*) Teflon (or polytetrafluoro ethylene), a polymer of tetrafluoroethylene is used for coating cookwares to make them non-sticky.

16 (*a*) Nylon-6, 6 is a condensation polymer of adipic acid and hexamethylene diamine.

$$nHOOC-(CH_2)_4-COOH + nH_2N-(CH_2)_6-NH_2 \xrightarrow[\text{High pressure}]{553\,K} \underset{\text{Nylon-6, 6}}{\left[\overset{O}{\overset{\|}{C}}-(CH_2)_4-\overset{O}{\overset{\|}{C}}-\overset{H}{\overset{|}{N}}-(CH_2)_6-\overset{H}{\overset{|}{N}}\right]_n}$$

17 (*b*) Lexan is a thermoplastic polycarbonate produced from bisphenol and phosgene. It is used for making bullet- resistant (proof) window glasses.

18 (*b*) Glyptal or alkyl resin is a polymer of ethylene glycol and phthalic acid.

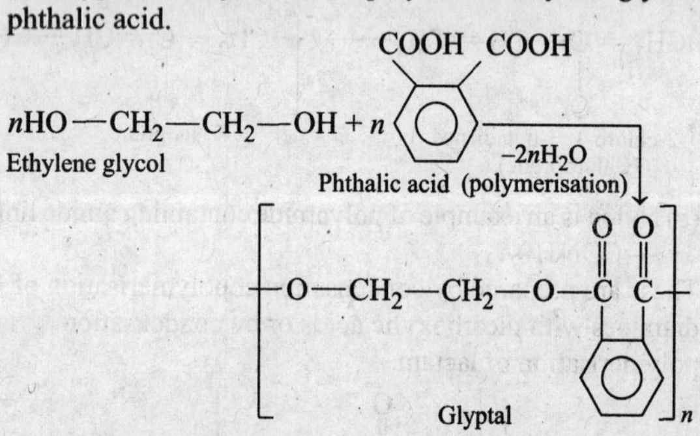

$$\underset{\text{Ethylene glycol}}{nHO-CH_2-CH_2-OH} + n\,\underset{\text{Phthalic acid}}{C_6H_4(COOH)_2} \xrightarrow[\text{(polymerisation)}]{-2nH_2O} \underset{\text{Glyptal}}{\left[O-CH_2-CH_2-O-\overset{O}{\overset{\|}{C}}-C_6H_4-\overset{O}{\overset{\|}{C}}\right]_n}$$

19 (*d*) Esterification of terephthalic acid with glycol produces terylene or dacron.

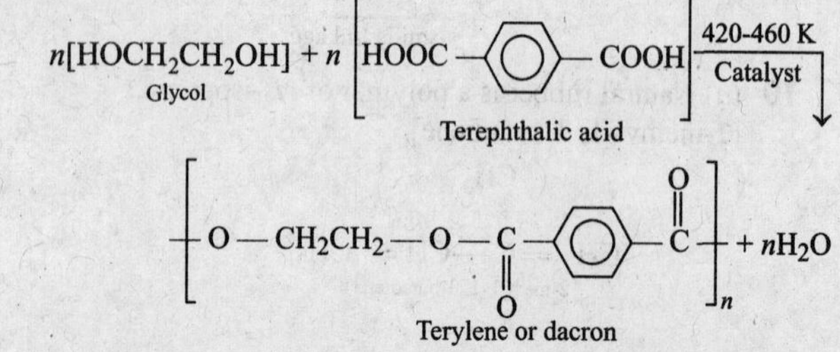

$$\underset{\text{Glycol}}{n[HOCH_2CH_2OH]} + n\,\underset{\text{Terephthalic acid}}{\left[HOOC-C_6H_4-COOH\right]} \xrightarrow[\text{Catalyst}]{420\text{–}460\,K} \underset{\text{Terylene or dacron}}{\left[O-CH_2CH_2-O-\underset{\underset{O}{\|}}{C}-C_6H_4-\overset{O}{\overset{\|}{C}}\right]_n} + nH_2O$$

20 (*b*) The correct structure of neoprene is

$$\left(-CH_2-\underset{\underset{Cl}{|}}{C}=CH-CH_2-\right)_n$$

Option (b) is incorrectly matched.

21 (*b*) Rubber, vulcanised with 3-10% sulphur is more rigid and hence, used for manufacturing tyres while the rubber, vulcanised with 1-3% sulphur is soft and stretchy, so used to make rubber bands.

22 (*d*) Buna-N (nitrile rubber or butadiene rubber), a copolymer of 1,3-butadiene and acrylonitrile, being resistant to the action of petrol, lubricating oil and organic solvents, is used for making petrol pump hose pipes, used for delivering petrol.

23 (*c*) Nylon-6, 6 is a polymer of hexamethylene diamine and adipic acid.

$$nHOOC(CH_2)_4COOH + nH_2N(CH_2)_6NH_2 \xrightarrow[-nH_2O]{\text{Polymerisation}} \underset{\text{Nylon-6, 6}}{\left[\overset{O}{\overset{\|}{C}}-(CH_2)_4-\overset{O}{\overset{\|}{C}}-\overset{H}{\overset{|}{N}}-(CH_2)_6-NH\right]_n}$$

24 (*e*) Polyvinyl polythene is obtained by the 1,2-polymerisation of 1,3-butadiene.

$$\underset{\text{1,3-butadiene}}{nCH_2{=}CH-CH{=}CH_2} \xrightarrow{\text{1,2-polymerisation}} \underset{\text{Polyvinyl polythene}}{\left[CH_2-\underset{\underset{\underset{CH_2}{\|}}{CH}}{\underset{|}{CH}}\right]_n}$$

While 1,3-butadiene on 1,4-polymerisation gives *cis* or *trans* polybutadiene.

25 (*d*) PHBV (poly β-hydroxybutyrate-co-β-hydroxyvalerate), a copolymer of 3-hydroxybutanoic acid and 3-hydroxypentanoic acid, is used in orthopaedic devices and in controlled drug release as 3-hydroxybutanoic acid provides stiffness and 3-hydroxypentanoic acid provides flexibility to the polymer.

26 (*a*) *Ziegler-Natta* catalyst $[(C_2H_5)_3Al + TiCl_4]$ is used in linear polymerisation to prepare high density polyethylene (HDPE) from alkene (olefin).

27 (*d*) Acrylonitrile ($CH_2{=}CH-CN$) is used to produce orlon.

28 (*c*) Nylon-6 is obtained from caprolactam

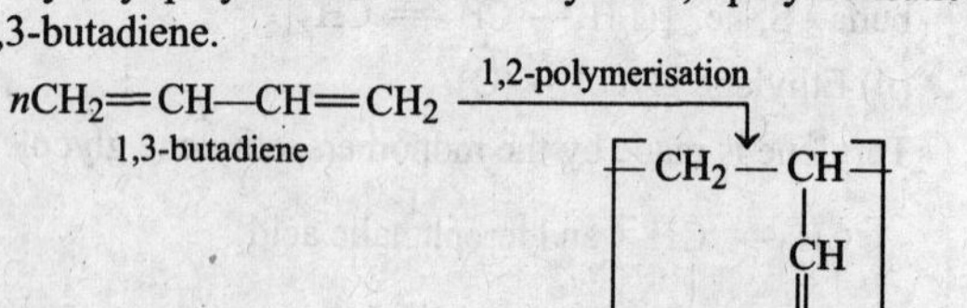

$$\underset{\text{Caprolactam}}{\text{Caprolactam ring (C=O, NH)}} \xrightarrow[H_2O]{533\text{–}593\,K} \underset{\text{Nylon-6}}{\left[\overset{O}{\overset{\|}{C}}-(CH_2)_5-\overset{H}{\overset{|}{N}}\right]_n}$$

29 (*b*) Natural rubber is *cis*-polyisoprene and is prepared from latex which is obtained from rubber tree (*Hevea brasiliensis*). Rest of the other statements are true.

30 (c) Nylon is a polymer which contains nitrogen. It has amide linkages $\left[\!-\overset{\displaystyle O}{\overset{\|}{C}}-NH-\!\right]$ and used in making bristles for brushes, in the manufacture of cords, sheets, ropes etc.

31 (a) Nylon-6, 6 is a polyamide. It has amide linkage $\left[\!-\overset{\displaystyle O}{\overset{\|}{C}}-NH-\!\right]$. It is prepared by the polymerisation of adipic acid and hexamethylene diamine.

$$\underset{\text{Adipic acid}}{nHO-\overset{\displaystyle O}{\overset{\|}{C}}-(CH_2)_4-\overset{\displaystyle O}{\overset{\|}{C}}-OH} + \underset{\text{Hexamethylene diamine}}{nH_2N-(CH_2)_6-NH_2}$$

$$\xrightarrow{-nH_2O} \underset{\text{Nylon 6, 6}}{\left[-\overset{\displaystyle O}{\overset{\|}{C}}-(CH_2)_4-\overset{\displaystyle O}{\overset{\|}{C}}-NH-(CH_2)_6-\overset{\displaystyle H}{\overset{|}{N}}-\right]_n}$$

32 (c) Buna-S rubber is also called SBR, i.e. styrene and butadiene rubber. 75% butadiene ($CH_2=CH-CH=CH_2$) and 25% styrene ($C_6H_5-CH=CH_2$) are its monomers.

$$\underset{\substack{\text{Buta 1, 3-diene}\\(75\%)}}{nCH_2=CH-CH=CH_2} + \underset{\text{Styrene (25\%)}}{n\,C_6H_5-CH=CH_2} \xrightarrow{\text{Addition copolymerisation}} \underset{\text{Buna-S or SBR}}{\left[CH_2-CH=CH-CH_2-CH_2-\underset{C_6H_5}{\underset{|}{CH}}\right]_n}$$

33 (c) Plexi glass is a commercial name of polymethylmethacrylate (PMMA). It is used in lenses, light covers, light shades, transparent domes, air craft windows etc.

34 (c) Orlon is polymer of acrylonitrile ($CH_2=CH-CN$). Thus, option (c) is incorrect match.

35 (a) Monomer of $\left[-\overset{\displaystyle CH_3}{\overset{|}{\underset{\displaystyle CH_3}{\underset{|}{C}}}}-CH_2-\right]_n$ polymer is 2-methylpropene or *iso*-butene, i.e. $H_3C-\underset{\displaystyle CH_3}{\underset{|}{C}}=CH_2$.

36 (d) 1,3-butadiene is the monomer unit of styrene-butadiene rubber or Buna-S (synthetic rubber). For natural rubber, monomer unit is isoprene. Ethylene, acrylic acid derivatives, vinyl derivatives, styrene, butadiene, isoprene and chloroprene are the examples of monomers which undergo free radical addition polymerisation. Examples of anionic addition polymerisation are vinylidene cyanide, vinylidene ester, derivatives of acrylonitrile, α-methylstyrene, etc.

Hence, both assertion and reason are incorrect.

37 (c) The polymer contains 30% molecules of mass 20000, 40% molecules of molecular mass 30000 and rest 30% molecules of molecular mass 60000. Thus,

$$\overline{M}_w = \frac{\Sigma N_i M_i^2}{\Sigma N_i M_i} = \frac{30(20000)^2 + 40(30000)^2 + 30(60000)^2}{30 \times 20000 + 40 \times 30000 + 30 \times 60000}$$

$$\overline{M}_w = 43333$$

38 (b) PTFE (polytetraflouro ethylene) is resistant towards heat and chemicals such as acids and bases. It is a bad conductor of electricity, hence it can be used as an insulator and lubricant.

39 (d) The vulcanised rubber has low water absorption, resistance to oxidation and good elasticity.

30

Chemistry in Everyday Life

Quick Review

Drugs

Drugs are the chemicals of low molecular mass (~100 – 500 u) that interacts with macromolecular targets and produces therapeutic biological response.

- When the biological response is therapeutic and useful, these chemicals are called **medicines**.
- **Chemotherapy** is the treatment of a disease with the help of chemicals.

Classification of Drugs

The classification of drugs are given in the flowchart below

Classification of Drugs

On the basis of pharmacological effect

- It provides the whole range of drugs available for the treatment of a particular kind of disease.
- e.g. analgesics–pain killing effect, antiseptic–kill or arrest the growth of micro-organisms.

On the basis of drug action

- It is based on the action of a drug on a particular biochemical process.
- e.g. antihistamines – inhibit the action of histamines.

On the basis of chemical structure

- It is based on the chemical structures of the drugs.
- e.g. sulphonamides have common structural features as shown below :

$H_2N-C_6H_4-SO_2-NH-R$ ($H_2N-C_6H_4-SO_2-NH-$: common; R : varies)

On the basis of molecular targets

- It is based on the interaction with biomolecules such as carbohydrates lipids and proteins.
- e.g. drugs with some common structural features may have the same mechanism of action on target.

Drug Target Interaction

The drug target interaction can be explained with the help of enzymes and receptors.

I. Enzymes as Drug Targets

Drugs interact with enzyme and perform the role of biological catalyst in the body. This interaction leads to formation of chemical compounds that help to cure the body.

1. **Catalytic Action of Enzymes**
   - Active sites of enzymes hold the substrate molecule, so that it can be attacked by reagent properly.
   - Substrate binds to the active site through ionic bonding, hydrogen bonding and van der Waals' interaction.

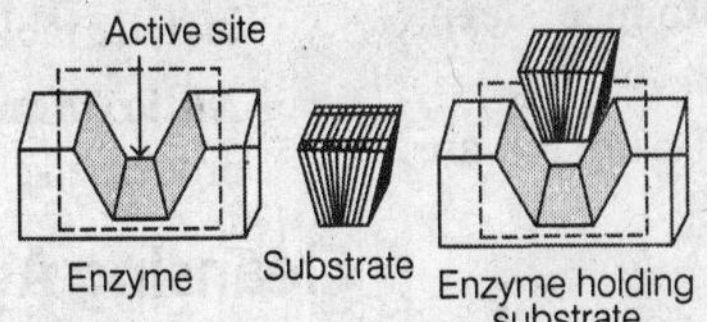

2. **Drug Enzyme Interaction**
   - Drug can block the binding site of the enzyme. It competes with the natural substrate for their attachment on the active site of enzymes. Such drugs are called **competitive inhibitors**.

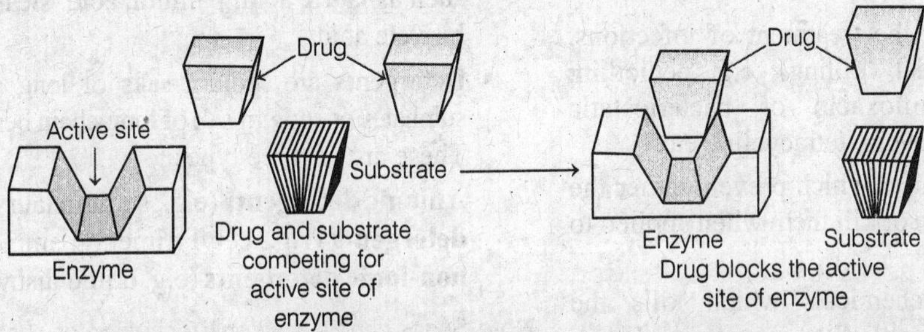

Drug and substrate competing for active site

- Some drugs bind at the allosteric site and changes the shape of active site in such a way that substrate cannot recognise it.

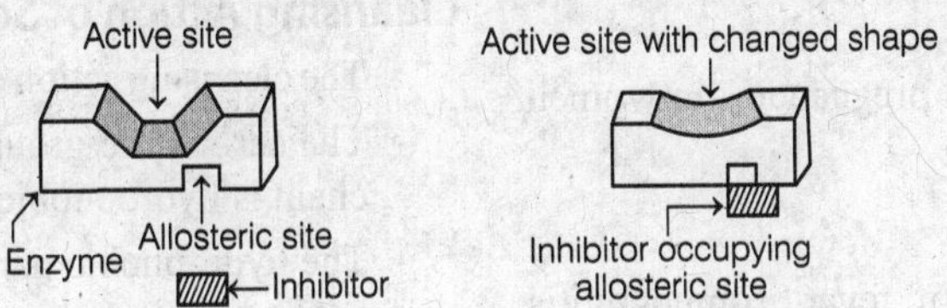

Non-competitive inhibitor changes the active site of enzyme after binding at allosteric site

II. Receptors as Drug Targets

- Sometimes drugs directly interact with receptors and message them to produce certain chemical compounds necessary to heal the body.
- Message between two neurons and between neurons to muscles is communicated through chemical messengers. These messengers are received at the binding site of receptor proteins.
- To accommodate a messenger, shape of the receptor site changes. This brings about the transfer of message into the cell.

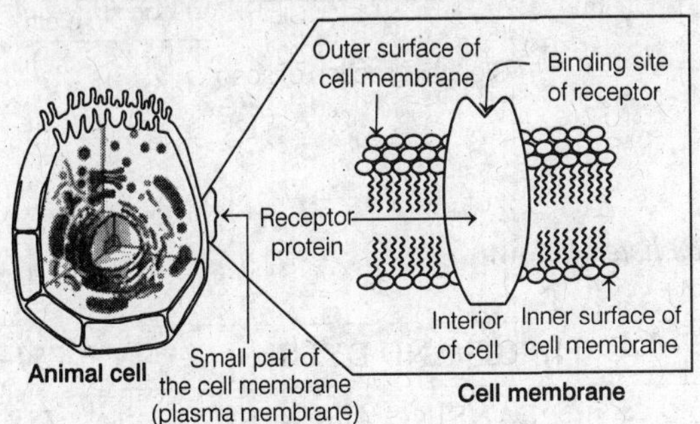

Receptor protein embedded in the cell membrane, the active site of the receptor opens on the outside region of the cell

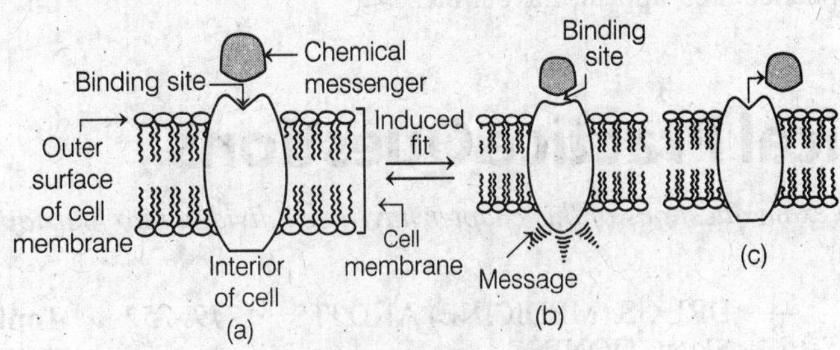

(a) Receptor receiving chemical messenger
(b) Shape of the receptor changed after attachment of messenger
(c) Receptor regains its original structure after the removal of chemical messenger

Neurologically Active Drugs

- **Tranquilizers** are used for the treatment of stress, fatigue, anxiety and mild or even severe mental diseases.

  They act on central nervous system and reduces mental stress. e.g. iproniazid and phenelzine
- **Analgesics** are used to reduce pain without causing impairment of consciousness, mental confusion.

  These are of two types :

  (*i*) **Narcotic analgesics** relieve pain and produce sleep, e.g. morphine, heroin and codeine.

  (*ii*) **Non-narcotic analgesics** relieve skeletal pain and are non-addictive, e.g. aspirin.

Antimicrobial Drugs

These drugs are used to cure diseases caused by microbes.

These are of following types :

(*i*) **Antibiotics** are used for the treatment of infections. These can be bactericidal (killing), e.g. penicillin, aminoglycosides and ofloxacin or bacteriostatic (inhibitory), e.g. erythromycin, tetracycline etc.

(*ii*) **Antiseptics** are the chemical which prevent either the growth of micro-organism or kill them when applied to living tissues, e. g. dettol.

(*iii*) **Disinfectants** are the chemicals which kills the micro-organism and are applied to inanimate objects like floors, instruments etc. e.g. lysol.

Antifertility Drugs

These are used to prevent unwanted pregnancies in women. e.g. norethindrone.

Antihistamines

These are used for the treatment of fever, conjunctivitis, sneezing and throat infection, e.g. brompheniramine.

Antacids

These are used to remove excess acid in the stomach and raise the pH at appropriate level, e.g. sodium hydrogen carbonate, cimetidine, ranitidine etc.

Chemicals in Food

- **Food additives** are added to food for their preservation and to enhance their appeal, flavour etc.
- **Artificial sweetening agents** are the chemical substances which provide sweetness to the food without increasing the calories in the body. e.g. sucralose and alitame.
- The first discovered artificial sweetener is saccharin which is 550 times as sweet as cane sugar.
- Alitame, an artificial sweetener is about 2000 times as sweet as cane sugar.
- **Food preservatives** are used to protect food against bacteria, yeasts and moulds. Common preservatives include table salt, sugar and sodium benzoate.
- **Antioxidants** are used to prevent oxidation of fats in processed food, e.g. BHA and BHT.

Cleansing Agents

Soaps and detergents are used as cleansing agents.

- **Soaps** are sodium or potassium salt of long chain fatty acids such as lauric acid, palmitic acid, stearic acid, oleic acid or linoleic acid.
- **Detergents** are sodium salts of long chain alkyl hydrogen sulphates or sodium salt of long chain benzene sulphonic acids. These are of three types :

  Anionic detergents (e.g., sodium lauryl sulphate), **cationic detergents** (e.g., cetyl trimethyl ammonium bromide) and **non-ionic detergents** (e.g. liquid dishwashing detergents).

Note Soaps can be used only for soft water whereas detergents can be used for both soft and hard water.

Cleansing Action of Soap

- The cleansing action of soap is due to affinity of soap anions.
- The carboxylic group is hydrophilic whereas hydrocarbon chain is hydrophobic.
- The hydrophobic part gets dissolved in the grease and thus leading to the formation of **micelle**.
- In micelles, the carboxylate groups form a negatively charged spherical surface, with hydrocarbon chains inside the sphere.

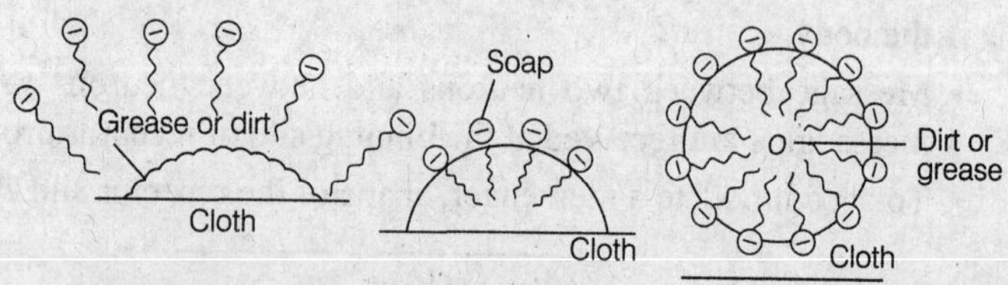

Cleansing action of soap

Topical Practice Questions

All the exam questions of this chapter have been divided into four topics as listed below.

Topic 1

Drugs (Medicine) and its Functioning

2019

1 Among the following, the narrow spectrum antibiotic is [NEET]

(a) ampicillin (b) amoxycillin
(c) chloramphenicol (d) penicillin G

2018

2 Which type of drugs come under anti-microbial drugs? [JIPMER]

(a) Antiseptics, antacids, antihistamines
(b) Tranquilizers, antiseptics, antifertility
(c) Tranquilizers, analgesics, antiseptics
(d) Antiseptics, antibiotics, disinfectants

2017

3 Mixture of chloroxylenol and terpineol acts as [NEET]

(a) analgesic (b) antiseptic
(c) antipyretic (d) antibiotic

2016

4 Which of the following is an analgesic? [NEET]

(a) Penicillin (b) Streptomycin
(c) Chloromycetin (d) Novalgin

2014

5 Which one of the following is a bacteriostatic drug? [Kerala CEE]

(a) Aminoglycosides (b) Penicillin-G
(c) Ofloxacin (d) Ampicillin
(e) Tetracycline

2013

6 Antiseptics and disinfectants either kill or prevent growth of microorganisms. Identify which of the following is not true? [NEET]

(a) A 0.2% solution of phenol is an antiseptic while 1% solution acts as a disinfectant
(b) Chlorine and iodine are used as strong disinfectants
(c) Dilute solutions of boric acid and hydrogen peroxide are strong antiseptics
(d) Disinfectants harm the living tissue

7 Salol is [AIIMS]

(a) acetylsalicylic acid (b) phenylsalicylate
(c) methyl salicylate (d) None of these

8 Paracetamol is used as an [Manipal]

(a) antibiotic (b) antimalarial
(c) antipyretic (d) arsenical

9 Which of the following destroys antigens? [Manipal]

(a) Insulin (b) Antibodies
(c) Chromoprotein (d) Phosphoprotein

2012

10 Chloramphenicol is an [CBSE AIPMT]

(a) antifertility drug (b) antihistamine
(c) antiseptic and disinfectant (d) broad spectrum antibiotic

11 The antiseptic present in dettol is [AIIMS]

(a) quinoline (b) chloroxylenol
(c) bithional (d) None of these

12 Parkinson's disease is linked to abnormalities in the level of dopamine in the body. The structure of dopamine is [Manipal]

(a) Benzene ring with CH_2NH_2, OH, OH
(b) Benzene ring with $CH_2CH_2CH_2NH_2$, OH, OH
(c) Benzene ring with $CH_2CH(NH_2)COOH$, OH, OH
(d) Benzene ring with $CH_2CH_2NH_2$, OH, OH

13 Which of the following antibiotics was first discovered? [OJEE]

(a) Ampicillin (b) Amoxycillin
(c) Penicillin (d) Chloramphenicol

2011

14 Which one of the following is employed as antihistamine? [CBSE AIPMT]

(a) Omeprazole (b) Chloramphenicol
(c) Diphenyl hydramine (d) Norethindrone

15 Terfenadine is commonly used as a/an [Kerala CEE]

(a) tranquilizer (b) antihistamine
(c) antimicrobial (d) antibiotic
(e) antifertility drug

16 Which one of the following has antiseptic property? [Kerala CEE]

(a) Dichloromethane (b) Trifluoromethane
(c) Triiodomethane (d) Tetrachloromethane
(e) Freon-12

17 Which of the following is pheromone? **[Guj CET]**

(a) Linalool (b) Disparlure
(c) BHA (d) Alitame

2010

18 Which one of the following is employed as a tranquilizer drug? **[CBSE AIPMT]**

(a) Mifepristone (b) Promethazine
(c) Valium (d) Naproxen

19 The chemical name of aspirin is **[UP CPMT, WB JEE]**

(a) methylbenzoate (b) hydroxybenzoic acid
(c) acetyl salicylic acid (d) ethylsalicylate

20 Arsenic drugs are mainly used in the treatment of **[BVP]**

(a) jaundice (b) typhoid
(c) syphilis (d) cholera

21 The following compound is used as **[RPMT]**

O
‖
O—C—CH_3
COOH

(a) an anti-inflammatory compound
(b) analgesic
(c) hypnotic (d) antiseptic

22 Which one of the following types of drugs reduces fever? **[RPMT]**

(a) Analgesics (b) Antipyretics
(c) Aspirin (d) Tranquilizers

2009

23 Which one of the following is employed as a tranquilizer? **[CBSE AIPMT]**

(a) Equanil (b) Naproxan
(c) Tetracycline (d) Chloropheninamine

24 The bacteriostatic antibiotic among the following is **[J&K CET]**

(a) erythromycin (b) penicillin
(c) aminoglycoside (d) ofloxacin

2008

25 Which of the following is not true for antibiotics? **[BHU]**

(a) Tetracycline is one of the broad spectrum antibiotics which is effective against a large number of harmful microorganisms.
(b) Streptomycin is highly effective against microorganisms which cause tuberculosis.
(c) Penicillin has a narrow spectrum and certain persons are sensitive to it.
(d) Penicillin may be administered without testing the patients for sensitivity to it.

26 Tranquilizers are also known as **[MHT CET]**

(a) psychosomatic drugs (b) psychotherapeutic drugs
(c) psychosystolic drugs (d) None of these

27 The environmental friendly method of killing harmful insects is through the use of **[Kerala CEE]**

(a) insecticides (b) sex attractants
(c) sex hormones (d) pesticides
(e) antibiotics

28 The functional groups present in 'salol' are **[Punjab PMET]**

(a) $—NH_2$ and $—OR$ (b) —OH and —COR
(c) $—NH_2$ and —COOH (d) —OH and —COOR

29 Which of the following is a local anaesthetic? **[AMU]**

(a) Diazepam (b) Procaine
(c) Chlorophenicol (d) Penicillin-G

30 Which of the following is used as an antibiotic? **[DUMET]**

(a) Ciprofloxacin (b) Paracetamol
(c) Ibuprofen (d) Tocopherol

2007

31 Chloramine-T is a **[AFMC]**

(a) disinfectant (b) antiseptic
(c) analgesic (d) antipyretic

32 Which of the following is considered to be an anti-cancer species? **[Manipal]**

(a) [Pt with Cl, Cl, Cl and $CH_2=CH_2$]
(b) [Pt with Cl, Cl, Cl, Cl]
(c) [Pt with H_3N, H_3N, Cl, Cl] (cis)
(d) [Pt with H_3N, Cl, Cl, NH_3] (trans)

33 Which of the following is used as a 'morning after pill'? **[Kerala CEE]**

(a) Norethindrone (b) Ethynylestradiol
(c) Mifepristone (d) Bithional
(e) Promethazine

2006

34 The pair whose both species are used in antacid medicinal preparations is **[AIIMS]**

(a) $NaHCO_3$ and $Mg(OH)_2$
(b) Na_2CO_3 and $Ca(HCO_3)_2$
(c) $Ca(HCO_3)_2$ and $Mg(OH)_2$
(d) $Ca(OH)_2$ and $NaHCO_3$

35 The reagent(s) used in the preparation of aspirin from salicylic acid is/are **[J&K CET]**

(a) $SOCl_2$, pyridine (b) $(CH_3CO)_2O, H^+$
(c) CH_3CO_2H, HCl (d) CH_3Cl, $AlCl_3$

36 Amphetamine is used as **[Punjab PMET]**

(a) anaesthetic (b) antidepressant
(c) antimalarial (d) analgesic

37 Which of the following compounds is used as broad spectrum antibiotics? **[Punjab PMET]**

(a) Ampicillin (b) Penicillin-G
(c) Penicillin-K (d) Tetracycline

2005

38 Phenacetin is used as **[RPMT]**

(a) antipyretics (b) antiseptics
(c) analgesic (d) antimalarials

39 Antiseptic chloroxylenol is **[KCET]**

(a) 4-chloro-3,5-dimethyl phenol
(b) 3-chloro-4,5-dimethyl phenol
(c) 4-chloro-2,5-dimethyl phenol
(d) 5-chloro-3,4-dimethyl phenol

40 An anaesthetic 'narcylene' is the commercial name of **[Haryana PMT]**

(a) C_2H_4 (b) C_2H_2
(c) $CHCl_3$ (d) $C_2H_5OC_2H_5$

41 Which of the following gives paracetamol on acetylation? **[EAMCET]**

(a) OH, NH_2 (b) OH, NH_2
(c) NH_2 (d) OH, NH_2

Answers

1 (d)	2 (d)	3 (b)	4 (d)	5 (e)	6 (c)	7 (b)	8 (c)	9 (b)	10 (d)
11 (b)	12 (d)	13 (c)	14 (c)	15 (b)	16 (c)	17 (b)	18 (c)	19 (c)	20 (c)
21 (b)	22 (b)	23 (a)	24 (a)	25 (d)	26 (b)	27 (b)	28 (d)	29 (b)	30 (a)
31 (b)	32 (c)	33 (c)	34 (a)	35 (b)	36 (b)	37 (a)	38 (a)	39 (a)	40 (b)
41 (d)									

Explanations

1 (*d*) Antibiotics which are effective mainly against either gram positive or gram negative bacteria are called narrow spectrum antibiotics.

Penicillin-G has a narrow spectrum. Ampicillin and amoxycillin are synthetic modifications of penicillin.

These have broad spectrum. Also, chloramphenicol is a broad spectrum antibiotic.

Hence, option (d) is correct.

2 (*d*) Antibiotics, antiseptics and disinfectants are antimicrobial drugs. An antimicrobial drug prevents the development or inhibit the pathogenic action of microorganisms such as bacteria (antibacterial drug), virus (antiviral drug), fungi (antifungal drug) or other parasite (antiparasitic drugs selectively).

3 (*b*) The chemicals which either prevent the growth of microorganisms or kill them but are not harmful to the living tissues are known as antiseptics. Mixture of chloroxylenol and α-terpineol is known as dettol and is an example of antiseptic.

4 (*d*) • Novalgin (Dipyrone) is a non-narcotic analgesic used as pain reliever.

- Penicillin is an antibiotic used for curing rheumatic fever.
- Streptomycin is an antibiotic drug.
- Chloromycetin is an antibiotic drug.

5 (*e*) Tetracycline is an antibiotic that fight against bacteria (bacteriostatic drug) in the body. Tetracycline is used to treat many different bacterial infections, like urinary tract infections etc.

6 (*c*) Both antiseptics and disinfectants either kill or prevent the growth of microorganisms. The main point of difference between these two is that the former (antiseptics) are used for living beings whereas disinfectants for non-living tissues. These are actually used for inanimate objects like floors, tiles etc.

A substance, like phenol in its lower concentration (0.2%) behaves as an antiseptic, whereas in higher concentration (1%) it behaves as a disinfectant. Chlorine and iodine are strong disinfectants, whereas dilute solution of boric acid and hydrogen peroxide are mild antiseptics.

7 (*b*) Salol is phenyl salicylate. It is used as an antiseptic.

It is obtained as shown below :

$$\underset{\text{Salicylic acid}}{C_6H_4(OH)COOH} + C_6H_5OH \xrightarrow{POCl_3} \underset{\text{Phenyl salicylate (salol)}}{C_6H_4(OH)COOC_6H_5} + H_2O$$

8 (*c*) Paracetamol is a drug used to decrease body temperature (antipyretic).

9 (*b*) The antibodies formed in the body destroy antigens.

10 (*d*) Chloramphenicol is a broad spectrum antibiotic (kill or inhibit wide range of gram positive and gram negative bacteria). It is used in the treatment of bacterial infections.

11 (*b*) Dettol contains chloroxylenol. It kills bacteria and provides protection against germs causing infection and illness.

12 (*d*) The structure of dopamine is

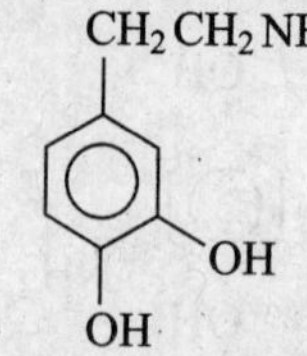

$CH_2CH_2NH_2$ – benzene ring – OH, OH

13 (*c*) The first discovered antibiotic was penicillin. Antibiotics are the compounds, produced by bacteria and fungi, capable of killing microbial species.

14 (*c*) Diphenyl hydramine is employed as an antihistamine. It interferes with the natural action of histamine by competing with histamine for binding sites of receptor where histamine exerts its effect.

15 (*b*) Terfenadine is commonly used as an antihistamine. It interferes with the natural action of histamine by competing with histamine for binding sites of receptor where histamine exerts its effect.

16. (*c*) Triiodomethane or iodoform has antiseptic property and it is applied to wounds.

17 (*b*) Disparlure is an example of pheromone (sex attractants).

18 (*c*) Valium is used as a tranquilizer drug.

19 (*c*) The chemical formula of aspirin is

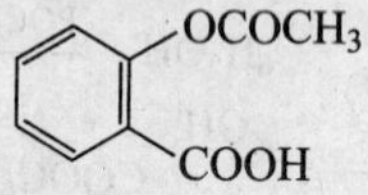

$OCOCH_3$, $COOH$

It is chemically known as acetyl salicylic acid.

20 (*c*) Arsenic drugs, such as salvarsan are used in the treatment of syphilis.

21 (*b*) It is used for the treatment of stress and mild or even severe mental diseases. The chemical substance used to relieve pain is known as analgesic.

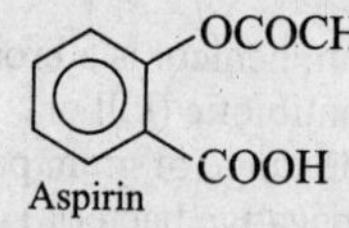

$OCOCH_3$, $COOH$

Aspirin

22 (*b*)

Type of drugs	Function
Antipyretics	Reduces fever
Analgesics	Relieve pain.
Tranquilizers	For the treatment of stress and mental diseases.

Note Aspirin is used as an analgesic as well as antipyretic.

23 (*a*) The drugs, which are used for the treatment of stress, fatigue, mild and severe mental diseases are called tranquilizers. Equanil is an example of tranquilizer, whereas naproxan, tetracycline and chloropheniramine are analgesic, antibiotic and antihistamine respectively.

24 (*a*) Antibiotics have either cidal (killing) effect or static (inhibitory) effect on microbes. Erythromycin is a bacteriostatic antibiotic.

25 (*d*) Penicillin has a narrow spectrum and is effective only against infections caused by various cocci or infections caused by some gram positive bacteria. Some persons have allergy to penicillin. Hence, it is very essential to test the sensitivity of the patient by giving a test dose before giving the full dose.

26 (*b*) Tranquilizers are the drugs which used to relieve mental ailments. These are also known as psychotherapeutic drugs because they act on the central nervous system.

27 (*b*) Sex attractant pheromones have been used for pest control (i.e. to kill harmful insects). This method is environmental friendly.

28 (*d*) Salol is phenyl salicylate. The functional group present in salol are —OH and —COO*R*. It's structure is given below :

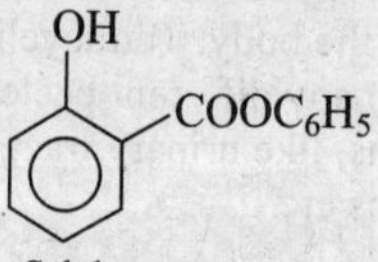

OH, $COOC_6H_5$

Salol

29 (*b*) General anaesthetic produces unconciousness all over the body, e.g. nitrous oxide (N_2O), cyclopropane, chloroform etc. Local anaesthetic affect only part of the body, e.g. xylocaine, procaine etc.

30 (*a*) Ciprofloxacin is used as an antibiotic while paracetamol, ibuprofen and tocopherol respectively, are antipyretic, pain killer and vitamin E.

31 (*b*) Chloramine-T is an antiseptic drug which causes destruction of microorganisms that produces septic disease, e.g. dettol, savlon, acriflavin, boric acid, phenol, iodoform, $KMnO_4$ and some dyes like methylene blue.

32 (*c*) *cis*-isomer of $[Pt(NH_3)_2Cl_2]$ is used as an anti-cancer drug for treating several types of malignant tumours.

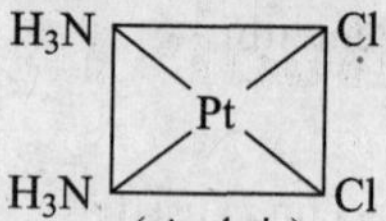

H_3N, Cl, Pt, H_3N, Cl

(*cis*-platin)

33 (*c*) Mifepristone is used as a "morning after pill".

34 (*a*) $NaHCO_3$ and $Mg(OH)_2$ are used in medicine to neutralise the acidity in the stomach. Magnesium hydroxide is basic in nature and dissolves in acids forming corresponding salts. So, both are used in antacid medicinal preparation.

35 (*b*) Aspirin (2-acetoxybenzoic acid) is an analgesic. It is obtained by acetylating salicylic acid with acetic anhydride and conc. H_2SO_4.

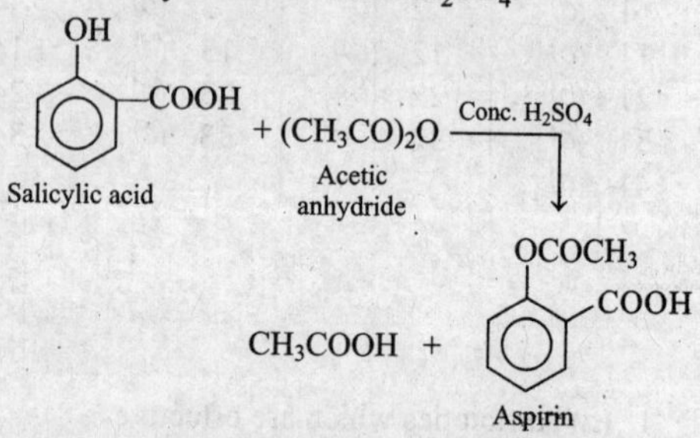

Salicylic acid (OH, COOH) $+ (CH_3CO)_2O$ (Acetic anhydride) $\xrightarrow{\text{Conc. } H_2SO_4}$ $CH_3COOH +$ Aspirin ($OCOCH_3$, COOH)

36 (*b*) Amphetamine is used as an antidepressant drug. These drugs inhibit the enzymes which catalyse the degradaiion of nor adrenaline.

37 (*a*) Ampicillin is widely used as broad spectrum antibiotics. It can kill or inhibit a wide range of gram positive and gram negative bacteria.

38 (*a*) Phenacetin is used as antipyretics (reduces fever).

39 (*a*)

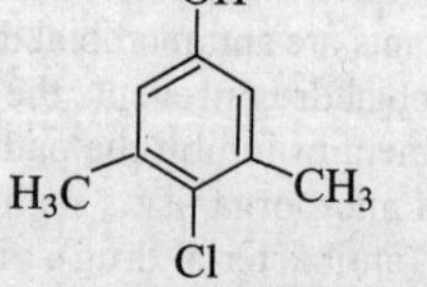

OH, H_3C, CH_3, Cl

Chloroxylenol
(4-chloro-3, 5-dimethylphenol)

40 (*b*) Acetylene (C_2H_2) acts as an anaesthetic and is commercially named as narcylene.

41 (*d*)

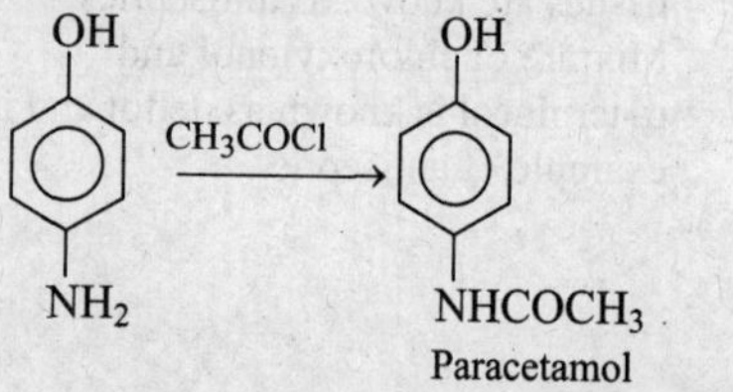

OH, NH_2 $\xrightarrow{CH_3COCl}$ OH, $NHCOCH_3$

Paracetamol

Topic 2

Chemicals in Food and Cosmetics

2019

1 The artificial sweetener stable at cooking temperature and does not provide calories is **[NEET (Odisha)]**

(a) saccharin (b) aspartame
(c) sucralose (d) alitame

2 Saccharin an artificial sweeterner is manufactured from **[JIPMER]**

(a) toluene (b) cyclohexane
(c) starch (d) cellulose

2018

3 Food preservatives prevent spoilage of food due to microbial growth. The most commonly used preservatives are **[AIIMS]**

(a) C_6H_5COONa
(b) table salt, sugar
(c) vegetable oils and sodium benzoate
(d) All of the above

2014

4 Butylated hydroxyl toluene as a food additive acts as **[KCET]**

(a) antioxidant (b) flavouring agent
(c) colouring agent (d) emulsifier

2012

5 Which of the following sweeteners is limited to cold foods and soft drinks? **[KCET]**

(a) Aspartame (b) Sucralose
(c) Alitame (d) None of these

2010

6 Potassium metabisulphite is a (an) **[MHT CET]**

(a) preservative (b) antioxidant
(c) artificial sweetener (d) Both (a) and (b)

7 Select the detergent that is used to prepare cosmetics. **[Guj CET]**

(a) DDBS
(b) Polyethylene glycol
(c) Cetyltrimethyl ammonium chloride
(d) LAS

2009

8 The sweetest artificial sugar among the following is **[AIIMS]**

(a) aspartame (b) sucralose (c) alitame (d) sucrose

2007

9 Heart patients can be given **[DUMET]**

(a) monosaturated fatty acid
(b) *trans* fatty acid
(c) polyunsaturated fatty acid
(d) polysaturated fatty acid

2006

10 Acrolein test is positive for **[KCET]**

(a) polysaccharides (b) proteins
(c) oils and fats (d) reducing sugars

Answers

1 (c)	2 (a)	3 (d)	4 (a)	5 (a)	6 (d)	7 (c)	8 (c)	9 (c)	10 (c)

Explanations

1 (*c*) Sucralose is a trichloro derivative of sucrose and is about 650 times sweeter than cane sugar. It is a zero calorie sugar and stable at cooking temperature.

Sucralose

2 (*a*) Saccharin is a low calorie sweetener manufactured from toluene.

Toluene $\xrightarrow[\text{(ii) } NH_3, \Delta]{\text{(i) conc. } H_2SO_4}$ o-toluenesulphonamide (CH_3, SO_2NH_2) $\xrightarrow{KMnO_2/OH^-}$ ($COOH$, SO_2NH_2) $\xrightarrow{\Delta}$ Saccharin (CO, NH, SO_2)

Saccharin

3 (*d*) The chemicals which are used to protect food from microbial action i.e. which inhibit the process of fermentation, acidification and any other decomposition of food are known as food preservatives. Table salt, sugar, vegetable oil, vinegar, sodium benzoate (C_6H_5COONa), sodium metabisulphite ($Na_2S_2O_5$), vitamin E. etc. are the common examples of food preservatives.

4 (*a*) Butylated *p*-hydroxyanisole (BHA), butylated *p*-hydroxy toluene (BHT), esters of gallic acid are examples of antioxidants. These chemicals retard the action of oxygen on the food material and help in its preservation.

5 (*a*) The use of aspartame is limited to cold foods and soft drinks because it is unstable at cooking temperature.

6 (*d*) Potassium metabisulphite, $K_2S_2O_5$, is a white crystalline solid with pungent odour of sulphur. It is used as an antimicrobial, preservative, antioxidant and bleaching agent in food.

7 (*c*) Cetylrimethyl ammonium chloride is a cationic detergent. It is used to prepare cosmetics becauses it processes germicidal properties.

8 (*c*) Among the given sugars, sucrose is the natural sugar while others are artificial. Among artificial sugars, alitame is about 2000 times as sweet as cane sugar.

9 (*c*) Polyunsaturated fatty acid is given to heart patients.

10 (*c*) Acrolein test is positive for oils and fats.

Topic 3

Fibres and Dyes

2011

1 Match metal ion (Column I) with colour (Column II) in presence of Alizarin.

Column I	Column II
A. Sr^{2+}	1. Blue
B. Mg^{2+}	2. Pink
C. Al^{3+}	3. Violet
D. Ba^{2+}	4. Red

[Guj CET]

Codes

	A	B	C	D
(a)	1	4	3	2
(b)	2	1	4	3
(c)	3	2	1	4
(d)	4	3	2	1

2010

2 Which type of dyes are not used to dye nylon and polyester fibres? [Guj CET]

(a) Vat dyes (b) Basic dyes
(c) Disperse dyes (d) Insoluble azo dyes

2009

3 A dye that imparts different colours to the fabric with different metal ions is called [Kerala CEE]

(a) mordant dye (b) disperse dye
(c) vat dye (d) direct dye
(e) acid dye

2008

4 Azo dye is prepared by the coupling of phenol and [AMU]

(a) diazonium chloride (b) *o*-nitroaniline
(c) benzoic acid (d) chlorobenzene

5 Benzaldehyde condenses with N,N-dimethylaniline in the presence of anhydrous $ZnCl_2$ to give [DUMET]

(a) Michler's ketone (b) azo dye
(c) malachite green (d) buffer yellow

2007

6 Which one is disperse dye? [AFMC]

(a) Congo red (b) Alizarin
(c) Celliton (d) None of these

7 An insoluble dye is reduced to a soluble colourless leuco form by an alkaline reducing agent. The fibre is soaked in the dye solution and then exposed to air to develop the colour. The dye is [Kerala CEE]

(a) mordant dye (b) vat dye
(c) azo dye (d) direct dye
(e) disperse dye

8 Select the basic dye from the following. [Guj CET]

(a) Congo red
(b) Methyl red
(c) Methyl orange
(d) Malachite green

2006

9 Fluoroscein is an example of [Punjab PMET]

(a) azo dye (b) phthalein dye
(c) triphenyl methane dye (d) nitro dye

10 Alizarin is a [Guj CET]

(a) nitro dye (b) azo dye
(c) anthraquinone dye (d) phthalein dye

Answers

1 (*d*)	2 (*a*)	3 (*a*)	4 (*a*)	5 (*c*)	6 (*c*)	7 (*b*)	8 (*d*)	9 (*b*)	10 (*c*)

Explanations

1 (*d*) Alizarin is used as a prominent red dye, principally for dyeing textile fabrics. The different metal ions gives the following colours in the presence of alizarin.

Column I	Column II
A. Sr^{2+}	4. Red
B. Mg^{2+}	3. Violet
C. Al^{3+}	2. Pink
D. Ba^{2+}	1. Blue

2 (*a*) Vat dyes are not used to dye nylon and polyester fibres but are used to dye cotton fibres. Basic dyes, disperse dyes and insoluble azo dyes, however, are used to dye nylon and polyesters.

3 (*a*) Mordant dyes are used for dyeing and imparting colour to fabrics in the presence of metal ions. In case of such dyes, the metal ion acts as binding agent between dye and fabric. A single mordant dye imparts different colours to the fabrics in the presence of different metal ions.

4 (*a*) Azo dye is prepared by the coupling of phenol and diazonium chloride.

Aniline (NH_2) $\xrightarrow[0-5°C]{NaNO_2 + HCl}$ Benzene diazonium chloride ($\overset{+}{N_2}Cl^-$)

Benzene diazonium chloride ($\overset{+}{N_2}Cl^-$) + Phenol (OH) ⟶ $C_6H_5-N{=}N-C_6H_4-OH$

p-hydroxy azobenzene (azo dye)

5 (*c*)

$C_6H_5CH{=}O$ + 2 H–C_6H_4–$N(CH_3)_2$ $\xrightarrow[\text{Anhydrous } ZnCl_2]{}$ $C_6H_5C(H)[C_6H_4N(CH_3)_2]_2 + H_2O$

Benzaldehyde; N, N-dimethyl aniline; Malachite green

6 (*c*) Celliton is a disperse dye. Disperse dye are usually applied in the form of dispersion of finely divided dye in a soap solution in the presence of phenol, cresol and benzoic acid etc. They are mainly used to dye dacron, nylon, synthetic fibre.

7 (*b*) Vat dyes are insoluble in water and cannot be but directly applied. It is reduced to soluble colourless leuco form by an alkaline reducing agent, e.g.

Indigo (blue, water insoluble) $\underset{}{\overset{\text{Reduction}}{\rightleftharpoons}}$ Indigo (white leuco base)

8 (*d*) Congo red — Direct dye
Methyl red — Acid dye
Methyl orange — Acid dye
Malachite green — Basic dye

9 (*b*) Fluorescein is an example of phthalein dye.

10 (*c*) Alizarin is an anthraquinone dye.

Alizarin

Topic 4

Cleansing Agents

2019

1 **Assertion** (A) For liquid dishwashing non-ionic type of detergent are used.

Reason (R) Remove grease and oil by micelle formation.

(a) Both A and R are correct and R is the correct explanation of A **[AIIMS 2019]**

(b) Both A and R are correct but R is not the correct explanation of A

(c) A is correct but R is incorrect

(d) Both A and R are incorrect

2018

2 Which one among the following is added to soap to impart antiseptic property? **[JIPMER]**

(a) Sodium lauryl sulphate
(b) Sodium dodecyl benzene sulphonates
(c) Rosin
(d) Bithional

2015

3 Bithional is generally added to the soaps as an additive to function as a/an **[CBSE AIPMT]**

(a) softener
(b) dryer
(c) buffering agent
(d) antiseptic

2014

4 Match the following Column I with Column II.

	Column I		Column II
A.	Sucralose	1.	Antioxidant
B.	Iodine	2.	Artificial sweetener
C.	Sodium benzoate	3.	Antacid
D.	Ranitidine	4.	Antiseptic
		5.	Food preservative

The correct answer is [EAMCET]

	A	B	C	D
(a)	2	4	1	3
(b)	2	4	5	3
(c)	2	3	5	1
(d)	2	1	3	4

2013

5 Hydrolytic reaction of fats with caustic soda is known as [KCET]

(a) acetylation
(b) carboxylation
(c) esterification
(d) saponification

2010

6 In the following which is soap? [MP PMT]

(a) CH_3COONa (b) CH_3ONa
(c) $C_{17}H_{35}COONa$ (d) $C_{17}H_{35}SO_3Na$

2009

7 The oxidant which is used as an antiseptic is [WB JEE]

(a) $KBrO_3$ (b) $KMnO_4$ (c) CrO_3 (d) KNO_3

8 Assertion (A) Sodium-2-dodecylbenzene sulphonate is a biodegradable detergent.
Reason (R) Detergents having highly branched chains are biodegradable. [AIIMS]

(a) Both A and R are correct and R is the correct explanation of A
(b) Both A and R are correct but R is not the correct explanation of A
(c) A is correct but R is incorrect
(d) Both A and R are incorrect

9 The role of phosphate in detergent powder is to [UP CPMT]

(a) control pH level of the detergent water mixture.
(b) remove Ca^{2+} and Mg^{2+} ions from the water that cause the hardness of water.
(c) provide whiteness to the fabrics.
(d) form solid detergents as phosphateless detergents are liquid in nature.

2008

10 Which of the following statement is not true? [Kerala CEE]

(a) Some disinfectants can be used as antiseptic at low concentration
(b) Sulphadiazine is a synthetic antibacterial
(c) Pheromones provide chemical means of establishing communication
(d) Aspirin is analgesic and antipyretic
(e) Norethindrone is a pheromone

2007

11 The saponification value of an oil or fat is measured in terms of [AIIMS]

(a) NH_4OH (b) NaOH (c) KOH (d) C_6H_5OH

12 Detergents are known to pollute rivers and waterways. However, detergents can be made biodegradable and pollution free by taking [Kerala CEE]

(a) cyclic hydrocarbon chain
(b) shorter hydrocarbon chain
(c) unbranched hydrocarbon chain
(d) hydrocarbon with more branching
(e) benzenoid hydrocarbons

2006

13 Which one of the following compounds is used as a body deodorant? [Kerala CEE]

(a) Aspirin
(b) Omeprazole
(c) Indigosol-O
(d) *p*-chlorometaxylenol
(e) Bithional

2005

14 Which one of the following forms micelles in aqueous solution above certain concentration? [CBSE AIPMT]

(a) Urea
(b) Dodecyltrimethylammonium chloride
(c) Pyridinium chloride
(d) Glucose

Answers

1 (a)	2 (d)	3 (d)	4 (b)	5 (d)	6 (c)	7 (b)	8 (d)	9 (b)	10 (e)
11 (c)	12 (c)	13 (d)	14 (b)						

Explanations

1 (*a*) Non-ionic detergents have groups at one end of the alkyl chain showing H-bonding that includes monoesters of polyhydric alcohols or polyethens derived from ethylene oxide. It is used as liquid dishwashing detergent. It removes grease and oil by micelle formation.
Hence, assertion and reason are correct and given reason is the correct explanation of the assertion.

2 (*d*) Bithional is an antiseptic. It is mixed with soap to impart antiseptic property.

3 (*d*) Bithional is added to soap to impart antiseptic properties. It reduces odour produced by bacterial decomposition of organic matter on the skin.

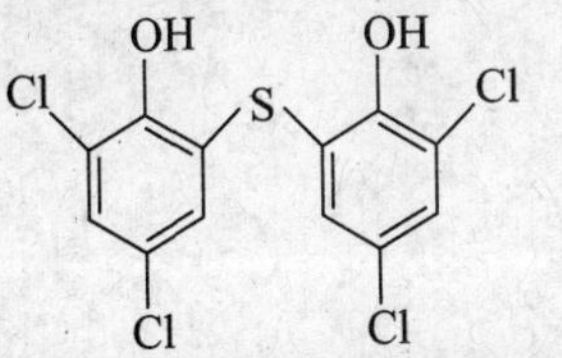

IUPAC Name: 2, 2 sulfanediylbis (4, 6-dichlorophenol).

4 (*b*) Sucralose is a low calorie artificial sweetener. Iodine is an antiseptic. Sodium benzoate is a food preservative. Ranitidine is used to prevent ulcers caused by the production of excess acid in the stomach.

5 (*d*) The hydrolytic reaction of fats with caustic soda is known as saponification.

$$\underset{\text{Glyceryl ester of stearic acid}}{\begin{array}{l} CH_2OCO\,C_{17}H_{35} \\ | \\ CHOCOC_{17}H_{35} \\ | \\ CH_2OCOC_{17}H_{35} \end{array}} + 3NaOH \longrightarrow \underset{\text{Glycerol}}{\begin{array}{l} CH_2OH \\ | \\ CHOH \\ | \\ CH_2OH \end{array}} + \underset{\text{Sodium stearate (Soap)}}{3C_{17}H_{35}CO\overset{-}{O}\overset{+}{Na}}$$

6 (*c*) Soaps are the sodium and potassium salts of higher fatty acids. $C_{17}H_{35}COONa$, sodium stearate is a soap.

7 (*b*) $KMnO_4$ is used as an oxidant and also act as antiseptic.

8 (*d*) Detergents with straight chains (unbranched chains) are biodegradable. Since, sodium-2-dodecylbenzene sulphonate has a branched chain, it is a non-biodegradable detergent.

9 (*b*) The role of phosphate in detergent powder is to remove Ca^{2+} and Mg^{2+} ions from the water that causes hardness of water.

10 (*e*) Norethindrone is not a pheromone. It is a progesterone hormone. It is used for treating certain menstrual and uterine problems. It works by altering the lining of uterus. All the other statements are true.

11 (*c*) Saponification value is the number of milligrams of KOH required to neutralise the fatty acid resulting from the complete hydrolysis of 1 g of oil or fat

12 (*c*) Detergent molecules associated with branched hydrocarbon tail are a source of water pollution. However, detergents can be made biodegradable and pollution free by taking unbranched hydrocarbon chain because unbranched chains are more prone to attack by bacteria.

13 (*d*) *p*-chlorometaxylenol is an antiseptic which is used as a body deodorant.

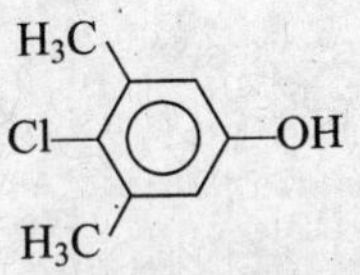

p-chlorometaxylenol

14 (*b*) Surfactant detergents form micelles in aqueous solution above their CMC (critical micelle concentration).

Dodecyltrimethylammonium chloride is an example of surfactant (cationic surfactant), so it shows the following phenomena.

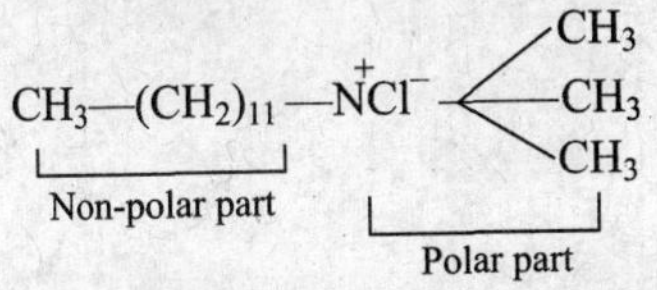

$$\underset{\text{Non-polar part}}{CH_3—(CH_2)_{11}}—\underset{\text{Polar part}}{\overset{+}{N}Cl^-(CH_3)_3}$$

NEET

SOLVED PAPER 2020

1. What is the change in oxidation number of carbon in the following reaction?

$CH_4(g) + 4Cl_2(g) \longrightarrow CCl_4(l) + 4HCl(g)$

(a) 0 to + 4 (b) – 4 to + 4
(c) 0 to – 4 (d) + 4 to + 4

2. On electrolysis of dilute sulphuric acid using platinum (Pt) electrode, the product obtained at anode will be

(a) oxygen gas (b) H_2S gas
(c) SO_2 gas (d) hydrogen gas

3. An increase in the concentration of the reactants of a reaction leads to the change in

(a) heat of reaction
(b) threshold energy
(c) collision frequency
(d) activation energy

4. Reaction between benzaldehyde and acetophenone in presence of dilute NaOH is known as

(a) Cannizzaro's reaction
(b) Cross Cannizzaro's reaction
(c) Cross aldol condensation
(d) Aldol condensation

5. Which of the following alkane cannot be made in good yield by Wurtz reaction?

(a) 2, 3-dimethylbutane (b) *n*-heptane
(c) *n*-butane (d) *n*-hexane

6. Which of the following is a natural polymer?

(a) Poly (Butadiene-styrene)
(b) Polybutadiene
(c) Poly (Butadiene-acrylonitrile)
(d) *Cis*-1, 4-polyisoprene

7. A mixture of N_2 and Ar gases in a cylinder contains 7 g of N_2 and 8 g of Ar. If the total pressure of the mixture of the gases in the cylinder is 27 bar, the partial pressure of N_2 is

[Use atomic masses (in g mol^{-1}) : N = 14, Ar = 40]

(a) 12 bar (b) 15 bar
(c) 18 bar (d) 9 bar

8. Match the following and identify the correct option.

A.	$CO(g) + H_2(g)$	(i)	$Mg(HCO_3)_2 + Ca(HCO_3)_2$
B.	Temporary hardness of water	(ii)	An electron deficient hydride
C.	B_2H_6	(iii)	Synthesis gas
D.	H_2O_2	(iv)	Non-planar structure

	A	B	C	D
(a)	(iii)	(ii)	(i)	(iv)
(b)	(iii)	(iv)	(ii)	(i)
(c)	(i)	(ii)	(ii)	(iv)
(d)	(iii)	(i)	(ii)	(iv)

9. For the reaction, $2Cl(g) \longrightarrow Cl_2(g)$, the correct option is

(a) $\Delta_r H > 0$ and $\Delta_r S < 0$ (b) $\Delta_r H < 0$ and $\Delta_r S > 0$
(c) $\Delta_r H < 0$ and $\Delta_r S < 0$ (d) $\Delta_r H > 0$ and $\Delta_r S > 0$

10. An element has a body centered cubic (bcc) structure with a cell edge of 288 pm. The atomic radius is

(a) $\frac{\sqrt{2}}{4} \times 288$ pm (b) $\frac{4}{\sqrt{3}} \times 288$ pm
(c) $\frac{4}{\sqrt{2}} \times 288$ pm (d) $\frac{\sqrt{3}}{4} \times 288$ pm

11. Urea reacts with water to form *A* which will decompose to form *B*. *B* when passed through Cu^{2+} (*aq*), deep blue colour solution *C* is formed. What is the formula of *C* from the following?

(a) $[Cu(NH_3)_4]^{2+}$ (b) $Cu(OH)_2$
(c) $CuCO_3 \cdot Cu(OH)_2$ (d) $CuSO_4$

12. Reaction between acetone and methylmagnesium chloride followed by hydrolysis will give

(a) secondary butyl alcohol
(b) *tert* butyl alcohol
(c) isobutyl alcohol
(d) isopropyl alcohol

13. The following metal ion activates many enzymes, participates in the oxidation of glucose to produce ATP and with Na, is responsible for the transmission of nerve signals

(a) copper (b) calcium
(c) potassium (d) iron

14. The number of protons, neutrons and electrons in $^{175}_{71}$Lu, respectively, are

(a) 104, 71 and 71
(b) 71, 71 and 104
(c) 175, 104 and 71
(d) 71, 104 and 71

15. Which of the following set of molecules will have zero dipole moment ?

(a) Boron trifluoride, hydrogen fluoride, carbon dioxide, 1,3-dichlorobenzene
(b) Nitrogen trifluoride, beryllium difluoride, water, 1,3-dichlorobenzene
(c) Boron trifluoride, beryllium difluoride, carbon dioxide, 1, 4-dichlorobenzene
(d) Ammonia, beryllium difluoride, water, 1,4-dichlorobenzene

16. Identify a molecule which does not exist.

(a) Li_2
(b) C_2
(c) O_2
(d) He_2

17. Identify the incorrect match.

Name	IUPAC official name
(A) Unnilunium	(i) Mendelevium
(B) Unniltrium	(ii) Lawrencium
(C) Unnihexium	(iii) Seaborgium
(D) Unununnium	(iv) Darmstadtium

(a) (B), (ii)
(b) (C), (iii)
(c) (D), (iv)
(d) (A), (i)

18. The rate constant for a first order reaction is $4.606 \times 10^{-3}\ s^{-1}$. The time required to reduce 2.0 g of the reactant to 0.2 g is

(a) 200 s
(b) 500 s
(c) 1000 s
(d) 100 s

19. Identify the correct statement from the following:

(a) Blister copper has blistered appearance due to evolution of CO_2.
(b) Vapour phase refining is carried out for nickel by van Arkel method.
(c) Pig iron can be moulded into a variety of shapes.
(d) Wrought iron is impure iron with 4% carbon.

20. Measuring zeta potential is useful in determining which property of colloidal solution?

(a) Solubility
(b) Stability of the colloidal particles
(c) Size of the colloidal particles
(d) Viscosity

21. Which of the following oxoacid of sulphur has —O—O— linkage?

(a) H_2SO_4, sulphuric acid
(b) $H_2S_2O_8$, peroxodisulphuric acid
(c) $H_2S_2O_7$, pyrosulphuric acid
(d) H_2SO_3, sulphurous acid

22. Elimination reaction of 2-bromo-pentane to form pent-2-ene is

1. β-elimination reaction.
2. Follows Zaitsev rule.
3. Dehydrohalogenation reaction.
4. Dehydration reaction.

(a) (1), (3), (4)
(b) (2), (3), (4)
(c) (1), (2), (4)
(d) (1), (2), (3)

23. Identify the correct statements from the following:

1. $CO_2(g)$ is used as refrigerant for ice-cream and frozen food.
2. The structure of C_{60} contains twelve six carbon rings and twenty five carbon rings.
3. ZSM-5, a type of zeolite, is used to convert alcohols into gasoline.
4. CO is colourless and odourless gas.

(a) (1) and (3) only
(b) (2) and (3) only
(c) (3) and (4) only
(d) (1), (2) and (3) only

24. An alkene on ozonolysis gives methanal as one of the product. Its structure is

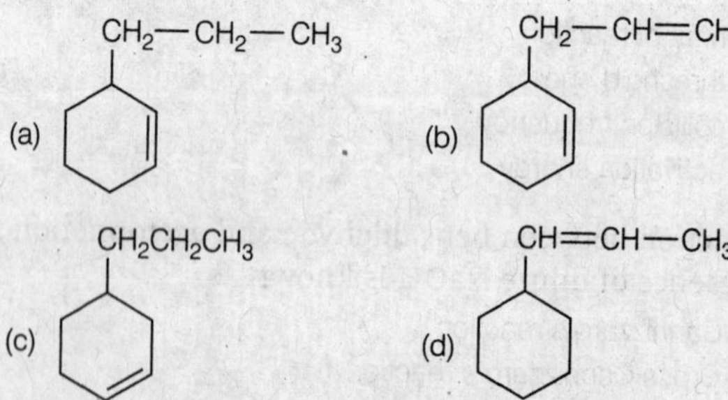

25. Paper chromatography is an example of

(a) partition chromatography
(b) thin layer chromatography
(c) column chromatography
(d) adsorption chromatography

26. Match the following.

Oxide	Nature
A. CO	(i) Basic
B. BaO	(ii) Neutral
C. Al_2O_3	(iii) Acidic
D. Cl_2O_7	(iv) Amphoteric

Which of the following is correct option?

	A	B	C	D
(a)	(ii)	(i)	(iv)	(iii)
(b)	(iii)	(iv)	(i)	(ii)
(c)	(iv)	(iii)	(ii)	(i)
(d)	(i)	(ii)	(iii)	(iv)

27. Which one of the followings has maximum number of atoms?

(a) 1 g of Mg(s) [Atomic mass of Mg = 24]
(b) 1 g of $O_2(g)$ [Atomic mass of O = 16]
(c) 1 g of Li(s) [Atomic mass of Li = 7]
(d) 1 g of Ag(s) [Atomic mass of Ag = 108]

28. Which of the following is a basic amino acid?

(a) Alanine (b) Tyrosine
(c) Lysine (d) Serine

29. The calculated spin only magnetic moment of Cr^{2+} ion is

(a) 4.90 BM (b) 5.92 BM
(c) 2.84 BM (d) 3.87 BM

30. Sucrose on hydrolysis gives

(a) α-D-glucose + β-D-glucose
(b) α-D-glucose + β-D-fructose
(c) α-D-fructose + β-D-fructose
(d) β-D-glucose + α-D-fructose

31. The mixture which shows positive deviation from Raoult's law is

(a) Benzene + toluene
(b) Acetone + chloroform
(c) Chlorethane + bromoethane
(d) Ethanol + acetone

32. A tertiary butyl carbocation is more stable than a secondary butyl carbocation because of which of the following?

(a) +*R*-effect of $—CH_3$ groups
(b) –*R*-effect of $—CH_3$ groups
(c) Hyperconjugation
(d) –*I*-effect of $—CH_3$ groups

33. Find out the solubility of $Ni(OH)_2$ in 0.1 M NaOH. Given, that the ionic product of $Ni(OH)_2$ is 2×10^{-15}.

(a) 2×10^{-8} M (b) 1×10^{-13} M
(c) 1×10^{8} M (d) 2×10^{-13} M

34. Which of the following is a cationic detergent ?

(a) Sodium stearate
(b) Cetyltrimethyl ammonium bromide
(c) Sodium dodecyl benzene sulphonate
(d) Sodium lauryl sulphate

35. The freezing point depression constant (K_f) of benzene is 5.12 K kg mol^{-1}. The freezing point depression for the solution of molality 0.078 m containing a non-electrolyte solute in benzene is (rounded off upto two decimal places)

(a) 0.80 K (b) 0.40 K
(c) 0.60 K (d) 0.20 K

36. Identify the incorrect statement.

(a) The transition metals and their compounds are known for their catalytic activity due to their ability to adopt multiple oxidation states and to form complexes.
(b) Interstitial compounds are those that are formed when small atoms like H, C or N are trapped inside the crystal lattices of metals.
(c) The oxidation states of chromium in CrO_4^{2-} and $Cr_2O_7^{2-}$ are not the same.
(d) Cr^{2+} (d^4) is a stronger reducing agent than Fe^{2+} (d^6) in water.

37. Which of the following statements is not correct about carbon monoxide?

(a) It reduces oxygen carrying ability of blood.
(b) The carboxyhaemoglobin (haemoglobin bound to CO) is less stable than oxyhaemoglobin.
(c) It is produced due to incomplete combustion.
(d) It forms carboxyhaemoglobin.

38. Hydrolysis of sucrose is given by the following reaction.

$$\text{Sucrose} + H_2O \rightleftharpoons \text{Glucose} + \text{Fructose}$$

If the equilibrium constant (K_C) is 2×10^{13} at 300 K, the value of $\Delta_r G^{\ominus}$ at the same temperature will be

(a) $8.314 \text{ J mol}^{-1} \text{K}^{-1} \times 300 \text{ K} \times \ln(2 \times 10^{13})$
(b) $8.314 \text{ J mol}^{-1} \text{K}^{-1} \times 300 \text{ K} \times \ln(3 \times 10^{13})$
(c) $-8.314 \text{ J mol}^{-1} \text{K}^{-1} \times 300 \text{ K} \times \ln(4 \times 10^{13})$
(d) $-8.314 \text{ J mol}^{-1} \text{K}^{-1} \times 300 \text{ K} \times \ln(2 \times 10^{13})$

39. Which of the following is the correct order of increasing field strength of ligands to form coordination compounds?

(a) $SCN^- < F^- < CN^- < C_2O_4^{2-}$
(b) $F^- < SCN^- < C_2O_4^{2-} < CN^-$
(c) $CN^- < C_2O_4^{2-} < SCN^- < F^-$
(d) $SCN^- < F^- < C_2O_4^{2-} < CN^-$

40. Identify compound *X* in the following sequence of reactions.

$$C_6H_5CH_3 \xrightarrow{Cl_2/h\nu} X \xrightarrow[373\text{ K}]{H_2O} C_6H_5CHO$$

(a) 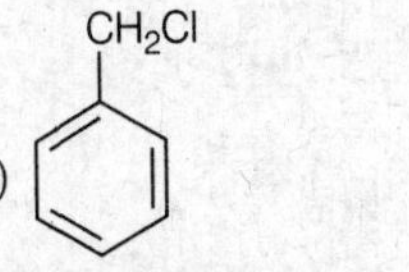

(b) 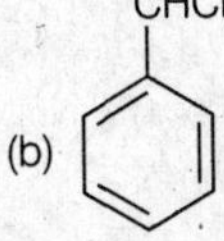

(c) 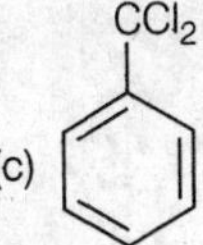

(d) 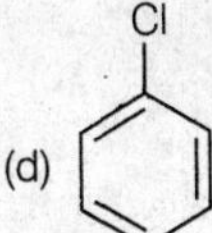

41. The correct option for free expansion of an ideal gas under the adiabatic condition is

(a) $q = 0, \Delta T < 0$ and $w > 0$
(b) $q < 0, \Delta T < 0$ and $w = 0$
(c) $q > 0, \Delta T < 0$ and $w > 0$
(d) $q = 0, \Delta T = 0$ and $w = 0$

42. The number of Faradays (*F*) required to produce 20 g of calcium from molten $CaCl_2$ (Atomic mass of Ca = 40 g mol^{-1}) is

(a) 2 (b) 3
(c) 4 (d) 1

43. HCl was passed through a solution of $CaCl_2$, $MgCl_2$ and NaCl. Which of the following compound(s) crystallise(s)?

(a) Only NaCl
(b) Only $MgCl_2$
(c) NaCl, $MgCl_2$ and $CaCl_2$
(d) Both $MgCl_2$ and $CaCl_2$

44. Anisole on cleavage with HI gives:

(a) I + CH_3OH
(b) I + C_2H_5I
(c) I + C_2H_5OH
(d) OH + CH_3I

45. Which of the following amine will give the carbylamine test?

(a) $NHCH_3$
(b) $N(CH_3)_2$
(c) NHC_2H_5
(d) NH_2

Answers

1.	(b)	2.	(a)	3.	(c)	4.	(c)	5.	(b)	6.	(d)	7.	(b)	8.	(d)	9.	(c)	10.	(d)
11.	(a)	12.	(b)	13.	(c)	14.	(d)	15.	(c)	16.	(d)	17.	(c)	18.	(b)	19.	(c)	20.	(b)
21.	(b)	22.	(d)	23.	(c)	24.	(b)	25.	(a)	26.	(a)	27.	(c)	28.	(c)	29.	(a)	30.	(b)
31.	(d)	32.	(c)	33.	(d)	34.	(b)	35.	(b)	36.	(c)	37.	(b)	38.	(d)	39.	(d)	40.	(b)
41.	(d)	42.	(d)	43.	(a)	44.	(d)	45.	(d)										

Answer *with* Explanations

1. ***(b)*** $\overset{x}{C}H_4(g) + 4Cl_2(g) \longrightarrow \overset{y}{C}Cl_4(l) + 4HCl(g)$

$x + 4(+1) = 0 \Rightarrow x = -4$ $\qquad$ $y + 4(-1) = 0 \Rightarrow y = +4$

Change in oxidation number ($x \rightarrow y$) of carbon in the reaction is -4 to $+4$.

2. ***(a)*** Dilute H_2SO_4 contains H_2SO_4 and H_2O and they show electrolytic dissociation as,

$$\underset{\text{Strong electrolyte as it is dilute}}{H_2SO_4} \longrightarrow 2H^+ + SO_4^{2-}$$

$$H_2O \rightleftharpoons H^+ + OH^-$$

Reaction at cathode (Pt)

$$2H^+ + 2e^- \longrightarrow H_2\uparrow$$

Reaction at anode (Pt)

$$4O\bar{H} - 4e^- \longrightarrow O_2\uparrow + 2H_2O$$

We get, O_2 gas at anode.

3. ***(c)*** An increase in the concentration of the reactants of a reaction leads to change in collision frequency. If the concentration of one or more reactants is increased, the rate of reaction increases. This happens because higher concentration of a reactant leads to more collisions of that reactant with in a particular time period.

4. ***(c)*** Dilute NaOH is the reagent for aldol condensation. Dilute NaOH process enolate ion from acetophenone which attacks benzaldehyde to give aldol.

$$\underset{\text{Benzaldehyde}}{Ph{-}CH{=}O} + \underset{\text{Acetophenone}}{CH_3{-}\overset{O}{\overset{\|}{C}}{-}Ph} \xrightarrow{\text{Dil. NaOH}}$$

$$Ph{-}\overset{OH}{\overset{|}{C}H}{-}CH_2{-}\overset{O}{\overset{\|}{C}}{-}Ph \xrightarrow{-H_2O} \underset{(Cis + trans)}{PhCH{=}CH{-}\overset{O}{\overset{\|}{C}}{-}Ph}$$

It is cross aldol condensation or Claisen-Schmidt reaction or Claisen reaction.

Mechanism

(i) $Ph{-}\overset{O}{\overset{\|}{C}}{-}CH_2{-}H \xrightarrow{^{\ominus}OH} \left[Ph{-}\overset{O}{\overset{\|}{C}}{-}\overset{\ominus}{\ddot{C}}H_2 \longleftrightarrow Ph{-}\overset{:\ddot{O}:^{\ominus}}{\overset{|}{C}}{=}CH_2 \right]$ Enolate ion

Tautomerism

$Ph{-}\overset{O{-}H}{\overset{|}{C}}{=}CH_2 \xrightarrow[-OH^{\ominus}]{H_2O}$ $Ph{-}\overset{:\ddot{O}:^{\ominus}}{\overset{|}{C}}{=}CH_2$

(ii) $Ph{-}\overset{O^{\delta-}}{\overset{\|}{C}}H^{\delta+} + \overset{\ominus}{C}H_2{-}\overset{O}{\overset{\|}{C}}{-}Ph \xrightarrow[-OH^{\ominus}]{H_2O}$

$$\underset{\text{Aldol}}{Ph{-}\overset{OH}{\overset{|}{C}H}{-}\underset{H}{\underset{|}{C}H}{-}\overset{O}{\overset{\|}{C}}{-}Ph} \xrightarrow{-H_2O} Ph{-}CH{=}CH{-}COPh$$

5. ***(b)*** In Wurtz reaction, an alkyl halide ($R{-}X$) give a symmetrical alkane ($R{-}R$) of even number of carbon atom with 100% yield.

$$2R{-}X \xrightarrow[-2NaX]{2Na/ether} R{-}R\ (100\%)$$

An unsymmetrical alkane ($R{-}R'$) with odd number of carbon atom can be obtained with 33% yield only, if we take a mixture of two different alkyl halides, $R{-}X$ and $R'{-}X$.

$$R{-}X + R'{-}X \longrightarrow \underbrace{R{-}R + R'-R'}_{67\%} + \underbrace{R-R'}_{33\%}$$

So, here *n*-heptane (C_7H_{16}) cannot be obtained with good yield. Hydrocarbons in options (a), (c) and (d) have even number of carbon atom (symmetrical, alkanes).

6. ***(d)*** Natural polymer (soft) is an addition homopolymer of isoprene which is a conjugated diene.

Isoprene shows 1, 4-addition with themselves to give *cis*-1, 4-polyisoprene or natural rubber.

$$\text{----}\overset{1}{C}H_2{=}\overset{CH_3}{\overset{|}{\underset{2}{C}}}{-}\underset{3}{C}H{=}\underset{4}{C}H_2\ \underset{1'}{C}H_2{=}\overset{CH_3}{\overset{|}{\underset{2'}{C}}}{-}\underset{3'}{C}H{=}\underset{4'}{C}H_2\text{----}$$

$\downarrow$ 1, 4-addition polymerisation

$$\sim\!\!\sim \underset{1}{C}H_2{-}\overset{H_3C}{\underset{2}{C}}{=}\overset{H}{\underset{3}{C}}{-}\underset{4}{C}H_2{-}\underset{1'}{C}H_2{-}\overset{H_3C}{\underset{2'}{C}}{=}\overset{H}{\underset{3'}{C}}{-}\underset{4'}{C}H_2 \sim\!\!\sim$$

Natural rubber

All polymers mentioned in options (a), (b) and (c) are synthetic 1,4-addition polymers. Where (a) and (c) are buna-S and buna-N respectively.

7. ***(b)*** From Dalton's law of partial pressure of gases. We know,

$$\boxed{p_i = \chi_i \times p}$$

where,

p_i = partial pressure of *i*th component

χ_i = mole-fraction of *i*th component

p = total pressure = 27 bar

$$(\text{partial pressure})_{N_2} = (\text{mole-fraction})_{N_2} \times p$$

$$= \frac{n_{N_2}}{n_{N_2} + n_{Ar}} \times p$$

$$= \frac{\frac{7}{28}}{\frac{7}{28} + \frac{8}{40}} \times 27\,\text{bar} = 15\,\text{bar}$$

$\therefore$ Partial pressure of N_2 in the mixture is 15 bar.

8. ***(d)*** So, correct combinations are:

(a)—(iii), (b)—(i), (c)—(ii), (d)—(iv)

(a) Water gas ($CO + H_2$) is also known as synthesis gas (iii).

(b) Temporary hardness of water is due to the presence of HCO_3^- radicals of Mg^{2+} and/or Ca^{2+} ion(s) (i).

(c) Boron atoms of B_2H_6 are sp^3-hybridised but due to the presence of two B—H—B bonds ($3C{-}2e^-$), B_2H_6 becomes as an electron deficient hydride (ii).

(d) H_2O_2 has a book-shaped non-planar structure (iv).

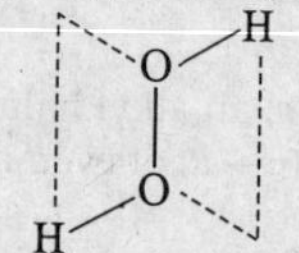

Non-planar structure

9. *(c)* In this reaction, combination of two Cl atoms takes place to give more stable Cl_2 molecule. So, the reaction is exothermic, i.e, $\Delta_r H < 0$.
Here, $\Delta n_g = 1 - 2 = -1$
So, entropy change of the reaction will be, $\Delta_r S < 0$.

10. *(d)* In bcc crystal,

$\because \quad 4r = \sqrt{3}a$

$$r = \frac{\sqrt{3}a}{4} = \frac{\sqrt{3} \times 288}{4} \text{ pm}$$

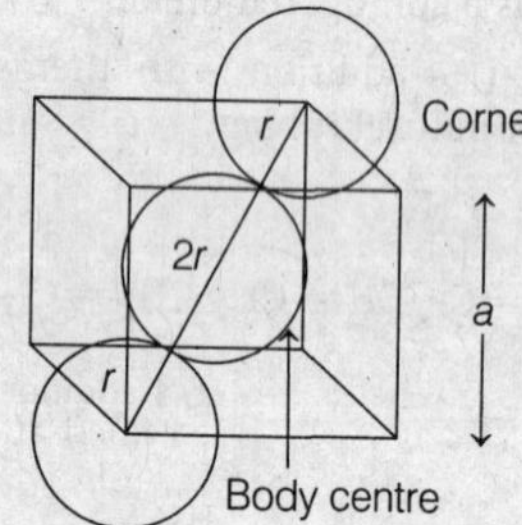

where, r = radius of atoms,
a = edge length of the unit cell.

11. *(a)* Complete reaction is

$$\underset{\text{Urea}}{H_2N—\overset{O}{\overset{\|}{C}}—NH_2} + H_2O \longrightarrow \underset{\underset{\text{Ammonium carbonate}}{A}}{H_2N—\overset{O}{\overset{\|}{C}}—\overset{\ominus\oplus}{ONH_4}} \longrightarrow CO_2(g) + \underset{B}{NH_3(g)}$$

$$\underset{\underset{\text{Deep blue solution}}{C}}{[Cu(NH_3)_4]^{2+}(aq)} \xleftarrow{Cu^{2+}(aq)} B$$

12. *(b)* A ketone on reaction with Grignard reagent followed by hydrolysis produces a tertiary or *tert*. or 3° alcohol.

$$\underset{CH_3}{\overset{CH_3}{>}}\overset{\delta+}{C}=\overset{\delta-}{O} \xrightarrow{\overset{\ominus}{CH_3}\overset{\oplus}{MgCl}} \underset{CH_3}{\overset{CH_3}{>}}C\underset{O—MgCl}{\overset{CH_3}{<}} \xrightarrow[H_2O]{-Mg(OH)Cl} CH_3—\underset{CH_3}{\overset{CH_3}{\underset{|}{\overset{|}{C}}}}—OH$$

(H : OH)

Tertiary butyl alcohol

13. *(c)* The ionic-gradients between two sides of a cell membrane, is operated by Na—K pump and consumes one-third of the ATP used by a resting animal.

Potassium ion (K^+) present in synapse helps transmission of nerve signals from one neuron to another.

14. *(d)* In $^{175}_{71}Lu$,

Mass number (A) = 175 = $n + p$
Atomic number (Z) = 71 = $p = e^-$

$\therefore$ Number of protons = 71
Number of neutrons = $A - Z = 175 - 71 = 104$
Number of electrons = 71

15. *(c)* In option (c), for all molecules, [i, vi, iii, viii]$\mu = 0$.

The structure of all compounds are as follows :

(i) Boron trifluoride (BF_3) $\Rightarrow$ F—B(F)(F) ; $\mu = 0$

(ii) Hydrogen fluoride (HF) $\Rightarrow$ H—F; $\mu \neq 0$

(iii) Carbon dioxide (CO_2) $\Rightarrow$ O=C=O ; $\mu = 0$

(iv) 1,3-dichloro benzene (m-$C_6H_4Cl_2$) $\Rightarrow$; $\mu \neq 0$

(v) Nitrogen trifluoride (NF_3) $\Rightarrow$ N(F)(F)(F) ; $\mu \neq 0$

(vi) Beryllium difluoride (BeF_2) $\Rightarrow$ F—Be—F ; $\mu = 0$

(vii) Water (H_2O) $\Rightarrow$ H—O—H ; $\mu \neq 0$

(viii) 1,4-dichloro benzene (p=$C_6H_4Cl_2$) $\Rightarrow$; $\mu = 0$

(ix) Ammonia (NH_3) $\Rightarrow$ N(H)(H)(H) ; $\mu \neq 0$

[$\because \mu$ = Dipole moment]

16. *(d)* If bond order of a molecules becomes zero, the molecule will not exist.

$$\text{Bond order} = \frac{\text{Number of bonding electrons} - \text{Number of antibonding electrons}}{2} = \frac{N_b - N_a}{2}$$

$Li_2(6e^-) \Rightarrow \sigma_{1s}^2\ \sigma_{1s}^{*2}\ \sigma_{2s}^2$; BO = $\frac{4-2}{2} = 1$

$C_2\ (12e^-) \Rightarrow \sigma_{1s}^2\ \sigma_{1s}^{*2}\ \sigma_{2s}^2\ \sigma_{2s}^{*2}\ \pi_{2p_x} = \pi_{2p_y}^2$; BO = $\frac{8-4}{2} = 2$

$O_2\ (16e^-) \Rightarrow \sigma_{1s}^2\ \sigma_{1s}^{*2}\ \sigma_{2s}^2\ \sigma_{2s}^{*2}\ \sigma_{2p_z}^2\ \pi_{2p_x}^2 = \pi_{2p_y}^2\ \pi_{2p_x}^{*1} = \pi_{2p_y}^{*1}$;

BO = $\frac{10-6}{2} = 2$

$He_2(4e^-) = \sigma_{1s}^2\ \sigma_{1s}^{*2}$; BO = $\frac{2-2}{2} = 0$

So, He_2 does not exist.

17. *(c)*

Name	Atomic number (Z)	IUPAC official name
(A) Unnilunium	101	(i) Mendelevium (Md)
(B) Unniltrium	103	(ii) Lawrencium (Lr)
(C) Unnilhexium	106	(iii) Seaborgium (Sg)
(D) Unununnium	111	(iv) Roentgenium (Rg) [but (iv) Darmstadtium (Ds), Given] [Z=110]

So, D-(iv) is the incorrect match.

18. *(b)* For a first order reaction,

Rate constant $(k) = 4.606 \times 10^{-3}\ s^{-1}$

Initial amount $(a_0) = 2g$

Final amount $(a) = 0.2$ g

So, time required,

$$t = \frac{2.303}{k} \log \frac{a_0}{a} = \frac{2.303}{4.606 \times 10^{-3}} \times \log \frac{2}{0.2} = 500 \text{ s}$$

19. *(c)* (a) Matte on auto-reduction produces blister copper, which has blistered appearance due to evolution of SO_2 (not CO_2).

$$\underset{\text{Matte}}{Cu_2S} + 2Cu_2O \longrightarrow \underset{\text{Blister copper}}{6Cu} + SO_2\uparrow$$

(b) Vapour phase refining is carried out for Ni by Mond's process (not by van Arkel method).

$$\underset{\text{Impure}}{Ni} \xrightarrow[80°C]{4CO} Ni(CO)_4 \xrightarrow[-4CO]{200°C} \underset{\text{Pure}}{Ni}$$

(c) Pig iron can be moulded into variety of shapes.

(d) Wrought iron the purest form of iron which contains 0.2-0.5% carbon (not 4%).

So, option (c) is correct.

20. *(b)* Stability of a colloidal solution is explained by zeta potential. The particles of colloid carry an electric charge, i.e. acquire positive or negative charge by preferential adsorption of positive or negative ions from dispersion medium. The combination of two layer of positive and negative charges around the colloid is called Helmholtz electrical double layer and the potential difference of this double layer is called zeta potential.

21. *(b)* The structure of given sulphur oxyacids are :

- H_2SO_4 (Sulphuric acid) ⇒ HO—S(=O)(=O)—OH
- $H_2S_2O_8$ (Peroxodisulphuric acid) ⇒ HO—S(=O)(=O)—O—O—S(=O)(=O)—OH (Peroxy linkage: —O—O—)
- $H_2S_2O_7$ (Pyrosulphuric acid) ⇒ HO—S(=O)(=O)—O—S(=O)(=O)—OH
- H_2SO_3 (Sulphurous acid) ⇒ HO—S(=O)—OH

22. *(d)*

CH_3CH_2—CH(H)—CH(Br)—CH_2(H) (β, α, β′) $\xrightarrow[-HBr]{\text{Strong base}}$

Zaitsev or Saytzeff elimination centre for β-H (two β-H atoms)

Hoffmann elimination centre for β′-H (three β′-H atoms)

$\underset{\substack{\text{Pent-1-ene} \\ \text{(Hofmann product)} \\ \text{[Minor]}}}{CH_3CH_2—CH_2—CH{=}CH_2}$ + $\underset{\substack{\text{Pent-2-ene } (cis+trans) \\ \text{(Zaitsev product)} \\ \text{[Major]}}}{CH_3CH_2—CH{=}CH—CH_3}$

In the above reaction, β-elimination takes place *via* E_2 mechanism (anti-elimination).

According to Zaitsev rule, β-carbon carrying lesser number of H-atoms get involved in the elimination to give a more substituted alkene (pent-2-ene) as the major product.

Here, loss of HBr, i.e. dehydrobromination (dehydrohalogenation) takes place.

So, 1, 2 and 3 are correct combination.

23. *(c)* 3 and 4 are correct statements, whereas 1 and 2 are incorrect.

1. Dry ice or $CO_2(s)$ [not $CO_2(g)$] is used as refrigerant for ice-cream and frozen food.
2. C_{60} contains 20 hexagones (not 12) and 12 pentagones (not 20).
3. ZSM-5, a type of zeolite, is used to convert alcohols directly into gasoline. It is true.
4. CO is a colourless and odourless gas. It is true.

24. *(b)* Let us identity the ozonolysis [(i) O_2/THF, (ii) Zn/H_2O] products from each of the following :

(a) 1-propylcyclohexene ($-CH_2CH_2CH_3$) ⟶ open-chain dicarbonyl compound (ring opened), $-CH_2CH_2CH_3$

(b) $C_6H_{11}-CH_2CH{=}CH_2$ ⟶ $C_6H_{11}-CH_2-CH{=}O + CH_2{=}O$ (Methanal)

(c) 3-propylcyclohexene ($-CH_2CH_2CH_3$) ⟶ open-chain dialdehyde, $-CH_2CH_2CH_3$

(d) $C_6H_{11}-CH{=}CH-CH_3$ ⟶ $C_6H_{11}-CH{=}O + CH_3-CH{=}O$

We get, methanal from the hydrocarbon in option (b) only.

25. *(a)* Based on the principle involved, chromatography is of two types :

Adsorption chromatography and partition chromatography. In adsorption chromatography, adsorbents are silica gel and alumina (Al_2O_3), which act as stationary phase. A mobile phase is allowed to move over the stationary phase.

e.g. Column chromatography and thin layer chromatography (TLC).

In partition chromatography, a continuous portion of components takes place between stationary phase and mobile phase. e.g. Paper chromatography, in which a special type of chromatography paper containing water acts as a stationary phases.

26. ***(a)*** The correct matching is :

(A)-(ii), (B)-(i), (C)-(iv), (D)-(iii)

(A) **CO** It is a neutral oxide and almost insoluble in water.

(B) **BaO** It is basic oxide.

$$BaO + H_2O \longrightarrow Ba(OH)_2$$

(C) $\mathbf{Al_2O_3}$ It is an amphoteric oxide, because it reacts with both acids and alkalis.

$$Al_2O_3 + 6HCl \longrightarrow 2AlCl_3 + 3H_2O$$

$$Al_2O_3 + 2NaOH \longrightarrow 2NaAlO_2 + H_2O$$

(D) $\mathbf{Cl_2O_7}$ It is an acidic oxide and produces a very strong acid, perchloric acid in H_2O.

$$Cl_2O_7 + H_2O \longrightarrow 2HClO_4$$

27. ***(c)*** Number of atoms (n)

$$= \frac{\text{Mass in g (1 g)} \times \text{Atomicity of the molecule}}{\text{Gram molar mass } (M)} \times N_A$$

[$\because N_A$ = Avogadro's number]

$$\Rightarrow n \propto \frac{\text{Atomicity}}{M}$$

(a) $n_{Mg} = \frac{1}{24}$

(b) $n_O = \frac{2}{32} = \frac{1}{16}$

(c) $n_{Li} = \frac{1}{7}$

(d) $n_{Ag} = \frac{1}{108}$

So, $n_{Li} > n_O > n_{Mg} > n_{Ag}$

28. ***(c)***

(a) Alanine $\Rightarrow CH_3—CH\begin{smallmatrix} NH_2 \\ COOH \end{smallmatrix}$

(b) Tyrosine $\Rightarrow$ HO—C_6H_4—$CH_2—CH\begin{smallmatrix} NH_2 \\ COOH \end{smallmatrix}$

(c) Lysine $\Rightarrow H_2N—(CH_2)_4—CH\begin{smallmatrix} NH_2 \\ COOH \end{smallmatrix}$

(d) Serine $\Rightarrow HO—CH_2—CH\begin{smallmatrix} NH_2 \\ COOH \end{smallmatrix}$

Since, lysine contains more number of $—NH_2$ groups as compared to —COOH groups, hence it is a basic amino acid.

29. ***(a)*** Electronic configuration of Cr^{2+} ion is

Cr^{2+} : $[Ar]3d^4$ or [Ar] | 1 | 1 | 1 | 1 | | ($3d^4$)
(22e^-)

It has four (n = 4) unpaired electrons.

$\therefore$ Spin only magnetic moment $(\mu) = \sqrt{n(n+2)}$ BM

$= \sqrt{4\,(4+2)}$BM

$= 4.90$BM

30. ***(b)*** Sucrose (invert sugar) is a disaccharide made of α-D-glucose and β-D-fructose by 1, 2-linkage. Sucrose undergoes inversion during hydrolysis to give α-D-glucose and β-D-fructose in 1 : 1 mole ratio.

$$\underset{\text{Sucrose}}{C_{12}H_{22}O_{11}} \xrightarrow[\text{Hydrolysis}]{H_3O^+} \underset{\alpha\text{-D-glucose}}{C_6H_{12}O_6} + \underset{\beta\text{-D-fructose}}{C_6H_{12}O_6}$$

31. ***(d)*** Let us study the nature of binary solutions made of two volatile liquids:

(a) **(Benzene + Toluene)** Ideal solution, obeys Raoult's law.

(b) **(Acetone + Chloroform)** Non-ideal solution, shows negative deviation from Raoult's law.

(c) **(Chloroethane + Bromoethane)** Ideal solution, obeys Raoult's law.

(d) **(Ethanol + Acetone)** Non-ideal solution, shows positive deviation from Raoult's law.

32. ***(c)***

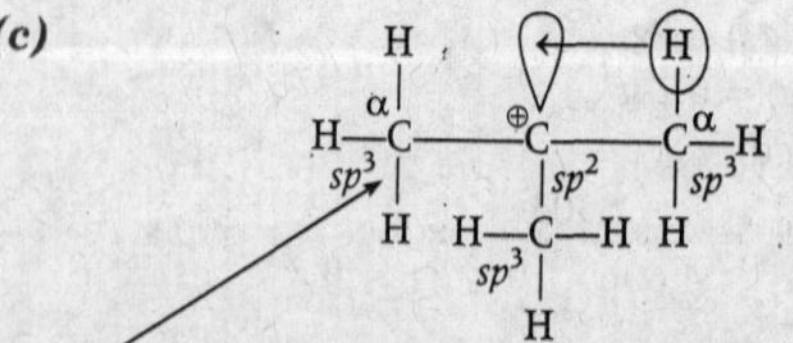

It is tertiary or 3°-butyl carbocation, it has nine α-hydrogen atoms. So, it will give nine hyperconjugative structures.

But, is secondary or 2°-butyl carbocation, only six hyperconjugations are possible because it has six α-H atoms only.

Higher the number of hyperconjugations, more stable will be the carbocation.

So, stability: $(CH_3)_3C^{\oplus} > (CH_3)_2CH^{\oplus}$

33. ***(d)*** $\underset{(0.1\text{ M})}{NaOH(aq)} \longrightarrow Na^+(aq) + \underset{(0.1\text{ M})}{OH^-(aq)}$

$$Ni(OH)_2(s) \rightleftharpoons \underset{S'}{Ni^{2+}(aq)} + \underset{0.1 + 2S'}{2OH^-(aq)}$$

Ionic product $= (S')\,(0.1 + 2S')^2$ ($\because 2S'$ is very small)

$$2\times10^{-15} = S'\,(0.1)^2$$

$$S' = 2\times10^{-13}\text{ M}$$

34. ***(b)*** (a) Solution stearate, $C_{17}H_{35}COONa$ is a soap.

(b) Cetyltrimethyl ammonium bromide,

$CH_3—(CH_2)_{15}—\overset{\oplus}{N}(CH_3)_3\overset{\ominus}{Br}$ is a cationic detergent.

(c) and (d) are anionic detergents.

Sodium dodecyl benzene sulphonate :

$$p\text{-}CH_3(CH_2)_{11}—C_6H_4—\overset{\ominus}{SO_3}\overset{\oplus}{Na}$$

Sodium lauryl sulphate:

$$CH_3—(CH_2)_{10}—CH_2—OS\overset{\ominus}{O_3}\overset{\oplus}{Na}$$

35. ***(b)*** The expression of freezing point depression is,

$$K_f = 5.12\text{ K kg mol}^{-1}$$

Molality $(m) = 0.078$ molal,

$i = 1$, for non-electrolyte solute

$$\Delta T_f = K_f \times m \times i$$
$$= 5.12 \times 0.078 \times 1$$
$$= 0.39936 \simeq 0.40\ \text{K}$$

36. ***(c)*** Statements in options (a), (b) and (d) are correct.
Statement in option (c) is incorrect, because oxidation states of Cr in CrO_4^{2-} (chromate) and $Cr_2O_7^{2-}$ (dichromate) are same and it is +6.

i.e., $\overset{x}{Cr}O_4^{2-} \Rightarrow x + 4(-2) = 2 \Rightarrow x = +6$

$\overset{y}{Cr_2}O_7^{2-} \Rightarrow 2y + 7(-2) = -2 \Rightarrow y = +6$

37. ***(b)*** Statements (a), (c) and (d) are correct about carbon monoxide (CO).
Statement (b) is not correct about CO, because carboxyhaemoglobin (haemoglobin bound to CO) is about 300 times more stable than oxyhaemoglobin complex.

38. ***(d)*** Sucrose + $H_2O \rightleftharpoons$ Glucose + Fructose

For this equilibrium,

$\Delta_r G^\ominus = -RT \ln K_C$

Given, $K_C = 2 \times 10^{13}$ and $T = 300$ K

$\Rightarrow \Delta_r G^\ominus = -(8.314\ \text{J mol}^{-1}\text{K}^{-1}) \times (300\ \text{K}) \times \ln(2 \times 10^{13})$

39. ***(d)*** Increasing field strength of ligands to form coordination compounds, we have to follow the spectrochemical series.

$I^- < Br^- < SCN^- < Cl^- < S^{2-} < F^- < OH^- < C_2O_4^{2-} < H_2O < NCS^- < EDTA^{4-} < NH_3 < en < CN^- < CO$

So, the order given in option (d):

$SCN^- < F^- < C_2O_4^{2-} < CN^-$ is correct.

40. ***(b)*** An 1, 1-*gem*-dihalide on hot hydrolysis (H_2O/373 K) can produce an aldehyde.

Toluene (CH_3) $\xrightarrow[h\nu]{2Cl_2}$ $CHCl_2$-benzene (X) $\xrightarrow[373\ \text{K}]{H_2O}$ CHO-benzene

41. ***(d)*** For adiabatic process, $q = 0$

For adiabatic free expansion of an ideal gas, no work will be done, because, $dV = 0$.

$\therefore w = pdV = 0$

For adiabatic free expansion of an ideal gas, no change in internal energy.

So, $dU = 0$ and $dT = 0$ $\quad [\because dU = nC_V dT]$

So, option (d) is correct.

42. ***(d)*** $\underset{\text{Molten}}{CaCl_2} \rightleftharpoons Ca^{2+} + 2Cl^-$

At cathode $Ca^{2+} + 2e^- \longrightarrow Ca$

(Reduction)

According to Faraday's first law,

Charge passed in Faraday = Gram equivalent of product

$$= \frac{\text{Given mass}}{\text{Atomic mass}} \times \text{no. of } e^- \text{ released}$$
$$= \frac{20}{40} \times 2 = 1\ \text{F}$$

So, one Faraday (F) is required for the process.

43. ***(a)*** Let us explain the crystallisation process by a flow-sheet diagram.

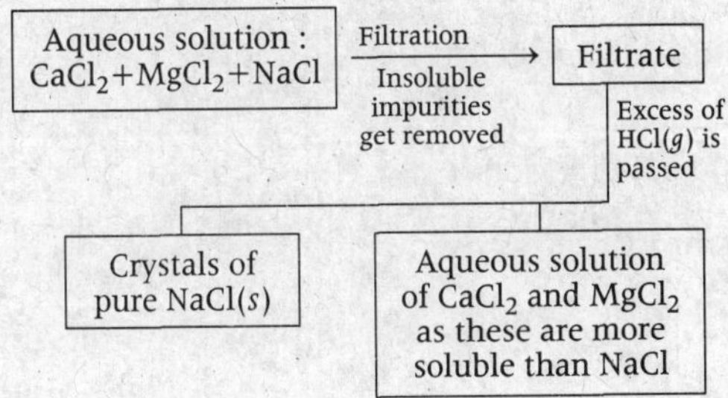

44. ***(d)***

Anisole (C_6H_5—$\ddot{O}$—CH_3) $\xrightarrow[-I^\ominus]{H—I}$ C_6H_5—$\overset{H}{\overset{|}{O^\oplus}}$—$CH_3$ $I^\ominus$ $\xrightarrow{S_N2 \text{ attack}}$ C_6H_5—OH + CH_3I

(Anisole)

No S_N2-attack of $I^\ominus$ to the aryl carbon is possible

Option (d)

So, even with excess of HI anisole will give always phenol and methyl iodide (as in option-d)

45. ***(d)*** Carbylamine test is responded by primary or 1°-amine (aliphatic or aromatic) only.

$R—NH_2 \xrightarrow[KOH/\Delta]{CHCl_3} R—NC + KCl + H_2O$

$Ar—NH_2 \xrightarrow[KOH/\Delta]{CHCl_3} \underset{\text{Carbyl amine}}{Ar—NC} + KCl + H_2O$

Options

(a) Ph—NH—CH_3; 2° amine

(b) Ph—N$(CH_3)_2$; 3° amine

(c) Ph—NH—C_2H_5; 2° amine

(d) Ph—NH_2; 1° amine (aniline)

It responds to carbylamine test.

NEET SOLVED PAPER 2021

Instruction

- This question paper contains of 50 Multiple Choice Questions of Chemistry, divided into two Sections; section A and section B.
- Section A contains 35 questions and all questions are compulsory.
- Section B contains 15 questions out of which only 10 questions are to be attempted.
- Each question carries 4 marks.

Section-A

1. Given below are two statements.

Statement I Aspirin and paracetamol belong to the class of narcotic analgesics.

Statement II Morphine and heroin are non-narcotic analgesics.

In the light of the above statements, choose the correct answer from the options given below.

(a) Both Statement I and Statement II are true.
(b) Both Statement I and Statement II are false.
(c) Statement I is true but Statement II is false.
(d) Statement I is false but Statement I is true.

2. The correct structure of 2,6-dimethyl-dec-4-ene is

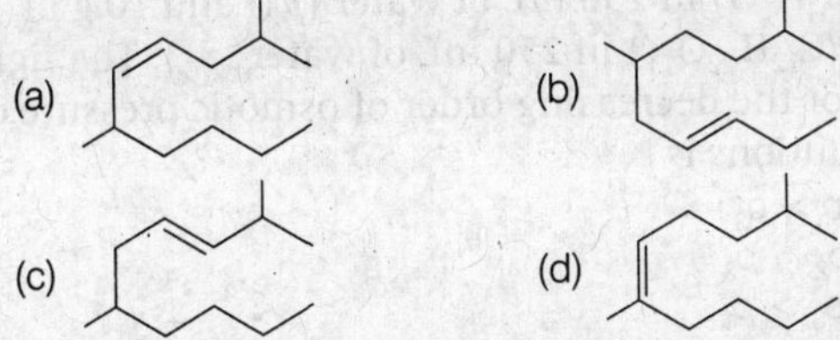

3. BF_3 is planar and electron deficient compound. Hybridisation and number of electrons around the central atom, respectively are

(a) sp^3 and 4 (b) sp^3 and 6
(c) sp^2 and 6 (d) sp^2 and 8

4. Noble gases are named because of their inertness towards reactivity. Identify an incorrect statement about them.

(a) Noble gases are sparingly soluble in water.
(b) Noble gases have very high melting and boiling points.
(c) Noble gases have weak dispersion forces.
(d) Noble gases have large positive values of electron gain enthalpy.

5. The molar conductance of NaCl, HCl andCH_3COONa at infinite dilution are 126.45, 426.16 and 91.0 S cm^2 mol^{-1} respectively. The molar conductance of CH_3COOH at infinite dilution is
Choose the right option for your answer.

(a) 201.28 S cm^2 mol^{-1} (b) 390.71 S cm^2 mol^{-1}
(c) 698.28 S cm^2 mol^{-1} (d) 540.48 S cm^2 mol^{-1}

6. The right option for the statement "Tyndall effect is exhibited by", is

(a) NaCl solution (b) glucose solution
(c) starch solution (d) urea solution

7. The RBC deficiency is deficiency disease of

(a) vitamin-B_{12} (b) vitamin-B_6 (c) vitamin-B_1 (d) vitamin-B_2

8. Dihedral angle of least stable conformer of ethane is

(a) 120° (b) 180° (c) 60° (d) 0°

9. The incorrect statement among the following is

(a) actinoid contraction is greater for element to element than lanthanoid contraction.
(b) most of the trivalent lanthanoid ions are colourless in the solid state.
(c) lanthanoids are good conductors of heat and electricity.
(d) actinoids are highly reactive metals, especially when finely divided.

10. The major product formed in dehydrohalogenation reaction of 2-bromo pentane is pent-2-ene. This product formation is based on

(a) Saytzeff's rule (b) Hund's rule
(c) Hoffmann rule (d) Huckel's rule

11. Which one among the following is the correct option for right relationship between C_p and C_V for one mole of ideal gas?

(a) $C_p + C_V = R$ (b) $C_p - C_V = R$
(c) $C_p = RC_V$ (d) $C_V = RC_p$

12. Which one of the following polymers is prepared by addition polymerisation?

(a) Teflon (b) Nylon-66 (c) Novolac (d) Dacron

13. What is the IUPAC name of the organic compound formed in the following chemical reaction ?

$$\text{Acetone} \xrightarrow[\text{(ii) } H_2O, H^+]{\text{(i) } C_2H_5MgBr, \text{ Dry ether}} \text{product}$$

(a) 2-methyl propan 2-ol (b) pentan-2-ol
(c) pentan-3-ol (d) 2-methyl butan-2-ol

14. Match List-I with List-II.

	List-I		List-II
A.	PCl_5	I.	Square pyramidal
B.	SF_6	II.	Trigonal planar
C.	BrF_5	III.	Octahedral
D.	BF_3	IV.	Trigonal bipyramidal

Choose the correct answer from the options given below

	A	B	C	D
(a)	IV	III	I	II
(b)	II	III	IV	I
(c)	III	I	IV	II
(d)	IV	III	II	I

15. Which one of the following methods can be used to obtain highly pure metal which is liquid at room temperature?

(a) Electrolysis
(b) Chromatography
(c) Distillation
(d) Zone refining

16. The major product of the following chemical reaction is

$$(CH_3)_2CH—CH{=}CH_2 + HBr \xrightarrow{(C_6H_5CO)_2O_2} ?$$

(a) $(CH_3)_2CH—CH_2—CH_2Br$
(b) $(CH_3)_2CHCH_2—CH_2OCOC_6H_5$
(c) $(CH_3)_2CH—CH(Br)—CH_3$
(d) $(CH_3)_2CBr—CH_2—CH_3$

17. Tritium, a radioactive isotope of hydrogen, emits which of the following particles?

(a) Beta (β^-)
(b) Alpha (α)
(c) Gamma (γ)
(d) Neutron (n)

18. The correct sequence of bond enthalpy of 'C—X' bond is

(a) $CH_3—F < CH_3—Cl < CH_3—Br < CH_3—I$
(b) $CH_3—F > CH_3—Cl > CH_3—Br > CH_3—I$
(c) $CH_3—F < CH_3—Cl > CH_3—Br > CH_3—I$
(d) $CH_3—Cl > CH_3—F > CH_3—Br > CH_3—I$

19. Right option for the number of tetrahedral and octahedral voids in hexagonal primitive unit cell are

(a) 8, 4
(b) 6, 12
(c) 2, 1
(d) 12, 6

20. Which of the following reactions is the metal displacement reaction ? Choose the right option.

(a) $2KClO_3 \xrightarrow{\Delta} 2KCl + 3O_2$
(b) $Cr_2O_3 + 2Al \xrightarrow{\Delta} Al_2O_3 + 2Cr$
(c) $Fe + 2HCl \longrightarrow FeCl_2 + H_2\uparrow$
(d) $2Pb(NO_3)_2 \longrightarrow 2PbO + 4NO_2 + O_2\uparrow$

21. Choose the correct option for graphical representation of Boyle's law, which shows a graph of pressure *vs* volume of a gas at different temperatures

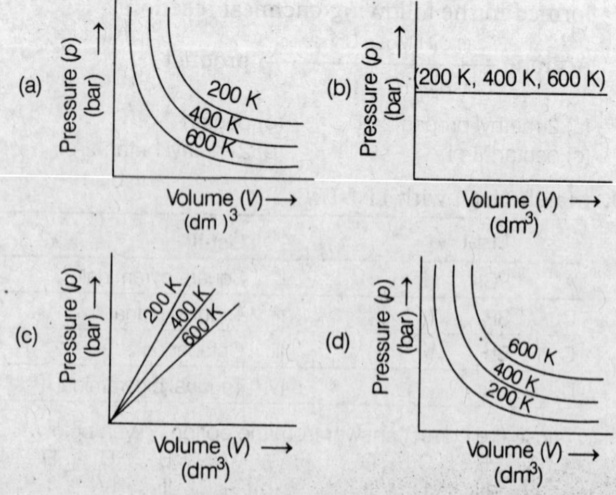

22. The pK_b of dimethyl amine and pK_a of acetic acid are 3.27 and 4.77 respectively at T(K). The correct option for the pH of dimethyl ammonium acetate solution is

(a) 8.50
(b) 5.50
(c) 7.75
(d) 6.25

23. Among the following alkaline earth metal halides, one which is covalent and soluble in organic solvents is

(a) calcium chloride
(b) strontium chloride
(c) magnesium chloride
(d) beryllium chloride

24. The maximum temperature that can be achieved in blast furnace is

(a) upto 1200 K
(b) upto 2200 K
(c) upto 1900 K
(d) upto 5000 K

25. Ethylene diaminetetraacetate (EDTA) ion is

(a) hexadentate ligand with four O and two N donor atoms
(b) unidentate ligand
(c) bidentate ligand with two N donor atoms
(d) tridentate ligand with three N donor atoms

26. The following solutions were prepared by dissolving 10 g of glucose ($C_6H_{12}O_6$) in 250 mL of water (p_1), 10 g of urea (CH_4N_2O) in 250 mL of water (p_2) and 10 g of sucrose ($C_{12}H_{22}O_{11}$) in 250 mL of water (p_3). The right option for the decreasing order of osmotic pressure of these solutions is

(a) $p_2 > p_1 > p_3$
(b) $p_1 > p_2 > p_3$
(c) $p_2 > p_3 > p_1$
(d) $p_3 > p_1 > p_2$

27. **Statement I** Acid strength increases in the order given as

$$HF << HCl << HBr << HI.$$

Statement II As the size of the elements F, Cl, Br and HI increases down the group. the bond strength of HF, HCl, HBr and HI decreases and so the acid strength increases.

In the light of the above statements, choose the correct answer from the options given below.

(a) Both Statement I and Statement II are true.
(b) Both Statement I and Statement II are false.
(c) Statement I is true but Statement II is false.
(d) Statement I is false but Statement II is true.

28. The structures of beryllium chloride in solid state and vapour phase, are

(a) chain and dimer, respectively
(b) linear in both
(c) dimer and linear, respectively
(d) chain in both

29. For a reaction, $A \rightarrow B$, enthalpy of reaction is -4.2 kJ mol^{-1} and enthalpy of activation is 9.6 kJ mol^{-1}. The correct potential energy profile for the reaction is shown in option.

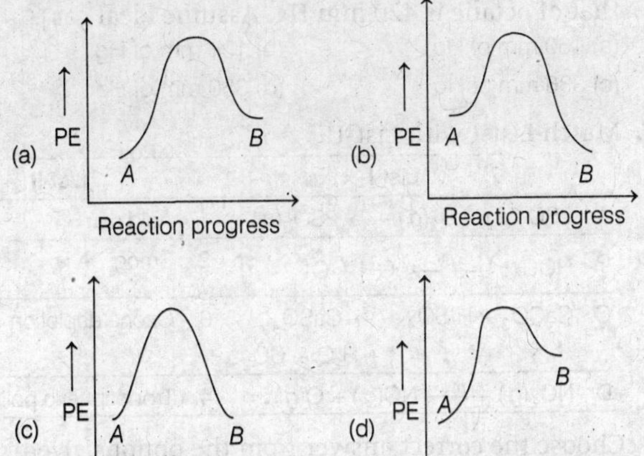

30. Zr $(Z = 40)$ and Hf $(Z = 72)$ have similar atomic and ionic radii because of

(a) belonging to same group
(b) diagonal relationship
(c) lanthanoid contraction
(d) having similar chemical properties

31. A particular station of All India Radio, New Delhi, broadcasts on a frequency of 1,368 kHz (kilohertz). The wavelength of the electromagnetic radiation emitted by the transmitter is [Speed of light, $c = 3.0 \times 10^3$ ms^{-1}]

(a) 219.3 m (b) 219.2 m
(c) 2192 m (d) 21.92 cm

32. An organic compound contains 78% (by wt.) carbon and remaining percentage of hydrogen. The right option for the empirical formula of this compound is [At. wt. of C is 12, H is 1]

(a) CH (b) CH_2 (c) CH_3 (d) CH_4

33. The compound which shows metamerism is

(a) C_5H_{12} (b) C_3H_8O
(c) C_3H_6O (d) $C_4H_{10}O$

34. Identify the compound that will react with Hinsberg's reagent to give a solid which dissolves in alkali.

(a) 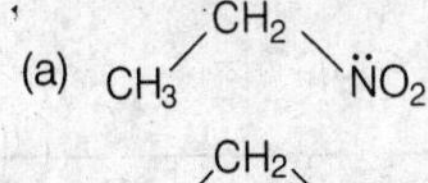

(b) 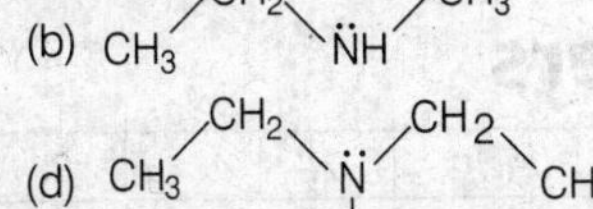

(c) $CH_3-CH_2-\ddot{N}H_2$

(d) $CH_3-CH_2-\ddot{N}(CH_3)-CH_2-CH_3$

35. The correct option for the number of body centred unit cells in all 14 types of Bravais lattice unit cell is

(a) 7 (b) 5 (c) 2 (d) 3

Section-B

36. Match List-I with List-II.

	List-I		List-II
A.	$[Fe(CN)_6]^{3-}$	1.	5.92 BM
B.	$[Fe(H_2O)_6]^{3+}$	2.	0 BM
C.	$[Fe(CN)_6]^{4-}$	3.	4.90 BM
D.	$[Fe(H_2O)_6]^{2+}$	4.	1.73 BM

Choose the correct answer from the options given below

	A	B	C	D
(a)	4	2	1	3
(b)	2	4	3	1
(c)	1	3	4	2
(d)	4	1	2	3

37. Choose the correct option for the total pressure (in atm) in a mixture of 4g O_2 and 2 g H_2 confined in a total volume of one litre at 0°C is [Given, $R = 0.082$ L atm $mol^{-1}K^{-1}$, $T = 273K$]

(a) 2.518 (b) 2.602 (c) 25.18 (d) 26.02

38. $CH_3CH_2COO^-Na^+ \xrightarrow[\text{Heat}]{\text{NaOH}+?} CH_3CH_3 + Na_2CO_3$

Consider the above reaction and identify the missing reagent/chemical.

(a) B_2H_6 (b) Red phosphorus
(c) CaO (d) DIBAL-H

39. For irreversible expansion of an ideal gas under isothermal condition the correct option is

(a) $\Delta U = 0, \Delta S_{total} = 0$ (b) $\Delta U \neq 0, \Delta S_{total} \neq 0$
(c) $\Delta U = 0, \Delta S_{total} \neq 0$ (d) $\Delta U \neq 0, \Delta S_{total} = 0$

40. In which one of the following arrangements the given sequence is not strictly according to the properties indicated against it?

(a) $HF < HCl < HBr < HI$: Increasing acidic strength
(b) $H_2O < H_2S < H_2Se < H_2Te$: Increasing pK_a values
(c) $NH_3 < PH_3 < AsH_3 < SbH_3$: Increasing acidic character
(d) $CO_2 < SiO_2 < SnO_2 < PbP_2$: Increasing oxidising power

41. The molar conductivity of 0.007 M acetic acid is 20 S cm^2 mol^{-1}. What is the dissociation constant of acetic acid ? Choose the correct option.
$[\lambda^\circ_{H^+} = 350$ S cm^2 mol^{-1}, $\lambda^\circ_{CH_3COO^-} = 50$ S cm^2 $mol^{-1}]$

(a) 1.75×10^{-4} mol^{-1} L^{-1} (b) 2.50×10^{-4} mol^{-1} L^{-1}
(c) 1.75×10^{-5} mol^{-1} L^{-1} (d) 2.50×10^{-5} mol^{-1} L^{-1}

42. The slope of Arrhenius plot $\left(\ln k \text{ vs } \frac{1}{T}\right)$ of first order reaction is -5×10^3K. The value of E_a of the reaction is [Given, $R = 8.314$ JK^{-1} mol^{-1}]

(a) 41.5 kJ mol^{-1} (b) 83.0 kJ mol^{-1}
(c) 166 kJ mol^{-1} (d) -83 kJ mol^{-1}

43. The product formed in the following chemical reaction is

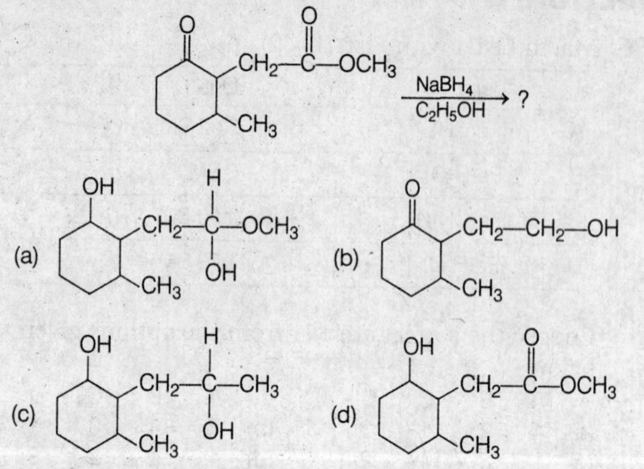

44. Match List-I with List-II.

List-I	List-II
A. Benzene $\xrightarrow[\text{Anhyd. } AlCl_3/CuCl]{CO,\ HCl}$	1. Hell-Volhard-Zelinsky reaction
B. $R—\overset{O}{\overset{\Vert}{C}}—CH_3 + NaOX \longrightarrow$	2. Gattermann-Koch reaction
C. $R—CH_2—OH + R'COOH \xrightarrow{\text{Conc. } H_2SO_4}$	3. Haloform reaction
D. $R—CH_2—COOH \xrightarrow[\text{(ii) } H_2O]{\text{(i) } X_2/\text{Red P}}$	4. Esterification

Choose the correct answer from the options given below.

	A	B	C	D		A	B	C	D
(a)	4	1	2	3	(b)	3	2	1	4
(c)	1	4	3	2	(d)	2	3	4	1

45. Which of the following molecules is non-polar in nature?

(a) $POCl_3$ (b) CH_2O (c) $SbCl_5$ (d) NO_2

46. From the following pairs of ion which one is not an iso-electronic pair?

(a) O^{2-}, F^- (b) Na^+, Mg^{2+}

(c) Mn^{2+}, Fe^{3+} (d) Fe^{2+}, Mn^{2+}

47. The correct option for the value of vapour pressure of a solution at 45°C with benzene to octane in molar ratio 3 : 2 is

[At 45°C vapour pressure of benzene is 280 mm Hg and that of octane is 420 mm Hg. Assume ideal gas].

(a) 160 mm of Hg (b) 168 mm of Hg

(c) 336 mm of Hg (d) 350 mm of Hg

48. Match List-I with List-II.

List-I	List-II
A. $2SO_2(g) + O_2(g) \longrightarrow 2SO_3(g)$	1. Acid rain
B. $HOCl(g) \xrightarrow{h\nu} \dot{O}H + \dot{C}l$	2. Smog
C. $CaCO_3 + H_2SO_4 \longrightarrow CaSO_4 + H_2O + CO_2$	3. Ozone depletion
D. $NO_2(g) \xrightarrow{h\nu} NO(g) + O(g)$	4. Tropospheric pollution

Choose the correct answer from the options given below

	A	B	C	D		A	B	C	D
(a)	1	2	3	4	(b)	2	3	4	1
(c)	4	3	1	2	(d)	3	2	4	1

49. The reagent '*R*' in the given sequence of chemical reaction is

2,6-dibromo-4-bromoaniline (NH_2, Br, Br, Br) $\xrightarrow[0\text{-}5°C]{NaNO_2,\ HCl}$ ($\overset{+}{N_2}Cl^-$, Br, Br, Br) $\xrightarrow{R}$ 1,3,5-tribromobenzene (Br, Br, Br)

(a) H_2O (b) CH_3CH_2OH

(c) HI (d) CuCN/KCN

50. The intermediate compound '*X*' in the following chemical reaction is

$C_6H_5CH_3 + CrO_2Cl_2 \xrightarrow{CS_2} X \xrightarrow{H_3O^-} C_6H_5—\overset{O}{\overset{\Vert}{C}}—H$

(a) $C_6H_5CH(OCrOHCl_2)_2$ (b) $C_6H_5CH(OCOCH_3)_2$

(c) $C_6H_5CHCl_2$ (d) $C_6H_5CH(Cl)(H)$

Answers

1.	(b)	2.	(a)	3.	(c)	4.	(b)	5.	(b)	6.	(c)	7.	(a)	8.	(d)	9.	(b)	10.	(a)
11.	(b)	12.	(a)	13.	(d)	14.	(a)	15.	(c)	16.	(a)	17.	(a)	18.	(b)	19.	(d)	20.	(b)
21.	(d)	22.	(c)	23.	(d)	24.	(b)	25.	(a)	26.	(a)	27.	(a)	28.	(a)	29.	(b)	30.	(c)
31.	(a)	32.	(c)	33.	(d)	34.	(c)	35.	(d)	36.	(d)	37.	(c)	38.	(c)	39.	(c)	40.	(b)
41.	(c)	42.	(a)	43.	(d)	44.	(d)	45.	(c)	46.	(d)	47.	(c)	48.	(c)	49.	(b)	50.	(a)

Answer *with* Explanations

1. ***(b)*** **Narcotic analgesics** They are the analgesics drugs that are used to reduce pain. They are obtained from opium poppy, so they are also called opiates. They are addictive in nature. Morphine and heroin are narcotic analgesics.

Non-narcotic analgesics They are non-addictive in nature and are not obtained from opium poppy. Aspirin and paracetamol are non-narcotic analgesics. So, both statements I and II are false.

2. ***(a)*** Structure of 2,6-dimethyl-dec-4-ene is

The structure can be identified with the help of branches at 2 and 6 positions and a double bond at 4 position.

3. ***(c)*** Hybridisation of a central atom can be calculate by using the formula :

$$\text{Hybridisation} = \frac{1}{2}[\text{number of valence electrons} + \text{Number of side atoms} - \text{Positive charge} + \text{Negative charge}]$$

Electronic configuration of $B = 1s^2, 2s^2, 2p^1$

Number of valence electrons in B = 3 electrons in last shell, $n = 2$

Number of side atoms in BF_3 = 3F-atoms.

$$\text{So, hybridisation} = \frac{1}{2}(3+3) = \frac{1}{2} \times 6 = 3.$$

Hybridisation of B in BF_3 is sp^2.

Number of electrons around central atom, B in BF_3 is equal to the number of electrons in three sigma bonds (B—F) i.e.

= 3 B—F bonds × 2 electrons in one σ-bond. = 6 electrons

4. ***(b)*** (a) Noble gases or inert gases are sparingly soluble in water as they are non-polar in nature. For solubility the thumb rule is "Like dissolves like".

∴ Statement (a) is correct.

(b) Nobles gases have weak interatomic forces (van der Waals' forces). So, they have low melting and boiling points.

∴ Statement (b) is incorrect.

(c) Noble gases have weak London dispersion forces which is weaker than all other intermolecular forces.

∴ Statement (c) is correct.

(d) The last shell of noble gas have 8 electrons. They have stable electronic configuration. So, addition of an electron is difficult. Hence, they have large positive values of electron gain enthalpy.

∴ Statement (d) is correct.

5. ***(b)*** Molar conductance of NaCl, $\lambda_{NaCl} = 126.45 \text{ S cm}^2 \text{ mol}^{-1}$

Molar conductance of HCl, $\lambda^\circ_{HCl} = 426.16 \text{ S cm}^2 \text{ mol}^{-1}$

Molar conductance of $CH_3CO\overset{-}{O}\overset{+}{Na}$,

$$\lambda^\circ_{CH_3COONa} = 91.0 \text{ S cm}^2 \text{ mol}^{-1}$$

According to Kohlrausch's law;

$$\lambda^\circ_{HCl} = \lambda^\circ_{H^+} + \lambda^\circ_{Cl^-} \quad \text{...(i)}$$

$$\lambda^\circ_{NaCl} = \lambda^\circ_{Na^+} + \lambda^\circ_{Cl^-} \quad \text{...(ii)}$$

$$\lambda^\circ_{CH_3COONa^+} = \lambda^\circ_{Na^+} + \lambda^\circ_{CH_3COO^-} \quad \text{...(iii)}$$

$$\lambda^\circ_{CH_3COOH} = \lambda^\circ_{CH_3COO^-} + \lambda^\circ_{H^+}$$

$$\lambda^\circ_{CH_3COOH} = (\lambda^\circ_{CH_3COO^-} + \lambda^\circ_{Na^+}) + (\lambda^\circ_{H^+} + \lambda^\circ_{Cl^-}) - (\lambda^\circ_{Na^+} + \lambda^\circ_{Cl^-})$$

$$\lambda^\circ_{CH_3COOH} = \lambda^\circ_{CH_3CO\overset{-}{O}Na^+} + \lambda^\circ_{HCl} - \lambda^\circ_{NaCl}$$

$$\lambda^\circ_{CH_3COOH} = 91.0 + 426.16 - 126.45$$

$$\lambda^\circ_{CH_3COOH} = 390.71 \text{ S cm}^2 \text{ mol}^{-1}$$

6. ***(c)*** Tyndall effect is shown by colloidal solution in which particles having larger size scatters the light.

NaCl, glucose and urea do not form a colloidal solution. Only starch solution is colloidal solution. So, Tyndall effect is exhibited by starch solution.

7. ***(a)***

- Vitamin B_{12} deficiency disease-RBC deficiency (anaemia).
- Vitamin B_6 deficiency disease–Dermatitis, epilepsy.
- Vitamin B_1 deficiency disease – Beri-beri
- Vitamin B_2 deficiency disease – Ariboflavinesis.

8. ***(d)*** Conformations of ethane are

Staggered Eclipsed

Eclipsed conformer of ethane having dihedral angle (∠H—C—C—H) of 0° is least stable conformer. In eclipsed conformer, H-atom of back carbon lies just behind the H-atom of front carbon. So, there is maximum repulsion between H-atoms resulting in angular strain.

9. ***(b)*** The shielding effect of $5f$-orbitals in actinoids is poor than the shielding effect of $4f$-orbitals. So, the effective nuclear charge on valence electrons is more in actinoids. Hence, actinoid contraction is greater than lanthanoid contraction.

∴ Statement (a) is correct.

Trivalent lanthanoid ions are coloured in the solid state due to presence of f-electrons.

∴ Statement (b) is incorrect.

Lanthanoids are inner transition metals. So, they are good conductors of heat and electricity.

∴ Statement (c) is correct.

The surface area increases when actinoids are finely divided which results in exposure of more reactant molecules to react. Hence, rate increases and so, actinoids are highly reactive metals when finely divided.

∴ Statement (d) is correct.

10. ***(a)*** Saytzeff's rule states that more substituted alkene is formed in a dehydrohalogenation reaction.

In dehydrohalogenation of 2-bromopentane, pent-2-ene is formed as major product which is a more substituted alkene.

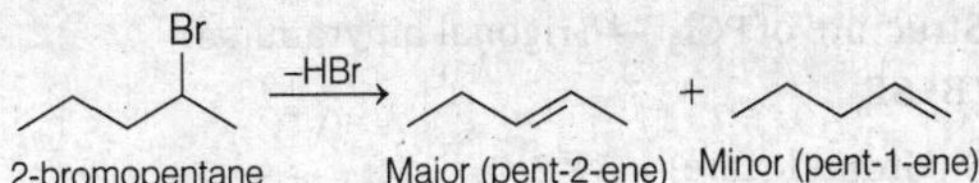

11. ***(b)*** For an ideal gas, $C_p - C_V = nR$

(where, n = number of moles of gas,

C_p, C_V = specific heat at constant pressure and volume, R = universal gas constant)

As $n = 1$, so $C_p - C_V = R$

12. *(a)* **Addition polymerisation** Monomers are added one after other in addition polymerisation.

Teflon Addition polymerisation.

$n\ F_2C{=}CF_2 \longrightarrow (\!-CF_2-CF_2-\!)_n$

Tetrafluoro ethene Teflon

Nylon-6, 6 Condensation polymerisation.

$HO-\overset{O}{\overset{\|}{C}}-(CH_2)_4-\overset{O}{\overset{\|}{C}}-OH + H_2N-(CH_2)_6-NH_2$

Adipic acid Hexamethylene diamine

$\xrightarrow{-H_2O} (\!-\overset{O}{\overset{\|}{C}}-(CH_2)_4-\overset{O}{\overset{\|}{C}}-NH-(CH_2)_6-NH-\!)_n$

Nylon-6, 6

Novolac Condensation polymerisation.

Phenol + HCHO (Formaldehyde) $\underset{OH^-}{\overset{H^+}{\rightleftharpoons}}$ o-hydroxymethylphenol (CH_2OH) $\longrightarrow$ Novolac

Dacron Condensation polymerisation.

Glycol (HO–CH₂CH₂–OH) + Terephthalic acid $\xrightarrow{-H_2O}$ $(\!-O-(CH_2)_2-O-\overset{O}{\overset{\|}{C}}-C_6H_4-\overset{O}{\overset{\|}{C}}-\!)_n$

Dacron

13. *(d)* Acetone on reaction with Grignard reagent and on further hydrolysis gives 2-methyl butan-2-ol as follows

$CH_3-\overset{O}{\overset{\|}{C}}-CH_3 \xrightarrow[\text{Dry ether}]{\text{(i) } C_2H_5MgBr} CH_3-\underset{C_2H_5}{\underset{|}{\overset{\overset{-\ \ +}{OMgBr}}{\overset{|}{C}}}}-CH_3 \xrightarrow{\text{(ii) } H_2O, H^+} CH_3-\underset{CH_2CH_3}{\underset{|}{\overset{OH}{\overset{|}{C}}}}-CH_3$

Acetone (Product)

IUPAC name of product is 2-methylbutan-2-ol.

14. *(a)* (A) $\mathbf{PCl_5}$

P (Ground state) = $3s^2 3p^3$

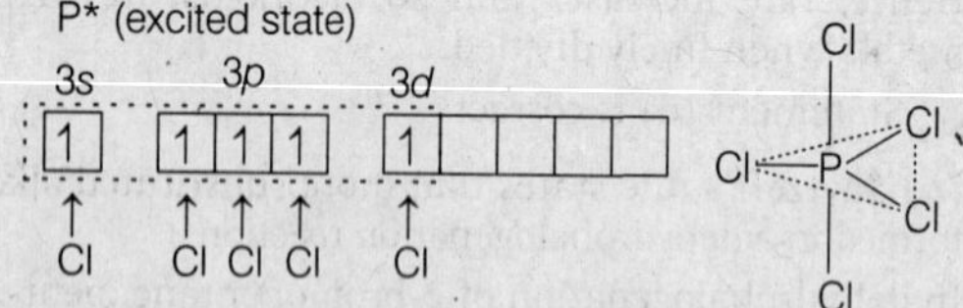

Hybridisation of P $\rightarrow sp^3d$

Structure of PCl_5 $\rightarrow$ Trigonal bipyramidal

(B) $\mathbf{SF_6}$

S (Ground state) = $3s^2 3p^4$

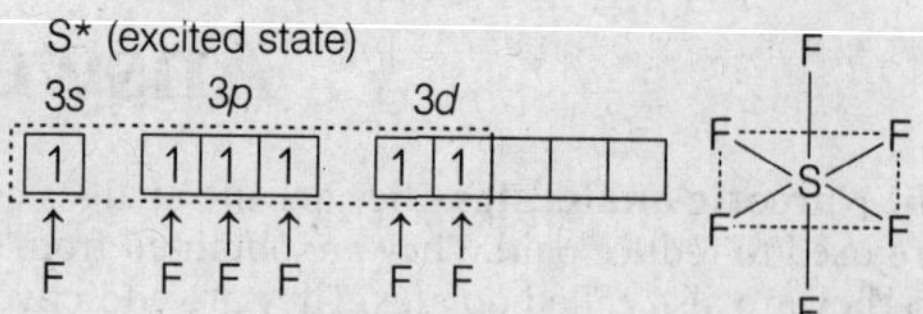

Hybridisation of S $\rightarrow sp^3d^2$

Structure of SF_6 $\rightarrow$ Octahedral

(C) $\mathbf{BrF_5}$

Br (Ground state) = $3s^2 3p^5$

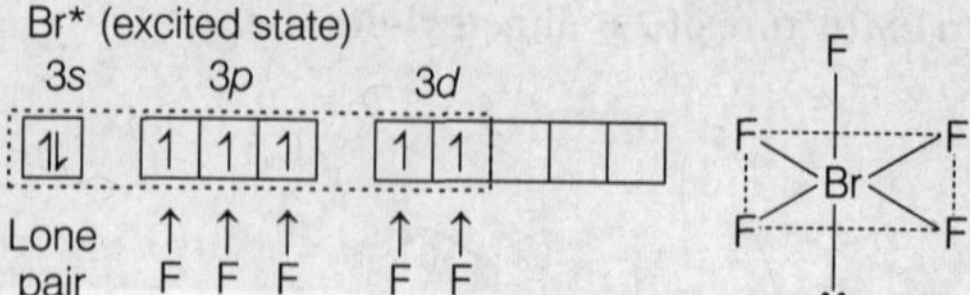

Hybridisation of Br $\rightarrow sp^3d^2$

Structure of BrF_5 $\rightarrow$ Square pyramidal

(D) $\mathbf{BF_3}$

B (Ground state) = $2s^2 2p^1$

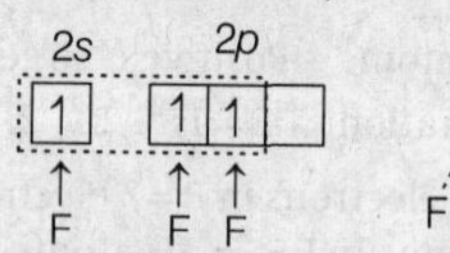

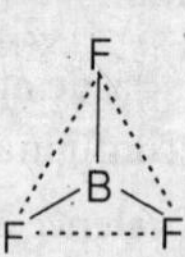

Hybridisation of B $\rightarrow sp^2$

Structure of BF_3 $\rightarrow$ Trigonal planar

$\therefore$ Correct match is

(A)-(IV); (B)-(III); (C)-(I); (D)-(II)

15. *(c)* Mercury is the only metal which is liquid at room temperature. Impure mercury metal is evaporated to obtain highly pure mercury metal as distillate. This method is known as distillation.

16. *(a)* Addition of HBr to an alkene in presence of a peroxide (benzoyl peroxide $[(C_6H_5CO)_2O_2]$ gives an anti-Markownikoff's product.

Anti-Markownikoff's rule states that hydrogen is added to a more substituted carbon atom of an unsymmetrical alkene.

$(CH_3)_2CH-CH{=}CH_2 + HBr \xrightarrow{(C_6H_5CO)_2O_2}$

3-methylbutene

$(CH_3)_2CH-CH_2-CH_2-Br + (CH_3)_2CH-\underset{Br}{\underset{|}{CH}}-CH_3$

1-bromo-3-methyl butane (Major) 2-bromo, 3-methyl butane (Minor)

17. *(a)* Tritium (^3_1H) is an isotope of hydrogen. It is a radioactive isotope and decays by emitting beta-particle (β^-) to form $^3_2He^+$.

$$\underset{\text{Tritium}}{^3_1H} \longrightarrow {}^3_2He^+ + \underset{\beta\text{-particle }(\beta^-)}{e^-} + 18.6 \text{ keV}$$

18. *(b)* On moving down the group from F to I, the size of atom increases. Order of the size of halogen atoms is I > Br > Cl > F. So, the bond length of C—X bond also increases from F to I and hence, the bond enthalpy decreases from F to I.

Correct order of bond length of C—X bond is

$$H_3C-I > H_3C-Br > H_3C-Cl > H_3C-F.$$

Correct order of bond enthalpy is

$H_3C—F > H_3C—Cl > CH_3—Br > H_3C—I$.

19. ***(d)*** Number of octahedral and tetrahedral voids are equal to N and $2N$ respectively, where N is the number of atoms in unit cell.

Number of atoms per unit cell in hexagonal primitive unit cell = 6.

Number of tetrahedral voids = $2N = 2 \times 6 = 12$.

Number of octahedral voids = $N = 6$.

20. ***(b)*** (a) $2KClO_3 \xrightarrow{\Delta} 2KCl + 3O_2$; (Decomposition reaction)

(b) $Cr_2O_3 + 2Al \xrightarrow{\Delta} Al_2O_3 + 2Cr$; (Metal displacement reaction)

(c) $Fe + 2HCl \xrightarrow{\Delta} FeCl_2 + H_2$; (Displacement reaction)

(d) $2Pb(NO_3)_2 \longrightarrow 2PbO + 4NO_2 + O_2$; (Decomposition reaction)

Metal displacement reaction is a displacement reaction in which a more reactive metal displaces/replaces the less reactive metal. In option (c), hydrogen is a non-metal. So, it is displacement reaction but not a metal displacement reaction.

21. ***(d)*** Boyle's law states, that at constant temperature, pressure of a gas of fixed amount varies inversely with volume.

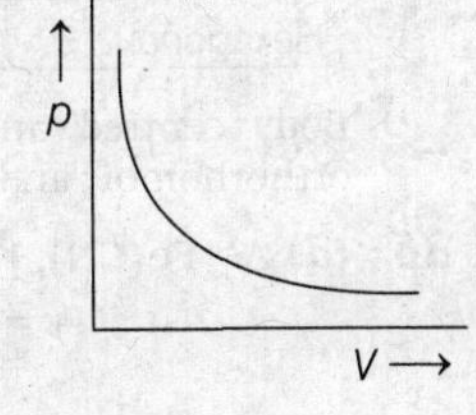

$$p \propto \frac{1}{V}$$

$$p = \frac{\lambda}{V}, \text{ (}\lambda\text{ is a constant)}$$

$$pV = \lambda$$

As temperature increases, gas expands i.e. volume of gas increases.

So, the product pV increases and the p *vs* V curve of Boyle's law shifts upwards.

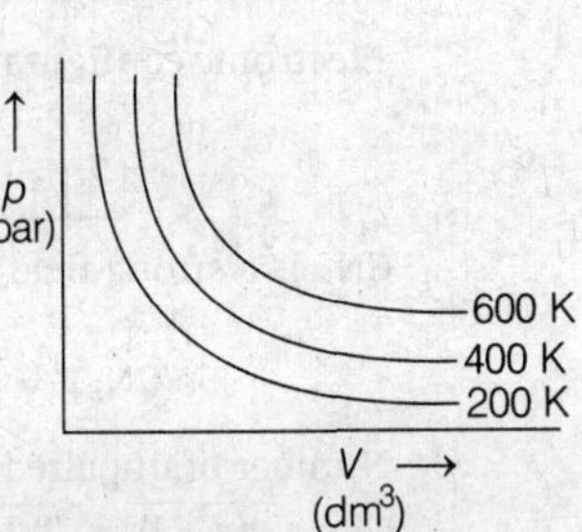

22. ***(c)*** Dimethyl ammonium acetate $[CH_3COONH_2(CH_3)_2]$ is a salt of weak acid (CH_3COOH) and weak base $[(CH_3)_2NH]$. pH of dimethyl ammonium acetate salt solution can be calculated using formula :

$$pH = 7 + \frac{1}{2}(pK_a - pK_b)$$

pK_a of acetic acid = 4.77

pK_b of dimethyl amine = 3.27

$$pH = 7 + \frac{1}{2}(4.77 - 3.27)$$

$$pH = 7 + \frac{1}{2} \times 1.50$$

$$\Rightarrow \quad pH = 7 + 0.75$$

$$pH = 7.75$$

23. ***(d)*** On moving down the group, the ionic size of alkaline earth metals increases. So, due to small size of Be^{2+} ion, Be has highest polarising power [ability to attract the electron cloud of anion (Cl^-)].

$\therefore$ $BeCl_2$ is more covalent than other alkaline earth metal halides. Organic molecules are covalent in nature. Rule for solubility is "Like dissolves like". So, $BeCl_2$ is soluble in organic solvents as both are covalent in nature.

24. ***(b)*** A blast furnace is generally used for reduction of iron oxides but it can be used for extraction of other metals like Pb from PbO, etc.

In a blast furnace, hot air is blown from the bottom of furnace. This bottom surface has the maximum temperature of upto 2200 K.

25. ***(a)*** Ethylene diaminetetraacetate (EDTA) ion.

EDTA is a hexadentate ligand with four 'O' and two 'N' donor atoms.

26. ***(a)*** van't Hoff factor for glucose, urea and sucrose is one as all are non-ionic.

- Mass of glucose = 10 g

  Molar mass of glucose = 180 g mol^{-1}

  Number of moles of glucose = $\frac{10}{180} = \frac{1}{18}$ mol = 0.056 mol

- Mass of urea = 10 g

  Molar mass of urea = 60 g mol^{-1}

  Number of moles of urea = $\frac{10}{60} = \frac{1}{6}$ mol = 0.167 mol

- Mass of sucrose = 10 g

  Molar mass of sucrose = 342 g mol^{-1}

  Number of moles of sucrose = $\frac{10}{342}$ = 0.029 mol

Osmotic pressure is a colligative property which depends on the amount of solute present in the solution. As the amount of urea is more than that of glucose and sucrose.

Amount of solute : Urea > Glucose > Sucrose

$\therefore$ Osmotic pressure, $p_2 > p_1 > p_3$

27. ***(a)*** The order of acidic strength is

$$HF << HCl << HBr << HI$$

As we move down the group, the size of atom increases. Thus, the bond length also increases and bond enthalpy decreases. So, it becomes easier to break H—X bond on moving down the group. This results the increase in the acidic strength.

So, both statements I and II are true.

28. ***(a)*** Beryllium chloride ($BeCl_2$) is an electron deficient compound. So, it does not exist in its monomer form.

In solid state and vapour phase, $BeCl_2$ exists in chain and dimer forms respectively.

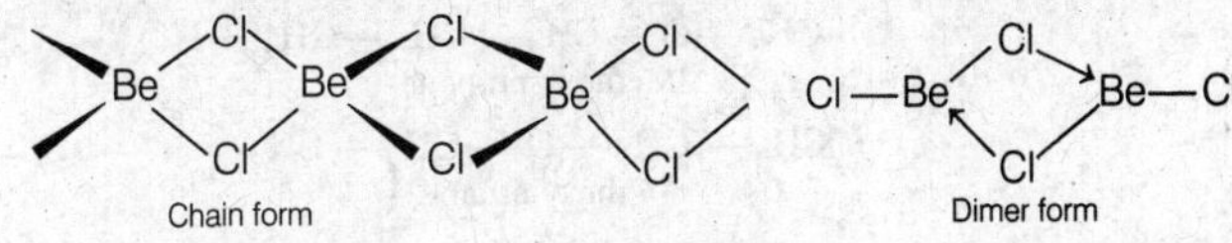

29. *(b)* The enthalpy of reaction is negative, -4.2 kJ mol^{-1}. The reaction is an exothermic reaction i.e. the energy of product *B*, is less than the energy of reactant *A*. So, the potential energy profile for the reaction is

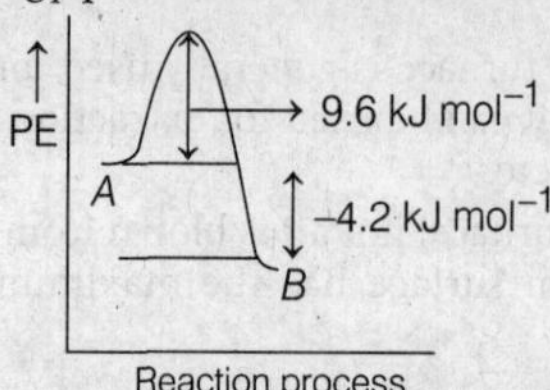

30. *(c)* $Zr (Z = 40) \rightarrow 1s^2, 2s^2 2p^6 3s^2 3p^6, 3d^{10}, 4s^2 4p^6 4d^2, 5s^2$

$Hf (Z = 72) \rightarrow 1s^2, 2s^2 2p^6, 3s^2 3p^6 3d^{10}, 4s^2 4p^6 4d^{10}, 5s^2 5p^6 4f^{14} 5d^2, 6s^2$

Hf is a post lanthanoid element. Due to presence of $4f$-orbitals which have poor shielding effect, the effective nuclear charge on valence shell electrons is more which result in the decrease of the size of Hf. This effect is known as lanthanoid contraction.

31. *(a)* Frequency of electromagnetic radiation

$$\nu = 1368 \text{ kHz} = 1368 \times 10^3 \text{ s}^{-1}$$

Speed of light, $c = 3 \times 10^8 \text{ ms}^{-1}$

Wavelength of electromagnetic radiation, $\lambda = \dfrac{c}{\nu}$

$$\lambda = \frac{3 \times 10^8 \text{ ms}^{-1}}{1368 \times 10^3 \text{ s}^{-1}} = 219.3 \text{ m}$$

32. *(c)*

Element	%	Atomic mass	Relative number of moles	Simple ratio of moles	Simplest whole number ratio
C	78	12	$\frac{78}{12} = 6.5$	$\frac{6.5}{6.5} = 1$	1
H	22	1	$\frac{22}{1} = 22$	$\frac{22}{6.5} = 3.3$	3

The empirical formula of the organic compound is CH_3.

33. *(d)* **Metamerism** compound which have same molecular formula but different number of carbon atoms on either sides of functional group are known as metamers and this phenomenon is known as metamerism.

(a) C_5H_{12} contains no functional group. So, it cannot show metamerism.

(b) C_3H_8O has ether functional group in which only one arrangement is possible. So, it does not show metamerism.

$$CH_3—O—CH_2—CH_3$$

(c) C_3H_6O has carbonyl functional group in which following two arrangements are possible. $CH_3—\overset{\overset{\large O}{\|}}{C}—CH_3, CH_3CH_2CHO$

So, it shows functional group isomerism and does not show metamerism.

(d) $C_4H_{10}O$ has ether functional group in which following two arrangements are possible. So, it shows metamerism.

$$\underset{\text{Methoxy propane}}{CH_3—O—CH_2—CH_2—CH_3}$$

$$\underset{\text{Ethoxy ethane}}{CH_3—CH_2—O—CH_2—CH_3}$$

34. *(c)* Hinsberg test is used to test the amine compounds. Only 1° and 2° amines give product after reacting with Hinsberg reagent (benzene sulphonyl chloride). 3° amines do not react. The product formed can be distinguished by dissolving in alkali. If it dissolves, then amine is 1° otherwise the reactant is secondary amine.

$$\underset{\text{Ethyl Amine}}{CH_3—CH_2NH_2} + \underset{\text{Hinsberg reagent}}{C_6H_5SO_2Cl} \longrightarrow C_6H_5SO_2NHCH_2CH_3 + HCl$$

$$C_6H_5SO_2NHCH_2CH_3 \xrightarrow{\text{Alkali KOH}} \underset{\text{Soluble in alkali medium}}{C_6H_5SO_2\overset{\ominus}{N}CH_2CH_3K^{\oplus}}$$

35. *(d)*

Crystal system	Bravais lattice
Cubic	Primitive, body centred, face centred, end centred
Orthorhombic	Primitive, body centred, face centred, end centred
Tetragonal	Primitive, body centred
Monoclinic	Primitive, end centred
Triclinic	Primitive
Rhombohedral	Primitive
Hexagonal	Primitive

Body centred unit cell exists in three systems, i.e. cubic, orthorhombic and tetragonal.

36. *(d)* A. $[Fe(CN)_6]^{3-}$ Oxidation number of

$$Fe = x + 6(-1) = -3$$
$$x - 6 = -3 \Rightarrow x = +3$$

Electronic configuration of $Fe \rightarrow [Ar]\, 3d^6 4s^2$

Electronic configuration of $Fe^{3+} \rightarrow [Ar]\, 3d^5 4s^0$

3d⁵: | 1 | 1 | 1 | 1 | 1 | 4s⁰: | |

CN^- is a strong field ligand so, pairing of electrons occurs.

$[Fe(CN)_6]^{3-}$ = 3d⁵: | 1↓ | 1↓ | 1 | | | 4s⁰: | |

Number of unpaired electrons = 1

$$\mu_s = \sqrt{n(n+1)} = \sqrt{1(1+2)} = \sqrt{3} = 1.73 \text{ BM}$$

B. $[Fe(H_2O)_6]^{3+}$ Oxidation state of Fe is +3.

Water is weak field ligand, so pairing of electron do not take place.

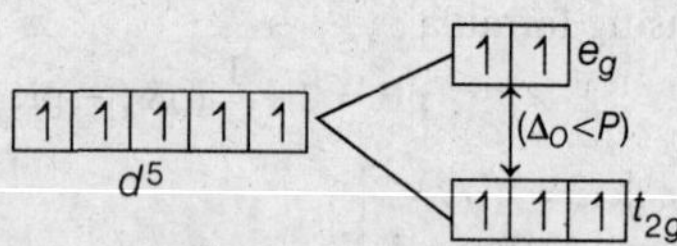

Number of unpaired electrons = 5.

$$\mu_s = \sqrt{n(n+2)} = \sqrt{5 \times (5+2)}$$
$$= \sqrt{5 \times 7} = \sqrt{35} = 5.92 \text{ BM}$$

C. $[Fe(CN)_6]^{4-}$ Oxidation state of Fe is +2.

Electronic configuration of $Fe^{2+} = [Ar]\, 3d^6 4s^0$

CN^- is a strong field ligand, so pairing of electrons take place.

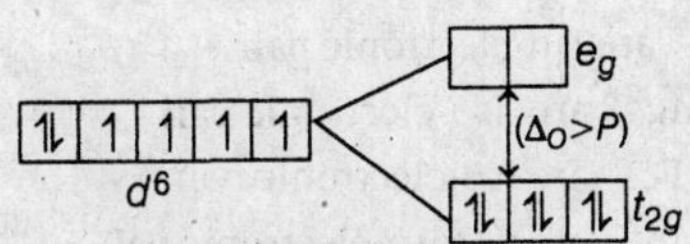

Number of unpaired electrons = 0

$$\mu_s = \sqrt{0(0+1)} = 0 \text{ BM}$$

D. $[Fe(H_2O)_6]^{4-}$ Oxidation state of Fe is +2 ($3d^6$).

Water is weak field ligand, so pairing of electron do not take place.

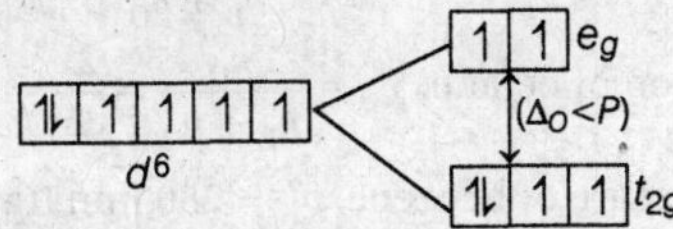

Number of unpaired electrons = 4

$$\mu_s = \sqrt{4(4+2)} = \sqrt{4 \times 6} = \sqrt{24} = 4.90 \text{ BM}$$

Hence, correct match is

A → 4, → B → 1, C → 2, D → 3.

37. *(c)* Given, mass of $O_2 = 4$ g

Molar mass of $O_2 = 32 \text{ g mol}^{-1}$

Number of moles of O_2,

$$n_{O_2} = \frac{\text{Mass of } O_2}{\text{Molar mass of } O_2} = \frac{4}{32} = \frac{1}{8} \text{ mol}$$

Given, mass of $H_2 = 2$ g

Molar mass of $H_2 = 2 \text{ g mol}^{-1}$

Number of moles of H_2,

$$n_{H_2} = \frac{\text{Mass of } H_2}{\text{Molar mass of } H_2} = \frac{2}{2} = 1 \text{ mol}$$

Total number of moles of mixture,

$$n_T = n_{O_2} + n_{H_2} \Rightarrow n_T = \frac{1}{8} + 1 = \frac{9}{8} \text{ mol}$$

Ideal gas equation;

$$pV = nRT \left(\begin{array}{l} \text{Given, } R = 0.082 \text{ L atm mol}^{-1} \text{ K}^{-1} \\ T = 0^\circ\text{C} = 273 \text{ K}, V = 1 \text{ L} \end{array} \right)$$

$$p \times 1 = \frac{9}{8} \times 0.082 \times 273 \Rightarrow p = 25.18 \text{ atm}$$

38. *(c)* In this reaction, removal of carbon dioxide takes place. So, this is a decarboxylation reaction. A decarboxylation reaction takes place with soda lime (NaOH + CaO).

So, missing reagent is CaO.

39. *(c)* The change in internal energy depends on the temperature. For isothermal process, $\Delta T = 0$.

So, $\Delta U = 0$.

With an expansion of an ideal gas, more space is available for the gaseous particles.

∴ Entropy of gas increases so, entropy of system is not zero.

i.e. $\Delta S \neq 0$

40. *(b)* HF < HCl < HBr < HI; Down the group, size of atom increases, bond length decreases and bond enthalpy decreases. So, acidic strength increases.

∴ The given sequence is correct

$H_2O > H_2S > H_2Se > H_2Te$, pK_a is inversely proportional to acidic strength. So, pK_a decreases.

∴ The given sequence is incorrect.

$NH_3 < PH_3 < AsH_3 < SbH_3$; Acidic character increases down the group,

∴ The given sequence is correct.

$CO_2 < SiO_2 < SnO_2 < PbP_2$; on moving down the group oxidising power increases.

∴ The given sequence is correct.

41. *(c)* $\lambda_{CH_3COOH} = 20 \text{ S cm}^2 \text{ mol}^{-1}$

Concentration of CH_3COOH, $C = 0.007$ M

$$\lambda^\circ_{H^+} = 350 \text{ S cm}^2 \text{ mol}^{-1}$$

$$\lambda^\circ_{CH_3COO^-} = 50 \text{ S cm}^2 \text{ mol}^{-1}$$

According to Kohlrausch's law,

$$\lambda^\circ_{CH_3COOH} = \lambda^\circ_{H^+} + \lambda^\circ_{CH_3COO^-}$$

$$\lambda^\circ_{CH_3COOH} = 350 + 50 = 400 \text{ S cm}^2 \text{ mol}^{-1}$$

$$\text{Degree of dissociation, } \alpha = \frac{\lambda_{CH_3COOH}}{\lambda^\circ_{CH_3COOH}}$$

$$\alpha = \frac{20}{400} = \frac{1}{20} = 0.05 = 5 \times 10^{-2}$$

	$CH_3COOH \rightleftharpoons$	CH_3COO^-	$+ H^+$
$t = 0$	C	–	–
$t = t_{eq}$	$C - C\alpha$	$C\alpha$	$C\alpha$

$$\text{Equilibrium constant, } k = \frac{C^2\alpha^2}{C(1-\alpha)} = \frac{C\alpha^2}{1-\alpha}$$

As $\alpha << 1; 1 - \alpha \approx 1$

$$k = C\alpha^2 = 0.007 \times (0.05)^2$$

$$= 0.007 \times 25 \times 10^{-4} = 1.75 \times 10^{-5} \text{ mol L}^{-1}$$

42. *(a)* Arrhenius equation,

$$k = Ae^{-E_a/RT}$$

$$\ln k = \ln A - \frac{E_a}{R}\left(\frac{1}{T}\right)$$

$\frac{-E_a}{R}$ is the slope of Arrhenius plot $\left(\ln k \text{ vs } \frac{1}{T}\right)$

$\ln A$ is the intercept

$$\text{Slope} = -5 \times 10^3 \text{ K}$$

$$R = 8.314 \text{ J K}^{-1} \text{ mol}^{-1}$$

So, $-\frac{E_a}{R} = -5 \times 10^3$ K

$\Rightarrow$ $E_a = 5 \times 10^3 \times R = 5 \times 10^3 \times 8.314$

$$= 41.57 \times 10^3 \text{ J mol}^{-1} = 41.5 \text{ kJ mol}^{-1}$$

43. *(d)* $NaBH_4$ is a weak reducing agent. It can reduce aldehyde/ketone to alcohol but cannot reduce ester group.

(2-oxo-cyclohexyl with CH_2–C(=O)–OCH_3 and CH_3) $\xrightarrow[C_2H_5OH]{NaBH_4}$ (2-hydroxy-cyclohexyl with CH_2–C(=O)–OCH_3 and CH_3)

44. *(d)* A. **Gattermann-Koch reaction** Benzene or its derivatives are treated with CO and HCl in presence of anhydrous $AlCl_3$/CuCl.

Benzene $\xrightarrow[\text{Anhy. } AlCl_3/CuCl]{CO, HCl}$ Benzaldehyde (CHO)

B. **Haloform reaction** Treatment of carbonyl compound having atleast one methyl group attached to the C ═O with X_2/NaOH or NaOX.

$$\underset{\text{Aldehyde}}{R—\overset{O}{\overset{\|}{C}}—CH_3} + NaOX \longrightarrow R—\overset{O}{\overset{\|}{C}}—O^{\ominus}Na^{\oplus} + CHX_3$$

C. **Esterification** Carboxylic acid reacts with an alcohol in acidic medium.

$$\underset{\text{Alcohol}}{R—CH_2—OH} + \underset{\text{Acid}}{R'COOH} \xrightleftharpoons{\text{Conc. } H_2SO_4} \underset{\text{Ester}}{RCH_2O—\overset{O}{\overset{\|}{C}}—R'}$$

D. **Hell-Volhard Zelinsky reaction** Treatment of carboxylic acid having α-hydrogen with PX_3 or X_2/Red P.

$$\underset{\text{Carboxylic acid}}{R—CH_2—\overset{O}{\overset{\|}{C}}—OH} \xrightarrow[\text{(ii) } H_2O]{\text{(i) } X_2\text{/ Red P}} \underset{\alpha\text{-halocarboxylic acid}}{R—\underset{X}{\underset{|}{CH}}—\overset{O}{\overset{\|}{C}}—OH}$$

Hence, correct match is A → 2, B → 3, C → 4, D → 1.

45. *(c)* (a) **POCl$_3$** Hybridisation $= \frac{1}{2} \times 8 = 4\ (sp^3)$

Shape = Tetrahedral
Dipole moment, $\mu \neq 0$
$POCl_3$ is polar in nature.

(b) **CH$_2$O** Hybridisation $= \frac{1}{2}(6) = 3\ (sp^2)$

Shape = Trigonal planar.
Dipole moment, $\mu \neq 0$
CH_2O is polar in nature.

(c) **SbCl$_5$** Hybridisation $= \frac{1}{2} \times 10 = 5 (sp^3d)$

Shape = Trigonal bipyramidal
Dipole moment, $\mu = 0$
$SbCl_5$ is non-polar in nature.

(d) **NO$_2$** Hybridisation $= \frac{1}{2} \times (4+2) = \frac{1}{2} \times 6 = 3$ (sp^2).

Shape = Trigonal planar
Dipole moment, $\mu \neq 0$
NO_2 is polar in nature.

46. *(d)*

Ion	Number of electrons
O^{2-}	10
F^-	10
Na^+	10
Mg^{2+}	10
Mn^{2+}	23
Fe^{3+}	23
Fe^{2+}	24
Mn^{2+}	23

O^{2-} and F^- are iso-electronic pair.
Na^+ and Mg^{2+} are iso-electronic pair.
Mn^{2+} and Fe^{3+} are iso-electronic pair.
Fe^{2+} and Mn^{2+} are not iso-electronic pair.

47. *(c)* Molar ratio of benzene to octane, $\frac{n_B}{n_O} = \frac{3}{2}$

Let $n_B = 3x$ mol, $n_O = 2x$ mol
Total number of moles $= n_B + n_O = 3x + 2x = 5x$ mol
Mole fraction of benzene, $\chi_B = \frac{n_B}{n_B + n_O} = \frac{3x}{5x} = \frac{3}{5}$.

Mole fraction of octane, $\chi_O = \frac{n_O}{n_B + n_O} = \frac{2x}{5x} = \frac{2}{5}$

Vapour pressure of benzene, $p_B^\circ = 280$ mm Hg
Vapour pressure of octane, $p_O^\circ = 420$ mm Hg
Total vapour pressure of solution,

$$p_S = \chi_B p_B^\circ + \chi_O p_O^\circ$$
$$= \frac{3}{5} \times 280 + \frac{2}{5} \times 420 = 3 \times 56 + 2 \times 84$$
$$= 168 + 168 = 336 \text{ mm of Hg}$$

48. *(c)* A. **Tropospheric pollution** Sulphur oxides are the main cause of tropospheric pollution.

$$2SO_2(g) + O_2(g) \longrightarrow 2SO_3(g)$$

B. **Ozone depletion** Free radical generated in atmosphere depletes the ozone layer.

$$HOCl(g) \xrightarrow{h\nu} \dot{O}H + \dot{C}l$$

C. **Acid rain** Rock ($CaCO_3$) reacts with H_2SO_4 to give $CaSO_4$, water and CO_2.

$$CaCO_3 + H_2SO_4 \longrightarrow CaSO_4 + H_2CO_3 \longrightarrow H_2O + CO_2$$

D. **Smog** It contains/composed of nitrogen oxides, sulphur oxide, smoke, etc.

Smog = Smoke + Fog

$$NO_2(g) \xrightarrow{h\nu} NO(g) + O(g)$$

Hence, correct match is A → 4, B → 3, C → 1, D → 2.

49. *(b)* Mild reducing agents like alcohol are used to reduce diazonium salts to arene. Alcohol (ethanol is oxidised to aldehyde (ethanal).

2,4,6 tribromoaniline $\xrightarrow[0\text{-}5^\circ C]{NaNO_2 + HCl}$ (2,4,6-tribromobenzenediazonium chloride, $\overset{\oplus}{N_2}\overset{\ominus}{Cl}$) $\xrightarrow{CH_3CH_2OH}$ 1,3,5.-tribromobenzene

∴ Reagent used is CH_3CH_2OH (ethanol).

50. *(a)* This is Etard reaction in which reaction of toluene with chromyl chloride in CCl_4 followed by hydrolysis gives benzaldehyde.

Toluene reacts with chromyl chloride to form a precipitate called the Etard complex.

Toluene ($C_6H_5CH_3$) $+ CrO_2Cl_2 \xrightarrow{CS_2}$ (X) $C_6H_5CH(OCrOHCl_2)_2 \xrightarrow{H_3O^+}$ Benzaldehyde (C_6H_5CHO)

NEET SOLVED PAPER 2022

Instruction

- This question paper contains 50 Multiple Choice Questions of Chemistry, divided into two Sections; section A and section B.
- Section A contains 35 questions and all questions are compulsory.
- Section B contains 15 questions out of which only 10 questions are to be attempted.
- Each question carries 4 marks.

Section-A

1. The given graph is a representation of kinetics of a reaction.

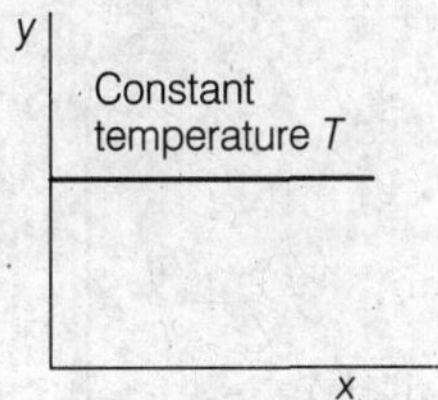

The y and x axes for zero and first order reactions, respectively are

(a) zero order (y = concentration and x = time), first order (y = rate constant and x = concentration).

(b) zero order (y = rate and x = concentration), first order ($y = t_{1/2}$ and x = concentration).

(c) zero order (y = rate and x = concentration), first order (y = rate and $x = t_{1/2}$).

(d) zero order (y = concentration and x = time), first order ($y = t_{1/2}$ and x = concentration).

2. Which compound amongst the following is not an aromatic compound?

(a) 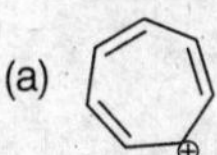 (b)

(c) 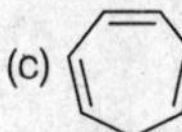 (d)

3. $RMgX + CO_2 \xrightarrow[\text{ether}]{\text{Dry}} Y \xrightarrow{H_3O^+} RCOOH$

What is Y in the above reaction ?

(a) $R_3CO^-Mg^+X$

(b) $RCOO^-X^+$

(c) $(RCOO)_2Mg$

(d) $RCOO^-Mg^+X$

4. Which of the following statement is not correct about diborane?

(a) The four terminal B—H bonds are 2-centre-2 electron bonds.

(b) The four terminal hydrogen atoms and the two boron atoms lie in one plane.

(c) Both the boron atoms are sp^2-hybridised.

(d) There are two 3-centre-2-electron bonds.

5. Gadolinium has a low value of third ionisation enthalpy because of

(a) high exchange enthalpy

(b) high electronegativity

(c) high basic character

(d) small size

6. Which one is not correct mathematical equation for Dalton's law of partial pressure? Here p = total pressure of gaseous mixture

(a) $p = n_1\frac{RT}{V} + n_2\frac{RT}{V} + n_3\frac{RT}{V}$

(b) $p_i = x_i p$, where p_i = partial pressure of ith gas x_i = mole fraction of ith gas in gaseous mixture.

(c) $p_i = x_i p_i^o$, where x_i = mole fraction of ith gas in gaseous mixture, p_i^o = pressure of ith gas in pure state.

(d) $p = p_1 + p_2 + p_3$

7. Given below are two statements.

Statement I The boiling points of the following hydrides of group 16 elements increases in the order

$$H_2O < H_2S < H_2Se < H_2Te$$

Statement II The boiling points of these hydride increases with increase in molar mass.

In the light of the above statements, choose the most appropriate answer from the options given below.

(a) Both statement I and statement II are incorrect.

(b) Statement I is correct but statement II is incorrect.

(c) Statement I is incorrect but statement II correct.

(d) Both statement I and statement II are correct.

8. Given below are two statements.

Statement I The acidic strength of monosubstituted nitrophenol is higher than phenol because of electron withdrawing nitro group.

Statement II *o*-nitrophenol, *m*-nitrophenol and *p*-nitrophenol will have same acidic strength as they have one nitro group attached to the phenolic ring.

In the light of the above statements, choose the most appropriate answer from the options given below.

(a) Both statement I and statement II are incorrect.
(b) Statement I is correct but statement II is incorrect.
(c) Statement I is incorrect but statement II is correct.
(d) Both statement I and statement II are correct.

9. The Kjeldahl's method for the estimation of nitrogen can be used to estimate the amount of nitrogen in which one of the following compounds?

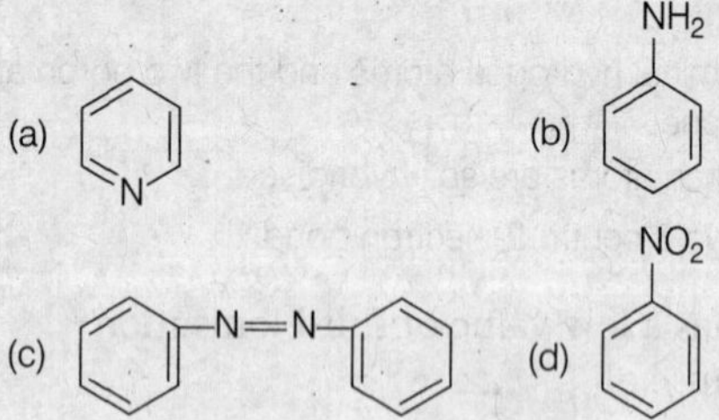

10. Match List-I with List-II.

	List-I (Drug class)		List-II (Drug molecule)
(A)	Antacids	(i)	Salvarsan
(B)	Antihistamines	(ii)	Morphine
(C)	Analgesics	(iii)	Cimetidine
(D)	Antimicrobials	(iv)	Seldane

Choose the correct answer from the options given below

(a) (A) - (iii), (B) - (iv), (C) - (ii), (D) - (i)
(b) (A) - (i), (B) - (iv), (C) - (ii), (D) - (iii)
(c) (A) - (iv), (B) - (iii), (C) - (i), (D) - (ii)
(d) (A) - (iii), (B) - (ii), (C) - (iv), (D) - (i)

11. The IUPAC name of an element with atomic number 119 is

(a) unnilennium
(b) unununnium
(c) ununoctium
(d) ununennium

12. Amongst the following which one will have maximum 'lone pair - lone pair' electron repulsions?

(a) IF_5
(b) SF_4
(c) XeF_2
(d) ClF_3

13. Which of the following sequence of reactions is suitable to synthesise chlorobenzene?

(a) Phenol, $NaNO_2$, HCl, CuCl
(b) [benzene], HCl
(c) [aniline, NH_2], HCl, Heating
(d) Benzene, Cl_2, anhydrous $FeCl_3$

14. Which of the following *p-V* curve represents maximum work done?

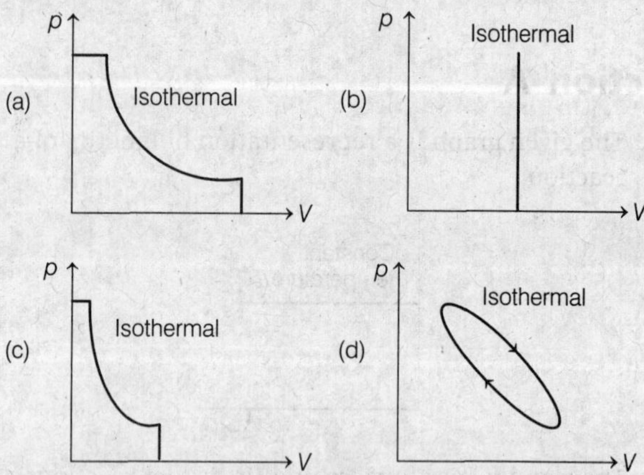

15. Given below are half-cell reactions

$$MnO_4^- + 8H^+ + 5e^- \longrightarrow Mn^{2+} + 4H_2O,$$
$$E^\circ_{Mn^{2+}/MnO_4^-} = -1.510 \text{ V}$$
$$\frac{1}{2}O_2 + 2H^+ + 2e^- \longrightarrow H_2O, \; E^\circ_{O_2/H_2O} = +1.223 \text{ V}$$

Will the permanganate ion, MnO_4^- liberate O_2 from water in the presence of an acid?

(a) No, because $E^\circ_{cell} = -0.287$ V
(b) Yes, because $E^\circ_{cell} = +2.733$ V
(c) No, because $E^\circ_{cell} = -2.733$ V
(d) Yes, because $E^\circ_{cell} = +0.287$ V

16. The IUPAC name of the complex $[Ag(H_2O)_2][Ag(CN)_2]$ is

(a) diaquasilver (II) dicyanidoargentate (II)
(b) dicyanidosilver (I) diaquaargentate (I)
(c) diaquasilver (I) dicyanidoargentate (I)
(d) dicyanidosilver (II) diaquaargentate (II)

17. Identify the incorrect statement from the following.

(a) The oxidation number of K in KO_2 is + 4.
(b) Ionisation enthalpy of alkali metals decreases from top to bottom in the group.
(c) Lithium is the strongest reducing agent among the alkali metals.
(d) Alkali metals react with water to form their hydroxides.

18. What mass of 95% pure $CaCO_3$ will be required to neutralise 50 mL of 0.5 M HCl solution according to the following reaction?

$$CaCO_3(s) + 2HCl(aq) \longrightarrow CaCl_2(aq) + CO_2(g) + H_2O(l)$$

[Calculate upto second place of decimal point]

(a) 1.32 g
(b) 3.65 g
(c) 9.50 g
(d) 1. 25 g

19. Given below are two statements.

Statement I Primary aliphatic amines react with HNO_2 to give unstable diazonium salts.

Statement II Primary aromatic amines react with HNO_2 to form diazonium salts which are stable even above 300 K.

In the light of the above statements, choose the most appropriate answer from the options given below.

(a) Both statement I and statement II are incorrect.
(b) Statement I is correct but statement II is incorrect.
(c) Statement I is incorrect but statement II is correct.
(d) Both statement I and statement II are correct.

20. Which statement regarding polymers is not correct?

(a) Fibers possess high tensile strength.
(b) Thermoplastic polymers are capable of repeatedly softening and hardening on heating and cooling respectively.
(c) Thermosetting polymers are reusable.
(d) Elastomers have polymer chains held together by weak intermolecular forces.

21. The incorrect statement regarding chirality is

(a) the product obtained by S_N2 reaction of haloalkane having chirality at the reactive site shows inversion of configuration.
(b) enantiomers are superimposable mirror images on each other.
(c) a racemic mixture shows zero optical rotation.
(d) S_N1 reaction yields 1 : 1 mixture of both enantiomers.

22. Given below are two statements.

Statement I In the coagulation of a negative sol, the flocculating power of the three given ions is in the order

$$Al^{3+} > Ba^{2+} > Na^+$$

Statement II In the coagulation of a positive sol, the flocculating power of the three given salts is in the order

$$NaCl > Na_2SO_4 > Na_3PO_4$$

In the light of the above statements, choose the most appropriate answer from the options given below.

(a) Both statement I and statement II are incorrect.
(b) Statement I is correct but statement II is incorrect.
(c) Statement I is incorrect but statement II is correct.
(d) Both statement I and statement II are correct.

23. Match List-I with List-II.

List-I (Hydrides)	List-II (Nature)
(A) MgH_2	(i) Electron precise
(B) GeH_4	(ii) Electron deficient
(C) B_2H_6	(iii) Electron rich
(D) HF	(iv) Ionic

Choose the correct answer from the options given below

(a) (A) - (iii), (B) - (i), (C) - (ii), (D) - (iv)
(b) (A) - (i), (B) - (ii), (C) - (iv), (D) - (iii)
(c) (A) - (ii), (B) - (iii), (C) - (iv), (D) - (i)
(d) (A) - (iv), (B) - (i), (C) - (ii), (D) - (iii)

24. Match List-I with List-II.

List-I	List-II
(A) Li	(i) Absorbent for carbon dioxide
(B) Na	(ii) Electrochemical cells
(C) KOH	(iii) Coolant in fast breeder reactors
(D) Cs	(iv) Photoelectric cell

Choose the correct answer from the options given below

(a) (A) - (iii), (B) - (iv), (c) - (ii), (D) - (i)
(b) (A) - (i), (B) - (iii), (c) - (iv), (D) - (ii)
(c) (A) - (ii), (B) - (iii), (c) - (i), (D) - (iv)
(d) (A) - (iv), (B) - (i), (c) - (iii), (D) - (ii)

25. Given below are two statements one is labelled as Assertion (A) and the other is labelled as Reason (R).

Assertion (A) In a particular point defect, an ionic solid is electrically neutral, even if few of its cations are missing from its unit cells.

Reason (R) In an ionic solid, Frenkel defect arises due to dislocation of cation from its lattice site to interstitial site, maintaining overall electrical neutrality.

In the light of the above statements, choose the most appropriate answer from the options given below.

(a) Both A and R are correct but R is not the correct explanation of A.
(b) A is correct but R is not correct.
(c) A is not correct but R is correct.
(d) Both A and R are correct and R is the correct explanation of A.

26. The incorrect statement regarding enzymes is

(a) like chemical catalysts enzymes reduce the activation energy of bio processes.
(b) enzymes are polysaccharides.
(c) enzymes are very specific for a particular reaction and substrate.
(d) enzymes are biocatalysts.

27. Match List-I with List-II.

List-I (Products formed)	List-II (Reaction of carbonyl compound with)
(A) Cyanohydrin	(i) NH_2OH
(B) Acetal	(ii) RNH_2
(C) Schiff's base	(iii) Alcohol
(D) Oxime	(iv) HCN

Choose the correct answer from the options given below

(a) (A) - (ii), (B) - (iii), (C) - (iv), (D) - (i)
(b) (A) - (i), (B) - (iii), (C) - (ii), (D) - (iv)
(c) (A) - (iv), (B) - (iii), (C) - (ii). (D) - (i)
(d) (A) - (iii), (B) - (iv). (C) - (ii), (D) - (i)

28. In one molal solution that contains 0.5 mole of a solute, there is

(a) 500 g of solvent
(b) 100 mL of solvent
(c) 1000 g of solvent
(d) 500 mL of solvent

29. Choose the correct statement.

(a) Diamond is covalent and graphite is ionic.
(b) Diamond is sp^3-hybridised and graphite is sp^2-hybridised.
(c) Both diamond and graphite are used as dry lubricants.
(d) Diamond and graphite have two dimensional network.

30. Which amongst the following is incorrect statement?

(a) C_2 molecule has four electrons in its two degenerate π-molecular orbitals.
(b) H_2^+ ion has one electron.
(c) O_2^+ ion is diamagnetic.
(d) The bond orders of O_2^+, O_2, O_2^- and O_2^{2-} are 2.5, 2, 1.5 and 1 respectively.

31. Given below are two statements one is labelled as Assertion (A) and the other is labelled as Reason (R).

Assertion (A) ICl is more reactive than I_2.

Reason (R) I—Cl bond is weaker than I—I bond.

In the light of the above statements, choose the most appropriate answer from the options given below .

(a) Both A and R are correct but R is not the correct explanation of A.
(b) A is correct but R is not correct.
(c) A is not correct but R is correct.
(d) Both A and R are correct and R is the correct explanation of A.

32. Given below are two statements.

Statement I The boiling points of aldehydes and ketones are higher than hydrocarbons of comparable molecular masses because of weak molecular association in aldehydes and ketones due to dipole-dipole interactions.

Statement II The boiling points of aldehydes and ketones are lower than the alcohols of similar molecular masses due to the absence of H-bonding.

In the light of the above statements, choose the most appropriate answer from the options given below

(a) Both statement I and statement II are incorrect.
(b) Statement I is correct but statement II is incorrect.
(c) Statement I is incorrect but statement II is correct.
(d) Both statement I and statement II are correct.

33. The pH of the solution containing 50 mL each of 0.10 M sodium acetate and 0.01 M acetic acid is [Given pK_a of $CH_3COOH = 4.57$]

(a) 3.57 (b) 4.57
(c) 2.57 (d) 5.57

34. Identify the incorrect statement from the following.

(a) All the five 4*d*-orbitals have shapes similar to the respective 3*d*-orbitals.
(b) In an atom, all the five 3*d*-orbitals are equal in energy in free state.
(c) The shapes of d_{xy}, d_{yz}, and d_{zx} orbitals are similar to each other; and $d_{x^2-y^2}$ and d_{z^2} are similar to each other.
(d) All the five 5*d*-orbitals are different in size when compared to the respective 4*d*-orbitals.

35. At 298 K, the standard electrode potentials of Cu^{2+}/Cu, Zn^{2+}/Zn, Fe^{2+}/Fe and Ag^+/Ag are 0.34 V, −0.76 V, −0.44 V and 0.80 V, respectively. On the basis of standard electrode potential, predict which of the following reaction can not occur?

(a) $CuSO_4(aq) + Fe(s) \longrightarrow FeSO_4(aq) + Cu(s)$
(b) $FeSO_4(aq) + Zn(s) \longrightarrow ZnSO_4(aq) + Fe(s)$
(c) $2CuSO_4(aq) + 2Ag(s) \longrightarrow 2Cu(s) + Ag_2SO_4(aq)$
(d) $CuSO_4(aq) + Zn(s) \longrightarrow ZnSO_4(aq) + Cu(s)$

Section-B

36. The order of energy absorbed which is responsible for the colour of complexes

(A) $[Ni(H_2O)_2(en)_2]^{2+}$
(B) $[Ni(H_2O)_4(en)]^{2+}$ and
(C) $[Ni(en)_3]^{2+}$ is

(a) (C) > (B) > (A) (b) (C) > (A) > (B)
(c) (B) > (A) > (C) (d) (A) > (B) > (C)

37. A 10.0 L flask contains 64 g of oxygen at 27°C. (Assume O_2 gas is behaving ideally). The pressure inside the flask in bar is
(Given, $R = 0.0831\,\text{L bar K}^{-1}\,\text{mol}^{-1}$)

(a) 498.6 (b) 49.8
(c) 4.9 (d) 2.5

38. Which one of the following is not formed when acetone reacts with 2-pentanone in the presence of dilute NaOH followed by heating?

(a) 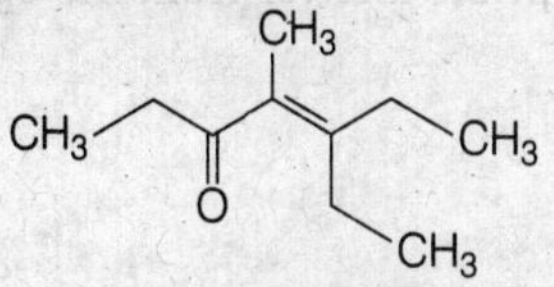 CH_3 CH_3 O CH_3 CH_3

(b) 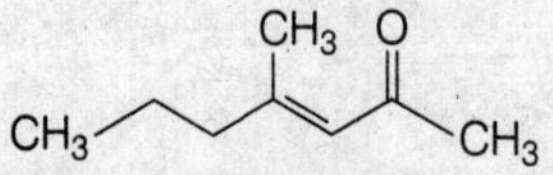 CH_3 O CH_3 CH_3

(c) 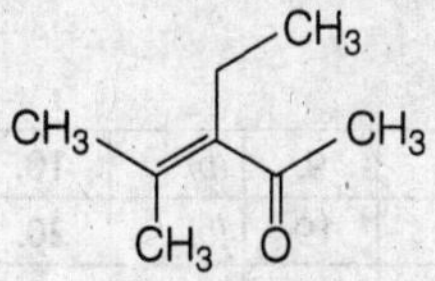 CH_3 CH_3 CH_3 CH_3 O

(d) 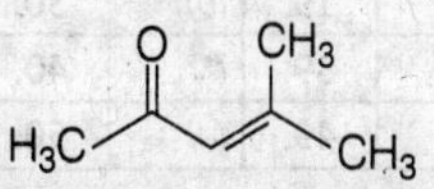 O CH_3 H_3C CH_3

39. Find the emf of the cell in which the following reaction takes place at 298 K

$Ni(s) + 2Ag^+ (0.001\text{ M}) \longrightarrow Ni^{2+} (0.001\text{ M}) + 2Ag(s)$

(Given that, $E^\circ_{cell} = 10.5$ V, $\dfrac{2.303\,RT}{F} = 0.059$ at 298 K)

(a) 1.385 V (b) 0.9615 V
(c) 1.05 V (d) 1.0385 V

40. The product formed from the following reaction sequence is

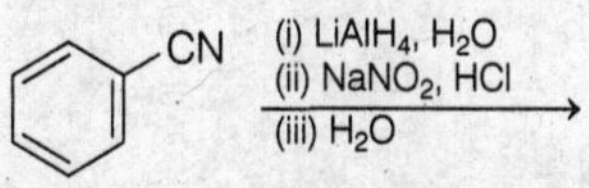

CN (i) $LiAlH_4$, H_2O (ii) $NaNO_2$, HCl (iii) H_2O

(a) 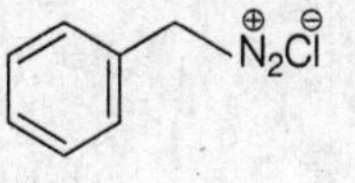 $\overset{\oplus}{N_2}\overset{\ominus}{Cl}$ (b) 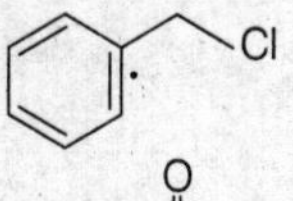 Cl

(c) 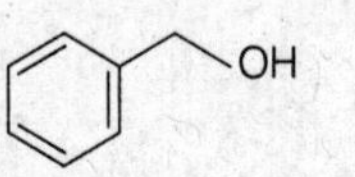 OH (d) 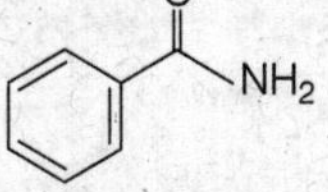 O NH_2

41. Copper crystallises in fcc unit cell with cell edge length of 3.608×10^{-8} cm. The density of copper is 8.92 g cm^{-3}. Calculate the atomic mass of copper.

(a) 31.55 u (b) 60 u
(c) 65 u (d) 63.1 u

42. $3O_2(g) \rightleftharpoons 2O_3(g)$

For the above reaction at 298 K, K_C is found to be 3.0×10^{-59}. If the concentration of O_2 at equilibrium is 0.040 M then concentration of O_3 in M is

(a) 1.9×10^{-63}
(b) 2.4×10^{31}
(c) 1.2×10^{21}
(d) 4.38×10^{-32}

43. Given below are two statements.

Statement I In Lucas test, primary, secondary and tertiary alcohols are distinguished on the basis of their reactivity with conc. HCl + $ZnCl_2$, known as Lucas reagent.

Statement II Primary alcohols are most reactive and immediately produce turbidity at room temperature on reaction with Lucas reagent.

In the light of the above statements, choose the most appropriate answer from the options given below.

(a) Both statement I and statement II are incorrect.
(b) Statement I is correct but statement II is incorrect.
(c) Statement I is incorrect but statement II is correct.
(d) Both statement I and statement II are correct.

44. In the neutral or faintly alkaline medium, $KMnO_4$ oxidises iodide into iodate. The change in oxidation state of manganese in this reaction is from

(a) + 6 to + 4
(b) + 7 to + 3
(c) + 6 to + 5
(d) + 7 to + 4

45. Match List-I with List-II.

List-I (Ores)	**List-II** (Composition)
(A) Haematite	(i) Fe_3O_4
(B) Magnetite	(ii) $ZnCO_3$
(C) Calamine	(iii) Fe_2O_3
(D) Kaolinite	(iv) $[Al_2(OH)_4Si_2O_5]$

Choose the correct answer from the options given below

(a) (A) - (iii), (B) - (i), (C) - (ii), (D) - (iv)
(b) (A) - (iii), (B) - (i), (C) - (iv), (D) - (ii)
(c) (A) - (i), (B) - (iii), (C) - (ii), (D) - (iv)
(d) (A) - (i), (B) - (ii), (C) - (iii). (D) - (iv)

46. The correct IUPAC name of the following compound is

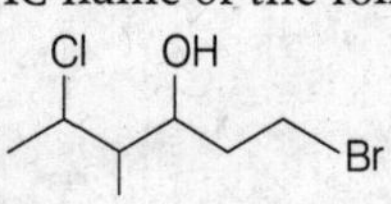

Cl OH Br

(a) 6-bromo-2-chloro-4-methylhexan-4-ol
(b) 1-bromo-4-methyl-5-chlorohexan-3-ol
(c) 6-bromo-4-methyl-2-chlorohexan-4-ol
(d) 1-bromo-5-chloro-4-methyhexan-3-ol

47. If radius of second Bohr orbit of the He^+ ion is 105.8 pm, what is the radius of third Bohr orbit of Li^{2+} ion?

(a) 15.87 pm (b) 1.587 pm
(c) 158.7 Å (d) 158.7 pm

48. Compound X on reaction with O_3 followed by Zn/H_2O gives formaldehyde and 2-methyl propanal as products. The compound X is

(a) 2-methylbut-1-ene
(b) 2-methylbut-2-ene
(c) Pent-2-ene
(d) 3-methylbut-1-ene

49. For a first order reaction $A \rightarrow$ products, initial concentration of A is 0.1 M, which becomes 0.001 M after 5 minutes. Rate constant for the reaction in min^{-1} is

(a) 0.9212 (b) 0.4606
(c) 0.2303 (d) 1.3818

50. The pollution due to oxides of sulphur gets enhanced due to the presence of

(I) particulate matter
(II) ozone
(III) hydrocarbons
(IV) hydrogen peroxide

Choose the most appropriate answer from the options given below

(a) (I),(II),(IV) only
(b) (II), (III), (IV) only
(c) (I), (III), (IV) only
(d) (I), (IV) only

Answers

1.	(b)	2.	(c)	3.	(d)	4.	(c)	5.	(a)	6.	(c)	7.	(a)	8.	(b)	9.	(b)	10.	(a)
11.	(d)	12.	(c)	13.	(d)	14.	(a)	15.	(d)	16.	(c)	17.	(a)	18.	(a)	19.	(b)	20.	(c)
21.	(b)	22.	(b)	23.	(d)	24.	(c)	25.	(a)	26.	(b)	27.	(c)	28.	(a)	19.	(b)	30.	(c)
31.	(d)	32.	(d)	33.	(d)	34.	(c)	35.	(c)	36.	(b)	37.	(c)	38.	(a)	39.	(*)	40.	(c)
41.	(d)	42.	(d)	43.	(b)	44.	(d)	45.	(a)	46.	(d)	47.	(d)	48.	(d)	49.	(a)	50.	(a)

Note *(*) None of the option is correct.*

Answer *with* Explanations

1. (b)

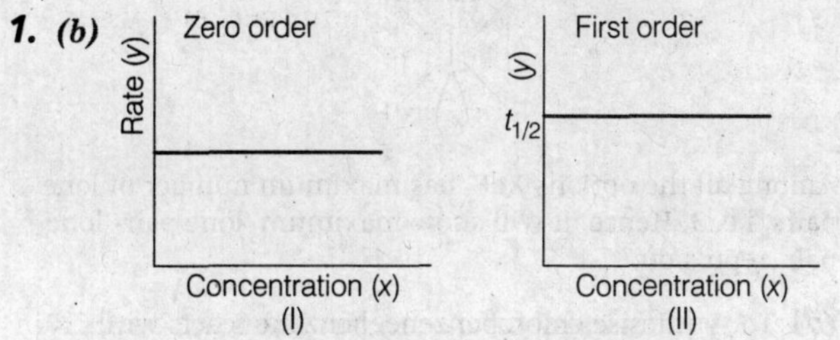

Here, graph I is of zero order if y-axis is representing rate and x represents concentration. For zero order, reaction rate is independent of concentration and remains constant.

While II graph represents first order if y is half-life ($t_{1/2}$) and x is concentration. Here $t_{1/2}$ is independent of concentration.

Hence, option (b) is correct, i.e. zero order (y = rate and x = concentration), first order ($y = t_{1/2}$ and x = concentration).

2. (c)

or CH=CH—CH, CH, CH, CH—CH_2

sp^3 hybridised carbon

The given structure follows the Huckel's rule $(4n + 2)\pi$ electrons as it has 6π electrons. But the given structure is non-planar due to the presence of sp^3 hybridised carbon atom as shown in the structure. Hence, it is non-aromatic compound. While other three options are planar and follow Huckel's rule. Hence they are aromatic.

So, option (c) is correct.

3. (d) The alkyl group of Grignard reagent have partial negative charge while magnesium will have partial positive charge. The alkyl group will attack carbon atom of CO_2 and will form the salts of carboxylic acids, which on hydrolysis will form carboxylic acids.

The reaction takes place is as follows

$$\overset{-\delta}{R}\,Mg\,\overset{\delta+}{X} + O{=}C{=}O \xrightarrow[\text{ether}]{\text{Dry}} R{-}\overset{O}{\overset{\|}{C}}{-}O^-\,Mg^+\,X\ (Y) \xrightarrow{H_3O^{\oplus}} R{-}\underset{O}{\underset{\|}{C}}{-}OH$$

Hence 'Y' in the reaction is $RCOO^-Mg^+X$.

4. (c) The incorrect statement about diborane is option (c) because boron has sp^3-hybridisation and it is non-planar.

H, H, B, H, H, B, H, H; sp^3, sp^3

5. (a) The electronic configuration of Gadolinium is

$$Gd = [Xe]4f^7 5d^1 6s^2.$$
$$Gd^{3+} = [Xe]\,4f^7$$

After removal of 3rd electron, it will attain half-filled electronic configuration. Due to which $4f$ will have high exchange energy. So, Gd has low value of third ionisation energy. Hence, option (a) is correct.

6. (c) According to Dalton's law of partial pressure

Partial pressure of gas = mole fraction of gas in gaseous mixture × total pressure of gaseous mixture.

So,
$$p_1 = x_1 p$$
$$p_2 = x_2 p$$
$$p_3 = x_3 p$$

Then, the total pressure is $p = p_1 + p_2 + p_3$.

Hence, statement (c) is incorrect.

7. (a) Statement I The correct order of boiling points of group 16th hydride is

$$H_2S < H_2Se < H_2Te < H_2O$$

Boiling point; H_2O, H_2Te, H_2Se, H_2S; Hydrides (16th group)

Statement II Boiling point increases with increase in molar mass but H_2O has a higher boiling point due to presence of hydrogen bond.

Hence, both statement I and statement II are incorrect.

So, option (a) is correct.

8. (b) Statement I is correct but statement II is incorrect because, the order of acidic strength is as follows.

p-nitrophenol (OH, NO_2) > o-nitrophenol (OH, NO_2) > m-nitrophenol (OH, NO_2) > phenol (OH)

—NO_2 group at *ortho* and *para*-position withdraws electrons of the O—H bonds towards itself by the stronger $-R$-effect while the NO_2 group at *meta* position withdraws electrons of O—H bond by the weaker $-I$-effect. Thus, *ortho* and *para*-nitrophenol are more acidic than *meta*-nitrophenol. Among *ortho* and *para*-nitrophenols, *o*-nitrophenol is less acidic due to intramolecular hydrogen bonding which makes loss of proton a little more difficult.

Hence option (b) is correct.

9. *(b)* Kjeldahl's method is not applicable to the compounds containing nitrogen as nitro and azo groups and nitrogen present in the ring (Pyridine). It is because nitrogen of these compounds does not change into ammonium sulphate. Hence in option (a), (c) and (d) Kjeldahl's method is not applicable. It is applicable only in compound (b), where —NH_2— group can be converted into ammonium sulphate.

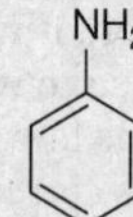

Hence correct option is (b).

10. *(a)* The correct match is

A-(iii), B-(iv), C-(ii), D-(i)

Explanation

- **Cimetidine** is an antacid, used to prevent the interaction of histamine with the receptors present in the stomach wall, due to which less amount of acid is released.
- **Seldane** is an antihistamine. It interferes with the natural action of histamine by competing with histamine for binding sites of receptor where histamine exerts its effect.
- **Morphine** is an analgesic. They are chiefly used for the relief of pain, cardiac pain etc.
- **Salvarsan** is an antimicrobial. It mainly affects the bacteria spirochete which causes syphilis in human being.

11. *(d)* The roots for 1, 1 and 9 are un, un and enn respectively. Hence the symbol and name respectively are uue and ununennium.

12. *(c)* SF_4

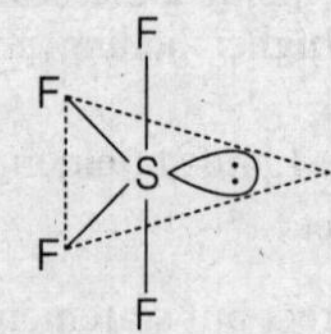

SF_4 contain 1 lone-pair

XeF_2

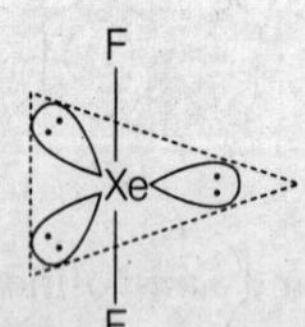

XeF_2 contain 3 lone-pairs

ClF_3

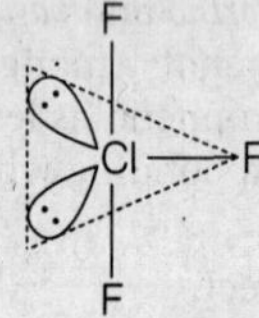

ClF_3 contains 2 lone-pairs

IF_5

Among all the options XeF_2 has maximum number of lone pairs, i.e. 3. Hence, it will show maximum 'lone pair- lone pair' repulsion.

13. *(d)* To synthesise chlorobenzene, benzene reacts with Cl_2 in the presence of $FeCl_3$. The reaction taking place is as follows

$$\text{Benzene} \xrightarrow[\text{Anhydrous } FeCl_3]{+Cl_2} \text{Chlorobenzene} + HCl$$

14. *(a)* In *p*-*V* graph, the area under the curve represents the magnitude of work. The maximum area is covered in graph(a).

Hence, it represents maximum work done.

15. *(d)*

$$MnO_4^- + 8H^+ + 5e^- \xrightarrow{\text{Reduction}} Mn^{2+} + 4H_2O$$

$$E^\circ_{Mn^{2+}/MnO_4^-} = -1.510 \text{ V}$$

$$1/2O_2 + 2H^+ + 2e^- \xrightarrow{\text{Reduction}} 2H_2O$$

$$E^\circ_{O_2/H_2O} = 1.223 \text{ V}$$

Reaction at cathode (reduction)

$$2MnO_4^- + 16H^+ + 10e^- \longrightarrow 2Mn^{2+} + 8H_2O$$

$$E^\circ_{RP} = 1.510 \text{ V}$$

Reaction at anode (oxidation)

$$5H_2O \longrightarrow \frac{5}{2}O_2 + 10H^+ + 10e^-$$

$$E^\circ_{OP} = -1.223 \text{ V}$$

The overall reaction is

$$2MnO_4^- + 6H^+ \longrightarrow 2Mn^{2+} + \frac{5}{2}O_2 + 3H_2O$$

$$E^\circ = E^\circ_{MnO_4^-/Mn^{2+}} - E^\circ_{O_2/H_2O}$$

$$E^\circ = 1.510 - 1.223 = 0.287 \text{ V}$$

Here, since the value of E° is positive, the reaction is spontaneous. Hence, MnO_4^- will liberate O_2.

16. *(c)* The complex $[Ag(H_2O)_2][Ag(CN)_2]$ has coordination number 2 and oxidation state is Ag^+ in both cationic and anionic parts.

Hence, its IUPAC name is diaquasilver (I) dicyanidoargentate (I).

17. ***(a)*** The incorrect statement among the given option is option (a).

The oxidation number of K in KO_2 is + 1 because in this compound oxygen is present as superoxide ion $K^+O_2^-$ (O_2^- superoxide ion).

18. ***(a)*** $CaCO_3(s) + 2\,HCl(aq) \longrightarrow CaCl_2(aq) + CO_2(g) + H_2O(l)$

Number of moles of $CaCO_3$ (pure) $= 1/2 \times$ number of moles of HCl

[Moles = Molarity × Volume (in L)]

$$= \frac{1}{2} \times 0.5 \times \frac{50}{1000} = 0.0125$$

Weight of $CaCO_3$ (pure) = Mole × Molecular weight

$$= 0.0125 \times 100 = 1.25\text{ g}$$

$$\%\text{ Purity} = \frac{\text{Weight of pure substance}}{\text{Weight of impure sample}} \times 100$$

$$95 = \frac{1.25}{\text{Weight of impure sample}} \times 100$$

$$\text{Weight of impure sample} = \frac{1.25 \times 100}{95} = 1.32\text{ g.}$$

Hence, weight of impure sample is 1.32 g.

19. ***(b)*** $R—NH_2 \xrightarrow{HNO_2} R—\overset{\oplus}{N_2}$

1° aliphatic amines → Alkyl diazonium ion (unstable)

NH_2 (benzene ring) $\xrightarrow{HNO_2}$ $\overset{\oplus}{N}≡N$ (benzene ring)

1° aromatic amines → Aryl diazonium ion (Stable at low temperature, i.e. 0-5°C)

Hence, statement I is correct but statement II is incorrect. So, option (b) is correct.

20. ***(c)*** The incorrect statement regarding polymers is option (c). It is because thermosetting polymers are not reusable due to presence of cross linking in them. This cross-linking makes the thermosetting polymer more resistant to high temperature and prevent remelting while all other options are correct.

21. ***(b)*** The incorrect statement regarding chirality is option (b). It is because enantiomers are non-superimposable mirror images of each other.

22. ***(b)*** **Statement I** According to Hardy Schulze rule for negative sol coagulation, greater the charge on cation, greater is its flocculation power. Hence, this statement is correct.

Statement II For positive sol coagulation, the greater the charge on anion, greater is its flocculating power.
Hence the correct order is

$$NaCl < Na_2SO_4 < Na_3PO_4.$$

So, statement II is incorrect.
Hence option (b) is correct.

23. ***(d)*** The correct answer from the given options is A-(iv), B-(i), C-(ii), D-(iii)

Hydride	Nature
MgH_2	Ionic
GeH_4	Electron precise
B_2H_6	Electron deficient
HF	Electron rich

- Electron deficient hydride contains less than 8 electrons.
- Electron precise hydride contains 8 electrons without lone pair.
- Electron rich hydride contains 8 electrons along with lone pair(s).

24. ***(c)*** The correct match from the given options is option (c), i.e. A-(ii), B-(iii), C-(i), D-(iv)

Li — Electrochemical cell
Na — Coolant in fast breeder reactors
KOH — Absorbent for CO_2
Cs — Photoelectric cell

- Lithium is used in electrochemical cells. These cells generate electrical energy from chemical reactions.
- Coolants are used to fill the engine's cooling system, to act as a heat exchange fluid. Sodium is one of its constituent.
- KOH is a strong base and CO_2 is slightly acidic. It absorbs CO_2 readily at room temperature.
- Caesium is used in photoelectric cells.

25. ***(a)*** **Assertion (A)** is correct because in point defects of ionic solids, electrical neutrality is an essential condition.

Reason (R) is also correct because cation dislocates from lattice site to interstitial position in Frenkel defect.

Hence, both (A) and (R) are correct but (R) is not the correct explanation of (A).

26. ***(b)*** The incorrect statement about enzymes is option (b) because enzymes are protein in nature and comprised of amino acids that are linked together in one or more polypeptide chains. Rest all other given options are correct.

27. ***(c)*** The correct match is option (c), i.e.
(A)-(iv), (B)-(iii), (C)-(ii), (D)-(i)

Products formed	Reaction of carbonyl compound with
Cyanohydrin	HCN
Acetal	Alcohol
Schiff's base	RNH_2
Oxime	NH_2OH

The reactions involved are as follows

$$>C=O + HCN \xrightarrow{OH^-} >C<^{OH}_{CN} \quad \text{Cyanohydrin}$$

$$^{R}_{H}>C=O + 2ROH\ (\text{Alcohol}) \xrightarrow{OH^-} ^{R}_{H}>C<^{OR}_{OR} \quad \text{Acetal}$$

$$>C=O + R\text{—}NH_2 \xrightarrow{H^+} ^{R}_{H}>C=N\text{—}R \quad \text{Schiff's base}$$

$$>C=O + NH_2OH \xrightarrow{H^+} ^{R}_{H}>C=N\diagdown OH \quad \text{Oxime}$$

28. *(a)* We know that,

$$\text{Molality} = \frac{\text{number of moles of solute}}{\text{weight of the solvent (g)}} \times 1000$$

Given that molality = 1

Moles of solute = 0·5

$$1 = \frac{0.5}{\text{Weight of the solvent (g)}} \times 1000$$

Weight of the solvent (g) = 500 g of solvent.

Hence, option (a) is correct.

29. *(b)* The correct statement is option (b). It is because in diamond, each carbon is bonded with four other carbon atoms. So, hybridisation of carbon atom is sp^3. In graphite each carbon atom is bonded with three other carbon atoms. So, hybridisation of carbon atom in graphite is sp^2.

Hence diamond is sp^3-hybridised and graphite is sp^2-hybridised. Rest all other options are incorrect. It is because only graphite is used as dry lubricants. Diamond has 3-D network structure. Both diamond and graphite are covalent.

30. *(c)* Among the given options, the incorrect statement is option (c).

$$O_2^+ = \sigma 1s^2 \sigma^* 1s^2 \sigma 2s^2 \sigma^* 2s^2 \sigma 2p_z^2\ \pi 2p_x^2 \pi 2p_y^2 \pi^* 2p^1$$

O_2^+ ions have 15 electrons, so it contains one unpaired electron. Hence, it is paramagnetic in nature.

31. *(d)* In interhalogen compound of group 17th, ICl is more reactive than I_2 due to polar bonds. Also, X—X' bond is weaker than X—X bond except F_2. So I— Cl bond is weaker than I—I bond.

Hence, both A and R are correct and R is the correct explanation of A.

32. *(d)* Boiling point of comparable molecular mass molecules is as follows

R—OH > aldehyde-ketone > alkane.

The order followed above is due to presence of hydrogen bonding (strong molecular association) in alcohol. In aldehyde-ketone, dipole-dipole interactions are present (weak molecular association) while in alkane it is non-polar hence, have lowest boiling point among all three.

Hence, both statement I and statement II are correct. So, the correct option is (d).

33. *(d)* Given that, pK_a of CH_3COOH = 4.57

Concentration of acetic acid (CH_3COOH) = 0.01 M

Concentration of sodium acetate (CH_3COONa) = 0.10 M

Weak acid (CH_3COOH) and salt of weak acid (i.e. strong base, CH_3COONa) forms an acidic buffer.

pH of acidic buffer solution is given by

$$\text{pH} = \text{p}K_a + \log\frac{[\text{Salt}]}{[\text{Acid}]}$$

$$= 4.57 + \log\left(\frac{0.1}{0.01}\right)$$

$$= 4.57 + 1 = 5.57.$$

Hence, the given solution has a pH 5.57.

34. *(c)* The incorrect statement is option (c) because the shape of first four orbitals, i.e. d_{xy}, d_{yz}, d_{zx} and $d_{x^2-y^2}$ are similar to each other, that is, double dumb bell shape, whereas the fifth one, i.e. dz^2 is different from other.

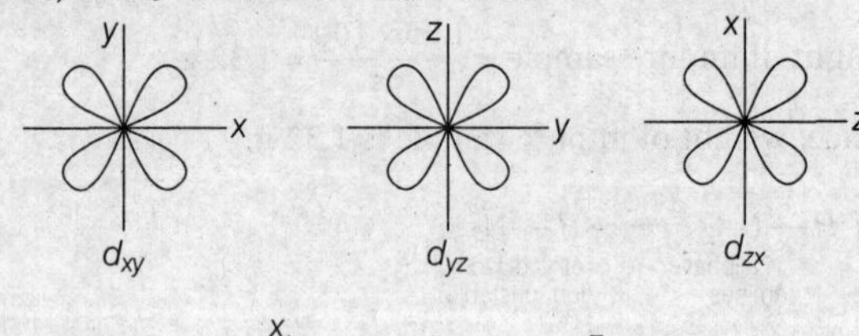

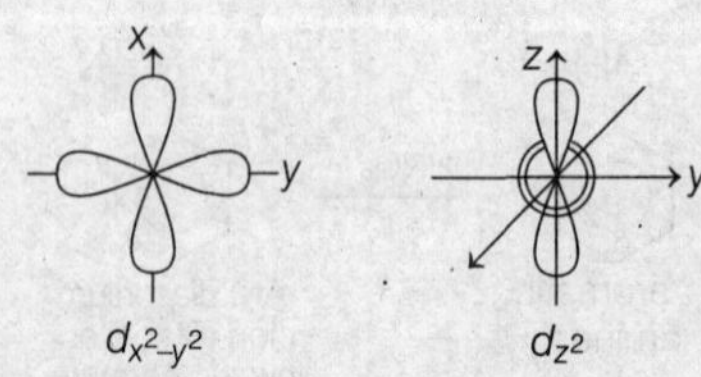

35. *(c)* Standard reduction potential values is given to us which can be arranged as follows

$$E^\circ_{Zn^{2+}/Zn} < E^\circ_{Fe^{2+}/Fe} < E^\circ_{Cu^{2+}/Cu} < E^\circ_{Ag^+/Ag}.$$

So, the reactivity order will be Zn > Fe > Cu > Ag.

The reactions given in the options are displacement reaction. In case of displacement reaction, more reactive metals (i.e., low SRP) can displace less reactive metals (higher SRP) from their salt solution.

So, $CuSO_4(aq) + 2Ag(s) \longrightarrow Cu(s) + Ag_2SO_4(aq)$ is not possible. As Ag is less reactive as compared to Cu.

Hence, the correct option is (c).

36. *(b)* en is a strong field ligand. As the number of en (strong field ligand) increases, splitting also increases. So, Δ_o increases. Hence, $[Ni(en)_3]^{2+}$ will have highest energy due to presence of 3 en ligands followed by $[Ni(H_2O)_2(en)_2]^{2+}$ and $[Ni(H_2O)_4en]^{2+}$. So, the correct order is (C) > (A) > (B).

37. *(c)* Given

$V = 10$ L

$W_{O_2} = 64$ g

$T = 27°C = 27 + 273 = 300$ K

$R = 0.0831 \text{ L bar K}^{-1} \text{ mol}^{-1}$

$n_{O_2} = 2$

Using, ideal gas equation

$$pV = nRT$$

$$\Rightarrow \quad p = \frac{nRT}{V}$$

Substituting the values

$$p = \frac{2 \times 0.0831 \times 300}{10}$$

$$p = 4.986 \approx 4.9 \text{ bar}$$

Hence option (c) is correct.

38. ***(a)*** When acetone reacts with 2-pentanone in presence of dilute NaOH followed by heating then the products will be formed according to aldol condensation.

Self aldol

$$CH_3-\overset{O}{\overset{\|}{C}}-CH_3 + CH_3-\overset{O}{\overset{\|}{C}}-CH_3 \xrightarrow[\Delta]{NaOH} CH_3-\underset{CH_3}{\underset{|}{C}}=CH-\overset{O}{\overset{\|}{C}}-CH_3$$

Cross aldol

$$CH_3-\overset{O}{\overset{\|}{C}}-CH_3 + CH_3CH_2CH_2COCH_3 \xrightarrow[\Delta]{NaOH} CH_3-\underset{CH_3}{\underset{|}{C}}=C(CH_2CH_3)-\overset{O}{\overset{\|}{C}}-CH_3$$

$$CH_3-\overset{O}{\overset{\|}{C}}-CH_3 + CH_3CH_2CH_2COCH_3 \xrightarrow[\Delta]{NaOH} CH_3CH_2CH_2C(CH_3)=CH-\overset{O}{\overset{\|}{C}}-CH_3$$

$CH_3CH_2C(=O)C(CH_3)=C(CH_2CH_3)CH_2CH_3$ will not form.

Hence, (a) is the correct option.

39. ***(*)*** Given,

$E^\circ_{cell} = 10.5 \text{ V}$

$$\frac{2.303\,RT}{F} = 0.059$$

$[Ni^{2+}] = 0.001 \text{ M} = 10^{-3} \text{ M}$

$[Ag^+] = 0.001 \text{ M} = 10^{-3} \text{M}$

Using Nernst equation

$$E_{cell} = E^\circ_{cell} - \frac{0.059}{n} \log \frac{[Ni^{+2}]^1}{[Ag^+]^2}$$

$$= 10.5 - \frac{0.059}{2} \log \frac{(10^{-3})}{(10^{-3})^2}$$

$$= 10.5 - \frac{0.059}{2} \log 10^3$$

$$= 10.5 - \frac{0.059}{2} \times 3 = 10.5 - 0.0885$$

$$E_{cell} = 10.4115 \text{ V}$$

40. ***(c)***

$$C_6H_5CN \xrightarrow{LiAlH_4,\ H_2O} C_6H_5CH_2-NH_2$$

Cyanobenzene → Benzyl amine

$$C_6H_5CH_2-NH_2 \xrightarrow{NaNO_2,\ +HCl} C_6H_5CH_2-\overset{\oplus}{N_2}\overset{\ominus}{Cl}$$

Benzyl amine → Diazonium salt (unstable)

$$C_6H_5CH_2-\overset{\oplus}{N_2}\overset{\ominus}{Cl} \xrightarrow{H_2O} C_6H_5CH_2-OH + N_2\uparrow + HCl$$

Diazonium salt (unstable) → Benzyl alcohol

In this reaction cyanobenzene reacts with strong reducing agent, i.e. $LiAlH_4$ to yield benzyl amine which on further reaction with $NaNO_2$ + HCl will give diazonium salt. This salt on reaction with H_2O will yield benzyl alcohol. Hence, the correct option is (c).

41. ***(d)*** Given

$a = 3.608 \times 10^{-8} \text{ cm}$

$d = 8.92 \text{ g / cm}^3$

fcc unit cell,

Hence, $Z = 4$

Atomic mass = ?

Using the formula of density,

$$d = \frac{Z \times M}{N_A \times a^3}$$

where, d = density

M = atomic mass

a = edge length

N_A = Avogadro's number

Z = number of atoms in unit cell

Now, substituting the values in the above formula,

$$8.92 = \frac{4 \times M}{6.022 \times 10^{23} \times (3.608 \times 10^{-8})^3}$$

$$M = 63.1 \text{ g / mol(Molar atomic mass)}$$

Or Atomic mass (M) = 63.1 u.

Hence, option (d) is correct.

42. ***(d)*** Given, $K_C = 3 \times 10^{-59}$

$[O_2] = 0.040 \text{ M}$

$3O_2(g) \rightleftharpoons 2O_3(g)$

$$K_C = \frac{[O_3]^2}{[O_2]^3}$$

Substituting the values,

$$3 \times 10^{-59} = \frac{[O_3]^2}{(4 \times 10^{-2})^3}$$

$$[O_3]^2 = 3 \times 10^{-59} \times (4 \times 10^{-2})^3$$

$$[O_3]^2 = 19.2 \times 10^{-64}$$

$$[O_3] = 4.38 \times 10^{-32} \text{ M}$$

Hence, the correct option is (d).

43. ***(b)*** 1°, 2°, 3° alcohols can be distinguished by using Lucas reagents (conc. HCl + anhy. $ZnCl_2$) on the basis of the time taken for turbidity to appear, i.e. $R—CH_2—OH \xrightarrow{\text{Lucas reagent}} R—CH_2—Cl$

1° alcohol (Turbidity in 30 min)

$\underset{R}{\overset{R}{>}}CH—OH \xrightarrow[\text{reagent}]{\text{Lucas}} \underset{R}{\overset{R}{>}}CH—Cl$

2° alcohol (Turbidity in 5 min)

$R_3C—OH \xrightarrow[\text{reagent}]{\text{Lucas}} R_3C—Cl$

(Turbidity appears immediately)

Hence the order of reactivity of alcohol towards Lucas reagent is in the order 3° > 2° > 1°.

So, statement I is correct but statement II is incorrect. Option (b) is correct.

44. *(d)* The reaction that takes place in the given condition is as follows

$$\underset{+7}{KMnO_4} + I^- \xrightarrow[\text{Weak alkaline medium}]{\text{Neutral}} \underset{+4}{MnO_2} + IO_3^-$$

So, the change in oxidation state of manganese in this reaction is from + 7 to + 4.

Hence, option (d) is correct option.

45. *(a)* The correct match is

A-(iii), B-(i), C-(ii), D-(iv)

- Haematite is an ore of iron. its composition is Fe_2O_3.
- Magnetite also, is an ore of Iron. Its composition is Fe_3O_4.
- Calamine is an ore of zinc. Its composition is $ZnCO_3$.
- Kaolinite is a clay mineral with chemical formula $[Al_2(OH)_4Si_2O_5]$.

46. *(d)*

Cl OH, 6 5 4 3 2 1, Br

The IUPAC name of the given compound is 1-bromo-5-chloro-4 methylhexan-3-ol.

47. *(d)* According to Bohr's atomic model

$$r \propto \frac{n^2}{Z}$$

For 2nd orbit of He^+ $n_2 = 2$

$$z_2 = 2$$

for 3rd orbit of Li^{2+} $n_1 = 3$

$$z_1 = 3$$

From the above equation

$$\frac{(r_3)_{Li^{2+}}}{(r_2)_{He^+}} = \frac{n_1^2 \times z_2}{n_2^2 \times z_1}$$

$$\frac{(r_3)_{Li^{2+}}}{105 \cdot 8 \text{ pm}} = \frac{3 \times 3 \times 2/3}{2 \times 2}$$

$$(r_3)_{Li^{2+}} = \frac{3 \times 3 \times 2 \times 105 \cdot 8}{4 \times 3}$$

$$(r_3)_{Li^{2+}} = 158.7 \text{ pm.}$$

Hence, the radius of third Bohr orbit of Li^{2+} ion is 158.7 pm.

48. *(d)* The compound '*X*' that reacts with O_3 followed by reaction with Zn/H_2O gives formaldehyde and 2-methyl propanal as products is 3-methyl but-l-ene. The ozonolysis reaction that involved in this is as follows

$$CH_3—\underset{CH_3}{\underset{|}{CH}}—CH{=}CH_2 \xrightarrow[\text{(ii) } Zn+H_2O]{\text{(i) } O_3} \underset{\text{2-methyl propanal}}{(CH_3)_2CH—CH{=}O} + \underset{\text{Formaldehyde}}{H—CHO}$$

49. *(a)* Given,

Initial concentration $[A_0] = 0.1$ M

Conc, after 5 min $[A_t] = 0.001$ M

$t = 5$ minutes

Using rate constant formula for 1st order reaction

$$K = \frac{2.303}{t} \log\left(\frac{A_0}{A_t}\right)$$

$$= \frac{2.303}{5} \log\left(\frac{0.1}{0.001}\right)$$

$$K = \frac{2.303 \times 2}{5} = 0.9212 \text{ min}^{-1}$$

Hence, the rate constant for the reaction is $K = 0.9212 \text{ min}^{-1}$.

50. *(a)* The pollution due to oxides of sulphur gets enhanced due to the presence of particulate matter, ozone and hydrogen peroxide.

The particulate matter present in polluted air catalyses the oxidation of sulphur dioxide to sulphur trioxide

$$2SO_2(g) + O_2(g) \longrightarrow 2SO_3(g)$$

Similarly, the reaction is also promoted by ozone and hydrogen peroxide.

$$SO_2(g) + O_3(g) \longrightarrow SO_3(g) + O_2(g)$$

$$SO_2(g) + H_2O_2(l) \longrightarrow H_2SO_4(aq)$$

Hence, option (a) is correct.

NEET

SOLVED PAPER

2023

NEET SOLVED PAPER 2023

Instruction

- This question paper contains 50 Multiple Choice Questions of Chemistry, divided into two Sections; section A and section B.
- Section A contains 35 questions and all questions are compulsory.
- Section B contains 15 questions out of which 10 questions are to be attempted.
- Each question carries 4 marks.

CHEMISTRY

Section-A

1. The relation between n_m, (n_m = the number of permissible values of magnetic quantum number (m)) for a given value of azimuthal quantum number (l), is

(a) $l = 2n_m + 1$ (b) $n_m = 2l^2 + l$

(c) $n_m = l + 2$ (d) $l = \frac{n_m - 1}{2}$

2. Amongst the given options which of the following molecules/ions acts as a Lewis acid?

(a) H_2O (b) BF_3

(c) OH^- (d) NH_3

3. Which of the following statements are not correct?

A. Hydrogen is used to reduce heavy metal oxides to metals.

B. Heavy water is used to study reaction mechanism.

C. Hydrogen is used to make saturated fats from oils.

D. The H—H bond dissociation enthalpy is lowest as compared to a single bond between two atoms of any element.

E. Hydrogen reduces oxides of metals that are more active than iron.

Choose the **most appropriate** answer from the options given below:

(a) B, D only (b) D, E only

(c) A, B, C only (d) B, C, D, E only

4. Which one of the following statements is correct?

(a) All enzymes that utilise ATP in phosphate transfer require Ca as the cofactor.

(b) The bone in human body is an inert and unchanging substance.

(c) Mg plays roles in neuromuscular function and interneuronal transmission.

(d) The daily requirement of Mg and Ca in the human body is estimated to be 0.2-0.3 g.

5. Homoleptic complex from the following complexes is

(a) diamminechloridonitrito-N-platinum (II)

(b) pentaamminecarbonatocobalt (III) chloride

(c) triamminetriaquachromium (III) chloride

(d) potassium trioxalatoaluminate (III)

6. Identify product (A) in the following reaction.

$\xrightarrow[\text{Conc.HCl}]{\text{Zn-Hg}}$ (A) + $2H_2O$

(a)

(b)

(c)

(d)

7. Identify the product in the following reaction.

$\xrightarrow[\text{(iii) } H_2O]{\text{(i) } Cu_2Br_2/HBr \text{ (ii) Mg/dry ether}}$ Product

(a) (b)

(c) 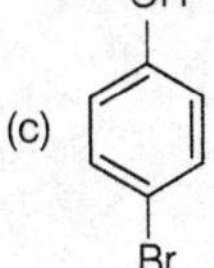

(d)

8. The correct order of energies of molecular orbitals of N_2 molecule, is

(a) $\sigma 1s < \sigma^* 1s < \sigma 2s < \sigma^* 2s < \sigma 2p_z < (\pi 2p_x = \pi 2p_y) < (\pi^* 2p_x = \pi^* 2p_y) < \sigma^* 2p_z$

(b) $\sigma 1s < \sigma^* 1s < \sigma 2s < \sigma^* 2s < \sigma 2p_z < \sigma^* 2p_z < (\pi 2p_x = \pi 2p_y) < (\pi^* 2p_x = \pi^* 2p_y)$

(c) $\sigma 1s < \sigma^* 1s < \sigma 2s < \sigma^* 2s < (\pi 2p_x = \pi 2p_y) < (\pi^* 2p_x = \pi^* 2p_y) < \sigma 2p_z < \sigma^* 2p_z$

(d) $\sigma 1s < \sigma^* 1s < \sigma 2s < \sigma^* 2s < (\pi 2p_x = \pi 2p_y) < \sigma 2p_z < (\pi^* 2p_x = \pi^* 2p_y) < \sigma^* 2p_z$

9. For a certain reaction, the rate $= k[A]^2[B]$, when the initial concentration of A is tripled keeping concentration of B constant, the initial rate would

(a) increase by a factor of six.
(b) increase by a factor of nine.
(c) increase by a factor of three.
(d) decrease by a factor of nine.

10. Given below are two statements: one is labelled as Assertion (A) and the other is labelled as Reason (R).

Assertion (A) In equation $\Delta_r G = -nFE_{cell}$, the value of $\Delta_r G$ depends on n.

Reason (R) E_{cell} is an intensive property and $\Delta_r G$ is an extensive property.

In the light of the above statements, choose the correct answer from the options given below:

(a) Both A and R are true and R is not the correct explanation of A.
(b) A is true but R is false.
(c) A is false but R is true.
(d) Both A and R are true and R is the correct explanation of A.

11. The given compound

C_6H_5—CH = CH = CH—CH_2CH_3 (X attached to the third carbon)

is an example of

(a) aryl halide
(b) allylic halide
(c) vinylic halide
(d) benylic halide

12. Which amongst the following molecules on polymerisation produces neoprene?

(a) $H_2C = C(Cl) - CH = CH_2$
(b) $H_2C = CH - C \equiv CH$
(c) $H_2C = C(CH_3) - CH = CH_2$
(d) $H_2C = CH - CH = CH_2$

13. Consider the following reaction and identify the product (*P*).

$CH_3-CH(CH_3)-CH(OH)-CH_3 \xrightarrow{HBr}$ Product (*P*)

3-methylbutan-2-ol

(a) $CH_3CH = CH - CH_3$
(b) $CH_3 - CH(CH_3) - CH(Br) - CH_3$
(c) $CH_3 - C(CH_3)_2 - CH_2Br$
(d) $CH_3 - C(Br)(CH_3) - CH_2 - CH_3$

14. The conductivity of centimolar solution of KCl at 25°C is 0.0210 ohm^{-1}cm^{-1} and the resistance of the cell containing the solution at 25°C is 60 ohm. The value of cell constant is

(a) 3.28 cm^{-1} (b) 1.26 cm^{-1}
(c) 3.34 cm^{-1} (d) 1.34 cm^{-1}

15. Match List-I with List-II.

	List-I		List-II
A.	Coke	I.	Carbon atoms are sp^3-hybridised.
B.	Diamond	II.	Used as a dry lubricant.
C.	Fullerene	III.	Used as a reducing agent.
D.	Graphite	IV.	Cage like molecules.

Choose the correct answer from the options given below:

(a) A-IV, B-I, C-II, D-III (b) A-III, B-I, C-IV, D-II
(c) A-III, B-IV, C-I, D-II (d) A-II, B-IV, C-I, D-III

16. The element expected to form largest ion to achieve the nearest noble gas configuration is

(a) F (b) N
(c) Na (d) O

17. Which of the following reactions will not give primary amine as the product?

(a) $CH_3CN \xrightarrow[\text{(ii) } H_3O^+]{\text{(i) } LiAlH_4}$ Product

(b) $CH_3NC \xrightarrow[\text{(ii) } H_3O^+]{\text{(i) } LiAlH_4}$ Product

(c) $CH_3CONH_2 \xrightarrow[\text{(ii) } H_3O^+]{\text{(i) } LiAlH_4}$ Product

(d) $CH_3CONH_2 \xrightarrow{Br_2/KOH}$ Product

18. The number of σ bonds, π bonds and lone pair of electrons in pyridine, respectively are

(a) 12, 3, 0 (b) 11, 3, 1
(c) 12, 2, 1 (d) 11, 2, 0

19. Given below are two statements.

Statement I A unit formed by the attachment of a base to 1′-position of sugar is known as nucleoside.

Statement II When nucleoside is linked to phosphoric acid at 5′-position of sugar moiety, we get nucleotide.

In the light of the above statements, choose the correct answer from the options given below:

(a) Both Statement I and Statement II are false.
(b) Statement I is true but Statement II is false.
(c) Statement I is false but Statement II is true.
(d) Both Statement I and Statement II are true.

20. Complete the following reaction:

[A] (cyclohexanone, =O) $\xrightarrow{HCN}$ [B] (cyclohexane with OH and CN) $\xrightarrow[\Delta]{conc. H_2SO_4}$ [C]

is____

(a) cyclohexane–COOH (b) cyclohexene–CHO
(c) cyclohexene–COOH (d) cyclohexane–OH

21. Taking stability as the factor, which one of the following represents correct relationship?

(a) $InI_3 > InI$ (b) $AlCl > AlCl_3$
(c) $TlI > TlI_3$ (d) $TlCl_3 > TlCl$

22. Some tranquilisers are listed below. Which one from the following belongs to barbiturates?

(a) Meprobamate
(b) Valium
(c) Veronal
(d) Chlordiazepoxide

23. Given below are two statements: one is labelled as Assertion (A) and the other is labelled as Reason (R).

Assertion (A) Helium is used to dilute oxygen in diving apparatus.

Reason (R) Helium has high solubility in O_2.

In the light of the above statements, choose the correct answer from the options given below:

(a) Both A and R are true and R is not the correct explanation of A.
(b) A is true but R is false.
(c) A is false but R is true.
(d) Both A and R are true and R is the correct explanation of A.

24. The right option for the mass of CO_2 produced by heating 20 g of 20% pure limestone is (Atomic mass of Ca = 40)

$$[CaCO_3 \xrightarrow{1200\text{ K}} CaO + CO_2]$$

(a) 1.76 g (b) 2.64 g (c) 1.32 g (d) 1.12 g

25. In Lassaigne's extract of an organic compound, both nitrogen and sulphur are present, which gives blood red colour with Fe^{3+} due to formation of

(a) NaSCN (b) $[Fe(CN)_5NOS]^{4-}$
(c) $[Fe(SCN)]^{2+}$ (d) $Fe_4[Fe(CN)_6]_3 \cdot xH_2O$

26. Given below are two statements: one is labelled as Assertion (A) and the other is labelled as Reason (R).

Assertion (A) A reaction can have zero activation energy.

Reason (R) The minimum extra amount of energy absorbed by reactant molecules so that their energy becomes equal to threshold value, is called activation energy.

In the light of the above statements, choose the correct answer from the options given below:

(a) Both A and R are true and R is not the correct explanation of A.
(b) A is true but R is false.
(c) A is false but R is true.
(d) Both A and R are true and R is the correct explanation of A.

27. A compound is formed by two elements *A* and *B*. The element *B* forms cubic close packed structure and atoms of *A* occupy 1/3 of tetrahedral voids. If the formula of the compound is A_xB_y, then the value of $x + y$ is in option

(a) 4 (b) 3
(c) 2 (d) 5

28. The stability of Cu^{2+} is more than Cu^{+} salts in aqueous solution due to

(a) enthalpy of atomisation
(b) hydration energy
(c) second ionisation enthalpy
(d) first ionisation enthalpy

29. Select the correct statements from the following:

A. Atoms of all elements are composed of two fundamental particles.
B. The mass of the electrons is 9.10939×10^{-31} kg.
C. All the isotopes of a given element show same chemical properties.
D. Protons and electrons are collectively known as nucleons.
E. Dalton's atomic theory, regarded the atom as an ultimate particle of matter.

Choose the correct answer from the options given below:
(a) C, D and E only
(b) A and E only
(c) B, C and E only
(d) A, B and C only

30. Which amongst the following options is correct graphical representation of Boyle's Law?

(a)
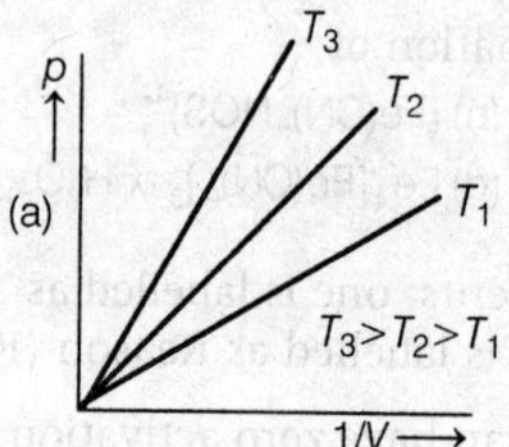

(b)
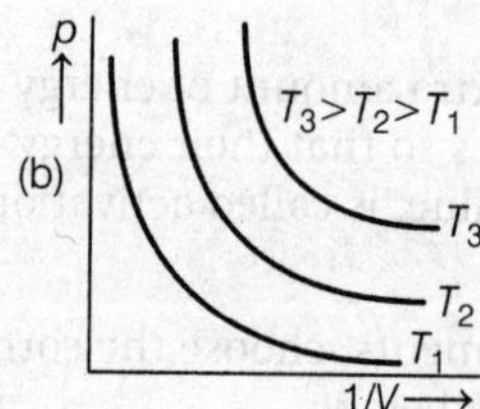

(c)
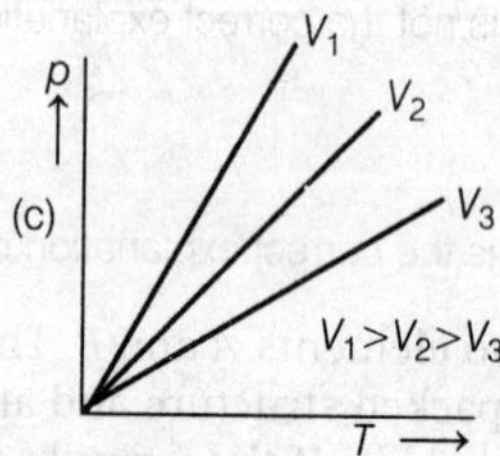

(d)
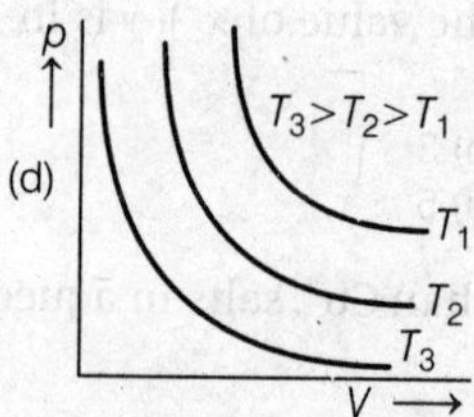

31. Intermolecular forces are forces of attraction and repulsion between interacting particles that will include;

A. dipole-dipole forces
B. dipole-induced dipole forces
C. hydrogen bonding
D. covalent bonding
E. dispersion forces

Choose the most appropriate answer from the options given below
(a) A, B, C , D are correct.
(b) A, B, C , E are correct.
(c) A, C, D, E are correct.
(d) B, C, D, E are correct.

32. Weight (g) of two moles of the organic compound, which is obtained by heating sodium ethanoate with sodium hydroxide in presence of calcium oxide is
(a) 32
(b) 30
(c) 18
(d) 16

33. Which one is an example of heterogeneous catalysis?
(a) Hydrolysis of sugar catalysed by H^+ ions.
(b) Decomposition of ozone in presence of nitrogen monoxide.
(c) Combination between dinitrogen and dihydrogen to form ammonia in the presence of finely divided iron.
(d) Oxidation of sulphur dioxide into sulphur trioxide in the presence of oxides of nitrogen.

34. Given below are two statements: one is labelled as Assertion (A) and the other is labelled as Reason (R).

Assertion (A) Metallic sodium dissolves in liquid ammonia giving a deep blue solution, which is paramagnetic.

Reason (R) The deep blue solution is due to the formation of amide.

In the light of the above statements, choose the correct answer from the options given below:
(a) Both A and R are true and R is not the correct explanation of A.
(b) A is true but R is false.
(c) A is false but R is true.
(d) Both A and R are true and R is the correct explanation of A.

35. Amongst the following, the total number of species not having eight electrons around central atom in its outer most shell, is

NH_3, $AlCl_3$, $BeCl_2$, CCl_4, PCl_5
(a) 2
(b) 4
(c) 1
(d) 3

Section-B

36. Identify the major product obtained in the following reaction

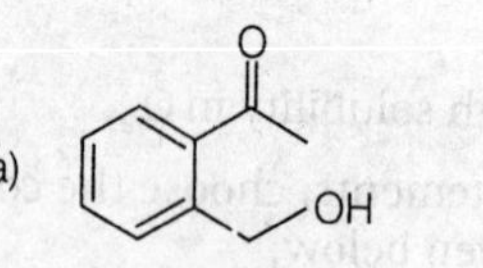

(a)
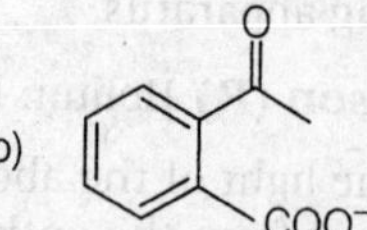

(b)

(c)
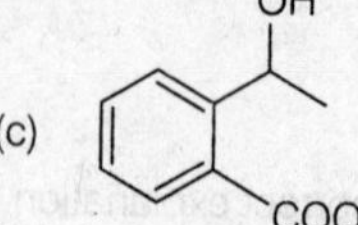

(d)
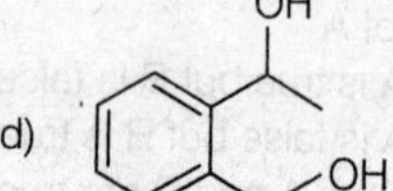

37. Match List-I with List-II.

List-I (Oxoacids of sulphur)		List-II (Bonds)	
A.	Peroxodisulphuric acid	I.	Two S—OH, four S=O, one S—O—S
B.	Sulphuric acid	II.	Two S—OH, one S=O
C.	Pyrosulphuric acid	III.	Two S—OH, Four S=O, one S—O—O—S
D.	Sulphurous acid	IV.	Two S—OH, two S=O

Choose the correct answer from the options given below.

(a) A-III, B-IV, C-I, D-II
(b) A-I, B-III, C-IV, D-II
(c) A-III, B-IV, C-II, D-I
(d) A-I, B-III, C-Ii, D-IV

38. Consider the following compounds/species.

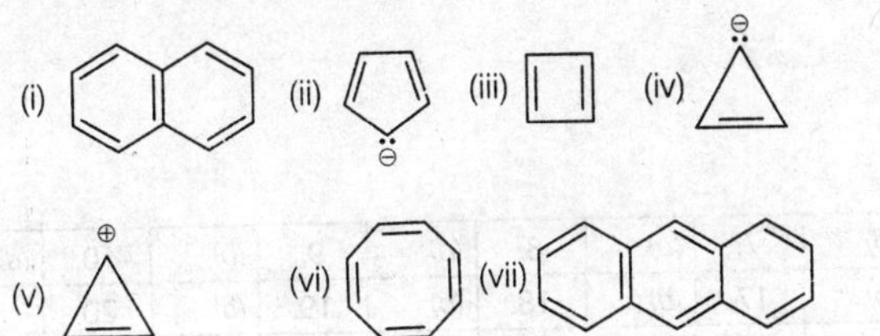

The number of compounds/species which obey Huckel's rule is ______.

(a) 6 (b) 2
(c) 5 (d) 4

39. Pumice stone is an example of

(a) gel (b) solid sol
(c) foam (d) sol

40. Which amongst the following options is the correct relation between change in enthalpy and change in internal energy?

(a) $\Delta H = \Delta U + \Delta n_g RT$
(b) $\Delta H - \Delta U = -\Delta nRT$
(c) $\Delta H + \Delta U = \Delta nR$
(d) $\Delta H = \Delta U - \Delta n_g RT$

41. Which amongst the following will be most readily dehydrated under acidic conditions?

(a) H_3C (OH, OH, H)
(b) (NO_2, H, OH, OH)
(c) (NO_2, OH)
(d) (NO_2, HO, H, CH_3)

42. Consider the following reaction.

C_6H_5—CH_2—O—C_6H_5 $\xrightarrow[\Delta]{HI}$ A + B

Identify products A and B.

(a) A = C_6H_5—CH_2OH and B = C_6H_5—I
(b) A = C_6H_5—CH_2I and B = C_6H_5—OH
(c) A = C_6H_5—CH_2I and B = C_6H_5—I
(d) A = C_6H_5—CH_3 and B = C_6H_5—OH

43. On balancing the given redox reaction,

$$aCr_2O_7^{2-} + bSO_3^{2-}(aq) + cH^+(aq) \longrightarrow$$
$$2aCr^{3+}(aq) + bSO_4^{2-}(aq) + \frac{c}{2}H_2O(l)$$

the coefficients a, b and c are found to be, respectively

(a) 3, 8, 1 (b) 1, 8, 3 (c) 8, 1, 3 (d) 1, 3, 8

44. Which complex compound is most stable?

(a) $[Co(NH_3)_3(NO_3)_3]$ (b) $[CoCl_2(en)_2]NO_3$
(c) $[Co(NH_3)_6]_2(SO_4)_3$ (d) $[Co(NH_3)_4(H_2O)Br](NO_3)_2$

45. What fraction of one edge centred octahedral void lies in one unit cell of *fcc*?

(a) 1/3 (b) 1/4
(c) 1/12 (d) 1/2

46. Which of the following statements are incorrect?

A. All the transition metals except scandium form *MO* oxides which are ionic.
B. The highest oxidation number corresponding to the group number in transition metal oxides is attained in Sc_2O_3 to Mn_2O_7.
C. Basic character increases from V_2O_3 to V_2O_4 to V_2O_5.
D. V_2O_4 dissolves in acids to give VO_4^{3-} salts.
E. CrO is basic but Cr_2O_3 is amphoteric.

Choose the correct answer from the options given below:

(a) B and D only (b) C and D only
(c) B and C only (d) A and E only

47. The equilibrium concentrations of the species in the reaction, $A + B \rightleftharpoons C + D$ are 2, 3, 10 and 6 mol L^{-1}, respectively at 300 K, $\Delta G°$ for the reaction is ($R = 2$ cal/mol K)

(a) −137.26 cal (b) −1381.80 cal
(c) −13.73 cal (d) 1372.60 cal

48. Identify the final product [*D*] obtained in the following sequence of reactions.

$$CH_3CHO \xrightarrow[\text{(ii) } H_3O^+]{\text{(i) LiAlH}_4} [A] \xrightarrow[\Delta]{H_2SO_4} [B]$$

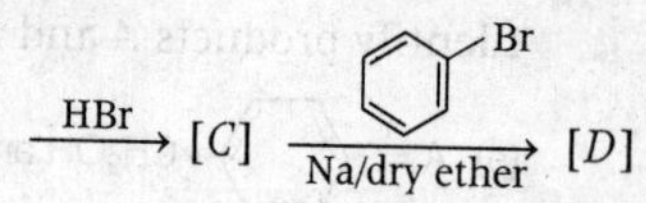

$$\xrightarrow{HBr} [C] \xrightarrow[\text{Na/dry ether}]{\text{Br}} [D]$$

(a)

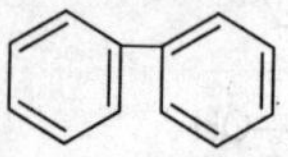

(b) C_4H_{10}

(c) $HC \equiv C^-Na^+$

(d)

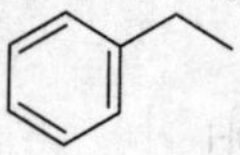

49. Given below are two statements.

Statement I The nutrient deficient water bodies lead to eutrophication.

Statement II Eutrophication leads to decrease in the level of oxygen in the water bodies.

In the light of the above statements, choose the correct answer from the options given below:

(a) Both statement I and statement II are false.
(b) Statement I is true but statement II is false.
(c) Statement I is false but statement II is true.
(d) Both statement I and statement II are true.

50. The reaction that does not take place in a blast furnace between 900 K to 1500 K temperature range during extraction of iron is

(a) $FeO + CO \longrightarrow Fe + CO_2$
(b) $C + CO_2 \longrightarrow 2CO$
(c) $CaO + SiO_2 \longrightarrow CaSiO_3$
(d) $Fe_2O_3 + CO \longrightarrow 2FeO + CO_2$

Answers

1.	(d)	2.	(b)	3.	(b)	4.	(d)	5.	(d)	6.	(d)	7.	(a)	8.	(d)	9.	(b)	10.	(d)
11.	(b)	12.	(a)	13.	(d)	14.	(b)	15.	(b)	16.	(b)	17.	(b)	18.	(b)	19.	(b)	20.	(c)
21.	(c)	22.	(c)	23.	(b)	24.	(a)	25.	(c)	26.	(c)	27.	(d)	28.	(b)	29.	(c)	30.	(a)
31.	(b)	32.	(a)	33.	(c)	34.	(b)	35.	(d)	36.	(b)	37.	(a)	38.	(d)	39.	(b)	40.	(a)
41.	(a)	42.	(b)	43.	(d)	44.	(b)	45.	(b)	46.	(b)	47.	(b)	48.	(d)	49.	(c)	50.	(d)

Answer *with* Explanations

1. *(d)* We know that, $n_m = 2l + 1$.

$$\therefore \quad 2l = n_m - 1 \text{ and } l = \frac{n_m - 1}{2}$$

2. *(b)* Among the given option BF_3 molecule acts as a Lewis acid. As it is an electron deficient molecule and has vacant orbital to accept the electron pair.

F — B(F)(F)

BF_3 has six electrons around central atom B that means its octet is not complete.

3. *(b)* Among the given statements, D and E are not correct because H—H bond dissociation enthalpy is not the lowest because bond formed between hydrogen atom is due to overlapping of 1s-1s orbital. So, it has smaller bond length and higher, bond enthalpy. There are also many other bond which are less stable then H—H and thus have less bond dissociation enthalpy.

Next, hydrogen does not reduces oxides of metals that are more active than iron. It can reduces oxides of elements like copper, mercury, silver, gold etc. as these metals are less reactive than hydrogen.

4. *(d)* Among the given options. Only option (d) is correct while other options are incorrect. The correct form of other statements are as follows.

(a) All enzymes that utilise ATP in phosphate transfer require Mg as the co-factor.

(b) The bone in human body is not inert and unchanging substance. It changes throughout the life.

(c) Ca plays roles in neuromuscular function and interneuronal transmission.

5. *(d)* Among the given option potassium trioxalatoaluminate (III) is an example of homoleptic complex while all other are examples of hetroleptic complex.
Complexes in which a metal is bound to only one kind of donor groups are known as **homoleptic complexes**.
Complexes in which a metal is bonded to more than one kind of donor groups are known as hetreroleptic complexes.

6. *(d)* The final reaction is as follows.

$\xrightarrow[\text{conc. HCl}]{\text{Zn-Hg}}$ (A) + $2H_2O$

This reaction is an example of Clemmensen reduction reaction.

7. *(a)*

Benzene diazonium chloride ($\overset{+}{N_2}Cl^-$) $\xrightarrow{\text{(i) } Cu_2Br_2/HBr}$ Bromobenzene (Br) $\xrightarrow{\text{(ii) Mg/dry ether}}$ MgBr $\xrightarrow{\text{(iii) } H_2O}$ Benzene

8. *(d)* The correct order of energies of molecular orbitals of N_2 molecule is,

$\sigma 1s < \sigma^* 1s < \sigma 2s < \sigma^* 2s < (\pi 2p_x = \pi 2p_y) < \sigma 2p_z$
$< (\pi^* 2p_x = \pi^* 2p_y) < \sigma^* 2p_z$

N_2 has total of 14 electrons. Thus, electrons can be filled as
$\sigma 1s^2 < \sigma^* 1s^2 < \sigma 2s^2 < \sigma^* 2s^2 < (\pi 2p_x^2 = \pi 2p_y^2) < \sigma 2p_z^2$

9. *(b)* Given, rate $(r) = k[A]^2\,[B]$ ...(i)

$$r_1 = k[3A]^2\,[B] \quad \text{...(ii)}$$

Dividing Eq (i) by (ii), we get

$$\frac{r}{r_1} = \frac{k\,[A]^2\,[B]}{k\,[3A]^2\,[B]}$$

$$\frac{r}{r_1} = \frac{1}{9}$$

$$\Rightarrow \quad r_1 = 9r$$

The initial rate would increase by a factor of nine.

10. *(d)* Both (A) and (R) are correct and (R) is the correct explanation of (A). The given relation i.e. $\Delta_r G = -nFE^\circ_{cell}$ is correct. Thus, according to this relation $\Delta_r G$ depends on n.
Also as ΔG depends on n i.e. number of mole, thus it is an extensive property and E_{cell} is independent of the amount of substance thus, it is an intensive property. As extensive properties are dependent on the amount of the substances.

11. *(b)* The given compound

C_6H_5—CH═CH—CH(X)—CH_2—CH_3

is an example of allylic halides. As in this the halogen is bonded to the sp^3-hybridised carbon atom next to the carbon-carbon double bond, which is called as allylic halides.

Benzylic halides In these halides, the halogen atom is bonded to the sp^3-hybridised carbon atom next to an aromatic ring.

Vinylic halide In these halides, the halogen atom is bonded to the sp^2-hybridised carbon of one of the carbon atoms of a double bond.

Aryl halide In these halides, the halogen atom is bonded to the sp^2-hybridised carbon atom of an aromatic ring.

12. *(a)* Chloroprene $[CH_2{=}C(Cl){-}CH{=}CH_2]$ is the monomer of neoprene.

$$xCH_2{=}\underset{\text{Chloroprene}}{C(Cl)}{-}CH{=}CH_2 \xrightarrow{\text{Polymerisation}} \underset{\text{Neoprene}}{[-CH_2-C(Cl){=}CH-CH_2-]_n}$$

13. *(d)*

$$\underset{\text{3-methylbutan-2-ol}}{CH_3CH(CH_3)-CH(OH)-CH_3} \xrightarrow{H^+} \underset{\substack{2^\circ\text{ carbocation}\\ \text{(Less stable)}}}{CH_3-CH(CH_3)-\overset{+}{C}H-CH_3}$$

$$\xrightarrow{\text{Hydride shift}} \underset{3^\circ\text{ carbocation (More stable)}}{CH_3-\overset{+}{C}(CH_3)-CH_2-CH_3} \xrightarrow{Br^-} \underset{\text{2-bromo-2-methyl butane}}{CH_3-C(Br)(CH_3)-CH_2-CH_3}$$

14. *(b)* Given, conductivity $(\kappa) = 0.0210\ \Omega^{-1}\text{cm}^{-1}$

Resistance = $60\ \Omega$

Cell constant = ?

We know that, $\kappa = \frac{1}{R} \times \frac{l}{a}$

Cell constant $= \frac{l}{a} = \kappa \times R$

$= 0.0210 \times 60$

$= 1.26\ \text{cm}^{-1}$

15. *(b)* The correct match is A—III, B—I, C—IV, D—II.

16. *(b)*

Given elements	Na	N	O	F
Formed ions to attain by nearest nobel gas configuration	Na^+ $(10e^-)$	N^{3-} $(10e^-)$	O^{2-} $(10e^-)$	F^- $(10e^-)$

Thus, all are isoelectronic species. In case of isoelectronic species, more is the negative charge on the ion, lesser is the effective nuclear charge, more will be the radius. Hence, N^{3-} has the largest radius among the above ions.

17. *(b)* Among the given reactions, primary amine will not form in case of 2nd reaction.

- $CH_3NC \xrightarrow[H_2O]{LiAlH_4} \underset{(2^\circ\text{ amine})}{CH_3-NH-CH_3}$
- $CH_3-CN \xrightarrow[H_2O]{LiAlH_4} \underset{\text{(Primary amine)}}{CH_3CH_2NH_2}$
- $CH_3-\overset{O}{\overset{\|}{C}}NH_2 \xrightarrow[H_2O]{LiAlH_4} \underset{\text{(Primary amine)}}{CH_3CH_2NH_2}$
- $CH_3CONH_2 \xrightarrow{Br_2/NaOH} \underset{\text{(Primary amine)}}{CH_3NH_2}$

18. *(b)*

In pyridine the number of σ, π and lone pair are 11, 3 and 1 respectively.

19. *(b)* Statement I is correct while statement II is incorrect. The correct form of statement II is — When nucleoside is linked to phosphoric acid at 5′-position of sugar moiety, we get nucleoside.

20. *(c)*

$$\underset{[A]}{\text{Cyclohexanone}} \xrightarrow{HCN} \underset{[B]}{\text{1-hydroxycyclohexane-1-carbonitrile (OH, CN)}} \xrightarrow[\Delta]{\text{conc. } H_2SO_4} \underset{[C]}{\text{Cyclohex-1-ene-1-carboxylic acid (COOH)}}$$

21. *(c)* Among the given relation $TlI > TlI_3$ is correct. As in group 13 element +1 oxidation state becomes more and more stable as we go down the group i.e. Al < Ga < In < Tl.

This is because of the presence of intervening *d* and *f*-orbitals which do not shield the nucleus efficiently. Consequently effective nuclear charge increases, that hold the *ns* electron tightly, so that they do not participate in bonding (inert pair effect). Thus, in Tl +1 oxidation state is more predominent whereas the +3 is strongly oxidising in nature.

22. *(c)* Among the given tranquilisers, veronal belongs to barbiturates.

23. *(b)* (A) is true while (R) is false. This is because at normal temperature and pressure helium is practically insoluble in oxygen. However under extreme conditions very small amount of helium dissolve in oxygen.

24. *(a)* Given reaction,

$$CaCO_3 \xrightarrow{\Delta} CaO + CO_2$$

Molar mass = 100 g/mol

20 g CO_2 of 20% pure limestone on heating gives $\frac{20 \times 20}{100} = 4$ g

$$\text{Mole} = \frac{4}{100} = 0.004$$

Mass of CO_2 produces = Mole × Molecular mass of CO_2
= 0.004 × 44 = 1.76 g

25. *(c)* If the compound contains sulphur and nitrogen both, sodium sulphocyanide is formed in Lassaigne's extract, which gives blood red colouration of $Fe(SCN)_3$ with $FeCl_3$.

$$Fe^{3+} + SCN^- \longrightarrow \underset{\text{Blood red}}{Fe[(SCN)]^{2+}}$$

26. *(c)* (A) is false but (R) is true. When a reaction have zero activation energy, the initial energy of the reactant will be equal to the activation energy of the reaction. That means every collision results into a chemical reaction which is not possible.

Mathematically, If $E_a = 0$, the according to Arrhenius equation

$$k = Ae^{-E_a/RT} = Ae^0 = A$$

27. *(d)* The element *B* forms cubic close packed structure = 4

Atom *A* occupy $\frac{1}{3}$ tetrahedral voids $= \frac{1}{3} \times 8$

[∵ Tetrahedral voids = 2of atom occupy by *B*]

∴ The formula of the compound is $A_8 B_4$ or A_2B_3

∴ The value of $x + y = 2 + 3 = 5$.

28. *(b)* In aqueous solution, copper (I) undergoes disproportionation reaction.

$$2Cu^+(aq) \longrightarrow Cu^{2+} + Cu(s)$$

The highest stability of Cu^{2+} ion in aqueous solution is due to negative enthalpy of hydration.

29. *(c)* Among the given statements (B), (C) and (E) are correct while remaining are incorrect. The correct form of (A) and (D) are as follows.

(A) Atoms of all elements are composed of three fundamental particles i.e. electrons, protons and neutrons.

(B) Protons and neutrons are collectively known as nucleons.

30. *(a)* According to Boyle's law, at constant temperature, the pressure of a fixed amount of a gas varies inversely with its volume.

$$p \propto \frac{1}{V} \text{ or } p = (nRT)\frac{1}{V}$$

Compare it with straight line equation, $y = mx + C$

we will get,

$$y = p,\ x = \frac{1}{V} \text{with } C = 0$$

and slope $(m) = T$

Thus, From the given options we can clearly see that, the correct option is given in option (a) i.e. p *vs* $1/V$ is a straight line with $T_3 > T_2 > T_1$.

31. *(b)* Among the given options covalent bonding is not an intermolecular force. It is the bond which is formed by mutual sharing of electrons between the combining atoms of the same or different element.

Whereas dipole-dipole forces, dipole-induced dipole forces, hydrogen bonds and dispersion forces are intermolecular forces.

32. *(a)*

$$\underset{\text{Sodium ethanoate}}{CH_3-\overset{\overset{O}{\|}}{C}-\overset{-}{O}\overset{+}{Na}} + NaOH \xrightarrow[\text{Decarboxylation}]{CaO,\ \Delta} CH_4 + Na_2CO_3$$

The product formed in above reaction is CH_4. Thus, weight of two moles of CH_4 is 2×12 i.e. 32.

33. *(c)* Among the given cases, option (c) is an example of heterogeneous catalysis as in this case the reactant and the catalyst are present in different phase.

Whereas all other are example of homogeneous catalysis as in respective reaction the reactants and the catalyst are present in same phase.

(a) $\underset{\text{Sugar solution}}{C_{12}H_{22}O_{11}(aq)} + H_2O(l) \xrightarrow{H_2SO_4(l)} \underset{\text{Glucose}}{C_6H_{12}O_6(aq)} + \underset{\text{Fructose}}{C_6H_{12}O_6(aq)}$

(b) $NO(g) + O_3(g) \longrightarrow O_2(g) + NO_2(g)$

$NO_2(g) + O(g) \longrightarrow NO(g) + O_2(g)$

[These reactions are involve in ozone depletion through nitrous oxide.]

(c) $N_2(g) + 3H_2(g) \xrightarrow{Fe(s),\ Mo(s)} 2NH_3(g)$

(d) $2SO_2(g) + O_2(g) \xrightarrow{NO(g)} 2SO_3(g)$

34. *(b)* (A) is true but (R) is false.

(A) is correct because all alkali metals gives deep blue solution by giving electrons. When sodium metal dissolved in liquid ammonia following reaction takes place.

$$Na + (x+y)\,NH_3 \longrightarrow \underset{\text{Ammoniated cations}}{[Na(NH_3)_x]^+} + \underset{\text{Ammoniated electrons}}{2[e^-(NH_3)_y]^-}$$

Thus, the correct (R) statement is:

The ammoniated electrons are responsible for the blue colour of the solution as they absorb the energy from visible region of light and, thus impart blue colour to the solution.

35. *(d)*

Given species	NH_3	$AlCl_3$	$BeCl_2$	CCl_4	PCl_5
Number of electrons central atom	8	6	4	8	10

Thus, among the given species $AlCl_3$, $BeCl_2$, PCl_5 does not have eight electrons around the central atom.

36. *(b)* The complete given reaction is as follows.

$$\text{(Phthalaldehyde-type keto-aldehyde)} + 2[Ag(NH_3)_2] + 3\,\bar{O}H \xrightarrow[H_2O]{\Delta}$$

[Tollen's reagent]

$$H_2O + NH_3 + \text{(2-acetylbenzoate, } COO^-) + Ag\downarrow$$

(Major) Silver

Tollen's reagent oxidises only the aldehyde group in the above reaction not the ketonic group.

37. *(a)* The correct match is A—III, B—IV, C—I, D—II.

Structure of given oxoacids of sulphur are as follows

HO—S(=O)₂—O—O—S(=O)₂—OH ; HO—S(=O)₂—OH

Peroxodisulphuric acid [Two S—OH, four S=O, one S—O—S bonds.]

Sulphuric acid [Two S—OH, two S=O bonds.]

HO—S(=O)₂—O—S(=O)₂—OH ; HO—S(=O)—OH

Pyrosulphuric - acid [Two S—OH, four S=O bond, one S—O—S bonds]

Sulphrous acid [Two S—OH, one S=O bond.]

38. *(d)* Among the given species that follows Huckel rule are given as

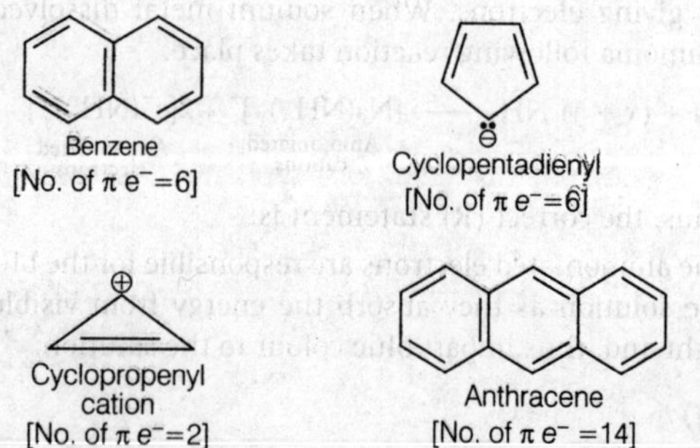

Whereas all other are non-aromatic and does not follows Huckel rule, as (iii), (iv) and (vi) have 4, 4 and 8 π electrons respectively.

39. *(b)* Pumice stone is an example of solid sol. In this dispersion phase is gas and dispersion medium is solid.

40. *(a)* Among the given option the correct relation between change in enthalpy (ΔH) and change in internal energy (ΔU) is,

$$\Delta H = \Delta U + \Delta n_g RT$$

41. *(a)* Among the given alcohols, (pentane-2,4-diol, OH OH) will most readily dehydrated under acidic conditions to give (1,3-pentadiene) as a product, in which double bonds are present in conjugation.

42. *(b)* Benzyl phenyl ether on heating with HI gives benzyl iodide (A) and phenol (B). The complete reaction is as follows.

$$C_6H_5-CH_2-O-C_6H_5 \xrightarrow[\Delta]{HI} C_6H_5-CH_2I + C_6H_5OH$$

Benzyl phenyl ether → (A) Benzyliodide + (B) Phenol

43. *(d)* The value of a, b and c is 1, 3, 8 the complete balanced equation is as follows.

$$Cr_2O_7^{2-} + 3SO_3^{2-}(aq) + 8H^+(aq) \longrightarrow$$

$$2Cr^{3+}(aq) + 3SO_4^{2-}(aq) + \frac{8}{2}H_2O(l)$$

44. *(b)* Among the given complex $[Co(Cl_2)(en)_2]NO_3$ is most stable because it is a chelating complex.

It coordinates with central metal atom to form a ring compound. Due to this reason, there is more force of attraction between the central metal ion and the chelating agent therefore it is more stable.

45. *(b)* As we know that, octahedral voids are present at the centre of edge length of the cube. Also, if any atom is present at the edge length then it divide into $\frac{1}{4}$ parts. Thus, fraction of one edge centred octahedral void lies in one unit cell of *fcc* is $\frac{1}{4}$

46. *(b)* Among the given statements C and D statements are incorrect. Their correct forms are as follows.

(C) Basic character decreases from V_2O_3 to V_2O_4 to V_2O_5. In general, the oxides in lower oxidation states of metals are basic and in their higher oxidation states they are acidic.

(D) V_2O_4 dissolves in acids to give VO_2^+ salts.

47. *(b)* According to given, general equation

$$A + B \rightleftharpoons C + D$$

$$\text{Equilibrium constant } (K_{eq}) = \frac{(10)(6)}{(2)(3)} = \frac{60}{6}$$

$$K_{eq} = 10$$

We know that,

$$\Delta G^\circ = -2.303\ RT \log K_{eq}$$

$$\therefore \quad \Delta G^\circ = -2.303 \times 2 \times 300 \times \log (10)$$

$$= -1381.8\ \text{cal}$$

48. *(d)*

$$\underset{\text{Ethanal}}{CH_3C{-}\overset{O}{\overset{\|}{C}}{-}H} \xrightarrow[\text{(ii) } H_3O^+]{\text{(i) LiAlH}_4} CH_3{-}CH_2OH \xrightarrow[\Delta]{H_2SO_4}$$

$$\underset{\substack{\text{Ethene}\\(B)}}{CH_2{=}CH_2} \xrightarrow{HBr} \underset{\substack{[C]\\\text{Bromoethane}}}{CH_3CH_2Br} \xrightarrow[\text{Na/Dry ether}]{C_6H_5Br} \underset{\substack{\text{Ethyl benzene}\\[D]}}{C_6H_5CH_2CH_3}$$

49. *(c)* Statement I is false but statement II is true. The correct statement I is : The nutrient rich water bodies lead to eutrophication.

The process in which nutrient enriched water bodies support a dense population, which kills animals life by depriving it of oxygen and results in subsequent loss of biodiversity is known as eutrophication.

50. *(d)* Among the given reaction,

$$Fe_2O_3 + CO \longrightarrow 2FeO + CO_2$$

reaction does not occur between 900 K to 1500 K temperature range in the blast furnace during extraction of iron. This reaction occur in temperature range of about 500-800 K (i.e. reduction zone).